Contemporary Authors

NEW REVISION SERIES

Contemporary Authors

A Bio-Bibliographical Guide to
Current Writers in Fiction, General Nonfiction,
Poetry, Journalism, Drama, Motion Pictures,
Television, and Other Fields

**ANN EVORY
LINDA METZGER**
Editors

PETER M. GAREFFA
DEBORAH A. STRAUB
Associate Editors

NEW REVISION SERIES volume 8

GALE RESEARCH COMPANY • THE BOOK TOWER • DETROIT, MICHIGAN 48226

EDITORIAL STAFF

Christine Nasso, *General Editor, Contemporary Authors*

Ann Evory and Linda Metzger, *Editors, New Revision Series*

Peter M. Gareffa and Deborah A. Straub, *Associate Editors*

James G. Lesniak and Thomas Wiloch, *Senior Assistant Editors*

Stewart R. Hakola, Kerry L. Lutz, Margaret Mazurkiewicz, Donna Olendorf, Heidi A. Tietjen, Marian Walters, and Michaela Swart Wilson, *Assistant Editors*

Melissa J. Gaiownik, Ellen Koral, Mary Alice Rattenbury, and Susan Salter, *Editorial Assistants*

Jean W. Ross and Walter W. Ross, *Interviewers*

Frederick G. Ruffner, *Publisher*   James M. Ethridge, *Editorial Director*

Copyright © 1962, 1963, 1964, 1965, 1966, 1967, 1968, 1969, 1970, 1973, 1974, 1975, 1976, 1977, 1978, 1979, 1980, 1983 by
GALE RESEARCH COMPANY

Library of Congress Catalog Card Number 81-640179
ISBN 0-8103-1937-3
ISSN 0275-7176

No part of this book may be reproduced in any form without permission in writing from the publisher, except by a reviewer who wishes to quote brief passages or entries in connection with a review written for inclusion in a magazine or newspaper. Manufactured in the United States of America.

Authors and Media People Featured in This Volume

Edward Albee—American playwright, producer, and director; his plays "The Zoo Story," "Who's Afraid of Virginia Woolf?," "The American Dream," "A Delicate Balance," and "Seascape" have earned numerous awards, including two Pulitzer Prizes, an Obie Award, Tony Award, New York Drama Critics Circle Award, and the Vernon Rice Memorial Award. (Sketch includes interview.)

Kingsley Amis—British novelist, poet, and nonfiction and short-story writer; *Lucky Jim, The Anti-Death League,* and *Russian Hide-and-Seek* are among his published work; entries for his wife, Elizabeth Jane Howard, and son Martin Amis also appear in this volume. (Sketch includes interview.)

Frank O. Braynard—American writer and artist who conceived of and organized Operation Sail, the "tall ships" festival of the American Bicentennial; author of books on ships and the sea, including a multi-volume maritime history, *Leviathan: The World's Greatest Ship.*

James M. Cain—American journalist and writer who died in 1977; his novels *The Postman Always Rings Twice, Double Indemnity,* and *Mildred Pierce* were adapted for films.

John William Corrington—American professor, attorney, and former head writer for the television serials "Search for Tomorrow," "Texas," and "General Hospital"; besides television scripts, he has written poetry, novels, and short stories (most of which have Southern settings and themes), screenplays (such as "The Red Baron," "The Omega Man," and "Killer Bees"), and critical essays. (Sketch includes interview.)

John Creasey—British novelist who died in 1973; author of approximately six hundred books under his own name or twenty-five pseudonyms; best known for his mystery series featuring Gideon, the Toff, the Baron, and Inspector West.

Helen Cresswell—British writer of children's books that have been lauded by critics for their humor and realistic language; among her books are *The Piemakers, The Nightwatchmen, Up the Pier,* and *The Bongleweed,* all of which have been nominated for the prestigious Carnegie Medal.

Stanley Elkin—American professor and writer; known for his use of parody and comic fantasy in such works of fiction as *Searches and Seizures, The Franchiser,* and *The Living End.* (Sketch includes interview.)

F.M. Esfandiary—Belgian-born futurist who foresees a world without schools, national governments, conventional family units, or print media, as outlined in his nonfiction books *Optimism One, Up-Wingers,* and *Telespheres.*

Doris Faber—American author of juvenile and adult nonfiction; her extensively researched biography *The Life of Lorena Hickok: E.R.'s Friend,* which raised questions about Hickok's relationship with Eleanor Roosevelt, attracted considerable critical attention.

Walter Farley—American writer of juvenile books about animals, including *The Black Stallion,* which was adapted into a popular film; over five million copies of his books have been sold in the United States alone.

Northrop Frye—Canadian literary critic; in his controversial and influential essay collection *Anatomy of Criticism,* he develops a schematic, nonjudgmental theory of literature that relates each genre, myth, and symbol to its place in literature as a whole.

Paul Fussell—American professor and writer; author of popular nonfiction works, including *The Great War and Modern Memory,* which won a National Book Award and National Book Critics Circle Award.

Gerald Green—American writer and television producer; among his works are the Emmy Award-winning television miniseries "Holocaust" and such novels as *The Last Angry Man* and *Murfy's Men.*

Jim Harrison—American poet and novelist; his fiction, often revolving around the themes of revenge and wilderness survival, "celebrates a fantasy of masculine self-sufficiency," according to *Newsweek* reviewer Peter S. Prescott; among Harrison's works are *A Good Day to Die, Legends of the Fall,* and *Warlock.* (Sketch includes interview.)

Joseph Heller—American novelist, playwright, and screenwriter; best known for his novels *Catch-22,* with over ten million copies now in print, *Something Happened,* and *Good as Gold.* (Sketch includes interview.)

Abbie Hoffman—American activist and former Yippie; *Steal This Book, To america with Love: Letters from the Underground, Soon to Be a Major Motion Picture,* and *Square Dancing in the Ice Age* are among his books, some written pseudonymously while he was a fugitive.

Justin Kaplan American free lance nonfiction writer and editor; received a Pulitzer Prize and National Book Award in 1967, for *Mr. Clemens and Mark Twain,* and an American Book Award in 1981, for *Walt Whitman: A Life.*

Arthur Laurents—Award-winning American playwright, screenwriter, and director; author of the books for the musicals "West Side Story," "Gypsy," "Hallelujah Baby!," and "My Mother Was a Fortune Teller"; also author of the screenplays "The Way We Were" and "The Turning Point." (Sketch includes interview.)

John Lehmann—British editor and author of poetry, autobiographies, and other nonfiction; developed a series of New Writing journals and anthologies in which the works of W.H. Auden, Christopher Isherwood, Jean-Paul Sartre, Saul Bellow, and Gore Vidal were first introduced to the public; founder of the publishing firm John Lehmann Ltd. and founding editor of *London* magazine; an entry for his sister Rosamond Lehmann also appears in this volume. (Sketch includes interview.)

F. Ray Marshall—American economist, professor, and secretary of labor under President Carter; called "an expert on the problems of minorities and employment" by *Newsweek;* author of numerous books in his field.

George S. McGovern—Former U.S. senator and 1972 Democratic presidential candidate; chairman of Americans for Common Sense; author of nonfiction, including *Grassroots,* an autobiography.

Iris Murdoch—Irish-born novelist, playwright, and nonfiction writer; among her widely reviewed novels are *Under the Net, A Word Child,* and *Nuns and Soldiers.* (Sketch includes interview.)

George Oppen—American Objectivist poet who uses words sparingly to achieve a pure statement of the subject itself rather than comment on the subject; his poetry collection *Of Being Numerous* received a Pulitzer Prize in 1969.

Mary Rodgers—American novelist, screenwriter, composer, and lyricist; *Freaky Friday, A Billion for Boris,* and *Summer Switch* are among her notable books for children. (Sketch includes interview.)

Walt W. Rostow—American economist, historian, professor, and former presidential advisor; best known for such economic texts as *The Stages of Economic Growth* and *The World Economy* and for his role as an advisor on Vietnam to President Lyndon Johnson. (Sketch includes interview.)

Ramon Sender—Spanish-born American novelist and nonfiction writer who died in 1982; although exiled from Spain in 1937, he continued to write in Spanish about his native land, notably in the novels translated into English as *Chronicle of Dawn* and *The Sphere.*

Alan Sillitoe—British writer who, in his novels, short stories, and plays, focuses on the British working-class individual who is isolated from society; best known for the novel *Saturday Night and Sunday Morning* and the short-story collection *The Loneliness of the Long-Distance Runner;* an entry for his wife, Ruth Fainlight, also appears in this volume.

Peter Singer—Australian philosophy professor who writes about speciesism and a lack of respect for nonhuman life, as outlined in his book *Animal Liberation.*

Robert Kimmel Smith—American novelist who at age forty left his position as an advertising executive to become a full-time writer; *Sadie Shapiro's Knitting Book* and *Sadie Shapiro, Matchmaker* are among his popular novels.

Theodore Solotaroff—American editor, essayist, and short-story writer; best-known as the editor of *New American Review* and *American Review,* prestigious literary quarterlies, and currently a senior editor with Harper & Row; his essays were collected and published as *The Red Hot Vacuum, and Other Pieces on the Writing of the Sixties.* (Sketch includes interview.)

W.A. Swanberg—American biographer whose scrupulously detailed and entertaining studies include the Pulitzer Prize-winning *Luce and His Empire* and the National Book Award winner *Norman Thomas: The Last Idealist.*

Calvin Tomkins—American art critic known for his ability to make art, especially the avant-garde, comprehensible to the general public; author of *The Scene, Off the Wall,* and other books on art and artists; currently a *New Yorker* staff writer. (Sketch includes interview.)

Rene Wellek—Austrian-born American professor and literary critic; advocate of the "intrinsic" critical method, which denigrates political and social influences and stresses the content of the work itself. (Sketch includes interview.)

Elie Wiesel—Romanian-born American professor and writer; his autobiographical novels, notably *Night, Dawn,* and *The Town beyond the Wall,* and nonfiction stem from his experiences during the Holocaust. (Sketch includes interview.)

Preface

The *Contemporary Authors New Revision Series* provides completely updated information on authors listed in earlier volumes of *Contemporary Authors*. Entries for active individual authors from *any* volume of *CA* may be included in a volume of the *New Revision Series*. The sketches appearing in *New Revision Series* Volume 8, for example, were selected from more than ten previously published *CA* volumes.

As always, the most recent *Contemporary Authors* cumulative index continues to be the user's guide to the location of an individual author's listing.

Compilation Methods

The editors make every effort to secure information directly from the authors. Clippings of all sketches in selected *CA* volumes published several years ago are sent to the authors at their last-known addresses. Authors mark material to be deleted or changed, and insert any new personal data, new affiliations, new books, new work in progress, new sidelights, and new biographical/critical sources. All author returns are assessed, additional research is done, if necessary, and those sketches with significant change are published in the *New Revision Series*.

If, however, authors fail to reply, or if authors are now deceased, biographical dictionaries are checked for new information (a task made easier through the use of Gale's *Biography and Genealogy Master Index* and other volumes in the "Gale Biographical Index Series"), as are bibliographical sources, such as *Cumulative Book Index* and *The National Union Catalog*. Using data from such sources, revision editors select and revise nonrespondents' entries which need substantial updating. Sketches not personally reviewed by the authors are marked with a dagger (†) to indicate that these listings have been revised from secondary sources believed to be reliable, but they have not been personally reviewed for this edition by the authors sketched.

In addition, reviews and articles in major periodicals, lists of prestigious awards, and requests from *CA* users are monitored so that authors on whom new information is in demand can be identified and revised listings prepared promptly.

Comprehensive Revision

All listings in this volume have been revised and/or augmented in various ways, though the amount and type of change vary with the author. Revised entries include additions of or changes in such information as degrees, mailing addresses, literary agents, career items, career-related and civic activities, memberships, work in progress, and biographical/critical sources. They may also include the following:

1) Major new awards—Playwright Edward Albee and biographers Justin Kaplan and W.A. Swanberg are only three of the numerous award-winning authors with revised entries in this volume. Added to Albee's already extensive awards section are a 1975 Pulitzer Prize for "Seascape" as well as a 1980 American Academy and Institute of Arts and Sciences Gold Medal and two honorary degrees. Justin Kaplan's original entry, which listed a Pulitzer Prize and National Book Award, was updated for this volume to include, among other new items, the American Book Award he received in 1981 for *Walt Whitman: A Life*. And W.A. Swanberg's revised sketch now credits him with a 1973 Pulitzer Prize for *Luce and His Empire* and a 1977 National Book Award for *Norman Thomas: The Last Idealist*.

2) Extensive bibliographical additions—Novelist John Creasey wrote nearly six hundred books before he died in 1973; his entry in this volume of the *New Revision Series* provides a comprehensive bibliography that includes approximately two hundred and fifty titles previously unlisted in *CA*. Alan Sillitoe has been actively writing in a number of genres as reflected in his updated sketch, which notes the following new works: four novels, two short-story collections, three juvenile books, a volume of memoirs, and collected plays and essays. Fewer than twenty titles were cited in Jane Werner Watson's former *CA* entry; her revised sketch, however, lists two hundred additional works of fiction and nonfiction for adults and children.

3) Informative new sidelights—Numerous *CA* sketches contain sidelights, which provide personal dimensions to the listings, supply information about the critical reception the authors' works have received, or both. Novelist and screenwriter Gerald Green, for example, commented upon some of the negative reaction to his Emmy Award-winning screenplay "Holocaust," which was viewed by millions of people worldwide. Green noted in his letter to *CA* that despite attacks on the artistic merit of the drama, its political and social impact cannot be denied: "Was this [critic] around to re-think his rancor when 'Holocaust' was directly responsible for changing the laws of West Germany so that Nazi war criminals could be prosecuted? Or when German schools began including Holocaust studies in their curricula?...Or when West German TV—as a direct result of 'Holocaust'—first broadcast documentaries on the Nazi era and German anti-Semitism?" Green's response to the critics and anecdotes he provided complement the critical overview assistant editor Stewart R. Hakola presents in sidelights.

Although his work is often compared to that of his father, Kingsley Amis, British novelist Martin Amis has firmly established a literary reputation of his own. Most Americans probably first became familiar with the younger Amis when he charged that his novel *The Rachel Papers* had been plagiarized by another writer. A summary of this issue appears in the sidelights section compiled by senior assistant editor James G. Lesniak.

These sketches, as well as others with sidelights compiled by *CA*'s editors, provide informative and enjoyable reading.

Writers of Special Interest

CA's editors make every effort to include in each *New Revision Series* volume a substantial number of revised entries on active authors and media people of special interest to *CA*'s readers. Since the *New Revision Series* also includes sketches on noteworthy deceased writers, a significant amount of work on the part of *CA*'s editors goes into the revision of entries on important deceased authors. Some of the prominent writers, both living and deceased, whose sketches are contained in this volume are noted in the list headed "Authors and Media People Featured in This Volume" immediately preceding the preface.

Exclusive Interviews

CA provides exclusive, primary information on certain authors in the form of interviews. Prepared specifically for *CA*, the never-before-published conversations presented in the section of the sketch headed *CA INTERVIEW* give *CA* users the opportunity to learn the authors' thoughts, in depth, about their craft. Subjects chosen for interviews are, the editors feel, authors who hold special interest for *CA*'s readers.

Authors and journalists in this volume whose sketches include interviews are Edward Albee, Kingsley Amis, John William Corrington, Stanley Elkin, Jim Harrison, Joseph Heller, Arthur Laurents, John Lehmann, Iris Murdoch, Mary Rodgers, Walt W. Rostow, Theodore Solotaroff, Calvin Tomkins, Rene Wellek, and Elie Wiesel.

Retaining *CA* Volumes

As new volumes in the series are published, users often ask which *CA* volumes, if any, can be discarded. Since the *New Revision Series* does not supersede any specific volumes of *CA*, all of the following must be retained in order to have information on all authors in the series:

- all revised volumes
- the two *Contemporary Authors Permanent Series* volumes
- *CA* Volumes 45-48 and subsequent original volumes

The chart on the following page is designed to assist users in keeping their collection as complete as possible.

Cumulative Index Should Always Be Consulted

The key to locating an individual author's listing is the *CA* cumulative index bound into the back of alternate original volumes (and available separately as an offprint). Since the *CA* cumulative index provides access to *all* entries in the *CA* series, the latest cumulative index should always be consulted to find the specific volume containing an author's original or most recently revised sketch.

(Preface continues on page following chart)

IF YOU HAVE:	YOU MAY DISCARD:
1-4 First Revision (1967)	1 (1962) 2 (1963) 3 (1963) 4 (1963)
5-8 First Revision (1969)	5-6 (1963) 7-8 (1963)
Both 9-12 First Revision (1974) AND *Contemporary Authors Permanent Series,* Volume 1 (1975)	9-10 (1964) 11-12 (1965)
Both 13-16 First Revision (1975) AND *Contemporary Authors Permanent Series,* Volumes 1 and 2 (1975, 1978)	13-14 (1965) 15-16 (1966)
Both 17-20 First Revision (1976) AND *Contemporary Authors Permanent Series,* Volumes 1 and 2 (1975, 1978)	17-18 (1967) 19-20 (1968)
Both 21-24 First Revision (1977) AND *Contemporary Authors Permanent Series,* Volumes 1 and 2 (1975, 1978)	21-22 (1969) 23-24 (1970)
Both 25-28 First Revision (1977) AND *Contemporary Authors Permanent Series,* Volume 2 (1978)	25-28 (1971)
Both 29-32 First Revision (1978) AND *Contemporary Authors Permanent Series,* Volume 2 (1978)	29-32 (1972)
Both 33-36 First Revision (1978) AND *Contemporary Authors Permanent Series,* Volume 2 (1978)	33-36 (1973)
37-40 First Revision (1979)	37-40 (1973)
41-44 First Revision (1979)	41-44 (1974)
45-48 (1974) 49-52 (1975) 53-56 (1975) 57-60 (1976) ↓ ↓ 106 (1982)	NONE: These volumes will not be superseded by corresponding revised volumes. Individual entries from these and all other volumes appearing in the left column of this chart will be revised and included in the *New Revision Series.*
Volumes in the *Contemporary Authors New Revision Series*	NONE: The *New Revision Series* does not replace any single volume of *CA*. All volumes appearing in the left column of this chart must be retained to have information on all authors in the series.

Those authors appearing in the *New Revision Series* are listed in the *CA* cumulative index with the designation **CANR-** in front of the specific volume number. For the convenience of those who do not have *New Revision Series* volumes, the cumulative index also notes the specific earlier volume of *CA* in which the sketch appeared. Below is a sample *New Revision Series* index citation:

> Vonnegut, Kurt, Jr. 1922- CANR-1
>   Earlier sketch in CA 3R
>   See also CLC 1, 2, 3, 4, 5, 8, 12
>   See also AITN 1

For the most recent information on Vonnegut, users should refer to Volume 1 of the *New Revision Series,* as designated by "CANR-1"; if that volume is unavailable, refer to *CA* 1-4 First Revision, as indicated by "Earlier sketch in CA 3R," for his 1968 listing. (And if *CA* 1-4 First Revision is unavailable, refer to *CA* 3, published in 1963, for Vonnegut's original listing.)

Sketches not eligible for inclusion in a *New Revision Series* volume because the author or a revision editor has verified that no significant change is required will, of course, be available in previously published *CA* volumes. Users should always consult the most recent *CA* cumulative index to determine the location of these authors' entries.

For the convenience of *CA* users, the *CA* cumulative index also includes references to all entries in three related Gale series—*Contemporary Literary Criticism* (CLC), which is devoted entirely to current criticism of the works of today's novelists, poets, playwrights, short story writers, filmmakers, screenwriters, and other creative writers, *Something About the Author* (SATA), a series of heavily illustrated sketches on authors and illustrators of books for young people, and *Authors in the News* (AITN), a compilation of news stories and feature articles from American newspapers and magazines covering writers and other members of the communications media.

As always, suggestions from users about any aspect of *CA* will be welcomed.

Contemporary Authors

NEW REVISION SERIES

† *Indicates that a listing has been revised from secondary sources believed to be reliable, but has not been personally reviewed for this edition by the author sketched.*

AARON, Chester 1923-

PERSONAL: Born May 9, 1923, in Butler, Pa.; son of Albert (a grocer and farmer) and Celia (Charleson) Aaron; married Margaurite Kelly (a self-employed jeweler), April 17, 1954 (divorced, 1973); stepchildren: Louis Daniel Segal. *Education:* Attended University of California, Los Angeles; University of California, Berkeley, B.A., 1966; San Francisco State University, M.A., 1972. *Home:* 3531 Hillcrest Ave., Sebastopol, Calif. 95472. *Agent:* Curtis Brown Ltd., 575 Madison Ave., New York, N.Y. 10022. *Office:* Department of English, St. Mary's College of California, Moraga, Calif. 94575.

CAREER: St. Mary's College of California, Moraga, assistant professor of English. *Military service:* U.S. Army, 1943-46. *Member:* East Bay Association of X-Ray Technicians (president). *Awards, honors:* Huntington Hartford Foundation grant; Chapelbrook Foundation grant; National Endowment for the Arts grant.

WRITINGS: About Us (novel), McGraw, 1967; *Better Than Laughter* (juvenile novel), Harcourt, 1972; *An American Ghost,* Harcourt, 1973; *Hello to Bodega,* Atheneum, 1976; *Spill,* Atheneum, 1978; *Catch Calico!,* Dutton, 1979.

Gideon, Lippincott, 1982; *Duchess,* Lippincott, 1982; *Lackawana,* Lippincott, 1983. Also author of play produced at University of California, Berkeley, 1955. Contributor of short stories to *Coastlines* and *North American Review.*

WORK IN PROGRESS: Two novels; a book of short stories; a play.

SIDELIGHTS: Chester Aaron said that the writing style he likes "is almost archaic. I insist upon simplicity. I do not philosophize but engage my characters in action. I am uncomfortable with complicated story lines. My themes are unorthodox but not intellectually pretentious. I do tend toward exotic characters."

* * *

ABEL, Elie 1920-

PERSONAL: Born October 17, 1920, in Montreal, Quebec, Canada; naturalized U.S. citizen in 1952; son of Jacob and Rose (Savetsky) Abel; married Corinne Adelaide Prevost, January 28, 1946; children: Mark, Suzanne. *Education:* McGill University, B.A., 1941; Columbia University, M.A., 1942. *Office:* Department of Communication, Stanford University, Stanford, Calif. 94305.

CAREER: Windsor Star, Windsor, Ontario, reporter, 1941; *Montreal Gazette,* Montreal, Quebec, assistant city editor, 1945-46; North American Newspaper Alliance, foreign correspondent in Berlin, Germany, 1946-47; Overseas News Agency, United Nations correspondent in New York City, 1947-49; *New York Times,* reporter in Detroit, Mich., Washington, D.C., Europe, and India, 1949-59; *Detroit News,* bureau chief in Washington, D.C., 1959-61; National Broadcasting Co., New York City, 1961-69, chief of London Bureau, 1966-67, diplomatic correspondent in Washington, D.C., 1967-69; Columbia University, New York City, Godfrey Lowell Cabot Professor of Journalism and dean of Graduate School of Journalism, 1969-79; Stanford University, Stanford, Calif., Chandler Professor of Communication, 1979—. Member of board of governors, American Stock Exchange, 1972—; chairman of board of trustees, Greater Washington Educational Television Association. *Military service:* Royal Canadian Air Force, 1942-45; served as radar man aboard flying boats based in Scotland and as combat correspondent.

MEMBER: Sigma Delta Chi, Century Club (New York). *Awards, honors:* George Foster Peabody Award, 1968, for outstanding radio interpretation of foreign news.

WRITINGS: The Missile Crisis, Lippincott, 1966 (published in England as *The Missiles of October: The Story of the Cuban Missile Crisis, 1962,* MacGibbon & Kee, 1966); (with Marvin Kalb) *Roots of Involvement: The U.S. in Asia, 1784-1971,* Norton, 1971; (with Averell Harriman) *Special Envoy to Churchill and Stalin,* Random House, 1975; (editor) *What's News: The Media in American Society,* Institute for Contemporary Studies, 1981.

SIDELIGHTS: After World War II, Elie Abel covered the Nuremberg war crimes trials for his agency and also witnessed the first attempts at four-power government in Germany. After he had toured the Soviet Union, he was arrested in Poland by security police. *Avocational interests:* Music.

BIOGRAPHICAL/CRITICAL SOURCES: New York Times, December 20, 1969.

* * *

ABERNETHY, Francis Edward 1925-

PERSONAL: Born December 3, 1925, in Altus, Okla.; son of

Talbot and Aileen (Cherry) Abernethy; married Hazel Shelton, May 20, 1948; children: Luanna, Robert, Sarah, Margaret, Benjamin. *Education:* Stephen F. Austin State College (now University), B.A., 1949; Louisiana State University, M.A., 1951, Ph.D., 1956. *Politics:* Democrat. *Religion:* Methodist. *Home:* 210 South Lanana St., Nacogdoches, Tex. 75961. *Office:* Department of English, Stephen F. Austin State University, Nacogdoches, Tex. 75961.

CAREER: High school teacher, Woodville, Tex., 1951-53; Lamar State College of Technology (now Lamar University), Beaumont, Tex., assistant professor, 1956-59, associate professor of English, 1959-65; Stephen F. Austin State University, Nacogdoches, Tex., professor of English, 1965—. *Military service:* U.S. Navy, 1943-46. *Member:* American Folklore Society, College Conference of Teachers of English, South Central Renaissance Society, South Central Modern Language Association, Texas Herpetological Society, Texas Folklore Society (secretary-editor; president), Texas Institute of Letters, East Texas Historical Association, Association of Mexican Cave Studies.

WRITINGS: (With Nossen and Emmons) *How to Write a Theme,* McCutchan, 1961; (contributor) *The Golden Log,* Southern Methodist University Press, 1962; *Tales from the Big Thicket,* University of Texas Press, 1966; *J. Frank Dobie,* Steck, 1967.

(Editor) *Observations and Reflections on Texas Folklore,* Encino Press, 1972; *The Folklore of Texan Cultures,* Encino Press, 1974; *Some Still Do,* Encino Press, 1975; *What's Going On?,* Encino Press, 1976; *Paisanos,* Encino Press, 1978; *Built in Texas,* E-Heart, 1979.

Legendary Ladies of Texas, E-Heart, 1981; *T for Texas,* E-Heart, 1982. Contributor to *Modern Drama, Sing Out, Studies in English Renaissance,* publications of Texas Folklore Society, and other journals.

WORK IN PROGRESS: Singin' Texas, for E-Heart Press.

AVOCATIONAL INTERESTS: Speleology, herpetology, playing guitar, raising horses, hunting, fishing.

* * *

ABRAMSON, Paul R(obert) 1937-

PERSONAL: Born November 28, 1937, in St. Louis, Mo.; son of Harry B. J. (a printer and businessman) and Hattie (Lewin) Abramson; married Janet Schwartz, September 11, 1966; children: Lee Jacob, Heather Lyn. *Education:* Washington University, St. Louis, Mo., B.A., 1959; University of California, Berkeley, M.A., 1961, Ph.D., 1967. *Home:* 2697 Linden Dr., East Lansing, Mich. 48823. *Office:* Department of Political Science, Michigan State University, East Lansing, Mich. 48824.

CAREER: Michigan State University, East Lansing, assistant professor, 1967-71, associate professor, 1971-77, professor of political science, 1977—. *Military service:* U.S. Army, 1960-62. U.S. Army Reserve, 1962-64; became captain. *Member:* American Political Science Association, American Sociological Association, Phi Beta Kappa. *Awards, honors:* Woodrow Wilson fellow, 1961; Ford Foundation faculty research fellow, 1972-73.

WRITINGS: Generational Change in American Politics, Heath, 1975; *The Political Socialization of Black Americans,* Free Press, 1977; (with John H. Aldrich and David W. Rohde) *Change and Continuity in the 1980 Elections,* Congressional Quarterly, 1982.

WORK IN PROGRESS: Political Attitudes in America, a study of changing political attitudes during the postwar years, for W. H. Freeman.

ABSHIRE, David M. 1926-

PERSONAL: Born April 11, 1926, in Chattanooga, Tenn.; son of James Ernest (a businessman) and Edith (Patten) Abshire; married Carolyn Lamar Sample (an importer), September 7, 1957; children: Lupton, Anna Lamar, Mary Lee, Phyllis, Caroline. *Education:* U.S. Military Academy, B.S., 1951; Georgetown University, Ph.D. (with honors), 1959. *Politics:* Republican. *Religion:* Episcopalian. *Home:* 311 South St. Asaph St., Alexandria, Va. 22314. *Office:* Center for Strategic and International Studies, Georgetown University 1800 K St., Washington, D.C. 20006.

CAREER: U.S. Army, cadet, 1946-51, regular officer, 1951-55, served as platoon leader, intelligence officer, and company commander, retired as first lieutenant, became captain, U.S. Army Reserve; U.S. House of Representatives, Washington, D.C., member of staff, 1959-60; American Enterprise Institute for Public Policy Research, Washington, D.C., director of special projects, 1961-62; Georgetown University, Washington, D.C., Center for Strategic and International Studies, co-founder, 1962, executive director, 1962-70, chairman, 1973—, adjunct professor in School of Foreign Service; U.S. Department of State, Washington, D.C., assistant secretary of state for congressional relations, 1970-73. Member of congressional committee on Organization of the Government for the Conduct of Foreign Policy, 1974-76; chairman of U.S. Board for International Broadcasting, 1974-77; director of National Security Group (including Department of State, Department of Defense, and Central Intelligence Agency), 1979-80; member of President's Foreign Intelligence Advisory Board; member of advisory board of Long Range Planning for Chief of Naval Operations; member of Trilateral Commission and of Council on Foreign Relations. Director of AIUO Insurance, Ltd. (Bermuda), Ogden Corp. (New York), and World Airways, Inc. Member of board of National Park Foundation; former member of advisory board of Naval War College; trustee of Baylor Preparatory School (Chattanooga, Tenn.); vice-chairman of board of Youth for Understanding; director of Tinker Foundation (New York) and of Atlantic Council of the United States. Consultant to *Reader's Digest* and to American International Group, Inc. *Member:* International Army and Navy Club, Foreign Policy Association, Academy of Political and Social Science, International Club (Washington, D.C.; member of board), Alfalfa Club (Washington, D.C.), Metropolitan Club (Washington, D.C., and New York), Phi Alpha Theta, Gold Key Society. *Awards, honors*—Military: Bronze Star Medal (twice), Commendation Ribbon, Combat Infantryman Badge (all for service in Korea.)

WRITINGS: (Editor with Richard Allen) *National Security: Political, Military and Economic Strategies in the Decade Ahead,* Praeger, 1963; (contributor) *Detente: Cold War Strategies in Transition,* Praeger, 1965; *The South Rejects a Prophet: The Life of Senator D. M. Key, 1824-1900,* Praeger, 1967; (editor with M. Samuels) *Portuguese Africa: A Handbook,* Praeger, 1969; *International Broadcasting: A New Dimension of Western Diplomacy,* Sage Publications, 1976; *Foreign Policy Makers: President vs. Congress,* Sage Publications, 1979; (contributor) Dante B. Fascell, editor, *International News: Freedom under Attack,* Sage Publications, 1979.

Also editor of *The Growing Power of Congress.* Contributor to *Annals of the American Academy of Political and Social Science* and to *U.S. Naval Institute Proceedings;* editor of proceedings of Conference on Plans and Needs for International Strategic Studies, 1969. Contributor of articles to magazines, newspapers, and scholarly journals, including *New York Times, Times of London, Reader's Digest,* and *American Political Science Review.* Founder and co-editor of *The Washington Quarterly: A Journal of Strategic and International Studies.*†

* * *

ACHTEMEIER, Elizabeth (Rice) 1926-

PERSONAL: Born June 11, 1926, in Bartlesville, Okla.; daughter of Francis Edgar (a petroleum engineer) and Ida (Schafer) Rice; married Paul John Achtemeier (a professor), June 11, 1952; children: Paul Mark, Marie Louise. *Education:* Stephens College, A.A., 1946; Stanford University, B.A. (with great distinction), 1948; Union Theological Seminary, New York, N.Y., M. Div. (summa cum laude), 1951; additional study at University of Heidelberg, 1952-53, and University of Basel, 1953-54; Columbia University, Ph.D., 1959. *Home:* 1508 Brookland Parkway, Richmond, Va. 23227. *Office:* Union Theological Seminary, 3401 Brook Rd., Richmond, Va. 23227.

CAREER: Ordained minister of United Church of Christ. Lancaster Theological Seminary of the United Church of Christ, Lancaster, Pa., visiting lecturer, 1959-71, adjunct professor of Old Testament, 1971-73; Union Theological Seminary in Virginia, Richmond, visiting professor of homiletics, 1973—. Visiting professor at Gettysburg Lutheran Theological Seminary, 1968, Pittsburgh Theological Seminary, 1976-77, Presbyterian School of Christian Education, 1979, 1980, 1982, and Duke University Divinity School, 1981. Lecturer and preacher for church groups and conferences. *Member:* Society of Biblical Literature, Phi Beta Kappa.

WRITINGS: (With husband, Paul J. Achtemeier) *The Old Testament Roots of Our Faith,* Abingdon, 1962, reprinted, Fortress, 1979; *The Feminine Crisis in Christian Faith,* Abingdon, 1965; (with P. J. Achtemeier) *To Save All People,* United Church Press, 1967; *The Old Testament and the Proclamation of the Gospel,* Westminster, 1973; (with P. J. Achtemeier) *Ephiphany,* Fortress, 1973; (contributor) Howard N. Bream, R. D. Heim, and C. A. Moore, editors, *A Light unto My Path: Old Testament Studies in Honor of Jacob M. Myers,* Temple University Press, 1974.

The Committed Marriage, Westminster, 1976; *Deuteronomy, Jeremiah: Proclamation Commentaries,* Fortress, 1978; (editor) *Proclamation II,* Fortress, 1979; (contributor) *Issues in Sexual Ethics,* UCPBW, 1979; *Creative Preaching,* Abingdon, 1980; (contributor) James W. Cox, editor, *The Twentieth Century Pulpit,* Volume II, Abingdon, 1981; *The Community and Message of Isaiah 56-66,* Augsburg, 1982; (editor) *Proclamation III,* Fortress, 1984.

Author of homiletical tapes for Thesis Theological Cassettes, Kerygma II, and Catalyst; contributor to *Interpreter's Dictionary of the Bible.* Contributor to numerous theological, biblical, and denominational journals and periodicals, including *Theology and Life, Interpretation, United Church Herald, Discovery, Lutheran Women,* and *Presbyterian Outlook.*

WORK IN PROGRESS: Commentary on Nahum-Malachi.

* * *

ACHTEMEIER, Paul J(ohn) 1927-

PERSONAL: Born September 3, 1927, in Lincoln, Neb.; son of Arthur R. (a pastor) and Clara (Barnstein) Achtemeier; married Elizabeth Rice (a professor), June 11, 1952; children: Paul Mark, Marie Louise. *Education:* Elmhurst College, A.B. (summa cum laude), 1949; Union Theological Seminary, New York, N.Y., B.D. (magna cum laude), 1952, Th.D., 1958; additional study at Princeton Theological Seminary, 1950, University of Heidelberg, 1952-53, and University of Basel, 1953-54. *Politics:* Liberal Republican. *Home:* 1508 Brookland Parkway, Richmond, Va. 23227. *Office:* Union Theological Seminary, 3401 Brook Rd., Richmond, Va. 23227.

CAREER: Ordained minister of United Church of Christ. Elmhurst College, Elmhurst, Ill., instructor in biblical literature and Greek, 1956-57; Lancaster Theological Seminary, Lancaster, Pa., assistant professor, 1957-59, associate professor, 1959-61, Kunz Professor of New Testament, 1961-73; Union Theological Seminary, Richmond, Va., professor of New Testament, 1973-79, Herbert Worth and Annie H. Jackson Professor of Biblical Interpretation, 1979—. Tutor, Ecumenical Institute of World Council of Churches, 1963-64; visiting professor, Pittsburgh Theological Seminary, 1968, Lutheran Theological Seminary, Gettysburg, Pa., 1970-71 and 1971-72; Staley Foundation Distinguished Christian Scholar, Rollins College, 1972, 1982, and Northwest Christian College, 1973; Rosenstiel Fellow, University of Notre Dame, 1974. Member of Committee on Faith and Order, Pennsylvania State Council of Churches, 1961-73; member of board of directors, Scholars Press, 1977—. Lecturer and preacher for church groups and conferences. *Member:* American Theological Society, Catholic Biblical Association (member of executive committee, 1975-77), Society of Biblical Literature (executive secretary, 1977-80), Studiorum Novi Testamenti Societas.

WRITINGS: (With wife, Elizabeth Achtemeier) *The Old Testament Roots of our Faith,* Abingdon, 1962, reprinted, Fortress, 1979; (with E. Achtemeier) *To Save All People,* United Church Press, 1967; (translator and contributor) R. Funk, editor, *History and Hermeneutics,* Harper, 1967; *An Introduction to the New Hermeneutic,* Westminster, 1969; (translator) Willi Marxsen, *The Beginnings of Christology: A Study in Its Problems,* Fortress, 1969; (translator and contributor) R. Kraft and G. Krodel, editors, *Orthodoxy and Heresy in Earliest Christianity,* Fortress, 1971; (with E. Achtemeier) *Ephiphany,* Fortress, 1973; (contributor) Herman G. Stuempfle, Jr., editor, *Preaching in the Witnessing Community,* Fortress, 1973.

Mark, Fortress, 1975; (contributor) E. S. Fiorenza, editor, *Aspects of Religious Propaganda in Judaism and Early Christianity,* University of Notre Dame Press, 1976; (author of introduction and annotations) *The New English Bible: Oxford Study Edition,* Oxford University Press, 1976; *Invitation to Mark,* Doubleday, 1978; *The Inspiration of Scripture: Problems and Proposals,* Westminster, 1980; (with J. L. Mebust) *Advent, Christmas,* Fortress, 1981; (contributor) C. H. Talbert, editor, *Perspectives on Luke: Acts,* Mercer University Press, 1981; (contributor) J. L. Mays, editor, *Interpreting the Gospels,* Fortress, 1981; (contributor) E. E. Shelp and R. Sunderland, editors, *A Biblical Basis for Ministry,* Westminster, 1981.

Author of tape cassette, "A New Perspective on Reality," Thesis Theological Cassettes, 1972; contributor to recording, "The Bible Today: An Open-Ended Discussion by Biblical Scholars, Ministers, and Laymen," United Church Press, 1967; translator and contributor to *God and Christ, Existence and Province.* Editor of *Society of Biblical Literature Seminar Papers,* 1977-80, and *Society of Biblical Literature Abstracts,* 1977-80; co-editor of *Biblical Scholarship in North America,* 1978—; New Testament editor, *Interpretation: Biblical Commentaries for Teaching and Preaching,* 1979—; member of editorial committee, *Centennial Publications of the Society of Biblical Literaute,* 1980—. Contributor to proceedings of U.S. Lutheran-Catholic Dialogue panel investigations, *Peter in the*

New Testament, Paulist Press/Augsburg, 1973, and *Mary in the New Testament*, Paulist/Newman and Fortress, 1978; also contributor to *Interpreter's Dictionary of the Bible*.

Contributor to numerous theological and biblical journals, including *Journal of Biblical Literature, Theology and Life, Interpretation, Perspective, Catholic Biblical Quarterly,* and *Theology Today*. Book review editor, *Theology and Life*, 1958-65; *Interpretation*, member of editorial board, 1973-81, associate editor, 1981—; member of editorial board, *Journal of Biblical Literature*, 1973-77, 1980—; member of editorial advisory committee, *Religious Studies Review*, 1975-76; associate editor, *Catholic Biblical Quarterly*, 1981—.

WORK IN PROGRESS: *Commentary on Romans*, for John Knox Press; *Commentary on 1 Peter*, for Fortress.

SIDELIGHTS: Paul J. Achtemeier is fluent in German and has a reading knowledge of French and New Testament Greek, and a working knowledge of Hebrew and Latin. *Avocational interests:* Woodworking, sailing, gardening, financial affairs on national scene.

* * *

ADAMS, Charles J(oseph) 1924-

PERSONAL: Born April 24, 1924, in Houston, Tex.; son of Joseph Edward (a barber) and Viola (Terry) Adams; married Joanna Zofia Teslar, August 18, 1963. *Education:* Baylor University, B.A., 1947; graduate study at McGill University, 1952-55; University of Chicago, Ph.D., 1955. *Religion:* Protestant. *Home:* 515 Francois, Apt. 311, Nun's Island, Montreal, Quebec, Canada. *Office:* Institute of Islamic Studies, McGill University, Sherbrooke St., Montreal, Quebec, Canada.

CAREER: Princeton University, Princeton, N.J., instructor in the history of religions, 1953-54; McGill University, Institute of Islamic Studies, Montreal, Quebec, assistant professor, 1957-59, assistant director, 1959-63, professor and director, 1963—. Visiting professor at University of California, Berkeley, summer, 1964, University of California, Santa Barbara, summer, 1967, University of Rochester, summer, 1970, University of Isphahan, winter and spring, 1977, and in Alexandria, Egypt, 1979; American Council of Learned Societies Lecturer in the History of Religions, 1971. Member of National Seminar on Pakistan, and UNESCO Commission for Establishment of an Institute of Higher Education in the Arab Countries, 1974-75. Consultant to National Selection Committee for Foreign Area Fellowship, Social Science Research Council, 1970, and American Council of Learned Societies Selection Committee for South Asia Awards, 1971. Trustee, Obor Foundation, 1976—. *Military service:* U.S. Army Air Forces, airborne radio operator, 1942-45.

MEMBER: American Society for the Study of Religion (treasurer; vice-president; president), American Oriental Society, American Academy of Religion, Middle East Studies Association (founding member; vice-president, 1971), Association for Asian Studies. *Awards, honors:* Ford Foundation foreign training and research fellowship, 1954-57; Rockefeller Foundation research fellowship, 1958-59; Canada Council senior leave award, 1968-69.

WRITINGS: (Editor) *A Reader's Guide to the Great Religions*, Free Press, 1965, 2nd edition, 1976; (editor) *The Ethico-Religious Concepts in the Qur'an*, McGill University Press, 1966; (with Janet O'Dea and Thomas F. O'Dea) *Religion and Man: Judaism, Christianity and Islam*, Harper, 1972; (editor) *Iranian Civilization and Culture: Essays in Honor of the 2500th Anniversary of the Founding of the Persian Empire*, McGill-Queens University Press, 1973; (author of preface) Jean Rene Milot, *L'Islam et les Musulmans*, Fides, 1975; (author of foreword) Mihr Afroz Murad, *Intellectual Modernism of Shibli Nucmani: An Exposition of His Religious and Political Ideas*, Institute of Islamic Culture (Lahore), 1976.

Contributor: Joseph M. Kitagawa, editor, *Modern Trends in World Religions*, [LaSalle, Illinois], 1959; Donald E. Smith, editor, *South Asian Politics and Religion*, Princeton University Press, 1966; Kitagawa, editor, *History of Religions*, University of Chicago Press, 1967; Aziz Ahmad and G. E. von Grunebaum, editors, *Muslim Self-Statement in India and Pakistan*, Otto Harrossowitz (Wiesbaden), 1970; Richard Comstock, editor, *Religion and Man*, Harper, 1971; G. Parrinder, editor, *Man and His Gods: Encyclopaedia of the World's Religions*, Hamlyn Publishing, 1971; Roger Savory, *History of Islamic Civilization*, Cambridge University Press, 1975; Donald P. Little, editor, *Essays on Islamic Civilization Presented to Niyazi Berkes*, E. J. Brill, 1976; Leonard Binder, editor, *The Study of the Middle East*, Wiley, 1976.

Contributor to journals, including *Journal des Notaires, Christian Outlook, New Values, Arab Journal,* and *Religious Studies Review*. Contributor of articles to encyclopedias, including *Encyclopaedia Britannica, Encyclopedia Americana,* and *World Book Encyclopedia*. Editor of "McGill Islamic Series," and *Religious Studies Review;* co-editor of *Hikmat-i-Irani*, sixteen volumes.

SIDELIGHTS: Charles J. Adams is proficient in Arabic, French, German, and Urdu. *Avocational interests:* Woodworking and travelling.

* * *

AERS, David 1946-

PERSONAL: Born October 3, 1946, in Lahore, India; son of Ian and Pamela (Ridgeway) Aers. *Education:* Cambridge University, B.A., 1968, M.A., 1972; University of York, Ph.D., 1971. *Office:* School of English and American Studies, University of East Anglia, Norwich, England.

CAREER: University of East Anglia, Norwich, England, lecturer, 1971—.

WRITINGS: (Editor with Mary Ann Radzinowicz) John Milton, *Paradise Lost*, Books VII-VIII, Cambridge University Press, 1974; *Piers Plowman and Christian Allegory*, St. Martin's, 1975; *Chaucer, Langland, and the Creative Imagination*, Routledge & Kegan Paul, 1980; (with Jon Cook and David Punter) *Romanticism and Ideology*, Routledge & Kegan Paul, 1981; (with Bob Hodge and Gunter Kress) *Literature, Language and Society in England, 1580-1680*, Barnes & Noble, 1981. Contributor of articles to scholarly journals.

WORK IN PROGRESS: "Working on a further study of Chaucer and a study on literature, religion, and ideology from the late Middle Ages into the seventeenth century."

SIDELIGHTS: David Aers wrote *CA*: "I see the activity of writing and teaching as indissolubly bound up with one's social and political aspirations, one's central convictions about the overall project of human emancipation—at the moment the chief task of all humanists and responsible religious people seems to be the active involvement in the rapidly growing international peace movement in opposition to the massive increase of weapons and mass slaughter so cultivated by United States and USSR today."

AINSLIE, Tom
See CARTER, Richard

* * *

AINSWORTH, Mary D(insmore) Salter 1913-
(Mary D. Salter)

PERSONAL: Born December 1, 1913, in Glendale, Ohio; daughter of Charles Morgan (president of Aluminum Goods Ltd.) and Mary (Hoover) Salter; married Leonard H. Ainsworth, June 10, 1950 (divorced, 1960). *Education:* University of Toronto, B.A., 1935, M.A., 1936, Ph.D., 1939. *Office:* Department of Psychology, Gilmer Hall, University of Virginia, Charlottesville, Va. 22901.

CAREER: University of Toronto, Toronto, Ontario, instructor, 1938-41, lecturer in psychology, 1941-42; Canadian Government, Department of Veterans' Affairs, Ottawa, Ontario, superintendent of women's rehabilitation, 1945-46; University of Toronto, assistant professor of psychology and co-director of research project evaluating security, Institute for Child Study, 1946-50; Tavistock Clinic, London, England, senior research psychologist, 1950-54; East African Institute for Social Research, Kampala, Uganda, senior research fellow, 1954-55; Johns Hopkins University, Baltimore, Md., lecturer, 1956-59, associate professor, 1959-63, professor of psychology, 1963-75; University of Virginia, Charlottesville, professor of psychology, 1975—. Psychology assistant, Department of Veteran Affairs, Canada, 1947-50; psychologist, Sheppard and Enoch Pratt Hospital, 1956-61. *Military service:* Canadian Womens Army Corps, 1942-46; consultant to director of personnel selection; became major.

MEMBER: American Psychological Association, British Psychological Society, Society for Research in Child Development, Association for Child Psychology and Psychiatry, American Association for the Advancement of Science, Eastern Psychological Association, Sigma Xi. *Awards, honors:* Fellow of Center for Advanced Study in the Behavorial Sciences, 1967-68; Distinguished Contribution Award, Maryland Psychological Association, 1973; fellow of Center for Advanced Study, University of Virginia, 1975-77.

WRITINGS: (Under name Mary D. Salter, with A. W. Ham) *Doctor in the Making,* Lippincott, 1943; (with B. Klopfer, W. G. Klopfer, and R. R. Holt) *Developments in the Rorschach Technique,* Volume I, World Book Co., 1954; (with Leonard H. Ainsworth) *Measuring Security in Personal Adjustment,* University of Toronto Press, 1958; (with J. Bowlby) *Child Care and the Growth of Love,* 2nd edition (Ainsworth was not associated with first edition), Penguin, 1965; *Infancy in Uganda: Infant Care and the Growth of Love,* Johns Hopkins Press, 1967; (with M. C. Blehar, E. Waters, and S. Wall) *Patterns of Attachment: A Psychological Study of the Strange Situation,* Erlbaum, 1978.

Contributor: (With S. M. Bell) A. Ambrose, editor, *Stimulation in Early Infancy,* Academic Press, 1969; (with Bell and D. V. Stayton) H. R. Schaffer, editor, *The Origins of Human Social Relations,* Academic Press, 1971; J. L. Gewirtz, editor, *Attachment and Dependency,* V. H. Winston, 1972; B. M. Caldwell and H. W. Ricciuti, editors, *Review of Child Development Research,* University of Chicago Press, 1974; (with Bell and Stayton) M.P.M. Richards, editor, *The Integration of a Child into a Social World,* Cambridge University Press, 1974; (with Bell) K. J. Connolly and J. Bruaer, editors, *The Growth of Competence,* Academic Press, 1974; (with I. Bretherton) M. Lewis and L. A. Rosenblum, editors, *The Origin of Fear,* Wiley, 1974.

P. H. Leiderman, S. R. Tuekin, and A. Rosenfeld, editors, *Culture and Infancy: Variations in the Human Experience,* Academic Press, 1977; J. M. Tanner, editor, *Developments in Psychiatric Research: Essays Based on the Sir Geoffrey Vickers Lectures of the Mental Health Foundation,* Hodder & Stoughton, 1977; J. S. Rosenblatt, R. A. Hindi, C. Beer, and M. Busnel, editors, *Advances in the Study of Behavior,* Volume IX, Academic Press, 1979; (with Bretherton) M. A. Roy, editor, *Species Identity and Attachment: A Phylogenetic Evaluation,* Garland Publishing, 1979; G. Gerbner, C. J. Ross, and E. Zigler, editors, *Child Abuse: An Agenda for Action,* Oxford University Press, 1980; C. M. Parkes and J. Stevenson-Hindi, editors, *The Place of Attachment in Human Behavior,* Basic Books, 1982.

WORK IN PROGRESS: Research into the development of infant-mother attachment.

* * *

ALBEE, Edward (Franklin III) 1928-

PERSONAL: Surname pronounced *All*-bee; born March 12, 1928, probably in Virginia; adopted son of Reed A. (part-owner of Keith-Albee theatre circuit) and Frances (Cotter) Albee. *Education:* Attended Trinity College, Hartford, Conn., 1946-47. *Religion:* Christian. *Home address:* 14 Harrison St., New York, N.Y. 10013; and Box 697, Mountauk, Long Island, N.Y. 11954.

CAREER: Writer, producer, and director of plays. Worked as continuity writer for WNYC-radio, office boy for Warwick & Legler (advertising agency), record salesman for G. Schirmer, Inc. (music publishers), and counterman in luncheonette of Manhattan Towers Hotel; messenger for Western Union, 1955-58. Producer, with Richard Barr and Clinton Wilder, New Playwrights Unit Workshop, 1963—; director of touring retrospective of his one-act plays including, "The Zoo Story," "The American Dream," "Fam and Yam," "The Sandbox," "Box," "Quotations from Chairman Mao Tse-Tung," "Counting the Ways," and "Listening," produced as "Albee Directs Albee," 1978-79; co-director of Vivian Beaumont Theatre at Lincoln Center for the Performing Arts, New York, N.Y., 1979—. Founder of William Flanagan Center for Creative Persons in Montauk, N.Y., 1971. Member of National Endowment grant-giving council; member of governing commission of New York State Council for the Arts. Lecturer at college campuses. Cultural exchange visitor to U.S.S.R. and Latin American countries for U.S. State Department.

AWARDS, HONORS: Berlin Festival Award, 1959, for "The Zoo Story," and 1961, for "The Death of Bessie Smith"; Vernon Rice Memorial Award, and Obie Award, 1960, and Argentine Critics Circle Award, 1961, all for "The Zoo Story"; "The Death of Bessie Smith" and "The American Dream" chosen as best plays of the 1960-61 season by Foreign Press Association, 1961; Lola D'Annunzio Award, 1961, for "The American Dream"; selected as most promising playwright of 1962-63 season by New York Drama Critics, 1963; New York Drama Critics Circle Award, Foreign Press Association Award, Antoinette Perry ("Tony") Award, Outer Circle Award, *Saturday Review* Drama Critics Award, and *Variety* Drama Critics' Poll Award, 1963, and *Evening Standard* Award, 1964, all for "Who's Afraid of Virginia Woolf?"; with Richard Barr and Clinton Wilder, recipient of Margo Jones Award, 1965, for encouraging new playwrights; Pulitzer Prize, 1967, for "A Delicate Balance," and 1975, for "Seascape"; D.Litt., Emerson College, 1967, and Trinity College, 1974; American Academy and Institute of Arts and Letters Gold Medal, 1980.

WRITINGS—Plays, except as indicated: *The Zoo Story, The Death of Bessie Smith, The Sandbox: Three Plays* ("The Zoo Story," first produced [in German] in Berlin at Schiller Theater Werkstatt, September 28, 1959, produced Off-Broadway at Provincetown Playhouse, January 14, 1960; "The Death of Bessie Smith," first produced in Berlin at Schlosspark Theater, April 21, 1960, produced Off-Broadway at York Playhouse, February 28, 1961; "The Sandbox," first produced in New York, N.Y. at Jazz Gallery, May 15, 1960, produced Off-Broadway at Cherry Lane Theatre, February, 1962, directed by author), Coward, 1960, published with "The American Dream" (also see below) as *The Zoo Story and Other Plays*, J. Cape, 1962; (author of libretto with James Hinton, Jr.) "Bartleby" (opera; adaptation of story by Herman Melville; music by William Flanagan), produced Off-Broadway at York Playhouse, January 24, 1961; *The American Dream*, with introduction by the author (produced Off-Broadway at York Playhouse, January 24, 1961), Coward, 1961; *Fam and Yam* (produced in Westport, Conn. at White Barn Theatre, August 27, 1960), Dramatists Play Service, 1961; *Who's Afraid of Virginia Woolf?* (produced on Broadway at Billy Rose Theatre, October 13, 1962), Atheneum, 1962; *The Ballad of the Sad Cafe* (adaptation of novella of same title by Carson McCullers; produced on Broadway at Martin Beck Theatre, October 30, 1963), Houghton, 1963; *Tiny Alice* (produced on Broadway at Billy Rose Theatre, December 29, 1964), Atheneum, 1965.

Malcolm (adaptation of novel of same title by James Purdy; produced on Broadway at Sam S. Shubert Theatre, January 11, 1966), Atheneum, 1966; *A Delicate Balance* (produced on Broadway at Martin Beck Theatre, September 22, 1966), Atheneum, 1966; "Breakfast at Tiffany's" (musical; adaptation of story of same title by Truman Capote; music by Bob Merrill), produced in Philadelphia, 1966, produced on Broadway at Majestic Theatre, December, 1966; *Everything in the Garden* (based on play by Giles Cooper; produced on Broadway at Plymouth Theatre, November 29, 1967), Atheneum, 1968; *Box* [and] *Quotations from Chairman Mao Tse-Tung* (two interrelated plays; first produced at Studio Arena Theater, Buffalo, N.Y.; produced on Broadway at Billy Rose Theatre, September 30, 1968), Atheneum, 1969.

All Over (produced on Broadway at Martin Beck Theatre, January 26, 1971; produced in London by Royal Shakespeare Co. at Aldwych Theatre, January 31, 1972), Atheneum, 1971; *Seascape* (produced on Broadway at Sam S. Shubert Theatre, January 26, 1975, directed by author), Atheneum, 1975.

Counting the Ways [and] *Listening: Two Plays* ("Counting the Ways," first produced in London by National Theatre Co., 1976, produced by Hartford Stage Co., Hartford, Conn., January 28, 1977; "Listening: A Chamber Play" [produced as radio play by British Broadcasting Corp. (BBC), 1976], first produced on stage by Hartford Stage Co., Hartford, January 28, 1977), Atheneum, 1977; *The Lady from Dubuque* (produced on Broadway at Morosco Theatre, January 31, 1980), Atheneum, 1979.

"Lolita" (adaptation of novel of same title by Vladimir Nabokov), first produced in Boston at Wilbur Theatre, January 15, 1981, produced on Broadway at Brooks Atkinson Theatre, March 19, 1981; "The Man Who Had Three Arms," first produced in Miami, Fla., at New World Festival, June 10, 1982, directed by the author, produced in Chicago, Ill. at Goodman Theater, October 4, 1982, directed by the author.

Author of introduction: Noel Coward, *Three Plays by Noel Coward: Blithe Spirit, Hay Fever,* [and] *Private Lives,* Delta, 1965; Phyllis Johnson Kaye, editor, *National Playwrights Directory,* 2nd edition, Eugene O'Neill Theater Center (Waterford, Conn.), 1981; (with Sabina Lietzmann) *New York,* Vendome Press, 1981; *Louise Nevelson: Atmospheres and Environments,* Clarkson N. Potter, Inc., 1981.

Also author of screenplays, including an adaptation of *Le Locataire* (title means "The Tenant"), a novel by Roland Topor, an adaptation of his "The Death of Bessie Smith," one about the life of Nijinsky, and one about Stanford White and Evelyn Nesbitt. Also contributor of articles to magazines.

WORK IN PROGRESS: Two plays, "Attila the Hun" and "Quitting."

SIDELIGHTS: Reviewing the numerous commentaries written about Edward Albee's plays, C.W.E. Bigsby notes in *Edward Albee: A Collection of Critical Essays* that in comparison to Albee "few playwrights . . . have been so frequently and mischievously misunderstood, misrepresented, overpraised, denigrated, and precipitatedly dismissed." Capsulizing the changing tone of Albee criticism since the early sixties (when his first play appeared), Bigsby offers this overview: "Canonized after . . . *The Zoo Story,* [Albee] found himself in swift succession billed as America's most promising playwright, leading dramatist, and then, with astonishing suddenness, a 'one-hit' writer. . . . The progression was essentially that suggested by George in [Albee's] *Who's Afraid of Virginia Woolf?,* 'better, best, bested.'"

To symbolize the curve of Albee's reputation as a dramatist, Bigsby chooses this phrase from a play designated by many critics as a dividing line in the playwright's career. T. E. Kalem, for example, in *Time* remarks: "Albee almost seems to have lived through two careers, one very exciting, the other increasingly depressing. From *The Zoo Story* through *The American Dream* to *Who's Afraid of Virginia Woolf?,* he displayed great gusto, waspish humor and feral power. In the succeeding . . . years, he has foundered in murky metaphysics, . . . dabbled in adaptations, . . . and gone down experimental blind alleys." Stanley Kauffmann gives a similar evaluation in *New Republic:* "Ever since . . . *Virginia Woolf*—Albee's last good play—all we've been getting . . . are abortions: two plays and three adaptations that are all varyingly bad and two one-act plays [as of 1971] that are Absurdist imitations."

However, many critics have praised these same plays. Albee continues to win awards; he received two Pulitzer Prizes since *Virginia Woolf,* one in 1967 for *A Delicate Balance,* and one in 1975, for *Seascape.* Walter Wagner in *The Playwrights Speak* notes, "[Albee] is a successful dramatist because of his intelligence, perceptions, talent and willingness to treat questions that few American playwrights examined before him." Brian Way, in *American Theatre,* while conceding what he judges to be limitations in the scope of Albee's writing, also praises the dramatist: "It is only fair that one should return to an assertion of the importance of Albee's good qualities in the American theatre. If it is true that he inhabits a finite world, he does so with brilliance, inventiveness, intelligence, and moral courage." And, according to Ruby Cohn in *Dialogue in American Drama,* Albee is "the most skillful composer of dialogue that America has produced."

Bigsby offers an explanation of the ongoing critical attacks on Albee's ability as a playwright: "There is no doubt that the Broadway production of . . . *Virginia Woolf* provided the basis for Albee's amazing popular reputation; . . . equally certainly, it was also the primary reason for the suspicion with which some reviewers and critics approached his work. . . . The success of . . . *Virginia Woolf* established Albee's reputation around the world. . . . And now, public and reviewers alike expected him to repeat his earlier success. [But] the truth was that Albee has remained at heart a product of Off-Broadway, claiming the same freedom to experiment and, indeed, fail, which is the special strength of that theatre."

The playwright, in spite of negative criticism, has not been "bested" by the critics. He continues in his role as dramatist, writing usually one play a year. In a *Washington Post* interview with David Richards, Albee explains his own reaction to the critics: "I have been both overpraised and underpraised. I assume by the time I finish writing—and I plan to go on writing until I'm ninety or gaga—it will all equal itself out. . . . You can't involve yourself with the vicissitudes of fashion or critical response. I'm fairly confident that my work is going to be around for a while."

Although stylistically varied, Albee's plays are thematically connected. Gerald Weales in *The Jumping Off Place: American Drama in the 1960's* notes: "Each new Albee play seems to be an experiment in form, in style . . . , and yet there is unity to his work as a whole. This is apparent in the devices and the characters that recur, modified according to context, but it is most obvious in the repetition of theme, in the basic assumptions about the human condition that underlie all his work."

Reviewing Albee's touring retrospective of eight of his one-act plays, "Albee Directs Albee," Sylvie Drake of the *Los Angeles Times* observes: "This condensation of work reveals Albee's consistent and enduring concern with loss. . . . 'Pain is understanding,' says someone in [Albee's play] 'Counting the Ways.' 'It's really loss.' Yes. These plays are *all* about loss." In her analysis of Albee's plays Drake also discovers the following themes: "the chasm between people, [and] their inability to connect except through pain."

John MacNicholas, writing in *Dictionary of Literary Biography,* says the development of these themes in Albee's plays started with his very first play, *The Zoo Story.* According to Way, this play, a tale of a fairly prosperous married man and his confrontation on a Central Park bench with a totally alienated young drifter, "is an exploration of the farce and agony of human isolation."

George Wellwarth, in *The Theater of Protest and Paradox,* explains the play's thematic content in more detail: "[Albee] is exemplifying or demonstrating a theme. That theme is the enormous and usually insuperable difficulty that human beings find in communicating with each other. More precisely, it is about the maddening effect that the enforced loneliness of the human existence condition has on the person who is cursed (for in our society it undoubtedly is a curse) with an infinite capacity for love."

Albee's thematic preoccupation with loss of contact between individuals is tied to the playwright's desire to make a statement about American values, as Weales points out. "In much of his work," according to the critic, "there is a suggestion . . . that the emptiness and loneliness of the characters are somehow the result of a collapse of values in the Western world, in general, in the United States, in particular." Albee finds the feelings of loss and emptiness prevalent in the society that surrounds him.

Howard Schneider elaborates on this idea in a *Pittsburgh Press* article: "[Albee] hammers incessantly [at this theme] when he talks at college campuses. The 'disengagement' of the population. The passivity of Americans drawn to a television set six hours a day. The religious, political and social structures that men have created to 'illusion' themselves from the world and each other." Schneider quotes Albee's own explanation of the themes present in his work: "People who are passive and who are careless contribute to the decline of the system, especially in a democracy. . . . People still refuse to think and act honorably with each other. They are still mean and vicious and these are the subjects of my plays."

Following *The Zoo Story,* three Albee plays opened in New York during 1960-61. All of these—*The Sandbox, The American Dream,* and *The Death of Bessie Smith*—"attack certain features in American society," according to MacNicholas. *The Death of Bessie Smith,* for example, deals with the death of the black singer who bled to death after an automobile accident, apparently because she was denied care at a nearby all-white hospital. *The American Dream* and *The Sandbox* share the same characters—Mommy, Daddy, and Grandma. MacNicholas feels that these two plays "form a continuum in subject matter and technique; both attack indifference to love, pity, and compassion. In both . . . , the characters . . . live in a kind of moral narcosis."

Allen Lewis, in *American Plays and Playwrights of the Contemporary Theatre,* comments: "*The American Dream* is a wildly imaginative caricature of the American family. . . . [In this play] Albee is the angry young man, tearing apart the antiseptic mirage of American middle-class happiness."

The American family of the play is comprised of characters known only as "Mommy" (a domineering shrew), "Daddy" (a weak hen-pecked husband), and "Grandma" (an older version of "Mommy"). Set in the family's stuffy apartment, the play includes the story of the couple's adoption of a "bumble of joy" whom they destroy after discovering his various defects. (For example, they cut out his tongue when he says a dirty word.) As he grows up, Mommy and Daddy complain that the baby has no head on his shoulders, is spineless, and has feet of clay. They complain again when he dies after having already been paid for. Near the end of the play, the baby's twin appears. He is a handsome young man who describes himself as a "clean-cut midwest farm boy type, almost insultingly good-looking in a typically American way." "The young man," as Frederick Lumley notes in *New Trends in Twentieth Century Drama,* "feels that he is incomplete, he doesn't know what has happened to something within him, but he has no touch, he is unable to make love, to see anything with pity; in fact he has no feeling."

Continuing his interpretation of the play, Lewis states: "The American Dream [of the title] is the young man who is all appearance and no feelings. . . . He says: 'I cannot touch another person and feel love . . . I have no emotions. . . . I have now only my person . . . my body, my face. . . . I let people love me. . . . I feel nothing.'"

In his preface to *The American Dream,* Albee explains the play's content: "The play is an examination of the American Scene, an attack on the substitution of artificial for real values in our society, a condemnation of complacency, cruelty, emasculation and vacuity; it is a stand against the fiction that everything in this slipping land of ours is peachy-keen."

According to MacNicholas, Albee continues his critique of American society in his first three-act play, *Who's Afraid of Virginia Woolf?.* Critics note a relationship between this play and *The American Dream.* Martin Esslin, writing in *The Theatre of the Absurd,* comments: "A closer inspection reveals elements which clearly . . . relate [*Virginia Woolf*] to Albee's earlier work. . . . George and Martha [a couple in the play] (there are echoes here of George and Martha Washington) have an imaginary child which they treat as real, until in the cold dawn of that wild night [in which the action of the play takes place] they decide to 'kill' it by abandoning their joint fantasy. Here the connection to *The American Dream* with its horrid dream-child of the ideal all-American boy becomes clear. . . . Is the dream-child which cannot become real among people torn by ambition and lust something like the American ideal itself?"

Drake finds George and Martha of *Virginia Woolf* directly related to Mommy and Daddy of *The American Dream*. Lumley describes this evolution: "The Mommy and Daddy of . . . *Virginia Woolf* are this time given names, Martha and George, thus becoming individuals instead of abstract characters. . . . They have been unable to have children; so that their love is mixed-up sexual humiliation, a strong love-hate relationship which makes them want to hurt and claw and wound each other because they know each other and cannot do without one another."

In the *Arizona Quarterly*, James P. Quinn describes the combination of social criticism and the theme of human isolation in *Virginia Woolf:* "In [the play] the author parodies the ideals of western civilization. . . . Thus, romantic love, marriage, sex, the family, status, competition, power all the 'illusions' man has erected to eliminate the differences between self and others and to escape the . . . burden of his freedom and loneliness come under attack."

Critics also note a continuation of theme and social awareness in Albee's more recent plays. For example, Harold Clurman, in his *Nation* review of *All Over*, writes: "Albee is saying [in this play] that despite all the hasty bickering, the fierce hostility and the mutual misunderstandings which separate us, we need one another. We cry out in agony when we are cut off." Bigsby, commenting on the same play, concludes: "Albee's concern in *All Over* is essentially that of his earlier work. He remains intent on penetrating the bland urbanities of social life in an attempt to identify the crucial failure of nerve which has brought individual men and whole societies to the point of not merely soulless anomie but even of apocalypse."

Bigsby also finds similar characteristics in Albee's play *Box*, calling it "a protest against the dangerously declining quality of life—a decline marked . . . by the growth of an amoral technology with a momentum and direction of its own." And, MacNicholas notes Albee's preoccupation with loss in *A Delicate Balance:* "[The play] concerns itself with loss: not loss which occurs in one swift traumatic stroke, but that which evolves slowly in increments of gentle and lethal acquiesence."

Although Albee has not achieved commercial success with all his plays, his impact on twentieth-century American drama is undeniable, according to Richards. He comments, "Despite what [the playwright] calls 'the ritual slaughter of Albee' each time he unveils a new play, he remains one of the key reference points of American theater." Alan Schneider, in *Tulane Drama Review*, finds that Albee's impact is due to his ability to touch people emotionally with his plays. The critic remarks, "Anyone who has read any portion of any play [Albee] has ever written surely must sense the depth of his purpose and recognize . . . the power of the talent which is at his disposal; certainly no . . . individual today can fail to recognize somewhere in Albee's characters and moods the stirring of his own viscera, the shadow of his own self-knowledge." In conclusion, MacNicholas writes, "Albee's ideals about man and art and his formidable technical skills representing them on stage unquestionably place him in the first rank of the dramatists of this century."

MEDIA ADAPTATIONS: *Who's Afraid of Virginia Woolf* was adapted and filmed by Warner Bros. in 1966.

AVOCATIONAL INTERESTS: Travel, playing the harpsichord.

CA INTERVIEW

CA interviewed Edward Albee by phone August 4, 1981, at his home in Montauk, N.Y.

CA: You wrote poetry and fiction for more than ten years before turning to playwriting. Although the poetry and fiction went largely unpublished, was the experience of writing them helpful to you in specific ways?

ALBEE: It goes back more than ten years before I started writing plays, because I started writing poetry when I was about six, and didn't write a play until I was twenty-nine. I'm sure it was useful, since it made me decide when I was six or whatever that I was a writer, and I kept on doing it—not terribly well, I must say—until I hit upon playwriting, and then I did that better. I'm sure it was useful to me since it convinced me there was no other way to live.

CA: When you're not directing your own plays, what sort of working relationship do you have with the director?

ALBEE: In theory and ideally the relationship is a good one because it is based upon a great deal of contact before rehearsals begin, to make sure the director and I are working on exactly the same play, that his or her goals are exactly the same as mine, that we are in mutual agreement on casting, though I retain for my own right absolute veto of casting and absolute approval. I must have the full cooperation of the director on interpretation of the play, on casting, on set and costumes, and a lot of discussions before rehearsals begin, and then a close relationship once rehearsals have begun, never stepping on the director's toes, of course, never talking to an actor without the director's permission about a matter of interpretation, and letting the director be the conduit between the author and the actor. This is all theory and all ideal.

It has worked out quite often, with people such as Alan Schneider and Peter Hall. Every once in a while the communication breaks down, or the director feels that he has rights and obligations, or the producer intrudes, and this perfectly healthy relationship is destroyed. One of the reasons I direct a lot of my own plays is to avoid this breakdown of communication.

CA: In these discussions that precede the actual beginnings of putting the play together, do you ever find that the director has some kind of insight into the play that you didn't intend or didn't have?

ALBEE: Quite often. If it's an intention that I think diminishes the play, then the director is wrong. If it's an insight that makes the play far more interesting than I had intended, I instantly pretend that it was my idea to begin with.

CA: Do you attend rehearsals?

ALBEE: I stay away for the first ten days and let them all work privately. Then I start coming in before things get to a point when they can't be changed.

CA: You have done a great deal personally to subsidize the work of playwrights you felt were deserving of an audience but were unlikely to get commercial backing. How do you feel about government subsidy for playwrights?

ALBEE: What government subsidy for playwrights? I think the Reagan administration has destroyed government participation in the health of the arts in this country, so it's an academic question. But we do have an extraordinary opportunity in this country. We are one of the few countries that can, at its healthiest, subsidize creative artists without censoring creative artists. It's an amazing opportunity. I've sat on the National Endowment grant-giving council, and presently I'm on the governing commission of the New York State Council for the Arts. I've watched very carefully, and I've never seen any censorship involved in the subsidy of the arts. The money can be given (in theory) to Trotskyites, to neofascists, to anybody who seems artistically worthy. It's an amazing opportunity, and it's one of the things that saddens me so much about the Reagan administration's decision to get the government out of subsidy for the arts. It's always seemed to me that education in the arts is part of public education. Since our government is determined to see that our people are educated up through high school, then I believe the government also has the responsibility to educate people in the arts.

CA: Do you think business or any other private interest will manage to fill the gap that's now being widened by recent budget cuts?

ALBEE: I suppose, if the federal government makes the tax basis more advantageous for private industry or private foundations or public foundations to aid the arts, they will. That's fine, and there's a good deal of money floating around that could be used for that purpose, but I don't understand why the government wants to get out of it. The reason that it's cut so heavily is that it's conspicuous; the vast majority of people who don't avail themselves of string quartets or Samuel Beckett or Jackson Pollock are going to be pleased.

CA: The critics have applied numerous labels to your work for purposes of discussion and assessment. Do you think this practice has narrowed the usefulness of critical writing about your work, or has it been illuminating in some way?

ALBEE: I was reading just the other day—to get some quotes for a reissue of four of my plays that are being done in a continuing reissue of all of my plays—some of the criticism of my work going back to 1960 and 1961, and I'm startled by it. There's no relationship to my memory of what the work was like; there's no relationship to any reality that I've ever come across. Critical labeling is a kind of shorthand that succeeds in cutting off thought. Back in the days when I was first beginning my playwriting, Martin Esslin was coming out with his book called *Theater of the Absurd*. Every new American and European playwright whose work was being done in the equivalent of Off-Broadway was labeled as part of the Theater of the Absurd. It was far easier for critics to do that than to think. And I don't think the critics have changed much.

CA: Why do you think there was so much critical misunderstanding of Who's Afraid of Virginia Woolf? *when it was first produced?*

ALBEE: I think there's been critical misunderstanding of just about every one of my plays. I read the reviews of *The Lady from Dubuque*, for example, and of *Seascape*, and there's just as much critical misunderstanding and confusion as to what I was about in those as there was with *Virginia Woolf*. There wasn't really *misunderstanding* about *Virginia Woolf* except from Walter Kerr, who didn't understand the basic metaphor of the play. But some of the critics were so deeply offended by the language of the play, by hearing onstage the same language that they used in their own living rooms, that they fell apart. That was . . . when? Kennedy was already in office; I'm surprised that we were filled with such self-delusion at that point. I'd be less surprised if I wrote *Virginia Woolf* next year and had the same response. It seems to me, given the repressive attitude of our government these days and the Moral Majority and all this dangerous neofascist nonsense that's coming to the fore in this country, I wouldn't be surprised if we had that particular kind of high-falutin', self-righteous, critical attitude again.

CA: Is there, in your opinion, any intelligent theater criticism being written now?

ALBEE: The simplest answer to that, of course (and it's the same answer that every playwright believes, although I'm one of the few foolhardy enough to state it), is that if a critic says something favorable about you, he's being intelligent, and if he's saying something unfavorable, he's being dumb. We all think this; we all believe it; when we get together in the Dramatists Guild, this is our concerted opinion; but I'm the only one stupid enough to say it.

CA: What role do you think the critics should play in theater?

ALBEE: They *should* be a useful conduit between the audience and the play. But they far too often set themselves up as a barrier, given the limitations of their own aesthetic and their own intelligence. Plus the fact that a number of them think they should *reflect* the taste of their readers rather than *create* the taste of their readers. I tell audiences who come to my lectures that there's absolutely nothing wrong with reading a critic, *any* critic, no matter how bright he is or how stupid he is, as long as you know the limits of that critic's perceptions. All criticism is an act of prejudice. It's either informed prejudice or uninformed prejudice, and you damned well, before you commit yourself to reading a critic, should know what his aesthetic is. You should know whether he's intelligent or stupid, whether he's avant-garde or mainstream, what his limitations are, because the only information you're going to get from a critic is information based upon his limits. People should never read what a critic says as fact. If people stopped doing that, I would have no argument about any critic any place.

CA: A lot of people who don't have direct access to much theater rely on the critics' writing to find out what's going on.

ALBEE: They should go one step further. If they are misinformed by a critic—"Gee, I went to see this because Frank Rich said it was high art"—and they finally come to the conclusion that what Frank Rich says is high art is quite often middlebrow, then they should begin to understand the difference between high art and middlebrow, at least as far as that critic is concerned. If they don't have the opportunity to see the play, they're not affecting the state of the theater, so it doesn't matter. A theoretical grasp is of absolutely no use. These people don't go to the theater and they don't affect what the producers are willing to do. Unfortunately, it's those people who *do* go to the theater who basically, at least in the commercial theater, want to escape rather than engage, to have a "good time" rather than a serious time, who are destroying our theater.

CA: What are the greatest difficulties in doing adaptations?

ALBEE: Probably that unfortunate electrical-chemical connection of the brain that persuades you to do the adaptation in the first place, that moment of insanity that persuades you that it's a good idea.

CA: Will you continue to do adaptations?

ALBEE: Considering what's happened to the last couple, I probably shouldn't. I don't have any plans to at the moment. *Lolita* went badly primarily because the production got out of hand, I think. The script wasn't bad, but the production was appalling.

CA: Would you comment on regional theater in this country —what role it should play, whether it is playing the role it should, and how it might be improved?

ALBEE: Ideally, regional theater should be an educational and entertainment instrument informing people around the country of what our best serious world theater is all about, so that people can start making intelligent decisions when they happen by some mischance to stumble upon new work in the theater. And a lot of our regional theaters are living up to this challenge. Some of them, however, are interested in catching the brass ring, of doing those plays which commercial managers will pick up and take to Broadway. They're misusing their function, they're becoming tryouts for commercial managements, and they're doing plays of lesser magnitude and less adventuresomeness only because they think if they do more middlebrow plays, they'll get transferred to Broadway. That's happening more and more in our regional theaters, and it's very sad. There's practically no new American play put on Broadway any more that hasn't been "tried out," as it's put, in regional theater. And that's pretty sad, too.

CA: Several times in past interviews and articles you've listed playwrights you liked. Are there new or very recent ones whose work you find exceptionally good?

ALBEE: Yes, there are, but I was reading over some old scrapbooks the other day and I saw myself giving this list of young playwrights whom I admired, and I was startled by the fact that two-thirds or three-quarters of them have sunk without a trace since I mentioned their names. I've come to the conclusion that if I mention anybody's name, it's going to be very bad for his career. I've stopped doing it.

CA: Many young playwrights are turning to movies; they seem to feel they can make a better living in that way.

ALBEE: They're turning to movies because they want to make a lot of money, and they don't seem to care much that they become hired hands. The nice thing about the theater *still* is that it's *still* possible to be your own man. You're not an employee; you're not owned by your bosses. It's still possible in the theater; in movies it's not possible. Writers look at the movies that gross three hundred million and see themselves tacked onto one-half of a percent of that gross, and they sell their souls to Hollywood.

CA: What questions are you asked most frequently on lecture tours to colleges and universities?

ALBEE: There are three that I get asked all the time, to the point that when I begin the question-and-answer period following the lecture, I always say that there are three questions that you must not ask me because they cannot be answered. They are: why do you write, how do you write, and where do your ideas come from? Those are the three most frequently asked questions.

CA: Has the nature of the questions changed over the years?

ALBEE: It varies from college to college, alarmingly. At some, where you least expect it, the students are profoundly informed and intellectually alert; other places where you would think, even though you know better, that they *should* be bright and informed, they're all asleep in the head. I don't know that there's been a basic shift. I'm a little distressed by the lack of social and political involvement that's afflicted our college students in the past eight or ten years. Their goals seem to be graduating, getting a good job, and vanishing into society. There are very few outlaws anymore, and it's too bad.

CA: In 1962 you commented in the New York Times Magazine: *"The health of a nation, a society, can be determined by the art it demands." In the nearly twenty years since that remark, have our demands improved?*

ALBEE: Maybe they did for a short period of time, but now it's come back about to where it was, I think. I think we're just as much into self-deception, into middlebrowism, into easy questions and easy answers as we ever were.

CA: How would you assess the effect of the theatrical experimentation that's been done in those years?

ALBEE: Like all things of any profound moment, the arts affect only a terribly minuscule portion of the people who see them. Those people who matter, who are affected by them, will go right on, their perceptions enlarged by the infection they've received. There are some people who, every time they come out of a safe experience in the theater, who happen to have had a dangerous experience in the past, turn their backs on the dangerous experience in preference to the safe one; but somewhere deep in their subconscious they're saying, "Oh, so you're compromising again, are you?"

CA: In a March, 1980, article in the New Yorker *you said you were getting ready for a cultural exchange program visit to Colombia and Venezuela. Did you make the trip?*

ALBEE: I got as far as Venezuela, and the day I was supposed to leave for Colombia all of the diplomats in Bogota were taken hostage. The State Department didn't want me to go on to Colombia, so I spent an extra week in Venezuela with the theater people. I've only been to Brazil and Argentina and Venezuela in South America. Argentina, when I was there a very long time ago, was even then under the most appalling military dictatorship. Brazil was fairly naive but enthusiastic about international theater in those days. Venezuela seems to be a hotbed of rationalism.

CA: Can you assess the effects of government repression on writers in other countries?

ALBEE: I've traveled around the world a lot—the Soviet Union, South Korea, Argentina, various other countries where the government has come to the conclusion that the arts are disruptive to the order of government—and I've seen an awful lot of brave people in the arts who fight for the right to create as they wish to; I've also seen instances where whole areas of society have been left completely in the dark about what the artistic aesthetic experience is. Any of us who have been to these totalitarian societies, whether they're totalitarian to the right or to the left, come back to this country more and more observant, more and more aware of what could possibly happen here in this country with government control and interference in the arts. Thirty-one thousand intellectuals have been forced out of the Soviet Union in the past ten years—writers, scientists, philosophers. They've found homes in various other countries; but if it ever happens in this country, where will anyone go? There aren't that many places left. We may all have to go to the barricades.

CA: Are there any current or future plans you'd like to talk about?

ALBEE: Contrary to the preference of a number of critics, I'm writing two more plays.

CA: You mentioned earlier the reissues of your plays.

ALBEE: It's a reissue of all of my plays to get them together in four or five volumes rather than various editions all over the place. It'll be easier for the burning.

CA: Don't be a cynic.

ALBEE: No, I'm an optimist. Better burned than unread.

BIOGRAPHICAL/CRITICAL SOURCES—Books: Edward Albee, *The American Dream,* Coward, 1961; George Wellwarth, *The Theater of Protest and Paradox: Development in the Avant-Garde Drama,* New York University Press, 1964; Richard Kostelanetz, *On Contemporary Literature,* Avon, 1964; Allan Lewis, *American Plays and Playwrights in the Contemporary Theatre,* Crown, 1965; Alan S. Downer, editor, *American Drama and Its Critics,* University of Chicago Press, 1965; Walter Wagner, editor, *The Playwrights Speak,* Delacorte, 1967; John Russell Brown and Bernard Harris, editors, *American Theatre,* Edward Arnold, 1967; Gilbert Debusscher, *Edward Albee: Tradition and Renewal,* American Studies Center (Brussels), 1967; Martin Esslin, *The Theatre of the Absurd,* Doubleday, 1969; Michael E. Rutenberg, *Edward Albee: Playwright in Protest,* Avon, 1969; Ruby Cohn, *Edward Albee,* University of Minnesota Press, 1969; Richard E. Amacher, *Edward Albee,* Twayne, 1969; Gerald Weales, *The Jumping Off Place: American Drama in the 1960's,* Macmillan, 1969.

Cohn, *Dialogue in American Drama,* Indiana University Press, 1971; Frederick Lumley, *New Trends in Twentieth Century Drama,* 4th edition, Oxford University Press, 1972; Anne Paolucci, *From Tension to Tonic: The Plays of Edward Albee,* Southern Illinois University Press, 1972; *Contemporary Literary Criticism,* Gale, Volume I, 1973, Volume II, 1974, Volume III, 1975, Volume V, 1976, Volume IX, 1978, Volume XI, 1979, Volume XIII, 1980; *Authors in the News,* Volume I, Gale, 1976; Catharine Hughes, *American Playwrights, 1945-75,* Pitman, 1976; *Dictionary of Literary Biography,* Volume VII: *Twentieth-Century American Dramatists,* Part I, Gale, 1981.

Periodicals: *Theatre Arts,* March, 1961; *New York Times Magazine,* February 25, 1962; *Tulane Drama Review,* spring, 1963, summer, 1965; *Transatlantic Review,* summer, 1963; *New York Times,* December 27, 1964, January 21, 1965, January 13, 1966, August 16, 1966, September 18, 1966, September 24, 1966, October 2, 1966, August 20, 1967, November 26, 1967, April 4, 1971, April 18, 1971, January 27, 1975, February 4, 1977, May 23, 1978, January 27, 1980, March 1, 1981, March 20, 1981, March 29, 1981; *Newsweek,* January 4, 1965, March 18, 1968, April 5, 1971, February 10, 1975, March 30, 1981; *Commonweal,* January 22, 1965; *New Republic,* January 23, 1965, April 17, 1971, February 2, 1975, April 11, 1981; *Hudson Review,* spring, 1965, winter, 1966-67; *Atlantic,* April, 1965; *Prairie Schooner,* fall, 1965.

New Yorker, January 22, 1966, April 3, 1971, March 3, 1980, May 30, 1981; *Saturday Review,* June 4, 1966, April 17, 1971, March 8, 1975, May, 1981; *Books,* July, 1966; *New York World Journal Tribune,* September 22, 1966, October 2, 1966;

Life, October 28, 1966, May 26, 1967, February 2, 1968; *Paris Review,* fall, 1966; *National Observer,* December 4, 1967; *Village Voice,* December 7, 1967, March 21, 1968, October 31, 1968; *New Leader,* December 18, 1967, April 19, 1971; *Nation,* December 18, 1967, March 25, 1968, April 12, 1971, February 23, 1980, April 18, 1981; *Reporter,* December 28, 1967; *Contemporary Literature,* spring, 1968; *Observer Review,* January 19, 1969; *London Magazine,* March, 1969.

New Statesman, January 23, 1970; *Newsday,* March 26, 1971; *Time,* April 5, 1971, February 10, 1975; *Pittsburgh Press,* February 3, 1974; *Arizona Quarterly,* autumn, 1974; *Los Angeles Times,* October 18, 1978; *Washington Post,* February 18, 1979; *Chicago Tribune,* March 26, 1979, September 26, 1982.

People, February 25, 1980, April 6, 1981; *Writer's Digest,* October, 1980; *Detroit News,* June 27, 1982; *Chicago Tribune Book World,* September 26, 1982.

[Sketch reviewed by Edward Albee's assistant, Glyw O'Malley]

—Sketch by Marian Walters
—Interview by Jean W. Ross

* * *

ALBERT, Burton, Jr. 1936-
(Brooks Healey)

PERSONAL: Born September 25, 1936, in Pittsfield, Mass.; son of Burton and Isabel (Deming) Albert; married Lois Bent, June 27, 1963; children: Heather Leigh, Kelley Lynn. *Education:* North Adams State College, B.S. (magna cum laude), 1958; Duke University, M.A., 1962. *Home and office:* 3 Narrow Brook Rd., Weston, Conn. 06883.

CAREER: Elementary school teacher in Greenwich, Conn., 1958-60, 1962-63; high school teacher of English in Greenwich, 1963-64; Harcourt Brace Jovanovich, Inc., New York, N.Y., assistant editor in language arts, 1964-66; *Reader's Digest,* Educational Division, Pleasantville, N.Y., senior editor and product developer, 1966-76, editorial director, 1976-77; Albert Communications, Weston, Conn., educational consultant to businesses and schools, 1977—. *Member:* International Reading Association, National Council of Teachers of English.

WRITINGS: (Contributor) Melissa Costello and Reginold Fickett, editors, *Essays in American and English Literature,* M.S.S. Information, 1976; *Sure Steps to a New Job,* Learning Pyramid, Inc., 1981.

Juveniles: *Codes for Kids,* Albert Whitman, 1976; *Monster Riddles,* Firefly Book Club, 1976; *More Monster Riddles,* Firefly Book Club, 1976; *Puzzle Fun,* Firefly Book Club, 1976; *Mine, Yours, Ours,* Albert Whitman, 1977; *More Codes for Kids,* Albert Whitman, 1979; *Sharks and Whales,* Platt, 1979; *Secrets of Hiding,* Macmillan, 1983; *Clubs for Kids,* Ballantine, 1983.

Textbooks and classroom materials: (Ghostwriter) *Language for Daily Use Workbook,* Harcourt, 1965; (ghostwriter) *Language for Daily Use,* Harcourt, 1966; (contributor) Ronald Noland, Jone Wright, and Elizabeth Allen, editors, *An Introduction to Elementary Reading: Selected Materials,* M.S.S. Information, 1971; (with Donald M. Murray) *Write to Communicate: The Language Arts in Process* (multimedia kit), Levels 3-6, Reader's Digest Educational Division, 1973-74; *Reader's Digest Reading Skills Practice Pads,* Level 3 and Advanced, Reader's Digest Educational Division, 1976; *Reader's Digest Reading Skill Builders,* Reader's Digest Educational Division, 1977; *Holiday Part Panels,* three sets, Instructor Curriculum

Materials, 1978; *Houghton Mifflin Reading Program*, Levels 6-8, Houghton, 1980; *Houghton Mifflin Spelling Series*, Levels 2-3, Houghton, 1981; *Teacher Time Savers*, Random House, 1980; *Our Country's History*, Scholastic Book Services, 1981.

Under pseudonym Brooks Healey; all juveniles; all published by Firefly Book Club: *The Giggles and Games Puzzle Book*, 1977; *It's True, by George!*, 1978; *Star Words*, 1978; *The Stranger and the Scarecrow*, 1978; *Maze Daze*, 1979.

Monthly columnist for *Early Years*, 1980-81. Contributor of articles and poems to education and literature journals, and to children's magazines, including *Instructor, Early Yeears, Today's Education, Jack and Jill, Bitterroot International Poetry Quarterly*, and *Language Arts*.

WORK IN PROGRESS: Hark 'n Mark Reading Games; Carlo: Ship's Boy on the Santa Maria; Celebrity Riddles; Dad's Crumb Catcher; Foolish Ghoulish Monster; Shing-Shang, Fing-Fang and Foo; Skeeter's Big Tiny Surprise; What Makes My Daddy Cry?; Wheeee! A Cartwheel Spree; Willie's Wink-on-the-Brink.

* * *

ALBINSKI, Henry Stephen 1931-

PERSONAL: Born December 31, 1931, in Chicago, Ill.; son of Stephen (a chemical engineer) and Josephine (Wieczorek) Albinski; married Barbara Van Why, January 30, 1954; married second wife, Ethel Bisbicos (a psychologist), September 2, 1967; children: (first marriage) Lawrence; (second marriage) Gillian, Allison. *Education:* University of California, Los Angeles, B.A. (summa cum laude), 1953, M.A., 1955; University of Minnesota, Ph.D., 1959. *Home:* 803 Cornwall Dr., State College, Pa. 16801. *Office:* Department of Political Science, Pennsylvania State University, University Park, Pa. 16802.

CAREER: University of Minnesota, Minneapolis, instructor in political science, 1959; Pennsylvania State University, University Park, instructor, 1959-61, assistant professor, 1961-65, associate professor, 1965-68, professor of political science, 1968—, director of Office of Australian Studies, 1980-81, director of Australian Studies Center, 1982—. Visiting fellow, Australian National University, Research School of Pacific Studies, 1963-64, 1978-79; visiting professor, University of Western Ontario, 1969, University of Queensland, 1970, University of Sydney, and Flinders University of South Australia, both 1974-75. Consultant, Research Analysis Corp., 1968-70, Institute for Defense Analyses, 1969, Georgetown University Center for Strategic and International Studies, 1972-73, and U.S. Department of State.

MEMBER: American Political Science Association, Australasian Political Studies Association, New Zealand Political Studies Association, Association for Canadian Studies in the United States, Canadian Political Science Association, American Association of University Professors, Hansard Society. *Awards, honors:* Rockefeller Foundation grant, 1963-64; Institute of Humanistic Studies of Pennsylvania State University fellowship, 1968; senior Fulbright scholar, 1974-75, 1979.

WRITINGS: Australia and the China Problem during the Korean War Period, Department of International Relations, Australian National University, 1964; *Australian Policies and Attitudes toward China*, Princeton University Press, 1965; *The Australian Labor Party and the Aid to Parochial Schools Controversy*, Pennsylvania State University Press, 1966; (contributor) *Writings on Canadian-American Studies*, Committee on Canadian-American Studies, Michigan State University, 1967; (editor with L. K. Pettit) *European Political Processes: Essays and Readings*, Allyn & Bacon, 1968, 2nd edition, 1974; (contributor) Jan Prybyla, editor, *Communism at the Crossroads*, Pennsylvania State University Press, 1968; (contributor) Richard Preston, editor, *Contemporary Australia: Studies in History, Politics and Economics*, Duke University Press, 1969.

(Contributor) *American Studies Conference Proceedings*, New South Wales Department of Education, 1970; *Politics and Foreign Policy in Australia*, Duke University Press, 1970; *Australia in Southeast Asia: Interest, Capacity, and Acceptability*, Research Analysis Corp., 1970; (editor and contributor) *Asian Political Processes*, Allyn & Bacon, 1971; (contributor) Arthur Stahnke, editor, *China's Trade with the West*, Praeger, 1972; *Canadian and Australian Politics in Comparative Perspective*, Oxford University Press, 1973; (contributor) Prybyla, editor, *The Pentagon of Power*, Pennsylvania State University Press, 1973; (contributor) Roy Forward, editor, *Public Policy in Australia*, F. W. Cheshire, 1974; *Australian External Policy under Labor*, University of Queensland Press and University of British Columbia Press, 1977; (contributor) Preston, editor, *Perspectives on Revolution and Evolution*, Duke University Press, 1979.

(Contributor) John Henderson and others, editors, *Beyond New Zealand: The Foreign Policy of a Small State*, Methuen, 1980; (contributor) R. Hayburn and B. Webb, editors, *Economic Strategies and Foreign Policy*, University of Otago, 1980; (contributor) James Roherty, editor, *Defense Policy Formation*, Carolina Academic Press, 1980; (contributor) Larry Bowman and Ian Clark, editors, *The Indian Ocean in Global Politics*, Westview Press, 1981; (contributor) Haus Indorf and others, editors, *Lines of Communication and Security*, National Defense University Press, 1981; (contributor) Ramon Myers, editor, *An American Foreign Policy for Asia*, Hoover Institution Press, 1982; (contributor) William Tow and William Feeney, editors, *U.S. Alliance System in the Indo-Pacific Region*, Westview Press, 1982; *The Australian-American Security Relationship*, University of Queensland Press and St. Martin's Press, 1982.

Contributor of articles and reviews to professional journals in the United States, Australia, Canada, and New Zealand.

WORK IN PROGRESS: ANZUS Alliance and the Indian Ocean; U.S.-Australian Relations.

* * *

ALCALDE, E. L.
See CHAIJ, Fernando

* * *

ALDAN, Daisy 1923-

PERSONAL: Born September 16, 1923, in New York, N.Y.; daughter of Louis (a designer) and Esther (an actress; maiden name, Edelheit) Aldan. *Education:* Hunter College (now Hunter College of the City University of New York), B.A., 1943; Brooklyn College (now Brooklyn College of the City University of New York), M.A., 1948; graduate study, New York University. *Home:* 103-26 68th Rd., Forest Hills, N.Y. 11375; and Dornach 4143, Switzerland.

CAREER: Actress on a regular dramatic program, Columbia Broadcasting System, 1930-57; also actress in stock theater, playing many classical roles; School of Art and Design, New York, N.Y., teacher of English, creative writing, literature, speech, and films, 1948-73; Ecole Libre des Hautes Etudes (French University of New York), member of Faculte des Lettres; publisher of small press, 1953—. Teacher of creative writing, Emerson College, Sussex, England, summer, 1971, Rudolf

Steiner Institute, Spring Valley, N.Y., summer, 1973, 1974, and 1980, and Goetheanum, Switzerland, 1974. Has lectured and given performances in major universities and art centers in the United States, Switzerland, India, France, and Germany. Member of board of directors, Folder Editions. *Member:* P.E.N., World Congress of Poets, Poetry Society of America (former member of executive board), Academy of American Poets, Poetry Forum, Film-Makers' Cooperative.

AWARDS, HONORS: Herman Ritter award; Plymouth Drama Festival award; DeWitt American Lyric Poetry Award, 1967; National Endowment for the Arts, poetry prize, 1968, grant, 1979, to publish novella *A Golden Story;* first prize for poetry, Rochester Festival of the Arts, 1969; Poetry Forum award, 1970; Litt.D., University of Karachi, 1970; Pulitzer Prize nomination, for *Between High Tides;* Hall of Fame Award, Hunter College of the City University of New York, 1981.

WRITINGS—Poetry, except as indicated: *Poems, by Daisy Aldan* (pamphlet), Rumyon Press, 1946; *The Destruction of Cathedrals and Other Poems,* preface by Anais Nin, Two Cities Press, 1963; *The Masks Are Becoming Faces* (pamphlet), Goosetree Press, 1964; (with Stella Snead) *Seven: Seven* (poems and photographs), Folder Editions, 1965; *Or Learn to Walk on Water,* Folder Editions, 1970; *Journey,* Folder Editions, 1970; *+1=1: An ESP Poetry Experience with Elaine Mendlowitz,* Folder Editions, 1970; *Breakthrough: Poems in a New Idiom,* Folder Editions, 1971; *Love Poems of Daisy Aldan,* Barlenmir House, 1972; *Stones,* Folder Editions, 1973; *Between High Tides,* Folder Editions, 1978; *Poetry and Consciousness* (nonfiction), St. George Books, 1978; *A Golden Story* (novella), Folder Editions, 1979; *Contemporary Poetry and the Evolution of Consciousness* (nonfiction), St. George Books, 1981; *The Art and Craft of Poetry* (nonfiction), North River Press, 1981.

Translator: Stephane Mallarme, *A Throw of the Dice Never Will Abolish Chance,* Tiber Press, 1959; Albert Steffen, *Selected Poems,* Volume I, Folder Editions, 1968; *Some Poems of Albert Steffen,* Satyabrata Pal (Calcutta), 1969; (with Elly Simons) Steffen, *The Death Experience of Manes* (a play in verse), Folder, 1970; Rudolf Steiner, *The Soul Calendar,* Anthroposophic Press, 1974; Herbert Witzenmann, *The Virtues,* Folder Editions, 1977; Steiner, *The Foundation Stone,* St. George Books, 1981.

Editor: *A New Folder: Americans: Poems and Drawings,* foreword by Wallace Fowlie, Folder Editions, 1959; *Poems from India,* Crowell, 1969.

Poetry is represented in major anthologies, including: *New Orlando Poetry Anthology,* edited by A. Vrbovska and others, New Orlando Publications, 1968; *Adam among the Television Trees: An Anthology of Verse by Contemporary Christian Poets,* edited by Virginia R. Mollenkott, Word Books, 1971; *Fifty-Three American Poets of Today,* edited by Ruth W. Diamant, R. West, 1973; *Twentieth-Century American Women Poets,* edited by Laura Chester, Rising Tides, 1974.

Essays are represented in anthologies, including: *Books as Art,* Magic Circle Press, 1973; *Publish It Yourself Handbook,* Pushcart Press, 1976; *The Little Magazine in America Today,* Pushcart Press, 1978.

Contributor of poems to *Botteghe Oscure, Trace, Epos, Literary Review, Poetry, New York Times, Locus Solus, Between Worlds, Massachusetts Review, Beat Coast East, Coastlines, Proteus Quarterly, Dimension, Imago, Poet and Critic, Two Cities,* and other periodicals. Contributor of translations to anthologies. Translator, into French, of the short stories of Anais Nin, published in Canada, Belgium, and France. Editor, *Folder Magazine of Literature and Art,* 1953-59; American editor, *Two Cities* (Paris-New York), 1961-62; member of reviewing staff, *World Literature Today;* member of board of advisors, *New York Quarterly.*

WORK IN PROGRESS: Translating from Swedish the work of Edith Sodergran; a novel.

SIDELIGHTS: Daisy Aldan's major interests are contemporary international poetry, philosophy (particularly metaphysics), criticism, teaching, and travel. She has studied painting and eurythmy. Many of her poems have been presented in programs with eurythmists in new experimental art forms. Aldan told *CA* that her primary motivation is "to bring a renewal of the WORD into the world." She advises aspiring writers: "Be responsible for what you publish. Don't add to the destruction of the WORD."

Although she is not well-known outside literary circles, Aldan's poetry has been praised by reviewers. Writing in *World Literature Today,* Doris Earnshaw states: "Aldan deserves increased recognition as a major poet in her own right. . . . The beauty of Aldan's work is its fine delicacy in expressing human and natural events." A *Choice* critic calls her "a gigantic talent" who "makes the reader see his world in a new way." Aldan was chosen by Cornell University's literary magazine, *Epoch,* as one of the fifty best poets writing in America today. She was also included in the Doubleday ballot of the five hundred greatest living American writers.

Aldan lectures extensively and has given poetry readings in the United States, France, Switzerland, and India. She has written, photographed, and directed two original films and has given an extensive course in films. She may be heard on five recordings in the Library of Congress collection of American poets, as well as on recordings of her own poems in the Lamont Poetry Collection of Harvard University, including "To Let the Light In: Selected Poems of Daisy Aldan," Black Box Series.

BIOGRAPHICAL/CRITICAL SOURCES: Mademoiselle, January, 1961; *New York Times Book Review,* March 8, 1964; *India News,* October 20, 1964; *India Morning Standard,* November 20, 1964; Valerie Harms, editor, *Celebration with Anais Nin,* Magic Circle Press, 1973; *Choice,* October, 1973; *The Little Magazine in America Today,* Pushcart Press, 1978; *World Literature Today,* spring, 1980.

* * *

ALIBER, Robert Z. 1930-

PERSONAL: Born September 19, 1930, in Keene, N.H.; son of Norman H. and Sophie (Becker) Aliber; married Deborah Baltzly, September 9, 1955; children: Jennifer, Rachel, Michael. *Education:* Williams College, B.A., 1952; Cambridge University, B.A., 1954, M.A., 1957; Yale University, Ph.D., 1962. *Home:* 5638 South Dorchester Ave., Chicago, Ill. 60637. *Office:* Graduate School of Business, University of Chicago, Chicago, Ill.

CAREER: Commission on Money and Credit, New York, N.Y., staff economist, 1959-61; Committee for Economic Development, Washington, D.C., staff economist, 1961-64; Agency for International Development, Washington, D.C., senior economic adviser, 1964-65; University of Chicago, Graduate School of Business, Chicago, Ill., 1965—, began as associate professor, currently professor of economics and director of program of international studies. *Military service:* U.S. Army, 1956-64. *Member:* American Economic Association, Royal Economic Society, Academy of International Business, Canadian Economics Association, Association for Public Policy Analysis and Management.

WRITINGS: The Management of the Dollar in International Finance, Princeton University Press, 1963; *The Future of the Dollar as an International Currency,* Praeger, 1966; (editor with George P. Shultz) *Guidelines, Informal Controls, and the Market Place,* University of Chicago Press, 1966; *The International Money Game,* Basic Books, 1973, 3rd edition, 1979; (editor) *National Monetary Policies and the International Financial System,* University of Chicago Press, 1974; *World Inflation and Monetary Reform,* Sage Publications, 1974; (editor) *The Political Economy of Monetary Reform,* Macmillan, 1976; *Exchange Risk and Corporate International Finance,* Halsted Press, 1978; *Your Money and Your Life,* Basic Books, 1982. Also author of *Money, Banking and Economic Activity,* 1981.

* * *

ALLRED, G. Hugh 1932-

PERSONAL: Born May 22, 1932, in Hill Spring, Alberta, Canada; came to United States in 1948, naturalized citizen in 1956; son of Golden and Josephine (Leavitt) Allred; married Carolyn Crapo, June 27, 1951; children: Steven Hugh, Lynnette (Mrs. Keele Johnson), Sharlene, Gregory Hugh, Jennifer. *Education:* Attended Yale University, 1951-52; Brigham Young University, B.A., 1957, M.A., 1960; University of Alberta, graduate study, summers, 1962-63; University of Oregon, Ed.D., 1966. *Politics:* Independent. *Religion:* Church of Jesus Christ of Latter-day Saints (Mormons). *Home:* 1400 Cherry, Provo, Utah 84604. *Office:* Department of Family Science, Brigham Young University, Provo, Utah 84602.

CAREER: Licensed marriage and family therapist in Utah; Utah State Hospital, Provo, psychiatric aide, 1955-57; high school social studies teacher in Provo, Utah, 1957-60; high school guidance counselor in Lethbridge, Alberta, 1960-64; University of Oregon, Eugene, supervisor of secondary school student teachers, 1964-65; Portland Community Parent Teacher Education Center (family counseling center), Portland, Ore., co-director, 1965; University of Oregon, counseling intern, 1965-66; Eugene Community Parent Teacher Education Center, Eugene, Ore., co-director, 1965-66; Brigham Young University, Provo, Utah, assistant professor of educational psychology, 1966-68, assistant professor, 1968-69, associate professor of child development and family relationships in marriage and family therapy, 1969—. Member of Mormon Tabernacle Choir, 1968—. Director and senior therapist for open forum family counseling programs in several Utah communities, 1968-72; member of examining board for licensing marriage and family counselors in Utah, 1973-82. *Military service:* U.S. Air Force, Chinese linguist, 1952-55; served in Japan and Korea.

MEMBER: American Association for Marriage and Family Therapy (fellow and approved supervisor), National Council on Family Relationships, American Society of Adlerian Psychology, Utah Parent Teacher Association (life member), Utah Association for Marriage and Family Therapy (president, 1974-76), Phi Delta Kappa.

WRITINGS—Published by Brigham Young University Press, except as indicated: *Mission for Mother: Guiding the Child,* Bookcraft, 1968; *The Challenge to Be One,* 1974; *On the Level with Self, Family, Society,* 1974; *How to Strengthen Your Marriage and Family,* 1976; (with son, Steve H. Allred) *How to Make a Good Mission Great,* Deseret, 1979; (with Thomas T. Graff) *CHEC: Couples Handbook for Effective Communication,* 1979; (with Graff) *Leader's Guide to CHEC,* 1979. Contributor to counseling and education journals and to church publications.

WORK IN PROGRESS: Developing interaction analysis instruments for counselors, husbands and wives, and parents and children.

SIDELIGHTS: G. Hugh Allred writes, "The major objectives in my writing have been to help relieve the pain and suffering of people in marriage and families and provide them with alternatives which will increase the possibilities for them to achieve serenity and happiness."

* * *

ALTMANN, Alexander 1906-

PERSONAL: Born April 16, 1906, in Kassa, Hungary; became a British subject in 1946; son of Adolf (a rabbi) and Malvine (Weisz) Altmann; married Judith Frank, December 20, 1932; children: Fay Aviva (Mrs. Alan Amias), Michael, Eve (Mrs. Yigal Yardeni). *Education:* University of Berlin, Dr.Phil., 1931; Rabbinical Seminary, Berlin, Rabbi, 1931. *Home:* 126 Glen Ave., Newton Center, Mass. 02159.

CAREER: Rabbi in Berlin, Germany, 1931-38; Rabbinical Seminary, Berlin, professor of Jewish philosophy, 1932-38; communal rabbi in Manchester, England, 1938-59; Institute of Jewish Studies, Manchester, director, 1953-58; Brandeis University, Waltham, Mass., Philip W. Lown Professor of Jewish Philosophy and History of Ideas, 1959-76, Philip W. Lown Professor Emeritus, 1976—. Honorary president, Institute of Jewish Studies, University College, University of London, 1959—. *Member:* American Academy of Arts and Sciences (fellow), American Academy of Jewish Research (fellow; past vice-president), Medieval Academy of America (fellow). *Awards, honors:* M.A., University of Manchester, 1943; D.H.L., Hebrew Union College-Jewish Institute of Religion, 1967, and Brandeis University, 1979; Th.D., University of Munich, 1972; Ph.D., University of Trier, 1980.

WRITINGS: Moses Mendelssohn's Fruehschriften zur Metaphysik, Mohr (Tuebingen), 1969; *Studies in Religious Philosophy and Mysticism,* Cornell University Press, 1969; *Moses Mendelssohn: A Biographical Study,* University of Alabama Press, 1973; *Essays in Jewish Intellectual History,* University Press of New England, 1981; *Die trostvolle Aufklaerung,* [Stuttgart], 1982; *Essays in Judaism* (in Hebrew), [Tel-Aviv], 1982.

Editor; published by Harvard University Press, except as indicated: *Between East and West: Essays Dedicated to the Memory of Bela Horowitz,* East & West Library, 1958; *Biblical and Other Studies,* 1963; *Studies in Nineteenth-Century Jewish Intellectual History,* 1966; *Biblical Motifs: Origins and Transformations,* 1966; *Jewish Medieval and Renaissance Studies,* 1967.

Translator: (From the Arabic; author of introduction and notes and abridger) Saadiah ben Joseph, *The Book of Doctrines and Beliefs,* East & West Library, 1946, published in *Three Jewish Philosophers,* Harper, 1965; (and co-author of commentary) *Isaac Israeli: A Neoplatonic Philosopher of the Early Tenth Century,* Oxford University Press, 1958, reprinted, Greenwood Press, 1979.

General editor, *Moses Mendelssohn Gesammelte Schriften: Jubilaeumsausgabe,* F. Fromman-G. Holzboog (Stuttgart), 1971—. Editor, *Journal of Jewish Studies,* 1954-59, and *Scripta Judaica,* 1957-65.

* * *

AMARY, Issam B(ahjat) 1942-

PERSONAL: Born July 11, 1942, in Jerusalem, Palestine (now

Israel); U.S. citizen; son of Bahjat K. (a merchant) and Essaf (Khaimi) Amary; married Wilma Blinn (a teacher), August 20, 1967; children: Jason Issam, Jarred Jamal, Dax Tallal. *Education:* Missouri Valley College, B.S., 1968; University of Missouri—Rolla, certificate in hospital management, 1973; Central Missouri State University, M.S., 1974. *Religion:* Christian. *Home:* 711 Plaza Dr., Marshall, Mo. 65340. *Office:* Marshall State School, East Slater, Marshall, Mo. 65340.

CAREER: Marshall State School and Hospital, Marshall, Mo., activity therapist, 1969-71, recreation therapist and coordinator of activity therapy staff, 1971-75, unit program director, 1975—. Registered master therapeutic recreation specialist. Missouri Special Olympics, assistant state director, 1969-70, executive state director, 1970-72, chairman of board of directors, 1970-73. Founding member and member of advisory committee, Betterment of Youth Program. *Member:* National Recreation and Park Association, National Therapeutic Recreation Society, Alpha Psi Omega (vice-president), Alpha Phi Omega, Masonic Lodge, International Club (Marshall, Mo.), Optimist Club (member of board of directors, 1971-72), Community Theatre, Valley Players.

WRITINGS—Published by C. C Thomas, except as indicated: *Creative Recreation for the Mentally Retarded,* 1975; *A Taste of Lebanon: An Exotic Gourmet Experience in Lebanese Foods* (cookbook), Wallsworth, 1975; *Effective Meal Planning and Food Preparation for the Mentally Retarded/Developmentally Disabled,* 1979; *The Rights of the Mentally Retarded/Developmentally Disabled to Treatment and Education,* 1980; *Social Awareness, Hygiene and Sex Education for the Mentally Retarded/Developmentally Disabled,* 1980.

SIDELIGHTS: Issam B. Amary writes *CA:* "Through close association with the Special Olympics program I was convinced of the need to provide the mentally retarded with constructive activities that would contribute toward their positive development. I was also convinced that the mentally retarded need guidance and understanding so that they might meet the challenge of life."

AVOCATIONAL INTERESTS: Travel (United States, Middle East, southern Europe, North Africa), reading, fishing, gourmet cooking.

*   *   *

AMIS, Kingsley (William)   1922-
   (Robert Markham)

PERSONAL: Born April 16, 1922, in London, England; son of William Robert (an office clerk) and Rosa Annie (Lucas) Amis; married Hilary Ann Bardwell, 1948 (divorced, 1965); married Elizabeth Jane Howard (a novelist), 1965; children: (first marriage) Philip Nicol William, Martin Louis, Sally Myfanwy. *Education:* St. John's College, Oxford, B.A. (with first class honors in English), 1947, M.A., 1948. *Home:* 186 Leighton Rd., London N.W.5, England. *Agent:* Jonathan Clowes Ltd., 19 Jeffrey's Pl., London NW1 9PP, England.

CAREER: University College of Swansea, Swansea, Glamorganshire, Wales, lecturer in English, 1949-61; Cambridge University, Peterhouse, Cambridge, England, fellow, 1961-63; full-time writer, 1963—. Visiting fellow in creative writing, Princeton University, 1958-59; visiting professor of English, Vanderbilt University, 1967-68. *Military service:* British Army, Royal Signal Corps, 1942-45; became lieutenant. *Member:* Authors' Club (London), British Channel Yacht Club. *Awards, honors:* Somerset Maugham Award, 1955, for *Lucky Jim;* M.A., Cambridge University, 1961; Booker Prize nomination and *Yorkshire Post* Book of the Year Award, both 1974, for *Ending Up;* John W. Campbell Memorial Award, 1977, for *The Alteration;* Commander of the British Empire, 1981.

WRITINGS: Socialism and the Intellectuals, Fabian Society (London), 1957; (author of introduction) Oscar Wilde, *Essays and Poems,* Norton, 1959; *New Maps of Hell: A Survey of Science Fiction,* Harcourt, 1960, reprinted, Arno, 1975; *My Enemy's Enemy* (short stories), Gollancz, 1962, Harcourt, 1963; *The James Bond Dossier,* New American Library, 1965; *Lucky Jim's Politics,* Conservative Political Centre (London), 1968; *What Became of Jane Austen? and Other Questions* (essays), J. Cape, 1970, Harcourt, 1971; *Dear Illusion* (short stories), Covent Garden Press, 1972; *On Drink,* J. Cape, 1972, Harcourt, 1973; *Rudyard Kipling and His World,* Scribner, 1975; (author of introduction) Arthur Hutchings, *Mozart: The Man, the Music,* Schirmer, 1976; *Interesting Things,* edited by Michael Swan, Cambridge University Press, 1977; *The Darkwater Hall Mystery,* Tragara Press, 1978; *Arts Policy?,* Centre for Studies in Social Policy, 1979; *Collected Short Stories,* Hutchinson, 1980.

Novels: *Lucky Jim,* Doubleday, 1954 (though title page of first printing reads 1953), reprinted, Queens House, 1976, edited and abridged by K. W. Swan, Longmans, 1963; *That Uncertain Feeling,* Gollancz, 1955, Harcourt, 1956, reprinted, Panther Books, 1975; *I Like It Here,* Harcourt, 1958, reprinted, Panther Books, 1975; *Take a Girl Like You,* Gollancz, 1960, Harcourt, 1961, reprinted, Penguin, 1976; *One Fat Englishman,* Gollancz, 1963, Harcourt, 1964; (with Robert Conquest) *The Egyptologists,* J. Cape, 1965, Random House, 1966; *The Anti-Death League,* Harcourt, 1966; (under pseudonym Robert Markham) *Colonel Sun: A James Bond Adventure,* Harper, 1968; *I Want It Now,* J. Cape, 1968, Harcourt, 1969; *The Green Man,* J. Cape, 1969, Harcourt, 1970; *Girl, 20,* J. Cape, 1971, Harcourt, 1972; *The Riverside Villas Murder,* Harcourt, 1973; *Ending Up,* Harcourt, 1974; *The Alteration,* J. Cape, 1976, Viking, 1977; *Jake's Thing,* Hutchinson, 1978, Viking, 1979; *Russian Hide-and-Seek,* Hutchinson, 1980.

Poetry: *Bright November,* Fortune Press, 1947; *A Frame of Mind,* School of Art, Reading University, 1953; *Kingsley Amis,* Fantasy Press, 1954; *A Case of Samples: Poems, 1946-1956,* Gollancz, 1956, Harcourt, 1957; (with Dom Moraes and Peter Porter) *Penguin Modern Poets 2,* Penguin, 1962; *The Evans Country,* Fantasy Press, 1962; *A Look Round the Estate: Poems 1957-1967,* J. Cape, 1967, Harcourt, 1968; *Collected Poems: 1944-1979,* Hutchinson, 1979, Viking, 1980.

Editor: (With James Michie) *Oxford Poetry, 1949,* Basil Blackwell, 1949; (with Conquest) *Spectrum: A Science Fiction Anthology,* Volume I, Gollancz, 1961, Harcourt, 1962, Volume II, Gollancz, 1962, Harcourt, 1963, Volume III, Gollancz, 1963, Harcourt, 1964, published as *Spectrum III: A Third Science Fiction Anthology,* Berkeley Publishing, 1965, Volume IV, Harcourt, 1965, Volume V, Gollancz, 1966, Harcourt, 1967; *Selected Short Stories of G. K. Chesterton,* Faber, 1972; *Tennyson,* Penguin, 1973; *The New Oxford Book of English Light Verse,* Oxford University Press (New York), 1978 (published in England as *The New Oxford Book of Light Verse,* Oxford University Press, 1978); *Harold's Years: Impressions from the "New Statesman" and the "Spectator,"* Quartet Books, 1978; *The Faber Popular Reciter,* Faber, 1978; *The Golden Age of Science Fiction,* Hutchinson, 1981.

Contributor: *Winter's Tales 1,* St. Martin's, 1955; Conquest, editor, *New Lines: An Anthology,* Macmillan (London), 1956, St. Martin's, 1957; Donald Hall and others, editors, *New Poets of England and America,* Meridian, 1957, 2nd edition, 1962; Paul Engle and Joseph Langland, editors, *Poet's Choice,* Dial,

1962; Malcolm Brinnan and Bill Read, editors, *The Modern Poets,* McGraw, 1963; C. B. Cox and A. E. Dyson, editors, *Fight for Education: A Black Paper,* Critical Quarterly Society, 1968; *Penguin Modern Stories 11,* Penguin, 1972; Cox and Dyson, editors, *Black Paper 1975: The Fight for Education,* Dent, 1975.

Also author of a science fiction radio play, "Something Strange," and of television plays "A Question about Hell," 1964, "The Importance of Being Harry," 1971, "Dr. Watson and the Darkwater Hall Mystery," 1974, and "See What You've Done," 1974. Author of recordings, "Reading His Own Poems," Listen, 1962, and with Thomas Blackburn, "Poems," Jupiter, 1962. Author of column on beverages in *Penthouse.* Contributor to periodicals, including *Spectator, Encounter, New Statesman, Listener, Observer,* and *London Magazine.*

WORK IN PROGRESS: A detective story.

SIDELIGHTS: "I think of myself like a sort of mid- or late-Victorian person," says Kingsley Amis in *Contemporary Literature,* "not in outlook but in the position of writing a bit of poetry (we forget that George Eliot also wrote verse), writing novels, being interested in questions of the day and occasionally writing about them, and being interested in the work of other writers and occasionally writing about that. I'm not exactly an entertainer pure and simple, not exactly an artist pure and simple, certainly not an incisive critic of society, and certainly not a political figure though I'm interested in politics. I think I'm just a combination of some of those things." Though an eclectic man of letters, Amis is best known as a prolific novelist who, in the words of Blake Morrison in the *Times Literary Supplement,* has the "ability to go on surprising us." He won critical acclaim in 1954 with the publication of his first novel, *Lucky Jim,* and after producing three other comic works was quickly characterized as a comic novelist writing in the tradition of P. G. Wodehouse and Evelyn Waugh. Since his early works, however, Amis has produced a spate of novels that vary radically in genre and seriousness of theme. He keeps "experimenting with ways of confounding the reader who hopes for a single focus," claims William Hutchings in *Critical Quarterly,* though Clancy Sigal suggests in *National Review* that Amis simply "has the virtue, rare in England, of refusing to accept an imposed definition of what a Serious Writer ought to write about."

Amis, who admits in *Contemporary Literature* that he considers poetry a "higher art" than prose writing, was publishing poems before novels; yet, it was through his early novels that he originally became known and respected as a writer. When *Lucky Jim* first appeared, it attracted unusually wide review attention and led to a Somerset Maugham Award, a successful film, and a paperback sale of over a million copies in America. Edmund Fuller praised it in the *New York Times* as "written with the cool, detached, sardonic style which is the trademark of the British satirical novelist. *Lucky Jim* is funny in something approaching the Wodehouse vein, but it cuts a bit deeper." Other critics also likened it to P. G. Wodehouse's works, and Walter Allen in *The Modern Novel* called it "the funniest first novel since [Evelyn Waugh's] *Decline and Fall.*" William Van O'Connor summed up the book's virtues this way in *The New University Wits and the End of Modernism,* "The characterizations are extremely good, the dialogue is natural, the narrative pacing is excellent, and Jim himself is not only a wonderfully funny character, he is almost archetypal."

Jim Dixon, the protagonist, is, according to Anthony Burgess in *The Novel Now,* "the most popular anti-hero of our time." Though a junior lecturer at a provincial university, Jim has no desire to be an intellectual, a "gentleman," because of his profound, almost physical, hatred of the social and cultural affectations of university life. This characteristic of Jim's has led several critics to conclude that he is a philistine and, moreover, that beneath the comic effects, Amis is really attacking culture and is himself a philistine. Brigid Brophy, for example, writes in *Don't Never Forget* that the "apex of philistinism" is reached "when Jim hears a tune by the composer whom either he or Mr. Amis . . . thinks of as 'filthy Mozart.'"

Ralph Caplan, however, claims in *Contemporary British Novelists* that *Lucky Jim* "never [promises] anything more than unmitigated pleasure and insight, and these it keeps on delivering. The book [is] not promise but fulfillment, a commodity we confront too seldom to know how to behave when it is achieved. This seems to be true particularly when the achievement is comic. Have we forgotten how to take humor straight? Unable to exit laughing, the contemporary reader looks over his shoulder for Something More. The trouble is that by now he knows how to find it."

Amis himself states in a *Publishers Weekly* interview that to see *Lucky Jim* as a polemic on culture is to misinterpret it: "'This is the great misunderstanding of it. People said I was part of an emergent group of angry young men writing novels of protest. But the idea that Jim was an "outsider" just won't do. He was an *insider.* This still eludes people, especially Americans.'" As to the charges of philistinism, Amis says to Dale Salwak in *Contemporary Literature:* "Jim and I have taken a lot of bad mouthing for being philistine, aggressively philistine, and saying, 'Well, as long as I've got me blonde and me pint of beer and me packet of fags and me seat at the cinema, I'm all right.' I don't think either of us would say that. It's nice to have a pretty girl with large breasts rather than some fearful woman who's going to talk to you about Ezra Pound and hasn't got large breasts and probably doesn't wash much. And better to have a pint of beer than to have to talk to your host about the burgundy you're drinking. And better to go to the pictures than go to see nonsensical art exhibitions that nobody's really going to enjoy. So it's appealing to common sense if you like, and it's a way of trying to denounce affectation."

Critics generally see the three novels that followed *Lucky Jim* as variations on this theme of appealing to common sense and denouncing affectation. Discussing *Lucky Jim, That Uncertain Feeling, I Like It Here,* and *Take a Girl Like You* in the *Hudson Review,* James P. Degnan states: "In the comically outraged voice of his angry young heroes—e.g., Jim Dixon of *Lucky Jim* and John Lewis of *That Uncertain Feeling*—Amis [lampoons] what C. P. Snow . . . labeled the 'traditional culture,' the 'culture of the literary intellectuals,' of the 'gentleman's world.'" James Gindin notes in *Postwar British Fiction* that the similarity of purpose is reflected in a corresponding similarity of technique: "Each of the [four] novels is distinguished by a thick verbal texture that is essentially comic. The novels are full of word play and verbal jokes. . . . All Amis's heroes are mimics: Jim Dixon parodies the accent of Professor Welch, his phony and genteel professor, in *Lucky Jim;* Patrick Standish, in *Take a Girl Like You,* deliberately echoes the Hollywood version of the Southern Negro's accent. John Lewis, the hero of *That Uncertain Feeling,* also mimics accents and satirically characterizes other people by the words and phrases they use."

The heroes in these four novels are in fact so much alike that Brigid Brophy charges Amis with "rewriting much the same novel under different titles and with different names for the characters," although Walter Allen insists that the "young man recognizably akin to Lucky Jim, the Amis man as he might be called, . . . has been increasingly explored in depth." Consistent with her assessment of Jim Dixon in *Lucky Jim,* Brophy sees the other three Amis heroes also as "militant philistines," a view that is not shared by Ralph Caplan, Anthony Burgess, or James P. Degnan. Caplan explains that though the Amis hero in these novels is seemingly anti-intellectual, he is nonetheless "always cerebral," and Burgess points out that the hero "always earns his living by purveying culture as teacher, librarian, journalist, or publisher." Representing a commonsensical approach to life, the Amis protagonist, according to Degnan, is an inversion of a major convention of twentieth-century literature: the convention of the hero "as 'sensitive soul,' the convention of the 'alienated' young man of artistic or philosophical pretensions struggling pitifully and hopelessly against an insensitive, middle-class, materialistic world. . . . In place of the 'sensitive soul' as hero, Amis creates in his early novels a hero radically new to serious contemporary fiction: a middle-class hero who is also an intellectual, an intellectual who is unabashedly middlebrow. He is a hero . . . whose chief virtues, as he expresses them, are: 'politeness, friendly interest, ordinary concern and a good natured willingness to be imposed upon.' . . . Suspicious of all pretentiousness, of all heroic posturing, the Amis hero . . . voices all that is best of the 'lower middle class, of the non-gentlemanly' conscience."

Degnan, however, does believe that Patrick Standish in *Take a Girl Like You* comes dangerously close to "the kind of anti-hero—e.g., blase, irresponsible, hedonistic—that Amis's first three novels attack," and that this weakens the satirical aspect of the novel. Echoing this assessment in *The Reaction against Experiment in the English Novel, 1950-1960,* Rubin Rabinovitz detects an uncertainty as to what "vice and folly" really are and who possesses them: "In *Take a Girl Like You* Amis satirizes both Patrick's lechery and Jenny's persistence in preserving her virginity. . . . The satire in *Lucky Jim* is not divided this way: Jim Dixon mocks the hypocrisy of his colleagues in the university and refuses to be subverted by it. [In *Lucky Jim*] the satire is more powerful because the things being satirized are more boldly defined."

After *Take a Girl Like You,* Amis produced several other "straight" novels, as *Time*'s Christopher Porterfield describes them, as well as a James Bond spy thriller, written under the pseudonym of Robert Markham, called *Colonel Sun;* a work of science fiction, *The Anti-Death League;* and a ghost story, *The Green Man.* When Gildrose Productions, the firm to which the James Bond copyright was sold after Ian Fleming's death, awarded the first non-Fleming sequel to Amis, the literary world received the news with a mixture of apprehension and interest. Earlier, Amis had done an analysis of the nature of Fleming's hero, *The James Bond Dossier,* and he appeared to be a logical successor to Bond's creator. But the reactions to *Colonel Sun* have been mixed. Though Clara Siggins states in *Best Sellers* that Amis has "produced an exciting narrative with the expertise and verve of Fleming himself," S. K. Oberbeck claims in the *Washington Post Book World* that the changes Amis makes "on Bond's essential character throw the formula askew. . . . In humanizing Bond, in netting him back into the channel of real contemporary events, Amis somehow deprives him of the very ingredients that made his barely believable adventures so rewarding." Similarly, David Lodge, discussing the book in *The Novelist at the Crossroads and Other Essays on Fiction and Criticism,* considers *Colonel Sun* "more realistic" yet "duller" than most of the Fleming novels, because "the whole enterprise, undertaken, apparently, in a spirit of pious imitation, required Amis to keep in check his natural talent for parody and deflating comic realism."

Amis's comic spirit, so prominent in his first four novels and muted in *Colonel Sun,* is noticeably absent from *The Anti-Death League,* which was published two years before the Bond adventure. Bernard Bergonzi comments in *The Situation and the Novel* that in *The Anti-Death League* Amis "has written a more generalised kind of fiction, with more clearly symbolic implications, than in any of his earlier novels. There is still a trace of sardonic humor, and his ear remains alert to the placing details of individual speech; but Amis has here abandoned the incisive social mimicry, the memorable responses to the specificity of a person's appearance or the look of a room that have previously characterized his fiction."

The story concerns a British army officer who becomes convinced that a nonhuman force of unlimited malignancy, called God, is responsible for a pattern of seemingly undeserving deaths. Bergonzi views the work as a provocative, anti-theological novel of ideas, and maintains that it "represents Amis's immersion in the nightmare that flickers at the edges of his earlier fiction." He does, however, find one shortcoming in the novel: "*The Anti-Death League* . . . is intensely concerned with the questions that lead to tragedy—death, cruelty, loss of every kind—while lacking the ontological supports—whether religious or humanistic—that can sustain the tragic view of life." A *Times Literary Supplement* reviewer admits that the rebellion against the facts of pain and death "seems rather juvenile, like kicking God's ankle for doing such things to people," but asserts: "[Amis] takes the argument to more audacious and hopeful lengths. . . . We do care about his creatures; the agents intrigue us and the victims concern us. The handling is vastly less pompous than the theme: oracular yes, but eloquent and earthly and even moving."

Christopher Porterfield believes *The Green Man* "undoubtedly will make people mad. Nearly everything about Amis does. One sizable body of readers has never forgiven him for not devoting his career to rewriting other versions of *Lucky Jim,* an understandable complaint considering the skill and savage glee with which that book [skewers] bores, snobs, and all the petty conspiracies of circumstance that can stand in the way of a fellow simply getting on with a job, a girl, a few drinks." Described by Amis in the *Paris Review* as a ghost story "combined with a reasonably serious study of human relations, in this case the problem of selfishness," *The Green Man* is, according to Melvin Maddocks in the *Christian Science Monitor,* "a desperate book" which marks a clear departure from Amis's earlier novels. Maddocks sees a "chilling fatalism" permeating the novel, "as though everything was predestined—jokes and all." Anthony Burgess, writing in *Life,* notes a thematic similarity between *The Anti-Death League* and *The Green Man:* "They both posit the existence of a malign ultimate reality, against which there is little defense."

Jonathan Yardley, however, claims in the *New Republic* that though "balleyhooed as a new departure . . . , [*The Green Man*] is strictly old hat. That means it is frequently funny, tedious when the dialogue turns weighty, determinedly suave, [and] a shade too nimble in plot." Other critics also see a continuity with Amis's earlier work. Porterfield characterizes the book as "an Amis novel with ghosts," adding, "Its tensions are dissipated at crucial moments by cold dashes of caustic humor. . . . It remains pretty high-grade Amis." And Burgess, who recognizes the philosophical preoccupation with a malign universe in the novel, says: "If admirers of *Lucky Jim* are puzzled as to how Amis has, after that uproarious first novel, arrived at this position, perhaps they ought to read *Lucky Jim* again. . . . Amis knows how to chill us as much as he knows how to make us laugh."

Amis followed *The Green Man* with *Girl, 20,* a comic novel with serious overtones. Like Burgess's assessment of the former, Paul Schleuter views the latter as a harmonious addition to Amis's body of work. He writes in *Saturday Review* that in *Girl, 20* Amis's "talent for creating humorous situations, characters, and dialogue is as fresh as ever.... Amis also has a distinct undercurrent of pathos, darkness, and trauma. The result is not really a 'new' Amis so much as a more mature examination of human foibles and excesses than was the case in his earlier novels." But Amis's next novel, *The Riverside Villas Murder,* "offers no comfort to those who look for consistency in [his] work," according to a *Times Literary Supplement* reviewer.

A departure from Amis's previous works, *The Riverside Villas Murder* is a detective story, though there is some debate among critics whether it is to be read "straight" or as a parody of the genre. Patrick Cosgrave, for example, claims in *Saturday Review/World* that the book is "a straight detective story, with a murder, several puzzles, clues, a great detective, and an eminently satisfying and unexpected villain. So bald a statement is a necessary introduction in order to ensure that nobody will be tempted to pore over *The Riverside Villas Murder* in search of portentousness, significance, ambiguity, or any of the more tiresome characteristics too often found in the work of a straight novelist who has turned aside from the main road of his work into the byways of such subgenres as crime and adventure. More, the book is straight detection because Amis intended it to be such: It is written out of a great love of the detective form and deliberately set in a period—the Thirties—when that form was ... most popular." The *Times Literary Supplement* reviewer, however, considers the book "something more and less than a period detective story. Mr. Amis is not one to take any convention too seriously, and on one plane he is simply having fun." Patricia Coyne, writing in the *National Review,* and *Time*'s T. E. Kalem express similar opinions. Coyne describes the story as "a boy discovers sex against a murder-mystery backdrop," and Kalem concludes that by making a fourteen-year-old boy the hero of the novel, "Amis cleverly combines, in mild parody, two ultra-British literary forms—the mystery thriller with the boyhood adventure yarn."

Some critics consider the plot of *The Riverside Villas Murder* weak, but the characterization and style particularly strong. Angus Wilson writes in the *New York Times Book Review* that the "mechanism of the murder, who did it and how, is at once creaky, obvious, and entirely improbable," yet he believes that the book contains "an almost perfect creation of the character of a young adolescent boy." Moreover, Wilson lauds Amis's prose as "probably the most pleasant to read of any good writers of English today. I know no other writer who can forgo all ornament without either aridity or pseudo-simplicity.... Each sentence, each paragraph, each chapter is organized to do its job, and the whole is therefore always satisfactory within its limits." Patricia Coyne, who also maintains that the mystery is not engaging enough, finds the characterization and style of the highest quality: "[Amis's] may be the best secondary characters—most notably, his old men—since Dickens. And equally satisfying is his style, the often complex sentences falling clear and true with that deceptive ease that marks the master craftsman."

John Vaizey states in *Listener* that stylistic grace is one feature Amis "connoisseurs" expect, and they will find it in *Ending Up*. "There is no writer now alive, other than Anthony Powell," asserts Vaizey, "who writes such classically pure English which is at the same time accurately and exactly idiomatic. This is a very rare gift that Mr. Amis has cultivated, so that there is nothing he cannot say economically and precisely if he wants to." What surprises Vaizey, among others, about *Ending Up* is "the quite extraordinary degree of compassion that Mr. Amis shows towards his characters and that they show towards each other.... Each person has a ghastly problem, derived from the fact of being old, and nobody—except the spinster—really feels deeply about anybody else. Nevertheless, they do not only put up, on the whole, with each other; for the most part, they make a go of it, which, of course, most people do. It is a kind of celebration of ordinariness."

Ironically, other critics see a lack of compassion in Amis's treatment of his five protagonists—all over seventy years old—who suffer from a variety of diseases. Roger Sale argues in the *Hudson Review* that the "characters exist only so Amis can wound them, and when he tires of the fun he just kills them off with casual carelessness." In the *National Review,* Charles Nicol compares reading *Ending Up* to "watching a clock run down. When there is nothing more to be exploited from the interactions of his five old people, Amis squeezes out a final drop of humor by killing them all off [almost simultaneously]." And *Time*'s Timothy Foote writes: "Somewhere before a surprise ending with more deaths than Act V of *Hamlet,* it becomes evident that Author Amis is enjoying his caricatured geriatrics in some way that might be appropriate to Goneril and Regan in *King Lear* but is simply hateful in Tuppenny-hapenny Cottage."

Vaizey admits that *Ending Up* has a "brooding sense of disaster, of evil even," one that reminds him of *The Green Man;* but he nevertheless maintains that there "seems to be added a new depth of human feeling." Matthew Hodgart reaches a similar conclusion in the *New York Review of Books:* "[*Ending Up*] describes the futility and meaninglessness of life as it must sooner or later appear to many old people. Despite his continual joking, and sometimes apparently callous indifference, Amis has written a very moving study of the pain of old age."

Almost as if to befuddle readers searching for consistency in his work, Amis followed his detective story *The Riverside Villas Murder* and straight novel *Ending Up* with *The Alteration,* which *Time*'s Paul Gray says "flits quirkily between satire, science fiction, boy's adventure, and travelogue. The result is what *Nineteen Eighty-Four* might have been like if Lewis Carroll had written it: not a classic, certainly, but an oddity well worth an evening's attention." According to Bruce Cook in *Saturday Review, The Alteration* belongs to a rare subgenre of science fiction: "the so-called counterfeit- or alternative-world novel." Though set in the twentieth century (1976), the book has as its premise that the Protestant Reformation never occurred and, as a result, that the world is essentially Catholic. The plot centers on the discovery of a brilliant boy soprano, the Church's plans to preserve his gift by "altering" his anatomy through castration, and the debate on the justice of this decision.

Thomas R. Edwards notes in the *New York Review of Books* that though "Amis isn't famous for his compassion," in *The Alteration* he "affectingly catches and respects a child's puzzlement about the threatened loss of something he knows about only from descriptions." John Carey insists in the *New Statesman* that the book "has almost nothing expectable about it, except that it is a study of tyranny." What Carey refers to is the destructive power of the pontifical hierarchy to emasculate life and art, which he sees as the theme of the novel. Bruce Cook shares this interpretation. Calling *The Alteration* "the most overtly and specifically theological of all [Amis's] books," Cook argues: "Fundamentally, *The Alteration* is another of Kingsley Amis's angry screeds against the Catholic faith and the Catholic idea of God. And it is not just what Amis sees as the life-hating, sex-hating aspect of High Christianity—something that made possible such monstrous phenomena as the castrati—that concerns him here [but] . . . Christianity itself. At the end of *The Anti-Death League,* his oddest and most extreme book and in some ways his best, Amis allows some talk of reconciliation, of forgiving God the wrongs He has done humanity. But there is none of that in *The Alteration.* It is an almost bitter book by a man grown angry in middle age.''

W. Hutchings, however, does not regard the novel as an attack on Catholicism. Despite sharing Cook's conviction that Amis's concern in his works since *The Anti-Death League* has been increasingly metaphysical, even theological, Hutchings maintains that the novel presents Amis with a way of making sense of a world ''both absurd and threatening. Death, which dominates much of his fiction (for example, *The Anti-Death League, The Green Man,* and *Ending Up*), may be meaningless, but it cannot be viewed dispassionately. If death is horrible and God, should he exist, is either cruel or teasing, life has all the more to be lived for its present values. If we don't want it now, we'll never get it. . . . It is here that *The Alteration* represents a fascinating new step in Amis's career. If art is to have any value in such a world, then it must be part of the reason for wanting it now. The structure of the novel and its use of a musically talented main character bring a consciousness of the importance of art directly into its presentation of some problems of life.''

From *The Alteration* to *Jake's Thing,* Amis again made the transition from science fiction to ''comic diatribe,'' according to V. S. Pritchett in the *New York Review of Books.* Pritchett considers *Jake's Thing* ''a very funny book, less for its action or its talk than in its prose. . . . Mr. Amis is a master of laconic mimicry and of the vernacular drift.'' A reviewer writes in *Choice* that this is ''the Amis of *Lucky Jim,* an older and wiser comic writer who is making a serious statement about the human condition.''

The story focuses on Jake Richardson, a sixty-year-old reader in Early Mediterranean History at Oxford who in the past has been to bed with well over a hundred women but now suffers from a loss of libido. Referred to sex therapist Dr. Proinsias (Celtic, pronounced ''Francis'') Rosenberg, Jake, says *Nation's* Amy Wilentz, ''is caught up in the supermarket of contemporary life. The novel is filled with encounter groups, free love, women's liberation, and such electronic contrivances as the 'nocturnal mensurator,' which measures the level of a man's arousal as he sleeps.'' Christopher Lehmann-Haupt of the *New York Times* notes that Amis ''makes the most of all the comic possibilities here. Just imagine sensible, civilized Jake coming home from Dr. Rosenberg's office with . . . assignments to study 'pictorial pornographic material' and to 'write out a sexual fantasy in not less than six hundred words.' Consider Jake struggling to find seventy-three more words, or contemplating the nudes in *Mezzanine* magazine, which 'had an exotic appearance, like the inside of a giraffe's ear or a tropical fruit not much prized even by the locals.'''

But for all the hilarity, there is an undercurrent of seriousness running through the novel. ''It comes bubbling up,'' writes Lehmann-Haupt, ''when Jake finally grows fed up with Dr. Rosenberg and his experiments.'' Wilentz argues that the novel expresses ''outrage at, and defeat at the hands of, modernity, whose graceless intrusion on one's privacy is embodied in Dr. Rosenberg's constantly repeated question, 'I take it you've no objection to exposing your genitals in public?''' Malcolm Bradbury shares this interpretation, writing in the *New Statesman:* ''Amis, watching [history's] collectivising, behaviourist, depersonalizing progress, would like nice things to win and certain sense to prevail. Indeed, a humanist common sense—along with attention to farts—is to his world view roughly what post-Heideggerian existentialism is to Jean-Paul Sartre's.''

John Updike, however, offers another interpretation. Reviewing the book in the *New Yorker,* he calls the satire ''more horrifying than biting, more pathetic than amusing.'' Updike claims that the book does not demonstrate that Dr. Rosenberg, in peddling the ideas and techniques of sex therapy, is a charlatan, ''though Jake comes to believe so, and the English reader might be disposed to expect so. To an American, conditioned to tolerance of all sorts of craziness on behalf of the soul, the exercises of group therapy seem at least a gallant attack upon virtually intractable forms of human loneliness and mental misery.'' Updike views *Jake's Thing* as a portrait of a man infuriated by the times in which he lives. As such, he concludes it is ''satisfyingly ambiguous, relentless, and full. Jake has more complaints than the similarly indisposed Alexander Portnoy [in *Portnoy's Complaint* by Philip Roth]. . . . He suffers from moments of seeing 'the world in its true light, as a place where nothing had ever been any good and nothing of significance done.' He is in a rage. Yet he is also dutiful, loyal in his fashion, and beset; we accept him as a good fellow, an honest godless citizen of the late twentieth century, trying hard to cope with the heretical possibility that sex isn't everything.''

After the problems of libido in *Jake's Thing,* writes Blake Morrison in the *Times Literary Supplement, Russian Hide-and-Seek* ''signals the return of the young, uncomplicated, highly sexed Amis male; . . . the more important connection, however, is with Amis's earlier novel, *The Alteration.*'' Another example of the ''alternative-world'' novel, *Russian Hide-and-Seek* depicts an England, fifty years hence, that has been overrun by the Soviet Union; oddly enough, though, the Soviets have abandoned Marxism and returned to the style of Russia under the czars. Paul Binding describes the book in the *New Statesman* as ''at once a pastiche of certain aspects of nineteenth-century Russian fiction and an exercise in cloak-and-dagger adventure. The two genres unite to form a work far more ambitious than those earlier *jeux*—a fictional expression of the author's obsessive conviction that, whatever its avatar, Russian culture is beastly, thriving on conscious exploitation, enamoured of brutality.''

Binding considers the indictment of Russian culture only moderately successful, citing as a weakness Amis's characterizations: ''For the most part he has accorded his twenty-first-century Russians only the outward rituals and attitudes—and indeed attitudinisings—of their ancestors. . . . If Amis believes that [the ideologies and social structure of the Soviet Union] now contain the germinating seeds of reversion, then—even in a fictional parable—evidence should be given.'' Morrison admits *Russian Hide-and-Seek* ''is not all it might be'' but maintains it is a novel ''of interest and subtlety.'' He believes that along with *The Alteration, Russian Hide-and-Seek* confirms in Amis's body of work ''a development away from the provincial, lower-middle class comic novels of the 1950s and the metropolitan, upper-middle, satirical ones of the 1960s and early 1970s towards an interest in serious politico-historical fiction (*The Anti-Death League* was an early forerunner).''

Amis's versatility, particularly apparent in his attempts at genre fiction, makes categorizing him as a novelist difficult. Though some critics share Morrison's perception of an increasing seriousness in his work, others continue to see him primarily as a comic novelist with some serious overtones. Hutchings, a member of the former group, suggests one reason for the conflict: ''A disturbing co-existence of [farce and seriousness] is often to be found in an Amis novel.'' Hutchings points out that this quality of alternating the farcical with the serious has even led some critics to claim that Amis belongs to a line of English novelists exemplified by Henry Fielding: "Tom Jones, like many of Amis's heroes, finally gets the girl in a triumph of goodheartedness over hypocrisy and meanness." But he argues that despite the similarity, "we are really in a different mode of writing with Amis: What has he to substitute for Fielding's exact relation to past values and literary norms in his use of picaresque and mock-epic? Amis's points of reference are uncompromisingly modern: hence the ghost story of *The Green Man* or (loosely) the science fiction of *The Alteration*."

Amis continues to elude categorization partly because he actively fights it. "'I agree with Kipling,'" he explains in a *Publishers Weekly* interview, that "'as soon as you find you can do something, try something you can't. As a professional writer one should range as widely as possible.'" Reflecting on efforts to categorize him and on his excursions into new areas of fiction, Amis muses in *Contemporary Literature*: "So I'm a funny writer, am I? [*Ending Up*], you'll have to admit, is quite serious. Oh, so I'm primarily a comic writer with some serious overtones and undertones? Try that with *The Anti-Death League* and see how that fits. So I'm a writer about society, twentieth-century man and our problems? Try that one on *The Green Man*. Except for one satirical portrait, that of the clergyman, it is about something quite different. So there is a lot of sex? Try that on [*Ending Up*], in which sexual things [are] referred to, but they've all taken place in the past because of the five central characters the youngest is seventy-one. So you dislike the youth of today, Mr. Amis, as in *Girl, 20*? Try that on [*Ending Up*] where all the young people are sympathetic and all the old people are unsympathetic. This can be silly, but I think it helps to prevent one from repeating oneself, and [Robert] Graves [said] the most dreadful thing in the world is that you're writing a book and you suddenly realize you're writing a book you've written before. Awful. I haven't quite done that yet, but it's certainly something to guard against."

MEDIA ADAPTATIONS: British Lion filmed *Lucky Jim* in 1957 and *That Uncertain Feeling,* renamed "Only Two Can Play" and starring Peter Sellers, in 1961. Columbia produced *Take a Girl Like You* in 1971.

AVOCATIONAL INTERESTS: Music (jazz, Mozart), thrillers, television, science fiction.

CA INTERVIEW

CA interviewed Kingsley Amis by phone May 21, 1981, at his home in London, England.

CA: You've written fiction, poetry, biography, criticism, a magazine column, television scripts. What's led you to take on such a variety of challenges?

AMIS: I started off with poetry, and I would have been a poet entirely if I had had my way. But of course one's way doesn't come into it. My second choice was fiction, and then I just got the other ideas. These things happen bit by bit; there was no policy. The chance of writing a small biography arrived and it seemed easy to take it on. The old idea of a challenge, it's got quite a lot in it, I think.

CA: In a 1975 Paris Review *interview you described how writing had gotten easier in certain ways over the years. Has it in any way become more difficult?*

AMIS: Oh yes, I think so. Any obligation to give any kind of report on today, as it were, makes for difficulty, and I think most writers who are writing about their own time do feel that. They can't help it. They will be making some sort of statement about the life around them, whether they want to or not, and I think that gets harder as one gets older. For instance, if anybody wants to know what is happening in London these days, whatever that means, they'd be much better off asking my son than asking myself. Also, one has a restricted number of favorite situations, favorite characters, favorite kinds of events. So the difficulty of not repeating oneself obviously becomes more acute.

CA: Are you writing much for television now?

AMIS: No, I haven't for some time. Again, that's very much a question of when one is asked. I've done five television plays, but none very recently. That, I think, is the result of internal difficulties in England today.

CA: Did you enjoy the television writing when you were doing it?

AMIS: Oh yes, very much. It's much nicer than writing fiction; the two things work in different ways. For a television script, I and the producer and the director would agree on an outline, and then I would just go off and write it. That sounds easy, and it is easy. When the order of events is determined, there's not much more to be done than the job of writing the dialogue, which I find comparatively straightforward, much easier than description and narrative, which to me is much harder work.

CA: Have you had a hand in the film productions based on your books?

AMIS: No. I chatted and conferred, but I didn't write the screenplays.

CA: You've written science fiction and a study of science fiction, New Maps of Hell: A Survey of Science Fiction *(1960). Do you follow science-fiction writing closely now?*

AMIS: Not anymore, no. It's all collapsed, it's gone to pot. The older writers are usually doing something else now; they're writing other kinds of fiction or nonfiction or they've stopped writing altogether, or some of them—I won't mention their names—are repeating themselves, writing just what they were writing before. And I see no younger writers coming out that please me at all.

CA: Do you miss teaching?

AMIS: Teaching is a drain on the energy, of course, and it goes with a lot of things that aren't necessarily associated with it but somehow always are, like sitting on committees and attending formal dinners and things like that which I didn't like so well. What I do miss, just occasionally, is the chance of discussing specific literary points with one other person or a small number of other persons. You can't really do that in ordinary conversation. You can't really discuss Shakespeare for half an hour. After ten seconds people get restless and say, "Can I get you another drink?" You can only do that sort of discussion if you're teaching or being taught, and I do miss that occasionally.

CA: Were the teaching position at Princeton and the semester at Vanderbilt helpful to you in any specific way in the writing?

AMIS: I don't know. I can't really say about that. I don't know if the teaching helps me at all, but meeting two very different kinds of life that weren't familiar to me may have been. I think it's a good thing for a novelist to move about. Jane Austen gained a lot sitting still, but we can't all be like her, and we shouldn't be. I think the profession has changed, and it's a good thing.

CA: Do you feel any literary kinship with any writers in the United States?

AMIS: There's one, Peter De Vries. I think he's a wonderful writer, but he does seem to be very different from other American writers. I think there was a brief period when I thought that I saw some things the same way J. D. Salinger did, but that time has passed. They are the only ones.

CA: Have you found American publishers fairly easy to work with?

AMIS: I have to say no to that. They're not impossible or terrible, but not easy to work with. All publishers are bad in the same sort of way. They tend to regard themselves as the professionals and the authors merely as amateurs: the author delivers an unshaped hunk of work which the publishers, the professionals, then proceed to lick into shape, and then they publish it. But I think American publishers are worse than British publishers because they're more energetic, not so lazy. What I particularly notice is that they make more changes without consulting the author. There are some writers, obviously, who are more or less illiterate and who can't punctuate. It's probably a kindness to people like that to put things in order for them. But I consider that I do know about commas, and when I put one in or leave it out, it's on purpose. I don't like the wholesale removal or putting in of commas. Some kinds of books need to be heavily punctuated and others lightly punctuated. Editors are trying to impose some sort of standard, and the authors, of course, are all fighting to be individual.

CA: Do you ever do promotional tours in either country?

AMIS: Never in the United States, and I can't really call them commercial tours in England—just getting on the train to Manchester or somewhere and appearing on local television or local radio, all that in a day, that type of thing, but on a very small scale.

CA: Do you have the book signings where all the ladies come in and have you sign their books?

AMIS: A few of the ladies, yes. I've been to several of those.

CA: Do you hear a lot from readers?

AMIS: I don't know what a lot is. I think I get about two or three letters a week, that's all. When a new book comes out, it sometimes increases. I get more letters after remarks to the press. If I'm fool enough, incautious enough, to say, as I did about two months ago, that there don't seem to be any good new poets about, I get deluged with stuff.

CA: Do you continue to get letters about the earlier books?

AMIS: Yes. *Lucky Jim* still raises an occasional question.

CA: Music has been a very important part of your life. What kind of music do you most enjoy now?

AMIS: The music of the eighteenth and nineteenth centuries, really, and jazz of a particular period, between about 1925 and around 1955—from early Louis Armstrong. . . . I suppose Ruby Braff is about the newest musician that I've enjoyed.

CA: You've described golf as "a game I hope fervently to go to my grave without once having had to play." Do you exercise or participate in any kind of sport?

AMIS: No, none whatever.

CA: Is there a lot of jogging in England?

AMIS: Oh yes, a tremendous amount. You cannot go a quarter of a mile in a taxi without seeing somebody.

CA: You're concerned about language. Is English in England being corrupted by technological and sociological jargon as badly as it is in this country?

AMIS: Yes, probably. A lot of new words for technology I can't mind, a specialized vocabulary. Sociology, yes. There's a general sense that the use of the language is becoming dull, conventional, routine. That's one thing, and bad enough it is. But also there is a growth of what I would call illiteracy. People no longer know very closely what words mean, and of course wouldn't dream of looking in the dictionary. That habit was built into me and into my generation very firmly. People no longer want to get the right word or get the best version. I think the problem is in education. The tendency here now is not to teach foreign languages. If you learn a foreign language, you're always wondering, "Have I got the right word?" The habit of wondering if you've got the right word is indispensable in producing something readable.

CA: Do you think dropping Latin from the curricula of most schools has been a big factor?

AMIS: I think the problem goes back further than that. Certainly some knowledge of Latin is very useful, or can be very useful. But I think it's more important to inculcate that habit of wondering what a word originally meant, even in English perhaps, or really means now. If you take the word *dilapidated,* to most people that's a mere synonym for "in a bad state" or "in a reduced state." But when you remember that it's to do with the stones of a house being pulled away from the house or falling from it on top of one another, then you can use the word more vigorously.

CA: Did you set out to do something in Rudyard Kipling and His World *that hadn't been done in previous Kipling biographies?*

AMIS: No. The ground had been worked over so thoroughly there that to get something new would have been impossible. As I say in my introduction, everything about Kipling is in print by now, but some of it is less well known, and I think one can find a few connections that other people have missed.

CA: Was the Penthouse *column fun to do?*

AMIS: Yes, I hope to return to doing that very soon. In a way you can run out of material, but in another way there's always something fresh to say about drinks, because there's always a change—fashions come and go.

CA: Was it a difficult process to select the poems to be included in your new book, Collected Poems, 1944-1979?

AMIS: The difficult part was hardening my heart and throwing out some of the ones that I had already published earlier. There aren't many of those. What I wrote early on is very much cut down and shortened in the collection. I should think that four-fifths of all the poems I've written over about the last thirty years are in that book, perhaps even a little more.

CA: You seem to have enjoyed your work a lot. Is there anything you wish you had done or anything different you plan to do in the future?

AMIS: I always wish that I had done what I have done more carefully, but then there's the law of diminishing returns. I think I could have made *Lucky Jim* five percent better by spending another six months on it, but then one wants to get on to the next one, and that always applies. I wish it were better, that's all. There are one or two kinds of books I hope one day that I still will write. For example, I'd like to write a detective story, nothing to do with spying except perhaps in a very indirect way, but I think such things have to be set in the nineteenth century. That's the sort of thing I have in mind that I would *like* to write, adventure, when the world was not as small a place as it is now—the sort of thing that might remind people of John Buchan or Rider Haggard. I don't know that I ever will get around to that.

BIOGRAPHICAL/CRITICAL SOURCES—Books: Kenneth Allsop, *The Angry Decade*, P. Owen, 1958; Gene Feldman and Max Gartenberg, editors, *The Beat Generation and the Angry Young Men*, Citadel, 1958.

James Gindin, *Postwar British Fiction*, University of California Press, 1962; Frederick R. Karl, *The Contemporary English Novel*, Farrar, Straus, 1962; Howard Nemerov, *Poetry and Fiction: Essays*, Rutgers University Press, 1963; William Van O'Connor, *The New University Wits and the End of Modernism*, Southern Illinois University Press, 1963; Walter Allen, *The Modern Novel*, Dutton, 1964; Charles Shapiro, editor, *Contemporary British Novelists*, Southern Illinois University Press, 1965; Edmund Wilson, *The Bit between My Teeth: A Literary Chronicle of 1950-1965*, Farrar, Straus, 1965; David Lodge, *Language of Fiction*, Columbia University Press, 1966; Brigid Brophy, *Don't Never Forget*, Holt, 1967; Rubin Rabinovitz, *The Reaction against Experiment in the English Novel, 1950-1960*, Columbia University Press, 1967; Anthony Burgess, *The Novel Now: A Guide to Contemporary Fiction*, Norton, 1967.

Bernard Bergonzi, *The Situation of the Novel*, University of Pittsburgh Press, 1970; Lodge, *The Novelist at the Crossroads and Other Essays on Fiction and Criticism*, Cornell University Press, 1971; *Contemporary Literary Criticism*, Gale, Volume I, 1973, Volume II, 1974, Volume III, 1975, Volume V, 1976, Volume VIII, 1978, Volume XIII, 1980; *Authors in the News*, Volume II, Gale, 1976.

Periodicals: *Spectator*, January 29, 1954, September 2, 1955, January 17, 1958, September 23, 1960, October 11, 1969; *Nation*, January 30, 1954, August 20, 1955, April 28, 1969, May 5, 1969, October 5, 1970, April 7, 1979; *New Statesman*, January 30, 1954, August 20, 1955, January 18, 1958, September 24, 1960, November 28, 1963, July 7, 1967, December 1, 1967, October 11, 1968, November 21, 1975, October 8, 1976, September 15, 1978, April 13, 1979, May 23, 1980; *New York Times*, January 31, 1954, February 26, 1956, February 23, 1958, April 25, 1967, April 25, 1968, March 12, 1969, August 17, 1970, January 6, 1972, May 11, 1979; *Manchester Guardian*, February 2, 1954, August 23, 1955, November 30, 1956; *Times Literary Supplement*, February 12, 1954, September 16, 1955, January 17, 1958, September 21, 1962, November 23, 1967, March 28, 1968, September 24, 1971, April 6, 1973, October 8, 1976, September 22, 1978, May 16, 1980, October 24, 1980, November 27, 1981; *Saturday Review*, February 20, 1954, May 7, 1955, February 25, 1956, July 27, 1957, March 8, 1958, April 6, 1963, April 5, 1969, February 5, 1977; *New Yorker*, March 6, 1954, March 24, 1956, March 24, 1958, April 26, 1969, September 13, 1969, October 21, 1974, August 20, 1979; *Atlantic*, April, 1956, April, 1958, July, 1965, June, 1968, June, 1970; *Christian Science Monitor*, January 16, 1958, September 24, 1970; *Commonweal*, March 21, 1958; *New Republic*, March 24, 1958, September 19, 1970, October 12, 1974; *Wilson Library Bulletin*, May, 1958, May, 1965.

New York Times Book Review, April 28, 1963, July 25, 1965, April 28, 1968, May 19, 1968, March 23, 1969, August 23, 1970, November 11, 1973, October 20, 1974, April 18, 1976, January 30, 1977, May 13, 1979; *Newsweek*, March 2, 1964, May 8, 1967, May 6, 1968, September 14, 1970, September 30, 1974; *Books and Bookmen*, December, 1965, July, 1968, January, 1969, September, 1969, October, 1978; *Critique*, spring-summer, 1966, Volume IX, number 1, 1968; *New York Review of Books*, October 6, 1966, August 1, 1968, March 9, 1972, March 20, 1975, April 15, 1976, March 3, 1977, May 17, 1979; *Listener*, November 9, 1967, January 11, 1968, November 26, 1970, May 30, 1974; *Observer Review*, November 12, 1967, October 6, 1968; *London Magazine*, January, 1968, August, 1968, October, 1968, January, 1970; *Punch*, April 24, 1968, August 28, 1968, October 12, 1968, October 22, 1969, November 18, 1970; *Life*, May 3, 1968, March 14, 1969, August 28, 1970; *Washington Post Book World*, May 5, 1968, August 8, 1968, October 20, 1968; *Best Sellers*, May 15, 1968, April 1, 1969; *Poetry Review*, spring, 1968; *National Review*, June 18, 1968, June 3, 1969, August 25, 1970, October 27, 1973, February 1, 1974, March 14, 1975; *Poetry*, July, 1969; *National Observer*, September 15, 1969; *Yale Review*, autumn, 1969, summer, 1975.

Library Journal, July, 1970; *Time*, August 31, 1970, September 10, 1973, September 30, 1974, June 12, 1978; *New Leader*, September 21, 1970; *Bookseller*, November 11, 1970; *Hudson Review*, summer, 1972, winter, 1973-74, winter, 1974-75; *Saturday Review/World*, May 8, 1973; *Publishers Weekly*, October 28, 1974; *Encounter*, November, 1974, January, 1979; *Contemporary Literature*, winter, 1975; *Paris Review*, winter, 1975; *Critical Quarterly*, summer, 1977; *Choice*, November, 1979; *Los Angeles Times Book Review*, May 4, 1980; *Times* (London), May 15, 1980, December 31, 1980.†

—Sketch by James G. Lesniak

—Interview by Jean W. Ross

* * *

AMIS, Martin 1949-

PERSONAL: Born August 25, 1949, in Oxford, England: son of Kingsley William (the writer) and Hilary (Bardwell) Amis. *Education:* Oxford University, B.A. (with honors), 1971. *Home:* 14 Kensington Gardens Sq., London W.2, England. *Agent:* Jonathan Cape Ltd., 30 Bedford Square, London WC1B 3EL, England.

CAREER: Times Literary Supplement, London, England, editorial assistant, 1972-75; *New Statesman*, London, assistant literary editor, beginning 1975; currently full-time writer. *Awards, honors:* Somerset Maugham Award, National Book League, 1974, for *The Rachel Papers*.

WRITINGS: The Rachel Papers (novel), J. Cape, 1973, Knopf, 1974; *Dead Babies* (novel), J. Cape, 1975, Knopf, 1976; (with others) *My Oxford,* edited and introduced by Ann Thwaite, Robson Books, 1977; *Dark Secrets,* Panther, 1977; *Success* (novel), J. Cape, 1978; *Other People: A Mystery Story* (novel), Viking, 1981. Contributor to periodicals, including *Times Literary Supplement, Observer, New Statesman, New York Times,* and *Sunday Telegraph.*

SIDELIGHTS: The son of English novelist Kingsley Amis, Martin Amis has firmly established a reputation of his own, having created in such novels as *The Rachel Papers, Dead Babies, Success,* and *Other People* a recognizable fictional world, one described by Michiko Kakutani of the *New York Times* as "a place defined by Swiftian excess and metropolitan satire, a place where variously shabby characters partake of lust and violence and guilt in hopes of being allowed a second chance." Blake Morrison of the *Times Literary Supplement* notes that Martin "has certainly not been afraid to borrow either [his father's] favourite phrases ('All fixed,' 'How about you?,' 'I want you . . . Now') or his oldest jokes. But in doing so he has indicated the difference in their approaches. When in *The Rachel Papers* ['Lucky Jim'] Dixon's commonsensical 'nice things are nicer than nasty ones' was altered to 'Surely, nice things are dull, and nasty things are funny,' the revision was a calculated one: Martin Amis was making clear that 'nastiness,' the comedy of the grotesque, was to be his specialty."

Morrison points out that in Amis's first three novels the objects of satire are familiar to readers of contemporary fiction: adolescent sex in *The Rachel Papers,* drugs and communal living in *Dead Babies,* and bisexuality and incest in *Success.* Jerome Charyn concludes in the *New York Times Book Review* that Amis is "so horrified by the world he sees in the process of formation that he feels compelled to warn us all about it." With *Other People,* however, Morrison sees a slight shift away from contemporary satire to "the contemplation of more universal verities. In an unprogrammatic way the novel explores notions of time, identity and self-responsibility; and it creates its own bleak universe in which lost souls wander vainly in search of the perfect match, the 'other people' who might make them whole."

According to Kakutani, many American readers first became aware of Martin Amis as the British author who charged that his novel *The Rachel Papers* had been plagiarized by Jacob Epstein, an American. Amis alleged in an October 19, 1980, article in the *London Observer* that some fifty sizable chunks of Epstein's first novel, *Wild Oats,* were virtual duplications of wording from *The Rachel Papers,* which had been published six years earlier in 1973. Susan Heller Anderson of the *New York Times* writes that when Amis first made the discovery, he "pondered what action to take. 'My own resentment was largely one of embarrassment,' he said. 'I am no real admirer of my first novel or indeed my second, regarding them as a mixture of clumsy apprenticeship and unwarranted showing off. It shamed me to see sentences exhumed for reinspection ten years on.'" Anderson reports that the *London Observer* article was Amis's only revenge and quotes him as saying: "'I'm not terrifically indignant, but just feel it ought to be made public. . . . The saddest thing about the case is that *Wild Oats* is the work of a genuinely talented writer.'"

Two days after Amis's article appeared, Jacob Epstein verbally admitted that he had indeed copied passages and images from Amis, as well as from other writers. Epstein then explained in the October 26, 1980, issue of the *London Observer* that out of admiration and a desire to learn his craft, he had copied passages from *The Rachel Papers* and from books by Nabokov, Turgenev, and Goethe into several notebooks. "After several rewrites and homogenizations," writes Anderson, "Mr. Epstein . . . assumed he was now working with virtually original wording." When Epstein discovered in June of 1979 that several phrases and images in his novel had come verbatim from *The Rachel Papers,* he asked his editor at Little, Brown & Co. about making revisions. Though this was impossible for the first printing, Epstein did make thirteen deletions for the second American edition and asked that the British publisher work from the revision. The letter to the British publisher, however, went astray.

Embarrassed by the British edition, Amis was infuriated by the revised American edition, because Epstein, who had recognized and regretted his error, only made thirteen deletions. According to an interview quoted by Anderson, Amis replied: "'There aren't thirteen bits, there are fifty odd bits from my book. Looking at his revisions, he had lost track of what he'd taken from me. How do you rewrite a novel and leave word-for-word passages?'"

BIOGRAPHICAL/CRITICAL SOURCES: *New Statesman,* November 16, 1973; *Times Literary Supplement,* November 16, 1973, October 17, 1975, April 14, 1978, March 6, 1981; *Encounter,* February, 1974, September, 1978; *Newsweek,* May 6, 1974; *New York Times Book Review,* May 26, 1974, February 8, 1976, April 5, 1981, July 26, 1981; *New Yorker,* June 24, 1974; *Times Educational Supplement,* July 12, 1974; *New York Review of Books,* July 18, 1974; *Contemporary Literary Criticism,* Gale, Volume IV, 1975, Volume IX, 1978; *New York Times,* January 16, 1976, October 21, 1980, October 28, 1980, August 20, 1981; *London Observer,* October 19, 1980, October 26, 1980.†

* * *

AMON, Aline 1928-

PERSONAL: Surname rhymes with "salmon"; born October 15, 1928, in Paris, France; daughter of U.S. citizens, Will Rice (an architect) and Aline (Halstead) Amon; married Laurance Villers Goodrich (an attorney), October 31, 1953; children: Nielsen Halstead, Lauren Aline. *Education:* Wellesley College, B.A., 1950; additional study at Art Student's League of New York, 1952, 1953. *Politics:* Democratic. *Religion:* None. *Home:* 295 Henry St., Brooklyn, N.Y. 11201.

CAREER: Appleton-Century-Crofts, Inc., New York, N.Y., secretary in college text department, 1950-51; U.S. Air Force, Paris, France, executive secretary in military liaison office, 1951-52; free-lance writer and illustrator, 1966—. Director of playground safety program, Brooklyn Heights, N.Y., 1963-64. *Member:* Authors Guild, Authors League of America. *Awards, honors:* New York Public Library listed *Talking Hands* as one of the ten best Christmas gift books, 1968; Outstanding Children's Science Book Award, National Science Teachers Association and Children's Book Council, for *Reading, Writing, Chattering Chimps* and *Roadrunners and Other Cuckoos.*

WRITINGS—All juveniles; all self-illustrated: *Talking Hands: How to Use Indian Sign Language,* Doubleday, 1968; *Reading, Writing, Chattering Chimps* (Junior Literary Guild selection), Atheneum, 1975; *Orangutan, Endangered Ape,* Atheneum, 1977; *Roadrunners and Other Cuckoos,* Atheneum, 1978; (contributor) G. G. Duffy and L. R. Roehler, editors, *Building Reading Skills,* McDougal, Littell, 1979; (contributor) Z. Sutherland, editor, *Close to the Sun,* Open Court, 1979; (contributor) *Reading Lanterns,* American Book Co., 1980; *The Earth Is Sore: Native Americans on Nature,* Atheneum, 1981.

WORK IN PROGRESS: A book of satiric verse and a novel, both for adults.

SIDELIGHTS: Aline Amon told *CA:* "I combined my concern for endangered wildlife with [my interest in] Native Americans for *The Earth Is Sore: Native Americans on Nature,* a collection of Indian quotations that decry, with great eloquence, what white people have done to this country. It is illustrated with collages of prints from natural materials—leaves, flowers, rocks—even a few insects and a fish.

"The depressed nature of the market for children's nonfiction, plus the fact that each book I wrote seemed to be for older readers than its predecessor, led me to start an adult novel. However, I missed the challenge of illustrating, so I postponed that briefly to write a book of satiric verses, a 'picture book' for adults.... The challenge of putting words and pictures together—building a book rather than just writing it—is too satisfying to permit me to become an author for adults only."

Reading, Writing, Chattering Chimps was translated into Japanese.

AVOCATIONAL INTERESTS: Watercolor painting, photography, gardening, travel.

* * *

ANDERSEN, Richard 1931-

PERSONAL: Born August 23, 1931, in Kansas City, Kan.; son of Marius Teodor (a carpenter) and Ellen K. (Christensen) Andersen; married Lois Jeannette Petersen (a music teacher), June 9, 1957; children: Kristyn, Deryk, Jennifer. *Education:* Dana College, B.A., 1953; Trinity Theological Seminary (now Wartburg Theological Seminary), B.D., 1960; California Graduate School of Theology, Ph.D., 1972. *Home:* 2863 Heather Rd., Long Beach, Calif. 90815. *Office:* Our Saviour's Lutheran Church, 370 Junipero Ave., Long Beach, Calif. 90815.

CAREER: Dana College, Blair, Neb., public relations assistant, 1951-53; University of Dubuque, Dubuque, Iowa, public relations assistant, 1957-60; ordained Lutheran minister, 1960; associate pastor of Lutheran church in North Hollywood, Calif., 1960-62; founding pastor of Lutheran church in Ojai, Calif., 1962-64; senior pastor of Lutheran churches in Rancho Cordova, Calif., 1964-68, and La Habra, Calif., 1968-73; Community Church of Joy, Glendale, Ariz., founding pastor, 1973-78; Our Saviour's Lutheran Church, Long Beach, Calif., pastor, 1978—. Executive director of Lutheran schools in Hacienda Heights, Calif., 1973. Member of Lutheran campus council at Arizona State University; member of Office of Communication and Mission Support Standing Committee, American Lutheran Church, 1972-80; member of board of regents, Dana College, 1978-82. *Military service:* U.S. Army, 1954-56. *Member:* Glendale Samaritan Hospital Chaplain's Organization.

WRITINGS—Published by Concordia, except as indicated: *Devotions Along the Way,* Augsburg, 1972; *Loving in Forgiveness,* 1973; *Your Keys to the Executive Suite,* 1973; *Flights of Devotion,* 1973; *Roads to Recovery,* 1974; *For Those Who Mourn,* 1974; *Now for the Good Wine,* 1974; *The Love Formula: Living in Forgiveness,* 1974; *Living Lenten Portraits,* 1975; *Devotions for Church School Teachers,* 1979; (with Roy Barlag) *They Were There,* 1977; (with Donald L. Deffner) *For Example,* 1977; *Inspirational Meditations for Sunday School Teachers,* 1980; *A Little Library of Inspiration for Sunday School Teachers,* 1982; *The Positive Power of Christian Partnership,* 1982. Contributor to religious periodicals.

WORK IN PROGRESS: New devotional publications and two novels.

SIDELIGHTS: Richard Andersen wrote *CA:* "When I sit at the typewriter and the thoughts begin to pour upon the page, I believe I sense what thrills the conductor has who awakens a still orchestra to the beauty of sound. And when I convey a thought that has a source beyond me, but has injected itself in the fluency of the Spirit, I sense what creative joy emanated from the commands of God. There is a distinctive sacramental wonder to the enfleshment of words; a breaking of bread, a savor of wine that can only come from a loving God. For me, writing is one of the sublimest of joys."

AVOCATIONAL INTERESTS: International travel, photography.

* * *

ANDERSON, Bernhard Word 1916-

PERSONAL: Born September 25, 1916, in Dover, Mo.; son of Arthur Lincoln and Grace (Word) Anderson; married Joyce Griswold, September 22, 1936; children: Carol Joyce, Sylvia Joan, Ronald Bernhard, Ruth Anne. *Education:* University of the Pacific, B.A., 1936; Pacific School of Religion, M.A., 1938, B.D., 1939; Yale University, Ph.D., 1945. *Home:* Laurel Lane, Charlemont, Mass. 01339. *Office:* Princeton Theological Seminary, Princeton, N.J. 08540.

CAREER: Ordained minister of United Methodist Church, 1939; pastor in Pittsburg, Calif., 1936-37, Sunnyvale, Calif., 1937-41, Connecticut, 1942-44, Millbrae, Calif., 1944-46, and Columbus, N.Y., 1946-48; Colgate University, Hamilton, N.Y., instructor in religion, 1946-48; University of North Carolina at Chapel Hill, James A. Gray Associate Professor of Bible, 1948-50; Colgate-Rochester Divinity School, Rochester, N.Y., Joseph B. Hoyt Professor of Old Testament Interpretation, 1950-54; Drew University, Theological Seminary, Madison, N.J., Henry Anson Buttz Professor of Biblical Theology, 1954-68, dean, 1954-63; Princeton Theological Seminary, Princeton, N.J., professor of Old Testament theology, 1968-82. Chairman of Study Department of United Student Christian Council, 1951-54; Annual Professor of Archaeology, American School of Oriental Research, Jerusalem, 1963-64; Lund Lecturer, North Park Theological Seminary, 1965; Burns Memorial Lecturer, University of Otago, 1969; Haskel Lecturer, Oberlin College, 1970; Francis Youngker Vosburgh Lecturer, Drew University, 1977; Alexander Clinton Zabriskie Lecturer, Virginia Theological Seminary, 1978. Active in Y.M.C.A., Y.W.C.A., and Student Christian Movement.

MEMBER: Society of Biblical Literature, American Academy of Religion, Bible Theologians, American Theological Society, Pi Gamma Mu. *Awards, honors:* D.D., Pacific School of Religion, 1960, Colgate University, 1965; S.T.D., University of the Pacific, 1961.

WRITINGS: *Rediscovering the Bible,* Association Press, 1951; *The Unfolding Drama of the Bible: Eight Studies Introducing the Bible as a Whole,* Association Press, 1953, revised edition, 1971; *Understanding the Old Testament,* Prentice-Hall, 1957, 3rd edition, 1975; *The Living World of the Old Testament,* Longmans, Green, 1958, 2nd edition, 1967; (editor with Walter Harrelson, and contributor) *Israel's Prophetic Heritage: Essays in Honor of James Muilenburg,* Harper, 1962; (editor) *The Old Testament and Christian Faith: A Theological Discussion,* Harper, 1963; *The Beginning of History: Genesis,* Abingdon, 1963; *Creation versus Chaos: The Reinterpretation of Mythical Symbolism in the Bible,* Association Press, 1967; *Out of the Depths: Studies into the Meaning of the Book of Psalms,* Westminster, 1974; (editor and contributor) Will Herburg, *Faith Enacted as History,* Westminster, 1976; *The Eighth-*

Century Prophets, Fortress, 1978; *The Living Word of the Bible,* Westminster, 1979. Contributor to *Interpreter's Bible* and to journals in his field. Chairman of editorial board, *Christian Scholar,* 1956-58; member of editorial board, *Old Testament Library,* 1974—.

WORK IN PROGRESS: Commentary on the Book of Genesis, for Fortress; a book on Old Testament theology; editing essays on Creation, for Fortress.

* * *

ANDREE, R(ichard) V(ernon) 1919-

PERSONAL: Born December 16, 1919, in Minneapolis, Minn.; son of Richard A. and Marguerite (Eigner) Andree; married Josephine Peet, December 16, 1944; children: David D., Peter, Suzanne, Jeanne. *Education:* University of Chicago, B.S., 1942; University of Wisconsin, Ph.M., 1945, Ph.D., 1949. *Home:* 627 East Boyd St., Norman, Okla. 73069. *Office:* Department of Mathematics, University of Oklahoma, Norman, Okla. 73071.

CAREER: University of Oklahoma, Norman, assistant professor, 1949-54, associate professor, 1954-57, professor of mathematics, 1957—, professor of information and computing sciences, 1972—, chairman of mathematics department, 1961-69, acting director of Computer Laboratory, 1958, director of Mathematical Computer Consultants, 1962—. Visiting associate professor at Haverford College, 1955-56; visiting professor at Oklahoma State University and Montana State University, both 1956-57; distinguished lecturer at Canadian Mathematics Institute of University of Alberta, 1959; principal lecturer at Karnataki University, 1965. Fellow of National Bureau of Standards, spring, 1959; member of board of governors of Center for Research in College Instruction of Science and Mathematics; director of Computer Systems Engineers; director of Oklahoma Educational Computer Users Program; co-director of Project Crypto; member of advisory panel for computer applications in research, National Science Foundation; research councilor for Oklahoma University's Research Institute.

MEMBER: American Association for the Advancement of Science (fellow), American Mathematical Society, American Society for Engineering Education, Association for Computing Machinery (sponsor of student chapter), Association of Educational Data Systems, Association of Symbolic Logic, COMMON Computer Users Group, Computer Assisted Instruction in Mathematics (member of national committee), Data Processing Management Association (member of Oklahoma City board of directors), Mathematical Association of America, Society for Industrial and Applied Mathematics (visiting lecturer), National Council of Teachers of Mathematics, Oklahoma Council of Teachers of Mathematics, Oklahoma Computing Consortium, Oklahoma Association for Gifted, Creative, and Talented (vice-president), Sigma Xi, Mu Alpha Theta, Pi Mu Epsilon.

AWARDS, HONORS: Carnegie Foundation grant, 1955-56, for research at Haverford College; C. C. MacDuffee Distinguished Service Award, Pi Mu Epsilon, 1966; named to DeMolay Legion of Honor, 1967; Her Majesty's Mint, 1973, for outstanding contributions to international civic leadership with youth groups (England); Outstanding Educator Award, National Council of Teachers of Mathematics, 1973.

WRITINGS: (With J. C. Brixey) *Fundamentals of College Mathematics,* Holt, 1954, revised edition, 1961; *Matrices and Congruences,* Summer Conference for Mathematics Teachers, 1954; *Survey of Abstract Algebra,* Mathematics Teacher's Institute, 1955; *The Need for Modern Mathematics,* National Science Foundation Institute, 1955; *Programming the IBM 650, Magnetic Drum Computer Extension Division,* University of Oklahoma, 1955; (with Brixey) *Modern Trigonometry,* Holt, 1955; *Boolean Algebra,* Department of Electrical Engineering, Oklahoma State University, 1955; *Calculus for Secondary School Science Teachers,* National Science Foundation Year Institute, 1956; *Modern Mathematics for High School Science Teachers,* National Science Foundation Summer Institute, 1957; *Calculus for Mature Students,* McGraw, 1958; *Selections from Modern Abstract Algebra,* Holt, 1958, revised edition, 1971; *Programming the IBM 650 Computer,* Department of Mathematics, University of Oklahoma, 1958; *Preparing a Questionnaire for Punched Card Analysis,* Computing Center, Oklahoma University, 1959.

A Table of Indices and Power Residues for All Primes and Prime Powers below 2000, Norton, 1962; *Introductory Calculus with Analytical Geometry,* McGraw, 1963; *Computer Programming and Related Mathematics for the IBM 1620,* Wiley, 1966; *Introduction a l'Algebre,* Gauthier Villars, 1968, 2nd edition, Mouton, 1970; *Twentieth-Century Algebra in High School,* National Council of Teachers of Mathematics, 1968; (with wife, J. P. Andree, and son, D. D. Andree) *Computer Programming: Techniques, Analysis, and Mathematics,* Prentice-Hall, 1973; (with J. P. Andree) *Cryptarithms,* National Council of Teachers of Mathematics, 1978; *Logic Unlocks,* Mu Alpha Theta, 1979; (with J. P. Andree) *Explore Computing with the TRS-80: With Programming in Basic,* Prentice-Hall, 1982.

Also author, *RAJA Cryptarithms 1,* 1976, *Pattern and Non-Pattern Words of 7-8 Letters,* 1977, *RAJA Cryptarithms 2,* 1979, *Secret Ciphers,* 1979, *Solving Ciphers,* 1979, *Pattern and Non-Pattern Words of 9-10 Letters,* 1979, *RAJA Puzzles 3,* 1980, *RAJA Puzzles 4,* 1980, *RAJA Puzzles 5,* 1980, *Sophisticated Ciphers,* 1980, *Pattern and Non-Pattern Words of 11-12-13 Letters,* 1980, *Logic Unlocks Puzzles,* 1981, *RAJA Crossword Puzzles 8,* 1982, *RAJA Computer Problem 10,* 1982, *Pattern and Non-Pattern Words of 2-6 Letters.* Contributor to *Show and Tell MicroComputer Proceedings,* 1978, 1979, 1980, 1981, 1982.

Contributor to *New Catholic Encyclopedia.* Contributor of more than two hundred fifty articles and reviews to a variety of professional journals. Editor of *Math Log;* founder and former editor of *Oklahoma University Mathematics Letter;* former editor of *Journal of the Mathematical Association of America.*

WORK IN PROGRESS: Problem Solving; Computers Are for You; Numerical Analysis; Computer Literacy; Computers in the Humanities; Cryptographic Frequency Counts.

SIDELIGHTS: R. V. Andree told *CA:* "My wife and I work together on educational projects, particularly those related to gifted/creative/talented in mathematics and computing. Every now and then one of our projects spills over onto paper and we publish it."

* * *

ARDIZZONE, Edward (Jeffrey Irving) 1900-1979

PERSONAL: Born October 16, 1900, in Haiphong, French Indochina (now Vietnam); died November 8, 1979, in London, England; son of Auguste (served in Far East with Eastern Extension Telegraph Co.) and Margaret (Irving) Ardizzone; married Catherine Anderson, April 4, 1928; children: Christianna, Philip, and Nicholas. *Education:* Educated in England. *Religion:* Catholic. *Home:* 130 Elgin Ave., London W. 9, England.

CAREER: Painter, illustrator, and author of children's books. Went into clerical work originally, ending this phase of his career as a statistical clerk with Eastern Telegraph Co. First exhibition in 1928; pictures in Tate Gallery, London, and other major public galleries. Visiting tutor, Royal College of Art, London, 1953-61. *Military service:* British Army, Royal Artillery, 1939-40; served as official war artist in France, North Africa, Sicily, Germany, and Italy, 1940-45. *Member:* Royal Academy (associate), Royal College of Art (honorary associate), Society of Industrial Artists (fellow), Double Crown Club (past president). *Awards, honors:* Kate Greenaway Medal from Library Association of Great Britain, 1956, for *Tim All Alone;* Commander, Order of the British Empire, 1971.

WRITINGS—All self-illustrated: *Little Tim and the Brave Sea Captain,* Oxford University Press, 1936, reprinted, 1978, redrawn version, Walck, 1955; *Lucy Brown and Mr. Grimes,* Oxford University Press, 1937, reprinted, Walck, 1971; *Tim and Lucy Go To Sea,* Oxford University Press, 1938, redrawn version, Walck, 1958; *Baggage to the Enemy* (adult), J. Murray, 1941; *Nicholas and the Fast-Moving Diesel,* Eyre & Spottiswoode, Penguin, 1947, redrawn version, Walck, 1959; *Paul the Hero of the Fire,* Penguin, 1948, revised edition, Walck, 1963; *Tim to the Rescue,* Walck, 1949.

Tim and Charlotte, Walck, 1951; *Tim in Danger,* Walck, 1953, Oxford University Press, 1979; *Tim All Alone,* Walck, 1956; *Johnny the Clockmaker,* Walck, 1960; *Tim's Friend Towser,* Walck, 1962; *Peter the Wanderer,* Walck, 1964; *Diana and Her Rhinoceros,* Walck, 1964, reprinted, Oxford University Press, 1979; *Sarah and Simon and No Red Paint,* Constable, 1965, Delacorte, 1966; *Tim and Ginger,* Walck, 1965; (with granddaughter, Aingelda Ardizzone) *The Little Girl and the Tiny Doll,* Delacorte, 1967; *Tim to the Lighthouse,* Walck, 1968.

The Wrong Side of the Bed, Doubleday, 1970; *Johnny's Bad Day,* Bodley Head, 1970; *Young Ardizzone: An Autobiographical Fragment,* Macmillan, 1970; *Tim's Last Voyage,* Bodley Head, 1972, Walck, 1973; *Diary of a War Artist,* Bodley Head, 1974; *Ship's Cook Ginger,* Bodley Head, 1977, Macmillan, 1978; (compiler and illustrator) *Ardizzone's Hans Andersen: Fourteen Classic Tales,* Deutsch, 1978, Atheneum, 1979; (compiler and illustrator) *Ardizzone's Kilvert: Selections from the Diary of the Reverend Francis Kilvert, 1870-79,* Merrimack Book Service, 1980.

Illustrator: Sheridan Le Fanu, *In a Glass Darkly,* Constable, 1929; George Crabbe, *The Library,* De La Mare Press, 1930; Paul Bloomfield, *A Mediterranean Anthology,* Cassell, 1935; Neil Lyons, *Tom, Dick, and Harriet,* Cresset, 1937; Maurice Gorham, *The Local,* Cassell, 1939; Charles Dickens, *Great Expectations,* Heritage Press, 1939, reprinted, 1967; H. E. Bates, *My Uncle Silas,* J. Cape, 1939; H. J. Kaiser, *Mimff,* Oxford University Press, 1939.

Dennis Freeman and Douglas Cooper, *The Road to Bordeaux,* Cresset, 1941; McCaskie, *Poems by Francois Villon,* Cresset, 1946; Walter de la Mare, *Peacock Pie,* Faber, 1946; Margaret Black, *Three Brothers and a Lady,* Acorn, 1947; Noel Langley, *Desbarollda, the Waltzing Mouse,* Lindsey Drummond, 1947; John Bunyan, *Pilgrim's Progress,* Faber, 1947; *Hey Nonny Yes,* Saturn, 1947; Dickens, *Charles Dicken's Birthday Book,* Faber, 1948; *Jubilee Book,* Camberwell School of Arts and Crafts, 1948; Cecil Day-Lewis, *The Otterbury Incident,* World Publishing, 1948, reprinted, 1969; Kaiser, *Mimff in Charge,* Oxford University Press, 1949; *Ali Baba,* Limited Editions, 1949; Gorham, *Back to the Local,* Percival Marshall, 1949.

Gorham, *Showmen and Suckers,* Percival Marshall, 1951; Gorham, *The Londoners,* Percival Marshall, 1951; Anthony Trollope, *The Warden,* Oxford University Press, 1952; Trollope, *Barchester Towers,* Oxford University Press, 1952; James Reeves, *The Blackbird in the Lilac,* Oxford University Press, 1952; *The Fantastic Tale of the Plucky Sailor and the Postage Stamp,* Faber, 1954; Kaiser, *Mimff Takes Over,* Oxford University Press, 1954; William M. Thackeray, *The Newcomes,* Limited Editions, 1954; Dickens, *David Copperfield,* Clarendon Press, 1954; Dickens, *Bleak House,* Clarendon Press, 1954; Kenward, *The Suburban Child,* Cambridge University Press, 1955; G. W. Stonier, *Pictures of the Pavement,* M. Joseph, 1955; Ann Phillippa Pearce, *The Minnow on the Say,* Oxford University Press, 1955, reprinted, 1975; Eleanor Frajeon, *The Little Bookroom,* Oxford University Press, 1955, published as *The Little Bookroom: Eleanor Farjeon's Short Stories for Children Chosen by Herself,* Puffin, 1978; Meriol Trevor, *Sun Slower, Sun Faster,* Collins, 1955; *Hunting with Jorrocks,* Oxford University Press, 1956; Reeves, *Pigeons and Princesses,* Heinemann, 1956, reprinted, Bequer Books, 1976; Reeves, *The Wandering Moon,* Heinemann, 1956; Tackeray, *Henry Esmond,* Limited Editions, 1956; *Stockful of Onopareil,* Cambridge University Press, 1956; *St. Luke's Gospel,* Collins, 1956; Bates, *Sugar for the Horse,* M. Joseph, 1957; Joan Goldman, *The School in Our Village,* Batsford, 1957; Percy Young, *Ding Dong Bell,* Dobson, 1957; John Symonds, *Lottie,* Bodley Head, 1957; Reeves, *Prefabulous Animiles,* Heinemann, 1957; Estes, *Pinky Pye,* Harcourt, 1958; Farjeon, *Jim at the Corner,* Oxford University Press, 1958; de la Mare, *The Story of Joseph,* Faber, 1958; Kaiser, *Mimff Robinson,* Oxford University Press, 1958; *Shakespeare's Comedies,* Heritage Press, 1958; Henry Cecil, *Brief to Counsel,* M. Joseph, 1958, reprinted, 1972; G. K. Chesterton, *The Adventures of Father Brown,* Folio, 1959; Ballantyne, *Holiday Trench,* Thomas Nelson, 1959; Reeves, *Titus in Trouble,* Bodley Head, 1959; Reeves, adaptor, *The Adventures of Don Quixote,* Blackie & Son, 1959; John Symonds, *Elfrida and the Pig,* Harrap, 1959; Ursual Moray-Williams, *The Nine Lives of Island MacKenzie,* Chatto & Windus, 1959, reprinted, 1979; de la Mare, *The Story of Moses,* Faber, 1959.

T. H. White, *The Godstone and the Blackymore,* J. Cape, 1960; Cyril Ray, *Merry England,* Vista Books, 1960; Naomi Mitchison, *The Rib of the Green Umbrella,* Collins, 1960; Gough, *Boyhoods of the Great Composers,* Oxford University Press, 1960; de la Mare, *The Story of Samuel and Saul,* Faber, 1960, Knopf, 1961; de la Mare, *Stories from the Bible,* Faber, 1960; Ballantyne, *Kidnappers at Coombe,* Nelson, 1960; Farjeon, *Eleanor Farjeon's Book: Stories, Verses, Plays,* Puffin, 1960, published as *A Book for Eleanor Farjeon,* Walck, 1966; Farjeon, *Italian Peepshow,* Oxford University Press, 1960; Robert Graves, *A Penny Fiddle,* Cassell, 1960; Estes, *The Witch Family,* Harcourt, 1960; *Folk Songs of the British Isles,* Doubleday, 1961; Mark Twain, *Tom Sawyer,* Heinemann School Edition, 1961; Nicholas Stuart Grey, *Down in the Cellar,* Dobson, 1961; Reeves, *Sailor Rumbelow,* Dutton, 1962; James Matthew Barrie, *Peter Pan: The Story of the Play,* Scribner, 1962; Farjeon, *Mrs. Malone,* Oxford University Press, 1962; Crozier, *Making an Opera,* Oxford University Press, 1962; Graham, adaptor, *Peter Pan,* Brockhampton Press, 1962; Eva Lis Wuorio, *The Island of Fish in the Trees,* World Publishing, 1962; Dana Faralla, *The Singing Cupboard,* Blackie & Son, 1962; Betjeman, *A Ring of Bells,* J. Murray, 1962; Christianna Brand, editor, *Naughty Children: An Anthology,* Gollancz, 1962; Clive King, *Stig of the Dump,* Penuin, 1962; Farjeon, *Kaleidoscope,* Oxford University Press, 1963; Gough, *Boyhoods of the Great Composers Book,* Book II, Oxford University Press, 1963; Reeves, *Hurdy Gurdy,* Heinemann, 1963.

Reeves, *The Story of Jackie Thimble,* Dutton, 1964; Brand, *Nurse Matilda,* Brockhampton Press, 1964; Jan Wahl, *Hello*

Elephant, Holt, 1964; Dana Faralla, *Swanhilda-of-the-Swans,* Blackie & Son, 1964; Buchan, *The Thirty-Nine Steps,* Dutton, 1964; Wuorio, *The Land of Up and Down,* World Publishing, 1964; Reeves, *Three Tall Tales,* Abelard, 1964; Graves, *Anne at Highwood Hall,* Cassell, 1964, Doubleday, 1966; Diana Ross, *Old Perisher,* Faber, 1964; Lederer, *Timothy's Song,* Norton, 1965; John Walsh, *The Truants,* Heinemann, 1965; Leonard Clark, *The Year Round,* Hart-Davis, 1965; Cecil, *Know about the Law,* Blackie & Son, 1965, revised edition published as *Learn about English Law,* William Luscombe, 1974; Freda Nichols, *The Milldale Riot,* Ginn, 1965; Farjeon, *The Old Nurse's Stocking Basket,* Walck, 1965; Langley, *The Land of Green Ginger,* Penguin, 1966, revised edition, Puffin, 1975; Archibald Marshall, *The Dragon,* Dutton, 1966; Wahl, *The Muffletumps,* Holt, 1966; Paul Claudel, *A Group of Apostles,* Dolman Press, 1966; Noel Streatfield, *The Growing Summer,* Collins, 1966; Reeves, *The Secret Shoemakers,* Abelard, 1966; Paula Fox, *A Likely Place,* Macmillan, 1966; Jean Webster, *Daddy Long Legs,* Brockhampton Press, 1966; John Symonds, *The Stuffed Dog,* Dent, 1967; Wuorio, *Kali and Her Golden Mirror,* World Publishing, 1967; Lewis, *Nurse Matilda Goes to Town,* Brockhampton Press, 1967; Estes, *Miranda the Great,* Harcourt, 1967; Reeves, *Rhyming Will,* Hamish Hamilton, 1967, McGraw, 1968; Streatfield, *The Magic Summer,* Random House, 1967; R. L. Stevenson, *Travels with a Donkey,* Folio, 1967; Forothy Clewes, *Upsidedown Willie,* Hamish Hamilton, 1967; Clewes, *Special Branch Willie,* Hamish Hamilton, 1968; Daniel Defoe, *Robinson Crusoe,* F. Watts, 1968; Reeves, *The Angel and the Donkey,* Hamish Hamilton, 1969, McGraw, 1970; Jean Chapman, *Do You Remember What Happened?,* Angus & Robertson, 1969.

Kathleen Lines, *Dick Whittington,* Walck, 1970; Clewes, *Fire-Brigade Willie,* Hamish Hamilton, 1970; Dickens, *The Short Stories of Charles Dickens,* Limited Editions, 1971; Estes, *The Tunnel of Hugsy Goode,* Harcourt, 1971; Shirley Morgan, *Rain, Rain, Don't Go Away,* Dutton, 1972; Mary Lavin, *The Second Best Children in the World,* Houghton, 1972; Reeves, adaptor, *Exploits of Don Quixote,* Blackie & Son, 1972; *The Old Ballad of the Babes in the Wood,* Walck, 1972; Graham Greene, *The Little Fire Engine,* Doubleday, 1973; Reeves, *Complete Poems for Children,* Heninemann, 1973; Aingelda Ardizzone, *The Night Ride,* Longman, 1973, Windmill Books, 1975; Greene, *The Little Horse Bus,* Doubleday, 1974; Greene, *The Little Steamroller,* Doubleday, 1974; Greene, *The Little Train,* Doubleday, 1974; Reeves, *The Lion that Flew,* Chatto & Windus, 1974; Reeves, *More Prefabulous Animiles,* Heinemann, 1975; Reeves, *The James Reeves Story Book,* Heinemann, 1978. Also illustrator of *The Alley,* 1964.

SIDELIGHTS: "Edward Ardizzone is a story-teller on the grand scale," a *Times Literary Supplement* critic once explained. "He asks us to believe the most amazing things and we do, cheerfully, because his books offer us, in a thoroughly matter-of-fact way, both excitement and a vision of a world where children are competent to cope with and live through hair-raising experiences, a world where goodness and integrity always triumph."

As author of over twenty-five books and illustrator of almost two hundred more, Ardizzone was frequently praised for his ability to couple his splendid art work with engaging story plots. For example, Shirley Toulson reported in the *New Statesman* that "no one else has such skill at interweaving text and pictures." "Small boys who like to make things will love [*Johnny the Clockmaker*] told in big print with many expressive pictures drawn with Edward Ardizzone's genius for indicating feelings and action with economy of line," wrote M. S. Libby in the *New York Herald Tribune Book Review.* Also writing of the same book, a critic for *Kirkus Reviews* pointed out that "Ardizzone's lyrical water colors blend appealingly with the wistfulness of his text." And a writer for the *Times Literary Supplement* remarked that Ardizzone's books have "distinction, not least in the peculiarly intimate linking of text (very simple but tuneful and various) and the pictures themselves."

Quentin Bell, writing in the British magazine *Studio,* once said of Ardizzone that he is "the best [illustrator], I think, that we have in the country, and a worthy scion of that great British family that is rooted in Hogarth. . . . Ardizzone looks at life with tenderness, sensuous enjoyment and considerable amusement [and] every stroke of the brush is applied with the deliberate purpose of creating an individual." Bell continued to explain that Ardizzone "draws like a painter, indicating masses with great scribbled areas of shadow which are punctuated by swiftly stated accents [and he] delights in the flow and collision of rotund curvilinear forms across his picture space."

Ardizzone's books have been immensely popular with his youthful readers. One reason for his great success, Susan Drysdale of the *New York Times Book Review* believes, was Ardizzone's talent for relating to children and their feelings. Drysdale wrote that Paul of *Paul, the Hero of the Fire* becomes "a hero in a way that seems most unlikely to adults. But then Mr. Ardizzone has always had the knack of making the improbable probable to his young readers. This is almost as endearing as his way of treating children as grown-ups." "Few picture books for the young tell a good story anymore," noted M. S. Libby in the *New York Herald Tribune.* "It is as if publishers, authors and parents all had forgotten how they loved good plots when they were young (and still do). Or perhaps they all know this but very few writers can be found with the gift of narrative, so mood books and descriptively poetic fancies are produced instead. But, Mr. Ardizzone has the gift." And L. S. Bechtel commented in the *New York Herald Tribune Book Review* that "the continuous charm of the work of this famous English illustrator lies partly in his remarkably living people, partly in his delightful use of color, and, for children, in his way of telling the tale mostly in pictures."

Although well-known for his illustrations for children's books, Ardizzone spent five years as an official war artist during World War II. According to the *New York Times,* "he recorded the fall of France, the bombing of London and then followed the dangerous route of the British Eighth Army from Alamein to Tunisia. Later he accompanied the tanks of the Eighth Hussars to Sicily, the Anzio landing, the Normandy beaches, and on into Germany."

Ardizzone once told *CA* a little about himself. He explained. "I came to England when five years old and have been domiciled here ever since. From 1919 to 1926 I worked as a clerk in London. However, owing to my mother's influence, I was interested in art and during this period of clerkship spent four evenings a week in classes learning to draw the figure. At weekends and during holidays I painted.

"In 1926 my father gave me a small sum of money, on receipt of which I threw up my job and set out to make my living as a professional artist. In 1926 I illustrated my first book and was married on the strength of it. I wrote and illustrated my first children's book, *Little Tim and the Brave Sea Captain,* in 1935. It developed from an impromptu tale told to my own children. The pictorial background of this book, like many of my other 'Tim' books, was based on nostalgic memories of the docks at Ipswich, in which I used to play as a boy before the 1914 war, and of the little coastal steamers that visited it, also of Deal on the Kent coast with its long pebbly beaches.

"With regard to writing for little children, I have no hard and fast theories. I do think, however, that great care should be taken to make the language euphonic and that the books should be easy for the adult to read aloud. I find that the books of mine which I like best have, in many cases, developed from tales I have told off the cuff to my own children in the past, and to my grandchildren. When it comes to illustration, I think it is very important not to draw down to children, but to draw up to please oneself. I like to regard a small illustration in the same way as I would a picture for an exhibition."

One of Ardizzone's best-known paintings, *Magic Carpet*, was reproduced by UNICEF for its collection of international Christmas cards. More than three hundred of Ardizzone's drawings are exhibited at the Imperial War Museum.

BIOGRAPHICAL/CRITICAL SOURCES: *New York Herald Tribune Book Review*, November 18, 1951, November 13, 1960; *Studio*, May, 1955; *Kirkus Reviews*, October 1, 1960; *Times Literary Supplement*, June 1, 1962, December 8, 1972; *New York Times Book Review*, May 5, 1963; *New York Herald Tribune*, May 12, 1963; *New Statesman*, November 10, 1972; *Edward Ardizzone: A Preliminary Hand-list of His Illustrated Books, 1929-1970*, Private Libraries Association, 1972; *Children's Literature Review*, Volume III, Gale, 1978.

OBITUARIES: *New York Times*, November 9, 1979; *Time*, November 19, 1979; *AB Bookman's Weekly*, December 24, 1979.†

* * *

**ARMSTRONG, Henry H.
See ARVAY, Harry**

* * *

ARNETT, Harold E(dward) 1931-

PERSONAL: Born January 20, 1931, in Hegeler, Ill.; son of Dumous Clay (a watchman) and Amie (Netherton) Arnett; married Betty Jo Anne Carter, August 31, 1952; children: John, Carl, Melia. *Education:* University of Illinois, B.S., 1955, M.S., 1958, Ph.D., 1962; Certificate of Management Accounting, National Association of Accountants, 1975. *Politics:* Conservative Republican. *Religion:* Presbyterian. *Home:* 2113 Delaware Dr., Ann Arbor, Mich. 48103. *Office:* 734 Graduate School of Business Administration, University of Michigan, Ann Arbor, Mich. 48109.

CAREER: Certified public accountant, state of Illinois, 1960; University of Illinois at Urbana-Champaign, instructor in accounting, 1955-60; American Institute of Certified Public Accountants, New York, N.Y., research associate, 1960-62; University of Michigan, Ann Arbor, assistant professor, 1962-66, associate professor, 1966-70, professor of accounting, 1970—, head of department, 1970-72. Faculty consultant, Federal Taxation Committee of American Institute of Certified Public Accountants, 1966-67. *Military service:* U.S. Navy, 1948-52.

MEMBER: American Accounting Association, Financial Executives Institute, American Institute of Certified Public Accountants, National Association of Accountants (international vice-president, 1981-82; member of executive committee, 1981-82), Stuart Cameron McCleod Society, Michigan Association of Certified Public Accountants, Phi Eta Sigma, Beta Gamma Sigma, Beta Alpha Psi, Sigma Iota Epsilon, Chi Gamma Iota. *Awards, honors:* Certificate of Merit, National Association of Accountants, 1978.

WRITINGS: (With others) *Reporting the Financial Effects of Price-Level Changes*, American Institute of Certified Public Accountants, 1963; (with R. Lee Brummet) *Business and Economic Evaluation of the Metal Finishing Industry* (monograph), Bureau of Business Research, University of Michigan, 1967; (contributor) *The Dental Clinics of North America* (readings), Saunders, 1967.

(Contributor) R. L. Dixon, editor, *The Executive's Accounting Primer*, McGraw, 1971; (with Donald Smith) *Financial and Economic Evaluation of the Tool and Die Industry,* Bureau of Business Research, University of Michigan, 1975; (with Smith) *The Metal Finishing Industry: A Framework for Success*, Bureau of Business Research, University of Michigan, 1977; *Proposed Funds Statement for Managers and Investors*, National Association of Accountants, 1979; (with Paul Danos) *CPA Firm Viability: A Study of Major Environmental Factors Affecting Firms of Various Sizes and Characteristics*, Bureau of Business Research, University of Michigan, 1979.

Contributor to journals, including *Journal of Contemporary Business, Mergers and Acquisitions, Management Accounting, Accounting Review, Australian Accountant,* and *Financial Analysts' Journal*. Member of editorial advisory board, *Journal of Accountancy*, 1969-74.

* * *

**ARVAY, Harry 1925-
(Henry H. Armstrong)**

PERSONAL: Given name Heinz; born December 21, 1925, in Graz, Austria; son of Geza (a traveling salesman) and Magda (Leschziner) Arvay; married Esther Hassoun (a secretary), November 2, 1953; children: Ronit, Ruth. *Education:* Cambridge University, University Diploma of English Studies, 1954; attended Israeli Government Institute for Productivity, 1962-64. *Politics:* "Conservative/Democrat." *Religion:* Jewish. *Home:* 6, Yaldei Teheran St., Givatayim 53484, Tel Aviv, Israel. *Office:* United Appeal in Israel, 11 Shapira St., Tel Aviv, Israel.

CAREER: Free-lance writer, 1947-49; *Life in Israel* (English-language monthly), Tel Aviv, Israel, assistant editor, 1949-53; high school teacher of English, 1953-56; MALBEN-American Joint Distribution Committee, Tel Aviv, worked in public relations department, 1956-60; Tel Aviv Exhibitions & International Trade Fair, Tel Aviv, public relations director, 1961-63; United Jewish Appeal in Israel, Tel Aviv, head of Tel Aviv fund raising department, 1964-76. Did public relations work for National Rehabilitation Council for Handicapped, 1960-63, World War II Disabled Veterans Committee, 1960-64, and Institute for Deaf Children, 1963-64. *Military service:* British Army, 1943-46. Australian Army Education Corps, 1947. *Member:* Israel Public Relations Association (secretary, 1963-67).

WRITINGS—Published by Corgi Books, except as indicated: (Under pseudonym Henry H. Armstrong) *A Warrior Never Dies,* Kenkyusha (Tokyo), 1952; *Rehov Allenby* (title means "Allenby Road"), Twersky (Tel Aviv), 1956; *Eleven Bullets for Mohammed*, Bantam, 1975; *Operation Kuwait*, Bantam, 1975; *The Piraeus Plot*, Bantam, 1975; *The Moscow Intercept*, Bantam, 1975; *The Meirovitz Plan,* 1975; *Damascus Countdown,* 1975; *The Swiss Deal,* 1976; *Togo Command,* 1976; *Stranglehold,* 1976; *Blow the Four Winds,* 1977; *Triad-21*, New English Library, 1977; *Society of Fear*, New English Library, 1979. Also translator of A. Negev's *Caesarea*, Lewin-Epstein.

WORK IN PROGRESS: "Further books on espionage completed; memoirs completed."

SIDELIGHTS: Harry Arvay told CA: "The subject of terrorism and counter terrorist activity has been a favourite of mine since age 12, when Hitler invaded Austria and I joined the resistance movement. During the war I qualified for British Military Intelligence. In India, Hong Kong, China, and Japan I was able to put these qualifications to good use. My mother and most relatives were killed by the Germans. My father got out of a concentration camp alive and fled to Shanghai. I escaped to England, in 1939, alone. With the great help of British military authorities, I was able to find my father in China in 1946."

Arvay continues: "I saw Hitler—in person. I saw Hiroshima—just after the bomb. I saw revolution and intestine war in Austria, India, and China; [I also saw] Chiang Kai-shek and Mao Tse-tung. I saw terrorism and heroism, Nazism and Communism. I lost everything twice, and almost everything more often than that. It's invigorating to begin again!

"I once loved Austria, liked England, loved Scotland, relished Japan and China, pitied India. Nowadays I *share* Israel."

Arvay adds: "After fifteen books (English, Japanese, Dutch, and Hebrew), my advice to young writers is: Learn how to SELL well, not merely to WRITE well. Find an enthusiastic young agent and pay him well. Remember: The publisher is always right. And if the above advice is not to your liking—consider the writing business a part-time hobby, no more."

* * *

ASHE, Gordon
See CREASEY, John

* * *

ASHENFELTER, Orley C(lark)   1942-

PERSONAL: Born October 18, 1942, in San Francisco, Calif.; son of Galen Orley and Frieda (McCullough) Ashenfelter; married Virginia Wilson, 1965; children: Theresa, Bevin, Gillian. *Education:* Claremont Men's College, B.A., 1964; Princeton University, Ph.D., 1970. *Home:* 30 Mercer St., Princeton, N.J. 08540. *Office:* Industrial Relations Section, Princeton University, Princeton, N.J. 08540.

CAREER: Princeton University, Princeton, N.J., lecturer, 1968-70, assistant professor, 1970-71, associate professor, 1971-73, professor of economics, 1973—, director of Industrial Relations Section, 1971—. Visiting scholar, Federal Reserve Bank of Philadelphia, 1979-80. Member of National Manpower Policy Task Force Associates, 1968-72; member of advisory board of Institute of Labor-Management Relations, Rutgers University, 1972—, and Project on Women, Urban Institute, 1975—. Director of Office of Evaluation, U.S. Department of Labor, 1972-73. Member of panel of statisticians, National Commission on Employment and Unemployment Statistics, 1978-81. *Member:* American Economic Association, American Statistical Association, Econometric Society (fellow), Industrial Relations Research Association. *Awards, honors:* Woodrow Wilson fellowships, 1964-65 and 1967-68; Guggenheim fellowship, 1976-77.

WRITINGS—Editor: (With Albert Rees, and contributor) *Discrimination in Labor Markets*, Princeton University Press, 1973; (with W. G. Bowen) *Labor and the National Economy*, Norton, 1975; (with L. Hausman, B. Rustin, R. Schubert, and D. Slaiman) *Equal Rights and Industrial Relations*, Industrial Relations Research Association, 1977; (with W. Oates) *Essays in Labor Market Analysis*, Halsted, 1978; (with J. Blum) *Evaluating the Labor Market Effects of Social Programs*, Industrial Relations Section, Princeton University Press, 1976.

Contributor: Ronald Wykstra, editor, *Human Capital Formation and Manpower Development*, Free Press, 1971; Glen Cain and Harold Watts, editors, *Income Maintenance and Labor Supply*, Markham, 1973; Lloyd Reynolds, Stanley Masters, and Collette Moser, editors, *Readings in Labor Economics and Labor Relations*, Prentice-Hall, 1971; T. W. Schultz, editor, *Economics of the Family*, National Bureau of Economic Research, 1974; Michael Intriligator and David Kendrick, editors, *Frontiers of Quantitative Economics*, North-Holland Publishing, 1974; Daniel Hamermesh, editor, *Labor in the Public and Nonprofit Sectors*, Princeton University Press, 1975; J. M. Artis and A. R. Nobay, editors, *Contemporary Economic Analysis*, Association of University Teachers of Economics, 1978; J. Palmer and J. Pechman, editors, *Welfare in Rural Areas: The North Carolina-Iowa Maintenance Experiment*, Brookings Institution, 1978; R. Stone and W. Peterson, editors, *Econometric Contributions to Public Policy*, Macmillan, 1978; *Supplementary Papers from the Conference on Youth Unemployment: Its Measurement and Meaning*, U.S. Government Printing Office, 1978; Sherwin Rosen, editor, *Studies in Labor Markets*, University of Chicago Press, 1981; *Aging: A Challenge to Science and Society*, Oxford University Press, 1981.

Contributor of numerous articles and reviews to various economic, labor, and finance journals. Member of board of editors, *Journal of Urban Economics*, and *Journal of Labor Research*.

* * *

ATKINS, Thomas R(adcliffe)   1939-

PERSONAL: Born April 5, 1939, in Mobile, Ala.; son of Jack R. (an importer) and Sadie B. (Daves) Atkins; married Mary Ellen O'Brien (a director and actress), April 14, 1964; children: Shawn, Mark. *Education:* Duke University, B.A., 1961; Yale University, M.F.A., 1964. *Office:* Department of Drama and Communications, University of New Orleans, New Orleans, La. 70148.

CAREER: Vassar College, Poughkeepsie, N.Y., lecturer in drama, 1964-65; Hollins College, Hollins College, Va., instructor, 1965-67, assistant professor, 1967-70, associate professor, 1970-81, professor of drama, 1981—, chairman of department of theatre arts, 1971-82; University of New Orleans, New Orleans, La., professor of drama and communications, and chairman of department, 1982—. Part-time lecturer at City College of the City University of New York, spring, 1971. *Member:* Authors Guild, Dramatists Guild, Mystery Writers of America, Associated Writing Programs. *Awards, honors:* Woodrow Wilson fellowship, 1961-62; John Golden fellowship, Yale University School of Drama, 1963-64.

WRITINGS: *Circus Maximus* (play), Row, Peterson, 1959; (co-author) *The Fire Came By* (nonfiction), Doubleday, 1975; *The Blue Man* (novel), Doubleday, 1978; *Pigeons* (play), Haunted Book Shop, in press.

Editor; published by Simon & Schuster, except as indicated; all 1976: *Sexuality in the Movies*, Indiana University Press; *Science Fiction Films; Graphic Violence on the Screen; Frederick Wiseman; Ken Russell*.

Contributor: Frank N. Magill, editor, *Contemporary Literary Scene, 1973*, Salem Press, 1974; Magill, editor, *Literary Annual, 1973*, Salem Press, 1974; Gerald Peary, editor, *The Classic American Novel and the Movies*, Ungar, 1977; Lewis Jacobs, editor, *The Documentary Tradition*, Norton, 1979.

General editor of Monarch Film series for Simon & Schuster, 1974—. Contributor of plays and articles to film and literary journals, including *Cinefantastique, Sight and Sound, Southern Humanities Review, Mill Mountain Review,* and *Kenyon Review.* Founder, editor, and publisher of *Film Journal,* 1971—; editor and publisher with wife, Mary Ellen O'Brien, of *Scripts South,* 1981—.

WORK IN PROGRESS: A novel, *A Darker Wave.*

SIDELIGHTS: Thomas R. Atkins told *Library Journal:* "My love of writing goes back at least as far as the fifth grade, when I was poring through Edgar Rice Burroughs's Martian novels and just beginning to attempt to put my own stories on paper. A teacher happened to see these early efforts and gave me an hour of class time each week to read my work aloud to my fellow students. This got me hooked, I believe, on the pleasure of storytelling.

"My first published works were chiefly plays and short stories, but now I am drawn to the novel for its creative freedom, the possibilities of multiple viewpoints, and the flexibility of time and space. In *The Blue Man,* for instance, I follow a large cast of characters, both real and imaginary, spread out from California to Virginia; and the mood ranges from stark realism to black comedy."

AVOCATIONAL INTERESTS: Travel, collecting art and books, photography.

BIOGRAPHICAL/CRITICAL SOURCES: Library Journal, June 15, 1978; *Roanoker,* November-December, 1978; *Azalea City News & Review* (Mobile, Alabama), July 31, 1981.

* * *

AUERBACH, Stevanne 1938-
(Stevanne Auerbach Fink)

PERSONAL: Born September 22, 1938, in New York, N.Y.; daughter of Nathan and Jean (Rosen) Stockheim; married Arthur Auerbach, November 24, 1961 (divorced November, 1970); married Donald Fink (a physician), February 4, 1972 (divorced, 1979); children: (first marriage) Amy. *Education:* Queens College of the City of New York (now Queens College of the City University of New York), B.A., 1960; graduate study, University of Maryland, 1961-65; George Washington University, M.A., 1965; Union Graduate School, Ph.D., 1973. *Residence:* San Francisco, Calif. *Agent:* Elizabeth Pomada, 1029 Jones St., San Francisco, Calif. 94109. *Office:* Institute for Childhood Resources, 1169 Howard St., San Francisco, Calif. 94103.

CAREER: Teacher of recreation and swimming in New York, N.Y., 1958-60; elementary school teacher in Silver Spring, Md., 1960-61; American Personnel and Guidance Association, Washington, D.C., professional assistant, 1961-63; B'nai B'rith Vocational Service, Washington, D.C., professional assistant, 1963-64; teacher of retarded children in Washington, D.C., 1965-66; Council for Exceptional Children, Washington, D.C., research associate, 1966-67; elementary school teacher in Washington, D.C., 1968; U.S. Department of Health, Education and Welfare, Washington, D.C., education program specialist, 1968-69, child care researcher, 1970-71; Far West Laboratory for Educational Research and Development, Berkeley, Calif., intern in childhood development, 1971-78; Institute for Childhood Resources, San Francisco, Calif., founder and director, 1978—. Lecturer throughout the United States.

MEMBER: Association for Childhood Education International, Council for Exceptional Children, American Personnel and Guidance Association (life member), National Vocational Guidance Association, National Education Association, National Association for Education of Young Children, American Association of University Women, Washington Independent Writers Group, Media Alliance of San Francisco.

WRITINGS: (Editor) *Counselor Education: A Progress Report on Standards,* American Personnel and Guidance Association, 1962; (editor) *NVGA Bibliography of Current Occupational Information,* American Personnel and Guidance Association, 1963; (contributor) Pamela Roby, editor, *Child Care: Who Cares?: Foreign and Domestic Infant and Early Childhood Development Policies,* Basic Books, 1973; (contributor) Roy Fairfield, editor, *Humanizing the Workplace,* Prometheus Press, 1974; (under name Stevanne Auerbach Fink) *Parents and Child Care,* Far West Laboratory for Educational Research and Development, 1974; (editor) *Child Care: A Comprehensive Guide,* four volumes, Human Sciences, 1975-76; *Confronting the Child Care Crisis,* Beacon Press, 1979; *The Whole Child: A Sourcebook,* Putnam, 1981; *Choosing Child Care: Parents' Guide to Child Care,* Dutton, 1982. Also author of *Petals* (poems), 1974. Contributor to journals and magazines. Editor, *Counselor's Information Service,* 1963-64, and *Physical Education for the Mentally Retarded.*

WORK IN PROGRESS: The Toy Chest; other publications.

SIDELIGHTS: Stevanne Auerbach told *CA:* "Writing has been a perfect way for me to synthesize learning, experience, and philosophy. I have been pleased to be able to develop 'breakthrough' books and articles in the specific areas. I have worked to be a writer from undergraduate classes at Queens College where as an education major, inspired by many excellent professors, I wrote papers which continued to be consistent with my life's philosophy and work expression—service to children and families.

"While working in various professional activities in Washington, D.C., I helped produce publications: *Opportunities in the Peace Corps—A Fact Booklet, Physical Education for the Mentally Retarded, Counselor Education Standards,* and *The NVGA Guide to Occupational Literature,* and others in the Dramatic Arts in Education. While at HEW I produced reviews of model programs and many papers related to National Title I, child care, and other areas in education.

"During graduate school I began writing a personal journal, articles, and a unique cross-cultural study on child care. Later I began publishing my own books and found each one made a contribution which has resulted in great satisfaction. I did learn the art of producing a book by self-publishing one and later selling it to a major publisher. I now lecture and appear on television and radio throughout the United States on child-related topics and am pleased to be able to impact on helping to raise children in the '80s."

* * *

AVICE, Claude 1925-
(Pierre Barbet, David Maine, Olivier Sprigel)

PERSONAL: Born May 16, 1925, in Le Mans, France; son of Leon (a pharmacist) and Renee (Bardet) Avice; married Marianne Brunswick (a pharmacist), July 23, 1952; children: Brigitte Avice Newman, Patrick, Olivier. *Education:* University of Paris, Docteur en pharmacie, 1954. *Home:* 4 Square de l'Avenue du Bois, Paris 75116, France.

CAREER: Science fiction writer. Pharmacist in Paris, France, 1957-81. Director of laboratory for medical analysis, 1955—. *Member:* European Society of Science Fiction (coordinator, 1979), Science Fiction Writers of America (overseas director), Society of Doctors in Pharmacy, French Society of Astronomy.

Awards, honors: Gold medal from International Institute of Science Fiction (Poznan).

WRITINGS—All science fiction; under pseudonym Pierre Barbet; published by Presses de la Cite (Paris), except as indicated: *Vers un avenir perdu* (title means "Towards a Lost Future"), Gallimard, 1962; *Babel 3,805*, Gallimard, 1963; *Les Limiers de l'infini* (title means "Bloodhounds of the Infinite"), 1966; *Les Cavernicoles de Wolf* (title means "Cave Inhabitants of Wolf"), 1966; *L'Etoile du neant* (title means "The Star of Nought"), 1967; *L'Enigme des quasars* (title means "The Secret of Quasars"), 1967; *Hallali cosmique* (title means "Cosmic Death"), 1967; *La Planete des cristophons* (title means "Planet of Cristophons"), 1968; *Evolution magnetique* (title means "Magnetic Evolution"), 1968; *Vikings de l'espace* (title means "Space Vikings"), 1969; *Les Chimeres de Seginus* (title means "The Chimeras of Seginus"), 1969; *L'Exile du temps* (title means "Exile of Time"), 1969.

Etoiles en perdition (title means "Stars in Distress"), 1970; *Les Maitres des pulsars* (title means "Masters of Pulsars"), 1970; *Les Grognards d'Eridan*, 1970, translation by Hochman published as *The Napoleons of Eridanus*, DAW Books, 1976; *L'Agonie da la Voie Lactee* (title means "The Agony of the Milky-Way"), 1970; *Les Conquistadores d'Andromede* (title means "The Conquistadors of Andromeda"), 1971; *Le Transmetteur de Ganymede* (title means "Ganymede's Transmitter"), 1971; *Azraec de Virgo* (title means "Azraec of Virgo"), 1971; *A quoi songent les psyborgs?*, 1971, translation by Wendane Ackerman published as *Games Psyborgs Play*, DAW Books, 1973; *L'Empire du Baphomet*, 1972, translation by Bernand Kay published as *Baphomet's Meteor*, DAW Books, 1972; *Les Insurges de Laucor* (title means "Insurgents of Laucor"), 1972; *La Planete empoisonnee* (title means "Poisoned Planet"), 1972; *Tremplins d'etoiles* (title means "Springboard of the Stars"), 1972.

La Planete enchantee, 1973, translation by C. J. Richards published as *Enchanted Planet*, DAW Books, 1975; *Liane de Noldaz*, 1973, translation by Hochman published as *The Joan-of-Arc Replay*, DAW Books, 1978; *Les Bioniques d'Atria* (title means "Bionics of Atria"), 1973; *Le Batard d'Orion* (title means "The Bastard of Orion"), 1973; *Magiciens galactiques* (title means "Galactic Magicians"), 1974; *L'Univers des Geons* (title means "The Universe of Geons"), 1974; *Croisade stellaire* (title means "Stellar Crusade"), 1974; *Les Mercenaires de Rychna* (title means "The Mercenaries of Rychna"), 1974; *La Nymphe de l'espace* (title means "Nymph of Space"), 1975; *Patrouilleur du neant* (title means "Patrol of Nought"), 1976; *A Problem in Bionics*, DAW Books, 1977; *Commandos sur commande*, 1978; *Odyssee galactique*, 1978; *Irafic stellaire*, 1979; *Oasis de l'espace*, 1979.

Periple galactique, 1980; *Cite des Asteroides*, 1980; *Stellar Crusaders*, DAW Books, 1980; *Le Marechal rebelle*, 1981; *Les Psychos de Logir*, 1981; *Survivants de l'apocalypse*, 1982; *L'Empereur d'Eridan*, 1982.

Under pseudonym David Maine; all published by Albin Michel: *Les Disparus du club Chronos* (title means "Club Chronos is Missing"), 1972; *Guerillero galactique* (title means "Galactic Guerrillas"), 1976; *Renaissance planetaire*, 1980; *Invasion Cosmique*, 1982.

Under pseudonym Olivier Sprigel; all published by Librairie des Champs Elysees: *Cepuscule de futur*, 1975; *Venusine*, 1977; *Lendemains incertains*, 1978.

Also author (with others) of *La Grande Encyclopedie de la Science Fiction*, Del Drago (Italy), and *L'homme est-il seul dans l'univers?*, La Bionique. Work represented in anthologies, including *Toxico Futuris*, edited by Michel Demuth, Opta (Paris), 1975, and *European Anthology*, edited by Donald A. Wollheim, Doubleday, 1976. Contributor of science fiction short stories to French periodicals, including *Policier Mystere Magazine* and *Horizons du Fantastique*.

WORK IN PROGRESS: Two more science fiction works.

B

BAARS, Conrad W(alterus)   1919-1981

PERSONAL: Born January 2, 1919, in the Netherlands; died October 18, 1981, in San Antonio, Tex.; son of Walter F. C. (a lawyer) and Constance (de Groot) Baars; married Virginia Kennedy, April 3, 1948; children: Michael Conrad, Sue Mary, Eleanor Constance. *Education:* University of Amsterdam, M.D., 1945. *Religion:* Roman Catholic. *Home and office:* 326 Highview Dr., San Antonio, Tex. 78228.

CAREER: Psychiatric residency training in Chicago, Ill., Minneapolis, Minn., and in California, 1945-52; Rochester State Hospital, Rochester, Minn., director of psychiatric education, 1952-60; private practice of medicine, Rochester, 1960-73; International Therapeutic Center for Clergy and Religion, Whitinsville, Mass., founder and director, 1973-75; private practice in psychiatry, Whitinsville, 1975-76; private practice in psychiatry, San Antonio, Tex., 1976-81. Consultant to Human Life Foundation. *Military service:* Royal Dutch Army, 1938-40. Fought with underground in Netherlands, Belgium, and France, 1940-43. U.S. Army Reserve, Medical Corps, 1951-52; became captain; received Croix du Combattant de l'Europe.

MEMBER: World Federation of Doctors Who Respect Human Life (member of board of directors of U.S. section), American Medical Association, American Psychiatric Association, American Society of Clinical Hypnosis, Massachusetts Medical Society, Massachusetts Psychiatric Society. *Awards, honors:* Christian Culture Award, Assumption University, 1980.

WRITINGS: The Psychology of Obedience, Herder, 1965; (with Jordan Aumann and Philip Roets) *Sex, Love, and the Life of the Spirit,* Priory, 1966; *A Priest for All Seasons: Masculine and Celibate,* Franciscan Herald, 1972; *How to Treat and Prevent the Crisis in Priesthood,* Franciscan Herald, 1972; (with Anna A. Terruwe) *Loving and Curing the Neurotic,* Arlington House, 1972, revised edition published as *Healing the Unaffirmed,* Alba House, 1976; (contributor) Ratibor-Ray M. Jurjevich, editor, *Direct Psychotherapy,* University of Miami Press, 1973; *Born Only Once,* Franciscan Herald, 1975; *The Homosexual's Search for Happiness,* Franciscan Herald, 1976; *Feeling and Healing Your Emotions,* Logos International, 1979; (with Terruwe) *Psychic Wholeness and Healing,* Alba House, 1981.

Also author of cassette tapes, "Affirmation and Psychic Incarnation," 1975, "Fear Is Useless—What Is Needed Is Trust," 1980, "Speak Lord—An Aid to Meditation," 1980, and "Premature Forgiving—When to Forgive and How," 1980. Contributor to *New Catholic Encyclopedia.*

SIDELIGHTS: Conrad W. Baars once told *CA* that his career was based on "new discoveries and interpretations of clinical observations based on the Aristotelian-Thomistic understanding of the nature of man. This led to ability to cure obsessive-compulsive neurotics and discovery of new psychiatric syndrome: deprivation neurosis in adults. My two years in Buchenwald concentration camp (1943-45) contributed to my disenchantment with utilitarian philosophy in my specialty and the poor clinical results of psychoanalytic therapy. The syndrome of the non-affirmed individual led to the discovery of the non-Freudian deprivation neurosis, requiring affirmation therapy without probing into the unconscious. Its incidence is huge (in the millions) and increases steadily in a non-affirming, denying society."†

*   *   *

BABBAGE, Stuart Barton   1916-

PERSONAL: Born January 4, 1916, in Auckland, New Zealand; son of Gordon Swaine (a clerk) and Florence (Rutherfurd) Babbage; married Elizabeth King, May 26, 1943; children: Veronica, Malcolm, Christopher, Timothy. *Education:* University of New Zealand, B.A., 1935, M.A., 1936; University of London, Ph.D., 1942. *Religion:* Protestant Episcopal. *Office:* New College, Anzac Parade, University of New South Wales, Kensington, New South Wales, Australia 2033.

CAREER: Collegiate School, Wanganui, New Zealand, tutor, 1937; Oak Hill College, Southgate, London, England, tutor, 1939-42; St. Andrew's Cathedral, Sydney, Australia, dean, 1946-53; St. Paul's Cathedral, Melbourne, Australia, dean, 1953-62; University of Melbourne, Ridley College, Melbourne, president, 1953-63; Columbia Theological Seminary, Decatur, Ga., professor of Christian apologetics, 1963-67; Temple University, Conwell School of Theology, Philadelphia, Pa., president, 1967-69; Gordon-Conwell Theological Seminary, South Hamilton, Mass., vice-president and dean, 1970-73; University of New South Wales, New College, Kensington, Australia, master, 1973—. President, Melbourne College of Divinity, 1960-63. Leader of evangelistic missions for university students in America, Australia, and New Zealand. Regular panel member for television program, "On the Spot." President, New South Wales Council of Churches, 1949, Father and Son Welfare Movement, 1953-63, and Scripture Union,

1953-63. *Military service:* Royal Air Force, senior chaplain, 1942-46. *Member:* Congress of Cultural Freedom (vice-patron), Inter-Varsity Fellowship (vice-president), Australian Teachers Christian Fellowship (vice-president), Council of Mental Hygiene (vice-president). *Awards, honors:* Th.D., Australian College of Theology, 1950; Fulbright Scholar in United States, 1961-62.

WRITINGS: *Hauhauism*, A.H. and A.W. Reed, 1936; *Man in Nature and in Grace*, Eerdmans, 1957; *Light beneath the Cross*, Doubleday, 1960; *Puritanism and Richard Bancroft*, S.P.C.K., 1962; *Christianity and Sex*, Inter-Varsity, 1963; *Sex and Sanity: A Christian View of Sexual Morality*, Hodder & Stoughton, 1965, Westminster, 1967; *The Mark of Cain*, Eerdmans, 1965; *The Light of the Cross: A Look at the Persons Who Stood at the Cross*, Zondervan, 1966; *The Vacuum of Unbelief*, Zondervan, 1969. Contributing editor, *Christianity Today* (United States), *The Churchman* (United Kingdom), and *Ecumenical Review* (Geneva). Joint editor, *Reformed Theological Review.*

WORK IN PROGRESS: Three books, *Death in Literature*, *Christianity and Literature*, and *Albert Camus.*

SIDELIGHTS: Stuart Barton Babbage pioneered marriage guidance in Australia and has traveled extensively in Africa and Asia.†

* * *

BABBIE, Earl (Robert) 1938-

PERSONAL: Born January 8, 1938, in Detroit, Mich.; son of Herman Octave (an automobile body mechanic) and Marion (Towle) Babbie; married Sheila Trimble (a project assistant for Erhard Seminars Training), May 17, 1965; children: Aaron Robert. *Education:* Harvard University, A.B. (cum laude), 1960; University of California, Berkeley, M.A., 1966, Ph.D., 1969. *Politics:* "Active, reformist, civil libertarian." *Religion:* None. *Home and office:* 91 La Verne Ave., Mill Valley, Calif. 94941.

CAREER: University of California, Berkeley, research sociologist at Survey Research Center, 1966-68, assistant director of center, 1967-68; University of Hawaii, Honolulu, assistant professor, 1968-70, associate professor, 1970-74, professor, 1974-80, affiliate professor of sociology, 1980—, chairman of department, 1973-74, 1977-79, program director for survey research at Social Science Research Institute, 1968-69, director of Institutional Research Office, 1970, director of Survey Research Office, 1970-73, associate director of Social Science Research Institute, 1972-73; Babbie Enterprises, Mill Valley, Calif., president, 1976—. University of California, Berkeley, visiting scholar, 1975, visiting professor, 1980. Partner, Pacific Poll Co., 1968-70; member of Hawaii State Census Tract Committee, 1969-74; president of Save Wawamalu Association, 1971-73; member of research committee of Hawaii Visitors Bureau, 1972-74; vice-president of Hawaii Center for Environmental Education, 1973-74; Erhard Seminars Training of Hawaii, vice president, 1975-76, member of national advisory board, 1976—; member of board of directors of Citizens for Hawaii, 1972-74, Policy Research Institute, 1976—, Holiday Project and Zero Population Growth, 1981—; member of planning committee of University of Hawaii Gerentology Center, 1977-78. Member of research advisory committee of Hawaii Commission on Children and Youth, 1972-74; member of advisory council of Hunger Project, 1978—. *Military service:* U.S. Marine Corps, 1960-66; active duty, 1960-63; became first lieutenant.

MEMBER: American Sociological Association, American Association for Public Opinion Research, American Civil Liberties Union, Zero Population Growth, Life of the Land, Pacific Sociological Association, Hawaii Statistical Association (vice-president, 1971). *Awards, honors:* Grant from Haas Community Fund, 1973, for the writing of *The Practice of Social Research;* grant from Erhard Seminars Training of Hawaii, 1975.

WRITINGS: (With Charles Y. Glock and Benjamin B. Ringer) *To Comfort and to Challenge*, University of California Press, 1967; (with William Nicholls) *Oakland in Transition: A Summary of the 701 Household Survey* (monograph), Survey Research Center, University of California, 1969; *Science and Morality in Medicine*, University of California Press, 1970; *A Profile of the Honolulu Model Neighborhoods: 1969* (monograph), Honolulu Model Cities Project, 1970; *Hubris: Hawaii Uniform Bank and Remote Interactive System* (monograph), Survey Research Office, University of Hawaii, 1971; *The Maximillion Report* (monograph), Citizens for Hawaii, 1972; *Survey Research Methods*, with instructor's manual, Wadsworth, 1973; (contributor) Glock, editor, *Religion in Sociological Perspective*, Wadsworth, 1973.

The Practice of Social Research, Wadsworth, 1975, 2nd edition, 1979; (with Robert Huitt) *Practicing Social Research* (manual), Wadsworth, 1975, 2nd edition, 1979; *Society by Agreement*, Wadsworth, 1977, 2nd edition published as *Sociology: An Introduction*, 1980; *Understanding Sociology: A Context for Action*, Wadsworth, 1981; *Social Research for Consumers*, Wadsworth, 1982. Contributor to academic journals, including *Review of Religious Research*, *Journal for the Scientific Study of Religion*, *American Sociological Review*, *Social Forces*, *American Journal of Correction*, and *Graduate Review*. Editorial reader for *Sociology of Education*, 1967.

WORK IN PROGRESS: *You Make the Difference; People Making a Difference; Social Problems* and *The Computer Society*, both for Wadsworth.

SIDELIGHTS: Earl Babbie writes: "I have only recently begun seeing myself as a writer rather than a professor who also writes. As things have turned out, I am able to write textbooks that both instructors and students seem to enjoy and get value from. That's a nice feeling, plus I've discovered you get paid for that."

AVOCATIONAL INTERESTS: "Saving the world."

* * *

BABLADELIS, Georgia 1931-

PERSONAL: Surname is pronounced *Bab*-le-delis; born January 30, 1931, in Manistique, Mich.; daughter of Alex N. and Bertha (Prokas) Babladelis. *Education:* University of Michigan, B.A. (honors in psychology), 1953; University of California, Berkeley, M.A., 1955; University of Colorado, Ph.D., 1959. *Office:* Department of Psychology, California State University, Hayward, Calif. 94542.

CAREER: Alameda County Probation Department, Oakland, Calif., clinical psychologist, 1959-60; senior clinical psychologist and training supervisor, 1960-63; California State University, Hayward, assistant professor, 1965-67, associate professor, 1967-72, professor of psychology, 1972—. Dissertation consultant and chairperson, California School for Professional Psychology, 1980—. Manuscript reader for publishers. *Member:* American Psychology Association (fellow). *Awards, honors:* Research grants and fellowships from National Institute of Mental Health, National Science Foundation, American Association for the Advancement of Science, and United Nations Educational, Scientific and Cultural Organization.

WRITINGS: (With Suzanne Adams) *The Shaping of Personality,* Prentice-Hall, 1967; (contributor) Krech, Crutchfield, and Livson, editors, *Elements of Psychology,* Knopf, 1974; *The Study of Personality,* Allyn & Bacon, 1983. Contributor to *International Zoo Yearbook.* Also contributor to *Journal of Abnormal and Social Psychology, Psychological Reports, Perceptual and Motor Skills, International Journal of Psychology,* and *Psychological Record.* Editor, *Journal of the Psychology of Women.*

WORK IN PROGRESS: Research on an article on a cross-national study of sex roles.

SIDELIGHTS: Georgia Babladelis told *CA:* "Among the many reasons for writing textbooks about personality is that of attempting to make a complex and sometimes isolated and esoteric topic of study part of the mainstream of psychological research and knowledge. Despite the efforts of contemporary researchers and writers, the study of personality remains enshrined in college offerings as the historical study of personality theories only. Many of us aspire to introduce the undergraduate student to the current and stimulating study of personality."

AVOCATIONAL INTERESTS: Travel, reading.

* * *

BAILEY, Raymond H(amby) 1938-

PERSONAL: Born January 31, 1938, in Athens, Tex.; son of Raymond G. and Ada Ann (in restaurant business; maiden name, Prince) Bailey; married Patricia Lawson (a teacher), December 21, 1962; children: Ramona Holland, Sarah Elizabeth. *Education:* Baylor University, B.A., 1959; Texas Technological College (now Texas Tech University), M.A., 1964; Northwestern University, additional graduate study, summers, 1965-66; Southern Baptist Theological Seminary, M.Div., 1967, Ph.D., 1973. *Home:* 228 Stilz Ave., Louisville, Ky. 40206. *Office:* Southern Baptist Theological Seminary, Louisville, Ky. 40280.

CAREER: Ordained Baptist minister, 1958; speech teacher in high school in Orange, Tex., 1960-63; Sul Ross State College (now University), Alpine, Tex., instructor in speech, 1964-65; Hardin-Simmons University, Abilene, Tex., assistant professor of speech and theater, 1965-67; Bellarmine College, Louisville, Ky., associate professor of theology and communications, 1967-73, member of board of trustees, 1971, director of Thomas Merton Study Center, 1973-74; First Baptist Church, Newport, Ky., pastor, 1974-77; First Baptist Church, Plantation, Fla., pastor, 1977-79; Southern Baptist Theological Seminary, Louisville, Ky., associate professor of communications and preaching, 1979—. Member of board of governors of St. Meinrad School of Theology and Seminary, 1972-74. *Member:* Phi Kappa Phi.

WRITINGS: (Contributor) DeWitte Holland, editor, *Preaching in American History,* Abingdon, 1969; (contributor) Holland, editor, *Sermons in American History,* Abingdon, 1971; *Thomas Merton on Mysticism,* Doubleday, 1975; *Destiny and Disappointment: Religion in America, 1900-1950,* Consortium, 1977; (contributor) *Illustrating the Gospel of Matthew,* Broadman, 1982; *The Sermon as Drama,* Broadman, 1983. Contributor to religious magazines.

* * *

BAILYN, Bernard 1922-

PERSONAL: Born September 10, 1922, in Hartford, Conn.; son of Charles Manuel and Esther (Schloss) Bailyn; married Lotte Lazarsfeld, June 18, 1952; children: Charles David, John Frederick. *Education:* Williams College, A.B., 1945; Harvard University, M.A., 1947; Ph.D., 1953. *Home:* 170 Clifton St., Belmont, Mass. 02178. *Office:* Department of History, Harvard University, Cambridge, Mass. 02138.

CAREER: Harvard University, Cambridge, Mass., instructor in education, 1953-54, assistant professor, 1954-58, associate professor, 1958-61, professor, 1961-66, Winthrop Professor of History, 1966-81, Adams University Professor of History, 1981—. Trevelyan Lecturer at Cambridge University, 1971. *Military service:* U.S. Army, 1943-46. *Member:* American Historical Association (president, 1981), American Academy of Arts and Sciences, American Antiquarian Society, National Academy of Education, American Philosophical Society, Royal Historical Society, Massachusetts Historical Society.

AWARDS, HONORS: Harvard Faculty Prize, 1965, for Volume I of *Pamphlets of the American Revolution;* Pulitzer Prize in history and Bancroft Prize, both 1967, for *The Ideological Origins of the American Revolution;* Robert H. Lord Award from Emmanuel College, 1967; National Book Award in history, 1975, for *The Ordeal of Thomas Hutchinson.* Honorary degrees from Lawrence University, 1967, Bard College, 1968, Williams College, 1969, Clark University, 1975, Yale University, Fordham University, and Rutgers University, 1976, and from Grinnell College, 1979.

WRITINGS: *The New England Merchants in the Seventeenth Century,* Harvard University Press, 1955; (with wife, Lotte Bailyn) *Massachusetts Shipping, 1697-1714: A Statistical Study,* Belknap Press of Harvard University Press, 1959; *Education in the Forming of American Society: Needs and Opportunities for Study,* University of North Carolina Press, 1960; (editor and author of introduction) *Pamphlets of the American Revolution, 1750-1776,* Volume I, Belknap Press of Harvard University Press, 1965; (editor) *The Apologia of Robert Keayne,* Harper, 1965; *The Ideological Origins of the American Revolution,* Belknap Press of Harvard University Press, 1967; *The Origins of American Politics,* Knopf, 1968; (editor with Donald Fleming) *The Intellectual Migration: Europe and America, 1930-1960,* Belknap Press of Harvard University Press, 1969.

(Editor with Donald Fleming) *Law in American History,* Little, Brown, 1972; *The Ordeal of Thomas Hutchinson,* Belknap Press of Harvard University Press, 1974; (with others) *The Great Republic,* Heath, 1977; (editor with John B. Hench) *The Press and the American Revolution,* American Antiquarian Society, 1980. Also author of *Religion and Revolution: Three Biographical Studies,* 1970.

Editor-in-chief, "John Harvard Library," 1962-70; editor with Donald Fleming, *Perspectives in American History,* annual of Charles Warren Center for Studies in American History, Harvard University, 1967-77. Contributor to symposia, proceedings, and professional journals, including *American Historical Review* and *William & Mary Quarterly.*

SIDELIGHTS: In the foreword to his Pulitzer Prize-winning *The Ideological Origins of the American Revolution,* Bernard Bailyn writes that the book is an attempt to "trace back into the early eighteenth century—and back into the European sources, wherever possible—the specific attitudes, conceptions, formulations, even in certain cases particular phrases, which together form the ideology of the American Revolution." According to the *New York Times Book Review,* what the author has contributed "is not so much a new viewpoint as a brilliantly persuasive analysis of the current viewpoint, bolstered by a thorough knowledge of the sources and an impressive grasp of the intellectual setting in which they were produced." *Book*

Week reviewer Staughton Lynd notes that the book is valuable to both historians and casual readers and that it "avoids the stereotypes and cliches and allows us to see more clearly the real nature of the American Revolution." Lynd also believes that "apart from the fullness of its documentation, the excellence of Bailyn's argument lies in its painstaking effort to grasp eighteenth-century political rhetoric." John Lustig, writing in *Library Journal*, concludes that "this excellent scholarly work will help us to determine the success of that venture which introduced the words consent and equality to our political process."

Bailyn's *The Ordeal of Thomas Hutchinson*, a 1975 National Book Award winner, is unique for its mostly sympathetic portrayal of the Royalist governor of Massachusetts (1771-1774), who became a well-known target of many statesmen of the day, including Samuel Adams, John Adams, and John Quincy Adams. D. B. Little, in a *Christian Science Monitor* review, explains Bailyn's position: "[Hutchinson] was a loyal British subject devoted to the welfare of the empire and believed firmly that America's well-being depended upon close ties with a strong Great Britain." In the *New York Review of Books*, E. S. Morgan writes: "In the concluding pages of [the book] Bailyn points out that Hutchinson never understood the forces that destroyed him. . . . And in the opening pages he tells us that his own instinctive sympathies remain with the revolutionists, that he is simply showing us how it was possible for a good man to take the other side. But in between the opening and closing pages he succeeds so well that he leaves the American Revolution looking a pretty shabby affair." *New Republic* reviewer Steven Kelman makes the point that the book is, to a large extent, based on Hutchinson's own papers "(which no doubt introduces an inevitable bias), and the author, while aware of the limitations of Hutchinson's political thought, is unsympathetic to most of the imputations of malice his contemporaries made against him." Still, Kelman finds that "Bailyn's approach—history written from the viewpoint of the losers—challenges us to imagine ourselves in Hutchinson's position and to ask ourselves how we would have acted in the America of the 1770s."

BIOGRAPHICAL/CRITICAL SOURCES: *Library Journal*, April 15, 1967; *Book Week*, May 7, 1967; *New York Times Book Review*, June 25, 1967, June 2, 1974; *Times Literary Supplement*, October 12, 1967, June 13, 1975; *New York Review of Books*, March 21, 1974; *Christian Science Monitor*, April 17, 1974; *New Republic*, May 4, 1974; *National Review*, June 7, 1974.

* * *

BAIRSTOW, Jeffrey N(oel) 1939-

PERSONAL: Born December 18, 1939, in Bradford, England; son of George and Mabel (Lee Hainsworth) Bairstow; married Susan C. Jones (a biologist), July 14, 1962; married Karen G. Salling (an editor), November 21, 1980; children: (first marriage) Anne-Marie, Timothy Michael; (second marriage) Sarah Elizabeth, Rachel Laura. *Education:* University of Birmingham, B.Sc., 1960; Fordham University, M.B.A., 1972. *Home address:* 150 South St., Fairfield, Conn. 06430. *Office:* International Telephone & Telegraph Co., 1000 Oronoque Lane, Stratford, Conn. 06497.

CAREER: *Tennis* Magazine, Norwalk, Conn., managing editor, 1973-81; International Telephone & Telegraph Co., Stratford, Conn., manager of communications, 1981—.

WRITINGS: (With Barry Tarshis) *All about Tennis*, Rand McNally, 1975; (with Tarshis) *Tennis*, Signet Books, 1975; (with Pancho Gonzalez) *Tennis Begins at Forty*, Dial, 1976; *Tennis Strokes and Strategies*, Simon & Schuster, 1976; *Tennis: How to Play, How to Win*, Tennis Magazine, 1978; (with Charles Brumfield) *Off the Wall*, Dial, 1978; (with George Lott) *Doubles Tactics and Strategies*, Tennis Magazine, 1979; (with Herb Fitz Gibbon) *The Complete Racquet Sports Player*, Simon & Schuster, 1980; (with Edward Fox and Donald Mathews) *I.T.—Interval Training for Lifetime Fitness*, Dial, 1980; *The Four Seasons Outdoor Guide*, Random House, 1982; (with Brumfield) *Roll-Out Racquetball*, Dial, 1982.

AVOCATIONAL INTERESTS: Tennis, racquetball, squash, running, backpacking, camping, skiing, soaring, flying.

* * *

BAKER, Eleanor Z(uckerman) 1932-

PERSONAL: Born February 14, 1932, in New York, N.Y.; daughter of William (a physician) and Sarah (Aranow) Zuckerman; married Roger M. Baker (an educational diagnostician); children: Susan Ellen (Mrs. Paul L. Mitchell), Cindy Ann, Mary Jane, Roger M. II. *Education:* Syracuse University, B.A., 1951; Stephen F. Austin State University, M.A., 1960; University of Texas at Austin, Ph.D., 1977. *Religion:* Presbyterian. *Home:* 1310 Wendel St., El Campo, Tex. 77437. *Office:* Department of English, Wharton County Junior College, 911 Boling Highway, Wharton, Tex. 77488.

CAREER: University of Houston, Houston, Tex., lecturer in English, 1960-62; University of Texas at Austin, teaching assistant in English, 1962-66; Stephen F. Austin State University, Nacogdoches, Tex., assistant professor of English and Asian studies, 1967-72; Firestone Plantations Co., Harbel, Liberia, English and social studies teacher at company school, 1972-74; University of Houston, member of English faculty, 1974-77; Wharton County Junior College, Wharton, Tex., instructor in English, 1977—. Junior high school English and social studies teacher in Houston, Tex., 1960-61; Carnegie Foundation consultant and guest lecturer at Stillman College, 1966-67; visiting research fellow at Australian National University, 1967. *Member:* Association of Asian Studies, American Association of University Women, American Association of University Professors, Phi Alpha Theta.

AWARDS, HONORS: Fulbright scholar at University of Hawaii, summer, 1965; United Nations Award, UNESCO, 1969, for *The Australian Aborigines*; Maverick Award, Piney Woods Writers Conference, 1970, for *New Guinea: A Journey into Yesterday*; Texas Writers Award nomination, 1971, for *New Zealand Today*; National Endowment for the Humanities scholar at Harvard University, summer, 1982.

WRITINGS: (Editor) *Australian-Japanese Documents*, Department of External Affairs, Government of Australia, 1967; *The Australian Aborigines*, Steck, 1968; *New Guinea: A Journey into Yesterday*, Steck, 1968; *Australia Today*, Steck, 1969; *New Zealand: Land of the Mighty Maori*, Steck, 1971; *Japanese Counterfeit Trademarks* (classified monograph), U.S. State Department, 1971; *New Zealand Today*, Steck, 1972; *The Wolderts: A Story of Texas and Texans*, [Tyler, Tex.], 1979. Also author of papers presented at learned societies.

WORK IN PROGRESS: A social commentary; a musical; United Methodist Committee on Relief self-help projects in Haiti.

SIDELIGHTS: Eleanor Z. Baker has traveled in Europe, Asia, Australia, Africa, and the Pacific Islands, with a strong interest in emerging nations, assimilation practices, and maintaining cultural values of tribal peoples. *Avocational interests:* Reading, travel, knitting, square dancing, collecting primitive art and artifacts.

* * *

BAKER, Michael H(enry) C(hadwick) 1937-

PERSONAL: Born June 19, 1937, in Croydon, Surrey, England; son of Leonard Chadwick (a chauffeur) and Elsie (a cook; maiden name, Knight) Baker; married Maeve Finucane (a teacher), August 17, 1968; children: William, Daniel, Samuel. *Education:* Attended Croydon Art School, 1958-61; Chelsea Art School, diploma in design, 1962; Liverpool Art College, art teacher's diploma, 1963. *Politics:* "Socialist (member of Labour Party)." *Religion:* Christian. *Home:* 75 Northmoor Way, Wareham, Dorsetshire BH20 4EG, England. *Office:* Swanage Middle School, Swanage, Dorsetshire, England.

CAREER: Newspaper reporter and photographer, 1954-55; industrial and commercial photographer, 1955-58; Southport School of Art, Southport, Lancashire, England, lecturer in photography, 1964-66; art teacher in elementary schools in Huyton, England, 1967-68, and Croydon, England, 1968-73; Oxted County Comprehensive School, Oxted, England, art teacher in secondary school, 1973-77; Purbeck Teachers Centre and Swanage Middle School, Swanage, Dorsetshire, England, art teacher, 1977—. *Military service:* Royal Air Force, senior aircraftsman, 1956-58. *Member:* Amnesty International (Poole Group), Great Western Society, Society of Authors, Irish Railway Record Society.

WRITINGS: Irish Railways since 1919, Ian Allen, 1972; *Journey to Katmandu* (travel book), David & Charles, 1974; *Railways in the Republic of Ireland: A Pictorial Survey of the G.S.R. and C.I.E., 1925-1975,* D. B. Barton, 1975; *Sussex Villages,* R. Hale, 1977; *Sussex Scenes,* R. Hale, 1978; *Vintage Train,* Great Western Society, 1980. Also author of *The Changing Southern Scene, 1948-1981,* 1981. Contributor to periodicals, including *Railway World, Modern Railways, Railway Magazine,* and *Dorset County Magazine.* Editor of *Heritage Education News* and *Great Western Echo.*

WORK IN PROGRESS: The Changing London Midland Scene, for Ian Allen; three children's books; books on the Great Western Railway and on Wessex.

AVOCATIONAL INTERESTS: Travel, Ireland, industrial archaeology, children.

* * *

BALANDIER, Georges (Leon) 1920-

PERSONAL: Born December 21, 1920, in Aillevillers, France; son of Andre and Lucienne (Andre) Balandier; married Claire Tron, September 11, 1947; children: Claude, Ann. *Education:* Lycee Colbert, Paris, Ph.B., 1937; Sorbonne, University of Paris, Ph.D., 1954. *Home:* 13 rue du Square Carpeaux, Paris 18, France. *Office:* 12 rue Cujas, Paris 5, France.

CAREER: Overseas Office of Scientific and Technological Research, in charge of research in Senegal, Guinea, and in the Congo (now Zaire), 1946-52; Paris Institute of Political Studies, Paris, France, professor, 1952-62; Sorbonne, University of Paris, Paris, professor of sociology, 1962—. Engaged in research at National Center for Scientific Research, Paris, 1952-54. *Member:* International Association of French Speaking Sociologists (honorary president), Acade'mie Royale de Belgique, Academy of Athens, American Philosophical Society.

WRITINGS: Tous Comptes Faits, Editions du Pavois, 1948; (with Jean-Claude Pauvert) *Les villages gabonais: Aspects de-mographiques, economiques, sociologiques, projets de modernisation,* [Brazzaville], 1952; (with Paul Mercier) *Les pecheurs Lebou du Senegal: Particularisme et evolution,* Centre IFAN-Senegal, 1952; *Sociologie actuelle de l'Afrique Noire: Dynamique des changements sociaux en Afrique centrale,* Presses universitaires de France, 1955, 2nd edition, augmented and updated, published as *Sociologie actuelle de l'Afrique noire: Dynamique sociale en Afrique centrale,* 1963, 3rd edition, 1971, translation by Douglas Garman published as *The Sociology of Black Africa: Social Dynamics in Central Africa,* Praeger, 1970; *Sociologie des Brazzavilles Noires,* A. Colin, 1955; *L'anthropologie appliquee aux problemes des pays sous-developpes,* Cours de droit, 1955; *Le "tiers-monde": Sous-developpement et developpement,* Presses universitaires de France, 1956, new edition (augmented and updated by Alfred Sauvy), 1961; *Afrique ambigue,* Plon, 1957, translation by Helen Weaver published as *Ambiguous Africa: Cultures in Collision,* Pantheon, 1966; *Les pays "sous-developpes": Aspects et perspectives,* Cours de droit, 1959.

(Contributor) *Economic Development and Its Social Implications: Technological Change and Industrialization,* Presses universitaires de France, 1962; *Les pays en voie de developpement: Analyse sociologique et politique,* Cours de droit, 1964; *La vie quotidienne au royaume de Kongo du XVI au XVIII siecle,* Hachette, 1965, translation by Helen Weaver published as *Daily Life in the Kingdom of the Kongo from the Sixteenth to the Eighteenth Century,* Pantheon, 1968; *Anthropologie politique,* Presses universitaires de France, 1967, 3rd revised edition, 1978, translation by A. M. Sheridan Smith published as *Political Anthropology,* Pantheon, 1970; (with Jacques Maquet) *Dictionnaire des civilisations africaines,* F. Hazan, 1968; (editor with others) *Perspectives de la sociologie contemporaine: Hommage a Georges Gurvitch,* Presses universitaires de France, 1968; (contributor) *Social, Economic and Technological Change: A Theoretical Approach,* Presses universitaires de France, 1968.

El concepto de "situacion" colonial, Editorial Jose de Pineda Ibarra (Guatemala), 1970; *Sens et puissance: Les dynamiques sociales,* Presses universitaires de France, 1971, 2nd edition, 1981; *Gurvitch,* Presses universitaires de France, 1972; *Anthropo-lognes,* Presses universitaires de France, 1974; *Histoire d'Auties,* Stock, 1977.

Le pouvoir du scenes, Balland, 1980; *Au tour de Georges Balandier,* Fondation d'Hautvillers, 1981. Also editor of *Sociology des mutations,* proceedings of the International Association of French Speaking Sociologists, 1970. Contributor of articles to professional journals. Director, *Cahiers Internationaux de Sociologie.*

* * *

BALDWIN, Joyce G(ertrude) 1921-

PERSONAL: Born August 1, 1921, in Wembley, Middlesex, England; daughter of Gilbert and Gertrude (Clarke) Baldwin. *Education:* University of Nottingham, B.A. (with honors), 1942; Cambridge University, teaching certificate, 1943; London Bible College, Dip. Th., 1949, B.D., 1958. *Address:* 18 Bibury Crescent, Bristol B59 4PW, England.

CAREER: Teacher of modern languages in Liverpool, England, 1945-47, and in Lancashire, England, 1952-56; Dalton House, Bristol, England, lecturer in Old Testament, 1956-58, vice-principal, 1958-71; Trinity College, Bristol, lecturer in biblical studies, 1971-82, principal, 1981-82.

WRITINGS: (Contributor) Donald Guthrie and J. A. Motyer, editors, *New Bible Commentary,* revised edition, Inter-Varsity

Press, 1970; *Haggai Zechariah Malachi*, Inter-Varsity Press, 1972; *Women Likewise* (booklet), Falcon, 1973; (contributor) *The New International Dictionary of New Testament Theology*, Paternoster, 1975; (contributor) *Moral Questions*, Falcon, 1977; *Daniel*, Inter-Varsity Press, 1978; *Literary Affinities of Daniel*, Tyndale Bulletin, 1979; (contributor) *The Illustrated Bible Dictionary*, Inter-Varsity Press, 1980. Also author of *The Role of the Ten Commandments*, 1981.

* * *

BALL, John C. 1924-

PERSONAL: Born May 14, 1924, in Lexington, Ky.; son of Charles Joseph (a journalist) and Gertrude Katherine (Kranz) Ball; married Marion E. Jokl (a computer analyst), August 1, 1959; children: Charles, Elizabeth. *Education:* Central Connecticut State College, B.S., 1949; George Peabody College for Teachers (now George Peabody College for Teachers of Vanderbilt University), M.A., 1950; additional study at University of Connecticut and Harvard University; Vanderbilt University, Ph.D., 1955. *Office:* Special Action Office for Drug Abuse Prevention, 726 Jackson Pl. N.W., Washington, D.C. 20500.

CAREER: University of Kentucky, Lexington, began as instructor, became associate professor, professor of sociology, 1967-70; Temple University, Philadelphia, Pa., professor of psychiatry, 1970-72; Special Action Office for Drug Abuse Prevention, Washington, D.C., member of staff, 1972—. Chief of sociology unit, Addiction Research Center, National Institute of Mental Health, U.S. Public Health Service Hospital, Lexington, Ky., 1962-70. Delegate, White House Conference on Drug Addiction, 1962. Director of grants, Social Science Research Council. Consultant in areas of drug addiction, juvenile delinquency, and criminology. *Military service:* U.S. Army, 1943-46. *Member:* American Sociological Association (fellow), Southern Sociological Society, Ohio Valley Sociological Society. *Awards, honors:* Ford Foundation fellow; two grants from the Kentucky Research Foundation.

WRITINGS: Social Deviancy and Adolescent Personality, University of Kentucky Press, 1962; (editor with John A. O'Donnell) *Narcotic Addiction*, Harper, 1966; (with Richard W. Snarr) *Involvement in a Drug Subculture*, Eastern Kentucky University and Temple University, 1969; (editor) *The Epidemiology of Opiate Addiction in the United States*, C. C Thomas, 1970. Contributor of articles to criminology, law, psychology, and sociology journals.

WORK IN PROGRESS: Several major studies of narcotic addiction in United States and Puerto Rico.†

* * *

BAN, Joseph D(aniel) 1926-

PERSONAL: Born April 12, 1926, in Homestead, Pa.; son of Joseph (a building contractor) and Suzannah (Petrusan) Ban; married Arline June Chapman (a writer for children), March 31, 1951. *Education:* University of Pittsburgh, B.S. in C.E., 1950; Colgate Rochester Divinity School, B.D., 1953; graduate study at University of Rochester, 1951, and Union Theological Seminary, New York, N.Y., 1956-58; University of Oregon, Ph.D., 1974. *Office:* Divinity College, McMaster University, Hamilton, Ontario, Canada L85 4KI.

CAREER: Baptist clergyman. Associate pastor in Rochester, N.Y., 1950-53, and Dayton, Ohio, 1953-56; pastor in New Brunswick, N.J., 1956-58; American Baptist Home Mission Societies, New York, N.Y., and Valley Forge, Pa., program associate in Division of Evangelism, 1958-64; Pennsylvania State University, University Park, executive director of University Christian Association, 1964-66, campus minister, 1967; Linfield College, McMinnville, Ore., associate professor, 1967-74, professor of religious studies and history, 1974-78, chaplain, 1967-73; McMaster University, Divinity College, Hamilton, Ontario, professor of Christian ministry and director, master of religious education programme, 1978—. *Member:* American Academy of Religion, American Baptist Historical Society, American Association of University Professors, Association of Professors and Researchers in Religious Education, Canadian Society of Church History. *Awards, honors: Education for Change* was named American Baptist "Best Book of the Year," 1968; Association of Theological Schools in United States and Canada grant.

WRITINGS: (Contributor) *The Church's Educational Ministry: A Curriculum Plan*, Bethany Press, 1965; *Education for Change*, Judson, 1968; (contributor) Charles L. Wallis, editor, *The Minister's Manual for 1970*, Harper, 1969; *Facing Today's Demands*, Judson, 1970; *Jesus Confronts Life's Issues*, Judson, 1972; (editor with Paul R. Dekar) *In the Great Tradition*, Judson, 1982.

With wife, Arline J. Ban; published by Christian Board of Publication, except as indicated: *Jesus Makes the Difference*, Judson, 1966; *God's Gift of Life*, 1969; *As Wide as the World*, Judson, 1971; *The New Disciple*, Judson, 1975; *Celebrating God's Gift of Life, Vacation Ventures*, 1982; *Long Journey to Freedom: Old Testament*, 1982; *Living the Word*, 1982.

Author of Baptist manuals and booklets, one in Spanish. Contributor and consulting editor of "Makers of Modern Thought" series, Judson, 1972. Contributor to *Biographical Dictionary of British Radicals in the Seventeenth Century*, Harvester, 1981; contributor of more than one hundred articles, book reviews, and sermons to religious periodicals.

WORK IN PROGRESS: Long Journey to Freedom: New Testament; The Bible: Who? What? When? Where? Why?; In Jesus's Day; additional volumes of "Living the Word" series for Christian Board of Publication; *Christology*, for Judson.

SIDELIGHTS: Joseph D. Ban told *CA:* "Writing, for me, is primarily a means of creative expression. This remains true though much of what has been published of my work is quite practical in nature. Time for writing comes on weekends and days off from a full schedule of classroom and other academic duties. My research has been made possible primarily through the inter-library loan system, a great boon to a serious writer.

"In recent years, much of my time has been spent writing with my wife, Arline. While she, too, has had several books of her own published, we enjoy writing together most of the time. It is a 'we' experience when we co-author a text. It involves numerous conferences, writing individually, editing each other's contributions, more consultation and, finally, a completed product where it is difficult for either of us to recall who wrote exactly which paragraph. We have also benefitted from skilled editors who have made the end result look far better than the raw manuscript."

* * *

BARBER, William Joseph 1925-

PERSONAL: Born January 13, 1925, in Abilene, Kan.; son of Ward Seymour Henry and Esther (Roop) Barber; married Sheila Mary Marr, April 16, 1955; children: Thomas, John, Charles. *Education:* Harvard University, A.B., 1949; Oxford University, B.A., 1951, M.A., 1955, D.Phil., 1957. *Home:* 306 Pine

St., Middletown, Conn. 06457. *Office:* Department of Economics, Wesleyan University, Middletown, Conn. 06457.

CAREER: Kansas State University, Manhattan, assistant professor, 1951-52; Oxford University, Balliol College, Oxford, England, lecturer, 1956; Wesleyan University, Middletown, Conn., 1957—, professor of economics, 1965-72, Andrews Professor of Economics, 1972—. American secretary of Rhodes Scholarship Trust, 1970-81; member of board of electors of Eastman professorship, Oxford University, 1970—. *Military service:* U.S. Army, 1943-46. *Member:* American Economics Association, Royal Economics Society, African Studies Association, American Association of Rhodes Scholars, Phi Beta Kappa. *Awards, honors:* Rhodes Scholar, 1949-51; Ford Foundation foreign area fellow in Africa, 1955-56; M.A., Wesleyan University, 1965.

WRITINGS: The Economy of British Central Africa: A Case Study of Economic Development in a Dualistic Society, Stanford University Press, 1961; *A History of Economic Thought,* Praeger, 1967; (contributor) Gunnar Myrdal, *Asian Drama: An Inquiry into the Poverty of Nations,* Twentieth Century Fund, 1968; *British Economic Thought and India, 1600-1858: A Study in the History of Development Economics,* Oxford University Press, 1975; (co-author) *Exhortation and Controls,* Brookings Institution, 1975; *Energy Policy in Perspective,* Brookings Institution, 1981. Contributor of articles to professional journals.

SIDELIGHTS: A History of Economic Thought has been translated into Swedish, Spanish, Italian, Japanese, and Portuguese.

* * *

BARBET, Pierre
See AVICE, Claude

* * *

BARBOUR, Ian G(raeme) 1923-

PERSONAL: Born October 5, 1923, in Peking, China; son of George Brown (a dean) and Dorothy (Dickinson) Barbour; married Deane Kern, November 29, 1947; children: John Dickinson, Blair Winn, David Freeland, Heather Deane. *Education:* Swarthmore College, B.A., 1943; Duke University, M.A., 1946; University of Chicago, Ph.D., 1950; Yale University, B.D., 1956. *Home:* 106 Winona St., Northfield, Minn. 55057. *Office:* Carleton College, Northfield, Minn. 55057.

CAREER: Kalamazoo College, Kalamazoo, Mich., assistant professor, 1949-51, associate professor and chairman of department of physics, 1951-53; Carleton College, Northfield, Minn., assistant professor of religion, 1955-57, associate professor, 1957-65, professor of religion and physics, 1965—. Lilly Visiting Professor of Science, Theology, and Human Values, Purdue University, 1973-74. *Member:* American Academy of Religion, Phi Beta Kappa, Sigma Xi. *Awards, honors:* Ford faculty fellow, 1953; Harbison award of Danforth Foundation, 1953; American Council of Learned Societies fellowship, 1963-64; Guggenheim and Fulbright fellowships, 1967-68; National Humanities Center fellow, 1980-81.

WRITINGS: Christianity and the Scientist, Association Press, 1960; *Issues in Science and Religion,* Prentice-Hall, 1966; (editor) *Science and Religion: New Perspectives on the Dialogue,* Harper, 1968; *Science and Secularity: The Ethics of Technology,* Harper, 1970; (editor) *Earth Might Be Fair,* Prentice-Hall, 1971; (editor) *Western Man and Environmental Ethics,* Addison-Wesley, 1972; *Myths, Models, and Paradigms,* Harper, 1974; (editor) *Finite Resources and the Human Future,* Augsburg, 1976; *Technology, Environment and Human Values,* Praeger, 1980; (co-author) *Energy and American Values,* Praeger, 1982. Contributor to scientific and religious journals. Member of editorial boards of *Process Studies, Zygon,* and *Journal of Science and Religion.*

* * *

BARCLAY, Oliver R(ainsford) 1919-
(A. N. Triton)

PERSONAL: Born February 22, 1919, in Kobe, Japan; son of Joseph Gurney (a missionary) and Gwendoline (a missionary; maiden name, Watney) Barclay; married Dorothy Knott, June 30, 1949 (died May 19, 1964); married Daisy Hickey, October 31, 1965; children: (first marriage) Janet (Mrs. Anthony Johnston), Andrew, Stephen, John. *Education:* Attended Cambridge University, 1938-41. *Religion:* Church of England. *Home:* 8 Southland Rd., Leicester LE2 3RJ, England. *Office:* Universities and Colleges Christian Fellowship of Evangelical Unions, 38 DeMontfort St., Leicester LE1 7GP, England.

CAREER: Cambridge University, Cambridge, England, research zoologist and part-time teacher, 1941-45; Universities and Colleges Christian Fellowship of Evangelical Unions, London, England, staff member, 1945—.

WRITINGS—All published by Inter-Varsity Press: *Guidance,* 1956, revised edition, 1978; *Christian Approach to University Life,* 1963; *Time to Embrace,* 1964; (under pseudonym A. N. Triton) *Whose World?,* 1970; (under pseudonym A. N. Triton) *Living and Loving,* 1972; *Reasons for Faith,* 1974; *Whatever Happened to the Jesus Lane Lot?,* 1977; (contributor) B. N. Kaye and G. J. Wenham, editors, *Law, Morality, and the Bible,* 1978; (under pseudonym A. N. Triton) *Salt to the World,* 1978.

* * *

BARCLAY, Virginia
See McDONNELL, Virginia B(leecker)

* * *

BARRON, Frank (Xavier) 1922-

PERSONAL: Born June 17, 1922, in Lansford, Pa.; son of Francis (a builder) and Sarah Ellen (Dougherty) Barron; married Nancy Jean Camp (an artist), January 20, 1961; children: Francis Charles Xavier, Brigid Jessica Sarah, Anthea. *Education:* LaSalle College, B.A., 1942; Cambridge University, additional study, 1946; University of Minnesota, M.A., 1948; University of California, Berkeley, Ph.D., 1950. *Politics:* Independent. *Religion:* Roman Catholic. *Home:* 206 Florence Dr., Aptos, Calif. 95003. *Office:* Department of Psychology, University of California, Santa Cruz, Calif. 95064.

CAREER: Bryn Mawr College, Bryn Mawr, Pa., lecturer in psychology, 1950-51; University of California, Berkeley, professor of psychology, 1951-74, research psychologist, 1962-74; University of California, Santa Cruz, professor of psychology, 1974—, faculty research lecturer, 1982-83. Lecturer in psychology, Harvard University, 1956 and 1960-61; visiting professor, Wesleyan University, 1958; fellow, Center for Advanced Study, Palo Alto, Calif., 1959. Research director, Berkeley Institute of Psychological Research. Co-director, Heims Fund for Creative Children. *Military service:* U.S. Army, 1943-46; became sergeant. *Member:* International Council of Psychologists (member of board of directors), American Psychological Association (fellow). *Awards, honors:* Ford Foundation grant for basic research in behavioral sciences, 1957-62; outstanding research award, American Personnel and Guidance Association, 1964; Social Science Research Council faculty research fellow, 1964-65; Guggenheim fellowship, 1968-69; Richardson Creativity Award, American Psychology Association, 1969; honorary Doctor of Science, LaSalle College, 1979.

WRITINGS: (Co-editor with Calvin Taylor) *Scientific Creativity: Its Recognition and Development*, Wiley, 1963; *Creativity and Psychological Health*, Van Nostrand, 1963; (with William Dement) *New Directions in Psychology II*, Holt, 1965; *Innovators and Innovation in Ireland*, Human Sciences Council, 1966; *An Eye More Fantastical*, National Art Education Association, 1967; *LSD, Man and Society*, Wesleyan University Press, 1967; *Creative Person and Creative Process*, Holt, 1968; *Creativity and Personal Freedom*, Van Nostrand, 1968.

Artists in the Making, Seminar Press, 1972; *The Shaping of Personality: Conflict, Choice, and Growth*, Harper, 1979. Contributor of articles to *Encyclopaedia Britannica*, *Encyclopedia of Mental Health*, *Scientific American* and *Science*. Also contributor of articles to psychology journals.

WORK IN PROGRESS: Varieties of Personal Philosophy, a study of philosophical beliefs of contemporaries; *To Kill a Twin*.

* * *

BASSETT, T(homas) D(ay) Seymour 1913-

PERSONAL: Born December 21, 1913, in Burlington, Vt.; son of Samuel Eliot (a professor of Greek) and Bertha (Raymond) Bassett; married Patricia Reynolds, December 26, 1942 (died November 23, 1959); married Mary Jane Gray (a physician specializing in obstetrics and gynecology), June 15, 1963 (divorced February 22, 1979); married Alice Fisher Cook, May 12, 1979; children: (first marriage) John Eliot, Elizabeth (Mrs. Ramiro Chacon), Miriam (Mrs. Douglas Clark French), Margot (deceased). *Education:* Yale University, A.B., 1935, graduate study, 1935-36; University of California, Berkeley, graduate study, 1936-37; Harvard University, graduate study, 1937-39, Ph.D., 1952. *Religion:* Society of Friends. *Home:* 11 Bilodeau Parkway, Burlington, Vt. 05401.

CAREER: National Archives, Washington, D.C., various posts, 1942-43; Princeton University, Princeton, N.J., research associate in American civilization program, 1946-48; Earlham College, Richmond, Ind., assistant professor, 1948-56, associate professor of history, 1956-57, college archivist, 1956-57; University of California, Riverside, lecturer, 1957-58; University of Vermont, Burlington, associate professor of history, 1958-65, Wilbur librarian, 1958-77, university archivist, 1962-77. Acting chief of archives, United Nations, summers, 1957, 1959; lecturer, University of California, Berkeley, summer, 1958. Trustee of Moses Brown School, Providence, R.I., 1961-71, Lincoln School, Providence, 1961-71, Farm and Wilderness Foundation, 1971-75, and Sheldon Museum, Middlebury, Vt., 1971—. *Member:* Friends Historical Association (Philadelphia), Friends Historical Society (London), Vermont Historical Society (trustee, 1961-66). *Awards, honors:* Social Science Research Council faculty grant, 1952-53.

WRITINGS: (Co-author, Volume I, and bibliographer, Volume II) Stow Persons and Donald D. Egbert, editors, *Socialism and American Life*, Princeton University Press, 1952; (editor) *Outsiders inside Vermont*, Greene, 1967, 2nd edition, Phoenix Publishing, 1976; *A History of the Vermont Geological Surveys and State Geologists*, Vermont Geological Survey, 1976; (editor with John D. Haskell, Jr.) *New Hampshire: A Bibliography of Its History*, G. K. Hall, 1979; (editor) *Vermont: A Bibliography of Its History*, G. K. Hall, 1981. Author of column "Burlington in History," *Burlington Free Press*, 1976-79. Contributor to *Vermont History*, *New England Quarterly*, and *Quaker History*.

WORK IN PROGRESS: A history of religion in Vermont.

* * *

BAWDEN, Nina
See KARK, Nina Mary (Mabey)

* * *

BECKMANN, David M(ilton) 1948-

PERSONAL: Born February 22, 1948, in Kearney, Neb.; son of Milton W. (a professor) and Leona (a teacher; maiden name, Lange) Beckmann; married Janet Williams (an English teacher) June 17, 1972. *Education:* Yale University, B.A., 1969; Joint Project for Theological Education (Seminex), St. Louis, Mo., M.Div., 1974; London School of Economics and Political Science, University of London, M.Sc., 1975. *Politics:* Democrat. *Home:* 517 Hilltop Ter., Alexandria, Va. 22301.

CAREER: Ordained minister of Lutheran Church, 1974; parochial high school English teacher in Accra, Ghana 1969; Lincoln Technical College, Lincoln, Neb., director of adult civic education, 1970-71; vicar in Omaha, Neb., 1972-73; Ranjpur/Dinajpur Rehabilitation Service of Lutheran World Federation, Dacca, Bangladesh, administrative assistant, 1976; World Bank, Washington, D.C., affiliated with Young Professionals Program, 1976-77, economist, Urban Projects, 1977-81, speechwriter, 1982—. *Member:* Phi Beta Kappa. *Awards, honors:* Woodrow Wilson fellow, 1971; Rockefeller Foundation fellow, 1971.

WRITINGS: Eden Revival: Spiritual Churches in Ghana, Concordia, 1975; *The Overseas List*, Augsburg, 1980; *Where Faith and Economics Meet*, Augsburg, 1981. Contributor to *Concordia Theological Monthly*, *Afro-American Studies*, *Christian Century*, *Currents in Theology and Mission*, *Cresset*, and *Missiology*.

WORK IN PROGRESS: Studies on the relationship between spiritual values and economic development, focusing on Christian understanding of economic life, with an interest in the perspectives of other religions and ethical traditions.

AVOCATIONAL INTERESTS: Travel.

* * *

BEDFORD, A. N.
See WATSON, Jane Werner

* * *

BEDFORD, Annie North
See WATSON, Jane Werner

* * *

BEECHER, John 1904-1980

PERSONAL: Born January 22, 1904, in New York, N.Y.; died May 11, 1980, of lung fibrosis, in San Francisco, Calif.; son of Leonard Thurlow (a U.S. Steel executive) and Isabel (Garghill) Beecher; married Virginia St. Clair Donovan, September 20, 1926 (divorced, 1946; died, 1965); married fourth wife,

Barbara Marie Scholz (a painter), August 16, 1955; children: (previous marriage) David, Leonard, Joan (Mrs. John Eichrodt), Michael, Thomas Edward. *Education:* Attended Cornell University, 1921-23; University of Alabama, A.B., 1926; graduate study, Harvard University, 1926-27, University of Paris, 1928; University of Wisconsin, M.A., 1930; graduate study, University of North Carolina, 1933-34. *Residence:* San Francisco, Calif.

CAREER: Poet and civil rights activist. U.S. Steel Corp., Birmingham, Ala., chemist, 1918-19, steelworker, 1920-21, 1923-24, open hearth metallurgist, 1928-29; Dartmouth College, Hanover, N.H., instructor in English, 1927; University of Wisconsin—Madison, instructor in English in Experimental College, 1929-33; Federal Emergency Relief Administration, 1934-43, district relief administrator in North Carolina, social research supervisor in Mississippi, manager of resettlement communities in Alabama, and state director of migratory labor camps in Florida; manager of resettlement projects and migrant camps, U.S. Department of Agriculture, 1935-40; *Birmingham Age-Herald and News,* Birmingham, assistant editor and editorial writer, 1940-41; Southern regional director of Fair Employment Practices Commission, 1941-43; *New York Post,* New York, N.Y., staff writer, 1943; UNRRA, Stuttgart, Germany, director of Displaced Persons Program, 1945; National Institute of Social Relations, Washington, D.C., chief editor, 1945-46; San Francisco State College (now University), San Francisco, Calif., assistant professor of sociology, 1948-50; founder, with wife Barbara, of Morning Star Press, and rancher, raising sheep and poultry, and growing fruit, Sebastopol, Calif., 1952-58; Arizona State University, Tempe, lecturer in English, 1959-61; University of Santa Clara, Santa Clara, Calif., poet-in-residence, 1963-65; reporter on Southern civil rights movement, *San Francisco Chronicle* and *Ramparts* (magazine), 1964-65; North Shore Community College, Beverly, Mass., poet-in-residence, 1969-71; St. John's University, Collegeville, Minn., poet-in-residence, 1970; Assumption College, Worcester, Mass., poet-in-residence, 1971; San Francisco State University, San Francisco, member of faculty, beginning 1977. Visiting professor, Miles College, 1966-67; campus visitor, Association of American Colleges Arts Program, 1969-72; visiting scholar, Duke University, 1973-75. Has given numerous poetry readings throughout the country. *Military service:* U.S. Merchant Marine, served aboard S. S. *Booker T. Washington* (first integrated unit in U.S. Merchant Marine), 1943-45; became ensign. *Member:* American Association of University Professors.

AWARDS, HONORS: L.H.D., Illinois College, 1948; Ford fellowship, 1951; Fund for the Advancement of Education fellow, 1951-52; Western Books Award, Huntington Library, 1960, 1961, 1963; National Endowment for the Arts award; May 1, 1974, was declared "Beecher Day" in Birmingham, Alabama; manuscript collection housed in William R. Perkins Library, Duke University.

WRITINGS—Poetry, except as indicated: *And I Will Be Heard: Two Talks to the American People,* Twice a Year Press, 1940; *Here I Stand,* Twice a Year Press, 1941; *All Brave Sailors* (war experiences), Fischer, 1945; *Land of the Free: A Portfolio of Poems on the State of the Union,* Morning Star, 1956; *Observe the Time: An Everyday Tragedy in Verse,* Morning Star, 1956; *Just Peanuts,* Morning Star, 1957; *Inquest,* Morning Star, 1957; *Moloch,* Morning Star, 1957.

In Egypt Land, Rampart, 1960; *Phantom City,* Rampart, 1961; *Homage to a Subversive,* Rampart, 1961; *Undesirables,* Rampart, 1962; *Report to the Stockholders, and Other Poems, 1932-1962,* Monthly Review Press, 1962; *Bestride the Narrow World,* Rampart, 1963; *Conformity Means Death,* Rampart, 1963; *On Acquiring a Cistercian Breviary,* Rampart, 1963; *Yours in the Bonds,* Rampart, 1963; *An Air That Kills,* Rampart, 1963; *A Humble Petition to the President of Harvard,* Rampart, 1963; *To Live and Die in Dixie, and Other Poems,* Red Mountain Editions, 1966; *Hear the Wind Blow!: Poems of Protest and Prophecy,* International Publishers, 1968.

(Contributor) Studs Terkel, editor, *Hard Times,* Pantheon, 1970; *Collected Poems, 1924-1974,* Macmillan, 1974; *Tomorrow Is a Day* (study of farm labor movement in Minnesota), Vanguard, 1979. Also author of Volume I of his autobiography, *The Vital I.* Author of recordings, "To Live and Die in Dixie," Folkways, 1968, "Report to the Stockholders," 1977, and of other recordings for Library of Congress; author of microfilm, "John Beecher Papers, 1899-1972," Microfilming Corp. of America, 1973. Contributor to numerous periodicals, including *Harper's, New Republic, Nation, Social Forces, Negro Digest, Science and Society, Coastlines,* and *Fellowship.* Editor, *Morning Star Quartos* (poetry); associate editor, *Ramparts* (magazine), 1959-63, 1964-67.

WORK IN PROGRESS: Additional volumes of his autobiography.

SIDELIGHTS: Civil rights crusader, poet, rancher, termed "the conscience of the people" by American poet William Carlos Williams and "an authentic American folk hero" by Robert Steinbrook in the *Philadelphia Bulletin,* John Beecher dedicated his life to eradicating racism and inequality, especially among blacks and steelworkers. The great-great nephew of abolitionists Henry Ward Beecher and Harriet Beecher Stowe (the author of *Uncle Tom's Cabin*), he fought for integrity and honesty from the age of sixteen, when he was expelled from Virginia Military Institute for refusing to inform upon his roommates. Beecher was proud of his ancestry, which also included Irish nationalists on his mother's side. He explained to Penelope Moffet in the *Los Angeles Times Book Review:* "All my life I've been a superpatriot. . . . It was in my lineage. My grandmother instilled all this in me."

Beecher's "superpatriot" actions defined him as a leader in twentieth-century freedom-fighting. According to Chet Fuller in the *Atlanta Journal,* Beecher "spent his life championing unpopular causes, turning out fire-edged poems and work songs that have been the cries of the downtrodden." Moffet sums up Beecher's life as "a life full of ups and downs, a public disgrace brought on by commitment to out-of-favor democratic principles and of grace achieved by a refusal to abandon those principles. A life in which John Beecher always managed, like the proverbial cat, to land on his feet."

His youthful stints in European cities, including Paris and Florence, convinced Beecher to return to the United States to obtain "the living experience of American life, as much as [could] be crammed in," he told Moffet. Beecher further explained that his personal creed—"do what the spirit say do" (from an old black spiritual)—dictated his actions. Beecher's jobs, especially his early employment, kept him aware of the vast discrepancies in America. He saw, first-hand, Ku Klux Klan attacks on black sharecroppers, lynchings, men broken by gruelling twelve-hour shifts in steel mills. His first attempts at poetry stemmed perhaps from his own realization of the injustice of inequality and of America's disinterest in righting such situations. "Spontaneously, I started to write," he explained to Steinbrook, in a *Philadelphia Bulletin* interview. "I hadn't even heard of Marx or Lenin, but violent and revolutionary poems started coming out."

Despite his numerous jobs and his especially time-consuming work with Franklin Delano Roosevelt's New Deal, Beecher never abandoned his writing. He used his bleak and discouraging moments in the South as fuel for his pen, as an outlet for his anger. He told Moffet: "I would have a weekend and I'd be in some God-awful little town at the crossroads of South Carolina and so I would write. I was involved in these jobs and I would write to blow off steam, to deal with the frustration and pain."

Throughout his life, Beecher remained true to his own principles regardless of possible adverse consequences. In 1950, while teaching at San Francisco State College, he refused to sign the Levering Act loyalty oath, a McCarthy-inspired oath of allegiance to the U.S. government, which was later found to be unconstitutional and rescinded in 1967. The first California professor to deny the authorities his signature, Beecher was fired from his teaching position and subsequently blacklisted for nine years. During those nine years, Beecher raised cattle and poultry and cultivated fruit on a Sonoma County, California, ranch. He continued writing poetry as well, and when he couldn't locate a publisher for his work, he and his wife founded Morning Star Press. Beecher taught himself to print and published his own poems, beginning with *Land of the Free: A Portfolio of Poems on the State of the Union* in 1956.

Beecher's work, which some critics have compared to that of Walt Whitman, focuses on daily events and actual experiences. John Druska commented in *Commonweal* that "Beecher's poetry is his recurrent act of telling stories and talking common sense about things that have happened and are happening." Druska pointed out that "throughout his work he attends to America's need to become American, to allow each of its people a real stake in the land." In his introduction to *Hear the Wind Blow!: Poems of Protest and Prophecy*, Maxwell Geismar described Beecher as "an authentic 'proletarian' poet . . . one who writes directly from the experience of the people, from the depths of poor people's lives, and mainly poor black people; a poet who speaks their language and whose poetry in turn can be understood by these people."

Beecher concentrated primarily on activist content in his poetry reflecting his passionate beliefs. Druska noted: "There isn't much development in method or theme through Beecher's poetry; he appears more concerned with the replication of themes that have mattered to him all along, voiced in the natural rhythms of everyday speech. He counts on the moral quality of his voice, rather than its music, and on his evocation of real scenes to move us." Peter Meinke of *New Republic* concurred with Druska's observations, commenting: "There is not much soul-searching, not much mystery in either his language or his subject matters. What holds one's interest is the plain facts of the stories he tells." Steinbrook perceived a sincere concern underlying Beecher's surface intensity: "While Beecher's poems are often angry and violent, they are more fundamentally dedicated to a sense of love and trust necessary for the preservation of the original American ideals. He speaks of courage, freedom and human dignity as part of a continuing American revolution."

Beecher's work embodies the plain language and common feelings of the working man. According to Steinbrook: "Beecher has written poems of everyday life, its injustices, its tribulations, its glories. He has written in the language of the people he writes about, eschewing indirection and metaphor to the chagrin of many critics unable to confront his poems on their own terms." Beecher explained his feelings about *Report to the Stockholders* to Moffett, stating: "[It is] contrary to everything I'd been taught about poetry being indirect, illusive, elusive, delusive, metaphorical. I used all nouns and verbs, almost no adjectives, very stark, as stark as I could make it because what I was trying to say was stark."

Along with his championing the rights of blacks and steelworkers, poetry seemed the most constant thread throughout Beecher's life. He told Moffet, however: "I don't think of myself primarily as a poet and I don't think I ever did. I thought I was primarily whatever I was doing at the moment. I would become so interested that the writing would become secondary. Although, it is true that I did want to be a poet from the time at which I started working in the steel mills." While Beecher's work lacked recognition during his blacklisted years, Steinbrook observed that "within academic and literary communities, some throw around superlatives like 'the best poet the South has ever produced.'" Druska identified what was possibly Beecher's greatest aim in his life's work: "Beecher's poetry, addressed as it is to a grassroots audience, might be just what we need to bring poetry closer to the public arena, to get people speaking the truth to each other, to begin putting people back in touch with themselves."

BIOGRAPHICAL/CRITICAL SOURCES: *Time,* October 14, 1940, July 22, 1974; *Atlanta Journal,* August 26, 1945, August 22, 1974; *New York Times,* August 26, 1945; *New Republic,* February 18, 1946, December 7, 1974; *Mainstream,* September, 1962; *Point West,* September, 1962; *San Jose Mercury,* April 7, 1963; *Show,* June, 1963; *Social Digest,* March-April, 1965; *Saturday Review,* February 11, 1967; John Beecher, *Hear the Wind Blow!: Poems of Protest and Prophecy,* International Publishers, 1968; *Nation,* July 7, 1969; *Philadelphia Bulletin,* June 28, 1974; *Commonweal,* April 25, 1975; *Contemporary Literary Criticism,* Volume VI, Gale, 1976; *Authors in the News,* Volume I, Gale, 1976; *Los Angeles Times Book Review,* August 26, 1979.

OBITUARIES: *New York Times,* May 15, 1980.†

—Sketch by Michaela Swart Wilson

* * *

BEHLMER, Rudy 1926-

PERSONAL: Born October 13, 1926, in San Francisco, Calif.; son of Rudy H. (a brewer) and Helen (McDonough) Behlmer; married Sandra Lee Wightman, 1959 (divorced, 1966); children: Curt. *Education:* Attended Pasadena Playhouse College, 1946-49, and Los Angeles City College, 1949-50. *Residence:* Studio City, Calif. *Office:* Leo Burnett Co., Inc., 6255 Sunset Blvd., Hollywood, Calif. 90028.

CAREER: KLAC-Television, Hollywood, Calif., television director, 1952-56; free-lance television director for networks based in Hollywood, 1956-59; Grant Advertising, Hollywood, director of television and radio, 1959-60; KCOP-Television, Hollywood, executive producer, 1960-63; Leo Burnett Co., Inc. (advertising firm), Los Angeles, Calif., producer, 1963—, vice-president. Lecturer at Art Center College of Design, 1967—. *Military service:* U.S. Navy, Air Corps, 1944-46; served as aviation radioman. *Member:* Directors Guild of America.

WRITINGS: (With Tony Thomas and Clifford McCarty) *The Films of Errol Flynn,* Citadel, 1969; *Memo from David O. Selznick,* Viking, 1972; (with Thomas) *Hollywood's Hollywood,* Citadel, 1975; (editor) *The Adventures of Robin Hood,* University of Wisconsin Press, 1979; *Behind the Scenes,* Ungar, 1982; (editor) *The Sea Hawk,* University of Wisconsin Press, 1982.

Author, producer, and director of "Movies' Golden Age," a television special production, for syndication, 1961; also author of notes for record series, "Classic Film Scores," and of "Warner

Brothers: Fifty Years of Film Music," a booklet accompanying a record album, 1973. Contributor to film journals.

AVOCATIONAL INTERESTS: Photographing and editing personal movies, travel (trips down the Colorado River; camera safaris in Africa).

* * *

BEHRENS, June York 1925-

PERSONAL: Born April 25, 1925, in Maricopa, Calif.; daughter of Mark Hanna and Aline (Stafford) York; married Henry W. Behrens (a school principal), August 23, 1947; children: Terry Lynne, Denise. *Education:* University of California, Santa Barbara, B.A., 1947; University of Maryland (Overseas Program), Munich, Germany, additional study, 1955; University of Southern California, M.A., 1961; additional study at University of California, Los Angeles, and University of London. *Religion:* Protestant. *Home:* 2732 San Ramon Dr., Rancho Palos Verdes, Calif. 90274.

CAREER: Elementary teacher in California, 1947-54, 1956-63, in overseas schools, 1954-56; vice-principal in Los Angeles, Calif., 1966; reading specialist in Los Angeles City Schools, 1966—. *Member:* National Education Association, American Association of University Women, California Teachers' Association.

WRITINGS—Juvenile books, all published by Elk Grove Press, except as indicated: *Soo Ling Finds a Way* (Junior Literary Guild selection), Golden Gate, 1965; *A Walk in the Neighborhood,* 1968; *Who Am I?,* 1968; *Where Am I?,* 1969.

Air Cargo, 1970; *Look at the Zoo Animals,* 1970; *Truck Cargo,* 1970; *Earth Is Home: The Pollution Story,* 1971; *Look at the Farm Animals,* 1971; *Ship Cargo,* 1971; *How I Feel,* 1973; *Look at the Desert Animals,* 1973; *Look at the Forest Animals,* 1974; *Train Cargo,* 1974; *Look at the Sea Animals,* 1975.

All published by Childrens Press: *Together,* 1975; *True Book of Metric Measurement,* 1975; *What I Hear,* 1976; *Can You Walk the Plank,* 1976; *Twisters,* 1976; *Jimmy Carter,* 1977; *Whalewatch!,* 1978; *Fiesta: Other Lands, Other Places,* 1978; *The Manners Book,* 1980; *Ronald Reagan,* 1981.

"Adventures in Art" series; published by Childrens Press: *Looking at Horses,* 1976; *Looking at Children,* 1977; *Looking at Beasties,* 1978.

"Childhood Awareness" series; published by Childrens Press: *My Brown Bag Book,* 1974; *My Favorite Thing,* 1975; *What Is a Seal?,* 1975.

"Holiday Play" series; published by Childrens Press: *Feast of Thanksgiving: The First American Holiday,* 1975; *A New Flag for a New Country,* 1975; *The Christmas Magic-Wagon,* 1975; *Martin Luther King: The Story of a Dream,* 1979; *Gung Hoy Fat Choy,* 1982; *Hanukkah,* 1983.

"Living Heritage" series; all with Pauline Brower; published by Childrens Press: *Colonial Farm,* 1976; *Algonquian Indians: At Summer Camp,* 1977; *Pilgrims Plantation,* 1977; *Canal Boats West,* 1978; *Lighthouse Family,* 1979; *Death Valley,* 1980.

Also author of films: "Children of the World," media series produced by Barr Films, 1978; "The Mediterranean" (four filmstrips), 1978; "Northern Africa" (four filmstrips), 1978, "Asia" (four filmstrips), 1978.

SIDELIGHTS: June York Behrens wrote *CA:* "My need to write started in elementary school. Our fifth grade teacher Mrs. Otis was in love with books. That love spilled over into the classroom and touched those of us who adored her. I wrote my first book for Mrs. Otis. She said it was one of her favorite stories. The book was about horses, illustrated with cut-outs from magazines. Many years later I did another book, *Looking at Horses.* I thought about Mrs. Otis when the book came back from the printer.

"Writing plays for young children is an exciting new adventure for me. What a thrill to see children become the characters and change into completely different personalities!

"Whatever the form of written expression—manuscripts, plays or scripting for filmstrips, my greatest joy comes from learning that the work has provided entertainment and learning experiences for young children."

* * *

BELL, Joyce 1920-
(Jean Colin)

PERSONAL: Born December 11, 1920, in Nuneaton, Warwickshire, England; daughter of William Henry (a craftsman potter) and Elizabeth (Randle) Bell; married J. Ziemba, 1943 (divorced, 1962); children: Michael, Julie, Anthony. *Education:* Educated in Nuneaton, England; attended evening classes at University of Warwick. *Politics:* "I belong to no political party." *Religion:* None. *Home:* Cobble Cottage, 129 New St., Baddesley Ensor, Near Atherstone, Warwickshire, England. *Agent:* Laurence Pollinger, Ltd., 18 Maddox St., Mayfair, London W1R 0EU, England.

CAREER: Worked in factory office in Nuneaton, England, 1934-36; employed in hosiery factory in Hinckley, Leicestershire, England, 1936-40; Dunlop Aircraft Factory, Coventry, England, shorthand typist, 1940-44; worked at various jobs including supervising a typing pool and newspaper reporting, beginning 1962; free-lance writer. *Member:* P.E.N. International, Society of Authors, Society of Women Writers and Journalists. *Awards, honors:* Two Nuneaton Festival of Arts short story prizes, both 1955.

WRITINGS: Garden of the Sun (mystery romance), R. Hale, 1971; *Farmhouse by the Sea* (mystery romance), R. Hale, 1972; (under pseudonym Jean Colin) *Never Had It So Good* (autobiographical), Gollancz, 1974; *Draw down the Dark Moon,* R. Hale, 1982. Work represented in anthologies including *New Stories 5,* Hutchinson, 1980. Contributor to *Birmingham Post* and to other periodicals.

WORK IN PROGRESS: A novel "dealing with the lives of an ordinary family in a town near Coventry over the past fifty years, including the thirties' depression, World War II, and the Coventry blitz, and the changes of the post-war period."

SIDELIGHTS: Joyce Bell's *Never Had It So Good* is an autobiographical account of the ten-year period following her divorce. Bell tells of her struggle to pull herself and her life back together and make a new life with her three children. A reviewer for the *Times Literary Supplement* believes that "what is exceptional about Mrs. Colin's story is the picture it gives of what it means for this kind of family, in this kind of situation, not just at one moment in time but for year after grinding year. Her style couples a pugnacious irony with an occasional bitter humour, and this makes what is in some ways a sad and discomfiting story enjoyable to read."

AVOCATIONAL INTERESTS: Travel, country and wild life.

BIOGRAPHICAL/CRITICAL SOURCES: Times Literary Supplement, August 9, 1974.

BELLAIRS, John 1938-

PERSONAL: Born January 17, 1938, in Marshall, Mich.; son of Frank Edward and Virginia (Monk) Bellairs; married Priscilla Braids, June 24, 1968; children: Frank. *Education:* University of Notre Dame, A.B., 1959; University of Chicago, M.A., 1960. *Politics:* Democrat. *Religion:* Episcopal. *Home:* 28 Hamilton Ave., Haverhill, Mass. 01830. *Agent:* Richard Curtis, 340 East 66th St., New York, N.Y. 10021.

CAREER: Free-lance writer. College of St. Teresa, Winona, Minn., instructor in English, 1963-65; Shimer College, Mount Carroll, Ill., member of humanities faculty, 1966-67; Emmanuel College, Boston, Mass., instructor in English, 1968-69; Merrimack College North Andover, Mass., member of English faculty, 1969-71. *Member:* Authors League, Authors Guild. *Awards, honors:* Woodrow Wilson fellowship; Utah Childrens Book Award, 1981.

WRITINGS: St. Fidgeta, and Other Parodies, Macmillan, 1966; *The Pedant and the Shuffly,* Macmillan, 1968; *The Face in the Frost,* Macmillan, 1969; *The House with a Clock in Its Walls,* Dial, 1973; *The Figure in the Shadows,* Dial, 1975; *The Letter, the Witch, and the Ring,* Dial, 1976; *The Treasure of Alpheus Winterborn,* Harcourt, 1978; *The Curse of the Blue Figurine,* Dial, 1983.

WORK IN PROGRESS: A sequel to *The Curse of the Blue Figurine.*

SIDELIGHTS: John Bellairs is a fantasy writer "of amazing brilliance and charm," as Lin Carter states in *Imaginary Worlds.* "[Bellairs'] style," *A Reader's Guide to Fantasy* notes, "is light and funny, full of puns; his brand of magic is lighthearted."

"A sure sign of Bellairs' enormous potential," Darrell Schweitzer of *Science Fiction Review* believes, "is his ability to shift from . . . scenes of sheer horror to wacky humor and back again without ever ruining the other." Bellair's first novel, *The Face in the Frost,* for instance, "is, in many places, a very scarey book," *A Reader's Guide to Fantasy* states. "It is also a very funny book." *Fantasy Literature* describes the novel as being "genuinely frightening at times and quite serious about its magic, but a playfully humorous tone is rarely absent. Occasionally, in fact, one suspects the author of writing a parody of fantasy." Carter finds *The Face in the Frost* "rich, hilarious, inventive, filled with infectious good humor, grisly horrors, slithering Evil, bumbling monarchs, and . . . Various and Sundry Menaces of the supernatural variety. . . . Bellairs is a marvelous writer who has obviously read all the right books with enthusiasm, and his own venture into the genre [of fantasy] is one of the most exciting debuts in a long time."

BIOGRAPHICAL/CRITICAL SOURCES—Periodicals: *Library Journal,* September 1, 1966; *Commonweal,* November 18, 1966, November 23, 1973; *Booklist,* July 1, 1969, May 15, 1975, October 1, 1976; *New York Times Book Review,* June 10, 1973, July 8, 1973, May 4, 1975, April 30, 1978; *National Observer,* December 25, 1976; *Changing Times,* November, 1978; *Science Fiction Review,* March-April, 1979; *Thrust,* summer, 1979; *West Coast Review of Books,* July, 1979; *Times Literary Supplement,* March 28, 1980.

Books: Lin Carter, *Imaginary Worlds: The Art of Fantasy,* Ballantine, 1973; Marshall B. Tymn, Kenneth J. Zahorski, and Robert H. Boyer, *Fantasy Literature: A Core Collection and Reference Guide,* Bowker, 1979; Baird Seales, Beth Meacham, and Michael Franklin, *A Reader's Guide to Fantasy,* Avon, 1982.

* * *

BENET, James 1914-

PERSONAL: Born January 7, 1914, in Port Washington, N.Y.; son of William Rose (a writer and editor) and Teresa (Thompson) Benet; married Mary Liles, December 13, 1938 (divorced, 1952); married Jane Gugel (a food editor), September 16, 1954; children: Judith (Mrs. Philip Richardson), Mary Kathleen (Mrs. Julian Hale), Peter. *Education:* Stanford University, B.A., 1935. *Politics:* Democrat. *Home:* 181 Edgehill Way, San Francisco, Calif. 94127.

CAREER: Correspondent for *New Republic* (magazine), 1936-39, and TASS, New York, N.Y., 1939-46; *San Francisco Chronicle,* San Francisco, Calif., copy editor and reporter, 1948-68; San Francisco State College (now University), San Francisco, associate professor of journalism, 1959-69; KQED (public television), San Francisco, education reporter, 1968-77; instructor at San Francisco State University, San Francisco, and University of California, Berkeley, 1977—. *Military service:* Spanish Republican Army, International Brigades, 1937-38. *Member:* Newspaper Guild, National Association of Broadcast Employees and Technicians, United Professors of California. *Awards, honors:* First prize in broadcast division, National Council for Advancement of Education Writing, 1974, for television documentary "Sunnyhills."

WRITINGS: A Private Killing, Harper, 1948; *The Knife behind You,* Harper, 1950; *A Guide to San Francisco and the Bay Area,* Random House, 1963, revised edition, 1967; *SCSD: The Project and the Schools,* Ford Foundation, 1967; (editor with Arlene Daniels and Gaye Tuchman and contributor) *Hearth and Home: Images of Women in Mass Media,* Oxford University Press, 1977; (with Daniels) *Education: Straitjacket or Opportunity?,* Transaction Books, 1980.

Author and producer of documentaries for KQED Television: "Hunters Point II," 1972; "Sunnyhills," 1974; "Peninsula School," 1974; "Nueva," 1974; "Oakland Street Academies," 1974; "The New Teaching," 1975.

WORK IN PROGRESS: On-going research on imagery in the mass media.

AVOCATIONAL INTERESTS: Gardening, skin-diving.

* * *

BEN-EZER, Ehud 1936-

PERSONAL: Born April 3, 1936, in Petah Tikva, Palestine (now Israel); son of Binyamin (an agriculturist) and Devora (Lipsky) Ben-Ezer; married Anat Fienberg, August 31, 1969 (divorced, 1972); married Yehudit Tomer (a nurse), September 24, 1974; children: (second marriage) Binyamin. *Education:* Hebrew University of Jerusalem, B.A., 1963. *Religion:* "Jew, Secular." *Address:* 20 Hakalir, P.O. Box 22135, Tel Aviv, Israel.

CAREER: Free-lance writer, lecturer, and editor. Member of Kibbutz Ein Gedi on shore of Dead Sea, Israel, 1956-58; teacher in night school for adults, near Jerusalem, Israel, 1959-66. *Military service:* Israeli Army, Nahal troops, 1955-56. Israeli Army Reserve, 1959—; served in first aid unit in Six Day War, 1967. *Member:* P.E.N., Hebrew Writers Association. *Awards, honors:* Israeli Prime Minister Prize for creativity, 1975.

WRITINGS: Hamahtzeva (novel; also see below; title means "The Quarry"), Am Oved, 1963; "Hamahtzeva" (two-act play; based on his novel of the same title), first produced in Tel Aviv at Zuta Theatre, April, 1964; *Anshei Sedom* (novel; title means "The People of Sodom"), Am Oved, 1968; *Lo Lagiborim Hamilhama* (novel; title means "Nor the Battle to the Strong"), Levin-Epshtien, 1971; *Laila Beginat Hayerakot Hanirdamim* (juvenile; title means "Night in the Sleeping Vegetable Garden"), Massada, 1971; (editor) *Unease in Zion* (interviews), Quadrangle, 1974.

Hapri Ha'asur (short stories; title means "The Forbidden Fruit"), Achiasef, 1977; *Oferit Blofferit* (juvenile; title means "Offerit the Bluffer"), Yavneh, 1977; *Efrat* (short stories), Tarmil, 1978; *Hasheket Hanafshi* (novel; title means "Peace of Mind"), Zmora, Bitan, Modan, 1979; *Bein Holot Vekhol Shamaim* (title means "Sand Dunes and Blue Sky"), illustrations by Nachum Gutman, Yavneh, 1980; *Mi Mesaper Et Hasaparim?* (juvenile; title means "Who Barbers the Barbers?"), Yavneh, 1982; *Otzar Habe'er Harishona* (juvenile; title means "The Treasure of the First Well"), Schocken, 1982. Contributor of weekly column to *Ha'aretz* (daily newspaper), 1970-78. Contributor to periodicals.

WORK IN PROGRESS: Research on the image of the Arab in Hebrew literature since the 1880's; a book of poems; a saga about the life of a family in Palestine since the 1830's; a lexicon of articles about more than two hundred Hebrew books; three children's books.

SIDELIGHTS: Ehud Ben-Ezer writes: "The Ben-Ezer (Raab) family has been living in Palestine since 1876. Yehuda Raab (Ben-Ezer), my grandfather, was one of the first settlers of Petah-Tikva in 1878, when that first Jewish colony in Palestine was founded." *Media adaptations:* Ben-Ezer's novel, *Hamahtzeva*, was adapted and broadcast on the Israel National Broadcasting Service, Kol Israel, in 1964, and again in six installments on the "Popular Hebrew" radio program in 1969.

*   *   *

BENSON, Charles S(cott) 1922-

PERSONAL: Born May 20, 1922, in Atlanta, Ga.; son of Marion Trotti (a physician) and Sallie (Bagley) Benson; married Dorothy Merrick, June 8, 1946; children: Michele, Scott, Sally. *Education:* Princeton University, A.B. (with honors), 1943; Columbia University, M.A., 1948, Ph.D., 1955. *Office:* School of Education, University of California, Berkeley, Calif.

CAREER: Bowdoin College, Brunswick, Me., instructor, 1950-52, assistant professor of economics, 1952-55; Harvard University, Cambridge, Mass., assistant professor of education, 1955-57, research associate, Center for Field Studies, 1955-62, member of department of economics, 1957-59, lecturer on education, 1957-62; University of California, Berkeley, associate professor, 1964-68, professor of education, 1968—, research associate, Institute of Governmental Studies, 1965-66. Consultant on finance to committees and organizations, including U.S. Office of Education and Ministry of Education, Colombia. Member, President's Advisory Panel on Financing Elementary and Secondary Education, 1979. Former secretary and trustee of New England Economic Education Council. *Military service:* U.S. Navy, 1943-46; commanding officer of minesweeper in western Pacific; became lieutenant junior grade.

MEMBER: American Economic Association, American Association for the Advancement of Science, American Academy of Political and Social Science, American Association of School Administrators, Econometric Society, American Educational Finance Association (president, 1977-78), Regional Science Association, California Association of School Administrators, Phi Delta Kappa. *Awards, honors:* Ford Foundation grant for investigation of finance of education in England and Wales, 1962-63.

WRITINGS: Teachers' Salaries: The Process of Change in 43 Metropolitan School Systems, New England School Development Council, 1959; *The Economics of Public Education,* Houghton, 1961, 3rd edition, 1978; *Are School Debt Finance Costs Too High?,* New England School Development Council, 1962; (editor) *Perspectives on the Economics of Education,* Houghton, 1963.

State and Local Fiscal Relationships in Education in California, California State Senate (Sacramento), 1965; *The Cheerful Prospect: A Statement on the Future of American Education,* Houghton, 1965; *The School and the Economic System,* Science Research Associates, 1966; *The Rhode Island Comprehensive Foundation and Enhancement State Aid Program for Education,* Rhode Island Special Commission on Education, 1966; (editor) *Citizens for the 21st Century: Long-Range Considerations for California Elementary and Secondary Education,* California State Board of Education, 1968; (with James W. Guthrie) *An Essay on Federal Incentives and Local and State Educational Initiative,* University of California, Berkeley, 1968; (with Peter B. Lund) *Neighborhood Distribution of Local Public Services,* University of California Institute of Governmental Studies, 1969.

(Staff director) *Report of the New York State Commission on the Quality, Cost and Financing of Elementary and Secondary Education,* three volumes, Viking, 1972; (with others) *Planning for Educational Reform: Financial and Social Alternatives,* Dodd, 1974; (with H. L. Hodgkinson) *Implementing the Learning Society,* Jossey-Bass, 1974; *Education Finance in the Coming Decade,* Phi Delta Kappa Foundation, 1975.

(With Guy Benveniste) *From Mass to Universal Education: The Experience of the State of California and Its Relevance to European Education in the Year 2000,* Nijhoff, 1976; (with Irene Blumenthal) *Educational Reform in the Soviet Union: Implications for Developing Countries,* World Bank (Washington, D.C.), 1978; *Education Finance and Organization: Research Perspectives for the Future,* U.S. Government Printing Office, 1980.

Contributor: *Educational Needs for Economic Development of the South,* Agricultural Policy Institute, North Carolina State College, 1962; *The Internship in Administrative Preparation,* University Council for Educational Administration, Ohio State University, 1963; Jesse Burkhead, *Public School Finance,* Syracuse University Press, 1964; S. Harris, editor, *Change and Challenge in American Education,* McCutchan, 1965; *Trends in Financing Public Education,* Committee on Educational Finance, National Education Association, 1965; *Challenges in Municipal-School Relations,* American Association of School Administrators and International City Managers' Association, 1965.

Education Is Good Business, American Association of School Administrators, 1966; Robert E. Doherty, Joan R. Egner, and William T. Lowe, editors, *The Changing Employment Relationship in Public Schools,* New York State School of Industrial and Labor Relations, 1966; John Minter, editor, *Campus and Capital,* Western Interstate Commission for Higher Education, 1966; Stanley Scott, editor, *Local Government in a Changing World,* Institute of Governmental Studies, 1967; *Institutional Research and Academic Outcomes,* Association for Institutional Research, 1968; Donald J. Eberly, editor, *National Service,* Russell Sage Foundation, 1968; *The Schools and the Challenge of Innovation,* Committee for Economic Development, 1969.

Joseph Fischer, editor, *The Social Sciences and the Comparative Study of Educational Systems,* International Textbook, 1970; Roe L. Johns and others, editors, *Economic Factors Affecting the Financing of Education,* National Educational Finance Project, 1970; (and author of foreword) John E. Coons and Stephen D. Sugarman, *Family Choice in Education: A Model State System for Vouchers,* Institute of Governmental Studies, 1971; Dennis L. Roberts II, editor, *Planning Urban Education,* Educational Technology Publications, 1972; (with others) *Tax and Expenditure Limitation by Constitutional Amendment,* Institute of Governmental Studies, 1973; *The Elementary School in the United States,* National Society for the Study of Education, 1973; John Pincus, editor, *School Finance in Transition,* Ballinger, 1974.

C. Benson and others, editors, *Future Research Directions for the Federal Government,* National Institute of Education, 1978; *Restoring Confidence in Public Education: An Agenda for the 1980's,* National Urban Coalition, 1979; (with E. Gareth Hoachlander) *Needs of Elementary and Secondary Education in the 1980's,* U.S. Government Printing Office, 1980; James W. Guthrie, editor, *School Finance Policies and Practices in the 1980's: A Decade of Conflict,* Ballinger, 1980; Walter W. McMahon and Terry G. Geske, editors, *Financing Education: Overcoming Inefficiency and Inequity,* University of Illinois Press, 1981.

Contributor of articles to periodicals and scholarly journals, including *Harvard Educational Review, International Social Science Journal, School and Society, Phi Delta Kappan, Educational Administration Quarterly, Nation, Review of Educational Research,* and *Administrator's Notebook.* Former member of board of editors, *Educational Administration Quarterly;* member of editorial advisory board, *Journal of Education Finance;* member of editorial board, *Economics of Education Review.*

* * *

BENTEEN, John
See HAAS, Ben(jamin) L(eopold)

* * *

BENVENISTE, Guy 1927-

PERSONAL: Born February 27, 1927, in Paris, France; son of Raphael Benveniste and Lucy de Botton. *Education:* Harvard University, B.S., 1948, M.S., 1950; Stanford University, Ph.D., 1968. *Office:* Department of Education, University of California, Berkeley, Calif. 94720.

CAREER: Stanford Research Institute, Stanford, Calif., research economist, 1954-60; U.S. Department of State, Washington, D.C., special assistant in Office of Education and Cultural Affairs, 1960-61; International Bank for Reconstruction and Development, Washington, D.C., economist in Education Division, 1961-62; UNESCO, Paris, France, senior staff member, 1962-65; University of California, Berkeley, professor of education, 1968—.

WRITINGS: Handbook of African Development, Praeger, 1962; *Agents of Change: Professionals in Developing Countries,* Praeger, 1969; *Bureaucracy and National Planning,* Praeger, 1970; *Politics of Expertise,* Glendessary, 1972, 2nd edition, Boyd & Fraser, 1977; *From Mass to Universal Education,* Nijhoff, 1976; *Bureaucracy,* Boyd & Fraser, 1977, 2nd edition, 1982; *Regulation and Planning: The Case of Environmental Politics,* Boyd & Fraser, 1981.

BERARDO, Felix M(ario) 1934-

PERSONAL: Born February 7, 1934, in Waterbury, Conn.; son of Rocco and Maria (Gurrera) Berardo; married; wife's name, Donna H.; children: (previous marriage) Marcellino Antonio, Benito Antonio (sons). *Education:* University of Connecticut, B.A., 1961; Florida State University, Ph.D., 1965. *Religion:* Roman Catholic. *Home:* 2026 Northwest 27th St., Gainesville, Fla. 32605. *Office:* Department of Sociology, University of Florida, Gainesville, Fla. 32611.

CAREER: Washington State University, Pullman, assistant professor of sociology and assistant rural sociologist, 1965-69; University of Florida, Gainesville, associate professor, 1969-73, professor of sociology, 1973—, associate chairman of department, 1972-77. *Military service:* U.S. Air Force, 1952-56.

MEMBER: American Sociological Association (secretary of family section, 1976-79; section organizer, 1979), Rural Sociological Society (member of membership committee, 1969-72), National Council on Family Relations (section chairman, 1970; member of publications board, 1972-76; chairman of publications board, 1974-76), Gerontological Society of America, Southeastern Council on Family Relations, Southern Sociological Society (section chairman, 1971; chairman of Florida membership committee, 1972; member of program committee, 1973; chairman of program committee, 1975), Pacific Sociological Association (section chairman, 1968), Pacific Northwest Council on Family Relations, Florida Council on Family Relations, Phi Beta Kappa, Phi Kappa Phi, Alpha Kappa Delta.

WRITINGS: (Editor with F. Ivan Nye and contributor) *Emerging Conceptual Frameworks in Family Analysis,* Macmillan, 1966, reprinted, Praeger, 1981; (with Nye) *The Family: Its Structure and Interaction,* Macmillan, 1973; (editor) *Decade Review: Family Research, 1970-1979,* National Council on Family Relations, 1980.

Contributor: Benjamin Schlessinger, editor, *The One-Parent Family,* University of Toronto Press, 1969; Jeffrey K. Hadden and Marie L. Borgatta, editors, *Marriage and the Family: A Comprehensive Reader,* F. E. Peacock, 1969; Raymond J.R. King, editor, *Family Relations: Concepts and Theories,* Glendessary Press, 1969; Howard Bahr, editor, *Disaffiliated Man: Essays and Bibliography on Skid Row, Vagrancy, and Outsiders,* University of Toronto Press, 1970; Jacquelin P. Wiseman, editor, *People as Partners: Individual and Family Relationships in Today's World,* Canfield Press, 1971; Marcia E. Lasswell and Thomas E. Lasswell, editors, *Love-Marriage-Family: A Developmental Approach,* Scott, Foresman, 1973; Daniel H. Carson, editor, *Man-Environment Interactions: Evaluations and Applications,* Environmental Design Research Association, 1974; Joann D. Delora and Jack R. Delora, editors, *Intimate Life Styles: Marriage and Its Alternatives,* 2nd edition, Goodyear Publishing, 1975; Anthony H. Richmond and Daniel Kubat, editors, *International Migration: The New World and the Third World,* Sage Publications, 1976; Thomas Burch, Luis Felipe Lira, and Valdecir F. Lopes, editors, *La familia como unidad de estudio demografico,* Centro Latino Americano de Demografia, 1976; Susan Thomas, editor, *Education for Family Living: Who Is Responsible?,* Department of Home and Family Life, Florida State University, 1978; Donald Light, Jr. and Suzanne Keller, editors, *The Professional Resource Book for Sociology,* Knopf, 1979; Jill S. Quadagno, editor, *Aging in Modern Society: Readings in Social Gerontology,* St. Martin's, 1980; Man Singh Das and Clinton J. Jesser, editors, *The Family in Latin America,* Vikas Publishing, 1980.

Also author of numerous professional papers presented at conferences and seminars. Contributor of articles and reviews to journals in United States and Brazil. Associate editor, *International Journal of Sociology of the Family*, 1970—, *Family Coordinator*, 1972-75, *Social Forces*, 1976-79, and *Death Education*, 1979—. *Journal of Marriage and the Family*, associate editor, 1972-75, editor, 1976-81. Guest editor for special issues, *Journal of Marriage and the Family*, November, 1971, and *Family Coordinator*, January, 1972. Member of editorial advisory board of *Population and Policy Review*, 1980—, and *Sage Family Studies Abstracts*, 1981—. Referee, *American Sociological Review, Human Organization*, and *Journal of Comparative Family Studies*.

WORK IN PROGRESS: Writing an article for *Medical Aspects of Human Sexuality*; research on "age-discrepant marriages, the training of family life specialists, widowhood, and the impact of institutionalization on families of death-row prisoners."

* * *

BERG, Stephen 1934-

PERSONAL: Born August 2, 1934, in Philadelphia, Pa.; son of Harry Sidney (a businessman) and Hilda (Wachansky) Berg; married Millie Lane, August 26, 1959; children: Clair, Margot. *Education:* Attended University of Pennsylvania, Boston University, and University of Indiana, School of Letters; State University of Iowa, B.A., 1959. *Office:* Philadelphia College of Art, Philadelphia, Pa.

CAREER: Temple University, Philadelphia, Pa., instructor in English, beginning 1963; currently a professor at Philadelphia College of Art, Philadelphia. *Awards, honors:* Frank O'Hara Poetry Prize, 1970; Guggenheim fellow, 1974-75; National Endowment for the Arts fellow, 1977; Pennsylvania Council grant, 1979; Rockefeller fellow.

WRITINGS: *Berg-Goodman-Mezey*, New Ventures Press (London), 1957; *Bearing Weapons* (poems), Cummington Press, 1963; (contributor of translations) Jorge Guillen, *Cantico: A Selection*, Atlantic-Little, Brown, 1965; (editor with Robert Mezey, and contributor) *Naked Poetry: Recent American Poetry in Open Forms*, Bobbs-Merrill, 1969; *The Queen's Triangle: A Romance*, Cummington Press, 1970; *The Daughters: Poems*, Bobbs-Merrill, 1971; (compiler and contributor) *Between People: A Reader for Open Learning*, Scott, Foresman, 1972; (translator with Steven Polgar and S. J. Marks) Miklos Radnoti, *Clouded Sky*, Harper, 1972; *Nothing in the Word: Versions of Aztec Poetry*, Grossman, 1972; (compiler with Marks) *About Women: An Anthology of Contemporary Fiction, Poetry, and Essays*, Fawcett, 1973; (editor with Marks) *Doing the Unknown*, Dell, 1974; *Grief: Poems and Versions of Poems*, Viking, 1975; (translator with Diskin Clay) Sophocles, *Oedipus the King*, Oxford University Press, 1978; *With Akhmatora at the Black Gates: Variations*, University of Illinois Press, 1981.

Contributor of poems to *Paris Review, New Yorker, Yale Review, Poetry, Prairie Schooner, Chicago Review*, and *Mademoiselle*. Poetry editor, *Saturday Evening Post*, 1961-62; co-editor, *American Poetry Review*.

WORK IN PROGRESS: A book of poems and prose.

SIDELIGHTS: Stephen Berg, writes Linwood C. Powers in *The Dictionary of Literary Biography*, "is not a conventional poet. Full of free associations, surrealistic imagery, and harsh rhythms, his poetry is sensitive, imaginative, ambitious, and revelatory. His work requires careful scrutiny, but it frequently rewards that effort with a sudden awareness that compensates for any frustrations the reader may feel at its often difficult and elliptic nature." In a review of *The Daughters*, Laurence Lieberman of *Yale Review* finds that "Berg seems to be . . . taken with the sound of his own voice and the exhilarating process of juggling images . . . but his commitment to the tools of his craft, as well as to the most central human concerns, is total; and when these two rival espousals are balanced and matched, . . . he can write masterful whole poems."

Berg's collection *Grief*, containing poems about the death of his father, has been particularly well received. Richard Howard writes in *Yale Review* that in this book Berg "is demonstrably a man of explicit affections, a husband and father of exemplary devotion [and] a compassionate teacher. . . . He cares, he mourns, he praises." In similar terms, Stanley Plumley of *Nation* states: "Berg is perhaps the most passionate of his contemporaries." Plumley also finds that Berg's "rhythms are free, searching, almost abrasive; they reveal the hard-working impatience of a poet determined to get down to it, no nonsense." Speaking of the book as a whole, Plumley maintains that "Berg's power builds line by line, poem by peom, and is really only achieved in the aggregate, when the poems' power to be beautiful transcends the local emotion."

BIOGRAPHICAL/CRITICAL SOURCES: *Poetry*, December, 1958, April, 1970, March, 1973, April, 1973, February, 1977, April, 1978; *Southwest Review*, autumn, 1969, spring, 1974; *Western Humanities Review*, spring, 1972; *Yale Review*, December, 1972, March, 1976; *Nation*, May 28, 1973, December 4, 1976; *The Dictionary of Literary Biography*, Volume V: *American Poets since World War II*, Gale, 1980; *Washington Post Book World*, August 2, 1981; *New York Times Book Review*, September 6, 1981; *Times Literary Supplement*, May 28, 1982.

* * *

BERGONZI, Bernard 1929-

PERSONAL: Born April 13, 1929, in London, England; son of Charles Ernest and Louisa (Lloyd) Bergonzi; married Gabriel Wall, April 19, 1960; children: Benet, Clarissa, Lucy. *Education:* Wadham College, Oxford, B.Litt., 1961, M.A., 1962. *Religion:* Roman Catholic. *Agent:* A. D. Peters, 10 Buckingham St., Adelphi, London WC2N 6BU, England. *Office:* Department of English, University of Warwick, Coventry, West Midlands, England.

CAREER: University of Manchester, Manchester, England, 1959-66, began as assistant lecturer, became lecturer in English; University of Warwick, Coventry, England, senior lecturer, 1966-71, professor of English, 1971—, pro-vice-chancellor, 1979-82. Visiting lecturer, Brandeis University, 1964-65; Beckman Summer Lecturer, University of California, Berkeley, 1965.

WRITINGS: *Descartes and the Animals: Poems 1948-54*, Platform, 1954; *The Early H. G. Wells: A Study of the Scientific Romances*, Manchester University Press, 1961; *Heroes' Twilight: A Study of the Literature of the Great War*, Constable, 1965, Coward, 1966, 2nd edition, Humanities, 1980; *The Situation of the Novel*, Macmillan (London), 1970, University of Pittsburgh Press, 1971, 2nd edition, Macmillan, 1979; *T. S. Eliot*, Macmillan, 1972, 2nd edition, 1978; *The Turn of a Century: Essays on Victorian and Modern English Literature*, Humanities, 1973; *Hopkins the Englishman*, Hopkins Society (Enfield, England), 1975; (editor) George Gissing, *New Grub Street*, Penguin, 1976; *Gerard Manley Hopkins*, Macmillan (New York), 1977; *Reading the Thirties: Texts and Contexts*,

University of Pittsburgh Press, 1978; *Yeats: Sixteen Poems*, Mandeville Press, 1979; *The Roman Persuasion* (novel), Weidenfeld & Nicolson, 1981. Contributor to *Encounter, Observer*, and other periodicals.

SIDELIGHTS: "My life falls into a number of categories; as an academic teacher and administrator, as a literary critic, and occasionally, when I have time and inspiration, as a writer of fiction and poetry," Bernard Bergonzi told *CA*. In his first novel, *The Roman Persuasion*, Bergonzi focused on a period that he had previously explored in his critical writing—the years before and after the Spanish Civil War. The book describes the reactions of an English Catholic family to events in the years 1935-1937. Through this story, says Gilliam Wilce of *New Statesman*, the reader learns how "people of goodwill could, seeing their church under attack, support Franco's rebels, agonize over whether they should support Franco's rebels and become divided from each other over the issue."

While critics find the book fair and informative, some, such as *Listener*'s Peter Kemp, complain that it is lacking in imagination. "The big weakness," he says, "is that the characters too obviously stand for varying points of view. . . . There is a typically reactionary Spanish priest, a typically 'advanced' Dominican, a typical socialist, a typical Fascist, and so on. Static specimens arranged into significant tableaux, Bergonzi's characters—the obvious result of patient and intelligent research—have everything except individuality." And Marigold Johnson, writing in the *Times Literary Supplement*, expresses a similar view. "*The Roman Persuasion*," she writes "is . . . somehow too cerebral to work simply as a novel, even of ideas. This is partly because the idealists—Dominica, Crispin, Father Giles—remain sketchy figures, types rather than individuals." Nonetheless Johnson, among others, acknowledges that the book makes a historical contribution and suggests that "at its descriptive best," it is a good and "evocative" record of the Spanish Civil War.

BIOGRAPHICAL/CRITICAL SOURCES: *New York Times Book Review*, May 1, 1977; *Times Literary Supplement*, June 3, 1977; March 20, 1981; *New Republic*, June 18, 1977; *Listener*, March 19, 1981; *New Statesman*, March 20, 1981; *Contemporary Review*, July, 1981.

* * *

BERKEBILE, Don(ald) H(erbert) 1926-

PERSONAL: Born November 21, 1926, in Johnstown, Pa.; son of Arthur William and Edythe Odell (Isenberg) Berkebile. *Education:* Attended Columbia Union College, 1944 and 1948, and University of Pittsburgh at Johnstown, 1949.

CAREER: Worked as steelworker and carpenter at various periods, 1947-54; Smithsonian Institution, Division of Transportation, Washington, D.C., exhibits specialist, 1955-60, museum specialist, 1960-73, assistant curator, 1973-74, associate curator, 1974-81. *Military service:* U.S. Army, 1945-46. *Member:* Company of Military Historians (fellow; life member), Military Order of Saint Barbara.

WRITINGS: (With Smith Hempstone Oliver) *The Smithsonian Collection of Automobiles and Motorcycles*, Random House, 1968; (with Smith Hempstone Oliver) *Wheels and Wheeling*, Smithsonian Institution Press, 1974; *American Carriages, Sleighs, Sulkies, and Carts*, Dover, 1977; *Carriage Terminology: An Historical Dictionary*, Smithsonian Institution Press, 1978; *American Commercial Horsedrawn Vehicles*, Dover, in press. Contributor to *Encyclopedia Americana, Cowles Comprehensive Encyclopedia*, and to publications of the Smithsonian Institution.

AVOCATIONAL INTERESTS: Mechanical arts (especially gunsmithing and carriage building; has restored and built replicas for museums).

* * *

BERRY, Wallace Taft 1928-

PERSONAL: Born January 10, 1928, in La Crosse, Wis.; son of Edward Carl and Louise (George) Berry; married Maxine Metzner (a painter), May 11, 1954. *Education:* University of Southern California, B.Mus., 1949, Ph.D., 1956; studied at National Conservatory of Music, Paris, France, 1953-54. *Religion:* None. *Office:* Department of Music, University of British Columbia, Vancouver, British Columbia, Canada V6T 1W5.

CAREER: University of Southern California, Los Angeles, lecturer in music, 1956-57; University of Michigan, Ann Arbor, instructor, 1957-60, assistant professor, 1960-63, associate professor, 1963-66, professor of music, 1966-78, director of music honors program, 1960-68, chairman of department of music theory, 1968-74; University of British Columbia, Vancouver, chairman of department of music, 1978—. Recital pianist and composer. *Military service:* U.S. Army, 1954-56. *Member:* American Society of Composers, Authors and Publishers, Society for Music Theory, American Association of University Professors (president, 1982-85). *Awards, honors:* University of Michigan Distinguished Faculty Award, 1963; American Society of Composers, Authors and Publishers Composer Award, 1966, and 1974; Outstanding Music Alumnus Award, University of Southern California, 1973; Composer Award, American Academy and Institute of Arts and Letters, 1978.

WRITINGS: *Form in Music*, Prentice-Hall, 1966; (with E. Chudacoff) *Eighteenth Century Imitative Counterpoint: Music for Analysis*, Appleton, 1969; *Structural Functions in Music*, Prentice-Hall, 1975.

Musical works: "Duo for Violin and Piano," Carl Fischer, 1964; "Five Pieces for Small Orchestra," Carl Fischer, 1965; "Two Canons for Two Clarinets," Elkan-Vogel, 1966; "Eight 20th-Century Miniatures for Piano," Carl Fischer, 1967; "String Quartet No. 2," Elkan-Vogel, 1967; "Divertimento for Wind Quintet, Piano, and Percussion," Elkan-Vogel, 1967; "Trio for Piano, Violin, and Cello," Composers Recordings, Inc., 1977; "Sonata for Piano," Composers Recordings, Inc., 1979; "Duo for Violin and Piano," Opus One, 1979. Recording of "String Quartet No. 2," "Duo for Flute and Piano," "Canto Lirico for Viola and Piano," Composers Recordings, Inc., 1972.

Contributor to *Journal of Music Theory, Perspectives in New Music*, and *Music Theory Spectrum*.

WORK IN PROGRESS: *Structure and Interpretation in Music;* a revised edition of *Form in Music*.

SIDELIGHTS: Wallace Taft Berry speaks French and Italian, and some German. He has traveled extensively in Europe, 1953-54, 1960, 1963-64. *Avocational interests:* Swimming, cooking.

* * *

BETTS, James
See HAYNES, Betsy

* * *

BICKHAM, Jack M(iles) 1930-
(Jeff Clinton, John Miles, George Shaw)

PERSONAL: Born September 2, 1930, in Columbus, Ohio;

son of John Robert (a manufacturing executive) and Helen E. (Miles) Bickham; married Janie R. Wallace, November 23, 1952; children: Robert, Daniel, Stephen, Lise. *Education:* Ohio State University, B.A., 1952; University of Oklahoma, M.A., 1960. *Politics:* Democrat. *Religion:* Roman Catholic. *Home:* 2603 Beaurue Dr., Norman, Okla. 73069. *Agent:* Diane Cleaver, Sanford J. Greenburger Associates, Inc., 825 Third Ave., New York, N.Y. 10022. *Office:* School of Journalism, University of Oklahoma, Norman, Okla. 73069.

CAREER: Norman Transcript, Norman, Okla., reporter, 1956-60; Oklahoma Publishing Co., Oklahoma City, Okla., assistant Sunday editor on *Daily Oklahoman* (newspaper), 1960-66; *Oklahoma Courier* (newspaper), Oklahoma City, managing editor, 1966-69; University of Oklahoma School of Journalism, Norman, 1969—, began as assistant professor, became professor of journalism. Oklahoma City University, part-time teacher of journalism, 1963-66. *Military service:* U.S. Air Force, 1952-54; became first lieutenant. *Member:* Authors Guild, Western Writers of America. *Awards, honors:* Editor of the Year, Sigma Delta Chi, 1969; trophy for best novel, Oklahoma Writers Federation, 1969, 1971; Oklahoma writing award, 1971; named outstanding professor, University of Oklahoma, 1972.

WRITINGS—Published by Doubleday, except as indicated: *Gunman's Gamble,* Ace Books, 1958; *Feud Fury,* Ace Books, 1959; *Killer's Paradise,* Ace Books, 1959; *The Useless Gun,* Ace Books, 1960; (under pseudonym John Miles) *Dally with a Deadly Doll,* Ace Books, 1960; *Hangman's Territory,* Ace Books, 1960; *Gunmen Can't Hide,* Ace Books, 1961; (under pseudonym John Miles) *Trouble Trails,* Bouregy, 1963; *Trip Home to Hell,* Berkley Publishing, 1965.

The Padre Must Die, 1967; *The War on Charity Ross,* 1967; *The Shadowed Faith,* 1968; *Target: Charity Ross,* 1968; *Decker's Campaign,* 1970; *The Apple Dumpling Gang,* 1970; *Jilly's Canal,* 1972; *Goin',* Paperback Library, 1972; *Dopey Dan,* 1972; *Katie, Kelly and Heck,* 1973; *Baker's Hawk* (Reader's Digest Condensed Book selection), 1973; (under pseudonym John Miles) *The Night Hunters,* Bobbs-Merrill, 1973; *Emerald Canyon,* 1974; *The Silver Bullet Gang,* Bobbs-Merrill, 1974; *The Blackmailer,* Bobbs-Merrill, 1974; *A Boat Named Death,* 1975; *Showdown at Emerald Canyon,* 1975; *Operation Nightfall,* Bobbs-Merrill, 1975.

Twister, 1977; *The Winemakers,* 1977; *The Excalibur Disaster,* 1978; *A Question of Ethics,* Pocket Books, 1979; *Dinah, Blow Your Horn,* 1979; *The Regensburg Legacy,* 1980; *All the Days Were Summer,* 1981.

Under pseudonym Jeff Clinton; published by Berkley Publishing, except as indicated: *The Fighting Buckaroo,* 1961; *Range Killer,* 1962; *Wildcat's Rampage,* 1962; *Wildcat against the House,* 1963; *Wildcat's Revenge,* 1964; *Killer's Choice,* 1964; *Wildcat Takes His Medicine,* 1966; *Wanted: Wildcat O'Shea,* 1967; *Wildcat on the Loose,* 1967; *Watch Out for Wildcat,* 1968; *Kane's Odyssey,* Laser Books, 1976. Also author of other "Wildcat" books. Contributor of short stories and articles to *Journalism Quarterly, Sporting News, Explicator, Sports Illustrated, Time, Life,* and *Official Detective.*

SIDELIGHTS: Jack Bickham, a licensed private pilot, told *CA,* "People who say they lack time to write amuse me." He adds that his writing emphasis is changing from westerns to mystery and contemporary comedy. *Media adaptations:* Several of Bickham's books have been made into motion pictures, including *The Apple Dumpling Gang,* produced by Walt Disney Productions, *Baker's Hawk, Katie, Kelly and Heck,* and *Dinah, Blow Your Horn.*

AVOCATIONAL INTERESTS: Tropical fish, organic gardening, playing guitar.

BIOGRAPHICAL/CRITICAL SOURCES: New York Times Book Review, August 11, 1968, May 11, 1980; *Washington Post Book World,* April 20, 1980.

* * *

BIDERMAN, Albert D. 1923-

PERSONAL: Born July 10, 1923, in Paterson, N.J.; son of Isaac and Celia (Silberstein) Biderman; married Sumiko Fujii, November 9, 1951; children: David Taro, Joseph Shiro, Paula Kei. *Education:* New York University, A.B., 1947; University of Chicago, M.A., 1952, Ph.D., 1964. *Home:* 6247 N. Kensington St., McLean, Va.

CAREER: Illinois Institute of Technology, Chicago, instructor in sociology, 1948-52; U.S. Air Force, Maxwell Air Force Base, Ala., research social psychologist, 1952-57; Bureau of Social Science Research, Washington, D.C., senior research associate, beginning 1957. Consultant to Advisory Committee to Secretary of Defense on Prisoners of War, 1954, Agency for International Development, 1960, and 1966-68, President's Commission on Law Enforcement and Administration of Justice, 1965-67, Bureau of Census, 1969-76, and President's Commission on Federal Statistics, 1971. Active in community, civic, and recreational organizations. *Military service:* U.S. Army, 1943-45. *Member:* American Sociological Association, American Association for Public Opinion Research, Society for the Study of Social Problems, District of Columbia Sociological Society (president, 1965-66). *Awards, honors:* Research fellowship, Human Ecology Fund, 1957-58.

WRITINGS: (Editor with Herbert Zimmer) *The Manipulation of Human Behavior,* Wiley, 1961; *March to Calumny: The Story of American POW's in the Korean War,* Macmillan, 1963, reprinted, Arno, 1979; (contributor) *Human Reactions to the Threat of Impending Disaster,* M.I.T. Press, 1964; (contributor) *The New Military: Changing Patterns of Organization,* Russell Sage Foundation, 1964; (contributor) *Social Indications,* M.I.T. Press, 1966; (co-editor) *Mass Behavior in Battle and Captivity,* University of Chicago Press, 1968; (with Elisabeth T. Crawford) *The Political Economics of Social Research: The Case of Sociology,* Bureau of Social Science Research, 1968; (compiler with Crawford) *Social Scientists and International Affairs,* Wiley, 1969; (editor with Thomas F. Drury) *Measuring Work Quality for Social Reporting,* Robert E. Krieger, 1976.

Also author of numerous research papers on indoctrination of American prisoners of war, coercive interrogation, and captivity situations published by the U.S. Air Force. Contributor of articles to professional journals.

WORK IN PROGRESS: The Communist Soldier and Authority; chapter for *International Encyclopaedia of the Social Sciences,* for Crowell-Collier.†

* * *

BIERMANN, Lillian
See WEHMEYER, Lillian (Mabel) Biermann

* * *

BLANCHARD, William H(enry) 1922-

PERSONAL: Born March 25, 1922, in St. Paul, Minn.; son of Charles Edgar (a jeweler) and Ethel R. (Gurney) Blanchard;

married Martha I. Lang, August 22, 1947; children: Gregory, Mary. *Education:* Iowa State University of Science and Technology, B.S., 1944; University of Southern California, Ph.D., 1954. *Politics:* Democrat. *Religion:* None. *Home:* 4307 Rosario Rd., Woodland Hills, Calif. 91364. *Office:* Planning Analysis and Research Institute, Santa Monica, Calif.

CAREER: Chemist, Goodrich Chemical Co., 1946-47; University of Southern California, Medical School, Los Angeles, research chemist, 1947; U.S. Veterans Administration Hospital, Los Angeles, clinical psychology trainee, 1950-54; California Youth Authority, Norwalk, clinical psychologist, 1954-57; social scientist, RAND Corp., 1958-60; System Development Corp., Santa Monica, Calif., social scientist, 1960-70; University of Southern California, consulting psychologist and lecturer, 1970-75; Planning Analysis and Research Institute, Santa Monica, senior research fellow, 1975—. Court psychologist, Los Angeles County General Hospital, 1954; clinical associate, University of Southern California, 1955-56; instructor in psychology of revolution, California School of Professional Psychology, 1976-77. President, Parents and Friends of Mentally Ill Children (nonprofit foundation), 1966-68. *Military service:* U.S. Marine Corps, 1944-45. *Member:* American Psychological Association, American Association for the Advancement of Science, Western Psychological Associaiton.

WRITINGS: *Rousseau and the Spirit of Revolt,* University of Michigan Press, 1967; *Aggression American Style,* Goodyear Publishing, 1978; *Apostles of Revolution,* American Bibliographical Center-Clio Press, 1983. Contributor to professional journals and newspapers.

SIDELIGHTS: William H. Blanchard wrote to *CA:* "Admire Freud, Sartre, Camus, Darwin, Marx, Kafka. Would like to do something to improve the quality of American life which I consider lacking in emotional range and in intellectual depth."

* * *

BLASER, Robin (Francis) 1925-

PERSONAL: Born May 18, 1925, in Denver, Colo.; naturalized Canadian citizen, 1972; son of Robert Augustus (a trucker) and Ina May Celestine (McCready) Blaser. *Education:* Attended Northwestern University, 1943, and College of Idaho, 1943-44; University of California, Berkeley, B.A., 1952, M.A., 1954, M.L.S., 1955. *Politics:* Socialist. *Religion:* "Imagination." *Home:* 1636 Trafalgar, Vancouver, British Columbia, Canada V6K 3R7. *Office:* Department of English, Simon Fraser University, Burnaby, British Columbia, Canada.

CAREER: Harvard University Library, Cambridge, Mass., librarian, 1955-59; California Historical Society, San Francisco, librarian, 1960; San Francisco State College (now University) Library, San Francisco, librarian, 1961-65; Simon Fraser University, Burnaby, British Columbia, lecturer, 1966-70, professor of English, 1970—, professor in the Centre for the Arts, 1981—. Reader for Canada Council. *Awards, honors:* New York Poetry Society Award, 1962; National Endowment for the Arts grant, 1968; Canada Council Arts Award, 1970-71.

WRITINGS—Poetry: *The Moth Poem,* Open Space, 1964; *Les Chimeres* (versions of Gerard de Nerval), Open Space, 1965; *Cups,* Four Seasons Foundation, 1968; *The Holy Forest Section,* Caterpiller, 1970; *Image-Nations 1-12* [and] *The Stadium of the Mirror,* Ferry Press, 1974; *Image-Nations 13-14,* Cobblestone, 1975; *Syntax,* Island, 1982.

Editor and contributor: *The Collected Books of Jack Spicer,* Black Sparrow Press, 1975; *Troilus: A Play by Jack Spicer,* Black Sparrow Press, 1975; George Bowering, *Particular Accidents: Selected Poems,* Talonbooks, 1980.

Work appears in anthologies, including: *New Writing in the U.S.A.,* edited by Donald M. Allen and Robert Creeley, Penguin, 1967; *The Poetics of the New American Poetry,* edited by Allen and Warren Tallman, Grove, 1973; *The Long Poem Anthology,* edited by Michael Undaatje, Coach House Press, 1979; *The Postmoderns,* edited by Allen and George F. Butterick, Grove, 1982. Also author of poems recorded on videotape. Editor, *Pacific Nation,* 1967-69.

WORK IN PROGRESS: *The Holy Forest; Astonishments.*

SIDELIGHTS: Robin Blaser writes: "With 'Image-Nation 12,' my own poetry has turned a corner where I work blindly and uneasily—toward an entangling that is the world and the beloved. Recently, with a few friends and poets, I've begun a book called *Astonishments.* It is taped in order to have a prose which is direct speech. This is really about the poets I've known—Spicer, Duncan, Wieners, Olson, Creeley, and I mix them with Dante or whatever astonishment."

* * *

BLOOMFIELD, Masse 1923-

PERSONAL: First name sounds like "macy"; born August 20, 1923, in Franklin, N.H.; son of Harry and Ida (Steinberg) Bloomfield; married Fay Koenigsberg, February 21, 1954; children: Beth, Ellen, Dina. *Education:* University of New Hampshire, B.S., 1948; Carnegie Institute of Technology (now Carnegie-Mellon University), M.L.S., 1951. *Politics:* Democrat. *Religion:* Jewish. *Home:* 20733 Stephanie Dr., Canoga Park, Calif. 91306. *Office:* Technical Library, Hughes Aircraft Co., El Segundo, Calif. 90245.

CAREER: Librarian for U.S. Department of Agriculture, Washington, D.C., 1951-52, U.S. Naval Ordnance Test Station, China Lake, Calif., 1952-55, and Atomics International, Canoga Park, Calif., 1955-62; Hughes Aircraft Co., supervisor of Culver City Library, Culver City, Calif., and of Technical Library, El Segundo, Calif., 1962—. President of M. Bloomfield & Co. (trade publishing house), 1975-77. Chairman of West Valley Division of United Jewish Welfare Fund, Canoga Park, 1962-64. *Military service:* U.S. Army Air Forces, 1942-45; received Distinguished Flying Cross and Air Medal with four clusters. U.S. Air Force Reserve, 1945-71; retired as lieutenant colonel. *Member:* Special Libraries Association, West Valley Folk Dancers.

WRITINGS: (With F. G. Bennett) *Reactor Kinetics: A Bibliography,* Atomics International, 1959; *Role of the Technical Library in Support of an Information Center,* Hughes Aircraft Co., 1964; (contributor) *Progress in Information Science and Technology,* Adrian Press, 1966; (with others) *Bibliography of Scientific and Technical Bibliographies,* Hughes Aircraft Co., 1968; *How to Use a Library,* Mojave Books, 1970; (with Harvey J. Wolf) *Man in Transition,* Mojave Books, 1973; (contributor) J. Lubans, editor, *Educating the Library User,* Bowker, 1974. Also author of *Project Fearless Fosdic: U.S. Air Force in the 1980's,* for 9339th Air Reserve Squadron. Contributor to library journals. Member of editorial board of *Current Contents—Chemical Sciences,* 1967; book review editor of *Sci-Tech News,* 1970-82; book reviewer for *Special Libraries,* 1972-76.

WORK IN PROGRESS: Several papers, including "What Is a Jew?," "Proposal on Crime and Education," "Evolution: A Basis for Planning," and "The Large Industrial Library as a Mail Order House."

BOA, Kenneth 1945-

PERSONAL: Born July 22, 1945, in Kearney, Neb.; son of Kenneth (a bus driver) and Ruthelaine (a driver; maiden name, Kelley) Boa; married Karen Powelson, December 29, 1967; children: Heather Robin. *Education:* Case Institute of Technology (now Case Western Reserve University), B.S., 1967; Dallas Theological Seminary, Th.M., 1972; New York University, doctoral candidate. *Religion:* Biblical Christianity. *Home and office:* 45 Willow Springs Lane, Roswell, Ga. 30075.

CAREER: University of Plano, Plano, Tex., instructor in mathematics, 1969-72; New Life, Inc., Knoxville, Tenn., writer and director of publications and research, 1972-75; King's College, Briarcliff Manor, N.J., instructor in biblical studies and college pastor, 1976-79; Walk thru the Bible, Atlanta, Ga., writer and teacher, 1979-82; Search Ministries, Atlanta, director of research and development, 1982—. *Member:* Evangelical Theological Society, Creation Research Society.

WRITINGS: God, I Don't Understand, Victor, 1975; *Cults, World Religions, and You,* Victor, 1977; *The Return of the Star of Bethlehem,* Doubleday, 1980; *Talk thru the Old Testament,* Tyndale, 1980; *Talk thru the New Testament,* Tyndale, 1981; *I'm Glad You Asked,* Victor, 1982; *Seeds of Change,* Crossway Books, 1982. Contributor to *New Life Newsletter* and to *Bibliotheca Sacra.*

WORK IN PROGRESS: A two-volume theology text for the layman; Ph.D. dissertation.

SIDELIGHTS: Kenneth Boa writes: "I am interested in showing that biblical Christianity, more specifically, the claims and credentials of Jesus Christ, has relevance for people and their problems today." *Avocational interests:* Music, art, films.

* * *

BOBROW, Edwin E. 1928-

PERSONAL: Born April 8, 1928; son of Abraham David (a sales manager) and Emma (Goldstein) Bobrow; married Gloria Lefkowitz, May 3, 1954; children: Mark David. *Education:* Long Island University, B.Sc., 1949; New York University, advanced study at Graduate School of Business Administration. *Home:* 4465 Douglas Ave., Riverside, N.Y. 10471. *Office:* Bobrow Sales Associates, Inc., 175 Fifth Ave., New York, N.Y. 10010.

CAREER: Decro Wall Corp., Elmsford, N.Y., former director of marketing; Bobrow Sales Associates, Inc., New York, N.Y., chairman of the board, 1955—; principal in Niesi Fitzmaurice Bobrow Sales, Inc., and in Bobrow/Hallmark, Inc. President of Bobrow Consulting Group, Inc.; vice-president of Bobrow Realty Co. Adjunct assistant professor at New York University and program coordinator for marketing management program, Management Institute; guest lecturer at Fairleigh Dickinson University, Long Island University, and University of Wisconsin; member of board of directors of Business Games Group, Graduate School of Business Administration, Long Island University; conductor of workshops; lecturer to business groups and at conferences. United Jewish Appeal of Greater New York, member of Leadership Council, past chairman of Hardware, Housewares, Paint, Garden and Outdoor Living Division; committee member of Israel Bond Drive; committee member, 1978 National United Nations Day; member of board of directors, Solidaridad Humana, Inc. Consultant to several firms, including Honeywell, Dow Corning, General Electric, and Toro; member of advisory boards of American Tack & Hardware Co., Hercules Chemical Co., and of Institute for Mass Marketing; member of Volunteer Urban Consulting Group.

MEMBER: International Platform Association, American Marketing Association, Manufacturers' Agents National Association, National Council of Salesmen's Organizations (past vice-president), Association for Sales through Representatives and Agents (member of advisory board), Automotive Affiliated Representatives, Automotive Accessories Parts Association, Mass Merchandising Distributors' Association (co-founder), Institute of Management Consultants, Society of Professional Management Consultants (member of board of directors), Authors Guild, Authors League of America, Hardware Boosters, Sales Executives Club of New York. *Awards, honors:* State of Israel Leadership Award; United Jewish Appeal Scroll of Honor and Leadership Citation; Manufacturers' Agents Associations Special Award; Distinguished Alumnus Award, Long Island University; Certificate of Highest Achievement in Teaching, University of Wisconsin (twice); Distinguished Service Marketing Award, Sales Executives Club of New York; Hardware Retailing Magazine Industry Service Award; numerous citations from the Institute for Mass Marketing.

WRITINGS: How to Make Big Money as an Independent Sales Agent, Parker Publishing, 1967; *Selling the Volume Retailer: A Practical Plan for Success,* Chain Store Publishing, 1975; *How to Sell Your Way into Your Own Business with Little or No Capital,* Bill Communications, 1977; *Marketing through Manufacturers' Agents,* Bill Communications, 1978; (editor with others) *Sales Manager's Handbook,* Dow Jones-Irwin, 1983. Author of a booklet, *Is the Independent Sales Agent for You?,* for the U.S. Government Small Business Administration; co-author of two booklets, *Checklist for Marketing Hardlines through Mass Merchandisers* and *Checklist for Successfully Marketing New Products.* Columnist for *Housewares Review,* two years, *Income Opportunities,* and for a number of other business publications. Contributor of more than one hundred articles on marketing and sales to trade journals. Editor of *Selling through Reps;* contributing editor of *Income Opportunities Magazine;* member of editorial advisory board of *The Journal of Applied Management.*

* * *

BOCCA, Al
See WINTER, Bevis (Peter)

* * *

BORNSTEIN, Diane (Dorothy) 1942-

PERSONAL: Born April 22, 1942, in New York, N.Y.; daughter of Irving (a teacher) and Ruth (Vogel) Fox; married Barry Bornstein (a lithographer), April 2, 1960 (divorced, 1979). *Education:* Hunter College of the City University of New York, B.A. (summa cum laude), 1966; New York University, M.A., 1967, Ph.D. (with distinction), 1970. *Home:* 56-56 220th St., Bayside, N.Y. 11364. *Office:* Department of English, Queens College of the City University of New York, Flushing, N.Y. 11367.

CAREER: Hunter College of the City University of New York, New York, N.Y., lecturer in English, 1970-71; Queens College of the City University of New York, Flushing, N.Y., instructor, 1971-73, assistant professor, 1973-77, associate professor, 1977-82, professor of English, 1982—. *Member:* Modern Language Association of America, Mediaeval Academy of America, Linguistic Society of America, Early English Text Society, Medieval Club of New York, Phi Beta Kappa. *Awards, honors:* American Council of Learned Societies grants, 1973-74, 1975-

76, and 1981-82; National Endowment for the Humanities fellowship, 1979.

WRITINGS: (With John F. Fisher) *In Forme of Speche Is Chaunge,* Prentice-Hall, 1974; *Mirrors of Courtesy* (nonfiction) Shoe String, 1975; (editor) *Readings in the Theory of Grammar,* Winthrop, 1975; (editor) Sir William Segar, *Book of Honor and Armes* [and] *Honor: Military and Civil,* Scholars' Facsimiles & Reprints, 1975; *An Introduction to Transformational Grammar,* Winthrop, 1977; *The Middle English Translation of Christine de Pizan's "Livre du corps de policie,"* Carl Winter, 1977; *Distaves and Dames: Renaissance Treatises for and about Women,* Scholars' Facsimiles and Reprints, 1978; *The Feminist Controversy of the Renaissance,* Scholars' Facsimiles and Reprints, 1980; *Ideals for Women in the Works of Christine de Pizan,* Medieval Monographs, 1981; *The Lady in the Tower,* Shoe String, 1982. Contributor to *Shakespeare Studies, Comparative Literature Studies, Studies in Scottish Literature,* and other journals.

WORK IN PROGRESS: An annotated bibliography of didactic literature for women, 100-1500; an edition of Philippe de Mornay's *Excellent discours de la vie et de la mort.*

* * *

BORNSTEIN-LERCHER, Ruth 1927-

PERSONAL: Born April 28, 1927, in Milwaukee, Wis.; daughter of Adolph and Bertha (Friedman) Lercher; married Harry Bornstein (a designer and builder), January 7, 1951 (divorced, 1981); children: Noa, Jonah, Adam, Jesse. *Education:* University of Wisconsin, Madison, B.S., 1948; graduate study at Art Students League, 1949, and at Cranbrook Academy of Art, 1951. *Home:* 2820 Highland Ave., Santa Monica, Calif. 90405.

CAREER: Teacher of children's book illustration at University of Southern California and University of California, Los Angeles.

MEMBER: Society of Children's Book Writers, Southern California Council on Literature for Children and Young People. *Awards, honors:* Southern California Council on Literature for Children and Young People award for significant contribution to illustration, 1974, for *Son of Thunder,* and 1977, for *Little Gorilla.*

WRITINGS—Juvenile fiction; all self-illustrated: *Indian Bunny,* Childrens Press, 1973; *Little Gorilla* (Junior Literary Guild selection), Seabury, 1976; *The Dream of the Little Elephant,* Seabury, 1977; *The Dancing Man* (Junior Literary Guild selection), Seabury, 1978; *Jim,* Seabury, 1978; *Annabelle,* Crowell, 1978; *I'll Draw a Meadow,* Harper, 1979; *Of Course a Goat,* Harper, 1980.

Illustrator: Ethel K. McHale, *Son of Thunder,* Children's Press, 1974; *Your Owl Friend,* Harper, 1977; *Flocks of Birds,* Crowell, 1981; *Mama One, Mama Two,* Harper, 1982; *Summer Is,* Crowell, 1983.

SIDELIGHTS: Ruth Bornstein has had several exhibitions of her paintings. *Avocational interests:* Singing, dancing, walking, travel, growing vegetables.

* * *

BOTTNER, Barbara 1943-

PERSONAL: Born May 25, 1943, in New York, N.Y.; daughter of Irving (a business executive) and Elaine (Schiff) Bottner. *Education:* Attended Boston University, 1961-62, and Ecole des Beaux Arts, 1963-64; University of Wisconsin, B.S., 1965; University of California, Santa Barbara, M.A., 1966. *Home:* 803 North Citrus Ave., Los Angeles, Calif. 90038. *Office:* Otis Art Institute of Los Angeles County, 2401 Wilshire Blvd., Los Angeles, Calif. 90057.

CAREER: Free-lance writer. Actress, kindergarten teacher, animation producer, writer, and artist; Parsons School of Design, New York, N.Y., instructor, beginning 1973; instructor at Otis Art Institute of Los Angeles County. Work has been represented in film festivals in London, Melbourne, Ottawa, and New York City. *Awards, honors:* Best Film for Television award from International Animation Festival, Annecy, France, 1973, for "Goat in a Boat"; Cine Golden Eagle for animated film "Later That Night."

WRITINGS—Juvenile: *What Would You Do with a Giant?,* Putnam, 1972; *Fun House,* Prentice-Hall, 1975; *Eek, a Monster,* Macmillan, 1975; *The Box,* Macmillan, 1975; *What Grandma Did on Her Birthday,* Macmillan, 1975; *Big Boss! Little Boss!,* Pantheon, 1978; *Jungle Day,* Delacorte, 1978; *There Was Nobody There,* Macmillan, 1978; *Messy,* Delacorte, 1979; *Dumb Old Casey Is a Fat Tree,* Harper, 1979; *Myra,* Macmillan, 1979; *Horrible Hannah,* Crown, 1980; *Mean Maxine,* Pantheon, 1980. Author of films "Goat in a Boat" and "Later That Night." Children's book reviewer for *New York Times* Sunday section. Contributor to *Cosmopolitan* and *Playgirl.*

WORK IN PROGRESS: A screenplay.

AVOCATIONAL INTERESTS: Dancing, cooking, jogging, travel.

BIOGRAPHICAL/CRITICAL SOURCES: Rita Xanthoudakis, "All about Time and No Time" (film), New York University, 1974.

* * *

BOULDING, Elise (Biorn-Hansen) 1920-

PERSONAL: Born July 6, 1920, in Oslo, Norway; daughter of Joseph (an engineer) and Birgit (Johnsen) Biorn-Hansen; married Kenneth Boulding (a professor), August 30, 1941; children: John Russell, Mark David, Christine Ann, Philip Daniel, William Frederick. *Education:* Douglass College, B.A., 1940; Iowa State University, M.S., 1949; University of Michigan, Ph.D., 1969. *Religion:* Society of Friends. *Office:* Department of Sociology, Dartmouth College, Hanover, N.H. 03755.

CAREER: University of Michigan, Ann Arbor, research associate at Survey Research Center, 1957-58, secretary for seminar on research development, Center for Research on Conflict Resolution, 1960-63; editor, *International Peace Research Newsletter,* 1963-67; University of Colorado, Boulder, lecturer, 1967-68, assistant professor, 1968-69, associate professor, 1969-73, professor of sociology, 1973-78; Dartmouth College, Hanover, N.H., professor of sociology and chairman of department, 1978—. International chairperson, Women's International League for Peace and Freedom, 1968-70; member of board of directors, Institute for World Order, 1972—; member of Commission on U.S. Peace Academy, 1980-81, and UNESCO Peace Prize and Peace Education Commission, 1982—.

MEMBER: International Peace Research Association, International Sociological Association (co-chairman, research committee on sex roles in society, 1973—), International Studies Association, American Association for the Advancement of Science (member of executive committee, 1970-72), American Association of University Professors, American Sociological Association (chairman of committee on status of women in the profession, 1970-72, and committee on sociology of world conflicts, 1972-74; member of council, 1976-79), National Council of Family Relations, World Future Society. *Awards, honors:* Danforth fellow, 1965-67; distinguished alumni award, Douglass College; University of Colorado faculty grant, 1974; Ted Lentz Peace Price, 1976; National Woman of Conscience Award, 1980.

WRITINGS: (Translator) Fred Polak, *Image of the Future*, two volumes, Oceana, 1961, abridged edition edited by Boulding, Jossey-Bass, 1972; (editor with Robert Kahn) *Power and Conflict in Organizations*, Basic Books, 1964.

(Author of introduction) Eric Graham Howe, *War Dance: A Study of the Psychology of War*, Garland Publishing, 1972; (author of introduction) Mark May, *A Social Psychology of War and Peace*, Garland Publishing, 1972; *From a Monastery Kitchen*, Harper, 1976; *The Underside of History: A View of Women through Time*, Westview, 1976; (with Shirley Nuss and Dorothy Carson) *Handbook on International Data on Women*, Sage Publications, 1976; *Women in the Twentieth-Century World*, Sage Publications, 1977; *Children's Rights and the Wheel of Life*, Transaction Press, 1979; (with Robert Passmore and Scott Gassler) *Bibliography on World Conflict and Peace*, Westview, 1979; *Family Wholeness: New Conceptions of Family Roles*, Sage Publications, 1979.

(Author of foreword) Natalie Sokoloff, *Between Money and Love: The Dialectics of Women's Home and Market Work*, Praeger, 1980; (with others) *Environmental and Societal Consequences of a Possible CO2-Induced Climate Change: A Research Agenda*, Volume I, Carbon Dioxide Effects Research and Assessment Program, U.S. Department of Energy, 1980; (with husband, Kenneth Boulding, and Guy Burgess) *The Social System of the Planet Earth*, Addison-Wesley, in press.

Contributor: Reuben Hill, *Families under Stress*, Macmillan, 1949; M. Schwebel, editor, *Behavioral Science and Human Survival*, Science and Behavior Books, 1965.

Magoroh Maruyama and James A. Dator, editors, *Human Futuristics*, Social Science Research Institute, University of Hawaii, 1971; Marvin Sussman and Betty Cogswell, editors, *Cross-National Family Research*, E. J. Brill, 1972; Nobuo Shimahara, editor, *Educational Reconstruction: Promise and Challenge*, C. E. Merrill, 1973; Sylvan Kaplan and Evelyn Kivy-Rosenberg, editors, *Ecology and the Quality of Life*, C. C Thomas, 1973; Christoph Wulf, editor, *Handbook on Peace Education*, International Peace Association, 1974; Robert Bundy, editor, *Images of the Future*, Prometheus Books, 1975; Shimahara and Adam Scrupski, editors, *Social Forces and Schooling*, McKay, 1975.

Theo F. Lentz, editor, *Humatriotism: Human Interest in Peace and Survival*, Futures Press, 1976; R. J. Akkerman, P. J. Van Krieken, and C. O. Pannenborg, editors, *Declarations on Principles: A Quest for Universal Peace*, Sijthoff, 1977; William Loehr and John P. Powelson, editors, *Economic Development, Poverty and Income Distribution*, Westview, 1977; Dennis L. Meadows, editor, *Alternative to Growth I: A Search for Sustainable Futures*, Ballinger, 1977; *A Critical Economic Balance: Water—Land—Energy—People*, Federal Energy Administration, 1977; Michael Katz, William P. Marsh, and Gail Gordon Thompson, editors, *Earth's Answer: Explorations of Planetary Culture at Lindisfarne Conferences*, Harper, 1978; Terrell J. Minger, editor, *The Future of Human Settlements in the Rocky Mountain West*, The Printery, 1978; Louis Rubin, editor, *Educational Reform for a Changing Society: Anticipating Tomorrow's Schools*, Allyn & Bacon, 1978; Abdul Azig Said, editor, *Human Rights and World Order*, Transaction Books, 1978; D. John Grove, editor, *Global Inequality: Politics and Socioeconomics*, Westview, 1979; Louis Kriesberg, editor, *Research in Social Movements, Conflict or Change*, JAI Press, 1979.

Stein Rokkan, editor, *A Quarter Century of International Social Science*, UNESCO, 1980; Helen Lopata, editor, *Research in the Interweave of Social Roles*, JAI Press, 1980; *Visions of Desirable Societies*, World Futures Federation, 1980; Roslyn Dauber and Melinda Cain, editors, *Impact of Technological Change on Women*, Westview, 1980; *Violence and Its Causes: Theoretical Methodological Aspects of Recent Research on Violence*, UNESCO, 1980; Magnus Haavelsrud, editor, *Approaching Disarmament Education*, IPC Science and Technology Press, 1981; Erich Jantsch, editor, *The Evolutionary Vision: Toward a Unifying Paradigm of Physical, Biological and Sociocultural Evolution*, Westview, 1981; Jerome Perlinski, editor, *The Spirit of Earth: Essays for the Teilhard Centennial*, Seabury Press, 1981; *Proceedings of the Conference on Women in Poverty: What Do We Know?*, Johns Hopkins Press, 1982; Raimo Vayrinen, editor, *Studies on Military Research and Development: The Arms Race and the Scientific Community*, UNESCO, 1983.

Author of booklets published by Society of Friends. Contributor to annals and proceedings. Contributor of articles and reveiws to *Marriage and Family Living, Human Relations, War/Peace Report, Japan Christian Quarterly, New Era, Journal of World Education, Contemporary Sociology*, and other journals. *International Peace Research Newsletter*, editor, 1963-68, North American editor, 1968-73; guest editor of *Journal of Social Issues*, January, 1967, and *Journal of Conflict Resolution*, December, 1972; associate editor of *American Sociologist*, 1970-73, and *International Interactions*, 1973—; member of board of editors, *Peace and Change: A Journal of Peace Research*, 1971—.

WORK IN PROGRESS: With Elizabeth Moen, Jane Lilleydahl, and Rise Palm, *Women and Social Costs of Development: Two Case Studies*.

* * *

BOWDEN, Edwin T(urner), Jr. 1924-

PERSONAL: Born June 5, 1924, in Milledgeville, Ga.; son of Edwin T. and Allie (Myrick) Bowden; married, 1948; children: Elisabeth, Susan, Edwin Eric, James, Margaret. *Education:* Harvard University, B.A., 1948; Yale University, M.A. and Ph.D., 1952. *Office:* Department of English, University of Texas, Austin, Tex. 78712.

CAREER: Yale University, New Haven, Conn., instructor in English, 1952-56; University of Texas at Austin, began as assistant professor, became associate professor, 1956-66, professor of English, 1966—. Visiting professor, University of New Mexico, summer, 1965. Secretary of English Institute, 1955. *Military service:* U.S. Army Air Forces, 1943-46. *Member:* Modern Language Association of America, Texas Institute of Letters. *Awards, honors:* Fulbright scholar, Cambridge University, 1949-50.

WRITINGS: The Themes of Henry James, Yale University Press, 1956, published as *The Themes of Henry James: A System of Observation through the Visual Arts*, Archon Books, 1969; *An Introduction to Prose Style*, Holt, 1956; *The Dungeon of the Heart: Human Isolation and the American Novel*, Macmillan, 1961; (editor) *The Satiric Poems of John Trumbull*, University of Texas Press, 1962, published as *The Satiric Poems of John Trumbull: "The Progress of Dulness" and "M'fingal,"* 1971;

(editor) Washington Irving, *A History of New York*, Twayne, 1964; (textual editor) *The Complete Works of Washington Irving*, University of Wisconsin Press, 1968; (compiler) *James Thurber: A Bibliography*, Ohio State University Press, 1969.

The Holy Bible at the University of Texas (originally published as *The Holy Bible: An Exhibit*), revised edition, University of Texas, Humanities Resource Center, 1971; (compiler) *The First Hundred Publications of the Humanities Research Center*, University of Texas, Humanities Research Center, 1971; *Peter De Vries: A Bibliography, 1934-1977*, University of Texas, Humanities Research Center, 1978. Co-editor of *Texas Studies in Literature and Language*, 1967—.†

* * *

BOWEN, Howard R(othmann) 1908-

PERSONAL: Born October 27, 1908, in Spokane, Wash.; son of Henry G. (a musician) and Josephine (Menig) Bowen; married Lois B. Schilling, August 24, 1935; children: Peter Geoffrey, Thomas Gerard. *Education:* State College of Washington (now Washington State University), B.A., 1929, M.A., 1933; University of Iowa, Ph.D., 1935; postdoctoral study at Cambridge University and London School of Economics and Political Science, 1937-38. *Home:* 916 West Harrison, Claremont, Calif. 91711. *Office:* Claremont Graduate School, Claremont, Calif. 91711.

CAREER: University of Iowa, Iowa City, instructor, 1935-38, assistant professor, 1938-40, associate professor of economics 1940-42; U.S. Government, Washington, D.C., chief of the Business Structure Unit, Department of Commerce, 1942-44, chief economist, Joint Congressional Committee on Internal Revenue Taxation, 1944-45; Irving Trust Co., New York, N.Y., economist, 1945-47; University of Illinois at Urbana-Champaign, professor of economics and dean of School of Commerce and Business Administration, 1947-52; Williams College, Williamstown, Mass., professor of economics, 1952-55; Grinnell College, Grinnell, Iowa, president, 1955-64; University of Iowa, Iowa City, president, 1964-69; Claremont Graduate School, Claremont, Calif., professor of economics, 1969-70; Claremont University Center, Claremont, president and chancellor, 1970-74; Claremont Graduate School, R. Stanton Avery Professor of Economics and Education, 1974—. Resident scholar, Bellagio Study Center, Rockefeller Foundation, 1973. Member of government missions to Japan, 1949, Thailand, 1961, and Yugoslavia, 1962; member of Committee for Economic Development, 1955-59, National Committee on Government Finance of the Brookings Institution, 1960-65, Federal Advisory Commission on Intergovernmental Relations, 1961-64, National Commission on Non-Traditional Study, 1970-72, National Board of Graduate Education, 1973-74, and National Council of Independent Colleges and Universities, 1973-74; chairman of National Commission on Technology, Automation and Economic Progress, 1966-67; chairman of Governor's Commission on Economic and Social Trends in Iowa, 1958, and National Citizen's Committee for Tax Revision and Reduction, 1963. Consultant to National Council of Churches, 1949-53, and to a number of federal and state agencies.

MEMBER: American Economic Association, American Finance Association (president, 1950), National Academy of Education, Royal Economic Society (London), Western Economic Association (president, 1977), Phi Beta Kappa, Phi Kappa Phi, Beta Gamma Sigma, University Club (Chicago), Des Moines Club.

AWARDS, HONORS: Social Science Research Council fellowship in England, 1937-38; Distinguished Alumnus Award from Washington State University and University of Iowa; National Council of Independent Colleges and Universities award, 1975, for "outstanding leadership in American higher education and unique contribution to independent colleges and universities"; New York Association of Colleges and Universities award, 1976, for educational leadership; National Association of Student Personnel Administrators award, 1981. LL.D. from Cornell College, Mount Vernon, Iowa, 1956, Knox College, Galesburg, Ill., 1964, Drake University, 1968, and Carnegie-Mellon University, 1973; L.H.D. from Loras College, 1963, Coe College, 1965, and Marycrest College, 1968; D.Litt., Grinnell College, 1964; also received honorary degrees from University of Illinois, University of the Pacific, Union College, Williams College, College of Santa Fe, Loyola University of Chicago, Ohio State University, Towson State University, and University of Tulsa.

WRITINGS: English Grants-in-Aid, University of Iowa Press, 1939; *Toward Social Economy*, Rinehart, 1948; *Social Responsibilities of the Businessman*, Harper, 1953; *Graduate Education in Economics*, American Economic Association, 1953; *Christian Values and Economic Life*, Harper, 1954.

(Editor with Garth L. Mangum) *Automation and Economic Progress*, Prentice-Hall, 1967; (with Gordon Douglass) *Efficiency in Liberal Education: A Study of Comparative Instructional Costs for Different Ways of Organizing Teaching-Learning in a Liberal Arts College*, McGraw, 1971; (editor and contributor) *Evaluating Performance for Accountability*, Jossey-Bass, 1974; *Investment in Learning*, Jossey-Bass, 1977.

The Costs of Higher Education, Jossey-Bass, 1980; *The State of the Nation and the Agenda for Higher Education*, Jossey-Bass, 1982. Also author of *The Finance of Higher Education*, 1969. Contributor of more than 100 monographs and articles relating to economics, finance, and education to economics journals. Member of editorial boards, *Journal of Higher Education*, 1972-81, and *Change*, 1979—.

* * *

BOWEN, J(ean) Donald 1922-

PERSONAL: Born March 19, 1922, in Malad, Idaho; son of John David (a railroad agent) and Lillian (Larsen) Bowen; married Catherine Holley, May 27, 1948; children: David James, Douglas Ray, Dale Eugene, Christina Lee, Karen Lucy. *Education:* Brigham Young University, B.A., 1944; Columbia University, M.A., 1949; University of New Mexico, Ph.D., 1952. *Religion:* Church of Jesus Christ of Latter-day Saints (Mormon). *Home:* 3055 Corda Dr., Los Angeles, Calif. 90049. *Office:* Department of English, University of California, 405 Hilgard Ave., Los Angeles, Calif. 90024.

CAREER: Duke University, Durham, N.C., instructor, 1952-53; U.S. Department of State Foreign Service Institute, Washington, D.C., linguistic scientist, 1953-58; University of California, Los Angeles, co-director of Philippine Center for Language Study and visiting associate professor, 1958-63, associate professor, 1963-66, professor of English, 1966—. Visiting professor at American University of Cairo, 1974-77, and Ain Shams University, 1976-77. Has conducted seminars in Poland, Czechoslovakia, Uruguay, Ecuador, Finland, and Romania. Consultant to U.S. Office of Education, State of California, Agency for International Development, U.S. Information Agency, Ford Foundation, and Center for Applied Linguistics. *Military service:* U.S. Army, 1943-46. *Member:* Modern Language Association of America, Linguistic Society of America, Teachers of English to Speakers of Other Languages, California Teachers of English to Speakers of Other Languages.

WRITINGS: (With Robert Stockwell) *Patterns of Spanish Pronunciation,* University of Chicago Press, 1960; (with Dwight Bolinger and others) *Modern Spanish,* Harcourt, 1960, 3rd edition, 1973; (with Stockwell) *The Sounds of English and Spanish,* University of Chicago Press, 1965; (with Stockwell and John Martin) *The Grammatical Structures of English and Spanish,* University of Chicago Press, 1965; *Patterns of English Pronunciation,* Newbury House, 1975; (with Harold S. Madsen) *Adaptation in Language Teaching,* Newbury House, 1978; (with Madsen and Ann Hilferty) *TESOL Techniques and Procedures,* Newbury House, in press; (with Ely Marquez) *Advanced Language Study,* Newbury House, in press.

Editor: Fe Dacanay, *Techniques and Procedures in Second Language Teaching,* Phoenix House, 1963; *Basic Readers for English Teaching,* Phoenix House, 1965; *Beginning Tagalog: A Course for Speakers of English,* University of California Press, 1965; *Intermediate Readings in Tagalog,* University of California Press, 1968; (with others, and contributor) *Linguistics in Oceana,* Mouton, 1971; (with Jacob Ornstein, M. L. Bender, R. L. Cooper, and C. A. Ferguson, and contributor) *Language in Ethiopia,* Oxford University Press, 1976; *Teaching English to Arabic Speaking Students,* Central Agency for University and School Books (Cairo, Egypt), Volume I: *A Guide for the Preparatory Stage,* Volume II: *A Guide for the Secondary Stage,* both 1977. Also editor of elementary school guide and textbook series, Philippine Government, 1960-66.

WORK IN PROGRESS: Advanced Language Study: ESOL, with E. J. Marquez.

* * *

**BOWES, Anne LaBastille
See LaBASTILLE, Anne**

* * *

BRADLEY, Virginia 1912-

PERSONAL: Born December 2, 1912, in Omaha, Neb.; daughter of Stephen (a lawyer) and Anne (a secretary; maiden name, Healy) Jonas; married Gerald Bradley (a business executive), June 8, 1940; children: Stephen, Michael, Betty (Mrs. Alfred Ramsey), Patricia (Mrs. James Curtis). *Education:* University of Nebraska, B.F.A., 1933. *Home:* 425 15th St., Santa Monica, Calif. 90402.

CAREER: Omaha World Herald, Omaha, Neb., member of classified advertising staff, 1937-38; workshop director of Los Angeles Schools, Adult Division, 1963-78, Southern California Woman's Press Club, 1974—, and Santa Monica Emeritus College, 1975—. *Member:* P.E.N., Educational Theatre Association, Society of Children's Book Writers, American Film Teachers Association, California Writers Guild, Santa Monica Writers Club (president, 1954-55).

WRITINGS: Is There an Actor in the House? (collection of dramatic material), Dodd, 1975; *Stage Eight* (plays), Dodd, 1977; *Bend to the Willow* (novel), Dodd, 1979; *Holidays on Stage* (plays), Dodd, 1981. Contributor to *Yankee, Young Miss, McCall's, Girltalk, Southland, Scouting, Western Family,* and religious journals.

WORK IN PROGRESS: A young adult novel.

SIDELIGHTS: Virginia Bradley told *CA:* "Always a dreamer, I lived in a world of 'let's pretend' throughout my childhood. Many a summer afternoon my friends and I created a makeshift stage in the backyard and put on a show for the neighborhood.

"This interest in drama, along with my love for the magic of words, took me to the theater arts and creative writing departments at college. Then during my single life I taught English and journalism and even had a brief stint with a repertory company. Finally, with marriage and a family, I turned to writing plays for Cub Scouts, Brownies, and school functions. Since I was inept at handicraft—for me the glue would never hold—the young people who joined my groups provided the entertainment. Many of the skits and sketches in my first book came from those performances.

"Plays are not my only interest. I am a storyteller. And because I am from the Midwest and remember how it was on the prairie, my young adult novel is set in a small Nebraska town in 1935."

BIOGRAPHICAL/CRITICAL SOURCES: Ms, December, 1978.

* * *

BRAND, Eugene L(ouis) 1931-

PERSONAL: Born November 22, 1931, in Richmond, Ind.; son of Oscar K. and Alice (Nolte) Brand. *Education:* Capital University, A.B., 1953; Lutheran Theological Seminary, B.D., 1957; University of Heidelberg, Dr. Theol., 1959. *Home:* 42, Ch. Chevillarde, 1208 Geneva, Switzerland. *Office:* Lutheran World Federation, 150 Rte. de Ferney, 1211 Geneva, Switzerland.

CAREER: Ordained minister of Lutheran Church in America, 1960; Lutheran Theological Seminary, Columbus, Ohio, professor of theology and worship, 1960-71; Lutheran Church in America, New York, N.Y., director of commission on worship, 1971-74; Inter-Lutheran Commission on Worship, New York, project director, 1975-78; director of Office on Studies, Lutheran World Ministries, 1978-81; Lutheran World Federation, Geneva, Switzerland, secretary for worship, 1982—. *Member:* National Academy of American Liturgists, Societas Liturgica.

WRITINGS: The Rite Thing, Augsburg, 1970; *Baptism: A Pastoral Perspective,* Augsburg, 1975; *A Lutheran Agenda for Worship,* Lutheran World Federation, 1979.

Contributor: *Reime Gottesdienst,* Lutherisches Verlagshaus, 1976; C. Halter and C. Schalk, editors, *A Handbook of Church Music,* Concordia, 1978; James Schmleser, editor, *Anglican Book Centre,* 1978; S. Anita Stauffer, editor, *By Water and the Holy Spirit,* Parish Life Press, 1979.

* * *

BRANDT, Leslie F. 1919-

PERSONAL: Born February 12, 1919, in Morris, Minn.; son of Elmer F. and Clara (Johnson) Brandt; married Edith Tokle (a junior high school teacher), August 30, 1942; children: Sonia Marie, Daniel Leslie, Donald Mark. *Education:* Augsburg College, B.A., 1941; further study at Lutheran Bible Institute, Minneapolis, Minn., 1941-42, Augsburg Theological Seminary, 1942-45, College of Chinese Studies, Peking, China, 1947-48, and American Institute of Family Relations, 1959-61. *Home:* 204 Hoihoi Way, Kula, Maui, Hawaii 96790.

CAREER: Ordained to ministry of American Lutheran Church, 1945; pastor in Pukwana, S.D., 1945-46; missionary in Peking and Shanghai, China, 1946-48; evacuated from Shangai in Communist take-over, 1948; pastor in Minneapolis, Minn., 1949-51; service pastor (as civilian) in Taiwan and Japan, 1951-54, establishing service centers and acting as auxiliary chaplain on Navy ships in port; pastor in Williston, N.D., 1954-58, Westminster, Calif., 1958-63, and Los Angeles, Calif., 1963-

67; Valley Lutheran Church, North Hollywood, Calif., pastor, 1967-73; Trinity Lutheran Church, Victorville, Calif., pastor, 1973-77.

WRITINGS—Published by Concordia, except as indicated: *Good Lord, Where Are You?*, 1967; *Great God, Here I Am*, 1969; *God Is Here: Let's Celebrate!*, 1969.

Contemporary Introits and Collects for the Twentieth Century, C.S.S. Publishing, 1970; *Can I Forgive God?*, 1970; *The Lord Rules: Let Us Serve Him*, 1971; *Meditations of a Radical Christian*, C.S.S. Publishing, 1973; *Psalms/Now*, 1973; *Living through Loving: Reflections on Letters of the New Testament*, 1974; *Book of Christian Prayer*, Augsburg, 1974, revised edition, 1980; (with wife, Edith Brandt) *Growing Together: Prayers for Married People*, Augsburg, 1975; *Contemporary Introits for the Revised Church Calendar*, 1975; *Epistles/Now*, 1976; *Why Did This Happen to Me?: God's Answer to Human Suffering*, 1978; *Jesus/Now*, 1978; *Prophets/Now*, 1979.

Christ in Your Life: What God's Good News Can Do for You, 1980; *A Battle Manual for Christian Survival*, 1980; *Meditations on a Loving God*, 1983. Contributor to religion publications. Former weekly newspaper columnist in Williston, N.D., and Westminster, Calif.

* * *

BRANSCUM, Robbie 1937-

PERSONAL: Born June 17, 1937, in Arkansas; daughter of Donnie H. (a farmer) and Blanch (Balitine) Tilley; married Duane Branscum (divorced, 1969); married Lesli J. Carrico, July 15, 1975 (divorced); children: Deborah. *Home address:* P. O. Box 387, Eufaula, Okla. 74432.

WRITINGS—All juvenile: *Me and Jim Luke*, Doubleday, 1971; *Johnny May*, Doubleday, 1975; *The Three Wars of Billy Joe Treat*, McGraw, 1975; *Toby, Granny, and George*, Doubleday, 1976; *The Saving of P.S.*, Doubleday, 1977; *Three Buckets of Daylight*, Lothrop, 1978; *To the Tune of a Hickory Stick*, Doubleday, 1978; *The Ugliest Boy*, Lothrop, 1978; *For Love of Jody*, Lothrop, 1978; *Toby Alone*, Doubleday, 1978; *Toby and Johnny Joe*, Doubleday, 1978.

* * *

BRASCH, Rudolph 1912-

PERSONAL: Born November 6, 1912, in Berlin, Germany; son of British citizens, Gustav and Hedwig (Mathias) Brasch; married Liselott Buchbinder, February 16, 1952. *Education:* Attended University of Berlin, 1931-35; University of Wurzburg, Ph.D. (summa cum laude), 1936; Jewish Theological Seminary, Berlin, Rabbi (with highest honors), 1938. *Home:* 14 Derby St., Vaucluse, Sydney, New South Wales, Australia.

CAREER: Rabbi of Progressive synagogues in London, England, 1938-48, and Dublin, Ireland, 1946-47; Johannesburg Reform Congregations, Johannesburg, South Africa, rabbi and director of public relations, 1948-49; Temple Emanuel, Woollahra, New South Wales, Australia, chief minister, 1949-79. Guest professor, University of Sydney, 1952-53; visiting rabbi in Montgomery, Ala., 1980; visiting professor at University of Hawaii, 1981. Lecturer on cruise ships. Life Vice-president and chairman of ecclesiastical board, Australian and New Zealand Union for Progressive Judaism; member of governing body, World Union for Progressive Judaism; director of education, Liberal Education Board of New South Wales; justice of the peace, New South Wales. *Military service:* Padre to Civil Defence during London blitz; received Coronation Medal (Queen Elizabeth II) for his work. *Member:* Royal Australian Historical Society, Society of Religious History (founding member), Rotary Club (Sydney). *Awards, honors:* D.D., Hebrew Union College-Jewish Institute of Religion, Los Angeles, 1959; made Officer of the British Empire, 1967; awarded Order of Australia, 1979; Peace Media Medal, Australian Association of United Nations, 1979; made lieutenant-colonel in the Alabama militia.

WRITINGS: (With Lily M. Montagu) *A Little Book of Comfort for Jewish People in Times of Sorrow*, [London], 1948; *The Star of David*, Angus & Robertson, 1955; *The Eternal Flame*, Angus & Robertson, 1958; *General Sir John Monash* (biography), Royal Australian Historical Society, 1959; *How Did It Begin?*, Longmans, Green, 1965, McKay, 1966; *Mexico: A Country of Contrasts*, McKay, 1966; *Judaic Heritage*, McKay, 1969; *The Unknown Sanctuary: The Story of Judaism, Its Teachings, Philosophy, and Symbols*, Angus & Robertson, 1969; *How Did Sports Begin? A Look at the Origins of Man at Play*, McKay, 1970; *How Did Sex Begin?: The Sense and Nonsense of the Customs and Traditions that Have Separated Men and Women Since Adam and Eve*, McKay, 1973; *The Supernatural and You!*, Cassell, 1976; *Strange Customs and How They All Began*, McKay, 1976; *Australian Jews of Today and the Part They Have Played*, Cassell, 1977; *There's a Reason for Everything*, Fontana, 1982.

Also author of *The Midrash Shir Ha-shirim Zuta*, 1936, *The Jewish Question Mark*, 1945, *The Symbolism of King Solomon's Temple*, 1954. Contributor to *This Is Australia*, Hamlyn, 1975, 1977, 1982, and to *The Australian Beef Eater's Diary*, 1977. Scriptwriter for Australian Broadcasting Commission. Regular columnist, "Religion and Life" in Australia's *Sun-Herald*. Contributor to *Mankind* and *Commentary* (both United States), and other magazines and newspapers in Australia, Europe, and Africa. Editor, *Progressive Jew*, Johannesburg, 1948-49.

SIDELIGHTS: Rudolph Brasch is a master of twelve languages, among them Babylonic-Assyrian (Cuneiform), Syriac, Arabic, and Persian. From his early days, he has been active in interfaith relations: in Ireland he stayed at a Franciscan monastery; in London he conducted Hindu-Jewish service; in South Africa he addressed Bantus and held Dutch Reformed-Jewish service; in Australia he has spoken in the Unitarian and Catholic churches of Sydney and at the Inland Mission Church at Alice Springs in the heart of the interior.

Several of Brasch's books have been translated into Japanese and German.

* * *

BRASHERS, H(oward) C(harles) 1930-

PERSONAL: Born December 11, 1930, in Martin County, Tex.; son of George A. (a farmer and carpenter) and Sallie Louise (Whitaker) Brashers; married Kerstin Birgitta Brorson, June 13, 1959; children: Erik, Bart, Per. *Education:* University of California, Berkeley, B.A., 1956; San Francisco State College (now University), M.A., 1960; University of Denver, Ph.D., 1962. *Politics:* "Liberal Democrat, more or less." *Office:* Department of English, San Diego State University, San Diego, Calif. 92182.

CAREER: Maxwell Union High School, Maxwell, Calif., teacher, 1957-59; University of Denver, Denver, Colo., instructor in English, 1961-62; University of Stockholm, Stockholm, Sweden, Fulbright lecturer at English Institute, 1962-65; University of Michigan, Ann Arbor, assistant professor of

English, 1965-68; San Diego State University, San Diego, Calif., assistant professor of English, 1968-70, associate professor, 1970-73, professor of literature, 1973—. *Military service:* U.S. Army, 1953-55.

WRITINGS: *The Other Side of Love* (two novellas), A. Swallow, 1963; *An Introduction to American Literature for European Students,* Svenska Bokforlaget, 1965; (with Vincent Petti and Dennis Gotobed) *An Anthology of British and American Authors,* Svenska Bokforlaget, 1966; *The Life of America,* Natur och Kultur, 1966; *Creative Writing: Fiction, Drama, Poetry and the Essay,* Van Nostrand, 1968; *Creative Writing for High School Students,* Bureau of School Services, University of Michigan, 1968.

The Structure of Essays, Prentice-Hall, 1972; *Developing Creativity,* Helix House, 1974; *The Vision Quest of Charlie Stonecrust,* Blue Cloud, 1976; *A Snug Little Purchase,* Associated Creative Writers, 1979; *Creative Writing Handbook,* Associated Creative Handbook, 1982. Contributor to *Sewanee Review, Moderna Sprak,* and other journals.

WORK IN PROGRESS: *Under the Dawn Star: A California Indian Family Chronicle, 1832-1973; The Education of a Prairie Boy,* autobiographical stories.

AVOCATIONAL INTERESTS: Art, especially painting; collecting rocks, fossils, and minerals; hunting and fishing; the mountains; psychology; publishing.

* * *

BRAYNARD, Frank O. 1916-

PERSONAL: Born August 21, 1916, in Sea Cliff, Long Island, N.Y.; married; wife's name Doris. *Education:* Duke University, A.B., 1939; Columbia University, A.M., 1940. *Home:* 98 DuBois Ave., Sea Cliff, N.Y. *Office:* Office of the Curator, American Merchant Marine Museum, U.S. Merchant Marine Academy, Kings Point, N.Y. 11024.

CAREER: Writer and artist. School teacher in Poughkeepsie, N.Y., 1941-42; American Merchant Marine Institute, Bureau of Information, New York City, assistant director, 1943-48, director, 1951-60, editor of weekly *Bulletin; New York Herald Tribune,* New York City, assistant ship news editor, 1948-51; Moran Towing Co., New York City, director of public relations and editor of *Towline* magazine, 1961-70; South Street Seaport Museum, New York City, co-founder, 1967-68, program director, 1970-73; U.S. Department of Commerce, Maritime Administration, New York City, press specialist and writer, 1970; Operation Sail, New York City, general manager, 1973-76; founder and director of New York Harbor Festival, 1978-80; U.S. Merchant Marine Academy, American Merchant Marine Museum, Kings Point, N.Y., part-time curator, 1979—; Operation Ship, Ltd. (nautical marketing company), New York City, chairman, 1980—. *Member:* Steamship Historical Society of America (president, 1953-54), Veteran Wireless Operators Association (honorary member), Council of American Master Mariners (honorary member). *Awards, honors:* LL.D., C. W. Post Center of Long Island University, 1977.

WRITINGS: *Lives of the Liners,* Cornell Maritime, 1947; *Famous American Ships,* Hastings, 1957; *The Story of Ships,* Grosset, 1962; *SS Savannah: The Elegant Steam Ship,* University of Georgia Press, 1963; *A Tugman's Sketchbook: Pen and Ink Impressions of New York Harbor and the Ships that Use It, Big and Small,* DeGraff, 1965; *Fire Island to Venice: A Tugman's Holiday Sketchbook,* DeGraff, 1966; *One Square Mile: A Sea Cliff Sketchbook,* privately printed, 1967; *By Their Works Ye Shall Know Them: The Life of William Francis Gibbs,* privately printed, 1968; *Leviathan: The World's Greatest Ship,* South Street Seaport Museum, Volume I, 1972, Volume II, 1974, Volume III, 1976, Volume IV, 1978, Volume V, 1980; *Search for the Tall Ships,* Operation Ship, 1978; *The Big Ship: The Story of the SS United States,* Mariners Museum, 1981; *Fifty Famous Liners,* Patrick Stephens (Cambridge, England), 1982. Editor of *Steamboat Bill,* 1945-49.

WORK IN PROGRESS: Volume VI of *Leviathan: The World's Greatest Ship; Speed Queens of the Atlantic; Cunyard's Sixteen Paddlers,* with W. North.

SIDELIGHTS: On July 4, 1976, sailing ships from around the world converged on New York City Harbor. The gathering of 228 "tall ships," fifty warships, and thousands of smaller vessels was one of the most spectacular events of the American Bicentennial celebrations, as well as the realization of a dream for Frank O. Braynard.

Braynard conceived of the "tall ships" festival—known officially as Operation Sail—in 1964 and spent five years travelling around the world searching out the vessels, seeking support, and orchestrating the event. By the time the ships met in New York City Harbor after a race from Bermuda to Newport, Rhode Island, thirty-one countries, four thousand crew members, five million spectators, and over seventy million dollars were involved. According to *Newsweek,* Operation Sail formed "the greatest armada under canvas since the Battle of Navarino off the coast of Greece in 1827.... [The gathering in New York City was] a vision of a world now vanished, as well as a remarkably appropriate tribute to a nation that was settled from the sea." A *New Yorker* reporter, who was on a pleasure boat watching the ships as they sailed up the Hudson River, observed: "For a while no one said anything. Everyone just looked at the ships. There were tall ones and short ones, a few almost four hundred feet long and one under thirty feet, some with four masts and some with one. On all sides, sails fluttered in the breeze as they were hauled up masts.... Everywhere there were flags. Color, color, color! New York had never looked or felt more festive to me."

Despite such difficulties as a prolonged calm that cut short the Bermuda-to-Newport race, collisions that shattered the masts of two of the vessels and injured several sailors, and accusations of foul play by the crew of one ship against that of another, Operation Sail was one of the most highly praised events of the Bicentennial. Before the ships gathered in the harbor, Braynard said to a *Newsweek* reporter: "We are going to show that thirty-five thousand seamen from all over the world can get along happily in New York on the Fourth of July.... We are all sailors on the spaceship Earth."

Braynard's romance with the sea and its ships is evident in all his work, including his multi-volume maritime history, *Leviathan: The World's Greatest Ship.* "Any number of people think Frank O. Braynard is an extraordinary New Yorker because of the balance of fun and grandeur that he brought billowing to our waters under the name of Operation Sail," comments *New York Times* reviewer Francis X. Clines. "But those who truly know Mr. Braynard realize that the harbor extravaganza, which he conceived and directed out of pure deep love of the sea and its ships, was only a distraction from the day-to-day maritime passion of his life." That passion is the ocean liner *Leviathan,* one of the most luxurious passenger ships in the world until it was scrapped in 1938. In his review of *Leviathan: The World's Greatest Ship,* Clines calls Braynard as "methodical as he is romantic," noting that the book traces the voyages and operational details of the *Leviathan,* as well as recounts the lives and fortunes of the men and women who sailed on her. It also contains sketches of the *Leviathan* by

Braynard, including one he did when he was seven years old. "What the writer is doing with the departed 59,956 gross tons of the *Leviathan* is etching each detail with a measurable buoyant quality of human history," says Clines. Braynard, the critic concludes, has "come to view [ships] as people."

BIOGRAPHICAL/CRITICAL SOURCES: *New Yorker*, June 21, 1976, July 19, 1976; *Newsweek*, July 4, 1976; *Savannah News Press*, August 7, 1977; *New York Times*, January 9, 1979, February 12, 1980; *Kings Pointer*, winter, 1981; *Newsday*, May 23, 1982.

* * *

BREDEMEIER, Harry Charles 1920-

PERSONAL: Born January 26, 1920, in Cincinnati, Ohio; son of Charles F. and Etta (Day) Bredemeier; married Mary Elizabeth Robertson (a teacher and writer), November 16, 1953; children: Suzanne, Richard Boots. *Education:* University of Cincinnati, B.A., 1943; Columbia University, Ph.D., 1955. *Home:* 150 Emerson Rd., Somerset, N.J. 08873. *Office:* Department of Sociology, Douglass College, Rutgers University, New Brunswick, N.J. 08903.

CAREER: American University, Washington, D.C., instructor, 1943-44; Princeton University, Princeton, N.J., instructor, 1946-49; Rutgers University, Douglass College, New Brunswick, N.J., assistant professor, 1949-55, currently professor of sociology, chairman of department, 1958-62, 1976—, executive officer of graduate sociology program, 1965-66, chairman of sociology section, 1966-67, director of graduate sociology program, 1968-74. Director of Youth Opportunities Project, 1962-65. *Member:* American Sociological Association, American Association of University Professors (treasurer, 1961-63), Eastern Sociological Society (chairman of committee on papers, 1968-69), Phi Beta Kappa.

WRITINGS: (With Jackson Toby) *Social Problems in America*, Wiley, 1960, revised edition, 1972; (with R. M. Stephenson) *Analysis of Social Systems*, Holt, 1962; (contributor) *Law and Sociology*, edited by William Evan, Free Press of Glencoe, 1962; (editor with Judith Getis) *Environments, People, and Inequalities: Some Current Problems*, Wiley, 1973; (with wife, Mary E. Bredemeier) *Social Forces in Education*, Alfred Publishing, 1978; *The Federal Public Housing Movement: A Case Study of Social Change*, Arno, 1980. Also author of *Human Beings and Social Systems*, 1978. Contributor of numerous articles to professional journals. Co-editor, *Modern American Society*, 1949.†

* * *

BRETSCHER, Paul G(erhardt) 1921-

PERSONAL: Born November 29, 1921, in Milwaukee, Wis.; son of Paul M. (a professor) and Minnie (Spohn) Bretscher; married Marguerite Melcher, August 4, 1946; children: Prisca, Bethel, Paul, Jr., Sarah, Monica, Rachel, Joel, Seth, Nathan, Matthew. *Education:* Concordia Seminary, St. Louis, Mo., B.D., 1945, S.T.M., 1964, Th.D., 1966; Washington University, St. Louis, Mo., M.A., 1946. *Home:* 752 Dove Dr., Valparaiso, Ind. 46383.

CAREER: Ordained minister in Lutheran Church, 1945; Concordia Seminary, Springfield, Ill., instructor in mathematics and science, 1946-47; Lutheran High School, St. Louis, Mo., instructor in languages and history, 1947-48; pastor in New Orleans, La., 1948-58; Valparaiso University, Valparaiso, Ind., assistant professor, 1958-66, associate professor of theology, 1966-69; Immanuel Lutheran Church, Valparaiso, pastor, 1969—. Member of Missouri Synod Commission on Theology and Church Relations of the Lutheran Church, 1967-75. *Member:* Society of Biblical Literature, Lutheran Academy for Scholarship.

WRITINGS: *The World Upside Down or Rightside Up?*, Concordia, 1965; *The Holy Infection*, Concordia, 1969; *After the Purifying*, Lutheran Education Association, 1975; *Cain, Come Home!*, Clayton Publishing, 1976; *The Sword of the Spirit*, Evangelical Lutherans in Mission, 1979; *The Mystery of Oneness*, Parish Leadership Seminars, 1980; *The Foolishness of God*, Immanuel Curriculum, 1981. Contributor to *Concordia Theological Monthly*, *Currents in Theology and Mission*, *Journal of Biblical Literature*, and *Lutheran World*.

SIDELIGHTS: Paul G. Bretscher has reading competence in Latin, German, Hebrew, Greek, and French.

* * *

BRIN, Ruth Firestone 1921-

PERSONAL: Born May 5, 1921, in St. Paul, Minn.; daughter of Milton P. and Irma (Cain) Firestone; married Howard B. Brin (a business executive), August 6, 1941; children: Judith, Arthur, David, Deborah. *Education:* Vassar College, B.A., 1941; University of Minnesota, M.A., 1972. *Religion:* Jewish. *Home:* 2861 Burnham Blvd., Minneapolis, Minn. 55416.

CAREER: Writer. Has taught at Macalester College and University of Minnesota. *Member:* National Council of Jewish Women, Urban League, League of Women Voters, Phi Beta Kappa.

WRITINGS: *A Time to Search*, Jonathan David, 1959; *Interpretations for the Weekly Torah Reading*, Lerner, 1965; *A Rag of Love*, Emmett, 1969; *Butterflies Are Beautiful* (juvenile), Lerner, 1974; *The Story of Esther* (juvenile), Lerner, 1976; *David and Goliath* (juvenile), Lerner, 1977; *Contributions of American Women: Social Reform*, Dillon, 1977; *The Shabbat Catalogue*, KTAV, 1978; *Minnesota Wildflowers* (juvenile), Nodin, 1982.

Work appears in anthologies. Contributor of articles and book reviews to *Minneapolis Star and Tribune* and *Reconstructionist;* also contributor of verse, articles, and fiction to Jewish and secular magazines.

SIDELIGHTS: Prayers from *Interpretations* have been reprinted in prayer books published by both the Conservative and Reform Jewish movements in the United States.

* * *

BRISCOE, Jill (Pauline) 1935-

PERSONAL: Born June 29, 1935, in Liverpool, England; came to United States in 1970; daughter of William A. (a motor trader) and Peggy (Pont) Ryder; married Stuart Briscoe (a clergyman), July 26, 1958; children: David, Judith, Peter. *Education:* Homerton College, Cambridge, teacher's diploma, 1958. *Religion:* Christian. *Residence:* Brookfield, Wis. *Office:* Elmbrook Church, Waukesha, Wis. 53186.

CAREER: Writer and lecturer. Grade school teacher in Liverpool, England, 1958-60; Capernwray Missionary Fellowship of Torch Bearers, Lancaster, England, missionary with youth mission, 1960-70, superintendent of youth club and nursery school, 1965-70; director of "Telling the Truth," a multimedia ministry.

WRITINGS: *There's a Snake in My Garden* (autobiography of work among British teenagers), Zondervan, 1975; *Prime Rib and Apple,* Zondervan, 1979; *Here Am I, Send Aaron,* Victor Books, 1979; *Hush, Hush,* Zondervan, 1979; *A Time for Giving,* Ideals Publishing, 1979; *A Time for Living,* Ideals Publishing, 1980; *Thank You for Being a Friend,* Doubleday, 1981; *Fight for the Family,* Zondervan, 1981; *How to Fail Successfully,* Revell, 1982. Also author of greeting cards and taped lectures.

SIDELIGHTS: Jill Briscoe writes: "After twelve years working full time with European youth . . . my heart is with those who will live in the somewhat frightening but challenging future. I want to challenge them to a philosophy of Christian discipleship I believe is the answer to the world's problems." *Avocational interests:* "Travelling round the world talking to kids and parents wherever they are and wherever I can."

* * *

BRISTOW, Allen P. 1929-

PERSONAL: Born July 11, 1929, in Kearney, Neb.; son of George P. and Mary (Nye) Bristow; married Patricia Ann DeWeber; children: Bradley, Scott, Teresa. *Education:* Los Angeles Valley College, A.A., 1952; Los Angeles State College of Applied Arts and Sciences (now California State University, Los Angeles), B.S., 1952; University of Southern California, M.S., 1957. *Home address:* P.O. Box 941, Palos Verdes Estates, Calif. 90274.

CAREER: San Fernando Police Department, San Fernando, Calif., police officer, 1952-53; Los Angeles County Sheriff's Department, Los Angeles, Calif., 1953-59, began as deputy, became sergeant; California State University, Los Angeles, 1959—, began as assistant professor, professor of police science, 1967—. Part-time or visiting professor at University of Hawaii, University of Southern California, Los Angeles Harbor College, and Orange Coast College. Developer and director of police training institutes, 1960—; consultant to President's Commission on Law Enforcement and Administration of Justice, 1966. *Military service:* U.S. Army, Corps of Military Police, 1950-51. *Member:* International Association of Polygraph Examiners (vice-president, 1962), Academy of Criminal Justice Sciences, Southern California Police Training Officers Association, California State Peace Officers Association.

WRITINGS: Police Decision Making, Donner Foundation, University of Southern California, 1957; *Field Interrogation,* C. C Thomas, 1958, 2nd edition, 1964; *Analysis of Chart and Graph Tests,* Davis Publishing (San Francisco), 1959; (with E. Carol Gabard) *Decision Making in Police Administration,* C. C Thomas, 1961; (with G. Douglas Gourley) *Patrol Administration,* C. C Thomas, 1961; *Police Film Guide,* Police Research Associates, 1962, 2nd edition, 1968; (editor) *Readings in Police Supervision,* Los Angeles State College Foundation, 1963; (with John B. Williams) *Criminal Procedure and the Administration of Justice,* Police Research Associates, 1964, 2nd edition, Glencoe, 1966; *Effective Police Manpower Utilization,* C. C Thomas, 1969; (with Willis Roberts) *Introduction to Modern Police Firearms,* Glencoe, 1969.

Police Supervision, C. C Thomas, 1971; *Police Disaster Operations,* C. C Thomas, 1972; *Search for an Effective Police Handgun,* C. C Thomas, 1973; *You and the Law Enforcement Code of Ethics,* Davis Publishing, 1976; *Police Unusual Occurrence Management,* Trident Publishers, 1979; *Rural Law Enforcement,* Allyn & Bacon, 1982. Contributor of articles to law enforcement publications. Member of board of editors, *Police,* 1961-72.

WORK IN PROGRESS: The development of visual aids for police science curriculum; *Famous Western Manhunts.*

AVOCATIONAL INTERESTS: Big game bow hunting, fishing.

* * *

BRODERICK, Robert C(arlton) 1913-

PERSONAL: Born June 4, 1913, in North Fond du Lac, Wis.; son of Francis Martin (a railroad conductor) and Martha Agnes (Wheir) Broderick; married Virginia Joanne Gaertner (an artist), July 3, 1941. *Education:* St. Francis Seminary (now St. Francis Seminary School of Pastoral Ministry), Milwaukee, Wis., B.A., 1934, M.A., 1936. *Politics:* "Generally Republican." *Religion:* Roman Catholic. *Home and office:* 660 Parkmoor Dr., Brookfield, Wis. 53005.

CAREER: Bruce Publishing Co., Milwaukee, Wis., fiction editor, 1936-44; managing editor, *Church Property Administration* (magazine), 1945; free-lance writer, 1945—. Currently editorial director, Catholic Publishers, Nashville, Tenn. Member of lecture bureau, National Council of Catholic Men, 1936—; president of board of directors, Catholic Interracial Council, 1963-65. Adviser-consultant to Postal Church Service, Inc., Youngstown, Ohio.

WRITINGS: (With W. Campbell) *Knight of the North,* Bruce, 1943; *Catholic Concise Dictionary,* Bruce, 1944, 2nd revised edition, Franciscan Herald and Catholic Publishers, 1967; *Paul of St. Peter's* (juvenile), Bruce, 1947; *Wreath of Song* (fictional biography of Francis Thompson), Bruce, 1948; *Inside the Bible,* Catechetical Guild Press, 1955; *Catholic Concise Encyclopedia,* Catechetical Guild Press and Golden Books, 1957; *Catholic Layman's Book of Etiquette,* Cathechetical Guild Press, 1957; *Historic Churches of the United States,* Funk, 1958.

Liturgical Renewal and Catholic Devotion, Franciscan Herald and Catholic Publishers, 1966; *The Parish Council Handbook,* Franciscan Herald, 1968; *Encyclopedia Subject Index of the Bible,* Catholic Publishers, 1968; *Your Parish Comes Alive,* Franciscan Herald, 1970; *Your Parish: Where the Action Is,* Franciscan Herald, 1974; *Catholic Encyclopedia,* Thomas Nelson, 1976; *Days of Praise,* Franciscan Herald, 1977; *Pray the Rosary,* Leaflet Missal Press, 1982. General editor, *Catholic Family Liturgical Bible,* Catholic Publishers, 1966—. Contributor to numerous church and general magazines.

WORK IN PROGRESS: A novel, tentatively entitled *The Great Prayer.*

SIDELIGHTS: Robert C. Broderick told *CA:* "Two elements of good writing, both of which are too often missing from present day literary efforts, are good research and good thought. By good thought is meant elevated, meditative thinking, for nothing gives quality to writing as does clear, profound thought."

* * *

BRODIE, Sally
See CAVIN, Ruth (Brodie)

* * *

BROKHOFF, John R(udolph) 1913-

PERSONAL: Born December 19, 1913, in Pottsville, Pa.; son of John H. (a businessman) and Gertrude (Heiser) Brokhoff; married Barbara Barnett (a minister), June 9, 1972. *Education:* Muhlenberg College, A.B., 1935; University of Pennsylvania, M.A., 1938; Lutheran Theological Seminary, Philadelphia, Pa., B.D., 1938. *Home:* 6 Belleview Blvd., A/501, Clearwater, Fla. 33515.

CAREER: Ordained minister of Lutheran Church in America, 1938; assistant pastor in Richmond, Va., 1938-40; pastor in

Marion, Va., 1940-42, Roanoke, Va., 1942-45, Atlanta, Ga., 1945-55, Charlotte, N.C., 1955-62, and Lanadale, Pa., 1962-65; Emory University, Candler School of Theology, Atlanta, professor of homiletics, 1965-79. Guest professor, Emory University, 1950-54; lecturer, Gammon Theological Seminary, 1966. Chairman, United Lutheran Radio Committee, 1948-54; moderator of youth program, Radio WSB, Atlanta, 1953-54, Radio WBT, Charlotte, 1955-56, and WSOC-TV, Charlotte, 1957-59; member of answer panel, "Pastors Face Your Questions," WBTV, Charlotte, 1956-62. Member of executive committee, Lutheran Synod of North Carolina, 1959-62; member of executive board, North Carolina Council of Churches, 1962. Member of board of trustees, Lutheran Children's Home of the South, 1951-54; secretary of board of trustees, Protestant Radio Center, Inc., 1959-62; member of board of directors, Academy of Preachers, Philadelphia Lutheran Seminary. Councillor, National Lutheran Council, 1951-55; member of advisory board, Juvenile Court, Atlanta, 1954; member of consulting committee, United Lutheran Church Department of Architecture, 1956-62.

MEMBER: Evangelical Ministers Association of Atlanta (president, 1948), Atlanta Christian Council (president, 1950-52), Atlanta Lutheran Pastors' Association (president, 1953), Mecklenburg Christian Ministers' Association (president, 1960), Charlotte Lutheran Pastors' Association (president, 1957-59), Omicron Delta Kappa, Tau Kappa Alpha, Alpha Kappa Alpha. *Awards, honors:* George Washington Medal from Freedoms Foundation for sermon, "Human Rights or Duties?"; D.D., Muhlenberg College, 1951.

WRITINGS—Published by C.S.S. Publishing, except as indicated: *Read and Live: A Study Dealing with How to Use the Bible,* Muhlenberg Press, 1953; *This Is Life,* Revell, 1959; *This Is the Church,* Lutheran Church Press, 1964; *Defending My Faith,* two volumes, Lutheran Church Press, 1966; *Table for Lovers,* 1974; (contributor) Charles L. Wallis, compiler, *Eighty-Eight Evangelistic Sermons,* Baker Book, 1974; *If Your Dearest Should Die,* 1975; *Wrinkled Wrappings,* 1975; *Lectionary Preaching Workbook,* Series C, 1979; *Lectionary Preaching Workbook,* Series A, 1980; *Lectionary Preaching Workbook,* Series B, 1981; *The Case of the Missing Body,* 1982; *Luther Lives,* 1982.

Also author of *Youth's World, Christ in the Gospels, Why?,* and *Christian Strategy,* published by Lutheran Church Press; contributor to *Notable Sermons from Protestant Pulpits* and *Preaching the Nativity.* Contributor of articles to *Christian Century Pulpit, Pulpit Digest,* and *New Pulpit Digest.*

* * *

BRONER, E(sther) M(asserman) 1930-

PERSONAL: Born in 1930 in Detroit, Mich.; daughter of Paul and Beatrice Masserman; married Robert Broner (a printmaker); children: Sari, Adam and Jeremy (twins), Nahama. *Education:* Wayne State University, B.A., 1950, M.A., 1962; Union Graduate School, Ph.D., 1978. *Office:* Department of English, Wayne State University, Detroit, Mich. 48202.

CAREER: Wayne State University, Detroit, Mich., 1962—, began as instructor in creative writing, currently associate professor and writer in residence. Visiting professor at Haifa University, 1972 and 1975, Hebrew University, Oberlin College, and University of California, Los Angeles. Has conducted writers workshops at Indiana University and State University of New York College at Brockport; has given readings at Sarah Lawrence, Drew University, University of Tulsa, University of California, Los Angeles, University of Southern California, and Pratt Institute; invited to United Nations Institute for research, Oslo, Norway, 1980. Convener of Conference for a Concerned Jewish Faculty, Wayne State University. *Awards, honors:* Two Wayne State University faculty research grants for creative work; Emma Lazarus Shaver Fund grant; O. Henry Awards, second prize, 1968; writing fellowships from *Esquire* magazine, National Endowment for the Arts in literature, 1980, Michigan Council for the Arts, summer, 1981, and Michigan Foundation for the Arts, 1982.

WRITINGS—Fiction, except as indicated: *Journal-Nocturnal and Seven Stories,* Harcourt, 1968; *Her Mothers,* Holt, 1975; *A Weave of Women,* Holt, 1978; (editor with Cathy N. Davidson) *The Lost Tradition: Mothers and Daughters in Literature* (essays), Ungar, 1981.

Plays: *Summer Is a Foreign Land* (first produced at Studio Theatre, Wayne State University, 1962), Wayne State University Press, 1966; "Wait Till I Swallow My Saliva" (television play) broadcast on WXYZ-TV, Detroit, Mich., 1968. Also author of film script "Dilatory Ship," and of several one-act plays performed at Raven's Theatre in Birmingham, Mich.

Contributor of numerous short stories, book reviews, and articles to literary magazines, including *North American Review, Commentary, Story Quarterly, Nimrod,* and *New Letters.*

WORK IN PROGRESS: A novel on women in the labor movement, the first book in a trilogy.

SIDELIGHTS: Esther Masserman Broner's early short stories were rejected by male editors who, according to *Monthly Detroit*'s Henrietta Epstein, offered "condescending advice about 'masculine experience' or 'male characterization.'" But, says Epstein, once Broner replaced her given name with the initials E. M. she "discovered she could write on virtually any topic she chose and have her stories accepted for publication." This experience led Broner to make a clear distinction between Esther—"a loving wife, a giving mother, a caring teacher"—and E. M.—a disciplined artist who cuts herself off from "all ordinary contacts and connections." In her writing, as in her life, Broner maintains a feminist point of view: "My work is largely about the unchartered course of women: their history, geneology, pilgrimage, literature, connections, and holidays," she told *CA*.

Each of these subjects is addressed in *A Weave of Women,* which Broner describes in her opening chapter as "the story of sanity and madness in the house of women." A "militant feminist novel," according to *Washington Post*'s Michele Slung, the story concerns the exploits and tribulations of fifteen women who share a communal home in the Old City of Jerusalem. Together the women, who come from all parts of the world, invent new ceremonies, which include ways of exorcising demons, getting married, and burying the dead. In all their actions, the women oppose the state and the rabbinate for what official politics and religion have done to women.

New York Times critic John Leonard describes the novel as "an astonishment," in which Broner "seeks nothing less than to achieve, in a kind of epic poem, a recapitulation of the rhythms of female consciousness." Though he notes similarities between her work and that of eminent feminists Marge Piercy, Doris Lessing, and Monique Wittig, he points out one crucial difference: "Miss Broner is interested in health; she proposes a myth of nurture." Praising her ability to create a "geography" as well as an ideology, Leonard continues: "Not the least of her accomplishments is this sense of place, of fact, on which the mysticism drapes itself.... When such ... a way with detail joins with a sneaky sense of humor, we are no longer in the countries of Marge Piercy, Monique Wittig, and Doris Lessing. War and madness yield to healing and music. Humor is subversive, just as beauty is beyond discussion. [The story's] rhythm, its heartbeat, is renewal."

Nation's Sheila Schwartz also offers high praise for the book: "*A Weave of Women* is an extraordinary novel, an original and beautiful work, musical in its conception, dreamlike in form, terrible, wonderful, and haunting." Describing the book as "an extended epic poem," she postulates that it "should become a classic."

Not all the reviewers are so unequivocal in their praise. *New York Times Book Review* writer Jane Larkin Crain admires *A Weave of Women*'s "narrative drive," but ultimately dismisses the work as "an essentially silly book, stuffed with all the cant of contemporary sexual politics." Michele Slung of the *Washington Post*, on the other hand, accepts Broner's treatment of subject but criticizes the way she has structured the story. "The presence of so many equal characters is distracting and the movement is not always smooth," Slung says. Despite these flaws, she commends Broner's efforts, concluding that the book has "enough moments of vulnerability, triumph and epiphany so that a woman reader may find herself, in spite of herself, being won over to the sensibility of its motley sisterhood."

BIOGRAPHICAL/CRITICAL SOURCES: New York Times Book Review, September 29, 1968, August 13, 1978; *Saturday Review*, November 23, 1968; *Detroit News*, October 23, 1975; *Washington Post*, June 3, 1978; *New York Times*, July 25, 1978; *Nation*, November 4, 1978; *Monthly Detroit*, February, 1980; *Contemporary Literary Criticism*, Volume XIX, Gale, 1981.

* * *

BROOMSNODDER, B(radley) MacKinley 1940-

PERSONAL: Born April 1, 1940, in Pittsborough, N.D.; son of MacKinley (a silkworm breeder) and Bertha (Pansy) Broomsnodder; married Ducilla Farnsworth (a ballet dancer), April 1, 1962 (divorced, 1981); children: Bradley MacKinley, Jr. *Education:* Attended public schools in Pittsborough, N.D. *Religion:* Animist. *Home:* 221 Lewiston Rd., Grosse Pointe Farms, Mich. 48236.

CAREER: Worked as assistant silk collector in father's silkworm factory, Pittsborough, N.D., 1957-60; wrote, illustrated, and edited own newspaper, *Pittsborough Weekly Sentinel* (now defunct), Pittsborough, 1958-61; silk farmer and free-lance writer in Michigan, 1961—. Part-time assistant to the manager of the shell collection, Pittsborough Museum of Natural History, 1958-61.

WRITINGS: The Art of Shell Collection and Classification, Peabody, 1961; *Humbert and Hubert: A Tale of Two Silkworms* (juvenile), Peabody, 1961; *Oneness: The Reality of the Psychedelic Soul*, privately printed, 1962; *The Soul and the Silkworm* (a fantasy), privately printed, 1963; *Perhaps to Dream: An Inspiration*, privately printed, 1965; *Shell We Dance?: Shell Collecting for All Ages*, Peabody, 1968; *The Silkworm Breeder's Handbook*, Pittsborough Museum of Natural History, 1970; *Conqueror Worm: The Story of Silk through the Ages*, Pittsborough Museum of Natural History, 1973, revised edition published as *Silk of Ages*, Peabody, 1977; (with D. Smither) *Silk in the Home: Theoretical Bases and Practical Applications*, Homesteaders Press, 1976; (contributor with Ernie Schwartz) Smither, editor, *The Silkman: Essays in Honor of Ned Schwartz*, Peabody, 2nd edition published as *Man of Silk*, two volumes, 1979; (with Sara Wooley) *Silk Education: One Hundred Uses and Abuses of Nature's Homespun Fun*, Stimulus Corp., 1981; (with Ducilla F. Broomsnodder) *Silk, Sin, and Eros: An Exchange*, Homesteaders Press, 1982. Contributor to professional journals.

WORK IN PROGRESS: More research into unusual uses of silk and silk-based products; a monograph, *Silk and Migrant Labor*, for Pittsborough Museum of Natural History.

SIDELIGHTS: B. MacKinley Broomsnodder told *CA* that he has been fascinated with silk since his boyhood on his father's farm. "People don't realize how important silk has been throughout our cultural history," Broomsnodder writes. "Perhaps my books will help enlighten the educated public as to this fact. If one person learns anything about silk, my work, I feel, will have been of value."

AVOCATIONAL INTERESTS: Shell collecting, doodling, dancing.

* * *

BROSSARD, Chandler 1922- (Daniel Harper)

PERSONAL: Born July 18, 1922, in Idaho Falls, Idaho; married, 1948 (divorced, 1978); married, 1978; children: (first marriage) two; (second marriage) one. *Education:* Self-educated (left school at age 11). *Residence:* New York, N.Y.

CAREER: Novelist and playwright. *Washington Post*, Washington, D.C., reporter, 1940-42; *New Yorker*, New York City, writer and editor, 1942-43; *Time*, New York City, senior editor, 1944; *Coronet*, New York City, assistant managing editor, 1944-45; *American Mercury*, New York City, executive editor, 1950-51; *Look*, New York City, senior editor, 1956-67; Old Westbury College, Oyster Bay, Long Island, N.Y., associate professor, 1968-70; University of Birmingham, Birmingham, England, visiting professor, 1970-71; New School for Social Research, New York City, lecturer, 1971-72; Schiller College, Paris, France, lecturer, 1975-76; University of California, Riverside, writer-in-residence, 1977; San Diego State University, San Diego, Calif., writer-in-residence, 1977-78. Adjunct professor at Fairleigh Dickinson University and C. W. Post College, spring, 1968.

WRITINGS—Novels, except as indicated: *Who Walk in Darkness*, New Directions, 1952; *The Bold Saboteurs*, Farrar, Straus, 1953; *All Passion Spent*, Popular Library, 1954, published as *Episode with Erika*, Belmont Books, 1963; (under pseudonym Daniel Harper) *The Wrong Turn*, Avon, 1954; (under pseudonym Daniel Harper) *The Double Vision*, Dial, 1960; *The Girls in Rome*, New American Library, 1961; *The Insane World of Adolf Hitler* (nonfiction), Fawcett, 1966; *Love Me, Love Me*, Fawcett, 1966; *The Spanish Scene* (nonfiction), Viking, 1968; *A Man for All Women*, Sphere Books, 1971; *Wake Up, We're Almost There*, Baron, 1971; *Did Christ Make Love?*, Bobbs-Merrill, 1973; *Dirty Books for Little Folks* (stories), Cointe (Paris), 1978; *Raging Joys, Sublime Violations* (fiction), Cherry Valley, 1981.

Editor: *The Scene Before You: A New Approach to American Culture*, Rinehart, 1955; *Eighteen Best Stories by Edgar Allan Poe*, Dell, 1965.

Plays—All produced in St. Louis, Mo.: "Harry the Magician," 1961; "Some Dreams Aren't Real," 1962; "The Man with Ideas," 1962; "The Test of True Friendship," 1962.

BIOGRAPHICAL/CRITICAL SOURCES: Max Gartenberg and Gene Feldman, editors, *The Beat Generation and the Angry*

Young Men, Citadel, 1958; Seymour Krim, editor, *The Beats,* Fawcett, 1960.

* * *

BROWN, Arthur Wayne 1917-

PERSONAL: Born April 20, 1917, in Sheslequin, Pa.; son of Arthur Linwood and Helen (LeClair) Brown; married Dorothy Johnston. *Education:* University of Scranton, A.B., 1937; Cornell University, M.A., 1938; Syracuse University, Ph.D., 1950. *Home:* 4425 Monserrate St., Coral Gables, Fla. 33146. *Office:* College of Arts and Science, University of Miami, Coral Gables, Fla.

CAREER: Monmouth College, West Long Branch, N.J., member of faculty, 1940-46, chairman of English department, 1940-45, assistant dean, 1945-46; Syracuse University, Syracuse, N.Y., instructor in English, 1946-48; Utica College, Utica, N.Y., professor of English, 1948-63, chairman of department, 1948-62, chairman of division of languages, 1960-62; Adelphi University, Garden City, N.Y., professor, chairman of English department, and director of Institute of Humanities, 1963-65, president, 1965-67; Fordham University, Bronx, N.Y., dean of Graduate School, 1967-69, vice-president of academic affairs, 1968-69; Marygrove College, Detroit, Mich., president, 1969-72; Bernard M. Baruch College of the City University of New York, New York, N.Y., professor of English and dean of School of Liberal Arts and Sciences, 1972-77; University of Miami, Coral Gables, Fla., dean of College of Arts and Science, 1977—. *Member:* Modern Language Association of America, American Association of University Professors, College English Association, American Studies Association. *Awards, honors:* American Council of Learned Societies grant-in-aid, 1961; L.H.D., University of Scranton, 1965; LL.D., Hofstra University, 1966.

WRITINGS: Always Young for Liberty, Syracuse University Press, 1956; *William Ellery Channing,* Twayne, 1961; *Margaret Fuller,* Twayne, 1964; *Puritanism in America, 1620-1750,* G. K. Hall, 1977; *Albion Small,* G. K. Hall, 1978; *Karl Marx,* G. K. Hall, 1978. Co-editor of "Great American Thinkers" series, sixteen volumes, Washington Square Press, 1963-68. Editor of "World Leaders" series, twenty-one volumes, G. K. Hall, 1968-82.

* * *

BROWN, David
See MYLLER, Rolf

* * *

BROWN, Theo W(atts) 1934-

PERSONAL: Born October 11, 1934, in Melbourne, Australia; son of Albert Henry (a radio technician) and Constance (Chapman) Brown. *Education:* Educated in Australia. *Home:* 21 Woodlands Rd., East Lindfield, New South Wales 2070, Australia. *Office:* Australian Division, World Life Research Institute, P.O. Box 26, Newport Beach, New South Wales 2106, Australia; and P.O. Box 125, Roseville, New South Wales 2069, Australia.

CAREER: Police officer and diver for Western Australian Police and Northern Territory Police Forces, 1954-57, 1959; Australian Deep Sea Diving and Salvage Service, Roseville, New South Wales, Australia, founder and director, 1957-77; World Life Research Institute, Colton, Calif., research associate, 1968—, director designate of Australian Division, Newport Beach, New South Wales, 1976—. Research associate, Medical Oceanographic Branch, Institute of Medical Research, Papeete, Tahiti, 1967—, and Academy of Applied Science, Boston, Mass., 1978—; research affiliate, School of Biological Sciences, University of Sydney, 1969-73. Consultant to South Pacific Commission and United Nations. *Military service:* Australian Army, 1954-56; received Silver Medal for Bravery. *Member:* Australian Surf Life Saving Association, Australian Society of Authors.

WRITINGS: Crown of Thorns: The Death of the Great Barrier Reef?, Angus & Robertson, 1972; *Sharks: The Search for a Repellent,* Angus & Robertson, 1973, published as *Sharks: The Silent Savages,* Little, Brown, 1975; *The Boy and the Shark,* Atarku Publishing, 1979. Contributor of about a thousand articles to scientific publications, popular magazines, and newspapers.

WORK IN PROGRESS: Three books, *The Creatures of Loch Ness, The Oceans: Man's Last Frontier on Planet Earth,* and *Egypt: The Past, Present and Future;* research on shark repellents, including a sonic approach to shark and fish attractants and repellents, on marine pollution, Crown of Thorns starfish infestation of the Indo-Pacific region, aquaculture, and scientific investigations at Loch Ness, Northern Scotland.

SIDELIGHTS: Theo Brown lists his major concerns as "protection of human life at sea; assisting man to meet future food requirements; protection, preservation and conservation of the marine environment." He told *CA:* "Originally I started writing to keep the general public informed of possible or existing environmental problems, together with scientific research projects within the scope of my expertise, that could directly or indirectly alter their way of life, or affect their physical or mental well-being. I soon encountered strong opposition to this approach from the 'scientific establishment,' a body of influential academics seeking to maintain a veil of secrecy over much of their activities. Publicity seemed to be a dirty world, and to be subject to public scrutiny, unthinkable, perhaps because any blunders one might make could be safely hidden from the ill-informed public sector. The royalties from my books and other literary efforts were soon making a significant contribution to the funding of my scientific research projects, and I was tempted to move into fiction writing, a plan that was quickly abandoned. The documentation of fact is a relatively easy literary pursuit, whereas to conceive and complete a novel requires considerable creative talents."

Brown explains his involvement in a recent Loch Ness project: "During 1978, I received a grant from the Literature Board of the Australia Council to visit Northern Scotland and undertake background research for a book on the legendary creatures of Loch Ness. This, in turn, led to an ongoing scientific project to establish the existence, or otherwise, of the so-called 'Loch Ness Monsters'. An entirely new approach was subsequently developed to probe the mystery of Loch Ness. Pressure-sensitive underwater corridors are being established across the loch, in the areas where the greatest numbers of 'monster' sightings have been recorded. The data obtained from the underwater sensing units will be transmitted to specially programmed computer banks for analysis. Being a passive kind of research, life forms in the loch will be unable to detect and avoid the pressure-sensitive corridors, which will remain activated for at least a year. This should provide sufficient quantitative and other data to determine if unknown life forms do frequent Loch Ness."

Brown also informed *CA* of his plans for work in another field: "Before entering the marine sciences in 1960 I was studying Egyptology, a field that has always held a great fascination for me. It now appears that the wheel is about to complete a full turn as I commence the final negotiations for a research programme with the Egyptian government's Institute of Oceanic Sciences and Fisheries.''

* * *

BROWNING, Norma Lee 1914-

PERSONAL: Born November 24, 1914, in Spickard, Mo.; daughter of Howard R. and Grace (Kennedy) Browning; married Russell J. Ogg, June 12, 1938. *Education:* University of Missouri, B.J. and A.B. (with distinction), both 1937; Radcliffe College, M.A., 1938. *Home:* 226 Morongo Rd., Palm Springs, Calif. 92262.

CAREER: Writer. *Chicago Tribune*, Chicago, Ill., reporter and feature writer, 1944-66, Hollywood correspondent, 1966-75. News and travel lecturer for Colston Leigh Bureau, 1957-67. Faculty adviser at Interlochen Arts Academy and editorial consultant to National Music Camp (Interlochen, Mich.), 1960-67. *Member:* Mortar Board (president, 1937), Theta Sigma Phi, Kappa Tau Alpha, Alpha Chi Omega. *Awards, honors:* E. S. Beck Award in reporting from *Chicago Tribune*, 1949.

WRITINGS: City Girl in the Country and Other Stories, Regnery, 1955; *Joe Maddy of Interlochen*, foreword by Van Cliburn, Regnery, 1963; (with W. Clement Stone) *The Other Side of the Mind*, Prentice-Hall, 1964; *The Psychic World of Peter Hurkos*, Doubleday, 1970; (with Louella Dirksen) *The Honourable Mr. Marigold: My Life with Everett Dirksen*, Doubleday, 1972; (with Ann Miller) *Miller's High Life*, Doubleday, 1972; *Peter Hurkos: I Have Many Lives*, Doubleday, 1976; *The Borderline World of Sydney Omar*, Doubleday, 1977; (with George Masters) *The Masters Way to Beauty*, Dutton, 1977; (with Russell Ogg) *He Saw a Hummingbird*, Dutton, 1978; (with Florence Lowell) *Be a Guest at Your Own Party*, M. Evans, 1980; *Facelifts: Everything You Always Wanted to Know*, Doubleday, 1982. Contributor to national magazines, including *Saturday Evening Post* and *Reader's Digest*.

BIOGRAPHICAL/CRITICAL SOURCES: Editor & Publisher, August 6, 1949; *Time*, December 12, 1949.

* * *

BUBB, Mel
See WHITCOMB, Ian

* * *

BUBE, Richard H. 1927-

PERSONAL: Born August 10, 1927, in Providence, R.I.; son of Edward Neser and Ella (Baltteim) Bube; married Betty Jane Meeker, October 9, 1948; children: Mark Timothy, Kenneth Paul, Sharon Elizabeth, Meryl Lee. *Education:* Brown University, Sc.B., 1946; Princeton University, M.A., 1948, Ph.D., 1950. *Politics:* Independent. *Religion:* Evangelical Christian. *Home:* 753 Mayfield Ave., Stanford, Calif. 94305. *Office:* Department of Materials Science, Stanford University, Stanford, Calif. 94305.

CAREER: Radio Corporation of America Laboratories, Princeton, N.J., member of research staff, 1948-62; Stanford University, Stanford, Calif., associate professor, 1962-64, professor of materials science and electrical engineering, 1964—, chairman of materials science and engineering, 1975—. Frequent speaker on science and Christianity at colleges and universities. Consultant to many industrial and government electronic laboratories. *Member:* American Physical Society (fellow), American Association for the Advancement of Science (fellow), American Society for Engineering Education, American Scientific Affiliation (fellow; member of executive council, 1964-68; vice-president, 1967; president, 1968), Sigma Xi. *Awards, honors:* Achievement awards for research at Radio Corporation of America Laboratories, 1952, 1957.

WRITINGS: A Textbook of Christian Doctrine, Moody, 1955; *Photoconductivity of Solids*, Wiley, 1960; (editor) *The Encounter between Christianity and Science*, Eerdmans, 1968; *The Human Quest: A New Look at Science and Christian Faith*, Word Books, 1971; *Electronic Properties of Crystalline Solids: An Introduction to Fundamentals*, Academic Press, 1974; *Electrons in Solids: An Introductory Survey*, Academic Press, 1981; *Fundamentals of Solar Cells*, Academic Press, 1983. Contributor of more than two hundred articles, chiefly in fields of photoconductivity, luminescence, and photoelectronic properties of materials, to professional journals; contributor of articles on science and Christianity to magazines. Editor, *Journal of American Scientific Affiliation*, 1969—; associate editor, *Annual Review of Materials Sciences* and *Materials Letters*; member of editorial board, *Solid-State Electronics*.

WORK IN PROGRESS: Science and the Whole Person, for American Scientific Affiliation.

SIDELIGHTS: Richard H. Bube told *CA:* "I started writing when my mother taught me to typewrite at the age of nine, and my friends have sometimes said that a blank piece of paper is an affront to me. A large portion of my writing has been in the professional area of solid-state physics, both in research reporting and in book writing. Because of the symbiotic relationship between myself and the typewriter, I write easily and quickly—how well must be judged by others.

"The written word fascinates me, and I can barely stand to have an idea without writing it down. A main concern of my writing is directed toward the integration of an authentic scientific view of life and an authentic Christian view of life based on the historic Christian faith. This means not only recognizing that the scientific method has its limitations in dealing with life's significant questions and still is a valid and reliable procedure for understanding God's work in the created universe, but also working out in one's person the implications of scientific knowledge and Christian faith in all of the areas of life. We live in a day when the religious tend to reject science, and when the scientific no longer see the relevance of authentic Christian faith. I would serve, with whatever skill I have, to tear down that false dichotomy and thereby to attempt to live out what it means to be a disciple of my Lord and Savior Jesus Christ here and now.''

* * *

BUCHMAN, Dian Dincin

PERSONAL: Born in New York; daughter of Herman B. (a doctor) and Renee (Meyerovici) Dincin; married Herman Buchman (a professor, film makeup man, and writer), February 20, 1949; children: Caitlin Dincin. *Education:* New York University, B.S., 1943, Ph.D., 1978. *Home:* 640 West End Ave., New York, N.Y. 10024. *Agent:* Anita Diamant, 51 East 42nd St., New York, N.Y. 10017.

CAREER: Producer and interviewer for radio show, "Tomorrow's People,'' WABF-FM, New York, N.Y.; researcher, Louis de Rochemont Films; in public relations for Prentice-Hall and Dick Taplinger associates; currently free-lance journalist. Teaches two preventive health courses at State University of New York College at Purchase; instructor and lecturer in alternative health at College of New Rochelle, New Rochelle, N.Y. Participant, health conferences, Harvard Medical School and Seoul, Korea, both 1975. Has made television and radio appearances nationally on health topics, particularly natural and herb aspects. *Member:* American Television Society (executive secretary), American Society of Journalists and Authors (member of executive council; co-chairman of nonfiction workshops, three years; past president), National Association of Science Writers. *Awards, honors:* Outstanding Service Award from Society of Magazine Writers, 1972.

WRITINGS: (Co-author) *Trips: New York City Classes,* New York City Board of Education, 1968; *The Sherlock Holmes of Medicine: Doctor Joseph Goldberger,* Messner, 1969; *The Complete Herbal Guide to Natural Health and Beauty,* Doubleday, 1973; *Organic Makeup,* Ace Books, 1975; *Feel Good/ Look Great,* Scholastic Book Services, 1976; *How to Make Your Dreams Work for You,* Scholastic Book Services, 1978; *The Complete Book of Water Therapy: Five Hundred Ways to Use Our Oldest and Safest Medicine,* Dutton, 1979; *Herbal Medicine: The Natural Way to Get Well and Stay Well,* McKay, 1979. Also author of *SOS: Don't Panic Book,* Scholastic Book Services. Narration writer for series of education films. Contributor of articles to magazines.

SIDELIGHTS: Dian Buchman has interviewed over two hundred individuals for "Tomorrow's People" radio program. *Avocational interests:* Film, travel (has been throughout Europe and much of the Far East).

* * *

BUELL, Victor P(aul) 1914-

PERSONAL: Born October 18, 1914, in McAlester, Okla.; son of Victor Paul (in insurance) and Genevieve (Keller) Buell; married Virginia Stevens, May 16, 1942; children: Elizabeth, Nancy, Victor III. *Education:* Pennsylvania State University, A.B., 1938. *Home:* 9 Bridle Path, Amherst, Mass. 01002. *Office:* School of Business Administration, University of Massachusetts, Amherst, Mass. 01003.

CAREER: Real Silk Hosiery Mills, Indianapolis, Ind., 1938-51, became regional sales manager, marketing research manager, and operations manager; McKinsey & Co., New York, N.Y., marketing consultant, 1951-55; Hoover Co., North Canton, Ohio, manager of Marketing Division, 1955-59; Archer Daniels Midland, Minneapolis, Minn., vice-president, marketing, 1960-64; American Standard, Inc., New York, N.Y., vice-president, marketing, 1964-70; University of Massachusetts—Amherst, professor of marketing, 1970—. Lecturer on marketing and marketing management. Member of board of trustees, Graduate School of Sales Management and Marketing, Syracuse University, 1963-67; director, L. R. Nelson Corp., Peoria, Ill., 1972-80; member of board of governors, Parlin Foundation, 1973-79. Consultant to several corporations including Continental Can, Gulf & Western, and American Standard. *Military service:* U.S. Army, 1941-46; became major.

MEMBER: American Marketing Association (director, 1957-59; vice-president, 1960-61; president, 1968-69), Association of National Advertisers (director), American Management Association (member of planning council, 1970—), Sales and Marketing Executives International, Beta Gamma Sigma, Advertising Club of New York, Union League Club of New York. *Awards, honors:* Alpha Kappa Psi award, 1975, for best article in *Journal of Marketing.*

WRITINGS: (Contributor) *Effective Marketing Action,* Harper, 1958; (contributor) *The Marketing Job,* American Management Association, 1961; *Marketing Management in Action,* McGraw, 1966; (contributor) *Handbook of Business Administration,* McGraw, 1967.

(Editor-in-chief) *Handbook of Modern Marketing,* McGraw, 1970, revised edition, in press; (contributor) Robert Ferber, editor, *Readings in Marketing Research,* Herrero Hermanos Sucesores, 1970; *Changing Practices in Advertising Decision-Making and Control,* Association of National Advertisers, 1973; *The British Approach to Improving Advertising Standards and Practice,* School of Business Administration, University of Massachusetts, 1977; (contributor) *Encyclopedia of Professional Management,* McGraw, 1978; *Organizing for Marketing/Advertising Success in a Changing Business Environment,* Association of National Advertisers, 1982; *Marketing Management and Strategic Planning* (textbook), McGraw, 1983.

Contributor to journals. Editorial adviser, *Journal of Marketing,* 1958-80, and *Industrial Marketing,* 1969-78.

* * *

BULLARD, Oral 1922-

PERSONAL: Born January 24, 1922, in Vassar, Kan.; son of Elvin Lee and Lois Marcia (Howland) Bullard; married Suzanne Stapleford, February 16, 1946; children: Randall, Tracy, Eric Lee. *Politics:* Independent. *Religion:* "I believe in God." *Home:* 12964 Southwest Fifth, Beaverton, Ore. 97005. *Office:* Touchstone Press, 7775 Southwest Cirrus, Beaverton, Ore. 97005.

CAREER: Arcady Press, Portland, Ore., vice-president, 1956-64, president, 1964-66; Irwin-Hodson Co. (printers), Portland, vice-president, 1966-70; Touchstone Press, Beaverton, Ore., founder and president, 1965—. Honorary president, Oregon Printing Industry, 1965. *Military service:* 383rd AAA (AW) Bn., 1943-45; served in United States, Australia, New Guinea, Moluccas, and Philippines.

WRITINGS: Crisis on the Columbia, Touchstone, 1968; *Short Trips and Trails: The Columbia Gorge,* Touchstone, 1974; *The Second Parting,* Lochan Experience, 1980; *Lancaster's Road: The Historic Columbia River Scenic Highway,* T.M.S. Book Service, 1982. Contributor to magazines and newspapers.

WORK IN PROGRESS: A guide to the Columbia River Gorge, for T.M.S. Book Service.

AVOCATIONAL INTERESTS: Travel, conservation, the human potential movement.

* * *

BUNTING, Bainbridge 1913-1981

PERSONAL: Born November 23, 1913, in Kansas City, Mo.; died February 13, 1981; son of William Miller (a merchant) and Ernestine (Bainbridge) Bunting; married Dorelen Feise, 1948; children: Emily, Meredith, Findlay. *Education:* University of Illinois, B.S., 1937; Harvard University, Ph.D., 1952. *Home:* 5021 Guadalupe Tr., Albuquerque, N.M. 87107. *Office:* Department of History, University of New Mexico, Fine Arts Center, Albuquerque, N.M. 87131.

CAREER: University of New Mexico, Albuquerque, assistant professor, 1943-53, associate professor, 1953-60, professor of architectural history, beginning 1960. Director of survey of Cambridge architecture, Cambridge Historical Commission, Cambridge, Mass., summers, 1964-74; trustee, Museum of Albuquerque, beginning 1969; member of Old Town Architectural Review Board, Albuquerque, 1965-75. *Member:* Society of Architectural Historians (member of board of directors), Colonial Art Association of America. *Awards, honors:* Fund for the Advancement of Education faculty grant, 1953-54.

WRITINGS: *Taos Adobes,* Museum of New Mexico Press, 1962; *Houses of Boston's Back Bay: An Architectural History,* Harvard University Press, 1967; *Take a Trip with NMA: An Architectural Guide to Northern New Mexico,* New Mexico Society of Architects, 1970; *Historic Architecture in Cambridge: Old Cambridge,* Cambridge Historical Commission, 1973; *Of Earth and Timbers Made: New Mexico Architecture,* University of New Mexico Press, 1973; *Early Architecture in New Mexico,* University of New Mexico Press, 1976.

WORK IN PROGRESS: *History of Harvard University Architecture,* to be edited, footnoted, and illustrated by Margaret Floyd.†

* * *

BURI, Fritz 1907-

PERSONAL: Born November 4, 1907, in Kernenried, Bern, Switzerland; son of Fritz and Rosalie (Rutschi) Buri; married Elsa Richard, August 7, 1931; children: Ursula, Samuel, Barbara, Dorothea. *Education:* Attended Universities of Basel, Marburg, and Berlin; University of Bern, D.Th., 1934. *Religion:* Evangelical Reform. *Home:* Auf der Alp 3, Basel, Switzerland.

CAREER: Former assistant professor at University of Bern, Bern, Switzerland, and professor of systematic theology at University of Basel, Basel, Switzerland. Guest professor at Drew University, Madison, N.J., 1966-67, International Christian University, Tokyo, 1968-69, Syracuse University, N.Y., 1971, and Iliff School of Theology, Denver, Colo., 1982. Dudleian Lecturer at Harvard University, 1967. Lecturer at universities and institutions in Australia, 1969, Korea, 1978, India, 1979, and China, 1981. Fellow of the Japan Foundation, Kyoto, Japan, 1978-79. Rector, Basler Cathedral. *Military service:* Chaplain. *Awards, honors:* Haller medal.

WRITINGS: *Die Bedeutung der neutestamentlichen Eschatologie fuer die neuere protestantische Theologie,* Max Niehans, 1934; *Clemens Alexandrinus und der paulinische Freiheitsbegriff,* Max Niehans, 1939; *Gottfried Kellers Glaube,* Paul Haupt (Bern), 1944; *Prometheus und Christus: Groesse uns Grenzen von Carl Spittelers religioeser Weltanschauung,* A. Francke, 1945; *Kreuz und Ring: Die Kreuzestheologie des jungen Luther und die Lehre von der ewigen Wiederkunft in Nietzsches "Zarathustra",* Paul Haupt, 1947.

Albert Schweitzer und Karl Jaspers, Artemis, 1950; *Christlicher Glaube in dieser Zeit,* Paul Haupt, 1952, translation by Edward Allen published as *Christian Faith in Our Time,* Macmillan, 1966; *Theologie der Existenz,* Paul Haupt, 1954, translation by Harold H. Oliver and Gerhard Onder published as *Theology of Existence,* Attic Books, 1966; *Theologie der Existentia,* Gaade, 1955; *Dogmatik als Selbstverstaendnis des christlichen Glaubens,* Paul Haupt, Volume I: *Vernunft und Offenvarung,* 1956, Volume II: *Der Mensch und die Gnade,* 1962, Volume III: *Die Transzendenz der Verantwortung in der dreifachen Schoepfung des dreieinigen Gottes,* 1978; *Die Reformation geht weiter,* Paul Haupt, 1956; *Das lebendige Wort,* Herbert Reich (Hamburg), 1957; *Unterricht im christlichen Glauben,* Paul Haupt, 1957; *Der Weg des Glaubens,* Ernst Reinhardt, 1958; *Basler Bekenntnis heute,* Evangelischer Verlag A. G. Zollikon, 1959; *Die Predigt der Saeulen,* Phoebus, 1959.

Gebot und Gebet, Evangelischer Verlag A. G. Zollikon, 1960; *Die Bilder und das Wort am Basler Muenster,* Phoebus, 1961; *Das dreifache Heilswerk Christi und seine Aneignung im Glauben,* Herbert Reich, 1962; *Vermaechtnis der Vaeter: Die Vorsteher der Basler Kirche seit der Reformation,* Pharos (Basel), 1963; *Von Sinn des Leidens: Eine Auslegung des Liedes von leidenden Gottesknecht,* Friedrich Reinhardt, 1963; *Bildnerische Kunst und Theologie,* Basilius Presse, 1964; *Wie koennen wir heute noch verantwortlich vont Gott reden?,* Mohr (Tuebingen), 1967, translation published as *How Can We Speak Responsibly of God?,* Fortress, 1968; *Hoffnung, Wesen und Bewaehrung,* Herbert Reich, 1967; *Denkender Glaube,* Paul Haupt, 1967, translation by Harold H. Oliver published as *Thinking Faith: Steps on the Way to a Philosophical Theology,* Fortress, 1968; *Der Pantokrator: Ontologie und Eschatologie als Grundlage der Lehre von Gott,* Herbert Reich, 1969.

Gott in Amerika, Paul Haupt, Volume I: *Amerikanische Theologie seit 1960,* 1970, Volume II: *Religion, Theologie, und Philosophie seit 1969,* 1972; *Zur Theologie der Verantwortung,* edited by Guenther Hauff, Paul Haupt, 1971; (with Lochman and Ott) *Dogmatik im Dialog,* three volumes, Guettersloh, 1973-76; *Der Buddha-Christus als der Herr des wahren Selbst: Die Religions-philosophie der Kyoto-Schule und das Christentum,* Paul Haupt, 1982.

* * *

BURMAN, Ben Lucien 1896-

PERSONAL: Born December 12, 1896, in Covington, Ky.; son of Sam and Minna B. Burman; married Alice Caddy (illustrator of nineteen of his books), September 19, 1927 (died August 3, 1977). *Education:* Harvard University, A.B., 1920. *Address:* Fifth Avenue Hotel, 24 Fifth Ave., New York, N.Y. 10011.

CAREER: Author. Reporter, *Boston Herald,* 1920; assistant city editor, *Cincinnati Times Star,* 1921; special writer, *New York Sunday World,* 1922; staff contributor, Newspaper Enterprise Association (Scripps-Howard), 1927; war correspondent in Africa and Middle East, 1941. *Military service:* U.S. Army, Field Artillery, World War I; severely wounded at Soissons, France, July, 1918. *Member:* Authors League (former member of board of directors), P.E.N. (former member of board of directors), Overseas Press Club, Dutch Treat Club, Saville Club (London), Players Club.

AWARDS, HONORS: Southern Authors Prize for the most distinguished Southern book of the year, 1938, for *Blow for a Landing;* Thomas Jefferson Memorial Prize, 1945, for *Rooster Crows for Day;* French Legion of Honor for wartime reporting from Africa, 1947; German Young People's Book Festival prize for *High Water at Catfish Bend,* also chosen by New York Public Library as favorite American book of the year for young people; Dutch Treat Club's Gold Medal, 1969, for "distinguished service to American literature"; Donald T. Wright Marine Award from University of Illinois, 1975; named honorary citizen of New Orleans and Natchez, 1979; named honorary ambassador of St. Louis, 1979.

WRITINGS—Many illustrated by wife, Alice Burman: *Mississippi,* Cosmopolitan Book Corp., 1929; *Steamboat Round the Bend,* Farrar & Rinehart, 1933; *Blow for a Landing,* Houghton, 1938; *Big River to Cross: Mississippi Life Today,* John Day, 1940; *Miracle on the Congo: Report from the Free French Front,* John Day, 1942; *Rooster Crows for Day,* Dutton, 1945; *Everywhere I Roam,* Doubleday, 1949.

Children of Noah: Glimpses of Unknown America, Messner, 1951; *High Water at Catfish Bend,* Messner, 1952; *The Four*

Lives of Mundy Tolliver, Mundy, 1953; *Seven Stars for Catfish Bend*, Funk, 1956; *It's a Big Country: America Off the Highways*, Reynal, 1956; *The Street of the Laughing Camel*, McGraw, 1959; *It's a Big Continent*, McGraw, 1961; *The Owl Hoots Twice at Catfish Bend*, Taplinger, 1961; *The Generals Wear Cork Hats*, Taplinger, 1963; *The Sign of the Praying Tiger*, New American Library, 1966; *Blow a Wild Bugle for Catfish Bend*, Taplinger, 1967.

Look Down that Winding River, Taplinger, 1975; *The High Treason at Catfish Bend*, Vanguard Press, 1977; *The Strange Invasion of Catfish Bend*, Vanguard Press, 1980. Regular contributor to *Reader's Digest* and *Saturday Review*.

SIDELIGHTS: The great rivers of America have always played an important role in the life and writings of Ben Lucien Burman. He was born and grew up in Covington, Kentucky, a city located on the banks of the Ohio River, and he later spent much of his time travelling up and down American waterways. Following graduation from college, Burman decided to become a writer. After working several years for newspapers, he returned home and began his successful career of chronicling adventure and life on the Mississippi.

Burman explains to the *New Orleans States* that his books are "my means of looking at the world and having fun with it. We are all children, trying to find our way." He continues: "Twain used exaggeration and I like to needle. I see myself as a genial cynic or a cynical optimist. . . . I've given up on the human race, but I love them."

Expressing his feelings on life as a writer, Burman told *CA*: "The novelist is a curious, cud-chewing animal, unlike the rarest found in any zoo. One moment he must have an ear and skin sensitive as the needle of some super-scientific instrument to record the impulses of his fellows; the next, when others would change or misinterpret his writing, he must possess ears of stone and an elephant's skin.

"Perhaps first of all he must have the eyes of the dragonfly, who, I have heard it said, can see in a thousand directions. Without this power to stand watch upon humanity as it goes its way in folly or wisdom, there is nothing. All is without depth, without universality. For the thousand-eyed novelist, the materials of drama are everywhere. But he must not be like the American tourists I have seen so often cruising in state to Casablanca or Algiers, who stop always in the same fashionable hotels and play bridge each night with the same dull companions, then return home thinking they know North Africa. The pursuit of true knowledge requires discomfort. I think it would be very difficult to be a snob and a good novelist. A bus is closer to the people of a country than a train; a buggy or a horse is closer than a bus. Walking is the closest of all. Out of the mosquito bites, the fleas, the hard beds in a tourist court, and all the varied accidents of the road, there gradually emerges a picture of a region, and an understanding of its inhabitants' philosophy.

"The novelist is a creature of many moods and professions, a jack of every trade. With his characters he must be at once doctor, priest, and devil's advocate. He is comedian, tragedian, villain, clown. He must know when to make his audience laugh and when to make it mourn; he must know when the play is ended and it is the hour to go home.

"As he writes and observes he cannot help but become a philosopher, with his own interpretation of the absurd but ever-fascinating pageant that is the human comedy. He need not hope to alter the universe. But he can hold a mirror up to life, so that men may study their reflections and laugh at their childish vanities.

"The mirror he uses may be of many sorts. His hope can be only one—to make the reflection true."

Burman was the first correspondent during World War II to reach the Free French capital at Brazzaville in French Equitorial Africa. A river light near Baton Rouge has been named in Burman's honor by the Lighthouse Service of the U.S. Coast Guard. His books have been translated into many languages, including Urdu and Vietnamese.

MEDIA ADAPTATIONS: *Mississippi* was made into a film entitled "Heaven on Earth" by Universal in 1929; *Steamboat Round the Bend* was filmed by Twentieth Century-Fox in 1935. The film rights to many of the Catfish Bend books have been sold to Disney Productions. *High Water at Catfish Bend* was chosen by the puppeteer Lou Bunin for his first full-length motion picture since "Alice in Wonderland."

BIOGRAPHICAL/CRITICAL SOURCES: *New York Herald Tribune Book Review*, November 2, 1955; *Miami Herald*, May 25, 1958; *New York Times Book Review*, May 13, 1973; *New Orleans States*, May 31, 1980.

* * *

BURNS, Richard Dean 1929-

PERSONAL: Born June 16, 1929, in Des Moines, Iowa; son of Richard B. (a teacher) and Luella E. Burns; married Frances Regina Sullivan, January 14, 1950; children: Richard Dean III. *Education:* University of Illinois, B.S. (honors), 1957, M.A., 1958, Ph.D., 1960. *Residence:* Claremont, Calif. *Office:* Department of History, California State University, Los Angeles, Calif. 90032; and Regina Books, P.O. Box 280, Claremont, Calif. 91711.

CAREER: Served in U.S. Air Force, 1947-56; California State University, Los Angeles, 1960—, professor of history, 1970—, chairman of department, 1969-72. Publisher, Regina Books. *Member:* Phi Kappa Phi.

WRITINGS: (With Donald Dewey, Eugene Fingerhut, and Samuel McSeveney) *The Continuing Dialogue*, two volumes, Pacific Books, 1964; (editor with Walter R. Fisher) *Armament and Disarmament*, Wadsworth, 1964; (with Donald Urquidi) *Disarmament in Historical Perspective, 1919-1941*, four volumes, Government Printing Office, 1968.

(Compiler with Milton Leitenberg) *The Vietnam Conflict*, Clio, 1973, revised edition (with Milton Leitenberg), 1983; (editor with Edward M. Bennett) *Diplomats in Crisis, 1919-1941*, Clio, 1974; (compiler) *Arms Control and Disarmament: A Bibliography*, Clio, 1977; (editor) *Guide to American Foreign Relations since 1700*, Clio, 1982. Editor of "War/Peace" series, Clio, 1972—. Contributor to political and history journals.

WORK IN PROGRESS: *Harry S. Truman: The Man and the President*.

* * *

BUSCH, Briton Cooper 1936-

PERSONAL: Born September 5, 1936, in Los Angeles, Calif.; son of Niven (an author) and Phyllis (Cooper) Busch; married Deborah Stone, 1958; children: Philip, Leslie. *Education:* Stanford University, A.B., 1958; University of California, Berkeley, M.A., 1960, Ph.D., 1965. *Address:* P.O. Box 154, Hamilton, N.Y. 13346. *Office:* Department of History, Colgate University, Hamilton N.Y. 13346.

CAREER: Colgate University, Hamilton, N.Y., instructor and assistant professor, 1963-68, associate professor, 1968-73, professor of history, 1978, William R. Kenan, Jr., Professor, 1978—, chairman of department, 1980—. *Member:* American Historical Association, Middle East Institute, Royal Central Asian Society (fellow), Middle East Studies Association (fellow), American Association of University Professors, North American Society for Oceanic History, Phi Alpha Theta. *Awards, honors:* Woodrow Wilson fellow, 1962-63; National Humanities Research Foundation fellow, 1968; Social Science Research Council fellow, 1969.

WRITINGS: Britain and the Persian Gulf, 1894-1914, University of California Press, 1967; *Britain, India, and the Arabs, 1914-1921,* University of California Press, 1971; *Mudros to Lausanne: Britain's Frontier in West Asia, 1918-1924,* State University of New York Press, 1976; *Hardinge of Penshurst: A Study in the Old Diplomacy,* Archon Press, 1980; *Master of Desolation: The Reminiscences of Captain Joseph J. Fuller,* Mystic Seaport Museum, 1980; *Alta California, 1840-1842: The Journal of William Dane Phelps, Master of the "Alert,"* Arthur H. Clark, in press. Contributor of articles and reviews to historical journals.

WORK IN PROGRESS: The Sealers: A History of the North American Sealing Industry.

* * *

BUTCHER, Russell Devereux 1938-

PERSONAL: Born February 8, 1938, in Bryn Mawr, Pa.; son of Devereux (a writer) and Mary Frances (Taft) Butcher; married Carol Lynne Dunn, February 1, 1958 (divorced March, 1967); married Pamela Richards (a manuscript editor), April 12, 1967; children: (first marriage) Pamela Marie (deceased), Neill D.; (second marriage) Wendy Nan. *Education:* University of Colorado, B.A., 1960; University of Michigan, graduate study of law, 1960-61. *Home and office address:* Box 67, Cottonwood, Ariz. 86326.

CAREER: Sierra Club, San Francisco, Calif., research editor, 1961-65; Save-the-Redwoods League, San Francisco, publicity writer, 1963-65; National Audubon Society, New York, N.Y., conservation specialist and publicity writer, 1965-66; Museum of New Mexico, Santa Fe, chief of public relations and publications, 1967-69; free-lance writer, editor, photographer, and public relations representative, 1970-80; Southwest regional representative, National Parks and Conservation Association, 1980—. *Member:* Save-the-Redwoods League (life member), Sierra Club (life member).

WRITINGS: (Self-illustrated) *Maine Paradise: Mount Desert Island and Acadia National Park,* Viking, 1973; *New Mexico: Gift of the Earth,* Viking, 1975; *The Desert,* introduction by Morris K. Udall, Viking, 1976; *Field Guide to Acadia National Park, Maine,* Reader's Digest Press, 1977. Contributor to periodicals, including *Down East* and *New York Times.*

SIDELIGHTS: Russell Devereux Butcher writes: "Travel, geography, and natural history are my main interests, with protection of the environment an underlying motivation. All my articles and books at least 'soft-sell' the need to conserve the environment, and many of my articles and editorials focus exclusively on some particular conservation problem. I have traveled throughout the United States and to the parks and nature reserves of the Alps region of Europe. Also . . . Canada, the West Indies, and Mexico.

"My current work—with my wife Pam hired as Assistant Southwest Regional Representative—takes us to most of the seventy-seven units of the National Park System in the Southwest and California, striving to further the goals of the private nonprofit National Parks and Conservation Association: to help promote the protection and public understanding of the national parks."

AVOCATIONAL INTERESTS: Hiking, canoeing, bird-watching, identification of wildflowers and all forms of plant life.

* * *

BUTLER, Richard 1925-

PERSONAL: Born April 29, 1925, in Liverpool, England; son of Arthur Odessa (an insurance salesman) and Elizabeth (Buck) Butler; married Patricia Lee Holden (a bank officer), January 28, 1956; children: Miles John, Charles Richard. *Education:* Attended Chester College, 1948-50. *Residence:* Victoria, Australia.

CAREER: Writer. Teacher of English and French in schools in England and Australia, 1950-73; professional television actor. *Military service:* Royal Air Force, 1943-47; became flight lieutenant. *Member:* Fellowship of Australian Writers, Australian Society of Authors.

WRITINGS—Novels: Fingernail Beach, John Long, 1964; *More Dangerous Than the Moon,* Walker & Co., 1967 (published in England as *South of Hell's Gates,* John Long, 1967); *Sharkbait,* John Long, 1970; *The Buffalo Hook,* Hutchinson, 1974; *The Men That God Forgot,* Hutchinson (Melbourne), 1975, St. Martin's, 1976; *And Wretches Hang,* Hyland House (Melbourne), 1977, St. Martin's, 1979; *Lift-Off at Satan,* John Long, 1978, St. Martin's, 1979; *Against the Wind,* Corgi Books, 1978, Dell, 1979; *A Blood-Red Sun at Noon,* Collins (Sydney), 1980; *The Devil's Coachman,* Collins, 1981. Also author of "The Doll," a play for television, produced by Crawford Productions, Melbourne, Australia, 1970.

WORK IN PROGRESS: Researching little-known aspects of Australian colonial history.

SIDELIGHTS: Several of Richard Butler's works have been translated into Swedish and Italian.

* * *

BUTZER, Karl W(ilhelm) 1934-

PERSONAL: Born August 19, 1934, in Mulheim-Rhur, Germany; became Canadian citizen; son of Paul A. and Wilhelmine (Hansen) Butzer; married Elisabeth Schloesser, May 12, 1959. *Education:* McGill University, B.Sc. (with honors), 1954, M.Sc., 1955; University of Bonn, Dr. rer. nat. (D.Sc. equivalent), 1957. *Residence:* Flossmoor, Ill. *Office:* Department of Geography, University of Chicago, Chicago, Ill. 60637.

CAREER: Academy of Science and Literature, Germany, research associate in geography, 1957-59; University of Wisconsin—Madison, assistant professor, 1959-62, associate professor of geography, 1962-66; University of Chicago, Chicago, Ill., professor of anthropology and geography, 1966-81; Swiss Federal Institute of Technology, Zurich, Switzerland, chairman of human geography, 1981-82; University of Chicago, Henry Schultz Professor of Environmental Archaeology, 1982—. Director, Alexanders Fontein Project, Kimberley, South Africa, 1974-75, and Beniali Research Project, Valencia, Spain, 1981-83. *Awards, honors:* Citation, Association of American Geographers, 1968, for *Environment and Archaeology;* Busk Medal, Royal Geographical Society; Fryxell Medal, Society for American Archaeology; Stopes Medal, Geologists Association of London, 1982.

WRITINGS: Environment and Archeology, Aldine, 1964; (with Carl L. Hansen) *Desert and River in Nubia,* University of

Wisconsin Press, 1969; *Recent History of an Ethiopian Delta*, University of Chicago Press, 1971; *Geomorphology from the Earth*, Harper, 1976; *Early Hydraulic Civilization in Egypt*, University of Chicago Press, 1976; *Dimensions of Human Geography*, University of Chicago Press, 1977; *Archaeology as Human Ecology*, Cambridge University Press, 1982. Contributor of more than 200 articles to scientific journals in North America, Europe, and South Africa. Editor, *Prehistoric Archaeology and Ecology* and *Journal of Archaeological Science*.

WORK IN PROGRESS: An adaptational paradigm for human geography.

SIDELIGHTS: Karl W. Butzer has done field research or been a member of expeditions in Egypt, 1956, Spain, 1957, East Africa, 1967, South Africa, 1969, and Illinois, 1971.

C

**CAGNEY, Peter
    See WINTER, Bevis (Peter)**

*   *   *

CAIN, James M(allahan) 1892-1977

PERSONAL: Born July 1, 1892, in Annapolis, Md.; died October 27, 1977, of a heart attack in University Park, Md.; son of James William (a former president of Washington College) and Rose Cecilia (Mallahan) Cain; married Mary Rebecca Clough, 1920 (divorced); married Elina Sjosted Tyszecka, 1927 (divorced); married Aileen Pringle, 1944 (divorced); married Florence Macbeth Whitwell (an opera singer), 1947 (deceased). *Education:* Washington College, A.B., 1910, A.M., 1917. *Politics:* Democrat. *Home:* 6707 44th Ave., University Park, Hyattsville, Md. 20782.

CAREER: Journalist and writer. *Baltimore American,* Baltimore, Md., staff member, 1917-18; *Baltimore Sun,* Baltimore, reporter, 1919-23; St. John's College, Annapolis, Md., professor of journalism, 1923-24; *New York World,* New York City, editorial writer, 1924-31; *New Yorker,* New York City, managing editor, beginning 1931; screenwriter in Hollywood, Calif., 1932-48. *Military service:* U.S. Army, American Expeditionary Forces, 1918-19; served as editor-in-chief of *Lorraine Cross,* official newspaper of the 79th Division.

WRITINGS—Novels, except as indicated: *Our Government* (sketches), Knopf, 1930; *The Postman Always Rings Twice* (also see below), Knopf, 1934, reprinted, Lightyear, 1981; *Serenade* (also see below), Knopf, 1937, reprinted AMS Press, 1981; *Mildred Pierce* (also see below), Knopf, 1941, reprinted, Lightyear, 1981; *Love's Lovely Counterfeit,* Knopf, 1942, reprinted, Vintage Books, 1979; *Double Indemnity* (also see below), Avon, 1943, reprinted Vintage Books, 1978; *Three of a Kind* (also see below; includes "Career in C Major," "The Embezzler," and "Double Indemnity"), Knopf, 1943; *Cain Omnibus: The Postman Always Rings Twice, Serenade, Mildred Pierce,* World, 1946; *The Embezzler* (also see below), New Avon Library, 1944; (editor) *For Men Only* (short stories), World, 1944; *Past All Dishonor,* Knopf, 1946; *The Butterfly,* Knopf, 1947, reprinted, Vintage Books, 1979; *Sinful Woman* (also see below), Avon, 1947; *The Embezzler* [and] *Double Indemnity,* Triangle Books, 1948; *The Moth,* Knopf, 1948, abridged edition, New American Library, 1950; *Jealous Woman* (also see below), Avon, 1950; *Galatea,* Knopf, 1953; *The Root of His Evil,* R. Hale, 1954, published as *Shameless,* Avon, 1979; *Jealous Woman* [and] *Sinful Woman,* R. Hale, 1955.

Mignon, Dial, 1962; *The Magician's Wife,* Dial, 1965; *Cain x 3: Three Novels* (*The Postman Always Rings Twice, Mildred Pierce,* and *Double Indemnity;* a Book-of-the-Month selection), introduction by Tom Wolfe, Knopf, 1969; *Three Novels by James M. Cain: Double Indemnity, The Postman Always Rings Twice, Serenade,* Bantam, 1973; *Rainbow's End,* Mason/Charter, 1975; *The Institute,* Mason/Charter, 1976; *Hard Cain* (includes *Sinful Woman, Jealous Woman,* and *The Root of His Evil*), introduction by Harlan Ellison, Gregg, 1980; *The Baby in the Icebox and Other Short Fiction,* edited by Roy Hoopes, Holt, 1981.

Plays: "The Postman Always Rings Twice," (based on his novel of the same title), first produced on Broadway, February 25, 1936.

Also author of "Two Can Sing," 1938, published as "Career in C Major" in *Three of a Kind,* Knopf, 1943.

WORK IN PROGRESS: An autobiography.

SIDELIGHTS: When James M. Cain moved to Hollywood to become a screenwriter, he had already run the gamut of writing careers. Behind him lay stints as a newspaper reporter, a professor of journalism at St. John's College, an editorial writer for Walter Lippmann, and the managing editor of the *New Yorker* magazine. And yet none of his efforts had fully taken hold; his career in journalism had been "fragmented and inconclusive," according to Kevin Starr, who reported in *New Republic* that Cain "was on the way to becoming just another hard-drinking Irish-American journalist with baffled aspirations in the direction of literature." And then, in 1934, having been fired by Paramount Pictures and in desperate need of money, the 42-year-old writer published his first novel, *The Postman Always Rings Twice.* Described by Cain biographer Roy Hoopes as "one of those rarest of literary achievements in America: a phenomenal best seller that received the highest acclaim from critics," *Postman* brought Cain "out of obscurity and into the literary limelight where he remained for fourteen years."

After *Postman,* Cain wrote *Double Indemnity, Mildred Pierce,* and *Serenade.* These four books earned him a reputation as a "tough-guy" writer or, as David Madden called him in *James M. Cain,* "the twenty-minute egg" of the "hard-boiled" school. "Cain and other hard-boiled writers," Madden explained in his critical study, "wrote not only *about* but mainly *to* the masses, giving violent impetus to their forbidden dreams, dramatizing their darkest temptations and their basic physical drives." His protagonists were the kind of people you read about "almost every day in the newspapers," according to William Rose Benet in *Saturday Review*. "They are chiefly stupid, slightly pathetic, capable of rape, arson, or murder in a sort of dumb, driven way. They have glimmers of decency, passions that overcome them, and are chiefly selfish and morally composed of gelatin while being big, husky brutes to outward view."

Cain resented such categorization. "I don't know what they're talking about—'tough,' 'hard-boiled.' I tried to write as people talk," he told David Zinsser of *Paris Review*. When asked to describe his work, he said: "I, so far as I can sense the pattern of my mind, write of the wish that comes true, for some reason a terrifying concept, at least to my imagination. . . . I think my stories have some quality of the opening of a forbidden box."

What Cain's "forbidden box" contains, according to W. M. Frohock in his *The Novel of Violence in America: 1920-1950*, "invariably turns out to be sex, experienced with perfect animal intensity, sometimes with a little hint of the abnormal or the forbidden about it." Though Cain repeatedly insisted to Zinsser and other interviewers that he took no interest in violence, Frohock argued that "sex, so conceived, is inseparable from violence. Violence is at once associated with the sexual act itself, and made an inevitable accompaniment of anything which tends to frustrate the sexual experience. In addition violence stimulates sexual activity, as in the scene of Nick's murder [in *The Postman Always Rings Twice*]. For Cain, sex and violence are not so much subjects as necessary accessories of the plot." And plot, Frohock continued, is "the essence of the Cain novel."

Chicago Tribune Book World critic David Mamet observed that "the understanding of plot that Cain embraced goes back . . . to Aristotle: Cain discovered the dramatic/tragic plot—discarding narration, exposition, and characterization in favor of event." But unlike the Greek dramas, Cain's books, Frohock argued, do *not* strike a tragic note "because the violence in them is not endowed with any sort of moral significance. We are aware of his violence not as something which we must accept because it is a part of Man's Fate, but as something for a clever writer to play tricks with." For these reasons, Frohock maintained that "nothing he has ever written has been entirely out of the trash category." But Ross Macdonald, writing in the *New York Times Book Review*, disagreed. Citing Cain's ability to transmute "blood into symbol" as the "stuff of art," he concluded that Cain was "a conscious and deliberate artist" whose novel *The Postman Always Rings Twice* had "moral and symbolic overtones."

James T. Farrell in his *Literature and Morality* expressed still another point of view: "Writers like Cain stand between the work of a serious and tragic character which has been fathered in America by such men as [Theodore] Dreiser and the work derived from the more-or-less forgotten writings of Robert W. Chambers, Gene Stratton-Porter, or Harold Bell Wright. And in this in-between, neither-fish-nor-fowl literary medium, James M. Cain has become the master. He is a literary thrill producer who profits by the reaction against the sentimentality of other years and, at the same time, gains from the prestige of more serious and exploratory writing."

While the argument over the seriousness of Cain's work continues, so too does his popularity. *Cain x 3*, a 1969 reprint of his most popular works, *Postman, Double Indemnity*, and *Mildred Pierce*, found a wide audience, as Ross Macdonald observed. "There is," he said, "a new generation of readers for Cain's stories—*Cain x 3* should make its way into the universities." And W. M. Frohock wrote that "in spite of the cheapness which sooner or later finds its way into his novels, an inordinate number of intelligent and fully literate people have read him. He has been translated in many parts of the world, and writers whose stature makes him look stunted have paid him the compliment of imitating him—as Albert Camus did, for example, in *The Stranger*."

In his *Nation* review of *Cain x 3*, Kenneth Lamott explained Cain's continued appeal: "There is the remembered tautness of structure, the absolute control of the well-articulated plot, the cold eye for the essential truth about men and women. The language is spare and clean, only occasionally breaking down into cliche. It is hardly an original observation, but watching Cain at work can still give the reader that particular pleasure that comes from watching a master craftsman, a cabinetmaker fitting a joint, or a potter throwing a pot. I would not go as far as Tom Wolfe, who in his introduction to this book suggests that Norman Mailer might well sit at Cain's feet to learn how to become a *real* novelist, but the spirit of the suggestion is not without merit."

Despite the success of what David Mamet called the "California novels," Cain experienced many bouts of failure in his fiction-writing career. His first effort to write a novel, for example, was a vain attempt as Cain explained to *Paris Review*: "In 1922 when I was still on the *Baltimore Sun*, I took the winter off to go down and work in the mines. I tried to write the Great American Novel, and wrote three of them, none of them any good. I had to come slinking back to work admitting that the Great American Novel hadn't been written."

Six years passed before Cain sold his first piece of fiction—a short story published by H. L. Mencken in the *American Mercury*. Entitled "Pastorale," it was a humorous rendering of a grisly murder, told—according to Roy Hoopes—in the Ring Lardner manner and significant for reasons which he outlined in his *Chicago Tribune Book World* review: "In the first place, Cain now found that he could tell a story in the first person, preferably in the voice of some 'lowlife character,' as his mother called that type. [And in the second,] he also found his favorite theme: Although two people may get away with committing a crime, they cannot live with it."

Encouraged by the success of "Pastorale," Cain continued to write short fiction and his name eventually came to the attention of several Hollywood producers who invited him to California. Since he was unhappy in New York, Cain accepted the offer, moving west in 1931. But his efforts at screenwriting were failures and, as Hoopes reported in his introduction to *The Baby in the Icebox and Other Short Fiction*, "within six months of his arrival in Hollywood, Cain was out of a job in the middle of the Depression, forty years old, and supporting a second wife . . . and her two young children."

Unwilling to return east, Cain took up free-lance writing and, Hoopes reported, "as he drove around in his 1932 Ford roadster, he began to feel more and more that California and its people provided a natural milieu for his writing. And there was one gas station, where he regularly stopped, that provided a spark that would eventually ignite Cain's phenomenal career as a writer of controversial best-sellers. 'Always this bosomy-looking thing comes out—commonplace, but sexy, the kind you have ideas about,' he later told an interviewer. 'We always talked while she filled up my tank. One day I read in the paper where a woman who runs a filling station knocked off her husband. Can it be this bosomy thing? I go by and sure enough the place is closed. I inquire. Yes, she's the one—this appetizing but utterly commonplace woman.'

"He began to think: What about a novel in which a woman and a typical California automobile tramp kill the woman's husband to get his gas station and car? Cain and [his wife] Elina discussed the idea for months, but he was still not ready for a long story. At the same time, he only felt comfortable in his writing when he pretended to be someone else, telling his story in the first person, in the manner of Ring Lardner. . . . So Cain put his idea for a novel in the back of his mind and decided to try another short story. The result was 'The Baby in the Icebox,' and like 'Pastorale,' . . . it was written in the first person, Ring Lardner style. But unlike his earlier stories, 'The Baby in the Icebox' was set in the West and had characters who were western in origin. Suddenly Cain found something happening in his fiction." As Cain reported to *Paris Review*, "Out there in California I began writing in the local idiom. Everything broke for me."

Paramount bought the movie rights to "Icebox" and produced the story as "She Made Her Bed"—the first in a succession of nine Cain stories and novels that would be adapted to the screen. Meanwhile, in New York, H. L. Mencken had shown "Icebox" to Alfred A. Knopf, a prominent publisher, who liked it so much that he encouraged Cain to try his hand at a novel. Cain did, and just six months later, in June 1933, he had a 159-page manuscript which would eventually become *The Postman Always Rings Twice*.

In an interview with *Paris Review*, Cain discussed the origins of the story: "It was based on the Snyder-Grey case, which was in the papers about then. . . . Grey and this woman Snyder killed her husband for the insurance money. Walter Lippmann went to that trial one day and she brushed by him. . . . Walter said it seemed very odd to be inhaling the perfume or being brushed by the dress of a woman he knew was going to be electrocuted. So the Snyder-Grey case provided the basis. The bit influence in *how* I wrote *The Postman Always Rings Twice* was this strange guy, Vincent Lawrence, who had more effect on my writing than anyone else. He had a device which he thought was so important—the 'love rack' he called it. . . . What he meant by the 'love rack' was the poetic situation whereby the audience felt the love between the characters. He called this 'the one, the two, and the three.'"

One time, reported Roy Hoopes in the *Washington Post*, "when Lawrence was talking about his 'love rack,' Cain asked: 'Why couldn't the whole thing be a love rack; why such attention to the one episode where they fall in love?' Cain asked why every episode in the story could not be written with a view to its effect on the love story. Lawrence thought that this had possibilities." So Cain wrote a story about Frank Chambers, a young drifter, who wanders into a diner run by a Greek named Nick and his restless wife, Cora, who is disgusted by Nick's "greasiness." After seeing Cora, Frank agrees to work in the restaurant and they become lovers. Soon Cora convinces Frank to help her murder Nick so that she will inherit his property. Although the first attempt is unsuccessful, their second effort succeeds. But, according to Hoopes, "the murder eventually becomes their love rack, and they are brought to justice when Cora is killed in an automobile accident and Frank is wrongly found guilty of her murder."

The first version of the story was called *Bar-B-Q*, and Knopf turned it down. "At that point," Cain told *Publishers Weekly*, "Lippmann wanted to see the book. He thought he could do something with it. He took it to Macmillan and Macmillan turned it down. Then Lippmann took it back to Knopf and they decided to publish it." But there was one final problem—Knopf did not like the title and wanted it changed. In his *Washington Post* article, Hoopes explained how *Bar-B-Q* was renamed: "Around this time Cain and Lawrence were musing about the agony of sweating out the publication of a first novel and Lawrence told him about sending his first play to a New York producer. Lawrence had been living in Boston then and would go to the window every day to watch for the postman; when he could not stand the waiting, he would go into the back yard, but always listening for the ring. 'And no fooling about that ring. The son-of-a-bitch always rang twice, so you'd know it was the postman.'" Lawrence's story reminded Cain of the old Irish tradition that the postman must always ring—or in olden days, knock—twice. He turned to Lawrence and said, "Vincent, I think I've got my title," Hoopes reported. And Vincent Lawrence's response to Cain's suggestion of *The Postman Always Rings Twice* was "Hey, that is a title. He sure did ring twice for [Frank] Chambers, didn't he?" (Though Chambers did kill Nick, his first attempt was unsuccessful, thus exemplifying how, as Ross Macdonald notes, "everything that happens in this novel happens twice, the first time with a twist [the cat dies instead of the Greek], the second time with a reverse twist.")

Like "Icebox," *Postman* was sold to a movie studio, though it was not filmed for more than ten years. "Mr. Cain's subject matter at the time he wrote was shocking," explained *New York Times* critic John Leonard. "The book was tried for obscenity in Boston, and his own Hollywood did not dare make a movie of it until 10 years after publication, with Lana Turner and John Garfield. And the movie makers dared only after the box-office successes of 'Double Indemnity,' directed by Billy Wilder, and 'Mildred Pierce,' for which Joan Crawford won an Academy Award." Though the success of *Postman* got Cain back into the studios as a writer, he was never invited to do the adaptations of his own books. Furthermore, he considered his efforts totally unsuccessful: "I want it understood that I consider I have a record of failure unmatched in Hollywood's history," he told *Publishers Weekly*.

In the early 1940's, Cain attempted to establish an authority headed by what he called "a tough mug," to whom authors would turn over their copyrights. "The authority," explained John Leonard, "would have protected authors' rights in courts and legislative halls, represented writers in litigation, negotiated contracts, and lobbied in Washington." While Leonard believed that Cain may have been motivated by the discrepancy between the $12 million that Hollywood made on his books and the $100,000 he received, some of Cain's contemporaries interpreted the project as a "Communist plot" or a "totalitarian attempt to control and manipulate creative talent." Cain's efforts failed.

Shortly afterwards, in 1947, Cain returned to Maryland where he lived until his death in 1977. "During those twenty-nine years," reported Joe Flaherty in the *New York Times Book Review*, "he wrote nine novels. Three found a publisher; none found a public. Why he left California (he called it El Dorado) and went back to the Eastern Shore is a psychological mystery." In assessing his contribution to modern literature, David Madden, writing in his *James M. Cain*, concluded: "Certainly Cain's art, more than anything else, moves even the serious reader to almost complete emotional commitment to the traumatic experiences Cain renders; and this artistic control convinces me that without his finest novels—*The Postman, Serenade, Mildred Pierce*, and *The Butterfly*—the cream of our twentieth-century fiction would be thinner. Straddling realism and expressionism, he often gives us a vivid account of life on the American scene as he has observed and experienced it; and, in his best moments, he provides the finer vibrations afforded by the esthetic experience. Cain . . . takes us through experiences whose special quality is found in no other writer's work."

MEDIA ADAPTATIONS: Two of Cain's short stories have been filmed: "The Baby in the Icebox" was released as "She Made Her Bed," by Paramount in 1934; "Career in C Major" was filmed as "Wife, Husband, Friend," by Twentieth Century-Fox in 1938. The Embezzler was filmed as "Money and the Woman" by Warner Bros. in 1940; Double Indemnity was filmed by Paramount in 1944; Mildred Pierce was filmed by Warner Bros. in 1945; Serenade was filmed by Warner Bros. in 1956; Loves' Lovely Counterfeit was filmed as "Slightly Scarlet" by Benjamin Beaugeus, 1956; The Root of His Evil was filmed as "Interlude" by Universal in 1957. In 1938 an authorized version of The Postman Always Rings Twice was made in France by Gladiator Films, with the title "Le Dernier Tourant," because Metro-Goldwyn-Mayer, the American owner of the film rights, decided that the film could not be released in the United States. In 1939, G. Musso of Italy released "Obsessione" (a Cocinor-Marcean release of ICI Productions), also based on The Postman Always Rings Twice. M.G.M. and Gladiator Films then filed a joint suit against the Italian producers, charging plagiarism. In 1946 the U.S. censorship of the film was lifted and the M.G.M. production was released. Critics agreed, however, that the Italian version was superior to both the American and the French efforts. A Lorimar production of The Postman Always Rings Twice was also released in the United States in 1981. In addition, Postman was adapted and performed as opera by the Opera Theatre of St. Louis, 1982. Butterfly was adapted for the screen by John Goff and Matt Climber and released in 1982.

AVOCATIONAL INTERESTS: Music.

BIOGRAPHICAL/CRITICAL SOURCES—Books: James T. Farrell, Literature and Morality, Vanguard, 1947; Edmund Wilson, Classics and Commercials, Farrar, Straus, 1950; W. M. Frohock, The Novel of Violence in America: 1920-1950, University Press in Dallas, 1950; David Madden, editor, Tough Guy Writers of the Thirties, Southern Illinois University Press, 1968; David Madden, James M. Cain, Twayne, 1970; Contemporary Literary Criticism, Gale, Volume III, 1975, Volume XI, 1979; Authors in the News, Volume I, Gale, 1976; Roy Hoopes, Cain: The Biography of James M. Cain, Holt, 1982.

Periodicals: Saturday Review, October 4, 1941, August 14, 1965; New Republic, October 6, 1941; Nation, May 22, 1943, June 16, 1969; New York Times Book Review, August 8, 1965, March 2, 1969, April 22, 1976, December 13, 1981; Time, August 27, 1965; New Yorker, January 8, 1966; Washington Post, January 19, 1969, November 8, 1981; Publishers Weekly, July 24, 1972; Village Voice, April 8-14, 1981; Chicago Tribune Book World, October 4, 1981; New York Times, February 5, 1982.

OBITUARIES: New York Times, October 29, 1977; Washington Post, October 29, 1977; Newsweek, November 7, 1977; Time, November 7, 1977.†

—Sketch by Donna Olendorf

* * *

**CAIRNCROSS, Alec
    See CAIRNCROSS, Alexander Kirkland**

* * *

**CAIRNCROSS, Alexander Kirkland 1911-
    (Alec Cairncross)**

PERSONAL: Born February 11, 1911, in Lesmahagow, Scotland; son of Alexander Kirkland and Elizabeth Andrew (Wishart) Cairncross; married Mary Frances Glynn, May 29, 1943; children: Frances Anne, Philip Wishart, Alexander Messent, David John, Elizabeth Mary. Education: University of Glasgow, M.A., 1933; Trinity College, Cambridge, Ph.D., 1936. Home: 14 Staverton Rd., Oxford OX2 6XJ, England.

CAREER: University of Glasgow, Glasgow, Scotland, lecturer in political economy, 1935-39; West of Scotland Agricultural College, Ayr, lecturer in agricultural economics, 1935-39; War Cabinet Office, London, England, staff member of economic section, 1939-41; administrative assistant of Board of Trade, 1941; Ministry of Aircraft Production, London, staff member of directorate of programs and planning, 1941-45; Economist, London, staff member, 1946; economic adviser to Board of Trade, 1946-49; Organization for European Economic Cooperation, Paris, France, director of Economic Division, 1949-50; University of Glasgow, professor of applied economics, and director of department of social and economic research, 1951-61; British Government, London, economic adviser, 1961-64, head of Economic Service, 1964-69; Oxford University, Oxford, England, master of St. Peter's College, 1969-78. Member of Court of Governors of London School of Economics and Political Science, University of London; chancellor of University of Glasgow, 1972—; fellow of St. Antony's College, Oxford University, 1978—. Director of Ailsa and Alva Investment Trusts, 1959-61; trustee of Urwick Orr & Partners, 1970-81; president of Girls Public Day School Trust, 1972—. Member of Wool Working Party, 1946; director of Economic Development Institute, Washington, D.C., 1955-56. Head of economic advisory panel, British Element, Control Commission for Germany, Berlin, 1945-46; advisory committee chairman to Houblon-Norman Trustees.

MEMBER: Royal Economic Society (president, 1968-70; vice-president, 1970—), National Institute of Social and Economic Research, British Association for the Advancement of Science (section F president, 1969; president, 1970-71), British Academy (fellow), American Academy of Arts and Sciences (foreign honorary member), Scottish Economic Society (president, 1969-73; vice-president, 1973—), United Oxford and Cambridge University Club.

AWARDS, HONORS: Named to Order of St. Michael and St. George, 1950, named knight commander, 1966; honorary degrees include LL.D. from Mount Allison University, 1962, University of Glasgow, 1966, and University of Exeter, 1969; D.Litt. from University of Reading, 1968, and Heriot Watt University, 1969; D.Sc. from University of Wales, 1971, and Queen's University, Belfast, 1972; D.Univ. from Stirling University, 1973; honorary fellow of St. Peter's College, Oxford University, and of Literary Society of England.

WRITINGS—All under name Alec Cairncross: Introduction to Economics, Butterworth, 1944, 6th edition, 1981.

Home and Foreign Investment, 1870-1913: Studies in Capital Accumulation, Cambridge University Press, 1953, Kelley, 1974; (editor) The Scottish Economy: A Statistical Account of Scottish Life by Members of the Staff of Glasgow University, Cambridge University Press, 1954; Some Problems of Economic Planning, Foreign Trade Research Institute, 1957; The International Bank for Reconstruction and Development, International Finance Section, Department of Economics and Sociology, Princeton University, 1959.

Monetary Policy in a Mixed Economy, Almqvist & Wiksell, 1960; Economic Development and the Atlantic Provinces, Atlantic Provinces Research Board, 1961; Factors in Economic Development, Praeger, 1962, Beekman, 1972; The Short Term *and the Long in Economic Planning*, Economic Development Institute (Washington, D.C.), 1966; (editor) *The Managed Economy*, British Association for the Advancement of Science, 1969, Barnes & Noble, 1970.

(Editor) *Papers on Planning and Economic Management*, Manchester University Press, 1970; (editor) *Britain's Economic Prospects Reconsidered*, Allen & Unwin, 1971, State University of New York Press, 1972; *Essays in Economic Management*, Allen & Unwin, 1971, State University of New York Press, 1972; (contributor) G.D.N. Woswick, editor, *Uses of Economics*, Barnes & Noble, 1972; *Learning to Learn*, University of Glasgow Press, 1972; *Control of Long-Term International Capital Movements: A Staff Paper*, Brookings Institution, 1973; *Control over International Capital Movements*, University of Reading, 1973; (editor with others, and contributor) *Economic Policy for the European Community*, Macmillan (London), 1974, Holmes & Meier, 1975; *Inflation, Growth, and International Finance*, Allen & Unwin, 1975; (editor with Mohinde Puri) *H. W. Singer: The Strategy of International Development*, Macmillan, 1975; (editor with Puri) *Employment, Income Distribution, and Development Strategy: Essays in Honor of H. W. Singer*, Macmillan, 1976; (editor) R.W.B. Clarke, *Public Expenditure, Management, and Control*, Macmillan, 1978.

Snatches (poems), Smythe Ltd., 1980; (contributor) Frances Anne Cairncross, editor, *Changing Perceptions of Economic Policy*, Methuen, 1981; (contributor) *The Economic History of Britain since 1700*, Cambridge University Press, 1981; (editor) Clarke, *Anglo-American Collaboration in War and Peace*, Oxford University Press, 1982. Also author of Radcliffe report, *The Working of the Monetary System*, 1959, and report on the Channel Link, 1982. General editor of "Social and Economic Studies" series, Department of Social and Economic Research, University of Glasgow, 1953-61. Co-author of script for phonotape, "The British Economy," Holt Information Systems, 1972. Editor, *Scottish Journal of Political Economy*, 1954-61.

AVOCATIONAL INTERESTS: Color photography, travel.

* * *

CAMERON, Alan (Douglas Edward) 1938-

PERSONAL: Born March 13, 1938, in Egham, Surrey, England; son of A. D. Cameron; married Averil Sutton, 1962 (divorced, 1980); children: one son, one daughter. *Education:* Oxford University, B.A., 1961, M.A., 1963. *Home:* 454 Riverside Dr., New York, N.Y. 10027. *Office:* 601 Hamilton Hall, Columbia University, New York, N.Y. 10027.

CAREER: Brunswick School, Haywards Heath, England, assistant master, 1956-57; University of Glasgow, Glasgow, Scotland, assistant lecturer, 1961-63, lecturer in humanity, 1963-64; University of London, London, England, lecturer, 1964-71, reader in Latin at Beford College, 1971-72, professor of Latin language and literature at King's College, 1972-77; Columbia University, New York, N.Y., Anthen Professor of Latin Language and Literature, 1977—. Visiting professor at Columbia University, 1967-68. *Member:* British Academy (fellow), American Academy of Arts and Sciences (fellow). *Awards, honors:* N. H. Baynes Prize, 1967; John Conington Prize, 1968.

WRITINGS: Claudian: Poetry and Propaganda at the Court of Honorius, Clarendon Press, 1970; (contributor) Arnold H. Jones, J. Morris, and J. R. Martindale, editors, *Prosopography of the Later Roman Empire*, Cambridge University Press, Volume I, 1971, Volume II, 1980; *Porphyrius the Charioteer*, Clarendon Press, 1973; *Circus Factions: Blues and Greens at Rome and Byzantium*, Clarendon Press, 1976; *The Greek Anthology: From Meleager to Planudes*, Clarendon Press, 1983; *Learning and Research in Eighth Century Byzantium: The Parastaseis Syntomai Chronikai*, E. J. Brill, 1983; *Essays in Late Antiquity*, Variorium, 1983. Also author of *The Last Pagans of Rome*. Contributor to scholarly journals.

* * *

CAMERON, D. A.
See CAMERON, Donald (Allan)

* * *

CAMERON, Donald (Allan) 1937-
(D. A. Cameron, Silver Donald Cameron)

PERSONAL: Born June 21, 1937, in Toronto, Ontario, Canada; son of Maxwell A. (a professor of education) and Hazel (Robertson) Cameron; married Catherine Ann Cahoon (divorced, 1973); married Lulu Terrio-Cameron; children: (first marriage) Maxwell, Ian, Leslie (daughter), Steven; (second marriage) Mark Patrick. *Education:* University of British Columbia, B.A., 1960; University of California, Berkeley, M.A., 1962; University of London, Ph.D., 1967. *Politics:* New Democratic Party. *Home:* D'Escousse, Nova Scotia, Canada.

CAREER: High school teacher in British Columbia public schools, 1957-58, principal, 1958-59; University of British Columbia, Vancouver, lecturer in English, 1962-64; Dalhousie University, Halifax, Nova Scotia, postdoctoral fellow, 1967-68; University of New Brunswick, Fredericton, associate professor of English, 1968-71; free-lance writer, broadcaster, and photographer in D'Escousse, Nova Scotia, 1971—. Writer-in-residence at College of Cape Breton and University of Prince Edward Island. *Member:* Writers Union of Canada, Canadian Civil Liberties Association.

AWARDS, HONORS: Woodrow Wilson fellowship, 1960-61; British Council scholar, 1965-66; Canadian Centennial Commission Author's Award, 1966-67; Killam fellowship, Dalhousie University, 1967-68; Prix Italia nominee, 1980, for radio play "The Sisters"; recipient of numerous National Magazine Awards for cultural reporting and travel writing; finalist in ACTRA Award competitions.

WRITINGS: Faces of Leacock (critical study), Ryerson, 1967; *Conversations with Canadian Novelists* (interviews), Macmillan, 1973.

Under name Silver Donald Cameron: *The Education of Everett Richardson: The Nova Scotia Fishermen's Strike, 1970-71* (nonfiction), McClelland & Stewart, 1977; *Season in the Rain* (essays), McClelland & Stewart, 1978; *Dragon Lady* (novel), McClelland & Stewart, 1980; *The Baitchopper* (children's fiction), James Lorimer & Company, 1982.

Author of material presented on Canadian Broadcasting Corporation radio and television, including "The Sisters" (radio play); also author of scripts for Cable Television (CTV). Contributor of articles under the names D. A. Cameron and Silver Donald Cameron to numerous journals, including *Holiday, Commonweal, Atlantic Monthly,* and *Nation.* Founding editor of *Mysterious East* magazine, 1969-71; contributing editor of *Weekend*, 1974-77.

WORK IN PROGRESS: A children's book; a novel; a film script for CBC-TV and National Film Board of Canada.

AVOCATIONAL INTERESTS: Woodworking, sailing, skiing, diving.

CAMERON, Kenneth Walter 1908-

PERSONAL: Born October 12, 1908, in Martins Ferry, Ohio; son of Albert Ernest (an executive) and Zoe Shockley (Barker) Cameron. *Education:* West Virginia University, A.B., 1930, A.M., 1931; General Theological Seminary, S.T.B., 1935; Yale University, Ph.D., 1940. *Politics:* Republican. *Home:* 23 Wolcott St., Hartford, Conn. 06106. *Office address:* Transcendental Books, Box A, Station A, Hartford, Conn. 06106.

CAREER: Ordained Episcopal priest, 1935. North Carolina College of Agriculture and Mechanic Arts (now North Carolina State University at Raleigh), Raleigh, instructor in English, 1938-43; Temple University, Philadelphia, assistant professor of English, 1945-46; Trinity College, Hartford, Conn., assistant professor, 1946-58, associate professor of English, 1958—. Manager of Transcendental Books, Hartford. Archivist and historiographer of Diocese of Connecticut. *Member:* Modern Language Association of America, Modern Humanities Research Association, Melville Society, Thoreau Society, Emerson Society (executive secretary, 1955—).

WRITINGS—Published by Transcendental Books, except as noted: *Authorship and Sources of "Gentleness and Nobility,"* Thistle Press, 1941; *Background of John Heywood's "Witty and Wittless,"* Thistle Press, 1941; *John Heywood's "Play of the Wether,"* Thistle Press, 1941; *Ralph Waldo Emerson's Reading,* Thistle Press, 1941, reprinted, Haskell, 1973, revised edition, Transcendental Books, 1962; *Emerson the Essayist: An Outline of His Philosophical Development through 1836,* two volumes, Thistle Press, 1945.

The Presbury Family of Maryland and the Ohio Valley, 1950; *Genesis of Hawthorne's "The Ambitious Guest,"* Thistle Press, 1955; *The Genesis of Christ Church, Stratford, Connecticut,* Christ Church, 1957; *The Transcendental Workbook,* 1957; *An Emerson Index; or, Names, Exempla, Sententiae, Symbols, Words, and Motifs in Selected Notebooks of Ralph Waldo Emerson,* 1958; *The Transcendentalists and Minerva,* three volumes, 1958; *Emerson and Thoreau as Readers* (selected chapters from *The Transcendentalists and Minerva*), 1958, 2nd edition, 1972; *Index of the Pamphlet Collection of the Diocese of Connecticut,* The Historiographer, 1958.

A Commentary on Emerson's Early Lectures, 1833-1836, with Index-Concordance, 1961; *Centennial History of Trinity Episcopal Church, Bridgeport, Connecticut,* Trinity Episcopal Church, 1963; *The Catholic Revival in Episcopal Connecticut, 1850-1925,* Trinity Episcopal Church, 1963; *Companion to Thoreau's Correspondence,* 1964; *Emerson's Workshop: An Analysis of His Reading in Periodicals through 1836,* 1964; *The Pardoner and His Pardons: Indulgences Circulating in England on the Eve of Reformation,* 1965; *Transcendental Epilogue,* 1965; *Thoreau's Harvard Years,* 1966; *Transcendental Climate,* 1967; *Hawthorne Index,* 1968.

Transcendental Reading Patterns: Library Charging Lists, 1970; *Young Emerson's Transcendental Vision: An Exposition of His World View with an Analysis of the Structure, Backgrounds, and Meaning of Nature,* 1971; *Emerson the Essayist: An Outline of His Philosophical Development through 1836 with Special Emphasis on the Sources and Interpretation of Nature, also Bibliographical Appendices,* 1972; *Letter-book of the Reverend Henry Caner, S.P.G. Missionary in Colonial Connecticut and Massachusetts until the Revolution,* 1972; *Longfellow's Reading in Libraries: The Charging Records of a Learned Poet Interpreted,* 1973; *Response to Transcendental Concord,* 1974; *Young Thoreau and the Classics,* 1975; *Transcendental Apprenticeship,* 1976; *Anglicanism in Early Connecticut and New England,* 1977; *Young Reporter of Concord: A Checklist of F. B. Sanborn's Letters,* 1978; *The Papers of Loyalist Samuel Peters,* 1978.

Strictly Personal: A Teacher's Reminiscences, 1980; *Transcendentalists in Transition,* 1980; *An Anglican Library in Colonial New England,* 1980; *The Younger Doctor William Smith (1754-1820),* 1980; *Samuel Seabury among His Contemporaries,* 1981; *Parameters of American Romanticism and Transcendentalism,* 1981; *The Episcopal Church in Connecticut and New England,* 1981; *Correspondence of Franklin Benjamin Sanborn the Transcendentalist,* 1982; *Abraham Jarvis: Connecticut's Second Anglican Bishop,* 1982.

Compiler: *Early Anglicanism in Connecticut,* 1962; *Index-Concordance to Emerson's Sermons,* 1963; (and author of notes, and editor) *Over Thoreau's Desk: New Correspondence 1838-1861,* 1965; *Emerson among His Contemporaries: A Harvest of Estimates, Insights, and Anecdotes from the Victorian Literary World and an Index,* 1967; *Research Keys to the American Renaissance: Scarce Indexes of "The Christian Examiner," "The North American Review," and "The New Jerusalem Magazine," for Students of American Literature, Culture, History, and New England Transcendentalism,* 1967; *Connecticut Churchmanship: Records and Historical Papers Concerning the Anglican Church in Connecticut in the Eighteenth and Early Nineteenth Centuries,* 1969; *The Massachusetts Lyceum during the American Renaissance: Materials for the Study of the Oral Tradition in American Letters,* 1969; *Concord Harvest: Publications of the Concord School of Philosophy and Literature,* 1970; *Contemporary Dimension—An American Renaissance Literary Notebook of Newspaper Clippings,* [and] *Victorian Notebook: Literary Clippings from Nineteenth-Century American Newspapers,* 1970; *The Anglican Episcopate in Connecticut: A Sheaf of Biographical and Institutional Studies for Churchmen and Historians (1784-1899),* 1970; *American Episcopal Clergy: Registers of Ordinations in the Episcopal Church in the United States,* 1970; *Transcendental Log,* 1973; *Anglican Climate in Connecticut: Historical Perspectives from Imprints of the Late Colonial and Early National Years,* 1974; *Ammi Rogers and the Episcopal Church in Connecticut, 1790-1832: His Memoirs and Documents Illuminating Historical, Religious, and Personal Backgrounds,* 1974.

Editor: (And author of introduction) Ralph Waldo Emerson, *Nature* (1836 edition), Scholars' Facsimiles Reprints, 1940; John Heywood, *Gentleness and Nobility,* Thistle Press, 1941.

Emerson, *Indian Superstition,* Friends of the Dartmouth Library, 1954, 2nd edition, 1963; *Emerson, Thoreau, and Concord in Early Newspapers,* 1957.

Thoreau's Literary Notebook in the Library of Congress, 1964; *Thoreau and His Harvard Classmates with Henry William's Memorials of the Class of 1837,* 1965; *Poems of Jones Very,* 1965; *Thoreau's Fact Book in the Harry Elkins Widener Collection in the Harvard College Library,* three volumes, 1966; *The Works of Samuel Peters of Hebron, Connecticut, New England Historian, Satirist, Folklorist, Anti-patriot, and Anglican Clergyman, 1735-1826, with Historical Indexes,* 1967.

Facsimiles of Early Episcopal Church Documents (1759-1789), 1970; *Phiothea or Plato against Epicurus: A Novel of the Transcendental Movement,* 1975; *Whitman, Bryant, Melville and Holmes among Their Contemporaries,* 1976; *The Church of England in Pre-Revolutionary Connecticut,* 1976; Samuel Hart, *Old Connecticut: Historical Papers,* 1976; *Romanticism and the American Renaissance,* 1977; *The Episcopal Church of the American Renaissance,* 1977; *Literary Comment in*

American Renaissance Newspapers, 1977; *Scholars' Companion to the American Renaissance*, 1977; *Lowell, Whittier, Very and the Alcotts among Their Contemporaries*, 1978; *Longfellow among His Contemporaries*, 1978; *American Renaissance and Transcendentalism: Historical, Cultural, and Bibliographical Dimensions*, 1978; *Samuel Seabury's Ungathered Imprints: Historical Perspectives*, 1978; *Samuel Seabury (1729-1796): His Election, Consecration and Reception*, 1978.

The New England Writers and the Press, 1980; *Ethos of Anglicanism in Colonial New England and New York*, 1981; *Further Response to Transcendental Concord*, 1982; *Anglican Church Music in America, 1763-1830*, 1982.

Editor of books by F. B. Sanborn: *Lectures on Literature and Philosophy*, 1975; *Transcendental and Literary New England*, 1975; *Sixty Years of Concord: 1855-1915*, 1976; *The Transcendental Eye*, 1981; *Ungathered Poems and Transcendental Papers*, 1981; *Table Talk*, 1981.

Editor of *Emerson Society Quarterly, Historiographer of the Episcopal Diocese of Connecticut,* and *American Transcendental Quarterly.*

WORK IN PROGRESS: The Seabury Years: The Journal of Connecticut's First Diocesan Reconstructed.

* * *

CAMERON, Silver Donald
See CAMERON, Donald (Allan)

* * *

CAMPBELL, Rita Ricardo
See RICARDO-CAMPBELL, Rita

* * *

CAMPBELL, Robert 1922-1977

PERSONAL: Born January 20, 1922, in Hagerstown, Md.; died October 2, 1977, of brain tumor, in Boonton, N.J.; son of Robert L. (a shoe manufacturer) and Adelaide (McBride) Campbell; married third wife, Nancy Van Arsdel, October 9, 1959; children: (third marriage) Thomas Scott, Stephen McBride. *Education:* St. John's College, Annapolis, Md., B.A., 1944. *Politics:* Independent. *Religion:* "Nonspecific." *Address:* R.D. 2, Box 212, Boonton, N.J. 07005.

CAREER: Life, New York, N.Y., reporter and writer, 1945-57; free-lance writer, industrial and documentary film maker, composer, assistant producer, 1957-77. *Military service:* U.S. Army, 1941-42. *Member:* American Society of Composers, Authors and Publishers, American Bugatti Club. *Awards, honors:* American Medical Association citation, 1966, for *Life* article on viruses; recipient of numerous film awards.

WRITINGS: (Editor) *Skeet Shooting with D. Lee Braun*, Rutledge Books, 1967; (editor) *Trapshooting with D. Lee Braun*, Rutledge Books, 1969; (contributor) Joseph Comprone, editor, *From Experience to Expression* (college textbook), W. C. Brown, 1974; *The Chasm: The Life and Death of a Great Experiment in Ghetto Education* (nonfiction), introduction by James Baldwin, Houghton, 1974; (with the editors of *Life*) *The Enigma of the Mind*, Time-Life Books, 1976; *The Golden Years of Broadcasting: A Celebration of the First Fifty Years of Radio and TV on NBC*, Rutledge Books, 1976. Contributor to *Sports Illustrated.*

WORK IN PROGRESS: An environmental picture for National Film Board of Canada; an American opera.

OBITUARIES: New York Times, October 4, 1977; *AB Bookman's Weekly*, January 30, 1978.†

* * *

CANE, Melville (Henry) 1879-1980

PERSONAL: Born April 15, 1879, in Plattsburg, N.Y.; died March 10, 1980; son of Henry William (a merchant) and Sophia (Goodman) Cane; married Florence Naumbury, December 23, 1909 (died, 1953); children: Katherine Detre, Mary (Mrs. Arthur Robinson). *Education:* Columbia University, A.B., 1900, LL.B., 1903. *Office:* Ernst, Cane, Berner & Gitlin, 7 West 51st St., New York, N.Y. 10019.

CAREER: Lawyer in New York, N.Y., 1905-80. Founding partner of law firm of Ernst, Cane, Berner & Gitlin. Member of board of directors of Harcourt Brace Jovanovich, Inc., 1940-80. *Member:* Association of the Bar (New York), Poetry Society of America, Columbia University Club, Phi Beta Kappa (honorary member). *Awards, honors:* Columbia University medal for conspicuous alumni service, 1933, and medal for excellence in law and literature, 1948; Poetry Society of America annual poetry award established by Harcourt Brace Jovanovich named in his honor, 1960; Poetry Society of America gold medal, 1971.

WRITINGS—Poems, except as indicated; published by Harcourt, except as indicated: *January Garden*, 1926; *Behind Dark Spaces*, 1930; *Poems: New and Selected*, 1938.

A Wider Arc, 1947; *Making a Poem* (prose), 1953; (editor with Harry E. Maule) *The Man from Main Street: A Sinclair Lewis Reader* (anthology), Random House, 1953; *And Pastures New*, 1956.

Bullet-Hunting and Other New Poems, 1960; (editor with John Farrar and Louise Townsend Nicholl) *The Golden Year: The Poetry Society of America Anthology*, Books for Libraries, 1960; *To Build a Fire: Recent Poems and a Prose Piece* (includes six translations by the author of poetry by Evgeny Vinokurov), 1964; *So That It Flower: A Gathering of Poems*, 1966; *All and Sundry: An Oblique Autobiography*, 1968; *Eloquent April: New Poems and Prose*, 1971; *The First Firefly: New Poems and Prose*, 1974; *Snow Toward Evening*, 1974.

Work included in anthologies. Contributor of poems, articles, and stories to magazines, including *American Scholar, Southwest Review, Sporting News,* and *Saturday Review.*

SIDELIGHTS: Melville Cane first became interested in writing while practicing law. Beginning early in his career he represented many prominent authors, including Upton Sinclair, Thomas Wolfe, William Saroyan, and Sinclair Lewis. At Columbia University two of his classmates were Alfred Harcourt and Donald Brace and, in 1919, he drew up incorporation papers for their publishing concern, Harcourt Brace (now Harcourt Brace Jovanovich). As a member of the board of directors of that firm, he often advised on legal matters as well as literary ones.

The relationship between law and literature in Cane's life influenced his ideas on writing. According to a *New York Times* article by Ian T. Macauley, Cane once wrote: "You have to be accurate in law, and you have to be accurate in a poem. . . . In both fields there has to be a precise inspection of the object." This interest in precision was noted by critics, and they praised Cane's poetry for its simplicity. For example, E. H. Walden, in *Library Journal*, noted, "There is a spontaneity in his verse, yet when analyzed, constraint and craftsmanship show through."

Although Cane's legal work required a great degree of seriousness and restraint, he felt free to let his sense of humor come to the fore in his poetry. Critics such as L. T. Nicholl and Gorham Munson commended Cane for the lightheartedness evident in his poetry. In the *New York Herald Tribune Book Review,* Nicholl wrote: "Mr. Cane is unique for the technical control which serves deep emotional need and also [for his] mad and merry wit." Munson, reviewing *And Pastures New* in *Saturday Review,* commented: "[Cane] is truly a serious poet, but he is saved from gravity by his playfulness, the playfulness that makes his light verse delightful and his serious verse springy in spirit." He expressed in his poetry, according to Harcourt Brace Jovanovich chairman William Jovanovich, as noted by Macauley, "the saving characteristic of finding life too serious to be viewed seriously."

BIOGRAPHICAL/CRITICAL SOURCES: *New York Times,* March 4, 1956; *New York Herald Tribune Book Review,* March 11, 1956; *Saturday Review,* June 16, 1956; *New York Times Book Review,* December 20, 1964; Melville Cane, *All and Sundry: An Oblique Autobiography,* Harcourt, 1968; *American Scholar,* autumn, 1968.

OBITUARIES: *New York Times,* March 11, 1980; *Publishers Weekly,* March 21, 1980; *Newsweek,* March 24, 1980.†

* * *

CAREY, Omer L. 1929-

PERSONAL: Born January 24, 1929, in Ellsworth, Ill.; son of George Franklin (a railroad telegrapher) and Nola (Thompson) Carey; married Carol Grant, June 20, 1954; children: Gayle, Craig, Dale, Bryan, Grant. *Education:* Illinois Wesleyan University, B.A., 1954; graduate study at Illinois State University, 1955-56, Southern Illinois University, 1957-59, and University of Illinois, 1957; Indiana University, M.B.A., 1960, D.B.A., 1962. *Politics:* Republican. *Religion:* Methodist. *Home:* 7625 Island Dr., Anchorage, Alaska 99504. *Office:* Department of Business Administration, Anchorage Senior College, University of Alaska, Anchorage, Alaska 99504.

CAREER: State Farm Mutual Automobile Insurance Co., Bloomington, Ill., staff member in accounting department, 1947-49, 1952-55; Illinois Power Co., Havana, accountant, 1949-52, 1955; high school teacher in Bethalto, Ill., 1956-59; Indiana University at Bloomington, instructor in business, 1959-62; Idaho State University, Pocatello, assistant professor of business administration and assistant director of Bureau of Business Research, 1962-64; Washington State University, College of Economics and Business, Pullman, 1964-73, began as assistant professor, became professor of business administration, chairman of department, 1968-73; University of Alaska, Anchorage, professor of business administration, 1973—, Harold T. Caven Professorship in Business and Finance, 1977—, associate dean, 1977-79, dean of School of Business and Public Administration, 1979-80, graduate program director, 1980-82. Visiting assistant professor of finance, University of Washington, Seattle, summer, 1966. Expert witness and business appraiser for Paul Dirksen Appraisal Co. and Alaska Valuation; expert witness for Alaska Gas & Pipeline Co. Member of board of directors of C.T. Management Services, Inc., and Alaska Food Co. Consultant to Bristol Bay Regional Development Council, Kenai Native Association, and Cook Inlet Region, Inc. Active at local, state, and national levels of Association for Retarded Citizens. *Member:* National Education Association, Financial Management Association, American Finance Association, Western Finance Association (secretary-treasurer, 1965-70), Western Economic Association, Phi Kappa Phi, Beta Gamma Sigma, Blue Key.

WRITINGS: (With Frank Seelye, Harold White, and Donald Carrell) *Personnel Policies of Small Business,* Small Business Administration and Idaho State University, 1964; (contributor) *Trends in Distribution, Services and Transportation,* Bureau of Economic and Business Research, Washington State University, 1966; (editor) *Military-Industrial Complex and United States Foreign Policy,* Washington State University, 1969; (contributor) *Management and Public Policy,* School of Management, State University of New York at Buffalo, 1971; (with Green) *Bristol Bay: Its Potential and Development,* State of Alaska, Department of Commerce and Economic Development, 1976; *Forty Niners Ski Club,* Intercollegiate Case Clearing House, 1978; *Teaching Note for Forty Niners Ski Club,* Intercollegiate Case Clearing House, 1977; *Bestway Mill and Lumber Co., Inc.,* Intercollegiate Case Clearing House, 1978; *Teaching Note for Bestway Mill and Lumber Co., Inc.,* Intercollegiate Case Clearing House, 1978; (contributor with Dean Olson) Karl Vesper, editor, *The Pacific Northwest: Small Business and Entrepreneurship in Region Ten,* University of Oregon, 1979; (with Olson) *Financial Tools for Small Businesses,* Reston, 1982. Contributor to journals.

* * *

CARFAX, Catherine
See FAIRBURN, Eleanor

* * *

CARLINSKY, Dan 1944-

PERSONAL: Born March 9, 1944, in Holyoke, Mass.; son of Louis H. and Ethel (Mag) Carlinksy; married Nancy Cooperstein, August 25, 1972. *Education:* Columbia University, B.A., 1965, M.S., 1966. *Home and office:* 301 East 78th St., New York, N.Y. 10021.

CAREER: Freelance writer and journalist.

WRITINGS: (With Edwin Goodgold) *Trivia,* Dell, 1966; (with Goodgold) *More Trivial Trivia,* Dell, 1966; *Rock 'n' Roll Trivia,* Popular Library, 1970; (compiler) *A Century of College Humor,* Random House, 1971; (with David Heim) *Bicycle Tours in and around New York,* Hagstrom, 1975; (with Goodgold) *Trivia and More Trivia,* Book Sales, Inc., 1975; *Typewriter Art,* Price, Stern, 1977; *Do You Know Your Husband?,* Price, Stern, 1979; *Do You Know Your Wife?,* Price, Stern, 1979; *The Great Bogart Trivia Book,* Fawcett, 1980; *Are You Compatible?,* Price, Stern, 1981; *Do You Know Your Mother?,* Price, Stern, 1981; *Do You Know Your Father?,* Price, Stern, 1981; *Celebrity Yearbook,* Price, Stern, 1982; *College Humor,* Harper, 1982; *Do You Know Your Boss?,* Price, Stern, 1983.

Quiz books: (With Goodgold) *The Compleat Beatles Quiz Book,* Warner Books, 1975; (with Goodgold) *The World's Greatest Monster Quiz,* Berkley Publishing, 1975; *The Complete Bible Quiz Book,* Berkley Publishing, 1976; *The Great 1960s Quiz,* Harper, 1978; *The Jewish Quiz Book,* Doubleday, 1979. Author of syndicated newspaper column, "It's On the Tip of My Tongue." Contributor to periodicals, including *New York Times, Travel and Leisure, Playboy,* and *T.V. Guide.*

* * *

CARLSEN, G(eorge) Robert 1917-

PERSONAL: Born April 15, 1917, in Bozeman, Mont.; son of Charles E. (an attorney) and Carolyn (Mason) Carlsen; married Ruth Christoffer (a writer), April 5, 1941; children: Christopher, Kristin, Peter, Jane. *Education:* University of Minnesota, B.A., 1939, B.S., 1940, M.A., 1943, Ph.D., 1948. *Home:* 817 North Gilbert, Iowa City, Iowa 52240. *Office:* N280 Lindquist Center, University of Iowa, Iowa City, Iowa 52240.

CAREER: University of Minnesota, Minneapolis, instructor in English and education, 1942-47; University of Colorado, Boulder, associate professor of English and education, 1947-52; University of Texas at Austin, associate professor of curriculum and instruction, 1952-58; University of Iowa, Iowa City, professor of English and education, 1958—. Faculty member at University of Colorado, summers, 1953, 1955, 1958, and University of Hawaii, 1957, 1970. *Member:* National Council of Teachers of English (second vice-president, 1959; first vice-president, 1961; president, 1962), Phi Beta Kappa, Phi Delta Kappa.

AWARDS, HONORS: Award for distinguished contributions in secondary school teaching, 1957, and Distinguished Service Award, 1970, both National Council of Teachers of English; Distinguished Service Award, Assembly of Literature for Adolescents, 1974; Distinguished Service Award, Iowa Council of English Teachers, 1975.

WRITINGS: Brown-Carlsen Test of Listening Comprehension, World Publishing, 1952; (with Richard Alm) *Social Understanding through Literature,* National Council for Social Studies, 1954; (editor with wife, Ruth C. Carlsen) *The Great Auto Race, and Other Stories of Men and Cars,* Scholastic Book Services, 1965; (editor with R. C. Carlsen) *Fifty-two Miles to Terror* (collection), Scholastic Book Services, 1966; *Books and the Teenage Reader: A Guide for Teachers, Librarians, and Parents,* Harper, 1967, 2nd revised edition, 1980.

General editor, "Themes and Writers" series, McGraw; six volumes, 1967—; also editor of the volumes in the series: (With others) *Western Literature: Themes and Writers,* with teacher's manual, 1967, 2nd edition (with Gabriele L. Rico), 1973, 3rd edition (with Miriam Gilbert) published as *British and Western Literature,* 1979; (with R. C. Carlsen and others) *American Literature: Themes and Writers,* 1967, 2nd edition (with R. C. Carlsen, Edgar H. Schuster, and Anthony Tovatt), 1973, 3rd edition, 1979; (with R. C. Carlsen and others) *Insights: Themes in Literature,* 1967, 3rd edition, 1979; (with R. C. Carlsen) *Encounters: Themes in Literature,* 1967, 3rd edition, 1979; (with R. C. Carlsen and others) *Perception: Themes in Literature,* 1969, 3rd edition, 1979; (with R. C. Carlsen, A. Tovatt, and Patricia O. Tovatt) *Focus: Themes in Literature,* 1969, 3rd edition, 1978. Also author, with R. C. Carlsen of teacher's manual for 2nd edition of *Perception: Themes in Literature,* McGraw, 1975.

WORK IN PROGRESS: Fourth edition of volumes in "Themes and Writers" series; editing two books with wife, R. C. Carlsen, and Miriam Gilbert, *Survey of American Literature* and *Survey of British Literature;* monograph on "what happens to people and their reading as they grow up in the American culture."

SIDELIGHTS: G. Robert Carlsen told *CA:* "I had a delightful time with books in the elementary schools: *Heidi, Hans Brinker, Tom Swift.* But in adolescence I was forced to read classics which I hated: *Ivanhoe, As You Like It, Evangeline, Silas Marner.* As I taught high school English classes, I became more and more conscious of the gap between children's books and the mature classics. So I constantly strove to map out a path leading from one to the other that would be less painful than my passage had been.

"Later as a college teacher, in my course called 'Literature for the Adolescent,' I have always asked my students who usually plan on being either an English teacher or a librarian, to write a reading autobiography detailing only their reading experiences from early childhood to the present day. As time moved on, I became impressed with the predictability of the pattern the group of individuals followed in becoming avid readers. At each age, one can predict with great accuracy the type of books that the majority will read by choice with certain differences made for male and female tastes. For this class I also developed lists of books leading from the junior novel centered on the teen age experiences to the popular adult novel to the classics. To put this material into a format that would be useful for parents as well as those professionally interested in helping todays' youngsters become readers, I wrote *Books and the Teenage Reader.*"

BIOGRAPHICAL/CRITICAL SOURCES: Los Angeles Times, March 26, 1980.

* * *

CARLSEN, Ruth C(hristoffer) 1918-

PERSONAL: Born February 21, 1918, in Milwaukee, Wis.; daughter of Carl Severin (a railroad official) and Lydia (Diefenthaeler) Christoffer; married George Robert Carlsen (a professor at University of Iowa), April 5, 1941; children: Christopher, Kristin, Peter, Jane. *Education:* University of Minnesota, B.A. (cum laude), 1939. *Religion:* Unitarian. *Home:* 817 North Gilbert, Iowa City, Iowa 52240.

CAREER: Writer. *Member:* Author's Guild, National P.E.N. Women's League, Athens Historical Circle, P.E.O. Sisterhood, Theta Sigma Phi.

WRITINGS—Children's fiction; published by Houghton: *Mr. Pudgins,* 1953; *Henrietta Goes West,* 1966; *Hildy and the Cuckoo Clock,* 1966; *Monty and the Tree House,* 1967; *Sam Bottleby,* 1968; *Ride A Wild Horse,* 1970; *Sometimes It's Up,* 1971; *Half Past Tomorrow,* 1973.

Editor, with husband, G. Robert Carlsen; published by McGraw, except as indicated: *The Great Auto Race, and Other Stories of Men and Cars,* Scholastic Book Services, 1965; *Fifty-Two Miles to Terror* (collection), Scholastic Book Services, 1966; (and others) *American Literature: Themes and Writers,* 1967, 2nd edition (Edgar H. Schuster, and Anthony Tovatt), 1973, 3rd edition, 1979; (and others) *Insights: Themes in Literature,* 1967, 3rd edition, 1979; *Encounters: Themes in Literature,* 1967, 3rd edition, 1979; (and others) *Perception: Themes in Literature,* 1969, 3rd edition, 1979; (A. Tovatt, and Patricia O. Tovatt) *Focus: Themes in Literature,* 1969, 3rd edition, 1978. Also author, with G. R. Carlsen, of teacher's manual for 2nd edition of *Perception: Themes in Literature,* McGraw, 1975.

WORK IN PROGRESS: Fourth edition of volumes in "Themes and Writers" series; editing two books with husband, G. R. Carlsen, and Miriam Gilbert, *Survey of American Literature* and *Survey of British Literature.*

SIDELIGHTS: Ruth C. Carlsen writes *CA:* "I have always felt that laughter is a very precious and a much too scarce experience in children's lives. And so, I have written my stories hoping to catch my audience unaware and surprise them into giggles and snorts. To hear children laughing out loud when one of my stories is read to them is one of the delights of my life.

"My first book, *Mr. Pudgins,* was immediately accepted on first reading by Houghton Mifflin which gave me super-confidence that my next books would cause as few birth pangs. How wrong I was proved. My next attempts were either aborted or stillborn. I had no other books published until fifteen years after Mr. Pudgin's appearance and then I was doubly blessed when *Hildy and the Cuckoo Clock* and *Henrietta Goes West* both came out in 1966.

"I have always tried to have real children living in a real world experience fantastic incidents which can almost but not quite be explained by the knowledge of the real world. It gives me the sensation of walking a tightrope, and keeping my balance is not easy.

"Now I have reached another plateau. My mind is filled with stories, but I never seem to have the time to type them down on paper. Instead I work away at my husband's literary series which keeps me writing, but not in the old way. Have I simply reached another 'season' of life?"

AVOCATIONAL INTERESTS: Travel, refinishing antiques, quilt making, needlepoint.

* * *

CARLSON, Marvin 1935-

PERSONAL: Born September 15, 1935, in Wichita, Kan.; son of Roy Edward (an accountant) and Gladys (Nelson) Carlson; married Patricia McElroy, August 20, 1961; children: Geoffrey Albert, Richard James. *Education:* University of Kansas, B.S.Ed., 1957; Cornell University, Ph.D., 1961. *Religion:* Presbyterian. *Home:* 514 North Washington, Bloomington, Ind. 47401. *Office:* Department of Theatre and Drama, Indiana University, Bloomington, Ind. 47401.

CAREER: Cornell University, Ithaca, N.Y., instructor, 1961-62, assistant professor, 1962-66, associate professor, 1966-72, professor of theatre arts, 1972-79, chairman of department, 1966-68, 1974-77; Indiana University at Bloomington, professor of theatre, 1979—. *Member:* American Theatre Association (fellow), American Society for Theatre Research, National Collegiate Players (second vice-president, 1963-67), American Association of University Professors, Phi Kappa Phi. *Awards, honors:* Guggenheim fellowship, 1969.

WRITINGS: (Translator) *Andre Antoine's Memories of the Theatre-Libre*, University of Miami Press, 1964; *The Theatre of the French Revolution*, Cornell University Press, 1966; *The French Stage in the Nineteenth Century*, Scarecrow, 1972; *The German Stage in the Nineteenth Century*, Scarecrow, 1972; *Goethe and the Theatre in Weimar*, Cornell University Press, 1977; *The Italian Stage in the Nineteenth Century*, McFarland Publications, 1980. Contributor to periodicals, including *Comparative Literature, Modern Drama, Educational Theatre Journal, Scandinavian Studies, Drama Review, Revue d'histoire du Theatre,* and *Players*.

WORK IN PROGRESS: A History of Theatre Theory.

* * *

CARR, Raymond 1919-

PERSONAL: Born April 11, 1919, in Bath, England; son of Reginald Henry and Ethel (Graham) Carr; married Sara Strickland. *Education:* Christ Church, Oxford, B.A. (with first class honors), 1941. *Politics:* Conservative. *Religion:* Church of England. *Home:* 29 Charlbury Rd., Oxford, England. *Office:* St. Antony's College, Oxford University, Oxford, England.

CAREER: Oxford University, Oxford, England, fellow of All Souls College, 1945-52, fellow of New College, 1952-65, St. Antony's College, professor of Latin American history and director of Latin American Centre, 1965-68, warden, 1968—. *Member:* Royal Historical Society (fellow).

WRITINGS: (Contributor) *European Nobility of the XVIII Century*, Adam Black, 1954; (contributor) M. Howard, *Soldiers and Politics*, Eyre & Spottiswoode, 1957; (contributor) *New Cambridge Modern History*, Cambridge University Press, 1965; *Spain 1808-1939*, Oxford University Press, 1966, revised edition, 1982; (contributor) *Cuba and the United States*, Brookings Institution, 1968; (editor) *The Republic and the Spanish Civil War*, Macmillan, 1971; *English Fox Hunting*, Weidenfeld & Nicolson, 1976; *The Spanish Tragedy*, Weidenfeld & Nicolson, 1977; (with J. P. Fusi) *Spain: Dictatorship to Democracy*, Allen & Unwin, 1979. Contributor of reviews to *New York Review of Books* and to professional journals; also contributor to *Economic History Review* and *Observer*.

WORK IN PROGRESS: A survey of United States-Puerto Rican relationships.

SIDELIGHTS: Raymond Carr knows Swedish, Norwegian, Danish, Italian, Spanish, French, and German.

* * *

CARROLL, John Millar 1925-

PERSONAL: Born December 6, 1925, in Philadelphia, Pa.; son of William (an engineer) and Mary Ann (Millar) Carroll; married Beryl Lois Skuce, October 28, 1944; children: William James, John, Jr., William Kingsley, Robert Loren, Richard Alan, Sandra Joy, Robert Alexander. *Education:* Lehigh University, B.S., 1950; Hofstra University, M.A., 1955; New York University, D.Eng.Sc., 1968. *Office:* Department of Computer Science, University of Western Ontario, London, Ontario, Canada ON N6A 5B8.

CAREER: National Bureau of Standards, Washington, D.C., and White Sands, N.M., radio engineering aide, 1947-48; *Electronics*, New York, N.Y., assistant editor, 1952-54, associate editor, 1954-57, managing editor, 1957-64; Lehigh University, Bethlehem, Pa., associate professor of industrial engineering, 1964-68; University of Western Ontario, London, Ontario, professor of computer science, 1968—. Secretary of field-test panel, National Stereophonic Radio Committee, 1959-60; member of committee on information handling, English Service Library, 1964-68; trustee of English Index, 1968-71. Consultant to Canadian Privacy and Computer Task Force, 1971; advisor on computer security to Royal Canadian Mounted Police, 1975-76. *Military service:* U.S. Navy, 1944-47, 1950-52; became ensign.

MEMBER: Institute of Electrical and Electronics Engineers (senior member, chairman of symbols committee, 1962-64, vice-chairman, information retrieval committee, 1964—, executive vice-chairman, engineering societies library committee on information handling), Tau Beta Pi, Alpha Pi Mu, Pi Tau Sigma, Sigma Pi Sigma, Pi Delta Epsilon.

WRITINGS: Mechanical Design for Electronics Production, McGraw, 1956; *Electron Devices and Circuits,* McGraw, 1962; *Careers and Opportunities in Electronics,* Dutton, 1963; *The Story of the Laser,* Dutton, 1964, revised edition, 1970. *Secrets of Electronic Espionage,* Dutton, 1966; *Careers and Opportunities in Computer Science,* Dutton, 1967; *The Third Listener: Personal Electronic Espionage,* Dutton, 1969; *Confidential Information Sources: Public and Private,* Security World Publishing, 1975; *Data Base and Computer Systems Security,* edited by Robert M. Curtice, Q.E.D. Information Sciences, 1976; *Computer Security,* Butterworth, 1977.

Editor; published by McGraw, except as indicated: *Transistor Circuits and Applications*, 1957; *Modern Transistor Circuits*, 1959; *Design Manual for Transistor Circuits*, 1961; *Tunnel-Diode and Semi-conductor Circuits*, 1963; *Microelectronic Circuits and Applications*, 1965. Also contributor to *McGraw-Hill Science and Technology Yearbook*.†

* * *

CARTER, Richard 1918-
(Tom Ainslie)

PERSONAL: Born January 24, 1918, in New York, N.Y.; married Gladys Chasins, October 20, 1945; children: Nancy Jane, John Andrew. *Education:* City College (now City College of the City University of New York), B.A., 1938. *Home:* 165 Pinesbridge Rd., Ossining, N.Y. 10562.

CAREER: Billboard magazine, New York City, music editor, 1940-46; New York Newspaper Guild, New York City, staff organizer, 1946-47; writer for *New York Daily Mirror*, 1947-49, *New York Daily Compass*, 1949-52, both New York City; writer, 1952—. *Military service:* U.S. Army Air Forces, 1942-45; Pacific theater of operations. *Member:* Authors Guild, National Association of Science Writers, National Association for the Advancement of Colored People. *Awards, honors:* George Polk award, 1952.

WRITINGS: (With William J. Keating) *The Man Who Rocked the Boat*, Harper, 1956; *The Doctor Business*, Doubleday, 1958, revised edition, 1961; *The Gentle Legions*, Doubleday, 1961; *Your Food and Your Health*, Harper, 1964; *Breakthrough: The Saga of Jonas Salk*, Trident, 1966; *Superswine*, Trident, 1966; (with Curt Flood) *The Way It Is*, Trident, 1971.

Under pseudonym Tom Ainslie: *The Compleat Horseplayer*, Simon & Schuster, 1966; *Ainslie on Jockeys*, Simon & Schuster, 1967, revised edition, 1975; *Ainslie's Complete Guide to Thoroughbred Racing*, Trident, 1968, revised edition, 1979; *The Handicapper's Handbook*, Trident, 1969; *Theory and Practice of Handicapping*, Simon & Schuster, 1969; *Ainslie's Complete Guide to Harness Racing*, Simon & Schuster, 1970, revised edition published as *Ainslie's New Complete Guide to Harness Racing*, 1980; *Ainslie's Complete Hoyle*, Simon & Schuster, 1975; *Ainslie's Encyclopedia of Thoroughbred Handicapping*, Morrow, 1978; *How to Gamble in a Casino: The Most Fun at the Least Risk*, Morrow, 1979; (with Bonnie Ledbetter) *The Body Language of Horses: Revealing the Nature of Equine Needs, Wishes, and Emotions and How Horses Communicate Them—For Owners, Breeders, Trainers, Riders, and All Other Horse Lovers—Including Handicappers*, Morrow, 1980.

SIDELIGHTS: Richard Carter writes *CA*: "It always astonishes me to discover that an aspiring writer has done little serious reading. When I can do so without starting an argument, I advise such persons to stop abusing themselves and the typewriter and begin patronizing the library. Literary development begins with avid reading, preferably in childhood but better late than never. No amount of perseverance in the accumulation of rejection slips can compensate for the lack of such background. Of course, it can be demonstrated that writers of undeveloped or absent ability land from time to time on the bestseller list. But we were talking about aspiring writers, not would-be accidents."

BIOGRAPHICAL/CRITICAL SOURCES: Book World, July 14, 1968; *Washington Post*, October 18, 1978; *Los Angeles Times Book Review*, August 17, 1980.

CARTTER, Allan Murray 1922-1976

PERSONAL: Born June 17, 1922, in Westfield, N.J.; died August 4, 1976, of cancer, in Beverly Hills, Calif.; son of Allan Murray and Bertha (Baker) Cartter; married Marietta Macklin, June 26, 1943 (divorced May, 1972); married Jill Warburg Maass, March 30, 1973; children: six stepchildren. *Education:* Colgate University, A.B., 1946; Yale University, A.M., 1949, Ph.D., 1952; Cambridge University, postgraduate student, 1950-52. *Religion:* Episcopalian. *Residence:* Beverly Hills, Calif.

CAREER: Colgate University, Hamilton, N.Y., instructor in economics, 1946-48; Duke University, Durham, N.C., 1952-58, began as assistant professor, became associate professor of economics, dean of graduate school, 1959-62; American Council on Education, Washington, D.C., vice-president, 1963-66; New York University, New York, N.Y., chancellor and executive vice-president, 1966-72; Carnegie Commission on Higher Education, Berkeley, Calif., senior research associate, 1972-74; University of California, Los Angeles, professor at Graduate School of Education and director of Laboratory of Research on Higher Education, 1974-76. Program associate, Ford Foundation, 1958-59. Member of board of directors of Theological Fund, 1966-72, and Teachers Insurance Annuity Association, 1967-71; vice-president and treasurer of Higher Education Research Institute, 1973-76. Member of numerous research commissions, including Inter-University Commission on Economic Development of the South, 1960-64, President's Economic Survey Team, Indonesia, 1961-62, Task Force on Manpower for President's Science Advisory Committee, 1963-64, Commission on Plans and Objectives for Higher Education, 1963-66, Commission on Human Resources, 1963-70, N.Y. Governor's Council of Economic Advisers, 1968-72, and National Board on Graduate Education, 1972-75; member of visiting committee of Harvard Graduate School, 1973-76. Director of studies for various foundations and for Government of Iran on the future of higher education. *Military service:* U.S. Army, 1942-45; became sergeant. *Member:* American Economic Association, Industrial Relations Research Association, American Association for the Advancement of Science, Cosmos Club (Washington, D.C.), Century Club (New York).

WRITINGS: The Redistribution of Income in Postwar Britain, Yale University Press, 1955, reprinted, Kennikat, 1973; *Theory of Wages and Employment*, Irwin, 1959, reprinted, Greenwood Press, 1976.

(With others) *Indonesia: Perspectives and Proposals for United States Economic Aid*, Yale University Southeast Asia Studies, 1963; (editor) *American Universities and Colleges*, American Council on Education, 1964; *Graduate Education: A Study in the Assessment of Quality*, American Council on Education, 1966; (with F. Ray Marshall) *Labor Economics: Wages, Employment and Trade Unionism*, Irwin, 1966, (with Marshall and Allan G. King) 3rd edition, 1976.

(Editor) *Assuring Academic Progress without Growth*, Jossey-Bass, 1975; *Ph.D.'s and the Academic Labor Market: A Report Prepared by the Carnegie Commission on Higher Education*, McGraw-Hill, 1976. Contributor to economic journals.

SIDELIGHTS: Allan Murray Cartter served as chancellor and executive vice-president of New York University during six years marked by both deepening financial problems for the institution and wide-spread student unrest over national issues, including minority rights and the Vietnam War. At the time Cartter resigned from this position, Iver Peterson noted in a

New York Times article: "Cartter's colleagues admire him above all for his handling of the student upheavals between 1968 . . . and the spring of 1970. . . . In his dealings with the students, Dr. Cartter was considered firm but understanding. He is credited with having kept several highly volatile political and racial episodes at the university from getting out of hand."

In his books, Cartter often correctly predicted trends in education. For example, in the seventies, Cartter first warned against an overabundance of Ph.D.s on the job market. Although "severely criticized by other academicians," according to Pranay Gupte writing in the *New York Times*, Cartter's warning "proved prophetic." Gupte added that Cartter was considered "one of the nation's authorities on academic manpower" at the time of his death.

BIOGRAPHICAL/CRITICAL SOURCES: *New York Times*, March 15, 1972.

OBITUARIES: *New York Times*, August 6, 1976.†

*   *   *

CAVIN, Ruth (Brodie) 1918-
(Sally Brodie, Jennie Soble)

PERSONAL: Born October 15, 1918, in Pittsburgh, Pa.; daughter of Abraham Jacob (a salesman) and Jennie (Soble) Brodie; married Bram Cavin (a writer and editor), November 26, 1946; children: Anthony, Emily, Nora. *Education:* Carnegie Institute of Technology (now Carnegie-Mellon University), B.S., 1941. *Politics:* Independent Socialist. *Religion:* None. *Home:* 2 Upland Ter., White Plains, N.Y. 10604. *Agent:* John Schaffner Associates, 425 East 51st St., New York, N.Y. 10022. *Office:* Walker & Co., 720 Fifth Ave., New York, N.Y. 10019.

CAREER: Employed as newsletter editor, public relations writer, researcher for dictionary publisher, and vacuum tube handler, 1942-68; administrative assistant, Longacre Press, 1968-73; Two Continents Publishing Group, New York City, editorial director, 1973-76, vice-president in charge of publicity, 1976-78; Walker & Co., New York City, senior editor, 1979—. *Member:* Authors League of America, Authors Guild.

WRITINGS—Juveniles, except as indicated: *Complete Party Dinners for the Novice Cook* (adult), Macmillan, 1965; *Best Restaurants of the United States* (adult), revised edition, Sun River Press, 1970; (adapter) Hans Manz, *Wheeler!*, illustrations by Werner Hofmann, Quist, 1971; (adapter) Ilse Noor, *The House on the Hill*, translated by Carola Lepping, Quist, 1971; *Timothy the Terror*, Quist, 1973; *1 Pinch of Sunshine, ½ Cup of Rain: Natural Food Recipes for Young People*, illustrations by Frances Gruse Scott, Atheneum, 1973; *Picnic Pickles*, Sun River Press, 1974; *The Day It Snowed Colored Snow*, Two Continents, 1974; (adapter under pseudonym Sally Brodie) *Litter, Rubbish, Trash*, Sun River Press, 1975; (adapter under pseudonym Jennie Soble) *Houses Keep the Weather Out*, Sun River Press, 1975; *Trolleys: Riding and Remembering the Electric Interurban Railways* (adult), Hawthorn, 1976; *A Matter of Money: What Do You Do with a Dollar?*, S. G. Phillip's, 1978; (adapter under pseudonym Sally Brodie) *The Tree outside My Window*, Cypress, 1978; (adapter under pseudonym Jennie Soble) *Presto!*, Cypress, 1978; *Crossing the Puddle*, Cypress, 1978; (ghost writer) *New York Divorce Book* (adult), Delacorte, 1980.

Also contributor to *Feasting on Raw Foods*, Rodale; adapter of "Great To-Do" series, Quist. Contributor of articles to *Good Housekeeping*.

SIDELIGHTS: Ruth Cavin told *CA*: "I am—or at least have been up to this point—a 'commercial' writer, in that I write what I think I can sell, rather than that great novel I have in my head. I particularly enjoy making a difficult subject interesting and understandable to a wide public. Of the work I've published, I most enjoyed doing *Trolleys: Riding and Remembering the Electric Interurban Railways;* the subject fascinated me and the research was most interesting and rewarding. I'm particularly good at popularizing science, but I have done cookbooks, juveniles, what-have-you. My motivation is one of perfecting a craft; I am a great respecter of the English language."

AVOCATIONAL INTERESTS: Travel, printing and production, drawing, the theatre.

*   *   *

CAWS, Peter (James) 1931-

PERSONAL: Born May 25, 1931, in Southall, England; son of Geoffrey Tulloh (an insurance man) and Olive (Budden) Caws; married Mary Ann Rorison (a professor of French), June 2, 1956; children: Hilary, Matthew. *Education:* University of London, B.Sc., 1952; Yale University, M.A., 1954, Ph.D., 1956. *Home:* 140 East 81st St., New York, N.Y. 10028. *Office:* Department of Philosophy, George Washington University, Washington, D.C. 20052.

CAREER: Michigan State University, East Lansing, instructor in natural science, 1956-57; University of Kansas, Lawrence, assistant professor of philosophy, 1957-60, associate professor, 1960-62, chairman of department, 1961-62; Carnegie Corp. of New York (educational foundation), New York City, executive associate, 1962-65, consultant, 1965-67; City University of New York, New York City, Hunter College, professor of philosophy, 1965-82, and chairman of department, 1965-67, Graduate School and University Center, executive officer of doctoral program in philosophy, 1967-70 and 1981-82; George Washington University, Washington, D.C., professor of philosophy, 1982—. Visiting professor and lecturer at Wilmington College, 1956, and University of Costa Rica, 1961; Rose Morgan Visiting Professor at University of Kansas, 1963.

MEMBER: Federation Internationale des Societies de Philosophie (chair of commission on general policy, 1979—), American Philosophical Association (member of board, 1974—), American Association for the Advancement of Science (vice-president, 1967; fellow), Philosophy of Science Association, Society for General Systems Research (president, 1966-67). *Awards, honors:* American Council of Learned Societies fellowship, 1972-73; Rockefeller humanities fellowship, 1979-80.

WRITINGS: *The Philosophy of Science: A Systematic Account*, Van Nostrand, 1965; (translator) J. M. Bochenski, *The Methods of Contemporary Thought*, Reidel (Netherlands), 1965; *Science and the Theory of Value*, Random House, 1967; *Sartre*, Routledge & Kegan Paul, 1979; (editor) *Two Centuries of Philosophy in America*, Blackwell, 1980; *Structuralism: The Art of the Intelligible*, Humanities, 1983.

Contributor: *Measurement: Definition and Theories*, Wiley, 1959; *Six Studies in Nineteenth-Century Literature and Thought*, University of Kansas Press, 1962; *The Little Magazine and Contemporary Literature*, Modern Language Association, 1966; *The Concept of Order*, University of Washington Press, 1968; *The Arts on Campus*, New York Graphic Society, 1970; *The Enlightened University*, Braziller, 1970; *Philosophy and Political Action*, Oxford University Press, 1972; *The Bankruptcy of Academic Policy*, Acropolis, 1972; *The History and Philosophy of Technology*, University of Illinois Press, 1979. Also contributor to philosophy journals.

SIDELIGHTS: Peter Caws told CA: "[I] have spent much of [my] spare time in the last decade on restoration and enlargement of a small stone house in the south of France."

* * *

CERVON, Jacqueline
See MOUSSARD, Jacqueline

* * *

CHAIJ, Fernando 1909-
(E. L. Alcalde)

PERSONAL: Born February 23, 1909, in San Fernando, Argentina; son of Gabriel (a carpenter) and Agustina (Saman) Chaij; married Sara Ramos (an editor), February 19, 1942. Education: Attended Colegio Adventista del Plata, 1931; National University of Buenos Aires, Ph.D. (with honors), 1942. Politics: "No affiliation." Religion: Seventh Day Adventist. Home: 1711 Cherrytree Lane, Mountain View, Calif. 94040. Office: 1350 Villa St., Mountain View, Calif. 94040.

CAREER: Colegio Adventista del Plata, Villa Libertador S. Martin, E. Rios, Argentina, teacher and president of the college, 1942-47; Casa Editora Sudamericana, Buenos Aires, Argentina, head of editorial department, 1948-60; Pacific Press Publishing Association, Mountain View, Calif., editor-in-chief and book editor of Spanish department, 1961-77; free-lance writer, 1977—. Member: American Academy of Political and Social Science.

WRITINGS—Published by Pacific Press Publishing Association, except as indicated: *El Desenlace del Drama Mundial*, Casa Editora Sudamericana, 1950, Pacific Press Publishing Association, 1956; *Hacia una Vida Mejor*, Casa Editora Sudamericana, 1951; *Paz en la Angustia*, Casa Editora Sudamericana, 1956, Pacific Press Publishing Association, 1959; *Potencias Supranormales que Actuan en la Vida Humana*, 1963; (with Braulio Perez Marcio and Hector Pereyra) *Libertad del Temor*, 1964.

Preparation for the Final Crisis, 1966; *Glossolalia: A New Pentecost?*, 1970; *El Dilema del Hombre*, 1972; *Un Solo Camino*, 1975; *Exploring the World of Psychic Powers*, Southern Publishing, 1971; *Como liberarse del Temor*, 1979; *The Key to Victory*, Southern Publishing, 1979; *The Impending Drama*, Southern Publishing, 1979. Contributor, sometimes under pseudonym E.L. Alcalde, to periodicals, including *El Centinela* and *Vida Feliz*. Chairman of editorial council, *El Centinela*.

SIDELIGHTS: Fernando Chaij told CA: "Although for me writing has always been a very delightful activity, the main reason for producing manuscripts for publication has been to convey a Christian and Biblical message of peace and happiness centered in Christ, whose presence in human life is the source of a meaningful existence."

* * *

CHAMBERS, William Nisbet 1916-

PERSONAL: Born November 30, 1916, in Joplin, Mo.; son of William Lionel (a lawyer and businessman) and Lucy (Matthews) Chambers; married Susan Jane Ross, April 16, 1941; children: Mary Reid, William David, Catherine Jane. Education: Harvard University, Sc.B. (magna cum laude), 1939; Washington University, St. Louis, Mo., Ph.D., 1949. Politics: "Critical Democrat." Home: 18 South Kings Highway, St. Louis, Mo. 63108; and R.F.D. 1, Box 37, Chester, N.H. 03036.

CAREER: Washington University, St. Louis, Mo., 1949-65, began as lecturer, professor of political science, 1957-65, professor of history and chairman of department, 1965-67, Edward Mallinckrodt Distinguished University Professor, 1968-78. Harvard University, visiting fellow in general education, 1956-57, and fellow at Charles Warren Center for Studies in American History, 1967-68; visiting professor of political history, Columbia University, 1959; visiting scholar, Center for Advanced Study in the Behavioral Sciences, Palo Alto, Calif., 1960. Chairman of conferences, including McDonnell Aircraft Foundation Conference on Democracy in the Mid-Twentieth Century, 1958, and Washington University and Social Science Research Council Conference on American Political Party Development, 1965-66. Co-founder, director, and member of board of directors of New City School (St. Louis). Military service: U.S. Army, 1943-45; official news correspondent, Army Forces Headquarters in western Pacific, Manila, and Philippines.

MEMBER: American Political Science Association (chairman, American government and politics section, 1963), American Historical Association, Organization of American Historians, Phi Beta Kappa, Pi Sigma Alpha, Omicron Delta Kappa, University Club of St. Louis. Awards, honors: Senior research award in governmental affairs, Social Science Research Council, 1962-63; research award in constitutional democracy, Rockefeller Foundation, 1963-64; grants from Carnegie Corp., Ford Foundation, American Council of Learned Societies, and American Philosophical Society.

WRITINGS: *Old Bullion Benton: Senator from the New West, 1782-1858*, Little, Brown, 1956, reprinted, Russell, 1970; (with Stuart A. Queen and Charles M. Winston) *The American Social System: Social Control and Individual Choice*, Houghton, 1956; (editor with Thomas H. Eliot and Robert H. Salisbury) *American Government: Readings and Problems for Analysis*, Dodd, 1959, new edition published as *American Government: Problems and Readings in Political Analysis*, 1965; (editor with Salisbury) *Democracy in the Mid-Twentieth Century: Problems and Prospects*, Washington University Press, 1960; (editor with Salisbury) *Democracy Today*, Collier, 1962; (contributor) *America's Ten Greatest Presidents*, Rand McNally, 1962; *Political Parties in a New Nation: The American Experience, 1776-1809*, Oxford University Press, 1963; *The Democrats, 1789-1964: A Short History of a Popular Party*, Van Nostrand, 1964, 2nd edition published as *The Democrats in American Politics: A Short History of a Popular Party*, 1972; (editor with W. Burnham) *American Party System*, Oxford University Press, 1967, 2nd edition, 1975; (compiler) *The Party System: Federalists and Republicans*, Wiley, 1972. Contributor to *St. Louis Post-Dispatch*, *Encyclopaedia Britannica*, *Encyclopedia Americana*, *Collier's Encyclopedia*, and professional journals.†

* * *

CHAMPION, John C(arr) 1923-

PERSONAL: Born October 13, 1923, in Denver, Colo.; son of Lee Rogers (a judge) and Alice Champion; married Madelon F. Green, January 27, 1951; children: John, Jr., Robert, Gina. Education: Attended Stanford University, 1941-42, 1945; additional study at Wittenburg College. Home: 16157 Morrison, Encino, Calif. 91316. Agent: David Shapira, 15301 Ventura Blvd., Sherman Oaks, Calif. 91403.

CAREER: Independent writer and producer for motion pictures and television, 1946—. Formerly employed in radio field, as a stock actor for Metro Goldwyn Mayer Studios, and as a co-pilot for Western Airlines; also worked as writer and producer for Allied Artists, vice-president in charge of production for Commander Films Corp., president, Champion Pictures, Inc., and as writer and producer for Metro Goldwyn Mayer, Warner Brothers, and Paramount; executive writer and producer of "Laramie" series for Universal-National Broadcasting Co., 1959-62; creator of "McHale's Navy" for Universal-American Broadcasting Co., 1963; director of "Oregon Trail" for Universal, 1976. *Military service:* U.S. Army Air Forces, Air Transport Command, 1943-45; became flight officer. *Member:* National Academy of Television Arts and Sciences, Screen Writers Guild, Screen Producers Guild, Society of Independent Motion Picture Producers, Screen Actors Guild.

WRITINGS: The Hawks of Noon (novel), McKay, 1965; *Mustang Country* (novel), Pocket Books, 1975.

Screenplays: "Panhandle," Allied Artists, 1948; "Stampede," Allied Artists, 1949; "Hellgate," Allied Artists, 1952; "Dragonfly Squadron," Allied Artists, 1954; "Shotgun," Allied Artists, 1955; (with Arthur Hailey and Hall Bartlet) "Zero Hour," Paramount, 1958; "The Texican," Columbia, 1966; "Attack on the Iron Coast," United Artists, 1968; "Submarine X-1," United Artists, 1969; "The Last Escape," United Artists, 1970; "Brother of the Wind," Sun International, 1972; (also director) "Mustang Country" (based on his novel of the same title), Universal, 1976.

WORK IN PROGRESS: A screenplay.

SIDELIGHTS: John C. Champion told *CA,* "I like to write about people who believe in something strongly enough to overcome their natural inclination to do nothing about it."

* * *

CHAN, Loren Briggs 1943-

PERSONAL: Born September 10, 1943, in Palo Alto, Calif.; son of S. Wing (a professor) and Anna Mae (Chin) Chan; married Frances A. Chow (a dietitian), April 19, 1975. *Education:* Stanford University, A.B., 1965, A.M., 1966; University of California, Los Angeles, M.A., 1967, C.Phil., 1969, Ph.D., 1971; Technical Training Center, diploma in computer technology, 1982. *Home:* 6182 Ocho Rios Dr., San Jose, Calif. 95123. *Office:* Nicolet Paratronics Corp., 201 Fourier Ave., Bldg. A, Fremont, Calif. 94539.

CAREER: San Fernando Valley State College (now California State University, Northridge, Los Angeles), lecturer in history, 1970-71; San Jose State University, San Jose, Calif., lecturer, 1971-72, assistant professor, 1972-76, associate professor of history, 1976-80; California State University, Hayward, lecturer in history, 1980-81; Nicolet Paratronics Corp., Fremont, Calif., electronics technician, 1982—. Member of Institute of Pacific Studies. *Member:* Chinese Historical Society of America (member of executive committee, 1972-75), American Radio Relay League, Nevada State Historical Society. *Awards, honors:* D.D., Universal Life Church of Arizona, 1969.

WRITINGS: Sagebrush Statesman: Tasker L. Oddie of Nevada, University of Nevada Press, 1973; *Chinese-American History Reader and Workbook,* Spartan Bookstore, 1976; (contributor) Thomas W. Chinn and others, editors, *Proceedings of the National Conference on the Life, Influence, and Role of the Chinese in the United States, 1776-1960,* Chinese Historical Society of America, 1976; *New Light on a New Land: Recent Research in Western History,* Spartan Bookstore, 1977; (contributor) Robert Sobel, editor, *The Biographical Directory of the Governors of the United States, 1789-1978,* four volumes, Meckler, 1978. Contributor of articles and reviews to journals.

WORK IN PROGRESS: Research on Chinese-American history and on digital electronics.

* * *

CHANDONNET, Ann 1943-

PERSONAL: Surname is pronounced Shan-doe-*nay;* born February 7, 1943, in Lowell, Mass.; daughter of Leighton D. (a farmer) and Barbara (Cloutman) Fox; married Fernand Chandonnet (a radio announcer), June 11, 1966; children: Yves, Alexdre Jules. *Education:* Lowell State College, B.S. (magna cum laude), 1964; University of Wisconsin, M.S., 1965; graduate study at Boston University, 1967. *Home address:* P.O. Box A, Chugiak, Alaska 99567-0903.

CAREER: Dog-walker, housepainter, secretary; high school English teacher in the public schools of Kodiak, Alaska, 1965-66; Lowell State College, Lowell, Mass., instructor in English, 1966-69; Security National Bank, Oakland, Calif., secretary to manager, 1970-71; First Enterprise Bank, Oakland, administrative assistant to president, 1971-72; *Anchorage Daily News,* Anchorage, Alaska, food editor, beginning 1975, children's book reviewer, 1979—; free-lance writer. *Member:* Literary Artists Guild of Alaska, Alaska Press Women, Mayflower Descendants in the State of Alaska. *Awards, honors:* First place award from Alaska Press Women, 1975, for a feature article, "Keeping an Ancient Art Alive," a profile of one of the last surviving Aleut basketweavers.

WRITINGS: Incunabula (poems), Quixote Press, 1967; *The Complete Fruit Cookbook,* 101 Productions, 1972; *The Cheese Guide and Cookbook,* Nitty Gritty Productions, 1973; *The Wife & Other Poems,* privately printed, 1977, 2nd edition, 1980; *The Wife: Part 2* (poems), privately printed, 1979; (self-illustrated) *The Once & Future Village of Ikluat-Eklutna,* privately printed, 1979; *At the Fruit-Tree's Mossy Root,* Wings Press, 1980; *Ptarmigan Valley* (poems), Lightning Tree, 1980. Contributor to *California Girl, Venus, Early American Life, Anchorage Daily News, Great Lander, Women's Circle: Home Cooking, Christian Science Monitor,* and *Alaska Journal.* Food editor, *Diablo Valley Voice,* 1971-72.

WORK IN PROGRESS: Auras, Tendrils, a collection of poems; a history of the Athapascan Indians of Cook Inlet.

AVOCATIONAL INTERESTS: Conducting living history interviews, skindiving, backpacking, sewing, gardening.

* * *

CHAPMAN, J. Dudley 1928-
(Jay Dudley)

PERSONAL: Born April 29, 1928, in Moline, Ill.; son of Joseph Dudley (a salesman) and Illian Caroline (Pruder) Chapman; married Mary Kay Sartini, June 15, 1948; married Virginia Helene Milius (a laboratory technician), June 17, 1958; children: (first marriage) Mary Jo, Nancy Jo. *Education:* Attended University of Illinois, 1946-48; Roosevelt University, B.S., 1949; College of Osteopathic Medicine and Surgery, D.O., 1953, D.S., 1968; University of California, Irvine, M.D., 1962. *Politics:* "Ambivalent." *Religion:* Lutheran. *Home:* 6374 Lake Rd., North Madison, Ohio 44057. *Office address:* P.O. Box 340, North Madison, Ohio 44057.

CAREER: Diplomate and member of American Osteopathic Board of Obstetrics and Gynecology. College of Osteopathic

Medicine and Surgery, Still Osteopathic Hospital, Des Moines, Iowa, associate professor of obstetrics and gynecology, 1956-58, chairman of department, 1957-58; private practice of obstetrics and gynecology in Ohio, 1958—; Brentwood Hospital, Cleveland, Ohio, chief of obstetrics and gynecology, 1958-61; Bayview Hospital, Bay Village, Ohio, senior obstetrician and gynecologist, 1961-63, consultant, 1963—; Northeastern Ohio General Hospital, Madison, chief of staff, 1967—. Member of faculty and academic board, Institute for Advanced Study of Human Sexuality, San Francisco, 1976—; clinical associate professor, College of Osteopathic Medicine, Ohio University, 1979—; lecturer at professional meetings, seminars, and conferences. Aviation medical examiner, Federal Aviation Agency.

MEMBER: International Society of Comprehensive Medicine (charter member; member of national scientific advisory council; member of editorial board), American College of Osteopathic Obstetricians and Gynecologists (fellow; president, 1966-67; member of editorial board), American Osteopathic Association, Society of Psychosomatic Medicine (executive secretary), Academy of Psychosomatic Medicine (fellow), American Medical Writers' Association, Aerospace Medical Association, Ohio Society of Osteopathic Obstetricians and Gynecologists (past president), Ohio Osteopathic Association of Physicians and Surgeons.

WRITINGS: *The Feminine Mind and Body,* Philosophical Library, 1967; (contributor) Nat Lehrman, *Masters and Johnson Explained,* Playboy Press, 1976; *The Sexual Equation: Man; Woman; Socially; Sexually,* Philosophical Library, 1977; (contributor) Leslie Kaslof, editor, *Wholistic Dimensions in Healing,* Doubleday, 1978. Contributor of articles and reviews to osteopathic and other journals of medicine and health. Editor-in-chief, *Osteopathic Physician,* 1968; member of editorial board, *Penthouse* "Forum."

WORK IN PROGRESS: *The Feminine Existant; My Devil Fear;* research in process thought as it affects feminine behavior and function, psychosexual problems relative to rapid management, and psychedelic agents and their relationship to hypnoidal phenomena.

SIDELIGHTS: J. Dudley Chapman believes that "writing memorializes our existence and delineates our contributions. *Avocational interests:* Aviation (holds commercial pilot's license with instrument rating), swimming, diving.

*   *   *

CHAPPELL, Fred 1936-

PERSONAL: Surname rhymes with "apple"; born May 28, 1936, in Canton, N.C.; son of James Taylor (a furniture retailer) and Anne (Davis) Chappell; married Susan Nicholls, August 2, 1959; children: Heath (son). *Education:* Duke University, B.A., 1961, M.A., 1964. *Politics:* Democrat. *Home:* 305 Kensington Rd., Greensboro, N.C. *Agent:* Peter Matson, 32 West 40th St., New York, N.Y. 10018.

CAREER: Brown Supply Co., Candler, N.C., general manager, 1957-59; Candler Furniture Co., Candler, credit manager, 1959-60; Duke University Press, Durham, N.C., proofreader, 1961; University of North Carolina at Greensboro, professor of English, 1964-72. *Member:* Southeastern Renaissance Association.

AWARDS, HONORS: Woodrow Wilson fellow; National Defense Act fellow; Rockefeller Foundation grant, 1966; National Institute of Arts and Letters grant, 1967; National Institute and American Academy awards in literature, 1968; Prix de Meilleur des Lettres Etrangers, French Academy, 1971, for *Dagon;* Roanoke-Chowan Poetry Cup, 1972, for *The World between the Eyes,* 1978, for *River: A Poem,* and 1979, for *Bloodfire: A Poem;* Sir Walter Raleigh Award, 1973, for *The Gaudy Place.*

WRITINGS—Novels: *It Is Time, Lord,* Atheneum, 1963; *The Inkling,* Harcourt, 1965; *Dagon,* Harcourt, 1968; *The Gaudy Place,* Harcourt, 1973.

Poetry; published by Louisiana State University Press, except as indicated: *The World between the Eyes,* 1971; *River: A Poem,* 1975; *The Man Twice Married to Fire,* Unicorn Press, 1977; *Bloodfire: A Poem,* 1978; *Wind Mountain: A Poem,* 1979; *Awakening to Music,* Briarpatch Press, 1979; *Earthsleep: A Poem,* 1980; *Midquest: A Poem* (contains *River: A Poem, Bloodfire: A Poem, Wind Mountain: A Poem,* and *Earthsleep: A Poem*), 1981.

Other: (Contributor) William Blackburn, editor, *Under Twenty-five: Duke Narrative and Verse, 1945-1962,* Duke University Press, 1963; *Moments of Light* (short story collection), New South Company, 1980.

Contributor to *Sewanee Review, Saturday Evening Post, American Review,* and other periodicals. Contributing editor, *Skyhook* and *Red Clay Reader;* advisory editor, *Greensboro Review, Appalachian Heritage,* and *Brown Bag;* editor, *Archive* and *Fly by Night.*

SIDELIGHTS: Novelist Fred Chappell has been praised as a skilled writer by critics in both the United States and Europe. His novels of the modern American South are concerned with characters who, David Paul Ragan of *The Dictionary of Literary Biography* writes, "have been displaced by a new society which has usurped an older, more stable culture. Chappell's books unfold during the period in which the traditional mountain culture is disintegrating." Each of Chappell's novels, Ragan believes, "creates a minutely detailed world in which image and symbol unite to form a densely woven fabric of meaning."

Employing the conventions of the Southern gothic novel, Chappell's stories explore a world of violence, illicit sex, and degradation, relating these social phenomena to the destruction of traditional Southern society. "As Chappell grew up," Ragan explains, "he observed a culture undergoing a transition from a primarily agrarian economy to a society in which one's ties with the land and the stability this connection instills became more and more distant. This upheaval underlies all of Chappell's work."

It Is Time, Lord, Chappell's first novel, concerns James Christopher, a weak and despondent man whose personality disintegrates as he drifts through a number of superficial relationships. The book's narrative structure combines chapters set in the present with the protagonist's unreliable journal entries about past events. Because of these conflicting narratives, the reality of the situation becomes unclear, echoing the protagonist's own mental state. R. A. Francoeur of *Best Sellers* finds that Chappell "skillfully interweaves memory and consciousness to produce an intriguing blend of fantasy and reality." He finds that "the main merit of this book lies in the simplicity of its style and the sharpness of its descriptions. With clean verbal strokes Chappell brings his characters into focus." Nelson Aldrich of the *New York Herald Tribune Book Review* agrees with Francoeur. Although thinking the protagonist's life story to be "a tedious thing," Aldrich nonetheless judges "the descriptions of a farming childhood and the portraits of [Christopher's] grandparents and father [to be] done with a hard, sure talent."

In his second novel, *The Inkling,* Chappell again uses a complex narrative structure, this one cyclical, beginning and ending the novel with the same scene. Set in North Carolina and involving five characters in the same family, the story concerns the young boy Jan and his struggle to develop self-control in the face of his sister's growing insanity, his mother's death, and his own seduction by an aunt. It is another story of failure and personality disintegration. Kenneth Lamott of *Book Week* admits that "Chappell writes like a whiz" but states: "I cannot promise to keep the peace if I am exposed to another bright young Southern writer who is hooked on incest, barnyard sadism, imbecility, and domestic bloodletting." In similar terms, the reviewer for the *Times Literary Supplement* writes: "If Mr. Chappell's considerable powers are to be used satisfactorily he must break away from or perhaps redirect the, by now, stale Southern myth of Carson McCullers and Tennessee Williams." In contrast to these opinions, C. P. Collier of *Best Sellers* judges *The Inkling* to be "a short, complex novel with a fine sense of dramatic assurance, disarming simplicity, and disquieting perception." He calls it "a wondrous piece of fresh and vigorous writing. Mr. Chappell moves smoothly from passions and cruelties to the beautiful imagery of dreams and the musings of a deluded mind. . . . For those readers who like good writing, in spite of the subject or the incidents, this is a small masterpiece."

Dagon, Chappell's third novel and winner of the French Academy's Prix de Meilleur des Lettres Etrangers, borrows settings and themes from the Southern gothic but includes elements from horror fiction, surrealism, and mysticism, as well. It is the first of Chappell's novels to use a conventional narrative structure and his only novel to date to have a transcendent ending. Like Chappell's previous books, *Dagon* deals with the destruction of personality. Its protagonist is Peter Leland, a minister who returns to his family estate in North Carolina to research pagan beliefs in America. He soon comes under the influence of Mina, a teenage girl who is both a sadist and nymphomaniac. She slowly destroys Leland's self-esteem, causes him to murder his wife, brutalizes and tortures him, and finally kills him in a sacrificial ritual to the pagan god Dagon. But Leland's personality survives even his physical death and metamorphoses into a new form of life in a realm where, as Ragan states, "metaphor and substance become one." Although advised by friends to omit the conclusion of the novel, Chappell believes his ending to be, according to Ragan, "a conscious effort 'to alleviate the agony of [the novel]'."

Critical response in the United States found the book well-written but lacking in motivation and believability. Robert B. Nordberg of *Best Sellers,* for example, calls the novel "absorbing" and Chappell's prose "skilled writing." "Nevertheless," Nordberg concludes, "it doesn't, somehow, make much sense." Peter Buitenhaus of the *New York Times Book Review* holds a similar opinion. Although he finds that "the style of the novel is of a very high order [and] its precise, dry elegance contrasts piquantly with its sleazy material," Buitenhaus believes "Chappell does not show adequately why Peter [Leland] suddenly nosedives from melancholy to mayhem and from scholarship to sadomasochism. Peter's lack of motivation makes him seem a mechanical figure, and it is hard to get excited by the systematic brutalization and torture that is meted out to him." The reviewer for the *Virginia Quarterly Review* sees the same fault in the novel. "Credulity is sometimes lost for the reader," he maintains, "as a result of the author's failure to elaborate upon the weaknesses inherent in the minister's character and to develop even further than he has the element of doom." But he concludes that "whatever defects the story may possess in a technical sense are far outweighed by the brilliance and sureness of the writing."

Dagon's reception in Europe, particularly in France where the book met with critical and commercial success, was highly favorable. "The warmth of [Chappell's] French reception," writes Ragan, "recalls that of William Faulkner, whose reputation as a novelist was very high in France while his work was being virtually ignored in this country."

With *The Gaudy Place,* Chappell decided to write a different kind of novel than he had previously published. A novel in which, as Ragan quotes Chappell, "all the pieces fitted together, and that had a latitude of characterization in it." The result is a book that relies far more on plot than did Chappell's previous works, and that depends on a carefully-developed sequence of events for its tragic ending.

The story is set in the seamy district of a North Carolina city where a prostitute, her pimp, and a teenage gambler briefly cross paths with a respectable professor and his family. Divided into five chapters, each told from a different character's perspective, the novel is, the reviewer for *New Republic* believes, "a series of character studies connected by an unpretentious plot." Writing in the *New York Times Book Review,* Jonathan Yardley argues that the novel's only fault is this use of character studies. The novel "is told from five points of view," he states, "and in shifting from one to another Chappell does not maintain a consistent flow." Despite this problem, Yardley finds that "the novel has considerable strengths: sharp, precise prose; several fine comic scenes; good dialogue; and, most important, an accurate feel for the new urban South." The *Choice* critic judges it "an almost perfectly executed, modest novel."

In evaluating Chappell's accomplishment as a novelist, Ragan notes that "Chappell's work has won reviewers' praise and the respect of fellow writers" and points out that "an even more important gauge of Chappell's significance is the strength of his international reputation." Yardley concludes that "Chappell is a serious and uncommonly skillful writer."

BIOGRAPHICAL/CRITICAL SOURCES: Saturday Review, August 10, 1963; *Best Sellers,* August 15, 1963, August 15, 1965, September 1, 1968; *New York Herald Tribune Book Review,* August 18, 1963; *New York Times Book Review,* September 8, 1963, September 29, 1968, May 13, 1973; *Book Week,* August 15, 1965; *Times Literary Supplement,* November 10, 1966; *Virginia Quarterly Review,* winter, 1969, summer, 1973; *Sewanee Review,* April, 1970, July, 1976; George Garrett, editor, *Craft So Hard to Learn: Conversations with Poets and Novelists about the Teaching of Writing,* Morrow, 1972; *Library Journal,* February 15, 1973; *Georgia Review,* spring, 1973; *Hollins Critic,* April, 1973; *New Republic,* June 2, 1973; *Choice,* October, 1973; *Hudson Review,* spring, 1976; *Southern Review,* October, 1976; *Mississippi Quarterly,* fall, 1978; *The Dictionary of Literary Biography,* Volume VI: *American Novelists since World War II,* 2nd series, Gale, 1980; *American Book Review,* July-August, 1981.

—*Sketch by Thomas Wiloch*

* * *

CHAPPELL, Warren 1904-

PERSONAL: Born July 9, 1904, in Richmond, Va.; son of Samuel M. (a railway clerk) and Mary L. (Hardie) Chappell; married Lydia A. Hatfield, August 28, 1928. *Education:* University of Richmond, B.A., 1926; studied art at Art Students League, New York, N.Y., 1926-28, Offenbacher Werkstatt in Germany, 1931-32, and Colorado Springs Fine Arts Center,

1935-36. *Politics:* Independent. *Religion:* Protestant. *Home:* 500 Court Sq., Charlottesville, Va. 22901.

CAREER: Designer, graphic artist, and illustrator. Art Students League, New York City, member of board of control, 1927-31 and instructor, 1933-35; Colorado Springs Fine Arts Center, Colorado Springs, Colo., instructor, 1935-36; lecturer at New York University, New York City. Artist-in-residence, University of Virginia, 1979. Consultant to Book-of-the-Month Club, 1944-77. *Member:* Phi Beta Kappa. *Awards, honors:* Doctor of Fine Arts, University of Richmond, 1968; Goudy Award from Rochester Institute of Technology, 1970.

WRITINGS: The Anatomy of Lettering, Loring & Mussey, 1935; *They Say Stories*, Knopf, 1960; *A Short History of the Printed Word: A New York Times Book*, Knopf, 1970; *The Living Alphabet*, University Press of Virginia, 1975. Contributor of articles and illustrations to periodicals, including *Virginia Quarterly Review* and *Dolphin*.

Adapter: *The Nutcracker* (music by Tchaikovsky), Knopf, 1958; *The Sleeping Beauty* (music by Tchaikovsky), Knopf, 1961; *Coppelia* (music by Delibes), Knopf, 1965.

Illustrator: Miguel de Cervantes, *The Adventures of Don Quixote de la Mancha*, Knopf, 1939, new edition, 1960; Sergei Prokofiev, *Peter and the Wolf*, Knopf, 1940; Corinne B. Lowe, *Knights of the Sea*, Harcourt, 1941; Julian David, *Three Horses*, Little, Brown, 1942; Mark Twain, *A Connecticut Yankee in King Arthur's Court*, Heritage House, 1942; Elizabeth Yates, *Patterns on the Wall*, Dutton, 1943, new edition, 1953; Henry Fielding, *Tom Jones*, Illustrated Modern Library, 1943, new edition, 1982; *The Comedies and Tragedies of Shakespeare*, Random House, 1944; Grimm Brothers, *Hansel and Gretel*, Knopf, 1944; Catherine Besterman, *Quaint and Curious Quest of Johnny Longfoot, the Shoe King's Son*, Bobbs-Merrill, 1947; Edward C. Wagenknecht, editor, *The Fireside Book of Ghost Stories*, Bobbs-Merrill, 1947; Babette Deutsch, adapter, *Reader's Shakespeare*, Messner, 1947; Wagenknecht, editor, *A Fireside Book of Yuletide Tales*, Bobbs-Merrill, 1948; Besterman, *Extraordinary Education of Johnny Longfoot in His Search for the Magic Hat*, Bobbs-Merrill, 1949.

Jane Austen, *The Complete Novels of Jane Austen*, two volumes, Random House, 1950; Regina Z. Kelly, *Young Geoffrey Chaucer*, Lothrop, 1952; Vincent Sheean, *Thomas Jefferson*, Random House, 1953; Thomas B. Costain, *Mississippi Bubble*, Random House, 1955; Manuel Komroff, *Mozart*, Knopf, 1956; Walter De La Mare, *Come Hither*, Knopf, 1957; Irving Kolodin, *Musical Life*, Knopf, 1958.

Charles Perrault, *The Sleeping Beauty*, Knopf, 1961; William McCleery, *Wolf Story*, Simon & Schuster, 1961; John Updike, *The Magic Flute*, Knopf, 1962; Updike, *Ring*, Knopf, 1964; Sid Fleischman, *The Ghost in the Noonday Sun*, Little, Brown, 1965; Conrad Richter, *The Light in the Forest*, Knopf, 1966; Kate Douglas Wiggin and N. A. Smith, *The Fairy Ring*, Doubleday, 1967; Paul Delarue, compiler, *French Fairy Tales*, Knopf, 1968; Geoffrey Household, *Prisoner of the Indies*, Little, Brown, 1968; Updike, *Bottom's Dream*, Knopf, 1969.

Charles B. Hawes, *Dark Frigate*, Little, Brown, 1971; Herman Melville, *Moby Dick*, Norton, 1976; Charles Dickens, *A Dicken's Christmas*, Oxford University Press, 1976; Jonathan Swift, *Gulliver's Travels*, Oxford University Press, 1977; Mark Twain, *Tom Sawyer* [and] *The Adventures of Huckleberry Finn*, Harper, 1978. Also illustrator of *The Temptation of Saint Anthony*, Limited Editions Club, 1942, and *All the King's Men*, Harcourt, 1981.

BIOGRAPHICAL/CRITICAL SOURCES: American Artist, October, 1944; *Publishers Weekly*, October 1, 1955; *Illustrators of Children's Books: 1946-1956*, Horn Book, 1958; Norma Fryatt, editor, *A Horn Book Sampler*, Horn Book, 1959; Diana Klemin, *The Art of Art for Children's Books*, Clarkson Potter, 1966; *Illustrators of Children's Books: 1957-1966*, Horn Book, 1968; Elinor W. Field, *Horn Book Reflections*, Horn Book, 1969; Klemin, *The Illustrated Book*, Clarkson Potter, 1970; *Horn Book*, October, 1971; de Montreville and Hill, editors, *Third Book of Junior Authors*, H. W. Wilson, 1972.

* * *

CHATHAM, Doug(las) M. 1938-

PERSONAL: Born November 24, 1938, in Monroe, La.; son of Bert and Hazel (May) Chatham; married Jackie Reed, June 5, 1959; children: Teresa, Douglas, Jr. *Education:* Mississippi College, B.S., 1964; New Orleans Baptist Theological Seminary, M.R.E., 1968; Christian International University, D.D. *Residence:* Conyers, Ga. *Office:* Conyers Academy, 1004 Green St., Conyers, Ga. 30207.

CAREER: Pastor in Greenville, Miss., 1965-67, New Orleans, La., 1968-69, Milton, Fla., 1969-72, and Stone Mountain, Ga., beginning 1972; affiliated with Conyers Academy, Conyers, Ga. Assistant to president of New Orleans Baptist Theological Seminary, 1968-69. Member of archaeological expedition to Beersheba, Israel, 1969. Frequent speaker in charismatic Christian movement. *Member:* Smithsonian Institution.

WRITINGS: Notes on the Rapture, Daniels Publishers, 1973; *The Rapture Book*, Whitaker House, 1974; *The Shepherd's Touch*, Cross Roads Publications, 1975; *The Shepherd's Church*, Cross Roads Publications, 1976; *Signs*, Our Shepherd's Books, 1978; *The Joseph Principle*, Our Shepherd's Books, 1981; (ghost writer) Frank Ford, *The Coming Food Crisis*, Chosen Books, 1982.

WORK IN PROGRESS: The Emerging Christian Counter-Economy; Living in the Supernatural.

SIDELIGHTS: Doug M. Chatham writes that he was saved at age eighteen while in jail in New Orleans and was called to preach at the same moment. Prior to receiving a pardon from the governor in 1959, he pastored his first church in 1958, while still on probation.

About his writing, Chatham told *CA:* "My writing is an extension of my speaking. I usually write to communicate more clearly what I feel my audiences receive enthusiastically but partially. In the beginning there was a great deal of interest in the theology of the Second Coming of Christ; then in the Renewal movement; and more recently, in preparation for the coming hard times." He adds: "I continue my interest in travel to remote cultures and in archaeology, as well as an active involvement in the Christian Embassy at Jerusalem. I hope to produce some day a serious historical or anthropological work out of these interests."

AVOCATIONAL INTERESTS: Archaeology, travel.

* * *

CHENEY, Ted
See CHENEY, Theodore Albert

* * *

CHENEY, Theodore A. Rees
See CHENEY, Theodore Albert

CHENEY, Theodore Albert 1928-
(Ted Cheney, Theodore A. Rees Cheney)

PERSONAL: Born January 1, 1928, in Milton, Mass.; son of Ralph Albert and Ruth (Rees) Cheney; married Dorothy Catherine Bates, September 3, 1949; children: Glenn Alan, Ralph Hunter, Bonnie Bates, Burke Adams. *Education:* Boston University, A.B., 1951, M.A. (geography), 1952; Fairfield University, M.A. (communication), 1973. *Politics:* "Progressive Conservative." *Religion:* Protestant. *Home:* 399 Round Hill Rd., Fairfield, Conn. 06430. *Office:* Graduate School of Corporate and Political Communication, Fairfield University, Fairfield, Conn. 06430.

CAREER: Photogrammetrist for Park Aerial Surveys, Inc., 1952-54; Cornell University, Ithaca, N.Y., assistant professor of photogrammetry, 1954-58; Geotechnics & Resources, Inc., White Plains, N.Y., vice-president, 1958-64; Dunlap & Associates ("think tank"), Darien, Conn., senior scientist, 1964-69; Fairfield University, Fairfield, Conn., lecturer in writing and director of professional writing program, 1969—, acting dean, 1981, 1982. *Military service:* U.S. Navy, 1945-47. *Member:* Authors Guild, Authors League of America.

WRITINGS: (Editor) *Burma: Landforms, Forestry, Geology*, Cornell University Press, 1956; *Fort Churchill, Manitoba, Canada: An Environmental Analysis*, Cornell University Press, 1957; (under name Ted Cheney) *Land of the Hibernating Rivers* (juvenile), Harcourt, 1968; *Camping by Backpack and Canoe*, Harper, 1970; (editor) Howard Smith and Paul Brourer, *Performance Appraisal and Human Development*, Addison, 1980; (under name Theodore A. Rees Cheney) *Day of Fate* (novel), Ace Books, 1981; *Cut, Revise, and Edit*, Writer's Digest, in press;

WORK IN PROGRESS: Research for a book about creativity and problem solving, *Soft Logic*.

SIDELIGHTS: Theodore Albert Cheney says he volunteered "to go to Little America, Antarctica at age seventeen while in the U.S. Navy, which led to a life-long interest in polar matters—out of which came my first book, [*Land of the Hibernating Rivers*]. Camping and canoeing as a Boy Scout leader over the years led to the second book."

* * *

CHEYNEY, Arnold B. 1926-

PERSONAL: Born February 23, 1926, in Massillon, Ohio; son of Ray A. and Viola May (Zurcher) Cheyney; married Jeanne Smith, September 3, 1948; children: Steven, Timothy. *Education:* Kent State University, B.S., 1944, M.Ed., 1951; Ohio State University, Ph.D., 1964. *Religion:* Baptist. *Home:* 5861 Southwest 51st Ter., Miami, Fla. 33155. *Office:* School of Education, University of Miami, Coral Gables, Fla. 33124.

CAREER: Elementary teacher in public schools of Suffield, Ohio, 1949-50, Canton, Ohio, 1950-55; elementary principal in Canton, 1955-58, supervisor of elementary education, 1958-61; Ohio State University, Columbus, instructor in education, 1961-64; University of Miami, Coral Gables, Fla., 1964—, began as associate professor, currently professor of elementary education. *Military service:* U.S. Marine Corps, 1944-46; served in South Pacific, Okinawa, and China; received Purple Heart. *Member:* International Reading Association, Association for Childhood Education International, National Council of Teachers of English, National Education Association (life member), National Committee on the Education of Migrant Children. *Awards, honors:* American Library Association Outstanding Academic Book award, 1973, for *The Ripe Harvest*.

WRITINGS: Teaching Culturally Disadvantaged in the Elementary School: A Language Approach, C.E. Merrill, 1967, 2nd edition published as *Teaching Children of Different Cultures in the Classroom: A Language Approach*, 1976; *Teaching Reading Skills through the Newspaper*, International Reading Association, 1971; (editor) *The Ripe Harvest: Educating Migrant Children*, University of Miami Press, 1972; *Puppet Enrichment Program*, Ideal School Supply Company, 1973; *Curriculum for Grades Two and Three*, Baptist Publications, 1973; *Press: A Handbook Showing the Use of Newspaper in the Elementary Classroom*, Educational Service, 1978; *The Writing Corner*, Scott, Foresman, 1979; *Video: A Handbook Showing the Use of Television in the Elementary Classroom*, Educational Service, 1980; *The Poetry Corner*, Scott, Foresman, 1982. Contributor of over 100 articles to periodicals.

WORK IN PROGRESS: The Map Corner, for Scott, Foresman.

* * *

CHIARA, Piero 1913-

PERSONAL: Born March 23, 1913, in Luino, Varese, Italy; son of Eugenio and Virginia (Maffei) Chiara; married Jula Scherb (divorced, 1972); married Irma Buzzetti, 1975; children: (first marriage) Marco. *Education:* Attended Scuole Medie Superiori. *Religion:* Roman Catholic. *Home:* Via Metastasio, 19, 21100 Varese, Italy. *Agent:* Avv. Giorgio Moscon, Via Settembrini 7, Rome, Italy.

CAREER: Writer. Began publishing a literary journal independently in 1942; after an order was issued for his capture for anti-fascist activities, sought refuge in Switzerland, escaping a fifteen-year sentence; held position of professor of letters, history, and philosophy at an Italian school in Zug, Switzerland, and was affiliated with Istituto Montana. *Member:* Rotary (Varese).

AWARDS, HONORS: "Silver-Caffe" prize, 1962, for *Il piatto piange;* Accademia del Ceppo di Pistoia Prize for best story of the year, 1964; Alpi-Apuane-Pea Prize and Campiello Prize, both 1964, for *La spartizione;* Veillon Prize (Switzerland), 1965, for *Con la faccia per terra;* Officiel des Palmes Academiques (Paris), 1967; Bagutta Prize, 1968, for *Il balordo;* Knight Commander of Republic of Italy, 1971; "Nastro d'argento" Prize for best screenplay of the year, Sindicato Nazione Giornalisti, 1971, for collaboration on "Venga a prendere il caffe da noi"; Rustichello da Pisa Prize, *Il Corriere della Sera* (newspaper), 1971, for an article; Ambrogino d'oro and citation as "Cittadino benemerito" from city of Milan, both 1973; Campione d'Italia journalism prize, 1974, for *Il pretore di Cuvio;* Napoli Prize, 1976, Efebo d'Oro Prize, 1979, both for *La stanza del Vescovo;* Giacomo Casanova-Venise Prize, 1978; Bancarella Prize and Mediterraneo Prize, both 1979, for *Vita di Gabriele D'Annunzio*.

WRITINGS: Incantavi (poetry), Poschiavo, 1945; *Itinerario svizzero* (travelog), Edizioni del "Giornale del Popolo," 1950; *Dolore del tempo* (short stories), Rebellato, 1959; (author of preface and notes) Giovan Pietro Olina, *L'uccelliera*, Ferriani, 1960; *L'opera grafica di Giuseppe Viviani*, Rebellato, 1960; *Il piatto piange* (novel), Mondadori, 1962; *Mi fo coragio da me* (prose), Scheiwiller, 1963; *La spartizione* (novel), Mondadori, 1964, 6th edition, 1974, translation by Julia Martinez published as *A Man of Parts*, Little, Brown, 1968; (author of introduction) Cesare Colombo, *La Prealpi varesine* (photographs), Editore L.E.A., 1964; *La sostanza della cose, con 18 disegni di Tabusso*, G. Ferrari, 1965; *Con la faccia per terra* (novel), Vallecchi, 1965, published as *Con la faccia per terra e altre storie*, Mondadori, 1972; *Ti sento, Giuditta* (short story), Scheiwiller, 1965; *Il povero Turati* (short fiction), Renzo Sommaruga, 1966; *I ladri* (short stories), Scheiwiller, 1967; *Il balordo* (novel), Mondadori, 1967; *Un racconto di P. Chiara, con 10 litografie di A. Possenti*, E.L.B., 1968; *L'ora esatta, con una acquaforte di Tabusso*, G. Ferrari, 1969; *L'uovo al cianuro e altre storie* (short stories), Mondadori, 1969.

I giovedi della signora Giulia, Mondadori, 1970; *Un turco tra noi* (short fiction), Scheiwiller, 1970; *Ella signor giudice . . .* (short story), Scheiwiller, 1971; *Il pretore di Cuvio* (novel), Mondadori, 1973; *Sotto la Sua mano, La Banca di Monate, Il giocatore Coduri* (short stories), Mondadori, 1974; (author of text) *Un'altra Lombardia*, Dolmine, 1975; *La stanza del Vescovo* (novel), Mondadori, 1976; (author of preface and text) *Il Decameron di G. Boccaccio*, S.E.E.D., 1976; (author of text) *Lario* (photographs), E.P.I., 1976; (author of text) *Verbano*, E.P.I., 1977; *Il vero Casanova*, edited by C. Ravizzoli, Mursia, 1977; (author of text) Roberto Carlo Kuenzli, *Les temps reviennent* (photographs), Silvana, 1977; *La settimana di Aldo Patocchi*, Cantini, 1978; *Le corna del diavolo e altri racconti* (short stories), Mondadori, 1978; *Il cappotto di astrakan* (novel), Mondadori, 1978; *Vita di Gabriele D'Annunzio* (biography), Mondadori, 1978; *Una spina nel cuore* (novel), Mondadori, 1979; *4 litografie con un racconto di P. Chiara*, Forum Jani, 1979; *Ora ti conto un fatto* (short stories), Mondadori, 1980; *Le avventure di Pierino al mercato di Luino* (short stories), Mondadori, 1980; (author of text) *Idea di Bergamo*, Bergamo, 1980; *Vedro Singapore?* (novel), Mondadori, 1981; *Helvetia, salve-racconti*, Casagrande, 1982; *Viva Migliavacca* (short stories), Mondadori, 1982.

Editor: (With Luciano Erba) *Quarta generazione: antologia della poesia italiana del depoguerra*, Magenta, 1954; Giacomo Casanova, *Lettere a un maggiordomo*, Ferriani, 1960; Casanova, *Storia della mia vita*, seven volumes, Mondadori, 1964-65; Casanova, *Saggi, libelli e satire*, Longanesi, 1968; *Disegni di Giovanni Carnovali, dello Il Piccio*, Scheiwiller, 1968; *Nuovi disegni di Giovanni Carnovali*, Scheiwiller, 1969; Casanova, *Epistolario*, Longanesi, 1969; *Il Satiricon di Petronio Arbitro*, Mondadori, 1969.

Lamberto Vitali, *Dodici acquarelli o disegni di Alberto Duerer*, Scheiwiller, 1970; *Dodici disegni di Giuseppe Viviani*, Scheiwiller, 1971; (and author of introductory essay and notes) *Quaranta sonetti di Giorgio Baffo*, Luigi Maestri, 1972; Stefano Franscini, *La Svizzera italiana*, Luigi Maestri, 1973; Giorgio Baffo, *Poesie*, Mondadori, 1974; *Sulla onde del Lago Maggiore*, Luigi Maestri, 1975; Bernardino Luini, *Sacro e profano nella pittura di Bernardo Luini*, Silvana, 1975; S. Colombo, *Acque Terre Civilta della provincia varesina*, Bramante, 1976; Casanova, *Storia della mia fuga dai Piombi*, Mondadori, 1976; *Quattordici lettere inedite di G. D'Annunzio a Barbara Leoni*, numbered edition, Mondadori, 1976; F. Menghini, *Poesie*, Luigi Maestri, 1977; *Battelli e capitani del Lago Maggiore*, Luigi Maestri, 1977; (with Federico Roncoroni) *Tamara De Lempicka*, F. M. Ricci, 1977; (with A. Oliva; and translator and author of introduction) *Casanova di G. Crepax e B. Madaudo*, F. M. Ricci, 1977.

Translator: (And author of note) Luis de Gongora y Argote, *I sonetti funebri*, Scheiwiller, 1955, new edition, translated, edited, and with commentary by Chiara, published as *I sonetti funebri e altre composizioni*, Einaudi, 1970; (and author of preface and notes) Marianna Alcoforado, *Lettere portoghesi*, Ferriani, 1960; (and author of introduction) Johann Jacob Weitzel, *Viaggio pittoresco al Lago Maggiore e al Lago di Lugano*, Il polifilo, 1973.

Author of television scripts, "I giovedi della signora Giulia" (based on his work of the same title), and "Un curioso uomo," both for R.A.I.-T.V. Italia, and "I capitani forse," for Televisione della svizzera Italiana. Co-author of screenplay for film "Venga a prendere il caffe da noi" (based on his novel *La spartizione*), 1970.

SIDELIGHTS: Some of Piero Chiara's works have been published in the United States, Germany, France, England, Spain, Romania, Yugoslavia, Hungary, Poland, Czechoslovakia, and Argentina. *Media adaptations:* "Venga a prendere il caffe da noi" (based on his novel *La spartizione*), produced by Mars Film (Rome); "Il piatto piange" (based on his novel of the same title), produced by Euro Internationale Film (Rome); "La stanza del Vescovo" (based on his novel of the same title), produced by Merope Film (Rome); "La Banca di Monate" (based on his story of the same title), produced by Euro Internationale Film; "Il balordo" (based on his novel of the same title), produced by R.T.V.; "Il cappotto di astrakan" (based on his novel of the same title), produced by Vides (Rome).

BIOGRAPHICAL/CRITICAL SOURCES: Patrizio Toni, *Piero Chiara*, Universita degli Studi di Urbino, 1974; Giuseppe Freni, *Piero Chiara: tra bozzettismo e avventura narrativa*, Universita degli Studi di Messina, 1974; Ornella De Carli, *Aspetti della provincia lombarda in Piero Chiara*, Universita Cattolica del Sacro Cuore di Milano, 1974; Carla Ravizzoli, *L'itinerario narrativo di Piero Chiara*, Universita Cattolica del Sacro Cuore di Milano, 1975; Maria Zito, *Piero Chiara*, Universita degli Studi di Napoli, 1975; Patrizia Biganzoli, *La provincia lombarda nell'opera narrativa di Piero Chiara*, Universita Cattolica del Sacro Cuore di Milano, 1976; Juliette Feliciani, *Traduction francaise des cent-sept premieres pages de "Il cappotto di astrakan" de Piero Chiara*, Universite de l'Etat a Nons (Belgium), 1978.

*   *   *

CHILCOTE, Ronald H. 1935-

PERSONAL: Born February 20, 1935, in Cleveland, Ohio; son of Lee A. (a businessman) and Katherine (Hodell) Chilcote; married Frances Tubby, January 6, 1961; children: Stephen, Edward. *Education:* Dartmouth College, B.A., 1957; Stanford University, M.B.A., 1959, M.A., 1963, Ph.D., 1965; University of Lisbon, Diploma Superior, 1960; University of Madrid, Diploma Estudios Hispanicos, 1961. *Home:* 1940 San Remo Dr., Laguna Beach, Calif. 92651. *Office:* Department of Political Science, University of California, Riverside, Calif. 92502.

CAREER: Stanford University, Stanford, Calif., assistant director of Institute of Hispanic American and Luso-Brazilian Studies, 1961-63; University of California, Riverside, 1963—, began as assistant professor, currently professor of political science, coordinator of Latin American research program, 1964-70. *Member:* Latin American Studies Association, African Studies Association, American Political Science Association. *Awards, honors:* University of California faculty fellowship, 1965; Haynes Foundation fellowship, 1966; Organization of American States grant, 1971; Social Science Research Council grants, 1971 and 1974-75.

WRITINGS: *The Press in Spain, Portugal, and Latin America: A Summary of Recent Developments*, Institute of Hispanic American and Luso-Brazilian Studies, Stanford University, 1963; *Portuguese Africa*, Prentice-Hall, 1967; *Spain's Iron and Steel*

Industry (monograph), Bureau of Business Research, University of Texas, 1968; *Emerging Nationalism in Portuguese Africa: A Bibliography of Documentary Ephemera through 1965*, Hoover Institution on War, Revolution, and Peace, 1969.

Revolution and Structural Change in Latin America: A Bibliography on Ideology, Development, and the Radical Left (1930-1965), two volumes, Hoover Institution on War, Revolution, and Peace, 1970; (compiler) *Protest and Resistance in Angola and Brazil*, University of California Press, 1972; (compiler) *Emerging Nationalism in Portuguese Africa* (documents), Hoover Institution on War, Revolution, and Peace, 1972; *The Brazilian Communist Party: Conflict and Integration, 1922-1972*, Oxford University Press, 1974; (editor with Joel C. Edelstein) *Latin America: The Struggle with Dependency and Beyond*, Schenkman, 1974.

(Compiler) *Brazil and Its Radical Left: An Annotated Bibliography, 1922-1972*, Kraus International, 1981; *Theories of Comparative Politics: The Search for a Paradigm*, Westview, 1981; (editor) *Dependency and Marxism: Toward a Resolution of the Debate*, Westview, 1982; *O Partido Comunista Brasileiro*, Edicoes Graal, 1982. Editor of volume on "The Americas," *Worldmark Encyclopedia of Nations*, 1963. Contributor to encyclopedias and yearbooks. Contributor of about sixty articles and reviews to journals and newspapers, including *Nation*, *New Republic*, *Journal of Modern African Studies*, *International Journal of Comparative Sociology*, and *Los Angeles Times*. Assistant editor of *Hispanic American Report*, 1961-63; managing editor of *Latin American Perspectives*, 1974—.

WORK IN PROGRESS: *Power and Ruling Classes in Two Communities of Backlands Brazil*.

* * *

CHILTON, John (James) 1932-

PERSONAL: Born July 16, 1932, in London, England; son of Thomas W. (a singer) and Eileen (Burke) Chilton; married Teresa Macdonald (a bookseller); children: Jennifer, Martin, Barnaby. *Education:* Attended schools in England. *Residence:* London, England. *Office:* 3 Great Ormond St., London W.C.1, England.

CAREER: Employed in advertising, and with the *Daily Telegraph*, 1953-57; professional musician, band-leader, 1957-59, member of Bruce Turner's Jump Band, 1959-63; worked in public relations and free-lance writing, 1963-67; Bloomsbury Book Shop, London, England, co-manager, 1967-73; full-time musician, band leader, 1973— . Jazz historian and composer. *Military service:* Royal Air Force, 1950-52; became senior aircraftsman. *Member:* National Union of Journalists, Musicians Union, Performing Rights Society.

WRITINGS: (With Max Jones) *Salute to Satchmo*, International Publishing, 1970; (with Jones) *Louis: The Louis Armstrong Story*, Little, Brown, 1971; *Who's Who of Jazz*, Bloomsbury Book Shop, 1970, Chilton, 1971; *Billie's Blues*, Stein & Day, 1975; *McKinney's Music*, Bloomsbury Book Shop, 1978; *Teach Yourself Music*, McKay, 1979; *A Jazz Nursery*, Bloomsbury Book Shop, 1980; (contributor) *Giants of Jazz*, Time-Life, 1981-82; (contributor) *A Biographical Dictionary of Modern Thought*, Fontana Books, 1982.

SIDELIGHTS: John Chilton's band, The Feetwarmers, began accompanying singer George Melly in 1974. They toured the United States in 1974, 1978, 1979, and 1980, and in 1982 they toured Australia. The band has recorded eight albums.

CHRISTENSON, Larry 1928-

PERSONAL: Born March 10, 1928, in Northfield, Minn.; son of Ade Leonard (a coach) and Mimi (Donhowe) Christenson; married Nordis Evenson, December 18, 1951; children: Timothy, Laurie, Stephen, Arne. *Education:* St. Olaf College, B.A. (magna cum laude), 1952; Luther Theological Seminary, B.D. (honors), 1959; Institute for Ecumenical and Cultural Research, additional study, 1971-72. *Office:* Trinity Lutheran Church, 1450 West Seventh St., San Pedro, Calif. 90732.

CAREER: Ordained minister of American Lutheran Church, 1960; Pacific Finance Corp., Los Angeles, Calif., technical writer, 1953-55; Augsburg Publishing House, Minneapolis, Minn., advertising writer, 1955-59; Trinity Lutheran Church, San Pedro, Calif., pastor, 1960—. *Military service:* U.S. Army, Airborne Division, 1946-48. *Member:* Phi Beta Kappa.

WRITINGS—Published by Bethany Fellowship, except as indicated: *The Heartless Troll* (libretto), Denison, 1960; *Speaking in Tongues and Its Significance for the Church*, 1968; *The Christian Family*, 1970; *The Trinity Bible Series*, 1971; *A Message to the Charismatic Movement*, 1972; *A Charismatic Approach to Social Action*, 1974; *The Renewed Mind*, 1974; (translator from the German) Basilea Schlink, *Realities*, Zondervan, 1966; (translator from the German) Schlink, *None Would Believe It*, Zondervan, 1967; (translator from the German) Schlink, *For Those Who Love Him*, Zondervan, 1969; *The Charismatic Renewal Among Lutherans*, 1976; (with wife Nordis Christenson) *The Christian Couple*, 1977; *Back to Square One*, 1979; *Larry Christenson's Financial Record System*, 1980; *The Wonderful Way That Babies Are Made* (children's book), Bethany House, 1982. Also author of numerous booklets, cassettes, and articles.

* * *

CLARK, Colin (Grant) 1905-

PERSONAL: Born November 2, 1905, in England; son of James (a merchant and manufacturer) and Marion Nellie (Jolly) Clark; married Marjorie Tattersall, July 27, 1935; children: Gregory, Nicholas, Christopher, Antony, Bernard, Maurice, Oliver, David, Cecily. *Education:* Oxford University, M.A., 1931; Cambridge University, M.A., 1931. *Office:* Department of Economics, University of Queensland, St. Lucia, Australia 4067.

CAREER: New Survey of London Life and Labour, London, England, staff member, 1928-29; Social Survey of Liverpool, Liverpool, England, deputy director, 1929-30; Cabinet Offices, London, assistant secretary of Economic Advisory Council, 1930-31; Cambridge University, Cambridge, England, lecturer in statistics, 1931-37; Government of Queensland, Australia, state statistician, 1938-46, Under-Secretary of State for Labour and Industry, 1946-52, financial adviser to state treasury and director of Bureau of Industry, 1938-52; Oxford University, Oxford, England, director of Institute for Research in Agricultural Economics, 1953-69; Econometric Institute of New York, New York, N.Y., supervisor of research, 1958-61; Monash University, Clayton, Victoria, Australia, research fellow of faculty of economics and politics, 1969-78; University of Queensland, St. Lucia, Australia, research consultant, 1978—. Visiting lecturer, University of Sydney, University of Melbourne, and University of Western Australia, 1937-38; visiting professor, University of Chicago, 1952.

MEMBER: Econometric Society (fellow), International Statistical Institute, Royal Statistical Society, Academy of Agriculture of France (corresponding member), Johnsonian Club (Brisbane, Australia). *Awards, honors:* Frances Wood Prizeman of Royal Statistical Society, 1928; Sc.D., University of Milan, 1957; D.Econ., University of Tilburg, 1962; D.Litt., Oxford University, 1971.

WRITINGS: *The National Income, 1924-1931,* Macmillan, 1932, reprinted, Augustus M. Kelley, 1965; (editor) George T. Jones, *Increasing Return: A Study of the Relation between the Size and Efficiency of Industries, with Special Reference to the History of Selected British and American Industries, 1850-1910,* Cambridge University Press, 1933; *The Control of Investment,* Gollancz, 1933; *Investment in Fixed Capital in Great Britain,* London & Cambridge Economic Service, 1934; *A Socialist Budget,* Gollancz, 1935; (with Arthur C. Pigou) *The Economic Position of Great Britain, 1935,* London & Cambridge Economic Service, 1936; *National Income and Outlay,* Macmillan, 1937, reprinted, Augustus M. Kelley, 1965; (with John G. Crawford) *The National Income of Australia,* Angus & Robertson, 1938; *Australian Economic Progress against a World Background,* Hassell Press (Adelaide), 1938; *A Critique of Russian Statistics,* Macmillan, 1939.

The Conditions of Economic Progress, Macmillan, 1940, 3rd edition, St. Martin's, 1957; *The Economics of 1960,* Macmillan, 1942; *The Advance to Social Security,* Melbourne University Press, 1943.

Principles of Public Finance and Taxation, Federal Institute of Accountants (Brisbane), 1950; *The Have and the Have-Not Countries,* University of Leeds, 1953; *Free Trade: An Immediate Remedy for Britain's Economy,* City Press Newspaper, 1954; *Welfare and Taxation,* Catholic Social Guild (Oxford), 1954; *Population Trends,* Manchester Statistical Society, 1956; *India's Capital Requirements: An Essay,* Eastern Economist (New Delhi), 1956; *The Cost of Living,* Hollis & Carter, 1957; *International Comparison of Rates of Economic Progress,* U.S. Industrial College of the Armed Forces, 1958; *Australian Hopes and Fears,* Hollis & Carter, 1958, Dufour, 1963.

The Economics of Irrigation in Dry Climates, Oxford University, Institute for Research in Agricultural Economics, 1960, 2nd edition, revised and enlarged, published as *The Economics of Irrigation,* Pergamon, 1970, revised edition, with Ian Carruthers, Liverpool University Press, 1981; *Growthmanship: A Study in the Mythology of Investment,* Barrie & Rockliff, 1961, 2nd edition, Institute of Economic Affairs (London), 1962; *The Real Productivity of Soviet Russia: A Critical Evaluation,* U.S. Government Printing Office, 1961; (with Henryk Frankel and Lynden Moore) *The Common Market and British Trade,* Praeger, 1962 (published in England as *British Trade in the Common Market: Plain Facts about the Common Market,* Stevens & Sons, 1962); *Taxmanship: Principles and Proposals for the Reform of Taxation,* Institute of Economic Affairs, 1964, 2nd edition, 1970; (with Margaret Haswell) *The Economics of Subsistence Agriculture,* St. Martin's, 1964, 4th edition, 1970; *Population Growth and Land Use,* St. Martin's, 1967.

Starvation or Plenty?, Taplinger, 1970; (with Eugene Csocsan de Varallja) *Measurement of Reproduction and Fertility of the Developed Countries,* Oxford University, Institute of Agricultural Economics, 1970; *Why Prices Rise,* Hawthorn Press, 1971; (with G. T. Jones) *The Demand for Housing,* Centre for Environmental Studies (London), 1971; *The Value of Agricultural Land,* Pergamon, 1973; *Poverty before Politics,* Institute of Economic Affairs, 1977.

Regional and Urban Location, University of Queensland Press, 1982. Author of numerous pamphlets. Contributor of articles to professional journals. Editor, *Review of Economic Progress* (Australian monthly), 1952—.

SIDELIGHTS: In addition to pursuing his career as an economist, Colin Clark contested seats in the British Parliament as a Labour Party candidate in North Dorset, 1929, Wavertree (Liverpool), 1931, and South Norfolk, 1935. *Avocational interests:* Walking and gardening.

* * *

CLARK, Donald E. 1933-

PERSONAL: Born April 25, 1933, in Silverton, Ore.; son of Harold Edward and Vera (Lang) Clark; married Barbara June Bollen (a dental hygienist), September 27, 1952; married Shirley Paulus, May 5, 1971; children: (first marriage) Donald E. II, Donna Kim. *Education:* Vanport College, student, 1951-53; San Francisco State College (now University), A.B., 1956; Portland State College (now University), graduate courses, 1958-60, master's program, beginning 1966. *Politics:* Democrat. *Home:* 811 Southwest Broadway Dr., Portland, Ore. 97201. *Office:* Office of the County Executive, Rm. 136, County Courthouse, Portland, Ore. 97204.

CAREER: Multnomah County (Ore.) Sheriff's Office, deputy, 1956-62, sheriff (elected), 1963-66; Portland State University, Portland, Ore., assistant professor of law enforcement and associate director of Law Enforcement Programs, 1967—. County commissioner, Multnomah County, 1969-74; chairman of board of county commissioners, Multnomah County, 1975-79; county executive, Multnomah County, 1979-83. Member of Vice-President's Task Force on Order and Justice, 1968, and Oregon Criminal Law Revision Commission. U.S. Civil Service investigator, 1957; elementary teacher in Portland, 1959-62. Advisor, President's Commission of Law Enforcement and Administration of Justice, 1968; director and consultant, Police Design Associates; special consultant to Public Administration Service, Chicago, Ill., and National Council on Crime and Delinquency, New York, N.Y. Member of board of directors, Boys' Club of Portland, Boys and Girls Aid Society, and local chapters of National Association for the Advancement of Colored People and Urban League.

MEMBER: American Correctional Association, International Association of Chiefs of Police, International Association of Police Professors, National Sheriffs' Association (life member; Oregon state director, 1964-65), American Society of Criminology, American Association of University Professors, Navy League (member of board of directors), Oregon Historical Society, City Club (Portland).

WRITINGS: (With Samuel G. Chapman) *A Forward Step: Educational Backgrounds for Police,* C.C Thomas, 1966; (contributor) *Municipal Police Administration,* International City Management Association, 6th edition, 1969.

* * *

CLARK, Henry B(alsley) II 1930-

PERSONAL: Born December 9, 1930, in Winston-Salem, N.C.; son of Henry Balsley and Marian (Wray) Clark; married second wife, Evelyn Simone Leeds, May 28, 1967; children: (first marriage) Wray Gregor, Wesley Hurst. *Education:* Duke University, B.A., 1953; Union Theological Seminary, B.D., 1959; Yale University, M.A., 1961, Ph.D., 1963. *Office:* Department of Religion, University of Southern California, Los Angeles, Calif. 90007.

CAREER: Minister, Methodist Church. Howard University, Washington, D.C., instructor in social ethics in School of Religion, 1962-63; Union Theological Seminary, New York, N.Y., assistant professor, 1963-66; Duke University, Durham, N.C., associate professor of religion, 1966-75; University of Southern California, Los Angeles, professor of social ethics and coordinator of humanities and professions, 1975—. Served on National Council of Churches, 1966-67. *Military service:* U.S. Navy, supply officer, 1953-56; became lieutenant junior grade. *Member:* Religious Research Association, Society for the Scientific Study of Religion, Society for Religion in Higher Education (Cross-Disciplinary fellow, 1973-74), American Society for Christian Ethics (task force on white racism), World Future Society, American Academy of Religion. *Awards, honors:* Woodrow Wilson fellow, 1953-54; Danforth fellow, 1953-62; Rotary fellow, 1957-58; Union Theological Seminary traveling fellow, 1959; Christopher Book Award, 1972, for *Ministries of Dialogue.*

WRITINGS: (Co-translator) *How To Serve God in a Marxist Land,* by Karl Barth and Johannes Hamel, Association Press, 1959; *The Ethical Mysticism of Albert Schweitzer,* Beacon Press, 1962; *The Church and Residential Desegregation: A Case Study of an Open Housing Covenant Campaign,* College & University Press, 1965; *The Christian Case against Poverty,* Association Press, 1965; *Human Values on the Spaceship Earth,* National Council of the Churches of Christ in the U.S.A., 1966; *The Irony of American Morality,* College & University Press, 1971; *Ministries of Dialogue,* Association Press, 1971; *Escape from the Money Trap,* Judson, 1973; (editor) *Religion and Social Sciences,* American Academy of Religion, 1973. Also author of *Manpower for Mission,* 1967. Editorial writer for *Christianity and Crisis;* member of editorial board of *Soundings.*†

*   *   *

CLARK, Mavis Thorpe (Mavis Latham)

PERSONAL: Born in Melbourne, Victoria, Australia; daughter of John Thorpe (a contractor) and Rose Matilda (Stanborough) Clark; married Harold Latham; children: Beverley Jeanne (Mrs. Ralph Henderson Lewis), Ronda Faye (Mrs. Peter Hall). *Education:* Attended Methodist Ladies' College, Melbourne. *Home:* 2 Crest Ave., Balwyn, Victoria 3103, Australia.

CAREER: Writer. *Member:* International P.E.N. (Australia Centre; vice-president of Melbourne branch, 1968, 1971, 1973, 1974; president of Melbourne branch, 1969, 1980, 1981), Australian Society of Authors (chairman of promotions committee of national book council), Fellowship of Australian Writers.

AWARDS, HONORS: Commendation by Children's Book Council of Australia for *The Brown Land Was Green,* 1956, and *Blue above the Trees,* 1968, and Book of the Year Award for *The Min-Min,* 1967; *The Min-Min* was chosen as an American Library Association "notable book," 1969; *Spark of Opal,* 1971, and *Iron Mountain,* 1973, were placed on Deutscher Jugendbuchpreis (German Youth Book Award) list.

WRITINGS—Novels for young teens, except as noted: *Dark Pool Island,* Oxford University Press, 1949; *The Twins from Timber Creek,* Oxford University Press, 1949.

Home Again at Timber Creek, Oxford University Press, 1950; *Jingaroo,* Oxford University Press, 1951; *Missing Gold,* Hutchinson, 1951; *The Brown Land Was Green,* Heinemann, 1956, special school edition, Heinemann, 1957, published with new illustrations, Lansdowne Press, 1967; *Gully of Gold,* Heinemann, 1958, published with new illustrations, Lansdowne Press, 1969; *Pony from Tarella,* Heinemann, 1959, published with new illustrations, Lansdowne Press, 1969.

They Came South, Heinemann, 1963, published with new illustrations, Lansdowne Press, 1971; (as Mavis Latham) *Fishing* (textbook), Oxford University Press, 1963; *The Min-Min,* Lansdowne Press, 1966, Macmillan (New York), 1969, published as *Armada Lions,* Collins, 1975; *Blue above the Trees,* Lansdowne Press, 1967, Meredith Press, 1969, published with new illustrations, Hodder & Stoughton, 1975; *Spark of Opal,* Lansdowne Press, 1968, Macmillan (New York), 1973; *The Pack-Tracker* (textbook), Oxford University Press, 1968; *The Opal Miner* (textbook), Oxford University Press, 1969; *Nowhere to Hide,* Lansdowne Press, 1969.

Iron Mountain, Lansdowne Press, 1970, Macmillan (New York), 1971, published as *If the Earth Falls In,* Seabury Press, 1975; *Iron Ore Mining* (textbook), Oxford University Press, 1971; *New Golden Mountain,* Lansdowne Press, 1973; *Wildfire,* Hodder & Stoughton, 1973, Macmillan (New York), 1974; *The Sky Is Free,* Macmillan, 1976; *The Hundred Islands,* Macmillan, 1977; *Spanish Queen* (remedial reader), Hodder & Stoughton, 1977; *The Boy from Cumeroogunga* (biography), Hodder & Stoughton, 1979; *The Lilly-Pilly,* Magpie Press, 1979.

The Stranger Came to the Mine, Hutchinson, 1980; *Solomon's Child,* Hutchinson, 1981; *Soft Shoe,* Magpie Press, 1982.

Adult biographies: (Under name Mavis Latham) *John Batman,* Oxford University Press, 1962; *Pastor Doug: The Story of an Aboriginal Leader,* Lansdowne Press, 1965, revised edition published as *Pastor Doug: The Story of Sir Douglas Nicholls, Aboriginal Leader,* 1972; *Joan and Betty Rayner: Strolling Players,* Lansdowne Press, 1972.

Readers published by Mount Gravat College of Advanced Education: *Joey,* 1980; *Boo to a Goose,* 1981; *The Thief Who Came Quietly,* 1981.

Contributor to anthologies: *Australian Bushrangers,* Casell (Australia), 1973; *Australians at War,* Casell (Australia), 1974; *Australian Escape Stories,* Casell (Australia), 1976; *A Handful of Ghosts,* Hodder & Stoughton, 1976; *Accents* (textbook), Houghton, 1978.

Also author of radio-script adaptations of *The Brown Land Was Green,* 1961, *Gully of Gold,* 1962, and *They Came South,* 1965, for Australian Broadcasting Commission, each broadcast as fifty-two episode serials.

WORK IN PROGRESS: A collection of stories.

SIDELIGHTS: Mavis Thorpe Clark told *CA:* "I started to write while still at school and, at fourteen, wrote a full-length children's book. . . . Many of my novels are set against some particular Australian background. . . . I have travelled thousands of miles in search of material, criss-crossing this vast country from east to west and north to south. I've travelled to Europe and Asia, too, but the spell of my own wide red land lures me continually and sets me on the lonely dusty outback track. Here again is the tremendous reward of friends in out-of-the-way places and glimpses of lives that are lived so simply yet so richly with the earth of the world's oldest continent. These intangible joys are the real reward of the writer."

For the background of her novel, *The Min-Min,* Clark chooses the stark beauty of the Australian desert region. Critics praise this book both for the author's painstaking sketch of the Australian landscape and the poignant portrait of adolescence which it contains. In *Library Journal,* S. M. Budd writes: "This is a powerful book. Sylvie's [the story's heroine] quest is the universal quest of adolescence, here set against the vivid background of the arid, sweltering Australian desert." Jane Manthorne also calls attention to the author's descriptive powers.

Manthorne states in the *New York Times Book Review:* "Clark paints the harsh land down under and the people and wild things which survive there. Her strong, terse prose . . . evokes tears. Her images are pragmatic and original."

The geographical and cultural details found in Clark's novels echo the deep love she feels for her native Australia and give insight into that country to those who have never been there. As a *Junior Bookshelf* critic, commenting on *The Min-Min,* notes: "[Clark's] characters are real people, so [much so] that along with them one can feel the heat and the thirst . . . out in the Australian desert. . . . All ages will appreciate this story because it will mirror their own lives, . . . and yet give them a glimpse into a completely different way of life."

MEDIA ADAPTATIONS: In 1976, film and television rights for *The Sky Is Free* were purchased by Walt Disney Productions.

BIOGRAPHICAL/CRITICAL SOURCES: *Junior Bookshelf,* June, 1967; *Library Journal,* December 15, 1969; *New York Times Book Review,* January 25, 1970; *Contemporary Literary Criticism,* Volume XII, Gale, 1980.

* * *

CLARKE, Mary Stetson 1911-

PERSONAL: Born December 27, 1911, in Melrose, Mass.; daughter of Horace (a manufacturers' representative) and Mabel Pitts (Russell) Stetson; married Edwin L. Clarke (an electrical engineer), June 8, 1937; children: Edwin Stetson, Susan E. Perry, Joyce Russell (Mrs. David M. Hockman). *Education:* Boston University, A.B., 1933; Columbia University, graduate study, 1937-38. *Religion:* Protestant. *Home:* 333 West Emerson St., Melrose, Mass. 02176.

CAREER: Writer. *Christian Science Monitor,* Boston, Mass., advertising copywriter, 1933-37; Boston Center for Adult Education, Boston, teacher of creative writing, 1959-60; Hilltop Press, Melrose, Mass., owner, 1974-83. Trustee of Melrose Public Library; director of Melrose Historical Society, and Stetson Kindred of America, Inc. Has served as member of Melrose Conservation Commission, member of executive board of Experiment in International Living, and director of Community Council. *Member:* American Association of University Women, Boston Authors Club (director, 1966-67), Society for the Preservation of New England Antiquities, Middlesex Canal Association (director, 1969—).

WRITINGS: *Petticoat Rebel,* Viking, 1964; *The Iron Peacock,* Viking, 1966; *The Limner's Daughter,* Viking, 1967; *Pioneer Iron Works,* Chilton, 1968; *The Glass Phoenix* (Junior Literary Guild selection), Viking, 1969; *Piper to the Clan,* Viking, 1970; *Bloomers and Ballots: Elizabeth Cady Stanton and Women's Rights,* Viking, 1972; *Immigration in Colonial Times,* Grossman, 1974; *The Old Middlesex Canal,* Hilltop Press, 1974; *A Visit to the Ironworks,* U.S. National Park Service, 1975; *Women's Rights in the U.S.,* Grossman, 1974; *Iron in Colonial Times,* Eastern National Park & Monument Association, 1981; (editor) Arnold Williams, *Trinity Episcopal Church, Melrose, Massachusetts, 1856-1981,* Trinity Parish, 1982.

WORK IN PROGRESS: *The Ancestors and Descendants of William David Russell.*

SIDELIGHTS: Mary Stetson Clarke writes *CA*: "The desire to make history come alive for young readers compelled me to write five novels about early New England between 1964 and 1970. The research for the novels was useful in the writing of three non-fiction works: *Pioneer Iron Works, Immigration in Colonial Times,* and *The Old Middlesex Canal,* my first history for adult readers.

"When asked by Viking to write about the women's rights movement, I chose a biography rather than a novel because I thought that the lives of early feminists contained drama enough without fictionalization. My heroine was Elizabeth Cady Stanton, and the title of my book: *Bloomers and Ballots.*

"The biography led to the compilation of *Women's Rights in the U.S.* that traced the development of the movement from colonial days to the present, with facsimile reproductions of early documents, sheet music, letters, newspaper accounts, photographs, etc.

"I am now working on a history of my mother's family, the Russells, who were among the early settlers of Cambridge, Massachusetts. Their story is that of countless others in their continual departure from familiar scenes, establishment of new homes, and making of new friendships in their westward trek.

"Because we Americans have so rich a heritage, I try to give my readers a sense of the courageous souls who dreamed and despaired and fought for survival on this continent. With this knowledge they may be better prepared, I hope, to face the complexities of today's world."

* * *

CLAY, Marie M(ildred) 1926-

PERSONAL: Born January 3, 1926, in Wellington, New Zealand; daughter of Donald Leolin (a public accountant) and M. Blanche (a musician; maiden name, Godier) Irwin; married Warwick V. Clay (a civil engineer), June 14, 1952; children: Alan V., Jennifer L. *Education:* Victoria University of Wellington, B.A., 1947, M.A., 1949; University of Minnesota, additional graduate study, 1951-52; University of Auckland, Ph.D., 1966. *Office:* Department of Education, University of Auckland, Private Bag, Auckland 1, New Zealand.

CAREER: Teacher in Wellington, New Zealand, 1947-49; school psychologist in Wellington and Auckland, New Zealand, 1949-50, 1956-59; teacher in Wanganui, New Zealand, 1953-54; University of Auckland, Auckland, lecturer and senior lecturer, 1960-74, professor of education, 1975—, head of department, 1975-77, 1981-82. *Member:* International Reading Association, New Zealand Psychological Society, British Psychological Society, International Association for Applied Psychology, Society for Research in Child Development. *Awards, honors:* Fulbright scholarship, University of Minnesota, 1951-52; International Citation of Merit, International Reading Association, 1978; Distinguished Research Award, National Council of Teachers of English, 1979; named to Reading Hall of Fame, 1982.

WRITINGS—Published by Heinemann Educational Books, except as indicated: *Sentence Imitation* (monograph), Society for Research in Child Development, 1971; *Reading: The Patterning of Complex Behaviour,* International Publications Service, 1972, 2nd edition, 1979; *The Early Detection of Reading Difficulties and Reading Recovery Procedures,* 1972, 2nd edition, 1979; *What Did I Write,* 1975; (with others) *Record of Oral Language,* 1976, 2nd edition, 1982; (with Dorothy Butler) *Reading Begins at Home,* 1979; *Observing Young Readers,* 1982; (contributor) G. Wells and B. Kroll, editors, *Explorations in Children's Writing,* Wiley, 1983.

WORK IN PROGRESS: *Round-about Twelve,* a report of eleven surveys of extracurricular activities and attitudes of twelve-year-old children.

SIDELIGHTS: Marie Clay writes: "My field is really the study of how children develop and the relationships of what we do to children to the kind of citizens we will have in the next generation." *Avocational interests:* Arts and crafts.

* * *

CLEVENGER, Ernest Allen, Jr. 1929-
(Ben Rovin)

PERSONAL: Born October 30, 1929, in Chattanooga, Tenn.; son of Ernest Allen, Sr. (a company president) and Mary Ellen (Fridell) Clevenger; married Glenda Willoughby (a high school registrar), December 17, 1950; children: Ernest Allen III, Elisabeth Anne. *Education:* David Lipscomb College, A.B., 1951; McKensie College, additional study, 1953; Harding Graduate School of Bible and Religion, M.A., 1967; Alabama Christian School of Religion, B.Th., 1971; Alabama Christian College of Biblical Studies, M.R.E., 1974, M.Th., 1975; University of Tennessee at Knoxville, additional study. *Home:* 8617 Clearwood Rd., Chattanooga, Tenn. 37421. *Office:* Brainerd Church of Christ, 4626 Bonnieway Dr., Chattanooga, Tenn. 37411.

CAREER: Ordained minister of Church of Christ, 1949; minister of Ohio Avenue Church of Christ, Athens, Tenn., 1951-53, West End Church of Christ, Birmingham, Ala., 1963-76, and Hunter Station Church of Christ, Montgomery, Ala., 1976-79; affiliated with Brainerd Church of Christ, Chattanooga, Tenn., 1979—. Teacher of general and physical science, Russellville High School, Russellville, Ala., 1959-63; Alabama Christian School of Religion, Montgomery, professor of Bible, 1968-76, director, 1969-76, president, 1973-76, academic dean, 1976-79; president, Boyd-Buchanan School, Chattanooga, 1979—. Conducted teacher training courses, leadership training courses, personal evangelism courses, and men's training courses for congregations, organizations, and learning institutions, 1952—. Guest lecturer at David Lipscomb College, Alabama Christian College of Biblical Studies, Abilene Christian College (now University), and Freed-Hardeman College. Director and member of board of trustees, Central Alabama Christian Youth Camp, 1958—; member of board of trustees, Childhaven Orphan Home, 1961-66; member of board of directors, Alabama Christian School of Religion, 1969-73. Director of Christian Campers Workshops, David Lipscomb College, 1974 and 1975. Owner and manager of Parchment Press, 1963—; executive vice-president, Bible Learning Materials, Inc., 1974-81.

MEMBER: American Schools of Oriental Research, Creation Research Society, Bible-Science Association, American Scientific Affiliation, Southern Association of Marriage Counselors (life member), Sons of the American Revolution, Franklin County Conservation Club (founder and president, 1957—). *Awards, honors:* American Chemical Society research grant, 1962; S.L.D. from Berean Christian College and Seminary, 1972.

WRITINGS—All published by Parchment Press: *The Bible*, 1960; *Lesson Commentary Index*, 1963, 3rd edition, 1973; *The History of God's People*, 1963; *Leadership Training Course*, 1964; *A Condensed Harmony of the Gospels*, 1964; *Bible Geography*, 1965; *A Pocket Bible Ready Reference*, 1965, revised edition published as *A Pocket Bible Ready Reference for Personal Workers*, 1970; *Jesus of the Bible*, 1965, 2nd edition, 1972; *Wisdom Books of the Bible*, 1966; *Bible Doctrine*, 1967; *The Church Usher's Guide*, 1967, 2nd edition published as *The Art of Greeting and Seating*, 1970; *Bible Evidences*, 1968, revised edition, 1973; (editor) *Bible Survey*, 1969.

Bible Characters, 1970; *History of the Bible Church*, 1971; *Then and Now: A History of the West End Church of Christ and Her Ministers*, 1973; *Psychology of Jesus*, 1975; *Men's Leadership Training Course*, 1975; *Directory of Alabama Churches of Christ*, 1976; *Parchment Notes of the New Testament*, 1976.

Weekly columnist, *Ledger and Times* (Murray, Ky.), 1954-59, and under pseudonym Ben Rovin, *Franklin County Times*, 1958-63. Contributor to religious publications, including *Firm Foundation*, *Gospel Advocate*, *Power for Today*, *World Evangelist*, and *Bible Foundations*. *Christian Bible Teacher Magazine*, contributing editor, 1964-70, high school editor, 1970—.

AVOCATIONAL INTERESTS: Photography, archaeology, fishing, hunting, archery.

* * *

CLINE, C(harles) Terry, Jr. 1935-

PERSONAL: Born July 14, 1935, in Birmingham, Ala.; son of Charles Terry (in the Red Cross) and Mildred (Vann) Cline; married Linda Street (a writer), October 23, 1959 (divorced December, 1977); married Judith Richards (a writer), June 30, 1979; children: (first marriage) Cabeth, Blaise Meredith, Charles Terry III, Marc Andrew. *Education:* Attended Florida State University, 1957. *Politics:* "Against." *Home and office:* 115 North Ave., Fairhope, Ala. 36532. *Agent:* Harvey Klinger, Inc., 301 West 53rd St., New York, N.Y. 10019.

CAREER: Writer. Worked at a variety of radio and television jobs, including those of announcer, disc-jockey, newsman, and manager in the southeastern United States; House of Chimpions, Thomasville, Ga., owner, 1960-63; Colonial Educational Exhibits, Dothan, Ala., owner, 1964-69; Land Alive Foundation, Mobile, Ala., executive director, 1970-72. *Military service:* U.S. Army, 1960.

WRITINGS: *Damon*, Putnam, 1975; *Death Knell*, Putnam, 1979; *Cross Current*, Doubleday, 1981; *Missing Persons*, Arbor House, 1981; *The Attorney Conspiracy*, Arbor House, 1983. Also author of a children's play, a musical, and several articles.

WORK IN PROGRESS: Mysteries.

SIDELIGHTS: C. Terry Cline told *CA* that both his ex-wife, Linda, and his second wife, Judy, work on the books with him. "We write because we are compelled," he said. "It is not altogether enjoyable, but in ways beyond money, it is always profitable."

* * *

CLINTON, Jeff
See BICKHAM, Jack M(iles)

* * *

CLINTON, Richard Lee 1938-

PERSONAL: Born September 20, 1938, in Cookeville, Tenn.; son of Howard C. (a salesman) and Nelva Dee (Webb) Clinton; married Susan Jeffries, September 17, 1964; children: Lara, Lisa. *Education:* Vanderbilt University, B.A., 1960, M.A. (history) and M.A. (Latin American studies), both 1964; attended Instituto Tecnologico y de Estudios Superiores de Monterrey, summer, 1960, Universidad Nacional Mayor de San Marcos, summer, 1961, and Gothe Institute, summer, 1963; University of North Carolina, Ph.D., 1971. *Politics:* "Democratic (for want of a better alternative)." *Religion:* "Pantheism." *Home:* 2335 Northwest Arthur Ave., Corvallis, Ore. 97330. *Office:* Department of Political Science, Oregon State University, Corvallis, Ore. 97331.

CAREER: First National City Bank of New York, loan officer in Overseas Division, 1964-68; University of North Carolina at Chapel Hill, assistant professor of political science and research associate of Carolina Population Center, 1971-76, member of faculty of graduate curriculum in ecology, 1974-76; Oregon State University, Corvallis, assistant professor, 1976-77, associate professor of political science, 1978—, assistant dean for research and faculty development, 1976-77, associate dean of College of Liberal Arts, 1978—. Referee for Burgess Publishing Co., Cambridge University Press, Harper & Row Publishers, Inc., and W. H. Freeman & Co. Has participated in numerous scholarly and civic conferences. Member of advisory board, United Campus Ministry, Oregon State University, 1978—; consultant to numerous governmental and private agencies, including Ford Foundation, United Nations Education, Cultural and Scientific Organization, National Institute of Child Health and Human Development, U.S. Department of State, and Smithsonian Institution.

MEMBER: International Population Policy Consortium (coordinator, 1971-72; executive secretary, 1972-75), American Political Science Association, American Association for Higher Education, Latin American Studies Association, American Civil Liberties Union, Environmental Defense Fund, Common Cause, Public Citizen, Pacific Coast Council on Latin American Studies. *Awards, honors:* National Institute of Health Centers grant, 1974-77; National Institute of Child Health and Human Development grant, 1976-79; Oregon Committee for the Humanities grant, 1978-79; Association of American Colleges Project QUILL grant, 1980-81.

WRITINGS: Problems of Population Policy Formation in Peru, Carolina Population Center, University of North Carolina, 1971; (editor with William S. Flash and R. Kenneth Godwin) *Political Science in Population Studies,* Heath, 1972; (editor with Godwin) *Research in the Politics of Population,* Heath, 1973; (editor) *Population and Politics: New Directions in Political Science Research,* Heath, 1973.

Contributor: Lewis Hanke, editor, *History of Latin American Civilization: Sources and Interpretations,* revised edition, Little, Brown, 1973; Se-Jin Kim, editor, *Afro-Asian World in Transition,* North Carolina Central University, 1974; Terry McCoy, editor, *The Dynamics of Population Policy in Latin America,* Ballinger, 1974; Godwin, editor, *Comparative Policy Analysis: The Study of Population Policy Determinants in Developing Countries,* Heath, 1975; David W. Orr and Marvin S. Soroos, editors, *The Global Predicament: Ecological Perspectives on World Order,* University of North Carolina Press, 1979; (with Godwin) John D. Martz and Lars Schoultz, editors, *Latin America, the United States, and the Inter-American System,* Westview Press, 1980.

Contributor of articles and reviews to numerous professional journals, including *Perspective, American Political Science Review, Library Journal, World Affairs, Bulletin of Atomic Scientists,* and *Inter-American Economic Affairs.* Referee for numerous professional journals, including *Journal of Developing Areas, Latin American Research Review, Social Science Quarterly, Western Political Quarterly, American Political Science Review,* and *Demography.*

WORK IN PROGRESS: Research on the concept of eco-development and on political implications of demographic and ecological realities.

SIDELIGHTS: Richard Lee Clinton writes: "My studies have convinced me that the current predicament of mankind is unprecedented and desperate, that the next few generations will quite certainly experience a steady deterioration in their quality of life, and that the survival of civilization and perhaps of our species is becoming increasingly unlikely. Man's technological cleverness has far outrun his wisdom and ability to cope with human and social problems. Present values and institutions—such things as capitalism, materialism, individualism, nationalism, bureaucratic organization, and reliance on continuous growth—must undergo radical alteration if the future is to hold any promise whatever."

* * *

CLOUDSLEY-THOMPSON, J(ohn) L(eonard) 1921-

PERSONAL: Born May 23, 1921, in Murree, India; son of A.G.G. (a medical doctor) and M. E. (Griffiths) Thompson; married J. Anne Cloudsley (a physiotherapist), 1944; children: John Hugh, Timothy, Peter Leslie. *Education:* Pembroke College, Cambridge, B.A., 1946, M.A., 1948, Ph.D., 1950. *Religion:* Church of England. *Home:* 4 Craven Hill, London W2 3D5, England; and Little Clarkes, Little Sampford, Saffron Walden, Essex CB10 2SA, England. *Office:* Department of Zoology, Birkbeck College, University of London, Malet St., London WC1E 7HX, England.

CAREER: King's College, University of London, London, England, lecturer in zoology, 1950-60; University of Khartoum, Khartoum, Sudan, professor of zoology and keeper of Sudan Natural History Museum, 1960-71; Birkbeck College, University of London, professor of zoology, 1972—. Visiting professor, University of Kuwait, 1978, and University of Nigeria, 1981. Member of expeditions to Iceland, 1947, southern Tunisia, 1954, and various parts of central Africa, 1960-73. Delegate to international congresses on entomology, zoology, biological rhythms, and bioclimatology. Honorary captain, Freeman of the City of London; liveryman, Worshipful Company of Skinners. *Military service:* British Army, 1940-44; wounded, 1942, but rejoined regiment for D-Day offensive in Normandy; became captain.

MEMBER: World Academy of Art and Science (fellow), Institute of Biology (fellow), Linnean Society (London; fellow; vice-president, 1975-76, and 1977-78), Royal Entomological Society (London; fellow), British Arachnological Society (president, 1982—), British Naturalists' Association, Biological Council, Zoological Society (London; fellow). *Awards, honors:* D.Sc., University of London, 1960; Royal African Society Medal, 1969; National Science Foundation fellow, University of New Mexico, 1969; Silver Jubilee gold medal and D.Sc., University of Khartoum, both 1981.

WRITINGS: (Editor) *Biology of Deserts,* Institute of Biology, 1954; *Spiders, Scorpions, Centipedes, and Mites,* Pergamon, 1958.

Animal Behaviour, Oliver & Boyd, 1960, Macmillan, 1961; (with John Sankey) *Land Invertebrates,* Methuen, 1961; *Rhythmic Activity in Animal Physiology and Behaviour,* Academic Press, 1961; (with Michael J. Chadwick) *Life in Deserts,* Dufour, 1964; *Animal Conflict and Adaptation,* Dufour, 1965; *Desert Life,* Pergamon, 1965; *Animal Twilight: Man and Game in Eastern Africa,* Dufour, 1967; *Microecology,* St. Martin's, 1967; *The Zoology of Tropical Africa,* Norton, 1969; *Animals of the Desert,* Bodley Head, 1969, McGraw, 1971.

(With F. T. Abushama) *A Guide to the Physiology of Terrestrial Arthropoda,* Khartoum University Press, 1970; *The Tem-*

perature and Water Relations of Reptiles, Merrow, 1971; Spiders and Scorpions, Bodley Head, 1973, McGraw, 1974; Desert Life, Danbury, 1974; Bees and Wasps, Bodley Head, 1974, McGraw, 1976; Terrestrial Environments, Halsted, 1975; Insects and History, Weidenfeld & Nicolson, 1975, St. Martin's, 1976; Crocodiles and Alligators (juvenile), Bodley Head, 1975, McGraw, 1977; The Ecology of Oases, Merrow, 1975; Tortoises and Turtles, Bodley Head, 1976; (co-editor) Environmental Physiology of Animals, Blackwell, 1976; Evolutionary Trends in the Mating of Arthropoda, Meadowfield Press, 1976; Man and the Biology of Arid Zones, E. J. Arnold, 1977; The Desert, Putnam, 1977; Dietary Adaptations in Animals, Meadowfield Press, 1977; The Size of Animals, Meadowfield Press, 1977; The Water and Temperature Relations of Woodlice, Meadowfield Press, 1977; Animal Migration, Putnam, 1978; Why the Dinosaurs Became Extinct, Meadowfield Press, 1978; Wildlife of the Desert, Hamlyn, 1979.

Biological Clocks: Their Functions in Nature, Weidenfeld & Nicolson, 1980; Tooth and Claw: Defensive Strategies in the Animal World, Dent, 1980; (contributor) David M. Burn, editor, The Complete Encyclopedia of the Animal World, Octopus, 1980; Form and Function in Animals, Meadowfield Press, 1980; Camels (juvenile), Wayland, 1980; Seals and Sea Lions (juvenile), Wayland, 1981.

Also author of monographs. Contributor to reference works, including Encyclopaedia Britannica and Encyclopedia Americana. Contributor to science journals. Editor of Journal of Arid Environments; member of editorial board of Environmental Research, Journal of Herpetology, Journal of Interdisciplinary Cycle Research, Comparative Physiology and Ecology, and International Journal of Biometeorology.

WORK IN PROGRESS: Research on the ecology and physiology of desert animals, thermal physiology, and biological rhythms; editing Sahara Desert, for Pergamon.

SIDELIGHTS: J. L. Cloudsley-Thompson told CA: "The only real justification for writing, research, or any other creative endeavour is that it is interesting and fun. If the work helps others, or gives them pleasure, so much the better, but these are merely 'spin offs.'"

Cloudsley-Thompson's philosophy that research and writing should be "interesting and fun" has been noted by reviewers. They praise the author for his easily understood prose written for the non-specialist. Commenting on one of Cloudsley-Thompson's books about animal life, David Graber in the Los Angeles Times states: "Animal Migration is a solid, challenging book, far from dry. All the 'gee wow' anybody could need is provided by [photographs of the] animals themselves, while the author simply tells it, straight and true." John R. Krebs, in a Nature review of Tooth and Claw: Defensive Strategies in the Animal World, observes: "The book touches on some issues without trying to discuss them in their full. . . . However, it would be churlish to criticize a popular book for not exploring recondite details. The main aim of Cloudsley-Thompson's book is to entertain and stimulate the reader. In this it succeeds."

AVOCATIONAL INTERESTS: Music, particularly opera; travel, photography.

BIOGRAPHICAL/CRITICAL SOURCES: Los Angeles Times, December 22, 1978; Times Literary Supplement, September 19, 1980; Nature, November 6, 1980.

*　　*　　*

CLOWNEY, Edmund P(rosper) 1917-

PERSONAL: Born July 30, 1917, in Philadelphia, Pa.; son of Edmund P. and Elizabeth (Barr) Clowney; married Jean Wright, 1941; children David, Deborah, Paul, Rebecca, Anne. Education: Wheaton College, Wheaton, Ill., A.B, 1939; Westminster Theological Seminary, B.D., 1942; Yale Divinity School, S.T.M., 1944; Wheaton College, D.D. Home: 520 Grant Ave., Willow Grove, Pa. 19090. Office: Westminster Theological Seminary, Chestnut Hill, Philadelphia, Pa. 19118.

CAREER: Ordained minister of Orthodox Presbyterian Church; pastor of Orthodox Presbyterian churches in Hamden, Conn., 1942-46, La Grange and Westchester, Ill., 1946-50, and Westfield, N.J., 1950-52; Westminster Theological Seminary, Chestnut Hill, Philadelphia, Pa., lecturer in practical theology, 1952-53, instructor, 1953-54, assistant professor, 1954-59, associate professor, 1959-63, professor, 1963—, president, 1963-82.

WRITINGS: Eutychus and His Pin, Eerdmans, 1961; Preaching and Biblical Theology, Eerdmans, 1962; Called to the Ministry, Inter-Varsity Press, 1964; Another Foundation: The Presbyterian Confessional Crisis, Presbyterian & Reformed, 1965; The Doctrine of the Church, Presbyterian & Reformed, 1969; Christian Meditation, Presbyterian & Reformed, 1979.

*　　*　　*

COCHRAN, Thomas C(hilds) 1902-

PERSONAL: Born April 29, 1902, in New York, N.Y.; son of Thomas (a teacher) and Ethel (Childs) Cochran; married Rosamond Beebe, May 26, 1938. Education: New York University, B.S., 1923, M.A., 1925; University of Pennsylvania, Ph.D., 1930. Politics: Democrat. Religion: Episcopalian. Home: 428 Gulph Creek Rd., Radnor, Pa. 19087. Office: History Department, University of Pennsylvania, Philadelphia, Pa. 19174.

CAREER: New York University, New York, N.Y., instructor, 1927-36, assistant professor, 1936-43, associate professor, 1943-44, professor of history, 1944-50; University of Pennsylvania, Philadelphia, professor of American history, 1950-68, Benjamin Franklin Professor of History, 1968-72, Benjamin Franklin Emeritus Professor of History, 1972—, director of Bicentennial College, 1975-77. Visiting lecturer, Research Center in Entrepreneurial History, Harvard University, 1948-50; visiting professor, Research Center of Social Sciences, University of Puerto Rico, 1955-56; Walgren Lecturer, University of Chicago, 1957; Pitt Professor, Clare College, Cambridge University, 1965-66; visiting fellow, St. Antony's College, Oxford University, 1970; Bailey Professor of History, University of North Carolina, 1973-74; visiting professor, University of Delaware, 1973-74; visiting senior scholar, Eleutherian Mills-Hagley Foundation, 1973-75; also visiting professor at Johns Hopkins University and University of California, Los Angeles. Chairman of board, Benjamin Franklin Papers, 1969—. Consultant, National City Bank, 1942-43, American Hawaiian Steamship Co., 1943-44; consulting editor, Scholarly Resources, Inc., 1972—; Bicentennial consultant, St. Regis Paper Co., 1973-74.

MEMBER: American Philosophical Society, American Academy of Arts and Letters, American Historical Association (member of council, 1965-68; president, 1972), Organization of American Historians (member of executive board, 1958-66, member of executive committee and vice-president, 1964-65; president, 1965-66), American Studies Association (member of council, 1968-72), American Association of University Professors, Economic History Association (secretary-treasurer, 1942-46; president, 1958-60), American Civil Liberties Union, National Records Management Council (chairman and president,

1948-50), National Bureau of Economic Research (director, 1949-52), Social Science Research Council (member of board and executive committee, 1962-65), Pennsylvania Historical Association, Historical Society of Pennsylvania (member of council, 1961—), Philadelphia Museum of Art, Philadelphia Art Alliance, Fairmount Park Art Association, Radnor Historical Society. *Awards, honors:* M.A., Cambridge University, 1965; LL.D., University of Pennsylvania, 1972; Thomas Newcomen Award in Business History from Newcomen Society of North America, 1973, for *Business in American Life: A History;* Litt.D., Ryder College, 1976.

WRITINGS: *New York in the Confederation,* University of Pennsylvania Press, 1932; (editor with Jesse D. Clarkson) *War as a Social Institution: The Historian's Perspective,* Columbia University Press, 1941; (with William Miller) *The Age of Enterprise: A Social History of Industrial America,* Macmillan, 1942, revised edition, Harper, 1961; *The Pabst Brewing Company: The History of an American Business,* New York University Press, 1948, reprinted, Greenwood Press, 1975.

Railroad Leaders: The Business Mind in Action, 1845-1890, Harvard University Press, 1953; *The American Business System: A Historical Perspective, 1900-1955,* Harvard University Press, 1957, published as *American Business in the Twentieth Century,* 1972; *The Puerto Rican Businessman: A Study in Cultural Change,* University of Pennsylvania Press, 1959; *A Basic History of American Business,* Van Nostrand, 1959, revised edition, 1969.

(With Thomas E. Brewer) *Views of American Economic Growth,* two volumes, McGraw, 1960; (editor with Wayne Andrews) James Truslow Adams, *Concise Dictionary of American History,* Scribner, 1961, abridged edition, 1962; (with Ruben Reina) *Entrepreneurship in Argentine Culture: Torcuato DiTella and S.I.A.M.,* University of Pennsylvania Press, 1963, published as *Capitalism in Argentine Culture: Torcuato DiTella and S.I.A.M.,* 1971; (editor and author of introduction) *Wealth against Commonwealth,* Prentice-Hall, 1963; *The Inner Revolution: Essays on the Social Sciences and History,* Harper, 1964; (with Arthur Bining) *The Rise of American Economic Life,* 4th edition (Cochran was not associated with earlier editions), Scribner, 1964; *The Great Depression and World War II, 1929-1945,* Scott, Foresman, 1968.

Social Change in America: The Twentieth Century, Harper, 1972 (published in England as *Social Change in Industrial Society,* Allen & Unwin, 1972); *Business in American Life: A History,* McGraw, 1972; *The Uses of History,* Scholarly Resources, 1973; (editor) *Business Enterprise in American Life: Selected Readings,* Houghton, 1974; *Two Hundred Years of American Business,* Basic Books, 1977; *Pennsylvania: A Bicentennial History,* American Association for State and Local History and Norton, 1978; *Frontiers of Change: Early Industrialism in America,* Oxford University Press, 1981.

Contributor: Allan Nevins and John Krout, editors, *The Greater City: New York, 1898-1948,* Columbia University Press, 1948; *Change and the Entrepreneur,* Harvard University Press, 1949; *An American History,* two volumes, Harper, 1950; Robert E. Spiller and Eric Larrabee, editors, *American Perspectives,* Harvard University Press, 1961; Raymond C. Miller, editor, *Twentieth Century Pessimism and the American Dream,* Wayne State University Press, 1961; (author of foreword) Sidney Goldstein, editor, *The Norristown Study,* University of Pennsylvania Press, 1961; Bruce Mazlish, editor, *The Railroads and Space Progress,* M.I.T. Press, 1965; Carleton C. Qualey, editor, *Thorstein Veblen: The Carleton College Seminar Essays,* Columbia University Press, 1968; (author of introduction) Francis Adams, Jr., editor, *Railroads: Their Origins and Problems,* Harper, 1969; Marvin Meyers, editor, *The Meanings of American History,* Scott, Foresman, 1972.

Editor, "Business History" series, New York University Press, 1945-50, and "The New American State Papers" series, Scholarly Resources, 1972—. Member of editorial board, *American Year Book* of American Historical Association, 1945-51. Contributor of more than thirty articles to professional journals, including *American Historical Review, Journal of American History, Journal of Economic History, Mississippi Valley Historical Review,* and *American Quarterly. Journal of Economic History,* co-editor, 1945-50, editor, 1950-55; *American Historical Review,* guest editor, 1973-74, advisory editor, 1973—; advisory editor, *Direction,* 1938-43.

WORK IN PROGRESS: *Challenges to American Culture: An Historical View.*

SIDELIGHTS: Thomas C. Cochran was one of the first scholars to undertake in-depth research into the history of industrial production in America, according to Elting E. Morison in a *Times Literary Supplement* review. "Starting . . . with the history of a brewing company," notes Morison, "[Cochran] has since moved through many rewarding areas—railroads, the movement of technical ideas, managerial personalities, and his dominant concern, American business systems. . . . He has laid out many new paths for others to follow, and in the sustained quality of his work—painstaking, but resourceful—he has established a standard for all to repair to."

Business in American Life: A History and *Frontiers of Change: Early Industrialism in America* reflect Cochran's interest in American business systems. While the author discusses the effect of these systems on American life in general in the first book, in the latter he explores their early development. Both books receive praise from critics for their content as well as their style.

A *Choice* reviewer calls *Business in American Life: A History* "an admirable fusion of the study of entrepreneurs, and their organizations, with the history of the larger society within which they functioned and which they . . . transformed." A *New York Times Book Review* critic similarly praises the book, calling it "innovative and important." Observes the critic: "None of Mr. Cochran's themes, or his sources, is absolutely novel, but his cooly detached style . . . makes his indictment of business's domination of our society more effective than the preachings of many contemporary . . . historians."

Morison, in his review of *Frontiers of Change: Early Industrialism in America,* also mentions Cochran's innovative thinking. Morison comments that the book contains "refreshingly new perspectives." The critic continues: "For this brief, authoritative summary all of Cochran's colleagues in history must be grateful. He aims, however, at a good deal more than a solid historical account. . . . It seems clear that his purpose is to relate . . . [his explanations for American industrial growth] to current conditions."

Cochran, himself, suggests that his purpose in writing is to show more clearly the relationship between business and society, not only currently but since the beginnings of American history. He states: "The principal aim of some fifty years of writing history has been to convince readers that business has been the most important American social institution from the Colonial period on. My aim has always been to write cultural, not narrowly economic, history, to place business as a social force as important as politics, or religion."

BIOGRAPHICAL/CRITICAL SOURCES: *New York Times Book Review,* August 6, 1972, June 7, 1981; *Choice,* December, 1972; *Times Literary Supplement,* November 27, 1981.

COFFIN, Geoffrey
See MASON, F(rancis) van Wyck

* * *

COLBERT, Edwin Harris 1905-

PERSONAL: Born September 28, 1905, in Clarinda, Iowa; son of George Harris (a professor of mathematics) and Mary (Adamson) Colbert; married Margaret Mary Matthew (a scientific draftsman of fossils), July 8, 1933; children: George Matthew, David William, Philip Valentine, Daniel Lee, Charles Diller. *Education:* Attended Northwest Missouri State Teachers College (now University), 1923-26; University of Nebraska, B.A., 1928; Columbia University, M.A., 1930, Ph.D., 1935. *Politics:* Democrat. *Home address:* Route 4, Box 721, Flagstaff, Ariz. 86001. *Office address:* Museum of Northern Arizona, Route 4, Box 720, Flagstaff, Ariz. 86001.

CAREER: American Museum of Natural History, New York, N.Y., research assistant to paleontologist Henry Fairfield Osborn, 1930-33, assistant curator, 1933-42, acting curator, 1942-43, curator of vertebrate paleontology, 1943, chairman of department of amphibians and reptiles, 1943-45, curator of fossil reptiles and amphibians, 1945-70, curator emeritus, 1970—, chairman of department of geology and paleontology, 1958-60, chairman of department of vertebrate paleontology, 1960-66, created Hall of Early Dinosaurs, 1952, and Hall of Late Dinosaurs, 1956; Museum of Northern Arizona, Flagstaff, curator, 1970—. Columbia University, lecturer, 1938-39, professor, 1945-69, professor emeritus, 1969—; lecturer at University of Pennsylvania, 1938-42, Bryn Mawr College, 1939-42, and University of California, 1945. Academy of Natural Sciences, Philadelphia, Pa., associate curator, 1937-48, research associate, 1949—; research associate at Northern Arizona Society of Science and Art, 1949-69; member of New Jersey museum advisory council, 1964-69. Major field work has been conducted in the western and southwestern United States, and in Nebraska, South Dakota, and Florida; he has also worked in Mexico, Brazil, Argentina, Israel, South Africa, Lesotho, India, Australia, New Zealand, Antarctica, England, Switzerland, and Germany.

MEMBER: National Academy of Sciences, American Association for the Advancement of Science (fellow), Geological Society of America (fellow), Paleontological Society (fellow; vice-president, 1962-63), Society of Vertebrate Paleontology (president, 1946-47), American Society of Mammalogists, Society of Ichthyology and Herpetology, Society of Systematic Zoology, Society for the Study of Evolution (president, 1958), Paleontological Society of India (honorary fellow), Academia Nacional de Ciencias (Argentina; corresponding member), New York Zoological Society (fellow), Rochester Museum of Arts and Sciences (fellow), Sigma Xi.

AWARDS, HONORS: Daniel Giraud Elliot Medal from National Academy of Sciences, 1935; medal from American Museum of Natural History, 1970; Sc.D. from University of Nebraska, 1973, and University of Arizona, 1976.

WRITINGS—Published by American Museum of Natural History, except as indicated: *Siwalik Mammals in the American Museum of Natural History*, American Philosophical Society, 1935; *The Origin of the Dog: Wild Dogs and Tame, Past and Present*, 1939.

Triumph of the Mammals, 1942; *The Dinosaur Book: The Ruling Reptiles and Their Relatives* (juvenile), 1945, 2nd edition, McGraw, 1951; *Dinosaurs*, 1947, 10th edition, 1961; *The Mammal-Like Reptile "Lycaenops,"* 1948.

(With Charles Craig Mook) *The Ancestral Crocodilian "Protosuchus,"* 1951; *A Pseudosuchian Reptile from Arizona*, 1952; (with Dirk Albert Hooijer) *Pleistocene Mammals from the Limestone Fissures of Szechwan, China*, 1953; *Evolution of the Vertebrates: A History of the Backboned Animals through Time*, Wiley, 1955, 3rd edition, 1980; (with John Imbrie) *Triassic Metoposaurid Amphibians*, 1956; *Millions of Years Ago: Prehistoric Life in North America* (juvenile), Crowell, 1958; (with John H. Ostrom) *Dinosaur Stapes*, 1958; (with Donald Baird) *Coelurosaur Bone Casts from the Connecticut Valley Triassic*, 1958.

A New Triassic Procolophonid from Pennsylvania, 1960; (with William A. Burns) *Digging for Dinosaurs* (juvenile), Children's Press, 1960, new edition, 1967; *Dinosaurs: Their Discovery and Their World*, Dutton, 1961; *The Triassic Reptile "Poposaurus,"* Chicago Natural History Museum, 1961; *The World of Dinosaurs*, Home Library Press, 1961; *The Weights of Dinosaurs*, 1962; *Fossils of the Connecticut Valley: The Age of Dinosaurs Begins*, Connecticut State Geological and Natural History Survey, 1963, 2nd edition, 1970; *Relationships of the Saurischian Dinosaurs*, 1964; *The Triassic Dinosaur Genera Podokesaurus and Coelophysis*, 1964; *A Phytosaur from North Bergen, New Jersey*, 1965; (with George Marshall Kay) *Stratigraphy and Life History*, Wiley, 1965; *The Age of Reptiles*, Norton, 1965; *New Adaptations of Triassic Reptiles*, Israel Academy of Sciences and Humanities, 1967; *Men and Dinosaurs: The Search in Field and Laboratory*, Dutton, 1968; *A Jurassic Pterosaur from Cuba*, 1969; (with Dale A. Russell) *The Small Cretaceous Dinosaur Dromaeosaurus*, 1969; (with others) *Getting Acquainted with Science* (juvenile), Ferguson, 1969.

The Triassic Gliding Reptile Icarosaurus, 1970; *A Saurischian Dinosaur from the Triassic of Brazil*, 1970; *Antarctic Fossils and the Reconstruction of Gondwanaland*, Natural History Press, 1972; *Wandering Lands and Animals*, Dutton, 1973; *Continental Drift and the Distribution of Fossil Reptiles*, Academic Press, 1973; (with John W. Cosgriff) *Labyrinthodont Amphibians from Antarctica*, 1974; *Lystrosaurus from Antarctica*, 1974; (with James W. Kitchening) *The Triassic Reptile Procolophon in Antarctica*, 1975; *Early Triassic Tetrapods and Gondwanaland*, Musee d'histoire naturele (Paris), 1975; *La Vita sui continenti alla Deriva*, Mondadori (Milan), 1975; (with Kitchening) *Triassic Cynodont Reptiles from Antarctica*, 1977; *The Year of the Dinosaur*, illustrations by wife, Margaret Colbert, Scribner, 1977; *The Dinosaur World* (juvenile), Stravon, 1977.

A Fossil Hunter's Notebook: My Life with Dinosaurs and Other Friends (autobiography), Dutton, 1980; (with Kitchening) *Scaloposaurian Reptiles from the Triassic of Antarctica*, 1981; *A Primitive Ornithiscian Dinosaur from the Kayenta Formation of Arizona*, Museum of Northern Arizona Press, 1981.

Contributor: George MacGurdy, editor, *Early Man*, Lippincott, 1937; Glenn Jepsen, George Simpson, and Ernst Mayr, editors, *Genetics, Paleontology, and Evolution*, Princeton University Press, 1949; Emil Haury, *Stratigraphy and Archaeology of Ventana Cave Arizona*, University of New Mexico Press, 1950; T. S. Westoll, editor, *Studies on Fossil Vertebrates*, Athlone Press, 1958; Anne Roe and Simpson, editors, *Behavior and Evolution*, Yale Univesity Press, 1958; L. D. Leet and F. J. Leet, editors, *The World of Geology*, McGraw, 1961; J. J. White, editor, *Study of the Earth: Readings in Geological Science*, Prentice-Hall, 1962; A.E.M. Nairn, editor, *Problems in Palaeoclimatology*, Interscience, 1964; Paul Ehrlich, Richard Holm, and Peter Raven, compilers, *Papers on Evolution*,

Little, Brown, 1969; Preston Cloud, editor, *Adventures in Earth History*, W. H. Freeman, 1970; Brainerd Mears, Jr., editor, *The Nature of Geology: Contemporary Readings*, Van Nostrand, 1970; Louis Quan, editor, *Research in the Antarctic*, American Association for the Advancement of Science, 1971; T. Dobzhansky, M. K. Hecht, and W. C. Steere, editors, *Evolutionary Biology*, Volume 6, Appleton, 1971; D. H. Tarling and S. Runcorn, editors, *Implications of Continental Drift to the Earth Sciences*, Academic Press, 1973; Eugenio de Rosa, editor, *La Riscoperta del Terra*, Mondadori, 1975.

Author of over 350 scientific papers. Contributor of articles to professional journals. Editor of *Bulletin of the Society of Vertebrate Paleontology*, 1943-45, *Evolution*, 1950-52, and *Curator*, 1958-63.

SIDELIGHTS: Among Edwin Harris Colbert's personal discoveries are fifty new species of fossils and ten genera, including a six-foot long dinosaur Coelophysis, and indications that dinosaurs could hear. He regards his vocation as interesting work and has said: "You have to care more about life in the prehistoric ages than fame or wealth. There isn't much money in the study of extinct vertebrates. It's just pure research, without any practical application whatsoever."

AVOCATIONAL INTERESTS: Reading, nature study, music, history of the American Civil War.

BIOGRAPHICAL/CRITICAL SOURCES: *Saturday Evening Post*, August 6, 1946; *New Yorker*, August 4, 1956; *New York Times Book Review*, November 24, 1968; *Instructor*, January, 1969; *Natural History*, December, 1969; *Science*, May 15, 1970, May 15, 1981; *Economist*, March 23, 1974; *Books and Bookmen*, June, 1974; *Earth Science*, Summer, 1978; Edwin Harris Colbert, *A Fossil Hunter's Notebook: My Life with Dinosaurs and Other Friends*, Dutton, 1980; Louis L. Jacobs, editor, *Aspects of Vertebrate History: Essays in Honor of Edwin Harris Colbert*, Museum of Northern Arizona Press, 1980.

* * *

COLEGATE, Isabel 1931-

PERSONAL: Born September 10, 1931, in London, England; daughter of Sir Arthur Colegate (a member of Parliament) and Lady Colegate Worsley; married Michael Briggs (director of an engineering firm), September 12, 1953; children: Emily, Barnaby, Joshua. *Education:* Attended three boarding schools in England. *Home:* Midford Castle, Bath, Somersetshire, England. *Agent:* Harold Matson Co., Inc., 276 Fifth Ave., New York, N.Y. 10001.

CAREER: Novelist and critic. *Awards, honors:* W. H. Smith Literary Award, 1981, for *The Shooting Party*.

WRITINGS—All novels: *The Blackmailer*, Anthony Blond, 1958; *A Man of Power*, Anthony Blond, 1960; *The Great Occasion*, Anthony Blond, 1962; *Statues in a Garden*, Bodley Head, 1964, Knopf, 1966; *Orlando King*, Knopf, 1968; *Orlando at the Brazen Threshold*, Bodley Head, 1971; *Agatha*, Bodley Head, 1974; *News from the City of the Sun*, Hamish Hamilton, 1979; *The Shooting Party*, Hamish Hamilton, 1980, Viking, 1981. Contributor to literary journals.

WORK IN PROGRESS: Another novel.

SIDELIGHTS: Isabel Colegate's metier is writing historical novels that rely less upon events than upon ambience; her books, full of precise and detailed descriptions, intimately portray the lives of the British aristocracy in the first half of the twentieth century. *Statues in a Garden*, writes *New York Times Book Review*'s Frank Littler, "[weaves] documentary details so adroitly into [the] story that the century in its teens is given a reality at once recognizable and fresh." In a *Times Literary Supplement* review of *Agatha*, a critic notes that Colegate "writes with beautiful calm and assurance" and offers "a good deal of evocative social detail."

While most of Colegate's books reflect her ability to recreate the spirit of past eras, it is her award-winning novel *The Shooting Party* that has received the greatest critical acclaim. *The Shooting Party*, remarks Charles Champlin in the *Los Angeles Times*, "is not only about events in England of 1913, it might somehow have—in the best sense—come forward from the literature of 1913, a lost manuscript by a fine author, let us say, published at last after being found beneath some linens in the ancestral armoire."

Through the use of meticulous detail in *The Shooting Party*, Colegate captures the aura of Edwardian England. Linda Barrett Osborne writes in the *Washington Post* that the novel "unfolds like an album of sepia photographs, its people recognizable yet muted, set in formal clothing and poses that bespeak the manners and attitudes of another age." Colegate, states a *Virginia Quarterly Review* critic, "has an eye and an ear for a time and place she can never have seen or heard, . . . [and] she wraps up the reader in her own time warp."

The impact of *The Shooting Party* stems not only from its style, but also from its story. As well as presenting "a stunning picture of the British upper classes at the pinnacle of their evolution," as John Naughton comments in *Listener*, the novel also presages the demise of those classes in the social upheaval following the First World War. The story of a pleasant weekend gone awry, *The Shooting Party* serves as "a metaphor for the workings of polite society, just as it might serve as a metaphor for the movement of Europe toward war," notes Osborne. "At each level there are disturbing forces underlying the civilized order." Thus, as the weekend closes with an accidental shooting and death, so the era in which the story takes place ends with the first shots of the war. Francis King writes in *Spectator* that Colegate "invests the beauty of the Oxfordshire estate in autumn with a grave, poetic melancholy. The same melancholy seems, like an autumnal mist, to cling about [the] characters even at their most buoyant and boisterous—as they play childish hide-and-seek, consume lavish meals, or carry on their intrigues with each other. The leaves are already falling; and this privileged order is about to fall, too."

BIOGRAPHICAL/CRITICAL SOURCES: *New Statesman*, August 21, 1964, September 20, 1968, July 13, 1979, September 12, 1980; *Times Literary Supplement*, October 28, 1964, September 19, 1968, May 20, 1971, October 5, 1973, December 4, 1979, September 12, 1980; *New York Times Book Review*, March 20, 1966, May 25, 1969; *Harper's*, April, 1966, May, 1969; *Library Journal*, April 1, 1966, April 15, 1969; *Best Sellers*, May 1, 1969; *Observer*, July 1, 1969; *Listener*, October 2, 1973, August 2, 1979, September 4, 1980; *Books and Bookmen*, October, 1979; *London Times*, February 18, 1980, February 12, 1981; *Spectator*, September 13, 1980; *Saturday Review*, May, 1981; *New York Times*, May 16, 1981; *New Yorker*, May 25, 1981; *Los Angeles Times*, May 29, 1981; *Time*, July 6, 1981; *Washington Post*, July 13, 1981; *Virginia Quarterly Review*, autumn, 1981.

* * *

COLEMAN, Kenneth 1916-

PERSONAL: Born April 28, 1916, in Devereux, Ga.; son of John Amoss (a merchant) and Nolia (Lee) Coleman. *Education:* University of Georgia, A.B., 1938, M.A., 1940; University of Wisconsin, Ph.D., 1952. *Politics:* Democrat. *Religion:* Methodist. *Home:* 220 Dearing St., Athens, Ga. 30605. *Office:* University of Georgia, Athens, Ga. 30602.

CAREER: University of Georgia, 1949-55, began as instructor, became assistant professor at Atlanta Campus, assistant professor at Athens Campus, 1955-61, associate professor, 1961-68, professor of history, 1968-76, professor emeritus, 1976—. Member of Athens-Clarke Heritage Foundation board of directors and of Georgia Bicentennial Commission. *Military service:* U.S. Army Reserve, 1941-56; active duty, 1941-46; served in European theater; became lieutenant colonel. *Member:* American Historical Association, Southern Historical Association, Georgia Historical Society, Athens Historical Society (past president).

WRITINGS—Published by University of Georgia Press, except as indicated: *Georgia History in Outline*, Georgia State College of Business Administration, 1955, 2nd edition, 1960, 3rd edition, 1978; *The American Revolution in Georgia*, 1958; (contributor) Horace Montgomery, editor, *Georgians in Profile: Historical Essays in Honors of Ellis Merton Coulter*, 1958; (with Sarah B. Gover Temple) *Georgia Journeys: Being an Account of the Lives of Georgia's Original Settlers and Many Other Early Settlers from the Founding of the Colony in 1732 until the Institution of Royal Government in 1754*, 1961; *Confederate Athens*, 1968; *Athens, 1861-1865: As Seen Through Letters in the University of Georgia Libraries*, 1969; *Colonial Georgia: A History*, Scribner, 1976; (with Numan V. Bartley, F. N. Boney, William F. Holmes, Phinizy Spalding, and Charles E. Wynes and general editor) *A History of Georgia*, 1977.

Editor with Milton Ready: *Colonial Records of the State of Georgia*, University of Georgia Press, Volume XXVII: *Original Papers of Governor John Reynolds, 1754-1756*, 1976, Volume XXVIII, Part I: *Original Papers of Governors Reynolds, Ellis, Wright, and Others, 1757-1763*, 1976, Volume XXVIII, Part II: *Original Papers of Governor Wright, President Habersham, and Others, 1764-1782*, 1979, Volume XXIX: *Original Papers, Correspondence to the Trustees, James Oglethorpe, and Others, 1732-1735*, 1982.

Contributor to *Agricultural History* and regional history journals.

WORK IN PROGRESS: Co-editing *Dictionary of Georgia Biography*, with Charles Stephen Gurr.

AVOCATIONAL INTERESTS: Architecture and how it reflects life of the period in which a house was built.

* * *

COLIN, Jean
  See BELL, Joyce

* * *

COLLINS, Carvel 1912-

PERSONAL: First name rhymes with marvel; born June 14, 1912, in West Union, Ohio; son of John Edgar (a professor) and Ina (Treber) Collins; married Mary Brewster, November 17, 1939 (divorced, 1956); married Ann Green, October 1, 1960; children: (first marriage) Lucy Collins. *Education:* Miami University, Oxford, Ohio, B.S., 1933; University of Chicago, M.A., 1937, Ph.D., 1944. *Home:* 142 Mason Rd., Vista, Calif. 92083.

CAREER: Instructor in English at Colorado State College (now University of Northern Colorado), Fort Collins, 1938-39, Stephens College, Columbia, Mo., 1939-40, and Harvard University, Cambridge, Mass. 1942-45; assistant professor of English at Swarthmore College, Swarthmore, Pa., 1945-46, and Harvard University, 1946-50; Massachusetts Institute of Technology, Cambridge, associate professor, 1950-56, professor of English, 1956-67; University of Notre Dame, Notre Dame, Ind., professor of English, 1967-78. Visiting professor at University of California, Berkeley, 1949, Salzburg Seminar in American Studies, 1955, University of Aix-Marseille, 1955, University of Tokyo, 1961-62, and University of Colorado, 1962. Chief content consultant for film "Faulkner: A Life on Paper," Public Broadcasting System, 1979. *Military service:* U.S. Naval Reserve, 1942; became lieutenant junior grade.

MEMBER: Modern Language Association of America. *Awards, honors:* Library of Congress fellowship, 1946; American Philosophical Society research grant, 1963; Fidelis Foundation research grant, 1963; Bollingen Foundation fellowship, 1964-65; O'Brien Fund grant, 1970.

WRITINGS: The American Sporting Gallery, Harvard University Press, 1949; *Sam Ward in the Gold Rush*, Stanford University Press, 1949; (editor and author of introduction) Frank Norris, *McTeague*, Rinehart, 1950, new edition, Holt, 1968; (with others) *Trends in Research in American Literature*, Modern Language Association of America, 1951; (with others) *Literature in the Modern World*, George Peabody College Press, 1954; (editor and author of introduction) William Faulkner, *New Orleans Sketches*, Rutgers University Press, 1958, revised and expanded edition, Random House, 1968; (author of introduction) Faulkner, *The Unvanquished*, Signet Books, 1959; (editor and author of introduction) Erskine Caldwell, *Men and Women*, Little, Brown, 1961; (editor and author of introduction) *William Faulkner's University Pieces*, Kendyusha Press, 1962; (editor and author of introduction) Faulkner, *Early Prose and Poetry*, Atlantic-Little, Brown, 1962; (editor and author of introduction) Faulkner, *Mayday*, University of Notre Dame Press, 1977, revised edition, 1980; (author of introduction) Jack Cofield and Lawrence Wells, *William Faulkner: The Cofield Collection*, Yoknapatawpha Press, 1978; (author of introduction) A. I. Bezzerides, *William Faulkner: A Life on Paper*, University Press of Mississippi, 1980; (editor and author of introduction) Faulkner, *Helen: A Courtship*, Tulane University and Yoknapatawpha Press, 1981.

Contributor: *English Institute Essays, 1952*, Columbia University Press, 1954; Malcolm Cowley, editor, *Writers at Work*, Viking, 1958; K. Hunt and P. Stoakes, editors, *Our Living Language*, Houghton, 1961; Irving Malin, editor, *Psychoanalysis and American Fiction*, Dutton, 1965; Wallace Stegner, editor, *The American Novel from James Fenimore Cooper to William Faulkner*, Basic Books, 1965; Charles F. Madden, editor, *Talks with Authors*, Southern Illinois University Press, 1968; Michael Cowan, editor, *Twentieth-Century Interpretations of "The Sound and the Fury*," Prentice-Hall, 1968; Harrison Hayford and Hershel Parker, editors, *"Moby-Dick" as Doubloon: Essays and Extracts, 1851-1969*, Norton, 1970; James Meriwether, editor, *Studies in "The Sound and the Fury*," C. E. Merrill, 1970; Jay Martin, editor, *Twentieth-Century Views of Nathanael West*, Prentice-Hall, 1971; M. Thomas Inge, editor, *The Frontier Humorists: Critical Views*, [Hamden, Conn.], 1975; Thomas Bonner, Jr., *William Faulkner: The Wisdom Collection*, Tulane University Libraries, 1980. Also contributor to "American Novel" series, Voice of America, 1964.

WORK IN PROGRESS: A biographical-critical volume on William Faulkner, for Farrar, Straus.

COLLINS, Philip (Arthur William) 1923-

PERSONAL: Born May 28, 1923, in London, England; son of Arthur Henry and Winifred (Bowmaker) Collins; married Mildred Lowe, November 1, 1952 (divorced, 1963); married Joyce Dickins, August 18, 1965; children: two sons, one daughter. *Education:* Emmanuel College, Cambridge, M.A., 1947. *Home:* 26 Knighton Dr., Leicester LE2 3HB, England. *Office:* University of Leicester, University Rd., Leicester LE1 7RH, England.

CAREER: University of Leicester, Leicester, England, staff tutor in adult education, 1947-54, warden of Vaughan College, 1954-62, senior lecturer in English, 1962-64, professor of English literature, 1964-82, head of English department, 1971-76, 1981-82. Visiting professor at University of California, Berkeley, 1967, Columbia University, 1969, and Victoria University (New Zealand), 1974. Lecturer on Charles Dickens, 1975-78, and 1980—; has given several international lecture tours. Member of drama panel of Arts Council of Great Britain, 1970-75, and board of directors of National Theatre, 1976-82. Secretary to board of directors, Leicester Theatre Trust Ltd., 1963—. *Military service:* British Army, 1942-45; served in Royal Army Ordnance Corps and Royal Norfolk Regiment; became lieutenant. *Member:* Tennyson Society, Dickens Fellowship (vice-president), Victorian Society.

WRITINGS: James Boswell, Longsmans, Green, 1956; *Dickens and Crime,* Macmillan, 1962, 2nd edition, 1964; *Dickens and Education,* Macmillan, 1963.

Editor: *English Christmas,* Gordon Fraser Gallery, 1956; (with others) *Letters of Charles Dickens,* Oxford University Press, 1960-63.

A Dickens Bibliography, Cambridge University Press, 1970; *Dickens: The Critical Heritage,* Barnes & Noble, 1971; *A Critical Commentary on Dickens's "Bleak House",* Macmillan (London), 1971; *The Public Readings of Charles Dickens,* Clarendon Press, 1975; Charles Dickens, *David Copperfield,* Dynamic Learning Corp., 1977; *Dickens: Interviews and Recollections,* two volumes, Barnes & Noble, 1981; *William Thackeray: Interviews and Recollections,* Barnes & Noble, 1982.

Also author of "The Canker and the Rose," performed in London, at Mermaid Theatre, 1964. Also author of talks and scripts for radio and television. Contributor to *Encyclopaedia Britannica;* also contributor to journals, including *Dickensian, Essays and Studies, Notes and Queries, Listener, Review of English Studies,* and *Times Literary Supplement.* Member of editorial board of *Dickens Studies.*

SIDELIGHTS: In the *London Times* Peter Davalle notes that Philip Collins's numerous books on the English nineteenth-century novelist Charles Dickens have "turned [Collins] into something of a one-man Dickens industry." Critics praise *Dickens: Interviews and Recollections,* Collins's two-volume set of reminiscences of Dickens recorded by his contemporaries. Davalle, for example, urges readers to "dip into Professor Collins's . . . volumes into which you will find some fascinating or half-forgotten tidbit about Dickens beckons to be savoured." An *Economist* reviewer comments: "No better editor than Professor Collins could be found for this compendium: his expertise on Victorian literature and society, on all levels, is unchallengeable. The major testimonies are here, with enlightening and scholarly annotations."

BIOGRAPHICAL/CRITICAL SOURCES: Economist, January 23, 1971, January 16, 1982; *Times Literary Supplement,* March 5, 1971; *Modern Language Review,* October, 1979; *London Times,* January 28, 1982.

* * *

COMINS, Ethel M(ae)

PERSONAL: Born in Clayton, N.Y.; daughter of Hayes and Alice (Burnham) Comins. *Education:* Attended Plattsburgh State Normal School (now State University of New York College at Plattsburgh), 1919; Syracuse University, B.S., 1930; New York University, M.S., 1936; additional study at Institute de Allende, San Miguel de Allende, Mexico. *Home:* R.F.D. 1, Steele's Point, Clayton, N.Y. 13624.

CAREER: High school teacher in Margaretville, N.Y., 1919-20, Carthage, N.Y., 1920-22, Syracuse, N.Y., 1922-30, and Queens, N.Y., 1930-61; author and artist. Evening school instructor in secretarial studies, Queens College (now Queens College of the City University of New York), 1955-61. Member of the board and art director, Thousand Islands Museum.

MEMBER: National League of American Pen Women (Queens branch president, 1956-58; New York State president, 1960-62; national contest chairman, 1962-64), North Country Artists Guild, Jefferson County Historical Society, Art League of Manatee County, Thousand Islands Museum Artists (president, 1970-72), Delta Kappa Gamma.

AWARDS, HONORS: Awards from National League of American Pen Women, 1956, for "Disqualified," 1957, for "A Quiet Evening," and 1968, for *A Cloak of Pride;* Deep South Writers Conference first prizes, 1964, for "Outdoor Art Show," 1967, for feature article, and 1970, for column "Addie Barton Explores Art," and of honorable mention, 1968, for *A Cloak of Pride;* award from British Amateur Press Association, 1970, for short story; awards from Tupper Lake, Jefferson County Fair, and Cranberry Lake, all 1973, Old Forge (N.Y.), 1973 and 1975, and North Country Artists Guild, 1974 and 1975, all for artistic work.

WRITINGS—Young adult novels; all published by Bouregy: *The Magic School House,* 1964; *Cloth of Dreams,* 1967; *Island Castle,* 1968; *Beyond the Night,* 1969; *Her Father's Daughter,* 1970; *The Black Jade Filly,* 1971; *Mystery Island,* 1973; *Moon Goddess,* 1974; *Under a Dancing Star,* 1977; *Love's Tangled Web,* 1978; *Ancestral Dilemma,* 1982.

Also author of novels, *Yankee Boy,* serialized in *Thousand Island Sun,* 1981, *Carolyn: The Enigmatic Bonaparte,* serialized in *Town and Country,* 1981-82, and *A Cloak of Pride,* not yet published; author of plays, "Disqualified" (one-act) and "A Quiet Evening" (one-act), of column, "Addie Barton Explores Art," and of coloring book, *Jeffrey Donaldson's Visit to Watertown in 1869.* Contributor of articles to *York State Tradition, Thousand Island Sun,* and *Jefferson County Historical Bulletin.*

SIDELIGHTS: Ethel Comins told *CA:* "My childhood was spent on a farm on the banks of the Saint Lawrence River. I was allowed to ride horseback when I was only four years old and still recall my beloved little horse, Fanny, with affection. We owned a rowboat which I learned to row, and I enjoyed fishing. Swimming was another pleasure from an early age.

"My love for the Saint Lawrence River has always been a part of my life. After I left the farm to begin my career as a teacher, I always returned to the river for summer vacations. I now own a home on the Saint Lawrence where I can watch the big boats move slowly by on the Seaway."

Four of Comins's novels, *Moon Goddess*, *Mystery Island*, *Black Jade Filly*, and *Island Castle*, have been sold to *Grit* newspaper serialization.

AVOCATIONAL INTERESTS: Vacationing by the Saint Lawrence River, international travel, fishing, swimming, ceramics, and gardening.

* * *

CONANT, Howard (Somers) 1921-

PERSONAL: Surname is pronounced *Co*-nunt; born May 5, 1921, in Beloit, Wis.; son of Rufus P. (a typewriter dealer) and Edith (Somers) Conant; married; wife's name, Florence; children: Judith Lynne, Jeffrey Scott. *Education:* University of Wisconsin—Milwaukee, B.S., 1946; University of Wisconsin—Madison, M.S., 1947; State University of New York at Buffalo, Ed.D., 1950; also attended Art Students League, New York, N.Y., 1944-45. *Residence:* Tucson, Ariz. *Office:* Department of Art, University of Arizona, Tucson, Ariz. 85721.

CAREER: University of Wisconsin—Madison, instructor in art, 1946-47; State University of New York at Buffalo, assistant professor, 1947-50, professor of art, 1950-55; New York University, New York, N.Y., professor of art education, chairman of department, and chairman of art collection, 1955-76; University of Arizona, Tucson, professor of art and head of department, 1976—. Artist, with work exhibited at a number of one-man shows, including those in Washington, D.C., New York, Buffalo, Milwaukee, Philadelphia, and Mexico City, and in group shows; has done murals in Henrietta, N.Y., and Phoenix, Ariz. Moderator of art programs on WBEN-TV, Buffalo, 1951-55; lecturer in India on modern American art under auspices of U.S. Department of State, 1964; director of Seminar on Education in Visual Arts, U.S. Office of Education, 1964-65. Consultant and participant, Girl Scouts of America-National Broadcasting Corp. television and film series on hand arts, 1958-59. *Military service:* U.S. Army Air Forces, 1943-46; became first lieutenant.

MEMBER: International Association of Art Critics, College Art Association, National Committee on Art Education (member of council, 1951-65; chairman, 1962-63), National Art Education Association (member of council, 1961-65), Institute for the Study of Art in Education (president, 1965-68), New York State Art Teachers Association, Washington Square Torch Club (president, 1964-65).

WRITINGS: Art Workshop Leaders Planning Guide, Davis Publications, 1958; (with Arne Randall) *Art in Education*, Bennett, 1959, 2nd edition, 1964; (editor) *Masterpieces of the Arts*, Parents Institute, 1959, 2nd edition, 1964; *Art Education*, Center for Applied Research in Education, 1964; *Seminar on Elementary and Secondary Education in the Visual Arts*, New York University, 1965; (contributor) Gregory Battcock, editor, *New Ideas in Art Education*, Dutton, 1973; (contributor) *Festschrift*, Syracuse University Press, 1974; *Art in the Environment*, Bowling Green University, 1975; *Art in Public Places in the United States*, Bowling Green University, 1976. Also author of evaluation reports for Guggenheim Museum and New York University Center for Educational Research; author and editor of chapters in a two-volume work, published by Lincoln Library of the Arts. Contributor to *Encyclopedia of Higher Education*, 1976. Contributor to *Saturday Review*, *Art News*, and to journals of art and art education. Associate editor, *Arts*, 1973-75; art editor, *Intellect*, 1975-78, and *U.S.A. Today*, 1978—.

SIDELIGHTS: In a pamphlet distributed by the Northern Arizona University Art Gallery, Howard Conant writes: "The paintings and drawings I have created in Arizona are of special importance to me. They have all been created during the new segment of my life in the beautiful, clean, healthy and upbeat Southwest, where my work and my total being have undergone welcome and marked changes.

"The softly toned and incredibly varied greens, yellows and tans of the Sonoran Desert have helped me develop a more subtle and actually sand-textured palette; at the same time the incredible sunrises and sunsets, as well as the ultramarine moonlit skies of night, have caused me to see and use bright colors in new combinations and permutations. My newly evolved fascination with ancient Indian art forms, most particularly with those of the Mayan culture, has markedly changed the iconography as well as the technique of my work.

"These important stimuli coupled with timely advice from San Francisco painter Ursula Schneider to free myself from painterly inhibitions, caused me to abruptly terminate my twenty-year-old-and-growing-stale love affair with hard edged, geometric abstract painting, to scoop up a pailful of sand from the arroyo near my studio, and to begin painting my own edges again, this time with sand-textured acrylics. The resultant paintings are much less mechanical, more personal, they convey at moderate distance the effect of clean cut, hard edges on the geometric abstract shapes which I so admire.

"I believe artists are products both of their genetic inheritance and of their environment. For me to say that my recent work is based upon Maynan designs and desert colors and textures, therefore, is to cite only the most recent influences. Among previous inspirational sources which have not as yet been sublimated into my subconscious are Etruscan, Medieval, African and South Pacific sculpture, Greek architecture, Pompeiian interiors, Corbusier's *Chandigarh*, and the art of Signorelli, Carlo Crivelli, Matisse, Picasso, Mondrian, the Delaunays and Frank Stella.

"But whereas I do not believe that art is created out of a vacuum, I feel it is the individual artist's primary mission to strive with all possible energy and courage to evolve a unique and significant style of artistic expression. After more than thirty-five years of diligently striving toward this goal, I honestly feel that I am only now beginning to come within its reach."

* * *

CONSTANTELOS, Demetrios J. 1927-
(Dimitris Stachys)

PERSONAL: Born July 27, 1927, in Spilia, Messenia, Greece; became U.S. citizen in 1958; son of John B. (a farmer) and Christine (Psilopoulos) Constantelos; married Stella Croussouloudis, August 15, 1954; children: Christine, John, Helen, Maria. *Education:* Holy Cross Greek Orothodox Theological School, Diploma in Theology, 1951, B.A. in Th., 1958; Princeton Theological Seminary, Th.M., 1959; Rutgers University, M.A., 1963, Ph.D., 1965. *Home:* 304 Forest Dr., Linwood, N.J. 08221. *Office:* Arts and Humanities, Stockton State College, Pomona, N.J. 08240.

CAREER: St. Demetrios Greek Orthodox Church, Perth Amboy, N.J., pastor, 1955-64; Dumbarton Oaks Research Library, Washington, D.C., junior fellow, 1964-65; Holy Cross Greek Orthodox Theological School, Brookline, Mass., assistant professor, 1965-67, associate professor of history, 1967-71; Stockton State College, Pomona, N.J., professor of history and religious studies, 1971—. Visiting lecturer in history, Boston College, 1967-68. Representative of Greek Orthodox Archdiocese of North and South America at national and international congresses. *Member:* American Historical Association, American Society of Church History, Mediaeval Academy of America, American Academy of Religion, Orthodox Theological Society of American (president, 1968-71), U.S. National Committee for Byzantine Studies.

WRITINGS: An Old Faith for Modern Man, Greek Orthodox Archdiocese (New York), 1964; *The Greek Orthodox Church: History, Faith and Practice,* Seabury, 1967; *Byzantine Philanthropy and Social Welfare,* Rutgers University Press, 1968; *Marriage, Sexuality, and Celibacy: A Greek Orthodox Perspective,* Light & Life Press, 1975.

Editor: *Encyclicals and Documents of the Greek Orthodox Archdiocese,* Institute for Patristic Studies, 1975; (with C. J. Efthymiou) *Greece: Today and Tomorrow,* Krikos, 1979; *Orthodox Theology and Diakonia: Trends and Prospects,* Hellenic College Press, 1981; *Understanding the Greek Orthodox Church,* Seabury, 1982.

Contributor: Bruce M. Metzger, editor, *The Oxford Annotated Apocrypha,* Oxford University Press, 1977; A. E. Laiou-Thomadakis, editor, *Charanis Studies,* Rutgers University Press, 1980; G. H. Anderson and T. F. Stransky, editors, *Christ's Lordship and Religious Pluralism,* Orbis, 1981; J. J. Allen, editor, *Orthodox Synthesis: The Unity of Theological Thought,* St. Valdimir's Seminary Press, 1981.

Also contributor of more than thirty studies, essays, articles, and reviews to theology and history journals, and numerous articles and reviews of a more popular nature to U.S. and Greek publications, some under pseudonym Dimitris Stachys.

* * *

COOKE, M. E.
 See CREASEY, John

* * *

COOKE, Margaret
 See CREASEY, John

* * *

COOMBS, Philip H(all) 1915-

PERSONAL: Born August 15, 1915, in Holyoke, Mass.; son of Charles Gilmore and Nellie (Hall) Coombs; married Helena Brooks, October 18, 1941; children: Peter Brooks, Helena Hall. *Education:* Amherst College, B.A., 1937; graduate study at University of Chicago, 1937-39, and Brookings Institution, 1939-40. *Politics:* Democrat. *Home address:* River Road, Essex, Conn. 06426. *Office address:* International Council for Educational Development, P.O. Box 217, Essex, Conn. 06426.

CAREER: Williams College, Williamstown, Mass., instructor in economics, 1939, 1940-41; U.S. government, Washington, D.C., economist in Office of Price Administration, 1941-42, economic adviser in Office of Economic Stabilization, 1945-46; Amherst College, Amherst, Mass., professor of economics, 1947-49; President's Materials Policy Commission (Paley Commission), Washington, D.C., executive director, 1950-52; Ford Foundation, New York, N.Y., program director for education, and director of research, Fund for the Advancement of Education, 1952-60; U.S. Department of State, Washington, D.C., assistant secretary of state for international educational and cultural affairs, 1961-62; International Institute for Educational Planning, Paris, France, director, 1963-68, director of research, 1969-70; International Council for Educational Development, Essex, Conn., vice-chairman, 1970—. Chairman of U.S. delegation to UNESCO Conferences on Economic Growth and Educational Development in Addis Ababa, 1961, and Santiago, 1962; chairman of Organization for Economic Co-operation and Development Conference on Educational Investment and Economic Growth, Washington, D.C., 1962. Consultant on education and economic planning to governments of India, 1953-55, Turkey, 1957, and Spain, 1967-71. Visiting lecturer, Harvard University, Graduate School of Education, 1969; visiting professor, Yale University, Institute of Social Science, 1970-71. Co-founder, Center for Educational Enquiry, 1970. *Military service:* U.S. Army, Office of Strategic Services, 1943-45; received Legion of Merit.

MEMBER: International Society for Public Administration, American Economic Association, Council on Foreign Relations, Phi Beta Kappa, Century Association (New York). *Awards, honors:* L.H.D., Amherst College, 1962; LL.D., Brandeis University and Monmouth College, 1962; Council on Foreign Relations fellowship, 1962-63; Brookings Institution guest fellow, 1963.

WRITINGS: The Fourth Dimension of Foreign Policy—Educational and Cultural Affairs, Council on Foreign Relations and Harper, 1964; *Education and Foreign Aid,* Harvard University Press, 1965; *The New Media: Memo to Educational Planners,* UNESCO, 1967; *The World Educational Crisis: A Systems Analysis,* Oxford University Press, 1968; *What Is Educational Planning?,* UNESCO, 1970; (editor) *Psychological Aspects of Medical Training,* C. C Thomas, 1971; *Managing Educational Costs,* Oxford University Press, 1972; *New Paths to Learning for Rural Children and Youth,* International Council for Educational Development, 1973; *Attacking Rural Poverty: How Nonformal Education Can Help,* Johns Hopkins Press, 1974; (editor) *Education for Rural Development: Case Studies for Planners,* Praeger, 1975; (editor) *Meeting the Basic Needs of the Rural Poor: The Integrated, Community-Based Approach,* Pergamon, 1980; *Future Critical World Issues in Education: A Provisional Report of Findings,* International Council for Educational Development, 1981; *New Strategies for Improving Rural Family Life,* International Council for Educational Development, 1981. Contributor to journals.

AVOCATIONAL INTERESTS: Sailing, fishing, swimming, touring, reading, house repairs, community service.

* * *

COOPER, Henry St. John
 See CREASEY, John

* * *

COPEMAN, George H(enry) 1922-

PERSONAL: Born February 19, 1922, in Brisbane, Australia; son of Arthur B(radby) and Ellen (Briggs) Copeman; married Rita Ward, September 23, 1944; children: Gillian Ann, Brian Arthur, Frances Ellen. *Education:* University of Queensland, B.A., 1949; University of London, Ph.D., 1953. *Home:* Sheridan, Woodland Way, Kingswood, Tadworth, Surrey KT20 6NA, England.

CAREER: Daily Telegraph, London, England, financial journalist, 1950-51; *Director,* London, assistant editor, 1951-53; *Business,* London, editor, 1953-58; Business Publications Ltd., London, editorial director, 1958-64; Copeman Paterson Ltd., London, managing director, 1964-69; Business Intelligence Services, London, chairman, 1969-74. Former chairman of

Julian Gibbs Financial Incentives Ltd. *Military service:* Royal Australian Air Force, 1941-45; became squadron leader. *Member:* Wider Share Ownership Council (honorary secretary).

WRITINGS: Leaders of British Industry, Gee, 1955; *Promotion and Pay for Executives*, Business Publications, 1957; *The Challenge of Employee Shareholding*, Business Publications, 1958; *The Role of the Managing Director*, Business Publications, 1959; *Laws of Business Management and the Executive Way of Life*, Business Publications, 1962, 2nd edition, 1963; (with H. Luijk and F. de P. Hanika) *How the Executive Spends His Time*, Business Publications, 1963.

The Chief Executive and Business Growth: A Comparative Study in the United States, Britain and Germany, Leviathan House, 1971; (with Tony Rumble) *Capital as an Incentive*, Leviathan House, 1972; *What Every Director Wants to Know about the Business*, Leviathan House, 1973; *Employee Share Participation in Nationalized and Other Industries*, Aims of Industry, 1974; *Employee Share Ownership and Industrial Stability*, Institute of Personnel Management, 1975; *The Managing Director*, David & Charles, 1978.†

*   *   *

CORRINGTON, John William 1932-

PERSONAL: Born October 28, 1932, in Memphis, Tenn.; son of John Wesley (an insurance adjuster) and Viva (Shelley) Corrington; married Joyce Elaine Hooper (a chemistry professor and writer), February 6, 1960; children: Shelley, John, Robert, Thomas. *Education:* Centenary College of Louisiana, B.A., 1956; Rice University, M.A., 1960; University of Sussex, D.Phil., 1964; Tulane University, J.D., 1975. *Politics:* Independent. *Religion:* Catholic. *Home:* 1724 Valence St., New Orleans, La. 70115.

CAREER: Spent about two years in Europe as foreign correspondent for *Houston Post* and as lecturer in contemporary literature; Louisiana State University, Baton Rouge, instructor, 1960-65, assistant professor of English, 1965-66; Loyola University, New Orleans, La., associate professor of English, 1966-73, chairman of department, 1966-68, and 1969-70; private practice of law in New Orleans, 1975-79; headwriter, with wife, Joyce Hooper Corrington, of television series for Columbia Broadcasting Systems, Inc., "Search for Tomorrow," 1978-80, "Texas," 1980-81, "General Hospital," 1982, and "Capitol," 1982—. Visiting professor of modern literature, University of California, Berkeley, 1968. *Awards, honors:* Charioteer Poetry Prize, 1962, for *Where We Are;* National Endowment for the Arts Award, 1968, for short story "To Carthage Then I Came."

WRITINGS—Poetry: *Where We Are*, Charioteer Press, 1962; *The Anatomy of Love and Other Poems*, Roman Books, 1964; *Mr. Clean and Other Poems*, Amber House Press (San Francisco), 1964; *Lines to the South and Other Poems*, Louisiana State University Press, 1965.

Poems represented in anthologies, including *Poets of Today*, edited by Walter Lowenfels, International Publishers, 1964; *19 Poetas de hoy en los Estados Unidos*, edited by Miller Williams, Ministerio de Educacion Publica (Chile), 1966; *Black and White Culture in America*, University of Massachusetts Press, 1969; *"Mandala": Literature for Critical Analysis*, edited by W. L. Guerin and others, Harper, 1970; *Contemporary Poetry in America*, edited by Williams, Random House, 1973.

Fiction: *And Wait for the Night* (novel), Putnam, 1964; *The Upper Hand* (novel), Putnam, 1967; *The Lonesome Traveler and Other Stories*, Putnam, 1968; *The Bombardier* (novel), Putnam, 1970; *The Actes and Monuments* (collection of short stories), University of Illinois Press, 1978; *The Southern Reporter* (collection of short stories), Louisiana State University, 1981.

Short stories represented in anthologies, including *Best American Short Stories*, edited by Martha Foley, Houghton, 1973, 1976, 1977 and *Prize Stories: The O. Henry Awards*, edited by William Abrahams, Doubleday, 1976.

Nonfiction; published by Louisiana State University Press, except as indicated: (Contributor) D. E. Stanford, editor, *Nine Essays in Modern Literature*, 1965; (with Miller Williams, editor and author of introduction) *Southern Writing in the Sixties*, two volumes, 1966-67; (contributor) Clive Hart, editor, *James Joyce's "Dubliners": Critical Essays*, Viking, 1969; (contributor) *Recherches anglaises et nord americaines, 4*, University of Strasbourg, 1971; (contributor) Stephen A. McNight, editor, *Eric Voegelin's Search for Order in History*, 1978.

Screenplays; with wife, Joyce H. Corrington: "Von Richthofen and Brown," United Artists, 1970 (later released as "The Red Baron," 1971); "I Am Legend," Warner Brothers, 1971 (later released as "The Omega Man," 1971); "Box Car Bertha," American International Production, 1972; "Battle for the Planet of the Apes," Twentieth Century-Fox, 1973; "The Arena," New World Pictures, 1973; "Killer Bees," Worldvision Enterprises, 1974.

Television series; head writer, with J. H. Corrington; for Columbia Broadcasting Systems, Inc.: "Search for Tomorrow," 1978-80; "Texas," 1980-81, "General Hospital," 1981-82, and "Capitol," 1982—.

Contributor of poetry, fiction, and criticism to *Kenyon Review, Massachusetts Review, Outsider, Georgia Review, James Joyce Quarterly, Southern Literary Journal, Dalhousie Review, Sewanee Review, Southern Review*, and numerous other periodicals.

WORK IN PROGRESS: Final versions of novels, *The Man Who Slept with Women* and *Asylum;* beginning another novel, *Down to Ilium;* continuing work on a collection of essays, *Toward the Skandalon*.

SIDELIGHTS: John William Corrington is a writer "of little fame but much talent," according to Sylvia Shorris in *Nation*. Corrington's "reputation rests largely on his achievements in poetry and short fiction," as James D. Wilson notes in *Dictionary of Literary Biography*, and he also demonstrated his talent as a novelist.

Corrington is generally labeled a Southern writer by critics; most of his poetry and fiction deal with the South, and he is interested in Southern culture and literature. Corrington and Miller Williams, his co-editor on *Southern Writers in the Sixties*, give a definition of a Southern writer in the introduction to their book. According to Granville Hicks in *Saturday Review*, this definition includes "four qualities that they regard as characteristically Southern: a strong concern with religion of the Calvinist variety; a deep awareness of the past; a pervasive feeling for the land; [and] a powerful sense of responsibility, not only to others but also for the self."

Hicks finds all these elements in Corrington's own work, but that quality most often mentioned by reviewers is the author's "awareness of the past." Hicks continues: "Corrington, perhaps more than most Southern writers, is preoccupied with the past." This emphasis, coupled with the author's Southern heritage, has often led critics to make a comparison between Corrington and another Southern writer also noted for his tendency to dwell on past events, William Faulkner. David Montrose explains the basis for this comparison in a *Times Literary Supplement* review: "Corrington's principal preoccupation is the Faulknerian one of the past intruding into the present. Typically, his protagonists are old, unable to come to terms with the modern world." James R. Frakes, in *New York Times Book Review,* suggests an even stronger affiliation between Corrington and Faulkner, listing a number of themes common to both men, including "the weight of time, the comedy of pure honor, the inescapable burden of the past, [and] the agony of loss." Frakes states that the use of so many Faulknerian themes by a Southern author invites a "hopeless comparison" to Faulkner. However, Frakes praises Corrington for taking this chance and obtaining favorable results: "[Corrington] runs all the risks, . . . even echoes style and characterization. And somehow he remains his own man throughout."

Barry Targan in *Washington Post Book World* also notes the similarities of theme between Corrington and Faulkner but emphasizes the originality of Corrington's work. Targan writes: "One is surprised by the freshness with which he uses an old and honorable tradition. Just when we think that the Southern Voice of Faulkner . . . has been played out or attenuated by innumerable mimics, along comes Corrington to wring from it a familiar but invigorated music."

ause of his interest in the past, the focus of Corrington's writing is often on "that supremely important event in Southern history, the War Between the States," according to Hicks. Many of Corrington's stories as well as his nonfiction works deal with the Civil War period or with the effects of the war on even contemporary Southern life. Summarizing the author's attitude, Frakes quotes a line from one of Corrington's stories: "'That war shaped all our destinies. . . . The years only diminish the influence; they do not erase it.'"

In his first novel, *And Wait for the Night,* the author's sympathetic portrayal of the Southern role during the Civil War "earned [him] the reputation of traditional Southern apologist," notes Wilson. Critics felt that in the novel Corrington was attempting to defend the Confederate position. A *Times Literary Supplement* reviewer, for instance, called the book "violently partisan" and remarked: "It is one of Mr. Corrington's passionate beliefs that [the Civil War] drags on still, with the South at the mercy of Yankee domination and exploitation." According to Hicks, in *And Wait for the Night* "Corrington is still trying to demonstrate that the Confederacy should have won the War Between the States."

The South cannot be entirely separated from a discussion of Corrington's writing. However, some critics take issue with the idea that Corrington is only a Southern writer. Arguing against the placement of geographical boundaries on the author's work, they feel that the scope of Corrington's writing is universal. Montrose notes: "Corrington is no more a regional writer than was Faulkner; his South functions like Yoknapatawpha County, as a backdrop against which wider themes are played." Wilson explains this idea further: "Admittedly Corrington's fiction . . . focuses on the South and attempts to capture the spiritual quality of a region he knows well. . . . But Corrington's real concerns are psychological and metaphysical. . . . Corrington presents in his most characteristic fiction a portrayal of the soul's metaphoric quest for spiritual wholeness." For example, Corrington's second novel, *The Upper Hand,* according to Wilson, "explores the dimensions and ambiguities of evil. . . . [It] traces the spiritual progression of its central character." Shorris refers to Corrington's collection of short stories, *The Actes and Monuments,* as "moral tales. . . . [In them] Corrington makes his characters as well as his readers squirm."

Born in the southern United States and writing about the South as he does, Corrington cannot escape the label of "Southern writer." But, many would also agree, as Hicks points out, that Corrington is "not only a good Southern writer, but a very good writer."

AVOCATIONAL INTERESTS: American history, sports, travel, music, philosophy and religion of India.

CA INTERVIEW

CA interviewed John William Corrington by phone September 4, 1981, at his home in New Orleans.

CA: You began your college years as a music student. Did you plan at that point to be a musician rather than a writer?

CORRINGTON: Yes. I had planned to be a big-band trumpet player, but just about the time I graduated from college the big bands vanished. But I always loved music; it was my first love, and I expect it will be my last.

CA: You told Contemporary Poets *that your early work in poetry gave you "a far greater sensitivity to form and style than an apprenticeship in prose fiction would have produced." Did you plan in the beginning to move from poetry to fiction?*

CORRINGTON: Yes. It seemed to me that since poetry is shorter, you could execute even a fairly long poem reasonably quickly and concentrate on the individual words, the lines, the rhythms. You just couldn't undertake to write a novel when you were under the pressure of being in graduate school. You're not going to be able to hold that much in your head while you're being interfered with by literary history and criticism courses and that sort of thing. It was a very deliberate decision because I figured, look, why not start with the shortest and most intense form with the ideal of one day writing a page of prose so that if somebody threw open my book at page 301, they'd say, "Hell, what a page." You master the smallest units then you don't have to think about them any longer. You can afford to think about the longer form because you know through your self-training in the short form that the small units are taken care of.

CA: Why did you choose to go to England, to the University of Sussex, for a Ph.D.?

CORRINGTON: I wanted to study with David Daiches, and furthermore I was sick and tired of the American graduate system—the endless English courses one takes that one either doesn't need or doesn't believe in and the refusal to allow one further courses in music, history, and philosophy. The farther I went in the American system, the narrower it got. I was forced to take more and more courses in areas that I had no interest in and which I could've picked up by careful reading anyhow. In England you simply write a dissertation; if it is considered publishable in its present state, you go up for examination. There are only two examiners: an interior examiner who'll be your dissertation director and an exterior examiner from another university. I had Matthew Hodjart of Cambridge on my committee, and he and Professor Daiches examined me. When you go up you don't go only for a D. Phil. They evaluate your writing, evaluate your oral examination, and then give you one of three degrees. You could get a bachelor of literature, a master of philosophy, or a doctor of philosophy; and I got the D. Phil.

CA: So it really is dependent on your doing good work.

CORRINGTON: Yes, instead of all this classroom time. They figure it's up to *you* to determine what you need, but when you get up in front of them, *they'll* determine what you've got.

CA: You've cited Eric Voegelin as an important influence on your writing. How did you come to Voegelin's work?

CORRINGTON: Well, Professor Voegelin had taught at LSU when I was an undergraduate there, but I didn't know him. When I went to LSU as a faculty member, I was reading manuscripts for the LSU Press. They couldn't pay you money so they gave you books. The director of the LSU Press at that time, Dick Wentworth, offered me the three volumes of *Order and History*. I was very much interested in Southern history then and said, "Ah, Dick, I don't want these." He said, "Listen, everybody says they're great; you ought to read them." So I went home and I read *Israel and Revelation* and thought it was the greatest book I'd read on any subject, and then read the other two and spent the rest of my time finding everything I could by Professor Voegelin. I would say his work is probably the greatest influence on my intellectual life.

CA: What was Voegelin's primary influence on your life and work?

CORRINGTON: It's very hard to say, really. When I finished *Israel and Revelation*, I had the distinct feeling that Professor Voegelin had shown me how God did it—through the Jewish people, the symbolic structure, the representation of reality in the Old Testament, the cosmological empires, and the rest. It was just that the world looked different, less arbitrary and more intelligible. And it has stayed that way.

CA: That kind of influence doesn't often come along.

CORRINGTON: No, it doesn't. I think you have to be prepared for it. But Dr. Edward Murray Clark of Centenary College had prepared me by excellent courses in the scripture, and I prepared myself by reading Latin and Greek classics. I was more ready for Voegelin's work than most people since nobody gets a decent classical education anymore; you either luck into it or you just don't have it. Since I happened to be ready, his work pulled together all the things that interested me: theology, literary criticism, symbolic studies, even psychology—everything I knew a little bit about fed into and was made coherent by Voegelin's work. And it's still going on.

CA: You've been called a Catholic writer and, not just a Southern writer, but a traditional apologist for the South. How do you feel about those labels?

CORRINGTON: I really don't think about them much at all. I figure that history will determine what I was, and I needn't put a label on myself. Those who do that generally want to set up something they can attack. I am Catholic and I am a Southerner; I love my country—the South—and if that constitutes a justification of the labels, fine. As a critic I never found it necessary to create labels because the works stand by themselves. I don't think anybody would spot a syllable of Catholicism in my most recent novel, *The Man Who Slept with Women*, which is going around to the publishers now.

CA: You've been working on that for several years?

CORRINGTON: Actually, ten years of thinking and four months of writing. It's produced a nine-hundred-page novel. It's so vast that anything I'd say about it would be a cartoon of the book itself. I'm happy with it and proud of it.

CA: There are writers who resent having any mention made of regionalism in their work. I gather from your work, your comments about it, and the comments you made in the preface to Southern Writing in the Sixties *that you don't feel it's necessary to apologize for that.*

CORRINGTON: If someone said, "Are you an American writer or a Southern writer?" I'd say very clearly, "I'm a Southern writer." I have no desire to represent or even fiddle around with New York and California or the rest of it. They appear in my work simply because I've been there and I've had encounters there and the experience is useful. But I would maintain I am a Southern writer, and if nobody else wants to be, that's fine; then we would have only one: me.

CA: Most of the critics consider The Upper Hand *your best novel. Do you agree?*

CORRINGTON: No, the best novel I ever wrote is *The Man Who Slept with Women*. By the way, a number of characters from *The Upper Hand* show up in *The Man Who Slept with Women*. It was fun to evoke them again after fifteen years.

CA: In The Bombardier *you presented, through the six main characters, a look at the diversity of American society and the violence that permeates our history. How did this book begin in your mind?*

CORRINGTON: That book was really almost a philosophical meditation. It was dedicated to Barbara Steinberg and my students at the University of California because I was there in 1968, pretty much at the height of all the activity of the '60s. I had gone there with the full expectation of having to defend myself with a machine gun because I disagreed with every single idea I thought they had. I didn't like dope, I was absolutely opposed to the anti-Vietnam business, and I figured it was going to be a rough term. To my astonishment, they loved me. And I loved them. I remember Tom Parkinson, who was a professor of English at Berkeley, came up to me at the end of the semester and said, "Is it true that you have had three standing ovations in your lectures on modern literature?" And I said, "Yeah, it was really spooky." And he said, "Well, that's one more than any professor at this campus has ever received." It was a strange time. Many of my students were screwed up emotionally, they had no sense of history, no sense of humor to speak of, but they were brilliant. If intellect alone made a human being, they would have been supermen and superwomen. They were incredible kids, but what they lacked made them miserable. They saw in me (and ironically, in my Southern past) serenity and a sense of a deeper knowledge than all their intellect could provide. One of them told me, "God, I wish I'd been born in the South." And I said, "Son, I'm not sure you mean that." Because it takes a certain kind of person to be happy here. You've always got your Tom Wickers and your Willy Morrises trotting up to New York to kiss somebody's fanny and get paid for denouncing their own country. Then there're the rest of us like Faulkner and Walker Percy and Flannery O'Conner and me. Hell, I wish I had a buck for every time I've been asked to go to California or New York. In fact we got an offer last night and I said no again. It used to be that I just didn't want to go, but now I'm getting kind of proud of saying no. *The Bombardier* was my attempt to explain the present as it rose from the past—for my Berkeley students. And perhaps, through Boileau, to explain part of myself to me.

CA: You became a lawyer in 1975. What led you to the decision to study and practice law?

CORRINGTON: Well, I was sick of academia, so I got out of that in '72 and started law school at Tulane. I think part of it was the fact that my dad had been a lawyer and had always wanted me to be one and I had always said, "No, I'm going my own way." But then I had a little bit of spare time and we were financially OK and why not do that for him, even if it was posthumously? There was one other reason: when I told my father I had a job at LSU, he said, "Well, son, teaching at LSU for a while is OK, but when are you going to get a job?" He didn't regard teaching school or writing novels—or doing movies, God knows—as serious work fit for a responsible and bright man. But when I became a lawyer, you see, I had a place in the social order just like everybody else.

CA: And then you could write in your spare time.

CORRINGTON: That's right. And that's fine, because, remember, Faulkner always said he was a farmer whose writing was a hobby; that was because people understood what a farmer was, and if a farmer had a crazy and eccentric hobby, that was all right.

CA: What kind of law do you specialize in?

CORRINGTON: Well, because we write for television I haven't been able to practice for a couple of years. But I may go back to it one day. My favorite work is appellate work; that's where you go before the appeals court to argue either to defend a case you won or to overturn a lower-court decision if you lost. I feel this is where I'm really at my best because I can marshal the facts and present oral argument and written argument perhaps at a more sophisticated level than the average working lawyer who, after all, is not a specialist in legal thinking, philosophical thinking, or in writing. So it just seems that what I like best and what one would presume would be my best area come together.

CA: You and your wife, Joyce Hooper Corrington, have collaborated on several screenplays and have written for television for several years. How did the collaboration begin?

CORRINGTON: Jo worked with me from the first. Roger Corman, who used to be called the king of the B-movies, wanted me to do a screenplay on Baron von Richthofen, who, as it happened, I really knew a lot about. Jo is a superb organizer so we got together and organized and wrote that one, and one led to the next. Then along came the TV stuff, and once again her first-rate organizational abilities and the fact that she is a good writer, too, helped. Even though she has her Ph.D. in chemistry, she had taken writing courses in college and is pretty much a natural writer. She doesn't have the same drive toward it that I do, but if she wanted to write you a movie script, or a novel, boy could she ever do it.

CA: Does the television work require you to travel much?

CORRINGTON: We've never left our home, wherever we were living with the children. We never set up shop in a place outside Louisiana. But, for example, when we were working regularly in television we would go up to New York about every two months and stay three days or so. Actually, it's all right to go to New York five or six times a year for a few days. We'd go to the opera, we'd go to a couple of plays, we'd look in the book shops and the record shops and go to nice restaurants and see friends. It was a real party. But I would never want to stay in New York more than a week. When I'm away from the boys more than three days or so I start getting worried and concerned and unhappy.

CA: How old are your children?

CORRINGTON: My eldest is nineteen, my next is fifteen, and my baby is fourteen. It's hard to believe I have a child nineteen because it seems like yesterday I picked him up at the hospital. I refuse to allow myself to become sentimental about this because it could really make me very unhappy. Some people say, oh boy, when our kids are gone we're going to do this and that or the other thing. I say when your kids are gone you're going to look around and you're going to be dead. I don't want my kids to leave. I know that they have to; I know it's proper that they do so; but I'll miss them every single day for the rest of my life.

CA: Do you find it difficult to switch back and forth between writing fiction and writing for movies or television?

CORRINGTON: No. There's an absolute difference. Joyce says it's funny because when I write for television or movies I always use a typewriter. And when I finished my latest book, there before me were 1,982 pages of handwritten manuscript. There's such a difference. *The Great Gatsby* was written in 1925; they've made three movies of it (the middle one was pretty good). All are out of general circulation, and nobody except on a late-night program would even consider showing them, but the novel is selling very well, thank you. I didn't start out to make money; I started out with the express purpose of being one of the finest American writers of the twentieth century, knowing that I would never know if I had won or not. The movies and TV are a way to keep eating. Nobody pays for quality writing today.

CA: It takes the perspective of time, doesn't it?

CORRINGTON: Sure. I love to ask people who was the best-selling novelist in England in the nineteenth century. The unsophisticated say Charles Dickens; the more sophisticated say George Meredith or Thackeray, and then you can name the Brontes and Jane Austen and everybody. And I say, "No, I'm sorry, the best-selling novelist in England in the nineteenth century was Lord Bulwer-Lytton. You may know of one of his books, *The Last Days of Pompeii*." Seriously, he sold more books than anybody—Trollope, Disraeli, any of the dozens of names you could come up with of really top-notch nineteenth-century British novelists. Bulwer-Lytton was the Harold Robbins of the nineteenth century, and nobody has reprinted one of his books since he died. Except possibly *The Last Days of Pompeii*.

CA: You've proven yourself able in many fields. Has it been difficult to decide where to concentrate your energy?

CORRINGTON: Yes. Not early on, but now. I'm getting tired, and I can tell I'm getting old because it used to be I was like a young gunfighter—not only was I going to win, but the other guy probably wouldn't even get clear of the leather. When you get older, you find out you can't expend yourself in so many directions. Maybe the reason is I was uncritical when I was young and just producing whatever came into my mind, but as I got older and learned more, I stopped letting something get out of hand the way I used to.

For example, I just got some reviews of my new book of short stories, *The Southern Reporter*. The *Washington Post Book World* review was the best review I have ever gotten on anything. The review concludes that if you want a masterpiece, you want *The Southern Reporter*. And the fact is, I wasn't terribly happy with the book in the sense that I felt at least the title story, which is the one that the reviewer liked a lot, was really unfinished and needed maybe six months of thinking and fiddling with it before it was satisfactory.

Well, hell, maybe as I get older, I'm holding things too long or trying to get a measure of perfection which won't even matter—now or later. It's very hard to know because unfortunately I am not a genius of Mozart's order. All Mozart had to do was sit down with a pen and write whatever came into his mind and it was a masterpiece, period, and everyone knows it. But most of us would be pretentious fools to try that. It's not that I'm getting scared or doubting my capacities as I get older; I've just perhaps become wiser to the fact that this is a very heavy game, and the heavier I realize it is, the more I've got to take my time.

CA: You want to do it better.

CORRINGTON: Yes, I want to be better. But better for me is not necessarily better for an audience. What audiences want today seems gibberish to me. My fiction is almost never translatable into a film. I think it speaks well for the books as fiction because any book that translates immediately into a film is obviously garbage. Not because there's something wrong with film but because the book must be simpleminded if you can do a really first-rate film of it. For example, take *Heart of Darkness* by Conrad; you can't make a film out of that because you must see Kurtz, but you mustn't see Kurtz. That's one little technical problem. But this goes on and on. To me Conrad's greatest book is a novel called *Victory,* a dynamite, wild adventure story that reminds me of *Sanctuary* by Faulkner, but you couldn't turn it into a film. Only the lurid part would be filmic.The part that matters is in the hearts of the characters, and it would be hell to try to reveal this. If they want to do a film of my new novel, it will be fine with me, but it'll be a completely different thing. The farce elements and the yokel jokes would be the primary stuff, and somebody will say, "Hey, this is a 200-IQ version of the 'Dukes of Hazzard.' " And this would be true—you'd lose the central story. You'd think of it only as a different, alternate form of entertainment, metaphysical and spiritual contemplation for imbeciles.

CA: Are there future projects you'd like to talk about?

CORRINGTON: I'm always looking forward to the next thing. Right now I've blocked out one new novel; I've sort of blocked out a couple of short stories, though I haven't yet gotten the call to sit down and write them. I'm very much hoping that we'll be in a financial position for me just to go ahead and devote full time to the writing now. I feel like this decade, my fifties, is *my* time, and if I can find time to do it, I swear I could turn out at least ten novels. Well, if it's going to get done, now is it because I'm not going to get any smarter to speak of and I'm certainly not going to get any younger.

BIOGRAPHICAL/CRITICAL SOURCES: Saturday Review, May 23, 1964, December 21, 1968; *New York Times Book Review,* July 26, 1964, December 15, 1968, February 25, 1979; *Christian Science Monitor,* July 30, 1964; *Times Literary Supplement,* November 19, 1964, September 18, 1981; John William Corrington and Miller Williams, editors, *Southern Writing in the Sixties,* two volumes, Louisiana State University Press, 1966-67; *Poetry,* April, 1966; *Contemporary Poets,* Macmillan, 1970, 3rd edition, 1980; *Nation,* February 10, 1979; *Dictionary of Literary Biography,* Volume VI: *American Novelists since World War II,* 2nd series, Gale, 1980; *Washington Post Book World,* August 30, 1981.

—Sketch by Marian Walters
—Interview by Jean W. Ross

CORTES, Carlos E(liseo) 1934-

PERSONAL: Born April 6, 1934, in Oakland, Calif.; married; wife's name Laurel; children: Alana. *Education:* University of California, Berkeley, B.A., 1956; Columbia University, M.S. (journalism), 1957; American Institute for Foreign Trade, B.F.T., 1962; University of New Mexico, M.A. (Portuguese), 1965, Ph.D. (history), 1969. *Office:* Department of History, University of California, Riverside, Calif. 92502.

CAREER: Jensen-Salsbery Chemical Co., Kansas City, Mo., laboratory assistant, summer, 1952; Whitaker Cable Corp., North Kansas City, Mo., cable splicer, summers, 1953-54; *Boxoffice* (magazine), Kansas City, general assistant, summer, 1956; American Shakespeare Festival, Stratford, Conn., assistant to the director of public relations, 1957; *Phoenix Sunpapers,* Phoenix, Ariz., executive editor, 1959-61; Associated Press, Phoenix, reporter, 1961; American Institute for Foreign Trade, Phoenix, assistant to the director of area studies, 1961-62; University of California, Riverside, acting assistant professor, 1968-69, assistant professor, 1969-72, associate professor, 1972-76, professor of history, 1976—, chairman of department, 1982—, chairman of Latin American studies program, 1969-71, chairman of Chicano studies program, 1972—, assistant to vice-chancellor for academic affairs, 1970-72. Programmer of teaching machines for Learning, Inc., 1961-62. Member of executive board, California Council for the Humanities, 1982—. Member of advisory panels of California State Commission for Teacher Preparation and Licensing, 1974-75; member of advisory board of Summer Institute for Chicano Studies at California State College (Long Beach), 1970; consultant to Far West Laboratory for Educational Research and Development, National Endowment for the Humanities, National Institute of Education, U.S. Commission on Civil Rights, Ford Foundation, Educational Testing Service, Council of State Governments. *Military service:* U.S. Army, information specialist, 1957-59.

MEMBER: International Association for Audio-Visual Media in Historical Research and Education, National Association for Chicano Studies, National Chicano Council on Higher Education, Society for the Study of Multi-Ethnic Literature of the United States, Association of Borderlands Scholars, American Historical Association, American Association of University Professors, Association for Supervision and Curriculum Development, Conference on Latin American History, Historians Film Committee, Latin American Studies Association, National Council for the Social Studies, Social Science Education Consortium, Immigration History Society, Western History Association, Pacific Coast Council on Latin American Studies, California Council for the Social Studies, Association of California Intergroup Relations Educators, Southern California Social Science Association, Phi Beta Kappa, Phi Kappa Phi, Phi Alpha Theta.

AWARDS, HONORS: Haynes Foundation summer fellowship, 1969; Ford Foundation grant, 1969-70; National Endowment for the Humanities education program grant, 1971-72; Hubert Herring Memorial Award, Pacific Coast Council on Latin American Studies, 1974, for *Gaucho Politics in Brazil: The Politics of Rio Grande do Sul, 1930-1964;* Eleanor Fishburn Award, Washington EdPress Association, 1977, for *Curriculum Guidelines for Multiethnic Education;* Distinguished California Humanist Award, California Council for the Humanities, 1980.

WRITINGS: (With Richard Kornweibel) *Bibliografia da Historia do Rio Grande do Sul: Periodo Republicano* (title means

"Bibliography of the History of Rio Grande do Sul: Republicano Period"), Edicoes da Faculdade de Filosofia, Universidade Federal do Rio Grande do Sul, 1967; (editor with Alfredo Castaneda, Manuel Ramirez III, and Mario Barrera, and contributor) *Mexican Americans and Educational Change,* Mexican-American Studies Program, University of California, Riverside, 1971; (with Pastora Montoro de Lopez-Roman, Leslie S. Offutt, and others) *Research Guide to the Godoi-Diaz Perez Collection in the Library of the University of California, Riverside,* Latin American Studies Program, University of California, Riverside, 1973; (contributor) James A. Banks, editor, *Teaching Ethnic Studies: Concepts and Strategies,* National Council for the Social Studies, 1973; *Gaucho Politics in Brazil: The Politics of Rio Grande do Sul, 1930-1964,* University of New Mexico Press, 1974; *The Mexican American* (reprints), twenty-one volumes, Arno, 1974.

(With Leon G. Campbell and Robert Pinger) *Latin America: A Filmic Approach,* Latin American Studies Program, University of California, Riverside, 1975; (with Arlin Ginsburg, Alan Green, and James Joseph) *The Ethnic Underclass: Blacks, Chicanos, and Native Americans—Three Perspectives on Ethnicity in America,* Putnam, 1976; *Understanding You and Them: Tips for Teaching about Ethnicity,* Educational Resources Information Center (ERIC) Clearinghouse for Social Studies and Social Science Education, 1976; (with Campbell and Alan Curl) *A Filmic Approach to the Study of Historical Dilemmas,* Latin American Studies Program, University of California, Riverside, 1976; *The Chicano Heritage* (reprints), fifty-five volumes, Arno, 1976; (with Banks, Geneva Gay, Ricardo L. Garcia, and Anna S. Ochoa) *Curriculum Guidelines for Multiethnic Education,* National Council for the Social Studies, 1976; *Mexico in the Study of Mexican Americans: An Analysis of Transnational Linkages,* Center for Teaching International Relations, University of Denver, 1976; (with Campbell) *Race and Ethnicity in the History of the Americas: A Filmic Approach,* Latin American Studies Program, University of California, Riverside, 1979; *Hispanics in the United States* (reprints), thirty volumes, Arno, 1980.

Teacher training aids: "A Bicultural Process for Developing Mexican-American Heritage Curriculum" (manual), Systems and Evaluation in Education, University of California, Riverside, 1971; "Using Local History: Resources in Social Studies" (two videotapes), Systems and Evaluation in Education, privately printed, 1972; "Concepts and Strategies for Teaching the Mexican-American Experience" (manual with three videotapes), Dissemination Center for Bilingual Bicultural Education, 1974.

Also co-author and co-producer of documentary film, "Northwest from Tumacacori," Matrix Media, 1972. Contributor to *Encyclopedia of Latin America.* Contributor of articles and reviews to professional journals. Contributing editor, *Aztlan-International Journal of Chicano Studies Research,* 1969—.

WORK IN PROGRESS: *A History of California,* for Scholastic; *Mexican Americans,* for Free Press.

* * *

CORWIN, Ronald Gary 1932-

PERSONAL: Born June 14, 1932, in Waterloo, Iowa; son of Leonard John and Beuhlah (Morris) Corwin; married Bonnie Titus, June 20, 1954; children: Cheryl, Marcia, Blair. *Education:* State College of Iowa (now University of Northern Iowa), B.A. (with high honors), 1954; University of Iowa, graduate study, 1956; University of Minnesota, M.A., 1958, Ph.D., 1960. *Home:* 2006 Collingswood Rd., Columbus, Ohio 43221. *Office:* Department of Sociology, Ohio State University, Columbus, Ohio 43210.

CAREER: University of Minnesota, Minneapolis, instructor in sociology, research fellow, and project director, 1959-60, assistant professor of education and research associate in sociology, 1960-61; Ohio State University, Columbus, assistant professor, 1961-65, associate professor, 1965-69, professor of sociology, 1969—. Visiting summer lecturer, Columbia University, 1965. Acting branch chief, Bureau of Research, U.S. Office of Education, 1967. *Military service:* U.S. Army, served in Japan, 1954-56; became sergeant. *Member:* American Educational Research Association (vice-president, 1969-71), American Sociological Association (fellow), North Central Sociological Association. *Awards, honors:* U.S. Public Health Service grant, 1960-61; U.S. Office of Education grant, 1962-68; Ford Foundation and National Education Association grant, 1968-73.

WRITINGS: (With M. J. Taves and J. Eugene Haas) *Role Conception and Success and Satisfaction,* Bureau of Business Research, Ohio State University, 1963; *A Sociology of Education: Emerging Patterns of Class, Status and Power in the Public Schools,* Appleton-Century-Crofts, 1965; (with Williard Lane and William Monahan) *Foundations of Administration in Education: A Behavioral Analysis,* Macmillan, 1966, revised edition, 1967; *Militant Professionalism: A Study of Conflict in High Schools,* Appleton-Century-Crofts, 1970; *Reform and Organizational Survival: The Teacher Corps as an Instrument of Educational Change,* Wiley, 1973; *Education in Crisis: A Sociological Analysis of Schools and Universities in Transition,* Wiley, 1974; (with Roy Edelfelt) *Lessons from the Teacher Corps,* National Education Association, 1974; (with Edelfelt) *Perspectives on Organizations,* Vol. I: *Viewpoints for Teachers,* American Association of Colleges for Teacher Education, 1976; *The Entrepreneurial Bureaucracy,* Jai Press, 1982.

Contributor: (With Taves) Howard Freeman and others, editors, *Handbook of Medical Sociology,* Prentice-Hall, 1963; Haas, *Role Conception and Group Consensus,* Ohio State University, 1964; Donald Hansen, editor, *Counseling in Society,* Houghton, 1966; Hansen and Joel Gerst, editors, *On Education: Sociological Perspectives,* Wiley, 1967; Bruce Eckland, editor, *Perspectives on Human Deprivation,* National Child Health Institute, U.S. Public Health Service, Department of Health, Education and Welfare, 1968; R. J. Havighurst, editor, *Readings,* Allyn & Bacon, 1968; Harold I. Goodwin and Patrick W. Carlson, editors, *The Collective Dilemma: Negotiations in Education,* Charles Jones Publishing, 1969; Hansen, editor, *Explorations in the Sociology of Counseling,* Houghton, 1969.

Simon Marcson, *Decentralization and Community Control in Urban Areas,* Rutgers University, 1971; (and editor with Saad Nagi) *The Social Contexts of Research,* Wiley, 1972; Alfred Lightfoot, editor, *Inquiries into the Social Foundations of Education,* Rand McNally, 1972; Jerald T. Hage and Koya Azumi, editors, *Sociological Study of Organizations,* Heath, 1972; Rudolph Moos and Paul Insel, editors, *Issues in Social Ecology,* National Press, 1973; Sam Sieber and David Wilder, editors, *The School in Society: Studies in the Sociology of Education,* Free Press, 1973; Jack Culbertson and others, editors, *Social Science Content for Preparing Educational Leaders,* C. E. Merrill, 1973; Donald Gerwin, editor, *The Employment of Teachers: Some Analytical Views,* McCutchan, 1974; John Carroll, editor, *Review of Research in Education,* 1974, F. E. Peacock, 1974; Monahan, editor, *Theoretical Dimensions of Educational Administration,* Macmillan, 1975; J. Cistone, editor, *Understanding School Boards: Problems and Prospects,*

Heath, 1975; Peter Schmidt, editor, *Innovation: Diffusion Von Neuerungen im Sozialen Bereich*, Hoffman and Compe Verlag, 1975; K. Ryan, editor, *Teacher Education*, National Society for the Study of Education, 1975.

M. Jacobs, editor, *Flexible Education for the Health Professions*, Wiley, 1976; M. Martinez, Jr. and J. M. Weston, editors, *School and Community: Issues and Alternatives*, Kendall/Hunt, 1976; (and editor) *Sociology of Education and Socialization*, Jai Press, Volume I, 1980, Volume II, 1982.

Contributor to *Encyclopedia of Education*. Contributor to numerous journals, including *Social Forces, Sociology of Education, Journal of Applied and Behavioral Science, International Review of Education*, and *Administrative Science Quarterly*.

* * *

COUGER, J(ames) Daniel 1929-

PERSONAL: Born October 20, 1929, in Olney, Tex.; son of James Larry Rogers (an engineer) and Faye Schly (Saylors) Couger; married Shirley Anne Thomas, March 4, 1951; children: Daniel Ray, Todd David, Timothy Lee, Julie Anne. *Education:* Phillips University, B.A., 1951; University of Kansas City (now University of Missouri—Kansas City), M.A., 1958; University of Colorado, D.B.A., 1964. *Politics:* Republican. *Religion:* Presbyterian. *Home:* 2611 Northridge Dr., Colorado Springs, Colo. 80907. *Office:* School of Business, University of Colorado, Cragmor Rd., Colorado Springs, Colo. 80907.

CAREER: Industrial engineer, National Gypsum Co., 1953-54; Hallmark Cards, Inc., Kansas City, Mo., industrial engineering department supervisor, 1954-58; Martin Marietta Corp., Littleton, Colo., computer department section chief, 1958-65; University of Colorado, Colorado Springs, professor of computer and management science, 1965—. Member of affiliate faculty of Japan American Institute of Management Science. Has lectured in twenty-three countries. President of Gethsemane Christian Church, Colorado Springs, 1972-73. Consultant to International Business Machines Corp., Dow Chemical Corp., and Hewlett Packard Co. *Military service:* U.S. Air Force, 1951-53; became lieutenant.

MEMBER: Operations Research Society of America, Institute of Management Sciences, Society for Management Information Systems (secretary; member of executive council), Association for Computing Machinery (chairman of lectureship series), American Institute for Decision Sciences (vice-president), Association for Systems Management, Data Processing Management Association, Christian Churches of Colorado and Wyoming (chairman of new church development, 1969-71), Boy Scouts of America (cubmaster, Denver Area Council, 1965-66). *Awards, honors:* National award from American Association for Collegiate Schools of Business, for curriculum innovation; distinguished service award, 1966, from Association for Systems Management; University of Colorado, Distinguished Faculty Award, 1976, and Chancellor's Award, 1977; U.S. Computer Science Man of the Year award, 1977, from Data Processing Management Association.

WRITINGS: Computers and the Schools of Business, Business Research Division, School of Business Administration, University of Colorado, 1967; (with Loren E. Shannon) *FORTRAN IV: A Programmed Instruction Approach*, Irwin, 1968, 3rd edition, 1976; (with Shannon) *FORTRAN: A Beginner's Approach*, with programmed learning aid, Irwin, 1971; (editor with Robert W. Knapp) *Systems Analysis Techniques*, Wiley, 1974; *Acts of the Holy Spirit*, Full Gospel Business Men's Fellowship, 1974; (with Fred McFadden) *Introduction to Computer-Based Information Systems*, Wiley, 1975; (with McFadden) *A First Course in Data Processing*, Wiley, 1977. Editor, "Business Data Processing" series, Wiley, 1965—. Columnist, *Computerworld*, 1970—. Contributor of over fifty articles to professional journals. Editor, *Computing Newsletter for Schools of Business*, 1967—.

WORK IN PROGRESS: Research on the use of the computer for application of management sciences and on the design of computer-based management information systems.†

* * *

COWAN, Ian Borthwick 1932-

PERSONAL: Born April 16, 1932, in Dumfries, Scotland; son of William McAuley (a banker) and Annie (Borthwick) Cowan; married Anna Little Telford, July 16, 1954; children: Gillian Alexandra, Susan Jane, Ingrid Kirsten. *Education:* University of Edinburgh, M.A. (with honors), 1954, Ph.D., 1961. *Home:* 119 Balshagray Ave., Glasgow G11 7EG, Scotland. *Office:* Department of Scottish History, University of Glasgow, Glasgow G12 8QH, Scotland.

CAREER: University of Edinburgh, Edinburgh, Scotland, assistant lecturer in Scottish history, 1956-59; Newbattle Abbey College, Dalkeith, Scotland, lecturer in Scottish history, 1959-62; University of Glasgow, Glasgow, Scotland, lecturer, 1962-70, senior lecturer, 1970-77, reader in Scottish history, 1977—. *Military service:* Royal Air Force, 1954-56; became flying officer. *Member:* Historical Association (vice-president, 1981—), Scottish History Society, Scottish Church History Society (president, 1971-74).

WRITINGS: Blast and Counterblast: Contemporary Writings on the Scottish Reformation, Saltire Society, 1960; *The Parishes of Medieval Scotland*, Scottish Record Society, 1967; (editor with A. I. Dunlop) *Calendar of Scottish Supplications to Rome*, Scottish History Society, 1970; *The Enigma of Mary Stuart*, St. Martin's, 1971; *The Scottish Covenanters: 1660-1689*, Gollancz, 1976; (reviser) D. E. Easson, *Medieval Religious Houses in Scotland* (1st edition, 1957), Longmans, 1976; *Regional Aspects of the Scottish Reformation*, Historical Association, 1978; *The Scottish Reformation: Church and Society*, Weidenfeld & Nicolson, 1982; (editor with D. Shaw) *Reformation and Renaissance in Scotland*, Scottish Academic Press, 1982; (editor with H. McKay and A. Macquarrie) *The Knights of St. John*, Scottish History Society, 1983. Contributor to history journals.

WORK IN PROGRESS: Heads of Medieval Religious Houses in Scotland, for Scottish Record Society.

SIDELIGHTS: Ian Borthwick Cowan writes: "I feel it most desirable that the history of Scotland should be given universal prominence. My main interest is in medieval ecclesiastical history and to this end I have spent at least four weeks each year for the past decade travelling in Italy and studying in the Vatican archives."

* * *

COWELL, Frank Richard 1897-

PERSONAL: Born November 16, 1897, in London, England; son of William Frank (a manager) and Emma (Pearce) Cowell; married Lilian Margaret Palin (an artist), September 1, 1937 (died, 1970); children: John Richard, Robert Adrian. *Education:* King's College, London, B.A., 1921, London School of Economics and Political Science, B.Sc. (first class honors),

1927, Ph.D., 1938. *Politics:* "Aristotelian." *Address:* Crowdleham House, Kensington, Kent, England.

CAREER: Government of England, London, civil servant with Admiralty, 1917-19, H. M. Stationery Office, 1921-39, Foreign Office, 1939-46, United Kingdom National Commission for UNESCO, 1946-58. *Military service:* British Army, 1916-17. *Member:* Society for the Promotion of Roman Studies (member of council, 1950), British Society for Aesthetics, Mind Association, Classical Association, Garden History Society, Royal Horticultural Society, Private Libraries Association, Athenaeum Club. *Awards, honors:* Rockefeller Foundation research fellowship in the social sciences, 1929-31; named Companion of the Most Noble Order of St. Michael and St. George, 1952.

WRITINGS: Cicero and the Roman Empire, Pitman, 1948, 6th edition, Penguin, 1972; *History, Civilization, and Culture: An Introduction to the Historical and Social Philosophy of Pitirim A. Sorokin*, A. & C. Black, 1952, reprinted, Hyperion Press, (Westport, Conn.), 1978; *Culture in Public and Private Life*, Beacon Press, 1959; *Everyday Life in Ancient Rome*, Putnam, 1961, 7th edition, 1972; *Revolutions of Ancient Rome*, Thames & Hudson, 1962; *The Dominance of Rome*, Paul Hamlyn, 1969; *Values in Human Society: The Contributions of Pitirim A. Sorokin to Sociology*, Sargent, 1970; *The Athenaeum Club and Social Life of London: 1824-1974*, Heinemann, 1974; *Measuring Inequality: Techniques for the Social Sciences*, Wiley, 1977; *The Garden as a Fine Art: From Antiquity to Modern Times*, Houghton, 1978.

Contributor: *Les Ecrivains Celebres* (title means "Renowned Writers"), Mazerod, 1951; *Weltgeschichte des Abenlandischen Kultur*, Westermann Verlag, 1963; Michael Grant, editor, *The Birth of Western Civilization*, Thames & Hudson, 1965; Philip J. Allen, editor, *Pitirim A. Sorokin in Review*, Duke University Press, 1965; Timothy Raison, editor, *Founding Fathers of Social Science*, Penguin, 1969; Harold Osborne, editor, *Oxford Companion to Art*, Oxford University Press, 1970.

Contributor to *Collier's Encyclopedia*. Contributor of articles and reviews to magazines, including *Economist, Journal of Public Administration, Times Literary Supplement, History Today,* and *British Journal of Aesthetics*.

SIDELIGHTS: Frank Richard Cowell told *CA*: "Roman history in England suffered, it seemed to me, because it was written by professors of classics unfamiliar with economic, political, administrative, [and] sociological theory such as I had studied at the London School of Economics. Professor Jeremy Frank of Johns Hopkins was the only historian to study economic life. I tried to cross-familiarlise the study, aided also by having read *Social and Cultural Dynamics* by Professor P. A. Sorokin of Harvard. His works stimulated my other work and I endeavoured to make his theories better known."†

* * *

COX, Richard Howard 1925-

PERSONAL: Born March 3, 1925, in Hammond, Ind.; son of Roy Howard and Elsie (Schoenbaum) Cox; married Margaret Merle Deems, 1953. *Education:* Northwestern University, B.S., 1949, M.A., 1952; graduate study at Ur.iversite de Lyon, 1949-50; University of Chicago, Ph.D., 1955. *Home:* 328 Woodbridge Ave., Buffalo, N.Y. *Office:* Department of Political Science, 685 Baldy Hall, State University of New York at Buffalo, Amherst, N.Y. 14260.

CAREER: Harvard University, Cambridge, Mass., instructor in government, 1955-57; University of California, Berkeley, assistant professor of political science, 1957-67; State University of New York at Buffalo, Amherst, 1963—, began as associate professor, currently professor of political science. Nimitz Chair Visiting Professor, U.S. Naval War College, 1967-68. *Military service:* U.S. Army, 1943-46. *Member:* American Political Science Association, Phi Beta Kappa.

WRITINGS: Locke on War and Peace, Clarendon Press, 1960; (contributor) C. J. Friedrich and J. W. Chapman, editors, *Nomos VI: Justice*, Atherton, 1963; (editor) *The State in International Relations*, Chandler Publishing, 1965; (editor) *Ideology, Politics, and Political Theory*, Wadsworth, 1969; (contributor) B. Barber and M.J.G. McGrath, editors, *The Artist and Political Vision*, Transaction Books, 1981; (editor) John Locke, *Second Treatise of Government*, AHM Publishing, 1982. Contributor to journals, including *Social Research, William and Mary Quarterly,* and *University of Chicago Law Review*.

* * *

COYSH, Victor 1906-

PERSONAL: Born April 24, 1906, in Guernsey, Channel Islands; son of Frederick William and Florence (Guppy) Coysh; married Leila Carey, September 7, 1939. *Education:* Attended Elizabeth College, Guernsey, Channel Islands, 1920-23. *Religion:* Church of England. *Home:* Clos de Saumarez, Delancey, Guernsey, Channel Islands.

CAREER: Secretary, John Mowlem & Co., Ltd., 1923-25; Bournemouth Gas & Water Co., Bournemouth, Hampshire, England, accountant, 1926-45; Guernsey Gas Co., Guernsey, Channel Islands, salesman, 1945-47; *Guernsey Evening Press*, Guernsey, feature writer, 1947—, chief reporter, 1955-71. Parochial officer in Guernsey, 1975—. Has appeared on British Broadcasting Corp. (BBC) radio and television. *Military service:* British Army, Home Guard, 1940-45. *Member:* Alderney Society (life member), La Societe Guernesiase (former president), Guernsey Society (member of council), Guernsey National Trust (former member of council), La Societe Serquiaise (life member).

WRITINGS: Unknown Guernsey, Guernsey Press, 1934; *Elizabeth College Register*, Volume III, Guernsey Press, 1950; *Guernsey*, Guernsey Press, 1960; *Alderney*, David & Charles, 1974; (editor) *The Channel Islands: A New Study*, David & Charles, 1977; *Royal Guernsey*, Guernsey Press, 1977; *Guernsey through the Lens*, Phillimore, 1978; *Guernsey through the Lens Again*, Phillimore, 1982. Editor for La Societe Guernesiase.

WORK IN PROGRESS: Research in Channel Islands history.

AVOCATIONAL INTERESTS: Travel, history, prehistory, Channel Islands.

* * *

CRAWFORD, Charles W(ann) 1931-

PERSONAL: Born October 12, 1931, in Ravenden, Ark.; son of Kermit (a farmer) and Elizabeth (Deyling) Crawford; married Margaret L. Bryant, April 10, 1954; children: Robert L., Charles R. *Education:* Harding College, B.A., 1953; University of Arkansas, M.A., 1958; University of Mississippi, Ph.D., 1968. *Home:* 512 Peabody Sq., Memphis, Tenn. 38104. *Office:* Oral History Research Office, Memphis State University, Memphis, Tenn. 38152.

CAREER: Lewisville High School, Lewisville, Ark., head of social studies department, 1956-59; Memphis State University,

Memphis, Tenn., assistant professor, 1962-70, associate professor of history, 1970—, director of Oral History Research Office, 1962—. Member, Tennessee Historical Commission, 1971-75, and Memphis Bicentennial Commission; chairman, Memphis Heritage Survey, 1974-75. *Military service:* U.S. Army, 1954-55. *Member:* Organization of American Historians, Society of American Archivists, Oral History Association (president, 1973-74), Omicron Delta Kappa (national secretary, 1972-75), Phi Alpha Theta. *Awards, honors:* Omicron Delta Kappa meritorious service certificate, 1972.

WRITINGS: Cal Alley, Memphis State University Press, 1973; *Yesterday's Memphis,* E. A. Seemann, 1976; *Stanley F. Horn: Editor and Publisher,* Forest History Society, 1978; (editor) *Governors of Tennessee: 1790-1835,* Memphis State University Press, 1979; *Memphis: Metropolis of the American Nile,* Windsor Books, 1982; *Old Memphis,* University of Tennessee Press, 1982. Contributor of articles to professional journals.

WORK IN PROGRESS: Research on the history of Memphis.

* * *

CRAWFORD, Robert
See RAE, Hugh C(rauford)

* * *

CRAZ, Albert G. 1926-

PERSONAL: Born June 26, 1926, in New York, N.Y.; son of Albert G. and Louise (Gottlock) Craz; married Joan-Carol McMunn, September 10, 1949; children: Lynda Constance, Peter Bruce. *Education:* Middlebury College, A.B., 1950, A.M., 1955; graduate study at Columbia University, Cornell University, Boston University, and other schools. *Politics:* Democrat. *Religion:* Protestant.

CAREER: Teacher in Boston and New York, 1950-57 and 1959-66, in Army schools in Germany, 1957-59; Patchogue-Medford (N.Y.) public schools, supervisor of English, 1966—. Chairman of English council, Columbia Teachers College Metropolitan School Study Council, 1964-66; adjunct professor at Dowling College, Oakdale, N.Y., 1967-68; chairman of English department at Northport High School, Northport, N.Y. Semi-professional (bass) singer. *Military service:* U.S. Army Air Forces, 1944-46. *Member:* New York State English Council's English Chairmen's Association (director, 1970-75), Westchester English Council (vice-president, 1964-66), Teachers Association of Tarrytown (president, 1964-66). *Awards, honors:* National Endowment for the Humanities fellow, summer, 1980.

WRITINGS: Getting to Know Liberia, Coward, 1958; *Getting to Know Italy,* Coward, 1961; (editor) Joseph Conrad, *Lord Jim,* with teacher's manual, Macmillan, 1962; *Getting to Know the Mississippi River,* Coward, 1965; *A Study of Drama,* with teacher's manual, McCormick-Mathers, 1965, revised edition, 1977; *A Study of Nonfiction,* with teacher's manual, McCormick-Mathers, 1965, revised edition, 1977; (contributor) *English Literature, I-V,* five volumes, McCormick-Mathers, 1967; *Writing the Business Letter,* Competency Press, 1980; *Writing the Report,* Competency Press, 1980; *Writing the Composition,* Competency Press, 1980. Contributor to journals.

WORK IN PROGRESS: A twelfth-grade English textbook, covering the period from John Donne to Oliver Goldsmith.

CREASEY, John 1908-1973
(Gordon Ashe, M. E. Cooke, Margaret Cooke, Henry St. John Cooper, Credo, Norman Deane, Elise Fecamps, Robert Caine Frazer, Patrick Gill, Michael Halliday, Brian Hope, Colin Hughes, Kyle Hunt, Abel Mann, Peter Manton, J. J. Marric, James Marsden, Richard Martin, Rodney Mattheson, Anthony Morton, Ken Ranger, William K. Reilly, Tex Riley, Jeremy York; Charles Hogarth, a joint pseudonym)

PERSONAL: Born September 17, 1908, in Southfields, Surrey, England; died June 9, 1973, of congestive heart failure, in Bodenham, Salisbury, England; buried in Bodenham churchyard; son of Joseph (a cabinet maker and coach builder) and Ruth (Creasey) Creasey; married Margaret Elizabeth Cooke, 1935 (divorced, 1939); married (Evelyn) Jean Fudge, February 16, 1941 (divorced, 1970); married Jeanne Williams (a writer), October, 1970 (divorced, 1973); married Diana Hamilton Farrell, May, 1973; children: (first marriage) Colin John; (second marriage) Martin John, Richard John. *Education:* Attended London elementary and secondary schools. *Politics:* Liberal. *Home and office:* New Hall, Bodenham, Salisbury, England. *Agent:* Hughes Massie Ltd., 31 Southampton Row, London WC1B 5HL, England; and Harold Ober Associates, 40 East 49th St., New York, N.Y. 10017.

CAREER: Writer. Held various clerical jobs, London, England, 1926-35. Publisher, Jay Books, 1957-59; director of Robert Sommerville Ltd. (literary agency) and of Salisbury Arts Theatre. Member of governing body of Liberal Party, 1945-50; Liberal Party candidate for Parliament, 1950; founder of All Party Alliance Movement, 1967; All Party Alliance Movement candidate for Parliament, 1967-68. Chairman of fund-raising committees for famine relief and refugee organizations, including National Savings Movement, United Europe, and Oxford Committee for Famine Relief.

MEMBER: Crime Writers Association (founder; chairman, 1953-57), Mystery Writers of America (chairman, 1966-67), Western Writers of America, Authors' League, Society of Authors (London), P.E.N., National Liberal Club, Paternosters (chairman, 1967), Rotary International, Westerners Club (Tucson, Arizona), Royal Automobile Club (London). *Awards, honors:* Member, Order of the British Empire (M.B.E.), 1946; Mystery Writers of America, Edgar Allan Poe Award, 1962, for *Gideon's Fire,* and Grand Master Award, 1969, for outstanding contributions to the mystery novel genre.

WRITINGS: Seven Times Seven (mystery novel), Melrose, 1932, reprinted, Arrow Books, 1970; *Men, Maids, and Murder* (mystery novel), Melrose, 1933, reprinted, Arrow Books, 1972; (contributor) *The Evening Standard Detective Book,* Gollancz, 1950; *Four of the Best* (also see below; contains *The Department of Death, Inspector West Alone, The Prophet of Fire,* and *Hunt the Toff),* Hodder & Stoughton, 1955; (contributor) Rex Stout, editor, *Eat, Drink, and Be Buried,* Viking, 1956 (published in England as *For Tomorrow We Die,* Macdonald & Evans, 1958); (contributor) Elizabeth Ferrars, editor, *Planned Departures,* Hodder & Stoughton, 1958; (editor and contributor) *Mystery Bedside Book,* six volumes, Hodder & Stoughton, 1960-65; *The Mountain of the Blind* (mystery novel), Hodder & Stoughton, 1960; *The Foothills of Fear* (mystery novel), Hodder & Stoughton, 1961; (editor) *Crimes across the Sea* (anthology), Harper, 1964; *The Masters of Bow Street* (mystery novel), Hodder & Stoughton, 1972, Simon & Schuster, 1974.

Juvenile fiction: *The Men Who Died Laughing*, Thompson, 1935; *The Killer Squad*, George Newnes, 1936; *Blazing the Air Trail*, Low, 1936; *The Jungle Flight Mystery*, Low, 1936; *The Mystery 'Plane*, Low, 1936; *Murder by Magic*, Amalgamated Press, 1937; *The Mysterious Mr. Rocco*, Mellifont Press, 1937; *The S.O.S. Flight*, Low, 1937; *The Secret Aeroplane Mystery*, Low, 1937; *The Treasure Flight*, Low, 1937; *The Air Marauders*, Low, 1937; *The Black Biplane*, Low, 1937; *The Mystery Flight*, Low, 1937; *The Double Motive*, Mellifont Press, 1938; *The Doublecross of Death*, Mellifont Press, 1938; *The Missing Hoard*, Mellifont Press, 1938; *Mystery of Manby House*, Northern News Syndicate, 1938; *The Fighting Flyers*, Low, 1938; *The Flying Stowaways*, Low, 1938; *The Miracle 'Plane*, Low, 1938; *Dixon Hawke: Secret Agent*, Thompson, 1939; *Documents of Death*, Mellifont Press, 1939; *The Hidden Hoard*, Mellifont Press, 1939; *The Blue Flyer*, Mellifont Press, 1939; *The Jumper*, Northern News Syndicate, 1939; *The Mystery of Blackmoor Prison*, Mellifont Press, 1939; *The Sacred Eye*, Thompson, 1939; *Mottled Death*, Thompson, 1939; *Peril by Air*, George Newnes, 1939; *The Flying Turk*, Low, 1939; *The Ship of Death*, Thompson, 1939; *The Monarch of the Skies*, Low, 1939.

Dazzle—Air Ace No. One, George Newnes, 1940; *Five Missing Men*, George Newnes, 1940; *The Poison Gas Robberies*, Mellifont Press, 1940; *The Cinema Crimes*, T. A. & E. Pemberton, 1945; *The Missing Monoplane*, Low, 1947.

Nonfiction: (Ghost writer) *Jimmy Wilde: Fighting Was My Business*, M. Joseph, 1938; (compiler and editor) *Action Stations!: An Account of the H.M.S. Dorsetshire and Her Earlier Namesakes*, John Long, 1942; (with Walter Hutchinson) *The Printer's Devil: The History of a Printer's Charity*, Hutchinson, 1943; *Heroes of the Air: A Tribute to the Courage, Sacrifice and Skill of the Men of the R.A.F.*, Dorset "Wings for Victory" Campaign Committee, 1943; (with John Lock) *Log of a Merchant Airman*, Stanley Paul, 1943; (under pseudonym Credo) *Man in Danger*, Hutchinson, 1948; (with Jean Creasey) *Round the World in 465 Days*, R. Hale, 1953; *Round the Table: The First Twenty-Five Years of the English Goodwill Association*, National Association of Round Tables of Great Britain and Ireland, 1953; (with Jean Creasey and sons, Martin and Richard Creasey), *Let's Look at America*, R. Hale, 1956; *They Didn't Mean to Kill: The Real Story of Road Accidents, Their Cause, Costs and Cure*, Hodder & Stoughton, 1960; (with Jean, M., and R. Creasey) *Optimists in Africa*, Howard Timmins (Capetown), 1963; *African Holiday*, illustrations and captions by M. Creasey, Howard Timmins, 1963; *Good, God and Man: An Outline of the Philosophy of Self-ism*, illustrations by M. Creasey, Hodder & Stoughton, 1968, Walker & Co., 1971; *Evolution to Democracy*, Hodder & Stoughton, 1969, revised edition, White Lion, 1972.

"Department Z" mystery series: *The Death Miser*, Melrose, 1933; *Redhead*, Hurst & Blackett, 1933, revised edition, Arrow Books, 1971; *First Came a Murder*, Melrose, 1934, revised edition, John Long, 1969, McKay, 1972; *Death round the Corner*, Melrose, 1935, revised edition, Popular Library, 1970; *The Mark of the Crescent*, Melrose, 1935, revised edition, John Long, 1970, Popular Library, 1972; *Thunder in Europe*, Melrose, 1936, reprinted, Arrow Books, 1968, revised edition, John Long, 1970, Popular Library, 1972; *The Terror Trap*, Melrose, 1936, revised edition, Arrow Books, 1969, Popular Library, 1972; *Carriers of Death*, Melrose, 1937, revised edition, Popular Library, 1968; *Days of Danger*, Melrose, 1937, reprinted, Arrow Books, 1968, revised edition, John Long, 1970, Popular Library, 1972; *Death Stands By*, John Long, 1938, revised edition, Arrow Books, 1966, Popular Library, 1972; *Menace!*, John Long, 1938, revised edition, Popular Library, 1971; *Murder Must Wait*, Melrose, 1939, revised edition, John Long, 1969, Popular Library, 1972; *Panic!*, John Long, 1939, reprinted, Arrow Books, 1969, Popular Library, 1972.

Death by Night, John Long, 1940, revised edition, Arrow Books, 1970, Popular Library, 1972; *The Island of Peril*, John Long, 1940, reprinted, Arrow Books, 1968, revised edition, John Long, 1970, Popular Library, 1976; *Sabotage*, John Long, 1941, revised edition, Arrow Books, 1971, Popular Library, 1976; *Go away Death*, John Long, 1941, revised edition, 1969, Popular Library, 1976; *The Day of Disaster*, John Long, 1942, reprinted, Arrow Books, 1968, revised edition, John Long, 1969; *Prepare for Action*, Stanley Paul, 1942, revised edition, Arrow Books, 1966, Popular Library, 1975; *No Darker Crime*, Stanley Paul, 1943, reprinted, Arrow Books, 1969, Popular Library, 1976; *Dark Peril*, Stanley Paul, 1944, revised edition, John Long, 1969, Popular Library, 1975.

The Peril Ahead, Stanley Paul, 1946, revised edition, John Long, 1969, Popular Library, 1974; *The League of Dark Men*, Stanley Paul, 1947, revised edition, John Long, 1968, Popular Library, 1975; *The Department of Death*, Evans Brothers, 1949, Popular Library, 1979; *The Enemy Within*, Evans Brothers, 1950, Popular Library, 1977; *Dead or Alive*, Evans Brothers, 1951, reprinted, Arrow Books, 1969, Popular Library, 1974; *A Kind of a Prisoner*, Hodder & Stoughton, 1956, reprinted, Arrow Books, 1972, Popular Library, 1975; *The Black Spiders*, Hodder & Stoughton, 1957, reprinted, Arrow Books, 1972, Popular Library, 1975.

"Sexton Blake" mystery series; published by Amalgamated Press: *The Case of the Murdered Financier*, 1937; *The Great Air Swindle*, 1939; *The Man from Fleet Street*, 1940; *The Case of the Mad Inventor*, 1942; *Private Carter's Crime*, 1943.

"The Toff" mystery series: *Introducing the Toff*, John Long, 1938, revised edition, 1954; *The Toff Goes On*, John Long, 1939, revised edition, 1955; *. . . Steps Out*, John Long, 1939, revised edition, 1955.

Here Comes . . . , John Long, 1940, Walker & Co., 1967, revised edition, Sphere Books, 1969; *. . . Breaks In*, John Long, 1940, revised edition, 1955; *Salute the Toff*, John Long, 1941, Walker & Co., 1971; *. . . Proceeds*, John Long, 1941, Walker & Co., 1968; *. . . Goes to Market*, John Long, 1942, Walker & Co., 1967; *. . . Is Back*, John Long, 1942, revised edition, Corgi Books, 1971, Walker & Co., 1974; *. . . Among Millions*, John Long, 1943, revised edition, Panther Books, 1964, Walker & Co., 1976; *Accuse . . .* , John Long, 1943, revised edition, Corgi Books, 1972, Walker & Co., 1975; *. . . and the Curate*, John Long, 1944, Walker & Co., 1969 (published in England as *. . . and the Deadly Parson*, Lancer Books, 1970); *. . . and the Great Illusion*, John Long, 1944, Walker & Co., 1967; *Feathers for . . .* , John Long, 1945, revised edition, Hodder & Stoughton, 1964, Walker & Co., 1970; *. . . and the Lady*, John Long, 1946, reprinted, Sphere Books, 1970, Walker & Co., 1975; *. . . on Ice*, John Long, 1946, revised edition, Corgi Books, 1976, published as *Poison for . . .* , Pyramid Publications, 1976; *Hammer . . .* , John Long, 1947, reprinted, Corgi Books, 1975; *. . . in Town*, John Long, 1948, reprinted, Sphere Books, 1969, revised edition, Walker & Co., 1977; *. . . Takes Shares*, John Long, 1948, revised edition, Corgi Books, 1971, Walker & Co., 1972; *. . . and Old Harry*, John Long, 1949, revised edition, Hodder & Stoughton, 1964, Walker & Co., 1970; *. . . on Board*, Evans

Brothers, 1949, revised edition, Corgi Books, 1971, Walker & Co., 1973.

Fool . . ., Evans Brothers, 1950, Walker & Co., 1966; *Kill . . .*, Evans Brothers, 1950, Walker & Co., 1966, revised edition, Corgi Books, 1972; *A Knife for . . .*, Evans Brothers, 1951, Pyramid Publications, 1964, revised edition, Corgi Books, 1971; *. . . Goes Gay,* Evans Brothers, 1951, published as *A Mask for . . .*, Walker & Co., 1966; *Hunt . . .*, Evans Brothers, 1952, Walker & Co., 1969, revised edition, Corgi Books, 1972; *Call . . .*, Hodder & Stoughton, 1953, Walker & Co., 1969; *. . . down Under,* Hodder & Stoughton, 1953, Walker & Co., 1969 (published in England as *Break . . .*, Lancer Books, 1970); *Murder out of the Past, and Under-Cover Man* (short stories), Barrington Gray, 1953; *. . . at Butlin's,* Hodder & Stoughton, 1954, reprinted, Corgi Books, 1974, Walker & Co., 1976; *. . . at the Fair,* Hodder & Stoughton, 1954, Walker & Co., 1968; *A Six for . . .*, Hodder & Stoughton, 1955, Walker & Co., 1969 (published in England as *A Score for . . .*, Lancer Books, 1972); *. . . and the Deep Blue Sea,* Hodder & Stoughton, 1955, Walker & Co., 1967; *Make-Up for . . .*, Hodder & Stoughton, 1956, Walker & Co., 1967 (published in England as *Kiss . . .*, Lancer Books, 1971); *. . . in New York,* Hodder & Stoughton, 1956, Pyramid Publications, 1964; *Model for . . .*, Hodder & Stoughton, 1957, Pyramid Publications, 1965; *. . . on Fire,* Hodder & Stoughton, 1957, Walker & Co., 1966; *. . . and the Stolen Tresses,* Hodder & Stoughton, 1958, Walker & Co., 1965; *. . . on the Farm,* Hodder & Stoughton, 1958, Walker & Co., 1964, published as *Terror for . . .*, Pyramid Publications, 1965; *Double for . . .*, Hodder & Stoughton, 1959, Walker & Co., 1965; *. . . and the Runaway Bride,* Hodder & Stoughton, 1959, Walker & Co., 1964, reprinted, Severn House, 1980.

A Rocket for . . ., Hodder & Stoughton, 1960, Pyramid Publications, 1964, reprinted, Severn House, 1980; *. . . and the Kidnapped Child,* Hodder & Stoughton, 1960, Walker & Co., 1965; *Follow . . .*, Hodder & Stoughton, 1961, Walker & Co., 1967; *. . . and the Teds,* Hodder & Stoughton, 1961, published as *. . . and the Toughs,* Walker & Co., 1968; *A Doll for . . .*, Hodder & Stoughton, 1963, Walker & Co., 1965; *Leave It to . . .*, Hodder & Stoughton, 1963, Pyramid Publications, 1965; *. . . and the Spider,* Hodder & Stoughton, 1965, Walker & Co., 1966; *. . . in Wax,* Walker & Co., 1966; *A Bundle for . . .*, Hodder & Stoughton, 1967, Walker & Co., 1968; *Stars for . . .*, Walker & Co., 1968; *. . . and the Golden Boy,* Walker & Co., 1969.

. . . and the Fallen Angels, Walker & Co., 1970; *Vote for . . .*, Walker & Co., 1971; *. . . and the Trip-Trip-Triplets,* Walker & Co., 1972; *. . . and the Terrified Taximan,* Walker & Co., 1973; *. . . and the Sleepy Cowboy,* Hodder & Stoughton, 1977. Also author of *. . . on the Trail,* published by Everybody's Books between 1953-55.

"Roger West" mystery series: *Inspector West Takes Charge,* Stanley Paul, 1942, revised ediiton, Pan Books, 1963, Scribner, 1972; *. . . Leaves Town,* Stanley Paul, 1943, published as *Go Away Murder,* Lancer Books, 1972; *. . . at Home,* Stanley Paul, 1944, reprinted, Coronet Books, 1972, Scribner, 1973; *. . . Regrets,* Stanley Paul, 1945, revised edition, Hodder & Stoughton, 1965; *Holiday for Inspector West,* Stanley Paul, 1946, reprinted, Coronet Books, 1974; *Battle for . . .*, Stanley Paul, 1948; *Triumph for . . .*, Stanley Paul, 1948, published as *The Case against Paul Raeburn,* Harper, 1958; *. . . Kicks Off,* Stanley Paul, 1949, reprinted, Coronet Books, 1971, published as *Sport for . . .*, Lancer Books, 1971.

. . . Alone, Evans Brothers, 1950, reprinted, Lythway Press, 1972, Scribner, 1975; *. . . Cries Wolf,* Evans Brothers, 1950, reprinted, Lythway Press, 1973, published as *The Creepers,* Harper, 1952; *A Case for . . .*, Evans Brothers, 1951, reprinted, Lythway Press, 1973, published as *Figure in the Dusk,* Harper, 1952; *Puzzle for . . .*, Evans Brothers, 1951, reprinted, Lythway Press, 1972, published as *The Dissemblers,* Scribner, 1967; *. . . at Bay,* Evans Brothers, 1952, published as *. . . The Blind Spot,* Harper, 1954, published as *The Case of the Acid Throwers,* Avon, 1960; *A Gun for . . .*, Hodder & Stoughton, 1953, reprinted, Ulverscroft Large Print Books, 1972, published as *Give a Man a Gun,* Harper, 1954; *Send . . .*, Hodder & Stoughton, 1953, revised edition, Coronet Books, 1972, Scribner, 1976, published as *Send Superintendent West,* Pan Books, 1965; *A Beauty for . . .*, Hodder & Stoughton, 1954, reprinted, 1972, published as *The Beauty Queen Killer,* Harper, 1956, published as *So Young, So Cold, So Fair,* Dell, 1958; *. . . Makes Haste,* Hodder & Stoughton, 1955, published as *The Gelignite Gang,* Harper, 1956, published as *Night of the Watchman,* Berkley Publishing; *Two for . . .*, Hodder & Stoughton, 1955, reprinted, Pan Books, 1969, published as *Murder: One, Two Three,* Scribner, 1960, published as *Murder Tips the Scales,* Berkley Publishing, 1962.

Parcels for . . ., Hodder & Stoughton, 1956, reprinted, 1971, published as *Death of a Postman,* Harper, 1957; *A Prince for . . .*, Hodder & Stoughton, 1956, published as *Death of an Assassin,* Scribner, 1960; *Accident for . . .*, Hodder & Stoughton, 1957, reprinted, 1972, published as *Hit and Run,* Scribner, 1959; *Find . . .*, Hodder & Stoughton, 1957, reprinted, Lythway Press, 1977, published as *The Trouble at Saxby's,* Harper, 1959, published as *Doorway to Death,* Berkley Publishing, 1961; *Murder, London—New York,* Hodder & Stoughton, 1958, Scribner, 1961, reprinted, Hutchinson, 1976; *Strike for Death,* Hodder & Stoughton, 1958, published as *The Killing Strike,* Scribner, 1961; *Death of a Racehorse,* Hodder & Stoughton, 1959, Scribner, 1962; *The Case of the Innocent Victims,* Hodder & Stoughton, 1959, Scribner, 1966.

Murder on the Line, Hodder & Stoughton, 1960, Scribner, 1963; *Death in Cold Print,* Hodder & Stoughton, 1961, Scribner, 1962; *The Scene of the Crime,* Hodder & Stoughton, 1961, Scribner, 1963; *Policeman's Dread,* Hodder & Stoughton, 1962, Scribner, 1964; *Hang the Little Man,* Scribner, 1963; *Look Three Ways at Murder,* Hodder & Stoughton, 1964, Scribner, 1965; *Murder, London—Australia,* Scribner, 1965; *Murder, London—South Africa,* Scribner, 1966; *The Executioners,* Scribner, 1967; *So Young to Burn,* Scribner, 1968; *Murder, London—Miami,* Scribner, 1969.

A Part for a Policeman, Scribner, 1970; *Alibi,* Scribner, 1971 (published in England as *Alibi for . . .*, Coronet Books, 1973); *A Splinter of Glass,* Scribner, 1972; *The Theft of Magna Carta,* Scribner, 1973; *The Extortioners,* Hodder & Stoughton, 1974, Scribner, 1975; *A Sharp Rise in Crime,* Scribner, 1978.

"Dr. Palfrey" mystery series: *Traitors' Doom,* John Long, 1942, reprinted, 1968, Walker & Co., 1970; *The Valley of Fear,* John Long, 1943, published as *The Perilous Country,* 1949, revised edition, Arrow Books, 1966, Walker & Co., 1973; *The Legion of the Lost,* John Long, 1943, Steven Daye, 1944, revised edition, John Long, 1968, Walker & Co., 1974; *Dangerous Quest,* John Long, 1944, revised edition, Arrow Books, 1965, Walker & Co., 1974; *Death in the Rising Sun,* John Long, 1945, revised edition, 1970, Walker & Co., 1976; *The Hounds of Vengeance,* John Long, 1945, revised edition, 1969; *Shadow of Doom,* John Long, 1946, revised edition, 1970; *The House of Bears,* John Long, 1946, revised edition, 1962, Walker & Co., 1975; *Dark Harvest,* John Long, 1947, revised edition, Arrow Books, 1962, Walker & Co., 1977; *The Wings of Peace,* John Long, 1948, revised edition, 1969, Walker

& Co., 1978; *Sons of Satan*, John Long, 1948, revised edition, 1972; *The Dawn of Darkness*, John Long, 1949; *The League of Light*, Evans Brothers, 1949, revised edition, 1969.

The Man Who Shook the World, Evans Brothers, 1950, revised edition, John Long, 1972; *The Prophet of Fire*, Evans Brothers, 1951, Walker & Co., 1978; *The Children of Hate*, Evans Brothers, 1952, published as *The Children of Despair*, Jay Books, 1958, revised edition, John Long, 1970, published as *The Killers of Innocence*, Walker & Co., 1971; *The Touch of Death*, Hodder & Stoughton, 1954, Walker & Co., 1968; *The Mists of Fear*, Hodder & Stoughton, 1955, reprinted, Hodder Paperbacks, 1970, Walker & Co., 1977; *The Flood*, Hodder & Stoughton, 1956, Walker & Co., 1969; *The Plague of Silence*, Hodder & Stoughton, 1958, Walker & Co., 1968; *The Drought*, Hodder & Stoughton, 1959, Walker & Co., 1967 (published in England as *Dry Spell*, New English Library, 1967).

The Terror: The Return of Dr. Palfrey, Hodder & Stoughton, 1963, Walker & Co., 1966; *The Depths*, Hodder & Stoughton, 1963, Walker & Co., 1966; *The Sleep*, Hodder & Stoughton, 1964, Walker & Co., 1968; *The Inferno*, Hodder & Stoughton, 1965, Walker & Co., 1968; *The Famine*, Hodder & Stoughton, 1967, Walker & Co., 1968; *The Blight*, Walker & Co., 1968; *The Oasis*, Hodder & Stoughton, 1969, Walker & Co., 1970.

The Smog, Hodder & Stoughton, 1970, Walker & Co., 1971; *The Unbegotten*, Hodder & Stoughton, 1971, Walker & Co., 1972; *The Insulators*, Hodder & Stoughton, 1972, Walker & Co., 1973; *The Voiceless Ones*, Hodder & Stoughton, 1973, Walker & Co., 1974; *The Thunder-Maker*, Walker & Co., 1976; *The Whirlwind*, Hodder & Stoughton, 1979.

Plays: *Gideon's Fear* (adaptation of his novel *Gideon's Week* [see below under pseudonymn J. J. Marric]; first produced in Salisbury, England, 1960), Evans Brothers, 1967; "Strike for Death," first produced in Salisbury, 1960; *The Toff: A Comedy Thriller in Three Acts*, Evans Brothers, 1963; "Hear Nothing, Say All," first produced in Salisbury, 1964.

Under pseudonym Gordon Ashe; mystery novels: *Who Was the Jester?*, George Newnes, 1940, published as *The Masked Gunman; The Man Who Stayed Alive*, John Long, 1955, reprinted, Corgi Books, 1975; *No Need to Die*, John Long, 1956, reprinted, Corgi Books, 1975.

Under pseudonym Gordon Ashe; "Patrick Dawlish" mystery series: *The Speaker*, John Long, 1939, reprinted, Transworld (London), 1966, published as *The Croaker*, Holt, 1972; *Death on Demand*, John Long, 1939, reprinted, Transworld (London), 1967; *Terror by Day*, John Long, 1940; *The Secret Murder*, John Long, 1940, revised edition, Corgi Books, 1972; *'Ware Danger!*, John Long, 1941, reprinted, Corgi Books, 1972; *Murder Most Foul*, John Long, 1942, revised edition, Corgi Books, 1973; *There Goes Death*, John Long, 1942, revised edition, Corgi Books, 1973; *Death in High Places*, John Long, 1942, revised edition, Corgi Books, 1973; *Death in Flames*, John Long, 1943, revised edition, Corgi Books, 1973; *Two Men Missing*, John Long, 1943, revised edition, Corgi Books, 1971; *Rogues Rampant*, John Long, 1944, revised edition, Corgi Books, 1973.

Death on the Move, John Long, 1945, reprinted, Corgi Books, 1969; *Invitation to Adventure*, John Long, 1945, reprinted, Corgi Books, 1969; *Here Is Danger*, John Long, 1946, reprinted, Corgi Books, 1970; *Give Me Murder*, John Long, 1947, reprinted, Corgi Books, 1966; *Murder Too Late*, John Long, 1947, reprinted, Corgi Books, 1968; *Engagement with Death*, John Long, 1948, reprinted, Corgi Books, 1970; *Dark Mystery*, John Long, 1948, reprinted, Corgi Books, 1971; *A Puzzle in Pearls*, John Long, 1949, revised edition, Corgi Books, 1971.

Kill or Be Killed, Evans Brothers, 1950, reprinted, Lythway Press, 1973; *The Dark Circle*, Evans Brothers, 1950, reprinted, Corgi Books, 1969; *Murder with Mushrooms*, Evans Brothers, 1950, revised edition, Corgi Books, 1971, Holt, 1974; *Death in Diamonds*, Evans Brothers, 1951, reprinted, Corgi Books, 1968; *Missing or Dead*, Evans Brothers, 1951; *Death in a Hurry*, Evans Brothers, 1952; *The Long Search*, John Long, 1953, reprinted, Corgi Books, 1974, published as *Drop Dead*, Ace Books, 1954; *Sleepy Death*, John Long, 1953; *Double for Death*, John Long, 1954, Holt, 1969; *Death in the Trees*, John Long, 1954, reprinted, Corgi Books, 1975, published as *You've Bet Your Life*, Ace Books, 1957; *The Kidnapped Child*, John Long, 1955, Holt, 1971, published as *The Snatch*, Corgi Books, 1965; *Day of Fear*, John Long, 1956, Holt, 1978; *Wait for Death*, John Long, 1957, Holt, 1972; *Come Home to Death*, John Long, 1958, published as *The Pack of Lies*, Doubleday, 1959; *Elope to Death*, John Long, 1959, Holt, 1977; *The Man Who Laughed at Murder*, Doubleday, 1960 (published in England as *Don't Let Him Kill*, 1960, reprinted, Corgi Books, 1975).

Under pseudonym Gordon Ashe; "Crime Haters" mystery series, a continuation of "Patrick Dawlish" series: *The Crime Haters*, Doubleday, 1960; *Rogue's Ransom*, Doubleday, 1961; *Death from Below*, John Long, 1963, Holt, 1968; *The Big Call*, John Long, 1964, Holt, 1975; *A Promise of Diamonds*, Dodd, 1964; *A Taste of Treasure*, Holt, 1966; *A Clutch of Coppers*, John Long, 1967, Holt, 1969; *A Shadow of Death*, John Long, 1968, Holt, 1976; *A Scream of Murder*, John Long, 1969, Holt, 1970; *A Nest of Traitors*, John Long, 1970, Holt, 1971; *A Rabble of Rebels*, Holt, 1972; *A Life for a Death*, Holt, 1973; *A Herald of Doom*, John Long, 1974, Holt, 1975; *A Blast of Trumpets*, Holt, 1975; *A Plague of Demons*, John Long, 1976, Holt, 1977.

Under pseudonym M. E. Cooke; mystery novels; published by Mellifont Press, except as indicated: *Fire of Death*, Fiction House, 1934; *The Black Heart*, Gramor Publications, 1935; *The Casino Mystery*, 1935; *The Crime Gang*, 1935; *The Death Drive*, 1935; *Number One's Last Crime*, Fiction House, 1935; *The Stolen Formula Mystery*, 1935; *The Big Radium Mystery*, 1936; *The Day of Terror*, 1936; *The Dummy Robberies*, 1936; *No One's Last Crime*, Fiction House, 1936; *The Hypnotic Demon*, Fiction House, 1936; *The Moat Farm Mystery*, Fiction House, 1936; *The Secret Fortune*, Fiction House, 1936; *The Successful Alibi*, 1936; *The Hadfield Mystery*, 1937; *The Moving Eye*, 1937; *The Raven*, Fiction House, 1937; *The Mountain Terror*, 1938; *For Her Sister's Sake*, Fiction House, 1938; *The Verrall Street Affair*, George Newnes, 1940.

Under pseudonym Margaret Cooke; romance novels; published by Fiction House, except as indicated: *For Love's Sake*, Northern News Syndicate, 1934; *Troubled Journey*, 1936; *False Love or True?*, Northern News Syndicate, 1937; *Fate's Playthings*, 1938; *Web of Destiny*, 1938; *Whose Lover?*, 1938; *A Mannequin's Romance*, 1938; *Love Calls Twice*, Northern News Syndicate, 1938; *The Road to Happiness*, 1938; *The Turn of Fate*, 1939; *Love Triumphant*, 1939; *Love Comes Back*, 1939; *Crossroads of Love*, Mellifont Press, 1939; *Love's Journey*, 1940.

Under pseudonym Henry St. John Cooper; romance novels; published by Low: *Chains of Love*, 1937; *Love's Pilgrimage*, 1937; *The Tangled Legacy*, 1938; *The Greater Desire*, 1938; *Love's Ordeal*, 1939; *The Lost Lover*, 1940.

Under pseudonym Norman Deane; mystery novels: *Play for Murder*, Hurst & Blackett, 1946, revised edition, Arrow Books,

1975; *The Silent House*, Hurst & Blackett, 1947, revised edition, Arrow Books, 1973; *Why Murder?*, Hurst & Blackett, 1948, revised edition, Arrow Books, 1975; *Intent to Murder*, Hurst & Blackett, 1948, revised edition, Arrow Books, 1973; *The Man I Didn't Kill*, Hurst & Blackett, 1950, reprint published under pseudonym Michael Halliday (see below), revised edition, Arrow Books, 1972; *No Hurry to Kill*, Hurst & Blackett, 1950, revised edition, Arrow Books, 1973; *Double for Murder*, Hurst & Blackett, 1951, revised edition, Arrow Books, 1972; *Golden Death*, Hurst & Blackett, 1952; *Look at Murder*, Hurst & Blackett, 1952, revised edition, Arrow Books, 1974; *Murder Ahead*, Hurst & Blackett, 1953, revised edition, Arrow Books, 1974; *Death in the Spanish Sun*, Hurst & Blackett, 1954, reprint published under name Michael Halliday (see below); *Incense of Death*, Hurst & Blackett, 1954, reprinted, New English Library, 1969.

Under pseudonym Norman Deane; "Bruce Murdoch" mystery series: *Secret Errand*, Hurst & Blackett, 1939, revised edition published under author's own name, New English Library, 1968, McKay, 1974; *Dangerous Journey*, Hurst & Blackett, 1939, revised edition published under author's own name, Arrow Books, 1971, McKay, 1974; *Unknown Mission*, Hurst & Blackett, 1940, revised edition, McKay, 1972; *The Withered Man*, Hurst & Blackett, 1940, revised edition published under author's own name, Arrow Books, 1971; *I Am the Withered Man*, Hurst & Blackett, revised edition published under author's own name, Arrow Books, 1971, McKay, 1973; *Where Is the Withered Man?*, Hurst & Blackett, 1942, revised edition, McKay, 1972.

Under pseudonym Norman Deane; "Liberator" mystery series; *Return to Adventure*, Hurst & Blackett, 1943, revised edition, John Long, 1974; *Gateway to Escape*, Hurst & Blackett, 1944, revised edition, Arrow Books, 1973; *Come Home to Crime*, Hurst & Blackett, 1945, revised edition, John Long, 1974.

Under pseudonym Elise Fecamps; romance novels; published by Fiction House: *Love of Hate*, 1936; *Love's Triumph*, 1936; *True Love*, 1937.

Under pseudonym Robert Caine Frazer; "Mark Kirby" mystery series; published by Pocket Books, except as indicated: *Mark Kirby Solves a Murder*, 1959 (published in England as *R.I.S.C.*, Collins, 1962, and as *The Timid Tycoon*, Fontana Books, 1966); *. . . and the Secret Syndicate*, 1960 (published in England as *The Secret Syndicate*, Collins, 1963); *. . . and the Miami Mob*, 1960 (published in England as *The Miami Mob* with *Mark Kirby Stands Alone* [also see below], Collins, 1965); *The Hollywood Hoax*, 1961; *. . . Stands Alone*, 1962 (published in England as *. . . and the Manhattan Murders*, Fontana Books, 1966); *. . . Takes a Risk*, 1962.

Under pseudonym Patrick Gill; juvenile fiction; published by Mellifont Press: *The Fighting Footballers*, 1937; *The Laughing Lightweight*, 1937; *The Battle for the Cup*, 1939; *The Fighting Tramp*, 1939; *The Mystery of the Centre-Forward*, 1939; *The £10,000 Trophy Race*, 1939; *The Secret Supercharger*, 1940.

Under pseudonym Michael Halliday; mystery novels: *Four Find Danger*, Cassell, 1937; *Three for Adventure*, Cassell, 1937, revised edition, Corgi Books, 1976; *Two Meet Trouble*, Cassell, 1938, reprinted, Corgi Books, 1975; *Murder Comes Home*, Stanley Paul, 1940; *Heir to Murder*, Stanley Paul, 1940; *Murder by the Way*, Stanley Paul, 1941, reprinted, Lythway Press, 1973; *Who Saw Him Die?*, Stanley Paul, 1941; *Foul Play Suspected*, Stanley Paul, 1942; *Who Died at the Grange?*, Stanley Paul, 1942; *Five to Kill*, Stanley Paul, 1943; *Murder at Kings's Kitchen*, Stanley Paul, 1943, reprinted, Lythway Press, 1972; *Who Said Murder?*, Stanley Paul, 1944; *No Crime More Cruel*, Stanley Paul, 1944; *Crime with Many Voices*, Stanley Paul, 1945; *Murder Makes Murder*, Stanley Paul, 1946; *Mystery Motive*, Stanley Paul, 1947, revised edition published under pseudonym Jeremy York in "Superintendent Folly" series (see below); *Lend a Hand to Murder*, Stanley Paul, 1947, reprinted, Lythway Press, 1973; *First a Murder*, Stanley Paul, 1948, revised edition published under pseudonym Jeremy York in "Superindendent Folly" series (see below); *No End to Danger*, Stanley Paul, 1948, reprinted, Lythway Press, 1972; *Who Killed Rebecca?*, Stanley Paul, 1949; *The Dying Witnesses*, Evans Brothers, 1949, reprinted, Lythway Press, 1973.

Dine with Murder, Evans Brothers, 1950; *Murder Week-End*, Evans Brothers, 1951, reprinted, Lythway Press, 1974; *Quarrel with Murder*, Evans Brothers, 1951, revised edition, Corgi Books, 1975; *Murder at End House*, Hodder & Stoughton, 1955; *Murder Assured*, Hodder & Stoughton, 1958; *Hate to Kill*, Hodder & Stoughton, 1962; *The Guilt of Innocence*, Hodder & Stoughton, 1964; *The Man I Didn't Kill*, reprinted, Mayflower Dell, 1965; *Death in the Spanish Sun*, reprinted, Mayflower Dell, 1968.

Under pseudonym Michael Halliday; mystery novels; published in United States under pseudonym Jeremy York: *Death out of Darkness*, Hodder & Stoughton, 1954, World Publishing, 1971; *Out of the Shadows*, Hodder & Stoughton, 1954, World Publishing, 1971; *Cat and Mouse*, Hodder & Stoughton, 1955, reprinted, White Lion, 1974, published as *Hilda, Take Heed*, Scribner, 1957; *Death of a Stranger*, Hodder & Stoughton, 1957, reprinted, White Lion, 1972, published as *Come Here and Die*, Scribner, 1959; *Runaway*, Hodder & Stoughton, 1957, World Publishing, 1971; *Missing from Home*, Hodder & Stoughton, 1959, published as *Missing*, Scribner, 1960; *Thicker than Water*, Hodder & Stoughton, 1959, Doubleday, 1962; *Go ahead with Murder*, Hodder & Stoughton, published as *Two for the Money*, Doubleday, 1962; *How Many to Kill?*, Hodder & Stoughton, 1960, published as *The Girl with the Leopard-Skin Bag*, Scribner, 1961; *The Edge of Terror*, Hodder & Stoughton, 1961, Macmillan, 1963; *The Man I Killed*, Hodder & Stoughton, 1961, Macmillan, 1963; *The Quiet Fear*, Hodder & Stoughton, 1963, Macmillan, 1968.

Under pseudonym Michael Halliday; "Fane Brothers" mystery series: *Take a Body*, Evans Brothers, 1951, revised edition, Hodder & Stoughton, 1964, World Publishing, 1972; *Lame Dog Murders*, Evans Brothers, 1952, World Publishing, 1972; *Murder in the Stars*, Hodder & Stoughton, 1953, World Publishing, 1973; *Man on the Run*, Hodder & Stoughton, 1953, World Publishing, 1972.

Under pseudonym Michael Halliday; published in United States under pseudonym Kyle Hunt; "Dr. Emmanuel Cellini" mystery series: *Cunning as a Fox*, Hodder & Stoughton, 1965, Macmillan, 1965; *Wicked as the Devil*, Hodder & Stoughton, 1966, Macmillan, 1966; *Sly as a Serpent*, Hodder & Stoughton, 1967, Macmillan, 1967; *Cruel as a Cat*, Hodder & Stoughton, 1968, Macmillan, 1968; *Too Good to Be True*, Hodder & Stoughton, 1969, Macmillan, 1969; *A Period of Evil*, Hodder & Stoughton, 1970, World Publishing, 1971; *As Lonely as the Damned*, Hodder & Stoughton, 1971, World Publishing, 1972; *As Empty as Hate*, Hodder & Stoughton, 1972, World Publishing, 1972; *As Merry as Hell*, Hodder & Stoughton, 1973, Stein & Day, 1974; *This Man Did I Kill?*, Hodder & Stoughton, 1974, Stein & Day, 1974; *The Man Who Was Not Himself*, Hodder & Stoughton, 1976, Stein & Day, 1976.

Under pseudonym Brian Hope; mystery novel: *Four Motives for Murder*, George Newnes, 1938.

Under pseudonym Colin Hughes; mystery novel: *Triple Murder*, George Newnes, 1940, published as *What Dark Motive?*,

Under pseudonym Kyle Hunt; mystery novels; published by Simon & Schuster, except as indicated: *Kill Once, Kill Twice,* 1956; *Kill a Wicked Man,* 1957; *Kill My Love,* 1958, reprinted, White Lion, 1973; *To Kill a Killer,* Random House, 1960.

Under pseudonym Abel Mann; mystery novel: *Danger Woman,* Pocket Books, 1966.

Under pseudonym Peter Manton; mystery novels, except as indicated; published by Wright & Brown, except as indicated: *Murder Manor,* 1937; *The Grey Vale School Mystery* (juvenile fiction), Low, 1937; *Stand by for Danger,* 1937; *The Circle of Justice,* 1938, revised edition, New English Library, 1959; *Three Days' Terror,* 1938, reprinted, New English Library, 1969; *The Crime Syndicate,* 1939, revised edition, New English Library, 1969; *Death Looks On,* 1939; *Murder in the Highlands,* 1939, reprinted, Lythway Press, 1973; *The Midget Marvel* (juvenile fiction), Mellifont Press, 1940; *Policeman's Triumph,* 1949; *Thief in the Night,* 1950, reprinted, Lythway Press, 1973; *No Escape from Murder,* 1953; *The Crooked Killer,* 1954; *The Charity Murders,* 1954.

Under pseudonym J. J. Marric; "Gideon" mystery series; published by Harper, except as indicated: *Gideon's Day* (also see below), 1955, reprinted, Popular Library, 1979, published as *Gideon of Scotland Yard,* Berkley Publishing, 1958; *Gideon's Week* (also see below), reprinted, F. A. Thorpe, 1970; . . . *Night* (also see below), 1957, reprinted, Popular Library, 1978; . . . *Month,* 1958, reprinted, F. A. Thorpe, 1975; . . . *Staff,* 1959, reprinted, Coronet Books, 1975; . . . *Risk,* 1960; . . . *Fire,* 1961; . . . *March* (also see below), 1962, reprinted, Popular Library, 1977; . . . *Ride,* 1963, reprinted, Popular Library, 1979; *Gideon at Work* (contains *Gideon's Day, Gideon's Week,* and *Gideon's Night*), 1964 (published in England as *The Gideon Omnibus,* Hodder & Stoughton, 1964); . . . *Vote,* 1964; . . . *Lot,* 1964, reprinted, Popular Library, 1979; . . . *Badge,* 1966; . . . *Wrath* (also see below), 1967; . . . *River* (also see below), 1968; . . . *Power,* 1969; . . . *Sport,* 1970; . . . *Art,* 1971; . . . *Men,* 1972; . . . *Press,* 1973; . . . *London Omnibus* (contains *Gideon's March, Gideon's Wrath,* and *Gideon's River*), Hodder & Stoughton, 1973; . . . *Fog,* 1974; . . . *Drive,* 1976.

Under pseudonym James Marsden; juvenile fiction: *Ned Cartwright—Middleweight Champion,* Mellifont Press, 1935.

Under pseudonym Richard Martin; mystery novels, except as indicated: *Keys to Crime,* William Earl & Co., 1947, reprinted, Lythway Press, 1973; *Vote for Murder,* William Earl & Co., 1948, reprinted, Lythway Press, 1973; *Adrian and Jonathon* (non-mystery novel), Hodder & Stoughton, 1954, reprinted, Lythway Press, 1972.

Under pseudonym Anthony Morton; mystery novels; published by Low: *Mr. Quentin Investigates,* 1943, reprinted, Lythway Press, 1973; *Introducing Mr. Brandon,* 1944, reprinted, Lythway Press, 1973.

Under pseudonym Anthony Morton; "Baron" mystery series: *The Man in the Blue Mask,* Lippincott, 1937 (published in England as *Meet the Baron,* Harrap, 1937, reprinted, Corgi Books, 1971); *The Return of Blue Mask,* Lippincott, 1937 (published in England as *The Baron Returns,* Harrap, 1937, reprinted, Corgi Books, 1974); *Salute Blue Mask!,* Lippincott, 1938 (published in England as *The Baron Again,* Low, 1938, reprinted, Corgi Books, 1969); *Blue Mask at Bay,* Lippincott, 1938 (published in England as *The Baron at Bay,* Low, 1938); *Alias Blue Mask,* Lippincott, 1939 (published in England as *Alias the Baron,* Low, 1939, reprinted, Transworld [London], 1966); *Challenge Blue Mask!,* Lippincott, 1939 (published in England as *The Baron at Large,* Low, 1939), revised edition published as *The Baron at Large,* Corgi Books, 1972, Walker & Co., 1975.

Blue Mask Strikes Again, Lippincott, 1940 (published in England as *Versus the Baron,* Low, 1940, reprinted, Lythway Press, 1972); *Blue Mask Victorious,* Lippincott, 1940 (published in England as *Call for the Baron,* Low, 1940, reprinted, Corgi Books, 1973), revised edition published as *Call for the Baron,* Walker & Co., 1976; *The Baron Comes Back,* Low, 1943, reprinted, Corgi Books, 1973; *A Case for the Baron,* Low, 1945, Duell, Sloan & Pearce, 1949, reprinted, Corgi Books, 1968; *Reward for the Baron,* Low, 1945, reprinted, Corgi Books, 1970; *Career for the Baron,* Low, 1946, Duell, Sloan & Pearce, 1950, reprinted, Lythway Press, 1974; *The Baron and the Beggar,* Low, 1947, Duell, Sloan & Pearce, 1950, reprinted, Corgi Books, 1974; *Blame the Baron,* Low, 1948, Duell, Sloan & Pearce, 1951; *A Rope for the Baron,* 1948, Duell, Sloan & Pearce, 1949, reprinted, Corgi Books, 1975; *Books for the Baron,* Low, 1949, Duell, Sloan & Pearce, 1952.

Cry for the Baron, Low, 1950, Walker & Co., 1970; *Trap . . . ,* Low, 1950, Walker & Co., 1971; *Attack . . . ,* Low, 1951, revised edition, Corgi Books, 1972; *Shadow . . . ,* Low, 1951, reprinted, Lythway Press, 1976; *Warn . . . ,* Low, 1952; *The Baron Goes East,* Low, 1953, reprinted, White Lion, 1973; *. . . in France,* Hodder & Stoughton, 1953, reprinted, Hodder Paperbacks, 1970, Walker & Co., 1976; *Danger for . . . ,* Hodder & Stoughton, 1953, reprinted, Hodder Paperbacks, 1971, Walker & Co., 1974; *. . . Goes Fast,* Hodder & Stoughton, 1954, Walker & Co., 1972; *Nest-Egg for . . . ,* Hodder & Stoughton, 1954, reprinted, Hodder Paperbacks, 1972, published as *Deaf, Dumb, and Blonde,* Doubleday, 1961; *Help from . . . ,* Hodder & Stoughton, 1955, reprinted, White Lion, 1973, Walker & Co., 1977; *Hide . . . ,* Hodder & Stoughton, 1956, Walker & Co., 1978; *Frame . . . ,* Hodder & Stoughton, 1957, reprinted, White Lion, 1976, published as *The Double Frame,* Doubleday, 1961; *Red Eye for . . . ,* Hodder & Stoughton, 1958, published as *Blood Red,* Doubleday, 1960; *Black for . . . ,* Hodder & Stoughton, 1959, reprinted, Coronet Books, 1974, published as *If Anything Happens to Hester,* Doubleday, 1962.

Salute for . . . , Hodder & Stoughton, 1960, Walker & Co., 1973; *A Branch for . . . ,* Hodder & Stoughton, 1961, published as *. . . Branches Out,* Scribner, 1967; *Bad for . . . ,* Hodder & Stoughton, 1962, published as *. . . and the Stolen Legacy,* Scribner, 1967; *A Sword for . . . ,* Hodder & Stoughton, 1963, published as *. . . and the Mogul Swords,* Scribner, 1966; *. . . on Board,* Hodder & Stoughton, 1964, Walker & Co., 1968; *. . . and the Chinese Puzzle,* Hodder & Stoughton, 1965, Scribner, 1966; *Sport for . . . ,* Hodder & Stoughton, 1966, Walker & Co., 1969; *Affair for . . . ,* Hodder & Stoughton, 1967, Walker & Co., 1968; *. . . and the Missing Old Masters,* Hodder & Stoughton, 1968, Walker & Co., 1969; *. . . and the Unfinished Portrait,* Hodder & Stoughton, 1969, Walker & Co., 1970.

Last Laugh for . . . , Hodder & Stoughton, 1970, Walker & Co., 1971; *. . . Goes A-Buying,* Hodder & Stoughton, 1971, Walker & Co., 1972; *. . . and the Arrogant Artist,* Hodder & Stoughton, 1972, Walker & Co., 1973; *Burgle . . . ,* Hodder & Stoughton, 1973, Walker & Co., 1974; *. . . , King-Maker,* Walker & Co., 1975; *Love for . . . ,* Hodder & Stoughton, 1979.

Under pseudonym Ken Ranger; western novels; published by Low: *One-Shot Marriott,* 1938; *Roaring Guns,* 1939.

Under pseudonym William K. Reilly; western novels: *Range War,* Stanley Paul, 1939; *Two Gun Texan,* Stanley Paul, 1939;

Gun Feud, Stanley Paul, 1940; *Stolen Range,* Stanley Paul, 1940; *War on Lazy-K,* Stanley Paul, 1941, Phoenix Press, 1946; *Outlaw's Vengeance,* Stanley Paul, 1941; *Guns over Blue Lake,* Jenkins, 1942; *Riders of Dry Gulch,* Jenkins, 1943; *Long John Rides the Range,* Jenkins, 1944; *Miracle Range,* Jenkins, 1945; *The Secret of the Range,* Jenkins, 1946; *Outlaw Guns,* William Earl & Co., 1949; *Range Vengeance,* Ward, Lock, 1953.

Under pseudonym Tex Riley; western novels; published by Wright & Brown, except as indicated: *Two-Gun Girl,* 1938; *Gun-Smoke Range,* 1938; *Gunshot Mesa,* 1939; *The Shootin' Sheriff,* 1940; *Rustler's Range,* 1940; *Masked Riders,* 1940; *Death Canyon,* 1941, reprinted, Lythway Press, 1974; *Guns on the Range,* 1942; *Range Justice,* 1943; *Outlaw Hollow,* 1944; *Hidden Range,* William Earl & Co., 1946; *Forgotten Range,* William Earl & Co., 1947; *Trigger Justice,* William Earl & Co., 1948; *Lynch Hollow,* William Earl & Co., 1949.

Under pseudonym Jeremy York; mystery novels: *By Persons Unknown,* Bles, 1941, reprinted, Lythway Press, 1972; *Murder Unseen,* Bles, 1943; *No Alibi,* Melrose, 1943, reprinted, Lythway Press, 1972; *Murder in the Family,* Melrose, 1944, revised edition published in "Superintendent Folly" series (see below); *Yesterday's Murder,* Melrose, 1945; *Wilful Murder,* McNaughton, 1946; *Death to My Killer,* Melrose, 1950, Macmillan, 1966; *Sentence of Death,* Melrose, 1950, Macmillan, 1964; *Voyage with Murder,* Melrose, 1952, reprinted, Lythway Press, 1975; *Safari with Fear,* Melrose, 1953, reprinted, Lythway Press, 1974; *So Soon to Die,* Stanley Paul, 1955, Scribner, 1957; *Seeds of Murder,* Stanley Paul, 1956, Scribner, 1958; *Sight of Death,* Stanley Paul, 1956, Scribner, 1958; *My Brother's Killer,* John Long, 1958, Scribner, 1959; *Hide and Kill,* John Long, 1959, Scribner, 1960; *To Kill or to Die,* John Long, 1960, Macmillan, 1966, published as *To Kill or Die,* Panther Books, 1965.

Under pseudonym Jeremy York; "Superintendent Folly" mystery series: *Find the Body,* Melrose, 1945, revised edition, Macmillan, 1967; *Murder Came Late,* Melrose, 1946, revised edition, Macmillan, 1969; *Let's Kill Uncle Lionel,* Melrose, 1947, revised edition, Corgi Books, 1973, McKay, 1976; *Run Away to Murder,* Melrose, 1947, Macmillan, 1970; *Close the Door on Murder,* Melrose, 1948, revised edition, Corgi Books, 1971, McKay, 1973; *The Gallows Are Waiting,* Melrose, 1949, revised edition, Corgi Books, 1972, McKay, 1973; *First a Murder,* revised edition, Corgi Books, 1970, McKay, 1972; *Mystery Motive,* revised edition, Corgi Books, 1970, published in United States under author's own name, McKay, 1974; *Murder in the Family,* revised edition, McKay, 1976.

Under joint pseudonym Charles Hogarth, with Ian Bowen; mystery novel: *Murder on Largo Island,* Selwyn & Blount, 1944.

Also author of juvenile fiction *One Glorious Term* and *The Captain of the Fifth,* published by Low between 1933-39; *The Fear of Felix Corder, John Brand: Fugitive,* and *The Night of Dread,* for Fleetway Press; *Dazzle and the Red Bomber,* for George Newnes. Also author under pseudonym Rodney Mattheson of *The Dark Shadow* and *The House of Ferrars,* both for Fiction House. Contributor to numerous magazines, including *Ellery Queen's Mystery Magazine* and *Armchair Detective.* Editor of *John Creasey Mystery Magazine,* 1956-65.

SIDELIGHTS: "'If such a man were created in a novel, no one could possibly believe in him. In real life he is almost unbelievable; it is hardly surprising that his English publishers call him 'a legend in his own lifetime.''' John Creasey thus summarized his career in an autobiographical article which he wrote in the third person for *Armchair Detective.*

Creasey had reason to speak in superlatives; a retelling of his life actually sounds like a not-too-believable work of fiction. Facts concerning his literary output are astonishing: The author of nearly six hundred books, Creasey was the world's most prolific writer of crime fiction in English. He once estimated that between three and four thousand different editions of his books had appeared in a total of twenty-six languages. At the time of his death nearly sixty million copies of his books had been sold worldwide.

Creasey's popular success allowed him to live a life as colorful as that of one of his characters. He lived in a forty-two room manor, virtually commuted between England and the United States, traveled twice around the world, married four times, started his own political party, ran for the British Parliament several times, and owned a Rolls-Royce marked with the symbol of his "Toff" character—a monocled gentleman sporting a top hat.

His success, while based on reader acceptance of his novels, was largely a product of his own determination. For example, although Creasey began submitting articles for publication when only ten, by age seventeen he had also collected an amazing total of 743 rejection slips from publishers. Although he had had his first novel published by the time he was twenty-seven, it was actually the tenth he had written and during the same period of time he had been fired from twenty-five jobs—often for writing on his employer's time. But Creasey did not believe in defeat. *Armchair Detective*'s editor, Allen J. Hubin, once wrote: "I was greatly struck . . . with [Creasey's] confidence and determination. 743 rejection slips without a sale!—the imagination boggles. . . . But as John says, 'It was never a question of "if," it was only a question of "when." '"

This determined attitude remained with Creasey throughout his life; he did not accept setbacks, he fought them. When told by many acquaintances that he would "never be able to sell" in the United States, Creasey responded by personally visiting nineteen U.S. publishers and editors in an attempt to discover the reason for lack of positive reader response to the previous U.S. editions of his books. Unsatisfied with the various explanations he received, he developed his own theory. Unlike their British counterparts, American readers of crime novels, he believed, needed a protagonist with whom they could more readily identify. He purposely set out to change his style, making his novels more acceptable to the American audience.

In 1951, Creasey spent six months in the United States attempting to convince American companies to accept his books for publication. Again, he received rejection slips—sixty-eight—but finally obtained a contract from Harper to publish *Inspector West Cries Wolf* (appearing under the U.S. title *The Creepers*). As in the past, Creasey's persistence led to success. The novel was well received in the United States, and the entire collection of Inspector West books became one of his most popular series among U.S. readers.

Although this series was also one of Creasey's own favorites, his "Gideon" books, written under the pseudonym J. J. Marric, most favorably impressed reviewers. Under this pseudonym, according to a *London Times* article, "[Creasey] received far better reviews than he was accustomed to get under his own name."

In the *Detroit News,* for example, Richard Werry noted, "Marric's characters have real personal problems which make them more substantial than the papier-mache stereotypes common in most mystery fiction." Julian Symons also commented on the high quality of J. J. Marric's writing. In *Mortal Consequences* Symons wrote: "Creasey's Gideon books, written as

J. J. Marric, are his best work.... His stories are notable for the ingenuity of the ideas with which he overflows." The *New York Times Book Review*'s Anthony Boucher added: "[Creasey's 'Gideon' books] are marked by the technically dazzling handling of a large number of plots in small compass.... All of the Creasey avatars are skilled at telling an exciting story; Marric, in addition, can *write*."

Not all reviewers, however, had such high regard for Creasey's work. A *New York Times* writer observed: "Mr. Creasey had his detractors among professional critics, some of whom described his writing as undistinguished." Critics, believing that quick production diminished the quality of his writing, belittled Creasey for his rapid rate of publication. A *New York Times Book Review* writer, for example, described Creasey as "a sort of homicide computer—punch a button and out comes a book." Lewis Nichols, also writing in the *New York Times Book Review*, saw Creasey more as a business concern than as an author and referred to him as "Syndicate C."

Creasey, later in life, was able to shrug off such criticism. In *Writer*, he once jokingly called himself "a hackneyed old professional . . . suspected . . . by so many to have invented the computer first and Creasey and pen-names later." Early in his career, however, a critic who accused him of being more interested in quickly-completed than well-written prose caused Creasey to re-evaluate his writing method. Claiming in a *Newsweek* article, "I need to write with speed or it's no good," Creasey had attempted to write two books a week, with one day off between for playing cricket. After realizing the truth behind the critic's comments, Creasey decided to slow his pace to a pattern consistently followed until his death.

He began to take greater care in the production of his books. Each was written in longhand first, then scrutinized and revised five or six times before going to the publisher—often up to twelve months after being originally written. Creasey also began the practice of revising his earlier novels to make them more contemporary as well as to polish his style. He had a staff of readers instructed to "tear to bits" each of the novels due to be revised. Using these critical reports, Creasey made the necessary revisions and then had the book retyped and reread by other assistants. Some books were so extensively rewritten that the original detective was completely replaced by another character.

At times, revision also meant that a novel would appear under a different Creasey pseudonym than the one under which it had originally appeared. While several of his early pen names were chosen for him by his publishers, others, like J. J. Marric, originated with Creasey. J. J. Marric was chosen deliberately for the "Gideon" series; the name derived from the initials of the given names of Creasey and his second wife, Jean, combined with the first syllables of the given names of their two sons: *Mar*tin and *Ric*hard. Creasey once gave the reason for both his use of pseudonyms and his enormous number of books in *Newsweek*. He explained: "When I began writing, I discovered that the only way to make a living at the craft was to publish more than two books a year. Since, at that time, no publishers wanted to print more than two books a year from one author, I just changed names; then, too, different pen names permit me to write in different tones."

No matter which pseudonym was used, there was always a "special stamp" of a Creasey book, according to Hubin in the *New York Times Book Review*. These distinguishing characteristics, as Hubin saw them, were "uncluttered plotting, and emphasis . . . on the basic goodness of most people involved." Newgate Callendar referred to "the Creasey formula" in a *New York Times Book Review* article. In Callendar's analysis, a typical Creasey novel had "a fairly rat-tat-tat style—short sentences, lots of padding, emphasis on plot gimmicks, [and] very little in the way of characterization." William Vivian Butler had yet another enumeration of Creasey literary characteristics. He listed the following points in a *Spectator* review: "The driving narrative, the subtley understated heroics, the simple humanity, the strident small-l liberalism, the all-embracing love of London—and, above all, the dogged vulnerable heroes."

Creasey devoted the last year of his life to the production of a novel telling the history of London's Metropolitan Police. "He meant this . . . to be," according to the *London Times*, "a vindication of his claim to be a serious writer." Creasey's avid readers never doubted this claim. A *London Times* writer noted, "His business, he believed, was to sell books and to entertain." Creasey accomplished both these aims. As reviewer Butler stated in *Spectator*, "[His career was an] incredible forty-year, six hundred book feast . . . [for] his fans."

MEDIA ADAPTATIONS: John Creasey's books have been adapted for two British television series, "Gideon" and "The Baron." A number of his novels have also been adapted for films, including "Salute the Toff," 1951, and "Hammer the Toff," 1952, by Butcher; "Gideon's Day," by Columbia Production Ltd., 1958; and "Cat and Mouse," by Eros, 1958.

BIOGRAPHICAL/CRITICAL SOURCES: Newsweek, February 2, 1958; *New York Times Book Review*, November 28, 1958, January 22, 1961, March 18, 1962, July 28, 1968, September 1, 1968, November 3, 1968, January 19, 1969, June 1, 1969, April 11, 1976; *Life*, April 27, 1962; *Publishers Weekly*, February 8, 1965; *Armchair Detective*, October, 1968; *Times Literary Supplement*, September 18, 1969, January 22, 1970, October 22, 1971; *Variety*, June 10, 1970; *Newsday*, December 12, 1970; *Detroit News*, November 28, 1971, June 4, 1972; Julian Symons, *Mortal Consequences: A History—From the Detective Story to the Crime Novel*, Harper, 1972; *New York Times*, July 22, 1972; *Writer*, September, 1972; *Spectator*, March 22, 1975; *Contemporary Literary Criticism*, Volume XI, Gale, 1979.

OBITUARIES: New York Times, June 10, 1973; *London Times*, June 11, 1973; *Publishers Weekly*, June 18, 1973; *Newsweek*, June 25, 1973; *AB Bookman's Weekly*, October 1, 1973.†

—Sketch by Marian Walters

* * *

CREDO
　See CREASEY, John

* * *

CRENSHAW, Mary Ann

PERSONAL: Born in Montgomery, Ala.; daughter of Jack (an attorney) and Catherine (Westcott) Crenshaw. *Education:* Vanderbilt University, B.A., 1951; also attended University of Havana (Cuba), and Parsons School of Design. *Politics:* Democrat. *Religion:* Episcopalian. *Residence:* New York, N.Y. *Agent:* Henry Morrison, Inc., 58 West 10th St., New York, N.Y. 10011. *Office:* 211 East 70th St., New York, N.Y. 10021.

CAREER: Writer. Assistant to couturier Charles James, New York City, 1958; *Vogue Magazine*, New York City, member of merchandising department staff, 1959-62; boutique manager for designer "Tiger" Morse, and publicist for Adolfo, both New York City, 1962; fashion coordinator for Ohrbach's, New York City, 1962-65; *New York Times*, New York City, fashion and beauty reporter, 1965-76. Contributor of material to *New York Times* promotion department.

WRITINGS: The Natural Way to Super Beauty, McKay, 1974; *Shape-up for Super Sex*, Delacorte, 1976; *End of the Rainbow*, Macmillan, 1981. Contributor to *Cosmopolitan, Harper's Bazaar, Family Circle,* and *Esquire.*

WORK IN PROGRESS: A diet book, for Macmillan.

SIDELIGHTS: Mary Ann Crenshaw's career in the fashion and newspaper business was almost destroyed by her addiction to both alcohol and prescription drugs. In *End of the Rainbow* Crenshaw tells the story of her struggle to regain emotional stability in her life and to continue in her occupation as a writer.

The "rainbow" in the title of her book refers to the multicolored prescription drugs the author took to relieve the pressures of her fast-paced professional and social life. After Crenshaw had suffered a physical collapse, a physician and a psychiatrist prescribed even more drugs to help her through this difficult period. Crenshaw credits her participation in a hospital detoxification program and her four week stint in a rehabilitation clinic for returning normalcy to her life. According to a *Los Angeles Times* review of *End of the Rainbow*, Crenshaw describes how she "found the fabled pot of gold in the form of restored physical health and renewed creative energy."

Intended not only as a volume of autobiography but also as a warning to users (and abusers) of drugs, *End of the Rainbow* is recommended by a *Publishers Weekly* reviewer as "reading for addicts and potential ones." Revealing how even legal drugs—those available with a prescription or from behind the bar—can be detrimental to their users' physical and emotional health, Crenshaw's book, notes the *Los Angeles Times* critic, "is sure to make many . . . take a good look at the contents of the family medicine cabinet."

AVOCATIONAL INTERESTS: Needlepoint, gymnastics, dance, travel, collecting antiques, primitive paintings, and quilts.

BIOGRAPHICAL/CRITICAL SOURCES: Publishers Weekly, January 9, 1981; *Los Angeles Times,* April 9, 1981.

* * *

CRESSWELL, Helen

PERSONAL: Born July 11, in Nottinghamshire, England; daughter of J. E. (an electrical engineer) and A. E. (Clarke) Cresswell; married Brian Rowe (in textiles), April 14, 1962; children: Caroline Jane, Candida Lucy. *Education:* Kings College, University of London, B.A. (with honors), 1955. *Religion:* Church of England. *Home:* Old Church Farm, Eakring, Newark, Nottinghamshire NG22 0DA, England. *Agent:* A. M. Heath & Co. Ltd., 40-42 William IV St., London WC2N 4DD, England.

CAREER: Writer, mainly of books for children. Career up to marriage was varied, including periods as literary assistant to a foreign author, fashion buyer, and teacher, and television work for British Broadcasting Corp. *Member:* International P.E.N., Society of Authors.

AWARDS, HONORS: Nottingham Poetry Society Award for best poem submitted in annual competition, 1950; runner-up, Carnegie Medal, Library Association (United Kingdom), 1967, for *The Piemakers,* 1969, for *The Nightwatchmen,* 1971, for *Up the Pier,* and 1973, for *The Bongleweed;* runner-up for best children's original television drama, Television Writers Guild of Great Britain, 1972, for "Lizzie Dripping"; *Absolute Zero: Being the Second Part of the Bagthorpe Saga* was named "best book" by School Library Journal, 1978; "Book of the Year" award, Child Study Association, 1978, for *Ordinary Jack: Being the First Part of the Bagthorpe Saga; Ordinary Jack* was listed in Horn Book Fanfare, 1978; *Up the Pier, The Winter of the Birds, Ordinary Jack, Absolute Zero,* and *Bagthorpes Unlimited: Being the Third Part of the Bagthorpe Saga,* were named "notable books of the year" by American Library Association.

WRITINGS: Sonya-by-the-Shore, Dent, 1961; *Jumbo Spencer,* Brockhampton Press, 1963, Lippincott, 1966; *The White Sea Horse,* Oliver & Boyd, 1964, Lippincott, 1965; *Jumbo Back to Nature,* Brockhampton Press, 1965; *Pietro and the Mule,* Oliver & Boyd, 1965, Bobbs-Merrill, 1970; *Jumbo Afloat,* Brockhampton Press, 1966; *Where the Wind Blows,* Faber, 1966, Funk, 1968; *The Piemakers,* Faber, 1967, Lippincott, 1968; *A Day on Big O,* Benn, 1967, Follett, 1968; *A Tide for the Captain,* Chatto & Windus, 1967; *The Signposters,* Faber, 1968; *The Sea Piper,* Chatto & Windus, 1968; *Jumbo and the Big Day,* Brockhampton Press, 1968; *Rug Is a Bear,* Benn, 1968; *Rug Plays Tricks,* Benn, 1968; *The Nightwatchmen,* Faber, 1969, Macmillan, 1970; *A Game of Catch,* Chatto & Windus, 1969; *A Gift from Winklesea,* Brockhampton Press, 1969; *A House for Jones,* Benn, 1969; *Rug Plays Ball,* Benn, 1969; *Rug and a Picnic,* Benn, 1969.

The Outlanders, Faber, 1970; *The Wilkses,* B.B.C. Publications, 1970; *Rainbow Pavement,* Benn, 1970; *John's First Fish,* Macmillan, 1970; *Up the Pier,* Macmillan, 1971; *The Weather Cat,* Benn, 1971; *The Bird Fancier,* Benn, 1971; *At the Stroke of Midnight,* Collins, 1971; *The Beachcombers,* Macmillan, 1972; *Jane's Policeman,* Benn, 1972; *The Long Day,* Benn, 1972; *Short Back and Sides,* Benn, 1972; *Blue Birds over Pit Row,* Benn, 1972; *Roof Fall,* Benn, 1972; *Lizzie Dripping,* B.B.C. Publications, 1972; *The White Sea Horse and Other Stories from the Sea,* Chatto & Windus, 1972; *The Bongleweed,* Macmillan, 1973; *The Bower Bird,* Benn, 1973; *The Key,* Benn, 1973; *The Trap,* Benn, 1973; *The Beetle Hunt,* Longman, 1973; *More Lizzie Dripping,* B.B.C. Publications, 1974; *The Two Hoots,* Benn, 1974; *The Two Hoots by the Sea,* Benn, 1974; *Cheap Day Return,* Benn, 1974; *The Shady Deal,* Benn, 1974; *The Winter of the Birds,* Faber, 1975, Macmillan, 1976; *Ordinary Jack: Being the First Part of the Bagthorpe Saga,* Macmillan, 1976; *Absolute Zero: Being the Second Part of the Bagthorpe Saga,* Macmillan, 1978; *Bagthorpes Unlimited: Being the Third Part of the Bagthorpe Saga,* Macmillan, 1979; *Bagthorpes versus the World: Being the Fourth Part of the Bagthorpe Saga,* Macmillan, 1979.

Dear Shrink, Macmillan, 1982; *The Secret World of Polly Flint,* Faber, 1982, Penguin, 1983.

Contributor: A. D. Maclean, editor, *Winters Tales,* Macmillan, 1969; *World Book of Ballet,* Collins, 1970; Eileen Colwell, editor, *Bad Boys,* Puffin, 1972; *Authors' Choice,* Hamish Hamilton, Number 2, 1973; Garfield, editor, *Bakers Dozen,* Ward, Lock, 1973; Richard Church and others, *My England,* Heinemann, 1973; Noel Streatfeild, *Christmas Holiday Book,* Dent, 1973; Streatfeild, *Summer Holiday Book,* Dent, 1973; Streatfeild, *Birthday Book,* Dent, 1975.

Television screenplays; all produced by British Broadcasting Corp., except as indicated: "Lizzie Dripping" series, six episodes, 1973, five episodes, 1975; "Dick Whittington," 1974; "Jumbo Spencer" series, five episodes, 1976; "For Bethlehem Read Little Thraves," 1976; "The Secret World of Polly Flint" series, seven episodes, ITV Central Television, 1983.

SIDELIGHTS: Helen Cresswell, four-time nominee for the prestigious Carnegie Medal, is one of Great Britain's foremost children's authors. Cresswell's work, says one *Times Literary Supplement* critic, "speaks the authentic language of childhood" and "shows a major talent in the making." Gillian Cross, also writing in *Times Literary Supplement*, states that Cresswell has "the two great virtues of originality and versatility. Her pen spawns new and unexpected worlds."

Nearly all of Cresswell's books have received critical acclaim. The *Times Literary Supplement* reviewer of *The Beachcombers* calls Cresswell "the most divinely discontented of modern writers for the young," and *Horn Book*'s Gregory Maguire contends that she "clearly . . . has no shortage of strings to her bow." A *Times Literary Supplement* critic comments on the difficulty some children may have understanding *The Outlanders* but also notes its impact: "For the rare child who can penetrate the heart of the story [*The Outlanders*] is likely to become a lasting formative influence. The book induces . . . a gentle melancholy born of loneliness and deep pondering. The memory of it is haunting, returning unexpectedly to the reader. Its persistent effect is some measure of the stature of a very remarkable book." The *Times Literary Supplement* reviewer of *The Piemakers* calls that book "singularly flawless." Leon Garfield in *Spectator* concludes: "I once heard Miss Cresswell liken her work humorously to a brussels sprout. I would have to say it is more like a Cos lettuce—having many crisp leaves and a good, strong heart."

Cresswell's popularity stems in part from her ability to appeal to children of all ages. She has written adaptations of fairy stories for preschoolers as well as novels for older children. "Helen Cresswell is one of those rare souls who can write angelically well for the child in the child," writes Garfield. Katherine Patterson in *Washington Post Book World* notes that her thirteen-year-old son loved *Ordinary Jack*. Patterson says, "The plot and characters [of the book] are strong enough to delight younger children who might not . . . catch on to the batting about of literary allusions, but there is plenty of humor for all."

As Patterson points out, humor is a crucial element in Cresswell's writing. Maguire calls Cresswell "a master humorist," and Patterson recounts that after her son read *Ordinary Jack*, "at least one All-American Boy found himself laughing out loud, . . . which was a problem, actually, because he was sneak reading after lights-out and didn't want to be discovered." Another *Horn Book* reviewer comments that "seldom, if ever, has there been such consistently funny writing for children as in the Bagthorpe chronicles." The comedy in Cresswell's books ranges from the slapstick and nonsensical, as it is in the Bagthorpe stories, to the whimsical and poignant, like that in *The Nightwatchmen* and *The Piemakers*. Says a *Times Literary Supplement* reviewer: "Miss Cresswell is . . . that rarest of children's writers, a master of high comedy. As in the best comedy, too, there is in these books [*The Nightwatchmen* and *The Piemakers*] a hint of sadness and a vein of genuine poetry."

Some reviewers, however, criticize Cresswell's comic inventions. Margaret F. O'Connell in *New York Times Book Review* contends that "whimsey is extravagantly thick" in *The White Sea Horse and Other Stories from the Sea* and that "capricious and contrived events happen at the convenience of the storytelling and a magical horse that remains so docile and physically powerless is hardly credible." Others find the madcap characters in the Bagthorpe saga tiresome. Marie Messenger writes in *Listener*: "Comedy needs straight men and, with all the supporting cast busy being humorous, . . . the poor hero [of *Ordinary Jack*] has to do the straight-man's job himself."

The combination of whimsey and humor in Cresswell's books has prompted many critics to classify them as fantasies. Cresswell's novels "rank with the finest examples of fantasy written in recent years," comments a *Times Literary Supplement* critic in a review of *The Bongleweed*. Maguire states that *The Winter of the Birds*, "more than any other children's book I know of, brings together the words *epic* and *fantasy*. . . . [Cresswell's novels] are fantasies which evoke morality plays, dream journeys, and vacation stories."

On the other hand, some critics are unsure if the stories actually are fantasies. In a *Times Literary Supplement* review of *The Beachcombers*, the critic asks: "Is it fantasy? There are none of the conventional trappings of fantasy, no magic, no bending of natural laws." As Gillain Cross mentions in her review of *Ordinary Jack* and *Absolute Zero*, Cresswell displays "a sane appreciation of ordinary human values." The *Times Literary Supplement* reviewer of *The Nightwatchmen* says: "*The Piemakers* has been called a fantasy, but while this enchanting tale strains credulity in the pleasantest fashion, there is nothing in it which breaches the ordinary laws of nature. . . . *The Nightwatchmen* [also] treads delicately on the brink of wonderland, yet it is planted in reality, in a close and affectionate observation of the ordinariness of backstreets and holes in the ground and the extraordinariness of human beings."

The division between fantasy and reality in Cresswell's work is not always distinct because, as one *Times Literary Supplement* reviewer says, the author continually explores "the frontiers of reality." After questioning whether or not *The Beachcombers* is a fantasy, the same critic continues: "Slowly, as the plot works its intricate way out, the flesh seems to fall from the bones of the Beachcombers and they become as ghostly as their old ship and as timeless as the wind that blows through them. . . . Not for the first time Miss Cresswell's imaginings are more real than reality." *New Statesman* critic Nicholas Tucker calls *The Bongleweed* "a balance of the surreal and the earthy."

Other critics, who consider Cresswell's work fantasies, also recognize the importance "ordinary human values" play in the stories. The *Times Literary Supplement* reviewer of *The Bongleweed* notes that "there is an unmistakably individual voice to her prose with its beautiful cadences, and the stories, however strange they may seem on the surface, have at their best the ability to touch on the most profound aspects of human experience. . . . They are never cosy or escapist, but deal with the problems of moral choice and the darker sides of ourselves." In a review of *The Piemakers*, the *Times Literary Supplement* critic observes: "[Cresswell is able to] treat an essentially comic (or impossible) idea with complete seriousness. [She is] consistent in the use of detail, filling in the framework of [her] inventions as if [she] were [a] master of the Dutch school. These are, one feels, not happily fantastic imaginings but studies from life. . . . [Further], there is a warmth, a richness of humor, an inner truthfulness in *The Piemakers* which puts this apparently slight tale in the select company of books which make nonsense credible, which make the reader laugh and cry and delight in a job exceedingly well done."

Whether or not Cresswell's books are fantasies, they do stress the power of the imagination. Sally Emerson writes in a *Books and Bookmen* review of *The Winter of the Birds* that "whether the birds actually exist or not is irrelevant, the story exemplifies the truth of the imagination. . . . This is the glory of the book: it is set in the here and now—the characters are flesh and blood, the dialogue and plot romp along—and yet it's also a poem of a book, rejoicing in the unexpectedness of life." In *The Beachcombers* "there is no neat ending to the story," observes Gladys Williams in *Books and Bookmen*. "A child is left to wonder, to speculate, to imagine." A *Horn Book* reviewer says that with *The Nightwatchmen,* Cresswell has "woven another fantasy whose elusive threads of meaning form a spiderweb of substance depending on the sophistication and imagination of the reader. . . . The actual details of the story are relatively unimportant; the author has created a mood picture and has left it up to the reader to find his own treasure in the work." Also writing about *The Nightwatchmen,* a *Times Literary Supplement* critic concludes: "What [the hero of the story] has gained from the wild and crazy and beautiful adventure is heightened sensitivity. He will never take a tree or a tramp or a lemon-meringue pie for granted again."

Cresswell herself acknowledges the importance imagination—both that of her characters and of her readers—plays in the success of her stories. She writes to *CA:* "I think much of what I write is ancient, in the sense that there is nothing new under the sun, but modern in that it embodies the attitudes not of the present establishment of technology, reason and materialism, but of the underground resistance to it. . . . Experts do not like to be confronted by the inexplicable . . . but children do, because they have not yet been fixed into conventional stances, because they have not yet been forced to make false boundaries and divisions, because they are still aware that [the world] *is* 'incorrigibly plural,' and [they] glory in the knowledge, instead of forcing it away as an unpalatable truth."

MEDIA ADAPTATIONS: The Bagthorpe saga was adapted for television by James Andrew Hall and produced by British Broadcasting Corp., 1981.

AVOCATIONAL INTERESTS: Philosophy, walking, gardening, and collecting coincidences.

BIOGRAPHICAL/CRITICAL SOURCES: New York Times Book Review, January 2, 1966, November 8, 1970; *Times Literary Supplement,* May 25, 1967, June 6, 1968, April 4, 1969, June 26, 1969, July 7, 1970, December 3, 1971, November 3, 1972, November 23, 1973, December 5, 1975, April 7, 1978, July 23, 1982; *Books and Bookmen,* February, 1973, November, 1975, June, 1980; *Horn Book,* February, 1973, October, 1978, April, 1981; *Spectator,* October 20, 1973, December 10, 1977; *New Statesman,* November 9, 1973, November 3, 1978; *Listener,* November 10, 1977; *Washington Post Book World,* April 9, 1978; *Chicago Tribune Book World,* October 10, 1982.

—Sketch by Heidi A. Tietjen

* * *

CRIPE, Helen 1932-

PERSONAL: Born March 2, 1932, in Vincennes, Ind.; daughter of Robert Rhodes (a printer) and Helen (a teacher; maiden name, Dixon) Petts; married Herbert R. Cripe, Jr., August 10, 1957 (died January 21, 1970). *Education:* Vincennes University Junior College, A.A., 1951; Maryville College, B.A., 1954; University of Notre Dame, M.A., 1968, Ph.D., 1972. *Home:* 133 Lovering Ave., Wilmington, Del. 19806. *Office:* Trolley Laundry, 33A Trolley Sq., Wilmington, Del. 19806.

CAREER: Former high school teacher of social studies in public schools in Indiana; American Antiquarian Society, Worcester, Mass., field director of *Index to the Manuscripts of Prominent Americans, 1763-1815,* 1973-76; Scholarly Resources, Inc., Wilmington, Del., acquisitions editor, 1976-79; Trolley Laundry and Cannery Laundry, both Wilmington, co-owner and manager, 1980—. Visiting lecturer at Madison College, Indiana University, University of Virginia, Atlantic Union College, Southern Illinois University at Carbondale, Maryville College, Wichita State University, and American Antiquarian Society. Workshop panelist, National Automatic Laundry and Cleaning Council, 1982. Member, board of directors, Salisbury Singers, Worcester, 1975. Consultant to Salisbury Singers, 1973-75, Delaware Musica Viva, 1976, Worcester Consortium for Higher Education, Eleutherian Mills Historical Library in Greenville, Del., for a special exhibit, and Collegium Antiquarium at University of Delaware on harpsichord technique and literature.

WRITINGS: Thomas Jefferson and Music, University Press of Virginia, 1974; (with Diane Campbell) *American Manuscripts 1763-1815: An Index to Documents Described in Auction Records and Dealers' Catalogues,* Scholarly Resources, 1977. Book reviewer for *Worcester Sunday Telegram,* 1974-75. Contributor of articles to *American Coin-Op,* 1982—. Editorial fellow, *Review of Politics* (University of Notre Dame), 1970-71.

WORK IN PROGRESS: Further research on Jefferson's music collection, and a social history of Jefferson's family and what happened to them after his death; research on other areas of music history in the United States, particularly the history of the manufacture of musical instruments and individuals connected with their manufacture; articles and handbooks pertinent to the coin-operated laundry business.

SIDELIGHTS: Helen Cripe told *CA:* "My career change in 1980 was a somewhat bizarre interpretation of alternative careers for historians. One simply must face the fact that a graduate degree in history, however intellectually satisfying, is not economically viable. I thoroughly enjoy the challenges of the coin-op laundry business and I particularly enjoy the income. Rich laundry owners have more time to write history than starving scholars." *Avocational interests:* Music (especially choral singing and study of piano, harpsichord, and baroque theory), sewing, knitting, needlepoint, reading, bowling.

BIOGRAPHICAL/CRITICAL SOURCES: Commercial Merchandiser, December, 1981.

* * *

CROISE, Jacques
See SCHAKOVSKOY, Zinaida

* * *

CRUMP, Barry (John) 1935-

PERSONAL: Born May 16, 1935, in Auckland, New Zealand; son of Walter William (a farmer) and Lilly (Hendry) Crump; married Fleur Adcock (a librarian and poet), 1961 (separated). *Education:* Attended Otahuhu Technical College, Auckland, New Zealand. *Politics:* "Politically irresponsible." *Religion:* Baha'i. *Address:* Box 13940, Auckland, New Zealand. *Office address:* Crump Productions, Ltd., P.O. Box 5040, Auckland, New Zealand.

CAREER: Worked at more than seventy jobs since leaving school and has continued his wandering ways ("no fixed abode") since becoming a writer, 1960—; affiliated with Crump Productions, Ltd., Auckland, New Zealand. Experiences as a professional deer shooter, employed by the New Zealand Forest Service, 1951-56, led to his first book, *A Good Keen Man,* and professional crocodile hunting in Queensland, Australia, 1956-64, led to another book, *Gulf;* film actor in "Runaway," produced in New Zealand, 1964; radio reader of his own works, New Zealand; currently host of "Radio Pacific," Auckland. *Member:* P.E.N. *Awards, honors:* Hubert Church Award for prose, P.E.N., 1963, for *One of Us.*

WRITINGS—Published by A. H. & A. W. Reed: *A Good Keen Man*, 1960; *Hang On a Minute, Mate*, 1961; *One of Us*, 1962; *There and Back*, 1963; *Gulf*, 1964; *Scrapwaggon*, 1965; *The Odd Spot of Bother*, 1967; *Warm Beer and Other Stories*, 1969; *A Good Keen Girl*, 1970; *No Reference Intended*, 1971.

Published by Crump Productions: *Bastards I Have Met: An ABC of Bastardry*, 1971; *Fred*, 1973; *The Best of Barry Crump*, 1974; *Shorty*, 1980; *Puha Road*, 1981.

Contributor of short stories and articles to New Zealand and Australian periodicals.

SIDELIGHTS: Barry Crump's first book was an instant success and has gone into twelve printings in five years; sales of that book and the three novels that followed it (featuring a Kiwi vagabond, Sam Cash) have passed the 200,000 mark.

BIOGRAPHICAL/CRITICAL SOURCES: Ron Helmer, *Stag Party*, Whitcombe & Tombs, 1964.

* * *

CRUMRINE, N(orman) Ross II 1934-

PERSONAL: Born May 22, 1934, in Beaver, Pa.; son of Norman Ross (a physician) and Elizabeth (Seiple) Crumrine; married Lynne Scoggins (an anthropologist), August 29, 1959 (died, April, 1969); married M. Louise Hobson, August 14, 1971; children: (first marriage) Juli Maria; (second marriage) Monica Louise, Norman Ross III. *Education:* Northwestern University, B.A., 1957; University of Washington, Seattle, graduate study, 1957-58; University of Arizona, M.A., 1962, Ph.D., 1968; University of Chicago, graduate study, 1962-63. *Home:* 1670 Earlston Ave., Victoria, British Columbia, Canada V8P 2Z7. *Office:* Department of Anthropology, University of Victoria, Victoria, British Columbia, Canada V8W 2Y2.

CAREER: California State University, Hayward, assistant professor of anthropology, 1965-68; University of Victoria, Victoria, British Columbia, assistant professor, 1968-71, professor of anthropology, 1971—. *Member:* American Anthropological Association, American Ethnological Society, American Folklore Association, Society for the Scientific Study of Religion, Latin American Studies Association, Canadian Ethnological Society, Canadian Latin American Studies Association.

WRITINGS: *El Ceremonial de Pascua y la Identidad de los Mayos de Sonora*, Instituto Nacional Indigenista (Mexico), 1974; *The Mayo Indians of Sonora, Mexico: A People Who Refuse to Die*, University of Arizona Press, 1977; (editor and contributor) *Ritual Symbolism and Ceremonialism in the Americas: Studies in Symbolic Anthropology*, Museum of Anthropology, University of Northern Colorado, 1979.

Contributor: Norman K. Denzin, editor, *The Values of Social Science*, Aldine, 1970; (with B. June Macklin) Ino Rossi, editor, *The Unconscious in Culture*, Dutton, 1974; *Annual Editions: Readings in Anthropology*, Dushkin, 1974; Thomas B. Hinton and Phil C. Weigand, editors, *Anthropological Papers of the University of Arizona*, University of Arizona Press, 1981.

Contributor of monographs to *Anthropological Papers of the University of Arizona*, 1964, and University of Northern Colorado Ethnological Series, 1979; contributor to acts of Congreso Internacional de Americanistas, 1972 and 1976. Contributor of articles to professional journals, including *Anthropological Quarterly*, *Journal for the Scientific Study of Religion*, *Comparative Studies in Society and History*, *Anthropos*, *Journal of Latin American Folklore*, and *Anthropologica*.

CUMMINGS, Paul 1933-

PERSONAL: Born January 24, 1933, in Detroit Lakes, Minn. *Education:* Attended University of Minnesota and Goldsmiths' College, London. *Office:* 945 Madison Ave., New York, N.Y. 10021.

CAREER: Louis Alexander Gallery, New York City, director, 1962-63; *New York Arts Calendar*, New York City, editor, 1963-65; *Gallery Guide*, New York City, editor and publisher, 1965-67; Smithsonian Institution, Archives of American Art, New York City, interviewer, 1968-70, director of oral history program, 1970-78. Adjunct curator of drawing, Whitney Museum of American Art, 1976—. Founder and publisher, *Print Collector's Newsletter*. *Member:* Drawing Society (member of executive committee; president, 1979—).

AWARDS, HONORS: *Fine Arts Market Place* named book of the year, American Library Association, 1973.

WRITINGS: *A Dictionary of Contemporary American Artists*, St. Martin's, 1966, 3rd edition, 1976; (editor) *Fine Arts Market Place*, Bowker, 1973, 3rd edition, 1977; *American Drawings: Twentieth Century*, Viking, 1976; *David Smith: The Drawings*, Whitney Museum of American Art, 1979; *Twentieth Century Drawings: Selections from the Whitney Museum of American Art*, Dover, 1981. Editor of "Documentary Monographs in Modern Art" series, seven books, Praeger. Editor, *Archives of American Art Journal*, 1973-78, and *Drawing*, 1979.

* * *

CUNNINGHAM, Dale S(peers) 1932-

PERSONAL: Born May 27, 1932, in Elmira, N.Y.; son of Arthur G. and Aletha (Speers) Cunningham; divorced. *Education:* Hamilton College, A.B., 1954; graduate study at Sorbonne, University of Paris, 1954, and Johann Wolfgang Goethe-Universität, 1954-55; Columbia University, A.M., 1959; graduate study at Princeton University, 1961-62, and Bryn Mawr College, 1962-65. *Home address:* Box 401, Main Office, Camden, N.J. 08101.

CAREER: Renssalaer Polytechnic Institute, Troy, N.Y., instructor in English and German, 1960-61; Rutgers University, Camden Campus, Camden, N.J., instructor in German, 1961-65; Smith, Kline & French Laboratories, Philadelphia, Pa., medical writer, 1965; Uniworld Languages, Haddonfield, N.J., translator and writer, beginning 1965; Management Information Corp., Cherry Hill, N.J., editor, technical writer, and director of translation services, 1981—. Free-lance editor, translator, and translations consultant.

MEMBER: Modern Language Association of America, American Translators Association (secretary, 1963-64; director, 1965-69; president, 1969-71; past president, 1971—), American Association of University Professors, Delaware Valley Translators Association (vice-chairman, 1962-63; chairman, 1963-64), P.E.N. (honorary member of translations committee), Bund Deutscher Uebersetzer, Verband Deutscher Uebersetzer (honorary member), Chambre Belge des Traducteurs, Interpretes, et Philologues (honorary member). *Awards, honors:* Fulbright assistantship in Germany, 1954-55.

WRITINGS—All published by Sterling: *Pioneers in Science*, 1962; *Picture Book of Music and Its Makers*, 1963.

Translator and adapter: (With Margrete Cunningham) Walter Sperling, *How to Make Things out of Paper*, 1961; (with M.

Cunningham) Gerhard Gollwitzer, *The Joy of Drawing,* 1961; Bruno Knobel, *Camping-Out Ideas and Activities,* 1961; Gollwitzer, *Abstract Art,* 1962; Harald Doering, *A Bee Is Born,* 1962; (with Marianne Das) Dieter Krauter, *Experimenting with the Microscope,* 1963; (with Ida H. Washington) Rudolf Dittrich, *Juggling,* 1963; Dittrich, *Tricks and Games for Children,* 1964; Susanne Strose, *Making Paper Flowers,* 1970; Lita Fischer-Munstermann, *Jazz Dance and Jazz Gymnastics,* 1978.

Contributor of articles, translations, reviews, and notes to learned journals, including *Meta;* contributor of articles to newspapers, including *Philadelphia Inquirer.* Former contributing editor, *Babel.*

WORK IN PROGRESS: Translations; research in the history and theory of translation; muckraking books on the Federal Bureau of Investigation and the American Telephone and Telegraph Co.

SIDELIGHTS: Dale S. Cunningham writes to *CA:* "I began to translate as a high school language student and continued the practice in college, but with a view towards eventual publication. My first original book was a 'work-for-hire' (i.e., no royalties) for the publisher of my first book-length translations. Like all of my early books, translations, and adaptations, I was concerned primarily with teaching something of value, or otherwise informing and/or entertaining my readers. My first work-for-hire was paid for as piecework, resulting in a 'wage' of almost 10 cents per hour.

"Close reading of my bibliography will reveal a [long] hiatus in published works; this occurred because I had become involved with peace activists during the final years of the Viet Nam war. The F.B.I. manipulated a money-hungry Judas/informer whom they paid to finance a draft-board raid resulting in arrests of a group that came to be known as the 'Camden 28.' Acting on incorrect information without a thorough check on the source, the F.B.I. staged an incident of intimidation for which I was arrested and which resulted in an indictment that was based on F.B.I.-agent perjury; the false charges were not dismissed until two-and-one-half years later in 1973. The rest of the decade was lost in only partially successful litigation against the government in an attempt to restore my good name, my lost business, and my expenses incurred in the morass of legal delays. (For the nineteenth-century equivalent, see Charles Dickens' *Bleak House.*)

"Having achieved some legal victories while acting as my own attorney, and being recognized for the actions in the newspapers, I returned to translating and writing on a full-time basis. Although some of the best (in the sense of potentially most productive) years of my life were wasted because of the essentially criminal activities initiated by J. Edgar Hoover and his clones under the direction of Nixon and former attorney general John Mitchell (only the latter having served time for his illegal activities in the course of Watergate), I feel that some of my moral victories have set me on the road to recovery, and I hope once again to be a productive writer and translator, albeit with a somewhat altered focus.

"Law enforcement is a necessary evil of modern civilization, for we have yet to achieve the bliss of perfect anarchy or the return of paradise. Consequently, I believe that my role as a writer/translator/communicator should be one of an educator and reformer, and the way I know best is through writing.

"If asked for advice to aspiring writers, I can merely caution them that such gratuitous pontification is probably not worth much more that it costs them. Nevertheless, insofar as a 1981 study showed that most free-lance writers trying to support themselves in that way earned less than $5,000 a year, my advice is that aspirants to the trade/art/profession of scribbling for pay emulate Geoffery Chaucer and obtain a sinecure like his tax collecting job; this tradition of government subsidization of worthy writers and thinkers was a common practice even in nineteenth-century America.

"As a translator, I feel a particular affinity for predecessors like John Wycliffe and Martin Luther, both of whom were outspoken and persisted in spite of opposition and persecution, and a writer hero is Sinclair Lewis, whose muckraking has saved countless lives, if only by leading to the availability of clean, wholesome meat on our tables."

* * *

CURRY, Kenneth 1910-

PERSONAL: Born October 24, 1910, in Orlando, Fla.; son of W. K. and Corinne (Sias) Curry. *Education:* Rollins College, A.B., 1932; Yale University, Ph.D., 1935. *Religion:* Episcopalian. *Office:* Department of English, University of Tennessee, Knoxville, Tenn. 37916.

CAREER: University of Tennessee, Knoxville, began as instructor, became assistant professor, 1935-46, associate professor, 1946-60, professor of English, 1960-68, professor emeritus, 1979—. *Member:* International Association of University Professors of English, Modern Language Association of America, Modern Humanities Research Association.

WRITINGS: (Editor) *New Letters of Robert Southey,* two volumes, Columbia University Press, 1965; *Southey,* Routledge & Kegan Paul, 1975; *Sir Walter Scott's Edinburgh Annual Register,* University of Tennessee Press, 1977; *Robert Southey: A Reference Guide,* G. K. Hall, 1977; *Robert Southey's Contributions to The Morning Post,* University of Alabama Press, 1982. Contributor to learned journals.

WORK IN PROGRESS: A chapter on *The Monthly Magazine* in *British Literary Magazines,* for Greenwood Press.

* * *

CUTTER, Robert Arthur 1930-

PERSONAL: Born July 4, 1930, in New York, N.Y.; son of Arthur J. and Letitia A. (Pray) Cutter. *Education:* St. John's University, B.A., 1952; graduate study at New York University, 1956-58, and New School for Social Research, 1969. *Home and office:* 340 Old Battery Rd., Bridgeport, Conn. 06605.

CAREER: Weider Publications, Jersey City, N.J., associate editor, 1952-54; St. John's University, Brooklyn, N.Y., assistant to director of public relations, 1954-56; U.S. Rubber Co., New York City, public relations manager, 1956-60; D'Arcy Advertising Co., New York City, public relations account executive, 1960-64; General Dynamics Corp., New York City, public relations executive, 1964-68; Hudson River Valley Commission, Tarrytown, N.Y., director of public relations and publications, 1968-69; public relations consultant to business and industry, 1970-75; public relations manager, Renault U.S.A., Inc., 1975-76; communications manager, General Electric Co., 1977-82. Free-lance writer.

MEMBER: International Motor Press Association (vice-president, 1972; member of board of directors, 1970-71, 1973-74), Federation Internationale des Associations de Journalistes de l'Automobile, American Auto Racing Writers and Broadcasters Association, American Aviation Historical Society, Society of World War One Aero Historians, U.S. Naval Institute,

New-York Historical Society (life member), New York State Historical Association (life member).

WRITINGS: (Editor and contributor) *Sherlockian Studies,* privately printed, 1948; *The Rocky Marciano Story,* William Allen Publishing, 1954; (with Robert Fendell) *Encyclopedia of Auto Racing Greats,* Prentice-Hall, 1973; *The New Guide to Motorcycling,* Arco, 1974; *The Model Car Handbook,* TAB Books, 1979. Also contributor to *True's Baseball Yearbook,* and to *True's Boxing Yearbook.* Author of "The Steering Column" in *Long Island Sunday Press,* 1958-79, and in *Business Journals,* 1981-82; author of "Motosports" in *Saga,* 1972-77. Contributor of more than one hundred articles to sports and men's magazines, including *Saga, Baseball Illustrated, Sport, Americana, Competition Car,* and *Impact.* Editor of *Redman* (of St. John's University), 1954-56; associate editor of *U.S.* (of U.S. Rubber Co.), 1956-60, and of *Dynamis* (of General Dynamics Corp.), 1964; U.S. editor of *Competition Car International,* 1973-75; automotive editor of *Saga,* 1973-79.

WORK IN PROGRESS: Two books, tentatively entitled *Fort Jefferson,* about the south-of-Florida National Historic Site, and *The Islands Called Wake.*

SIDELIGHTS: Robert Arthur Cutter told *CA:* "While much of my work seems to be about 'things'—machines like airplanes and automobiles, technologies like microelectronics, etc.—I spend a lot of effort in trying to relate them to people. This keeps the work from being just of interest to specialists. In fact, that is why my range of interests is so catholic. I like writing about different things and relating one to another. It makes all my work more interesting and better." *Avocational interests:* Collecting (books, political memorabilia, scale model cars, stamps), travel (has been to Europe, the Caribbean, and England), cars, motion pictures, sports, aviation, ships and naval matters, history, biography.

D

DANA, Barbara 1940-

PERSONAL: Born December 28, 1940, in New York, N.Y.; daughter of Richard (a writer and actor) and Mildred (an actress; maiden name, Ferry) Dana; married Alan Arkin (an actor), June 16, 1964; children: Anthony, Matthew, Adam. *Education:* Quintano's School for Young Professionals, high school diploma.

CAREER: Stage and television actress; writer. Broadway appearances include roles in "Who's Afraid of Virginia Woolf?," "Where's Daddy?," and "Enter Laughing"; on television has appeared in "Daughter of the Mind," an original movie for television, "As the World Turns," "New York Television Theatre," "N.E.T. Playhouse," and over 100 network shows; films include "The In-Laws," "P.J.," "Fire Sale," and "Popi."

WRITINGS: Spencer and His Friends (juvenile), Atheneum, 1966; *Rutgers and the Water-Snouts* (juvenile), Harper, 1969; *Crazy Eights* (young adult), Harper, 1978; "Chu Chu and the Philly Flash" (screenplay), Twentieth Century-Fox, 1981; *Zucchini* (juvenile), Harper, 1982.

WORK IN PROGRESS: A young adult book on Joan of Arc; a screenplay.

* * *

DANCE, Stanley (Frank) 1910-

PERSONAL: Born September 15, 1910, in Braintree, England; son of Frank Albert (in tobacco trade) and Violet Mary (Shead) Dance; married Helen Oakley, January 30, 1947; children: Teresa Mary Violet, Rupert Stanley Frank, Francis John Edward, Cynthia Maria Paula. *Education:* Attended Framlingham College, 1925-28. *Religion:* Roman Catholic. *Home:* 1745 Bittersweet Hill, Vista, Calif. 92083.

CAREER: F. A. Dance Ltd. (wholesale tobacconists), Braintree, England, director, 1928-58; currently free-lance writer specializing in jazz. Member of board of trustees, New York Jazz Museum, 1972-74; director, New York Jazz Repertory Company, 1974-75. *Military service:* Royal Observer Corps, 1935-45. *Member:* National Academy of Recording Arts and Sciences. *Awards, honors:* Grammy Award for best liner notes, National Academy of Recording Arts and Sciences, 1963, for "The Ellington Era."

WRITINGS: (Editor) *The Jazz Era,* MacGibbon & Kee, 1961; *The World of Duke Ellington,* Scribner, 1970; (with Dicky Wells) *The Night People,* Crescendo, 1971; *The World of Swing,* Scribner, 1974; *The World of Earl Hines,* Scribner, 1977; (with Mercer Ellington) *Duke Ellington in Person,* Houghton, 1978; *The World of Count Basie,* Scribner, 1980. Author of liner notes for recording "The Ellington Era"; also author of narratives for CBS television special, "Ailey Celebrates Ellington," and for New York Jazz Repertory Co. production on Louis Armstrong, both 1974. Regular columnist for *Jazz Times.*

WORK IN PROGRESS: Clap Hands, Here Comes Charlie, with Charlie Barnet; *Jazz Jungle,* an anthology.

SIDELIGHTS: Stanley Dance told *CA:* "Interest in medieval history has only been pushed into the background by the necessity to make a living. My interest in jazz continues, however, especially in documenting the first fifty years of its history." Editions of Dance's books have appeared in France, Sweden, Germany, and Argentina.

* * *

DANIELS, Roger 1927-

PERSONAL: Born December 1, 1927, in New York, N.Y.; son of George Roger (an author) and Eleanor (Lustig) Daniels; married Judith Marcia Mandel, October 2, 1960; children: Richard John, Sarah Elizabeth. *Education:* University of Houston, B.A., 1957; University of California, Los Angeles, M.A., 1958, Ph.D., 1961. *Office:* Department of History, State University of New York College at Fredonia, Fredonia, N.Y.

CAREER: Wisconsin State College and Institute of Technology, Platteville (now University of Wisconsin—Platteville), assistant professor, 1961-62, associate professor of history, 1962-63; University of California, Los Angeles, assistant professor of history, 1963-68; University of Wyoming, Laramie, associate professor, 1968-71, professor of history, 1971; State University of New York College at Fredonia, professor of history, 1971—. *Military service:* U.S. Army, 1952-54; became sergeant. *Member:* American Historical Association, Economic History Association, Organization of American Historians, American Association of University Professors.

WRITINGS: The Politics of Prejudice: The Anti-Japanese Movement in California and the Struggle for Japanese Exclusion, University of California Press, 1962, 2nd edition, 1977; (with Harry H. L. Kitano) *American Racism: Exploration of the Nature of Prejudice,* Prentice-Hall, 1969.

Concentration Camps USA: Japanese Americans and World War II, Holt, 1971; *The Bonus March: An Episode of the Great Depression*, Greenwood Press, 1971; (compiler with Spencer C. Olin, Jr.) *Racism in California: A Reader in the History of Oppression*, Macmillan, 1972; *The Decision to Relocate the Japanese Americans*, Harper, 1975; (editor) *Three Short Works on Japanese Americans*, Arno, 1978; *Anti-Chinese Violence in North America: An Original Anthology*, Arno, 1979; (editor) *Citizen 13660*, Arno, 1979; (editor) *Reports of the Royal Commission on Chinese Immigration*, Arno, 1979; (editor) *Two Monographs on Japanese Canadians*, Arno, 1979. Contributor of articles to history journals.†

* * *

DAS, Manmath Nath 1926-

PERSONAL: Born January 5, 1926, in Balasore, India; son of Madhu Sudan and Kadambini (Samal) Das; married, 1944; wife's name, Rajasri; children: Sanghamitra (daughter), Siddhartha (son). *Education:* Ravenshaw College, B.A. (with honors), 1946; Allahabad University, M.A., 1948; University of London, Ph.D., 1956. *Residence:* Sankhari, District Balasore, Orissa, India. *Office:* Department of History, Utkal University, Bhubaneswar, Orissa, India.

CAREER: F. M. College, Balasore, India, lecturer, 1948-53; S.C.S. College, Puri, India, lecturer, 1953-54; Ravenshaw College, Cuttack, India, reader, 1957-59; University of London, School of Oriental and African Studies, London, England, research associate, 1960-61; Utkal University, Bhubaneswar, Orissa, India, professor of history and head of department, 1961—. Government of India, member of advisory board for archaeology. Member of Indian History Congress, Indian Council of World Affairs, and of advisory council of Institute of Historical Studies, Calcutta.

WRITINGS: Glimpses of Kalinga History, Century (Calcutta), 1949; *The Substance behind India's New Constitution*, Orissa (Balasore, India), 1951; *Economic and Social Development of Modern India, 1848-56*, K. L. Mukhopadhyay, 1959; *Political Philosophy of Jawaharlal Nehru*, Day, 1961; *India under Morley and Minto*, Allen & Unwin, 1964; *Keep the Story Secret*, Vidyapuri, 1968; *Social, Economic, and Cultural History of India*, Macmillan, 1971; *Indian National Congress versus the British*, Ajanta International, 1977. Contributor of research papers to journals.

* * *

DAVIES, Evelyn 1924-

PERSONAL: Born April 2, 1924, in Brockenhurst, Hampshire, England; daughter of George William Stanley (a shoemaker) and Ethel Jane (James) Brown; married David John Davies (a publican; died, 1972); children: Claire Evelyn (Mrs. Jonathan Douglas Blake Tagart), Robert John. *Education:* Attended private and secondary schools in Brockenhurst. *Religion:* Church of England. *Home:* 2 Saxonford Rd., Friars Cliff, Christchurch BH2 34ES, England.

CAREER: Writer. Former landlady at Haven House Inn, Christchurch, England.

WRITINGS—All for young people; all published by Hamish Hamilton: *Little Bear's Feather*, 1973; *Run for Home*, 1974; *Joseph's Bear*, 1975; *Little Bear the Brave*, 1976; *The Little Foxes*, 1977; *Sailor Bill*, 1978; *Little Bear's Journey*, 1979; *The Big Old Horse*, 1979; *Cam*, 1980.

SIDELIGHTS: Evelyn Davies commented: "I have always had a great interest in the American Indian and American pioneering days. One of my earliest memories is of standing on a chair to recite 'Hiawatha' as a small child, which is perhaps where my interest first started. And in my stories I like to portray the Indians as having similar feelings of children the world over and to show they were not the 'bad men' films and television would have us believe." *Little Bear's Feather*, *Joseph's Bear*, and *Little Bear the Brave* have been translated into German.

* * *

DAVIS, Kingsley 1908-

PERSONAL: Born August 20, 1908, in Tuxedo, Tex.; son of Joseph Dyer (a physician) and Winifred (Kingsley) Davis; children: Jo Ann (Mrs. Charles Daily), Jefferson K., Laura Isabelle. *Education:* University of Texas, A.B., 1930, M.A., 1932; Harvard University, M.A., 1933, Ph.D., 1936. *Home:* 735 Vernal Way, Redwood City, Calif. 94062. *Office:* University of California, 2234 Piedmont Ave., Berkeley, Calif. 94520.

CAREER: Smith College, Northampton, Mass., instructor in sociology, 1934-36; Clark University, Worcester, Mass., assistant professor of sociology, 1936-37; Pennsylvania State University, University Park, associate professor of sociology and chairman of department, 1937-42; Princeton University, Princeton, N.J., associate professor of anthropology and sociology, 1942-48; Columbia University, New York, N.Y., director of Bureau of Applied Social Research, 1949-55, professor of sociology, 1952-55; University of California, Berkeley, professor of sociology, 1955-71, Ford Professor of Sociology and Comparative Studies, 1971-77, director of international population and urban research, 1957-77, chairman of department, 1961-63. Distinguished Professor of Sociology, University of Southern California, Los Angeles, beginning 1977. Chairman, visiting committee of social scientists to Africa, Carnegie Foundation, 1951-52; has conducted research in India, Europe and Latin America. Vice-president of Population Reference Bureau, 1952-55, trustee, 1952-75; U.S. representative, United Nations Population Commission, 1954-61. Member of National Committee on Marriage and Divorce Law, American Bar Association, 1950-53, U.S. Ad Hoc Committee on the International Biological Program, 1963-64, committee on the sonic boom, American Academy of Arts and Sciences, 1964-65, and Governor's Population Study Commission, State of California, 1966-67; Behavioral Science Division, National Research Council, member, 1963—, chairman, 1966-68. Consultant for population studies, Conservation Foundation, 1951-54; member of Advisory Council on Science and Technology and chairman of panel on population, State of California, 1970-71; U.S. Bureau of the Census, advisory committee on population, member, 1973-76, chairman, 1975-76.

MEMBER: World Academy of Art and Science, International Union for the Scientific Study of Population, American Sociological Association (president, 1959), Sociological Research Association (president, 1960), Population Association of America (president, 1962-63), American Association for the Advancement of Science (fellow; vice-president, 1963; chairman of section K, 1963, and 1980), American Academy of Arts and Sciences, American Statistical Association (fellow; liason member of council, 1968-69), American Philosophical Society, National Academy of Sciences (council member, 1970-73), Inter-American Statistical Institute (constituent member), American Eugenics Society (director, 1953-55), American Association of University Professors (council member, 1962-64), Regional Science Association. *Awards, honors:* Post-doctoral fellowship, Social Science Research Council, 1940-41; felowship Center for Advanced Study in the Behavioral Sciences,

1956-57; senior postdoctoral fellow, National Science Foundation, 1964-65.

WRITINGS: Youth in the Depression, University of Chicago Press, 1935; (editor) *World Population in Transition,* American Academy of Political and Social Science, 1945; (with Ana Casis) *Urbanization in Latin America,* Milbank Memorial Fund, 1946; *Human Society,* Macmillan, 1949, reprinted, 1967; (editor with Marion J. Levy, Jr. and Harry C. Bredeneuer) *Modern American Society,* Rinehart, 1949; (with Julius Issac) *People on the Move,* UNESCO, 1950; *Population of India and Pakistan,* Princeton University Press, 1951; (editor) *A Crowding Hemisphere: Population Change in the Americas,* American Academy of Political and Social Science, 1958; (with others) *The World's Metropolitan Areas,* University of California Press, 1959.

(With Judith Blake and J. Myone Stycos) *Family Structure in Jamaica,* Free Press of Glencoe, 1961; (with Roy Turner, Richard L. Park, and Catherine Bauer Wurster) *India's Urban Future,* University of California Press, 1962; (with Eleanor Langlois) *The Future Demographic Growth of the San Francisco Bay Area,* University of California Press, 1963; *World Urbanization, 1950-70,* Institute of International Studies, University of California, Volume I: *Basic Data for Cities, Countries, and Regions,* 1969, Volume II: *Analysis of Trends, Relationships, and Development,* 1972; (editor with Frederick Styles) *California's Twenty Million: Research Contributions to Population Policy,* Institute of International Studies, University of California, 1971; (compiler and author of introduction) *Cities: Their Origin, Growth, and Human Impact; Readings from Scientific American,* W. H. Freeman, 1973.

Also author of population studies and sociology papers. Member of senior editorial board, *New Encyclopedia of the Social Sciences,* 1962-68; member of board of editors for atlas published by Hammond, 1971—. Contributor to professional journals. Member of editorial board, *Proceedings of the National Academy of Sciences,* 1972—. Associate editor, *Journal of Legal and Political Sociology,* 1942-44; American member, board of editors, *Current Sociology,* 1953-63; member, international advisory board, *Population Review,* 1957-70; member, editorial board, *Economic Development and Cultural Change,* 1958, and *International Journal of Comparative Sociology,* 1960—.

SIDELIGHTS: Kingsley Davis told *CA:* "My interest lies in the comparative study of population structure and change, urbanization, marriage and the family, in countries around the world. I have travelled extensively in all continents, particularly Latin America, Africa, and South Asia. My work is primarily concerned with the causes and consequences of population change. It is thus theoretical and analytical rather than descriptive or applied." Davis speaks Spanish and French and has some fluency in Russian, Portuguese, and German.

BIOGRAPHICAL/CRITICAL SOURCES: American Sociological Review, Volume XVIII, August, 1953; Charles P. and Zona K. Loomis, *Modern Social Theories: Selected American Writers,* Van Nostrand, 2nd edition, 1965.

* * *

DAVIS, William C(harles) 1946-

PERSONAL: Born September 28, 1946, in Kansas City, Mo.; son of Eual Edward (a salesman) and Martha (an accountant; maiden name, Joan) Davis; married Pamela S. McIntyre, July 22, 1969 (divorced); children: M. Jefferson, Rebecca M. *Education:* California State College, Sonoma, A.B., 1968, M.A., 1969. *Politics:* Democrat. *Home and office:* 240 Gettysburg Rd., Mechanicsburg, Pa.

CAREER: Historical Times, Inc., Harrisburg, Pa., magazines editor, 1969-82; writer. *Member:* Manuscript Society, Southern Historical Association. *Awards, honors: Breckinridge: Statesman, Soldier, Symbol* received Jules F. Landry Award from Louisiana State University Press, 1973, for the best book on Southern history, literature, and biography, and the Jefferson Davis Award from Museum of the Confederacy and the Confederate Memorial Literary Society, 1974, for the best book on Confederate history; Pulitzer Prize nomination, 1977, for *Battle at Bull Run;* Fletcher Pratt Award, 1977; honorary doctor of humane letters, Lincoln Memorial University, 1977.

WRITINGS—Published by Doubleday, except as indicated: (Author of introduction) E. Porter Thompson, *History of the Orphan Brigade,* Morningside Press, 1973; *Breckinridge: Statesman, Soldier, Symbol,* Louisiana State University Press, 1974; *The Battle of New Market,* 1975; *Duel between the First Ironclads,* 1975; *Battle at Bull Run,* 1977; *The Orphan Brigade: The Kentucky Confederates Who Couldn't Go Home,* 1980; (editor) *Shadows of the Storm,* 1981; *Deep Waters of the Proud,* 1982; (editor) *The Guns of '62,* 1982; (editor) *The Embattled Confederacy,* 1982. Editor, *American History Illustrated,* 1972-80, and *Civil War Times,* 1972—.

WORK IN PROGRESS: Completion of a three-volume general narrative of the Civil War; a biography of Jefferson Davis.

SIDELIGHTS: William C. Davis's *The Orphan Brigade: The Kentucky Confederates Who Couldn't Go Home* chronicles the Civil War activities of those Kentucky soldiers who, unlike most of their fellow Kentuckyians, elected to side with the Confederacy. Robert Kirsch of the *Los Angeles Times* notes, "William C. Davis's intimate account captures the pride and loyalty of the regiments, brings individuals alive, draws heavily on the records and narratives left by the brigade under encouragement by Capt. Ed Porter Thompson, an amateur historian." Rory Quirk writes in the *Washington Post* that "the battles are rich with detail," yet criticizes the book's lack of maps: "This absence of detailed maps is a regrettable omission in an otherwise informative, comprehensive and colorful account."

BIOGRAPHICAL/CRITICAL SOURCES: Los Angeles Times, April 18, 1980; *Washington Post,* May 30, 1980.

* * *

DAY, A(rthur) Grove 1904-

PERSONAL: Born April 29, 1904, in Philadelphia, Pa.; son of Arthur Sinclair (a salesman) and Clara Tomlinson (Hogeland) Day; married Virginia T. Molina (a college instructor), July 2, 1928. *Education:* Stanford University, A.B., 1926, M.A., 1942, Ph.D., 1944. *Home:* 1434 Punahou St., Apt. 1223, Honolulu, Hawaii 96822. *Agent:* Paul R. Reynolds, Inc., 12 East 41st St., New York, N.Y. 10017.

CAREER: Columbia University, New York, N.Y., research assistant at Institute of Educational Research, 1926-27; freelance writer, 1927-30; Stanford University, Stanford, Calif., research assistant, 1932-36, assistant director of engineering, science, and management war training, 1943-44; University of Hawaii, Honolulu, assistant professor, 1944-46, associate professor, 1946-50, professor, 1950-61, senior professor of English, 1961-69, professor emeritus, 1969—, chairman of department, 1948-53. Proprietor, White Knight Press (private press), 1940—. Fulbright senior research fellow in Australia, 1955; Smith-Mundt Visiting Professor of American Studies,

University of Barcelona, 1957-58; Fulbright visiting professor of American studies, University of Madrid, 1961-62. Chairman of publications committee, Tenth Pacific Science Congress, 1977. Occasional lecturer aboard cruise ships. *Member:* Modern Language Association of America, Phi Beta Kappa, Phi Kappa Phi, Elks, Adventurers' Club of Honolulu. *Awards, honors:* Hawaii State Award for Literature, 1980.

WRITINGS: *Tommy Dane of Sonora* (juvenile fiction), Century, 1929; (with Fred J. Buenzle) *Bluejacket: An Autobiography,* Norton, 1939; *Coronado's Quest: The Discovery of the Southwestern States,* University of California Press, 1940, revised edition, 1982; (with Ralph S. Kuykendall) *Hawaii: A History,* Prentice-Hall, 1948, revised edition, 1978; *The Sky Clears: Poetry of the American Indians,* Macmillan, 1951, new edition, 1964; *Hawaii and Its People,* Duell, Sloan & Pearce, 1955, revised edition, 1969; (with James A. Michener) *Rascals in Paradise,* Random House, 1957; *Hawaii, Fiftieth Star,* Duell, Sloan & Pearce, 1960, 2nd edition, Meredith, 1969; *The Story of Australia,* Random House, 1960; *James A. Michener,* Twayne, 1964, revised edition, 1977; *They Peopled the Pacific,* Duell, Sloan & Pearce, 1964; *Louis Becke,* Twayne, 1966; *Explorers of the Pacific,* Duell, Sloan & Pearce, 1966; *Coronado and the Discovery of the Southwest,* Meredith, 1967; *Pirates of the Pacific,* Meredith, 1968; *Adventures of the Pacific,* with foreword by James A. Michener, Meredith, 1969.

Jack London in the South Seas, Four Winds Press, 1971; *Pacific Islands Literature: One Hundred Basic Books,* University Press of Hawaii, 1971; (with Edgar C. Knowlton, Jr.) *V. Blasco Ibanez,* Twayne, 1972; *What Did I Do Right?* (auto-bibliography), privately printed, 1974; *Robert D. Fitzgerald,* Twayne, 1974; *Kamehameha, First King of Hawaii,* edited by Dorothy Hazama, Hogarth Press, 1974; *Eleanor Dark,* Twayne, 1976; *Books about Hawaii: Fifty Basic Authors,* University Press of Hawaii, 1977; *Captain Cook and Hawaii,* Hogarth Press, 1977; (with Amos P. Leib) *Hawaiian Legends in English: An Annotated Bibliography,* University Press of Hawaii, 1979; *Modern Australian Prose, 1901-1975: A Guide to Information Sources,* Gale, 1980.

Editor: *Fernando Cortes: Despatches from Mexico* (Spanish textbook), American Book Co., 1935; (with Carl Stroven) *The Spell of the Pacific: An Anthology of Its Literature,* Macmillan, 1949; (with William F. Bauer) *The Greatest American Short Stories,* McGraw, 1953, published as *The Greatest American Short Stories: Twenty Classics of Our Heritage,* 1970; (with Stroven) *A Hawaiian Reader,* with introduction by James A. Michener, Appleton, 1959; (with Stroven) *Best South Sea Stories,* Appleton, 1964; Jack London, *Stories of Hawaii,* Appleton, 1965; *Mark Twain's Letters from Hawaii,* Appleton, 1966; (with Stroven) *True Tales of the South Seas,* Appleton, 1966; Louis Becke, *South Sea Supercargo,* University Press of Hawaii, 1967; (with Stroven) *The Spell of Hawaii,* Meredith, 1968; (and author of introduction) *Melville's South Seas: An Anthology,* Hawthorn, 1970; *The Art of Narration: The Novella,* McGraw, 1971; *The Art of Narration: The Short Story,* McGraw, 1971; (and author of introduction) Robert L. Stevenson, *Travels in Hawaii,* University Press of Hawaii, 1973.

Contributor to *Encyclopedia of Poetry and Poetics,* 1965, and *Encyclopaedia Britannica,* 1968; also contributor of short stories and articles to national magazines. Editor-in-chief, *Pacific Science,* 1947-48.

SIDELIGHTS: A. Grove Day told *CA*: "I do not remember any time when I did not wish to publish books. [I am] especially interested in history and biography of Hawaii and Pacific region; James A. Michener has termed me 'the world's foremost authority on Pacific literature.' [I] retired from [the] university in 1969 but still write every morning." *Avocational interests:* Travel, swimming.

BIOGRAPHICAL/CRITICAL SOURCES: *New Statesman,* June 23, 1967.

*   *   *

DAY, Douglas (Turner III) 1932-

PERSONAL: Born May 1, 1932, in Colon, Republic of Panama; son of Douglas Turner, Jr. (an officer in the U.S. Navy) and Bess (Turner) Day; married Mary Hill Noble, July 3, 1954; children: Douglas T. IV, Ian Christopher, Emily Forsyth. *Education:* University of Virginia, B.A., 1954, M.A., 1959, Ph.D., 1962. *Politics:* Democrat. *Religion:* Episcopal. *Home:* 1616 King Mountain Rd., Charlottesville, Va. 22901. *Agent:* Peter Matson, Harold Matson Co., Inc., 22 East 40th St., New York, N.Y. 10016. *Office:* Department of English, University of Virginia, Charlottesville, Va. 22901.

CAREER: Washington and Lee University, Lexington, Va., instructor in English, 1960-62; University of Virginia, Charlottesville, 1962—, began as assistant professor, became professor of English, Commonwealth Professor of English, 1977—. Fulbright visiting professor, University of Zaragoza, 1965-66; Center for Advanced Research fellow, 1969-70 and 1976-77. *Military service:* U.S. Marine Corps, naval aviator, 1954-57; became first lieutenant. *Member:* Modern Language Association of America, Phi Beta Kappa. *Awards, honors:* Fellowships or grants from Folger Shakespeare Library, American Philosophical Society, Guggenheim Foundation, and American Council of Learned Societies; National Book Award, 1974, for *Malcolm Lowry: A Biography*; Rosenthal Fiction Award, American Academy of Arts and Letters, 1978.

WRITINGS: *Swifter Than Reason: The Poetry and Criticism of Robert Graves,* University of North Carolina Press, 1963; *The Stranger: A Critical Commentary,* American Research Development Corp., 1965; (editor with Margaret Lowry) Malcolm Lowry, *Dark as the Grave Wherein My Friend Is Laid,* New American Library, 1968; (editor) *Flags in the Dust,* Random House, 1973; *Malcolm Lowry: A Biography,* Oxford University Press, 1973; *Journey of the Wolf* (novel), Atheneum, 1977. Contributor of articles to scholarly journals. Former editor of *Shenandoah.*

SIDELIGHTS: After receiving the National Book Award in 1974 for his biography of Malcolm Lowry and publishing four other academic works, Douglas Day wrote his first novel, *Journey of the Wolf,* in 1977. This story takes place in Spain in 1973 when Sebastian Rosales returns to his home in Andalucia after an absence of thirty-four years. (He had left home as a teenager to fight as a sergeant in the Spanish Civil War.) Rosales finds great changes have taken place over the years. Tourism has become the all-important, major industry of this part of Spain.

"In *Journey of the Wolf,* Douglas Day seems to be saying that Spain has 'progressed' from the tragedy of poverty to the tragedy of tourism," Anatole Broyard comments in the *New York Times.* "Tourism, as he sees it, brings about a poverty of the spirit. Instead of starving for food or the ordinary comforts of life, the Spanish peasant or worker now starves for meaning. He has put his life into his new refrigerator and substituted for it a counterfeit image of the television set. According to Mr. Day, technology is the new dictator of Spain and each tourist is its traveling salesman. The remaining function of the Spaniard is to serve up his past to foreigners as a folk festival."

Richard Freedman of the *New York Times Book Review* writes: "Narrated in lean, efficient prose, with unobtrusive flashbacks to the war, this first novel is a taut adventure story of an exile's return to danger, disillusionment and death. . . . Day has done his research well." However, *Newsweek*'s Mark Stevens believes that "Day sprinkles his text with too many Spanish words—an unimaginative way to add local color—and he sets up too many straw men, including a foolish American who shakes Rosales's hand for fighting in the last 'pure' war. But Rosales himself does not become a stock figure and Day . . . writes in a simple, understated manner well suited to his hero's stoicism."

BIOGRAPHICAL/CRITICAL SOURCES: *New York Times Book Review*, November 4, 1973, November 29, 1973, December 2, 1972, December 13, 1973, March 27, 1977; *New York Times*, November 8, 1973, February 18, 1977; *Times Literary Supplement*, April 19, 1974; *Newsweek*, February 14, 1977; *Christian Science Monitor*, April 13, 1977.

* * *

DEAKIN, James 1929-

PERSONAL: Born December 3, 1929, in St. Louis, Mo.; son of Rogers (a surgeon) and Dorothy (Jeffrey) Deakin; married Doris Kanter (a free-lance writer), April 14, 1956; children: David Andrew. *Education:* Washington University, St. Louis, Mo., B.A., 1951, graduate study, 1951-52. *Politics:* Independent. *Home:* 6406 Whittier Ct., Bethesda, Md. 20817. *Office:* George Washington University, Washington, D.C. 20006.

CAREER: *St. Louis Post-Dispatch*, 1951-81, member of staff of Washington Bureau, Washington, D.C., 1954-81, White House correspondent, 1965-81; George Washington University, Washington, D.C., adjunct associate professor of journalism and faculty associate for political communications, 1981—. *Member:* White House Correspondents' Association (president, 1974-75). *Awards, honors:* Distinguished Alumnus Citation, Washington University, 1973; Merriman Smith Award for White House reporting, 1977; Woodrow Wilson International Center for Scholars fellow, 1980-81; Markle Foundation grant, 1981.

WRITINGS: *The Lobbyist*, Public Affairs Press, 1966; *Lyndon Johnson's Credibility Gap*, Public Affairs Press, 1968; (coauthor) *Smiling through the Apocalypse*, L.B.J. School of Public Affairs, University of Texas at Austin, 1971; *The Presidency and the Press*, L.B.J. School of Public Affairs, University of Texas at Austin, 1977. Contributor to periodicals, including *New Republic*, *Esquire*, and *Washingtonian*.

* * *

DEANE, Norman
See CREASEY, John

* * *

de BLIJ, Harm J(an) 1935-

PERSONAL: Surname is pronounced *duh-Blay*; born October 9, 1935, in Schiedam, Netherlands; son of Hendrik and Nelly (Erwich) de Blij; married Katherine Powers (divorced, 1971); married Bonnie Doughty, 1977. *Education:* University of the Witwatersrand, B.Sc., 1955; Northwestern University, M.A., 1957, Ph.D., 1959. *Home:* 4850 Biltmore Dr., Coral Gables, Fla. *Office:* Department of Geography, University of Miami, Coral Gables, Fla. 33124.

CAREER: University of Natal, Pietermaritzburg, South Africa, lecturer in geology and geography, 1959-60; Michigan State University, East Lansing, assistant professor, 1961-63, associate professor, 1964-67, professor of geography, 1967-69, associate director of African Studies Center, 1964-69; University of Miami, Coral Gables, Fla., chairman of geography department, 1969-76, associate dean of College of Arts and Sciences, 1976-78, professor of geography, 1978—. Northwestern University, visiting lecturer, spring, 1959, visiting assistant professor, 1960-61, visiting associate professor, 1963-64; visiting professor of geography, Institute for Shipboard Education, University of Colorado, autumn, 1978, and University of Hawaii, autumn, 1979; Visiting Presidential Professor, Colorado School of Mines, 1981-82. Visiting geographical scientist, Association of American Geographers, 1967-70. Representative for Miami University to board of directors, Organization for Tropical Studies. Host of annual meeting of Southeastern Division of Association of American Geographers, 1971. Founder of Miami Geographical Society. Member, wine tasting panel, *Miami Herald*, 1980—. Consultant to Encyclopaedia Britannica Films, Inc., 1963-65, Bobbs-Merrill Reprint Series in Geography, 1966-72, and Encyclopaedia Britannica Educational Corp., 1980—; member of editorial advisory board, John Wiley & Sons, Inc. (publishers), 1968-72 and 1975-78, and Hamilton Publishing Co., 1972-75; member of editorial advisory board for cartography, Hammon, Inc. (publishers), 1974—; consultant on African maps and text, Atlas project, National Geographic Society, 1979-80. Sometime professional violinist.

MEMBER: Association of American Geographers (councillor, 1970-72; member of steering committee, Southeastern Division, 1970-73; secretary, 1972-75), National Council for Geographic Education (member of executive board, 1970-74), National Geographic Society, Royal African Society, American Geographical Society, African Studies Association, American Association of University Professors, Florida Society of Geographers, Society of Wine Educators, Phi Kappa Phi, Sigma Xi, Gamma Theta Upsilon.

AWARDS, HONORS: Recipient of grants from Ford Foundation, 1962 and 1966, Midwest Consortium for International Assistance, 1967, and Association of American Geographers, 1975; Presidential Scholar, University of Miami.

WRITINGS: *Africa South*, Northwestern University Press, 1962; (contributor) O. Williams and N. Hurvitz, editors, *Economic Framework of South Africa*, Shuter and Shooter (Pietermaritzburg, South Africa), 1962; *Subsaharan Africa*, Michigan State University Continuing Education Service, 1963; *Dar Es Salaam: A Study in Urban Geography*, Northwestern University Press, 1963; *A Geography of Subsaharan Africa*, Rand McNally, 1964; *Political Geography*, University of the Air, Michigan State University, 1965, *Systematic Political Geography*, Wiley, 1967, 3rd edition, with Martin Ira Glassner, 1981; *A Guide to Subsaharan Africa*, Michigan State University Continuing Education Service, 1968; *Mombasa: An African City*, Northwestern University Press, 1968; (contributor) J. Kritzeck and W. H. Lewis, editors, *Islam in Africa*, Van Nostrand, 1969.

Geography: Regions and Concepts, Wiley, 1971, 3rd edition, 1981; *Instructor's Manual to Geography: Regions and Concepts*, Wiley, 1971; *A Glossary and Study Guide to Geography*, Wiley, 1971; *Essentials of Geography*, Wiley, 1973; *Man Shapes the Earth*, Hamilton Publishing, 1974; (contributor) C. G. Knight and J. L. Newman, editors, *Contemporary Africa*, Prentice-Hall, 1976; (contributor) *CBS News Almanac*, Hammond, 1977; (with Alan C. G. Best) *African Survey*, Wiley, 1977; (with David Greenland) *The Earth in Profile: A Physical Geography*, Canfield Press, 1977; *Human Geography: Culture, Society, and Space*, Wiley, 1977, 2nd edition, 1982; (contributor) P. E. James and G. J. Martin, editors, *The Association of American*

Geographers: The First Seventy-five Years, Association of American Geographers, 1979.

The Earth: A Topical Geography, Wiley, 1980; *Geography of Viticulture*, Miami Geographical Society, 1981; (editor, with Esmond Bradley Martin, and contributor) *African Perspectives: An Exchange of Essays on the Economic Geography of Nine African States*, Metheun, 1981.

Also author of television series, "Subsaharan Africa," for Michigan State University Continuing Education Service, 1963, and "Political Geography," for University of the Air, Michigan State University, 1964. Contributor to *Encyclopaedia Britannica*, 1974; also contributor to *Proceedings of the Second University of Manitoba Conference on Commonwealth Affairs*, 1962. Contributor of articles and reviews to professional journals, including *Economic Geography, Canadian Journal of African Studies, Professional Geographer, South African Journal of Science*, and *Journal of Geography*; contributor of articles to *Miami News* and *Museum*. Editor, *Journal of Geography*, 1970-74; member of editorial board, *Comparative Urban Research*, 1972-74; member of editorial committee, *Southeastern Geographer*, 1980—.

WORK IN PROGRESS: *Wines and Wine Regions of the Southern Hemisphere; Viticulture and Viniculture in Japan; Geographic Aspects of Oenology.*

SIDELIGHTS: Harm J. de Blij spent ten years in Africa and has continued research there at intervals since leaving. He visited the Soviet Union in 1964 and the People's Republic of China in 1981. De Blij is fluent in Afrikaans, Dutch, and German. A generalist by temperament, he is also interested in the arts.

* * *

DELTON, Judy 1931-

PERSONAL: Born May 6, 1931, in St. Paul, Minn.; daughter of A. F. (a plant engineer) and Alice (Walsdorf) Jaschke; married Jeff J. Delton (a school psychologist), June 14, 1958; children: Julie, Jina, Jennifer, Jamie. *Education:* Attended School of Associated Arts, 1950, and College of St. Catherine, 1954-57. *Home:* 1694 Van Buren, St. Paul, Minn. 55104.

CAREER: Elementary school teacher in parochial schools of St. Paul, Minn., 1957-64; free-lance writer. Teacher of writing at University of Minnesota, Metropolitan State University, and other local colleges and universities, beginning 1972. *Member:* Authors Guild of America. *Awards, honors: Two Good Friends* was named an American Library Association Notable Book, 1975.

WRITINGS: *Two Good Friends* (Junior Literary Guild selection), Crown, 1974; *Rabbit Finds a Way*, Crown, 1975; *Two Is Company*, Crown, 1976; *Three Friends Find Spring* (Junior Literary Guild selection), Crown, 1977; *Penny Wise Fun Foolish*, Crown, 1977; *My Mom Hates Me in January*, Albert Whitman, 1977; *It Happened on Thursday*, Albert Whitman, 1978; *Brimhall Comes to Stay*, Lothrop, 1978; *Brimhall Turns to Magic* (Junior Literary Guild selection), Lothrop, 1979; *On a Picnic*, Doubleday, 1979; *The New Girl at School*, Dutton, 1979; *Rabbit's New Carpet*, Parents Magazine Press, 1979; *The Best Mom in the World*, Albert Whitman, 1979; *Kitty in the Middle*, Houghton, 1979.

Kitty in the Summer, Houghton, 1980; *Lee Henry's Best Friend*, Albert Whitman, 1980; *My Mother Lost Her Job Today*, Albert Whitman, 1980; *Groundhog's Day at the Doctor*, Parents Magazine Press, 1981; *I Never Win*, Carolrhoda, 1981; *Blue Ribbon Friends*, Houghton, 1982; *A Walk on a Snowy Night*, Harper, 1982; *I'm Telling You Now*, Arthur Ray, Dutton, 1982; *The Goose Who Wrote a Book*, Carolrhoda, 1982; *Only Jody*, Houghton, 1982; *A Pet for Bear and Duck*, Albert Whitman, 1982.

Contributor of over two hundred essays, articles, poems, and short stories to popular magazines including *Wall Street Journal, Saturday Review, Humpty Dumpty, Instructor*, and *Highlights for Children*.

WORK IN PROGRESS: Three novels—one for adults and two for children.

SIDELIGHTS: A prolific writer, Judy Delton has published more than twenty-five books and over two hundred essays, articles, and short stories in just under ten years. She tells Kathryn Boardman of the *St. Paul Dispatch:* "I really resent it when people ask me when I am going to write a novel for adults. Children's fiction is a special field. In my opinion it is as important as any other kind of writing. I like to do it and my publishers think I am good at it."

Delton further explains her feelings on being an author to *CA:* "Someone once said that an author is fortunate, in that he gets to live his life twice, once in the doing and once in the telling. I find that to be true, since I am always reliving my life from some new aspect, often not knowing what is truth and what is illusion. After reliving my life in the 'Kitty' books (growing up Catholic in the 40s), I went on to do it again in an adult novel in progress. From there I encroached on my son's life in *Only Jody*, the story of an only boy in a family of four women. Right now I'm borrowing from my daughter's life, but some way or other, I am always in the book.

"I began writing in 1971 and since then have published twenty-five books. In the early years I wrote poetry, verse, articles and essays; then [I] branched out into children's books where I've stayed comfortably ever since. If I move into adult fiction it will not be because it 'comes after' juvenile literature, but because I get restless and want to try a new form.

"I have given up teaching but do lecture around the country at libraries, colleges, universities, and enjoy it tremendously since writing is basically a very solitary occupation."

BIOGRAPHICAL/CRITICAL SOURCES: *St. Paul Dispatch*, April 2, 1977; *St. Paul Pioneer Press*, May 31, 1981.

* * *

De MENTE, Boye 1928-

PERSONAL: Born November 12, 1928, in Redford, Mo.; son of Elza Lafayette and Ruby (Bounds) De Mente; married Margaret Warren, September 29, 1958; children: Dawn Rubi, Demetra (both daughters). *Education:* Studied at American Institute of Foreign Trade (now American Graduate School of International Management), BFT, 1953; Jochi University, Tokyo, Japan, B.S., 1956. *Residence:* Paradise Valley, Ariz.

CAREER: In military service with U.S. Navy, 1946-48, and U.S. Army Security Agency, 1948-52, became sergeant; worked in public relations for Japan Travel Bureau, Tokyo, 1953-54; editor in Tokyo, Japan, of *Kembun* (weekly newspaper), 1954-55, *Today's Japan* (cultural magazine), 1955-57, and *Importer* (trade journal), 1958-62; free-lance writer, 1962—. Member of board of directors, *Importer*, 1975—. Executive advisor, East Asia Publishing Co., 1975—. *Member:* Arizona Authors Association (founder and president, 1978—).

WRITINGS: *Japanese Manners and Ethics in Business*, East Asia Publishing, 1961, 2nd revised edition, Simpson-Doyle &

Co., 1975; *The Tourist and the Real Japan*, Tuttle, 1961, revised edition, 1966; *Bachelor's Japan*, Tuttle, 1962, revised edition, 1966; *How Business Is Done in Japan*, Simpson-Doyle & Co., 1963, revised edition published as *How to Do Business in Japan: A Guide for International Businessmen*, Center for International Business, 1972; *Oriental Secrets of Graceful Living*, Wilshire, 1963; *Once a Fool: From Tokyo to Alaska by Amphibious Jeep*, Simpson-Doyle & Co., 1964; *Bachelor's Hawaii*, Tuttle, 1964, revised edition, 1966; *Mizu Shobai: The Pleasure Girls and Fleshpots of Japan*, Medco Books, 1966; *Some Prefer Geisha: The Lively Art of Mistress-Keeping in Japan*, Wayward Press, 1966; *Faces of Japan: Twenty-Three Critical Essays*, Simpson-Doyle & Co., 1966; *Bachelor's Mexico*, Tuttle, 1967; (with Fred Thomas Perry) *The Japanese as Consumers: A General Description of Asia's First Mass Market*, Weatherhill/Walker, 1968; *Face-Reading for Fun and Profit*, Bachelor Books, 1968; *International Businessman's After-hours Guide to Japan*, East Asia Publishing, 1968, revised edition, Phoenix Books, 1975; *Girl-Watcher's Guide to the Far East*, Bachelor Books, 1969; *Aphrodisiac Recipes for Swingers*, Bachelor Books, 1969, revised edition published as *Cookbook for Lovers*, Phoenix Books, 1975.

Insiders' Guide to Phoenix, Scottsdale and Tucson, Phoenix Books, 1972, 4th edition, 1980; *Retiring in Arizona: Senior Citizen's Shangri La*, Phoenix Books, 1973, 4th edition, 1980; (with Mario De La Guente) *I Like You, Gringo—But!*, Phoenix Books, 1973; *Fifteen Ways to Kick the Smoking Habit*, Phoenix Books, 1974; *P's and Cues for Travelers in Japan*, Japan Publications, 1974; *Insiders' Guide to Rocky Point, Guaymas, Mazatalan and La Paz*, Phoenix Books, 1975; *Exotic Japan: The Land, the People, the Places, the Pleasures*, Phoenix Books, 1975; *Visitor's Guide to Arizona's Indian Reservations*, Phoenix Books, 1978.

Eros' Revenge: The 'Brave New World' of American Sex (novel), Phoenix Books, 1980; *The Japanese Way of Doing Business: The Psychology of Management in Japan*, Prentice-Hall, 1982; *How to Order Chinese Food*, Phoenix Books, 1982. Contributor to magazines in United States and Asia. Founding editor of *ASA Star* (Pacific), 1950-52.

WORK IN PROGRESS: A collection of short stories, *Hai-ior no Sekai* (title means "The Grey World"); a novel about a Japanese-American orphan growing up in Tokyo, *The Mixed-Blood*; an "A to Z introduction to Japan, from the abacus to Zen," *The Whole Japan Book*.

SIDELIGHTS: Boye De Mente told *CA*: "Having arrived in Japan shortly after the end of World War II [in 1948], studied the language and the people and thereafter serving as an interpreter, a go-between and a consultant, I have spent most of my adult life trying to help resolve the cross-cultural problems that inevitably occur when Americans and Japanese come together. My first two books were pioneer works on Japanese management and the unique way the Japanese do business, and for the first seven years I had the field entirely to myself. Now, more than twenty years later, and dozens of similar books on Japan by other authors, I am chagrined to note that American politicians and many American businessmen still do not know how to deal with the Japanese. I am now trying to reach the grassroots level of Americans through a basic educational type of book on Japan, along with a novel and a collection of short stories in which I attempt to delineate and explain the character and ambitions of the Japanese."

In 1957, De Mente and Australian adventurer Ben Carlin made a four month journey across the Pacific Ocean in an amphibious jeep called Half-Safe. De Mente recounted the adventure in *Once a Fool: From Tokyo to Alaska by Amphibious Jeep*.

DEMI
See HITZ, Demi

* * *

de MONTFORT, Guy
See JOHNSON, Donald McI(ntosh)

* * *

DENMAN, D(onald) R(obert) 1911-

PERSONAL: Born April 7, 1911, in London, England; son of Robert Martyn and Letitia Kate Denman; married Jessica Hope, 1941; children: two sons. *Education:* University of London, B.Sc., 1938, M.Sc., 1940, Ph.D., 1945. *Home:* Pembroke College, Cambridge University, 12 Chaucer Rd., Cambridge, England.

CAREER: Cambridge University, Cambridge, England, university lecturer, 1948-68, professor of land economy, 1968-78, head of department, 1962-78, fellow of Pembroke College, 1962-78. Adviser on development of land economy to the University of Science and Technology, Ghana, and the University of Nigeria, 1963—; member of governing board, Commonwealth Human Ecology Council, 1970—; member of National Commission of UNESCO, 1972—; advisor to the Iranian Government. *Wartime service:* Cumberland War Agricultural Executive Committee, deputy executive officer, 1939-46.

MEMBER: Istituto di Diritto Agrario Internazionale e Comparato (Florence; standing committee member, 1960—), Ghana Institution of Surveyors (honorary fellow), Royal Swedish Academy of Forestry and Agriculture (fellow), Royal Institution of Chartered Surveyors (fellow), Carlton Club, Farmer's Club. *Awards, honors:* M.A., Cambridge University, 1948; gold medal, Royal Institution of Chartered Surveyors, 1972; holder of Ivory Horn (Ofo) of Ozo Order of Nobility of Iboland (Nigeria); Distinguished Order of Homayoun (Iran).

WRITINGS: *Tenant-Right Valuation in History and Modern Practice*, Heffer, 1942; *Tenant-Right Valuation and Current Legislation: Being a Supplement to Tenant-Right Valuation in History and Modern Practice Dealing with the Relevant Provisions of the Agricultural Act, 1947, and the Agricultural Holdings Act, 1948*, Heffer, 1948; *First Footprints* (religious tales), S.P.C.K., 1949.

Estate Capital: The Contribution of Landownership to Agricultural Finance, foreword by the Duke of Northumberland, Verry, 1957; (with O.H.M. Sawyer and J.F.Q. Switzer) *Bibliography of Rural Land Economy and Landownership, 1900-1957: A Full List of Works Relating to the British Isles and Selected Works from the United States and Western Europe*, Department of Estate Management, Cambridge University, 1958; *Origins of Ownership: A Brief History of Land Ownership and Tenure in England from Earliest Times to the Modern Era*, Allen & Unwin, 1958; (with V. F. Stewart) *Farm Rents: A Comparison of Current and Past Farm Rents in England and Wales*, Allen & Unwin, 1959; *Land Ownership and Resources: A Course of Lectures Given at Cambridge in June, 1958*, Bury St. Edmund's Borough Council, c. 1959.

Land in the Market: A Fresh Look at Property, Land, and Prices, Institute of Economic Affairs (London), 1964; (with R. A. Roberts and H.J.F. Smith) *Commons and Village Greens: A Study in Land Use, Conservation, and Management Based on a National Survey of Commons in England and Wales, 1961-*

66, Leonard Hill, 1967; (contributor) Norman Macrae, *Homes for the People*, Economic Research Council, 1967.

(With Sylvio Prodano) *Land Use: An Introduction to Proprietary Land Use Analysis*, Verry, 1972; *The King's Vista: A Land Reform Which Has Changed the Face of Persia*, Geographical Publications, 1973; *Prospects of Cooperative Planning*, Geographical Publications, 1973; (editor) *Government and the Land, Volume XIII: Land Nationalization: A Way Out?*, Institute of Economic Affairs, 1974; *Land Economy: An Education and a Career*, Geographical Publications, 1975; *The Place of Property*, Geographical Publications, 1978.

Land in a Free Society, Centre of Policy Studies (London), 1980; *The Fountain Principle*, NEI (Rome), 1982. Author of monographs and research papers. Contributor to conference proceedings and to journals and newspapers in Britain and abroad.

AVOCATIONAL INTERESTS: Travel.

* * *

DENNIS-JONES, H(arold) 1915-
(Paul Hamilton, Dennis Hessing)

PERSONAL: Born December 2, 1915, in Mauritius; son of Harold Richard (a master mariner) and Helen Marjory (a piano teacher; maiden name, Small) Jones; married Kathleen Jean Nelson (a health visitor), March 18, 1953 (divorced, 1977); children: Esther Caroline, Helen Clare. *Education:* Attended Dulwich College; St. John's College, Oxford, M.A., 1938. *Politics:* None. *Religion:* None. *Residence:* Kent, England. *Office:* Tourplan Ltd., 14/38 Broadwater Down, Tunbridge Wells, Kent TN2 5NX, England.

CAREER: Kemsley Newspapers, London, England, member of news staff, 1945-48; free-lance journalist and photographer, 1948-53; senior classics master in various grammar schools in England, 1953-60; *Guide Kleber*, Paris, France, United Kingdom editorial representative, 1964-72; Tourplan Ltd. (copyright-handling agency and travel and editorial consultants), Tunbridge Wells, Kent, England, managing director, 1974—. Chairman of board of trustees, Children's Relief International, 1962-69. *Military service:* Served with Civil Defence in London, Royal Air Force, and Royal Artillery, 1939-45. *Member:* Society of Authors, Guild of Travel Writers.

WRITINGS: (Contributor of translations under pseudonym Dennis Hessing) Fred Marnau, editor, *New Roads*, Grey Walls Press, 1955; (under pseudonym Dennis Hessing; translator with Reginald Snell) Alois Jalkotzy, *School for Parents*, Galley Press, 1963; *Your Guide to the Dalmatian Coast (of Yugoslavia)*, International Publication Service, 1963; *Your Guide to Denmark*, International Publication Service, 1963; *Your Guide to Brittany (in France)*, Redman, 1964, International Publication Service, 1965; *Your Guide to Morocco*, International Publication Service, 1965; *Romania*, Horizon Press, 1969; *Bulgaria*, Horizon Press, 1969.

Israel, McGraw, 1970, 3rd edition, 1975; *Portugal*, Letts, 1974, 5th edition, 1981; *Costa Del Sol and Southern Spain*, Letts, 1974, 5th edition, 1981; *Majorca and the Balearic Islands*, Letts, 1974, 5th edition, 1981; *Costa Brava (of Spain)*, Letts, 1974, 5th edition, 1981; *Morocco & Tunisia*, Letts, 1974, 3rd edition, 1979; *Holland*, Letts, 1975, 5th edition, 1981; *Denmark*, Letts, 1975, 5th edition, 1981; *France*, Letts, 1975, 5th edition, 1981; *Northern Spain*, Letts, 1975, 5th edition, 1981; *Amsterdam*, Letts, 1977, 3rd edition, 1981; *Letts Speak French*, Letts, 1977; *Letts Speak Italian*, Letts, 1977; *Letts Speak Spanish*, Letts, 1977.

Contributor to "Fodor's Modern Guides" series occasionally under pseudonym Paul Hamilton: *Italy; Yugoslavia; Morocco; Scandinavia; Europe; Budget Guide to Europe; Youth Guide to Europe*. Regular contributor to Letts Guides to *Greece: The Mainland, Greek Islands, Germany, Yugoslavia, Norway and Sweden, Austria, Italy*, and *England and Wales*. Contributor to radio programs broadcast on British Broadcasting Corp. Contributor to *Times* (London), *Guardian, Daily Telegraph* (London), *Times Educational Supplement, Vogue, La Revue des Voyages*, and many other periodicals. Regional editor for Fodor for countries of Yugoslavia, 1965-78, Morocco, 1969-72, Romania, 1972-73, and Bulgaria, 1972-73. Assistant editor of *Travel Asia Pacific*, 1977-78.

WORK IN PROGRESS: Railway travel in Europe, Romania, and others; a foreign language learning system employing printed material and tape cassettes.

SIDELIGHTS: H. Dennis-Jones told *CA:* "I was born into travel-addicted families (both mother's and father's) who, till recently, had members in every continent of the world. My relatives were in India from the eighteenth century on, in New Zealand from the 1840s, in the New World by 1900. My father served his apprenticeship at sea in the China Seas. I myself was born in Mauritius, my sister in what was British India and later became first Pakistan and now Bangladesh, and my brother in Ceylon, now Sri Lanka, etc. etc. Though very highly qualified academically, I am far more interested in communicating with ordinary people than with remoter academics. If my relatively simple travel books, guides, and articles help people of one country to learn about another nation's ways I am very happy.

"In the last few years I've developed another main interest. I was brought up with music. My mother was an extremely able and highly qualified pianist, and I was educated at Dulwich College, one of the first great schools in Britain to take music seriously. Sir Jack Westrup was on the classical teaching staff until he became professor of music at Oxford. I learned piano, cello, and organ for a time and sang for six years in our large school choir, giving concerts with Sir Thomas Beecham, etc. In recent years I've become quite obsessed with the traditional folk music that still survives in various European countries, especially in Eastern Europe, and with traditional (non-composed) Orthodox Church music. Some of what I've recorded goes back literally thousands of years. Much is extremely beautiful. Much is historically very important. Yet very little sensible attention is paid to it in the prosperous industrialized countries. I'm doing what I can to alter that, and I'm enjoying it. I also enjoy doing things like devising, translating, and arranging a full sequence of traditional Romanian carols, totally unknown outside their own country, which my choir sang, with me conducting, at our 1981 Christmas concert. I've discovered thousands of Spanish carols, most of which have never been heard outside their own villages, though many are very lovely indeed."

* * *

DESMOND, Adrian J(ohn) 1947-

PERSONAL: Born October 6, 1947, in Guildford, Surrey, England; son of William John and Barbara (Dew) Desmond. *Education:* University of London, Chelsea College of Science and Technology, B.Sc., 1969, M.Sc. (history and philosophy of science), 1971, University College, M.Sc. (vertebrate palaeontology), 1973; graduate study, Harvard University, 1973-76. *Home:* 8 Albert Terrace Mews, London NW1, England.

CAREER: Writer, science historian, and paleontologist. *Member:* British Society for the History of Science, Society of Vertebrate Paleontology.

WRITINGS: The Hot-Blooded Dinosaurs: A Revolution in Palaeontology, Blond & Briggs, 1975, Dial, 1976; *The Ape's Reflexion,* Dial, 1979; *Archetypes and Ancestors: Palaeontology in Victorian London, 1850-1875,* Blond & Briggs, 1982. Contributor to scientific journals and to newspapers.

WORK IN PROGRESS: Research on pre-Darwinian transmutation theories, their structure, and social production, concentrating on following up the teaching of evolution at the infant London University in the 1830s.

SIDELIGHTS: About *The Ape's Reflexion,* David Burns comments in the *Washington Post Book World* that Adrian J. "Desmond, a British science historian and paleontologist (author of *The Hot-Blooded Dinosaurs*) writes with wit and vigor." The book, which examines research and experimentation in teaching primates human communication, "is an entertaining look at a fascinating aspect of animal intelligence," according to Burns.

Desmond told *CA:* "I move freely between academic and more popular work; indeed, one generally sends me scurrying towards the other. But I wouldn't have it any other way. Unlike institutionalised academics, however, I do have to resort to the publishing marketplace for funding. The upshot of this is that I have tended to look more deeply into the financial predicaments of my Victorian subjects, producing as a result more materialistic interpretations of their scientific work (vide *Archetypes and Ancestors,* Chapter 1)."

Desmond's work has been translated into German, Japanese, Italian, Spanish, Swedish, and Dutch.

BIOGRAPHICAL/CRITICAL SOURCES: Financial Times, December 11, 1975; *Observer Review,* December 28, 1975; *New Scientist,* August 23, 1979; *Washington Post Book World,* October 28, 1979; *Contemporary Psychology,* November, 1980.

* * *

DETERLINE, William A(lexander) 1927-

PERSONAL: Born December 2, 1927, in Palmerton, Pa.; son of Harold A. (a banker) and Alexandra (Stedman) Deterline; married Lynne E. McHugh, February 3, 1962; children: Kimberly, Mark. *Education:* University of Pittsburgh, B.S., 1953, M.S., 1955, Ph.D., 1958. *Home:* 1990 Scott Lane, Los Altos, Calif. 94104. *Office address:* Deterline Associates, Inc., P.O. Box 10245, Palo Alto, Calif. 94303.

CAREER: University of Pittsburgh, Pittsburgh, Pa., instructor in psychology, 1955-57; Alma College, Alma, Mich., assistant professor of psychology, 1957-60; American Institutes for Research, Pittsburgh, research scientist, 1960-63; Trinity University, San Antonio, Tex., associate professor of psychology, 1963-64; General Programmed Teaching Corp., Los Altos, Calif., president, 1964-69; Deterline Associates, Inc. (research and development company), Palto Alto, Calif., president, 1969—. Director and president, Programmed Instruction, Inc., San Antonio, Tex., 1963-64; president, Sound Education, Inc., 1972—. Consultant, Air Training Command, U.S. Air Force, Randolph Air Force Base, Tex., 1962-65. *Military service:* U.S. Army, 1946-48, 1950-52; became first lieutenant; received Commendation Medal. *Member:* American Psychological Association, National Society for Programmed Instruction (president, 1964-65), American Educational Research Association, American Association for the Advancement of Science, Sigma Xi, Psi Chi.

WRITINGS: (With D. J. Klaus) *Atomic Physics: An Auto-Instructional Program,* American Institutes for Research, 1961; (with Klaus) *Elementary Electronics,* American Institutes for Research, 1961; *An Introduction to Programmed Instruction,* Prentice-Hall, 1962; *Characteristics of Programmed Instruction,* Programmed Instruction, Inc., 1963; *Instructional Programming Procedures,* U.S. Office of Education, 1964; (with Robert Branson) *An Empirical Course Development Model,* Sound Education, Inc., 1972; *Instructional Accountability: Philosophy and Methodology,* Sound Education, Inc., 1972. Contributor to education yearbooks and journals.

WORK IN PROGRESS: A textbook in applied educational psychology; a revision of *Instructional Programming Procedures;* an audiovisual program on techniques of instructional design.

AVOCATIONAL INTERESTS: Water sports, golf, skiing.†

* * *

DEVLIN, Harry 1918-

PERSONAL: Born March 22, 1918, in Jersey City, N.J.; son of Harry George (general manager of Savarin Co.) and Amelia (Crawford) Devlin; married Dorothy Wende (an artist and writer), August 30, 1941; children: Harry Noel, Wende Elizabeth (Mrs. Geoffrey Gates), Jeffrey Anthony, Alexandra Gail (Mrs. James Eldridge), Brion Phillip, Nicholas Kirk, David Matthew. *Education:* Syracuse University, B.F.A., 1939. *Religion:* Congregationalist. *Home:* 443 Hillside Ave., Mountainside, N.J. 07092.

CAREER: Artist, 1939—. Lecturer at Union College (Cranford, N.J.), 1966, chairman of Tomasulo Art Gallery; New Jersey State Council on the Arts, member, 1970-81; vice-chairman of grants committee, 1976-81; member of Rutgers University's advisory council on children's literature; president of board of trustees of Mountainside Library, 1968-70; member of board of directors, Summit Art Center, 1981—. *Military service:* U.S. Naval Reserve, 1942-46; served as artist for Office of Naval Intelligence; became lieutenant.

MEMBER: Society of Illustrators, National Cartoonists Society (past president; honorary president; life member), Authors Guild, Authors League of America, Artists Equity Association (New Jersey), Associated Artists of New Jersey, Dutch Treat Club. *Awards, honors:* New Jersey Teachers of English award, 1970, for *How Fletcher Was Hatched!;* Award of Excellence from Chicago Book Fair, 1974, for *Old Witch Rescues Halloween;* New Jersey Institute of Technology award, 1976, for *Tales of Thunder and Lightning;* Arents Award for Art and Literature, Syracuse University, 1977; Chairman's Award, Society of Illustrator's, 1981.

WRITINGS—Juveniles, except as indicated; all self-illustrated: *To Grandfather's House We Go,* Parents' Magazine Press, 1967; *The Walloping Window Blind,* Van Nostrand, 1968; *What Kind of House Is That?,* Parents' Magazine Press, 1969; *Tales of Thunder and Lightning,* Parents' Magazine Press, 1975; *Portraits of American Architecture* (adult), East View Editions, 1982.

With wife, Wende Devlin: *Old Black Witch,* Encyclopaedia Britannica Press, 1963; *The Knobby Boys to the Rescue,* Parents' Magazine Press, 1965; *Aunt Agatha, There's a Lion under the Couch,* Van nostrand, 1968; *How Fletcher Was Hatched!,* Parents' Magazine Press, 1969; *A Kiss for a Warthog,* Van Nostrand, 1970; *Old Witch and the Polka Dot Ribbon,* Parents' Magazine Press, 1970; *Cranberry Thanksgiving,* Parents' Magazine Press, 1971; *Old Witch Rescues Halloween,* Parents' Magazine Press, 1973; *Cranberry Christmas,* Parents' Magazine Press, 1976; *Hang on Hester*, Lothrop, 1980; *Cranberry Halloween*, Four Winds Press, 1982.

Also author and host of four films entitled "Fare You Well Old House," 1976, 1979, 1980, 1981, and of films, "Houses of the Hackensack," 1976, and "To Grandfather's House We Go," 1981, all for New Jersey Public Broadcasting Corp.

SIDELIGHTS: Harry and Wende Devlins' first book sold over a million copies, "which beguiled us," wrote Harry Devlin, "into the belief that we could write. Wende writes more and better than I can. I write only about those things that I think may fascinate and pay no heed to trends or styles."

MEDIA ADAPTATIONS: *Old Black Witch* was adapted by Gerald Herman as the film, "The Winter of the Witch," Parents' Magazine Films, 1972.

BIOGRAPHICAL/CRITICAL SOURCES: *New York Times Book Review*, May 9, 1965, January 4, 1970; *Library Journal*, May 15, 1969, May 15, 1970.

* * *

DEVLIN, (Dorothy) Wende 1918-

PERSONAL: Born April 27, 1918, in Buffalo, N.Y.; daughter of Bernhardt Philip (a veterinarian) and Elizabeth (Buffington) Wende; married Harry Devlin (an artist and writer), August 30, 1941; children: Harry Noel, Wende Elizabeth (Mrs. Geoffrey Gates), Jeffrey Anthony, Alexandra Gail (Mrs. James Eldridge), Brion Phillip, Nicholas Kirk, David Matthew. *Education:* Syracuse University, B.F.A., 1940. *Politics:* Independent. *Religion:* Congregationalist. *Home and office:* 443 Hillside Ave., Mountainside, N.J. 07092. *Agent:* Dorothy Markinko, McIntosh & Otis, Inc., 475 Fifth Ave., New York, N.Y. 10017.

CAREER: Free-lance writer and portrait painter. Member of Rutgers University's advisory council on children's literature. *Member:* Authors Guild, Authors League of America, Woman Pays Club. *Awards, honors:* New Jersey Teachers of English award, for *How Fletcher Was Hatched!*; Award of Excellence from Chicago Book Fair, 1974, for *Old Witch Rescues Halloween*; Arents Award for Art and Literature, Syracuse University, 1977.

WRITINGS—All juveniles, with husband, Harry Devlin; all illustrated by Harry Devlin: *Old Black Witch*, Encyclopaedia Britannica Press, 1963; *The Knobby Boys to the Rescue*, Parents' Magazine Press, 1965; *Aunt Agatha, There's a Lion under the Couch*, Van Nostrand, 1968; *How Fletcher Was Hatched!*, Parents' Magazine Press, 1969; *A Kiss for a Warthog*, Van Nostrand, 1970; *Old Witch and the Polka Dot Ribbon*, Parents' Magazine Press, 1970; *Cranberry Thanksgiving*, Parents' Magazine Press, 1971; *Old Witch Rescues Halloween*, Parents' Magazine Press, 1973; *Cranberry Christmas*, Parents' Magazine Press, 1976; *Hang on Hester*, Lothrop, 1980; *Cranberry Halloween*, Four Winds Press, 1982. Author of poem feature page, "Beat Poems for a Beat Mother," *Good Housekeeping*, 1963-71.

SIDELIGHTS: Wende Devlin writes: "My husband and I became children's book oriented when we had seven of our own. We had a built in sounding board for ideas and I can't think of more worthwhile work than pleasing and developing a child's mind and imagination."

MEDIA ADAPTATIONS: *Old Black Witch* was adapted by Gerald Herman as the film, "The Winter of the Witch," Parents' Magazine Films, 1972.

BIOGRAPHICAL/CRITICAL SOURCES: *New York Times Book Review*, May 9, 1965, January 4, 1970; *Library Journal*, May 15, 1969, May 15, 1970.

* * *

DILES, Dave 1931-

PERSONAL: Born October 14, 1931, in Middleport, Ohio; son of Lisle Desmond (a railroader) and Lucille (Bowman) Diles; married Jean Schweiger, May 22, 1954 (divorced, 1970); children: Beverly Susan, David Lisle. *Education:* Ohio University, A.A., 1951. *Religion:* Protestant. *Residence:* Racine, Ohio.

CAREER: *Gallipolis Tribune* and *Gallia Times*, Gallipolis, Ohio, news and sports reporter, 1947-49; *Pomeroy Daily Sentinel*, Pomeroy, Ohio, sports editor, 1948-49; *Athens Messenger*, Athens, Ohio, reporter, 1949-51; Associated Press, correspondent in Columbus, Ohio, 1949-51, writer-reporter in Louisville, Ky., 1951, writer-editor in Columbus, 1951-56, sports editor in Detroit, Mich., 1956-61; WXYZ, Inc., Detroit, radio and television sports director, 1961-72; American Broadcasting Corp., New York, N.Y., network sportscaster and commentator on "ABC Wide World of Sports," 1961-82; WJR-Radio, Detroit, sports commentator, 1973-75; WDEE-Radio, Detroit, sports commentator, 1975; WXYZ, Inc., television sports director, 1979-82; free-lance writer. Commentator for Detroit Lions' football on radio, 1973-74, Detroit Pistons' basketball on television, 1973-75.

WRITINGS: *Duffy*, Doubleday, 1974; *Nobody's Perfect*, Dial, 1975; *Twelfth Man in the Middle*, Word, 1976; *Archie*, Doubleday, 1977; *Terry Bradshaw—Man of Steel*, Zondervan, 1979.

WORK IN PROGRESS: Two books, as yet untitled; a book on Willie Nelson.

* * *

DILKS, David (Neville) 1938-

PERSONAL: Born March 17, 1938, in Coventry, England; son of Neville Ernest and Phyllis (Follows) Dilks; married Jill Medlicott, 1963; children: Richard Neville. *Education:* Oxford University, B.A., 1959. *Home:* Wits End, Long Causeway, Leeds LS16 8EX, England. *Office:* School of History, University of Leeds, Leeds LS2 9JT, England.

CAREER: University of London, London School of Economics and Political Science, Aldwych, England, assistant lecturer, 1962-65, lecturer in international history, 1965-69; University of Leeds, Leeds, England, professor of international history, 1969—, chairman of School of History, 1974-79, dean of Faculty of Arts, 1975-77. Research assistant to Earl of Avon, 1960-62, to Marshal of the Royal Air Force, 1963-65, and to Harold Macmillan, 1964-67. Chairman of Commonwealth Youth Exchange Council, 1968-73. Host of television series, "The Lovliest Job," 1977, and interviewer on "The Twentieth Century Remembered," 1982, both for British Broadcasting Corp. Consultant, Commonwealth Youth Program, 1974-75.

MEMBER: Royal Commonwealth Society, Royal Historical Society (fellow), Royal Society for the Protection of Birds, Shropshire Ornithological Society, Shropshire Naturalists Trust, Yorkshire Naturalists Trust, Severn Valley Railway Society, Leeds Defense Studies Dining Club (chairman), Rolls-Royce Enthusiasts Club.

WRITINGS: *Sir Winston Churchill*, Hamish Hamilton, 1965; *Curzon in India*, Volume I: *Achievement*, Hart-Davis, 1969, Volume II: *Frustration*, Taplinger, 1970; (editor) *The Diaries of Sir Alexander Cadogan, O.M., 1938-1945*, Cassell, 1971,

Putnam, 1972; (contributor) Butler, editor, *The Conservatives,* Allen & Unwin, 1977; (editor and author of introduction) *Britain and Canada,* Commonwealth Foundation, 1980; (editor, author of introduction, and contributor) *Retreat from Power: Studies in Britain's Foreign Policy of the Twentieth Century,* two volumes, Macmillan, 1981. Also author of biography of Neville Chamberlain, 1983. Writer for television series, "The Lovliest Job," for British Broadcasting Corp., 1977. Contributor to learned journals.

WORK IN PROGRESS: Editor, with Christopher Andrew, and contributor to a volume of essays on the gathering and use of intelligence services by the Great Powers in the twentieth century, for Macmillan.

SIDELIGHTS: In a review of Volume I of David Dilks's *Curzon in India,* a *Times Literary Supplement* critic states that the book "promises to be a major biographical achievement." *Curzon in India: Achievement,* the reviewer continues, "is not only a highly professional historical study but a very well-written book which can be read for pleasure as well as instruction.... [It is] a distinguished book, as a biography, as an essay in diplomatic history, and as a contribution to the history of India."

In another *Times Literary Supplement* article, a reviewer calls Dilks's second volume, *Curzon in India: Frustration,* "a major achievement. Not only does it present a portrait, in considerable detail, of the most brilliant of Indian Viceroys [Lord George Curzon]; it analyses, with the utmost care, some very important aspects of British diplomacy during that peculiar period when both alliances and enmities were in a highly fluid state and the Russian 'menace,' always slightly fictitious, was being replaced by a very real German one. Dr. Dilks, indeed, has made a very great contribution to our understanding both of [Curzon] and of the circumstances."

While the *Times Literary Supplement* critic praises Dilks for his thoroughness in *Curzon in India: Frustration,* noting the author's "meticulous attention to the details of diplomatic history" and "massive documentation," other reviewers find that Dilks becomes bogged down in administrative details. J. H. Plumb in the *New York Times Book Review,* for instance, calls the two volumes "painstaking, pedestrian and preoccupied with the minutiae of dispatches, telegrams, council minutes, cabinet memoranda. Had the book been half as long, twice as analytical, and written with style, it might have reached a wide public.... This rather leaden effort will not." Nevertheless, Plumb concludes, "Anyone deeply concerned about America's ... plight [in Southeast Asia] would do well to read [*Curzon in India*]. It stresses two useful lessons: imperialism is rarely popular; diplomacy obsessed by chimeras and military power, not firmly responsible to its constituency, is highly dangerous."

Dilks edited and contributed an article and introduction to each volume of *Retreat from Power: Studies in Britain's Foreign Policy of the Twentieth Century.* An *Economist* critic considers *Retreat from Power* "a mixed and various collection [with] no common theme or argument to it, ... more for the experts than for the general reader or student." However, Paul Kennedy in *Times Literary Supplement* feels "Dilks's two introductions *are* worth recommending to anyone interested in learning about [Great Britain's] diplomacy in the post-Victorian age." The *Economist* reviewer also commends Dilks's work: "Professor Dilks does a valiant job as editor, not only in contributing a useful article to each of these volumes, but also by providing two introductions which link the various essays and comment upon the broader trends. [Dilks's] comments on the long-standing British problem of achieving military security without forfeiting economic stability are especially good."

BIOGRAPHICAL/CRITICAL SOURCES: *Economist,* August 2, 1969, January 24, 1970, February 28, 1981; *Spectator,* August 2, 1969, January 31, 1970; *Guardian Weekly,* August 7, 1969, January 31, 1970; *New Statesman,* August 8, 1969; *Times Literary Supplement,* August 14, 1969, February 12, 1970, March 20, 1981; *Observer,* August 17, 1969, January 18, 1970; *American Historical Review,* October, 1970; *New York Times Book Review,* October 4, 1970; *English Historical Review,* January, 1971; *Journal of Modern History,* June, 1972; *History Today,* May, 1981.

* * *

DILLON, Richard H(ugh) 1924-

PERSONAL: Born January 16, 1924, in Sausalito, Calif.; son of William Tarleton and Alice Mabel (Burke) Dillon; married Barbara A. Sutherland, June, 1950; children: Brian, David, Ross. *Education:* University of California, Berkeley, A.B., 1948, A.M., 1949, B.L.S., 1950. *Politics:* Independent. *Religion:* Independent.

CAREER: Sutro Library, San Francisco, Calif., assistant librarian, 1950-53, librarian, 1953-79. Member, California History Commission, 1964—. *Military service:* U.S. Army, 1943-46; received Purple Heart. *Member:* Western History Association, California Historical Society, California Library Association, California Writers Club, Phi Beta Kappa, Phi Alpha Theta, Roxburghe Club.

AWARDS, HONORS: James D. Phelan Award in literature, 1960, for *Embarcadero;* Gold Medal of Commonwealth Club of California for best nonfiction book by a Californian, 1965, for *Meriwether Lewis;* Silver Medal of Commonwealth Club of California for best nonfiction book by a Californian, 1968, for *Fool's Gold;* Spur Award, Western Writers of America, for best nonfiction book in Western America, 1973, for *Burnt-Out Fires.*

WRITINGS: *Embarcadero,* Coward, 1959; (editor) W. H. Boyle, *Personal Observations on the Conduct of the Modoc War,* Dawsons, 1959; (editor) Benjamin B. Harris, *The Gila Trail,* University of Oklahoma Press, 1960; *Shanghaiing Days,* Coward, 1961; (editor) C. C. Loveland, *California Trail Herd,* Talisman Press, 1961; *The Hatchet Men,* Coward, 1962; *Meriwether Lewis* (biography), Coward, 1965; *J. Ross Browne,* University of Oklahoma Press, 1965; *The Legend of Grizzly Adams,* Coward, 1966; *Fool's Gold: The Biography of John Sutter,* Coward, 1967; *Wells Fargo Detective,* Coward, 1969.

Humbugs and Heroes: A Gallery of California Pioneers, Doubleday, 1970; *Burnt-Out Fires,* Prentice-Hall, 1973; *Exploring the Mother Lode Country,* Ritchie, 1974; *Siskiyou Trail,* McGraw, 1975; *We Have Met the Enemy,* McGraw, 1978; *High Steel,* Celestial Arts, 1979; *Great Expectations,* Benicia Heritage, 1980; *Delta Country,* Presidio Press, 1982. Contributor of articles and reviews to popular and scholarly journals.

* * *

DINNEEN, Betty 1929-

PERSONAL: Born August 28, 1929, in London, England; naturalized U.S. citizen in 1975; daughter of Albert Ernest and Edith Louise (Taylor) Newark; married Barry Dinneen, March 2, 1957 (divorced, 1971); children: Penelope Jane, Hugh Martin. *Education:* Educated at Tiffin Girls School. *Home:* 148 Newman St., San Francisco, Calif. 94110. *Office:* 300 Montgomery St., Suite 700, San Francisco, Calif. 94104.

CAREER: Times Book Club, London, England, assistant librarian, 1945-47; South African Embassy, London, secretary, 1947-54; Government of Sarawak, Kuching, secretary, 1954-56; Government of Tanganyika, Department of Lands and Surveys, Dar es Salaam, secretary, 1956-58; Government of Kenya, Ministry of Defence, Nairobi, secretary, 1958-63; African Medical and Research Foundation (Flying Doctor Service), Nairobi, secretary, 1963-64; Thacher, Jones, Casey & Ratcliff, San Francisco, Calif., legal secretary, 1970—.

WRITINGS—Juveniles: *Lions and Karen,* Dent, 1965; *A Lurk of Leopards,* Walck, 1972; *Lion Yellow,* Walck, 1975; *Make Way for the Ark,* McKay, 1977; *Tale of Three Leopards,* Doubleday, 1980; *The Family Howl,* Macmillan, 1981; *Striped Horses,* Macmillan, 1982.

SIDELIGHTS: Betty Dinneen told *CA:* "Living in Africa impelled me to write, and all my published stories have concerned African animals. I feel I may be helping to record a part of life that is on the wane." *Avocational interests:* Conservation, gardening, cooking.

* * *

DOBRIN, Arthur 1943-

PERSONAL: Born August 22, 1943, in Brooklyn, N.Y.; son of Moe (a truck driver) and Anne (Slavin) Dobrin; married Lyn Fradkin (a writer of children's books, artist, and model), August 30, 1964; children: Eric Simba, Kikora Anana. *Education:* City College of the City University of New York, B.A., 1965; New York University, M.A., 1971; additional graduate study at Nathan Ackerman Family Institute, 1973-75. *Religion:* Ethical Humanist. *Home:* 613 Dartmouth St., Westbury, N.Y. 11590. *Office:* Ethical Humanist Society, 38 Old Country Rd., Garden City, N.Y. 11530.

CAREER: Poet. U.S. Peace Corps, volunteer in Kenya, 1965-67; Ethical Humanist Society of Long Island, Garden City, N.Y., leader, 1968—. Initiator of The Learning Tree (experimental school); summer director of Encampment for Citizenship, Great Falls, Mont., and Tucson, Ariz., 1968, 1969, 1970, 1972; director of Institute for Leadership Development, 1971-72; teacher at Westbury Experimental High School, 1973-74. Board member of Westbury League of Women Voters, 1974-75. *Member:* World Poetry Society, American Association of Marriage and Family Therapists (clinical member), Poetry Society of America.

WRITINGS: The Role of Cooperatives in the Development of Rural Kenya (monograph), Rutgers University Press, 1970; (with Kenneth Briggs) *Getting Married the Way You Want,* Prentice-Hall, 1974; *Sunbird: Poems of East Africa,* Cross-Cultural Communications, 1976; *Saying My Name Out Loud,* Xanadu Press, 1978; *Gentle Spears,* Cross-Cultural Communications, 1979; *Lace: Poetry from the Poor, Homeless, Aged, Physically and Emotionally Handicapped,* Cross-Cultural Communications, 1979; (editor with wife, Lyn Dobrin, and Thomas Liotti) *Convictions: Political Prisoners—Their Stories,* Orbis, 1981; *Out of Place,* Backstreet Press, 1982. Contributor of poems to *Bitterroot, Chelsea, Dark Waters, Street Cries, Compass, Poet, Ocarina, Xanadu,* and *East Africa Journal.*

BIOGRAPHICAL/CRITICAL SOURCES: Family Circle, June, 1974.

* * *

DODGE, Richard Holmes 1926-

PERSONAL: Born May 22, 1926, in Lawrence, Mass.; son of Israel Rogers (a salesman) and Ann (McCarthy) Dodge; married Margaret Hangen, March 11, 1952 (divorced, 1978); married Corinne Ann Ising, February 17, 1978; children: (first marriage) Ashley (daughter), Jason. *Education:* University of New Hampshire, B.A., 1951; University of California, Los Angeles, M.A., 1955. *Politics:* Democrat. *Religion:* Unitarian Universalist. *Home:* 466 Cresthill Dr., Agoura, Calif. 91301. *Office:* Department of English, Santa Monica College, Santa Monica, Calif. 90405.

CAREER: University of California, Los Angeles, instructor in English, 1955; Santa Monica College, Santa Monica, Calif., professor of English, 1956—. Co-founder and co-director of University of California, Los Angeles/California Writing Project, 1977—. *Military service:* U.S. Army, Infantry, 1944-46; 1951-53, served in Korean War, became first lieutenant. *Member:* Modern Language Association of America, National Council of Teachers of English.

WRITINGS: How to Read and Write in College, Harper, *Form 1,* 1962, revised edition, 1982, *Form 2,* 1964, *Form 3,* 1967, *Form 4,* 1969, *Form 5,* 1973, *Form 6,* 1979; *The Shorter Harper Handbook,* Harper, 1965; *The Shorter Harper Workbook* (two forms), Harper, 1965; *Divided We Stand,* Canfield Press, 1970; *Of Time and Experience,* Winthrop, 1972; (with Leonard Nimoy) *I Am Not Spock,* Celestial Arts, 1975; (with John Wooden and Bill Sharman) *The Wooden-Sharman Method,* McMillan, 1976; *Players Handbook,* Project Basketball, 1976; *Coaches Handbook,* Project Basketball, 1976; (with Alan Casty) *The Writing Project,* Wadsworth, 1982.

WORK IN PROGRESS: Confessions of a Born Again Writing Teacher: A Professional Memoir.

* * *

DOLL, Ronald C. 1913-

PERSONAL: Born March 14, 1913, in Mehoopany, Pa.; son of H. Stanley (a salesman) and Florence (Carpenter) Doll; married Ruth E. Paul, June 16, 1940; children: Cheryl R. *Education:* Columbia University, B.A., 1934, M.A., 1935, Ed.D., 1951. *Religion:* Presbyterian. *Home:* 1081A Argyle Cir., Lakewood, N.J. 08701. *Office:* Richmond College of the City University of New York, 130 Stuyvesant Pl., Staten Island, N.Y. 10301; and Department of Curriculum, Georgian Court College, Lakewood, N.J. 08701.

CAREER: Teacher, counselor, and acting principal, Dallas, Pa., and Cranford, N.J., public schools, 1935-43; West Orange (N.J.) Public Schools, administrative assistant and director of guidance, 1944-52; Columbia University, New York City, Citizenship Education Project, curriculum specialist, 1952-53; Montclair (N.J.) Public Schools, director of instruction, 1953-57; New York University, New York City, professor of education, 1957-61; City University of New York, Hunter College, New York City, professor of education, 1961-67, Richmond College (now College of Staten Island), Staten Island, N.Y., dean of teacher education, 1967-68, professor of education, 1968-76, professor emeritus of the university, 1976—; Georgian Court College, Lakewood, N.J., professor of curriculum, 1976—. Consultant to school systems, state departments of education, and publishers.

MEMBER: Association for Supervision and Curriculum Development, National Association of Secondary School Principals, National Society for the Study of Education, Phi Delta Kappa, Kappa Delta Pi.

WRITINGS: (With others) *Organizing for Curriculum Improvement,* Horace Mann-Lincoln Institute of School Experimentation, Teachers College, Columbia University, 1953; (with T. C. Pollack and others) *The Art of Communicating* (textbook), Macmillan, 1955, 2nd edition, 1961; (contributor) B. M. Harris, editor, *Supervisory Behavior in Education*, Prentice-Hall, 1963; *Curriculum Improvement: Decision-Making and Process*, Allyn & Bacon, 1964, 5th edition, 1982; (editor with R. S. Fleming) *Children Under Pressure: A Collection of Readings about Scholastic Pressure*, C. E. Merrill, 1966; (contributor) William Van Til, editor, *Curriculum: Quest for Relevance*, Houghton, 1971, 2nd edition, 1974; *Leadership to Improve Schools*, Charles A. Jones Publishing, 1972; (with Ruth C. Cook) *The Elementary School Curriculum*, Allyn & Bacon, 1972; (contributor) *Issues in Secondary Education: Seventy-fifth Yearbook, Part II*, Society for the Study of Education, 1976; *Supervision for Staff Development: Ideas and Application*, Allyn & Bacon, 1982. Also author of survey reports and industrial manuals. Editor and contributor to yearbooks of the Association for Supervision of Curriculum Development; contributor to *Educational Leadership*.

AVOCATIONAL INTERESTS: Fishing, golf, history, gardening, and theology.

SIDELIGHTS: Ronald C. Doll told *CA*: "Caught in the Great Depression, I was frustrated in my original plan to become a journalist. Nevertheless, my second love, the education of children and youth, soon provided me with serious content for my writing. I've spent happy days in teaching and administration, but even happier ones in describing what teachers and administrators can do to make youngsters' learning easier and more productive."

* * *

DOSKOCILOVA, Hana 1936-

PERSONAL: Born July 11, 1936, in Jihlava, Czechoslovakia; daughter of Jan (a lawyer) and Maria (Juraskova) Doskocil; married Miroslav Sekyrka (a bookseller), September 21, 1961. *Education:* Attended public schools in Znojmo, Czechoslovakia. *Home:* Praha 10-Vrsovice, Madridska 4/820, Czechoslovakia. *Office:* Albatros, Na Perstyne 1, Prague 1, Czechoslovakia.

CAREER: Clerk in coal store in Jihlava, Czechoslovakia, 1954-56; Academy of Sciences, Prague, Czechoslovakia, clerk, 1956-59; Albatros (publishers for children and young people), Prague, press editor, 1959-61, proofreader, 1961-64, editor in department for small children, 1964-72; free-lance writer, 1972—.

WRITINGS—All juvenile: *Pohadky pro deti, mamy a taty* (title means "Fairy Tales for Children, Mothers, and Fathers"), Statni Nakladatelstvi Detske Knihy (Prague), 1961; *Psanicko pro tebe—O hrackach* (title means "A Letter for You—About Toys"), Statni Nakladatelstvi Detske Knihy, 1964; *Bydlim doma* (title means "I Live at Home"), Statni Nakladatelstvi Detske Knihy, 1966; *Kajetan the Magician* (translated from the German), Artia (Prague), 1967; *Cervena lodicka* (title means "The Little Red Ship"), Mlada fronta (Prague), 1968; *Modern Czech Fairy Tales* (English translation from the Czech), Artia, 1969; *Animal Tales*, translations from the Czech by Eve Merriam, adapted by William Howard Armstrong, Doubleday, 1970; *Ukradeny orloj* (title means "Rob of Astronomical Clock"), Materidouska (Prague), 1973; *Basama bernardyn a Vendulka* (title means "St. Bernard Dog Named Basama and a Girl Vendulka"), Orbis (Prague), 1973; *Jelen se zlatymi parohy* (title means "The Hart with Golden Antlers"), Artia, 1978; *Chaloupka z perniku* (title means "Little Cottage of Gingerbread"), Artia, 1982.

All published by Albatros (Prague): *Micka z trafiky a kocour Pivoda* (title means "Pussy Cat from the Tobacconist's and Tomcat Pivoda"), 1971; *Zviratka z celeho sveta* (title means "The Animals from the Whole World"), 1971; *Kudy chodi maly lev* (title means "Where the Little Lion Walks"), 1972; *Medvedi pohadky* (title means "The Bear Fairy Tales"), 1973; *Zviratka z lesa* (title means "The Animals from the Wood"), 1974; *Drak Barborak a Ztraceny kral Kulajda* (title means "Dragon Barborak and the Lost King Kulajda"), 1974; *Posledniho kousne pes: A dalsich ctyriadvacet prislovi v pohadkach* (title means "The Last Will Be Bitten by the Dog: Proverbial Fairy Tales"), 1974; *Eliska a tata Kral* (title means "Elizabeth and Her Father King"), 1977; *Dva dedecci z Dlouhe mile* (title means "Two Grandfathers from Long Mile"), 1978; *Jak se vychovava papousek* (title means "How Is Educated the Parrot"), 1979; *Fanek a Vendulka* (title means "Small Francis and a Girl Vendulka"), 1980; *Pohadky na dobry den* (title means "Tales for a Good Day"), 1982; *Krtek v sedmem nebi* (title means "The Mole in Seventh Heaven"), 1982.

Author of juvenile television scripts, 1963-73, animated cartoons, 1969-71, and of a puppet play. Member of editorial council, *Materidouska* (children's monthly), 1966-72.

WORK IN PROGRESS: *Diogenes v sudu a dalsich dvacet nejzajmejsich pribehu* (title means "Diogenes in the Barrel and Twenty Other Well-known Stories"), for Albatros.

SIDELIGHTS: Many of Hana Doskocilova's books have been translated into Russian, German, French, Dutch, Japanese, and English.

* * *

DOTY, Roy 1922-

PERSONAL: Born September 10, 1922, in Chicago, Ill.; son of E. Roy (a salesman) and Dorothy (Schroeder) Doty; married Louise Hall, April 10, 1949 (divorced, 1954); married Jean Slaughter (a writer), July 19, 1955 (divorced, 1981); married Nan Dameron King, January 2, 1982; children: Debbie (Mrs. David Levinson), Jeffrey, Christopher, Didi. *Education:* Attended Columbus School of Art. *Politics:* Independent liberal. *Religion:* Methodist. *Home and office:* Grey Hollow Rd., Norwalk, Conn. 06851.

CAREER: Free-lance writer, artist, cartoonist, and illustrator, 1946—. *Military service:* U.S. Army, 1942-46; became technical sergeant. *Member:* National Cartoonist Society. *Awards, honors:* Named Illustrator of the Year by National Cartoonist Society, twice; also received three art director awards; United Way of America graphics award, 1978; Advertising Council Silver Bell Award, 1979.

WRITINGS: (With Richard Wolters) *Instant Dog*, Dutton, 1968; *Rowan & Martin's Laugh-In #2: Mod, Mod World* (based on his *Laugh-In* comic strip), New American Library, 1969; (with Robert Stevenson) *The Popular Science Illustrated Almanac for Home Owners*, Popular Science, 1972; (with Norma Klein) *Girls Can Be Anything*, Dutton, 1973; *Puns, Gags, Quips, and Riddles: A Collection of Dreadful Jokes* (also see below), Doubleday, 1974; (with Stevenson) *Almanac for Home Makers*, Grosset, 1974; (with Barbara Rinkoff) *No Pushing, No Ducking*, Lothrop, 1974; *Q's Are Weird O's: More Puns, Gags, Quips, and Riddles* (also see below), Doubleday, 1975.

Where Are You Going with That Tree?, Doubleday, 1976; *Where Are You Going with That Oil?*, Doubleday, 1976; *Gunga, Your Din-Din Is Ready: Son of Puns, Gags, Quips, and Riddles* (also see below), Doubleday, 1976; *Puns, Gags, Quips, and Riddles* [and] *Q's Are Weird O's* (collection), Archway, 1976;

(with Esther R. Hautzig) *Life with Working Parents*, Macmillan, 1976; *Pinocchio Was Nosey: Grandson of Puns, Gags, Quips, and Riddles* (also see below), Doubleday, 1977; (with Lee Polk) *The Incredible Television Machine*, Macmillan, 1977; (with Leonard Maar) *Where Are You Going with That Coal?*, Doubleday, 1977; (with Maar) *Where Are You Going with That Energy?*, Doubleday, 1977; *Old One-Eye Meets His Match*, Lothrop, Lee & Shepard, 1978; *Gunga, Your Din-Din Is Ready* [and] *Pinocchio Was Nosey* (collection), Archway, 1978; *King Midas Has a Gilt Complex*, Doubleday, 1979; (with Patrick F. McManus) *Kid Camping from Aaaaiii! to Zip*, Lothrop, Lee & Shepard, 1979; (with Maar) *How Much Does America Cost?*, Doubleday, 1979.

Tinkerbell Is a Ding-a-Ling, Doubleday, 1980; (with Jean S. Doty) *Macmillan's Children's Calendar 1981*, Macmillan, 1980; *Children's Calendar 1982*, Macmillan, 1981; *Children's Calendar 1983*, Macmillan, 1982; (with D. Reuther) *Fun to Go*, Macmillan, 1982. Author and illustrator of *Laugh-In* comic strip, 1968-71.

Illustrator: Harry Walton, editor, *Wordless Workshop*, Taplinger, 1967; Robert M. Herhold, *Funny, You Don't Look Christian*, Weybright & Talley, 1969; Judy Blume, *Tales of a Fourth Grade Nothing*, Dell, 1972; Frank R. Donovan, *Let's Go Metric*, Weybright & Talley, 1974; Eleanor S. Clymer, *Take Tarts as Tarts Is Passing*, Dutton, 1974; Clymer, *Hamburgers—and Ice Cream for Dessert*, Dutton, 1978; Alvin Silverstein, *Itch, Sniffle, and Sneeze*, Four Winds Press, 1978; Don L. Wulffson, *How Sports Came to Be*, Lothrop, 1980; Rhoda Blumberg, *The First Travel Guide to the Moon*, Scholastic Book Service, 1980. Contributor to periodicals, including *Popular Science*, *Business Week*, *Newsweek*, and *New York Times*.†

*   *   *

DOUGHERTY, Joanna Foster
   See FOSTER, Joanna

*   *   *

DOUGLAS, Thorne
   See HAAS, Ben(jamin) L(eopold)

*   *   *

DUDLEY, Jay
   See CHAPMAN, J. Dudley

*   *   *

DUFFY, John 1915-

PERSONAL: Born March 27, 1915, in Barrow-in-Furness, England; son of James (a ship-plater) and Ethel (Hough) Duffy; married Florence Corinne Cook, June 13, 1942; children: James Norman, John, Jr. *Education:* Louisiana State Normal College (now Northwestern State University of Louisiana), B.A., 1941; Louisiana State University, M.A., 1943; University of California, Los Angeles, Ph.D., 1946. *Politics:* Democrat. *Home:* 4401 College Heights Dr., Hyattsville, Md. 20782. *Office:* Department of History, University of Maryland, College Park, Md. 20742.

CAREER: Northwestern State College of Louisiana (now Northwestern State University of Louisiana), Natchitoches, assistant professor of history, 1946-47; Southeastern Louisiana College (now University), Hammond, associate professor of history, 1947-49; Northwestern State College of Louisiana (now Northwestern State University of Louisiana), associate professor of history, 1949-53; Louisiana State University, Baton Rouge, associate professor, 1953-60; University of Pittsburgh, Graduate School of Public Health, Pittsburgh, Pa., associate professor, 1960-64, professor of public health history, 1965; Tulane University, New Orleans, La., professor of history of medicine, with dual appointment in Medical School and history department, 1965-72; University of Maryland, College Park, Priscilla Alden Burke Professor of History, 1972—. Consultant to New York City Health Department.

MEMBER: American Association for the History of Medicine (member of executive council, 1963-66; vice-president, 1974-76; president, 1976-78), American Historical Association, Organization of American Historians, American Association of University Professors, Southern Historical Association (member of executive council, 1962-65), Louisiana Historical Association, Maryland Historical Society. *Awards, honors:* Ford Foundation fellow, 1951-52; Louisiana Library Association Literary Award, 1958, for Volume I of Matas work.

WRITINGS: *Epidemics in Colonial America*, Louisiana State University Press, 1953; (editor) *Parson Clapp of the Strangers' Church of New Orleans*, Louisiana State University Studies, 1957; (editor) Rudolph Matas, *History of Medicine in Louisiana*, Louisiana State University Press, Volume I, 1958, Volume II, 1962; *Sword of Pestilence: The New Orleans Yellow Fever Epidemic of 1853*, Louisiana State University Press, 1966; *A History of Public Health in New York City, 1625-1866*, Russell Sage, 1968; *A History of Public Health in New York City, 1866-1966*, Russell Sage, 1974; *A History of American Medicine*, McGraw, 1975; (editor) *Ventures in World Health: The Memoirs of Fred Lowe Soper*, Pan American Health Organization, 1977; *The Healers: A History of American Medicine*, University of Illinois Press, 1979. Contributor to *Mississippi Valley Historical Review*, *Bulletin of the History of Medicine*, *Journal of the American Medical Association*, *Journal of Southern History*, and other professional journals. Interim editor, *American Historical Review*, 1975.

SIDELIGHTS: John Duffy told *CA*: "As a historian, I feel an obligation to make history of interest to the general reader. Only a few individuals have creative talent, but writing is a craft that can be learned. I stress to my students that the essence of good writing is clarity, brevity, and precision, qualities that can be acquired by any intelligent individual. I also point out that while there may be a few inspired souls who can quickly whip out great prose or poetry, for the vast majority of us writing is sheer hard work. When I am writing on a full-time basis, I set a goal of five or six pages a day, and I do not stop until I have at least met my quota. Had I awaited inspiration, my list of publications would be much shorter."

*   *   *

DUNHAM, H(enry) Warren 1906-

PERSONAL: Born January 24, 1906, in Omaha, Neb.; son of Henry Warren and Elizabeth Marie (Cowan) Dunham; married Vera Sandomirsky (a professor of Slavic languages), November 1, 1942; children: Eugenie. *Education:* Attended University of Omaha (now University of Nebraska at Omaha), 1924-26; University of Chicago, Ph.B., 1928, M.A., 1935, Ph.D., 1941. *Home:* 15 Stephens Path, Port Jefferson, N.Y. *Office:* Department of Psychiatry, State University of New York, Stoney Brook, N.Y. 11790.

CAREER: Vanderbilt University, Nashville, Tenn., instructor, 1940; Wayne State University, Detroit, Mich., instructor, 1940-42, assistant professor, 1943-48, associate professor, 1948-54, professor of sociology, 1954-70, professor of sociological psychiatry, 1971-76, professor emeritus, 1976—; State University of New York at Stoney Brook, professor of psychiatry, 1976—. Information research analyst, U.S. Office of War Information, 1944-45. Resident director, Michigan State Psychiatric Research Clinic, 1950; director of epidemiology laboratory, Lafayette Clinic, Detroit, 1959-64. Special lecturer, Howard University, 1944-45; visiting professor at Stanford University, summer, 1947, New York University, summer, 1948, Columbia University, 1970-71. Member of review committee of Center for Epidemiological Studies, 1969-71. Speaker at International Congress on Social Psychiatry and International Congress of Psychotherapy, London, England, 1965. Consultant, National Institute of Mental Health, 1949-53.

MEMBER: American Sociological Association (chairman, section on social psychiatry, 1947), Michigan Academy of Science, Arts and Letters (chairman, sociology section, 1949), American Association of University Professors, Michigan Sociological Society (vice-president, 1943-44; executive committee, 1947-48; president, 1948-49), Ohio Valley Sociological Society (vice-president, 1946-47; president, 1949-50), Sigma Xi, Alpha Kappa Delta.

AWARDS, HONORS: Leo M. Franklin Memorial Chair, Wayne State University, 1955-56; Fulbright scholar and lecturer at University of Amsterdam, 1956-57, and at University of Ain Shams, Cairo, United Arab Republic (now Egypt), 1966-77; research grants from National Institute of Mental Health, 1959-62, and Michigan State Department of Mental Health, 1964; Rema Lapouse Memorial Award, American Public Health Association, 1972.

WRITINGS: (With R.E.L. Faris) *Mental Disorders in Urban Areas*, University of Chicago Press, 1939; (with S. W. Waldfogel) *A Healthy Mind: It's Yours for the Doing*, Wayne State University Press, 1943; (contributor) O. J. Kaplan, editor, *Mental Disorders in Later Life*, Stanford University Press, 1945.

(With Francis E. Merrill, Arnold Rose, and Paul W. Tappan) *Social Problems*, Knopf, 1950; *Crucial Issues in the Treatment and Control of Sexual Deviation*, Michigan State Department of Mental Health, 1951; (contributor) M. Caldwell and L. Foster, editors, *Analysis of Social Problems*, Stackpole, 1954; (editor) *The City in Mid-Century*, Wayne State University Press, 1957; *Sociological Theory and Mental Disorder*, Wayne State University Press, 1959; (with S. K. Weinberg) *The Culture of the State Mental Hospital*, Wayne State University Press, 1960; *Community and Schizophrenia: An Epidemiological Analysis* (monograph), Wayne State University Press, 1965; (contributor) Marshall Clinard, editor, *Anomie and Deviant Behavior*, Free Press, 1964.

Social Realities and Community Psychiatry, Behavioral Publications, 1976; *Social Systems and Schizophrenia: Selected Papers*, Praeger, 1980.

Contributor of articles to five books. Contributor of more than eighty articles and papers to psychiatry and sociology journals and conference reports, including *Social Forces, Marriage and Family Living, International Journal of Social Psychiatry*, and *Archives of General Psychiatry*.

* * *

DURNBAUGH, Donald F. 1927-

PERSONAL: Born November 16, 1927, in Detroit, Mich.; son of Floyd D. (an office worker) and Ruth E. (Tombaugh) Durnbaugh; married Hedwig T. Raschka (a librarian), July 10, 1952; children: Paul, Christopher, Renate. *Education:* Manchester College, B.A., 1949; University of Michigan, M.A., 1953; University of Pennsylvania, Ph.D., 1960. *Politics:* Independent. *Religion:* Church of the Brethren. *Home:* 18W647 22nd St., Lombard, Ill. 60148. *Office:* Bethany Theological Seminary, Oak Brook, Ill. 60521.

CAREER: Brethren Voluntary Service, relief worker in Austria and Germany, 1949-51; Brethren Service Commission, director of program in Austria, 1953-56; Juniata College, Huntingdon, Pa., instructor, 1958-60, assistant professor of history, 1960-62; Bethany Theological Seminary, Oak Brook, Ill., associate professor, 1962-69, professor of church history, 1969—. European director in Marburg and Strasbourg, Brethren Colleges Abroad, 1964-65; Menno Simons Lecturer, Bethel College, 1974. Participant in Conference on Faith and History. *Member:* American Historical Association, American Society of Church History, Organization of American Historians, North American Academy of Ecumenists, Brethren Journal Association.

AWARDS, HONORS: Colonial Society of Pennsylvania Award, 1957, for best essay on colonial heritage by graduate student at University of Pennsylvania; Association of Theological Schools fellowship, 1971-72; National Endowment for the Humanities senior fellowship, 1976-77.

WRITINGS: *European Origins of the Brethren*, Brethren Press, 1958; (with Lawrence W. Shultz) *A Brethren Bibliography, 1713-1963*, Brethren Press, 1964; *The Brethren in Colonial America*, Brethren Press, 1967; *The Believers' Church: The History and Character of Radical Protestantism*, Macmillan, 1968; *The Church of the Brethren: Past and Present*, Brethren Press, 1971; (editor) *Every Need Supplied: Mutual Aid and Christian Community in the Free Churches, 1525-1675*, Temple University Press, 1974; (editor) M. R. Zigler and others, *To Serve the Present Age: The Brethren Service Story*, Brethren Press, 1975; (contributor) F. Ernest Stoeffler, editor, *Continental Pietism and Early American Christianity*, Eerdmans, 1976; (editor) *On Earth Peace*, Brethren Press, 1978; (contributor) W. J. Boney and G. A. Igleheart, editors, *Baptists and Ecumenism*, Judsen, 1980; (editor) *The Brethren Encyclopedia*, three volumes, Brethren Press, 1983. Contributor to church and historical journals.

WORK IN PROGRESS: Research on German-American religious communities in the United States, American civil religion, and peace churches in the American revolution; editing a major reference work on all aspects of all religious denominations stemming from the Schwarzenan Brethren in 1708, especially the Brethren Church, Church of the Brethren, Dunkard Brethren, Fellowship of Grace Brethren Churches, and Old German Baptist Brethren.

SIDELIGHTS: Donald F. Durnbaugh's extensive travel in western Europe has provided him opportunities to study European-founded church groups such as the peace churches and Moravians, and to trace interrelationships back and forth across the Atlantic.

* * *

DURRELL, Donald D(e Witt) 1903-

PERSONAL: Born December 18, 1903, in Fergus Falls, Minn.; son of William Benmore and Fanny (Richardson) Durrell; married Katharine Moore, August 20, 1929; children: Suzanne, Elizabeth. *Education:* University of Iowa, A.B., 1926, A.M., 1927; Harvard University, Ed.D., 1930. *Politics:* Republican. *Religion:* Unitarian Universalist. *Home:* 19 Orchard Dr., Durham, N.H. 03824. *Office:* Department of Education, Boston University, Boston, Mass.

CAREER: Harvard University, Cambridge, Mass., instructor, 1927-30; Boston University, Boston, Mass., assistant professor, 1930-33, associate professor, 1933-35, professor of education, 1935-69, professor emeritus, 1969—, dean of School of Education, 1942-52. U.S. Air Force, director of operations analysis, Third Air Force, 1945-46. Adjunct professor, University of New Hampshire, 1973—. Member of Research Advisory Council, U.S. Office of Education, 1962-65; consultant on current national study of first-grade reading. *Member:* International Reading Association, American Educational Research Association, American Association for the Advancement of Science (vice-president, 1952), National Society for the Study of Education. *Awards, honors:* L.H.D., Boston University, 1969; Citation of Merit, International Reading Association, 1970.

WRITINGS: Improving Reading Instruction, Harcourt, 1956; *Durrell Reading Analysis,* Harcourt, 1957; (with Helen A. Murphy) *Speech-to-Print Phonics,* Harcourt, 1964; (editor with B. Alice Crossley) *Favorite Plays for Classroom Reading,* Plays, 1965, revised edition, 1971; (editor with Crossley) *Thirty Plays for Classroom Reading,* Plays, 1966, 2nd edition, 1968; *Phonics Practice Program,* Harcourt, 1969.

Plays for Echo Reading, Harcourt, 1970; (compiler) *Teen-Age Plays for Classroom Reading,* Plays, 1971; *Learning Letter Sounds,* Borg-Wagner, 1972; *Beginning Language Concepts,* Borg-Wagner, 1974; *Learning Letters through Sounds,* Borg-Warner, 1974; *Vocabulary Improvement Program,* Harcourt, 1974; *Sound Start,* Curriculum Associates, 1982; *Vocabulary Fluency,* Curriculum Associates, 1982. Also author of more than one hundred articles on reading and elementary education.

WORK IN PROGRESS: Prereading skills instruction; learning programs to improve reading skills.

SIDELIGHTS: Donald D. Durrell wrote *CA:* "What components of reading and language arts instruction increase the amount and quality of learning? This has been the focus of our fifty years of direction of graduate theses. There are still a large number of high-yield components that *should* appear in textbooks, but will not until publishers feel that the market is ready for them. During the past twelve years, Dr. Helen A. Murphy and I have built and evaluated small units of instruction in critical areas in the hope that the components will find their way into future textbooks. We still hope to eliminate reading failures from American schools!"

* * *

DWIGGINS, Don 1913-

PERSONAL: Born November 15, 1913, in Plainfield, N.J.; son of Clare Victor (a cartoonist) and Betsey (Lindsay) Dwiggins; married Olga Arabsky; children: Don Lindsay, Toni Kay. *Education:* Attended Los Angeles Junior College, 1932-33. *Home:* 3816 Paseo Hidalgo, Malibu, Calif.

CAREER: Commercial pilot; *Los Angeles Daily News,* Los Angeles, Calif., aviation editor, 1947-54; *Los Angeles Mirror News,* Los Angeles, aviation editor, 1956-62; station KTTV, Los Angeles, news writer, 1964; Disney Studios, Burbank, Calif., editor of "Mickey Mouse Newsreel," 1965; senior editor, *Plane & Pilot* (magazine), 1974-82; free-lance writer. Space technology consultant, Lockheed Aircraft Co., 1964. *Military service:* U.S. Army Air Forces, 1942-43; became master sergeant. *Member:* Aviation Aerospace Writers Association, Writers Guild of America, West.

AWARDS, HONORS: Award for best California news story of 1960, for coverage of Chessman execution; Aviation Aerospace Writers Association award for best aviation feature in metropolitan newspaper, 1961, and award for best aviation book, 1968, for *Hollywood Pilot; The Eagle Has Landed* was selected as one of the Child Study Association's Books of the Year, 1970.

WRITINGS: "Frankie" (a biography of Frank Sinatra), Paperback Library, 1961; *The S. O. Bees,* New American Library, 1963; *They Flew the Bendix Race,* Lippincott, 1965; *The Air Devils,* Lippincott, 1966; *Hollywood Pilot,* Doubleday, 1967; *The SST: Here It Comes, Ready or Not,* Doubleday, 1968; *The Barnstormers,* Grosset & Dunlap, 1968; *Space and the Weather,* Golden Gate, 1968; *Bailout,* Crowell, 1969; *Famous Flyers and the Ships They Flew,* Grosset & Dunlap, 1969; *Voices in the Sky,* Golden Gate, 1969.

On Silent Wings, Grosset & Dunlap, 1970; *The Eagle Has Landed,* Golden Gate, 1970; *Spaceship Earth,* Golden Gate, 1970; *Into the Unknown,* Golden Gate, 1971; *Robots in the Sky,* Golden Gate, 1972; *The Sky Is Yours,* Childrens Press, 1973; *Riders of the Winds,* Hawthorn Books, 1973; *The Search for Energy,* Childrens Press, 1974; *Build Your Own Sports Plane,* Hawthorn Books, 1974; *Restoration of Antique and Classic Planes,* TAB Books, 1975; *Aircraft Metal Work,* TAB Books, 1976; *Why Airplanes Fly* (juvenile), Childrens Press, 1976; *The Asteroid War* (juvenile), Childrens Press, 1978; *Jimmy Fox and the Flying Falcon* (juvenile), Childrens Press, 1978; *Jimmy Fox and the Mountain Rescue* (juvenile), Childrens Press, 1979; *Low-Horsepower Fun Aircraft You Can Build,* TAB Books, 1979; *Man-Powered Aircraft,* TAB Books, 1979.

Thirty-One Practical Ultralight Aircraft You Can Build, TAB Books, 1980; *Flying the Frontiers of Space,* Dodd, 1982. Also author of other books; also author of television material. Contributor of more than one thousand articles to numerous periodicals, including *Saturday Evening Post, Reader's Digest, Collier's, True, Argosy, This Week,* and *Parade.*

WORK IN PROGRESS: The Next Ten Years in Space, for Childrens Press; *Pilots' Bible,* for Doubleday.

BIOGRAPHICAL/CRITICAL SOURCES: Christian Science Monitor, May 1, 1969, May 7, 1970; *New York Times Book Review,* August 9, 1970.

E

ECHERUO, Michael J(oseph) C(hukwudalu) 1937-

PERSONAL: Born 1937, in Umunumo, Imo State, Nigeria; son of J. M. and Martha N. Echeruo; married Rose N. Ikwueke, 1968; children: Ikechukwu, Okechukwu, Ijeoma, Chinedu, Ugonna. *Education:* Attended Stella Maris College; University College of Ibadan (now University of Ibadan), B.A., 1960; Cornell University, M.A., 1963, Ph.D., 1965. *Office:* Vice Chancellor's Office, Imo State University, Owerri, Nigeria.

CAREER: Lecturer in English at the University of Nigeria (now University of Ibadan), Nsukka, until the outbreak of the Biafran civil war in 1967, returned to his post after the fighting ended in 1970, became professor of English and head of department, dean of postgraduate school, 1978-80; Imo State University, Owerri, Nigeria, president, 1981—.

WRITINGS: Mortality: Poems, Longmans, Green, 1968; (editor) *Igbo Traditional Life, Culture, and Literature*, Conch Magazine Ltd., 1971; *Joyce Cary and the Novel of Africa*, Africana Publishing, 1973; *Distanced: Poems*, I. K. Imprints, 1976; *The Conditional Imagination from Shakespeare to Conrad*, Macmillan, 1979; *Victorian Lagos*, Macmillan, 1979; *The Dimensions of Order*, Macmillan, 1980; (editor) William Shakespeare, *The Tempest*, Longman, 1981.

Work represented in anthologies, including *Modern Poetry from Africa*, edited by Gerald Moore and Ulli Beier, Penguin, 1963, *West African Verse: An Anthology*, edited by Donatus I Nwoga, Longmans Green, 1967, and *New African Literature and the Arts*, edited by Joseph Okpaku, Crowell, 1970. Contributor of poems to *Black Orpheus*.

SIDELIGHTS: Michael J.C. Echeruo directed the first production of John Pepper Clark's "Song of a Goat" at Enugu, Nigeria, in 1962.

* * *

EDDISON, John 1916-

PERSONAL: Born September 7, 1916, in Derbyshire, England; son of Frederick William (a clergyman) and Dorothea (Buchanan-Dunlop) Eddison. *Education:* Trinity College, Cambridge, M.A., 1939. *Home:* Durham Lodge, Crowborough, Sussex, England.

CAREER: Ordained minister in Church of England, 1939; St. John's, Tunbridge Wells, England, curate, 1939-43; Scripture Union, London, England, traveling secretary, 1943—. Honorary chaplain to Bishop of Rochester, 1947-59. Member of board of directors of school companies. *Member:* National Club, Marylebone Cricket Club.

WRITINGS—Published by Scripture Union, except as indicated: *Search Party*, 1960; *The Troubled Mind*, 1963, Concordia, 1972; *Christian Answers about Doctrine*, 1966; *Christian Answers to Contemporary Problems*, 1967; *Who Died Why*, 1970; *God's Frontiers*, 1972; *To Tell You the Truth*, 1972; *It's a Great Life*, 1973; *What Makes a Leader*, 1974; *Understanding Bible Topics*, 1977; *Step by Step*, Walters, 1977; *Talking to Children*, Walters, 1978; *Your Money and Your Life*, Walters, 1979; *What Christians Believe*, Hodder & Stoughton, 1981; *Towards Confirmation*, Marshall, 1982.

* * *

**EDWARDS, Elwyn Hartley 1927-
(Edward Leyhart)**

PERSONAL: Born April 17, 1927; son of Edward Hartley (an army officer) and May (Kent-Hartley) Edwards; married Mary Purnelle Hodgson; children: Sarah Elizabeth, Louise Mary. *Education:* Attended Indian Military Academy, 1944-45. *Religion:* Church of England. *Home:* Park Stud Cottage, Dedham, Essex, England. *Office: Riding* Magazine, 189 High Holborn, London W.C. 1, England.

CAREER: British Army, Brigade of Ghurkas, 1945-56, retired as major; Gibson Saddlery Co., Newmarket, England, director, 1956-64; IPC Magazine Division, London, England, editor of *Riding*, 1964-81, consultant editor of *Horse and Hound* and *Riding*, 1981—. *Member:* Institute of Journalists, British Horse Society, Welsh Pony and Cob Society, British Show Jumping Association, Arab Horse Society; also member of other horse societies. *Awards, honors:* Military Cross.

WRITINGS: Saddlery, Country Life, 1963; *Horseman's Guide*, Hamlyn, 1969; *Owning a Pony*, Thomas Nelson, 1970; *From Paddock to Saddle*, Thomas Nelson, 1972; (editor) *Horse and Rider Review*, Ian Allan, 1973; (editor with Candida Geddes) *Complete Book of the Horse*, Ward, Lock, 1973, Arco, 1974; *Go Riding*, Hamlyn, 1975; *Horses and Ponies*, W. H. Allen, 1975; *The Larousse Guide to Horses and Ponies of the World*, Larousse, 1979 (published in England as *The Hamlyn Guide to Horses and Ponies of the World*, illustrations by David Nockels, Hamlyn, 1979); (editor) *A Standard Guide to Horse and Pony Breeds*, McGraw, 1980; *Know Your Horses*, Methuen, 1980. Editor of Thomas Nelson's "Horsemaster" series; also editor of *Encyclopaedia of Riding and Problem Horses*. Contributor to numerous animal periodicals.

* * *

EGGLESTON, Wilfrid 1901-

PERSONAL: Born March 25, 1901, in Lincoln, England; son of Samuel (a farmer) and Ellen (Cowham) Eggleston; married Magdalena Raskevich, June 28, 1928; children: Anne Elisabeth. *Education:* Queen's University at Kingston, B.A., 1926. *Home:* 234 Clemow Ave., Ottawa, Ontario, Canada.

CAREER: Toronto Star and *Star Weekly*, Toronto, Ontario, 1926-33, began as reporter, became head of Ottawa bureau; correspondent for Reuter's (news service), 1934-36; press secretary, Royal Commission on Federalism, 1937-39; press censor for Canada, 1940-43, director of censorship, 1944; Carleton University, Ottawa, Ontario, professor of journalism and director of School of Journalism, 1947-66, professor emeritus, 1966—. *Awards, honors:* Order of the British Empire, 1943, for war services in censorship; LL.D., Carleton University, 1966; D.Litt., University of Western Ontario, 1967; National Press Club Award, 1968; Alex Award, Media '75, 1975.

WRITINGS: The High Plains (fiction), Macmillan, 1938; *The Road to Nationhood*, Oxford University Press, 1946; *Scientists at War*, Oxford University Press, 1950; *The Frontier and Canadian Letters*, Ryerson, 1957; (editor) *The Green Gables Letters*, Ryerson, 1960; *The Queen's Choice: A Story of Canada's Capital*, Queen's Printer, 1961; *Canada's Nuclear Story*, Clarke, Irwin, 1965; *While I Still Remember* (autobiography), Ryerson, 1968; *Newfoundland: The Road to Confederation*, Queen's Printer, 1974; *Prairie Symphony* (fiction), Borealis Press, 1978; *Research in Canada, 1916-1966*, Clarke, Irwin, 1978; *Literary Friends*, Borealis Press, 1980; *Homestead on the Range* (autobiography), Borealis Press, 1982. Contributor to newspapers.

WORK IN PROGRESS: An anthology of articles from Canadian newspapers.

SIDELIGHTS: Wilfrid Eggleston founded Canada's first school of journalism at Carleton University.

* * *

EHRLICH, Anne (Fitzhugh) Howland 1933-

PERSONAL: Born November 17, 1933, in Des Moines, Iowa; daughter of Winston D. and Virginia (Fitzhugh) Howland; married Paul Ralph Ehrlich (a population biologist and writer), December 18, 1954; children: Lisa Marie. *Education:* Attended University of Kansas, 1952-55. *Home:* Pine Hill, Stanford, Calif. 94305. *Office:* Department of Biological Sciences, Stanford University, Stanford, Calif. 94305.

CAREER: Stanford University, Stanford, Calif., research assistant and biological illustrator, 1959-75, senior research associate in biological sciences, 1975—.

WRITINGS: (With husband, Paul R. Ehrlich, and others) *How to Know the Butterflies*, W. C. Brown, 1961; (illustrator) P. R. Ehrlich and Richard W. Holm, *The Process of Evolution*, McGraw, 1963; (with P. R. Ehrlich) *Population, Resources, Environment: Issues in Human Ecology*, W. H. Freeman, 1970, 2nd edition, 1972; (with P. R. Ehrlich and John P. Holdren) *Human Ecology: Problems and Solutions*, W. H. Freeman, 1973; (with P. R. Ehrlich) *The End of Affluence: A Blueprint for Your Future*, Ballantine, 1974; (with P. R. Ehrlich and Holdren) *Ecoscience: Population, Resources, Environment*, W. H. Freeman, 1977; (with P. R. Ehrlich) *Extinction: The Causes and Consequences of the Disappearance of Species*, Random House, 1981; (with P. R. Ehrlich and Loy Bilderback) *The Golden Door: International Migration, Mexico, and the United States*, Wideview, 1981. Contributor to *Compton Yearbook* and *Brittanica Book of the Year*, 1971. Contributor to scientific journals and periodicals, including *Saturday Review, American Naturalist, New York Times Magazine*, and *Nature in Focus*.

SIDELIGHTS: Reviewing *The Golden Door: International Migration, Mexico, and the United States, Washington Post Book World*'s Christopher Dickey writes, "[This] book brings into focus virtually all the crucial problems [of immigration] and explains, as must be done, why some of the most troubling issues related to international migration remain blurred by ignorance." The reviewer admires the authors' "skill and patience" in examining immigration and commends the book's "many virtues." Robert Sherrill of the *New York Times Book Review* terms the work a "fascinating book," adding: "The solutions to the immigration crisis that [the authors] offer as possibilities are vague and not very hopeful. But never mind. In most respects, *The Golden Door* is a first-rate book, an excitingly scary book that sizes up a mammoth problem that the politicians appear determined to ignore for as long as possible."

In *Extinction: The Causes and Consequences of the Disappearance of Species*, Anne and Paul Ehrlich alert readers to the hazards of allowing any species of life to die out, and in particular, identify potential dangers to mankind when other species become extinct. The *New York Times Book Review*'s Bayard Webster observes, "In *Extinction*, Paul and Anne Ehrlich, members of Stanford University's department of biological sciences, explain in dramatic, definitive, and entertaining fashion the reason for the general alarm, and then present their strategy for the prevention of further extinctions, including our own." Webster concludes that the Ehrlichs "have produced a very readable volume that, in addition to demonstrating the importance of preserving species, is an invaluable compendium of facts, events, and theories of evolution, biology, environmental history, and ecology."

BIOGRAPHICAL/CRITICAL SOURCES: Donald W. Cox, *Pioneers of Ecology*, Hammond, 1971; *New York Times Book Review*, November 18, 1979, June 21, 1981; *Washington Post Book World*, December 16, 1979.

* * *

EHRLICH, Paul R(alph) 1932-

PERSONAL: Born May 29, 1932, in Philadelphia, Pa.; son of William (a salesman) and Ruth (a Latin teacher; maiden name, Rosenberg) Ehrlich; married Anne Fitzhugh Howland (a biological research associate and writer), December 18, 1954; children: Lisa Marie. *Education:* University of Pennsylvania, B.A., 1953; University of Kansas, M.A., 1955, Ph.D., 1957. *Politics:* Independent. *Home:* Pine Hill, Stanford, Calif. 94305. *Office:* Department of Biological Sciences, Stanford University, Stanford, Calif. 94305.

CAREER: Field officer on Northern Insect Survey, summers, 1951-52; associate investigator on United States Air Force research project in Alaska, 1956-57; Chicago Academy of Science, Chicago, Ill., research associate, 1957-58; University of Kansas, Lawrence, research associate, 1958-59; Stanford University, Stanford, Calif., assistant professor, 1959-62, associate professor, 1962-66, professor of biological sciences, 1966—, Bing Professor of Biological Sciences, 1976—, director of biological science graduate study department, 1966-

69, 1974-76. Editor in population biology and consultant in biology, McGraw Hill, 1964—. Has conducted field work in Africa, Latin America, Antarctica, Australia, and in Southeast Asia. Associate of Center for the Study of Democratic Institutions. Consultant, Behavioral Research Laboratories, 1963-67.

MEMBER: International Association for Ecology, Zero Population Growth (founder; president, 1969-70), Society for the Study of Evolution (vice-president, 1970), American Institute of Biological Science, Society of Systematic Zoology, American Society of Naturalists, Lepidopterists Society (secretary, 1957-63), American Museum of Natural History (honorary life member), American Association of University Professors, Airplane Owners and Pilots Association, California Academy of Sciences (fellow), Sigma Xi, Royal Aero Club of New South Wales. *Awards, honors:* National Science Foundation fellow at University of Sydney, 1965-66; Bestseller's Paperback of the Year Award, 1970, for *The Population Bomb.*

WRITINGS: (With wife, Anne H. Ehrlich, and others) *How to Know the Butterflies,* W. C. Brown, 1961; (with Richard W. Holm) *The Process of Evolution,* McGraw, 1963, 2nd edition, also with Dennis R. Parnell, 1974; *Principles of Modern Biology,* Addison-Wesley, 1968; (compiler with Holm and Peter H. Raven) *Papers on Evolution,* Little, Brown, 1968; *The Population Bomb,* Ballantine, 1968, revised and expanded edition, 1971.

(With A. H. Ehrlich) *Population Resources, Environment: Issues in Human Ecology,* W. H. Freeman, 1970, 2nd edition, 1972; (with others) *How to Be a Survivor,* Ballantine, 1970; (editor and compiler with John P. Holdren) *Global Ecology: Readings toward a Rational Strategy for Man,* Harcourt, 1971; (compiler with Holdren and Holm) *Man and the Ecosphere: Readings from Scientific American,* W. H. Freeman, 1971; (with A. H. Ehrlich and Holdren) *Human Ecology: Problems and Solutions,* W. H. Freeman, 1973; (with Holm and Michael E. Soule) *Introductory Biology,* McGraw, 1973; (with A. H. Ehrlich) *The End of Affluence: A Blueprint for Your Future,* Ballantine, 1974; (with Dennis Pirages) *Ark II: Social Response to Environmental Imperatives,* W. H. Freeman, 1974; (with Holm and Irene L. Brown) *Biology and Society,* McGraw, 1976; (with S. Shirley Feldman) *The Race Bomb: Skin Color, Prejudice, and Intelligence,* New York Times Co., 1977; (with A. H. Ehrlich and Holdren) *Ecoscience: Population, Resources, Environment,* W. H. Freeman, 1977.

(With A. H. Ehrlich) *Extinction: The Causes and Consequences of the Disappearance of Species,* Random House, 1981; (with A. H. Ehrlich and Loy Bilderback) *The Golden Door: International Migration, Mexico, and the United States,* Wideview, 1981.

Contributor: Garrett DeBell, editor, *The Environmental Handbook,* Ballantine, 1970; Harold W. Helfrich, Jr., editor, *The Environmental Crisis,* Yale University Press, 1970. Also author of, with others, *The Collected Papers: Index and Bibliography,* Volume IV, Pergamon. Contributor of articles to periodicals. Member of editorial board, *Systematic Zoology,* 1964-67, and *International Journal of Environmental Science,* 1969—.

SIDELIGHTS: See preceding sketch, Anne (Fitzhugh) Howland Ehrlich, for "Sidelights."

MEDIA ADAPTATIONS: Metro-Goldwyn-Mayer purchased documentary film rights to *The Population Bomb.*

BIOGRAPHICAL/CRITICAL SOURCES: Donald W. Cox, *Pioneers of Ecology,* Hammond, 1971; *New York Times Book Review,* July 17, 1977, November 18, 1979, June 21, 1981; *New York Times,* October 1, 1977; *Washington Post Book World,* December 16, 1979.

* * *

ELBERT, Virginie Fowler 1912-
(Virginie Fowler)

PERSONAL: Born February 8, 1912, in Brooklyn, N.Y.; daughter of Fred C. and Anna (Wolsey) Fowler; married George A. Elbert (a writer and editor); children: Steven, Suzanne. *Education:* Attended art school; also studied book design, pottery, and jewelry-making privately and with American Institute of Graphic Arts. *Home and office:* 801 West End Ave., New York, N.Y. 10025.

CAREER: Doubleday Book Shop, New York City, employee, 1939-40; Charles Scribner's Sons, New York City, assistant juvenile editor, 1941-51; Holt, Rinehart & Winston, Inc., New York City, children's book editor and head of department, 1951-57; Alfred A. Knopf, Inc., New York City, children's book editor and head of department, 1958-72; writer, editor, and photographer, 1972—. Has worked as free-lance newspaper and advertising artist; instructor at Institute of Study for Older Adults, New York City Community College (now New York City Community College of Applied Arts and Sciences), and at Interior Design Division of School of Continuing Education, New York University.

MEMBER: Children's Book Council (president), American Institute of Graphic Arts, Indoor Light Gardening Society of America (president of metropolitan chapter), American Crafts Council (craftsman member). *Awards, honors:* Silver Medal Award, Massachusetts Horticultural Society, 1978, for contributions to horticultural literature.

WRITINGS: (With Stanley Chin) *Two Lands for Ming* (juvenile novel), Scribner, 1945; (contributor of photographs) *The Wild Flowers of the United States,* McGraw, 1966; (with husband, George A. Elbert) *Simple Cooking for Sophisticates,* Hearthside, 1968; (with G. A. Elbert) *Fun with Terrarium Gardening,* Crown, 1973; (with G. A. Elbert) *Fun with Growing Herbs Indoors,* Crown, 1974; (with G. A. Elbert) *Plants That Really Bloom Indoors,* Crown, 1974; *Potterymaking,* Doubleday, 1974; (with Gloria R. Mosesson) *Jewelry Craft for Beginners,* Bobbs-Merrill, 1975; (with G. A. Elbert) *Fun with Growing Odd and Curious House Plants,* Crown, 1975; *Easy Enameling on Metal,* Lothrop, 1975; (with G. A. Elbert) *The Miracle Houseplants,* Crown, 1976; *Grow a Pet Plant,* Doubleday, 1977; *Shellcraft,* Bobbs-Merrill, 1977; (with G. A. Elbert) *The House Plant Decorating Book,* Dutton, 1977; (under name Virginie Fowler) *Folk Arts around the World,* Prentice-Hall, 1981; (under name Virginie Fowler) *Paperworks,* Prentice-Hall, 1982. Frequent contributor to *Ladies' Home Journal, Gourmet,* and *Woman's Day.*

WORK IN PROGRESS: Orchids of the World Coloring Book, for publication by Dover; a fictionalized biography; a novel.

SIDELIGHTS: Virginie Fowler Elbert commented: "There is a strong need in our mechanized world to return to the use of our hands and eyes to create and make our own personal objects. Without an apprentice system, formal or informal, the beginning skills are lost, and the relearning process can be long and frustrating."

AVOCATIONAL INTERESTS: International travel (especially Italy and France), photographing wild flowers, buildings, and landscapes, Byzantine and Renaissance art and history, tumbling beach stones gathered in the summer, all crafts.

ELGIN, (Patricia Anne) Suzette Haden 1936-

PERSONAL: Born November 18, 1936, in Louisiana, Mo.; daughter of Gaylord Lloyd (a lawyer) and Hazel (a teacher; maiden name, Lewis) Wilkins; married Peter Haden, 1955 (deceased); married George Elgin (a sales manager), 1964; children: (first marriage) Michael, Rebecca, Patricia; (second marriage) Benjamin. *Education:* Attended University of Chicago, 1954-56; Chico State College (now California State University, Chico), B.A., 1967; University of California, San Diego, M.A., 1970, Ph.D., 1973. *Home and office address:* Route 4, Box 192-E, Huntsville, Ariz. 72740. *Agent:* James Byron, P.O. Box 2389, Hollywood, Calif. 90028. *Office:* Department of Linguistics, San Diego State University, San Diego, Calif. 92182.

CAREER: Writer. ETV (channel 9), Redding, Calif., performer on folk music show and folk guitar instruction show, 1966-68; Chico Conservatory of Music, Chico, Calif., instructor, 1967-68; adult education teacher of French, 1968-69; teacher of guitar and music theory, 1969-70; University of California at San Diego, La Jolla, teacher of basic linguistics for Apache field methods, summer, 1971; San Diego State University, San Diego, Calif., associate professor of linguistics, 1972-80, associate professor emeritus, 1980—; Ozark Center for Language Studies, Huntsville, Ariz., founder and director, and publisher of newsletter, *The Lonesome Node,* 1980—. Worked as translator and interpreter for American Bar Association Committee on World Peace through Law. Has worked as a consultant. *Member:* Science Fiction Writers of America, Science Fiction Poetry Association, Association of Women in Psychology, National Council of Teachers of English, Lovingkindness (president). *Awards, honors:* Academy of American Poets Award, University of Chicago, 1955; Eugene Saxon Memorial Trust fellowship in poetry from *Harper's,* 1958.

WRITINGS—Published by Prentice-Hall, except as indicated: (Contributor) John Kimball, editor, *Syntax and Semantics,* two volumes, Academic Press, 1972; *What Is Linguistics?,* 1973, 2nd edition, 1979, workbook published as *Beginning Linguistics Workbook,* 1974; *Pouring Down Words* (English textbook), 1975; *The Gentle Art of Verbal Self-Defense,* 1980, Book II, in press.

Science fiction novels: *The Communipaths* (also see below), Ace Books, 1970; *Furthest* (also see below), Ace Books, 1971; *At the Seventh Level* (also see below), Daw Books, 1972; *Star-Anchored, Star-Angered,* Doubleday, 1979; *Communipath Worlds* (collection including *The Communipaths, Furthest,* and *At the Seventh Level*), Pocket Books, 1981; *The Ozark Trilogy* (includes *Twelve Fair Kingdoms, The Grand Jubilee,* and *And Then There'll Be Fireworks;* Science Fiction Book Club alternate selection), Doubleday, 1981. Contributor of articles and reviews to linguistics journals and to *Mother Earth News.*

WORK IN PROGRESS: A novel, *Native Tongue;* a nonfiction book on the uses of linguistics; a monograph on a case-grammar analysis of Ozark English; a medical case study, in fictional form; a book investigating the hypothesis that existing languages are not adequate to express the perceptions of women.

SIDELIGHTS: Suzette Haden Elgin writes: "A great deal of my time, and much of my writing, is devoted to an attempt to destroy the Romantic Love Ethic of our culture, which I see as the major barrier to male/female communication, the major obstacle to women's liberation, and a blasted nuisance generally." Her linguistic specialty is Amerindian languages, especially Navajo, Kumeyaay (a California Indian language), and Hopi.

AVOCATIONAL INTERESTS: Theology ("particularly seen as a discipline . . . religious language, for example"), guitar, singing.

* * *

ELKIN, Stanley L(awrence) 1930-

PERSONAL: Born May 11, 1930, in New York, N.Y.; son of Phil (a salesman) and Zelda (Feldman) Elkin; married Joan Marion Jacobson, February 1, 1953; children: Philip Aaron, Bernard Edward, Molly Ann. *Education:* University of Illinois, A.B., 1952, M.A., 1953, Ph.D., 1961. *Religion:* Jewish. *Home:* 225 Westgate, University City, Mo. 63130. *Agent:* Georges Borchardt, Inc., 136 East 57th St., New York, N.Y. 10022. *Office:* Department of English, Washington University, St. Louis, Mo. 63130.

CAREER: Washington University, St. Louis, Mo., instructor, 1960-62, assistant professor, 1962-66, associate professor, 1966-69, professor of English, 1969—. Visiting professor at Smith College, 1964-65, University of California, Santa Barbara, 1967, University of Wisconsin—Milwaukee, 1969, University of Iowa, 1974, Yale University, 1975, and Boston University, 1976. *Military service:* U.S. Army, 1955-57. *Member:* Modern Language Association of America, American Academy and Institute of Arts and Letters.

AWARDS, HONORS: Longview Foundation award, 1962; *Paris Review* humor prize, 1964; Guggenheim fellow, 1966-67; Rockefeller Foundation grant, 1968-69; National Endowment for the Arts and Humanities grant, 1972; American Academy of Arts and Letters award, 1974; Richard and Hinda Rosenthal Award, 1980; *Sewanee Review* prize, 1981, for *Stanley Elkin's Greatest Hits.*

WRITINGS: Boswell: A Modern Comedy (novel), Random House, 1964, reprinted, Warner Books, 1980; *Criers and Kibitzers, Kibitzers and Criers* (stories), Random House, 1966, reprinted, Warner Books, 1980; *A Bad Man* (novel), Random House, 1967, reprinted, Warner Books, 1980; *The Dick Gibson Show* (novel), Random House, 1971; *The Making of Ashenden* (novella; also see below), Covent Garden Press, 1972; *Searches and Seizures* (contains "The Bailbondsman," "The Making of Ashenden," and "The Condominium"), Random House, 1973 (published in England as *Eligible Men: Three Short Novels,* Gollancz, 1974), published as *Alex and the Gypsy: Three Short Novels,* Penguin, 1977; *The Franchiser* (novel), Farrar, Straus, 1976; *The Living End* (contains three contiguous novellas, "The Conventional Wisdom," "The Bottom Line," and "The State of the Art," which first appeared, in slightly different form, respectively in *American Review, Antaeus,* and *TriQuarterly*), Dutton, 1979; *Stanley Elkin's Greatest Hits,* foreword by Robert Coover, Dutton, 1980; (editor with Shannon Ravenel and author of introduction) *The Best American Short Stories, 1980,* Houghton, 1980; *The First George Mills* (novel), Pressworks, 1981; *George Mills,* Dutton, 1982.

Also author of film scenario "The Six-Year-Old Man," published in *Esquire,* December, 1968. Stories appear in *The Best American Short Stories,* Houghton, 1962, 1963, 1965, and 1978. Contributor to *Epoch, Views, Accent, Esquire, American Review, Antaeus, TriQuarterly, Perspective, Chicago Review, Journal of English and Germanic Philology, Southwest Review, Paris Review, Harper's, Oui,* and *Saturday Evening Post.*

SIDELIGHTS: "'What happens next?' is a question one doesn't usually ask in Stanley Elkin's [works]," writes Christopher Lehmann-Haupt of the *New York Times.* "Plot is not really Mr. Elkin's game. His fiction runs on language, on parody, on comic fantasies and routines. Give him conventional wisdom and he will twist it into tomfoolery. . . . Give [him] cliche and jargon and he will fashion of it a kind of poetry." Long recognized and praised for his extraordinary linguistic vitality and comic inventiveness, Elkin, though he dislikes these terms, has been described as a "stand-up literary comedian" and a "black humorist" who invites us to laugh at the painful absurdities, frustrations, and disappointments of life. His books "aren't precisely satires," according to Bruce Allen in the *Chicago Tribune Book World,* but rather are "unillusioned yet affectionate commemorations of rascally energy and ingenuity." Ironically, in the view of some critics, Elkin's strength has often been his weakness as well, for he is sometimes criticized for carrying his high-energy rhetoric and comic monologues to extremes. Nonetheless, Josh Greenfeld, who considers Elkin "at once a bright satirist, a bleak absurdist, and a deadly moralist," declares in the *New York Times Book Review,* "I know of no serious funny writer in this country who can match him."

Searches and Seizures, a collection of three novellas, "should provide the uninitiated with an ideal introduction to [Elkin's] art even as it confirms addicts like me in our belief that no American novelist tells us more about where we are and what we're doing to ourselves," claims Thomas R. Edwards in the *New York Times Book Review.* "This is an art that takes time—his scenes are comic turns that build cunningly toward climax in deflative bathos, and in the novels there's an inclination toward the episodic, the compulsive storyteller's looseness about connections and logic. [The first novella,] 'The Bailbondsman,' . . . is just about perfectly scaled to Elkin's imagination; we have a tight focus, one day in the life of an aging Cincinnati bondsman of Phoenician descent, which nevertheless accommodates an astonishing thickness of texture, a weaving of events and psychic motifs that is as disturbing as it is funny."

The other two stories in *Searches and Seizures* are "The Making of Ashenden" and "The Condominium." The former is, in the words of Clancy Sigal in the *New Republic,* "a fantasy satirizing Brewster Ashenden, an idle wastrel in love with Jane Loes Lipton, a kind of Baby Jane Holzer with a Schweitzerian yen to do good. The 'shocking' climax, within the dream landscape of a rich Englishman's private zoo, has Brewster interminably screwing a bear." The man-bear sex scene "is vigorous, raunchy, painful, smelly—and downright *touching,*" exclaims Bruce Allen in the *Hudson Review,* and it forces Brewster, humbly and hilariously, to admit his animal nature.

"The Condominium" is a tale about a graduate student who inherits his father's Chicago condominium and "then gets fatally drawn into the numbing quality of its community life," notes Christopher Lehmann-Haupt. Though the pieces of these stories seem to be always "flying apart," Lehmann-Haupt concludes: "In some subtle way that defies all equations—metaphorical, symbolical, allegorical, or otherwise—everything connects with everything else. And tells us in a way that lies just beyond explanation, in crazy poetic searches and seizures, much about loneliness, sex, and mortality."

According to Michael Wood in the *New York Review of Books,* "the real subject of the three short novels contained in *Searches and Seizures* is a complicated invention of character by means of snowballing language. The writer invents characters who invent themselves as they talk and thereby invent him, the writer." The protagonist of "The Bailbondsman," for example, introduces himself as "Alexander Main the Bailbondsman. I go surety. . . . My conditions classic and my terms terminal. Listen, I haven't much law—though what I have is on my side, binding as clay, advantage to the house—but am as at home in replevin, debenture, and gage as someone on his own toilet seat with the door closed and the house empty." "The motive force of Elkin's writing," says William Plummer in the *New Republic,* "is 'the conventional wisdom' itself. His aggressive, high energy rhetoric comes into being under the pressure of cliche, which is not to suggest that his *metier* is either satire or camp. Rather, he seems to share with Emerson the vaguely platonic idea that the hackneyed is 'fossil poetry'—the Truth in tatters, in its fallen condition."

Thomas R. Edwards claims the first story "shows that an art founded on aggression, on assaults against the reader's habits of association and sense of good manners, can be both wrenchingly funny and oddly moving." Plummer concurs, calling "The Bailbondsman" "one of the great works in the language—right up there, perhaps, with [Faulkner's] 'The Bear' and [Melville's] 'Bartleby.'" He adds, however, one qualification: "But you must grant Elkin his premises. He has no interest in 'the arduous, numbing connections' in plot or even structure. He's not anti-story, . . . but rather has an insatiable 'sweet tooth for instance,'" which he treats with gags, interpolated tales, catalogues and assorted pieces. Like *Tristram Shandy,* he believes in progress by digression."

But Clancy Sigal, also writing in the *New Republic,* will not grant Elkin's premises: "Elkin's monologues, at which he excels, are the alienated patter of a brilliant, but turned off, stand-up literary comic. I'm very suspicious of it in large doses." Moreover, L. J. Davis charges in the *Washington Post Book World* that Elkin's focus on language weakens the characterization. "Elkin's characters," declares Davis, "are artifacts, superbly sculptured statuary adorned with rich garlands of prose. Sedentary, separate from us, their gestures frozen, they are meant to be observed but not experienced, admired but not touched. The strength of the writing imbues them with a kind of static life, but it does not bestow upon them either an autonomous vitality or a poignant humanity. They exist to prove a point. The way in which they are written about is more important than the way they react to their surroundings, and they are trundled from place to place like demonstration models, more for the purpose of description than for faltering and imperfect reasons of their own. In a way, the prose itself becomes a hero."

Far from seeing Elkin's characters as passive instruments, however, Jonathan Raban argues in *Encounter* that the heroes in *Searches and Seizures* are tragic, in the classical sense: "They build up glittering verbal palaces around themselves, in cascading rhetorical monologues, in dreams, in deep wordy caverns of introspection. Their worlds are perfected right down to the final bauble on the last minaret. Then the crunch comes. They discover that no one else is living there but them. The brilliant talker is the proprietor and sole inhabitant of his universe, and he might as well be adrift in outer space. His fatal proficiency in language has taken him clean out of the world of other people. This is the central theme."

The Dick Gibson Show, Elkin's third novel, "contains enough comic material for a dozen nightclub acts," notes R. Z. Sheppard in *Time,* "yet it is considerably more than an entertainment." Joseph McElroy claims in the *New York Times Book Review* that this "absolutely American compendium . . . may turn out to be our classic about radio." The hero of the book is a disc jockey who has worked for dozens of small-town radio stations across the country. "As the perpetual apprentice, whetting his skills and adopting names and accents to suit geography," says Sheppard, "he evolves into part of American folklore. As Dick Gibson, the paradox of his truest identity is that he is from Nowhere, U.S.A."

A radio talk-show host, Gibson is the principal listener for a bizarre cast of callers: Norman, the "caveman from Africa," whose linguistic equivalent for "chief" is "Aluminum Siding Salesman"; a rich orphaned boy—his skydiving parents accidentally parachuted into a zoo's tiger den—who has fears of being adopted for his money; a woman who wants to trade a bow and arrow, and in exchange will accept nothing but used puppets. Sheppard surmises that Gibson is "a McLuhan obfuscation made flesh—a benevolent witch doctor in an electronic village of the lonely, the sick, and the screwed up." McElroy concurs, arguing that Elkin "unites manic narrative and satiric wit to ensure that we know Dick Gibson [as] . . . receiver of an America whose invisibility speaks live into the great gap of doubt inside him, itinerant listener in this big-hearted country where it's so hard to get anyone to listen."

Christopher Lehmann-Haupt, however, believes that while it could be argued that Dick Gibson is "the sound of American silence, . . . this is forcing things somewhat. . . . The bittersweet and seriocomic truth is that Stanley Elkin is [merely] stringing routines together. . . . Which is not to say that I didn't love . . . passages like 'the wide laps beneath her nurse's white uniform with its bas-relief of girdle and garter like landmarks under a light snow.' Or that I didn't sink to my knees from laughing time and again. It's just that after a while one gets tired, can predict the patterns, begins to look for more than gags, and can't really find much."

But Geoffrey Wolf of Newsweek finds that the novel's loose structure is patterned after that of radio itself. Acknowledging that the book "flies straight in the teeth of fiction's decorums," Wolff concludes that Elkin "insists on his freedom, radio's freedom to wander, and seems to accept radio's risk, the risk that the audience's attention will wander." McElroy, too, is convinced that Elkin's digressions enhance the thematic concerns of the novel: "Far from seeming prolix, Mr. Elkin's expansiveness—notably in the lunatic monologues of one horrendous talk-show night fourteen years after [World War II]—proves a rich and anxious means of further surrounding his theme."

John Leonard, writing in *Saturday Review*, considers *The Franchiser* to be the closest of Elkin's novels to *The Dick Gibson Show*; he also deems it Elkin's best. "It is a brilliant conceit—the franchising of America on the prime interest rate; manifest destiny on credit," states Leonard. "It is also considerably more than a conceit. It is a frenzied parable, rather as though the Wandering Jew and Willy Loman had gotten together on a vaudeville act. Who, after all, is displaced by the franchise? Ben Flesh, [the protagonist,] knows: 'Kiss off the neighborhood grocers and corner druggists and little shoemakers.' Kiss off, in other words, ethnicity, roots. Assimilate. Homogenize. What's in the melting pot? Campbell's soup, Kraft cheese, Kool-Aid. . . . The immigrants who shortened their names, the Jews who changed them, the slaves who borrowed new ones from their masters, were consequently diminished. They tailored who they were to the specifications of a culture that wanted someone else, insofar as the culture knew anything at all about what it wanted."

Despite Leonard's explication and the fact that his assessment is shared by other reviewers, some critics fault the book for its digressiveness—a common flaw in Elkin's novels according to Lehmann-Haupt, Robert Towers, and John Irving. Towers says in the *New York Times Book Review:* "While he can invent wonderful scenes full of madness and power, Elkin seems unable to create a sustaining comic action or plot that could energize the book as a whole and carry the reader past those sections where invention flags or becomes strained. Without the onward momentum of plot—no matter how zany—we are left with bits, pieces and even large chunks that tend to cancel each other out and turn the book into a kind of morass. . . . The need is especially felt in a book as long as *The Franchiser*, where the potentials of situation, character, and theme—very rich potentials—are never fully mobilized into a truly memorable novel." Novelist John Irving, also writing in the *New York Times Book Review*, declares that the "rap against Elkin is that he's too funny, and too fancy with his prose, for his own good. . . . It is brilliant comedy, but occasionally stagnant: the narrative flow is interrupted by Elkin's forays into some of the best prose-writing in English today; it is extraordinary writing, but it smacks at times of showing off—and it is digressive. Despite the shimmering language, the effect is one of density; I know too many readers who say they admire Stanley Elkin as a writer, but they haven't finished a single Elkin novel."

Anthony Heilbut, however, maintains that as in *Searches and Seizures* and *The Dick Gibson Show*, Elkin's "stylistic pyrotechnics" clearly have a thematic function: "The novel's bravado is to set itself against cultural illiteracy of the untellable in all its forms; when the untellable is the truly monstrous disease of multiple sclerosis, [with which Elkin himself is afflicted,] Elkin's verbal triumph is very moving. It may not be an insight into our public mess, but when Ben Flesh observes that his multiple sclerosis is 'always incurable but only generally fatal' his grammatical trickery is literally lifesaving." Michael Wood of the *New York Review of Books* shares Heilbut's belief. He writes that jokes and "gags for Elkin seem to represent some sort of hold on randomness, serve both to clarify and to stave off the dizzying sense that nothing has to happen the way it does, and they afford Elkin and his heroes a recurring, cheerfully defeated stance."

The Living End is, in the opinion of many critics, Elkin's best work. John Irving, for example, calls it a "narrative marvel [with] a plot and such a fast pace that a veteran Elkin reader may wonder about the places where he lost interest, or lost his way, in reading Elkin before." The book consists of three contiguous novellas, "The Conventional Wisdom," "The Bottom Line," and "The State of the Art," which provide the kind of conventional, "beginning-middle-end," structure often lacking in Elkin's other novels. The titles of the novellas also reflect Elkin's characteristic attention to cliche, according to Harold Robbins in the *Washington Post Book World*. Echoing William Plummer's comment on *Searches and Seizures*, Robbins points out that Elkin "knows that cliches are the substance of our lives, the coinage of human intercourse, the ways and means that hold our messy selves and sprawling nation intact. To exploit their vigor and set them forth with unexpected force has been the basis of his success as a novelist; no writer has maneuvered life's shoddy stock-in-trade into more brilliantly funny forms."

In addition to the strenuous language and the book's structural balance, "in *The Living End* Elkin has finally found a subject worthy of him," writes Geoffrey Stokes in the *Village Voice*. "No more does he diddle with the surrogates, no more leave us wiping the laughter from our eyes and wondering if we really care quite all that much about One-Hour Martinizing. This time, Elkin goes directly for the big one: God, He Who, etc." *Time*'s R. Z. Sheppard believes that with *The Living End* "Elkin must finally be recognized as the grownup's Kurt Vonnegut, the Woody Allen for those who prefer their love, death, and cosmic quarrels with true bite and sting."

With a vision that is sometimes blasphemous, the book begins with Ellerbee, a Minneapolis liquor-store owner and "the nicest of guys," notes Sheppard, who goes to Heaven after being gunned down behind the counter during a robbery. His surprise at Heaven's unsurprising sights, sounds, and smells—pearly gates, angels with harps, ambrosia, manna, and a choir that sings "Oh dem golden slippers"—however, turns to shock when St. Peter tells him, "beatifically," to go to Hell. The "ultimate ghetto," Hell also gives Ellerbee a sense of *deja vu*, with the devils' horns and pitchforks, and the sinners raping and mugging each other endlessly and pointlessly; moreover, there is cancer, angina, indigestion, headache, toothache, earache, and a painful, third-degree burning itch everywhere. "What Ellerbee discovers," declares Irving, "is that everything [about the afterlife] is true.... It's like life itself, of course, but so keenly exaggerated that Elkin manages to make the pain more painful, and the comedy more comic."

After several years God visits Hell, and Ellerbee asks why he, a good man, has been condemned. A mean-spirited and petty God charges him with selling the demon rum, keeping his store open on the Sabbath, uttering an occasional oath, having impure thoughts, and failing to honor his parents, even though he was orphaned as an infant. Sheppard infers that Ellerbee "ignored what Elkin labels 'the conventional wisdom.' The corollary: in a cosmos ruled by an unforgiving stickler, 'one can never have too much virtue.'"

Jeffrey Burke points out in *Harper's* that Elkin "founds his irreverence on the truths of contemporary religion, that is, on the myriad inconsistencies, cliches, superstitions, and insanities derived from centuries of creative theology," but claims that Elkin's purpose lies beyond satire. Harold Robbins explains: "Unlike others of his generation,... Elkin does not identify with the laughter of the gods, he does not dissociate himself from the human spectacle by taking out a franchise on the cosmic joke. Hard and unyielding as his comic vision becomes, Elkin's laughter is remission and reprieve, a gesture of willingness to join the human mess, to side with the damned, to laugh in momentary grace at whatever makes life Hell."

The remainder of the story leads up to the Day of Judgment, when God appears before the Heavenly Host to reveal that the purpose of creation was theatrical, though He never found His audience: "'Goodness? Is that what you think?... Were you born yesterday? You've been in the world. Is that how you explain trial and error, history by increment, God's long Slap and Tickle, His Indian-gift wrath? *Goodness?* No. It was Art! It was always Art. I work by the contrasts and metrics, by beats and the silences. It was all Art. *Because it makes a better story is why.*'" "Precisely because it's God talking," surmises Geoffrey Stokes, "the question of why He does what He does is genuinely important—especially when it turns out that Elkin is ultimately addressing the obligations of all creators. And suddenly—when the eternally-disfigured Christ learns that his suffering occurred solely because God thought it would make a better story—the laughter stops, and the very funny, very serious Elkin goes deeper than he's ever gone before. *The Living End* makes it at once possible to forgive God, and unnecessary to forgive Stanley Elkin."

MEDIA ADAPTATIONS: Of his novellas, "The Bailbondsman" was filmed as "Alex and the Gypsy." The film rights to *Boswell* and *A Bad Man* have been purchased.

CA INTERVIEW

CA interviewed Stanley Elkin by phone July 30, 1981, at his home in St. Louis, Mo.

CA: "Inspiration is real," you believe. "It's real as digestion." Do you find inspiration usually available, or is it very much influenced by moods, pressures, other vicissitudes the writer can't control?

ELKIN: Sounds like something a Jesus freak might say. All I mean is that once in a while you get lucky, you get an idea. But the impetuous idea, the idea that will start you on the career of a novel, you *do* have to wait for. You can't sit down and say, "Well, I think I'll write a novel." And once you have the good idea, you can't sit back and wait for the muses to sing to you again. You've got to pursue it; search and destroy; that's where the work comes in. When I said that about inspiration, I was just talking about the thing that gets you off the dime.

CA: Is it likely to be futile, then, for a writer to force himself to write if he doesn't have an idea, a situation, *to begin with?*

ELKIN: I take back the word *inspiration*.

CA: When did you begin to be interested in writing?

ELKIN: About the time I was toilet trained. I wasn't any good, but it was something I wanted to do. I really got the idea from my father's business letterhead. He'd bring back letterhead from his firm—this might have been before I could read, I don't remember—and I was charged by the fact that every page looked like the page preceding it. I remember scribbling on that stuff.

CA: Did you get much encouragement from parents or teachers?

ELKIN: Yes, both. My teachers would give me assignments—I wasn't writing novels, I was writing compositions—and there were one or two teachers back in grammar school who said that I had some talent. My mother always felt the best writing I ever did were the skits I wrote in high school.

CA: You've said that you wrote like Faulkner until you began to find your own style in writing the story "On a Field, Rampant." Do you find in teaching creative writing that most students have a similar problem?

ELKIN: I wish they did. It would be a lot more fun to read stuff that was vaguely reminiscent of Faulkner or any other real writer.

CA: Are most of them unread, as many teachers now complain of their students?

ELKIN: There are two kinds of students we're talking about. I teach a course to graduate students, and they're *not* unread. The undergraduates, of course, are.

CA: You've indicated that students need help in recognizing what makes a good situation for fiction. Are you able to help them with this?

ELKIN: Mostly I help by saying, "No, that ain't it."

CA: Do you still feel that personal experience is tricky to work with in fiction?

ELKIN: Yes.

CA: Do most students try to write out of their own personal experience?

ELKIN: They used to. I don't know that *I've* talked them out of it—maybe the very difficulty itself has talked them out of it—but it seems I'm getting fewer stories now, both by undergraduates and by graduates, that have anything to do not only with *their* real life, but with *anybody's* real life.

CA: Sounds discouraging.

ELKIN: Not really. We have a writers' program here at Washington University. There are perhaps nine people currently in the program, and a full third of those are first-rate writers. That's not bad. You're batting three hundred and thirty-three; that could get you a good contract next year. Of the three I'm talking about, two have already published and one is clearly on the way.

CA: Teaching and writing seem to be a productive combination for you. Does each activity help the other in some way?

ELKIN: No. What helps is the fact that I don't have to work as hard when I'm teaching a writing class. I don't have to work as hard as a teacher, since it's essentially an art that can't be taught. So I have more time for my own writing even without short-circuiting the folks who are there to learn.

CA: Do you often have a problem of time?

ELKIN: Since I've been doing nothing but teaching writing—and, this past semester, doing nothing but my own writing, since I'm off the entire year—there's no problem. I know that when I teach a literature class, just *one* literature class, it's impossible for me to get any work done. Say it meets Monday, Wednesday, and Friday; that's only three hours, but it's impossible for me to get any work done because I'm studying the stuff myself. But I haven't taught literature for three years now; I just teach the writing. That's not only fun, it's easy to disengage and get back to the typewriter—or in my case, the word processor.

CA: Is that how you write now?

ELKIN: For a year, yes. I love it.

CA: The critics and reviewers often mention the vitality *of your writing. From its exuberance the reader might imagine that it leaps from your head onto the paper in final form. But you're a careful reviser, aren't you?*

ELKIN: I am. That's what I'm doing right now.

CA: What have you found to be the greatest difficulties in writing?

ELKIN: That's hard. It seems to me that all fiction is or ought to be a piece of logic. I guess not allowing fiction's phony arguments to get in the way of the real solutions to the particular plot you're working on is the hard part.

CA: What do you mean by "fiction's phony arguments?"

ELKIN: I mean spectacular scenes. I'm revising one right now which I'm thinking of throwing out. It's a wonderful idea for a scene, but it gets in the way of the novel's logic.

CA: Aside from going to the word processor, have your working patterns changed much over the years?

ELKIN: Yes, I work harder now than I used to, I think. With the word processor, I spend more time just seated at the desk. I can go for six hours, and that's a long stretch. Before I got the word processor, I couldn't do that.

CA: You like to read your own writing out loud to people, you've said. Do you read it to other people while it's still in progress?

ELKIN: I don't like reading anything that's been published. I like being invited places and giving readings and being paid for them. I mean, I don't go up to people and say, "Hey, you want to hear something?" The word processor's too heavy.

CA: Your wife is a painter. Does she ever ask your help with opinions of something she's working on?

ELKIN: Yes, I help her out with the reds and greens.

CA: Do you ever read your work to her while you're working on it?

ELKIN: She goes to sleep.

CA: You've felt a steady progress in your writing, an improvement with each book.

ELKIN: Every writer likes to think that's so, but I think it *is* so, in my case. Sure, you're always trying to do things better. I want every sentence to be as good as it possibly can be. I'm involved in episodic structure, and those episodes are part of a pattern. I hope that when one reads them, or when one reads them intelligently, I connect the dots and they spell *mother*.

CA: You are fortunate to have several other good writers near you in St. Louis. Do you see each other often?

ELKIN: Indeed.

CA: When you get together, do you talk about writing, or everything but writing?

ELKIN: Advances; we talk a lot about advances and sales. We talk about money. We talk about people behind their backs. We certainly don't talk about art. We talk about who fell on his face.

CA: Unlike many other writers, you say you love the excesses of America, the "overstatement of the neon signs on our Broadways." Doesn't it seem to you, though, that many of our regional distinctions are being lost through those excesses?

ELKIN: All you have to do is go twelve miles out of the way and there's still frontier. I mean that quite literally. You're driving along an interstate, and suddenly it says "Detour" and you're lost. America has a very thin geological and sociological crust that is immediately recognized as American, but if you get off the beaten track, you don't see that anymore. This last spring I was up in a place called Houghton Hancock, Mi., giving a reading at Michigan Technological University. My God, I could have been in Wales!

CA: Have you found much of the academic criticism of your work good?

ELKIN: No, bad. I read the pieces about my work in those books that I find myself in, and if I hadn't known that I wrote what they're writing about, I wouldn't recognize their decoding of the work. That's what they're trying to do—decode it. They think literature is written in Ultra.

CA: Although you write to please yourself, as you've said, you do respond to mail from readers, don't you?

ELKIN: Yes.

CA: Do you get letters mostly from people who like what you've written?

ELKIN: Yes, but most of the time they tend to be madmen. I was on "The Dick Cavett Show" in April or May, and I thought, well, I should be getting some mail. And I did, but except for letters from old friends who happened to see the show, they were all crazy. That's understandable. I've never written a letter to anybody I've seen on television or whose book I've read. Two categories of fan—the mad and the wanters.

CA: Did any of the viewers send you their novels to read and help them get published?

ELKIN: Somebody did write to say he was out west but would come to St. Louis, Mo. He had seen me on the Cavett show, and he wanted to talk about his novel with me. Now that's crazy.

CA: Are there plans to produce any of the screenwriting you've done?

ELKIN: The Living End has been optioned now for the third year in a row. *The Franchiser* has just been optioned. For every ten options, maybe one thing gets made. Only one of my books has been made into film; a novella called "The Bailbondsman" was made into a movie called "Alex and the Gypsy."

CA: If either of those novels is made into a movie, will you have a hand in it?

ELKIN: No. The script for "The Living End" has already been written, and I did not do it.

CA: Do you want to discuss George Mills?

ELKIN: I'm still working on it, and I have two more chapters to write. That doesn't sound like much, but they've got to be very good chapters or the book will fall on its face. I know what's going to be in those two chapters, but I don't think I'll finish the book until maybe the middle of November. I go back to teaching in January.

BIOGRAPHICAL/CRITICAL SOURCES—Books: Stanley Elkin, *The Dick Gibson Show*, Random House, 1971; Allan Guttman, *The Jewish Writer in America: Assimilation and the Crisis of Identity*, Oxford University Press, 1971; Naomi Lebowitz, *Humanism and the Absurd in the Modern Novel*, Northwestern University Press, 1971; Tony Tanner, *City of Words*, J. Cape, 1971; Raymond M. Olderman, *Beyond the Waste Land: A Study of the American Novel in the 1960s*, Yale University Press, 1972; Elkin, *Searches and Seizures*, Random House, 1973; *Contemporary Literary Criticism*, Gale, Volume IV, 1975, Volume VI, 1976, Volume IX, 1978, Volume XIV, 1980; *Dictionary of Literary Biography*, Gale, Volume II: *American Novelists since World War II*, 1978, *Yearbook: 1980*, 1981; Elkin, *The Living End*, Dutton, 1979; Doris G. Bargen, *The Fiction of Stanley Elkin*, Lang, 1980.

Periodicals: *Book Week*, June 21, 1964; *New York Times Book Review*, July 12, 1964, January 23, 1966, October 15, 1967, February 21, 1971, October 21, 1973, June 13, 1976, June 10, 1979; *Saturday Review*, August 15, 1964, January 15, 1966, November 18, 1967, May 29, 1976; *Times Literary Supplement*, October 22, 1964, August 27, 1971, January 18, 1980; *Library Journal*, January 15, 1966; *New York Review of Books*, February 3, 1966, January 18, 1967, March 21, 1974, August 5, 1976, August 16, 1979; *Christian Science Monitor*, May 12, 1966; *Choice*, October, 1966; *Washington Post Book World*, October 22, 1967, October 29, 1967, March 7, 1971, October 28, 1973, June 13, 1976, January 7, 1979, July 1, 1979; *Life*, October 27, 1967; *Time*, October 27, 1967, March 1, 1971, October 29, 1973, May 24, 1976, June 4, 1979, November 10, 1980; *Nation*, November 27, 1967, August 28, 1976; *New Leader*, December 4, 1967; *Commonweal*, December 8, 1967; *New Yorker*, February 24, 1968; *Punch*, March 27, 1968, January 1, 1969; *Listener*, March 28, 1968; *Books and Bookmen*, May, 1968.

New York Times, February 17, 1971, October 9, 1973, May 21, 1976, May 25, 1979; *Newsweek*, April 19, 1971, June 18, 1979; *Publishers Weekly*, October 22, 1973; *New Republic*, November 24, 1973, March 23, 1974, June 12, 1976, June 23, 1979; *Hudson Review*, spring, 1974; *Studies in Short Fiction*, fall, 1974; *Encounter*, February, 1975; *Contemporary Literature*, spring, 1975; *TriQuarterly*, spring, 1975; *Paris Review*, summer, 1976; *New York*, June 18, 1979; *Harper's*, July, 1979; *Chicago Tribune Book World*, July 8, 1979; *Los Angeles Times Book Review*, July 15, 1979; *Village Voice*, August 20, 1979; *Critique*, Volume XXI, number 2, 1979; *Esquire*, November, 1980.

—Sketch by James G. Lesniak

—Interview by Jean W. Ross

*   *   *

ELLIOTT, Janice 1931-

PERSONAL: Born October 14, 1931, in Derby, England; daughter of Douglas John (an advertising executive) and Dorothy (Wilson) Elliott; married Robert Cooper (a public affairs adviser for an oil company), April 11, 1959; children: Alexander. *Education:* Oxford University, B.A. (with honors), 1953. *Residence:* England. *Agent:* Richard Scott Simon, Ltd., 32 College Cross, London N1 1PR, England.

CAREER: Journalist in London, England, 1954-62; novelist, free-lance journalist, and critic, 1962—. *Member:* P.E.N. (England), Society of Authors.

WRITINGS—Novels: *Cave with Echoes*, Secker & Warburg, 1962; *The Somnambulists*, Secker & Warburg, 1964; *The Godmother*, Secker & Warburg, 1966, Holt, 1967; *The Buttercup Chain*, Secker & Warburg, 1967; *The Singing Head*, Secker & Warburg, 1968; *Angels Falling*, Knopf, 1969.

The Kindling, Knopf, 1970; *The Birthday Unicorn* (children's novel), Gollancz, 1970; *A State of Peace* (first novel in trilogy), Knopf, 1971; *Private Life* (second novel in trilogy), Hodder & Stoughton, 1972; *Alexander in the Land of Mog* (children's novel), Brockhampton Press, 1973; *Heaven on Earth* (third novel in trilogy), Hodder & Stoughton, 1975; *A Loving Eye*, Hodder & Stoughton, 1977; *The Honey Tree*, Hodder & Stoughton, 1978.

Summer People, Hodder & Stoughton, 1980; *Secret Places*, Hodder & Stoughton, 1981, St. James Press, 1982; *The Country of Her Dreams*, Hodder & Stoughton, 1982.

Contributor to anthologies: A. D. Maclean, editor, *Winter's Tales*, Macmillan, 1966; Derwent May, editor, *Good Talk*, Gollancz, 1968; Judith Burnley, editor, *Penguin Modern Stories 10*, Penguin, 1972; A. S. Burack, editor, *Techniques of Novel Writing*, Writer, Inc., 1973; James Hale, editor, *The Midnight Ghost Book*, Barrie & Jenkins, 1978; Caroline Hobhouse, editor, *Winter's Tales 25*, Macmillan, 1979; Hale, editor, *The After Midnight Ghost Book*, Hutchinson, 1980; Hale, editor, *The Twilight Book*, Gollancz, 1981.

Regular book reviewer for *Sunday Telegraph*, 1969—. Contributor of short stories to *Harper's Bazaar*, *Transatlantic Review*, *Nova*, and *Queen*; contributor of articles to newspapers and magazines, including *Sunday Times* and *Twentieth Century*; contributor of book reviews to *Sunday Times*, *London Times*, *New York Times*, and *New Statesman*. Former member of editorial staff, *House and Garden*, *House Beautiful*, *Harper's Bazaar*, and *Sunday Times*.

WORK IN PROGRESS: A novel.

SIDELIGHTS: Janice Elliott's novels have been praised by many reviewers for the authenticity of their atmosphere and mood. According to a *Times Literary Supplement* review of *A State of Peace*, Elliott is "now firmly establishing herself as a novelist with notable talent for recreating times past. . . . [Her books] capture a remarkably authentic, solid and evocative background." David Haworth, reviewing the same book for *New Statesman*, comments: "To write of very recent history is a more formidable job than it might seem. Janice Elliott is not in the least daunted. . . . She evokes the immediate postwar world with accuracy and panache." *Secret Places*, Elliott's highly acclaimed account of a girls' school in World War II England, is, according to Gillian Greenwood of *Spectator*, a "tight, self-contained story [which draws] the reader inside school walls. . . . That England is at war is made evident from the perfectly executed period detail." And Piers Brendon in *Books and Bookmen* describes *A State of Peace* as "an imaginative and deeply felt account of the vissitudes of an upper middle class family in the London of the immediate post-war years. The atmosphere of demob drabness, poverty and points, bomb-sites and black marketeers is well conveyed. . . . I found this an involving and moving book—one which transmits life instead of trying to explain it."

William Boyd, however, finds the futuristic setting in Elliott's *Summer People* "puzzling." In the *Times Literary Supplement*, Boyd states: "The book's post-1984 world consists of a few layabout hippies on the beach, wandering stray dogs, hints that essential services are not all they could be, and dark talk of violence in the cities. The apocalyptic doom-laden atmosphere that's so patently striven for just doesn't emerge and odd references to the oil running out and planes called Super-Jumbos strike one merely as afterthoughts." A *Listener* critic is more impressed with Elliott's scenario: "*Summer People* is a perceptive, witty and disturbing book. The use of the present tense and the way places are described like paintings . . . produce a sultry, threatening atmosphere, like the lull before a cosmic storm." And Peter Tinniswood of the *London Times* believes the book is "perfection. . . . Gradually a complex and beautifully modulated picture is built up of a society crumbling in on itself. . . . It is a brilliantly imaginative work. Everything about it shimmers with quality of the highest order."

Several critics comment on Elliott's economical use of language and images and how this helps to convey theme. "She builds meaning from snatches of conversation, exact portrayals of scene and mood," Mary Borg says in *New Statesman*. In a review of *The Kindling*, Borg writes: "One is deeply impressed with the reverberations of the story. The effect is of gradual osmosis." But Anne Duchene, reviewing *The Honey Tree* for the *Times Literary Supplement*, finds "the author's taste for elegant, allusive incisiveness . . . has taken a . . . regrettable turn into a rather clogged, portentous shorthand. . . . A great deal [, however,] is still enjoyable." Finally, John Naughton, appraising *Secret Places* for *Listener*,

asserts: "The beauty of it all is that nothing much happens. Ms. Elliott has succeeded in etching her characters, and their story, with a gossamer touch. Her book is full of eloquent understatement, the kind that communicates with the reader as surely as the half-finished sentences of an old friend. One was glad to receive her so loud and clear."

MEDIA ADAPTATIONS: "The Buttercup Chain" was produced by Columbia Pictures in 1969.

AVOCATIONAL INTERESTS: Sailing.

BIOGRAPHICAL/CRITICAL SOURCES: Times Literary Supplement, July 21, 1966, July 11, 1970, July 23, 1971, October 13, 1978, April 18, 1980, March 13, 1981, March 19, 1982; *Saturday Review*, April 8, 1967; *Nation*, September 11, 1967; *New Statesman*, June 12, 1970, July 16, 1971; *Book World*, November 8, 1970; *Books and Bookmen*, September, 1971; *Spectator*, March 15, 1975, March 28, 1981; *London Times*, April 3, 1980, March 18, 1982; *Listener*, April 10, 1980, March 5, 1981.

* * *

EMME, Eugene M(orlock) 1919-

PERSONAL: Born November 3, 1919, in Evanston, Ill.; son of Earle Edward (a psychologist) and Ada (Morlock) Emme; married Ruth Rance, June 18, 1942; children: Sandra Jean, Stephen Rance, Stuart Morlock. *Education:* Morningside College, A.B., 1941; University of Iowa, M.A., 1946, Ph.D., 1949. *Religion:* Protestant. *Home and office:* 11308 Cloverhill Dr., Silver Spring, Md. 20902.

CAREER: Civilian pilot prior to World War II, and flight instructor for U.S. Army; University of Iowa, Iowa City, instructor in practice teaching of social studies at University High School, 1946-47, university instructor in history, 1947-48; Air University, Montgomery, Ala., assistant professor, 1949-50, associate professor, 1950-52, professor of international politics, 1952-57, director of graduate study group of Air War College, 1953-56; U.S. Office of Civil and Defense Mobilization, Battle Creek, Mich., director of Operations Research project, 1958; National Aeronautics and Space Administration (NASA), Washington, D.C., chief historian, 1959-78; currently free-lance historian for Clio Research Associates and consultant to Time-Life, Inc. Lecturer at military staff colleges and to academic groups. *Military service:* U.S. Navy, aviator, World War II. U.S. Air Force Reserve, 1948-73, became colonel.

MEMBER: International Academy of Astronautics, American Astronautical Society (fellow; member of board of directors, two terms), Organization of American Historians, Society for the History of Technology (founding member; member of advisory board), American Association for the Advancement of Science (fellow), Air Force Historical Foundation, American Institute of Aeronautics and Astronautics (founder of History Manuscript Award), Air Force Association, British Interplanetary Society (fellow), National Space Club (founder and sponsor of annual Robert H. Goddard Historical Essay Competition, 1962—), National Space Institute (life member).

AWARDS, HONORS: Commendation for Meritorious Civilian Service, U.S. Air Force, 1958; Apollo Award and Outstanding Performance Award, both NASA, 1969; Distinguished Alumni Award, Morningside College, 1972; Tsiolkovsky History Award, State Museum of Cosmonautics, Kaluga, U.S.S.R., 1981.

WRITINGS: International Politics and National Air Power, Air University, 1951; *Hitler's Blitzbomber*, Air University, 1951; (editor) *The Impact of Air Power: National Security and*

World Politics, Van Nostrand, 1959; *Aeronautics and Astronautics: An American Chronology of Science and Technology in the Exploration of Space, 1915-1960,* National Aeronautics and Space Administration, 1961, and editor of annual supplement, *Astronautics and Aeronautics: Chronology on Science, Technology and Policy,* 1961-73; (editor) *The History of Rocket Technology,* Wayne State University Press, 1964; *A History of Space Flight,* Holt, 1965; (author of foreword) Shirley Thomas, *Men of Space,* Volume VII, Chilton, 1965; (contributor) Melvin Kranzberg and C. W. Pursell, editors, *Technology in Western Civilization,* two volumes, Oxford University Press, 1967; (editor) *Two Hundred Years of Flight in America: A Bicentennial Survey,* American Astronautical Society, 1977; (editor) *Twenty-Five Years of the American Astronautical Society, 1954-1979,* Univelt, 1980. Editor of history series for American Astronautical Society. Contributor of articles and reviews to periodicals. Member of editorial board of *Aerospace Historian* and *Journal of the British Interplanetary Society.*

WORK IN PROGRESS: Editing *Science Fiction Space Futures: Past and Present,* for American Astronautical Society; *The White House and the Cosmos;* lectures and articles.

SIDELIGHTS: "Writing about one's own work surely will not be useful to eliminate the sheer torture, inefficiency, and hard work in my experience," Eugene M. Emme told *CA.* "Upon reflection perhaps writing aerospace history was my academic salvation as it was later a professional necessity enforced by learning a lot about a significant field of high interest to others. If I began as a loner among historians, such was an intellectual challenge which truly assisted any scholarship I may have exhibited. If my writing has any style it is letting documented facts speak for themselves—there were few historians worth quoting in my field until lately. Majoring in European history dictated stricter standards of precision as well as influential contrasts in conflicting cultures in evolution. Any art in my writing was largely the product of continuous reflection and much rewriting, helped by some good teachers and sometimes the skill of good editors helping one to express himself to others. For historians research is the trigger. Historians cannot use single sources like journalists, while memoirs are always hindsight views.

"Upon examination I note few of my writings garnered royalties of any note, and as a public servant much more was written which has never been published (not all memoranda to be sure). During my first week in the civil service I had the pleasure of hearing a Secretary of the Air Force quote one of my academic articles, while one essay with an attached anthology was read by a [United States] president.

"Getting started writing is happenstance out of schooling and personal reading until one's name is in print as the author of something. . . . But it was my father, a professor of psychology, who had insisted that I co-author with him an article on educational attitudes. As an undergraduate I first got my name in print, other [than in] some items I had written for the college newspaper. At that time, Abigail Van Buren and Ann Landers wrote the weekly gossip column at Morningside College so my name often appeared in print [but in] other than any authorship. In a senior reading course I discovered the first airplane flight in the state of Iowa was in Sioux City, and not in Iowa City as claimed, a first lesson in embarking on critical historical writing.

"Out of government thirty years later, I am still doing most of my writing after midnight, have too many meetings to go to, much research to complete, and so much to write. Somehow I had best get one of those books written first. My greatest satisfaction has been helping solid young historians pick up good pieces of the action. My greatest fans were my parents and my wife. My greatest pleasure is that some things written decades ago seem of interest to others today."

* * *

EPSTEIN, Charlotte 1921-

PERSONAL: Born February 18, 1921, in Brooklyn, N.Y.; daughter of Morris (a house painter) and Pauline (a garment worker; maiden name, Sobel) Epstein. *Education:* Brooklyn College (now Brooklyn College of the City University of New York), B.A., 1945; University of Miami, Coral Gables, Fla., M.A., 1953; University of Pennsylvania, Ph.D., 1956; postdoctoral study at San Francisco State College (now University). *Residence:* Philadelphia, Pa. *Office:* College of Education, Temple University, Philadelphia, Pa. 19122.

CAREER: High school teacher of English, Latin, French, and social studies in Miami Beach, Fla., 1946-51, assistant principal, 1951-53; National Conference of Christians and Jews, Philadelphia, Pa., assistant director for eastern Pennsylvania and southern New Jersey, 1955-57; University of Pennsylvania, Philadelphia, assistant professor of human relations and staff associate of Greenfield Center for Human Relations, both 1957-61; Philadelphia Police Department, Philadelphia, social scientist, 1961-66; Temple University, Philadelphia, associate professor, 1966-69, professor of curriculum and instruction, 1969-75, professor of early childhood and elementary education, 1975—. Adjunct professor of nursing, Temple University, 1969-72. Conducted clinic in human relations for police officers at Michigan State University, 1963; director of Coppin State College Intergroup Relations Institute, summers, 1969, 1970; staff member, Institute for Teacher Corps Leadership, summer, 1969; taught English to scientists in China, 1981-82. Special examiner for Philadelphia Civil Service Commission to select human relations representative for Center of Human Relations, 1958; research analyst for American Friends Service Committee, 1961. Member of Fellowship Commission's committee on community tensions, 1955-68; member of Philadelphia Board of Education's sub-committee on non-discrimination, 1964.

WRITINGS: Intergroup Relations for Police Officers, Williams & Wilkins, 1961; (contributor) Alvin Vaughn and Robert A. Shultheis, editors, *Changing Undergraduate Business Teacher Education Programs to Prepare Teachers for Culturally Different Youth,* Center for Vocational and Technical Education, Temple University College of Education, 1968; *Intergroup Relations for the Classroom Teacher,* Houghton, 1968; *Affective Subjects in the Classroom: Exploring Race, Sex, and Drugs,* Intext Publishers Group, 1972; *Effective Interaction in Contemporary Nursing,* Prentice-Hall, 1974; *Nursing the Dying Patient,* Reston, 1975; *Learning to Care for the Aged,* Reston, 1977; *Classroom Management and Teaching: Persistent Problems and Rational Solutions,* Reston, 1979; *An Introduction to the Human Services,* Prentice-Hall, 1981; *The Nurse Leader: Philosophy and Practice,* Reston, 1982; *Mainstreaming Skills for Classroom Teachers,* Reston, in press.

WORK IN PROGRESS: A novel, *Murder by Law.*

SIDELIGHTS: Charlotte Epstein writes: "Most of my writing (based on empirical data) deals with relationships between antagonistic groups—primarily racial groups. My aim has been to develop strategies for conflict resolution in productive ways so that people may be free to become all they can be. I write because sometimes I get tired of conflict."

ESFANDIARY, F. M.

PERSONAL: Born in Brussells, Belgium; son of A. H. Sadigh (a diplomat) and Mohtaram Esfandiary. *Education:* Attended schools in the Middle East, Europe, and the United States. *Agent:* Curtis Brown Ltd., 575 Madison Ave., New York, N.Y. 10022. *Office address:* P.O. Box 24421, Los Angeles, Calif. 90024.

CAREER: Member of Conciliation Commission for Palestine, United Nations, 1952-54; did research on social problems in Iran, 1961-62. Writer, 1954—. Worked at various times as counselor in camps for children in New York and California. Lecturer in futurist philosophy, New School for Social Research, Smithsonian Institution, Extension Division, University of California, Los Angeles, and elsewhere. *Awards, honors:* Farfield Foundation grant, 1965; Bread Loaf Writers Conference fellowship, 1966; Rockefeller Foundation grant, 1966.

WRITINGS: Day of Sacrifice (novel), Obolensky, 1959; *The Beggar* (novel), Obolensky, 1965; *Identity Card* (novel), Grove, 1966; *Optimism One* (nonfiction), Norton, 1970; *Up-Wingers* (nonfiction), John Day, 1973; *Telespheres* (nonfiction), Fawcett, 1977.

Work represented in anthologies, including *Essays Today,* edited by William Moynihan, Harcourt, 1968; *Dimensions of the Future,* edited by Maxwell Norman, Holt, 1974; *Woman Year 2000,* edited by Maggie Tripp, Arbor House, 1974. Contributor to *Nation, New York Times Sunday Magazine, Science Digest, New York Times,* and other periodicals.

WORK IN PROGRESS: Three nonfiction books.

SIDELIGHTS: "Most books are too long, too wordy, too slow," F. M. Esfandiary told *Futurist* interviewer Mico Delianova. Believing that "modern readers do not have the patience to slush through a mass of verbiage," Esfandiary contends that "any book over 100 or 150 pages is not worth reading. The author has not crystallized the ideas effectively," he explains. That is why Esfandiary's nonfiction books are concise publications that read, in Delianova's words, "like rapid printouts." A futurist who maintains that "we are now moving beyond the age of print," Esfandiary tries to "approximate the rhythms of electronics" in his prose. Nor is that the most radical feature of his writing. According to critics, the content of Esfandiary's books is even more controversial than his style. Writing in the *Los Angeles Times,* William Overend observes that "Esfandiary sees a world where there will be no schools, national governments, conventional family units or traditional parent-child relationships. And that's just for openers."

Esfandiary has detailed his ideas in three books—*Optimism One, Up-Wingers,* and *Telespheres*—which together, he told Dielianova, "constitute the synthesis of a triumphant new philosophy of the future." Unlike doomsayers and cynics who see mankind heading into an era of shrinking resources and spiraling costs, Esfandiary foresees a prosperous future for humanity. "We are at the beginning of an age of limitless abundance," he remarked in a *New York Times* interview. "This energy scare is a total fabrication. There is no scarcity; there is only the psychology of scarcity. People . . . brought up in the puritan old world of sacrifice and privation . . . believe they don't really deserve abundance, leisure and pleasure; . . . and yet that's exactly what we're moving toward."

Not only will we be creatures of leisure, we will also live forever, Esfandiary maintains. "This very day we are outgrowing the confinements of our microplanet and opening up the fantastic potentials of our Universe," he told the *Futurist.* "We are also breaking out of the limitations of our mortal animal bodies to extend each human life indefinitely. We are on our way to becoming Universal and Immortal." This feat will be accomplished, reports *New York Times* writer Leslie Bennetts, "through the gradual evolution of these 'gawky, fragile animal bodies' into more durable, even eternal alternatives. Malfunctioning parts will be replaced with 'durable, versatile components'; nonflesh implants will be substituted for original parts. . . . The result will be what Mr. Esfandiary calls 'telebodies,' comprising many micro-electronic parts."

Esfandiary believes social structures will also be transformed. Schools will be abolished and replaced by teleducation; cities, which are already "obsolete," will become museums, and people will move from one instant community (called mobilias) to another; globalism and space colonies will supersede nations and people will abandon their national identities to become "Universal." The nuclear family and even marriage itself will disappear. Writes Overend, "Among the specifics in Esfandiary's future world would be sperm and egg banks where geneticists would select the children to be born—all very computerized and scientific. Children would be raised in Child Center Homes (learning via TV and computers) where adults who liked children would visit. There wouldn't be just one Mom and Dad; there would be hundreds of them."

While Esfandiary has many supporters, he also has his critics. Associated Press writer Kay Bartlett reports that "he gets the most adverse reaction when he calls for the complete abandonment of the family and describes motherhood as a cop-out for women who are afraid to get involved with the world." ("Parenthood," he told *CA,* "is the ultimate chauvinism.") To his adversaries Esfandiary offers the reassurance that in time his theories will seem acceptable—even normal. Besides which, he told the *New York Times,* "the thrust of history and evolution is incontrovertible and irreversible, and no government can stop or even slow down the cumulative force of change."

AVOCATIONAL INTERESTS: World affairs, United Nations, global planning, normative philosophy, post-industrial world, space, physical immortality, the future.

BIOGRAPHICAL/CRITICAL SOURCES: New York Herald Tribune Book Review, August 30, 1959; *New Yorker,* September 12, 1959; *New York Times Book Review,* November 14, 1965; *Time,* December 24, 1965; *New York Times,* July 24, 1966, August 31, 1966, November 8, 1966, July 11, 1979; *Washington Post,* December 30, 1973, January 27, 1978; *Wisconsin State Journal,* March 19, 1978; *Los Angeles Times,* March 20, 1978; *Detroit News,* March 22, 1978; *Futurist,* June, 1978; *Los Angeles Reader,* April 2, 1982.

* * *

ESLER, Anthony (James) 1934-

PERSONAL: Born February 20, 1934, in New London, Conn.; son of James Arthur (an artist, sheetmetal worker, and shipfitter) and Helen (a teacher; maiden name, Kreamer) Esler; married Carol Clemeau (a college professor and novelist), 1961; children: Kenneth Campbell, David Douglas. *Education:* University of Arizona, B.A., 1956; Duke University, M.A., 1958, Ph.D., 1961; University of London, postdoctoral study, 1961-62. *Office:* Department of History, College of William and Mary, Williamsburg, Va. 23185.

CAREER: College of William and Mary, Williamsburg, Va., assistant professor, 1962-67, associate professor, 1967-72, professor of history, 1972—. Visiting associate professor, Northwestern University, 1968-69. American Council of Learned Societies research fellow, Chicago, 1969-70; College of William and Mary research fellow, 1975-76. *Member:* Amnesty International, American Historical Association, Authors Guild, Authors League of America. *Awards, honors:* Fulbright scholar in London, 1961-62.

WRITINGS: The Aspiring Mind of the Elizabethan Younger Generation, Duke University Press, 1966; *Bombs, Beards and Barricades,* Stein & Day, 1971; *The Youth Revolution,* Heath, 1974; *The Blade of Castlemayne,* Morrow, 1974; *Hellbane,* Morrow, 1975; *Lord Libertine,* Morrow, 1976; *Forbidden City,* Morrow, 1977; *The Freebooters,* Futura (London), 1978, revised edition published as *Pirate,* Morrow, 1979; *Generational Studies: A Basic Bibliography,* privately printed, 1979; *Babylon,* Morrow, 1980; *Bastion,* Jade Books (London), 1981.

WORK IN PROGRESS: A History of the World, two volumes, for Prentice-Hall; *Generations in History: An Introduction to the Concept.*

SIDELIGHTS: Anthony Esler told *CA:* "As a novelist and historian, I have always wanted to lead vicariously—through writing—as wide a variety of interesting lives as I could find or invent. Every book I do is therefore a new challenge. A new subject, of course, new characters, a new setting in time and space, and a new story—true or fictional—to tell. But also and every bit as important, new themes, new formal problems to solve, new genres to explore.

"I have thus written about political revolutionaries and religious zealots, about romantic young men and women and cynical older ones, about people in love with power, in love with ideas, in love with money, in love with love. I have set these stories—and found these histories—in the Americas, in Europe, in the Near and Far East, from the sixth century B.C. to the 1960s A.D. And I have presented this gallery of human lives in what seemed to me to be an appropriate range of literary forms: in romantic and ironic adventure, stark tragedy, picaresque comedy, monographic and semi-popular history.

"There have of course been underlying continuities. Perennials like love and death, faith and fanaticism, and the eternal conflicts of cultures, social types, and generations have permeated almost all my writing. But mostly it is the variety that fascinates me when I sit down to meditate on ancient Mesopotamia or ask myself what the *last* President of the United States might be like. I write for the same reason that I travel: to see what I can of the world we all live in—a village-eye view of East Africa, a spiritual seeker's vision of the Ganges, or Moscow through the eyes of a young Russian woman who set out to be a mathematician and got lost along the way.

"Infinite variety within the bounds of one man's finite life is the point of writing for me."

AVOCATIONAL INTERESTS: Drawing, travel, islands and mountains, sea-beaches, ruins, serious talk, and a very few people.

*   *   *

ETTER, Dave 1928-

PERSONAL: Born March 18, 1928, in Huntington Park, Calif.; son of Harold Pearson and Judith (Goodenow) Etter; married Margaret Cochran, August 8, 1959; children: Emily Louise, George Goodenow. *Education:* University of Iowa, B.A., 1953. *Politics:* Independent. *Home and office:* 414 Gates St., Elburn, Ill. 60119.

CAREER: Before 1961, did odd jobs in Iowa, Indiana, Illinois, Massachusetts, and California; Northwestern University Press, Evanston, Ill., editor, 1961-63; *Encyclopaedia Britannica,* Chicago, Ill., editor and writer, 1964-73; Northern Illinois University Press, De Kalb, Ill., editor, 1974-80; free-lance writer and editor, 1980—. *Military service:* U.S. Army, 1953-55. *Member:* Illinois State Historical Society.

AWARDS, HONORS: Bread Loaf Writers Conference fellow in poetry, 1967; Midland Poetry Award, 1967, and Friends of Literature poetry award, 1967, both for *Go Read the River;* Illinois Sesquicentennial Poetry Prize, 1968, for *The Last Train to Prophetstown;* Theodore Roethke Poetry Prize, 1971.

WRITINGS—Poetry, except as indicated: *Go Read the River,* University of Nebraska Press, 1966; *The Last Train to Prophetstown,* University of Nebraska Press, 1968; *Strawberries,* Juniper Press, 1970; *Voyages to the Inland Sea* (also includes prose), University of Wisconsin, 1971; *Crabtree's Woman,* BkMk Press, 1972; *Well You Needn't,* Raindust Press, 1975; *Bright Mississippi,* Juniper Press, 1975; *Central Standard Time: New and Selected Poems,* BkMk Press, 1978; *Alliance, Illinois,* Kylix Press, 1978, 2nd edition, Spoon River Poetry Press, 1983; *Open to the Wind,* Uzzano, 1978; *Riding the Rock Island through Kansas,* Wolfsong Press, 1979; *Cornfields,* Spoon River Poetry Press, 1980; *West of Chicago,* Spoon River Poetry Press, 1981; *Boondocks,* Uzzano, 1982.

Contributor: Lucien Stryk, editor, *Heartland: Poets of the Midwest,* Northern Illinois University Press, 1967; R. Schreiber, editor, *31 New American Poets,* Hill & Wang, 1969; M. Williams, compiler, *Contemporary Poetry in America,* Random House, 1973; Robert Killoren, editor, *Late Harvest: Plains and Prairie Poets,* BkMk Press, 1977; Dan Jaffe and John Knoepfle, editors, *Frontier Literature: Images of the American West,* McGraw, 1979; David R. Pichaske, editor, *Beowulf to Beatles and Beyond: The Variations of Poetry,* Macmillan, 1981.

Also contributor to more than sixty anthologies and textbooks. Contributor to more than 140 literary magazines, including *Prairie Schooner, Massachusetts Review, Midwest, Choice, Poetry Northwest, Beloit Poetry Journal, Saturday Review, Poetry, Nation,* and *North American Review.*

WORK IN PROGRESS: Main Street Blues, a book of poems.

SIDELIGHTS: Dave Etter told *CA:* "I have always written about the small town and rural Midwest because that is all I know well, all I have a real feel for, all I really care about deeply. There is an endless wealth of poem material right in my hometown; I will never be forced to look elsewhere. It is not easy to say for sure what authors have influenced me the most but I would surely have to list Walt Whitman, Sherwood Anderson, Carl Sandburg, Mark Twain, George Ade, Thomas Hardy, William Faulkner, and Richard Bissell. Recently, I have been considerably influenced by some of America's jazz greats, particularly Thelonious Monk, Dizzy Gillespie, and Miles Davis—they have shown me new rhythms, new ways to break the line, new structures."

Of Etter's work, the *Milwaukee Journal*'s Norbert Blei writes: "Whatever it is that characterized the Midwest—cows, crows, cicadas, hollyhocks, the back screen door banging real good— Etter has made a poem of it. . . . He knows the lay of the land and the junctions, loves the sleepy, small-town life, and records it all as carefully as the village clerk."

BIOGRAPHICAL/CRITICAL SOURCES: Panorama (Chicago Daily News), July 16, 1966; *Poetry,* February, 1967, February, 1971; *Chicagoland,* November, 1968, March, 1969; *Milwaukee Journal,* October 7, 1979.

F

FABER, Doris (Greenberg) 1924-

PERSONAL: Born January 29, 1924, in New York, N.Y.; daughter of Harry and Florence (Greenwald) Greenberg; married Harold Faber (a writer for *New York Times*), June 21, 1951; children: Alice, Marjorie. *Education:* Attended Goucher College, 1940-42; New York University, B.A., 1943. *Home address:* R.D.1, Ancram, N.Y. 12502.

CAREER: New York Times, New York, N.Y., reporter, 1943-51; writer.

WRITINGS—Juveniles: *Elaine Stinson: Campus Reporter*, Knopf, 1955; *The Wonderful Tumble of Timothy Smith*, Knopf, 1958; *Printer's Devil to Publisher: Adolph S. Ochs of the New York Times* (Junior Literary Guild selection), Messner, 1963; *Luther Burbank: Partner of Nature*, Garrard, 1963; *The Life of Pocahontas*, Prentice-Hall, 1963; *Behind the Headlines: The Story of Newspapers*, Pantheon, 1963; *The Miracle of Vitamins*, Putnam, 1964; *Horace Greeley: The People's Editor*, Prentice-Hall, 1964; *Robert Frost: America's Poet* (Junior Literary Guild selection), Prentice-Hall, 1964.

Clarence Darrow: Defender of the People, Prentice-Hall, 1965; *Captive Rivers: The Story of Big Dams*, Putnam, 1966; *Enrico Fermi: Atomic Pioneer*, Prentice-Hall, 1966; *John Jay*, Putnam, 1966; *Rose Greenhow: Spy for the Confederacy*, Putnam, 1967; *Petticoat Politics: How American Women Won the Right to Vote*, Lothrop, 1967; (with husband, Harold Faber) *American Heroes of the 20th Century*, Random House, 1967; *Anne Hutchinson*, Garrard, 1970; *I Will Be Heard: The Life of William Lloyd Garrison*, Lothrop, 1970; *Lucretia Mott*, Garrard, 1971; *Enough! The Revolt of the American Consumer*, Farrar, Straus, 1972; *Harry Truman*, Abelard, 1972; *Oh, Lizzie! The Life of Elizabeth Cady Stanton*, Lothrop, 1972; *Nationalism*, Harper, 1973; *The Perfect Life: The Shakers in America*, Farrar, Straus, 1974; *Franklin Roosevelt*, Abelard, 1975; *Wall Street: A Story of Fortunes*, Harper, 1979.

Adult nonfiction: *The Mothers of American Presidents*, New American Library, 1968; *The Presidents' Mothers*, St. Martin's, 1978; (with H. Faber) *The Assassination of Martin Luther King, Jr.*, F. Watts, 1978; *The Life of Lorena Hickok: E.R.'s Friend* (Book-of-the-Month Club alternate selection), Morrow, 1980. Contributor of occasional feature stories to newspapers, 1951—.

WORK IN PROGRESS: Several biographical and historical books.

SIDELIGHTS: Doris Faber was doing routine research for a commissioned book on the life of Eleanor Roosevelt when she made a startling discovery. A bundle of letters, previously unavailable to scholars, suggested that the first lady may have been, as *Los Angeles Times Book Review* critic Carolyn See suggests, "'in love,' perhaps even in a physical sense" with Lorena Hickok, one of the foremost women journalists of the time. Faber's first reaction, reports Kenneth S. Lynn of the *Times Literary Supplement*, was "to have the Hickok papers sealed up again until at least the year 2,000. When this proved impossible, she decided that she simply could not walk away from a biographical discovery of such magnitude. She would turn the papers into a book." Abandoning her original project, Faber instead produced *The Life of Lorena Hickok: E.R.'s Friend*.

Though critics speculate that Hickok's biography would never have been written were it not for her friendship with Eleanor Roosevelt, they find her an interesting woman in her own right. "She reminds one of those brave young women in a Dreiser novel who, in shirtwaist and long skirt, struggled determinedly in the early years of this century to escape the dreariness of small-town life in the Middle West and seek their fortunes in the great city," Arthur Schlesinger, Jr., writes in the *New York Times Book Review*. Born to a poverty-stricken family, Hickok was abused by her father and neglected by her mother, who died when Lorena was only thirteen. After her mother's death, Hickok became a domestic servant in a boarding house. Eventually, she worked her way through college and got a job at the *Battle Creek Journal*. "Fifteen years later," Schlesinger says, "she was a top reporter for the Associated Press in New York, chain-smoking and hard-drinking, covering events such as the sinking of the Vestris and the Lindberg kidnapping and reputed to be the first woman whose byline appeared above a page-one story in the *New York Times*."

It was as a journalist that Hickok first came in contact with Eleanor Roosevelt in 1932. Lynn writes: "While waiting to learn whether the Democratic convention in Chicago had nominated her husband for president, Eleanor Roosevelt invited two reporters from the Associated Press to have breakfast with her in the Executive Mansion in Albany. As they left the mansion a short time later, one of the reporters turned to the other and said, 'That woman is unhappy about something.' The speaker was Lorena Hickok who knew something of unhappiness herself."

Sylvia Jukes Morris writes in *Washington Post Book World* that Hickok was "immediately attracted to Eleanor Roosevelt's patrician qualities. She also felt a special empathy with her plainness, ungainly height and poor dress sense. For her part, Eleanor Roosevelt was drawn to Hickok's directness, humor, quick intelligence and imagination. She envied women of achievement and longed to be one of them." Though she had already spent twenty-three years in the public eye by the time her husband became president, Eleanor Roosevelt felt inadequate to assume the role of first lady. She feared that she would be unfavorably compared to her Uncle Theodore's wife, Edith, whom, Faber reports, she considered "one of the most successful and admired hostesses the White House had ever had." She had also learned of her husband's affair with his secretary, Lucy Mercer, and felt despondent that she "had not been able to hold the attention of a man she loved," Lynn says.

Soon after Roosevelt was inaugurated president, Hickok quit her Associated Press job and went to work for Harry Hopkin's Federal Emergency Relief Administration. There, as a chief field investigator, she filed reports of bureaucratic bungling and deception, which *Los Angeles Times Book Review* writer Walter Wells calls "among the most vivid records we have of that time of not-so-quiet depression." Her work sometimes took her out of Washington, D.C. for months at a time; nevertheless, she and Eleanor wrote to one another daily. Critics say the intimate tone of their correspondence suggests that the two women were deeply in love. "Hick darling," Eleanor Roosevelt wrote in a letter dated March 7, 1933, "All day long I've thought of you & another birthday I *will* be with you . . . Oh! I want to put my arms around you. I ache to hold you close. Your ring is a great comfort. I look at it & I think she does love me or I wouldn't be wearing it." Over a year later, on September 1, 1934, Eleanor Roosevelt wrote, "I wish I could lie down beside you tonight & take you in my arms."

Though evidence indicates that Eleanor Roosevelt's infatuation with Lorena Hickok diminished as her self-confidence increased, her friend's ardor never cooled. Elizabeth Cleland notes in the *Washington Star* that after election night Hickok "all but ceased being a reporter. She was Mrs. Roosevelt's confidant; her love for Eleanor Roosevelt was the most important thing in her life, then and for the next thirty years."

The correspondence that the women exchanged during this time was entrusted to Hickok. Though she destroyed those letters she deemed too private to be seen by others, over 3000 still remain. In noting what she calls the "sensational tinge" of this writing, Faber arouses her readers' curiosity. "What we want to know—to put it less decorously than Mrs. Faber ever does: Were Hick and Mrs. Roosevelt actually lovers?" writes Christopher Lehmann-Haupt of the *New York Times*.

According to Elizabeth Ollen of the *Cincinnati Enquirer*, that question can never be answered. "The exact nature of Hickok's friendship with Eleanor Roosevelt," she writes, "will never be known for sure." The uncertainty persists, not because of any flaw in Faber's "carefully written and thoroughly researched" biography, but rather because it is difficult to interpret the evidence correctly. "The language of their correspondence is warm and intense," explains Ollen, "but since the general public was far less informed and far less paranoid about homosexuality, and colloquial English permitted more effusiveness some forty years ago, it was permissible then for women to walk arm in arm and to use terms of endearment that would raise eyebrows today." But Sylvia Jukes Morris argues that it may be misleading to see the content of these letters in "some innocent historic context." Regardless of the general public's awareness, Morris believes Hickok and Roosevelt were too "well-read and well-traveled" to be so naive.

Florence Mouckley, on the other hand, believes that Faber has "threaded her way carefully through fact and inference insofar as it was possible." She suggests that to read the book for sensationalism is to miss the point. "The book is serious biography, not pulp disclosure," she writes in her *Christian Science Monitor* review.

If Faber's intention was to downplay the sensational, why, wonder several reviewers, does she invest the issue with so much significance? Lehmann-Haupt thinks the omnipresence of the question "throws a glaring spotlight on the middle chapters of the book—those covering the period when the two protagonists were closest to each other—and makes everything that comes before and after seem as relatively unimportant as a prologue and an afterword." Arthur Schlesinger, Jr., suggests that what Faber should have explored is "the light Hickok's life cast on the times—the problems of a female reporter in a male-dominated profession, for instance, or the significance of Hickok's work for Hopkins." And Kenneth S. Lynn of the *Times Literary Supplement* thinks Faber could have explored more fully the "significant implications of her subject," but tempers this criticism by applauding her responsible presentation of evidence. "Thanks to her," he says, "future historians will be able to write vastly more believable appraisals of Eleanor Roosevelt than those we now have."

Elizabeth Cleland of the *Washington Star* also praises the careful job of reporting that Faber has done: "She assumed nothing. She checked and rechecked every date, every event. She sought out, with difficulty, people who knew Hickok, or knew about her and her friendship with Mrs. Roosevelt. The copious notes at the back of the book justify every statement. If the story 'had to come out,' Doris Faber was the one to tell it."

BIOGRAPHICAL/CRITICAL SOURCES: *New York Times*, February 5, 1980; *Newsday*, February 10, 1980; *Los Angeles Times Book Review*, February 10, 1980; *New York Times Book Review*, February 17, 1980; *Washington Post Book World*, February 17, 1980; *Cincinnati Enquirer*, March 16, 1980; *Christian Science Monitor*, April 9, 1980; *Times Literary Supplement*, July 11, 1980.

—Sketch by Donna Olendorf

* * *

FABER, Harold 1919-

PERSONAL: Born September 12, 1919, in New York, N.Y.; son of Charles and Anna (Glassman) Faber; married Doris Greenberg (a writer), June 21, 1951; children: Alice, Marjorie. *Education:* City College (now City College of the City University of New York), B.S., 1940. *Home address:* R.D.1, Ancram, N.Y. 12502. *Office:* New York Times, 229 West 43rd St., New York, N.Y.

CAREER: *New York Times*, New York, N.Y., reporter and war correspondent, 1940-52, day national news editor, 1952-68, editorial director of Book and Educational Division, 1968-72, upstate New York correspondent, 1972—. *Military service:* U.S. Army, 1942-46; awarded Purple Heart for war injuries received as correspondent in Korea, 1950-51.

WRITINGS: (Editor) *New York Times Election Handbook—1964*, McGraw, 1964; *George C. Marshall, Soldier and Statesman*, Farrar, Straus, 1964; (editor) *The Kennedy Years*, Viking, 1964; (editor) *The Road to the White House*, McGraw, 1965; (with wife, Doris Faber) *American Heroes of the 20th Century*, Random House, 1967; *From Sea to Sea: The Growth of the United States*, Farrar, Straus, 1967; (editor) *New York Times*

Election Handbook—1968, New American Library, 1968; (editor) *New York Times Guide for New Voters,* Quadrangle Books, 1972; (editor) *Luftwaffe: A History,* Times Books, 1977; (with D. Faber) *The Assassination of Martin Luther King, Jr.,* F. Watts, 1978; *The Book of Laws,* Times Books, 1979.

* * *

FAINLIGHT, Ruth (Esther) 1931-

PERSONAL: Born May 2, 1931, in New York, N.Y.; daughter of Leslie Alexander and Fanny (Nimhauser) Fainlight; married Alan Sillitoe (a writer), November 19, 1959; children: David Nimrod, Susan (adopted). *Education:* Attended schools in United States and England until the age of sixteen, then studied two years at Birmingham and Brighton Colleges of Arts and Crafts, England. *Religion:* Jewish. *Home:* 14 Ladbroke Ter., London W11 3PG, England. *Agent:* Tessa Sayle, 11 Jubilee Pl., London SW3 3TE, England.

CAREER: Poet, writer, and translator.

WRITINGS—Poetry, except as indicated: *A Forecast, A Fable,* Outposts Publications, 1958; *Cages,* Dufour, 1966; *18 Poems from 1966,* Turret Books, 1967; *To See the Matter Clearly,* Macmillan (London), 1968, Dufour, 1969; (translator and adapter with Alan Sillitoe) Lope de Vega, *All Citizens Are Soldiers* (two-act play; first produced in Stratford, England, at Theatre Royal, 1967), Macmillan (London), 1969, Dufour, 1970; (contributor) *Poems* [by] *Ruth Fainlight, Ted Hughes, Alan Sillitoe,* Rainbow Press, 1971; *Daylife and Nightlife* (short stories), Deutsch, 1971; *The Region's Violence,* Hutchinson, 1972; *21 Poems,* Turret Books, 1973; *Another Full Moon,* Hutchinson, 1976; *Sibyls and Others,* Hutchinson, 1980; *Climates,* Bloodaxe Books, 1982; (translator) *Coral* (poems of Sophia de Mello Breyner), Carcanet, 1982. Also translator of Spanish poetry.

Poetry is represented in anthologies, including *Holding Your Eight Hands,* edited by E. Lucie-Smith, Doubleday, 1969, *Poetry Dimension No. 2,* edited by D. Abse, Abacus, 1974, *Contemporary Women Poets,* edited by T. Kneale, Rondo, 1975, *New Poems 76-77* (P.E.N. anthology), edited by H. Sergeant, Hutchinson, 1976, *New Poetry 2,* edited by K. Crossley-Holland and P. Beer, Arts Council, 1976, *New Poetry 3,* edited by A. Brownjohn and M. Duffy, Arts Council, 1977, *Poetry Dimension No. 5,* edited by Abse, Robson Books, 1978, *The Poetry Anthology,* edited by Daryl Hine and J. Parisi, Houghton, 1978, *New Poetry 5,* edited by P. Redgrove and J. Silkin, Arts Council, 1979, *Voices within the Ark,* edited by H. Schwartz and A. Rudolf, Avon, 1980, *How Strong the Roots,* edited by Sergeant, M. Evans, 1981, and *Bread and Roses,* edited by Diana Scott, Virago, 1982.

Short stories are represented in anthologies, including *Penguin Modern Stories,* Volume IX, edited by Judith Burnley, Penguin, 1971, *Bananas,* edited by Emma Tennant, Quartet, 1977, *Stories by Famous Women Writers,* edited by D. Val Baker, W. H. Allen, 1978, and *New Stories 4* (Arts Council anthology), edited by E. Feinstein and F. Weldon, Hutchinson, 1979.

Translations are represented in anthologies, including *The Other Voice,* edited by Bankier, Cosman, Earnshaw, Keefe, Lashgari, and Weaver, Norton, 1976, *The Contemporary World Poets,* edited by D. Junkins, Harcourt, 1976, *Contemporary Portuguese Poetry,* edited by H. Macedo and E. M. Melo e Castro, Carcanet, 1978, and *Literature from the World,* edited by W. Carrier and B. Neumann, Scribner, 1981.

WORK IN PROGRESS: A new collection of poems.

SIDELIGHTS: Ruth Fainlight told *CA:* "I enjoy slow travel, by which I mean going somewhere and living there a while. So far I have only done this in France, Spain, Morocco, Israel, and England. . . . My main interests apart from literature are in the fields of sociology, psychology, anthropology, religion, history, animal behaviour, biology, cosmology—in fact, every area of science I am capable of understanding, having had no scientific education at all."

BIOGRAPHICAL/CRITICAL SOURCES: New Statesman, March 12, 1976, May 9, 1980; *Times Literary Supplement,* April 8, 1977, May 23, 1980; *Poetry,* February, 1978.

* * *

FAIRBURN, Eleanor 1928-
(Catherine Carfax, Emma Gayle, Elena Lyons, Anna Neville)

PERSONAL: Born February 23, 1928, in Ireland; became British subject, 1953; daughter of Michael John and Mary Josephine (Clarke) Lyons; married Brian G. Fairburn (an analytical chemist), 1950; children: Anne Marie Miller. *Politics:* None. *Religion:* Roman Catholic. *Home and office:* 199 Oxford Rd., Linthorpe, Middlesbrough, Cleveland TS5 5EG, England. *Agent:* Rosemary Guild, Laurence Pollinger Ltd., 18 Maddox St., London W1R 0EU, England.

CAREER: Free-lance fashion designer for various magazines, 1954-61; novelist, 1961—.

WRITINGS—Historical novels: *The Green Popinjays,* Hodder & Stoughton, 1962; *The White Seahorse,* Heinemann, 1964; *The Golden Hive,* Heinemann, 1966; *Crowned Ermine,* R. Hale, 1968.

"Rose" series: *The Rose in Spring,* R. Hale, 1971, Pinnacle Books, 1973; *White Rose, Dark Summer,* R. Hale, 1972; *The Rose at Harvest End,* R. Hale, 1975, Reader's Digest Press, 1976; *Winter's Rose,* R. Hale, 1976.

Romantic/crime novels; under pseudonym Catherine Carfax: *A Silence with Voices,* Macmillan, 1969; *The Semper Inheritance,* R. Hale, 1972; *To Die a Little,* R. Hale, 1972, published as *The Locked Tower,* Fawcett, 1974; *The Sleeping Salamander,* Stein & Day, 1973.

Light romantic fiction: (Under pseudonym Anna Neville) *The House of the Chestnut Trees,* Woman's Weekly Library, 1977; (under pseudonym Emma Gayle) *Cousin Caroline,* Mills & Boon, 1980; (under pseudonym Elena Lyons) *The Haunting of Abbotsgarth,* Piatkus Books, 1980; (under pseudonym Emma Gayle) *Frenchman's Harvest,* Mills & Boon, 1980; (under pseudonym Elena Lyons) *A Scent of Lilacs,* Woman's Weekly Fiction Series, 1982. Contributor of short stories and articles to periodicals.

SIDELIGHTS: Eleanor Fairburn told *CA:* "The poetess Sylvia Plath once wrote (during a period when she was overwhelmed by domestic chores): 'Who asks why there's no great she-poet, / Come live with me and he will know it.' I think that women writers, in particular, understand this situation as they deal with their thousand and one other jobs.

"When my first book was published, I imagined that the ultimate achievement was to become recognised as a writer. Now—twenty years and several pseudonyms later—I find that time for creative work becomes scarcer through even the most localised or limited advance in 'fame.' Letters and phone-calls demand answers; other authors' books and typescripts need to be read; literary gatherings must be attended from time to time. So is it possible, I nervously ask myself, that being 'known as writers' eventually turns people into non-writers?

"Preparatory to taking entirely to the hills, I'm hoping not. Difficult and frustrating though the business of fiction-writing may be, I believe it gives much-needed respites from reality to both authors and readers. The former must be forgiven, however, if they wish for a little more uninterrupted time to fantasise, research, and re-draft."

Some of Fairburn's books have been translated into Dutch, French, Swedish, Finnish, Norwegian, and Greek.

BIOGRAPHICAL/CRITICAL SOURCES: G. W. Grubb, *The Grubbs of Tipperary*, Mercier Press, 1972; Bernard Knight, *Lion Rampant*, R. Hale, 1972; Alan Falconer, *The Cleveland Way*, H.M.S.O. for the Countryside Commission, 1972; Ian Postlethwaite, *Richard, Third Duke of York*, Richard the Third Society, 1974.

* * *

FARER, Tom J. 1935-

PERSONAL: Born July 28, 1935, in New York, N.Y.; son of Louis and Lola (Garfink) Farer; married Mika Ignatieff (a social worker), December 26, 1964. *Education:* Princeton University, A.B. (magna cum laude), 1957; University of Glasgow, graduate study, 1957-58; Harvard University, LL.B. (magna cum laude), 1961. *Home:* 22 East Oak Ave., Moorestown, N.J. 08056. *Office:* Department of Law, Rutgers Law School, Camden, N.J. 08102.

CAREER: Agency for International Development, Washington, D.C., program officer, 1962; U.S. Department of Defense, Washington, D.C., special assistant to general counsel, 1962-63; Somali Police Force, Republic of Somalia, legal adviser, 1963-64; Massachusetts Institute of Technology, Cambridge, research associate, 1964-65; Davis, Polk, Wardwell, Sunderland, & Kiendl (law firm), New York City, attorney, 1965-66; Columbia University, New York City, assistant professor, 1966-69, associate professor of law, 1969-71; Rutgers Law School, Camden, N.J., professor, 1971-74, distinguished professor of law, 1974—. Visiting professor at Princeton University, 1982-83. Lecturer at New York University, 1966, and at Naval War College, 1971. Assistant counsel to Temporary Committee for Revision of New York Constitution, 1966. Special assistant to Assistant Secretary of State, 1975. Inter-American Commission on Human Rights of the Organization of American States, member, 1976—, president, 1981-82. *Member:* American Bar Association, American Society of International Law (member of board of review and development, 1971-74), Council on Foreign Relations, Cosmos Club, Phi Beta Kappa. *Awards, honors:* Fulbright scholar to University of Glasgow; Carnegie Endowment senior fellow, 1974; Council on Foreign Relations senior fellow, 1975.

WRITINGS: (Editor) *Financing African Development*, M.I.T. Press, 1965; (with Jack B. Weinstein) *State Credit Card Crime Act*, [New York], 1966; *The Laws of War 25 Years after Nuremberg*, Carnegie Endowment for International Peace, 1971; *War Clouds on the Horn of Africa*, Carnegie Endowment, 1976, revised edition, 1980; (editor) *The Future of the Inter-American System*, Praeger, 1979; (editor) *Toward a Humanitarian Diplomacy*, New York University Press, 1980. Contributor to *Foreign Affairs, Foreign Policy*, and *New York Review of Books*. Member of board of editors, *American Journal of International Law*, 1980—.

* * *

FARLEY, Walter

PERSONAL: Born in Syracuse, N.Y.; son of Walter and Isabelle (Vermilyea) Farley; married Rosemary Lutz, 1945; children: Pamela, Alice, Steve, Tim. *Education:* Attended Mercersburg Academy and Columbia University. *Residence:* Pennsylvania and Florida.

CAREER: Writer and Arabian horse breeder. Copywriter for a New York advertising agency, 1941. *Military service:* U.S. Army, 1942-46; reporter for *Yank*, an army publication.

WRITINGS—Published by Random House, except as indicated: *The Black Stallion* (Junior Literary Guild selection; also see below), 1941 (adapted as *Big Black Horse* under supervision of Josette Frank, 1953); *Larry and the Underseas Raider*, 1942; *The Black Stallion Returns* (Junior Literary Guild selection; also see below), 1945, reprinted, 1977; *Son of the Black Stallion* (Junior Literary Guild selection), 1947; *The Island Stallion* (Junior Literary Guild selection), 1948; *The Black Stallion and Satan* (Junior Literary Guild selection; also see below), 1949; *Blood Bay Colt*, 1950; *The Island Stallion's Fury*, 1951; *The Black Stallion's Filly*, 1952; *The Black Stallion Revolts* (Junior Literary Guild selection), 1953, reprinted, 1977; *The Black Stallion's Sulky Colt*, 1954; *The Island Stallion Races*, 1955; *The Black Stallion's Courage*, 1956; *The Black Stallion Mystery* (also see below), 1957; *The Horse-tamer*, 1959, reprinted, 1980.

The Black Stallion and Flame, 1960; *Little Black, a Pony*, 1961; *Man o' War*, 1962; *Little Black Goes to the Circus*, 1963; *The Black Stallion Challenged!*, 1964; *The Horse That Swam Away*, 1965; *The Great Dane, Thor*, 1966; *The Little Black Pony Races*, 1968; *The Black Stallion's Ghost*, 1969; *The Black Stallion and the Girl*, 1971; *The Black Stallion Picture Book*, 1979; *Walter Farley's Black Stallion Books*, four volumes (includes *The Black Stallion, The Black Stallion Returns, The Black Stallion and Satan*, and *The Black Stallion Mystery*), 1979; *How to Stay Out of Trouble with Your Horse*, Doubleday, 1981.

SIDELIGHTS: "My great love was, and still is, horses," Walter Farley writes. "I wanted a pony as much as any boy or girl could possibly want anything—but I never owned one. I tried selling subscriptions to win a pony, which was offered as a prize to the kid who sold the most subscriptions. Then my uncle with a flock of show horses and jumpers moved from the West Coast to Syracuse, and I was deliriously happy. I was at the stables every chance I could get."

Farley's now-famous children's book, *The Black Stallion*, "did not emerge all of a sudden, over a single evening and bottle of beer," wrote *Young Wings* critic Lewis Nichols. "He began it as a student at Erasmus High, wrote another version while a student at Mercersburg, . . . wrote other versions as class assignments at Columbia. His first editor told him he never could make a living writing children's books, which was one of the misstatements of the age. . . . Sales of the books have gone over the five million copy mark in the United States alone, and all are in print in 14 other countries."

Farley's *The Great Dane, Thor*, "atypically, . . . is not a boy-animal love affair, as so many children's books about horses and dogs tend to be," commented Taliaferro Boatwright in *Book Week*. "Lars Newton, its fifteen-year-old hero, does not like his father's Great Dane, Thor, and is happy when their new colt outwits the dog. . . . It's an exciting climax, but it's a little too pat for belief. . . . Nevertheless, the knowledge and the love of nature that permeate the book and the understanding of a boy's behavior and wellsprings, as well as those of horses and dogs, make it well worth while."

MEDIA ADAPTATIONS: *The Black Stallion* was filmed by United Artists in 1979. *The Black Stallion Returns* has been optioned by United Artists.

BIOGRAPHICAL/CRITICAL SOURCES: *Young Wings,* September, 1945; *New York Times Book Review,* November 2, 1947, November 6, 1966; *Book Week,* April 30, 1967; *Atlantic Monthly,* December, 1969; *Contemporary Literary Criticism,* Volume XVII, Gale, 1981.

* * *

FARMER, Richard Neil 1928-

PERSONAL: Born August 19, 1928, in California; son of George A. and Alice (Mellin) Farmer; married Barbara Jean Flaherty (a writer), September 18, 1951; children: Christine, Geoffrey, Sarah, Daniel. *Education:* University of California, Berkeley, B.A., 1950, M.A., 1951, Ph.D., 1957. *Home:* 1115 East Wylie, Bloomington, Ind. 47401. *Agent:* Arthur Pine Associates, 1780 Broadway, New York, N.Y. 10019. *Office:* Indiana University, Bloomington, Ind. 47401.

CAREER: American University of Beirut, Beirut, Lebanon, assistant professor of business, 1957-59; General Contracting Co., Al Khobar, Saudi Arabia, general manager, 1959-61; University of California, Davis, lecturer in economics, 1961-62; University of California, Los Angeles, assistant professor of business, 1962-64; Indiana University at Bloomington, professor of international business administration, 1964—. *Military service:* U.S. Army, 1951-53; became sergeant. *Member:* Academy of International Business, Society for International Development, Association for Education in International Business, American Economic Association, Academy of Management.

WRITINGS: Technical Studies in Transportation: Cost Finding (booklet), Department of Engineering, University of California, Los Angeles, 1963; (with Barry M. Richman) *Comparative Management and Economic Progress,* Irwin, 1965, revised edition, Cedarwood Press, 1971; (with Richman and William G. Ryan) *Incidents in Applying Management Theory,* Wadsworth, 1966; (with Richman) *International Business: An Operational Theory,* Irwin, 1966, 3rd edition, Cedarwood Press, 1974; *Management in the Future,* Wadsworth, 1967; *Incidents in International Business,* Irwin, 1967, revised edition, Cedarwood Press, 1975; *International Management,* Dickenson, 1968; (editor with John D. Long and George J. Stolnitz) *World Population: The View Ahead,* Bureau of Business Research, Indiana University, 1968; *New Directions in Management Information Transfer,* Gottlieb Duttweiler Institute for Economic and Social Studies, 1968; *Incidents for Introduction to Business,* Wadsworth, 1969.

(With Richman and Ryan) *Incidents for Studying Management and Organization,* Wadsworth, 1970; *Introduction to Business: Systems and Environment,* Random House, 1972; (compiler with Robert W. Stevens and Hans Schoelhammer) *Readings in International Business,* Dickenson, 1972; *Benevolent Aggression,* McKay, 1972; *Farmer's Law: Junk in the World of Affluence,* Stein & Day, 1973; *The Real World of 1984,* McKay, 1973; (with W. Dickerson Hogue) *Corporate Social Responsibility,* Science Research Associates, 1973; (with Richman) *Leadership, Goals, and Power in Higher Education,* Jossey-Bass, 1974; *Why Nothing Works Anymore,* Regnery, 1977. Also author of technical reports and case studies.

Contributor: B. Prasad, editor, *Management in International Perspective,* Appleton-Century-Crofts, 1967; Walter Krause and F. John Mathis, editors, *International Economics and Business: Selected Readings,* Houghton, 1968; *International Business: An Introduction to the World of the Multinational Firm,* Prentice-Hall, 1972; *Issues in Business and Society,* Random House, 1972; Farris and McElhiney, editors, *Modern Transportation,* 2nd edition, Houghton, 1973; Stefan H. Robock and Kenneth Simmons, editors, *International Business and Multinational Enterprises,* Irwin, 1973; Lawrence A. Klatt, editor, *Small Business Management: Essentials of Entrepreneurship,* Wadsworth, 1973; Joseph W. McQuire, editor, *Contemporary Management: Issues and Viewpoints,* Prentice-Hall, 1974. Also contributor to conference proceedings. Contributor of more than fifty articles and reviews to professional journals, including *Business Horizons, California Management Review, Overdrive,* and *Foreign Trade Review.*

SIDELIGHTS: Management in the Future has been translated into Spanish, Japanese, and Italian. *International Management* has been translated into Japanese.

* * *

FARMILOE, Dorothy Alicia 1920-

PERSONAL: Born September 8, 1920, in Toronto, Ontario, Canada; daughter of Thomas and Beatrice Daisy (Archer) Roach; married Ray Edwin Farmiloe, September 16, 1939 (died October, 1963); children: Dan, Judith (Mrs. John Long), Linda. *Education:* University of Windsor, B.A., 1967, M.A., 1969. *Home address:* P.O. Box 94, Elk Lake, Ontario, Canada P0J 1G0.

CAREER: Long Point Lodge, Elk Lake, Ontario, owner and operator, 1955-63; St. Clair College, Windsor, Ontario, teacher of English, 1969-78. Member, Windsor Poetry Movement, 1966; organizer of poetry readings in libraries and schools, 1966—; former publisher, Sesame Press. *Member:* League of Canadian Poets, Writer's Union of Canada, Detroit Women Writers. *Awards, honors:* Metropolitan Society prize, 1975, for poem "Heritage."

WRITINGS—Poetry, except as indicated: *The Lost Island, and Other Poems,* Gryphon, 1966; (with Len Gaspari and Edward McNamara) *21 X 3,* Gryphon, 1967; *Poems for Apartment Dwellers,* Fiddlehead Press, 1970; (editor and contributor) *Contraverse,* Concorde Press, 1971; *Winter Orange Mood,* Fiddlehead Press, 1973; *Blue Is the Colour of Death,* Fiddlehead Press, 1973; *And Some in Fire* (novel), Alive Press, 1974; *Creative Communication* (nonfiction), Holt, 1974; *Elk Lake Diary Poems,* Highway Book Shop Press, 1976; *Adrenalin of Weather,* York Press, 1978; *How to Write a Better Anything* (writer's handbook), Black Moss, 1979; *Words for My Weeping Daughter,* Penumbra Press, 1981. Also author of play, "What Do You Save from a Burning Building?," 1973.

Poems represented in anthologies, including *Temper of the Times,* edited by Ronald Side and Ralph Greenfield, McGraw, 1969, and *Visions 20-20: Fifty Canadians in Search of a Future,* edited by Stephen Clarkson, Hurtig, 1970. Contributor of articles, poems and reviews to professional journals. Former editor, *Mainline.*

WORK IN PROGRESS: A novel; another collection of poetry; a biography of Isabella Valancy Crawford.

* * *

FAULKNOR, Cliff(ord Vernon) 1913-
(Pete Williams)

PERSONAL: Born March 3, 1913, in Vancouver, British Columbia, Canada; son of George Henry and Rhoda Anne Faulknor; married Elizabeth Harriette Sloan, August 21, 1943; children: Stephen Edward Vernon, Noreen Elizabeth. *Education:* University of British Columbia, B.S.A. (with honors), 1949. *Politics:* "A little right of centre." *Religion:* Protestant. *Home:*

2919 14th Ave. N.W., Calgary, Alberta, Canada. *Office:* Alberta Land Compensation Board, Suite 202, Lavalin Centre, 909 Fifth Ave. S.W., Calgary, Alberta, Canada.

CAREER: Affiliated with Royal Bank of Canada, beginning 1929; later worked with lumber companies, and as an assistant ranger for British Columbia Forest Service; British Columbia Department of Lands and Forests, Land Utilization Research and Survey Division, Victoria, land inspector, 1949-54; *Country Guide* (national farm monthly), associate editor in Calgary, Alberta, 1954-75; accredited appraiser, 1976—; member of Alberta Land Compensation Board, 1978—. *Military service:* Canadian Army, Water Transport, 1939-45; became sergeant. *Member:* Agricultural Institute of Canada, Appraisal Institute of Canada, Writers Union of Canada, Canadian Farm Writers' Federation, Alberta Farm Writers' Association (past president).

AWARDS, HONORS: Awards from Canadian Farm Writers Federation, 1961, 1962, 1968, 1969, 1973, 1974, and 1975; Pacific Northwest Writers Conference award, 1963, for short story; Canadian Children's Book Award, Little, Brown & Co., 1964, for *The White Calf; Pen and Plow* was named best nonfiction book by an Alberta writer, 1976; Vicky Metcalf Award, 1979, for contributions to Canadian literature.

WRITINGS—Juveniles, except as indicated: *The White Calf,* Little, Brown, 1965; *The White Peril,* Little, Brown, 1966; *The In-Betweener,* Little, Brown, 1967; *The Romance of Beef* (adult), Public Press, 1967; *The Smoke Horse,* McClelland & Stewart, 1968; *West to Cattle Country,* McClelland & Stewart, 1975; *Pen and Plow* (adult), Public Press, 1976; *Turn Him Loose!* (adult), Western Producer Prairie Books, 1977; *Alberta Hereford Heritage* (adult), Advisor Graphics, 1981; *Johnny Eagleclaw,* John LeBel Enterprises, 1982.

Contributor to anthologies: *Chinook Arch,* Co-op Press, 1967; *Western Profiles,* Alberta Education, 1979; *Transitions,* Alberta Education, 1979; *The Alberta Diamond Jubilee Anthology,* Hurtig, 1979. Former author of national column for *Country Guide,* under pseudonym Pete Williams; former free-lance columnist for *Victoria Times.* Also contributor of articles and short stories to numerous magazines and newspapers, including *Toronto Star Weekly, Liberty, Canadian Geographic Journal,* and *Cattlemen.*

WORK IN PROGRESS: The Gentle Prophet, an adult novel.

SIDELIGHTS: Cliff Faulknor told *CA:* "When I was a youth, I could idle away a whole summer's day on some beach without a twinge of conscience, just listening to the music of the waves or watching galleon-like cumulus clouds moving across the sky. Later, I was somehow inveigled into taking what is often referred to as 'higher education' and soon fell prey to the work ethic demon. In that grinding process and the various careers which followed, the boy on the beach was lost. But I found him again, or at least a part of him, when I began to write adventure stories for juveniles. I did not plan any of these stories. My daily journalistic chores gave me about all the planning I could stomach. With my juveniles, I just sat down at my typewriter and put my characters into motion. If any new ones appeared I tossed them into the pot and stirred. The characters themselves did the rest. As they went about their lives they took me with them. I recommend this as a cure to those who feel that they are growing old in heart."

* * *

FECAMPS, Elise
See CREASEY, John

FEIWEL, George R(ichard) 1929-

PERSONAL: Born July 4, 1929, in Cracow, Poland; son of Herman (a lawyer) and Resia (Wang) Feiwel; married Ida Rieger (a research associate), May 19, 1957. *Education:* McGill University, B.Com., 1955, M.A., 1961, Ph.D., 1963; University of California, Berkeley, graduate study, 1961-62. *Home:* 5507 Holston Hills Rd., Knoxville, Tenn. 37914. *Office:* Department of Economics, University of Tennessee, Knoxville, Tenn. 37916.

CAREER: University of Alberta, Edmonton, associate professor of economics, 1962-66; University of Tennessee, Knoxville, professor, 1966-76, alumni distinguished service professor of economics, 1977—. Visiting faculty member, Cambridge University, 1965, 1969, 1972; research associate, Harvard University, 1966, 1967, 1971, 1975, Clare Hall, Cambridge, England, 1972, University of California, Berkeley, 1976, 1977; visiting professor, Instituto di Studi per lo Sviluppo Economico, 1969, 1970, University of Stockholm, 1973, University of California, Berkeley, 1977, 1979, Harvard University, 1978. Chancellor's research scholar, University of Tennessee, 1976. Member of American Economic Association's search committee for editors of *American Economic Review* and *Journal of Economic Literature,* 1977-78. *Member:* American Economic Association, Eastern Economic Association, Southern Economic Association.

AWARDS, HONORS: Guggenheim fellow, 1968-69; fellowships and grants from American Council of Learned Societies, Social Science Research Council, American Philosophical Society, Canada Council, and National Science Foundation; elected Phi Kappa Phi university lecturer and macebearer, University of Tennessee, 1970.

WRITINGS: The Economics of a Socialist Enterprise, Praeger, 1965; *The Soviet Quest for Economic Efficiency,* Praeger, 1967, revised edition, 1972; *New Economic Patterns in Czechoslovakia,* Praeger, 1968; (editor) *New Currents in Soviet-Type Economies: A Reader,* International Textbook Co., 1968; (contributor) G. Franco, editor, *Studi sulle politiche monetarie le creditizie per lo sviluppo economico,* Edizioni Cedam, 1970; *Industrialization and Planning under Polish Socialism,* two volumes, Praeger, 1971; *Recent Developments in the Polish Financial System,* Arms Control and Disarmament Agency, 1971; (author of introduction) Michal Kalecki, *The Last Phase in the Transformation of Capitalism,* Monthly Review Press, 1972; *Essays on Planning in Eastern Europe,* Instituto di Studi per lo Sviluppo Economico, 1973; *The Intellectual Capital of Michal Kalecki: A Study in Economic Theory and Policy,* University of Tennessee Press, 1975; *Growth in a Supply Constrained Economy,* Instituto di Studi per lo Sviluppo Economico, 1975; *Growth and Reforms in Centrally Planned Economies: Lessons of Bulgarian Experience,* Praeger, 1977; *Samuelson and Neoclassical Economics,* Kluwer Boston, 1981.

Also author of booklet on the meanings of cost. Contributor of articles to *Collier's Encyclopedia, Economia Internazionale, Ricerche Economiche, Indian Economic Journal, Rendiconti, Keio Economic Studies, Soviet Studies, Osteuropa Wirtschaft, Scientia,* and numerous other journals. Member of editorial board, *Journal of Economic Literature,* 1976-78.

WORK IN PROGRESS: Research on contemporary economic theory, and growth planning and marketing.

AVOCATIONAL INTERESTS: Travel.

FELD, Werner (Joachim) 1910-

PERSONAL: Born April 10, 1910, in Dusseldorf, Germany; son of Bruno and Irma (Loebl) Feld; married Betty Tandy, October 1, 1957. *Education:* University of Berlin, LL.B., 1933; Tulane University of Louisiana, Ph.D., 1962. *Religion:* Episcopalian. *Home:* 2362 Killdeer St., New Orleans, La. 70122. *Office:* Department of Political Science, University of New Orleans, New Orleans, La., 70122.

CAREER: Dixie Specialty Co., Inc., Mobile, Ala., president, 1947-61; North Georgia College, Dahlonega, assistant professor of political science, 1961-62; Moorhead State College, Moorhead, Minn., 1962-65, began as assistant professor, became professor of political science; University of New Orleans, New Orleans, La., professor of political science, 1965—. Civil Defense director, Mobile, Ala., 1956-57; consultant to U.S. Department of State, 1965-70. *Military service:* U.S. Army Reserve, 1943-63, with active duty in World War II and Korean War; became lieutenant colonel. *Member:* American Political Science Association, International Studies Association (executive committee, 1966-67), Southern Political Science Association (secretary, 1966-67).

WRITINGS: Reunification and West German-Soviet Relations, Nijhoff, 1963; *The Court of the European Communities: New Dimension in International Adjudication,* Nijhoff, 1964; *The European Common Market and the World,* Prentice-Hall, 1967; (editor with others) *The Enduring Questions of Politics,* Prentice-Hall, 1969, revised edition, 1974; *Transnational Business Collaboration among Common Market Countries,* Praeger, 1970; *Non-governmental Forces and World Politics,* Praeger, 1972; (with John K. Wildgen) *Domestic Political Realities and European Integration,* Westview, 1976; *The European Community in World Affairs,* Alfred Publishing, 1976; *International Relations: A Transnational Approach,* Alfred Publishing, 1976; *Multinational Corporations and U.N. Politics,* Pergamon, 1980; (with Gavin Boyd) *Comparative Regional Systems,* Pergamon, 1980; *West Germany and the European Community,* Praeger, 1981; (with Wildgen) *NATO and the Atlantic Defense,* Praeger, 1982. Contributor to political science, law, and other journals.

WORK IN PROGRESS: With Robert S. Jordan, *International Organization: A Comparative Approach,* for Praeger; *American Foreign Policy: Aspirations and Reality,* for Wiley.

* * *

FELKENES, George T(heodore) 1930-

PERSONAL: Born November 19, 1930, in Dayton, Ohio; son of Theodore (a barber) Felkenes; married Sandra Weeks Hartness (a professor), March 24, 1961. *Education:* University of Maryland, B.S., and J.D., 1961; California State University, Long Beach, M.A., 1968; University of California, Berkeley, D.Crim., 1970. *Home:* 5214 Calderwood St., Long Beach, Calif. 90815.

CAREER: Federal Trade Commission, Washington, D.C., attorney and investigator, 1961; Olmsted Air Force Base, Middletown, Pa., deputy chief of security and law enforcement, 1961-64; California State University, Long Beach, assistant professor, 1964-68, associate professor, 1968-69, professor of criminology, 1969-71, chairman of department, 1964-71; University of Alabama in Birmingham, professor of criminology, 1971-77; Michigan State University, East Lansing, director of School of Criminal Justice; California State University, Long Beach, dean of School of Applied Arts and Sciences. Consultant to private and governmental agencies on criminal justice. *Military service:* U.S. Army, served in counterintelligence and law enforcement, 1951-57; became first lieutenant. *Member:* International Association of Chiefs of Police, American Society of Criminology, Academy of Criminal Justice Sciences (president, 1975-76), California Peace Officers Association, Phi Alpha Delta.

WRITINGS: (With Paul Whisenand and Harold Becker) *New Dimensions in Criminal Justice,* Scarecrow, 1968; (with Becker) *Law Enforcement: A Selected Bibliography,* Scarecrow, 1968, 2nd edition, 1977; (with Whisenand) *Police Patrol Operations,* McCutchan, 1972; (with Whisenand and James Cline) *Police-Community Relations,* Goodyear Publishing, 1974; *Rules of Evidence,* Delmar Publishers, 1975; *The Criminal Justice System: Its Functions and Personnel,* Prentice-Hall, 1975; *Criminal Law and Procedure: Text and Cases,* Prentice-Hall, 1976; *Effective Police Supervision,* Justice Systems Development, 1977; *Constitutional Law for Criminal Justice,* Prentice-Hall, 1978; (contributor) *Principles of Investigation,* West Publishing, 1979; (contributor) *Fundamentals of Law Enforcement,* West Publishing, 1980; *Michigan Criminal Justice Law Manual,* West Publishing, 1982. Case decisions editor of *Journal of California Law Enforcement,* 1967-71.

WORK IN PROGRESS: Researching several articles on police ethics.

SIDELIGHTS: George T. Felkenes writes: "Criminal justice education was a comparatively new field of study when I entered the teaching profession. There were few books on the market devoted to the study of the criminal justice system. I wanted to be deeply involved in the development of a new academic field by exposing my ideas to future criminal justice academicians and practitioners. Writing was the best way to do this. I hope I have helped in sharpening perspectives, transferring knowledge, and shaping the future." *Avocational interests:* Travel, reading.

* * *

FERGUSON, John 1921-

PERSONAL: Born March 2, 1921, in Manchester, England; son of Allan Hitchen (a scientist) and Nesta (Thomas) Ferguson; married Elnora Dixon (a lecturer), July 25, 1950. *Education:* Attended Bishop's Stortford College; St. John's College, Cambridge, B.A., 1942, M.A., 1947; University of London, B.D., 1944. *Politics:* Independent. *Religion:* "Christianity—nonconformist Protestant." *Home and office:* Selly Oak Colleges, Birmingham B29 6LQ, England.

CAREER: University of Durham, King's College, Newcastle upon Tyne, England, lecturer in classics, 1948-53; University of London, Queen Mary College, London, England, senior lecturer in classics, 1953-56; University of Ibadan, Ibadan, Nigeria, professor of classics, 1956-66, dean of arts, 1958-59, 1960-61, master of Kuti Hall, 1960-66, member of University Council, 1964-66; University of Minnesota, Minneapolis, Hill Visiting Professor in Classics, 1966-68, professor, 1968-69; Open University, Walton, England, dean of arts and director of studies in arts, 1969-79; Selly Oak Colleges, Birmingham, England, president, 1979—. Old Dominion Visiting Professor of Humanities, Hampton Institute, 1968-69; visiting professor, University of Florida, 1977, and Ohio Wesleyan University, 1978. Governor, Queen's Theological College. Lecturer on tour of United States, 1956, and Republic of South Africa, 1961. Emily Hobhouse Memorial Lecturer, 1961. Lay preacher in pulpits of all denominations. Chairman of British Fellowship of Reconciliation, 1953-56; vice-chairman of Christian Economic and Social Research Foundation, 1979—.

MEMBER: Royal Institute of Philosophy, Royal Society of Arts (fellow), Historical Association, British Association for Advancement of Science, British United Nations Association (chairman, 1979—), British Council of Churches (chairman of division of community affairs, 1974-77), British and Foreign Schools Society (chairman, 1977—), Classical Association of Nigeria (chairman, 1957-60), Hellenic Society, Roman Society, London Missionary Society (associate), London Society for the Study of Religion (chairman, 1977-79), Athenaeum. *Awards, honors:* Kaye Prize, Cambridge University, 1951, for *Pelagius;* International Institute of Arts and Letters fellow, 1962; knight of Mark Twain.

WRITINGS: *The Enthronement of Love,* Fellowship of Reconciliation, 1950, 4th edition, 1959; *Pelagius,* Heffer, 1956; *Christian Faith for Today,* Source, 1956; (with Ian Pitt-Watson) *Letters on Pacifism,* S.C.M. Press, 1956; *The Camp* (play), Epworth, 1956; *Roma Aeterna,* Ibadan University Press, 1957, 2nd edition, 1961; *The Trial* (play), Epworth, 1957; *The United Nations and the World's Needs,* Regency, 1957; *The Road to Heaven* (play), Epworth, 1958; *Moral Values in the Ancient World,* Methuen, 1958.

(With A. Olubummo) *The Emergent University,* Longmans, Green, 1960; *Job* (play), Epworth, 1961; *The Challenge of the Cross,* Society of Friends (Johannesberg), 1961; *Foundations of the Modern World,* Cambridge University Press, 1963; (contributor) E. Dunn, editor, *Alternatives to War and Violence,* John Clarke, 1963; *Quiz Book for West Africa,* Collins, 1964; (with M. Marioghae) *Nigeria Under the Cross,* Highway Press, 1965; (with O. Esan and M. M. Laycock) *The Enduring Past,* Cambridge University Press, 1965; *Ibadan Verses,* privately printed, 1966; *The Wit of the Greeks and Romans,* Leslie Frewin, 1968; *Christian Byways,* Ibadan Daystar Press, 1968; (with L. Thompson) *Africa in Classical Antiquity,* Ibadan University Press, 1969.

Socrates: A Source Book, Macmillan, 1970; *Religions of the Roman Empire,* Thames & Hudson, 1970; *American Verses,* privately printed, 1971; *Some Nigerian Church Founders,* Ibadan Daystar Press, 1971; *Sermons of a Layman,* Epworth, 1972; *The Place of Suffering,* James Clarke, 1972; *A Companion to Greek Tragedy,* University of Texas Press, 1972; *Aristotle,* Twayne, 1972; *The Heritage of Hellenism,* Thames & Hudson, 1973; *The Politics of Love,* James Clarke, 1973; *Clement of Alexandria,* Twayne, 1974; *Utopias of the Classical World,* Thames & Hudson, 1975; *The Open University from Within,* University of London Press, 1975; *Danilo Dolci,* S.C.M. Press, 1975; *An Illustrated Encyclopaedia of Mysticism and the Mystery Religions,* Thames & Hudson, 1976; *O My People,* Oliphants, 1977; *War and Peace in the World's Religions,* Sheldon, 1977; *Religions of the World,* Lutterworth, 1978; (with Kitty Chisholm) *Political and Social Life in the Great Age of Athens,* Ward, Lock, 1978.

Greek and Roman Religion: A Source Book, Noyes, 1980; *Jesus in the Tide of Time,* Routledge & Kegan Paul, 1980; *The Arts in Britain in World War I,* Stainer & Bell, 1980; *Callimachus,* Twayne, 1980; (with Chisholm) *Rome: The Augustan Age,* Oxford University Press, 1981; *Gods Many and Lords Many,* Lutterworth, 1982; *Disarmament: The Unanswerable Case,* Heinemann, 1982.

Editor: *Studies in Christian Social Commitment,* Independent Press, 1954; Plato, *Republic X,* Methuen, 1957; *Studies in Cicero,* Centro di Studi Ciceroniani, 1962; *Ibadan Versions,* Taylor & Francis, 1967; *War and the Creative Arts,* Macmillan, 1973; *Juvenal: The Satires,* Macmillan, 1979; *Christianity, Society and Education,* S.P.C.K., 1981. Also editor of *Nigeria and the Classics,* Volumes I-IX. Nigerian editor, *Encyclopedia of African Personalities.* Contributor of about fifty articles on classical subjects, theology, and current affairs to journals.

WORK IN PROGRESS: *An Encyclopaedia of Graeco-Roman Theatre; Animals in Ancient Religion; Numbers in Ancient Religion.*

SIDELIGHTS: John Ferguson wrote *CA:* "I write because I have something to say. Very often books emerge from teaching, preaching or public speaking. My first book, *The Enthronement of Love,* and my latest, *Disarmament,* both arose from lectures. Always, or almost always, I have been mulling over a subject, consciously or unconsciously, sometimes for years, often noting relevant material as I go along. When the thing is ready it comes out very quickly. I seldom have to do much rewriting; it may not be any good but it is as good as I can make it. I don't make much money from writing and do not write for that reason."

AVOCATIONAL INTERESTS: Drama, music, travel, hockey, cricket, mountain climbing.

* * *

FESHBACH, Norma Deitch 1926-

PERSONAL: Born September 5, 1926, in New York, N.Y.; married Seymour Feshbach (a professor of psychology), August 16, 1947; children: Jonathan Stephen, Laura Elizabeth, Andrew David. *Education:* City College (now City College of the City University of New York), B.S., 1947, M.S., 1949; University of Pennsylvania, Ph.D., 1956. *Home:* 743 Hanley Ave., Los Angeles, Calif. 90049. *Office:* Department of Education, University of California, 405 Hilgard Ave., Los Angeles, Calif. 90024.

CAREER: Yale University, New Haven, Conn., teacher at Betsy Ross Nursery School, 1947-48, clinical psychologist at Seizure Clinic, 1948; Junior College of Physical Therapy, New Haven, lecturer in child development, 1948-49; George Washington University, Washington, D.C., research assistant in Human Resources Research Office, 1951-52; Youth Services, Inc., Philadelphia, Pa., clinical and research consultant, 1955-61; Stanford University, Stanford, Calif., visiting assistant professor, 1961-62; University of California, Berkeley, lecturer in psychology, 1962-63; University of Colorado, Boulder, research associate at Institute of Behavioral Science, 1963-64; University of California, Los Angeles, associate research psychologist, 1964-65, lecturer at Neuropsychiatric Institute, 1965, assistant professor, 1965-68, associate professor, 1969-74, professor of educational psychology in department of psychology and Graduate School of Education, 1974—, program director at Center for the Study of Evaluation, 1966-69, head of program in early childhood and developmental studies, 1968-80. Certified clinical psychologist in Pennsylvania; licensed clinical and school psychologist in California; diplomate in school psychology, from American Board of Professional Psychology. Psychology intern at Philadelphia General Hospital, 1955-56; clinical psychologist for California Department of Mental Hygiene, 1965; National Institutes of Mental Health, director of training program, 1972—, member of psychology training review committee, 1974-79. University of Pennsylvania, research associate, 1956-57, 1959-61, lecturer, 1956-57; University of California, Los Angeles, co-director of Bush Foundation training program, 1978—, member of extended faculty of school of nursing; member of faculty of National Academy of Professional Psychologists. National Science Foundation, researcher on field projects, 1976-79, co-principal investigator of research grants and projects, 1976-81. Has presented papers to a number of professional conferences. Trustee of committee to End Violence against the Next Generation; member of board of Professional Psychologists, Western Region, 1974-77, and of Higher Education Research Institute, 1980—. Adviser on early childhood education to California legislature, 1972-73; also member of advisory boards, committees, task forces, and councils on early childhood education and development, women's issues, and minority rights; consultant to universities, research and development institutes, laboratories, public councils, film companies, children's television programs, language programs, and several publishing companies.

MEMBER: International Society for Research on Aggression, International Society for the Study of Behavioral Development, International Association of Applied Psychology, American Association for the Advancement of Science, American Association of University Professors, American Educational Research Association, American Psychological Association (fellow; chairperson of Task Force on Children's Rights, 1975-77), National Association for the Education of Young Children, National Register of Health Services Providers in Psychology, National Society for the Study of Education, Association for the Advancement of Psychology (trustee), Society for the Psychological Study of Social Issues (member of council, 1975-77), Society for Research in Child Development, Western Psychological Association (president, 1979-80), California Association for the Education of Young Children, California Educational Research Association, California Professors of Early Childhood Education, California State Psychological Association, University of California, Los Angeles, Association of Academic Women, Sigma Xi, Delta Phi Upsilon.

AWARDS, HONORS: National Institutes of Mental Health training grant, 1971-82; named Woman of the Year by Hadassah, Los Angeles, 1973; sabbatical award, James McKeen Cattell Fund, 1980-81.

WRITINGS: (With M. Frances Klein, J. M. Novotney, and others) *Guide to the Appraisal of Nursery Schools*, Institute for the Development of Educational Activities, 1970; (with John I. Goodlad and Avima Lombard) *Early Schooling in England and Israel*, McGraw, 1973; (with husband, Seymour Feshbach, M. Fauvre, and M. Campbell) *Affective Communication Skills*, Scott, Foresman, in press. Also author of a report on the use of graphics in conveying nutritional information, for the United States Senate, 1977, and of numerous technical reports, manuals, and guides.

Contributor: B. S. Greenberg and E. B. Parker, editors, *The Kennedy Assassination and the American Public*, Stanford University Press, 1965; W. J. Gnagey, editor, *Readings in the Psychology of Classroom Learning*, Holt, 1969; M. B. Miles and W. W. Charters, Jr., editors, *Learning in Social Settings*, Allyn & Bacon, 1970; M. L. Silberman, editor, *The Experience of Schooling*, Holt, 1971; W. W. Hartup, editor, *The Young Child*, Volume II, National Association for the Education of Young Children, 1972; Gardner Lindzey, Calvin S. Hall, and Martin Manosevitz, editors, *Theories of Personality: Primary Sources and Research*, 2nd edition, Wiley, 1973; Judy F. Rosenblith, Wesley Allinsmith, and Joanna P. Williams, editors, *Readings in Child Development*, Allyn & Bacon, 1973; Anne E. Pick, editor, *Minnesota Symposia on Child Psychology*, Volume VII, University of Minnesota Press, 1973; Paul H. Mussen and M. R. Rosenweig, editors, *Concepts in Psychology*, Heath, 1974; P. H. Mussen, John J. Conger, and Jerome Kagan, editors, *Basic and Contemporary Issues in Child Development*, Harper, 1975; Conger, editor, *Contemporary Issues in Adolescent Development*, Harper, 1975; J. DeWit and Hartup, editors, *Determinants and Origins of Aggressive Behavior*, Mouton, 1975; B. J. Wishart and L. C. Reichman, editors, *Modern Sociological Issues*, Part VII, Macmillan, 1975.

Gerald Koocher, editor, *Children's Rights and the Mental Health Professions*, Wiley, 1976; M. L. Kramer, editor, *The Socialization Process*, Xerox Individualized Publishing, 1976; V. Allen, editor, *Children as Tutors: Theory and Research on Tutoring*, Wisconsin University Press, 1976; (with S. Feshbach) R. Takanishi, editor, *Public Policy for Children and Families: Who Shall Decide?*, University of California, Los Angeles, 1977; B. A. Maher, editor, *Progress in Experimental Personality Research*, Volume VIII, Academic Press, 1978; David G. Gil, editor, *Child Abuse and Violence*, AMS Press, 1979; C. Kopp and M. Kirkpatrick, editors, *Becoming Female: Perspectives on Development*, Plenum, 1979; S. Feshbach and A. Fraczek, editors, *Aggression and Behavior Change: Biological and Social Processes*, Praeger, 1979; G. Gerbner, C. Ross, and E. Zigler, editors, *Child Abuse: An Agenda for Action*, Oxford University Press, 1980; H. Kornadt, editor, *Aggression und Frustration als Psychologisches Problem*, Wissenschaftliche Buchgesellschaft, 1981; N. Eisenberg-Berg, editor, *The Development of Prosocial Behavior*, Academic Press, 1982; R. M. Kaplan, V. J. Konecni, and R. Novoco, editors, *Aggression in Children and Youth*, Sijthoff/Noordhoff International Publisher (Netherlands), 1982.

Also contributor to *Inter-age Interaction in Children: Theory and Research on the Helping Relationship*, edited by Vernon Allen, University of Wisconsin Press. Contributor to *International Encyclopedia of Neurology, Psychiatry, Psychoanalysis, and Psychology*, edited by B. B. Wolman, 1976, and to *Policy Studies Review Annual*, Volume IV, edited by Bertram H. Raven, Sage Publications, 1980. Also contributor to conference proceedings of the International Symposium on Violence towards Children, Radda Barnen (Stockholm), 1980.

Contributor of numerous articles and book reviews to education and psychology journals. Member of editorial board of *Journal of Social Issues, Developmental Review, Merrill-Palmer Quarterly,* and *Policy Studies Review Annual*. Consulting editor of *Developmental Psychology, Psychology of Women Quarterly,* and *Review of Educational Research;* consultant to numerous journals, including *American Psychologist, Child Development, Journal of Abnormal Psychology, Human Development,* and *Psychology Bulletin.*

WORK IN PROGRESS: Topics in Early Childhood Special Education, with R. Takanishi.

*　　*　　*

FESHBACH, Seymour 1925-

PERSONAL: Born June 21, 1925, in New York, N.Y.; son of Joseph (a furrier) and Fannie (Katzman) Feshbach; married Norma Deitch (a professor), August 16, 1947; children: Jonathan Stephen, Laura Elizabeth, Andrew David. *Education:* City College (now City College of the City University of New York), B.S., 1947; Yale University, M.A., 1948, Ph.D., 1951. *Politics:* Democrat. *Religion:* Hebrew. *Home:* 743 Hanley Ave., Los Angeles, Calif. 90049. *Office:* Department of Psychology, University of California, 405 Hilgard Ave., Los Angeles, Calif. 90024.

CAREER: University of Pennsylvania, Philadelphia, assistant professor, 1952-57, associate professor of psychology, 1957-63; University of Colorado, Boulder, professor of psychology, 1963-64; University of California, Los Angeles, professor of psychology, 1964—, chairman of department, 1977—, director of Fernald School, 1964-73. Chairman of Psychology Training Grant Committee and member of national panel, National Institutes of Mental Health. Consultant to Columbia Broadcasting System educational television. *Military service:* U.S. Army, Infantry, served in Pacific Theatre of Operations, 1943-46; project director, Attitude Assessment Branch, 1951-52; became first lieutenant.

MEMBER: International Applied Psychology Association, International Society for Study of Aggression, International Society for Study of Behavior Development, American Psychological Association (fellow), American Association for the Advancement of Science, Society for Research in Child Development, Western Psychological Association (president, 1976-77), Phi Beta Kappa, Sigma Xi. *Awards, honors:* Townsend Harris Medal, Alumni Association of the City College of the City University of New York, 1972; grants from National Institutes of Mental Health and National Science Foundation.

WRITINGS: (Editor with Richard Jessor) *Cognition, Personality and Clinical Psychology,* Jossey-Bass, 1967; *The Remediation of Learning Problems in Culturally Disadvantaged Children: Some Issues and Data* (monograph), Office of Compensatory Education (Los Angeles), c. 1967; (with Robert D. Singer) *Television and Aggression,* Jossey-Bass, 1970; (contributor) Paul Henry Mussen, editor, *Carmichael's Manual of Child Psychology,* Volume II, Wiley, 1970; (contributor with wife, Norma Deitch Feshbach) R. Takanishi, editor, *Public Policy for Children and Families: Who Shall Decide?,* University of California, Los Angeles, 1977; (editor with A. Fraczek) *Aggression and Behavior Change: Biological and Social Processes,* Praeger, 1979; (with Bernard Weiner) *Personality,* Heath, 1982; (with N. D. Feshbach, M. Fauvre, and M. Campbell) *Affective Communication Skills,* Scott, Foresman, in press. Also co-author of *Psychology: An Introduction,* 1977. Contributor to psychology journals. Consulting editor, *Journal of Abnormal Psychology,* 1973—, and *Developmental Psychology.*

WORK IN PROGRESS: Research on children's aggression, and on sex and aggression.

AVOCATIONAL INTERESTS: Politics, theater, history, European travel.†

*   *   *

FEUERWERKER, Albert 1927-

PERSONAL: Born November 6, 1927, in Cleveland, Ohio; son of Martin and Gizella (Feuerwerker) Feuerwerker; married Yitsi Mei (a lecturer in literature at University of Michigan), June 11, 1955; children: Alison, Paul M. *Education:* Harvard University, A.B. (magna cum laude), 1950, Ph.D., 1957. *Home:* 1224 Ardmoor Ave., Ann Arbor, Mich. 48103. *Office:* Department of History, University of Michigan, Ann Arbor, Mich. 48104.

CAREER: University of Toronto, Toronto, Ontario, lecturer in history, 1955-58; Harvard University, Center for East Asian Studies, Cambridge, Mass., research fellow, 1958-60; University of Michigan, Ann Arbor, associate professor, 1960-63, professor of history, 1963—, director of Center for Chinese Studies, 1961-67, 1974—. Research fellow, American Council of Learned Societies and Social Science Research Council, both 1962-63. Director d'etudes, Ecole des Hautes Etudes en Sciences Sociales, Paris, 1981; visiting scholar, Shanghi Academy of Social Sciences, 1982. Lecturer on contemporary Chinese affairs at numerous universities and institutes, including Harvard and Stanford Universities. Chairman and president of Chinese Materials and Research Aids Service Center, 1964-74; vice-chairman of modern China section of XXVII International Congress of Orientalists, 1967; chairman of U.S. delegation of Sino-American Symposium on Social and Economic History of China from the Song Dynasty to 1900, 1980. Member of numerous committees on various aspects of contemporary Chinese and Asian life; member of national screening committee of Foreign Area Fellowship Program, 1964-65, of nominating committee of American Historical Association, 1972-75, and of research grants panel of National Endowment for the Humanities, 1973-76. Also member of executive board of Horace A. Rackham School of Graduate Study, 1968-71, chairman of Academic Affairs Advisory Committee, Senate Assembly, 1970-71, and member of executive committee of College of Literature, Science, and the Arts, 1979—, all at University of Michigan. *Military service:* U.S. Army, 1945-46.

MEMBER: American Historical Association, Association for Asian Studies, American Association of University Professors, American Academy of Arts and Sciences (fellow), Phi Beta Kappa. *Awards, honors:* National Endowment for the Humanities senior fellowship, 1971-72; Fulbright-Hays award, 1981-82.

WRITINGS: China's Early Industrialization: Sheng Hsuan-huai (1894-1916) and Handarin Enterprise, Harvard University Press, 1958; (with S. Cheng) *Chinese Communist Studies of Modern Chinese History,* Harvard University Press, 1961; *The Chinese Economy, 1912-1949,* University of Michigan Center for Chinese Studies, 1968; *The Chinese Economy, ca. 1870-1911,* University of Michigan Center for Chinese Studies, 1969; *Rebellion in Nineteenth-Century China,* University of Michigan Center for Chinese Studies, 1975; *State and Society in Eighteenth-Century China: The Ch'ing Empire in Its Glory,* University of Michigan Center for Chinese Studies, 1976; *The Foreign Establishment in China in the Early Twentieth-Century,* University of Michigan Center for Chinese Studies, 1976; *Economic Trends in the Republic of China, 1912-1949,* University of Michigan Center for Chinese Studies, 1977; *Chung-kuo chin pai-nien ching-chi shih (1870-1949)* (title means "China's Economic History of the Last Hundred Years"), Hua-shih Publishers, 1978.

Editor and contributor: *Modern China,* Prentice-Hall, 1964; (with R. Murphey and M. C. Wright) *Approaches to Modern Chinese History,* University of California Press, 1967; *History in Communist China,* M.I.T. Press, 1968.

Contributor: H. L. Boorman, editor, *Men and Politics in Modern China,* [New York], 1960; C. S. Cowan, editor, *The Economic Development of China and Japan,* Allen & Unwin, 1964; Ping-ti Ho and Tang Tsou, editors, *China in Crisis,* Volume I, University of Chicago Press, 1968; Michel Oksenberg, editor, *China's Developmental Experience,* Academy of Political Science, 1973; Paul A. Cohen and John E. Schrecker, editors, *Reform in Nineteenth-Century China,* Harvard University Press, 1976; *Conference on Modern Chinese Economic History,* Institute of Economics, 1978; Leo Orleans, editor, *Science in Contemporary China,* Stanford University Press, 1980; *The Cambridge History of Modern China,* Cambridge University Press, Volume XI, 1980, Volume XII, 1982; Robert Dernberger, editor, *China's Development Experience and the Other Developing Countries,* Harvard University Press, 1980; *Quingmo Minchu Zhongguo shehui,* Fudan University Press, 1982.

Also contributor to *Encyclopedia Americana, Revue Bibliographique de Sinologie, Bibliographical Dictionary of Republican China,* and to *The Annals of the American Academy of Political and Social Science,* July 1972. Contributor of book reviews to history journals, including *American Historical Review, Journal of Asian Studies,* and *China Quarterly.* Associate editor, *Journal of Asian Studies,* 1959-62; member of editorial board of *Comparative Studies in Society and History,* 1964—, *China Quarterly,* 1967—, and *American Historical Review,* 1970-75.

WORK IN PROGRESS: Editing, with J. K. Fairbank, Volume XIII of *The Cambridge History of China.*

* * *

FIELDING, Raymond E. 1931-

PERSONAL: Born January 3, 1931, in Brockton, Mass.; son of Walter Howard (an engineer) and Irma (Nelson) Fielding; married Carole Behrens, October 11, 1963. *Education:* University of California, Los Angeles, B.A., 1953, M.A., 1956; University of Southern California, Ph.D., 1961. *Home:* 3010 Cedar Knolls Dr., Kingwood, Tex. 77339. *Office:* School of Communication, University of Houston, Houston, Tex. 77004.

CAREER: University of California, Los Angeles, lecturer, 1957-61, assistant professor, 1961-65, associate professor of theater arts, 1965-66; University of Iowa, Iowa City, associate professor of speech and dramatic arts, 1966-69; Temple University, Philadelphia, Pa., professor of radio-television-film, 1969-78; University of Houston, Houston, Tex., professor of communication, 1978—. University of Southern California, visiting lecturer, summer, 1960, visiting assistant professor, summer, 1961, visiting director of cinema studies, 1980-81; visiting associate professor and director of motion picture workshop, New York University, summer, 1965. Founder and curator of Theater Arts Film Archive, 1958-65. Vice-president, International Congress of Schools of Cinema and Television, 1967-70. Birmingham Educational Film Festival, judge, 1972-73, member of advisory board, 1972—. Director of research and development, Zoetrope Studios, Francis Coppola Company, 1980-81. Consultant to National Aeronautics and Space Administration, 1966-67, Compton Encyclopedia, 1971, Hoover Institution for War, Peace, and Revolution, 1975, Smithsonian Institution, 1975, and to various corporations. *Military service:* U.S. Air Force Reserve, 1955-63.

MEMBER: American Film Institute (former trustee), American Science Film Association (trustee), American Center of Films for Children (trustee), Industry Film Producers Association (president, 1961-62), University Film Association (president, 1967-68), University Film Foundation (trustee), Society for Cinema Studies (president, 1972-74), Society of Motion Picture and Television Engineers (fellow), Academy of Motion Picture Arts and Sciences.

AWARDS, HONORS: University of California research grants, 1961-62 and 1964-65, for research in the history of the motion picture newsreel, 1962-63, for research in special cinematographic techniques. Lion of St. Marc, Venice International Film Festival, 1968, for *A Technological History of Motion Pictures and Television;* Frank Luther Mott Research Award Citation, 1973; Pulitzer Prize nomination, 1973, for *The American Newsreel, 1911-1967.*

WRITINGS: (Editor)*The Wills of the Presidents,* Oceana, 1958; *The Technique of Special Effects Cinematography,* Hastings House, 1965, revised edition, 1972; (editor) *A Technological History of Motion Pictures and Television,* University of California Press, 1967; (author of introduction) Kemp R. Niver, *Motion Pictures from the Library of Congress Paper Print Collection, 1894-1912,* University of California Press, 1967; *The American Newsreel, 1911-1967,* University of Oklahoma Press, 1972; (contributor) Ronald Gottesman and Harry Geduld, editors, *Guidebook to Film,* Holt, 1972; (contributor) *The American Cinema,* United States Information Agency, 1974; *The March of Time, 1935-51,* Oxford University Press, 1978; *A Bibliography of Theses and Dissertations on the Subject of Film, 1916-1979,* University Film Association, 1979; (contributor) *Sound and the Cinema,* Redgrave, 1980.

Filmscripts: (And director) "The Honorable Mountain," Columbia Broadcasting System, 1953; "The American Newsreel," Public Broadcasting Service, 1974; "Yesterday's Witness," Public Broadcasting Service, 1975; "Eyewitness to Yesterday," Walt Disney Studios, 1978.

Author of papers for film symposiums and conferences. Contributor of articles to *Focal Encyclopedia of Film and Television Techniques, Encyclopaedia Britannica, Smithsonian Journal of History, Western Political Quarterly, American Archivist, Journal of the University Film Association, Journal of the University Film Producers Association, Cinema Journal Society for Cinema Studies, Journal of the Society of Motion Picture and Television Engineers,* and other film and television journals. Associate editor, *Journal of the University Film Association;* advisory editor, *Quarterly Review of Film Studies;* member of editorial boards, *Cinema Journal.*

* * *

**FINK, Stevanne Auerbach
See AUERBACH, Stevanne**

* * *

FISCHER, LeRoy H(enry) 1917-

PERSONAL: Born May 19, 1917, in Hoffman, Ill.; son of Andrew Leroy (a physician) and Effie (Risby) Fischer; married Martha Gwendolyn Anderson, June 20, 1948; children: Barbara Ann, James LeRoy, John Andrew. *Education:* University of Illinois, B.A., 1939, M.A., 1940, Ph.D., 1943; postdoctoral study at Columbia University, 1941, and Oxford University and Cambridge University, 1945. *Religion:* Methodist. *Home:* 1010 West Cantwell Ave., Stillwater, Okla. 74074. *Office:* Department of History, Oklahoma State University, Stillwater, Okla. 74078.

CAREER: Ithaca College, Ithaca, N.Y., assistant professor of history, 1946; Oklahoma State University, Stillwater, assistant professor, 1946-49, associate professor, 1949-60, professor of history, 1960-72, Oppenheim Regents Professor of History, 1973—, executive director of honors program, College of Arts and Science, 1959-61. Member, Oklahoma Civil War Centennial Commission, 1958-65, Oklahoma Chisholm Trail Centennial Commission, 1966-67; Oklahoma State Historic Preservation Review Commission, member, 1978—, chairman, 1981—. *Military service:* U.S. Army, Signal Corps, 1943-45.

MEMBER: American Historical Association, American Association of University Professors, Organization of American Historians, Western History Association, Southern Historical Association, Oklahoma Historical Society (member of board of directors), Illinois State Historical Society, Oklahoma Westerners (past president), Oklahoma City Civil War Round Table (past president), Faculty Club (past president), Phi Alpha Theta (past president), Pi Gamma Mu (past president), Omicron Delta Kappa.

AWARDS, HONORS: Literary Award of Loyal Legion of the United States for best book-length study on the Civil War, 1963, for manuscript of *Lincoln's Gadfly, Adam Gurowski;* research grants from Merrick Foundation and American Association for State and Local History; named Oklahoma State University Teacher of the Year by Oklahoma Education Association, 1969.

WRITINGS: *Lincoln's Gadfly, Adam Gurowski,* University of Oklahoma Press, 1964; *The Civil War Era in Indian Territory,* Lorrin L. Morrison, 1974; *Oklahoma's Governors, 1890-1978,* four volumes, Oklahoma Historical Society, 1975-1983; *The Western States in the Civil War,* Lorrin L. Morrison, 1975; *The Western Territories in the Civil War,* Sunflower University Press, 1977; *Civil War Battles in the West,* Sunflower University Press, 1981.

Contributor to *Dictionary of American Biography, Encyclopaedia Britannica,* and *Encyclopedia of Southern History.* Also contributor of articles to *Chronicles of Oklahoma, Civil War History, Journal of American History, Journal of the West, Arkansas Historical Quarterly,* and other professional journals.

WORK IN PROGRESS: "Books and articles on Oklahoma history and on Civil War and Reconstruction history."

AVOCATIONAL INTERESTS: Gardening, hiking, travel.

* * *

FISHER, Laine
See HOWARD, James A(rch)

* * *

FITZGERALD, Arlene J.
(Monica Heath)

PERSONAL: Born in Orleans, Neb.; daughter of William Franklin and Laura Mae (Sell) Daily; married Ralph L. Fitzgerald (a safety engineer); children: Ralph A., Fawn J. (Mrs. David M. Machado), Dawn A. (Mrs. Michael L. McGuire). *Education:* Attended Southern Oregon College. *Home:* 4520 Foots Creek Rd., Gold Hill, Ore. 97525. *Agent:* Donald MacCampbell, Inc., 12 East 41st St., New York, N.Y. 10017.

CAREER: Professional writer and artist.

WRITINGS: *Northwest Nurse,* Ace Books, 1964; *Young Nurse Rayburn,* Pyramid Books, 1964; *Harbor Nurse,* Avon, 1964; *Daredevil Nurse,* Pyramid Books, 1964; *Log Camp Nurse,* Avon, 1966; *Volunteer Nurse,* Avon, 1967; *Double Duty Nurse,* Belmont, 1968; *Pamela's Palace,* Manor, 1971, 2nd edition, 1975; *Everything You Always Wanted to Know about Sorcery (But Were Afraid),* Manor, 1973; *Satanic Sex,* Manor, 1973; *House of Tragedy,* Manor, 1973; *Numbers for Lovers,* Manor, 1974; *The Devil's Gate,* Popular Library, 1975; *Windfire,* Zebra Books, 1983. Contributor of historical articles to western magazines.

Under pseudonym Monica Heath; published by Signet Books, except as indicated: *Falconlough,* 1966; *Dunleary,* 1967; *Secrets Can Be Fatal,* 1967; *The Secret of the Vineyard,* 1968; *Clerycastle,* 1969; *Return to Clerycastle,* 1970; *Mistress of Ravenstone,* 1973; *Chateau of Shadows,* 1973; *Duncraig,* 1974; *The Legend of Crownpoint,* 1974; *Woman in Black,* 1974; *The Secret Citadel,* 1975; *Calderwood,* 1975; *The Legend of Blackhurst,* 1976; *Raneslough,* 1976; *House of the Strange Woman,* 1977; *Marshwood,* 1977; *Castlereagh,* 1978; *Clancumara's Keep,* 1978; *Hawkshadow,* Playboy Press, 1980.

WORK IN PROGRESS: *Reap the Wind,* the Saga of Comstock Lode.

* * *

FOLLETT, Robert J(ohn) R(ichard) 1928-

PERSONAL: Born July 4, 1928, in Oak Park, Ill.; son of Dwight W. (an executive) and Mildred (Johnson) Follett; married Nancy L. Crouthamel, December 30, 1950; children: Brian L., Kathryn R., Jean A., Lisa W. *Education:* Brown University, A.B., 1950; Columbia University, graduate study, 1950-51. *Home:* 508 North Oak Park Ave., Oak Park, Ill. 60302. *Office:* 1000 West Washington Blvd., Chicago, Ill. 60607.

CAREER: Follett Publishing Co., Chicago, Ill., editor, 1951-55, sales manager, 1955-58, general manager of educational division, 1958-68, president, 1968-78, president of Follett International, 1972—, chairman and director of Follett Corp., 1979—. President, Alpine Research Institute, 1968—; member of Illinois Governor's Commission on Schools, 1972, and National Advisory Council on Educational Statistics, 1975-77; chairman, Book Distribution Task Force on the book industry, beginning 1978. Member of board of directors, Community Foundation of Oak Park and River Forest, 1959—, Village Manager Association of Oak Park, 1964—, and Fund for Justice, 1974-77; trustee, Institute for Educational Data Systems, 1965—. Republican State Committeeman, Illinois Seventh Congressional District, 1982—. *Military service:* U.S. Army, Psychological Warfare School, 1951-53. *Member:* Association of American Publishers (director, 1972-79), Chicago Publishers Association (president, 1976—), Sierra Club, Cliff Dwellers, River Forest Tennis Club.

WRITINGS: *Your Wonderful Body,* Follett, 1962; *How to Keep Score in Business,* Follett, 1978; *What to Take Backpacking—And Why,* Alpine Guild, 1978; *The Financial Side of Book Publishing,* Association of American Publishers, 1982. Contributor to numerous professional journals.

WORK IN PROGRESS: *Financial Feasibility in Book Publishing; Financial Report Fundamentals.*

SIDELIGHTS: Robert J.R. Follett wrote *CA:* "All of my books have a single impetus. They were written to help someone learn about something. I get great pleasure from helping people to learn.

"Each book I have written has been sparked by the inquiry of a potential reader. The subjects have been ones in which I already had an interest, of course, but the spark from a potential reader was essential.

"Writing involves making decisions. What shall the topic be? How shall it be organized? In what mode of expression shall it be presented? Where to begin? What sentences should be in the paragraph? In what order? What words shall be chosen for the sentences? How shall they be ordered? Is this a place for a conjunction, a comma, a semi-colon? Or should there be a period and another sentence? These, and many other choices must constantly be made by writers. The choices are made in terms of the objectives the writer has. For some writers, the primary objective is emotional impact. For others, it is maximum understanding. Other writers have other objectives. Objectives guide choices.

"Some writers make decisions unconsciously. The result is great if they are truly gifted. Most of us have to make the decisions and choices more consciously. I find this process a very satisfying aspect of writing.

"The act of writing is more pleasurable for me than the event of publication. The process gives more joy than the product. When my children grew up and left home I had the time to write. I have tried to use that time and have something in work constantly. I can't write as well as Will Durant. I hope I can write as long."

AVOCATIONAL INTERESTS: Running, skiing, reading, music, painting, sculpture, and sewing.

FONSECA, John R. 1925-

PERSONAL: Born March 13, 1925, in New Bedford, Mass.; son of Joseph R. and Mary (Vicente) Fonseca; married Joan Fagan, August 27, 1949; children: Kathleen, Patricia, Gwendolyn. *Education:* Harvard University, A.B. (cum laude), 1949, J.D., 1952. *Home:* El Rancho Valley Rd., Greenfield Center, N.Y. 12833. *Office:* Department of Business Law, State University of New York, Albany, N.Y. 12222.

CAREER: Attorney and counsellor at law; admitted to Bars of the States of New York and Massachusetts, to Bar of Oneida County, and to Bar of the U.S. Supreme Court. Dun & Bradstreet, financial analyst in Boston, Mass., and Brazil, 1952-53; Chase Manhattan Bank, New York, N.Y., editor and trust and estate administrator, 1953-56; State University of New York at Utica, head of department of banking and insurance, 1956-65; Hamilton Research Associates, New Hartford, N.Y., president, 1965; Syracuse University, Utica College, Utica, N.Y., professor of law, 1966-68; State University of New York at Albany, professor of law and banking, 1968—. Licensed insurance broker in State of New York. *Military service:* U.S. Army, 1943-46; served on Okinawa and in Korea; became staff sergeant; received battle star. *Member:* American Bar Association, Judge Advocates Association, New York Bar Association, American Business Law Association, Harvard Faculty Club, Scribes.

WRITINGS: (Editor) *Bank Operations Manual*, three volumes, Chase Manhattan Bank, 1955; *Law of Contracts*, Addison-Wesley, 1965; *Fire Insurance*, Addison-Wesley, 1966; *Law of Sales* (Uniform Commercial Code), Addison-Wesley, 1967; *Law of Commercial Paper* (Uniform Commercial Code), Addison-Wesley, 1967; *Law of Business Organizations* (casebook), two volumes, State University of New York, 1971; *Law and Society* (casebook), three volumes, State University of New York, 1972; (with Barkley Clark) *Handling Consumer Credit Cases*, Bancroft-Whitney, 1972, revised edition, 1981; *Environmental Law* (casebook), State University of New York, 1972; (reviser with Alphonse Squillante) Samuel Williston, *Williston on the Law of Sales*, 4th edition, Bancroft-Whitney, 1974; *Automobile Insurance and No-Fault Law*, Lawyers Co-Operative Publishing Co., 1974; *Consumer Credit Compliance Manual*, Lawyers Co-Operative Publishing Co., 1975.

Contributor to annual supplements of *Law of Modern Commercial Practices*, *Proof of Cases in Massachusetts*, and *New York Evidence: Proof of Cases*, all published by Lawyers Co-Operative Publishing Co.

Editor of *Banking Law Journal Digest*, supplements, 1967-72, *Encyclopedia of Commercial Laws*, supplements, 1968-71, *Encyclopedia of Banking Law*, supplements, 1968-71, *Brady on Bank Checks*, supplements, 1968 and 1969. Editor, *Banking Law Journal*, 1967-72; editor-in-chief, *Uniform Commercial Code Law Journal*, 1968-72; associate editor, *Criminal Law Bulletin*, 1969-71.

* * *

FOSTER, David William (Anthony) 1940-

PERSONAL: Born September 11, 1940, in Seattle, Wash.; son of William Henry (a mechanic) and Rosamond (Pepin) Foster; married Virginia Maria Ramos (a professor), May 31, 1966. *Education:* University of Washington, Seattle, B.A. (magna cum laude), 1961, M.A., 1963, Ph.D., 1964. *Politics:* Democrat. *Religion:* Roman Catholic. *Home:* 928 West Palm Lane, Phoenix, Ariz. 85007. *Office:* Department of Foreign Languages, Arizona State University, Tempe, Ariz. 85281.

CAREER: University of Missouri—Columbia, assistant professor of Spanish, 1964-66; Arizona State University, Tempe, assistant professor, 1966-68, associate professor, 1968-71, professor of Spanish, 1971—. Fulbright lecturer in linguistics, Universidad de la Plata and Instituto Nacional de Lenguas Vivas, Argentina, 1967 and 1973; Inter-American Development Bank Visiting Professor, Universidad Catolica de Chile, 1975.

MEMBER: American Association of Teachers of Spanish and Portuguese, Modern Language Association of America, Hispanic Institute, Linguistic Society of America, Instituto Internacional de Literatura Iberoamericana, American Association of University Professors, Philological Association of the Pacific Coast, Rocky Mountain Council for Latin American Studies, Phi Sigma Iota.

WRITINGS: (Co-author) *Research on Language Teaching: An Annotated International Bibliography for 1945-1961*, University of Washington Press, 1962, revised edition, 1965; *Forms of the Novel in the Work of Camilo Jose Cela*, University of Missouri Press, 1967; *The Myth of Paraguay in the Fiction of Augusto Roa Bastos*, University of North Carolina Press, 1969.

(Compiler with wife, Virginia Ramos Foster) *Manual of Hispanic Bibliography: An Annotated Handbook of Basic Sources*, University of Washington Press, 1970; (with Virginia Ramos Foster) *Research Guide to Argentine Literature*, Scarecrow, 1970; *Christian Allegory in Early Hispanic Poetry*, University Press of Kentucky, 1971; *The Early Spanish Ballad*, Twayne, 1971; *The Marques de Santillana*, Twayne, 1971; (with Virginia Ramos Foster) *Luis de Gongora*, Twayne, 1973; *Unamuno and the Novel as Expressionistic Conceit*, Inter American University Press, 1973; (with Gary L. Brower) *An Annotated Bibliography of Haiku in Western Languages*, American Haiku Press, 1974.

Currents in the Contemporary Argentine Novel, University of Missouri Press, 1975; (compiler) *A Dictionary of Contemporary Latin American Authors*, Center for Latin American Studies, Arizona State University, 1975; (compiler) *Latin American Government Leaders*, 2nd edition, Center for Latin American Studies, Arizona State University, 1975; (editor with Virginia Ramos Foster) *Modern Latin American Literature*, two volumes, Ungar, 1975; *The Twentieth Century Spanish-American Novel: A Bibliographic Guide*, Scarecrow, 1975; *Chilean Literature: A Working Bibliography of Secondary Sources*, G. K. Hall, 1978; *Studies in the Contemporary Spanish American Short Story*, University of Missouri Press, 1979; *Augusto Roa Bastos*, Twayne, 1979.

Peruvian Literature: A Bibliography of Secondary Sources, Greenwood Press, 1981; *Mexican Literature: A Bibliography of Secondary Sources*, Scarecrow, 1981; (compiler with Roberto Reis) *A Dictionary of Contemporary Brazilian Authors*, Center for Latin American Studies, Arizona State University, 1982. Contributor of over one hundred articles to professional journals. Editor of *Rocky Mountain Review of Language and Literature*, 1980—.

WORK IN PROGRESS: *Puerto Rico: A Bibliography of Secondary Sources*; *Cuba: A Bibliography of Secondary Sources*; *Argentine Popular Culture*; editing *The Major Texts of the Argentine Teatro Independiente*; *Ensayos semiologicos sobre teatro mexicano*; *Aproximaciones estructurales y semiologicos al ensayo hispanoamericano*; *Studies on Latin American Countercultural Literature*.

FOSTER, Joanna 1928-
(Joanna Foster Dougherty)

PERSONAL: Born July 30, 1928, in Chicago, Ill.; daughter of Orrington C. (an engineer) and Genevieve (an author and artist; maiden name, Stump) Foster; married Paul Dougherty, May 21, 1960 (divorced, 1965); children: Genevieve. *Education:* Attended School of the Chicago Art Institute and Stanford University; Vassar College, B.A., 1950. *Religion:* Unitarian Universalist.

CAREER: Charles Scribner's Sons, New York City, assistant children's editor, 1950-52; Field Enterprises, Inc., Chicago, Ill., editor of music volume of *Childcraft*, 1952-53; Harcourt, Brace & World, Inc., New York City, associate children's book editor, 1953-57; Children's Book Council, Inc., New York City, executive director, 1958-61; The Ready Pen (a freelance service for publishers, editors, and organizations), New York City, staff member, 1962—; *Publishers Weekly*, New York City, editor for children's books, 1962-64; *Scholastic Teacher*, New York City, book editor, 1965-67; vice-president, Connecticut Films, Inc., 1966—. *Member:* American Institute of Graphic Arts (secretary, 1960-61).

WRITINGS: Pete's Puddle (juvenile), Houghton, 1950, reprinted, Harcourt, 1969; *Pages, Pictures and Print*, Harcourt, 1958; *Recipe for a Book Fair* (booklet), Children's Book Council, 1962; (compiler) *How to Conduct Effective Picture Book Programs: A Handbook*, Westchester Library System, 1967; *Home: Shelter and Living Space*, Parents Magazine Press, 1972; *Dogs Working for People* (juvenile), National Geographic Society, 1972. Columnist, *Publishers Weekly* and *Scholastic Teacher*. Biography editor, *Illustrators of Children's Books*, 1957-66.

Wrote and directed films: "The Lively Art of Picture Books" and "The Pleasure is Mutual."

WORK IN PROGRESS: Several films; a filmstrip and manual.†

*   *   *

FOWLER, Charles B(runer) 1931-

PERSONAL: Born May 12, 1931, in Peekskill, N.Y.; son of Charles B. (a conductor) and Mabel (Ackerman) Fowler. *Education:* State University Teachers College (now State University of New York College at Potsdam), B.S.Mus.Ed., 1952; Northwestern University, M.M., 1957; Boston University, D.M.A., 1964. *Home and office:* 320 Second St. S.E., Washington, D.C. 20003.

CAREER: Vocal music supervisor in elementary schools in Rochester, N.Y., 1952-56; Mansfield State College, Mansfield, Pa., assistant professor of music, 1957-62; Northern Illinois University, DeKalb, associate professor of music, 1964-65; Music Educators National Conference, Washington, D.C., editor of *Music Educators Journal*, 1965-71, director of publications, 1970-71; journalist and consultant in the arts, 1971—. Writer and consultant, Walt Disney Productions, 1971—; writer and creative consultant to the executive producer, Radio City Music Hall Productions, Inc., 1979; communications designer for opening events of Epcot Center, Walt Disney World, October, 1982.

MEMBER: Music Educators National Conference (life member), Music Critics Association, Society for Ethnomusicology, Educational Press Association of America (member of board of directors of District of Columbia chapter, 1969-71), Friends of the Kennedy Center, Kappa Delta Pi, Pi Kappa Lambda, Phi Mu Alpha Sinfonia (honorary life member). *Awards, honors:* Danforth grants, 1962-63, 1963-64; certificate of excellence in educational journalism, Educational Press Association of America, 1970, for editorial "Facing the Music in Urban Education."

WRITINGS: (With Robert W. Buggert) *The Search for Musical Understanding*, Wadsworth, 1973; *The Arts Process*, Pennsylvania State Department of Education, 1973.

Dance Is (booklet and slide/tape presentation), National Dance Association, 1978; "Careers in Entertainment" (videotape), Walt Disney Productions, 1979; "Arts Education: A Promise" (slide/tape presentation), John F. Kennedy Center, 1980; "Carmen Opera Box" (multi-media teaching tool), The Metropolitan Opera, 1980; "Porgy and Bess Opera Box" (multi-media teaching tool), Metropolitan Opera, 1981; "First Flights: The Kennedy Center's Programs for Children and Youth" (slide/tape presentation), John F. Kennedy Center, 1981; "Alaska 1984" (live and televised production), Radio City Music Hall Productions, 1981; (author of narration) "The Glory of Christmas: A Living Nativity," The Crystal Cathedral, 1981; (author of narration) "Encore: The Fiftieth Anniversary Show," Radio City Music Hall, 1982; (author of narration) "Carnival de Lumiere," Walt Disney Productions, 1982.

Author of education column in *Musical America*, 1974—. Contributor to *Encyclopedia of Education*. Contributor of numerous articles to music and education journals. Editor-in-chief, *Parks and Recreation*, and manager of publications for National Recreation and Parks Association, 1973-75.

AVOCATIONAL INTERESTS: Painting, theater, gardening, exercise, overseas travel.

*   *   *

FOWLER, Virginie
See ELBERT, Virginie Fowler

*   *   *

FOX, John H(oward) 1925-

PERSONAL: Born October 1, 1925; son of William and Mabel (Morgan) Fox; married Jacqueline Meunier, July 10, 1947; children: Brian Henry, Roland Paul, Graham Richard. *Education:* University of London, B.A., 1946; University of Paris, Doctorat de l' Universite de Paris (mention tres honorable), 1948. *Home:* 6, Hill Close, Exeter, Devonshire, England. *Office:* Department of French, University of Exeter, Queen's Drive, Exeter, Devonshire, England.

CAREER: Civil Service Commission, London, England, assistant principal, 1946; University of Exeter, Exeter, England, lecturer in French language and literature, 1948—. *Member:* Societe de Linguistique Romane, Society for French Studies.

WRITINGS: Robert de Blois: Son oeuvre didactique et narrative, Nizet, 1950; *The Poetry of Villon*, Nelson, 1962; (with Robin Wood) *A Concise History of the French Language: Phonology and Morphology*, Blackwell, 1968, Barnes & Noble, 1969; *The Lyric Poetry of Charles d'Orleans*, Clarendon Press, 1969; *The Rhetorical Tradition in French Literature of the Late Middle Ages: An Inaugural Lecture Delivered in the University of Exeter on 17 January 1969*, University of Exeter, 1969; *The Middle Ages*, Barnes & Noble, 1974; (editor with others) *Studies in Eighteenth Century French Literature: Presented to Robert Niklaus*, University of Exeter, 1975. Contributor to language journals in United States and in Europe.

BIOGRAPHICAL SOURCES: *Times Educational Supplement,* January 18, 1963.†

* * *

FRASER, J(ulius) T(homas) 1923-

PERSONAL: Born May 7, 1923, in Budapest, Hungary; came to United States in 1946, naturalized in 1953; son of Francis (an attorney) and Olga (Szigethy) Fraser; married Margaret Cameron (a musician), 1948 (divorced, 1970); married Jane Hunsicker (a school teacher), 1973; children: Thomas C. Fraser, Anne-Marie C. Fraser, Carol Hunsicker, Margaret C. Fraser, Ann Hunsicker. *Education:* Cooper Union School of Engineering, B.E.E., 1951; Technische Universitaet Hannover, Ph.D., 1970. *Politics:* "A Jeffersonian independent." *Religion:* "Christian by private creed." *Office address:* International Society for the Study of Time, P.O. Box 815, Westport, Conn. 06881.

CAREER: Worked as a machinist, technician, and draftsman in Budapest, Hungary, 1941-44; Allied Control Commission, Rome, Italy, English correspondent, 1945-46; cataloger at Columbia University Libraries, contract inspector for Electrolux Vacuum Cleaners, and laboratory foreman at North American Philips, Inc., 1947-50; Rangertone, Inc., Newark, N.J., design draftsman, 1950-51; Westinghouse Electric Corp., Baltimore, Md., junior engineer, 1951-53; General Precision Laboratory (now Singer-Kearfott, Inc.), Pleasantville, N.Y., staff member, 1955-57, senior staff member, 1957-62, senior scientist in physics department of Research Division, 1962-71; independent researcher in study of time, 1971—. Visiting lecturer at Massachusetts Institute of Technology, 1966-67, and Mt. Holyoke College, 1967-69; visiting professor at University of Maryland, 1969-70; adjunct professor at Fordham University, 1971—. *Member:* International Society for the Study of Time (founder and secretary).

WRITINGS: Of Time, Passion, and Knowledge: Reflections on the Strategy of Existence, Braziller, 1975; *Time as Conflict: A Scientific and Humanistic Study,* Birkhaeuser, 1978; *The Genesis and Evolution of Time: A Critique of Interpretation in Physics,* University of Massachusetts Press, 1982.

Editor and contributor; published by Springer-Verlag, except as indicated: *The Voices of Time: A Cooperative Survey of Man's Views of Time as Expressed by the Sciences and the Humanities,* Braziller, 1966, 2nd enlarged edition, University of Massachusetts Press, 1981; (with F. C. Haber and G. H. Mueller) *The Study of Time I,* 1972; (with N. Lawrence) *The Study of Time II,* 1975; *The Study of Time III,* 1978; *The Study of Time IV,* 1981.

Contributor to *Britannica Yearbook of Science and the Future.* Also contributor of numerous articles to scientific and literary journals.

WORK IN PROGRESS: Revolt of the Caged Mind, a novel; *The Study of Time V.*

SIDELIGHTS: "As a young child growing up in the Hungarian countryside, I liked to tell people that I would be a blacksmith, explorer, and everyone's friend," J. T. Fraser told *CA.* "The 'blacksmith' progressed through technician, draftsman, engineer, inventor, physicist and philosopher to the writer of both fiction and nonfiction. The 'explorer' still travels around the world, in search of ideas and feelings. The 'friend' is manifest in a profound empathy for people, and in an unremitting concern with the responsibility of being human.

"All three parts are joined in my dedication to the study of time which spans over thirty-five years. In my early writings I formulated a new system of natural philosophy—the theory of time as conflict. In my subsequent writings I have been working out the practical significance of the new philosophical system for our understanding of matter, life, mind, and society.

"The moving power of this single passion—the analysis of time—to which I have given my life, is, not surprisingly, experiential. As an adolescent in World War II, I watched the clash of cultures and the attendant release of primordial emotions. As a young man I observed America, this land of promise, through extensive travels—but always returning in body and spirit to my home along the Hudson.

"Integrating these two families of impressions, I could not help but note how thoroughly the spectacular achievements of science and industry have undermined all traditional assessments of the position of man in the scheme of things. The consequent absence of ideals, inspiring as well as intelligible to the majority of people, makes our epoch an uninformed one.

"An analysis of the social forces at work, carried out through the theory of time as conflict suggests that this regression is, metaphorically, a withdrawal before the leap. We are witnessing around the earth a 'revolt of the caged mind,' a radical alteration in the texture of human life itself. The march is not to the tune of Dies Irae, not even to that of the Communist Internationale, but to a more elemental call. We have reached an evolutionary dead-end, comparable in its dynamics to the one that was reached by inorganic evolution just before the birth of life, and by organic evolution just before the emergence of the human mind.

"As a writer, philosopher and scientist I see my task as one of chronicling and interpreting these profound changes, becoming a part of the motive forces behind them, and pursuing them toward their unknown end."

Of Fraser's *The Voices of Time: A Cooperative Survey of Man's Views of Time as Expressed by the Sciences and the Humanities,* critic Philip Toynbee writing in the *Observer Review* says: "Nearly all the contributors to this compendium are scientists of one kind or another, and for a non-scientist reader a principal source of pleasure comes from having his mind stretched to the uttermost limits of its capacity. . . . In these furthest reaches of their subjects, scientists are involved in the most heady metaphysical speculations, not merely retrospectively but as an immediate, intrinsic and unavoidable element in all that they think and write." It is, he concludes, "one of the most fascinating books I have read for a long time."

BIOGRAPHICAL/CRITICAL SOURCES: Observer Review, February 18, 1968; *International Herald Tribune,* August 30-31, 1975.

* * *

FRAZER, Robert Caine
See CREASEY, John

* * *

FREDRICKSON, George M(arsh) 1934-

PERSONAL: Born July 16, 1934, in Bristol, Conn.; son of George (a merchant) and Gertrude (Marsh) Fredrickson; married Helene Osouf, October 16, 1956; children: Anne Hope, Laurel, Thomas, Caroline. *Education:* Harvard University, B.A., 1956, Ph.D., 1964; University of Oslo, graduate study, 1956-57. *Home:* 1215 Judson Ave., Evanston, Ill. 60202. *Office:* Department of History, Northwestern University, Evanston, Ill. 60201.

CAREER: Harvard University, Cambridge, Mass., instructor in history, 1963-66; Northwestern University, Evanston, Ill., 1966—, associate professor, 1966-71, professor of history, beginning 1971, currently William Smith Mason Professor of American History. *Military service:* U.S. Navy, 1957-60; became lieutenant junior grade. *Member:* American Historical Association, Southern Historical Society, Organization of American Historians. *Awards, honors:* Annisfield Wolf Award in race relations, 1972, for *The Black Image in the White Mind;* Ralph Waldo Emerson Award, from Phi Beta Kappa, 1981, for *White Supremacy.*

WRITINGS: The Inner Civil War: Northern Intellectuals and the Crisis of the Union, Harper, 1965; (editor) Albion Tourgee, *A Fool's Errand,* Torchbooks, 1966; (editor) Hinton R. Halper, *The Impending Crisis of the South,* Harvard University Press, 1968; (editor) *William Lloyd Garrison,* Prentice-Hall, 1968; *The Black Image in the White Mind,* Harper, 1971; (contributor) Huggins, Kilson, and Fox, editors, *Key Issues in the Afro-American Experience,* Harcourt, 1971; (editor) *A Nation Divided: Problems and Issues of the Civil War and Reconstruction,* Burgess, 1975; *White Supremacy,* Oxford University Press, 1981. Contributor to *American Historical Review, Journal of Southern History, Civil War History, New York Review of Books,* and other periodicals.

WORK IN PROGRESS: A book on the transformation of American society, 1865-1900.

SIDELIGHTS: In *White Supremacy,* his comparative history of race relations in the United States and South Africa, George M. Fredrickson systematically analyzes the similarities and differences between the two countries. Although *New York Times Book Review* critic David Brion Davis believes that such a comparison "evokes resistance," Robert Dawidoff of the *Los Angeles Times Book Review* suggests that "*White Supremacy* illustrates how clarifying and absorbing and how challenging comparative history can be. [Fredrickson] has written about white European domination of native and imported, slave and otherwise, unfree nonwhite people in South Africa and the United States." And, in doing so, says *Washington Post Book World* writer Jim Hoagland, Fredrickson "deftly picks apart the tangled threads of two brands of white power and traces them back to their sources."

In both countries, white supremacy began in the 1600's with the subjugation of natives who were not black and, in both cases, reactions to these native groups were preceded by "rehearsals" elsewhere on the part of the parent nations. "In England," explains C. Vann Woodward in the *New York Review of Books,* "the brutal subjugation of the 'Wild Irish' . . . was such a rehearsal. At the same time the Dutch commercially exploited the East Indies with the milder motives of trade, without the need for expropriation of the land or extermination of the natives. The English repeated their experience in colonizing America, treating the Indians as they had the 'Wild Irish.' The Dutch repeated theirs at the Cape of Good Hope." Neither the English nor the Dutch considered the indigenous populations their social or intellectual equals, and both groups found the natives unsuitable as sources of cheap labor or slaves.

By the early 1700's, writes Kathryn Marshall in *Commonweal,* "both the Cape and the American tidewater colonies had become slave societies. In each region whites relied on imported rather than indigenous labor; Americans bought West African slaves, white Cape colonists obtained slaves from East Africa, Madagascar, and the East Indies. Fredrickson points out that the institution of racial slavery was intimately linked to tensions within the white social order, with the dehumanization of blacks creating a basis for inter-class unity among whites. For both the Cape and North American colonies were essentially frontiers, lacking the cohesiveness imparted by a metropolitan authority." Eventually both slave societies developed an ideology of what Fredrickson calls "*Herrenvolk* democracy"—or as Woodward explains it, "the equality of all white males—to justify white supremacy, and each developed its own style of patriarchalism."

Despite these and other similarities, there were also important differences in the way the countries developed. The descendants of the Dutch settlers, for instance, were primarily herdsmen, while the white Americans were farmers who wanted to clear, cultivate and claim title to the land. Responsive to the demands of its citizens, the American government committed itself to the spread of "civilization" and did little to protect helpless minorities. According to *New York Times Book Review* critic Davis, "these distinctive conditions of American settlement and expansion, when compared with those of South Africa, led at first to a more ruthless dispossession of the indigenes, to a more thoroughgoing commitment to Negro slavery and to a much earlier insistence on a rigid and impermeable color line." On the other hand, writes *Washington Post Book World* reviewer Hoagland, "South Africans will also have to register Fredrickson's conclusions that for all its imperfections and fitful halts, the United States has since the Civil War worked hard at eliminating the legalized 'dominative racism' while a new central government in South Africa has moved in exactly the opposite direction, with disastrous results."

Despite the temptation to moralize, Fredrickson restrains himself "and thereby fuels the reader's thinking on the issues he raises," *Los Angeles Times Book Review* critic Dawidoff says. "Without saying what should or will happen, he does show what can happen here, because it did. He also suggests . . . that it might all have been different and therefore may yet be."

BIOGRAPHICAL/CRITICAL SOURCES: New York Times Book Review, January 25, 1981; *Washington Post Book World,* March 1, 1981; *New York Review of Books,* March 5, 1981; *Los Angeles Times Book Review,* March 29, 1981; *Chicago Tribune Book World,* April 5, 1981; *Commonweal,* June 5, 1981.

* * *

FREE
See HOFFMAN, Abbie

* * *

FREED, Alvyn M. 1913-

PERSONAL: Born June 19, 1913, in Philadelphia, Pa.; son of Jesse (a merchant) and Amy (Jacobs) Freed; married Margaret De Haan (a teacher and writer), May 22, 1947; children: Lawrence Douglas, Jesse Mark. *Education:* Temple University, B.S., 1938, M.A., 1948; University of Texas at Austin, Ph.D., 1955; also studied at University of California, Los Angeles, University of Miami, and Claremont College. *Home:* 1129 Commons Dr., Sacramento, Calif. 95825. *Office:* Psychological Services Inc., 1820 Professional Dr., Sacramento, Calif. 95825.

CAREER: Former physical education teacher in public schools in Philadelphia, Pa.; school psychologist in Ventura, Calif., 1949-52; RAND Corp., Santa Monica, Calif., human factors scientist, 1955-57; System Development Corp., Santa Monica, human factors scientist, 1957-61; private practice in Sacramento, Calif., 1960—; Aerojet-General Corp., Sacramento, employed in quality and reliability division, 1961-64; San Juan Unified School District, Sacramento, school psychologist, 1964-

67; Jalmar Press, Inc., Sacramento, president and owner, 1973-81; currently president of Psychological Services Inc., Sacramento. Lecturer at University of California, Riverside, 1956-59, and Sacramento State College (now California State University, Sacramento), 1961-63. *Military service:* U.S. Army Air Forces, 1940-46.

MEMBER: International Transactional Analysis Association, American Pyschological Association, American Society for Clinical Hypnosis, California Psychological Association, Sacramento Psychological Association, Association for Past Life Regression and Therapy. *Awards, honors:* Cindy Award from Industrial Film Producers Association, 1963, for film "Power of the Individual."

WRITINGS—All published by Jalmar Press: (With Herb Michelson) *Please Keep on Smoking: We Need the Money,* 1980.

"Transactional Analysis for Everybody" series: (With Barbara Freed) *T.A. for Kids (and Grown Ups Too),* 1971, 3rd revised edition, 1977; *T.A. for Tots (and Other Prinzes),* 1973; *T.A. for Teens (and Other Important People),* 1976; *T.A. for Tots Coloring Book,* 1976; *T.A. for Tots II,* 1980.

Also author of screenplay "Power of the Individual," produced by Aerojet-General Corp., 1962. Contributor to journals.

SIDELIGHTS: Alvyn M. Freed's wife, Margaret, told *CA:* "Over 6,000 schools and churches all over the world have adopted transactional analysis techniques in their group work and teaching. It is being applied in prisons, hospitals, and seminaries, and is highly effective. The T.A. books have been translated into Spanish, French, German, and Portuguese and are widely distributed in Canada, Australia, and New Zealand, as well as throughout the United States."

MEDIA ADAPTATIONS: Several of Freed's books have been developed for audio-visual packages, including "Tot Pac," which was adapted from *T.A. for Tots,* and "Kid Pac," which was adapted from *T.A. for Kids.*

* * *

**FREED, Barry
See HOFFMAN, Abbie**

* * *

FREEMAN, Jo 1945-

PERSONAL: Born August 26, 1945, in Atlanta, Ga.; daughter of William Maxwell and Helen Claire (a history teacher; maiden name, Mitchell) Freeman. *Education:* University of California, Berkeley, B.A. (with honors), 1965; University of Chicago, Ph.D., 1973; New York University, J.D., 1982. *Home:* 1738 Riggs Pl. N.W., Washington, D.C. 20009. *Office:* 433 Tenth St. N.W., Brooklyn, N.Y. 11215.

CAREER: U.S. Navy Department, Washington, D.C., clerk-typist for Bureau of Ships, 1962; staff member of "Cranston for Senate" campaign in Oakland, Calif., 1964; Southern Christian Leadership Conference, fieldworker and research director in Alabama, Georgia, Illinois, and Mississippi, 1965-66; *West Side Torch* (community newspaper), Chicago, Ill., co-editor and photographer, 1967; *Modern Hospital,* Chicago, assistant editor, 1967-68; member of national staff of "McCarthy for President" campaign, 1968; University of Chicago, Department of Urban Studies, Chicago, intermittant work as research associate, 1968-70, extension lecturer in political science, autumn, 1971; State University of New York College at Old Westbury, assistant professor of American studies, 1973-74; State University of New York College at Purchase, assistant professor of political science, 1974-77; staff associate in employment policy at Brookings Institution and for Employment and Training Administration, Department of Labor, both Washington, D.C., 1977-78; law clerk, eastern district of New York, 1982-83. Civil rights activist, 1963-67; free-lance photographer, 1967-68; lecturer. Visiting professor, California State University, Chico, 1977. Member of Twentieth Century Fund's task force on women and employment, 1970; organizer of feminist groups and activities, 1967—; alternate delegate to Democratic National Convention, 1972; reporter at 1964, 1968, 1976, and 1980 Democratic Conventions, and at 1976 and 1980 Republican Conventions; delegate to International Women's Year meeting in Houston, 1977. Has served as consultant to General Motors, Columbia University, Canadian ministry for women's programs, Dutch ministry for social welfare, Office of Federal Contract Compliance Programs, Eagleton Institute, and various periodicals, task forces, and commissions on women's and minority rights.

MEMBER: American Bar Association, American Political Science Association, Women's Caucus for Political Science (former national treasurer), National Organization for Women, Manhattan Women's Political Caucus. *Awards, honors:* National Institute of Mental Health fellow, 1968-73; national finalist in White House fellows competition, 1975; prize for best scholarly work on women in politics, American Political Science Association, 1975, for *The Politics of Women's Liberation;* grant from State University of New York Research Foundation, 1975-76; American Political Science Association congressional fellow, 1978-79.

WRITINGS: (Editor) *Women: A Feminist Perspective,* Mayfield, 1975, 2nd edition, 1979; *The Politics of Women's Liberation: A Case Study of an Emerging Social Movement and Its Relation to the Policy Process,* Longman, 1975; (editor) *Social Movements of the Sixties and Seventies,* Longman, 1982.

Contributor: Robin Morgan, editor, *Sisterhood Is Powerful,* Random House, 1970; June Sochen, editor, *The New Feminism in Twentieth Century America,* Heath, 1971; *Discrimination against Women,* U.S. Government Printing Office, 1971; Anne Koedt and Ellen Levine, editors, *Notes from the Third Year,* privately printed, 1971; Michele Garskof, editor, *Roles Women Play: Readings toward Women's Liberation,* Brooks/Cole, 1971; Hans Peter Dreitzel, editor, *Recent Sociology Number Four: Family, Marriage, and the Struggle of the Sexes,* Macmillan, 1972; Karlyn K. Campbell, editor, *Critique of Contemporary Rhetoric,* Wadsworth, 1972; Anne Koedt, Ellen Levine, and Anita Rapone, editors, *Radical Feminism,* Quadrangle, 1972; Diana Riesche, editor, *Women and Society,* H. W. Wilson, 1972; William Feigelman, editor, *Sociology Full Circle,* Praeger, 1972; P. Denain, M. Lecomte, and C. Thomas, editors, *Protest U.S.A.,* Masson Et Cie (Paris, France), 1972; Joan Huber, editor, *Changing Women in a Changing Society,* University of Chicago Press, 1973; Jerome Skolnick and Elliot Currie, editors, *Crisis in American Institutions,* Little, Brown, 2nd edition, 1973, 3rd edition, 1976; Eleanor S. Morrison and Vera Borosage, editors, *Human Sexuality: Contemporary Perspectives,* National Press Books, 1973; Elliot Aronson and Robert Helmreich, editors, *Social Psychology,* Van Nostrand, 1973; Helena A. Lopata, editor, *Marriages and Families,* Van Nostrand, 1973; Alice Rossi and Ann Calderwood, editors, *Academic Women on the Move,* Russell Sage, 1973.

Douglas Ehringer, editor, *Influence, Belief and Argument,* Scott, Foresman, 1974; Arlene Skolnick and Jerome Skolnick, editors, *Intimacy, Family and Society,* Little Brown, 1974; Diane Gersoni-Stavn, editor, *Sexism and Youth,* Bowker, 1974; Andrew Scott and Earle Wallace, editors, *Politics, U.S.A.,* Macmillan, 1974; Jane Jaquette, editor, *Women in Politics,* Wiley, 1974; Scott McNall, editor, *The Sociological Perspective,* Little, Brown, 4th edition, 1977; R. Serge Denisoff, editor, *The Sociology of Dissent,* Harcourt, 1974; Helen Icken Safa and Gloria Levitas, editors, *Social Problems in Corporate America,* Harper, 1975; Rinah Sheleff, Sara Sikes, and others, editors, *Woman, Women, Womanliness: An Anthology of Feminist Writings,* Feminist Movement of Israel, 1975; Ruby Rohrlich-Leavitt, editor, *Women Cross Culturally: Change and Challenge,* Mouton, 1975.

Lawrence Habermehl, editor, *Morality in the Modern World: Ethical Dimensions of Contemporary Human Problems,* Dickenson, 1976; Richard G. Braungart, editor, *Society and Politics: Readings in Political Sociology,* Prentice-Hall, 1976; Ritchie P. Lowry and Robert P. Rankin, editors, *Sociology: Social Science and Social Concern,* Heath, 1976; Barbara Bellow Watson, editor, *Women's Studies: The Social Realities,* Harper's College Press, 1976; *Impact ERA: Limitations and Possibilities,* edited by the California Commission on the Status of Women Equal Rights Amendment Project, Les Femme Publishing, 1976; Roberta Ash Garner, *Social Change,* Rand McNally, 1977; David Popenoe, editor, *Sociology,* Prentice-Hall, 3rd edition, 1977; *Creative Career Development: A Workbook,* Alexander Menthven and Associates, 2nd edition, 1977; Ann Beaudry and Kim Yonkers, editors, *Women in the Economy: Policies and Strategies for Change,* Institute for Policy Studies, 1978; John McCarthy and Mayer Zald, editors, *Dynamics of Social Movements,* Winthrop Publishing, 1979; Catherine Stimson and others, editors, *Women and the American City,* University of Chicago Press, 1981; Ellan Boneparth, editor, *Women Power and Policy,* Pergamon, 1982.

Contributor to *Collier's Encyclopedia* and *Merit Students Encyclopedia.* Also contributor to proceedings of the colloquium on legislation for women's rights in the Netherlands and the United States. Contributor of 45 articles and numerous book reviews to academic journals, feminist publications, and popular magazines, including *Nation* and *Ms.*

WORK IN PROGRESS: Co-authoring *Women and the Democratic Party;* researching a book on social movements and public policy.

SIDELIGHTS: Jo Freeman has been active in politics since 1962, participating in national and local campaigns. She is also active in the feminist movement and has organized conferences, newsletters, women's centers, and speakers programs. Some of her books have been translated into Japanese, Spanish, and Hebrew.

Freeman's history of the feminist movement, *The Politics of Women's Liberation,* traces the political theory behind the movement. Writing in *Political Science Quarterly,* Kathryn B. Yatrakis comments that Freeman's book "will make a significant contribution to the literature of the women's liberation movement.... The author has succeeded in taking the potentially unwieldy topic ... and has firmly grounded it in social-movement theory. To this extent the book goes well beyond much of the literature in this area." Joyce T. Macrorie, reviewing the book for *Antioch Review,* complains that as a published doctoral thesis, "it is unreadable.... It suffers from the author's fear of cheating her sources, of coming on with too much self." *Ms.* writer Joan Peters also is "somewhat disappointed in [The] *Politics of Women's Liberation*" but does point to Freeman's "fine documentation of the Women's Movement." Carol Anne Douglas states in *Off Our Backs* that Freeman's book will help "fill in the gaps" in most women's "vague ideas about the origins of our movement."

AVOCATIONAL INTERESTS: Martial arts, photography, collecting political buttons.

BIOGRAPHICAL/CRITICAL SOURCES: Off Our Backs, August, 1975; *Ms.,* August, 1975; *New York Times Book Review,* October 5, 1975; *Political Science Quarterly,* winter, 1975-76; *Antioch Review,* spring, 1976; *Contemporary Issues Criticism,* Volume I, Gale, 1982.

* * *

FREGLY, Bert 1922-

PERSONAL: Born August 19, 1922, in Patton, Pa.; son of Alphonse Francis (a merchant) and Mary (Vaccario) Fregly; married Violet Elizabeth Milovich, April 26, 1952 (died October 7, 1957). *Education:* National Electronic Institute, B.S. (physics), 1948; San Diego City College, A.A., 1966; San Diego State University, B.S. (business administration), 1970, M.A., 1976. *Politics:* Democrat. *Religion:* Roman Catholic. *Home:* 9350 Bolsa Ave., Westminster, Calif. 92683.

CAREER: WFAH-Radio, Alliance, Ohio, broadcast engineer, 1948-51; WFMT-Radio, Chicago, Ill., broadcast engineer, 1951-52; Packard Bell Electronics, San Diego, Calif., technician, field engineer, and member of public relations staff, 1952-54; U.S. Naval Air Station, North Island, Calif., electronic technician in guided missile program, 1955-56; Electro Instruments, Inc., San Diego, packaging designer and research and development technician, 1956-63; real estate salesman in residential property and raw land, at various times, 1959—; Toy Giant, Inc., San Diego, owner and manager, 1963-66; White Front Discount Department Stores (residential interiors), San Diego, branch manager, 1971-72; San Diego Community Colleges, San Diego, instructor in vocational guidance training, career development, and business education, 1973-79; Small Business Administration, Los Angeles, Calif., management assistance officer, 1979—; Santa Ana College, Santa Ana, Calif., instructor in business, 1980—. Free-lance writer and lecturer; vocational guidance counselor. President, Allied Gardens Merchants Association, 1963-64; volunteer police reserve officer and probation officer in San Diego. Business and management consultant. *Military service:* U.S. Navy, 1943-45; served in European, Atlantic, and South Pacific theaters.

WRITINGS: How to Get a Job, E.T.C. Publications, 1974; *How to Cast Your Own Horoscope,* Ashley Books, 1975; *How to Be Self Employed,* E.T.C. Publications, 1975; *Help Wanted,* E.T.C. Publications, 1979. Contributor of about forty articles on electronics, astrology, business, economics, and social science to periodicals; contributor of articles to trade journals.

WORK IN PROGRESS: Astrological data and reference encyclopedia; *How to Manage in the Eighties, Nineties, and the Twenty-first Century; Management by Common Sense; Civil Justice: A Shocking Revelation; Why Business in the U.S.A.?*

SIDELIGHTS: Bert Fregly writes to *CA:* "My whole concept centers on the improvement of mankind in the areas of business, employment, family, and social life. To this end I have devoted my energies to help solve the problems of the unemployed, the underemployed, the unsuccessful business person, the test taker trying to compete in the world of mental discrimination, and the depressed people who are lacking in the skills that enable them to compete in our social environment.

"I have but one desire in life, to bring about an equality in business, employment, and personal achievement. I want everyone to have an equal chance at success. For those who lack the necessary skills and techniques I hope to create an equality through the medium of my classrooms, my books, my lectures and seminars, and counseling techniques."

AVOCATIONAL INTERESTS: Square dance calling, amateur radio.

* * *

FREIDSON, Eliot 1923-

PERSONAL: Born February 20, 1923, in Boston, Mass.; son of Joseph (a merchant) and Grace Margaret (Backer) Freidson; married Marion Elizabeth Facinger, April 26, 1950; children: Jane Beatrice, Oliver Eliot. Education: Attended University of Maine, 1941-42; University of Chicago, Ph.B., 1947, M.A., 1950, Ph.D., 1952. Home: 325 Park Ave., Leonia, N.J. Office: Department of Sociology, New York University, 822 Main, New York, N.Y.

CAREER: University of Illinois at Urbana-Champaign, research fellow, 1952-54; City College of the City University of New York, New York City, assistant professor of sociology, 1956-61; New York University, New York City, associate professor, 1961-63, professor of sociology, 1963—, head of department, 1975-78. Research sociologist, Montefiore Hospital. Military service: U.S. Army, 1943-46, became technical sergeant; received Bronze Star. Member: American Anthropological Association (liaison fellow), Society for the Study of Social Problems, American Association of University Professors, American Sociological Association (fellow; chairman of section of medical sociology, 1963-64), Eastern Sociological Society.

WRITINGS: (Editor) Student Leaders, Student Government and the American College, U.S. National Student Association, 1955; Patients' Views of Medical Practice, Russell Sage, 1961, reprinted, University of Chicago Press, 1980; (editor) The Hospital in Modern Society, Free Press of Glencoe, 1963; Profession of Medicine: A Study of the Sociology of Applied Knowledge, Dodd, 1970; Professional Dominance: The Social Structure of Medical Care, Atherton, 1970; (editor with Judith Lorber) Medical Men and Their Work, Aldine, 1972; (editor) The Professions and Their Prospects, Sage Publications, 1973; Doctoring Together: A Study of Professional Social Control, Elsevier-North Holland, 1975. Contributor to professional journals.†

* * *

FRINGS, Manfred S. 1925-

PERSONAL: Surname rhymes with "rings"; born February 27, 1925, in Cologne, Germany (now West Germany); U.S. citizen; son of Gottfried (a teacher) and Maria (Over) Frings; married Emma J. Broussard, 1960; children: one. Education: University of Cologne, Ph.D., 1953, and staatsexamen in English and Philosophy, State Teacher Training Diploma, postdoctoral study, 1953-55. Religion: Roman Catholic. Office: Department of Philosophy, DePaul University, 2322 North Kenmore, Chicago, Ill. 60614.

CAREER: University of Detroit, Detroit, Mich., assistant professor of philosophy, 1958-61; Gymnasium of Monchen-Gladbach, Monchen-Gladbach, Germany, school master, 1961-63; Duquesne University, Pittsburgh, Pa., associate professor of philosophy, 1963-66; DePaul University, Chicago, Ill., associate professor, 1966-68, professor of philosophy, 1968—. Founder of Heidegger Conference, 1966—. Member: American Association of University Professors, American Philosophical Association, Husserl Society (secretary, 1971-72).

Awards, honors: Fulbright grant, 1958-59; American Council of Learned Societies grant, 1973.

WRITINGS: (Editor) Readings in the Philosophy of Science, University of Detroit Press, 1960; Max Scheler: A Concise Introduction into the World of a Great Thinker, Duquesne University Press, 1965; Person und Dasein: Zur Frage der Ontologie des Wertseins, Nijhoff, 1969; Zur Phanomenologie der Lebensgemeinschaft, Anton Hain, 1970; (contributor) Phenomenology in Perspective, Nijhoff, 1970; (contributor) Linguistic Analysis and Phenomenology, Macmillan, 1972; (cotranslator) Scheler, Formalism in Ethics and Non-Formal Ethics of Values, Northwestern University, 1973; (contributor) Grundprobleme der Grossen Philosophen, Vandenhoeck & Ruprecht, 1973.

Also editor of The German Collected Works of Max Scheler, and co-editor of The German Collected Works of M. Heidegger. Contributor to numerous international journals.

SIDELIGHTS: "I believe that writing a book should be a creative process coming from one's own imagination, preferably from the spur of the moment," Manfred S. Frings told CA. "Having been born with perfect pitch, I am at heart a musician. I improvised and created music (piano) from my fourth year of life. I am completely self-taught, playing almost exclusively Chopin. I have tried to convey creating music to writing. At times it works, but only for a short while. I feel that at those moments I might have reached the essence of writing which I hold should have only a minimum of planning ahead. In philosophy this is very difficult to do and yields mostly fragments or jottings."

* * *

FRYE, (Herman) Northrop 1912-

PERSONAL: Born July 14, 1912, in Sherbrooke, Quebec, Canada; son of Herman Edward and Catherine Maud (Howard) Frye; married Helen Kemp, August 24, 1937. Education: University of Toronto, B.A., 1933; Emmanuel College, ordained, 1936; Merton College, Oxford, M.A., 1940. Religion: United Church of Canada. Home: 127 Clifton Rd., Toronto, Ontario, Canada M4T 2G5. Office: Massey College, University of Toronto, Toronto, Ontario, Canada M5S 2E1.

CAREER: University of Toronto, Victoria College, Toronto, Ontario, lecturer in English, 1939-41, assistant professor, 1942-46, associate professor, 1947, professor of English, 1948—, chairman of department, 1952-59, principal, 1959-67, University Professor, 1967—. Chancellor, Victoria University, Toronto, 1978—. Visiting professor at Harvard University, Princeton University, Columbia University, Indana University, University of Washington, University of British Columbia, Cornell University, University of California, Berkeley, and Oxford University. Andrew D. White Professor-at-Large, Cornell University, 1970-75; Charles Eliot Norton Poetry Professor, Harvard University, 1974-75. Member of board of governors, Ontario Curriculum Institute, 1960-63; chairman of Governor-General's Literary Awards Committee, 1962. Advisory member, Canadian Radio Television and Telecommunications Commission, 1968-77. Member: Modern Language Association of America (executive council member, 1958-62; president, 1976), English Institute (former chairman), Royal Society of Canada (fellow), American Academy of Arts and Sciences (foreign honorary member), British Academy (corresponding fellow), American Philosophical Society (foreign member), American Academy and Institute of Arts and Letters (honorary member).

AWARDS, HONORS: Guggenheim fellow, 1950-51; Lorne Pierce Medal of the Royal Society of Canada, 1958; Canada Council medal, 1967; Pierre Chauveau Medal of the Royal Society of Canada, 1970; Canada Council Molson Prize, 1971; Companion of the Order of Canada, 1972; honorary fellow, Merton College, Oxford, 1974; Civic Honour, City of Toronto, 1974; Royal Bank Award, 1978. Thirty honorary degrees from colleges and universities in Canada and the United States, including Dartmouth College, Harvard University, Princeton University, and University of Manitoba.

WRITINGS: Fearful Symmetry: A Study of William Blake, Princeton University Press, 1947; *Anatomy of Criticism: Four Essays,* Princeton University Press, 1957; (with others) *The English and Romantic Poets and Essayists: A Review of Research and Criticism,* Modern Language Association of America, 1957; *Culture and the National Will,* Carleton University, for Institute of Canadian Studies, 1957; (with Kluckhohn and Wigglesworth) *Three Lectures,* University of Toronto, 1958; *By Liberal Things,* Clarke, Irwin, 1959; (editor) Shakespeare, *The Tempest,* Penguin, 1959.

(Editor) *Design for Learning,* University of Toronto Press, 1962; (with L. C. Knights and others) *Myth and Symbol: Critical Approaches and Applications,* edited by Bernice Slote, University of Nebraska Press, 1963; *The Developing Imagination* (published together with an essay by A. R. MacKinnon), Harvard University Press, 1963; *The Well-Tempered Critic,* Indiana University Press, 1963; *T. S. Eliot,* Grove, 1963, reprinted, University of Chicago Press, 1982; *Fables of Identity: Studies in Poetic Mythology,* Harcourt, 1963; (editor) *Romanticism Reconsidered,* Columbia University Press, 1963; *The Educated Imagination,* Indiana University Press, 1964; *A Natural Perspective: The Development of Shakespearean Comedy and Romance,* Columbia University Press, 1965; *The Return of Eden: Five Essays on Milton's Epics,* University of Toronto Press, 1965; (editor) *Blake: A Collection of Critical Essays,* Prentice-Hall, 1966; *Fools of Time: Studies in Shakespearean Tragedy,* University of Toronto Press, 1967; *The Modern Century* (Whidden Lectures), Oxford University Press, 1967; *A Study of English Romanticism,* Random House, 1968.

The Stubborn Structure: Essays on Criticism and Society, Methuen, 1970; *The Bush Garden: Essays on the Canadian Imagination,* House of Anansi Press, 1971; *The Critical Path: An Essay on the Social Context of Literary Criticism,* Indiana University Press, 1971; *The Secular Scripture: A Study of the Structure of Romance,* Harvard University Press, 1976; *Spiritus Mundi: Essays on Literature, Myth and Society,* Indiana University Press, 1976; *Northrop Frye on Culture and Literature: A Collection of Review Essays,* edited by Robert Denham, Chicago University Press, 1978; *Creation and Recreation,* University of Toronto Press, 1980; *The Great Code: The Bible and Literature,* Harcourt, 1982; *Divisions on a Ground: Essays on Canadian Culture,* House of Anansi Press, 1982; *The Myth of Deliverance: Reflections on Shakespeare's Problem Comedies,* University of Toronto Press, 1982. Has written educational radio and television programs for the Canadian Broadcasting Co. Contributor to professional journals. *Canadian Forum,* literary editor, 1947-49, editor, 1949-52.

WORK IN PROGRESS: Second volume of a two volume work on the Bible.

SIDELIGHTS: Northrop Frye's most important book, *Anatomy of Criticism: Four Essays,* "forced itself" on him when he was trying to write something else. Frye had just completed a comprehensive study of William Blake and was determined to apply Blake's principles of literary symbolism and Biblical analysis to the poet Edmund Spenser. But "the introduction to Spenser became an introduction to the theory of allegory, and that theory obstinately adhered to a much larger theoretical structure," Frye explains in *Anatomy*'s preface. "The basis of argument became more and more discursive, and less and less historical and Spenserian. I soon found myself entangled in those parts of criticism that have to do with such words as 'myth,' 'symbol,' 'ritual,' and 'archetype'. . . . Eventually, the theoretical and the practical aspects of the task I had begun completely separated." But rather than abandon the project, Frye simply shifted his focus, writing not about Spenser in particular, but about literature in general. When he finished, he had produced four essays of what he calls "pure critical theory." Published together in 1957, these essays comprise *Anatomy of Criticism,* a schematic, non-judgmental theory of literature and the first, according to David Schiller in *Commentary,* "which enables a student to tell where, in the totality of his literary experiences, an individual experience belongs."

One of Frye's motives for writing *Anatomy of Criticism* was to bring some sense of order to the field of literary criticism, an art he considered not only misunderstood, but also in disarray. He found the lack of communication among critics appalling. Each school had its own specific theory, but there was no general framework to measure it by. "It is all very well for Blake to say that to generalize is to be an idiot," Frye writes in his study, "but when we find ourselves in the cultural situation of savages who have words for ash and willow and no word for tree, we wonder if there is not such a thing as being *too* deficient in the capacity to generalize." To remedy the problem, Frye set out to develop "a coordinating principle, a central hypothesis which, like the theory of evolution in biology, will see the phenomena it deals with as parts of a whole."

His idea was to approach poetry (and by poetry Frye means all literature) the way Aristotle did—"as a biologist [approaching] a system of organisms, picking out its genera and species, formulating the broad laws of literary experience and, in short, writing as though . . . there is a totally intelligible structure of knowledge attainable about poetry which is not poetry itself, or the experience of it, but poetics." To figure out what these "poetics" were, Frye surveyed the whole phenomena of literary experience, isolating each genre, myth and archetypal literary symbol and then relating it to literature as a whole. Frye organized his finding into categories and came up with the four critical approaches that would eventually form the basis of his essays. They are: historical criticism (theory of modes), ethical criticism (theory of symbols), archetypal criticism (theory of myths), and rhetorical criticism (theory of genres). Although Frye allots each of these approaches a place in his hypothetical structure, his own particular emphasis is on literary archetypes and how they relate to myths.

When Frye speaks of archetypes, he is referring not to the Jungian concept of a racial consciousness, but to certain "typical" images that recur in poetry. In literature, the repetition of such common images of physical nature as the sea or the forest cannot be explained away as "coincidence," Frye argues. Instead, he says, each is an "archetype" or "symbol which connects one poem with another and thereby helps to unify and integrate our literary experience." When we study a masterpiece, Frye explains in his study, the work "draws us to a point at which we seem to see an enormous number of converging patterns of significance. We begin to wonder if we cannot see literature, not only as complicating itself in time, but as spread out in conceptual space from some kind of center that criticism could locate." That center represents the primitive myths from which archetypes spring.

Frye contends that archetypal criticism provides an effective means of deriving the structural principles of literature because it assumes a larger context of literature as a whole. Employing an analogy, Frye compares literature to painting, showing that just as the structural principles of painting are related to plane geometry, so too are the structural principles of literature related to religion and mythology. The Biblical archetypes of the "city," the "garden," and the "sheepfold" are as pervasive in religious writing as gods and demons are in myths, Frye maintains. Thus Frye turns to the symbolism of the Bible and to classical mythology, employing both as "a grammar of literary archetypes" to use his words.

Harold Bloom, writing in the *New York Times Book Review*, calls Frye's theory of myths "the richest and most persuasive of [his] investigations. . . . He mapped four seasonal myths: Spring or Comedy, Summer or Romance, Autumn or Tragedy, Winter or Irony and Satire. Working entirely from what he took to be the internal characteristics of thousands of literary texts, Frye produced a coherent account of the ways in which themes, ideas and metaphors tended to repeat themselves in each of his seasonal myths."

Although post-classical literature rarely seems mythic, Frye argues that the myth has simply been "displaced" or covered over with a veneer of realism, making the new work "credible, logically motivated, or morally acceptable" to its audience. In Nathaniel Hawthorne's *The Marble Faun*, for example, there is a girl of singular purity and gentleness who lives in a tower surrounded by doves. Writes Frye: "The doves are very fond of her; another character calls her his 'dove,' and remarks indicating some special affinity with doves are made about her by both author and characters. If we were to say that [she] is a dove-goddess like Venus . . . we should not be reading the story quite accurately in its own mode; we should be translating it into straight myth." But, Frye argues, to recognize that Hawthorne employs an archetypal pattern is not irrelevant, or unfair. In fact, he postulates that a person "can get a whole liberal education simply by picking up one conventional poem and following its archetypes as they stretch out into the rest of literature."

One of the most controversial features of Frye's schema is the role it assigns critics. The historical function of criticism, from the time of Samuel Johnson to T. S. Eliot, has been to provide a means of discriminating good writing from bad. But Frye's interest is in what makes works of literature similar to one another, not what makes them different, and he adamantly rejects the notion of critic as judge. It is not, he maintains, the critic's responsibility to evaluate poetry or to say that one poem is better than another because his judgment, while informed, is really nothing more than a reflection of taste. And, "the history of taste is no more a part of the structure of criticism than the Huxley-Wilberforce debate is part of the structure of biological science," Frye writes. Matters of judgment are best left to book reviewers, not critics, in Frye's point of view.

But W. K. Wimsatt, in an essay in *Northrop Frye in Modern Criticism*, charges Frye with inconsistency: "He can and is willing to distinguish 'ephemeral rubbish,' mediocre works, random and peripheral experience, from the greatest classics, the profound masterpieces in which may be discerned the converging patterns of the primitive formulas. At other moments, however, he says that criticism has nothing whatever to do with either the experience of the judging of literature. The direct experience of literature is *central* to criticism, yet somehow this center is excluded from it." The effect, Wimsatt concludes, is that the reader remains unsure whether Frye "wishes to discredit all critical valuing whatever, or only the wrong kinds of valuing."

Another important feature of Frye's schema is his view of art in general and poetry in particular. According to A. Walton Litz, writing in the *Harvard Guide to Contemporary American Writing*, Frye "shares with his modern predecessors a post-Romantic view of the poem as an autonomous organism, which exists independently from the intentions of its creator." And in his study, Frye employs a metaphor that bears out Litz's supposition. "The poet," Frye says, "who writes creatively rather than deliberately, is not the father of his poem; he is at best a midwife, or, more accurately still, the womb of Mother Nature herself. . . . The fact that revision is possible, that a poet can make changes in a poem not because he likes them better, but because they are better, shows clearly that the poet has to give birth to the poem as it passes through his mind. He is responsible for delivering it in as uninjured a state as possible, and if the poem is alive, it is equally anxious to be rid of him, and screams to be cut loose from all the navel-strings and feeding-tubes of his ego."

If the poet is the "midwife" of the poem, the critic, according to Frye, may be conceived of as the nurse who presents the creation to the world. And in this role as a describer and classifier of literature, the critic assumes a position that is not subservient, but equal to that of the artist, as Litz explains: "If *Anatomy of Criticism* is a major work of enduring importance, as I believe it to be, then it is the first great work of English or American literary criticism not produced by a practicing artist, and signals a decisive turn toward the continental model. The critic is no longer the servant of the artist but a colleague, with his own special knowledge and powers. . . . [Frye] provides a system which tempts the critic to interpose himself between the artist and the audience as an independent creative force." Despite his admiration for *Anatomy*, Litz says that Frye's system "when manipulated by less subtle minds— tend[s] to homogenize literature and give the critic a spurious authority."

Nor is this the only objection that has been raised against Frye's theory. Some critics charge that Frye's preoccupation with myth and convention isolates literature from its social context, while others accuse him of ignoring history and imprisoning literature in a timeless vacuum of archetypal myths. W. K. Wimsatt perhaps best articulates this objection when he says: "The Ur-Myth, the Quest Myth, with all its complications, its cycles, acts, scenes, characters, and special symbols, is not a historical fact. And this is so not only in the obvious sense that the stories are not true, but in another sense, which I think we tend to forget and which mythopoeic writing does much to obscure: that such a coherent, cyclic, and encyclopedic system, such a monomyth, cannot be shown ever to have evolved actually either from ritual, anywhere in the world, or ever anywhere to have been entertained in whole or even in any considerable part. We are talking about the myth of myth. As Frye himself, in his moments of cautionary vision, observes, the 'derivation' of the literary genres from the quest myth is 'logical,' not historical. [But,] if we take Frye at his word and attempt to deduce his system 'logically,' we will reject it, for the structure which he shows us is . . . divided between truism and *ad libitum* fantasy."

As a way of countering these charges, Frye, in his subsequent writings, frequently employs subtitles that insist upon the social reference of his criticism, according to Scott Sanders in *Cambridge Review*. Frye's 1970 publication, *The Stubborn Structure: Essays on Criticism and Society* is one such example, and *The Critical Path: An Essay on the Social Context of Literary Criticism*, which appeared the following year, is another. Sanders says that in such publications, however, Frye is "less concerned with the communal *sources* of literature

... than he is with the potential role of the humanities, informed by literature, in directing social change."

In addition to addressing issues raised by his adversaries, Frye's later writing also elucidates his original theory, and offers some of the practical criticism that was absent in his masterwork. In *A Natural Perspective: The Development of Shakespearean Comedy and Romance,* for instance, Frye turns to Shakespeare to demonstrate his belief that art does not imitate life directly, but instead art imitates art. Writing in the *Times Literary Supplement,* a reviewer explains: "These essays elaborate the thesis that Shakespearean comedy, like modern painting, represents a deliberate departure from the conventions of realism, a distortion or stylization of the subject which indicates an interest in more purely self-contained artistic values. The comedies and romances, so the argument runs, do not hold up the mirror to nature: their *raison d'etre* must be sought in the comic structure itself, as that of music in the musical structure. Indeed, Shakespeare's thematic images and words, echoing, calling, responding, have the same function as similar repeated patterns in music, and sometimes, as in music, a new theme or second subject will be introduced which our ear accepts without explanation—as when Leonte's jealousy burst out unheralded and unforeseen."

In the years that have passed since Frye published his seminal piece, critics have continued to search for its flaws. One common objection, expressed by Morris Dickstein in *Partisan Review,* is that "Frye always establishes a distance, at once heuristic and self-protective between himself and his subject. He aims at the precision of outline rather than the intimacy or concreteness of detail." Another is the point, raised by W. K. Wimsatt, that the analogies Frye depends on to make his major points are not logically valid. Notwithstanding this criticism, many scholars are attracted by the nonjudgmental quality of Frye's system and his genuinely humanistic approach (which proclaims that an understanding of literature is indeed of great human importance). This group has embraced Frye's theories and introduced his methods into the university classroom. And, as Murray Krieger notes in his introduction to *Northrop Frye in Modern Criticism,* "whatever the attitude toward Northrop Frye's prodigious scheme, one cannot doubt that . . . he has had an influence—indeed an absolute hold—on a generation of developing literary critics greater and more exclusive than that of any one theorist in recent critical history." Summarized Harold Bloom in the *New York Times Book Review:* "Frye is the legitimate heir of a Protestant and Romantic tradition that has dominated much of British and American literature, the tradition of the Inner Light, by which each person reads Scripture for himself or herself without yielding to a premature authority imposed by Church or State or School. This is Frye's true greatness, and all who teach interpretations are indebted to him for precept and for example."

BIOGRAPHICAL/CRITICAL SOURCES—Periodicals: *Commonweal,* September 20, 1957; *Yale Review,* autumn, 1957, spring, 1964, spring, 1967, summer, 1967, March, 1971; *Book Week,* July 19, 1964; *Times Literary Supplement,* August 12, 1965, July 2, 1982; *South Atlantic Quarterly,* spring, 1967; *Criticism,* summer, 1967; *Fiddlehead,* summer, 1967; *Commentary,* September, 1968; *Partisan Review,* winter, 1969; *Cambridge Review,* May 7, 1971; *New York Times Book Review,* April 18, 1976, April 11, 1982; *New York Review of Books,* April 14, 1977; *Washington Post Book World,* May 16, 1982.

Books: Murray Krieger, editor, *Northrop Frye in Modern Criticism: Selected Papers from the English Institute,* Columbia University Press, 1966; Robert Denham, *Northrop Frye and Critical Method,* Pennsylvania State University Press, 1978; Daniel Hoffman, editor, *Harvard Guide to Contemporary American Writing,* Belknap Press, 1979.

—Sketch by Donna Olendorf

* * *

FUSSELL, Paul 1924-

PERSONAL: Surname rhymes with "Russell"; born March 22, 1924, in Pasadena, Calif.; son of Paul (an attorney) and Wilhma (Sill) Fussell; married Betty Harper (a teacher), June 17, 1949; children: Rosalind, Martin. *Education:* Pomona College, B.A., 1947; Harvard University, M.A., 1949, Ph.D., 1952. *Home:* 2 Nassau St., Princeton, N.J. 08540. *Office:* Department of English, Rutgers University, New Brunswick, N.J. 08903.

CAREER: Connecticut College, New London, instructor in English, 1951-54; Rutgers University, New Brunswick, N.J., assistant professor, 1955-59, associate professor, 1959-64, professor of English, 1964—. Fulbright lecturer, University of Heidelberg, 1957-58. Regional chairman, Woodrow Wilson National Fellowship Foundation, 1962-64. Consulting editor, Random House, Inc., 1964-65. *Military service:* U.S. Army, Infantry, 1943-47; became first lieutenant; received Bronze Star and two Purple Hearts. *Member:* Modern Language Association of America, Academy of Literary Studies, English Institute (secretary, 1964-70).

AWARDS, HONORS: James D. Phelan Award, 1965, for nonfictional prose; Lindsack Foundation Award, 1971; National Endowment for the Humanities senior fellowship, 1973-74; National Book Critics Circle Award and National Book Award, both 1976, both for *The Great War and Modern Memory;* American Academy and Institute of Arts and Letters award, 1980, for excellence in literature; *Abroad: British Literary Traveling between the Wars* was nominated for a National Book Critics Circle Award, 1980; Litt.D., Pomona College, 1981.

WRITINGS: Theory of Prosody in Eighteenth-Century England, Connecticut College Press, 1954; (co-author) *The Presence of Walt Whitman,* Columbia University Press, 1962; *The Rhetorical World of Augustan Humanism,* Oxford University Press, 1965; *Poetic Meter and Poetic Form,* Random House, 1965; *Samuel Johnson and the Life of Writing,* Harcourt, 1971; *The Great War and Modern Memory,* Oxford University Press, 1975; *The Ordeal of Alfred M. Hale,* Leo Cooper, 1975; *Abroad: British Literary Traveling between the Wars,* Oxford University Press, 1980; *The Boy Scout Handbook and Other Observations* (collection of essays on literary topics), Oxford University Press, 1982. Contributor of reviews and essays to *Saturday Review, Encounter, Virginia Quarterly Review, Partisan Review,* and other periodicals. Contributing editor to *Harper's* and *New Republic.*

WORK IN PROGRESS: A book about the Second World War.

SIDELIGHTS: It was not until Paul Fussell "got tired of writing" what he was "supposed to write" that he became a successful author. Before publication of *The Great War and Modern Memory,* Fussell wrote critical works on poetic theory and eighteenth-century English literature, none of which sold more than 8,000 copies, according to *Publishers Weekly.* But with his foray into modern history came the realization that he could reach general audiences: *The Great War* sold almost 40,000 copies and won him two prestigious awards. Fussell doubts he will ever write a book as good as that again. "It was the perfect moment in a writer's life," he explained to *Publishers Weekly,* "the right subject, the right time. It was an accidental masterpiece." Nevertheless, he has continued to write for less specialized audiences.

As Fussell explains in the preface, *The Great War and Modern Memory* is about "the British experience of the Western Front from 1914 to 1918 and some of the literary means by which it has been remembered." In *Abroad: British Literary Traveling between the Wars*, Fussell's subject is still England and his purpose, according to *Los Angeles Times Book Review* critic Richard Rodriguez, still to describe "the mood of an era through an examination of its literature." But in *Abroad*, Fussell's focus has moved forward in history to the years 1918-1939.

"Specifically," says Rodriguez, "*Abroad* is concerned with British travelers and travel writing in the years between the wars. The '20's and '30's were, argues Fussell, the great years of modern travel. After wartime gray, cold, deprivation and confinement, 'imaginative and sensitive' Englishmen sought release in travel to the glittering regions of the sun: the Mediterranean, the Middle East, Africa, and Latin America." Writing in the *Washington Post Book World*, Peter Stansky observes that Fussell is "not so much interested in travelers who write as in writers who travel," and he devotes chapters to D. H. Lawrence, Graham Greene, Norman Douglas, Evelyn Waugh, and Robert Byron. Although it is almost unknown to Americans, Byron's *The Road to Oxiana* is a masterpiece—the "*Ulysses* or *Wasteland*" of travel writing—according to Fussell.

Fussell's intention, say critics, is to demonstrate that travel writing is an independent genre, worthy of a place alongside poetry or the novel as a distinct literary form. Many reviewers applaud his position. "As a reward for merely knocking on the door of this establishment in literature's red-light district, Paul Fussell deserves a laurel or two," writes *New York Times Book Review* critic Jonathan Raban. He calls *Abroad* "an exemplary piece of criticism. It is immensely readable. It bristles with ideas. It disinters a real lost masterpiece from the library stacks. It admits a whole area of writing—at last!—to its proper place in literary history." Stansky agrees, "It is hard to imagine the case for travel writing, as a genre worthy of a place alongside poetry and the novel, being made more impressively." Michael Ratcliffe of the *London Times*, on the other hand, considers this Fussell's weakest proposition "for everything he tells us about it argues its diversity and binds it more tightly to other forms and to the central intellectual crisis of the age."

In her *New York Times* review, Sarah Ferrell notes that "Fussell's last chapters are elegiac. He quotes Waugh, whom he describes as 'shocked and embittered by [World War II], which, by destroying Europe and the Orient and multiplying controls on people and producing the jet aircraft engine, effectively ended travel in the old sense.'" Fussell maintains that in today's world tourism has replaced travel and that tourists, by definition, cannot write travel books.

"Nonsense," says Raban, who suggests that "two of the best books ever written in the genre, Mark Twain's *Innocents Abroad* and Evelyn Waugh's own *Labels*, happen to be about tourists on a package holiday." Raban maintains that instead of performing a "burial service" over the remains of a genre he has just resurrected, Fussell should have come to a different conclusion. The one essential condition of travel writing isn't "a private income, rough terrain, English imperial hauteur, tramp steamers . . . or any other of the incidentals on which Mr. Fussell dwells with valedictory nostalgia; it is the experience of living among strangers, away from home." Stansky expresses a similar view. "The spirit of travel," he writes, "will prove inextinguishable: the space ship is waiting, the hotel is on Mars."

BIOGRAPHICAL/CRITICAL SOURCES: Criticism, winter, 1967; *New York Times Book Review*, August 31, 1980, August 29, 1982; *New York Times*, September 11, 1980, November 2, 1980, December 16, 1980, October 8, 1982; *Washington Post Book World*, September 21, 1980, June 27, 1982, September 6, 1982; *Chicago Tribune*, October 1, 1980; *Publishers Weekly*, October 3, 1980; *Los Angeles Times*, November 23, 1980; *London Times*, March 19, 1981; *Times Literary Supplement*, March 20, 1981; *Washington Post*, September 28, 1982.

G

**GATTI, Enzo
See GATTI, Vincenzo**

* * *

**GATTI, Vincenzo 1942-
(Enzo Gatti)**

PERSONAL: Born February 21, 1942; son of Giovanni Battista and Maggiorina (Riccabone) Gatti. *Education:* Gregorianum, M.A. (theology), 1969; Biblicum, M.A. (Biblical literature), 1972; Gregorian University, Ph.D., 1977. *Religion:* Roman Catholic. *Home:* Dopschstrasse 20/1/7, A-1210 Vienna, Austria.

CAREER: Xaverianum, Parma, Italy, professor of Biblical theology, 1976-79; visiting professor and dean of theology faculty at Urbanian University, Rome, and at Istituto Pastorale Lombardo, Milan. Lecturer in various Third World countries. Has worked as translator of scientific works on Biblical literature and on history of Christian thought into Italian from English, German, French, and Spanish.

WRITINGS: Colui che sa il Doloreo dell'Uomo, Editrice Missionaria Italiana (Bologna, Italy), 1972, translation by Matthew O'Connell published as *Rich Church—Poor Church?,* Orbis, 1974; *Atti degli Apostoli: Il libro della Missione,* Editrice Missionara Italiana, 1975, 2nd edition, 1977; *La chiesa della Beatitudini,* Dehoniane (Bologna), 1980; *Temi biblici sulla Missione,* E.M.I. (Bologna), 1980; *Il discorso di Paolo ad Atene, uno studio di Act. 17, 22-31,* Paideia Editrice (Brescia, Italy), 1982. Also contributor to *La Bibbia, parola di Dio scritta per noi,* three volumes, Marietti (Torino, Italy). Founder and editor, *Missione Oggi,* 1978—.

WORK IN PROGRESS: Research on the intertestamentary period and the hellenistic world, and on early Christian institutions and diffusion.

* * *

**GAULDEN, Ray 1914-
(Wesley Ray)**

PERSONAL: Born June 27, 1914, in Fort Worth, Tex.; son of Herman Alan and Jessie (Maddin) Gaulden; married Thelma Fells, May 3, 1940; children: Marsha (Mrs. John F. Messner). *Politics:* Independent. *Religion:* Baptist. *Home:* 1699 South Zenobia Way, Denver, Colo. 80219.

CAREER: Writer. During early career was a sign painter, hotel clerk, hospital admittance clerk, and parts expediter in a munitions factory. *Member:* Western Writers of America (vice-president, 1969). *Awards, honors:* Twice awarded Colorado Authors' League Top-hand Award for best western short story.

WRITINGS—All novels: *The Rough and Lonely Land,* Rich & Cowan (London), 1956; *Shadow of the Rope,* Pocket Books, 1957; *The Vengeful Men* (originally serialized in *Ranch Romances,* under title "Red Sundown," 1954), Pocket Books, 1958; *Rita,* Zenith Books, 1959 (published in England as *A Good Place to Die,* R. Hale, 1965); (under pseudonym Wesley Ray) *Damaron's Gun,* New American Library, 1958; *High Country Showdown,* Monarch Books, 1961; *Action at Alameda,* Avalon, 1962; *The Devil's Deputy,* Avalon, 1963; *McVey's Valley,* Doubleday, 1965; (under pseudonym Wesley Ray) *Long Day in Latigo,* Paperback Library, 1965; *Glory Gulch,* Berkeley, 1967, published as *Five Card Stud,* 1968; *Lawless Land,* Berkley, 1968; *Time to Ride,* Ballantine, 1969; *Shoot To Kill,* Ballantine, 1970; *Rage at Red Butte,* Berkley, 1971; *Wicked Women of Lobo Wells,* Belmont, 1971; *Deputy Sheriff,* Ballantine, 1972; *A Man Named Murdo* [and] *Rough Road to Denver,* Zebra Books, 1981. Also author of *Legend of the Silver Belle* and *Manhunt at Morada.* Contributor of over two hundred short stories to magazines.

MEDIA ADAPTATIONS: Gaulden's novel *Glory Gulch* was made into the film "Five Card Stud."

* * *

GAY, Kathlyn 1930-

PERSONAL: Born March 4, 1930, in Zion, Ill.; daughter of Kenneth Charles and Beatrice (Anderson) McGarrahan; married Arthur L. Gay (an elementary teacher), August 28, 1948; children: Martin, Douglas, Karen. *Education:* Attended Northern Illinois University, two years. *Politics:* Registered Democrat. *Religion:* Unitarian Universalist. *Home and office:* 1711 East Beardsley Ave., Elkhart, Ind. 46514.

CAREER: Editor and public relations writer in Elkhart, Ind., and New York, N.Y., 1962-66; free-lance writer, 1966—; partner in rental business, 1971—. Writing consultant to Lyons & Carnahan, 1969-70, Ginn & Co., 1971, and Science Research Associates, 1972-73; community relations director for Americana Healthcare Center, 1976-79; instructor in creative writing, Elkhart Area Career Center. Staff writer, Mayor Richard J. Daley's political campaign in Chicago, 1967. *Member:* Authors Guild, Authors League of America. *Awards, honors:* Honorable mention in *Writer's Digest* short story contest, 1962; first prize in literary section, Northern Indiana Arts Festival, 1965, for one-act play.

WRITINGS: Girl Pilot, Messner, 1966; *Money Isn't Everything: The Story of Economics*, Delacorte, 1967; *Meet the Mayor of Your City*, Hawthorn, 1967; *Beth Speaks Out*, Messner, 1968; *Careers in Social Service*, Messner, 1969; *Where the People Are: Cities and Their Future*, Delacorte, 1969; *Core English: English for Speakers of Other Languages*, Ginn, 1972; *A Family Is for Living*, Delacorte, 1972; *Body Talk*, Scribner, 1974; *Be a Smart Shopper*, Messner, 1974.

(With Ben E. Barnes) *The River Flows Backward*, Ashley Books, 1975; *What's in a Name?*, Elkhart Community Schools, 1975; *Care and Share: Teenagers and Volunteerism*, Messner, 1977; *Look Mom! No Words!*, Houghton, 1977; (with Martin and Marla Gay) *Get Hooked on Vegetables*, Messner, 1978; (co-author) *English around the World*, Scott, Foresman, 1979; (with Martin Gay) *Eating What Grows Naturally*, And Books, 1980; (with Barnes) *Your Fight Has Just Begun*, Messner, 1980; (with Barnes) *Beginner's Guide to Better Boxing*, McKay, 1980; (co-author) *I Like English*, Scott, Foresman, 1981; *Boxes and More Boxes*, Houghton, 1981; (co-author) *Family Living*, Prentice-Hall, 1982; *Junkyards*, Enslow, Ridley, 1982; (with Douglas Gay) *Road Racing*, Harvey House, 1983.

Also author of teaching manuals, including activities and stories for Ginn & Co., Science Research Associates, Lyons & Carnahan, Scott, Foresman & Co., and Prentice-Hall. Contributor of articles to *American Home, Ebony, Women's World, Women in Business, Popular Medicine, Family Digest,* and other periodicals; contributor of short stories to *Highlights for Children, Child Life, Instructor,* and other magazines.

WORK IN PROGRESS: Books for young people on sports superstitions, "sign" language (various ways people communicate through many different types of signs from billboards to wayside pulpits to graffiti), and several picture books; *Acid Rain*, for F. Watts; *The Love Cycle*, an adult book showing the way people experience love or its deprivation through the life cycle.

SIDELIGHTS: Kathlyn Gay told *CA:* "Writing, for me, is a way of life, and I could not imagine trying to function as an individual without exercising this form of communication. I have always considered myself a rather shy person, but also one who can 'walk in another's shoes.' These traits, more than any others, have probably motivated me to write both fiction and non-fiction.

"For as long as I can remember I have been concerned about the way people get along with each other I believe we are all of one humankind, but have differences that we can learn to respect. So, much of my writing has been about our pluralistic society—the variety of different cultures and backgrounds which shape people in this country.

"Besides human relationships, other interests have determined some types of writing I do. Since my husband has been a teacher, counselor and principal in elementary schools, I have had many first-hand experiences with new educational programs. Much of this has been shared in textbooks and teaching materials I've helped prepare.

"Also, my husband and I have been active in amateur theater groups and I have been involved in some sort of drama ever since childhood when I staged my own plays in our basement or backyard. This has led to writing a few plays and a variety of articles on how dramatic skills can be used in teaching, the way our bodies and facial expressions are used to send silent messages, and how to use speech effectively.

"Of course, being a part of the development of my three children—and now grandchildren—has provided material for articles and stories, too. In recent years, I have become increasingly concerned about our total environment and this had led to involvement in various social action groups. In addition, I have been able to write about various social and environmental issues such as changing family life, protection of civil rights, better nutrition, recycling scrap metals, and the effects of acid rain on the environment.

"Finally, I consider it a real privilege to write—to share with others what arouses my curiosity and elicits my concern. I have always been eager to learn and to understand. I hope I never lose that desire to investigate and try to make sense out of one's discoveries. That is the stuff from which one keeps developing not only as a writer, but also as a productive human being."

* * *

**GAYLE, Emma
 See FAIRBURN, Eleanor**

* * *

GEIS, Florence L(indauer) 1933-

PERSONAL: Born April 3, 1933, in Oakland, Calif.; daughter of Earl S. (a farm owner) and Alma (Dahm) Lindauer; married H. Jon Geis (divorced, 1960). *Education:* University of Arizona, B.A., 1956; Columbia University, M.A., 1961, Ph.D., 1964. *Residence:* Landenberg, Pa. *Office:* Department of Psychology, University of Delaware, Newark, Del. 19711.

CAREER: New York University, New York, N.Y., assistant professor of psychology, 1964-67; University of Delaware, Newark, assistant professor, 1967-71, associate professor of psychology, 1971—. Adjunct assistant professor, Columbia University, 1964.

MEMBER: International Council of Psychologists, American Psychological Association, Association for Women in Psychology, American Association of University Professors, Eastern Psychological Association, Delaware Psychological Association. *Awards, honors:* National Science Foundation grants, 1963 and 1965; New York University Seed Funds grant, 1969; grants from University of Delaware, 1970, 1972, 1974, 1975, and 1978; U.S. Department of Education grant, 1980.

WRITINGS: (With Richard Christie) *Studies in Machiavellianism*, Academic Press, 1970; *Personality Research Manual*, with instructor's guide, Wiley, 1978; (with M. Carter and D. Butler) *Seeing and Evaluating People* (pamphlet), Educational Development Center (Newton, Mass.), 1981.

Contributor: (With Christie) E. F. Borgatta and W. W. Lambert, editors, *Handbook of Personality Theory and Research*, Rand McNally, 1968; (with K. Bogart and M. Levy) *The Cognitive Control of Motivation*, Scott, Foresman, 1969; (with Christie) K. J. Gergen and D. Marlowe, editors, *Personality and Social Behavior*, Addison-Wesley, 1970; (with Christie) E. P. Hollander and R. Hunt, editors, *Current Perspectives in Social Psychology*, Oxford University Press, 1971, 4th edition, 1976; Carter, editor, *The Role of Women in Politics*, Delaware Humanities Forum, 1974; H. London and J. Exner, editors, *Dimensions of Personality*, Wiley, 1978; London, editor, *Personality: A New Look at Metatheories*, Hemisphere Press, 1978;

L. H. Eckensberger and Y. H. Poortinger, editors, *Cross-Cultural Contributions to Psychology*, Lisse (Netherlands), 1979; (with N. Porter) C. Mayo and N. Henley, editors, *Androgyny, Gender and Nonverbal Behavior*, Springer Verlag, 1981.

Author of papers presented to conventions of the American Psychological Association, 1964-81; author of papers presented to numerous conferences and colloquia, including International Communication Association annual conference, Montreal, 1973, International Association of Cross-Cultural Psychology research conference, Munich, 1978, and International Council of Psychologists conference, Oslo, 1978. Contributor to proceedings of the American Psychological Association, 1968 and 1972. Contributor to professional journals, including *Annual Review of Psychology, Journal of Personality and Social Psychology, Psychiatric Spectator, Sex Roles,* and *Contemporary Psychology*.

* * *

GEIST, Valerius 1938-

PERSONAL: Born February 2, 1938, in Nikolajew, Russia; moved to Canada, 1953; naturalized Canadian citizen, 1959; son of Alexander Schutov and Olga Geist; married wife, Renate (a scientist), 1961; children: Rosemarie, Karl, Harald. *Education:* University of British Columbia, B.S. (with honors), 1960, Ph.D., 1967. *Office:* Faculty of Environmental Design, University of Calgary, Calgary, Alberta, Canada T2N IN4.

CAREER: University of Calgary, Calgary, Alberta, assistant professor and research scientist in Environmental Science Centre, 1968-71, associate professor and director for environmental sciences of faculty of environmental design, 1971-75, professor of environmental sciences and biology, 1976—, associate dean, 1977—. *Member:* Wildlife Society, Canadian Society of Zoology, Canadian Society of Wildlife and Fishery Biology. *Awards, honors:* National Research Council fellowship at Max Planck Institute for the Physiology of Behavior, 1967-68; publication award from Wildlife Society, 1971, for *Mountain Sheep*.

WRITINGS: Mountain Sheep: A Study in Behavior and Evolution, University of Chicago Press, 1971; (editor with F. Walther) *The Behavior of Ungulates and Its Relation to Management,* International Union for the Conservation of Nature (Morges, Switzerland), 1974; *Mountain Sheep and Man in the Northern Wilds,* Cornell University Press, 1975; *Life Strategies, Human Evolution, Environmental Design,* Springer-Verlag, 1978; (contributor) J. L. Schmidt and D. L. Gilbert, editors, *Big Game of North America,* Stackpole, 1978; (contributor) *Wild Animals of North America,* National Geographic Society, 1979; (contributor) J. Theberge, editor, *Pinnacle of Canada,* Doubleday (Canada), 1980; (contributor) O. C. Wallmo, editor, *Mule and Black-Tailed Deer of North America,* University of Nebraska Press, 1981; (contributor) Sheridan Baker, *The Practical Stylist,* 5th edition, Harper, 1982. Also contributor of papers to scientific symposium volumes.

WORK IN PROGRESS: Two books, *Seven Steps to Man* and *Deer: A Study in Behavior and Evolution*.

SIDELIGHTS: Valerius Geist told *CA:* "Science is great fun! I love rummaging around not only in my own discipline, but even more in others because I always find new, startling insights. As a zoologist with one eye on humans, often both, I see in man a remarkable creature, and my only despairs are the ignoramuses that want to improve on him. Science has a way of shedding light on man that is just too good to be kept secret. What option, but to write?"

Geist's book *Mountain Sheep: A Study in Behavior and Evolution* has been translated into Japanese.

GELLERMAN, Saul W(illiam) 1929-

PERSONAL: Born January 8, 1929, in Brooklyn, N.Y.; son of Louis (a sales manager) and Yetta (Perlman) Gellerman; married Frances Thompson, June 27, 1953; children: Henry, Peter, Gracie. *Education:* University of Missouri, B.A., 1949, M.A., 1950; University of Pennsylvania, Ph.D., 1956. *Office address:* Gellerman Consulting, Inc., P.O. Box 205, Ho-Ho-Kus, N.J. 07423.

CAREER: Personnel Laboratory, Inc., New York City, director of psychological services, 1956-59; International Business Machines Corp., personnel research associate in White Plains, N.Y., 1959-62, manager of personnel research, IBM World Trade Corp., New York City, 1962-67; Gellerman Consulting, Inc. (management consulting firm), Ho-Ho-Kus, N.J., president, beginning 1967. Trustee, Harrington Park Organization for Public Education, 1965—. *Military service:* U.S. Army, Medical Service Corps, 1951-53; became first lieutenant. *Member:* American Psychological Association, Harrington Park Swim Club (financial secretary, 1961-63).

WRITINGS: People, Problems and Profits, McGraw, 1960, published as *The Uses of Psychology in Management,* Macmillan, 1970; *Motivation and Productivity,* American Management Association, 1963; *The Management of Human Relations,* Holt, 1966; *Management by Motivation,* American Management Association, 1968; *Gellerman on Productivity* (monograph), American Management Association, 1973; *Behavioral Science in Management,* Penguin, 1974; *Managers and Subordinates,* Dryden, 1976. Contributor to professional journals.†

* * *

GELLES, Richard J. 1946-

PERSONAL: Born July 7, 1946, in Newton, Mass.; son of Sidney S. (a neckwear manufacturer) and Clara (Goldberg) Gelles; married Judy S. Isacoff (a research assistant), July 4, 1971; children: Jason Charles. *Education:* Bates College, B.A., 1968; University of Rochester, M.A., 1970; University of New Hampshire, Ph.D., 1973. *Politics:* "Independent pragmatist." *Religion:* Jewish. *Home:* 81 Stonehenge Rd., Kingston, R.I. 02881. *Office:* Department of Sociology, University of Rhode Island, Kingston, R.I. 02881.

CAREER: University of New Hampshire, Durham, instructor in sociology, 1970-73; University of Rhode Island, Kingston, assistant professor, 1973-76, associate professor of sociology, 1976—. Research director, Louis Harris & Associates, 1981—. Lecturer at University of Rochester, summer, 1970 and 1971; lecturer on pediatrics at Harvard University Medical School, 1979—. Consultant to Family Development Study of Children's Hospital Medical Center, Emma Pendleton Bradley Hospital, and Child and Family Services of Newport.

MEMBER: International Society for Research on Aggression, American Association of University Professors, American Sociological Association, National Council on Family Relations, Eastern Sociological Association, New England Social Psychological Association. *Awards, honors:* National Institute of Mental Health grants, 1973-82; U.S. Department of Health, Education and Welfare grants, 1975-80; Distinguished Contribution to Teaching Award, American Sociological Association, Section on Undergraduate Education, 1979; National Institute of Justice grant, 1980.

WRITINGS: The Violent Home: A Study of Physical Aggression between Husbands and Wives, Sage Publications, 1974; *Family*

Violence, Sage Publications, 1979; (with Murray A. Straus and Suzanne K. Steinmetz) *Behind Closed Doors: Violence in the American Family*, Doubleday-Anchor, 1980; *Sociology: An Introduction*, Random House, 1980; *Social Problems*, Harcourt, 1982.

Contributor: Steinmetz and Straus, editors, *Violence in the Family*, Dodd, 1974; Stella Chess and Alexander Thomas, editors, *Annual Progress in Child Psychology and Child Development*, Brunner, 1974; *Violence against Children*, Rowohlt Taschenbuch Verlag, 1975; *Nursing Digest 1975 Review of Maternal-Child Health*, Contemporary Publishing, 1975; *Review of Psychiatry and Mental Health and Review of Community Health*, Contemporary Publishing, 1975.

Editor of "Teaching Sociology" series, Sage Publications, 1973-82. Contributor to professional journals. Associate editor, *Journal of Applied Communications Research*, 1974—, *Journal of Marriage and the Family*, 1977—, *International Journal of Child Abuse and Neglect*, 1978—, *Sage Family Studies Abstracts*, 1978—, *Focus on Women*, 1980.

BIOGRAPHICAL/CRITICAL SOURCES: *Washington Post Book World*, March 23, 1980; *New York Times Book Review*, April 6, 1980.

* * *

GERASSI, John 1931-

PERSONAL: Born July 12, 1931, in Paris, France; son of Fernando (an artist) and Stepha (Awdykowicz) Gerassi; married Marysa Navarro (a historian), October 12, 1958 (divorced); children: Nina. *Education:* Lycee Francais de New York, Baccalaureat es Lettres, 1949, Baccalaureat es Philosophie, 1950; Columbia University, B.A., 1952, M.A., 1954; London School of Economics, Ph.D., 1977. *Office:* Queens College of City University of New York, Flushing, N.Y. 11367.

CAREER: *Time*, New York City, Latin American editor, 1957-61; *New York Times*, New York City, correspondent, 1961-62; free-lance writer, 1962-63; Latin American editor, *Newsweek*, 1963-66; Latin American editor, *Ramparts*, 1966-71; 20former instructor in international relations at San Francisco State College (now San Francisco State University), San Francisco, Calif., and at University of Paris, Paris, France; currently instructor in political science, Queens College of the City University of New York, New York City. *Military service:* U.S. Army, Psychological Warfare Department, 1955-56.

WRITINGS: *The Great Fear*, Macmillan, 1963, published as *The Great Fear in Latin America*, P. Collier, 1965; *The Boys of Boise: Furor, Vice and Folly in an American City*, Macmillan, 1966; *North Vietnam: A Documentary*, Bobbs-Merrill, 1968; (editor) Che Guevara, *Venceremos!*, Macmillan, 1968; (editor with Irving Louis Horowitz and Josue de Castro) *Latin American Radicalism: A Documentary Report on Left and National Movements*, Random House, 1968; *The Coming of the New International*, World, 1971; (editor) *The Revolutionary Priest*, Randon House, 1971; (editor and author of introduction) *Towards Revolution*, Weidenfeld & Nicholson, 1971; *Fidel Castro: A Biography*, Doubleday, 1973; (with Frank Browning) *The American Way of Crime*, Putnam, 1980. Contributor to *New Republic*, *Les Temps Modernes*, *Atlantida*, *Asia-Africa*, *Social Policy*, *Geo*, and other magazines.

WORK IN PROGRESS: *The First Volunteers*, an oral history of the American volunteers in the Spanish Civil War, 1936-39, for MIT Press; the authorized biography of Jean-Paul Sartre, for Knopf.

SIDELIGHTS: Former Latin American editor for *Time*, *Newsweek*, and *Ramparts* magazines, journalist John Gerassi is a harsh critic of the United States' "imperialist" power structure and an outspoken advocate of violent change. "Human progress," Gerassi declares in *Towards Revolution*, "has always come about as a result of confrontation—and revolution." Mao Tse-tung, Fidel Castro, and Che Guevera are not only the subjects of his books, they are also his personal heroes, according to an *Observer* critic who writes that Gerassi supports "the new strategy of guerilla warfare" and sees "revolutionary violence as not only necessary but also existentially liberating, cleansing, and manhood-building." His is a "'villain' interpretation of history," notes *Saturday Review* critic Albert Lauterback and, regardless of what country Gerassi is writing about, his "villain" is always the United States.

In *Latin American Radicalism: A Documentary Report on Left and Nationalist Movements*, Gerassi and his co-editors offer a collection of essays and documents that help define the role of the left in Latin America. *Nation* reviewer Robert F. Smith calls the volume "a significant addition to the bookshelf of dissident views," because "in assembling these materials from a wide variety of sources, the editors have vastly simplified the task of locating relevant literature for the many non-specialists who need to see the Latin American experience through the critical lenses of intelligent radicals." Other critics charge, however, that the selections are biased: "Instead of a balanced analysis of *all* the roots of existing social evils the reader is offered an assortment of stereotypes in pseudo-revolutionary phraseology," says Lauterback. "Thus the term imperialism in this book always refers to the U.S. . . . Never is Soviet expansionism mentioned, let alone the armed intervention of certain Latin American nations into the affairs of others. Just what the United States could do to please this kind of critic, short of committing hara-kiri or adopting *their* ideology and institutions, is rarely made clear."

Gerassi's tendency to "wax eloquent with diagnosis and remain mute as to prescription" is also a fault with *The American Way of Crime*, according to *Washington Post Book World* reviewer Michael C. Blumenthal. In this analysis of the nature of crime in America, Gerassi and co-author Frank Browning propose that control over social policies and the administration of public order lies in the hands of power-money elites. Under their scrutiny behavior that threatens the establishment is branded criminal. Thus, the argument runs, over the years, the United States has acquired a fifth and sixth estate, in addition to the four inherited from the French revolution. The fifth estate is made up of the federal intelligence agencies, the sixth, professional and organized crime. "If America is to change," Gerassi warns the reader, "the inordinate power that all the other [estates] share with the sixth must be curtailed—by an estate not yet established." While acknowledging Gerassi and Browning's "brilliantly organized and well-articulated presentation of . . . evidence," Blumenthal expresses his hope that "in their sequel to this less-than-optimistic volume—the authors will give us a hint of where and how that curtailment is to begin."

BIOGRAPHICAL/CRITICAL SOURCES: *New York Times Book Review*, May 5, 1963, May 5, 1968; *Saturday Review*, July 20, 1963, June 7, 1969; *Newsweek*, May 13, 1968; *Partisan Review*, winter, 1969; *National Review*, January 14, 1969; *Nation*, March 3, 1969; *New Leader*, April 28, 1969; *Observer*, May 9, 1971; *Washington Post Book World*, August 12, 1980.

GIBSON, James L(awrence) 1935-

PERSONAL: Born August 10, 1935, in Junction City, Ky.; son of James Patrick (a railroad employee) and Lucille (Case) Gibson; married Dianne Richardson, January 24, 1960; children: Steven Patrick, Kimberly Dawn. *Education:* Centre College of Kentucky, A.B., 1957; University of Kentucky, M.B.A., 1959, Ph.D., 1962. *Home:* 408 North Fourth St., Danville, Ky. *Office:* College of Business and Economics, University of Kentucky, Lexington, Ky. 40506.

CAREER: University of Kentucky, Lexington, instructor, 1962; University of Texas at Arlington, assistant professor of management, 1962-63; Centre College of Kentucky, Danville, assistant professor, 1963-64, associate professor of economics and chairman of department of business administration, 1964-66; University of Kentucky, associate professor of business administration, 1966—. *Military service:* Kentucky National Guard, 1953-62; became staff sergeant. *Member:* American Accounting Association, American Economic Association, Academy of Management, Beta Gamma Sigma.

WRITINGS: (With James W. Martin) *State and Large City Administration of Petty Cash Funds,* Bureau of Business Research, University of Kentucky, 1960; *Accounting in Small Business Decisions,* University of Kentucky Press, 1963; (compiler with James H. Donnelly) *Fundamentals of Management,* Business Publications, 1971, 3rd edition, 1978; (with Donnelly and John M. Ivancevich) *Organizations: Structure, Processes, Behavior,* Business Publications, 1973, 3rd edition, 1979; (editor with others) *Readings in Organizations,* Business Publications, 1973, 3rd edition, 1979; *Accountability in Urban Society,* Sage Publications, 1978; (with Ivancevich) *Managing for Performance,* Business Publications, 1980. Contributor to accounting journals.

* * *

GIESSLER, Phillip Bruce 1938-

PERSONAL: Born May 27, 1938, in Fort Wayne, Ind.; son of Benjamin (a welder) and Loretta (Eicks) Giessler; married Janet Lynne Dienes (a teacher and organist), August 5, 1961; children: David William. *Education:* Concordia Teachers College, River Forest, Ill., B.S., 1961; Concordia Seminary, M.A.R., 1965; Westminster Theological Seminary, Th.M., 1974; Concordia Theological Seminary, M.Div., 1975. *Residence:* Rocky River, Ohio. *Office:* St. Thomas Lutheran Church, Rocky River, Ohio 44116.

CAREER: Parochial high school teacher of religion in St. Louis, Mo., 1962-63; ordained minister of Lutheran Church, 1967; pastor in Croydon, Pa., 1969-71; St. Thomas Lutheran Church, Rocky River, Ohio, pastor, 1971—. Visiting professor at Concordia Theological Seminary, Fort Wayne, Ind., 1978—.

WRITINGS: Christian Love: Campus Style, Dillon/Liederbach, 1974, published as *Love, Phil,* C.S.S. Publishing, 1975; *To Nathan and Nancy with Luv,* C.S.S. Publishing, 1975; *Christian Nursery School Guidebook for Religion Readiness,* C.S.S. Publishing, 1975; *Referred by Luke, M.D.,* C.S.S. Publishing, 1976; (editor) *The Holy Bible: An American Translation,* Leader Press, 1976; (editor) *A Short Explanation of Luther's Small Catechism,* Leader Press, 1977; *Preparing Laymen for the 1980's,* A/D/Z Press, 1980; (editor) *Know the Truth,* A/D/Z Press, 1980; *Milliennialisticitis: What if Hal Lindsey Is Wrong?,* A/D/Z Press, 1981; *Significant Sermons for the 1980's,* A/D/Z Press, 1982.

* * *

GILL, Patrick
See CREASEY, John

* * *

GILLON, Adam 1921-

PERSONAL: Born July 17, 1921; son of Jacob and Rachel (Perelman) Gillon; married Isabella Zamojre (an architect); children: Joseph (deceased), Iris. *Education:* Hebrew University of Jerusalem, M.A., 1948; Columbia University, Ph.D., 1954. *Home:* Lake Illyria, 450 Route 299 West, New Paltz, N.Y. 12561. *Office:* Department of English, State University of New York College at New Paltz, New Paltz, N.Y. 12561; and Department of English, University of Haifa, Haifa, Israel.

CAREER: University of Kansas, Lawrence, instructor in English language and literature, 1956-57; Acadia University, Wolfville, Nova Scotia, Canada, teacher of English literature and head of department of English, 1958-62; State University of New York College at New Paltz, 1962—, began as professor of English and world literature, currently professor emeritus; professor of English literature, University of Haifa, Haifa, Israel. Manager, American Development Corp. Member of editorial board of Institute for Textual Studies, Texas Tech University. Fund raiser and public speaker for organizations in United States and Canada.

MEMBER: Modern Language Association of America, Authors League of America, English Graduate Union (Columbia University), Comparative Literature Association, National Council of Teachers of English, Joseph Conrad Society of America (president, 1975—), State University of New York Association. *Awards, honors:* Summer research grants from State University of New York; Alfred Jurzykowski Foundation Award, 1967, for translations of Polish literature; has also received numerous awards from the Joseph Fels Foundation, New York State University Research Foundation, Fulbright Foundation, British Council, and Canada Council.

WRITINGS: The Eternal Solitary: A Study of Joseph Conrad, Bookman Associates, 1960; *Cup of Fury* (novel), Astra Books, 1962; *Selected Poems and Translations,* Astra Books, 1962; (translator and editor with Ludwik Krzyzanowski) *Introduction to Modern Polish Literature,* Twayne, 1964; (translator and editor) *Poems of the Ghetto: A Testament of Lost Men,* Twayne, 1969; *In the Manner of Haiku: Seven Aspects of Man,* Astra Books, 1967, 2nd edition, 1970; (translator) Julian Tuwim, *The Dancing Socrates,* Twayne, 1968; *Daily New and Old: Poems in the Manner of Haiku,* Astra Books, 1971; *Strange Mutations in the Manner of Haiku,* Astra Books, 1973; *Summer Morn . . . Winter Weather: Poems Twixt Haiku and Senryu,* Hippocrene Books, 1976; *Conrad and Shakespeare,* Hippocrene Books, 1976; *Joseph Conrad,* Twayne, 1982.

Also author of two plays, broadcast by Canadian Broadcasting Corp., and several educational programs. Contributor of more than seventy short stories, articles, poems, and reviews to periodicals in America, Canada, and overseas. Educational consultant and editor for Polish and Hebrew sections of Twayne's "World Authors" series, 1963-72. Regional editor, *Conradiana,* 1968-72. Editor, *Joseph Conrad Today.*

* * *

GINZBERG, Eli 1911-

PERSONAL: Born April 30, 1911, in New York, N.Y.; son

of Louis (a Talmudist) and Adele (Katzenstein) Ginzberg; married Ruth Szold, July 14, 1946; children: Abigail, Jeremy, Rachel. *Education:* Attended University of Heidelberg and University of Grenoble, 1928-29; Columbia University, A.B., 1931, A.M., 1932, Ph.D., 1934. *Home:* 845 West End Ave., New York, N.Y. *Office:* Graduate School of Business, Columbia University, New York, N.Y. 10027.

CAREER: Columbia University, Graduate School of Business, New York, N.Y., member of faculty, 1935—, A. Barton Hepburn Professor of Economics, 1967-79, professor emeritus, 1979—, director of Research Economists on Group Behavior, 1939-42 and 1948-49, Staff Studies of National Manpower Council, 1941-61, Conservation of Human Resources Project, 1950—, and Revson Fellows Program on the Future of New York City, 1979—. Honorary member of faculty, Industrial College of the Armed Forces, 1971—. Chairman of board, Manpower Demonstration Research Corp. Research director, United Jewish Appeal, 1941; member of Committee on Wartime Requirements for Scientific and Specialized Personnel, 1942; special assistant to chief statistician, U.S. Department of War, 1942-47; director of Resources Analysis Division, Surgeon General's Office, 1944-46; U.S. Representative, Five Power Conference on Reparations for Non-Repatriable Refugees, 1946; member of medical advisory board, Secretary of War, 1946-48; director, New York State Hospital Study, 1948-49; member of board of governors, Hebrew University of Jerusalem, 1953-59; member, National Advisory Mental Health Council, 1959-63, and National Advisory Allied Health Professions Council, 1969-72; chairman of studies committee, White House Conference on Children and Youth, 1960; National Commission for Manpower Policy, chairman of advisory committee, 1962-74, chairman of Commission, 1974-79; chairman of task force on manpower research, Defense Science Board, 1970-71; member of scientific advisory board, U.S. Air Force, 1970-74; chairman, National Commission for Employment Policy, 1979—. Consultant to U.S. Department of the Army, 1946-70, Department of State, 1953, 1956, 1965-69, Department of Labor, 1954—, Department of Defense, 1964-71, Department of Commerce, 1965-66, General Accounting Office, 1973—, and Department of Health, Education, and Welfare; consultant to General Electric, Western Electric, du Pont, and International Business Machines; consultant to Federation of Jewish Philanthropies of New York, Rockefeller Foundation, Robert Wood Johnson Foundation, Ford Foundation, and McKinsey Foundation for Management Research; medical consultant, Hoover Commission, 1952.

MEMBER: American Association for the Advancement of Science (fellow), American Economic Association, Academy of Political Science, American Academy of Arts and Sciences (fellow), American Association of University Professors, Society of Medical Consultants to the Armed Forces (associate member), Industrial Relations Research Association, Institute of Medicine, Allen O. Whipple Surgical Society (honorary member), National Academy of the Sciences, Phi Beta Kappa, Beta Gamma Sigma.

AWARDS, HONORS: U.S. Department of War Medal, 1946, for exceptional civilian service; International University of Social Studies Medal (Rome), 1957, for research contributions to the study of human resources; McKinsey Management Journal Award, University of California, 1964; D. Litt., Jewish Theological Seminary of America, 1966; LL.D., Loyola University (Chicago), 1969; certificate of merit, U.S. Department of Labor, 1972.

WRITINGS: Studies in the Economics of the Bible, Jewish Publication Society, 1932; *The House of Adam Smith,* Columbia University Press, 1934, reprinted, Octagon, 1964, new edition published as *The House of Adam Smith Revisited,* Temple University Press, 1977; *The Illusion of Economic Stability,* Harper, 1939; *Grass on the Slag Heaps: The Story of the Welsh Miners,* Harper, 1942; *Report to American Jews on Overseas Relief, Palestine, and Refugees in the United States,* Harper, 1942; (with Ethel L. Ginsberg, Dorothy L. Lynn, and others) *The Unemployed,* Harper, 1943; (with Joseph Carwell) *The Labor Leader,* Macmillan, 1948; *Program for the Nursing Profession,* Macmillan, 1949; *A Pattern for Hospital Care,* Columbia University Press, 1949.

Agenda for the American Jews, King's Crown Press, 1950; (with others) *Occupational Choice,* Columbia University Press, 1951; (with John L. Herma and Sol W. Ginsburg) *Psychiatry and Military Manpower Policy: A Reappraisal of the Experience in World War II,* King's Crown Press, 1953; (with Douglas W. Bray) *The Uneducated,* Columbia University Press, 1953; (with others) *What Makes an Executive?* (symposium), Columbia University Press, 1955; (with Bray, James K. Anderson, and Robert W. Smuts) *The Negro Potential,* Columbia University Press, 1956; (with Ewing W. Reilley, Bray, and Herma) *Effecting Change in Large Organizations,* Columbia University Press, 1957; *Human Resources: The Wealth of a Nation,* Simon & Schuster, 1958, reprinted, Greenwood Press, 1973; (with Anderson) *Manpower for Government: A Decade's Forecast,* Public Personnel Association (Chicago), 1958; (with Anderson and others) *The Ineffective Soldier: Lessons for Management and the Nation,* Volume I: *The Lost Divisions,* Volume II: *Breakdown and Recovery,* Volume III: *Patterns of Performance,* Columbia University Press, 1959, reprinted, Greenwood Press, 1975.

(With Peter Rogatz) *Planning for Better Hospital Care,* King's Crown Press, 1961; (with Anderson and Herma) *The Optimistic Tradition and American Youth,* Columbia University Press, 1962; (with Ivar E. Berg) *Democratic Values and the Rights of Management,* Columbia University Press, 1963; (with Hyman Berman) *The American Worker in the Twentieth Century: A History through Autobiographies,* Free Press of Glencoe, 1963; (with Alfred S. Eichner) *The Troublesome Presence: American Democracy and the Negro,* Free Press of Glencoe, 1964; (with Herma) *Talent and Performance,* Columbia University Press, 1964; (with Dale L. Hiestand and Beatrice G. Reubens) *The Pluralistic Economy,* McGraw, 1965; *Louis Ginzberg: Keeper of the Law,* Jewish Publication Society, 1966; (with others) *Life Styles of Educated Women* (also see below), Columbia University Press, 1966; (with Alice M. Yohalem) *Educated American Women: Self-Portraits* (also see below), Columbia University Press, 1966; (with Herbert A. Smith) *Manpower Strategy for Ethiopia,* Central Press (Addis Abada), 1966, enlarged edition published as *Manpower Strategy for Developing Countries: Lessons from Ethiopia,* Columbia University Press, 1967; *The Development of Human Resources,* McGraw, 1966; (with others) *The Middle-Class Negro in a White Man's World,* Columbia University Press, 1967; (with Carol A. Brown) *Manpower for Library Services,* Columbia University Press, 1967; (with Hiestand) *Mobility in the Negro Community: Guidelines for Research on Social and Economic Progress,* U.S. Commission on Civil Rights, 1968; *Manpower Agenda for America,* McGraw, 1968; (with others) *Manpower Strategy for the Metropolis,* Columbia University Press, 1968; *People and Progress in East Asia,* Columbia University Press, 1968; *One Fifth of the World: Manpower Reports on Iran and South Asia,* Conservation of Human Resources Project, Columbia University, 1969; (with Miriam Ostow) *Men, Money, and Medicine,* Columbia University Press, 1969.

Manpower for Development: Perspectives on Five Continents, Praeger, 1971; *Educated American Women: Life Styles and Self-Portraits* (contains *Life Styles of Educated Women* and *Educated American Women: Self-Portraits*), Columbia University Press, 1971; *Career Guidance: Who Needs It, Who Provides It, Who Can Improve It,* McGraw, 1971; *Perspectives on Indian Manpower, Employment and Income,* [New Delhi], 1971; (with others) *Urban Health Services: The Case of New York,* Columbia University Press, 1971; *Manpower Advice for Government,* U.S. Department of Labor, 1972; *The Outlook for Educated Manpower,* Engineering Manpower Commission (New York), 1972; *Federal Manpower Policy in Transition,* U.S. Department of Labor, 1974; *The Manpower Connection: Education and Work,* Harvard University Press, 1975; *The Human Economy,* McGraw, 1976; *The Limits of Health Reform: The Search for Realism,* Basic Books, 1977; *Health Manpower and Health Policy,* Allanheld, Osmun, 1978; *Good Jobs, Bad Jobs, No Jobs,* Harvard University Press, 1979; *The One-One School Work Nexus,* Phi Delta Kappa, 1980.

Editor: *The Nation's Children,* Columbia University Press, 1960, Volume I: *The Family and Social Change,* Volume II: *Development and Education,* Volume III: *Problems and Perspectives; Values and Ideals of American Youth,* foreword by John W. Gardner, Columbia University Press, 1961, new edition, Books for Libraries, 1972; *The Negro Challenge to the Business Community,* McGraw, 1964; *Technology and Social Change,* Columbia University Press, 1964; *Business Leadership and the Negro Crisis,* McGraw, 1968; (with Yohalem) *Corporate Lib: Women's Challenge to Management,* Johns Hopkins Press, 1973; *New York Is Very Much Alive: A Manpower View,* McGraw, 1973; (with Robert M. Solow) *The Great Society: Lessons for the Future,* Basic Books, 1974; (with Yohalem) *The University Medical Center and the Metropolis,* Josiah Macy, Jr. Foundation, 1974; *The Future of the Metropolis: People, Jobs, Income,* Olympus, 1975; *Economic Impact of Large Public Programs: The NASA Story,* Olympus, 1976; *Jobs for Americans,* Prentice-Hall, 1976; *Regionalization and Health Policy,* U.S. Department of Labor, 1977; *Employing the Unemployed,* Basic Books, 1980.

Also author of *The Skilled Work Force of the United States,* 1955, *The Negro and His Work,* 1961, *Kavim le-heker haye ha-kalkalah shel Yehude ha-tefutsot,* 1972, and *American Jews: The Building of a Voluntary Community,* 1979. Author of manpower studies for Israeli Ministry of Labor, 1961, 1964, and 1968, for Industrial College of the Armed Forces, 1964, and for National Commission on Productivity, 1971. Contributor to *Public Interests.*

BIOGRAPHICAL/CRITICAL SOURCES: Book World, January 26, 1969; *New York Review of Books,* December 17, 1970, December 16, 1971; *New York,* May 7, 1973; *New Leader,* December 9, 1974; *New Republic,* December 8, 1979; *American Journal of Sociology,* March, 1981.†

* * *

GITIN, Maria (Brians) 1946-

PERSONAL: Born April 21, 1946, in Petaluma, Calif.; married David Daniel Gitin (a poet and teacher), March 27, 1969 (divorced, 1978); married Edgardo Antonio Moncada, 1979 (divorced, 1982). *Education:* Attended San Francisco State College (now University), 1968, and University of Wisconsin—Madison, 1972-73; Antioch University, B.A., 1979. *Home:* 410 Central, No. 1, Pacific Grove, Calif. 93950.

CAREER: Poet. Has worked as librarian and as executive secretary; University for Man, Monterey, Calif., teacher of English, 1975—. Director of Crisis Line for Battered Women, Monterey, 1979-80; executive director of Y.W.C.A. of Monterey Peninsula, 1980-82. *Awards, honors:* Writer's award from International P.E.N., 1975, for *Little Movies.*

WRITINGS: Little Movies (poems), Ithaca House, 1975; *The Melting Pot* (cookbook), Crossing Press, 1977; *Night Shift* (poems), Blue Wind Press, 1978. Contributor to literary magazines, including *Epoch, Greenfield Review,* and *New.*

WORK IN PROGRESS: Another collection of poems.

* * *

GLAAB, Charles N(elson) 1927-

PERSONAL: Born December 19, 1927, in Williston, N.D.; son of Reuben and Betty (Nelson) Glaab; married Mary Ellen Anderson, November 5, 1949; children: Martha Ann, John Reuben. *Education:* Attended Colorado Agriculture and Mechanical College (now Colorado State University), 1945-46; University of North Dakota, B.Ph., 1951, M.A., 1952; University of Missouri, Ph.D., 1958. *Home:* 3021 Hopewell Pl., Toledo, Ohio 43606. *Office:* Department of History, University of Toledo, Toledo, Ohio 43606.

CAREER: University of Chicago, Chicago, Ill., History of Kansas City Project, research associate in urban history, 1956-58; Kansas State University, Manhattan, assistant professor of American history, 1958-60; University of Wisconsin—Milwaukee, associate professor, 1960-63, professor of American history, 1964-68; University of Toledo, Toledo, Ohio, professor of history, 1968—. State Historical Society of Wisconsin, director of urban history section, 1960-63, director of Fox Valley research project, 1963-64. Member of Milwaukee Landmarks Commission, 1965-68, Toledo Landmark Commission, 1968-71, and State of Ohio Historic Preservation Board, 1978-81. *Military service:* U.S. Army, 1946-48. *Member:* Organization of American Historians, American Historical Association, Phi Beta Kappa.

WRITINGS: Kansas City and the Railroads, State Historical Society of Wisconsin, 1962; (editor) *The American City: A Documentary History,* Dorsey, 1963; (contributor) Philip M. Hauser and Leo F. Schnore, editors, *The Study of Urbanization,* Wiley, 1965; (with A. Theodore Brown) *A History of Urban America,* Macmillan, 1968, 3rd edition, 1982; (with Lawrence H. Larsen) *Factories in the Valley: Neenah-Menasha, 1870-1915,* State Historical Society of Wisconsin, 1969; (contributor) Thomas W. Howard, editor, *The North Dakota Political Tradition,* Iowa State University Press, 1981; (with Morgan Barclay) *Toledo: Gateway to the Great Lakes,* Continental Heritage, 1982.

Contributor to *Encyclopaedia Britannica* and to journals. *Urban History Group Newsletter,* editor, 1962-68, co-editor, 1968-70; member of board of editors of *Urban Affairs Quarterly,* 1966-74, and *Journal of Urban History,* 1973—.

WORK IN PROGRESS: Nineteenth-Century Conceptions of the American City.

* * *

GLAZE, Andrew (Louis III) 1920-

PERSONAL: Born April 21, 1920, in Nashville, Tenn.; son of Andrew Louis, Jr. (a physician) and Mildred (Ezell) Glaze; married Dorothy Elliott; married second wife, Adriana Keathley (a dancer), August 12, 1962; children: (first marriage) Betsy, Peter. *Education:* Harvard College, A.B. (cum laude), 1942; Stanford University, additional study, 1946-47. *Politics:* Independent. *Religion:* None. *Home:* 803 Ninth Ave., New York, N.Y. 10019. *Agent:* Victor Chapin, John Schaffner Literary Agency, 425 East 51st St., New York, N.Y. 10021.

CAREER: Birmingham Post-Herald, Birmingham, Ala., staff-writer, 1949-56; British Tourist Authority, New York, N.Y., press officer, beginning 1958; free-lance writer, 1982—. Member of faculty, Breadloaf Writer's Conference, 1969. Participant in workshops held at Brown University, Martha Washington College, University of Alabama in Birmingham, and New York University. Has given poetry readings at numerous universities, organizations, and institutions. *Military service:* U.S. Army Air Forces, ground communications, 1942-46; became first lieutenant. *Member:* Author's Guild. *Awards, honors:* Eunice Tietjens Award, *Poetry* magazine, 1951; American Library Association Notable Books List, 1966, for *Damned Ugly Children;* Hackney Literary Award, 1968 and 1975.

WRITINGS—All poetry: *Lines,* Editions Heraclita, 1964; *Damned Ugly Children,* Trident, 1966; (contributor) *New Yorker Book of Poems,* Viking, 1969; *Masque of Surgery,* Menard Press, 1974; *The Trash Dragon of Shensi,* Copper Beech Press, 1978; *I Am the Jefferson County Courthouse,* Thunder City, 1981. Also author of *76th Street* and *Dog Dancing.*

Produced plays: "Who Stole the Lollipop," performed by the Tullio Garzone Company, 1962; "Miss Pete," first produced Off-Broadway at the American Place Theatre, 1966; "Kleinhoff Demonstrates Tonight," first produced at the Texas Summer Drama Festival, 1971; "The Man-Tree," first produced at the New York Shakespeare Festival, 1975. Also author of seven nonproduced plays and an operetta.

Author of two unpublished novels, *Spectacular Travelers* and *Decisions.* Poems represented in numerous anthologies, including: *New Directions 26,* New Directions, 1973; *Western Wind,* Random House, 1974; *The Doctor Generosity Poets,* Damascus, 1975; *Contemporary Southern Poetry,* Louisiana State University Press, 1979; *Best Loved Poems,* Merit Publications, 1980. Contributor to many periodicals, including *New Yorker, Saturday Review, Audience, Tri-Quarterly, Folio, Open Places* and *Occasional Windhover.*

SIDELIGHTS: Andrew Glaze wrote *CA:* "I speak, write, read, and translate French, I study ballet, my major interests are in anthropology, philosophy, psychology and music. [Since I retired I have devoted] myself entirely to writing, doing readings, and teaching."

* * *

GLAZER, Tom 1914-

PERSONAL: Born September 3, 1914, in Philadelphia, Pa.; son of Jacob Glazer; married Miriam Reed Eisenberg (a remedial reading teacher), June 25, 1944; children: John Prescott, Peter Reed. *Education:* Attended City College (now City College of the City University of New York). *Politics:* Independent. *Religion:* Ecumenical. *Address:* Box 102, Scarborough, N.Y. 10510. *Agent:* Julian Bach, Jr., Julian Bach Literary Agency, 747 Third Ave., New York, N.Y. 10017; and other agents.

CAREER: Folksinger, songwriter, and composer. *Member:* American Federation of Musicians, American Guild of Authors and Composers, American Society of Composers, Authors, and Publishers, Screen Actors Guild, Coffee House Club (New York). *Awards, honors:* Silver Medal of U.S. Treasury Department for war bond work during World War II; other awards and prizes for radio, television, and films, and from American Society of Composers, Authors, and Publishers.

WRITINGS—Compiler: *A New Treasury of Folk Songs,* Bantam, 1961; *Tom Glazer's Treasury of Songs for Children* (arranged for piano, with guitar chords), Grossett, 1964; *Songs of Peace, Freedom, and Protest,* Fawcett World, 1972; *Eye Winker, Tom Tinker, Chin Chopper: Fifty Musical Fingerplays* (arranged for piano, with guitar chords), Doubleday, 1973; *Do Your Ears Hang Low?: Fifty More Musical Fingerplays,* Doubleday, 1980; *On Top of Spaghetti,* Doubleday, 1982; *Music for Ones and Twos: Songs and Games for the Very Young Child,* Doubleday, 1983.

Recordings sung, or sung and played, include: "Activity and Game Songs," two albums; "Music for Ones and Twos"; "Children's Songs from Latin America" (sung in English and Sapnish); "The Musical Heritage of America," three albums; "The Twelve Days of Christmas"; "Do Not Go Gentle . . ." (song-settings of lyrics of Dylan Thomas, Yeats, Shakespeare, and other poets). Also author of poetry and liner notes for albums.

SIDELIGHTS: Tom Glazer told *CA* that one of his prime motivations is "to provide instruction and/or entertainment to as many people as can find my efforts useful. The most vital thing I know of today is to prevent violence while changing the world for the better if possible. All else is secondary, certainly books. Next we must preserve the remaining beauty of the world. I have had a long drawn out love affair with the French language, but the more I study it, the more I realize how few people master their own tongue."

* * *

GLICK, Edward Bernard 1929-

PERSONAL: Born February 12, 1929, in Brooklyn, N.Y.; son of Louis (a butcher) and Ray (Schwartz) Glick; married Florence Joy Wolfson (a public school teacher), June 18, 1950; children: Reuven (son), Marnina (daughter). *Education:* Attended New York University, 1946-48; Brooklyn College (now Brooklyn College of the City University of New York), B.A. (cum laude), 1950; University of Florida, M.A., 1952, Ph.D., 1955. *Religion:* Jewish. *Office:* Department of Political Science, Temple University, Ambler, Pa. 19002.

CAREER: University of Florida, Gainesville, instructor in political science, 1955-56; American Jewish Congress, New York, N.Y., director of Commission on International Affairs, 1956-59; System Development Corp., human factors scientist in Paramus, N.J., and Falls Church, Va., 1959-64; Bendix Corp., Office of National Security Studies, Washington, D.C., senior political scientist, 1964-65; Temple University, Ambler, Pa., associate professor, 1965-68, professor of political science, 1968—. Consultant to U.S. Office of Naval Research, 1964-67, Bendix Corp., 1965-70, and Voice of America, 1977—. *Member:* International Studies Association, American Political Science Association, American Association of University Professors, Inter-University Seminar on Armed Forces and Society (fellow), Association of Canadian Studies in the United States. *Awards, honors:* Stackpole Award for "the most significant contribution to military thinking," 1967, for *Peaceful Conflict: The Non-Military Use of the Military.*

WRITINGS: Latin America and the Palestine Problem, Herzl Press, 1958; *Straddling the Isthmus of Tehuantepec,* University of Florida Press, 1959; *Peaceful Conflict: The Non-Military Use of the Military,* Stackpole, 1967; *Soldiers, Scholars, and Society: The Social Impact of the American Military,* Goodyear Publishing, 1971; *Between Israel and Death,* Stackpole, 1974; *Israel and Her Army: The Influence of the Soldier on the State,* Labor Zionist Alliance, 1977; *The Triangular Connection:*

America, Israel, and American Jews, Allen & Unwin, 1982. Contributor to *Commonweal, Congress Weekly, Midstream, Military Review, Jewish Frontier, Americas,* and other journals.

SIDELIGHTS: Edward Bernard Glick told *CA:* "I remain convinced that substance cannot be divorced from style. I am even more convinced that scholars should write in readable English, not jargon, and that they have an obligation to write well for the intelligent layman. If this means that they must learn to be wordsmiths as well as scholars, then so be it."

Glick speaks Spanish, French, modern Hebrew, Yiddish, and German.

AVOCATIONAL INTERESTS: Travel (has visited Israel and Latin America).

BIOGRAPHICAL/CRITICAL SOURCES: *Washington Post,* April 28, 1964; *Philadelphia Inquirer* (Northwest edition), October 1, 1967; *Philadelphia Jewish Exponent,* June 7, 1974; *New York Times,* November 17, 1977; *Philadelphia Bulletin,* December 21, 1979.

* * *

GLOVER, Michael 1922-

PERSONAL: Born May 20, 1922, in London, England; son of James Alison (a physician) and Katharine (Merriam) Glover; married Daphne Bowring, September 1, 1945; children: Stephanie. *Education:* St. John's College, Cambridge, M.A., 1947. *Religion:* Church of England. *Address:* Bidcombe, France Lynch near Stroud, Glostershire, England.

CAREER: British Council, London, England, director of educational aids department, 1947-70. Writer. *Military service:* British Army, Sherwood Foresters, 1941-46; served in North Africa and Italy; taken prisoner of war. British Army Reserve, London Rifle Brigade Rangers, 1948-63; became major. *Member:* Society for Army Historical Research, Royal United Service Institution.

WRITINGS: *Wellington's Peninsular Victories,* Macmillan, 1963; *Wellington as Military Commander,* Van Nostrand, 1968; *Britannia Sickens: Sir Arthur Wellesley and the Convention of Cintra,* Leo Cooper, 1970; *Legacy of Glory: The Bonaparte Kingdom of Spain,* Scribner, 1971; *1815,* Cardinal, 1973; *Assemblage of Indian Army Soldiers and Uniforms from the Paintings by the Late Chater Paul Chater,* P. Perpetua, 1973; *The Peninsular War, A Concise History,* David & Charles, 1974.

Rorke's Drift: A Victorian Epic, Cooper Ltd., 1975; *General Burgoyne in Canada and America,* Gordon & Cremonesi, 1976; *Wellington's Army in the Peninsula,* David & Charles, 1977; *A Very Slippery Fellow: Sir Robert Wilson, 1777-1849,* Oxford University Press, 1978; *The Napoleonic Wars: An Illustrated History,* Batsford, 1979; *A Gentleman Volunteer: George Hennell, 1812-13,* Heinemann, 1979; *Warfare from Waterloo to Mons,* BCA Publications, 1980; *Warfare in the Age of Bonaparte,* BCA Publications, 1980; *The Velvet Glove: The Decline and Fall of Moderation in War,* Hodder & Stoughton, 1982. Also author of radio scripts. Contributor of articles to *History Today* and *Journal of the Society of Army Historical Research.*

* * *

GOITEIN, S(helomo) D(ov) 1900-
(Solomon Dob Fritz Goitein)

PERSONAL: Born April 3, 1900, in Burgkunstadt, Germany; came to United States in 1957; son of Eduard E. (a rabbi) and Frida (Braunschweiger) Goitein; married Theresa Gottlieb (a teacher of eurhythmics), July 16, 1929; children: Ayala (Mrs. Amirav Gordon), Ofra (Mrs. Baruch Rosner), Elon. *Education:* University of Frankfurt on the Main, Ph.D., 1923. *Religion:* Jewish. *Home:* 284 Hamilton Ave., Princeton, N.J. 08540. *Office:* School of History, Institute for Advanced Study, Princeton, N.J. 08540.

CAREER: School teacher in Haifa, Israel, 1923-27; Hebrew University, Jerusalem, Israel, instructor, 1928-32, assistant professor, 1933-46, associate professor, 1947-48, professor of Islamic history, 1949-57, director of School of Oriental Studies, 1949-56; University of Pennsylvania, Philadelphia, professor of Arabic, 1957-71; Institute for Advanced Study, School of History, Princeton, N.J., visitor, 1971—. Senior education officer of Mandatory Government of Palestine, 1938-48.

MEMBER: American Philosophical Society, Mediaeval Academy of America (fellow), American Academy for Jewish Research (fellow), American Oriental Society (president, 1969-70), Conference on Jewish Social Studies, Middle Eastern Studies Association, Israel Oriental Society (president, 1949-57).

AWARDS, HONORS: Recipient of grants from American Philosophical Society, 1958, 1961, Ulmann Foundations, 1959, Social Science Research Council, 1962, 1968-69, and Guggenheim Memorial Foundation, 1965-66, 1971-73; L.H.D., University of Chicago, 1971, University of Pennsylvania, 1982, and Gratz College; D.H.L., Jewish Theological Seminary of America, 1973; Haskins Medal, Mediaeval Academy of America, 1973; Ben-Zvi Institute Prize, 1973; Levi Della Vida Medal, University of California, 1975; Harvey Prize, Technion, Haifa, 1980.

WRITINGS: *From the Land of Sheba: Tales of the Jews of Yemen,* translation by Christopher Fremantle, Schocken, 1947, revised edition, 1973; *Jews and Arabs: Their Contacts through the Ages,* Schocken, 1955, revised edition, 1974; *Studies in Islamic History and Institutions,* E. J. Brill, 1966; *A Mediterranean Society: The Jewish Communities of the Arab World as Portrayed in the Documents of the Cairo Geniza,* University of California Press, Volume I: *Economic Foundations,* 1968, Volume II: *The Community,* 1971, Volume III: *The Family,* 1978, Volume IV: *Daily Life,* in press; *Letters of Medieval Jewish Traders,* Princeton University Press, 1974; *Palestinian Jewry in Early Islamic and Crusader Times,* Ben Zvi Institute (Jerusalem), 1980; *The Yemenites: History, Communal Organization, Spiritual Life,* Ben Zvi Institute, 1982.

Under name Solomon Dob Fritz Goitein: *Jemenica: Sprichwoerter und Redensarten aus Zentral-Jemen,* Kommissionsverlag von O. Harrassowitz, 1934; *Baladhuri: Arab Historian,* Hebrew University Press, 1936; *Travels in Yemen,* Hebrew University Press, 1941; *Hora-at ha-ivrit be-Erets Yisrael,* Yavneh Publishing, 1945; *Ha-Islam shel Muhammad,* Hebrew University, 1956; (author of introduction) Carl Rathjens, *Jewish Domestic Architecture in San'a, Yemen,* Luzac & Co., 1957; *The Mentality of the Middle Class in Mediaeval Islam,* Centre pour l'Etude des Problems du Monde Musulman Contemporain (Brussels, Belgium), 1961.

Also author of *Hora-at ha-TaNakh be-vet ha-sefer,* 1942, *Shete masot al sefer Yirmiyah,* 1952, *Umanut ha-sipur ba-Mikra,* 1955, *Iyunim be-Mikra,* 1957, *Ha-Mishpat ha-muslimi bi-Medinat Yisrael,* 1957, *Hora-at ha-TaNaKH,* 1957, *The Geniza Collection at the University Museum of the University of Pennsylvania,* 1958, *Sidre hinnukh,* 1962, *Hora-at ha-Ivrit,* 1967 and *Iyunim ba-Mikra,* 1967. Also editor and translator of *Masa'ot Habshush,* by Hayyim Habshush, 1939.

WORK IN PROGRESS: Documents from the Cairo Geniza on the India Trade during the High Middle Ages.

SIDELIGHTS: According to Charles Issawi in *Commentary*, Volume I of S. D. Goitein's series *A Mediterranean Society* is a "particularly valuable" study. "It is based on one of the richest archieval sources available on medieval Islam, the Geniza documents. . . . The existence of the Geniza has been known since 1864, and its contents have been scattered over four continents, but it remained for Professor Goitein to realize its potential value for economic history. . . . Ten years of intensive work in libraries ranging from Leningrad and Jerusalem to Cambridge and New York, and a lifetime devoted to Semitic studies and research on Oriental Jewish communities, have enabled Goitein to make one of the most important contributions to medieval Islamic and Jewish history." Goitein's series, Issawi continues, is "an incomparable mine of information and a rich storehouse of historical interpretation." In a review of Volume II of the series for *Commentary*, Erich Isaac writes that Goitein's "monumental researches" have resulted in a "fascinating recounting" of Mediterranean society. And a *Commonweal* reviewer believes Goitein's *Jews and Arabs* "is the kind of book one should have read years ago. . . . There are many historical indications in these pages as to why Jews and Arabs are so similar in some areas, so dissimilar in others."

"My lifework has had one main purpose," Goitein told *CA*, "[namely,] to help Jews and Arabs to understand their own civilizations, as well as the relations between the two, more completely. My occupation with the gigantic work of the Muslim historian al-Baladhuri provided me with an excellent opportunity to penetrate into the life of a most genuine Arab society. My study of the Jews of Yemen, those most Jewish and most Arab of all Jews, revealed important aspects of Judaec-Arabic symbiosis. Research in the Cairo Geniza (letters and documents from the tenth through the thirteenth centuries written mostly in Judaec-Arabic) has resulted thus far in seven [books], portraying a Mediterranean, mostly middle class, world of almost modern mobility and lively contacts between the various religious and racial groups. However, the increasingly oppressive discrimination of non-Muslims and all that went with it led to the eclipse of that society by the end of the thirteenth century." In all these studies, Goitein concludes, "My lifelong preoccupation with biblical literature, society, and thought provided a firm foundation."

AVOCATIONAL INTERESTS: Calisthenics, hiking.

BIOGRAPHICAL/CRITICAL SOURCES: Commentary, May, 1968, September, 1973; *Journal of Economic History*, June, 1969; *Speculum*, July, 1973, July, 1976; *Economist*, March 9, 1974; *American Historical Review*, April, 1974, June, 1975, October, 1979; *Commonweal*, December 6, 1974; Robert Attal, *A Bibliography of the Writings of Professor S. D. Goitein*, Institute of Asian and African Studies, Hebrew University, 1975; *Archaeology*, January, 1979.

* * *

GOITEIN, Solomon Dob Fritz
See GOITEIN, S(helomo) D(ov)

* * *

GOLD, Sharlya

PERSONAL: Given name is pronounced to rhyme with "Carla"; born in Los Angeles, Calif.; daughter of Albert Hyman (an accountant) and Selma (a pianist and concert singer; maiden name, Mayer) Isenberg; married Leonard Gold (an elementary school principal), 1951; children: Alison, Sheridan, Hilary, Darien. *Education:* San Bernardino Valley College, A.A., 1949; University of California, Berkeley, B.A., 1951; San Jose State University, M.L.S., 1977, M.A., 1981. *Religion:* Jewish. *Home:* 805 Sir Francis Ave., Capitola, Calif. 95010.

CAREER: Former elementary school teacher in Klamath, Calif., and Rialto, Calif., beginning 1951; reading specialist; instructor of adult classes in writing for children and of children's classes in bookbinding; Watsonville High School, Watsonville, Calif., library media specialist, 1979—. Part-time instructor in adolescent literature, University of Santa Clara. Has taught English to Spanish-speaking women volunteer services in Santa Cruz, Calif.

MEMBER: Authors Guild, Society of Children's Book Writers, National Writers Club, National League of American Pen Women (writer's conference chairperson, 1974, 1976). *Awards, honors:* National League of American Pen Women, first prize in juvenile short story contest conducted by Southern California branch, and first prize for juvenile short story, at Biennial Convention, 1976, for *Time to Take Sides*.

WRITINGS: The Potter's Four Sons, Doubleday, 1969; *Amelia Quackenbush* (juvenile), Seabury, 1973; (contributor) *The Porcupine Storybook*, Concordia, 1974; *Time to Take Sides* (juvenile; Junior Literary Guild selection), Seabury, 1976. Author of bilingual (Spanish and English) book review column in Watsonville (Calif.) *Register-Pajaronian*. Contributor of numerous short stories to magazines, including *Cricket*, *Instructor*, and *Jack and Jill*.

WORK IN PROGRESS: "I don't like to talk about books in progress, subject, or date of completion. One is in progress."

SIDELIGHTS: Sharlya Gold told *CA*: "I became a writer, I think, when I learned to read. Often I would stop in the middle of a story and wonder, 'How did the writer know *that* was going to happen? How could the writer possibly tell what a person was thinking?' When I grew to understand that imagination can invent the future and describe the thoughts and feelings of another, then I wanted to be the imaginer of happenings and the people they happened to. But on the other hand, I sometimes feel that the people I write about exist without me. My typewriter merely strips off their covering and allows them to reveal themselves."

AVOCATIONAL INTERESTS: "Nuts about photography, especially darkroom."

* * *

GOLDFEDER, Cheryl
See PAHZ, (Anne) Cheryl Suzanne

* * *

GOLDFEDER, James
See PAHZ, James Alon

* * *

GOLDFEDER, Jim
See PAHZ, James Alon

* * *

GOLDMAN, Michael (Paul) 1936-

PERSONAL: Born May 11, 1936, in New York, N.Y.; son of Julius David (a dentist) and Rose (Pollens) Goldman; married

Eleanor Bergstein (an author), January 17, 1965. *Education:* Columbia University, A.B., 1956; Clare College, Cambridge, B.A., 1958; Princeton University, M.A., 1960, Ph.D., 1962. *Office:* Department of English, Princeton University, Princeton, N.J. 08544.

CAREER: Princeton University, Princeton, N.J., instructor in English, 1961-63; Columbia University, New York, N.Y., instructor, 1965-66, assistant professor of English, 1966-72; Queens College of the City University of New York, Flushing, N.Y., associate professor of English, 1972-75; Princeton University, professor of English, 1975—. *Member:* Phi Beta Kappa. *Awards, honors:* Jennie Tane Prize in Poetry; George Jean Nathan Award for Dramatic Criticism, 1976, for *The Actor's Freedom: Toward a Theory of Drama;* Guggenheim Fellowship, 1977-78; American Council of Learned Societies fellowship, 1981-82.

WRITINGS: First Poems, Macmillan, 1965; (contributor) Ned O'Gorman, editor, *Prophetic Voices,* Random House, 1969; *At the Edge* (poems), Macmillan, 1969; *Shakespeare and the Energies of Drama,* Princeton University Press, 1972; *The Actor's Freedom: Toward a Theory of Drama,* Viking, 1975. Poems anthologized in *Of Poetry and Power,* edited by E. A. Gilkes and P. Schwaber, Basic Books, 1964, and *The New Yorker Book of Poems,* Viking, 1969. Contributor to *Nation, Massachusetts Review, New Yorker, Kenyon Review,* and *Poetry.* Poetry editor, *Nation,* 1965-68.

SIDELIGHTS: Arvin Brown writes in *New Republic* that "there is probably no artistic medium in which the gap between practitioner and theoretician is more profound than in theater. That is why it is a delight to encounter Michael Goldman's *The Actor's Freedom,* a new exercise in dramatic theory that places its emphasis from first to last squarely on the actor and his audience, and on that peculiar and sometimes exhilarating event that is an evening in the theater. . . . The pleasure one has in reading *The Actor's Freedom* remains one's recognition of Goldman's intelligent, informed enthusiasm for the medium; what a rare treat to discover a perceptive work of theory written by a man stimulated rather than intimidated by an actual evening in the theater."

BIOGRAPHICAL/CRITICAL SOURCES: Commonweal, September 24, 1965; *Library Journal,* May 1, 1975; *New Republic,* October 4, 1975; *Nation,* November 8, 1975.

* * *

GOLDMAN, Peter L(ouis) 1933-

PERSONAL: Born February 8, 1933, in Philadelphia, Pa.; son of Walter (a sales representative) and Dorothy (Semple) Goldman; married Helen Dudar (a writer), July 16, 1961. *Education:* Williams College, A.B., 1954; Columbia University, M.S., 1955. *Religion:* Jewish. *Home:* 36 Gramercy Pk., New York, N.Y. 10003. *Agent:* JCA Literary Agency, Inc., 242 West 27th St., New York, N.Y. 10001. *Office: Newsweek,* 444 Madison Ave., New York, N.Y. 10022.

CAREER: St. Louis Globe-Democrat, St. Louis, Mo., reporter, 1955-62; *Newsweek,* New York, N.Y., associate editor, 1962-64, general editor, 1965-68, senior editor, 1969—. *Member:* American Civil Liberties Union, Phi Beta Kappa. *Awards, honors:* Nieman fellow, Harvard University, 1960-61; Sigma Delta Chi award for magazine reporting, 1963; National Headliners award, 1963, for coverage of riot at University of Mississippi, 1962; Robert F. Kennedy Journalism Award, 1972; American Bar Association Silver Gavel Award, 1972, for a report on criminal justice in America; National Magazine Award, 1982, for *Newsweek* issue on Vietnam veterans.

WRITINGS: Civil Rights: The Challenge of the Fourteenth Amendment, Coward, 1965, revised edition, 1967; *Report from Black America,* Simon & Schuster, 1970; *The Death and Life of Malcolm X,* Harper, 1973, revised edition, 1979; (contributor) John Hope Franklin and August Meier, editors, *Black Leadership of the Twentieth Century,* University of Illinois, 1982; (with Tony Fuller) *Charlie Company: What Vietnam Did to Us,* Morrow, 1983.

WORK IN PROGRESS: Researching a book on basketball as a subculture in black American life.

SIDELIGHTS: Peter L. Goldman told *CA:* "I am a career journalist, fulfilling an early boyhood ambition. I write about U.S. affairs, with subspecialties in national politics and the black American situation; and, as an avocation, about sports—particularly basketball. An area of current interest is the probability that two of the three men convicted of the assassination of Malcolm X are innocent, as I have argued in several articles and in the revised edition of my biography of Malcolm."

* * *

GOLENBOCK, Peter 1946-

PERSONAL: Born July 19, 1946, in New York, N.Y.; son of Jerome (an attorney and art dealer) and Annette (Sklarin) Golenbock. *Education:* Dartmouth College, B.A. (with honors), 1967; New York University, J.D., 1970. *Agent:* Edward J. Acton, 17 Grove St., New York, N.Y. 10014.

CAREER: Writer. Sport columnist for newspapers in Stamford, Conn., 1968-70, and in New York, N.Y., 1970; Prentice-Hall, Inc., Legal Department, Englewood Cliffs, N.J., editor, 1972; *North Bergen Suburbanite,* Englewood, N.J., political reporter, 1975; *Bergen Record,* Bergen, N.J., reporter and editor, 1975-78.

WRITINGS: Dynasty: The New York Yankees, 1949-1964, Prentice-Hall, 1975; (with Sparky Lyle) *The Bronx Zoo,* Crown, 1979; (with Ron Guidry) *Guidry,* Prentice-Hall, 1980; (with Billy Martin) *Number 1,* Delacorte, 1980; *The Boss: George Steinbrenner's Story,* Crown, 1982.

WORK IN PROGRESS: Bums: The Brooklyn Dodgers, 1947-1957, for Delacorte.

SIDELIGHTS: Peter Golenbock's books *Dynasty, The Bronx Zoo,* and *Number 1* have all appeared on the *New York Times Book Review* best-seller list. "Sports has become an integral part of American society," Golenbock told *CA.* "With the public interest in *Dynasty, The Bronx Zoo,* and *Number 1,* I would hope that publishers would begin to take books on sports more seriously than in the past."

BIOGRAPHICAL/CRITICAL SOURCES: Best Sellers, August, 1975; *Book World,* April 22, 1979; *New York Times Book Review,* November 2, 1980; *Times Literary Supplement,* February 27, 1981.

* * *

GOOD, Thomas L(indall) 1943-

PERSONAL: Born October 4, 1943, in Owensboro, Ky.; son of Thomas Edison (a store owner) and Bessie (Howard) Good; married Suzanne R. Fischer, June 24, 1967; children: Heather Lynn, Jeffrey Thomas, Kate Elizabeth, Molly Ann. *Education:* University of Illinois, A.B., 1965; University of Michigan, graduate study, 1966; Indiana University, M.S., 1967, Ph.D., 1968. *Home:* 112 Parkhill, Columbia, Mo. 65201. *Office:* Department of Curriculum and Instruction, University of Missouri, Columbia, Mo. 65202.

CAREER: University of Texas at Austin, assistant professor of educational psychology and project director of Research and Development Center for Teacher Education, 1968-71; University of Missouri—Columbia, Department of Curriculum and Instruction, associate professor, 1971-73, professor of curriculum and instruction, 1974—, research scientist at Center for Research in Social Behavior, 1971—. Visiting lecturer at numerous universities, including Indiana University, Michigan State University, and University of California, Los Angeles. Assistant director at Southeastern Educational Service Center, 1967-68; staff development coordinator for Early Childhood Education Program at Southwest Educational Development Laboratory, 1970-71. Member of advisory panel, Northeast Regional Laboratory, and Institute for Research in Teaching, Michigan State University; consultant to National Child Development Associate Program, 1972, U.S. Office of Child Development, National Commission of the States, and Texas Education Agency.

MEMBER: American Educational Research Association, American Association of University Professors, American Psychological Association, Phi Kappa Phi. *Awards, honors:* National Institute of Mental Health grants, 1969, 1970; Hogg Foundation grant, 1970; National Academy of Education Spencer fellow, 1972; Spencer Foundation grant, 1972; National Institute of Education grant, 1973, 1976, and 1979; National Science Foundation grant, 1978.

WRITINGS: (With B. Dollar and P. Scott) *Psychological Foundations of Elementary Education*, University of Texas, 1971; (with Gordon Greenwood and B. Siegel) *Problem Situations in Teaching*, Harper, 1971; (with others) *Teaching Skills*, College of Education, University of Missouri, 1972; (with J. E. Brophy) *Looking in Classrooms*, Harper, 1973, 2nd edition, 1978; (with Brophy) *Teacher-Student Relationships: Causes and Consequences*, Holt, 1974; (with B. J. Biddle and Brophy) *Teachers Make a Difference*, Holt, 1975; (with S. E. Nedler and Brophy) *Teaching in the Preschool*, Harper, 1975; (with Brophy) *Educational Psychology: A Realistic Approach*, Holt, 1977, 2nd edition, 1980; (with H. Cooper) *Pygmalion Grows Up*, Academic Press, in press.

Contributor: A. Simon and E. G. Boyer, editors, *Mirrors for Behavior: An Anthology of Observation Instruments Continued, 1970 Supplement*, Volumes A and B, Research for Better Schools, 1970; (with Brophy) H. C. Lindgren and F. Lindgren, editors, *Current Readings in Educational Psychology*, 2nd edition (Good was not associated with earlier edition), Wiley, 1971; (with Brophy) J. F. Rosenblith, W. Allensmith, and J. P. Williams, editors, *The Causes of Behavior*, 3rd edition (Good was not associated with earlier editions), Allyn & Bacon, 1972; (with Brophy) U. Bronfenbrenner, editor, *Influence on Human Development*, Dryden, 1972; (with Brophy) R. Coop and K. White, editors, *Psychological Concepts in the Classroom*, Harper, 1973; (with Brophy) R. A. Magoon, editor, *Educational Psychology: Past, Present, and Future*, C. E. Merrill, 1973; J. M. Palardy, editor, *Teaching Today*, Macmillan, 1973; P. C. Stetson, editor, *Educational Psychology Reader*, MSS Educational Publishing, 1974; Murphey and others, *Educational Psychology Reader*, Simon & Schuster, 1974; (with Brophy) M. D. Gall, editor, *Educational Psychology Reader*, Little, Brown, 1975; H. Stub, editor, *The Sociology of Education*, Dorsey, 1975; H. Clarizio, R. Craig, and W. Mehrens, editors, *Contemporary Readings in Educational Psychology*, Allyn & Bacon, 1977; (with D. Grouws) G. Borich, editor, *The Appraisal of Teaching: Concepts and Process*, Addison-Wesley, 1977.

J. McMillan, editor, *The Social Psychology of School Learning*, Academic Press, 1980; D. MacMillan, editor, *Management of Resources in Schools*, Deakin University (Victoria, Australia), 1981; *Resource Management*, Deakin University, 1981; K. Howey and R. Dykstra, editors, *Research and Development in Teacher Education*, University of Minnesota Press, in press; (with Grouws) E. Fennema, editor, *Implications of Research in Mathematics Education for the Curriculum of the 80's*, Association for Supervision and Curriculum Development, in press.

Also author of thirty-five technical reports for Center for Research in Social Behavior and four reports for Research and Development Center for Teacher Education. Member of editorial board, "Research on Teaching" monograph series, Longman. Contributor of articles and book reviews to professional journals, including *Journal of Educational Psychology, American Educational Research Journal, Contemporary Psychology, Educational Leadership, Journal of Personality and Social Psychology,* and *Journal of School Psychology.* Editor, *Elementary School Journal;* advisory editor, *Journal of Educational Psychology* and *Journal of Teacher Education.*

WORK IN PROGRESS: A research monograph; a textbook; book chapters for *Research and Policy Implications in Education,* edited by M. Sykes and L. Shuman, and for *Teacher and Student Perceptions: Implications for Learning,* edited by J. Levine and M. Wang.

* * *

GOODSELL, Charles T(rue) 1932-

PERSONAL: Born July 23, 1932, in Kalamazoo, Mich.; son of Charles T. (a professor) and Frances (Comee) Goodsell; married Mary Elizabeth MacKintosh, June 13, 1959; children: Holly Delight, Amanda Joy. *Education:* Kalamazoo College, A.B., 1954; Harvard University, M.P.A., 1958, M.A., 1959, Ph.D., 1961. *Politics:* Independent Democrat. *Religion:* Presbyterian. *Home:* 509 College View Dr., Blacksburg, Va. 24060. *Office:* Center for Public Administration and Policy, Virginia Polytechnic Institute and State University, Blacksburg, Va. 24061.

CAREER: U.S. Bureau of the Budget, Washington, D.C., management intern, summers, 1957-59; University of Puerto Rico, Rio Piedras, assistant professor of public administration, 1961-64; Princeton University, Princeton, N.J., research associate at Woodrow Wilson School, 1964-66; Southern Illinois University, Carbondale, associate professor, 1966-72, professor of political science, 1972-78; Virginia Polytechnic Institute and State University, Blacksburg, professor of public administration and public affairs, 1978—. Visiting professor, University of Texas, 1978. *Military service:* U.S. Army, 1954-56. *Member:* American Political Science Association, American Society for Public Administration, Midwest Political Science Association, Southern Political Science Association.

WRITINGS: *Administration of a Revolution*, Harvard University Press, 1965; *American Corporations and Peruvian Politics*, Harvard University Press, 1974; *The Public Encounter*, Indiana University Press, 1981; *The Case for Bureaucracy*, Chatam House, 1982. Contributor to professional journals.

SIDELIGHTS: Charles T. Goodsell wrote *CA*, "My current interests include reevaluation of bureaucracy in America, comparative bureaucratic behavior, and semiotic study of political and administrative settings."

* * *

GOODWIN, Stephen 1943-

PERSONAL: Born October 20, 1943, in Pennsylvania; son of

Claudius Lee and Jeannette (Levy) Goodwin; married Lucia Stanton, June 16, 1964 (divorced, 1977); children: Eliza. *Education:* Harvard University, A.B., 1965; University of Virginia, M.A., 1969. *Home:* 2022 Columbia Rd., Washington, D.C. 20009. *Agent:* Russell & Volkening, 551 Fifth Ave., New York, N.Y. 10017. *Office:* Department of English, George Mason University, Fairfax, Va.

CAREER: Washington and Lee University, Lexington, Va., instructor in English, 1969-73; Bryn Mawr College, Bryn Mawr, Pa., assistant professor of English, 1973-78; University of Virginia, Charlottesville, lecturer, 1978-79; George Mason University, Fairfax, Va., associate professor of English, 1979—. *Military service:* U.S. Army, 1966-68. *Awards, honors:* National Endowment for the Arts literary fellowship, 1973.

WRITINGS: Kin, Harper, 1975; *The Blood of Paradise,* Dutton, 1979. Contributor to journals.

WORK IN PROGRESS: A novel, *Luther Pie, American.*

SIDELIGHTS: The Blood of Paradise is "a scrupulous, poignant novel—the work of an apprentice to the trade, but a very skilled one," according to James Atlas writing in the *New York Times.* Steven Goodwin's second novel receives similar praise from other reviewers.

Both Julian Moynahan in *New York Times Book Review* and Anne Tyler in *Washington Post Book World,* for example, note that Goodwin's growth as a novelist becomes evident when a comparison between *The Blood of Paradise* and *Kin,* his first novel, is made. Moynahan says that *The Blood of Paradise* "has a much richer physical ambience and a more forlorn sense of human possibility." Tyler states: "*The Blood of Paradise* . . . will strike Goodwin-watchers as a kind of flowering. It's not merely a step forward; it'a a leap—a book that seems laden, rich, powerful."

While Atlas describes *Kin,* Goodwin's novel of a Southern white who brings a black fellow-soldier home for a visit, as a "Gothic tale of rural violence, racism, and suicide," the reviewer comments, "*The Blood of Paradise* has a more substantial subject: men and women in conflict." Atlas sees flaws in both the plot and the characters presented in *The Blood of Paradise,* but believes that Goodwin's superior writing ability makes the novel a success. After describing the book's plot and characters, Atlas continues: "How . . . does the author salvage this rather unpromising material? Simply by writing well. . . . He has mastered an austere voice that encompasses passion; so many scenes in the novel shine forth with a restrained, but deeply felt emotion."

A *Chicago Tribune Book World* review written by Charles Larson sums up the critical response to *The Blood of Paradise.* Larson comments: "When a rare novel like Stephen Goodwin's *The Blood of Paradise* comes along, one feels like shouting out the news or banging a drum—anything to drown out the din announcing the lesser rivals. . . . This is a superbly rewarding novel."

BIOGRAPHICAL/CRITICAL SOURCES: Washington Post Book World, May 27, 1979; *New York Times,* June 14, 1979; *Chicago Tribune Book World,* June 17, 1979; *New York Times Book Review,* June 24, 1979; *Detroit News,* July 22, 1979.

* * *

GOSTELOW, Mary 1943-

PERSONAL: Surname is accented on first syllable; born July 23, 1943, in London, England; daughter of Sir James Macdonald and Lorna Mary (Marlow) Cobban; married Martin Gostelow (a photographer), July 20, 1968. *Education:* Educated in England and New York. *Home:* 43 Milton Abbas, Blandford Forum, Dorsetshire, England. *Agent:* Ann Borchardt, 136 East 57th St., New York, N.Y. 10022.

CAREER: Book researcher, editorial assistant, journalist, 1964-68; free-lance travel and arts writer, based in Beirut, Lebanon, 1968-72; free-lance writer, journalist, and lecturer on decorative arts in Dorsetshire, England, 1972—. Lecturer in the United States, Canada, Australia, and South Africa. *Member:* National Association of Decorative and Fine Arts Societies, Embroiderers Guild of America, National Standards Council of American Embroiderers.

WRITINGS: A World of Embroidery, illustrations by the author and Janet Watson, Scribner, 1975; *The Fan,* Gill & Macmillan (Dublin), 1976; *Embroidery South Africa,* Mills & Boon, 1976; *Blackwork,* Van Nostrand, 1976; *The Complete International Book of Embroidery,* Simon & Schuster, 1977; *Embroidery of All Russia,* illustrations by the author and John E. Damsell, Scribner, 1978; *The Coats Books of Embroidery,* illustrations by the author and husband, Martin Gostelow, David & Charles, 1978; *Embroidery: Traditional Designs, Techniques and Patterns from All over the World,* Cavendish, 1978; *Mary Gostelow's Embroidery Book,* illustrations by the author and Martin Gostelow, Dutton, 1979; *Art of Embroidery: Great Needlework Collections of Britain and the United States,* Dutton, 1979; *Mary Gostelow's Book of Embroidery Projects,* illustrations by Martin Gostelow, David & Charles, 1981. Also author of *The Cross-Stitch Book.*

AVOCATIONAL INTERESTS: Travel (has been to Africa, Soviet Union, Middle East), food and wine, sports, and all forms of art.

* * *

GOULDEN, Joseph C. (Jr.) 1934-

PERSONAL: Surname is pronounced "Golden"; born May 23, 1934, in Marshall, Tex.; son of Joseph C. (a book dealer) and Lecta Mahon (Everett) Goulden; married Emily Jo Corns, July 15, 1961; married Leslie Cantrell Smith, June 21, 1979; children: (first marriage) Joseph III, James Craig. *Education:* Attended University of Texas, 1952-56. *Home:* 2500 Que St. N.W., Washington, D.C. 20007. *Agent:* Carl Brandt, Brandt & Brandt Literary Agents, Inc., Paramount Bldg., 101 Broadway, New York, N.Y. 10036.

CAREER: Free-lance writer. Molybdenum miner in Colorado, 1953; reporter for newspaper in Marshall, Tex., 1956; *Dallas News,* Dallas, Tex., reporter, 1958-61, *Philadelphia Inquirer,* Philadelphia, Pa., reporter, 1961-68. *Military service:* U.S. Army, 1956-58. *Awards, honors:* Recipient of numerous journalistic awards, including reporting awards from State Bar of Texas, 1960, and Pennsylvania and Philadelphia Press Associations, 1964; national magazine award, 1969, for *Nation* issue on the Law Enforcement Assistance Administration; Carr P. Collins Award, Texas Institute of Letters, 1972.

WRITINGS: The Curtis Caper, Putnam, 1965; *Monopoly,* Putnam, 1968; *Truth Is the First Casualty: The Gulf of Tonkin Affair, Illusion and Reality,* Rand McNally, 1969; *The Money Givers,* Random House, 1971; *Meany: The Unchallenged Strong Man of American Labor,* Atheneum, 1972; *The Superlawyers: The Small and Powerful World of the Great Washington Law Firms,* Weybright, 1972; *The Benchwarmers: The Small and Powerful World of the Great Federal Judges,* Weybright, 1974; *The Best Years* (Book-of-the-Month Club selection), Atheneum, 1976; (editor) *Mencken's Last Campaign,* New Republic

Books, 1976; *The Million Dollar Lawyers,* Putnam, 1978; *Korea: The Untold Story of the War,* Times Books, 1982; *Jerry Wurf: Labor's Last Angry Man,* Atheneum, 1982. Contributor to periodicals, including *Harper's, National Review, Nation, Penthouse, Texas Monthly,* and *Texas Observer.*

SIDELIGHTS: A *Nation* critic describes Joseph C. Goulden as "one of the country's best investigative reporters." Goulden, a former newspaperman, told *CA* that he has made "a gradual transition from journalist to historian." In such works as *The Superlawyers* and *Truth Is the First Casualty,* Goulden has carefully researched and written history designed for the general reader.

The Superlawyers, described by John M. Blair in *Nation* as an "excellent pioneering expose," presents a behind-the-scenes view of the most powerful Washington law firms. "Goulden, an old hand at muckraking . . . , has looked into the . . . activities of Superlawyer and found numerous cases of conflict-of-interest, wire-pulling, Establishment collusion, and influence-peddling," a *New York Review of Books* article states. "Goulden shows how the Superlawyers dominate the federal regulatory agencies, are in cahoots with congressmen . . . and are constantly violating the public interest if not the public law," the article continues. "[The Superlawyers] is a fascinating book."

Truth Is the First Casualty, as critics have observed, is a comprehensive study of the Gulf of Tonkin incidents which sparked the Vietnam War. Goulden's balanced treatment of this controversial subject has been praised by such differing editorial voices as the *Armed Forces Journal* and the *New York Review of Books.* "As I grow older," he told *CA,* "I find myself more opinionated in private, less argumentative in print. I feel that a reader is entitled to get mad of his own accord, and that a writer who tries to shape public events should enter either politics or an institution."

In the *New York Review of Books,* Peter Dale Scott calls *Truth Is the First Casualty* a "fascinating book. . . . Goulden has made good use of his years of experience in Washington. . . . His method is to stick closely to the official documents (above all the neglected Fulbright Committee Hearing of 1968) and first-hand interviews with witnesses the Committee failed to call. . . . The result is devastating. It is now even more clear that the Tonkin Gulf Resolution (in his words) 'contains the fatal taint of deception.' The [Johnson] Administration had withheld much vital information in formulating the simple story of 'unprovoked attack' by which that resolution was pushed through Congress." According to Richard J. Walton in *Nation,* Goulden's study "is of the first importance. . . . This book poses [deeply serious questions] about the American system of government in the postwar years." Goulden "has given us vital facts about one of the crucial events, or nonevents, in American history," Walton concludes. "Future historians will be grateful."

BIOGRAPHICAL/CRITICAL SOURCES: *Saturday Review,* November 1, 1969; *Nation,* November 17, 1969, June 26, 1972, November 6, 1972; *New York Review of Books,* January 29, 1970, May 4, 1972; *New York Times Book Review,* May 28, 1972, June 26, 1976, April 11, 1982; *New York Times,* July 27, 1976; *Washington Post Book World,* September 14, 1978, February 21, 1982, August 1, 1982; *Los Angeles Times Book Review,* August 29, 1982.

*   *   *

GRAHAM, A(lexander) John 1930-

PERSONAL: Born March 9, 1930, in Lowestoft, England; son of Godfrey Michael (a naturalist) and Edith (Meek) Graham; married Jenny Fitter, July 6, 1963; children: William Richard, Oliver James. *Education:* King's College, Cambridge, B.A. (with first class honors), 1952, Ph.D., 1957. *Office:* Department of Classical Studies, 720 Williams Hall C.U., University of Pennsylvania, Philadelphia, Pa. 19104.

CAREER: University of London, Bedford College, London, England, assistant lecturer in classics, 1955-57; University of Manchester, Manchester, England, assistant lecturer, 1957-59, lecturer, 1959-70, senior lecturer in history, 1970-77; University of Pennsylvania, Philadelphia, professor of classical studies and Allen Memorial Professor of Greek, 1977—. Member, British School at Athens. *Military service:* British Army, 1948-49. *Member:* Association Internationale d'Epigraphie Grecque et Latine, American Philological Association, Archaeological Institute of America, Classical Association (secretary of Manchester branch, 1959-62), Hellenic Society (member of council, 1960-63, 1974—).

WRITINGS: *Colony and Mother City in Ancient Greece,* Barnes & Noble, 1964, revised edition, 1971; (co-editor) V. L. Ehrenberg, *Polis und Imperium,* Artemis Press, 1965; (contributor) *Oxford Classical Dictionary,* 2nd edition, Oxford University Press, 1970; (contributor) Hildegard Temporini, editor, *Aufstieg und Niedergang der roemischen Welt,* de Gruyter, 1972; (contributor) M.R.D. Foot, editor, *War and Society: Essays in Honor and Memory of John Western,* Paul Elek, 1973; (co-author) *An Attic Country House,* Thames & Hudson, 1973; (contributor) *Cambridge Ancient History,* 2nd edition, Cambridge University Press, 1982. Contributor of articles to *Historica, Journal of Hellenic Studies, Journal of Roman Studies, Annual of the British School at Athens,* and other periodicals.

WORK IN PROGRESS: Studies in early Greek history, epigraphy, colonization, horses, and aspects of ancient beekeeping.

SIDELIGHTS: A. John Graham is competent in Latin, classical and modern Greek, and the major modern European languages. *Avocational interests:* Archaeology, especially Greek and Roman, including excavation; canoeing, cricket, photography, travel in Mediterranean countries.

*   *   *

GRAHAM, Ilse 1914-

PERSONAL: Born July 4, 1914, in Berlin, Germany; daughter of Paul (a businessman) and Else Martha (Henschel) Appelbaum; married Gerald Graham (a consulting physician); children: Nina, Martin. *Education:* Bedford College, London, B.A. (with first class honors), 1939, Ph.D., 1951. *Home:* 60 Northway, London N.W.11, England.

CAREER: University of London, London, England, assistant lecturer in German at Queen Mary College, 1942-46, assistant lecturer at University College, 1946-49, lecturer in German, 1949-51, part-time lecturer at King's College, 1954-57, lecturer, 1957-65, reader in German, 1965-75, professor of German, 1975, emeritus professor, 1975—. *Member:* International Goethe Society, Wiener Goethe-Verein (honorary life member), English Goethe Society, Modern Humanities Research Association (member of council). *Awards, honors:* Modern Humanities Research Association prize, 1972, for *Schiller: A Master of the Tragic Form;* Medal of Distinction, Wiener Goethe-Verein, 1978, for services to Goethe; D.Litt., University of London, 1978.

WRITINGS: *Goethe and Lessing: The Wellsprings of Creation,* Elek, 1973; *Schiller's Drama: Talent and Integrity,* Barnes &

Noble, 1974; *Schiller: Ein Meister der Tragischen Form*, Wissenschaftliche Buchgesellschaft, 1974, translation by Klaus Boerner and Graham published as *Schiller: A Master of the Tragic Form*, Dusquesne University Press, 1975; *Goethe: Portrait of the Artist*, De Gruyter, 1977; *Kleist: Word into Flesh: A Poet's Quest for the Symbol*, De Gruyter, 1977; (contributor) H. J. Maehl and E. Mannack, editors, *Studien zur Goethezeit. Erich Trunz zum 75. Geburtstag*, [Heidelberg], 1981; *Auf der Spur des Herrn: Zehn Versuche zu Goethes "Faust,"* De Gruyter, in press.

Contributor to *Akten des VI. Internationalen Germanisten-Kongresses Basel 1980*. Contributor to professional journals, including *German Life and Letters*.

WORK IN PROGRESS: *Goethe: Schauen und Glauben*, for De Gruyter.

SIDELIGHTS: Ilse Graham writes to *CA*: "I do not believe in any hard and fast distinction between creative writing and literary criticism. The best criticism we have undoubtedly comes from the pen of creative artists such as T. S. Eliot, H. von Hofmannsthal or Thomas Mann (which, however, is far from implying that there is not much excellent criticism without such a tie-up). In my own modest instance, the writing of poetry has steadily gone hand in hand with my critical work; indeed, the latter would be unthinkable without the former. My own writing of verse has provided an invaluable source of insight into the poetic process as such. (Even the writing of bad verse is capable of doing so.) Besides, being a woman writer, my 'creative' work has opened my eyes to the extraordinarily close connection between biological and mental creativity, between the events of conception, gestation and labour on the physical and on the spiritual levels. Such a continuum of experience is by no means exclusive to my own sex. On the contrary, it is my firm conviction—and my critical studies have amply borne this out—that the creative man, being endowed with an unusually rich admixture of femininity, can and does fully share in the essential Oneness of the diverse manifestations of creativity. It is these insights regarding the nature of the poetic process, this intimate link with biological process and the affinity, in this important respect, between the sexes, that have informed the slant of my critical work from beginning to end.

"All in all, I would say that what Rilke writes to a young poet about his poetry-making is equally applicable to the literary critic: 'Don't write unless you absolutely must.' On the whole, I absolutely must!"

* * *

GRANGER, Clive W(illiam) J(ohn) 1934-

PERSONAL: Born September 4, 1934, in Swansea, Glamorganshire, Wales; son of Edward John (a divisional sales manager) and Evelyn (Hessey) Granger; married Patricia Anne Loveland, May 14, 1960; children: Mark William John, Claire. *Education:* University of Nottingham, B.A. (first class honors), 1955, Ph.D., 1959. *Office:* Department of Economics, University of California, San Diego, La Jolla, Calif.

CAREER: University of Nottingham, Nottingham, England, reader in economics, 1956-64, professor of economics, 1964-74, head of department, 1968-69, director of Statistical Forecasting Project, 1970-74; University of California, San Diego, La Jolla, professor of economics, 1974—, chairman of department, 1982—. Research associate, Econometric Research Program, Princeton University, beginning 1960; visiting assistant professor of statistics, Stanford University, 1963; visiting professor of economics, University of California, San Diego, 1969, Institute for Advanced Studies in the Social Sciences, Vienna, Austria, 1971, and Australian National University, 1977; external examiner, University of the West Indies, 1972—. Consultant, Pricing Research Ltd., 1971. Co-director, Nottingham Consumer Group, 1962-74. *Member:* Royal Statistical Society (fellow), Institute of Mathematical Statistics. *Awards, honors:* Harkness fellow, Commonwealth Fund, 1960.

WRITINGS: (With Michio Hatanaka) *Spectral Analysis of Economic Time Series*, Princeton University Press, 1964; *Investigating the Future: Statistical Forecasting Problems* (lecture), University of Nottingham, 1967; (with Morgenstern) *Predictability of Stock Market Prices*, Lexington Books, 1970; (with Walter C. Labys) *Speculation Hedging and Commodity Price Forecasts*, Lexington Books, 1970; *Statistical Forecasting of Economic Series: A Review of Techniques*, University of Surrey, 1973; (editor and contributor) *Trading in Commodities*, Woodhead-Faulkner, 1974, published as *Getting Started in London Commodities*, Investor Publications, 1975, 3rd edition, 1980; *Forecasting Economic Time Series*, Academic Press, 1977; (with Andre Gabor) *Pricing, Principles and Practices*, Heinemann Educational, 1977; *An Introduction to Bilinear Time Series Models*, Vandenhoeck & Ruprecht, 1978; *Forecasting in Business and Economics*, Academic Press, 1980.

Also author of approximately fifty research papers. Contributor to academic journals in Europe and America, including *Information and Control, Kyklos*, and *L'Industria*. Joint editor, *Applied Economics*, 1969—; associate editor, *Journal of Financial Economics*, 1975-79, *Journal of Econometrics*, 1977—, *Journal of the American Statistical Association*, 1978-80, *Journal of Time Series Analysis*, 1980—, and *Energy*, 1980—.

SIDELIGHTS: Clive W. J. Granger once told *CA*: "I have the usual Englishman's interest in travel combined with incompetence in other people's languages." Granger camped his way around the United States in 1960.

* * *

GRAY, Ralph D(ale) 1933-

PERSONAL: Born October 13, 1933, in Otwell, Ind.; son of Lee M. (a grocer) and Voris R. (Gray) Gray; married Janice R. Everett, September 2, 1956; children: Karen David, Sarah. *Education:* Hanover College, B.A., 1955; University of Durham, 1955-56; University of Delaware, M.A., 1958; University of Illinois, Ph.D., 1962. *Home:* 1724 West 73rd Pl., Indianapolis, Ind. 46260. *Office:* Department of History, Indiana University—Purdue University at Indianapolis, 1219 West Michigan Ave., Indianapolis, Ind. 46202.

CAREER: Ohio State University, Columbus, instructor in history, 1961-64; Indiana University, Kokomo Regional Campus, assistant professor, 1964-67, associate professor of history, 1967-68; Indiana University—Purdue University at Indianapolis, associate professor, 1968-72, professor of history, 1972—. Special consultant to Monon Railroad, 1966, and Cabot Corp., 1971. *Member:* Society for Historians of Early American Republic, Organization of American Historians, Business History Conference, Indiana Historical Society, Indiana Oral History Roundtable (president, 1975-76), Marion County/Indianapolis Historical Society (director, 1981—). *Awards, honors:* Fulbright scholar in England, 1955-56; Dickerson Award, University of Illinois, 1966, for *The National Waterway*; McKean Cup, Antique Automobile Club of America, 1980, for *Alloys and Automobiles: The Life of Elwood Haynes*.

WRITINGS: *The National Waterway: A History of the Chesapeake and Delaware Canal, 1769-1965*, University of Illinois

Press, 1967; (editor) *Gentlemen from Indiana: National Party Candidates, 1840-1940*, Indiana Historical Bureau, 1977; *Alloys and Automobiles: The Life of Elwood Haynes*, Indiana Historical Society, 1979; (editor and author of introduction) *The Hoosier State: Readings in Indiana History*, Eerdmans, 1981. Also author of *Stellite: A History of the Stellite Company, 1912-1972*, 1974. Contributor to *Encyclopedia of World Biography*, McGraw, 1973, *Dictionary of American Biography*, Supplement V, 1977, and to *Encyclopedia of Southern History*, 1979. Contributor of articles and reviews to business history and regional history journals. Founder and editor, *Journal of the Early Republic*, 1981—.

WORK IN PROGRESS: A study of the life of Henry D. Gilpin of Philadelphia, 1801-1860.

AVOCATIONAL INTERESTS: All sports, woodworking, photography.

* * *

GREEN, Gerald 1922-

PERSONAL: Name legally changed; born April 8, 1922, in Brooklyn, N.Y.; son of Samuel (a doctor) and Anna (Matzkin) Greenberg; married Maria Pomposelli, November 9, 1950 (died, November 14, 1979); married Marlene M. Eagle, October 19, 1980; children: (first marriage) Nancy, Theodore, David. *Education:* Columbia University, A.B., 1942, M.S. (journalism), 1947. *Politics:* Democrat. *Religion:* Jewish. *Residence:* New Canaan, Conn. *Agent:* Scott Meredith Literary Agency, Inc., 845 Third Ave., New York, N.Y. 10022.

CAREER: Writer. International News Service, New York City, editor, 1947-50; National Broadcasting Co., Television News, New York City, producer and writer, 1950—, with programs including "Today," "Wide Wide World," "Chet Huntley Reporting," and a number of documentaries. Columbia University, John Jay Associate. *Military service:* U.S. Army, Ordnance Corps, 1942-46; served with Armed Forces Network in Germany; became sergeant. *Member:* Authors League of America, Writers Guild of America—East, P.E.N., Phi Beta Kappa.

AWARDS, HONORS: Alumni Award, Columbia University School of Journalism, 1957; Emmy Award nominations, Academy of Television Arts and Sciences, 1967, for "Toscanni, The Maestro Revisited," and 1972, for "The Cave People of the Philippines"; Emmy Award for best dramatic script, Academy of Television Arts and Sciences, 1978, for mini-series, "Holocaust"; Prix International Dag Hammarskojd for Literature, 1979, for novel, *Holocaust;* awards from various organizations, including American Jewish Committee, Brith Sholem, and Hadassah, for series, "Holocaust."

WRITINGS—Novels, except as indicated: (With L. Klingman) *His Majesty O'Keefe*, Scribner, 1948; *The Sword and the Sun*, Scribner, 1950; *The Last Angry Man*, Scribner, 1957; *The Lotus Eaters*, Scribner, 1959; *The Heartless Light*, Scribner, 1961; *The Portofino PTA* (nonfiction), Scribner, 1962; *The Legion of Noble Christians; or, The Sweeney Survey*, Trident, 1965; (with Drew Pearson) *The Senator*, Doubleday, 1968; *To Brooklyn with Love* (Book-of-the-Month Club selection), Trident, 1968; *The Artists of Terezin* (nonfiction), Hawthorn, 1969; *Faking It; or, The Wrong Hungarian*, Trident, 1971; *The Stones of Zion: A Novelist's Journal in Israel* (nonfiction), Hawthorn, 1971; *Blockbuster*, Doubleday, 1972; *Tourist*, Doubleday, 1973; *The Hostage Heart*, Playboy Press, 1974; *An American Prophet*, Doubleday, 1975; *Girl*, Doubleday, 1976; *Holocaust* (novelization of screenplay of same name), Bantam, 1978; *The Healers*, Putnam, 1978; *Cactus Pie* (short story collection), Houghton, 1979; *The Chains*, Seaview, 1980; *Murfy's Men*, Seaview, 1981.

Screenplays: "The Last Angry Man" (based on novel of same title), Columbia Pictures, 1959, television presentation (based on 1959 screenplay), Columbia Pictures Television, 1974; "Holocaust" (television mini-series), Titus Productions, broadcast by the National Broadcasting Corporation, 1978; (with Richard Kramer) "Kent State" (television movie), Interplanetary Productions, broadcast by the National Broadcasting Corporation, 1980.

Also author of documentaries for NBC. Contributor to periodicals, including *Reader's Digest, Kenyon Review, Travel and Leisure, Playboy, Penthouse,* and *Good Housekeeping.*

SIDELIGHTS: Gerald Green is best known for his novel *The Last Angry Man* and for the television screenplay "Holocaust," for which he received an Emmy Award in 1978. Both works reflect Green's desire to root his fiction in social history, applying his journalistic background to produce well-researched stories which shed light on historical experiences.

"At rare intervals a novel comes along which manages to focus the sparkle of its facets in one steady gleam of light. Such a novel is *The Last Angry Man*," James Kelly writes in *Saturday Review*. In this account of an idealistic doctor torn by the realities of life in a Brooklyn slum, Kelly continues, "Green achieves a significant social document about the dilemmas that divide us. He does it without losing sight of his novelist's obligation to provide a dramatic and brightly written story in which truly motivated and warmly regarded people resolve the blurred pattern of their lives." In the *Chicago Sunday Tribune*, Robert Molloy comments: "[The doctor's] progress from a poor Jewish boy to a gruff, coarse Schweitzer of the Brooklyn jungle makes a good story. . . . Green tells a story well enough. . . . His writing is generally heavy, journalistic, and undistinguished. . . . But even a lack of stylistic elegance need not keep a sturdy novel from artistic . . . success." And in a *New York Herald Tribune* article, F. T. Marsh finds that "*The Last Angry Man* is not a subtly-written novel. But for its many appeals as a big story involving many little stories it is certain to find thousands and thousands of readers. More important than the plotted story line is the fact that it has moral stature."

Green's screenplay "Holocaust" has created enormous political and critical controversy. Even before the show was broadcast, one-and-a-half million copies of Green's novelization of his screenplay had been sold. An estimated 120 million American viewers watched the documentary-drama, and its premiere in foreign countries generated sharp controversy and attracted millions of additional viewers. West Germany, especially, experienced much turmoil over the presentation of "Holocaust." Amid fears that, as Guy Stern notes in *Columbia*, "the spate of historical errors, inaccurate visual details, and improbabilities in the series would only fuel the Big Lie that the Holocaust had not taken place," the program was rejected by the major West German networks. The series was eventually carried via regional television to an estimated thirteen million German viewers, and heated discussion of its accuracy and merit was featured on national phone-in shows, during which a solid majority of callers applauded the presentation. Largely as a result of the showing of "Holocaust," the statute of limitations on Nazi war criminals was annulled by the West German parliament.

In addition to the political issues stirred up by "Holocaust," reviewers of the drama have criticized both its quality and its supposed oversimplification—some, such as Elie Wiesel, would say "trivialization"—of its subject.

Several critics, including James Lardner of the *New Republic,* have argued that "the show's creators aggravated the inherent difficulties of their assignment by resolving to tell not just one story of Jews under Nazism, but *the* story. From that decision, it follows that no character can be just a character. Each must stand for a whole category of people, or for a way of thinking. . . . Being a cipher is hard work. It is not easy to do simultaneous duty as a mere human being. Perhaps that is why these characters don't speak to each other. They speak to history." In the same review, Lardner comments: "Perhaps this is material so appalling and so colossal as to confound the skills of the most brilliant writer. It has, at any rate, confounded those of Gerald Green. . . . 'Holocaust' is a minefield of banalities. Whole scenes roll by without even a fleeting moment of originality." In *Commonweal,* Philip Terzian is also critical of the show's treatment of its subject matter: "It was clear from the beginning what was going to happen to [the Weiss family], and whatever drama there might have been was discarded at the beginning. This then, lies at the heart of what is wrong with 'docu-dramas.' They throw away their subject. . . . 'Holocaust' is the sort of thing that makes dramatization seem trivial. And, in a commercial enterprise, tragicomic. The networks ought to be wary of cutting from scenes of the ovens of Auschwitz to the ovens of Elm City, USA. They ought to realize that while commerce can be oppressive, history is overwhelming, and the two do not always mix well, and sometimes explode on impact. That is the potential harm of 'docu-dramas': not so much the banality of evil, but the evil of banality."

Peter Sourian of *Nation* takes a different view on the issue of oversimplification: "The mission of 'Holocaust,' as I perceive it, was to inform those without any desire to be informed, at least not during prime time when we generally use TV as a cheap way to escape realities, not to face them. So, Gerald Green as author of 'Holocaust' had to attract people in an escapist frame of mind to a real and repellent business. And thus, ironically, contradictorily, he had to make it in some sense or other *attractive*—itself and not his contemplation of it. Since he was constrained . . . by the nature of his behemoth audience from using poetical or documentary means, he was forced to be cheap and to cheapen. Green's 'Holocaust' is thus, finally, false, yet it gets some of the important facts across, because in its falseness it moves the prime-time viewer who is otherwise uninterested, and carries him to the end. If it were not false, it could not do so." Similarly, Frank Rich of *Time* asserts that the "exhaustively researched" show "demonstrates that TV's built-in limitations can become assets: they can make difficult material more accessible to a mass audience. It is hard to imagine 'Holocaust' being so effective in another format. . . . The authors have forced themselves to be equally responsive to the demands of both prime-time show biz and historical accuracy. They prove that such a marriage of commerce and art can bear remarkable fruit."

Commenting specifically on Green's screenplay, Rich continues: "Green does everything in his power to keep the audience transfixed. Once some early exposition is out of the way, his narrative races along at a relentless pace, spinning off subplots and love stories as it goes. Green knows the drama speaks for itself, so he never bothers to halt the action for gratuitous sermons. . . . He is also shrewd enough to give the audience a wide assortment of characters with which to identify. 'Holocaust's' Jews are religious and non-religious, Zionist and non-Zionist. . . . Perhaps the finest achievement is the depiction of the Germans. . . . They, too, invite audience identification—and so force us to wonder whether we might ever colloborate with an immoral government for the sake of opportunism and self-preservation." In an interview with *Time,* Green explains that "we felt it was dramatically important that the audience be able to recognize people whose religion is not a nationality, but whose nationality was a place of birth. . . . I wanted a real German family, the equivalent of American Jews who think of themselves first as Americans. We didn't want to do 'Fiddler on the Roof' Jews, although they were the prime victims of the Holocaust. We were afraid they would vitiate what we were trying to do—appeal to a broad audience." Green's attempt to create identifiable characters, in Rich's view, succeeded: "'Holocaust' attaches human faces to the inhuman statistics of mass murder. It envelops the audience in grief and suffering, and long after the show has ended, the pain does not easily go away."

In Green's opinion, the arguments concerning the artistic merit of the drama ignore the more important issue—the impact the broadcast had on the laws of West Germany and, especially, the thinking of West Germans and others. According to *Society,* a poll taken before the airing of "Holocaust" in West Germany revealed that fifteen percent of the Germans surveyed supported the continued prosecution of Nazi war criminals. After the series was presented, the survey recorded thirty-nine percent in favor of extending the statute of limitations on Nazi offenders. Stern, noting a "dramatic turnabout in attitude on the statute of limitation" in the German public and the Bundestag after the showing of "Holocaust," feels "the inherent power of drama to render a mass tragedy comprehensible by portraying the suffering and grief on an individual was demonstrated anew. That effect of 'Holocaust,' especially on postwar generations of Germans, to whom the extirpation of the Jews was at most a page in a history text, outweighed all its shortcomings." And historian John Toland, in an article in *TV Guide,* writes: "Atrocity is a human, all too human, crime and not the sole franchise of Adolf Hitler. He is dead, as is Nazi Germany, but the atrocities continue. Television must not let us forget that."

In a letter to *CA,* Gerald Green replies at length to the critics of "Holocaust," beginning by relating his producer's comments: "'Just imagine the impact the presentation would have had,' said our producer, Herbert Brodkin, 'if it had been any good.'

"I read again, with glazed eyes, the vituperation and apoplectic outbursts of the intellectual critics who detested our program. How [does one] explain these outbursts? 'The evil of banality.' 'Contemptible.' 'Cheap and cheapening.' and the favorite, 'trivialization.'

"I have my own theory. Intellectuals, particularly those of the left, and many Jewish intellectuals (sad to say), are characterized by three distressing traits—ineptitude, envy and cowardice. In the face of the onslaught of the Holocaust, they have been the essence of ineffectuality, both in resisting the mass murder of the Jews, and what is worse, in failing to make the facts known to the world. As Lucy Davidowicz points out in her recent work *The Holocaust and the Historians,* the scholars on whom we depended to explain, or more simply, to report the Final Solution, failed miserably. Why was the world still in darkness until our much-condemned 'trivialization' made three hundred million people aware of the event? Why? *Because intellectuals and elitists talk to one another; they keep little secrets; deep down they are governed by fear.* They failed; TV's 'Holocaust' succeeded. Therefore we must be denounced, excoriated, ridiculed. One deep thinker, writing in *Midstream*—one of three articles filled with condemnations usually reserved for SS *Sturmbahnfuhrers*—asked rhetorically, 'Has this program a single redeeming feature?' And responded, 'No.'

Was this fellow around to re-think his rancor when 'Holocaust' was directly responsible for changing the laws of West Germany so that Nazi war criminals could be prosecuted? Or when German schools began including Holocaust studies in their curricula? Or when German teachers began taking their students to Auschwitz? Or when West German TV—as a direct result of 'Holocaust'—first broadcast documentaries on the Nazi era and German anti-Semitism?

"It is noteworthy that in most of the general American press, magazines and newspapers, the program was praised. And why not? Journalists are keener than intellectuals. They understand the need to reach *masses* of people, to state issues in understandable terms, to personalize history. It is only when the elitists of publications like the *Nation*, the *New Republic*, *Commonweal*, etc. reviewed the program—after Wiesel's diatribe in the *New York Times*—that it was decided that the program was 'banal,' 'evil,' a comfort to the enemies of the Jews. How say they now, when the polls in West Germany show a magnum leap in anti-Nazi sentiments and in sympathy for the victims after the telecast?

"Professor Guy Stern of Wayne State University, writing in the alumni magazine of Columbia University, reveals how in his capacity as adviser to a West German group seeking to annul the statute of limitations, he counseled *against* showing the program on West German TV. *After* it ran, and created shock waves, a national surge of self-awareness, an unforeseen willingness to confront the past, Stern decided that *it had been worthwhile after all*. Indeed, it is unlikely, he says, that the laws would ever have been changed, or that Germans would *ever* have known the truth, without 'Holocaust.'

"James Shenton, the American historian, informed me—at a seminar attended by West German political scientists and journalists—that no work of fiction in history had so changed the thinking of vast groups of people, and with such impact, as did 'Holocaust,' with the possible exception of *Uncle Tom's Cabin*.

"But our intellectuals, notably those on the left, keep up their mindless attacks. As for admitting they might have been wrong, that is too much to hope for. How dare crass commercial American TV tell the world the facts of the Holocaust, when they, *they alone*, knew the truth—and managed to hide it under a welter of words, argument, vaporizing, analysis and dreary speculation.

"I have not given up all hope. Tony Schwartz, writing in the *New York Times*—a paper whose critics ran a dozen separate articles denouncing the program—recently conceded that 'Holocaust' 'did compellingly evoke . . . a very personal, very accessible portrait of the brutality of the Nazis, the horror visited on their victims, and the heartbreaking futility of most resistance.' Progress, progress.

"One need only thumb through the *New German Critique*'s special issue on 'Holocaust' (Number 19, Winter, 1980) to realize the dimensions of the wrong-headedness of American intellectuals and elitists. I could choose a score of quotes from German scholars, but this by Jean-Paul Bier sets the tone of the articles: 'More than in other countries, 'Holocaust' was an important event in the Federal Republic of Germany. Having destroyed a taboo and created a climate favorable to discussing it in the family, at school or at work, what, until now, had been repressed, it has seemingly permitted the realization that it is less a question of assuming the past than of preventing a future through recollection of the past.'

"A final surrealistic note, which perhaps illustrates most vividly the maladroit efforts of intellectual journals to destroy 'Holocaust.' I had occasion to meet the editor of the *New Republic*, Martin Peretz, some weeks after the series was aired. He, in fact, sought me out (it was a White House reception), pumped my hand eagerly and congratulated me lavishly on the program, my contributions to understanding, the way it had riveted the world's attention on the Final Solution, etc., etc.

"I thanked him, and he then said, a bit shyly, 'Of course we're giving you a bad review.' They did."

BIOGRAPHICAL/CRITICAL SOURCES: *New York Times*, October 11, 1953, February 3, 1957, April 16, 1978, April 23, 1978, April 30, 1978, October 12, 1979, February 16, 1982; *New York Herald Tribune Book Review*, February 21, 1954, February 3, 1957, April 1, 1962; *Saturday Review*, February 2, 1957, February 3, 1968, July 31, 1971, June 23, 1979; *Chicago Sunday Tribune*, February 10, 1957, April 23, 1961, March 25, 1962; *New Yorker*, March 16, 1957, September 19, 1959.

New York Times Book Review, May 27, 1962, January 9, 1966, January 28, 1968, May 16, 1971, July 11, 1971, April 10, 1977, April 16, 1978, May 6, 1979, July 22, 1979, May 11, 1980, June 7, 1981; *Atlantic*, January, 1966; *Book Week*, January 2, 1966; *Harper's*, February, 1968; *Time*, February 2, 1968, August 2, 1971, April 17, 1978, February 5, 1979; *Newsweek*, February 12, 1968, April 10, 1978, February 5, 1979; *Book World*, April 30, 1978; *New Republic*, May 13, 1978; *Commonweal*, May 26, 1978; *National Review*, May 26, 1978; *Nation*, June 24, 1978; *Washington Post*, March 17, 1979; *Times Literary Supplement*, May 9, 1980; *New German Critique*, winter, 1980; *Los Angeles Times*, June 12, 1981; *Columbia*, February, 1982; *TV Guide*, February 13-19, 1982.

—Sketch by Stewart R. Hakola

* * *

GREENBERGER, Martin 1931-

PERSONAL: Born November 30, 1931, in Elizabeth, N.J. *Education:* Harvard University, A.B. (summa cum laude), 1955, A.M., 1956, Ph.D., 1958. *Home:* 336 F St. N.E., Washington, D.C. 20002. *Office:* Department of Mathematical Sciences, Johns Hopkins University, Baltimore, Md. 21218.

CAREER: Harvard University, Cambridge, Mass., member of staff of computation laboratory, 1954-56; International Business Machines (IBM), Cambridge, manager of the applied science Cambridge group, 1956-58; Massachusetts Institute of Technology, Alfred P. Sloan School of Management, Cambridge, assistant professor, 1958-61, associate professor of management, 1961-67; Johns Hopkins University, Baltimore, Md., professor of computer science, 1967-71, professor of mathematical sciences, 1971—, chairman of chairman of computer science and director of information processing, both 1967-71. Visiting professor, University of California, Berkeley, 1965-66, and Stanford University, 1980; Isaac Taylor Visiting Professor of Energy, Technion-Israel Institute of Technology, 1978. Chairman of council and member of board of trustees, Interuniversity Communications Council, 1968-73; organizer of Hopkins-Brookings symposium, Computers, Communications, and the Public Interest, 1969, and of National Science Foundation workshop, Computer Networks in Research and Education, 1973; member of visiting committee, Office for Information Technology, 1975-81; manager of systems program, Electric Power Research Institute, 1976-78. Witness before Committee on Science and Technology, U.S. House of Representatives, June, 1981. Chairman of advisory committee, Brookhaven National Center for Analysis of Energy Systems,

1977-80; consultant to Brookings Institution and the National Science Foundation.

MEMBER: Association for Computing Machinery, National Academy of Sciences (member of computer science and engineering board, 1970-73), American Association for the Advancement of Science (fellow; chairman of Section on Information, Computing, and Communications, 1974-76), Phi Beta Kappa, Sigma Xi.

AWARDS, HONORS: National Science Foundation fellowship, 1955-56; Guggenheim fellowship, 1965-66; National Science Foundation grants, 1968-75, 1971-72, 1972-73, and 1975; International Business Machines grant, 1968-75; American Federation of Information Processing Societies grant, 1969-71; Alfred P. Sloan Foundation grant, 1969-71; National Institute of Health grant, 1970-72; Russell Sage Foundation grant, 1972-73; Rockefeller Foundation grant, 1978-81.

WRITINGS: (With Guy H. Orcutt, John Korbel, and Alice M. Rivlin) *Microanalysis of Socioeconomic Systems*, Harper, 1961; (editor) *Management and the Computer of the Future*, M.I.T. Press, 1962, published as *Computers and the World of the Future*, 1964; (with Malcolm Jones, James R. Morris, and David N. Ness) *On-Line Computation and Simulation: The OPS-3 System*, M.I.T. Press, 1965; (editor) *Computers, Communications, and the Public Interest*, Johns Hopkins Press, 1972; (editor with Julius Aronofsky, James L. McKenny, and William F. Massy) *Computer Networks in Research and Education: Sharing Information Resources Nationwide*, M.I.T. Press, 1974; (with Matthew A. Crenson and Brian L. Crissey) *Models in the Policy Process: Public Decision Models in the Computer Era*, Russell Sage Foundation, 1976. Also author, with others, of *Caught Unawares: Mobilization of Analysis for Energy Policy*, in press.

Contributor: (With Robert K. Guthrie) *Drilling and Production Practice*, American Petroleum Institute, 1955; J. N. Buxton, editor, *Simulation Programming Languages*, North-Holland, 1967; James M. Beshers, editor, *Computer Methods in the Analysis of Large-Scale Social Systems*, M.I.T. Press, 1967; Charles R. Walker, editor, *Technology, Industry, and Man: The Age of Acceleration*, McGraw, 1968; Zenon W. Pylyshyn, editor, *Perspectives on the Computer Revolution*, Prentice-Hall, 1970; *The Financing and Organization of Computing in Higher Education*, Educom (Princeton, N.J.), 1971; M. Marois, editor, *Man and Computer*, North-Holland, 1975; Robert H. Haveman and Kevin Hollenbeck, editors, *Microeconomic Simulation Models for Public Policy Analysis*, Volume I, Academic Press, 1980; Saul I. Gass, editor, *Validation and Assessment of Energy Models*, National Bureau of Standards, 1981; Rudy Yaksick, editor, *Workshop on Nonfuels Minerals Demand Modeling*, two volumes, National Research Council, 1981; R. Amit and M. Avriel, editors, *Perspectives on Resource Policy Modeling: Energy and Minerals*, Ballinger, 1982.

Author of special reports for Harvard University, RAND Corporation, U.S. Navy, International Business Machines, Columbia Broadcasting System, Federal Reserve System, and Massachusetts Institute of Technology. Contributor to proceedings of International Conference on Operational Research, 1961, National Automation Conference, 1965, International Federation for Information Processing, 1965, Computer Simulation Conference, 1975, and Energy Technology Conference, 1979. Contributor to *Encyclopedia Americana*, 1967. Contributor to *Atlantic Monthly*, *Scientific American*, *Science*, *Baltimore Sun*, and *Johns Hopkins Magazine*; contributor to professional journals, including *Industrial Management Review*, *Mathematics of Computation*, *Technology Review*, *Management Science*, *Law and Computer Technology*, and *Sloan Management Review*.

* * *

GREENE, Constance C(larke) 1924-

PERSONAL: Born October 27, 1924, in New York, N.Y.; daughter of Richard W. (a newspaper editor) and Mabel (a writer; maiden name, McElliott) Clarke; married Philip M. Greene (a radio station owner), June, 1946; children: Sheppard, Philippa, Stephanie, Matthew, Lucia. *Education:* Attended Skidmore College, 1942-44. *Politics:* Democrat. *Religion:* Roman Catholic. *Residence:* East Hampton, Long Island, N.Y., 11937. *Agent:* Marilyn Marlow, Curtis Brown Ltd., 575 Madison Ave., New York, N.Y. 10022.

CAREER: Writer.

WRITINGS—Juveniles; published by Viking: *A Girl Called Al*, 1969; *Leo the Lioness*, 1970; *Good Luck Bogie Hat*, 1971; *Unmaking of Rabbit*, 1972; *Isabelle the Itch*, 1973; *The Ears of Louis*, 1974; *I Know You, Al*, 1975; *Beat the Turtle Drum*, 1976; *Getting Nowhere*, 1977; *I and Sproggy*, 1978; *Your Old Pal, Al*, 1979; *Dotty's Suitcase*, 1980; *Double-Dare O'Toole*, 1981; *Al(exandra) the Great*, 1982.

WORK IN PROGRESS: A story about a girl who lives in Maine.

SIDELIGHTS: "I started writing when I was ten," Constance C. Greene told *CA*. "I aim to entertain, not to instruct. I also aim to make children laugh, not only at others, but at themselves, a much harder thing to do. I would also like children to feel, to have some emotion aroused by my books. I don't care what emotion it is, but I would like them to feel something when they've finished—preferably a little bit better, or happier than they were before they started, but any emotion beats none at all."

MEDIA ADAPTATIONS: Beat the Turtle Drum was filmed as an after-school special by American Broadcasting Co.

BIOGRAPHICAL/CRITICAL SOURCES: Saturday Review, April 19, 1969; *New York Times Book Review*, November 4, 1973, November 15, 1975, February 15, 1981.

* * *

GREER, Herb 1929-

PERSONAL: Born August 22, 1929, in Santa Fe, N.M. *Education:* Fresno State College (now California State University, Fresno), B.A. (honors), 1950; additional study at University of Washington, Seattle, at University College, London, and at Bristol Old Vic Theatre School. *Agent:* Anthony Sheil Associates Ltd., 2-3 Morwell St., London WC1B 3AR, England.

CAREER: Actor, composer, photo-journalist, and writer.

WRITINGS: A Scattering of Dust, Hutchinson, 1962; *The Trip*, Hutchinson, 1963; *Mud Pie*, Parrish, 1964; *Hard Journey*, Parrish, 1964, published as *The Short Cut*, Roy, 1965; *All Change and Other Plays*, Calder & Boyars, 1973.

Also author of plays: "Free Forever," 1967; "Kill, Kill," 1968; "To Kill Barbarians," 1969; "Po Miss Julie" (produced in London at the Hampstead Theatre Club, 1972), 1971; "Embers," 1971; "Kill the Kids," 1972; "The New Forever Robe," 1973; "Roger, Bart, and Mackie," 1974; "Spartan Broth," 1975; "Act of Triumph," 1976; "Rosie," 1977. Contributor to *New Directions 13*, *Observer*, *New Statesman*, *Spectator*, *Transatlantic Review*, *Toronto Star*, to other periodicals, and to British Broadcasting Corp.

WORK IN PROGRESS: Three novels, *The Enemy, A Circling Fire,* and an untitled satirical work; plays.

SIDELIGHTS: Herb Greer speaks French, German, Spanish, Italian, Polish. *Avocational interests:* Scuba diving, underwater photography.†

*   *   *

GREGORY, Violet L(efler)   1907-

PERSONAL: Born January 19, 1907, in Ontario, Canada; daughter of Lewis (a farmer) and Alice (a music teacher; maiden name, Hughes) Lefler; married Allen Shelby Pruett, August 2, 1927 (divorced March 1, 1933); married Walter B. Gregory, August 9, 1947 (died July 18, 1963); children: (first marriage) Gerald Allen Pruett. *Education:* Attended University of California, San Diego, 1961-66; San Diego City College, A.A., 1967; San Diego State College (now University), B.A., 1972. *Religion:* Protestant. *Home:* 1401 North Flower, Apt. 511, Santa Ana, Calif. 92706.

CAREER: Western Union Telegraph Co., Detroit, Mich., file clerk, 1925-27; Harper Hospital, Detroit, nurse's aide, 1931-38; Lady Madison Hosiery Co., Detroit, store manager, 1938-40; Palmer House Restaurant, Detroit, receptionist, 1940-41; Jewel Tea Co., Detroit, route manager, 1941-46; Grace Holmes Club Plan, Newark, N.J., correspondent, 1949-53; Little Corner Store, Lyndhurst, N.J., owner, 1953-55; Star Market, San Diego, Calif., owner, 1956-59; Gregory Distributors, San Diego, owner, 1961-64; tutor in literature interpretation and free-lance writer, 1972—.

MEMBER: World Poetry Society (India), International Poetry Society (fellow), National League of American Pen Women (vice-president of San Diego branch, 1966-68; president, 1970-72), California Federation of Chaparral Poets, California State Poetry Society, Pennsylvania Poetry Society. *Awards, honors:* Sweepstake prize, Forest Lawn Foundation and California Federation of Chaparral Poets, 1966, for "No Questions Asked," and 1967, for "In Myriad Containers"; recipient of about forty additional awards for poetry, 1961—.

WRITINGS—Poems: *Mixed Bouquet,* Centro Studi E Scambi Internazionale (Rome), 1966; *The Silver Link,* Dorrance, 1969; *Full Circle,* Branden Press, 1974; *Toward New Plateaus,* Pierce Publishing, 1978; *Etchings on the Sand,* Friis-Pioneer Press, 1980.

Contributor of poems to anthologies: Lilith Lorraine, editor, *The Minds Create,* Different Press, 1961; Lincoln B. Young, editor, *Poetry Parade,* Young Publications, 1963; Young, editor, *Rhymetime for the Very Young,* Young Publications, 1964; B. K. Shaw, editor, *Spring Anthology,* Mitre Press, 1968; Evelyn Petry, editor, *Clover Collection of Verse,* Clover Publishing, 1972; Ernest Kay, editor, *International Who's Who in Poetry Anthology,* Melrose Press, 1973; Robin Gregory, editor, *Ipso Facto: An I.P.S. Anthology,* Hub Publications, 1975. Contributor of 450 articles and poems to periodicals.

WORK IN PROGRESS: Kaleidoscope, a prose manuscript; research on modern poetry and on poets' works and techniques.

SIDELIGHTS: Violet L. Gregory's *Full Circle* has been described by Edward L. Meyerson of *Poet* as "a circumscribed concept of life, bounded by horizons of unravelings and fulfillments; [a] sphere of calm seas and turbulent storms, and inevitable anchorage. . . . Emotionally and structurally, *Full Circle* traverses the symbolic circle and emerges whole."

The poet writes to *CA:* "I began writing poems and stories when a small child, often using a composition book as combined journal and scrapbook. Not until 1960 was any attempt made to publish. Now there are 2000 copies of my books in various homes or libraries, all poetry!

"What happened to the prose that started out on equal footing? Part of it is in assorted envelopes, many of them packed and re-packed through all the various moves a fully rounded life contains. Ironically, part of the blame can rest on the success of the poems I *did* write and submitted to contests; then editors compounded the problem by paying me cash (from thirty-five cents to one dollar a line) in those early days.

"These creative happenings have brought floods of inner happiness, even smoothing away the sharp edges of loss and pain. Because I wanted to share this unexplained joy with others, I assembled certain poems in a book manuscript and [published them]. Many of the letters I received testify that this sharing had been a bonus in other lives as well; some writers even sending extra money 'toward your next book.' So another manuscript of poetry was prepared, another publisher was secured, then a repeat performance for more books.

"Life moves along, so irrevocably! Over a year ago I promised myself: I will work on *prose* only. Difficulties appeared almost week after week (none having to do with writing). But now I can actually say that a manuscript of 'mood pieces' is in process. Since these pieces stem from [a long] exercise with words, I am tempted to grieve over all the childish or teen-age spontaneity lost forever; I am not alone in this for very few writers see all of their dreams fulfilled. There is an old saying, something along these lines: 'Our stars always exceed our reach.' That's what stars are for!"

BIOGRAPHICAL/CRITICAL SOURCES: Poet (India), December, 1978.

*   *   *

GRENE, Marjorie (Glicksman)   1910-

PERSONAL: Born December 13, 1910, in Milwaukee, Wis.; daughter of Harry (a professor of English) and Edna (Kerngood) Glicksman; divorced; children: Ruth, Nicholas. *Education:* Wellesley College, B.A., 1931; graduate study at University of Freiburg, 1931-32, and at University of Heidelberg, 1932-33; Radcliffe College, M.A., 1934, Ph.D., 1935. *Home:* 206 Ridgedale Rd., Ithaca, N.Y. 14850. *Office:* Department of Philosophy, University of California, Davis, Calif. 95616.

CAREER: Monticello College, Godfrey, Illinois, instructor, 1936-37; University of Chicago, Chicago, Ill., instructor in philosophy, 1937-44; University of Manchester, Manchester, England, research assistant, 1957-58; University of Leeds, Leeds, England, research fellow in education, 1958-59, lecturer in philosophy, 1959-60; The Queen's University of Belfast, Belfast, Northern Ireland, lecturer in philosophy, 1960-65; University of California, Davis, professor of philosophy, 1965-78, professor emeritus, 1978—, faculty research lecturer, 1971. Alice Freeman Palmer Fellow, Wellesley College, 1935-36; Lucy Martin Donnelloy Fellow, Bryn Mawr College, 1960-61; visiting professor, University of Texas at Austin, 1967-68, Boston University, 1972, and University of Goettingen, 1973; Mellon Professor of Humanities, Tulane University, fall, 1978; visiting professor, Temple University, spring, 1979, Rutgers University, fall, 1979, University of California, Berkeley, spring, 1980, Yale University, fall, 1980, and University of Waterloo, spring, 1981; U.S. University Professor, Boston University, spring, 1982.

MEMBER: American Academy of Arts and Sciences (fellow), American Association for Advanced Science (fellow), Metaphysical Society of America (president, 1975—), Society for Phenomenology and Existential Philosophy, American Philosophical Association (president of Pacific Division, 1971-72). *Awards, honors:* D.H.L., Tulane University, 1980.

WRITINGS: Dreadful Freedom, a Critique of Existentialism, University of Chicago Press, 1948, published as *Introduction to Existentialism,* University of Chicago Press, 1959; *Heidegger,* Hillary, 1957; *A Portrait of Aristotle,* University of Chicago Press, 1963; *The Knower and the Known,* Basic Books, 1969; *Approaches to a Philosophical Biology,* Basic Books, 1971; *Sartre,* F. Watts, 1973; *The Understanding of Nature,* Reidel, 1974; *Philosophy in and out of Europe and Other Essays,* University of California Press, 1976.

Editor: (With Thomas Vernor Smith) *From Descartes to Kant,* University of Chicago Press, 1940; (with Smith) *Philosophers Speak for Themselves,* University of Chicago Press, 1957; *Toward a Unity of Knowledge,* International University Press, 1969; *The Anatomy of Knowledge,* University of Massachusetts Press, 1969; Michael Polanyi, *Knowing and Being,* Routledge & Kegan Paul, 1969; *Interpretations of Life and Mind: Essays around the Problem of Reduction,* Humanities, 1971; *Spinoza,* Doubleday, 1973; (with E. Mendelsohn) *Topics in the Philosophy of Biology,* Reidel, 1976.

Also translator of a book by Helmuth Plessner. Contributor of articles and reviews to philosophy journals.

* * *

GRESHAM, Claude Hamilton, Jr. 1922-
(Grits Gresham)

PERSONAL: Born June 21, 1922, in Spartanburg County, S.C.; son of Claude Hamilton and Belle (Hill) Gresham; married Mary Ellen Ryan, February 8, 1944; children: Barbara Lea, Thomas Hamilton, Gary Kent. *Education:* Attended University of North Carolina, 1941-43, and Vanderbilt University; Louisiana State University, B.S. in Forestry, 1949, M.S. in Game Management, 1950. *Religion:* Presbyterian. *Home:* 942 Williams Ave., Natchitoches, La. 71457.

CAREER: Free-lance writer-photographer. U.S. Fish and Wildlife Service, Paris, Tenn., refuge manager, 1950-51; Arizona Game and Fish Commission, Phoenix, chief of Information-Education Division, 1951-52; Louisiana Wild Life and Fisheries Commission, New Orleans, editor of *Louisiana Conservationist,* 1953-55; *Shreveport Times,* Shreveport, La., outdoor editor, 1955-73; field host and producer of "The American Sportsman" series, American Broadcast Companies (ABC), 1966-79; currently host of "Sports Afield" syndicated television series. Owner-operator of hunting and fishing resort in Natchitoches, La., 1955-57. Member of executive board, Victor Recreation Products Group. Lecturer at banquets, sport shows, and conventions. Former consultant to Braniff Airlines; consultant to outdoor industries, manufacturers of recreational vehicles, and producers of outdoor television commercials. *Military service:* U.S. Army Air Forces, 1943-46; served as electronics officer; became first lieutenant.

MEMBER: Outdoor Writers Association of America (president, 1962-63; chairman of board, 1963-64), Society of American Foresters, National Rifle Association, Wildlife Society, Louisiana Outdoors Writers Association (president, 1955), Louisiana Forestry Association (member of board of directors, 1961—), African Safari Club of New York, Phi Kappa Phi. *Awards, honors:* Outstanding Conservationist of the Year in Louisiana, 1959; Winchester Outdoorsman of the Year, 1978; Alumnus of the Year, School of Forestry and Wildlife Management, Louisiana State University, 1979.

WRITINGS—Under name Grits Gresham: *Fishing and Boating in Louisiana,* Tam Publications, 1958; *Fishes & Fishing in Louisiana,* Claitor's Book Store, 1965; *The Complete Book of Bass Fishing,* Harper, 1966; *The Sportsman and His Family Outdoors,* Dutton, 1969; *The Complete Wildfowler,* Winchester Press, 1973.

Contributor: *The Compact Book of Hunting,* J. Lowell Pratt, 1963; *The Compact Book of Fresh Water Fishing,* J. Lowell Pratt, 1963; *Fishing Moments of Truth,* Winchester Press, 1973; *Hunting Moments of Truth,* Winchester Press, 1973; *Hunting America's Game Animals and Birds,* Winchester Press, 1975.

Contributor of photographs and articles to periodicals, including *Sports Illustrated, Gentlemen's Quarterly, Field and Stream, Argosy, True,* and *Outdoor Life.* Shooting editor, *Sports Afield,* 1974—.

WORK IN PROGRESS: A novel about Natchitoches, the oldest town in the Louisiana Purchase.

SIDELIGHTS: Grits Gresham has participated in numerous pro-am gold tournaments and has appeared in television commercials for Lite beer. *Avocational interests:* Golf, music, boating, fishing, hunting.

BIOGRAPHICAL/CRITICAL SOURCES: Shreveport Magazine, October, 1962.

* * *

GRESHAM, Grits
See GRESHAM, Claude Hamilton, Jr.

* * *

GRIFFITHS, Richard M(athias) 1935-

PERSONAL: Born June 21, 1935, in Barry, Glamorganshire, Wales; son of William Thomas (a solicitor) and Evelyn (Hill) Griffiths; married Patricia Youles, June 26, 1971; children: Dominic, Hilary, Katharine. *Education:* Attended Lancing College, 1948-53; King's College, Cambridge, B.A., 1957, M.A. and Ph.D., 1961. *Politics:* Conservative. *Religion:* Anglican. *Office:* Department of French, University College, Cardiff, Wales.

CAREER: Cambridge University, Selwyn College, Cambridge, England, fellow in modern languages, 1960-66, dean of College, 1962-65; Oxford University, Oxford, England, fellow in modern languages at Brasenose College, 1966-74, lecturer at Queen's College, 1966-74; University College, Cardiff, Wales, professor of French and head of department, 1974—. Governor, Lancing College, 1962-80; fellow, Corporation of St. Mary and St. Nicholas (Woodard Schools), 1962—; member, Welsh Arts Council, 1980—. City councillor, Oxford, 1968-72. *Member:* Society for French Studies, Honourable Society of Cymmrodorion, Societe Huysmans (member of committee), Coningsby Club, Carlton Club, Athenaeum Club.

WRITINGS: (Translator and author of introduction and notes) *Parisian Sketches* (translation of Joris Karl Huysmans' *Croquis Parisiens*), Fortune Press, 1961; *The Reactionary Revolution: The Catholic Revival in French Literature, 1870-1914,* Constable, 1966; (editor) *Claudel: A Reappraisal,* Rapp & Whiting, 1968; *Marshal Petain,* Constable, 1970, published as *Petain,* Doubleday, 1972; *The Dramatic Technique of Antoine de Montchrestien,* Clarendon Press, 1970; *Montherlant: Port-Royal,* Basil Blackwell, 1976; *Impersonation,* University College, Cardiff, 1977; *Fellow Travellers of the Right: British Enthusiasts for Nazi Germany, 1933-1939,* Constable, 1980. Contributor to periodicals, including *Spectator, Times Literary*

Supplement, Sunday Times, French Studies, and *Modern Language Review.* Editor, *Cambridge Review,* 1962-63.

WORK IN PROGRESS: Research on religion and literature in France, French Renaissance tragedy, and French public opinion and England, 1880-1980.

SIDELIGHTS: Richard M. Griffiths's *Fellow Travellers of the Right* is a survey of the range of pro-German sentiment in England immediately before the Second World War. "Griffiths is splendidly equipped to examine British attitudes in a wider context," Stephen Koss writes in the *Times Literary Supplement.* "His knowledge compels him to reject conspiracy theories, and to recognize 'the very variety of motivation . . . which creates the difficulty of making too many generalisations' about contemporaries who pleaded the case for Hitler's Germany. Many of them prove to have been well-meaning individuals, determined above all else to avoid the dreaded prospect of war," Kos continues. "Others derived their sympathies from a despondency with democracy, which had revealed its apparent incapacity to sustain a healthy capitalism and promote a vigorous patriotism." In *Listener,* Anthony Howard notes that the list of Nazi sympathizers included "members of the Royal House, pillars of the Church, leaders of the British Legion—to say nothing of the more populist-minded Tory MPs." Griffiths's "singular achievement," Koss believes, "has been to make [these pro-German] attitudes credible, if hardly creditable. In an enthralling survey, . . . he deals with the men, women, fringe organizations, periodicals, all obstensibly qualifying as 'fellow travellers of the right.' Tracing the evolution of their thought and contacts . . . , he points up the inconsistencies and often utter illogic of his subjects."

"What now seems extraordinary is the willingness on the part of these lofty-principled people to excuse and play down the evil sides of Hitler's Reich," Hugh Cecil observes in *Spectator.* Koss points out that most of these sympathizers "hurriedly disembarked" when Hitler's expansionism became evident. "Strategic considerations, and not German persecution of the Jews nor any other aspect of Hitler's domestic policy, were . . . the decisive factor," Koss states. "The thought is sobering and, as documented here, wholly convincing." And in the *London Times,* Michael Radcliffe concludes: "Throughout Richard Griffiths's absorbing and scholarly disentanglement of hindsight and myth . . . we never lose sight of two things. The first is that . . . to the vast majority of the British population, struggling to work and play and live, the Nazis were foreign and of remote concern. The second is hindsight's cruellest deception of all. It is the flattery that had we been present at the time we [would] have handled matters very differently. Nobody could read this sobering . . . book and be quite sure of that."

AVOCATIONAL INTERESTS: Conservative politics, music, jazz, lawn bowls, wine, food, conversation.

BIOGRAPHICAL/CRITICAL SOURCES: *Times Literary Supplement,* September 25, 1969, October 23, 1970, March 12, 1971, October 24, 1980; *Economist,* November 7, 1970; *Spectator,* November 7, 1970, October 25, 1980; *Book World,* April 16, 1972; *New York Times Book Review,* May 14, 1972; *Modern Age,* summer, 1978; *New Statesman,* September 5, 1980; *London Times,* September 11, 1980; *Listener,* October 23, 1980.

* * *

GRIMM, Reinhold 1931-

PERSONAL: Born May 21, 1931, in Nuremberg, Germany (now West Germany); came to United States in 1967; son of Eugen (a laborer) and Anna (Kaeser) Grimm; married Anneliese E. Schmidt, September 25, 1954; children: Ruth Sabine. *Education:* Attended University of Colorado, 1952-53; Erlangen University, Ph.D., 1956. *Home:* 3983 Plymouth Circle, Madison, Wis. 53705. *Office:* Department of German, University of Wisconsin, Madison, Wis. 53706.

CAREER: Erlangen University, Erlangen, West Germany, assistant professor of German literature, 1957-61; Frankfurt University, Frankfurt, West Germany, assistant professor of German literature, 1961-67; University of Wisconsin—Madison, Alexander Hohlfeld Professor of German, 1967-80, Vilas Professor of Comparative Literature and German, 1980—. Visiting professor, New York University and Columbia University, both 1967, University of Florida, 1973, and University of Virginia, 1978. *Member:* Modern Language Association of America, American Association of Teachers of German (president, 1974-75). *Awards, honors:* Foerderungspreis der Stadt Nuernberg, 1964; Guggenheim fellow, 1969-70; Institute for Research in the Humanities fellow, 1981.

WRITINGS: *Gottfried Benn: Die farbliche Chiffre in der Dichtung* (title means "Gottfried Benn: The Color-Emblem in Literature"), H. Carl (Nuremberg), 1958, 2nd edition, 1962; *Bertolt Brecht: Die Struktur seines Werkes* (title means "Bertolt Brecht: The Structure of His Work"), H. Carl, 1959, 6th edition, 1972; *Bertolt Brecht,* J. B. Metzler, 1961, 3rd revised edition, 1971; *Bertolt Brecht und die Weltliteratur* (title means "Bertolt Brecht and World Literature"), H. Carl, 1961; (with Heinz Otto Burger) *Evokation und Montage: Drei Beitraege zum Verstaendnis moderner deutscher Lyrik* (title means "Evocation and Montage: Three Contributions towards an Understanding of Modern German Poetry"), Sachse & Pohl, 1961, revised edition, 1967; *Strukturen: Essays zur deutschen Literatur* (title means "Structures: Essays on German Literature"), Sachse & Pohl, 1963; (author of afterword) Denis Diderot, *Das Paradox ueber den Schauspieler* (title means "The Paradox of the Comedian"), Insel Verlag, 1964.

(With others) *Romanticism Today: Friedrich Schlegel, Novalis, E.T.A. Hoffmann, Ludwig Tieck,* Inter Nationes (Bonn), 1973; *Nach dem Naturalismus: Essays zur modernen Dramatik,* Athenaeum Verlag, 1978; *Brecht und Nietzsche oder Gestandnisse eiues Dichters,* Suhrkamp, 1979; *Von der Armut und vom Regen: Rilkes Autwort auf die soziale Frage,* Athenaeum Verlag, 1981.

Editor or compiler: (With Wolf-Dieter Marsch) *Die Kunst im Schatten des Gottes: Fuer und wider Gottfried Benn,* Sachse & Pohl, 1962; (with Viktor Zmegac) Iwan Goll, *Methusalem oder Der ewige Buerger: Ein satirisches Drama* (title means "Methusalah or the Eternal Bourgeois: A Satiric Drama"), de Gruyter, 1966; *Episches Theater* (title means "Epic Theater"), Kiepenheuer & Witsch, 1966, 3rd edition, 1972; *Zur Lyrik-Diskussion* (title means "Concerning the Lyric"), Wissenschaftliche Buchgesellschaft, 1966, 2nd edition, 1974; (and author of introduction) *Deutsche Romantheorien: Beitraege zu einer historischen Poetik des Romans in Deutschland* (title means "German Theories of the Novel: Essays towards a Historical Poetics of the Novel in Germany"), Athenaeum Verlag, 1968, 2nd edition, 1974; *Bertolt Brecht: Leben Eduards des Zweiten von England; Vorlage, Texte und Materialien* (title means "Bertolt Brecht: The Life of Edward II of England; Sources, Texts and Materials"), Suhrkamp, 1968; (with Conrad Wiedemann) *Literatur und Geistesgeschichte: Festgabe fuer Heinz Otto Burger* (title means "Literature and History: A Congratulatory Volume for Heinz Otto Burger"), E. Schmidt, 1968; (with Jost Hermand and author of introduction) *Deutsche*

Revolutionsdramen (title means "German Dramas of Revolution"), Suhrkamp, 1969.

(With Henry J. Schmidt) *Brecht Fibel* (title means "Brecht Primer"), Harper, 1970; (and author of introduction) *Deutsche Dramentheorien: Beitraege zu einer historischen Poetik des Dramas in Deutschland* (title means "German Theories of the Drama: Essays towards a Historical Poetics of the Drama in Germany"), Athenaeum Verlag, 1971, 3rd edition, 1981; (with Klaus L. Berghahn) *Schiller: Zur Theorie und Praxis der Dramen* (title means "Schiller: Theory and Practice of His Plays"), Wissenschaftliche Buchgesellschaft, 1972, 2nd edition, 1981; (with Hermand) *Methodenfragen der deutschen Literaturwissenschaft* (title means "Methodological Problems in German Literary Criticism"), Wissenschaftliche Buchgesellschaft, 1973; (with Helene Scher) Friedrich Duerrenmatt, *Die Ehe des Herrn Mississippi: Eine Komoedie* (title means "The Marriage of Mr. Mississippi: A Comedy"), Holt, 1973; (with Peter Spycher and Richard Zipser) *From Kafka and Dada to Brecht and Beyond*, University of Wisconsin Press, 1982.

Editor, with Jost Hermand, of thirteen volumes sponsored by Deutsche Abtelung of University of Wisconsin, including *Die sogenannten Zwanziger Jahre* (title means "The So-Called Twenties"), Gehlen, 1970, *Die Klassik-Legende* (title means "The Myth of Classicism"), Athenaeum Verlag, 1971, and *Exil und innere Emigration* (title means "Exile and Inner Emigration"), Athenaeum Verlag, 1972. Editor or co-editor of yearbooks and journals, mainly on German and comparative literature, including *Monatshefte*, 1967—, *German Studies*, 1969—, and *Text und Kontext*, 1978—.

WORK IN PROGRESS: A book on research on the black man in German literature.

* * *

GROL, Lini R(icharda) 1913-

PERSONAL: Born October 7, 1913, in Nijmegen, the Netherlands; daughter of Johannes and Catharine (Engel) Grol. *Education:* Trained in the Netherlands for R.N. and public health nursing; writing courses at McMaster University, Brock University, and Columbia University. *Politics:* Conservative. *Religion:* Christian. *Home and studio:* Fonthill Studio, 53 South Pelham St., Fonthill, Ontario, Canada L0S 1E0.

CAREER: Free-lance writer and artist. Formerly employed as a nurse in the Netherlands and Ontario, Canada. Instructor and lecturer in scissorcraft; has exhibited scissor-cut illustrations in the Netherlands and at art gallerys and libraries in Ontario; has hosted two local television programs on arts and crafts. Has read her poetry for audiences in the Netherlands, Canada, and the United States.

MEMBER: Canadian Authors Association, Professional Association of Women Writers, Canadian Association for the Advancement of Netherlands Studies, St. Catharines Arts Council, Hamilton Arts Council, Niagara Falls Arts Association (Ontario), Media Club. *Awards, honors:* Molson Award, for illustration of *Lelawala: The Maid of the Mist*.

WRITINGS—Published by Trillium Books (Fonthill Studio), except as indicated: *Repetiuorium* (title means "Referendum for the Mental Nursing Student"), De Bussy, 1950; (self-illustrated) *Silent Thoughts and Silhouettes* (poems), 1967; (self-illustrated) *Scissorcraft*, Sterling, 1970; *The Bellfounder's Sons* (juvenile), Bobbs-Merrill, 1971; (self-illustrated) *Lelawala: The Maid of the Mist* (juvenile), 1972; (self-illustrated) *Tales from the Niagara Peninsula*, 1973; *De Overjas* (serialized novel in Dutch), Courant, 1973; (self-illustrated) *Three Fables* (juvenile), 1974; (self-illustrated) *Insiders or Outsiders* (poems), 1974; (self-illustrated) *Mix and Match* (short stories), 1975; (self-illustrated) *Magic Gifts* (Christmas stories), 1975; *Midnight Musings*, 1978; *Pelham as It Is and Was*, 1980; *Heartsongs*, Baker Book, 1980. Also author of *Mine and Thine*, a volume of poems.

Editor and illustrator of *Cameos, 1, 2, 3*, by D. C. Smith, *Weeds and Other Flowers*, by J. Kinsella, *Yesterday's Moons*, by W. Blizzard, and *We and You: An Anthology of Canadian Poetry*. Book reviewer, *Pelham Herald*. Contributor of stories, articles, poems, and illustrations to magazines in the Netherlands, England, Canada, and the United States.

WORK IN PROGRESS: Two novels, *Out of the Dark* and *The Stepmother*.

SIDELIGHTS: Lini R. Grol writes: "My viewpoints can be found in my writing and depend very much on the audience, age or theme I try to convey. I am a Christian and rather conservative in my views. Consideration of the fellowmen, especially the children, is my main theme in life."

Three of Grol's poems were read at the National Arts Center in Ottawa on May 17, 1970, as part of the program marking the 25th anniversary of the liberation of the Netherlands. The celebration was organized by Canadians from the Netherlands.

BIOGRAPHICAL/CRITICAL SOURCES: The St. Catharine's Standard, May 25, 1972.

* * *

GROSS, Harvey S(eymour) 1922-

PERSONAL: Born March 6, 1922, in Cleveland, Ohio; son of Jack and Sadie (Gross) Gross; married Virginia La Rue (a teacher), June 25, 1949; children: Joseph Warren, Daniel La Rue. *Education:* University of California, Los Angeles, B.A., 1947, M.A., 1949; attended University of Vienna, 1951-52; University of Michigan, Ph.D., 1955. *Home:* 5 Hilltop Rd., Stony Brook, N.Y. 11790. *Office:* Program in Comparative Literature, State University of New York at Stony Brook, Stony Brook, N.Y. 11794.

CAREER: Hofstra College (now University), Hempstead, N.Y., instructor in English, 1954-57; University of Denver, Denver, Colo., 1957-65, began as assistant professor, became professor of English; University of California, Irvine, associate professor of English, 1965-74; State University of New York at Stony Brook, professor of comparative literature, 1974-. Visiting professor at University of Southern California, Irvine, 1978-79. *Military service:* U.S. Army Air Forces, 1942-45; became staff sergeant. *Member:* Modern Language Association of America, National Council of Teachers of English, American Comparative Literature Association, Michigan Academy of Science, Arts, and Letters. *Awards, honors:* Fulbright award to Austria, 1951-52; Avery and Jule Hopwood Award in creative writing, University of Michigan, 1953; Folger Library fellow, 1964; American Council of Learned Societies fellow, 1965-67; Rockefeller Foundation grant, 1967; Huntington Library fellow, 1977; National Endowment for the Humanities grant, 1981; National Humanities Center fellow, 1981-82.

WRITINGS: Sound and Form in Modern Poetry, University of Michigan Press, 1964; (editor and author of introduction) *The Structure of Verse: Modern Essays on Prosody*, Fawcett, 1966, revised edition, Ecco Press, 1979; *Plans for an Orderly Apocalypse and Other Poems*, University of Michigan Press, 1968; *The Contrived Corridor: History and Fatality in Modern Literature*, University of Michigan Press, 1971; (editor with Myron Simon) *Teacher and Critic*, Plantin, 1976; (editor) *Eras-*

mus, *The Praise of Folly,* [Malibu], 1979. Contributor to *Encyclopaedia Britannica,* 1974. Contributor to *Centennial Review, Commentary, Prairie Schooner,* and other journals.

* * *

GROSSU, Sergiu 1920-

PERSONAL: Born November 14, 1920, in Cubolta, Rumania; son of Ion and Maria (Cudalbu) Grossu; married Nicole-Valerie Bruteanu, April 24, 1957. *Education:* Bucharest University, B.A., 1947. *Religion:* Orthodox. *Office:* Catacombes, B.P. 79, 92405 Courbevoie, France.

CAREER: Journalist in Rumanian Ministry of Propaganda, 1941-43; employed as civil servant, 1950-58, 1962-69; *Catacombes,* Paris, France, editor, 1971—. Preacher on Rumanian religious program broadcast in Paris, 1971—. *Military service:* Rumanian Army Reserve, 1943-45; became lieutenant. *Member:* Arts et Lettres de France, La Chaine, Presence de Gabriel Marcel.

WRITINGS: Nous attendons une nouvelle terre (title means "We Look for a New Earth"), La Pensee Universelle, 1971; *La Chaine* (poems; title means "The Chain"), Les Paragraphes litteraires de Paris, 1971, 2nd edition, 1973; *Un rayon de soleil* (poems; title means "A Beam of Sunshine"), Debresse-Poesie, 1971; (editor) *The Church in Today's Catacombs,* Arlington House, 1975; *Derriere le rideau de Bambou* (title means "Behind the Bamboo Curtain"), Editions des Catacombes, 1975; *Au fond de l'abime,* Apostolat des Editions, 1976; *Vania Moisseieff le jeune martyr de Volontirovka,* Editions des Catacombes, 1976; *Les enfants du Goulag,* Editions France-Empire, 1979. Also editor of *Les Camps de travail en U.R.S.S.* (title means "U.S.S.R. Labor Camps") and *L'en fer chinois.* Contributor to French periodicals.

WORK IN PROGRESS: Terre des miracles; Le calvaire de la Roumanie chretienne; Plaidoyer pous l'Eglise du Silence; Lettres d'U.R.S.S.

SIDELIGHTS: Sergiu Grossu writes that he wishes "to defend Jesus's cause in the free world, after three years of prison in communist Rumania, solely for my religious fight as leader of the 'unlawful' orthodox organization, 'The Army of the Lord,' and to inform against the persecution of the Christians behind the iron and bamboo curtain."

* * *

GRUBER, Martin Jay 1937-

PERSONAL: Born July 15, 1937, in Brooklyn, N.Y.; son of Samuel (an executive) and Betty (a teacher; maiden name, Coronell) Gruber; married Eleanor Cohen, August 13, 1961; children: Jonathan Holmes, Stacey Lynne. *Education:* Massachusetts Institute of Technology, S.B., 1959; Columbia University, M.B.A., 1961, Ph.D., 1966. *Home:* 454 George St., Ridgewood, N.J. 07450. *Office:* Graduate School of Business Administration, New York University, 100 Trinity Pl., New York, N.Y. 10006.

CAREER: New York University, Graduate School of Business Administration, New York, assistant professor, 1965-68, associate professor, 1968-72, professor of finance, 1972—. Senior research fellow at International Institute of Management, 1972-74. *Member:* European Finance Association (member of board of directors, 1973—), American Finance Association, American Economic Association, American Statistical Association, Institute of Management Sciences, New York Society of Security Analysts (member of advisory board on computer applications, 1970—).

WRITINGS: (Editor with Reynold Sachs) *Pension Funds,* 1966, Investors Publishing Co., 1966; *The Determinants of Common Stock Prices,* Center for Research of the College of Business Administration, Pennsylvania State University, 1971; (compiler with Edwin J. Elton) *Security Evaluation and Portfolio Analysis,* Prentice-Hall, 1972; (with Elton) *Finance as a Dynamic Process,* Prentice-Hall, 1975; (with Elton) *International Capital Markets: Studies in Financial Economics,* Volume I, North-Holland, 1975; (editor with Elton) *Portfolio Theory, 25 Years After: Essays in Honor of Harry Markowitz,* North-Holland, 1979; (editor with Elton) *Modern Portfolio Theory and Investment Analysis,* Wiley, 1981.

Contributor of articles to professional journals. Associate editor, *Journal of Finance,* 1971-73.†

* * *

GRUEN, John 1926-

PERSONAL: Born September 12, 1926, in Enghien-les-Bains, France; married Jane Wilson (a painter), March 28, 1948; children: Julia. *Education:* Attended City College (now City College of the City University of New York), 1944-45; University of Iowa, B.A., 1948, M.A., 1949. *Home:* 317 West 83rd St., New York, N.Y. 10024.

CAREER: Brentano's Bookstore, New York City, assistant book buyer, 1950-54; Grove Press, New York City, publicity director, 1955-56; Rapho-Guillumette Pictures, New York City, agent for photographers, 1956-59; Martha Jackson Gallery, New York City, director, 1960; *New York Herald Tribune,* New York City, associate critic of music and art, 1960-66; *New York World Journal Tribune,* New York City, chief art critic, 1966-69; *New York Magazine,* New York City, art critic, 1969-71; free-lance writer, 1971—; *Soho Weekly News,* New York City, art critic, 1974-75. Host of weekly program "The Sound of Dance" on WNCN-FM, 1975—.

WRITINGS: The New Bohemia: The Combine Generation, Shorecrest, 1966; *Close-Up,* Viking, 1968; *The Private World of Leonard Bernstein,* Viking, 1968; *The Party's Over Now,* Viking, 1972; *The Private World of Ballet,* Viking, 1974; *Menotti, A Biography,* Macmillan, 1978; *Erik Bruhn: Danseur Noble,* Viking, 1979; *The World's Great Ballets,* Abrams, 1981; *Objects,* Knopf, 1981.

Author of play, "Never Tell Isabel," first produced in New York at La Mama Experimental Theatre Club, January 22, 1969, published in *The Best Short Plays of 1981,* selected and edited by Stanley Richards, 1981. Composer of art songs, and film and theater music. Contributing editor, *Art News Magazine,* 1975—; associate editor, *Dance Magazine,* 1976—; cultural contributor, *New York Times.*

WORK IN PROGRESS: A book, *Dance Dictionary,* with Andrew Mark Wentink, for Doubleday.

SIDELIGHTS: In *Erik Bruhn: Danseur Noble,* dance enthusiast John Gruen focuses on a man he calls "one of the twentieth century's greatest classical male dancers." Based upon hundreds of hours of interviews with its subject, the biography "reveals Bruhn the person more than Bruhn the artist," *Library Journal* critic Joseph E. Heubner says. But, in allowing the artist to speak for himself, Gruen also allows Bruhn to reveal more of himself than he might have wished, according to Caroline Seebohm in the *New York Times Book Review.* "I am thinking," she says, "of the examples of ruthlessness that mar the dancer's career—for instance, his desertion of his fiancee . . . in favor of Blevins Davis and Ballet Theatre (later American Ballet Theatre) in New York [and] his subsequent expressions of ingratitude to Mr. Davis, who paid for the trip. . . . These and other faintly petulant episodes lend an air of hollowness to the man—a hollowness that ultimately drains the book of stature." A *Choice* reviewer, on the other hand, praises Gruen's handling of the subject matter: "He reports emotional turmoil such as the Bruhn-Nureyev encounter without becoming gossipy and shows Bruhn's achievements without becoming a sycophant." The book, the critic concludes, "is a joy to read."

BIOGRAPHICAL/CRITICAL SOURCES: *New York Times Book Review,* May 4, 1975, June 18, 1978, November 18, 1979; *Choice,* December, 1978, March, 1980; *Library Journal,* November 1, 1979; *Los Angeles Times Book Review,* January 31, 1982.

* * *

GULLASON, Thomas A(rthur) 1924-

PERSONAL: Born July 1, 1924, in Watertown, Mass.; son of Sarkis (a businessman) and Rebecca (Sahagian) Gullason; married Elizabeth Bakalian, June 26, 1955; children: Edward. *Education:* Suffolk University, B.A., 1948; University of Wisconsin, M.A., 1949, Ph.D., 1953. *Politics:* Independent. *Religion:* Protestant. *Office:* Department of English, University of Rhode Island, Kingston, R.I. 02881.

CAREER: Instructor in English at Heidelberg College, Tiffin, Ohio, 1952-53, and Wisconsin State College (now University of Wisconsin—Eau Claire), 1953-54; University of Rhode Island, Kingston, instructor, 1954-57, assistant professor, 1957-60, associate professor, 1960-64, professor of English, 1964—. Vice-president of board of trustees, Kingston Free Library, 1965-67. *Military service:* U.S. Army, Signal Corps, 1943-46. *Member:* Modern Language Association of America.

WRITINGS: (Editor with Leonard Casper) *The World of Short Fiction: An International Collection,* Harper, 1962, 2nd edition, 1971; (editor and author of introduction) *The Complete Short Stories and Sketches of Stephen Crane,* Doubleday, 1963; (editor and author of introduction) *The Complete Novels of Stephen Crane,* Doubleday, 1967; *Stephen Crane: Perspectives and Evaluations of His Art,* New York University Press, 1972; (contributor) *American Literary Naturalism: A Reassessment,* Carl Winter University, Press, 1975; (editor and contributor) Stephen Crane, *Maggie: A Girl of the Streets,* critical edition, Norton, 1979; (contributor) *Critical History of the Modern Short Story,* G. K. Hall, 1983; *Stephen Crane,* Ungar, 1984.

Contributor of more than thirty articles to professional journals; book reviewer for *American Literature, Studies in Short Fiction,* and *Boston Sunday Herald.* Member of editorial committee, *Studies in Short Fiction.*

SIDELIGHTS: Thomas Gullason told *CA*: "I make it a habit—more so these days—to read and reread good poems and good stories (Chekhov still remains my favorite) in order to preserve whatever literary taste I have accumulated. I also make it a habit to listen to light classical music, to angle strenuously for fish by the ocean's edge (though I may not catch a thing), to maintain a garden with many flowers and bushes in it, to play tennis and ping-pong, and to collect stamps—all to keep my pores open.

"I would like to reacquaint myself with languages I knew better before—Armenian, Spanish, and French."

* * *

GUSTAFSON, Ralph (Barker) 1909-

PERSONAL: Surname is pronounced Gus-*taf*-son; born August 16, 1909, in Lime Ridge, Quebec, Canada; son of Carl Otto (a photographer) and Gertrude (Barker) Gustafson; married Elisabeth Renninger, October 4, 1958. *Education:* Bishop's University, B.A. (with first class honors), 1929, M.A., 1930; Oxford University, B.A. (with honors), 1933, M.A., 1963. *Address:* P.O. Box 172, North Hatley, Quebec, Canada.

CAREER: Bishop's College School, Lennoxville, Quebec, music master, 1930; St. Alban's School, Brockville, Ontario, master, 1934; lived in London, England, 1934-38; worked for British Information Service in Canada, 1942-46; writer in New York, N.Y., 1946-63; Bishop's University, Lennoxville, lecturer, 1963-64, assistant professor, 1965-66, associate professor, 1967-71, professor of English, 1971-79, poet in residence, 1965-69. Poetry delegate to United Kingdom, 1972, to U.S.S.R., 1976, to Washington, D.C., 1977, and to Italy, 1981-82. Music critic, frequently broadcasting for Canadian Broadcasting Corp. *Member:* Association of Canadian University Teachers of English (life member), Keble Association, Oxford League of Canadian Poets.

AWARDS, HONORS: Prix David from Quebec Government, 1935, for *The Golden Chalice;* Canada Council senior fellowship, 1959-60, 1971-72; D.Litt., Mount Allison University, 1973; Governor General's Award for Poetry, 1974, and A.J.M. Smith Award, Michigan State University, 1974, both for *Fire on Stone;* D.C.L., Bishop's University, 1977; Queen's Silver Jubilee Medal, 1978.

WRITINGS—Poetry: *The Golden Chalice,* Nicholson & Watson, 1935; *Alfred the Great* (poetic drama), M. Joseph, 1937; *Epithalamium in Time of War,* privately printed, 1941; *Lyrics Unromantic,* privately printed, 1942; *Flight into Darkness,* Pantheon, 1944; *Rocky Mountain Poems,* Klanak Press, 1960; *Rivers among Rocks,* McClelland & Stewart, 1960; *Sift in an Hourglass,* McClelland & Stewart, 1966.

Ixion's Wheel, McClelland & Stewart, 1969; *Theme and Variations for Sounding Brass,* privately printed, 1972; *Selected Poems,* McClelland & Stewart, 1972; *Fire on Stone,* McClelland & Stewart, 1974; *Corners in the Glass,* McClelland & Stewart, 1977; *Soviet Poems,* Turnstone Press, 1978; *Sequences,* Sono Nis Press, 1979; *Landscape with Rain,* McClelland & Stewart, 1980; *Conflicts of Spring,* McClelland & Stewart, 1981; *At the Ocean's Verge,* Black Swan, 1982; *Gradations of Grandeur,* Sono Nis Press, 1982; *Selected Poems,* McClelland & Stewart, 1983. Contributor of poems to anthologies, including *The Best Poems of 1961, Oxford Modern Canadian Verse,* 1967, and *Canadian Poetry,* 1974 and 1983. Contributor of poetry to literary magazines.

Editor: *Anthology of Canadian Poetry,* Penguin, 1942; *A Little Anthology of Canadian Poets,* New Directions, 1943; *Canadian Accent* (collection of stories and poems by contemporary writers from Canada), Penguin, 1944; *The Penguin Book of Canadian Verse,* Penguin, 1958, 2nd revised edition, 1975. Also editor of Canadian poetry issue of *Voices,* 1943.

Other: *Poetry and Canada,* Canadian Legion Educational Services, 1945; *The Brazen Tower* (short stories), Roger Ascham Press, 1975; *The Vivid Air* (short stories), Sono Nis Press, 1980. Short stories included in *The Best American Short Stories,* 1948, 1950, *Canadian Short Stories,* 1960, and *A Book of Canadian Stories,* 1962. Contributor of short stories, and critical articles to literary periodicals and journals in Canada, the United States, and abroad.

WORK IN PROGRESS: Poetry.

SIDELIGHTS: Ralph Gustafson, according to David MacFarlane in a *Books in Canada* article, "can be ranked among the very best of our poets." Gustafson is often praised for the beauty of the imagery in his poems and for his skillful use of the English language.

In a review of *Flight into Darkness*, Gustafson's 1944 collection, Darrel Abel of *Poetry* wrote: "[Gustafson's] poems about the war are the excellently pointed and finely sympathetic observations of an imaginative bystander. He has a poignant and well controlled elegiac note." And in a *Springfield Republican* article, C. M. Sauer said that *Flight into Darkness* "contains a sensitive Canadian's reactions to this present day world—reactions passionately, ironically and realistically expressed. This is a volume for readers who delight in discovering modern poetry with singing strength, original phrasing, excellent technique, and fullness of vocabulary."

Commenting on a lengthy poem included in *Sequences*, Rosemary Aubert, in a *Quill & Quire* review, says that "the rich imagery (especially images of taste and smell), and the sustained tone make this a poem of beauty reminiscent of some of Pound's cantos." And Barry Dempster, also writing in *Quill & Quire*, states that in *Landscape with Rain* Gustafson "is in fine form, probing beyond history and mythology to the present imbued with all the magic of the past. . . . Gustafson is a cultured man, a complete poet."

AVOCATIONAL INTERESTS: Music ("have a collection of piano records since the inception of the gramophone"), travel.

BIOGRAPHICAL/CRITICAL SOURCES: Springfield Republican, February 19, 1945; *New York Times*, February 25, 1945; *Poetry*, May, 1945; C. Klinck, editor, *Literary History of Canada*, University of Toronto Press, 1965; Wendy Keitner, *Ralph Gustafson*, Twayne, 1979; *Quill & Quire*, January, 1980, May, 1980; *Books in Canada*, April, 1980; Dermot McCarthy, *Ralph Gustafson*, E.C.M. Press, 1982.

* * *

GUTKIND, Erwin A(nton) 1886-1968

PERSONAL: Born, 1886; died, 1968; married A. Gutkind-Bulling (a Chinese scholar); children: two.

CAREER: Architect and city planner. Member, British Control Commission for Germany, 1946-47; former research professor of urban studies, Institute for Urban Studies, University of Pennsylvania. *Member:* Royal Geographical Society (fellow), British Town Planning Institute.

WRITINGS: Creative Demobilisation, two volumes, K. Paul, Trench, Trubner, 1943; *Revolution of Environment*, K. Paul, Trench, Trubner, 1946; *Our World from the Air: An International Survey of Man and His Environment*, Doubleday, 1952; *The Expanding Environment*, Freedom Press, 1953; *Community and Environment*, Philosophical Library, 1954, reprinted, Haskell House, 1974; *The Twilight of Cities*, Free Press of Glencoe, 1962.

"International History of City Development" series; published by Free Press: *Urban Development in Central Europe*, 1964; *. . . the Alpine and Scandinavian Countries*, 1965; *. . . Southern Europe: Spain and Portugal*, 1966; *. . . Southern Europe: Italy and Greece*, 1969; *. . . Western Europe: France and Belgium*, 1970; *. . . Western Europe: The Netherlands and Great Britain*, 1971; *. . . East-Central Europe: Poland, Czechoslavia, and Hungary*, 1972; *. . . Eastern Europe: Bulgaria, Romania, and U.S.S.R.*, 1972. Contributor of numerous articles to various professional journals.†

GUTTENTAG, Marcia 1932-1977

PERSONAL: Name legally changed; born November 9, 1932, in Brooklyn, N.Y.; died November 4, 1977; daughter of Morris and Flora (Kaufman) Blumberg; married Paul Frank Secord (a professor of urban studies), September 21, 1972; children: Lisa Andra, Michael Daniel. *Education:* University of Michigan, B.A. (with honors), 1953; additional study at University of Freiburg, 1953-54, and Harvard University, 1954-55; Adelphi University, Ph.D., 1960. *Office:* Graduate School of Education, Harvard University, Cambridge, Mass. 02138.

CAREER: Queens College of the City University of New York, Flushing, N.Y., instructor in psychology, 1960-64; State University of New York at Stony Brook, assistant professor of psychology, 1964-65; Yale University, New Haven, Conn., visiting fellow at Social Interaction Laboratories, 1965-66; Queens College of the City University of New York, assistant professor of social psychology, 1966-70; City University of New York, Graduate Center, New York, N.Y., 1970-73, began as associate professor, became professor of psychology, director of Harlem Research Center, 1970-72; Harvard University, Cambridge, Mass., Richard Clarke Cabot Visiting Professor of Social Ethics, 1972-73, developmental social psychologist at Graduate School of Education, 1973-77. Professor of psychology, University of Massachusetts—Boston. Visiting lecturer at Hebrew University of Jerusalem, Ohio State University, University of Southern California, Cornell University, and other universities. Member of social sciences research review panel, National Institute of Mental Health, 1971-75; trustee, Research for Social Change; member of ethics committee, Department of Health, Education, and Welfare. Evaluation consultant to UNESCO, Office of Child Development, National Institute of Mental Health, and other agencies.

MEMBER: American Psychological Association (fellow; president of Division 9, 1971-72; founder of Public Interest Coalition, 1974; president of Division 8, beginning 1974), Society for the Psychological Study of Social Issues (fellow; member of council, 1968; president, 1971-72), American Sociological Association (fellow), American Association for the Advancement of Science (fellow), Association for the Advancement of Psychology (member of board of trustees; chairman of committee on policy and planning), Association for Women Psychologists, Psychonomic Society, Evaluation Research Society (founder; president, 1976-77), Bayesian Society, New York Academy of Sciences, Emily Dickinson House, Harvard Club (New York).

AWARDS, HONORS: Fulbright scholar at University of Freiburg, 1953-54; Distinguished Scientific Contribution Award, New York State Psychological Association, 1970; Distinguished Woman in Science Award, University of Michigan, 1973; Distinguished Alumna Award, Adelphi University, 1974; grants from U.S. Office of Education, 1965-66, National Institute of Mental Health, 1965-66, 1969-71, 1973, 1974, 1975, National Science Foundation, 1968-70, Carnegie Foundation, 1970-71, Carnegie Corp. and Rockefeller Foundation, 1971, Ford Foundation, 1973, and National Academy of Sciences, 1974.

WRITINGS: (Translator from the German) *Farbpyramiden Test Manual*, Hans Huber, 1955; (with F. Denmark and R. Riley) *Communications Patterns in Integrated Classrooms and Pre-Integration Subject Variables as They Affect the Academic Achievement and Self-Concept of Previously Segregated Children* (monograph), U.S. Office of Education, 1967; (editor)

The Poor: Impact on Research and Theory, [Ann Arbor, Mich.], 1970; (editor) *Professionals and the Poor,* [Ann Arbor], 1970; (with Marilyn Gittell and others) *Local Control of Education,* Praeger, 1972; (with T. Kiresuk and M. Oglesby) *The Evaluation of Training in Mental Health,* Behavioral Publications, 1974; (editor with E. L. Struening and contributor) *Handbook of Evaluation Research,* two volumes, Sage Publications, 1975; *Undoing Sex Stereotypes: Research and Resources for Educators,* McGraw, 1976; (editor with Shalom Saar) *Evaluation Studies Review Annual,* Volume II, Sage Publications, 1977; *Evaluating Community Mental Health Services,* U.S. Department of Health, Education, and Welfare, 1977; (editor with others) *The Mental Health of Women,* Academic Press, 1980.

Contributor: Harry Rivlin and V. Robinson, editors, *The Preparation of Urban Teachers,* National Defense Education Act National Institute, 1968; Nathaniel N. Wagner and M. J. Haug, editors, *Chicanos: Social and Psychological Perspectives,* Mosby, 1971; Marvin Leiner, editor, *Children of the Cities: Education of the Powerless,* New American Library, 1974; Ronald Krage, editor, *Social Issues in Human Development,* Praeger, 1974.

Also author of *Principles and Practices of Community Mental Health Center Evaluation,* 1976, *Public Policies for Women,* 1977, and *Familes Abandoned: Mental Health in Today's Society,* 1977. Author of a number of research reports. Contributor of articles and reviews to psychology and sociology journals. Editor, *Newsletter* of Division of Personality and Social Psychology, American Psychological Association, beginning 1972; member of editorial board, *Journal for the Theory of Social Behavior,* beginning 1970, *Basic Readings in Social Psychology,* beginning 1972, and *Journal of Homosexuality,* beginning 1974; member of publications committee, *Personality and Social Psychology Bulletin,* beginning 1974; editorial reviewer, *Journal of Personality and Social Psychology.*

WORK IN PROGRESS: Evaluating Social, Health and Educational Programs: The United Nations Handbook.†

H

HAAS, Ben(jamin) L(eopold) 1926-1977
(John Benteen, Thorne Douglas, Richard Meade)

PERSONAL: Born July 21, 1926, in Charlotte, N.C.; died October 27, 1977; son of Otto (a realtor) and Lorena Jo (Michael) Haas; married Douglas Thornton Taylor, March 31, 1950; children: Joseph Elliott, Benjamin Michael, John Douglas. *Education:* Attended schools in Charlotte, N.C. *Politics:* Democrat. *Religion:* Presbyterian. *Home:* 2818 Bedford Ave., Raleigh, N.C. 27607. *Agent:* Paul R. Reynolds, Inc., 12 East 41st St., New York, N.Y. 10017. *Office:* Box 5332, Raleigh, N.C. 27607.

CAREER: Charlotte News, Charlotte, N.C., proofreader, 1947; American Oil Co., Charlotte, clerk in engineering department, 1947-52; Southern Engineering Co., Charlotte, steel estimator, 1952-56; B. L. Montague Co., Inc., Sumter, S.C., chief estimator and assistant sales manager, 1956-59; Raleigh Metal Products, Inc., Raleigh, manager, 1959-61; full-time writer, 1961-77. *Military service:* U.S. Army, 1945-46; became sergeant. *Member:* Authors Guild, Western Writers of America, North Carolina Writer's Conference.

WRITINGS: The Foragers, Simon & Schuster, 1962, reprinted, 1978; *KKK: A Study of the Ku Klux Klan,* Regency, 1963; *Look Away, Look Away* (Literary Guild selection), Simon & Schuster, 1964; *The Last Valley,* Simon & Schuster, 1966; *Summer Always Ends,* Dell, 1966; *The Troubled Summer,* Bobbs-Merrill, 1966; *The Chandler Heritage* (Literary Guild alternate selection; Doubleday Book Club selection), Simon & Schuster, 1971; *Daisy Canfield,* Simon & Schuster, 1973; *The House of Christina* (Literary Guild alternate selection; Doubleday Book Club selection), Simon & Schuster, 1977.

Under pseudonym John Benteen; published by Nordon, except as indicated: *Sharpshooters,* Tower, 1974; *Overkill,* 1976; *War Trail,* 1976; *Gunbelt,* 1977; *Ride the Man Down,* 1977; *Riding Shotgun,* 1977; *Fargo Bandolero,* Tower, 1977; *Shotgun Man,* Tower, 1977; *Silent Enemy,* 1977; *Dakota Badlands,* Tower, 1977; *Fargo and the Texas Rangers,* Tower, 1977; *Taps at Little Big Horn,* 1978; *The Ghost Dancers,* 1978; *Manhunt,* 1978; *Bring Me His Scalp,* 1978; *Run for Cover,* 1978; *Blood on the Prairie,* 1978; *The Pistoleros,* 1979; *Bounty Killer,* 1979; *Dakota Territory,* 1979; *Dead Man's Canyon,* 1979; *Death in the Lava,* 1979; *The Wild Stallions,* 1979; *Apache Raiders,* Tower, 1980; *Fargo,* Tower, 1980; *Panama Gold,* Tower, 1980; *Alaska Steel,* Tower, 1980; *Massacre River,* Tower, 1980; *Valley of Skulls,* Tower, 1982.

Under pseudonym Thorne Douglas: *Night Riders,* Fawcett, 1975; *Killraine,* Hodder & Stoughton, 1977, Fawcett, 1979; *The Mustang Men,* Fawcett, 1977; *Calhoon,* Fawcett, 1978.

Under pseudonym Richard Meade: *Beyond the Danube,* P. Davies, 1967, published as *The Danube Runs Red,* Random House, 1968, published as *The Gun Runner,* New English Library, 1969; *Big Bend,* Doubleday, 1968; *The Lost Fraulein,* Random House, 1969 (published in England as *A Score of Arms,* P. Davies, 1969); *Exile's Quest,* New American Library, 1970; (with Jay Rutledge) *The Belle from Catscratch,* Fawcett, 1972; *Cartridge Creek,* Doubleday, 1973; *Gaylor's Badge,* Doubleday, 1975; *Swimming the Channel,* Story Press, 1981.

SIDELIGHTS: Ben L. Haas once told *CA:* "I grew up in a family which believed in reading, and my German-born father, during the Depression, would bid on hundreds of books of all sorts at a time at unclaimed freight auctions, through which my two brothers and I were allowed to wade uncensored. Simultaneously, I heard stories of the Civil War and Reconstruction from my grandmother, who had lived through them.

"Our home was on the edge of the city, with countless miles of open farmland, woods, fields and creeks to explore. We hunted, fished, trapped, collected Indian relics; and our lives were interwoven with those of the black sharecroppers, tenant farmers, and hired hands of the area, as well as the poor whites and the cotton mill workers. We backpacked into the Smoky Mountains long before progress had erased the old-time mountaineer and, in our very early youth, knew Confederate veterans and ex-slaves. Because my father, before the Depression, had been a pioneer operator of motion picture theaters, we had free access to every theater in Charlotte and saw countless films. Early on, we were hooked not only on the lore of our own South, but on the Old West, too, and Western history and lore has remained one of my major interests.

"By the age of fourteen, I had decided I wanted to be a professional writer and at eighteen sold my first story to a Western pulp. Immediately after, I was drafted, sent to the Philippines, and added a certain amount of knowledge of the military, World War II, and the tactics of Communist guerilla warfare as used by the Hukbalahap rebels to my store of material. Returning home, I continued to write in my spare time while working at other jobs; in 1961, I broke into the paperback field, received several contracts and acquired the services of . . . an agent; he promptly sold *The Foragers,* which was already finished, to Simon & Schuster, and I became a full-time professional writer.

"My writing is compartmented into several levels and categories. As a compulsive writer who's uncomfortable without working every day, I spin off minor ideas and themes into lesser works under pen names. When a major subject or theme seizes me, I then spare no effort or sacrifice to develop it under my own name, with all the force, clarity, and honesty at my command. I have consciously tried to develop a style which puts the reader into the novel itself, where he can know intimately its characters and himself feel the impact of the events which touch their lives. I believe that any major novel which leaves the reader mentally, emotionally and perhaps psychologically unchanged has failed. I try to follow the same precept in lesser works, but they require less effort. My novels under my own name are those important to me, and I try to transmit this importance to the reader, striving as hard as possible to capture the texture of time, place, events, and character."

AVOCATIONAL INTERESTS: Outdoor activities.

BIOGRAPHICAL/CRITICAL SOURCES: Commonweal, May 26, 1967.

OBITUARIES: New York Times, October 29, 1977; AB Bookman, March 20, 1978.†

* * *

HAGAN, William T(homas) 1918-

PERSONAL: Born December 19, 1918, in Huntington, W.Va.; son of William Fleming (a building contractor) and Verna (Grass) Hagan; married Charlotte Nix, January 31, 1943; children: Thomas M., Martha D., Daniel B., Sarah E. Education: Marshall College (now Marshall University), A.B., 1941; University of Wisconsin, Ph.D., 1950. Office: History Department, State University of New York College at Fredonia, Fredonia, N.Y. 14063.

CAREER: North Texas State University, Denton, 1950-65, began as assistant professor, became professor of history; State University of New York College at Fredonia, professor, 1965-75, distinguished professor of history, 1975—, chairman of department. President, American Indian Ethnohistoric Conference, 1963. Member of advisory committee of Newberry Library's Center for the History of the American Indian, 1972—. Military service: U.S. Army, Artillery, 1942-45; became first lieutenant. Member: American Historical Association, American Society for Ethnohistory, Organization of American Historians, Western History Association (president, 1980).

WRITINGS: The Sac and Fox Indians, University of Oklahoma Press, 1958, reprinted, 1980; American Indians, University of Chicago Press, 1961, revised edition, 1979; The Indian in American History, American Historical Association, 1963, revised edition, 1971; Indian Police and Judges: Experiments in Acculturation and Control, University of Nebraska Press, 1966, reprinted, 1980.

(Contributor) Francis Paul Prucha, editor, American Indian Policy, Indiana Historical Society, 1971; United States-Comanche Relations: The Reservation Years, Yale University Press, 1976; Longhouse Diplomacy and Frontier Warfare: The Iroquois Confederacy in the American Revolution, New York State American Revolution Bicentennial Commission, 1976. Member of editorial board of Western Historical Quarterly, 1973; editorial consultant, Arizona & West, 1978—.

WORK IN PROGRESS: A book on the Indian Rights Association.

HALL, Elvajean 1910-

PERSONAL: Born May 30, 1910, in Hamilton, Ill.; daughter of Nelson (a clergyman) and Nellie Jean (Hyer) Hall. Education: Oberlin College, A.B., 1930; University of Wisconsin, graduate study, 1931-32; Columbia University, M.L.S., 1941. Politics: Independent Republican. Religion: Protestant. Office: 4010 Camelot Dr., Raleigh, N.C. 27609.

CAREER: Milwaukee University School, Milwaukee, Wis., teacher and librarian, 1937-42; Jackson (Mich.) public schools, school library supervisor, 1942-44; Stephens College, Columbia, Mo., head librarian, 1944-46; Newton (Mass.) public schools, supervisor of School Library Services, 1946-75. Library consultant, Chung Chi College, The Chinese University of Hong Kong, 1962-63; visiting lecturer in children's literature, University College, Dublin, summers, 1967-69.

MEMBER: American Library Association, National Education Association, American Association of School Librarians, Association for Supervision and Curriculum Development, Authors Guild, Authors League of America, National League of American Pen Women (president, Boston chapter, 1970-72), Women's National Book Association (president, Boston chapter, 1957-59; national secretary, 1959-61), New England School Library Association, Massachusetts School Library Association, Boston Authors Club (member of board, 1973—), Delta Kappa Gamma, Kappa Delta.

WRITINGS: Books to Build On, Bowker, 1954, 2nd edition, 1957; Land and People of Argentina, Lippincott, 1960, 2nd edition, 1972; Pilgrim Stories, Rand McNally, 1961; Land and People of Norway, Lippincott, 1963, 2nd edition, 1973; Pilgrim Neighbors, Rand McNally, 1964; The Volga: Lifeline of Russia, Rand McNally, 1965; Land and People of Czechoslovakia, Lippincott, 1966; Hong Kong, Rand McNally, 1967; The Psalms, F. Watts, 1968; (with Calvin L. Criner) Picture Map of Eastern Europe, Lippincott, 1968; The Proverbs, F. Watts, 1970; (with R. J. Houlehen) Battle for Sales, Lippincott, 1973; Careers in Marketing and Distribution, Lothrop, 1974; Today in Old Boston, Children's Press, 1975; Today in Old New York, Children's Press, 1975; Today in Old Philadelphia, Children's Press, 1976. Contributor of articles to educational and library journals, and of cartoons and reviews to library journals.

WORK IN PROGRESS: A study of American colonial and nineteenth-century history; English biographies.

AVOCATIONAL INTERESTS: Cartooning, world travel (has been to Hong Kong three times, Japan five times, Korea twice, Philippines three times, Taiwan twice, Ireland seven times, Norway five times, British Isles thirty-two times, and has visited, at least once, every country of Europe except Albania).

* * *

HALL, Peter (Geoffrey) 1932-

PERSONAL: Born March 19, 1932, in London, England; son of Arthur Vickers and Bertha (Keefe) Hall. Education: Attended St. Catharine's College, Cambridge. Politics: Labour. Home: 5 Bedford Rd., London W4 1JD, England. Office: Department of Geography, University of Reading, Whiteknights, Reading, Berkshire RG6 2AB, England.

CAREER: University of London, London, England, assistant lecturer in geography, Birkbeck College, 1957-60, lecturer in geography, Birkbeck College, 1960-65, reader in geography with special reference to regional planning, London School of Economics and Political Science, 1966-67; University of Reading, Reading, England, professor of geography, 1968—. Associate, Economics Associates Ltd., London; member of executive committee, Regional Studies Association. *Member:* Royal Geographical Society.

WRITINGS: *The Industries of London*, Hutchinson, 1962; *London 2000*, Faber, 1963, revised edition, 1969; (editor) *Labour's New Frontiers*, Deutsch, 1964; (editor) *Land Values*, Sweet & Maxwell, 1965; *The World Cities*, World University, 1966, 2nd edition, McGraw, 1979; (editor) J. H. von Thuenen, *Isolated State*, Pergamon, 1966; (with others) *An Advanced Geography of North-West Europe*, Hulten, 1967.

Theory and Practice of Regional Planning, Pemberton Publishing, 1970; (with others) *The Containment of Urban England*, Allen & Unwin, 1973, Volume I: *Urban and Metropolitan Growth Processes*, Volume II: *The Planning System: Objectives, Operations, Impacts;* (with Marion Clawson) *Planning and Urban Growth: An Anglo-American Comparison*, Johns Hopkins University Press, 1973; *Urban and Regional Planning: An Introduction*, Penguin, 1974, new edition, 1980; (with Roger Sammons) *Urban Activity Patterns and Modal Split in the Journey to Work*, Department of Geography, University of Reading, 1974; (with Edward Smith) *Better Use of Railways*, University of Reading, 1976; (editor) *Europe 2000*, Columbia University Press, 1977; (editor with Ross Davies) *Issues in Urban Society*, Penguin, 1978; (editor) *The New Penguin World Atlas*, Penguin, 1979.

(With Dennis Hay) *Growth Centres in the European Urban System*, Heinemann Educational, 1980; (editor) *Radical Agenda for London*, Fabian Society, 1980; *Great Planning Disasters*, Weidenfeld & Nicolson, 1980. Also editor of *The Inner City in Context*, 1981. Regular contributor to *New Society*. Editor, *Regional Studies*.

WORK IN PROGRESS: Editing *Forecasts and Decisions*, a study in planning theory and practice.

BIOGRAPHICAL/CRITICAL SOURCES: *Times Literary Supplement*, September 3, 1974, July 4, 1980; *Listener*, February 9, 1978; *Economist*, March 4, 1978, April 5, 1980; *Observer*, March 30, 1980.

* * *

HALLIDAY, Michael
See CREASEY, John

* * *

HALMOS, Paul 1911-1977

PERSONAL: Born December 19, 1911, in Budapest, Hungary; died October 18, 1977; son of Maurice (a civil servant) and Ethel (Soos) Halmos; married Edith Molnar, July 18, 1937; married Ena Edwards, February 18, 1972; children: (first marriage) Anthony Michael. *Education:* University of Budapest, Doctor Juris, 1935; University of London, B.A. (with honors), 1945; London School of Economics and Political Science, Ph.D., 1950. *Office:* Open University, Bletchley, Buckinghamshire, England.

CAREER: Master at various grammar schools in Britain, 1941-47; Southwest Essex Technical College, lecturer in social psychology, 1947-56; University of Keele, Keele, England, senior lecturer and tutor in charge of social studies, 1956-65; University of Wales, University College, Cardiff, professor of sociology, 1965-74; Open University, Bletchley, England, professor of sociology, beginning 1974. Distinguished Visiting Professor, Wayne State University, 1972. Editorial adviser to Constable & Co. Ltd. *Member:* British Sociological Association.

WRITINGS: *Solitude and Privacy*, Routledge & Kegan Paul, 1952, Philosophical Library, 1953, published as *Solitude and Privacy: A Study of Social Isolation, Its Causes and Therapy*, Greenwood Press, 1969; *Towards a Measure of Man*, Humanities, 1957; *The Faith of the Counsellors*, Constable, 1965, published as *The Faith of the Counsellors: A Study of the Theory and Practice of Social Casework and Psychotherapy*, Schocken, 1966; *The Personal Service Society*, Constable, 1965, Schocken, 1971; *Introduction to Welfare: Concepts and History*, Open University Press, 1978; *The Personal and the Political: Social Work and Political Action*, Hutchinson, 1978.

Editor of "Sociological Review" monograph series; published by the University of Keele: *The Teaching of Personality Development*, 1958; *The Problems Arising from the Teaching of Personality Development*, 1959; *Moral Issues in the Training of Teachers and Social Workers*, 1960; *The Teaching of Sociology to Students of Education and Social Work* 1961; *Sociology and Medicine: Studies within the Framework of the British Health Service*, 1962; *The Canford Families: A Study in Social Casework and Group Work*, 1962; *The Development of Industrial Societies*, 1964; *Sociological Studies in British University Education*, 1965; *Sociological Studies in the British Penal System*, 1965; *Japanese Sociological Studies*, 1966; *Latin-American Sociological Studies*, 1967; *Sociological Studies in Economics and Administration*, 1969; *The Sociology of Mass-Media Communications*, 1970; *The Sociology of Sociology*, 1970; *The Sociology of Science*, 1972; *Hungarian Sociological Studies*, 1972; *Stochastic Processes in Sociology*, 1973; *Professionalism and Social Change*, 1973.

Also editor of "Sociology and Social Welfare" series, beginning 1966. Member of editorial board, *Sociological Review*.

AVOCATIONAL INTERESTS: Philately, painting, mosaics.†

* * *

HALSBAND, Robert 1914-

PERSONAL: Born March 22, 1914, in New York, N.Y.; son of Max (a contractor) and Bertha (Locker) Halsband; married Ruth Alice Norman Weil, December 30, 1954 (died, 1971). *Education:* New York University, B.S., 1934; Columbia University, M.A., 1936; Northwestern University, Ph.D., 1948. *Religion:* "Lapsed Jew." *Residence:* Pasadena, Calif.

CAREER: New York public schools, New York City, high school teacher, 1938-43; Northwestern University, Evanston, Ill., instructor in English, 1944-47; Hunter College (now Hunter College of the City University of New York), New York City, assistant professor, 1949-57, associate professor of English, 1958-60; Columbia University, New York City, adjunct professor of English, 1963-71; University of California, Riverside, professor of English, 1971-73; University of Illinois at Urbana-Champaign, professor of English, 1973-82. National Book Awards judge, 1960 and 1972. *Member:* Century Association, P.E.N. (vice-president of American branch, 1966-67; president, 1967-69), Morgan Library (member of council, 1965-68), Phi Beta Kappa, Grolier Club (member of council, 1962-67). *Awards, honors:* Guggenheim fellowship, 1968-69; Huntington Library-National Endowment for the Humanities fellowship, 1981-82.

WRITINGS: (Editor) *The Nonsense of Common-Sense, 1737-1738*, Northwestern University Press, 1947; *The Life of Lady*

Mary Wortley Montagu, Oxford University Press, 1956; (editor) *The Complete Letters of Lady Mary Wortley Montagu,* Oxford University Press, Volume I, 1965, Volume II, 1966, Volume III, 1967; (editor) *Selected Letters of Lady Mary Wortley Montagu,* Longman, 1970, St. Martin's, 1971; *Lord Hervey: Eighteenth-Century Courtier,* Oxford University Press, 1974; (co-editor) *Essays and Poems of Lady Mary Wortley Montagu,* Oxford University Press, 1977; *The Rape of the Lock and Its Illustrations,* Oxford University Press, 1980.

SIDELIGHTS: In a review of Robert Halsband's *Lord Hervey: Eighteenth-Century Courtier,* Alan Bell of *Listener* writes: "Lord Hervey had a short life, of 47 years, but it was an interesting one—as courtier, politician, pamphleteer and literary victim. Mr. Halsband has treated him well. . . . Halsband handles the political and literary scenes with a commendable sureness of touch." A *New Yorker* critic describes the biography as "an exceptionally enjoyable book. Professor Halsband's sense of the period is perfect." "Moving with practised and expert tread through tangled thickets of manuscripts, memoirs, and anonymous pamphlets, Professor Halsband has succeeded admirably in the formidable task of producing the first detailed life of Hervey," a *Times Literary Supplement* reviewer notes. "[Halsband's] judgment is as sound as his conclusions are careful and sensible. . . . His achievement in supplying a reliable account of Hervey's life and career is considerable." Finally, a *New York Times Book Review* critic states, "Once tucked into [Halsband's book], I doubt whether anyone would hear the call of the hills or the sea, no matter how brilliant the summer's day."

BIOGRAPHICAL/CRITICAL SOURCES: *New Statesman,* November 2, 1973; *Times Literary Supplement,* November 2, 1973, November 7, 1980; *New York Times Book Review,* June 2, 1974; *Yale Review,* autumn, 1974; *American Historical Review,* June, 1975; *Virginia Quarterly Review,* autumn, 1981.

* * *

HAMBURGER, Robert (A., Jr.) 1943-

PERSONAL: Born May 30, 1943, in Brooklyn, N.Y.; son of Robert A. and Mary Jo (Epstein) Hamburger. *Education:* Cornell University, A.B. (cum laude), 1964; University of Chicago, M.A., 1965, Ph.D., 1969. *Home:* 825 West End Ave., Apt. 11-G, New York, N.Y. 10025.

CAREER: Writer. City College of the City University of New York, New York City, lecturer, 1968-70, assistant professor of English, 1970-76; William Paterson College, Wayne, N.J., lecturer, 1976, associate professor of Afro-American Studies, 1978; University of Paris, Paris, France, Fulbright lecturer in American studies, 1977-78; MacDowell Colony, New York City, writer-in-residence, 1977, 1979; Ossabaw Island Project, Ossabaw Island, Ga., writer-in-residence, 1980. Writer and co-director of half-hour radio show based on *Our Portion of Hell,* WBAI. *Member:* P.E.N. *Awards, honors:* National Endowment for the Humanities research grant, 1980-81.

WRITINGS: *Our Portion of Hell: An Oral History of the Civil Rights Movement in Fayette County, Tennessee,* Links Books, 1973; *The Thirties,* Links Books, 1975; (contributor) Stanley Kutler, editor, *Looking for America: The People's History,* Canfield Press, 1976; *A Stranger in the House: Personal Narratives from Twelve Black Household Workers,* Macmillan, 1978; (contributor) Linda Kerber and Jane Mathews, editors, *Women's America: Refocusing the Past,* Oxford University Press, 1981; *A Journal of the Plague Years,* Tichner & Fields, 1983. Contributor to *Southern Exposure, Mimo* (Belgium), and *Vrij Nederland.*

SIDELIGHTS: Robert Hamburger says his books are attempts to make a general reading audience aware of how racial and economic oppression affect the consciousness of minority peoples and contradict the positive ideals of American life.

The tapes, transcriptions, notes, and edited manuscripts from *Our Portion of Hell* and *A Stranger in the House* are part of the permanent collection in the history archives of the Schomberg Center for Research in Black Culture.

MEDIA ADAPTATIONS: *Our Portion of Hell* was produced as a television documentary by WBAI, Memphis.

BIOGRAPHICAL/CRITICAL SOURCES: *Nation,* April 13, 1974; *Reviews in American History,* September, 1975, March, 1980.

* * *

HAMILTON, Paul
See DENNIS-JONES, H(arold)

* * *

HANCOCK, Maxine 1942-

PERSONAL: Born September 2, 1942, in Calgary, Alberta, Canada; daughter of Max E. (a salesman) and Ruth (Woods) Runions; married Campbell Hancock (a farmer), July 7, 1962; children: Geoffrey, Camille, Heather, Mitchell. *Education:* University of Alberta, Ed.B. (with distinction), 1964. *Religion:* Protestant Evangelical. *Residence:* Marwayne, Alberta, Canada.

CAREER: Bonnie Doon Composite High School, Edmonton, Alberta, English teacher, 1964-65; Marwayne Jubilee School, Marwayne, Alberta, English teacher in shared appointment with husband, Campbell Hancock, 1979—; School of Christian Writing, Minneapolis, Minn., faculty member, 1981, 1982—; writer. Conference and convention speaker. *Member:* Canadian Authors' Association.

WRITINGS: *Love, Honor and Be Free,* Moody, 1975; *Living on Less and Liking It More,* Moody, 1977; *The Forever Principle,* Revell, 1980; *Confident, Creative Children,* Christian Herald, 1981; *Giving and Receiving,* Harvest House, 1983. Also author of radio scripts for Alberta School Broadcasts, and of educational media scripts. Contributor of short stories, articles, and criticism to professional journals; contributor of articles to religion magazines, including *Decision, Eternity, Moody Monthly, Christian Herald,* and *Christian Life.*

* * *

HANNA, William John 1931-

PERSONAL: Born October 30, 1931, in Cleveland, Ohio; son of William Henry (a businessman) and Anne (a teacher; maiden name, Dobrin) Hanna; married Judith Lynne Selmont (a writer and lecturer), December 16, 1960; children: Shawn Harrison, Aaron Evan. *Education:* University of California, Los Angeles, B.A., 1957, M.A., 1960, Ph.D., 1962. *Home:* 8520 Thornden Ter., Bethesda, Md. 20817. *Office:* Comparative Urban Research, Marie Mount Hall, University of Maryland, College Park, Md. 20742.

CAREER: Michigan State University, East Lansing, instructor, 1961-62, assistant professor of political science, 1962-65, member of faculty at African Studies Center, 1961-65; American University, Washington, D.C., associate professor, 1965, professor of political science, 1965-68, research scientist, 1965, senior research scientist, 1965-68; City University of New York,

New York, N.Y., professor of political science and urban studies at Herbert H. Lehman College and at Graduate School, 1968-78, director of Comparative Urban Studies Program, 1972-76; University of Texas at Dallas, professor of political science, 1976-78; University of Maryland, College Park, professor of community development, 1978—. Visiting associate of Institute of African Studies at University of Ibadan, 1960, 1963; adjunct professor at New York University, 1970. Senior partner of Hanna & Hanna Associates, 1965—. Consultant to United Nations, U.S. Department of Housing and Urban Development, and U.S. Department of State. *Military service:* U.S. Army, 1953-54.

MEMBER: International Political Science Association, International Sociological Association, International Studies Association, American Planning Association, National Association of Social Workers, American Political Science Association, American Society for Public Administration, American Sociological Association (fellow), Society for Applied Anthropology (fellow).

AWARDS, HONORS: Ford Foundation fellowship for Michigan State University's Overseas Program in Black Africa, 1962-63; U.S. Office of Education international programs grant, 1972-74; Social Science Research Council and American Council of Learned Societies grant, 1973-74; National Science Foundation grant, 1975; U.S. Office of Education neighborhood training program grant, 1979-80.

WRITINGS: (With Douglas Steen) *Precision Power Bidding,* Coffin, 1956; (editor and contributor) *Independent Black Africa: The Politics of Freedom,* Rand McNally, 1964; *Politics in Black Africa,* Michigan State University Press, 1964; (with wife, Judith Lynne Hanna) *Polyethnicity and Political Integration in Umuahia and Mbale,* American Society for Public Administration, 1968; *The University Students of Black Africa,* American Institutes of Research, 1970; (with J. L. Hanna) *Urban Dynamics in Black Africa: An Interdisciplinary Approach,* Aldine, 1971, 2nd edition, 1981; *Comparative Urban Politics,* two volumes, Sage Publications, 1972; *University Students and African Politics,* Africana Publishers, 1975; *Equity for the Disabled,* Montgomery Co., 1980. Contributor to professional journals. Editor and publisher of *Comparative Urban Research,* 1972—.

WORK IN PROGRESS: Urban Service Equity.

SIDELIGHTS: William John Hanna writes: "Over the past five years, I have become increasingly interested in the issue of equity. What, I want to know, is fair? This has led me to conduct research and to write on questions such as these: What is an equitable distribution of services among socioculturally contrasting neighborhoods? To what extent should resources be devoted to minimizing the environmental handicaps that disabled citizens face—for instance, curb barriers? Is the 'Fair Housing' program fair to homeseeking minority group members and also to old-timer neighborhood residents? My purpose is not to reveal the answer, for I think that there is no single answer. Rather, I am trying to clarify the questions and demonstrate the subjective or personal nature of the answers."

* * *

HANRIEDER, Wolfram F. 1931-

PERSONAL: Born May 9, 1931, in Munich, Germany; naturalized U.S. citizen; son of Josef and Barbara (Laubmeier) Hanrieder. *Education:* University of Chicago, B.A., 1958, M.A., 1959; University of California, Berkeley, Ph.D., 1963. *Home:* 4812 Winding Way, Santa Barbara, Calif. 93111.

CAREER: Princeton University, Princeton, N.J., research associate, Center of International Studies, 1963-64; assistant professor of political science, 1964-67; University of California, Santa Barbara, associate professor, 1967-71, professor of political science, 1971—. Visiting professor at University of California, Berkeley, 1966, University of Kiel, 1974, and School of Advanced International Studies, Johns Hopkins University, 1974. Milton R. Merrill Professor of Political Science, Utah State University, 1973. Fulbright professor, University of Munich and University of Braunschweig, 1969-70. *Awards, honors:* NATO research fellow.

WRITINGS: West German Foreign Policy, 1949-1963: International Pressure and Domestic Response, Stanford University Press, 1967; (editor with R. A. Falk and contributor) *International Law and Organization,* Lippincott, 1968; (contributor) Roy C. Macridis, editor, *Modern European Governments: Cases in Comparative Policy Making,* Prentice-Hall, 1968.

The Stable Crisis: Two Decades of German Foreign Policy, Harper, 1970; (editor and contributor) *Comparative Foreign Policy: Theoretical Essays,* McKay, 1971; (editor and contributor) *The United States and Western Europe: Political, Economic and Strategic Perspectives,* Winthrop Publishing, 1974; (contributor) W. Link and W. Feld, editors, *The New Nationalism: Implications for Transatlantic Relations,* Pergamon, 1979; (contributor) *America's Transformation from Kennedy to Carter,* ICA, 1979; (with Graeme Auton) *The Foreign Policies of Germany, France, and Britain,* Prentice-Hall, 1979; (with Larry V. Buel) *Words and Arms: Dictionary and Data of National Security and Defense Policy,* Westview, 1979; (editor and contributor) *Arms Control and Security: Current Issues,* Westview, 1979; (editor and contributor) *West German Foreign Policy, 1949-1979,* Westview, 1979.

(Editor and contributor) *Economic Issues and the Atlantic Community,* Praeger, 1980; (editor and contributor) *Helmut Schmidt: Perspectives on Politics,* Praeger, 1982. Contributor of numerous articles to *Policy Studies Journal, Western Political Quarterly, American Political Science Review, Journal of Common Market Studies,* and other periodicals.

WORK IN PROGRESS: A book on German foreign policy.

* * *

HANSER, Richard (Frederick) 1909-1981

PERSONAL: Born December 15, 1909, in Buffalo, N.Y.; died December 7, 1981, in Port Chester, N.Y.; son of Adolf T. (a minister) and Caroline (Feiertag) Hanser; married Anne Golcar, November 29, 1931; children: David Karl. *Education:* Attended Concordia Lutheran Collegiate Institute (now Concordia College), Bronxville, N.Y., 1923-29. *Politics:* Democrat. *Home:* 420 Grant Terr., Mamaroneck, N.Y. 10543. *Agent:* Bill Cooper Associates, 16 East 52nd St., New York, N.Y. 10022.

CAREER: Free-lance writer. *Buffalo Times,* Buffalo, N.Y., reporter and feature writer, 1929-33; *Cleveland Press,* Cleveland, Ohio, reporter and rewrite man, 1933-34; *Buffalo Times,* columnist and feature writer, 1934-36; Fawcett Publications, Inc., New York City, associate editor, 1937-41; *PM,* New York City, city editor, 1941-42; RKO Pathe, Inc., New York City, documentary script writer, 1946-52; National Broadcasting Co. Television, New York City, documentary script writer, 1952-74, chief writer for "Project 20" documentary series, 1959-74. Consultant to National Endowment for the Humanities, 1971-74. *Wartime service:* U.S. Office of War Information, Psychological Warfare Section, London, England, 1942-43; worked as civilian specialist on psychological war. U.S. Army, 12th Army Group, European Theatre, 1944-45; attached to psychological warfare detachment. *Member:* Television Academy (member of New York board of governors, 1962-66), Writers Guild of America East (member of council, 1961-65), Overseas Press Club (New York City).

AWARDS, HONORS: George Foster Peabody Award, for "Victory at Sea"; Robert E. Sherwood Award for Television Documentary, 1959, for "Meet Mr. Lincoln"; Emmy Award nominations, Academy of Television Arts and Sciences, 1960, 1961, 1962, and 1963; Writers Guild of America Award for Television Documentary, 1961, for "Mark Twain's America"; Western Heritage Award, 1970, for "The West of Charles Russell"; recipient of other awards for "Victory at Sea."

WRITINGS: (With Henry Saloman) *Victory at Sea* (based on television documentary of same title), Doubleday, 1959; (with Donald B. Hyatt) *Meet Mr. Lincoln* (based on television documentary of same title), Ridge, 1960; (compiler) *True Tales of Hitler's Reich*, Crest Books, 1962; (with Hyatt) *The Coming of Christ*, Cowles Publications, 1963; *Putsch! How Hitler Made Revolution*, Wyden Books, 1970 (published in England as *Prelude to Terror: The Rise of Hitler, 1919-1923*, Hart-Davis, 1971); *Jesus: "What Manner of Man Is This?,"* Simon & Schuster, 1972; *The Glorious Hour of Lt. Monroe*, Atheneum, 1976; *A Noble Treason: The Revolt of the Munich Students against Hitler*, Putnam, 1979.

Author of television documentaries, including "Life in the Thirties," "Not So Long Ago," "He Is Risen," "Mirror of America," "Meet George Washington," "Meet Mr. Lincoln," "Strange and Terrible Times," "Mark Twain's America," "The West of Charles Russell," "That War in Korea," "The Island Called Ellis," "The Law and the Prophets," and, with Saloman, "Victory at Sea" series. Also author of other television documentaries for NBC's "Project 20" series.

Translator from German: Hans Habe, *Aftermath,* Viking, 1947; Habe, *Walk in Darkness,* Putnam, 1948; H. M. Mons, *The Sword of Satan,* McKay, 1952.

Contributor to anthologies. Contributor of articles to periodicals, including *Saturday Review, New York Times Magazine, Esquire, London Opinion, Reader's Digest,* and *Theatre Arts.* Member of editorial board, *Television Quarterly,* beginning 1963, and *American-German Review,* 1965-69.

SIDELIGHTS: In the *New Leader,* Richard C. Hottelet wrote of Richard Hanser's *Putsch! How Hitler Made Revolution:* "This pungent and powerful book is the anatomy of a nightmare. It goes beyond its title . . . to sketch the tragedy of a nation unhinged. And yet it tells its story—the fateful conjunction of public confusion and fanatic, gifted personality—in colorful detail and with a strong grasp of essentials. Hanser thoroughly understands his material and is fascinated by it, drawing his reader into a shared experience. *Putsch!* is historical journalism at its best." Hanser's account of the rise of Nazism in Germany focused on the social conditions and the individual events that propelled Adolph Hitler—a "crashing nonentity" as of 1919, Richard M. Watt notes—to national prominence.

In 1919, when Hitler first attended a meeting of the German Workers, an obscure political party, "Germany was a bedlam of political uprisings, street battles and local wars, compounded by the French occupation of the Ruhr and a demoralizing inflation," Hottelet commented. "There were only 46 people at the meeting," Watt wrote in the *New York Times Book Review.* "The party was so desperate for adherents that without Hitler's applying they sent him a membership card. Even Hitler found this ludicrous. But he joined, [and] . . . shortly afterwards, [he] had 50,000 dedicated followers and was influential enough to be an authentic menace to the state. How this came to be is the story Mr. Hanser tells, and he tells it vividly."

Hanser's chronicle builds up to the events of November 9, 1923, when Hitler made his first attempt to seize power. Hottelet said of the thwarted Beer Hall Putsch: "Observers have, quite properly, concentrated on the center ring of [the] dismal circus—the national scene, where the power lay. And the time came when one sinister set of local clowns moved in to usurp it. Hanser looks closely at the sideshow in an earlier phase to demonstrate how much and how little of an accident their later victory was. He does so economically and with the professional's eye for illuminating detail, while keeping the larger picture in focus."

Hanser's *A Noble Treason* tells the story of Hans and Sophie Scholl and the White Rose movement, one of the few organized voices of opposition to Hitler within Nazi Germany. "The question will not go away," Mayo Mohs stated in *Time.* "When the cattle cars with their human cargo rumbled off for Auschwitz, where were the righteous in the Third Reich?" *A Noble Treason,* Mohs continued, "unfolds with compassion and craft the story of the White Rose conspiracy, whose name was a symbol of purity and whose work was one of the most selfless acts of resistance in the entire war."

"As he demonstrated in his previous book, *Putsch! How Hitler Made Revolution,* the author has a genuine flair for recreating a place and time by way of a revealing incident," Gary Walther wrote in the *New Leader.* "*A Noble Treason* is popular history at its best—accurate, lively, readable." In *America,* Jerome Donnely remarked: "Using diaries, letters and accounts of surviving friends and family, Hanser builds a detailed, compelling account of the White Rose movement and its setting, and especially of the Scholl family. Hanser's account is masterly; his understatement only enhances the stature of the students' words and acts." "Hanser's intense admiration for this brother and sister team leaps from the pages," Walther observed. "They were attractive youngsters in their 20s when they were discovered as the authors and disseminators of anti-Hitler leaflets, were summarily judged, and guillotined. . . . The countless tales of Nazi atrocities have been repeated many times; only a few lacunae have to be filled in. The rare stories of heart, passion, conscience and courage have been slow in coming. That of the White Rose and the Scholls is one of them. It is fortunate that a man of Hanser's skill, moderation, and sympathy has told it." Concluded Donnely: "Sophie Scholl, so vibrant in the photographs accompanying the text, epitomizes the manner of the group in her clear, calm demeanor. As she told the enraged judge who sentenced her, 'Somebody, after all, had to make a start.' Richard Hanser has nobly captured their start in a wise and wonderful book."

Hanser traveled extensively in Europe, particularly to Germany to make documentary films and research his books.

BIOGRAPHICAL/CRITICAL SOURCES: New York World-Telegram, February 7, 1959; *New York Times,* March 25, 1961; *New York Times Book Review,* January 17, 1971, December 10, 1972; *Wall Street Journal,* January 28, 1971; *Washington Post Book World,* June 13, 1971; *New Leader,* December 14, 1971, November 19, 1979; *Commonweal,* November 19, 1976; *Time,* July 16, 1979; *New Yorker,* September 3, 1979; *Los Angeles Times Book Review,* September 23, 1979; *Atlantic,* October, 1979; *National Review,* April 4, 1980; *America,* May 3, 1980.

OBITUARIES: New York Times, December 10, 1981.†

HANSON, Norwood Russell 1924-1967

PERSONAL: Born August 17, 1924, in West New York, N.J.; died April, 1967; son of Samuel Norwood (a salesman) and Hannah Helen (Proper) Hanson; married Frances Fay Kenney, August 14, 1948; children: Trevor Russell, Leslie Fay. *Education:* Attended Curtis Institute, 1941; University of Chicago, B.A., 1946; Columbia University, B.Sc., 1948, M.A., 1949; Oxford University, B.Phil., 1951, D.Phil., 1955; Cambridge University, M.A., 1953, Ph.D., 1955. *Politics:* "(Manchester) *Guardian* Liberal." *Religion:* Atheist. *Home:* 47 Deepwood Dr., Hamden, Conn. 06514.

CAREER: Cambridge University, Cambridge, England, university lecturer in philosophy of science, 1952-57, fellow of St. John's College, 1956; Indiana University at Bloomington, professor of philosophy, 1957-62, professor of the history and logic of science, 1962-63, chairman of department of the history and logic of science, 1960-63; Yale University, New Haven, Conn., professor of philosophy, 1963-67. Silliman Lecturer, Yale University, 1961; visiting lecturer, Oxford University, 1961; visiting professor, University of Colorado, 1961; faculty member, Oak Ridge Institute of Nuclear Studies, 1963-64. Consultant to E. I. du Pont de Nemours & Co. *Military service:* U.S. Marine Corps, fighter pilot, 1942-46; became major; received Air Medal, Distinguished Flying Cross. *Member:* American Association for the Advancement of Science (fellow; vice-president, 1961; secretary of Section L), History of Science Society (member of council).

AWARDS, HONORS: Fulbright fellow at Oxford University, 1951; Nuffield Foundation fellow for work at Institute of Advanced Study, Princeton, N.J., and California Institute of Technology; Ford Foundation fellow, 1957; American Council of Learned Societies fellow, 1958; research fellow at Center for Philosophy of Science, University of Minnesota, 1959; Rockefeller Foundation fellow, 1959; American Philosophical Society grant, 1961; Distinguished Alumni Award, Columbia University, 1962; honorary M.A., Yale University, 1963; National Science Foundation grants, 1964-66; Carnegie Corp. fellow, 1967.

WRITINGS: Patterns of Discovery: An Inquiry into the Conceptual Foundations of Science, Cambridge University Press, 1958; *The Concept of the Positron: A Philosophical Analysis,* Cambridge University Press, 1963; *A History of Science,* Dell, 1965; *Perception and Discovery: An Introduction to Scientific Inquiry,* edited by Willard C. Humphreys, Freeman, Cooper, 1969; *Observation and Explanation: A Guide to the Philosophy of Science,* Harper, 1971; *Why I Do Not Believe and Other Essays,* edited by Stephen Toulmin and Harry Woolf, Dordrecht Reidel, 1972; *Constellations and Conjectures,* edited by Humphreys, Dordrecht Reidel, 1973.

Contributor: P.A. Schilpp, editor, *The Philosophy of C. D. Broad,* Tudor, 1960; *A Physics Anthology,* Reinhold, 1960; Sidney Hook, editor, *Dimensions of Mind,* New York University Press, 1961; Herbert Feigl and Grover Maxwell, editors, *Current Issues in the Philosophy of Science,* Holt, 1961; (author of introduction) John Maynard Keynes, *Treatise on Probability,* Torchbooks, 1962; Robert Garland Colodny, editor, *Beyond the Edge of Certainty,* Prentice-Hall, 1965; R. S. Cohen and M. W. Wartofsky, editors, *Boston Studies in the Philosophy of Science,* Humanities Press, 1968.

Also contributor to proceedings of Oxford University International Congress for the History of Science, 1962, and Wesleyan Conference on Induction, 1962; contributor to *International Encyclopedia of Philosophy.* Contributor of more than one hundred articles and reviews to periodicals, including *Cambridge Review, Listener, Analysis, Physics Today, Saturday Review, Rationalist, Scientia, American Bar Association Journal,* and to philosophy journals in the United States, Europe, and Australia.

WORK IN PROGRESS: Explanation and Prediction in the History of Planetary Theory, for Cambridge University Press; *A History of Aerodynamic Theory,* for Northwestern University Press; *Notes Towards a Logic of Discovery; Thirteen Dialogues on Necessity.*

SIDELIGHTS: Norwood Russell Hanson started garnering kudos with a science medal in grammar school, Philharmonic music scholarships and a scholarship to Curtis Institute of Music. Hanson owned a Navy fighter plane and flew in air shows with aerobatic teams such as the "Blue Angels."†

* * *

HARCLEROAD, Fred F(arley) 1918-

PERSONAL: First syllable of surname rhymes with "lark"; born November 22, 1918, in Cheyenne, Wyo.; son of Fred F. and Ina Mary (Livermore) Harcleroad; married Moyne Payne, December 20, 1942; children: Patricia Irene, Fred Douglass. *Education:* Colorado State College (now University of Northern Colorado), B.A., 1939, M.A., 1942; Stanford University, Ph.D., 1948. *Home:* 840 Via Linterna, Tucson, Ariz. 85718.

CAREER: High school teacher and principal in Ault, Colorado, 1939-43; Menlo Junior College, Menlo Park, Calif., teacher, counselor, and director of dormitory, 1943-46; San Diego State College (now University), San Diego, Calif., 1946-52, began as assistant professor, professor of education, 1951-52, director of audiovisual services, 1947-50, director of secondary education, 1949-51, chairman of Division of Education, 1951-52; San Jose Junior College, San Jose, Calif., dean of instruction, 1952-53; San Jose State College (now University), San Jose, dean of instruction, 1952-57, dean of college, 1957-59; California State University, Hayward, Calif., professor of higher education and president, 1959-67; University of Iowa, Iowa City, professor of higher education, 1968-74; University of Arizona, Tucson, professor of higher education, 1974—, director of Center for the Study of Higher Education, 1974-80. Assistant and acting instructor, Stanford University, summers, 1944, 1945; visiting professor, University of Southern California, summers, 1951, 1958, California State University, San Diego, summer, 1954, Pennsylvania State University, summer, 1956, University of Hawaii, summer, 1961, and University of Washington, summer, 1969. Member of State of California Advisory Committee on Real Estate Education and Research, 1956-59; member of Committee on Intercultural Education, 1966-69; Education Commission on the States, member of advisory committee on higher education, 1966-68, vice-chairman of advisory committee on higher education, 1967-68, member of planning board, Kellogg In-Service Education Project, 1976-79; president of American College Testing Program, 1967-74; member of advisory panel of Southern California Community College Study, 1971-72; member of National Commission on Accrediting Study, 1971-72; member of advisory board of ERIC Clearinghouse for Junior Colleges, 1973-77; member of ERIC Clearinghouse on Higher Education, 1973-79; member of Task Force on Interagency Cooperation for Council on Postsecondary Accreditation, 1976-78; National Home Study Council Accrediting Commission, public commissioner, 1976-82, chairman, 1977-81. Consultant to McGraw-Hill Book Co., 1959-63, U.S. Department of Health and Human Services, 1964, 1966-67, 1969, Los Angeles Times-Mirror Corp., 1967, Education Commission of the States, 1972-73, 1977-80, and American Association of State Colleges and Universities Research Center for Planned Change, 1979-80.

MEMBER: National Education Association, American Council on Education, American Association for Higher Education, Association of Professors of Higher Education (member of executive committee, 1973-76; president, 1974-75), American Association of Community and Junior Colleges (president, 1975-76), Association for Educational Communications and Technology, Foundation for Educational Communications and Technology (member of board of directors, 1971-78, 1980-82), Association for the Study of Higher Education, Western College Association (member of board of directors and executive committee, 1963-67), Higher Education Colloquium, Commonwealth Club of California, Pi Kappa Delta, Kappa Delta Pi, Phi Mu Alpha, Phi Kappa Phi, Phi Alpha Theta, Phi Delta Kappa. *Awards, honors:* Trailblazer Award, University of Northern Colorado, 1970.

WRITINGS: (With William Allen) *Audio-Visual Administration,* W. C. Brown, 1951; (with James W. Brown and Richard B. Lewis) *Audio-Visual Instruction, Technology, Media and Methods,* McGraw, 1959, 6th revised edition, 1983.

(Editor) *Learning Resources in Colleges and Universities,* U.S. Office of Education, 1964; *Need for Fiscal Authority and Responsibility in the California State Colleges,* California State Colleges, 1967; *The Historical Background, Current Status, and Future Plans of the Developing State Colleges and Universities,* U.S. Office of Education, 1969.

(With Robert J. Armstrong) *New Dimensions of Continuing Studies Programs in the Massachusetts State College System,* American College Testing Program, 1972; (with Frank Dickey) *Educational Auditing and Voluntary Institutional Accrediting,* ERIC, 1975; *Institutional Efficiency in State Systems of Public Higher Education,* American Association of State Colleges and Universities, 1975; (with C. Theodore Molen, Jr., and Suzanne Van Ort) *The Regional State Colleges and Universities in the Middle 1970's,* American Association of State Colleges and Universities, 1976; *Educational Auditing and Accountability,* Council on Postsecondary Accreditation, 1976; (editor) *The Study of Higher Education: Some Papers on Administrative Theory and Practice,* Association of Professors of Higher Education, 1976; (with T. Harry McKinney and S. V. Martorana) *Postsecondary Education in North Dakota: An Agenda for 1977-78,* North Dakota Postsecondary Education Commission, 1977; (with Brown and Lewis) *Instructor's Manual to Accompany Audio-Visual Instruction: Technology, Media and Methods,* 5th edition, 1977

Accreditation: History, Process, and Problems, ERIC, 1980; *Voluntary Organizations in America and the Development of Educational Accreditation,* Council on Postsecondary Accreditation, 1980. Also author of *Audio-Visual Instructional Technology Manual for Independent Study,* with Brown and Lewis, and of *International Education in the Developing State Colleges and Universities,* with Alfred Kilmartin, 1966.

Editor and contributor; published by American College Testing Program, except as indicated: *Issues of the 70's: The Future of Higher Education,* Jossey-Bass, 1970; *New Directions in Higher Education,* 1971; (with Jean H. Cornell) *Assessment of Colleges and Universities,* 1971; *Comprehensive Information Systems for Statewide Planning in Higher Education,* 1971; *Planning for State Systems of Postsecondary Education,* 1971; *Administration of Statewide Systems of Higher Education,* 1975; *Financing Postsecondary Education in the 1980's,* University of Arizona, 1979.

Contributor: *Audio-Visual Instructional Materials Manual,* McGraw, 1959; William J. McKeefery, *Parameters of Learning,* Southern Illinois University Press, 1970; *New Horizons in Admissions Excellence,* Brigham Young University, 1970; *Target for the 70's,* American Association of State Colleges and Universities, 1970; G. Kerry Smith, editor, *New Teaching, New Learning,* Jossey-Bass, 1971; Roy Trout, *Exploring Non-Traditional Degree Programs in Higher Education,* American College Testing Program, 1971; Paul L. Dressel and Frances H. Delisle, *Blueprint for Change: Doctoral Programs for College Teachers,* American College Testing Program, 1972; Richard M. Millard, *Vocation: Central Aim of Education,* American College Testing Program, 1973; *Exploring the Case for Low Tuition in Public Higher Education,* American College Testing Program, 1974.

Berdahl, *Evaluating Statewide Boards,* Jossey-Bass, 1975; *Community College Staff Development,* National Board on Graduate Education, 1975; Martorana and Eileen Kuhns, *Managing Academic Change,* Jossey-Bass, 1975; *Academic Program Evaluation,* Jossey-Bass, 1980; Jedamus, Peterson and others, *Improving Academic Management: A Handbook of Planning and Institutional Research,* Jossey-Bass, 1980; Hample and others, *New Directions in Institutional Research,* Jossey-Bass, 1981; Altbach and Berdahl, *Higher Education and American Society,* Pergamon, 1981; Young, Kenneth and others, *Understanding Accreditation: A Practical Guide to Self-Regulation in Postsecondary Education,* Jossey-Bass, 1982. Also contributor to *Academic Program Evaluation, New Directions for Institutional Research,* 1980, and to *The Changing Nature of Rehabilitation Administration and Supervision,* with Amos Sales, 1981.

Contributor to *Proceedings* of Northwest Association of Secondary and Higher Schools Annual Convention, 1970, and to *Summer 1970 Philosophic Exchange Annual Proceedings,* 1970. Contributor of articles and reviews to higher education journals. Audio-visual editor of *California Journal of Secondary Education,* 1952-55; member of editorial board, *Audio-Visual Communication Review,* 1959-65.

* * *

HARDESTY, Nancy A(nn) 1941-

PERSONAL: Born August 22, 1941, in Lima, Ohio; daughter of Byron Tapscott (a tool and die maker) and Ruth Lucille (a bank clerk; maiden name, Parr) Hardesty. *Education:* Wheaton College, Wheaton, Ill., A.B., 1963; Northwestern University, M.S.J., 1964; University of Chicago, Ph.D., 1976. *Politics:* Democrat. *Religion:* Episcopalian. *Home:* 2534 Bradford Sq. N.E., Atlanta, Ga. 30345.

CAREER: Lima News, Lima, Ohio, reporter, 1961-63; *Christian Century,* Chicago, Ill., editorial assistant, 1964-65; *Eternity,* Philadelphia, Pa., assistant editor, 1966-69; Trinity College, Deerfield, Ill., assistant professor of English and sports information director, 1969-73; Emory University, Candler School of Theology, Atlanta, Ga., assistant professor of American church history, 1976-80; Central Gwinnett High School, Lawrenceville, Ga., English teacher, 1980—. Founding member, Evangelical Women's Caucus.

WRITINGS: (Contributor) Robert G. Clouse and others, editors, *The Cross and the Flag,* Creation House, 1972; (with Letha Scanzoni) *All We're Meant To Be: A Biblical Approach to Women's Liberation,* Word Books, 1974; (contributor) Gary R. Collins, editor, *It's O.K. to Be Single,* Word Books, 1976; (contributor) Helen Gray Crotwell, editor, *Women and the Word,* Fortress, 1978; (contributor) Rosemary Ruether and

Eleanor McLaughlin, editors, *Women of Spirit,* Simon & Schuster, 1979; *Great Women of Faith,* Baker Book, 1980; (contributor) Jim Towns, editor, *Solo Flight,* Tyndale, 1980; (contributor) Theodore Runyon, editor, *Sanctification and Liberation,* Abingdon, 1981; (contributor) Hilah F. Thomas and Rosemary Skinner Keller, *Women in New Worlds,* Abingdon, 1981.

WORK IN PROGRESS: A revision of doctoral dissertation, "*Your Daughters Shall Prophesy*": *Revivalism and Feminism in the Age of Finney.*

SIDELIGHTS: Nancy A. Hardesty writes: "I have been reared, educated and employed within a conservative, 'evangelical' Christian context. There I have seen first-hand the discrimination practiced against women and have felt the frustration when such oppression is buttressed with biblical and religious arguments. I decided to fight back. My goal is to learn more about Christian women of the past, their work and their beliefs, and then to communicate their inspiring stories to people today."

* * *

HARDY, David A(ndrews) 1936-

PERSONAL: Born April 10, 1936, in Birmingham, England; son of Arthur (a violinist) and Lilian (Andrews) Hardy; married Ruth Margaret Fearn (a music teacher), 1975; children: Karen Dawn. *Education:* Attended schools in England. *Religion:* Church of England. *Home:* 99 Southam Rd., Hall Green, Birmingham B28 0AB, England. *Office:* Astro Art, 99 Southam Rd., Hall Green, Birmingham B28 0AB, England.

CAREER: Employed as laboratory technician, 1952-54; Cadbury Bros. Ltd., Bournville, England, artist, 1956-65; Astro Art, Birmingham, England, artist and writer, 1965—. Has designed and illustrated book jackets. *Military service:* Royal Air Force, 1954-56. *Member:* Royal Astronomical Society (fellow), British Interplanetary Society (associate fellow), British Astronomical Association, Lincoln Astronomical Society (president, 1969-72; vice-president, 1972—). *Awards, honors:* Hugo Award nomination for best professional artist, 1979.

WRITINGS—Published by World's Work, except as indicated: (With Patrick A. Moore) *The Challenge of the Stars: A Forecast of the Future Exploration of the Universe,* Rand McNally, 1972; (self-illustrated) *The Solar System,* 1975; (self-illustrated) *Rockets and Satellites,* 1976; (self-illustrated) *Air and Weather,* 1977; (self-illustrated) *Light and Sight,* 1977; (self-illustrated) *Energy and the Future,* 1979; (self-illustrated) *Atlas of the Solar System,* 1982. Contributor of articles on science and art to various publications.

Illustrator: M. T. Bizony, general editor, *The Space Encyclopedia: A Guide to Astronomy and Space Research,* Dutton, 1957, revised edition, 1960; Patrick Moore, *Astronomy,* Oldbourne, 1961, published as *Story of Astronomy,* Macdonald, 1972; George H. Gopsill and Frank Beesley, *Practical Geography,* Macmillan, 1964; Colin Ronan, *The Stars,* Bodley Head, 1965; Ronan, *The Universe,* Oxford University Press, 1966; W. E. Swinton, *The Earth Tells Its Story,* Bodley Head, 1967; J. Petrie, *The Earth,* Oxford University Press, 1967; Moore, *Space,* Lutterworth, 1968; Moore, *Astronomy for "O" Level,* Duckworth, 1970; Brenda Thompson, editor, *Volcanoes,* Sidgwick & Jackson, 1974; Thompson, editor, *Spaceship Earth,* Sidgwick & Jackson, 1975; (with Bob Shaw) *Galactic Tours: Thomas Cook Out of This World Vacations,* Proteus, 1982. Also illustrator of various children's books, including "Outlines" series, Metheun, 1957-61, of science fiction books published in the United States, Britain, and Germany, and of filmstrips.

SIDELIGHTS: "My chief motivation, since the early 1950's," David A. Hardy told *CA,* "has been to present an *accurate* picture of space and astronomy—in fact any science, as so many bad books, cheaply illustrated, have been on sale.

"In addition, I firmly believe that Man's future lies in space. Apart from his traditional pioneering spirit—the 'outward urge,' his need to expand, the challenge and joy of pure exploration, and the exciting possibilities of scientific discoveries—there are very practical reasons to go into space. Energy is there in abundance, there is 'free' heat, cold, vacuum, zero gravity, and the pollution from industrial centers can be taken away from Earth. In my writing and painting I try to show how such a future could benefit all."

BIOGRAPHICAL/CRITICAL SOURCES: Science in Action, February 6, 1969; *Canvas,* June, 1969; *Spaceflight,* January, 1970; *Pictures & Prints,* spring, 1970.

* * *

HARMON, Robert Bartlett 1932-

PERSONAL: Born November 29, 1932, in Helper, Utah; son of John Harold (a salesman) and Winnie Ethlynn (Bartlett) Harmon; married Merlynn Swensen, August 18, 1961; children: Marriner John, Jane Anne, David Wright, James Bartlett, Nancy Louise. *Education:* Brigham Young University, B.A., 1958, M.A., 1960; Rutgers University, M.L.S., 1962; graduate study at San Jose State University, 1966-68. *Politics:* Republican. *Religion:* Church of Jesus Christ of Latter-day Saints. *Home:* 964 Chapel Hill Way, San Jose, Calif. 95122. *Office:* Library, San Jose State University, San Jose, Calif. 95192.

CAREER: San Jose State University, San Jose, Calif., librarian II, 1962-65, senior assistant librarian, 1969-75, associate librarian, 1975—, reference librarian, 1979—, Library Education and Assistance Program lecturer in Graduate School of Librarianship, head of acquisitions department, 1969-79. Editor and publisher, Dibco Press, 1966—; founder and research bibliographer, Bibliographic Research Library, 1970—.

MEMBER: American Library Association (founder and director of Bibliographic Information Center for the Study of Political Science, 1970—), Bibliographical Society of America, American Printing History Association, Hemingway Society, John Steinbeck Society of America, Mormon History Association, Bibliographical Society of Canada, Bibliographical Society of the University of Virginia, California Library Association, Kappa Delta Pi.

WRITINGS: The Cole Family: A Brief Bibliography, privately printed, 1964; *A Preliminary Checklist of Materials on Harman-Harmon Genealogy,* privately printed, 1964; *Political Science: A Bibliographical Guide to the Literature,* four volumes, Scarecrow, 1965-74; (with John Ray Harmon) *Descendants of Charles Claymore Bartlett and Annie Katrine Jensen,* Harmonart, 1965; *Sources and Problems of Bibliography in Political Science,* Dibco, 1966.

Suggestions for a Basic Political Science Library, Bibliographic Information Center for the Study of Political Science, 1970; *Political Science Seminar Research Methods Manual,* Bibliographic Information Center for the Study of Political Science, 1970; *Imperialism as a Concept of Political Science: Essay and Bibliography,* Bibliographic Information Center for the Study of Political Science, 1971; *Art and Practice of Diplomacy,* Scarecrow, 1971; *Methodology and Research in Po-*

litical Science: An Annotated Bibliography, Bibliographic Information Center for the Study of Political Science, 1972; *Elementary Cataloging Manual for Small Libraries*, Dibco, 1972; *Earthquakes: Toward a Bibliography of Bibliographies*, Dibco, 1972; *John Steinbeck: Toward a Bibliography of Bibliographies*, Dibco, 1973; *Georgette Heyer: A Preliminary Checklist*, Dibco, 1974; *The Ghostly Bibliography*, Dibco, 1975; *Selected Guide to Annotated Sources of Information in Political Science*, General Learning Press, 1975; *Simplified Cataloging Manual for Small Libraries and Private Collections*, Bibliographic Research Library, 1975; *Developing the Library Collection in Political Science*, Scarecrow, 1976; (with Margaret A. Burger) *An Annotated Guide to the Works of Dorothy L. Sayers*, Garland, 1977; *Understanding Ernest Hemingway: A Study and Research Guide*, Scarecrow, 1977; *Elements of Bibliography: A Simplified Approach*, Scarecrow, 1981.

Published by Hermes in 1978: *The First Editions of Ernest Hemingway; The First Editions of William Faulkner; The First Editions of John Steinbeck; The First Editions of Robinson Jeffers; The First Editions of Gertrude Stein; The First Editions of F. Scott Fitzgerald.*

Also author of bibliographies for "Public Administration and Architecture" series, Vance Bibliographies, 1974. Editor, *The Steinbeck Collector*, 1979—.

WORK IN PROGRESS: *An Annotated Index to Bibliographical Sources Related to Steinbeck Studies;* bibliographical projects related to Hemingway and Steinbeck studies, political science, and architecture.

SIDELIGHTS: Robert Bartlett Harmon writes to *CA*: "To many people libraries are simply repositories for books and other materials. For me the library is my laboratory—a place where, like the chemist or physicist, I can experiment, explore and discover new and exciting knowledge. My primary tools are bibliographic instruments that provide me with the information I need for my projects. New ideas and concepts are constantly being generated and refined from encounters with students and others at the library reference desk which is an unlimited source for motivation and enlightenment. The ultimate goal of my writing is to provide works that will direct users to new and unsuspected resources so that their minds will be stimulated by new ideas, and their conception of their subject enriched by the indication of new areas as yet unexplored."

* * *

HARMS, Leroy Stanley 1928-

PERSONAL: Born December 3, 1928, in Spink County, S.D.; son of Henry (a rancher) and Mollie Kristina (Barness) Harms; married Joan Yuhas (an evaluation specialist for Hawaii Open Program), April 11, 1966; children: John, William, Kathleen, Kristina. *Education:* Sorbonne, University of Paris, diploma in French and phonetic science, 1954; University of Florida, B.A., 1955; Ohio State University, M.A., 1957, Ph.D., 1959. *Home:* 165 Nawiliwili St., Honolulu, Hawaii 96825. *Office:* Department of Communication, University of Hawaii at Manoa, Honolulu, Hawaii 96822.

CAREER: Louisiana State University, Baton Rouge, assistant professor of speech, 1959-62; University of Kansas, Lawrence, associate professor of speech and communication, 1962-65; University of Hawaii at Manoa, Honolulu, associate professor, 1965-74, professor of communication, 1974—, senior specialist at East-West Center, 1965-66. Member of board of directors of United Nations Association—Hawaii; conference chairman of Major Issues in World Communication; organizer and chairman of Speech Communication Association of Communication Rights Commission. *Military service:* U.S. Army, 1947-50.

MEMBER: International Communication Association, International Broadcast Institute, World Future Society, Speech Communication Association of America, Asian Mass Communication Research and Information Center.

WRITINGS: (With L. B. Rabby) *The Effect of Stage Lighting on Audience Comprehension*, University of Kansas, 1963; (with M. Scheib) *Toward a Generalized Self-Instructional System for Speech Sound Acquisition*, University of Kansas, 1963; *Phonetic Transcription*, Scott, Foresman, 1964; (with Paul Heinberg and June Yamada) *Speech Communication Learning Systems*, International Learning Systems, 1970; *International Studies of National Speech-Education Systems*, Burgess, 1970; *Intercultural Communication*, Harper, 1973; (contributor) Kgzuo Nakano, editor, *Phonetic Papers for Masao Onishi*, Phonetic Society of Japan, 1974; *Human Communication*, Harper, 1974; (editor with Jim Richstad) *Evolving Perspectives on the Right to Communicate*, East-West Communication Institute, 1977; (editor with Richstad and Kathleen A. Kie) *Right to Communicate: Collected Papers*, University of Hawaii at Manoa, 1977.

Also author, with Robert Eugene Dunham, of *Index and Table of Contents of Southern Speech Journal, 1935-60*, Central States Speech Journal, 1949-60 and *Today's Speech*, 1953-60. Editor, with Richstad, of *World Communication: Population Communication, Communication Technology, Communication in the Future*, University of Hawaii at Honolulu, 1973.†

* * *

HARPER, Daniel
See BROSSARD, Chandler

* * *

HARRIS, Del(mer William) 1937-

PERSONAL: Born June 18, 1937, in Orleans, Ind.; son of Elmer W. (a barber) and Wilma (Whitten) Harris; married Joyce A. Crites, June 20, 1958; children: Larry, Alex, Stanley, Carey Ann. *Education:* Milligan College, A.B. (cum laude), 1959; Indiana University, M.A., 1964.

CAREER: Teacher of psychology and history and athletic coach in high schools in Indiana, 1959-65; Earlham College, Richmond, Ind., associate professor, athletic director, and basketball coach, 1965-74; European Pro League, Barcelona, Spain, head coach, 1974-75; Utah Stars (professional basketball team), Salt Lake City, Utah, assistant coach, 1975-76; Houston Rockets (professional basketball team), Houston, Tex., assistant coach, 1976-79, head coach, 1979—. Summer coach for Puerto Rico Pro League, 1969-75; charter builder of Indiana Basketball Hall of Fame.

WRITINGS: *Multiple Defenses for Winning Basketball*, Parker Publishing, 1971; *Coaching Basketball's Zone Offenses*, Parker Publishing, 1975; *Playing the Game* (sports novel), Harco, 1982.

WORK IN PROGRESS: Research for a book set in the 1890's.

SIDELIGHTS: Del Harris gives motivational talks and self-image lectures to conventions, corporations, and business groups. In 1980, Harris guided his Houston Rockets basketball team to the final series in the National Basketball Association playoffs. He writes to *CA*: "*Playing the Game* is a sports novel for teenagers and adults illustrating how to use a positive thinking program to go from losing to winning in life. The story line is about three boys who play on the high school basketball team. Basically, it's a beginner's book on positive thinking—a very good message for young people."

* * *

HARRIS, Philip R(obert) 1926-

PERSONAL: Born January 22, 1926, in Brooklyn, N.Y.; son of Gordon Rodger and Esther E. (Delahanty) Harris; married Dorothy Lipp (a professor and associate dean at U.S. International University), July 3, 1965. *Education:* St. John's University, Jamaica, N.Y., B.B.A., 1949; Fordham University, M.S., 1952, Ph.D., 1956; special courses at St. Francis College, Brooklyn, N.Y., Syracuse University, New York University, Catholic University of America, and University of Notre Dame. *Politics:* Independent. *Religion:* Christian. *Home:* 2702 Costebelle Dr., La Jolla, Calif. 92037.

CAREER: Licensed psychologist, State of New York, 1959. St. Francis College, Brooklyn, N.Y., 1956-63, became director of student personnel and vice-president; Association for Human Emergence, Inc., State College, Pa., executive director, 1964-66; Pennsylvania State University, College of Education, University Park, lecturer in counselor education, 1965-66; Leadership Resources, Inc., Washington, D.C., senior associate, 1966-69; Copely International Corp., San Diego, Calif., vice-president, 1970-71; Harris International, Ltd., La Jolla, Calif., president, 1971—. Fulbright lecturer in India, 1962-63; visiting professor, Temple University, 1967-69, University of California, San Diego, 1971-79, University of North Colorado, 1973-74, and Pepperdine University, 1975; lecturer and conductor of human and management relations and leadership institutes throughout North America. Delegate to UNESCO Conference, Paris, 1962. Publications director for International Consultants Foundation, 1980. Consultant to Fe Y Algeria School System, Caracas, Venezuela, 1960-69, Temple University, 1967-69, and Trikon Productions, 1978.

MEMBER: International Consultants Foundation, World Future Society, American Psychological Association, American Society for Training and Development. *Awards, honors:* Named Young Man of the Year, New York City Junior Chamber of Commerce, 1959; mental health grant, U.S. Department of Health, Education, and Welfare, 1959; National Training Laboratories scholarship, National Education Association, 1965; Office of Naval Research grant, 1972-74.

WRITINGS: Change in the Military Justice System through Professional Development of Correctional Personnel, National Technical Information Service, 1972; (with wife, Dorothy L. Harris) *Leadership Effectiveness with People,* Harris International, 1978; *New Worlds, New Ways, New Management,* American Management Association, 1982; *Improving Leadership Effectiveness,* University Associates, 1982.

"Insight" series, with William J. McMahon and James J. Cribbin; published with instructor's manuals by Harcourt, 1959, revised edition, 1965; *It's Your Life; It's Your Education; It's Your Personality; It's Your Future.*

"Increasing Managerial Effectiveness" series: *Organization Dynamics,* Tam's Books, 1974; *Effective Management of Change,* Westinghouse Learning Corp., 1976; (with D. L. Harris) *Improving Management Communication Skills,* Westinghouse Learning Corp., 1978.

"International Management Productivity" series, with Robert T. Moran; published by Gulf Publishing: *Managing Cultural Differences,* 1979; *The Cosmopolitan Manager,* 1981; *Transnational Managers as Cultural Change Agents,* 1981; *Understanding Cultural Differences,* 1981; *Family Relocation Coping Skills,* 1981; *Improving Productivity of International Managers,* 1981; *Managing Cultural Synergy,* 1982.

Editor: *Republic Study Guide for Regents Scholarship Preparation,* Republic Book Co., 1955; *Readings for Catholic Counselors,* [New York], 1958; *NCWC Guide to Catholic Education Institutions,* National Catholic Welfare Conference, 1959; (with Garld H. Malin) *Innovations in Global Consultation: Macro Perspectives on the Consulting Relationship,* International Consulting Foundation (Washington, D.C.), 1980.

Also author of "Organizational Effectiveness with People" series, Harris International. Author of column, "Tools for Training," for *Successful Meetings,* 1975-78. Contributor of 160 articles to professional journals. Editor, *Catholic Counselor,* 1955-59.

WORK IN PROGRESS: A novel on the subject of the industrialization of space, *Launch Out.*

AVOCATIONAL INTERESTS: Travel (including extensive tours of five continents), reading, swimming, golfing.

* * *

HARRISON, James (Thomas) 1937-
(Jim Harrison)

PERSONAL: Born December 11, 1937, in Grayling, Mich.; son of Winfield Sprague (an agriculturist) and Norma Olivia (Wahlgren) Harrison; married Linda King, October, 1960; children: Jamie Louise, Anna Severin. *Education:* Michigan State University, B.A., 1960, M.A., 1964. *Religion:* "Zennist." *Home address:* Box 120A, Lake Leelanau, Mich. 49653.

CAREER: Writer. Assistant professor of English, State University of New York at Stony Brook, 1965-66. Screenwriter for Warner Brothers and other film companies. *Member:* Trout Unlimited, Grouse Society. *Awards, honors:* National Endowment for the Arts grants, 1967-69; Guggenheim fellowship, 1969-70; two awards from National Literary Anthology.

WRITINGS—Under name Jim Harrison, except as indicated; poems: (Under name James Harrison) *Plain Song,* Norton, 1965; *Locations,* Norton, 1968; *Walking,* Pym Randall Press (Cambridge, Mass.), 1969; *Outlyer and Ghazals,* Simon & Schuster, 1971; *Letters to Yesinin,* Sumac Press, 1973; *Returning to Earth,* Ithaca House, 1977; *Selected Poems,* Delacorte, 1982.

Novels, except as indicated: *Wolf: A False Memoir,* Simon & Schuster, 1971; *A Good Day to Die,* Simon & Schuster, 1973; *Farmer,* Viking, 1975; *Legends of the Fall* (collection of three novellas, "Revenge," "The Man Who Gave Up His Name," and "Legends of the Fall"), Delacorte, 1979; *Warlock,* Delacorte, 1981.

Contributor of poems to anthologies: *Out of the War Shadow,* War Resisters League (New York City), 1967; Coralie Howard, editor, *Lyric Poems,* F. Watts, 1968; Ron Schreiber, editor, *Thirty-One New American Poets,* Hill & Wang, 1969; A. Poulin, Jr., editor, *Contemporary American Poetry,* Houghton, 1971; Louis Untermeyer, editor, *Fifty Modern American and British Poets,* McKay, 1973.

Also author of screenplays for Warner Brothers and other film studios. Contributor to other anthologies. Contributor of poems, stories, articles, and reviews to periodicals, including *New York Times Book Review, Sports Illustrated, Partisan Review, Esquire, American Poetry Review,* and *Nation.*

WORK IN PROGRESS: A novel, *The Foreman;* poems; screenplays.

SIDELIGHTS: "[Jim] Harrison's stories tend to be powered by myth," Stuart Schoffman writes in the *Los Angeles Times Book Review.* "Underneath, the ingredients are staple: nature, adultery, violence." With this mix of ingredients, Harrison has created "a holy American mythology," Jerome Klinkowitz asserts. In a *Chicago Sun-Times* review of *Legends of the Fall,* Harrison's widely-acclaimed collection of novellas, Klinkowitz finds that "so much of American legend is packed into these brief pages that Jim Harrison must be admired as an almost sacred writer."

Before 1979, the year when the publication of *Legends of the Fall* brought him great commercial success, Harrison "had averaged a scanty $10,000 a year writing award-winning . . . poetry (five volumes) and three other novels which had never quite taken off," Gordon Chaplin notes in the *Washington Post.* "For years he wrote beautiful poems that everyone said were 'beautiful poems' and made no money," Kathleen Stocking states in the *Detroit News Magazine.* "Surprise. Jim Harrison has become rich and famous." Harrison, who recently completed a contract with Warner Brothers, is currently working on the screenplay adaptations of the novellas in *Legends of the Fall.* He told *CA* that the motion picture rights to each of the three novellas have been purchased by a major studio but that he has "decided not to give out any information on my film work as it is not central to my career (pure money work) and has caused dozens of unwarranted invasions of privacy." Harrison writes screenplays, he says, only "in order to buy farm land and swamps."

Legends of the Fall reveals Harrison "at the height of his powers," Raymond Carver writes in the *Washington Post Book World.* According to Carver, the novella "The Man Who Gave Up His Name" is an "extraordinary piece of writing covering what might seem all-too-familiar territory: a change in life for a man in his early 40s. But I think this novella can stand with the best examples the form has to offer—those by Conrad, Chekhov, Mann, James, Melville, Lawrence, Isak Dinesen." "I can't begin to do justice to the nuances of character and honest complexities of plot in this work," Carver continues. "The writing is precise and careful—and sings withal." "*Legends of the Fall* is a good Harrison sampler," Klinkowitz writes, "three short novels about revenge, redemption, and sorrow, all primal acts of strong men in profile against an even more demanding world."

Legends of the Fall is inhabited by "men to whom life reveals itself in primitive ways, through primitive acts of will," an *Atlantic* reviewer declares. "These violent, compelling novellas startled, angered, and disturbed me," Garrett Epps comments in the *Washington Post Book World.* "They also fascinated me, kept me thinking afterwards. They are, beyond question, the work of a gifted and accomplished writer. They tell of men who seek vengeance on their enemies . . . , [men for whom] vengeance brings a kind of religious ecstasy." Chaplin remarks that "an almost mystical faith and fascination in the efficacy of violence as nature's own solution" underlies the three novellas. And in *Nation,* Keith Opdahl says that *Legends of the Fall* is "full of silent men and lovely women who desire to be ravaged. The bad guys are nightmare figures with names like 'Slats' who just don't listen to reason. You have to zap them hard."

Because of his harsh, often violent subject matter and his one-dimensional portrayals of female characters, Harrison has been criticized, as Jonathan Yardley writes in the *New York Times Book Review,* for being "extravagantly free-male, male animal" in his fiction. Epps believes that *Legends of the Fall* "is not for everyone. Harrison writes about—and, I think, almost completely for—men." "In fact," Epps continues, "it seems fair to say that *Legends of the Fall* is a collection of fairy tales for men. That is not to disparage its craft, power or worth—such tales have always been a sophisticated form of literature, important for their exemplary role in teaching people how to overcome evil and enjoy goodness," but "because these men are everything most men wish to be, their stories have a terrible power. They speak to the reader's deepest hopes and fears about himself." Epps feels that in the novellas Harrison "is holding up a view of manhood—self-sufficient, violent, strong, antisocial—that seems to be losing currency in this country. I happen to think that the passing of these values is, on the whole, a good thing."

The title novella of *Legends of the Fall* tells the story of Tristan, a Montana farmer who, along with his two brothers, enlists to fight in World War I. When his gentle younger brother is killed in the war, Tristan goes mad, scalping every German he can capture, and is locked away. In the *National Review,* Laurie Prothro says of Tristan: "His obsessive fury and quest for vengeance cause him to inflict terrible agonies on others, and on himself. He escapes the hospital to spend his life in tortured search of the reason why there is no fair system of rewards and punishments on earth. We share his limitless grief when he realizes that there is no way to even the score with the world." "Tristan's is a shatteringly tragic story," Prothro concludes. "Harrison tells it brilliantly." "Harrison takes a terrible pleasure in himself as a moral creature," James Whitehead concludes in the *Saturday Review.* "Man and beast in the rounds of their dying—Harrison can tolerate it. He can celebrate it." As Harrison told Stocking, "You can't be a writer unless you are willing to face up to every unpleasant aspect of the human experience." "It is a matter of 'not withholding the evidence,'" Stocking adds, "of telling the truth about life."

Despite his praise for Harrison's "extraordinary talent," Yardley feels that Harrison "manufactures a fraternity of he-men who use women in the fashion of town pumps and romanticize about an ecologically balanced utopia where, fishing pole in hand and Rover by his side, a man can be a man—while the rest of the world staggers on in its lamentable, but inescapably real, way." Peter S. Prescott of *Newsweek* believes that Harrison's fiction "celebrates a fantasy of masculine self-sufficiency" in which "a woman is a smooth-skinned primate who, by virtue of her domesticity and enervating sexuality, is incapable of understanding a man's need to blaze his solitary path in a senseless world. A woman is something a man must leave behind, preferably pregnant, with the suggestion that he may return in a year or two; the woman, of course, waits." "Has Harrison seen too many gangster movies, too many Westerns, too much TV?," Opdahl asks. "He seems to *believe* all this," Opdahl continues, "though I would guess that he is either doing movie scenarios, attempting to tap into the great American Dream Machine, . . . or has trained himself as a poet to be too honest, too direct to soften these American fantasies."

According to M. L. Rosenthal, "Harrison is one of our finest young poets." In the *New York Times Book Review,* Rosenthal says that in his verse Harrison is "relentlessly hard on himself; his past life, his present plights, his character in general. But he redeems the poems from grimness by a buffoonery of anguish and by something else that is more elusive." "The something else," Rosenthal explains, "is an open, volatile atmosphere. It involves a sense of comic slovenliness originating in the self-ironies of folkspeech and unexpectedly convertible into an almost physical precision, that of a workman who knows just how to use his tools. . . . All the poetic faces and voices make themselves felt [in *Outlyer and Ghazals*]. It is sometimes exasperating, sometimes cheaply facile, often heartbreaking, often exquisitely beautiful as the waves of language and sense-impressions and uncontrollably black moods and randy philosophizing and esthetic balancings sweep over the pages.'' ''This is poetry worth loving, hating, and fighting over,'' Rosenthal concludes, ''a subjective mirror of our American days and needs.'' In *Harper's*, Hayden Carruth calls *Letters to Yesinin* ''a minor masterpiece'' but finds that *Returning to Earth* ''seems not quite so successful . . . but still notable. . . . It is hard-boiled poetry, some of the best of its kind. . . . [Harrison's] poetic vision is at the heart of it all. To stay alive now is primitivism. And that is the hard best that we can know.'' Finally, a *Publishers Weekly* reviewer describes *Selected Poems* as the work of ''untrammeled renegade genius.'' (''I made a T-shirt out of this quote,'' Harrison says.)

In the *New York Times*, Christopher Lehmann-Haupt calls Harrison's first novel, *Wolf: A False Memoir*, ''a poet's novel, adding up to nothing but its boisterous and eloquent self.'' H. L. Van Brunt, writing in the *Saturday Review*, asserts that Harrison and other poets-turned-novelists have ''a conspicuous advantage. For while they may have to learn a new and very different discipline, they came to their task equipped with copious imagination and, of course, a trained command of the language. . . . Humor, irony and, above all, energy animate Harrison's prose.''

The main character of *Wolf* is Swanson, ''a one-man pioneer movement looking for a new country,'' Van Brunt writes. A bitter and restless thirty-three-year-old drifter, Swanson abandons the decadence of urban life for the renewing atmosphere of the northern Michigan woods. According to Yardley, Swanson is ''a loner, an anachronism, a wolf.'' During his stay in the forest, Swanson becomes obsessed with spotting a wolf, a kindred spirit. He says that ''there are only three or four hundred native wolves left in the United States. I felt that if I could see one all my luck would change.'' Swanson's quest for the wolf, Van Brunt comments, ''may be seen as a symbolic pursuit of lost wildness and freedom. . . . Swanson bristles into being—a man mean in the fashion of a child or an animal, a creature who snarls and spits at would-be tamers who hold out the meat of mediocrity and uniformity as he struggles to keep open all the possibilities his free-wheeling youth once afforded.'' Despite his longing for freedom, Swanson doesn't remain in the forest for long; ''he is bitten by insects, he gets lost, he worries about snakes, and he desperately misses liquor and cigarettes,'' Lehmann-Haupt observes. ''Swanson is not very wolflike,'' Joyce Carol Oates points out in the *Partisan Review*. ''He is lost in the wilderness, and, we assume, he has always been lost; his life is as shapeless as nature itself.'' As Swanson says in the book: ''Driving out of the woods I felt a new and curious calm but doubted it would last. . . . When I reached the main road I would stop at a gas station and make a reservation at a hotel in Ishpeming and when I got there I knew I would shower and go down to the bar and drink myself into the comatose state I knew I deserved.'' Swanson's story, Yardley concludes, ''sharply portray[s] the conflict between the urge to live—fully, meaningfully, exuberantly—and the circumstances we have created for life.'' ''The effect of the whole,'' Lehmann-Haupt states, ''is touching and slightly fearsome.''

A *Choice* critic describes *A Good Day to Die* as ''a fine novel,'' a ''black comedy of three modern misfits.'' This tale of disaffected youth, of two men and a woman who travel west to dynamite a government dam, is ''a poet's book,'' according to William Crawford Woods. ''Its metaphors are sharp as jagged bone. Its long cadences plead to be read aloud. Its language as a whole is a half-mad harvest of technical vocabularies.'' Writing in the *Washington Post Book World*, Woods is critical of the novel's development but believes that Harrison is ''the real thing, and his work is absolutely genuine. . . . [He] has several gifts it would be hard to overpraise. Bright, dizzying language aside, he can swiftly characterize certain rural and urban types with a precision close to paradigm.'' In a *New York Times* review, Lehmann-Haupt commends Harrison's ''jagged and cutting'' perceptions in this ''remarkably well-plotted story,'' but hopes that Harrison will learn to ''more skilfully match [his] themes to the underlying myths they rely on.''

Harrison's third novel, *Farmer*, is the story of Joseph, a middle-aged schoolteacher in rural Michigan who finds himself torn between two women—his steady girlfriend Rosealee and a racy high school senior. ''Joseph . . . has been planning for several years to marry his fellow teacher Rosealee,'' Raymond Sokolov observes in *Newsweek*. ''Stolidly and regularly, on appointed days of the week, they sleep together in the dark. Sometime soon, they will wed and Joseph will farm her acreage. It is a joyless plan. Joseph, meanwhile, dreams of the ocean, of breaking out of the landlocked world.'' As a *Booklist* reviewer notes, Joseph's young lover Catherine offers ''a more tantalizing yet not clearly marked trail.'' ''She comes from the outside world that Joseph craves,'' Sokolov points out. ''Harrison cannily fractures his story and reveals each treasured facet only gradually . . . [to form] an artfully disjointed meditation on a complicated person.'' Sokolov finds that Harrison's patient unraveling of his main character succeeds in putting ''the reader inside Joseph's head.'' ''Harrison gives us a man, an environment, an attitude,'' Webster Schott writes. ''The man is a wanter, usually fondling a dream, often on the edge of failure, endowed with an ability to survive. The environment is Michigan bursting. The attitude is stoic.'' In the *New York Times Book Review*, Schott concludes that Harrison ''writes beautifully. He sees life going on and on, its meaning in its pattern, its outcome uncertain except in ending. He moves us rather than overwhelms us. He creates an art small except in its grace.''

''What a joy it is to discover Jim Harrison,'' Schoffman declares in a review of *Warlock*, Harrison's fourth novel. Schoffman says that Harrison ''has written a rich and sparkling novel about a tired theme: the mid-life *angst* of the American male.'' This account of the adventures of Johnny ''Warlock'' Lundgren, an unemployed executive who dabbles in detective work, is laced with ''tender irony, a touch of absurdity,'' Schoffman remarks. ''Man in mid-stream, seeking transformation, will realize that the river moves, not he,'' Schoffman observes, ''but the dream of change is the vital counterweight to the omnipresent dream of death. Between clenched teeth, in *Legends of the Fall*, in the Faulknerian reveries of *Farmer* and now in Warlock's baying to [his beautiful wife], goddess of the Michigan moon, Harrison proves himself master of American theme and style.'' In the *Times Literary Supplement*, T. O. Treadwell says that ''*Warlock* is a comic novel which rests on the premise that beneath the slick and sophisticated surface of American life the old nature gods still exercise their capricious power. This . . . territory has been explored before, . . . [but] to it Jim Harrison has brought a fresh and original eye.'' Treadwell believes that ''what satisfies most, perhaps, is the author's vigorous and often acerbic wit.'' ''Harrison scores well on the firing range,'' J. D. Reed comments in *Time*. ''His humor usually strikes in the killing zone.''

In the *Saturday Review*, John Buckley finds that *Warlock* is ''flawed in its timing, taking forever to start and then no time to end." Similarly, John D. Casey writes in the *New York Times Book Review:* "The only flaw in this book is its pacing. Mr. Harrison takes the first lap too slowly and the last lap too fast." Yet Casey contends that "the flaw is noticeable mainly because of the affection one develops for the novel's characters. Warlock is an engaging fellow, and his wife is a pretty nifty woman. I even liked his old dad and his mutt of a dog. So I didn't want to see these good creatures get so roughly tumbled about for the sake of the novel's big finish." "For all its unevenness of pacing," Casey concludes, "there are pleasures of all sorts to be had—farcical, reflective, luscious, gritty—in this stylish entertainment."

Harrison's ability to create realistic characters and settings, especially his landscapes of northern Michigan, has been praised by several reviewers. "Few writers can surpass Harrison at rendering vividly the sights, smells, and sounds of this world— the pleasures of dancing and hunting, the angular beauty of the American Midwest," Epps states. In the *Christian Science Monitor,* Parkman Howe finds that *Farmer*'s "true touches" are its "descriptive passages . . . , such as the almost indiscernible, relentless coming on of seasons in upstate Michigan," and Prothro believes that Harrison "records the facts like an omnipresent reporter: details of the natural world as well as what his heroes feel, smell, see." Finally, a *New Yorker* reviewer praises the "graceful descriptions of rural northern-Michigan life and robust, empathetic portraits of country people" in *Farmer.* Concludes the reviewer: "Harrison . . . is at his best when he is telling us about hunting and fishing, about the swoop of a hawk, or about the way the light falls on a horse's flanks or the side of a barn."

AVOCATIONAL INTERESTS: Hunting, fishing, cooking, wine.

CA INTERVIEW

CA interviewed Jim Harrison by phone October 7, 1981, at his home in Lake Leelanau, Michigan.

CA: You've been away recently. Were you out promoting your new book, Warlock?

HARRISON: No, I've been out to Los Angeles figuring out how I'm going to make this year's living. I don't like to do any book promotion; I've never done any.

CA: Being at home on your Michigan farm seems to be very important to you, yet you travel a lot, both for work and for pleasure. Is the contrast necessary to your writing?

HARRISON: I think so. I live in northern Michigan, where I was born and raised. It's where I feel the best in the world, and it's the only place I've ever been able to write—I've never been able to write in transit. Also, I have a place further north here, a cabin on a river in the Upper Peninsula. My nearest neighbor there is five miles away. I like that sort of thing. If you have to go to Los Angeles and New York a lot where everything's enervating, it's nice not to have anything to do with that during other times.

CA: In his Washington Post *article, Gordon Chaplin wrote about how much you enjoy telling stories. Was there a storytelling tradition in your family?*

HARRISON: To a certain extent, I would say, on both sides of the family. The families were large and basically rural, and such people are always storytellers. My dad could never bear to say the same thing the same way. You know, when people spend a lot of their lives based in some kind of oral tradition, they're much more careful about the words and they make a much greater attempt to make what they say interesting. They also have a lot of time to talk if everyone is poor and there's no television. I think you have the same thing in any rural region, even in the countryside of, say, northern France.

CA: How did your early interest in writing begin?

HARRISON: I guess with a ninth-grade teacher who started giving me books that I couldn't ordinarily have gotten. But I didn't have anything specific in mind. Even when I ran off to New York and California when I was nineteen, I still didn't know what I wanted to write, so I wrote short stories at that time and then started writing poems. I wrote poems until I was thirty-one or thirty-two, then I wrote my first novel.

CA: Was writing poetry a kind of deliberate apprenticeship, as it is for some writers?

HARRISON: Usually it is, almost inadvertently. For instance, the houseguest I have now from Alabama just gave me William Faulkner's first book of poems. Even Hemingway wrote poems; Sherwood Anderson did. I suppose it's partly because you have so many hormones in your twenties and thirties that you can't sit down for that long haul that's known as writing a novel, yet your feelings are inexpressibly intense at the time, so you take it out on poetry. I still write poetry. In fact, Delacorte is going to publish my selected poems next year. About a third of the poems will be new ones.

CA: You've been described as something of a nonconformist as an undergraduate at Michigan State. Was it hard for you to stay on for your M.A.?

HARRISON: It was hideous. As an undergraduate I think I had quit half a dozen times. But the man in the scholarship office was sympathetic with my desire to be an author. I think he was Michigan State's first Rhodes scholar; he was interested in literature. So he'd always give my scholarship back to me when I came back. But then I sort of flunked out of the M.A. program. They rearranged the degree requirements for me when I published my first book of poems with Norton. They had to waive the language exams. I'm the only person I know of who actually got an F in a graduate course.

CA: Has the M.A. been worthwhile at all in your writing?

HARRISON: Not at all. I never took any writing courses, except a course in writing essays when I was a sophomore. The teacher had the odd idea that the way to get people to write essays was to have them imitate other people, so we wrote essays in the fashion of Henry James and so on. That was good teaching. If you don't have an incredible playfulness about language, I think you tend to write boring novels. Auden talked about that. Being a writer requires an intoxication with language, an obsession with language. You get the meaning later, because you don't have a great sense of meaning when you're first finding this out—it's the hormones again.

CA: Very young children are fascinated by the sounds of language before they have any real sense of meaning, but that seems to be educated out of us.

HARRISON: Oh, for sure. That's because of the banality of the school system. And literature isn't now and never was nor ever will be a popular taste. It's all a mistake to think that literacy has any real meaning other than a very functional one; most quasi-literate people only read the comic strips or the sports page. The importance of literacy in the United States is basically for people to know what they're signing so they won't be swindled.

CA: I noticed that A Good Day to Die *had been published in Spain. Have you gotten much mail or other response from readers of the translation?*

HARRISON: Really quite a bit. I got an enormous sheaf of Spanish reviews, which I've never read because I don't read Spanish. That novel in particular seems to be perfect for them. *Legends of the Fall* sold better in England than it did here, oddly enough. One thing, I guess, is that Bernard Levin gave it a huge review in the *Times* in London, and his reviews have a lot of authority. It was certainly a more interesting review than I've ever gotten in America.

CA: Legends of the Fall *brought financial success the earlier books had failed to bring. How were you affected by the rush of publicity that came with it?*

HARRISON: It was a real mess for a while, because I had been poor for about forty years, you know, and then I got really *not* poor. That was confusing for about two and a half years until I started spending a lot of my time with my family; then the confusion went away and I became sane again. But before I became sane again, I made a lot of dumb investments. I made no investment that I wasn't able to halve in one year—English gambling stock, Australian oil stock, a charter boat in Key West, a lot of personal loans to indigent friends, unsecured, written off for ever and ever. I don't care now.

CA: You've helped a lot of friends who were trying to get established as writers, haven't you?

HARRISON: You try to, but it's very difficult. The only novel I think I ever helped immediately get published was Tom McGuane's *The Sporting Club,* just because I knew someone at Simon and Schuster. Tom had fired his agent suddenly. I took it to Richard Locke, who was then at Simon and Schuster, and he only took twenty-four hours to get it accepted there. That was fun.

CA: Commenting on the style of the title novella of Legends of the Fall, *Vance Bourjaily wrote in the* New York Times Book Review, *"In compression, unexpectedly, lies credibility." Did it take a lot of revision to achieve the narrative leanness of "Legends of the Fall"?*

HARRISON: That's the one about which an unnamed publisher asked me wouldn't it be wonderful if I had written that in a 400-page form. Long books are popular because people think they're getting a good deal. It didn't take a lot of revision; I only took out one sentence after the first draft. That novella came sort of pouring out. I wanted to tell a tale like a romance, sort of like "Once upon a time. . . ." What you do is create the illusion in the first paragraph that this actually happened. You're very matter-of-fact about it.

CA: How are plans proceeding for the movie version of "Revenge"?

HARRISON: "Revenge" is still owned by Warner, and they've got John Huston on it now. I think he's a fine director, when you consider the number of really good pictures he's done. He's not terribly popular with the studios, because he's such a wonderfully arrogant, powerful human being. He can get away with wearing a cape. I've had dinner a number of times with Orson Welles, and I like him too. "Legends" is owned by Twentieth Century-Fox. "The Man Who Gave Up His Name" is owned by Columbia.

CA: You've been writing screenplays on contract for Warner Brothers now for several years. Are you enjoying the work?

HARRISON: I've finished my Warner Brothers contract. But the way it works for me is that after I finish a novel I have a big overflow of energy for about a year and a half, and that's the time I feel I can write screenplays with impunity. And they're actually sort of fun to write, because I've tried a number of times to write a play for the theater but have never been able to. I'm still trying, in fact; I've started another one this year. I suppose screenplays are an overflow too of that passion that started on my senior trip to New York when I saw Eugene O'Neill's "The Iceman Cometh."

CA: Would you like to respond to the criticism that you sometimes portray women shallowly and in a chauvinistic way?

HARRISON: It's OK as long as you don't say the word *macho,* which has literally driven me up the tree. No, I think in *Warlock* that's definitely not true. Someone told me, at least, that that was my first major woman. It's just that I don't suppose I ever knew them well enough. Certainly no one could present women as shallow as women novelists often do. Feminism as such has too many didactic tenets to expect novelists to follow now. Novelists write stories; they don't write tracts. When I've presented a shallow woman, it was because she *was* a shallow woman; she was no more shallow than the man—as in *A Good Day to Die.* Also, I certainly don't want to pretend to more knowledge about women than I have, just to curry favor. Most women are still like Tibet to me; though I've studied Tantric Buddhism at some length, I still don't feel I comprehend it. The only thing I really resent is *macho.* I know a lot about Mexican culture, and as I've pointed out, macho is when you throw a rattlesnake in a baby carriage or bite off your mother's toe—some kind of overpowering violence.

CA: You work in a very concentrated way—long hours—on a specific project, then rest when it's done. Are you able to free your mind of writing during the periods of rest?

HARRISON: Of course not, but generally you're so exhausted that you can't write any longer. Since I was born and raised here a lot of my preoccupations are with hunting, fishing, things like that. (And that may be one reason I'm so highly criticized by the feminist press.) Some New York critic said that the people in *Farmer* couldn't have actually existed. That's because people on America's dream coasts—both East and West—don't largely have any comprehension of the Midwest. Or the deep South; the fashionable opinion is that any white Southerner is ipso facto a bigot.

CA: You care a great deal about nature. In an Esquire *article you wrote, "If the next good country doesn't exist it's because we pillaged the last one we so stridently walked through." Do you play an active role in any organized conservation movement?*

HARRISON: No, I don't, because I can't bear them, but I just won a big environmental suit that cost me in the five figures personally. I didn't take donations because I just wanted to win the suit and I didn't want it to be messy.

CA: What kind of suit was it—or do you want to talk about it?

HARRISON: Not really, because it's a sore point up here. It was about an illegal and totally unwarranted dredging activity. So I pursue conservation to that extent. But I find that conservation groups are very busy with language: they think if they get the language right, then everything's OK. But that's not what it takes. You have to have power, and you have to have power resources equal to those of your opponent; so you have to organize yourself some way, either with cash or dynamite, to win. There's no sense sitting around convincing the convinced. You have to go after them with usually every legal means possible, and very immediately—there's not much time for meetings.

CA: Are there present or future projects you'd like to discuss? Anything you'd like to say for the record that's gotten left out of other interviews?

HARRISON: I have started another novel, but it's a long one, my first long one, so it takes a long time.

CA: I know you've been unhappy with some of your interviews. Is there anything you'd like to add to this one?

HARRISON: No, I don't think so. It never was any kind of inclusive or specific thing. I don't think I actually enjoy talking about myself. I don't mind talking about my work, but I've consistently turned down interviews that were based on personality. That's why I have a big sign in my front driveway that says, "Do not stop here without calling. This means *you*." I don't understand writers who want to be in some publicity-oriented limelight, because it's never based on people who are actually interested in the work.

BIOGRAPHICAL/CRITICAL SOURCES: Saturday Review, February 19, 1966, December 18, 1971, December 25, 1971, August 21, 1976, October, 1981; *Virginia Quarterly Review,* summer, 1966; *Poetry,* July, 1966, February, 1971; Jim Harrison, *Wolf: A False Memoir,* Simon & Schuster, 1971; *New York Times Book Review,* July 18, 1971, December 4, 1971, September 9, 1973, October 10, 1976, June 17, 1979, November 22, 1981; *New York Times,* November 24, 1971, September 13, 1973, July 26, 1976; *Western Humanities Review,* spring, 1972; *Detroit Free Press,* April 16, 1972; *Partisan Review,* summer, 1972; *Washington Post Book World,* September 9, 1973, May 13, 1979, July 8, 1979, November 29, 1981.

Contemporary Literary Criticism, Gale, Volume VI, 1976, Volume XIV, 1980; *New Yorker,* August 30, 1976, July 30, 1979; *Newsweek,* August 30, 1976, July 9, 1979; *Christian Science Monitor,* January 27, 1977, September 5, 1979; *Harper's,* June, 1978; *Nation,* July 7, 1979; *Chicago Sun-Times,* July 15, 1979; *Best Sellers,* September, 1979; *Atlantic,* September, 1979; *Booklist,* November 1, 1979; *Listener,* February 28, 1980; *Washington Post,* March 2, 1980; *National Review,* March 7, 1980; *Times Literary Supplement,* March 21, 1980, January 15, 1982; *Detroit News Magazine,* August 17, 1980; *Los Angeles Times Book Review,* October 25, 1981; *Time,* November 9, 1981; *Detroit News,* December 15, 1981; *London Times,* January 7, 1982; *Publishers Weekly,* June 25, 1982.

—Sketch by Stewart R. Hakola

—Interview by Jean W. Ross

* * *

**HARRISON, Jim
See HARRISON, James (Thomas)**

**HARTEL, Klaus Dieter
See VANDENBERG, Philipp**

* * *

HARVEY, John F(rederick) 1921-

PERSONAL: Born August 21, 1921, in Maryville, Mo.; son of Abraham Frederick and Lois Ernestine (Glenn) Harvey. *Education:* Dartmouth College, A.B., 1943; University of Illinois, B.S., 1944; University of Chicago, Ph.D., 1949. *Address:* P.O. Box 122, Lyndonville, Vt. 05851.

CAREER: John Crerar Library, Chicago, Ill., assistant cataloger, 1944-45, assistant medical reference librarian, 1945-47; University of Chicago Library, Chicago, Ill., administrative assistant, 1949-50; Parsons College, Fairfield, Iowa, librarian and professor of library science, 1950-53; Kansas State Teachers College of Pittsburg (now Pittsburg State University), Pittsburg, professor, head librarian, and chairman of department of library science, 1953-58; Drexel Institute of Technology (now Drexel University), Philadelphia, Pa., director of libraries, 1958-63, Graduate School of Library Science, dean and professor, 1958-67; University of Tehran, Tehran, Iran, professor of library sciences, 1967-71, chairman of department, 1967-68; Iranian Documentation Centre and Tehran Book Processing Centre, Tehran, founder, technical director, 1968-71; University of New Mexico, Albuquerque, dean of School of Library Services, 1972-74; Hofstra University, Hempstead, N.Y., dean of School of Library Services, 1974-76; writer, editor, and consultant, 1976-78; visiting professor at Mottahedin University, Tehran, 1978-80. Pennsylvania director, National Library Week, 1960-62. Consultant to organizations, including World Health Organization. *Military service:* U.S. Army, 1942-43.

MEMBER: American Library Association, American Association of University Professors, American Society of Information Science, Association of College and Research Libraries, Church and Synagogue Library Association, Library Administration and Management Association, American Institute of Iranian Studies, British Institute of Persian Studies, Institute of Information Scientists (London), Iranian Library Association, Middle East Librarians Association, New England Association of Schools and Colleges, Library Public Relations Association of Philadelphia, Phi Kappa Phi, Melvil Dui Chowder and Marching Association (New York), La Societe des Amities Francaises (Tehran), Archons of Colophon (New York), Brothers Three of Moriarity (Santa Fe). *Awards, honors:* Library Binding Institute Silver Book Award, 1965; Fulbright grant, 1967-71.

WRITINGS: Action Manual for Library Recruiters (monograph), Joint Committee on Library Work as a Career, 1956; *The Librarian's Career: A Study of Mobility,* University of Rochester Press, for Association of College and Research Libraries, 1957; (compiler with Phillips Temple) *A Directory of Library Periodicals in the Continental United States,* State College Library (Pittsburg, Kan.), 1957; *Report to Chancellor Torab Mehra Covering Recommendations for the Development of Jundi Shapur University Library Services,* University of Tehran, 1968.

Iranian Senior College Library Standards, Educational Resources Information Center, 1971; *Comparative and International Library Science,* Scarecrow, 1977; *Church and Synagogue Libraries,* Scarecrow, 1980; (editor with Peter Spyers-Duran) *Austerity Management in Academic Libraries,* Scarecrow, 1983; (editor with Frances Laverne Carroll) *Internationalizing Library Education,* Greenwood Press, in press.

Also author of *Toward a Definition of International and Comparative Library Science*, 1972. Contributor to *Encyclopedia Americana*, 1963, *Bowker Library Annual*, 1963, *American Educator Encyclopedia*, United Educators, and proceedings of Southwest Asian Documentation Centre Conference, 1970. Editor, "Drexel Library School" series, 1960—, "Monthly Recruitment" series, "Drexel Information Science" series, Spartan Press, 1964—. Contributor of articles and reviews to professional journals. Editor of *Library Journal*, 1962, and of newsletters.

SIDELIGHTS: *Toward a Definition of International and Comparative Library Science* has been translated into Chinese.

* * *

HASTINGS, Phyllis (Dora Hodge) (Julia Mayfield)

PERSONAL: Born in Bristol, England; daughter of William and Dora Rosina (Miles) Hodge; married Philip Norman Hastings, August 20, 1938; children: Kerry. *Education:* Attended Edgebaston Church of England College for Girls. *Politics:* Tory. *Home:* The Abbot's Cottage, Upper Lake, Battle, East Sussex TN33 OAN, England.

CAREER: Was a ballet dancer as a child; owned and operated a dairy farm in 1953; runs an antiquarian bookshop with her husband, Philip Norman Hastings, in Battle, East Sussex, England.

WRITINGS: *As Long as You Live*, Jenkins, 1951; *Far from Jupiter*, Jenkins, 1952; *Crowning Glory*, Jenkins, 1952; *Rapture in My Rags*, Dutton, 1954, published as *Scarecrow Lover*, Pan Books, 1960; *Dust Is My Pillow*, Dutton, 1955; *The Field of Roses*, Dent, 1955, published as *Her French Husband*, Dutton, 1956; *The Black Virgin of the Gold Mountain*, Dent, 1956; *The Signpost Has Four Arms*, Dent, 1957; *The Happy Man*, Hutchinson, 1958; *Golden Apollo*, Hutchinson, 1958; *The Fountain of Youth*, Hutchinson, 1959; *Sandals for My Feet*, Hutchinson, 1960; *Long Barnaby*, Hodder & Stoughton, 1961, published as *Hot Day in High Summer*, May Fair Books, 1962; *The Night the Roof Blew Off*, Hodder & Stoughton, 1962; *All Earth to Love* (part one of "The Sussex Saga"), Howard Baker, 1969; *Day of the Dancing Sun* (part two of "The Sussex Saga"), Corgi Books, 1971; *The Candles of Night*, Collier Macmillan, 1977; *Field of the Forty Footsteps*, St. Martin's, 1978; *The Feast of the Peacock*, Cassell, 1978. Also author of *London Quartet*.

Published by R. Hale: (Under pseudonym Julia Mayfield) *The Forest of Stone*, 1957; *Their Flowers Were Black*, 1967; *The Swan River Story*, 1968; *An Act of Darkness*, 1969, published as *The House on Malador Street*, Putnam, 1970; *The Stars Are My Children*, 1970; *The Temporary Boy*, 1971; *When the Gallows Is High*, 1971; *The Conservatory*, 1973; *Bartholomew Fair*, 1974; *House of the Twelve Caesars*, 1975; *The Gates of Morning*, 1976; *The Image-Maker*, 1976; *The Death-Scented Flower*, 1977; *The Stratford Affair*, 1978; *Running Thursday*, 1980; *Buttercup Joe*, 1980. Also author of about 450 short stories published in magazines in numerous countries, of stories and plays for radio, and of poems.

WORK IN PROGRESS: A third part of "The Sussex Saga"; *Tiger's Heaven; A Delight of Angels; The Overlooker*.

SIDELIGHTS: Phyllis Hastings told *CA*: "My chief interest is country life, pure air, and escaping from crowds. I dabble in painting and musical composition and study seriously the history of agriculture. In collecting, I am the complete magpie. I collect dogs, old and rare books, pictures, and every bit of Victorian curiosa on which I can lay my hands.

"In the garden I grow flowers, trees, and vegetables and try to raise from seed everything from a violet to a cedar."

Hastings lives in the thirteenth-century house wherein the last abbot of Battle Abbey retired and died. Her books have appeared in a variety of European editions.

BIOGRAPHICAL/CRITICAL SOURCES: *Best Sellers*, February 1, 1970.

* * *

HAWKINS, Arthur 1903-

PERSONAL: Born April 9, 1903, in Cumberland, Md.; son of Arthur Hanson (a surgeon) and Louise (Price) Hawkins; married Patricia Laporte, 1930; married Nancy Pilson (a writer), June 28, 1940; children: Arthur III, Barbara (Mrs. Julian Palmore III), Nancy (Mrs. Richard N. Field), Gilbert Huston. *Education:* University of Virginia, B.S., 1925; attended Art Students League of New York, 1925-27. *Politics:* Independent Democrat. *Religion:* Episcopalian. *Home and office:* 396 Allaire Ave., Leonia, N.J. 07605.

CAREER: Designer, painter, art director; consulting art director in book publishing and advertising sales promotion fields. Speaker on advertising arts and judge of exhibitions. *Member:* Society of Illustrators (life member), Art Directors Club (New York; life member; past president), Authors Guild, Authors League of America.

WRITINGS: (Editor with Edward N. Gotshall) *Advertising Directions: Trends in Visual Advertising*, Art Directions Book Co., 1959; (editor) *Illustrators '59*, Hastings House, 1959; (editor) *The Art Director at Work: How Fifteen Medal-Winning Exhibits Were Conceived and Executed*, Hasting House, 1959; *The Steak Book*, Doubleday, 1966; *Who Needs a Cookbook: How to Make 222 Delicious International Dishes with a Minimum of Direction*, Prentice-Hall, 1968; *The Antisocial Cookbook*, Madison Laboratories, 1968.

The Complete Seafood Cookbook, Prentice-Hall, 1970; (with Aileen Paul) *Kids Cooking*, Doubleday, 1970; *Cook It Quick: 203 Delicious Half-Hour Recipes*, Prentice-Hall, 1971; (co-author) *Chef's Special*, Prentice-Hall, 1972; (co-author) *Chef's Magic*, Prentice-Hall, 1972; (with wife, Nancy Hawkins) *The Low Cost Meat Book: First Class Fare with Economy Meats*, Doubleday, 1974; (with Paul) *Candies, Cookies, Cakes*, Doubleday, 1974; (with N. Hawkins) *American Bi-Centennial Cookbook*, Prentice-Hall, 1975; *The Architectural Cookbook*, Architectural Record, 1975; (with N. Hawkins) *The American Regional Cookbook: Recipes from Yesterday & Today for the Modern Cook*, Prentice-Hall, 1976; (with N. Hawkins) *Nantucket and Other New England Cooking*, Hastings House, 1976; (with N. Hawkins) *The Shellfish Cookbook*, Hastings House, 1981.

Designer of more than one thousand book jackets. Contributor of articles about art to trade journals.

SIDELIGHTS: Arthur Hawkins told *CA*: "I write—and paint—as a means of escape. Escape from what? From the every day, day-in-and-day-out monotony. It is most gratifying if my books are useful and enjoyable—and if my paintings give some degree of pleasure to others—but for me the escape is the thing."

* * *

HAWKINS, John Noel 1944-

PERSONAL: Born May 18, 1944, in Sterling, Ill.; son of Noel

James (a salesman) and Kathryn (Denison) Hawkins; married Judith Ayami Takata (a graphic designer), August 12, 1967; children: Marisa Harumi, Larina Yasuko. *Education:* University of Hawaii, B.A. (with honors), 1967; University of British Columbia, M.A., 1969; Vanderbilt University, Ph.D., 1972. *Home:* 6509 Penfield Ave., Woodland Hills, Calif. 91367. *Office:* Graduate School of Education, University of California, 405 Hilgarde Ave., Los Angeles, Calif. 90024.

CAREER: Vanderbilt University, Nasville, Tenn., instructor in education and Asian studies, 1969-70; University of California, Los Angeles, professor of comparative education, 1973—. Visiting lecturer at University of Hawaii, 1968-69; has lectured throughout People's Republic of China; involved in China Exchange Program at University of California, Los Angeles. *Member:* Comparative and International Education Society (secretary, 1975-77; vice-president, 1982-85), American Educational Studies Association, Phi Delta Kappa.

WRITINGS: Educational Theory in the People's Republic of China: The Report of Chien Chu-jui, University of Hawaii Press, 1970; *Mao Tse-tung and Education: His Thoughts and Teachings,* Shoe String, 1973; *Small Hydroelectric Projects for Rural Development,* Pergamon, 1981; *Food and Agricultural Waste Projects,* Pergamon, 1982; *Human Resource Development and Food and the City: The Case of Shanghai,* East-West Center Publications, 1982; *Education and Social Change in the People's Republic of China,* Praeger, in press.

SIDELIGHTS: John Noel Hawkins is competent in both Chinese and Japanese. *Avocational interests:* Travel (has travelled to Japan, Hong Kong, and the People's Republic of China).

*   *   *

HAY, Robert D(ean) 1921-

PERSONAL: Born November 17, 1921, in La Porte, Ind.; married, 1944; children: Sue Ann, Carol Lynn. *Education:* Attended University of Indiana, 1940-42; University of Oklahoma, B.S., 1949, M.B.A., 1950; Ohio State University, Ph.D., 1954; postdoctoral study at Williams College, 1957 and 1962, Carnegie Institute of Technology (now Carnegie-Mellon University), 1963, University of California, Los Angeles, 1973, and University of Michigan, 1974. *Home:* 740 Huntsville Rd., Fayetteville, Ark. 72701. *Office:* College of Business Administration, University of Arkansas, Fayetteville, Ark. 72701.

CAREER: University of Arkansas, Fayetteville, instructor, 1949-51, assistant professor, 1951-55, associate professor, 1955-59, professor of management, 1959—, chairman of department, 1955-74. Instructor at Ohio State University, 1952-54. Certified public accountant by American Institute of Accountants, 1949. Has served on eight Senate committees. Consultant to business and industry. *Military service:* U.S. Army Air Forces, 1942-47; became captain. U.S. Air Force Reserve, 1947-71; became lieutenant colonel.

MEMBER: American Business Communications Association (fellow; president, 1967), American Business Communication Association, Academy of Management, Ozarks Economic Association, Case Research Association, Beta Gamma Sigma, Delta Pi Epsilon (charter member of Sigma chapter), Beta Alpha Psi, Sigma Iota Epsilon, Phi Eta Sigma. *Awards, honors:* Plaque of recognition from American Numismatics Association, 1965; distinguished faculty-researcher award, University of Arkansas Alumni Association, 1976; outstanding teacher of management award, University of Arkansas, 1979.

WRITINGS: (With Raymond V. Lesikar) *Business Report Writing,* Irwin, 1957; *Written Communications for Business Administrators,* Holt, 1965; *Introduction to Business,* with instructor's manual, Holt, 1968, programmed instruction workbook, 1969; (editor with Ed Gray and contributor) *Business and Society: Text and Cases,* with instructor's manual, Southwestern Publishing, 1976, 2nd edition, 1981; (with Frank Broyles) *Athletic Administration: A Management Approach,* with instructor's manual, Prentice-Hall, 1979.

Monographs: *Managerial Staffing and Training Problems of Arkansas Sawmills,* Industrial Research and Extension Center, University of Arkansas, 1961; *Management Audit for Small Business,* Arkansas Duplicating Service (Fayetteville), 1962; (co-author) *A Study of the Feasibility of Using Programmed Instruction in Teaching,* University of Arkansas, 1963.

Contributor: J. K. Lasser, editor, *Standard Handbook for Accountants,* McGraw, 1956; Merwyn Hargrove, Ike Harrison, and Gene Swearingen, editors, *Business Policy Cases,* Irwin, 1963; John Champion and Francis J. Bridges, editors, *Critical Incidents in Management,* Irwin, 1963; Frank Greenwood, editor, *Casebook for Management and Business Policy: A Systems Approach,* International Textbook Co., 1967; H. N. Broom, editor, *Business Policy and Strategic Action,* Prentice-Hall, 1969; Joseph L. Massie and Warren Haynes, editors, *Management: Analysis, Concepts, and Cases,* Prentice-Hall, 1969; Preston Le Breton, editor, *New Issues and Directions in Business Administration,* Southwestern Publishing, 1969; Hicks and Powell, *Management, Organization, and Human Resources,* McGraw, 1976; Archie Carroll, *Managing Corporate Social Responsibility,* Little, Brown, 1977; Edgar F. Huse and James L. Bowditch, *Behavior in Organizations: A Systems Approach to Management,* Addison-Wesley, 1977; James A. Stoner, editor, *Management,* Prentice-Hall, 1978; Dolan, *Basic Economics: Understanding Prices and Markets,* Dryden, 1978; Thompson and Strickland, editors, *Strategy and Policy: Concepts and Cases,* Business Publications, 1978; *Contemporary Business,* Holt, 1979; William G. Glueck, editor, *Management,* 2nd edition, Dryden, 1980; Louis E. Boone and David L. Kurtz, editors, *Contemporary Marketing,* Dryden, 1980.

Also contributor to other business and management books. Author of papers presented to business associations. Contributor to professional journals, including *Journal of Accounting, Business Education World, Accounting Review, Advanced Management, Journal of Business Communication,* and *Athletic Administrator.*

AVOCATIONAL INTERESTS: Golf, playing bass fiddle in a faculty music group.

*   *   *

HAYNES, Betsy 1937-
(James Betts)

PERSONAL: Born October 20, 1937, in Benton, Ill.; daughter of Paul DeWitte (a musician) and Marounah Lee (a secretary; maiden name, Phillips) Shadle; married James Monroe Haynes (a manager for General Telephone and Electronics Corp.), October 8, 1960; children: Craig Johnasen, Stephanie Jo. *Education:* Attended University of Illinois, 1955-57; Southern Illinois University, B.Journalism, 1962. *Home address:* Route No. 2, Newton, Iowa 50208.

CAREER: Writer. Has worked as clerk, switchboard operator, insurance claims examiner, classified advertising manager for a newspaper, and secretary. *Member:* Authors Guild, Authors League of America, Society of Children's Book Writers, Children's Reading Round Table. *Awards, honors:* Book for Brotherhood award, National Conference of Christians and Jews,

1974, for *Cowslip;* Journalism Alumnus Award, School of Journalism, Southern Illinois University, 1978.

WRITINGS—Juveniles, except as indicated: *Cowslip,* Nelson, 1973, published in paperback as *Slave Girl,* Scholastic Book Services, 1973; *Spies on the Devil's Belt,* Nelson, 1974; *The Against Taffy Sinclair Club,* Nelson, 1976; *The Ghost of the Gravestone Hearth,* Nelson, 1977; *The Shadows of Jeremy Pimm* (young adult), Beaufort Book Co., 1981; *The Power* (young adult), Dell, 1982; (with husband, James Haynes, under joint pseudonym James Betts) *Demon Wheels* (young adult), Dell, 1983; *Taffy Strikes Again,* Bantam, 1983.

SIDELIGHTS: Betsy Haynes writes: "As a writer of historical fiction for young people in these days of rapid advance and transition, I believe that it is important to help children see themselves as a part of the whole historical perspective, not just the future but the past as well."

Cowslip has been translated into French and German; *Spies on the Devil's Belt* has been translated into French.

* * *

HAYNES, William Warren 1921-

PERSONAL: Born March 10, 1921, in Berkeley, Calif.; son of Earll (clerk) and Marguerite (Gateley) Haynes; married Catharine Kennedy, January 29, 1950; children: Douglas, Kenneth, Carolyn. *Education:* University of California, A.B., 1942; Harvard University, M.B.A., 1947, D.C.S., 1952. *Politics:* Democrat.

CAREER: Ohio University, Athens, instructor in statistics, economics and business organization, 1947-48; University of Kentucky, College of Commerce, Lexington, assistant professor, 1948-52, associate professor, 1952-57, professor, 1957-63; Harvard University, Harvard Business School of Indian Institute of Management, Ahmedubud, India, project director, 1963-65, Harvard Business School, Boston, Mass., director of Division of International Activities, beginning 1966. Visiting associate professor, University of California, Berkeley, 1953. Director, Franklin Printing Co., Louisville, Ky.; consultant to Tennessee Valley Authority and other government agencies and to private firms. *Military service:* U.S. Army, administrative, personnel and executive officer, 1943-46; became first lieutenant. *Member:* American Economic Association, American Association of University Professors, Southern Economic Association, Phi Beta Kappa. *Awards, honors:* Fulbright award for study in Great Britain, 1950-51; Ford Foundation fellowship for study in Great Britain, 1956-57.

WRITINGS: *Nationalization in Practice: British Coal Industry,* Harvard Business School, 1953; *The Present and Prospective Markets for West Kentucky Coal,* University of Kentucky Press, 1955.

(With J. L. Massie) *Management: Analysis, Concepts, and Cases,* Prentice-Hall, 1961, 3rd edition, 1975; *Pricing Decisions in Small Business,* University of Kentucky Press, 1962; (with J. L. Gibson) *The Role of Accounting in Small Business Decisions,* University of Kentucky Press, 1963; (with Mary Jean Bowman) *The East Kentucky Coal Industry: Post-War Problems and Prospects,* Johns Hopkins Press, 1963; *Managerial Economics: Text and Cases,* Dorsey Press, 1963, 4th edition, Business Publications, 1979; (with John T. Masten) *Programmed Text in Money and Banking,* Prentice-Hall, 1969.

(With Thomas Mason Hill) *Institution Building in India,* Harvard University, 1973; (compiler) *Readings in Managerial Economics,* Business Publications, 1973, revised edition, 1977. Contributor to professional journals.†

HAZO, Samuel (John) 1928-

PERSONAL: Born July 19, 1928, in Pittsburgh, Pa.; son of Sam and Lottie (Abdou) Hazo; married Mary Anne Sarkis (a legal secretary), June 11, 1955. *Education:* University of Notre Dame, B.A. (magna cum laude), 1948; Duquesne University, M.A., 1955; University of Pittsburgh, Ph.D., 1957. *Politics:* Independent. *Religion:* Roman Catholic. *Home:* 785 Somerville Dr., Pittsburgh, Pa. *Office:* Department of English, Duquesne University, Pittsburgh, Pa.

CAREER: *Pittsburgh Post-Gazette,* Pittsburgh, Pa., assistant financial editor, 1949; Shady Side Academy, Pittsburgh, teacher of Latin, 1953; Duquesne University, Pittsburgh, instructor, 1955-58, assistant professor, 1958-60, associate professor, 1960-61, professor of English, 1964—, associate dean of college, 1961-66. Director of International Poetry Forum at Carnegie Library, Pittsburgh. Lectures and poetry readings at more than 200 colleges and universities, 1960—; weekly broadcast, "Bookmark," for KDKA. *Military service:* U.S. Marine Corps, 1950-53; became captain. *Awards, honors:* James V. Mitchell Memorial Award for Playwriting, 1948, for a one-act play; nominated for Pulitzer Prize and National Book Award, 1962, both for *The Quiet Wars;* D. Litt., Seton Hill College, 1965; National Book Award nomination, 1973, for *Once for the Last Bandit.*

WRITINGS—Poetry; published by University of Pittsburgh Press, except as indicated: *Discovery and Other Poems,* Sheed, 1959; *The Quiet Wars,* Sheed, 1962; *Listen with the Eye,* photographs by James P. Blair, 1964; *My Sons in God: Selected and New Poems,* 1965; *Blood Rights,* 1968; (co-author) *The Blood of Adonis,* 1971; (with George Nama) *Twelve Poems,* Byblos Press, 1972; *Seascript: A Mediterranean Logbook,* Byblos Press, 1972; *Once for the Last Bandit,* 1972; *Quartered,* University of Pittsburgh Press, 1974; *Inscripts,* Ohio University Press, 1975; *To Paris,* New Directions, 1981.

Other: *Hart Crane: An Introduction and Interpretation,* Barnes & Noble, 1963, revised edition published as *Smithereened Apart: A Critique of Hart Crane,* Ohio University Press, 1978; (editor) *The Christian Intellectual: Studies in the Relation of Catholicism to the Human Sciences,* Duquesne University Press, 1963; (editor) *A Selection of Contemporary Religious Poetry,* Paulist Press, 1963; (translator with Beth Luey) Denis de Rougement, *The Growl of Deep Waters,* University of Pittsburgh Press, 1976; *The Very Fall of the Sun,* (novel), Popular Library, 1978.

SIDELIGHTS: Suffering, aging, and death are recurring themes in Samuel Hazo's poetry, and many reviewers suggest that his sincerity and honesty in dealing with these subjects are what attract readers to his work. A critic for *Virginia Quarterly Review* notes that *Blood Rights,* one of Hazo's more popular collections, "established him as one of the most honest and gifted of modern poets.... Hazo's poems are both strong and true, the poems of a deeply religious man facing up to the hard realities of the skull beneath the skin, the suffering of a fallen world.... Hazo boldly dares to be himself in this book." Many reviewers conclude that Hazo's seemingly natural ability to deal with issues in a honest, open way stems from the fact that he often draws from his own experiences to write his poetry. "What emerges is a portrait of a reflective, somewhat self-centered man who writes candidly about his experiences," explains Elizabeth Knies in *Commonweal.*

A number of reviewers, however, interpret Hazo's soul-searching manner as self-indulgent. J. C. Sorensen notes in *Library Journal* that Hazo "has a tendency to identify with legendary and emblematic images." And a writer for *Choice* believes that some of Hazo's poetry "suffers from self-conscious refinement. Post-romantic poets are acutely aware of themselves in the creative process and often tell us how they write in their poems. For Hazo, this 'poet-in-process' is the major motif throughout the poems." However, this same reviewer praises works like *Once for the Last Bandit* because it "contains enough good poems to make it worthwhile."

While the themes of Hazo's poetry have remained the same, the form of his poetry has changed over the years. His earlier poems were noted for their highly technical mastery and traditional style. With the publication of *Listen with the Eye*, Hazo began composing poetry in iambic free verse. Still considered a master of the technical aspects of poetry by many of his fans, Hazo no longer writes in the structured, rhythmic style of his earlier collections *Discovery* and *The Quiet Wars*.

Once for the Last Bandit contains several of Hazo's new poems and a number of older pieces. Karl Malkoff of *Commonweal* notices that "Hazo's earlier poems are more technically proficient than his later work." Malkoff continues: "The handling of formal elements is more evident, easier to judge, intellectual structures are tighter, there is often a sharp neo-metaphysical wit working, the frequent sense of tour de force. But these rules are arbitrary. The later poems have a power of their own; and it seems obvious that in them Hazo has managed to master the form that most accurately expresses his vision of reality." Reviewer Peter Dollard, however, says in *Library Journal* that "though some of the poems are successful," in the collection, "too many are weakened by the poet's continuing reliance on lessons rather than poetry. Hazo can indeed write a striking phrase, but too often his lines are flat and his diction downright bad."

Like Dollard, Sorensen praises certain aspects of Hazo's work while expressing disappointment with others. Reviewing *Quartered* in *Library Journal*, Sorensen writes: "Hazo sets up situations which could be explored poetically, but he too often settles for a clever and superficial use of sonics within story outlines.... However, there are revealing and effective pieces. In 'The Mexican Panels' Hazo gains personal identity and control; 'Breakfasting with Sophomores' is calm, fluid, precise in its reflections, unhampered by extraneous details."

AVOCATIONAL INTERESTS: Tennis.

BIOGRAPHICAL/CRITICAL SOURCES: Minnesota Review, May/July, 1965; *Saturday Review*, October 9, 1965; *New York Times Book Review*, November 21, 1965; *Library Journal*, March 15, 1972, October 15, 1974; *Choice*, December, 1972, March, 1975; *Commonweal*, January 5, 1973, July 4, 1975; *Poetry*, June, 1973, July, 1975.

* * *

HEADY, Earl O(rel) 1916-

PERSONAL: Born January 25, 1916, in Imperial, Neb.; son of Orel C. (a farmer) and Jessie (Banks) Heady; married Marian R. Hoppert, March 1, 1941; children: Marilyn (Mrs. Timothy Kling), Stephen, Barbara. *Education:* University of Nebraska, B.Sc., 1939, M.Sc., 1940; Iowa State University of Science and Technology, Ph.D., 1945. *Politics:* Independent. *Home:* 919 Gaskill, Ames, Iowa 50010. *Office:* Iowa State University of Science and Technology, Ames, Iowa 50010.

CAREER: Iowa State University of Science and Technology, Ames, instructor, 1940-43, assistant professor, 1944-46, associate professor, 1946-49, professor of economics, 1949—, Curtis Distinguished Professor of Economics, 1956—, executive director, Center for Agricultural and Economic Development, 1958—, director of planning projects in Thailand, 1972—, and Indonesia, 1979—. Visiting professor at North Carolina State University, 1952, and Harvard University, 1956; lecturer at universities and research academies in United States and abroad. Member, White House Advisory Group on Domestic Affairs, 1964—, Economic Institute, 1969-74, Agency for International Development committee, 1971—, United Nations Food and Agricultural Organization, 1971—, Research Advisory Committee of the U.S. State Department, 1971—, and National Water Commission, 1971-72; chairman, East-West Seminar on Econometric Models, 1968—. Consultant to President's Commission on Food and Fiber, Organization for European Cooperation and Development, U.S. Department of Agriculture, Tennessee Valley Authority, Ford Foundation, and governments of Greece, India, Thailand, Mexico, and Ethiopia.

MEMBER: International Economic Association, Econometric Society (fellow), American Economic Association, American Farm Economic Association (fellow; vice-president, 1954), American Agricultural Economics Association (fellow), American Association for the Advancement of Science (fellow), American Academy of Arts and Sciences (fellow), American Statistical Association (fellow), Canadian Agricultural Economics Society (vice-president, 1957), Hungarian Academy of Science (honorary member), Royal Swedish Academy of Science (honorary member), Alpha Zeta, Phi Kappa Phi, Gamma Sigma Delta, Sigma Xi, Phi Beta Kappa.

AWARDS, HONORS: American Farm Economic Association awards, 1949, 1953, 1956, 1959, 1973, 1974, 1976, and 1980, for outstanding research, and, 1953, for *Economics of Agricultural Production and Resource Use;* Social Science Research Council faculty award, 1950-53; Center for Advanced Study in the Behavioral Sciences fellow, 1960-61; D.Sc., University of Nebraska, 1960, University of Uppsala and Agricultural College of Sweden, both 1965, and University of Debrecem and Warsaw Agricultural University, both 1979; Gamma Sigma Delta Distinguished Service Award, 1962 and 1974, for outstanding contributions to agriculture; American Agricultural Editors Association National Award, 1965, for services to American agriculture; Browning Medal, American Agronomy Society, 1977; Iowa State University Distinguished Service Award, 1977; Henry A. Wallace Award, 1979.

WRITINGS—Published by Iowa State University Press, except as indicated: (With John A. Hopkins) *Farm Records*, Iowa State College Press, 1949, 5th edition published as *Farm Records and Accounts*, 1962; *Economics of Agricultural Production and Resource Use*, Prentice-Hall, 1952; (with Harold R. Jensen) *Farm Management Economics*, Prentice-Hall, 1954; (editor with Glenn L. Johnson and Lowell S. Hardin) *Resource Productivity, Returns to Scale, and Farm Size*, Iowa State College Press, 1956; (editor with others) *Agricultural Adjustment Problems in a Growing Economy*, Iowa State College Press, 1958; (with Wilfred Chandler) *Linear Programming Methods*, Iowa State College Press, 1958.

(With John L. Dillon) *Agricultural Production Functions*, 1961; (with Alvin C. Egbert) *Regional Adjustments in Grain Production*, U.S. Government Printing Office, 1961; (editor with others) *Agricultural Supply Functions*, 1961; *Agricultural Policy under Economic Development*, 1962; (with Luther G. Tweeten) *Resource Demand and Structure of the Agricultural Industry*, 1963; (with others) *Roots of the Farm Problem*, 1965; *Problems and Policies of Agriculture in Developed Countries*, [Norway], 1967; *A Primer on Food, Agriculture and Public Policy*, Random House, 1967.

(Editor) *Economic Models and Quantitative Methods for the Transformation of Agriculture,* 1971; (with Ramesh C. Agrawal) *Operations Research Methods for Agricultural Decisions,* 1972; (with others) *Future Farm Programs,* 1972; (with Alan R. Ball) *Size, Structure, and Future of Farms,* 1972; *World Food Production, Demand and Trade,* 1973; *Spatial Sector Programming Models for Agricultural Policy and Land Use,* 1974; *Use of Food Aid in Economic Development,* 1974; (with Ference Feheto) *Economics of Cooperative Farming,* Academia Press (Budapest), 1975; (with Larry Whiting) *Externalities in Agricultural Development: Problems in Equity,* 1975; (with others) *Land Use: Ongoing Developments in the North Central Region,* 1975; (with Harold G. Halcrow and Melvin Cotner) *Land Use and Soil Conservation Policies,* Soil Conservation Society of America, 1982; (with Shashanka Bhide) *Livestock Response Functions,* 1982. Also author, with Keneth Nical, of *Agricultural Development Planning in Thailand.*

Contributor: Hughes and others, editors, *Forages,* Iowa State College Press, 1950; Halcrow, editor, *Contemporary Readings in Agricultural Economics,* Prentice-Hall, 1955; C. R. Hoglund, editor, *Nutritional and Economic Aspects of Feed Utilization on Dairy Cows,* Iowa State University Press, 1959; S. May, editor, *Mechanization of Agriculture,* North-Holland Publishing, 1961; A.S. Manne and H. M. Markowitz, editors, *Studies in Process Analysis: Economy Wide Production Capabilities,* Wiley, 1963. Contributor of sections to more than twenty other Iowa State University Press books on agriculture and economics, and more than 750 articles to journals.

WORK IN PROGRESS: Research on econometric analysis, national agricultural policy, the structure of the farm industry, resource use and the environment, and agricultural development.

SIDELIGHTS: Economics of Agricultural Production and Resource Use has been published in five languages, and three other books by Earl O. Heady have been published in eight languages. Heady has traveled in forty-four countries, largely in Southeast Asia, the Middle East, and Europe.

* * *

HEALEY, Brooks
See ALBERT, Burton, Jr.

* * *

HEARSEY, John E(dward) N(icholl) 1928-

PERSONAL: Born May 25, 1928, in Eastbourne, Sussex, England; son of Lionel Douglas William (a major in the Indian Army) and Dorothy Maud (Nicholl) Hearsey. *Education:* Studied architecture in a private school in England and under tutors. *Politics:* Conservative. *Religion:* Church of England. *Home:* Ross Cottage, Station Rd., Angmering, Littlehampton, West Sussex, England. *Agent:* Campbell Thomson & McLaughlin Ltd., 31 Newington Green, London N16 9PU, England.

CAREER: Writer. Makes architectural models to scale, with two in a U.S. museum. *Member:* Society of Authors.

WRITINGS: The Tower, MacGibbon & Kee, 1960; *Bridge, Church and Palace,* J. Murray, 1961; *City of Constantine,* J. Murray, 1963; *London and the Great Fire,* Dufour, 1965; *Marie Antoinette,* Heron Books, 1968; *Elizabeth I,* Heron Books, 1969; *Men of Power* (school history), Granada, 1970; *Young Mr. Pepys,* Dutton, 1973; *Voltaire,* Scribner, 1976. Author of scripts for British Broadcasting Corp. television and radio. Contributor to numerous periodicals, including *Country Life, Field, East Anglian Magazine, Yachting World,* and *Lady.*

WORK IN PROGRESS: A book on his family in India, covering the years 1765-1865, based largely on diaries and letters.

SIDELIGHTS: John E. N. Hearsey, who speaks French and Swedish, told *CA:* "I feel that the seeds of my future interests must have been sown at a very early age, judging by the vividness with which I remember such cathedrals as Cologne and Friburg and such cities as Bruges and Lausanne, visited when not yet in double figures. That interest grew into a fascination for old buildings and history, and perhaps above all for English parish churches, which is today stronger than ever. But a career as an architect was abandoned while still a student after contracting polio. After turning to writing I found I could combine history and architecture (and to a lesser degree, people) in my first four books, before being edged, painlessly, into biography in the two periods I seem to know most about: seventeenth-century England and eighteenth-century France. What do I hope to achieve through the books I write? 1) To make some money. 2) To share my enthusiasm with others, whether for places or for people."

BIOGRAPHICAL/CRITICAL SOURCES: London Times, November 30, 1961; *Daily Telegraph,* July 5, 1963; *Observer,* July 2, 1972; *Sunday Times,* September 24, 1972, February 29, 1976; *New Yorker,* July 22, 1974.

* * *

HEATH, Monica
See FITZGERALD, Arlene J.

* * *

HEIMLER, Eugene 1922-

PERSONAL: Born March 27, 1922, in Szombathely, Hungary; son of Ernest (an attorney) and Maria (Lax) Heimler; first wife killed at Auschwitz; married Livia Salgo, November 30, 1946; children: (second marriage) George Ernest, Susan Maria. *Education:* Academy of Social Science, Budapest, Hungary, Diploma in Social Science, 1947; University of Manchester, Diploma in Psychiatric Social Work, 1953; also attended University of London. *Religion:* Jewish. *Agent:* Curtis Brown Ltd., 575 Madison Ave., New York, N.Y. 10022. *Office:* Heimler Foundation, Elmhurst, High St., Great Missenden, Buckinghamshire, England.

CAREER: Prisoner in German concentration camps during World War II; returned to Hungary after the war and worked as journalist (while studying) until he went to England in 1947; trained as psychiatric social worker at Bexley Mental Hospital, Kent, England; Middlesex City Council, London, England, psychiatric social worker 1953-60, psychiatric social work organizer, 1960-65; Hounslow Project (community care), Hounslow, England, director, beginning 1965; University of Calgary, Calgary, Alberta, professor of human social functioning, 1970—. Affiliated with Heimler Foundation, Buckinghamshire, England; director of community care course, University of London, 1960-80. Speaker on mental health on U.S. tour, 1964. Consultant to World Health Organization, 1964 and U.S. government, 1964; adviser to ministry of Social Security of England, 1965-67. *Member:* British Association of Psychiatric Social Workers; also member of other social work organizations in Britain.

WRITINGS: Eternal Dawn (poems) [Hungary], 1939; *Confession to the World* (poems), [Hungary], 1943; *Night of the Mist* (experiences in Nazi concentration camps), Vanguard, 1960, reprinted Greenwood, 1978; *A Link in the Chain* (experiences under Communist regime in Hungary), Bodley Head, 1962;

Prison, Horizon, 1964; (editor) *Resistance against Tyranny: A Symposium*, Routledge & Kegan Paul, 1966, Praeger, 1967; *Mental Illness and Social Work*, Penguin, 1967, 2nd edition, 1969; *Survival in Society*, Halstead, 1975; *The Storm: The Tragedy of Sinai*, translation and introduction by Anthony Rudolf, Menard, 1976. Contributor to newspapers and to professional journals.

WORK IN PROGRESS: *The Hendon Experiment*, dealing with his 1954 experiment with forty-one individuals unable to get and hold a job (half were returned to productive permanent work through psychiatric social work counseling).

* * *

HEINTZ, Ann Christine 1930-

PERSONAL: Born July 25, 1930, in Blue Island, Ill.; daughter of Fred H. (a sales representative and buyer) and Hazel (Hobbs) Heintz. *Education:* Mundelein College, B.A., 1952; Marquette University, M.A., 1962. *Politics:* "Independent; member of 'Network,' national religious women's lobby for social justice." *Home:* 7064 North Damen, Chicago, Ill. 60645.

CAREER: Roman Catholic nun, entered Sister of Charity, Beata Virgo Maria (means Blessed Virgin Mary), 1952; high school teacher in parochial schools in Clinton, Iowa, 1955-65, and Cedar Rapids, Iowa, 1966-68; St. Mary's Center for Learning (high school), Chicago, Ill., teacher of journalism and developer of media program, 1968-76; founder and adviser, Youth Communication/Chicago Center, Chicago, 1977—. Summer instructor at St. Cloud State College, 1968-71, and University of Minnesota, 1972-73. Member of Robert F. Kennedy Commission of Inquiry into High School Journalism; member of national communication committee of the U.S. Catholic Conference. *Member:* Journalism Education Association, UNDA-USA.

AWARDS, HONORS: Carl Towley Award from Journalism Education Association, 1967, for contributions to journalism education; named journalism teacher of the year by newspaper fund of *Wall Street Journal*, 1971; centennial award from Academy of Our Lady, 1974; Ford Foundation grant, 1974-76, to study the potential role of popular television programs in the learning process; Maxi Award from *Media and Methods*, 1975, for *Mass Media*.

WRITINGS—Published by Ginn, except as indicated: *Persuasion*, Loyola University Press, 1970, revised edition, 1974; (with Elizabeth Conley and Lawrence Reuter) *Mass Media*, Loyola University Press, 1972; (contributor) *Captive Voices*, Schocken, 1974; (with Patricia Fitzgerald and Margaret Fieweger) *Independent Learning*, 1975; (with Elaine Schuster and Lester Angene) *Experiencing*, 1975; (with Schuster and Arlene Larson) *Explaining*, 1975; (with Schuster and Isidore Levine) *Analysing*, 1975; (with Schuster and Florence Nolte) *Organizing*, 1975; (with Schuster and John Ashmead) *Synthesizing*, 1975; (with Schuster and Bernard McCabe) *Recognizing*, 1975; *Me and My TV*, Journalism Education Association, 1977.

Author and producer of television videotapes "What If?" on alternative education, and "To Know Ourselves," for National Council of Teachers of English. Contributor to religious publications and literature journals. Contributing editor of *Communication: Journalism Education Today*.

SIDELIGHTS: Ann Christine Heintz founded Youth Communication/Chicago Center to expose high school students to the world of journalism. She told *CA*: "I took a chance that Chicago kids—street kids—would like the idea of running their own city-wide newspaper. They do. Their newspaper (circulation 70,000) is not a great financial success because they give it away, but it does seem to be a strong forum for youth in this brawling city where citizens need to be very noisy or very well-connected in order to be heard.

"What I've learned after five years of playing adviser to the newspaper is that teenaged writers need a refuge from term papers and vocabulary tests. They need a better reason to write than getting an 'A' in English, especially those students who were never fated to compete for 'A's. I've also learned that the chance to write for a big community audience is a compelling reason for them to accept the pain of writing well, even for those who come from the city's toughest housing projects.

"Now this Youth Communication concept is being tested in New York, Philadelphia, Los Angeles and Cleveland. It's becoming a happy gamble."

* * *

HEISERMAN, David L(ee) 1940-

PERSONAL: Born July 11, 1940, in Fostoria, Ohio; son of Leland H. (a laborer) and Maudine (Needles) Heiserman; married Judith Hopewell, February 5, 1965; children: Paul. *Education:* Attended Ohio State University, 1961-67. *Politics:* Conservative Republican. *Religion:* "Fundamentalist Christian." *Home:* 1814 Walden Dr., Columbus, Ohio 43229. *Office:* Ohio Institute of Technology, Columbus, Ohio 43219.

CAREER: Franklin University, Columbus, Ohio, instructor in electronics and mathematics, 1969-74; Ohio Institute of Technology, Columbus, associate professor of electronics and mathematics, 1974—. Consulting engineer on technical education systems. *Military service:* U.S. Navy, 1958-61.

WRITINGS—Published by TAB Books, except as indicated: *Handbook of Small Appliance Troubleshooting and Repair*, Prentice-Hall, 1974; *Radio Astronomy for the Amateur*, 1975; *Build Your Own Working Robot*, 1976; *Handbook of Major Appliance Troubleshooting and Repair*, Prentice-Hall, 1977; *Miniprocessors*, 1977; *How to Design and Build Your Own Custom TV Games*, 1978; *How to Build Your Own Self-Programming Robot*, 1978; *Handbook of Digital IC Applications*, Prentice-Hall, 1980; *Pascal*, 1980; *Robot Intelligence*, 1981; *How to Design and Build Your Own Custom Robot*, 1981; *Programming in Basic for Personal Computers*, Prentice-Hall, 1981; *Beginner's Handbook of IC Projects*, Prentice-Hall, 1981; *Projects in Machine Intelligence for Your Home Computer*, 1982; *Intermediate Programming for the TRS-80 (Model I)*, Sams, 1982; *Microprocessor Instruction Sets and Software Principles*, Prentice-Hall, 1982; *Art and Animation for the TRS-80*, Prentice-Hall, 1982. Contributor of about sixty articles to electronics and science journals.

SIDELIGHTS: David L. Heiserman writes: "I suppose I would be considered a science and technical writer; however I want to do more than simply interpret things of science for the general reading public. My book on radio astronomy not only explains what radio astronomy is and how to build a radio telescope—it also tells the amateur experimenter how he can carry out some sophisticated projects that have a great deal of potential value as far as professional radio astronomy is concerned.

"Every nonfiction book should have an impact upon the reader's life and way of thinking—it is far more important to build positive attitudes and motivate a reader to action than it is to feed him facts."

Build Your Own Working Robot has been translated into Russian.

HEITLER, Walter (Heinrich) 1904-1981

PERSONAL: Born January 2, 1904, in Karlsruhe, Germany (now West Germany); died November 15, 1981, in Zurich, Switzerland; son of Adolf (a professor of engineering) and Ottilie (Rudolf) Heitler; married Kathleen Nicholson, March, 1942; children: Eric. *Education:* Attended University of Berlin, 1921-22; University of Munich, Ph.D., 1926. *Home:* Am Guggenberg 5, 8053 Zurich, Switzerland. *Office:* Institute for Theoretical Physics, University of Zurich, Zurich, Switzerland.

CAREER: University of Goettingen, Goettingen, Germany (now West Germany), privatdocent for theoretical physics, 1929-33; University of Bristol, Bristol, England, research fellow, 1933-41; Dublin Institute for Advanced Science, Dublin, Ireland, professor of theoretical physics, 1941-49, director of School of Theoretical Physics, 1945-49; University of Zurich, Institute for Theoretical Physics, Zurich, Switzerland, professor of theoretical physics, beginning 1949, dean of Philosophical Faculty, 1962-64.

MEMBER: Royal Society (London; fellow), Royal Irish Academy, Academy of Science (Uppsala), Akademie Leopoldina (Halle), Akademie der Wissenschaften und der Literatur (Mainz). *Awards, honors:* University of Zurich research fellowship, 1927; Max Planck Medal; Marcel Benoist prize; D.Sc., National University of Ireland; Dr. rer. nat., University of Goettingen; Dr. phil., University of Uppsala; Foundation for Western Thinking Literary Prize, for *Die Natur und das Goettliche*.

WRITINGS: Quantum Theory of Radiation, Oxford University Press, 1936, 3rd edition, 1954; *Elementary Wave Mechanics*, Oxford University Press, 1945, 2nd edition, 1956, published as *Elementary Wave Mechanics with Applications to Quantum Chemistry*, 1969; *Der Mensch und die Naturwissenchaftliche Erkenntnis*, Vieweg, 1961, translation by Robert Schlapp published as *Man and Science*, Basic Books, 1963, 4th edition, 1966; *Lectures on Problems Connected with the Finite Size of Elementary Particles*, Tata Institute of Fundamental Research (Bombay), 1961; *Naturphilosophische Streifzuege: Vortraege und Aufsaetze*, Vieweg, 1970; *Warheit und Richtigkeit in den Akademie der Wissenschaften*, F. Steiner (Wiesbaden), 1972; *Die Natur und das Goettliche*, Klett & Balmer, 1974; *Ueber die Komplementaritaet von lebloser und lebender Materie*, F. Steiner, 1976; *Gottesbeweise? und weitere Vortraege*, Klett & Balmer, 1977; *Schoepfung, die Oeffnung der Naturwissenschaft zum Goettlichen*, Verlag der Arche (Zurich), 1979; *Toward a Man-Centered Medical Science*, edited by K. E. Schaefer, Futura Publishing, 1979. Also author, with F. London, of *Theory of Chemical Bond*, 1927.

SIDELIGHTS: In the *London Times*, Sir Nevill Mott writes of Walter Heitler: "[He] was one of the generation of theoretical physicists who quickly achieved international reputations by applying the new quantum mechanics . . . to some of the established concepts of physics and of chemistry, and showing how they could be derived from more general laws." In 1927 Heitler and his colleague F. London published their theory on the homopolar chemical bond that exists between two negative atoms. Fifty years later this theory, as Mott notes, "must be known to every undergraduate in physics and chemistry. It gave the kind of understanding that had to await the new quantum theory of matter." Late in his career, Mott continues, Heitler "sought particularly to find a synthesis between Christian belief and natural science." This subject was the theme of many of his later books, including the prize-winning *Die Natur und das Goettliche*.

BIOGRAPHICAL/CRITICAL SOURCES: Weekly Book Review, May 19, 1946; *Journal of Physical Chemistry*, July, 1946; *Helvetiea Physica Acta* (Basel), December 22, 1964; *Archives Internationales d'Histoire des Sciences*, 30, 163, 1980.

OBITUARIES: London Times, December 11, 1981.†

* * *

HELLER, Erich 1911-

PERSONAL: Born March 27, 1911, in Komotau, Bohemia (now Czechoslovakia); naturalized British citizen in 1947. *Education:* Charles University, Prague, Czechoslovakia, D.Jur. (with distinction), 1935; Cambridge University, Ph.D., 1948. *Office:* Department of German, Northwestern University, Evanston, Ill. 60201.

CAREER: University of London, London School of Economics and Political Science, London, England, assistant lecturer in German, 1943-45; Cambridge University, Peterhouse College, Cambridge, England, lecturer in German and director of studies in modern languages, 1945-48; University of Wales, University College, Swansea, professor of German, 1948-60; Northwestern University, Evanston, Ill., professor of German, 1960-66, professor of the humanities, 1966-68, Avalon Professor of Humanities, 1968—. Visiting lecturer at universities in Germany, 1947-48, at Harvard University, Yale University, Brown University, and other American universities, 1953-54, 1957-58; Ziskind Visiting Professor at Brandeis University, 1957-58; visiting professor at University of Heidelberg, spring, 1963; Carnegie Visiting Professor of Humanities at Massachusetts Institute of Technology, fall, 1963. *Member:* German Academy for Language and Literature, Bavarian Academy of Fine Arts, P.E.N. (Germany and Austria), American Academy of Arts and Sciences (fellow). *Awards, honors:* Gold Medal, Goethe Institut (Munich); Great Crown of Merit, Federal Republic of Germany.

WRITINGS: Die Flucht aus dem zwanzigsten Jahrhundert (essay), Saturn Verlag, 1938; *The Disinherited Mind* (essays), Bowes, 1952, Farrar, Straus, 1957, enlarged edition, Harcourt, 1975; *The Hazard of Modern Poetry*, Bowes, 1953; *The Ironic German, a Study of Thomas Mann*, Little, Brown, 1958, revised edition published as *Thomas Mann: The Ironic German*, Regnery/Gateway, 1979; *Studien zur Modernen Literatur*, Suhrkamp Verlag, 1963; *Nietzsche-Drei Essays*, Suhrkamp Verlag, 1964; *The Artist's Journey into the Interior, and Other Essays*, Random House, 1965; *Franz Kafka*, Heimeran (Munich), 1969, Viking, 1974; *Essays Uber Goethe*, Insel Verlag, 1970; (editor with Juergen Born and author of introduction) Franz Kafka, *Letters to Felice*, Schocken, 1973; *Nirgends wird Welt sein: Rilke*, Suhrkamp Verlag, 1975; *The Poet's Self and the Poem*, Athlone Press, 1976; *Die Weiderkehr der Unschuld*, Suhrkamp Verlag, 1977.

Author of introductions to the Everyman's Library *Thomas Mann*, to the German edition of *Works of Ludwig Wittgenstein*, Suhrkamp Verlag, 1960, and to *The Basic Kafka*, Pocket Books, 1979. Contributor to three volumes of *Jahresring* (an annual survey of contemporary German literature and art), Deutsche Verlags-Anstalt, 1956-59, to *New Cambridge Modern History*, Volume X, 1960. Contributor of essays on German writers and philosophers to *Cambridge Journal, Times Literary Supplement* (London), *Sewanee Review, Forum, Der Monat, Merkur*, and other journals.

SIDELIGHTS: Erich Heller adapted and translated three of his books, *The Disinherited Mind, The Ironic German*, and *The Artist's Journey into the Interior* for publication in Germany.

HELLER, Joseph 1923-

PERSONAL: Born May 1, 1923, in Brooklyn, N.Y.; son of Isaac (a truck driver) and Lena Heller; married Shirley Held, September 3, 1945 (divorced); children: Erica Jill, Theodore Michael. *Education:* Attended University of Southern California; New York University, B.A., 1948; Columbia University, M.A., 1949; graduate study, Oxford University, 1949-50. *Residence:* New York City. *Agent:* Candida Donadio & Associates, 111 West 57th St., New York, N.Y. 10019.

CAREER: Novelist. Pennsylvania State University, University Park, instructor in English, 1950-52; *Time* magazine, New York City, advertising writer, 1952-56; *Look* magazine, New York City, advertising writer, 1956-58; *McCall's* magazine, New York City, promotion manager, 1958-61; former teacher of fiction and dramatic writing at Yale University and University of Pennsylvania; City College of the City University of New York, New York City, Distinguished Professor of English, until 1975; full-time writer, 1975—. Has worked in the theater, in movies, and in television. *Military service:* U.S. Army Air Forces, World War II; served as B-25 wing bombardier; flew sixty missions; became first lieutenant. *Member:* Phi Beta Kappa. *Awards, honors:* Fulbright scholar, 1949-50; National Institute of Arts and Letters grant in literature, 1963.

WRITINGS: (Contributor) *Nelson Algren's Own Book of Lonesome Monsters*, Lancer, 1960; *Catch-22* (novel; also see below; chapter one originally published in *New World Writing*, 1955), Simon & Schuster, 1961, critical edition, edited by Robert M. Scotto, Dell, 1973; *Something Happened* (novel; excerpt originally published in *Esquire*, September, 1966), Knopf, 1974; *Good as Gold* (novel; Literary Guild selection), Simon & Schuster, 1979.

Plays: *We Bombed in New Haven* (two-act; first produced in New Haven, Conn., at the Yale School of Drama Repertory Theater, December 4, 1967, produced on Broadway at the Ambassador Theater, October 16, 1968), Knopf, 1968; *Catch-22: A Dramatization* (one-act play based on novel of same title; first produced in East Hampton, N.Y., at the John Drew Theater, July 23, 1971), Samuel French, 1971; *Clevinger's Trial* (based on chapter eight of novel *Catch-22;* produced in London, 1974), Samuel French, 1973.

Screenplays: (With David R. Schwartz) "Sex and the Single Girl" (based on book of same title by Helen Gurley Brown), Warner Brothers, 1964; (uncredited) "Casino Royale" (based on novel of same title by Ian Fleming), Columbia Pictures, 1967; (with Tom Waldman and Frank Waldman) "Dirty Dingus Magee" (based on novel *The Ballad of Dingus Magee* by David Markson), Metro-Goldwyn-Mayer, 1970; (contributor) "Of Men and Women" (television drama), American Broadcasting Companies, 1972. Also author, under pseudonym, of other television screenplays during the 1960s.

Contributor of short stories to periodicals, including *Atlantic Monthly*, *Esquire*, and *Cosmopolitan;* contributor of reviews to periodicals, including *New Republic*.

WORK IN PROGRESS: A novel.

SIDELIGHTS: "There was only one catch . . . and that was Catch-22," Doc Daneeka informed Yossarian. As Yossarian, the lead bombardier of Joseph Heller's phenomenal first novel, soon learns, this one catch is enough to keep him at war indefinitely. After pleading with Doc Daneeka that he is too crazy to fly any more missions, Yossarian is introduced to Catch-22, a rule which stipulates that anyone rational enough to want to be grounded could not possibly be insane and therefore must return to his perilous duties. The novel *Catch-22* is built around the multifarious attempts of Captain John Yossarian to survive the Second World War, to escape the omnipresent logic of a regulation which somehow stays one step ahead of him.

At the time of its publication in 1961, Heller's antiwar novel met with modest sales and lukewarm reviews. But by mid-decade, the book began to sell in the American underground, becoming a favored text of the counter-culture. "[*Catch-22*] came when we still cherished nice notions about WW II," Eliot Fremont-Smith recalls in the *Village Voice*. "Demolishing these, it released an irreverence that had, until then, dared not speak its name." With more than ten million copies now in print, *Catch-22* is generally regarded as one of the most important novels of our time. It "is probably the finest novel published since World War II," Richard Locke declares in the *New York Times Book Review*. "*Catch-22* is the great representative document of our era, linking high and low culture." The title itself has become part of the language, and its "hero" Yossarian, according to Jack Schnedler of the *Newark Star-Ledger*, "has become the fictional talisman to an entire generation."

In the *New York Times Book Review*, Heller cites three reasons for the success of *Catch-22*: "First, it's a great book. I've come to accept the verdict of the majority. Second, a whole new generation of readers is being introduced to it. . . . Third, and most important: Vietnam. Because this is the war I had in mind; a war fought without military provocation, a war in which the real enemy is no longer the other side but someone allegedly on your side. The ridiculous war I felt lurking in the future when I wrote the book." "There seems no denying that though Heller's macabre farce was written about a rarefied part of the raging war of the forties during the silent fifties," Josh Greenfeld wrote in a 1968 *New York Times Book Review* article, "it has all but become the chapbook of the sixties." As Joseph Epstein summarizes in *Book World*, *Catch-22* "was a well-aimed bomb."

In his *Bright Book of Life*, Alfred Kazin finds that "the theme of *Catch-22* . . . is the total craziness of war . . . and the struggle to survive of one man, Yossarian, who knows the difference between his sanity and the insanity of the system." After his commanding officer repeatedly raises the number of bombing missions required for discharge, Yossarian decides to "live forever or die in the attempt." "Yossarian's logic becomes so pure that everyone thinks him mad," Robert Brustein writes in the *New Republic*, "for it is the logic of sheer survival, dedicated to keeping him alive in a world noisily clamoring for his annihilation." Brustein continues: "According to this logic, Yossarian is surrounded on all sides by hostile forces. . . . [He] feels a blind, electric rage against the Germans whenever they hurl flak at his easily penetrated plane; but he feels an equally profound hatred for those of his own countrymen who exercise an arbitrary power over his life."

"The urgent emotion in Heller's book is . . . every individual's sense of being directly in the line of fire," Kazin believes. In the *Dictionary of Literary Biography*, Inge Kutt views Pianosa, the fictional island in the Mediterranean Sea which is the setting of the novel, as a microcosm of "the postwar world which not only includes the Korean and Vietnam wars but also the modern mass society." "Heller's horrifying vision of service life in World War II is . . . merely an illustration of the human condition itself," Jean E. Kennard asserts in *Mosaic*. "The world has no meaning but is simply there [, and] man is a creature who seeks meaning," Kennard elaborates. "Reason and language, man's tools for discovering the meaning of his existence and describing his world, are useless."

Language, as presented in *Catch-22*, is more than useless; it is dangerous, a weapon employed by the authorities to enslave individuals in a world of institutionalized absurdity, a world where pilots lose their lives because their commanding officer wants to see prettier bombing patterns or his name in the *Saturday Evening Post*. Language, in the form of Catch-22, is the mechanism which transforms military doublethink into concrete reality, into commands which profoundly affect human life and death. Catch-22, as the novel states, is the rule "which specified that a concern for one's safety in the face of dangers that were real and immediate was the process of a rational mind. Orr was crazy and could be grounded. All he had to do was ask; and as soon as he did, he would no longer be crazy and would have to fly more missions." As Jerry H. Bryant notes in his book *The Open Decision*: "Only the insane voluntarily continue to fly. This is an almost perfect catch because the law is in the definition of insanity. . . . The system is closed." In the *Arizona Quarterly*, Marcus K. Billson III examines Catch-22: "There is no way out of the tautological absurdity of [this] regulation. . . . The will of authority predominates by the force of language. Man is caught in an unrelenting cycle of oppression and brutality disguised in the convolutions of Catch-22." "Catch-22," Billson continues, "is law deriving its power from a universal faith in language as presence. . . . The world of the novel projects the horrific, yet all too real, power of language to divest itself from any necessity of reference, to function as an independent, totally autonomous medium with its own perfect system and logic. That such a language pretends to mirror anything but itself is a commonplace delusion which Heller satirizes masterfully throughout the novel. Yet, civilization is informed by this very presence, and Heller shows how man is tragically and comically tricked and manipulated by such an absurdity."

The acquiescence of men to language in *Catch-22*, Carol Pearson observes, is rooted in their failure to find any "transcendental comfort to explain suffering and to make life meaningful. . . . People react to meaninglessness by renouncing their humanity, becoming cogs in the machine. With no logical explanation to make suffering and death meaningful and acceptable, people renounce their power to think and retreat to a simple-minded respect for law and accepted 'truth.'" Writing in the *CEA Critic*, Pearson cites one of the book's many illustrations of this moral retreat: "The M.P.'s exemplify the overly law-abiding person who obeys law with no regard for humanity. They arrest Yossarian who is AWOL, but ignore the murdered girl on the street. By acting with pure rationality, like computers programmed only to enforce army regulations, they have become mechanical men." This incident, this "moment of epiphany," Raymond M. Olderman writes in *Beyond the Waste Land*, symbolizes "much of the entire novel's warning—that in place of the humane, . . . we find the thunder of the marching boot, the destruction of the human, arrested by the growth of the military-economic institution."

In the novel, the character Milo Minderbinder is the personification of this military-economic system. An enterprising mess officer, Minderbinder creates a one-man international syndicate whose slogan, "What's good for M&M Enterprises is good for the country," is used to justify a series of war-profiteering schemes. Minderbinder forms a private army of mercenaries (available to the highest bidder), corners the market on food and makes enormous profits selling it back to army mess halls, and convinces the U.S. government that it must buy up his overstock of chocolate-coated cotton balls in the interest of national security. Milo's empire soon stretches across Europe and North Africa. "His deals have made him mayor of every town in Sicily, Vice-Shah of Oran, Caliph of Baghdad, Imam of Damascus, and the Sheik of Araby," Brustein notes. Minderbinder's ambitions culminate in one final economic boom. As Olderman observes: "His wealth, influence, and sphere of action become enormous, until he and his profit-seeking are omnipotent and omnipresent. For business purposes he takes gas pellets from life jackets and morphine from first aid kits, leaving the drowning and the wounded without aid, but with the comforting message that 'what's good for M & M Enterprises is good for the country.' The ultimate inversion comes when Milo bombs and strafes his own camp for the Germans, who pay their bills more promptly than some, and kills many Americans at an enormous profit. In the face of criticism, he reveals the overwhelming virtue of his profit." In the *Canadian Review of American Studies*, Mike Franks concludes that "for Milo, contract, and the entire economic structure and ethical system it embodies and represents, is more sacred than human life."

"The military-economic institution rules, and the result is profit for some, but meaningless, inhuman parades for everyone else," Olderman writes. Confronted with this "totally irrelevant and bureaucratic power that either tosses man to his death or stamps out his spirit," Yossarian must make a moral decision. Olderman surveys Yossarian's alternatives: "He can be food for the cannon; he can make a deal with the system; or he can depart, deserting not the war with its implications of preserving political freedom, but abandoning a waste land, a dehumanized inverted, military-economic machine."

Yossarian, whose only wish is to stay alive, will not stand still for the "cannon." Kennard recounts Yossarian's second alternative: "[He] is given the chance to save his own life if he lies about Colonels Cathcart and Korn to their superior officers. He will, in accepting the offer, probably act as an incentive to his fellow officers to fly more missions in which many of them may be killed. He is given a chance . . . to join forces with the pestilences. After accepting the offer he is stabbed by Nately's whore and realizes that by joining those who are willing to kill, he has given them the right to kill him." Nately's whore, who shadows Yossarian after his fellow pilot Lt. Nately is killed in action, "pops out of every bush and around every corner to attack him because of Nately's death," Olderman writes. "However guiltless Yossarian may be of that one death, he is not guiltness—he has suffered as a victim, but has also been a victimizer. So Nately's whore will follow him forever, a kind of universal principle reminding him that he will always be unjustly beset and will probably always deserve it." In the book, Yossarian sympathizes with his determined pursuer: "Someone had to do something. Every victim was a culprit, every culprit a victim, and somebody had to stand up and do something and break the lousy chain of inherited habit that was imperiling them all."

As Bryant notes, "The only way that the circular justification of Catch-22 can be dealt with is by breaking out of the circle." Yossarian's friend Orr had broken free by sailing off into the Mediterranean in a rowboat, bound for neutral Sweden. Guided by Orr's example and by the wisdom imparted by the death of a young gunner named Snowden, Yossarian reneges on his agreement with the colonels and decides to desert. "In the course of the narrative," Olderman says, "occasional references are made to Snowden, . . . whose insides are shot out as his plane flies over Italy and who dies in Yossarian's arms. The experience profoundly affects Yossarian. As the narrative advances, the reader is given longer and longer glimpses of the incident. But not until Yossarian decides to try another way of getting out of combat than to agree with Korn and

Cathcart do we get Snowden's full story. As the boy whimpers, 'I'm cold,' Yossarian, horrified, sees his entrails slither to the floor. There is a message in those entrails that teaches Yossarian, finally, what he must do. The message reads: 'Man was matter, that was Snowden's secret. Drop him out of a window and he'll fall. Set fire to him and he'll burn. Bury him like other kinds of garbage and he'll rot. The spirit gone, man is garbage.'" Yossarian refuses to discard his spirit; he heads for Sweden, the only place left in the world, he believes, which is free of mob rule. The impossibility of reaching Scandinavia via rowboat does not deter him. What is important is the act, the attempt, not the destination, Ronald Wallace observes in *The Last Laugh.* As Frank concludes, "The Sweden he aims for is located, perhaps, not so much in the real world as in the geography of the moral imagination." And Yossarian "is still at large," Heller surmises in an interview in the *Newark Star-Ledger.* "He hasn't been caught."

In the *Partisan Review,* Morris Dickstein comments: "The insanity of the system . . . breeds a defensive counter-insanity. . . . [Yossarian is] a protagonist caught up in the madness, who eventually steps outside it in a slightly mad way." Heller remarks in *Pages* that much of the humor in his novel arises out of his characters' attempts to escape, manipulate, and circumvent the logic of Catch-22. Before deserting, Yossarian tries to outwit Catch-22 in order to survive; he employs "caution, cowardice, defiance, subterfuge, strategem, and subversion, through feigning illness, goofing off, and poisoning the company's food with laundry soap," Brustein writes. "He refuses to fly, goes naked, walks backward," adds Olderman.

"Heller's comedy is his artistic response to his vision of transcendent evil, as if the escape route of laughter were the only recourse from a malignant world," Brustein states. "[He] is concerned with that thin boundary of the surreal, the borderline between hilarity and horror. . . . Heller often manages to heighten the macabre obscenity of war much more effectively through its gruesome comic aspects than if he had written realistic descriptions. And thus, the most delicate pressure is enough to send us over the line from farce to phantasmagoria." "I never thought of *Catch-22* as a comic novel," Heller says in the *New York Times.* "[But] . . . I wanted the reader to be amused, and . . . I wanted him to be ashamed that he was amused. My literary bent . . . is more toward the morbid and the tragic. Great carnage is taking place and my idea was to use humor to make ridiculous the things that are irrational and very terrible." Dickstein cites the profiteering of Minderbinder as one example of the tragic underpinning of Heller's comedy: "[Milo's] amoral machinations, so hilarious at first, become increasingly sombre, ugly and deadly—like so much else in the book—that we readers become implicated in our own earlier laughter." "Below its hilarity, so wild that it hurts, *Catch-22* is the strongest repudiation of our civilization, in fiction, to come out of World War II," Nelson Algren states in *Nation.* As Brustein concludes, Heller is "at war with much larger forces than the army. . . . [He] has been nourishing his grudges for so long that they have expanded to include the post-war American world. Through the agency of grotesque comedy, Heller has found a way to confront the humbug, hypocrisy, cruelty, and sheer stupidity of our mass society. . . . Through some miracle of prestidigitation, Pianosa has become a satirical microcosm of the macrocosmic idiocies of our time."

Heller's subsequent novels have continued this "war," extending the field of battle to governmental and corporate life. *Good as Gold,* Fremont-Smith notes in the *Village Voice,* is "touted . . . as doing for the White House what *Catch-22* did for the military," while the absurdity and alienation of the American business community is the focus of *Something Happened,* the story of Bob Slocum, a middle-level manager who describes himself as "one of those many people . . . who are without ambition already and have no hope."

"He is restless," Kurt Vonnegut, Jr., writes of Slocum in the *New York Times Book Review.* "He mourns the missed opportunities of his youth. He is itchy for raises and promotions, even though he despises his company and the jobs he does. He commits unsatisfying adulteries now and then at sales conferences in resort areas, during long lunch hours, or while pretending to work late at the office. He is exhausted," Vonnegut concludes. "He dreads old age." In the *New Republic,* William Kennedy analyzes Heller's restless protagonist: "Bob Slocum is no true friend of anybody's. He is a woefully lost figure with a profound emptiness, a sad, absurd, vicious, grasping, climbing, womanizing, cowardly, sadistic, groveling, loving, yearning, anxious, fearful victim of the indecipherable, indescribable malady of being born human." John W. Aldridge describes Slocum as "a man raging in a vacuum." In the *Saturday Review/World,* Aldridge examines Slocum's plight: "His mental state is shaped by chronic feelings of loss divorced from an understanding of what precisely has been lost. . . . The elements that are most real in Slocum's life are precisely those that might be considered conducive to peace of mind: material affluence and comfort, abundant leisure time, professional success, satisfactory marital relations, and considerable extracurricular sex with a number of attractive women. Yet these are the primary sources of his suffering because he is forever searching them for meaning and can find none." Aldridge continues: "He is haunted by the sense that at some time in the past something happened to him, something that he cannot remember but that changed him from a person who had aspirations for the future, who believed in himself and his work, who trusted others and was able to love, into the person he has since unaccountably become, a man who aspires to nothing, believes in nothing and no one, least of all himself, who no longer knows if he loves or is loved."

Slocum's loss of meaning is symbolized by his search for Virginia, for the lost dreams of his youth. "As Yossarian kept flashing back to that primal, piteous scene in the B-25 where his mortally wounded comrade, Snowden, whimpered in his arms, so Slocum keeps thinking back, with impacted self-pity and regret, to the sweetly hot, teasing, slightly older girl in the insurance office where he worked after graduating from high school, whom he could never bring himself to 'go all the way' with," Edward Grossman writes in *Commentary.* "He blew it," D. Keith Mano remarks in the *National Review,* "and this piddling missed opportunity comes to stand for loss in general. He makes you accompany him again and again, and again and again to the back staircase for a quiet feel that never matures." As Mano notes, "Slocum becomes semi-obsessed: telephones the insurance company to ascertain if his . . . girlfriend is still employed there, if *he* is still employed there. And he isn't." Instead, Slocum finds that this haunting figure of a girl, like his own spirit, has committed suicide.

"What he wants now is to want something the way he once wanted Virginia," Kennedy declares. "Why can't some things other than stone remain always as they used to be, he wonders. Sad. What happened is that something happened. . . . [Slocum] spends the whole book trying to recreate what was and what is, speculating endlessly on what caused the ruin of such glorious innocence, such exciting desire. He has no more desire, only a stale, processed lust."

Clearly, something happened to create such unhappiness. "Something happened indeed," Benjamin DeMott finds, "namely the death of the heart." In the novel, Slocum says he wants "to continue receiving my raise in salary each year, and a good cash bonus at Christmastime . . . to be allowed to take my place on the rostum at the next company convention . . . and make my three minute report to the company of the work we have been doing in my department." In the *Atlantic Monthly,* DeMott attributes Slocum's pain to the fact that "caring at levels deeper than these is beyond him." Melvin Maddocks points out that "it is not what has happened, but what has not happened to Slocum that constitutes his main problem." In a *Time* review, Maddocks describes Slocum as "a weightless figure with no pull of gravity morally or emotionally" who can love only his nine-year-old son, and then only for "brief, affecting moments."

Slocum's life revolves around his office and home; in both of these worlds he folds, under the weight of external pressures and inner fears, into a helpless state of alienation. "Money and power and the corporation [are] for Bob Slocum what war and death and the Air Force had been for Yossarian," John Leonard notes in the *New York Times.* Just as Yossarian feared his own commanders and compatriots, so does Slocum, in the more secure confines of the business organization, live in fear of his associates. "He's afraid of closed doors and of accident reports. He's afraid of five people in his office," Jerome Klinkowitz observes. "At home Slocum fears and distrusts his family, although he loves them in his way," Aldridge says. "Slocum's wife is attractive and intelligent but bored and without a sense of meaning in her life. She has begun to drink in the afternoon and to flirt at parties." The Slocums, as Kennedy details, are the parents of "an insecure and nasty 16-year-old daughter whose shins [Slocum] wants to kick, an idiot son he is sick of and would like to unload, another son, aged nine, who is the principal joy of his life and whom he ruins by allowing the company's values (get to the top, don't give your money away, compete, compete) smother the boy's wondrously selfless and noncompetitive good nature." "One cannot but recognize that many of the pressures on Slocum are generated by the nuclear family itself and by the establishments in which the family is trained," Elaine Glover writes in *Stand.* With the exception of Derek, the mentally retarded son, none of Slocum's family have names, Fremont-Smith points out. "All of them are unhappy in various ways, and Slocum knows it is largely his fault." "Slocum does his deadly best to persuade us, with his tap-tap-tapping of facts, that he is compelled to be as unhappy as he is, not because of . . . flaws in his own character, but because of the facts," Vonnegut states.

However much the "facts" may conspire against Slocum, the real pressure is exerted from within. As Heller comments in the *Newark Star-Ledger:* "All the threats to Bob Slocum are internal. His enemy is his own fear, his own anxiety." According to an *America* review, "Heller has replaced the buzzing, booming world of an army at war with the claustrophobic universe of Bob Slocum's psyche, where all the complications, contradictions and absurdities are generated from within. . . . Like Yossarian, Slocum always feels trapped—by his wife, by his children, but mostly by himself." Slocum, who giggles inwardly at the thought of rape and glances over his shoulder for sodomists, confesses, "Things are going on inside me I cannot control and do not admire." "Within and without, his world is an unregenerate swamp of rack and ruin," Pearl K. Bell asserts in the *New Leader.* "Pathologically disassociated from himself, Slocum is a chameleon, taking on the gestures and vocabularies of whichever colleague he is with; even his handwriting is a forgery, borrowed from a boyhood friend." This disassociation is more than a middle-age malaise; it is symptomatic of a deeper affliction, a crippling of the spirit that leaves Slocum barely enough strength to lament, "I wish I knew what to wish."

As the novel draws to a close, Slocum finally and tragically expresses his love for his favorite son. As the boy lies bleeding after being struck by a car, someone yells, "Something happened!" Slocum rushes towards the child, horrified: "He is dying. A terror, a pallid, pathetic shock more dreadful than any I have been able to imagine, has leaped into his face. I can't stand it. He can't stand it. He hugs me. He looks beggingly at me for help. His screams are piercing. I can't bear to see him suffering such agony and fright. I have to do something. I hug his face deeper into the crook of my shoulder. I hug him tightly with both my arms. I squeeze. 'Death,' says the doctor, 'was due to asphyxiation. The boy was smothered. He had superficial lacerations of the scalp and face, a bruised face, a deep cut on his arm. That was all.'"

According to *Playboy, Something Happened* "unleashed a fusillade of violently mixed reviews. . . . Nearly three quarters of the critics viewed Heller's looping, memory-tape narrative as a dazzling, if depressing, literary tour de force." Fremont-Smith, for instance, calls *Something Happened* a "very fine, wrenchingly depressing" novel. "It gnaws at one, slowly and almost nuzzlingly at first, mercilessly toward the end. It hurts. It gives the willies." In his *New York Times Book Review* article, Vonnegut finds that the book is "splendidly put together and hypnotic to read. It is as clear and hard-edged as a cut diamond." Maddocks, however, labels Heller's second novel "a terrific letdown," while Grossman believes it is "a lump compared with *Catch-22.*" L. E. Sissman of the *New Yorker,* who calls *Something Happened* "a painful mistake," cites a frequent criticism of the novel: "[Heller] indulges in overkill. When we have seen Bob Slocum suffer a failure of nerve (or a failure of common humanity) in a dozen different situations, we do not need to see him fail a dozen times more." Mano asserts that "you can start *Something Happened* on page 359, read through to the end, and still pass a multiple choice test in plot, character, style. . . . [It] is overlong, a bit of an imposition."

Slocum's repetitive monologue has been criticized by certain reviewers, but, as George J. Searles points out in *Critique,* "Slocum, a businessman rather than a man of letters, is by necessity a limited narrator. Although articulate and aware of the fundamentals of language . . . , he is not a *writer.* His mode of speech—and the book has the feel of being spoken, rather than written—is flat, ordinary, and unexciting, and is an accurate reflection of his personality." Caroline Blackwood is uncomfortable with the narrative voice of the story for a different reason. In the *Times Literary Supplement,* she asks: "Is it possible [that such a man as Slocum] would be capable of viewing himself, his values, his work, and his relationship with his family, with the brutal and humorous introspection of Mr. Heller's central character? . . . Slocum asks for an enormous suspension of disbelief. Quite often he appears schizophrenic; the superior wit, insights, and sensibilities of his creator are superimposed so erratically and unsuitably on this commonplace and tiresome man." Schroth, however, finds Slocum a convincing narrator. He writes in *Commonweal:* "Who can read the paranoid utterances of Robert Slocum . . . and not recognize to some degree his own share in the competitive madness and chronic anxiety of American life? . . . [*Something Happened* is] a book which sums up the spiritual emptiness of the 1970s so excruciatingly that it may be another decade before many critics adequately appreciate it and most Americans can read it with sufficient detachment." Finally, Aldridge believes Heller "has discovered and possessed new territories of the imagination, and he has produced a major work of fiction, one that is as distinctive of its kind as *Catch-22* but more ambitious and profound, an abrasively brilliant commentary on American life that must surely be recognized as the most important novel to appear in this country in at least a decade.''

Heller's third novel ''indicts a class of clerks,'' Leonard writes in the *New York Times*. *Good as Gold* is a fictional expose of the absurd workings of the machinery of government, of a politics reduced to public relations, of a President who spends most of his first year in office penning *My Year in the White House,* of an administrative aide who mouths such wisdom as ''Just tell the truth . . . even if you have to lie'' and ''This President doesn't want yes-men. What we want are independent men of integrity who will agree with all our decisions after we make them.'' Into this world stumbles Bruce Gold, a professor of English who is called to public service after writing a favorable review of the Presidential book. Gold is rewarded for his kind words with a ''spokesman'' position but yearns for higher duty; specifically, he wants to be Secretary of State, more specifically, he wants to be the first *real* Jewish Secretary of State (Gold is convinced that Henry Kissinger, who prayed with Richard Nixon and ''made war gladly,'' cannot possibly be Jewish). For his part, Gold chips in by coining such expressions as ''You're boggling my mind'' and ''I don't know,'' phrases that enter the lexicon of the press conference and earn Gold the admiration of his superiors. As *Time*'s R. Z. Sheppard observes: ''[Gold] is no stranger to double-think. A literary hustler whose interest in government is a sham, he does not even vote, a fact 'he could not publicly disclose without bringing blemish to the image he had constructed for himself as a radical moderate.''' Gold was schooled in absurdity during his tenure at a New York City university, where he devised a curriculum such that ''it was now possible . . . for a student to graduate with an English major after spending all four years of academic study watching foreign movies in a darkened classroom.'' With this experience as a huckster of the academy, Gold, it would appear, is ready for Washington.

In the beginning, Gold flourishes in his new environment, where, according to Sheppard, ''catch-22 is now Potomac newspeak.'' He meets the Important People, elbows his way onto a Presidential Commission, and prepares to exchange his homey Jewish wife for the promiscuous daughter of a wealthy bigot in order to ease his advance to the upper echelons of the Administration. Along the way he is more than willing to endure the anti-Semitic prattle of his potential father-in-law and others, learning, as Leonard says, ''to lick the boots that specialize in stepping on you.''

Like *Something Happened, Good as Gold* is ''another painful portrait of a bright but almost empty man watching his soul melt in his hands,'' writes Schroth. ''The book is essentially about Jews, especially those like Gold, who wants to escape his identity while exploiting it, particularly by making a lot of money on a big book about Jews,'' Leonard Michaels comments in the *New York Times Book Review*. (Gold, despite his ignorance of his heritage, has received a substantial advance from a publisher for a book on ''The Jewish Experience in America.'') ''It is one of the main themes of *Good as Gold* that Jews violate themselves in their relations with such unreal creatures of their own minds, especially when Jews yearn for tall blondes and jobs in Washington, where successful Jews are slaves,'' Michaels continues. ''Gold yearns to escape what he is so that he can become what he isn't, which is precisely what he hates. He nearly succeeds, nearly becomes a Washington non-Jewish Jew, a rich, powerful slave with a tall blonde wife.'' Gold, unlike other characters in the story, is very much aware of his moral degeneration; a passage from the book reads:

''How much lower would he crawl to rise to the top? he asked himself with wretched self-reproval. Much, much lower, he answered in improving spirit, and felt purged of hypocrisy by the time he was ready for dinner.'' ''Unlike Heller's earlier hero, Yossarian, Gold pants to embrace the insanity of our time,'' Peter S. Prescott observes in *Newsweek*. ''His need for money and the chance to escape his suffocating family prick his ambition.''

''He is totally out of sync with his family,'' Alex Taylor says in the *Detroit Free Press*. In the *Los Angeles Times Book Review*, Darryl Ponicsan explains: ''He's got two sons away at college and he's not crazy about them. . . . He won't let them come home for a weekend. He's afraid of his daughter, who lives at home. He's bored with his wife, Belle. He has an older brother, Sid, who sets him up at every opportunity. . . . He has four older sisters and their mates harping about, an aged father who admits to having liked him briefly when he was a baby and a stepmother who suffers—if that's the word, and it isn't—insanity, ceaselessly knitting wool and talking just like a Joseph Heller character.'' Jack Beatty finds that ''the scenes of the Golds at dinner belong to the heights of comedy. . . . These family dinners are torture for Gold. Yet underneath [all the eating] and the practiced taunts, the feverish intimacy of the Gold family, there are some abiding values at work which Heller wants us to recognize and, I think, celebrate.'' In the *New Republic,* Beatty sees Gold's brother Sid as an example of such values: ''Sid, a prosperous businessman, is no hero; he's just a good man. He hated his father, yet bailed the old man out of his last business, and still pays the bills for his Florida retirement. He resented his smarter kid brother but paid his way through Columbia nonetheless. Sid has done his duty.'' ''The scenes with the family might at first seem disconnected from the Washington scenes,'' Ronald Hayman points out, ''but the pivotal joke is that someone who can fly so high as Gold should be treated with such savage contempt by his family, should be so inept at defending himself, and so incapable of staying away.''

In his *New York Times* article, Leonard elaborates on Gold's dilemma: ''What is being proposed is that being brought up lower middle-class Jewish in this country means being humiliated by your own family; that you assimilate, by groveling, a vacuum and a lie; that you have masturbatory dreams of acquiring the power to exact revenge on the father who disdains you; that to acquire such power you will be willing to mortgage every morsel of your capacity for critical discrimination; that you lick the boots that specialize in stepping on you, and hate yourself in the morning.'' Leonard adds: ''Those critics who, over the years, have suggested that [Heller] be more Jewish in his fiction are going to be sorry they asked.''

Indeed, Heller's treatment of ''The Jewish Experience in America'' has aroused criticism, including accusations that *Good as Gold* is anti-Semitic. According to Sheppard, the book ''is a savage, intemperately funny satire on the assimilation of the Jewish tradition of liberalism into the American main chance. It is a delicate subject, off-limits to non-Jews fearful of being thought anti-Semitic and unsettling to successful Jewish intellectuals whose views may have drifted to the right in middle age. Heller, who is neither a Gentile or a card-carrying intellectual, goes directly for the exposed nerve.'' Lyons observes that ''it was not so long ago . . . when a book dealing in such cultural stereotypes as Heller employs throughout would have been closely scrutinized by a self-appointed committee of rabbis and Jewish intellectuals to determine whether, on the balance, the portraits presented were 'good for the Jews' or 'bad for the Jews'. . . . Such stereotypes are nothing but peasant superstition and ought to be dismissed as such.'' In *Books and*

Bookmen, Hayman points out that the Gentiles in Heller's satirical novel are "even more obnoxious" than the Jewish characters. "Both, fortunately, are extremely entertaining." But Fremont-Smith asserts in the *Village Voice* that *Good as Gold* is not "without offensiveness. It does bore. It is also anti-Semitic. If Heller believes (and I'm willing to think he thinks he does) that everything is rotten to the core, this goes double for the Jews.... The Jews in *Good as Gold* are uniformly portrayed as snivelling, deceitful, self-aggrandizing, and ambitious beyond their worth: *Much, much lower, he answered in improving spirit.*"

In the novel, Heller depicts Henry Kissinger as the epitome of the "non-Jewish Jew" and examines, as Schroth notes, "the germ of Kissingerism within each of us." "Gold's real tension comes from the fact that his own morality dangles barely a ledge above his enemy's. He knows the corrupting tendency within himself, in every intellectual and journalist to become corrupted by the mere smell of power, to become a Kissinger...and, worst of all," Schroth adds, "to forsake his heritage, to forget or deny he is a Jew." In the *New York Review of Books,* Thomas R. Edwards finds that Gold's political aspirations have "one distinct drawback. Gold hates everything connected with Henry Kissinger, sees him as a loathsomely pushy cartoon-Jew and a closet Nazi.... Whatever the merits of this view of Kissinger's character, Gold's assault on his good name ... is exhileratingly energetic and winning. Its single-mindedness serves the purposes not only of comedy and moral outrage but also gives the novel its structure." Similarly, Jack Beatty of the *New Republic* comments: "The risk Gold runs in trying to become the first real Jewish Secretary of State is that he will be forced to act like Henry Kissinger, and that would mean his moral destruction.... *Good as Gold* is a cultural event. A major novelist takes on our greatest celebrity with all the wit and language at his command, and ... a central historical figure [has] been ... intimately castigated by the Word. Score one for literature." Gene Lyons in *Nation,* however, believes that the attack on Kissinger is only "occasionally funny, [and] often slides over into what seems like simple malice, and pretty much for its own sake.... Satirizing the man by presenting clippings from Anthony Lewis is not very funny or effective. They were much better the first time around."

In the end, Gold is finally offered his alter ego's former cabinet position but, as Beatty observes, "is recalled to New York and to himself" by the death of his brother Sid. Like Yossarian, Gold decides to "desert" his absurd world; he refuses the coveted post, choosing instead to preside over the funeral of his brother, the grief of his family, and, finally, the restoration of his own integrity. "He is a man with a profound moral sense," William McPherson asserts in *Book World.* "Once in a while he is reminded of it, and reminds us."

The critical reaction to *Good as Gold* has been divided. Edwards remarks that "*Good as Gold,* if hardly a perfect novel, is continuously alive, very funny, and finally coherent.... Like Heller's other novels, [it] is a book that takes large risks: it is sometimes rambling, occasionally self-indulgent, not always sure of the difference between humor and silliness. But this time the risks pay off.... Heller is among the novelists of the last two decades who matter." The *Hudson Review* describes it as a "big, ugly book," and Aram Bakshian, Jr., of the *National Review* calls it "an embarrassing flop.... The best [Heller] has to offer us in his latest novel is fool's gold." Hayman finds the novel is flawed but says that "nothing is unforgivable when a book makes you laugh out loud so often," and McPherson concludes: "When I didn't hate it, I loved it. Joseph Heller, of all people, would understand that." Finally, Mel Brooks in *Book World* rates *Good as Gold* as "somewhere between *The Brothers Karamazov* and those dirty little books we used to read.... It's closer to *Karamazov.*"

Despite the success of *Something Happened* and *Good as Gold,* Heller remains best known as the author of *Catch-22,* a book that captured and helped shape the longings of a generation. Now at work on a fourth novel, Heller "continues to probe with the skill, the patience, and the precision of a scientist beneath the camouflage of everyday life," Kutt writes. "In one sense," Schroth says, "we can never have enough of Joseph Heller. We need him to articulate our common secret fears." Concludes Peter Ackroyd in *Spectator*: "Someone must make chaos out of our order and Mr. Heller has done it."

MEDIA ADAPTATIONS: Catch-22 was produced as a motion picture by Paramount in 1970. The film was directed by Mike Nichols, adapted by Buck Henry, and starred Alan Arkin as Yossarian.

CA INTERVIEW

CA interviewed Joseph Heller by phone March 7, 1981, at his home in New York City.

CA: You worked for several years as an advertising writer and promotion manager. Did that work contribute greatly to your sense of the absurd?

HELLER: No, it didn't contribute to my sense of the absurd. It helped me a great deal with *Catch-22* because I think, fortuitously, much of what's in *Catch-22* has the same dynamics that advertising writing has—the emphasis on novel ideas, for example. But no, I didn't find anything absurd about working in advertising. It was the best job I could find, and I didn't see anything absurd about working at something I had to work at.

CA: You've also been a teacher. Why did you decide to leave teaching?

HELLER: Because I didn't enjoy it and didn't have to do it anymore. I left as soon as *Something Happened* was coming out: that's the first time I had enough income from writing to enable me not to do any other work.

CA: You've said you consider yourself a writer of burlesque rather than black humor.

HELLER: I don't know what black humor is.

CA: Several critics have called you a black humorist, and you seemed not to like that.

HELLER: It's not that I dislike it. It just has little meaning to me as a literary concept, a literary description.

CA: Is your work stimulated much by contact with other writers?

HELLER: No.

CA: Do you see much of other writers?

HELLER: I see them. Living where I do, I meet many of them, but there's very little in the way of any real relationships between us. I don't see anything like what I would call deep friendships. And I don't seem to have any with people whom I've met since I became a writer. My friendship with Mario Puzo goes back to the time when neither one of us was a writer.

CA: During the long period between Catch-22 *and* Something Happened, *were you under much outside pressure to produce another novel?*

HELLER: No, I wasn't. Once I had written a section of *Something Happened*, I signed a contract and took an advance on it. So I had the choice of either finishing the book or returning the money. But that was the only pressure, and that wasn't even pressure. I wanted to write a book anyway, so even if I hadn't had a contract I would have been writing it.

CA: You've admitted to a tendency to procrastinate. When you're not writing, are you thinking about writing?

HELLER: Yeah. I won't say always, but most of my thoughts have to do with the book I'm working on.

CA: You said in a recent U.S. News and World Report *article, "I have a feeling I'm not a natural writer, although I do have a writer's imagination." Why do you feel you aren't a natural writer?*

HELLER: Oh, I think I'm not very secure with literary language. It does not come as easily to me as I *imagine* it comes to other people. Maybe my imagination is a form of masochistic fantasy. But listening to someone like Gore Vidal speak, I get a sense that his oral vocabulary is very close to his literary vocabulary. I think there are very few writers who are that way. But I can't help feeling that the prose of John Updike comes more easily to him than literary language comes to me. It may just be a feeling, just an expression of certain feelings of inadequacy I have. I have very little trouble getting ideas, but I seem to have much work in getting them down on paper in prose form.

CA: When you say you have a writer's imagination, then, you mean that the ideas come easily?

HELLER: Yes.

CA: Do you find a great deal that's positive in contemporary fiction?

HELLER: I don't know what you mean by positive, but I don't even think that's an important consideration. What *do* you mean by positive?

CA: Let's switch to negative. Some critics are complaining that much contemporary fiction has no form, is too experimental.

HELLER: That's fine. I don't think that's negative; I think that's marvelous. And along with that, we have so much fiction that has too much form. I think that the very diversity of fiction, American fiction, is a sign of great health, and it's what I enjoy.

CA: Do you read a great deal?

HELLER: I don't know what a great deal is. When I'm writing I don't seem to have much time to read. But I read *about* novels more than I read novels. I read reviews, and if a book comes out that I think will appeal very strongly to me, then I buy it.

CA: Are there specific writers whose work you read?

HELLER: Writers all of whose works I would read? No.

CA: You've described in the past your method of writing as it relates to the lack of chronological order in your books.

HELLER: I think there's a misunderstanding there. The events in my books are not usually told in the traditional sequence of chronological order. But I *write* the books in chronological order. I do a lot of introspection, a lot of meditation, in the course of a day, in walking or jogging or whatever I'm doing, and my thoughts get on ideas for the book. Generally I am thinking ahead about the section I'm doing at the time. And if something occurs to me that I think I don't want to forget, I will jot it down on a card.

CA: These ideas fit into an outline in your mind, at least?

HELLER: Yes. And fit into an outline in folders. I start with a small file cabinet, and the next step is to get a sequence of folders. If I know exactly in which chapter certain thoughts are going to go in dialogue, I drop them into the right folder.

CA: You seem to express in your writing a concern with the way people use and misuse language to obscure and confuse and build barriers.

HELLER: It seems to be true. There's an unconscious expression of some kind of philosophy. In all three of my novels, my characters do seem to get preoccupied with words and the way words are either misused or corrupted, or the way words contradict themselves. Slocum speculates on words very often. There is much about it in my writing. I don't know what it means, frankly. I've read pieces by somebody on the hollowness of language, particularly on certain prize cliches that I seem to dwell on in my writing, and it is true. But I was not aware of it until I read it.

CA: Has scholarly or critical writing been very helpful to you?

HELLER: Usually it is, and it may not be about my own work, but about other people's work. While I'm writing a book I may read an interpretation of another book or read something about the modern novel and realize I'm doing something close to what I'm reading about. That happened when I was writing *Something Happened*. When it does, I just make more use of it.

CA: What do you think of the tendency among academics to categorize writers?

HELLER: I don't think it's bad. I think the most intelligent comments on fiction come from academics or professional critics rather than reviewers. The more discussion the better. I seldom read anything about any of my books, even the very derogatory pieces, that I would say were inaccurate. It comes down to matters of taste.

CA: About Something Happened, *Eliot Fremont-Smith wrote in* New York *magazine, "It hurts, it gives the willies." Is that what you wanted it to do?*

HELLER: Yes, I did.

CA: Were you very happy with that book yourself?

HELLER: Oh, and how! Extremely!

CA: I've read that Good as Gold *has been particularly popular in Germany. Have you any indication, through fan mail or critical writing, why that's so?*

HELLER: I didn't know that. No. Normally I would see letters, but the arrangements with this particular book allow the publisher to handle the foreign rights, so any communications and royalty checks from foreign publishers go directly to the publisher. They don't keep me informed. I didn't know it had done that well in Germany. I'm sorry I don't read German.

CA: Does Bruce Gold in Good as Gold *reflect your own concerns more than Bob Slocum of* Something Happened?

HELLER: No. I would say he is a reflection of certain concerns, a reflection of certain attitudes. I think in both cases, though, the characters are presented as being somewhat inferior to the reader I assume. Neither character is intended to be admired. But Slocum is not intended to be laughed at and derided, whereas Bruce Gold is. Bruce Gold is a comic intellectual in the sense that he's capable of handling none of the predicaments he finds himself in. Many of the attitudes are mine, particularly the reflections on society. But these attitudes don't represent my entire outlook, just as they don't represent his. I think he comes close to being able to see both sides of a question, and he's able to regard certain situations as almost surely hopelessly resistant to solutions. I make him a fool, but he's a fool only in his ambitions and social aspirations. I guess he's of sound mind in other areas. And his cynicism is mine. His hypocrisy, I hope, isn't.

CA: In his review of Good as Gold *in* Harper's *magazine, John Aldridge said, "The horror is that the time may soon come when the conditions Heller depicts will no longer seem to us either funny or the least bit odd." Do you think this is happening?*

HELLER: Yes, but I think it was also true by the time that Aldridge was writing his review. I don't think things are much worse under Reagan than they were under Carter. It's too soon to judge. But that reminds me of a line in *Good as Gold:* "Gold knew that the most advanced and penultimate stage of a civilization was attained when chaos masqueraded as order, and he knew we were already there."

CA: Are you working on something you'd like to talk about?

HELLER: I'm working on another novel I'd rather not talk about. Writing fiction is all I want to do, and novels are the only kind of fiction I want to write.

BIOGRAPHICAL/CRITICAL SOURCES—Books: Joseph Heller, *Catch-22,* Simon & Schuster, 1961; Harry T. Moore, editor, *Contemporary American Novelists,* Southern Illinois University Press, 1964; Richard Kostelanetz, editor, *On Contemporary Literature,* Avon, 1964; Norman Podhoretz, *Doings and Undoings: The Fifties and After in American Writing,* Farrar, Straus, 1964; Bruce Jay Friedman, editor, *Black Humor,* Bantam, 1965; *New American Arts,* Horizon Publishing, 1965; Thomas B. Whitbread, editor, *Seven Contemporary Authors,* University of Texas Press, 1966; Anthony Burgess, *The Novel Now: A Guide to Contemporary Fiction,* Norton, 1967; John Colmer, editor, *Approaches to the Novel,* Rigby (Adelaide), 1967; James E. Miller, Jr., *Quests Surd and Absurd: Essays in American Literature,* University of Chicago Press, 1967; Jesse Bier, *The Rise and Fall of American Humor,* Holt, 1968; Nathan A. Scott, editor, *Adversity and Grace: Studies in Recent American Literature,* University of Chicago Press, 1968; *American Novels of the Second World War,* Mouton, 1969.

Literary Horizons: A Quarter Century of American Fiction, New York University Press, 1970; Bernard Bergonzi, *The Situation of the Novel,* University of Pittsburgh Press, 1970; Wayne Charles Miller, *An Armed America, Its Face in Fiction: A History of the American Military Novel,* New York University Press, 1970; David Littlejohn, *Interruptions,* Grossman, 1970; Jerry H. Bryant, *The Open Decision: The Contemporary American Novel and Its Intellectual Background,* Free Press, 1970; Moore, editor, *American Dreams, American Nightmares,* Southern Illinois University Press, 1970; Richard Boyd Hauck, *A Cheerful Nihilism: Confidence and the Absurd in American Humorous Fiction,* Indiana University Press, 1971; Tony Tanner, *City of Words,* Harper, 1971; Charles B. Harris, *Contemporary American Novelists of the Absurd,* College and University Press, 1971.

Gerald B. Nelson, *Ten Versions of America,* Knopf, 1972; Raymond M. Olderman, *Beyond the Waste Land: The American Novel in the Nineteen-Sixties,* Yale University Press, 1972; Gilbert A. Harrison, editor, *The Critic as Artist: Essays on Books, 1920-1970,* Liveright, 1972; Alfred Kazin, *The Bright Book of Life: American Novelists and Storytellers from Hemingway to Mailer,* Little, Brown, 1973; *A Dangerous Crossing,* Southern Illinois University Press, 1973; Frederick Kiley and Walter McDonald, editors, *A Catch-22 Casebook,* Crowell, 1973; *Contemporary Literary Criticism,* Gale, Volume I, 1973, Volume III, 1975; Volume V, 1976, Volume VIII, 1978, Volume XI, 1979; Robert M. Scotto, editor, *A Critical Edition of Catch-22,* Delta, 1973.

James Nagel, editor, *Critical Essays on Catch-22,* Dickenson, 1974; D. H. Richter, *Fable's End: Completeness and Closure in Rhetorical Fiction,* University of Chicago Press, 1974; Heller, *Something Happened,* Knopf, 1974; *Number and Nightmare: Forms of Fantasy in Contemporary Fiction,* Archon, 1975; Peter Aichinger, *The American Soldier in Fiction, 1880-1963,* Iowa State University Press, 1975; Matthew J. Bruccoli and C. E. Frazer Clark, Jr., editors, *Pages: The World of Books, Writers, and Writing,* Gale, 1976; *Authors in the News,* Volume I, Gale, 1976; *Dictionary of Literary Biography,* Gale, Volume II: *American Novelists since World War II,* 1978, *Yearbook: 1980,* 1981; Heller, *Good as Gold,* Simon & Schuster, 1979; Ronald Wallace, *The Last Laugh,* University of Missouri Press, 1979.

Periodicals: *Saturday Review,* October 14, 1961, August 31, 1968, February 6, 1971; *New York Times Book Review,* October 22, 1961, September 9, 1962, March 3, 1968, October 6, 1974, February 2, 1975, May 15, 1977, March 11, 1979; *New York Times,* October 23, 1961, December 3, 1967, December 7, 1967, June 19, 1970, October 1, 1974, March 5, 1979; *Time,* October 27, 1961, February 1, 1963, June 15, 1970, October 14, 1974, March 12, 1979; *Nation,* November 4, 1961, October 19, 1974, June 16, 1979; *New Republic,* November 13, 1961, October 19, 1974, March 10, 1979; *New Yorker,* December 9, 1961, November 25, 1974, April 16, 1979.

Atlantic Monthly, January, 1962, October, 1974, March, 1979; *Spectator,* June 15, 1962, October 26, 1974, May 5, 1979; *Critique,* Volume V, number 2, 1962, Volume VII, number 2, 1964-65, Volume IX, number 2, 1967, Volume XXII, number 2, 1970, Volume XVII, number 1, 1975, Volume XVIII, number 3, 1977; *Vogue,* January 1, 1963; *Mademoiselle,* August, 1963; *Book Week,* February 6, 1966; *Twentieth Century Literature,* January, 1967, October, 1973; *Books,* October, 1967; *Life,* January 1, 1968; *Motive,* February, 1968; *Mosaic,* fall, 1968, spring, 1971.

Studies in the Novel, spring, 1971, spring, 1972; *Midwest Quarterly,* winter, 1974; *Paris Review,* winter, 1974; *New York,* September 30, 1974; *Book World,* October 6, 1974, March 11, 1979, December 9, 1979; *Newark Star-Ledger,* October 6, 1974; *Christian Science Monitor,* October 9, 1974,

March 28, 1979, April 9, 1979; *Newsweek,* October 14, 1974, December 30, 1974, March 12, 1979; *New York Review of Books,* October 17, 1974, April 5, 1979; *Saturday Review/World,* October 19, 1974; *Listener,* October 24, 1974, May 10, 1979; *New Statesman,* October 25, 1974; *Times Literary Supplement,* October 25, 1974; *America,* October 26, 1974, May 19, 1979; *New Leader,* October 28, 1974, March 26, 1979; *CEA Critic,* November, 1974; *Commentary,* November, 1974, June, 1979; *National Review,* November 22, 1974, July 20, 1979; *Commonweal,* December 5, 1974, May 11, 1979; *Richmond Times-Dispatch,* December 8, 1974; *Playboy,* June, 1975.

Yale Review, summer, 1975; *Stand,* Volume XVI, number 3, 1975; *Partisan Review,* Volume XLIII, number 2, 1976; *Canadian Review of American Studies,* spring, 1976; *Book Digest,* May, 1976; *Harper's,* March, 1979; *New York Times Sunday Magazine,* March 4, 1979; *Village Voice,* March 5, 1979; *Chicago Tribune Book World,* March 18, 1979; *Detroit Free Press,* March 18, 1979; *Los Angeles Times Book Review,* March 25, 1979; *U.S. News and World Report,* April 9, 1979; *Books and Bookmen,* June, 1979; *Hudson Review,* winter, 1979-80; *Arizona Quarterly,* winter, 1980; *Rolling Stone,* April 16, 1981.†

—Sketch by Stewart R. Hakola

—Interview by Jean W. Ross

* * *

HENDRICK, George 1929-

PERSONAL: Born March 30, 1929, in Stephenville, Tex.; son of Hoyt (a rancher) and Bessie Lea (Sears) Hendrick; married Willene Lowery, January 23, 1955. *Education:* Texas Christian University, B.A., 1948, M.A., 1950; University of Texas, Ph.D., 1954. *Office:* Department of English, University of Illinois at Urbana-Champaign, Urbana, Ill. 61810.

CAREER: Southwest Texas State College, San Marcos, assistant professor of English, 1954-56; University of Colorado, Boulder, member of English department faculty, 1956-60; Johann Wolfgang Goethe-Universitat (University of Frankfurt), Frankfurt am Main, West Germany, professor of American literature and culture, 1960-65, co-director of English seminar, and director of Amerika-Institut; University of Illinois at Chicago Circle, professor of English, 1965-67; University of Illinois at Urbana-Champaign, professor of English, 1967—, head of department, 1971-76, associate dean of graduate college, 1967-71. Visiting professor, University of Illinois at Chicago Circle, 1964-65. *Member:* Modern Language Association of America, Midwest Modern Language Association.

WRITINGS: (With Donna Gerstenberger) *Director of Periodicals Publishing Articles in English and American Language and Literature,* A. Swallow, 1959, 4th edition, 1974; (editor) *1785 Bhagavad-Gita,* translation by Charles Wilkins, Scholars' Facsimiles, 1959; (with Gerstenberger) *The American Novel: A Checklist of Twentieth Century Criticism,* A. Swallow, 1960; *Katherine Anne Porter,* Twayne, 1965.

Mazo de la Roche, Twayne, 1970; *A Checklist of American Literary Manuscripts in Australia, Canada, India, Israel, Japan and New Zealand,* Bull Publishing, 1972; (with Lynn Altenbernd) *The Sandburg Roots,* University of Illinois Library Friends, 1976; *Henry Salt, Humanitarian Reformer and Man of Letters,* University of Illinois Press, 1977; (with J. A. Robbins and others) *American Literary Manuscripts,* University of Georgia Press, 1977; *Remembrances of Concord and the Thoreaus: Letters of Horace Hosmer to Dr. S. A. Jones,* University of Illinois Press, 1977; (editor with Fritz Oehlschleger) *Toward the Making of Thoreau's Modern Reputation: Selected Correspondence of S. A. Jones, A. W. Hosmer, H. S. Salt, H.G.O. Blake and D. Ricketson,* University of Illinois Press, 1979; (editor with Willene Hendrick) *On the Illinois Frontier: Dr. Hiram Rutherford, 1840-1848,* Southern Illinois University Press, 1981.

* * *

HERMAN, Walter
See WAGER, Walter H(erman)

* * *

HERNON, Peter 1944-

PERSONAL: Born August 31, 1944, in Kansas City, Mo.; son of Robert M. (a geologist) and Ethel (Grazier) Hernon; married Elinor Griffith (a librarian), December 30, 1972; children: Alison. *Education:* University of Colorado, B.A., 1966, M.A. (history), 1969; University of Denver, M.A. (library science), 1971; Indiana University, Ph.D., 1978. *Politics:* Liberal independent. *Home:* 4 Belmore Park, Newton, Mass. 02162. *Office:* Simmons College, Boston, Mass. 02115.

CAREER: University of Nebraska at Omaha, reference librarian, 1971-75, instructor, 1971-74, assistant professor of library science, 1974-75; Indiana University at Bloomington, associate instructor, 1975-78; Simmons College, Boston, Mass., assistant professor, 1978-81, associate professor, 1981—. *Member:* American Library Association.

WRITINGS: (Editor with others) *Municipal Government Reference Sources: Publications and Collections,* Bowker, 1978; *Use of Government Publications by Social Scientists,* Ablex Publishing, 1979; *Microfilms and Government Information,* Microform Review, 1981; (editor with Bernard M. Fry) *Government Publications: Key Papers,* Pergamon, 1981; (with Ching-Chih Chen) *Information Seeking: Assessing and Anticipating,* Neal-Schuman, 1981; (with Gary R. Purcell) *Developing Collections of U.S. Government Publications,* Jai Press, in press; (with Charles R. McClure) *Improving Access to Government Information,* Ablex Publishing, in press; (with McClure) *Improving Reference Service for Government Publications,* American Library Association, in press.

Editor of proceedings of first annual Conference on Library Government Documents. Contributor of articles and reviews to library journals.

AVOCATIONAL INTERESTS: Tennis, walking, vegetable gardening.

* * *

HESKETT, J(ames) L(ee) 1933-

PERSONAL: Born May 8, 1933, in Cedar Falls, Iowa; son of Gail Stewart (a farmer) and Leone (Stein) Heskett; married Marilyn Louise Taylor (a teacher), July 13, 1955; children: Sarah Louise, Charles Taylor, Benjamin. *Education:* Iowa State Teachers College (now University of Northern Iowa), A.B., 1954; Stanford University, M.B.A., 1958, Ph.D., 1960. *Home:* 233 Prospect St., Belmont, Mass. 02178. *Office:* Graduate School of Business Administration, Harvard University, Boston, Mass. 02163.

CAREER: Ohio State University, Columbus, assistant professor, 1960-63, associate professor of business organization, 1963-65; Harvard University, Graduate School of Business Administration, Boston, Mass., associate professor, 1965-69, professor of business logistics, 1969—. President, Logistics Systems, Inc., 1968-69; director, Distribution Centers, Inc., Community Music Center, Boston, Mass., and The Window Shop, Inc. Consultant to industry. *Military service:* U.S. Army, 1954-56; served in Europe. *Member:* Society of Logistics and Engineers (director), American Marketing Association, American Association of University Professors, National Council on Physical Distribution Management, American Society of Traffic and Transportation, Transportation Research Forum (board of trustees). *Awards, honors:* M.A., Harvard University, 1970; Alumni Achievement Award, University of Northern Iowa, 1971; John Drury Shehan Award, National Council on Physical Distribution Management, 1974.

WRITINGS: (With Donald Peery Cottrell) *Supplement to Education for Business*, Chapman, Evans & Delehanty, 1962; (with Gayton E. Germane and Nicholas A. Glaskowsky, Jr.) *Highway Transportation Management*, McGraw, 1963; (with Robert M. Ivie and N. A. Glaskowsky, Jr.) *Business Logistics*, Ronald, 1964, 2nd edition, 1973; *Case Problems in Business Logistics*, Wiley, 1973; *Marketing*, Macmillan, 1976; *Student Resource Manual to Accompany Marketing*, Macmillan, 1976. Contributor to marketing and transportation journals. Member of board of editors, *Journal of Marketing Research*, and *Journal of Business Logistics*.†

* * *

HESSING, Dennis
See DENNIS-JONES, H(arold)

* * *

HEUSSLER, Robert 1924-

PERSONAL: Born August 11, 1924, in Buffalo, N.Y.; son of Herman Koerner and Carlotta (Morgan) Heussler; married Ten Broeck Jackson, January 12, 1957; children: Morgan Ten Broeck, Lowry Elizabeth, Sarah Stuyvesant, Ann Bayard (daughters). *Education:* Dartmouth College, B.A., 1948; College of Chinese Studies, Peking, additional study; Princeton University, M.A., 1959, Ph.D., 1961. *Politics:* "Tend to vote Democrat." *Residence:* Strafford, Vt. *Office:* Department of History, State University of New York College at Geneseo, Geneseo, N.Y. 14454.

CAREER: Standard-Vacuum Oil Co., aviation executive in China, Hong Kong, and Philippines, 1948-50; Central Intelligence Agency, Washington, D.C., intelligence officer, 1952; Cinerama Productions Corp., overseas representative of company president, Lowell Thomas, 1952-55; University of Vermont, Burlington, lecturer in political science and executive director of World Affairs Council, 1955-57; Princeton University, Princeton, N.J., instructor of political science, 1958-59; Syracuse University, Syracuse, N.Y., assistant professor of political science and executive director of Africa-Asia Program, 1961-62; Ford Foundation, New York, N.Y., program associate, 1962-64; University of Vermont, associate professor of history, 1966-68; Trenton State College, Trenton, N.J., president, 1968-70; State University of New York College at Geneseo, professor of history, 1973—, chairman of department, 1973-75. Visiting fellow, Center for International Studies, Princeton University, 1970-71; national fellow, Hoover Institution, Stanford University, 1971-72; research associate, St. Antony's College, Oxford University, 1972-73. Consultant to Foreign Area Training Program, London, 1965—. *Military service:* U.S. Army Air Forces, pilot, 8th Air Force, Europe, 1944; became first lieutenant, flew thirty-seven combat missions; received Distinguished Flying Cross, Air Medal with three oak leaf clusters, battle stars, Presidential Unit Citation.

MEMBER: Royal Commonwealth Society (London). *Awards, honors:* Fulbright Fellow, St. Antony's College, Oxford University; Theodore F. Sanxay Fellow in Practical Ethics, Princeton University; American Philosophical Society grants, 1964, 1965, 1967; Social Science Research Council grants, 1965 and 1972.

WRITINGS: *Yesterday's Rulers: The Making of the British Colonial Service*, Syracuse University Press, 1963; *The British in Northern Nigeria*, Oxford University Press, 1968; *British Tanganyika*, Duke University Press, 1971; (contributor) *France and Britain in Africa*, Yale University Press, 1971; (contributor) *Contemporary Africa*, Prentice-Hall, 1976; *British Rule in Malaya: The Malayan Civil Service and Its Predecessors, 1867-1942*, Greenwood Press, 1981; *British Malaya: A Bibliographical and Biographical Compendium*, Garland Publishing, 1981; (editor) Sir Donald Cameron, *My Tanganyika Service and Some Nigeria*, University Press of America, 1982. Contributor to British and American journals.

* * *

HIEATT, Constance B(artlett) 1928-

PERSONAL: Born February 11, 1928, in Boston, Mass.; daughter of Arthur Charles and Eleonora (Very) Bartlett; married Allen Kent Hieatt (a college professor and writer), October 25, 1958. *Education:* Attended Smith College, 1945-47; Hunter College (now Hunter College of the City University of New York), A.B., 1953, M.A., 1957; Yale University, Ph.D., 1959. *Religion:* Episcopalian. *Home:* 2 Grosvenor St., London, Ontario, Canada N6A 1Y4. *Office:* University of Western Ontario, London, Ontario, Canada N6A 3K7.

CAREER: Held various positions of a secretarial or editorial nature in publishing and teaching, 1948-57; City College of New York (now City College of the City University of New York), New York, N.Y., lecturer in English, 1959-60; Queensborough Community College of the City University of New York, Bayside, N.Y., assistant professor, 1960-64, associate professor of English, 1964-65; St. John's University, Jamaica, N.Y., associate professor, 1965-67, professor of English, 1967-69; University of Western Ontario, London, professor of English, 1969—. *Member:* International Arthurian Society, International Saga Society, Association of Canadian University Teachers of English, Societe Rencesvals, Children's Literature Association, Royal Society of Canada (fellow), Modern Language Association of America, Mediaeval Academy of America.

WRITINGS: (With husband, A. Kent Hieatt) *The Canterbury Tales of Geoffrey Chaucer* (adaptation for young readers), Golden Press, 1961; (translator) *Sir Gawain and the Green Knight* (adaptation for young readers), Crowell, 1967; (compiler) *Beowulf, and Other Old English Poems*, Odyssey, 1967; *The Realism of Dream Visions: The Poetic Exploitation of the Dream-Experience in Chaucer and His Contemporaries*, Mouton, 1967; (adapter) *The Knight of the Lion*, Crowell, 1968; *Essentials of Old English*, Crowell, 1968; (adapter) *The Knight of the Cart*, Crowell, 1969.

(Editor) *The Miller's Tale of Geoffrey Chaucer*, Odyssey, 1970; (editor with A. K. Hieatt) *Edmund Spenser: Selected Poetry*, Appleton-Century-Crofts, 1970; (adapter) *The Joy of the Court*, Crowell, 1971; (adapter) *The Sword and the Grail*, Crowell, 1972; (adapter) *The Castle of Ladies*, Crowell, 1973; (adapter) *The Minstrel Knight*, Crowell, 1974; (translator) *Karlamagnus Saga: The Saga of Charlemagne and His Heroes*, Pontifical

Institute of Medieval Studies, Volume I, 1975, Volume II, 1975, Volume III, 1980; (with Sharon Butler) *Pleyn Delit: Medieval Cookery for Modern Cooks,* University of Toronto Press, 1976, revised edition, 1979.

WORK IN PROGRESS: *Curye on Inglysch: Fourteenth-Century English Cookery Books,* with Sharon Butler, for publication by Early English Text Society; a translation, with Minette Grunmann-Gaudet, of *Guillaume de Marchaut's Dit de l'Alerion.*

SIDELIGHTS: *Pleyn Delit: Medieval Cookery for Modern Cooks* has been published in French.

BIOGRAPHICAL/CRITICAL SOURCES: *Book Week,* May 21, 1967; *New York Times Book Review,* October 20, 1968.

* * *

HIGGINS, Dick
See HIGGINS, Richard C(arter)

* * *

HIGGINS, Richard C(arter) 1938-
(Dick Higgins)

PERSONAL: Born March 15, 1938, in Cambridge, England; son of Carter Chapin Higgins (a steel manufacturer) and Katharine (Bigelow) Higgins Doman; married Alison Knowles (a silk screen technician and artist), May 30, 1960 (divorced, 1970); children: Hannah and Jessie (twins). *Education:* Attended Yale University, 1955-57; studied music with John Cage, Henry Cowell, and others, 1957-59; Columbia University B.S., 1960; Manhattan School of Printing, C.P.O. certificate, 1961; New York University, M.A., 1977. *Politics:* Progressive Republican. *Address:* P.O. Box 27, Station Hill Rd., Barrytown, N.Y. 12507.

CAREER: Writer; publisher; graphics designer. Zaccar Offset (printers), New York City, cameraman, 1963; Book Press, New York City, technician and member of production staff, 1963-64; Russell & Russell (publishers), New York City, member of production staff, beginning 1964; Something Else Press, New York City, founder, designer, and U.S. manager, 1964-73; Printed Editions (formerly Unpublished Editions), New York City, founder, 1973—. Instructor in publishing at California Institute of the Arts, 1970-71; fellow of Center for Twentieth-Century Studies, University of Wisconsin—Milwaukee, 1977; member of literature panel, New York State Council on the Arts, 1979—; lecturer. Operator of Something Else Gallery, 1966-69; has had one-man shows, in a number of media, in the United States, Canada, Brazil, Argentina, Germany, Sweden, Iceland, and Italy; has participated in many other shows, festivals, and exhibitions in the United States and abroad. *Member:* Film Makers' Co-op, New York Audio-Visual Society (co-founder; vice-president), Broadway Opera Company. *Awards, honors:* New York State Council on the Arts grant, 1968; Deutscher Akademischer Austauschdienst grants to Berlin, 1975 and 1981-82.

WRITINGS: *What Are Legends* (essay), Bern Porter, 1960; *Jefferson's Birthday* (plays) [and] *Postface* (essay), Something Else, 1964; *A Book about Love and War and Death,* Canto 1, Something Else, 1965, Cantos 2 and 3, Nova Broadcast, 1969, Cantos 1-3, published in one volume, Something Else, 1972; *Towards the 1970's,* Abyss Publications, 1969; *foew&ombwhnw: A Grammar of the Mind and a Phenomenology of Love and a Science of the Arts as Seen by a Stalker of the Wild Mushroom,* Something Else, 1969; (with Wolf Vostell) *Pop Architektur,* Droste (Dusseldork), 1969, translation published as *Fantastic Architecture,* Something Else, 1971; *Die fabelhafte Getraume von Taifun-Willi,* Relection Press (Stuttgart), 1969, Abyss Publications, 1970.

Computers for the Arts, Abyss Publications, 1970; *amigo,* Unpublished Editions, 1972; *The Ladder to the Moon,* Unpublished Editions, 1973; *for eugene in germany,* Unpublished Editions, 1973; *Le Petit Cirque au Fin du Monde: Un Opera Arabasque,* Aarevue/Aafondation, 1973; *Spring Game,* Unpublished Editions, 1973; *City with All the Angles,* Unpublished Editions, 1974; *Modular Poems,* Unpublished Editions, 1975; *classic plays,* Unpublished Editions, 1976; *Legends and Fishnets,* Unpublished Editions, 1976; *Cat Alley,* Tuumba Press, 1976; *The Epitaphs,* Studio Morra (Naples), 1977; *Everyone Has Sher Favorite (His or Hers),* Unpublished Editions, 1977; *George Herbert's Pattern Poems: In Their Tradition,* Unpublished Editions, 1977; *The Epickall Quest of the Brothers Dichtung and Other Outrages,* Printed Editions, 1978; *A Dialectic of Centuries: Notes towards a Theory of the New Arts,* Printed Editions, 1978, 2nd edition, 1979; *Hymns to the Night,* Treacle Press, 1978; *some recent snowflakes (and other things),* Printed Editions, 1979.

of Celebration of morning, Printed Editions, 1980; *Ten Ways of Looking at a Bird,* Printed Editions, 1981; *26 mountains for viewing the sunset from,* Printed Editions, 1981; *1959/60,* Pari & Dispari, 1981.

Musical compositions: *Graphis 144: "Wipeout for Orchestra"* and *Graphis 143: "Softly for Orchestra,"* Something Else, 1967; *Suggested by Small Swallows,* Dorn Editions, 1973; *Emmett Williams's Ear,* Pari & Dispari, 1977; *Piano Album: Short Pieces, 1962-1984,* Printed Editions, 1980. Also composer of music for records, reel-to-reel tapes and cassettes.

Author of "Stacked Deck," the first "electronic opera," with music by Richard Maxfield, 1958; creator of graphics and "multiples," "postcards and miniatures," and "sound poems"; also author of a number of films, including "A Tiny Movie," 1959; "For the Dead," 1965, "Scenario," 1968, and "Mysteries," 1969.

Contributor: Fred McDarra, editor, *The Beat Scene,* Corinth Books, 1959; La Monte Young, editor, *An Anthology,* La Monte Young & Jackson Mac Low, 1963, 2nd edition, Heinger Friedrich, 1970; Wolf Vostell and Juergen Becker, editors, *Happenings,* Rowohlt Verlag (Hamburg), 1966; Richard Kostelanetz, editor, *The Young American Writers,* Funk, 1967; Eugene Wildman, editor, *An Anthology of Concretism,* Swallow Press, 1968; Mary Ellen Solt, editor, *Concrete Poetry: A World View,* Indiana University Press, 1968; Jean-Francois Bory, editor, *Once Again,* New Directions, 1968; Andre Balthazar and Pol Bury, editors, *Qui Who Etes Are Vous You,* Daily Bul (Brussels), 1968; Jean-Jacques Lebel, editor, *El Happening,* Ediciones Nueva Vision (Buenos Aires), 1968; John Cage, editor, *Notations,* Something Else, 1969; Dieter Roth, editor, *Anekdoten zu einer Topographie des Zufalls von Daniel Spoerri mit Emmett Williams,* Luchterhand Verlag (Neuwied), 1969.

Richard Kostelanetz, editor *John Cage,* Praeger, 1970; Wolf Vostell, editor, *Aktionen,* Rowohlt Verlag, 1970; Dana Atchley, editor, *Space Atlas,* Ace Space Co., 1971; Jean-Marc Poinsot, editor, *Mailart Communication: A Distance Concept,* Editions Cedic (Paris), 1971; Barry McCallion, *Prepare to Publish,* Aleatory Press, 1971; David Mayor, editor, *Fluxshoe,* Beau Geste Press, 1972; Kostelanetz, editor, *Breakthrough Fictioneers,* Something Else, 1973; Jan Herman, editor, *Something Else Yearbook,* Something Else, 1973; Jerome Rothenberg and George Quasha, editors, *America, a Prophecy: A New Reading of American Poetry from Pre-Columbian Times to the Present*, Random House, 1973; Ronald Gross and others, editors, *Open Poetry*, Simon & Schuster, 1973; Bill Henderson, editor, *The Publish-It-Yourself Handbook*, Pushcart, 1973; Bill Katz, editor, *Library Lit 4: The Best of 1973*, Scarecrow, 1974; Milton Klonsky, editor, *Speaking Pictures*, Harmony Books, 1975; Kostelanetz and Beth Learn, editors, *Language and Structure in North America*, Kensington Arts Association (Toronto), 1975.

Endre Tot, editor, *Total Questions by Tot*, Edition Hundertmark (Berlin), 1976; Kostelanetz, editor, *Essaying Essays*, Out of London Press, 1976; Harry Smith, editor, *X-1*, The Smith, 1976; Terry Reid, editor, *Mask Media Profile*, Sunnyland Press, 1976; Daigon and Weisskoff, editors, *Live and Learn*, Prentice-Hall, 1977; Walter Zanini and Julio Plaza, editors, *Poeticas Visuais*, Museu do Arte Contemporanea da Universidade de Sao Paulo, 1977; Kostelanetz, editor, *Esthetics Contemporary*, Prometheus Books, 1978; Sarenco, editor, *Poesie e Prosa delle Avanguardia*, Museo di Castelvecchio (Verona), 1978; Michael Gibbs, editor, *Deciphering America*, Kontexts Publications (Amsterdam), 1978; Gabor Toth, editor, *Reflections*, Onga Press (Budapest), 1978; Steve McCaffery and B.P. Nichol, editors, *Sound Poetry: A Catalogue*, Underwhich Editions (Toronto), 1978; Robert Fillious, *Six Fillious*, Membrane Press, 1978; Jonathan Greene, editor, *A 50th Birthday Celebration for Jonathan Williams*, Truck/Gnomon, 1979; James Laughlin, editor, *New Directions 38*, New Directions, 1979; Carolee Schneemann, *More Than Meat Joy*, edited by Bruce McPherson, Documentext, 1979; Nichol, *Translating Translating Apollinaire*, Membrane Press, 1979; Umberto Romano, editor, *Great Men*, Dial, 1979.

Richard Kostelanetz, editor, *Text-Sound-Texts*, Morrow, 1980; Roger Johnson, editor, *Scores*, Schirmer Books, 1981; Kostelanetz, editor, *Scenarios*, Assembling Press, 1981. Contributor to numerous periodicals, including *Chelsea Review*, *Arts in Society*, *Los Angeles Free Press*, *Panache*, *General Schmuck*, *West Coast Review*, *Performing Arts Journal*, and *Mouth of the Dragon*.

U.S. editor of *Fluxus*, beginning 1961, and *De-collage*, 1962—; editor of *Something Else Newsletter*, 1964—.

SIDELIGHTS: Dick Higgins was one of the founders and early promoters of the "Happenings" movement (other noteworthy proponets included Allan Kaprow, who coined the term, Claes Oldenburg, Robert Whitman, and John Cage). Happenings are staged events that are intended to bring drama and reality as close together as possible. They have little formal structure: groups of participants assemble—on stages, in lofts, at galleries, on streetcorners, or in parking lots—and react to each other and to stimuli provided by the organizers of the Happening or by other persons or occurrences.

The object of a Happening is to affect participants and spectators on an unconscious rather than rational level. They are not improvisations, since a good deal of the necessary stimulation—usually both visual and aural—is planned and provided by the organizers, but, like improvisations, Happenings are meant to be single-performance phenomena; they are not usually recorded or preserved (although a number of them have been described in scholarly works).

Early Happenings were somewhat elitist events, consisting of a rather small group of participants and performed before small audiences. Eventually, however, the term Happening came to be applied to mass gatherings in which everyone present participated: "Love-ins" and "Be-ins."

In addition to being involved in the founding of the movement, Higgins participated in Fluxus Festivals, 1962-64, which introduced the new art form to Europe.

BIOGRAPHICAL/CRITICAL SOURCES: *Village Voice*, August 17, 1967; Hanns Sohm, editor *Happenings and Fluxus*, Koelner Kunstverein (Cologne), 1970; *Rolling Stone*, April 27, 1972; Michael Nyman, *Experimental Music: Cage and Beyond*, Studio Vista (London), 1974; Richard Kostelanetz, *The End of Intelligent Writing*, Sheed, 1975; *West Coast Poetry Review*, No. 18, 1977; Peter Frank, editor, *In Meta-Print: The Art of Dick Higgins and the Something Else Press*, DocumenText, 1979.

* * *

HILDEBRAND, George H(erbert) 1913-

PERSONAL: Born July 7, 1913, in Oakland, Calif.; son of George Herbert and Irene (Colegrove) Hildebrand; married Margaret Boardman, August 28, 1937; children: George C., Richard W., Stephen B. *Education:* University of California, Berkeley, B.A. (with honors), 1935; Harvard University, M.A., 1941; Cornell University, Ph.D., 1942. *Religion:* Congregationalist. *Office:* 651 Phillips Hall, University of Iowa, Iowa City, Iowa 52242.

CAREER: University of Texas, Main University (now University of Texas at Austin), assistant professor of economics, 1941-43; National War Labor Board, Washington, D.C., principal economist, 1943-44; director of Wage Stabilization Division in Colorado, Regional War Labor Board, 1944-45; University of California, Berkeley, assistant professor of social institutions, 1945-47; University of California, Los Angeles, assistant professor, 1947-49, associate professor, 1949-54, professor of economics, 1954-60, director of Institute of Industrial Relations, 1956-60; Cornell University, Ithaca, N.Y., professor of economics and industrial and labor relations, 1960-70, Maxwell M. Upson Professor of Economics and Labor Relations, 1970-80, professor emeritus, 1980—; University of Iowa, Iowa City, Ralph L. Sheets Professor of Industrial Relations, 1981—. Visiting professor at University of California, Berkeley, 1959-60, and Massachusetts Institute of Technology, 1964-65. Labor arbitrator, 1951—. Consultant to Office of Strategic Services, 1942, Department of Labor, 1959-60, and Department of Health, Education, and Welfare, 1961-62. Member of board of directors, Social Science Research Council, 1961-67; member of foreign service board, U.S. Department of State, 1969-71; deputy undersecretary of labor for international affairs, U.S. Department of Labor, 1969-71.

MEMBER: American Economic Association, National Academy of Arbitrators, Industrial Relations Research Association (member of executive board, 1964-67; president, 1971), Phi Beta Kappa. *Awards, honors:* Fulbright fellowship to Italy, 1952-53; Guggenheim fellowships, 1952-53 and 1957-58; Ford Foundation research professorship, 1962-63.

WRITINGS: (Author of introduction) F. J. Teggart, *The Idea of Progress*, revised edition, University of California Press, 1949; (co-author) *Pacific Coast Maritime Shipping Industry, 1930-1948*, two volumes, University of California Press, 1952, 1954; *Growth and Structure in the Economy of Modern Italy*, Harvard University Press, 1965; (with Ta-Chung Liu) *Manufacturing Production Functions in the United States, 1957: An Inter-Industry and Interstate Comparison of Productivity*, School of Industrial and Labor Relations, Cornell University, 1965; *Growth and Structure in the Economy of Modern Italy*, Harvard University Press, 1965; *Poverty, Income Maintainance, and the Negative Income Tax*, Cornell University, 1967; *American Unionism: An Historical and Analytical Survey*, Addison-Wesley, 1979; *Borax Pioneer: Francis Marion Smith*, Howell-North Books, 1982.

Contributor: Neil W. Chamberlain and others, editors, *A Decade of Industrial Relations Research, 1946-56*, Harper, 1958; Joseph Shister and others, editors, *Public Policy and Collective Bargaining*, Harper, 1962; J. L. Meij, editor, *Internal Wage Structure*, North-Holland Publishing Co., 1963; Jack Stieber, editor, *Employment Problems of Automation and Advanced Technology: An International Perspective*, St. Martin's, 1966; Robert Aaron Gordon and Margaret S. Gordon, editors, *Prosperity and Unemployment*, Wiley, 1966.

Also author of *Postwar Italy: A Study in Economic Contrasts*, University of California. Contributor to proceedings and professional journals. Member of board of editors, *American Economic Research*, 1954-57, and publications committee, 1961—.

SIDELIGHTS: George H. Hildebrand wrote *CA:* "My last book, *Borax Pioneer*, tells the story of the man who founded the borax industry and opened Death Valley to the world! It fills an important gap in western American history. It also reflects a long-standing interest entirely independent of my professional work." *Avocational interests:* Railroads and western U.S. history.

* * *

HILL, Monica
See WATSON, Jane Werner

* * *

HILTON, Bruce 1930-

PERSONAL: Born June 3, 1930, in Plymouth, Wis.; son of Vernon Emmett (a clergyman) and Mary Alice (Soper) Hilton; married Virginia Ann Young, December 27, 1952; children: Stephen, Philip, Thomas, Paul. *Education:* Indiana Central College, A.B., 1953, D.D., 1975; United Theological Seminary, B.D., 1956. *Politics:* Independent.

CAREER: *Rochester Post-Bulletin*, Rochester, Minn., reporter, 1948; *Indianapolis News*, Indianapolis, Ind., reporter, assistant city editor, religious news editor, 1948-52; *Dayton Journal Herald*, Dayton, Ohio, reporter, 1952-55; ordained minister in United Methodist Church; Evangelical United Brethren Church, Board of Publications, Dayton, editor of youth publications, 1955-65; National Council of Churches, director of interpretation, Delta Ministry, 1965-67, director of interpretation and research, Intermedia, 1967-71; associate for publication, Institute of Sociology, Ethics, and the Life Sciences, 1971-73; National Center for Bioethics, Leonia, N.J., director, 1973—. Member of board of directors, National Transplant Information Center, 1972—; member of task force on human life and the New Genetics, National Council of Churches, 1974—. Member of Civil Air Patrol. *Member:* Editors of Church Magazines for Children and Youth (chairman, 1963), American Society of Human Genetics, National Association of Science Writers, Soar Heads (flying club), Torch Club. *Awards, honors:* LL.D., Westmar College, 1976.

WRITINGS: (Editor) *Personal Christian Living*, Otterbein, 1960; (editor) *Growing Together in Faith*, Otterbein, 1961; (editor) *Facing Frontiers*, Otterbein, 1962; (editor) *One Lord, One Faith*, Otterbein, 1963; *My Brother Is a Stranger*, Friendship, 1963; *The Delta Ministry*, Macmillan, 1969; *Highly Irregular*, Macmillan, 1969; (editor with others) *Ethical Issues in Human Genetics: Genetic Counseling and the Use of Genetic Knowledge*, Plenum, 1973. Also author of *Knowing the Unborn*, 1974.

WORK IN PROGRESS: A book on the civil rights movement in Mississippi, 1964-66; a novel about mountain-climbing; a book of essays on the church in Europe.

AVOCATIONAL INTERESTS: Mountain-climbing, private flying, photography.

BIOGRAPHICAL/CRITICAL SOURCES: Christian Century, February 18, 1970.†

* * *

HILTON, Lewis B. 1920-

PERSONAL: Born November 21, 1920, in Saskatchewan, Canada; U.S. citizen; son of George W. (a farmer) and Myra (Bozarth) Hilton; married Mary Jean O'Banion, March 22, 1943. *Education:* Attended University of Nancy, 1939, Ohio State University, 1941, and Johns Hopkins University, 1943-44; Iowa State Teachers College (now University of Northern Iowa), B.A., 1942; Columbia University, M.A., 1946, Ed.D., 1951. *Politics:* Independent. *Home:* 1485 Memoli Lane, No. 1 S., Fort Myers, Fla. 33907. *Office:* Department of Music, Edison Community College, Fort Myers, Fla. 33907.

CAREER: Elementary school teacher in public and private schools of Belleville, N.J., 1945-46, and Des Moines, Iowa, 1946-48; professional clarinetist and oboist in New York, Des Moines, and St. Louis, 1945-46, 1949-51; Drake University, Des Moines, member of faculty, 1946-49; Washington University, St. Louis, Mo., assistant professor, 1951-53, associate professor, 1953-59, professor of music, 1959-80, chairman of department and director of music education, 1951-80; Edison Community College, Fort Myers, Fla., instructor in woodwind instruments, 1980—. Professional musician and conductor of woodwind instruments in New York, Chicago, Des Moines, St. Louis, and in other locations. Editor, Roger Dean Co., Macomb, Ill. Chairman of board of directors of Young Audiences, St. Louis, Mo., 1971-73; member of board of directors of Community Music School, St. Louis, 1970-72, and Community Association of Schools for the Arts, St. Louis, 1972-80. *Military service:* U.S. Coast Guard, 1942-45. *Member:* International Society for the Study of Music Education, Music Educators National Conference (member of board of research council, 1968-72), Council for Research in Music Education, Missouri Music Education Association (research chairman, 1962-77), Phi Mu Alpha Sinfonia.

WRITINGS: Learning to Teach through Playing: The Woodwinds, Addison-Wesley, 1971; (contributor) *Music Teacher Education*, Music Educators National Conference, 1973.

Music, published by Roger Dean Co.: (Arranger) Wolfgang Mozart, *La Ci Darem la Mano*, 1975; (arranger and editor) Ludwig van Beethoven, *Duo for Two Flutes: Minuet and Allegretto*, 1976; (arranger and editor) Beethoven, *Duo for Two Clarinets: Minuet and Allegretto*, 1976; *Polarities* (brass quintets), 1977; *Etudes for the Intermediate Clarinetist*, 1978; *From Bass to Tenor Clef for the Bassoon*, 1978; *Adagio for Bassoon and Piano*, 1978.

Also composer of performed but unpublished works, *Glen and Katja, Yet Do I Marvel, Piece for Solo Clarinet, Bassoon Quartet, Eight Bagatelles for Woodwind Trio, Polarities II*, and *Trio for Five Flutes*; arranger of *Piano Sonatine: First Movement*, by D. Kabalevsky. Author of *From Bass to Tenor Clef for the Cello*; translator of *Instrumentos Musicales Precortesianos*, by Samuel Marti. Contributor to proceedings of Midwest Symposium on Music Education, 1978. Contributor of articles to music education journals, including *Music Educators Journal* and *Missouri Journal of Research and Music*

Education. Editor of *Missouri Journal of Research in Music Education,* 1962-76; member of editorial board of *Journal of Research in Music Education,* 1970-78.

AVOCATIONAL INTERESTS: Travel.

* * *

HINSON, E(dward) Glenn 1931-

PERSONAL: Born July 27, 1931, in St. Louis, Mo.; son of Allen Lloyd and Docia F. Hinson; married Martha Ann Burks, September 1, 1956; children: Christopher Glenn, Elizabeth Leora. *Education:* Washington University, St. Louis, Mo., B.A., 1954; Southern Baptist Theological Seminary, B.D., 1957, Th.D., 1962; Oxford University, D.Phil., 1974. *Politics:* Democrat. *Home:* 120 Heady Ave., Louisville, Ky. 40207. *Office:* Southern Baptist Theological Seminary, 2825 Lexington Rd., Louisville, Ky. 40206.

CAREER: Baptist clergyman. Southern Baptist Theological Seminary, Louisville, Ky., instructor in New Testament, 1959-60, instructor in church history, 1960-62, assistant professor, 1962-66, associate professor, 1966-73, David T. Porter Professor of Church History, 1973—. *Member:* North American Academy of Liturgy, American Catholic Historical Association, American Society of Church History. *Awards, honors:* American Association of Theological Schools fellowship to Oxford University, 1966-67; Association of Theological Schools in the United States and Canada fellowship, 1975-76.

WRITINGS: The Church: Design for Survival, Broadman, 1967; (with Frank Stagg and Wayne E. Oates) *Glossolalia: Tongue Speaking in Biblical, Historical and Theological Perspectives,* Abingdon, 1967; *Seekers after Mature Faith,* Word Books, 1968; *A Serious Call to a Contemplative Lifestyle,* Westminster, 1974.

Soul Liberty, Convention Press, 1975; *Jesus Christ,* Consortium, 1977; *The Integrity of the Church,* Broadman, 1978; (editor) *Doubleday Devotional Classics,* three volumes, Doubleday, 1978; *The Reaffirmation of Prayer,* Broadman, 1979; *A History of Baptists in Arkansas,* Arkansas Baptist State Convention, 1979; *The Early Church Fathers,* Broadman, 1980; *The Evangelization of the Roman Empire,* Mercer House, 1981; *The Priesthood of All Believers,* Sunday School Board, Southern Baptist Convention, 1981; *Are Southern Baptists Evangelicals?,* Mercer House, 1982.

Contributor: George Torney, editor, *Towards Creative Urban Strategy,* Word Books, 1970; Clifton J. Allen, general editor, *Broadman Bible Commentary,* Volume XI, Broadman, 1971; Watson Mills, editor, *Tongue Speaking: Let's Talk about It,* Word Books, 1974; Claude A. Frazier, editor, *What Faith Has Meant to Me,* Westminster, 1975; Bob E. Patterson, editor, *Science, Faith, and Revelation,* Broadman, 1979; Glenn Igleheart and William Jerry Boney, editors, *Baptists and Ecumenism,* Judson, 1980; Patrick Hart, editor, *The Message of Thomas Merton,* Cistercian Publications, 1981; *A Matter of Faith,* Sojourner, 1981; E. A. Livingstone, editor, *Proceedings of the Eighth International Patristics Conference,* Pergamon, 1981. Contributor to periodicals, including *Christian Century, Cistercian Studies, Catholic Historical Review, Church History, Ecumenical Trends,* and *One in Christ.*

WORK IN PROGRESS: A textbook on the history of Christianity; a study of prayer in Christian history.

SIDELIGHTS: E. Glenn Hinson is competent in Latin, Greek, German, French, Italian, and Biblical Hebrew.

HITZ, Demi 1942- (Demi)

PERSONAL: Born September 2, 1942, in Cambridge, Mass.; daughter of William Morris (an architect, actor, and entrepreneur) and Rosamond (an artist; maiden name, Pier) Hunt; married John Rawlins Hitz (a teacher and writer), December 18, 1965; children: John. *Education:* Attended Instituto Allende and Rhode Island School of Design; Immaculate Heart College, B.A., 1962; University of Baroda, M.S., 1963; additional graduate study at China Institute. *Home and office:* 325 Riverside Dr., New York, N.Y. 10025. *Agent:* Julian Bach, Inc., 747 Third Ave., New York, N.Y. 10017.

CAREER: Artist; murals, paintings, mosaics, and silk screen prints have been exhibited in museums and galleries in California, New York, N.Y., and Massachusetts, as well as in India. Speaker at colleges, universities, libraries, and children's events. *Member:* China Institute. *Awards, honors:* Fulbright scholarship to India, 1962; awards from *Boston Globe* scholastic competitions, 1961, California State Fair, 1962, Los Angeles County Museum, 1962, California Arts and Science Fair, 1962, and Los Angeles Outdoor Art Festival, 1962.

WRITINGS—Under name Demi, except as indicated; all juveniles; all self-illustrated: *The Book of Moving Pictures,* Knopf, 1979; *Under the Shade of the Mulberry Tree,* Prentice-Hall, 1979; *Where Is It?,* Doubleday, 1980; *Liang and the Magic Paint Brush,* Holt, 1980; *The Leaky Umbrella,* Prentice-Hall, 1980; *Where's Willie Worm?,* Random House, 1981; *The Elephant Book,* Random House, 1981; *Follow the Line* (wordless story), Holt, 1981; *Book of Opposites,* Intervisual Communications, Metropolitan Museum of Art, 1981; *Six Performances,* Intervisual Communications, Metropolitan Museum of Art, 1981; *The Adventures of Marco Polo,* Holt, 1981; *Peek-A-Boo,* Random House, 1982; *Cinderella on Wheels,* Holt, 1982.

Illustrator: (Under name Demi Hitz) Partap Sharma, *The Surangini Tales,* Harcourt, 1973; (under name Demi Hitz) Lu Yu, *The Classic of Tea,* translation by Francis Ross Carpenter, Little, Brown, 1974; (under name Demi Hitz) Smith and Wardhough, *Feelings,* Macmillan, 1975; (under name Demi Hitz) *The Wild, Wild World of Animals: The Cats,* Vineyard Books, 1976; (under name Demi Hitz) Tom Glazer, *The Tom Glazer Guitar Book,* Warner Brothers, 1976; Augusta Goldin, *The Shape of Water,* Doubleday, 1979; Yushin Yoo, *Bong Nam and the Pheasants,* Prentice-Hall, 1979; June Yolan, *Dragon Night and Other Lullabies,* Methuen, 1980; Ann S. McGrath, *Tony's Tunnel,* Prentice-Hall, 1981; Miriam Chaikin, *Light Another Candle,* Clarion Books, 1981. Also illustrator of *Lu Pan,* Prentice-Hall, 1978.

Illustrator of "All about Your Name" series, by Tom Glazer; published by Doubleday, 1978: *All about Your Name, Anne;* *...Elizabeth; ...Mary; ...Susan; ...William; ...James;* *...John; ...Joseph; ...David; ...Katherine.*

Contributor of illustrations and stories to periodicals, including *New Yorker, Young Children, New York Times, Christian Science Monitor, Art News, China Trade Journal,* and *House and Garden.*

WORK IN PROGRESS: Illustrations for *Purim,* by Miriam Chaikin, for Clarion, and for *Fat Gopal,* by Jacqueline Singh, for Harcourt.

SIDELIGHTS: Demi Hitz has painted murals in Mexico, walls for modern homes, and the dome of St. Peter's & Paul's Church in Wilmington, Calif. A filmstrip, "Making Mosaics," about her work was shown in Boston on CBS-TV in 1963. *Avocational interests:* Travel (has been to Mexico, Guatemala, Brazil, Chile, England, and Japan).

BIOGRAPHICAL/CRITICAL SOURCES: *New York Times Book Review,* April 25, 1982.

* * *

HODGETTS, Richard M(ichael) 1942-

PERSONAL: Born March 10, 1942, in Bronx, N.Y.; son of Harold Thomas (a postal employee) and Regina (McDermott) Hodgetts; married Sara J. Fontana, August 1, 1970; children: Steven Michael, Jennifer Anne. *Education:* New York University, B.S., 1963; Indiana University, M.B.A., 1964; University of Oklahoma, Ph.D., 1968. *Home:* 3930 Durango, Coral Gables, Fla. 33134. *Office:* School of Business and Organizational Sciences, Florida International University, Miami, Fla. 33199.

CAREER: University of Nebraska, Lincoln, assistant professor, 1968-70, associate professor, 1970-73, professor of management, 1973-75; Texas Tech University, Lubbock, visiting professor of management, 1975-76; Florida International University, Miami, professor of management, 1976—. Management consultant to businesses and hospitals. *Member:* Academy of Management (secretary, History of Management Division), Academy of International Business, Southern Management Association.

WRITINGS: *Top Management Simulation,* D. H. Mark, 1970; (with Fred Luthans and Kenneth A. Thompson) *Social Issues in Business,* Macmillan, 1972, 4th edition, 1984; *Readings on the Current Social Issues in Business: Poverty, Civil Rights, Ecology, and Consumerism,* Macmillan, 1972; (with Henry Albers) *Cases and Incidents on the Basic Concepts of Management,* Wiley, 1972; (with Luthans) *Study Guide to Accompany Organizational Behavior,* McGraw, 1973, 2nd edition, 1977; *Management: Theory, Process and Practice,* Saunders, 1975, 3rd edition, Dryden, 1982; (with Richard L. Howe and Ronald Greenwood) *Study Guide to Accompany Management: Theory, Process and Practice,* Saunders, 1975, 3rd edition, Dryden, 1982; (editor with A. Thomas Hollingsworth) *Readings in Basic Management,* Saunders, 1975; (with Max S. Wortman) *Administrative Policy: Text and Cases in the Policy Sciences,* Wiley, 1975, 2nd edition, 1980.

American Business: Social Challenge, Social Response, Saunders, 1977; (with Terry Smart) *The American Free Enterprise System,* Addison-Wesley, 1978; (with Steve Altman) *Readings in Organizational Behavior,* Saunders, 1979; (with Altman) *Organizational Behavior,* Saunders, 1979; (with C. Edward Cavert) *Study Guide to Accompany Organizational Behavior,* Saunders, 1979.

Human Relations, Dryden, 1980, 2nd edition, 1984; (with Ruth de Bliek) *Study Guide to Accompany Human Relations,* Dryden, 1980; *Introduction to Business,* 2nd edition, Addison-Wesley, 1980; (with Charles Beavins and Karen Brinkman) *Study Guide to Accompany Introduction to Business,* 2nd edition, Addison-Wesley, 1980; (with Pamela Keel) *Topics in Small Business Management,* Kendall/Hunt, 1980; *Introduction to Management,* Dryden, 1981; (with Regina and R. Greenwood) *Management Fundamentals: Study Guide,* Dryden, 1981; (with Smart) *Economics and the Free Enterprise System,* Addison-Wesley, 1982; *Effective Small Business Management,* Academic Press, 1982; (with Dorothy Cascio) *Modern Health Care Administration,* Academic Press, 1983; *Personal Finance,* Addison-Wesley, 1983; *Management,* Academic Press, 1984.

Contributor: Luthans, editor, *Cases, Readings and Review Guide for Principles of Management,* Wiley, 1969; *Business Games Handbook,* American Management Association, 1969; William H. Klein and Darrel C. Murphy, editors, *Policy: Concepts in Organizational Guidance,* Little, Brown, 1973; *Fremtiden Er Naermere End Vi Tror!,* Danish Marketing Association (Copenhagen), 1976; Donald D. White and H. William Vroman, editors, *Action in Organizations: Cases and Experiences in Organizational Behavior,* 2nd edition, Holbrook, 1977.

Consulting editor of management series for Academic Press. Contributor to *Academy of Management Proceedings,* 1973, 1976, and 1978, and to *Proceedings of the Second National ABSEL Conference,* 1975. Contributor of articles and reviews to numerous management and business journals and periodicals, including *Business Inquiry, Personnel Journal, Management Horizons, Accounting Review, Simulation,* and *Personnel Psychology.* Member of review board of *Journal of Management.*

SIDELIGHTS: Richard M. Hodgetts told *CA:* "I write because I believe knowledge should be conveyed in an up-to-date, interesting fashion; and what field changes more than business? So there is always a new development to be related and the challenge of trying to do this in an entertaining, yet substantive, manner. Too much of business literature is dull and dry. I like to think that every now and then I am able to convey business-related ideas the way they are actually brought to fruition in the 'real' world: excitingly, interestingly, factually, pragmatically, and—when the occasion merits—humorously."

* * *

HOFFMAN, Abbie 1936-
(Free, Barry Freed, George Metesky)

PERSONAL: Born November 30, 1936, in Worcester, Mass.; son of John (founder of Worcester Medical Supply Co.) and Florence (Schanberg) Hoffman; married, 1960 (divorced, 1966), wife's name Sheila; married Anita Kushner, June 10, 1967; children: (first marriage) Andrew, Amy; (second marriage) america. *Education:* Brandeis University, B.A., 1959; University of California, Berkeley, M.A., 1960. *Home address:* Barry Freed, Thousand Islands, N.Y. 13640. *Agent:* (Literary) Elaine Markson, 44 Greenwich Ave., New York, N.Y. 10011; (lectures) Jack Hoffman, P.O. Box 15, Worcester, Mass. 01613.

CAREER: Worcester State Hospital, Worcester, Mass., psychologist, 1960-62; pharmaceuticals salesman, 1963-65; founder of Prospect Community House, Worcester; civil rights worker for the Student Non-Violent Coordinating Committee (SNCC) in Mississippi, 1964-66; founder of Liberty House, New York, N.Y., 1966; co-founder of the Youth International Party (Yippies), 1968; founder of Save the River, Thousand Islands, N.Y., 1978.

WRITINGS: *F--- the System* (pamphlet), privately printed, 1968; (under pseudonym Free) *Revolution for the Hell of It,* Dial, 1968; *Woodstock Nation: A Talk-Rock Album,* Vintage Books, 1969; *Steal This Book,* Pirate Editions, 1971; (with Jerry Rubin and Ed Sanders) *Vote!,* Warner Paperback, 1972; (with wife, Anita Hoffman) *To america with Love: Letters from the Underground,* Stonehill Publishing, 1976; *Soon to Be a Major Motion Picture,* Putnam, 1980; *Square Dancing in the Ice Age,* Putnam, 1982. Also author of *Son of Steal This Book.* Contributor of articles, some under pseudonyms, to *East Village Other, Village Voice, Los Angeles Free Press, Eye, Realist, Harper's, Esquire, Parade,* and *Sports Illustrated.* Former travel editor, *Crawdaddy.*

SIDELIGHTS: Described by *Time* as the "Puck of the 1960s underground [and] the frizzy-haired, war-painted Yippie leader who preached revolution against the American establishment," Abbie Hoffman personified the youthful rebellion of the late 1960s with his outlandish guerrilla theatrics, political pranks, and colorful lifestyle. His activities against the Vietnam War combined the revolutionary perspective of the New Left with the cultural exuberance of the hippies.

Hoffman first became politically active in the civil rights movement of the early 1960s, working as an organizer for several civil rights organizations and founding Liberty House, a store selling the products of the poor people's co-ops of Mississippi. With the decline of the civil rights movement and the increasing U.S. military presence in Vietnam, Hoffman turned his attention to the fledgling peace movement, organizing opposition to the Vietnam War among the hippies of New York's East Village. Hoffman's brand of political opposition took its cue from Madison Avenue. "Again and again," Morris Dickstein writes in the *New York Times Book Review,* "[Hoffman] describes himself as a super salesman for radical ideas." This "selling" of radical ideas was done by grabbing as much media attention as possible through wild political pranks, guerilla theater, and media events. "[Hoffman] was engaging," writes Eva Hoffman in the *Washington Post,* "in an 'image war' in which symbolic desecrations were the weapons and sanctified institutions were the targets." "Even Hoffman's most outrageous performances. . . ," Dickstein points out, "had a clear political goal: to remove the aura of legitimacy from what he saw as unjust and oppressive authority."

One of Hoffman's most successful events involved dumping a flurry of dollars into the midst of the New York Stock Exchange during a busy trading day. The resulting mad scramble by stockbrokers for the money garnered worldwide media attention and made a political statement about the American economic system. When appearing as a guest on the "Merv Griffin" television program, Hoffman showed up wearing an American flag shirt, causing the network censors to blank out his half of the television screen. Despite the success of Hoffman's media events in attracting national attention and making statements about what he perceived as societal shortcomings, Hoffman "never for a moment [believed] guerrilla theater . . . could alone stop the war in Vietnam," he writes in *Soon to Be a Major Motion Picture.* "But it did extend the possibilities of involving the senses and penetrating the symbolic world of fantasy." Hoffman maintains that the modern revolutionary movement must concentrate "on infiltrating and changing the image system." And, of course, "one of the greatest mistakes any revolution can make is to become boring."

In his early books, Hoffman presented the ideas that motivated his unorthodox and dramatic political behavior. Irreverent, humorous, provocative—and sometimes soberingly thoughtful—Hoffman's writings have inspired a very mixed critical reaction. Jack Newfield, writing in the *New York Times Book Review,* finds *Revolution for the Hell of It* "a serious manifesto for the growing counter-culture of mind drugs, rock bands, sexual freedom, mixed media, communes, Free Stores, astrology, colorful costumes, and casual nudity. . . . It is a recipe for private amusement and public catastrophe." Describing the same book as a "disjointed but somehow engaging nonbook" and "a slender, acid-infused account of the rise of the non-violent yippies," a *Time* reviewer goes on to find that "the book trips along most gaily on currents of aphorism and imagination. Between its often outrageous put-ons and put-downs lies much that is of significance." Hoffman's books have sold over three million copies.

In 1968, Hoffman founded the Youth International Party with Jerry Rubin in order, as a *Saturday Night* writer states, to "bring together the hippies who were beginning to turn political and the New Left types who were getting bored with picket lines and parades." Known as Yippies, supporters of the party had no official membership rolls, no platform, and no leaders. They supported the hippie lifestyle while denouncing the Vietnam War and the American political and economic system. They called for the replacement of the present system with an anarchistic, communal society. The party first tested its strength at the Democratic Party National Convention in Chicago in 1968, where the Yippies were one of several groups to organize demonstrations against the war. These demonstrations ended in a bloody street battle between protesters and police in what many observers labeled a "police riot." The fighting was so chaotic that television newsmen sent to the scene found themselves being beaten by police. As a result of the violence, eight radicals, including Hoffman, were arrested and charged with "conspiring to cross state lines to incite a riot" for their roles in organizing the demonstrations. Though it was not the first time Hoffman had been arrested—he had been arrested some thirty times before for various civil rights and antiwar activities—it was the most serious charge he had faced and, with the national media focused on the trial, the one that made his name synonymous with radical activism.

Popularly termed the Chicago Conspiracy Trial, the court proceedings were "as spectacular and outrageous as anything seen in an American courtroom," James Gleick states in *New Times.* Defendant Bobby Seale of the Black Panther Party was bound and gagged in the courtroom; former Attorney General Ramsey Clark was refused permission to testify before the jury on behalf of the accused; FBI agents were discovered with eavesdropping equipment outside of a private meeting between the defendants and their lawyers. *Newsweek* reported that "the trial . . . was a landmark in American life and law—and not just for its almost daily pyrotechnics. It had produced the most devastating use of a judge's contempt-of-court power that any lawyer could remember, raised questions about the proper limits on that power and opened up the possibility that the trial system itself might have to be modified in order to cope with defendants and lawyers who refuse to observe its fragile rules of decorum. It had offered the first court test of the controversial 'Rap Brown law' which makes it a crime simply to cross a state line with riotous intent. And it had locked Attorney General John Mitchell's Justice Department into its starkest confrontation with the radical movement, prompting charges from radicals and some liberals that the Administration was embarked on a campaign of political repression against the militant left." All of the defendants, and their lawyers, were found guilty of contempt charges; Hoffman was sentenced to five years in prison. The convictions were appealed and, with the aid of documents obtained under the Freedom of Information Act, eventually dismissed. Defense attorney William Kunstler states in the *Nation* that the government had tapped their phones, opened their mail, and either bugged or infiltrated their private meetings. The judge and the F.B.I. regularly met in collusion. These actions, together with such things as the jury selection process, which higher courts ruled was "unconstitutional," were grounds for the defendants to be acquitted.

At the conclusion of a drug deal on August 28, 1973—a deal involving Hoffman, $36,000 worth of cocaine, and two undercover police officers—Hoffman again found himself in trouble with the law. Hoffman claimed he had been framed but was arrested and charged with possession of cocaine, a charge that carried a minimum sentence of fifteen years in prison. The *New Yorker* noted at the time of the arrest that Hoffman was "in the worst trouble of his life. . . . Although many medical authorities regard cocaine as a non-narcotic drug, relatively innocuous in comparison to heroin, the laws of New York State make no distinction." Despite Hoffman's charges of a frame-up (both buyer and seller of the drug were police officers; Hoffman acted as their middleman), his chances for a fair trial seemed slim, and he jumped bail to avoid standing trial. Hoffman explained his decision to go underground: "We didn't have the money to put on an adequate defense." Hoffman told CA: "I was the Devil's naughty son charged with selling the Devil's dandruff."

For the next seven years Hoffman's whereabouts were unknown, although he granted clandestine interviews to several national magazines, served as by-mail travel editor for *Crawdaddy* magazine, and published two books and some thirty-five articles. After he surfaced in 1980, it was learned that Hoffman had lived the previous four years under the alias "Barry Freed," working as an environmental activist in Thousand Islands, New York. As Freed, Hoffman had appeared on local television and radio, been commended by the governor of New York for his conservation work, testified before a U.S. Senate subcommittee on the environment, and been appointed to a federal water resources commission. After serving a year in prison on a reduced charge relating to his drug arrest, Hoffman was released in early 1982 and returned to Thousand Islands where, adopting his old alias of Barry Freed, he continues to work against the transporting of nuclear waste material on the St. Lawrence River. He has also become a popular speaker on college campuses.

Hoffman's life underground has somewhat modified his political views. The hippie culture he once found revolutionary has become absorbed into mainstream America, while the radical critique of society still seems valid to him. Although he is less theatrical than he once was, Hoffman still works towards the radical ideals he has long held. Speaking of *Square Dancing in the Ice Age*, Don Lessem writes in the *Nation* that "Hoffman can still raise important issues." Dickstein finds that "isolation and flight cut Abbie off from his 'image,' like the man in the fable who lost his shadow. This brought out the more serious and thoughtful self that always lurked just behind the clownish facade. . . . I hope Abbie Hoffman makes his peace with the law and is able to function again as a community organizer, for his old colleagues are a dispirited lot and there is much in the community that still needs mending." Hoffman describes himself in *Square Dancing in the Ice Age* as "the most famous relatively poor person in America who hasn't killed a whole bunch of people or assassinated a political candidate." He told CA that he is "just a person who wants to make America a better place for all."

BIOGRAPHICAL/CRITICAL SOURCES: New York, September, 1968; *Time,* December 20, 1968, September 15, 1980; *New York Times Book Review,* December 29, 1968, February 22, 1970, July 12, 1970, July 18, 1971, September 21, 1980, August 15, 1982; *Eye,* January, 1969; *New York Times,* January 10, 1969, November 5, 1969, September 1, 1980; *National Observer,* January 13, 1969; *Washington Post,* January 30, 1969, October 5, 1971, September 5, 1980; *Commonweal,* February 7, 1969; *National Review,* March 25, 1969, April 7, 1970, June 1, 1971; *Saturday Night,* July, 1969; *Progressive,* November, 1969; *Variety,* November 19, 1969; *New Republic,* November 29, 1969; *Saturday Review,* December 13, 1969; *Newsweek,* March 2, 1970, July 13, 1970, September 15, 1980; *Nation,* January 11, 1971, September 29, 1979, May 3, 1980, June 19, 1982; *Newsday,* November 6, 1971; *Life,* December 31, 1971; *Harper's,* May, 1974, September, 1980; *New Yorker,* May 6, 1974; *New Times,* May 30, 1975; *Esquire,* April, 1976; *Playboy,* May, 1976; *Washington Monthly,* June, 1976; *Village Voice,* December 10, 1979; Abbie Hoffman, *Soon to Be a Major Motion Picture,* Putnam, 1980; *Chicago Tribune,* June 9, 1980; *Wall Street Journal,* September 5, 1980; *Los Angeles Times,* September 5, 1980; *People,* September 22, 1980; *New York Daily News,* October 5, 1980; *Chicago Tribune Book World,* October 26, 1980; *New York Review of Books,* November 6, 1980; *Los Angeles Times Book Review,* December 7, 1980, June 20, 1982; Hoffman, *Square Dancing in the Ice Age,* Putnam, 1982.

—Sketch by Thomas Wiloch

* * *

HOGARTH, Charles
See CREASEY, John

* * *

HOLTJE, Herbert F(ranklin) 1931-

PERSONAL: Surname is pronounced *Holt*-jay; born February 24, 1931, in Englewood, N.J.; son of Herbert F. (a marine designer) and Irma Holtje; married Adrienne Ruth Kriebel (a free-lance artist), June 23, 1956; children: James Peter. *Education:* Fairleigh Dickinson University, B.S., 1962, M.A., 1968; graduate study at New School for Social Research, 1969-70. *Home:* 151 Sunset Lane, Tenafly, N.J. 07670.

CAREER: Tek-Mark, Inc. (advertising and public relations), Westwood, N.J., president, 1960-81; James Peter Associates, Inc. (book producers and communications consultants), Tenafly, N.J., president, 1972—. Trustee, Tenafly, N.J. Community Chest. *Military service:* U.S. Navy, 1949-53. *Member:* American Psychological Association, American Marketing Association, Public Relations Society of America, American Society for Training and Development, Nyack Boat Club, Tenafly Swim Club.

WRITINGS: How To Borrow Everything You Need to Build a Great Personal Fortune, Prentice-Hall, 1974; (with John Stockwell) *How To Be a Fix-It Genius Using Seven Simple Tools,* McGraw, 1975; *One Hundred Ways to Make Money in Your Spare Time, Starting with Less Than One Hundred Dollars,* Prentice-Hall, 1976; *The New Homeowner's Illustrated Handbook,* illustrations by wife, Adrienne Holtje, Parker Publishing Co., 1977; *Schaum's Outline of Theory and Problems of Advertising,* McGraw, 1978; (with A. Holtje) *Cardcraft,* Chilton, 1978; (editor) *National Directory of Manufacturers' Representatives,* McGraw, 1978; *The Parker Lifetime Treasury of Wealth-Building Secrets,* Parker Publishing Co., 1978; *Handbook of Exterior Home Repairs: A Practical Illustrated Guide,* illustrations by A. Holtje, Parker Publishing Co., 1979; *Schaum's Outline of Marketing,* McGraw, 1980; (with Abe Finkelstein) *Handbook of Woodworking,* Parker Publishing Co., 1980; (with Stockwell) *The Photographer's Business Handbook,* McGraw, 1980. Contributor to *Personal Development Newsletter* and scientific journals.

WORK IN PROGRESS: A book on graphic arts for McGraw; a self-improvement book for Parker Publishing Co.

* * *

HONNOLD, John Otis, Jr. 1915-

PERSONAL: Born December 5, 1915, in Kansas, Ill.; son of John Otis and Louretta (Wright) Honnold; married Annamarie Kunz, June 26, 1939; children: Carol (Mrs. Vinton Deming),

Heidi (Mrs. David Spencer), Edward E. *Education:* University of Illinois, A.B., 1936; Harvard University, LL.B., 1949, converted to J.D. *Politics:* Democrat. *Religion:* Society of Friends. *Office:* School of Law, University of Pennsylvania, Philadelphia, Pa. 19104.

CAREER: Wright, Gordon, Zachry & Parlin, New York City, attorney, 1939-41; U.S. Securities and Exchange Commission, Washington, D.C., attorney, 1941; U.S. Office of Price Administration, Washington, D.C., chief of court review, 1942-46; University of Pennsylvania, Philadelphia, assistant professor, 1946-49, associate professor, 1949-52, professor of constitutional law, sales, and sales financing, 1952-69; United Nations, New York City, Office of Legal Affairs, secretary of Commission on International Trade Law, 1969-74, chief of International Trade Law Branch, 1969-74; University of Pennsylvania, School of Law, Philadelphia, professor of law, 1974—. Salzburg Seminar in American Studies, faculty member, 1960, chairman, 1963, 1966; Goodhart Professor of Science of Law, University of Cambridge, 1982-83. Diplomatic Conference on Uniform Law for International Sales, member of U.S. delegation and drafting committee, The Hague, 1964, co-chairman of U.S. delegation, Vienna, 1980. Consultant to New York Law Revision Commission, 1954-56. *Member:* American Bar Association, American Friends Service Committee, (member of board and executive committee, 1967-69), Phi Beta Kappa, Phi Kappa Phi. *Awards, honors:* Fulbright research scholar, University of Paris, 1957-58; Guggenheim fellow, 1958.

WRITINGS—Published by Foundation Press, except as indicated: (Editor) *Cases and Materials on the Law of Sales and Sale Financing,* 1954, 4th edition, 1976; (editor with Edward L. Barrett, Jr. and Paul W. Bruton) *Cases and Materials on Constitutional Law,* 1959, 3rd edition, 1968; (editor) *The Life of the Law: Readings on the Growth of Legal Institutions,* Free Press of Glencoe, 1964; (with Edward Allan Farnsworth) *Cases and Materials on Commercial Law,* 1965, 3rd edition, 1976; *Unification of the Law Governing International Sales of Goods,* Librairie Dalloz (Paris), 1966.

Cases and Materials on the Law of Credit Transactions and Consumer Protection, 1976; *Manual for Teachers to Accompany Cases and Materials on the Law of Credit Transactions and Consumer Protection,* 1977; *Manual for Teachers to Accompany Cases and Materials on the Law of Sales and Sales Financing,* 4th edition, 1977; (with Edward Allan Farnsworth) *Manual for Teachers to Accompany Cases and Materials on Commercial Law,* 3rd edition, 1977; *Uniform Law for International Sales under the 1980 United Nations Convention,* 1982.

Member of editorial board, *American Journal of Comparative Law,* 1955—.

* * *

**HOPE, Brian
See CREASEY, John**

* * *

HORELICK, Arnold L(awrence) 1928-

PERSONAL: Born March 24, 1928, in New York, N.Y.; son of David and Celia (Schneiderman) Horelick; children: Lisa Joy, Andrew Louis. *Education:* Rutgers University, B.A. (magna cum laude), 1948; graduate study at Columbia University, 1948; Harvard University, M.A., 1950; graduate study at University of California, Los Angeles. *Home:* 11625 Texas Ave., Unit 301, Los Angeles, Calif. 90025. *Office:* RAND Corp., 1700 Main St., Santa Monica, Calif. 90406.

CAREER: U.S. Government, Washington, D.C., Foreign Broadcast Information Service, political affairs analyst and head of Soviet Division, 1951-52, 1954-58; RAND Corp., Santa Monica, Calif., senior staff member in social science department, 1959-77; U.S. Government, Intelligence Community, national intelligence officer for the U.S.S.R. and Eastern Europe, 1977-80; RAND Corp., senior social scientist in the social science department, associate director of the international studies program, and director of Soviet and East European studies, 1980—. Visiting lecturer, Cornell University, 1965, California Institute of Technology, 1976, and Columbia University, 1972; visiting professor, Hunter College of the City University of New York, 1972, and University of California, Los Angeles, 1975; occasional lecturer on U.S. national security, international relations, and Soviet affairs at numerous institutions, including Harvard University, National War College, Columbia University, International Institute of Strategic Studies, London, and Institute of the U.S.A. and Canada, Moscow. Member of panel, Security Conference on Asia and the Pacific, New Alternatives Workshop, Aspen Consortium, California Seminar on International Security and Foreign Policy, California Workshop on American Foreign Defense Policy in the 1980s, and Political-Military Advisory Panel to the National Intelligence Council of the Central Intelligence Agency. Vice-president of Transport-a-Child Foundation. *Military service:* U.S. Army, 1952-54.

MEMBER: International Institute of Strategic Studies, European-American Institute for Security Research, Council on Foreign Relations, American Political Science Association, American Association for the Advancement of Slavic Studies, American Institute of Aeronautics and Astronautics, Phi Beta Kappa. *Awards, honors:* Distinguished Intelligence Medal, 1980.

WRITINGS: (With Myron Rush) *Strategic Power and Soviet Foreign Policy,* University of Chicago Press, 1966; (with A. R. Johnson and J. Steinbruner) *The Study of Soviet Foreign Policy: Decision-Theory-Related Approaches,* Sage Publications, 1975.

Contributor: Joseph M. Goldsen, editor, *Outer Space and World Politics,* Praeger, 1963; H. A. Kissinger, D. Brodie, and others, editors, *La Guerre Nucleaire,* Editions Stock, 1965; Samuel Merlin, editor, *The Big Powers and the Present Crisis in the Middle East,* Fairleigh Dickinson University Press, 1968; R. V. Burks, editor, *The Future of Communism in Europe,* Wayne State University Press, 1968.

W. R. Duncan, editor, *Soviet Policy in Developing Countries,* Ginn-Blaisdell, 1970; M. D. Hancock and D. A. Rustow, editors, *American Foreign Policy in International Relations,* Prentice-Hall, 1971; R. A. Divine, editor, *The Cuban Missile Crisis,* Quadrangle, 1971; E. P. Hoffman and F. J. Fleron, editors, *The Conduct of Soviet Foreign Policy,* Aldine, 1971; DeAnne Sobul, editor, *Encounters with American History,* Holt, 1972; P. Y. Hammond and S. S. Alexander, editors, *Political Dynamics in the Middle East,* Elsevier, 1972; G. R. Hess, editor, *America and Russia: From Cold War Confrontation to Coexistence,* Crowell, 1973; F. N. Trager and P. S. Kronenburg, editors, *National Security and American Society,* University of Kansas Press, 1973; B. Horton, editor, *Comparative Defense Policy,* Johns Hopkins Press, 1974; *East Asia and the Major Powers,* Kyung Nam University Press (South Korea), 1975; *Military Aspects of the Israeli-Arab Conflict,* University Publishing (Tel Aviv), 1975.

Also author of papers presented to international conferences; author of monographs and studies for RAND Corp. Contributor to professional journals, including *Problems of Communism,*

Soviet Union/Union Sovietique, Asian Survey, Studies in Comparative Communism, World Affairs, and *Policy Sciences.*

* * *

HORN, George F(rancis) 1917-

PERSONAL: Born September 21, 1917, in Baltimore, Md.; son of William Thomas (a contractor) and Mazie (Snyder) Horn; married Nancy Mowery, May 30, 1941; children: George Michael, John William. *Education:* Pennsylvania State University, B.S., 1939; University of Maryland, M.Ed., 1954. *Politics:* Republican. *Religion:* Presbyterian.

CAREER: Baltimore public schools, Baltimore, Md., art teacher, 1939-54, art supervisor, 1954—. *Military service:* U.S. Navy, 1942-46; became lieutenant. *Member:* National Art Education Association, Eastern Arts Association (member of council, 1962-64), Maryland Art Association (president, 1959-62).

WRITINGS—Published by Davis Publications, except as indicated: *Bulletin Boards,* Reinhold, 1962; *How to Prepare Visual Materials for School Use,* 1963; *Posters: Designing, Making, Reproducing,* 1964; *Cartooning,* 1965; *Art for Today's Schools,* 1967; *Crayon: A Versatile Medium for Creative Expression,* 1969; (with Grace Sands Smith) *Experiencing Art in the Elementary Schools,* 1971; *Crafts for Today's Schools,* 1972; *Visual Communication: Bulletin Boards, Exhibits, Visual Aids,* 1973; *Texture: A Design Element,* 1974; *Balance and Unity,* 1975; *Contemporary Posters: Design and Techniques,* 1976; (with Gerald F. Brommer) *Art in Your World,* 1977; (with Brommer) *The Art of Collage,* 1978; *Art for Today,* 1979.

Also author of series of six filmstrips, "Teaching with Visual Materials," McGraw, 1963. Contributor of monthly articles to *Seventeen-at-School.* Contributor of numerous articles to art and education journals.†

* * *

HOSIER, Helen Kooiman 1928-
(Helen W. Kooiman)

PERSONAL: Surname is pronounced *Hoe*-sher; middle name is pronounced *Koy*-man; born January 26, 1928, in Hull, Iowa; daughter of Henry and Hattie (Brunsting) Westra; married Virgil J. Kooiman, January 26, 1947 (divorced, 1971); married Herman R. Hosier (a school principal), February 14, 1974; children: Barry John, Tonia Kooiman Thompson, Rhonda Kooiman Petrillo, Kraig Peter. *Education:* Attended high school in Sibley, Iowa. *Religion:* Protestant. *Residence:* Sunnyvale, Calif.

CAREER: Writer. Gospel Book and Gift Shop, Bellflower, Calif., co-owner and manager, 1951-68; Bible Book Store, Buena Park, Calif., co-owner and manager, 1964-70; Christian Freedom Foundation, Buena Park, editorial assistant, 1970-71; Thomas Nelson Publishers, Nashville, Tenn., editor, 1977-81; Christian Women's National Concerns, Fort Worth, Tex., director of publications, beginning 1981. Director of communications for radio program "Haven of Rest," Hollywood, Calif., 1971-72.

WRITINGS: The Other Side of Divorce: A Christian's Plea for Understanding and Compassion, Hawthorn, 1975; *The Caring Jesus: A Woman's View of the Gospel of John,* Hawthorn, 1975, published as *Jesus: Love in Action,* Ronald N. Haynes, 1982; *Profiles: Men and Women Who Are Helping Change the World,* Hawthorn, 1976; *Kathryn Kuhlman: The Life She Led, the Legacy She Left,* Revell, 1976; (with Jean G. Wade) *Eating Your Way to Good Health,* Revell, 1977; *Suicide: A Cry for Help,* Harvest House, 1979; (with Richard O. Brennan), *Coronary? Cancer? God's Answer: Prevent It,* Harvest House, 1979; (with Frances Kelly) *Better Than I Was,* Thomas Nelson, 1979; (with Wilma Stanchfield) *Struck by Lightning, Then by Love,* Thomas Nelson, 1979; (with Nell Maxwell) *Never Say Never to God,* G. R. Welch, 1980; *How to Know When God Speaks,* Harvest House, 1980; (with Judy Mamou) *I Can Hear My Baby Crying,* Zondervan, 1983.

Ghostwriter: Pederson, *One Lonely Street with God,* Hawthorn, 1973; Pat Boone, *Dr. Balaam's Talking Mule,* Bible Voice, Inc., 1974, published as *My Brother's Keeper,* 1975; Morrow Coffey Graham, *They Call Me Mother Graham,* Revell, 1977; Anita Bryant, *The Anita Bryant Story,* Revell, 1977; Bryant, *At Any Cost,* Revell, 1978; Marie Brady Roloff, *Lester Roloff: Living by Faith,* Thomas Nelson, 1978; Donna Axum, *The Outer You . . . The Inner You,* Word, 1978, published as *How to Be and Look Your Best Every Day,* 1980; Ellen de Kroon Stamps, *My Years with Corrie,* Revell, 1978; J. Harold Smith, *Fast Your Way to Health,* Thomas Nelson, 1979; Margaret Jean Jones, *The World in My Mirror,* Abingdon, 1979; Ernst Schmidt, *Choose to Win,* Abingdon, 1979; Paul E. Freed, *Let the Earth Hear,* Thomas Nelson, 1980; Gladys Lindberg and Judy Lindberg McFarland, *Take Charge of Your Health,* Harper, 1982; Sandy McKasson and Karen Davis, *Behind Closed Doors,* Thomas Nelson, in press.

Under name Helen W. Kooiman: *Joyfully Expectant: Meditations before Baby Comes,* Revell, 1966, published under name Helen Kooiman Hosier as *Joyfully Expectant,* 1981; *Please Pray for the Cabbages: Pint-Size Parables for Grownups,* Revell, 1967; *Cameos: Women Fashioned by God,* Tyndale, 1968, 2nd edition published under name Helen Kooiman Hosier, Harvest House, 1979; *Small Talk,* Tyndale, 1968; *Living Words of Comfort and Cheer,* Tyndale, 1969; *Transformed: Behind the Scenes with Billy Graham,* Tyndale, 1970; *Silhouettes: Women behind Great Men,* Word, 1972; *Walter Knott: Keeper of the Flame,* Plycon Press, 1973; *Forgiveness in Action,* Hawthorn, 1973, published under name Helen Hosier as *It Feels Good to Forgive,* Harvest House, 1980; (with Duane Pederson) *Going Sideways: Hope, Love, Life versus Suicide,* Hawthorn, 1974; (with Pederson) *Day of Miracles,* Hawthorn, 1974.

Author of radio and television scripts. Contributor to religious periodicals.

* * *

HOSLEY, Richard 1921-

PERSONAL: Born March 13, 1921, in New York, N.Y.; son of McDowell and Marian (Manley) Hosley; married Diana Adams Crawford, June 9, 1945; children: Pamela, Deborah, Diana. *Education:* Yale University, B.A., 1942, Ph.D., 1950; attended University of Lausanne, 1946-47. *Home:* 7021 Optatas Pl., Tucson, Ariz. *Office:* Department of English, University of Arizona, Tucson, Ariz. 85721.

CAREER: Instructor in English at U.S. Naval Academy, Annapolis, Md., 1945-46, New Haven State Teachers College (now Southern Connecticut State College), New Haven, Conn., 1950-52, University of Virginia, Charlottesville, 1952-55; University of Missouri—Columbia, associate professor of English, 1955-63; University of Arizona, Tucson, professor of English, 1963—, chairman of department, 1972-76. *Military service:* U.S. Naval Reserve, 1943-46; became lieutenant. *Member:* Modern Language Association of America, Shakespeare Association of America, Bibliographical Society of University of Virginia, Malone Society. *Awards, honors:* Honorary fellow of the Shakespeare Institute, Stratford-upon-Avon,

1957-58; Guggenheim fellowship, 1957-58; Huntington Library fellowship, 1961-62; Folger Shakespeare Library summer research fellowships.

WRITINGS: *Corrupting Influence of the Bad Quarto on the Received Text of Romeo and Juliet,* Folcroft, 1953, reprinted, 1978; *The Use of the Upper Stage in Romeo and Juliet* (monograph), Folcroft, 1954, reprinted, 1978; (editor) Shakespeare, *Romeo and Juliet,* Yale University Press, 1954, revised edition, 1961; (editor) *Essays on Shakespeare and Elizabethan Drama in Honor of Hardin Craig,* University of Missouri Press, 1962; (editor) Shakespeare, *The Taming of the Shrew,* Penguin, 1964, revised edition, 1970; *Romeo and Juliet: An Outline Guide to the Play,* Barnes & Noble, 1965, (adaptation by others published as *William Shakespeare: Romeo and Juliet,* Barnes & Noble, 1968); (editor) *Shakespeare's Holinshed,* Putnam, 1968; *Cymbeline,* New American Library, 1968; (co-author) *Shakespeare Variorum Handbook,* Modern Language Association of America, 1971; (contributor) *Revels History of Drama in English, 1576-1613,* Barnes & Noble, 1975. Also editor of studies in Shakespeare. Contributor to scholarly journals. Member of editorial board, *Shakespeare Quarterly,* 1962—.†

* * *

HOUGH, Lindy Downer 1944-

PERSONAL: Surname is pronounced Huff; born July 4, 1944, in Denver, Colo.; daughter of Henry W. (a journalist and publisher) and Frances (Downer) Hough; married Richard Grossinger (a writer), June 21, 1966; children: Robin (son), Miranda. *Education:* Smith College, B.A., 1966; Goddard College, M.A., 1971. *Home and office:* 635 Amador St., Richmond, Calif. 94805.

CAREER: Teacher at Eastern Michigan University, Ypsilanti, 1966-69, University of Maine at Portland-Gorham, 1970-71, and Goddard College, Plainfield, Vt., 1972-73; director, Poetry-in-the-Schools Program, Vermont Council on the Arts, 1974-75; arts administrator and development consultant, Lindy Hough Associates, 1975-81; currently West Coast editor and publicist, Shambhala Publications, Inc., Richmond, Calif. Editor and publisher, with husband Richard Grossinger, of *Io* (literary magazine), Io Publications, and North Atlantic Books, 1968—. *Awards, honors:* Vermont Council on the Arts grant, 1974, for *The Sun in Cancer;* grants from National Endowment on the Arts, Coordinating Council on the Arts, and California Arts Council.

WRITINGS—All poetry: *Changing Woman,* Io Publications, 1971; *Psyche,* North Atlantic Books, 1974; *The Sun in Cancer,* North Atlantic Books, 1975; *Outlands and Inlands,* Truck Press, 1980. Contributor to literary magazines.

WORK IN PROGRESS: *Blood on My Hands,* a collection of essays on contemporary culture.

SIDELIGHTS: Lindy Hough told CA: "Whether in poetry, short prose, or non-fiction essay, my work has been an attempt to write about a struggle to refuse roles, both of life and feeling, commonly assigned to men and women. My concern is first with language and then with subject matter, not so much in telling stories or developing perception on my part and the reader's part. My work has become more accessible over the years as I have become interested in reaching a wider audience; I hope it still has the careful crafted quality of the early books of poems but takes on a wider informational and sometimes subtly political world."

HOUSTON, R. B.
See RAE, Hugh C(rauford)

* * *

HOWARD, D(erek) L(ionel) 1930-

PERSONAL: Born May 6, 1930, in Brighton, Sussex, England; son of William Naylor and Lavinia (Rason) Howard; married Elisabeth Katharine Ree (a social worker), September 10, 1958. *Education:* London School of Economics and Political Science, London, B.Sc. (honors), 1955; Cambridge University, postgraduate certificate in education, teaching diploma, 1959. *Religion:* Christian. *Office:* Newham Voluntary Agencies Council, Durning Hall, Earlham Grove, London E7, England.

CAREER: British Centre in Sweden, Stockholm, lecturer in English, 1955-56; Eastchurch Prison, Kent, England, education officer, 1956-58; Cranbrook Secondary Boys' School, Cranbrook, Kent, head of English department, 1959-62; British Prison and Borstal Service, education organizer working on educational program for disturbed delinquent teen-age boys, 1963-66; Brighton College of Education, Brighton, England, lecturer in sociology, beginning 1966; currently director of Newham Voluntary Agencies Council, London, England. Visiting lecturer at several British and Swedish universities. Assistant education secretary, National Marriage Guidance Council. Member, Howard League for Penal Reform. *Military service:* British Army, Service Corps, 1949-51; became lieutenant. *Member:* Society of Authors, British Society of Criminology.

WRITINGS: *The Life of Britain,* Natur och Kultur, 1957, 6th edition, 1963; *John Howard: Prison Reformer,* Johnson Publications, 1958; *The English Prisons: Their Past and Future,* Methuen, 1960; (with H. C. Brashers) *The Life of America,* Natur och Kultur, 1966; (editor) *Man and Society* (anthology), Natur och Kultur, 1966; *Trouble with the Law,* National Association of Youth Clubs, 1971; (compiler) *The Education of Offenders: A Select Bibliography on Education in Relation to Prisons and Other Institutions for the Custodial Treatment of Offenders,* Institute of Criminology, University of Cambridge, 1972.

Also author of radio scripts for the British Broadcasting Corp. Contributor to *Times Literary Supplement, Daily Telegraph, Education, Social Service Quarterly, Times Educational Supplement,* and other periodicals.

WORK IN PROGRESS: A novel; a book on adolescent psychology; a book on non-directive teaching methods in English secondary schools.

SIDELIGHTS: *The Life of Britain* has been issued in German, Norwegian, and Dutch editions. *Avocational interests:* The countryside, poetry.†

* * *

HOWARD, Elizabeth Jane 1923-

PERSONAL: Born March 26, 1923, in London, England; daughter of David Liddon and Katharine Margaret (Somervell) Howard; married Peter Scott, 1942 (divorced); married James Douglas Henry, 1960 (divorced); married Kingsley Amis (the author), 1965; children: (first marriage) Nicola Scott. *Home:* 186 Leighton Rd., London N.W. 5, England. *Agent:* Jonathan Clowes Ltd., 19 Jeffrey's Pl., London NW1 9PP, England.

CAREER: Writer. Actress in Stratford-on-Avon, England, and in repertory theater in Devon, England; model and broadcaster for British Broadcasting Corp., 1939-46; editor for various publishers, including Chatto & Windus and Weidenfeld & Nicolson. Director of Cheltenham Literary Festival, 1962, and of Salisbury Festival, 1973. Member of awards committee for John Llewelyn Rhys Memorial Prize and for Somerset Maugham Award. *Awards, honors:* John Llewelyn Rhys Memorial Prize, 1951, for *The Beautiful Visit.*

WRITINGS: The Beautiful Visit (novel), Random House, 1950, reprinted, Penguin, 1976; (with R. Aickman) *We Are for the Dark* (ghost stories), J. Cape, 1951; *The Long View* (novel), J. Cape, 1956, reprinted, Penguin, 1976; (with A. Helps) *Beltina* (biography), Chatto & Windus, 1957; *The Sea Change* (novel), Harper, 1959, reprinted, Penguin, 1975; *After Julius* (novel), J. Cape, 1965, Viking, 1966; *Something in Disguise* (novel), J. Cape, 1969, Viking, 1970; *Odd Girl Out* (novel), Viking, 1972; *Mr. Wrong* (short stories), Viking, 1975; (editor) *The Lover's Companion,* David & Charles, 1978; *Getting It Right* (novel), Hamish Hamilton, 1982. Also author of television plays "After Julius" and "Something in Disguise" (both based on her novels), as well as scripts for "Upstairs Downstairs." Contributor to *Encounter, Sunday Times, Daily Express, New Yorker,* and *Town and Country.*

WORK IN PROGRESS: A play.

SIDELIGHTS: National Observer's Robert Ostermann places Elizabeth Jane Howard in the same class with "Rosamond Lehmann and Elizabeth Bowen: female novelists of impressive intelligence and sensibilities that respond to every nuance in human relationships." Called a "remarkably seductive writer" by a *New Yorker* critic, Howard has "from the start been recognized as a fine technician," according to Harry Keyishian in the *Washington Post Book World.* "She has a talent for compressing detail into phrases which repay close reading," writes a reviewer for the *Times Literary Supplement,* and Daniel George echoes this assessment. Reviewing Howard's *The Long View* in *Spectator,* George remarks: "Not many novels deserve to be read twice. This one does—preferably, the second time, from finish to start."

Howard is also known for her shorter fiction, and *Mr. Wrong,* her first collection of stories, has received much praise. "Howard's characterizations of alienated people," notes V. L. Fetscher in *Library Journal,* "are chilling and touching, her descriptive passages deft and evocative, and her timing is almost impeccable." Writing in the *New Statesman,* Victoria Glendinning believes that Howard "writes most confidently and touchingly at very close range, about momentary doubts, unspoken anxieties, fleeting perceptions, intense good moments and equally intense bad ones, all inextricably bound up with a natural or domestic setting." Jerome Charyn concludes in the *New York Times Book Review* that indeed Howard's "special grace" is "delineating the little corrosions of tight family structures—the bickering husbands and wives, the cruel, secretive world of children in a country house, the territorial squabbles of mothers and daughters, the bonds of jealousy between a beautiful girl and her grandmother."

BIOGRAPHICAL/CRITICAL SOURCES: Spectator, March 16, 1956, April 8, 1972, July 26, 1975; *Times Literary Supplement,* March 23, 1956, November 20, 1959, November 4, 1965, November 6, 1969, March 24, 1972, July 11, 1975, May 14, 1982; *New York Times Book Review,* January 31, 1960, January 9, 1966, February 1, 1970, February 22, 1976; *Saturday Review,* February 20, 1960, February 14, 1970; *Book Week,* January 30, 1966; *New Yorker,* April 16, 1966, February 26, 1972; *National Observer,* February 23, 1970; *Washington Post Book World,* January 30, 1972; *New Statesman,* July 11, 1975; *Library Journal,* December 1, 1975; *Newsweek,* December 29, 1975; *Contemporary Literary Criticism,* Volume VII, Gale, 1977.

HOWARD, James A(rch) 1922-
(Laine Fisher)

PERSONAL: Born May 8, 1922, in Delavan, Ill.; son of Arch Clark (a contractor) and Claudine (Boyd) Howard; married second wife, Nancy C. Thompson, 1966; children: one. *Education:* Heidelberg College, Tiffin, Ohio, A.B., 1948; Columbia University, M.A., 1949; University of California, Los Angeles, Ph.D., 1957. *Residence:* Fallbrook, Calif. *Agent:* James M. Fox, Roberto Dr., Palm Springs, Calif. *Office:* Mesa Vista Hospital, 7850 Vista Hill Ave., San Diego, Calif. 92123.

CAREER: Alabama Polytechnic Institute (now Auburn University), Auburn, Ala., instructor, 1949-51; Los Angeles State College of Applied Arts and Sciences (now California State University, Los Angeles), lecturer in creative writing, 1956-57; Office of Vocational Rehabilitation, Long Beach, Calif., research director, 1957-60; Southwestern Mental Health Center, Luverne, Minn., clinical psychologist, 1961-65; private practice as clinical and consulting psychologist in Luverne, 1961-65, and in San Diego, Calif., 1965—; Mesa Vista Hospital, San Diego, clinical psychologist, 1965—; San Diego State University, San Diego, lecturer, 1966-72. Writer. U.S. Public Health Service fellow, Los Angeles Psychiatric Service, 1956-57; dean for administrative affairs, California School of Professional Psychology, 1972. *Military service:* U.S. Army Air Forces, 1942-43.

MEMBER: American Psychological Association, National Rehabilitation Association, Mystery Writers of America. *Awards, honors:* Tuberculosis and Health Association Merit Award, 1960; Community Rehabilitation Industries Merit Award, 1960.

WRITINGS: I Like It Tough, Popular Library, 1955; *I'll Get You Yet,* Popular Library, 1956; *Blow Out My Torch,* Popular Library, 1956; *Die on Easy Street,* Popular Library, 1957; *Murder Takes a Wife,* Dutton, 1958; *Murder in Mind,* Dutton, 1959; (under pseudonym Laine Fisher) *Fare Prey,* Ace Books, 1959; *Bullet Proof Martyr,* Dutton, 1961; *The Ego Mill: 5 Cases in Clinical Psychology,* Cowles, 1971; *Death Audit,* Raven House, 1982; *Friday Is a Killing Day,* Raven House, 1982; *Grave Injury,* Raven House, in press; *A Well Rehearsed Death,* Raven House, in press. Also author of *The Flesh-Colored Cage,* Hawthorn. Author of television plays for "Alfred Hitchcock Presents." Contributor of short stories to mystery magazines.

AVOCATIONAL INTERESTS: Flying, avocado and citrus ranching, woodworking and construction, design, acting and directing in local theatre productions.

* * *

HUANG, Ray (Jen-yu) 1918-

PERSONAL: Born June 25, 1918, in Changsha, China; son of Cheng-pai and Chang-shun (Li) Huang; married Gayle Bates, September 20, 1966; children: Jefferson. *Education:* Attended U.S. Command and General Staff College, 1947; University of Michigan, B.A., 1954, M.A., 1957, Ph.D., 1964. *Home:* 10 Bonticou View Dr., New Paltz, N.Y. 12561.

CAREER: Chinese National Army, served in India, Burma and Manchuria, 1941-50, leaving service as major; Southern Illinois University, Edwardsville, assistant professor of history, 1964-66; Columbia University, New York, N.Y., visiting associate professor of history, 1966; State University of New York College at New Paltz, associate professor, 1967-71, professor of Chinese history, 1971-80. Research fellow at Harvard

University, 1970-71. *Member:* PEN. *Awards, honors:* American Council of Learned Societies fellowships, 1966, 1972; National Science Foundation grant, 1973; Guggenheim fellowship, 1975-76; nomination for history category of American Book Awards, 1982, for *1587, A Year of No Significance: The Ming Dynasty in Decline.*

WRITINGS: *Taxation and Governmental Finance in Sixteenth-Century Ming-China,* Cambridge University Press, 1974; (with Joseph Needham) *The Nature of Chinese Society: A Technical Interpretation,* East & West Library, 1974; *1587, A Year of No Significance: The Ming Dynasty in Decline,* Yale University Press, 1981; *Wan-li Shih-wu-nian,* Chung-hua Book Co. (Peking), 1982. Contributor to *Ming Biographical Dictionary.*

WORK IN PROGRESS: A general introduction to Chinese history and culture; collaborating with Joseph Needham on *Science and Civilisation in China,* Volume VII: *Conclusions.*

BIOGRAPHICAL/CRITICAL SOURCES: *New York Times Book Review,* June 21, 1981.

* * *

**HUGHES, Colin
     See CREASEY, John**

* * *

HUMPHREY, James H(arry)   1911-

PERSONAL: Born February 26, 1911, in Marietta, Ohio; son of Harry and Nellie (Pugh) Humphrey; married Frances Drokopil, March 29, 1945; children: Joy Nell. *Education:* Denison University, B.S., 1933; Western Reserve University (now Case Western Reserve University), M.S., 1946; Boston University, Ph.D., 1951. *Religion:* Protestant. *Home:* 9108 St. Andrews Place, College Park, Md. 20740. *Office:* Department of Physical Education, University of Maryland, College Park, Md. 20740.

CAREER: Bedford Board of Education, Bedford, Ohio, director of health and physical education, 1937-49; Michigan State University, East Lansing, assistant professor of health and physical education, 1951-53; University of Maryland, College Park, associate professor, 1953-56, professor of physical education and health, 1956—. Distinguished visiting scholar, University of Delaware, 1965; distinguished visiting professor, University of Texas at Austin, 1971; lecturer to learned societies and educational groups. Member, International Compendium of Eminent People in the Field of Exceptional Education, 1973. *Military service:* U.S. Naval Reserve, 1943-45.

MEMBER: American Academy of Physical Education, American Alliance for Health, Physical Education, and Recreation, American School Health Association (fellow; past chairman of research council), Society for Research in Child Development (fellow), Society of Children's Book Writers, Science for the Handicapped Association, Association for Anthropological Study of Play. *Awards, honors:* American Alliance for Health, Physical Education, Recreation National Honor Award, 1972, and R. Tait McKenzie Award, 1976.

WRITINGS: (With Harris F. Beeman) *Intramural Sports: A Text and Study Guide,* W. C. Brown, 1954, 3rd edition, Princeton Book, 1980; (with Leslie W. Irwin) *Principles and Techniques of Supervision in Physical Education,* Mosby, 1954, 3rd edition, Princeton Book, 1980; (with Irwin and Warren R. Johnson) *Methods and Materials in School Health Education,* Mosby, 1956; (with W. R. Johnson and Granville Bradley Johnson) *Your Career in Physical Education: An Introduction to the Profession for Young Men and Women,* Harper, 1957; *Elementary School Physical Education: With Emphasis upon Its Integration in Other Curriculum Areas,* Harper, 1958; (editor with Edwina Jones and Martha J. Haverstick) *Readings in Physical Education for the Elementary School,* National Press, 1958, 2nd edition, 1960.

(With W. R. Johnson and Virginia D. Moore) *Elementary School Health Education: Curriculum, Methods, Integration,* Harper, 1962; (with W. R. Johnson and others) *Health Concepts for College Students,* Ronald, 1962; (compiler with Doris E. Terry and Howard S. Slusher) *Readings in Health Education: A Collection of Selected Articles for Use in Personal Health and Health Education Courses,* W. C. Brown, 1964; *Child Learning through Elementary School Physical Education,* W. C. Brown, 1966, 2nd edition (with daughter, Joy N. Humphrey), 1974; (with Anne Gayle Ingram) *Introduction to Physical Education for College Students,* Holbrook, 1969.

(With Dorothy D. Sullivan) *Teaching Slow Learners through Active Games,* C. C Thomas, 1970; (with Sullivan) *Teaching Reading through Motor Learning,* C. C Thomas, 1973; (with J. N. Humphrey) *Learning to Listen and Read through Movement,* Kimbo Educational, 1974; (contributor) Loyda M. Shears and Eli M. Bower, editors, *Games in Education and Development,* C. C Thomas, 1974; *Teaching Elementary School Science through Motor Learning,* C. C Thomas, 1975; *Education of Children through Motor Activity,* C. C Thomas, 1975; (with others) *Health Teaching in Elementary Schools,* C. C Thomas, 1975; (with R. B. Ashlock) *Teaching Elementary School Mathematics through Motor Learning,* C. C Thomas, 1976; *Improving Learning Ability through Compensatory Physical Education,* C. C Thomas, 1976; *Physical Education as a Career,* C. C Thomas, 1978.

With J. N. Humphrey, except as indicted; published by C. C Thomas, except as indicated: *Help Your Child Learn the 3 R's through Active Play,* 1980; *Sports Skills for Boys and Girls,* 1980; *How Teachers Can Cope with Stress,* [College Park, Md.], 1980; (sole author) *Child Development through Physical Education,* 1980; *Reducing Stress in Children through Creative Relaxation,* 1981; (contributor) Hans Selye, editor, *Selye's Guide to Stress Research,* in press.

Recordings; all produced by Kimbo Educational: "Teaching Children Mathematics through Games, Rhythms and Stunts," 1968; "Stunts and Tumbling for Elementary School Children," 1969; (with others) "Teaching Reading through Creative Movement," 1969; (with J. N. Humphrey) "Helping Children Understand about Stress," 1980.

Author, with Moore, of "Read and Play" series, six books, Muller, 1965. Contributor to proceedings of professional organizations, including International Reading Association, International Seminar on Play, and National Science Teachers Association. Contributor to professional journals, including *Stress, Perceptual and Motor Skills, Research Quarterly,* and *Academic Therapy.* Member of board of associate editors, *Research Quarterly,* 1954-59 and 1960-63; research editor, *Journal of School Health,* 1962-65.

* * *

HUNDLEY, Norris (Cecil), Jr.   1935-

PERSONAL: Born October 26, 1935, in Houston, Tex.; son of Norris Cecil (an engineer) and Helen (Mundine) Hundley; married Carol Marie Beckquist, June 8, 1957; children: Wendy, Jacqueline. *Education:* Mount San Antonio College, A.A., 1956; Whittier College, A.B., 1958; University of California,

Los Angeles, Ph.D., 1963. *Office:* Department of History, University of California, Los Angeles, Calif. 90024.

CAREER: University of Houston, Houston, Tex., instructor in American history, 1963-64; University of California, Los Angeles, assistant professor, 1964-69, associate professor, 1969-73, professor of American history, 1973—, member of executive committee of Consortium on Mexico and the United States, 1981—. Visiting assistant professor, Whittier College, summer, 1964. *Member:* American Historical Association (member of Pacific Coast Branch executive council, 1969—), Institute of American Culture (chairman of executive committee, 1977—), Organization of American Historians, Western History Association, California Historical Association (member of board of editorial consultants, 1980—). *Awards, honors:* Winther Award, Western History Association, 1973 and 1979; Guggenheim fellow, 1978-79; award of merit, California Historical Society, 1979.

WRITINGS: John Walton Caughey, Dawson's, 1961; *Dividing the Waters: A Century of Controversy between the United States and Mexico,* University of California Press, 1966; *The American West: Frontier and Region,* Ward Ritchie, 1969; (editor) *The American Indian,* Clio Press, 1974; *Water and the West: The Colorado River Compact and the Politics of Water in the American West,* University of California Press, 1975; *The Chicano,* Clio Press, 1975; *The Asian American,* Clio Press, 1975; (co-author) *California: History of a Remarkable State,* 4th edition (Hundley was not associated with earlier editions), Prentice-Hall, 1982.

Co-editor of "Golden State" series, 1978—. Contributor to *Notable American Women.* Contributor to journals, including *Foreign Affairs, Pacific Historical Review, Western Historical Quarterly,* and *California Historical Quarterly.* Managing editor, *Pacific Historical Review,* 1968—; member of board of editors, *Journal of San Diego History,* 1970—.

* * *

HUNT, Irene 1907-

PERSONAL: Born May 18, 1907, in Newton, Ill.; daughter of Franklin Pierce and Sarah (Land) Hunt. *Education:* University of Illinois, A.B., 1939; University of Minnesota, M.A., 1946. *Home:* 2587 Roy Hanna Dr. S., St. Petersburg, Fla. 33712.

CAREER: Oak Park (Ill.) public schools, teacher of French and English, 1930-45; University of South Dakota, Vermillion, instructor in psychology, 1946-50; Cicero (Ill.) public schools, teacher, 1950-65, consultant, director of language arts, beginning 1965. *Awards, honors.* Charles W. Follett Award, 1964, American Notable Book Award, 1965, and sole runner-up for the Newbery Medal, 1965, all for *Across Five Aprils;* Newbery Medal, 1967, for *Up a Road Slowly;* Friends of Literature Award and Charles W. Follett Award, both 1971, both for *No Promises in the Wind.*

WRITINGS: Across Five Aprils, Follett, 1964; *Up a Road Slowly,* Follett, 1966; *Trail of Apple Blossoms,* Follett, 1968; *No Promises in the Wind,* Follett, 1970; *The Lottery Rose,* Scribner, 1976; *William,* Scribner, 1978; *Claws of a Young Century,* Scribner, 1980.

WORK IN PROGRESS: The Everlasting Hills, for Scribner.

SIDELIGHTS: "The true-to-life happens in Irene Hunt's stories," writes Adrienne Richard in the *New York Times Book Review.* "Heroes and heroines bear flaws and scars; friends die. A mother may be a hard drinker, and a father thoughtless and cruel."

In *Up a Road Slowly,* her 1967 Newbery Medal winner, Hunt chronicled ten years in the life of a young girl who suffers the loss of her mother and goes to live with her spinster aunt. The novel grew out of an experience that has remained vivid in the author's memory—the death of her father when she was a child. The Newbery-Caldecott committee described the book as "a work of poignant fiction which concerns itself with the timeless problems of all young people groping for independence and maturity. The young heroine, Julia, . . . is susceptible to a whole range of influences. . . . The many diverse characters who shape her life and emotional growth are beautifully realized with great perception and sensitivity and a happy absence of sentimentality."

New York Times Book Review critic D. M. Broderick praised the book for similar reasons: "The adult who chooses to write a first-person novel about the child he once was faces two serious problems: the danger of over-sentimentalizing his material, and the difficulty of sustaining a young reader's interest in a past-tense narrative. The author has surmounted both obstacles triumphantly. . . . Those who follow Julie's growth—from a tantrum-throwing seven-year-old to a gracious young woman of seventeen—will find this book has added a new dimension to their lives."

Though her writing appeals to a youthful audience, Hunt says she did not set out to capture the children's market. "I didn't plan my first book for a certain age group," she told *Publisher's Weekly.* "I don't want to aim at a special age of reader. I write when I have something to say."

Several of Hunt's books have been translated into German, Italian, Norwegian, Danish, and French.

BIOGRAPHICAL/CRITICAL SOURCES: New York Times Book Review, November 6, 1966, March 19, 1967, April 14, 1968, April 5, 1970, May 16, 1976; *Publisher's Weekly,* March 13, 1967; *Commonweal,* May 24, 1968; *Young Readers' Review,* June, 1968; *New Yorker,* December 14, 1968; Nancy Larrick, *A Parent's Guide to Children's Reading,* 3rd edition, Doubleday, 1969; *The Writer,* March, 1970; *Hornbook,* June, 1970; *Children's Literature Review,* Volume I, Gale, 1976.

* * *

HUNT, Kyle
See CREASEY, John

* * *

HUNTER, Sam 1923-

PERSONAL: Born January 5, 1923, in Springfield, Mass.; son of Morris and Lottie (Sherman) Hunter; married Edys Merrill, July 22, 1954 (divorced, 1976); children: Emily, Alexa. *Education:* Williams University, A.B., 1943; University of Florence, Certificate of Studies, 1951. *Home:* 146 Mercer St., Princeton, N.J. 08540. *Office:* Department of Art and Archaeology, McCormick Hall, Princeton University, Princeton, N.J. 08540.

CAREER: New York Times, New York City, art critic, 1947-49; Harry N. Abrams, Inc. (publisher of art books), New York City, editor, 1952-53; *Arts* (magazine), New York City, editor, 1953-54; University of California, Los Angeles, associate professor, 1955-56; Museum of Modern Art, New York City, curator, 1956-58; Minneapolis Institute of Arts, Minneapolis, Minn., chief curator and acting director, 1958-60; Brandeis University, Waltham, Mass., associate professor of fine arts, director of Rose Art Museum, and director of Poses Institute of Fine Arts, 1960-65; Jewish Museum, New York City, director, 1965-68; Princeton University, Princeton, N.J., professor of art and archaeology and curator of modern art at Princeton University Art Museum, 1969—. Lecturer, Barnard College, 1955-57, and New School for Social Research, 1967-68; visiting professor, Cornell University, 1967-69; director, studies in visual arts, Massachusetts Board of Higher Education, 1968-69; Regent's Professor and visiting critic, University of California, Riverside, 1968; visiting critic, State University of New York, 1968-69; lecturer on contemporary American art, United States Information Agency tour of Japan, 1975; Robert Sterling Clark Visiting Professor, Clark Art Institute and Williams College, 1976; lecturer and senior member, cultural exchange delegation in Bulgaria, U.S. Department of State and Institute of Cultural Affairs, 1979; director, National Endowment for the Humanities summer seminar, 1980.

Exhibition director of American Art since 1950, Seattle World's Fair, 1962; International Art juror, Thirty-Second Venice Biennale, 1964; critic's choice program director, New York State Council of the Arts, 1968-69; director, Monumenta outdoor sculpture exhibition, Newport, R.I.; director of exhibition, "Post-Modernism: Narrative and Decorative Art," art gallery, Squibb & Sons world headquarters, 1982; member, State of Michigan Commission on Art in State Buildings, 1976; member, arts and humanities task force, Carter-Mondale campaign, 1976. Harry N. Abrams, Inc., consulting editor, 1969—, vice-president and editor-in-chief, 1971-72. Consultant to circulating exhibition, Commodities Corp. collection, 1981-82; member of advisory board, Modarco, S.A., art investment group, London. *Military service:* U.S. Navy, 1943-46; became lieutenant junior grade; received five battle stars. *Member:* College Art Association, Phi Beta Kappa. *Awards, honors:* Guggenheim fellowship, 1971-72.

WRITINGS: *Henri de Toulouse-Lautrec*, Abrams, 1953; *Raoul Dufy*, Abrams, 1953; *Jackson Pollock*, New York Museum of Modern Art, 1956; *Modern French Painting, 1855-1956*, Dell, 1956, 2nd edition, 1964; *Picasso: Cubism to the Present*, Abrams, 1957; *Mondrian*, Abrams, 1958; (editor) *Modern American Painting and Sculpture*, Dell, 1959; (editor) *European Art Today*, [Minneapolis], 1959; *Joan Miro: His Graphic Work*, Abrams, 1959; (co-author) *Art since 1945*, Abrams, 1959; *Motherwell*, Berggruen (Paris), 1961; *Hans Hofmann*, Abrams, 1963; *James Brooks*, Praeger for Whitney Museum of American Art, 1963; (with others) *New Art around the World: Painting and Sculpture*, Abrams, 1966; *Action Painting: La generazione eroica*, Fabbri (Milan), 1967; *Sculptures*, M. Knoedler, 1968.

Larry Rivers, Abrams, 1970, 2nd edition, with supplement, 1971; *La pittura americana del dupoguerra*, Gabbri, 1970; *Modern American: Op, Pop, and the School of Color*, Fabbri, 1970; *Monumenta: A Biennial Exhibition of Outdoor Sculpture*, Monumenta Newport Inc., 1974; (with Rosalind Krauss and Marcia Tucker) *Critical Perspectives in American Art: An Exhibition*, The Gallery (Amherst), 1976; (with John Jacobus) *Modern Art from Post-Impressionism to the Present: Painting, Sculpture, Architecture*, Abrams, 1976; *The Dada/Surrealist Heritage*, Clark Art Institute, 1977; *Isamu Noguchi*, Abbeville Press, 1978; (with Edward Lucie-Smith) *Kunst der Gegenwart*, Propylaen Verlag (Frankfurt), 1978; *Art in Business: The Philip Morris Story*, Abrams, 1979; *Masters of Twentieth Century Art*, Abbeville Press, 1980; *Twentieth Century Painting*, Abbeville Press, 1980; *Seymour Lipton: Recent Sculpture*, Mint Museum of Art, 1982; *Rivers*, New American Library, in press.

Also author of *American Art since 1960*, 1970, *Josef Albers: Paintings and Graphics, 1917-1970*, 1971, *The Port Authority Art Collection*, 1982, and of exhibition catalogues.

AVOCATIONAL INTERESTS: Tennis.

* * *

HUSTON, Mervyn James 1912-

PERSONAL: Born September 4, 1912, in Ashcroft, British Columbia, Canada; son of William Mervyn (a pharmacist) and Irene (Gray) Huston; married Helen Margaret McBryan, December 18, 1938; children: Bryan Mervyn, Dorna Helen (Mrs. David Thomas Young). *Education:* University of Alberta, B.Sc., 1934, M.Sc., 1938; University of Washington, Seattle, Ph.D., 1941. *Religion:* United Church of Canada. *Home:* 11562 80th Ave., Edmonton, Alberta, Canada. *Office:* Faculty of Pharmacy, University of Alberta, Edmonton, Alberta, Canada.

CAREER: University of Alberta, Edmonton, assistant professor, 1943-44, professor of pharmacy, 1944-78, professor emeritus, 1978—, dean of faculty of pharmacy and pharmaceutical sciences, 1948-78; writer. *Member:* Canadian Conference on Pharmacy Faculties (chairman, 1948), Canadian Pharmaceutical Association (president, 1969), Canadian Foundation for the Advancement of Pharmacy (president, 1970), Association of Deans of Pharmacy of Canada (president, 1972), Sigma Xi, Phi Sigma, Rho Chi, Phi Delta Theta, Kiwanis Club, Masonic Lodge, Al Azhar Temple, Edmonton Burns Club, Mayfair Golf and Country Club. *Awards, honors:* Centennial Medal from Government of Canada, 1968, Dr. E. R. Squibb Award from Canadian Pharmaceutical Association, 1971, and Alta Achievement Award from Government of Alberta, 1971, all for contributions to the pharmaceutical profession.

WRITINGS: Textbook of Pharmaceutical Arithmetic, Canadian Pharmaceutical Association, 1959; *Test and Improve Your Scientific Word Power*, Canadian Pharmaceutical Association, 1960; *The Great Canadian Lover*, Musson, 1964; *Text and Dictionary of Scientific Words*, Canadian Pharmaceutical Association, 1965; *Toasts to the Bride and How to Propose Them*, Tuttle, 1968; *Canada, Eh to Zed: A Further Contribution to the Continuing Quest for the Elusive Canadian Identity*, Hurtig, 1973; *Great Golf Humour*, Hurtig, 1977; *Golf and Murphy's Law*, Hurtig, 1981; *Gophers Don't Pay Taxes*, Tree Frog Press, 1981. Contributor to journals in his field. Editor-in-chief of *Canadian Journal of Pharmaceutical Sciences*, 1965-78.

WORK IN PROGRESS: More Gophers, for publication by Tree Frog Press.

* * *

HUTCHINSON, Peter 1943-

PERSONAL: Born August 24, 1943, in London, England; married Maite Lores; children: Fabian. *Education:* University of Wales, B.Sc., 1965; King's College, London, Ph.D., 1970. *Home:* 120 Oxford Rd., Abingdon, Oxfordshire, England.

CAREER: Elsevier International Projects Ltd., Oxford, England, editor of popular scientific books, 1970—. Part-time researcher in department of zoology, Cambridge University.

WRITINGS: Evolution Explained, David & Charles, 1974.

Editor of encyclopedias; all published by Elsevier: *How Invertebrates Live*, 1975; *How Birds Live*, 1975; *How Mammals Live*, 1975; *How Insects Live*, 1975; *The Mating Game*, 1976; *How Fishes Live*, 1976; *Bird Life*, 1976; *Planet Earth*, 1977. Also editor of *Elsevier's Animal Encyclopedia*.

Consultant editor to *Manwatching*, by Desmond Morris, 1977. Contributor to scientific journals, including *Paleontology*.

WORK IN PROGRESS: Research on the early evolution of fish.

HYAMS, Edward (Solomon) 1910-1975

PERSONAL: Born September 30, 1910, in London, England; died November 25, 1975, in Besancon, France; son of Arthur and Dolly (Hart) Hyams; married Hilda Mary Aylett, 1933 (divorced); married Mary Patricia Bacon, 1973. *Education:* Attended University College School, London, England, and Lycee Jacquard, Lausanne, Switzerland; University of Lausanne, license es lettres. *Home:* The Old School House, Brampton, Beccles, Suffolk, England. *Agent:* Hughes Massie, 21 Southampton Row, London W.C.1, England; Harold Ober Associates, Inc., 40 East 49th St., New York, N.Y. 10017.

CAREER: Writer and translator. Worked in advertising and as manual laborer, 1930-39. *Military service:* Royal Air Force, 1939-41; Royal Navy, 1941-46; became lieutenant. *Awards, honors:* Atlantic Award in Literature, 1948; Scott-Moncrieff Prize, 1964.

WRITINGS—Fiction: *The Wings of the Morning*, Little, Brown, 1939; *A Time to Cast Away*, Methuen, 1942; *To Sea in a Bowl*, Methuen, 1942; *Blood Money*, Lane, 1948; *William Medium*, Lane, 1948; *Not in Our Stars*, Longmans, Green, 1949; *The Astrologer*, Longmans, Green, 1950; *Sylvester*, Longmans, Green, 1951, published as *998*, Pantheon, 1952; *Gentian Violet*, Longmans, Green, 1953; *Stories and Cream*, Longmans, Green, 1954; *The Slaughterhouse Informer*, Longmans, Green, 1955; *Into the Dream*, Longmans, Green, 1957; *The Unpossessed*, Simon & Schuster, 1958; *Taking It Easy*, Longmans, Green, 1958, published as *Tillotson*, Simon & Schuster, 1961; *All We Possess*, Longmans, Green, 1961; *A Perfect Stranger*, Simon & Schuster, 1964; *The Last Poor Man*, Simon & Schuster, 1966; *The Irish Garden*, Macdonald, 1966; *Cross Purposes: Four Stories of Love*, Longmans, Green, 1967; *The Mischief Makers*, Longmans Green, 1968; *The Death Lottery*, Longman, 1971; *The Final Agenda*, Allen Lane, 1973; *Prince Habib's Iceberg*, Allen Lane, 1974; *Morrow's Ants*, Allen Lane, 1975.

Nonfiction: *Metropolitan Verses*, Gale & Polden, 1934; *The Grape Vine in England*, Bodley Head, 1949; *From the Waste Land*, Turnstile Press, 1950; *Soil and Civilization*, Thames & Hudson, 1952, reprinted, Harper, 1976; *Grapes under Cloches*, Faber, 1952; *Melons under Cloches*, Faber, 1952; (with Harold John Massingham) *Prophecy of Famine: A Warning and the Remedy*, Thames & Hudson, 1953; *Strawberry Cultivation*, Faber, 1953, revised edition published as *Strawberry Growing Complete: A System of Procuring Fruit throughout the Year*, 1962; (editor) *Vineyards in England*, Faber, 1953; *The Speaking Garden*, Longmans, Green, 1957; *Vin: The Wine Country of France*, Newnes, 1959, published as *The Wine Country of France*, Lippincott, 1960; *Odhams' Fruit Growers' Encyclopaedia*, Odhams, 1960; (editor with A. A. Jackson) *The Orchard and Fruit Garden: A New Pomona of Hardy and Sub-Tropical Fruits*, Longmans, Green, 1961; (author of introduction and commentary) *English Heritage in Color*, Hastings House, 1963; (with George Ordish) *The Last of the Incas*, Simon & Schuster, 1963; *The New Statesman: The History of the First Fifty Years, 1913-1963*, Longmans, Green, 1963; (editor) *New Statesmanship: An Anthology*, Longmans, Green, 1963, Books for Libraries, 1970; *The English Garden*, Abrams, 1964; *Dionysus: A Social History of the Wine Vine*, Macmillan, 1965; *Ornamental Shrubs for Temperate Zone Gardens*, Volume 1-2, Macdonald, 1965, A. S. Barnes, 1968.

Irish Gardens (not the same as similar title above), Macdonald, 1967; *An Englishman's Garden*, Macdonald, 1967; (with Jan De Graaff) *Lilies*, Thomas Nelson, 1967, Funk, 1968; (with George Elbert) *House Plants*, Thomas Nelson, 1967, Funk, 1968; *The Gardener's Bedside Book*, Faber, 1968; *Great Botanical Gardens of the World*, Macmillan, 1969; *Of Gardens and Gardeners*, A. S. Barnes, 1969; *Killing No Murder: A Study of Assassination as a Political Means*, Thomas Nelson, 1969, Panther Books, 1970; *English Cottage Gardens*, Thomas Nelson, 1970; (with Mary Bacon) *The Traveller's Bedside Book*, Faber, 1970; *Capability Brown and Humphry Repton*, Scribner, 1971; *A History of Gardens and Gardening*, Praeger, 1971; *Plants in the Service of Man: 10,000 Years of Domestication*, Dent, 1971, Lippincott, 1972; *Animals in the Service of Man: 10,000 Years of Domestication*, Lippincott, 1972, new edition published as *Working for Man: Domestication of Animals*, Kestrel Books, 1975; *A Dictionary of Modern Revolution*, Taplinger, 1973; *The Changing Face of England*, Kestrel Books, 1974, revised edition published as *The Changing Face of Britain*, Paladin Books, 1977; *The Millennium Postponed: Socialism from Sir Thomas More to Mao Tse-tung*, Taplinger, 1974; *Survival Gardening: How to Grow Vegetables, Herbs, Fruits, Nuts, Wine, and Tobacco in Garden or Allotment*, J. Murray, 1975; *Terrorists and Terrorism*, St. Martin's, 1975; (with Neil Treseder) *Growing Camellias*, Thomas Nelson, 1975; *The Story of England's Flora*, Kestrel Books, 1978; *Pierre-Joseph Proudhon: His Revolutionary Life, Mind and Works*, Taplinger, 1979.

Translator: Roger Peyrefitte, *Diplomatic Conclusions*, Thames & Hudson, 1954; Jules Moch, *Human Folly: To Disarm or Perish*, Gollancz, 1955; Zoe Oldenbourg, *Cornerstone*, Pantheon, 1955; Henri Cartier-Bresson, *China in Transition*, Thames & Hudson, 1956; Gabriel Chevallier, *Wicked Village*, Simon & Schuster, 1956; Maurice de LaFuye and E. A. Babeau, *Apostle of Liberty: A Life of Lafayette*, Yoseloff, 1956; Jean Reverzy, *Crossing*, Pantheon, 1956; Peyrefitte, *Keys of St. Peter*, Criterion, 1957; Oldenbourg, *Awakened*, Pantheon, 1957; (and author of introduction) Hippolyte Adolphe Taine, *Notes on England*, Thames & Hudson, 1957; Jules Renard, *Sponger*, Longmans, Green, 1957; Tibor Meray, *Enemy*, Secker & Warburg, 1958; Tibor Dery, *Niki: The Story of a Dog*, Doubleday, 1958; Peyrefitte, *Special Friendships*, Secker & Warburg, 1958; Jean Denys, *Shouting Dies Away*, Longmans, Green, 1958; Roger Grenier, *Party Is Over*, Eyre & Spottiswoode, 1959; Peyrefitte, *Knights of Malta*, Criterion, 1959; Alexis Curvers, *Tempo di Roma*, McGraw, 1959; Michel Droit, *Pueblo*, Eyre & Spottiswoode, 1959; Michel Landa, *The Cactus Grove*, Longmans, Green, 1960; Georges Blond, *Admiral Togo*, Macmillan, 1969; Regine Pernoud, *Joan of Arc*, Macdonald, 1964; Philippe Ceillier, *To See the White Cliffs*, Longmans, Green, 1965; Phillipe Erlanger, *Margaret of Anjou: Queen of England*, University of Miami Press, 1970.

Former author of regular column for *Illustrated London News*, *New Statesman*, and *Financial Times*. Contributor to *Punch* and other periodicals; contributor to horticulture journals in England and France.

SIDELIGHTS: "Edward Hyams is an excellent translator, the author of some splendid comic novels, a charming writer on gardening and horticulture and the author of an official—but by no means tame—biography of that Dutch uncle the *New Statesman*. A man of parts." With this statement, a *Nation* critic sums up the work of Edward Hyams, who, at the time of his death in 1975, had written or translated more than ninety books on subjects ranging from herbal gardens to political terrorism.

Hyams's early work consisted primarily of short novels and horticultural studies, both of which have attracted critical attention. In a review of the novel *A Perfect Stranger* for *Book Week,* Cade Ware writes: "Mr. Hyams has vast and wonderful abilities. He can write as well as Thackeray, Dickens, Waugh, Ian Fleming and Maugham. . . . [But] his fictional world is a kaleidoscope of other writers' worlds, and if he envisions a Hyams world, he has yet to see the center of it clearly. *A Perfect Stranger* is carefully polished, intelligent, civilized, insightful and absorbing." In *Saturday Review,* R. A. Cordell describes *The Wings of the Morning* as "a very strange novel—baffling, irritating, and intellectually exciting. It is baffling because the reader is never quite sure what it is about, irritating because one suspects that the author himself is uncertain, but intellectually exciting because of the acute and subtle—sometimes passionate and breath-taking—analyses of the problems of modern man."

Described by E. C. Hall of *Library Journal* as "one of the great contemporary authorities on gardens and gardening," Hyams has written more than twenty-five books on various aspects of horticultural technique and history. A *Times Literary Supplement* reviewer comments on *A History of Gardens and Gardening:* "This is a thorough and scholarly piece of research, packed with true history. Edward Hyams's style is orderly, lucid, and entertaining and it compels the reader's attention throughout. . . . In a book of this quality it is hard to pick out highlights. . . . The book is outstanding, both as a piece of historical research and as an illustration of how the art of gardening has always formed part of the progress of civilization." *Capability Brown and Humphry Repton,* Hyams's study of the two famous English landscape artists, is "of inestimable value, both to the scholar . . . and to the general reader," according to a *New Statesman* critic. It is "an enjoyable melange of contemporary characters, whims and criticisms," the reviewer continues. "At the hands of their latest biographer, an expert gardener and an accomplished historian, both [Brown and Repton] have fared extraordinarily well."

In such works as *Killing No Murder* and *Terrorists and Terrorism,* Hyams, as Mervyn Jones observes in the *New Statesman,* has advocated the view that "the swift removal of an unjust ruler is a short cut to needed social change; and, internationally, that killing an opponent like Hitler is a method of combat both more humane and efficient than mass slaughter." "*Killing No Murder* is Mr. Hyams at his most madly logical, eccentrically learned and passionately humane," Lewis Bates says in *Punch.* "If killing millions in war is laudable, [Hyams] argues, why shouldn't preventing a war by assassinating a bellicose statesman be laudable too?" In *Books and Bookmen,* Richard Whittington-Egan summarizes Hyams's argument: "If a woman sticks a knife into the merciless heart of the husband whose regular Saturday night recreation is to beat up her and her children, she is guilty of murder. But if, at the height of that communal insanity which we call war, you or I go out and slaughter some unfortunate person whom we have never seen before in our life, . . . not only is this killing no murder, but we are quite likely to get a medal for it. The act of killing, it would seem, is not wrong *per se* in our culture. Circumstances alter cases. . . . How then, on that premise, Hyams asks, can a society which condones war morally condemn assassination?"

"One should be grateful to Edward Hyams for sparing some time from his novels and his gardens to raise this stern ghost," Bernard Crick states in his review of *Killing No Murder.* "And he raises it in the most lively possible manner." In his *Observer Review* article, however, Crick points out: "Tyrannicide is a sensible and can be a just political force in societies which in fact depend for their character on the will of one man. . . . Oppression is greater and more comprehensive in industrial civilization, and so must be the remedies. One admires the ancient spirit of Mr. Hyams, but the theory is simply wrong." "A considerable complication is that one man's tyrant is another man's hero," Whittington-Egan asserts. In his review of *Killing No Murder,* Whittington-Egan concludes: "In reality, the death of one man is qualitatively no less terrible than the death of ten. Every man's death diminishes the slayer."

AVOCATIONAL INTERESTS: Garden design, gardening, travel, conversation.

BIOGRAPHICAL/CRITICAL SOURCES: Times Literary Supplement, January 7, 1939, September 24, 1964, January 23, 1969, September 3, 1971, December 31, 1971, June 2, 1972; *New York Times,* June 17, 1939, March 30, 1952, September 27, 1979; *Saturday Review,* June 17, 1939, June 18, 1966; *New Republic,* June 28, 1939, April 11, 1964; *New York Times Book Review,* April 12, 1964, December 14, 1975; *Book Week,* April 19, 1964, July 17, 1966; *New Statesman,* September 25, 1964, November 11, 1966, June 13, 1969, April 16, 1971; *Books and Bookmen,* November, 1968, September, 1969, July, 1974, August, 1979; *Punch,* June 25, 1969; *Observer Review,* July 20, 1969; *Horticulture,* April, 1970, October, 1972; *Library Journal,* July, 1971; *New Yorker,* November 13, 1971, October 22, 1979; *Listener,* August 30, 1973; *Nation,* November 15, 1975; *New York Review of Books,* September 16, 1976.

OBITUARIES: AB Bookmen's Weekly, January 5, 1976.†

I

IDYLL, C(larence) P(urvis) 1916-

PERSONAL: Born February 10, 1916, in Edmonton, Alberta, Canada; son of A. Charles (a salesman) and Annabelle (Purvis) Idyll; married Marion Janet Daniels (a music teacher), June 28, 1941; children: Marilyn Judith (Mrs. Richard Dana Hamly), Janice Leah (Mrs. John Francis Barr III), Jacqueline, Margaret (Mrs. Charles Lee Beem). *Education:* University of British Columbia, B.A. (first class honors), 1938, M.A., 1940; University of Washington, Seattle, Ph.D., 1951. *Religion:* Protestant. *Home:* 9116 Kirkdale Rd., Bethesda, Md. 20817.

CAREER: Biologist, International Pacific Salmon Fisheries Commission, 1941-48; University of Miami, Coral Gables, Fla., assistant professor of zoology, 1948-50, associate professor, 1950-54, professor of marine science, 1948-72, chairman of Division of Fisheries and Estuarine Ecology, Institute of Marine Science, 1964-71; Food and Agriculture of the United Nations, Rome, Italy, fishery research advisor, 1971-74; U.S. Department of Commerce, National Oceanic and Atmospheric Administration, study director of ocean policy, 1974-78, chief of Division of International Fisheries Development and Ser0vices, 1978-80. Gulf Caribbean Fisheries Institute, executive secretary, 1949-58, chairman, 1958-72. Consultant on conservation, government of British Honduras, 1958; consultant to United Nations Development Program, 1963, 1968, and 1969; senior marine advisor to National Advisory Committee on Oceans and Atmosphere, 1980-82.

MEMBER: American Institute of Biological Sciences, Marine Technology Society, American Institute of Fishery Research Biologists, American Institute of Ichthyologists and Herpetologists, American Fisheries Society, American Association for Advancement of Science, Florida Academy of Science, Sigma Xi, Phi Sigma, Friends of the University Library (member of editorial board), Friends of Chamber Music of Miami (vice-president, 1965-72). *Awards, honors:* Conservation award from Florida Wildlife Federation, 1967.

WRITINGS: The Commercial Shrimp Industry of Florida, Marine Laboratory, University of Miami, 1950; (with Charles E. Dawson) *Investigations on the Florida Spiny Lobster, Panulirus argus,* (Florida) State Board of Conservation, 1951; (with William Saenz) *Preliminary Report on the Marine Fisheries of Honduras,* Marine Laboratory, University of Miami, 1957; (with Edwin S. Iversen) *The Tortugas Shrimp Fishery: The Fishing Fleet and Its Method of Operation,* State Board of Conservation, 1959; *Commercial Fishery of St. John, Virgin Islands,* Marine Laboratory, University of Miami, 1959.

(With John E. Randall) *Addendum to Sport and Commercial Fisheries Potential of St. John, Virgin Islands,* Marine Laboratory, University of Miami, 1960; *Abyss: The Deep Sea and the Creatures That Live in It,* Crowell, 1964, 3rd edition, 1976.

(Editor and contributor) *Exploring the Ocean World: A History of Oceanography,* Crowell, 1970, revised edition, 1972; *The Sea Against Hunger: Harvesting the Oceans to Feed a Hungry World,* Crowell, 1970, revised edition, 1978; (editor) *The Science of the Sea: A History of Oceanography,* Crowell, 1970. Contributor to Smithsonian Institution *Annual Report,* 1959, and *Transactions* of American Fisheries Society, 1957, 1960; contributor to encyclopedias, magazines, and professional journals.

WORK IN PROGRESS: A book on migrations of marine animals; scientific and popular articles on marine science.

* * *

IFKOVIC, Edward 1943-

PERSONAL: Born June 16, 1943, in North Branford, Conn.; son of Anthony J. (a pattern maker) and Anna (Farkash) Ifkovic. *Education:* Southern Connecticut State College, B.S. (magna cum laude), 1965; University of North Carolina, M.A., 1966; University of Massachusetts, Ph.D., 1972. *Home:* 462 Broadview Terrace, Hartford, Conn. 06106. *Office:* Department of English, Tunxis Community College, Farmington, Conn. 06032.

CAREER: High school English teacher in Branford, Conn., 1966-69; University of Massachusetts, Amherst, part-time lecturer in English, 1969-72; Tunxis Community College, Farmington, Conn., assistant professor, 1972-74, professor of English, 1974—, chairman of department, 1974-77. Member of World Education Fellowship. *Member:* Modern Language Association of America, Popular Culture Association, Multi-Ethnic Literature in the United States.

WRITINGS: (Editor) *American Letter: Immigrant and Ethnic Writing,* Prentice-Hall, 1975; *The Yugoslavs in America,* Lerner, 1977; *For Love of Country: The Development of an American Identity in the Popular Novel, 1893-1913,* Revisionist Press, 1977; *Anna Marinkovich* (novel), Manyland Books, 1980; *Dream Street: The American Movies and the Popular Imagination,* Revisionist Press, 1980; *Mr. Dooley and Mr. Dunne,*

Revisionist Press, 1982; (editor with Robert Di Pietro) *New Perspectives in American Literature: The European Contribution*, Modern Language Association of America, 1982. Contributor to literary magazines, including *America, Review of Comparative Literature, American Notes and Queries, Journal of Popular Culture, Whitman Review, Crescent Review, Matica,* and *Zajednicar.*

WORK IN PROGRESS: *Suppertime*, a novel.

SIDELIGHTS: Edward Ifkovic writes: "While I was a graduate student I met a woman from Zagreb, Croatia, in Yugoslavia, and she brought me back to my own Croatian roots. Not only did I explore the history of my family in America—dating from grandparents who arrived at Ellis Island around 1907—but I explored the history, literature, and language of the Old Country. In the process I came home to myself as an American with a particular ethnic history.... I saw ethnicity not as a divisive chauvinistic force but, instead, a force that leads out of diversity into unity.... I have been especially excited by the rise of the 'unmelted' white ethnics—the Polish, the Italian, the Jews, etc.—following after the new Black and Red consciousness."

BIOGRAPHICAL/CRITICAL SOURCES: *Library Journal*, June 15, 1981.

* * *

IGNOTUS, Paul 1901-1978

PERSONAL: Given name in Hungarian: Pal; born July 1, 1901, in Budapest, Hungary; naturalized British citizen; died April 1, 1978, in London, England; son of Hugo (a writer) and Johanna (Steinberger) Ignotus; married Olga Florence Matay (a marketing executive), June 22, 1956; children: Paul Imre. *Education:* Attended University of Budapest. *Politics:* Liberal Socialist; supporter of labor movement. *Religion:* "By religion, a Calvinist; by taste, a Catholic; by conviction, an atheist; on top of all, a Jew." *Home:* 33 Prince of Wales Mansions, Prince of Wales Dr., London S.W. 11, England.

CAREER: *Esti Kurir* (daily newspaper), Budapest, Hungary, leader writer, 1923-38; *Szep Szo* (literary magazine), Budapest, founder and co-editor, 1936-38; *Nepszava* (daily newspaper), Budapest, correspondent in London, England, 1939, 1945-47; British Broadcasting Corp., London, intelligence assistant, 1939-45, program assistant, 1945-47; Hungarian Legation, London, press counselor, 1947-49; imprisoned in Hungary as alleged British spy, 1949-56; remained in Hungary as free-lance writer and research fellow of Hungarian Institute of Literary History for six months after release; free-lance writer in London, England, beginning 1957. *Member:* Hungarian Writers' Association (member of Presidential board, 1956; president of association abroad, 1957), P.E.N. (English center), Society of Authors, Societe Europeenne de Culture (British center).

WRITINGS: *Bortonnaplom: Proza Dalban Elbeszelve*, Latohatar (Munich), 1957; *Political Prisoner* (autobiography), Routledge & Kegan Paul, 1959, Macmillan, 1960, revised edition published with epilogue, Collier, 1964; (contributor) George Mikes, editor, *Prison*, Routledge & Kegan Paul, 1963, Horizon, 1964; *The Paradox of Maupassant*, University of London Press, 1967, Funk, 1968; *Hungary*, Praeger, 1972.

Also author of *Czechs, Magyars, Slovaks*, 1969. Author of radio scripts for British Broadcasting Corp. and Voice of America. Contributor to periodicals, including *Encounter, Socialist Commentary, New Statesman, Times Literary Supplement, Political Quarterly,* and *Irodalmi Ujsag* (Paris).

SIDELIGHTS: After the Second World War, Hungarian-born journalist Paul Ignotus, a liberal socialist, decided to collaborate with the new Communist state in Hungary and work as an official press attache in London. Upon returning to Budapest in May of 1949, Ignotus was accused of being a British spy, arrested, and sentenced to fifteen years hard labor for "rehabilitation." During these years in prison, he wrote in his book *Political Prisoner*, he learned it was "comparatively easy under torture to confess lies and conceal the truth." After the Hungarian Revolution of 1956, Ignotus was released from prison and later emigrated to the West to resume, as Robert Ray notes in *Books and Bookmen*, a writing career of "high caliber."

In *Spectator*, T. R. Fyvel says that the "special merit" of Ignotus's prison chronicle is "to throw light on this phase of Communist history from the inside.... Though in parts Mr. Ignotus's story could hardly be more gruesome, it yet has a curious note of hope.... In spite of what happened in ... prison, he is still able to look back on it with human understanding." "The principal value of Mr. Ignotus's book is in its account of how a courageous and resourceful man can endure hunger, torture, and degradation and yet remain indomitably human, able to laugh, retain hope, and resist embitterment," Emanuel Litvinoff asserts in *Guardian*. *Political Prisoner*, Litvinoff concludes, is "a moving affirmation of life in a society which seeks to destroy all that is free, spontaneous, and joyous in the human spirit."

Ignotus once told *CA* that he had decided "to turn away from politics" to concentrate on other subjects. His study of the nineteenth-century French writer Guy de Maupassant and his comprehensive history of Hungary for Benn's Nations of the Modern World series have both drawn critical acclaim. A *Choice* reviewer believes Ignotus's *The Paradox of Maupassant* "has no real equivalent among the various biographical and critical studies of Maupassant.... The book is well documented, well written, and entertaining." And Ray describes *Hungary* as "an extremely engrossing work.... Where Mr. Ignotus comes into his own is the detailed description of [Hungarian] life and values."

BIOGRAPHICAL/CRITICAL SOURCES: *Encounter*, April, 1957; *Time*, June 10, 1957; *Guardian*, October 16, 1959; *Spectator*, October 16, 1959; *Times Literary Supplement*, October 30, 1959, March 30, 1967, February 25, 1972; *New Statesman*, November 7, 1959, June 9, 1967, July 21, 1972; *Canadian Forum*, December, 1959; Paul Ignotus, *Political Prisoner*, Macmillan, 1960; *Foreign Affairs*, January, 1961; *Observer Review*, March 12, 1967; *Choice*, November, 1968, July, 1972; *Books and Bookmen*, April, 1972; *Journal of Modern History*, March, 1973; *Jewish Social Studies*, summer, 1978.

OBITUARIES: *New York Times*, April 2, 1978.†

* * *

INCIARDI, James A(nthony) 1939-

PERSONAL: Born November 28, 1939, in Brooklyn, N.Y.; son of James A. (a physician) and Marie (Craig) Inciardi; married Carolyn Jo Kincaid, June 20, 1975. *Education:* Fordham University, B.S., 1961; New York University, M.A., 1971, Ph.D., 1973. *Office:* Division of Criminal Justice, University of Delaware, Newark, Del. 19711.

CAREER: New York City Department of Welfare, New York City, caseworker, 1961-62; New York State Division of Parole, Special Narcotic Project, New York City, parole officer, 1962-68; New York State Narcotic Addiction Control Commission, New York City, research associate, 1968-70, deputy director of research, 1970-71; Metropolitan Dade County Comprehensive Drug Program, Miami, Fla., associate director of research,

1971-73; University of Miami, School of Medicine, Miami, Division of Addiction Sciences, research associate, 1971-73, project director of National Center for the Study of Acute Drug Reactions, 1975-76, Department of Psychiatry, assistant professor, 1972-73 and 1975-76, Department of Epidemiology and Public Health, adjunct assistant professor, 1973-75; University of Delaware, Division of Criminal Justice, Newark, associate professor, 1976-79, professor, 1979—, director, 1976—.

Therapist in peer groups, New York City Addiction Services Agency, 1966-67, and Daytop Village, Staten Island, N.Y., 1966-68; supportive counselor, New York State Division of Parole, 1966-68; counselor, Alcohol Intervention Program, Wright State University, 1981. Instructor at City College of the City University of New York, 1969, and New York University, 1969-71; faculty member, U.S. Office of Education Regional Drug Abuse Training Program, Miami, 1972-73, and National Institute of Mental Health Drug Abuse Training Center, Miami, 1972-74; visiting professor, Ibero Americana University, 1974, and Pepperdine University, 1975; visiting lecturer, Georgia State University, 1975; adjunct associate professor, Institute for Public Health Research, Antioch College, 1976-77. Resource Planning Corp., Miami, senior associate, 1972-73, vice-president, 1974-75; project director of Metropolitan Dade County Manager's Office, 1974-75; member of National Task Force on Drug Use and Criminal Behavior, U.S. Department of Health, Education and Welfare, 1974-75; National Institute on Drug Abuse, investigator, 1977—, member of Drug Abuse Resource Development Review Committee, 1979-81. Consultant to numerous social service agencies, hospitals, drug addiction, correction, and rehabilitation groups, publishing firms, school systems, Congressional committees, governmental organizations, and police departments. *Member:* American Society of Criminology (member of executive board, 1975-81), American Sociological Association, Alpha Kappa Delta. *Awards, honors:* National Institute on Drug Abuse grants, 1974, 1977-79, 1979-81, and 1982-84.

WRITINGS: (Editor with Carl D. Chambers and contributor) *Drugs and the Criminal Justice System*, Sage Publications, 1974; *Careers in Crime*, Rand McNally, 1975; (with Harvey A. Siegal and Chambers) *Chemical Coping: A Report on Legal Drug Use in the United States*, Spectrum, 1975; (editor with Siegal) *Emerging Social Issues: A Sociological Perspective*, Praeger, 1975; (editor with Siegal) *Crime: Emerging Issues*, Praeger, 1977; (with Alan A. Block and Lyle A. Hallowell) *Historical Approaches to Crime: Research Statistics and Issues*, Sage Publications, 1977.

Reflections on Crime: An Introduction to Criminology and Criminal Justice, Praeger, 1978; (editor with Kenneth C. Haas) *Crime and the Criminal Justice Process*, Kendall/Hunt, 1978; (editor with Anne E. Pottieger) *Violent Crime: Historical and Contemporary Issues*, Sage Publications, 1978; (with Duane C. McBride, Brian R. Russe, Pottieger, and Siegal) *Legal and Illicit Drugs: Acute Reactions of Emergency Room Populations*, Holt, 1978; (editor) *Radical Criminology: The Coming Crises*, Sage Publications, 1980; (editor with Charles E. Faupel) *History and Crime: Implications for Criminal Justice Policy*, Sage Publications, 1980; (editor) *The Drugs-Crime Connection*, Sage Publications, 1981; *Criminal Justice: An Introduction*, Academic Press, in press.

Contributor: (With Daniel Glaser and Dean V. Babst) P. A. Healy and J. P. Manak, editors, *Drug Dependence and Abuse Reference Book*, National District Attorneys Association, 1971; (with Chambers) W. Keup, editor, *Drug Abuse: Current Concepts and Research*, C. C Thomas, 1972; F. Adler and G.O.W. Mueller, editors, *Politics, Crime and the International Scene: An Inter-American Focus*, North-South Center for Technical and Cultural Interchange (Hato Rey, Puerto Rico), 1972; Edward Sagarin and Donald E. J. MacNamara, editors, *Corrections: Problems of Punishment and Rehabilitation*, Praeger, 1973; Leon Brill and Chambers, editors, *Methadone: Experiences and Issues*, Behavioral Publications, 1973.

Glaser, editor, *Handbook of Criminology*, Rand McNally, 1974; (with Chambers) Vernon Shorty, Harold Alksne, and Edward Senay, editors, *Developments in the Field of Drug Abuse*, Schenkman, 1975; Emilio Viano, editor, *Victims and Society*, Visage Press, 1976; Robert S. Weppner, editor, *The Street Ethnography of Crime and Drugs*, Sage Publications, 1977; (with McBride and Pottieger) Daniel J. Lettieri, editor, *Drugs and Suicide: When Other Coping Strategies Fail*, Sage Publications, 1978; Frank R. Scarpitti and Susan K. Datesman, editors, *Drugs and the Youth Culture*, Sage Publications, 1980; Scarpitti and Datesman, editors, *Women, Crime and Criminal Justice*, Oxford University Press, 1980.

Author of eight monographs for governmental organizations. Editor of "Sage Annual Reviews of Drug and Alcohol Abuse" series, Sage Publications, 1976-80, "Sage Research Progress in Criminology" series, Sage Publications, 1976-80, and "Issues and Research in Substance Abuse" series, Praeger, 1979-82.

Contributor to *Encyclopedia of Crime and Justice*, Free Press, 1983. Contributor of articles to professional journals, including *Journal of Research in Crime and Delinquency, Federal Probation, Journal of Drug Issues, Journal of Psychoactive Drugs, International Journal of the Addictions,* and *Victimology: An International Journal;* contributor of book reviews to *Sociology: Reviews of New Books, Contemporary Society, Crime and Delinquency, Journal of Criminal Law and Criminology,* and *Society.* Member of editorial staff, *International Journal of Current Therapeutic and Applied Pharmacology Reviews, International Journal of the Addictions, Society, Criminology, Addictive Diseases, Chemical Dependencies, Social Problems, Crime and Delinquency, Journal of Crime and Delinquency, Review of Public Data Use,* and *Deviant Behavior,* 1972—; editor, *Criminology: An Interdisciplinary Journal,* 1978-81.

* * *

INGLIS, R(obert) M(orton) G(all) 1910-1975

PERSONAL: Born February 6, 1910, in Edinburgh, Scotland; died June, 1975; son of James Gall and Charlotte (Kinmont) Inglis; married Vera Evelyn Murray Johnstone, July 2, 1943; children: Evelyn, Jean. *Education:* Attended Edinburgh Academy, 1920-28. *Home:* 19 Dalrymple Crescent, Edinburgh, Scotland. *Office:* Gall & Inglis, 62 Buckstone Ter., Edinburgh EH10 6RQ, Scotland.

CAREER: Gall & Inglis (publishers), Edinburgh, 1932-75, senior partner, 1939-75, managing director of Gall & Inglis (Reckoners), Ltd., 1964-75. Lay reader, Church of Scotland. *Military service:* British Army, 1943-46; became sergeant. *Member:* British Astronomical Association (president, 1971-73), Edinburgh Astronomical Society, Scottish Mountaineering Club (librarian, 1960; vice-president, 1971-73).

WRITINGS—Published by Gall & Inglis, except as indicated: *Northern and Southern Constellations and How to Find Them,* 1940; *The Presto Decimals of an Hour, and Minutes Calculator,* 1943; *The Swift Specific Gravity Reckoner,* 1948; (with father, James Gall Inglis) *The Express Foreign Exchange Reckoner,* 1948; *The 'Long Range' 40-hour Wages Reckoner,* 1949; (with J. G. Inglis) *The "Express" Profit on Cost and Per-*

centage on Returns Reckoner, 1949; (with J. G. Inglis) *British Weights Expressed in Lbs. and Kilos,* 1949; (with J. G. Inglis) *Easy Guide to the Constellations,* revised edition, 1949.

Popular Star Atlas, 1950, second edition published as *A New Popular Star Atlas,* 1958; *The 'Presto' Purchase Tax Reckoner,* 1950; (general editor) Sir Hugh T. Munro, *Munro's Tables of the 3000-Feet Mountains of Scotland,* 1953; *The Swift Every Farthing Reckoner,* 1954; *The Presto Grosses and Dozens into Units Reckoner,* 1954; *The "Express" Salary, Monthly Wages and Per Hour Wages Reckoner,* 1955; *The 'Presto' Pounds and Ounces Pricing Card,* 1955; *The "Express" Sterling to Dollars Reckoner for American and Canadian Dollars,* 1955; *Decimal Equivalents Reckoner,* 1955; *The Presto Decimals of an Hour and Minutes Calculator,* 1956.

(With Harry Robert Gall Inglis) *Hill Path Contours of the Chief Mountain Passes in Scotland,* 1963, 25th edition, 1975; *The "Express' Universal Decimal Coinage Reckoner,* 1964; (editor) *A Star Atlas and Reference Handbook,* 15th edition, Sky Publishing Corp., 1964; *The 'Ideal' Decimal Coinage Reckoner,* 1966; *Profit Reckoner,* 1967; *The "Express" Dollars Exchange Reckoner,* 1968; *Pocket Pricer for Fixing Selling Prices,* 1969.

The "Express" Decimals of a Penny Reckoner, 1970; *On and Off Cost Percentage Reckoner,* 1970; *Speedy Ready Reckoner,* 1970; *Foreign Exchange Reckoner,* 1971; *The "Express" Unit Cost and Division Reckoner,* 1971; *The Long Range Three Place Decimal Reckoner for Wages and General Calculations,* 1971; *Per Tonne or Per 1000 Kilogram Reckoner,* 1972; *Per Tonne and 1000Kg. to £56 Reckoner,* 1973; *The Long Range 1 to 200% and Per 100 Reckoner,* 1973; (with A. P. Norton and others) *Norton's Star Atlas,* 1973, 17th edition, 1978; *Chrichton's Total Weight Reckoner and Multiplication Tables,* 1974; *Multiplication of Metres Reckoner,* 1975; *The Long Range Superficial Measurement Reckoner for Calculating Areas in Metric Measure,* 1976.

Also reviser and contributor to many other "ready reckoners" published by Gall & Inglis. Editor of "Guidebooks" series for Scottish Mountaineering Club, 1946-59.†

* * *

IYENGAR, K(odaganallur) R(amaswami) Srinivasa 1908-
(Rajaram, R. R.)

PERSONAL: Born April 17, 1908, in Sattur, Tamil Nadu, India; son of Ramaswami (a farmer) and Lakshmi (Ammal) Iyengar; married Padmasani Krishna, March 31, 1930; children: Ambirajan (son), Prema (Mrs. M. S. Nandakumar). *Education:* Attended Hindu College, Tirunelveli, India, 1916-25, and St. Xavier's College, Palamcottah, India, 1925-27; University of Madras, B.A., 1927, M.A., 1932, D.Litt., 1939. *Politics:* Indian Nationalist. *Religion:* Hindu. *Home:* "Matri Bhaven," 152 Kutchery Rd., Mylapore, Madras, Tamil Nadu 600 004, India.

CAREER: Chidambara Vidyalaya, Valvettiturai, Ceylon (now Sri Lanka), teacher of English and mathematics, 1928-31, vice-principal, 1929-31; Lingaraj College, Belgaum, India, assistant professor, 1933-35, professor of English, 1935-44; Basaveshvar College, Bagalkot, India, professor of English and vice-principal, 1944-47; Andhra University, Waltair, India, professor of English, 1947-61, president of Faculty of Arts, 1961-66, vice-chancellor, 1966-68; Sahitya Akademi (National Academy of Letters), New Delhi, India, vice-president, 1969-77, acting president, 1977-78; Indian Institute of Advanced Study, Simla, India, member of governing body, 1970-79. Visiting professor, University of Leeds, 1959; lecturer at Puri College, Parlakimedi College, Balasore College, Balangir College, and Annamalai University; lecturer on literary subjects, A.I.R. radio stations. Delegate, World P.E.N. Congress and UNESCO Symposium, Tokyo and Kyoto, 1957, and World Conference on Religion and Peace, Belgium, 1974. Member of governing body, Central Institute of English and Foreign Languages, Hyderabad, 1970-74, 1977—. Spiritual advisor to Sri Aurobindo Ashram, New Delhi, 1969—.

MEMBER: International Association of University Professors of English, P.E.N. (executive member of All-India Centre, 1944-47, 1951-57), Association of Commonwealth Literature and Languages Studies, National Council of Educational Research and Training, All-India English Teachers Conference (president, 1963), Indian Association for English Studies (life member; president, 1963), Sri Aurobindo Society (member of executive council, 1977—), Eighteen Nineties Society (vice-president, 1963—), Andhra English Teachers Conference (president, 1950). *Awards, honors:* D.Litt., Andhra University, 1978, and Sri Venkateswara University, 1982; Sahitya Akademi (National Academy of Letters) Award for most outstanding work in English published during 1978-80, 1978, for *On the Mother: The Chronicle of a Manifestation and a Ministry.*

WRITINGS: Lytton Strachey: A Critical Study, Chatto & Windus, 1938, Kennikat, 1967; (with S. S. Basawanal) *A Handbook of Indian Administration,* Karnatak Publishing House (Bombay), 1939; *S. Srinivasa Iyengar: The Story of a Decade of Indian Politics,* Basel Mission Press, 1939; *Indo-Anglian Literature,* P.E.N. (Bombay), 1943; *Literature and Authorship in India,* Allen & Unwin, 1943; *Sri Aurobindo: A Biography and a History,* Arya Publishing House, 1945, 3rd edition published in two volumes, Sri Aurobindo International Centre of Education (Pondicherry), 1972; *On Beauty,* Padmaja Publications (Baroda), 1945; *The Indian Contribution to English Literature,* Karnatak Publishing House, 1945; *Gerard Manley Hopkins: The Man and the Poet,* Oxford University Press, 1948, reprinted, Norwood, 1977; *A New Deal for Our Universities,* Orient Longmans, Green (Calcutta), 1951; *On the Mother,* Sri Aurobindo Ashram (Pondicherry), 1952, 2nd edition published as *On the Mother: A Chronicle of a Manifestation and a Ministry,* two volumes, Sri Aurobindo International Centre of Education, 1978, Auromere, 1979; *A Jubilee Miscellany,* Porunai, 1954; *The Mind and Heart of Britain,* Orient Longmans, Green, 1955.

Indian Writing in English, Asia Publishing House, 1962, 3rd edition, Sterling Publishers (New Delhi), 1982; *The Adventure of Criticism,* Asia Publishing House, 1962; *Francois Mauriac: Novelist and Moralist,* Asia Publishing House, 1964; *Shakespeare: His World and His Art,* Asia Publishing House, 1964; (with others) *Shakespeare Number,* Sahitya Akademi (New Delhi), 1964; *Rabindranath Tagore,* Popular Prakashan (Bombay), 1965; (with Prema Nandakumar) *Introduction to the Study of English Literature,* Asia Publishing House, 1967, 2nd edition, 1969; *Education and the New India,* Prasaranga (Mysore), 1968; *Mainly Academic: Talks to Students and Teachers,* Asia Publishing House, 1968; *Two Cheers for the Commonwealth: Talks on Literature and Education,* Asia Publishing House, 1969; *A Big Change: Talks on the Spiritual Revolution and the Future of Man,* Sri Aurobindo Ashram, 1971; *Tryst with the Divine,* Sabda (Pondicherry), 1974; *Dawn to Greater Dawn: Six Lectures on Sri Aurobindo's Savitri,* Indian Institute of Advanced Study (Simla), 1975; *Sri Aurobindo's World-Vision,* Bombay University Press, 1976; *Microcosmographia Poetica,* Writers Workshop (Calcutta), 1976; *Religion, Peace and a*

World Community, WCRP Madras, 1978; *Leaves from a Log: Fragments of a Journey,* Heinemann, 1979; *Religion and Social Concern,* Parichay Trust, 1981.

Editor: John Dryden, *Absalom and Achitopel,* Karnatak Publishing House, 1943; William Congreve, *The Way of the World,* Karnatak Publishing House, 1943; Samuel Taylor Coleridge, *Christabel,* Educational Publishing House, 1944; *Indian Writers in Council,* International Book House, 1947; Henry David Thoreau, *Walden,* Andhra University Press, 1953; (with C. B. Young) *Standard English Poems,* Oxford University Press, 1955; (and author of introduction) *Drama in Modern India and the Writer's Responsibility in a Rapidly Changing World,* P.E.N. (Bombay), 1961; (and author of introduction) Cattamanchi Ramalinga Reddy, *Essays and Addresses,* Andhra University Press, 1966; (and author of introduction) *Indian Literature since Independence,* Sahitya Akademi, 1973; (and author of introduction) *Guru Nanak: A Homage,* Sahitya Akademi, 1973; (and author of introduction) *Sri Aurobindo: A Homage,* Sri Aurobindo Ashram, 1974.

Other: (Translator with S. S. Basawanal and co-author of introduction) Basava, *The Musings of Basava: A Free Rendering,* Basel Mission Press, 1940. Also author of a novella, "Topsy Turvy"; author of plays, including "Suniti and Her Spouse," "The Battle of the Optionals," "The Beast of Berlin," and "The Education of Dina Cockroach"; author of a biography of Sardar Raja Lakhamagauda Basawaprabhu; translator of Sankaracharya's *Atma Bodha;* translator from the Tamil of selections from *Tirumandirum* and *Tiru-Arutpa;* translator from the Sanskrit of selections from *Devi Mahatmyam* and *Sundara Kanda* written by Valmiki Ramayana.

Contributor to encyclopedias, including *New Encyclopaedia of Catholic Literature on Indian Writing, Encyclopaedia of World Literature, Contemporary Indian Literature,* and *History and Culture of the Indian People;* contributor to commemoration volume presented to Sardar Raja Lakhamagauda Basawaprabhu, 1941. Contributor, sometimes under pseudonyms Rajaram and R. R., of poems, short stories, articles, and reviews to periodicals, including *Human Affairs, Hindu, Indian Express, Indian Literature, Mother India,* and *Illustrated Weekly.* Member of editorial board, *Indian Journal of English Studies,* and *Shakespeare Quarterly*'s annual Shakespeare bibliography.

WORK IN PROGRESS: Australia Helix, a collection of "verse sequences" recording impressions of a visit to Australia; revising a poem, "Zero Hour," for publication in a new volume of poetry; English verse rendering from the Sanskrit of part of "India's supreme national epic," the *Ramayana* of Valmiki; English verse translation from the Tamil of *Tirukkural.*

SIDELIGHTS: K. R. Srinivasa Iyengar has earned praise for his professional activities in India. As the first professor of English at Andhra University, he founded the university's School of English Studies and introduced to Indian scholars new areas of investigation, including Indo-Anglian literature, American literature, and Commonwealth literature. During his brief tenure as vice-chancellor at Andhra University, he started the Postgraduate Center in Guntar which later became Nagarjuna University.

Iyengar told *CA* that although he has retired from active participation in academic life, he still occasionally gives talks and lectures. Currently, he is very interested in participating in inter-religious dialogues and expresses concern about the armament race.

BIOGRAPHICAL/CRITICAL SOURCES: Indian P.E.N., 1969; M. K. Naik, editor, *Aspects of Indian Writing in English: Essays in Honour of Professor K. R. Srinivasa Iyengar,* Macmillan (New Delhi), 1979.

J

JACKSON, Basil 1920-

PERSONAL: Born April 3, 1920, in Swansea, Wales; emigrated to Canada in 1948; son of Harry and Pauline (Zeltzer) Jackson; divorced; children: Pauline, David. *Education:* Attended Merchant Venturers' Technical College, University of Bristol. *Home:* 216-8040 Blundell Rd., Richmond, British Columbia, Canada.

CAREER: Bristol Aeroplane Co. (now British Aircraft Corp.), Bristol, England, plant errand boy, rivet sorter, and airframe assembler, 1937-39; Fairey Aviation Co., London, England, draftsman, 1939-46; Airspeed Ltd. (aircraft engineering firm), London, senior design draftsman, 1946-48; technical writer, de Havilland Aircraft Co., and A. V. Roe of Canada Ltd., 1948-61; *Financial Post,* Toronto, Ontario, science editor, 1961—. *Member:* Authors League (New York), Royal Aeronautical Society (London; associate member).

WRITINGS—Novels; all published by Norton: *Epicenter,* 1971; *Rage under the Arctic,* 1974; *Supersonic,* 1975; *Flameout,* 1976; *The Night Manhattan Burned,* 1979; *State of Emergency,* 1982.

WORK IN PROGRESS: A novel.

SIDELIGHTS: Basil Jackson told *CA:* "Most of my novels (which are *not* science fiction) are based on the philosophy that however cleverly a high-technology product is made and tested, the human element often leads to disaster, e.g., Apollo 13 didn't make it to the moon because someone on the ground, during a routine test, plugged in a 56 volt input instead of 28 volts. As a result Apollo's oxygen tank leaked and set off a chain of events that nearly caused the deaths of the three astronauts."

Jackson's novels have been translated into Japanese, Swedish, and Norwegian.

* * *

JACKSON, (William) Keith 1928-

PERSONAL: Born September 5, 1928, in Colchester, Essex, England; son of William James (a businessman) and Alice Beatrice (Hill) Jackson; married Mary Diane Robertson, January 18, 1960 (separated, 1980); children: Benjamin Giles, Nigel James, Matthew Guy. *Education:* University of Nottingham, B.A., (with first class honors), 1952; University of Otago, Ph.D., 1967. *Home:* 92 Hinau St., Christchurch, New Zealand. *Office:* Department of Political Science, University of Canterbury, Christchurch, New Zealand.

CAREER: J. & P. Coats, Glasgow, Scotland, management trainee, 1954-55; Ministry of Defense, London, England, research officer, 1955-56; University of Otago, Dunedin, New Zealand, assistant lecturer, 1956-58, lecturer, 1959-62, senior lecturer in political science, 1963-67; University of Canterbury, Christchurch, New Zealand, professor of political science, 1967—, head of department, 1967-80. Lecturer, Radio New Zealand. Election planning consultant. *Military service:* Royal Air Force, 1945-47. *Member:* New Zealand Institute of International Affairs, New Zealand Political Studies Association, New Zealand Institute of Public Administration, New Zealand Historical Association, Australasian Political Science Society. *Awards, honors:* Mobil Award, Radio New Zealand, 1979, for best spoken current affairs program.

WRITINGS: (With Austin V. Mitchell and Robert M. Chapman) *New Zealand: Politics in Action,* Oxford University Press, 1962; (with John Harre) *New Zealand,* Walker & Co., 1969; (editor) *Fight for Life: New Zealand, Britain, and the European Economic Community,* New Zealand Institute of International Affairs, 1971; *New Zealand Legislative Council,* University of Otago Press and University of Toronto Press, 1972; *New Zealand: Politics of Change,* Reed, 1973; (editor with John Henderson and Richard Kennaway) *Beyond New Zealand: The Foreign Policy of a Small State,* Metheun, 1980; (contributor) H. Penniman, editor, *New Zealand at the Polls II,* American Enterprise Institute, 1983.

Author of political commentaries for Radio New Zealand and New Zealand Television. Contributor to professional journals. Editorial advisor to *Journal of Commonwealth and Comparative Politics* (formerly *Journal of Commonwealth Political Studies*), 1972—, *Political Science,* 1975—, and *Politics,* 1981—.

WORK IN PROGRESS: Research on various aspects of New Zealand political parties; a comparative study of the New Zealand Parliament, "with a view to assessing its adequacy to meet modern-day needs."

SIDELIGHTS: Keith Jackson writes to *CA:* "Having emigrated to New Zealand, I have become absorbed by small nations, laboratory-scale politics, and the belated but rapid evolution of New Zealand self-consciousness in the context of the just-emerging Pacific Basin. New Zealand has proven an ideal nation in which to bring up children and practice the craft of political science."

"New Zealand provides in microcosm many of the problems which currently concern much larger countries—labour, environment, race and development. It is a nation which falls between the developed and underdeveloped and for these reasons has a fascination all its own. But in addition it has undergone in the past twenty years a transformation which amounts to a decolonisation process. My writings have been concerned with aspects of these changes in both the domestic and international spheres.

"My writing career is essentially a pleasurable aspect of my work as a university teacher. It began after I arrived in New Zealand and was struck by the fact that a separate system of representation existed for the Maori race and that the upper house of Parliament had been abolished by a conservative rather than a radical government. These practical problems started my writing career. I write mainly to satisfy my curiosity, but growingly over the years I have also found myself writing books to fill specific gaps—to meet the needs of students. The topic, however, must be something that interests me. Too many political scientists, I believe, tend towards the esoteric—towards jargon and dullness. I suppose that I am a frustrated novelist—a person who lacks the time and confidence to become a true writer."

BIOGRAPHICAL/CRITICAL SOURCES: *Best Sellers,* November 1, 1969; *Christian Science Monitor,* November 28, 1969; *Current History,* April, 1970; *Booklist,* April 1, 1970; *Pacific Affairs,* fall, 1971.

* * *

JACOBSON, Nolan Pliny 1909-

PERSONAL: Born March 27, 1909, in Hudson, Wis.; son of Jacob Albert and Lena (Engen) Jacobson; married Grace Webb (a teacher), November 24, 1939; children: Albert Page, Susan Faye. *Education:* Attended University of Wisconsin, 1930-32; Emory University, A.B., 1940, B.D., 1942; University of Chicago, Ph.D., 1946. *Home:* 812 South Laurel Ave., Adel, Ga. 31620.

CAREER: Huntingdon College, Montgomery, Ala., professor of philosophy, 1946-49; University of Oregon, Eugene, interim head of department of religion, 1949-51; University of Florida, Gainesville, associate professor of religion, 1951-54; Winthrop College, Rock Hill, S.C., professor of philosophy, 1954-74, distinguished professor, 1962-63, chairman of department, 1954-74. Summer visiting professor at Emory University, 1948, and University of Denver, 1957; lecturer at University of Florida, 1961; visiting professor, Queens College, Charlotte, N.C., 1974-79. *Military service:* U.S. Navy, chaplain, 1943-46; participated in invasion of Okinawa.

MEMBER: International Association of Buddhist Studies, Association For Asian Studies, American Philosophical Association, Society for Asian and Comparative Philosophy, Societe Europeenne de Culture, Philosophy of Education Society (past president, Southeastern region), Southern Society for Philosophy of Religion (past president), South Carolina Philosophy Society (past president), South Carolina Committee for Non-Western Studies (chairman), Phi Kappa Phi, Phi Sigma Tau. *Awards, honors:* Ford Foundation grant for research at International Institute for Advanced Buddhistic Studies, Rangoon, Burma, 1961-62; Swearinger grant for study in Japan, 1972.

WRITINGS: (Contributor) John Nordskog, editor, *Social Change,* University of Southern California Press and McGraw, 1960; *Buddhism: The Religion of Analysis,* Allen & Unwin, 1966, Southern Illinois University Press, 1970; (contributor) Nicholas Steneck, editor, *Science and Society: Past, Present and Future,* University of Michigan Press, 1975; *Nihon-do: The Japan Way,* Risosha (Tokyo), 1977; *Life Sciences in an Oriental Culture,* Kyoritsu-Shuppan (Tokyo), 1977; *Buddhism in the Contemporary World: Change and Self-Correction,* Southern Illinois University Press, 1982. Contributor of essay to souvenir volume presented to President Radhakrishnan of India on his sixty-seventh birthday, 1965. Contributor to professional journals in India, France, Mexico, England, the United States, and Japan.

WORK IN PROGRESS: *The Politics of Aesthetic Power: The Deep Heart of Japan.*

SIDELIGHTS: Nolan Pliny Jacobson told *CA:* "It is easier for me to be published in Japanese. In the deeper life-commitments about which I write, American thinking is as slow to change as the weathering of rock. The Japanese are more flexible, leaning out of their own culture to learn other options from the community of humankind."

* * *

JAGER, Okke 1928-

PERSONAL: Born April 23, 1928, in Delft, The Netherlands; son of Johann Coenraad (a surveyor) and Anna Wouterina (Wingerden) Jager; married Antje Lagerwerf, October 1, 1952; children: Ruth, Judith, Job. *Education:* Free University of Amsterdam, D.D., 1962. *Religion:* Reformed Church. *Home:* Jacob Catsstraat 433, Kampen, The Netherlands.

CAREER: Clergyman in The Netherlands, in Vrouwenpolder, 1952-56, Almelo, 1956-60, and Haarlem, 1960-65; broadcaster of religious radio and television, Hilversum, The Netherlands, 1965-73; Theological University, Kampen, The Netherlands, teacher, 1973—. *Member:* Society of Dutch Literature.

WRITINGS: *Poezie en religie* (title means "Poetry and Religion"), Zomer & Keuning (Wageningen, The Netherlands), 1952; *Feest op feest* (title means "Feast after Feast"), Zomer & Keuning, 1956; *Interview met de tijdgeest* (title means "Interview of the Spirit of the Times"), J. H. Kok (Kampen, The Netherlands), 1956; *Worden als een kind* (title means "To Become Like a Child"), J. H. Kok, 1956; *Jeugd en evangelie* (title means "Youth and Gospel"), Zomer & Keuning, 1957; *Op de man af* (title means "Straight from the Shoulder"), J. H. Kok, 1958; *De humor van de Bijbel in het Christelijk leven* (title means "The Humor of the Bible"), J. H. Kok, 1958; *Uw wil geschiede,* Bosch & Keuning, 1958, translation by M. E. Osterhaven published as *What Does God Want, Anyway?,* Judson, 1972; *Kom haastig! Gedichten over de wederkomst van Jezus* (poetry; title means "The Come-back of Jesus"), J. H. Kok, 1959; *Zegen u zelf: Tien radio-spreken* (sermons; title means "Bless Yourself"), J. H. Kok, 1959.

Parade of paradijs (title means "Parade or Paradise"), J. H. Kok, 1960; *Wij mogen van geluk spreken* (title means "Happiness for Us"), Zomer & Keuning, 1961; *Het eeuwige leven: Met name in verband met de verhouding van tijd en eeuwigheid* (title means "The Everlasting Life: Time and Eternity"), J. H. Kok, 1962; *Achter een glimlach* (title means "Behind a Smile"), J. H. Kok, 1964; *Een groene pasen* (title means "Green Easter"), Zomer & Keuning, 1964; *Geloven na kerktijd: Een nieuwe bundel televisie-dagsluitingen* (title means "Belief After Church Hours"), Zomer & Keuning, 1965; *Daglicht: Bijbels dagboek* (title means "Daylight: Exegesis"), J. H. Kok, 1967; *Eigentijdse verkondiging: Beschouwingen over de vertolking van het Evangelie in het taaleigen van der moderne mens* (title means

"Timely Preaching of the Gospel for Modern Man"), J. H. Kok, 1967; *Een witte kerst* (title means "White Christmas"), Zomer & Keuning, 1968; *Het klagen wordt gezang* (title means "Topics of the Church"), J. H. Kok, 1969; *Land van Jahwe* (title means "Land of Jahwe"), Zomer & Keuning, 1969; *Om razend te worden* (title means "It's Enough to Drive You Mad"), J. H. Kok, 1969.

Liefde doet wonderen (title means "Love Does Wonders"), Zomer & Keuning, 1970; *Hoedjes met voetjes* (title means "Ironical Stories"), J. H. Kok, 1970; *Verkondiging en massamedia* (title means "Preaching and Mass Media"), J. H. Kok, 1971; *Binnenpretjen om buitenbeentjes* (title means "Personalities of Television"), J. H. Kok, 1971; *Kruisweg* (title means "Via Dolorosa"), Zomer & Keuning, 1972; *Baas boven buis* (title means "Television: Theory and Practice"), J. H. Kok, 1973; *Bevrijde tijd* (title means "To a Culture of Leisure"), Zomer & Keuning, 1974; *Schrale troost im magere jaren: Theologische kritiek in maatschelijke krisse*, Ten Have (Baarn, The Netherlands), 1976; *Een tijd van twijfel: Preken over levensvargen*, J. H. Kok, 1977; *Wij zijn niet machteloos: Een tijdsbeeld met tegenwicht*, Ten Have, 1978.

Opklaring: Bijbellezen met verbeelding skracht, Zomer & Keuning (Ede, The Netherlands), 1980; *Het andere in het eendere: Over het denken van Cornelis Verhoeven*, Ambo (Baarn), 1982. Contributor to journals and periodicals.

* * *

JANIS, Irving L(ester) 1918-

PERSONAL: Born May 26, 1918, in Buffalo, N.Y.; son of M. Martin (in shoe business) and Etta (Goldstein) Janis; married Marjorie Graham (a research associate in child psychology), September 5, 1939; children: Cathy Janis Wheeler, Charlotte Janis Mervin. *Education:* University of Chicago, B.S., 1939, graduate study, 1939-40; Columbia University, Ph.D., 1948; New York Psychoanalytic Institute, postdoctoral study, 1948-53. *Home:* 1205 Race Brook Rd., Woodbridge, Conn. 06525. *Office address:* Department of Psychology, Yale University, Box 11A, Yale Station, New Haven, Conn. 06520.

CAREER: Library of Congress, Washington, D.C., research assistant, 1941; U.S. Department of Justice, Washington, D.C., senior social science analyst, 1941-43; Social Science Research Council, New York, N.Y., research associate, 1945-46, research fellow, 1946-47; Yale University, New Haven, Conn., assistant professor, 1947-51, associate professor, 1951-60, professor of psychology, 1960—. Participant in research panels of the National Science Foundation and National Institute of Mental Health. Research consultant, RAND Corp., 1948-60; member of Surgeon General's Scientific Advisory Committee on the Social Effects of Technology, 1969-72. *Military service:* U.S. Army, Research Branch, 1943-45.

MEMBER: American Psychological Association (fellow; chairman of committee on psychology in national and international affairs, 1965-66), American Association for the Advancement of Science (representative on council, 1965-70), American Academy of Arts and Sciences, Academy of Behavioral Medicine Research.

AWARDS, HONORS: Ford Foundation research grant, 1956; Fulbright research award to University of Oslo, 1957-58; Hofheimer Prize, American Psychiatric Association, 1959, for outstanding contribution in field of psychiatry and mental hygiene; faculty fellowships from Yale University and Social Science Research Council, 1961-62 and 1966-67, for research at Tavistock Clinic and Institute, London, England, and from Social Science Research Council, 1966-67, for research at La Jolla, Calif.; Socio-Psychological Prize, American Association for the Advancement of Science, 1967; Guggenheim fellow, 1973-74; Center for Advanced Study in the Behavioral Sciences fellow, 1973-74; Distinguished Scientific Contributions Award, American Psychological Association, 1981; Netherlands Institute for Advanced Study fellow, 1981-82.

WRITINGS: Air War and Emotional Stress: Psychological Studies of Bombing and Civilian Defense, McGraw, 1951; (with C. I. Hovland and H. H. Kelley) *Communication and Persuasion: Psychological Studies of Opinion Change*, Yale University Press, 1953; *Psychological Effects of Atomic Disasters*, Industrial College of the Armed Forces, 1954; *Psychological Stress*, Wiley, 1958; (editor with Hovland) *Personality and Persuasibility*, Yale University Press, 1959; (editor) *Personality: Dynamics, Development, and Assessment*, Harcourt, 1969; *Stress and Frustration*, Harcourt, 1971; *Victims of Groupthink: A Psychological Study of Foreign Policy Decisions and Fiascoes*, Houghton, 1972; (with L. Mann) *Decision-Making: A Psychological Analysis of Conflict, Choice, and Commitment*, Free Press, 1977; (editor) *Current Trends in Psychology: Readings from American Scientist*, William Kaufmann, 1977; (with D. Wheeler) *A Practical Guide for Making Decisions*, Free Press, 1980; (with others) *Counseling on Personal Decisions: Theory and Research on Short-Term Helping Relationships*, Yale University Press, 1981.

Contributor: S. Stouffer and others, editors, *The American Soldier: Combat and Its Aftermath*, Princeton University Press, 1949; Harold D. Lasswell and N. C. Leites, editors, *Language of Politics: Studies in Quantitative Semantics*, George W. Stewart, 1949; D. Katz and others, editors, *Public Opinion and Propaganda: A Book of Readings*, Dryden, 1954; (with R. L. Feierabend) Hovland, editor, *The Order of Presentation in Persuasion*, Yale University Press, 1957; E. E. Maccoby, T. M. Newcomb, and E. L. Hartley, editors, *Readings in Social Psychology*, 3rd edition (Janis was not associated with earlier editions), Holt, 1958; W. Muensterberger and S. Axelrad, editors, *Psychoanalysis and the Social Sciences*, Volume V, International Universities, 1958; G. Lindzey, editor, *Assessment of Human Motives*, Holt, 1958; M. R. Jones, editor, *Nebraska Symposium on Motivation*, University of Nebraska Press, 1959.

D. Chapman and G. Baker, editors, *Man and Society in Disaster*, Basic Books, 1962; W. Schramm, editor, *The Science of Human Communications*, Basic Books, 1963; (with others) J. Yudkin and J. McKenzie, editors, *Changing Food Habits*, MacGibbon & Kee, 1964; (with H. Leventhal) B. Wolman, editor, *Handbook of Clinical Psychology*, McGraw, 1965; S. Klausner, editor, *The Quest for Self Control*, Free Press, 1965; (with M. B. Smith) H. Kelman, editor, *International Behavior*, Holt, 1965; (with Leventhal) E. Borgatta and W. W. Lambert, editors, *Handbook of Personality Theory and Research*, Rand McNally, 1967; L. Berkowitz, editor, *Advances in Experimental Social Psychology*, Academic Press, 1967; D. Cartwright and A. Zander, editors, *Group Dynamics: Research and Theory*, 3rd edition (Janis was not associated with earlier editions), Harper, 1968; R. P. Abelson and others, editors, *Theories of Cognitive Consistency: A Sourcebook*, Rand McNally, 1968; (with L. Mann) A. Greenwald, T. Brock, and T. Ostrom, editors, *Psychological Foundations of Attitudes*, Academic Press, 1968; F. Redlich, editor, *Social Psychiatry*, Association for Research in Nervous and Mental Disease (New York), 1969.

N. Sanford and C. Comstock, editors, *Sanctions for Evil: Sources of Destructiveness*, Jossey-Bass, 1971; D. A. Hamburg and C. V. Coelho, editors, *Coping and Adaptation*, Academic Press, 1974; M. Deutsch and H. Hornstein, editors, *Problems of Ap-*

plying Social Psychology, Erlbaum (Hillsdale, N.J.), 1975; R. S. Lazurus, editor, Clues to the Riddle of Man, Prentice-Hall, 1975; S. S. Nagel, editor, Policy Studies and the Social Sciences, Heath, 1975; J. Howard and A. Strauss, editors, Humanizing Health Care, Wiley, 1976; (with J. Rodin) G. C. Stone, F. Cohen, and N. E. Adler, editors, Health Psychology, Jossey-Bass, 1979.

R. I. Evans, The Making of Social Psychology: Discussions with Creative Contributors, Gardner Press, 1980; H. Brandstetter, J. Davis, and C. Stocker-Kreichgauer, editors, Group Decision Making, Academic Press, 1981; S. Breznitz, editor, Stress and Denial, Plenum, in press; P. Defares, C. Spielberger, and I. Sarason, editors, Stress and Anxiety, Wiley, in press; D. Meichenbaum and M. Jaremko, editors, Stress Prevention and Management: A Cognitive-Behavioral Approach, Plenum, in press; D. Gentry, editor, Handbook of Behavioral Medicine, Guilford Press, in press; L. Goldberger and Breznitz, editors, Handbook of Stress, Free Press, in press; H. H. Blumberg and P. Hare, editors, Small Groups, Wiley, in press; (with P. Grossman and Defares) H. Selye, editor, Selye's Guide to Stress Research, Volume III, Van Nostrand, in press; (with L. Mann) N. Feather, editor, Expectations and Action: Expectancy-Value Models in Psychology, Erlbaum, in press; (with Mann) D. Johnson and D. Tjosvold, editors, Conflicts in Organizations, Irvington, in press; (with Rodin) H. S. Friedman and M. R. DiMatteo, editors, Interpersonal Issues and Health Care, Academic Press, in press.

Also author of seven government reports on social psychological surveys. Also contributor to Science and Social Structure: A Festschrift for Robert K. Merton, edited by T. F. Gieryn, New York Academy of Sciences; contributor to proceedings of XV International Congress of Psychology, Amsterdam, 1957, and of XVIII International Congress of Psychology, Moscow, 1966; contributor to International Encyclopedia of the Social Sciences, Macmillan, 1968. Contributor of more than fifty articles and research papers to professional journals, including Journal of Experimental Psychology, Public Opinion Quarterly, Psychometrika, Psychiatry, Journal of Personality, and Journal of Nervous and Mental Diseases. Former member of editorial board, American Scientist; associate editor, Sociometry, 1955-58; consulting editor, Journal of Abnormal and Social Psychology, 1955-65, Journal of Experimental Social Psychology, 1966-70, and Journal of Behavioral Medicine; chairman of editorial board, Journal of Conflict Resolution.

WORK IN PROGRESS: Stress, Attitudes, and Decisions: Selected Papers.

BIOGRAPHICAL/CRITICAL SOURCES: American Psychologist, January, 1982.

* * *

JANNER, Greville Ewan 1928-
(Ewan Mitchell)

PERSONAL: Born July 11, 1928, in Cardiff, South Wales; son of Lord Barnett (a solicitor and former member of Parliament) and Lady Elsie (Cohen) Janner; married Myra Louise Sheink, July 6, 1955; children: Daniel Joseph Mitchell, Marion Juliette, Laura Naomi. Education: Trinity Hall, Cambridge, M.A., 1952; Harvard University, graduate study in law, 1952-53. Politics: Labour. Religion: Jewish. Home: 2 Linnell Dr., London N.W.11, England. Agent: Winant Towers Ltd., Clerkenwell House, 45-47 Clerkenwell Green, London EC1R 0HT, England. Office: 1 Garden Ct. Temple, London E.C.4, England.

CAREER: Admitted to bar, 1954; Member of Parliament for Leicester West, 1970—; Queen's Counsel, 1971—. President of Board of Deputies of British Jews and of Association for British Youth. Military service: British Army, 1946-48; became sergeant. Member: National Union of Journalists (England), Society of Labour Lawyers, Fabian Society.

WRITINGS—Published by Business Books, except as indicated: Janner's Product Liability, 1979; Janner's Employment Forms, 1979; Janner's Compendium of Employment Law, 1979.

All under pseudonym Ewan Mitchell: The Businessman's Lawyer and Legal Lexicon, Business Publications, 1962, 2nd edition, 1965, portion published as The Businessman's Legal Lexicon, 1970; Farming and the Law, Farming Press, 1962; The Lawyer and His World, Gollancz, 1963; All You Need to Know about the Law, New English Library, 1963; The Retailer's Lawyer, Business Publications, 1963; Motorists—Know Your Law, Newnes, 1964; The Personnel Manager's Lawyer and Employer's Guide to the Law, Business Publications, 1964, 2nd edition, 1967; Your Office and the Law, Business Publications, 1964; You and the Law: A Guide for Young People, Parrish, 1964; Your Factory and the Law, Business Publications, 1966, 2nd edition, 1969; The Sales Executive's Lawyer and Businessman's Guide to the Laws of Buying and Selling, Business Publications, 1966; Your Property and the Law and Investor's Legal Guide, Business Publications, 1967; The Businessman's Guide to Speech-Making and to the Laws and Conduct of Meetings, 1968; The Director's Lawyer and Company Secretary's Legal Guide, 1968, 2nd edition, 1972; Coping with Crime, 1969.

The Executive's Guide to Successful Speechmaking, Vertex Books, 1970; Letters of the Law: The Businessman's Encyclopedia of Draft Letters with Legal Implications, 1970; The Businessman's Guide to Letter-Writing and to the Law on Letters, 1970; The Employer's Lawyer, 1971; The Business and Professional Man's Lawyer, 1971, 2nd edition, 1973; The Businessman's Guide to Travel and to Profits Abroad, 1971; Letters of Industrial Law: The Executive's Practical Guide to the Industrial Relations Act, 1972; The Businessman's Guide to Commercial Conduct and the Law, 1972; The Merchandiser's Lawyer, 1974; The Director's and Company Secretary's Handbook of Draft Contract Letters, 1975; The Director's and Company Secretary's Handbook of Draft Legal Letters, 1975; The Employer's Guide to the Law on Health, Safety, and Welfare at Work, 1975, 2nd edition, 1977; The Transport Manager's Lawyer and Transport Operator's Legal Guide, 1975; The Employer's Guide to the Law on Employment Protection and Sex and Race Discrimination, 1976; The Businessman's Guide to Speech Making and to the Laws and Conduct of Meetings, 1977.

Also author of Janner's Complete Speechmaker and RAC Motorist's Lawyer. Contributor of regular columns to Daily Mail, Building Design, Pulse, and Estates Times. Contributor of articles to other journals.

SIDELIGHTS: Greville Ewan Janner speaks French, Spanish, Hebrew, Yiddish, German, Italian and is learning Russian.

* * *

JASNER, W. K.
See WATSON, Jane Werner

* * *

JENNINGS, Elizabeth (Joan) 1926-

PERSONAL: Born July 18, 1926, in Boston, Lincolnshire, England; daughter of Henry Cecil Jennings (a physician). Education: St. Annes College, Oxford, M.A. (with honors). Religion: Roman Catholic. *Home:* 11 Winchester Rd., Oxford OX2 6NA, England. *Agent:* David Higham Associates Ltd., 5-8 Lower John St., Golden Square, London W1R 4HA, England.

CAREER: Oxford City Library, Oxford, England, assistant, 1950-58; Chatto & Windus (publishing firm), London, England, reader, 1958-60; poet and free-lance writer, 1961—. Guildersleeve Lecturer, Barnard College, Columbia University, 1974. *Member:* Society of Authors. *Awards, honors:* Arts Council award, 1953, for *Poems;* Somerset Maugham Award, 1956, for *A Way of Looking;* Arts Council bursary, 1965 and 1968; Richard Hillary Memorial Prize, 1966, for *The Mind Has Mountains;* Arts Council grant, 1972.

WRITINGS: Poems, Fantasy Press, 1953; *A Way of Looking: Poems,* Deutsch, 1955, Rinehart, 1956; (editor with Dannie Abse and Stephen Spender) *New Poems 1956: A P.E.N. Anthology,* M. Joseph, 1956; *A Child and the Seashell,* Poems in Folio, 1957; (editor) *The Batsford Book of Children's Verse,* Batsford, 1958; *A Sense of the World: Poems,* Deutsch, 1958, Rinehart, 1959; *Let's Have Some Poetry,* Museum Press, 1960; *Song for a Birth or a Death and Other Poems,* Deutsch, 1961, Dufour, 1962; (editor) *An Anthology of Modern Verse, 1940-60,* Metheun, 1961; *Every Changing Shape,* Deutsch, 1961; *Poetry Today,* Longmans, Green, 1961; (translator) *The Sonnets of Michaelangelo,* Folio Society, 1961, revised edition, Allison & Busby, 1969, Doubleday, 1970; (with Lawrence Durrell and R. S. Thomas) *Penguin Modern Poets I,* Penguin, 1962; *Recoveries: Poems,* Dufour, 1964; *Frost,* Oliver & Boyd, 1964, Barnes & Noble, 1965; *Christian Poetry,* Hawthorn, 1965 (published in England as *Christianity and Poetry,* Burns & Oates, 1965); *The Mind Has Mountains,* St. Martin's, 1966; *The Secret Brother and Other Poems for Children,* St. Martin's, 1966; *Collected Poems,* Dufour, 1967; *The Animals' Arrival,* Dufour, 1969.

Lucidities, Macmillan, 1970; (editor) *A Choice of Christina Rossetti's Verse,* Faber, 1970; *Hurt,* Poem-of-the-Month Club, 1970; (with others) *Folio,* Sceptre Press, 1971; *Relationships,* Macmillan, 1972; *Growing Points* (poems), Carcanet Press, 1975; *Seven Men of Vision: An Appreciation* (literary criticism), Harper, 1977; *Consequently I Rejoice* (poems), Carcanet Press, 1977; *After the Ark* (children's poems), Oxford University Press, 1978; *Selected Poems,* Carcanet Press, 1980; *Moments of Grace* (poems), Carcanet Press, 1980; (editor) *The Batsford Book of Religious Verse,* Batsford, 1981; *Celebrations and Elegies* (poems), Carcanet Press, 1982.

Contributor of poems and articles to periodicals, including *New Statesman, New Yorker, The Scotsman, Vogue, Encounter,* and *Spectator.*

SIDELIGHTS: Poet Elizabeth Jennings established her literary reputation during the 1950s as part of The Movement, a group of "angry young men" including such writers as Kingsley Amis, Thom Gunn, and Philip Larkin, who used literature as a means of social protest. Jennings "brought the 'sensitive' dimension to the no-nonsense Movement," Alan Brownjohn writes in the *New Statesman.* "Her work was . . . memorable in its quiet, unstrained way." Since then, Brownjohn notes, Jennings has "impressively increased the scope and richness, and the technical variety and command, of her writing."

Jennings has increasingly turned to religious themes in her verse; her "best and natural state is contemplation, and the poems tend to be about the debits and credits of the contemplative attitude," P. N. Furbank points out in a *Listener* review of *Recoveries.* In a review of *Moments of Grace* for *Listener,* Dick Davis finds that Jennings's title refers to the "intimations of a peace glimpsed beyond the fret and frustration of daily existence." "The poet herself," Davis adds, "seems suspended" between the natural and spiritual worlds. Andrew Motion of *New Statesman* finds that "although [Jennings] has always produced excellently-crafted poems, she has also tended to reduce their lyric force by including ruminatively philosophical material," while a *Books and Bookmen* reviewer of *Selected Poems* praises Jennings's attempt to "balance the mental and emotional demands of the priest and poet." And in *Spectator,* Emma Fisher asserts that Jennings is "looking earnestly" for moments of grace, "carefully examining pieces of life as if waiting for them to break open in revelations."

Jennings's manuscripts are in the collections of the Oxford City Library and the University of Washington, Seattle.

AVOCATIONAL INTERESTS: Travel, art, the theater, conversation.

BIOGRAPHICAL/CRITICAL SOURCES: Listener, July 23, 1964, January 31, 1980; *New Statesman,* October 13, 1967, May 30, 1975, November 2, 1979; Michael Schmidt and Grevel Lindop, editors, *British Poetry since 1960,* Carcanet Press, 1972; *Books and Bookmen,* December, 1972, February, 1980; *Contemporary Literary Criticism,* Gale, Volume V, 1976, Volume XIV, 1980; *Poetry,* March, 1977; *Times Literary Supplement,* December 30, 1977, February 1, 1980, July 16, 1982; *Spectator,* December 1, 1979.

* * *

JENSEN, Clayne R. 1930-

PERSONAL: Born March 17, 1930, in Gunnison, Utah; son of Alton H. (a stockman) and Arvilla (Roylance) Jensen; married Eloise Henrie, March 14, 1952; children: Craig, Michael, Blake, Chris. *Education:* University of Utah, B.S., 1952, M.S., 1956; Indiana University, Ph.D., 1962. *Religion:* Church of Jesus Christ of Latter-day Saints. *Home:* 1900 Oak Lane, Provo, Utah 84601. *Office:* Brigham Young University, Provo, Utah 84601.

CAREER: Utah State University, Logan, 1956-64, began as instructor, became associate professor of physical education; Brigham Young University, College of Physical Education, Provo, Utah, associate professor and coordinator of college programs, 1965-67; professor of physical education and assistant dean, 1968-74, dean of College, 1974—. Executive director and member of board of governors, Utah Recreation and Parks Association, 1958-63; executive director, Utah Inter-Agency Council for Recreation and Parks, 1962-65; chairman, National Conference on Inter-Agency Planning for Parks and Recreation, 1963-64, and National Conference on Outdoor Recreation and Education, 1969. Committee chairman, Logan-Cache Chamber of Commerce, 1961-64, Provo Chamber of Commerce, 1966-69 and 1970-71. Chairman of advisory committee, National Conference on State and Federal Inter-Agency Councils, 1964-65. *Military service:* U.S. Marine Corps, 1953-55; became captain.

MEMBER: National Recreation and Parks Association (chairman of Southwest district advisory board, 1965-66; member of board of governors, 1965-69), American Association for Health, Physical Education and Recreation (member of executive council, 1964-65 and 1967-68; vice-president of Southwest district, 1965-66), Utah Education Association, Utah Association for Health, Physical Education, Recreation and Athletics (vice-president, 1959-60; president, 1966-67), Western College Men's Physical Education Society (member of steering committee, 1963-64), Phi Beta Kappa, Kiwanis, Lion's

Club (Logan, Utah). *Awards, honors:* Annual award for outstanding contribution to recreation and park development in Utah, 1964.

WRITINGS: (With Mary Bee Jensen) *Square Dancing,* Wadsworth, 1965, published as *Square Dance,* Brigham Young University Press, 1973; (with M. B. Jensen) *Folk Dancing,* Wadsworth, 1965, published as *Folk Dance,* Brigham Young University Press, 1973; (contributor) J. B. Nash, *Recreation: Pertinent Readings,* W. C. Brown, 1965; (with Vernon Barney and Cynthia Hirst) *Conditioning Exercises—To Improve Body Form and Function,* Mosby, 1965, 3rd edition, 1972; *Manual of Kinesiology,* Multilith, 1966; (with Arthur Wilcox) *Outdoor Recreation in America—Trends and Problems,* Burgess, 1968, 3rd edition, 1977; (with Gordon Schultz) *Applied Kinesiology,* McGraw, 1970, 2nd edition, 1977; (contributor) Charles Bucher, *Administrative Dimensions of Health and Physical Education,* Mosby, 1971; (with Garth Fisher) *Scientific Basis of Athletic Conditioning,* Lea & Febiger, 1972; (with N. P. Nielsen) *Measurement and Statistics in Physical Education,* Wadsworth, 1972; (with Clark Thorstenson) *Issues in Outdoor Recreation,* Burgess, 1972, 2nd edition, 1977; (with Clarence Robison) *Modern Track and Field Coaching Technique,* Lea & Febiger, 1974.

Recreation and Leisure Time Careers, Vocational Guidance Manuals, 1976; (with Karl Tucker) *Skiing,* 3rd edition, W. C. Brown, 1977; *Leisure and Education in America: A Guide and Overview,* Lea & Febiger, 1977; *Winter Touring and Mountaineering,* Burgess, 1977; (with Hirst) *Measurement and Evaluation in Physical Education and Athletics,* Macmillan, 1979; *Backpacking,* Leisure Press, 1981; *Administrative Management of Physical Education and Athletics,* Lea & Febiger, 1982.

Writer of three Utah State University Extension pamphlets on recreation. Contributor to physical education periodicals, including *Athletic Journal, Physical Educator, Coach and Athlete,* and *Scholastic Coach.* Editor, *Utah Journal of Health, Physical Education and Recreation,* 1970-72.

AVOCATIONAL INTERESTS: Conservation and development of outdoor recreation resources, travel (including visits to forty-four states and eighteen countries), athletics.

* * *

JERVELL, Jacob 1925-

PERSONAL: Born May 21, 1925, in Fauske, Norway; son of Sverre (a pastor) and Thora (Mejdell) Jervell; married Kari Lange (a librarian), July 3, 1938; children: Stephen. *Education:* Attended Lund University, 1950; Oslo University, B.D., 1951, D.D., 1959; graduate study at Heidelberg University, 1953, and Goettingen University, 1954-55. *Religion:* Lutheran. *Home:* Silurveien 41 F, Oslo 3, Norway. *Office:* Oslo University, Blindern, Oslo 3, Norway.

CAREER: Oslo University, Oslo, Norway, lecturer, 1955-59, professor of biblical theology, 1960—, dean of faculty of theology, 1975-76, vice-chancellor, 1977-80. Visiting professor, Lund University, 1964, Yale University, 1970, and Aarhus University, 1973. Chairman of Norwegian Christian Student Movement, 1958-65. *Member:* Societe Royale des Lettres de Lund, Norwegian Academy of Science and Letters, Studiorum Novi Testamenti Societas, Norwegian Bible Society (member of board, 1966—). *Awards, honors:* D.D.h.c., Aarhus University, 1978.

WRITINGS: Imago Dei (title means "The Image of God"), Vandenhoeck & Ruprecht, 1960; *The Historical Jesus,* Forlaget Land og Kirke, 1962, 3rd revised edition, 1978; *Ikke bare ruiner* (title means "Not Only Ruins"), Forlaget Land og Kirke, 1967; *Da fremtiden begynte* (title means "When the Future Began"), Forlaget Land og Kirke, 1967, 2nd revised edition, 1976; *Studien zu den Testamenten der 12 Patriarchen* (title means "Studies in the Testaments of the 12 Patriarchs"), A. Toepelmann, 1969.

Luke and the People of God, Augsburg, 1972, 2nd edition, 1979; *Gud og hans fiender* (title means "God and His Enemies"), Oslo University Press, 1973, 2nd edition, 1978; ". . . bare all makt"* (title means ". . . Only All Power"), Gyldendal, 1975; (editor) *God's Christ and His People,* Universitetsforlaget, 1977; *Ingen har stoerre kjaelighet* (title means "Greater Love Has No Man"), Universitetsforlaget, 1979. Contributor to theology journals and periodicals.

WORK IN PROGRESS: Die Apostelgeschichte, for Vandenhoeck & Ruprecht; *The Unknown Paul; History of Early Christianity.*

* * *

JOHN, B.
See JOHN, Elizabeth Beaman

* * *

JOHN, Betty
See JOHN, Elizabeth Beaman

* * *

JOHN, Elizabeth Beaman 1907-
(B. John, Betty John; Beth St. John, Elizabeth St. John, Sinjun, pseudonyms)

PERSONAL: Born October 25, 1907, in Cincinnati, Ohio; daughter of Charles Worcester (a doctor) and Laura Zoe (Bogue) Beaman; married Henry J. John (a retired physician), October 9, 1928. *Education:* Attended University of Cincinnati, 1925-28; attended Cincinnati School of Art, 1926-28; attended Cleveland College of Western Reserve University (now Case Western Reserve University); attended Cleveland Institute of Art, 1950-51; has studied various literature and writing courses. *Politics:* Republican. *Religion:* Episcopalian.

CAREER: Designer, craftswoman, and writer. Camp Ho Mita Koda, Newbury, Ohio, co-founder and co-director with husband, 1929-42, 1946-48, director, 1956, now on board of trustees; Red Cross Blood Donor Service, Cleveland, Ohio, first executive secretary, 1942; director of Overseas Clubs, American Red Cross, 1942-44; *Cleveland News,* Cleveland, war correspondent, 1945; residential director and member of public relations staff, American Red Cross Fund Drive, 1945-46. One-woman art show at Dezign House, Cleveland. Member, camp advisory committee, Cleveland (Ohio) Welfare Federation.

MEMBER: American Camping Association (president, Great Lakes section, 1940-42), Maison Francaise (president, 1940-41), Academy of Medicine (president, women's auxiliary, 1953), Womens Overseas Service League (president, 1954), National League of American Pen Women (president, Cleveland branch, 1964-65), Cleveland Play House (member, board of the women's committee), Cleveland Institute of Art (member of executive board).

AWARDS, HONORS: Several first prizes in national writing contests, National League of American Pen Women, for a three-act drama, feature article, humor, television script, children's short story, and tiny tots' short story; Lakewood Little Theater drama prize for three-act play, "Starched White"; art awards for several Cleveland May Shows; most distinguished entry award, Smithsonian Fine Arts Gallery, 1958; first prize, North Atlantic regional art contests of National League of American Pen Women, for lucite and silver cloisonne box, 1961; walnut and enamel cross purchased by American Crafts Council for Coventry Cathedral, England.

WRITINGS: (Editor with Devon E. Francis; under name Betty John) *Flak Bait*, Duell, Sloane & Pearce, 1948; *Seloe*, World Publishing, 1956; *Hummingbirds*, Follett, 1961; *El Capitano Pelican Cafe*, Hummingbird Press, 1975; (under pseudonym Elizabeth St. John) *Sammy, the Christmas Adventure*, edited by Joanna Handel, Handel & Sons Publishing, 1976; (under pseudonym Elizabeth St. John) *Sammy, the White House Mouse*, edited by J. Handel, Handel & Sons Publishing, 1976; *Libby and the Pribilof Aleuts*, University of Alaska Press, 1977. Also author of three-act plays, "West of Linares" and "Starched White." Author of two-page column, "The Wife Line," in Cleveland Academy of Medicine *Bulletin*. Contributor to numerous magazines, including *Today's Health, Nature, Camping Magazine, Forecast, Carry On, The Explorer,* and *M.D.'s Wife*. Associate editor, Cleveland Academy of Medicine *Bulletin*.

WORK IN PROGRESS: A children's book about bridges, tentatively entitled *Billions of Bridges;* a children's historical novel about an Aleut boy; a children's book, *Ten Little Princes*, adapted from Sanskrit.

SIDELIGHTS: Elizabeth Beaman John is fluent in French. *Avocational interests:* Aviation, the biosciences with reference to human genetics and chemistry, animals and nature, arts and crafts (particularly enamels and wood sculpture), travel, cooking and entertaining.

BIOGRAPHICAL/CRITICAL SOURCES: *Cleveland Press*, October 30, 1944; *Cleveland Plain Dealer*, November 5, 1944, March 30, 1958, June 21, 1959, July 3, 1960; *Cleveland News*, June 2, 1948, January 30, 1952, November 24, 1959; *Washington Star*, April 8, 1958; *Penwoman*, February, 1959.†

* * *

JOHNSON, Ben E(ugene) 1940-

PERSONAL: Born August 16, 1940, in Storm Lake, Iowa; son of Jonas Birger (a laborer) and Bernice (Brown) Johnson; married Bonnie McPherson (a teacher), August 24, 1964 (divorced, 1977); children: Steven, Susan, Shelley. *Education:* Detroit Bible College (now William Tyndale College), B.R.E., 1962; Eastern Michigan University, M.A. (history), 1964, M.A. (English), 1967; Washington State University, doctoral study, 1968-69. *Residence:* Santa Barbara, Calif. *Office:* Preferred Administrators Corp., 14 State St., Santa Barbara, Calif. 93101.

CAREER: Pastor of Baptist church in Detroit, Mich., 1961-64; WBFG-FM, Detroit, radio announcer and disc jockey, 1962-64; Detroit Bible College (now Willian Tyndale College), Detroit, instructor in English and literature, 1964-68; Washington State University, Pullman, university librarian in archives, 1968-69; Trinity College, Deerfield, Ill., assistant professor of English, 1969-76, chairman of department, 1969-73; currently president of Preferred Administrators Corp., Santa Barbara, Calif. President of Achieving Greater Proficiency Inc. (learning skills firm), 1970—. *Member:* International Reading Association, National Council of Teachers of English.

WRITINGS: *Rapid Reading with a Purpose*, Regal Press, 1974; *Learn to Rapid Read*, Sams, 1974; *Learn to Rapid Write*, Sams, 1974; *What Was That Verse Again?*, Quill Publications, 1976; *Rapid Reading Naturally: What It Is, How to Teach It*, Quill Publications, 1976; *How to Rapid Read, Naturally*, Quill Publications, 1977; *Rapid Reading Resource Workbook*, Achieving Greater Proficiency, 1978; *How to Read Better and Enjoy It More*, Harvest House, 1980.

SIDELIGHTS: Ben E. Johnson writes: "My AGP (Achieving Greater Proficiency) courses are the most widely used instructor-taught courses on the college level in the area of rapid reading, memory, and speed writing. A dozen foreign countries also offer the courses.

"All of my writings reflect my fascination with learning skills. I keep wanting to find out *how* adults learn, and how that learning can be increased. This has naturally led to my researching and writing about such areas as memory improvement and rapid reading."

* * *

JOHNSON, Christopher 1931-
(Louis McIntosh)

PERSONAL: Born June 12, 1931, in London, England; son of Donald McIntosh (a publisher) and Christiane (Coussaert) Johnson; married Anne Robbins, January 4, 1958; children: James, Caroline, Victoria, Elizabeth. *Education:* Magdalen College, Oxford, demy, 1950-54 (with first class honors in philosophy, politics, and economics, 1953). *Office:* Group Economics Department, Lloyds Bank Ltd., 71 Lombard St., London EC3P 3BS, England.

CAREER: *Times Educational Supplement*, London, England, editorial assistant, 1954-57; *The Times*, London, assistant to foreign news editor, 1957-59, foreign sub-editor, 1958-59, assistant Paris correspondent, 1959-60; *Financial Times*, London, diplomatic correspondent in Paris, France, 1960-63, diplomatic correspondent, 1963-65, foreign editor, 1965-67, managing editor, 1967-70, managing director of Business Enterprises Division, 1970-76, main board director, 1973-76; Lloyds Bank Ltd., London, economic advisor, 1977-81, group economic advisor, 1981—. *Military service:* British Army, 1949-50; became captain.

WRITINGS: (Under pseudonym Louis McIntosh) *Oxford Folly*, Johnson Publications, 1955; *Firms and Their Exports*, Political & Economic Planning, 1964; *Anatomy of U.K. Finance*, Financial Times, 1976; *North Sea Energy Wealth*, Financial Times, 1979. Contributor to periodicals, including *London Times, The Banker, Mind, Crossbow,* and *Journal of Common Market Studies*.

SIDELIGHTS: Christopher Johnson is competent in French, German, Italian, Spanish, Russian, modern and ancient Greek, and Latin.

* * *

JOHNSON, David 1927-

PERSONAL: Born August 26, 1927, in Meir, Stoke on Trent, England; son of Robert Arthur and Winifred (Stewart) Johnson. *Education:* Attended schools in England. *Home:* 16 Belgrave Gardens, London NW8 0RB, England.

CAREER: Writer. *Military service:* British Army, Infantry, 1945, 1946-48; became lieutenant.

WRITINGS: *Sabre General*, Hodder & Stoughton, 1959, published as *The Proud Canaries*, Sloane, 1960; *Promenade in Champagne*, Hodder & Stoughton, 1960, Sloane, 1961; *Lan-*

terns in Gascony, Sidgwick & Jackson, 1964; *A Candle in Aragon: A Fragment of the Reconquista,* Jenkins, 1969; *Regency Revolution: The Case of Arthur Thistlewood,* Compton Russell, 1974; *Napoleon's Cavalry and Its Leaders,* Batsford, 1978.

Compiler: *Clive of India: A Collection of Contemporary Documents,* J. Cape, 1968; *The Monmouth Rebellion and the Bloody Assizes: A Collection of Contemporary Documents,* J. Cape, 1968; *The Tower of London: A Collection of Documents,* J. Cape, 1968; *Marlborough: A Collection of Contemporary Documents,* J. Cape, 1969; *Elizabeth Fry and Prison Reform: A Collection of Contemporary Documents,* Jackdaw Publications, 1969; *Alfred the Great,* Grossman, 1969; *The Anglo-Boer War: A Collection of Contemporary Documents,* J. Cape, 1969; *The American Revolution,* Grossman, 1970; *Clipper Ships and the Cutty Sark,* Grossman, 1971; *London's Peelers and the British Police,* Grossman, 1971; *The Civil War,* Grossman, 1971; *General Gordon at Khartoum,* J. Cape, 1971.

AVOCATIONAL INTERESTS: History, riding, travel.

* * *

JOHNSON, Donald McI(ntosh) 1903-
(Guy de Montfort, Odysseus)

PERSONAL: Born February 17, 1903, in Bury, Lancashire, England; son of Isaac Wellwood and Bertha Louise (Hall) Johnson; married Christiane Marthe Coussaert; married second wife, Betty Muriel Plaisted; children: (first marriage) Christopher Louis McIntosh; (second marriage) Norman McIntosh, Carol Eden. *Education:* Attended Cheltenham College; St. Bartholomew's Hospital Medical College, University of London, M.R.C.S. and L.R.C.P., 1925; Gonville and Caius College, Cambridge, M.B., B.Ch., 1926, M.A., 1927; Gray's Inn, barrister-at-law. *Politics:* Conservative. *Religion:* Church of England. *Home:* 55 Langley Park Rd., Sutton, Surrey, England. *Office:* Johnson Publications Ltd., 11/14 Stanhope Mews West, London S.W. 7, England.

CAREER: Called to Bar at Gray's Inn, 1930, but career has been devoted to general practice of medicine and publishing. Casualty and medical officer at hospitals in London, England; Cambridge University, Cambridge, England, medical officer of East Greenland expedition, 1926; Grenfell Mission, Labrador, Canada, medical officer, 1928-29; private medical practice in Thorton Heath, Croydon, England, 1930-37; Oxford University, Oxford, England, demonstrator in anatomy, 1937-39; Johnson Publications Ltd., London, founder, chairman, and managing director, 1946—. Liberal Party candidate in four elections, 1935-45; joined Conservative Party in 1948, adopted as candidate for Carlisle, 1954, elected to Parliament, 1955, re-elected, 1959, defeated, 1964. *Member:* British Medical Association, Oxford and Cambridge Club.

WRITINGS—Published by Johnson Publications, except as indicated: (Under pseudonym Odysseus) *Safer than a Known Way,* J. Cape, 1941; *A Doctor Regrets,* 1947; *Bars and Barricades,* 1952; *Indian Hemp: A Social Menace,* 1952; *The Hallucinogenic Drugs,* 1953; *A Doctor Returns,* 1956; *A Doctor in Parliament,* 1958; *The British National Health Service: Friend or Frankenstein?* 1962; (under pseudonym Guy de Montfort) *Welcome to Harmony,* Marlowe, 1962; *A Cassandra at Westminster,* 1967; *Ted Heath: A Latter Day Charlemagne: Europe, Slave or Free?,* 1971; *A Doctor Reflects: Miracles and Mirages,* 1975. Also author of *The End of Socialism.*†

JOHNSON, William C(lark, Jr.) 1945-

PERSONAL: Born March 5, 1945, in Portland, Ore.; son of William Clark (in business management) and Genevieve L. (Cotterel) Johnson; married Cheryl L. Ashby, August 19, 1967; children: Brendan, Suzanne, Stephen. *Education:* Attended University of Washington, Seattle, 1966; Whitworth College, B.A. (cum laude), 1967; State University of New York at Stony Brook, M.A., 1969; University of Denver, Ph.D., 1972. *Home:* 2621 Willow Dr., Lewiston, Idaho 83501. *Office:* Lewis-Clark State College, Lewiston, Idaho 83501.

CAREER: University of Denver, Denver, Colo., instructor in English, 1971-72; Stetson University, DeLand, Fla., assistant professor, 1972-77, associate professor, 1977-80, Carlton Professor of English, 1980-81, director of freshman English, 1974-76, chairman of admissions committee, 1978-79; Lewis-Clark State College, Lewiston, Idaho, associate professor of humanities, 1981—. Director of Florida Poetry Symposium, 1980-81. *Member:* Modern Language Association of America, National Council of Teachers of English, South Atlantic Modern Language Association, Rocky Mountain Modern Language Association. *Awards, honors:* Student-faculty award for leadership, scholarship, and publication, Stetson University, 1979.

WRITINGS: (Editor with L. C. Gruber and contributor) *New Views on Chaucer: Essays in Generative Criticism,* Society for New Language Study, 1973; (with Raymond P. Tripp, Jr.) *The Ladder of Language: An Introductory Structural Grammar,* Society for New Language Study, 1973, 3rd edition, 1979. Also author of poems and of *The Presence of "Beowulf": A Phenomenological View.*

Contributor: Gruber and D. Loganbill, editors, *In Geardagum: Essays on Old English Language and Literature,* Society for New Language Study, 1974; Tripp, editor, *Man's Natural Powers: Essays for and about C. S. Lewis,* Onny Press, 1975; *In Geardagum II,* [Denver, Colo.], 1977; V. Carrabino, editor, *The Power of Myth in Literature and Film,* University Presses of Florida, 1980; M. Green, editor, *Old English Elegy Collection,* Fairleigh Dickinson University Press, 1982.

Contributor of papers to meetings of professionals associations, including South Atlantic Modern Language Association, Rocky Mountain Modern Language Association, and Medieval Institute; contributor to professional journals, including *New Views on Chaucer, CEA Critic, English Language Notes, Poetica, Journal of Aesthetics and Art Criticism,* and *Philological Quarterly.*

WORK IN PROGRESS: In a Dark Range, a collection of lyric poems; an essay on Henry David Thoreau's *Walden.*

SIDELIGHTS: William C. Johnson writes to *CA:* "My energies move more and more into poetry. A writer, especially a poet, helps all of us keep the world awake—find and nurture its poetic life. Against all ever-accelerating technology, which must ultimately reduce and distort the qualitative world, poetic consciousness may be our last hope."

Johnson has a reading knowledge of Old English, Old Icelandic, Latin, French, and German.

AVOCATIONAL INTERESTS: Hiking, nature study, playing the guitar, coaching soccer.

* * *

JONAS, Doris F(rances) 1916-
(Doris F. Klein)

PERSONAL: Born May 21, 1916, in London, England; daughter of L. Edward (a manufacturer) and Gertrude (Froomberg) Warshaw; married Frank Klein, January 14, 1945 (divorced, 1970); married Adolphe David Jonas (a psychiatrist), June 17, 1970; children: (first marriage) Francis Charles, Jill Elise. *Education:* London School of Economics and Political Science, M.Sc. *Politics:* Conservative. *Home:* 24B Wellington Court, London SW1X 7PL, England.

CAREER: Writer. Editor and ghostwriter, 1937-39; Institute of Theoretical Medicine New York City, director of department of anthropology, 1956-72; family psychotherapist in New York City, 1965-72, and in Wuerzburg, German, 1974. *Wartime service:* Women's Voluntary Services, Department of Salvage Research, 1939-46. *Member:* Royal Anthropological Institute (fellow), Current Anthropology (associate), English-Speaking Union. *Awards, honors:* Pawlowski Peace Prize from Pawlowski Peace Foundation, 1974, for work on the evolutionary infantilization of man as a factor in violence.

WRITINGS: Man-Child, McGraw, 1970; *Young till We Die,* Coward, 1973; (contributor) L. Pawlowski, editor, *Paths to Permanent Peace,* Volume II, Pawlowski Peace Foundation, 1974; *Sex and Status,* Stein & Day, 1975; (contributor) Robin Deniston, editor, *Man's Concern with Life after Death,* Weidenfeld & Nicolson, 1976; *Other Senses, Other Worlds,* Stein & Day, 1976; *The Past Within Us,* Hippocrates, 1977; *The First Word,* Hoffmann & Campe, 1979; (contributor) *Woman and Power,* Fischer, 1979; (contributor) D. Lettieri, editor, *Theories on Drug Abuse,* National Institute on Drug Abuse, 1980; *Male Dominance: A Dead-End Path?,* Kosel, 1981. Also contributor to *Children of the Caves,* 1980. Contributor to professional anthropology and psychiatry journals and medical magazines.

AVOCATIONAL INTERESTS: Ethology, art history.

* * *

JONAS, Manfred 1927-

PERSONAL: Born April 9, 1927, in Mannheim, Germany; came to United States, 1937; naturalized U.S. citizen; son of Walter (a wine merchant) and Antonie (Dannheisser) Jonas; married Nancy Jane Greene (a teacher and counselor), July 19, 1952; children: Andrew Miles, Kathryn Leslie, Emily Susan, Matthew Greene. *Education:* City College (now City College of the City University of New York), B.S., 1949; Harvard University, A.M., 1950, Ph.D., 1959. *Office:* Department of History, Union College, Schenectady, N.Y. 12308.

CAREER: U.S. Department of Defense, Salzburg, Austria, intelligence analyst, 1950-53; Free University of Berlin, Berlin, Germany, visiting assistant professor of American history, 1959-62; Pennsylvania Military College (now Widener College of Widener University), Chester, associate professor of history, 1962-63; Union College, Schenectady, N.Y., assistant professor, 1963-64, associate professor, 1964-67, professor of history, 1967-81, Washington Irving Professor of Modern Literary and Historical Studies, 1981—, director of graduate program in American studies, 1964-74, chairman, department of history, 1970-81, director of transdisciplinary program in American studies, 1981—. Summer lecturer at City College (now City College of the City University of New York), 1950, University of Maryland Extension Division, 1954, and Northeastern University, 1958. Radio commentator and lecturer on American topics in Germany, 1960-62; conductor of discussion program on public issues, WMHT-TV, Schenectady, 1965. Member of board of directors, Freedom Forum, Inc., 1966-77. *Military service:* U.S. Naval Reserve, 1945-51, active duty, 1945-46.

MEMBER: American Historical Association, Organization of American Historians, American Association of University Professors, Society for Historians of American Foreign Relations, Torch. *Awards, honors:* Senior Fulbright-Hays lecturer at University of the Saarland, Germany, 1973; research fellow at Charles Warren Center for Studies in American History, Harvard University, 1977-78.

WRITINGS: Die Unabhaengigkeitserklaerung der Vereinigten Staaten, Hans Pfeiffer Verlag, 1965; *Isolationism in America, 1935-1941,* Cornell University Press, 1966; (editor) *American Foreign Relations in the Twentieth Century,* Crowell, 1967; (editor with F. L. Loewenheim and H. D. Langley) *Roosevelt and Churchill: Their Secret Correspondence,* Saturday Review Press, 1975; (general editor) *The Politics and Strategy of World War II,* nine volumes, Da Capo Press, 1976-77; (editor with R. V. Wells) *New Opportunities in a New Nation: The Development of New York after the Revolution,* Union College Press, 1982.

Contributor: Richard Wernicke, editor, *Welt im Prisma,* Agentur des Rauhen Hauses, 1962; *Die U.S.A. und Deutschland: Zeitgeschichtliche Fragen,* Albert Limbach Verlag, 1962; John Braeman and others, editors, *Twentieth-Century American Foreign Policy,* Ohio State University Press, 1971; Charles Chatfield, editor, *Peace Movements in America,* Schocken, 1973; (with wife, Nancy Jonas) Henry Steele Commager and Maldwyn A. Jones, general editors, *The American Destiny,* Danbury Press, 1976; David H. White, editor, *Proceedings of the Conference on War and Diplomacy 1976,* Citadel, 1976; Jules Davids, editor, *Perspectives in American Foreign Policy,* Arno, 1976; Dwight D. Eisenhower, *Crusade in Europe,* Da Capo Press, 1977; Alexander De Conde, editor, *Encyclopedia of American Foreign Policy,* Scribner, 1978; Hans L. Trefousse, editor, *Germany and America: Essays on Problems of International Relations and Immigration,* Brooklyn College Press, 1980. Contributor to historical periodicals in the United States and Germany. Member of board of editors, *Diplomatic History.*

WORK IN PROGRESS: A history of American-German relations between 1865 and 1955.

SIDELIGHTS: Manfred Jonas told *CA* he believes "the great age of narrative historical writing is long past (though C. Vann Woodward and others are trying hard to revive it), and historians now write largely for each other. I would like to think that my work aims at a larger audience. Those who do not know their past may not be doomed to repeat it, but they are surely the poorer for not recognizing what has come before them or seeing their place in a larger scheme of things."

AVOCATIONAL INTERESTS: Skiing, sailing, acting.

* * *

JONES, Oakah L., Jr. 1930-

PERSONAL: Born June 20, 1930, in Providence, R.I.; son of Oakah L. (president of Consumer's Natural Gas Co.) and Dorothy (Wilson) Jones; married Nancy Aline Andre, June 14, 1953 (divorced, 1976); children: Marcia Aline, Kathleen Ann (deceased), Christopher Andre. *Education:* Attended University of Tulsa, 1947-48, and University of Arkansas, 1948-49; U.S. Naval Academy, B.S., 1953; University of Oklahoma, M.A., 1960, Ph.D., 1964. *Religion:* Episcopalian. *Home:* 1945 Indian Trail Dr., West Lafayette, Ind. 47906. *Office:* Department of History, Purdue University, West Lafayette, Ind. 47907.

CAREER: Regular officer, U.S. Air Force, 1953-76, retired as lieutenant colonel; U.S. Air Force Academy, Colo., instructor, 1960-62, assistant professor, 1962-63, associate professor, 1964-65, tenure associate professor and professor of Latin American history, 1965-73; Florida State University, Canal Zone Branch, adjunct professor of Latin American history, 1973-77; Purdue University, West Lafayette, Ind., began as associate professor, currently professor of history, 1977—. Lecturer on Latin American history, University of Colorado, Extension Division, 1964-69. *Member:* Conference on Latin American History, Western History Association, Historical Society of New Mexico, Indiana Historical Society.

WRITINGS: Pueblo Warriors and Spanish Conquest, University of Oklahoma Press, 1966; *Santa Anna,* Twayne, 1968; *My Adventures in Zuni,* West Publishing, 1970; *Federal Control of the Western Apaches, 1848-1886,* University of New Mexico, 1970; (editor) *The Spanish Borderlands: A First Reader,* Lorrin L. Morrison, 1974; *Los Paisanos: Spanish Settlers on the Northern Frontier of New Spain,* University of Oklahoma Press, 1979. Contributor of articles and reviews to history journals. Regional editor, *Journal of the West;* member of board of editors of Colorado Historical Society and *New Mexico Historical Review.*

WORK IN PROGRESS: Nueva Vizcaya: Heart of the Spanish Frontier.

SIDELIGHTS: Oakah L. Jones, Jr. told *CA* that his purpose in writing scholarly books is "to portray as accurately as possible the extent and nature of the Spanish frontier experience from Zacatecas to New Mexico and from Texas to Alta California." Jones researches his books using manuscripts located in Spain, Mexico, and archival collections in the United States. "I am primarily interested in the Spanish experience in the Americas," he says, "but the nature of the sources requires a lengthy period between publications of my scholarly works. Since my major professor, Dr. Max L. Moorhead (deceased) of Oklahoma University, was a student of Dr. Herbert Eugene Bolton and has contributed greatly to the study of the Spanish frontier in North America, I tend to follow his example, but, as he noted tersely in evaluating my writing: 'Oakah, you seem to write like your sources, long sentences and wordy!' As a third generation student of the Spanish frontier, I hope that I can make contributions to our overall understanding of its nature in the same (although not equal) manner of my major professor and his."

AVOCATIONAL INTERESTS: Baseball, tennis, reading about American Indians.

* * *

JORDEN, Eleanor Harz

PERSONAL: Born in New York, N.Y.; daughter of William George and Eleanor (Funk) Harz; married William J. Jorden (a diplomat), March 3, 1944 (divorced); children: William Temple, Eleanor Harz, Jr., Marion Telva. *Education:* Bryn Mawr College, A.B., 1942; Yale University, M.A., 1943, Ph.D., 1950. *Home:* 333 North Sunset Dr., Ithaca, N.Y. 14850. *Office:* Department of Modern Language and Linguistics, 321 Morrill Hall, Cornell University, Ithaca, N.Y. 14853.

CAREER: Yale University, New Haven, Conn., instructor in Japanese, 1943-46, 1947-48; American Embassy, Tokyo, Japan, director of Foreign Service Institute Language School and of Japanese language program, 1950-55; U.S. Department of State, Foreign Service Institute, Washington, D.C., scientific linguist, 1959-61, acting head and chairman of Far Eastern languages division, 1961-67, 1969, chairman of Vietnamese language division, 1967-69; Cornell University, Ithaca, N.Y., visiting professor, 1969-70, professor of linguistics, 1970-74, Mary Donlon Alger Professor of Linguistics, 1974—, director of Japanese FALCON program, 1972—. Distinguished lecturer, Association for Asian Studies, 1979; visiting scholar, Japan Foundation, 1982; guest scholar, Smithsonian Institution, 1982. Member of Fulbright-Hays Committee on International Exchange of Scholars, 1972-75; chairman of Social Science Research Council Task Force on Japanese Language Teaching, 1976-78.

MEMBER: Linguistic Society of America, Association for Asian Studies (president, 1980-81), American Council of Teachers of Foreign Languages, Association of Teachers of Japanese (president, 1978—), National Association for Self-Instructional Language Programs (consultant and examiner, 1965—; president, 1977-78). *Awards, honors:* Superior Service Award, U.S. Department of State, 1965; Japanese Foundation and Social Science Research Council senior fellow, 1976; honorary Doctor of Letters, Williams College, 1982.

WRITINGS: (With Bernard Bloch) *Spoken Japanese,* Holt, 1945; *Written Japanese,* Institute of Far Eastern Languages, Yale University, 1947; *Syntax of Modern Colloquial Japanese,* Linguistic Society of America, 1955; *Beginning Japanese,* Yale University Press, Part I, 1962, Part II, 1963; (with Sheehan, Quang, and others) *Basic Vietnamese,* two volumes, Foreign Service Institute, U.S. Department of State, 1965; (with Quang) *Vietnamese Familiarization Course,* U.S. Department of State, 1969; (with Hamako Chaplin) *Reading Japanese,* Yale University Press, 1976. Also author of other teaching materials, including "Gateway to Russian" record set, Ottenheimer, 1960.

* * *

JOSEPHY, Alvin M., Jr. 1915-

PERSONAL: Surname is accented on second syllable, Jo-*seph*-y; born May 18, 1915, in Woodmere, N.Y.; son of Alvin M. (a businessman) and Sophia C. (Knopf) Josephy; married Elizabeth C. Peet, March 13, 1948; children: Diane, Alvin M. III, Allison, Katherine. *Education:* Attended Harvard University, 1932-34. *Politics:* Democrat. *Home:* 4 Kinsman Lane, Greenwich, Conn. 06830; and Box 62, Joseph, Ore. 97846. *Office:* American Heritage Publishing Co., 10 Rockefeller Plaza, New York, N.Y. 10020.

CAREER: New York Herald-Tribune, New York City, reporter and correspondent, 1937-38; WOR-Mutual, New York City, director of news and special features, 1938-42; Office of War Information, Radio Bureau, Washington, D.C., chief of special events, 1942-43; Metro-Goldwyn-Mayer Studios, Culver City, Calif., screenwriter, 1945-51; *Time,* New York City, associate editor, 1951-60; American Heritage Publishing Co., New York City, vice-president and senior editor of American Heritage Books, 1960-76, editor of *American Heritage* magazine, 1976-78, director and senior editor, 1978—. Commissioner of Indian Arts and Crafts Board, Department of the Interior, 1966-70; author of Report on Indian Affairs for President Nixon, 1969; trustee of National Resources Defense Council, 1977-81, Museum of the American Indian, 1977—, and Environmental Policy Center, 1978—. Democratic state central committeeman, Connecticut, 1956-60; Democratic candidate for Connecticut Legislature, 1958, and 1960. Consultant to National Congress of American Indians, 1958-65, Secretary of the Interior, 1963, and Public Land Law Review Commission, 1970; member of Connecticut Small Business Advisory Committee, 1961-63; member of National Advisory Committee on Indian Work, Episcopal Church. *Military service:* U.S. Marine Corps, combat correspondent, 1943-45; became master sergeant; received Bronze Star (action at Guam).

MEMBER: Institute of the American West (president of national council, 1981—), Association on American Indian Affairs (member of executive committee), Society of American Historians (member of executive committee, 1971—), American Antiquarian Society, U.S. Capitol Historical Association, Western History Association, New York Westerners, Third Marine Division Association, Harvard Club (New York City).

AWARDS, HONORS: Awards from National Cowboy Hall of Fame and Western Heritage Center, 1961 and 1965, for best books on the American West; Western Writers of America Golden Spur and Golden Saddleman Awards, 1965; New York Westerners Buffalo Award, 1965 and 1968, for best books on the American West; American Association for State and Local History national award of merit, 1966; Guggenheim fellowship, 1966-67; National Book Award nominee for history, 1968.

WRITINGS: (Co-author) *The U.S. Marines on Iwo Jima*, Dial, 1945; (contributor) *My Favorite War Story*, Whittlesey House, 1946; *The Long and the Short and the Tall: The Story of a Marine Combat Unit in the Pacific*, Knopf, 1946; (co-author) *Uncommon Valor*, Infantry Journal Press, 1946; (contributor) *Semper Fidelis*, Sloane, 1947; (co-author) *The American Heritage Book of the Pioneer Spirit*, American Heritage Publishing Co., 1959.

The Patriot Chiefs: A Chronicle of American Indian Leadership, Viking, 1961; *Chief Joseph's People and Their War*, Yellowstone Library and Museum Association, 1964; *The Nez Perce Indians and the Opening of the Northwest*, Yale University Press, 1965; (contributor) *The Red Man's West*, Hastings House, 1965; (co-author) *The American Heritage Pictorial Atlas of United States History*, American Heritage Publishing Co., 1966; (contributor) *The Mountain Men*, Volume III, Arthur H. Clark, 1966; (editor) *RFK: His Life and Death*, Dell, 1968; *The Indian Heritage of America*, Knopf, 1968; (contributor) *Great Adventures of the Old West*, American Heritage Press, 1969; (contributor) *The United States Marine Corps in World War II*, Random House, 1969.

The Artist Was a Young Man, Amon Carter Museum, 1970; *Red Power: The American Indians' Fight for Freedom*, American Heritage Press, 1971; (reviser) Oliver LaFarge, *The Pictorial History of the American Indian*, Crown, 1974; *History of the Congress of the United States*, McGraw, 1975; *Black Hills, White Sky*, New York Times Books, 1979; *On the Hill*, Simon & Schuster, 1979; *Now That the Buffalo's Gone*, Knopf, 1982.

Editor; all published by American Heritage Press: *The American Heritage Book of Indians*, 1961; *The American Heritage History of Flight*, 1962; *The American Heritage Book of Natural Wonders*, 1962; *The American Heritage History of World War I*, 1964; *The American Heritage History of the Great West*, 1965; *The Horizon History of Africa*, 1971; *American Heritage History of Business and Industry*, 1972; *The Horizon History of Vanishing Primitive Man*, 1973; *The Law in America*, 1974; *The Cold War*, 1982.

Also author of screenplays for Metro-Goldwyn-Mayer, 1945-51. Contributor to *Collier's Encyclopedia* and *Brand Book*. Contributor to periodicals, including *Life*, *Atlantic*, *New York Times Sunday Magazine*, *American West*, and *Audubon*.

WORK IN PROGRESS: An updated history of the Nez Perce Indians and their homeland, for the National Park Service; editing the journal of Astorian Alfred Seton; a tribal history of the Western Shoshone and Painte Indians of the Duck Valley Reservation in Nevada.

SIDELIGHTS: Alvin M. Josephy, Jr.'s historical studies of Indians in America have been praised for their value to scholars and general readers alike. Additionally, critics have commended Josephy's fair and compassionate treatment of the native American experience. In the *Washington Post Book World*, Morris Opler writes of *The Indian Heritage of America:* "The author is not a trained anthropologist or historian, but, . . . he has respect for scholarship and is trying to write something compact and flowing enough to attract the general reader without being too casual with facts and sources that the specialists are disgruntled. . . . The book has unusual touches and solid merits. . . . It breathes appreciation of [the Indians'] worth and indignation at their long travail."

Josephy, who helped shape the Nixon Administration's policy of Indian rights and self-determination, has also written of the recent political struggle of the Indians. Dee Brown comments in the *New York Times Book Review:* "In Alvin M. Josephy's *Red Power* . . . the most spirited statements are those made by the Indians. . . . They all stand far above the reports of task forces and commissions, important though the latter may be. When compared with the flat governmentalese of George McGovern and Richard Nixon, who are included, they fairly burn with eloquence." *Red Power*, Brown concludes, is "an essential handbook for anyone concerned with the never-ending struggle of native Americans to obtain freedoms that other Americans have long taken for granted."

BIOGRAPHICAL/CRITICAL SOURCES: Time, December 1, 1961, November 19, 1965; *New York Times Book Review*, November 7, 1965, February 15, 1970, August 29, 1971; *Washington Post Book World*, September 22, 1968; *Nation*, December 23, 1968; *American Historical Review*, June, 1969; *Books and Bookmen*, November, 1972; *Antioch Review*, summer, 1976.

* * *

JUERGENSEN, Hans 1919-

PERSONAL: Born December 17, 1919, in Myslowitz, Germany (now Myslowice, Poland); naturalized U.S. citizen; foster son of Hermann Anton and Dora (Grossmann) Juergensen; married Ilse Dina Loebenberg (a poet and teacher of poetry in elementary schools), October 27, 1945; children: Claudia Jeanne. *Education:* Upsala College, East Orange, N.J., B.A., 1942; Johns Hopkins University, Ph.D., 1951. *Religion:* Jewish. *Home:* 7815 Pine Hill Dr., Tampa, Fla. 33610. *Office:* Department of Humanities, University of South Florida, Tampa, Fla. 33620.

CAREER: University of Kansas, Lawrence, instructor in German, 1951-53; Quinnipiac College, Hamden, Conn., 1953-61, began as assistant professor, became associate professor of English and chairman of department; University of South Florida, Tampa, assistant professor, 1961-63, associate professor, 1963-68, professor of humanities, 1968—. Silvermine College of Art, lecturer in humanities, 1948-61, acting dean and member of board, 1960-61. Coordinator, Poetry in the Schools, Hillsborough County, Florida, 1972-76; member of nominating committee, Nobel Prize in literature, 1975—. Has exhibited his works of graphic art at a number of one-man shows. Special consultant to U.S. Holocaust Memorial Council, 1981. *Military service:* U.S. Army, 1942-45; served in three campaigns; wounded at Anzio; received Purple Heart and Unit Citation.

MEMBER: International Poetry Society (fellow), National Federation of State Poetry Societies (president, 1968-70), Poetry Society of America, Poetry Society of Florida, Connecticut Academy of Arts and Science (fellow). *Awards, honors:* Florida poet of the year, 1965; Stephen Vincent Benet Award, 1970 and 1974; award for services to American literature, Hayden Library, Arizona State University, 1970.

WRITINGS: *I Feed You from My Cup* (poems), Quinnipiac College Press, 1958; *In Need for Names* (poems), Linden Press, 1961; *Existential Canon, and Other Poems*, South & West, 1965; *Florida Montage* (poems), South & West, 1966; *Sermons from the Ammunition Hatch of the Ship of Fools*, Vagabond, 1968; *From the Divide* (poems), Olivant, 1970; *Hebraic Modes* (poems), Olivant, 1972; *Journey toward the Roots* (poems and drawings), Valkyrie Press, 1976; (translator) Heinrich von Kleist, *The Broken Jug*, Olivant, 1977; *California Frescoes* (poems and drawings), American Studies Press, 1980; *General George H. Thomas: A Summary in Perspective*, American Studies Press, 1980; *The Record of a Green Planet* (poems), Linden Press, 1982.

Contributor: *Where Is Vietnam?*, Doubleday, 1967; Robin Gregory, editor, *Ipso Facto* (poetry anthology), Hud Publications, 1975; Walter Lowenfels, editor, *For Neruda, For Chile*, Beacon Press, 1975; Alan F. Pater, editor, *The Anthology of American Magazine Verse*, Monitor, 1981.

Editor of *Children's Poetry Anthology*, 1975. Contributor of art criticism to *Tampa Times*, 1961-67. Co-editor, *Orange Street Poetry Journal*, 1958-62, and *University of South Florida Language Quarterly*, 1961-74; editor, *Gryphon* (University of South Florida), 1974—.

WORK IN PROGRESS: Essays on the political, social, and cultural events in Germany, 1918-1945, for U.S. Holocaust Memorial Council; new poems.

SIDELIGHTS: "The more I write and publish," observes Hans Juergensen, "the more reluctant I become about pronouncing artistic maxims. There is stark necessity in me to create. It is my hope that my skill complements that need." In addition to English and his native German, Juergensen is competent in French and has some knowledge of Latin and Hebrew.

BIOGRAPHICAL/CRITICAL SOURCES: *Choice*, September, 1977.

K

KACHRU, Braj Behari 1932-

PERSONAL: Born May 15, 1932, in Srinagar, Kashmir, India; came to United States in 1963; son of Shyam Lal (an educator) and Tulsidevi (Tutu) Kachru; married Yamuna Keskar (a professor), January 22, 1965; children: Amita, Shamit. *Education:* Jammu and Kashmir University, B.A. (with honors), 1952; Allahabad University, M.A., 1955; University of Edinburgh, Ph.D., 1961. *Religion:* Hindu. *Home:* 2016 Cureton Dr., Urbana, Ill. 61801. *Office:* Department of Linguistics, University of Illinois, Urbana, Ill. 61801.

CAREER: Deccan College Research Institute, Poona, India, fellow in linguistics, 1957-58; Lucknow University, Lucknow, India, assistant professor of English, in charge of linguistics program, 1962-63; University of Illinois at Urbana-Champaign, research associate, 1963-64, assistant professor, 1964-67, associate professor, 1967-70, professor of linguistics, 1970—, head of department, 1969-79, and associate of Center for Advanced Study, 1971-72, and 1979-80. Linguistic Institute, Linguistic Society of America, coordinator of Division of Applied Linguistics, 1976—, director, 1978. Member of South Asian study committees; co-director of summer program in South Asian study, 1967; member of board of trustees, American Institute of Indian Studies, 1980-82; chairman, International Committee for South Asian Languages and Linguistics, 1980—; chairman of seminars in linguistics. Consultant to American Institute of Indian Studies, 1972, and to Ford Foundation, 1974.

MEMBER: International P.E.N., Linguistic Society of America, American Oriental Society, Linguistic Society of India (life member), Linguistic Association of Canada and the United States, American Association of Applied Linguistics, Teachers of English to Speakers of Other Languages. *Awards, honors:* Grants from U.S. Department of Health, Education and Welfare's Institute of International Affairs, 1965-72, for *A Reference Grammar of Kashmiri*, and 1970-72, for *An Introduction to Spoken Kashmiri;* faculty research fellow of American Institute of Indian Studies, New Delhi, India, 1967-68, 1971-72, and 1982.

WRITINGS: A Reference Grammar of Kashmiri, U.S. Office of Education, 1969; (editor with H. W. Stahlke) *Current Trends in Stylistics*, Linguistic Research, Inc., 1972; (editor with others, and contributor) *Issues in Linguistics: Papers in Honor of Henry and Renee Kahane*, University of Illinois Press, 1973; *An Introduction to Spoken Kashmiri*, two parts, U.S. Office of Education, 1973; (editor with S. N. Sridhar) *Aspects of Sociolinguistics in South Asia*, Mouton, 1978; *Kashmiri Literature*, Otto Harrassowitz, 1981; *The Indianization of English: The English Language in India*, Oxford University Press, 1982; (editor and contributor) *The Other Tongue: English across Cultures*, University of Illinois Press, 1982.

Contributor: C. E. Bazell and others, editors, *In Memory of J. R. Firth*, Longmans, Green, 1966; John W. M. Verhaar, editor, *Foundations of Language*, Part III, Volume VIII, D. Reidel (Dordrecht, Netherlands), 1968; T. Sebeok and others, editors, *Current Trends in Linguistics*, Mouton, 1969; J. E. Alatis, editor, *International Dimensions of Bilingual Education*, Georgetown University Press, 1978; Ladislav Zgusta, editor, *Theory and Method in Lexicography: Western and Non-Western Perspective*, Hornbeam Press, 1980; L. Smith, editor, *English for Cross-Cultural Communication*, Macmillan (London), 1981; Charles Ferguson and Shirley B. Heath, editors, *Language in the U.S.A.*, Cambridge University Press, 1981; R. Kaplan, editor, *Annual Review of Applied Linguistics*, Rowley, 1981; B. Hartford and A. Baldman, editors, *Issues in International Bilingual Education*, Plenum, 1981; R. W. Bailey and Manfred Gorlach, editors, *English as a World Language*, University of Michigan Press, 1982. Also contributor to *Theoretical Foundations of Bilingualism*, edited by Henry Trueba.

Contributor of articles and reviews to language, education, and Oriental studies journals. Editor of *Studies in Language Learning;* co-editor of *Studies in Hindi Linguistics*, 1970; review editor of *Papers in Linguistics*, 1970-78; has been guest editor of South Asian issues of *International Journal of the Sociology of Language* and *Studies in the Linguistic Sciences*. Member of editorial board of *Studies in the Linguistic Sciences*. 1969—, *International Journal of the Sociology of Language, Papers in Linguistics, Studies in Language Learning*, 1976-77, *TESOL Quarterly*, 1978—, *English World-Wide: Journal of Varieties of English*, 1979—, *Journal of South Asian Literatures*, 1980—, and *World Language English*, 1981. Editorial director, *Annual Review of Applied Linguistics;* consultant to *Random House Dictionary of the English Language*, 1965-66.

WORK IN PROGRESS: Continuing research on non-native varities of English, and on Kashmiri language and literature; sociolinguistic research on bilingualism.

KALIN, Robert 1921-

PERSONAL: Born December 11, 1921, in Everett, Mass.; son of Benjamin (a grocer) and Celia (Kraff) Kalin; married Madelyn Pildish, August 17, 1962; children: Susan Leslie, John Benjamin, Sandra Kim, Richard Dean. *Education:* University of Chicago, B.S., 1947; Harvard University, M.A.T., 1948; Florida State University, Ph.D., 1961. *Home:* 1120 Cherokee Dr., Tallahassee, Fla. 32301. *Office:* Department of Mathematics Education, Florida State University, Tallahassee, Fla. 32306.

CAREER: High school mathematics teacher in Danvers, Mass., 1948-49, and St. Louis, Mo., 1949-52; Naval Air Technical Training Center, Norman, Okla., educational statistician, 1952-53; Educational Testing Service, Princeton, N.J., test specialist and associate in research, 1953-55; College Board's Commission on Mathematics, Princeton, N.J., executive assistant, 1955-56; Florida State University, Tallahassee, instructor, 1956-61, assistant professor, 1961-63, associate professor, 1963-65, professor of mathematics education, 1965—, chairman of mathematics education program, 1974-78. Chairman of Florida State Mathematics Curriculum Guide Committee, 1961-64; director of Florida State University Mathematics Television Project, 1965-66; chairman of Board of Regents Committee on Educational Television, 1966-68; member of advisory committee to Florida Committee on Mathematics Assessment, 1970-72. *Military service:* U.S. Army, 1943-46.

MEMBER: International Group for the Psychology of Mathematics Education, Mathematical Association of America, National Council of Teachers of Mathematics (Florida representative, 1957-64), School Science and Mathematics Association, Association of Teachers of Mathematics, Queensland Association of Mathematics Teachers, Australian Association of Mathematics Teachers, Florida Council of Teachers of Mathematics (president, 1960-61), Pi Mu Epsilon, Mu Alpha Theta (member of governing board, 1970-74; president, 1977-79).

WRITINGS: (With Henry S. Dyer and Frederick M. Lord) *Problems in Mathematical Education,* Educational Testing Service, 1956; (contributor) *Evaluation of Mathematics,* National Council of Teachers of Mathematics, 1961; (with Henry Garland and Eugene Nichols) *Introduction to Sets,* Holt, 1962; *The Arithmetic of Directed Numbers,* Holt, 1962; *Equations and Inequalities,* Holt, 1963; *Introduction to Coordinate Geometry,* Holt, 1963; (with Nichols, Frances Flournoy, and Leonard Simon) *Elementary Mathematics: Patterns and Structure,* eleven volumes, Holt, 1966, revised edition, 1968; (contributor) *Conference on Mathematics for Gifted Students,* School Mathematics Study Group, 1968; (with George Green) *Modern Mathematics for the Elementary School Teacher,* with video tapes, McGraw, 1969; (contributor) *Computer-Assisted Instruction and the Teaching of Mathematics,* National Council of Teachers of Mathematics, 1969.

(With Nichols) *Analytic Geometry,* Holt, 1973; (with Nichols, Flournoy, Simon, Paul A. Anderson, John Schluep, and Leslie A. Dwight) *Holt School Mathematics: Grades K-8,* Holt, 1974, revised edition, 1978; (co-author) *Holt Mathematics,* Holt, 1981. Also author of unpublished educational reports. Contributor to mathematics and education journals. Co-editor, referee, and reviewer of testing for *Mathematics Teacher,* 1957-61; book reviewer for Prentice-Hall.

WORK IN PROGRESS: Investigating the thinking strategies, memorization process, and levels of understanding of elementary school students in arithmetic, with emphasis on basic facts of division and other operations, in line with models suggested by William Brownell; research on teaching methods and school organizations in Germany, Great Britain, and the United States.

* * *

KALSTONE, Shirlee A(nn) 1932-

PERSONAL: Born September 2, 1932, in Pittsburgh, Pa.; daughter of Daniel C. (an actors' agent) and Irene (Mangold) Comoroda; married Milton C. Staude, December 1, 1953 (divorced, 1959); married Lawrence M. Kalstone (a manufacturer), May 5, 1961; children: (first marriage) Gary M. *Education:* Attended University of Pittsburgh. *Home and office:* 250 East 73rd St., New York, N.Y. 10021.

CAREER: Owner of "Poodle Boutique," 1953-60; Kalstone Studios Grooming School, Pittsburgh, Pa., director, 1961-70; Lambert Kay, Los Angeles, Calif., director of consumer relations, 1972-73; VO Toys, Inc., New York, N.Y., consultant to "Ring 5," 1974—. Has lectured on dog grooming in Japan, England, and in Scandinavian countries; conducted "All About Dogs" show on WQED-Television, 1963; volunteer worker for Fund for Animals and American Society for the Prevention of Cruelty to Animals. *Member:* Professional Groomers Association (former vice-president), National Dog Groomers Association of America (former director of public relations).

AWARDS, HONORS: Award for best technical book, Dog Writers Association of America, 1968, for *The Complete Poodle Clipping and Grooming Book,* and 1980, for *The Art of Handling Show Dogs;* outstanding grooming award, National Dog Groomers Association of America, 1974; founder's award, National Dog Groomers Association of America, 1975; "Dog Person of the Year" Award, National Retail Pet Supply and Groomers Association, 1976.

WRITINGS: The Complete Poodle Clipping and Grooming Book, Howell Book, 1968, revised edition, 1981; *Pet Poodle Grooming Made Easy,* Howell Book, 1972; *The Kalstone Guide to Grooming All Toy Dogs,* Howell Book, 1976; (with Frank T. Sabella) *The Art of Handling Show Dogs,* B & E Publications, 1980; (with Walter McNamara) *First Aid for Dogs,* Arco, 1980; *Dogs: Breeds, Care, and Training,* Dell, 1982. Also author of consumer booklets on pets. Writer of column "About Grooming" for *Pet/Supplies/Marketing* (magazine), and of columns for *Pure-Bred Dogs* and *American Kennel Gazette;* contributor to other pet magazines. Editor, *Professional Groomer,* 1970-72.

WORK IN PROGRESS: A book on cats; an encyclopedia of grooming for all dog breeds.

SIDELIGHTS: Shirlee Kalstone presently breeds and shows poodles and whippets.

* * *

KAMINSKI, Margaret (Joan) 1944-

PERSONAL: Born March 16, 1944, in Detroit, Mich.; daughter of John Joseph (a diemaker) and Gertrude (Malak) Kaminski; married Bruce Charles Bennett, May 30, 1967 (divorced, 1972). *Education:* Wayne State University, B.F.A., 1966, M.S.L.S., 1969. *Politics:* Feminist. *Religion:* Roman Catholic. *Home:* 720 East Second St., Royal Oak, Mich. 48067. *Office:* Detroit Public Library, 5201 Woodward Ave., Detroit, Mich. 48202.

CAREER: Detroit Public Library, Detroit, Mich., reference librarian in language, literature, philosophy, and fine arts department, 1969-73, assistant to coordinator of public relations, 1973-76, reference librarian in general information department,

1976—, adult program assistant for library branches, 1979—. Poet and diarist; owner and operator of Glass Bell Press, a poetry press for women. Radio interviewer, writer, and presenter; guest producer of "Dimension," poetry program on WDET-FM, "World of Books" and "Meet the Author" programs on WDEE-FM. Has given poetry readings on program, "The Ins and Outs of Love," for PBS-TV, during "High Noon Poetry Series" at Detroit Public Library, and at Wayne State University Miles Modern Poetry Committee readings.

WRITINGS: Martinis, White Light Press (Detroit), 1974; (editor) Moving to Antarctica: An Anthology of Women's Writing, Dustbooks, 1975; (editor and contributor) Ten Michigan Women Poets, Glass Bell Press, 1975; La Vida de la Mujer (title means "The Life of the Woman"), Fallen Angel Press, 1975; El Canon and Other Poems, Rhiannon Press, 1979; A Guatemalan Diary, Cumberland Journal, 1981.

Contributor to anthologies, including Free Women, edited by Judith McCombs, Red Hanrahan Press, 1971, A Change in Weather: Midwest Women Poets, edited by Peg Lauber, Concerns: Essays and Reviews, 1972-76, edited by Tom Montag, Pentagram, 1977, and The Greater Golden Hill Poetry Express National Issue, Feminist Poetry and Graphics Center.

Author of monograph, A Short History of the Woman Suffrage Movement in Detroit and Michigan, 1974. Writer of "Dame Philology," monthly column in Margins, 1974—. Contributor of poetry and articles to numerous journals, magazines, and newspapers, including University of Windsor Review, Wayne Literary Review, Detroit Discovery, Detroit News, Mainline, and Poetry Review. Editor of Detroit Public Library Staff News Bulletin, 1970-71; co-editor of Moving Out (feminist literary journal), 1971—.

WORK IN PROGRESS: Egyptian Diary; German Diary.

SIDELIGHTS: Margaret Kaminski told CA: "My experience in meeting and interviewing Anais Nin, Margaret Atwood, Marge Piercy, Audre Lorde, and other women has amplified my own life as a woman writer, editor, and publisher. Their encouragement and their work has made me realize that there have always been adventurous women. I read of Nin's handset and handprinted press in the Greenwich Village of the '40s, and started Glass Bell Press, named for her book, Under a Glass Bell and Other Stories. I also realized that I was not the only person eccentric enough to record my life's passage since the age of 12, and Nin became a model for me.

"Since 1975, my inner journey has been symbolized by my outer journeys. I have visited and photographed South and Central America: Macchu Pichu in Peru, Argentina, Brazil, Colombia, Venezuela, the Yucatan (Chichen-Itza and Tulum); I backpacked around Tikal and Lake Atitlan in Guatemala. I visited Egypt: the pyramids, Valley of the Kings and Queens, Edfu, Esna, Memphis, and Cairo, and the fantastic array of sites occupied by the peoples representing 8,000 years of civilization in Turkey. The European countries I have visited include Great Britain, France, Spain, Portugal, Italy, Germany, and Austria. I am now making a pilgrimage of Indian ruins and national parks in the United States, recording everything in my diary and camera.

"My diary and poetry have taken on a new meaning. It is as if my travels were equivalent to a journey of the soul. I live partly in the past, among the great societies which have come and gone, with their ruins, pottery shards and petroglyphs; among natural phenomena—vast geologic changes, rock formations, volcanos, fossils, the whole history of organic matter, and all the earth's movements. These pasts inspire me toward another future, which only the poetic imagination can envision."

AVOCATIONAL INTERESTS: Yoga, meditation, photography, printing, hiking, backpacking, and the fine arts.

BIOGRAPHICAL/CRITICAL SOURCES: Detroit Women's Voice, September, 1982.

*   *   *

KAPLAN, Howard B(ernard)   1932-

PERSONAL: Born March 17, 1932, in New York, N.Y.; son of Samuel (a businessman) and Esther (Schimmer) Kaplan; married Diane Gray, August 9, 1970; children: Samuel Charles, Rachel Esther. Education: New York University, A.B., 1953, M.A., 1954, Ph.D., 1958. Home: 2330 Bolsover, Houston, Tex. 77005. Office: Baylor College of Medicine, 1200 Moursund, Houston, Tex. 77030.

CAREER: New York University, New York, N.Y., instructor, 1955-57, assistant professor of sociology, 1958; Baylor College of Medicine, Houston, Tex., postdoctoral fellow, 1958-60, assistant professor, 1960-65, associate professor, 1965-70, professor of sociology, 1970—. University of Houston, visiting assistant professor, 1960-65, visiting professor, 1981—. Visiting associate professor at New York University, 1960, and Rice University, 1967-69. Senior sociologist, Sociological Research Section, Houston State Psychiatric Institute, 1958-67. Consultant to Veterans Administration Hospital, Houston, 1961—, Community Council of Houston and Harris County, 1964-66, and Southmore House, 1964-67. Member: International Sociological Association, American Sociological Association. Awards, honors: Russell Sage Foundation postdoctoral fellowship, 1958-60; Milbank faculty fellowship, 1965-72.

WRITINGS: The Sociology of Mental Illness, College & University Press, 1972; Self-Attitudes and Deviant Behavior, Goodyear Publishing, 1975; Deviant Behavior in Defense of Self, Academic Press, 1980.

Contributor: P. H. Leiderman and David Shapiro, editors, Psychological Approaches to Social Behavior, Stanford University Press, 1964; Earl Rubington and M. S. Weinberg, editors, Deviance: The Interactionist Perspective, Macmillan, 1968.

Erwin O. Smigel, editor, Handbook on the Study of Social Problems, Rand McNally, 1971; E. Gartly Jaco, editor, Patients, Physicians, and Illness, Free Press, 1972; Paul R. Patterson, Carolyn Denning, and Austin H. Kutscher, editors, Psychosocial Aspects of Cystic Fibrosis: A Model for Chronic Lung Disease, Columbia University Press, 1973; W. E. Fann, A. D. Pokorny, I. Karacan, and R. L. Williams, editors, Phenomenology and Treatment of Depression, Spectrum Publications, 1977; F. A. Seixas, editor, Currents in Alcoholism, Grune, Volume II, 1977, Volume IV, 1978; Fann, Pokorny, Karacan, and Williams, editors, Phenomenology and Treatment of Schizophrenia, Spectrum Publications, 1978; D. J. Lettieri, editor, Drugs and Suicide: When Other Coping Strategies Fail, Sage Publications, 1978; H. E. Freeman, S. Levine, and L. G. Reeder, editors, Handbook of Medical Sociology, Prentice-Hall, 1979; Fann, Pokorny, Karacan, and Williams, editors, Phenomenology and Treatment of Anxiety, Spectrum Publications, 1979.

S. B. Sells, M. Roff, J. Strauss, and Pollin, editors, Human Functioning in Longitudinal Perspective, Williams & Wilkins, 1980; Lettieri, Sayers, and H. W. Pearson, editors, Theories on Drug Abuse: Selected Contemporary Perspectives, U.S. Government Printing Office, 1980; Moffic and G. L. Adams, editors, *The Clinicians Manual on Mental Health Care: An Interdisciplinary Approach*, Addison-Wesley, 1982.

* * *

KAPLAN, Justin 1925-

PERSONAL: Born September 5, 1925, in New York, N.Y.; son of Tobias D. (a manufacturer) and Anna (Rudman) Kaplan; married Anne Bernays (a writer), July 29, 1954; children: Susanna Bernays, Hester Margaret, Polly Anne. *Education:* Harvard University, B.S., 1945. *Politics:* Democrat. *Religion:* Jewish. *Home:* 16 Francis Ave., Cambridge, Mass. 02138.

CAREER: Free-lance work for various New York publishers, 1946-54; Simon & Schuster, Inc., New York, N.Y., editor, 1954-59; full-time professional writer, 1959—. Lecturer at Harvard University, 1969, 1973, 1976, 1978. *Member:* American Academy of Arts and Sciences, Society of American Historians, Phi Beta Kappa. *Awards, honors:* National Book Award and Pulitzer Prize, 1967, both for *Mr. Clemens and Mark Twain;* Guggenheim fellow, 1975-76; American Book Award for Biography, 1981, for *Walt Whitman: A Life*.

WRITINGS: (Editor) *Dialogues of Plato*, Pocket Books, 1950; (editor) *With Malice Toward Women*, Dodd, 1952; (editor) *The Pocket Aristotle*, Pocket Books, 1958; (editor) *Mark Twain, The Gilded Age*, Trident, 1964; *Mr. Clemens and Mark Twain*, Simon & Schuster, 1966; (editor) *Great Short Works of Mark Twain*, Harper, 1967; *Mark Twain: A Profile*, Hill & Wang, 1967; *Lincoln Steffens, A Biography*, Simon & Schuster, 1974; *Mark Twain and His World*, Simon & Schuster, 1974; *Walt Whitman: A Life*, Simon & Schuster, 1980; (editor) *Walt Whitman: Complete Poetry and Collected Prose*, Library of America, 1982.

WORK IN PROGRESS: A biography of Charlie Chaplin.

SIDELIGHTS: "I'm an obscurantist," Justin Kaplan told *Newsweek* reporter James N. Baker. "I'm drawn to people whose lives have a certain mystery—mysteries that aren't going to be solved, that are too sacred to be solved." Mark Twain and Walt Whitman—the subjects of Kaplan's award-winning biographies—were two such enigmatic figures. In his treatment of both men, Kaplan says he consciously created a tension between himself and his subjects. This technique, which he employs in all his biographies, keeps his books from degenerating into dry accounts of someone's life. Attentive not only to scholarship but also to the requirements of a good story, Kaplan produces biographies that read like novels, critics say.

During his research for *Mr. Clemens and Mark Twain*, Kaplan discovered that he had found a subject who was "a mystery to himself." "The conflict," writes *Saturday Review*'s A. G. Day, "is the battle between 'Mark Twain'—. . . the exploder of sham—and the success-hunting Samuel Clemens, victim of the 'Gilded Age' that he himself named and satirized. Nowhere does Mr. Kaplan use the word 'schizophrenia,' but his book examines almost clinically the growing gap between the man and his mask."

Kaplan's insight into Twain, the man, as opposed to Twain, the legend, makes this book "unmistakably destined for classic status in its field," according to *Newsweek*. *Punch* reviewer Malcolm Bradbury expresses a similar view. "Kaplan," he writes, "gives us a better and deeper Mark Twain than we ever had, a Twain who carried the tensions of the age he lived in and felt his way into the possibilities, and the crudities, of his culture. The place of a mind in a culture is superbly caught, and the narrative remains throughout human and sympathetic while catching it. It redeems a writer who has been as badly served by excessive claims about his 'wisdom' or intelligence as by false claims about his 'primitivism.' It is altogether an admirable and important book."

Kaplan told *Library Journal* that his purpose in writing Twain's biography was "not only to explore the mystery of this man but also to respect it. . . . Two currents flowed through his life. One flowed away from Hannibal, Missouri, toward the world of wealth, fame and materialities. The other flowed back to Hannibal again. Out of the opposition of these currents, out of the turbulent dark waters, came one of the great styles and dazzling personalities of our literature, one of its undisputed masterpieces, and half a dozen of its major books." In his National Book Award acceptance speech, Kaplan added: "Mark Twain said he hated the past because it was so 'damned humiliating,' hated prying, hated to read over his old letters—'they make my flesh creep,' he said. His biographer is inevitably his enemy, and there were nights during the writing of this book when punishment from beyond the grave seemed perfectly possible. There were also, when this book was finished and its subject laid to rest once again, weeks of a very powerful emotion which I finally recognized as grief."

After exploring the man who was "a mystery to himself," Kaplan turned to a subject who was a mystery to others—the American poet Walt Whitman. But, as *Newsweek*'s Baker reports, Kaplan was so frustrated by "the 'disappearing act' of the poet's early years," that he turned out a life-and-times biography of Lincoln Steffens before committing himself to unravelling the Whitman legend. When *Walt Whitman: A Life* was finally published, most critics praised Kaplan's portrayal of the elusive poet who, in the words of *Washington Post Book World* critic Marcus Cunliffe, "covered his tracks and left false trails."

How was Kaplan able to establish the truth about the man *Nation*'s Phyllis Rose calls "the artful dodger of American Letters"? As Rose notes, it was never Kaplan's intention to "prove conclusively things about Whitman which Whitman himself did not know." She and other reviewers think the strength of Kaplan's biography lies rather in its convincing delineation of "Whitman's setting and context," which is accomplished through a deft juxtaposition of carefully-researched detail. "Kaplan," explains Donald Hall in *Saturday Review*, "shows us not one or two sources for Whitman's images and innovations but a thousand sources, amounting to a background. His method is not to analyze a poem for its origins . . . but to recount the dense days of a life, the incidents of a busy Manhattan—and then to juxtapose a relevant line from a poem; let the reader note and judge the connection." Comments *New York Times Book Review*'s Helen Vendler: "Justin Kaplan's excellent life of Whitman, a life for the general reader, if it does not solve 'the curious whether and how' of Whitman's power, does the next best thing and the thing most appropriate to a life. It puts the multiplicity of Whitman's mysterious selves on view."

In addition to its broad scope, Kaplan's biography also displays a narrative vigor which draws the reader into the story, critics say. "Even though his text runs to 421 pages, there is not really a dull one among them," writes Seymour Krim in the *Village Voice*. "If Kaplan's prose is slightly staccato compared to the patient straightforwardness of [Gay Wilson] Allen's [earlier] study, it seems fitting: he is giving us a Whitman for the '80s, and with our movie-eyes, we can actually see the old patriot through Kaplan's lens in a way that was not possible before." *Nation*'s Phyllis Rose comments: "I can hardly imagine a more satisfying literary biography. It is psychologically acute without being tendentiously analytic. It has the narrative density and historical breadth of a novel. It is artful sentence by sentence and in the structure of the whole. Making the best use of Whitman's own optimism and passion for the palpable, it is a buoyant, energizing book."

Instead of beginning, conventionally, with Whitman's childhood, the biography opens at the end of his life in what Erica Jong calls in the *Chicago Tribune Book World* "his days of poetic glory and physical decline." Reviewers are unanimous in their regard for this unusual organization: "By beginning the book toward the end of Whitman's life and by placing at the start an overview of Whitman's character and achievement, Kaplan refreshingly disrupts the usual pattern of biography and eases artfully into the treatment of the long foreground of *Leaves of Grass*," Rose says. This approach, observes *New York Times* reviewer Christopher Lehmann-Haupt, "allows him to close his book with Whitman still alive, riding 'contentedly at anchor on the waters of the past,' as the closing phrase of the biography puts it. To judge from this luminescent work, which far outshines Mr. Kaplan's previous study, 'Lincoln Steffens,' and rivals the splendor of his first book, 'Mr. Clemens and Mark Twain,' that is just the way Walt Whitman would have wanted his life to end."

AVOCATIONAL INTERESTS: Walking, swimming, Cape Cod, talk.

BIOGRAPHICAL/CRITICAL SOURCES: Saturday Review, June 18, 1966, November, 1980; *Punch*, March 1, 1967; *Newsweek*, March 20, 1967, November 10, 1980; *Library Journal*, April 1, 1967; *New York Times*, May 2, 1967, November 5, 1980; *Village Voice*, October 22, 1980; *Atlantic Monthly*, November, 1980; *Chicago Tribune Book World*, November 2, 1980; *Nation*, November 8, 1980; *New York Times Book Review*, November 9, 1980, April 25, 1982, June 6, 1982; *Washington Post Book World*, November 9, 1980; *Time*, November 17, 1980.

—Sketch by Donna Olendorf

* * *

KAPP, K(arl) William 1910-1976

PERSONAL: Born October 27, 1910, in Koenigsberg, Germany; died April 10, 1976, in Dubrovnik; son of August Wilhelm (a professor of mathematics) and Gertrud (Schrader) Kapp; married Lore L. Masur, October 27, 1937. *Education:* Attended universities of Berlin, Geneva, and Koenigsberg, 1929-32; law degree, 1932; Graduate Institute of International Studies, University of Geneva, graduate studies, 1933-36, Docteur es Sciences Politiques, 1936; postgraduate studies at London School of Economics. *Home:* 39 Oberer Batterieweg, Basel 4052, Switzerland. *Office:* University of Basel, Basel 4000, Petersgrabere 29, Switzerland.

CAREER: Economist and writer. Geneva Research Center, Geneva, Switzerland, fellow, 1937; New York University, New York City, instructor in economics, 1938-43; Columbia University, New York City, instructor in economics, 1944-46; Wesleyan University, Middletown, Conn., assistant professor of economics, 1946-50; Brooklyn College (now Brooklyn College of the City University of New York), New York City, associate professor, 1950-53, professor of economics, 1953-65; University of Basel, Basel, Switzerland professor of national economics, 1965-75, professor emeritus, 1975-76. Fulbright research professor, Gokhale Institute of Politics and Economics, Poona, India, 1957-58; Fulbright lecturer, University of Rajasthan, Jaipur, India, 1961-62; visiting Rockefeller professor, University of the Philippines, Diliman-Manila, 1964. Consultant, Economic Division, Office of Strategic Services, 1942. *Member:* American Economic Association, Association for Evolutionary Economics, Society for General Systems Research, Regional Science Association, List-Gesellschaft. *Awards, honors:* Fellow and grant recipient, Fund for the Advancement of Education, Ford Foundation, 1952-53.

WRITINGS: Planwirtschaft und Aussenhandel, Librairie de l'Universite (Geneva), 1936; *The League of Nations and Raw Materials, 1919-1939*, Geneva Studies, 1941; (co-editor) *Introduction to Contemporary Civilization in the West*, Columbia University Press, 1946; (with wife, Lore L. Kapp) *Readings in Economics*, Barnes & Noble, 1949, 2nd edition published as *History of Economic Thought: A Book of Readings*, 1963; *The Social Costs of Private Enterprise*, Harvard University Press, 1950, 2nd revised edition published as *The Social Costs of Business Enterprise*, Asia Publishing House, 1963, revised and enlarged edition, edited by Michael Barrett-Brown, Spokesman Books, 1978; (with L. Kapp) *A Graphic Approach to Economics*, Holt, 1951; *Toward a Science of Man in Society*, Nijhoff, 1961; *Hindu Culture; Economic Development and Economic Planning in India: A Collection of Essays*, Asia Publishing House, 1962; (with Fritz Vilmar) *Sozialisierung der Verluste? Die sozialen Kosten eines privatwirtschaftlichen Systems*, C. Hansert (Munich), 1972; (editor) *Neve Wege fur Bangladesh*, Institut fur Sozialwissenschaften, 1973; *Environmental Policies and Development Planning in Contemporary China and Other Essays*, Mouton, 1974; (with Hans Baumann and Peter Wachtl) *Staatliche Foerderung "umweltfreundlicher" Technologien*, Schwartz (Gottingen), 1976; *Economics in Institutional Perspective*, Lexington Books, 1977. Contributor to professional journals.

WORK IN PROGRESS: The Economics of Regional Development Projects; Social Economics: A Systematic Introduction.

SIDELIGHTS: K. William Kapp traveled widely in South America and Asia. *Avocational interests:* Skiing, hiking.

OBITUARIES: New York Times, April 26, 1976.†

* * *

KARGER, Delmar William 1913-

PERSONAL: Born May 9, 1913, in Cape Girardeau, Mo.; son of Ernest John (a foreman) and Clara M. (Hellewege) Karger; married Paula Miller, July 5, 1935 (died November, 1958); married Edith Kennedy, January 11, 1962 (died August 31, 1969); married Ruth Lounsberry Rivard, October 31, 1970; children: (first marriage) Bonnie E. (Mrs. Lloyd McCormack), Karin R. (Mrs. Douglas Van Slyke), Joyce P. *Education:* Valparaiso University, B.S. in E.E., 1935; University of Pittsburgh, M.S. in Gen.Eng., 1947. *Religion:* Presbyterian. *Home and office:* 506 Circle Dr., De Funiak Springs, Fla. 32433.

CAREER: International Harvester Co., Fort Wayne, Ind., assistant chief electrician, 1935-41, assistant plant engineer, 1941-42; Westinghouse Electric Corp., Pittsburgh, Pa., head manufacturing engineer, 1942-45, manager of cooperative education, 1945-47; Pennsylvania Electric Coil Corp., Pittsburgh, plant manager, 1947-48; Radio Corp. of America (now RCA Corp.), Camden, N.J., manager of organization and systems, 1948-49, chief industrial engineer of RCA Service Co., 1949-51; Magnavox Corp., Fort Wayne, chief plant and industrial engineer, 1951-56, manager of new product development, 1956-59; Rensselaer Polytechnic Institute, Troy, N.Y., professor and head of department of management engineering, 1959-63, dean of School of Management, 1963-70, Ford Foundation professor of management, 1970-78. Management and industrial engineering consultant, 1959—. Director of Fiber Glass Industries,

1961-82, Wellington Technical Industries, 1963—, Wellington Industries, Inc. (formerly Wellington Computer Graphics), 1969-75, 1977—, Bunker Ramo Corp., 1974-82, and Scott Fetzer, 1976-82. American Cancer Society, chapter president, 1963-64, director, 1964—; New York State Finance Committee, member, 1964-68, state director, 1965-72.

MEMBER: American Institute of Industrial Engineers (fellow; national vice-president, 1958-59), American Institute of Plant Engineers, American Society for Engineering Education, Council for International Progress in Management (member of board of directors, 1962-65), Methods Time Measurement Association for Standards and Research (fellow; president, 1958-60; chairman of research committee, 1962-70), Society for the Advancement of Management (fellow; vice-president and member of board of directors, 1977-79), Institute of Management Sciences, American Association of University Professors, Academy of Management, American Association for the Advancement of Science (fellow), Santa Rosa Beach and Golf Club.

WRITINGS: (With Franklin H. Bayha) *Engineered Work Measurement*, Industrial Press, 1957, 3rd edition, 1977; *The New Product*, Industrial Press, 1960; (with Robert G. Murdick) *Managing Engineering and Research*, Industrial Press, 1963, 3rd edition, 1977; (with A. B. Jack) *Problems of Small Business in Developing and Exploiting New Products*, Rensselaer Polytechnic Institute and U.S. Small Business Administration, 1963; (with Murdick) *New Product Venture Management*, Gordon & Breach, 1973; *How to Choose a Career*, F. Watts, 1978; (with W. Hancock) *Advanced Work Measurement*, Industrial Press, 1982; (with F. James) *Advanced Investment Decision-Making: The Technical Approach*, Prentice-Hall, 1983.

SIDELIGHTS: Delmar Karger's books have been published in French and Dutch.

* * *

KARK, Nina Mary (Mabey) 1925-
(Nina Bawden)

PERSONAL: Born January 19, 1925, in London, England; daughter of Charles Mabey and Ellalaine Ursula May (Cushing) Mabey; married Austen Steven Kark (an executive in Overseas Department of British Broadcasting Corp.), 1954; children: (prior marriage) Nicholas Bawden, Robert Humphrey Felix Bawden; (present marriage) Perdita Emily Helena Kark. *Education:* Somerville College, Oxford, B.A., 1946, M.A., 1951; additional graduate study at Salzburg Seminar in American Studies, 1960. *Home:* 22 Noel Rd., London N1 8HA, England. *Agent:* Curtis Brown Ltd., 575 Madison Ave., New York, N.Y. 10022.

CAREER: Writer. Assistant, Town and Country Planning Associates, 1946-47; Justice of the Peace, Surrey, 1968. *Member:* P.E.N., Royal Society of Literature (fellow), Society of Women Writers and Journalists (president), British Ski Club. *Awards, honors: Guardian* Award for Children's Fiction, 1975, for *The Peppermint Pig; Yorkshire Post* Novel of the Year Award, 1977, for *Afternoon of a Good Woman*.

WRITINGS—All under name Nina Bawden; adult novels: *Eyes of Green*, Morrow, 1953 (published in England as *Who Calls the Tune*, Collins, 1953); *The Odd Flamingo*, Collins, 1955; *The Solitary Child*, Collins, 1956; *Devil by the Sea*, Collins, 1957, Lippincott, 1959; *Change Here for Babylon*, Collins, 1957; *Glass Slippers Always Pinch*, Lippincott, 1960 (published in England as *Just Like a Lady*, Longmans, Green, 1960); *In Honour Bound*, Longmans, Green, 1961; *Tortoise by Candlelight*, Harper, 1963; *Under the Skin*, Harper, 1964; *A Little Love, A Little Learning*, Harper, 1966; *A Woman of My Age*, Harper, 1967; *The Grain of Truth*, Harper, 1968; *The Birds on the Trees*, Harper, 1970; *Anna Apparent*, Harper, 1972; *George Beneath a Paper Moon*, Harper, 1974; *Afternoon of a Good Woman*, Harper, 1977; *Familiar Passions*, Morrow, 1979; *Walking Naked*, St. Martin's, 1981.

Juveniles: *Secret Passage*, Gollancz, 1963, published as *The House of Secrets*, Lippincott, 1964; *On the Run*, Gollancz, 1964, published as *Three on the Run*, Lippincott, 1965; *The White Horse Gang*, Lippincott, 1966; *The Witch's Daughter*, Lippincott, 1966; *A Handful of Thieves*, Lippincott, 1967; *The Runaway Summer*, Lippincott, 1969; *Squib*, Lippincott, 1971; *Carrie's War*, Lippincott, 1973; *The Peppermint Pig*, Lippincott, 1975; *Rebel on a Rock*, Lippincott, 1978; *The Robbers*, Lothrop, 1979; *Kept in the Dark*, Lothrop, 1982.

Contributor to *Evening Standard* and *Daily Telegraph*.

SIDELIGHTS: Reviewing *Walking Naked* in the *Times Literary Supplement*, Peter Kemp remarks: "Fashionably, the book is partly about the function and genesis of fiction.... The impulse to make fiction, Nina Bawden indicates, can get crookedly snarled up with feelings of aggression. It can also constitute a defence-mechanism, offering some shelter from life's contingent assaults by its temporary meanings and brief patterns. People, she shows, often find it necessary to inhabit some tidily rearranged and comfortably furnished version of reality... in order to cope."

In her juvenile books, also written under the name Nina Bawden, Kark gives children this kind of comforting reassurance, according to Nicholas Tucker in *Children's Literature in Education*. Tucker says that all these books "end with a more or less satisfying round-up—the 'Day of Judgement' Chesterton once demanded for the final chapter of good children's literature, where obvious villains are despatched and the good regroup their forces, free now from danger. These are not necessarily the pat happy endings of romantic fiction—characters may be more suitably rewarded here by a change of attitude rather than fortune—but even so, Nina Bawden stays within a conventional framework when it comes to finishing a story.... Most children are not quite ready for the implications of a truly amoral universe, where natural justice can seem very scant; they need sustaining myths as well as glimpses of the truth, and so often Nina Bawden achieves this balance with great skill, for her books are both wise and immensely entertaining."

BIOGRAPHICAL/CRITICAL SOURCES: *New York Times Book Review*, June 3, 1973; *Children's Literature in Education*, Number 13, 1974; (under name Nina Bawden) *Children's Literature Review*, Volume II, Gale, 1976; *Times Literary Supplement*, April 17, 1981.

* * *

KATES, Robert W. 1929-

PERSONAL: Born January 31, 1929, in Brooklyn, N.Y.; son of Simon Jack and Helen Gordon (Brener) Kates; married Eleanor Clare Hackman, February 9, 1948; children: Kathy Ann, Jonathan Simon, Barbara Ellen. *Education:* Attended New York University, 1946-48, Indiana University, Gary (now Indiana University Northwest), 1957; University of Chicago, M.A., 1960, Ph.D., 1962. *Office:* Graduate School of Geography, Clark University, Worcester, Mass. 01610.

CAREER: Clark University, Graduate School of Geography, Worcester, Mass., assistant professor, 1962-65, associate professor, 1965-67, professor of geography, 1968—, university professor, 1974-81, Center for Technology, Environment and Development, research professor, 1981—. Staff member of Association of American Geographers summer geography institute for small southern colleges, 1966; lecturer, National Science Foundation summer institute in introductory college geography, 1966; University of Dar es Salaam, Tanzania, lecturer, 1967-68, honorary research professor, 1970-71; visiting scholar, University of Oklahoma, 1976. Director, Bureau of Resources Assessment and Land Use Planning, University College, Dar Es Salaam, 1967-69; Elm Park Center for Early Childhood Education, Inc., treasurer, 1972-78, clerk, 1979—.

U.S. National Committee on the Man and Biosphere Program, vice-chairman of directorate on perception of environmental quality, 1973, chairman of directorate and member of U.S. National Committee on the Man and Biosphere Program, 1974-76, member of directorate, 1977—; review coordinator, Project on Improving the Science of Climate Impact Assessment, Scientific Committee on Problems of the Environment, International Council of Scientific Unions, 1980—. Member of task group on human dimensions of the atmosphere, National Center for Atmospheric Research, 1966-67, study group on the societal consequences of weather modification, Southern Methodist University, 1971-73, human resources task force of Executive Office of Environmental Affairs, State of Massachusetts, 1972-73, energy task force, City of Worcester, 1974-75, and expert group on Climate Impact Studies, United Nations Environmental Program, 1980. Has conducted and supervised research on the impact of floods, droughts, climate fluctuation, and other environmental or technological hazards on human populations and on other climate-related topics, in the United States and Africa. Consultant to C. W. Thornwaite Associates, 1963-64, UNESCO Interdisciplinary Symposium on Man's Role in Changing the Environment: Architecture and Urbanism for Growth and Change, 1970, and Natural Hazard Research Assessment, Institute of Behavioral Science, 1972-74; member of technical advisory committee, Natural Disaster Studies, U.S. Home and Housing Finance Agency, 1966, and science advisory group, Connecticut River Basin Program, New England River Basin Commission, 1973; senior consultant to Scientific Committee on Problems of the Environment, 1974-77.

MEMBER: Academy of Independent Scholars, Academy of Arts and Sciences, National Academy of Sciences, American Association for the Advancement of Science, American Association of University Professors (Clark University Chapter, vice-president, 1965-66, president, 1966-67), Tanzania Society, Phi Beta Kappa (honorary member). Awards, honors: Woodrow Wilson International Center for Scholars, fellow, 1979.

WRITINGS: (Editor with Ian Burton) Readings in Resource Management and Conservation, University of Chicago Press, 1965; (author of introduction with R. J. Chorley) Water, Earth, and Man, Methuen, 1969; (with Clifford S. Russell and David Arney) Drought and Water Supply: Implications of the Massachusetts Experience for Municipal Planning, Johns Hopkins Press, 1970; (with Burton and Gilbert F. White) The Environment as Hazard, Oxford University Press, 1975; (with Roger Kasperson, Paul Slovic, Baruch Fischoff, Sarah Lichtenstein, and William Clark) Managing Technological Hazard: Research Needs and Opportunities, University of Colorado, 1978; (editor and contributor with Leonard Berry) Making the Most of the Least: Alternative Ways to Development, Holmes & Meier, 1980.

Contributor: J. G. Jenson, editor, Spatial Organization of Land Uses: The Willamette Valley, Oregon State University, 1964; Research and Education for Regional and Area Development, Iowa State University Press, 1966; M. E. Garnsey and J. R. Hibbs, editors, Social Science and the Environment, University of Colorado Press, 1967; (with W.R.D. Sewell and with W. J. Maunder) Human Dimensions of the Atmosphere, National Science Foundation, 1968; Regional Planning: Challenge and Prospects, Praeger, 1969; Student Resources: Geography in an Urban Age—Habitat and Resources, Macmillan, 1970; (with Duane Baumann) T. R. Detwyler and M. G. Marcus, editors, Urbanization and Environment: The Physical Geography of a City, Duxbury, 1972; (with L. Berry) W. P. Adams and F. N. Helleiner, editors, International Geography, 1972, Volume I, University of Toronto Press, 1972; Patterns and Perspectives in Environmental Science, National Science Foundation, 1972; (with J. Heijnen) G. F. White, editor, Natural Hazards: Local, National, Global, Oxford University Press, 1974; (with Ian Burton and Anne V. T. Kirkby) A. E. Utton and D. H. Henning, editors, Interdisciplinary Environmental Approaches, Educational Media Press, 1974.

Science Year, 1976, Field Educational Publications, 1975; Seymour Wapner, Saul Cohen, and Bernard Kaplan, editors, Experiencing the Environment, Plenum, 1976; The Golden Jubilee Volume, 1976, Indian Geographical Society (Madras), 1976; (with D. Johnson and K. Johnson Haring) Desertification: Its Causes and Consequences, Pergamon, 1977; Gerald J. Karaska and Judith B. Gertler, editors, Transportation, Technology and Society: Future Options, Clark University Press, 1978; (with R. C. Harris and C. Hohenemser) G. T. Goodman and W. D. Rowe, editors, Energy Risk Management, Academic Press (London), 1979, Natural Hazards in Australia, Australian Academy of Sciences (Canberra), 1979.

Also author of numerous scientific monographs and research papers, including ones published by Department of Geography, University of Chicago, Bureau of Resource Assessment and Land Use Planning, University College, National Academy of Sciences and National Research Council, and Center for Technology, Environment, and Development, Clark University. Contributor to World Book Encyclopedia, 1974. Contributor to Papers and Proceedings of the Regional Science Association, Volume II, 1963, Trends in Economics: Papers of the Fifth Conference of Pennsylvania Economists, edited by W. E. Everett, 1963, Proceedings of the University of East Africa Social Science Conference, 1968-69, 1970, Proceedings of the Conference on Rural Water Supply in East Africa, 1971, and Proceedings of the World Climate Conference, 1979. Also contributor to scientific and professional journals, including Bulletin of Atomic Scientists, Geographical Review, Ambio, Science, Environment, Economic Geography, The Professional Geographer, and International Social Sciences Journal. Assistant editor of Economic Geography, 1963-64; member of editorial board of Geographical Review, 1976-78.

*   *   *

KATSH, Abraham I(saac) 1908-

PERSONAL: Born August 10, 1908, in Poland; came to United States, 1925; naturalized U.S. citizen, 1932; son of Reuven (former chief rabbi of Petah Tikva, Israel, and member of Chief Rabbinate of Israel) and Rachel (Maskilleytan) Katz; married Estelle Wachtell, February 20, 1943; children: Ethan Maskett, Salem Michael, Rochelle Seena. Education: New York University, B.S., 1931, M.A., 1932, J.D., 1936; Princeton University, graduate study, 1941; Dropsie College for Hebrew and Cognate Learning (now Dropsie University), Ph.D., 1944. Religion: Jewish. Home: 45 East 89th St., New York, N.Y. 10028; and Kaumeonga Lake, N.Y. 12749.

CAREER: Institute of Jewish Studies for Adults, Brooklyn, N.Y., principal, 1933-36; New York University, New York, N.Y., instructor in modern Hebrew, beginning 1934, professor of Hebrew culture and education and chairman of department, 1937-59, Abraham I. Katsh Professor of Hebrew Culture and Education, 1962-67, distinguished research professor, 1967-68, professor emeritus, 1976—, founder and director of Jewish Culture Foundation, 1937-43, founder and curator of Library of Judaica and Hebraica, 1941-67, founder and director of American Israel Student and Professional Workshop, 1949-67, professor of Hebrew and Near Eastern studies in Graduate School of Arts and Sciences, 1959-62, founder, director, and professor of Hebrew and Near Eastern studies in Institute of Hebrew Studies, 1962-67; Dropsie University, Philadelphia, Pa., president, 1967-76, professor emeritus and distinguished research professor, 1976—. Lecturer at World Congress for Jewish Scholarship, Jerusalem, 1947-73, International Oriental Congress, Munich, 1957, Moscow, 1960, Congress of Linguistic and Hebrew Scholarships, Vienna, 1976, World Congress of Jewish Studies, Jerusalem, 1977, and at numerous American and European universities; visiting scholar, University of Georgia and Angus Scott College, 1967, Oxford Centre for Post Graduate Hebrew Studies, 1977-78, Mishkenot Shaanamin, 1978, and City of Jerusalem, 1978; Montague Burton Lecturer, University of Leeds and University of Copenhagen. Special examiner, New York City Board of Education, beginning 1956; member of reference board, Hadassah, beginning 1958; associate trustee, American School of Oriental Research in Jerusalem (now William F. Albright School of Archaeology), 1969-75; member of board of governors, Brit Ivrit Olamit, 1977—; member of international committee, Cultural Religious Commission of World Joint Distribution Committee, 1977—. Delegate to Congress International Des Linguistas, 1967. Former radio commentator on modern Hebrew. Former member of advisory board, Hadassah; consultant on Hebrew, National Association on Standard Medical Vocabulary; member of advisory board, Villanova Institute.

MEMBER: World Union of Jewish Studies (member of council, 1977—), World Hebrew Congress (member of advisory board, beginning 1956), International Congress of Orientalists, Jewish Academy of Arts and Sciences (former chairman of board of governors; president), American Association for Jewish Education (national chairman of board of licenses, 1958—), National Council for Jewish Education, American Jewish Congress (former member of Commission of Jewish Life and Culture), National Association of Professors of Hebrew (founder and honorary president, 1950—), American Academy for Jewish Research, Society of Biblical Literature, Conference on Jewish Relations, American Jewish Historical Society (member of academic council), Jewish Book Council (member of executive board, 1976—), Academy of Religion, Jewish National Fund (member of board of directors), Society for Jewish Documentation (member of committee, 1976—), American Oriental Society, Modern Language Association of America (chairman of evaluation for modern Hebrew materials, beginning 1962), Memorial Foundation of Jewish Culture (member of Commission on Formal Jewish Studies Program, 1973—), Histadrut Ivrit (member of board of directors), Jewish Culture Foundation (founder), American Association of University Professors, Phi Delta Kappa (member of board of directors).

AWARDS, HONORS: B'nai Zion Meritorious Key, 1944; Ernest O. Melby Award for Human Relations, New York University, 1952; B'rith Abraham Gold Medal, 1952, for Hebrew scholarship and learning; tercentenary citation, Jewish Book Council, 1954, for contributions to literature on Jewish American history; American Hebrew Academy Award, 1956, for *Judaism in Islam;* endowed professorship of Hebrew culture and education named in Katsh's honor by New York University, 1957; citations from State of Kentucky, Dropsie College Alumni, and National Association of Negro Business and Professional Women's Club, all 1957; American Association for Jewish Education award, 1959; festschriften in Katsh's honor were published in 1963, by the National Association of Professors of Hebrew, and in 1976; New York University Honor Society Award, 1963; Doctor of Hebrew Letters, Hebrew Union College and Jewish Institute of Religion, 1964; presidential citation, New York University, 1965; mayor's citation, City of New York, 1965; Moriah Literary Award for Hebrew Letters, 1965; Washington Square College Alumni Achievement Award, 1965; Scheiderman Prize, 1965; citation from Government of Israel, 1965; Brotherhood Award, Chapel of Four Chaplains, 1967; D.Litt., Spertus College of Judaica, 1968; D.D., Christian Theological Seminary, 1970, and University of Dubuque, 1971; L.L.D., Lebanon Valley College, 1971, and Dropsie University, 1976; Spiritual Leadership Award, Chapel of Four Chaplains, 1975; Morris J. Kaplun Prize, 1977, for distinguished research; D.H.L., Villanova University, 1977; Mechayil el Chayil Award, Board of Rabbis of Greater Philadelphia, 1977; Israel Solidarity Award, 1977; Rabbi Kaniel Prize, Municipality of Haifa, Israel, 1979, for *Ginze Mishnah* and *Ginze Talmud Babli;* Scroll of Honor, American Association for Jewish Education, 1979, for service on the board of licenses; Avodah Award, Jewish Teachers Association, 1980; Mordecai Ben David Distinguished Award, 1980; Charles Kramer research fellow, Institute for Jewish Policy and Planning, 1980; Middle East Studies Association of North America fellow; recipient of grants from American Council of Learned Societies, National Endowment for the Humanities, Rockefeller Foundation, Littauer Foundation, Matz Foundation, Kohut Foundation, Kaplun Foundation, Memorial Foundation for Jewish Culture, Hebrew Academy, William Liebermann Research Fund, Harold E. Beckman Fund, U.S. Department of Health, Education, and Welfare, and U.S. Office of Education.

WRITINGS: Torat Hayahasut Shel Einstein, Gutenberg Press, 1936; *Hebrew in American Higher Education,* New York University Book Store, 1941; *Hebraic Contributions to American Life,* New York University Book Store, 1941; *Syllabus in Modern Hebrew Language and Literature,* New York State Board of Regents, 1948; *Hebrew Language, Literature and Culture in American Institutions of Higher Learning,* Payne Foundation, 1950; *Hebraic Foundations of American Democracy,* Philosophical Library, 1951; *Judaism in Islam,* Bloch, 1954, 3rd edition, Sepher-Hermon Press, 1980; (editor) *Bar Mitzvah Illustrated,* Shengold, 1955, 7th edition, 1976; *Catalogue of the William and Ida Rosenthal Collection,* New York University, 1955; *ha-Yahadut ba-Islam,* [Jerusalem], 1957; *Catalogue of Hebrew Manuscripts in the USSR,* Library of Judaica and Hebraica, New York University, Volume I, 1957, Volume II, 1958, Volume III, 1963; (compiler) *Ginze russiyah,* Library of Judaica and Hebraica, New York University, 1958; *Judaism and the Koran,* New York University Press, 1962; (editor) *Yigal Hazon* (unpublished Hebrew poetry of the Spanish Golden Age), Neuman, 1963; *The Antonin Genizah Collection in Leningrad,* Institute of Hebrew Studies, New York University, 1963; (editor and translator) David ben Abraham, *Midrash David Hanagid* (thirteenth-century Arabic manuscripts on Genesis and Exodus), Mosad Harav Kook (Jerusalem), Volume I, 1964, Volume II, 1966; (contributor) Israel T. Naamani and David Rudavsky, editors, *Doron: Essays in Honor of Professor Abraham I. Katsh,* [New York], 1965; *National Association of Professors of Hebrew in American Institutions of Higher*

Learning, National Association of Professors of Hebrew, 1965; (editor and translator) *Scroll of Agony* (Chaim A. Kaplan's diary of the Warsaw ghetto), Macmillan, 1965, published as *The Warsaw Diary of Chaim A. Kaplan,* Collier, 1973, new edition, Macmillan, 1980; *Shemot,* Exodux, 1967; *Ginze Mishnah,* Mosad Harav Kook, 1971; *Ginze Talmud Babli,* Rubin Mass (Jerusalem), Volume I, 1976, Volume II, 1979; *Biblical Heritage of American Democracy,* Ktav, 1977; (editor with Leon Nemov) *Essays on the Occasion of the Seventieth Anniversary of the Dropsie University,* Dropsie University Alumni Association, 1979.

Also author of *Lamentations,* 1971; co-editor of *Israel through the Eyes of Its Leaders,* 1971. Contributor to books and festschriften; contributor to jubilee volumes and annals of the Jewish Academy of Arts and Sciences; contributor to proceedings of the International Oriental Congress, 1957, 1960, and 1964; contributor to encyclopedias, including *Hebrew Encyclopedia, Encyclopaedia Britannica, New International Encyclopedia, Encyclopedia of Religion,* and *Encyclopedia Judaica.* Contributor of several hundred articles and papers to journals, including *American Historical Review, Jewish Quarterly Review,* and *Modern Langauge Journal.* Co-editor, *Bar Mitzvah,* 1946-76; managing editor, *Journal of Educational Sociology,* beginning 1951; chairman of board of editors, *Hebrew Abstracts,* 1950-76, and *Hebrew Studies,* beginning 1976; assistant editor in charge of Hebrew section, *Modern Language Journal,* 1954-75; chairman of editorial board, *Jewish Apocryphal Literature,* beginning 1968; *Jewish Quarterly Review,* co-editor, 1968-78, editor, beginning 1978; member of editorial board, *Bitzaron.*

SIDELIGHTS: In 1956, scholar Abraham I. Katsh made an unprecedented trip to the Soviet Union to study the rare manuscripts of Judaica stored in the Antonin Geniza Collection in the Leningrad Library. During this and five subsequent visits, Katsh "established a rare scholarly rapport" with Soviet librarians and assembled hundreds of ancient Talmudic fragments that shed "new light from ancient sources," Richard F. Shepard writes in the *New York Times.* Katsh has published his findings in *Ginze Mishnah* and *Ginze Talmud Babli,* books now recognized as major reference sources for the restoration of the Talmud. Katsh told Shepard that his research "covers the whole Talmud. There are many variants, variations from printed text of the Talmud. The Geniza fragments were written in a very early period when study was by oral transmission." According to Katsh, his study offers a different version of the Talmud which will help to clarify problematic parts of the text.

Katsh's books have been translated into French, German, Swiss, Portuguese, Danish, and Japanese.

BIOGRAPHICAL/CRITICAL SOURCES: New York Times, October 12, 1977, July 4, 1979.

* * *

KELL, Richard (Alexander) 1927-

PERSONAL: Born November 1, 1927, in Youghal, County Cork, Ireland; son of George (a clergyman) and Florence Irene (Musgrave) Kell; married Muriel Adelaide Nairn, December 31, 1953 (died, 1975); children: Colin Richard, Carolyn Muriel, Timothy Patrick, Shelagh Patricia. *Education:* Studied at Methodist College, Belfast, Ireland, and Wesley College, Dublin, Ireland; Trinity College, University of Dublin, B.A. (with honors), 1952. *Home:* 18 Rectory Grove, Gosforth, Newcastle upon Tyne NE3 1AL, England. *Office:* Department of English, Newcastle upon Tyne Polytechnic, Newcastle upon Tyne NE1 8ST, England.

CAREER: Assistant teacher at Kilkenny College, Kilkenny, Ireland, then at Whinney Banks School, Middlesbrough, England; Luton Public Library, Luton, England, assistant librarian, 1954-56; Brunel College of Technology (now Brunel University), Acton, London, England, assistant librarian, 1956-59; Isleworth Polytechnic, Isleworth, Hounslow, England, assistant lecturer, 1960-65, lecturer in English, 1966-70; Newcastle upon Tyne Polytechnic, Newcastle upon Tyne, England, senior lecturer in English, 1970—. *Member:* British Society of Aesthetics, Critical Quarterly Society.

WRITINGS—Poetry: *Control Tower,* Chatto & Windus, 1962; *Differences,* Chatto & Windus, 1969; *Heartwood,* Northern House, 1978; *Humours,* Ceolfrith Press, 1978; *The Broken Circle,* Ceolfrith Press, 1981; (with Roger Garfitt, Frances Horovitz, and Rodney Pybus) *Wall,* LYC Press, 1982.

Poems represented in anthologies, including *New Poems* (P.E.N. anthology), Hutchinson, 1958, 1961, 1963; *Six Irish Poets,* Oxford University Press, 1962; *Modern Poetry for Schools,* Odhams, 1962; *New Poets of Ireland,* A. Swallow, 1963; *New Lines 2,* Macmillan, 1963; *Here Today,* Hutchinson, 1963; *Flash Point,* Arnold, 1964; *Mentor Book of Irish Poetry,* New American Library, 1965; *My Kind of Verse,* Burke Publishing, 1965; *Reading Poetry,* Harper, 1965; *Love Poems of the Irish,* Mercier Press, 1967; *Reading Poetry,* Harper, 1968; *New Irish Writing,* Dolmen Press, 1970; *Penguin Book of Irish Verse,* Penguin, 1970; *Irish Poets 1924-1974,* Pan Books, 1975; *Thoth,* Morden Tower, 1977; *Life Hungers to Abound,* Morrow, 1978; *New Poetry 5,* Arts Council, 1979.

Contributor of poems, essays, and short stories to *Listener, Observer, Critical Quarterly, Irish Writing, Poetry Ireland, Dubliner, New Statesman, London Magazine, British Journal of Aesthetics, Poetry Northwest, Icarus, Outposts,* and other periodicals. Reviewer of poetry, *Guardian,* 1960-69.

WORK IN PROGRESS: Poetry, short stories, and essays, for eventual collections.

* * *

KELLEY, Joseph J(ohn), Jr. 1914-

PERSONAL: Born May 31, 1914, in Philadelphia, Pa.; son of Joseph J. (a real estate broker) and Kathryne Madeleine (Hookey) Kelley; married Eleanor Eileen Dougan, June 11, 1949; children: Roger D., Janet E., Heather Ann (died, October 3, 1964). *Education:* La Salle College, B.S., 1937; attended University of Pennsylvania Law School, 1937-39; Temple University, J.D., 1941. *Home:* 15 North 27th St., Camp Hill, Pa. 17011.

CAREER: Attorney in private practice in Philadelphia, Pa., 1946-53; Pennsylvania Chamber of Commerce, Harrisburg, legislative counsel, 1953-66; secretary to Governor of Pennsylvania, Harrisburg, 1967; served as Secretary of the Commonwealth of Pennsylvania, Harrisburg, 1968-71; WITF-TV (public broadcasting service), Hershey, Pa., executive director of Division of American History and Culture, 1971-72; Pennsylvania District Attorneys Association, Camp Hill, executive director, 1973-77. Lecturer at Valley Forge Military College, 1947-48, and at Drexel University, 1952-53. *Military service:* U.S. Navy, 1941-46; became lieutenant commander.

MEMBER: Organization of American Historians, American Historical Association, Historical Society of Pennsylvania, Pennsylvania Historical Association, Historical Foundation of Pennsylvania (director, 1967—; president, 1980-82). *Awards, honors:* Freedoms Foundation awards, 1953, 1957; honorary citizen of Statesville, N.C., 1967, and of Texas, 1970; Admiral of Great Navy of the State of Nebraska, 1970; Pennsylvania Student Historians Award, 1982.

WRITINGS: Life and Times in Colonial Philadelphia, Stackpole, 1973; (with Sol Feinstone) *Courage and Candlelight: Feminine Spirit of '76*, Stackpole, 1974; *Pennsylvania: The Colonial Years, 1681-1776*, Doubleday, 1980; *Speechwriting: The Master Touch*, Stackpole, 1980, published as *Speechwriting: A Handbook for All Occasions*, New American Library, 1981. Author of script "Ten Days that Changed the World," for WITF-TV, 1971. Contributor to periodicals.

WORK IN PROGRESS: Pennsylvania and the Young Republic, for the National Park Service.

SIDELIGHTS: "I try to make the past come alive," Joseph J. Kelley, Jr. told *CA*, "without superimposing my twentieth-century judgment on men and women who did what they did in their own day, under given circumstances at a given time. Anything else is fiction.

"In all my writings I intersperse my prose with pertinent quotes from letters, documents, and contemporary newspapers, magazines, etc. Words written against the winds of an uncertain future best capture the pulse of the period."

* * *

KELLY, Lawrence C(harles) 1932-

PERSONAL: Born December 3, 1932, in Oklahoma City, Okla.; son of Charles Lawrence (an office manager) and Esther (Beavin) Kelly; married Mary Margaret Keating, August 2, 1955; children: Kathleen, Sean, Eileen, Sheila, Kevin. *Education:* Marquette University, B.S., 1954, M.A., 1959; University of New Mexico, Ph.D., 1961. *Politics:* Democrat. *Religion:* Catholic. *Home:* 2608 Emerson Dr., Denton, Tex. 76201. *Office:* Department of History, North Texas State University, Denton, Tex. 76203.

CAREER: Lewis College, Lockport, Ill., instructor, 1961-63, assistant professor of American history, 1963-64; Indiana University at Fort Wayne, assistant professor, 1964-66, associate professor of history, 1966-68; North Texas State University, Denton, associate professor, 1968-71, professor of American history, 1971—. Lecturer on Indian affairs at symposia. *Military service:* U.S. Naval Reserve, 1955-63; active duty, 1955-58; became lieutenant junior grade. *Member:* American Historical Association, Organization of American Historians.

AWARDS, HONORS: Grants from American Philosophical Society, 1964, Harry S. Truman Library, 1965, National Science Foundation, 1978-79, Rockefeller Archive, 1979, Smithsonian Institution, 1980, and Herbert Hoover Library, 1981; Commendation Award, American Association for State and Local History, 1969, for *The Navajo Indians and Federal Indian Policy, 1900-1935*, and 1972, for *The Navajo Roundup*; National Endowment for the Humanities fellow, 1970-71; Weatherhead scholar at School of American Research, 1982.

WRITINGS: The Navajo Indians and Federal Indian Policy, 1900-1935, University of Arizona Press, 1968; *The Navajo Roundup: Selected Correspondence of Kit Carson's Expedition against the Navajo Indians, 1863-1865*, Pruett Press, 1970; (contributor) Jane F. Smith and Robert M. Kvasnicka, editors, *Indian-White Relations: A Persistent Paradox*, Howard University Press, 1976; (contributor) Howard R. Lamar, editor, *Reader's Encyclopedia of the American West*, Crowell, 1978; (contributor) Kvasnicka and Herman J. Viola, editors, *The Commissioners of Indian Affairs, 1824-1977*, University of Nebraska Press, 1979; (contributor) *Academic American Encyclopedia*, Arete Publishing, 1980; *The Assault on Assimilation: John Collier and the Origins of Indian Policy Reform*, Volume I, University of New Mexico Press, 1983; *Pueblo Water Rights on the Rio Grande*, University of Arizona Press, 1984. Also contributor to *The Handbook of North American Indians*, Volume IV. Author of recorded lecture "Indians in the Twentieth-Century West," Everett Edwards, 1979. Contributor to periodicals, including *New Mexico Historical Review*, *Pacific Historical Review*, *Journal of the History of the Behavioral Sciences*, and *Chronicles of Oklahoma*.

WORK IN PROGRESS: The Origins of Applied Anthropology in the United States, 1930-1945, and *The Dream and the Reality: John Collier and the Indian New Deal*.

SIDELIGHTS: "In recent years," Lawrence C. Kelly told *CA*, "I have become increasingly involved in litigation on western water rights as an expert witness. My historical research has been increasingly concerned with the history of anthropology in the United States and with the personalities who popularized the Southwest in the 1920s, particularly those involved in the growth of Santa Fe, New Mexico."

* * *

KENT, Arden
See MARION, Frieda

* * *

KESLER, Jay 1935-

PERSONAL: Born September 15, 1935, in Barnes, Wis.; son of Herbert E. and Elsie (Campbell) Kesler; married Jane Smith, June 7, 1957; children: Laurie, Bruce, Terri. *Education:* Attended Ball State University, 1953-54; Taylor University, B.A., 1957. *Office:* Youth for Christ International, North Main St., Wheaton, Ill. 60187.

CAREER: Youth for Christ International, Wheaton, Ill., director of Marion, Ind. branch, 1955-58, crusade staff evangelist, 1959-60, director of Illinois-Indiana region, 1960-62, director of college recruitment, 1962-63, vice-president for personnel, 1963-68, vice-president for field coordination, 1968-73, president, 1973—, and member of board of directors. *Member:* Evangelicals for Social Action (member of board of directors), National Educators Fellowship (member of board of reference), Prison Fellowship International (member of board of directors).

WRITINGS: Let's Succeed with Our Teenagers, David Cook, 1973; *I Never Promised You a Disneyland*, Word, Inc., 1975; *The Strong Weak People*, Victor Books, 1976; *Outside Disneyland*, Word, Inc., 1977; *I Want a Home with No Problems*, Word, Inc., 1977; *Growing Places*, Revell, 1978; *Too Big to Spank*, Regal Books, 1978; *Breakthrough*, Zondervan, 1981. Also author of column, "I Never Promised You a Disneyland," *Campus Life* (magazine), 1974-75. Member of editorial review committee for *New King James Bible*.

* * *

KESSELMAN, Judi R.
See K-TURKEL, Judi

* * *

KESSELMAN-TURKEL, Judi
See K-TURKEL, Judi

KESSLER, Jascha (Frederick) 1929-

PERSONAL: Born November 27, 1929, in New York, N.Y.; son of Hyman (a furrier) and Rosella (Bronsweig) Kessler; married Julia Braun (a free-lance editor and writer), July 17, 1950; children: Margot Lucia Braun, Adam Theodore Braun, William Alessandro Braun. *Education:* New York University, B.A., 1950; University of Michigan, M.A., 1951, Ph.D., 1955. *Politics:* Independent. *Office:* Department of English, University of California, Los Angeles, Calif. 90024.

CAREER: New York University, New York City, instructor in English, 1954-56; Hunter College (now Hunter College of the City University of New York), New York City, instructor in English, 1955-56; Harcourt, Brace & Co. (now Harcourt, Brace, Jovanovich, Inc.; publishers), New York City, educational research director, 1956-57; Hamilton College, Clinton, N.Y., assistant professor of English, 1957-61; University of California, Los Angeles, assistant professor, 1961-64, associate professor, 1964-70, professor of English, 1970—, director of Institute of Government and Public Affairs research project, "Culture in Los Angeles: A Study of Its Problems, Resources, Potentialities," 1967-68. Fulbright professor of American literature, and director of American studies seminar at Centro di Studi Americani, Rome, Italy, 1970; Seminar Professor of American Literature, University of Urbino, Urbino, Italy, 1970; lecturer and translator of contemporary poetry, P.E.N. (Hungary), 1972, 1974, 1977, 1979; U.S. Department of State lecturer in Belgium and Iran, 1974; lecturer in Hungary, Israel, Austria, and Yugoslavia, 1979. Visiting poet, Seminar of the President of Israel, Haifa, Tel Aviv and Jerusalem, Israel, 1970; guest poet, XIXth Struga Festival of Poetry, Yugoslavia, 1980; speaker and participant at international writers conferences in Ireland, Israel, France, Finland, and Bulgaria. Reviewer, KUSC-FM, Los Angeles, 1968—. Program development writer, lecturer in western United States, and member of advisory panel of Western Center for Program Development, National Humanities Series, National Endowment for the Humanities, 1973-75; member of literature panel, California Council for the Arts, 1982-85.

AWARDS, HONORS: Avery and Jule Hopwood Award in Poetry, Major Division, University of Michigan, 1952; poetry prizes from Heptagon Club (New York), 1954, and Ellis Bush Foundation, 1958; writing fellowships from Yaddo Foundation, 1958, Danforth Foundation, 1960, Helene Wurlitzer Foundation, 1961, Institute for the Creative Arts, University of California, 1963-64, 1974, 1978, and National Endowment for the Arts, 1974-75; D. H. Lawrence fellowship, University of New Mexico, 1961; Fulbright research fellowship, 1963-64, to Florence, Italy; American Place Theater playwriting fellowship, 1967; Popular Panel Awards Prize, American Society of Composers, Authors, and Publishers, 1968-75; Academy Award ("Oscar") nomination, Academy of Motion Picture Arts and Sciences, 1970, for "A Long Way from Nowhere"; regents fellowship in the humanities, University of California, 1977; translation award, Translation Center of Columbia University, 1978, for *The Magician's Garden;* Rockefeller Foundation fellowship, 1978, to Bellagio, Italy; P.E.N. (Hungary) Memorial Medal, 1979, for "outstanding translation of Hungarian poetry and service to Hungarian literature in the United States"; Artisjus Award, Artisjus: Agence Litteraire, de Musique et Theatrale (Budapest), 1980, for work in Hungarian Literature.

WRITINGS: (Editor and author of introduction) *American Poems: A Contemporary Collection,* Southern Illinois University Press, 1964; (contributor of translations) David Ray, editor, *From the Hungarian Revolt* (poems), Cornell University Press, 1966; *An Egyptian Bondage and Other Stories,* Harper, 1967; *Whatever Love Declares* (poems), Plantin Press, 1969; *After the Armies Have Passed* (poems), New York University Press, 1970; *In Memory of the Future* (poems), Kayak, 1976; *Bearing Gifts: Two Mythologems,* Treacle Press, 1979; (translator from the Hungarian with Charlotte Rogers) Geza Csath, *The Magician's Garden* (stories), Columbia University Press, 1980; *Lee Mullican,* Galerie Schreiner, 1980; *Death Comes for the Behaviorist and Other Stories,* Lexis Press, 1982; (translator from the Persian with Amin Banani) Forugh Farrokhzad, *Bride of Acacias: The Selected Poems of Forugh Farrokhzad,* University of Texas Press, 1982; *Transmigrations: Eighteen Mythologems,* Jazz Press, 1982; (translator from the Hungarian) Miklo Radnoti, *Under Gemini: The Selected Poems of Miklo Radnoti,* Ohio University Press, in press. Also author of books of poems, *The Prisoner* and *Following the Sun.* Author of *Technology, Prometheus, and Future Human Values,* readings and commentary to accompany lecture series.

Plays: "Perfect Days" and "The Dummy" (one-acts), first produced at University of California, Los Angeles, August, 1965, "Perfect Days" published in *Modern Occasions,* edited by Philip Rahv, Farrar, Strauss, 1966; "Crane, Crane, Montrose and Crane" (one-act), first produced in New York at American Place Theatre, December, 1968. Also author of "The Cave" (libretto for an opera in two acts), 1963, and of "Exodus," 1966.

Films: "Autistic Children" (teaching film), 1968; "Reaching Them with Reward-Punishment Therapy" (teaching film), 1969; "The Tender Power" (documentary), 1969; "A Long Way From Nowhere" (documentary), 1970; "An American Family" (documentary), 1971; "The Fire of the Gods" (teaching film), 1974.

Contributor of poetry and short stories to periodicals, including *Encounter, Poetry, Kayak, Midstream, The Centennial Review, West Coast Poetry Review, The Southwest Review,* and *Saturday Review;* contributor of articles and reviews to *The Emerson Review, Los Angeles Times, Saturday Review, Parnassus: Poetry in Review,* and other periodicals; contributor of translations to *The Hungarian Pen, Mundis Artium, The New Hungarian Quarterly,* and *Modern Poetry in Translation.*

WORK IN PROGRESS: Poetry; plays; a novel.

SIDELIGHTS: Jascha Kessler, observes *New York Times Book Review* critic Laurence Lafore, "writes about the death of mice; simple domestic events. The simplicity is ironic, of course; mice and their deaths are subjects of infinite complexity."

In his short stories and in his poetry, Kessler endeavors to infuse the commonplace with "cosmic meanings," as Lafore points out in his review of *An Egyptian Bondage and Other Stories.* Kessler's subjects are ordinary people and ordinary events that, through some quirk of fate or idiosyncracy of character, become extraordinary. Writing about *Whatever Love Declares,* Jerome Cushman comments in *Library Journal* that Kessler's poems "speak of everyday things, love, family, the landscape, all within the framework of mildly philosophical argumentation." Kessler's ability to draw universal conclusions from the particulars of everyday occurrences leads Robert Kirsh to write in the *Los Angeles Times:* "[Kessler's] experience is individual; his evocation universal. . . . He celebrates the private voice, the individual history. And yet, its overtones seem to have resonance in us."

However, Kessler's attempts to imbue "simple domestic events" with deeper significance has caused some criticism. Lafore states that Kessler "shares . . . the conviction that excellence consists partly of the number of arcane and portenteous Meanings that can be crammed into a small space. . . . When he gets significance-conscious, the effect on his writing is that of a much overstuffed suitcase on the press of the pants." The problem arises in Kessler's work, says a *Choice* critic, because "the tension needed to develop insights into man's morality is missing. The stories are bland."

While he agrees that Kessler's stories "sometimes tend to reach too far for too little, or for too little that is defined," Eliot Fremont-Smith finds *An Egyptian Bondage* "never without interest." "That is not a backhanded compliment," Fremont-Smith continues in the *New York Times*. "The interest comes repeatedly as a surprise, and even the most tenuous of the stories keeps poking around inside one's head long after the book is done."

Commenting on his work, Kessler told *CA*: "I have always written down what has been given to me, and my word, such as it is, seems to be given over to past and future, the dead and the not-yet living. One listens, then, for it, and waits, more or less patiently, perhaps stoically. Force and violence are of little use, though they have been the means of too many of us scribblers in this long period of the last hundred years, though many of us are easily inclined towards such instruments, and tempted continually to avail ourselves of them. As for the present, the long present that is the lot of some of us, perhaps I am occasionally overheard. Certainly glad of it when I am, as who would not be? ('Wouldn't you?' The most powerful question asked in this time, and that is the motto and moral of Burroughs's *The Naked Lunch*. . . . 'Wouldn't you?' He should be remembered for that! It may be that some phrase of mine will be remembered as I remember his, something better and tending more towards hope, I pray.) At any rate, we are always in the present, the ever-present, and I can be found there these days."

Some of Kessler's poetry has been recorded for broadcast and for the National Poetry Archives. Kessler's work has been translated into Italian and Hungarian. He is competent in Italian, French, Hungarian, and German.

BIOGRAPHICAL/CRITICAL SOURCES: *Publishers Weekly*, July 17, 1967; *New York Times Book Review*, September 24, 1967; *New York Times*, November 10, 1967; *New Leader*, February 12, 1968; *Choice*, July/August, 1968; *Library Journal*, March 1, 1970; *Los Angeles Times*, March 13, 1970, December 8, 1971; *Contemporary Literary Criticism*, Volume IV, Gale, 1975.

* * *

KEYES, Kenneth S(cofield), Jr. 1921-

PERSONAL: Surname rhymes with "eyes"; born January 19, 1921, in Atlanta, Ga.; son of Kenneth S. (in real estate) and Lucille (Thomas) Keyes; children: Kenneth S. III, Clara Lucille. *Education:* Attended Duke University, 1938-40; University of Miami, Coral Gables, Fla., A.B., 1953. *Home:* Cornucopia, St. Mary, Ky. 40063.

CAREER: In real estate business, 1953-64; Keyes Realty International, Inc., Miami, Fla., vice-president, 1964-68; Keyes National Investors, Miami, president, 1968-71; Living Love Center, Berkeley, Calif., founder, 1973-77; founder of Cornucopia Institute, 1977—. *Military service:* U.S. Navy, 1941-45; became chief petty officer.

WRITINGS—Published by Living Love, except as indicated: *How to Develop Your Thinking Ability*, McGraw, 1951; *How to Live Longer-Stronger-Slimmer*, Fell, 1966, published as *Loving Your Body*, Living Love, 1974; (with Jacque Fresco) *Looking Forward*, A. S. Barnes, 1969; *Handbook to Higher Consciousness*, 1973; *Taming Your Mind*, 1975; (with Tolly Burkan) *How to Make Your Life Work; or, Why Aren't You Happy?*, 1976; *A Conscious Person's Guide to Relationships*, 1979; *How to Enjoy Your Life in Spite of It All*, 1980; *Prescriptions for Happiness*, 1981; *The Hundredth Monkey*, 1982.

AVOCATIONAL INTERESTS: Yachting, general semantics, classical music.

* * *

KIMBALL, Nancy
See UPSON, Norma

* * *

KING, Adele Cockshoot 1932-

PERSONAL: Born July 28, 1932, in Omaha, Neb.; daughter of Ralph Waldo (a lawyer) and Thera (Brown) Cockshoot; married Bruce A. King (a university professor), December 28, 1955; children: Nicole Michelle. *Education:* University of Iowa, B.A. (with highest distinction), 1954; graduate study at Sorbonne, University of Paris, 1954-55, and Washington University, St. Louis, 1955-56; University of Leeds, M.A., 1960; University of Paris, Doctorat d'Universite, 1970. *Home:* 67A Glandovey Rd., Christchurch 5, New Zealand.

CAREER: St. Luke's School and Allen Stevenson School, New York, N.Y., teacher of French, 1960-61; University of Alberta, Calgary, Alberta, instructor in French, 1961-62; University of Ibadan, Ibadan, Nigeria, lecturer in French, 1963-65; University of Lagos, Lagos, Nigeria, lecturer in French, 1967-70, head of French Division; University of Windsor, Windsor, Ontario, instructor in English literature, 1971-72; Ahmadu Bello University, Zaria, Nigeria, reader in French, 1973-76, head of French Section and chairman of committee on Arabic studies; University of Missouri—Columbia, visiting professor of French, 1976-77; Rangi Ruru School, Christchurch, New Zealand, teacher of French, 1980—. Part-time tutor in French, University of Bristol, 1967; part-time instructor in French, Wayne State University, 1970; lecturer in English literature, St. Clair College of Applied Arts and Technology, Windsor, 1971-72. *Member:* Phi Beta Kappa. *Awards, honors:* American Association of University Women postdoctoral fellow, 1977-78.

WRITINGS: *Albert Camus*, Grove, 1964 (published in Scotland as *Camus*, Oliver & Boyd, 1964), published as *Camus*, Barnes & Noble, 1965, new edition, Capricorn Books, 1971; *Proust*, Oliver & Boyd, 1968; *Paul Nizan: Ecrivain*, Didier (Paris), 1976; *The Writings of Camara Laye*, Heinemann, 1980.

Study guides; all published by Longman: *Camus's "L'Etranger,"* 1980; *Hemingway's "A Farewell to Arms,"* 1981; *Ibsen's "Ghosts,"* 1981.

Contributor: *A Celebration of Black and African Writing*, Oxford University Press, 1976; *Images of Man*, Deakin University (Geelong, Australia), 1978; *Artist and Audience: African Literature as a Shared Experience*, Three Continents Press, 1979.

Author of papers presented to African Literature Association Conference, 1977, Colloque, Critique et Reception des Litteratures, 1978, and Congress of the International Federation for Modern Languages and Literatures, 1978. Contributor to professional journals, including *French Studies, Modern Language Journal, Afrique Litteraire, Research in African Literature,* and *Language and Style*.

WORK IN PROGRESS: Co-editing "Modern Dramatists" series for Macmillan; a study of French women writers of the twentieth century; study guides, Laye's *"L'Enfant Noir"* and Graham Greene's *"The Power and the Glory"*; articles and essays on African writers.

AVOCATIONAL INTERESTS: Cooking, travel, Nigerian art.

* * *

KING, Robert R(ay) 1942-

PERSONAL: Born June 8, 1942, in Rock Springs, Wyo.; son of Edward C. and Elinor Marie (Smith) King; married Kay Atkinson (a linguist), December 30, 1969; children: Nathan Atkinson, James Robert, Daniel Edward. *Education:* Brigham Young University, B.A., 1966; Fletcher School of Law and Diplomacy, M.A., 1967, M.A.L.D., 1968, Ph.D., 1970. *Home:* 1216 Wildwood Cir., Boulder, Colo. 80303. *Office:* Tosco Corp., 1877 Broadway, Suite 405, Boulder, Colo. 80302.

CAREER: Radio Free Europe, Munich, West Germany, assistant director of research and senior analyst for Romania and Bulgaria, 1970-77; National Security Council Staff, Washington, D.C., member, 1977-78; writer and political consultant in Washington, D.C., 1979; Appalachian Regional Commission, Washington, D.C., special assistant to the federal co-chairman, 1980-81; currently manager of community development and socioeconomic planning, Tosco Corp., Boulder, Colo. Lecturer in international relations at Brigham Young University, Salzburg, Austria, 1971-77, and at University of Southern California, Munich, Germany, 1973-77. *Member:* American Political Science Association, Association for the Advancement of Slavic Studies.

WRITINGS: (With Stephen E. Palmer, Jr.) *Yugoslav Communism and the Macedonian Question,* Archon Books, 1971; *Minorities under Communism: Nationalities as a Source of Tension among Balkan Communist States,* Harvard University Press, 1973; (editor with Robert W. Dean) *East European Perspectives on European Security and Cooperation,* Praeger, 1974; (editor with J. F. Brown) *Eastern Europe's Uncertain Future,* Praeger, 1977; *A History of the Romanian Communist Party,* Hoover Institution, 1980. Editor and contributor to "Radio Free Europe Research" series, published by Radio Free Europe. Contributor to professional journals.

WORK IN PROGRESS: Research on the socioeconomic impact of large-scale energy development, organizational boundaries, organizational development and group cohesion.

* * *

KING, William R(ichard) 1938-

PERSONAL: Born December 24, 1938, in McKeesport, Pa.; son of Dewey Clark and Cambria (Jones) King; married Fay Eileen Bickerton, June 20, 1958; children: James David, Suzan Lorain. *Education:* Pennsylvania State University, B.S. (with honors), 1960; Case Institute of Technology (now Case Western Reserve University), M.S., 1962, Ph.D., 1964. *Office:* Graduate School of Business, University of Pittsburgh, Pittsburgh, Pa. 15260.

CAREER: Case Institute of Technology (now Case Western Reserve University), Cleveland, Ohio, assistant professor, 1964-65; Air Force Institute of Technology, Dayton, Ohio, assistant professor, 1965-67; University of Pittsburgh, Pittsburgh, Pa., associate professor, 1967-69, professor of business administration, 1969—. Professional staff member, U.S. Senate Committee on the Budget, 1976-77; director and president of Western Pennsylvania Montessori School; director of Pittsburgh Commerce Institute. Consultant to industrial firms and government agencies. *Military service:* U.S. Air Force, 1965-67; became first lieutenant.

MEMBER: World Future Society, American Association for the Advancement of Science (fellow), American Marketing Association, American Institute for Decision Science, Operations Research Society of America, North American Society for Corporate Planning, Society for Information Management, Institute of Management Sciences, Tau Beta Pi, Beta Gamma Sigma, Alpha Pi Mu, Sigma Tau. *Awards, honors:* McKinsey Foundation Book Award, 1969, for *Systems Analysis and Project Management.*

WRITINGS: Quantitative Analysis for Marketing Management, McGraw, 1967; *Probability for Management Decisions,* Wiley, 1968; (with D. I. Cleland) *Systems Analysis and Project Management,* McGraw, 1968, 3rd edition, 1983; (editor with Cleland) *Systems, Organizations, Analysis Management: A Book of Readings,* McGraw, 1968; (with Cleland) *Management: A Systems Approach,* McGraw, 1972; *Marketing Management Information Systems,* Van Nostrand, 1977; (with Cleland) *Strategic Planning and Policy,* Van Nostrand, 1978; (editor with G. Zaltman) *Marketing Scientific and Technical Information,* Westview, 1979; (with J. Grant) *The Logic of Strategic Planning,* Little, Brown, 1982; (editor with Cleland) *Project Management Handbook,* Van Nostrand, 1983. Contributor to journals. Associate editor, *Management Science,* 1974—, and *International Journal of Policy and Information,* 1982—; *MIS Quarterly,* associate editor, 1977-82, senior editor, 1982—.

WORK IN PROGRESS: A second edition of *Strategic Planning and Policy* and, with R. Wendell, *Management Science: Decision Problem Formulation, Solution, and Implementation.*

* * *

KIRALY, Bela (Kalman) 1912-

PERSONAL: Born April 14, 1912, in Kaposvar, Hungary; divorced. *Education:* Ludovika Military Academy, B.A., 1935; General Staff Academy, Budapest, Hungary, M.A., 1942; Columbia University, M.A., 1959, Ph.D., 1966. *Address:* P.O. Box 568, Highland Lakes, N.J. 07422. *Office:* Program on Society in Change, Brooklyn College of the City University of New York, Brooklyn, N.Y. 11210.

CAREER: General Staff Academy, Budapest, Hungary, professor of military history and superintendent of academy, 1950-51; lecturer in the United States, Europe, and Asia, 1957-68; Brooklyn College of the City University of New York, Brooklyn, N.Y., instructor, 1965-66, assistant professor, 1966-70, associate professor, 1970-71, professor of history, 1971-82, professor emeritus, 1982—, professor of history, City University of New York Graduate School, and chairman of East European Section of Center for European Studies, 1969-82. Adjunct associate professor, St. John's University, 1969-71; Columbia University, visiting professor, 1971-72, 1975-76, visitng scholar, 1972-73. Member of White House Conference on International Cooperation, 1964. *Military service:* Hungarian Army, commander-in-chief of Infantry, and chief of department of education, training, and sports of Ministry of Defense, 1947-50; became major-general.

MEMBER: American Historical Association, American Association for the Advancement of Slavic Studies, American Association for the Study of Hungarian History (president, 1981-82), P.E.N. *Awards, honors:* Named honorary member of staff and faculty of U.S. Army Command and General Staff

College, 1959; named Teacher of the Year, Brooklyn College of the City University of New York, 1968; American Philosophical Society research grant for research in Vienna and London, 1968; International Research and Exchange Board and American Council of Learned Societies grants, 1978-81; National Endowment for the Humanities research grant, 1978-84; Presidential Medal, Brooklyn College of the City University of New York, 1982.

WRITINGS: *The Hungarian Army under the Soviets* (in Japanese), Japan Institute of Foreign Affairs, 1950; *Hungary in the Late Eighteenth Century: The Decline of Enlightened Despotism,* Columbia University Press, 1969; (contributor) Joseph Held and others, editors, *Intellectual History of the Hapsburg Monarchy: 1806-1914,* Columbia University Press, 1975; *Ferenc Deak,* Twayne, 1975; (editor) *Tolerance and Movements of Religious Dissent in East Central Europe,* East European Quarterly and Columbia University Press, 1975; (contributor) Paul Teleki, editor, *Evolution of Hungary and Its Place in European History,* new edition, Academic International, 1975; *East Central European Perceptions of Early America,* Peter de Ridder Press (Lisse), 1977; (editor and contributor) *The Hungarian Revolution of 1956,* Columbia University Press, 1978; (editor and contributor) *War and Society in East Central Europe,* Brooklyn College Press, Volume I, 1978, Volume II, 1982, Volume III, 1983; *Az Elso Haboru Szocialista Orszagok Kozott* (title means, "The First War between Socialist States"), Bessenyei Club, 1981; (contributor) M. Palumbo and W. O. Shanahan, editors, *Nationalism: Essays in Honor of L. C. Snyder,* Greenwood Press, 1981. Director and editor-in-chief of "Brooklyn College Studies on Society in Change," 1978—. Contributor to history journals in the United States and abroad.

SIDELIGHTS: In 1951, Bela Kiraly was arrested, sentenced to death, and imprisoned in Budapest. He was paroled in 1956 and became the commander-in-chief of the National Guard of Hungary. He spent the years from 1957 to 1968 lecturing in European, Asian, and American colleges, universities, military academies, and war colleges on the subjects of the Hungarian Revolution, organization, training, and system of Soviet control of the People's Armies of East Central Europe.

* * *

KIRBY, Jean
    See McDONNELL, Virginia B(leecker)

* * *

KISMARIC, Carole 1942-

PERSONAL: Born April 28, 1942, in Orange, N.J.; daughter of John Joseph and Alice (Gruskos) Kismaric; married Charles Mikolaycak (a book illustrator and designer), October 1, 1970. *Education:* Pennsylvania State University, B.F.A., 1964. *Home:* 64 East 91st St., New York, N.Y. 10028. *Office:* Aperture, Millerton, N.Y. 12546.

CAREER: Time-Life, Inc., New York, N.Y., picture editor, 1969-73, assistant editor, 1973-75; Photo-200 (photo project to document United States bicentennial), assistant director, 1975-76; *Aperture,* Millerton, N.Y., managing editor, 1976-80, associate editor, 1980—.

WRITINGS: (Editor) Fred Freeman, *Duel of the Ironclads* (juvenile), Time-Life, 1968; (adapter with husband, Charles Mikolaycak) *The Boy Who Tried to Cheat Death* (juvenile), Doubleday, 1971; *On Leadership,* edited and designed by Mikolaycak, I.B.M., 1974; *Prelude to War,* edited and designed by Mikolaycak, Time-Life, 1976; *Blitzkrieg,* edited and designed by Mikolaycak, Time-Life, 1976; *The Battle of Britain,* edited and designed by Mikolaycak, Time-Life, 1976; (editor with Norman Snyder) *The Photography Catalogue,* Harper, 1976; (author of introduction) *Exposure: Ten Photographers' Work* (Creative Artists Public Service Exposure Project), Creative Artists Public Service, 1976; (author of introduction) George Krause, *Saints and Martyrs,* Photopia Gallery, 1976; (author of introduction) Andre Kertesz, *Andre Kertesz,* Aperture, 1977; (editor with Michael E. Hoffman) Ray Metzker, *Sand Creatures,* Aperture, 1979; (editor with Hoffman) Phillip Lopate, *Lisette Model,* Aperture, 1979; (editor with Hoffman) *Eugene Atget,* Aperture, 1980; (editor with Hoffman) *Man Ray,* Aperture, 1980. Picture editor, "Time-Life Photography" series, "Time-Life Old West" series, "Human Behavior" series. Contributor to *Camera* and *du Magazine* (Switzerland).

* * *

KITCHEN, Helen (Angell)

PERSONAL: Born in Fossil, Ore.; daughter of Lloyd Steiwer and Hilda (Miller) Angell; married Jeffrey C. Kitchen, August 12, 1944; children: Jeffrey Coleman, Jr., Erik, Lynn. *Education:* University of Oregon, B.A. (honors), 1942. *Home:* 4309 Embassy Park Dr. N.W., Washington, D.C. 20016. *Office:* Director of African Studies, Center for Strategic and International Studies, Georgetown University, Suite 400, 1800 K St. N.W., Washington, D.C. 20006.

CAREER: *Reader's Digest,* Pleasantville, N.Y., member of editorial staff, 1942-44; political researcher in Cairo, Egypt, 1944-47; *Middle East Journal,* Washington, D.C., assistant editor, 1948; U.S. Department of State, Washington, D.C., special assistant to director of research for Africa, Middle East, and South Asia, 1951-58; *Africa Report,* Washington, D.C., editor-in-chief, 1960-68; director, Africa Area Study, Commission on Critical Choices for Americans, 1974-76; executive director, United States-South Africa Leader Exchange Program, 1978-81; Georgetown University, Center for Strategic and International Studies, Washington, D.C., director of African studies, 1981—. Member of board of public advisers, U.S. Department of State, African Bureau, 1963-70. Consultant, RAND Corp., 1962-68. Trustee, Georgetown Day School, 1957-63. *Member:* African Studies Association of United States (trustee, 1964-67), Phi Beta Kappa. *Awards, honors:* Outstanding service award, U.S. Secretary of State, 1957.

WRITINGS: *The Press in Africa,* Ruth Sloan Associates, 1956; *Africa: Images and Realities,* UNESCO, 1962; *The Educated African: A Country-by-Country Survey of Educational Development in Africa,* Praeger, 1962; *A Handbook of African Affairs,* Praeger, 1964; *Footnotes to the Congo Story: An Africa Report Anthology,* Walker & Co., 1967; *Africa: From Mystery to Maze,* Lexington Books, 1976; *Where Is South Africa Headed?: Options for Americans,* Seven Springs Center, 1978; *AEI Foreign Policy and Defense Review,* American Enterprise Institute for Public Policy Research, 1979. Contributor to magazines and journals. Editor of fortnightly news analysis, *African Index,* 1978-82; editor, *CSIS Africa Notes,* 1982—.

WORK IN PROGRESS: *U.S. Interests in Africa in the 1980s and Beyond,* for Praeger.

* * *

KLEIN, Doris F.
    See JONAS, Doris F(rances)

KLINK, Johanna L. 1918-

PERSONAL: Born March 6, 1918, in Roermond, Netherlands; daughter of D.J. (an engineer) and C.J.W.F. (Davyt) Klink. *Education:* University of Leiden, Dr. Theology, 1947. *Home:* Bakenessergracht 107, 2011 JV Haarlem, Netherlands.

CAREER: Ordained minister of Remonstrant (Arminian) Church, 1948; served as minister in various parishes, 1948-68; freelance writer and lecturer on religious education, 1968—.

WRITINGS: De bijbel vandaag (title means "The Bible Today"), De Tijdstroom, 1951; *Het is als met* (parables), De Tijdstroom, 1952; *De bijbel voor de kindren* (title means "The Bible for Children"), Het Wereldvenster, Volume I: *O.T.*, 1958, Volume II: *N.T.*, 1961, translation by Patricia Compton published as *Bible for Children*, Westminster, Volume I: *Old Testament*, 1967, Volume II: *New Testament*, 1969; *Ter meerdere ere: Een gesprek met kerkgangers*, Het Wereldvenster, 1965.

Die Theologie van de kinderen (title means "The Theology of Children"), Amboboeken, Volume I: *Kind en geloof* (title means "Child and Religion"), 1970, translation by R.A. Wilson published as *Your Child and Religion*, John Knox, 1972, Volume II: *Kind en leven* (title means "Child and Life"), 1971, Volume III: *Kind op aarde* (title means "Child on Earth"), 1972, Volumes I-III published in one volume as *Geloven met kinderen* (title means "Believing with Children"), 1976; *Niet in de wind, niet in het vuur* (title means "Not in the Storm, Not in the Fire"), Amboboeken 1974, translation published as *The Still Small Voice*, S.C.M. Press, 1974; *De kleine mens en het grote boek* (title means "The Little Man and the Great Book"), Amboboeken, 1976; *Het huis in de wereld* (title means "The House in the World"), De Toorts, 1976; *Het geheim van de wereld* (title mans "The Mystery of the World"), De Toorts, 1976; *Naar de tred van de kinderen*, Callenbach, 1981.

WORK IN PROGRESS: Bible for Small People.

SIDELIGHTS: Johanna L. Klink writes: "Perhaps we now live in a period during which the Christian church will lose more and more influence in the world. It will lose ground among members of the younger generation, because it looks backward to often petrified theories about the Bible, God, and Jesus, theories which are still taught to young children in Sunday school. Parents are very critical and progressive in the education of their children, but when it comes to religion, often the critical awareness stops. One of the reasons might be that adults adhere to the ideas, images, and theories they learned as children in Sunday school.

"In this chaotic and menacing period it is of the utmost importance that we concentrate on the aim of our lives and the ground of our being. And we cannot come to that center of our life with the children when we let them sit in front of the television for the only inspiration in their lives. The Christian religion will have a grip on new generations only when we are willing to correct our age-old theories about God and the Bible—with the help of the wiser and more original children!—and when we look to the way in which Jesus himself lived and spoke out against his religious tradition, freely and critically, even though it was written in his 'Bible'! We must also concentrate more consciously on what we transfer to children and from which life-center we ourselves live and believe."

AVOCATIONAL INTERESTS: Painting with watercolors.

KNEESE, Allen V(ictor) 1930-

PERSONAL: Born April 5, 1930, in Fredricksburg, Tex.; married, 1956. *Education:* Southwest Texas State College (now University), B.S., 1951; University of Colorado, M.A., 1952; Indiana University, Ph.D., 1956. *Home:* 2420 Cameron Mills Rd., Arlington, Va. *Office:* Resources for the Future, 1755 Massachusetts Ave. N.W., Washington, D.C. 20036.

CAREER: University of New Mexico, Albuquerque, assistant professor of economics, 1956-58; Federal Reserve Bank of Kansas City, Kansas City, Mo., research associate, 1958-61; Resources for the Future, Washington, D.C., research economist, 1961-63, director of water resources program, 1963-67, director of Quality of the Environment Division, 1967-74; University of New Mexico, professor of economics, 1974-78; Resources for the Future, senior fellow in Quality of the Environment Division, 1978—. Visiting associate professor of economics, Stanford University, 1963; visiting professor of economics, University of New Mexico, 1968-69; Royer Visiting Professor of Political Economy, University of California, Berkeley, 1971; adjunct professor, University of New Mexico, 1978—. Member of program development and review board, New Mexico Water Resources Research Institute; member of advisory committee for the resources and environment area, International Institute for Applied Science Analysis. Consultant to numerous organizations, including World Health Organization, U.S. Environmental Protection Agency, Tennessee Valley Authority, and the Navajo tribe.

MEMBER: Association of Environmental and Resource Economists, American Association for the Advancement of Science, American Economic Association, American Academy of Arts and Sciences, National Science Foundation (member of policy research and analysis advisory committee), National Academy of Sciences (member of liaison committee on resources and the environment; member of Navajo cooperative committee), National Research Council (member of commission on nonfuel minerals demand; member of committee on minerals demand; member of executive committee of Commission on Natural Resources), Chemical Manufacturers Association (member of advisory panel on benefits from toxic chemicals regulation).

WRITINGS: Water Pollution: Economic Aspects and Research Needs, Johns Hopkins Press, 1962, 2nd edition, 1964; (coauthor) *A Water Quality Program for the Delaware Basin*, Delaware River Basin Commission, 1964; *The Economics of Water Quality Management*, Johns Hopkins Press, 1964; (coauthor) *Problems and Opportunities in Managing Environmental Quality*, Resources for the Future, 1965; (with Orris C. Herfindahl) *Quality of the Environment: An Economic Approach to Some Problems Using Land, Water, and Air*, Johns Hopkins Press, 1965; *The Economics of Regional Water Management*, Johns Hopkins Press, 1968; (with Blair T. Bower) *Managing Water Quality: Economics, Technology, Institutions*, Johns Hopkins Press, 1968; (with George O. G. Loef) *The Economics of Water Utilization in the Beet Sugar Industry*, Johns Hopkins Press, 1968; *Approaches to Regional Water Quality Management*, Japan Economics Research Institute (Tokyo), 1968; *Water Resources Development and Use*, Federal Reserve Bank of Kansas City, 1969.

(With Robert U. Ayres and Ralph C. d'Arge) *Economics and the Environment: A Materials Balance Approach*, Johns Hopkins Press, 1970; (with Robert C. Haveman and A. Myrick Freeman III) *The Economics of Environmental Policy*, Wiley, 1973; (with Herfindahl) *Economic Theory of Natural Re-*

sources, C. E. Merrill, 1974; (with Charles L. Schultze) *Pollution, Prices, and Public Policy,* Brookings Institution, 1975; *Economics and the Environment,* Penguin, 1976; (with others) *Environmental Improvement through Economic Incentives,* Johns Hopkins Press, 1978; (with Bower) *Environmental Quality and Residuals Management: Report of a Research Program on Economic, Technological, and Institutional Aspects,* Resources for the Future, 1979; (with F. Lee Brown) *The Southwest Region under Stress: National Resource Development Issues in a Regional Setting,* Johns Hopkins Press, 1981.

Editor: (With Stephen C. Smith) *Water Research,* Johns Hopkins Press, 1966; (with Sidney Rolfe and Joe Harned, and contributor) *Managing the Environment: International Cooperation for Pollution Control,* Praeger, 1972; (with Bower) *Environmental Quality Analysis: Theory and Method in the Social Sciences,* Johns Hopkins Press, 1972; (with Peter Bohm, and contributor) *The Economics of Environment: Papers from Four Nations,* Macmillan (London), 1972; (with Alfred T. Parker and Walter O. Spofford, Jr.) *Energy Development in the Southwest: Problems of Water, Fish, and Wildlife in the Upper Colorado River Basin,* two volumes, Resources for the Future, 1980; (with Henry M. Peskin and Paul Portney) *Environmental Regulation and the U.S. Economy,* Johns Hopkins Press, 1981.

Contributor: Harold L. Amoss, editor, *Water Measuring and Meeting Future Requirements,* University of Colorado Press, 1961; *The Value of Water in Alternative Uses,* University of New Mexico Press, 1963; Julius Margolis, editor, *The Public Economy of Urban Communities,* Resources for the Future, 1965; *A Ten-Year Program of Federal Water Resources Research,* U.S. Office of Science and Technology, 1966; Henry Jarrett, editor, *Environment Quality in a Growing Economy,* Johns Hopkins Press, 1966; *Water Pollution Control,* World Health Organization (Geneva), 1966; *Economics of Air Pollution,* Norton, 1966; Ted L. Willrich and N. William Hines, editors, *Water Pollution Control and Abatement,* Iowa State University Press, 1966; Earnest F. Gloyna and W. Wesley Eckenfelder, Jr., editors, *Advances in Water Quality Improvement,* University of Texas Press, 1967; *Social Sciences and the Environment,* University of Colorado Press, 1967.

Managing the Environment: International Economic Cooperation, Asaki (Tokyo), 1970; *Symposium on Air Pollution,* Da Capo Press, 1971; Selma J. Mushkin, editor, *Public Prices for Public Products,* Urban Institute (Washington, D.C.), 1972; *The Royer Lectures,* University of California, 1972; (with Herfindahl) *The Measurement of Economic and Social Performance,* Columbia University Press, 1973; (with Bower) Robert Dorfman and Nancy S. Dorfman, editors, *Economics of the Environment,* Norton, 1972; Joe S. Bain, editor, *Environmental Decay: Economic Causes and Remedies,* Little, Brown, 1973; Edward W. Erickson and Leonard Waverman, editors, *The Energy Question: An International Failure of Policy,* Volume I: *The World,* University of Toronto Press, 1974; Eugene Seskin and Peskin, editors, *Cost Benefit Analysis,* Urban Institute, 1975; *Energy Development in the Rocky Mountain States,* Federation of Rocky Mountain States (Denver), 1975; (with Jon Sonstelie and Portney) Edwin Haefele, editor, *The Governance of Common Property Resources,* Johns Hopkins Press, 1975; J. Rothenberg and Ian Heggie, editors, *Management of Water Quality and Environment,* Macmillan (London), 1975.

(With Ayres) Martin Pfaff, editor, *Frontiers in Social Thought: Essays in Honor of Kenneth E. Boulding,* American Elsevier, 1976; Rolf Steppacher, Brigette Zogg-Walz, and Herman Hatzfeldt, editors, *Economics in International Perspective: Essays in Honor of Professor K. William Kapp,* Heath, 1977; (with Bower) Bower, editor, *Regional Residuals: Environmental Quality Management Modeling,* Resources for the Future, 1977; (with Schultze) Stuart S. Nagel, editor, *Policy Studies Review Annual,* Sage Publications, 1978; Ann F. Friedlaender, editor, *Approaches to Controlling Air Pollution,* M.I.T. Press, 1978; Gideon Golany, editor, *Urban Planning for Arid Zones: American Experiences and Directions,* Wiley, 1978; (with Jennifer Zamora) Daniel Yaron, editor, *Salinity, Irrigation, and Water Resources,* Dekker, 1978; Walter Mead and Albert Utton, editors, *U.S. Energy Policy,* Ballinger, 1979; (with Bower) Horst Siebert, editor, *Umwelt und Wirtschaftliche Entwicklung,* Wissenschaftliche Buchesellschaft (Darmstadt, West Germany), 1979; Golany, editor, *Arid Zone Settlement Planning,* Pergamon, 1979; (with Michael Williams) Siebert and others, editors, *Environmental Policy: The Economic Issues,* New York University Press, 1979.

Western Water Resources, Westview, 1980; Peter Duignan and Alvin Rabushka, editors, *The United States in the 1980s,* Hoover Institution, 1981; (with d'Arge) Donald G. Hagman, editor, *Land Use and Environmental Law Review, 1982,* Boardman, 1981. Also contributor to *Waste Management and Control,* a report for the Federal Council for Science and Technology, 1966.

Contributor to proceedings, annals, and working papers of New York Academy of Science, 1969, Oak Ridge Conference, 1976, Electric Power Research Institute, 1976, and Commission of Environmental Decision Making, 1977. Contributor to professional journals, including *Southwestern Review, National Resource Journal, Third World Quarterly, Journal of Economic Literature, American Economic Review,* and *International Organization.* Editor, *Water Resources Research Journal,* 1964-67; co-editor, *Journal of Environmental Economics and Management,* 1972—; member of editorial board, *Journal of Environmental Ethics* and *Risk Analysis.*

* * *

KNOWLES, Alison 1933-

PERSONAL: Born April 29, 1933, in New York, N.Y.; daughter of Edwin B. (a professor) and Helen Lois (Beckwith) Knowles; married James Ericson, 1955; married Richard C. Higgins (a writer and publisher), May 31, 1960 (divorced, 1970); children: (second marriage) Hannah and Jessica (twins). *Education:* Attended Middlebury College, 1950-52; Pratt Institute, A.B., 1955. *Politics:* Liberal. *Religion:* "?" *Home:* 122 Spring St., New York, N.Y. 10012.

CAREER: Free-lance silk screen work (both technical and artistic) in New York, N.Y., 1959—. Had one-woman shows in New York at Nonagon Gallery, 1958, and Judson Gallery, 1962; also exhibitor in shows in New York, Los Angeles, Chicago, Amsterdam, Vienna, Italy, and Germany. Performer in Fluxus Festivals in New York and abroad, 1962-64; performer in numerous other festivals and stage productions in the United States and abroad.

WRITINGS: Alison Knowles Bean Rolls, Fluxus, 1964; (contributor) *The Four Suits,* Something Else Press, 1965; *By Alison Knowles,* Something Else Press, 1965; *The Big Book,* Something Else Press, 1967, 2nd edition, 1969; *The House of Dust* (computer poem), Konig Verlag, 1968; *Journal of the Identical Lunch,* Nova Broadcast Press, 1970; *More by Alison Knowles,* Printed Editions, 1976; *Gem Duck,* Pari & Dispari (Italy), 1977, Printed Editions, 1978; *Seven Days Running,* Edition after Hand (Denmark), 1978; *Natural Assemblages and the Crow,* Printed Editions, 1980. Also author of *Alison Knowles;* editor, with Anna Lockwood, of *Women's Work,* an anthology of performance pieces. Contributor to magazines, including *Yam, CC V TRE, V TRE,* and *Fluxus.*

WORK IN PROGRESS: New Pieces, for Something Else Press.

SIDELIGHTS: Alison Knowles' *The Big Book* is an eight-foot tall, one-ton reading structure equipped with a telephone, toilet, hot plate, art gallery, graffiti wall, and a four-foot sleeping tunnel lined with artificial grass. Her earlier book *Alison Knowles Bean Rolls* is a tin can full of bean recipes and lore written on scrolls.

* * *

KOLINSKY, Martin 1936-

PERSONAL: Born June 24, 1936, in Winnipeg, Manitoba, Canada; son of Harry (a businessman) and Esther (Promislow) Kolinsky; married Eva Heckel (a university teacher), November 1, 1969; children: Harry, Daniel. *Education:* University of Saskatchewan, B.A. (cum laude), 1960; London School of Economics and Political Science, Ph.D., 1966. *Politics:* Moderate. *Religion:* Jewish. *Home:* 12 Selly Wick Dr., Birmingham, England. *Office:* Department of Political Science, University of Birmingham, Birmingham B15 2TT, England.

CAREER: University of Birmingham, Birmingham, England, lecturer in sociology, 1966-70, senior lecturer in political science, 1972—; Hebrew University of Jerusalem, Jerusalem, Israel, lecturer in sociology, 1970-72.

WRITINGS: Continuity and Change in European Society, St. Martin's, 1974; (editor with William E. Paterson) *Social and Political Movement in Western Europe,* Croom Helm, 1976; (contributor) P. Sargant Florence, editor, *C. K. Ogden,* Elek, 1977; (editor) *Divided Loyalties,* Manchester University Press, 1978; (with Michalina Vaughan and Peta Sheriff) *Social Change in France,* St. Martin's, 1980; (contributor) L. Tivey, editor, *The Nation-State,* Martin Robertson, 1981. Contributor to professional journals in England, France, and Israel.

* * *

KOLODNY, Annette 1941-

PERSONAL: Born August 21, 1941, in New York, N.Y.; daughter of David (a dentist) and Esther (a teacher; maiden name, Rifkind) Kolodny; married Daniel James Peters (a novelist), June 14, 1970. *Education:* Brooklyn College of the City University of New York, B.A. (magna cum laude), 1962; University of California, Berkeley, M.A., 1965, Ph.D., 1969; also attended University of Oslo, summer, 1961. *Politics:* "Radical Feminist." *Home address:* R.F.D. 1, Lee Hook Rd., Newmarket, N.H. 03857. *Office:* Department of English, University of New Hampshire, Durham, N.H. 03824.

CAREER: Newsweek, New York, N.Y., associate to editor of international editions, 1962-63; Universtiy of California, Berkeley, teaching assistant in English, 1965-68; Yale University, New Haven, Conn., assistant professor of English and fellow of Ezra Stiles College, 1969-70; University of British Columbia, Vancouver, assistant professor of English, 1970-74, co-coordinator and member of faculty in Women's Studies Program, 1973-74; University of New Hampshire, Durham, 1974—, began as assistant professor, became associate professor of English, adjunct research scholar, 1980—. Master teacher in Upward Bound Program at University of California, Berkeley, 1966; consultant and visiting scholar, National Humanities Center, 1980; member of institute faculty, Yale University, 1982; has lectured and presented papers at numerous symposia and professional conferences. Member of President's Commission on the Status of Women, University of New Hampshire, 1974-75. Linguisitc consultant to RAND Corp., 1968; consultant to various schools in western Canada on the establishment of women's studies programs, 1972-74; consultant for awards and grants to Canada Council, 1974—, and to National Endowment for the Humanities, 1975—. *Member:* Modern Language Association of America, American Studies Association, American Society for Eighteenth Century Studies, National Women's Studies Association, Canadian Association for American Studies.

AWARDS, HONORS: Canada Council senior research grant, 1973-74; National Endowment for the Humanities younger humanist fellowship, 1974-75; Ford Foundation fellowship, 1975-76; Rockefeller Foundation humanities fellowship, 1978-79; Guggenheim Memorial Foundation fellowship, 1979-80; Florence Howe Essay Prize, Modern Language Association of America, 1979, for "Dancing through the Minefield: Some Observations on the Theory, Practice, and Politics of a Feminist Literary Criticism."

WRITINGS: The Lay of the Land: Metaphor as Experience and History in American Life and Letters, University of North Carolina Press, 1975; *Westering Women: Fantasies of the American Frontiers, 1630-1860,* University of North Carolina Press, 1983; *Dancing through the Minefield: Theory, Method, and Politics in Feminist Literary Criticism,* Indiana University Press, 1983; (editor and author of introduction) Nathaniel Hawthorne, *The Blithedale Romance,* Viking, 1983.

Contributor: Nancy Esther James, editor, *I, That Am Ever Stranger: Poems on Women's Experience* (anthology), Globe Printing, 1974; E. L. Epstein and Douglas R. Butturff, editors, *Women's Language and Style,* University of Akron Press, 1978; Cheryl L. Brown and Karen Olson, editors, *Feminist Criticism: Essays on Theory, Poetry and Prose,* Scarecrow Press, 1978; Wayne Fields, editor, *James Fenimore Cooper: A Collection of Critical Essays,* Prentice-Hall, 1979; Sally McConnell-Ginet, Ruth Borker, and Nelly Furman, editors, *Women and Language in Literature and Society,* Praeger, 1980; Estelle C. Jelinek, editor, *Women's Autobiography: Essays in Criticism,* Indiana University Press, 1980; Martin Tucker, editor, *The Critical Temper,* Ungar, 1980; Dale Spender, editor, *Men's Studies Modified: The Impact of Feminism on the Academic Disciplines,* Pergamon, 1981.

Also contributor to *Proceedings of the Conference on Feminist Literary Criticism,* 1981. Regular book reviewer for *American Literature, Journal of English and German Philology, In These Times,* and *Women's Studies International Quarterly.* Contributor of articles and reviews to professional journals, including *Feminist Studies, Critical Inquiry, New Literary History, South Atlantic Quarterly, American Literature,* and *Modern Fiction Studies.* Member of board of editors, *American Literature,* 1975-78; outside reader and consultant, *SIGNS: Journal of Women in Culture and Society,* 1975—; member of board of advisors, *Literary Classics of the United States,* 1980-82; member of editorial board, *Early American Literature,* 1981-84.

WORK IN PROGRESS: Contributing "A Map for Re-Reading: Gender and the Interpretation of Literary Texts," to *The M(Other) Tongue: Essays in Feminist Psychoanalystic Literary Interpretation,* edited by Madelon S. Gohlke, Shirley N. Garner, and Claire Kahane.

SIDELIGHTS: Annette Kolodny writes: "I fear that the human species is hell-bent on self-annihilation, with the United States rather blindly leading the way. We pollute our minds with trivia and our environment with carcinogens. The political and moral awakenings of the nineteen-sixties are now being dismissed—to our peril; and the current women's movement may run out of energy before it achieves the changes it envisions. The nation as a whole is in the hands of the blind, the selfish, and the mediocre."

* * *

KOOIMAN, Helen W.
See HOSIER, Helen Kooiman

* * *

KOVEL, Ralph

PERSONAL: Surname is pronounced Cove-*el;* born in Milwaukee, Wis.; son of Lester (a clothing manufacturer) and Dorothy (Bernstein) Kovel; married Terry Horvitz (a writer), June 27, 1950; children: Lee Ralph, Kim (daughter). *Education:* Attended Ohio State University, 1939. *Home:* 22000 Shaker Blvd., Shaker Heights, Ohio 44122.

CAREER: Writer on antiques, in collaboration with wife, 1952—; Ralph M. Kovel & Associates (food brokers), Cleveland, Ohio, president, 1958—. Short course instructor in American decorative arts, Cleveland College, Western Reserve University (now Case Western Reserve University), 1958-63. Co-host, with wife, of syndicated television series, "Kovels on Collecting," 1981—. President, East End Neighborhood House, Cleveland, 1962-63. *Member:* Union League Club of Chicago, Oakwood Club, Whitehall Club. *Awards, honors:* Cleveland Area Television Academy Award, 1971; National Antiques Show Annual Award, 1974; Louis S. Pierce Award for outstanding community service.

WRITINGS—All with wife, Terry Kovel; all published by Crown: *Dictionary of Marks: Pottery and Porcelain,* 1953; *Directory of American Silver, Pewter and Silver Plate,* 1961; *American Country Furniture,* 1965; *Know Your Antiques,* 1967, 3rd edition, 1981; *The Kovels' Collector's Guide to Limited Editions,* 1974; *The Kovel Book of American Art Pottery,* 1974; *Kovels' Price Guide for Collector Plates, Figurines, Paperweights and Other Limited Editions,* 1978; *Kovels' Illustrated Price Guide to Royal Doulton,* 1980; *Kovels' Illustrated Guide to Depression Glass and American Dinnerware,* 1980; *Kovels' Know Your Collectibles,* 1981. Also co-author of *Kovels' Antiques Price List,* 1968-81, and of *The Kovels' Bottle Price List,* 1971, 1973, 1975, 1977, 1979, and 1982.

Author, with T. Kovel, of monthly newsletter, "Ralph and Terry Kovel on Antiques," 1974—, and of monthly columns, "Know Your Antiques," Register and Tribune Syndicate, Des Moines, Iowa, 1954—, and "Your Collectibles," *House Beautiful,* 1979—. Contributor to magazines.

SIDELIGHTS: In 1950 Ralph and Terry Kovel were paying monthly installments on a $15 music box, their first antique. Today, according to a *New York Times Book Review* critic, their books on antiques and collectibles are regarded "as bibles in their field" and have sold more than one million copies. "There was an explosion in antiques in the 1950s," Ralph Kovel's wife and co-author Terry Kovel said in a *Publishers Weekly* interview with Robert Dahlin. "The United States was finally old enough to have a history and to have something to look back on."

Many of the Kovels' books are price guides—compilations of current prices for antiques and collectibles. Their first book, however, was an alphabetical listing of the marks on the bottom of glassware and pottery. "Terry was in New York with her parents, so I decided to put all the A's and B's [of the pottery marks] together in straight alphabetical order," Ralph Kovel told *Smithsonian* reporter Scott Eyman. "When my wife and her father came home and I showed them my work, he looked at me in disbelief and asked, 'Is that the best way you can spend a weekend of your time?'" The book, *Dictionary of Marks: Pottery and Porcelain,* is now in its thirty-second printing.

The Kovels and their staff of twelve gather information on prices quoted for items throughout the country and feed them into a computer. "We don't write books, we report prices," Ralph Kovel said in *Publishers Weekly.* Terry Kovel agrees. In *Smithsonian* she commented: "We are reporters and researchers; we never make value judgements. A lot of what we do is like biology, devising categories and subcategories for things that have never been categorized before. As far as prices go, we just tell people what's being asked and gotten; prices obviously out of line, we don't use."

The Kovels are themselves avid antique collectors. The basement of their home has been turned into a "country store" museum, writes Eyman, and their house is "furnished in a profusion of heavy styles that should, theoretically, clash [but instead] is a perfect representation of their personalities. Its air of lived in comfort is typical of the unpretentiousness familiar to anyone who has ever seen [the Kovels] on television." Terry Kovel remarked in *Publishers Weekly:* "Any antique dishes that can't go through my dish washer, I can't live with." The most valuable item they own is an eighteenth-century silver sugar castor made by Paul Revere's father. The Kovels bought it at a house sale for $12; it is actually worth close to $10,000, Ralph Kovel said.

"If you are destined to own an antique, it will wait for you," Ralph Kovel commented in *Smithsonian.* "It's really almost mystical, the sense of union you experience when you first see the antique you've been looking and waiting for. That satisfaction is very, very special. It's what makes all the hard work—the tramping through the woods and dirty shops—more than worthwhile. It's all part of the search for something forgotten and wonderful."

BIOGRAPHICAL/CRITICAL SOURCES: Smithsonian, November, 1980; *New York Times Book Review,* January 25, 1981; *Publishers Weekly,* September 25, 1981.

* * *

KOVEL, Terry 1928-

PERSONAL: Surname is pronounced Cove-*el;* born October 27, 1928, in Cleveland, Ohio; daughter of Isadore (a publisher) and Rix (Osteryoung) Horvitz; married Ralph Kovel (a writer and businessman), June 27, 1950; children: Lee Ralph, Kim (daughter). *Education:* Wellesley College, B.A., 1950; University of Illinois, graduate study, 1961. *Home:* 22000 Shaker Blvd., Shaker Heights, Ohio 44122.

CAREER: Writer on antiques, in collaboration with husband, 1952—; part-time teacher in Lyndhurst, Ohio, 1959-72. Short course instructor in American decorative arts, Cleveland College, Western Reserve University (now Case Western Reserve University), 1958-63. Co-host, with husband, of syndicated television series, "Kovels on Collecting," 1981—. *Member:* Ohio Newspaper Women's Association.

WRITINGS—All with husband, Ralph Kovel; all published by Crown: *Dictionary of Marks: Pottery and Porcelain,* 1953; *Directory of American Silver, Pewter and Silver Plate,* 1961; *American Country Furniture,* 1965; *Know Your Antiques,* 1967, 3rd edition, 1981; *The Kovels' Collector's Guide to Limited*

Editions, 1974; *The Kovel Book of American Art Pottery*, 1974; *Kovels' Price Guide for Collector Plates, Figurines, Paperweights and Other Limited Editions*, 1978; *Kovels' Illustrated Price Guide to Royal Doulton*, 1980; *Kovels' Illustrated Guide to Depression Glass and American Dinnerware*, 1980; *Kovels' Know Your Collectibles*, 1981. Also co-author of *Kovels' Antiques Price List*, 1968-81, and of *The Kovels' Bottle Price List*, 1971, 1973, 1975, 1977, 1979, and 1982.

Author, with R. Kovel, of monthly newsletter, "Ralph and Terry Kovel on Antiques," 1974—, and of monthly columns, "Know Your Antiques," Register and Tribune Syndicate, Des Moines, Iowa, 1954—, and "Your Collectibles," *House Beautiful*, 1979—. Contributor to magazines.

SIDELIGHTS: See CA entry for Ralph Kovel.

* * *

KRAUSS, Ellis S(aunders) 1944-

PERSONAL: Born January 8, 1944, in Memphis, Tenn.; son of Irving and Pearl (Kivel) Krauss; married Carol Draper (an audiologist/speech therapist), March 28, 1969; children: Jennifer Rachel. *Education:* Brooklyn College of the City University of New York, B.A. (cum laude), 1964; Stanford University, M.A., 1965, Ph.D., 1973. *Home:* 2915 Victor St., Bellingham, Wash. 98225. *Office:* Department of Political Science, Western Washington University, Bellingham, Wash. 98225.

CAREER: Western Washington University, Bellingham, lecturer, 1970-71, assistant professor, 1971-74, associate professor of political science, 1974—. Conducted research at Inter-University Center for the Study of the Japanese Language (Tokyo), 1968-69; visiting scholar at Institute of International Relations, Sophia University, 1969-70; visiting researcher, University of Kyoto, 1974-75, and University of Tokyo, 1978; honorary research associate, Harvard University, 1978-79.

MEMBER: American Council of Learned Societies (member of joint committee on Japanese studies), Social Science Research Council. *Awards, honors:* Grants from American Council of Learned Societies-Social Science Research Council, and Japan Foundation, 1974-75, all for research in Japan; Fulbright-Hays faculty research abroad award, 1978; Fulbright research grant, 1983, for research in Japan.

WRITINGS: *Japanese Radicals Revisited: Student Protest in Postwar Japan*, University of California Press, 1974; (editor with Kurt Steiner and Scott C. Flanagan) *Political Opposition and Local Politics in Japan*, Princeton University Press, 1980; (editor with Patricia G. Steinfoff and Thomas P. Rohlen) *Conflict in Japan: Studies of Postwar Society and Politics*, Princeton University Press, in press. Contributor of numerous articles and reviews to political science and Asian studies journals.

WORK IN PROGRESS: *The State and Opposition in Japan*; articles on politicians and bureaucrats in policymaking in Japan and on the Swedish and Japanese parliaments in the 1970s.

SIDELIGHTS: Ellis Krauss wrote CA: "In recent years, interest in Japan in the West has changed from considering it to be an exotic and unique but unimportant country to viewing it as a major model and competitor. This is a healthy trend, as long as we don't exchange indifference based on ignorance for admiration or fear based on ignorance. The function of Western experts on Japan today is to approach Japan realistically as an advanced industrial nation that can be compared with equivalent Western countries, and to see all such societies as facing universal problems but sometimes handling them in different ways. This is the approach I've tried to take in my own work."

KRESS, Robert (Lee) 1932-

PERSONAL: Born September 22, 1932, in Jasper, Ind.; son of Oscar Michael (a cabinetmaker) and Stella (Schutz) Kress. *Education:* St. Meinrad's College, B.A., 1954; University of Innsbruck, S.T.B., 1956, S.T.L., 1958; University of Notre Dame, M.A., 1964; Pontifical Gregorian University, graduate study, 1965-67; Pontifical University of St. Thomas Aquinas, S.T.D., 1968. *Politics:* Independent. *Home:* 620 Michigan Ave. N.E., Washington, D.C. 20064. *Office:* Theology Department, Catholic University of America, Washington, D.C. 20064.

CAREER: Ordained Roman Catholic priest, 1958; assistant pastor for Diocese of Evansville, Ind., 1958-64; Washington Catholic High School, Washington, Ind., superintendent, 1959-64; University of Vincennes, Vincennes, Ind., lecturer in religion, 1964; St. Meinrad College, St. Meinrad, Ind., lecturer in philosophy and theology, 1967-68; University of Evansville, Evansville, lecturer in philosophy and religion, 1967-70; Princeton Theological Seminary, Princeton, N.J., visiting fellow, 1970-71; St. Louis University, School of Divinity, St. Louis, Mo., assistant professor, 1971-73; University of Evansville, associate professor of philosophy and religion, 1973-79; Catholic University of America, Washington, D.C. associate professor of theology, 1979—. Visiting lecturer in biomedical ethics, School of Medicine, Indiana University at Bloomington, 1973-79; visiting professor, Lutheran Theological Seminary, Gettysburg, Pa., 1980, Princeton Theological Seminary, Princeton, N.J., 1981, and University of St. Michael's College, Toronto School of Theology, Toronto, Ontario, 1982. Auxiliary chaplain for U.S. Armed Forces in Europe, 1964-66; chaplain of Newman Center and University Christian Movement, 1967-70; director of Newman Foundation, 1967-70; producer and director of television program, "Moral View," WTVW, 1969; consultant and lecturer.

MEMBER: Catholic Campus Ministry Association, College Theology Society (member, board of directors, 1981-84), Catholic Theological Society of America, Religious Educators Association, Evansville Clergy Ecumenical Association, St. Louis Theological Consortium Inter-faculty Dialogue.

AWARDS, HONORS: Outstanding Book of the Year Award, College Theology Society, 1975, for *Whither Womankind?*; Danforth Foundation associate, 1976-82; National Endowment for the Arts fellow, 1977; Outstanding Teacher of the Year Award, University of Evansville, 1979; Ludwig von Mises fellow in Humanities, 1982-83.

WRITINGS: *The Sinful Member of the Holy Church*, Angelicum University Press (Rome), 1968; *Whither Womankind?*, Abbey Press, 1975; *Come, Pilgrim: Reconciliation Themes for the Holy Year*, Office of Religious Education, 1975; *Christian Roots: No Alien God*, Christian Classics, 1978; *The Difference that Jesus Makes: The Sacrament of the Forgiving God*, Franciscan Herald, 1981; *A Rahner Handbook*, John Knox, 1982; *The Church: Communion, Sacrament, Communication*, University Press, 1982; *Touching the Divine*, Cross Roads, 1983.

Translator: Hugo Rahner, editor, *The Parish*, Newman, 1957; A. Laepple, *Key Problems of Genesis*, Paulist Press, 1964. Also translator of articles for journals.

Contributor of 120 articles and reviews to scholarly and popular periodicals. Consulting editor of *Theology Digest*, 1971-75.

WORK IN PROGRESS: Studies in liberation theology, ecclesiology, ethics, and the history of ideas.

SIDELIGHTS: Robert Kress has knowledge of Greek, Latin, German, French, Italian, Spanish, and Dutch. He told *CA:* "I strive to help my students and readers critically examine their heritage and tradition and so to relate to it, whether negatively or positively. I urge them to operate on the basis of the classic question, 'What's it all about?'"

* * *

KRESSY, Michael 1936-

PERSONAL: Born December 25, 1936, in New York, N.Y.; son of Edmund F. (an artist) and Maryland (a writer-journalist; maiden name, Newcomb) Kressy; married Jean Gleichenhaus (an instructor in nursing and a writer) October 1, 1964; children: Peter, Sarah. *Education:* Boston University, B.A., 1959; University of Massachusetts, M.F.A., 1969. *Home:* Lane Village, Ashburnham, Mass. 01430. *Office:* Department of English, Mount Wachusett Community College, Gardner, Mass. 01440.

CAREER: *White Plains Reporter-Dispatch,* White Plains, N.Y., general reporter and feature writer, 1962-63; *New York Daily News,* New York City, assistant editor of employee magazine, 1963-65; Mount Wachusett Community College, Gardner, Mass., instructor in English, 1969-74; founder and editor of *North Country Pilot* and co-founder of *Leominster Tribune,* 1975—; Mount Wachusett Community College, associate professor of English, 1979—. Has given poetry readings in New England colleges. Gardening consultant to Sphagnum Peat Moss Information Bureau, New York City; consultant to Houghton Mifflin Co. *Military service:* U.S. Army, translator, 1959-62; served in Germany. *Member:* Garden Writers Association of America. *Awards, honors:* Grant from Corporation for Public Broadcasting, 1968, for experimental sight-sound play "Earth-Toil and Sesame"; first prize in poetry contest, Worcester County Poetry Association, 1982.

WRITINGS—Published by Meredith Corp., except as indicated: (Contributor) Nora Barraford, Kenneth Gibbs, and Stan Rubin, editors, *Working from Silence* (poems), Kendall/Hunt, 1971; *How to Grow Your Own Vegetables,* 1973, abridged edition, 1975; (author and editor) *Container Plants You Can Grow,* 1978; (contributor) *Complete Guide to Gardening,* 1979.

Author of "Race," a one-act play, first performed in New York, N.Y., at New York Theatre Ensemble, November, 1968, and "Earth-Toil and Sesame," a radio play, Corporation for Public Broadcasting, 1969. Contributor to *College English* and *Agora.*

WORK IN PROGRESS: *Petal Tones,* poems, with drawings by his twin brother, Christopher Kressy; *Emil and the Chocolate Chip Cookie* and *Emil and the Rainbow Balloon,* both for children.

SIDELIGHTS: Michael Kressy writes that since college he has been "haunted by question of man's relation to his environment—whether blight or blessing—and the purity of individual man versus obvious failure of collective man. As inveterate taker to the woods, I believe there are subtle clues communicable only by the poet who has few ulterior motives. Purpose in writing is to encourage real and unreal connections first for myself and by happy accident others."

* * *

KROETSCH, Robert 1927-

PERSONAL: Born June 26, 1927, in Heisler, Alberta, Canada; son of Paul (a farmer) and Hilda (Weller) Kroetsch; married Mary Jane Lewis, January 13, 1956; children: Laura Caroline, Margaret Ann. *Education:* University of Alberta, B.A., 1948; McGill University, graduate study, 1954-55; Middlebury College, M.A., 1956; University of Iowa, Ph.D., 1961. *Home:* 5-634 Kenaston Blvd., Winnipeg, Manitoba, Canada. *Agent:* Raines & Raines, 475 Fifth Ave., New York, N.Y. 10017. *Office:* Department of English, University of Manitoba, Winnipeg, Manitoba, Canada R3T 2N2.

CAREER: Yellowknife Transportation Co. (riverboats), Northwest Territories, Canada, laborer and purser, 1948-50; U.S. Air Force, Goose Bay, Labrador, civilian information and education specialist, 1951-54; State University of New York at Binghamton, assistant professor, 1961-65, associate professor, 1965-68, professor of English, 1968-78; University of Manitoba, Winnipeg, professor of English, 1978—. *Member:* Modern Language Association of America, American Association of University Professors. *Awards, honors:* Fellowship to Bread Loaf Writers' Conference, 1966; Governor General's Award for fiction, 1969.

WRITINGS—Novels, except as indicated: *But We Are Exiles,* St. Martin's, 1966; *The Words of My Roaring,* St. Martin's, 1966; *Alberta: Description and Travel* (nonfiction), St. Martin's, 1969; *The Studhorse Man,* Simon & Schuster, 1970; *Gone Indian,* New Press, 1973; *Badlands,* New Press, 1975; *What the Crow Said,* General Publishing, 1978; *Seed Catalogue: Poems,* Turnstone Press, 1978; *Ledger* (poems), Brick/Nairn, 1979; *The Crow Journals* (nonfiction), New West Press, 1980; *Field Notes* (poems), General Publishing, 1981.

WORK IN PROGRESS: A seventh novel.

SIDELIGHTS: "I'm interested in sharing with the reader the fact that I'm making a fiction," Canadian novelist and poet Robert Kroetsch told Geoff Hancock in an interview for *Canadian Fiction Magazine.* Abandoning what he calls "the old style realism," Kroetsch has adopted an approach that pulls the reader into the fiction-making process. Connie Harvey writing in *Essays on Canadian Writing* explains, "Kroetsch wants to force the reader into a direct perceptual approach to the material so that he, as well as the narrator, creates the work."

According to Harvey, Kroetsch's use of language helps create a "voice" that allows for this direct perceptual experience. "With gerunds and participles, verbals that operate as nouns, and adjectives, Kroetsch is able to list the details of a scene without interrupting the flow of action, thereby creating an immediate experience for the reader's perception," Harvey says. In thus engaging the reader, notes Louis MacKendrick in *Essays on Canadian Writing,* Kroetsch hopes to overcome "the tyranny of language." He breaks free of "the word's received meaning and absolutes into a contemporary world of fresh usage" by "demythologizing, deconstructing, unnaming, uncreating, or uninventing," MacKendrick says.

In an *Essays on Canadian Writing* interview, Kroetsch justifies this novel approach by pointing out that "creation and destruction go hand in hand." But, he continues, "my destruction takes the form of trying to make an old story work, for instance having almost to destroy the old story to tell it anew." According to Kroetsch, the old stories, instead of illuminating the world, sometimes stop people from seeing it. "It's like a pair of glasses that don't quite fit anymore," he explains later in that interview. To improve vision, Kroetsch has said he wants to "uninvent" a mythology and to set another one in its place.

The theme of Kroetsch's first novel *But We Are Exiles* is drawn from the ancient myth of Narcissus. (Son of a river-god, Narcissus was a vain creature who loved only himself. When the wood-nymph Echo fell in love with him, he scorned her, and, as punishment for his vanity Nemesis, goddess of law and justice, caused him to fall in love with his own reflection seen in a pool. Narcissus gazed at his image until he wasted away, becoming a flower of the same time.) In Kroetsch's story, protagonist Peter Guy pilots a work boat up Canada's MacKenzie River in search of the drowned body of the boat owner, Mike Hornyak. Accompanying him is Kettle Fraser, Hornyak's wife and Guy's former lover. Writing in *Canadian Literature*, Peter Thomas says that in loving both Hornyak and Guy, Fraser recognizes the two faces of Narcissus. The faceless condition in which Guy finds Hornyak's body is a revelation of his own emptiness, according to Thomas who writes that Guy "joins with the image he has tried to reject" when he climbs into the barge which holds the corpse. It is the myth of Narcissus, concludes Thomas now writing in *Essays on Canadian Writing*, which "provides the main structural symbolism in the relations of Peter Guy/Mike Hornyak, two faces of self-love embracing at the conclusion, and their Echo Kettle Fraser."

The Studhorse Man, described by Kroetsch as the *Odyssey* retold on dry land, is another example of an old tale that has been infused with new life. Narrated by Demeter Proudfoot, a lunatic who spends much of his time in an asylum bathtub, the story is an account of how the last of the studhorse men, Hazard Lepage, takes a perfect virgin stallion (named Poseidon) across Alberta in search of a perfect mare. Lepage's fiance, Martha Proudfoot, remains at home. By the book's end, the horse has trampled Lepage to death and Demeter has gone mad under the strain of knowing Lepage and trying to tell his story. Martha, however, survives. "The book's pattern is circular, as is Hazard's journey," observes *New York Times* book reviewer Paul West, "and the point—made in a manner that fuses prarie tall-tale with Odyssean myth—is that perfectionists procrastinate and thus waste their lives while life in general goes muddling on around them."

Despite the unhappy fate of its main character, *The Studhorse Man* is "flanked by bouts of farce," according to West. Writing in *Canadian Literature*, critic Peter Thomas describes the work as a "complex and essentially comic confabulation" and thinks this "tale told by an idiot" is an assault on realism: "The myths of Demeter and Poseidon . . . are fragmented and distorted schemes of reference in *The Studhorse Man*. Their order is mocked as it is realized." And yet, *Essays on Canadian Writing*'s MacKendrick observes, in this as in his other novels, "Kroetsch's unrestraint is more idea than performance, for he retains all the virtues of story and storytelling while imitating their conventions and parodying their devices. . . . In his hands, the possibilities and improbabilities of [this technique] have an exciting life."

BIOGRAPHICAL/CRITICAL SOURCES: New York Times Book Review, April 26, 1970; *Canadian Literature*, summer, 1974; *Contemporary Literary Criticism*, Volume V, Gale, 1976; *Canadian Fiction Magazine*, spring/summer, 1977; *Canadian Forum*, October-November, 1978, June-July, 1981; *Essays on Canadian Writing*, summer, 1978, summer/fall, 1980.

—Sketch by Donna Olendorf

* * *

KRULIK, Stephen 1933-

PERSONAL: Born May 1, 1933, in Brooklyn, N.Y.; son of Max and Sadie Krulik; married Gladys Olshan, December, 1959; children: Nancy, Jeffry. *Education:* Brooklyn College (now Brooklyn College of the City University of New York), B.A., 1954; Columbia University, M.A., 1955, Ed.D., 1961. *Office:* Department of Secondary Education, Temple University, Philadelphia, Pa. 19122.

CAREER: New York (N.Y.) Board of Education, teacher, 1954-69; Temple University, Philadelphia, Pa., professor of mathematics education, 1969—. Educational consultant to Anti-Poverty Program. *Member:* Phi Delta Kappa, Kappa Delta Pi, Pi Mu Epsilon.

WRITINGS: (With Irwin Kaufman) *Multi-Sensory Techniques in Mathematics Teaching*, Prentice-Hall, 1963; (with Kaufman) *High School Geometry Review Notes*, Monarch, 1964; (with Kaufman and Jerome Shostak) *The Handbook of College Entrance Examinations*, Pocket Books, 1965; (with Kaufman) *Elementary Algebra: High School Level*, Monarch, 1965; (with Kaufman) *How to Use the Overhead Projector in Mathematics Education* (booklet), National Council of Teachers of Mathematics, 1966.

(With Kaufman and Shostak) *The Civil Service Examination Handbook*, New American Library, 1970; *A Handbook of Aids for Teaching Junior-Senior High School Mathematics*, Saunders, 1971; *A Mathematics Laboratory Handbook for Secondary Schools*, Saunders, 1972; (with Ingrid B. Weise) *Teaching Secondary School Mathematics*, Saunders, 1975; (with Jesse A. Rudnick) *Problem Solving: A Handbook for Teachers*, Allyn & Bacon, 1980; (with Rudnick) *A Guidebook for Teaching General Mathematics*, Allyn & Bacon, 1982; (with Rudnick) *Problem Solving in Math*, Scholastic Book Services, 1982; *Problem Solving: A Sourcebook for Instruction*, Allyn & Bacon, 1983. Contributor to journals.

* * *

K-TURKEL, Judi 1934-
(Judi R. Kesselman, Judi Kesselman-Turkel, Pauline Turkel)

PERSONAL: Born January 3, 1934, in Bronx, N.Y.; daughter of Samuel S. and Pauline (Turkel) Rosenthal; children: Joseph Jay Kesselman, Jeffrey Peter Kesselman. *Education:* Brooklyn College (now Brooklyn College of the City University of New York), B.A. (cum laude), 1955. *Home and office:* 3006 Gregory St., Madison, Wis. 53711.

CAREER: Free-lance writer. *Screen Stories*, New York City, story editor, 1956-58; editor, Sterling Publications, New York City, 1959, Stern Publications, New York City, 1960-61, and K.M.R. Publications, New York City, 1961-62; senior editor at McFadden-Bartell, 1962; Dell Publishing Co., New York City, managing editor, 1964; contributing editor to *Pageant* magazine, 1967-68, and to *Physician's Management*, 1975-79; currently partner in P/K Associates, Inc., Madison, Wis. Instructor in adult communications and writing in Great Neck Public Schools, Great Neck, N.Y., 1974-76, and at University of Wisconsin Extension, 1976—. *Member:* American Society of Journalists and Authors, National Press Club, Authors Guild, Authors League of America, Wisconsin Council of Writers. *Awards, honors:* Jesse H. Neal Award for editorial achievement, American Business Press Association, 1977.

WRITINGS—Under name Judi R. Kesselman; with Franklynn Peterson, except as indicated: (Sole author) *Stopping Out: A Guide to Leaving College and Getting Back In*, M. Evans, 1976; *The Do-It-Yourself Custom Van Book*, Regnery, 1977; (with Peterson and Frank Konishi) *Eat Anything Exercise Diet*, Morrow, 1979; *Handbook of Snowmobile Maintenance and Repair*, Dutton, 1979; *Vans* (juvenile), Dandy Lion, 1979; *I Can Use Tools* (juvenile), Elsevier-Nelson, 1981; *Test-Taking Strategies*, Contemporary Books, 1981; *Study Smarts*, Contemporary Books, 1981.

Under name Judi Kesselman-Turkel, with Franklynn Peterson: *Good Writing*, F. Watts, 1980; *Homeowner's Book of Lists*,

Contemporary Books, 1981; *How to Improve Damn Near Everything around Your Home,* Prentice-Hall, 1981; *Author's Handbook,* Prentice-Hall, 1982; *Magazine Writer's Handbook,* Prentice-Hall, 1982; *Research Shortcuts,* Contemporary Books, 1982; *Grammar Crammer,* Contemporary Books, 1982; *Note-Taking Made Easy,* Contemporary Books, 1982; *Word Games to Build Word Power,* Contemporary Books, 1982.

Contributor to periodicals and newspapers, including *OMNI, Fortune, McCall's, New York Times, Playgirl,* and *Popular Mechanics.*

WORK IN PROGRESS: Several more study aids for high school and college students, for Contemporary Books; books on computer use for the general public; a play; a novel; several magazine articles.

SIDELIGHTS: Judi K-Turkel told *CA:* "I find that one of the hardest things I must deal with as a writer is frustration: the frustration of preparing what I know is the best book on the subject and seeing it die aborning because the publisher has decided not to publicize it, or has given it the wrong title, or has attempted to sell it in the wrong market; the frustration of having to abandon book projects or turn down magazine assignments that are extremely worthwhile because the publisher or editor can't or won't give enough of an advance or writing fee to enable me to undertake the project and still pay the bills. Being a full-time free-lance writer is itself a great frustration because publishers and editors won't pay an experienced author any more than the author of a first book or article—a situation that doesn't exist in *any* other field of work. Joining into a writing partnership six years ago immeasurably helped me cope with this frustration. In this lonely endeavor, writing, it's a great luxury not to have to slog along entirely alone."

AVOCATIONAL INTERESTS: Playing piano, travel, rare book collecting.

* * *

KYBURG, Henry (Guy) E(ly), Jr. 1928-

PERSONAL: Born October 9, 1928, in New York, N.Y.; son of Henry Guy Ely and Margherita (Abbey) Kyburg; married Sarah Randlev, February 4, 1967; children: (previous marriage) Robin Margherita, Christopher Ely, Alice Independence, Peter David; (current marriage) Henry Guy Ely III, Sarah Abbey. *Education:* Yale University, B.E., 1949; Columbia University, M.A., 1953, Ph.D., 1955. *Home:* Eyer Rd., Lyons, N.Y. 14489. *Office:* Department of Philosophy, University of Rochester, Rochester, N.Y. 14627.

CAREER: Combustion Engineering, Inc., New York City, worked in research and development, 1951-52; Wesleyan University, Middletown, Conn., assistant professor of mathematics, 1958-61; Rockefeller Institute, New York City, research associate, 1961-62; University of Denver, Denver, Colo., associate professor of mathematics and philosophy, 1962-63; Wayne State University, Detroit, Mich., associate professor of philosophy, 1963-65; University of Rochester, Rochester, N.Y., professor of philosophy, 1965—, chairman of department, 1967-81. *Military service:* U.S. Coast Guard, 1951. *Member:* Mathematical Association of America, American Mathematical Society, American Philosophical Association, American Association for Symbolic Logic, American Association for the Advancement of Science. *Awards, honors:* Grants from American Council of Learned Societies, 1962, and National Science Foundation, 1964-75.

WRITINGS: Probability and the Logic of Rational Belief, Wesleyan University Press, 1961; (editor with Ernest Nagel) *Induction: Some Current Issues,* Wesleyan University Press, 1963; (editor with Henry E. Smokler) *Studies in Subjective Probability,* Wiley, 1964, 2nd edition, Krieger, 1980; *Philosophy of Science: A Formal Approach,* Macmillan, 1968; *Probability Theory,* Prentice-Hall, 1969; *Induction and Probability,* Macmillan, 1970; *The Logical Foundations of Statistical Inference,* Reidel, 1974; (editor with Peter D. Asquith) *Current Research in Philosophy of Science: Proceedings of the P.S.A. Critical Research Problems Conference,* Philosophy of Science Association, 1979. Also author of *Epistemology and Inference.*

L

LaBASTILLE, Anne 1938-
(Anne LaBastille Bowes)

PERSONAL: Born November 20, 1938, in New York, N.Y.; daughter of Ferdinand Meyer (a professor) and Irma (a pianist and writer; maiden name, Goebel) LaBastille; divorced. *Education:* Attended University of Miami, Coral Gables, Fla.; Cornell University, B.S., Ph.D.; Colorado State University, M.S. *Agent:* Julian Bach, Julian Bach Literary Agency, 747 Third Ave., New York, N.Y. 10017.

CAREER: National Audubon Society, wildlife tour leader, Palm Beach, Fla., 1955-56; Caribbean Wildlife Tours, Miami, Fla., organizer and co-leader, winters, 1956-63; Covewood Lodge, Big Moose, N.Y., owner, co-manager, and naturalist, summers, 1956-64; Everglades National Park, Fla., ranger-naturalist, 1964; Cornell University, Ithaca, N.Y., assistant professor in department of natural resources and department of science and environmental education, 1969-71, research associate, Laboratory of Ornithology, 1971-73; free-lance wildlife ecologist, consultant, writer, and photographer, 1971—. Onwer of West of the Wind Publications, Inc. Field director and biologist in campaign to save endangered Atitlan grebe, Guatemala, between 1964-68; biologist and writer on National Geographic Society expedition in Guatemala, 1968; conducted wildlife studies on Atlantic Coast for Smithsonian Institution, 1972-74, and made other surveys for World Wildlife Fund, Defenders of Wildlife, and U.S. Environmental Protection Agency. Lecturer at Harvard University, Cornell University, State University of New York at Albany, and Philadelphia Academy of Natural Sciences. Juror, J. Paul Getty Wildlife Conservation Award, 1974-77; member and consultant, Survival Services Commission, International Union for Conservation of Nature and Natural Resources; member of scientific advisory board, Island Resources Foundation, U.S. Virgin Islands. Registered Adirondack guide. *Member:* Society of Women Geographers, American Women in Science, Association for Tropical Biology, Wildlife Society.

AWARDS, HONORS: World Wildlife Fund Gold Medal for conservation, 1974; research grants from International Union for Conservation of Nature and Natural Resources, Caribbean Research Institute, World Wildlife Fund, Smithsonian Institution, and other agencies; Literature award, New York State Outdoor Education Association, 1977; L.I.D., Union College, 1980.

WRITINGS: (Author and illustrator under name Anne LaBastille Bowes) *Birds of the Mayas* (folk tales and guide to birds of Yucatan and Guatemala), West of the Wind Publications, 1964; (under name Anne LaBastille Bowes) *Bird Kingdom of the Mayas* (folklore of birds), Van Nostrand, 1967; (author of appendix material) *Life of the Jungle,* McGraw, 1970; *Ecology and Management of the Atitlan Grebe, Guatemala* (monograph), Wildlife Society, 1974; *Woodswoman,* Dutton, 1976; (contributor) *Wildlife Country,* National Wildlife Federation, 1977; (contributor) *Wildlife '78,* Danbury Press, 1978; *Assignment: Wildlife,* Dutton, 1980; *Women and Wilderness,* Sierra Books, 1980; (contributor) *Orbits and Opportunities,* Ginn, 1980.

"Ranger Rick's Best Friends" series for young people; published by National Wildlife Federation: *White-Tailed Deer,* 1973; *The Seal Family,* 1974; *Wild Bobcats,* 1974; *The Opposums,* 1974.

Contributor to journals, juvenile magazines, and newspapers, including *Nature, Travel, Reader's Digest, Historia Natural y Pro Natura, Outdoor Life, Audubon, National Geographic, New York Times, Fauna, Chicago Tribune, Caribbean Journal of Science, Auk,* and *Biological Conservation.* Contributing editor in ecology, *Today's Girl,* 1971-72.

SIDELIGHTS: Following her divorce, Anne LaBastille bought twenty-two acres of lakefront forest land in New York State's Adirondack Park and there built the log cabin that has since been her home. *Woodswoman* is an account of her adventures living in the Adirondacks and of the plants and animals she has met in the woods.

BIOGRAPHICAL/CRITICAL SOURCES: Anne LaBastille, *Woodswoman,* Dutton, 1976; *New York Times,* November 3, 1977; LaBastille, *Assignment: Wildlife,* Dutton, 1980.

*   *   *

LACY, Norris J(oiner) 1940-

PERSONAL: Born March 8, 1940, in Hopkinsville, Ky.; son of Edwin Vermont (a cook) and Lillian (Joiner) Lacy; married Faye Tison (a communications specialist), December 21, 1962 (divorced, 1981). *Education:* Murray State University, A.B., 1962; Middlebury College, graduate study, summer, 1962; Indiana University, M.A., 1963, Ph.D., 1967. *Home:* 1904 Countryside Lane, Lawrence, Kan. 66044. *Office:* Department of French, University of Kansas, Lawrence, Kan. 66045.

CAREER: Indiana University at Bloomington, lecturer in French, 1965-66; University of Kansas, Lawrence, assistant professor, 1966-70, associate professor, 1970-75, professor of French language and literature, 1975—, assistant chairman of French and Italian, 1969-72, chairman of French and Italian, 1978—. Visiting professor at University of California, Los Angeles, 1975-76. Has worked as jazz musician and music teacher. *Member:* International Courtly Literature Society, International Arthurian Society, Mediaeval Academy of America, Modern Language Association of America, American Association of Teachers of French, Societe Rencesvals. *Awards, honors:* Woodrow Wilson fellowship, 1962-63; grants from American Philosophical Society, 1969, American Council of Learned Societies, 1973, and National Endowment for the Humanities, 1975.

WRITINGS: (Editor and contributor) *A Medieval French Miscellany*, University of Kansas, 1972; (editor and author of introduction) J. N. Carman, translator, *From Camelot to Joyous Guard: The Old French "La Mort le Roi Artu,"* University Press of Kansas, 1974; (editor) *26 Chansons d'amour de la Renaissance* (title means "26 Renaissance Love Songs"), University Press of Kansas, 1975; (editor and contributor) *The Comic Spirit in Medieval France*, Soler (Valencia), 1976; *The Craft of Chretien de Troyes: An Essay on Narrative Art*, E. J. Brill (Leiden), 1980; (co-editor and contributor) *Essays in Early French Literature*, French Literature Publishing Co. (York, S.C.), 1982; (editor) *L'Istoyre de Jehan Coquault*, French Literature Publishing Co., 1982. Contributor to language and literature journals.

WORK IN PROGRESS: Research leading to studies of French romances after Chretien de Troyes.

AVOCATIONAL INTERESTS: Photography, music.

* * *

LAIRD, Carobeth 1895-

PERSONAL: Born July 20, 1895, in Coleman, Tex.; daughter of James Harvey (an editor) and Emma Cora (Chaddock) Tucker; married John Peabody Harrington, 1916 (divorced, 1923); married George Laird, August 23, 1923 (died April 13, 1940); children: Elizabeth Dresser, Awona Harrington, Frances Georgia Culp, Rosaleen Ragsdale (died January 15, 1982), Oliver, Margaret, George Theodore. *Education:* "Very little formal education." *Politics:* "Liberal, present affiliation, Democrat." *Religion:* "Vital to my existence yet impossible to categorize; continually evolving; based largely on the Beatitudes, yet not altogether Christian at its roots." *Home and office:* 13761 Tobiasson Rd., Poway, Calif. 92064.

CAREER: Writer. Conducted workshop "The Gestalt of the Myth" at Southwestern Anthropological Association conference, April, 1982.

WRITINGS: *Encounter with an Angry God*, Malki Museum Press (Banning, Calif.), 1975; *The Chemehuevis*, Malki Museum Press, 1976; *Limbo*, Chandler & Sharp, 1979; *Mirror and Pattern: George Laird's World of Chemehuevi Mythology*, Malki Museum Press, 1982. Author of pamphlets. Contributor of poems and articles to *Christian Science Journal* and *Christian Science Sentinel*. Contributing editor, *Journal of California Anthropology*, 1974—.

WORK IN PROGRESS: The first volume of *Pilgrim and Stranger*, an open-ended autobiographical project.

SIDELIGHTS: Carobeth Laird told CA: "Although my first book was published when I was eighty, I am not a beginning author. I can never remember a time when I was not interested in writing and trying to teach myself the art of writing. My life appears to have been divided by abrupt dislocations into more or less unrelated segments; yet there is an inner continuity, and every phase has contributed to my development. I would not blot out any of it. I am glad to have traveled over most of the United States by car at a time when towns were less homogenized than they now are and rural areas comparatively untouched. In my adolescence I traveled with my parents in Mexico for several months each year and learned a little something of the country and the language. It was in Mexico that I first heard English spoken without Southern accent or flat Texas drawl and began my long love affair with the spoken as well as the written language.

"Since I sneaked into Academia by the backdoor without any of the usual credentials, I am amused to discover that three of my published books are in use as texts. Several courses on creative writing have employed *Encounter with an Angry God; The Chemehuevis* is used in native American studies and in anthropology classes; and *Limbo*, which seems to be the only book to have been written by a survivor of the nursing home experience, is required reading in a number of nursing schools in this country and Canada."

* * *

LAMBERT, John (Robin) 1936-

PERSONAL: Born February 4, 1936, in Surrey, England; son of Ralph (a company secretary) and Rhoda (Holland) Lambert. *Education:* Corpus Christi College Oxford, B.A., 1957, M.A. 1966; College of Europe, certificate, 1958. *Politics:* "Left."

CAREER: Agence Europe (specialized reporting on European economic communities), Luxembourg, Luxembourg, staff member, 1958-63; European Economic Community (Common Market), Brussels, Belgium, commission deputy spokesman, 1963-66; free-lance journalist, 1967—. *Member:* Former Students of the College of Europe (member of committee, 1960-63; vice-president, 1963-64; president, 1964-67).

WRITINGS: (With Michael Shanks) *The Common Market Today and Tomorrow*, Praeger, 1962 (published in England as *Britain and the New Europe: The Future of the Common Market*, Chatto & Windus, 1962); *Britain in a Federal Europe*, Chatto & Windus, 1969; (with John Augustine, Robert Holman, and Dipak Nandy) *Race in the Inner City: A Report from Handsworth, Birmingham*, Runnymede Trust, 1970; *What Is Man?*, Herald House, 1973; (with Chris Paris and Bob Blackaby) *Housing Policy and the State: Allocation, Access, and Control*, Macmillan (London), 1978. Contributor to *Spectator*, *World Today*, and *Journal of Common Market Studies*. Member of editorial board, *Agenor*, 1966—.

SIDELIGHTS: John Lambert speaks French, Italian, and German fluently, and he reads Spanish, Dutch, and Swedish. *Avocational interests:* Modern architecture, cooking.

* * *

LAMIRANDE, Emilien 1926-

PERSONAL: Born May 22, 1926, in Saint-Georges de Windsor, Quebec; son of Armand and Valentine (Boucher) Lamirande. *Education:* University of Ottawa, B.A., 1949, L.Ph., 1950, M.A., 1951, L.Th., 1955; Leopold-Franens Universitaet, D.Th., 1960; Union Theological Seminary, S.T.M., 1965. *Home:* 60 Cartier, Apt. 602, Ottawa, Ontario, Canada K2P 2E1. *Office:* Department of Religious Studies, University of Ottawa, Ottawa, Ontario, Canada K1N 6N5.

CAREER: University of Ottawa, Ottawa, Ontario, lecturer in theology, 1954-58, associate professor, 1960-64, titular professor, 1964-65; Saint Paul University (federated with the University of Ottawa), Ottawa, dean of the faculty of theology, 1967-69, titular professor of theology, 1970; University of Ottawa, titular professor of religious studies, 1970—, chairman of department, 1972-75. *Member:* Societe Canadienne de Theologie, Societe Canadienne de l'Histoire de l'Eglise Catholique, Societe Canadienne d'Etudes Patristiques (vice-president, 1979—).

WRITINGS: La Communion des Saints, Fayard, 1962, published as *The Communion of Saints,* Hawthorne, 1963; *Un siecle et demi d'etudes sur l'ecclesiologie de Saint Augustin* (bibliographical essay), Etudes Augustiniennes (Paris), 1962; *L'Eglise Celeste Selon Saint Augustin,* Etudes Augustiniennes, 1963; (author of introduction and notes) *Oeuvres de Saint Augustin,* Volume 32, Desclee de Brouwer, 1965; *Dieu chez les hommes: La signification du pavillon chretien de l'Expo 67,* Montreal, 1967; *Etudes sur l'ecclesiologie de saint Augustin,* Editions de l'Universite, 1969; *La situation ecclesiologique des Donatistes selon Saint Augustin,* Editions de l'Universite, 1972; *Church, State and Toleration: An Intriguing Change of Mind in Augustine,* Villanova University Press, 1975; *Le P.G. Simard: Un disciple de saint Augustine a l'Universite d'Ottawa,* Editions de l'Universite d'Ottawa, 1981; *Paulin de Milan et la "Vita Ambrosii,"* Bellarmin, 1982. Contributor of articles to theological journals in Europe and America.

WORK IN PROGRESS: Research on the history of the African Church, Augustine, ecclesiology, and the role of women in the early church.

SIDELIGHTS: Besides French, Emilien Lamirande has a "reading knowledge of English, German, Spanish, Italian, Portuguese, etc."

* * *

LANCASTER, Clay 1917-

PERSONAL: Born March 30, 1917, in Lexington, Ky.; son of John William, Jr. and Della (Clay) Lancaster. *Education:* University of Kentucky, A.B., 1938, M.A., 1939; graduate study at Columbia University, 1943-49.

CAREER: Columbia University, New York City, lecturer in department of fine arts and archaeology, 1948-49, 1951-53; Vassar College, Poughkeepsie, N.Y., lecturer, 1950-51; Cooper Union, New York City, lecturer, 1951-53; Metropolitan Museum of Art, New York City, lecturer, 1953; Prospect Park, Brooklyn, N.Y., curator, beginning 1966. Advisor to U.S. Department of State for film on American architecture, 1951-53. *Member:* National Trust for Historic Preservation, Phi Beta Kappa. *Awards, honors:* Guggenheim fellow, 1953 and 1964.

WRITINGS: Ante Bellum Suburban Villas and Rural Residences of Fayette County, Kentucky, and Some Outstanding Homes of Lexington, privately printed, 1955; *Back Streets and Pine Trees,* Bur Press, 1956; *Architectural Follies in America,* Tuttle, 1960; *The Periwinkle Steamboat,* Viking, 1961; *Old Brooklyn Heights: New York's First Suburb,* Tuttle, 1961, 2nd edition, Dover, 1979; *Ante Bellum Houses of the Bluegrass,* University of Kentucky Press, 1961; *The Japanese Influence in America,* Twayne, 1963; *Michiko; or, Mrs. Belmont's Brownstone on Brooklyn Heights,* Tuttle, 1965; *Prospect Park Handbook,* Rawls, 1967.

The Architecture of Historic Nantucket, McGraw, 1972; *The Far-out Island Railroad: Nantucket's Old Summer Narrow-Gauge, 1879-1918,* Pleasant Publications, 1972; (with Edmund Vincent Gillon) *Victorian Houses,* Dover, 1973; (with Joseph Byron) *New York Interiors at the Turn of the Century,* Dover, 1976; (editor with Lawrence Grow) *Waiting for the 5:05: Terminal, Station, and Depot in America,* Main Street, 1977; *Vestiges of the Venerable City: A Chronicle of Lexington, Kentucky, Its Architectural Development, and Survey of Its Early Streets and Antiquities,* Lexington-Fayette County Historic Commission, 1978; *Eutaw: The Builders and Architecture of an Ante-Bellum Southern Town,* Greene County Historical Society, 1979; *Nantucket in the Nineteenth Century,* Dover, 1979.

Contributor of articles to periodicals in the fields of art, architecture, and antiques, including *Art Quarterly, Antiques, Gazette Des Beaux-Arts, Journal of the Society of Architectural Historians, Archaeology, Marg* (India), *American Heritage, Art Bulletin, Artibus Asiae,* and *Plants and Gardens.*

WORK IN PROGRESS: Children's books.†

* * *

LANDAU, Jacob M. 1924-

PERSONAL: Born March 20, 1924, in Chisinau, Romania; taken to Palestine in 1935; son of Michael (a civil servant) and Maria (a teacher; maiden name, Abeles) Landau; married Zipora Marcus (a teacher), July 29, 1947; children: Ronnit (daughter), Iddo (son). *Education:* Hebrew University of Jerusalem, M.A., 1946; School of Oriental and African Studies, Ph.D., 1949. *Religion:* Jewish. *Home:* 5 Mishael St., Jerusalem, Israel. *Office:* 213 Kaplan Bldg., Hebrew University of Jerusalem, Jerusalem, Israel.

CAREER: Hebrew University of Jerusalem, Jerusalem, Israel, high school teacher, 1949-58, teaching fellow, 1958-62, senior lecturer, 1962-68, associate professor, 1968-74, professor of political science, 1974—. Visiting lecturer, Brandeis University, 1955-56; lecturer, University of Tel Aviv, 1956-59; visiting associate professor, University of California, Los Angeles, 1963-64; visiting professor, Wayne State University, 1968-69, Columbia University, 1969, University of Ankara, 1974, University of Texas at Austin, 1975, and Candido Mendes University, Rio de Janeiro. *Member:* Israel Oriental Society, American Oriental Society, Middle East Studies Association of North America, Israel Association for Political Science, Academy of Political Science (New York). *Awards, honors:* Fulbright travel grant, 1963; President Ben Zvi Memorial Award, 1968, for *Jews in Nineteenth-Century Egypt;* Itzhak Grunbaum Award, 1974, for *The Arabs in Israel: A Political Study.*

WRITINGS: Parliaments and Parties in Egypt, Praeger, 1954, reprinted, University Microfilm International, 1977; *Studies in the Arab Theater and Cinema,* University of Pennsylvania Press, 1958; *A Word Count of Modern Arabic Prose,* American Council of Learned Societies, 1958; (editor) *Teaching of Arabic as a Foreign Language* (in Hebrew), School of Education, Hebrew University, 1961; (editor) *Der Staat Israel,* Glock & Lutz (Nuernberg), 1964, 2nd edition, 1970; (with M. M. Czudnowski) *The Israel Communist Party and the Elections for the Fifth Knesset, 1961,* Hoover Institution, 1965; *ha-Yehudim be-Mitsrayim ba-me'ah hatesha'-'esreh,* Ben Zvi Institute, Hebrew University, 1967, revised edition translated and published as *Jews in Nineteenth-Century Egypt,* New York University Press, 1969; (with H.A.R. Gibb) *Arabische Literaturgeschichte,* Artemis (Zurich), 1968; *The Arabs in Israel: A Political Study,* Oxford University Press, for the Royal Institute of International Affairs, 1969.

The Hejaf Railway and the Muslim Pilgrimage: A Case of Ottoman Political Propaganda, Wayne State University Press,

1971; (editor) *Man, State and Society in the Contemporary Middle East,* Praeger, 1972; *Middle Eastern Themes: Papers in History and Politics,* Cass, 1973; *Radical Politics in Modern Turkey,* E. J. Brill, 1974; *The Arabs and the Histradut,* Department of Higher Education (Tel Aviv), 1976; *Politics and Islam: The National Salvation Party in Turkey,* University of Utah Press, 1976; *Abdul Hamid's Palestine,* Deutsch, 1979; *Pan-Turkism in Turkey: A Study of Irredentism,* Christopher Hurst, 1981. Contributor to several scholarly encyclopedias in Israel, Greece, England, and the United States.

Contributor to specialized journals, including *Middle Eastern Studies* (London), *Journal of Modern History* (Chicago), *Oriente Moderno* (Rome), *Western Political Quarterly* (Salt Lake City), *Bamah* (Tel Aviv), and *International Review of Social History* (Amsterdam).

SIDELIGHTS: Jacob M. Landau reads ten languages fluently: Hebrew, Arabic, Turkish, English, French, German, Italian, Spanish, Romanian, and Russian. *Studies in the Arab Theater and Cinema* has been translated into French and Arabic; *Arabische Literaturgeschichte* has been translated into Hebrew.

BIOGRAPHICAL/CRITICAL SOURCES: Times Literary Supplement, August 20, 1982.

* * *

LANE, Sylvia 1916-

PERSONAL: Born May 26, 1916, in New York, N.Y.; married Benjamin Lane (an engineering consultant), September 2, 1939; children: Leonard, Reese, Nancy. *Education:* University of California, Berkeley, A.B., 1934, M.A., 1936; graduate study at Columbia University, 1937; University of Southern California, Ph.D., 1957. *Home:* 3028 North El Macero Dr., El Macero, Calif. 95618. *Office:* Department of Agricultural and Resource Economics, University of California, Berkeley, Calif. 94720.

CAREER: Los Angeles City College, Los Angeles, Calif., instructor, 1940; commercial placement officer with U.S. Employment Service, 1941-42; manager of L., R., & S., Inc., 1945-49; University of Southern California, Los Angeles, 1947-60, began as lecturer, became assistant professor; East Los Angeles Junior College, Los Angeles, head of department of marketing, 1949-53; San Diego State College (now University), San Diego, Calif., associate professor of economics and finance, 1961-65; California State College (now University), Fullerton, associate professor of finance and associate director of Center for Economic Education, 1965-69, chairman of department, 1967-69; University of California, Davis, professor of agricultural economics, 1969-82; University of California, Berkeley, visiting professor of agricultural and resource economics, 1982—. Project economist, Los Angeles County Welfare Planning Council, 1956-59; chairman of Commission on Aging, San Diego Community Welfare Council, 1963-65; member of board of directors, Consumer Credit Counselors of Orange County, 1967-69; principal investigator, evaluation of Section 237 Counseling Programs, U.S. Department of Housing and Urban Development, 1971-73. Consultant in economics to Assembly Committee on Revenue and Taxation, State of California, 1964-66, President's Committee on Consumer Interests, 1966-74, National Defense Education Act, 1966-67, Advisory Committee on Tax Reform, State of California, 1968-69, Education Committee, Consumers Union, 1969-79, and to Advisory and Technical Committee, Western Region Area Development Research Center, 1972-82. *Wartime service:* Civilian instructor with U.S. Army Air Forces Supply, 1942-45.

MEMBER: American Economics Association, American Agricultural Economics Association, American Association of University Women, American Finance Association, American Council on Consumer Interests (member of executive board, 1972), Western Agricultural Economics Association, Western Economics Association (member of executive committee, 1965-67), Omicron Delta Epsilon (vice-president, 1971-72; president, 1972; chairman of board of trustees, 1982-84), Beta Gamma Sigma. *Awards, honors:* Ford Foundation fellow, 1963 and 1965; University of Chicago fellow, 1968.

WRITINGS: (Editor) Francis Loman Feldman, *The Family in a Money World,* Family Service Association of America, 1957; *Buying Intelligently,* University of Southern California Press, 1959; (with Elmo Bryant Phillips) *Personal Finance,* Wiley, 1963, 2nd edition published as *Personal Finance: Text and Case Problems,* 1969, 4th edition, 1980; *The Insurance Tax: A Major Tax Study,* Assembly, California Legislature, 1964; (with Norman Townshen-Zeller) *A Resource Document for a High School Course in the United States Economy,* California State Department of Education, 1967; (with Young P. Joun) *An Analytical Model of the Inter-Regional Flow of Funds,* California State College (Fullerton), 1968, published as *The Inter-Regional Flow of Mortgage Funds,* Division of Real Estate, State of California, 1968; (with Phillips) *How to Manage Your Personal Finances: A Short Course for Professionals,* Wiley, 1978.

Also author of economics tests for Houghton, 1971; contributor to *Strengthening Family Economic Functioning through Effective Counseling: Proceedings of an Institute under the Auspices of Consumer Credit Counselors of California and School of Social Work,* 1971, and to *Annals of Regional Science.* Contributor to periodicals, including *American Journal of Agricultural Economics, Journal of Consumer Affairs, Journal of Financial and Quantitative Analysis, Journal of American Institute of Planners, Business Inquiry, Quarterly Report,* and *Western Economics Journal.*

WORK IN PROGRESS: Evaluation of Egyptian food policy; research on the relationship between income and nutrition.

* * *

LANGE, John Frederick, Jr. 1931-
(John Norman)

PERSONAL: Born June 3, 1931, in Chicago, Ill.; son of John Frederick and Almyra D. (Taylor) Lange; married Bernice L. Green, January 14, 1956; children: John, David, Jennifer. *Education:* University of Nebraska, B.A., 1953; University of Southern California, M.A., 1957; Princeton University, Ph.D., 1963. *Office:* Department of Philosophy, Queens College of the City University of New York, Flushing, N.Y. 11367.

CAREER: Hamilton College, Clinton, N.Y., instructor in philosophy, 1962-64; Queens College of the City University of New York, Flushing, N.Y., assistant professor, beginning in 1964, professor of philosophy, 1976—. Former story analyst for Warner Bros., staff writer and technical editor for Rocketdyne Division of North American Aviation, and radio continuity writer. *Military service:* U.S. Army, personnel management specialist; became sergeant. *Member:* American Philosophical Association.

WRITINGS: (Editor) Clarence I. Lewis, *Values and Imperatives: Studies in Ethics,* Stanford University Press, 1969; *Cognitivity Paradox: An Inquiry Concerning the Claims of Philosophy,* Princeton University Press, 1970.

Under pseudonym John Norman: *Imaginative Sex*, DAW Books, 1974; *Time Slave*, DAW Books, 1975; *Ghost Dance*, DAW Books, 1979.

Under pseudonym John Norman; "The Chronicles of Counter-Earth" series; all science fiction novels: *Tarnsman of Gor*, Ballantine, 1966; *Outlaw of Gor*, Ballantine, 1967; *Priest-Kings of Gor*, Ballantine, 1968; *Nomads of Gor*, Ballantine, 1969; *Assassin of Gor*, Ballantine, 1970; *Raiders of Gor*, Ballantine, 1971; *Captive of Gor*, Ballantine, 1972; *Gor Omnibus: The Chronicles of Counter-Earth*, Sidgwick & Jackson, 1972; *Hunters of Gor*, DAW Books, 1974; *Marauders of Gor*, DAW Books, 1975; *Tribesmen of Gor*, DAW Books, 1976; *Slave Girl of Gor*, DAW Books, 1977; *Beasts of Gor*, DAW Books, 1977; *Explorers of Gor*, DAW Books, 1979; *Fighting Slave of Gor*, DAW Books, 1981; *Guardsman of Gor*, DAW Books, 1981; *Rogue of Gor*, DAW Books, 1981; *Savages of Gor*, DAW Books, 1982.

Also author of radio scripts. Contributor of articles to philosophy journals.

SIDELIGHTS: John Norman's best-selling science fiction series "The Chronicles of Counter-Earth" is set on the planet Gor, a primitive planet on the other side of the sun from Earth. Tarl Cabot is a former Earthling who has chosen to live on Gor, and his many adventures make up the exciting series. In a letter to *CA*, Norman describes the Gor books as "intellectual and philosophical novels, as well as adventure novels."

Many critics fail to see the intellectual or philosophical aspects of Norman's books, however. They instead criticize the series for what they see as its sexism and obsession with bondage and slavery. Richard E. Geis of *Science Fiction Review*, for example, writes that Norman "betrays an obsession, a compulsion, to dwell repeatedly, endlessly, minutely, on the subject of women slaves; how to use them, handle them, discipline them, dominate them, create them." Similarly, Theodore Sturgeon writes in the *New York Times Book Review* that *Hunters of Gor* "exhibits more of its author's total obsession with stripping, tying, whipping, and submission." He judges the book "good fare for kinks who find *The Story of O* too intellectual." Speaking of *Explorers of Gor*, a *Publishers Weekly* critic states that it "is an unsavory and oddball collection of sexist, misogynistic, and sadistic notions and fantasies."

In an article for *Extrapolation*, Mary Kenny Badami examines Norman's Gor series from a feminist perspective and finds that the books "blatantly pander to an audience which thrills at the imagined degradation of a woman by a man, a perversion of sexuality which is based on power and cruelty." She cites a chapter in *Priest-Kings of Gor* in which the male protagonist has captured the slave-girl Vika and "has ordered her head shaved and imprisoned her in a cage. . . . Vika acknowledges . . . that such humiliation is really what she has wanted all along." "Novels like this," Badami concludes, "play right into bondage fantasies and sadomasochism. Ultimately I believe they are dangerous because they foster a rape mentality."

Reviewers also criticize Norman's writing style. Reviewing *Fighting Slave of Gor*, Geis states: "Gor is only a device, a stage setting, on which to act out [the author's] power fantasy in exquisite, endlessly repetitive detail. As writing, this is simply terrible. As a novel, this is simply terrible." A *Publishers Weekly* critic calls *Explorers of Gor* "a story of a quest. . . . However, any similarity to Wagner or Tolkien ceases right there. . . . There's a fair adventure story buried in here somewhere; the question is whether one wants to look for it." Another *Publishers Weekly* critic finds *Time Slave* to be "a real treat for bondage fanciers who can work their way through the author's murky and repetitious prose; others are apt to find it disgusting."

"I have been personally belittled and slandered," Norman asserts in *Fantasy Voices 1*, "by individuals I do not even know, and who do not know me. Sometimes, I wonder seriously about the sanity and moral character of some of these individuals." Norman points out that his books have been best sellers. His publisher, Donald A. Wollheim, states in an interview with *Science Fiction Review* that readers "who dislike [the Gor books] are outnumbered more than ten to one by readers who find in John Norman's novels exactly what pleases their imaginations and makes daily life more bearable."

"I am well aware," Norman told *CA*, "that my views, which are based on history, tradition, and biology, may not concur with those of certain current political orthodoxies." He sees his work being unfairly judged partly because of the views he presents. As he states in *Fantasy Voices 1*, "The Gorean books have introduced new subject matter and new ideas to science fiction. They have plowed new conceptual furrows; they have altered, in the thinking of thousands, the conceptions and horizons of science fiction. The borders of science fiction have been extended by my work; new possibilities have been delineated and explored. It is natural that these changes would be felt as threatening to a vain, stale, insecure establishment."

BIOGRAPHICAL/CRITICAL SOURCES: *Amazing Stories*, June, 1967; *Times Literary Supplement*, October 16, 1969, April 9, 1970; *New Worlds*, April, 1970; *Worlds of If*, January/February, 1971, July/August, 1974; *Fantastic Stories*, November, 1973; *New York Times Book Review*, September 8, 1974; *Publishers Weekly*, November 11, 1974, October 13, 1975, February 6, 1978, January 29, 1979; *Galaxy*, July, 1976; *Extrapolation*, December, 1976; *Paunch*, No. 48, 1977; *Science Fiction Review*, November, 1979, May, 1980; Jeffrey M. Elliot, *Fantasy Voices 1*, Borgo, 1982.

* * *

LANGE, (Leo) Joseph (Jr.) 1932-

PERSONAL: Born December 12, 1932, in Wilmington, Del.; son of Leo Joseph (in insurance business) and Helen (Seiler) Lange. *Education:* Niagara University, B.S. (summa cum laude), 1956; Catholic University of America, M.S., 1958; Loyola University, M.A., 1966; University of Chicago, graduate study, 1965-68. *Home:* Island Ave., Peaks Island, Me. 04108.

CAREER: Roman Catholic priest of Oblate Fathers of St. Francis de Sales (O.S.F.S.). Northeast Catholic High School, Philadelphia, Pa., chemistry teacher, 1960-61; Cathedral Preparatory School, Erie, Pa., chemistry teacher, 1961-62; Salesianum School, Wilmington, Del., television science teacher, 1963-65, program director of educational television studio, 1964-65; Allentown College of St. Francis de Sales, Allentown, Pa., lecturer in philosophy, 1968-71; Center for Renewal, Allentown, director, 1970-77; editor of *Catholic Charismatic* magazine, Paulist/Newman, 1976-80; pastor of St. Christopher's Church, 1982—. *Member:* Sigma Xi.

WRITINGS: *A Christian Understanding of Existence*, Newman, 1965; *Renewing the Catholic Parish*, Dimension, 1980. Author of weekly newspaper column for *Church World*, Brunswick, Me.

"Living Christianity Community" series; with A. J. Cushing; all published by Dove Books: *Friendship with Jesus*, 1974; *Worshipping Community*, 1975; *Called to Service*, 1975; *Freedom and Healing*, 1976.

LANGLAND, Joseph (Thomas) 1917-

PERSONAL: Born February 16, 1917, in Spring Grove, Minn.; son of Charles M. (a farmer and legislator) and Clara (Hille) Langland; married Judith Gail Wood (an artist), June 26, 1943; children: Joseph, Jr., Elizabeth, Paul. *Education:* Santa Ana Junior College (now Santa Ana College), Associate of Arts, 1936; Bread Loaf School of English, summer student, 1940; State University of Iowa, B.A., 1940, M.A., 1941, postgraduate study, 1946-48. *Politics:* Democrat. *Home:* 16 Morgan Circle, Amherst, Mass. 01002. *Office:* Department of English, University of Massachusetts, Amherst, Mass. 01002.

CAREER: Farmer in Winneshiek County, Iowa, during the 1930s; rural school teacher, Winneshiek County, Iowa, 1936-38; Dana College, Blair, Neb., instructor in English, 1941-42; University of Wyoming, Laramie, 1948-59, began as assistant professor, became associate professor of English; University of Massachusetts—Amherst, associate professor, 1959-62, professor of English, 1962—. Guest lecturer at University of British Columbia, 1960, Poetry Center, San Francisco State College (now University), 1961, University of Washington, 1964, and University of Oregon, 1968 and 1969. *Military service:* U.S. Army, Infantry, and Military Government in Bavaria, 1942-46; became captain; received four European Theater battle stars.

AWARDS, HONORS: Fund for the Advancement of Education in Humanities fellow at Harvard and Columbia Universities, 1953-54; Amy Lowell travelling poetry fellow in Europe, 1955-56; Melville Cane Award, Poetry Society of America, 1964, for *The Wheel of Summer;* grant from National Council on the Arts, 1966-67; Litt.D., Luther College, 1974.

WRITINGS: For Harold (poems), [Augsburg], 1945; *The Green Town* (poems), Scribner, 1956; (editor and contributor with James B. Hall) *The Short Story,* Macmillan, 1956; *A Little Homily,* Apiary Press, 1960; (editor with Paul Engle) *Poet's Choice,* Dial, 1962; *The Wheel of Summer* (poems), Dial, 1963; (author of foreword) *Poems in Progress,* University of Washington, 1964; *Song and Half-Songs,* Dial, 1968; *Adlai Stevenson: 1900-1965* (long poem), [Laramie], 1966; (with Donald Hall and Randall Jarrell) *War, War, War* (poems), University of Iowa, 1968; (editor and translator with Tamas Aczel and Laszio Tikos) *Poetry from the Russian Underground: A Bilingual Anthology,* Harper, 1973; *An Interview and Fourteen Poems,* Clark University, 1974; *The Sacrifice Poems,* North American Review, University of Northern Iowa, 1975; *In the Shell of the Ear* (poems), Massachusetts Review, University of Massachusetts, 1977; *Any Body's Song* (poems), Doubleday, 1980.

Contributor of poetry to recordings for the Library of Congress, for a Folkways album, "Today's Poets 1," 1967, for a Canadian Broadcasting Corp. series, and for radio. Contributor of poetry, essays, articles, and reviews to periodicals, including *New Yorker, Paris Review, London Magazine, Nation, Atlantic, Harper's, Saturday Review, Poetry,* and *Accent.* Poetry editor, *Massachusetts Review,* 1960-66.

WORK IN PROGRESS: A full-length drama; a book-length series of dramatic poems based on Scandinavian proverbs and folk sayings.

SIDELIGHTS: William Pritchard writes in the *New York Times Book Review* that *Any Body's Song* "exhibits a range of sensibility and feeling that makes it altogether a weightier and more various thing than [Joseph Langland] has done before.... There is an admirably impersonal air about the poems, for all their featuring of an 'I.'" Richard Tillinghast, discussing the book in the *Sewanee Review,* says his favorite poem is "A Dream of Love," a seven-page "celebration of horses—an instant classic.... If Langland did not have a high old time writing this poem, I am much mistaken. The exuberance, the glee of poetic transport, shines through."

BIOGRAPHICAL/CRITICAL SOURCES: Book Week, December 29, 1963; *Poetry,* March, 1964; *Minnesota Review,* summer, 1964; *New York Times Book Review,* July 6, 1980; *Sewanee Review,* spring, 1981.†

* * *

LATHAM, Mavis
See CLARK, Mavis Thorpe

* * *

LAUGHLIN, Henry Prather 1916-

PERSONAL: Born June 25, 1916, in Hagerstown, Md.; son of John Royer (a doctor) and Myrtle Frances (Binkley) Laughlin; married Marion Page Durkee, June 2, 1941; children: Constance Ann Laughlin Kuhn, John Royer, Robert Scott, Barbara Hilton Laughlin Thornton, Deborah Page Laughlin Mayer. *Education:* Attended Johns Hopkins University, 1936 and 1938; Ursinus College, B.S., 1938; Temple University, M.D., 1941; Washington-Baltimore Psychoanalytic Institute, psychoanalytic training, 1947-52. *Home and office:* Freehold, 7977 Timmons Rd., Union Bridge, Md. 21791.

CAREER: Licensed to practice medicine in Pennsylvania, Maryland, and Washington, D.C.; certified by National Board of Examiners, 1942; diplomate of American Board of Psychiatry and Neurology, 1948. Intern at U.S. Navy Hospital, Washington, D.C. George Washington University Hospital, Washington, D.C., and U.S. Navy Hospital, National Naval Medical Center, Bethesda, Md., 1941-42; resident in psychiatry at U.S. Navy Hospital, Bethesda, 1942, and Saint Elizabeth Hospital, Washington, D.C., 1943; U.S. Public Health Service, Washington, D.C., director of Federal Employee Mental Health Clinic, 1947-49; private practice in psychotherapy and analysis in Washington, D.C., 1947-74, Frederick, Md., 1974-82, and Union Bridge, Md., 1982—. George Washington University, Medical School, 1946—, began as faculty member, became clinical professor of psychiatry and behavioral sciences, 1977. Lecturer at Saint Elizabeth's Hospital, 1956, and U.S. Navy Hospital, Bethesda, 1972-79; visiting professor at University of Cincinnati, Keio University, National University College of Medicine (Seoul), University of Taiwan, Royal Faculty of Medicine (Baghdad), American University (Beirut), University of Istanbul, all 1957, Institute of Living, 1959, University of Michigan, 1960 and 1972, University of Athens, 1966, National Navy Medical Center, 1969, 1975, and 1977, Walter Reed Army Medical Center, 1973, Puerto Rico Psychiatric Institute, 1973, Royal Hospital of Saint Bartholomew (London), 1973 and 1976, William S. Hall Psychiatric Institute, 1975, E. J. Brady Hospital, 1976, 1977, and 1979, University of Colorado, 1976, Veterans Administration Center, Togus, Maine, 1976, Taylor Manor Hospital, 1977, and Menninger Foundation, 1979; Beling-Englander Memorial Lecturer, New Jersey Neuropsychiatric Association and American Psychiatric Association, 1961; distinguished visiting professor, University of Louisville, 1974—. Member of attending staff of District of Columbia General Hospital, 1947-53, George Washington University Hospital, 1947-62, Walter Reed Hospital, 1949-58, Suburban Hospital (Bethesda), 1954-64, 1970-

71 (chief of psychiatry and neurology, 1954-64, consultant in psychiatry, 1970-77), and Frederick Memorial Hospital, 1976—.

Member of Montgomery County Medical Care Commission, 1951-61, chairman, 1955-60; member of Washington Area Council on Rehabilitation, 1957-59; member of board of directors of Foundation for Community Health, 1966-69. Member of board of trustees of Bethesda Community School, 1951-53; member of future planning committee of Landon School, 1960-62, chairman, 1961-62; member of board of directors of Ursinus College, 1966-67, director, 1967-77. Co-organizer of Alaska-North America Investment Corp., 1956-58, vice-president and member of board of directors, 1958-62; founder and director, Robert B. Luce Publishers, Inc., 1957-62; member of board of directors, Capitol Investment Corp., 1959-62; director, Information Services Corp., 1971-75; director emeritus, Digital Systems Corp., 1980—; secretary, Galaxy Conferences, Inc., 1982—. Consultant to numerous medical and governmental organizations, 1947—. *Military service:* U.S. Navy, 1942-47, chief of psychiatry at Special Augmented Hospital, 1944-45, professor in naval hospitals, 1942-47; served in African-European theater and Asiatic-Pacific theater; became lieutenant commander; received three combat stars.

MEMBER: World Association for Social Psychiatry (fellow), American Medical Association, American Psychiatric Association (fellow; founder of Metropolitan Washington branch, 1952; branch president, 1953-55; chairman of board of trustees of retirement fund, 1964-68), American Society of Psychoanalytic Physicians (fellow), American College of Psychiatrists (fellow; founder, 1949; president, 1963-65), American College of Psychoanalysts (fellow; founder, 1948; president, 1969-72 and 1976-77; historian-archivist, 1978-84; honorary life president, 1979—), American Association for Social Psychiatry (fellow; co-founder, 1968; vice-president, 1976-78), American Society of Physician Analysts (fellow; founder, 1950; president, 1962-65; historian, 1978—; honorary life president, 1982—), Modern Founders of the American Psychiatric Association (organizer, 1957-59; chairman, 1959-61), National Psychiatric Endowment Fund (founder, 1958; president, 1960—), American Academy of Psychoanalysis (founder, 1946), Foundation of the American College of Psychiatrists (co-founder, 1965; member of board of trustees, 1968—), Sons of the American Revolution (president, 1982—), Royal College of Psychiatrists (fellow), Royal Society of Medicine (fellow), Royal Medical-Psychological Association (honorary fellow), Southern Psychiatric Association (fellow; member of executive committee, 1972-75; chairman of board of regents, 1974-75; vice-president, 1976-77), Eastern Psychoanalytic Association (fellow; founder, 1954-62; president, 1962-65), Montgomery County Medical Society (member of executive board, 1952-73; president, 1959), Washington Medical and Surgical Society (fellow; life member), Washington Psychiatric Society (co-founder, 1947-49; president, 1953-54; president of Maryland chapter, 1968-70), Medical Council of the Washington Metropolitan Area (president, 1959-61), Medical Arts Society of Greater Washington (fellow; president, 1964-65; emeritus member, 1969, Medical and Chirurgical Faculty of Maryland (member of council, 1962-73; vice-president, 1964-65), Suburban Maryland Psychiatric Association (founder, 1949; president, 1968-70), Babcock Surgical Society (honorary member), Tau Kappa Alpha, Phi Chi.

AWARDS, HONORS: Montgomery County Medical Society, certificates of award, 1952, 1954, 1958, and 1961, presidential plaque, 1960; letter of commendation, Republic of Korea, 1957; certificates or citations for distinguished medical service and leadership, American Psychiatric Association, 1961, 1962, and 1974, Medical Council of Washington Metropolitan Area, 1961, Medical Arts Society of Greater Washington, 1961, 1963, and 1965, American Board of Psychiatry and Neurology, 1966, American Psychological Association, 1968, Washington Psychiatric Society, 1969, Eastern Psychoanalytic Association, 1972, and Frederick Community College, 1976; American College of Psychiatrists, Gold Medal Award, 1965 and 1976, Distinguished Lecturer Award, 1969, Presidential Leadership Medal, 1976; American Society of Physician Analysts, commendations, 1966 and 1972, Distinguished Lecturer Award, 1977; Ursinus College, Alumni Award, 1966, Sc.D., 1976; presented with key to the city, New Orleans, 1968, Baltimore, 1971, and Louisville, 1976 and 1979; Physicians Recognition Award, American Medical Association, 1969, 1973, and 1976; book selection, Behavioral Science Book Club, 1971, for *The Neuroses,* and 1974, for *The Ego and Its Defenses,* Psychotherapy and Social Science Book Club, 1979, for *The Ego and Its Defenses;* American College of Psychoanalysts, commendation certificate, 1971, 1974, and 1976, leadership plaque, 1974 and 1977, Laughlin Gold Medal Award, 1981; Order of the Palmetto, State of South Carolina, 1976; Sc.S.D., University of Louisville, 1978; honorary life commodore, U.S. Navy Psychiatrists, 1980; recipient of numerous other awards and honors.

WRITINGS: (With M. de G. Ruffin) *An Outline of Dynamic Psychiatry,* School of Medicine, George Washington University, 1949, 4th edition, 1954; *A Psychiatric Glossary,* American Psychiatric Association, 1952, 7th edition, 1976; *A Psychiatric Contribution to the Development of Executives: The Development of a Psychoanalytically Oriented Approach to Training in Human Relations,* National Institute of Health, 1953; *The Psychoneuroses,* School of Medicine, George Washington University, 1955; *The Neuroses in Clinical Practice,* Saunders, 1956; *The Depressions: Clinical Understanding and Management,* Bates, 1962; *Mental Mechanisms,* Butterworths, 1963; *The Emotional Reactions to Trauma,* Butterworths, 1967; *The Neuroses,* Butterworths, 1967, new edition, Appleton-Century-Crofts, 1976; *The Academy Movement: Historical Notes on the Origins and Founding of the American Academy of Psychoanalysis,* [Bethesda, Md.], 1970, revised edition, 1974; *The Ego and Its Defenses,* Appleton-Century-Crofts, 1970, new edition, Jason Aronson, 1984.

Editor: *Directory of Psychiatrists and Clinical Psychiatric Facilities in the Washington Area,* Washington Psychiatric Society, 1948, 5th edition, 1957, supplement, 1958; (with Alex Castro) *Handbook,* Washington Medical and Surgical Society, 1962, 3rd edition, 1967; *Psychiatry,* Volume VI, Butterworths, 1962; (and contributor) *The American College of Psychoanalysts Archives,* American College of Psychoanalysts, 1975, 5th edition, 1983; *The American College of Psychiatrists Archives,* 4th edition, American College of Psychiatrists, 1979.

Contributor: M. Belli, editor, *Trial and Tort Trends,* Bobbs-Merrill, 1962; Paul Cantor, editor, *Traumatic Medicine and Surgery for the Attorney,* Butterworths, 1962; *The American College of Psychiatrists Archives,* 2nd edition, American College of Psychiatrists, 1963; H. F. Conn, editor, *Current Therapy,* Saunders, 1972; L. Caswell, editor, *Attorney's Textbook of Medicine,* Matthew Bender, 1972; *Critique and Analysis with Six Related Concepts,* Endo Laboratories (Garden City, N.Y.), 1976. Also contributor to *On the Art of Psychotherapy: Useful Conceptions for the Clinician,* edited by Henry Krystal, 1972.

Also author of *Constitution of the Washington Psychiatric Society,* 1949, *Constitutional Drafts for the American Academy of Psychoanalysts,* 1952, *Constitution of the Eastern Psychiatric Association,* 1962, *Constitution of the American College* of Psychiatrists, 1963, and Constitution of the American College of Psychoanalysts, 1969; author of report for U.S. Personnel Administration, 1949. Contributor to Dorland's Pocket Medical Dictionary, 1957 and 1968, Encyclopaedia Britannica, 1975, and International Encyclopedia of Psychology, Psychiatry, Psychoanalysis, and Neurology, 1977. Contributor to professional journals, including Psychiatry Digest, American Journal of Psychiatry, and Current Medical Digest. Member of editorial board, Maryland State Medical Journal, 1960-66; manuscript reviewer, American Journal of Psychiatry, 1966-67; editor, The American College of Psychoanalysts Newsletter, 1969-79; advisory editor on psychoanalysis, Psychosomatics, 1977—.

WORK IN PROGRESS: A Contemporary Dictionary of Psychiatric Terms and Concepts.

AVOCATIONAL INTERESTS: Philately, history, biography, ecology, big game hunting and conservation, lawn care, designing, framing, mat cutting.

* * *

LAURENTS, Arthur 1918-

PERSONAL: Born July 14, 1918, in Brooklyn, N.Y.; son of Irving (a lawyer) and Ada (Robbins) Laurents. Education: Cornell University, B.A., 1937. Residence: Quogue, N.Y. Agent: Shirley Bernstein Paramuse, Paramuse Artists Associates, 1414 Sixth Ave., New York, N.Y. 10019.

CAREER: Playwright, writing primarily for radio, 1939-40, and for stage and screen, 1945—. Director of Broadway productions, "Invitation to a March," 1960, "I Can Get It for You Wholesale," 1962, and "Anyone Can Whistle," 1964; director of "The Enclave," 1973, of London production of "Gypsy," 1973, of National Company production of "Gypsy," 1974, of "My Mother Was a Fortune Teller," 1978, and of "So What Are We Gonna Do Now?," 1982; co-producer, with Herbert Ross, of film "The Turning Point," 1977. Director, Dramatists Play Service. Military service: U.S. Army, 1941-45; became sergeant. Member: Dramatists Guild (member of council), P.E.N., Screenwriters Guild, Authors League of America, Academy of Motion Picture Arts and Sciences.

AWARDS, HONORS: Variety Radio Award, 1945, for "Assignment Home" series; National Institute of Arts and Letters grant in literature, 1946; co-winner of Sidney Howard Memorial Award, 1946, for "Home of the Brave"; Antoinette Perry (Tony) Award, 1967, for "Hallelujah, Baby!"; Drama Desk Award, 1974, for revival of "Gypsy," and 1978, for "My Mother Was a Fortune Teller"; Writers Guild of America Award, 1978, Golden Globe Award, and National Board of Review Best Picture Award, all for "The Turning Point."

WRITINGS—Novelizations: The Way We Were (based on his screenplay of the same title; also see below), Harper, 1972; The Turning Point (based on his screenplay of the same title; also see below), New American Library, 1977.

Plays; published by Random House, except as indicated: Home of the Brave (first produced on Broadway at Belasco Theatre, December 27, 1945; produced in London under title "The Way Back," 1946), 1946; The Bird Cage (two-act; first produced on Broadway at Coronet Theatre, February 22, 1950), Dramatists Play Service, 1950; The Time of the Cuckoo (two-act comedy; also see below; first produced in New York at Empire Theatre, October 15, 1952), 1953, acting edition, Samuel French, 1954; A Clearing in the Woods (two-act; first produced on Broadway at Belasco Theatre, January 10, 1957), 1957, revised edition, Dramatists Play Service, 1960; West Side Story (musical; score by Leonard Bernstein, lyrics by Stephen Sondheim; first produced in Washington, D.C., at National Theatre, August 26, 1957; produced on Broadway at Winter Garden Theatre, September 26, 1957), 1958, published with Romeo and Juliet by William Shakespeare as Romeo and Juliet [and] West Side Story, Dell, 1965.

Gypsy (musical based on Gypsy, the memoirs of Gypsy Rose Lee; score by Jule Styne, lyrics by Sondheim; first produced on Broadway at Broadway Theatre, May 21, 1959; produced on West End at Picadilly Theatre, May 27, 1973), 1960; (also director) Invitation to a March (comedy; first produced on Broadway at Music Box Theatre, October 29, 1960), 1961; (also director) Anyone Can Whistle (musical; score and lyrics by Sondheim; first produced on Broadway at Majestic Theatre, April 4, 1964), 1965; Do I Hear a Waltz? (musical based on Laurents's The Time of the Cuckoo; score by Richard Rodgers, lyrics by Sondheim; first produced on Broadway at Forty-Sixty Street Theatre, March 15, 1965), 1966; Hallelujah, Baby! (two-act musical; score by Styne, lyrics by Betty Comden and Adolph Green; produced on Broadway at Martin Beck Theatre, April 27, 1967), 1967; (also director) The Enclave (first produced in Washington, D.C., at Theatre Club, February, 1973; produced in New York at Theatre Four, November 15, 1973), Dramatists Play Service, 1974; A Loss of Memory (one-act; first produced in Southampton, N.Y., at Southampton College Theatre, 1981), Chilton, 1983.

Unpublished plays: "Heartsong," first produced in New Haven, Conn., at Shubert Theatre, February 27, 1947; "Scream," produced in Houston, Tex., at Alley Theatre, 1978; (also director; co-author with Phyllis Newman) "My Mother Was a Fortune Teller" (musical comedy), first produced in New York at Hudson Guild Theatre, 1978, produced as "The Madwoman of Central Park West" in New York at Twenty-Two Steps Theatre, June 13, 1979.

Screenplays: (With Frank Partos and Millen Brand) "The Snake Pit" (based on novel by Mary Jane Ward), Twentieth Century-Fox, 1948; "Rope" (based on play by Patrick Hamilton), Warner Bros., 1948; "Caught" (based on Libbie Block's Wild Calendar), Enterprise Pictures, 1949; (with Philip Yordan) "Anna Lucasta" (based on Yordan's play), Columbia, 1949; "Anastasia" (based on play by Marcel Maurette), Twentieth Century-Fox, 1956; "Bonjour Tristesse" (based on novel by Francoise Sagan), Columbia, 1958; "The Way We Were," Columbia, 1973; "The Turning Point," Twentieth Century-Fox, 1977.

Radio plays: "Now Playing Tomorrow," 1939; "Western Electric Communicade," 1944; "The Last Day of the War," 1945; "The Face," 1945. Also author of radio plays for series, including "Hollywood Playhouse," "Dr. Christian," "The Thin Man," and "Manhattan at Midnight," 1939-40, and "The Man behind the Gun," "Army Service Force Presents," "Assignment Home," and "This Is Your FBI," 1943-45.

Plays collected in anthologies, including: Short Plays for Stage and Radio, edited by Carless Jones, University of New Mexico Press, 1939; Radio Drama in Action, edited by Erik Barnouw, Farrar & Rinehart, 1945; The Best One-Act Plays of 1944-45, edited by M. G. Mayora, Dodd, 1945; The Best One-Act Plays of 1945-46, edited by Mayora, Dodd, 1946; The Best Plays of 1945-46, edited by Burns Mantle, Dodd, 1946; Best Plays of the Modern American Theatre, 1939-1946, edited by John Gassner, Crown, 1947; The Best Plays of 1956-57, edited by Louis Kronenberger, Dodd, 1957; Broadway's Best, 1958, edited by John A. Chapman, Doubleday, 1958; Broadway's Best, 1959, edited by Chapman, Doubleday, 1959.

Also author of "The Light Fantastic: How to Tell Your Past, Present, and Future through Social Dancing," a television show produced in 1967.

SIDELIGHTS: After a brief period of writing for radio, Arthur Laurents caught the attention of theatre-goers in 1945 with "Home of the Brave," his first play and winner of a Sidney Howard Memorial Award. Since then, his other Broadway hits and a number of successful films have made him a widely respected dramatist, librettist, and screenwriter. Among his more famous works are the books for "West Side Story" and "Gypsy," which some critics consider to be among the best musicals ever produced on the Broadway stage, and his more recent screenplay "The Turning Point," which received a Golden Globe Award, a National Board of Review Best Picture Award, and a Writers Guild of America Award.

In 1950, choreographer Jerome Robbins suggested to Laurents the idea of creating a New York romance in the form of a danced musical play and basing it on Shakespeare's "Romeo and Juliet." Robbins' suggestion, Laurents told CA, was ingenious—except for the notion of having a Jewish girl and a Gentile boy as the main characters; to Laurents, that sounded too much like "Abie's Irish Rose" with the sexes switched. Instead, Laurents incorporated the phenomena of juvenile delinquency and racial prejudice into his libretto. The result was "West Side Story," a musical so successful that it played to sold-out houses on its three-week trial run in Washington, D.C., had an original Broadway run of 981 performances and a London production of 1,040, has since been produced throughout Europe, Australia, North and South America, has been filmed, and even adapted into novel form.

The parallels between "Romeo and Juliet" and "West Side Story" are readily apparent. The principal characters of both plays are two young lovers who are members of antagonistic groups. In Shakespeare's plot, Romeo and Juliet are members of families, the Montagues and Capulets; Laurents' factions are street gangs, the Puerto Rican Sharks and the Anglo Jets, who fatally stifle the love of Maria, sister of Sharks Leader Bernardo, and Tony, best friend of Jets Leader Riff. Richard L. Coe says in the Washington Post that Tony "is a reluctant fighter just as Romeo was, and [after Bernardo kills Riff in a switchblade rumble, Tony] will kill Bernardo, Maria-Juliet's kin, as impetuously and fatefully as Romeo killed Tybalt. By joining the roles of Friar Laurence and the apothecary into the part of Doc, the druggist, Laurents leads into a denouement close to Shakespeare's."

Despite the parallels, "Laurents has wisely chosen not to follow Shakespeare's plot slavishly," reports Henry Hewes in Saturday Review. "Rather, he concentrates on expressing the realities of an alarming contemporary situation: [the problem of juvenile delinquency]. From the beginning he faces the hard fact that today's teen-ager, who alternates between purposeless violence and sullen detachment, cannot really be explained by use of specific phrases like 'insufficient housing' and 'broken homes.' Rather, he implies that adults' sins of omission on the highest level of national and international policy create the vacuum which these teen-agers feel obliged to fill with cool and fierce bravado. [The show] leaves a telling reminder for us at the final curtain, when we see the two gangs temporarily allied against the law enforcement officers."

Harold Clurman notes in Nation that besides the problem of juvenile delinquency, the work also deals with "race prejudice in New York where the poor native-born live in uneasy proximity to the immigrants from Puerto Rico." Hewes believes "the Puerto Rican situation is a touchy one to present and 'West Side Story' does it without direct sermonizing. True, it does not emphasize the utter squalor in which many Puerto Rican immigrants live; [but] it does gain sympathy for the Puerto Ricans by showing the cops to be more viciously prejudiced than their gang-enemies, the Jets."

The musical's focus on these two social problems made it a "revolutionary show" when it premiered in 1957, writes Frank Rich in Time. "Its subject," says Rich, "was far more adventurous than the typical fluff of musicals; its language was tough and its ending downbeat." Though critics generally praised "West Side Story" for its serious attention to the matters of street gangs and racial prejudice, a few reviewers attacked the musical for violating what Allan Lewis calls in American Plays and Playwrights of the Contemporary Theatre "the sacred code of show business: Musicals are for nonthinking joy." Harold Clurman, for example, wrote of the original Broadway production: "The show, I repeat, is as professional as can be and all of the contributions are of a superior grade. [However,] people who want to see a Broadway musical do not particularly crave a 'tragedy' of social significance in which ugly sentiments and violence must play a major role. My sympathies in this case go with this lowbrow opinion. Although I appreciated the show's merits—and sat in a theatre echoing with 'bravos'— I did not enjoy it. In fact, I resented it: I thought it a phony. I am not above enjoying the phony on occasion, but I could not do so here. I do not like intellectual slumming by sophisticates for purposes of popular showmanship. It is vulgar, immature, unfeeling."

In 1980, the musical returned to Broadway in a hit revival, and in some ways the passage of twenty-three years altered response to the show. "Audiences and critics," states Rich, "were not so much shocked as charmed; the show's story, language, and sociological concerns now belong to a distant, tamer era." To Charles Michener, writing in Newsweek, the streets of Manhattan's Upper West Side "now seem almost idyllic. Teen-age blood is still spilled in the racial gangmanship between the white Jets and the Puerto Rican Sharks. But who's going to walk out on a bunch of kids who get together in the corner drugstore and order 'Cokes all around,' whose worst street obscenity is 'mother-love' and whose only crime against society seems to have been the stink-bombing of an old man's store? What is this, 'Happy Days'? . . . This revival points up what was always soft about the show—the hinges of its 'Romeo and Juliet' plot and the social comment of Arthur Laurents' book (Doc/Friar Laurence to the Jets: 'You make this world lousy!' Reply: 'That's the way we found it, Doc')."

Time's T. E. Kalem explains that even "the finest musicals are subject to sociocultural jet lag. The biorhythms of the societal clock seem organically out of kilter. No time machine can transport the audience to the 1943 spirit of Oklahoma! or the 1957 of West Side Story. Separate components (songs, dances, acting) can be marvelously exciting, but the core of the musical, what it is rather than what it does, recedes into an odd realm of detachment. The original galvanizing impact is dissipated." Nevertheless, John Simon maintains in New York that as a musical, "West Side Story" is "a summit achievement that can and should be savored both by those who have never seen it and by those who, mistakenly, think they have seen it often enough."

If "West Side Story" is "a work of art," as Richard L. Coe believes, then so too is "Gypsy," the musical based on the memoirs of stripper Gypsy Rose Lee. As Kenneth Tynan claims in the New Yorker, "nothing about it is superfluous; there is no display of energy for energy's sake. No effort is spared, yet none wasted. Book, lyrics, [and] music . . . seem not— as so often occurs—to have been conscripted into uneasy and unconvinced alliance but to have come together by irresistible mutual attraction, as if each could not live without the rest. With no strain or dissonance, a machine has been assembled that is ideally fitted to perform this task and no other. Since the task is worthwhile, the result is art.'' *Newsweek*'s Jack Kroll not only lauds it as ''one of the best musicals Broadway has ever created,'' but describes the original production of ''Gypsy,'' with its book by Laurents, music by Jule Styne, lyrics by Stephen Sondheim, direction and choreography by Jerome Robbins, and its ''shooting star'' Ethel Merman, as ''an encyclopedic definition of the form.''

Harold Clurman, who also considers ''Gypsy'' one of America's best musicals, says its ''basic merit is Arthur Laurents' 'book.' It has credible characters, honest writing, truthful atmosphere and background material, and its point is intelligent.'' The plot centers on Rose, a woman driven by the fury of frustrated ambition who tries to make stars of her daughters, June and Louise (later ''Gypsy''). ''Rose turns her kids into travesties,'' writes Kroll, ''and herself into a travesty of a mother. But they are *darling* travesties, and that's what makes 'Gypsy' a musical, and that's what makes the musical the most darling of all America's magnificent mutations of reality. Laurents' book gets all this, although there are a couple of perilous moments where his well-known solemnity threatens to jimmy its way into the theater. But his flow is marvelous and his details often brilliant and funny, as when Rose, trying to close a deal in her sleazy and overfilled hotel room, snaps, 'Children, go play in the alley.'''

Like Kroll, Robert Hatch calls ''Gypsy'' a ''soaring delight'' in *Nation* but notes that it is bitter and perceptive: ''What gives *Gypsy* depth and substance is the tension between its surface pleasures and the underlying bitterness of its story. It is, for a wonder, a musical based on an ugly state of affairs.'' George Oppenheimer states in *Saturday Review* that the dramatic scene ''when Rose bullies her daughter into stripping and the subsequent montage wherein Gypsy Rose Lee becomes the Queen of Minsky's, are the high spots of a superior show that could do with some pruning in a long first act, but is otherwise almost consistently entertaining, touching, and uncompromisingly real.'' Kenneth Tynan concludes: ''I don't see how anyone could deny that the show tapers off from perfection in the first act to mere brilliance in the second.''

Laurents has also achieved success with other Broadway hits, notably the Tony Award-winning ''Hallelujah, Baby!,'' and with a number of screenplays. His movie ''The Way We Were,'' starring Barbara Streisand—whom he ''discovered'' while directing ''I Can Get It for You Wholesale''—and Robert Redford, has won kudos from reviewers like Stephen Farber, who writes in the *New York Times:* '' 'The Way We Were' is almost a milestone because it's a thoughtful, believable love story for adults. For once, the characters are sharply defined, and their relationship develops and deepens persuasively. . . . The differences that attract them will ultimately separate them; but there is real electricity between them, and when they argue, we're involved because we can see that neither of them is wholly right.''

A more recent achievement is ''The Turning Point,'' named best picture of 1977 by the National Board of Review and winner of a Golden Globe Award and a Writers Guild of America Award. The story centers on two old friends, now in their forties, who once shared a dream of becoming ballerinas. Emma eventually became the prima ballerina of the American Ballet Company, but Deedee chose marriage and children (though she and her husband operate a highly successful ballet school). When Deedee's daughter, Emilia, joins the American Ballet Company and is a quick success, the former rivalry between the two women is rekindled. Besides fighting over who will coach Emilia, the two face mid-life crises brought on by their earlier life decisions and by their envy of each other's lifestyle.

Though an extremely popular film, critical reaction to ''The Turning Point'' has been mixed. Arlene Croce, writing in the *New Yorker,* wonders why the life decisions of the two ''self-involved heroines'' are irrevocable, pointing out that dancers have married, borne children, and gone on with their careers. Moreover, Croce claims the ''middle-age crisis stifles the interest we might have taken in the movie's one serious theme—the necessity for continuity in the ballet tradition—and in order to precipitate the crisis the movie concocts an outlandish story. . . . The goddaughter of the prima ballerina Emma, Emilia doesn't depend on the link to get ahead, and though she sleeps with Yuri, . . . that doesn't help her career, either. She succeeds, [all in one summer,] on merit. But was merit ever—in real life—so swiftly rewarded? . . . 'The Turning Point' is a Beverly Hills view of professional ballet.''

David Ansen admits in *Newsweek* that the movie ''has its flaws—some over-written scenes and lapses into staginess and sentimentality''—but asserts that these ''are easily forgiven, [because] this is not primarily a dance film; it's a warm and stormily human melodrama, and it belongs finally to Anne Bancroft and Shirley MacLaine as Emma and Deedee. . . . These are plum roles, and much of the excitement of 'The Turning Point' comes from watching these two superb actresses take large, juicy bites.'' Also noting that this is not a ballet film, Vincent Canby of the *New York Times* says the collective achievement of screenwriter Laurents and director Herbert Ross ''is in having found so much vitality in the sort of movie that demands that its audiences weep with sympathy for characters who have all they ever wanted but simply don't realize it yet.'' Canby concludes that ''The Turning Point'' is ''entertaining, not for discovering new material, but for treating old material with style and romantic feeling that, in this day and age, seem remarkably unafraid.''

MEDIA ADAPTATIONS: United Artists filmed *Home of the Brave* in 1949 and *The Time of the Cuckoo*—released as ''Summertime,'' starring Katherine Hepburn—in 1955. United Artists also produced a filmed version of *West Side Story,* starring Natalie Wood, in 1961, and Noble & Noble published Irving Shulman's *West Side Story: A Novelization of the Broadway Musical* in 1969. WNTA-TV (Newark, N.J.-New York, N.Y.) televised *A Clearing in the Woods* in 1961, and Warner Bros. filmed *Gypsy* in 1962.

CA INTERVIEW

CA interviewed Arthur Laurents by phone August 11, 1981, at his home in Quogue, N.Y.

CA: You started your career doing radio plays and then went on to write screenplays, stage plays, musicals, and novelizations. How early did you actually begin writing?

LAURENTS: When I was ten. I wrote a short story which, oddly enough, was all in dialogue. I don't know why, but it was.

CA: What was your major at Cornell?

LAURENTS: I majored in English. I took a playwriting course in which I learned never to begin a play with a telephone ringing. So I wrote a one-act play that began with a phone ringing, and if it hadn't there wouldn't have been any play.

CA: Was the radio writing good training for the writing that followed?

LAURENTS: Yes, it was, because of two things. I learned economy, and I learned what I call *action dialogue*. Instead of people just talking, there has to be some tension and conflict, I think, to move a scene along. Also I developed, without knowing it, a style in radio writing.

CA: Then the style you developed in writing for radio served you well in your later writing?

LAURENTS: Yes.

CA: You've written some memorable screenplays: among others "The Snake Pit," "Anna Lucasta," "Bonjour Tristesse," "Anastasia," "The Way We Were," and "The Turning Point." You also wrote the novelization of the latter two.

LAURENTS: The novelization of "The Way We Were" was written at the same time as the screenplay. *The Turning Point* was done afterwards.

CA: Do you find particular problems in adapting other people's work to the screen?

LAURENTS: No, there are no problems; it's just more satisfying to do something that's completely one's own work.

CA: Do you ever see any of the old films at festivals?

LAURENTS: I never go to festivals, I tell you that. I'm not a film buff. I don't use the word *film*; I call them movies. That's sort of a symbol to me. I think there have been very few movies which deserve to be called films. Film as an art form is much overrated. Because of the financial exigencies when you do a movie, there have to be elements that will reach a great many people. And the people who make movies in Hollywood are very conscious of that and go for that at the expense of what might be called art. Movie critics write great, long pieces, very often about trivial movies; even if it's a good movie, it's not worth all that space and dissection. And also the few pieces I've read in the esoteric so-called film magazines. . . . There was one about a movie I made with a director named Max Ophuls, who was deified after he died. He made some very interesting films in Europe and a few pictures here. The one I did with him was called "Caught," and I read some great dissertations on his psychological use of dark and shadow—among other people, Pauline Kael wrote about this. What they don't know is that the use of dark and shadow in this particular sequence in this particular picture was for economy. There wasn't enough money to have a real set. And that's typical of critics in both movies and theater. They don't know the reality of the situation. They don't know who does what or why. And they make all these great *pronunciamentos* based on ignorance.

CA: Have you seen any films or any movies lately that you consider indicative of better things to come?

LAURENTS: There are two movies I saw recently, "Kramer vs. Kramer" and "Ordinary People," that I think, instead of being the exception, are what Hollywood should be making a great many of—so-called small pictures about human problems. And I really think that's what people are interested in. It's not an exception that they went to see those two pictures; they were good movies. But then they make these blockbusters that they say have to appeal to an audience between the ages of two and three. In "The Turning Point" a great problem I had was that nobody wanted to do a ballet picture. There is a vast ballet audience, but it's not a movie audience. So the studios were not interested, and I had to come up with a story that I felt would have enough appeal to a movie audience so that they would not be put off by the ballet aspect. The ballet side had to be underplayed, frankly.

CA: Were you happy with "The Turning Point"?

LAURENTS: I'm never completely happy with anything I do, and certainly with no movies. I liked it moderately. I felt there were scenes that were not shot or that were cut that shouldn't have been.

CA: How did you like the ballet scenes?

LAURENTS: The ballet scenes were terribly well photographed. I thought the gala at the end was a mess. One of the things that bothered me was the whole treatment of the gay element. I thought it was slighted—it was cut out of the script. It is a part of the ballet world, but certain people connected with the picture—not the studio heads, by the way—said, oh, that doesn't exist anymore. Well, that's just nonsense. And there were things in the picture that, from the story point of view, didn't make complete sense. The other thing is that, so far as portraying a milieu honestly, the picture evaded it, and that bothered me.

CA: Do you prefer to direct your own plays, or would you rather have an outside director?

LAURENTS: It depends. The trouble is that there are so few good directors anymore in the theater, which is why I began to direct. And then there's this myth that authors shouldn't direct plays. It's actually historically rather recent in the theater that authors don't direct. Recently I was asked if I would direct somebody else's play. I would if I could find a good one. I am going to direct somebody else's musical next year. As a matter of fact, the first musical I directed I didn't write. That was called "I Can Get It For You Wholesale." That's where I found Barbra Streisand. And David Merrick, who produced it, was after me most of the time to fire her.

CA: He didn't think she was talented, or was she difficult to work with?

LAURENTS: He didn't think she was attractive enough in those days, and he didn't think she was funny.

CA: It's inconceivable now, isn't it?

LAURENTS: It is now, but it wasn't then. When she just came in off the streets to audition, I absolutely flipped. I'd never heard anybody sing like that. There was no part in the show for her, but there was a character who was supposed to be a fifty-year-old spinster, and I thought, "What difference does it make how old she is?" I let Barbra play it and kept building up the part during rehearsal, and she was, of course, wonderful.

CA: Have you done any acting?

LAURENTS: Years ago, right after I got out of college. I worked with some other young kids—there were five or six of us—who did a satirical nightclub act. I had to act to get paid. But I was so self-conscious about performing that I had to be drunk to go on. So I only acted for about three months.

CA: Do you think the experience in directing has affected your writing for the stage?

LAURENTS: Yes, it helps because you realize some of the problems actors have can come from not giving them something specific to play in the writing. This is a crude example, but if you have somebody doing a long monologue, that's all right if the person listening has some reaction; but if the listener is just there as a stooge, it's bad for the actor and it's not a good scene. So you learn something about actors' problems from directing, and I think it does help with writing.

CA: You've said you "suspect obscurantism of being the refuge of the vague, the uncommitted and the chic." Was this in reference particularly to some of the plays being done in the late 1960s and early 1970s?

LAURENTS: Yes, it was the period I call the Period of the Emperor's Clothes. It really was maddening to me because it was all style and no content, and I think content is more important than form or style.

CA: Do you think anything of lasting value to theater came out of the very experimental plays of that period?

LAURENTS: Yes, I think that almost any kind of experimentation has a value in that it shows there can be other ways of saying something or writing something or doing something. And it can evoke a freedom so that you don't feel you have to abide by the same old rules. In that sense it's helpful. Unfortunately, what happens during a period like that is the work that may break ground is so over-praised that it's disheartening. Instead of looking at it and saying, "Well, there is something I can learn from this, something that I can use," we give too much credit just for the novelty. As time goes by, of course, things settle down. Now there's a return to what I think are essentials in any dramatic medium—first of all, character. You're hard put to think of a good play that doesn't have a memorable character. And there is also a return to the story. It doesn't have to be linear, but there has to be a narrative thrust, I feel, in anything. Even "Waiting for Godot" has one.

CA: Are there young playwrights you consider promising?

LAURENTS: Yes, there are young playwrights that I consider promising, but I don't see them developing, by and large. When I began in the theater there was a good deal of discipline, a good deal of working to perfect one's craft, which meant, of course, rewriting and learning. And I don't see that going on with the young playwrights. There are early plays which show real talent and yet are flawed, as almost everything is flawed; but the same flaws continue, and they begin to get worse. I think it's because the playwrights don't go back and rewrite, and there aren't producers and directors as there used to be to encourage and say, "Yes, but . . . ." The word *but* is so important, and it is not said.

CA: "West Side Story" was produced again in 1980, twenty-three years after the beginning of the original production. Did the time lapse present special problems?

LAURENTS: First I must tell you I did not want it to be revived. I didn't think *enough* time had passed. Second, I thought it was a poor revival. Third, there is a thing going on today of reviving musicals as a duplication of what they were originally. Now one wouldn't do that with a play. You would have a contemporary look at it or a different look, a new look. And I don't want to see something done today exactly as it was done twenty-three years ago. I don't think the work should be changed, but I think the viewpoint on it should. It would be more interesting.

CA: The original dialogue of "West Side Story" was so authentic to the time and the characters. How did you manage to produce that authenticity?

LAURENTS: It was all made up. It seems authentic, but it wasn't. I felt at the time that if I used contemporary expressions they would be dated in six months because phrases go in and out of the vernacular so fast. So I made up a lanugage that sounded like street talk but actually wasn't. I mean the word *cool,* for example, wasn't used then. I think one has to be very careful about using current phraseology. You read plays now where they say something is *peachy* or *swell,* and you think it's quaint. It's the equivalent of *terrific* or *dynamite* today—though *dynamite* is disappearing, thank God. On the other hand, certain idiomatic phrases creep in that are so apt, one thinks, *that* will last, that's not just idiom, it's contemporary poetry.

CA: Do you have a favorite among the musicals you've done?

LAURENTS: Yes. "Gypsy."

CA: You haven't done much writing for television.

LAURENTS: I did one television show in 1967. It was called "The Light Fantastic." It was a musical of sorts, and the subtitle was "How to Tell Your Past, Present and Future Through Social Dancing." The funny part of it is, there is a correlation. For example, the waltz is always popular in periods of peace. So, of course, it's decidedly unpopular today. And it's curious, the Charleston came in at a period just before the Crash, and the frug, which is very close to the Charleston, came in just before the recession of the Nixon period. It has to do with people dancing together or apart, and with tempo. Hemlines, by the way, are also indicative.

CA: Do you think we're coming back into a time of people dancing together?

LAURENTS: I think so, because I think it's part of our coming out of the "me" period. When people were so obsessed with "self-development," they didn't realize that development is really relating to other people, not just to oneself.

CA: Yes. Whatever good that period may have done, it produced a very selfish outlook.

LAURENTS: Yes, because life is about relationships with people. Manners are not just manners. They are, I think, a kind of ritualistic expression of consideration for other people. Certainly they can be carried too far: one doesn't have to curtsy or wear white gloves. But certain politenesses are a sign of consideration. Just saying "thank you" means a great deal to almost anyone, whether they admit it or not. It seems that age-old theory is still very true, that the pendulum has to go all the way to the other extreme before we come back to a sane center.

CA: Of the kinds of writing you've done, is there one you've enjoyed more than the others?

LAURENTS: I like writing for the theater. That's partly because the playwright is respected in the theater, and the attitude toward the screenwriter is almost the same today as it was when I first went to Hollywood: the screenwriter, unfortunately, is low man on the totem pole and has very little control or say. It also doesn't make for the best writing because there is a tendency to say, "Well, what the hell, they're going to change it to suit themselves anyway, so why bother?'' As you get older, you pick and choose what is worth fighting for in every area of life.

CA: Is there any genre you haven't written in that you would like to try?

LAURENTS: I would like to write a novel. I don't know whether I'm capable. I seem to be so much of a dramatist that the whole interior side of novel writing is difficult for me. I'd like to try almost everything—except poetry; I'm totally incapable of that.

CA: Are you hopeful about theater in the near future?

LAURENTS: I'm an optimist, so I'm hopeful. I don't know about the near future because it seems to me we're going through a period where almost everything in this country is very second-rate. The second-rate is exalted and the goal is always material success, and when that's the aim, people aren't as willing to take chances. Mind you, I think the *audience* is. I'll always believe in them, if they're given the chance. It's perfectly true in the theater that if something gets good reviews, they run to see it and the minute there's a bad review they stay away, which is unfortunate. But, on the other hand, the prices are so high that one can't blame them for wanting somebody's approbation before they go. With good seats costing $25 to $35, and the babysitter and dinner. . . . And yet, on a percentage basis theater tickets have not gone up that much. Curiously enough, it's the expensive seats that sell first. All that means is that we do have a level of affluence, but those are not the people, the audience, to rely on. They're the people I think are so addicted to fashion. They will go to what's fashionable rather than decide for themselves.

BIOGRAPHICAL/CRITICAL SOURCES: Washington Post, August 27, 1957, January 6, 1980; *New Republic,* September 9, 1957; *New Yorker,* October 5, 1957, May 30, 1959, October 7, 1974, November 21, 1977; *Saturday Review,* October 5, 1957, June 6, 1959, April 3, 1965; *Newsweek,* October 7, 1957, October 7, 1974, November 28, 1977, February 25, 1980; *Time,* October 7, 1957, October 7, 1974, February 25, 1980, March 3, 1980; *Nation,* October 12, 1957, June 6, 1959, October 12, 1974; Allan Lewis, *American Plays and Playwrights of the Contemporary Theatre,* Crown, 1965; *New York Times Book Review,* April 16, 1972; *New York Times,* October 18, 1973, November 4, 1973, November 15, 1977, June 14, 1979, February 10, 1980; *New York,* March 3, 1980.

—Sketch by James G. Lesniak

—Interview by Jean W. Ross

* * *

LAURIE, Edward J(ames) 1925-

PERSONAL: Born November 21, 1925, in Sparks, Nev.; son of Albert Edward (a railroad conductor) and Margaret (Fraser) Laurie; married Patricia Jean Johnson, March 31, 1962; children: Katherine Louise, Margaret Dee, Elizabeth Ann. *Education:* University of California, Los Angeles, B.S., 1946, M.B.A., 1950, Ed.D., 1959. *Home:* 1287 Pampas Dr., San Jose, Calif. 95120. *Office:* School of Business, San Jose State University, San Jose, Calif.

CAREER: San Jose State University, San Jose, Calif., assistant professor, 1956-59, associate professor, 1959-63, professor of management, 1964-70, professor of marketing, 1971—, chairman of Marketing/Quantitative Studies, 1971—, associate dean of Academic Studies, 1974-81, acting dean, 1981. Instructor at Oregon State University, Washington State University, University of California, Los Angeles, Colorado State University and other teaching institutions. Faculty research fellow, International Business Machines, Systems Research Institute, 1962-63. *Military service:* U.S. Naval Reserve, active duty, 1943-45; became lieutenant junior grade. *Member:* American Marketing Association, American Association of University Professors, American Academy of Political and Social Sciences, Planetary Society, Newcomen Society in North America, Association of California State College Professors, Phi Kappa Phi, Phi Delta Phi, Beta Gamma Sigma, Tau Delta Pi, Pi Omega Pi.

WRITINGS—Published by South-Western, except as indicated: *Computer Systems in the United States,* 1960; *Computers and How They Work,* 1963; *Computers and Computer Languages,* 1966; *Modern Computer Concepts,* 1970; *Computers, Automation, and Society,* Irwin, 1979; *Today's Electronic Data Processing for Business,* 1983. Contributor to professional journals.

SIDELIGHTS: Edward J. Laurie told *CA:* ''I now use a micro computer word-processing program for most of my preliminary writing work. This permits me the luxury of revision and storage on disks. Most college texts do not make a great deal of money, but from time to time a student says he or she got excited because of what one of my books revealed, and I think that is sufficient reward for the effort.

''My goal in writing is simply to tell the truth in the clearest way possible. I believe one learns to write by reading! I'm one of those 'weird' people who loves to read; in fact, I generally prefer books to people (family excepted).

''Mostly one can write only to the degree he or she is willing to set schedules for day-to-day activity and stay with the work until it is done. Good editors, and they are legion, take care of the rest. After six books, I seem to have gotten 'the hang of it.'''

AVOCATIONAL INTERESTS: General history, Egyptology, history of science, astronomy.

* * *

LAVAN, Spencer 1937-

PERSONAL: Born December 31, 1937, in New York, N.Y.; son of Peter I. B. (an attorney) and Fay (a writer; maiden name, Collen) Lavan; married Susan Anthony Kohlberg, December 22, 1961; children: Johnathan Peter, Daniel Horton, Timothy Spencer, Joanna Be. *Education:* Tufts University, A.B. (cum laude), 1959; Harvard University, S.T.B., 1962; McGill University, M.A., 1966, Ph.D., 1970. *Religion:* Unitarian Universalist. *Home address:* R.F.D. 2, Box 2220, Brunswick, Me. 04011. *Office:* College of Osteopathic Medicine, University of New England, Biddeford, Me. 04005.

CAREER: Minister in Charleston, S.C., 1962-64, in Montreal, Quebec, 1965-67; Tufts University, Medford, Mass., assistant professor of religion, 1969-79, associate dean of liberal arts, 1973-78; program consultant, Maine Humanities Council, 1979-81; University of New England, College of Osteopathic Medicine, Biddeford, Me., associate professor of humanities, 1982—. Founder of Collegium: Liberal Religious Studies. Town meeting member, town of Lexington, Mass., 1973-77. *Member:* American Academy of Religion, Association of Asian Studies, Unitarian Historical Society (president, 1978-82), Society for Health and Human Values, American Society of Law and Medicine, Bengal Studies Association, Middle East Studies Association.

WRITINGS: (Editor with Barbara Thomas) *West Bengal and Bangladesh: Perspectives from 1972,* Michigan State University, 1973; *The Ahmadiyah Movement: A History and Perspective,* South Asia Books, 1974; (contributor) Jones and Gustafson, editors, *Sources on Punjab History,* [Delhi], 1975; *Unitarians and India: A Study in Encounter and Response,* Beacon Press, 1977; (editor with Peter I. Kaufman) *Alone Together: Essays in the History of Liberal Religion,* Beacon Press, 1978. Contributor to journals in his field.

* * *

LAWSON, Richard H(enry) 1919-

PERSONAL: Born January 11, 1919, in San Francisco, Calif.; son of Henry Porter and Alice (Hanchett) Lawson; married Eldene Laura Balcom, August 26, 1950. *Education:* Attended Multnomah College, 1937-39; University of Oregon, B.A., 1941, M.A., 1948; University of California, Los Angeles, Ph.D., 1956. *Home:* 72 Laurel Ridge Apts., Chapel Hill, N.C. 27514. *Office:* Department of Germanic Languages, University of North Carolina, Chapel Hill, N.C. 27514.

CAREER: Washington State University, Pullman, instructor in German, 1953-57; San Diego State University, San Diego, Calif., assistant professor, 1957-62, associate professor, 1962-66, professor of German, 1966-76, chairman of department of foreign languages, 1965, and department of German and Russian, 1966-68, chairman of Division of Humanities, 1968-69, acting associate or assistant dean of graduate studies, 1970-74; University of North Carolina at Chapel Hill, professor of German, 1976—, chairman of department of Germanic languages, 1976-79. *Military service:* U.S. Army Air Forces, 1941-46; became first lieutenant; received Air Medal. U.S. Air Force Reserve, 1946—; present rank, major.

MEMBER: International Arthur Schnitzler Research Association, Internationale Vereinigung fuer Germanische Sprach-und Literaturwissenschaft, Modern Language Association of America, American Comparative Literature Association, American Association of Teachers of German, Philological Association of the Pacific Coast, South Atlantic Modern Language Association.

WRITINGS: (With others) *Studies in Arthur Schnitzler,* University of North Carolina Press, 1963; (editor) *Novellen aus Wien,* Scribner, 1964; (with others) *Encyclopedia of World Literature in the Twentieth Century,* Ungar, 1969, revised edition, 1982; (with others) *Dichtung, Sprache, Gesellschaft,* Athenaeun Verlag, 1971; *Edith Wharton and German Literature,* Bouvier Verlag, 1974; *Edith Wharton,* Ungar, 1977; (with others) *Medicine and Literature,* Neale Watson, 1980. Editor of "University of North Carolina Studies in the Germanic Languages and Literature" series; consultant on etymologies to *Webster's New International Dictionary,* 1955-57. Contributor to language and other professional journals.

WORK IN PROGRESS: Studies on linguistics in Old High German; *Guenter Grass,* for Ungar.

SIDELIGHTS: Richard H. Lawson is competent in German, Spanish, Russian, French, Italian, and Latin.

* * *

LEE, Francis Nigel 1934-

PERSONAL: Born December 5, 1934, in Kendal, England; son of William Sydney (a company director) and Alice Maud (Smith) Lee; married Nellie Vander Westhuizen, December 7, 1963; children: Johanna, Annamarie. *Education:* University of Capetown, B.A., 1957, LL.B., 1960, M.A., 1966; Reformed Theological Seminary, Cand. Litt., 1959, Dip. Theol., 1962; University of Stellenbosch, B.D., 1962, L.Th., 1963, Th.M., 1964, Th.D., 1966; University of the Orange Free State, Ph.D., 1972; postdoctoral study at Potchefstroom University for Christian Higher Education. *Politics:* Conservative. *Home:* 3 Kenya St., Wavell, Australia 4012. *Office:* Department of Systematic Theology, Queensland Presbyterian Theological Seminary, Emmanuel College of Queensland University, Upland Rd., St. Lucia, Australia 4067.

CAREER: Licensed Presbyterian minister, 1963; Shelton College, Cape May, N.J., professor of philosophy, 1968-69; minister in Winterton, South Africa, 1969-73; Christian Studies Center, Memphis, Tenn., research professor, 1974-77; Queensland University, Queensland Presbyterian Theological Seminary, St. Lucia, Australia, professor of systematic theology, 1981—. Member of National Board for Anti-Communism, 1969-73; chairman of Natal State Board for Advancement of Protestantism, Natal, South Africa, 1971-73; Staley Distinguished Lecturer at Covenant Theological Seminary, 1974.

MEMBER: International Association for Calvinistic Philosophy, Association for Christian Higher Education, Calvinistic Students Association (chairman, 1962-63), South African Association for the Advancement of Christian Scholarship. *Awards, honors:* Ernest Oppenheimer Postgraduate Memorial scholarships, 1967, 1968, 1969.

WRITINGS—In English: *The Covenantal Sabbath,* Lord's Day Observance Society (London), 1966; *Culture: Its Origin and Development,* Shelton College Press, 1967; *Nationality and the Bible,* Shelton College Press, 1967; *Philosophy and the Bible,* Shelton College Press, 1967; *The Biblical Theory of Christian Education,* Shelton College Press, 1967; *Calvin on the Sciences,* Sovereign Grace Union (England), 1969; *A Christian Introduction to the History of Philosophy,* Craig Press, 1969; *Communism Versus Creation,* Craig Press, 1969.

Christian Philosophy in Twentieth-Century North America, SAVBCW-Potchestroom (South Africa), 1970; *The Westminster Confession and Modern Society,* Scottish Reformed Fellowship (Edinburgh, Scotland), 1972; *Communist Eschatology: A Christian Philosophical Analysis of the Post-Capitalistic Views of Marx, Engels, and Lenin,* Craig Press, 1974; *Are the Ten Commandments Relevant Today?,* Blue Banner, 1974; *The Origin and Destiny of Man,* Presbyterian and Reformed Publishing, 1974; *Effective Evangelism,* Renewal, 1975; *The Central Significance of Culture,* Craig Press, 1976; *What about Baptism?,* Scottish Reformed Fellowship, 1976; *About Sunday,* Lord's Day Observance Society, 1978, *The Office of All Believers,* Presbyterian Church of America Publications, 1978; *The Office of Deacon,* Presbyterian Church of America Publications, 1978; *The Ministry of the Word,* Presbyterian Church of America Publications, 1978.

Published by Jesus Saves: *Christocracy,* 1979; *Mount Sinai and the Sermon on the Mount,* 1979; *Are the Mosaic Laws for Today?,* 1979; *Creation and Commission,* 1979; *Have You Been Neglecting Your Baby?,* 1979; *Toward a Biblical Theology,* 1979; *Toward a Biblical Philosophy,* 1979; *Abraham Kuyper and the Rebirth of True Knowledge,* 1980; *John Calvin: True Presbyterian,* 1981; *Communism: A Christian Evaluation,* 1981; *Will Christ or Satan Win This World?,* 1981; *Our Life in This World,* in press; *A Biblical Approach to Church Architecture,* in press.

In Afrikaans: *Die Mens se Verantwoordelikheid Teenoor sy Gees* (title means "Man's Responsibility for His Soul"), Akos (South Africa), 1970; *Die Grondgedagtes van die Kommunisme en Hoedat Dit Gepropageer Word* (title means "The Basic Ideas of Communism and How They Are Propagated"), SAVBCW-Potchestroom, 1971; *Ras en Nasie: Wat se die Bybel?* (title means "Race and Nation: What Does the Bible Teach?"), Wever (South Africa), 1971; *Die Saligheid van Vroegsterwende Kindertjies* (title means "The Salvation of Those Dying during Infancy"), N. G. Uitgewers (South Africa), 1971; *Die Sendingtaak as Hart van die Kerk se Roeping* (title means "The Missionary Task as the Heart of the Church's Calling"), N. G. Uitgewers, 1971; *Julle Doop Mos Verkeerd!* (title means "Ye Baptise Incorrectly!"), N. G. Uitgewers, 1973; *Sondag die Sabbat* (title means "Sunday the Sabbath"), N. G. Uitgewers, 1976.

WORK IN PROGRESS: Onward, Christian Soldiers!; I Believe in the Holy Ghost!; Dorot Decrees Christian Conquest!

SIDELIGHTS: Francis Nigel Lee has traveled to eighty countries of the world and is competent in seven languages. He writes that the important circumstances of his life are "my conversion to Christ, my marriage, my overall viewpoint—the total Lordship of Jesus Christ over every atom of His universe and over everyone and everything in it."

BIOGRAPHICAL/CRITICAL SOURCES: H. J. Hegger, editor, *Jesus Arrested Me*, Velp (Netherlands), 1960.

* * *

LEE, Lucy
See TALBOT, Charlene Joy

* * *

LEES, Ray 1931-

PERSONAL: Born November 28, 1931, in England; son of Herbert (a bus driver) and Ivy (Gilks) Lees; married Sue Mullock (a lecturer), August 9, 1970; children: Sean, Daniel, Josie. *Education:* University of London, B.Sc. (with honors), 1969. *Home:* 9 Northolme Rd., London N. 5, England. *Office:* Department of Social Sciences, Polytechnic of Central London, Regent St., London, England.

CAREER: Recreation organizer at Leybourne Grange Hospital, 1956-61; probation officer, London Probation Service, 1961-65; lecturer at Ipswich Civic College, 1966-67, and at Polytechnic of Central London, 1969-72; University of York, Heslington, England, research fellow in sociology, 1972-75; Polytechnic of Central London, London, England, professor of applied social studies, 1975—, head of department, 1975—. *Member:* Association of Teachers of Social Administration, British Association of Social Workers, British Sociological Association.

WRITINGS: Politics and Social Work, Routledge & Kegan Paul, 1972; *Research Strategies for Social Welfare*, Routledge & Kegan Paul, 1975; (editor with George Smith) *Action Research in Community Development*, Routledge & Kegan Paul, 1975; (with wife, Sue Lees, and B. Heraud) *Studies in Community Development*, Polytechnic of North London, 1980, Volume I: *Final and Interproject Reports—Action Research*, Volume II: *Industry and Employment—Housing*, Volume III: *Advice and Community Work*; (with Nick Bailey and Marjorie Mayo) *Resourcing Communities: Evaluating the Experience of Six Area Resource Centres*, Polytechnic of Central London, 1981; (with E. Butterworth and P. Arnold) *The Challenge of Community Work*, University of York, 1981; *Politics and Community Action: Polarization in the 1980's*, Routledge & Kegan Paul, 1982. Contributor to social work journals.

WORK IN PROGRESS: Research on the role of politics and ideology in the formulation of social policy.

* * *

LEHMAN, David 1948-

PERSONAL: Born June 11, 1948, in New York, N.Y.; son of Joseph and Anne (Lusthaus) Lehman; married second wife, Stephanie Green (a graphic designer), December 2, 1978. *Education:* Columbia University, B.A. (magna cum laude), 1970, Ph.D., 1978; Cambridge University, B.A., M.A., 1972. *Politics:* "As legislators, poets are doomed to go unacknowledged." *Religion:* Jewish. *Home:* 159 Ludlowville Rd., Lansing, N.Y. 14882.

CAREER: Columbia University, New York City, preceptor in English, 1974-75; Brooklyn College of the City University of New York, Brooklyn, N.Y., instructor in English, 1975-76; Hamilton College, Clinton, N.Y., assistant professor of English, 1976-80; Cornell University, Ithaca, N.Y., fellow of Society for the Humanities, 1980-81; Wells College, Aurora, N.Y., lecturer in English, 1981-82. Karolyi Memorial Foundation poet-in-residence, Vence, France, summer, 1977. Co-producer and host of "The Only Poetry Show" on WKCR-FM Radio, 1972-73. *Member:* Phi Beta Kappa.

AWARDS, HONORS: Van Rennselaer Award, 1967 and 1970; Kellett fellow, 1970; Woodrow Wilson fellow, 1970; Book-of-the-Month Club creative writing fellow, 1970; Bennett A. Cerf Prize for Poetry, Columbia University, 1973, for "Baby Burning"; Academy of American Poets Prize, 1974, for "Threatening Weather"; Ingram Merrill Foundation grant, 1976 and 1982; National Endowment for the Humanities grant, summer, 1979.

WRITINGS: Some Nerve (poems), Columbia Review Press, 1973; *Day One* (poems), Nobadaddy Press, 1979; (editor) *Beyond Amazement: New Essays on John Ashbery*, Cornell University Press, 1980; (contributor) Lloyd Schwartz and Sybil Estes, editors, *Elizabeth Bishop and Her Art*, University of Michigan Press, in press.

Work represented in anthologies, including: *The Uses of Poetry*, Holt, 1975; *Ardis Anthology of New American Poetry*, Ardis, 1977; *The "Poetry" Anthology, 1912-1977*, Houghton, 1978; *Anthology of Magazine Verse and Yearbook of American Poetry*, Monitor, 1981. Contributor of poems and reviews to periodicals, including *Poetry, Paris Review, Partisan Review, Times Literary Supplement, Newsday, Epoch, Shenandoah, Prairie Schooner, Parnassus: Poetry in Review,* and *Washington Post.* Editor of *Columbia Review*, 1969-70, and *Poetry in Motion*, 1976—; contributing editor, *Columbia Today*, 1975; founding editor, Nobadaddy Press, 1976; poetry editor, *New York Arts Journal*, 1976-80.

WORK IN PROGRESS: James Merrill: Essays in Criticism, with Charles Berger; *An Alternative to Speech*, a collection of poems.

SIDELIGHTS: David Lehman told *CA:* "'I, too, dislike it,' Marianne Moore said of poetry, and this has always seemed to me the logical place for any poet to start. Even as they swing open their gates and bid the multitudes enter, . . . poems must *reject* things, influences, intrusions. In a way, poems are rejection slips issued to the world at large, though the yes of their existence tends to overshadow this opposing tendency. . . . The first poem I read that made me want to write out my own experience was Frank O'Hara's 'Why I Am Not a Painter' in my freshman year at college; Koch and Ashbery followed anon. . . . Perhaps it is revealing that my three favorite critics are the late W. H. Auden, the late Randall Jarrell, and the very with us William Gass. What I find particularly inspiring in Gass is his use of language as an intoxicant; in Jarrell, his enthusiasm, so genuine and immediate; in Auden, his absolute individuality, as though he had taught himself everything he knew."

AVOCATIONAL INTERESTS: Baseball.

BIOGRAPHICAL/CRITICAL SOURCES: Times Literary Supplement, June 5, 1981.

* * *

LEHMANN, (Rudolph) John (Frederick) 1907-

PERSONAL: Born June 2, 1907, in Bourne End, Buckinghamshire, England; son of Rudolph Chambers (a writer, editor of Punch, and member of Parliament) and Alice Marie (Davis) Lehmann. Education: Attended Eton College; Trinity College, Cambridge, B.A. Home: 85 Cornwall Gardens, London S.W.7, England. Agent: David Higham Associates Ltd., 5-8 Lower John St., London WIR 4HA, England; and A. Watkins, Inc., 77 Park Ave., New York, N.Y. 10016.

CAREER: Writer and editor. Hogarth Press, London, England, general manager, 1931-32; poet and journalist in Vienna, Austria, 1932-36, and Soviet Transcaucasia, 1935 and 1936; Hogarth Press, partner, general manager, and editor of New Writing, Penguin New Writing, Daylight, and New Writing and Daylight, 1938-46; John Lehmann Ltd. (publishers), London, founder and managing director, 1946-52; London Magazine, London, founding editor, 1953-61. Editor, "New Soundings," British Broadcasting Corp. Third Programme, 1952-53. Visiting professor, University of Texas at Austin, 1970-71, California State University, San Diego, 1971-72, University of California, Berkeley, 1974, and Emory University, 1977. Chairman of editorial advisory panel, British Council, 1952-58; president, Alliance Francaise in Great Britain, 1955-64, and Royal Literary Fund, 1967-76. Member: Royal Society of Literature (fellow), P.E.N.; Bath Club, Naval and Military Club (both London).

AWARDS, HONORS: Order of George I of Hellenes, 1954, Commander, 1961; Officier, Legion d'Honneur, 1958; Grand Officier, Etoile Noir, 1960; Prix du Rayonnement Francais, 1961; Commander, Order of the British Empire, 1964; William Foyle Poetry Prize, 1964; Officier, Ordre des Arts et des Lettres, 1965; Queen's Silver Jubilee Medal, 1977; D. Litt., University of Birmingham, 1980.

WRITINGS—Poems: A Garden Revisited and Other Poems, Leonard and Virginia Woolf, 1931; The Noise of History, Hogarth, 1934; Forty Poems, Hogarth, 1942; The Sphere of Glass and Other Poems, Hogarth, 1944; The Age of the Dragon: Poems, 1930-1951, Longmans, Green, 1951, Harcourt, 1953; The Secret Messages, Overbrook Press, 1958; Christ the Hunter, Eyre & Spottiswoode, 1965; Collected Poems, 1930-1963, Eyre & Spottiswoode, 1965; Photograph, Poem-of-the-Month Club (London), 1971; The Reader at Night and Other Poems, Basilike (Toronto), 1974. Also author of The Bud, Burial, Dawn, Grey Days, The Lover, The Mountain, Ruin, The Gargoyles, Turn Not, and Hesperides, ten broadsheets privately printed in 1928.

Nonfiction: Prometheus and the Bolsheviks, Cresset, 1937, Knopf, 1938; Down River: A Danubian Study, Cresset, 1939; New Writing in England, Critics' Group Press, 1939; New Writing in Europe, Penguin, 1940, reprinted, Century Bookbindery, 1977; The Open Night (essays), Harcourt, 1952; Edith Sitwell, Longmans, Green, 1952; Ancestors and Friends, Eyre & Spottiswoode, 1962; A Nest of Tigers: The Sitwells in Their Times, Little, Brown, 1968 (published in England as A Nest of Tigers: Edith, Osbert and Sacheverell Sitwell in Their Times, Macmillan, 1968; Holborn: An Historical Portrait of a London Borough, Macmillan (London), 1970; Lewis Carroll and the Spirit of Nonsense, University of Nottingham, 1974; Virginia Woolf and Her World, Thames & Hudson, 1975, Harcourt, 1976; Edward Lear and His World, Scribner, 1977; Thrown to the Woolfs: Leonard and Virginia Woolf and the Hogarth Press, Weidenfeld & Nicolson, 1978, Holt, 1979; Rupert Brooke: His Life and His Legend, Weidenfeld & Nicolson, 1980, published as The Strange Destiny of Rupert Brooke, Holt, 1981; English Poets of the First World War, Thames & Hudson, 1982.

Novels: Evil Was Abroad, Cresset, 1938; In a Purely Pagan Sense, Blond & Briggs, 1976.

Autobiographies: The Whispering Gallery: Autobiography I (also see below), Longmans, Green, 1955; I Am My Brother: Autobiography II (also see below), Reynal, 1960; The Ample Proposition: Autobiography III (also see below), Eyre & Spottiswoode, 1966; In My Own Time: Memoirs of a Literary Life (revised and condensed version of The Whispering Gallery, I Am My Brother, and The Ample Proposition), Little, Brown, 1969.

Editor: (With Denys Kilham Roberts and Gerald Gould) The Year's Poetry: A Representative Selection, three volumes, John Lane, 1934-36; (with T. A. Jackson and C. Day Lewis) Ralph Fox, A Writer in Arms, International Publishing, 1937; (with Stephen Spender) Poems for Spain, Hogarth, 1939; Demetrios Capetanakis: A Greek Poet in England, Lehmann, 1947, published as Shores of Darkness: Poems and Essays, Devin, 1949; (and author of introduction) Shelley in Italy: An Anthology, Lehmann, 1947; Orpheus: A Symposium of the Arts, Volume I, New Directions, 1948, Volume II, Lehmann, 1949, reprinted, Century Bookbindery, 1977.

(With Day Lewis, and contributor) The Chatto Book of Modern Poetry, 1915-1955, Chatto & Windus, 1956, revised edition, 1959, reprinted, Greenwood Press, 1978; The Craft of Letters in England: A Symposium, Cresset, 1956, Houghton, 1957, reprinted, Greenwood Press, 1974; Coming to London, Phoenix House, 1957, reprinted, Books for Libraries, 1971; (and author of introduction) Italian Stories of Today, Faber, 1959; Edith Sitwell, Selected Poems, Macmillan, 1965; (with Derek Parker) Edith Sitwell, Selected Letters, 1919-1964, Macmillan, 1970, Vanguard, 1971.

Editor of "New Writing" anthologies: New Writing: Spring, 1936, John Lane, 1936; New Writing: Autumn, 1936, John Lane, 1936; New Writing: Spring, 1937, Lawrence & Wishart, 1936, Knopf, 1937; New Writing: Fall, 1937, Knopf, 1973; New Writing: Spring, 1938, Lawrence & Wishart, 1938; (with Christopher Isherwood and Stephen Spender) New Writing: Fall, 1938, Knopf, 1938; (with Isherwood and Spender) New Writing: Spring, 1939, Hogarth, 1939; New Writing: Christmas, 1938, Hogarth, 1939.

The Penguin New Writing, Penguin, 1940, new edition, 1947, reprinted, Century Bookbindery, 1977; Folios of New Writing, four volumes, Hogarth, 1940-41; New Writing and Daylight: Summer, 1942, Hogarth, 1942; New Writing and Daylight: Winter, 1942-43, Hogarth, 1943; New Writing and Daylight: Summer, 1943, Hogarth, 1943, Transatlantic, 1944; New Writing and Daylight: Winter, 1943-44, Hogarth, 1944; New Writing and Daylight: Autumn, 1944, Hogarth, 1944, Transatlantic, 1945; New Writing and Daylight: 1945, Hogarth, 1945; New Writing and Daylight: 1946, Lehmann, 1946, New Directions,

1947; *Poems from New Writing, 1936-46*, Lehmann, 1946; *French Stories from New Writing*, Lehmann, 1947, published as *Modern French Stories*, New Directions, 1948.

Best Stories from New Writing, Harcourt, 1951 (published in England as *English Stories from New Writing*, Lehmann, 1951); *Pleasures of New Writing: An Anthology of Poems, Stories and Other Prose Pieces*, Lehmann, 1952, reprinted, Century Bookbindery, 1977.

Contributor: *Poems of Today*, third series, Macmillan, 1938; Elizabeth Jennings, editor, *An Anthology of Modern Verse, 1940-1960*, Metheun, 1961; *Penguin Book of Contemporary Verse*, Penguin, 1962; Patricia Beer and others, editors, *New Poems, 1963: A P.E.N. Anthology*, Hutchinson, 1963; Robin Skelton, editor, *Poetry of the Thirties*, Penguin, 1964; Brian Gardner, editor, *Terrible Rain: The War Poets, 1939-1945*, Metheun, 1966.

Advisory editor, *Geographical Magazine*, 1940-45; founder and editor, *Orpheus*, 1948-49.

SIDELIGHTS: John Lehmann, according to Max Cosman in *Commonweal*, is "England's dean of creative editors." After joining Leonard and Virginia Woolf's Hogarth Press in 1931, Lehmann developed a series of "New Writing" journals and anthologies in which the works of such writers as W. H. Auden, Christopher Isherwood, Jean-Paul Sartre, Saul Bellow, and Gore Vidal were first introduced to the public. "Mr. Lehmann's position in English letters has been unique," David Daiches comments in the *New York Times Book Review*. "As editor, anthologist, and publisher, he has been the prime encourager of new talent." "A good editor must be eagle-eyed, poised to swoop up the smallest mouse of talent from the vast and turbulent plain of literature," Julian Mitchell notes. Writing in the *New York Times Book Review*, Mitchell calls Lehmann "the greatest British literary editor of his time. . . . One whiff of talent and his head shoots forward, his eyes narrow to a penetrating blue, he listens, tense and still—then plummets for the prey. . . . There is scarcely a writer [of his generation] in Britain . . . who hasn't at one time or other been grateful for his passionate scrutiny."

"To explain Lehmann's effectiveness, one would, I think, have to invoke a set of specific historical circumstances and a wide range of personal gifts," Lawrence Graver remarks in the *New Republic*. The son of Rudolph Lehmann (the former editor of *Punch* magazine) and brother of novelist Rosamond Lehmann, "Lehmann was born with a silver pencil between his fingers," Mitchell states. In a review of Lehmann's autobiographical *In My Own Time*, Graver writes: "He spent an idyllic Edwardian childhood, thriving on the advantages of breeding, geniality, and clean air. . . . When in the late twenties Europe moved toward calamity, Lehmann in his early twenties moved toward manhood and an honorable place in the literary society of his time. Although he valued the solidities of tradition, he also understood the vulnerability of his inheritance and the threatening new facts of social and political experience. For many years afterward, he could defend *belles lettres* with the confidence of an 18th-century aristocrat, while at the same time printing incendiary works by a broad spectrum of modernist writers." "But sensitivity and serviceable connections would have counted for little if Lehmann did not have a fundamental fitness for his job," Graver continues. "In addition to his catholic taste and sharp eye for spotting talent, he had the ability to coax work out of blocked writers, and to convince a refractory novelist like Isherwood to press on. Not only did he recognize fine writing when it came into his office, but by traveling across Europe to seek it out, he gave his magazines a rare and bracing cosmopolitanism."

In his critical studies and three volumes of autobiography, Lehmann presents detailed accounts of his work at the Hogarth Press and his relationship with his formidable employers, Leonard and Virginia Woolf. As critics have observed, Lehmann's books, full of personal portraits of great writers, have considerable value as literary and cultural documents.

In the *Saturday Review*, Granville Hicks describes *I Am My Brother*, Lehmann's autobiographical study of literature and war, as "an important document." Daiches concurs, adding that "it provides a significant part of the record of British cultural life during World War II, and it captures with uncanny accuracy the shifting moods of younger writers and artists between 1939 and 1946. Lehmann, after all, had a supreme vantage point; the combination of gilded youth and embattled editor and publisher has its own rewards, not least that of being able to be at the same time both free and *engage*." Louis O. Coxe finds that "one of the triumphs" of *The Whispering Gallery* is that "the events, as he recounts and relives them, take on meaning and actuality." Writing in *Nation*, Coxe calls Lehmann's memoir of British cultural life before World War II "the portrait of a young man who found the world out of joint." "What emerges most forcibly," Coxe writes, "is the sense of commitment thrwarted by history, by the predicament of time and situation. Born into a prosperous family of considerable culture and position, the sensitive and imaginative boy finds the world he was trained to occupy changing all around him. . . . Bewilderment, a sense of impending disaster and of importance before it, coupled with an enormous zest for experience and the life of the spirit: I found all these in Mr. Lehmann's book." "It is impossible not to be moved by the unyielding faith in the power of the creative imagination which Lehmann showed even at the darkest time of the war," Mitchell says. In a review of *In My Own Time*, Mitchell asserts that "this autobiography is invaluable as general literary history" and that Lehmann deserves praise for "his extraordinary kindness to young writers . . . , his endless patience and encouragement."

Reviewers have also commented favorably on Lehmann's reminiscences of the Woolfs, especially his balanced portraiture of Leonard, with whom he frequently quarreled. "Lehmann labored on the forefront of the British literary scene and at close quarters with two of its star literati," Ann Hulbert comments in the *New Republic*. As Hulbert notes, Lehmann was "utterly devoted" to Virginia, but was "inclined to be testy with his touchy, sometimes tyrannical boss, Leonard." Woolf and Lehmann often argued over which authors to publish at Hogarth; "the partnership failed through a profound difference of literary taste," Simon Blow observes in *Spectator*. Richard Shone of *Books and Bookmen* finds that *Thrown to the Woolfs* "gives a most fair impression of [Leonard], as well as showing how remarkable he was and under what strain he lived. . . . But Lehmann's book does not simply concern itself with working for Leonard and Virginia. It describes in some detail the whole magnetic field of being at the Press. . . . This considerably increases the value of the memoir—its portraits of [Stephen] Spender and Isherwood, of [William] Sansom, [William] Plomer, Henry Green and Roy Fuller."

Lehmann's critical study *Virginia Woolf and Her World* has been described as "brilliant" by the *New York Review of Books*. "His commentaries on the novels are dispassionate and lucid, based on a first-hand experience of how [Woolf] wrote them," James Atlas writes in the *New York Times Book Review*. According to Atlas, Bloomsbury (the circle of writers surrounding Woolf) "has become our new literary myth." "Why does Bloomsbury continue to fascinate us?," Atlas asks in a *New York Times* review of *Thrown to the Woolfs*. "It is that Virginia

Woolf, Lytton Strachey and her friends cultivated a habit of grace and civility now largely vanished from the world? That they managed to seem both aristocratic and bohemian?" And William Abrahams comments in *Atlantic*, "Lehmann has written a straightforward, urbane, and sympathetic account of a life whose fascination remains undimmed, however often it be told, and which, in spite of its encroaching tragedy, is life-enhancing: so much courage, intelligence, and unstavable energy, and such a marvelous belief in the power of the word."

"For many American readers, aware as they may be of John Lehmann the editor and critic, this selection of his verse will introduce a new poet," M. L. Rosenthal writes of *The Age of the Dragon*. In the *New Republic*, Rosenthal says that readers "will notice the typical easy grace of language. . . . And, after that first pang, there will be another recognition, of warm bright sunlight filtering through orchard branches on remembered scenes of a rural childhood." Rosenthal finds that in Lehmann's verse "an ideal moment of peace, meaning, and security has been projected" which serves as a "contrast to everything that war and a machine-civilization represent. Folksong and folk-legendry, the small country cottage and the great country house, are in the same cluster of associations at whose heart, again and again, we find the sunlit trees of a child's memory." "Lehmann has composed most readable and usually objective poems, many of a fine order of competence," Richard Eberhart comments on the same book for the *New York Times Book Review*. But, Eberhart believes, "he has not invented a new language or way of saying things, some inescapable idiom of his own, nor reached for mystery and strangeness in form or thought."

"Was he publisher or poet," Blow asks in *Spectator*. "Could he be both?" In the *New York Times Book Review*, Mitchell comments on Lehmann's dilemma: "The chief crises of his life all seem to be about whether or not he should sacrifice his own poetry in order to publish other people's. The decisions can never have been easy. Lehmann is a distinguished minor poet and he has never had the time to write as much as he would like. Perhaps the poet, though, was an invaluable assistant, whether he knew it or not, to the editor. For all his direct involvement in the dramatic events of his own time, Lehmann's poetry has always been full of the river smells, fruit trees and sunshine of his happy boyhood by the Thames. While the editor was experiencing the Anschluss in Vienna, or the Blitz in London, the poet, I suspect, was keeping a sense of proportion, of permanent values, quietly contemplating a memory of light dancing on water. Yet we must be glad the editor won out."

"As an editor Mr. Lehmann has seen great talents drawn to him, blossoming in the warmth of his appreciation and the light of his advice," Neil Millar says in the *Christian Science Monitor*. "[He] mentions his remarkable editorial achievements modestly (he has published many of the greatest names in 20th century literature); his heartbreaks are gallantly dismissed." In a review of *In My Own Time,* Millar concludes: "[Lehmann's] story is a cultural cockleshell afloat on tides of literary, social, and political history. It is one man's rich, often sparkling world, lost now, precious, and tactfully preserved." And Daiches sums up Lehmann's life-work: "The claims of literature had to be repeatedly asserted in an increasingly violent world. . . . He helped to keep [literature] going, helped to keep the literary imagination alive. That was his great achievement."

Lehmann's poetry has been recorded for the archives of the British Council, the United States Library of Congress, and the Library of Harvard University. His manuscripts are collected at the Humanities Research Center of the University of Texas at Austin.

AVOCATIONAL INTERESTS: Reading, swimming, gardening.

CA INTERVIEW

John Lehmann answered *CA*'s questions by mail in October, 1981.

CA: In a lecture you delivered in Vienna in 1947, "The Poet in the Modern World," you said, "The idea shapes history; and it is my belief that in the creation of the idea the work of the poet is the prime generating spark." Has the course of poetry, of art, in the intervening years changed your view in any way?

LEHMANN: No. I still feel exactly the same, though such an idea is difficult to follow out.

CA: From early in your life your ambition and attention have been divided between writing and publishing. If the opportunity to work with Leonard and Virginia Woolf at the Hogarth Press hadn't come when it did, do you think your writing might have taken a different course?

LEHMANN: I think I would have written a great deal more.

CA: Your memoirs and biographies provide valuable information on the Woolfs, other figures associated with the Bloomsbury circle, and the literary climate of that period and beyond. Are you often consulted by other writers who are working on accounts of that time?

LEHMANN: Alas, all the time.

CA: How would you assess the growing body of writing on that period?

LEHMANN: There is a great deal of rubbish written nowadays, especially on feminist themes. Nothing that has been written compares with *The Diary of Virginia Woolf* and *The Letters of Virginia Woolf*, which have been coming out volume by volume, with the exception of Quentin Bell's biography.

CA: As editor of New Writing *and the similar publications that followed it or grew out of it, you provided a forum for promising young writers who later became famous—people such as Auden, Spender, and Isherwood in England. Is it much harder now than it was then for beginning writers in England to find such an outlet for their work?*

LEHMANN: There are fewer literary magazines in England now and therefore the outlets are more difficult to find. But I am inclined to think that a really good, promising writer will find someone to publish him nonetheless.

CA: Among the American writers whose early work you recognized and published were Saul Bellow and Gore Vidal. Have you maintained contact with them or with other American writers you published?

LEHMANN: Yes, I have maintained contact with American writers I published, and others. Two examples are Paul Bowles and Gore Vidal.

CA: Has regionalism been as much a factor in modern British fiction as it has in American?

LEHMANN: Britain is a very much smaller country than the United States, so regionalism is less evident. But I think that the Scots have become very conscious of their own tradition.

CA: As an editor, you were commended for encouraging your writers and coaxing work out of them. Were there any who were particularly hard to get work from or who needed unusual encouragement?

LEHMANN: They fell into two categories. First, those who were continually sending me their work without having their elbows jogged. And second, those I reminded that I would like more work of theirs.

CA: Reading some of your very lucid literary criticism, I wondered how you feel about the state of literary criticism today. Much of what I see that's being written in this country is narrow and obscure. How is it there?

LEHMANN: Literary criticism seems to be divided today between stuffy academic books and articles and rather vulgar popularizing ones. I miss the work of what Virginia (and Samuel Johnson) called the work to appeal to the Common Reader.

CA: You've described the decrease in British publication during World War II that was due in large part to the paper shortage, and the resulting "book hunger" among the reading public. Did any particular genre suffer disproportionately from the cut?

LEHMANN: Almost anything that was any good at all got published during the war, but the editions were often smaller and took a long time to come out.

CA: What are your major concerns for book and magazine publishing in England in the near future? How do you think the situation there compares with that here?

LEHMANN: My major concern is that books should get better. I think that both American and English publishers are in a bad way. The curious thing is that there are still a lot of small presses, particularly for poetry.

CA: Do you see new trends developing in British writing?

LEHMANN: Nothing to write home about; the novel is still very flourishing. Poetry, in my opinion, is in a very bad way, though there are outstanding exceptions. I think poetry has been influenced quite a lot by being spoken on the radio, which has on the whole made it less obscure.

CA: Did you encounter special problems of research, or other unusual problems, in writing the biographies and memoirs of the Woolfs, the Sitwells, Rupert Brooke, Edward Lear?

LEHMANN: Awful problems, but I suppose there always were such problems. As so much of the original material is on your side of the Atlantic, journeys to New York, Austin, and to institutions there always seem to be necessary—much more than in the past.

CA: Did you find it harder to write your autobiographies than the other biographical books?

LEHMANN: If I had not kept diaries, writing my autobiography would have been much harder.

CA: Have you enjoyed the visiting professorships in the United States?

LEHMANN: I did enjoy some of my visiting professorships, particularly my most recent to Emory University in Atlanta. I liked the place, I liked my colleagues, and I liked the work I was given.

CA: Is there anything you haven't done that you'd like to do?

LEHMANN: Yes, write a great deal more poetry. Also, a final volume of autobiography.

CA: What would you most like to be remembered for?

LEHMANN: I cannot answer for posterity, but I hope my work as a literary editor will not be forgotten.

BIOGRAPHICAL/CRITICAL SOURCES: *Times Literary Supplement,* July 10, 1937, September 30, 1955, February 12, 1960, September 12, 1980, January 29, 1982; *Manchester Guardian,* August 13, 1937, September 27, 1955; *Nation,* January 29, 1938, December 24, 1955; *Time,* July 5, 1948; *New York Times,* July 18, 1948, June 2, 1969, October 8, 1979, January 24, 1981, April 19, 1982; *San Francisco Chronicle,* November 7, 1948, September 13, 1953.

New York Times Book Review, April 26, 1953, March 20, 1960, September 22, 1968, July 27, 1969, April 11, 1976, November 4, 1979; *New Republic,* May 25, 1953, November 21, 1955, July 12, 1969, November 3, 1979; *New Statesman,* October 1, 1955, February 13, 1960, May 31, 1968; *Spectator,* October 7, 1955, February 12, 1960, September 13, 1975, December 9, 1978, September 12, 1981; *Saturday Review,* October 29, 1955, March 26, 1960, July 12, 1969; *Commonweal,* April 15, 1960; *Christian Science Monitor,* April 28, 1960, August 26, 1969; *Punch,* June 5, 1968; *Book World,* September 22, 1968, July 20, 1969, January 25, 1981.

Choice, March, 1970; *New Yorker,* March 29, 1976; *Atlantic,* May, 1976, February, 1981; *New York Review of Books,* July 15, 1976, September 24, 1981; *Economist,* October 21, 1978; *Books and Bookmen,* February, 1979; *Los Angeles Times,* March 17, 1981; *New Leader,* April 20, 1981; *National Review,* June 12, 1981; *Observer,* September 12, 1981; *Times Educational Supplement,* October 23, 1981.

—Sketch by Stewart R. Hakola
—Interview by Jean W. Ross

* * *

LEHMANN, Rosamond (Nina) 1901-

PERSONAL: Born February 3, 1901, in Bourne End, Buckinghamshire, England; daughter of Rudolph Chambers (a writer, editor of *Punch,* and member of Parliament) and Alice Marie (Davis) Lehmann; married Leslie Ruciman (divorced); married Wogan Philipps, 1928 (divorced, 1942); children: Hugo, Sally (died, 1958). *Education:* Attended Girton College, Cambridge, 1919-22. *Home:* 70 Eaton Square, London S.W.1, England.

CAREER: Writer. Co-director of John Lehmann Ltd. (a publishing company), 1946-53. *Member:* International P.E.N. (former president of English Centre; former international vice-president), Society of Authors (former member of council). *Awards, honors:* Commandeur dans l'Ordre des Arts et Lettres, 1968.

WRITINGS—Novels: *Dusty Answer,* Holt, 1927, reprinted, Collins & World, 1978; *A Note in Music,* Holt, 1930; *Invitation to the Waltz,* Holt, 1932, reprinted, Harcourt, 1975; *The Weather in the Streets,* Reynal, 1936; *The Ballad and the Source,* Reynal, 1945, reprinted, Harcourt, 1975; *The Echoing Grove,* Harcourt, 1953, reprinted, 1980; *A Sea-Grape Tree*, Collins & World, 1976.

Other: *A Letter to a Sister*, Hogarth, 1931, Harcourt, 1932; *No More Music* (play; first produced in London at the Duke of York's Theatre, 1938), Collins, 1939; (editor with others) *Orion: A Miscellany 1-3*, three volumes, Nicholson & Watson, 1945-46; *The Gipsy's Baby and Other Stories*, Collins, 1946, Reynal, 1947, reprinted, Collins, 1972; (translator from the French) Jacques Lemarchand, *Genevieve*, Lehmann, 1947; (translator from the French) Jean Cocteau, *Children of the Game*, Harvill, 1955, published as *The Holy Terrors*, New Directions, 1957; (with W. Tudor Pole) *A Man Seen Afar*, Spearman, 1965; *The Swan in the Evening: Fragments of an Inner Life*, Harcourt, 1967; (with Pole) *Zeuge im Leben Jesu*, Origo-Verlag (Zurich), 1969; (with Cynthia Hill Sandys) *Letters from Our Daughters*, two volumes, College of Psychic Studies, 1972; (editor with Sandys) *The Awakening Letters*, Spearman, 1978; (author of foreword) Pole, *My Dear Alexias: Letters to Rosamond Lehmann*, edited by Elizabeth Gaythorpe, Spearman, 1979. Contributor to *New Writing*.

SIDELIGHTS: Rosamond Lehmann was categorized early in her career as a "woman's writer." Along with Virginia Woolf and Elizabeth Bowen, she is heralded as the creator of the modern "feminine" novel, a term which connotes, James Gindin writes in *Contemporary Literature*, "the delicate, the perceptive, the working of insight in a smaller area often missed by the blunter, clumsier, 'masculine' sensibility." Primarily a romantic novelist, Lehmann explores the inner lives of a wide range of restless heroines; hers is "a world of young girls and women—growing up, falling in love, regretting, growing older," Diana E. LeStourgeon says. In her study *Rosamond Lehmann*, LeStourgeon adds that "Lehmann's world is a feminine world, whether 'she' be a child of ten listening intently to stories of a life she has yet to know, or an aristocratic dowager defending her rigid standards against the assault of her son's mistress. She is usually of the upper middle class, but she may be of the aristocracy, or she may be a prostitute. Whoever she is, Rosamond Lehmann knows the secret of her heart as few novelists do."

In her first novel, *Dusty Answer*, "Lehmann described relationships that hitherto had been discussed behind closed doors," Hope Hale Davis observes in the *New Leader*. With the publication of this delicate treatment of adolescent lesbianism, Lehmann "won fame overnight," Davis notes. "Readers welcomed with great relief the breaking of the taboo, and accorded Lehmann the awe due a revolutionary. A curiously delicate, sensitive revolutionary she was." "*Dusty Answer* is an extraordinary first novel, for the unfailingly certain creation of the characters, for the insistence and courage of its record, and for the rich monotony of its emotional tone," Stark Young writes in the *New Republic*. "As it moves from its beginning to its end, you feel in it that sort of progression and unity that your life has. And you get a sense that every emotion, experience, desire, however beautiful, blessed, dangerous or condemned, is, at its birth, innocent, as a human being is; and you are thus able to see more simply its nature and destiny."

Dusty Answer and Lehmann's subsequent novels have been praised for the beautiful, lyric quality of their prose and for the richness of their psychological insight. "It is a joy to read her prose," Eleanor Carroll Chilton comments on *Dusty Answer* in the *Saturday Review of Literature*, "for she has the poet's gift of making a new experience of every familiar beauty, without in any way brushing off the bloom of its familiarity." In the *New York Times Book Review*, Harold Strauss remarks that Lehmann "has few peers in the craftsmanship of writing."

In his review of *The Weather in the Streets*, Strauss, although he labels the plot commonplace, expresses admiration for the novelist's "technical brilliance, the impeccable style, the sensitivity and the deep, almost intuitive knowledge of the thought-processes of women." Isabelle Mallet, reviewing *The Ballad and the Source* for the *New York Times Book Review*, finds that in her "exquisite prose" Lehmann "broods delicately and beautifully over the past, turning the gaze inward." Lehmann, Mallet adds, "uses her uncanny insight as a weapon—having learned through a flamboyant career to uncover in those around her the insecurities and fears which render them powerless before her perception."

Lehmann's drawing of the character Sybil Jardine in *The Ballad and the Source* has been acclaimed as "a masterpiece of actuality" by Mallet. "Diagnosed to the last quivering sensibility, she still retains her original feminine flavor," Mallet states. "The impact of her personality never ceases to haunt and disturb long after mere acquaintance has deepened into apprehension." Lehmann's portrayal of the domineering Mrs. Jardine is "full of the psychological undertones we associate with the novels of [Henry] James," Hamilton Basso contends in the *New Yorker*. "Lehmann is an extremely skillful writer, with an acute insight into human behavior, and she makes all her characters real," Basso states. LeStourgeon calls Jardine "one of the most fascinatingly complex characters imaginable. . . . Without doubt this portrait is Miss Lehmann's masterpiece. Mrs. Jardine's very ambiguity insures her hold on the reader's imagination; for, when the book is finished and laid aside, she refuses to loosen her grip on the reader. Part of her power stems not merely from the complexity but from the elusiveness of her character—from her refusal to be pinned down to any simple interpretation. . . . She is of course vicious, egotistical, disagreeable; but she also possesses those qualities that make [other characters] love her. . . . It is possible both to admire her and to be horrified by her, even to pity her."

LeStourgeon believes that Lehmann's novels are marred by two major weaknesses: "The disillusionment implied in *nostalgia for lost youth* is her principle theme . . . [and] is indicative of one of Miss Lehmann's limitations. Disillusionment is, of course, a legitimate theme—perhaps it is *the* theme of the Age of Anxiety—but to use it time and time again, without comment and without *thought*, is to reveal a narrow view of human life. . . . A second limitation is in the range of her characterization. She seems unable to create a fully realized, three-dimensional male character. All of her protagonists are women. . . . The men who are there exist in the shadows." Richard Watts, reviewing *The Ballad and the Source* for *New Republic*, finds that "the men who appear in it are comparatively dim as contrasted with the vivid yet mysterious women who play its central roles." And Gindin comments, "Critics have always praised Miss Lehmann's prose, its clarity, its sensitivity, its 'beauty,' sometimes as a kind of minor compensation for the major limitations of her femininity and disillusionment."

"Much has been said about the limitations of Miss Lehmann's art," LeStourgeon says, "but, in the final analysis, it is fairer to judge her not by what she fails to do, but by what she succeeds in doing. Equipped with an understanding of family life and of social classes, and gifted with a beautiful prose style and an extraordinary insight into the thought processes of children and women, she has created out of her vision . . . novels [which attest] to the mark of the superior craftsman."

In *The Swan in the Evening*, Lehmann recounts her mystical experiences following the death of her only daughter. "It is an attempt to put into words a series of experiences which are ineffable," a *Times Literary Supplement* reviewer notes. The reviewer believes that "the mystical experience is incapable of being transmitted even by as fine a writer as Miss Lehmann.... [But *The Swan in the Evening*] is a courageous book, the more moving because the author was clearly reluctant to communicate to others what to herself was wonderful." In the *Washington Post Book World*, Jean Stafford writes: "She presents her case so gracefully, so unaggressively, with so fine a care to maintain her humor and her level head, that one feels rude in refusing her refreshments of nectar and ambrosia.... Nevertheless one feels oneself withdrawing, flushed, stammering an apology as if, in a house one had thought well-known, one had by accident opened the door to an altogether strange room and had confronted a scene that was none of one's business." Echoing Stafford's sentiments, V. S. Pritchett declares in *New Statesman* that "*The Swan in the Evening* embarrasses because it puts the reader into the position of being an intruder on a terrible private grief.... One is left tantalised, respectful but at a loss." D. C. Goddard in the *New York Times Book Review* finds the book "is witness to Miss Lehmann's reconciliation to a life in which death is implicit and which is thereby, paradoxically, enriched." Goddard maintains that "no one of any sensitivity is likely to remain unmoved, for there are few authors living who write more beautifully than Miss Lehmann."

In 1976, Lehmann published *A Sea-Grape Tree*, her first novel in twenty years. "She has been silent for too long, and her descriptive prose is more powerful than ever, her characters as enigmatic, as convincing," Margaret Drabble writes in the *Listener*. Drabble believes that after the mysticism of *The Swan in the Evening*, "it is fitting that *A Sea-Grape Tree* should present us with a timeless world, where past and present mingle strangely, in a place far removed from the vivid, fraught, emotional decor of her earlier works. The book has a strange, haunted quality." Writing in the *Spectator*, Nick Totton comments: "*A Sea-Grape Tree* is written in a high style which few writers now dare attempt; it describes a dream-reality where intuition and inspiration are the chief sources of knowledge—a world which, we slowly come to feel, is one that we inexplicably inhabit all the time, amphibians of the public and the subliminal. Rosamond Lehmann's honesty in showing us the dream world is preceded by an internal honesty, a clarity in grasping her own perceptions." Virginia Llewellyn Smith of the *Times Literary Supplement*, surveying the recent reprints of Lehmann's novels, welcomes "this renewal of interest" but asserts that "there is too much dream and not enough reality" in *A Sea-Grape Tree*. And Drabble concludes: "Lehmann has always written brilliantly of women in love, of mothers and daughters, of suffering. This novel seems to point to some hope of harmony, although many of its images are desolate.... One can only hope that Miss Lehmann will go on from this, into a world less ethereal, less removed: she must write more novels, for this is too full of life to be a swan song."

Miss Lehmann's manuscripts are collected at the University of Texas at Austin.

BIOGRAPHICAL/CRITICAL SOURCES—Books: Henry Reed, *The Novel since 1939*, Longmans, Green, 1946; Stephen Spender, *World within World*, Harcourt, 1948; R. A. Scott-James, *Fifty Years of English Literature: 1900-1950*, Longmans, Green, 1951, 2nd edition, 1956; Mark Longaker and Edwin C. Bolles, *Contemporary English Literature*, Appleton-Century-Crofts, 1953; John Lehmann, *The Whispering Gallery: Autobiography I*, Longmans, Green, 1955; J. Lehmann, editor, *The Craft of Letters in England: A Symposium*, Cresset, 1956, Houghton, 1957, reprinted, Greenwood Press, 1974; J. Lehmann, *I Am My Brother: Autobiography II*, Reynal, 1960; Diana E. LeStourgeon, *Rosamond Lehmann*, Twayne, 1965; J. Lehmann, *The Ample Proposition: Autobiography III*, Eyre & Spottiswoode, 1966; *Contemporary Literary Criticism*, Volume V, Gale, 1976.

Periodicals: *New York Times Book Review*, September 4, 1927, October 30, 1932, May 17, 1936, April 1, 1945, January 19, 1947, May 10, 1953, July 14, 1968, October 9, 1977; *Saturday Review of Literature*, September 10, 1927, November 5, 1932, March 31, 1945; *New Republic*, September 28, 1927, April 9, 1945, May 11, 1953; *Outlook*, December 7, 1927; *Nation*, June 3, 1936, April 14, 1945, January 19, 1947; *New Yorker*, April 7, 1945; *Commonweal*, May 4, 1945; *Times Literary Supplement*, April 20, 1946, April 17, 1953, November 2, 1967, August 28, 1981; *New York Herald Tribune Weekly Book Review*, January 19, 1947.

Saturday Review, May 16, 1953, June 1, 1968; *New Statesman*, December 22, 1967; *Washington Post Book World*, April 21, 1968; *Books and Bookmen*, April, 1973; *Contemporary Literature*, spring, 1974; *Listener*, November 4, 1976; *Spectator*, November 13, 1976, June 6, 1981; *New Leader*, November 7, 1977; *Virginia Quarterly Review*, winter, 1978; *Carleton Miscellany*, winter, 1980; *British Book News*, June, 1981; *Observer*, July 19, 1981; *Village Voice Literary Supplement*, December, 1981.

—Sketch by Stewart R. Hakola

* * *

LEIBOWITZ, Herschel W. 1925-

PERSONAL: Born February 21, 1925, in York, Pa.; son of Lewis (a salesman) and Nettie (Wolfson) Leibowitz; married Eileen Wirtshafter, June 12, 1949; children: Marjorie, Michael. *Education:* Attended University of Paris, 1945-46; University of Pennsylvania, B.A., 1948; Columbia University, M.A., 1950, Ph.D., 1951. *Religion:* Jewish. *Home:* 160 Sandy Ridge Rd., State College, Pa. 16801. *Office:* Department of Psychology, Pennsylvania State University, University Park, Pa. 16802.

CAREER: University of Wisconsin—Madison, 1951-61, began as instructor in psychology, professor, 1960-61, research associate, School of Medicine, 1953-56; Pennsylvania State University, University Park, professor of psychology, 1962—, Evan Pugh Professor, 1977—. Visiting lecturer at University of Maryland, 1960-62; visiting summer professor at University of Michigan, 1962, Massachusetts Institute of Technology, 1963, Florida State University, 1972; visiting scientist in Japan, 1965; visiting professor at University of Florida, 1977; visiting scholar at University of California, Berkeley, 1981-82. Advisory psychologist, International Business Machines Corp., 1960-62. Consultant to Veterans Administration, 1959—, Institute for Defense Analysis, 1964-80, U.S. Department of the Interior, 1965-67, U.S. Department of Defense, 1967—, and Institute of Environmental Medicine, 1970-75. Member of psychobiology review panel, National Science Foundation, 1962-65; member of National Academy of Sciences-National Research Council Armed Forces Vision Committee, 1963—; member of experimental psychology study section, National Institutes of Health, 1970-74. Member of advisory board, Applied Research Laboratory, 1973-76. *Military service:* U.S. Army, 1943-46; served in Europe with 75th Infantry Division.

MEMBER: American Psychological Association (fellow), American Association for the Advancement of Science (fellow), National Science Foundation (member of sensory physiology and perception panel, 1979-82), American Academy of

Optometry (fellow), Optical Society of America (fellow), Human Factors Society (fellow), Psychonomic Society. *Awards, honors:* Guggenheim fellowship, 1957; Heineman stipend, 1967.

WRITINGS: (Contributor) M. Marx, *Some Trends in Perceptual Theory*, 2nd edition, Macmillan, 1963; *Visual Perception*, Macmillan, 1965; (co-editor) *Psychology: From Research to Practice*, Plenum, 1978; (co-editor) *Handbook of Sensory Physiology*, Volume VIII (Leibowitz was not associated with earlier volumes), Springer Publishing Co., 1978; (co-editor and contributor) *Perception of Space and Motion*, Psychological Society, 1979; (co-editor and contributor) *Tutorials in Motion Perception*, Plenum, 1982; (contributor) *Organizations and Representation in Perception*, Erlbaum, 1982; (contributor) *Basic and Clinical Aspects of Binocular Vergence Eye Movements*, Butterworths, 1982.

Contributor of over 140 articles to professional journals. Member of editorial advisory board, *International Journal of Vision Research*, 1959-64, and 1970-79, *Psychologische Forschung*, 1965—, and *Perception and Psychophysics*, 1969—; consulting editor, *Journal of Experimental Psychology*, 1960-74, *Psychological Bulletin*, 1964-68, *Behavioral Research and Instrumentation*, 1970—, and *Contemporary Psychology*, 1973-79.

* * *

LERNER, Robert E. 1940-

PERSONAL: Born February 8, 1940, in New York, N.Y.; son of Oscar (a pharmacist) and Helene (Heyman) Lerner; married Erdmut Krumnack, October 25, 1963; children: Dietlind, Olivia. *Education:* University of Chicago, A.B., 1960; Princeton University, M.A., 1962, Ph.D., 1964. *Politics:* Independent. *Office:* Department of History, Northwestern University, Evanston, Ill. 60201.

CAREER: Princeton University, Princeton, N.J., instructor in history, 1963-64; Western Reserve University (now Case Western Reserve University), Cleveland, Ohio, assistant professor of history, 1964-67; Northwestern University, Evanston, Ill., assistant professor, 1967-71, associate professor 1971-76, professor of history, 1976—, director of Humanities Program, 1981—. *Member:* American Historical Association, Mediaeval Academy of America. *Awards, honors:* Woodrow Wilson fellow, 1960-61; Germanistic Society of America fellow, 1962-63; Fulbright research fellow, 1967-68; National Endowment for the Humanities research fellow, 1972-73; American Council of Learned Societies fellow, 1979-80.

WRITINGS: The Age of Adversity: The Fourteenth Century, Cornell University Press, 1968; *The Heresy of the Free Spirit*, University of California Press, 1972; (contributor) R.L. DeMolen, editor, *One Thousand Years: Western Europe in the Middle Ages*, Houghton, 1974; (with E.M. Burns and S. Meacham) *Western Civilizations*, 9th edition, Norton, 1980; (with Burns, Meacham, and P. Ralph) *World Civilizations*, 6th edition, Norton, 1982; *The Powers of Prophecy*, University of California Press, 1983. Advisory editor, *Dictionary of the Middle Ages*, 1976—. Contributor to periodicals, including *American Historical Review, Analecta Cisterciensia, Archiv fuer Kulturgeschichte, Catholic Historical Review, Church History, Deutsches Archiv, Dictionnaire d'histoire et de geographie ecclesiastiques, French Historical Studies, The Historian, Mediaeval Studies, Medievalia et Humanistica, Modern Philology, Past and Present, The Social Studies, Speculum, Theologische Realenzykopaedie,* and *Traditio*.

WORK IN PROGRESS: Approaches to understanding medieval mentalities.

SIDELIGHTS: Robert Lerner told *CA* that he studies and writes history because he gets "a kick out of it" and remains "slightly amazed" that he can make his main hobby his living. Lerner reads Latin, German, French, Italian, Dutch, and Catalan. *Avocational interests:* Music, "European culture, gardening—attempts to grow kohlrabi and melons against nearly insuperable odds."

* * *

LESKO, Leonard Henry 1938-

PERSONAL: Born August 14, 1938, in Chicago, Ill.; son of Matthew E. (a pharmacist) and Josephine Lesko; married Barbara Switalski (an Egyptologist and bibliographer), December 29, 1966. *Education:* Loyola University, Chicago, Ill., B.A., 1961, M.A., 1964; University of Chicago, Ph.D., 1969. *Office:* Department of Egyptology, Brown University, Providence, R.I. 02912.

CAREER: Teacher of Latin and Greek at a preparatory seminary in Chicago, Ill., 1961-64; University of Chicago, Epigraphic Survey of Oriental Institute, Luxor, Egypt, Egyptologist epigrapher, 1964-65; University of California, Berkeley, acting instructor, 1966-67, acting assistant professor, 1967-68, assistant professor, 1968-72, associate professor, 1972-77, professor of Egyptology, 1977-82, director of Center for Near Eastern Studies, 1973-75, chairman of department of Near Eastern studies 1975-77, 1979-81; Brown University, Providence, R.I., Charles Edwin Wilbour Professor of Egyptology and chairman of department, 1982—.

MEMBER: International Association of Egyptologists, American Research Center in Egypt (member of board of governors), American Oriental Society, Egypt Exploration Society, Foundation Egyptologique Reine Elisabeth, Explorers Club. *Awards, honors:* National Endowment for the Humanities, Younger Humanist fellowship, 1970-71; grant for a late Egyptian dictionary, 1975-79; American Council of Learned Societies grant, 1973-74, for computer-oriented research in the humanities.

WRITINGS: (Contributor with Charles F. Nims, George R. Hughes and others) *Medinet Habu VIII: The Eastern High Gate*, University of Chicago Press, 1970; *The Ancient Egyptian Book of Two Ways*, University of California Press, 1972; *Glossary of the Late Ramesside Letters*, privately printed, 1975; *King Tut's Wine Cellar*, B. C. Scribe Publications, 1977; *Index of the Spells on Egyptian Middle Kingdom Coffins and Related Documents*, B. C. Scribe Publications, 1979; (contributor) *The Tomb of Khernef*, University of Chicago Press, 1980; *Dictionary of Late Egyptian*, Volume I, B. C. Scribe Publications, 1982. Contributor to *Encyclopedia Americana* and *World Book Encyclopedia*. Contributor to professional journals.

SIDELIGHTS: Lesko writes: "My main interest is in ancient Egyptian religious literature. To some extent this means that I must translate and try to explain what the religious texts actually have to say, but I am particularly interested in trying to discover how and why these texts developed into the set forms in which we find them."

* * *

LESTER, Julius B. 1939-

PERSONAL: Born January 27, 1939, in St. Louis, Mo.; son of W. D. (a minister) and Julia (Smith) Lester; married Joan Steinau (a researcher), 1962 (divorced, 1970); married Alida Carolyn Fechner, March 21, 1979; children: (first marriage) Jody Simone, Malcolm Coltrane; (second marriage) Elena Milad (stepdaughter), David Julius. *Education:* Fisk University,

B.A., 1960. *Office:* University of Massachusetts, Amherst, Mass. 01002.

CAREER: Professional musician and singer, recorded with Vanguard Records; Newport Folk Festival, Newport, R.I., director, 1966-68; WBAI-FM, New York City, producer and host of live radio show, 1968-75; University of Massachusetts—Amherst, professor of Afro-American studies, 1971—. Lecturer at New School for Social Research, New York City, 1968-70; host of live television show, "Free Time," WNET-TV, New York City, 1971-73. *Awards, honors:* To Be a Slave was nominated for the Newberry Award; The Long Journey Home was named a National Book Award honor book.

WRITINGS: (With Pete Seeger) *The 12-String Guitar as Played by Leadbelly,* Oak, 1965; *Look Out Whitey! Black Power's Gon' Get Your Mama!,* Dial, 1968; *To Be a Slave,* Dial, 1969; *Black Folktales,* Baron, 1969; *Search for the New Land: History as Subjective Experience,* Dial, 1969; *Revolutionary Notes,* Baron, 1969; (editor) *The Seventh Son: The Thoughts and Writings of W.E.B. Du Bois,* two volumes, Random House, 1971; (compiler with Rae Pace Alexander) *Young and Black in America,* Random House, 1971; *The Long Journey Home: Stories from Black History,* Dial, 1972; *The Knee High Man and Other Tales,* Dial, 1972; *Two Love Stories,* Dial, 1972; (editor) Stanley Couch, *Ain't No Ambulances for No Nigguhs Tonight* (poems), Baron, 1972; *Who I Am* (poems), Dial, 1974; *All Is Well: An Autobiography,* Morrow, 1976; *This Strange New Feeling,* Dial, 1982.

Contributor of essays and reviews to numerous magazines and newspapers, including *New York Times Book Review, New York Times, Nation, Katallagete, Democracy,* and *Village Voice.* Associate editor, *Sing Out,* 1964—; contributing editor, *Broadside of New York,* 1964—.

SIDELIGHTS: Julius B. Lester is "foremost among young black writers who produce their work from a position of historical strength," according to critic John A. Williams writing in the *New York Times Book Review.* Drawing on old documents or folk tales, Lester fashions stories that proclaim the heritage of black Americans and, in the words of *New York Review of Books* critics Eric and Naomi Foner, "attempt to recreate the social life of the past." While historically accurate, Lester's tales are more than simple reportage. Their purpose, as the Foners point out, is "not merely to impart historical information, but to teach moral and political lessons." Because he feels that the history of minority groups has been largely ignored, Lester intends to furnish his young readers with what he calls "a usable past," and with what the Foners call "a sense of history which will help shape their lives and politics."

Lester's characters fall into two categories: those drawn from Afro-American folklore and those drawn from black history. The former are imaginary creatures, or sometimes animals, such as *The Knee-High Man*'s Mr. Bear and Mr. Rabbit; the latter are real people, "ordinary men and women who might appear only in . . . a neglected manuscript at the Library of Congress," according to William Loren Katz in *Washington Post Book World.* Critics find that Lester uses both types of characters to reveal the black man's struggle against slavery.

Black Folktales, Lester's first collection of folk stories, features larger-than-life heroes (including a cigar-smoking black God), shrewd animals, and cunning human beings. While some of the characters are taken from African legends and others from American slave tales, they all demonstrate that "black resistance to white oppression is as old as the confrontation between the two groups," Williams says. Most reviewers applaud Lester's view of Afro-American folklore and praise his storytelling skills, but a few object to what they perceive as the anti-white tone of the book. Zena Sutherland, writing in *Bulletin of the Center for Children's Books,* calls *Black Folktales* "a vehicle for hostility. . . . There is no story that concerns white people in which they are not pictured as venal or stupid or both."

Lester also deals with white oppression in his second collection of folktales, *The Knee-High Man.* Although these six animal stories are funny, *New York Times Book Review* critic Ethel Richards suggests that "powerfully important lessons ride the humor. In 'The Farmer and the Snake,' the lesson is that kindness will not change the nature of a thing—in this case, the nature of a poisonous snake to bite." A *Junior Bookshelf* reviewer points out that this story—as well as others in the book—reflects the relationship between owner and slave.

While pursuing the same theme, Lester moves into the realm of nonfiction with *The Long Journey Home,* a documentary collection of slave narratives, and *To Be A Slave,* a collection of six stories based on historical fact. Both books showcase ordinary people in adverse circumstances and provide the reader with a look at what Lester calls "history from the bottom up." *Black Like Me* author John Howard Griffin, writing in the *New York Times Book Review,* commends Lester's approach, saying that the stories "help destroy the delusion that black men did not suffer as another man would in similar circumstances," while the Foners applaud the fact that "Lester does not feel it is necessary to make every black man and woman a superhero." Writing in the *New York Times Book Review,* Rosalind K. Goddard recommends Lester's writing as both lesson and entertainment. "These stories point the way for young blacks to find their roots, so important to the realization of their identities, as well as offer a stimulating and informative experience for all."

BIOGRAPHICAL/CRITICAL SOURCES: New York Times Book Review, November 3, 1968, November 9, 1969, July 23, 1972, February 4, 1973, September 5, 1982; *Bulletin of the Center for Children's Books,* February, 1970; *Nation,* June 22, 1970; *New York Review of Books,* April 20, 1972; *Washington Post Book World,* September 3, 1972; Seymour Krim, *You and Me,* Holt, 1972; *Junior Bookshelf,* February, 1975; *Children's Literature Review,* Volume II, Gale, 1976; Julius B. Lester, *All is Well: An Autobiography,* Morrow, 1976.

* * *

LEVI, Lennart 1930-

PERSONAL: Born May 20, 1930, in Riga, Latvia; son of Sam (a merchant) and Debora (Lowenstein) Levi; married Isabella Weitman, August 16, 1957; children: Jan Richard, Georg Ragnar. *Education:* Karolinska Institute, M.D., 1959, Ph.D., 1972. *Home:* Solangsvagen 35, S-19154 Sollentuna, Sweden. *Office:* Laboratory for Clinical Stress Research, Box 60205, S-10401 Stockholm, Sweden.

CAREER: State Rehabilitation Clinic, Stockholm, Sweden, physician, 1956-58; Karolinska Hospital, Stockholm, research physician in departments of medicine and psychiatry, 1959-63, director of Laboratory for Clinical Stress Research and World Health Organization Psychosocial Centre, 1959—. Part-time industrial physician, Swedish AEG Concern. Director of National Institute for Psychosocial Factors and Health, 1980—. *Military service:* Swedish Army, surgeon, 1965—. *Member:* International Society of Psychoneuroendocrinology, International College of Psychosomatic Medicine, Swedish Medical Association, American Psychosomatic Society, Society for Psychophysiological Research.

WRITINGS: *Stress-Korper, Seele und Krankheit*, Musterschmidt-Verlag, 1964, translation published as *Stress: Sources, Management and Prevention*, Liveright, 1967; *Fran sjuksang till arbetsbank* (title means "From Sick-bed to Work-Table"), Swedish Personnel Administration Council, 1966; (editor) *Emotional Stress: Physiological and Psychological: Reactions—Medical, Industrial, and Military Implications*, American Elsevier, 1967; (with Kurt Bronner) *The Stress of Everyday Work*, Personnel Administration Council, 1967; *Psycho-Physiological Reactions During Emotional Stress*, American Elsevier, 1967.

(Editor) *Society, Stress and Disease*, Oxford University Press, Volume I: *The Psychosocial Environment and Psychosomatic Diseases*, 1971, Volume II: *Childhood and Adolescence*, 1975, Volume III: *Male/Female Roles and Relationships*, 1978, Volume IV: *Working Life*, 1981; *Stress and Disease in Response to Psychosocial Stimuli*, Pergamon, 1972; (with Lars Andersson) *Psychosocial Stress: Population, Environment, and Quality of Life*, Spectrum, 1975; (editor) *Emotions: Their Parameters and Measurement*, Raven Press, 1975; *Preventing Work Stress*, Addison-Wesley, 1981.

Contributor: W. Raab, editor, *Preventive Cardiology*, C. C Thomas, 1966; E. Bajusz, editor, *An Introduction to Clinical Neuro-endocrinology*, S. Karger, 1967; D. A. Hamburg and others, editors, *Healthy People*, U.S. Department of Health, Education and Welfare, 1979; Glen R. Elliott and Carl Eisdorfer, editors, *Stress and Human Health*, Springer Publishing Co., 1982. Contributor of research papers to medical journals in United States and Sweden.

* * *

LEVIN, David 1924-

PERSONAL: Born November 21, 1924, in York, Pa.; son of Louis and Rose (Braufman) Levin; married Patricia Marker, 1945; children: David, Jr., Rebecca. *Education:* Harvard University, A.B., 1947, A.M., 1949, Ph.D., 1955. *Office:* Department of English, University of Virginia, Charlottesville, Va. 22903.

CAREER: Stanford University, Stanford, Calif., instructor, 1952-55, assistant professor, 1955-59, associate professor, 1959-64, professor of English, 1964-71; University of Virginia, Charlottesville, Commonwealth Professor of English, 1971—, member of Center for Advanced Studies, 1971—. Fulbright lecturer in France, 1956-57. Fellow, Center for Advanced Study in Behavioral Sciences, 1962-63, 1980-81; Charles Warren Center fellow, Harvard University, 1976-77. *Military service:* U.S. Army Air Forces, navigator, 1943-46; became second lieutenant. *Member:* Modern Language Association of America, American Studies Association, American Association of University Professors, American Civil Liberties Union, National Association for the Advancement of Colored People. *Awards, honors:* National Endowment for Humanities Senior fellow, 1968-69; Virginia College Stores Award, 1979, for *Cotton Mather*.

WRITINGS: History as Romantic Art, Stanford University Press, 1959.

What Happened in Salem?, Harcourt, 1960; (editor) *The Puritan in the Enlightenment: Franklin and Edwards*, Rand McNally, 1963; *In Defense of Historical Literature*, Hill & Wang, 1967; (editor and author of introduction) Cotton Mather, *Bonifacius: An Essay upon the Good*, Harvard University Press, 1967; (editor) *Jonathan Edwards: A Profile*, Hill & Wang, 1969.

Cotton Mather: The Young Life of the Lord's Remembrancer, 1663-1703, Harvard University Press, 1978; (editor) *America in Literature*, Volume I, Wiley, 1978.

(Editor) Frances Parkman, *The Oregon Trail*, Viking, 1982; (editor) Parkman, *France and England in North America*, two volumes, Library of America, 1983. General editor, "Harbrace Sourcebooks," twenty volumes, 1961-71.

WORK IN PROGRESS; Two books, *Hawthorne and Faulkner* and *Exemplary Elders: Memoirs and Stories*.

* * *

LEVY, Sue 1936-

PERSONAL: Born December 20, 1936, in Washington, D.C.; daughter of Julius (a U.S. Air Force officer) and Amy (Behrend) Goldstein; married Mayer Levy (a dentist), August 30, 1959 (divorced March 11, 1975); children: Lon, Guy. *Education:* American University, B.A., 1959. *Politics:* Independent. *Religion:* Animist.

CAREER: Has worked in public relations. Levy adds that she has "done some deadly PR work for the Jewish Funeral Directors of America."

WRITINGS: The Daisy Book (poetry, prose, and illustrations), Acropolis Books, 1975; *From Every Pile of Shit That Falls My Way I Shall Make a Daisy Grow (New Life)*, Acropolis Books, 1975; *Susu's Daisy*, Ermine, 1975; *Daughter of Daisy*, Ermine, 1976.

WORK IN PROGRESS: "I write every day about me, my environment and the absurd—which may all be synonymous."

SIDELIGHTS: Sue Levy writes that *The Daisy Book* describes how she "went from Dependent Wife to Independent Person. Included are divorce, leaving my boys (whom I still see) with their father, living alone (for the first time), getting jobs (without a resume), overcoming credit discrimination, learning how to have fun (also first time)." Her book, she continues, "was originally designed as a poster, but ended up being a book jacket with the book written to go with it. . . . *The Daisy Book* seems to be something for everyone—a lovely bonus—because I had only intended it to be everything to me. I am most proud of the foreword that my children asked to write. . . ."

AVOCATIONAL INTERESTS: Dancing, "analyzing rocks and bringing them to life with a few lines of a black marker."

* * *

LEYHART, Edward
See EDWARDS, Elwyn Hartley

* * *

LIBERTY, Gene 1924-

PERSONAL: Born June 3, 1924, in Bronx, N.Y.; son of Charles and Lillian (Glaser) Liberty. *Education:* Polytechnic Institute of Brooklyn, B.S., 1950. *Politics:* Independent. *Religion:* Jewish. *Home:* 500 Kappock St., Bronx, N.Y. 10463.

CAREER: Writer. *Military service:* U.S. Army, World War II; served in Pacific; became sergeant. *Member:* Authors Guild, Authors League of America.

WRITINGS: First Book of Tools, F. Watts, 1960; *First Book of the Human Senses*, F. Watts, 1961; *Time: Seconds and Centuries*, Grosset, 1963; *The How and Why Wonder Book of Time*, Grosset, 1963; *Cycles of Nature*, Creative Education,

1968; (editor) Robert J. Lowenherz, *Population,* Creative Education, 1970; (editor) Joseph Alvarez, *Politics in America,* Creative Education, 1971; (editor) Joel Lugunn, *Motion,* Creative Education, 1971; (editor) Daniel Cohen, *Superstitions,* Creative Education, 1971; *The Continuation of Life,* AMSCO School Publications, 1975; *The Meaning of Life,* AMSCO School Publications, 1975; *The Support of Life,* AMSCO School Publications, 1975. Author of documenary film scripts and of many nonfiction articles, particularly in the field of science.

* * *

LIEBERMAN, Laurence 1935-

PERSONAL: Born February 16, 1935, in Detroit, Mich.; son of Nathan (a businessman) and Anita (Cohen) Lieberman; married Bernice Braun (an editor), June 16, 1956; children: Carla, Deborah, Isaac. *Education:* University of Michigan, B.A., 1956, M.A., 1958; University of California, Berkeley, graduate study, 1958-60. *Home:* 1304 Eliot, Urbana, Ill. 61801. *Office:* Department of English, University of Illinois at Urbana-Champaign, Urbana, Ill. 61801.

CAREER: Orange Coast College, Costa Mesa, Calif., instructor, 1960-64; College of the Virgin Islands, St. Thomas, assistant professor, 1964-66, associate professor of English, 1966-68; University of Illinois at Urbana-Champaign, associate professor, 1968-70, professor of English and creative writing, 1970—, editor of Poetry Books Program for university press, 1970—. *Awards, honors:* University of Michigan Hopwood Award in Poetry, 1958; Yaddo fellowship, 1963 and 1967; Huntington Hartford Foundation fellowship, 1964; National Endowment for Arts award, 1969, for poem "Tarpon"; University of Illinois Center for Advanced Study grants to write poetry in Japan, 1971-72, and to write Caribbean poems, 1981-82; Illinois Arts Council Creative Writing fellowship, 1982-83.

WRITINGS: (Contributor) Nolan Miller and Judson Jerome, editors, *New Campus Writing No. 4,* Grove, 1962; (contributor) Paris Leary and Robert Kelly, editors, *A Controversy of Poets,* Doubleday, 1965; *The Unblinding* (poems), Macmillan, 1968; *The Achievement of James Dickey,* Scott, Foresman, 1969; *The Osprey Suicides* (poems), Macmillan, 1973; *Unassigned Frequencies: American Poetry in Review (1964-77)* (criticism), University of Illinois Press, 1977; *God's Measurements* (poems), Macmillan, 1980; *Eros at the World Kite Pageant: Poems (1979-82),* Macmillan, 1982. Poetry reviewer for *Yale Review,* 1971-75. Contributor of poetry and critical articles to journals, including *Antioch Review, Hudson Review, Paris Review, New Republic, Atlantic,* and *New Yorker.* Poetry editor and contributing editor, *Orange County Illustrated,* 1964-65.

SIDELIGHTS: The images found in *The Osprey Suicides* are "raw and vicious . . . and have to do with the cheapening of our spiritual values," according to H. Leslie Wolfe in a *Daily Illini* review. Wolfe sees *The Osprey Suicides,* and more particularly the title poem, as a metaphor of the American experience. "[Lieberman] outlines America's particular state of despair, its ill-planned land development, its air pollution, its people specialized in professionalism," says the critic. "The American," Wolfe continues, "is not a majestic eagle. . . . He is a plucky osprey who dares too much always, even to the point of self-destruction. The osprey and the American have been driven a bit mad."

Vernon Young, in *Hudson Review,* notes the same theme of struggle between self and an imperfect environment in Lieberman's poems but sees this struggle more as a conflict between the poet and his world than as an image relating to one national group. Young writes: "[Lieberman's] book . . . subscribes to a comprehensive metaphor, with consistent, undulating motifs: the creative struggle of the poet towards *communion,* undergoing seasons in hell, . . . scanning the ether, stalled in the halfway region of domestic hope and alienation."

BIOGRAPHICAL/CRITICAL SOURCES: Daily Illini, May 17, 1973; *Hudson Review,* winter, 1973-74; *Contemporary Literary Criticism,* Volume IV, Gale, 1975; *Yale Review,* spring, 1978; *Times Literary Supplement,* September 1, 1978.

* * *

LIEBERMAN, Myron 1919-

PERSONAL: Born April 30, 1919, in St. Paul, Minn.; married Mary Elizabeth Arthur (a physician); children: Lawrence, Loren, Warren Louis, Rachel Elizabeth. *Education:* University of Minnesota, B.S. in Laws, 1941, B.S. in education, 1948; University of Illinois, M.A., 1950, Ph.D., 1952. *Office:* City College of the City University of New York, New York, N.Y. 10036.

CAREER: U.S. War Department, Tokyo, Japan, research analyst, civil intelligence section, 1946-47; Humboldt High School, St. Paul, Minn., teacher, 1948-49; University of Illinois at Urbana-Champaign, teaching assistant and instructor, 1949-52; Emory University, Atlanta, Ga., visiting lecturer, 1952; University of Oklahoma, Norman, assistant professor of education, 1953-56; Yeshiva University, New York City, chairman of department of education, 1956-59; Educational Research Council of Greater Cleveland, Cleveland, Ohio, director of basic research, 1959-60; Rand McNally Co., Skokie, Ill., editorial consultant, 1961; Hofstra College, Hempstead, N.Y., visiting professor of education, 1962-63; Rhode Island College, Providence, professor, 1963-69; City College of the City University of New York, New York City, professor of education, 1969—, director of teacher leadership program, 1971-74. Professor of education, University of Hawaii, summer, 1967. Coordinator, National Institute on Collective Negotiations by Teachers, 1966. Negotiator or consultant for collective negotiations to various school boards, teachers organizations, and school board organizations. Educational consultant, NAACP Legal Defense and Educational Fund, New Rochelle, N.Y., and New York School System. Lecturer at many universities and educational societies. *Military service:* U.S. Army Air Forces, 1942-46, became staff sergeant; served in Hawaii, Australia, New Guinea, Biak, Philippine Islands, Okinawa, and Japan. *Member:* American Arbitration Association (member of panel of arbitrators), National Education Association, American Federation of Teachers.

WRITINGS: Education as a Profession, Prentice-Hall, 1956; *The Future of Public Education,* University of Chicago Press, 1960; (co-author) *Social Forces Influencing American Education,* National Society for the Study of Education, 1961; (co-author) *Language and Concepts in Education,* Rand McNally, 1961; (with Michael H. Moskow) *Collective Negotiations by Teachers,* Rand McNally, 1966; (compiler with Stanley Munson Elam) *Readings on Collective Negotiations in Public Education,* Rand McNally, 1967; (with Thomas H. Patten, Jr.) *When School Districts Bargain,* Public Personnel Association, 1968.

Educational Accountability, West Virginia—Kanawha Valley Graduate Center, 1971; *The Impact of the Taylor Act upon the Governance and Administration of Elementary and Secondary Education,* City College of the City University of New York, 1971; *Bargaining: Before, During, and After,* Teach'em, 1979.

Public-Sector Bargaining: A Policy of Reappraisal, Lexington Books, 1980. Also author of several monographs. Contributor of numerous articles and reviews to professional journals. Issue editor, *Progressive Education*, July, 1957.†

* * *

LIENTZ, Bennet Price 1942-

PERSONAL: Born October 24, 1942, in Hollywood, Calif.; son of Beverly Price and Josephine (Palen) Lientz; married Martha Benson, August 29, 1964; children: Bennet P., Jr., Andrew Noll, Charles Sumner. *Education:* Claremont Men's College, B.A., 1964; University of Washington, Seattle, M.S., 1966, Ph.D., 1968. *Religion:* Presbyterian. *Home:* 229 21st Pl., Santa Monica, Calif. 90402. *Office:* Graduate School of Management, University of California, Los Angeles, Calif. 90024.

CAREER: System Development Corp., Santa Monica, Calif., department head and senior research scientist, 1968-70; University of Southern California, Los Angeles, assistant professor, 1970-73, associate professor of engineering, 1973-74; University of California, Los Angeles, professor of management and vice-chairman of department, 1974—, director of Office of Information Systems, 1977-80. Consultant to Atlantic Richfield, 1974—, U.S. Dept. of Navy, 1977—, and Security Pacific Bank, 1978—. *Member:* Institute of Management Science, Operations Research Society of America, American Statistical Association, Institute of Mathematical Statistics. *Awards, honors:* National Science Foundation research travel grant, 1972.

WRITINGS: *Computer Applications in Operations Analysis*, Prentice-Hall, 1975; *Systems in Action*, Goodyear Publishing, 1978; *Software Maintenance Management*, Addison-Wesley, 1980; *Distributed Systems*, Addison-Wesley, 1981. Contributor to journals in his field.

WORK IN PROGRESS: A study of computer networks, experiments, and economic trade-offs; research in computer security and system development procedures.

* * *

LIFSHIN, Lyn (Diane) 1944-

PERSONAL: Born in Burlington, Vt., July 12, 1944; daughter of Ben and Frieda (Lazarus) Lipman; married Eric Lifshin, 1963. *Education:* Syracuse University, B.A., 1960; University of Vermont, M.A., 1963. *Home:* 2142 Appletree Lane, Niskayuna, N.Y. 12309.

CAREER: Poet. State University of New York at Albany, teaching fellow, 1964-66; educational television writer, Schenectady, N.Y., 1966; State University of New York, Cobleskill, instructor, 1968, and 1970; New York State Mental Health Department, Albany, writing consultant, 1969; writing consultant, Empire State College of the State University of New York, 1973; Mansfield State College, Mansfield, Pa., poet-in-residence, 1974. *Awards, honors:* Hart Crane Award; Bread Loaf scholarship; Harcourt Brace poetry fellowship; Boulder poetry award; Millay fellowship; San Jose poetry award; Yaddo fellowship, 1970, 1971; MacDowell fellowship, 1973; New York Creative Artists Public Service grant, 1976.

WRITINGS: (Editor) *Tangled Vines: A Collection of Mother and Daughter Poems*, Beacon Press, 1978; *Doctors and Doctors of English*, Mudborn, 1981; (editor) *Ariadne's Thread*, Harper, 1982.

Poetry: *Why Is the House Dissolving?*, Open Skull Press, 1968; *Femina 2*, Abraxas Press, 1970; *Leaves and Night Things*, Baby John Press, 1970; *Black Apples*, New Books, 1971, revised edition, Crossing Press, 1973; *Lady Lyn*, Morgan Press, 1971; *I'd Be Jeanne Moreau*, Morgan Press, 1972; *The Mercurochrome Sun: Poems*, Charas Press, 1972; *Tentacles, Leaves*, Hellric Publications, 1972; *Moving by Touch*, Cotyledon Press, 1972; *Undressed*, Cotyledon Press, 1972; *Love Poems*, Zahir Press, 1972; *Forty Days, Apple Nights*, Morgan Press, 1972; *Museum*, Conspiracy Press, 1973; *The First Week Poems*, Zahir Press, 1973; *All the Women Poets I Ever Liked Didn't Hate Their Fathers*, Konglomerati, 1973; *The Old House on the Croton*, Shameless Hussy Press, 1973; *Poems*, Konglomerati, 1974; *Selected Poems*, Crossing Press, 1974; *Thru Blue Post, New Mexico*, Basilisk, 1974; *Blue Fingers*, Shelter Press, 1974; *Mountain Moving Day*, Crossing Press, 1974; *Plymouth Women*, Morgan Press, 1974; *Walking Thru Audley End Mansion Late Afternoon and Drifting into Certain Faces*, MAG Press, 1974.

Green Bandages, Hidden Springs, 1975; *Upstate Madonna: Poems, 1970-1974*, Crossing Press, 1975; *Old House Poems*, Capra Press, 1975; *Paper Apples*, Wormwood Review Press, 1975; *North Poems*, Morgan Press, 1976; *Shaker House Poems*, Sagarin Press, 1976; *Naked Charm*, Fireweed Press, 1976; *Some Madonna Poems*, White Pine Press, 1976; *Crazy Arms*, Ommation Press, 1977; *The January Poems*, Waters Journal of the Arts, 1977; *More Waters*, Waters Journal of the Arts, 1977; *Pantagonia*, Wormwood Review Press, 1977; *Mad Girl Poems*, Out of Sight Press, 1977; (contributor) *Six Poets*, Vagabond, 1978; *Leaning South*, Red Dust, 1978; *Glass*, Morgan Press, 1978; *Early Plymouth Women*, Morgan Press, 1978; *35 Sundays*, Ommation Press, 1979; *More Naked Charm*, Peter Schneider Press, 1979.

Lips on That Blue Rail, Lion's Breath, 1980; *Colors of Cooper Black*, Morgan Press, 1981; *In the Dark with Just One Star*, Morgan Press, 1982; *Want Ads*, Morgan Press, 1982; *Madonna Who Shifts for Herself*, Applezaba, 1982; *Mad Girl*, Blue Horse, 1982; *Reading Lips*, Morgan Press, 1982; *Hotel Lifshin*, Poetry Now, 1982; *Leaving the Bough*, New World Press, 1982.

Recordings: "Lyn Lifshin Reads Her Poems," Women's Audio Exchange, 1977; "Offered by Owner," with booklet of poems, Natalie Slohm Assos., 1978.

Work appears in anthologies, including: *New American and Canadian Poetry*, edited by John Gill, Beacon Press, 1971; *Writing While Young and Seeing thru Shucks*, Ballantine, 1972; *Rising Tides*, Simon & Schuster, 1973; *Psyche*, Dell, 1974; *In Youth*, Ballantine, 1974; *Pictures That Storm inside My Head*, Avon, 1975; *I Hear My Sisters Saying*, Corwell, 1976; *Editor's Choice*, Spirit That Moves Us, 1980; *Woman: An Affirmation*, D. C. Heath, 1980; *Contents under Pressure*, edited by Fred H. Laughter, Moonlight, 1981; *Poetry: Sight and Insight*, Random House, 1982.

Work has been published as broadsides and poetry postcards. Contributor of poems to many periodicals, including *December*, *Wormwood Review*, *Ms.*, *Rolling Stone*, and *American Poetry Review*.

BIOGRAPHICAL/CRITICAL SOURCES: *Road Apple Review*, summer-fall, 1971; *Library Journal*, June 1, 1971, December 15, 1972; *Wormwood Review*, Volume XII, number 3, 1971; *Northeast*, fall, 1971; *Minneapolis Star*, April 18, 1972; *Windless Orchard*, summer, 1972; *Little Magazine*, summer, 1972; *Ms.*, September, 1976, July, 1978; *Booklist*, April 1, 1978, July 15, 1978; *North American Review*, fall, 1978; *Village Voice*, September 24, 1979; *Poetry Now*, spring, 1980.

LILLARD, Charles (Marion) 1944-

PERSONAL: Born February 26, 1944, in Long Beach, Calif.; son of Donald George and Viola Katherine (Brooks) Lillard. *Education:* University of British Columbia, B.A., 1969, M.F.A., 1973. *Home:* 4609 Cordova Bay Rd., Victoria, British Columbia, Canada V8X 3V6.

CAREER: Writer. Has worked as a boom man in Alaska, and as a faller, machine operator, and crewboss for Environment Canada, 1960-72; University of British Columbia, Center for Continuing Education, Vancouver, lecturer in poetry and writing, 1971-74; University of Victoria, Victoria, British Columbia, instructor in creative writing, 1974-78; editor, Victoria Indian Cultural Centre, 1978-79; general editor, Gregson & Graham Ltd., 1979-81. Research assistant, National Film Board of Canada, 1973-74; lecturer, Matsqui Institution, 1973-74.

AWARDS, HONORS: Huntington Poetry Award, 1968; Book Promotion and Editorial Club award, 1972, for *Volvox: Poetry from the Unofficial Languages of Canada;* Canada Council grant, summer, 1973; Multi-Cultural Programme grant, 1974; Canada Council Explorations Programme grant, 1975; L.I.P. grant, 1975.

WRITINGS: Cultus Coulee (poems), Sono Nis Press, 1971; (editor with J. Michael Yates) *Volvox: Poetry from the Unofficial Languages of Canada,* Sono Nis Press, 1971; *Drunk on Wood* (poems), Sono Nis Press, 1973; (contributor) *A Guide to South East Alaska Trails,* Mountaineer Press, 1975; *Jabble* (poems), Kanchenjunga, 1975; (editor with George McWhirter) *Words from the Inside* (poems), Morriss, 1975; *Voice My Shaman* (poems) Sono Nis Press, 1976; (editor) *Mission to Nootka,* Gray's Publishing Ltd., 1977; (contributor) *Treasures of Canada,* Samuel-Stevens, 1980; (editor) *In the Wake of the War Canoe* (poems), Sono Nis Press, 1981.

Also author of play, "The Crossing," first produced in Vancouver, British Columbia, November, 1972. Poems represented in anthologies, including *Contemporary Poetry of British Columbia,* edited by J. Michael Yates, Sono Nis Press, 1970, and *Skookum Wawa,* edited by Gary Geddes, Oxford University Press, 1975.

Contributor of articles, reviews, fiction, translations, and poems to *Vancouver Magazine, Canadian Literature, Prism International, Contemporary Literature in Translation, Penumbra, West Coast Review,* and other periodicals. Editor, *Newsletter* of the Victoria Archaeology Society, 1975-76; associate editor, *Malahat Review,* 1975-80; guest editor, *Canadian Fiction Magazine,* summer, 1975.

WORK IN PROGRESS: Coastal Sanctus, a book of poems; editing *The Lost World of Robert Brown.*

AVOCATIONAL INTERESTS: The west coast, North Pacific Americana and literature.

* * *

LINDGREN, Alvin J. 1917-

PERSONAL: Born April 17, 1917, in Roxsbury, Kan.; son of Charles T. (a banker) and Isla (Tinsley) Lindgren; married Alma Huebscher, July 16, 1945; children: Patricia, Judith (Mrs. Richard Fasteson), James, John, Dianne. *Education:* McPherson College, B.A., 1937; Garrett Theological Seminary, B.D., 1940. *Home:* 1104 Duncan Ave., Lakeland, Fla. 33801.

CAREER: Ordained Methodist minister, 1940; minister of Methodist churches in Manawa, Green Bay, and Oshkosh, Wis., 1941-53; member of East Wisconsin Conference of United Methodist Church, 1953-57; Garrett Theological Seminary, Evanston, Ill., professor of church administration and director of field education, 1957-79; church management consultant and trainer, 1979—; member of Judicial Council of United Methodist Church, 1982—. *Awards, honors:* Swift fellowship, 1940-41; honorary D.D., McPherson College, 1958.

WRITINGS: Field Education Manual, Garrett Theological Seminary, 1963; *Foundations for Purposeful Church Administration,* Abingdon, 1965; (with Norman Shawchuck) *Management for Your Church,* Abingdon, 1977; (with Shawchuck) *Let My People Go,* Abingdon, 1980.

WORK IN PROGRESS: Completion of *Effective Multiple Staff Ministries,* for Abingdon.

* * *

LINDSAY, R(obert) Bruce 1900-

PERSONAL: Born January 1, 1900, in New Bedford, Mass.; son of Robert (a gas engineer) and Eleanora E. (Leuchsenring) Lindsay; married Rachel Tupper Easterbrooks, July 29, 1922; children: Robert III, Evelyn Tupper (Mrs. Richard Calvin Roberts). *Education:* Brown University, A.B. and M.S., 1920; University of Copenhagen, graduate study in theoretical physics, 1922-23; Massachusetts Institute of Technology, Ph.D., 1924. *Home:* 91 Indian Ave., Portsmouth, R.I. 02871. *Office:* Department of Physics, Brown University, Providence, R.I. 02912.

CAREER: Massachusetts Institute of Technology, Cambridge, instructor in physics, 1920-22; Yale University, New Haven, Conn., instructor, 1923-27, assistant professor of physics, 1927-30; Brown University, Providence, R.I., associate professor of theoretical physics, 1930-36, Hazard Professor of Physics, 1936-71, professor emeritus, 1971—, chairman of department, 1934-54, director of ultrasonics laboratory, 1946-60, dean of the Graduate School, 1954-66. Honorary fellow of British Institute of Acoustics, 1977—. Society of Sigma Xi, national lecturer, 1967-68, Bicentennial lecturer, 1975-77. *Military service:* U.S. Navy, 1918-21.

MEMBER: American Academy of Arts and Sciences (vice-president, 1957-59), Acoustical Society of America (president, 1956-57; editor-in-chief), American Institute of Physics (member of governing board, 1956-71; member of executive committee, 1959-71), American Association for the Advancement of Science (vice-president and section chairman, 1958, 1968), American Physical Society (chairman of New England section, 1935-36; member of council, 1943-46), American Association of Physics Teachers (member of executive committee, 1945-47), Philosophy of Science Association (member of governing board, 1958-59), History of Science Society, Society of Rheology, American Mathematical Society, Association of Graduate Schools in Association of American Universities (president, 1965-66), Phi Beta Kappa, Sigma Xi. *Awards, honors:* Ed.D., Rhode Island College, 1959; Gold Medal of Acoustical Society of America, 1963; Distinguished Service Citation, American Association of Physics Teachers, 1963; Sc.D., Southeastern Massachusetts University, 1968 and Brown University, 1978.

WRITINGS: (With George W. Stewart) *Acoustics,* Van Nostrand, 1930; *Physical Mechanics,* Van Nostrand, 1933, 3rd edition, 1961; (with Henry Margenau) *Foundations of Physics,* Wiley, 1936, reprinted, Ox Bow Press, 1980; *General Physics,* Wiley, 1940; *Physical Statistics,* Wiley, 1941; *Handbook of Elementary Physics,* Dryden Press, 1943; *Concepts and Methods of Theoretical Physics,* Van Nostrand, 1951; *Mechanical*

Radiation, McGraw, 1960; *The Role of Science in Civilization,* Harper, 1963; *The Nature of Physics,* Brown University Press, 1968; *Lord Rayleigh: The Man and His Work,* Pergamon, 1970; *Basic Concepts of Physics,* Van Nostrand, 1971; *Julius Robert Mayer: Prophet of Energy,* Pergamon, 1973.

Editor; published by Dowden, Hutchinson & Ross, except as indicated: *International Dictionary of Physics and Electronics,* Van Nostrand, 1956; *Proceedings of the Third International Congress on Acoustics,* American Institute of Physics, 1957; (of section) *American Institute of Physics Handbook,* McGraw, 1957; *Acoustics: Historical and Philosophical Development,* 1973; *Physical Acoustics,* 1974; *Applications of Energy: Nineteenth Century,* 1976; *The Control of Energy,* 1977.

Editor of "Benchmark Papers in Acoustics," and "Benchmark Papers in Energy" series. Consulting editor on acoustics for *McGraw-Hill Encyclopedia of Science and Technology,* 1977—. Contributor to *Encyclopaedia Britannica* and *Dictionary of Scientific Biography* published by American Council of Learned Societies; also contributor to professional journals. Editor of *Journal of the Acoustical Society of America,* 1957—.

WORK IN PROGRESS: Editing *Energy in Atomic Physics, 1925-1975,* and a series on the psychology of science, both for Hutchinson.

SIDELIGHTS: R. Bruce Lindsay tells *CA:* "I am reminded of the Ph.D. who was said not to be the kind of doctor who does anybody any good. I fear that I am the kind of author who does not do the bulk of the population any good!

"I feel that a large part of the purpose of my life is to do my best to combat the second law of thermodynamics, which certified the inevitable increase in the entropy and disorder of the universe. If life is a struggle, that principle is a worthy opponent."

Lindsay notes that his "intellectual autobiography" is on file at the American Institute of Physics and in the Archives of Brown University.

AVOCATIONAL INTERESTS: Collecting books on the history of science and biographies of scientists; walking, sawing wood, cutting grass.

BIOGRAPHICAL/CRITICAL SOURCES: Journal of the Acoustical Society of America, Volume XXXV, Number 1298, 1963; *Physics Today,* Volume XVI, Number 8, 1963; *American Journal of Physics,* Volume XXI, Number 455, 1963.

* * *

LIPSYTE, Robert (Michael) 1938-

PERSONAL: Born January 16, 1938, in New York, N.Y.; son of Sidney I. and Fanny (Finston) Lipsyte; married Marjorie L. Rubin (a novelist), 1966; children: two. *Education:* Columbia University, B.A., 1957, M.S., 1959. *Agent:* Lynn Nesbit, International Creative Management, 40 West 57th St., New York, N.Y. 10019. *Residence:* New Jersey.

CAREER: Writer. *New York Times,* New York, N.Y., sports columnist, 1957-71. Has also worked as radio commentator. *Military service:* U.S. Army, 1961. *Member:* Institute for Sports and Social Analysis (member of board of directors).

AWARDS, HONORS: Dutton Best Sports Stories Award from E. P. Dutton & Co., Inc., for news feature articles, "The Long Road to Broken Dreams," 1964, "Where the Stars of Tomorrow Shine Tonight," 1967, "Dempsey in the Window," 1971, for news coverage article, "The Incredible Cassius," 1965, and for magazine story, "Pride of the Tiger," 1976; Mike Berger Award from Columbia University, 1966, for distinguished reporting; Wel-Met Children's Book Award from Child Study Association of America, 1968, for *The Contender; One Fat Summer* was selected one of *New York Times*'s outstanding children's books of the year for 1977.

WRITINGS: (With Dick Gregory) *Nigger,* Dutton, 1964; *The Masculine Mystique,* New American Library, 1966; *The Contender,* Harper, 1967; *Assignment: Sports,* Harper, 1970; (with Steve Cady) *Something Going,* Dutton, 1973; *Liberty Two,* Simon & Schuster, 1974; *SportsWorld: An American Dreamland,* Quadrangle, 1975.

Published by Harper: *One Fat Summer,* 1977; *Free to Be Muhammed Ali,* 1978; *Summer Rules,* 1981; *Jock and Jill,* 1982; *The Summerboy,* 1982.

Also author of screenplays, including "That's the Way of the World," released by United Artists, 1975 (also released under title "Shining Star").

SIDELIGHTS: Robert Lipsyte was "for fourteen years . . . the most original and elegant writer on the sports staff of *The New York Times,*" according to Paul D. Zimmerman in *Newsweek.* As a journalist, notes Fred Rotondaro in a *Best Sellers* review, Lipsyte "was one of the first . . . who wrote critically about the sports world; for he knew that sports figures had blemishes just like the rest of us." More recently, as a novelist for adults and adolescents, Lipsyte has continued writing about sports and the people involved in sports activities in the same realistic manner.

His talent in accurately portraying the world of the adolescent, referred to by John S. Simmons in *Elementary English* as "Lipsyte's ability to produce a picture of life which is credible for today's adolescents," is perhaps due to events in the author's own childhood which enable him to better relate to the problems of young people. Like Bobby Marks, the main character of the teen-age novels *One Fat Summer, Summer Rules,* and *The Summerboy,* Lipsyte was overweight as a boy. At the age of fourteen, he slimmed down and began actively participating in sports. This experience of transformation is often echoed in Lipsyte's novels. For example, *One Fat Summer* tells the story of Bobby's struggle to lose weight during one summer, and in *The Contender* Lipsyte writes of the metamorphosis of Alfred, a boy who endures rigorous training in order to become a prize-winning boxer.

Critics have responded favorably to many of Lipsyte's books, including those featuring Bobby Marks. For instance, April Smith, commenting on *Summer Rules* in *New York Times Book Review,* calls the novel "witty and well-written." Stephen Krensky, in another *New York Times Book Review* article, notes that Bobby is "refreshingly . . . neither precocious nor offbeat, in the manner of so many teen-age protagonists, but simply a normal boy in abnormal circumstances." And Zena Sutherland, in *Bulletin of the Center for Children's Books,* comments that in *One Fat Summer* "the plot elements are nicely balanced and paced, the characterization is developed with insight, and the writing style is deft and polished."

Lipsyte believes participation in sports is one way in which young people can grow both physically and emotionally, and this idea is reflected in his writing. He hopes that by realistically portraying sports in books for young readers, he will encourage them to become involved in sports. He summarizes these ideas in a *Children's Literature in Education* article: "Trying to reform sports books for children is discouraging, but you've got to start somewhere. . . . We should be trying to write books that acknowledge kids' fears about sports and say that other people, even heroes, share them. [Books] in which making the team doesn't end all problems and the team doesn't win all the games. Books that integrate sports into the rest of life. If we write more truthfully about sports, perhaps we can encourage kids to relax, . . . to challenge themselves for the pleasure of it, without self-doubt and without fear."

BIOGRAPHICAL/CRITICAL SOURCES: *New York Times Book Review,* November 12, 1967, May 31, 1970, November 9, 1975, July 10, 1977, November 13, 1977, January 6, 1980, April 26, 1981, April 25, 1982; *English Journal,* April, 1971, September, 1977, February, 1979; *Elementary English,* January, 1972; *Best Sellers,* June 15, 1974; *Bulletin of the Center for Children's Books,* July-August, 1977; *Children's Literature in Education,* spring, 1980; *Contemporary Literary Criticism,* Volume XXI, Gale, 1982.

* * *

LISTER, Raymond (George) 1919-

PERSONAL: Born March 28, 1919, in Cambridge, England; son of Horace (an engineer) and Ellen (Arnold) Lister; married Pamela Brutnell, June 6, 1947; children: Rory Brian George, Delia Fionnuala. *Education:* Attended Cambridge schools until fifteen. *Home:* Windmill House, Linton, Cambridgeshire CB1 6NS, England. *Agent:* A. S. Knight, Wildacre, The Warren, Ashtead, Surrey, England. *Office:* George Lister & Sons Ltd., 120 Church End, Cherry Hinton, Cambridge, England.

CAREER: George Lister & Sons Ltd. (architectural metalworkers), Cambridge, England, director, 1939—; Golden Head Press Ltd., Cambridge, managing director and editor, 1952-72. Wolfson College, Cambridge University, honorary senior member, 1971-75, fellow, 1975—. Miniature painter, with work exhibited each summer at one-man shows in Federation of British Artists Galleries, London.

MEMBER: Royal Society of Arts, Royal Society of Miniature Painters, Sculptors and Engravers (treasurer, beginning 1958; president, 1970-80), Federation of British Artists (governor, 1972-80), Private Libraries Association (president, 1971-72), Liveryman of Worshipful Company of Blacksmiths, Sette of Odd Volumes (president, 1960), Atheneum Club, City Livery Club.

WRITINGS: Decorative Wrought Ironwork in Great Britain, G. Bell, 1957, Tuttle, 1970, 2nd edition, David & Charles, 1970; (translator from the French) V. I. Stepanov, *Alphabet of Movements of the Human Body,* Golden Head Press, 1958; *Decorative Cast Ironwork in Great Britain,* G. Bell, 1960; *The Craftsman Engineer,* G. Bell, 1960; *Private Telegraph Companies of Great Britain and Their Stamps,* Golden Head Press, 1961; *Great Craftsmen,* G. Bell, 1962; *Edward Calvert,* G. Bell, 1962; *The Miniature Defined* (booklet), Golden Head Press, 1963; *How to Identify Old Maps and Globes,* Archon Books, 1965; *Beulah to Byzantium: A Study of Parallels in the Works of W. B. Yeats, William Blake, Samuel Palmer and Edward Calvert,* Dolmen Press, 1965; *College Stamps of Oxford and Cambridge,* Golden Head Press, 1966; *The Craftsman in Metal,* G. Bell, 1966, A. S. Barnes, 1968; *Victorian Narrative Paintings,* C. N. Potter, 1966; *Great Works of Craftsmanship,* G. Bell, 1967, A. S. Barnes, 1968; *William Blake: An Introduction to the Man and to His Work,* G. Bell, 1968, Ungar, 1970; *Samuel Palmer and His Etchings,* Watson-Guptill, 1969; *Hammer and Hand: An Essay on the Ironwork of Cambridge* (booklet), privately printed, 1969.

Antique Maps and Their Cartographers, Archon Books, 1970; *British Romantic Art,* G. Bell, 1973; *Samuel Palmer: A Biography,* Faber, 1975; (editor) *The Letters of Samuel Palmer,* two volumes, Oxford University Press, 1975; *Infernal Methods: A Study of William Blake's Art Techniques,* G. Bell, 1975; *Samuel Palmer: A Vision Recaptured,* Victoria and Albert Museum, 1978; *George Richmond: A Biography,* R. V. Garton, 1981. Also author of *Apollo's Bird,* 1975, *For Love of Leda,* 1977, and *Great Images of British Printmaking,* 1978. Author of numerous pamphlets.

Contributor to *Connoisseur, Apollo, Journal of Royal Society of Arts, Irish Book, Blake Studies,* and *Blake Newsletter.*

AVOCATIONAL INTERESTS: Book collecting, mountaineering in the fens.

BIOGRAPHICAL/CRITICAL SOURCES: Simon Lissim, *The Art of Raymond Lister,* Gray, 1958; C. R. Cammell and others, *Raymond Lister: Five Essays,* Golden Head Press, 1963.

* * *

LIVINGOOD, James W(eston) 1910-

PERSONAL: Born July 5, 1910, in Birdsboro, Pa.; son of Howard Manwiller and Minnie (Potts) Livingood; married Alma Lawshe, June 19, 1937; children: James Weston, Jr., Richard Shafto. *Education:* Gettysburg College, B.S., 1932; Princeton University, M.A., 1934, Ph.D., 1937. *Religion:* Episcopalian. *Home:* 395 Shallowford Rd., Chattanooga, Tenn. 37411.

CAREER: Princeton University, Princeton, N.J., instructor in history, 1935-36; University of Tennessee at Chattanooga, 1937—, professor of history, 1951-75, Guerry Professor of History, 1962-75, distinguished research professor of history, 1969-75, distinguished professor emeritus, 1975—, chairman of Division of Social Sciences, 1951-52, dean of College of Arts and Sciences, 1957-66, dean of the university, 1966-69. Official Hamilton County historian and consultant to University of Tennessee Press. *Member:* American Historical Association, Southern Historical Association, Tennessee Historical Society, East Tennessee Historical Society, Tennessee College Association (president, 1967-68), Chattanooga Area Historical Society (charter member; past president), Chattanooga Civil War Roundtable (president, 1979-80), Phi Beta Kappa, Pi Gamma Mu, Phi Delta Theta.

WRITINGS: Philadelphia-Baltimore Trade Rivalry, 1780-1860, Pennsylvania Historical and Museum Commission, 1947, reprinted, Arno, 1970; (with Gilbert E. Govan) *The University of Chattanooga: Sixty Years,* University of Chattanooga Press, 1947; (with Govan) *The Chattanooga Country: From Tomahawks to T.V.A.,* Dutton, 1952, revised edition, University of Tennessee Press, 1977; (with Govan) *A Different Valor: The Story of General Joseph E. Johnston, C.S.A.,* Bobbs-Merrill, 1956, reprinted, Greenwood Press, 1974; (editor with Govan) *The Haskell Memoirs,* Putnam, 1960; (contributor) *Landmarks of Tennessee History,* Tennessee Historical Society and Tennessee Historical Commission, 1965; (with J. Leonard Raulston) *Sequatchie: A Story of the Southern Cumberlands,* University of Tennessee Press, 1974; *Chattanooga: An Illustrated History,* Windsor Publications, 1981; *Hamilton County,* University Press of Memphis State University, 1981. Also author, with Govan, of *Chronology: University of Chattanooga 1872-1961,* University of Chattanooga Press. Contributor to *Collier's Encyclopedia, Encyclopedia Americana,* and *Encyclopaedia Britannica.* Book reviewer for *Chattanooga Times;* contributor of articles and reviews to *Saturday Review, Tennessee Valley Perspective, Civil War Times Illustrated,* and numerous history journals.

SIDELIGHTS: James Livingood told *CA:* "I am a committed believer in scholarly-researched local history, which has too long been prepared [only] for patriotic speeches and chamber of commerce messages. It is the fundamental base for all state, regional, and national history. It's where the roots dig in."

* * *

LLOYD, Cynthia B(rown) 1943-

PERSONAL: Born March 24, 1943, in New York, N.Y.; married; children: one. *Education:* Bryn Mawr College, B.A. (cum laude), 1964; Columbia University, M.A., 1967, Ph.D. (with distinction), 1972. *Home:* 285 Riverside Dr., New York, N.Y. 10025. *Office:* Population Divison, United Nations, 799 United Nations Plaza, New York, N.Y. 10017.

CAREER: Federal Reserve Bank, New York City, research assistant in foreign research department, 1964-65; United Nations, New York City, associate social affairs officer in Population Division, summers, 1968-69; Columbia University, New York City, Barnard College, instructor, 1970-72, assistant professor of economics, 1972-79, Center for Social Sciences, Program in Sex Roles and Social Change, co-director, 1978-79; United Nations, Population Division, population affairs officer, 1979—. *Member:* American Economic Association, Population Association of America, American Association of University Professors, Eastern Economic Association.

WRITINGS: (Editor and contributor) *Sex, Discrimination, and the Division of Labor,* Columbia University Press, 1975; (with Beth T. Niemi) *The Economics of Sex Differentials,* Columbia University Press, 1979; (editor with others) *Women in the Labor Market,* Columbia University Press, 1979. Contributor to academic journals.

WORK IN PROGRESS: Cross-national analysis of world fertility survey data.

* * *

LLOYD, Marjorie 1909-

PERSONAL: Born September 4, 1909, in Haydock, Lancashire, England; daughter of John and Elizabeth (Ormrod) Lloyd. *Education:* University of Birmingham, B.Sc., 1931. *Home:* East High Green, Great Musgrave, Kirby Stephen, Cumbria CA17 4DW, England.

CAREER: Free-lance writer. *Member:* Society of Authors, National Book League, National Trust.

WRITINGS: Fell Farm Holiday, Penguin, 1951; *Fell Farm for Christmas,* Penguin, 1954, reprinted, Puffin Books, 1975; *The Farm in Mallerstang,* Methuen, 1956; *One Summer Term,* Methuen, 1959; *Fell Farm Campers,* Penguin, 1960; (with Ellatine Schulz and Gertrude Vogeley) *Junior Teacher's Guide, Year Three,* Augsburg, 1961; (with Schulz and Vogeley) *Junior Worksheets, Year Three,* Augsburg, 1961; *The Family at Foxy Beck,* Hutchinson, 1967; *One Silver Shilling,* Chatto & Windus, 1969; *Patch the Puppy,* Benn, 1970; *River Trail,* Hutchinson, 1970. Also author of *Kit* and *Fell Trek;* also author of stories and plays for children's programs, British Broadcasting Corp., and Radio Eireann. Contributor to *Guardian, Lady, Time and Tide, Field, Cumbria,* and to periodicals for children.

WORK IN PROGRESS: A children's book; short stories and articles.

SIDELIGHTS: One Silver Shilling has been translated into German.†

* * *

LONG, David F(oster) 1917-

PERSONAL: Born December 8, 1917, in Cleveland, Ohio; son of Roger and Christine (Foster) Long; married third wife, Susan Robinson (a teacher), June 6, 1969; children: Elisabeth B., Roger D., Craig R. *Education:* Dartmouth College, A.B., 1939; Columbia University, A.M., 1948, Ph.D., 1950. *Home:* 175 Concord Rd., Lee, Dover, N.H. 03820. *Office:* Department of History, University of New Hampshire, Durham, N.H. 03824.

CAREER: High school history teacher in New Hampshire and New York, 1939-48; University of New Hampshire, Durham, assistant professor, 1948-50, associate professor, 1950-60, professor of history, 1960—. Fulbright lecturer at University of Ceylon, 1956-57, 1958-59, and Makerere University, Uganda, 1965-66; U.S. State Department lecturer, Sierra Leone, 1966; U.S. Information Service lecturer in East Asia, Southeast Asia, and South Pacific, all 1974; visiting professor, University of Waikato, New Zealand, 1974, and "Semester at Sea" (affiliated with University of Pittsburgh) aboard S.S. *Universe,* around the world, spring, 1981; honorary professor of history, Hong Kong University, 1978.

MEMBER: American Association of University Professors, American Historical Association, Organization of American Historians, Society for the Historians of American Foreign Relations. *Awards, honors,* Rockefeller Foundation grant, 1958-59; Ford Foundation grant, 1960-61; U.S. State Department grant, 1966; Fulbright research grant, East Asia, 1974; honorary fellow of Australian National University, 1974.

WRITINGS: (With Robert E. Riegel) *The American Story,* two volumes, McGraw, 1955; *The Outward View: An Illustrated History of U.S. Foreign Relations,* Rand McNally, 1964; *Nothing Too Daring: A Biography of Commodore David Porter, 1780-1843,* U.S. Naval Institute, 1970; (contributor) *In Peace and War: American Naval Policies, 1776-1976,* Greenwood Press, 1978; (editor) *A Documentary History of U.S. Foreign Relations,* two volumes, University Press of America, 1980; *Ready to Hazard: A Biography of Commodore William Bainbridge, 1774-1833,* University Press of New England, 1981; (contributor) *New Aspects of Naval History,* Naval Institute Press, 1981; *Sailor-Diplomat: A Biography of Commodore James Biddle, 1783-1848,* Northeast University Press, 1983. Contributor to history journals.

WORK IN PROGRESS: Diplomatic Activities of U.S. Naval Officers, 1798-1883.

AVOCATIONAL INTERESTS: Foreign travel (has been to over 100 countries).

* * *

LOOMIS, Roger Sherman 1887-1966

PERSONAL: Born October 31, 1887, in Yokohama, Japan; died October 11, 1966, following a long illness; son of Henry and Jane Herring (Greene) Loomis (both American missionaries); married Gertrude Schoepperle, August 27, 1919; married second wife, Laura Hibbard (a professor of English at Wellesley College), June 6, 1925 (died, 1960); married Dorothy Bethurum. *Education:* Attended Hotchkiss School; Williams College, B.A., 1909; Harvard University, M.A., 1910; Oxford University, B.Litt., 1913. *Home:* 76 Great Neck Rd., Waterford, Conn.

CAREER: University of Illinois, Urbana, instructor, 1913-18; Columbia University, New York, N.Y., member of English faculty, 1919-58, professor emeritus, 1958-66. Oxford University, Oxford, England, Eastman Professor, 1955-56. *Wartime service:* World War I, editor of Army publication *Attenshun 21. Member:* International Arthurian Society (president of American branch, 1948-63), Modern Language Association,

Mediaeval Academy of America (fellow; second vice-president, 1961-64), Modern Humanities Research Association, American Humanist Association. *Awards, honors:* Rhodes Scholar at New College, Oxford University; Haskins Medal of Mediaeval Academy of America, 1951, for *Arthurian Tradition and Chretien de Troyes;* D.Litt., University of Wales, 1952, Columbia University, 1957, Williams College, 1957; Doct. hon. causa, University of Rennes, 1952.

WRITINGS: *Illustrations of Medieval Romance on the Tiles from Chertsey Abbey,* University of Illinois, 1916, reprinted, Johnson Reprint, 1967; (compiler) *Freshman Readings,* Houghton, 1925; *Celtic Myth and Arthurian Romance,* Columbia University Press, 1927, reprinted, Haskell House, 1967; (with others) *The Art of Writing Prose,* R. R. Smith, 1930, revised edition, Farrar & Rinehart, 1936; (editor) *Models for Writing Prose,* R. R. Smith, 1931, revised edition, Farrar & Rinehart, 1937; (editor with Donald L. Clark) *Modern English Readings,* Farrar & Rinehart, 1934, 6th edition, 1950, alternate edition of 6th edition published as *Readings in Biography and Exposition,* 1950, 7th edition, with Clark and John H. Middendorf, 1956, alternate edition of 7th edition published as *Readings in Exposition,* 1956, 8th edition, with Clark and Middendorf, published as *Modern English Readings: Essays, Biography, Plays, Stories, Poems,* Holt, 1963, alternate edition of 8th edition, with Clark and Middendorf, published as *Readings in Exposition,* 1963; *Arthurian Legends in Medieval Art* (Part II with wife, Laura H. Loomis), Oxford University Press, for Modern Language Association of America, 1938, reprinted, Kraus Reprint, 1966; (compiler) *Introduction to Medieval Literature, Chiefly in England,* Columbia University Press, 1939, 2nd edition, 1948.

(Editor and translator with Henry W. Wells) *Representative Medieval and Tudor Plays,* Sheed & Ward, 1942, reprinted, Books for Libraries, 1970; (editor with Gabriel M. Liegey) *The Fight for Freedom: College Readings in Wartime,* Farrar & Rinehart, 1943; (editor with Rudolph Willard) *Medieval English Verse and Prose in Modernized Versions,* Prentice-Hall, 1948; *Arthurian Tradition and Chretien de Troyes,* Columbia University Press, 1949; *The Romance of Tristram and Ysolt* (original translation of the 12th-century Anglo-Norman poem by Thomas), Columbia University Press, 1951, reprinted, Dynamic Learning Corp., 1979; *Lanzelet: A Romance of Lancelot* (translated from the Middle High German), Columbia University Press, 1951; *Wales and the Arthurian Legend,* University of Wales Press, 1956, reprinted, Folcroft, 1977; (editor with L. H. Loomis) *Medieval Romances,* Random House, 1957; (editor) *Arthurian Literature in the Middle Ages: A Collaborative History,* Oxford University Press, 1959; *The Grail, from Celtic Myth to Christian Symbol,* Columbia University Press, 1963; *The Development of Arthurian Romance,* Harper, 1963; (editor) *Studies in the Fairy Mythology of Arthurian Romance,* 2nd enlarged edition, B. Franklin, 1963; *A Mirror of Chaucer's World,* Princeton University Press, 1965; (editor) R. H. Fletcher, *The Arthurian Material in the Chronicles,* 2nd edition (Loomis was not associated with 1st edition), B. Franklin, 1966; *Studies in Medieval Literature: A Memorial Collection of Essays,* with bibliography of Loomis's writings by Ruth Roberts, B. Franklin, 1970.

WORK IN PROGRESS: *A Humanists' Anthology.*

SIDELIGHTS: Roger Sherman Loomis was recognized as one of the world's foremost authorities on the legends of King Arthur and his Knights of the Round Table. His book *A Mirror of Chaucer's World* is a pictorial presentation of drawings, sculpture, paintings, and other materials related to Chaucer and his age.

BIOGRAPHICAL/CRITICAL SOURCES: Roger Sherman Loomis, *Studies in Medieval Literature: A Memorial Collection of Essays,* with bibliography of Loomis's writings by Ruth Roberts, B. Franklin, 1970.

OBITUARIES: *New York Times,* October 12, 1966; *World Journal Tribune,* October 12, 1966.†

* * *

LOPSHIRE, Robert M(artin) 1927-

PERSONAL: Born April 14, 1927, in Sarasota, Fla.; son of Conrad A. and Jessie (Martin) Davidson; adopted, 1931, by Roy Howard and Dorothy (DeLaGrange) Lopshire; married Jane Haller Ingalls, October 21, 1946 (divorced); married Selma Dorothy Stefel, February 21, 1974; children: Robert Martin, Jr., Howard Clyde, Terri Jane, Victoria Anne. *Education:* Attended Vesper George School of Art, and School of Practical Art, both Boston, Mass., 1946-48. *Residence:* Keystone Heights, Fla.

CAREER: Free-lance artist and illustrator, Philadelphia, Pa., 1948-54, Boston, Mass., 1954-56, and New York City, 1956-59; Random House, New York City, creative art director, 1959-61; owner of advertising agency, Sergeantsville, N.J., 1961-64. Consultant art director for companies in New York. *Military service:* U.S. Coast Guard, 1944-45, served in Pacific theatre; Air Sea Rescue, 1945-46, combat photographer; awarded invasion awards.

WRITINGS: *Put Me in the Zoo,* Random House, 1960; *How to Make Flibbers, Etc.,* Random House, 1964, published as *The Beginner's Book of Things to Make: Fun Stuff You Can Make Yourself,* Beginner Books, 1977; *Beginner's Guide to Building and Flying Model Airplanes,* Harper, 1967; *I Am Better Than You!,* Harper, 1968; *It's Magic?,* Macmillan, 1969; *Radio Control Miniature Aircraft,* Macmillan, 1974; *How to Make Snop Snappers and Other Fine Things,* Greenwillow, 1977; *The Biggest, Smallest, Fastest, Tallest Things You've Ever Heard Of,* Crowell Collier, 1980.

Illustrator: Fred B. Phleger, *Ann Can Fly,* Random House, 1959; Kin Platt, *Big Max,* Harper, 1965; Betty Baker, *Pig War,* Harper, 1969; Richard Margolis, *Wish Again, Big Bear,* Macmillan, 1972; Bernard Wiseman, *Little New Kangaroo,* Macmillan, 1973; Margolis, *Big Bear to the Rescue,* Greenwillow, 1975; Platt, *Big Max in the Mystery of the Missing Moose,* Harper, 1977.

Contributor to *World Book Encyclopedia;* also contributor to magazines, including *Model Airplane News.*

WORK IN PROGRESS: Numerous children's book ideas; a novel.

SIDELIGHTS: Robert Lopshire told *CA:* "Two constant questions, when people find that I am a writer and artist, are: 'How did you get started?' and 'Where do you get your ideas?'

"There is no simple party-chatter answer to either question, as any writer or artist will be quick to admit. My feeling is that an artist or writer becomes so by a dedicated conviction that what boils within must be put down for others to see, study, and comment on. Many of us look forward to the acclaim—it bolsters our egos, or demolishes them so much that we try harder the next time if our work is snubbed.

"I would be dishonest if I said that I did not enjoy hearing that people like my work, but having chosen to write mainly for children, I have developed a bit different outlook. . . . I ignore the critics, be they kind or cutting. My audience is children—I write and draw for *them,* not the critics or any possible awards.

"I am personally offended by those writers I see pushing their books on television talk shows and the lecture circuits. (I turn down all such invitations.) A book, article, drawing, or painting should stand on its own for what it is . . . not as something sold by media or appearance hype. While I agree that the media should be used to inform of existing works, I find the public appearance of writers and artists promising more than they've done to be repugnant, just as I dislike the annual awards handed out to children's books that the children themselves never had a chance to vote for.

"Personally, the best award I've ever received was the news that one of my books was the most often stolen from a large metropolitan library system. I put a tremendous amount of effort into trying to give kids what *they* want . . . what better tribute could any writer ask for than that theft record? Of course, it would now seem only fitting that I do a book about why one should not go about stealing books from libraries!"

AVOCATIONAL INTERESTS: Model aircraft, painting, "stimulating young minds to think and go further than the immediate limits of their own small world."

* * *

LORD, Clifford L(ee) 1912-1980

PERSONAL: Born September 4, 1912, in Mount Vernon, N.Y.; died of cancer, October 22, 1980, in West Orange, N.J.; son of Charles Clifford (a salesman) and Bertha Eunice (Lee) Lord; married Elizabeth Sniffen Hubbard, June 12, 1937 (died, 1980); children: Charles Hubbard, Helen Patricia. *Education:* Amherst College, A.B., 1933, A.M., 1934; graduate study at Columbia University, 1934-36, Ph.D., 1943. *Residence:* West Orange, N.J.

CAREER: Columbia University, New York City, instructor in American history, 1936-41; State Historical Association, Cooperstown, N.Y., director, 1941-46; State Historical Society, Madison, Wis., director, 1946-58; Columbia University, School of General Studies, New York City, dean and professor of history, 1958-64; Hofstra University, Hempstead, Long Island, N.Y., president, 1964-72, chancellor, 1972-73; Hudson Institute, Croton-on-Hudson, N.Y., president, 1973-75; New Jersey Historical Society, Newark, 1977-80. Organizer of Farmer's Museum, 1942. Director of Circus World Museum, 1952-58, honorary director, 1958-80; vice-president of National Railroad Museum, 1958-62, honorary director, 1962-80. Member of board of directors of American Heritage, Inc., 1956-60, Hudson Tersesquicentennial Commission, 1959, and Columbia University Press, 1959-62; member of council, Smithsonian Institution, 1966-72, honorary member of council, 1972-80. Trustee of Rider College, 1977-80. Member of advisory bodies of National Union Catalog and Manuscript Collections, 1957-80, New Jersey Tercentenary Commission, 1961-64, and New Jersey State Museum, 1964. Consultant, Historical Records Survey of Works Progress Administration, New York City, 1936-39, and N.J., 1940-42, Western Heritage Center, 1960-64, National Archives, 1962-64, and Philadelphia Maritime Museum, 1976. *Military service:* U.S. Naval Reserve, active duty, 1942-46; administrative historian, Bureau of Aeronautics, 1943-45, head of Naval Aviation History Unit, 1945-46; became lieutenant commander.

MEMBER: American Association of Museums (member of council, 1944-48), American Historical Association, Organization of American Historians, American Association for State and Local History (member of council, 1950-52, 1960-64; chairman of advisory council of American History Research Center, 1950-59; vice-president, 1952-56; president, 1956-60; chairman of research and publications committee, 1960-64), Regional Plan Association (member of board of directors, 1967-80), New York State Historical Association, New Jersey Historical Society (member of board, 1963-64), Phi Beta Kappa, Century Club (New York), Rotary Club (Rock Springs). *Awards, honors:* LL.D., Lawrence College (now Lawrence University), 1948, University of Buffalo, 1962, Adelphi University, 1965; L.H.D., Amherst College, 1953, Rider College, 1970.

WRITINGS: Handbook of the Museum and Art Gallery of the New York State Historical Association, New York State Historical Association, 1942; *Atlas of Congressional Roll Calls, 1777-1789,* New York State Historical Association, 1943; (with wife, Elizabeth H. Lord) *Historical Atlas of the United States,* Holt, 1944, 2nd edition, 1953, reprinted, Johnson Reprint Corp., 1972; (compiler and author of introduction) *The State Historical Society of Wisconsin: A Century of Service,* State Historical Society of Wisconsin, 1948; (with Archibald Douglas Turnbull) *History of United States Naval Aviation,* Yale University Press, 1949, reprinted, Arno, 1972; (with Turnbull) *History of U.S. Ideas in Conflict: A Colloquium on Certain Problems in Historical Society Work,* 1958; (editor with Henry Graff) *John Allen Krout, American Themes,* Columbia University Press, 1963; *Teaching History With Community Resources,* Teachers College Press, 1964, 2nd edition, 1967, (editor) *Keepers of the Past,* University of North Carolina Press, 1965; (with Carl Ubbelohde) *Clio's Servant: The State Historical Society of Wisconsin, 1846-1954,* State Historical Society of Wisconsin, 1967; (editor) *List and Index of Presidential Executive Orders, 1789-1941,* Michael Glazier, 1980. Author of monographs on history.

General editor, "Localized History Series," Teachers College Press, 1964-80. Editor of *New York History* (quarterly), 1942-43, *Wisconsin Magazine of History* (quarterly), 1942-43, *Wisconsin Magazine of History* (quarterly), 1946-53; member of editorial advisory board, *America: History and Life,* 1964-68.

SIDELIGHTS: During Clifford L. Lord's presidency at Hofstra University, the university underwent a period of growth, both in terms of student enrollment and campus structures. Lord oversaw the construction of a nine-story library as well as six thirteen-story residential student buildings, and was instrumental in the opening of the university's School of Law.

BIOGRAPHICAL/CRITICAL SOURCES: Milwaukee Journal, July 1, 1956; *History News,* August, 1958, September, 1960; *New York Times,* April 8, 1964; *Columbia Owl,* April 15, 1964; *Hofstra Chronicle,* April 16, 1964; *Newsday,* April 30, 1964.

OBITUARIES: New York Times, October 23, 1980; *Chicago Tribune,* October 24, 1980; *AB Bookman's Weekly,* December 15, 1980.†

* * *

LOVELL, Mark 1934-
(Peter Rowlands)

PERSONAL: Born September 3, 1934, in London, England; son of Maurice Henry (a journalist) and Hilda (a teacher; maiden name, Rowland) Lovell; married Ann Scott-Buccleuch, August 8, 1959 (divorced, 1975); married Susi Hock, November 29, 1975; children: (first marriage) Frank, Sara, Simon, Stephen; (second marriage) Rebecca. *Education:* Jesus College, Cambridge, B.A. (honors), 1959. *Politics:* None. *Home:* 216 Percival Ave., Montreal West, Quebec, Canada H4X 1T9. *Office:*

Groupe Innova Inc., 2055 Peel St., Montreal, Quebec, Canada H3A 1V4.

CAREER: British Market Research Bureau, London, England, head of group, 1959-63; Marplan Ltd., London, director, 1963-66; Leo Burnett Ltd., London, director, 1966-75; Creative Research Group, Toronto, Ontario, vice-president, 1976—; general director, Groupe Innova Inc., Montreal, Quebec. Chairman of London Regional Society for Autistic Children, 1968-75. *Military service:* Royal Navy, 1953-55; became sub-lieutenant. *Member:* Professional Marketing Research Society (president, 1979-80). *Awards, honors:* Thomson silver medal, 1967, gold medals, 1968 and 1969, all for advertising and media research.

WRITINGS—All nonfiction: *How Children Grow,* two volumes, Routledge & Kegan Paul, 1975-76; (with Jack Potter) *Assessing the Effectiveness of Advertising,* Business Books, 1976; *Passing Examinations,* Faber, 1976.

Under pseudonym Peter Rowlands: *The Fugitive Mind,* Dent, 1972; *Children Apart,* Dent, 1973; *Saturday Parent,* Crossroad/Continuum, 1980; *Love Me: Love My Kids,* Crossroad/Continuum, 1982.

Regular columnist in *Esomar.* Contributor to advertising and business journals.

* * *

LOW, Alice 1926-

PERSONAL: Born June 5, 1926, in New York, N.Y.; daughter of Harold (in textiles) and Anna (a writer of children's books; maiden name, Epstein) Bernstein; married Martin Low (owner of a film studio), March 25, 1949; children: Andrew, Katherine, David. *Education:* Smith College, B.A., 1947; also attended Columbia University. *Residence:* Briarcliff Manor, N.Y. *Agent:* Russell & Volkening, Inc., 551 Fifth Ave., New York, N.Y. 10176.

CAREER: Warren Schloat Productions, Tarrytown, N.Y., writer and producer of educational filmstrips, 1968-72; Birch Wathen School, New York City, teacher of creative writing, 1972-73; Random House, New York City, free-lance editor, 1975—; Scholastic Book Services, New York City, editorial consultant to Children's Choice Book Club, 1978—. Guide at Museum of the City of New York. *Member:* Authors Guild, Authors League of America, American Society of Composers, Authors, and Publishers.

WRITINGS—Juveniles: *Open My Suitcase,* Simon & Schuster, 1954; *Out of My Window,* Random House, 1962; *Grandmas and Grandpas,* Random House, 1962; *Summer,* Random House, 1963; *Taro and the Bamboo Shoot* (adaptation of a folk tale), Pantheon, 1964; *A Day of Your Own, Your Birthday,* Random House, 1964; *What's in Mommy's Pocketbook?,* Golden Press, 1965; *Kallie's Corner,* Pantheon, 1966; *At Jasper's House and Other Stories,* Pantheon, 1968; *Witches' Holiday,* Pantheon, 1971; *Herbert's Treasure,* Putnam, 1971; *David's Windows,* Putnam, 1974; *The Witch Who Was Afraid of Witches,* Pantheon, 1978; *Genie and the Witch's Spells,* Knopf, 1982.

Work has been anthologized in *Captain Kangaroo's Read Aloud Book,* Random House, 1962, and *Captain Kangaroo's Sleepytime Book,* Random House, 1963.

Also author of scripts for filmstrips "Folk Songs and the American Flag," "Folk Songs and the Declaration of Independence," "Folk Songs and Abraham Lincoln," and "Folk Songs and Frederick Douglas," all for Warren Schloat Productions, 1968-70, "First Things, Social Reasoning" (series of eight filmstrips), Guidance Associates, 1973-74, "You Can Be Anything," Teaching Resource Films, 1975, and "A Houseful of Ocean," Guidance Associates, 1975; author of scripts and producer of "Folk Songs and the Railroad," "Cowboys," and "Whaling," all for Warren Schloat Productions, 1970-72, and "History of the City," Warren Schloat Productions, 1972.

Author of operetta for elementary school children and of material for UNICEF; author of lyrics for *Big and Little and Noisy and Quiet,* RCA Corp., 1962. Contributor of stories to young adult magazines, including *Ingenue* and *Seventeen.*

WORK IN PROGRESS: A children's book; short stories.

SIDELIGHTS: Alice Low writes: "My mother wrote children's books and . . . many of her friends were in the arts and publishing. Birch Wathen School also encouraged creativity. We made books, puppets, gave plays, painted, sang, etc. under the guidance of people in the arts." *Avocational interests:* "Painting and ceramics were my first interests, and I still make ceramics in between books, and sing in a local chorus. Travel stimulates, and many a line has come to me on a tennis court or a walk."

BIOGRAPHICAL/CRITICAL SOURCES: *New York Times Book Review,* November 6, 1966; *Christian Science Monitor,* November 11, 1971.

* * *

LOWE, Roberta (Justine) 1940-

PERSONAL: Born June 2, 1940, in Portland, Ore.; daughter of Robert Stuart and Noni (Ellingson) Long; married Donald Clark Lowe (a photographer), December 2, 1966. *Education:* Attended Reed College, 1958-60; Portland State University, B.A., 1969. *Home and office address:* P.O. Box 217, Sandy, Ore. 97055.

CAREER: Full-time writer. Professional dancer, 1961-63.

WRITINGS—All with photographs by husband, Donald Lowe; published by Touchstone, except as indicated: *One Hundred Oregon Hiking Trails,* 1969; *One Hundred Northern California Hiking Trails,* 1970; *One Hundred Southern California Hiking Trails,* 1972; *Eighty Northern Colorado Hiking Trails,* 1973; *Seventy Hiking Trails: Northern Oregon Cascades,* 1974; *Mount Hood,* Caxton, 1975; *Fifty West Central Colorado Hiking Trails,* 1976; *Sixty Hiking Trails: Central Oregon Cascades,* 1978; *Sixty-two Hiking Trails: Northern Oregon Cascades,* 1979; *Thirty-five Hiking Trails: Columbia George,* 1980; *Forty-one Hiking Trails: Northwestern California,* 1981. Monthly columnist on outdoors for *Oregon Times,* 1975-77, and *Willamette Week,* 1978-80; weekly columnist on hiking and cross-country skiing for *Oregon Journal,* 1978—. Contributor of articles to *Pacific Northwest, Northwest,* and other periodicals.

WORK IN PROGRESS: *Thirty-two Hiking Trails: Southwestern Washington Cascades,* for Touchstone; *Guide to the John Muir Trail,* for Caxton.

AVOCATIONAL INTERESTS: Ballet, piano, and music in general.

* * *

LOWENFELD, Andreas F(rank) 1930-

PERSONAL: Born May 30, 1930, in Berlin, Germany; son of Henry (a physician) and Yela (a physician; maiden name, Herschkowitsch) Lowenfeld; married Elena Machado, August 11, 1962; children: Julian, Marianna. *Education:* Harvard University, A.B., 1951, LL.B., 1955. *Office:* School of Law, New York University, New York, N.Y. 10003.

CAREER: Hyde & deVries, New York City, attorney, 1958-61; U.S. Department of State, Office of Legal Adviser, special assistant to the legal adviser, 1961-63, assistant legal adviser for economic affairs, 1963-65, deputy legal adviser, 1965-66; Harvard University, Cambridge, Mass., fellow of John F. Kennedy Institute of Politics, 1966-67; New York University, School of Law, New York City, professor of law, 1967—, Charles L. Denison Professor of Law, 1981—. *Military service:* U.S. Army, 1955-57. *Member:* American Society for International Law, American Bar Association, American Arbitration Association, American Law Institute, Council on Foreign Relations, Association of the Bar of the City of New York.

WRITINGS—Published by Matthew Bender, except as indicated: (With Abram Chayes and Thomas Ehrlich) *International Legal Process*, Little, Brown, Volume I, 1968, Volume II, 1969; (editor) *Expropriations in the Americas*, Dunellen, 1971; *Aviation Law*, 1972, 2nd edition, 1981; *International Economic Law*, 1975; *International Private Trade*, 1975, 2nd edition, 1981; *International Private Investment*, 1976, 2nd edition, 1982; *Trade Controls for Political Ends*, 1977; *International Monetary System*, 1977; *Public Controls on International Trade*, 1979. Contributor to law and foreign affairs journals.

* * *

LUEKER, Erwin L(ouis) 1914-

PERSONAL: Born December 15, 1914, near Dover, Ark.; son of Charles H. (a farmer) and Louise (Harms) Lueker; married Anna Marie Schick, May 2, 1942 (died, 1973); married Margaret A. Reimann, July 19, 1980; children: (first marriage) Erwin, Jr., Lisette, George, Jonathan. *Education:* Attended St. Paul's College, Concordia, Mo., 1933-35; Concordia Seminary, St. Louis, Mo., B.D., 1939; Washington University, St. Louis, Mo., M.A., 1940, Ph.D., 1942. *Home:* 7201 Waterman, University City, Mo. 63130.

CAREER: Ordained Lutheran minister, 1939; pastor in Richmond Heights, Mo., 1943-46; Concordia Seminary, St. Louis, Mo., instructor, 1945-46; St. Paul's College, Concordia, Mo., associate professor of languages and humanities, 1946-55; Concordia Seminary, professor of theology and philosophy, 1955-74, director of Correspondence School, 1957-73, acting director of graduate studies, 1965-66; Christ Seminary—Seminex, St. Louis, Mo., professor, 1974-80. Adjunct professor, St. Louis University and Eden Theological Seminary, 1974—. *Member:* American Philological Association.

WRITINGS—Published by Concordia, except as indicated: (Editor) *Lutheran Cyclopedia*, 1954, revised edition, 1975; (with O. E. Feucht, P. Hansen, and F. Kramer) *Engagement and Marriage*, 1959; *The Concordia Bible Dictionary*, 1963; (with Carl S. Meyer and others) *Moving Frontiers*, 1964; (with Richard Caemmerer) *Church and Ministry in Transition*, 1964; *Structured Musings of EL*, four volumes, privately printed, 1968-80; *Change and the Church*, 1969; *Development-Tension-Crisis: A Study of Interaction of Event and Thought in the Missouri Synod with Documents*, privately printed, 1980; *Chapel Musings*, privately printed, 1981; *Gospel Declared and Confirmed*, privately printed, 1982. Also author of numerous essays on religious subjects. Contributor of poetry and of articles to reference works and journals. Former member of editorial board, *Lutheran Witness*.

WORK IN PROGRESS: Study of synoptic problems and New Testament manuscripts; revisions of reference books; poetry.

SIDELIGHTS: Erwin Lueker told *CA:* "Religious language is symbolic language and the deepest religious perceptions are expressed poetically." The author also added that he "plans to make the study of poetry, classics, philosophy and theology [my] avocation during retirement. [I am] particularly interested in their interrelationships."

* * *

LYONS, Elena
See FAIRBURN, Eleanor

M

MACDONNELL, James Edmund 1917-
(James MacNell)

PERSONAL: Born November 3, 1917, in Mackay, Queensland, Australia; son of Harold Claude and Lilian (Northam) Macdonnell; married Valerie Comer; children: Beth Lilian. *Home and office:* 15 Bundabah Ave., St. Ives, New South Wales, Australia.

CAREER: Writer. On staff of *Sydney Bulletin*, Sydney, Australia, beginning 1948. *Military service:* Royal Australian Navy, fourteen years of service, ending 1948; became lieutenant. *Member:* Avalon R.S.L. Club, Mona Vale Golf Club.

WRITINGS—Published by Constable, except as indicated: *Fleet Destroyer*, illustrated by author, Book Depot (Melbourne, Australia), 1945; *Valiant Occasions*, 1952; *Gimme the Boats*, 1953; reprinted, Elmfield Press, 1975; *Wings off the Sea*, 1953; *Jim Brady: Leading Seaman*, 1954, reprinted, Corgi Books, 1970; (under pseudonym James MacNell) *Captain Mettle, V.C.*, 1955, reprinted, Horwitz, 1979 (under pseudonym James MacNell) *Mettle Dives Deep*, 1956; *Stand-by to Ram!*, Horwitz (Melbourne), 1957; *Battle Ensign*, Horwitz, 1957; *Coffin Island*, Horwitz, 1958; *Killer Ship*, Horwitz, 1959.

Published by Horwitz, except as indicated: *Saintsbury, V.C.*, 1960; *Subsmash!*, Constable, 1960; *Colt and Company in the Valley of Gold*, Dent, 1960; *Enemy in Sight*, Pyramid, 1960; *Frogman!*, Pyramid, 1960; (under pseudonym James MacNell) *Mettle at Woomera*, Children's Press, 1961; *Doctor Defiant*, 1962; *Foul Ground*, 1966; *Loom of Ice*, 1966; *The Convert*, New American Library, 1967; *Down the Throat*, New American Library, 1967; *South Pacific Fury*, Signet, 1968; *White Fury*, 1968; *Approved to Scrap*, 1968; *Attack and Be Damned*, 1968; *The Hammer of God*, 1968; *High Command*, 1968; *Judas Rat*, 1968; *Mission Hopeless*, 1968; *And the Heavens Spoke*, 1969; *Commander Brady*, 1969; *Operation Jackal*, 1969; *Strike Force*, 1969.

The Captain, 1971; *Damn the Torpedoes*, 1971; *Repel Boarders*, 1974; *Battle Hymn*, 1978; *Circle of Fire*, 1978; *Died Fighting*, 1978; *Fog Blind*, 1978; *For Valour*, 1978; *The Last Stand*, 1978; *Not Wanted on Voyage*, 1978; *Object Destruction*, 1978; *Blind into Doom*, 1979; *The Brave Men*, 1979; *Breaking Point*, 1979; *Chain of Violence*, 1979; *Close Up*, 1979; *False Colours*, 1979; *Fire Storm*, 1979; *First Command*, 1979; *The Iron Claw*, 1979; *Most Immediate*, 1979; *Northwest by North*, 1979; *Point Blank*, 1979; *Standing into Danger*, 1979; *This Ship Is Mine*, 1979; *The Trap*, 1979; *The Verge of Hell*, 1979; *Weapon Raid*, 1979; *The Worst Enemy*, 1979.

The Liberty Men, 1980; *Operational Immediate*, 1980; *The Shadow*, 1980; *Stand Off*, 1980; *Big Bill, the Bastard*, 1980; *Confirmed in Command*, 1980; *The Dark of the Night*, 1980; *Death of a Destroyer*, 1980.

AVOCATIONAL INTERESTS: Car racing, squash, reading.†

* * *

MacDOUGALL, Ruth Doan 1939-

PERSONAL: Born March 19, 1939, in Laconia, N.H.; daughter of Daniel (a writer) and Ernestine (Crone) Doan; married Donald K. MacDougall, October 9, 1957. *Education:* Attended Bennington College, 1957-59; Keene Teachers College (now Keane State College), B.Ed., 1961. *Agent:* Raines & Raines, 475 Fifth Ave., New York, N.Y. 10017.

CAREER: Writer.

WRITINGS: *The Lilting House*, Bobbs-Merrill, 1965; *The Cost of Living*, Putnam, 1971; *One Minus One*, Putnam, 1971; *The Cheerleader*, Putnam, 1973; *Wife and Mother*, Putnam, 1976; *Aunt Pleasantine*, Harper, 1978; *The Flowers of the Forest*, Atheneum, 1981; *A Lovely Time Was Had by All*, Atheneum, 1982.

WORK IN PROGRESS: A novel.

* * *

MacHORTON, Ian
See MACHORTON, Ian (Duncan)

* * *

MACHORTON, Ian (Duncan) 1923-
(Ian MacHorton)

PERSONAL: Surname originally MacHorton; born April 13, 1923, in Maidstone, Kent, England; son of William and Valentine E. (Rose) MacHorton; married Mary G. Fisher, November 10, 1945; married Gillian Mary Eustance, 1973; children: (first marriage) Sheena Mary, John Graeme Barrie. *Education:* Attended Indian Military Academy, Dehra Dun, India, 1941-42, and University of London, 1953-54. *Politics:* Conservative. *Religion:* Church of Scotland. *Home:* 14 Onslow

Sq., London S.W.7, England; and White Horse Cottage, Stow Beden, Norfolk, England. *Agent:* Peggy Maule Inc., Barn Cottage, Hampstead Norreys, Near Newbury, Berkshire, England. *Office:* 235 High Holborn, London W.C.1, England.

CAREER: Designer and organizer of management courses for British companies as chief executive of Training Services Ltd. (TSL). Director of Resettlement Course Programme of British Ministry of Defence and Metropolitan Police at the Polytechnic of Central London, 1964. Host of radio and television programs in England, including "Out of the Rut." *Military service:* Brigade of Gurkhas, served in 8th Gurkha Rifles as a Chindit in India and Burma, 1942-47; transferred to Cameronians (Scottish Rifles); invalided out with rank of major (honorary lieutenant colonel), 1957. *Member:* Naval and Military Club (London).

WRITINGS—Under name Ian MacHorton: *The Chindits,* Calcutta Press, 1947; *Three Came Back,* Odhams, 1953; *I Refused to Die,* John Bull, 1957; (with Henry Maule) *Safer Than the Known Way,* Odhams, 1958, published as *The One Hundred Days of Lt. MacHorton,* McKay, 1960; *How to Get a Better Job in Management,* Mercury Press, 1971. Also author of business games for senior and junior management, including the computerized game "Splosh" and "Atlas." Contributor of articles on business management to journals.

SIDELIGHTS: Ian Machorton told *CA* that his family "soldiered in India since the days of 'John Company' (the East India Company), including one ancestor who was a colonel under [Robert] Clive [founder of the empire of British India], and [my] father who commanded a squadron of the 1st Australian Light Horse at Gallipoli and Paschedaele in WWI." Machorton's war experiences have been portrayed on several radio and television programs in England, including "Forgotten Heroes," produced by Independent Television, "Chance in a Million," "Find the Link," and "This Is Your Life," all produced by British Broadcasting Corporation (BBC).

*   *   *

**MacNELL, James
    See MACDONNELL, James Edmund**

*   *   *

MACURA, Paul   1924-

PERSONAL: Born September 18, 1924, in Goleszow, Poland; son of Jan (a businessman) and Anna (Marosz) Macura; married Irene M. Pyrghes, January 1, 1959; children: Rene M. *Education:* University of Washington, Seattle, M.A., 1959. *Religion:* Lutheran. *Home:* 812 University Ter., Reno, Nev. 89507. *Office:* University of Nevada, Reno, Nev. 89507.

CAREER: High school teacher of Russian in Tucson, Ariz., 1960-61; University of Arizona, Tucson, instructor in Russian, 1961-63; University of Nevada, Reno, lecturer in Russian and German, 1963—. *Member:* American Association of Teachers of Slavic and East European Languages.

WRITINGS: (Editor with J. Malik) *A Supplementary Russian Reader,* University of Arizona Press, 1965; (compiler) *Russian-English Dictionary of Electrotechnology and Allied Sciences,* Wiley, 1971; (compiler) *Dictionary of Botany in English, French, German, Latin, Russian,* Elsevier (Amsterdam), Volume I: *Plant Names,* 1979, Volume II: *Dictionary of Botany: General Terms in English, French, German, Russian,* 1982; (compiler) *Russian-English Botanical Dictionary,* Slavica, 1982.

WORK IN PROGRESS: Russian-English Standard Dictionary, for Slavica.

*   *   *

MAESTRO, Betsy   1944-

PERSONAL: Surname is pronounced Ma-*es*-troh; born January 5, 1944, in New York, N.Y.; daughter of Harlan R. (a design consultant) and Norma (in education; maiden name, Sherman) Crippen; married second husband, Giulio Maestro (a free-lance writer and book illustrator), December 16, 1972; children: (second marriage) Daniela Marisa, Marco Claudio. *Education:* Southern Connecticut State College, B.S., 1964, M.S., 1970. *Politics:* Democrat. *Home and office:* 702 Summer Hill Rd., Madison, Conn. 06443.

CAREER: Writer. Deer Run School, East Haven, Conn., kindergarten teacher, 1964-75. *Member:* Authors Guild, Authors League of America, National Education Association, Connecticut Education Association. *Awards, honors:* Notable Book Award, American Library Association, 1981, for *Traffic: A Book of Opposites.*

WRITINGS—With husband, Giulio Maestro, except as indicated; published by Crown, except as indicated; all illustrated by G. Maestro: *A Wise Monkey Tale,* 1975; *Where Is My Friend?,* 1976; (sole author) *Fat Polka-Dot Cat and Other Haiku,* Dutton, 1976; (sole author) *In My Boat,* Crowell, 1976; *Harriet Goes to the Circus,* 1977; *Busy Day: A Book of Action Words,* 1978; *Lambs for Dinner,* 1978; *On the Go: A Book of Adjectives,* 1979; *Harriet Reads Signs and More Signs,* 1981; *Traffic: A Book of Opposites,* 1981; *The Key to the Kingdom,* Harcourt, 1982.

WORK IN PROGRESS: Two new word concept books for Crown.

SIDELIGHTS: Betsy Maestro writes: "When you work on picture books for young children, it is impossible to think of the story or concept separately from the illustration. The two are one. I have been very lucky in that, since Giulio and I work together most of the time, we both have a lot of input in each area and give each other suggestions and advice. I loved books as a child (and still do!) and enjoy sharing the ones I write with all the children we know."

AVOCATIONAL INTERESTS: Reading, cooking, gardening, photography, travel.

*   *   *

MAESTRO, Giulio   1942-

PERSONAL: Given name is pronounced *Jool*-yoh, and surname, Ma-*es*-troh; born May 6, 1942, in New York, N.Y.; son of Marcello (a writer) and Edna (Ten Eyck) Maestro; married Betsy Crippen (a kindergarten teacher and writer), December 16, 1972; children: Daniela Marisa, Marco Claudio. *Education:* Cooper Union, B.F.A., 1964; further study in printmaking at Pratt Graphics Center. *Home:* 702 Summer Hill Rd., Madison, Conn. 06443.

CAREER: Design Organization, Inc. (advertising design), New York City, assistant to art director, 1965-66; Warren A. Kass Graphics, Inc. (advertising design), New York City, assistant art director, 1966-69; free-lance writer and book illustrator, 1969—. *Member:* American Institute of Graphic Arts.

AWARDS, HONORS: Two books have been included in American Institute of Graphic Arts Children's Book Shows, *The Tortoise's Tug of War* in the 1971-72 show and *Three Kittens* in the 1973-74 show; artwork from *The Remarkable Plant in Apartment 4* was exhibited in the Society of Illustrators Show, New York, 1974; *Two Good Friends* was chosen an American Library Association Notable Book, 1974; Merit Award from Art Directors Club of New York, 1978, for *Harriet Goes to the Circus*; artwork from *The Tortoise's Tug of War* was included in the 14th Exhibition of Original Pictures of International Children's Books, Japan, 1979; Notable Book Award, American Library Association, 1981, for *Traffic: A Book of Opposites*.

WRITINGS—All self-illustrated: *The Tortoise's Tug of War*, Bradbury, 1971; *The Remarkable Plant in Apartment 4*, Bradbury, 1973; *One More and One Less* (Junior Literary Guild selection), Crown, 1974; (with wife, Betsy Maestro) *A Wise Monkey Tale*, Crown, 1975; (with B. Maestro) *Where Is My Friend?*, Crown, 1976; (with B. Maestro) *Harriet Goes to the Circus*, Crown, 1977; (with B. Maestro) *Busy Day: A Book of Action Words*, Crown, 1978; *Leopard Is Sick*, Greenwillow, 1978; (with B. Maestro) *Lambs for Dinner*, Crown, 1978; *Leopard and the Noisy Monkeys*, Greenwillow, 1979; (with B. Maestro) *On the Go: A Book of Adjectives*, Crown, 1979; (with B. Maestro) *Harriet Reads Signs and More Signs*, Crown, 1981; (with B. Maestro) *Traffic: A Book of Opposites*, Crown, 1981; (with B. Maestro) *The Key to the Kingdom*, Harcourt, 1982; *A Raft of Riddles*, Dutton, 1982.

Illustrator; juvenile picture books: Millie McWhirter, *A Magic Morning with Uncle Al*, Collins & World, 1969; Rudyard Kipling, *The Beginning of the Armadillos*, St. Martin's, 1970; Mirra Ginsburg, *What Kind of Bird Is That?*, Crown, 1973; Ginsburg, *Three Kittens* (Junior Literary Guild selection), Crown, 1973; Vicki Kimmel Artis, *Gray Duck Catches a Friend*, Putnam, 1974; Tony Johnston, *Fig Tale*, Putnam, 1974; Judy Delton, *Two Good Friends* (Junior Literary Guild selection), Crown, 1974; Harry Milgrom, *Egg-Ventures* (Junior Literary Guild selection), Dutton, 1974.

Eva Ibbotson, *The Great Ghost Rescue*, Walck, 1975; Maria Polushkin, *Who Said Meow?* (Junior Literary Guild selection), Crown, 1975; William R. Gerler, *A Pack of Riddles*, Dutton, 1975; B. Maestro, *Fat Polka-Dot Cat and Other Haiku*, Dutton, 1976; B. Maestro, *In My Boat*, Crowell, 1976; Delton, *Two Is Company*, Crown, 1976; Delton, *Three Friends Find Spring*, Crown, 1977; Delton, *Penny-Wise, Fun-Foolish*, Crown, 1977; Ruth Lerner Perle and Susan Horowitz, adapters, *Little Red Riding Hood with Benjy and Bubbles*, Holt, 1979; Perle and Horowitz, adapters, *The Fisherman and His Wife with Benjy and Bubbles*, Holt, 1979; Perle and Horowitz, adapters, *Rumpelstiltskin with Benjy and Bubbles*, Holt, 1979; Perle and Horowitz, adapters, *Sleeping Beauty with Benjy and Bubbles*, Holt, 1979; Ginsburg, *Kitten from One to Ten*, 1980; Delton, *Groundhog's Day at the Doctor*, Parents Magazine Press, 1980; Mike Thaler, *Moonkey*, Harper, 1981.

Illustrator: Katherine Cutler, *From Petals to Pinecones*, Lothrop, 1969; Cutler, *Creative Shellcraft*, Lothrop, 1971; (with others) Richard Shaw, editor, *The Fox Book*, Warner, 1971; Elyse Sommer, *The Bread Dough Craft Book*, Lothrop, 1972; Franklyn Branley, *The Beginning of the Earth*, Crowell, 1972; Jo Phillips, *Right Angles: Paper-Folding Geometry*, Crowell, 1972; Sommer, *Designing with Cutouts: The Art of Decoupage*, Lothrop, 1973; Sommer, *Make It With Burlap*, Lothrop, 1973; (with others) Shaw, editor, *The Cat Book*, Warner, 1973; Roma Gans, *Millions and Millions of Crystals*, Crowell, 1973; Mannis Charosh, *Number Ideas through Pictures*, Crowell, 1974; Carolyn Meyer, *Milk, Butter and Cheese: The Story of Dairy Products*, Morrow, 1974; Sarah Riedman, *Trees Alive*, Lothrop, 1974; Melvin Berger, *The New Air Book*, Crowell, 1974; (with others) Shaw, editor, *The Bird Book*, Warner, 1974.

Gans, *Oil: The Buried Treasure*, Crowell, 1975; John Trivett, *Building Tables on Tables: A Book about Multiplication*, Crowell, 1975; Elyse Sommer and Joellen Sommer, *A Patchwork, Applique, and Quilting Primer*, Lothrop, 1975; (with others) Shaw, editor, *The Mouse Book*, Warne, 1975; Sigmund Kalina, *How to Make a Dinosaur*, Lothrop, 1976; Gans, *Caves*, Crowell, 1976; Berger, *Energy from the Sun*, Crowell, 1976; Eve Barwell, *Make Your Pet a Present*, Lothrop, 1977; Caroline Anne Levine, *Knockout Knock Knocks*, Dutton, 1978; Gail Kay Haines, *Natural and Synthetic Poisons*, Morrow, 1978; Trivett and Daphne Trivett, *Time for Clocks*, Crowell, 1979; Vicki Cobb, *More Science Experiments You Can Eat*, Lippincott, 1979; Joanne E. Bernstein, *Fiddle with a Riddle: How to Write Riddles*, Dutton, 1979; Isaac Asimov, *Saturn and Beyond*, Lothrop, 1979; Boris Arnov, *Water: Experiments to Understand It*, Lothrop, 1980; Andrea G. Zimmerman, *The Riddle Zoo*, Dutton, 1981; Marvin Terban, *Eight Ate a Feast of Homonyn Riddles*, Clarion Books, 1981.

SIDELIGHTS: Giulio Maestro told *CA*: "I was born in New York City and lived in Greenwich Village most of my life. My family owned a house on Charlton Street, and I attended The Little Red School House from kindergarten through grade six. I started drawing and painting before I even went to school."

Some of Maestro's work has been published in Germany, England, and Japan.

AVOCATIONAL INTERESTS: Reading, painting, gardening, travel.

*   *   *

MAGARY, Alan 1944-

PERSONAL: Surname is pronounced Muh-*geh*-ree; born December 30, 1944, in San Francisco, Calif.; son of Frank A. (a foreign service officer) and Laura (a secretary; maiden name, Forsberg) Margary; married Kerstin Fraser (a writer and editor), April 8, 1972. *Education:* Middlebury College, B.A., 1966. *Home:* 1440 16th Ave., San Francisco, Calif. 94122. *Agent:* Max Gartenberg, 15 West 44th St., New York, N.Y. 10036.

CAREER: *Middletown Press*, Middletown, Conn., part-time reporter, 1964-71; free-lance writer, 1971-74; California Coastal Zone Conservation Commission, San Francisco, editor of coastal plan, 1974-75; proprietor of Editorial/Design, 1976-80; partner in Lexikos Publishing, 1980—. *Military service:* U.S. Army, 1967-70; received Bronze Star. *Member:* Sierra Club, Heritage, SPUR.

WRITINGS: (Editor with wife, Kerstin Fraser, and John Hirsch) *Fodor's Europe on a Budget*, Fodor/McKay, 1972, 4th revised edition, 1975; (with Fraser) *East Africa: A Travel Guide*, Harper, 1975; *Across the Golden Gate*, Harper, 1980.

WORK IN PROGRESS: *South of San Francisco: A Guide*.

SIDELIGHTS: Alan Magary writes, "I now work on the other side of the fence—that is, I'm a book publisher as well as author. Good perspectives!"

*   *   *

MAGGS, Peter B(lount) 1936-

PERSONAL: Born July 24, 1936, in Durham, N.C.; son of Douglas B. (a professor of law) and Dorothy (Mackay) Maggs; married Barbara Widenor, February 27, 1959; children: Bruce, Gregory, Stephanie, Katherine. *Education:* Harvard University, A.B., 1957, LL.B., 1961; Leningrad State University, exchange student, 1961-62. *Home:* 2011 Silver Ct. East, Urbana, Ill. 61801.

CAREER: University of Illinois at Urbana-Champaign, College of Law, assistant professor, 1964-67, associate professor, 1967-69, professor of law, 1969—. *Military service:* U.S. Army Reserve, active duty, 1957. *Member:* American Association for the Advancement of Slavic Studies. *Awards, honors:* Medal of Merit, U.S. Information Agency, 1959, for services at American Exhibition in Moscow; Fulbright Lecturer on U.S. Law, spring, 1977.

WRITINGS: (With Harold J. Berman) *Disarmament Inspection under Soviet Law,* Oceana, 1967; (with John Hazard and Issac Shapiro) *The Soviet Legal System,* 2nd edition (Maggs was not associated with earlier edition), Oceana, 1969, (with Hazard and William Butler), 3rd edition, 1977; (with Donald Barry, F.J.M. Feldbrugge, and George Ginsburgs) *Soviet Law after Stalin,* Volume I, Sijthoff (Leiden), 1977, Volume II, Sijthoff & Noordhoff International, 1978, Volume III, Sijthoff & Noordhoff International, 1979; (translator) Piers Beirne and Robert Sharlet, editors, *Pashukanis: Selected Writings on Marxism and Law,* Academic Press, 1979; (with Gordon Smith and Ginsburgs) *Soviet and East European Law and the Scientific and Technical Revolution,* Pergamon, 1981.

WORK IN PROGRESS: Research on computer application to law; *Soviet Economic Law.*

* * *

MAHONEY, Michael J(ohn) 1946-

PERSONAL: Born February 22, 1946, in Streator, Ill.; son of Daniel F. and Zita E. Mahoney; children: Sean. *Education:* Joliet Junior College, A.A., 1967; Arizona State University, B.A., 1969; Stanford University, Ph.D., 1972. *Religion:* Humanist. *Home:* 320 East Whitehall Rd., State College, Pa. 16801. *Office:* Department of Psychology, Pennsylvania State University, University Park, Pa. 16802.

CAREER: Palo Alto Veterans Hospital, Palo Alto, Calif., trainee in clinical psychology and instructor to nursing services, 1970-71; Learning House (delinquency program), Palo Alto, assistant director, 1971-73; Pennsylvania State University, University Park, professor of psychology, 1972—. Consultant to Laurelton State Hospital for the Retarded, 1972-74. *Member:* Association for the Advancement of Behavior Therapy, Association for Humanistic Psychology, Society for Social Studies of Science, Psychotherapy Research Society.

WRITINGS: (With Carl E. Thoresen) *Behavioral Self-Control,* Holt, 1974; (editor with Thoresen) *Self-Control: Power to the Person,* Brooks-Cole, 1974; *Cognition and Behavior Modification,* Ballinger, 1974; (with W. E. Craighead and A. E. Kazdin) *Behavior Modification: Principles, Issues, and Applications,* Houghton, 1976; (contributor) Harold Leitenberg, editor, *Handbook of Behavior Modification,* Prentice-Hall, 1976; *The Scientist as Subject: The Psychological Imperative,* Ballinger, 1976; (co-author) *Permanent Weight Control,* Norton, 1976; *Self-Change: Strategies for Solving Personal Problems,* Norton, 1979; (editor) *Psychotherapy Process: Current Issues and Future Directions,* Plenum (New York), 1980; *Abnormal Psychology: Perspectives on Human Variance,* with study guide and teacher's manual, Harper, 1980.

* * *

MAINE, David
See AVICE, Claude

MALI, Paul 1926-

PERSONAL: Born July 6, 1926, in Hartford, Conn.; married Mary S. Mammone (a general manager), June 28, 1948; children: Faith L., Dawn S. *Education:* University of Connecticut, B.S., 1953, M.S., 1962, Ph.D., 1966; Cornell University, certificate in manpower management, 1963. *Politics:* Independent. *Religion:* Christian. *Home:* 638 Pequot Ave., New London, Conn. 06320. *Office:* Paul Mali & Associates, Groton Shoppers Mart, Groton, Conn. 06340.

CAREER: Certified management consultant; certified psychological test specialist. Western Electric Corp., New York, N.Y., engineer, 1954-58; General Dynamics Corp., Electric Boat Division, Groton, Conn., director of education, 1960-66; University of Hartford, Hartford, Conn., beginning 1967, became professor of management; Paul Mali & Associates (management consultants), Groton, Conn., senior associate, 1967—. Has developed management by objectives systems in over 100 organizations in United States and Canada; has conducted seminars on a variety of subjects. Trustee of Connecticut Colleges, State of Connecticut. Diplomate of American Management Association, 1963. *Member:* Academy of Management, American Management Association, American Society of Training and Development, Tau Beta Pi, Eta Kappa Nu, Phi Delta Kappa.

WRITINGS: The Training and Development of Nuclear Technicians, Franklin Press, 1962; *Future Management for the Smaller Businessman,* University of Hartford Press, 1971; (contributor) *Handbook of Personnel Management,* McGraw, 1971; *Managing by Objectives,* Wiley Interscience, 1972; *How to Manage by Objectives,* Wiley Interscience, 1975; *Improving Total Productivity,* Wiley Interscience, 1978; *Management Handbook,* Wiley, 1981.

* * *

MALONEY, George A(nthony) 1924-

PERSONAL: Born October 29, 1924, in Green Bay, Wis.; son of George John (a paper-mill manager) and Catherine (Karbowski) Maloney. *Education:* Attended University of Wisconsin (now University of Wisconsin—Milwaukee), 1942-43; St. Louis University, B.A., 1948, Ph.L., 1951; Gregorian University, S.T.L., 1958; Pontifical Oriental Institute, Doctor of Oriental Ecclesiastical Sciences (summa cum laude), 1962; additional study at Fordham University. *Home and office:* John XXIII Institute for Eastern Christian Studies, Fordham University, Bronx, N.Y. 10458.

CAREER: Roman Catholic priest of Society of Jesus (Jesuit order), ordained in Russian Byzantine rite, 1957. Fordham University, John XXIII Ecumenical Center, Institute for Eastern Christian Studies, Bronx, N.Y., associate professor of theology, 1963—, founder and director of Institute. Visiting professor of theology, University of San Francisco, 1968. Member of Episcopal Commission on Ecumenism.

WRITINGS: (Editor and contributor) *The Byzantine Christian Heritage,* Fordham University Press, 1966; *The Cosmic Christ: From Paul to Teilhard,* Sheed, 1968.

Published by Dimension, except as indicated: *Russian Hesychasm,* Mouton, 1972; *The Breath of the Mystic,* 1973; *Man: The Divine Icon,* Dove, 1972; *Listen Prophets,* 1975; *The Mystic of Fire and Light,* 1975; *History of Byzantine: Slav Orthodox Theology from 1453 to the Present,* Nordland, 1975; *Inward Stillness,* 1975; *Mary: The Womb of God,* 1976; *Bright Darkness,* 1976; *Nesting in the Rock,* 1977; *A Theology of Uncreated*

Energies, Marquette University Press, 1978; *Jesus, Set Me Free*, 1978; *Inscape*, 1978; *Intoxicated By God: Fifty Spiritual Homilies of St. Macarius*, 1979; *The Everlasting Now*, Ave Maria Press, 1979.

Invaded by God, 1980; *Broken But Loved*, Alba, 1980; *Prayer of the Heart*, Ave Maria Press, 1981; *Alone with the Alone*, Ave Maria Press, 1981; *The First Day of Eternity: Resurrection Now*, Crossroad, 1982; *Centering on the Lord Jesus*, Michael Glazier, 1982; *The Return of the Sun*, Living Flame Press, 1982; *An Anthology of Eastern Christian Spirituality*, Harper, 1983. Contributor to encyclopedias and to journals, including *America* and *Catholic World*. Consulting editor, *New Catholic Encyclopedia*, 1964-65. Editor of *Diakonia* (ecumenical journal).

SIDELIGHTS: George Maloney speaks seven languages, including Russian and Greek and reads many others. *Avocational interests:* Swimming, the Green Bay Packers football team.

* * *

MALPASS, Leslie F(rederick) 1922-

PERSONAL: Born May 16, 1922, in Hartford, Conn.; son of John Fred and Lilly (Elmslie) Malpass; married Winona H. Cassin, May 17, 1946; children: Susan, Peter, Jennifer, Michael. *Education:* Attended University of Cincinnati and Cincinnati Conservatory of Music, 1940-42; Syracuse University, B.A., 1947, M.A., 1949, Ph.D., 1952. *Home:* 2001 North Wigwam Hollow Rd., Macomb, Ill. 61455. *Office:* Office of the President, Western Illinois University, Macomb, Ill. 61455.

CAREER: Onondaga County Child Guidance Center, Syracuse, N.Y., psychologist, 1948-52; lecturer at Syracuse University, Syracuse, and University of Buffalo (now State University of New York at Buffalo), Buffalo, N.Y., 1949-52; Southern Illinois University, Carbondale, assistant professor, 1952-55, associate professor of psychology, 1955-60, supervisor of Psychological Services Center, 1952-55; University of South Florida, Tampa, professor of psychology and chairman of Division of Behavioral Sciences, 1960-65; Virginia Polytechnic Institute and State University, Blacksburg, professor of psychology, 1965-74, dean of College of Arts and Sciences, 1965-68, vice-president for academic affairs, 1968-74; Western Illinois University, Macomb, president and professor, 1974—. Visiting professor, University of Florida, 1959-60. Member of board of directors, First National Exchange Bank of Virginia, and A. M. Showalter Memorial Hospital, both 1966—. Diplomate, American Board of Examiners in Professional Psychology. Consultant to numerous organizations, including Peace Corps, National Science Foundation, American Council on Education, Kennedy Foundation, and Cooperative Research Program of U.S. Office of Education. *Military service:* U.S. Army, Medical Corps, 1945-46.

MEMBER: American Association for the Advancement of Science, American Psychological Association (fellow), American Association of University Professors, American Association for Higher Education, American Council on Education, National Education Association, National Conference of University Research Administrators (executive committee, 1964-65), National Association of State Universities and Land Grant Colleges' Council on Academic Affairs (executive committee, 1970-74; president, 1972-73), Southern Association of Colleges and Schools' Conference of Provosts and Academic Deans (president, 1973-74), North Central Association of Colleges and Secondary Schools, Illinois Mental Health and Developmental Disabilities (region 1B advisory council, 1978—), CONVOCOM—Regional Educational Television, Community Coordinating Council (Hillsborough Co., Fla.), Citizens for Community Development (Blacksburg, Va.), Sigma Xi, Psi Chi, Phi Mu Alpha, Theta Chi Beta, Omicron Delta Kappa, Beta Gamma Sigma, United Fund, Salvation Army Citizens Advisory Board; Kiwanis and Rotary clubs. *Awards, honors:* Ellis Phillips Foundation fellow, 1962-63; Medallion of Recognition, Lord Fairfax Community College; Gold Medal and Diplome de Merite Agricole (Officier), Republic of Haiti.

WRITINGS: (With Chester J. Atkinson and Israel Goldiamond) *Perceptual and Response Abilities of Mentally Retarded Children*, Southern Illinois University Press, 1959; (with Neil Carrier and Kenneth Orton) *Responses of Bright, Normal and Retarded Children to Learning Tasks*, Southern Illinois University Press, 1961; (contributor) Norman R. Ellis, editor, *Handbook of Mental Deficiency*, McGraw, 1963; (with Alden Gilmore, Miles Hardy, and Charles Williams) *Comparison of Two Automated Procedures for Retarded Children*, Cooperative Research Program, U.S. Office of Education, 1963; (with Margaret B. Fisher) *A Comparison of Programmed and Conventional Textbooks for College Instruction*, Cooperative Research Program, U.S. Office of Education, 1964; (contributor) Joseph Roucek, editor, *Automated Teaching*, Philosophical Library, 1965; (editor and contributor) *Human Behavior: A Program for Self-Instruction* (textbook), McGraw, 1965.

(With Williams and Gilmore) *Programmed Reading Instruction for Culturally Deprived Slow Learners* (booklet), MacDonald Training Center Foundation (Tampa), 1966; (editor and contributor) *Social Behavior: A Program for Self-Instruction* (textbook), McGraw, 1966; (with Williams and Gilmore) *Further Development, Comparison, and Evaluation of Programmed Instruction for Retarded Children*, Bureau of Research, U.S. Office of Education, 1967; (contributor) A. Baumeister, editor, *Mental Retardation: Appraisal, Education, Rehabilitation*, Aldine, 1967; (contributor) *Classroom Management: The Successful Use of Behavior Modification*, Pergamon, 1972. Contributor to professional journals.

AVOCATIONAL INTERESTS: Tennis, racquetball, golf, swimming, waterskiing, travel, composing vocal and instrumental music; reading, especially biography, history, and fiction.

* * *

MANDELL, Betty Reid 1924-

PERSONAL: Born November 4, 1924, in Denver, Colo.; daughter of Aubrey W. (a farmer) and Ruth (Flint) Reid; married Marvin L. Mandell (a professor), 1954; children: Christine, Charlotte. *Education:* Colorado State University, B.S., 1945; Union Theological Seminary, M.A., 1947; Columbia University, M.S.W., 1952. *Politics:* Democratic socialist. *Religion:* None. *Home:* 102 Anawan Ave., West Roxbury, Mass. 02132. *Office:* Department of Social Work, Bridgewater State College, Bridgewater, Mass. 02324.

CAREER: University of Iowa, Iowa City, assistant professor of social work, 1964-67; Child and Family Services, Inc., Hartford, Conn., social worker, 1967-69; Northeastern University, Boston, Mass., assistant professor of social welfare, 1969-72; Boston State College, Boston, Mass., assistant professor of social welfare, 1972-82; Bridgewater State College, Bridgewater, Mass., associate professor of social work, 1982—.

WRITINGS: *Where Are the Children? A Class Analysis of Foster Care and Adoption*, Heath, 1973; (editor) *Welfare in America: Controlling the 'Dangerous Classes,'* Prentice-Hall, 1975; *An Introduction to Human Services*, Wiley, 1983; *Strategies of Intervention*, Wiley, 1983. Contributor to journals in her field. Member of editorial board, *Social Work*, 1967-72.

MANDER, Anica Vesel 1934-

PERSONAL: Given name is pronounced *An*-itsa; born October 21, 1934, in Sarajevo, Yugoslavia; daughter of Joseph (a lawyer) and Mela (Hofbauer) Vesel; married Jerry Mander (a writer), November 27, 1965; children: Yari Vesel, Kai Vesel. *Education:* University of California, Berkeley, B.A. (with honors), 1952, M.A., 1960. *Politics:* "Feminist." *Home:* 1166 Filbert St., San Francisco, Calif. 94109. *Office:* Antioch University West, 650 Pine St., San Francisco, Calif. 94108.

CAREER: Assistant to U.S. correspondent in Paris, 1960-62; Boston University, Boston, Mass., lecturer in French, 1962-65; San Francisco State College (now University), San Francisco, Calif., assistant professor of French, 1965-71; Alyssum, San Francisco, organizer and facilitator of women's studies program, 1972-73; Antioch University West, San Francisco, faculty coordinator for women's studies and feminist therapy, 1973—. Lecturer in Italian at Harvard University, 1962-63; coordinator of women's studies at Esalen Institute. Editor and co-publisher of Moon Books.

WRITINGS: (Contributor) Anne Ken Rush, editor, *Getting Clear: Bodywork for Women,* Bookworks/Random House, 1973; (with Rush) *Feminism as Therapy,* Bookworks/ Random House, 1974; (contributor) D. K. Carter and E. Rawlings, editors, *Psychotherapy for Women: Treatment toward Equality,* C. C Thomas, 1975; *Blood Ties,* Moon Books/Random House, 1976; (contributor) Nina Winter, editor, *Interview with the Muse,* Moon Books, 1978.

SIDELIGHTS: Anica Mander writes: I am a writer and a historian. I am working collectively with other women and reexamining past misinformation which has been imposed on us by a white, male-dominated society. I am interested in healing myself and society of hierarchical, imperialist, ego-motivated power structures. With other women I am learning to build a base of unity through collectivity and correct my identity from male identified to female identified." Mander speaks Italian and French in addition to English and her native Serbo-Croatian. She has lived in Yugoslavia, Italy, and France.

* * *

MANISCALCO, Joseph 1926-

PERSONAL: Born October 12, 1926, in San Francisco, Calif.; son of Vincent (a truck driver) and Linda (Montalbano) Maniscalco; married Shirley D'Arcy, 1951; children: Glen, Christine, John. *Education:* La Sierra College, B.A., 1950; San Jose State College (now University), M.A., 1952; attended Art Center School, Los Angeles, Calif., 1952. *Religion:* Seventh Day Adventist.

CAREER: Loma Linda Medical School (now Loma Linda University, College of Medicine), Loma Linda, Calif., medical artist, 1949-50; Pacific Union College, Angwin, Calif., art teacher, 1950-54; Pacific Press Publishing Association, Mountain View, Calif., staff artist, 1954-56; free-lance artist and writer, beginning 1956. *Military service:* U.S. Army, 1945-46; became staff sergeant. *Awards, honors:* First place in an international poster contest sponsored by *Liberty* magazine.

WRITINGS—Published by Pacific Press Publishing Association; except as indicated: *Nenook the Polar Bear,* 1957; *Animals of the Bible,* Southern Publishing, 1958.

Our Wonderful Birds, Southern Publishing, 1960; *Elmer the Squirrel,* 1962; *Marty the Marmot,* Southern Publishing, 1963; *Baby Animals of the Sierra,* 1963; *Birds of the Sierra,* 1963; *Bears of the World,* Grosset, 1963; *Bible Animals,* Warner, 1963; *Tantor the Elephant,* 1963; *Creatures of the Sea,* 1964; *God's Other Book,* Southern Publishing, 1965; *Birds,* Review & Herald, 1965; *Billy Bison,* 1965; *How to Draw Bears,* Foster, 1965; *Trees Every Child Should Know,* 1965; (self-illustrated) *The Waldenses,* Southern Publishing, 1966; *Creepy Crawly Creatures,* 1966; *Reptiles and Amphibians,* 1966; *Martin Luther,* Southern Publishing, 1966; *Happy Hippo,* Southern Publishing, 1967; *Flowers and Insects,* 1967.

Published by Standard Publishing; except as indicated: *The Art of Painting Portraits and Features,* M. Grumbacher, 1974; *The Story of the Good Shepherd,* 1974; *Paul,* 1975; *Jesus,* 1975; (self-illustrated) *Joseph,* 1975; *Moses,* 1975; *Bible Hero Stories,* 1975; *Nebuchadnezzar: Mighty King of Babylon,* Review & Herald, 1975; *Symbology—Pagan and Christian,* Pacific Union College, 1975; *Paul,* 1975; *David,* 1977.

Illustrator of over 200 books, including *Friends God Gave Us,* written by Charles Lee Paddock, Southern Publishing, 1967; *Bilibi and the Kangaroos,* written by Pearle Peden, Southern Publishing, 1968; and *The Wonderful World of Birds,* written by George H. Taggart, Review & Herald, 1970. Contributor of over 200 self-illustrated stories to periodicals.

AVOCATIONAL INTERESTS: Skiing, backpacking, lifting weights, gymnastics, photography, travel.†

* * *

MANN, Abel
See CREASEY, John

* * *

MANNIN, Ethel (Edith) 1900-

PERSONAL: Born October 11, 1900, in London, England; daughter of Robert (a post office sorter) and Edith (Gray) Mannin; married John A. Porteous, 1919 (deceased); married Reginald Reynolds (an author and poet), 1937 (died, 1958); children: (first marriage) Jean Porteous Faulks. *Education:* Self-educated after age of 14. *Politics:* "Left." *Home:* Overhill, Brook Lane, Shaldon, Teignmouth, Devonshire, England.

CAREER: Writer. Charles F. Higham, Ltd. (advertising agency), London, England, stenographer, 1915, copy writer, 1916-19.

WRITINGS—Novels; published by Jarrolds, except as indicated: *Martha,* Duffield, 1923, revised edition, Jarrolds, 1929; *Hunger of the Sea,* Duffield, 1924; *Sounding Brass,* 1925, Duffield, 1926, reprinted, Hutchinson, 1972; *Pilgrims,* Doran, 1927; *Green Willow,* Doubleday, 1928, reprinted, Severn House, 1976; *Crescendo: Being the Dark Odyssey of Gilbert Stroud,* Doubleday, 1929.

Children of the Earth, Doubleday, 1930; *Ragged Banners: A Novel with an Index,* Knopf, 1931, reprinted, Hutchinson, 1973; *Linda Shawn,* Knopf, 1932; *Love's Winnowing,* Wright & Brown, 1932; *Venetian Blinds,* Knopf, 1933, reprinted, Hutchinson, 1972; *Men Are Unwise,* 1934, Knopf, reprinted, Severn House, 1976; *Cactus,* 1935, revised edition, 1944; *The Pure Flame,* 1936; *Women Also Dream,* Putnam, 1937; *Rose and Sylvie,* 1938; *Darkness My Bride,* 1938.

Julie: The Story of a Dance-Hostess, 1940; *Rolling in the Dew,* 1940; *Red Rose: A Novel Based on the Life of Emma Goldman,* 1941; *Sleep after Love,* Ryerson, 1942; *Captain Moonlight,* 1942, reprinted, Morley-Baker, 1969; *The Blossoming Bough,* 1943; *Proud Heaven,* 1944; *Lucifer and the Child,* 1945, reprinted, Hutchinson, 1975; *The Dark Forest,* 1946; *Comrade,*

O Comrade: or, Low-Down on the Left, 1947; *Late Have I Loved Thee,* Putnam, 1948, reprinted, Hutchinson, 1974; *Everyman a Stranger,* 1949; *Bavarian Story,* 1949, Appleton-Century-Crofts, 1950, reprinted, Hutchinson, 1974.

At Sundown the Tiger, Putnam, 1951; *The Fields at Evening,* 1952; *Lover under another Name,* 1953, Putnam, 1954; *So Tiberius* (novella), 1954; *The Living Lotus,* Putnam, 1956; *Pity the Innocent,* Putnam, 1957, reprinted, Hutchinson, 1975; *Fragrance of Hyacinths,* 1958; *The Blue-Eyed Boy,* 1959.

Published by Hutchinson: *Sabishisa,* 1961; *Curfew at Dawn,* 1962; *The Road to Beersheba,* 1963, Regnery, 1964; *The Burning Bush,* 1965; *The Night and Its Homing,* 1966; *The Lady and the Mystic,* 1967; *Bitter Babylon,* 1968; *The Midnight Street,* 1969.

Free Pass to Nowhere, 1970; *The Curious Adventure of Major Fosdick,* 1972; *Mission to Beirut,* 1973; *Kildoon,* 1974; *The Late Miss Guthrie,* 1976.

Short stories; published by Jarrolds, except as indicated: *Green Figs,* 1931; *Tinsel Eden and Other Stories,* Wright & Brown, 1931; *Bruised Wings and Other Stories,* Wright & Brown, 1931; *Dryad,* 1933; *The Falconer's Voice,* 1935; *No More Mimosa,* 1943; *Selected Stories,* Maurice Fridberg, 1946; *The Wild Swans and Other Tales from the Irish,* 1952.

Nonfiction; published by Jarrolds, except as indicated: *Confessions and Impressions,* 1930, revised edition, Hutchinson, 1936; *Common-Sense and the Child: A Plea for Freedom,* introduction by A. S. Neill, 1931, Lippincott, 1932, 2nd edition, Jarrolds, 1937; *All Experience,* 1932; *Forever Wandering,* 1934, Dutton, 1935; *South to Samarkand,* 1936, Dutton, 1937; *Common-Sense and the Adolescent,* preface by A. S. Neill, 1937, revised edition, 1945; *Women and the Revolution,* Secker & Warburg, 1938, Dutton, 1939; *Privileged Spectator: A Sequel to "Confessions and Impressions,"* 1939, revised edition, 1947; *Christianity—or Chaos?: A Restatement of Religion,* 1941; *Castles in the Street,* Dent, 1942; *Commonsense and Morality,* preface by A. S. Neill, 1942; *Bread and Roses: An Utopian Survey and Blue-Print,* Macdonald & Co., 1944; *Connemara Journal,* Westhouse, 1947; *German Journey,* 1948; *Jungle Journey,* illustrated with photographs by daughter, Jean Porteous, 1950; *This Was a Man: Some Memories of Robert Mannin by His Daughter,* 1952; *Moroccan Mosaic,* 1953; *Two Studies in Integrity: Gerald Griffin and the Rev. Francis Mahoney,* Putnam, 1954; *Land of the Crested Lion: A Journey through Modern Burma,* 1955; *The Country of the Sea: Some Wanderings in Brittany,* 1957.

Published by Hutchinson, except as indicated: *Brief Voices: A Writer's Story,* 1959; *The Flowery Sword: Travels in Japan,* 1960; *A Lance for the Arabs: A Middle East Journey,* 1963; *Aspects of Egypt: Some Travels in the United Arab Republic,* 1964; *Rebels' Ride: A Consideration of the Revolt of the Individual,* 1964; *The Lovely Land: The Hashemite Kingdom of Jordan,* 1965; *Loneliness: A Study of the Human Condition,* 1966; *An American Journey,* 1967; *England for a Change,* 1968; *Practitioners of Love: Some Aspects of the Human Phenomenon,* 1969, Horizon Press, 1970; *England at Large,* 1970; *My Cat Sammy,* M. Joseph, 1971; *Young in the Twenties: A Chapter of Autobiography,* 1971; *England My Adventure,* 1972; *Stories from My Life,* 1973; *An Italian Journey,* 1974; *Sunset over Dartmoor: A Final Chapter of Autobiography,* 1977.

Juvenile fiction: *With Will Adams through Japan,* Muller, 1962; *The Saga of Sammy—Cat,* Pergamon, 1969.

"The Kennedys Abroad" series; published by Muller: *Ann and Peter in Sweden,* 1959; *Ann and Peter in Japan,* 1960; *Ann and Peter in Austria,* 1962.

Associate editor of *Pelican* (a theater and sports newspaper), 1917-1919.

SIDELIGHTS: In 1932, Ethel Mannin expressed a desire to produce two books per year, one fiction and one nonfiction. During her writing career, which has spanned seven decades, she has consistently met this goal. But she is not only an extremely prolific writer, she is also a highly diversified one, having produced books as varied as a novel/biography about Emma Goldman (who was widely known as "the mother of anarchy in America"), a children's story about a cat, and several volumes on child rearing.

Mannin relates her early success as a writer in the volume *Confessions and Impressions,* the first of her many books of memoirs. She began writing stories and poems while still very young, publishing her first story when she was ten years old. Later, she decided to write longer fictional works. In 1923, Mannin entered a first-novel competition, and her entry was subsequently published by the contest's sponsor. This novel, *Martha,* prompted some praise from reviewers. A *New York Evening Post Literary Review* writer, for example, called the book "a psychological novel of considerable merit" and found Mannin's writing "smooth" and "promising."

Discounting such early praise, Mannin considers her first eight novels immature works and prefers to concentrate on her later production. However, her third novel, *Sounding Brass,* was even more successful with readers and critics than *Martha.* In *Sounding Brass,* Mannin takes a satirical look at the world around her—in this case, London's advertising district—a characteristic tendency appearing in many of her later books. Several critics noted similarities between *Sounding Brass* and other satirical works published in England and in the United States during the same period.

In *Bookman,* a reviewer compared *Sounding Brass* to *Main Street* and *Babbitt,* two satires on American life during the early twenties, written by American novelist Sinclair Lewis. The reviewer stated, "Since *Main Street* and *Babbitt* I have read nothing so amusing, so caustic, so constantly entertaining as this novel of the advertising profession, its motives and its characters." Reviewer Edwin Clark also mentioned the resemblance between the work of Mannin and Lewis. Commenting in the *New York Times,* Clark said: "*Sounding Brass* is a novel of scope and lively entertainment. The character of this fatuous Babbitt [the main character in Lewis's novel of the same title] from abroad is fascinating. The satire of this novel is broad, harsh, but arresting and compelling." L. P. Hartley in the *Saturday Review* compared Mannin to another famous writer of the day, Aldous Huxley, whose sardonic look at British society *Antic Hay* had come out three years before the publication of *Sounding Brass.* Hartley commented: "The excellence of Miss Mannin's story lies chiefly in its execution. . . . She does not get out of her satirical pictures of Bohemians and Business Men the amusement that Huxley did. But for that very reason the satire is sharper."

Reviewers have praised Mannin's skill as a novelist, especially her ability to create memorable characters. *Green Willow* tells the story of a group of children who, after their mother's death, are reminded of her by a green willow tree to which she was very attached. Kathleen Field in the *New York Times* stated: "Besides being a rarely good story throughout, the early part of the book is brilliant with a steady illumination of the child mind." A *Saturday Review of Literature* reviewer wrote: "She tells an interesting story . . . of the conflict of personalities and the change of ideas."

Reviewers also commented on Mannin's superior character portrayal in *Linda Shawn.* This novel is the story of a farming family, with emphasis on one of the children, Linda. Peter Quennell, writing in *New Statesman and Nation,* wrote: "Miss Mannin charts with some skill the difficult passage through the narrows of adolescence." A *New York Times* reviewer noted: "Miss Mannin shows a remarkable gift of character study, each person of the book comes to life." And a *Saturday Review of Literature* critic added: "Miss Mannin writes not only the story of the little girl whose name gives the title to the volume, but that of the whole discouraged . . . family as well. Each character stands out as a whole and merges into the composite family portrait."

These two novels, while showing Mannin's skill at characterization, also point out another characteristic of her work. Many of her novels and nonfiction pieces spring from her personal interest in particular social issues. In *Green Willow* and *Linda Shawn,* for example, the author shows her interest in child psychology and progressive education. One of Mannin's first volumes of nonfiction *Common-Sense and the Child: A Plea for Freedom* also grew out of this concern. In her book, Mannin expresses thoughts on child rearing similar to those expounded by A. S. Neill, writer of the book's introduction. About ten years before *Common-Sense and the Child* was published, Neill and his wife founded Summerhill, the progressive school which Mannin's own daughter attended. Although Mannin's views were considered controversial, the book was well received by critics.

Bertrand Russell, a British philosopher whose ideas on education were similar to Mannin's, reviewed the book in *Saturday Review,* calling the volume "a most valuable and courageous book." A *Boston Transcript* reviewer agreed with this evaluation, saying: "To each problem she brings common sense and a freshness of viewpoint, as well as understanding. . . . Here is the sanest, most thought-provoking educational book published in many seasons." Dora Russell commented in *New York Herald-Tribune Books:* "Ethel Mannin is known as a writer of novels and not as a professional educationist. . . . Yet her book . . . is one that no educator can afford to miss."

Mannin's political views are also evident in her work. Her involvement with the Independent Labour Party, a revolutionary socialist organization, and participation in Emma Goldman's campaign for the Spanish Republican forces during the Spanish Civil War led to the publication of two books, *Women and the Revolution* and *Red Rose: A Novel Based on the Life of Emma Goldman.* Later Mannin's interest turned to pacifism, and she began to write novels dealing with war or post-war experiences, emphasizing the effect that conflict has on the people living through such uncertain times.

One criticism voiced by reviewers of Mannin's books was that often her concerns became more important than the story being related, which gave a propagandistic tone to her fiction. This is seen in *Pity the Innocent,* a novel following the life of a boy whose mother is executed for committing murder. Although the book was called "both absorbing and moving" by Edmund Fuller of the *New York Times,* he also felt that it was too opinionated. According to Fuller, "some passages . . . seem like a tract against capital punishment."

In his *Book Week* review, R. D. Spector similarly praised Mannin's novel *The Road to Beersheba* while criticizing the pro-Arab slant the volume takes. Spector called the book "an anti-Zionist tirade, an attack on what [Mannin] believes to have been an Israeli and British plot to oust the Arabs from their homeland. . . . Yet there was and is an injustice that [she] portrays in . . . her novel."

Forever Wandering, a book of travel memoirs, was comparably criticized and praised by E. H. Walton of *Forum* and E. F. Allen of the *New York Times.* Walton found the book "opinionated and sometimes provoking," but added, "It is infinitely more lively and more interesting than the conventional travel book." Allen commented: "This is the travel notebook of a British novelist, who takes for granted that the world is interested in her observations and reactions. . . . Although [she] is often opinionated to the point of irritation, she is honest in her attitudes and exuberant in her style of writing."

Although Mannin told *CA* that, at the age of eighty, she is "not likely to write anything more," she produced a large and varied collection of work during her active career. Her fifty novels, thirty-eight volumes of nonficton, and numerous other books assure something compatible with the tastes of every interested reader.

BIOGRAPHICAL/CRITICAL SOURCES: New York Evening Post Literary Review, November 3, 1923; *Times Literary Supplement,* November 13, 1924, April 27, 1933, September 12, 1936, April 2, 1938, August 31, 1967, May 14, 1970, August 25, 1972; *Saturday Review* (London), January 9, 1926, March 19, 1927, July 4, 1931, November 26, 1932; *New York Times,* June 20, 1926, October 7, 1928, June 26, 1932, June 16, 1935, July 25, 1937, October 10, 1948, September 1, 1957; *Boston Transcript,* July 24, 1926, December 8, 1928, March 2, 1932, June 15, 1935, July 24, 1937; *Saturday Review of Literature,* July 24, 1926, October 13, 1928, July 15, 1950; *Bookman,* August, 1926; *New Statesman and Nation,* January 10, 1932; *New York Herald-Tribune Books,* February 28, 1932, February 14, 1937; *Wilson Quarterly,* March, 1932; *Forum,* August, 1935; *Commonweal,* November 12, 1948; *Book Week,* August 30, 1964.

—Sketch by Marian Walters

* * *

**MANTON, Peter
See CREASEY, John**

* * *

MAQUET, Jacques Jerome Pierre   1919-

PERSONAL: Surname sounds like "McKay"; born August 4, 1919, in Brussels, Belgium; came to United States in 1967, naturalized in 1974; son of Jerome (a state administrator) and Jeanne (Lemoine) Maquet; married Emma de Longree, June 17, 1947 (divorced, 1969); married Gisele Cambresier, November 13, 1970; children: (first marriage) Bernard, Denis. *Education:* University of Louvain, LL.D., 1946, D.Phil., 1948; University of London, Ph.D., 1952. *Office:* Department of Anthropology, University of California, Los Angeles, Calif. 90024.

CAREER: Institute for Scientific Research in Central Africa, Astrida, Ruanda-Urundi (now Butare, Rwanda), field anthropologist, 1949-51, research director of Social Sciences Center, 1951-57; State University of Congo (now Universite Nationale du Zaire), Elisabethville, Congo (now Lubumbushi, Zaire), professor of anthropology, 1957-60; University of Paris, Ecole Pratique des Hautes Etudes, Paris, France, research director of anthropology, 1961-68; Case Western Reserve University, Cleveland, Ohio, professor of anthropology, 1968-70; University of California, Los Angeles, professor of anthropology, 1971—, chairman of department, 1978—. Visiting professor, Northwestern University, 1956, University of Brussels, 1963-68, Harvard University, 1964, University of Montreal, 1965, University of Pittsburgh, 1967, and Stanford University, 1976. Secretary, Inter-African Committee for the Social Sciences, 1953-56; consultant in museology, UNESCO, 1964-65.

MEMBER: Association internationale des sociologues de langue francaise, International Association for Buddhist Studies, International African Institute, Royal Anthropological Institute of Great Britain, Association for Asian Studies, Federation of American Scientists, Institute for Transcultural Studies (fellow), Current Anthropology (associate member), American Anthropological Association (fellow). *Awards, honors:* Emile Waxweiler Award from Royal Academy of Belgium, 1961, for *The Premise of Inequality in Ruanda;* Wenner-Gren Foundation grants, 1965 and 1973; best French book on African art award, 1966, for *Afrique: Les Civilisations noires;* D.Litt., University of Paris, 1973.

WRITINGS: Sociologie de la connaissance, sa structure et ses rapports avec la philosophie de la connaissance: Etude critique des systemes de Karl Mannheim et de Pitirim A. Sorokin, Institut de recherches economiques et sociales (Louvain, Belgium), 1949, 2nd edition, Institut de sociologie de l'universite libre de Bruxelles (Brussels), 1969, translation by John F. Locke published as *The Sociology of Knowledge, Its Structure and Its Relation to the Philosophy of Knowledge: A Critical Analysis of the Systems of Karl Mannheim and Pitirim A. Sorokin,* Beacon Press, 1951, reprinted, Greenwood Press, 1973.

Le Systeme des relations sociales dans le Ruanda ancien, Musee royal d'Afrique centrale (Tervuren, Belgium), 1954, translation by the author published as *The Premise of Inequality in Ruanda: A Study of Political Relations in a Central African Kingdom,* Oxford University Press for the International African Institute, 1961; *Aide-memoire d'ethnologie africaine* (title means "Manual of African Ethnology"), Academie royale des sciences d'outremer (Brussels), 1954; *Ruanda: Essai photographique sur une societe africaine en transition* (title means "Photographic Essay on an African Society in Transition"), Elsevier (Brussels), 1957; (with Marcel d'Hertefelt) *Elections en societe feodale: Une Etude sur l'introduction du vote populaire au Ruanda-Urundi* (title means "Elections in a Federal Society: A Study of the Introduction of Popular Vote in Ruanda-Urundi"), Academie royale des sciences d'outremer, 1959.

Afrique: Les Civilisations noires, Horizons de France (Paris), 1962, 2nd edition, 1968, published as *Les Civilisations noires: Histoire, techniques, arts, [et] societes,* Gerard (Verviers, Belgium), 1966, translation by Joan Rayfield published as *Civilizations of Black Africa,* Oxford University Press, 1972; *Africanite: Traditionnelle et moderne,* Presence africaine (Paris), 1967, translation by Joan Rayfield published as *Africanity: The Cultural Unity of Black Africa,* Oxford University Press, 1972; (editor with Georges Balandier) *Dictionnaire des civilisations africaines,* Hazan (Paris), 1968, translation by Mariska Caroline Peck, Beltina Wadia, and Peninah Heimark published as *Dictionary of Black African Civilization,* Leon Amiel, 1974.

Pouvoir et societe en Afrique, Hatchette (Paris), 1971, translation by Jeanette Kupfermann published as *Power and Society in Africa,* McGraw, 1971; *Introduction to Aesthetic Anthropology,* Addison-Wesley, 1971, 2nd revised edition, Undena, 1979; (editor) *On Linguistic Anthropology,* Undena, 1980; (editor) *On Symbols in Anthropology,* Undena, 1982.

Contributor: Daryll Forde, editor, *African Worlds,* Oxford University Press for the International African Institute, 1954; F.S.C. Northrop and Helen Livingston, editors, *Cross-Cultural Understanding: Epistemology in Anthropology,* Harper, 1964; Paul Alexandre, editor, *L'Heritage de l'homme,* Editions de la Grange-Bateliere (Geneva, Switzerland), 1967; Mary Douglas and Phyllis M. Kaberry, editors, *Man in Africa,* Tavistock Publications, 1969; Philip K. Bock, editor, *Cultural Shock: A Reader in Modern Cultural Anthropology,* Knopf, 1970; Ronald Cohen and John Middleton, editors, *From Tribe to Nation in Africa,* Chandler Publishing, 1970; Arthur Tuden and Leonard Plotnicov, editors, *Social Stratification in Africa,* Free Press, 1970; James A. Clifton, editor, *Applied Anthropology: Readings in the Use of the Science of Man,* Houghton, 1970; Hubert Deschamps, editor, *Histoire generale de l'Afrique noire,* Presses Universitaires de France (Paris), 1970.

Editor of "Other Realities" anthropological series, Undena, 1978—. Author of screenplay for motion picture, "Ruanda: Tableaux d'une feodalite pastorale," filmed in 1956. Contributor to *International Encyclopedia of the Social Sciences, Encyclopaedia Universalis* and of over 200 articles and reviews to scholarly journals. Editor of *Jeune Afrique,* 1958-60.

WORK IN PROGRESS: Research for books and journal articles on intentional communities, on comparative symbolism, and on aesthetics, in the South Asian context.

SIDELIGHTS: Jacques Jerome Pierre Maquet told *CA:* "A scholar in the social sciences writes but is not necessarily a writer, and I think I am one. To be a writer does not simply mean 'to write well' (which is what I try to do, but English is a second language for me!); it means that one's professional research and one's life are not two separate compartments. Shifts in my scholarly interests—from sociology to anthropology, from Black Africa to South Asia, from social stratification and power to aesthetics and symbolic thinking—reflect and are parallel to the unfolding of my personal itinerary. Commitments and experiences in turn give insight and depth to scholarly endeavors. This dimension makes the difference between a scholar who writes, and a scholar who is a writer."

* * *

MARION, Frieda 1912-
(Arden Kent, Friedl von Castelhun)

PERSONAL: Born October 17, 1912, in Rowley, Mass.; daughter of Fredric Karl (an electrical engineer) and Bertha (Burke) Castelhun; married Donald J. Marion (a sonar technician), October 17, 1934; children: Donna Marise Titus, Donald Theodor. *Education:* Studied art in Boston, Mass., two years, and in Rockport, Mass. *Religion:* Unitarian Universalist. *Home:* 155 West Clark St., No. 5, Manchester, N.H. 03104.

CAREER: Free-lance writer. Former teacher of art at private schools in Newburyport and Malden, Mass.; *Newburyport Daily News,* Newburyport, special feature writer and columnist, 1941-66. Public information chairperson, Haverhill Area Mental Health and Retardation Board, 1971-73. Joint curator (with husband), John Greenleaf Whittier Home, Amesbury, Mass., 1978-81. *Member:* Doll Collectors of America, United Federation of Doll Clubs, Merrimac Valley Writers' Club, First Religious Society, Study Club (Newburyport, Mass.).

WRITINGS: (Contributor) *Guideposts Christmas Treasury,* Guideposts Associates, 1972; (self-illustrated) *China Half-Figures Called Pincushion Dolls,* J. Palmer, 1974; (contributor) A. Christian Revi, editor, *Spinning Wheel's Complete Book of Dolls,* Hanover Press, 1975; (with Norma Werner) *Collector's Encyclopedia of Half-Dolls,* Collector Books, 1979; *Dresser Dolls and Other China Figurals,* Collector Books, in press.

Contributor of poetry, sometimes under pseudonym Friedl von Castelhun, to anthologies: *Book of American Verse,* edited by Harry Bristol Williams, American Publishing, 1930; *The Spring Anthology,* Mitre Press, 1930; *Principal Poets of the World,* Mitre Press, 1932; *The Muse of 1942,* edited by Ann A. Kurdt, Horizon House, 1942.

Author of newspaper column, "The Clinic," under pseudonym Arden Kent, 1941-42; and of "Salt and Pepper," 1949-52.

Contributor of articles and poems, sometimes under pseudonym Arden Kent, to *Pacific Weekly, The Poet, Author and Journalist, Woman's Day, New Hampshire Profiles, Ebony, Christian Science Monitor, Antiques Journal, Spinning Wheel, Boston Globe,* and other periodicals.

SIDELIGHTS: Frieda Marion writes: "I am in the position of having had close personal association with two generations which came before me, as well as being close to the two generations which have followed my own, and this expanded viewpoint covering the lives of five generations I consider to be one of the benefits of growing older."

AVOCATIONAL INTERESTS: Travel (has visited England, France, Germany, Turkey, and Spain, where she lived for about one year).

BIOGRAPHICAL/CRITICAL SOURCES: Lawrence Daily Eagle, August 1, 1957.

* * *

MARKER, Lise-Lone (Christensen) 1934-

PERSONAL: Born September 23, 1934, in Aalborg, Denmark; daughter of Henry M. (a medical doctor) and Gudrun (Haugen Johansen) Christensen; married Frederick J. Marker (a university professor), November 27, 1959. *Education:* Attended Vassar College, 1953-54; University of Copenhagen, Magister artium, 1961; Yale University, Ph.D., 1968. *Home:* 144 Banbury Rd., Don Mills, Ontario, Canada M3B 2L3. *Office:* Graduate Centre for Study of Drama, University of Toronto, Toronto, Canada M5S 2E1.

CAREER: Danish Royal Theatre, Copenhagen, Denmark, librarian of theater collection, 1955-65; Teaterdirek-toerforeningens Skuespillerskole (acting academy), Copenhagen, lecturer in theatre history, 1957-65; Folkeuniversitetet, Copenhagen, lecturer in theater history, 1958-60; University of Copenhagen, Copenhagen, assistant professor of theater history, 1961-65, research fellow, 1962-65; University of Toronto, Graduate Centre for Study of Drama, Toronto, Ontario, assistant professor, 1968-71, associate professor, 1971-77, professor of theatrical history, 1977—. Archives committee consultant, Stratford Shakespeare Festival, 1971-73.

MEMBER: International Federation for Theatre Research, American Society for Theatre Research, Canadian Assocation of University Teachers, Association for Canadian Theatre History, Association for the Advancement of Scandinavian Studies in Canada. *Awards, honors:* American-Scandinavian Foundation scholar at Vassar College, 1953-54; Canada Council research and publication grants, 1971, 1972, 1973; Nordisk Kulturfond grant, 1974; Canada Council leave fellowship, 1974-75.

WRITINGS—With husband, Frederick J. Marker, except as indicated: (Sole author) *David Belasco: Naturalism in the American Theatre,* Princeton University Press, 1972; (and Michael Booth and Robertson Davies) *Revels History of Drama in English,* Volume VI, *1750-1880,* Barnes & Noble, 1975; *The Scandinavian Theatre: A Short History,* Basil Blackwell, 1975, Rowman & Littlefield, 1976; *Edward Gordon Craig and 'The Pretenders': A Production Revisited,* Southern Illinois University Press, 1981; *Ingmar Bergman: Four Decades in the Theater,* Cambridge University Press, 1982.

Contributor: David Galloway, editor, *The Elizabethan Theatre,* Volume II, Macmillan of Canada, 1970; Daniel Haakonsen, editor, *Contemporary Approaches to Ibsen,* Volume II, Oslo university Press, 1971; Margret Dietrich, editor, *Regie in Dokumentation, Forschung, und Lehre,* Otto Mueller Verlag, 1975; *Das Theater und sein Publikum,* Verlag der Oester-reichischen Akademie der Wissenchaften, 1977; Errol Durbach, editor, *Ibsen and the Theatre,* Macmillan, 1980.

Contributor of drama criticism and reviews to *Roskilde Dagblad,* 1955-61, and *Roskilde Tidende,* 1961-65; also contributor to *Theatre Survey, Theatre Research, Quarterly Journal of Speech, Saturday Review, Theatre, Modern Drama,* and other journals. Associate editor, *Modern Drama,* 1972—, and *Scandinavian Studies,* 1973—.

WORK IN PROGRESS: Research in methodology of promptbook research, in theater audiences, and in theories of acting; *A Project for the Theatre* by Ingmar Bergman, "a commented edition of Bergman's scripts for his simultaneous production of Ibsen's 'A Doll House,' Strindberg's 'Miss Julie,' and the stage version of 'Scenes from a Marriage,' prepared in collaboration with husband, Frederick J. Marker."

* * *

MARKHAM, Robert
See AMIS, Kingsley (William)

* * *

MARKS, Peter
See SMITH, Robert Kimmel

* * *

MARRIC, J. J.
See CREASEY, John

* * *

MARRIS, Robin Lapthorn 1924-

PERSONAL: Born March 3, 1924, in London, England; son of Eric Denyer (a civil servant) and Phyllis (Lapthorn) Marris; married, 1949; married Jane Burney Ayres, June 24, 1954; married, 1972; children: Veronica, Sarah, Toby. *Education:* King's College, Cambridge, B.A., 1946, M.A., 1948, Sc.D., 1968. *Politics:* Socialist. *Office:* King's College, Cambridge University, Cambridge, England.

CAREER: Cambridge University, Cambridge, England, fellow at King's College, 1950, assistant lecturer, 1951-60, lecturer, 1960-72, reader in economics, 1972—, assistant director of research, 1955-58. Visiting professor at University of California, Berkeley, 1961-62, and Harvard University, 1967-68. Assistant principal at H. M. Treasury, 1947-50; editor for United Nations, 1950-52; staff member of Ministry of Overseas Development Ministry (London), World Economy Division, 1964-66. *Military service:* Royal Air Force, pilot, 1942-45; became flight lieutenant. *Member:* Royal Economic Society, Association of University Teachers.

WRITINGS: The Machinery of Economic Policy, Fabian Publications, 1954; reprinted, Nendelin/Liechenstein, Kraus Reprint, 1972; *Economic Arithmetic,* St. Martin's, 1958; *The Economics of Capital Utilisation,* Cambridge University Press, 1964; *The Economic Theory of Managerial Capitalism,* Free Press of Glencoe, 1964; (editor with Richard S. Rosenbloom) *Social Innovation in the City: New Enterprises for Community Development,* Harvard University Press, 1969; (editor with Arian Wood) *The Corporate Economy: Growth, Competition, and Innovative Potential,* Harvard University Press, 1971; (editor) *The Corporate Society,* Wiley, 1974; *The Theory and Future of the Corporate Economy and Society,* North-Holland

Publishing, 1979. Contributor to numerous economic journals, including *Review of Economic Studies, Quarterly Journal of Economics, Economica, Economic Journal,* and *American Economic Review.*†

* * *

**MARSDEN, James
    See CREASEY, John**

* * *

MARSHALL, (Sarah) Catherine 1914-

PERSONAL: Born September 27, 1914, in Johnson City, Tenn.; daughter of John Ambrose (a minister) and Leonara (Whitaker) Wood; married Peter Marshall (a minister), November 4, 1936 (died January, 1949); married Leonard Earle LeSourd (an editor and publisher), November 14, 1959; children: (first marriage) Peter John. *Education:* Agnes Scott College, B.A., 1936. *Religion:* Presbyterian. *Home:* 3003 Fernwood Dr., Boynton Beach, Fla. 33435.

CAREER: Full-time writer. National Cathedral School for Girls, Washington, D.C., member of faculty, 1949-50. Chosen Books Publishing Co., Lincoln, Va., treasurer and partner, 1968—. Trustee, Agnes Scott College. *Member:* National League of American Pen Women, Phi Beta Kappa.

AWARDS, HONORS: "Woman of the Year" Award in the field of literature from Women's National Press Club, 1953; D.Litt. from Cedar Crest College, 1954 and Westminster College, 1979; Paperback of the Year Award from *Bestsellers* magazine, 1969, for *Christy;* L.H.D. from Taylor University, 1973; American Book Award nomination, 1980, for *The Helper.*

WRITINGS—Published by McGraw: *A Man Called Peter: The Story of Peter Marshall,* 1951; (with husband, Peter Marshall) *God Loves You,* 1953; *To Live Again,* 1957; *Beyond Our Selves,* 1961; *Christy* (novel), 1967; *Something More,* 1974.

Published by Chosen Books: *Adventures in Prayer,* 1975; *The Helper,* 1978; (with husband, Leonard E. LeSourd) *My Personal Prayer Diary,* 1979; *Meeting God at Every Turn,* 1981; *Catherine Marshall's Story Bible,* 1982.

Editor and author of introduction; collections of sermons and prayers by P. Marshall; published by McGraw, except as indicated: *Mr. Jones, Meet the Master* (also see below), Revell, 1949, revised edition, Revell, 1950; *Let's Keep Christmas,* 1953; *Prayers of Peter Marshall,* 1954; *Heart of Peter Marshall's Faith* (excerpt from *Mr. Jones, Meet the Master*), Revell, 1956; *Friends with God: Stories and Prayers of the Marshall Family,* 1956; *First Easter,* 1959; *John Doe, Disciple: Sermons for the Young in Spirit,* 1963. Contributor to periodicals, including *Reader's Digest.* Woman's editor, *Christian Herald* magazine, 1958-60; roving editor, *Guideposts* magazine, 1960—.

WORK IN PROGRESS: A second novel, set in "a small town in western Pennsylvania during the 1930s, a period currently much in the public mind and eye."

SIDELIGHTS: Catherine Marshall's first book, *Mr. Jones, Meet the Master,* is a collection of sermons written by her husband, Peter Marshall, chaplain of the U.S. Senate from 1947 until 1949. The book, which appeared shortly after his death, attained a place on the bestseller list within a few weeks of publication and remained there for almost a year.

In 1951, Marshall wrote a biography of her husband, *A Man Called Peter.* Receiving favorable reviews from critics and remaining on the bestseller list for more than three years, this second book met with even greater success than Marshall's first. "The best stories are those that really happened," commented Clarence Seidenspinner in the *Chicago Sunday Tribune.* The critic continued: "None of the novels concerning the ministry, written during the last few years, touches the heart and appeals to the mind in the way that Catherine Marshall does in telling the story of her husband." A. P. Davies of the *New York Times* added: "Catherine Marshall writes extremely well. Those who do not accept her religious viewpoint will nevertheless admit that she presents it with grace and charm."

Recalling the experience of writing *A Man Called Peter,* Marshall told *McCall's:* "Literature, if it is accurately to reflect life, must at times reach past the reader's intellect to the emotional level. In order to achieve that the writer has to *feel* something as he writes. There were times during the writing of *A Man Called Peter* when reliving . . . my life with Peter was almost too much for me. . . . Particularly . . . [when] I wrote the chapter on Peter's death. Not only did I have to re-experience every vivid detail . . . , but there was [also] the necessity of holding that emotion in check. I am convinced that real communication in writing always has to be disciplined."

More recently, Marshall explained the writing of her first novel, *Christy,* to *CA:* "The idea for the novel was born from experiences in the life of [my] mother who, as a sheltered, nineteen-year-old girl went to live among and teach the inhabitants of the Great Smoky Mountains of eastern Tennessee. [She was] determined to make herself useful in any way possible and [in the manner] acceptable for young women of the early twentieth century. Readers of all ages can identify with Christy [the novel's heroine] because her spirit exists in everyone, whether young or old, male or female."

Calling the novel her "very special brain child," Marshall notes that *Christy* "delves into actual life" and "is enhanced by in-depth research into the mountain people's lives." There are over 250,000 hard-cover copies and four million paperback copies of Marshall's novel in print.

MEDIA ADAPTATIONS: A Man Called Peter was adapted and released as a film by Twentieth Century-Fox Film Corp. in 1955.

BIOGRAPHICAL/CRITICAL SOURCES: Chicago Sunday Tribune, October 7, 1951; *New York Times,* October 7, 1951; *New York Herald Tribune Book Review,* October 28, 1951; *Reader's Digest,* July, 1953; *McCall's,* August, 1953; *Look,* March 6, 1956; *New York Times Book Review,* October 22, 1967.

* * *

**MARSHALL, F(reddie) Ray 1928-
    (Ray Marshall)**

PERSONAL: Born August 22, 1928, in Oak Grove, La.; son of Thomas Jefferson (a farmer) and Virginia (Foster) Marshall; married Patricia Williams, November 27, 1946; children: Jill Ann, Susan Ray, John Thomas, Christopher Dow (deceased), Sarah Lee. *Education:* Hinds Junior College, student, 1946-48; Millsaps College, B.A., 1949; Louisiana State University, M.A., 1950; University of California, Berkeley, Ph.D., 1955. *Politics:* Democrat. *Religion:* Presbyterian. *Home:* 6400 Lost Horizon, Austin, Tex. 78759. *Office:* Department of Economics, University of Texas, Austin, Tex. 78712.

CAREER: Instructor in economics at Louisiana State University, Baton Rouge, 1950-51, and San Francisco State College (now University), San Francisco, Calif., 1953; University of Mississippi, Oxford, 1953-57, began as assistant professor, became associate professor of economics; Louisiana State University, professor of economics, 1957-62; University of Texas at Austin, Austin, professor of economics, 1962-67; University of Kentucky, Lexington, Alumni Professor of Economics and chairman of department, 1967-69; University of Texas at Austin, professor of economics, 1969-76, director of Center for the Study of Human Resources, 1969-76, chairman of department, 1970-72; U.S. Government, Washington, D.C., secretary of labor, 1977-81; University of Texas at Austin, Bernard Rapoport Centennial Professor of Economics and Public Affairs, 1981—. University of Helsinki, Fulbright research scholar, 1955-56. As U.S. Secretary of Labor: member of boards, committees, and official organizations, including Consumer Affairs Council, East-West Foreign Trade Board, President's Export Council, Special White House Committee of the Energy and Policy Planning Group, and Federal Council on the Arts and Humanities. President of National Rural Center, 1974-77, and National Policy Exchange. Chairman of U.S. Department of Labor subcommittee on research, development, and evaluation, 1973-76, and institution grant panel, 1974; Federal Committee on Apprenticeship, 1974—, and co-chair of U.N. Economic Policy Council's productivity panel. Member of board of directors of Mexican American Research Center, Inc., American Life Insurance Co., and Winthrop Rockefeller Foundation. Member of U.S. Department of Labor and U.S. Department of Health, Education, and Welfare committee on administration of training programs, 1967-68; member of National Manpower Task Force, 1969-76; member of U.S. Department of Labor Consortium on Rural Manpower Development, 1971-75; member of Binational Committee to Study the Border Region between United States and Mexico, U.N. Economic Policy Council steering committee, and Texas Comptroller of Public Accounts Grievance Review committee. Member of U.S. Department of Labor and U.S. Department of Health, Education, and Welfare manpower advisory committees, north central region, 1967-69, southwestern region, 1969-76, and chairman, 1969-72, and national, 1970-73; member of advisory council of Texas Employment Commission; member of board of advisors, John Grey Institute; senior advisor, Labor Policy Institute. Consultant to Chicago Board of Education, 1967, U.S. Department of Health, Education, and Welfare Bureau of Higher Education, 1968-69, review committee of graduate program in economics at Vanderbilt University, Ford Foundation's division of national affairs, Control Data Corp., and Westinghouse Corp. *Military service:* U.S. Navy, 1943-46, served as radioman with amphibious unit in Pacific. U.S. Naval Reserve, 1946-76; retired as commander.

MEMBER: American Economic Association (chairman of committee on hiring practices, 1972-74, committee on labor market statistics, 1973-74, and committee on political discrimination); Industrial Relations Research Association (member of board of directors, 1969-72; president), National Institute of Labor Education (board member, 1960), Association for Evolutionary Economics, National Academy of Sciences, American Arbitration Association (member of panel of labor arbitrators), National Council for Employment Policy, League for Industrial Democracy (member of board of directors), Joint Council on Economic Education (member of board of trustees), American Association of University Professors (president, Texas chapter, 1966-67), Southern Economic Association (member of executive committee, 1969-71 and 1975-76; president, 1973-74), Texas Association of College Teachers, Greater South Texas Cultural Basin Commission, Beta Gamma Sigma, Omicron Delta Kappa, Phi Kappa Phi.

AWARDS, HONORS: Rockefeller Foundation fellow, 1951-53; Wertheim fellow in industrial relations, Harvard University, 1960-61; Ford Foundation faculty fellow, 1964-65. Has received honorary degrees from universities and colleges, including Rutgers University, Millsaps College, St. Edwards University, Bryant College, University of Maryland, University of Kentucky, and Cleveland State University.

WRITINGS: (With Paul Norgren and Samuel Hill) *Toward Fair Employment,* Columbia University Press, 1964; (with Allan Murray Cartter) *Labor Economics: Wages, Employment and Trade Unionism,* Irwin, 1966, (with Cartter and Allan G. King) 3rd edition, 1976, (with King, and Vernon M. Briggs, Jr.) 4th edition, 1980; (with Briggs) *Negro Participation in Apprenticeship Programs,* University of Texas, Department of Economics, 1966; *Labor in the South,* Harvard University Press, 1967; (with Briggs) *The Negro and Apprenticeship,* Johns Hopkins Press, 1967; (with Briggs) *Equal Apprenticeship Opportunities: The Nature of the Issue and the New York Experience,* Institute of Industrial Relations, University of Michigan-Wayne State University, 1968; (with Lamond Godwin) *Cooperatives and Rural Poverty in the South,* Johns Hopkins Press, 1971; (with Sar Levitan and Garth Magnum) *Human Resources and Labor Markets,* Harper, 1972, 4th edition, 1980.

Under name Ray Marshall: *The Negro and Organized Labor,* Wiley, 1965; *The Negro Worker,* Random House, 1967; (with Robert W. Glover) *Compensation of Texas State Employees,* Texas Public Employees Association, 1972; (compiler with Richard Perlman) *An Anthology of Labor Economics,* Wiley, 1972; (with William S. Franklin and Glover) *A Comparison of Union Construction Workers Who Have Achieved Journeyman Status through Apprenticeship and Other Means,* National Technical Information Service, 1973; (with Franklin and Glover) *Training and Entry into Union Construction,* U.S. Government Printing Office, 1974; *Rural Workers and Rural Labor Markets,* Olympus, 1974; (with James L. Walker and R. Lynn Rittenoure) *Human Resource Development in Rural Texas,* Center for the Study of Human Resources, University of Texas at Austin, 1974.

(With Thomas E. Till and Alan Thompson) *Stages of Industrial Development and Poverty Impact in Nonmetropolitan Labor Markets of the South,* Center for the Study of Human Resources, University of Texas at Austin, 1975; *Increasing the Options,* Southern Regional Council, 1977; *Human Resources Dimensions of Rural Development,* Center for the Study of Human Resources, University of Texas at Austin, 1977; (editor with Christian) *Employment of Blacks in the South: A Perspective on the 1960s,* University of Texas at Austin Press, 1978, (with Brian Rungeling) *The Role of Unions in the American Economy,* Joint Council on Economic Education, 1978; (with Thompson) *Small Farmers,* Southern Regional Council, 1978; (with Liggett, Knapp, and Glover) *Employment Discrimination: The Impact of Legal and Administrative Remedies,* Praeger, 1978; *Illegal Immigration: Challenge to the U.S.,* Economic Policy Council of U.N. Association, 1981.

Contributor: Mark Perlman, editor, *Human Resources in the Urban Economy,* Johns Hopkins Press, 1963; Clyde Dankert, Floyd C. Mann, and Herbert Northrup, editors, *Hours of Work,* Harper, 1965; Northrup and Richard L. Rowan, editors, *The Negro and Employment Opportunity: Problems and Practice,* University of Michigan, 1965; Guy Hunter, editor, *Industrialization and Race Relations,* Oxford University Press, 1965; Walter Fogel and Archie Kliengarten, editors, *Contemporary Labor Issues,* Wadsworth, 1966; Lloyd Ulman, editor, *Challenges to Collective Bargaining,* Prentice-Hall, 1967; *Research in Apprenticeship Training,* Center for Studies in Vocational and Technical Education, University of Wisconsin, 1967; Julius Jacobsen, editor, *The Negro in the American Labor Movement*, Doubleday, 1968; (with Biggs) *Federal Programs for the Development of Human Resources*, U.S. Government Printing Office, 1968; Louis A. Ferman, Joyce L. Kornbluh, and J. A. Miller, editors, *Negroes and Jobs*, University of Michigan Press, 1968.

Michael Moskow, editor, *Collective Bargaining in the Public Sector*, Prentice-Hall, 1971; David Brody, editor, *The American Labor Movement*, Harper, 1971; Levitan, editor, *Blue-Collar Workers: A Symposium on Middle America*, McGraw, 1971; W. Ellison Charmers and Gerald W. Cormick, editors, *Racial Conflict and Negotiations*, Institute of Labor and Industrial Relations (Ann Arbor, Mich.), 1971; *Collective Bargaining Today*, Bureau of National Affairs (Washington, D.C.), 1971; Lloyd Zempel, editor, *The Disadvantaged Worker: Readings in Developing Minority Manpower*, Addison-Wesley, 1971; Harold L. Sheppard, Bennett Harrison, and William J. Spring, *The Political Economy of Public Service Employment*, Heath, 1972; Colette Moser, editor, *Labor Market Information in Rural Areas*, Center for Rural Manpower and Public Affairs, Michigan State University, 1972; Irving Howe, editor, *The World of the Blue-Collar Worker*, Quadrangle, 1972; H. Brandt Ayers and Thomas H. Naylor, editors, *You Can't Eat Magnolias*, McGraw, 1972; Harold G. Vatter and Thomas Palm, editors, *The Economics of Black America*, Harcourt, 1972; Seymour L. Wolfbein, editor, *Manpower Policy: Perspectives and Prospects*, Temple University, 1973; Donald C. Huffman and Garnett L. Bradford, editors, *Structure and Control of Southern Agriculture*, Southern Farm Management Research Committee, 1973.

Moser, editor, *Manpower Services in Rural America*, Center for Rural Manpower and Public Affairs, Michigan State University, 1974; *Developing the Nation's Work Force*, American Vocational Association, 1975; Ernest M. Lander, Jr. and Richard J. Calhoun, editors, *Two Decades of Change*, University of South Carolina, 1975; *Group Identity in the South*, Mississippi State University, 1975; *Technology, Human Values, and the Southern Future*, University of Alabama Press, 1976; David C. Warner, editor, *Toward New Human Rights: The Social Policies of the Kennedy and Johnson Administrations*, University of Texas at Austin, Lyndon B. Johnson School of Public Affairs, 1977; *Employment and Unemployment: Priorities for the Next Five Years*, Conference Board (New York, N.Y.), 1977; Stanley R. Ross, editor, *Views across the Border*, University of New Mexico Press, 1978; (with Karen Davis) *Research in Health Economics*, Volume I, Brookings Institute, Jai Press, 1979; Gordon I. Swanson and John Michaelson, editors, *Manpower Research and Labor Economics*, Sage Publications, 1979.

James Stern, editor, *Essays in Honor of Jack Barbash*, University of Wisconsin Press, 1981.

Contributor to numerous journals, including *Texas Business Review*, *American Federationist*, *Southern Economic Journal*, *American Economic Review*, and *Journal of Economic Literature*. Member of board of editors, *Southern Economic Journal*, 1967-70; member of editorial board, *Poverty and Human Resources*, 1971—; contributing editor, *Southern Voices*, 1974—.

SIDELIGHTS: According to a *Newsweek* profile written by Susan Fraker and Dennis A. Williams, F. Ray Marshall "is considered an expert on the problems of minorities and employment." Explaining more specifically Marshall's area of expertise, David E. Rosenbaum, in a *New York Times* article, notes that Marshall's "principal academic interest over the years has involved expansion of employment opportunities for women and members of minority groups."

Reflecting these interests, Marshall has written many books on the subject of disadvantaged workers that have been praised by critics as valuable aids in the study of labor history. B. L. Masse, for example, reviewing *The Negro and Organized Labor in America*, states: "This book [is] a major contribution to an understanding of relations between Negroes and unions. . . . Nowhere can the reader find a better resume of the history of the problem. . . . I cannot too highly recommend this carefully documented book." And, J. O. Morris, commenting on *Labor in the South* in *American Historical Review*, writes: "This is an excellent and ambitious study. The research is thorough. The depth of documented material on every major labor union and organizing effort in the South, since the later nineteenth century, makes the book highly valuable and assures it long life as a scholarly source in labor history."

Marshall's work attracted the attention of former-President Jimmy Carter, when Carter was governor of Georgia. During his years as governor, Carter called on Marshall frequently as an advisor on labor issues, and during the 1976 presidential campaign Marshall wrote position papers on manpower policies for Carter. After Carter's election, Marshall was named U.S. Secretary of Labor and continued in his role as chief presidential advisor on manpower and employment problems. Marshall also administered laws and programs in such areas as job training, union pension funds, occupational safety standards, and labor-management relations. Two of the first programs proposed by Marshall as head of the Labor Department were "Help through Industrial Retraining and Employment" (HIRE), a program designed to provide training to disabled veterans and Vietnam War era veterans which would enable them to obtain jobs in private industry, and a plan to furnish identification cards to every U.S. worker in order to thwart the employment of illegal aliens.

A *Time* article, published soon after Marshall's confirmation as U.S. labor secretary, offered the following summary of ideas which Marshall hoped to work on while serving in this new capacity: "Marshall calls for vastly expanding training programs, arguing that people should be trained for more than one job, so that in a recession they can find work outside their original field. . . . He challenges the contention that reducing unemployment need be inflationary. 'Which is the more inflationary,' he asks, 'paying unemployment insurance or putting people in work-training programs where they are producing for the economy?'"

BIOGRAPHICAL/CRITICAL SOURCES: *America*, June 19, 1965; *Annals of American Academy of Political and Social Science*, September, 1965; *American Economic Review*, December, 1965, September, 1968; *Reporter*, November 2, 1967; *Record*, March, 1968; *American Historical Review*, June, 1968; *New York Times*, December 22, 1976, January 15, 1977; *Newsweek*, January 3, 1977; *Time*, January 3, 1977.

* * *

MARSHALL, Ray
    See MARSHALL, F(reddie) Ray

* * *

MARTIN, James J(oseph)   1916-

PERSONAL: Born September 18, 1916, in St. Leonard, New Brunswick, Canada. *Education:* Attended University of Arizona, 1942; University of New Hampshire, A.B., 1942; University of Michigan, M.A., 1945, Ph.D., 1949. *Residence:* Palmer Lake, Colo.

CAREER: University of Michigan, Ann Arbor, teaching fellow and lecturer, 1946-50; Northern Illinois University, De Kalb, 1950-57, began as assistant professor, became associate professor; Hoover Institution, Stanford University, Stanford, Calif., researcher, 1957-58; San Francisco State College (now University), San Francisco, Calif., visiting professor, summer, 1958; free-lance research, writing, and editorial work, Seattle, Wash., 1958-59; Deep Springs College, Deep Springs, Calif., professor of history and economics, 1959-65; University of California, Los Angeles, researcher, 1965-66; Rampart College Graduate School, Larkspur, Colo., chairman of history department, beginning 1966. *Member:* Organization of American Historians, Society of American Historians. *Awards, honors:* John Tyler Award of Conservative Library Association for *American Liberalism and World Politics.*

WRITINGS: Men against the State, Adrian Allen Associates, 1953, reprinted, Ralph Myles, 1970; *Meditations on the Early Wisdom of John Foster Dulles,* privately printed, 1958; (contributor) *Dictionary of American Biography,* Scribner, 1958; (editor) Paul Eltzbacher, *Anarchism: Exponents of the Anarchist Philosophy,* Libertarian Book Club, 1960; (editor) *The Ego and His Own,* Libertarian Book Club, 1963; *American Liberalism and World Politics, 1931-41,* two volumes, Devin-Adair, 1964; (editor) Lysander Spooner, *No Treason,* Pine Tree Press, 1966; *Revisionist Viewpoints: Essays in Dissident Historical Tradition,* Ralph Myles, 1971; (editor with Leonard Liggio) *Watershed of Empire: Essays and New Deal Foreign Policy,* Ralph Myles, 1976; *The Saga of Hog Island and Other Essays in Inconvenient History,* Ralph Myles, 1977; *Raphael Lemkin and the Invention of Genocide,* Revisionist Press, 1981. Contributor to *Encyclopaedia Britannica,* 1961. Contributor of over fifty articles and reviews to journals.†

* * *

MARTIN, John Bartlow 1915-

PERSONAL: Born August 4, 1915, in Hamilton, Ohio; son of John Williamson (a building contractor) and Laura (Bartlow) Martin; married Frances Rose Smethurst, August 17, 1940; children: Cynthia (Mrs. Joseph Coleman), Daniel Bartlow, John Frederick. *Education:* De Pauw University, B.A., 1937. *Politics:* Democrat. *Religion:* Protestant. *Home:* 185 Maple Ave., Highland Park, Ill. *Agent:* Harold Ober Associates, 40 East 49th St., New York, N.Y. 10017.

CAREER: Free-lance writer, 1938-62; consultant on Caribbean Affairs to the Department of State, 1961; special envoy of U.S. President to Dominican Republic, 1961 and 1965; U.S. Ambassador to Dominican Republic, 1962-64, free-lance writer, 1964—. Wesleyan University, Center for Advanced Studies, Middletown, Conn., senior fellow, 1964-65; Princeton University, Princeton, N.J., visiting fellow in public affairs, 1966-67; Graduate School and University Center of the City University of New York, N.Y., visiting professor, 1968; Northwestern University, Medill School of Journalism, Evanston, Ill., professor of journalism, 1970-80, professor emeritus, 1980—. Staff member for Adlai Stevenson, 1952-56, John F. Kennedy, 1960, Lyndon B. Johnson, 1964, and Hubert H. Humphrey, 1968. *Military service:* U.S. Army, 1944-46. *Member:* Authors Guild, Century Association (New York), Arts Club (Chicago). *Awards, honors:* Sigma Delta Chi Magazine Award, 1950, 1957; Benjamin Franklin Magazine Award, 1954, 1956, 1957, and 1958; Indiana Authors' Day Award from Indiana University Writers' Conference, and Ohioana Book Award, both 1967, both for *Overtaken by Events.*

WRITINGS: Call It North Country, Knopf, 1944; *Indiana: An Interpretation,* Knopf, 1947, reprinted, Arno, 1972; *Butcher's Dozen,* Harper, 1950; *Adlai Stevenson,* Harper, 1952; *My Life in Crime,* Harper, 1952; *Why Did They Kill?,* Ballantine, 1953; *Break Down the Walls,* Ballantine, 1954; *The Deep South Says, Never,* Ballantine, 1957; *Jimmy Hoffa's Hot,* Dell, 1959; *The Pane of Glass,* Harper, 1959; *Overtaken by Events,* Doubleday, 1966; *The Life of Adlai Stevenson,* two volumes, Doubleday, 1976-77; *U.S. Policy in the Caribbean,* Westview, 1978; *The Televising of Heller,* Doubleday, 1980. Contributor to *Harper's, Reader's Digest, Saturday Evening Post,* and other magazines.

WORK IN PROGRESS: A memoir; two novels.

SIDELIGHTS: John Bartlow Martin has had a diverse career as a journalist and speech writer and has managed to serve on the staffs of two presidents and a presidential candidate in addition to producing nearly a dozen highly praised books. Martin has transferred these experiences into a novel describing the workings of a political campaign. Charles Peck writes in the *Washington Post* that *The Televising of Heller* "skillfully suggests the endless dispute over how much time and resources ought to be devoted to creating and projecting a candidate's image when he already has a good record of service.... [The book] is at its most perceptive in revealing the politics behind the cameras."

BIOGRAPHICAL/CRITICAL SOURCES: Chicago Sunday Tribune, February 22, 1959; *New York Times,* May 31, 1959; *New Statesman,* February 6, 1960; *Harper's,* November, 1965; *Washington Post,* February 5, 1980; *New York Times Book Review,* March 9, 1980; *Los Angeles Times,* March 27, 1980.

* * *

MARTIN, Paul Sidney 1899-1974

PERSONAL: Born November 20, 1899, in Chicago, Ill.; died January 20, 1974; son of Ellsworth Crandall and Adelaide (Sackett) Martin; foster children: Carl, Marshall, Roland, Paul. *Education:* University of Chicago, Ph.B., 1923, Ph.D., 1929.

CAREER: Public Museum, Milwaukee, Wis., assistant in anthropology, 1925; Carnegie Institution, Washington, D.C., archeologist in Yucatan, Mexico, 1926-28; State Museum, Denver, Colo., curator of archeology, 1928-29; Field Museum of Natural History, Chicago, Ill., assistant curator of North American archeology, 1929-34, acting curator of anthropology, 1934-35, head curator, 1935-64, emeritus chief curator of anthropology, 1964-74. Lecturer at University of Chicago, 1942-74, and Northwestern University, 1972-74. Director of archeology research for National Science Foundation-Undergraduate Research Participation Project, beginning 1965. Director of Field Museum of Natural History expeditions in American Southwest, 1930, 1931, 1933-39, 1941, 1946-66; other archeological field work in Wisconsin, Illinois, Yucatan, and Colorado. *Member:* American Anthropological Association (fellow), Society for American Archaeology, Sigma Xi.

WRITINGS: Berthold Laufer, *Archaeology of North America,* Field Museum of Natural History (Chicago), 1933; (with George I. Quimby, and Donald Collier) *Indians before Columbus: Twenty Thousand Years of North American History Revealed by Archaeology,* University of Chicago Press, 1947, reprinted, 1975; *Digging into History: A Brief Account of Fifteen Years of Archaeological Work in New Mexico,* Field Museum of Natural History, 1959; (with Fred Plog) *The Archaeology of Arizona: A Study of the Southwest Region,* Natural History Press, 1973. Contributor with others of numerous museum publications to

Fieldiana: Anthropology, including studies of Hooper Ranch Pueblo, late Mogollon communities, Higgins Flat Pueblo, SU site excavations, and Anasazi painted pottery. Contributor to *Anthropology Memoirs.* Assistant editor, *Field Museum of Natural History Bulletin,* 1935-64.†

* * *

MARTIN, Richard
See CREASEY, John

* * *

MASON, F(rancis) van Wyck 1901-1978
(Van Wyck Mason; pseudonyms: Geoffrey Coffin, Frank W. Mason, Ward Weaver)

PERSONAL: Born November 11, 1901, in Boston, Mass.; drowned August 28, 1978, off the coast of Bermuda; son of Francis Payne and Erma (Coffin) Mason; married Dorothy Louise Macready, 1927 (died March, 1958); married Jeanne-Louise Hand, October 3, 1958; children: (first marriage) F. van Wyck II, Robert A. *Education:* Student at Berkshire School, 1919-20; Harvard University, B.S., 1924. *Politics:* Republican. *Religion:* Protestant Episcopal. *Home and office:* Hampton Head, Southampton, Bermuda. *Agent:* Harold Matson Co., Inc., 276 Fifth Ave., New York, N.Y. 10001.

CAREER: Writer. Owner and operator of importing firm, 1925-27. Junior commander with Loyal Legion at Chicago Commandery, 1951. *Military service:* Twenty-six years of active and reserve duty: U.S. Army, 1918-19, served in France; became second lieutenant; received Medaille de Sauvetage. New York National Guard, Calvary, 1924-29; served as sergeant. Maryland National Guard, Field Artillery, 1930-33; became first lieutenant. Recalled to active duty, 1942-45, served as General Staff Corps officer and as chief historian, civil and military government section, Supreme Allied Headquarters, 1943-45; became colonel, received Croix de Guerre with two palms and made Officer in French Legion of Honor.

MEMBER: Society of Collectors and Historians (fellow), Boston University Libraries (fellow), American Society of Bermuda (president, 1960-78); Harvard Club and Racquet and Tennis Club (both New York); Army and Navy Club (Washington, D.C.), Devonshire Club (London), Royal Bermuda Yacht Club. *Awards, honors:* Valley Forge Foundation Medal, 1952, for *The Winter at Valley Forge;* Society of Colonial Wars in the State of New York Citation of Honour, 1960, for *The Young Titan.*

WRITINGS—Historical novels, except as indicated: (Under name Van Wyck Mason) *Captain Nemesis,* Putnam, 1931, reprinted, Pocket Books, 1957; (under name Van Wyck Mason) *Spider House* (mystery novel), Mystery League (New York), 1932, reprinted, R. Hale, 1959; *Three Harbours* (also see below), Lippincott, 1938; *Stars on the Sea* (also see below), Lippincott, 1940, reprinted, Pocket Books, 1964; *Rivers of Glory,* Lippincott, 1942; (editor and author of introduction) *The Fighting American: A War-Chest of Stories of American Soldiers* (anthology), Reynal, 1943; *Eagle in the Sky* (also see below; Literary Guild selection), reprinted, Grosset, 1961; *Cutlass Empire,* Doubleday, 1949; *Valley Forge: 24 December 1777,* Doubleday, 1950; *Proud New Flags,* Lippincott, 1951; *Golden Admiral: A Novel of Sir Francis Drake and the Armada,* Doubleday, 1953; *The Winter at Valley Forge* (young adult), Random House, 1953, published as *Washington at Valley Forge,* E. M. Hale, 1953; *Blue Hurricane,* Lippincott, 1954; *Silver Leopard,* Doubleday, 1955; *Captain Judas,* Pocket Books, 1955;

Our Valiant Few, Little, Brown, 1956 (published in England as *To Whom Be Glory,* Jarrolds, 1957); *Lysander,* Pocket Books, 1956; *The Young Titan,* Doubleday, 1959; *The Return of the Eagles,* Pocket Books, 1959; *The Battle of Lake Erie* (young adult), Houghton, 1960; *Manila Galleon,* Little, Brown, 1961; *The Sea 'Venture,* Doubleday, 1961; *The Battles for New Orleans* (young adult), Houghton, 1962; *Rascals' Heaven,* Doubleday, 1964; (editor and author of introduction) *American Men at Arms* (anthology of war stories), Little, Brown, 1964; *The Battle for Quebec* (young adult), Houghton, 1965; *Wild Horizon* (also see below), Little, Brown, 1966; *Harpoons in Eden,* Doubleday, 1969; *The Maryland Chronicle,* Crowell-Collier Press, 1969; *Brimstone Club,* Little, Brown, 1971; *Roads to Liberty* (contains *Three Harbours, Stars on the Sea, Eagle in the Sky,* and *Wild Horizon*), Little, Brown, 1972; *Log Cabin Noble,* Doubleday, 1973; *Trumpets Sound No More,* Little, Brown, 1975; *Guns for Rebellion,* Doubleday, 1977; *Armored Giants: A Novel of the Civil War,* Little, Brown, 1980. Also author of *Captain Renegade,* 1932, published as *Wild Drums Beat,* Pocket Books, 1954; author of *The Barbarian,* 1934, revised edition published as *The Barbarians,* Pocket Books, 1954.

"Hugh North" series; mystery novels, except as indicated; published by Doubleday, except as indicated: *Seeds of Murder,* 1930; *The Vesper Service Murders,* 1931; *The Fort Terror Murders* (also see below), 1931; *The Yellow Arrow Murders,* 1932; *The Branded Spy Murders,* 1932; *The Shanghai Bund Murders* (also see below), 1933, revised edition published as *The China Sea Murders,* Pocket Books, 1959; *The Sulu Sea Murders* (also see below), 1933; (under name Van Wyck Mason) *The Budapest Parade Murders,* 1935; (under name Van Wyck Mason) *The Washington Legation Murders* (also see below), 1935; *The Seven Seas Murders: Four Cases in the Career of Captain North* (novelettes), 1936; (under name Van Wyck Mason) *The Castle Island Case,* Reynal, 1937, published as *The Multi-Million Dollar Murders,* Pocket Books, 1960; *The Hongkong Airbase Murders* (also see below), 1937; (under name Van Wyck Mason) *The Cairo Garter Murders,* 1938; *The Singapore Exile Murders* (also see below), 1939; (under name Van Wyck Mason) *The Bucharest Ballerina Murders,* Frederick Stokes, 1940; (under name Van Wyck Mason) *Military Intelligence—Eight* (contains *The Washington Legation Murders, The Hongkong Airbase Murders,* and *The Singapore Exile Murders*), Frederick Stokes, 1941; *The Rio Casino Intrigue,* Reynal, 1941; *Oriental Division G-Two* (contains *The Fort Terror Murders, The Shanghai Bund Murders,* and *The Sulu Sea Murders*), Reynal, 1942.

(Under name Van Wyck Mason) *Saigon Singer,* 1946, reprinted, American Reprint Co. (Mattituck, N.Y.), 1976; *Dardanelles Derelict,* 1949; *Himalayan Assignment,* 1952; *Two Tickets for Tangier,* 1955, reprinted, American Reprint Co. (Mattituck, N.Y.), 1976; *The Gracious Lily Affair,* 1957; *Secret Mission to Bangkok,* 1960; (under name Van Wyck Mason) *Trouble in Burma,* 1962; *Zanzibar Intrigue,* 1963; *Maracaibo Mission,* 1965; (under name Van Wyck Mason) *The Deadly Orbit Mission,* 1968.

Under pseudonym Geoffrey Coffin; with H. Brawner; mystery novels: *Murder in the Senate,* Dodge Publishing, 1935; *The Forgotten Fleet Mystery,* Dodge Publishing, 1936.

Under pseudonym Frank W. Mason; published by Lippincott: *Q-Boat,* 1943; *Pilots, Man Your Planes!,* 1944; *Flight into Danger,* 1946.

Under pseudonym Ward Weaver: *Hang My Wreath,* Funk, 1941; *End of Track,* Reynal, 1943.

Author of stories serialized in magazines, including *Saturday Evening Post* and *Argosy;* contributor of short fiction and articles to magazines, including *Writer, Town and Country,* and *Country Life.*

SIDELIGHTS: F. van Wyck Mason once summed up his literary career saying, "Started writing in 1928. Still at it!" Even at age seventy-six, when most people have already retired, Mason was still writing, at work on *Armored Giants: A Novel of the Civil War* based on the first Naval battle during the American Civil War between two ironclads, the *Merrimac* and the *Monitor*. This book, left in final-draft stage when the author died, was subsequently published as Mason's last novel. In all, he wrote some fifty-eight novels, during a career spanning forty years.

Although Mason slowed down his writing pace during the latter years of his life, he had had a reputation for working on many writing projects at the same time and for completing them with great speed. In 1948 when Mason revealed that his "immediate projects" were a biographical novel and four books on the American Civil War, a writer for the *New York Times Book Review* marveled, "That is all, for the moment, that Mr. Mason plans, but this is only Sunday and there is a whole week ahead."

According to the *Washington Post,* Mason once listed the varieties of fiction included in his writing. He mentioned the following: "Foreign Legion stories, juveniles, historical romances, war stories, flying stories, and many types of adventure-action stories." Before concentrating on historical novels, Mason wrote many mystery stories with international settings. For these novels of intrigue he created Captain Hugh North (later Major and Colonel), an Army Intelligence officer. North, described as "a man of incisive thought as well as action" by Allen J. Hubin in the *New York Times Book Review,* appeared in over twenty-three Mason adventures. During his career, North traveled to Cuba, the Middle East, the Balkans, Africa, and to the Orient; readers were never sure where Mason's next novel would take them.

The background for each of these mystery tales is both colorful and exciting, usually a product of details gathered during the author's own extensive travels. For example, *The Deadly Orbit Mission* takes North to Tangier where he attempts to keep Chinese agents from taking control of a Russian nuclear-armed satellite. Another assignment, this time in *Secret Mission to Bangkok,* takes North to Thailand where he must act as a bodyguard for a famous space scientist searching for his errant wife. The complicated plots, coupled with Mason's vivid details, made the "Hugh North" series very popular with readers and critics.

Secret Mission to Bangkok, which features North as a colonel, received praise from Anthony Boucher of the *New York Times Book Review*. Boucher commented: "[Mason] continues to satisfy us . . . with the pyrotechnic exploits of Col. Hugh North. . . . It is a lively unflagging entertainment." A *New York Herald Tribune Book Review* critic noted: "The plot twists and doubles. . . . [The book] adds up to standard fare, perhaps, but of a very superior brand." Echoing the thoughts of many readers, Isaac Anderson wrote in the *New York Times,* "Van Wyck Mason and . . . North never let one down when it comes to mystery and adventure thrillers."

Although he continued to write mysteries until his late forties, Mason began later in life to concentrate on writing historical novels. For these works he delved mainly into American history, especially Colonial and Civil War America, with occasional forays afield—into the Crusades, for instance. One of his most popular novels, *Three Harbours* deals with the American Revolution. While colorful details contribute an exotic backdrop for Mason's mystery novels, historical details add notable realism to his writings based on historic events. For *Three Harbours,* and Mason's other works dealing with history, extensive research was done before the actual writing took place. Reportedly Mason read sixty-eight volumes of reference material before beginning *Three Harbours*. The resulting book was praised by critics, sold over 100,000 hardcover copies, and remained on the best-seller lists for nearly a year.

A reviewer from the *Boston Transcript* called *Three Harbours* "historically sound," while a *New Yorker* reviewer described the book as "authentic." Margaret Wallace in the *New York Times* wrote: "*Three Harbours* is a romance. . . . But the romantic events, which might have seemed unlikely in themselves, are set against a background of cold rationalism which gives *Three Harbours* its singular impact, which makes of it a very memorable novel."

The complicated plots of Mason's mystery novels and the battles and war stories of his historical novels are rivaled by events from the author's own life. Although born in Boston, he spent his first years in Berlin and Paris living with his grandfather who was the U.S. consul at various times in both cities. At the age of sixteen, Mason became actively involved in World War I as an ambulance driver in the Verdun region of France and later, being fluent in both Spanish and French, served as an interpreter. Although he had planned a diplomatic career, Mason started an importing business in 1925 and began buying embroidery, rugs, and rare books on trips to Europe, North Africa, and the Caribbean. He traveled throughout the world and on vacations engaged in big-game hunting. His last fifteen years were spent at his home in Bermuda, but he never lost his love of adventure and foreign lands. Through his novels he was able to share this avocation with many who by choice or circumstance had less colorful lives.

BIOGRAPHICAL/CRITICAL SOURCES: *New Yorker,* November 5, 1938, November 30, 1946; *Saturday Review of Literature,* November 12, 1938; *New York Times,* November 13, 1938, November 24, 1946, October 20, 1957; *Boston Transcript,* November 19, 1938; *New York Times Book Review,* February 15, 1948, June 21, 1959, January 31, 1960, February 26, 1961, May 19, 1968, September 30, 1973; *New York Herald Tribune Book Review,* May 27, 1951, September 27, 1959; *Chicago Sunday Tribune,* June 14, 1959; *New York Herald Tribune Lively Arts,* March 19, 1961; *Best Sellers,* September 1, 1969; *Los Angeles Times,* October 28, 1980.

OBITUARIES: *Washington Post,* August 30, 1978; *Time,* September 11, 1978; *Publishers Weekly,* September 11, 1978; *AB Bookman's Weekly,* November 6, 1978.†

—Sketch by Marian Walters

* * *

MASON, Frank W.
    See MASON, F(rancis) van Wyck

* * *

MASON, Van Wyck
    See MASON, F(rancis) van Wyck

* * *

MASSIALAS, Byron G. 1929-

PERSONAL: Born November 1, 1929, in Athens, Greece; son of George and Helen (Hidiroglou) Massialas; married Sara

Spentzos, June 9, 1957; children: George, James. *Education:* Greek Classical Gymnasium, diploma, 1948; Butler University, B.A. (cum laude), 1957; Indiana University, M.A., 1958, Ph.D., 1961. *Religion:* Greek Orthodox. *Home:* 2402 Killarney Way, Tallahassee, Fla. 32303. *Office:* College of Education, Florida State University, Tallahassee, Fla. 32306.

CAREER: Indiana University, University High School, Bloomington, instructor in social studies, 1959-61; University of Chicago, Chicago, Ill., assistant professor of education, 1961-65; University of Michigan, Ann Arbor, associate professor of education and director of research training program in social science education, 1965-70; Florida State University, Tallahassee, professor of education, 1970—. International consultant. *Member:* American Educational Research Association, National Council for the Social Studies (chairman of international relations committee, 1966-67), Comparative Education Society, American Academy of Political and Social Science, Middle East Institute, Modern Greek Studies Association.

WRITINGS: (Editor and contributor) *The Indiana Experiments in Inquiry,* School of Education, Indiana University, 1963; (editor with A. M. Kazamias) *Crucial Issues in the Teaching of Social Studies,* Prentice-Hall, 1964; (with Kazamias) *Tradition and Change in Education,* Prentice-Hall, 1965; (editor with F. R. Smith) *New Challenges in the Social Studies,* Wadsworth, 1965; (with C. B. Cox) *Inquiry in Social Studies,* McGraw, 1966; (with Jack Zevin) *Creative Encounters in the Classroom,* Wiley, 1967, revised edition published as *Teaching Creatively,* Robert E. Krieger, 1983; (editor with Cox) *Social Studies in the United States: A Critical Appraisal,* Harcourt, 1967; (editor) *Education and the Political System,* Addison-Wesley, 1969.

(Editor) *Political Youth, Traditional Schools,* Prentice-Hall, 1972; (with Nancy Sprague and Joseph Hurst) *Social Issues through Inquiry,* Prentice-Hall, 1975; (with Hurst) *Social Studies in a New Era,* Longman, 1978; *World Systems in Action,* EDAC/Lesley College, 1981; (with Samir Jarrar) *Education in the Arab World,* Praeger, 1983. Also author of monographs. Editor, Addison-Wesley's "Social and Behavioral Foundations of Education" series. Contributor to education journals.

* * *

MATHES, W(illiam) Michael 1936-

PERSONAL: Born April 15, 1936, in Los Angeles, Calif.; son of William C. (a U.S. district judge) and Rilla (Moore) Mathes. *Education:* Loyola University, Los Angeles, Calif., B.S. 1957; University of Southern California, M.A., 1962; University of New Mexico, Ph.D., 1966. *Religion:* Roman Catholic. *Home address:* P.O. Box 1227, Sonoma, Calif. 95476. *Office:* Department of History, University of San Francisco, San Francisco, Calif. 94117.

CAREER: University of New Mexico, Albuquerque, special collections librarian in Coronado Room, 1963-65; University of San Francisco, San Francisco, Calif., assistant professor, 1966-71, associate professor, 1971-75, professor of history, 1975—. Taught course at Universidad Autonoma de Guadalajara, 1978; visiting professor at "First History Week" observance at Universidade Federal do Acre (Brazil), 1978, and at Colegio de Michoacan (Mexico), 1981. Agente de canje, National Archives of Mexico, 1960-74; "Pablo L. Martinez" Historical Archives, La Paz, technical director, 1974-77, director of microfilming project, 1975-76; Commission of the Californias, archivist-historian, 1975—, and chairman of history committee, 1982—; Patronato para la Preservacion del Patromonio Historico-Cultural de Baja California Sur, assessor, 1975-77, secretary, 1977-78; cultural representative, Camara Nacional de Comercio, Ensenada, Baja California, 1977; special researcher, Centro de Investigaciones Historicas of Universidad Nacional Autonoma de Mexico and Universidad Autonoma de Baja California, 1977—; special representative to Archivo General de las Indias for Bancroft Library of University of Southern California, 1981; honorary curator of Mexican collection of California State Library—Sutro Branch, 1981—. California Historical Society, associate editor, 1967-69, review editor, 1981—; San Diego Historical Society, advisory editor, 1970-74, member of board of editors, 1981—; member of board of editors, Universidad de Baja California Sur, 1977—. Consultant, Oakland Museum, 1967-69; advisor-consultant, Automobile Club of Southern California, 1975-76.

MEMBER: American Historical Association, American Catholic Historical Association, Westerners International (member of executive board, 1978—), Western Historical Association, Associacion Cultural de las Californias, California Historical Society, San Diego Historical Society, Sigma Delta Pi (honorary member), Phi Alpha Theta. *Awards, honors:* Fulbright grant to Spain, 1962-63; Del Amo fellow in Spain, 1965-66; California Historical Society, award of merit, 1977, for contributions to California history, and Henry R. Wagner Memorial Award, 1979; Diploma de Merito, Universidade Federal do Acre (Brazil), 1978.

WRITINGS: (Editor) *Californiana* (in Spanish), seven volumes, J. Porrua Turanzas (Madrid), 1965-72; (editor) *Documentos para la historia de la demarcacion comercial de California, 1583-1632* (title means "Documents for the History of the Commercial Charting of California"), J. Porrua Turanzas, 1965.

(Transcriber, translator, and author of annotations) Juan Cavallero Carranco, *The Pearl Hunters in the Gulf of California, 1668,* Dawson's Book Shop, 1966; *Vizcaino and Spanish Expansion the the Pacific Ocean, 1580-1630,* California Historical Society, 1968; (editor) *Documentos para la historia de la explotacion comercial de California, 1611-1679* (title means "Documents for the History of the Commercial Exploitation of California"), J. Porrua Turanzas, 1968; (editor) Eusebio Francisco Kino, *First from the Gulf to the Pacific,* Dawson's Book Shop, 1969; (transcriber, translator, and author of annotations) *The Capture of the "Santa Ana," Cabo San Lucas, November, 1587: The Accounts of Francis Pretty, Antonio de Sierra, and Tomas de Alzola,* Dawson's Books Shop, 1969.

Reparo a errores de la navegacion espanola (title means "Correction of Errors in Spanish Navigation"), J. Porrua Turanzas, 1970; *To Save a City: The Desague,* Americas, 1970; *The Conquistador in California: The Voyage of Fernando Cortes to Baja California in Chronicles and Documents, 1535,* Dawson's Book Shop, 1973; *A Brief History of the Land of Calafia: The Californias, 1533-1795,* Gobierno del Territorio de Baja California Sur (La Paz, Mexico), 1974, 2nd edition, Patronato del estudiante sud-californiano, 1977; *Geographic and Hydrographic Descriptions of Many Northern and Southern Lands and Seas in the Indies: Specifically of the Discovery of the Kingdom of California (1632),* Dawson's Book Shop, 1974; *Spanish Approaches to the Island of California, 1628-1632,* Book Club of California, 1975.

(Contributor) *Some California Catholic Reminiscences for the United States Bicentennial,* Knights of Columbus (Los Angeles), 1976; *Piratas en la costa de Nueva Galicia en el siglo XVII* (title means "Pirates on the Coast of New Galicia during the Seventeenth Century"), Libreria Font (Guadalajara), 1976; *Las misiones de Baja California—The Missions of Baja California: Una resena historica-fotografica—An Historical-Pho-*

tographic Survey, Gobierno del Estado de Baja California Sur, 1977; *Cattle Brands of Baja California Sur, 1809-1885: Los registros de marcas de Baja California Sur,* Dawson's Book Shop-Archivo Historico de Baja California Sur "Pablo L. Martinez," 1978; *Cortes en California, 1535,* Universidad Autonoma de Baja California (Mexicali, Mexico), 1978; *Clemente Guillen: Explorer of the South,* Dawson's Book Shop, 1979; (contributor) *Cabrillo and His Compatriots: The Explorers and Their Expeditions,* Cabrillo Historical Association, 1979; *Baja California cartografica: catalogo de mapas, planos y disenos del siglo XIX que se encuentran en el Archivo Historico de Baja California Sur "Pablo L. Martinez"* (title means "Cartographic Baja California: A Catalog of Maps, Plans, and Designs from the Nineteenth Century Found in the 'Pablo L. Martinez' Historical Archives of Baja California Sur"), Gobierno del Estado de Baja California Sur, 1979.

Missions, with photographs by Stanley Truman, California Historical Society, 1980; *Obras californianas del Padre Miguel Venegas, S.J.,* Universidad Autonoma de Baja California Sur, five volumes, 1980; (co-editor) Miguel del Barco, *The Natural History of Baja California,* Dawson's Book Shop, 1980.

Contributor of articles and reviews to journals, including *Pacific Historian, Journal of San Diego History, Hispanic American Historical Review, California Quarterly,* and *Western Historical Quarterly.* Member of board of editors, *Calafia,* 1977—, *Meyibo,* 1977—, and *California History,* 1982—. Editorial consultant, *The Journal of San Diego History,* 1975-80.

WORK IN PROGRESS: Research on the history of California in the seventeenth century, on the history of drainage of lakes in Mexico, and on the history of convalescent hospitals in Mexico.

* * *

**MATTHESON, Rodney
See CREASEY, John**

* * *

MATTISON, Judith 1939-

PERSONAL: Born December 9, 1939, in Milwaukee, Wis.; daughter of Arthur D. (a salesman) and Junice (Magnuson) Nelson; married John K. Mattison (a minister), August 25, 1962 (divorced January, 1982); children: Theodore John, Michael Andrew. *Education:* University of Minnesota, B.S., 1961; graduate study at Luther Northwestern Seminary. *Home:* 5029 Oakland Ave. S., Minneapolis, Minn. 55417. *Office:* Richfield Lutheran Church, Minneapolis, Minn. 55419.

CAREER: Elementary school teacher in public schools in Hopkins, Minn., 1961-62, 1963-65, and in East Hartford, Conn., 1962-63; Minneapolis Public Schools, Minneapolis, Minn., volunteer, 1968-73, radio writer and producer, 1973-76; program director at Mt. Olivet Retreat Center, 1977-79; Richfield Lutheran Church, Minneapolis, director of social ministries, 1979—. Member of Centennial District school board, 1971-75; member of board, Luther Northwestern Seminary, 1980-82, and Office for Communications Management Committee, Lutheran Church in America, 1982—. Member of Minneapolis Aquatennial, 1960-61, and Minnesota Chorale, 1975—. *Member:* Alpha Gamma Delta.

WRITINGS—Published by Augsburg, except as indicated: *From a Woman's Heart,* 1969; *Prayers from a Woman's Heart,* 1972; *Prayers from a Mother's Heart,* 1975; *Who Will Listen to Me?,* 1977; *I'm Worried about Your Drinking,* 1978; *Facing Up,* Fortress, 1979; *Beginnings,* 1980; *Mom Has a Second Job,* 1980; *Help Me Adapt, Lord,* 1981. Contributor to *Lutheran, Lutheran Standard, Lutheran Women,* and *Scope.*

WORK IN PROGRESS: Prayer-Thoughts for Single Parents.

SIDELIGHTS: Judith Mattison told *CA:* "I write about feelings. . . . This brief, usually poetic form is a way of painting pictures of life. People see the event through words, and live it in their own feelings. We share the event, and hopefully come to know ourselves and others better."

* * *

**MAYFIELD, Julia
See HASTINGS, Phyllis (Dora Hodge)**

* * *

MAYHALL, Jane (Francis) 1921-

PERSONAL: Born May 10, 1921, in Louisville, Ky.; daughter of Howard Wesley and Loula (Bennett) Mayhall; married Leslie George Katz (a publisher), June 4, 1940. *Education:* Attended Black Mountain College, 1937-40, Middlebury Music School, 1939, Longy Music School, 1940-41, Black Mountain Music School, 1944, New School for Social Research, 1946-48, and Claremont (Calif.) College, summer, 1948. *Home:* 15 West 67th St., New York, N.Y. 10023.

CAREER: Writer. Member of faculty of New School for Social Research, New York, N.Y., 1948; guest lecturer at New School for Social Research and New York University, both 1950, and Ohio University, 1968; member of summer workshop faculty at Morehead (Ky.) State College, 1960-62, and Alice Lloyd College, Pippa Passes, Ky., 1968; member of staff of Hofstra University, 1977 and Hindman (Ky.) Writers Workshop, 1980-81; writer-in-residence at various times at Yaddo Foundation and MacDowell Colony. *Awards, honors:* Fletcher Pratt prose fellowship, Bread Loaf School of English, 1957; Yaddo fellow; Edward MacDowell fellow.

WRITINGS: "Ecologue" (verse play), produced by Poets' Company, 1954; *Cousin to Human,* Harcourt, 1960; *Ready for the Ha-Ha,* Eakins, 1966; *Givers and Takers: Poems,* Eakins, 1968.

Contributor to many anthologies, including: *The Prize Stories, 1973: The O. Henry Awards,* Doubleday, 1973; *Bitches and Sad Ladies,* edited by Pat Rotter, Harper's Magazine Press, 1975; *Treasury of American Poems,* Doubleday, 1978; *New York Poems,* Avon, 1980; *A Treasury of American Short Stories,* 1981. Translator, with Otto Guth, of opera libretto, "Die Kluege," for San Francisco Opera Co. Contributor of articles, poems, and short stories to numerous periodicals, including *Modern Language Quarterly, Paris Review, Nation, Partisan Review,* and *Harper's Bazaar.*

WORK IN PROGRESS: A book on American women writers, from Colonial times to the present; a book of feminist short stories.

SIDELIGHTS: Jane Mayhall told *CA:* "I began writing at the age of ten. I thought I was looking for a niche, but I was really looking for an escape (into other kinds of experience). Throughout my years of writing I've always felt an uneasiness. And now I realize that the lack of ease is my direction. Because art and society do not cohere, and even art and 'art' (the artist personified as he is now as a status symbol, with the same instincts as a businessman) these do not cohere. What I look for, in viewing the world, is the uncompromising individuality; everybody has it, though people are always trying to live according to stereotypes, such as 'the husband,' 'the wife,' 'the actor,' 'the terrorist,' 'the assassin,' 'the well-adjusted,' 'the neurotic,' and etc. Life is more interesting and complicated and I look for the revelation of that. Which is never a state of rest, acceptance, adjustment—but is the precious lack of certainty that, as Keats intimated, is the necessity and the groundsoil for the creative act. I try to find this in poems and fiction.''

AVOCATIONAL INTERESTS: Singing and composing music.

* * *

McCAULEY, Carole Spearin 1939-

PERSONAL: Born April 18, 1939, in Great Barrington, Mass.; daughter of Kenneth Waldo and Elizabeth (LaPrise) Spearin; married Arthur Leo McCauley (a technical writer), November 14, 1964; children: Brendan Spearin. Education: Attended University of Montpellier, 1959, and University of Besancon, 1959-60; Antioch College, A.B., 1962; graduate study at New School for Social Research, 1965-66, and at Manhattanville College, 1973-74. Politics: "Saddened liberal." Religion: "Saddened Catholic." Home: 23 Buena Vista Dr., Greenwich, Conn. 06830.

CAREER: Antioch College, Yellow Springs, Ohio, secretary-assistant in extramural department, 1962; Grailville, Loveland, Ohio, staff member, 1962-64; secretary-receptionist at Ann Dunn Real Estate, 1964-65; Grail Art and Bookshop, New York City, assistant, 1966-74, manager, 1972; Woman's Salon (writer's group), New York City, coordinator of public programs, 1976-80; medical editor, Southwest Connecticut Health Systems Agency, 1979; member of public relations staff, A. P. John Institute for Cancer Research, Greenwich, Conn.; staff writer, *Orthopaedic Index,* Long Island, N.Y.; editor of technical publications, IBM, White Plains, N.Y. Has conducted writing workshops at Dialogue House, 1974, 1977, and The Womanschool, 1976. Participant in computer conferences in data processing and APL and BASIC programming languages. Does public speaking on numerous topics. *Member:* Grail Movement, New England Small Press Association. *Awards, honors:* Short story prize, *Writer's Digest,* 1968, for "Monty Montgomery Knorr"; short story prize, *Analecta,* 1968, for "Hello to All My Readers"; short story prize, Contemporary Connecticut Writers, 1979.

WRITINGS: (Translator from the French) Pierre Babin, *Crisis of Faith,* Herder, 1963; (translator from the French) Maurice Bellet, *Facing the Unbeliever,* Herder, 1967; (contributor) *Women: Omen,* Connecticut Feminists in the Arts, 1971; (contributor) Richard Kostelanetz, editor, *In Youth,* Ballantine, 1972; *Six Portraits* (computer-assisted fiction), Cantz'sche, 1973; *Computers and Creativity* (nonfiction), Praeger, 1974; (contributor) Diane Kruchkow, editor, *Changes of the Day,* New England Small Press Association, 1975; (contributor) Joe David Bellamy, editor, *The New Fiction: Interviews with Innovative American Writers,* University of Illinois Press, 1975; (contributor) Adele Aldridge, editor, *Spaced Out* (computer prose), Magic Circle, 1975; *Happenthing in Travel On* (fiction with computerized sections), Daughters, Inc., 1975; *Pregnancy after Thirty-five* (medical nonfiction), Dutton, 1976; *Surviving Breast Cancer,* Dutton, 1979. Contributor of articles, interviews, poetry, stories, and reviews to over eighty periodicals, including *Partisan Review, North American Review, Creative Computing, Omni, Self, Our Sunday Visitor,* and *New Women's Times.* Associate editor, *Panache* (literary magazine), 1969-74.

WORK IN PROGRESS: Two novels, *The Honesty Tree,* a lesbian love story set in a New England town, and *Cold Steal,* a medical suspense story, involving bisexuality, about fraud in cancer research.

SIDELIGHTS: Carole Spearin McCauley told *CA:* "Although I earn a living writing or editing various kinds of nonfiction, the novel and fiction are my first love. By this time I have a core of people who care and understand what I am doing, whether experimentation in form (computer-assisted work) or in content (sexual variations), but it saddens me to see how addicted to 'blockbusters' most large publishers are and how eager to publish only their friends' work many small publishers are. How do 'tweenies'—fiction writers between these two categories—survive? Does anyone care?''

McCauley continues: "Because the characters in my books care passionately about vital topics (human cooperation and survival, honest medical research, better treatment of cancer patients, civil and personal rights for minorities, feminist consciousness), I hope to embed within exciting plots a variety of such characters who learn to cope with their worlds, even triumph above them. I want especially to construct characters with whom contemporary women can identify. Subjects, such as androgyny or better care in medical settings, seem to choose me, and I try to honor them by careful constructions because they will matter to the history of human thought and evolution. A century from now, for example, will we all be androgynous or bisexual? Will the human lifespan have doubled, reducing or at least postponing the degradation of chronic illness (cancer, stroke, etc.)?

"Although my books have received many reviews plus their share of media attention, a review that means much to me was written by Andrea Dworkin, feminist author and thinker, about my first novel, *Happenthing in Travel On:* 'This is a book about the struggle to survive—*in* the environment, not against it as its enemy; women with each other, not pitted against each other. . . . McCauley does not mythicize adventure or suffering or survival or physical pain or birth or death. Instead, she looks at these things with an underlying ethic, a sense of justice. . . . She sees the way women at our most whole do see: with compassion, without sentimentality, the discreteness of things, the rhythms of daily life, the work of maintaining and nourishing life. . . . This is an adventury story full of woods and work, home and the body, weather, objects, human sensibilities, touch and feel, danger and tenderness.'"

McCauley adds: "My computer texts have appeared in art shows in the United States, Canada, and Germany. I give illustrated talks on computer arts to school groups and speak on women's writing to suburban groups, writers' conferences, and book fairs."

* * *

McCLOSKEY, Donald N(ansen) 1942-

PERSONAL: Born September 11, 1942, in Ann Arbor, Mich.; son of Robert Green (an academician) and Helen (a singer; maiden name, Stueland) McCloskey; married Joanne Comi (a nurse), June 19, 1965; children: Daniel. Education: Harvard University, B.A. (magna cum laude), 1964, Ph.D., 1970. Politics: "Anarchist, registered Democrat." Religion: None. Home: 320 Melrose Ave., Iowa City, Iowa 52240. Office: Department of Economics, University of Iowa, Iowa City, Iowa 52242.

CAREER: University of Chicago, Chicago, Ill., assistant professor, 1968-73, associate professor of economics, 1973-80, associate professor of history, 1979-80; University of Iowa, Iowa City, professor of history and chairman of department of economics, 1980—. *Member:* American Economic Association, American Economic History Association, Economic History Society (England).

WRITINGS: (Editor) *Essays on a Mature Economy: Britain after 1840*, Princeton University Press, 1972; *Economic Maturity and Entrepreneurial Decline: British Iron and Steel, 1870-1913*, Harvard University Press, 1973; *Enterprise and Trade in Victorian Britain: Essays in Historical Economics*, Allen & Unwin, 1981; (editor with Roderick Floud) *The Economic History of Britain since 1700*, Cambridge University Press, 1981, Volume I: *1700-1860*, Volume II: *1860 to the 1970s*; *The Applied Theory of Price*, Macmillan, 1982. Contributor to professional journals. Editor of *Journal of Economic History*, 1981—.

WORK IN PROGRESS: *How the Gold Standard Worked*; *Open Fields and Enclosures in England*.

SIDELIGHTS: Donald N. McCloskey's books, dealing with the economic history of Britain, are characterized by views contrary to those held by many British historians. For example, according to a *Times Literary Supplement* reviewer, in *Economic Maturity and Entrepreneurial Decline: British Iron and Steel, 1870-1913*, McCloskey "mounts a vigorous attack on the views of that historical school which has argued that a failure of entrepreneurship fostered the decline of the British iron and steel industries."

Many reviewers mention McCloskey's prose style, although as an economist he deals mainly with statistical data, concentrating on the content and not the form of his writing. A *Choice* reviewer, commenting on McCloskey's work on Britain's iron industry, notes that he writes in a way "that makes the book both good economics and good literature. . . . It illustrates an exercise in creative thinking, reasoning, and writing." Sidney Pollard of the *Times Literary Supplement* states: "[McCloskey] is equally at home among the historical literature and the formulae of econometricians. He can . . . write elegantly and with wit."

AVOCATIONAL INTERESTS: Latin, folk music.

BIOGRAPHICAL/CRITICAL SOURCES: *Times Literary Supplement*, March 24, 1972, August 16, 1974, August 7, 1981; *Business History Review*, autumn, 1972, summer, 1974; *American Historical Review*, June, 1973, June, 1975; *Choice*, March, 1974; *Journal of Modern History*, March, 1974; *Journal of Economic History*, September, 1974.

* * *

McCREA, James (Craig, Jr.) 1920-

PERSONAL: Born September 12, 1920, in Peoria, Ill.; son of James Craig and Helen (Sloan) McCrea; married Ruth Dickinson Pirman, Jr. (a writer and illustrator), July 4, 1943; children: James Craig III, Ruth Dickinson, Claire. *Education:* Attended University of the South, 1938-40, and Ringling School of Art, 1940-41; special courses in book design, drawing, and printing at Pratt Institute, Brooklyn Museum, and New York University.

CAREER: Free-lance writer, illustrator, and book designer. U.S. Merchant Marine, purser, 1942-45; employed in ceramics studio, New York City, 1946; studio of Bernard Brussel-Smith, New York City, apprentice, 1947-48; Cooper Union, New York City, instructor in typography, 1954-64. Owner and operator, with wife, of Little Press, Bayport, N.Y.

WRITINGS—With wife, Ruth McCrea: *Goosie, Goosie!*, Little Press, 1960; *The King's Procession* (Junior Literary Guild selection), illustrations by the authors, Atheneum, 1963; *The Story of Olaf* (Junior Literary Guild selection), illustrations by the authors, Atheneum, 1964; *The Magic Tree* (Junior Literary Guild selection), illustrations by the authors, Atheneum, 1965; *The Birds*, illustrations by the authors, Atheneum, 1966; *The Marvelous Machine of Monsieur Le Duc*, Holt, 1973; *The Beautiful Egg*, Holt, 1973.

Illustrator with R. McCrea: Kirkpatrick and Goodfellow, *Poetry with Pleasure*, Scribner, 1965; Clyde Robert Bulla, *Stories of Gilbert and Sullivan Operas*, Crowell, 1968; Ann McGovern, *Shakespearean Sallies, Sullies, and Slanders*, Crowell, 1969; Judy Hawes, *What I Like About Toads*, Crowell, 1969; Patricia P. Mintz, editor, *America, the Melting Pot*, Scribner, 1969; Sylvia Louise Engdahl, *Journey between Worlds*, Atheneum, 1970; John J. Loeper, *Men of Ideas*, Atheneum, 1970; Barbara K. Walker, *The Courage of Kazan*, Crowell, 1970; Stanley A. Werner, Jr., editor, *The American Dream in Literature*, Scribner, 1970; Molly Cone, *The Ringling Brothers*, Crowell, 1971; Laurence Pringle, *Cockroaches: Here, There, and Everywhere*, Crowell, 1971; Jane J. Srivastava, *Computers*, Crowell, 1972; Judith Thurman, editor, *I Became Alone: Five Women Poets*, Atheneum, 1975; Carl V. Morrison and Dorothy Nafus Morrison, *Can I Help How I Feel?*, Atheneum, 1976.

SIDELIGHTS: James and Ruth McCrea have worked together as designers since their marriage. They operate their own press, The Little Press, in the basement of their home, using it largely for block prints, an annual Christmas book that they turn out, and sometimes for jacket assignments.

BIOGRAPHICAL/CRITICAL SOURCES: *American Artist*, December, 1962.†

* * *

McCREA, Ruth (Pirman) 1921-

PERSONAL: Born May 28, 1921, in Jersey City, N.J.; daughter of Ernest James and Ruth (Dickinson) Pirman; married James Craig McCrea, Jr. (a free-lance writer, illustrator, and book designer), July 4, 1943; children: James Craig III, Ruth Dickinson, Claire. *Education:* Attended Ringling School of Art, 1938-41, 1942-43; special courses in book design at New York University, drawing at Brooklyn Museum, and writing at Columbia University.

CAREER: Free-lance writer and illustrator. Painter, mainly of water colors for sale through galleries, 1943-47. Owner and operator, with husband, of Little Press, Bayport, N.Y.

WRITINGS—With husband, James McCrea, except as indicated: (Sole author) *A Present for Molly*, Aladdin, 1949; (sole contributor) *Spooks and Spirits and Shadowy Shapes*, Aladdin, 1949; *Goosie, Goosie!*, Little Press, 1960; *The King's Procession* (Junior Literary Guild selection), illustrations by the authors, Atheneum, 1963; *The Story of Olaf* (Junior Literary Guild selection), illustrations by the authors, Atheneum, 1965; *The Magic Tree* (Junior Literary Guild selection), illustrations by the authors, Atheneum, 1965; *The Birds*, illustrations by the authors, Atheneum, 1966; *The Marvelous Machine of Monsieur Le Duc*, Holt, 1973; *The Beautiful Egg*, Holt, 1973.

Illustrator with J. McCrea: Kirkpatrick and Goodfellow, *Poetry with Pleasure*, Scribner, 1965; Clyde Robert Bulla, *Stories of Gilbert and Sullivan Operas*, Crowell, 1968; Ann McGovern, *Shakespearean Sallies, Sullies, and Slanders*, Crowell, 1969; Judy Hawes, *What I Like about Toads*, Crowell, 1969; Patricia P. Mintz, editor, *America, the Melting Pot*, Scribner, 1969; Sylvia Louise Engdahl, *Journey between Worlds*, Atheneum, 1970; John J. Loeper, *Men of Ideas*, Atheneum, 1970; Barbara K. Walker, *The Courage of Kazan*, Crowell, 1970; Stanley A. Werner, Jr., editor, *The American Dream in Literature*, Scribner, 1970; Molly Cone, *The Ringling Brothers*, Crowell, 1971;

Laurence Pringle, *Cockroaches: Here, There, and Everywhere,* Crowell, 1971; Jane J. Srivastava, *Computers,* Crowell, 1972; Judith Thurman, editor, *I Became Alone: Five Women Poets,* Atheneum, 1975; Carl V. Morrison and Dorothy Nafus Morrison, *Can I Help How I Feel?,* Atheneum, 1976.

BIOGRAPHICAL/CRITICAL SOURCES: *American Artist,* December, 1962.†

* * *

McDONALD, Elvin 1937-

PERSONAL: Born February 17, 1937, in Gray, Okla.; son of J. D. (a rancher) and Lillian (King) McDonald; married Edith Deardeuff, June 6, 1958 (divorced); children: Mark Elvin, Steven Douglas, Jeannene Louise. *Education:* Attended Conservatory of Music, Kansas City, Mo., 1956-58, Mannes College of Music, New York, N.Y., 1958-60, University of Missouri, Kansas City, 1965-67. *Politics:* Republican. *Religion:* "Protestant/Buddhist." *Home:* 225 East 57th St., New York, N.Y. 10022.

CAREER: Writer and lecturer on plants. American Gloxinia Society (now American Gloxinia and Gesneriad Society), Gray, Okla., editor, *Gloxinian,* 1950-60; Mid-America Publishing Corp., Kansas City, Mo., editor, *Flower and Garden,* 1956-62; McDonald/Bourke/Associates, Kansas City, Mo., editorial director, 1962-66; Elvin McDonald & Associates, Grandview, Mo., partner, 1966-67; *House Beautiful* magazine, New York, N.Y., garden editor and senior editor, 1967-79. Teacher of "Urban Gardening: Success by Design," Pratt Institute, spring, 1982; member of teaching staff of Horticultural Society of New York, New York Botanical Garden, and Brooklyn Botanic Garden. Minister of music at Armour Heights Baptist Church. *Member:* American Gloxinia and Gesneriad Society (founder), American Begonia Society, African Violet Society of America, Garden Writers Association of America. *Awards, honors:* Elvin McDonald Research Fund of the American Gloxinia and Gesneriad Society named in his honor.

WRITINGS: *Miniature Plants for Home and Greenhouse,* Van Nostrand, 1962, revised edition published as *Little Plants for Small Spaces: How to Select and Grow Mini Plants and Trees Indoors and Out,* M. Evans, 1974; *The World Book of House Plants,* World Publishing, 1963.

(Editor) *Handbook for Greenhouse Gardeners,* Lord & Burnham, 1966, 4th edition, 1974; *The Complete Book of Gardening Under Lights,* Doubleday, 1966; *The Flowering Greenhouse Day by Day,* Van Nostrand, 1966, revised edition published as *Greenhouse Gardener,* New American Library, 1976.

Garden Ideas A to Z, Doubleday, 1970; (with Lawrence Power) *The Low-Upkeep Book of Lawns and Landscape,* Hawthorn, 1971; (editor with Ralph S. Bailey) *Good Housekeeping Basic Gardening Techniques,* Hearst Books, 1974; *Miniature Gardens,* Grosset, 1975; *The World Book of House Plants,* Funk, 1975; (producer) Jacqueline Heriteau, editor, *The Hyponex Handbook of House Plants,* Wentworth Press, 1975; (editor with Heriteau and Francesca Morris) *The Color Handbook of House Plants,* Hawthorn, 1975; *Gardening in Containers,* Grosset, 1975; *The House Plant Answer Book,* Popular Library, 1975; *House Plants to Grow if You Have No Sun,* Popular Library, 1975.

Hanging Gardens: Indoors and Outdoors, Grosset, 1976; *How to Grow House Plants from Seeds,* Van Nostrand, 1976; *How to Grow Vegetables and Herbs from Seeds,* Van Nostrand, 1976; *Plants as Therapy: A Natural Alternative,* Praeger, 1976; *Making Your Lawn and Garden Grow,* Dorison House, 1977; *Stop Talking to Your Plants and Listen,* Funk, 1977; *Decorative Gardening in Containers,* Doubleday, 1978; *Easy Gardens: A Weed Eater Book,* Dorison House, 1978; (with C. Z. Guest) *C. Z. and Elvin's Weekly Garden Planner: 1979,* Chelsea House, 1978; *How to Grow Flowers from Seeds,* Van Nostrand, 1979; (with Guest) *C. Z. and Elvin's Week-by-Week Garden Guide,* Chelsea House, 1980.

Executive editor of *Good Housekeeping Illustrated Encyclopedia of Gardening,* Book Division, Hearst Magazines, 1972. Author and illustrator of twice-weekly syndicated column, "Plants in the Home," appearing in King Features Syndicate newspapers in United States, Canada, Sweden, and Portugal, 1975—. Contributor of over 200 articles to journals, including *New York Times* and *Flower and Garden.* Editor of *Gloxinian,* 1950-60, *Flower and Garden,* 1956-62, *Park's Floral Magazine,* 1963—, and *Pride,* 1963-64; associate editor, *Under Glass,* 1959—, and *Popular Gardening and Living Outdoors,* 1963-64; garden editor and senior editor of *House Beautiful* magazine, 1967-79. Gardening consultant, *Family Circle* magazine, 1980—.

WORK IN PROGRESS: *Serious Agriculture for Amateur Gardeners.*

SIDELIGHTS: Besides his numerous books explaining what one can do for plants to make them grow better, Elvin McDonald has also written one volume, *Plants as Therapy,* which, as he explains, "is . . . about what growing plants can do for you." In this book, McDonald supports the following thesis: "If you live in an urban environment, as I do, your alienation from the earth is real, and it really increases the higher up you live in an apartment house. . . . If you live and work with plants around you, there is always something that needs to be done for them and that will simultaneously help you get through everyday anxieties. As you wait for an important telephone call or recover from a difficult personal or professional confrontation, picking off dead leaves . . . , watering a plant, or cleaning its leaves with a damp tissue can reduce anxiety far better than chain smoking, a stiff drink, or a tranquilizer."

BIOGRAPHICAL/CRITICAL SOURCES: Elvin McDonald, *How to Grow Houseplants from Seeds,* Van Nostrand, 1976; McDonald, *Plants as Therapy: A Natural Alternative,* Praeger, 1976.

* * *

McDONNELL, Jinny
See McDONNELL, Virginia B(leecker)

* * *

McDONNELL, Virginia B(leecker) 1917-
(Jinny McDonnell; pseudonyms: Virginia Barclay, Jean Kirby)

PERSONAL: Born November 24, 1917; daughter of J. Barclay (a real estate broker) and Helen Borden (Farley) Bleecker; married John H. McDonnell (a utility employee and free-lance writer); children: Gordon R. *Education:* Samaritan Hospital School of Nursing, Troy, N.Y., R.N.; also attended Russell Sage College. *Religion:* Episcopalian. *Home:* 79 Hudson Park Rd., New Rochelle, N.Y. *Agent:* Richard Curtis Associates, Inc., 340 East 66th St., New York, N.Y. 10021.

CAREER: Surgical nurse in New York City during World War II; former director, with husband, of Gore Mountain Ski School, North Creek, N.Y.; *Knickerbocker News,* Albany, N.Y., sports columnist, 1956-58; Free and Accepted Masons, New York

City, assistant to director of publications, 1957; *Standard Star* (daily newspaper), New Rochelle, N.Y., reporter, feature writer, and columnist, 1958-62; *Daily Argus*, Mount Vernon, N.Y., women's news editor, 1963; free-lance writer, 1963—. *Member:* Authors Guild, Authors League of America, Mystery Writers of America, National Academy of Television Arts and Sciences, Writers Guild East.

WRITINGS: *Your Future in Nursing*, Richards Rosen, 1963; *The Nurse with the Silver Skates*, Ace Books, 1964; *West Point Nurse*, Macfadden, 1965; *Annapolis Nurse*, Macfadden, 1965; (under pseudonym Jean Kirby) *Olympic Duty*, Whitman Publishing, 1965; (under pseudonym Jean Kirby) *Tracy's Little People*, Whitman Publishing, 1965; *Dee O'Hara, Astronauts' Nurse*, Thomas Nelson, 1965; *Dixie Cline, Animal Doctor*, Thomas Nelson, 1966; *The Ski Trail Mystery*, Macrae, 1966; *Foster Pups*, Thomas Nelson, 1966; *Aerospace Nurse*, Messner, 1966; *County Agent*, Messner, 1968; *The Irish Helped Build America*, Messner, 1969; *Storm over Garnet*, Golden Press, 1969; *Careers in Hotel Management*, Messner, 1971; *Miscalculated Risk*, Western Publishing, 1972; *Silent Partner*, Western Publishing, 1972; *The Deep Six*, Western Publishing, 1973; *The Long Shot*, Western Publishing, 1974; *The Accident*, Western Publishing, 1975.

"Mid-City Hospital" series; all novels; all published by New American Library: *Emergency*, 1981; *High Risk*, 1981; *Trauma*, 1981; *Crisis*, 1982; *Double Face*, 1982; *Life-Support*, 1982. Also author of other books in the series.

Author of television scripts for daytime dramas "The Guiding Light," 1977-78, 1982—, and "The Young and the Restless," 1980. Contributor of over three hundred articles and short stories, sometimes under name Jinny McDonnell, to magazines and newspapers.

SIDELIGHTS: Virginia McDonnell won a house, completely furnished, in 1948, for a jingle entered in a national contest sponsored by *Photoplay*. When she and her son were recovering from polio, McDonnell took up skiing and became an instructor. *Avocational interests:* Boating, swimming, reading.

* * *

McGEACHY, D(aniel) P(atrick) III 1929-

PERSONAL: Born November 19, 1929, in Atlanta, Ga.; son of Daniel Patrick, Jr. (a clergyman) and Beth (McClure) McGeachy; married Alice Neely (a teacher-counselor), August 28, 1952; children: Daniel, Elizabeth, Martin. *Education:* Davidson College, A.B., 1951; Union Theological Seminary in Virginia, B.D. (cum laude), 1954, Th.M., 1955; San Francisco Theological Seminary, S.T.D., 1982. *Politics:* Democrat. *Home address:* Songwood, P.O. Box 3151, Nashville, Tenn. 37219. *Office:* Downtown Presbyterian Church, 154 Fifth Ave. N., Nashville, Tenn. 37219.

CAREER: Ordained Presbyterian minister, 1954; pastor of churches in Sylva, N.C., 1955-59, Gainesville, Ga., 1959-66, and Nashville, Tenn., 1966-72; A New Song (consultants in liturgical renewal), Nashville, director, 1973—; Rockvale Cumberland Presbyterian Church, Rockvale, Tenn., pastor, 1975-81; Downtown Presbyterian Church, Nashville, pastor, 1981—.

WRITINGS: *A Matter of Life and Death*, John Knox, 1966; *Common Sense and the Gospel*, John Knox, 1969; *Beyond the Facts, Acts*, Friendship, 1973; *The Gospel According to Andy Capp*, John Knox, 1973; *A New Song*, A New Song, 1973; *Traveling Light*, Abingdon, 1975; *Help Lord*, John Knox, 1978; *The Folk Psalm Book*, A New Song, 1980.

WORK IN PROGRESS: An illustrated children's book.

* * *

McGOVERN, George S(tanley) 1922-

PERSONAL: Born July 22, 1922, in Avon, S.D.; son of Joseph C. (a Methodist minister) and Frances (McLean) McGovern; married Eleanor Faye Stegeberg, October 31, 1943; children: Ann McGovern Mead, Susan McGovern Rowen, Teresa, Steven, Mary. *Education:* Dakota Wesleyan University, B.A. (magna cum laude), 1945; Northwestern University, M.A., 1949, Ph.D., 1953. *Religion:* Methodist. *Office:* Americans for Common Sense, 1825 Connecticut Ave., N.W., Washington, D.C. 20009.

CAREER: Dakota Wesleyan University, Mitchell, S.D., assistant professor of history and political science, 1949-53; South Dakota Democratic Party, Pierre, executive secretary, 1953-55; U.S. Congress, Washington, D.C., representative from South Dakota, 1956-60; director of Food for Peace Program and special assistant to President John F. Kennedy, 1961-62; U.S. Congress, Washington, D.C., senator from South Dakota, 1963-80, served on the Senate Foreign Relations Committee, the Senate Joint Economic Committee, and the Senate Committee on Agriculture, Nutrition, and Forestry; Democratic Party presidential candidate, 1972; Americans for Common Sense, Washington, D.C., chairman, 1980—. U.S. delegate to North Atlantic Treaty Organization (NATO) Parliamentarians Conference, 1958, and 1959; U.S. delegate to United Nations Food and Agriculture Organization Conference, 1961. *Military service:* U.S. Army Air Forces, 1943-45; bomber pilot; flew thirty-five combat missions in European Theatre; became 1st lieutenant; received Distinguished Flying Cross and Air Medal with Oak Leaf Clusters. *Member:* American Historical Association, American Legion, Veterans of Foreign Wars, Masons, Elks, Kiwanis. *Awards, honors:* William Randolph Hearst fellowship, 1949-50; LL.D., Wilmington College, 1962.

WRITINGS: *War against Want: America's "Food for Peace Program,"* Walker & Co., 1964; (editor) *Agricultural Thought in the Twentieth Century*, Bobbs-Merrill, 1967; *A Time of War, a Time of Peace*, Random House, 1968; (author of introduction) Joseph L. Sax, *Defending the Environment: A Strategy for Citizen Action*, Knopf, 1971; (with Leonard Guttridge) *The Great Coalfield War*, Houghton, 1972; *McGovern: The Man and His Beliefs*, edited by Shirley Maclaine, Norton, 1972; *An American Journey: The Presidential Campaign Speeches of George McGovern*, Random House, 1974; (with Richard Stilwell) *Withdrawal of U.S. Troops from Korea?*, American Enterprise Institute for Public Policy Research, 1977; *Grassroots: The Autobiography of George McGovern*, Random House, 1977. Contributor to *Atlantic, Saturday Review, Look, Commentary, New Republic*, and other periodicals.

SIDELIGHTS: George McGovern served as U.S. Senator from South Dakota for 18 years, building a reputation as a prominent liberal spokesman and a skilled political organizer. His support of important social legislation, his building of the South Dakota Democratic Party, and his winning of the presidential nomination in 1972, made McGovern one of the leading figures in the Democratic Party.

McGovern first entered the political arena in 1952 when, impressed by Adlai Stevenson's acceptance speech for the Democratic nomination, he wrote a letter to a local newspaper praising Stevenson. The letter caught the attention of the South Dakota Democratic Party chairman who suggested that McGovern, then an assistant professor of history at Dakota

Wesleyan University, become the party's executive secretary. McGovern took the job. Although his previous political involvement had only extended to serving as a delegate to Henry Wallace's Progressive Party in 1948, McGovern took on his new position with enthusiasm and skill, spending the next three years travelling throughout South Dakota building the almost-nonexistent Democratic Party, a party that held no major state office and had only two members in the 110-member state legislature. During this period of intense political organizing, Bernard A. Weisberger of the *Washington Post Book World* writes, McGovern was "living on doughnuts and coffee furnished at receptions; painstakingly building [his] files of past and potential local workers; [and] even peddling campaign buttons on the street to raise the price of a tankful of gas or a hotel room." In 1956 the organizing work paid off when McGovern ran for U.S. representative and won with 52% of the vote, becoming the first Democratic representative from South Dakota in 22 years. In 1958 he won reelection, this time garnering 53% of the vote. In his years as a representative, McGovern pushed hard for price supports for food products (a popular position in rural South Dakota), for federal aid to public schools and small business, and for medical aid for the aged.

After John F. Kennedy's election as president in 1960, McGovern was appointed director of the Food for Peace Program, a program designed to feed America's poorer allies by providing them with credit to buy our surplus crops. The idea for the program came from McGovern, who felt it would help the American farmer as well as strengthen the nation's allies. In his two years as director of Food for Peace, McGovern became an expert on the problem of world hunger. His book *War against Want* describes the program and his work as its director.

In 1962, McGovern left the Food for Peace Program to run for the U.S. Senate in South Dakota. Strongly supporting the liberal reforms of President Kennedy, McGovern fought a hard campaign against Republican Joseph H. Bottum, who held that Kennedy's administration was spending too much money. Slowed by a bout with hepatitis brought on by a dirty needle during a vaccination, McGovern campaigned only a minimal amount, relying on his wife Eleanor to make public appearances for him. Despite the handicap, McGovern won the election, by 597 votes, and became the first Democratic senator from South Dakota in 26 years. Running for reelection in 1968 against Archie M. Gubbard, McGovern won with a handy 56% of the vote.

As a U.S. senator, McGovern worked for a number of legislative measures of liberal interest. He supported the Civil Rights Act, Medicare, the nuclear test ban treaty, anti-poverty legislation, and the Housing and Urban Development Act. He also strongly supported a number of bills relating to the nation's agriculture and proposed increases in the export of agricultural products. In his position on the Senate Committee on Agriculture, Nutrition, and Forestry, McGovern became one of the Senate's strongest and most consistent voices for the nation's farmers. In an evaluation of McGovern's work as senator, the *New Republic* notes that he was "stubbornly concerned for the poor, the hungry, the jobless [and wanted] a substantially bigger investment in social services. . . . [His] record shows a scrupulous respect for civil liberties . . . and civil rights, a devotion to raising economic and educational opportunities, and a partiality for liberalized foreign trade and foreign aid."

In matters of foreign policy, McGovern showed a consistent interest in the easing of world tensions and the establishing of peaceful relations between East and West. He criticized America's obsession with anti-Communism and proposed that the nation concentrate its attention on building an example of a better life as a counterweight to the Communist appeal. He urged recognition of Cuba and mainland China, expansion of trade between Communist and noncommunist nations, and the ending of the Cold War. He joined Senator Hubert Humphrey in proposing a special commission to convert the nation's war industries to peacetime production.

An early opponent of the Vietnam War, McGovern emerged in the 1960s as a major spokesman for anti-war congressmen. He delivered his first speech against the war, and the first speech against the war to be delivered by any senator, in September of 1963. At that time he defined the war as a "moral debacle and political defeat" and called upon President Kennedy to withdraw American advisors from Vietnam. McGovern was concerned that the war was diverting attention and resources from important programs at home while needlessly killing many young Americans. He also saw it as an extension of the nation's obsessive anti-Communism. "Vietnam," McGovern once said, "is just the most grevious manifestation of a world view that is based on what we're afraid of rather than what we stand for." He criticized the dictatorial nature of our South Vietnamese allies and questioned the morality of American support for such a regime. He urged the settlement of the war by negotiation and stressed that the Vietnamese should play the primary role in such a settlement. With Senator Mark Hatfield of Oregon, McGovern sponsored the McGovern-Hatfield Amendment, a Senate bill which set a date for withdrawal of American troops from Vietnam. Although presented to the Senate on several occasions, the amendment was never passed.

Out of his concern over America's involvement in the Vietnam War and the resultant problems the war had caused at home, McGovern announced his candidacy for the Democratic Party's presidential nomination in January of 1971. The *New Republic* notes that upon hearing McGovern's announcement, "his colleagues smiled, the press yawned, the public didn't know who he was, [and] the polls left him out of their preference ratings." *Time* referred to McGovern's chances of winning the presidential nomination as "a gigantic if" and called his attempt "a brash swim against a powerful tide." Oddsmaker Jimmy the Greek gave McGovern a 200 to 1 chance of winning the nomination. But the *Nation* editorialized that "McGovern is one of the rare good men in national politics. . . . His decency as a human being, let it be confessed, is a distinct liability. But times are changing; perhaps today a good man—particularly if he runs against a candidate who has the opposite image—has a better chance of winning than in the past."

By announcing his candidacy a year before the primaries began, McGovern hoped to overcome the odds by making his name better known to the public. As *Time* pointed out, "for a McGovern candidacy, it is not a question of staying alive but striking the initial spark of life." During 1971 McGovern travelled some 100,000 miles and delivered over 1,500 speeches. Although he made all the traditional stops expected of a Democratic presidential hopeful—courting ethnic voters, labor union members, and farmers, for example—McGovern was best received on the nation's college campuses where his stand against the Vietnam War was popular. It was from this base of young people, along with peace activists and the liberal wing of the party, that McGovern pieced together a powerful grassroots organization. By primary day in Wisconsin, for example, McGovern's people had 35 storefront offices, a chapter in each of the 72 counties, and 10,000 volunteers to canvass every precinct in the state.

Although he emphasized his opposition to the Vietnam War and sought to make the war the major issue of the campaign,

McGovern spoke out on a number of other issues too, taking positions to the left of most of his opponents. He called for drastic reductions in military spending and the cancellation of military projects he felt to be wasteful or unneeded. He proposed changes in the nation's tax laws to benefit those with low incomes and sought to close a number of tax loopholes used by the wealthy. Instead of a welfare system, McGovern suggested a minimum income grant of $1,000 per person, an idea, sometimes called a "negative income tax," that had been discussed by such politicians as Barry Goldwater since the early 1960s. McGovern tied all these issues to the central issue of the Vietnam War. "When we talk about the war," he told a press conference on September 24, 1971, "when we talk about a defense budget which goes up $4 billion while [President Nixon] preaches economy, we are talking about all of the other issues."

McGovern had the popularity of his ideas tested in the first primary of 1972, held in New Hampshire on March 7th. It was an important primary for McGovern because he needed an early show of strength to be considered a serious contender for the nomination. It was a hard contest. McGovern had only a 6% standing in the opinion polls. Most New Hampshire Democratic Party officials had endorsed Senator Edmund Muskie of neighboring Maine, and media observers expected the favored Muskie to win an easy victory with at least 50% of the vote. McGovern campaigned hard against Muskie, attacking his cautious positions on most issues and publicly asking him why he had only recently come out against the war. These tactics, combined with McGovern's organization of the state, did much to bring him into the spotlight. When the votes were counted, McGovern came in a close second to Muskie, 46% to 37%, and established himself as a surprisingly viable contender for the nomination.

It was in the Wisconsin and Massachusetts primaries that McGovern first took a substantial lead over his opponents. In Wisconsin, Muskie enjoyed the endorsements of most of the local Democratic Party, while former vice-president Hubert Humphrey, a perennially popular Democratic politician, was favored in the black and working-class districts of the state. Alabama governor George Wallace and New York mayor John Lindsay were also in the race. McGovern's major advantage was, again, his organization. While Muskie and Humphrey had contented themselves with the endorsements of established politicians and groups, McGovern's campaign had gone to the people, gathering volunteers, passing out literature, and setting up local offices throughout the state.

The major issue of the Wisconsin primary was the state property tax which, having risen to the highest levels Wisconsin had ever known, was now becoming a source of widespread resentment among the voters. Accordingly, all the candidates spoke out against the property tax and railed against tax loopholes and giveaways. With complete agreement on the major issue, all the candidates sounded the same and so McGovern's extensive organization, able to reach and motivate more voters than were the organizations of his rivals, tipped the scales in his favor. McGovern won the Wisconsin primary, garnering 30% of the vote and carrying seven of the state's nine congressional districts. Wallace and Humphrey were virtually tied for second place, Wallace with 22% and Humphrey with 21%, while Muskie trailed far behind with 10%.

With his Wisconsin victory and his strong showing in New Hampshire, McGovern was now seen as the front-runner for the Democratic presidential nomination. This position was extremely important to the outcome of the Massachusetts primary three weeks later. A liberal, Democratic state with a large student population, Massachusetts was solidly behind McGovern. The goal of McGovern's campaign staff was not to win the Massachusetts primary—they were assured of victory—but to win a landslide victory that would put McGovern far ahead of the pack. With the win in Wisconsin they were able to turn Massachusetts into the landslide they needed. As Morris S. Dees, Jr., the direct-mail chairman for McGovern, explains: "In McGovern's campaign each primary financed the next primary." And the day after the Wisconsin win, according to McGovern Massachusetts campaign chairman John McKean, "our switchboard lit up like a Christmas tree."

The Massachusetts primary was a landslide victory for McGovern, who won 52% of the vote in a field of four candidates. McGovern's new momentum enabled him to confront Humphrey in the Ohio primary a week later and come within 2% of winning it from him, despite the fact that media observers had long conceded the state to Humphrey. With the other presidential contenders lagging far behind, McGovern went on to win primaries in Nebraska, Oregon, Rhode Island, California, New Jersey, South Dakota, New Mexico, and New York, gathering enough delegates in these contests to virtually insure a first ballot nomination at the Democratic Party convention in July. "Within the Democratic Party," Theodore H. White maintains in *The Making of the President, 1972,* "no political strategy had been more astonishingly successful than [McGovern's] in recent times." *Time* called it "one of the most extraordinary success sagas in U.S. politics."

Though McGovern won the Democratic nomination on the first ballot, there were two major mistakes made at the convention which hurt his chances to win the general election against Richard Nixon in November. One of these was the unrestrained nature of the convention itself. Some of McGovern's supporters used the opportunity to avenge themselves on the conservative, old-line wing of the party—refusing to seat Chicago mayor Daley's delegation, for example—and caused irreparable damage to much-needed party unity. The delegates also engaged in so much frivolity on the night of McGovern's nomination—nominating a host of make-believe characters for vice-president, for instance—that McGovern's acceptance speech was delayed until 3 A.M., long after most of the convention's television viewing audience had gone to bed. The image of a disorganized and frivolous Democratic Party did not help McGovern's image. Nor did the popular impression that McGovern's supporters included many radicals who had somehow "captured" the party, this idea being fostered by the blacks, women, and young people who made up the McGovern delegation. More serious was McGovern's choice of Thomas Eagleton, a Missouri senator, as his running mate. Shortly after the convention it was learned that Eagleton had suffered a nervous breakdown some years before and had undergone shock therapy treatments. Speculation about Eagleton's suitability for the job of vice-president was widespread. At first promising to stand by Eagleton "1,000 percent," McGovern was forced to reverse his decision, remove Eagleton from the ticket, and replace him with R. Sargent Shriver. This reversal hurt McGovern's image, making him appear to be indecisive.

In contrast to McGovern, Republican Richard Nixon had several important advantages. He was an incumbent president, his peace-making overtures to China and the Soviet Union were well-publicized and served to enhance his image as a statesman, and his standing in the public opinion polls was consistently higher than McGovern's. But Nixon had certain weak points, too, and McGovern sought every opportunity to bring them to public attention. There was the matter of ten million dollars in unaccounted-for Nixon campaign funds, the unpopular U.S.-Soviet grain deal, the embarrassing I.T.T. scandal and, of course, the Watergate affair, which eventually caused Nixon's resignation from office some two years later. Add to this a high unemployment rate, inflation, Nixon's controversial appointments to the Supreme Court, and the unpopular Vietnam War, and McGovern had plenty of issues to use to his advantage.

But McGovern's public mistakes kept media attention focused on his own affairs, and he too often found himself defending his own actions instead of discussing the shortcomings of his opponent. Nixon refused to debate McGovern or to make any public acknowledgement of the charges McGovern made against him. "McGovern's image," Paul R. Wieck of *New Republic* maintains, "was so bad in so many segments of society that Nixon was never required to come forward and explain himself." McGovern's campaign floundered, unable to find a way to successfully debate the issues.

As the campaign drew to an end, McGovern, according to Peter Goldman and Richard Stout of *Newsweek,* "turned more furiously evangelical than any major-party candidate since William Jennings Bryan, . . . trying in his low-decibel style to preach his way to the Presidency on the . . . proposition that this election is a contest between good and evil—and that if he loses, evil will have won." McGovern's opposition to the Vietnam War also became more strident. Whereas his previous statements had been calm ("To say," McGovern stated at one point during the campaign, "that we are doing fairly well in foreign policy except for Vietnam is very much like a man saying 'I feel pretty well except for the cancer in my lungs.'"), McGovern began to personally attack Nixon over the war. "Why, Mr. Nixon," McGovern asked in the last week of the campaign, "was it necessary to kill another 20,000 young Americans [in Vietnam]? What did you gain by killing or wounding or driving out of their homes 6 million [Vietnamese] by this incredible bombing that's gone on the last four years?" McGovern's strident approach proved unpopular with the voters, perhaps because, as *Time* points out, "what he is trying to tell America is too hot."

The results of the November election were overwhelmingly against McGovern. Nixon won 61% of the vote and carried 49 states in an unprecedented landslide. McGovern carried only Massachusetts and the District of Columbia. "I want every single one of you to remember," McGovern told his supporters in his concession speech, ". . . that if we pushed the day of peace just one day closer, then every minute and every hour and every bone-crushing effort in this campaign was worth the entire sacrifice." McGovern pledged to support Nixon in his work toward "peace abroad and justice at home."

After the 1972 election, McGovern returned to his seat in the U.S. Senate where he served until 1980. In that year, "targeted" by right-wing political action groups and caught in the conservative landslide of Republican Ronald Reagan, he lost his Senate seat. Angered that during the 1980 campaign the right wing labeled him everything from "a pawn of Castro," for his support of normalized relations with Cuba, to a "baby killer," for his support of abortion rights, McGovern founded Americans for Common Sense, a public interest organization opposing the tactics and ideas of the resurgent right wing and issuing position papers on issues of the day. Speaking to *Newsweek* about his activities since leaving government office, McGovern maintains: "This has been the happiest year of my life."

BIOGRAPHICAL/CRITICAL SOURCES—Periodicals: *New York Times,* March 31, 1961, July 30, 1966, January 16, 1978; *Christian Science Monitor,* December 6, 1962, January 8, 1963; *America,* December 19, 1964; *New Yorker,* August 24, 1968, February 20, 1978; *Newsweek,* August 26, 1968, June 5, 1972, June 19, 1972, July 10, 1972, July 24, 1972, September 11, 1972, November 6, 1972, November 13, 1972, November 17, 1980, February 15, 1982; *Saturday Review,* November 23, 1968, July 1, 1972; *Carleton Miscellany,* spring, 1969.

Nation, January 25, 1971, May 15, 1982; *Time,* January 25, 1971, May 8, 1972, July 10, 1972, August 21, 1972, October 16, 1972, October 23, 1972, October 30, 1972, October 6, 1980, November 17, 1980; *New York Times Magazine,* May 2, 1971, May 6, 1973; *Washington Post,* September 24, 1971; *National Review,* February 18, 1972, December 23, 1977; *New Republic,* May 6, 1972, November 18, 1972, October 25, 1980; *Business Week,* May 27, 1972; *U.S. News & World Report,* June 19, 1972, June 26, 1972, July 24, 1972, August 21, 1972; *Life,* July 7, 1972; *New York Review of Books,* July 20, 1972; *New Statesman,* July 28, 1972; *Ramparts,* September, 1972; *Fortune,* September, 1972; *Ladies' Home Journal,* October, 1972; *Harper's,* November, 1972, October, 1980; *Christian Century,* November 1, 1972; *Progressive,* September, 1974, April, 1978; *American Opinion,* October, 1974, February, 1979; *Washington Post Book World,* January 8, 1978; *Village Voice,* January 23, 1978; *Political Science Quarterly,* summer, 1978; *Commonweal,* October 13, 1978; *Current,* January, 1979; *Politics Today,* March-April, 1980; *Atlantic,* June, 1980; *In These Times,* October 15-21, 1980.

Books: Robert Sam Anson, *McGovern: A Biography,* Holt, 1972; Shirley Maclaine, editor, *McGovern: The Man and His Beliefs,* Norton, 1972; Ernest R. May and Janet Fraser, editors, *Campaign '72,* Harvard University Press, 1973; Theodore H. White, *The Making of the President, 1972,* Atheneum, 1973; Gordon L. Weil, *Long Shot: George McGovern Runs for President,* Norton, 1973; Richard Dougherty, *Goodbye, Mr. Christian: A Personal Account of McGovern's Rise and Fall,* Doubleday, 1973; Gary Warren Hart, *Right from the Start: A Chronicle of the McGovern Campaign,* Quadrangle, 1973; George McGovern, *An American Journey: The Presidential Campaign Speeches of George McGovern,* Random House, 1974; Kristi Witker, *How to Lose Everything in Politics Except Massachusetts,* Mason & Lipscomb, 1974; Eleanor McGovern and Mary Finch Hoyt, *Uphill: A Personal Story,* Houghton, 1974; McGovern, *Grassroots: The Autobiography of George McGovern,* Random House, 1977.

—Sketch by Thomas Wiloch

* * *

McGOWEN, Thomas 1927-
(Tom McGowen)

PERSONAL: Born May 6, 1927, in Evanston, Ill.; son of William Robert (a salesman) and Helene (Nelson) McGowen; married Loretta Swok; children: Alan, Gayle, Maureen, Kathleen. *Education:* Attended Roosevelt College of Chicago (now Roosevelt University), 1947, 1948, and American Academy of Art, 1948-49. *Home:* 4449 North Oriole Blvd., Norridge, Ill. 60656.

CAREER: Sidney Clayton & Associates (advertising), Chicago, Ill., production manager, 1949-53; Justrite Manufacturing Co., Chicago, advertising manager, 1953-54; National Safety Council, Chicago, sales promotion director, 1954-59; Hensley Co. (advertising), Chicago, creative director, 1959-69; World Book, Inc. (publishers), Chicago, senior editor, 1969—. *Military service:* U.S. Navy, hospital corpsman, World War II. *Member:* Authors Guild, Society of Children's Book Writers, Children's Reading Round Table.

WRITINGS—Under name Tom McGowen; juveniles: (Self-illustrated) *The Only Glupmaker in the U.S. Navy*, Albert Whitman, 1966; *The Apple Strudel Soldier*, Follett, 1968; *Dragon Stew*, Follett, 1969; *Last Voyage of the Unlucky Katie Marie*, Whitman, 1969.

Published by Rand McNally, except as indicated: *The Biggest Toot in Toozelburg*, Reilly & Lee, 1970; *Hammet and the Highlanders*, Follett, 1970; *Sir MacHinery*, Follett, 1970; *The Fearless Fossil Hunters*, Whitman, 1971; *Album of Dinosaurs*, 1972; *Album of Prehistoric Animals*, 1974; *Odyssey from River Bend*, Little, Brown, 1975; *Album of Prehistoric Man*, 1975; *The Spirit of the Wild*, Little, Brown, 1976; *Album of Sharks*, 1977; *Album of Reptiles*, 1978; *Album of Astronomy*, 1979.

Album of Whales, 1980; *Album of Rocks and Minerals*, 1981; *Encyclopedia of Legendary Creatures*, 1981; *Album of Birds*, 1982; *Album of Space Flight*, 1983.

SIDELIGHTS: Tom McGowen told *CA:* "I began writing books for children in 1964, when in my late thirties, with the feeling that this was the most meaningful and important work I could possibly do. Now, I still feel the same. My fiction, mainly fantasy, is designed to entertain; my non-fiction, mainly in the area of general science, is intended to both entertain and to help children understand the reasons for things, whether the behavior of a particular kind of wild animal or the twinkle of a star. I believe that if children can come to understand the why and how of things going on around them, from the interrelated activities of animals and plants to the unseen movement of molecules, they'll be more likely to grow into comfortable, confident, *civilized* adults, unencumbered by superstition and irrationality. If one of my fiction books can turn just *one* child on to the imagination-stimulating world of fantasy; if one of my non-fiction books can make just *one* child aware of the equally stimulating world of nature and natural science, I'll have achieved my personal goal."

*   *   *

McGOWEN, Tom
See McGOWEN, Thomas

*   *   *

McGUIGAN, F(rank) J(oseph) 1924-

PERSONAL: Born December 7, 1924, in Oklahoma City, Okla.; son of Francis Leo and Edith Louise (Whiting) McGuigan; married Elizabeth Spieler, August 16, 1982; children: (previous marriage) Joan (Mrs. Broaddus C. Fitzpatrick), Constance, Richard. *Education:* University of California, Los Angeles, B.A., 1945, M.A., 1949; attended Harvard University, 1945, Columbia University, summer, 1947; University of Southern California, Ph.D., 1950; further studies at University of Colorado, 1951. *Office:* Performance Research Laboratory, University of Louisville, Louisville, Ky. 40208.

CAREER: Pepperdine College (now University), Los Angeles, Calif., instructor, 1949-50; University of Nevada, Reno, assistant professor, 1950-51; George Washington University, Washington, D.C., research scientist and director of Human Resources Research Office, 1951-55; Hollins College, Roanoke, Va., professor of psychology and chairman of department, 1955-76; University of Louisville, Louisville, Kentucky, research professor at graduate school, professor of psychiatry at school of medicine, and director of performance research laboratory at Institute of Advanced Study, 1977—. Part-time lecturer at University of Louisville and U.S. Armed Forces Institute, 1952-55; visiting professor at University of Hawaii, summer, 1965, and University of California, Santa Barbara, 1966; adjunct research professor at Adult Learning Center of North Carolina State University, 1970-72. Part-time research associate, Psychological Corp., 1950-51. Director of evaluation project for Encyclopaedia Britannica, 1961-67. President of Roanoke Mental Health Association, 1968. *Military service:* U.S. Naval Reserve, 1942-46; served in Pacific.

MEMBER: International Stress and Tension Control Society (executive vice-president, 1981—), American Association for Advancement of Tension Control (executive director, 1973-81), American Psychology Association (fellow), American Physiological Society, Psychonomic Society, Pavlovian Society (president, 1975-76), Inter-American Society for Psychology, Biofeedback Research Society, Society for Psychophysiology Research, Sigma Xi. *Awards, honors:* American Psychology Foundation award, 1973, for outstanding contributions to education in psychology; Medal of Honor from Tours, France, 1981; Medal for Scientific Achievement from Bulgarian Academy of Sciences, 1981; Medal of Award from Hiroshima University, 1982.

WRITINGS: (With A. D. Calvin) *Current Studies in Psychology*, Appleton-Century-Crofts, 1958; *Experimental Psychology*, Prentice-Hall, 1960, 4th edition, 1983; (with others) *Psychology*, Allyn & Bacon, 1961; *The Biological Basis of Behavior*, Prentice-Hall, 1963; (editor) *Thinking: Studies of Covert Language Processes*, Appleton-Century-Crofts, 1966.

(With Paul J. Woods) *Contemporary Studies in Psychology*, Appleton-Century-Crofts, 1972; (with others) *A National Field-Test of Selected Programmed Reading Materials for Undereducated Adults*, North Carolina State University, Adult Learning Center, 1972; (editor with D. Barry Lumsden) *Contemporary Approaches to Conditioning and Learning*, V. H. Winston, 1973; (editor) *The Psychophysiology of Thinking*, Academic Press, 1973; *Cognitive Psychophysiology: Principles of Covert Behavior*, Prentice-Hall, 1978; (editor) *Tension Control*, American Association for the Advancement of Tension Control, 1978; *Psychophysiological Measurement of Covert Behavior: A Guide for the Laboratory*, Halsted, 1979; (editor with Wesley E. Sime and J. Macdonald Wallace) *Stress and Tension Control*, Plenum, 1980; *Calm Down: A Guide to Stress and Tension Control*, Prentice-Hall, 1981. Contributor to journals.

*   *   *

McINTOSH, Louis
See JOHNSON, Christopher

*   *   *

McKELVEY, John J(ay), Jr. 1917-

PERSONAL: Born July 16, 1917, in Albany, N.Y.; son of John Jay (a lawyer) and Louise (Brunning) McKelvey; married Josephine Faulkner (a librarian), June 28, 1941; children: John Jay III, Richard Drummond, Edward Faulkner, Laurence Brunning. *Education:* Oberlin College, A.B., 1939; Virginia Polytechnic Institute and State University, M.S., 1941; Cornell University, Ph.D., 1945. *Politics:* "Unimportant." *Religion:* "Unimportant." *Home:* 12 Barnes Ter., Chappaqua, N.Y. 19514. *Office:* Rockefeller Foundation, 1133 Avenue of the Americas, New York, N.Y.

CAREER: Investigator for New York State Agricultural Experiment Station, 1942-45; Rockefeller Foundation, New York, N.Y., associate deputy director, 1945-59, associate director, 1959—, deputy director of agricultural sciences, 1966-68, Latin

American fellowship grant and fellowship officer, 1952-59, African grants and fellowships officer, 1959—. Trustee, International Insitute for Tropical Agriculture, Ibadan, Nigeria, 1971—; member of board of governors, Institute for Agricultural Research, Ahmadu Bello University, Zaria, Nigeria, 1971-74. *Member:* American Association for the Advancement of Science, Entomological Society of America, Association for the Advancement of Agricultural Sciences in Africa (charter member).

WRITINGS: Man against Tsetse: Struggle for Africa, Cornell University Press, 1973; (with R. L. Metcalf) *The Future of Insecticides,* Wiley Inter-science, 1976; (with H. Shorey) *Chemical Control of Insect Behavior,* Wiley Inter-science, 1977; (with L. H. Miller and John A. Pino) *Immunity of Blood Parasites of Animals and Men,* Plenum, 1977; (with Bruce F. Eldridge and Karl Maramorosch) *Vectors of Disease Agents,* Praeger, 1981.

WORK IN PROGRESS: Selected trends in the history of agricultural research in the United States.

SIDELIGHTS: John J. McKelvey told *CA:* "I find writing to be more demanding than any other activity. It forces one to be accurate and truthful. It is also extremely humbling because one usually find the things he thinks he knows to be erroneous unless he checks and re-checks. There really is no use in trying to write 'off-the-cuff,' so to speak. No one, not even the writer himself, will be impressed. The English language is a beautiful language, replete with possibilities for describing one's thoughts and emotions."

AVOCATIONAL INTERESTS. Beekeeping, farming, building.

*   *   *

McKILLOP, Susan Regan 1929-

PERSONAL: Born April 20, 1929, in Woodland, Calif.; daughter of William Michael (a professor) and Susan (a university administrator; maiden name, Cobb) Regan; married Allan A. McKillop (a professor), June 30, 1954; children: Mary Alexis, Allan Michael. *Education:* University of Missouri, A.B. (with honors) and B.Journalism, both 1951; University of California, Berkeley, M.A., 1953; Harvard University, Ph.D., 1966. *Home:* 535 Miller Dr., Davis, Calif. 95616. *Office:* Department of Art, Sonoma State University, Rohnert Park, Calif. 94928.

CAREER: University of California, Davis, assistant professor of art history, 1964-71, assistant dean of College of Letters and Science, 1966-67; California State University, Sacramento, lecturer in art history, 1971-75; Sonoma State University, Rohnert Park, Calif., lecturer, 1975-76, assistant professor, 1976-81, associate professor of art history, 1981—, chairperson of department of art, 1980—. Member of board of directors of Crocker Art Gallery Association, E. B. Crocker Art Gallery, Sacramento, 1972-78. *Member:* College Art Association. *Awards, honors:* Best catalog citation, Western Association of Museums and Museum Directors, 1975, for *Jerald Silva, His World.*

WRITINGS: Robert Bechtle, E. B. Crocker Art Gallery, 1973; *Franciabigio,* University of California Press, 1974; (editor with Wilma Beatty Cox) *Jerald Silva, His World,* E. B. Crocker Art Gallery, 1975; (editor with Cox) *The Chicago Connection, West Coast '76,* E. B. Crocker Art Gallery, 1976.

WORK IN PROGRESS: Research on Medici symbolism and the political aspects of Medici visual commissions, particularly Cosimo the Elder's patronage at San Mario, as well as a study of the underlying pattern of Medici artistic patronage.

McLURE, Charles E., Jr. 1940-

PERSONAL: Born April 14, 1940, in Sierra Blanca, Tex.; son of Charles E. (a retailer) and Dessie (Evans) McLure; married Patsy Nell Carroll, September 17, 1962. *Education:* Attended Texas Western College (now University of Texas at El Paso), 1961; University of Kansas, B.A., 1962; Princeton University, M.A., 1964, Ph.D., 1966. *Home:* 250 Yerba Santa Ave., Los Altos, Calif. 94022. *Office:* Hoover Institution, Stanford University, Stanford, Calif. 94022.

CAREER: Rice University, Houston, Tex., assistant professor, 1965-69, associate professor, 1969-72, professor of economics, 1972-73, Allyn R. and Gladys M. Cline Professor of Economics and Finance, 1973-79; National Bureau of Economic Research, Cambridge, Mass., executive director for research, 1977-78, vice-president, 1978-81; Stanford University, Hoover Institution, Stanford, Calif., senior fellow, 1981—. Honorary research associate, Harvard University, 1967-68, 1977-79, and University of California, Berkeley, 1975; senior staff economist, Council of Economic Advisers, 1969-70; adjunct scholar, American Enterprise Institute, 1972—. Visiting lecturer, St. Thomas University, 1968-70; John S. Bugas Visiting Distinguished Lecturer in Economics, University of Wyoming, 1972; visiting professor, Stanford University, 1973. Organizer of economics conferences. Consultant to private and governmental agencies. *Member:* American Economic Association, National Tax Association (board of directors, 1978-81), Phi Beta Kappa, Omicron Delta Kappa. *Awards, honors:* Woodrow Wilson fellowship, 1962-63; Ford Foundation fellowship, 1964-65, 1967-68.

WRITINGS: Fiscal Failure: Lessons of the Sixties, American Enterprise Institute, 1972; (with Norman B. Ture) *Value Added Tax: Two Views,* American Enterprise Institute, 1972; (with others) *Inflation in the 1960s,* American Enterprise Institute, 1972; (with others) *A New Look at Inflation,* American Enterprise Institute, 1973; (with others) *Perspectives on Tax Reform: Death Taxes, Tax Loopholes, and the Value Added Tax,* Praeger, 1974; (with Malcolm Gillis) *La reforma tributaria colombiana de 1974* (title means "The Colombian Tax Reform of 1974"), Biblioteca Banco Popular (Bogata), 1977; *Once Is Enough: The Taxation of Corporate Equity Income,* Institute for Contemporary Studies, 1977; *Must Corporate Income Be Taxed Twice?,* Brookings Institution, 1979.

Contributor: Gillis, editor, *Fiscal Reform for Colombia: The Final Report and Staff Papers of the Colombian Commission on Tax Reform,* Part II, Harvard Law School, 1971; Richard A. Musgrave, editor, *Broad-Based Taxes: New Options and Sources,* Johns Hopkins Press, 1973; *La politica tributaria como instrumento del desarrollo* (title means "Tax Policy as an Instrument of Development"), Organization of American States, 1973; *The Impact of Multinational Corporations on Development and on International Relations,* United Nations, 1974; Richard M. Bird and Oliver Oldham, editors, *Readings on Taxation in Developing Countries,* 3rd edition (McLure was not associated with earlier editions), Johns Hopkins Press, 1975; Erwin N. Griswold and Michael J. Graetz, editors, *Cases and Materials on Federal Income Taxation,* Foundation Press (Mineola, N.Y.), 1975.

Amacher, Tollison, and Willett, editors, *The Economic Approach to Public Policy,* Cornell University Press, 1976; Wallace E. Oates, editor, *The Political Economy of Fiscal Federalism,* Lexington Books, 1977; Joseph A. Pechman, editor, *Comprehensive Income Taxation,* Brookings Institution, 1977;

Tax Policies in the 1979 Budget, American Enterprise Institute, 1978; (with J. Gregory Ballentine) *1978 Compendium of Tax Research,* U.S. Government Printing Office, 1978; Roy W. Bahl, editor, *The Taxation of Urban Property in Less Developed Countries,* University of Wisconsin Press, 1979; John R. Moroney, editor, *Income Inequality: Trends and International Comparisons,* Lexington Books, 1979; Sijbren Cnossen, editor, *Beschouwingen over het verrekingsstelsel* (title means "Reflections on the Imputation System"), Kluwer (Netherlands), 1979.

R. Albert Berry and Ronald Soligo, editors, *Economic Policy and Income Distribution in Colombia,* Westview, 1980; Henry J. Aaron and Michael J. Boskin, editors, *The Economics of Taxation,* Brookings Institution, 1980; Felicity Skidmore, editor, *Financing Social Security,* M.I.T. Press, 1981; Wayne Thirsk and John Whalley, editors, *Tax Policy Options in the 1980s,* Canadian Tax Foundation, 1982. Also contributor to *Budgetwirkungen und Budgetpolitik,* edited by Klaus Mackscheidt, Gustave Fischer Verlag (West Germany).

Contributor to journals, including *National Tax Journal, Canadian Journal of Economics, Public Finance Quarterly,* and *American Economic Review.* Referee for numerous journals, including *Public Policy, American Economic Review, Journal of Political Economy, Growth and Change, Journal of Public Economics,* and *Journal of Money, Credit, and Banking.* Invited reader, *Quarterly Journal of Economics,* 1972-77. Member of editorial advisory board, *National Tax Journal,* 1972—; member of editorial board, *Public Finance Quarterly,* 1975-77, and *Southern Economic Journal,* 1977-79.

WORK IN PROGRESS: Research on tax policy, tax reform in developing countries, taxation of natural resources, and tax incidence; contributing to numerous volumes on taxation.

AVOCATIONAL INTERESTS: Backpacking, ski touring, canoeing.

* * *

McWILLIAMS, Margaret (Ann Edgar) 1929-

PERSONAL: Born May 26, 1929, in Osage, Iowa; daughter of Alvin R. (a professor) and Mildred Irene (Lane) Edgar; married former husband, Don A. McWilliams (a physicist), September 20, 1953; children: Roger, Kathleen. *Education:* Iowa State University of Science and Technology, B.S., 1951, M.S., 1953; Oregon State University, Ph.D., 1968. *Home address:* P.O. Box 220, Redondo Beach, Calif. 90277. *Office:* California State University, 5151 State College Dr., Los Angeles, Calif. 90032.

CAREER: California State University, Los Angeles, assistant professor, 1961-66, associate professor, 1966-68, professor of home economics, 1968—, and chairman of department, 1968-76.

MEMBER: Institute of Food Technologists, American Home Economics Association, College Teachers of Food and Nutrition, American Dietetic Association, Society for Nutrition Education, Phi Kappa Phi, Phi Upsilon Omicron (nation founders fellow, 1964, 1967), Omicron Nu, Iota Sigma Pi, Sigma Alpha Iota, Sigma Delta Epsilon. *Awards, honors:* Iowa State University of Science and Technology, Alumni Centennial Award, 1971, and Professional Achievement Award, 1977; Outstanding Professor Award, California State University, Los Angeles, 1976.

WRITINGS: Food Fundamentals, Wiley, 1966, 3rd edition, 1979; *Nutrition for the Growing Years,* Wiley, 1967, 3rd edition, 1980; (with Lendal Kotschevar) *Understanding Food,* Wiley, 1969; (with Linda Davis) *Food for You,* Ginn, 1971, 2nd edition, 1972; *Illustrated Guide to Food Preparation,* Plycon, 2nd edition, 1972, 4th edition, 1982; (with Fredrick Stare) *Living Nutrition,* Wiley, 1973, 3rd edition, 1981; *Meatless Cookbook,* Plycon, 1973; (with Stare) *Nutrition for Good Health,* Plycon, 1974, 4th edition, 1982; (with Harriett Paine) *Modern Food Preservation,* Plycon, 1977; *Fundamentals of Meal Management,* Plycon, 1978.

* * *

MEADE, Richard
See HAAS, Ben(jamin) L(eopold)

* * *

MEHDI, M(ohammed) T(aki) 1928-

PERSONAL: Surname is pronounced *Meh-dee;* born January 6, 1928, in Baghdad, Iraq; son of Al-Haj M. and Zahra (Moeni) Mehdi; came to United States, 1949; married Beverlee Turner (a teacher), June 20, 1953; children: Anisa, Janan, Laila. *Education:* University of California, Berkeley, B.A., 1953, M.A., 1954, Ph.D., 1961. *Office address:* American-Arab Relations Committee, P.O. Box 416, New York, N.Y. 10017.

CAREER: Arab Information Center, San Francisco, Calif., 1959-62; American-Arab Relations Committee, New York, N.Y., secretary-general, 1964-76, executive director and publisher, *Action* (Arabic-English newspaper), 1969—, president, 1977—. Lecturer on Arab and Middle East affairs, 1960—; advisor to Arab delegations to the United Nations, 1963-64. *Member:* American Political Science Association, American Association for Legal and Political Philosophy, Federation of American-Arab Organizations (founder and secretary-general), Arab Anti-Defamation League (executive director), Arab People to American People (secretary-general, 1980—). *Awards, honors:* Book of the Year award from Friends of Literature (Beirut), 1963, for *A Nation of Lions . . . Chained.*

WRITINGS—Published by New World Press, except as indicated: *Constitutionalism—Western and Middle Eastern,* 1961; *The Question of Palestine,* Arab Information Center, 1962; *A Nation of Lions . . . Chained,* 1963; (translator into Arabic) Hans Kelsen, *General Theory of Law and State,* University of Baghdad, 1967; *Peace in the Middle East,* 1967; *Kennedy and Sirhan: Why?,* 1968; (editor) *Palestine and the Bible,* 1970. Also author of *Peace in Palestine,* 1976. Author of pamphlets. Contributor of articles to journals.

SIDELIGHTS: M. T. Mehdi writes: "I am an Arab who is interested in Thomas Jefferson and Alexander Hamilton. My interest in contemporary philosophy is within the field of logical empiricism. [I am] concerned with better American-Arab relations. Have coined the expression 'anti-Gentile-ism,' which refers to the prejudices of the Jews toward the Gentiles, much as the expression 'anti-Semitism' refers to the prejudices of the Gentiles toward the Jews."

Mehdi's personal interest in Arab-U.S. relations has kept him constantly active. He has traveled throughout the Arab world, meeting with heads of state, including the late King Khaled of Saudi Arabia and President Qaddafi of Libya. He has met several times with Yasir Arafat, chairman of the Palestine Liberation Organization (PLO), discussing with him the question of peace in Palestine. Mehdi has also met with many prime ministers, ambassadors, and high-ranking officials in the Arab world and the United States and has appeared on numerous radio and television programs in order to bring his message to as many people as possible.

Mehdi describes the activities and goals of his American-Arab Relations Committee in an interview in *Middle East International:* "We are unorthodox in our approach, concerned primarily with civil rights, human rights. We have publicly opposed America giving arms to Israel or selling arms to Jordan, Saudi Arabia, Kuwait and other Arab countries. We do this because it is ultimately to the detriment of all parties. Peace in the Middle East will not come through Arab armament. It will come through Israeli disarmament and our activities in America are directed towards suspending American military aid to Israel." Mehdi comments to *CA* that ending American military aid to the Arabs and to Israel is "the most vital step towards peace" in the Middle East.

BIOGRAPHICAL/CRITICAL SOURCES: Middle East International, August, 1975.

* * *

MEHROTRA, S(ri) Ram 1931-

PERSONAL: Born June 23, 1931, in Etawah, Uttar Pradesh, India; son of Hari Narain and Manno Devi (Tandon) Mehrotra; married Eva Ganguli (a teacher), July 24, 1957. *Education:* Allahabad University, B.A. (first class honors), 1948, M.A., 1950; School of Oriental and African Studies, Ph.D., 1960. *Religion:* Hindu. *Home:* "Seva," Kenfield Estate, Simla 171 004, India. *Office:* Himachel Pradesh University, Simla 171 005, India.

CAREER: Saugar University, Saugar, Madhya Pradesh, India, lecturer in history, 1950-58; University of London, London, England, research fellow at Institute of Commonwealth Studies, 1960-61, School of Oriental and African Studies, research fellow, 1961-62, lecturer in politics, 1962-71; Indian Institute of Advanced Study, Simla, India, fellow, 1971-79; Himachel Pradesh University, Simla, professor of history, 1972—.

WRITINGS—Published by Vikas Publishing: *India and the Commonwealth, 1885-1929,* Praeger, 1965; *The Emergence of the Indian National Congress,* 1971; *The Commonwealth and the Nation,* 1978; *Towards India's Freedom and Partition,* 1979. Contributor to *India Quarterly, Indian Economics and Social History Review, Journal of Commonwealth Political Studies,* and *Journal of Development Studies.*

* * *

MEIDEN, Walter 1907-

PERSONAL: Born July 12, 1907, in Grand Haven, Mich. *Education:* University of Michigan, A.B., 1931; Ohio State University, M.A., 1933, Ph.D., 1945. *Home:* 2949 Neil Ave., Apartment 301-C, Columbus, Ohio 43202.

CAREER: Ohio State University, Columbus, 1931—, began as graduate assistant, professor of Romance languages, 1966-74, professor emeritus, 1974—. *Military service:* U.S. Naval Reserve, 1943-46. *Member:* Modern Language Association of America, U.S. Chess Federation.

WRITINGS: (With W. S. Hendrix) *Beginning French,* Houghton, 1940, 5th edition, 1978; (with Richard Armitage) *Beginning Spanish,* Houghton, 1953, 4th edition, 1978; (editor with Olin Moore) *Onze Contes,* Houghton, 1957; (with Max Euwe) *Chess Master vs. Chess Amateur,* McKay, 1963, 2nd edition, 1971; *Contes de Michelle Maurois,* Houghton, 1966; (with Euwe) *The Road to Chess Mastery,* McKay, 1966; (with Charles Carlut) *French for Oral and Written Review,* Holt, 1968, 2nd edition, 1976; (editor with Diane Birckbichler and Ann Dube) Jean Anouilh, *Le voyageur sans bagage,* Holt, 1973; (with Mario Iglesias) *Spanish for Oral and Written Review,* Holt, 1975, 2nd edition, 1981; (with Euwe) *Chess Master vs. Chess Master,* McKay, 1977. Author of monthly column with Norman Cotter, "Back to Basics," *Chess Life and Review,* 1973-77.

WORK IN PROGRESS: Critical edition of the Old French versions of *La Descente de Saint-Paul en enfer,* with Alison Elliott; 3rd edition of *French for Oral and Written Review,* with Charles Carlut.

SIDELIGHTS: Walter Meiden writes *CA:* "Dr. Max Euwe (former world chess champion) and I wrote our chess books to indicate to the amateur exactly how a master would take advantage of an error or of a weak move. In these books we try to penetrate more deeply than anyone has done up to this time into the essential nature of chess play. Whenever an appropriate position arises, we explain what the strategic plan at that moment should be. And at every point of the game where other moves also come into consideration we show what would happen if those moves had been played. Thus, these books are a practical exposition of the art of chess analysis."

* * *

MEINTJES, Johannes 1923-1980

PERSONAL: Surname is pronounced Main-cheese; born May 19, 1923, in South Africa; died July 7, 1980; son of Ernest Frederick (a farmer) and Valerie (Keyter) Meintjes; married Ronell Rossouw (his secretary), March 25, 1960; children: Lynn (stepdaughter). *Education:* University of Capetown, B.A., 1943; studied art in London, Amsterdam, and Paris, 1946-47, 1958. *Home:* "Grootzeekoegat," Molteno, Cape Province, South Africa. *Agent:* Blanche C. Gregory, 2 Tudor City Pl., New York, N.Y. 10017. *Office address:* Box 125, Molteno, Cape Province, South Africa.

CAREER: Writer and professional painter, 1944-80; art work shown in one-man exhibitions in major cities of South Africa, and in group exhibitions nationally and abroad, also displayed in public and private collections throughout the world. Librarian at George Vice Memorial Library, Molteno, South Africa, 1967-80. Lecturer in fine art, 1945, 1947-49; honorary curator, Molteno Museum, 1967-80; member of board of control, Burgersdorp Museum, 1973-76. *Member:* South African P.E.N., South African Academy for Arts and Science. *Awards, honors:* Award as most original South African painter, 1949.

WRITINGS—In English: *Anton Anreith, Sculptor* (monograph), Juta & Co., 1951; *Frontier Family: A Chronicle of a South African Farm, Its Homestead, and Its People* (autobiographical), Central News Agency, 1955.

Complex Canvas: A South African Approach, Afrikaanse Pers Boekhandel (Johannesberg), 1960; (editor) Ambrose Lomax, *Portrait of a South African Village* (bilingual edition), Bamboesberg, 1964; *Manor House,* Delacorte, 1964 (published in England as *The Silent Conspiracy,* M. Joseph, 1965); *Olive Schreiner: Portrait of a South African Woman,* Hugh Keartland (Johannesberg), 1965; *De la Rey—Lion of the West* (biography), Hugh Keartland, 1966; *Sword in the Sand: The Life and Death of Gideon Scheepers,* Tafelberg-Uitgewers (Cape Town), 1969; *President Steyn* (also see below), Nasionale Boekhandel (Cape Town), 1969; *Stormberg: A Lost Opportunity, the Anglo Boer War in the North Eastern Cape Colony, 1899-1902,* Nasionale Boekhandel, 1969.

General Louis Botha (biography), Casell, 1970; *The Commandant-General: The Life and Times of Petrus Jacobus Joubert of the South African Republic, 1831-1900,* Tafelberg-Uitgewers, 1971; *Sandile: The Fall of the Xhosa Nation,* T. V. Bulpin (Cape Town), 1971; *The Voortrekkers: The Story of the Great Trek and the Making of South Africa,* Cassell, 1973; *President Paul Kruger* (biography), Cassell, 1974; *SASOL: 1950-1975* (history of South African Coal, Oil, and Gas Corporation), Tafelberg-Uitgewers, 1976; *The Anglo-Boer War, 1899-1902: A Pictorial History* (also published in Afrikaans; see below), C. Struik (Cape Town), 1976, Hippocrene, 1979. Also author of *The Round Table in South Africa,* 1970.

In Afrikaans: *Maggie Laubser* (monograph), Hollands-Afrikaanse Uitgewersmaatskappy, 1944; *Kamerade* (short stories), Anreith Press, 1947; *Die Blanke Stilte* (play), Holloway, 1952; *Stormsvlei* (romance novel), Afrikaanse Pers Boekhandel, 1955; *Die Soekendes* (play), Afrikaanse Pers Boekhandel, 1958; *Dagboek I* (diary), Bamboesberg, 1961; *Die Singende Reen* (romance novel), Bamboesberg, 1962; *Gister is Vandag* (romance novel), Afrikaanse Pers Boekhandel, 1963; *Jeugjare* (autobiography), Bamboesberg, 1963; *Mallemeule* (romance novel), Afrikaanse Pers Boekhandel, 1964; *Vader van sy Volk* (biography; based on his *President Steyn*), Tafelberg-Uitgewers, 1970; *Siembamba* (short stories and essays), Afrikaanse Pers Boekhandel, 1971; *Dagboek 2* (diary), Bamboesberg, 1972; *Dorp van Drome: Die Geskiedenis van Molteno, 1874-1974* (history), Minisipaliteit Molteno, 1974; *Die Anglo-Boere Oorlog in Beeld, 1899-1902,* C. Struik, 1976; *Eeu van Genade: Die Geskiedenis van die N. G. Kerk in Molteno, 1881-1981* (history of the Dutch Reformed Church), Nasionale Koerante (Port Elizabeth, South Africa), 1981. Also author of *Dagboek 3* (diary), 1975.

WORK IN PROGRESS: Several sketches dealing with figures of the Boer War; an autobiography; introductions to "Anglo-Boer War Reprint Library" series books, for C. Struik.

SIDELIGHTS: Johannes Meintjes's widow, Ronell Meintjes, writes *CA* that her husband was as "indefatigable a writer as he was a painter, firmly [believing] that the one complimented the other. This belief is evident in reading his books, be they fiction or nonfiction.

"Painting was his first love," she continues. "He had an individualistic style, often depicting studies of the human face (mostly imaginary), with emphasis on the hands and eyes. More often [his paintings depicted] coloured fishermen, thatched white cottages, colourful landscapes, the exotic. His inspiration lay close at hand—sometimes in a skull of a sheep, dandelions arranged in a vase, full blown flowers of an onion plant, a shell, a branch loaded with lemons. But mostly, the beauty of his surroundings, the compelling charm which emanates from this old homestead in which he lived, the peace and quiet that surrounded him, inspired the drive to continue in both fields in which he had succeeded so admirably.

"Meintjes may have insisted that he was a painter first and foremost, but there is no doubt that if he didn't sandwich writing in between all his other activities, South Africa would have been poorer for it. The fruits of his talents are very much in demand—some of his books are Africana and hard to come by, but they're there.

"The National English Literary Museum in Grahamstown, South Africa, under the leadership of Prof. Andre de Villiers, is, with [my] approval and assistance, creating a Johannes Meintjes Room and all his letters, documents, manuscripts, some books, furniture, even paintings, etc., will be housed there for everyone to see."

Meintjes appeared in three South African Television specials, "Meintjes—The Artist and His Work," "Meintjes and His Milieu," and "On the Stormberg."

AVOCATIONAL INTERESTS: Reading, walking, collecting books (mainly Africana) and Cape Colonial furniture.

BIOGRAPHICAL/CRITICAL SOURCES: Pieter Marincowitz, *Meintjes—Lyrical Work* (monograph), Anreith Press, 1948; *Tydskrif vir Letterkunde,* September 1951, June, 1961, September, 1962; *Lantern,* March, 1963; Esme Berman, *Art and Artists of South Africa,* Balkema, 1970; *Panorama,* July, 1974; *Die Huisengoot,* October, 1975.†

[Sketch verified by wife, Ronell Meintjes]

* * *

MELENDY, H(oward) Brett 1924-

PERSONAL: Born May 3, 1924, in Eureka, Calif.; son of Howard Burton (an assessor) and Pearl (Brett) Melendy; married Marian Robinson, March 29, 1952; children: Brenda Dale, Darcie Brett, Lisa Marie. *Education:* Attended Humboldt State College (now University), 1942-45; Stanford University, A.B., 1946, M.A., 1948, Ph.D., 1952. *Politics:* Democrat. *Religion:* Presbyterian. *Home:* 2010 University Ave., San Jose, Calif. 95128. *Office:* Office of Undergraduate Studies, San Jose State University, San Jose, Calif. 95192.

CAREER: High school teacher, Fresno, Calif., 1950-54; Fresno Junior College, Fresno, instructor, 1954-55; San Jose State University, San Jose, Calif., faculty member, 1955-70, chairman of history department, 1958-69, professor of history, 1961-70; University of Hawaii, Honolulu, professor of history, 1970-79, vice-president for community colleges, 1970-73; San Jose State University, professor of history emeritus, 1979—. College Entrance Examination Board, visiting representative of Council on College-Level Examinations, 1965-66. *Member:* American Historical Association, National Education Association, Masons. *Awards, honors:* American Philosophical Society grant, 1962 and 1974; American Council on Education fellowship, 1967-68.

WRITINGS: (With Benjamin F. Gilbert) *The Governors of California,* Talisman, 1965; *The Oriental Americans,* Twayne, 1972; *Asians in America,* Twayne, 1977.

Contributor: Roger Daniels and Spencer C. Olin, Jr., *Racism in California,* Macmillan, 1972; Norris Hundley, Jr., editor, *The Asian American,* CLIO Book, 1976; Emma Gee, editor, *Counterpoint: Perspectives on Asian America,* Asia American Studies Center, University of California, Los Angeles, 1976; Dennis L. Cuddy, editor, *Contemporary American Immigration,* Twayne, 1982. Contributor to *Encyclopaedia Britannica, Encyclopedia Americana, Harvard Encyclopedia of American Ethnic Groups,* and to historical journals.

WORK IN PROGRESS: History of the Territory of Hawaii, 1898-1959.

* * *

MERRILL, Dean 1943-

PERSONAL: Born December 17, 1943, in Los Angeles, Calif.; son of D. Raymond (a minister) and Mary Lucille (Frantz) Merrill; married Grace LaVonne Danielson, June 25, 1966; children: Nathan, Rhonda, Tricia. *Education:* Chicago Bible College, Th.B., 1964; Syracuse University, M.A., 1970. *Religion:* Christian. *Office: Leadership* Magazine, 465 Gundersen Dr., Carol Stream, Ill. 60187.

CAREER: Campus Life (magazine), Carol Stream, Ill., various editorial positions, 1965-69 and 1971-73; Oral Roberts University, Tulsa, Okla., director of university information, 1970-

71; Creation House, Inc, (publishers), Carol Stream, executive editor, 1973-74; David C. Cook Publishing Co., Elgin, Ill., various editorial positions, 1974-81; *Leadership* magazine, Carol Stream, senior editor, 1981— . Visiting lecturer in communications, Graduate School, Wheaton College, Wheaton, Ill., 1973-75. *Member:* Evangelical Press Association, Association for Supervision and Curriculum Development.

WRITINGS: (With Ken Taylor) *The Jesus Book,* Tyndale, 1971; (with Taylor) *The Way,* Tyndale, 1972; (with Harold Myra) *Rock, Bach, and Superschlock,* A. J. Holman, 1972; (with Janet Lynn) *Peace and Love,* Creation House, 1973; (editor with Clayton Baumann) *125 Crowdbreakers,* Regal Books, 1974; *The Husband Book,* Zondervan, 1977, published as *How to Really Love Your Wife,* 1980; (with Bonnie Thielmann) *The Broken God,* David Cook, 1979; *Another Chance,* Zondervan, 1981. Contributor to religious periodicals including *Eternity, Christian Life, New Wine, Christian Reader, Reflections,* and *Logos Journal.*

SIDELIGHTS: Dean Merrill writes: "*How to Really Love Your Wife* is an attempt to apply the Christian message and principles to a very specific area of modern living. It emerged from my own struggle to be and do what I understood the Scriptures to mandate. Good books, it seems to me, often come from what the author has lived through, not just studied about. I hope mine has the ring of authenticity to it."

* * *

METESKY, George
See HOFFMAN, Abbie

* * *

MIKOLAYCAK, Charles 1937-

PERSONAL: Surname is pronounced *Mike*-o-lay-chak; born January 26, 1937, in Scranton, Pa.; son of John Anthony and Helen (Gruscelak) Mikolaycak; married Carole Kismaric (an editor and writer), October 1, 1970. *Education:* Pratt Institute, B.F.A., 1958; attended New York University, 1958-59. *Home:* 64 East 91st St., New York, N.Y. 10028.

CAREER: Free-lance illustrator and designer. Du Crot Studios, Hamburg, Germany, illustrator and designer, 1959; Time-Life Books, New York, N.Y., designer, 1963-76; Syracuse University, Syracuse, N.Y., guest instructor, 1976— . *Military service:* U.S. Army, 1960-62; became sergeant. *Member:* American Institute of Graphic Arts.

AWARDS, HONORS: Books Mikolaycak designed or illustrated were included among the fifty best books of the year in American Institute of Graphic Arts Shows, 1967, 1968, 1970, 1973, 1974, 1977, 1980, and in Chicago Book Clinic Best of the Year Show, 1967, 1971, 1972; Printing Industries of America Graphic Design Awards, 1967, for *Great Wolf and the Good Woodsman,* 1970, for *Mourka, the Mighty Cat,* 1971, 1972, and 1973; Society of Illustrators Gold Medal for book art direction, 1970; *How the Hare Told the Truth about His Horse* was among the twenty-one books from which American Institute of Graphic Arts selected illustrations to enter in Biennial of Illustrations, Bratislava, 1973; *Shipwreck* and *The Feast Day* were included in American Institute of Graphic Arts Children's Book Show for 1973-74; *Shipwreck* was among twenty-seven books selected for Children's Book Showcase of Children's Book Council, 1975; Brooklyn Museum Art Books for Children citations, 1976, 1978, and 1979, for *Great Wolf and the Good Woodsman;* New York Graphics award, 1980, for *The Surprising Things Maui Did.*

WRITINGS: (Adapter with wife, Carole Kismaric, from Norwegian folktale, and illustrator) *The Boy Who Tried to Cheat Death* (juvenile), Doubleday, 1971.

Illustrator of adult books, published in Japanese: Feodor Dostoevski, *Crime and Punishment,* Kawade Shobo (Tokyo), 1966; Feodor Dostoevski, *The Brothers Karamazov,* Kawade Shobo, 1967.

Illustrator and designer of children's books: Helen Hoover, *Great Wolf and the Good Woodsman,* Parents' Magazine Press, 1967; Jacob Grimm and Wilhelm Grimm, *Little Red Riding Hood,* C. R. Gibson, 1968; J. Grimm and W. Grimm, *Grimm's Golden Goose,* Random House, 1969; Jane Lee Hyndman (under pseudonym Lee Wyndham), *Mourka, the Mighty Cat,* Parents' Magazine Press, 1969; Hyndman (under pseudonym Lee Wyndham), *Russian Tales of Fabulous Beasts and Marvels,* Parents' Magazine Press, 1969.

Cynthia King, *In the Morning of Time,* Four Winds, 1970; Barbara Rinkoff, *The Pretzel Hero,* Parents' Magazine Press, 1970; Eric Sundell, *The Feral Child,* Abelard-Schuman, 1971; Margaret Hodges, reteller, *The Gorgon's Head,* Little, Brown, 1972; Barbara K. Walker, *How the Hare Told the Truth about His Horse,* Parents' Magazine Press, 1972; Edwin Fadiman, Jr., *The Feast Day,* Little, Brown, 1973; Vera Cumberlege, *Shipwreck,* Follett, 1974; Mirra Ginsburg, translator, *How Wilka Went to Sea and Other Tales from West of the Urals,* Crown, 1975; Marion L. Starkey, *The Tall Man from Boston,* Crown, 1975; Jerzy Ficowsky, *Sister of the Birds,* Abingdon, 1976; Doris Gates, *A Fair Wind for Troy,* Viking, 1976; Norma Farber, *Six Impossible Things before Breakfast,* Addison-Wesley, 1977; Farber, *Three Wanderers from Wapping,* Addison-Wesley, 1978; Barbara Cohen, *Binding of Isaac,* Norman Lathrop, 1978; Ewa Reid and Barbara Reid, *The Cobbler's Reward,* Macmillan, 1978; Richard Kennedy, *Delta Baby and Two Sea Songs,* Addison-Wesley, 1979; Jay Williams, *The Surprising Things Maui Did,* Four Winds, 1979; Elizabeth Winthrop, *Journey to the Bright Kingdom,* Holiday House, 1979; William Armstrong, *Tale of Tawny and Dingo,* Harper, 1979; Ginsburg, *Twelve Clever Brothers and Other Fools,* Lippincott, 1979.

Ernestine Long, *Johnny's Egg,* Addison-Wesley, 1980; Barbara Cohen, *I Am Joseph,* Norman Lathrop, 1980; Anne Pellowski, *Nine Crying Dolls,* Philomel, 1980; Loretta Holz, *Christmas Spider,* Philomel, 1980; Anne Laurin, *Perfect Crane,* Harper, 1981; Bernard Evslin, *Signs and Wonder,* Four Winds, 1981; Sergei Prokofiev, *Peter and the Wolf,* Viking, 1982; Jan Wahl, *Tiger Hunt,* Harcourt, 1982; *A Child Is Born,* Holiday House, 1983; *The Highwayman,* Norman Lathrop, 1983.

Editor and designer; published by Time-Life, except as indicated: Ken Dallison, *When Zeppelins Flew,* 1969; Fred Freeman, *Duel of the Ironclads,* 1969; Paul Williams, *The Warrior Knights,* 1969; Carole Kismaric, *On Leadership,* I.B.M., 1974; Kismaric, *Prelude to War,* 1976; Kismaric, *Blitzkrieg,* 1976; Kismaric, *The Battle of Britain,* 1976.

Contributor to *Parent's Choice.*

SIDELIGHTS: Charles Mikolaycak writes: "I am an illustrator because I must illustrate, and I am a book designer because I love books. Obviously the field in which the two meet is the one which makes me most happy—children's books. I can usually find something in most stories which makes me excited; be it a locale or period of time requiring great research, or a sense of fantasy which permits me to exercise my own fantasies pictorially, or great writing which forces me to try to match it in visual images.

"I am particularly fond of epics and folk tales. I care not how many times they have been illustrated before; the challenge is to find the truth for myself and depict it. When I illustrate I am aware of many things; storytelling, graphic design, sequence of images and my own interests in which I can indulge. I never 'draw-down' to a projected audience. I feel children are most surprisingly capable of meeting a challenge and instinctively understand a drawing. Perhaps it will lead them to ask a question or wonder in silence—either will help them to learn or to extend themselves. I have experienced that if I am satisfied with one of my books, both children and adults will often get from it more than I ever realized I was putting into it."

Three of Mikolaycak's children's book illustrations are in Kerlan Collection at University of Minnesota; several of his illustrations are in permanent collection of International Youth Library, Munich, Germany.

AVOCATIONAL INTERESTS: Reading, theatre, films, travel.

BIOGRAPHICAL/CRITICAL SOURCES: Sam L. Sebesta and William Iverson, *Literature for Thursday's Child*, Science Research Associates, 1975; Zena Sutherland, *Children and Books*, Scott, Foresman, 1981; *Language Arts*, October, 1981; Sally Holmes Holtze, *Fifth Book of Junior Authors and Illustrators*, Wilson, 1983.

* * *

MILD, Warren (Paul) 1922-

PERSONAL: Born March 22, 1922, in Minneapolis, Minn.; son of Lawrence Albert (a bus driver) and Clara (Kumm) Mild; married Phyllis Jensen (an orders processor), August 21, 1943; children: David, Samuel, Joanne. *Education:* University of Minnesota, B.A., 1946, M.A., 1947, Ph.D., 1950. *Politics:* Democrat. *Religion:* American Baptist. *Home:* 1001 Wentz Rd., Blue Bell, Pa. 19422.

CAREER: Bethel College, St. Paul, Minn., instructor in English, 1948-50; University of Redlands, Redlands, Calif., instructor, 1950-51, assistant professor, 1951-55, associate professor of English, 1955-58, director of admissions, 1951-54; American Baptist Convention, Board of Education and Publications, Valley Forge, Pa., director of collegiate education, 1958-65; Ellen Cushing Junior College, Bryn Mawr, Pa., president, 1966-74; full-time writer, 1975—. Member of board of governors, Radnor Scholarship Committee, 1967-68. *Military service:* U.S. Army, 1942-46; became staff sergeant. *Member:* American Society for Eighteenth Century Studies. *Awards, honors:* Ford Foundation fellowship, 1954-55.

WRITINGS: What Do the Lions Eat When Daniel's Out to Lunch? (drama), Judson, 1964; *Strangers outside the Feast* (drama), Friendship, 1966; *Fractured Questions,* Judson, 1966; *The Drop-Ins,* Judson, 1968; *The Story of American Baptists,* Judson, 1976. Author of two series of church school curricula, 1980, 1982; also author of recording "Look Back and Dream."

Filmstrips; all produced by American Baptist Churches: "Seeking the Chosen," 1975; "Furthering the Ministry," 1975; "People with a Mission," 1980; "Together in Name," 1982.

WORK IN PROGRESS: A biography of Joseph Highmore of Holborn Row.

* * *

MILES, Dorien K(lein) 1915-
(Sylva Miles, a joint pseudonym)

PERSONAL: Born September 17, 1915, in Kimball, Neb.; daughter of Ben (a petroleum distributor) and Frances (a teacher; maiden name, Houston) Klein; married Delbert L. Miles (chief clerk of a post office), August 20, 1937; children: Rosalee (Mrs. James Hughes), William, Janis (Mrs. Douglas Worrell), Karen (Mrs. Edward Berney, Jr.), Kathleen (Mrs. Artur Hohl), Robert. *Education:* Attended Kearney State College, 1933-34, and Olympic Community College, 1955-56. *Politics:* "Democrat, not always following party line." *Religion:* Baptist. *Home:* 1623 Jacobsen Blvd., Bremerton, Wash. 98310.

CAREER: Writer. Manette Community Church, Bremerton, Wash., secretary, 1965-74; clerk at Manette Post Office, 1974-78. *Member:* Pacific Northwest Writers Conference, Washington Poets Association, Seattle Free Lances, Kitsap Writers Club (president, 1973-74). *Awards, honors:* Second place in novel competition, Pacific Northwest Writers Conference, 1970, for *Shadow over Beauclaire;* National League of American Pen Women, honorable mention in free verse, 1974, in children's poetry, 1975; also recipient of other local awards.

WRITINGS: (With Sylva Mularchy, under joint pseudonym Sylva Miles) *Shadow over Beauclaire* (novel), Bouregy, 1975; *Changing Seasons* (poems), Straub, 1977; *Terror of Heartbreak House* (mystery), Bouregy, 1979. Also author of historical novel *Jonathan Hunter,* 1982. Contributor of more than forty poems, short stories, and articles to *Parents Magazine* and other periodicals.

SIDELIGHTS: Dorien K. Miles told *CA:* "From the time I was a young girl, I wanted to be a writer. My father, who had educated himself by reading, encouraged me.

"I became published but was twenty-four when I received my first check. It is only since 1978 that I have been able to keep a regular schedule of writing in an office of my own. At nine a.m. four mornings a week I go upstairs and work for at least two hours. If I have a deadline I sometimes work for as long as six hours in one day but rarely more than that. I'm a slow but persistent writer."

Terror of Heartbreak House has been translated into Swedish.

* * *

MILES, John
See BICKHAM, Jack M(iles)

* * *

MILES, Sylva
See MILES, Dorien K(lein)

* * *

MILONAS, Rolf
See MYLLER, Rolf

* * *

MITCHELL, Alan 1922-

PERSONAL: Born November 4, 1922, in Ilford, Essex, England; son of Alec Duncan (a research chemist) and Marjorie (Fyson) Mitchell; married Marjorie Beryl Clark, October 5, 1946 (divorced, 1961); married Philippa Dunn, February 20, 1962; children: (second marriage) Clio, Julia. *Education:* Attended University of Liverpool, 1942-43; Trinity College, Dublin, B.A., 1951, B.A.Ag. (with first class honors), 1951. *Politics:* "Socialist, tinged with anarchy and very independent." *Religion:* "Positively nil." *Home:* "Rosemead" Rowledge, Farnham, Surrey, England. *Office:* Forestry Commission, Alice Holt Lodge, Wrecclesham, Farnham, Surrey, England.

CAREER: Forestry Commission, Farnham, England, assistant geneticist, 1953-63, silviculturist, 1963-70, dendrologist, 1970—. *Military service:* Royal Navy, 1941-45; became petty officer; served in Far East. *Member:* Royal Forestry Society, Institute of Foresters, British Trust for Ornithology, Royal Horticultural Society, National Trust, Surrey Bird Club, Surrey Naturalists. *Awards, honors:* Veitch Memorial Medal, Royal Horticultural Society, 1966; Victorian Medal of Honor, Royal Horticultural Society, 1971; Gold Medal, Royal Forestry Society, 1978; M.A., University of Surrey, 1978.

WRITINGS—Published by Collins, except as indicated: *Field Guide to Trees of Britain and Northern Europe,* 1974; *Birds of Gardens and Woodlands,* 1976; *Birds of Shore and Estuary,* 1978; *Hand Guide to Trees,* 1980; *The Gardener's Book of Trees,* Dent, 1981; *Trees of Britain and Northern Europe,* 1982. Author of fortnightly column, "Nature Notes," in *Farnham Herald,* and of occasional tree items in *The Guardian.* Contributor to *Guinness Book of Records* and to forestry and gardening journals.

WORK IN PROGRESS: *Field Guide to Trees of North America;* two more tree books.

SIDELIGHTS: Alan Mitchell writes that he has "no faith whatever in mankind's 'leaders' who are contemptible, ignorant hate-mongers ruining the world. I try to arouse interest in the delights of the natural world and show the utter evil of destroying life, people, forests, anything, for absurd temporary vague propaganda like 'the Western way of life' or any other and the lies and tortures excused by such partisan nonsense."

AVOCATIONAL INTERESTS: Astronomy, traditional jazz, evolution, steam engines, travel in North America, making love, watching children grow, good health, gardening, politics, arguing.

* * *

MITCHELL, Ewan
See JANNER, Greville Ewan

* * *

MOHLER, James A. 1923-

PERSONAL: Born July 22, 1923, in Toledo, Ohio; son of Edward Francis (a teacher and writer) and Gertrude (Aylward) Mohler. *Education:* Xavier University, Cincinnati, Ohio, Litt.B., 1946; Bellarmine School of Theology, Ph.L., 1949, S.T.L., 1956; Loyola University, Chicago, Ill., M.S.I.R., 1960; University of Ottawa, Ph.D., 1964, S.T.D., 1965. *Home and office:* John Carroll University, University Heights, Cleveland, Ohio 44118.

CAREER: Entered Society of Jesus, 1942, ordained Roman Catholic priest, 1955. St. Ignatius High School, Chicago, Ill., teacher of religion, mathematics, economics, and Latin, 1949-52; Jesuit Indian Mission, Sault Ste. Marie, Mich., teacher, 1954-56; John Carroll University, Cleveland, Ohio, instructor, 1960-65, assistant professor, 1965-69, associate professor, 1969-74, professor of religious studies, 1974—. Visiting scholar, Union Theological Seminary (N.Y.), 1966; research fellow, Yale University, 1978. *Member:* Catholic Theological Society of America, American Academy of Religion, College Theology Society, American Association of University Professors, Association for Asian Studies.

WRITINGS: *Man Needs God,* John Carroll University Press, 1966; (with others) *Speaking of God,* edited by D. Dirscherl, Bruce Publishing, 1967; *The Beginning of Eternal Life: The Dynamic Faith of Thomas Aquinas, Origins and Interpretation,* Philosophical Library, 1968; *Dimensions of Faith, Yesterday and Today,* Loyola University Press, 1969.

The Origin and Evolution of the Priesthood, Alba, 1970; *The Heresy of Monasticism: The Christian Monks, Types and Anti-Types,* Alba, 1971; *The School of Jesus,* Alba, 1973; *Cosmos, Man, God, Messiah,* John Carroll University Press, 1973; *Dimensions of Love: East and West,* Doubleday, 1975; *Sexual Sublimation and the Sacred,* John Carroll University Press, 1978; *The Sacrament of Suffering,* Fides/Claretian, 1979; *Love, Marriage, and the Family, Yesterday and Today,* Alba, 1982. Contributor to religious journals.

WORK IN PROGRESS: Books on eschatology and on prayer.

SIDELIGHTS: James A. Mohler is competent in Latin, Greek, French, Italian, and German. He spent 1968 abroad, doing research in Switzerland, France, Italy, and Israel. In 1972 and 1974 he traveled and studied in Japan, China and India.

* * *

MONSMAN, Gerald Cornelius 1940-

PERSONAL: Born March 3, 1940, in Baltimore, Md.; son of Gerald (a lawyer) and Diana (DeKryger) Monsman; married Nancy Weaver, March 25, 1972; children: two daughters. *Education:* Attended Calvin College, 1957-59; Johns Hopkins University, B.A., 1961, M.A., 1963, Ph.D., 1965. *Religion:* Presbyterian. *Office:* Department of English, 315 Carr Bldg., Duke University, Durham, N.C. 27706.

CAREER: Duke University, Durham, N.C., assistant professor, 1965-70, associate professor, 1970-81, professor of English, 1981—. *Member:* Modern Language Association of America, American Association of University Professors, Phi Beta Kappa. *Awards, honors:* Research faculty fellowship, Duke University, 1967, 1970; Blackwood Prize, 1967, 1969, for most outstanding short story; Guggenheim fellowship, 1982-83.

WRITINGS: *Pater's Portraits: Mythic Pattern in the Fiction of Walter Pater,* Johns Hopkins Press, 1967; *Walter Pater,* G. K. Hall, 1977; *Walter Pater's Art of Autobiography,* Yale University Press, 1980; (contributor) *Walter Pater: An Imaginative Sense of Fact,* Frank Cass & Co., 1981; (contributor) Richard A. Levine, editor, *The Victorian Experience: The Essayists,* Ohio University Press, 1982. Contributor to *Blackwood's Magazine, South Atlantic Quarterly, University of Toronto Quarterly,* and *Victorian Newsletter.*

WORK IN PROGRESS: A study of psychology and dream in nineteenth-century imaginative prose.

* * *

MOORE, Patrick (Alfred) 1923-

PERSONAL: Born March 4, 1923, in Pinner, Middlesex, England; son of Charles (an army officer) and Gertrude (White) Moore. *Education:* Educated at private schools in England. *Politics:* Conservative. *Home and office:* Farthings, West St., Selsey, Sussex, England. *Agent:* Hilary Rubinstein, A. P. Watt, Ltd., 26-28 Bedford Row, London WC1R 4HL, England.

CAREER: Free-lance writer. Lecturer in Europe and United States on astronomy topics. Regular broadcaster on British Broadcasting Corporation television program, "The Sky at

Night," 1957—; Armagh Planetarium, Armagh, Northern Ireland, director, 1965-68. *Military service:* Royal Air Force, Bomber Command, 1940-45; became first lieutenant.

MEMBER: International Astronomical Union, Royal Astronomical Society (fellow), British Astronomical Association (director of lunar section, 1965—; director of Mercury and Venus section, 1954-63), Royal Society of Arts (fellow), Children's Writers Group of London (chairman, 1964-65). *Awards, honors:* Lorimer Gold Medal, 1962, for services to astronomy; Goodacre Gold Medal, 1968; Officer Order of the British Empire, 1968; Guido Horn d'Arturo Medal, 1969; Amateur Astronomers' Medal, New York City, 1970; D.Sc., University of Lancaster, 1974; Jackson Gold Medal, 1979.

WRITINGS: (Translator) Gerard de Vaucouleurs, *Planet Mars*, Macmillan, 1950; *Master of the Moon*, Museum Press, 1952; *A Guide to the Moon*, Norton, 1953, revised edition, Collins, 1973; *Suns, Myths, and Men*, Muller, 1954, revised edition, 1968, Norton, 1969, published as *The Story of Man and the Stars*, Norton, 1955; (with A. L. Helm) *Out into Space*, Museum Press, 1954; *Island of Fear*, Museum Press, 1954; *Frozen Planet*, Museum Press, 1954; *The True Book about Worlds around Us*, Miller, 1954, published as *The World around Us*, Abelard, 1956; *A Guide to the Planets*, Norton, 1954, revised edition, 1960, published as *The New Guide to the Planets*, 1972; *Destination Luna*, Lutterworth, 1955; (with Hugh Percival Wilkins) *The Moon*, Macmillan, 1955, new edition, Mitchell Beazley, 1981; *Quest of the Spaceways*, Muller, 1955; *Mission to Mars*, Burke Publishing Co., 1955; (with Irving Geis) *Earth Satellite: The New Satellite Projects Explained*, Eyre & Spottiswoode, 1955, published as *Earth Satellites*, Norton, 1956, revised edition, 1958.

World of Mists, Muller, 1956; *Domes of Mars*, Burke Publishing Co., 1956; *The Boys' Book of Space*, Roy Publishers, 1956, 6th edition, Burke Publishing Co., 1963; *Wheel in Space*, Lutterworth, 1956; *The Planet Venus*, Faber, 1956, Macmillan, 1957, new edition (with Garry Hunt), 1981; (with Wilkins) *How to Make and Use a Telescope*, Norton, 1956 (published in England as *Making and Using a Telescope*, Eyre & Spottiswoode, 1956); *The True Book about the Earth*, Muller, 1956; *Guide to Mars*, Muller, 1956, new edition, Macmillan, 1960, revised edition, Muller, 1965; *Voices of Mars*, Burke Publishing Co., 1957; *The True Book about Earthquakes and Volcanoes*, Muller, 1957; *Isaac Newton*, A. & C. Black, 1957, Putnam, 1958; *Science and Fiction*, Harrap, 1957, Folcroft, 1970; *The Amateur Astronomer*, Norton, 1957, 5th revised edition, Lutterworth, 1964, revised edition, Norton, 1966, published as *Amateur Astronomy*, 1968, 7th revised edition, Lutterworth, 1974; *The Earth, Our Home*, Abelard, 1957; *Peril on Mars*, Burke Publishing, 1958, Putnam, 1965; *Your Book of Astronomy*, Faber, 1958, 2nd edition, 1964; *The Solar System*, Methuen, 1958, Criterion, 1961; (editor with David R. Bates) *Space Research and Exploration*, Sloane, 1958; *The Boys' Book of Astronomy*, Roy Publishers, 1958; *The True Book about Man*, Muller, 1959; *Rockets and Earth Satellites*, Muller, 1959, 2nd edition, 1960; *Raiders of Mars*, Burke Publishing Co., 1959.

Astronautics, Methuen, 1960; *Captives of the Moon*, Burke Publishing Co., 1960; *Guide to the Stars*, Norton, 1960; *Stars and Space*, A. & C. Black, 1960, 3rd edition, 1969; (with Henry Brinton) *Navigation*, Methuen, 1961; *Astronomy*, Oldbourne, 1961, 3rd revised edition, 1967, 4th revised edition published as *The Story of Astronomy*, Macdonald & Co., 1972, published as *The Picture History of Astronomy*, Grosset, 1961, 3rd edition, 1967; *Wanderer in Space*, Burke Publishing Co., 1961; *The Stars*, Weidenfeld & Nicolson, 1962; (with Brinton) *Exploring Maps*, Odhams, 1962, Hawthorn, 1967; (with Paul Murdin) *The Astronomer's Telescope*, Brockhampton Press, 1962; (with Francis L. Jackson) *Life in the Universe*, Norton, 1962; *The Planets*, Norton, 1962; *The Observer's Book of Astronomy*, Warne, 1962; *Crater of Fear*, Harvey, 1962; *Telescopes and Observatories*, Weidenfeld & Nicolson, 1962; *Invader from Space*, Burke Publishing Co., 1963; *Survey of the Moon*, Norton, 1963; *Space in the Sixties*, Penguin, 1963; (editor) *Practical Amateur Astronomy*, Lutterworth, 1963, published as *A Handbook of Practical Amateur Astronomy*, Norton, 1964; *Exploring the Moon*, Odhams, 1964; *The True Book about Roman Britain*, Muller, 1964; (with Brinton) *Exploring Weather*, Odhams, 1964; *Caverns of the Moon*, Ulverscroft, c.1964; *The Sky at Night*, Volume I, Eyre & Spottiswoode, 1964, Norton, 1965, Volume II, Eyre & Spottiswoode, 1968; (with Jackson) *Life on Mars*, Routledge & Kegan Paul, 1965, Norton, 1966.

Exploring the World, Oxford University Press, 1966, F. Watts, 1968; (with Hilary Rubinstein) *The New Look of the Universe*, Norton, 1966; *Exploring the Planetarium*, Odhams, 1966; *Legends of the Stars*, Odhams, 1966; *Naked-Eye Astronomy*, Norton, 1966; *Basic Astronomy*, Oliver & Boyd, 1967; (with Brinton) *Exploring Other Planets*, Hawthorn, 1967; (with Brinton) *Exploring Earth History*, Odhams, 1967; (with Peter J. Cattermole) *The Craters of the Moon*, Norton, 1967; *The Amateur Astronomer's Glossary*, Norton, 1967; *Armagh Observatory: A History, 1790-1967*, Armagh Observatory, 1967; *Exploring the Galaxies*, Odhams, 1968; *Exploring the Stars*, Odhams, 1968; *Space: The Story of Man's Greatest Feat of Exploration*, Lutterworth, 1968; Natural History Press, 1969, 3rd edition, Lutterworth, 1970; (author of revision) Mervyn A. Ellison, *The Sun and Its Influence*, 3rd edition (Moore was not associated with earlier editions), American Elsevier, 1968; *The Sun*, Norton, 1968; *Moon Flight Atlas*, Rand McNally, 1969 revised edition, Philip & Son, 1970; *Astronomy and Space Research*, National Book League (London), 1969; *The Development of Astronomical Thought*, Oliver & Boyd, 1969.

The Atlas of the Universe, Rand McNally, 1970, 4th edition, Mitchell Beazley, 1981; *Astronomy for O Level*, Duckworth, 1970, 2nd edition, 1974; *Seeing Stars*, Rand McNally, 1971; (author of introduction) Arthur C. Clarke, *Islands in the Sky*, Sidgwick & Jackson, 1971; *The Astronomers of Birr Castle*, Mitchell Beazley, 1971; *Can You Speak Venusian?*, David & Charles, 1972, Norton, 1973; (with David A. Hardy) *Challenge of the Stars*, Mitchell Beazley, 1972; (with Desmond Leslie) *How Britain Won the Space Race*, Mitchell Beazley, 1972; (with Laurence T. Clarke) *How to Recognize the Stars*, Corgi Books, 1972; *The Southern Stars*, Rigby, 1973; *Color Star Atlas*, Crown, 1973; *The Starlit Sky*, South African Broadcasting Co., 1973; *Man the Astronomer*, Priory, 1973; (with Charles A. Cross) *Mars*, Crown, 1973; (editor and contributor) *Astronomical Telescopes and Observatories for Amateurs*, David & Charles, 1973; (author of revision) James S. Pickering, *1001 Questions Answered about Astronomy*, Dodd, 1973; (translator) E. M. Antoniadi, *The Planet Mercury*, Keith Reid, 1974; *The Comets*, Keith Reid, 1974; *Watchers of the Stars*, Putnam, 1974.

(With P. Collins) *The Astronomy of Southern Africa*, Howard Timmins, 1979; *The Guinness Book of Astronomy Facts and Feats*, Guinness Superlatives, 1980; (with Hunt) *Jupiter*, Mitchell Beazley, 1981; *Pocket Guide to Stars and Planets*, Mitchell Beazley, 1981.

Also author of *Spy in Space*, *Planet of Fear*, *The Moon Raiders*, *Killer Comet*, and *The Secret of the Black Hole*, all published by Armada. Editor, *Yearbook of Astronomy*, Norton, 1962—.

SIDELIGHTS: Patrick Moore told *CA:* "I speak French as well as the average schoolboy, but otherwise I believe in speaking English! I particularly like Scandinavia, notably Iceland, which I know well. I have done an eclipse television broadcast from Yugoslavia." *Avocational interests:* Cricket, tennis, chess.

* * *

MORGAN, Bryan S(tanford) 1923-1978

PERSONAL: Born July 23, 1923, in London, England; died in 1978; son of Charles Leslie and Winifred (Lock) Morgan. *Education:* St. Catharine's College, Cambridge University, B.A., 1944. *Politics:* Tory. *Religion:* Anglo-Catholic.

CAREER: Free-lance author, journalist, and editor. *Awards, honors:* Atlantic Award in Literature; scholarship to Salzburg Seminar in American Studies.

WRITINGS: Vain Citadels, Heinemann, 1947; *Rosa,* Hodder & Stoughton, 1949; *Men and Discoveries in Electricity,* J. Murray, 1952; *The Business at Blanche Capel,* Hamish Hamilton, 1953; *The End of the Line,* Cleaver-Hume, 1955; (editor) *Golden Milestone,* Newman Neame, 1955; *Apothecary's Venture,* Newman Neame, 1959.

Fastness of France, Cleaver-Hume, 1962; *Men and Discoveries in Chemistry,* J. Murray, 1962; (editor) *The Railway-Lover's Companion,* Eyre & Spottiswoode, 1963; *Express Journey, 1864-1964: A Centenary History of the Express Dairy Company,* Newman Neame, 1964; *Andorra: The Country In Between,* Ray Palmer, 1964; *Playing with History,* Newman Neame, 1965; *Electrons at Work,* Macmillan (London), 1965, St. Martins, 1966; (with Joan Morgan) *Pepe's Island,* Oliver & Boyd, 1965, Criterion, 1966; *Acceleration,* Newman Neame, 1965; (editor) William Plenderbeith Knowles, *New Life through Breathing,* Allen & Unwin, 1966; *Sermons in Stone,* Newman Neame, 1966; *Explosion and Explosives,* Macmillan (London), 1967; (editor) Louis Rose, *Faith Healing,* Gollancz, 1968; *Railway Relics,* Ian Allen, 1969.

Civil Engineering: Railways, Longman, 1971; *The Rolls and Royce Story,* Collins, 1971; *Men and Discoveries in Mathematics,* J. Murray, 1972; *The Great Trains,* Stephens, 1974; *Navigation,* Viking, 1974; (editor) *Crime on the Lines: An Anthology of Mystery Short Stories with a Railway Setting,* Routledge & Kegan Paul, 1975; *Stories of the Railway,* Routledge & Kegan Paul, 1977.

Also author of *The Sacred Nursery,* 1951, *Total to Date,* 1953, and *Early Trains,* 1973. Author of television and radio scripts. Contributor to journals.

AVOCATIONAL INTERESTS: Travel, small boats, chess.†

* * *

MORRESSY, John 1930-

PERSONAL: Born December 8, 1930, in Brooklyn, N.Y.; son of John Emmett and Jeanette (Geraghty) Morressy; married Barbara Turner, August 11, 1956. *Education:* St. John's University, Jamaica, N.Y., B.A., 1953; New York University, M.A., 1961. *Residence:* East Sullivan, N.H. *Agent:* James Oliver Brown, Curtis Brown Assos., Ltd., 575 Madison Ave., New York, N.Y. 10022. *Office:* Department of English, Franklin Pierce College, Rindge, N.H. 03461.

CAREER: Teacher, intermittently, 1956-63; St. John's University, Jamaica, N.Y., instructor in English, 1963-66; Monmouth College, West Long Branch, N.J., assistant professor of English, 1966-67; Franklin Pierce College, Rindge, N.H., 1968—, began as associate professor and chairman of English department, currently professor of English and writer in residence. *Military service:* U.S. Army, 1953-55. *Member:* Science Fiction Writers of America, Authors Guild of the Authors League of America. *Awards, honors:* Bread Loaf Writers' Conference fellowship, 1968; University of Colorado Writers' Conference fellowship, 1970.

WRITINGS—All novels, except as indicated: *The Blackboard Cavalier,* Doubleday, 1966; *The Addison Tradition,* Doubleday, 1968; *Starbrat,* Walker & Co., 1972; *Nail Down the Stars,* Walker & Co., 1973; *The Humans of Ziax II* (juvenile), Walker & Co., 1974; *A Long Communion,* Walker & Co., 1974; *Under a Calculating Star,* Doubleday, 1975; *The Windows of Forever* (juvenile), Walker & Co., 1975; *A Law for the Stars,* Laser Books, 1976; *The Extraterritorial,* Laser Books, 1977; *Frostworld and Dreamfire,* Doubleday, 1977; *Drought on Ziax II* (juvenile), Walker & Co., 1978; *Ironbrand,* Playboy Press, 1980; *Graymantle,* Playboy Press, 1981; *Kingsbane,* Playboy Press, 1982; *The Mansions of Space,* Berkley Publishing, 1982; *The Corridor, and Other Stories,* Northern New England Review Press, 1983. Contributor to *Magazine of Fantasy and Science Fiction, Harper's, Esquire, Omni, Playboy,* and other magazines.

WORK IN PROGRESS: A novel set in eighteenth-century London; a fantasy novel; a short story collection.

SIDELIGHTS: John Morressy told *CA:* "Perhpas because I've spent so much of my life in and around classrooms, learning plays an important part in all my books. My characters all learn something in the course of their books, though what they learn is not always what they hope, or expect, to learn. Life is like that, too. I try to write about what one must know, and how it is to be learned, and how taught.

"Over the past decade, most of my writing has been in fantasy and science fiction, because in these genres, instead of writing about neurosis, failure, anxiety, loneliness, despair, cruelty, sexual frustration, anomie, loss of identity, and the other wonders of contemporary life, I am free to speculate on the future of the human race and the creation of myths and heroes. I spend my time not among the whiners, but among seekers. It is old fashioned, I suppose, but I find it very rewarding.

"I do not believe that the novel is dead, although a great many people—too many of them writers—are trying to kill it. The novel has simply moved to a more interesting neighborhood. I have tried to move with it."

BIOGRAPHICAL/CRITICAL SOURCES: Times Literary Supplement, February 2, 1967; *New York Times Book Review,* July 28, 1968; *Best Sellers,* August 15, 1968; *Christian Science Monitor,* August 29, 1968; *Choice,* November, 1968; *Virginia Quarterly Review,* winter, 1969; *Booklist,* October 1, 1977; *Newsday,* October 30, 1977; *Fantasy Newsletter,* September, 1980.

* * *

MORRISON, Dorothy Nafus

PERSONAL: Born in Nashua, Iowa; daughter of Roy A. (a merchant) and Edwinna (a teacher of Latin and German; maiden name, Bolton) Nafus; married Carl V. Morrison (a psychiatrist; deceased); married Robert C. Hunter (an attorney); children: (first marriage) James, Anne (Mrs. John Feighner), David, John. *Education:* University of Iowa, B.A. *Home:* 8600 Southwest 170th Ave., Beaverton, Ore. 97007.

CAREER: Teacher of stringed instruments in public schools in Beaverton, Ore., 1954-66; writer, 1965—.

WRITINGS—Juveniles: *The Mystery of the Last Concert,* Westminster, 1971; (with husband, Carl V. Morrison) *Can I Help How I Feel?* (nonfiction), Atheneum, 1976; *Ladies Were Not Expected: Abigail Scott Duniway and Women's Rights,* Atheneum, 1977; *The Eagle and the Fort: The Story of John McLoughlin,* Atheneum, 1978; *Chief Sarah: Sarah Winnemucca's Fight for Indian Rights,* Atheneum, 1980; (contributor) William Gentz, editor, *Writing to Inspire,* Writer's Digest, 1982.

WORK IN PROGRESS: A biography of Jessie Benton Fremont.

SIDELIGHTS: Dorothy Nafus Morrison writes: "When I moved to the West Coast, I became fascinated with the rich history of this area, which I am now trying to present by writing biographies for young readers. I have pictured the fur trade, the growth of women's rights in the West, the fight for Indian rights, and am now concerned with the Gold Rush. I make extensive use of primary sources, such as letters and journals of the time, and rather than invent scenes or dialogue, I quote brief passages from these. History is people."

* * *

MORROW, Patrick David 1940-

PERSONAL: Born October 1, 1940, in Inglewood, Calif.; son of Patrick Francis (an appraiser and writer) and Marilyn (a writer and teacher; maiden name, Keefe) Morrow; married Judith R. Spenceley, June 28, 1964 (divorced April 9, 1975); married Mary Elizabeth Vehrs (a special education teacher), August 19, 1975 (divorced September 1, 1980); children: (first marriage) Milan Elizabeth, Christopher Patrick. *Education:* Attended Sacramento State College (now California State University, Sacramento), 1958-61; University of Southern California, B.A., 1963; University of Washington, Seattle, M.A., 1965, Ph.D., 1969; also attended University of California, Berkeley, and Free University of Seattle. *Politics:* Democrat. *Religion:* Roman Catholic. *Home:* 423 Sanders St., Auburn, Ala. 36830. *Office:* Department of English, Auburn University, Auburn, Ala. 36849.

CAREER: Professional musician, 1957-62; U.S. Veterans Administration, Property Management Division, Sacramento, Calif., technical writer, 1963; University of Washington, Seattle, instructor in English, 1968-69; University of Southern California, Los Angeles, assistant professor of English and American studies, 1969-75; Auburn University, Auburn, Ala., associate professor, 1975-81, professor of English, 1981—. Visiting associate professor at University of New Mexico, summer, 1972; visiting lecturer at Idaho State University, summer, 1974; Fulbright senior lecturer at University of Canterbury, Christchurch, New Zealand, 1981; lecturer in American studies at universities in New Zealand, Australia, and Samoa, 1981. French interpreter for Eighth Winter Olympic Games (Squaw Valley, Calif.), 1960. Volunteer worker with retarded and handicapped children.

MEMBER: Modern Language Association of America, American Studies Association, Popular Culture Association, Western American Literature Association (member of executive council, 1972—), South Atlantic Modern Language Association. *Awards, honors:* National Endowment for the Humanities grant, 1974-75, for curriculum development and publication; Egan Foundation fellowships, 1971, 1974; Leo S. Bing fellowship from University of Southern California, 1971; Auburn University faculty fellowships, 1978, 1979.

WRITINGS: (Translator, editor, and author of introduction) *Porcelain Butterfly: Five French Symbolist Poets in Translation* (bi-lingual text), Red Hill Press, 1971; *Bret Harte* (pamphlet), Boise State University, 1972; (contributor) Edward F. Heenan, editor, *Mystery, Magic, and Miracle: Religion in a Post-Aquarian Age,* Prentice-Hall, 1973; *Radical Vistas: Eight Essays on American Literature,* Fault Press, 1974; *Bret Harte, Literary Critic,* Popular Press, 1978; (editor) *Growing Up in North Dakota,* University Press of America, 1979; *Tradition, Undercut, and Discovery: Eight Essays on British Literature,* Rodopi (Amsterdam), 1980. Contributor to academic journals. Member of editorial board of *Western American Literature, Journal of American Culture, Journal of Popular Culture,* and *Popular Music and Society;* associate editor of *Southern Humanities Review.*

WORK IN PROGRESS: Bret Harte, for Twayne; research on frontier literature of America and the British Commonwealth.

SIDELIGHTS: Patrick David Morrow writes: "I consider myself primarily a critic—of life, culture, human relationships, and art. To me the primary function of criticism is explication and not attack. My ideal critic strives to make clear what is obscure, not to pass moral judgments from on high. I strive for the personal voice and vision that the shared experience of reader and writer under these terms makes all concerned better able to understand life and cope with it." Morrow made a tape recording, "Bret Harte," for Everett/Edwards, 1974.

* * *

MORSE, Roger A(lfred) 1927-

PERSONAL: Born July 5, 1927, in Saugerties, N.Y.; son of Grant D. (a superintendent of schools) and Margery A. (a teacher; maiden name, Saxe) Morse; married Mary Lou Smith, October 6, 1951; children: Joseph G., Susan A., Mary Ann. *Education:* Cornell University, B.S., 1950, M.S., 1953, Ph.D., 1955. *Politics:* Republican. *Home:* 425 Hanshaw Rd., Ithaca, N.Y. 14850. *Office:* Department of Entomology, Cornell University, Ithaca, N.Y. 14853.

CAREER: State Plant Board of Florida, Gainesville, apiculturist, 1955-57; University of Massachusetts, Field Station, Amherst, assistant professor of horticulture, 1957; Cornell University, Ithaca, N.Y., assistant professor, 1957-64, associate professor, 1964-70, professor of apiculture, 1970—. Visiting professor of apiculture, University of the Philippines, 1968, and University of Sao Paulo, 1978; guest lecturer at colleges and universities. Former volunteer fire chief; member of Tompkins County Fair Board; member of Tompkins County Board of Representatives. Consultant to Food and Agriculture Organization of United Nations, 1982. *Military service:* U.S. Army, 1944-47; became staff sergeant.

MEMBER: International Union for the Study of Social Insects, International Bee Research Association (chairman, American committee), Entomological Society of America, American Association for the Advancement of Science (fellow), Philippine Association of Entomologists, Eastern Apicultural Society, Florida Entomological Society, New York Academy of Science, Sigma Xi, Delta Sigma Rho, Rotary International (former president, Ithaca section). *Awards, honors:* Thirteen travel and research grants from National Science Foundation, 1961—; research grant from U.S. Army, 1966; three research grants from National Institute of Health; two research grants from Environmental Protection Agency; Apimondia Gold Medal, 1979, for *Pests, Predators, and Diseases of Honey Bees;* Apimondia Silver Medal, 1981, for *Making Mead.*

WRITINGS: The Complete Guide to Beekeeping, Dutton, 1972, revised edition, 1974; *Bees and Beekeeping,* Comstock, 1975;

(contributor) Eva Crane, editor, *Honey*, Bee Research Association, 1975; (editor) *Pests, Predators, and Diseases of Honey Bees*, Cornell University Press, 1978; *Comb Honey Production*, Wicwas Press, 1979; *Rearing Queen Honey Bees*, Wicwas Press, 1980; *Making Mead*, Wicwas Press, 1981. Contributor of hundreds of articles to conservation, natural history, and beekeeping journals. Research editor of *Gleanings in Bee Culture*, 1959—.

WORK IN PROGRESS: *International Encyclopedia of Beekeeping*, with Ted Hooper; *Beeswax*, with William L. Coggshall; *Pheromone Language of the Honey Bee*.

SIDELIGHTS: Roger A. Morse has spent a total of nine months studying bees in Asia and has made numerous study trips to Europe, Africa, and South America. Morse holds a U.S. patent on a method of making wine from honey. *Avocational interests:* Farming.

* * *

MORTON, Anthony
See CREASEY, John

* * *

MOSELEY, Edwin M(aurice) 1916-1978

PERSONAL: Born September 12, 1916, in Orangeburg, S.C.; died December 5, 1978; son of John Pike and Blumah (Sorentrue) Moseley; married Catharine Fisher (a teacher), June 11, 1941; children: Stephen Fisher, Quentin Brown. *Education:* College of Charleston, A.B., 1937; Syracuse University, M.A., 1939, Ph.D., 1947.

CAREER: Syracuse University, Syracuse, N.Y., instructor in English, 1939-43, 1946-47, instructor in mathematics, Air Force and Army Specialized Training Program, 1943-45; Evansville College (now University of Evansville), Evansville, Ind., assistant professor of English, 1947-48; Washington and Jefferson College, Washington, Pa., assistant professor, 1948-49, associate professor, 1949-55, professor of English, 1955-61; Skidmore College, Saratoga Springs, N.Y., dean of faculty and professor of English, 1961-78. Intercollegiate Council of Cultural and International Exchange, delegate to international seminar, 1961. *Military service:* U.S. Army, Infantry, and Specialized Training Program (Japanese), 1945-46. *Member:* American Association of University Professors, Modern Language Association of America, College English Association, American Conference of Academic Deans, Eastern Deans Association.

WRITINGS: (Editor with Robert Paul Ashley) *Elizabethan Fiction*, Holt, Rinehart & Winston, 1953, 2nd edition, 1962; *Pseudonyms of Christ in the Modern Novel*, University of Pittsburgh Press, 1963; *F. Scott Fitzgerald: A Critical Essay*, Eerdmans, 1967; *The Outsider as Hero and Anti-Hero*, Skidmore College, 1967; *Renaissance and Modern*, Skidmore College, 1976. Also author of *Comparative Literature: Matter and Method*, 1969, *Czechoslovakia Past and Present*, 1970, and *Religion and Modern Literature: Essays in Theory and Criticism*, 1975.

Work appears in *Best American Short Stories of 1962*. Contributor of fiction and criticism to *Accent*, *Shenandoah*, and other publications. Founder, *Topic*.†

* * *

MOSS, C(laude) Scott 1924-

PERSONAL: Born May 17, 1924, in Newark, N.J.; son of Claude Scott (a newspaper columnist) and Leone (Dieter) Moss; married Bette L. Witty, September 23, 1956; children: Joel, Julie, Kevin. *Education:* University of Wisconsin, B.S., 1948; University of Illinois, M.S., 1951, Ph.D., 1953. *Religion:* Protestant. *Home:* 3180 Glengary Rd., Santa Ynez, Calif. 93460. *Office:* Federal Penitentiary, Lompoc, Calif. 93436.

CAREER: Licensed clinical psychologist in California; diplomate in clinical psychology, American Board of Examiners in Professional Psychology, and diplomate in psychological hypnosis, American Board of Examiners in Psychological Hypnosis. Veterans Administration Hospital, Jefferson Barracks, Mo., clinical psychologist, 1953-56; State Hospital, Fulton, Mo., chief psychologist, 1956-60; National Institute of Mental Health, San Francisco, Calif., consultant in mental health, 1961-67; University of Illinois at Urbana-Champaign, professor of psychology, 1967-70; Federal Penitentiary, Lompoc, Calif., mental health coordinator, 1970—, coordinator of Western Region, 1973-74. Instructor, Washington University, 1953-56; associate professor of psychology, University of Missouri—Columbia, 1956-60; visiting professor of psychology, University of Kansas, 1960-61; adjunct professor of counseling psychology, University of California, Santa Barbara, 1977—; former assistant professor, Lincoln University; former lecturer, William Woods College. Former member, Missouri State Civil Service Review Board; deputy to associate regional health director for mental health, State of California, 1965-67. Consultant to halfway house for emotionally disturbed juveniles, 1953-56, and San Francisco Regional Office, National Institute of Mental Health, 1971-76; former consultant to Missouri State Men's and Women's Prisons, and to community mental health programs in the western United States; member of research advisory committee, California Mental Health Hygiene Department, 1973-74. *Military service:* U.S. Army Air Forces, 1942-46.

MEMBER: International Council of Psychologists (fellow), American Psychological Association (fellow), Society for Clinical and Experimental Hypnosis (fellow), American Society of Clinical Hypnosis (fellow), Society for Psychophysiological Study of Sleep, American Academy of Psychotherapists, American Public Health Association (fellow), American Association for the Advancement of Science (member of Foundation for Science and the Handicapped), Western Psychological Association. *Awards, honors:* Alternate selection, Behavioral Sciences Book Club, 1968, for *The Hypnotic Investigation of Dreams;* book-of-the-month selection, Psychotherapy and Social Science Book Club, 1970, for *Dreams, Images and Fantasy*.

WRITINGS: *Hypnosis in Perspective*, Macmillan, 1965; *The Hypnotic Investigation of Dreams*, Wiley, 1967; *Dreams, Images and Fantasy: A Semantic Differential Casebook*, University of Illinois Press, 1970; *Black Rover, Come Over*, University of Illinois Press, 1970; *Recovery with Aphasia: The Aftermath of My Stroke*, University of Illinois Press, 1973; *The Crumbling Walls: Treatment and Counseling of The Adult Offender*, University of Illinois Press, 1975; *Research on est Training within a Correctional Institute* (monograph), American Psychological Association, 1982.

Contributor: J. R. Braun, editor, *Clinical Psychology in Transition*, World Publishing, 1966; O. Buros, editor, *The Mental Measurements Yearbook* (reviews), Rutgers University Press, 1966; Jesse Gordon, editor, *Handbook on Clinical and Experimental Hypnosis*, Macmillan, 1967; L. E. Abt and B. R. Reiff, editors, *Progress in Clinical Psychology*, Grune, 1969; J. G. Snider and C. E. Osgood, *Semantic Differential Technique*, Aldine, 1969; A. Katzenstein, editor, *Psychologische*

Aspekte der Hypnose in der slinischen Draxis, Veb Bustav Fisher Verlag (East Berlin), 1970; L. Diamant, editor, *Case Studies in Psychopathology,* C. E. Merrill, 1970.

Recovery from Aphasia, Swets & Zemlinger (the Netherlands), 1976; J. D. Krumboltz and C. E. Thoreson, editors, *Methods in Counseling,* Holt, 1976; *Abnormal Psychology,* Random House, 1976; R. Herink, editor, *Psychotherapy Handbook,* Jason Aronson, 1980; L. Yaukey and R. Greene, editors, *Early and Middle Childhood: Growth, Abuse, and Delinquency and Its Effect on the Individual, Family and Community,* Technomic Publishing (Westport, Conn.), 1981.

Also contributor to *People-to-People Mental Health Delegation, People's Republic of China,* edited by Jeanne Sloan, 1981. Author of papers presented to conferences, including International Congress of Experimental Psychology, Bonn, 1960, International Congress of Applied Psychology, Copenhagen, 1961, International Congress of Psychology, Moscow, 1966, and International Conference on Aphasia, Brussels, 1975; contributor to proceedings of professional organizations; contributor of tapes to American Academy of Psychotherapists Tape Library, 1970 and 1975, and Behavioral Sciences Tape Library, 1973. Contributor to psychology journals, including *International Psychologist, American Psychologist, Rehabilitation Psychology,* and *Journal of Counseling and Clinical Psychology.* Consulting editor, *Journal of Selected Documents in Psychology,* 1978—.

WORK IN PROGRESS: My Stroke: Recovery Is a Lifetime Affair; research on the predictability of violence within correctional institutions.

AVOCATIONAL INTERESTS: Travel, including extensive visits to Eastern Europe.

* * *

MOUSSARD, Jacqueline 1924- (Jacqueline Cervon)

PERSONAL: Born July 6, 1924, in Cervon, Nievre, France; daughter of Lucien (a cabinet maker) and Audree Sene; married Serje Moussard (in electronics), December 31, 1945; children: Catherine Moussard Berthet, Jean-Marc, Guillaumette Moussard Alami. *Education:* Lycee Paul Bert, Paris, licence d'enseignement es lettres classiques, 1944; also attended Sorbonne, University of Paris. *Home:* Cervon, 58800 Corbigny, France.

CAREER: Writer. Journalist, 1946-47, teacher, 1948-52, and secretarial director, 1953-54, all in Djibouti, East Africa.

AWARDS, HONORS: Prix de l'Academie Francaise, 1965, for *Ali, Jean-Luc et la gazelle;* Prix des parents d'eleves, 1967, for *Le Tresor de Nikos;* Prix Jeunesse, 1968, for *L'Aiglon d'Ouazazate;* Prix la joie par le livre, and Mention du prix europeen de la ville de Caorle (Italy), both 1968, for *Le Naufrage de Rhodes;* Prix Fantasia, 1970, for *Joao de Tintubal;* Prix la joie par le livre, 1971, for *Malik, le garcon sauvage;* diplome meilleur livre loisirs jeune, 1972, for *Le Nain et le Baobab,* and 1974, for *Coumba du pays oublie des pluies;* Prix de la jeunesse de la CRPFL (associated French, Swiss, and Belgian radio), 1973, for *Le Chasseur au lasso;* Selection 1000 jeunes lecteurs, 1973, for *Le Tambour des sables.*

WRITINGS—All under pseudonym Jacqueline Cervon: *Benoit, l'arbre et la lune,* Editions G.P., 1969.

Children's books; published by Editions G.P., except as indicated: *Ali, Jean-Luc et la gazelle,* 1963; *Quand la terre trembla a Skoplje,* 1965, translation by John Buchanan-Brown published as *The Day the Earth Shook,* Bodley Head, 1967;

Coward, 1969; *Le coquillage rose de Catissou,* Magnard, 1965; *Le Tresor de Nikos,* Magnard, 1966; *Selim, le petit marchand de bonheur,* 1967; *Belle Agao,* Magnard, 1967, *Le Naufrage de Rhodes,* 1968, translation by Thelma Niklaus published as *Castaway from Rhodes,* F. Watts, 1973; *L'Aiglon d'Ouazazate,* Editions de l'Amitie, 1968; *Les Pigeons d'Urgup,* Presses de la Cite (Paris), 1968; *Joao de Tintubal,* Magnard, 1969.

Le Defi au soleil, 1970; *Malik, le garcon sauvage,* Magnard, 1970; *Le Fouet et la cithare,* 1971; *Les Moissons du desert,* 1971; *Le Tambour des sables,* 1972; *Le Nain et le Baobab,* 1972; *Djinn la malice,* 1972; *Le Chasseur au lasso,* 1973; *Diango de l'ile verte,* 1973; *Coumba du pays oublie des pluies,* 1974; *La Jarre percee,* 1975; *La Griffe du fauve,* 1976; *La Seve de la terre,* 1977; *Le Feu aux poudres,* 1978; *Djilani et l'oiseau de nuit,* 1978; *La Marmite des cannibales,* Editions Duculot, 1979.

Alexandre le grand, Editions Duculot, 1980; *Le Dernier mirage,* Editions Duculot, 1981; *Et si j'etais un chien,* 1981; *Les Magiciens denaima,* 1982. Also author of *Les Chevaliers du Stromboli, Francesco,* and *Prince des Neiges,* all Editions G.P.

AVOCATIONAL INTERESTS: Travel.

BIOGRAPHICAL/CRITICAL SOURCES: Marc Soriano, *Guide de Litterature pour la jeunesse,* Flammarion, 1975.

* * *

MU, Yang
See WANG, C(hing) H(sien)

* * *

MURDOCH, (Jean) Iris 1919-

PERSONAL: Born July 15, 1919, in Dublin, Ireland; daughter of Wills John Hughes and Irene Alice (Richardson) Murdoch; married John Oliver Bayley (a novelist, poet, critic), 1956. *Education:* Somerville College, Oxford, B.A., 1942; Newnham College, Cambridge, Sarah Smithson studentship in philosophy, 1947-48. *Home:* Cedar Lodge, Steeple Aston, Oxfordshire, England.

CAREER: Writer. British Treasury, London, England, assistant principal, 1942-44; United Nations Relief and Rehabilitation Administration (UNRRA), administrative officer in London, Belgium, and Austria, 1944-46; Oxford University, St. Anne's College, Oxford, England, fellow and university lecturer in philosophy, 1948-63, honorary fellow, 1963—; Royal College of Art, London, lecturer, 1963-67. Member of Formentor Prize Committee. *Awards, honors:* Black Memorial Prize, 1974, for fiction; Whitehead Literary Award, 1974, for fiction; named Commander, Order of the British Empire, 1976.

WRITINGS—Novels; published by Viking, except as indicated: *Under the Net,* 1954, published with introduction and notes by Dorothy Jones, Longmans, Green, 1966; *The Flight from the Enchanter,* 1956; *The Sandcastle,* 1957; *The Bell,* 1958; *A Severed Head,* 1961; *An Unofficial Rose,* 1962; *The Unicorn,* 1963; *The Italian Girl,* 1964; *The Red and the Green,* 1965; *The Time of the Angels,* 1966; *The Nice and the Good,* 1968; *Bruno's Dream,* 1969; *A Fairly Honourable Defeat,* 1970; *An Accidental Man,* 1971; *The Black Prince,* 1973; *The Sacred and Profane Love Machine,* 1974; *A Word Child,* 1975; *Henry and Cato,* 1977; *The Sea, The Sea,* 1978; *Nuns and Soldiers,* 1980.

Nonfiction: *Sartre: Romantic Rationalist,* Yale University Press, 1953, 2nd edition, Barnes & Noble, 1980 (published in England as *Sartre: Romantic Realist,* Harvester Press, 1980);

(contributor) *The Nature of Metaphysics,* Macmillan, 1957; (author of foreword) Wendy Campbell-Purdie and Fenner Brockaway, *Woman against the Desert,* Gollancz, 1964; *The Sovereignty of Good over Other Concepts* (Leslie Stephen lecture, 1967), Cambridge University Press, 1967, published with other essays as *The Sovereignty of Good,* Routledge & Kegan Paul, 1970, Schocken, 1971; *The Fire and the Sun: Why Plato Banned the Artists* (based on the Romanes lecture, 1976), Clarendon Press, 1977.

Plays: (With J. B. Priestley) *A Severed Head* (three-act; based on her novel of the same title; first produced in London at Royale Theatre, October 28, 1964; produced in New York, 1964), Chatto & Windus, 1964, acting edition, Samuel French, 1964; (with James Saunders) *The Italian Girl* (based on her novel of the same title; first produced at Bristol Old Vic, December, 1967), Samuel French, 1968; *The Three Arrows* [and] *The Servants and the Snow* (both original plays; *The Servants and the Snow* first produced in London at Greenwich Theatre, September 29, 1970; *The Three Arrows* first produced in Cambridge at Arts Theatre, October 17, 1972), Chatto & Windus, 1973, Viking, 1974.

Poetry: *A Year of Birds,* Compton Press (Tisbury, England), 1978.

Many of Iris Murdoch's books have been translated into foreign languages, including Swedish, Spanish, Italian, French, Norwegian, Dutch, and German. Contributor to periodicals in United States and Great Britain, including *Listener, Yale Review, Chicago Review, Encounter, New Statesman, Nation,* and *Partisan Review.*

WORK IN PROGRESS: A novel.

SIDELIGHTS: Described by *Commonweal*'s Linda Kuel as "a philosopher by trade and temperament," Irish-born Iris Murdoch is better known as a serious and witty novelist. She began her writing career in 1953 with a well-received study of the French existentialist Jean-Paul Sartre, then launched into fiction with a picaresque novel, *Under the Net,* the following year. Since then she has continued to produce, at a remarkable rate, what critics refer to as "novels of ideas."

Murdoch's allegiance to the Existentialist movement may have been relatively short-lived, as *Publishers Weekly* reports; nonetheless, this philosophy had a lasting influence upon her work. Like Sartre, writes William Van O'Connor in *The New University Wits and the End of Modernism,* Murdoch views man as a "lonely creature in an absurd world . . . impelled to make moral decisions, the consequences of which are uncertain." Like Sartre, says Warner Berthoff in *Fictions and Events,* Murdoch believes that writing is "above all else a collaboration of author and reader in an act of freedom." And, continues Berthoff, "following Sartre she has spoken pointedly of the making of works of art as not only a 'struggle for freedom' but as 'a task which does not come to an end.'"

Despite these similarities, critics note some important differences between the two philosophers. Gail Kmetz writes in *Ms.* that Murdoch "rejected Sartre's emphasis on the isolation and anguish of the individual in a meaningless world . . . because she felt it resulted in a sterile and futile solipsism [, a belief that the self is the only existent thing]. She considers the individual always as a part of society, responsible to others as well as to herself or himself; and insists that freedom means respecting the independent being of others, and that subordinating others' freedom to one's own is a denial of freedom itself. Unlike Sartre, Murdoch sees the claims of freedom and love as identical: love is real only when one accepts the 'otherness' of other people, and only when one is capable of love is one free."

Kmetz postulates that this philosophical position is close to that of the religious existentialists—"without the theological element. . . . [Murdoch] calls herself a 'Christian fellow-traveler,' [but] feels we must act as if humanity were alone in the universe, without guidance from some realm 'beyond.'" For Murdoch, Kmetz continues, "morality is not a divinely given truth, but a process which occurs when we respect the reality of other people."

How best to respect the "reality" of others, i.e., how best to live "morally," is an issue that emerges in Murdoch's fiction again and again. Together with questions of "love" and "freedom," it comprises her major concern. "Miss Murdoch's pervasive theme has been the quest for a passion beyond any center of self," explains *New York Times Book Review* critic David Bromwich. "What her characters seek may go by the name of Love or God or the Good: mere physical love is the perilous and always tempting idol that can become a destroyer." "The basic idea," says Joyce Carol Oates writing in the *New Republic,* "seems to be that centuries of humanism have nourished an unrealistic conception of the powers of the will: we have gradually lost the vision of a reality separate from ourselves. . . . Twentieth-century obsessions with the authority of the individual, the 'existential' significance of subjectivity, are surely misguided, for the individual cannot be (as he thinks of himself, proudly) a detached observer, free to invent or reimagine his life." The consequences of trying to do so are repeatedly explored in Murdoch's fiction, beginning with her first published novel, *Under the Net.*

Drawn on Austrian philosopher Ludwig Wittgenstein's idea that we each build our own "net" or system for structuring our lives, *Under the Net* describes the wanderings of bohemian Jake Donaghue as he attempts to structure his. But, observes James Gindin in *Postwar British Fiction,* "planned ways of life are . . . traps, no matter how carefully or rationally the net is woven, and Jake discovers that none of these narrow paths really works." Only after a series of comic misadventures (which change his attitude rather than his circumstances) is Jake able to accept the contingencies of life and the reality of other people. He throws off the net, an act which takes great courage according to Kmetz, "for nothing is more terrifying than freedom."

Though situations vary from book to book, each of the protagonists in Murdoch's twenty novels fashions a "net" of some kind. It "may be a set of rules such as those adhered to by the community members in *The Bell:* always cover your head in church; no personal decorations in one's room; we never ask each other about our past lives," writes Kmetz. "It may be an ideology or a huge impersonal bureaucracy, like the Special European Labor Immigration Board in *The Flight from the Enchanter.* Or a role: loving wife, martyr, rake."

For Hilary Burde, protagonist of *A Word Child,* the net is a fixed routine. An unloved, illegitimate child, Hilary as a boy is a violent delinquent. Then, befriended by a teacher, he learns that he possesses a remarkable skill with words. In the rigid structure of grammar he seeks shelter from life's randomness. He is awarded a scholarship to Oxford and begins what should be a successful career. "But," as *New York Times* critic Bromwich explains, "the structure of things can bear only so much ordering: his university job ends disastrously with an adulterous love affair that is indirectly responsible for two deaths." The story opens twenty years later, when Gunnar—the husband of Hilary's former lover—appears in the government office where Hilary holds a menial job. "The novel's subject," explains

Lynne Sharon Schwartz in *Nation* "is what Hilary will do about his humiliation, his tormenting guilt and his need for forgiveness."

What he does, according to Schwartz, is the worst possible thing. "He attempts to order his friends and his days into the kind of strict system he loves in grammar," she says. "This rigid life is not only penance but protection as well, against chaos, empty time, and the unpredictable impulses of the self. The novel shows the breakdown of the system: people turn up on unexpected days, they refuse—sometimes comically—to act the roles assigned them, and Hilary's dangerous impulses do come forth and insist on playing themselves out." The tragedy of Hilary's early days is repeated. He falls in love with Gunnar's second wife; they meet in secret and are discovered. Once more by accident Hilary commits his original crime.

"At the novel's conclusion," writes *Saturday Review*'s Bruce Allen, "we must consider which is the illusion: the optimist's belief that we can atone for our crimes and outlive them or the nihilist's certainty (Hilary expresses it) that people are doomed, despite their good intentions, to whirl eternally in a muddle of 'penitence, remorse, resentment, violence, and hate.'" David Bromwich interprets the moral issue somewhat differently. "Hilary, the artist-figure without an art," he says, "wants to make the world (word) conform to his every design, and is being guided to the awareness that its resistance to him is a lucky thing. . . . Like the novelist in *The Black Prince* and the poet in *Bruno's Dream*, Hilary must consent at last to the arbitrariness of an order imposed on him."

Learning to accept the chaos of life without the aid of patterns or categories is a constant struggle for Murdoch's characters. In her novels it is artists who, in Bromwich's words, are "trying daily by their disinterestedness to create a world outside themselves," who most nearly succeed. The importance of their role in her novels reflects Murdoch's belief in the importance of art, as *Midwest Quarterly*'s Sohreh Tawakuli Sullivan explains. "If the sickness of the age, as Murdoch contends, is solipsism, lovelessness, neurosis, a fear of history, . . . she would hold that its manifestation in philosophy and art, for example, could be cured by a therapy of perception, a rebirth of imagination. The need to perceive the unique particularity of the other is for Murdoch a measure not only of virtue and love, but of the creative imagination." For Murdoch, writes Joyce Carol Oates in the *New Republic*, the highest art is "that which reveals and honors the minute, 'random' detail of the world, and reveals it together with a sense of its integrity, its unity and form."

The creation of art, Murdoch told *Publishers Weekly*, should be the novelist's goal. "I don't think a novel should be a committed statement of political and social criticism," she said in that interview. "Novelists do enlighten people, they are great sources of education, but that's just incidental. They should aim at being beautiful. The most important thing about art is that it tells you what nature is really like, as opposed to what people in their fantasy-ridden way vaguely imagine it's like. Art holds a mirror to nature, and I think it's a very difficult thing to do."

The way Murdoch mirrors nature is by creating what she calls "real characters"—in other words, says Warner Berthoff in *Fictions and Events*, "personages who will be 'more than puppets' and at the same time other than oneself." In Murdoch's novels, the emphasis is not on form, but on character, as Linda Kuehl writing in *Modern Fiction Studies* explains: "Form, Iris Murdoch warns, is the artist's consolation and his temptation: he is tempted to sacrifice the eccentric, contingent individual while he consoles himself with the secure boundaries of structure. As [Murdoch] sees it, this constitutes a crisis since the contemporary novelist tends to produce fiction in the shape of tiny, self-contained crystal-like objects. Diagnosing the tyranny of form as an ill that must be cured, she postulates a return to the novel of character as it is manifested in the works of Scott, Jane Austen, George Eliot and Tolstoy, for these nineteenth century writers were so capable of charity that they gave their people an independent existence in an external world."

Unfortunately, continues Kuehl, Murdoch fails in her attempt: "Miss Murdoch's enthusiasm for nineteenth century characters prompts her desire to give 'a lot of people' an existence separate from herself and to permit them to roam freely and cheerfully throughout her pages. [But,] she seems unable to do this, for in each successive novel there emerges a pattern of predictable and predetermined types. These include the enchanter or enchantress—occult, godly, foreign, ancient—who is torn between exhibitionism and introspection, egotism and generosity, cruelty and pity; the observer, trapped between love and fear of the enchanter, who thinks in terms of ghosts, spells, demons and destiny, and imparts an obfuscated view of life; and the accomplice, a peculiar mixture of diabolical intention and bemused charm, who has dealings with the enchanters and power over the observers. . . . All three groups—enchanters, observers and accomplices—make up a scheme symptomatic of the author's failure to break away from the tyranny of form. Though she produces many people, each is tightly controlled in a super-imposed design, each is rigidly cast in a classical Murdochian role."

Lawrence Graver, writing in the *New York Times Book Review*, expresses a similar view. Notwithstanding her theory of fiction, he says, "in practice, the more she talked about freedom and opaqueness the more over-determined and transparent her novels seemed to become. Thinking back now on books like *The Unicorn*, *The Red and the Green*, *A Fairly Honorable Defeat*, or *An Accidental Man*, one is likely to remember situations not characters, mechanisms not worlds. Despite the inventiveness of the situations and the brilliance of the design, Miss Murdoch's philosophy has recently seemed to do little more than make her people *theoretically* interesting."

The problem, says Oates, is that her novels are "structures in which ideas, not things, and certainly not human beings flourish." In *The Novel Now*, Anthony Burgess compares Murdoch to a puppeteer who exerts complete control: "[Murdoch's] characters dress, talk, act like ourselves, but they are caught up in a purely intellectual pattern, a sort of contrived sexual dance in which partners are always changing. They seem to be incapable of free choice; they are totally in the . . . hands of their creatrix." Because she creates symbols rather than personalities, few, if any, of her characters, says *Saturday Review/World*'s Barbara Harrison, "resonate in the mind." In the intellectual game she plays, observes William Van O'Connor, the real communication is "between Miss Murdoch and her reader, not between the reader and the characters." This is both her strength and her limitation from his point of view.

Despite the prodigious response her novels generate, Murdoch refuses to read her critics: "One never learns anything one doesn't know already from them," she told *Publishers Weekly*. "Any novelist worth her salt knows very clearly what is wrong with her work before it is ever published. Why else would she be writing her next novel except to try to correct in it the mistakes of her last?"

Despite Murdoch's implication that there is room for improvement in her work, many reviewers praise the writing she has done. "She wears her formidable intelligence with a careless swagger," writes *Encounter*'s Jonathan Raban, "and her astonishingly fecund, playful imagination looks as fresh and effortless as ever.... Part of the joy of reading Iris Murdoch is the implicit assurance that there will be more to come, that the book in hand is an installment in a continuing work which grows more and more important as each new novel is added to it." Concludes Raban, "At a time when fiction seems hard and harder to write with any confidence, Miss Murdoch makes it look as easy and natural as breathing."

MEDIA ADAPTATIONS: "A Severed Head" (based on her novel and play), was filmed by Columbia Pictures, 1971; the film rights to *A Fairly Honourable Defeat* were sold in 1972.

CA INTERVIEW

Iris Murdoch answered *CA*'s questions by mail in October, 1981.

CA: In both your philosophical writing and your fiction you are concerned with the nature and practice of love. As you described it in "The Sublime and the Good" [originally published in Chicago Review, *autumn, 1959], "love is the perception of individuals ... the extremely difficult realisation that something other than oneself is real." Has your concept of love evolved or become modified significantly since you thus described it?*

MURDOCH: No, I don't think so. Perhaps, in my philosophical studies, the idea has gained a little more background. One aspect of goodness is the purification of desire. Love is a spring of energy; one must purify the source.

CA: Your work has attracted a great deal of critical attention. Though you've said you don't read reviews, do you try to read and assess the more lengthy critical and scholarly writing about your work? Do you find much of it perceptive?

MURDOCH: No, I don't read critical stuff, even the long serious pieces. Articles I have glanced at seem on the whole unperceptive, including the friendly ones.

CA: Do you and your husband [author and literary critic John Oliver Bayley] discuss your work in progress with each other? Do you keep in close touch with other writers?

MURDOCH: No, I do not discuss my work with my husband, though we talk all the time about literature and art generally. I certainly do not talk to other writers about my work.

CA: You particularly admire the good nineteenth-century novelists. Are there any contemporaries whose writing you read and enjoy currently?

MURDOCH: I do not read much, indeed scarcely any, contemporary fiction. I admire Yukio Mishima. I liked a novel by Robbe-Grillet (*Les Gommes*), which I read lately.

CA: In an interview with the late W. K. Rose published in Harper's Bazaar, *May, 1969, you spoke of the careful thinking and plotting that precede the actual writing of your novels. Has the process changed at all?*

MURDOCH: No, I have always made a very careful plan of the whole novel before writing the first sentence. I want to keep the purely inventive stage (plot, characters) open as long as possible.

CA: Do you keep a journal or notebook for ideas, scraps of conversation, any material that might become a part of your writing?

MURDOCH: I keep a journal with all sorts of notes and observations, not just for novels.

CA: In the same interview you acknowledged an "alteration between a sort of closed novel, where my own obsessional feeling about the novel is very strong and draws it closely together, and an open novel, where there are more accidental and separate and free characters. I would like to write the second kind." Are you satisfied with your progress toward that goal? Have you become progressively more satisfied with your writing in general?

MURDOCH: I think the later novels are better (mostly considerably better) than the earlier ones. I am still far from my goal.

CA: You often have male narrators, and they don't seem to present any writing difficulties for you. Could you say something about this preference, if it is a preference?

MURDOCH: I find no difficulty in imagining men. I know quite a lot. I am very much concerned about the (still distant) liberation of women, which I think will come about through education, and generally joining intellectual, cultural, and political life. I do not want to write about "women's problems" in any narrow, specialized sense. I have female narrators, too. I just identify more with the men.

CA: Do you prefer doing adaptations of your novels to the stage, as with The Severed Head *and* The Italian Girl, *to starting from scratch, as with* The Servants *and* The Snow *and* The Three Arrows?

MURDOCH: I much prefer to invent the whole thing. Adapting to another medium may be a waste of time which could be spent on writing something new.

CA: Were you involved in the production of the plays?

MURDOCH: Not much.

CA: You have been highly respected as a teacher. Are you teaching now? Doing any visiting lectures?

MURDOCH: I am not teaching at Oxford now. I sometimes give lectures, and have done so in certain universities in America. I shall be lecturing in Edinburgh on moral philosophy next January and February. I miss the teaching.

CA: You've managed to balance two careers, teach, garden, and run your house. Has it been difficult to do all the things you've wanted to do?

MURDOCH: Yes, it has been difficult. There are many, many things I have not enough time to do.

CA: Are there works in progress or future plans of your own that you'd like to mention?

MURDOCH: I am writing the philosophy lectures for Edinburgh, and a novel.

BIOGRAPHICAL/CRITICAL SOURCES: Kenneth Allsop, *The Angry Decade,* P. Owen, 1958; James Gindin, *Postwar British Fiction,* University of California Press, 1962; William Van O'Connor, *The New University Wits, and the End of Modernism,* Southern Illinois University Press, 1963; *New York Times Book Review,* September 13, 1964, February 8, 1970, August 24, 1975, November 20, 1977, December 17, 1978, August

10, 1980, January 4, 1981, March 7, 1982; A. C. Ward, *Twentieth-Century English Literature, 1901-1960,* Methuen-University Paperbacks, 1964; *Harpers,* October, 1964; *Critique,* Volume X, number 1, and spring, 1964; *Times Literary Supplement,* September 10, 1964, November 25, 1977, September 5, 1980; A.S.D. Byatt, *Degrees of Freedom,* Barnes & Noble, 1965.

Peter Wolfe, *The Disciplined Heart,* University of Missouri Press, 1966; Anthony Burgess, *The Novel Now: A Guide to Contemporary Fiction,* Norton, 1967; Rubin Rabinowitz, *Iris Murdoch,* Columbia University Press, 1968; *Shenandoah,* winter, 1968; *Listener,* April 4, 1968; *Modern Fiction Studies,* Volume XV, number 3, 1969; *Commonweal,* March 28, 1969; *Saturday Review,* February 7, 1970; August 9, 1975; January 6, 1979; Warner Berthoff, *Fictions and Events: Essays in Criticism and Literary History,* Dutton, 1971; Malcolm Bradbury, *Possibilities: Essays on the State of the Novel,* Oxford University Press, 1973; *Contemporary Literary Criticism,* Gale, Volume I, 1973, Volume II, 1974, Volume III, 1975, Volume IV, 1975, Volume VI, 1976, Volume VIII, 1978, Volume XI, 1979, Volume XV, 1980, Volume XX, 1982; *Encounter,* July, 1974; *Saturday Review/World,* October 5, 1974; *Midwest Quarterly,* spring, 1975; *Nation,* March 29, 1975, October 11, 1975; *Publisher's Weekly,* December 13, 1976; *Ms.,* July, 1976; *New Republic,* November 18, 1978; *Washington Post,* December 21, 1980; *New York Times,* January 6, 1981; *Atlantic Monthly,* March, 1981; *New Yorker,* March 23, 1981; *World Literature Today,* summer, 1981.

—Sketch by Donna Olendorf

—Interview by Jean W. Ross

*   *   *

MURPHY, Buck
See WHITCOMB, Ian

*   *   *

MURPHY, James F(redrick) 1943-

PERSONAL: Born August 31, 1943, in Oakland, Calif.; son of Fredrick and Ruth (a nurse; maiden name, Thomson) Murphy; married Roxanne Howe, November 27, 1976; children: (previous marriage) Erin. *Education:* San Francisco State College (now University), B.A., 1966; Indiana University, M.S. (with honors), 1967; Oregon State University, Ph.D., 1972. *Politics:* Democrat. *Home:* 18335 Baylor Ave., Saratoga, Calif. 95070. *Office:* Department of Recreation and Leisure Studies, San Jose State University, San Jose, Calif. 95192.

CAREER: Community College of Baltimore, Baltimore, Md., instructor in recreation leadership, 1967-68; San Jose State University, San Jose, Calif., assistant professor, 1968-70, 1972-74, associate professor, 1974-78, professor of recreation and leisure studies, 1978-79; Northeastern University, Boston, Mass., professor of recreation and leisure studies and chairman of department, 1979-81; San Jose State University, professor of recreation and leisure studies, 1981—. Instructor at Oregon State University, summers, 1970-71; visiting associate professor at University of Illinois, summer, 1975, and University of North Carolina, summer, 1976. Administrative assistant at Camp Trinity, Hayfork, Calif., summers, 1963-65; playground director of Oakland Recreation and Park Department, 1965; recreation intern and coordinator of personnel and recruitment for Baltimore Bureau of Recreation, 1967-68; supervisor of Sunnyvale, Calif., Parks and Recreation Department, summers, 1968-69. Member of board of directors of recreation advisory committee at Ohlone College, 1972—, and Monterey Peninsula College, 1972-75; member of advisory board of New Games Foundation.

MEMBER: European Centre for Leisure and Education (Prague), National Recreation and Park Association, Society of Park and Recreation Educators (member of board of directors, 1974-77; president-elect, 1980-81; president, 1981-82; past-president, 1982-83), American Alliance for Leisure and Recreation, Academy of Leisure Sciences (charter fellow), Recreation and Park Educators of California. *Awards, honors:* Recreation literature special award of merit from Pi Sigma Epsilon, 1970; Professional Merit award from National Student Recreation and Park Society, National Recreation and Park Association, 1975, for literary contributions.

WRITINGS: (Editor with John A. Nesbitt and Paul D. Brown, and contributor) *Recreation and Leisure Service for the Disadvantaged: Guidelines to Program Development and Related Readings,* Lea & Febiger, 1970; (contributor) Larry Neal, editor, *Leisure and the Schools,* Center for Leisure Studies (Eugene, Ore.), 1972; (contributor) Thomas A. Stein and H. Douglas Sessoms, editors, *Recreation and Special Populations,* Holbrook, 1973, 3rd edition, in press; (contributor) Joseph J. Bannon, editor, *Outreach: Extending Community Service in Urban Areas,* C. C Thomas, 1973; (with Brown, William Niepoth, and John Williams) *Leisure Service Delivery System: A Modern Perspective,* Lea & Febiger, 1973; *Concepts of Leisure: Philosophical Implications,* Prentice-Hall, 1974, 2nd edition, 1981; *Recreation and Leisure Service: A Humanistic Perspective,* W. C. Brown, 1975; (with Dennis Howard) *Delivery of Community Leisure Services: A Holistic Perspective,* Lea & Febiger, 1977; (contributor) Tom Goodale and Peter Witt, editors, *Recreation and Leisure: Issues in an Era of Change,* 1980.

Also contributor to *Handbook of Social Intervention,* 1982. Regular reviewer for *Journal of Park Recreation Administration.* Contributor of articles and reviews to professional journals. Member of *Forum Newsletter* committee of Society of Park and Recreation Educators, 1969-70, 1971-72, member of research and scholarly publications committee, 1972-73; member of advisory board of *Leisure Today,* 1973-81; member of editorial board of *San Jose Studies,* 1974-78; associate editor, *Journal of Leisure Research,* 1975-77.

SIDELIGHTS: James F. Murphy sees a "need for people to work closely together in a non-threatening manner and assume more control over our own lives."

*   *   *

MYERS, Bernice

PERSONAL: Born in Bronx, N.Y.; daughter of Leonard (a jewelry designer) and Anna (a dressmaker; maiden name, Marer) Kaufman; married Lou Myers (a cartoonist and writer), June 5, 1947; children: Marc Lee, Danny Alan. *Education:* Attended Brooklyn College (now Brooklyn College of the City University of New York), 1966. *Home:* 58 Lakeview Ave. W., Peekskill, N.Y. 10566.

CAREER: After high school worked at various jobs in garment industry, including model, designer assistant, and sketcher, 1943-45; Columbia Pictures, New York, N.Y., employee in photostat department and illustrator of spots for movie ads, 1945-47; writer and illustrator of children's books. Occasional advertising illustrator. Judge, Golden Kite Award competition, Society of Children's Books Writers, 1982. *Member:* Authors Guild, Authors League of America.

WRITINGS—Juveniles; all self-illustrated: *Olivier, l'ours savant,* Hachette, 1956; *Voila le facteur,* Hachette, 1957; *Les*

Quatre Musiciens, Hachette, 1957; *Not This Bear!*, Four Winds, 1968; *My Mother Is Lost*, Scholastic Book Services, 1971; *Come Out Shadow, Wherever You Are*, Scholastic Book Services, 1971; *The Apple War*, Parents' Magazine Press, 1973; *Shhhh! It's a Secret*, Holt, 1973; *Chicken Feathers*, Holt, 1973; *The Safest Place*, Holt, 1973; *Nobody Knows Me*, Macmillan, 1974; *Where's a Dog?*, Holt, 1974; *A Lost Horse*, Doubleday, 1975; *Herman and the Bears Again*, Scholastic Book Services, 1976; *Sally's Secret*, Scholastic Book Services, 1977; *Giggles*, Scholastic Book Services, 1979; *Herman and the Bears behind Bars*, Scholastic Book Services, 1981; *My Diary*, Scholastic Book Services, 1981; *Not at Home*, Lothrop, 1981. Also author of stories for readers published by Holt, 1972, and Macmillan, 1973.

Illustrator: Benjamin Brewster (pseudonym for Mary Elting), *It's a Secret*, Grosset, 1950; Inez McClintock, *Billy and His Steam Roller*, Grosset, 1951; Burl Ives, *Sailing on a Very Fine Day*, Rand McNally, 1954; (with husband, Lou Myers) adapted from Charles Perrault, *Puss-in-Boots*, Rand McNally, 1955; Samuel Epstein and Beryl Williams, *First Book of Mexico*, F. Watts, 1955; Jane K. Lansing (pseudonym for Caroline Horowitz), *Being Nice Is Lots of Fun*, Hart, 1955; Rose Wyler, *First Book of Weather*, F. Watts, 1956; Rose Wyler and Gerald Ames, *What Makes It Go?*, McGraw, 1958; Margaret O. Hyde, *Off into Space!: Science for Young Space Travelers*, McGraw, 1959, 3rd edition, 1969; Irving A. Leitner, *Pear Shaped Hill*, Golden Press, 1960; John Lawrence Peterson, *How to Write Codes and Send Secret Messages*, Four Winds, 1970; *Tailspin*, Western Printing & Publishing, 1981.

Illustrator of science series by Tillie S. Pine and Joseph Levine; published by McGraw, except as indicated: *Sounds All Around*, 1958; *Water All Around*, 1959; *Air All Around*, 1960; *Friction All Around*, 1960; *Light All Around*, 1961; *Electricity All Around*, 1962; *Gravity All Around*, 1963; *Heat All Around*, 1963; *Simple Machines and How We Use Them*, Whittlesey House, 1965; *Weather All Around*, 1966; *Rocks and How We Use Them*, Whittlesey House, 1967; *Trees and How We Use Them*, 1969.

Illustrator of "Norman" series by Frank Gault and Claire Gault; published by Scholastic Book Services, 1975-81: *Norman Plays Soccer; . . . Plays Basketball; . . . Plays Baseball; . . . Plays Football; . . . Plays Ice Hockey*.

SIDELIGHTS: Bernice Myers told *CA*: "I rarely write with a theme in mind. I begin with an interesting sentence and let my typewriter take over. I never quite know where I'm going until the last sentence is written. If I feel that, at some point, the story is going nowhere, then the fingers automatically stop typing. And I begin another sentence. When I have actually written a satisfactory story the honing begins; rearranging the sentences, eliminating words where I know the illustrations will take over and always trying to make the wit and fun as good as it can get. Which means that even while the story is at the printer I am still rewriting."

AVOCATIONAL INTERESTS: Tennis.

MYLLER, Rolf 1926-
(David Brown, Rolf Milonas)

PERSONAL: Born October 13, 1926, in Germany; son of Ernest and Liselotte (Hirschmann) Myller; married June, 1956; children: Elise, Corinne. *Education:* Cornell University, Bachelor of Architecture, 1951; also attended New York University. *Religion:* Jewish. *Home and office:* 1165 Fifth Ave., New York, N.Y. 10029.

CAREER: Edward D. Stone (architect), New York, N.Y., draftsman, 1954-56; private practice as architect, New York, N.Y., 1958-1978. Assistant professor of architecture, Pratt Institute; instructor in architecture at New York School for Interior Design and New York Institute of Technology. *Military service:* U.S. Army. *Member:* American Arbitration Association, American Institute of Architects, P.E.N. *Awards, honors:* Award for design for Franklin D. Roosevelt Memorial in Washington, D.C.; other design awards.

WRITINGS: *How Big Is a Foot?*, Atheneum, 1962; *Rolling Round*, Atheneum, 1963; *The Design of the Small Public Library*, Bowker, 1966; *From Idea into House*, Atheneum, 1966, 2nd edition, 1974; (under pseudonym David Brown) *Someone Always Needs a Policeman*, Simon & Schuster, 1972; (under pseudonym Rolf Milonas) *Fantasex*, Grosset, 1975; *Mazes: 60 Beautiful and Beastly Labyrinths with Solutions*, Pantheon, 1976; *The Bible Puzzle Book*, Harper, 1977; *Symbols and Their Meaning*, Atheneum, 1978; *New Mazes*, Pantheon, 1979; *A Very Noisy Day*, Atheneum, 1981. Contributor of articles to magazines.†

* * *

MYRA, Harold L(awrence) 1939-

PERSONAL: Born July 19, 1939, in Camden, N.J.; son of John S. and Esther (Christensen) Myra; married Jeanette Austin (a registered nurse), May 7, 1966; children: Michelle, Todd, Gregory. *Education:* East Stroudsburg State College, B.S., 1961. *Home:* 1737 Marion Ct., Wheaton, Ill. 60187. *Office:* Christianity Today, Inc., 465 Gundersen Dr., Carol Stream, Ill. 60187.

CAREER: *Campus Life*, Wheaton, Ill., publisher, 1961-75; *Christianity Today*, Carol Stream, Ill., president and publisher, 1975—. *Military service:* U.S. Marine Corps Reserve, 1957-62. *Awards, honors:* Honorary doctorate, John Wesley College, 1977.

WRITINGS: *No Man in Eden*, Word, Inc., 1969; *Michelle, You Scallawag, I Love You*, John J. Benson, 1972; *The New You*, Zondervan, 1972; *Is There a Place I Can Scream?*, Doubleday, 1975; *Elsbeth*, Revell, 1976; *Santa, Are You for Real?*, Thomas Nelson, 1977; *Love Notes to Jeanette*, Victor Books, 1979; *Easter Bunny, Are You for Real?*, Thomas Nelson, 1980; *The Choice*, Tyndale House, 1981.

N

NAMIKAWA, Banri 1931-

PERSONAL: Born October 29, 1931, in Tokyo, Japan; son of Ryo and Hisako Namikawa. *Education:* Nihon University, graduate, 1952. *Home:* 2-13, 5-chome, Kugayama, Suginami-ku, Tokyo 168, Japan.

CAREER: Tokyo Broadcasting System, Tokyo, Japan, member of television news section, 1952-55; free-lance photographer, 1955—. Director and executive photographer, Reconstructive Borobudur (Indonesia), 1969; member and executive photographer, Asian Cultural Centre for UNESCO, 1970; executive photographer, EXPO '70 and EXPO '75. *Member:* Japan Professional Photographers Society, Photographic Society of Japan, New Modern Photographers Society, Japan Pen Club, Literary Men's Association of Japan, Japan-China Exchange Society, Borobudur Reconstruction Society, Japan-Turkey Society (permanent director).

AWARDS, HONORS: Frankfurt Photographers Society award, 1966; Photographic Cultural Prize, Spanish Government, 1967; Cultural Merits Prize, Guadalajara City, 1968, for photography; special prize, Turkish Journalists Association, 1969; International Prize, Photographic Society of Granada, 1970; Grand Prix, Photographic Society of Japan, 1971; Cultural Decoration, His Imperial Majesty Mohamad Reza Pahlavi Aryamehr, Shahanshah of Iran, 1972; Cultural Prize, Turkish Government, 1973: Art Grand Prix award, 7th Asian Games in Iran, 1974; Science Cultural Prize, Turkish Government, 1974; Mainchi Art Prize, 1976.

WRITINGS: Mexico, Kodan-sha, 1971; *Spain,* Kodan-sha, 1971; (with father, Ryo Namikawa) *Istanbul: Tale of Three Cities,* Kodan-sha, 1972; *Iran,* Kodan-sha, 1973; *Silk Road,* Shinjin-butsu-orai-sha, Volume I, 1975, Volume II, 1976; *Chichukai no nakano Spain* (title means "Spain in the Mediterranean Sea"), Tamagawa University, 1978; *Taiyo to senjyo no Silk Road* (title means "Burning and Great Sun in Silk Road"), Shincho-sha, 1979.

Photo albums: *Kamigami no iseki* (title means "The Lost Splendor of the Ancient Remains"), Mainichi Newspapers (Tokyo), 1966; *Chichyukai rekishi no tabi* (title means "Trip to the Mediterranean Historical Remains"), Shuei-sha, 1967; *Maya no shinden* (title means "Palaces in Maya"), Kodan-sha, 1968; *Islam no sekai* (title means "The World of Islam"), Kodan-sha, 1968; *Orient no haikyo* (title means "Dawn of the Orient"), Kodan-sha, 1968; *Nihobi no tenkai* (title means "Genealogy of Japanese Beauty"), Kodan-sha, 1969: *Girisha no shinden* (title means "The Greek Temples"), Kodan-sha, 1969. *Romanesque to Gothic no seidoo* (title means "The Romanesque and Gothic Cathedral"), Kodan-sha, 1970; *Bizantine no bijutu* (title means "The World of Byzantine Arts"), Kodan-sha, 1970; *Alhambra-kyuden* (title means "The Alhambra Palace"), Kodan-sha, 1970; *Darius no isan* (title means "Darius the Great"), Kawade-shobo, 1970; *Borobudor,* Heibon-sha, 1971; *Istanbul-bijutsukan* (title means "Istanbul Archaeological Museum"), Kodan-sha, 1971; *Kyuros no isan* (title means "The Legacy of Cyrus the Great"), Kawade-shobo, 1971; *Teioh no eikho* (title means "The Glory of the Persian Empire"), Shuei-sha, 1972; *Sabaku no hoshi to inori* (title means "The Cultural Inheritance in Iraq and Syria"), Shuei-sha, 1972; *Kareinaru Genzoh* (title means "The Magnificence of Turkey"), Shuei-sha, 1972; *Persia no shiho* (title means "The Great Treasures of Persia"), Mainichi Newspapers, 1972; *Kodai toshi no eikoo* (title means "The Great City of Ancient Times"), Koocho-sha, 1972; *Maboroshi no maya-bunmei* (title means "Phantasmal of the Great Civilization of Maya"), Keishoo-sha, 1972; *Silk Road no kenchiku to bijyutu* (title means "The Arts and Architecture of Silk Road"), Koocho-sha, 1973; *Toruko no shiho* (title means "The Great Treasures of Turkey"), Mainichi Newspapers, 1973; *Chugoku tojiki* (title means "Chinese Porcelains"), Heibon-sha, 1974.

Toroko no soshoku tile (title means "The Turkish Ceramics Tile Art"), Heibon-sha, 1975; *The Silk Road,* Shincho-sha, 1976; *Islam-sekai no tabi* (title means "The Trip to the Islam World"), Gakushu-kenkyu-sha, 1976; *Maya, Aztec no tabi* (title means "The Trip to Maya and Aztec"), Gakushu-kenkyu-sha, 1977; *Asia-koji junrei* (title means "Pilgrimage to an Ancient Asia Temple"), Gakushu-kenkyu-sha, 1977; *Harukanaru Silk Road* (title means "Remote Silk Road"), Gakusha-kenkyu-sha, 1977; *Islam no kaiga* (title means "Islamic Paintings"), Heibon-sha, 1978; *Chokoku kenchiku* (title means "Sculptures and Architectures"), Shinjinbutsu-orai-sha, 1978; *Kin, gin, dho-khi* (title means "Gold, Silver, and Copperware"), Shinjinbutsu-orai-sha, 1979; *Do, thoki, orimono* (title means "Earthenware, Pottery, and Textiles"), Shinjinbutsu-orai-sha, 1979; *Silk Road hakubutsukan* (title means "Silk Road Museums"), Kodan-sha, 1979; *Toruko-tile no hana-karakusa* (title means "Arabesque of Turkish Tiles"), Bunka-shuppan-kyoku, 1979.

Persia no seito (title means "Holy City of Persia"), Kodan-sha, 1980; *Persia no yakimono* (title means "Persian Ceramics"), Bunka-shuppan-kyoku, 1980; *Silk Road no accessories* (title means "Accessories of the Silk Road"), Bunka-shuppan-kyoku, 1980; *Silk Road 25-nen* (title means "Silk Road 25 Years"), Kodan-sha, 1980; *Persia no meitoh* (title means "Persian Famous Ceramics"), Heibon-sha, 1980; *Palestine no shishu* (title means "Embroideries of Palestine"), Bunka-shuppan-kyoku, 1981; *Silk Road no shugei* (title means "Handicrafts of Silk Road"), Bunka-shuppan-kyoku, 1981; *Tasho toshi* (title means "Caravan City"), Shincho-sha, 1981.

All published by Topkapi Sarayi Museum: *Houmotsu-kan* (title means "Treasure House"), 1980; *Harem no kenchiku* (title means "Architectures of Harem"), 1980; *Sultan no isho* (title means "Clothes of Sultan"), 1980; *Kyutei jyutan* (title means "Carpets of the Court"), 1980; *Saimitsu-ga* (title means "Miniature Paintings"), 1980; *Chugoku thojiki* (title means "Chinese Porcelains"), 1981; *Nihon thojiki* (title means "Japanese Porcelains"), 1981; *Istanbul thojiki* (title means "Istanbul Porcelains"), 1981; *Toruko thoki* (title means "Turkish Ceramics"), 1981; *Gun-gu, tokei, kinzoku-kogei* (title means "Arms, Watches, and Metal Works"), 1981.

Also collaborator on 42 other photo albums, 1967-1980.

* * *

NASH, Gerald D(avid) 1928-

PERSONAL: Born July 16, 1928, in Berlin, Germany; naturalized U.S. citizen; son of Alfred B. (a businessman) and Alice (Kantorowicz) Nash; married Marie Norris, August 19, 1967. *Education:* New York University, B.A., 1950; Columbia University, M.A., 1952; University of California, Berkeley, Ph.D., 1957. *Religion:* Jewish. *Home:* 9124 Princess Jeanne N.E., Albuquerque, N.M. 87112. *Office:* Department of History, University of New Mexico, Albuquerque, N.M. 87106.

CAREER: Stanford University, Stanford, Calif., instructor in history, 1957-58, visiting assistant professor, 1959-60; Northern Illinois University, De Kalb, assistant professor, 1958-59; Harvard University, Cambridge, Mass., research fellow at Center for the Study of Liberty, 1960-61; University of New Mexico, Albuquerque, assistant professor, 1961-63, associate professor, 1963-68, professor of history, 1968—, chairman of department, 1974-80. Visiting summer professor at University of California, Berkeley, 1959, and University of California, Davis, 1961; visiting summer lecturer at University of Maryland, 1962; visiting associate professor at New York University, 1965-66. Member of advisory board and director, Lincoln Educational Foundation.

MEMBER: American Historical Association, Business History Society, Agricultural History Society, Economic History Association, Organization of American Historians (chairman of membership committee, 1968-70), Western History Association, Phi Beta Kappa. *Awards, honors:* Newberry Library fellow, 1959; Huntington Library fellow, 1979; National Endowment for the Humanities, senior fellow, 1981, award on bicennial of the U.S. Constitution, 1983; Project '87 fellow, 1982.

WRITINGS: State Government and Economic Development, Institute of Governmental Studies, University of California, 1964, reprinted, Arno, 1979; (editor) *Issues in American Economic History: Selected Readings,* Heath, 1964, 3rd edition, 1980; (editor) *Franklin Delano Roosevelt,* Prentice-Hall, 1967; (editor) *Gifford Pinchot: The Fight for Conservation,* University of Washington Press, 1967; *U.S. Oil Policy, 1890-1964: Business and Government in 20th Century America,* University of Pittsburgh Press, 1968; *The Great Tradition: A Short History of 20th Century America,* Allyn & Bacon, 1971; *The American West in the 20th Century: A Short History of an Urban Oasis,* Prentice-Hall, 1973; (with others) *Herbert Hoover and the Crisis of American Liberalism,* Scheckman, 1973.

The Great Depression and World War II, St. Martin's, 1979; (editor) *The Urban West,* Sunflower, 1980; *World War II and the West,* Indiana University, 1983. Editor, *The Historian,* 1974—. Member of board of editors, *Business History Review,* 1964-68, *New Mexico Historical Review,* 1964—, *Journal of American History,* 1971-74, *Western Historical Quarterly,* 1971-74, *Agricultural History,* 1981, and *Journal of the West,* 1978-81.

WORK IN PROGRESS: World War II and the Economy of the West, for University of Nebraska Press; *A History of American Bureaucracy,* for University of Pittsburgh Press.

* * *

NASH, Ronald H. 1936-

PERSONAL: Born May 27, 1936, in Cleveland, Ohio; son of Herman and Violet (Pankratz) Nash; married Betty Jane Perry, June 8, 1957; children: Jeffrey Alan, Jennifer Anne. *Education:* Barrington College, A.B., 1958; Brown University, M.A., 1960; Syracuse University, Ph.D., 1964. *Politics:* Republican. *Religion:* Baptist.

CAREER: Barrington College, Barrington, R.I., instructor in philosophy, 1958-60; Houghton College, Houghton, N.Y., instructor in philosophy, 1960-62; Syracuse University, Syracuse, N.Y., instructor in philosophy, 1963-64; Western Kentucky University, Bowling Green, associate professor of philosophy and head of philosophy department, beginning 1964. Baptist minister in churches in Penn Yan, N.Y., and Fall River, Mass., five years; has lectured in England, Wales, Ireland, and Scotland.

WRITINGS: Dooyeweerd and the Amsterdam Philosophy, Zondervan, 1962; *The New Evangelicalism,* Zondervan, 1963; (editor) *The Philosophy of Gordon H. Clark: A Festschrift,* Presbyterian & Reformed, 1968; *The Light of the Mind: St. Augustine's Theory of Knowledge,* University of Kentucky Press, 1969; (editor) *Ideas of History,* Dutton, 1969; (contributor) *Christianity and the Counter-Culture,* I-V Press, 1973; *Freedom, Justice, and the State,* University Press of America, 1980.†

* * *

NAST, Elsa Ruth
See WATSON, Jane Werner

* * *

NAYLOR, Phyllis (Reynolds) 1933-

PERSONAL: Born January 4, 1933, in Anderson, Ind.; daughter of Eugene S. and Lura (Schield) Reynolds; married second husband, Rex V. Naylor (a speech pathologist), May 26, 1960; children: Jeffrey Alan, Michael Scott. *Education:* Joliet Junior College, diploma, 1953; American University, B.A., 1963. *Politics:* Independent. *Religion:* Unitarian Universalist. *Home:* 9910 Holmhurst Rd., Bethesda, Md. 20817.

CAREER: Elementary school teacher in Hazelcrest, Ill., 1956; Montgomery County Education Association, Rockville, Md., assistant executive secretary, 1958-59; National Education Association, Washington, D.C., editorial assistant with *NEA Journal,* 1959-60; full-time writer, 1960—. Active in civil rights and peace organizations. *Member:* Society of Children's Book Writers, Authors Guild, Authors League of America, Children's Book Guild (Washington, D.C.; president, 1974-75).

WRITINGS: Grasshoppers in the Soup, Fortress, 1965; *The Galloping Goat, and Other Stories,* Abingdon, 1965; *The New*

Schoolmaster, Silver Burdett, 1967; *A New Year's Surprise,* Silver Burdett, 1967; *Jennifer Jean, the Cross-Eyed Queen,* Lerner, 1967; *Knee Deep in Ice Cream,* Fortress, 1967; *To Shake a Shadow,* Abingdon, 1967; *What the Gulls Were Singing,* Follett, 1967; *When Rivers Meet,* Friendship, 1968; *The Dark Side of the Moon,* Fortress, 1969; *Private I,* Fortress, 1969; *To Make a Wee Moon,* Follett, 1969; *Meet Murdock,* Follett, 1969.

Making It Happen, Follett, 1970; *Ships in the Night,* Fortress, 1970; *Wrestle the Mountain,* Follett, 1971; *No Easy Circle,* Follett, 1972; *How to Find Your Wonderful Someone,* Fortress, 1972; *To Walk the Sky Path,* Follett, 1973; *An Amish Family,* J. Philip O'Hara, 1974; *Getting Along in Your Family,* Abingdon, 1976; *Crazy Love: An Autobiographical Account of Marriage and Madness,* Morrow, 1977; *Getting Along with Your Friends,* Abingdon, 1979; *A Change in the Wind,* Augsburg Press, 1979; *Revelations,* St. Martin's, 1979.

Getting Along with Your Teachers, Abingdon, 1981; *Never Born a Hero,* Augsburg Press, 1982.

All published by Atheneum: *Walking through the Dark,* 1976; *How I Came to Be a Writer* (autobiography), 1978; *In Small Doses,* 1979; *How Lazy Can You Get?,* 1979; *Eddie, Incorporated,* 1980; *Shadows on the Wall,* 1980; *All Because I'm Older,* 1981; *Faces in the Water,* 1981; *Footprints at the Window,* 1981; *The Boy with the Helium Head,* 1982; *A String of Chances,* 1982; *The Solomon System,* 1983.

"Witch" trilogy; published by Atheneum: *Witch's Sister,* 1975; *Witch Water,* 1977; *The Witch Herself,* 1978. Contributor of 2,000 short stories and articles to periodicals.

WORK IN PROGRESS: A Man of Choice; The Baby, the Bed, and the Rose; Carrying On; Night Cry; The Other Side of the Door.

SIDELIGHTS: Phyllis Naylor told *CA:* "I can never imagine myself writing only for children or only for adults. I like to follow up a mystery story for the nine-to-twelve set with a contemporary novel for adults; after that perhaps I will do a picture book, or a realistic novel for teens, or possibly a humorous book for children. The marvelous thing about writing is that I may play the part of so many different people—an old grandmother on one page, a young boy the next; a middle-aged man or a girl of fifteen. I feel most whole when I can look at a scene through the eyes of several different people. My biggest problem is that there are always four or five books waiting in the wings. Scarcely am I halfway through one book than another begins to intrude. I'm happy, of course, that ideas come so easily, but it is like having a monkey on my back. I am never quite free of it. Almost everything that happens to me or to the people I know ends up in a book at some time, all mixed up, of course, with imaginings. I can't think of anything else in the world I would rather do than write."

BIOGRAPHICAL/CRITICAL SOURCES: Phyllis Naylor, *Crazy Love: An Autobiographical Account of Marriage and Madness,* Morrow, 1977; Naylor, *How I Came to Be a Writer,* Atheneum, 1978; *New York Times Book Review,* December 2, 1979; *Washington Post Book World,* September 12, 1982.

* * *

NELSEN, Hart M(ichael) 1938-

PERSONAL: Born August 3, 1938, in Pipestone, Minn.; son of Noah I. (a teacher) and Nova (a college professor; maiden name, Ziegler) Nelsen; married Anne Kusener (a writer, researcher, and historian), June 13, 1964; children: Jennifer. *Education:* University of Northern Iowa, B.A., 1959, M.A., 1963; Princeton Theological Seminary, M.Div., 1963; Vanderbilt University, Ph.D., 1972. *Politics:* Democrat. *Religion:* United Presbyterian. *Office:* Department of Sociology, Catholic University of America, Washington, D.C. 20064.

CAREER: Western Kentucky University, Bowling Green, assistant professor, 1965-70, associate professor of sociology, 1970-73; Catholic University of America, Washington, D.C., associate professor, 1973-74, professor of sociology and chairman of department, beginning 1974. *Member:* American Sociological Association, Association for the Sociology of Religion (member of executive council, 1974-77), Society for the Scientific Study of Religion, Religious Research Association, British Sociological Association, Southern Sociological Society. *Awards, honors:* Presbyterian denominations grant, 1966-68, for research study in Appalachia; National Science Foundation faculty fellowship, 1969-71; National Institute of Mental Health grant, 1969-72, to study the Black church as a socializing and politicizing agency; Russell Sage Foundation grant, 1972-73, to study church involvement and voting.

WRITINGS: (With wife, Anne K. Nelsen, and James K. Miller) *Bibliography on Appalachia,* Office of Research and Services, Western Kentucky University, 1967; *The Appalachian Presbyterian: Some Rural-Urban Differences,* Office of Research and Services, Western Kentucky University, 1968; (with John L. Dec and Susan C. Westfall) *A Comparison of Religious Groupings in Appalachia,* Office of Research and Services, Western Kentucky University, 1968; *Strategy for Change: Presbyterians, Churches, and Education in Appalachia,* Appalachian Research Project, 1968; (editor with A. K. Nelsen and Raytha L. Yokley) *The Black Church in America,* Basic Books, 1971; (with A. K. Nelsen) *Black Church in the Sixties,* University Press of Kentucky, 1975; (with Raymond H. Potvin and Joseph Shields) *The Religion of Children,* Office of Research, Policy, and Program Development, U.S. Catholic Conference, 1977.

Contributor to *American Sociological Review, American Journal of Sociology, Social Forces, Journal for the Scientific Study of Religion, Sociological Analysis,* and *Review of Religious Research.*†

* * *

NELSON, Robert James 1925-

PERSONAL: Born March 29, 1925, in Woodside, Long Island, N.Y.; son of Norman (an electrician) and Irene (O'Leary) Nelson; married Olga Samios, August 4, 1947; children: Andrew Paul, Alexandra. *Education:* Columbia University, B.A., 1949, M.A., 1950, Ph.D., 1955. *Politics:* Democrat. *Office:* Department of French, University of Illinois at Urbana-Champaign, Urbana, Ill. 61822.

CAREER: Columbia University, New York, N.Y., instructor in French, 1953-55; Yale University, New Haven, Conn., instructor in French, 1955-58; University of Michigan, Ann Arbor, assistant professor of French, 1958-59; University of Pennsylvania, Philadelphia, associate professor, 1959-63, professor of romance languages, 1963-69; University of Illinois at Urbana-Champaign, professor of French and comparative literature, 1969—, head of Department of French, 1973—. *Military service:* U.S. Army, 1943-46.

MEMBER: Modern Language Association of America, American Association of Teachers of French, American Association of University Professors, Modern Humanities Research Association, American Council of Learned Societies, Phi Beta Kappa. *Awards, honors:* American Council of Learned Societies grant-in-aid, 1960; American Philosophical Society grant-in-aid, 1963; Chevalier, Palmes Academiques, 1972.

WRITINGS: *Play within a Play: The Dramatist's Conception of His Art,* Yale University Press, 1958; (with M. M. Guiney) *A Student's Manual to Accompany "Therese Desqueyroux" by F. Mauriac,* Department of Romance Languages, University of Michigan, 1958; (editor with Neal Oxenhnalder) *Aspects of French Literature,* Appleton, 1961; *Corneille: His Heroes and Their Worlds,* University of Pennsylvania Press, 1963; (editor) *Corneille and Racine: Parallels and Contrasts,* Prentice-Hall, 1966; *Immanence and Transcendence: The Theater of Jean Rotrou, 1609-1650,* Ohio State University Press, 1969; (editor with Gerald Weales) *Enclosure: A Collection of Plays,* McKay, 1975; (editor with Weales) *Revolution: A Collection of Plays,* McKay, 1975; *Pascal: Adversary and Advocate,* Harvard University Press, 1982.

Recordings: "Henry IV," Everett/Edwards, 1973; "Six Characters in Search of an Author," Everett/Edwards, 1973. Contributor of articles and reviews to *Denver Quarterly* and other journals.

BIOGRAPHICAL/CRITICAL SOURCES: *Times Literary Supplement,* July 30, 1982.†

* * *

NEVILLE, Anna
See FAIRBURN, Eleanor

* * *

NEWBURY, Colin (Walter) 1929-

PERSONAL: Born March 4, 1929, in Dunedin, New Zealand; son of W. L. and A. A. (Raven) Newbury; married Gertrude E. Setscheny, 1955; children: Jacqueline Louise. *Education:* University of Otago, B.A., 1951; University of New Zealand, M.A., 1952; Australian National University, Ph.D., 1956. *Politics:* Labour. *Religion:* Presbyterian. *Home:* 9 Carlton Rd., Oxford, England. *Office:* Institute of Commonwealth Studies, St. Giles, Oxford, England.

CAREER: University of Ibadan, Ibadan, Nigeria, lecturer in history, 1957-60; UNESCO, Paris, France, administrative officer in department of social sciences, 1961; Institute of Commonwealth Studies, Oxford, England, research officer, 1962-64, senior research officer, beginning 1965. Fellow of Linacre College, Oxford University. Lecturer at French universities and in Belgium; visiting professor, Duke University, 1963. *Member:* African Association (United Kingdom), Societe des Oceanistes (Paris), International African Institute.

WRITINGS: *John Davies: The History of the Tahitian Mission,* Cambridge University Press and Hakluyt Society, 1961; *The Western Slave Coast and Its Rulers,* Clarendon Press, 1961; *The West African Commonwealth,* Duke University Press, 1964; (editor) *British Policy Towards West Africa: Select Documents,* Clarendon Press, Volume I: *1786-1874,* 1965, Volume II: *1875-1914,* 1971; (editor) Sir Richard Burton, *A Mission to Gelele, King of Dahome,* Routledge & Kegan Paul, 1966; *Aspects of Cultural Change in French Polynesia: The Decline of the Ari'i,* Polynesian Society, 1967; (editor) Honore Laval, *Memoires pour servir a l'historie de Mangareva,* Musee de l'homme (Paris), 1968; (with wife, Gertrude E. Newbury) *Bibliography of Commonwealth Migrations: The Tropical Territories,* Institute of Commonwealth Studies, 1969; *Tahati Nui: Change and Survival in French Polynesia, 1767-1945,* University Press of Hawaii, 1980.

Contributor of articles and reviews to *Times Literary Supplement, Africa, Journal of the Royal Geographical Society, Journal de la Societe des Oeanistes, Revue d'histoire d'Outre-mer,* and other publications.†

* * *

NEWMAN, Jeremiah Joseph 1926-

PERSONAL: Born March 31, 1926, in County Limerick, Ireland; son of Joseph and Catherine (Kiely) Newman. *Education:* Attended St. Munchin's College; Maynooth College, B.A., 1946, M.A., 1947, B.D., 1949; University of Louvain, D.Ph., 1951; Oxford University, post-doctoral study, 1951-52. *Home:* St. Patrick's College, Maynooth, County Kildare, Ireland.

CAREER: Ordained Roman Catholic priest, 1950. Queen's University, Belfast, Ireland, lecturer in scholastic philosophy, 1952-53; Maynooth College, Maynooth, Ireland, professor of Catholic sociology, beginning 1953. *Member:* Malines Union of Social Studies, Statistical and Social Inquiry Society of Ireland, European Society for Rural Sociology (founder member), Geographical Society of Ireland, Irish Philosophical Club, National Institute for Physical Planning (chairman of planning and development committee).

WRITINGS: *Foundations of Justice,* Cork University Press, 1954; *A Time for Truth,* Browne & Nolan, 1955; *Co-Responsibility in Industry,* Newman, 1955; *What Is Catholic Action?,* Newman, 1958; *The Christian in Society,* Helicon, 1962; *Studies in Political Morality,* Scepter, 1962; (contributor) *Limerick Rural Survey,* 1963; *Principles of Peace,* Catholic Social Guild, 1964; *Change and the Catholic Church,* Helicon, 1965; *The Christian Layman,* Scepter, 1966; *Vatican II: The Christian Layman,* Scepter Books, 1966; *New Dimensions in Regional Planning: A Case Study of Ireland,* An Foras Forbartha, 1967; *Christianity and Race,* Helicon, 1967; *Race: Migration and Integration,* Helicon, 1968; *Conscience versus Law: Reflections on the Evolution of Natural Law,* Franciscan Herald Press, 1971; *Introduction to Sociology,* Talbot Press, 1972; *The State of Ireland,* Four Courts Press, 1977; *Maynooth and Georgian Ireland,* Kenny's Bookshops, 1979.

Editor, *Christus Rex;* correspondent, *Sociologia Ruralis;* member of scientific committee, *Social Compass.*†

* * *

NEWTON, Stu
See WHITCOMB, Ian

* * *

NICHOLSON, Geoffrey (George) 1929-

PERSONAL: Born April 11, 1929, in Croydon, England; son of George Llewellyn (a businessman) and Florence (Tucker) Nicholson; married Mavis Mainwaring (a free-lance advertising copywriter), August 16, 1952; children: Stephen, Lewis, Harry. *Education:* University College of Swansea, B.A. (with honors), 1952. *Politics:* Labour. *Home and office:* Aber-Rhaeadr Farmhouse, Llanrhaeadr-Ym-Mochnant, Powys SY10 DAX, Wales.

CAREER: Free-lance journalist and writer. W. S. Crawford Ltd. (advertising agents), London, England, copywriter, 1952-57; *Observer,* London, sports editor, 1976-78. *Military service:* British Army, 1947-49. *Member:* National Union of Journalists, Rugby Writers' Club.

WRITINGS: (With W. John Morgan) *Report on Rugby,* Heinemann, 1959; *The Professionals,* Deutsch, 1964, Transatlantic, 1965; (editor) *Touchdown, R.F.U.*, 1971; *The Great Bike Race,* Hodder & Stoughton, 1977; (with Clem Thomas) *Welsh Rugby: The Crowning Years,* Collins, 1980. Contributor to *Observer* and *Guardian.*

* * *

NITZSCHE, Jane Chance 1945-

PERSONAL: Born October 26, 1945, in Neosho, Mo.; daughter of Donald William (a U.S. Army lieutenant colonel) and Julia (Mile) Chance; married Dennis Carl Nitzsche, June, 1966 (divorced March, 1969); married Paolo Passaro, April 30, 1981; children: (first marriage) Therese Chance. *Education:* Purdue University, B.A. (with highest distinction), 1967; University of Illinois, A.M., 1968, Ph.D., 1971. *Home:* 3907 Riley, Houston, Tex. 77005. *Office:* Department of English, Rice University, Houston, Tex. 77001.

CAREER: University of Saskatchewan, Saskatoon, assistant professor of English, 1971-73; Rice University, Houston, Tex., assistant professor, 1973-77, associate professor, 1977-80, professor of English, 1980—. Lecturer at professional conferences. Judge of Poetry Society of Texas poetry contest, 1980. Consultant and reader on medieval literature.

MEMBER: International Association for Neo-Latin Studies, Modern Language Association of America (alternate delegate in old English Language and Literature Section, 1981—), American Association of University Professors (secretary-treasurer of Rice chapter, 1975-76), Mediaeval Academy of America, New Chaucer Society, Authors Guild, Authors League of America, P.E.N., Poets and Writers, Women's Caucus for the Modern Languages, South Central Modern Language Association, Southeastern Medieval Academy, Mortarboard (chapter editor and historian), Alpha Lambda Delta, Theta Sigma Phi, Delta Rho Kappa. *Awards, honors:* National Defense Education Act fellow, 1967-70; National Endowment for the Humanities research fellow, 1977-78; honorary research fellow, University College, London, 1977-78; Guggenheim fellow, 1980-81.

WRITINGS: The Genius Figure in Antiquity and the Middle Ages, Columbia University Press, 1975; *Tolkien's Art: A "Mythology for England,"* St. Martin's, 1979; (contributor) *Anthology of Magazine Verse and Yearbook of American Poetry,* Monitor Book, 1979; *Woman as Hero in Anglo-Saxon Literature,* Macmillan, 1983.

Author of papers on medieval literature for professional conferences. Contributor of poems to literary magazines, including *Dalhousie Review, Ariel, Icarus, Southern Humanities Review, Nimrod,* and *Wascana Review;* contributor of articles and reviews to professional journals, including *American Transcendental Quarterly, Chaucer Newsletter, Allegorica, English Miscellany, Studies in Medievalism,* and *Change;* contributor to *Houston Chronicle.*

WORK IN PROGRESS: The Mythological Tradition in the Middle Ages; An Anthology of Modern American Woman Poets.

SIDELIGHTS: Jane Chance Nitzsche told *CA:* "I began writing when I was eight, and I don't think I will ever stop. In the recent past most of my books have been written under pressure, to finish a Ph.D., to get a job, or to keep it and get promoted. They have also been squeezed into Christmas and summer vacations, or written during fellowships: teaching schedules aren't very accommodating. And they have generally grown out of smaller pieces that happened to reflect ideas in which I was interested—the Genius book from a seminar paper in a graduate class, and the Tolkien book from my lecture notes for a college course requested by interested students. What both books share is an interest in mythology, and the ways in which men make myths out of older heroic beliefs, be they Graeco-Roman or medieval, and the ways in which men interpret those myths after the makers have died.

"Of course I was originally interested in writing poetry and fiction, and somehow I got diverted into publishing books on myth and mythology and heroic literature, which brings me to my advice to other writers: don't confuse means and ends, but if you do, you were probably meant to."

BIOGRAPHICAL/CRITICAL SOURCES: Classical Outlook, June, 1976; *Speculum,* Number 52, 1977; *Times Literary Supplement,* January 18, 1980; *Choice,* February, 1980; *Modern Fiction Studies,* Number 26, 1980.

* * *

NOLL, Roger G(ordon) 1940-

PERSONAL: Born March 13, 1940, in Monterey Park, Calif.; son of Cecil Ray (a broadcaster and lawyer) and Hjordis A. (a realtor; maiden name, Westover) Noll; married Robyn R. Schreiber, August 25, 1962; children: Kimberlee Elizabeth. *Education:* California Institute of Technology, B.S. (with honors), 1962; Harvard University, A.M., 1965, Ph.D., 1967. *Office:* Division of Humanities and Social Sciences, California Institute of Technology, Pasadena, Calif. 91125.

CAREER: California Institute of Technology, Pasadena, instructor, 1965-67, assistant professor, 1967-69, associate professor, 1969-71, professor of economics, 1973—, chairman of the Division of Humanities and Social Sciences, 1978—. Visiting professor, Graduate School of Business, Stanford University, 1976-77. Senior staff economist for President's Council of Economic Advisers, 1967-68; member of committee, National Council on Marine Resources and Engineering, 1968, Office of Science and Technology, 1970-71, National Research Council, 1970-73, and National Academy of Sciences, 1975-76; secretary, President's Interagency Task Force on Income Maintenance, 1968; member, Federal Interagency Committee on Education, 1968, and President's Commission for a National Agenda for the Eighties, 1980; senior fellow and co-director of Studies in the Regulation of Economic Activity, Brookings Institution, 1970-73; chairman, Fourth Annual Conference on Telecommunications Policy Research, 1975-76, and Los Angeles School Monitoring Committee, 1978-79. Has testified on professional sports, drug regulation, airline regulation, and regulatory reform before several Congressional committees. Member, Commerce Technical Advisory Board Panel on Venture Capital, 1968-69; member of advisory council, National Science Foundation, 1975 and 1978-82, Senate Committee on Government Operations, 1975-77, Jet Propulsion Laboratory, 1976-81, National Aeronautics and Space Administration, 1978-81, and Committee for Economic Development, 1979-82. Consultant to numerous corporations and governmental agencies and commissions, including U.S. Department of Justice, 1974-77 and 1979-81, RAND Corp., 1974—, Federal Communications Commission, 1977-81, and Department of Energy, 1979. *Member:* American Economic Association, Sierra Club. *Awards, honors:* National Science Foundation fellow, 1963-64; book award, National Association of Educational Broadcasters, 1974, for *Economic Aspects of Television Regulation.*

WRITINGS: Reforming Regulation: An Evaluation of the Ash Council Report, Brookings Institution, 1971; (with Merton J. Peck and John J. McGowan) *Economic Aspects of Television Regulation,* Brookings Institution, 1973; (editor and contributor) *Government and the Sports Business,* Brookings Institution, 1974.

Contributor: *Increasing Understanding of Public Problems and Policies,* Farm Foundation, 1969; John P. Crecine, editor, *Financing the Metropolis: Public Policy in Urban Economics, the Urban Affairs Annual Reviews IV,* Sage Publications, 1970; (with Peck and McGowan) *On the Cable: Report of the Sloan Commission on Cable Communications,* McGraw, 1971; (with William Capron) Capron, editor, *Technological Change in Regulated Industries,* Brookings Institution, 1971; *Compendium on Price and Wage Controls: Now and the Outlook for 1973,* Joint Economic Committee, U.S. Congress, 1972; Rolla Edward Park, editor, *The Role of Analysis in Regulatory Decisionmaking: The Case of Cable Television,* Heath, 1973; *The Changing Role of the Public and Private Sectors in Health Care,* National Health Council, 1973; *Government Policies and Technological Innovation,* Volumes I and II, National Technical Information Service, 1974; *The Economics of Federal Subsidy Programs,* Part VIII: *Selected Subsidies,* U.S. Government Printing Office, 1974.

William G. Shephard, editor, *Public Policies toward Business: Readings and Cases,* Irwin, 1975; Neil H. Jacoby, editor, *The Business-Government Relationship in American Society: A Reassessment,* University of California Press, 1975; *Controls on Health Care,* National Academy of Sciences, 1975; W. B. Littrell and G. Sjoberg, editors, *Current Issues in Social Policy,* Sage Publications, 1976; Henry Owen and Charles L. Schultze, editors, *Setting National Priorities: The Next Ten Years,* Brookings Institution, 1976; (with Paul A. Thomas) *Research with Recombinant DNA,* National Academy of Sciences, 1977; (with others) Paul W. MacAvoy, editor, *Deregulation of Cable Television,* American Enterprise Institute, 1977; W. S. Moore, editor, *Regulatory Reform,* American Enterprise Institute, 1978; Robert F. Lanzillotti, editor, *Economic Effects of Government-Mandated Costs,* Public Policy Center, University of Florida, 1978; (with John A. Ferejohn and Robert E. Forsythe) Vernon L. Smith, editor, *Research in Experimental Economics,* Volume I, Jai Press, 1979; Michael L. Dertouzos and Joel Moses, editors, *The Future Impact of Computers and Information Processing,* M.I.T. Press, 1979; (with Ferejohn and Forsythe) Clifford S. Russell, editor, *Collective Decisionmaking,* Resources for the Future (Washington, D.C.), 1979; (with Alain Enthoven) Stuart H. Altman and Robert Blendon, editors, *Medical Technology: The Culprit behind Health Care Costs,* Sun Valley Forum on National Health, U.S. Department of Health, Education, and Welfare, 1979.

Stephen L. Feldman and Robert M. Wirtshafter, editors, *On the Economics of Solar Energy,* Heath, 1980; Walter Adams, editor, *The Structure of American Industry,* 6th edition, Macmillan, 1982.

Author of reports for the President and Attorney General of the United States, 1979; author of research reports for organizations, including Brookings Institution, National Science Foundation, Federal Communications Commission, Exxon Research Foundation, and Department of Energy. Contributor to numerous congressional reports and hearings; contributor to proceedings of Conference on Communications Policy Research, 1973, Conference on the Economics of Professional Sports, 1974, Future Planning Conference, 1976, and Symposium on Media Concentration, 1978. Contributor of articles to professional journals, including *Administrative Law Reform, American Economic Review, Review of Social Economics, Yale Law Journal, American Behavioral Scientist,* and *American Political Science Review;* contributor of reviews to *Engineering and Science, Journal of Economic Literature,* and *Science;* contributor of articles to *Pasadena Star-News, Los Angeles Times,* and *San Francisco Chronicle.*

WORK IN PROGRESS: Reforms of Environmental Regulation; Energy Policy Analysis; Group Decisionmaking Processes.

SIDELIGHTS: "Like many applied economists, I try to keep one foot in the professional literature and the other in communicating with non-economists," Roger G. Noll told *CA.* "Economic analysis provides a fascinating perspective from which to analyze how people and organizations behave in certain kinds of settings, and how our economic institutions can be made to produce better results. And, because so much of what government does amounts to allocating economic resources, economics also has something to say about political institutions. The old, nineteenth-century discipline of political economy—a marriage of politics and economics—is making a comeback, and I am lucky to witness the renaissance."

BIOGRAPHICAL/CRITICAL SOURCES: Washington Post, September 26, 1971.

* * *

NORMAN, John
See **LANGE, John Frederick, Jr.**

* * *

NOUVEAU, Arthur
See **WHITCOMB, Ian**

O

O'BRIEN, Darcy 1939-

PERSONAL: Born July 16, 1939, in Los Angeles, Calif.; son of George J. (a film actor) and Marguerite (Churchill) O'Brien; married Ruth Ellen Berke, August 26, 1961 (divorced, 1969); children: Molly Marguerite. *Education:* Princeton University, A.B., 1961; University of California, Berkeley, M.A., 1963, Ph.D., 1965; Pembroke College, Cambridge, graduate study, 1963-64. *Politics:* Independent. *Religion:* None. *Office:* Department of English, University of Tulsa, Tulsa, Okla. 74104.

CAREER: Pomona College, Claremont, Calif., instructor, 1965-66, assistant professor, 1966-70, associate professor, 1970-75, professor of English, 1975-78; University of Tulsa, Tulsa, Okla., graduate professor of English, 1978—. Resident fellow in Irish literature, Center for Advanced Study, 1969-70. *Member:* Modern Language Association of America, James Joyce Society, Authors Guild, Authors League of America, P.E.N. *Awards, honors:* Woodrow Wilson fellowship; Fulbright fellowship; Mellon Foundation grant; Guggenheim fellowship; Ernest Hemingway Award, 1978, for *A Way of Life, Like Any Other*.

WRITINGS: The Conscience of James Joyce, Princeton University Press, 1968; *W. R. Rodgers,* Bucknell University Press, 1971; *Patrick Kavanagh,* Bucknell University Press, 1975; *A Way of Life, Like Any Other,* Norton, 1978; *The Silver Spooner,* Simon & Schuster, 1981. Contributor to *Modern Fiction Studies, New York, New York Times Magazine,* and other publications.

WORK IN PROGRESS: A novel entitled *Only for a While.*

SIDELIGHTS: Darcy O'Brien's first novel, *A Way of Life, Like Any Other,* is a fictionalized account of his own boyhood as the son of two former Hollywood stars. "It's a half-comic, half-tragic memoir," O'Brien told Wayne Warga of the *Los Angeles Times.* "I used to say it was all made-up, but it's really half-autobiographical." The *New Yorker* critic calls the book "an eccentric, cynical, and sometimes exceedingly funny first novel" and "the most literate 'Hollywood novel' to have appeared in years."

O'Brien told *CA:* "It took me too many years to realize how much I am the child of my parents, who were both fine actors. Now I see my fiction as a performing art, written to please an audience and myself. I do not know who or what that audience is, so I imagine an audience of my friends and family, assuming that among us we know best."

BIOGRAPHICAL/CRITICAL SOURCES: Times Literary Supplement, April 24, 1969, October 21, 1977; *Sewanee Review,* July, 1969; *Observer,* August 21, 1977; *Listener,* September 22, 1977; *New Yorker,* February 6, 1978, October 5, 1981; *New York Times Book Review,* April 9, 1978; *Hudson Review,* summer, 1978; *Saturday Review,* August, 1981; *Los Angeles Times,* January 7, 1982.

* * *

O'BROIN, Leon 1902-

PERSONAL: Surname is pronounced "O'Brin"; born November 10, 1902, in Dublin, Ireland; son of J. P. and Mary (Killeen) Byrne; married Cait O'Reilly, August 19, 1925; children: Eimear, Coilin, Eithne O'Broin Winder, Noirin, Blanaid O'Broin MacGinty. *Education:* Attended University College, Dublin, 1922-23; and King's Inns, 1923-24. *Home:* St. Raphael, 128 Stillorgan Rd., Dublin 4, Ireland.

CAREER: Called to the Bar, Dublin, Ireland, 1924; associated with the Department of Finance, Ireland, 1924-47; Government of Irish Republic, Department of Posts and Telegraphs, Dublin, secretary general, 1947-67. *Member:* Royal Irish Academy (senior vice-president, 1976), Irish Historical Society (president, 1974-76), Military History Society of Ireland (vice-president). *Awards, honors:* J.D., National University of Ireland, 1966.

WRITINGS: The Unfortunate Mr. Robert Emmet, Clonmore & Reynolds, 1958; *Dublin Castle and the 1916 Rising,* Helicon, 1966, revised edition, New York University Press, 1971; *Chief Secretary: Augustine Birrell in Ireland,* Archon Books, 1969; *Fenian Fever: An Anglo-American Dilemma,* New York University Press, 1971; *The Prime Informer: A Suppressed Scandal,* Sidgwick & Jackson, 1971; *Revolutionary Underground: The Story of the Irish Republican Brotherhood,* Macmillan, 1976; *Michael Collins,* Macmillan, 1980; *Frank Dutt,* Macmillan, 1982; *Joseph Brennan: Civil Servant and Central Bank Governor,* Institute of Public Administration (Dublin), 1982.

* * *

ODYSSEUS
See JOHNSON, Donald McI(ntosh)

OGILVIE, Gordon (Bryant) 1934-

PERSONAL: Born May 8, 1934, in Christchurch, New Zealand; son of Maxwell Gordon (an orchardist) and Margaret (a nurse; maiden name, Bryant) Ogilvie; married Elisabeth Hanna (a librarian and writer), August 27, 1960; children: Frances Anne, Margaret Lynley, Susan Jennifer. *Education:* University of Canterbury, B.A., 1955; Victoria University of Wellington, M.A., 1956; Post Primary Teachers College, teaching certificate, 1957. *Religion:* Church of England. *Home and office:* 5 Centaurus Rd., Christchurch, Canterbury, New Zealand.

CAREER: Supply teacher in London, England, 1958-59; high school teacher in Christchurch, New Zealand, 1960-68; St. Andrew's College, Christchurch, teacher of English, 1969—, head of department, 1970—. *Member:* English Teachers Association, Post Primary Teachers Association, New Zealand Historical Association, New Zealand Association for Teachers of English, English Review Committee, Historic Places Trust, Aviation Historical Society, Museum of Transport and Technology, Highland Pipers Association.

WRITINGS: St. Mary's Heathcote Centennial History, Willis & Aiken, 1960; *Moonshine Country,* Caxton Press (Christchurch), 1971; *The Riddle of Richard Pearse,* Tuttle, 1974, revised edition, 1975; *The Christchurch Port Hills,* Reed, 1978; *Historic Buildings of the South Island,* Cassells, 1982; (contributor) *Introducing Denis Glover,* Longman Paul, 1982. Contributor to journals, and newspapers.

WORK IN PROGRESS: A history of Banks Peninsula, Canterbury; a biography of an early Canterbury pioneer; a children's novel based on life in pioneer times in Christchurch; poetry.

SIDELIGHTS: Gordon Ogilvie told *CA:* "Writing can be a lonely and frustrating job, but I work at it whenever I have a spare moment at the outer edges of the day, or in longer bursts during the school holidays. I can't afford to risk writing as my main breadwinner, so it has to remain an absorbing hobby. I write in a crabbed longhand and my wife, a history graduate and former librarian, helps with the proofreading. I'm particularly interested in historical and biographical writing, which gives me the chance to meet many fascinating people well outside my normal range of teaching contacts." Ogilvie's books have been adapted for television and radio documentaries.

* * *

OLCHESKI, Bill 1925-

PERSONAL: Born July 20, 1925, in Pennsylvania; son of Stanley (an electrician) and Julia (Gruzeski) Olcheski; married Rosemary Breslin, September 5, 1953; children: Julie (Mrs. James Stirling), Bill, Jr., Cathy A., Susan, James. *Education:* University of Missouri, B.J., 1950. *Politics:* Independent. *Religion:* Roman Catholic. *Home:* 6711 Moly Dr., Falls Church, Va. 22046. *Office:* Olcheski Enterprises, 450 West Broad St., Falls Church, Va. 22046.

CAREER: Elmira Star Gazette, Elmira, N.Y., feature writer, 1951; *Air Force Times,* Washington, D.C., associate editor, 1953-65; owner of B&W Stamp Co., 1956—; *Federal Times,* Washington, D.C., editor, 1965-72; Olcheski Enterprises (public relations firm), Falls Church, Va., president, 1972—; teacher of local adult education courses in public relations, 1975—; first vice-president of Falls Church (Va.) Chamber of Commerce, 1976—; senior editor/writer, Federal Deposit Insurance Corporation, 1980—. *Military service:* U.S. Army, Infantry, 1943-46; served in the Philippines and Okinawa. U.S. Air Force, information officer, 1951-53. *Awards, honors:* National University Extension Award, 1980.

WRITINGS: (Editor) Bernard Haldane, *Career Satisfaction and Success,* American Management Association, 1974; *Beginning Stamp Collecting,* McKay, 1976; *How to Specialize in Stamp Collecting,* McKay, 1981; *100 Trivia Quizzes for Stamp Collectors,* American Philatelic Society, in press. Also author of correspondence course in stamp collecting for Pennsylvania State University. Stamp editor, Army Times Publications, 1953-72. Contributor to *Stamp Collector, Stamp Wholesaler, Scott's Monthly Journal,* and *Reader's Digest.*

SIDELIGHTS: Bill Olcheski began collecting stamps in a military hospital in 1952. He told *CA* that he is "vitally interested in stamps and the people who collect them. I am kept busy on the lecture circuit and in work with clubs promoting stamp collecting as a family hobby."

* * *

OLSON, Alan M(elvin) 1939-

PERSONAL: Born January 7, 1939, in Minneapolis, Minn.; son of Melvin Olaf (a farmer and painter) and Luella (Randall) Olson; married Janet Pederson (a teacher and artist), July 1, 1961; children: Maren Kirsten, Sonja Astrid. *Education:* St. Olaf College, B.A., 1961; Luther Theological Seminary, M.Div., 1965; Nashotah House Episcopal Theological Seminary, additional graduate study, 1966-67; Boston University, Ph.D., 1973; Eberhard-Karls-Universitat Tubingen, Ph.D., 1982. *Politics:* Independent. *Home:* 20 Benjamin Rd., Belmont, Mass. 02178. *Office:* Department of Religious Studies, Boston University, 232 Bay State Rd., Boston, Mass. 02215.

CAREER: Ordained Lutheran minister, 1965. Vicar of Lutheran church in Garden Grove, Calif., 1963-64; assistant pastor of church in Oconomowoc, Wis., 1965-69; Boston University, Boston, Mass., assistant professor of philosophy and theology, 1969-71, lecturer in theology, 1972-73, assistant professor of philosophy and religion, 1973—, executive assistant to the dean of School of Theology, 1972-73, member of board of directors of Institute of Philosophy of Religion and Philosophy of Theology, 1973—, associate chairman of department of religion, 1980—. Lecturer at Emmanuel College, Boston, Mass., 1970-72. *Member:* American Philosophical Association, American Academy of Religion, Boston Theological Society.

WRITINGS: (Editor) *Disguises of the Demonic: Contemporary Perspectives on the Power of Evil,* Association Press, 1975; *Transcendence and Hermeneutics: An Interpretation of the Philosophy of Karl Jaspers,* Nijhoff (Amsterdam), 1979; (editor) *Myth, Symbol, and Reality,* University of Notre Dame Press, 1980; (editor) *Transcendence and the Sacred,* University of Notre Dame Press, 1981; (co-author) *The Seeing Eye: Hermeneutic Phenomenology in the Study of Religion,* Pennsylvania State University Press, 1982.

WORK IN PROGRESS: Mysticism and Modern Philosophy: The Hegelian Mediation.

SIDELIGHTS: Alan M. Olson writes: "As I am preoccupied with the philosophy of religion in practically everything I do, it is entirely natural for me to view the act of writing as the most demanding and also the most satisfying form of meditation possible—as the externalization, so to speak in Plato's words, of 'the soul's internal dialogue with itself,' for it is in just this externalization that this dialogue becomes *dia-logos* in the true sense of the word."

OLSON, Richard Paul 1934-

PERSONAL: Born July 19, 1934, in Rapid City, S.D.; son of Ole (a minister) and Hazel (a county auditor; maiden name, Doty) Olson; married Mary Ann Edland, June 3, 1957; children: Julie, Lisa, Laurie. *Education:* Sioux Falls College, B.A. (with honors), 1956; Andover Newton Theological School, B.D., 1959, S.T.M. (with honors), 1960; Boston University, Ph.D., 1972. *Residence:* Boulder, Colo. *Office:* First Baptist Church, 1237 Pine, Boulder, Colo.

CAREER: Ordained American Baptist minister in 1959; minister in Parker, S.D., 1960-63, and in Beaver Dam, Wis., 1963-67; associate minister in Lexington, Mass., 1967-71; First Baptist Church, Racine, Wis., senior pastor, 1971-80; First Baptist Church, Boulder, Colo., pastor, 1980—. Professor at Sioux Falls College, 1961-62; teacher at Beaver Dam Vocational Technical School, 1965-67; field education supervisor at Harvard Divinity School, 1970-71; lecturer at College of Racine, 1972-74, and Holy Redeemer College, 1973-74; counselor at Addiction Center of Racine, 1973-80. President of Downtown Cooperative Parish of Racine, 1974, 1979. Member of advisory committee on desegregation of Racine Unified School District, 1974-76, and of Funeral and Memorial Society of Racine and Kenosha, 1974-76. *Member:* American Society of Christian Ethics, Ministers Council of American Baptist Churches.

WRITINGS: A Job or a Vocation, Thomas Nelson, 1973; *Mid-Life: A Time to Discover, a Time to Decide,* Judson, 1980; *Changing Male Roles in Today's World,* Judson, 1982; (with Wayne G. Johnson) *Each Day a Gift,* Morrow, 1982. Contributor to *Directions 80, Christian Home, Baptist Leader, Adult Class, High Call,* and *Foundations.*

WORK IN PROGRESS: Two books on the church's ministry with remarried people, with Carole Pia-Terry and Dela Pia-Terry, for Judson.

* * *

OPPEN, George 1908-

PERSONAL: Born April 24, 1908, in New Rochelle, N.Y.; son of George A. and Elsie (Rothfeld) Oppen; married Mary Colby, August 11, 1928; children: Linda (Mrs. Alexander Mourelatos). *Education:* Attended public schools in California. *Home:* 2811 Polk St., San Francisco, Calif. 94109.

CAREER: Poet. Founder and publisher, with wife, Mary Oppen, of To Publishers, Paris, France, 1930-33; Objectivist Press Co-Op, New York, N.Y., member, 1934-36; Workers Alliance, Brooklyn, N.Y., and Utica, N.Y., organizer, beginning 1935; worked in factory in Detroit, Mich.; cabinet maker and building contractor in Los Angeles, Calif., late 1940s; moved to Mexico, 1950; operated furniture factory in Mexico City, Mexico, during the 1950s; returned to the United States, 1958. *Military service:* U.S. Army, 1942-45; wounded in combat; received the "normal 'decorations' and condolences." *Awards, honors:* Pulitzer Prize, 1969, for *Of Being Numerous;* American Academy and Institute of Arts and Letters award, 1980.

WRITINGS—Poetry, except as indicated: *Discrete Series,* Objectivist Press, 1934, reprinted, Asphodel Book Shop, 1966; *The Materials,* New Directions, 1962; *This in Which,* New Directions, 1965; *Of Being Numerous,* New Directions, 1968; *Alpine: Poems,* Perishable Press, 1969; (author of foreword) Paul Vangelisti, *Communion,* Red Hill, 1970; *Collected Poems,* Fulcrum Press, 1972; *Seascape: Needle's Eye,* Sumac Press (Fremont, Mich.), 1973; *The Collected Poems of George Oppen, 1929-1975,* New Directions, 1975; *Primitive,* Black Sparrow Press, 1978.

Work appears in anthologies, including: *An "Objectivists" Anthology,* edited by Louis Zukofsky, To Publishers, 1932; *Active Anthology,* edited by Ezra Pound, Faber, 1933; *Mark in Time: Portraits and Poetry/San Francisco,* edited by Robert E. Johnson and Nick Harvey, Glide, 1971. Contributor to *Poetry, Hound and Horn, San Francisco Review, Massachusetts Review, New Yorker, Nation,* and other periodicals.

SIDELIGHTS: "George Oppen," writes Michael Adams in *The Dictionary of Literary Biography,* "has had one of the most unusual careers of any American poet." Oppen published his first book of poetry in 1934, but didn't publish his second book until some 28 years later. Those intervening years were taken up with political activity, Oppen and his wife joining the Communist Party in 1935 and working as organizers for the party for a number of years. Oppen wrote no poetry while politically active. He "never believed," L. S. Dembo of the *Nation* writes, "that politics could be made into poetry or, conversely, that poetry could have any effect on social conditions." When, in 1950, Oppen faced government pressure to inform on his friends in the Communist Party, he moved to Mexico, where he stayed until 1958. Shortly after returning to the United States, Oppen began to write poetry again and has continued to write and publish ever since.

A member of the Objectivist school, Oppen concerns himself with the question, as Dick Allen of *Antioch Review* states, "How can the poet communicate a realization of the concrete object *as object* without drawing the reader's attention to *the way* in which he communicates?" Dembo believes that the "aesthetic qualities of objects or events—apprehended not in terms of their associations or conventional meaning but in terms of their form or motion—[are] considered by Oppen to be 'empirical.'" Oppen's writing career, Jonathan Galassi of *Poetry* believes, has been "a life-long confrontation between an unimpeachably free spirit's sense of order and 'a world of things.'" Irwin Ehrenpreis of the *New York Review of Books* sees this confrontation as "the effort of the mind to reach clarity of vision by turning always upon itself, travelling back and forth between things and words, reconsidering and correcting earlier impressions or ponderings." "Oppen," writes Michael Heller in *American Poetry Review,* "stands alone in this regard: that his poetry is not composed of the effects of modern life upon the self, but is rather our most profound investigation of it." Oppen has commented that he is "really concerned with the substantive, with the subject of the sentence, with what we are talking about, and not rushing over the subject matter in order to make a comment about it."

Because of this concern for clarity, Oppen's poetry is lean and precise. He has, according to several observers, a "distrust of language" that leads him to use words sparingly. "Nothing," writes Hugh Kenner in the *New York Times Book Review,* "better characterizes Oppen than his wariness about the language itself, this distrust of inherent fluency. In a review of *Seascape: Needle's Eye* for *Poetry,* Mark Perlberg comments: "Oppen seems here to distrust most of the processes of language. Perhaps in an attempt to achieve the purest kind of statement, perfect in its honesty, he seems wary of rhythm, of patterns of rhythm, of connections, [and] of the music a poem can make." Oppen's spare poems "are tightly wrought meditations," according to Paul Zweig of *Partisan Review,* "which do not so much define as surround their subject with tentative thrusts of meaning. Abstractions and carefully observed details mingle to produce a line that is almost sculptural in its precision."

Oppen's style works most successfully in his Pulitzer Prize-winning collection *Of Being Numerous,* an examination of the city as man's highest expression of himself. The title poem consists of 40 separate sections, "each virtually a poem in itself," David Ignatow comments in *New Leader,* "but related through subject and, primarily, by a transitional mode of writing. The poet progresses from self-doubt and self-searching through the artifacts of the city, to a moment in which his mind is revealed to itself as its own strength." *Of Being Numerous,* Zweig maintains, "contains some of the finest poetry Oppen has written, and presents a difficult challenge to the reader, for the poem proceeds by side leaps and deft associations. Single words are caught up from a preceding stanza, and expanded into a constellation of images. Sharply evoked cityscapes issue into elusive statements of feeling or philosophy." Galassi describes the book as "a serial meditation on man's situation as a social animal, as the member of a tribe. Characteristically, it is highly dense, allusive, [and] laden with historical references." Zweig concludes that the collection's title poem is "Oppen's major achievement to date, and one of the most important single poems to be written in recent years."

BIOGRAPHICAL/CRITICAL SOURCES: *Poetry,* July, 1934, August, 1966, August, 1969, January, 1975, June, 1975, October, 1976, December, 1976; *Hudson Review,* Volume XIX, number 1, 1966, summer, 1976; *Antioch Review,* Volume XXVI, number 2, 1966; *New Leader,* July 8, 1968; *Contemporary Literature,* spring, 1969, spring, 1970; *Stony Brook,* fall, 1969; *Nation,* November 24, 1969; *New York Times Book Review,* December 28, 1969, October 19, 1975, December 31, 1978.

Hugh Kenner, *The Pound Era,* University of California Press, 1971; *Iowa Review,* winter, 1972; *Encounter,* August, 1973; *Partisan Review,* Volume XL, number 2, 1973; Kenner, *A Homemade World: The American Modernist Writers,* Knopf, 1975; Michael Hamburger, *Art as Second Nature: Occasional Pieces, 1950-74,* Carcanet Press, 1975; *American Poetry Review,* March/April, 1975; *Ironwood,* #5, 1975; *New York Review of Books,* January 22, 1976; *Parnassus,* spring-summer, 1976; *Contemporary Literary Criticism,* Gale, Volume VII, 1977, Volume XIII, 1980; Mary Oppen, *Meaning a Life: An Autobiography,* Black Sparrow Press, 1978; *Paideuma,* winter, 1978; *Texas Quarterly,* spring, 1978; *The Dictionary of Literary Biography,* Volume V: *American Poets since World War II,* Gale, 1980; *Times Literary Supplement,* June 13, 1980; *George Oppen: Man and Poet,* Poetry Foundation, 1981.†

* * *

ORBAAN, Albert F.

PERSONAL: Born in Rome, Italy; became U.S. citizen, 1937; son of Jan A.F. and Alice (Baker) Orbaan; married Harriett Robertson (a fashion illustrator), November 7, 1945. *Education:* Attended University of Neuchatel. *Politics:* Democrat. *Home and office:* 102 East 22nd St., New York, N.Y.

CAREER: Author and illustrator. Rewrite man on the foreign news desks of Havas News Agency (French) and Aneta (Netherlands News Agency) in New York, N.Y., prior to World War II. *Military service:* U.S. Army, Intelligence Corps, World War II; served in European Theater; received two battle stars. *Awards, honors:* Boy's Club of America Gold Medal, 1965, for *Powder and Steel.*

WRITINGS—Author and illustrator: *With Banners Flying,* John Day, 1960; *Powder and Steel: Notable Battles and Campaigns of the 1800's from New Orleans to the Zulu War,* John Day, 1963; *Forked Lightning: The Story of General Philip H. Sheridan,* Hawthorn, 1964; *Duel in the Shadows: True Accounts of Anti-Nazi Underground Warfare during World War II,* Doubleday, 1965; *K-9 Alert,* John Day, 1967; *Dogs against Crime: True Accounts of Canine Training and Exploits in Worldwide Police Work, Past and Present,* John Day, 1968; *Rare and Rugged Sports,* Putnam, 1973.

Illustrator: Patricia Miles Martin, *A Long Ago Christmas,* Putnam, 1968; Jef Last, *The Bamboo School in Bali,* John Day, 1969; Arthur George Joseph Whitehouse, *The Laughing Falcon,* Putnam, 1969; Jean Muir, *The Adventures of Grizzly Adams,* Putnam, 1970; Helen Markley Miller, *The San Francisco Earthquake and Fire,* Putnam, 1970; Lorraine Henriod, *I Know a Grocer,* Putnam, 1970; Curtis W. Casewit, *The Adventures of Snowshoe Thompson,* Putnam, 1970.†

* * *

OSBORNE, Juanita Tyree 1916-

PERSONAL: Born August 31, 1916, in Irvine, Ky.; daughter of Charles G. (in railroad business) and Sally (Turpin) Tyree; married Harry C. Osborne (in insurance business), February 6, 1938; children: Jerry, Robert, Charles, Linda. *Education:* Attended Modesto Junior College. *Religion:* Presbyterian. *Home and office:* 1310 Stage Ave., Memphis, Tenn. 38127.

CAREER: Writer.

WRITINGS—Gothic novels; published by Bouregy, except as indicated: *Tornado,* Ace Books, 1954; *The Shrinking Pond,* 1974; *The Wind-Bells of Lovingwood,* 1974; *Rendezvous at the Hallows,* 1975; *The Cottage at Barron Ridge,* 1975; *Ashes of Windrow,* 1976; *Shadow over Wyndham Hall,* 1976; *The House on Hibiscus Hill,* 1977; *Dark Season at Aerie,* 1977; *Dwellers of Riven Oak,* 1978; *Peril at Dorrough,* 1979; *Fury of Fenlon,* 1979; *The Curse of Wayfield,* 1980; *The Dark Bayou,* 1980; *A Nest of Hawks,* 1980; *Terror at Tolliver Hall,* 1981; *Cry of the Whippoorwill,* 1981. Editor of *Scribblings* (literary magazine), Modesto Junior College, 1934-36.

WORK IN PROGRESS: *Web of Haefen;* another gothic novel.

SIDELIGHTS: A number of Juanita Osborne's gothic romances have been published in foreign markets, including Germany and Denmark.

* * *

OTT, David Jackson 1934-1975

PERSONAL: Born January 13, 1934, in Ft. Worth, Tex.; died May 19, 1975; son of William O. (a physician) and Margaret (Smith) Ott; married Mary Springer, June 23, 1956; married Attiat Farag (a professor of economics) July 2, 1964; children: Lisa. *Education:* North Texas State University, B.A., 1955, M.A., 1956; University of Maryland, Ph.D., 1961.

CAREER: Brookings Institution, Washington, D.C., economics fellow, 1959-60, research associate, beginning 1961; Southern Methodist University, Dallas, Tex., assistant professor, 1960-63, associate professor, 1963-68; Clark University, Worcester, Mass., professor of economics, 1969-75. Consultant, U.S. Treasury, 1962. Council of Economic Advisors, staff member, 1965. *Military service:* U.S. Army, 1956-57; became captain in reserve. *Member:* American Economic Association, American Finance Association, American Association of University Professors.

WRITINGS: (With Allan H. Meltzer) *Federal Tax Treatment of State and Local Securities,* Brookings Institution, 1963, reprinted, Greenwood Press, 1980; (with wife, Attiat F. Ott) *Federal Budget Policy,* Brookings Institution, 1965, 3rd edition, 1977; (with A. F. Ott) *Simulation of Revenue and Tax Structure Implications of Broadening the Federal Income Tax Base*, American Bar Foundation, 1968; (with A. F. Ott) *Personal Income Taxation*, General Learning Press, 1972; (with A. F. Ott and Jang H. Yoo) *Macroeconomic Theory*, McGraw, 1975.

Published by American Enterprise Institute for Public Policy Research: (With others) *Nixon, McGovern, and the Federal Budget*, 1972; (with others) *Public Claims on United States Output: Federal Budget Output Options in the Last Half of the Seventies*, 1973; (with others) *State and Local Finances in the Last Half of the Seventies*, 1975; (with A. F. Ott) *Projections of State-Local Expenditures*, 1975; (with A. F. Ott) *The 1976 Budget: Short-Run Stabilization and the Long-Run Budget Outlook*, 1975. Contributor to periodicals.†

P

PAGE, Norman 1930-

PERSONAL: Born May 8, 1930, in Kettering, England; son of Frederick Arthur and Theresa Ann (Price) Page; married Jean Hampton, March 29, 1958; children: Camilla, Benjamin, Barnaby, Matthew. *Education:* Emmanuel College, Cambridge, B.A., 1951, M.A., 1955; University of Leeds, Ph.D., 1968. *Office:* Department of English, University of Alberta, Edmonton, Alberta, Canada T6G 2E1.

CAREER: High school teacher of English in England, 1951-60; Ripon College of Education, Yorkshire, England, principal lecturer in English and head of department, 1960-69; University of Alberta, Edmonton, assistant professor, 1969-70, associate professor, 1970-75, professor of English, 1975—. *Awards, honors:* Canada Council research grants, 1971, 1973, and 1975; Guggenheim fellowship, 1979-80; University of Leicester honorary visiting research fellow, 1979-80, 1982; Royal Society of Canada fellow, 1982.

WRITINGS: (Editor) Charles Dickens, *Bleak House*, Penguin Books, 1971; *The Language of Jane Austen*, Blackwell, 1972; *Speech in the English Novel*, Longman, 1973; (editor) *Wilkie Collins: The Critical Heritage*, Routledge & Kegan Paul, 1974; *Thomas Hardy*, Routledge & Kegan Paul, 1977; *E. M. Forster's Posthumous Fiction*, University of Victoria, 1977; (editor) Thomas Hardy, *Jude the Obscure*, Norton, 1978; (editor) *Thomas Hardy: The Writer and His Background*, Bell & Hyman, 1980; (editor) *D. H. Lawrence: Interviews and Recollections*, Macmillan, 1981; (editor) *Nabokov: The Critical Heritage*, Routledge & Kegan Paul, 1982. Also contributor of chapters to scholarly books. Contributor of articles and book reviews to professional and scholarly journals.

WORK IN PROGRESS: A. E. Housman: A Critical Biography; A Dickens Companion; Tennyson: Interviews and Recollections; Henry James: Interviews and Recollections; A Kipling Companion; A Conrad Companion; a biography of Edward FitzGerald.

* * *

PAHZ, (Anne) Cheryl Suzanne 1949-
  (Cheryl Goldfeder; Zan Paz, a pseudonym)

PERSONAL: Original married name, Anne Cheryl Goldfeder; name legally changed; born January 29, 1949, in Ypsilanti, Mich.; daughter of Morris (a businessman) and Shirley (Bender) McConnell; married Kenneth James Goldfeder (name legally changed to James Alon Pahz; a consultant for programs for the deaf), August 27, 1969. *Education:* Attended Ringling Art School; University of Tennessee, B.A., 1972. *Religion:* Jewish. *Residence:* Shepherd, Mich.

CAREER: Illustrator, writer, and teacher. Knoxville County Library, Knoxville, Tenn., former technical assistant; co-founder, with husband James Alon Pahz, of Moondog Press. Poster designs are on display in the United States and abroad. *Member:* Society of Children's Book Writers, International Association of Parents of the Deaf, National Association of the Deaf, National Association of the Deaf and Mute in Israel, National Congress of Jewish Deaf. *Awards, honors:* First place in design, Jewish Agency in Israel, 1974, for a poster design made for World Union of Jewish Students Institute.

WRITINGS—Under name Cheryl Goldfeder; with husband, Jim Goldfeder: *The Girl Who Wouldn't Talk* (self-illustrated), National Association of the Deaf, 1975.

Under name Cheryl Suzanne Pahz; with husband, James Alon Pahz: *Robin Sees a Song*, National Association of the Deaf, 1977; *Will Love Be Enough?*, National Association of the Deaf, 1977; *Total Communication: The Meaning behind the Movement to Expand Educational Opportunities for Deaf Children*, C. C Thomas, 1978.

Author, with James Alon Pahz, of bi-weekly column, "Small Press Review," for the University of Tennessee's *Daily Beacon*, beginning 1976.

SIDELIGHTS: Cheryl Suzanne Pahz, with her husband, James Alon Pahz, is an advocate of the "total communication" method of educating deaf children. She writes: "Everywhere there are children [who,] despite all of the wishes of parents and the expectations of teachers, do not develop communication skills through auditory channels. But communication is the key word. It is communication that makes a small world larger—and, if communication cannot be achieved auditorily, then there is still another way: the language of signs and the manual alphabet."

BIOGRAPHICAL/CRITICAL SOURCES: Tennessee Alumnus, Volume 55, number 2, spring, 1975; *Deaf American*, April, 1975.†

PAHZ, James Alon 1943-
(James Goldfeder; Jim Goldfeder; A. Paz, a pseudonym)

PERSONAL: Original name, Kenneth James Goldfeder; name legally changed; born September 11, 1943, in Chattanooga, Tenn.; son of Abraham (a physician) and Katherine (Suggs) Goldfeder; married Cheryl McConnell (a writer, illustrator, and teacher), August 27, 1969. *Education:* Attended Ohio Wesleyan University, 1961-63; Tennessee Temple College, B.A., 1967; University of Tennessee, M.S., 1972, M.P.H., 1975, Ed.D. candidate. *Religion:* Jewish. *Residence:* Shepherd, Mich.

CAREER: Writer and teacher. Comprehensive Service for the Deaf, Nashville, Tenn., director, 1973-74; Tennessee School for the Deaf, Knoxville, coordinator of Title I projects, 1973-74; University of Tennessee, Knoxville, teaching assistant in public health, beginning 1975. Member of Tennessee Registry of Interpreters for the Deaf. Co-founder, with wife Cheryl Suzanne Pahz, of Moondog Press.

MEMBER: International Association of Parents of the Deaf, National Association of the Deaf, National Association of the Deaf and Mute in Israel, National Association of Hearing and Speech Agencies, Professional Rehabilitation Workers with Adult Deaf, Convention of American Instructors of the Deaf, Alexander Graham Bell Association for the Deaf, Congress of Jewish Deaf, American Public Health Association, Tennessee Registry of Interpreters for the Deaf. *Awards, honors:* Certificate of community service from Chattanooga Area Council on Alcoholism and Other Substance Abuse.

WRITINGS—Under name Jim Goldfeder; with wife, Cheryl Goldfeder: *The Girl Who Wouldn't Talk*, National Association of the Deaf, 1975.

Under name James Alon Pahz; with wife, Cheryl Suzanne Pahz: *Robin Sees a Song,* National Association of the Deaf, 1977; *Will Love Be Enough?*, National Association of the Deaf, 1977; *Total Communication: The Meaning behind the Movement to Expand Educational Opportunities for Deaf Children,* C. C Thomas, 1978.

Author, with Cheryl Suzanne Pahz, of bi-weekly column, "Small Press Review," for the University of Tennessee's *Daily Beacon,* beginning 1976. Contributor to professional journals. Tennessee editor of *Silent News,* beginning 1975.

BIOGRAPHICAL/CRITICAL SOURCES: Tennessee Alumnus, Volume 55, number 2, spring, 1975; *Deaf American,* April, 1975.†

* * *

PALLEY, Marian Lief 1939-

PERSONAL: Born June 28, 1939, in New York, N.Y.; daughter of Samuel (a teacher) and Frances (a teacher; maiden name, Levy) Lief; married Howard Palley (a professor), April 21, 1961; children: Stephen, Elizabeth. *Education:* Syracuse University, B.A., 1961, M.A., 1963; New York University, Ph.D., 1966. *Home:* 11 North Townview, Newark, Del. 19711. *Office:* Department of Political Science, University of Delaware, Newark, Del. 19711.

CAREER: High school social studies teacher in New York, N.Y., 1961-62, and Wayne, N.J., 1962-63; University of Wisconsin—Milwaukee, acting instructor in political science, spring, 1966; Rutgers University, New Brunswick, N.J., assistant professor of political science at Newark College of Arts and Sciences, 1967-70, assistant professor of political science at New Brunswick campus, 1969-70; University of Delaware, Newark, assistant professor, 1970-73, associate professor, 1973-77, professor of political science, 1977—, chairperson of department, 1980—. Visiting fellow at University of Pennsylvania, 1974-75, and at Jerusalem Institute for Federal Studies, 1978.

MEMBER: American Political Science Association, American Society for Public Administration, Policy Studies Association, Pi Sigma Alpha. *Awards, honors:* American Council on Education fellow, 1974-75.

WRITINGS: (Editor with Joyce Gelb) *Political Parties and Social Change,* Associated Educational Services Corp., 1969; (editor with Gelb) *The Politics of Social Change: A Reader for the Seventies,* Holt, 1971; (with Gelb) *Tradition and Change in American Party Politics,* Crowell, 1975; (with husband, Howard Palley) *Urban America and Public Policies,* Heath, 1977; (with Preston) *Race, Sex, and Policy Problems,* Heath, 1979; (with Hale) *The Politics of Federal Grants,* Congressional Quarterly, 1981; (with Gelb) *Women and Public Policies,* Princeton University Press, 1982. Contributor to political science and behavioral science journals.

* * *

PALMER, Roy (Ernest) 1932-

PERSONAL: Born February 10, 1932, in Leicestershire, England; son of George Herbert (a truck driver) and Gwendoline (Cooper) Palmer; married Patricia Madin (a teacher), August 1, 1953; children: Simon James, Adam George, Thomas Eric. *Education:* University of Manchester, B.A., 1953, M.A., 1955. *Politics:* "Left of centre; ecologist and unilateralist." *Religion:* None. *Home:* 4 Victoria Rd., Birmingham B17 0AN, England. *Office:* Dame Elizabeth Cadbury School, Birmingham, England.

CAREER: High school teacher, 1958-61, and grammar school teacher, 1961-63, both in Yorkshire, England; Shenley Court Comprehensive School, Birmingham, England, head of modern languages department, 1963-69, deputy headmaster, 1969-72; Dame Elizabeth Cadbury School, Birmingham, headmaster, 1972—. Producer and performer on recordings and in the theater. *Military service:* British Army, 1955-57. *Member:* English Folk Dance and Song Society, Society for Oral History.

WRITINGS—Editor, except as indicated: *French Travellers in England,* Hutchinson, 1960; *Room for Company,* Cambridge University Press, 1971; *The Painful Plough,* Cambridge University Press, 1972; *Songs of the Midlands,* Norwood, 1972; *The Valiant Sailor,* Cambridge University Press, 1973; (contributor) *Folklore: Myths and Legends of Britain,* Reader's Digest Association, 1973; *Love Is Pleasing,* Cambridge University Press, 1974; *Poverty Knock,* Cambridge University Press, 1974; *A Touch on the Times,* Penguin, 1974.

(With Jon Raven) *The Rigs of the Fair,* Cambridge University Press, 1976; *Warwickshire Folklore,* Batsford, 1976; *The Rambling Soldier,* Penguin, 1977; (with A. Adams and R. Leach) *Feasts and Seasons,* four volumes, Blackie & Son, 1977-78; (with R. Leach) *Folk Music in School,* Cambridge University Press, 1978; *A Ballad History of England,* Batsford, 1979; *Birmingham Ballads,* Birmingham Education Department, 1979; *Everyman's Book of English Country Songs,* Dent, 1979; *Everyman's Book of British Ballads,* Dent, 1981; *Manchester Ballads,* Manchester Education Department, 1982. Also author of eight radio programs on the subjects of street ballads, Wellington's Army, and the Battle of Waterloo, for British Broadcasting Corp., 1982, 1983. Contributor of articles and reviews to magazines. Member of editorial board of *Folk Music Journal.*

WORK IN PROGRESS: Editing a selection of folk songs from the collection of Ralph Vaughan Williams, for Dent; continuing research on the folk song, street ballad, and on folklore.

SIDELIGHTS: Roy Palmer has produced, and performed for, Topic Records albums, "The Wide Midlands," 1971, "The Painful Plough," 1972, and "Room for Company," 1972; he produced "George Dunn," 1974, and "Cecilia Costello," 1975, both for Leader Records. Palmer was musical director and performer for "The Wellesbourne Tree" (a documentary drama), first produced in Birmingham, England at Cannon Hill Arts Centre, March, 1972; he has also acted as advisor to theatres, including the Traverse in Edinburgh, and the Duke of York's Theatre in Lancaster.

Palmer told *CA:* "I hope to have commissions for further work, possibly including a series of songs and sailors' autobiographies dealing with life at sea in the age of sail."

* * *

PALMER, Tobias
    See WEATHERS, Winston

* * *

PAPENFUSE, Edward C(arl), Jr. 1943-

PERSONAL: Born October 15, 1943, in Toledo, Ohio; son of Edward C. (an engineer) and Ruth (Wilson) Papenfuse; married Sallie Fisher (a teacher), June 19, 1965; children: Eric, David. *Education:* American University, B.A., 1965; University of Colorado, M.A., 1967; Johns Hopkins University, Ph.D., 1973. *Home:* 206 Oakdale Rd., Baltimore, Md. 21210. *Office address:* Maryland Hall of Records, P.O. Box 828, Annapolis, Md. 21404.

CAREER: American Historical Review, Washington, D.C., associate editor-bibliographer, 1970-73; Maryland Hall of Records, Annapolis, assistant state archivist, 1973-75, state archivist, 1975—. Lecturer on Maryland archives and history. *Member:* American Historical Association, Society of American Archivists, Organization of American Historians, Association for State and Local History, Maryland Historical Society. *Awards, honors:* National Endowment for the Humanities grant, 1974-76.

WRITINGS: (Compiler with Jack Phillip Greene) *The American Colonies in the Eighteenth Century,* Appleton, 1968; (with Jane W. McWilliams and Carol Tilles) *Directory of Maryland Legislators: 1635-1789,* Maryland Bicentennial Commission, 1974; *Guide to the Microfilm Edition of the Papers of Thomas Sim Lee,* Maryland Historical Society, 1974; *In Pursuit of Profit: The Annapolis Merchants in the Era of the American Revolution,* Johns Hopkins Press, 1975; (with others) *Maryland: A New Guide to the Old Line State,* Johns Hopkins Press, 1976; (editor with others) *An Inventory to the Maryland State Papers: The Revolutionary War Era 1775-1789,* Part 1, Maryland Hall of Records, 1977; (illustrator) *The Decisive Blow Is Struck,* Maryland Hall of Records, 1977; (with others) *A Guide to the Maryland Hall of Records: Local Judicial and Administrative Records on Microform,* Volume I, Maryland Hall of Records, 1978; (editor with Gregory A. Stiverson, Jr.) *Maryland Manual: 1979-1980,* Maryland Hall of Records, 1979; (editor with others) *A Biographical Dictionary of the Maryland Legislature, 1635-1789,* Volume I, Johns Hopkins Press, 1979; *Historical Maps of Maryland, 1608-1908,* Johns Hopkins Press, 1982. Contributor of articles and reviews to professional journals.

WORK IN PROGRESS: In Search of Place and Pedigree, proceedings of the Second Conference on Maryland History.

* * *

PAPPAS, Lou Seibert 1930-

PERSONAL: Born August 1, 1930, in Corvallis, Ore.; daughter of Emil E. (a wholesale grocer) and Norma (Helgesson) Seibert; married Nicholas Pappas (a consultant), November 21, 1956; children: Derek, Alexis, Christian, Niko. *Education:* Oregon State University, B.S., 1952. *Home:* 1201 Bryant St., Palo Alto, Calif. 94301.

CAREER: Sunset (magazine), Menlo Park, Calif., staff home economist, 1952-58, 1964-71; De Anza College, Cupertin, Calif., instructor in home economics, 1972-78; food editor of *Peninsula Time Tribune,* 1978—. Consultant to western food firms, and to Ortho Books. *Member:* Home Economists in Business. *Awards, honors:* Hope Chamberlain Award, Oregon State University, 1975.

WRITINGS: Crossroads of Cooking, Ritchie, 1973; *Greek Cooking,* Harper, 1973; *Party Menus,* Harper, 1974; *Bread Baking,* Nitty Gritty Productions, 1975; *Crockery Pot Cookbook,* Nitty Gritty Productions, 1975; *Egg Cookery,* 101 Productions, 1976; *Casseroles/Salads,* Nitty Gritty Productions, 1977; *Gourmet Cooking the Slim Way,* Addison-Wesley, 1977; *International Fish Cookery,* 101 Productions, 1979; *Entertaining the Slim Way,* Addison-Wesley, 1979; *Cookies,* Nitty Gritty Productions, 1981; *Entertaining in the Light Style,* 101 Productions, 1982; *Vegetable Cookery,* H.P. Books, 1982.

SIDELIGHTS: Lou Seibert Pappas told *CA:* "Writing cookbooks, for me, is a great joy, an outpouring and sharing of great culinary discoveries. It is an intensive, well-disciplined time, brimming with working with great zeal. It is a way to consummate so many pleasures of travel and dining in one small compact volume. I write because I hope to bring pleasure to others with simple, sophisticated, delectable dishes.

AVOCATIONAL INTERESTS: Travel (has been to Europe and Mexico).

* * *

PASTINE, Maureen (Diane) 1944-

PERSONAL: Born November 21, 1944, in Hays, Kan.; daughter of Gerhard Walter and Ada (Hillman) Hillman; married Jerry Joel Pastine (an electrician), February 5, 1966. *Education:* Fort Hays Kansas State College (now University), A.B., 1967; Kansas State Teachers College (now Emporia State University), M.L.S., 1970; graduate study at Fort Hays Kansas State University and University of Nebraska at Omaha. *Home:* 5028 Trenary Way, San Jose, Calif. 95118. *Office:* Library, San Jose State University, San Jose, Calif. 95192.

CAREER: High school teacher in Kingman, Kan., 1967-69, and Palco, Kan., 1970-71; University of Nebraska at Omaha, University Library, assistant head of reference department, 1971-74, acting head of department, 1974-75, head of department, 1976-77, assistant professor at University, 1974-77; University of Illinois at Urbana-Champaign, University Library, undergraduate librarian, 1977-79, reference librarian, 1979-80, associate professor at University, 1977-80; San Jose State University, University Library, San Jose, Calif., library director, 1980—.

MEMBER: American Library Association, American Association of University Professors, National Women's Studies Association, Women Library Workers, California Library Association, California Academic and Research Librarians, Beta Phi Mu. *Awards, honors:* Outstanding Service to Academic Profession Award nomination, Emporia State University, 1981; recipient of travel grants from University of Nebraska at Omaha.

WRITINGS: (With Sara Lou Williams and Peter Hernon) *Library and Library Related Publications: A Directory of Publishing Opportunities in Journals, Series, and Annuals,* Libraries Unlimited, 1973; (compiler with others) *Women's Work and Women's Studies, 1973-1974,* Women's Center, Barnard College, 1975; (contributor) Rolland E. Stevens, editor, *Supervision of Employees in Libraries,* Graduate School of Library Science, University of Illinois, 1979; (contributor with Susan Bekiares and Lucille Wert) *Library Effectiveness: A State of the Art,* American Library Association, 1980; (contributor with Melissa Cain and Kate Hammell) Paula Treichler and others, editors, *Feminist Scholarship in the Eighties,* University of Illinois Press, 1981.

Author of papers presented to professional organizations; editor of transcripts of American Library Association conference, 1981. Contributor of articles to professional journals, including *Library College Experimenter, Journal of Education for Librarianship,* and *Library Review;* contributor of reviews to *American Reference Book Annual* and *RQ;* contributor of articles to *Women's Studies Newsletter* and *Women's Studies International Quarterly.*

WORK IN PROGRESS: Research on academic libraries, educational librarianship, women's studies, and small press magazines and underground newspapers.

* * *

PATTERSON, Ward L(amont) 1933-

PERSONAL: Born December 26, 1933, in Killbuck, Ohio; son of Raymond Floyd and Florence May (Crosby) Patterson. *Education:* Cincinnati Bible Seminary, A.B., 1956, M.A., 1958; Fort Hays Kansas State College (now Fort Hays State University), M.S., 1960; graduate study at University of Melbourne, 1961, and Indiana University at Bloomington, 1972—. *Religion:* Undenominational Christian. *Home and office:* 3649 Morningside Dr., Bloomington, Ind. 47401.

CAREER: Ordained minister of Christian Church, 1958; pastor of churches in Ohio and Indiana, 1955-58, and Hays, Kan., 1958-59; Fort Hays Kansas State College (now Fort Hays State University), Hays, instructor, 1959-60; professional artist specializing in archaeological designs from the Middle East, 1965—; Indiana University at Bloomington, associate instructor in speech, 1972-75, associate minister with Campus Christian Ministry, 1974-76, campus minister, 1976—. Exhibitor at art shows; cover artist for Standard Curriculum. *Member:* Lambda Iota Tau, Phi Kappa Phi. *Awards, honors:* Rotary International student exchange fellowship, 1960, for study in Australia.

WRITINGS—Published by Standard Publishing: *Yesterday/Today,* 1974; *Struggle, Crisis, and Victory,* 1975; *At the Testing Tree,* 1978; *Wonders in the Midst,* 1979; *The Morality Maze,* 1982. Also author of studies on ethics and leadership for Standard Publishing's "New Life Teen Studies" series. Creator of "The Adventures of Alan West," an illustrated comic strip for young people. Curriculum writer for Standard Publishing. Contributor to *Christian Standard, His, Outlook,* and *Seek.*

WORK IN PROGRESS: Research on early Egyptian, Persian, Mesopotamian, and Greek art; dissertation on Grady Nutt and religious humor.

SIDELIGHTS: Ward Patterson writes: "My interests concern religion, history, archeology, art, and travel. I spent nine years abroad, traveling for seven years on a 1946 motorcycle on which I visited over thirty countries of the Middle and Far East." He has trekked 500 miles into the high Himalayas of Nepal in order to reach Mount Everest, stayed in northern Afghan villages, climbed Mount Ararat, crewed on a yacht in the Mediterranean, worked as an extra in a movie being shot by Twentieth Century-Fox in Tunisia, and made a living as a "grave-rubber" in Egypt. He has acquired an extensive collection of rubbings of ancient Middle Eastern bas-reliefs.

More recently, Patterson combines his writing career with his duties as a minister at Indiana University. He continues: "I find that the students and the college atmosphere stimulate me and help keep me in tune with contemporary trends in our society.

"My writing centers on religious subjects, though I am very interested in communication and leadership research. My graduate research has taken me into the area of religious humor and I hope to write more extensively on this subject. I find much personal fulfillment in writing, though I also find it laborious. I spent this past summer in a small trailer littered with books and articles as I camped out in Ohio and New York in order to complete the manuscript for *The Mortality Maze.*"

BIOGRAPHICAL/CRITICAL SOURCES: Rotarian, October, 1972.

* * *

PAZ, A.
See PAHZ, James Alon

* * *

PAZ, Zan
See PAHZ, (Anne) Cheryl Suzanne

* * *

PEATTIE, Mark R(obert) 1930-

PERSONAL: Born May 3, 1930, in Nice, France; son of Donald Culross (a writer) and Louise (a writer; maiden name, Redfield) Peattie; married Alice Richmond, June 21, 1955; children: Victoria, Caroline, David. *Education:* Pomona College, B.A., 1951; Stanford University, M.A., 1952; Princeton University, Ph.D., 1972. *Politics:* Democrat. *Religion:* Protestant. *Office:* Department of History, University of Massachusetts, Harbor Campus, Boston, Mass. 02125.

CAREER: U.S. Information Agency, Washington, D.C., assistant cultural affairs officer at American Embassy in Phnom Penh, Cambodia (now Kampuchea), 1955-57; American Cultural Center, Sendai, Japan, director, 1958-60; American Embassy Japanese Language School, Tokyo, Japan, language officer, 1960-62; American Cultural Center, Kyoto, Japan, director, 1962-67; U.S. Information Agency, Washington, D.C., Japan-Korea desk officer, 1967-68; Pennsylvania State University, University Park, assistant professor, 1972-76, associate professor of history, 1976-79; University of California, Los Angeles, visiting associate professor of Japanese history, 1979-82; University of Massachusetts, Harbor Campus, Boston, associate professor of Japanese history and director of East Asian Studies Program, 1982—. *Military service:* U.S. Army, Counter Intelligence Corps, 1952-54. *Member:* Association for Asian Studies.

WRITINGS: (Contributor) *Princeton Papers on East Asia: Japan,* Volume I, Princeton University Press, 1972; *Ishiwara Kanji and Japan's Confrontation with the West,* Princeton University Press, 1975; (editor with Ramon Myers) *The Japanese Colonial Empire, 1895-1945,* Princeton University Press, in press; (contributor) *The Cambridge History of Japan,* Volume VI, Cambridge University Press, in press. Also contributor to *U.S. Naval Institute Proceedings,* 1977, *The Encyclopedia of Japan,* Kodansha International, and *The Encyclopedia of Military Biography,* Dupuy Associates.

WORK IN PROGRESS: *Pride and Dust: A History of the Kwantung Army, 1919-1945; The Rising Sun in the South Pacific: A History of the Japanese in Micronesia,* 1885-1945.

SIDELIGHTS: Mark R. Peattie told *CA:* "Ever since my father (writer and naturalist Donald Culross Peattie) introduced me to the wonders of history as a boy, it has been the intellectual passion of my life: reading it as a youngster and college student, seeing it made as a representative of my country in the Far East, and now, in my academic career, writing it and teaching it. My interest is the modern history of Japan and the way in which a country so isolated, with relatively few resources and a feudal tradition, should have risen within a mere half century to become a major industrial nation. In recent years I have become absorbed in the study of Japan's emergence as a colonial power. In assessing the attitudes, achievements, and human costs involved in that effort, I have sought less to praise or blame than to understand how they reflect the ambivalence and dilemmas of Japan's unique historical position in Asia."

* * *

PEIL, Margaret 1929-

PERSONAL: Born 1929, in Racine, Wis. *Education:* Milwaukee-Downer College, B.S., 1951; Fordham University, M.A., 1961; University of Chicago, Ph.D., 1963. *Office:* Centre of West African Studies, University of Birmingham, Birmingham 15, England.

CAREER: University of Ghana, Legon, lecturer in sociology, 1963-68; University of Birmingham, Birmingham, England, lecturer, 1968-71, senior lecturer, 1972-77, reader in sociology, 1978—. Senior lecturer at University of Lagos, 1971-72. *Member:* International Sociological Association, American Sociological Association.

WRITINGS: *The Ghanaian Factory Worker,* Cambridge University Press, 1972; *Nigerian Politics: The People's View,* Cassell, 1976; *Consensus and Conflict in African Societies: An Introduction to Sociology,* Longman, 1977; *Cities and Suburbs: Urban Life in West Africa,* Holmes & Meier, 1981; (with P. K. Mitchell and D. Rimmer) *Social Science Research Methods: An African Handbook,* Hodder & Stoughton, 1982. Contributor to journals. Editor of *Ghana Journal of Sociology,* 1966-68.

WORK IN PROGRESS: An urban sociology textbook for African universities, for Wiley.

* * *

PENTONY, DeVere Edwin 1924-

PERSONAL: Born September 10, 1924, in Manchester, Iowa; son of Joseph Clive and Amber (Davis) Pentony; married Isabel Hoag, November 23, 1955; children: Bryan, Elisabeth. *Education:* State University of Iowa, B.A., 1949, M.A., 1951, Ph.D., 1955. *Politics:* Democrat. *Home:* 15 Red Rock, No. 308, San Francisco, Calif. 94131. *Office:* School of Behavioral and Social Sciences, San Francisco State University, San Francisco, Calif. 94132.

CAREER: State University of Iowa, Iowa City, instructor, 1956-57; San Francisco State University, San Francisco, Calif., 1958—, professor of international relations, 1961—, chairman of department, 1961-66, dean of School of Behavioral and Social Sciences, 1966-82, associate of International Studies Project. Served with Peace Corps, 1962-66. Consultant and lecturer. *Military service:* U.S. Army, 1943-46. *Member:* International Studies Association, American Civil Liberties Union, American Federation of Teachers, American Association of University Professors, Association of California State College Professors, Phi Beta Kappa, Pi Sigma Alpha.

WRITINGS: (With Robert Smith) *By Any Means Necessary: The Revolutionary Struggle at San Francisco State,* Jossey-Bass, 1970; (with Smith and Richard Axen) *Unfinished Rebellions,* Jossey-Bass, 1971; (with Ralph Morris Goldman and Philip G. Schoner) *The Political Science Concept Inventory,* Clio Books, 1980.

Editor; all published by Chandler Publishing Co.: *United States Foreign Aid: Readings in the Problem Area of Wealth,* 1960; *The Underdeveloped Lands: A Dilemma of the International Economy,* 1960; *Soviet Behavior in World Affairs: Communist Foreign Policies,* 1962; *China, the Emerging Red Giant: Communist Foreign Policies,* 1962; *Red World in Tumult: Communist Foreign Policies,* 1962.

WORK IN PROGRESS: A book on communism and on communist foreign policies; research on appeals of communism in the underdeveloped countries and on teaching of communism in American schools.

* * *

PERKINS, Michael 1942-

PERSONAL: Born November 3, 1942, in Lansing, Mich.; son of William and Virginia (Davis) Perkins; married Renie McCune, June 20, 1960 (died, 1968); children: Leslie, Djuna, Zachary. *Education:* Ohio University, B.A., 1963; attended New School for Social Research and City College of New York (now City College of the City University of New York).

CAREER: Department of Welfare, New York City, case worker, 1963-66; Board of Education, New York City, corrective reading teacher, 1966-68; Milky Way Productions, New York City, 1969—, managing editor, 1969, currently contributing editor; editorial director, Croton Press Ltd., 1969-73; *Ulster Arts,* New Paltz, N.Y., editor, 1977-79. Editor, Tompkins Square Press, 1966-68. Co-founder and director, Artists' Cooperative, Woodstock, N.Y., 1973-75; co-director, Woodstock Poetry Festival, 1979-80. *Member:* Authors League of America, Authors Guild, National Book Critics Circle.

WRITINGS: *Third Street Poems,* [New York], 1965; *The Blue Woman, and Other Poems,* PN Press, 1966; *Blue Movie,* Essex House, 1968; *Queen of Heat,* Essex House, 1968; *Shorter Poems,* Croton Press, 1968; *Evil Companions,* Essex House, 1968; *The Tour: Hell's Heated Vacancies,* Essex House, 1969; *Renie Perkins: The Life and Work of a Young Artist Who Died by Her Own Hand at the Age of Twenty-five,* Croton Press, 1969; *Whacking Off,* Essex House, 1969; *Terminus,* Essex House, 1969; *Estelle,* Essex House, 1969; *Down Here* (short stories), Essex House, 1969; *The Secret Record: Modern Erotic Literature,* Morrow, 1976; (contributor) *Twentieth Century Science Fiction Writers,* Macmillan, 1982.

Also author of a play, "Death of the King of Harlem," produced in New York at One Sheridan Square by Theater 10009, 1964, and of a book of poems, *The Persistence of Desire;* also contributor to *Loose Change One,* Half-Ass Press, *Younger*

Critics of North America, edited by Richard Kostelanetz, 1977, *Turpentin on the Rocks*, edited by Charles Bukowski, 1978, and *Dictionary of Literary Biography: The Beats*, Gale. Contributor to *Wormwood Review* and *In New York*.

WORK IN PROGRESS: A book of poems, *Praise in the Ears of Clouds*, for R. Mutt Press; a novel, *Night Moves*.

* * *

PERVIN, Lawrence A. 1936-

PERSONAL: Born August 3, 1936, in Brooklyn, N.Y.; son of Murray (a businessman) and Mary (Reuthen) Pervin; married Barbara Zucker, June 21, 1958; children: David Joshua, Levi Jonathan. *Education:* Queens College (now Queens College of the City University of New York), B.A., 1957; Harvard University, Ph.D., 1962. *Office:* Department of Psychology, Livingston College, Rutgers University, New Brunswick, N.J. 08903.

CAREER: Princeton University, Princeton, N.J., lecturer, 1962-64, assistant professor of psychology, 1964-68; Rutgers University, Livingston College, New Brunswick, N.J., associate professor and associate dean, 1968-71, professor of psychology, 1971—. *Member:* American Psychological Association, American College Health Association, Phi Beta Kappa.

WRITINGS: (With L. E. Reik and W. Dalrymple) *The College Dropout and the Utilization of Talent*, Princeton University Press, 1966; *Personality: Theory and Assessment*, Wiley, 1970, 3rd edition, 1980; (editor with M. Lewis) *Perspectives in Interactional Psychology*, Plenum, 1978; *Current Controversies and Issues in Personality*, Wiley, 1978; (editor with S. Leiblum) *Principles and Practice of Sex Therapy*, Guilford, 1980.

WORK IN PROGRESS: Research on person-situation interaction.

* * *

PETRIE, Charles (Alexander) 1895-1977

PERSONAL: Born September 28, 1895, in Liverpool, England; died December, 1977; son of Sir Charles (first Baronet of Carrowcarden) and Hannah Lindsay (Hamilton) Petrie; married Ursula Gabrielle, 1920 (divorced, 1925); married Jessie Cecilia Mason (a former member of the London County Council), February 24, 1926; children: (first marriage) Richard; (second marriage) Peter. *Education:* Educated privately and at Corpus Christi College, Oxford. *Politics:* Tory. *Religion:* Presbyterian. *Home:* 190 Coleherne Court, London S.W.5, England. *Agent:* Curtis Brown Ltd., 575 Madison Ave., New York, N.Y. 10022.

CAREER: Member of secretariat of British War Cabinet Office, 1918-19; *Outlook*, London, England, member of staff, 1925-28; foreign editor, *English Review*, 1931-37; *Empire Review*, associate editor, 1940-41, editor, 1941-43; managing editor, *New English Review*, 1945-50; editor, *Household Brigade*, 1945-77; member of staff, *Illustrated London News*, 1958-77. Succeeded brother as third Baronet of Carrowcarden, 1929. Official lecturer, H.M. Forces, 1940-45. *Military service:* Royal Artillery, 1915-19.

MEMBER: Royal Historical Society (fellow), Royal Spanish Academy of History (corresponding member), Military History Society of Ireland (president), Hispanic Society of America, Institucion Fernando el Catolico (Spain; corresponding member); Authors Club (president), Carlton Club, and Hurlingham Club (all London); University Club (Dublin).

AWARDS, HONORS: Commander, Order of the British Empire, 1957; Knight Order of Civil Merit (Spain); Commander, Order of Isabella the Catholic (Spain); Commendatore, Order of the Crown (Italy); Commander, Order of George I (Greece); D.Phil., Universidad de Valladolid, 1964; D.Litt., National University of Ireland, 1971.

WRITINGS: *The Story of Government*, Little, Brown, 1929 (published in England as *The History of Government*, Methuen, 1929); *George Canning*, Eyre & Spottiswoode, 1930, 2nd edition, 1946; *Mussolini*, Holme Press, 1931; *The Jacobite Movement*, Eyre & Spottiswoode, 1932, published as *The Stuart Pretenders*, Houghton, 1933, revised edition published in two volumes, 1948-50, 3rd revised edition published under original title, Eyre & Spottiswoode, 1959; *Monarchy*, Eyre & Spottiswoode, 1933; *The British Problem*, Nicholson & Watson, 1934; (with Louis Bertrand) *The History of Spain*, Part 2, Appleton, 1934, 2nd edition, Eyre & Spottiswoode, 1956, Collier, 1971; *Spain*, Arrowsmith, 1934; (editor) *Letters, Speeches, and Proclamations of King Charles I*, Cassell, 1935, reprinted, Funk & Wagnalls, 1968; *The Four Georges: A Reevaluation of the Period from 1714-1830*, Eyre & Spottiswoode, 1935, Houghton, 1936, reprinted, Chivers, 1973; *William Pitt*, Duckworth, 1935; *Walter Long and His Times*, Hutchinson, 1935; *Bolingbroke*, Collins, 1937; *Lords of the Inland Sea*, Dickson, 1937; *The Stuarts*, Eyre & Spottiswoode, 1937, 2nd edition, 1958; *The Chamberlain Tradition*, Frederick Stokes, 1938; *Louis XIV*, Butterworth, 1938; *The Life and Letters of the Right Hon. Sir Austen Chamberlain, K.G.C., M.P.*, two volumes, Cassell, 1939-40.

Joseph Chamberlain, Duckworth, 1940; *Twenty Years' Armistice and After: British Foreign Policy since 1918*, Eyre & Spottiswoode, 1940; *When Britain Saved Europe*, Eyre & Spottiswoode, 1941; *Diplomatic History, 1713-1933*, Hollis & Carter, 1946, Macmillan, 1949; (translator) Paul Baudoin, *Private Diaries*, Eyre & Spottiswoode, 1948; *Earlier Diplomatic History, 1492-1713*, Macmillan, 1949; *Chapters of Life*, Eyre & Spottiswoode, 1950; (editor and author of introduction) F. Berwick, *The Duke of Berwick and His Son*, Eyre & Spottiswoode, 1951; *Monarchy in the Twentieth Century*, Dakers, 1952; *The Marshal Duke of Berwick*, Eyre & Spottiswoode, 1953; *Lord Liverpool and His Times*, J. Barrie, 1954; *The Carlton Club*, Eyre & Spottiswoode, 1955, revised edition, White Lion, 1972; (editor) Jose Pla, *Gibraltar*, Hollis & Carter, 1955; *Wellington: A Reassessment*, J. Barrie, 1956; *Daniel O'Connor Sligo: His Family and His Times* (pamphlet), National University of Ireland, 1958; *The Powers behind the Prime Ministers*, MacGibbon & Kee, 1958; *The Spanish Royal House*, Bles, 1958.

The Victorians, Eyre & Spottiswoode, 1960, McKay, 1962, reprinted, Greenwood Press, 1979; *The Modern British Monarchy*, Eyre & Spottiswoode, 1961; *King Alfonso XIII and His Age*, Chapman & Hall, 1963; *Philip II of Spain*, Norton, 1963; *The Edwardians*, Norton, 1965 (published in England as *Scenes of Edwardian Life*, Eyre & Spottiswoode, 1965); *Don John of Austria*, Norton, 1967; *Great Beginnings in the Age of Queen Victoria*, Macmillan (London), 1967; *The Drift to World War, 1900-1914*, Benn, 1968; *King Charles III of Spain: An Enlightened Despot*, John Day, 1971; *The Great Tyrconnel: A Chapter in Anglo-Irish Relations*, Mercier Press, 1972; *A Historian Looks at His World*, Sidgwick & Jackson, 1972; (editor) *King Charles, Prince Rupert, and the Civil War: From Original Letters*, Routledge & Kegan Paul, 1974; *A Short History of Spain*, Sidgwick & Jackson, 1975. Contributor to *Transactions of the Royal Historical Society* (London), 1931 and 1935.

AVOCATIONAL INTERESTS: "Anything and everything to do with Ireland and Spain."

OBITUARIES: AB Bookman's Weekly, March 6, 1978.†

PHILLIPS, (Elizabeth Margaret Ann) Barty 1933-

PERSONAL: Born May 4, 1933, in Dorking, England; daughter of Henry Lloyd (a headmaster) and Margaret (Strawn) Brereton; married Pearson Phillips (a journalist), April 16, 1955 (divorced, 1965); children: John, Jane, Charles. *Education:* Educated in Scotland, England, and Germany. *Home:* Cottage, Marden Hill, Hertfordshire, England. *Agent:* Patrick Seale Books Ltd., 2 Motcombe St., Belgrave Square, London SW1X 8JU, England. *Office: Observer*, 8 St. Andrew's Hill, London, England.

CAREER: Editor's secretary, *Nova Magazine;* sub-editor, *Good Housekeeping* (magazine), London, England; *Observer*, London, home editor, 1968—. Conducted occasional household television program, "Pebble Mill at One," for British Broadcasting Corp., 1975.

WRITINGS: How to Decorate without Going Broke, Doubleday, 1974; (contributor) Beverley Hilton and Maria Kroll, editors, *The House Book,* Mitchell Beazley, 1975; *Wonderworker* (home repair book), Sidgwick & Jackson, 1978; (with Nicholas Hills) *Setting Up Home,* Design Council, 1978; *Complete Book of Cleaning,* Sidgwick & Jackson, 1981; *The Bargain Book,* Pan Books, 1982. Also contributor to *Household Manual,* edited by Theo Hodges, Reader's Digest Press.

* * *

PHILLIPS, Robert (Schaeffer) 1938-

PERSONAL: Born February 2, 1938, in Milford, Del.; son of Thomas Allen and Katheryn Augusta (Schaeffer) Phillips; married Judith Anne Bloomingdale (a poet), June 16, 1962; children: Graham Van Buren. *Education:* Syracuse University, B.A., 1960, M.A., 1962. *Politics:* Republican. *Religion:* Episcopalian. *Home:* 603 Cross River Rd., Katonah, N.Y. 10536. *Agent address:* Wieser & Wieser Ltd., P.O. Box 608, Millwood, N.Y. 10546. *Office:* J. Walter Thompson, Inc., 466 Lexington Ave., 7th Floor, New York, N.Y. 10017.

CAREER: Syracuse University, Syracuse, N.Y., assistant director of admissions, 1962-64; Benton & Bowles, Inc. (advertising agency), New York City, copywriter, 1964-67; McCann-Erickson, Inc. (advertising agency), New York City, senior writer, 1967-69; Grey Advertising, Inc., New York City, vice-president and creative supervisor, 1969-76; J. Walter Thompson, Inc. (advertising agency), New York City, vice-president and creative director, 1977—. Vice-president and associate creative director, Gramm & Grey, Duesseldorf, West Germany, 1971-72. Instructor in creative writing, New School for Social Research; poetry judge, American Book Awards, 1981. Director of cultural events, Katonah Village Library; member, Katonah Village Improvement Society. *Member:* P.E.N. American Center, Authors Guild, Authors League of America, National Book Critics Circle, The Players. *Awards, honors:* Creative Artists Public Service fellow in literature, 1976.

WRITINGS: 8 & 8 (poems), J. J. Janos, 1960; *Inner Weather* (poems), Golden Quill, 1966; *The Achievement of William Van O'Connor* (bibliography), Syracuse University Library, 1969; *The Land of Lost Content* (fiction), Vanguard Press, 1970; *Aspects of Alice: Lewis Carroll's Dreamchild* (criticism), Vanguard Press, 1971, revised edition, Penguin, 1981; *The Confessional Poets* (criticism), Southern Illinois University Press, 1973; (editor) *Moonstruck: An Anthology of Lunar Poetry,* Vanguard Press, 1974; *Denton Welch* (criticism), Twayne, 1974; *The Pregnant Man* (poems), Doubleday, 1978; *William Goyen* (criticism), Twayne, 1979; (editor) *Last and Lost Poems of Delmore Schwartz,* Vanguard Press, 1979; *Running on Empty: New Poems,* Doubleday, 1981.

Contributor: Aage Jorgensen, editor, *Isak Dinesen: Storyteller,* Akademisk Boghandel, 1972; Ed Ochester, editor, *Natives: An Anthology of Contemporary American Poetry,* Quixote Press, 1973; Robert Morris and Irving Malin, editors, *The Achievement of William Styron,* University of Georgia Press, 1975; Morris, editor, *Old Lines: New Forces,* Fairleigh Dickinson University Press, 1975; Edward Butscher, editor, *Sylvia Plath: The Woman and the Work,* Dodd, 1978; Howard Moss, editor, *New York: Poems,* Avon, 1980; Robert Henderson, editor, *The Pushcart Prize IV: Best of the Small Presses,* Pushcart Press, 1979; Alan F. Pater, editor, *Anthology of Magazine Verse and Yearbook of American Poetry,* Monitor Book Co., 1981; William Jay Smith, editor, *A Green Place,* Delacorte, 1981.

Regular reviewer, *North American Review,* 1965-69. Contributor of poetry, fiction, and essays to the *New Yorker, Hudson Review, Partisan Review, Paris Review, Poetry, New American Review, American Poetry Review, New York Quarterly, Commonweal, Southwest Review, New York Times Book Review, Los Angeles Times Book Review, Saturday Review, Studies in Short Fiction,* and *Encounter.* Book review editor, *Modern Poetry Studies,* 1971-78; associate editor, *New Letters* and *Ontario Review;* contributing editor, *Paris Review.*

WORK IN PROGRESS: Editing *Selected Letters of Delmore Schwartz;* writing a fifth book of poems and a second collection of stories.

SIDELIGHTS: "I have always written," Robert Phillips told *CA*. "When I was very young, I composed 'books' and illustrated and bound them myself. These juvenilia were usually about stray horses and dogs—perhaps because I felt somewhat of a stray myself. Subsequently the serious study of art and music helped liberate my imagination.

"Growing up in a small town has been perhaps the greatest influence on my work. Most of my stories and some of my poems are about provincial characters. Several critics have accused me of a preoccupation with 'the mean, the maimed, the foolish.' True. I *am* fascinated by the eccentric and the outrageous, especially characters whose 'inner weather' is turbulent. Any physical grotesqueries of my characters are usually symbolic representations of their mental conditions.

"Since 1971, the large part of my creative work has been poetry, which has resulted in two volumes, *The Pregnant Man* and *Running on Empty.* The former featured a group of poems in which all human functions and emotions are imaged in terms of the body and bodily parts. The latter book was structured around a long sequence of poems based upon my childhood on the eastern shore of Delaware and Maryland. It is my hope that my poetry is deepening, and becoming a better balance of wit (in the metaphysical sense) and insight. In an age of disposable products, it is my aim to write a non-disposable poem."

BIOGRAPHICAL/CRITICAL SOURCES: North American Review, November, 1966; *New York Times,* December 2, 1971; *Saturday Review,* January 15, 1972; *New York Times Book Review,* January 30, 1972; *Newsday,* June 16, 1974; *Modern Poetry Studies,* March, 1978; *New Republic,* December 9, 1978; *Providence Journal,* December 10, 1978; *Hudson Review,* spring, 1979; *White Plains Reporter-Dispatch,* June 27, 1979; *Poetry,* March, 1980; *Commonweal,* March 14, 1980; *Lewisboro Ledger* (Katonah, N.Y.), September 2, 1981; *St. Louis Globe-Democrat,* November 14, 1981.

PICK, Robert 1898-1978
(Valentin Richter)

PERSONAL: Born March 1, 1898, in Vienna, Austria; came to United States in 1940; died April 7, 1978, in New York, N.Y.; son of Anton and Ida (Bell) Pick; married Priscilla Kennaday, March 4, 1957. *Education:* University of Vienna, doctorate. *Home:* 138 East 78th St., New York, N.Y.; and Woodstock, N.Y. *Agent:* Sanford Jerome Greenburger, 825 Third Ave., New York, N.Y. 10022.

CAREER: Novelist, editor, and translator. Editor and member of executive board, Alfred A. Knopf, Inc.; reviewer for Book-of-the-Month Club. *Member:* P.E.N. (member of executive board, 1946-64). *Awards, honors:* Guggenheim fellow, 1946.

WRITINGS: (Under pseudonym Valentin Richter) *Ein Leben und ein Augenblick,* Bermann-Fischer Verlag (Vienna), 1937; (author of introduction) Klaus Mann and Herman Kesten, editors, *Heart of Europe,* L. B. Fischer (New York), 1943; *The Terhoven File* (novel), Lippincott, 1944; *The Guests of Don Lorenzo* (novel), Lippincott, 1950; (author of introduction) Alexander Lernet-Holenia, *Count Luna,* Criterion Books, 1951; (translator) Theodor Plievier, *World's Last Corner,* Appleton, 1951; (editor) *German Stories and Tales,* Knopf, 1954; *The Escape of Socrates* (novel), Knopf, 1954; (translator with James Stern) Kesten, *Casanova,* Harper, 1955; (editor and author of introduction) Hermann Broch, *Briefe von 1929 bis 1951,* Rhein Verlag (Zurich), 1957; (compiler with others) *Schiller in England: A Bibliography, 1787-1960,* State Mutual Book, 1961; *Empress Maria Theresa: The Earlier Years, 1717-1757* (biography), Harper, 1966; (editor and translator with David Luke) Johann Wolfgang von Goethe, *Conversations and Encounters,* Regnery, 1966; *The Last Days of Imperial Vienna,* Weidenfeld & Nicolson, 1975, Dial, 1976.

Contributor to *Encyclopaedia Britannica.* Reviewer, *Saturday Review.* Contributor to periodicals.†

* * *

PIERS, Maria W(eigl) 1911-

PERSONAL: Born May 17, 1911, in Vienna, Austria; came to America in 1939, naturalized in 1944; daughter of Karl (a musicologist) and Elsa (Pazeller) Weigl; married Gerhart Piers (a psychiatrist), July 15, 1938 (deceased); children: Margaret Maria, Matthew Jakob. *Education:* University of Vienna, Ph.D., 1939; additional study at Northwestern University, 1942, and Chicago Institute of Psychoanalysis. *Religion:* Unitarian Universalist. *Home:* 5811 Dorchester Ave., Chicago, Ill. 60637.

CAREER: Department of Public Welfare, Vienna, Austria, staff member, 1934-38; social worker with Illinois Society for Mental Health, 1940-42, and Association for Family Living, 1941-50; Chicago Medical School, Chicago, Ill., assistant professor, 1949-52; Chicago Institute of Psychoanalysis, Chicago, professor, 1959-62; University of Chicago, Chicago, lecturer in psychology and psychiatry, 1962-68; Loyola University, Erikson Institute for Early Education, Chicago, dean, 1966-77, Distinguished Service Professor, 1977—. Member of Advisory Committee for Family Viewing, of board of directors, American Parents Committee, Inc., of board of advisors, Social Change Advocates, and of board of advisors, Chicago Children's Museum. Conducted radio program, "Childcaring," 1973-75. *Member:* Orthopsychiatric Association, Royal Society of Health, Psychoanalytic Child Care Alumni Association, Chicago Psychoanalytic Association.

AWARDS, HONORS: Received, with husband, Gerhart Piers, Immigrant of the Year Award, Immigrant Protective Association, 1964; Myrtle Wreath Award, Hadassah, 1971; Young Women's Christian Association leadership award, 1972; Operation Push award, 1975, for achievements in the field of education; D.H.L., Loyola University, Chicago, 1978.

WRITINGS: Growing Up with Children, Quadrangle, 1966; (with Robert Coles) *The Wages of Neglect,* Quadrangle, 1969; (editor) *Play and Development,* Norton, 1972; *Infanticide,* Norton, 1978; (with Genevieve Millet Landau) *The Wonderful World of Play: A Guide to Fun and Learning in the Romper Room Years,* Hasbro Industries, 1978; (with Landau) *The Gift of Play,* Walker & Co., 1980.

Also author of *How to Work with Parents,* 1952. Scriptwriter for national educational television programs, including "Children Growing" and "About People." Contributor to *International Encyclopedia of the Social Sciences.* Contributor of over thirty-five articles to professional journals. Advisory editor, Parents' Magazine Enterprises and Parents' Magazine Films.

BIOGRAPHICAL/CRITICAL SOURCES: Laura Fermi, *Illustrious Immigrants,* University of Chicago Press, 1968.

* * *

PILKINGTON, William T(homas, Jr.) 1939-

PERSONAL: Born June 29, 1939, in Fort Worth, Tex.; son of William Thomas, Sr. and Alice (Levey) Pilkington; married Betsy Walter (a teacher), January 20, 1968; children: Michael Thomas. *Education:* University of Texas at Arlington, B.A., 1961; Texas Christian University, M.A., 1963, Ph.D., 1968. *Politics:* Independent. *Home address:* Star Route, Box 101, Stephenville, Tex. 76401. *Office:* Department of English, Tarleton State University, Stephenville, Tex. 76402.

CAREER: Southwest Texas State University, San Marcos, instructor in English, 1965-68; Texas Christian University, Fort Worth, instructor in English, 1968-69; Tarleton State University, Stephenville, Tex., assistant professor, 1969-71, associate professor, 1971-77, professor of English, 1977—. *Member:* American Studies Association, Modern Language Association of America, South Central Modern Language Association, Western Literature Association (member of executive council, 1973-76), Texas Folklore Society.

WRITINGS: My Blood's Country: Studies in Southwestern Literature, Texas Christian University Press, 1973; *Harvey Fergusson,* Twayne, 1975; (co-editor) *Western Movies,* University of New Mexico Press, 1979; (editor) *Critical Essays on the Western American Novel,* G. K. Hall, 1980; *Imagining Texas: The Literature of the Lone Star State,* American Press, 1981. Contributor of articles to *Studies in Short Fiction, Western American Literature, New Mexico Quarterly, South Dakota Review,* and other jouranls.

WORK IN PROGRESS: Current research is in the novel of the American West and in the literary history of Texas.

SIDELIGHTS: William T. Pilkington told *CA:* "My main vocational and avocational interest is the literature of the American West and Southwest—primarily fiction. This interest is stimulated by nothing more complicated than a liking for these regions—topographically, culturally, literarily." *Avocational interests:* Reading, playing tennis, listening to country and western music, harvesting mesquite beans, drinking Lone Star beer ("not necessarily in that order").

PISTOLE, Elizabeth (Smith) 1920-

PERSONAL: Born February 4, 1920, in Halecenter, Tex.; daughter of Price C. and Sarah (Waller) Smith; married Hollis Sidney Pistole (a professor), February 14, 1941; children: Cynthia Poikonen, Carole Bagwell, David, John. *Education:* Anderson College, B.S., 1943; Ball State University, M.A., 1966. *Politics:* Republican. *Religion:* Protestant. *Home:* 3826 Middleway Dr., Anderson, Ind. 46011. *Office:* Anderson High School, Anderson, Ind.

CAREER: Anderson High School, Anderson, Ind., teacher of psychology, 1963—. *Member:* Sigma Tau Delta.

WRITINGS—All published by Warner Press: (With husband, Hollis Pistole) *The Church in Thy House*, 1959; *Confidentially, Girls*, 1961; *Food and Fellowship in the Christian Home* (cookbook), 1965.

With daughters, Cynthia Poikonen and Carole Bagwell: *Servings with Love: Main Course Foods from Which to Choose*, 1979; *Servings with Love: Desserts Galore and Much, Much More*, 1979; *Servings with Love: Entertaining Ways for Special Days*, 1981; *Servings with Love: Entertaining Designs with Seasons in Mind*, 1981.

* * *

PITRONE, Jean Maddern 1920-

PERSONAL: Born December 20, 1920, in Ishpeming, Mich.; daughter of William Courtney (a clerk) and Gladys (Beer) Maddern; married Anthony Peter Pitrone (a landscaper in civil service), October 26, 1940; children: Joseph, Jill, Anthony, Jr., Joyce, John, Janet, Julie, Jane, Cheryl. *Education:* Educated in public schools in Ishpeming, Mich. *Politics:* Independent. *Religion:* Roman Catholic. *Home:* 3878 Pare Lane, Trenton, Mich. 48183.

CAREER: Teacher of piano, 1950, and church organist, 1955, both in Dearborn Heights, Mich.; Oakland University, Rochester, Mich., staff member of annual writer's conference, 1962-80; teacher of magazine writing in adult education classes, Dearborn, Mich., 1963; editorial associate and writing instructor, Writer's Digest School, 1967—; teacher of writing for publication classes, Wayne County Community College extension division, 1977-81. Music director, St. Alfred Church, Taylor, Mich., 1975-81. *Member:* Women in Communications, Detroit Women Writers (past president). *Awards, honors:* First place award for juvenile literature, Friends of American Writers, 1970, for *Trailblazer*.

WRITINGS: *The Great Black Robe*, Daughters of St. Paul, 1964; *Trailblazer: Negro Nurse in the American Red Cross*, Harcourt, 1969; *The Touch of His Hand*, Alba, 1970; *Chavez: Man of the Migrants*, Alba, 1972; *Myra: The Life and Times of Myra Wolfgang, Trade Union Leader*, Calibre Books, 1980; (with Joan Potter Elwart) *The Dodges: Auto Family Fortune and Misfortune*, Icarus, 1981.

Author of monthly column in *Detroit Purchasor* and of monthly column "Writers' Corner" in *Downriver Magazine*, 1982—. Contributor of articles and short stories to newspapers and magazines, including *Extension*, *Columbia*, *Family Digest*, *Adult Teacher*, *Presbyterian Life*, *Catholic Digest*, and *Detroit News Sunday Magazine*.

WORK IN PROGRESS: A novel, tentatively entitled *Blood Relatives*.

SIDELIGHTS: Jean Maddern Pitrone told *CA:* "For those who want to write but are waiting for the children to become more self-sufficient or the job to become less demanding or, simply, for inspiration to strike, remember that tomorrows are not forever. The time to begin is now, and we begin by merely setting pen to paper. There is no magic formula. We learn by doing."

* * *

PLOTZ, Helen Ratnoff 1913-

PERSONAL: Born March 20, 1913, in New York, N.Y.; daughter of Hyman (a physician) and Ethel (Davis) Ratnoff; married Milton Plotz (a physician), September 4, 1933 (deceased); children: Elizabeth (Mrs. R. J. Wagman), Paul, Sarah (Mrs. Roy L. Jacobs), John. *Education:* Vassar College, A.B., 1933. *Politics:* Democrat. *Religion:* Jewish. *Home:* 80 Westminster Rd., Brooklyn, N.Y. 11218.

WRITINGS—Compiler, except as indicated; published by Crowell, except as indicated: *Imagination's Other Place: Poems of Science and Mathematics*, 1955; *Untune the Sky: Poems of Dance and Music*, 1957; Emily Dickinson, *Poems*, 1964; *The Earth Is the Lord's: Poems of the Spirit*, 1965; *Poems from the German*, 1967; *The Marvelous Light: Poets and Poetry*, 1970; Robert Louis Stevenson, *Poems*, Crowell, 1973; Thomas Hardy, *The Pinnacled Tower*, Macmillan, 1975; *As I Walked Out One Evening: A Book of Ballads*, Greenwillow, 1976; (editor) *The Gift Outright: America to Her Poets*, Greenwillow, 1977; (editor) *Life Hungers to Abound: Poems of the Family*, Greenwillow, 1978; *This Powerful Rhyme: A Book of Sonnets*, Morrow, 1979; *Gladly Learn and Gladly Teach: Poems of the School Experience*, Greenwillow, 1981; *Saturday's Children: Poems of Work*, Greenwillow, 1982. Contributor of a chapter to *Children's Bookshelf*, Bantam, and of articles to magazines.

* * *

POLE, J(ack) R(ichon) 1922-

PERSONAL: Born March 14, 1922, in London, England; son of Joseph (a playwright) and Phoebe (Rickards) Pole; married Marilyn Mitchell; children: Ilsa, Nicholas, Lucy. *Education:* Attended King's College, London; Queen's College, Oxford, B.A., 1949; Princeton University, Ph.D., 1953; Cambridge University, M.A. (by incorporation), 1963. *Office:* St. Catherine's College, Oxford University, Oxford, England.

CAREER: Princeton University, Princeton, N.J., instructor in history, 1952-53; University of London, University College, London, England, lecturer in American history, 1953-63; Cambridge University, Cambridge, England, reader in American history and government and fellow of Churchill College, 1963-79, member of university senate council, 1970-74, vice-master of Churchill College, 1975-78; Oxford University, Oxford, England, Rhodes Professor of American History and Institutions and fellow of St. Catherine's College, 1979—. University of California, Berkeley, visiting associate professor, 1960-61; Jefferson Memorial Lecturer, 1971; visiting professor, University of Ghana, 1966; professorial lecturer, University of Chicago, 1969; Richard B. Russell Lecturer, University of Georgia, 1981. Fellow, Center for Advanced Study in the Behavioral Sciences, 1969-70; guest scholar, Woodrow Wilson International Center, 1978-79. Member, International Commission for the History of Parliamentary and Representative Institutions. *Military service:* British Army, 1941-46; became captain.

MEMBER: Institut Europeenne d'Histoire, Royal Historical Society (fellow), Historical Society of Ghana (honorary fellow), Institute of Early American History and Culture (member of council, 1973-76), British Association for American Studies, American Historical Association, Trojan Wanderers Cricket Club (co-founder).

AWARDS, HONORS: Rockefeller Foundation research fellow, 1952 and 1960; Commonwealth Fund American studies fellow, 1956; American Philosophical Society award, 1957; Charles W. Ramsdell Award, Southern Historical Association, 1959, for articles in *Journal of Southern History;* American Council of Learned Societies grant, 1968; elected Knight of Mark Twain, 1980.

WRITINGS: (Contributor) H. C. Allen and C. P. Hill, editors, *British Essays in American History,* St. Martin's, 1957; *Abraham Lincoln and the Working Classes of Britain,* English-Speaking Union, 1959; *Abraham Lincoln,* Oxford University Press, 1964; *Abraham Lincoln and the American Commitment,* Cambridge University Press, 1966; *Political Representation in England and the Origins of the American Republic,* St. Martin's, 1966; (editor) *The Advance of Democracy,* Harper, 1967; (contributor) M. F. Cunliffe and R.W.E. Winks, editors, *Pastmasters,* Harper, 1969; *The Seventeenth Century: The Origins of Legislative Power,* University of Virginia Press, 1969.

The Revolution in America, 1754-1788: Documents and Commentaries, Stanford University Press, 1970; (editor with Marvin Meyers) *The Meanings of American History,* Scott, Foresman, 1971; *Foundations of American Independence, 1763-1815,* Bobbs-Merrill, 1972; (editor) *Slavery, Race and Civil War in America,* Harrap, 1974; *The Decision for American Independence,* Lippincott, 1975; (contributor) Esmond Wright, editor, *A Tug of Loyalties: Anglo-American Relations, 1765-85,* Athlone Press, 1975; *The Idea of Union,* [Alexandria, Va.], 1977; *The Pursuit of Equality in American History,* University of California Press, 1978; *Paths to the American Past,* Oxford University Press, 1979.

General editor, "American Historical Documents" series, Harrap, 1975; member of editorial committee, "Cambridge Studies in the History and Theory of Politics" series, Cambridge University Press, 1964—. Contributor to proceedings. Contributor of numerous essays, articles, and reviews to journals. Member of editorial board, *Journal of American Studies,* 1967-80, and *William and Mary Quarterly,* 1974-76.

AVOCATIONAL INTERESTS: History of ideas, race relations, cricket.

BIOGRAPHICAL/CRITICAL SOURCES: Times Literary Supplement, May 19, 1978, May 30, 1980; *Economist,* June 17, 1978; *Annals of the American Academy of Political and Social Science,* November, 1978; *Washington Post Book World,* December 16, 1979.

*　*　*

POMADA, Elizabeth 1940-

PERSONAL: Born June 12, 1940, in New York, N.Y.; daughter of Maxim (a businessman) and Rita (a social worker; maiden name, Ross) Pomada. *Education:* Cornell University, B.S., 1962. *Politics:* "Rational." *Religion:* Protestant. *Home and office:* Michael Larsen/Elizabeth Pomada Literary Agency, 1029 Jones St., San Francisco, Calif. 94109. *Agent:* Charlotte Sheedy Literary Agency, Inc., 145 West 86th St., New York, N.Y. 10024.

CAREER: Editorial assistant in New York City, 1962-63; promotion assistant in New York City for National Aeronautics Space Administration Institute for Space Studies, 1963-64, Holt, Rinehart & Winston, 1964-66, and David McKay, 1966-67; Dial Press, New York City, library promotion director, 1967-69; Bernard Kaplan Associates, New York City, account executive, 1969-70; free-lance writer, 1970-72; Michael Larsen/Elizabeth Pomada Literary Agency, San Francisco, Calif., partner, 1972—.

MEMBER: Women's National Book Association (vice president, San Francisco chapter, 1979-81), Authors Guild, Authors League of America, National Writers Club, Independent Literary Agents Association, Mystery Writers Guild, California Press Women, California Writers Club. *Awards, honors:* Best Book of the Year award, American Institute of Graphic Arts, 1978, for *Painted Ladies: San Francisco's Resplendent Victorians.*

WRITINGS: (Editor with Michael Larsen) *California Publicity Outlets,* Unicorn Systems, 1972; *Places to Go with Children in Northern California,* Chronicle Books, 1973, revised edition, 1980; (ghost writer) Dinesh Bahadur, *Come Fight a Kite,* Harvey House, 1978; *Painted Ladies: San Francisco's Resplendent Victorians,* Dutton, 1978. Book reviewer for *San Francisco Chronicle,* 1974-81; art columnist for *San Francisco Magazine,* 1974-75. Contributor of articles to various magazines and periodicals, including *McCall's, Bride's, California Living, ArtWest, Mankind,* and *Hughes Airwest Magazine.*

WORK IN PROGRESS: America's Left Bank: A Cultural History of Greenwich Village, for Little, Brown.

SIDELIGHTS: Elizabeth Pomada finds inspiration for writing in the pleasures of her life. She told *CA:* "Since I love books, food, and travelling, that's what I like to write about. I like to write about things I want to know more about—figuring that if it's interesting to me, then it will be of interest to my readers. For example, my favorite articles have been on ice cream and on lithographs. And a gourmet tour of France on my way to a Frankfurt Book Fair has inspired me to (a)Go back; (b)Write well so I can afford it; (c)Polish my French; and (d)Study this history of the place. That also led to my investigation of America's Left Bank—Greenwich Village."

As a literary agent, Elizabeth Pomada and her partner, Michael Larsen, have established what Patricia Holt, in *Publishers Weekly,* describes as "the oldest and so far the best-known" of all Bay Area literary agencies. "In eight years," reports Holt, "they have negotiated contracts for 104 books, and today they represent approximately 100 authors." Their list of clients includes several popular writers such as June Lund Shiplett, Robert McCammon, Joseph Torchia, and Karen Lustgarten.

BIOGRAPHICAL/CRITICAL SOURCES: Publishers Weekly, January 16, 1981; *Writer's Digest,* August, 1982.

*　*　*

PORTE, Joel (Miles) 1933-

PERSONAL: Born November 13, 1933, in Brooklyn, N.Y.; son of Jack and Frances (Derison) Porte; married Llana d'Ancona, June 17, 1962 (divorced, 1976); children: Susanna Maria. *Education:* City College (now City College of the City University of New York), A.B. (magna cum laude), 1957; Harvard University, A.M., 1958, Ph.D., 1962. *Residence:* Arlington, Mass. *Office:* Warren House, Harvard University, Cambridge, Mass. 02138.

CAREER: Harvard University, Cambridge, Mass., instructor, 1962-64, assistant professor, 1964-68, associate professor, 1968-69, professor of English and American literature, 1969—. Visiting lecturer, City College (now City College of the City University of New York), summer, 1958 and 1959, and American Studies Research Center, Hyderabad, India, 1976. Scholar-in-residence, Rockefeller Foundation Study Center, Bellagio, Italy, 1979. *Awards, honors:* Guggenheim fellow, 1981-82.

WRITINGS: *Emerson and Thoreau: Transcendentalists in Conflict,* Wesleyan University Press, 1966; *The Romance in America: Studies in Cooper, Poe, Hawthorne, Melville, and James,* Wesleyan University Press, 1969; *Representative Man: Ralph Waldo Emerson in His Time,* Oxford University Press, 1979; (author of introduction) Nathaniel Hawthorne, *The Scarlet Letter,* Dell, 1979; (author of introduction) Oliver Wendell Holmes, *Ralph Waldo Emerson,* Chelsea House, 1980; (editor) *Emerson in His Journals,* Harvard University Press, 1982; (editor) *Emerson: Prospect and Retrospect,* Harvard University Press, 1982; (editor) *Works of Ralph Waldo Emerson,* Library of America, 1983.

Contributor: Harry Levin, editor, *Veins of Humor,* Harvard University Press, 1972; Monroe Engel, editor, *Uses of Literature,* Harvard University Press, 1973; Matthew Bruccoli, editor, *The Chief Glory of Every People,* Southern Illinois University Press, 1973; Richard Thompson, editor, *The Gothic Imagination,* Washington State University Press, 1974; Daniel Aaron, editor, *Studies in Biography,* Harvard University Press, 1978.

Contributor of articles and reviews to *New England Quarterly, Christian Science Monitor, New Leader, New Boston Review, Forum, American Literature, Studies in Romanticism, Journal of American History, Criticism, American Literary Realism, Harvard Magazine,* and other periodicals and newspapers.

WORK IN PROGRESS: A study of American modernist writing, for Cambridge University Press.

SIDELIGHTS: According to Paul Zweig in the *New York Times Book Review,* Joel Porte's study of American essayist and poet Ralph Waldo Emerson, *Representative Man,* differs from conventional biographies in that it combines textual analyses with overviews of significant periods in Emerson's life. Explains the critic: "Porte refracts the crucial events through the prism of Emerson's journals, letters and essays, concentrating on a selection of images and ideas that seem fused with the internal heat of the life they represent. Each chapter centers on a series of textual analyses that Mr. Porte conducts with enormous precision but also with charm and wit. [He] seems to probe the very texture of Emerson's mind. . . . Although Mr. Porte proceeds chronologically, he doesn't attempt to tell a life story, nor does he work toward a comprehensive interpretation of Emerson's sensibility. His approach is episodic, rich with local insights. He doesn't pretend to exhaust his subject, but rather samples the Emersonian enterprise at moments of heightened complexity."

Harold Beaver, commenting in *Books and Bookmen,* finds *Representative Man* to be "an admirably lucid introduction to the sage of Concord." Yet he suggests that Porte might have examined Emerson from a somewhat more modern vantage point. "Nowhere [does the author consider Emerson's] notions in contemporary, structuralist terms," observes the critic. "Nor is the language of nineteenth century idealism ever tested against its twentieth century, phenomenological counterpart. . . . To use only Emerson's language in explicating Emerson runs the risk of marooning Emerson further in his own past." As a result, concludes Beaver, *Representative Man* "is mainly for those who have already fallen for the siren appeal of Emerson's voice."

In the *Nation,* Earl Rovit remarks that Porte's book is "an apt reminder of the cardinal importance that Emerson possesses for American culture." Obviously the "product of careful and sympathetic reading," he continues, it is nevertheless "a chastening example of the curious fact that although the challenge to understand Emerson is obligatory for the student of American culture, it is a challenge that cannot be wholly met. . . . [*Representative Man*] is worth adding to complementary studies. . . . But even as the Emersonian spirit suffuses Porte's book, it just as clearly evades it."

Alfred Kazin more or less agrees with Rovit's assessment, stating in his *New Republic* review that "Joel Porte's literary biography of Emerson is a perfectly sound book, has many delicate insights, and is armed on every page with lovely quotations. . . . [But] it will not bring Emerson back. . . . Emerson at his best actually creates the mood, the medium, by which to appreciate him. You will never think the 'spirit' so alive and bracing as when you read him."

Though Philip F. Gura would like to have seen Porte discuss Emerson's "relation to the Northern abolitionists and the traumas of the Civil War" in greater detail, he is for the most part highly impressed by *Representative Man.* As he writes in the *Virginia Quarterly Review:* "Any reader throwing up his arms in exasperation and railing that we simply do not need another book on Emerson would do well to secure a copy of Joel Porte's *Representative Man.* By my own count there are no fewer than four new studies of the Concord sage this season, and this volume is far and away the most interesting, primarily because it is the first account of Emerson since Stephen Whicher's *Freedom and Fate: An Inner Life of Ralph Waldo Emerson* (1953) which successfully treats the complex relationship between Emerson's writings (including the newly edited journals and notebooks) and Emerson the man. . . . As the title suggests, the vigor of this critical biography comes in good measure from a mind actively seeking to understand Emerson *in his time,* with tools well-tempered in the crucible of contemporary biographical and literary criticism."

Gura praises Porte for revealing Emerson "as a living presence, both challenged and confused by the demands his age made upon him, and displaying in his published works and private notebooks the ambivalence, the veritable inconsistencies, which make him one of the central figures in American intellectual history. . . . Porte is not afraid to challenge readers to a new understanding of Emerson's intellectual problems. . . . He successfully combines intellectual and social history with some well-parried psychological thrusts." In short, concludes the critic, "Porte ably and honestly turns this great American before our eyes so that new colors are struck from each angle. He also succeeds in showing how Emerson in his time speaks to our own."

BIOGRAPHICAL/CRITICAL SOURCES: *New York Times Book Review,* February 11, 1979; *New Republic,* February 24, 1979; *Nation,* March 31, 1979; *Books and Bookmen,* June, 1979; *Virginia Quarterly Review,* summer, 1979; *Sewanee Review,* April, 1980; *Washington Post Book World,* July 25, 1982; *Times Literary Supplement,* August 27, 1982.

* * *

PORTER, H(arry) Boone 1923-

PERSONAL: Born January 10, 1923, in Louisville, Ky.; son of Harry Boone and Charlotte (Wiseman) Porter; married Violet Monser, 1947; children: Charlotte, H. Boone III, Michael T., V. Gabrielle, Clarissa H., Nicholas T. *Education:* Yale University, B.A., 1947; Berkeley Divinity School, S.T.B., 1950; General Theological Seminary, S.T.M., 1952; Oxford University, D.Phil., 1954. *Office: The Living Church* Magazine, 407 East Michigan St., Milwaukee, Wis. 53029.

CAREER: Ordained priest of Episcopal Church, 1952; Nashotah House, Nashotah, Wis., assistant professor, 1954-60; General Theological Seminary, New York, N.Y., professor of liturgics, 1960-70; Roanridge Foundation, Kansas City, Mo., executive director, 1970-77; *The Living Church* Magazine, Milwaukee, Wis., editor, 1977—. Lecturer on tour in Asia, 1960. *Military service:* U.S. Army, 1943-46. *Member:* American Society of Church History, Anglican Society, Phi Beta Kappa, Elizabethan Club (Yale University). *Awards, honors:* Annual Latin translation prize of Christian Research Foundation, 1964, for manuscript, "Ordination Prayers of the Ancient Western Churches."

WRITINGS—Published by Seabury, except as indicated: (Contributor) *Viewpoints*, 1959; *The Day of Light*, 1960; (contributor) *Anglican Mosaic*, 1962; (contributor) D. M. Paton, editor, *New Forms of Ministry*, Edinburgh House Press, 1965; (contributor) *The Episcopal Church and Education*, Morehouse, 1966; *The Ordination Prayers of the Early Western Churches*, S.P.C.K., 1967; *Growth and Life in the Local Church*, 1968; *Keeping the Church Year*, 1977; (contributor) *Prayer Book Renewal*, 1978; *Jeremy Taylor: Liturgist*, S.P.C.K., 1979; (contributor) *Sacrifice of Praise*, Edizioni Litugiche, 1981; (contributor) *Worship Points the Way*, 1981. Regular contributor to religious periodicals.

WORK IN PROGRESS: Research on several religious and historical topics.

AVOCATIONAL INTERESTS: Painting, illustrating.

* * *

PORTER, Joyce 1924-

PERSONAL: Born March 28, 1924, in England; daughter of Joshua and Bessie Evelyn (Earlam) Porter. *Education:* King's College, London, B.A. (honors), 1944. *Politics:* "Unenthusiastic Conservative." *Religion:* None. *Home:* 68 Sand St., Longbridge Deverill, NR Warminster, Wiltshire, England. *Agent:* Curtis Brown Ltd., 1 Craven Hill, London W2 3EP, England.

CAREER: Flight officer, Women's Royal Air Force (WRAF), 1949-63; full-time writer, 1963—. *Member:* Mystery Writers of America, Crime Writers' Association.

WRITINGS: Dover One, Scribner, 1964; *Dover Two*, Scribner, 1965; *Dover Three*, J. Cape, 1965, Scribner, 1966; *Sour Cream with Everything*, Scribner, 1966; *Dover and the Unkindest Cut of All*, Scribner, 1967; *The Chinks in the Curtain*, J. Cape, 1967, Scribner, 1968; *Dover Goes to Pott*, Scribner, 1968; *Neither a Candle Nor a Pitchfork*, Weidenfeld & Nicolson, 1969, McCall Books, 1970.

Rather a Common Sort of Crime, McCall Books, 1970; *Dover Strikes Again*, Weidenfeld & Nicolson, 1970, McKay, 1973; *Only with a Bargepole*, Weidenfeld & Nicolson, 1971, McKay, 1974; *A Meddler and Her Murder*, Weidenfeld & Nicolson, 1972, McKay, 1973; *It's Murder with Dover*, McKay, 1973; *The Package Included Murder*, Weidenfeld & Nicolson, 1975; *Dover and the Claret Tappers*, Weidenfeld & Nicolson, 1977; *Who the Heck Is Sylvia?*, Weidenfeld & Nicolson, 1977; *Dead Easy for Dover*, Weidenfeld & Nicolson, 1978, St. Martin's, 1979; *The Cart before the Crime*, Weidenfeld & Nicolson, 1979; *Dover Beats the Band*, Weidenfeld & Nicolson, 1980.

SIDELIGHTS: Joyce Porter told *CA:* "Began writing in order to be able to retire from Air Force. Continue writing because it is easier than work. Consider sole duty of my type of writer is to entertain." Porter learned to speak fluent Russian while in the Air Force; she has a special interest in Imperial Russian history. In 1964, she toured the Soviet Union by car.

* * *

PORTER, Margaret Eudine 1905-1975

PERSONAL: Born June 1, 1905, in Rio Vista, Calif.; died April 17, 1975, in Belfast, Me.; daughter of James Henry and Mary Anne (McHugh) Preston; married James Aimsley, June 10, 1942 (died September 11, 1942); married Bernard Harden Porter (an author and publisher), August 27, 1955; children: Carole Aimsley Fohler Kassebaum. *Education:* Attended University of California, Berkeley, 1935, and Munson Business College, 1937. *Politics:* Republican. *Religion:* Catholic. *Home and office:* 22 Salmond Rd., Belfast, Me. 04915.

CAREER: U.S. Navy, Sausalito, Calif., member of special services staff, 1938-42; Pacific Gas and Light Co., San Francisco, Calif., member of special services staff, 1944-57; Bern Porter Books, Belfast, Me., director, beginning 1955; Institute of Advanced Thinking, Belfast, director and member of board of directors, beginning 1959. Correspondent, World Field Research, 1967. Consultant to Small Business Administration, 1968, and International Executive Service Corps, 1968. *Member:* Society for International Development. *Awards, honors:* Porter Conference Room in the Belfast (Me.) Public Library was set up in her memory by her husband, Bernard Harden Porter.

WRITINGS—Published by Bern Porter: (Editor) *Henry: An Anthology of World Poets*, 1970; *James Joyce and His Times*, 1973; *Vistiga: Notes on the Life of Janelle Viglini*, 1975; (editor) *Anthology of American Poets*, 1975; (editor) *Poets of the Pacific*, 1975.

SIDELIGHTS: Margaret Porter once told *CA* that she was concerned with the role of females in poetry and the problems of small press distribution and author relationships. *Avocational interests:* Interchange of cultural activities among nations.†

* * *

POST, Joyce A(rnold) 1939-

PERSONAL: Born January 10, 1939, in Harrisburg, Pa.; daughter of Lawrence W. (a sheet-metal worker) and Edna (Stutz) Arnold; married Jeremiah B. Post (a map librarian), April 15, 1967; children: Jonathan. *Education:* Susquehanna University, A.B., 1960; Drexel University, M.S.L.S., 1961. *Home:* 4613 Larchwood Ave., Philadelphia, Pa. 19143.

CAREER: Philadelphia Civic Center, Foreign Trade Library, Philadelphia, Pa., chief librarian, 1963-65; Pennsylvania State Library, Law Library Bureau, Harrisburg, assistant law librarian, 1965-67; Free Library of Philadelphia, Reader Development Program, Philadelphia, technical services librarian, 1967-68; Drexel University, Graduate School of Library Science, Philadelphia, research associate, 1971-75; Triangle Publications, Radnor, Pa., index consultant, 1976-77; Arete Publishing Co., Burbank, Calif., index editor and index supervisor, 1979-82. *Member:* American Library Association, American Society of Indexers (member, board of directors, 1979-82), American Society for Information Science, Beta Phi Mu.

WRITINGS: Index to Members' Collecting Interests, Private Libraries Association, 1968; *Let's Drink to That . . .* (nonfiction), Owlswick Press, 1970; (contributor) Guy Garrison, editor, *Total Community Library Service*, American Library Association, 1973; *Consolidated Index to the Hexamer General Surveys*, privately printed, 1974; (with Thomas Childers) *The*

Information Poor in America, Scarecrow, 1975; (with Childers) *The Blue Collar Adult's Information Needs, Seeking Behavior and Use,* Drexel University, 1976; *Index to the Private Library,* Private Libraries Association, Series 1, 1977, Series 2, 1980; *TV Guide 25 Year Index, by Author and Subject,* Triangle Publications, 1979; (with husband, Jeremiah B. Post) *Travel in the United States: A Guide to Information Sources,* Gale, 1981. Editor of *American Society of Indexers Newsletter,* 1981—.

SIDELIGHTS: Joyce A. Post told *CA:* "It's a shame that the potential usefulness of so many good nonfiction works is diminished by no or poorly done indexes. This is a heartfelt plea to all nonfiction authors and publishers to recognize that a good index can provide the reader with many different access points to the contents than the contents arrangement itself, and to view the index preparation as a definite and necessary phase of the production schedule and expense and not as a last-minute token gesture."

AVOCATIONAL INTERESTS: Travel, music, knitting.

* * *

POSTLETHWAIT, S(amuel) N(oel) 1918-

PERSONAL: Born April 16, 1918, in Willeysville, W.Va.; son of Frank and Etta Postlethwait; married Sara M. Cover, March 22, 1941; children: John, Robert. *Education:* Fairmont State College, A.B., 1940; University of West Virginia, M.S., 1947; University of Iowa, Ph.D., 1949. *Politics:* Democrat. *Religion:* Church of Christ. *Home:* 3180 Soldiers Home Rd., West Lafayette, Ind. 47906. *Office:* Department of Biological Sciences, Purdue University, West Lafayette, Ind. 47907.

CAREER: Public school teacher in West Virginia, 1940-41; University of Iowa, Iowa City, instructor in botany and biology, 1948-49; Purdue University, West Lafayette, Ind., assistant professor, 1949-56, associate professor, 1956-63, professor of botany and biology, 1963—. *Military service:* U.S. Naval Reserve, active duty, 1942-46; became lieutenant.

MEMBER: International Society of Plant Morphology, International Society for Sterology, International Platform Association, American Institute of Biological Sciences, Botanical Society of America, American Association for the Advancement of Science (fellow), American Genetic Association, American Society for Cell Biology, National Association of Biology Teachers, National Education Association, National Association for Research in Science Teaching, Community College Forum (member of advisory board), Indiana Science Teachers Association, Indiana Academy of Science (fellow; president, 1971), New York Academy of Sciences, Sigma Xi, Lambda Delta Lambda, Kappa Delta Pi, Omicron Delta Kappa (honorary member), Phi Eta Sigma (honorary member), Torrey Botany Club.

AWARDS, HONORS: National Science Foundation faculty fellowship, 1957-58; Purdue Student Government Best Teacher Award, 1965; Sigma Delta Chi Best Teacher Award, 1965; Audio-Visual Instruction Director's Award, 1965; Eastman Kodak Gold Medal Award, 1967; Fulbright Award, Macquarie University, 1968; Standard Oil Best Teacher Award, 1979; Indiana Academy of Science Speaker of the Year Award, 1978; Botanical Society of America Merit Award, 1979; Lilly Endowment faculty open fellowship, 1979; Postlethwait Award created in his honor by International Congress of Individualized Instruction, 1980; Doctor of Pedagogy, Doane College, 1982.

WRITINGS—Published by Burgess, except as indicated: *Workbook in Plant Science,* 1948; *Textbook of Intermediate Plant Science,* 1950; *Plant Science: A Workbook with an Audio Program Approach,* 1963, revised edition, 1966; (with J. Novak and H. T. Murray, Jr.) *An Integrated Experience Approach to Learning with Emphasis on Independent Study,* 1964, 2nd edition published as *The Audio-Tutorial Approach to Learning through Independent Study and Integrated Experiences,* 1969, 3rd edition, 1972; *The Audio-Tutorial System,* 1971; *Minicourses in Biology,* Saunders, 1976; *The World's Greatest Solar Energy Converters: Plants,* 1978; (editor) *Exploring Teaching Alternatives,* 2nd edition, 1978. Developer of minicourses in biology and of "Meiosis Action Text Pac" and "DNA Replication Text Pac," both for PRAMCOR, Inc., 1981. Contributor to *Encyclopaedia of Educational Media Communications and Technology* and *International Encyclopedia of Education, Research and Studies.*

* * *

POWELL, James M(atthew) 1930-

PERSONAL: Born June 9, 1930, in Cincinnati, Ohio; son of Matthew J. and Mary Loretta (Weaver) Powell; married Judith K. Davidorf, May 29, 1954; children: James J., Michael L., Mark E., Mary Helen E., Miriam T., John W.D.C. *Education:* Xavier University, Cincinnati, Ohio, A.B., 1953, M.A., 1955; University of Cincinnati, additional graduate study, 1954-56; Indiana University, Ph.D., 1960. *Politics:* Democrat. *Religion:* Roman Catholic. *Office:* Department of History, Syracuse University, Syracuse, N.Y. 13214.

CAREER: Kent State University, Kent, Ohio, instructor in history, 1959-61; University of Illinois at Urbana-Champaign, assistant professor of history, beginning 1961; Syracuse University, Syracuse, N.Y., assistant professor, 1965-67, associate professor, 1967-72, professor of history, 1972—. Visiting lecturer in medieval history, University of Wisconsin—Milwaukee, 1963-64. *Member:* American Historical Association, Mediaeval Academy of America, American Catholic Historical Association, Society for Italian Historical Studies (member of council, 1979-81), Midwest Medieval Conference. *Awards, honors:* Grants from American Philosophical Society, 1961, 1967, and 1981; summer faculty fellowship, University of Illinois, 1963; grant from Pontifical Institute of Medieval Studies, 1970.

WRITINGS: *Medieval Monarchy and Trade,* Centro Italiano di Studi sull'Alto Medioeva, 1962; (editor) *Innocent III: Vicar of Christ or Lord of the World?,* Heath, 1963; *The Civilization of the West,* Macmillan, 1967; *The Liber Augustalis,* Syracuse University Press, 1971; *Introduction to Medieval Studies,* Syracuse University Press, 1976. Also contributor to *Encyclopaedia Britannica, Dictionary of the Middle Ages,* and *New Catholic Encyclopedia.* Contributor to journals, including *Speculum, Church History, Catholic Historical Review, Medieval Studies,* and *Franciscan Studies.*

WORK IN PROGRESS: Research on the papacy and reform in the early thirteenth century; *The Fifth Crusade.*

SIDELIGHTS: James M. Powell knows Latin, Italian, French, German, and Greek.

* * *

POWELL, Lawrence Clark 1906-

PERSONAL: Born September 3, 1906, in Washington, D.C.; son of G. Harold and Gertrude (Clark) Powell; married Fay Ellen Shoemaker, March 26, 1934; children: Norman Jerrold, Wilkie Haines. *Education:* Occidental College, B.A., 1928; University of Dijon, Ph.D., 1932; University of California,

Berkeley, certificate of librarianship, 1937. *Politics:* Democrat. *Religion:* Quaker. *Home:* 6288 North Campbell Ave., Tucson, Ariz. 85718.

CAREER: Occidental College, Los Angeles, Calif., teaching assistant in English, 1929; Vroman's Bookstore, Pasadena, Calif., shipping clerk, 1929-30; worked for rare book stores in Los Angeles and for Western Publishers, 1934-36; University of California Press, Berkeley, editorial assistant, 1936-37; Los Angeles (Calif.) Public Library, employed in order department and associated with various branches, 1937-38; University of California, Los Angeles, junior assistant in acquisitions department of library, 1938-43, chief librarian, 1944-61, director of William Andrews Clark Memorial Library, 1944-66, professor and dean, School of Library Service, 1960-66; full-time writer, 1966—; University of Arizona, Tucson, professor-in-residence, 1971—. Randolph G. Adams Memorial Lecturer, University of Michigan, 1953; lecturer, University of Tennessee Library, and visiting professor, Columbia University, 1954; Trumbull Lecturer, Yale University, 1960; visiting professor, Simmons College, 1968. Conductor of workshops for U.S. Air Force librarians, Tokyo, Japan, 1960 and 1966. Fellow, Center for Advanced Studies, Wesleyan University, 1968.

MEMBER: American Library Association (honorary life member), Bibliographical Society of America (president, 1954-56), California Library Association (president, 1950), California Historical Society (fellow), Phi Beta Kappa, Phi Gamma Delta; Zamorano Club, Rounce Club, and Coffin Club (all Los Angeles); Grolier Club (New York City). *Awards, honors:* Guggenheim fellow in Great Britain, 1950-51 and 1967; Litt.D., Occidental College, 1955, and Juniata College, 1963; Clarence Day Award, 1960; L.H.D., Carnegie Institute of Technology, 1961; Doctor of Humanities, University of Arizona, 1971.

WRITINGS: An Introduction to Robinson Jeffers, Imprimerie Bernigaud & Privat (Dijon), 1932, 2nd edition published as *Robinson Jeffers: The Man and His Work,* Primavera Press, 1934, 3rd edition, San Pasquale Press, 1940; *Philosopher Pickett: The Life and Writings of Charles Edward Pickett,* University of California Press, 1942; *Islands of Books* (essays), Ritchie, 1951; *Land of Fiction* (bibliographical essay), Dawson's Book Shop, 1952; *The Alchemy of Books, and Other Essays and Addresses on Books and Writers,* Ritchie, 1954; (editor) *Libraries in the Southwest,* University of California Library (Los Angeles), 1955; *Books: West, Southwest* (essays), Ritchie, 1957; (reviser) Phil Townsend Hanna, *Libros Californianos; or, Five Feet of California Books,* Zeitlin & Ver Brugge, 1958; *A Passion for Books,* World Publishing, 1959.

Books in My Baggage: Adventures in Reading and Collecting, World Publishing, 1960; *Southwestern Book Trails: A Reader's Guide to the Heartland of New Mexico and Arizona,* Horn & Wallace, 1963; *The Little Package: Pages on Literature and Landscape from a Traveling Bookman's Life,* World Publishing, 1964; (compiler) Walt Whitman, *Leaves of Grass,* Crowell, 1964; *Bookman's Progress: Selected Writings,* Ritchie, 1968; *Fortune and Friendship: An Autobiography,* Bowker, 1968; *California Classics: The Creative Literature of the Golden State,* Ritchie, 1971; *Southwest Classics: The Creative Literature of the Arid Land,* Ritchie, 1974; *Arizona: A Bicentennial History,* Norton, 1976; *From the Heartland,* Northland Press, 1976; *The Blue Train* (novel), Capra, 1977; *The River Between* (novel), Capra, 1979; *Where Water Flows: The Rivers of Arizona,* Northland Press, 1980; *My Mozart Commonplace Book,* privately printed, 1980; *Susanna's Secret; or, The Lost Mozart Letters* (play), privately printed, 1981; *My Haydn Commonplace Book,* privately printed, 1982. Also author of monographs, occasional papers, and pamphlets on authors, books and book publishing, libraries, and regional literature.

Author of forewords and introductions for more than forty books, including: William Everson, *San Joaquin,* Ritchie, 1939; Lawrence Durrell, *A Landmark Gone,* [Los Angeles], 1949; *The Intimate Henry Miller,* Signet, 1959; Theodore Roosevelt, *The Rough Riders,* New American Library, 1961; George Wickes, editor, *Henry Miller and the Critics,* Southern Illinois University Press, 1963; *The Raymond Chandler Omnibus,* Knopf, 1964; Frances Clark Sayers, *Summoned by Books,* Viking, 1965; *Come Hither! Papers on Children's Literature and Librarianship,* Yeasayers Press, 1966; Ansel Adams, *Photographs of the Southwest,* New York Graphic Society, 1976; Bert Fireman, *History of Arizona,* Knopf, 1982.

Contributor of articles on books, librarianship and western history to a number of publications, including *Antiquarian Bookman, Arizona Highways, Library Journal, New York Times Book Review, Saturday Review, Westways,* and other library journals, scholarly quarterlies, and literary and book-collecting reviews.

SIDELIGHTS: "My literary life began in grammar school when I wrote 'The Purple Dragon,' a Fu Manchu-esque thriller, for the school paper," Lawrence Clark Powell told *CA.* "Years later as a graduate student in France, I wrote four drafts, increasingly bad, of a novel based on college experiences as a jazz musician. Then I went to work in earnest in the depths of the Depression, and during many years as a librarian, administrator, and educator, the essay form was all I had strength for after the regular day's work. When at age seventy I retired from active university life, I wrote two novels, *The Blue Train* and *The River Between,* one about Europe and the other about the Southwest; and then a literary geography of Arizona's rivers, *Where Water Flows,* [after] flying in a Cessna 170 with a pilot and photographer, both young graduate geologists unimpressed with my senior status. Now as I approach my eighties I find it harder and harder to sustain belief in my powers, yet am determined to finish at least one more novel and update my autobiography for the twenty years since I wrote *Fortune and Friendship.* My life has been a series of opening doors into wonderful new rooms—wonder not without fear, pain and sorrow and always [with] the voice of the Lord, reminding me that nothing is free and must be paid for by service to others in the realization of one's birthright gifts."

BIOGRAPHICAL/CRITICAL SOURCES: Gertrude Clark Powell (mother), *The Quiet Side of Europe,* [Los Angeles], 1959; Betty Rosenberg, *Checklist of the Published Writings of Lawrence Clark Powell,* School of Library Service, University of California, 1966; Lawrence Clark Powell, *Fortune and Friendship: An Autobiography,* Bowker, 1968; *New York Times Book Review,* August 18, 1968; *American Literature,* November, 1971; Donald C. Dickinson and others, editors, *Voices from the Southwest: A Gathering in Honor of Lawrence Clark Powell,* Northland Press, 1976.

* * *

POWELL, Marvin 1924-

PERSONAL: Born May 5, 1924, in Syracuse, N.Y.; son of William and Gussie (Chainov) Powell; married Rita Cohen, June 17, 1951; children: Jeffrey Arnold, Linda Beth, Laura Wendy. *Education:* Syracuse University, A.B., 1947, M.S. in Ed., 1949, Ph.D., 1952. *Home:* 417 Fairmont Dr., DeKalb, Ill. 60115. *Office:* Department of Learning, Development, and Special Education, Northern Illinois University, DeKalb, Ill. 60115; and Foundation for Individualized Evaluation and Research, Inc., 248½ East Lincoln Hwy., DeKalb, Ill. 60115.

CAREER: Western Reserve University (now Case Western Reserve University), Cleveland, Ohio, assistant professor of educational psychology, 1952-61, acting director of vocational counseling services, 1953-55; Willoughby-Eastlake Board of Education, Willoughby, Ohio, director of psychological services, guidance, and research, 1956-61; Northern Illinois University, DeKalb, professor of educational psychology, 1961—; Fundation for Individualized Evaluation and Research, Inc., DeKalb, president, 1973—. Has made several appearances on radio and television talk shows. Consultant, State of Illinois Mental Health Program. Registered psychologist and school psychologist, State of Illinois. *Military service:* U.S. Army Air Forces, 1943-46.

MEMBER: American Psychological Association (fellow), American Association for the Advancement of Science (fellow), Society for Research in Child Development, American Educational Research Association, Sigma Xi, Phi Delta Kappa, B'nai B'rith (president of Kishwaukee lodge, 1966-67).

WRITINGS: The Psychology of Adolescence, Bobbs-Merrill, 1963, 2nd edition, 1971; (editor with I. Frank) *Psychosomatic Ailments in Childhood and Adolescence,* C. C Thomas, 1967; (with M. Carroll and H. McNamara) *Individual Progression,* Bobbs-Merrill, 1970; (with R. Mangum) *Introduction to Educational Psychology,* Bobbs-Merrill, 1971; (editor with A. Frerichs) *Readings in Adolescent Development,* Burgess, 1971; *Youth: Critical Issues,* C. E. Merrill, 1973.

Contributor: R. G. Kuhlen, *The Psychology of Adolescent Development,* Harper, 1952; D. R. Cook, *A Guide to Educational Research,* Allyn & Bacon, 1965; Contributor to psychology and education journals. Editor (ad hoc), *Journal of Educational Psychology.*

SIDELIGHTS: Marvin Powell told *CA:* "My primary interest has been studying adolescents, but now I'm also back to an earlier interest—the study of aging. This appears to be an area where we know relatively little, and it's fascinating to find that many of the stereotypes are really myths. 'Older is indeed better' if you can stay physically fit."

* * *

POWICKE, Michael Rhys 1920-

PERSONAL: Born October 2, 1920, in Manchester, England; son of William Alfred (a minister) and Gwladys (Evans) Powicke; married Hilda Marie Benson (a dramatist), May 27, 1948; children: Helen Mary, Margaret Kristin, Elinor Janet. *Education:* Oxford University, M.A., 1944. *Religion:* Angelican. *Home:* 67 Lee Ave., Toronto, Ontario, Canada M4E 2P1. *Office:* Department of History, University of Toronto, Toronto, Ontario, Canada M5S 1A8.

CAREER: University of Toronto, Toronto, Ontario, lecturer, 1946-52, assistant professor, 1952-58, associate professor, 1958-65, professor of history, 1965—. *Military service:* British Army, 1941-46. *Member:* Royal Historical Society (fellow), Mediaeval Academy of America, Canadian Association of University Teachers.

WRITINGS: Military Obligation in Medieval England: A Study in Liberty and Duty, Clarendon Press, 1962; (co-author) *The Hundred Year War,* Macmillan, 1969; (editor and contributor) *Essays in Medieval History Presented to Bertie Wilkinson,* University of Toronto Press, 1969; *The Community of the Realm, 1154-1485,* Knopf, 1973. Contributor to *Speculum.*

WORK IN PROGRESS: The Age of the Lancastrians; Knighthood and War; Causes of Victory; two volumes of documents, *War and Politics, 500-1500,* and *Military Contracts of the 14th and 15th Centuries.*

* * *

PRABHAVANANDA, Swami 1893-1976

PERSONAL: Original name, Abani Ghosh; born December 26, 1893, in Vishnupur, India; came to United States in 1923; died July 4, 1976, in Hollywood, Calif.; son of Kumud Bihari (a lawyer) and Jnanada (Sarkar) Ghosh. *Education:* Calcutta University, B.A., 1914. *Home and office:* 1946 Vedanta Pl., Hollywood, Calif. 90068.

CAREER: Joined Ramakrishna Order of India, 1914, ordained swami (monastic religious teacher), 1923; assistant leader of Vedanta Society (followers of a system of Hindu philosophy), San Francisco, Calif., 1923-25; founder and leader of Vedanta Society, Portland, Ore., 1925-29; Vedanta Society of Southern California, Hollywood, 1929-76, founder, 1929, became senior minister. President of a Calcutta and Madras session of Vivekananda centenary celebration in India, 1963-64.

WRITINGS: (Translator) *Srimad Bhagavatam: The Wisdom of God,* Putnam, 1943, reprinted, Vedanta Press, 1978, 3rd edition, Sri Ramakrishna Math (Madras), 1964; *The Eternal Companion* (life and teachings of Swami Brahmananda), Vedanta Press, 1944, 5th edition, Sri Ramakrishna Math, 1971; (editor and translator with Christopher Isherwood) Shankara, *Crest-Jewel of Discrimination,* Vedanta Press, 1947, 3rd edition, 1978; (translator with Frederick Manchester) *The Upanishads: Breath of the Eternal,* Vedanta Press, 1948, reprinted, 1968; *Vedic Religion and Philosophy,* Sri Ramakrishna Math, 1950, reprinted, 1968; (translator with Isherwood) *The Song of God: Bhagavad-gita,* Harper, 1951, 3rd edition, Vedanta Press, 1965; (editor and translator with Isherwood and author of commentary) *How to Know God: The Yoga Aphorisms of Pantajali,* Vedanta Press, 1953, reprinted, 1971; (with Manchester) *The Spiritual Heritage of India,* Allen & Unwin, 1962, Doubleday, 1963; (author of part-by-part commentary) *The Sermon on the Mount according to Vedanta,* Vedanta Press, 1964; (editor with Clive Johnson) *Prayers and Meditations Compiled from the Scriptures of India,* Vedanta Press, 1968; (editor and translator) *Swami Premananda: Teachings and Reminiscences,* Vedanta Press, 1968; *Yoga and Mysticism: Four Lectures,* Vedanta Press, 1969; (translator) *Narada's Way of Divine Love: The Bhakti Sutras,* Vedanta Press, 1971.

SIDELIGHTS: Swami Prabhavananda's Vedanta Society of Southern California maintains a temple and monastic community in Hollywood, a temple and convent in Santa Barbara, and a monastery in Trabuco Canyon. Many well-known writers and philosophers studied under Prabhavananda during his long tenure as senior minister of the society, including Aldous Huxley, Christopher Isherwood, Gerald Heard, and John Van Druten.

BIOGRAPHICAL/CRITICAL SOURCES: John R. Yale, editor, *What Vedanta Means to Me,* Doubleday, 1961; Christopher Isherwood, *An Approach to Vedanta,* Vedanta Press, 1963; C. Muppathyil, *Meditation as a Path to God-Realization: A Study in the Spiritual Teachings of Swami Prabhavananda and His Assessment of Christian Spirituality,* Universita Gregoriana, 1979; Isherwood, *My Guru and His Disciple,* Farrar, Straus, 1980.†

* * *

PRESCOTT, Kenneth W(ade) 1920-

PERSONAL: Born August 9, 1920, in Jackson, Mich.; son of

Edward E. and Harriett (McInerney) Prescott; married Emma-Stina Johnsson, January 13, 1947; children: Kristina Lisen Fanaberia, Gertrude Mae. *Education:* Western Michigan College of Education (now Western Michigan University), B.S., 1942; University of Delaware, Ed.M., 1954; University of Michigan, M.A., 1948, Ph.D., 1950. *Home:* 2526 Tanglewood Trail, Austin, Tex., 78703. *Office:* Department of Art, University of Texas, Austin, Tex. 78712.

CAREER: Kansas City Museum, Kansas City, Mo., director, 1954-58; Academy of Natural Sciences, Philadelphia, Pa., managing director, 1958-63; Temple University, School of Graduate Studies, Philadelphia, adjunct professor, 1961-71; New Jersey State Museum Cultural Center, Trenton, director, 1963-71; Ford Foundation, New York, N.Y., program officer for visual arts, 1971-74; University of Texas at Austin, professor of art and head of department, 1974—. Member of board of directors of Urban League, Kansas City, Mo., 1957-58; chairman of Southeastern Pennsylvania Chapter of Junior Red Cross, 1959-62; member of executive committee of Trenton Symphony, 1963-65; member of White House Conference on Youth, 1971. Member of advisory board of U.S. Secretary of the Navy, 1972-75; consultant to Ford Foundation, Jewish Museum, Kennedy Galleries, Harry S Truman Library Museum, Andre Emmerich Gallery, and Meredith Long Gallery. *Military service:* U.S. Naval Reserve; served in Southwest Pacific theater, 1942-47, in Korea, 1951-54, and in Vietnam; recalled intermittently, 1960-70; retired as captain.

MEMBER: College Art Association of America, National Association of Arts Administration, National Council of Arts Administration (chairman, 1979-80), American Association of Museums, Midwest Museums Conference (president, 1957-58), Northeast Conference of Museums (president, 1961-62), Texas Association of Schools of Arts (member of coordinating board), Sigma Xi, Princeton Club.

WRITINGS: *Life History of the Scarlet Tanager,* New Jersey State Museum, 1965; (with Gustave von Groswitz) *Domjan the Woodcutter,* River Edge Press, 1966; *The Complete Graphic Works of Ben Shahn,* Quadrangle, 1973; *Paints and Posters of Ben Shahn,* Dover, 1982; *The Prints of Jack Levine,* Dover, 1982; *Burgoyne Diller, American Neoplasticist,* Smithsonian Institution Press, 1983. Author of exhibition catalogues on Ben Shahn, Jack Levine, Burgoyne Diller, Richard Hunt, and others. Contributor of articles on art, museology, and ornithology to periodicals.

WORK IN PROGRESS: *The Complete Sculpture of Dorothea Greenbaum.*

AVOCATIONAL INTERESTS. Travel, ornithology.

*   *   *

PRESTON, Dickson J(oseph)   1914-

PERSONAL: Born March 22, 1914, in Monticello, Ind.; son of Charles S. (an editor and teacher) and Helen (a teacher; maiden name, Hurst) Preston; married Janet Longley, June 17, 1939; children: Dickson Hurst. *Education:* DePauw University, B.A., 1936; attended University of Iowa, 1938-39. *Address:* R.D. 5, Box 607, Easton, Md. 21601.

CAREER: Writer. *Indianapolis Times,* Indianapolis, Ind., reporter and copy editor, 1937-38; Indiana Writers Project, Indianapolis, assistant state director, 1939-42; *Cleveland Press,* Cleveland, Ohio, world news editor, 1943-52; Scripps-Howard Newspapers, Washington, D.C., reporter, 1952-66. *Member:* Talbot County Historical Society (member of board of directors, 1976—), Delta Kappa Epsilon, Sigma Delta Chi. *Awards, honors:* Reporting award of Cleveland Newspaper Guild, 1955; best in show award in Blackwater wildlife photo contest, 1972.

WRITINGS: (Editor) *Indiana: A Guide to the Hoosier State,* Oxford University Press, 1941; *Wye Oak: The History of a Great Tree,* Tidewater, 1972; *Trappe: The Story of an Old-Fashioned Town,* Economy Co., 1976; *St. Luke's Parish: A History,* Wye Institute, 1978; *Young Frederick Douglass: The Maryland Years,* Johns Hopkins Press, 1980; *Memorial Hospital at Easton: The First 75 Years,* Memorial Hospital, 1982; *The Country Editors: Two Centuries of Journalism on the Maryland Eastern Shore,* Queen Anne Press, 1983.

WORK IN PROGRESS: Talbot: A Study in Liberty, a modern history of Talbot County, Md., for Tidewater.

SIDELIGHTS: Dickson J. Preston told *CA:* "I reject both the 'inspirational' and 'bunk' views of history; it seems to me we cannot possibly know where we are going unless we know where we have been. My method is to examine specific events of the past with a reporter's eye for detail and a writer's sense of the significance of seemingly small things."

*   *   *

PRICE, Nelson Lynn   1931-

PERSONAL: Born August 24, 1931, in Osyka, Miss.; son of Robert S. and Genevieve (Dykes) Price; married Trudy Knight, February 12, 1956; children: Lynn, Sharon. *Education:* Southeastern Louisiana University, B.S., 1953; New Orleans Baptist Theological Seminary, Th.M., 1957. *Home:* 1400 Beaumont Dr., Kennesaw, Ga. *Office:* 774 Roswell St., Marietta, Ga.

CAREER: Pastor in New Orleans, La., 1957-65; Roswell Street Baptist Church, Marietta, Ga., pastor, 1965—. Member of board of trustees of New Orleans Baptist Theological Seminary, 1963—; member of Georgia Board of Human Resources, 1974—; first vice-president of Georgia Baptist Convention, 1981. Broadcasts weekly over WXIA-TV, Atlanta, Ga.; broadcasts commentary daily over WYNX-Radio, Marietta, Ga. National trustee, Fellowship of Christian Athletes, 1978-82. *Awards, honors:* Cobb County Chamber of Commerce public service award, 1968; Liberty Bell Award from Cobb County Bar Association, 1968; Cobb County Citizen of the Year Award from *Marietta Daily Journal,* 1969.

WRITINGS—All published by Broadman Press: *I've Got to Play on Their Court,* 1976; *How to Find Out Who You Are,* 1978; *Supreme Happiness,* 1979; *Only the Beginning,* 1980; *The Destruction of Death,* 1982. Also author of *Shadows We Run From.* Contributor of weekly editorial to *Marietta Daily Journal,* 1966—.

SIDELIGHTS: Nelson Lynn Price told *CA:* "When I write, I begin at about 4:00 a.m. and crash on a topic until I have exhausted it or me. My latest work, *The Destruction of Death,* is related to the resurrection. The subject is approached as an apologetic stance with the ambition of affording inspiration."

*   *   *

PROTHRO, James W(arren)   1922-

PERSONAL: Born April 15, 1922, in Robeline, La.; son of Edwin Thomas (a railroad official) and Lillian Frances (Terry) Prothro; married Mary Frances Harris, October 17, 1943; children: Pamela, Barbara, Susan. *Education:* North Texas State Teachers College (now North Texas State University), B.A., 1943; University of Edinburgh, graduate study, 1946; Louisiana State University, M.A., 1947; Princeton University, M.A., 1949, Ph.D., 1952; Columbia University, postdoctoral study,

1954-55. *Politics:* Democrat. *Religion:* Protestant. *Home:* 306 Elliott Rd., Chapel Hill, N.C. 27514. *Office:* Department of Political Science, Hamilton Hall 070 A, University of North Carolina, Chapel Hill, N.C. 27514.

CAREER: Florida State University, Tallahassee, assistant professor, 1950-53, associate professor, 1953-57, professor of political science, 1957-61; University of North Carolina at Chapel Hill, visiting professor and visiting research professor, 1960-61, professor of political science, 1961—, Alumni Distinguished Professor, 1976—, Institute for Research in Social Science, research professor, 1961—, director, 1967-73, acting chairman of department of political science, 1964-66, chairman, 1980—. Consultant to National Broadcasting Co. (NBC) on election coverage, 1964; consultant to U.S. Commission on Civil Rights, 1964-65, and FLASCO, Santiago, Chile, 1966-67. *Military service:* U.S. Army, Infantry, 1943-46; became captain.

MEMBER: American Political Science Association (chairman of nominating committee, 1965; member of executive council, 1970-72), Southern Political Science Association (president, 1970-71), Inter-University Consortium for Political Research (council member and chairman). *Awards, honors:* Ford faculty fellow, Fund for Advancement of Education, Columbia University, 1954-55; Rockefeller Foundation grant, 1960-64; Social Science Research Council grant, 1963-64.

WRITINGS: The Dollar Decade: Business Ideas in the 1920s, Louisiana State University Press, 1954, reprinted, Greenwood Press, 1969; (with Marian D. Irish) *The Politics of American Democracy,* Prentice-Hall, 1959, 7th edition (with Irish and R. R. Richardson), 1981; (with Irish) *State and Local Supplement: The Politics of American Democracy,* Prentice-Hall, 1959, 2nd edition, 1962; (with Donald R. Matthews) *Negroes and the New Southern Politics,* Harcourt, 1966; (editor with Irish and R. L. Lineberry) *Readings on the Politics of American Democracy,* Prentice-Hall, 1969; (with David M. Kovenock and others) *Explaining the Vote: Presidential Choice in the Nation and the States, 1968,* Institute for Research in Social Science, University of North Carolina, 1973.

Contributor: *Cases in State and Local Government,* Prentice-Hall, 1961; *The American Political Arena,* Little, Brown, 1962; *Politics and Social Life,* Houghton, 1963; *Change in the Contemporary South,* Duke University Press, 1963; *The American South in the 1960s,* Praeger, 1964; *Essays on the American Constitution,* Prentice-Hall, 1965; *Comparative Politics and Political Theory,* University of North Carolina Press, 1966.

Contributor of articles to political science journals. Book review editor, *American Political Science Review;* member of editorial board, *Journal of Politics* and *Public Opinion Quarterly.*

* * *

PULKINGHAM, Betty (Jane) 1928-

PERSONAL: Born August 25, 1928, in Burlington, N.C.; daughter of Leo (a lawyer and judge) and Betty (Knott) Carr; married William Graham Pulkingham (an Episcopalian priest), September 1, 1951; children: William Graham III, Mary Graham, Nathan Carr, Elizabeth Jane, Martha Louise, David Earle. *Education:* University of North Carolina at Greensboro, B.S. (magna cum laude), 1949; graduate study at Eastman School of Music. *Religion:* Episcopalian. *Home:* Community of Celebration, Woodland Park, Colo. 80863. *Office address:* Celebration Services, United States Corp., Box FF, Woodland Park, Colo. 80863.

CAREER: Music theory instructor at University of Texas, 1949-52; Austin High School, Austin, Tex., choral music teacher, 1956-57; private piano teacher in Galveston, Tex., 1958-60; Church of the Redeemer, Houston, Tex., choir director, 1964-71; currently director of research and development, Celebration Services International, Ltd.

WRITINGS: (Arranger and compiler with Oressa Wise) *Songs of Fellowship,* privately printed, 1972, Net Music Co., 1975; (editor with Jeanne Harper) *Sound of Living Waters,* Eerdmans, 1974; *Little Things in the Hands of a Big God,* Word Publishers, 1977; (editor with Mimi Farra) *Cry Hosanna,* Hope Publishing, 1980.

Q-R

QUINLAN, Red
See QUINLAN, Sterling C(arroll)

*   *   *

**QUINLAN, Sterling C(arroll) 1916-
(Red Quinlan)**

PERSONAL: Born October 23, 1916, in Maquoketa, Iowa; son of Carroll and Lillian (Sterling) Quinlan; married Elizabeth Longton, September 15, 1942; married Mary Janda, February 23, 1963; children: (second marriage) Thomas. *Home:* 5121 South Harvey, Western Springs, Ill. 60558. *Office:* 303 East Ohio St., Chicago, Ill. 60611.

CAREER: Began writing for community newspapers in Chicago, Ill., 1930; WIND (radio station), Gary, Ind., host of "The Boy Reporter and His Community" program, 1930-35; National Broadcasting Co. (NBC), writer and lead player for documentary series on transient life in America, 1936, staff writer in Cleveland, Ohio, 1936-37; free-lance actor and writer in Chicago and in Hollywood, Calif., 1937-40; WBKB (radio station), Chicago, employee, 1947-67, vice-president, 1953-67; vice-president, American Broadcasting Co. (ABC), 1953-64; Field Communications Corp., Chicago, president until 1967; currently vice-president of Broadcast Services Division, IDC Service Industries, Inc., Chicago. Member of board of directors, Better Business Bureau. *Military service:* U.S. Navy, five years. *Member:* Defense Orientation Conference Association, Navy League, Broadcast Advertising Club (director), Tavern Club, M and M Club, Economics Club.

WRITINGS: The Merger, Doubleday, 1958; *Jugger,* Obolensky, 1960; *Muldoon Was Here,* Citadel, 1967; *The Hundred Million Dollar Lunch,* J. Philip O'Hara, 1974; *Inside ABC: American Broadcasting Company's Rise to Power,* Hastings House, 1979. Also author of a play, "The Day the Sun Caught Cold."

*   *   *

RABY, William L(ouis) 1927-

PERSONAL: Born July 16, 1927, in Chicago, Ill.; son of Gustave E. (a painter) and Helen (Burgess) Raby; married Norma Claire Schreiner, September 8, 1956; children: Burgess, Marianne, Marlene. *Education:* Northwestern University, B.S., 1949; University of Illinois, C.P.A., 1950; University of Arizona, M.B.A., 1961, Ph.D., 1970. *Office:* 2700 Valley Bank Center, Phoenix, Ariz. 85073.

CAREER: Swenson & Raby (certified public accountants), Rockford, Ill., partner, 1950-60; William L. Raby & Co. (certified public accountants), Tucson, Ariz., partner, 1961-69; Laventhol & Horwath (certified public accountants), Philadelphia, Pa., partner in Phoenix, Ariz., office, 1969-77; Touche Ross & Co., New York, N.Y., partner in Phoenix office, 1977—. Lecturer in accounting, Rockford College, Rockford, Ill., 1954-55, and University of Arizona, 1958-70; associate professor of accounting, Ohio University, 1962-65; adjunct professor of taxation, New York University, 1978-81. Member of Tax Court bar. *Military service:* U.S. Navy, 1942-45. *Member:* American Institute of Certified Public Accountants (chairman of Federal Tax Division), American Accounting Association (past president of American Taxation Association section).

WRITINGS: The Income Tax and Business Decisions, Prentice-Hall, 1964, 4th edition, 1978; *Building and Maintaining a Successful Tax Practice,* Prentice-Hall, 1964; (with Carl Riblet, Jr.) *The Reluctant Taxpayer,* Cowles, 1970; *Tax Practice Management,* American Institute of Certified Public Accountants, 1974; (with Victor Tidwell) *Introduction to Federal Taxation* (annual), Prentice-Hall, 1980—.

Author of tax columns in *National Law Journal, Arizona Daily Star,* and *Los Angeles Times.* Contributor to professional journals. Member of editorial board, *Taxation for Accountants* and *Tax Advisor.*

*   *   *

**RAE, Hugh C(rauford) 1935-
(Robert Crawford, R. B. Houston, Stuart Stern)**

PERSONAL: Born November 22, 1935, in Glasgow, Scotland; son of Robert Tennant (a carpenter) and Isobel (McNair) Rae; married Elizabeth Dunn, September 3, 1960; children: Gillian (daughter). *Education:* Attended school in Glasgow, Scotland. *Politics:* Conservative. *Religion:* Presbyterian. *Home:* Drumore Farm Cottage, Gartness Rd., Balfron Station, Stirlingshire, Scotland. *Agent:* Fraser & Dunlop Ltd., 91 Regent St., London W1R 8RU, England.

CAREER: John Smith & Son Ltd. (antiquarian booksellers), Glasgow, Scotland, assistant, 1952-65; full-time writer, 1965—. Lecturer in creative writing, University of Glasgow. *Military service:* Royal Air Force, National Service, 1954-56. *Member:*

P.E.N., Scottish Association of Writers (president, 1970-77), Scottish Arts Council (member of literature committee, beginning 1973).

WRITINGS: *Skinner*, Viking, 1965; *Night Pillow*, Viking, 1967; *A Few Small Bones*, Anthony Blond, 1968; *The House at Balnesmoor*, Coward, 1969; *The Interview*, Coward, 1969; *The Saturday Epic*, Coward, 1970; *The Marksman*, Coward, 1971; *The Shooting Gallery*, Coward, 1972; *The Rock Harvest*, Constable, 1973; *The Rookery*, Constable, 1974, St. Martin's, 1975; *Harkfast!: The Making of the King*, St. Martin's, 1976; (under pseudonym Stuart Stern with S. Ungar) *The Minotaur Factor*, Playboy Press, 1977; (under pseudonym Stuart Stern) *The Poison Tree*, Playboy Press, 1978; *The Travelling Soul*, Avon, 1978; *Sullivan*, Playboy Press, 1978; (editor) *Scottish Short Stories*, Collins, 1978; *The Haunting at Waverly Falls*, Constable, 1980; *Privileged Strangers*, Hodder & Stoughton, 1982.

Under pseudonym Robert Crawford: *Cockleburr*, Constable, 1969, Putnam, 1970; *The Shroud Society*, Putnam, 1969; *Kiss the Boss Goodbye*, Constable, 1970, Putnam, 1971; *The Badger's Daughter*, Constable, 1971; *Whip Hand*, Constable, 1972.

Also author of plays, television scripts, short stories, poems, and literary articles.

SIDELIGHTS: Hugh C. Rae wrote *CA*: "Compulsive writer.... No strong desire to travel. No foreign languages. No strong commitment to any specific cause through development of an 'innocent bystander' attitude. Boringly single-minded." As a novelist, he splits his interest between "Victorian history and contemporary America. The act of writing a novel has long ceased to be an adventure but the opportunity to research social history and contemporary power politics keeps the juice flowing."

AVOCATIONAL INTERESTS: The cinema and theater, television, reading, sports (tennis, golf, and basketball).

* * *

RAE, Milford Andersen 1946-
(Rusty Rae)

PERSONAL: Born October 5, 1946, in Sheridan, Wyo.; son of Joseph (a photographer) and Ruth (a receptionist; maiden name, Stutsman) Rae; married Claudia Jane Neubauer (a home economics teacher), May 23, 1970 (died October, 1980); children: Joseph Edward. *Education:* Attended Tacoma Community College, 1966-67, and University of Washington, Seattle, summer, 1969; Linfield College, B.A., 1970. *Politics:* Independent. *Religion:* Episcopalian. *Home and office address:* P.O. Box 486, Lafayette, Ore. 97127; and 8440 136th S.E., Renton, Wash. 98055.

CAREER: *Port Orchard Independent*, Port Orchard, Wash., news editor, 1970; *McMinnville News Register*, McMinnville, Ore., sports editor, 1970-73; American Motorcycle Association, Westerville, Ohio, photography editor, 1972-76; instructor at Nikon School, 1976-79; independent producer of visual communications (magazines, brochures, slide shows, films, and video presentations), 1979—. Sports information director at Linfield College, 1970-72. *Member:* National Press Photographers Association, American Power Boat Association. *Awards, honors:* First prize in National Association of Intercollegiate Athletics photography contest, 1972, and Federation Internationale Motorcyclists photography contest, 1974.

WRITINGS—Under name Rusty Rae: *Speed and Spray: The Story of Stock Outboard Power Boat Racing,* self-illustrated with photographs, Stackpole, 1975; *The World's Biggest Motorcycle Race: The Daytona 200*, Lerner, 1978; (with John Yaw) *Grand National Championship Races*, Lerner, 1978. Author, with John Yaw, of *Motocross Racing;* also author of material for Associated Press. Contributor to magazines and newspapers.

WORK IN PROGRESS: *Motorcycle Hill Climbing* and *Boatracing*, both for Lerner; a movie script.

SIDELIGHTS: Rusty Rae told *CA*: "I feel honored and just a little out of place by being included with all of these wordsmiths, since what I do best is not necessarily write (although that certainly is a part of what I do), but rather meld words and pictures together into stories so that the whole is greater than the sum of the parts.

"This is something that I guess I have always been interested in, since my father was a professional photographer, and from my earliest memory I have been fascinated by the power that photographs have in the communicative process. However, I also realize that in most cases photographs or picture stories become not only more interesting, but more complete, with the addition of the appropriate words."

AVOCATIONAL INTERESTS: Participating as a driver in boat races (stock outboards), many other sports, reading, travel.

* * *

RAE, Rusty
See RAE, Milford Andersen

* * *

RAFFAELE, Joseph A(ntonio) 1916-

PERSONAL: Born September 1, 1916, in New York, N.Y.; son of John and Frances Raffaele; married Pia Rossi (a professor of Romance languages); children: Piera, Joseph Mark. *Education:* City College (now City College of the City University of New York), B.A., 1939; Temple University, M.A., 1947; University of Pennsylvania, Ph.D., 1955. *Home:* 513 Midland Cir., St. Davids, Pa. 19087. *Office:* Department of Management, Drexel University, Philadelphia, Pa. 19104.

CAREER: Drexel University, Philadelphia, Pa., 1958—, currently professor of human resource development. Labor arbitrator. *Military service:* U.S. Army Reserve; present rank, major. *Member:* National Academy of Arbitrators.

WRITINGS: *Labor Leadership in Italy and Denmark*, University of Wisconsin Press, 1962; *The Economic Development of Nations*, Random House, 1971; *System and Unsystem: An Ethnic View of Organization and Society*, Schenkman, 1974; *The Mafia Principle*, University Press of America, 1979; *The Management of Technology: Change in a Society of Organized Advocacies*, University Press of America, 1979. Contributor of articles to labor journals and personnel magazines.

* * *

RAJARAM
See IYENGAR, K(odaganallur) R(amaswami) Srinivasa

* * *

RAMANUJAN, A(ttipat) K(rishnaswami) 1929-

PERSONAL: First two "a's" in surname are long vowels; born March 16, 1929, in Mysore, India; son of Attipat Asuri (a professor) and Seshammal Krishnaswami; married Molly Daniels, June 7, 1962; children: Krittika (daughter), Krishnaswami (son). *Education:* Mysore University, B.A. (with honors), 1949, M.A., 1950; Deccan College, graduate diplomas, 1958 and 1959; Indiana University, Ph.D., 1963. *Home:* 5629 South Dorchester Ave., Chicago, Ill. 60637. *Office:* South Asia Language and Area Center, University of Chicago, 1130 East 59th St., Chicago, Ill. 60637.

CAREER: Lecturer in English at colleges in India, 1950-58, including University of Baroda, 1957-58; University of Chicago, Chicago, Ill., research associate in Tamil, 1961, assistant professor of linguistics (Tamil and Dravidian languages), 1962-65, associate professor, 1966-68, professor of linguistics and Dravidian studies, 1968—, professor on committee on social thought, 1972—, chairman of department of South Asian languages and civilizations, 1980—. Visiting professor, University of Wisconsin, 1965 and 1971, University of California at Berkeley, 1966 and 1973, University of Michigan, 1970, and Carleton College, 1978.

AWARDS, HONORS: Fulbright travel fellowship and Smith-Mundt fellowship for study in United States, 1959-60; faculty research fellowship, American Institute of Indian Studies, 1963-64; fellow, Indiana School of Letters, 1963; Poetry Society recommendation, 1964, for *The Striders;* Tamil Writers' Association Award, 1969; Fulbright fellowship, 1969; American Council of Learned Societies fellowship, 1973; National Book Award nomination, 1974, for *Speaking of Siva;* National Endowment for the Humanities fellowships, 1976 and 1982; named Padma Sri by Government of India, 1976.

WRITINGS: Proverbs (in Kannada), Karnatak University (Dharwar, India), 1955; *Fifteen Poems from a Classical Tamil Anthology,* Writer's Workshop (Calcutta), 1965; (translator into Kannada) Molly Ramanujan (wife), *The Yellow Fish,* Manohar Granthmala (Dharwar), 1966; *The Striders* (poems), Oxford University Press, 1966; (translator) *The Interior Landscape: Love Poems from a Classical Tamil Anthology,* Indiana University Press, 1967; (translator with Michael Garman and Rajeev Taranath) M. Gopalakrishna Adiga, *The Song of the Earth and Other Poems,* Writer's Workshop, 1968; *No Lotus in the Navel* (poems; in Kannada), Manohar Granthmala, 1969; *Relations* (poems), Oxford University Press, 1972; (translator) *Speaking of Siva,* Penguin, 1973; (with E. C. Dimock and others) *The Literatures of India: An Introduction,* University of Chicago Press, 1975; (translator) U. R. Anantha Murthy, *Samskara* (novel), Oxford University Press, 1976; *And Other Poems* (in Kannada), [Dharwar], 1977; *Selected Poems,* Oxford University Press, 1977; *Mattobbana Atmakate* (novel), [Dharwar], 1978; (translator) *Hymns for the Drowning* (medieval Tamil religious poems), Princeton University Press, 1981.

Poems in English are represented in more than sixty anthologies and have been published in Indian, British, and American periodicals.

WORK IN PROGRESS: A book of poems; a book of translations from classical Tamil; a book of Indian folktales.

BIOGRAPHICAL/CRITICAL SOURCES: New York Times Book Review, November 20, 1966; *Poetry,* March, 1967.

* * *

**RANGER, Ken
See CREASEY, John**

* * *

RANUM, Orest Allen 1933-

PERSONAL: Born February 18, 1933, in Lyle, Minn.; son of Luther George (a carpenter) and Nada (Chaffee) Ranum; married Patricia McGroder (an editor and translator) July 4, 1955; children: Kristin Helena, Marcus James Aymar. *Education:* Macalester College, A.B., 1955; University of Minnesota, M.A., 1957, Ph.D., 1960. *Home:* 208 Ridgewood Rd., Baltimore, Md. 21210. *Office:* Department of History, Johns Hopkins University, Baltimore, Md. 21218.

CAREER: University of Strasbourg, Strasbourg, France, lecturer, 1959-60; University of Southern California, Los Angeles, assistant professor of history, 1960-61; Columbia University, New York, N.Y., assistant professor, 1961-64, associate professor of history, 1964-69; Johns Hopkins University, Baltimore, Md., professor of history, 1969—, chairman of department, 1969—. Fellow, Institute of Advanced Studies, 1973-74. *Member:* American Historical Association, French Historical Society. *Awards, honors:* Guggenheim fellow, 1968-69.

WRITINGS: Richelieu and the Councillor of Louis XIII: A Study of the Secretaries of State and Superintendents of Finance in the Ministry of Richelieu, 1635-1642, Oxford University Press, 1963; *Paris in the Age of Absolutism: An Essay,* Wiley, 1968; (editor) *Searching for Modern Times: Discussion Problems and Readings,* two volumes, Dodd, 1969.

(Editor with wife, Patricia Ranum) *The Century of Louis XIV,* Harper, 1972; (editor with Patricia Ranum) *Popular Attitudes Toward Birth Control in Pre-Industrial France and England,* Harper, 1972; (editor) *National Consciousness, History, and Political Culture in Early-Modern Europe,* Johns Hopkins University Press, 1975; (editor with Robert Forster) *Biology of Man in History,* Johns Hopkins University Press, 1975; (editor with Forster) *Family and Society,* Johns Hopkins University Press, 1976; (author of introduction) Jacques-Benigne Bossnet, *Discourse on Universal History,* University of Chicago, 1976; (with Forster) *Rural Society in France,* Johns Hopkins University Press, 1977; (contributor) Forster, editor, *Deviants and the Abandoned in French Society,* Johns Hopkins University Press, 1978; (editor with Forster) *Food and Drink in History,* Johns Hopkins University Press, 1979.

Artisans of Glory: Writers and Historical Thought in Seventeenth-Century France, University of North Carolina Press, 1980; (editor with Forster) *Medicine and Society in France,* Johns Hopkins University Press, 1980. Contributor of articles and reviews to journals.

SIDELIGHTS: In a review of *Paris in the Age of Absolutism,* J. H. Plumb writes in *Saturday Review*: "The story of Paris's growth, of its transmogrification from a small, largely mediaeval, highly clustered town into a city of Roman grandeur worthy of the Sun King, is told with admirable scholarship by Professor Ranum. His range is enviably wide. Most historians fight shy of literary matters, but Corneille, Racine and Moliere have no terrors for him. His sensitivity and knowledge of music, architecture and painting are equally great. He is as much at home with the complexity of the Parisian constitution as its tax system and economic life. Above all, he is a social historian with a keen sense of the importance of religion as well as politics. And in consequence he has written one of the best histories of an epoch in the life of a great city that I know."

BIOGRAPHICAL/CRITICAL SOURCES: Saturday Review, February 22, 1969; *Spectator,* March 21, 1969.

* * *

RAPOPORT, Rhona (Ross) 1927-

PERSONAL: Born January 29, 1927, in South Africa; daughter of Ely (a businessman) and Cecilia Ross; married Robert N. Rapoport (a sociologist), February 14, 1957; children: Lorna, Alin. *Education:* University of Capetown, B.Soc.Sci., 1946; London School of Economics and Political Science, Ph.D., 1951. *Home:* 7A Kidderpore Ave., London NW3 7SX, England. *Office:* Institute of Family and Environmental Research, London, England.

CAREER: Sociologist, East African Institute of Social Research, University College of East Africa, 1951-52; assistant psychologist, Tavistock Clinic, 1952-53; engaged in various research programs, 1953-59, including work as research associate for Joint Commission for the Study of Mental Illness and Health in the United States, 1957-59; Harvard University, Cambridge, Mass., lecturer on mental health at School of Public Health and Medical School and director of family research for Community Health Program, 1959-66; consulting sociologist, 1967-71; senior social scientist, Tavistock Institute of Human Relations, 1969-73; Institute of Family and Environmental Research, London, England, co-director, 1973—. Member of executive boards, International Scientific Commission on the Family and Human Resources Center of the Tavistock Institute, both 1970—. Consultant to Ford Foundation, 1982. *Member:* International Sociological Association, International Psychoanalytic Society, British Sociological Association, British Psychoanalytic Society, American Sociological Association.

WRITINGS: (With Michael Fogarty) *Sex, Career, and Family,* Sage Publications, 1971; *Dual Career Families,* Penguin, 1971, 2nd edition published as *Dual Career Families Reexamined,* Harper, 1977; *Leisure and the Family Life Cycle,* Routledge & Kegan Paul, 1975; *Fathers, Mothers, and Others,* Routledge & Kegan Paul, 1977; (with Michael Dower) *Leisure Provision and People's Needs,* H.M.S.O., 1981. Advisory editor of *Family Process,* 1966—.

*   *   *

RAU, Margaret   1913-

PERSONAL: Surname rhymes with "now"; born December 23, 1913, in Swatow, China; daughter of George Wright (a missionary) and Mary Victoria (a missionary; maiden name, Wolfe) Lewis; married Neil Rau (a writer), 1935 (died, 1971); children: Robert, Peter, Peggy, Frank, Thomas. *Education:* Studied under private tutor in China; attended University of Chicago, 1931, Columbia University, 1932, and University of Redlands, 1933-34; Riverside Library College, degree, 1934. *Home:* 5807 Topanga Canyon Blvd., No. B-303, Woodland Hills, Calif. 91367.

CAREER: Writer. *Member:* Photographic Society of America, United States-China People's Friendship Association, National Writers Guild, Authors Guild. *Awards, honors:* Notable Children's Trade Books in Social Studies Award, 1974, for *Our World: The People's Republic of China,* and 1981, for *Red Earth, Blue Sky;* Outstanding Science Books for Children Award, 1977, for *Musk Oxen, Bearded Ones of the North* and *The Giant Panda at Home,* and 1978, for *The Grey Kangaroo at Home;* Southern California Council on Literature for Children and Young People Award for a distinguished work of nonfiction published during 1979, for *The Snow Monkey at Home.*

WRITINGS—Juvenile books: *Band of the Red Hand,* Knopf, 1938; *Dawn from the West,* Hawthorn, 1964; *The Penguin Book,* Hawthorn, 1968; *The Yellow River,* Messner, 1969; *The Yangtze River,* Messner, 1970; (self-illustrated with photographs) *Jimmy of Cherry Valley,* Messner, 1973; *Our World: The People's Republic of China,* Messner, 1974, revised edition, 1981; *Musk Oxen, Bearded Ones of the North,* Crowell, 1976; *The Giant Panda at Home,* Knopf, 1977; *The Grey Kangaroo at Home,* Knopf, 1978; *The Snow Monkey at Home,* Knopf, 1979; *Red Earth, Blue Sky,* Crowell, 1981; *Young People of China,* Dutton, 1983.

Adult books; with husband, Neil Rau, except as indicated: *My Father, Charlie Chaplin,* Random House, 1960; *Act Your Way to Successful Living,* Prentice-Hall, 1966; *My Dear Ones,* Prentice-Hall, 1971; (sole author) *People of New China,* Messner, 1978, revised edition, 1980; (sole author) *Minority Peoples of China,* Messner, 1982. Author of six-part film strip series covering ancient and modern China, Activity Records, 1977; collaborator with husband on material used by Norman Lear for film, "Cold Turkey," United Artists, 1972. Also author of pamphlets on China. Contributor to *Parents' Magazine* and *Cricket.*

SIDELIGHTS: Margaret Rau told *CA:* "I grew up in China where I spoke Chinese for four years before learning English. I have always felt a deep and abiding love for the countryside in which I grew up and for the people among whom I found myself. Now with China taking a new and ever-growing role in the modern world I feel it imperative that our young people know something about this great country and the Chinese—their aims, dreams and hopes. In 1974 I paid a visit to the People's Republic of China. I returned again in 1978, 1979, 1980 and expect to go again in 1982. I have also spent 10 months in Australia where I gathered material for my kangaroo book and my *Red Earth, Blue Sky* about the Australian outback. I expect to return there too in the near future. I have also traveled in New England, Fiji, Japan, Europe, and the Soviet Union."

BIOGRAPHICAL/CRITICAL SOURCES: Washington Post Book World, January 13, 1980.

*   *   *

RAY, Wesley
See GAULDEN, Ray

*   *   *

REED, John R(obert)   1938-

PERSONAL: Born January 24, 1938, in Duluth, Minn.; son of John Sam and Josephine (Zuponcic) Reed; married Ruth Yzenbaard. *Education:* University of Minnesota, Duluth, B.A. (in music and English), 1959; University of Rochester, Ph.D., 1963. *Home:* 17320 Wildemere, Detroit, Mich. 48221. *Office:* Department of English, Wayne State University, Detroit, Mich. 48202.

CAREER: University of Cincinnati, Cincinnati, Ohio, instructor in English, 1962-64; University of Connecticut, Storrs, assistant professor of English, 1964-65; Wayne State University, Detroit, Mich., assistant professor, 1965-68, associate professor, 1968-71, professor of English, 1971—. *Member:* Modern Language Association of America, Midwest Victorian Studies Association (vice-president, 1979-80; president, 1981-82). *Awards, honors:* Leverhulme fellow, University of Warwick, 1966-67; Guggenheim fellow, 1971; Wayne State University faculty grants.

WRITINGS: Old School Ties: The Public Schools in British Literature, Syracuse University Press, 1964; *Perception and Design in Tennyson's "Idylls of the King,"* Ohio University Press, 1970; (contributor) Jerome Mazzaro, editor, *Profile of Robert Lowell,* C. E. Merrill, 1971; (contributor) Peter Lisca, editor, John Steinbeck, *The Grapes of Wrath* (critical edition),

Viking, 1972; *Hercules* (poetry), Fiddlehead Poetry Books, 1973; *Victorian Conventions,* Ohio University Press, 1975; *A Gallery of Spiders* (poetry), Ontario Review Press, 1980; *The Natural History of H. G. Wells,* Ohio University Press, 1982.

Contributor of articles to *Western Humanities Review, Victorian Poetry, English Literary History, Nineteenth-Century Fiction, Dickens Studies Annual,* and other periodicals, and of poems to *Sewanee Review, Poetry, Modern Poetry Studies,* and other journals.

WORK IN PROGRESS: Research on the will in nineteenth-century English literature and on decadent style in the arts.

SIDELIGHTS: John R. Reed told *CA:* "Working with Raymond Smith and Joyce Carol Oates in preparing *A Gallery of Spiders* for publication in their Ontario Review Press poetry series taught me much about being a professional poet, and since then I have become more serious in my ambitions and have devoted more of my attention to poetry. Jerome Mazzaro, reviewing *A Gallery of Spiders* in the *Michigan Quarterly Review,* writes: 'Reed commits himself to a view of the individual poet's voice as the "concrete universal" of society and, consequently, to views of greatness in art as being related to comprehensiveness of soul. *A Gallery of Spiders* makes a fine beginning toward such comprehensiveness, as Reed emerges intelligent, inquisitive, and alternately compassionate and angry.' Mazzaro's observation has helped me to understand better that what I wish to achieve in my poems is a union of ambiguous and ambivalent emotions with a manner of perception that treats experiences as problems to be solved, though not resolved, by intellect."

AVOCATIONAL INTERESTS: Writing poetry, music (plays trumpet), travel.

BIOGRAPHICAL/CRITICAL SOURCES: Michigan Quarterly Review, fall, 1981; *Times Literary Supplement,* August 20, 1982.

* * *

REESE, William Lewis 1921-

PERSONAL: Born February 15, 1921, in Jefferson City, Mo.; son of William Lewis (a minister) and Lillian (Fisher) Reese; married Louise Weeks (a librarian), June 11, 1945; children: Claudia, Patricia, William L. III. *Education:* Drury College, A.B., 1942; University of Chicago, B.D., 1945, Ph.D., 1947; Yale University, postdoctoral study, 1955-56. *Religion:* Unitarian Universalist. *Home:* Font Grove Road, Slingerlands, New York 12159. *Office:* Department of Philosophy, Humanities 257, State University of New York, 1400 Washington Ave., Albany, N.Y. 12222.

CAREER: Drake University, Des Moines, Iowa, assistant professor, 1947-49, associate professor of philosophy, 1949-57, head of department, 1954-57; Grinnell College, Grinnell, Iowa, associate professor of philosophy, 1957-60; University of Delaware, Newark, professor of philosophy and chairman of department, 1960-66, H. Rodney Sharp Professor of Philosophy, 1965-66; State University of New York at Albany, professor of philosophy, 1967—, chairman of department, 1968-74. Visiting professor, Iowa State University, 1958, and University of Mexico in Iztapalapa, 1980; Tully Cleon Knoles Lecturer, University of the Pacific, 1962; Fulbright lecturer in Argentina, summer, 1971; lecturer, University of Peking, Peking Academy of the Social Sciences, University of Nanking, and Fudan University, summer, 1979. Senior fellow, Institute for Humanistic Studies, 1977—. President and member of board of governors, Metaphilosophy Foundation, Inc.

MEMBER: Metaphysical Society of America (secretary-treasurer, 1962-65), American Philosophical Association, American Association of University Professors, Society for Iberian and Latin American Thought, Latin American Studies Association, Fulbright Alumni Association. *Awards, honors:* Ford Foundation fellow in Argentina, 1967; *Dictionary of Philosophy and Religion: Eastern and Western Thought* was named "outstanding reference work of 1980" by American Library Association.

WRITINGS: (Contributor) *Studies in C. S. Peirce,* Harvard University Press, 1952; (with Charles Hartshorne) *Philosophers Speak of God,* University of Chicago Press, 1953; *The Ascent from Below,* Houghton, 1959; (general editor) *Philosophy of Science,* Volumes I-II, Interscience, 1963; (contributing editor) *Philosophical Interrogations,* Holt, 1964; (editor with Eugene Freeman) *Process and Divinity: The Hartshorne Festschrift,* Open Court, 1964; (contributor) *Business and the Humanities: A Symposium,* Humanities Center for Liberal Education, 1965; (general editor) *Philosophy of Science,* Volume III (Reese was not associated with earlier editions), Springer-Verlag, 1967; *Dictionary of Philosophy and Religion: Eastern and Western Thought,* Humanities Press, 1980. Contributor to *Charles Hartshorne and Henry Nelson Wireman,* 1969, and *The Future of Metaphysics,* 1970. Also contributor to *Encyclopaedia Britannica,* 1974. Contributor to *Saturday Review* and to philosophy journals.

WORK IN PROGRESS: A study of religion that will try "to go behind the conceptual super-structures to the sub-structures of metaphor and myth," tentatively entitled *The Metaphorical Basis of Religious Structures; A Latin American Reader.*

SIDELIGHTS: "I write only to complete myself," William Lewis Reese told *CA.* "All else is beyond my control—publication, sales, influence. I learned this from my son when I was still working on my *Dictionary of Philosophy and Religion: Eastern and Western Thought,* the manuscript still not completed after eighteen years. My son explained to me that it didn't matter if the book were never published. The important fact was the mental activity I had been able to enjoy all those years. When I submitted the completed manuscript to my publisher the editors wanted me, because of [the book's] size to separate philosophy from religion, or Eastern from Western thought, publishing two separate books. But the manuscript was the way I wanted it. With my son's principle in mind, with utter lightness of heart I was able to withdraw the manuscript from the original publisher. At that time I had no conviction the book would ever be published. But if the important act lay in the writing, there was obviously no point in compromising such minor detail as its publication. Within months Humanities Press had come forward [and agreed] to publish the manuscript in the single volume format I had planned. Shortly, the book was named "outstanding reference work of 1980" by the American Library Association. What can I say? 'To thine own self be true.'"

* * *

REICH, Steve 1936-

PERSONAL: Born October 3, 1936, in New York, N.Y. *Education:* Cornell University, B.A. (with honors), 1957; graduate study, Juilliard School of Music, 1958-61; Mills College, M.A., 1963; additional graduate study, University of Ghana, 1970, and American Society for Eastern Arts, summers, 1973-74. *Religion:* Jewish. *Home:* 16 Warren St., New York, N.Y. 10007.

CAREER: Composer and performer in San Francisco, Calif., 1963-65; composer and performer in his own music ensemble in New York, N.Y., 1965—. Has made appearances at Carnegie Hall, Town Hall, and Museum of Modern Art. Collaborated on music and dance concerts throughout Europe and at New York University, 1972-73. *Awards, honors:* National Endowment for the Arts grant, 1974; New York State Council on the Arts grant, 1974; Rockefeller Foundation grants, 1975, 1979, and 1981; Guggenheim fellow, 1978; Koussevitzky International Recording Award, 1981.

WRITINGS: Writings about Music (essays), New York University Press, 1974, enlarged French translation published as *Ecrits et entretiens sur la musique,* Bourgois, 1981.

Also author of various recorded compositions, including "Come Out," Odyssey, 1967, "It's Gonna Rain" and "Violin Phase," Columbia Records, 1969, "Four Organs," Angel Records, 1973, "Drumming," "Six Pianos," and "Music for Mallet Instruments, Voices, and Organ," Deutsche Grammophon, 1974, "Music for Eighteen Musicians," ECM Records, 1978, "Octet," "Music for a Large Ensemble," and "Violin Phase," ECM Records, 1980, and "Tehillim," ECM Records, 1982. Author of other compositions, including "Phase Patterns," "Clapping Music," "Music for Pieces of Wood," and "Variations for Winds, Strings and Keyboards."

WORK IN PROGRESS: Composing works commissioned by the flutist Ransom Wilson, the Cologne Radio Symphony and Chorus, the St. Louis Symphony, the London Sinfonietta, and the San Francisco Symphony.

SIDELIGHTS: Described by *Newsweek*'s Annalyn Swan as one of today's leading composers of "stripped-down, hypnotically repetitive, so-called 'minimal' music," Steve Reich is committed to making an original and personally satisfying statement as he blends new musical forms with old. Explains Reich: "I didn't become a composer so that someone would pat me on the back and say, 'That's a pretty good twelve-tone piece, almost as good as third-rate Berio or Stockhausen,' which I think can be said of much serial music in America. Instead, I opted to do what came naturally. Basically I was after music with a strong, clear pulse, a clear tonal center, and that was clearly mine. . . . The listener I'm most concerned with is myself. I feel obliged to do something that's going to engage me."

Reich typically borrows and adapts elements from a wide variety of styles and composers. Bach and Stravinsky, for example, are among his more "traditional" sources of inspiration. As a teenager, however, he developed an interest in jazz, and later, in his twenties, he was intrigued by Terry Riley's innovative and repetitively patterned composition "In C." Reich's exposure to new forms of music continued throughout the 1970s. Early in the decade, he journeyed to Ghana to study with a master drummer of the Ewe tribe at the Institute of African Studies; in subsequent years, he received instruction in the cantillation (chanting) of Hebrew scripture and in the specialized tuned percussion music known as Balinese Gamelan Semar Pegulingan.

These diverse kinds of music have all made their mark on Reich's work, often to such an extent that, as Swan points out, "on first hearing, [his] music can seem maddeningly mindless and static to ears steeped in the classical and romantic traditions. . . . The initial effect is of a floating, somewhat amorphous cloud of sound. Gradually, however, you begin to distinguish the subtly varied patterns within the whole. . . . Like Eastern music, Reich's compositions use the most sophisticated of means to achieve the simplest of surfaces. They are at once exhilarating, because of the bright intensity of his timbres and musical colors, and tranquil, because of their seeming suspension in time."

After praising Reich's "lively percussion patterns," "gentle sustained chords," and "light, quick notes," Gregory Sandow declares in a *Village Voice* article that "surely Steve Reich is one of the best composers around. I can't agree with most of the critical remarks about him. I don't think his way of writing turns musicians into robots fit only to execute mechanical repeating patterns; not everyone might want to play his music, but the people who do play it sound inspired and at times even exalted. I don't worry that his pieces are too much like their African and Balinese influences or else not rhythmically complicated enough to be worthy of them; Reich is not writing African or Balinese music. To my ear—though he uses sounds taken from music he likes, just as any composer would, and for that matter is original in countless ways of his own—he is a *western* composer, working squarely in the tradition of western classical music."

"Reich's work has been called 'minimal music,'" observes the *New Yorker*'s Andrew Porter. "It is a label that can fairly be attached to some of his earlier compositions, . . . which are based on the rigorous working out of a single idea. It does not apply to his increasingly thoughtful and elaborately eloquent later pieces. The reflection that Beethoven and Reich seem to have worked at some of the same 'problems' can calm the uneasiness voiced [by those who feel the composer relies too heavily on simple harmonies and a steady beat]. His music has a joyful, very attractive surface; it may be that some of his admirers do not get beyond it. . . . But there is substance beneath."

Concludes Swan: "In the 1960s he was all but unheard of outside Manhattan's Soho district. In the '70s he was often dismissed as little more than a cult figure. But in the '80s Steve Reich . . . is emerging as one of the central influences in experimental music."

Reich's compositions have been performed by several orchestras in the United States and abroad, including the Boston Symphony Orchestra, the San Francisco Symphony, the South German Radio Symphony, and the New York Philharmonic.

BIOGRAPHICAL/CRITICAL SOURCES: New York, May 25, 1970; *Musical Times,* March, 1971; *New York Times,* October 24, 1971, March 14, 1982; *Washington Post,* February 24, 1972; *Artforum,* May, 1972; *New Yorker,* November 6, 1978; *Chicago Tribune,* March 4, 1979; *Village Voice,* March 10, 1980; *Musical America,* June, 1980; *Christian Science Monitor,* October 23, 1980; *Newsweek,* March 29, 1982.

* * *

REILLY, D(avid) Robin 1928-

PERSONAL: Born January 3, 1928, in Everton, Hampshire, England; son of Noel Edmund and Margaret Mary (Dearbergh) Reilly. *Education:* Attended Royal Military Academy, Sandhurst, England, 1947-48. *Politics:* None. *Religion:* Church of England. *Agent:* Curtis Brown Ltd., 1 Craven Hill, London W2 3EW, England.

CAREER: British Army, career service, 1945-52, retired as captain; London director, Josiah Wedgwood & Sons Ltd.; partner, Hogarth Galleries. Committee member, National Trust, 1960-76. *Member:* Glyndebourne Festival Society.

WRITINGS: Portrait Waxes, Batsford, 1953; *The Rest to Fortune: The Life of Major-General James Wolfe,* Cassell, 1960, Dufour, 1964, published as *Wolfe of Quebec,* White Lion Publishers, 1973; *The Sixth Floor,* Frewin, 1969; *Wedgwood Jasper,* World Publishing, 1972; *Wedgwood Portrait Medallions: An Introduction* (exhibition catalog), Barrie & Jenkins, 1973;

Wedgwood: The Portrait of Medallions, Barrie & Jenkins, 1973; *British Watercolours,* Letts, 1974; *The British at the Gates: The New Orleans Campaign in the War of 1812,* Putnam, 1974; *Pitt the Younger, 1759-1806,* Cassell, 1978, published as *William Pitt the Younger,* Putnam, 1979; *The Dictionary of Wedgwood,* Antique Collectors' Club, 1980; *The Collector's Wedgwood,* Portfolio Press, 1980.

Contributor of articles to *Encyclopaedia Britannica, Encyclopedia of Knowledge,* and *Dictionary of Business Biography* and to *Science Today, Design and Industry, House and Garden,* and other periodicals.

AVOCATIONAL INTERESTS: Music, art, tennis.

* * *

REILLY, William K.
See CREASEY, John

* * *

REISMAN, John M(ark) 1930-

PERSONAL: Born May 22, 1930, in Perth Amboy, N.J.; son of Harry (a plumber) and Frieda (Feuerman) Reisman; married Margo Sue Jacobson, June 19, 1955; children: Hope, David, Carl, Andrew. *Education:* Rutgers University, B.S., 1952; Michigan State University, M.A., 1955, Ph.D., 1958. *Home:* 730 Milburn St., Evanston, Ill. 60201. *Office:* Department of Psychology, De Paul University, Chicago, Ill. 60614.

CAREER: Children's Memorial Hospital, Chicago, Ill., staff psychologist, 1958-59; Northwestern University, Medical School, Chicago, instructor in psychology, 1958-59; Rochester Mental Health Center, Rochester, N.Y., chief psychologist in Children and Youth Division, 1959-69; Memphis State University, Memphis, Tenn., professor of psychology and director of psychology clinic, 1969-75; De Paul University, Chicago, professor of psychology and director of clinical training, 1975—. Clinical associate, University of Rochester. Consultant, Hillside Children's Center. *Military service:* U.S. Navy, 1952-54; became lieutenant junior grade. *Member:* American Psychological Association.

WRITINGS: The Development of Clinical Psychology, Appleton, 1966; *Toward the Intergration of Psychotherapy,* Wiley, 1971; *Principles of Psychotherapy with Children,* Wiley, 1973; *The History of Clinical Psychology,* Irvington, 1976; *Anatomy of Friendship,* Irvington, 1979; *P.S. Your Shrink Is Dead,* Leisure Books, 1979.

Contributor: A. Hess, editor, *Supervision in Psychotherapy,* Wiley, 1980; S. Duck and R. Gilmour, editors, *Developing Personal Relations,* Volume II, Academic Press, 1981; C. E. Walker, editor, *Clinical Practice of Psychology,* Pergamon, 1981. Contributor to professional journals.

WORK IN PROGRESS: Editing *Psychopathology of Children and Adolescents,* for Addison-Wesley.

SIDELIGHTS: John M. Reisman told *CA:* "I have learned that you should do what is intrinsically rewarding, that bitterness and disappointment imply the imposition of your own expectations upon a world that has no obligation to fulfill them, and that life should be savored."

* * *

RESTAK, Richard M(artin) 1942-

PERSONAL: Born February 4, 1942, in Wilmington, Del.; son of Lewis J. (a physician) and Alice (Hynes) Restak; married Carolyn Serbent, October 12, 1968; children: Jennifer, Alison. *Education:* Gettysburg College, A.B., 1962; Georgetown University, M.D., 1966. *Home:* 4737 Fulton St. N.W., Washington, D.C. 20007. *Agent:* Ann Buchvald, Washington, D.C.

CAREER: St. Vincent's Hospital, New York City, intern, 1966-67; Mount Sinai Hospital, New York City, psychiatric resident, 1967-68; Georgetown University Hospital, Washington, D.C., psychiatric resident, 1968-69; George Washington University Hospital, Washington, D.C., resident in neurology, 1970-73; neurologist and neuropsychiatrist in Washington, D.C., 1973—. Clinical instructor at Georgetown University, 1975—; visiting lecturer at Kenyon College, Wright State Medical School, University of Kentucky, and Ohio State University. Consultant to British Council for Science and Society, and Kennedy Institute for the Study of Human Reproduction and Bioethics.

WRITINGS: Premeditated Man: The Bioethics and Control of Future Human Life, Viking, 1975; *The Brain: The Last Frontier,* Doubleday, 1979; *The Self Seekers,* Doubleday, 1982. Contributor of articles and reviews to psychology journals and to newspapers and magazines, including *Saturday Review, New York Times,* and *Washington Post.*

WORK IN PROGRESS: Magazine articles for *Science Digest, Science '82,* and *Smithsonian.*

SIDELIGHTS: About Richard M. Restak's *The Brain: The Last Frontier, Washington Post* reviewer Maya Pines writes: "[This book is] a densely packed and conscientious compendium of everything you ever wanted to know about the human brain and its workings. It has something for everyone." Although critical of some chapter headings and Restak's lack of supporting evidence in certain instances, Pines concludes, "All in all, . . . *The Brain: The Last Frontier* is a noble effort to cover the entire range of developments in brain research during the past 20 years, showing its contributions as well as some of its dangers."

The Self Seekers deals with the range of narcissism inherent in humanity and its behavior manifestations. Bruce Mazlish of the *Washington Post Book World* states: "*The Self Seekers* makes depressing but very informative reading. Unduly repetitious—where was the editor of this book?—and sometimes name-dropping, Restak nevertheless offers as good or better a presentation of object relations and narcissistic theory for the general reader as one can find." Mazlish adds, "A merit of Restak's book is that he documents the line leading from normal to disturbed narcissism, and then to the borderline condition, and over it to psychotic behavior."

AVOCATIONAL INTERESTS: English literature.

BIOGRAPHICAL/CRITICAL SOURCES: Washington Post, June 21, 1979; *Washington Post Book World,* June 20, 1980.

* * *

REYNOLDS, Clark Winton 1934-

PERSONAL: Born March 13, 1934, in Chicago, Ill.; son of Lee Davis and Lilla (Hall) Reynolds; married Dorothy Floris, February 21, 1959 (divorced, 1972); married Nydia O'Connor Viales, April 10, 1977; children: (first marriage) Rebecca Lynn, Clark Winton III, Matthew Lee; (second marriage) Camila. *Education:* Claremont Men's College, A.B. (magna cum laude), 1956; graduate study at Massachusetts Institute of Technology, 1956-57 and 1958, and Harvard Divinity School, 1957-58; University of California, Berkeley, M.A., 1961, Ph.D., 1962. *Home:* 828 Esplanada Way, Stanford, Calif. 94305. *Office:*

Food Research Institute, Stanford University, Stanford, Calif. 94305.

CAREER: Occidental College, Los Angeles, Calif., assistant professor of economics, 1961-62; Yale University, New Haven, Conn., assistant professor, 1962-66, associate professor of economics, 1966-67; Stanford University, Food Research Institute, Stanford, Calif., associate professor, 1967-72, professor of economics, 1972—. Visiting professor, College of Mexico, 1964-65 and 1979, and National University of Mexico, summer, 1966; visiting lecturer, Stockholm School of Economics, 1968; Oxford University, visiting fellow, St. Anthony's College, and visiting scholar, Queen Elizabeth House, 1975; visiting research scholar, International Institute for Applied Systems Analysis, 1978. Member of Rockefeller Commission to Latin America, 1969. Brookings Institution, senior fellow, 1975-76, consultant, 1976-77; consultant to various companies and government agencies in the United States and Latin America. *Awards, honors:* Woodrow Wilson fellow, 1956-57; Danforth fellow, 1956-60; Rockefeller theological fellow, 1957-58; Doherty Foundation fellow, 1960-61; Norman Buchanan Award, 1964; Social Science Research Council grant, 1970-72.

WRITINGS: (With M. Mamalakis) *Essays on the Chilean Economy,* Irwin, 1965; *The Mexican Economy: Twentieth-Century Structure and Growth,* Yale University Press, 1970; (with Donald Nichols) *Principles of Economics,* Holt, 1971; (editor with Carlos Tello and contributor) *Las Relaciones Mexico-Estados Unidos,* Fondo de Cultura Economica, 1981.

Contributor: G. Ranis, editor, *Government and Economic Development,* Yale University Press, 1971; *El Mercado de capitales en Colombia,* Editorial Andes, 1971; Wayne A. Cornelius and Felicity M. Trueblood, editors, *Latin American Urban Research,* Volume V: *Urbanization and Inequality: The Political Economy of Urban and Rural Development in Latin America,* Sage Publications, 1975; Joseph Grunwald, editor, *Latin America and World Economy: A Changing International Order,* Volume II, Sage Publications, 1978; William Cline and Enrique Delgado, editors, *Economic Integration in Central America,* Brookings Institution, 1978; Jonathan Aronson, editor, *Debt and the Less Developed Countries,* Westview, 1978; Henrique Rattner, editor, *A Crise de ordem mundial,* Edicoes Simbolo, 1978; Jerry R. Ladman, Deborah J. Baldwin, and Elihu Bergman, editors, *U.S.-Mexican Energy Relationships: Realities and Prospects,* Lexington Books, 1981; Richard D. Erb and Stanley R. Ross, editors, *United States Relations with Mexico: Context and Content,* American Enterprise Institute, 1981. Contributor to proceedings and professional journals.

WORK IN PROGRESS: U.S.-Mexican Economic Relations, for University of Texas Press; coordinating U.S.-Mexico project on economic and social development.

* * *

REYNOLDS, Timothy (Robin) 1936-

PERSONAL: Born July 18, 1936, in Vicksburg, Miss.; son of Earle Landry (an anthropologist and activist) and Barbara (a writer and activist; maiden name, Leonard) Reynolds; married Mary Kay Crawford, 1961 (divorced); children: Anthony Felix. *Education:* Attended Antioch College, 1953-56; University of Wisconsin, B.A., 1961; Tufts University, M.A., 1962; graduate study at University of Texas at Austin, 1966. *Address:* c/o Stein, 914 Legal Research, University of Michigan, Ann Arbor, Mich. 48104.

CAREER: Writer. Pentucket Regional High School, Merrimac, Mass., teacher, 1963-64; University of Texas at Austin, associate professor of classics, 1966-68; National Translation Center, Austin, fellow, 1968; travelled in England, and worked in a pub and at odd jobs, 1970-76; worked as housepainter, garbage collector, woodcutter, and transcriber, all in Wilmington, Ohio, 1976-78; Irwin Auger Bit Factory, Wilmington, grinder, 1978; office worker and typist at Wordprocessors, Inc., 1979, University of Michigan, Ann Arbor, Mich., Department of Human Genetics, 1979, Department of Geology, 1979-80, and Law School, 1980, and Steno Service, New York, N.Y., 1980. *Military service:* U.S. Army language school, 1956-58.

MEMBER: Mystic Knights of Nowhere (Wilmington, Ohio). *Awards, honors:* Rockefeller Foundation grant, 1969, for study in Italy.

WRITINGS—Poetry: *Ryoanji: Poems,* Harcourt, 1964; *Catfish Goodbye: Poems,* Anubis Press, 1966; *Slocum,* Unicorn Press (Santa Barbara), 1967; *Tlatelolco: A Sequence from "Que,"* Phoenix Book Shop, 1970; *Que,* Halty Fergusen, 1971; *The Women Poem,* Phoenix Book Shop, 1973; *Dawn Chorus,* Ithaca House, in press.

Plays: (Author of book and lyrics) "Peace" (musical; translation of a play by Aristophanes; music by Al Carmines), first produced Off-Broadway at Astor Place Theatre, January 27, 1969, published in *The Tenth Muse: Classical Drama in Translation,* edited by Charles Doria, Swallow Press, 1980; "The Tightwad" (translation of a play by Moliere), first produced in Yellow Springs, Ohio, 1978.

Also author of *Ertanax, Halflife: Poems, 1962-64,* published by Pym-Randall, three books of "epistles," *The Hadron, Arnheim II,* and *Memnonia,* and of a "cyborg." Translator of *Mencius.*

WORK IN PROGRESS: Nod, with brother Ted Reynolds; a book on a western painting, for children; *Margaret Schecter;* continued exploration of modes of production and distribution of verbal artifacts.

SIDELIGHTS: Timothy Reynolds has varying degrees of fluency in French, German, Russian, Latin, and Greek.

BIOGRAPHICAL/CRITICAL SOURCES: Cue, February 8, 1969; *Variety,* February 12, 1969.

* * *

RICARDO-CAMPBELL, Rita

PERSONAL: Born in Boston, Mass.; daughter of David and Elizabeth (Jones) Ricardo; married Wesley Green Campbell (director of the Hoover Institution), September 15, 1946; children: Barbara Lee, Diane Rita, Nancy Elizabeth. *Education:* Simmons College, B.S., 1941; Harvard University-Radcliffe College, M.A., 1945, Ph.D., 1946. *Home:* 26915 Alejandro Dr., Los Altos Hills, Calif. 94022. *Office:* Hoover Institution, Stanford University, Stanford, Calif. 94305.

CAREER: Harvard University, Cambridge, Mass., instructor, 1947-48; Tufts University, Medford, Mass., assistant professor, 1948-51; Wage Stabilization Board, Washington, D.C., labor economist, 1951-53; U.S. House of Representatives, Ways and Means Committee, Washington, D.C., economist, 1953; consulting economist, 1957-60; Stanford University, Hoover Institution, Stanford, Calif., archivist and research associate, 1961-68, senior fellow, 1968—, lecturer in health services at Stanford Medical School, 1973-78. Visiting professor at San Jose State College (now University), 1960-61. Member of board of directors of Independent Colleges of Northern California, 1971—, Watkins-Johnson Co., 1974—, Simmons College,

1974-80, and Gillette Co., 1978—. Member of President's Economic Policy Advisory Board, 1981—. *Member:* American Economic Association, Mont Pelerin Society, Phi Beta Kappa. *Awards, honors:* National Endowment for the Humanities senior fellowship, 1971; Alumnae Achievement Award, Simmons College, 1972.

WRITINGS—Surname cited in bibliographic sources as Campbell: (With husband, Wesley Glenn Campbell) *Economics of Mobilization and War,* Irwin, 1952; *Economics of Health and Public Policy,* American Enterprise Institute for Public Research, 1971; (contributor) *Food Safety Regulation: Uses and Limitations of Cost-Benefit Analysis,* American Enterprise Institute—Hoover Institution Joint Study, 1974; *Drug Lag: Federal Government Decision Making,* Hoover Institution, 1976; *Social Security: Promise and Reality,* Hoover Institution, 1977; *The Economics and Politics of Health,* University of North Carolina Press, 1982. Contributor of articles and reviews to numerous journals.

* * *

RICE, James 1934-

PERSONAL: Born February 10, 1934, in Coleman, Tex.; son of James W. (a railroad worker) and Mary (Jennings) Rice; married Martha Oustad (a secretary/editor), June 4, 1954; children: Zel, Maria, Lyn, Patti, Jason. *Education:* University of Texas, B.F.A., 1959; Howard Payne College, M.Ed., 1960; Stephen F. Austin State University, M.F.A., 1982. *Address:* P.O. Box 373, Hico, Tex. 76457.

CAREER: Teacher of art and music in public schools of Kingsville, Tex., Hampton, Va., and the Canal Zone, 1959-64; Southeastern Louisiana University, Hammond, assistant professor of art, 1964-66; Louisiana State University, Baton Rouge, assistant professor of art, 1967-68; Southeastern Louisiana University, assistant professor of art, 1969-75; writer and illustrator, 1973—; teacher of art and music in Hico, Tex., 1979—. *Military service:* U.S. Army, 1955-56.

WRITINGS—Self-illustrated books for children, except as indicated: *Lyn and the Fuzzy,* Pelican, 1975; *Cajun Alphabet,* Pelican, 1976; *Cajun Night before Christmas Coloring Book,* Pelican, 1976; *Cowboy Alphabet,* Shoal Creek Publishers, 1977; *Prairie Christmas,* Shoal Creek Publishers, 1977.

"Gaston" series; all published by Pelican: *Gaston the Green-Nosed Alligator,* 1974; *... the Green-Nosed Alligator Coloring Book,* 1976; *... Goes to the Mardi Gras,* 1977; *... Goes to Texas,* 1978; *... Lays an Offshore Pipeline,* 1979; *... Drills on Offshore Oil Well,* 1981.

Illustrator: J. B. Kling, *Cajun Night before Christmas,* Pelican, 1973; Annie F. Johnson, editor, *The Little Colonel,* Pelican, 1974; Alice Durio, *Cajun Columbus,* Pelican, 1975.

WORK IN PROGRESS: Texas Night before Christmas; Hillbilly Night before Christmas.

AVOCATIONAL INTERESTS: Reading, chess, playing piano and woodwinds, motorcycling, painting, sculpture.

* * *

RICHARDS, Martin P(aul) M(eredith) 1940-

PERSONAL: Born January 26, 1940, in Cambridge, England; son of Paul Westmacott (a botanist) and Anne (a botanist; maiden name, Hotham) Richards. *Education:* Trinity College, Cambridge, B.A., 1962, M.A. and Ph.D., both 1965. *Home:* 57 Selwyn Rd., Cambridge, England. *Office:* Child Care and Development Group, Cambridge University, Cambridge, England.

CAREER: Princeton University, Princeton, N.J., visiting fellow in biology, 1966-67; Harvard University, Cambridge, Mass., visiting fellow at Center for Cognitive Studies, 1967; Cambridge University, Cambridge, England, research worker in medical psychology unit, 1967—, lecturer in social psychology, 1970—.

MEMBER: Zoological Society, British Society for Social Responsibility in Science, Society for the Study of Animal Behaviour, Society for Research in Child Development. *Awards, honors:* Postdoctoral fellowships from Science Research Council, 1965-67, Trinity College, Cambridge University, 1965-69, and Mental Health Research Fund, 1969-70.

WRITINGS: (Editor with Kenneth Richardson and David Spears) *Race, Culture and Intelligence,* Penguin, 1972; (editor) *The Integration of a Child into a Social World,* Cambridge University Press, 1974; (editor with Tim Chard) *Benefits and Hazards of the New Obstetrics,* Heinemann Medical, 1977; (editor with F.S.W. Brimblecombe and N.R.C. Roberton) *Separation and Special Care Nurseries,* Heinemann Medical, 1978; *Infancy: The World of the Newborn,* Harper, 1980. Contributor to scientific and popular journals. Member of editorial board of *Journal of Biosocial Science, Early Human Development, Birth and the Family Journal,* and *Infant Mental Health Journal.* Adviser to Penguin Books, Inc.

WORK IN PROGRESS: A book on the care of preterm babies, with J. Davis and Roberton; a book on fathers and fatherhood.

SIDELIGHTS: Martin P. M. Richards writes *CA:* "I have longstanding doubts about the effectiveness of scientific research for producing beneficial change. Through writing, teaching, and other activities I have attempted to both expose the weaknesses and dangers in current scientific work and to strive to find better methods and strategies through my own scientific research."

* * *

RICHIE, Donald (Steiner) 1924-

PERSONAL: Born April 17, 1924, in Lima, Ohio; son of Kent Hayes and Ona (Steiner) Richie; married Mary Evans (a writer), November, 1961 (divorced, 1965). *Education:* Attended Antioch College, 1942; Columbia University, B.S., 1953. *Home:* 304 Shato Nezo, Yanaka, 1, 1-18, Taito-ku, Tokyo 110, Japan.

CAREER: Japan Times, Tokyo, film critic, 1955-68; New York Museum of Modern Art, New York, N.Y., curator of film, 1968-73; literary critic, 1973— Advisor to Uni-Japan, Film, 1961-68. *Wartime service:* U.S. Maritime Service, 1942-45. *Member:* P.E.N. (Tokyo). *Awards, honors:* Citation from Japanese government, 1963, 1970; citation from U.S. National Film Critics' Society, 1970.

WRITINGS: (With J. L. Anderson) *The Japanese Film,* Grove, 1959, Princeton University Press, 1982; *The Japanese Movie: An Illustrated History,* Kodansha (England), 1965; *The Films of Akira Kurosawa,* University of California Press, 1965; *Companions of the Holiday,* Weatherhill (Tokyo), 1968; *George Stevens: An American Romantic,* Museum of Modern Art, 1970; *Japanese Cinema,* Doubleday, 1971; *The Inland Sea,* Weatherhill, 1971; *Ozu: The Man and His Films,* University of California Press, 1974; *The Japanese Tattoo,* Weatherhill, 1980; *Zen Inklings,* Weatherhill, 1982.

WORK IN PROGRESS: The Films of Shohei Imamura, with Robert Tranchin; *Modern Japan/Living Tradition,* for Kodansha.

SIDELIGHTS: Donald Richie told *CA:* "Living as I do in Japan, and having lived here well over half my life, I write mainly about this country and its people. It has become my subject, one which I seek to describe, understand, even perhaps to illuminate. The experience of attempting to limn an entire culture has given me, perhaps not so paradoxically, a deeper insight into my own and a consequent understanding of all cultures which I might not have otherwise had."

AVOCATIONAL INTERESTS: Music (criticism and composition).

* * *

**RICHTER, Valentin
See PICK, Robert**

* * *

RICOU, Laurence (Rodger)   1944-

PERSONAL: Born October 17, 1944, in Brandon, Manitoba, Canada; son of Reginald Thomas (an advertising agent) and Gladys (Hawke) Ricou; married Treva Carolyn Clendenning (a librarian), June 21, 1966; children: Marc Laurence, Liane Adele. *Education:* Brandon College, University of Manitoba, B.A., 1965; University of Toronto, M.A., 1967, Ph.D., 1971. *Home:* 3181 West 27th Ave., Vancouver, British Columbia, Canada V6L 1W6. *Office:* Department of English, University of British Columbia, No. 597, 1873 East Mall, Vancouver, British Columbia, Canada V6T 1W5.

CAREER: University of Lethbridge, Lethbridge, Alberta, assistant professor, 1970-75, associate professor of English, 1975-78, chairman of department, 1973-78; University of British Columbia, Vancouver, associate professor of English, 1978—.

MEMBER: Modern Language Association of America, Association of Canadian University Teachers of English, Canadian Association for Commonwealth Language and Literary Studies, Humanities Association of Canada, Association for Canadian and Quebec Literatures. *Awards, honors:* Humanities Research Council of Canada grant, 1973, for *Vertical Man/Horizontal World: Man and Landscape in Canadian Prairie Fiction;* Ontario Arts Council grant, 1976; Canada Council leave fellowship, 1976-77 and 1982-83.

WRITINGS: Vertical Man/Horizontal World: Man and Landscape in Canadian Prairie Fiction, University of British Columbia Press, 1973; (author of introduction) Patricia Blondal, *A Candle to Light the Sun,* McClelland & Stewart, 1976; (editor and author of introduction) *Twelve Prairie Poets* (anthology), Oberon Press, 1976; (contributor) S. M. Trofimenkoff, editor, *The Twenties in Western Canada,* National Museum of Man, 1972; (contributor) Dennis Cooley, editor, *RePlacing,* ECW Press, 1980; (contributor) Jeffrey M. Heath, editor, *Profiles in Canadian Literature 2,* Dundurn Press, 1980; (contributor) Terry Goldie and Virginia Harger-Grinling, editors, *Violence in the Canadian Novel since 1960,* Memorial University of Newfoundland, 1981.

Contributor of articles and reviews to literary journals, including *Essays on Canadian Writing, NeWest Review, Canadian Literature, Canadian Plains Studies 6: Man and Nature on the Praries, Mosaic,* and *Canadian Children's Literature.*

WORK IN PROGRESS: "Canadian Poetry, 1972-84," for *The Literary History of Canada;* a book on images of childhood in Canadian literature.

RIGGS, Robert E.   1927-

PERSONAL: Born June 24, 1927, in Mesa, Ariz.; son of Lyle Alton (a lawyer) and Goldie (Motzkus) Riggs; married Hazel Dawn Macdonald, September 1, 1949; children: Robert Macdonald, Richard Edwon, Russel Owen, Rodney Lyle, Raymond David, Reisa Dawn, Preston Joseph. *Education:* Brigham Young University, student, 1947; University of Arizona, B.A., 1952, M.A., 1953, LL.B., 1963; graduate study at Oxford University, 1952-53; University of Illinois, Ph.D., 1955. *Politics:* Democrat. *Religion:* Church of Jesus Christ of Latter-day Saints (Mormon). *Home:* 1158 South 350 West, Orem, Utah. *Office:* J. Reuben Clark Law School, Brigham Young University, Provo, Utah 84601.

CAREER: Brigham Young University, Provo, Utah, instructor, 1955-57, assistant professor of political science, 1957-60; University of Arizona, Tucson, government research associate, 1960-63; admitted to Bar of Arizona, 1963; Riggs & Riggs (law firm), Tempe, Ariz., attorney in private practice, 1963-64; University of Minnesota, Minneapolis, associate professor, 1964-68, professor of political science, 1968-75; Brigham Young University, J. Reuben Clark Law School, professor of law, 1975—. Mayor, Golden Valley, Minn., 1972-75. Member of board of trustees, Utah Legal Services, Inc., 1978-82. *Military service:* U.S. Army, 1945-47. *Awards, honors:* Ford Foundation fellow, 1957; Rockefeller Foundation research fellow at Columbia University, 1957-58.

WRITINGS: Politics in the United Nations, University of Illinois Press, 1958; *Arizona State Personnel Policies,* Bureau of Business and Public Research, University of Arizona, 1962; *The Movement for Administrative Reorganization in Arizona,* University of Arizona Press, 1964; *Vox Populi: The Battle of 103,* University of Arizona Press, 1964; (with Jack C. Plano) *Forging World Order,* Macmillan, 1967; *U.S./U.N.: Foreign Policy and International Organization,* Appleton, 1971; (with Plano) *Dictionary of Political Analysis,* Dryden Press, 1973, 2nd edition (with Plano and Helenan S. Robin), 1982; (with Plano, Milton Greenburg, Roy Olton) *Political Science Dictionary,* Dryden Press, 1973; (with I. Jostein Mykletun) *Beyond Functionalism: Attitudes toward International Organization in Norway and the United States,* University of Minnesota Press, 1979. Contributor of articles and reviews to law and political science journals.

WORK IN PROGRESS: Studies in the First Amendment.

SIDELIGHTS: Robert E. Riggs told *CA:* "I write primarily because research and writing have been part of my academic responsibility as a teacher of political science and now law. I also enjoy giving verbal form to ideas and seeing a finished product emerge. Although I have few illusions about the enduring significance of my work, the printed page does endure and one may always hope that readers will find some significance in it. I have no doubt that the larger scholarly endeavor, of which I am a small part, is of great and enduring significance."

* * *

**RILEY, Tex
See CREASEY, John**

* * *

**RIVIERE, Bill
See RIVIERE, William Alexander**

RIVIERE, William Alexander 1916-
(Bill Riviere)

PERSONAL: Born May 16, 1916, in Manchester, N.H.; son of Horace A. (a labor organizer) and Ernestine (Boudreau) Riviere; married Eleanor R. Robie, March 6, 1939; children: William A., Jr., Jo Anne. *Education:* Attended public schools in Manchester, N.H., and U.S. Immigration Border Patrol Training School, El Paso, Tex., 1943. *Politics:* "Republican inclinations." *Religion:* Episcopalian.

CAREER: Writer. S. C. Noyes Co. (timber owners), Rangeley, Me., publicity manager, two years; Harter's Inc. (mail order sporting goods), Waseca, Minn., publicity manager, two years; free-lance guide in Maine woods, Rangeley Lakes area, twelve years; *Herald-Journal,* Waseca, editor, 1958-61; *Waldoboro Press,* Waldoboro, Me., editor, 1962; managing editor, *Campfire Chatter,* New England Family Campers' Association.

WRITINGS—Under name Bill Riviere: *Squire Rangeley Slept Here,* S. C. Noyes, 1955; *The Camper's Bible,* Doubleday, 1961, revised edition, 1973; *How to Build and Operate Private Family Campgrounds,* Kalmbach, 1964; *The Gunner's Bible: The Complete Guide to Sporting Firearms,* Doubleday, 1965, revised edition, 1973; *Family Campers' Cookbook,* Holt, 1965; *Complete Guide to Family Camping,* Doubleday, 1966; *Pole, Paddle, and Portage,* Van Nostrand, 1969; *Backcountry Camping,* Doubleday, 1971; (with Thomas Lyman) *The Field Book of Mountaineering and Rock Climbing,* Winchester Press, 1975; *The Family Camper's Bible,* Doubleday, 1975; (with the staff of L. L. Bean) *The L. L. Bean Guide to the Outdoors,* Random House, 1981. Contributor to *Field and Stream.*

BIOGRAPHICAL/CRITICAL SOURCES: Hartford Courant, July 20, 1961; *Boston Herald,* April 15, 1963; *Worcester Evening Gazette,* April 23, 1963; *Worcester Sunday Telegram,* April 28, 1963.

* * *

ROBINSON, Douglas Hill 1918-

PERSONAL: Born July 9, 1918, in Columbia, Mo.; son of Gustavus Hill (a professor of law) and Sarah (Anderson) Robinson; married Margaret Rowan (divorced, 1951); married Merle Schmidt, February 14, 1953; children: (first marriage) Barbara (Mrs. Donald Barton), Bruce, Carol (Mrs. John Kanis); (second marriage) Joan Beth, Douglas H., Jr. *Education:* Harvard University, B.S., 1939, M.D., 1943. *Politics:* Republican. *Religion:* Protestant. *Home address:* P.O. Box 254B, R.R.1, Pennington, N.J. 08534.

CAREER: Engaged in full-time medical practice specializing in psychiatry in Trenton, N.J., 1947—. Director of special therapies, New Jersey State Hospital, 1947-53. St. Francis Hospital, member of staff, 1956-82, honorary member of staff, 1982—, chief of psychiatry, 1968-74. *Military service:* U.S. Navy, Medical Corps, 1943-47; became lieutenant. *Member:* American Aviation Historical Society, American Medical Association, American Psychiatric Association, Marine-Luftschiffer Kameradschaft (Hamburg, Germany; honorary member), Wingfoot Lighter-Than-Air Society, Cross and Cockade. *Awards, honors:* Silver "C" Soaring Achievement Award, 1972.

WRITINGS: (Translator) Eckener, *My Zeppelins,* Putnam, 1958; *The Zeppelin in Combat: A History of the German Naval Airship Division, 1912-1918,* Foulis, 1962, 4th edition, University of Washington Press, 1980; *Famous Aircraft: LZ 129 "Hindenburg,"* Arco, 1964; *The B-58 Hustler,* Arco, 1968; *The Dangerous Sky: A History of Aviation Medicine,* University of Washington Press, 1973; *Giants in the Sky: A History of the Rigid Airship,* University of Washington Press, 1973; (with Charles L. Keller) *"Upship!" A History of U.S. Navy Rigid Airships, 1919-1935,* U.S. Naval Institute Press, 1982. Contributor to aviation journals.

WORK IN PROGRESS: A biography of Heinrich Mathy, zeppelin captain; *The Golden Age of the Great Rigid Airships,* with Harold G. Dick.

AVOCATIONAL INTERESTS: Aviation history prior to 1935 (particularly lighter-than-air), military history of twentieth century, eighteenth-century ship model-building and research, flying (holds private pilot license), gliding and soaring.

* * *

ROBINSON, Maudie Millian Oller 1914-

PERSONAL: Born August 4, 1914, in Norris, Okla.; daughter of William Randolph (a farmer and merchant) and Fannie Elizabeth (Kimbrough) Oller; married William Cole Lewis, May 5, 1933 (divorced, 1940); married Charles Hugh Robinson (an educator and administrator of schools in New Mexico), September 6, 1942 (died, 1977); children: (first marriage) Betty Carole (Mrs. Tom Bell). *Education:* Attended Highlands University, 1950-58. *Politics:* Republican. *Religion:* Presbyterian. *Home and office:* 105 Torreon, Clovis, N.M. 88101. *Agent:* August Lenniger, Lenniger Literary Agency, Inc., 104 East 40th St., New York, N.Y. 10016.

CAREER: Free-lance writer. Worked as bookkeeper and secretary for businesses, Veteran's Administration, and Vaughan Municipal Schools in Vaughan, N.M., and Las Vegas, N.M., 1943-58; free-lance writer, 1958-63; Navajo Lodge, Las Vegas, N.M., manager, 1963-73. Member of Friends of the Clovis Library. *Member:* New Mexico Book League, Order of the Eastern Star.

WRITINGS: Children of the Sun: The Pueblos, Navajos, and Apaches of New Mexico (juvenile), Messner, 1973; *Grass Singing, Indian Bride of Kit Carson* (historical novel), Western Heritage Press, 1977; *How to Do Nothing after Sixty,* Thomas Printing & Publishing, 1978; *The Mystery of the Squash Blossom Necklace* (juvenile), Western Heritage Press, 1980. Contributor of articles and stories to popular magazines, including *She, Reader's Digest,* and *Homemaker.*

WORK IN PROGRESS: Two novels, *Unvarnished* and *Jimson Weed;* two juveniles, *Grass Singing's Home at Bent Fort* and *The Mystery of the White Wolf; The Proverbial Way.*

SIDELIGHTS: Maudie Robinson writes: "I grew up in a very close-knit family in the eastern hills of Oklahoma. The small place where I was born was originally called Bugscuffle! My father was a mixture of English and German and a perfectionist in all his endeavors. My mother was a delightful mixture of Irish and Cherokee. We grew up among the Choctaws and Cherokees, and my father was always their friend and champion.

"New Mexico has been my home since 1930, and for me, it is truly a Land of Enchantment. I am vitally interested in Southwest history and the Indians who inhabit the land now and those of long ago. I enjoy tramping through the hills and over the prairies, visiting old ruins, and searching through junk shops and second-hand stores for that rare Old West Book that has long been out of print."

RODGERS, Mary 1931-

PERSONAL: Born January 11, 1931, in New York, N.Y.; daughter of Richard (a composer) and Dorothy (an interior designer and author; maiden name, Feiner) Rodgers; married Julian B. Beaty, Jr., December 7, 1951 (divorced, 1957); married Henry Guettel (a theatrical executive), October 14, 1961; children: (first marriage) Richard R., Linda M., Constance P.; (second marriage) Adam, Alexander. *Education:* Attended Wellesley College, 1948-51. *Politics:* Liberal. *Religion:* Jewish. *Home:* 115 Central Park W., New York, N.Y. 10023. *Agent:* Shirley Bernstein, Paramuse Artists, Inc., 1414 Avenue of the Americas, New York, N.Y. 10019.

CAREER: Novelist, screenwriter, composer, and lyricist. Assistant to the producer of the New York Philharmonic's Young People's Concerts, 1957-71. Script writer, Hunter College Little Orchestra Society, 1958-59. Member of board of trustees, Brearley School, 1973-76, and Phillips Exeter Academy, 1977—. *Member:* Authors League, Dramatists Guild (member of council), Writers' Guild of America, Cosmopolitan Club. *Awards, honors: Book World* Spring Book Festival Award, 1972, Christopher Award, 1973, and American Library Association Notable Book Award, all for *Freaky Friday;* Christopher Award, 1975, for *A Billion for Boris.*

WRITINGS—Published by Harper, except as indicated: *The Rotten Book,* 1969; (with mother, Dorothy Rodgers) *A Word to the Wives,* Knopf, 1970; *Freaky Friday* (also see below), 1972; *A Billion for Boris,* 1974; *Summer Switch* (sequel to *Freaky Friday*), 1982.

Screenplays: "Freaky Friday" (based on Rodgers' book of the same title), Walt Disney Productions, 1977; (with Jimmy Sangster) "The Devil and Max Devlin," Walt Disney Productions, 1981.

Composer of music for musical plays: (Co-composer and author of book and lyrics) "Three to Make Music," first produced in New York City at Hunter College, 1959; "Once upon a Mattress," first produced on Broadway at Phoenix Theatre, 1959; "Hot Spot," first produced on Broadway at Majestic Theatre, 1963; "Mad Show," first produced Off-Broadway at New Theatre, 1966.

Also composer of numerous children's musicals, including "Davy Jones' Locker," performed with the Bill Baird Marionettes in New York City, 1959; "Young Mark Twain," 1964; "Pinocchio," performed with the Bill Baird Marionettes in New York City, 1973. Also author of television scripts, including "Mary Martin Spectacular," 1959, and "Feathertop," 1961. Co-author with Dorothy Rodgers of monthly column, "Of Two Minds," *McCall's,* 1971-78.

SIDELIGHTS: A woman of diverse talents, Mary Rodgers concentrated on composing music early in her career, working with many well-known lyricists (including Sammy Kahn) to create a number of songs and musical play scores for both adults and children. However, many critics feel Rodgers is even more talented as an author of children's books.

Her books for children have been noted for their imaginative plots and their traditional moral lessons. A *Kirkus Reviews* writer calls *Freaky Friday* "a conventional situation comedy in which 13-year-old Annabel, whose mother has switched 'bods' to teach her a lesson, tries unsuccessfully to cope with cooking, laundry, budgeting, and all that.... At the height of a company crisis mother switches back.... It all ends as a lesson in mother-knows-best, and the rest is like the silly TV show you hate yourself for laughing at . . . but can't stop." Writing in *Horn Book Magazine,* Virginia Haviland offers *A Billion for Boris* as another example of Rodgers' literary style. Haviland labels the book a "deliciously original, engaging and consistently inventive story told by Annabel Andrews of *Freaky Friday.* . . . The author adroitly resolves the ethical problem of Boris' success at the betting office, and she portrays with comedy and poignancy Boris' earnest endeavors to alter the life style of his mother."

Some critics point to Rodgers' ability to create believable and identifiable characters and place these subjects in captivating situations. One such reviewer, Jane Langton, writes in *Chicago Tribune Book World:* "Mary Rodgers has the knack of catching the sound of a real child talking. When Annabel [in *Freaky Friday*] says, 'Oh, wow,' it is because writer, character, page of print, and reader have all been catapulted into an Oh, wow mood. Plenty of other writers try to hit young readers with 'now' ideas and phrases. . . . You wish they hadn't. Why didn't they try to be, like, universal and timeless? But in this book the pages rush by . . . and it might all be happening in the apartment next door. *Freaky Friday* is unputdownable. It is a gem." Agreeing with Langton, Betsy Wade explains in the *New York Times Book Review* that Rodgers "appears to have a sharp ear for the peculiar tone adults use on children." Still another critic remarks in a *Publishers Weekly* review of *A Billion for Boris* that "this jubilant work is an engaging story and also a barometer of adolescent emotions and needs—real and imagined."

Humor also plays a major role in Rodgers' books for children. Reviewing *Freaky Friday* for *Horn Book Magazine,* Beryl Robinson calls the book as "bright and breezy as the title, a truly funny story about a girl who awakens one morning in her mother's body, and who—during an incredible day of revelation and opportunity—sees herself as others see her and faces her mixed-up adolescent problems squarely.... There is wisdom as well as humor in this fresh, original story, and the impact, despite the story's fantastic basis, is successful and convincing." "If it's a laugh you want . . . try [*Freaky Friday*]," P. M. Canham suggests in the *Christian Science Monitor.* "It really is freaky, but it's very funny, too. . . . Rodgers . . . has a deft touch. While she can make fun of the frictions in family life, and teen-age idiosyncrasies in particular, there is a kindness in her humor that takes away any sting. And she is funny. I laughed out loud; I really did." Alix Nelson writes in the *New York Times Book Review* that "it's too bad we don't reserve a special set of adjectives for books that really are commendable—witty, original, entertaining, well-plotted and well-wrought; as it is, copywriters . . . have so diluted those terms that when the genuine article [like *A Billion for Boris*] comes along it's like crying wolf. Wolf!"

Rodgers expanded her bibliography into another area in 1970 with the publication of *A Word to the Wives,* written with her mother, Dorothy Rodgers. This book, intended for adults, describes the advantages and disadvantages of living and raising children in New York City. Rodgers feels the benefits of big city life far outweigh the drawbacks. "Dorothy's advice is printed in black. Mary's in brown, so one always knows who is speaking," E. C. Howley explains in *Best Sellers.* "In any case, Mary's tone is less formal and breezier. This is a special book for a special reader/audience." V. Becher writes in *Library Journal* that "Dorothy Rodgers . . . offers her expertise as an interior decorator; her suggestions are quite formal. . . . Mary Rodgers Guettel is a mother of five; her thoughts are more to the point for the homemaker of the 1970's. . . . Most readers will find this personal narrative, interspersed with worthwhile suggestions, fun to read." The mother and daughter writing partnership that began with *A Word to the Wives* continued with the column "Of Two Minds," published monthly in *McCall's* from 1971 to 1978. The magazine pieces explored current life-style issues, with each woman bringing her own individual viewpoints and occasionally disagreeing with the other.

In 1977 Rodgers wrote the screenplay for "Freaky Friday," a venture that introduced her to still another different and larger audience. Janet Maslin comments in *Newsweek:* "This Disney production takes on a spooky, unexpected verisimilitude that ought to make it at least as interesting to adults as it is to children, perhaps even more so. Mary Rodgers' screenplay, based on her novel, . . . is delightfully flip and evenhanded." "Freaky Friday" was followed three years later by Rodgers' second screenplay, "The Devil and Max Devlin." A reviewer for the *Chicago Tribune* writes: "An altogether different kind of movie is 'The Devil and Max Devlin,' a Walt Disney comedy that is a surprising success. . . . This is a very funny little movie. . . . The laughs in [this film] are many and genuine. The screenplay and story are credited to Mary Rodgers and Jimmy Sangster, and those are two people who Disney should employ again. Immediately."

CA INTERVIEW

CA interviewed Mary Rodgers by phone October 15, 1981, at her home in New York City.

CA: Richard Rodgers, your father, wrote in his biography that he encouraged you and your sister [Linda Rodgers Breckir] musically but never gave you work in his own shows. Were you allowed as small children to watch rehearsals?

RODGERS: We went to the orchestra reading just before the show opened in New York, but that was our only involvement. We never actually expected to get any work in the shows. I think by the time we were old enough to be performers neither of us wanted to be one anyhow. We both took piano lessons; we were certainly encouraged as far as that was concerned.

CA: Did you have formal training in music besides piano lessons?

RODGERS: No. I'd studied piano from the time I was eight until I was about sixteen, and then I studied theory and counterpoint privately. Then I was a music major at Wellesley, where I would have graduated in 1952, but I left in my senior year and got married. So that was the extent of the formal training—not enough of stuff like orchestration, as a matter of fact, which I would have liked to study but wouldn't have been able to get satisfactorily at a place like Wellesley anyway.

CA: Your first published song was "Christmas Is Coming," written when you were about twenty. Were there earlier songs that didn't get published?

RODGERS: Actually, yes, I started writing when I was about sixteen. My parents acquired a second piano in the living room and I thought it was a wonderful opportunity, so I began to write two-piano things because my sister could play them with me. I wrote a whole series of little piano pieces called "Clean Sheets"—I don't know why; I guess I always thought clean sheets were a terrific thing to have. Then I wrote some very bad popular songs for a while. "Christmas Is Coming" was a children's song. And I did not write the lyric; it was written with another Wellesley friend. We auditioned it in the living room of the dorm we lived in at Wellesley, and people who were interested got a beautifully illustrated giant Christmas card with the song written on it, which took up all the time we had away from our studies. We sold them for something like two or three dollars apiece, I've forgotten exactly. It did quite a hefty business, and when I showed that to my father he said, "Well, now, I really think you ought to go ahead and see what you can do on your own," which is when I began to write kids' things.

CA: Later you collaborated with Sammy Kahn on the music for "Ali Baba," a recording. The collaboration was done by mail?

RODGERS: Yes, he sent me all the lyrics by mail, and I set the lyrics and recorded them on tape and sent the tape back to him—all in the space of a weekend, as a matter of fact. They needed everything in a hurry. Bing Crosby recorded it. Sammy Kahn and I didn't meet until quite a long time after that.

CA: You said at one point that you preferred to do the lyric first and then write to that. Do you still feel the same?

RODGERS: I prefer not writing any lyrics at all. I hate writing lyrics and only did them in self-defense when I was getting started, because I couldn't find anybody else who wrote lyrics that I thought were good enough for me to set—anybody who was willing to work with me, that is. But since then I've avoided writing them whenever possible.

CA: Several good things happened in 1959: "Once upon a Mattress," for which you had done the music, was first produced; so were "Three to Make Music" and "Davy Jones' Locker," a children's musical with marionettes. Had many years of work preceded that successful year?

RODGERS: Well, a number of years of working at Golden Records as a composer, and I did anything anybody would give me to do. I wrote scripts for the Little Orchestra Concerts; that's how "Three to Make Music" happened. Actually, that was not my music except for one song. It was a little musical revue about music, explaining music to kids, basically the theory that it takes three to make music: the man who writes it, the man who plays it, and the man who hears it. My sister wrote the music and I wrote the book and the lyrics. Then Mary Martin decided to use it on her show. She was traveling around the country doing an evening show and doing a children's show in the afternoon, and she used that and a little hunk of "Peter Pan" and Rodgers and Hammerstein's "Cinderella," which I rewrote for them so that it would accommodate Mary and one other performer instead of a whole cast. Then I wrote the scripts for both the television shows that were made from those Mary Martin shows. That was in Easter of 1959, so it was indeed a very busy year.

CA: What kind of work did you do primarily with the New York Philharmonic's Young People's Concerts?

RODGERS: I was assistant to the producer. Actually, I was kind of an editor to Lenny Bernstein. When he took over the Philharmonic he inherited the Young People's Concerts at the same time, and he was a little insecure about his ability to deal with children. He knew I had done a lot of writing for children and asked me if I would be interested in being his assistant. Actually, he knew perfectly well how to deal with children and wrote wonderfully for them, and I never wrote any of those scripts; I was just an editor and a good sounding board. I did those concerts for thirteen years, until he left.

CA: Are you still very active in the Dramatists Guild?

RODGERS: I'm very actively involved with the Dramatists Guild; I'm on the Dramatists Guild Council, the Dramatists Guild Fund, and the finance committee of the Dramatists Guild. I'm also on the Authors League Council, the Authors League Fund, and the board of a wonderful place called Symphony Space, which is what I refer to as the poor man's Lincoln Center, at Ninety-fifth and Broadway. And I'm a trustee of Phillips Exeter Academy.

CA: Did your own children have much to do with your deciding to write children's books?

RODGERS: Nothing. I had a terrible childhood. I *hated* being a child. I was bored to death. It was the longest prison sentence in the world. It's the only prison sentence from which there is no parole; you just have to wait until you grow out of it. I guess I have the mind of a child. I think it's much more fun thinking up fantasy "what-ifs" to take children out of their miseries than writing for adults. I'm in the middle of a second *Freaky Friday* sequel right now for Harper & Row.

CA: Even though you've had help with the children, haven't you often found it hard to write?

RODGERS: Very! Most of the time I've gone away. I go away for about three weeks at a time, or I used to, and leave my very benevolent, understanding husband and the housekeeper in charge. The kids are older now. The three big ones have got their own digs, and the other two are sixteen and thirteen. But when they were younger, I would just leave seven or eight pages of instructions and take off and work twelve hours a day until I got the job done. But the last time I went back to work, which was a few months ago when I went back to work on this final book, I thought, I'm just not going to work like that anymore. It's too much of a deprivation for me and for everybody else. Now I stay in New York; I get up at six or so and work until lunchtime, and it *is* difficult. The phone rings and it's a great temptation to pick it up, or people come and ask me things that they would figure out for themselves if I weren't there. It does make it difficult, so it takes me a little longer, that's all.

CA: In A Word to the Wives, *which was published in 1970, you and your mother discussed the pros and cons of living in New York City. You felt that, in spite of the problems, the city offered many advantages for children.*

RODGERS: I still think it's the best place to bring up kids. I think from many points of view kids are much safer, curiously enough, being brought up in a city than they are in the suburbs. For one thing, you always know where they are because you *have* to know where they are. Secondly, they don't get bored because a place like New York has a great deal to offer them.

CA: And you love the city?

RODGERS; Yes, I adore it.

CA: How did A Word to the Wives *evolve?*

RODGERS: The idea for it was originally suggested to my mother by Bob Gottlieb of Knopf. He submitted a whole list of topics which dealt largely with questions of etiquette, more or less, or life-style questions for wives of upwardly mobile executives. And a lot of it struck me as being so inappropriate for our time—silly, unimportant things—that I said, "Oh God, I'd love to get my mitts on all this, because so much of it seems unimportant compared to the things that are really important." My mother said, "Well, we could do it together—why not?" and that's how it happened. We took turns in the actual writing. For instance, having had slightly more experience with children than she, since she only had two and I had five, I wrote the whole chapter on children, and when I was finished I gave it to her. Then she would insert comments, jokes, whatever. She would do the same with me on the chapters that she was basically responsible for. It's more or less the technique that we continued when we did the column for *McCall's*.

CA: Did that column come from the book?

RODGERS: Yes, it did. It was a direct result of that. Pat Carbine, who was then at *McCall's*, really wanted us to answer some juicy, kind of important life-style questions. And we had a wonderful time the year that she was there, but then she left to found *Ms.* magazine. Bob Stein, the very nice guy who took over, was a terrific conservative, and I think he believed that the magazine should appeal to the most unimaginative element of middle-class society. It became less and less fun for us to write things about how to deal with your neighbor's dogs and the inequities of who gave the Thanksgiving dinner every year and things like that.

CA: Did you and your mother have to go through all of the questions that came in to select those to be answered?

RODGERS: The editor would select four, let's say, and then we would split them up, and I'd say, "Well, I think I have an answer to that one; let me try that one first." We'd alternate because it's always easier to be the first person to answer. Quite often we agreed; we're only twenty years apart in age, and my mother's a fairly sophisticated, savvy type. So, often we would have to talk a little bit about what our ideas were going to be in order to leave the other person something to say.

CA: Did you get a lot of mail in response to that column?

RODGERS: Yes, quite a lot. Certain topics were more highly charged than others. The first interesting question that we got was right at the beginning, and *McCall's* thought it was so interesting they took a full-page ad in the back of the *New York Times* about it. It was, "My nephew is coming to stay with me for a weekend and he's bringing with him the girl he's been living with for three months. What sleeping arrangements should we offer them?" And naturally I said, "Don't be hypocritical. Unless there's a terrifically shockable older person living in your house or an impressionable teenager with whom you haven't yet had a chance to discuss sexual relationships, I don't see any reason to force somebody to creep through the living room in the middle of the night." My mother said, "I accept the notion that premarital sex seems to be here to stay, but I see no reason to openly acknowledge it, and they should be given separate rooms." Well, she's the one that got the hate mail because they figured she should know better, that at her age she shouldn't be condoning premarital sex *period*. They didn't expect anything better of me.

She also got a whole bunch of hate mail on the subject of doggie bags, I remember, and she felt very badly about that. She had said she thought doggie bags were totally unnecessary and in very bad taste, and I defended them. She got some really sad, touching letters from little old ladies, for instance, around the country who said, "It's all very well for *you* to talk about taste, but imagine what it's like if you're on a limited income and you've bought more food than you can *possibly* eat; it seems so wasteful and terrible not to be able to take it home and eat it the next day, just because it may not be socially correct." And she felt really badly about that and was dying to write and say, "You're absolutely right. It was insensitive of me," but *McCall's* would never publish our apologies. I think it would have made an interesting addition to the column, because one's public deserves to get apologies when they're right.

CA: You've lately done screenplays, "Freaky Friday" in 1977 and "The Devil and Max Devlin" in 1981, both for Disney. Have you enjoyed that work?

RODGERS: I absolutely hated that work. It was terrible, because I've been brought up in the East, where you're spoiled by editors and publishers and the theater, where nobody's allowed to change anything of yours. They can say, "We won't produce your play if you don't take that song out or rewrite it," and that's your option, but they can't throw you out, they can't interpolate other people's material, and they can't change one word of your material. Any changes that are made are at your option.

Even though you know when you agree to do a screenplay that you're an employee and you have to join a union, there's somehow a difference between knowing it and the full realization when you've written what you think is a pretty good screenplay and it's *utterly* changed. It's awful. I finally quit in the middle of the last one. I did the two screenplays you mentioned. I did two others, for television, that never even got on, because they change horses in midstream at the networks all the time; the producer who was interested in your project and commissioned it to begin with suddenly moves to another network, and the new guy comes in and feels it incumbent upon him to loathe everything his predecessor set in motion. The money comes in in such dribs and drabs that you don't really feel as though you had anything, and the government's got a lot of it anyway, and you have this dead baby in a drawer—that's what it feels like. It's just hideous to have unproduced work. I was in the middle of my fifth screenplay for Warner Brothers, an original, and I found myself really almost unable to work and on the verge of having a nervous breakdown. I called my agent and said, "Get me out of this. If I have to pay them back, I'll pay them back. I'm not doing this ever again." And I'm very happy I did it.

CA: It's surely not worth the frustration.

RODGERS: Well, it is for some people. There are people I know and have a lot of respect for who are terrifically quick writers (they're usually men, so they don't have fourteen other little things to balance at the same time in their lives). They can have one project in stage A of development and another project in stage B of development. Everything is neatly overlapping and they're making a lot of money and the situation isn't highly charged emotionally; it's a craft and a business to them. But because I work very slowly to begin with and I only work on one thing at a time (because I only *can* with all the other interests that I have and the family and kids), it puts a tremendous amount of emphasis and pressure on that one piece of work.

CA: Have any of the children followed in your footsteps, in music or writing?

RODGERS: My oldest son is a teacher. I have a daughter who's a painter and a daughter who's an actress and a son who was a boy soprano opera singer until his voice changed. He sang with the Met and the Santa Fe Opera. He's now a musician and composer. He plays the double bass and is in France in school for the year. I'm quite sure he's going to end up as a musician. He also writes very well. And my youngest one is a super jock, so I don't know what he's going to do with his life yet; he's only thirteen. But so far nobody—nobody who's old enough, anyway—has decided to be a writer. They're in other areas of art.

CA: After the sequel to Freaky Friday, *are there any plans for the future you'd like to talk about?*

RODGERS: I haven't thought beyond this book. As I said, I only do one thing at a time, and that's as far as I've gotten at this point.

BIOGRAPHICAL/CRITICAL SOURCES: Cosmopolitan, June, 1960; *Kirkus Reviews,* September 1, 1969, March 1, 1972; *New York Times Book Review,* November 16, 1969, November 24, 1974; *Library Journal,* November 1, 1970; *Best Sellers,* December 15, 1970; *Christian Science Monitor,* May 1, 1972, November 6, 1974; *Chicago Tribune Book World,* May 4, 1972; *Horn Book Magazine,* August, 1972, October, 1974; *Publishers Weekly,* July 29, 1974; *Newsweek,* February 28, 1977; *Contemporary Literary Criticism,* Volume XII, 1980; *Chicago Tribune,* February 9, 1981; *New York Times,* March 6, 1981.

—Sketch by Margaret Mazurkiewicz

—Interview by Jean W. Ross

*   *   *

RODMAN, Hyman 1931-

PERSONAL: Born May 5, 1931, in Montreal, Quebec, Canada; son of Wolfe and Bertha (Cutler) Rodman; married Barbara Hilary Mahase, September 28, 1955; children: Kenneth, Derek, David, Gail. *Education:* McGill University, B.A., 1952, M.A., 1953; Harvard University, Ph.D., 1957. *Office:* Family Research Center, University of North Carolina, Greensboro, N.C. 27412.

CAREER: Boston Children's Service Association, Boston, Mass., Russell Sage Foundation resident, 1957-59; Boston University, Boston, 1958-61, began as lecturer, became assistant professor of sociology; Merrill-Palmer Institute, Detroit, Mich., sociologist, 1961-75; University of North Carolina at Greensboro, Excellence Fund Professor, 1975—, director of Family Research Center, 1977—. Adjunct professor, Wayne State University, 1966-75; member of research committee, Detroit Co-ordinating Council on Human Relations, 1965-68; Max Bell Lecturer, Vanier Institute of the Family, University of Calgary, 1971; guest scholar, Brookings Institution, 1972-73 and 1980-81. Consultant to President's Commission on Law Enforcement and the Administration of Justice, 1966, and National Advisory Commission on Civil Disorders, 1967.

MEMBER: International Sociological Association, American Sociological Association (former member of committee on public issues and the family), Society for the Study of Social Problems (chairman of committee on marriage, family, and divorce, 1962-64; chairman of editorial and publications committee, 1971-72), Canadian Sociology and Anthropology Association, National Council on Family Relations (member of board of directors, 1968-71 and 1981—; member of public policy committee, 1980-81; chairman of International Section, 1981—), American Association for the Advancement of Science (fellow). *Awards, honors:* U.S. Department of Health, Education, and Welfare research grants, 1962-75; Ford Foundation grants, 1972-73 and 1979-80; William T. Grant Foundation grant, 1977-81; American Council of Life Insurance social research grant, 1979.

WRITINGS: (Editor) *Marriage, Family, and Society: A Reader,* Random House, 1965; *Teaching about Families,* Doyle, 1970; *Lower-Class Families: The Culture of Poverty in Negro Trinidad,* Oxford University Press, 1971; (with Betty Sarvis) *The Abortion Controversy,* Columbia University Press, 1973, revised edition, 1974.

Contributor: Arthur B. Shostak and William Gomberg, editors, *Blue-Collar World,* Prentice-Hall, 1964; Alvin W. Gouldner and S. M. Miller, editors, *Applied Sociology: Opportunities and Problems,* Free Press, 1965; Shostak and Gomberg, editors, *New Perspectives on Poverty,* Prentice-Hall, 1965; Louis A. Ferman, Joyce Kornbluh, and Alan Haber, editors, *Poverty in America,* University of Michigan Press, 1965; (with Paul Grams) *Task Force Report: Juvenile Delinquency and Youth Crime,* President's Commission on Law Enforcement and the Administration of Justice, 1967; Marvin B. Sussman, editor, *Sourcebook in Marriage and the Family,* 3rd edition, Houghton, 1968; Raymond W. Mack, editor, *Race, Class, and Power,* 2nd edition, Van Nostrand, 1968; Nona Y. Glazer and Carol F. Creedon, editors, *Children and Poverty,* Rand McNally, 1968; Ivar Berg, editor, *The Business of America,* Harcourt, 1968; Robert W. Winslow, editor, *Juvenile Delinquency in a Free Society,* Dickenson, 1968; Stella Chess and Alexander Thomas, editors, *Annual Progress in Child Psychiatry and Child Development,* Brunner, 1969; J. Ross Eshleman, editor, *Perspectives in Marriage and the Family: Text and Readings,* Allyn & Bacon, 1969; Gerhard Neubeck, editor, *Extramarital Relations,* Prentice-Hall, 1969.

J. E. Veevers, editor, *Sociological Studies of Marriage and the Family,* Simon & Schuster, 1970; Andree Michel, editor, *La Sociologie de la Famille,* Mouton, 1970; (with Charles Lebeaux and Eleanor Wolf) *Comprehensive Planning Process for Women,* Wayne County Planning Commission (Wayne County, Mich.), 1970; Gunther Luschen and Eugen Lupri, editors, *Kolner Zeitschrift fur Soziologie und Sozialpsychologie,* Sonderheft, 1970; (with Grams) James E. Teele, editor, *Juvenile Delinquency: A Reader,* F. E. Peacock, 1971; Ira L. Weiss, editor, *Readings on the Family System,* Holt, 1972; Irwin Deutscher, *What We Say/What We Do: Sentiments and Acts,* Scott, Foresman, 1973; Bruce R. Ekstrand and Lyle E. Bourne, Jr., editors, *Principles and Meanings of Psychology: Readings,* Dryden, 1973; Joe R. Feagin, editor, *The Urban Scene: Myths and Realities,* Random House, 1973; Robert R. Bell, editor, *Studies in Marriage and the Family,* 2nd edition, Crowell, 1973; Jon M. Shepard, editor, *Spectrum on Social Problems: Society, Economy, and Man,* C. E. Merrill, 1973; (with James D. Bruce) Irving R. Stuart and Lawrence E. Abt, editors, *Interracial Marriage: Expectations and Realities,* Grossman, 1973; William H. Bruening, editor, *Self, Society, and the Search for Transcendence: An Introduction to Philosophy,* National Press Books (Palo Alto, Calif.), 1974; J. Joel Moss and Kenneth Cannon, editors, *Readings in Marriage and Family Interaction,* Child Development and Family Relations Department, Brigham Young University, 1974; Leonard Gross, editor, *Sexual Behavior: Current Issues,* Spectrum, 1974; Robert E. Winch and Graham B. Spanier, editors, *Selected Studies in Marriage and the Family,* 4th edition, Holt, 1974.

Nancy C. Ostheimer and John M. Ostheimer, editors, *Life or Death: Who Controls?,* Springer, 1976; Francis G. Caro, *Readings in Evaluation Research,* 2nd edition, Russell Sage, 1977; Arlene S. Skolnick and Jerome H. Skolnick, editors, *Family in Transition,* 2nd edition, Little, Brown, 1977; *Theoretical Perspectives on School Crime,* Volume I, Department of Health, Education, and Welfare, 1978; Everett D. Dyer, editor, *The American Family: Variety and Change,* McGraw, 1979; George Kurian, editor, *Cross-Cultural Perspectives of Mate-Selection and Marriage,* Greenwood Press, 1979.

Paul Sachdev, editor, *Abortion: Readings and Research,* Buttersworth (Toronto), 1981; Audrey Wipper, editor, *The Sociology of Work in Canada,* Macmillan, in press. Also contributor, with Constantina Safilios-Rothschild, to *Family and Work Roles in Comparative Perspective,* edited by M. Brinkerhoff, in press.

Contributor to *International Encyclopedia of the Social Sciences,* 1968. Contributor of articles and reviews to professional journals, including *Sociological Quarterly, American Sociological Review, Social Forces, Human Organization, American Sociologist,* and *Sociological Focus;* contributor to periodicals, including *Detroit News, Los Angeles Times, Christian Science Monitor, Washington Star-News, Nation,* and *Science.* Consulting editor, *Merrill-Palmer Quarterly,* 1963-80; *Social Problems,* editor, 1967-69, associate editor, 1969-74; associate editor, *Journal of Marriage and the Family,* 1975—, and *Journal of Applied Developmental Psychology,* 1978—.

WORK IN PROGRESS: Research on family organization and values, the relationships between researchers and practitioners, and family policy issues.

* * *

ROGERS, A(mos) Robert 1927-

PERSONAL: Born September 9, 1927, in Moncton, New Brunswick, Canada; naturalized U.S. citizen, November 18, 1965; son of Amos R. (a farmer) and Ethel (Lutes) Rogers; married Rhoda M. Page, December 18, 1960; children: Mark. *Education:* University of New Brunswick, B.A., 1948; University of Toronto, M.A., 1950; University of London, Academic Post Graduate Diploma in Librarianship, 1953; University of Michigan, Ph.D., 1964. *Politics:* Democrat. *Religion:* United Methodist. *Home:* 1965 Pine View Dr., Kent, Ohio 44240. *Office:* School of Library Science, Kent State University, Kent, Ohio 44242.

CAREER: University of New Brunswick, Fredericton, assistant librarian, 1951-55, executive librarian, 1955-56; Detroit Public Library, Detroit, Mich., adult assistant for home reading services, 1957-59; Bowling Green State University Library, Bowling Green, Ohio, assistant to director, 1959-61, acting director, 1961-64, director, 1964-69; Kent State University, Kent, Ohio, professor of library science, 1969—, School of Library Science, acting dean, 1977-78, dean, 1978—. Visiting professor of library science, Pahlavi University, Shiraz, Iran, 1976-77. Member of board of trustees, Ohio College Library Center, 1967-69, of evaluation committee for Community Services Staff Development Project of Akron Public Library, 1972-74, of planning committee of Governor's Conference on Library and Information Services, 1973-74, and of Ohio Valley Area Libraries Project Review Committee, 1980, 1981; Ohio White House Conference, member of planning committee, 1977-78, delegate, 1978; project director to update *Ohio Library Trustees Manual,* 1977-78; delegate, White House Conference on Library and Information Services, 1979. First Methodist Church, Bowling Green, member of official board, 1961-69, and of Commission on Education, 1965-69, and superintendent of church school, 1965-68; member of board of trustees of United Christian Fellowship, 1966-69 and of religious activities committee, 1968-69, both at Bowling Green State University; United

Methodist Church of Kent, Commission on Education, member, 1969—, chairman, 1973-76, 1978-80, administrative board, member, 1969—, chairman, 1980—, Council on Ministries, member, 1969—. Co-president, Wallis Elementary School Parent-Teacher Association, 1974-75. Member of advisory council, Federal Library Programs, 1971-76, 1978—, and Ohio-Morehead Project, 1974-76.

MEMBER: American Library Association (Ohio Chapter councillor, 1972-76), Canadian Library Association, Library Association of Great Britain, Ohio Library Association (member of board of directors, 1968-76, 1979-81; president, 1979-80; chairman of open hearings on proposed Ohio regional library and information system and supplemental state support for public libraries, 1980).

AWARDS, HONORS: Best article of the year award from Ohio Library Association, 1973, for "Some Impressions of Three Russian Libraries," *Ohio Library Association Bulletin;* Librarian-of-the-Year Award, Ohio Library Association, 1976.

WRITINGS: Books and Pamphlets by New Brunswick Writers, 1890-1950, [Frederickton, New Brunswick], 1953; *The White Monument,* Ryerson, 1955; *Revised Text of Survey Document,* Bowling Green State University Library, 1967; (contributor) A. F. Kuhlman, E. W. Erickson, and A. R. Rogers, editors, *Survey of the Libraries of Murray State University,* Murray State University, 1968; *The Humanities: A Selective Guide to Information Sources,* Libraries Unlimited, 1974, 2nd edition, 1980; *Evaluation of Project Outreach (Yo-Mah-Co-Co),* Public Library of Youngstown and Mahoning County, 1975; (contributor) Sidney L. Jackson, Eleanor B. Herling, and E. J. Josey, editors, *A Century of Service,* American Library Association, 1976; (contributor) Josey, editor, *Libraries in the Political Process,* Oryx, 1980; (editor) *Standards for the Public Libraries of Ohio,* revised edition, (Rogers was not associated with earlier editions), Ohio Library Association, 1980; (with Mary T. Kim) *Alternative Modes for Providing Graduate Education for Librarianship in Ohio,* Center for Library Studies, Kent State University School of Library Science, 1981.

Also author of unpublished reports, *Status Report on Academic Libraries in Ohio, Status Report on Public Libraries in Ohio,* and *Status Report on School Libraries in Ohio,* all with Susan Masirovits, all for State Library of Ohio, 1974. Contributor to *The American Library Association Yearbook,* 1976, and to *Encyclopedia of Library and Information Science,* Dekker, 1977. Also contributor to professional journals, including *International Library Review, Ohio Libraries Association Bulletin, Ohio Library Trustee, Library Journal, Humanities Association of Canada Bulletin, Journal of Education for Librarianship,* and *Journal of Library History, Philosophy, and Comparative Librarianship.* Guest editor of *Ohio Library Trustee,* April, 1981.

WORK IN PROGRESS: "A Comparison of Manual and Online Searches in the Preparation of Philosophy Pathfinders"; *The Library in Society,* with Kathryn McChesney, for Libraries Unlimited.

* * *

ROGERS, Katharine M(unzer) 1932-

PERSONAL: Born June 6, 1932, in New York, N.Y.; daughter of Martin (a business executive) and Jean (a psychiatrist; maiden name, Thompson) Munzer; married Kenneth C. Rogers (a college president), August 4, 1956; children: Margaret, Christopher, Thomas. *Education:* Barnard College, B.A. (summa cum laude), 1952; Columbia University, Ph.D., 1957. *Politics:* Liberal. *Home:* Hoxie House, Stevens Institute of Technology, Hoboken, N.J. 07030. *Office:* Department of English, Brooklyn College of the City University of New York, Brooklyn, N.Y. 11210.

CAREER: Instructor in English at Skidmore College, Saratoga Springs, N.Y., 1954-55, and Cornell University, Ithaca, N.Y., 1955-57; Brooklyn College of the City University of New York, Brooklyn, N.Y., instructor, 1958-64, assistant professor, 1965-70, associate professor, 1971-73, professor of English, 1974—, member of doctoral faculty, 1972—. *Member:* Modern Language Association of America, American Society for Eighteenth Century Studies, National Organization for Women, Phi Beta Kappa. *Awards, honors:* Fulbright fellow at Newnham College, Cambridge University, 1952-53.

WRITINGS: The Troublesome Helpmate: A History of Misogyny in Literature, University of Washington Press, 1966; *William Wycherley,* Twayne, 1972; (editor) *Signet Classic Book of Eighteenth and Nineteenth Century British Drama,* New American Library, 1979; (editor) *Before Their Time: Six Women Writers of the Eighteenth Century,* Ungar, 1979; (editor) *Selected Writings of Samuel Johnson,* New American Library, 1981; *Feminism in Eighteenth-Century England,* University of Illinois Press, 1982. Contributor of scholarly articles to professional journals.

WORK IN PROGRESS: A book on Elizabeth Cellier, *The Popish Midwife.*

SIDELIGHTS: Katharine Rogers told *CA:* "My intense concern with the status of women (spurred by some deplorable experiences in my professional life—e.g., being deprived of academic tenure with each pregnancy) provided a driving motive for writing my first book. Lately, I have been concerned with how women of the past perceived themselves and their situations. To a surprising extent, they anticipated the insights of the Women's Liberation Movement of today."

* * *

ROGNESS, Alvin N. 1906-

PERSONAL: Born May 16, 1906, in Astoria, S.D.; son of I. A. and Mina (Engelstad) Rogness; married Nora M. Preus, June 30, 1934; children: Michael, Stephen, Paul, Martha (Mrs. Wayne D. Vetter), Peter, Andrew. *Education:* Augustana College, Sioux Falls, S.D., B.A., 1927; Luther Theological Seminary, B.Th., 1932; University of Minnesota, graduate study, 1932-34. *Home:* 1555 Branston, St. Paul, Minn. 55108.

CAREER: Ordained to Lutheran ministry, 1934; pastor in Duluth, Minn., 1934-37, Ames, Iowa, 1937-42, Mason City, Iowa, 1942-51, Sioux Falls, S.D., 1951-54; Luther Theological Seminary, St. Paul, Minn., president, 1954-74. Member of Board of Christian Education, Evangelical Lutheran Church, 1950-60; delegate to World Council of Churches for American Lutheran Church, New Delhi, India, 1961. Trustee, St. Olaf College. *Awards, honors:* D.D., Pacific Lutheran University, 1949.

WRITINGS—Published by Augsburg, except as noted: *On the Way,* 1943; *If God Were King,* 1948; *The Age and You,* 1949; *Who Shall be God?,* 1954; *His Increasing Church,* 1957; *Why Bother with God?,* Thomas Nelson, 1965; *Captured by Mystery,* 1966.

Forgiveness and Confession: Keys to Renewal, 1970; *The Wonder of Being Loved: Messages for Lent and Every Season,* 1972; *Appointment with Death,* Thomas Nelson, 1972; *The Jesus Life: A Guide for Young Christians,* 1973; *The Touch of His Love: Devotions for Every Season,* 1973; *Signs of Hope in the*

Thunder of Spring, 1973; *Bridges to Hope,* 1975; *Remember the Promise,* 1978; *Book of Comfort,* 1979; *The Word for Every Day,* 1981. Contributor to *Lutheran Standard* and theological journals.

* * *

ROLLIN, Roger Best 1930-

PERSONAL: Born February 12, 1930, in McKeesport, Pa.; son of John W. and Hazel (Best) Rollin; married Marian Plants, December 19, 1952 (died May 21, 1982); children: Bruce Geoffrey, Lisa Ann. *Education:* Washington and Jefferson College, B.A., 1952; Yale University, M.A., 1957, Ph.D., 1960. *Politics:* Independent Democrat. *Religion:* Agnostic. *Home address:* Route 5, Box 233, Seneca, S.C. *Office:* Department of English, Clemson University, Clemson, S.C. 29631.

CAREER: Franklin and Marshall College, Lancaster, Pa., instructor, 1959-60, assistant professor, 1960-65, associate professor, 1965-72, professor of English, 1972-75; Clemson University, Clemson, S.C., William James Lemon Professor of Literature, 1975—. *Military service:* U.S. Army, 1952-55. *Member:* Modern Language Association of America, American Association of University Professors, National Council of Teachers of English, Milton Society, Popular Culture Association, American Civil Liberties Union, Phi Beta Kappa. *Awards, honors:* Faculty research grant, Franklin and Marshall College, 1965.

WRITINGS: Robert Herrick, Twayne, 1966; (editor) *Hero/Anti-Hero,* McGraw, 1973; (contributor) James D. Simmonds, editor, *Milton Studies,* Volume V, University of Pittsburgh Press, 1973; (contributor) Murray J. Levith, editor, *Renaissance and Modern: Essays in Honor of Edwin M. Moseley,* Syracuse University Press, 1976; (editor with J. Max Patrick) *'Trust to Good Versus': Herrick Tercentenary Reader,* University of Pittsburgh Press, 1977; (contributor) William B. Hunter, editor, *A Milton Encyclopedia,* Volume V, Bucknell University, 1979; Jack Salzman, editor, *Prospects: An Annual of American Cultural Studies,* Volume V, B. Franklin, 1980.

WORK IN PROGRESS: A book on self-education; a book on the role of popular culture in the context of contemporary society and culture.

SIDELIGHTS: "For me, writing is a way of knowing," Roger Best Rollin writes *CA.* "A way in which I can reduce—slightly, at least—my own ignorance, begin to understand what puzzles me, and give shape and structure to what previously was fuzzy, formless. Since a lot of things interest me, literature and the arts in particular, I have felt compelled to write pretty constantly for over twenty years now. Self-education, then, has been a chief aim of my writing, though it's also my aim (and my hope) that those who read what I write will further their own self-education by being challenged by my work. That challenge will arise either because they feel informed by what I have to say or because they disagree; either way their consciousness will be raised. Thus I try to enlarge readers or inflame them—either will do. Easy acquiescence or indifference means I have failed them.

"Most of my writing has been scholarly, intended for specialists in literature or for students, but as I have begun to investigate and write in the area known as Popular Culture, I've begun to feel that quantity as well as quality is important: *Paradise Lost,* written by John Milton for 'fit audience, though few,' is important, but so also is *Bonanza,* with its audience of millions. I have begun then to write for a wider, serious audience—thus my book-in-progress on how to up-grade one's educational level on one's own. Thus also a projected book on how all culture, from Dante and Picasso to Johnny Carson and *Peanuts,* constitutes a kind of mirror of society and how it is 'processed' and used by individuals in society."

AVOCATIONAL INTERESTS: Aviation, military history, amateur acting, collecting art, tennis.

* * *

ROMANO, Louis G. 1921-

PERSONAL: Born January 1, 1921, in Milwaukee, Wis.; son of Liborio and Maria (Pellegrino) Romano; married Shirley Mae Stevens, February 20, 1943; children: Jill Stevens (Mrs. Steven Styker), Pamela Ann Dilley. *Education:* Milwaukee State Teachers College (now University of Wisconsin—Milwaukee), B.S., 1943; University of Wisconsin—Madison, M.S., 1948, Ph.D., 1955. *Religion:* Methodist. *Home:* 4453 Manitou, Okemos, Mich. 48864. *Office:* Department of Administration and Higher Education, College of Education, Erickson Hall, Michigan State University, East Lansing, Mich. 48824.

CAREER: Shorewood (Wis.) public schools, teacher, 1944-54, assistant superintendent and director of instruction, 1954-64; Wilmette (Ill.) public schools, superintendent, 1964-66; Michigan State University, East Lansing, associate professor, 1966-71, professor of administration and higher education, 1971—. *Military service:* U.S. Army Air Forces, 1943-44.

MEMBER: National Education Association (life member), National Middle Schools Association (member of board of directors), Michigan Association of Middle School Educators (past executive secretary; executive director), Michigan Association for Individually Guided Education (member of board of directors), Michigan Association of Professors of Educational Administration, Phi Delta Kappa (chapter vice-president). *Awards, honors:* President's Award, National Middle School Association and Michigan Association of Middle School Educators, 1978; Outstanding Professor Award, Michigan State University College of Education Alumni Association, 1979.

WRITINGS—Adult nonfiction; with Nicholas P. Georgiady, except as indicated: (Sole author) *A Guide to Successful Parent-Teacher Conferences,* Franklin Publishers (Milwaukee), 1964; (sole author) *Challenge of the Fives,* Franklin Publishers, 1965; (contributor) Richard P. Klahn, editor, *The Evaluation of Teacher Competency,* Franklin Publishers, 1965; (editor, also with James E. Heald) *Selected Readings on General Supervision,* Macmillan, 1970; (editor, also with R. Featherstone and A. Kloster) *Personnel Management: Selected Readings on Human Management,* MSS Corp., 1971, revised edition, 1977; (compiler, also with Heald) *The Middle School: Selected Readings on an Emerging School Program,* Nelson-Hall, 1973. Also author of filmstrip and cassette presentations, "Changing a Junior High to A Middle School," with Georgiady, and "The Middle School: A Humanizing Effort," with Addie Kinsinger.

All juveniles; all with Georgiady; published by Franklin Publishers: *Wisconsin's First Settlers: The Indians,* 1966; *Wisconsin Women,* 1966; *Wisconsin Men,* 1966; (also with Rosella Linski) *Indians of Illinois,* 1966; *Illinois: Land of Lincoln,* 1966; *Wisconsin Historical Sights,* 1967; *Illinois Women,* 1967; *Illinois Men,* 1967; *Michigan's First Settlers: The Indians,* 1967; *Michigan Women,* 1967; *Michigan Men,* 1967; *Michigan Historical Sights,* 1967; *American Negro Musicians,* 1967; *The History of Our Nation's Capital,* 1968; *Monuments and Memorials in Our Nation's Capital,* 1968; *Famous People in the Early History of Our Capital,* 1968; *Important Buildings in Our Nation's Capital,* 1968; *Ohio Indians,* 1970; *Ohio Women,*

1970; *Ohio Men,* 1970; *Ohio Historical Sights,* 1970; *Know about Skyscrapers,* 1977; *Know about Computers,* 1977; *Know about Assembly Lines,* 1977; *Know about Shopping Centers,* 1977.

Series: "American Negro," with cassettes and filmstrips, sixty titles, 1969; (also with John Gauthier, James LeGoo, and George Haley) "The Defenders: From Peace Pipe to Tomahawk," with cassettes, 1973: *Introduction, Pope, King Philip, Tecumseh.*

Published by Follett: *Exploring Wisconsin,* 1957, 3rd edition, 1977; *Gertie the Duck,* 1959; *This Is a Department Store,* 1962; *Our Country's Flag,* 1963; *Our National Anthem,* 1963.

Published by Independence Publishers (Milwaukee), except as indicated: *Know about Money,* 1966, revised edition, Franklin, 1977; *Know about Banks,* 1966; *The Ironclads: The Monitor and the Merrimac,* 1966; *The Boston Tea Party,* 1966; *Events in the Life of Thomas Jefferson,* 1966.

Editor of *Michigan Middle School Journal;* guest editor of *Michigan Journal of Secondary Education,* summer, 1971, and of *Michigan Association of School Boards Journal,* September, 1972, March, 1973, and May, 1977.

SIDELIGHTS: *Gertie the Duck* has been translated into Spanish, French, Swedish, Danish, and German.

* * *

ROSE, Jerome G. 1926-

PERSONAL: Born July 4, 1926, in New York, N.Y.; son of Robert (a businessman) and Ida (Lippman) Rose; married Naomi Lichtman; children: Patricia, Elizabeth, Theodore. *Education:* Cornell University, A.B., 1948; Harvard University, LL.B. (cum laude), 1951; graduate study at New York University. *Home:* 21 Tyson Lane, Princeton, N.J. 08540. *Office:* Department of Urban Planning, Rutgers University, New Brunswick, N.J. 08903.

CAREER: Admitted to Bar of the State of New York, 1951; attorney-at-law, 1951-69; Rutgers University, New Brunswick, N.J., associate professor, 1969-72, professor of urban planning, 1972—; licensed as an urban planner in New Jersey, 1976. Director, Institute of Legal Knowledge, Inc., 1963-65; visiting lecturer, Rutgers University, 1967-68, 1968-69. *Military service:* U.S. Navy, 1944-46. *Member:* American Society for Public Administration, Phi Beta Kappa, Harvard Law School Club of Long Island.

WRITINGS: *The Legal Adviser on Home Ownership,* Institute of Legal Knowledge, 1964, 2nd edition, Little, Brown, 1967; *Landlords and Tenants: A Complete Guide to the Residential Rental Relationship,* Dutton, 1973; (with Melvin R. Laird and Joseph Slavet) *New Approaches to State Land Use Policies,* Lexington Books, 1974; *The Transfer of Development Rights,* Rutgers Center for Urban Policy Research, 1975; (editor with Robert Rothman) *After Mount Laurel: The New Suburban Zoning,* Rutgers Center for Urban Policy Research, 1977; *Legal Foundations of Land Use Planning: A Textbook-Casebook on Planning Law,* Rutgers Center for Urban Policy Research, 1979. Contributor of articles to *Modern Bride* and *House and Garden Plans Guide.*

WORK IN PROGRESS: *Legal Foundations of Environmental Planning.*

* * *

ROSENBERGER, Homer Tope 1908-

PERSONAL: Born March 23, 1908, in Lansdale, Pa.; son of Daniel Hendricks and Jennie (Markley) Rosenberger; married Pauline Richards, July 14, 1934 (died June, 1975); married Jean Hershey Richards, April, 1977; children: (first marriage) Arley Jane (Mrs. Harry C. Furminger), Lucretia Hazel (Mrs. Patrick R. Myers). *Education:* Albright College, B.Sc., 1929; Cornell University, M.A., 1930, Ph.D., 1932. *Religion:* United Methodist. *Office:* 1307 New Hampshire Ave. N.W., Washington, D.C. 20036.

CAREER: High school teacher in Pennsylvania, 1930-31, and night school instructor, 1933-35; U.S. Office of Education, Washington, D.C., member of educational research and administration staff, 1935-42; U.S. Department of Justice, Bureau of Prisons, Washington, D.C., supervisor of training, 1942-57; U.S. Department of Commerce, Bureau of Public Roads, Washington, D.C., chief of training, 1957-65; private consultant on personnel training to government and other agencies, including U.S. Department of Commerce, U.S. Agency for International Development, Pennsylvania Department of Highways, and United Hospitals of Newark (N.J.), 1965—. Chairman of U.S. Training Officers Conference, 1949-50, 1955-57; organizer and moderator of Rose Hill Seminars, 1963—. Member of Pennsylvania Historical and Museum Commission, 1972—, and Pennsylvania State Historic Preservation Board, 1980—; president of Bureau of Rehabilitation of the National Capital Area, 1958-61; chairman of Pennsylvania State Board of Private Correspondence Schools, 1972-73; member of board of directors and of grants committee of Historical Foundation of Pennsylvania, 1980—.

MEMBER: Pennsylvania Historical Association (president, 1967-69), Pennsylvania Historical Junto (founder; president, 1942-46, 1954-56), Columbia Historical Society (president, 1968—), Phi Delta Kappa, Pi Gamma Mu, Phi Alpha Theta, Alpha Pi Omega, Cosmos Club (Washington, D.C.; member of board of management). *Awards, honors:* LL.D., Albright College, 1955; Ford Foundation grant, 1963-64, for personnel advisory project in Western Nigeria; citations from U.S. Training Officers Conference, 1957, Pennsylvania Historical Junto, 1957, 1967, and Bureau of Rehabilitation of the National Capitol Area, 1968.

WRITINGS: *What Should We Expect of Education?,* National Association of Secondary School Principals, 1956; *Letters from Africa,* American Peace Society, 1965; *The Pennsylvania Germans, 1891-1965* (75th anniversary volume), Pennsylvania German Society, 1966; *Adventures and Philosophy of a Pennsylvania Dutchman: An Autobiography in a Broad Setting,* Pennsylvania Heritage, 1971; *Man and Modern Society,* Pennsylvania Heritage, 1972; *Mountain Folks: Fragments of Central Pennsylvania Lore,* Annie Halenbake Ross Library, 1974; *Grassroots Philosophy for the Modern Mind,* Rose Hill Press, 1976; *Vignettes of Philosophy: Thirty-five Vital Subjects,* Rose Hill Press, 1977; *The Enigma: How Shall History Be Written?,* Rose Hill Press, 1979; *A Paradise of One's Own: Perceptions Concerning Man's Relation to Nature,* Rose Hill Press, 1982. Also author of *The Philadelphia and Erie Railroad: Its Place in American Economic History,* 1974.

Author of numerous training courses, tests, and filmstrips for U.S. government agencies. Contributor of articles on history to periodicals, including a series for *Lock Haven Express,* Lock Haven, Pa.; also contributor to regional history journals and education and prison administration journals. Chairman of publications committee, Pennsylvania Historical Association.

WORK IN PROGRESS: *Excellence: Twentieth Century Examples.*

SIDELIGHTS: In his comments for the book jacket of *The Enigma: How Shall History Be Written?,* historian Louis B.

Wright notes that Homer Tope Rosenberger "is a philosopher and a historian with a fervent dedication to stimulating interest in the reading and writing of history. Not only is he concerned with the academic community but with the intelligent public, who, he believes, will benefit from increased enlightenment that history can provide."

Rosenberger has built and organized an extensive private collection of material on the history of Pennsylvania and the Pennsylvania Germans. His bibliographical record published by the Pennsylvania Historical Junto lists 170 items (up to 1959). However, Rosenberger has never accepted money for writing.

BIOGRAPHICAL/CRITICAL SOURCES: *Homer Tope Rosenberger: A Bibliographical Record,* Pennsylvania Historical Junto, 1958.

* * *

ROSS, Raymond S(amuel)   1925-

PERSONAL: Born April 14, 1925, in Milwaukee, Wis.; son of Samuel and Agnes (Thorkildsen) Ross; married Jean Joy Reichmann, June 19, 1948; children: Mark, Scott. *Education:* Attended University of Illinois, 1943; Marquette University, Ph.B., 1949, M.A., 1950; Purdue University, Ph.D., 1954. *Home:* 1714 Norfolk Dr., Birmingham, Mich. 48009. *Office:* Department of Speech Communication and Theatre, Wayne State University, Detroit, Mich. 48202.

CAREER: Marquette University, Milwaukee, Wis., instructor, 1950-51; Ohio State University, Columbus, 1954-58, began as instructor, became assistant professor of speech; Wayne State University, Detroit, Mich., 1958—, began as assistant professor, professor of speech, 1965—. Coordinator, University of Michigan-Wayne State University Institute of Industrial Relations, 1959—. *Military service:* U.S. Army, 1943-45. *Member:* International Communication Association, American Psychological Association, American Speech and Hearing Association, Speech Communication Association.

AWARDS, HONORS: Foundation for Economic Education (U.S. Steel Corp.) postdoctoral fellowship, 1955; distinguished alumni award of Marquette University School of Speech, 1963.

WRITINGS: (Co-author) *The Air Force Staff Officer,* U.S. Government Printing Office, 1961; *Speech Communication Fundamentals and Practice,* Prentice-Hall, 1965, 6th edition, 1983; (contributor) *The Communicative Arts and Sciences of Speech,* C. E. Merrill, 1967; *Persuasion: Communication and Interpersonal Relations,* Prentice-Hall, 1974; *Essentials of Speech Communication,* Prentice-Hall, 1979; (with son, Mark G. Ross) *Understanding Persuasion,* Prentice-Hall, 1981; (with M. G. Ross) *Relating and Interacting: An Introduction to Interpersonal Communication,* Prentice-Hall, 1982. Associate editor, *Speech Monographs* and *Communication Quarterly.*

WORK IN PROGRESS: A second edition of *Essentials of Speech Communication.*

SIDELIGHTS: *Persuasion: Communication and Interpersonal Relations* has been translated into Spanish.

* * *

ROSSI, Mario   1916-

PERSONAL: Born January 21, 1916, in Venice, Italy; son of Gino and Rita (Rava) Rossi; children: Richard. *Education:* Studied at Venice School of Economics and University of Geneva; New School for Social Research, Ph.D., 1953. *Home:* 61 Morton St., New York, N.Y. 10014. *Agent:* Sterling Lord Agency, Inc., 660 Madison Ave., New York, N.Y. 10021. *Office:* Room 486, United Nations, New York, N.Y.

CAREER: United Nations correspondent for *The Christian Science Monitor.* Lecturer on international issues. *Member:* United Nations Correspondents Association, Authors Guild.

WRITINGS: *Marx e la dialettica hegeliana,* Editori Riuniti, 1960; *The Third World: The Unaligned Countries and the World Revolution,* Funk, 1963; *Da Hegel a Marx,* Feltrinelli, 1970; *North Africa,* Doubleday, 1974; *Cultura e rivoluzione,* Editori Riuniti, 1974. Contributor to *New Republic, Virginia Quarterly Review, Foreign Policy Bulletin,* and *New York Review of Books.*†

* * *

ROSSITER, Ian
See ROSS WILLIAMSON, Hugh

* * *

ROSS WILLIAMSON, Hugh   1901-1978
(Ian Rossiter)

PERSONAL: Born January 2, 1901, in Romsey, Hampshire, England; died January 13, 1978; son of Hugh (a Congregational minister) and Grace Winifred (Walker) Ross Williamson; married Margaret Joan Cox (an educator and television producer), November 3, 1941; children: Julia Nesbyth, Hugh. *Education:* University of London, B.A. (honours), 1922. *Politics:* None. *Religion:* Roman Catholic. *Home:* 193 Sussex Gardens, London W2, England. *Agent:* John Johnson, Clerkenwell House, 45-17 Clerkenwell Green, London FC1R 0HT, England.

CAREER: Preparatory school master in Burgess Hill, Sussex, England, 1922-24; *Yorkshire Post,* Yorkshire, England, drama critic and assistant editor, 1925-30; *The Bookman,* London, England, editor, 1930-34; *The Strand Magazine,* London, acting editor, 1934-35; London General Press, London, director, 1935-42; clergyman of the Church of England, 1943-55; fulltime professional writer and actor, 1955—. *Member:* Royal Society of Literature (fellow), Savage Club.

WRITINGS—Plays: *Rose and Glove,* Chatto & Windus, 1934; *After the Event,* Baker International Play Bureau, 1935; *The Seven Deadly Virtues, In a Glass Darkly* [and] *Various Heavens* (sequence), Constable, 1936; *Cinderella's Grandchild,* Baker International Play Bureau, 1936; *Mr. Gladstone,* Constable, 1937; *Stories From History* (10 plays for school), Duckworth, 1938; *Paul, a Bondslave* (radio play), S.C.M. Press, 1945; *Queen Elizabeth,* Constable, 1947; *Fool's Paradise,* Evans, 1947.

"The Cardinal's Learning," in *Best One-Act Plays of 1948-49,* edited by J. W. Marriott, Harrap, 1950; "Conversation with a Ghost," in *Best One-Act Plays of 1950-51,* edited by J. W. Marriott, Harrap, 1950; "Gunpowder, Treason, and Plot," in *Plays of the Year,* edited by J. C. Trewin, Elek, 1951; "Diamond Cut Diamond," in *Plays of the Year,* edited by J. C. Trewin, Elek, 1952; *His Eminence of England,* Heinemann, 1953; "Heart of Bruce," in *Plays of the Year,* edited by J. C. Trewin, Elek, 1959; "Teresa of Avila," in *Plays of the Year,* edited by J. C. Trewin, Elek, 1961; *Pavane for a Dead Infanta,* Stourton Press, 1972.

Other writings: *The Poetry of T. S. Eliot,* Hodder & Stoughton, 1932, reprinted, Richard West, 1977; *John Hampden,* Hodder & Stoughton, 1933; *King James I,* Duckworth, 1935; *Gods and Mortals in Love,* Country Life, 1936; *Who Is for Liberty?,* M. Joseph, 1939.

George Villers, First Duke of Buckingham, Duckworth, 1940; *A.D. 33*, Collins, 1941; *Captain Thomas Schofield*, Collins, 1942, reprinted, M. Joseph, 1975; *Charles and Cromwell*, Duckworth, 1946; *The Arrow and the Sword*, Faber, 1947, 2nd edition, 1955; *The Story without an End*, Mowbray, 1947, 2nd edition, 1954; *The Silver Bowl*, M. Joseph, 1948, 2nd edition, New English Library, 1962; *The Seven Christian Virtues*, S.C.M. Press, 1949; *Four Stuart Portraits*, Evans, 1949.

The Gunpowder Plot, Faber, 1951; *Sir Walter Raleigh*, Faber, 1951, reprinted, Greenwood, 1978; *Jeremy Taylor*, Dobson, 1952, reprinted, Richard West, 1975; *Canterbury Cathedral*, Country Life, 1953; *The Ancient Capital: An Historian in Search of Winchester*, Muller, 1953; *The Children's Book of British Saints*, Harrap, 1953; *The Children's Book of French Saints*, Harrap, 1954; *Historical Whodunits*, Phoenix, 1955, Macmillan, 1956 (also see below); *James, By the Grace of God*, M. Joseph, 1955, Regnery, 1956; *The Children's Book of Italian Saints*, Harrap, 1955; *The Great Prayer*, Collins, 1955, Macmillan, 1956; *The Church of England and "The Great Prayer,"* Catholic League, 1955; *The Children's Book of Spanish Saints*, Harrap, 1956; *The Walled Garden* (autobiography), M. Joseph, 1956, Macmillan, 1957; *The Day They Killed the King*, Macmillan, 1957; *Enigmas of History*, Macmillan, 1957 (also see below); *The Beginning of the English Reformation*, Sheed & Ward, 1957; *The Sisters*, M. Joseph, 1958, published as *The Conspirators and the Crown*, Hawthorn, 1959; *The Children's Book of German Saints*, Harrap, 1958; *The Challenge of Bernadette*, Newman, 1958.

Sixty Saints of Christendom (collection), Harrap, 1960, published as *The Young People's Book of Saints*, Hawthorn, 1960; *A Wicked Pack of Cards*, M. Joseph, 1961, Guild Press, 1965; *The Day Shakespeare Died*, M. Joseph, 1962; *The Flowering Hawthorn*, Hawthorn, 1962; *Guy Fawkes*, Collins, 1964, Roy, 1966; *Te Kooti Rikirangi: General and Prophet*, Collins (Auckland, New Zealand), 1966; *The Butt of Malmsey*, M. Joseph, 1967; *The Marriage Made in Blood*, M. Joseph, 1968; *A Matter of Martyrdom*, M. Joseph, 1969; *The Cardinal in Exile*, M. Joseph, 1969.

The Cardinal in England, M. Joseph, 1970; *The Florentine Woman*, M. Joseph, 1970, St. Martin's, 1973; *The Last of the Valois*, M. Joseph, 1971, St. Martin's, 1973; *Paris Is Worth a Mass*, M. Joseph, 1971, St. Martin's, 1973; *Kind Kit: An Informal Biography of Christopher Marlowe*, M. Joseph, 1972, St. Martin's, 1973; *The Modern Mass*, Tan Books, 1972; *The Great Betrayal*, Tan Books, 1972; *Catherine de Medici*, Viking, 1973; *Lorenzo the Magnificent*, Putnam, 1974; *Letter to Julia*, Stourton Press, 1974, Mowbray, 1975; *Historical Enigmas* (contains *Historical Whodunits* and *Enigmas of History*), St. Martin's, 1974; *The Princess a Nun!: A Novel without Fiction*, M. Joseph, 1978.

Editor: Jack Waller, *Wild Grows the Heather*, Chappell, 1957; John Bunyan, *Pilgrim's Work*, Norton, 1959; (and author of introduction) William King, *An Historical Account of the Heathen Gods and Heroes Necessary for the Understanding of the Ancient Poets*, Southern Illinois University Press, 1965.

Author of introduction: Reginald Scot, *The Discoverie of Witchcraft*, Southern Illinois University Press, 1964.

Unpublished plays: "Monsieur Moi" (produced and subsequently televised as "The Magnificent Egoist"), 1935; "Odds Beyond Arithmetic," 1947; "The Mime of Bernadette," 1958; "The Test of Truth," 1958; (with Ian Burford) "Quartet for Lovers," 1962; "The Prisoner of Longwood," 1964.

SIDELIGHTS: Hugh Ross Williamson once told *CA*: "In 1933 [I] entered politics at suggestion of [my] cousin, Sir John (later Lord) Simon, then Foreign Secretary. Later joined Labour Party and was prospective Labour candidate for East Dorset from 1937 to 1941 when [I] was officially expelled for [my] book *Who Is for Liberty?* On becoming Anglican clergyman gave up political affiliations."

Ross Williamson used the pseudonym Ian Rossiter only for acting.

BIOGRAPHICAL/CRITICAL SOURCES: Hugh Ross Williamson, *The Walled Garden*, M. Joseph, 1956, Macmillan, 1957.†

* * *

ROSTOW, Walt W(hitman) 1916-

PERSONAL: Born October 7, 1916, in New York, N.Y.; son of Victor Aaron (a metallurgical engineer) and Lillian (Helman) Rostow; married Elspeth Vaughan Davies (a professor), June 26, 1947; children: Peter Vaughan, Ann Larner. *Education:* Yale University, B.A., 1936, Ph.D., 1940; Balliol College, Oxford, M.A., 1938. *Home:* 1 Wildwind Point, Austin, Tex. 78746. *Agent:* Julian Bach Literary Agency, Inc., 747 Third Ave., New York, N.Y. 10017. *Office:* Department of Economics, University of Texas at Austin, Austin, Tex. 78712.

CAREER: Columbia University, New York, N.Y., instructor in economics, 1940-41; U.S. Government, Department of State, Washington, D.C., assistant chief of German-Austrian Economic Division, 1945-46; Oxford University, Oxford, England, Harmsworth Professor of American History, 1946-47; United Nations Economic Commission for Europe, Geneva, Switzerland, assistant to executive secretary, 1947-49; Cambridge University, Cambridge, England, Pitt Professor of American History, 1949-50; Massachusetts Institute of Technology, Cambridge, professor of economic history, 1950-61, member of staff of Center for International Studies, 1951-61; U.S. Government, Washington, D.C., Office of the President, deputy special assistant for national security affairs, 1961, Department of State, counselor and chairman of Policy Planning Council, 1961-66, Office of the President, special assistant to the President on national security, 1966-69; University of Texas at Austin, professor of economics and history, 1969—. Lecturer, Cambridge University, 1958. Consultant to Eisenhower Administration and chairman of Quantico Panel that evolved President Eisenhower's "open skies" proposal at Geneva conference, 1955; U.S. representative, with rank of ambassador, on Inter-American Committee on the Alliance for Progress, 1964-66. Member of Board of Foreign Scholarships, 1969-71. *Military service:* U.S. Army, Office of Strategic Services, 1942-45; became major; received Legion of Merit and Order of the British Empire (honorary military division).

MEMBER: Royal Economic Society, Elizabethan Club, Cosmos Club. *Awards, honors:* Rhodes Scholar, 1936-38; Social Science Research Council fellow, 1939-40; Presidential Medal of Freedom, with distinction, 1969; LL.D., Carnegie Institute of Technology, 1962, University of Miami, 1965, University of Notre Dame, 1966, and Middlebury College, 1967; Doctor of Humane Letters, Jacksonville University, 1974.

WRITINGS: *The American Diplomatic Revolution*, Oxford University Press, 1947; *British Economy of the Nineteenth Century: Essays*, Oxford University Press, 1948, reprinted, Greenwood Press, 1982.

The Process of Economic Growth, Norton, 1952, revised edition, 1962; (with A. D. Gayer and A. J. Schwartz) *The Growth and Fluctuation of the British Economy, 1790-1850*, two volumes, Oxford University Press, 1953, 2nd edition, Barnes & Noble, 1975; (with A. Levin and others) *The Dynamics of*

Soviet Society, Norton, 1953, revised edition, 1967; (with others) *The Prospects for Communist China*, M.I.T. Press, 1953; (with R. W. Hatch) *An American Policy in Asia*, M.I.T. Press, 1955; (with M. F. Millikan) *A Proposal: Key to an Effective Foreign Policy*, Harper, 1957, reprinted, Greenwood Press, 1976.

The Stages of Economic Growth: A Non-Communist Manifesto, Cambridge University Press, 1960, 2nd edition, 1971; *The United States in the World Arena: An Essay in Recent History*, Harper, 1960; (contributor) Max F. Millikan and Donald L. M. Blackmer, editors, *The Emerging Nations: Their Growth and United States Policy*, Little, Brown, 1961; (editor) *The Economics of Take-Off into Sustained Growth* (proceedings of International Economic Association conference), St. Martin's, 1963; *View from the Seventh Floor*, Harper, 1964; *A Design for Asian Development* (speeches), Japan Council for International Understanding, 1965; (with William E. Griffith) *East-West Relations: Is Detente Possible?*, American Enterprise Institute for Public Policy Research, 1969.

Politics and the Stages of Growth, Cambridge University Press, 1971; *The Diffusion of Power: An Essay in Recent History*, Macmillan, 1972; *How It All Began: The Origins of the Modern Economy*, McGraw, 1975; (with W. L. Fisher and H. H. Woodson) *National Energy Policy: An Interim Overview*, Council on Energy Resources, University of Texas at Austin, 1977; *The World Economy: History and Prospect*, University of Texas Press, 1978; *Getting from Here to There*, McGraw, 1978.

Why the Poor Get Richer and the Rich Slow Down: Essays in the Marshallian Long Period, University of Texas Press, 1980; *British Trade Fluctuations, 1868-1896: Dissertations in European History II*, edited by Stuart Bruchey, Arno, 1981; *Pre-Invasion Bombing Strategy: General Eisenhower's Decision of March 25, 1944*, University of Texas Press, 1981; *The Division of Europe after World War II: 1946*, University of Texas Press, 1981; *Europe after Stalin: Eisenhower's Three Decisions of March 11, 1953*, University of Texas Press, 1982.

SIDELIGHTS: Walt Rostow first came to prominence in government circles as the author of *The Stages of Economic Growth: A Non-Communist Manifesto*, a book based on a series of lectures he gave at Cambridge University in 1958. Described by the *New Republic*'s Melville J. Ulmer as an attempt "to formulate a general theory that would at once explain economic growth throughout history, refute the dialectical materialism of Karl Marx, and serve as a model for current practice in today's developing countries," *The Stages of Economic Growth* furnished much of the ideological basis for U.S. foreign policy toward underdeveloped nations of Asia, Africa, and Latin America in the 1960s. Eventually, presidents Kennedy and Johnson turned to Rostow himself for advice; from 1961 to 1969, he received several government appointments, including chairman of the State Department Policy Planning Council and special assistant to the president for national security affairs. It is as one of President Johnson's chief advisors on economics as applied to foreign affairs that Rostow is best known to the American public.

In his study, Rostow depicts economic growth as a five-stage process many critics call "aerodynamic" because it is reminiscent of the movement of an airplane. During the first stage, a country, "untouched or unmoved by man's . . . capability for regularly manipulating his environment to his economic advantage," remains dependent on traditional means (such as agriculture and local commercial activity) for economic survival. It is a time (similar in many respects to medieval Europe) when man does not know how to make use of new technology to achieve sustained growth.

The second stage (symbolized for some by the starting of the plane's engine and a subsequent warm-up period) sees the emergence of certain "preconditions for development." In this phase, an economy exhibits an increase in commercial activity and a corresponding increase in productivity which, though modest, foreshadows the development to come.

Stage three is what Rostow terms the "take-off," the most important period of a country's economic growth. It is usually brief (twenty or thirty years long) and traumatic and occurs after "a particularly sharp stimulus" leads to technical innovations and, consequently, a rapid rise in productivity. Growth then becomes "self-sustaining," according to Rostow, who lists England in the late eighteenth century and America in the mid-nineteenth century as typical stage three economies.

After this "take-off" comes "the drive to maturity" (exemplified by the United States from 1865 to 1914), during which time the economy continues to expand and become more sophisticated and complex. It is followed by the stage now in progress in the United States, Western Europe, and Japan: "the age of high mass consumption."

Rostow devised his theory to demonstrate that countries still in the traditional stage can, as Ulmer notes, "duplicate the economic experience of the West, and *without* resort to Communist or other totalitarian methods" merely by establishing the appropriate "preconditions" for "take-off." (Taking issue with Ulmer's use of the word "duplicate," Rostow told *CA* that he never claimed underdeveloped countries could achieve "take-off" in exactly the same manner as the established economies; rather, each nation proceeds in its own fashion and at its own rate as determined by its own resource endowments and its capacity to absorb the pool of available technology.) In addition, Rostow insists that less time is needed to achieve "take-off" in this day and age, primarily because underdeveloped nations can take advantage of modern science and technology (and Western financial assistance) to speed up the process.

Though this theory strikes the *New York Review of Books*'s Anthony Lewis as "a threadbare piece of wishful thinking" from the vantage point of the 1980s, it was initially heralded as the solution to the economic and political problems facing underdeveloped nations in the 1960s. (Rostow, who disagrees with Lewis's assessment, maintains that economic data of the last thirty years demonstrates that growth and progress have indeed occurred in the pattern outlined in *The Stages of Economic Growth*. Furthermore, he states, the book continues to be read by officials in developing countries, including China and several nations of Eastern Europe.) Presidents Kennedy and Johnson, among others, interpreted Rostow to mean that the spread of Communism could be halted if the United States provided certain Asian, African, and Latin American countries with generous amounts of foreign aid. (The economist did, in fact, believe that Communist insurgencies were most successful in those countries on the verge of "taking off"—that is, countries already in a transitional state marked by discontent and imbalance.) Thus, declare Rostow's opponents, *The Stages of Economic Growth* not only inspired the optimistic expectations and extensive foreign aid programs of the early 1960s, it also contributed to the notion that developed nations (such as the United States) had a responsibility to hold off Communist challenges in underdeveloped nations until "take-off" could be achieved.

In the eyes of many observers, it was as an advisor to President Johnson on Vietnam strategy that Rostow exercised the most influence in government. But as he points out to Jean W. Ross in the following *CA* interview, he has often been misquoted and misunderstood on the subject of Vietnam. Remarks Rostow: "People sometimes refer to me as the architect of U.S. policy in Vietnam, which was not true. . . . The simple fact is that the fundamental decisions on Vietnam policy were made by President Johnson in July of 1965 when I was a planner in the State Department."

While serving in the State Department, Rostow wrote a report that outlined a course of action designed to apply to Vietnam-like situations wherever they might occur. As explained in Facts on File's book *Political Profiles: The Johnson Years,* the "Rostow thesis" (as the report came to be known in the months after its release) recommended destroying the means of external support such insurgencies often depend upon to survive. A combined physical and psychological assault would demonstrate to those supporting an insurgency from the outside that the consequences of their decision would be costly, resulting in an end to the support.

The Rostow thesis did not attract much attention until the summer of 1964, when, according to *Political Profiles,* it was widely circulated throughout the administration as a possible means of handling the widening conflict in Vietnam. (In keeping with his thesis, Rostow had called for the United States to use ground forces to block the Ho Chi Minh Trail in order to force the North to abandon its support of rebel forces in the South and in Laos.) Even though the plan was criticized by some Defense Department officials, who expressed doubts about the feasibility of military attacks on the North and pointed out that domestic and international response to such actions would probably not be favorable, it soon began to influence the president's policy decisions regarding Vietnam. Some of the measures Rostow recommended, such as the stationing of a large retaliatory force in the Pacific, the introduction of ground troops in South Vietnam and Laos, and the start of naval blockades and bombing assaults against North Vietnam, later became part of official U.S. strategy in the war.

In 1966, shortly after being named special assistant to the president for national security affairs, Rostow joined the inner circle of White House advisors, a group consisting of Secretary of State Dean Rusk, Secretary of Defense Robert S. McNamara, and the president's press secretary; Rostow soon urged Johnson to include the joint chiefs of staff and the director of the Central Intelligence Agency as well. In his new post, Rostow accompanied President Johnson on his trips abroad, sat in on meetings with foreign leaders, and, perhaps most importantly, determined which of the hundreds of reports and charts prepared by various government officials would be passed on to the chief executive. (Some observers have claimed that Rostow censored or suppressed information he did not agree with; as Lewis states, for example, Rostow "systematically interpreted intelligence reports for President Johnson in ways most likely to make the war seem to be going well. . . . As far as possible he kept dissenting views from the President." On the other hand, Rostow told *CA* that he arranged for Johnson to see more material than had ever before been made available to him.) According to several reports, he also continued to make specific recommendations regarding the conduct of the war. In mid-1966, Rostow spoke out on behalf of a plan to bomb petroleum and petroleum-product installations near Hanoi and Haiphong, and in 1967, he strongly advocated using U.S. ground forces to invade Laos. When President Johnson refused to order such an invasion, Rostow instead supported McNamara's proposal calling for the South Vietnamese army to take over a larger share of the fighting responsibility. Nevertheless, he remained firmly convinced throughout his years in the White House that the best way to bring the war to a close would be to block the Ho Chi Minh Trail on the ground and therefore cut off the major supply line to the South.

As one of the few whose loyalty to Johnson never wavered in the face of increasing opposition to the war, Rostow found himself unwelcome on many college campuses after leaving office with the president in 1969. That same year, however, he resumed his academic career at the University of Texas at Austin, teaching economics and history and helping the former chief executive edit his papers. Since then Rostow has also published nearly a dozen books, including *The World Economy,* which he considers his "magnum opus."

CA INTERVIEW

CA interviewed Walt Rostow by phone September 4, 1981, at his office at the University of Texas at Austin.

CA: You came into political prominence with the administration of John F. Kennedy after playing a major role in shaping his campaign.

ROSTOW: That's excessive. I had a serious job as deputy special assistant to the president, but I was not a cabinet member. I played a minor role in the campaign. I was not on the campaign train or plane. I gave my ideas to the senator through political slogans and worked on a wide range of position papers during the campaign, but I would not say I was prominent in it.

CA: You obviously did have something to do with shaping his ideas as he was getting ready for the presidency.

ROSTOW: I think many of the ideas for which I stood were ideas familiar to him and which he'd already taken a position on as a senator—for example, aid to the developing countries. It was on the issue of aid to India that we met in February 1958, and I first worked with him on economic development problems. My ideas on other aspects of foreign and military policy were congenial to him. I think the one idea where I had the strongest influence, in the sense that he may not have taken quite so firm a position if I hadn't argued for it as hard as I did, was, strangely enough, on domestic policy; namely, that before he went for a tax cut he had to find a way to nail down a linkage between the rate of increase of money wages and the rate of increase of productivity. I argued that during the 1960 campaign and I argued it in 1961. He then agreed to it; and we negotiated an agreement with Walter Reuther which was essentially this: a 2½% rise in auto and steel wages, no rise in the steel price, since steel productivity was increasing at about 2½% per annum. In early 1962 the Council of Economic Advisers put out the wage-price guideposts which validated that deal. President Kennedy was greatly concerned about the need to contain inflation before he expanded the economy in order to lift pressure from the balance of payments. I think it was in reinforcing and giving some operational shape to his instinct that I had the greatest identifiable influence on him.

CA: You will take credit for "The New Frontier" slogan?

ROSTOW: There's no doubt that I gave him "Let's get this country moving again." On "The New Frontier" the story is as follows: David Wise, who was then writing for the *New York Herald Tribune,* ran a story in 1961 saying that I was the source of the phrase "The New Frontier." I called him up and said "I gave the president 'Let's get this country moving again' but not 'The New Frontier.'" He said, "All right, then. I'll tell you what my evidence is. First, the president of the United

States told me you gave it to him. Second, he showed me a speech draft in which you used the phrase. And third, if you'd look on pages . . . (and he gave me two page references) of your *Stages of Economic Growth*, you will find the phrase 'The New Frontier' used." Nevertheless, Max Freedman, Washington correspondent of the *Manchester Guardian*, ran a story after Wise's. He said "The New Frontier" appeared in a speech draft done by Ted Sorensen. I have no doubt that both stories are quite true. I probably did do a draft with that phrase and I used it several times in my *Stages of Economic Growth* when I looked to the future of the world economy; but it may very well be that Ted Sorensen also put it in the draft.

The point I would emphasize strongly, however, is that the only serious responsibility for a campaign slogan of that kind is the responsibility of the politician who says, "Yes, I'm going to take the risk of using it." For example, I explained to him that "Let's get this country moving again" was appropriate because, from travels I'd done in the United States after a sabbatical year at Cambridge, England, I had a sense of rather diffuse uneasiness in the country. He said, "Well, I'm going to try it out in the Oregon primary." And then he said, "I like it," and used it. But it was *his* responsibility. So I was privileged to share the adventure of the 1960 campaign and privileged to have been able to serve President Kennedy and President Johnson during those eight years; but one shouldn't take advisors too seriously—there's a difference between advice and responsibility.

CA: You have had the enviable opportunity in your career to combine teaching and public service, to put your knowledge and capabilities into practice. Did you find it difficult in any way to leave teaching and venture more into public life?

ROSTOW: No, I never had trouble going in or going out of public life, because I went in only when issues were involved about which I felt deeply. After all, I began public service in the summer of 1941 before we were in World War II. I accepted a post in the Research and Analysis Branch of the Office of Strategic Services in Washington, a job that is reflected in a small book I did that is just out, called *Pre-Invasion Bombing Policy*. That was serious work, and after the war I felt a duty, when asked, to help on German-Austrian policy, and did a year in the State Department. I also felt European reconstruction needed support, so I did two years in the United Nations in Geneva helping start an institution (the Economic Commission for Europe) meant to hold a bridge between Eastern and Western Europe in a difficult time. My wife and I gave up attractive academic posts in the United States to make that kind of contribution for the long pull. Whenever I was in public life, I was doing something I believed in, as I did when I was a consultant in the Eisenhower administration and when I worked for President Kennedy and President Johnson.

On the other hand, I never had withdrawal pains or Potomac fever when I left because my academic life has had continuity from the age of seventeen to the present—almost a half century. I decided when I was seventeen what I would do in academic life, centered around two large ideas: one is the application of modern economic theory and statistical analysis to economic history; and the other is the relationship between economic factors and society as a whole. Both of these problems are much bigger than I am, so I have had more to do than I'll ever have time to do. For example, I decided when I was young that some day I would write a history of the world economy over the past two centuries. I had the grace to wait until 1972, when I had done a reasonable amount of homework. But I have done it now, and it consists of one big central book, *The World Economy: History and Prospect*, and three related books. Whenever I left Washington, I wished everyone well and knew exactly where I would pick up in the rhythm of my academic work. There's no virtue in any of this, simply extraordinary good fortune. I've had fun doing my academic work; and the truth is I had great fun as a public servant.

CA: In various prefaces and introductions you've credited your parents for encouraging all of you to find your own way and form your own judgments.

ROSTOW: That is absolutely true. They were always there in strong and steady support; but they knew we'd have to make our own way in the world and make up our own minds. As my father used to say, "You're entitled to your own opinion, you must form your own opinion, but I'm entitled to mine, too." We were very fortunate in our parents.

CA: Did they push you in the direction of public service in any way?

ROSTOW: The only time I was ever pushed in any direction was by my mother when I was a senior at Yale and she urged me to try out for a Rhodes scholarship. She leaned on me in a warm and amiable way, and I did it. That *was* important because that gave me two years (although I'd already been working on British economic history at Yale) to work in both economic theory and economic history at Oxford; and my doctoral thesis (which, incidentally, has just been published) was written at Oxford while I was a Rhodes scholar, while I was playing rugger for my college, playing tennis, and writing songs, and having a pleasant life. It was finished in 1939.

CA: In your work for the Johnson administration, you were a key advisor on Vietnam policy.

ROSTOW: Well, he'd already made his decisions on Vietnam policy when I came into his administration in 1966. People sometimes refer to me as the architect of U.S. policy in Vietnam, which was not true. I stated my views after the event, before the event, and during the event, so I'm not at all shy about my position. But the simple fact is that the fundamental decisions on Vietnam policy were made by President Johnson in July of 1965 when I was a planner in the State Department, including the way he proposed to fight the war in Vietnam, a way with which I did not wholly agree.

CA: You've said there's been a great deal of misunderstanding and misquoting of your comments and your role.

ROSTOW: There has been, of course. But what I urged was that we fight the war more decisively and fight the climactic phase primarily on the ground, not by bombing them back to the Stone Age. I thought the war could be foreshortened and the pain lifted from the peoples of Southeast Asia, the United States, and the world if we went into Laos on the ground and blocked off the infiltration trails. But I had nothing operationally to do with Vietnam and Southeast Asia when the key decisions were made in 1965. I was proud to support President Johnson in a very difficult period, and I don't regret for a minute that I did support him.

CA: Did your support of President Johnson set you at odds with your students in any way when you returned to teaching after Johnson left office?

ROSTOW: There was considerable controversy about my coming to the University of Texas, as there would have been if I had gone to any other American university. The university president, Mr. Hackerman, said I ought to have a press conference on my arrival in Austin, and I did. I was asked what my strategy was toward the Students for a Democratic Society. I said I had no strategy toward the SDS; it is a student organization, and my strategy toward students is that they have every right to ask a public servant about his stand on the issues when he comes to a university and that I would be pleased to meet with any student or student group in the university. The first term I must have had five sessions with students, the second term five, and then it fell off. None of these sessions went less than three hours, and most ran five or six. There were no problems about my teaching or meeting them, no violence or anything of that kind, although some students felt strongly indeed about the war in Southeast Asia. Among those to whom I talked, none said immediately, "I've had a revelation; I now agree with you." We would go through a protracted cycle; I could tell what we would be talking about an hour out, two hours, three hours; and we would end up discussing the domestic society, in which our views were much closer together. Some of them sought me out in my office and, in time, we became friends. I had no trouble, and I went about my teaching in a congenial setting. I am just putting to bed the eighth book I have written since I came here.

CA: What comprehensive written accounts of the period of the Johnson administration and the Vietnam War do you consider accurate and useful from a historical point of view?

ROSTOW: *The Vantage Point* (1971) by President Johnson was, as he said, written from his perspective; nevertheless, it is accurate and careful. It is going to hold up as a primary source to historians long after the controversies end. Although he was not a professional historian, he understood how faulty memory is and built the book around documents, so it can be used with confidence. I tried in my *Diffusion of Power* to provide an analytic account of the period 1958-1972, dealing with the Vietnam War as history. I have biases, a special perspective, but I tried to perform as a professional historian. I trust others will do better. I do believe my book has been the only effort made to examine objectively the nature of the political split in the United States over Vietnam. One problem in responding to your question is that, when I finished *The Diffusion of Power* in mid-1972, I went to work on (for me) the exciting project of writing a history of the world economy, which I had pledged to do; so I haven't kept up compulsively with the literature on Vietnam or, indeed, on the Johnson administration.

I think we are going to get some well-balanced studies of the Vietnam War a good many are now in progress—but, even though Max Taylor's book and Westmoreland's are as they saw the war, they have a right to set out their views because they were intimately involved and know the facts. Peter Braestrup's two-volume study of the press is an important scholarly work. A good many of the other books about the Johnson period are caught up in polemics, and most were written when little documentation was available. In fact, all the necessary documentary material still is not available.

CA: In the introduction to The United States in the World Arena *you said, "While patterns of events reminiscent of the past often recur, history is treacherous as a literal guide to the present." What do you think about the teaching of history, including economic history? Could it be greatly improved in our colleges and universities?*

ROSTOW: Yes, of course it could. But history and the evolution of any academic discipline have a kind of inner logic, almost a dialectic of their own. Academics go off in a particular direction, usually led by a major figure or a national mood. Their ideas become fashionable. Other scholars come along and develop them further. Then the central ideas, in effect, wear themselves out. Then some young fellow comes along and makes his reputation by going in another direction. And the academic pack is on to a new track. That is perhaps the best that imperfect human beings can do: explore one line of thought and say, "Well, that's getting pretty thin. I'm going to react against it." So the evolution of historiography is a history of successive revisionists, each scoring off his predecessors, but in so doing, opening up new materials, new insights, and gradually, as events get further and further away in time and more and more people have worked over the evidence, they get closer to a consensus. There still will be revisionists about George Washington or Abraham Lincoln or Thomas Jefferson. But there has been enough back and forth—turning of the subject around—with people making their reputations from going off in another direction; so that you have got a much more solid historical view of the pre-1860 period than you do of the 1960s.

At the moment I am trying to persuade my fellow economists that their methods and concepts developed in the 1950s and 1960s have to be substantially modified to deal successfully with the 1980s and 1990s. I have written a polite, even mildly humorous, but essentially serious blast at both the monetarists and the Keynesians for the *Economic Journal* of March 1982 in response to a group of articles published in March 1981.

I believe the biggest revision required in academic life is the restructuring of economics. It is now focused obsessively on the determinants of aggregate demand. There is virtually no serious linkage of that variable to problems of supply. I do not mean supply-side economics as the term is used in the Reagan administration. I mean problems like energy, food supply, pollution control, research and development, etc. All these problems, which are left out of what is often called *mainstream economics,* are central to the period we are living in and, in fact, central to the level of aggregate demand and changes in that level. We have, for example, a state Commission on Texas in the Year 2000. We have selected as the key subjects to deal with, the life and death issues for Texas in the next twenty years: energy, water, agriculture, transport, state finance, research and development, and relations with Mexico. These are the great issues. But what are high-level economists arguing about: whether you should control inflation by monetary or fiscal policy; or, are Keynesians or monetarists right? (Incidentally, neither monetary nor fiscal policy is sufficient to deal with the kind of inflation we confront.) The mainstream economists are arguing fine points in macroeconomics when we are not going to get our economy in shape until we deal with some of these key sectors, like water and energy, and approach inflation in a quite different way. I think revisionism in academic life is most needed in economics because politicians listen to economists, and both economists and politicians are in trouble. History and economic history can look after themselves in their own leisurely dialectical way.

CA: Do you think there's a tendency among economists to hold on to theories that just no longer apply practically?

ROSTOW: Yes. And it's an important and potentially tragic fact. Between the two world wars the mainstream economists remained committed to concepts and policies based on pre-1914 experience. They did not come to grips with the new problems of the interwar period until well along in the 1930s. That lag in thought helped contribute to the coming of the

Second World War by producing, for example, the Great Depression with thirty-odd percent unemployment in Germany. By the time new concepts and policies began to be effective, Hitler was in power and the Japanese military as well. Here is how Keynes closes *The General Theory of Employment, Interest and Money* (1936): ". . . the ideas of economists and political philosophers, both when they are right and when they are wrong, are more powerful than is commonly understood. Indeed the world is ruled by little else. Practical men, who believe themselves to be quite exempt from any intellectual influences, are usually the slaves of some defunct economist. Madmen in authority, who hear voices in the air, are distilling their frenzy from some academic scribbler of a few years back. I am sure that the power of vested interests is vastly exaggerated compared with the gradual encroachment of ideas. Not, indeed, immediately, but after a certain interval; for in the field of economic and political philosophy there are not many who are influenced by new theories after they are twenty-five or thirty years of age, so that the ideas which civil servants and politicians and even agitators apply to current events are not likely to be the newest. But, soon or late, it is ideas, not vested interests, which are dangerous for good or evil."

You asked if current economic theories are out of date. I am sure they are. They are fixed in the molds which emerged in the late 1930s and early postwar years. I believe the arguments on theory and policy that I am putting forward now will be accepted in time, not because economists and politicians read what I write and conclude: "By golly, he's right." They will emerge because economists and politicians will be driven by their own experiences and successive frustrations to a similar position. I am confident that I am essentially correct not because of higher intellect or virtue than my colleagues, but because I am both an economist and an economic historian. I have never been able to accept the conventional wisdom or mainstream economics of the past generation, which has been devoted to macroeconomics: the analysis and manipulation of aggregate demand. As an economic historian, I had to deal also with a world in which the price of wheat, cotton, timber, coal, oil, and everything else was always changing because of supply factors screened out in macroeconomics. I had to pay attention to new technologies and demographic changes. Therefore, I had to be, in my generation, a rather unconventional economist to be a good economic historian. And so, when we came upon a time when these supply-side issues (energy, food, raw materials, environment, water, new technologies, and so on) emerged as critically important, I was somewhat more intellectually at home than my colleagues. That is why I believe the policy work I have done in the course of writing a history of the world economy over the past two centuries is relevant; not because I, uniquely, escaped from being captured by the ideas I formed when I was twenty-five or thirty. They just happened to be a different set of ideas than those of the mainstream economists and freed me from the limitations of the reigning macrotheories, whether Keynesian or monetarist.

BIOGRAPHICAL/CRITICAL SOURCES: *Christian Science Monitor*, April 9, 1960; *New Statesman*, April 30, 1960; *Spectator*, May 6, 1960, April 7, 1979; *New York Times Book Review*, May 8, 1960, June 28, 1964, August 1, 1971, December 10, 1972, April 6, 1975; *New Republic*, May 9, 1960, July 25, 1964, September 4, 1971, October 28, 1972, May 17, 1975, June 17, 1978; *Guardian*, May 27, 1960; *Nation*, June 11, 1960, October 14, 1978; *Saturday Review*, July 9, 1960, July 11, 1964; *American Economic Review*, December, 1960; *American Political Science Review*, December, 1960; *Social Education*, December, 1960; *Annals of the American Academy of Political and Social Science*, January, 1961; *American Sociological Review*, February, 1961; *American Anthropologist*, April, 1961; *Book Week*, June 28, 1964; William L. O'Neill, *Coming Apart: An Informal History of America in the 1960s*, Quadrangle Books, 1971; *The Pentagon Papers: The Defense Deparment History of United States Decisionmaking on Vietnam—The Senator Gravel Edition*, four volumes, Beacon Press, 1971; *National Review*, September 24, 1971; Walt W. Rostow, *The Diffusion of Power: An Essay in Recent History*, Macmillan, 1972; David Halberstam, *The Best and the Brightest*, Random House, 1972; *Newsweek*, January 8, 1973; *New York Review of Books*, February 8, 1973; *Political Profiles; The Johnson Years*, Facts on File, 1976; *Times Literary Supplement*, December 1, 1978.

—Sketch by Deborah A. Straub
—Interview by Jean W. Ross

* * *

ROTENSTREICH, Nathan 1914-

PERSONAL: Born March 31, 1914, in Sambor, Poland; immigrated to Palestine (now Israel), 1932; son of Ephraim and Miriam (Eifermann) Rotenstreich; married Binah Metzger, March 3, 1936; children: Ephrat (Mrs. I. Bolberg), Noa (Mrs. D. Schindler). *Education:* Hebrew University of Jerusalem, M.A., 1936, Ph.D., 1938; University of Chicago, postdoctoral study, 1949. *Home:* 7 Marcus St., Jerusalem, Israel. *Office:* Department of Philosophy, Hebrew University of Jerusalem, Jerusalem, Israel.

CAREER: Youth Aliyah Teachers Training College, Jerusalem, Israel, principal, 1944-51; Hebrew University of Jerusalem, Jerusalem, research fellow, 1949, senior lecturer in philosophy, Ahad Ha'am Professor of Philosophy, 1955—, dean of humanities, 1957-61, rector of university, 1963-69, head of Institute of Philosophy, 1971-74. Center for the Study of Democratic Institutions, visiting fellow, 1970, associate, 1972; visiting professor, City College of the City University of New York, 1969-70, and Harvard University, 1980. *Member:* International Institute of Philosophy, Israel National Academy of Sciences and Humanities. *Awards, honors:* Tscernichowski prize, 1955, for translation of *Critique of Pure Reason*; recipient of awards from municipalities of Tel Aviv, 1960, and Haifa, 1961; Israel Prize for Humanities, 1963.

WRITINGS: Between Past and Present: An Essay on History, with foreword by Martin Buber, Yale University Press, 1958, 2nd edition, Kennikat, 1973; *The Recurring Pattern: Studies in Anti-Judaism in Modern Thought*, Weidenfeld & Nicolson, 1963, Horizon Press, 1964; *Humanism in the Contemporary Era*, Mouton & Co., 1963; *Basic Problems of Marx's Philosophy*, Bobbs-Merrill, 1965; *On the Human Subject: Studies in the Phenomenology of Ethics and Politics*, C. C Thomas, 1966; *Jewish Philosophy in Modern Times: From Mendelssohn to Rosenzweig*, Holt, 1968; *Tradition and Reality*, Random House, 1972; *Philosophy: The Concept and Its Manifestations*, Reidel, 1973.

All published by Nijhoff: *Spirit and Man: An Essay on Being and Value*, 1963; *Experience and Its Systemization: Studies in Kant*, 1965, 2nd edition, 1972; *From Substance and Subject: Studies in Hegel*, 1974; *Philosophy, History and Politics: Studies in Contemporary English Philosophy*, 1976; *Theory and Practice: An Essay in Human Intentionalities*, 1977; *Practice and Realization: Studies in Kant*, 1979.

Also author of more than twenty books in Hebrew on philosophy, politics, history, philosophy of Judaism, and problems in Israeli society, published in Israel, 1939—. Translator into

Hebrew, with S. H. Bergman, *Critique of Pure Reason, Critique of Practical Reason,* and *Critique of Judgement,* all by Immanuel Kant.

WORK IN PROGRESS: *Power and Its Mold: An Essay in Social and Political Philosophy: Reflection and Action; On the Dignity of Man,* for Magnes Press.

SIDELIGHTS: Of *Jewish Philosophy in Modern Times: From Mendelssohn to Rosenzweig,* Arthur A. Cohen writes in the *New Republic:* "It is to the complex rethinking of classic Judaism in the light of the Kantian revolution that Nathan Rotenstreich's brilliant book, *Jewish Philosophy in Modern Times,* is directed. Rotenstreich, a careful and scrupulous scholar, shows how Jewish thinkers, disarmed by Kant's critique of *religious* metaphysics, sought to salvage Judaism by making ethics its quasi-autonomous essence."

BIOGRAPHICAL/CRITICAL SOURCES: *New Republic,* March 15, 1969.

* * *

ROTHBLATT, Donald N(oah) 1935-

PERSONAL: Born April 28, 1935, in New York, N.Y.; son of Harry and Sophie (Chernofsky) Rothblatt; married Ann Vogel (a teacher), June 16, 1957; children: Joel M., Steven S. *Education:* City University of New York, B.Civil Engineering, 1957; Columbia University, M.S., 1963; Institute of Social Studies, The Hague, Netherlands, diploma in comprehensive planning, 1964; Harvard University, Ph.D., 1969. *Home:* 4051 Scripps Ave., Palo Alto, Calif. 94306. *Office:* Department of Urban and Regional Planning, San Jose State University, San Jose, Calif. 95192.

CAREER: New York City Planning Commission, New York City, planner, 1961-62; New York Housing and Redevelopment Board, New York City, planner, 1963-66; Harvard University, Center for Environmental Design Studies, Cambridge, Mass., research fellow, 1965-70, William F. Milton Research Fellow, 1970-71, assistant professor of city and regional planning, 1969-71; San Jose State University, San Jose, Calif., professor of urban and regional planning and chairman of department, 1971—. Lady Davis Visiting Professor of Urban and Regional Planning at Hebrew University of Jerusalem and at Tel-Aviv University, 1978; visiting scholar, Indian Association of Architects, Bombay and New Delhi, 1979; visiting faculty member at Graduate School of Design, Harvard University, 1981. Member of local citizens' community improvement committee. *Military service:* U.S. Army, Corps of Engineers, 1957-58; became first lieutenant.

MEMBER: American Institute of Certified Planners (member of task force on national urban policy, 1972-76), Association of Collegiate Schools of Planning (president, 1974-76), California Committee on Environmental Design Education (chairman, 1973-75). *Awards, honors:* Traveling fellowship from Dutch Government, 1964; faculty research grant from National Science Foundation, 1972-76; Innovative Teaching Grant, California State University and Colleges, 1975-76; Best of West Award for informational public television, Western Educational Society for Telecommunication, 1976.

WRITINGS: *Human Needs and Public Housing,* New York City Housing Library, 1964; *Thailand's Northeast,* Center for Environmental Design Studies, Harvard University, 1967; *Regional Planning: The Appalachian Experience,* Heath, 1971; *Allocation of Resources for Regional Planning,* Appalachian Regional Commission, 1972; (editor) *National Policy for Urban and Regional Development,* Heath, 1974; (editor) *Regional Advocacy Planning: Expanding Air Transport Facilities for the San Jose Metropolitan Area,* San Jose State University, 1975; (editor) *Metropolitan-Wide Advocacy Planning: Dispersion of Low and Moderate Cost Housing in the San Jose Metropolitan Area,* San Jose State University, 1975; (co-author) *The Suburban Environment and Women,* Praeger, 1979; *Regional-Local Development Policy Making: The Santa Clara Valley Corridor,* University of California, 1981; *Planning the Metropolis: The Multiple Advocacy Approach,* Praeger, 1982. Contributor to planning, urban studies, and regional studies journals.

WORK IN PROGRESS: *Suburbia: An International Perspective.*

* * *

ROTHENBERG, Albert 1930-

PERSONAL: Born June 2, 1930, in New York, N.Y.; son of Gabriel (a businessman) and Rose (Goldberg) Rothenberg; married Elissa Isaacson, September 6, 1953 (divorced, 1969); married Julia C. Johnson (an educator), June 28, 1970; children: (first marriage) Michael, Mora Ruth, Rina Susannah. *Education:* Harvard University, A.B., 1952; Tufts University, M.D., 1956. *Home:* Main St., Stockbridge, Mass. 01262. *Office:* Austen Riggs Center, Stockbridge, Mass. 01262.

CAREER: Pennsylvania Hospital, Philadelphia, intern, 1956-57; Yale University, School of Medicine, New Haven, Conn., resident in psychiatry, 1957-60, instructor, 1960-61, 1963-64, assistant professor, 1964-68, associate professor, 1968-74, clinical professor of psychiatry, 1974, assistant medical director of Yale Psychiatric Institute, 1964-65, attending psychiatrist at Yale New Haven Medical Center, 1964—; University of Connecticut, Farmington, professor of psychiatry, 1974-79; Austen Riggs Center, Stockbridge, Mass., director of research, 1979—. Senior attending physician at Puerto Rico Institute of Psychiatry, 1961-63. Visiting professor at Pennsylvania State University, 1971, Yale University, 1975-78. *Military service:* U.S. Army, 1961-63; became captain.

MEMBER: Pan-American Medical Association, American Psychiatric Association (fellow), American Society for Aesthetics, Society for Phenomenology and Existentialism, Royal Society of Health (fellow), Sigma Xi. *Awards, honors:* Research scientist career development program awards from National Institutes of Health, 1964, 1969; Guggenheim fellowship, 1974-75; American College of Psychoanalysts fellow, 1981.

WRITINGS: *Comprehensive Guide to Creative Writing Programs in American Colleges and Universities,* National Council of Teachers of English, 1970; (with B. R. Greenberg) *The Index of Scientific Writings on Creativity: Creative Men and Women,* Archon, 1974; *The Index of Scientific Writings on Creativity: General, 1566-1974,* Archon, 1975; (with C. R. Hausman) *The Creativity Question,* Duke University Press, 1976; *The Emerging Goddess: The Creative Process in Art, Science, and Other Fields,* University of Chicago Press, 1979.

Contributor: L.F.E. Lewis, editor, *Group Tensions and Mental Health,* Trinidad Government Printing, 1971; D. Carr and E. Casey, editors, *Explorations in Phenomenology,* Nijhoff, 1973; J. Leedy, editor, *Poetry the Healer,* Lippincott, 1973; S. Pasternak, editor, *Violence and Victims,* Halsted Press, 1975; V. K. Kar, editor, *Nepalese Short Stories,* Gallery Press, 1975; W. Muenster Berger, editor, *The Psychoanalytic Study of Society,* Yale University Press, 1976; A. Roland, editor, *Psychoanalysis, Creativity and Literature: A French-American Inquiry,* Columbia University Press, 1978.

Contributor to education, philosophy, and medical journals, and to *Saturday Review, Esquire, Psychology Today,* and other periodicals. Editorial consultant to *American Journal of Psychiatry*, *Archives of General Psychiatry*, and *Psychological Reports*.

WORK IN PROGRESS: *Creative Empathy*.

SIDELIGHTS: "I study the creative process," Albert Rothenberg told CA, "because of its importance to psychiatry, its applications to concepts of mental health and to the practice of psychotherapy. Also, I love the arts in all their forms and I have been privileged to glimpse some answers to their mysteries and those of creation in science as well." *Avocational interests:* Tennis, chess, painting, cross country skiing, walking.

* * *

ROTHENBERG, Gunther Eric 1923-

PERSONAL: Born July 11, 1923, in Berlin, Germany; son of Erich and Charlotte (Cohen) Rothenberg; married, 1952 (divorced, 1967); married, 1969. *Education:* University of Illinois, B.A., 1954, Ph.D., 1958; University of Chicago, M.A., 1956. *Home:* 210 East Lutz Ave., Lafayette, Ind. 47906. *Office:* Department of History, Purdue University, Lafayette, Ind. 47907.

CAREER: Served in British Army, 1941-46, and U.S. Air Force, 1949-55; Illinois State University, Normal, instructor in history, 1958; Southern Illinois University at Carbondale, assistant professor of modern European history, 1958-62; University of New Mexico, Albuquerque, associate professor, 1962-68, professor of military history, 1968-73; Purdue University, Lafayette, Ind., professor of military history, 1973—. Associate, Historical Evaluation and Research Organization (HERO), Washington, D.C.; member, United States Commission on Military History. *Member:* American Historical Association, Company of Military Collectors and Historians, American Military Institute, American Association for the Advancement of Slavic Studies. *Awards, honors:* American Philosophical Society grants, 1959, 1965, 1969, 1975; American Council of Learned Societies grant, 1962; Guggenheim fellowship, 1962-63.

WRITINGS: The Austrian Military Border in Croatia: 1522-1747, University of Illinois Press, 1960; *The Military Border in Croatia: 1740-1881*, University of Chicago Press, 1966; *The Army of Francis Joseph*, Purdue University Press, 1975; *The Art of Warfare in the Age of Napoleon*, Batsford, 1978, Indiana University Press, 1980; *The Anatomy of the Israeli Army*, Hippocrene, 1979; *Napoleon's Great Adversaries: The Archduke Charles and the Austrian Army*, Indiana University Press, 1979. Contributor to historical journals. Member of editorial board of *Military Affairs*, 1973-75, and *Austrian History Yearbook*, 1973-76; editor of *Indiana Journal of Military History*, 1981—.

WORK IN PROGRESS: *The Battle of Wagram*; *Fire and Movement: Tactics in the Age of the Repeating Rifle*.

SIDELIGHTS: Gunther Eric Rothenberg writes: "In recent years the approach to military history has tended to emphasize military history as a part of the overall history, stressing political and social considerations, and scorning the allegedly old-fashioned interest in battles and campaigns.

"The practitioners of this 'new military history' have, however, forgotten that military institutions exist for only one reason; that is to engage in conflict or in the implicit conflict of deterrence. To pretend, as has been done, that the study of conflict, including that of strategy, tactics, and weaponry, is not a worthy enterprise for an academic historian in an exercise in pretentiousness. In my recent works, I have increasingly concerned myself with the areas the 'new military history' has abandoned, and I have found that the response of publishers and readers has been overwhelmingly favorable.

"My working habits have remained the same. I have tried to assemble the materials as completely as possible, keeping in mind that all records of combat operations are more or less confused at best and that it has been common practice for such materials to be distorted for the sake of concealing mistakes. Here, perhaps, arises one of the real sources of the 'new military history.' Military men seldom possess the scholarly background or sometimes the detachment necessary to evaluate historical materials; professional historians lack familiarity with weapons, tactics, strategy, and combat operation. Having both a military background and an academic education has been of considerable help to me."

* * *

ROVIN, Ben
See CLEVENGER, Ernest Allen, Jr.

* * *

ROWLANDS, Peter
See LOVELL, Mark

* * *

R. R.
See IYENGAR, K(odaganallur) R(amaswami) Srinivasa

* * *

RUITENBEEK, Hendrik M(arinus) 1928-

PERSONAL: Born February 26, 1928, in Leiden, The Netherlands; came to United States, 1955; naturalized U.S. citizen, 1962; son of Johannes (a businessman) and Maria (de la Court) Ruitenbeek. *Education:* University of Leyden, B.A., 1948, Doctorandus degree, 1952, Ph.D., 1955.

CAREER: Psychoanalyst in private practice, New York City, 1960—. Instructor in psychology, New York University, 1963—; staff member of Community Guidance Service, New York City; faculty member of Institute of Practicing Psychotherapists, New York City. Editorial adviser to Dell Publishing Company. *Member:* American Sociological Association, Institute of Practicing Psychotherapists, Association of Existential Psychology and Psychiatry, Society for the Scientific Study of Sex.

WRITINGS: *Het ontstaan van de Partij van de Arbeid*, De Arbeiderspers, 1955.

(Editor) *Psychoanalysis and Existential Philosophy*, Dutton, 1962; (editor) *Psychoanalysis and Social Science*, Dutton, 1962; (editor) *Varieties of Classic Social Theory*, Dutton, 1963; (editor) *Varieties of Modern Social Theory*, Dutton, 1963; (editor) *The Problem of Homosexuality in Modern Society*, Dutton, 1963; (editor) *The Dilemma of Organizational Society*, Dutton, 1963; *The Individual and the Crowd*, Nelson, 1964; (editor) *Psychoanalysis and Contemporary American Culture*, Dell, 1964; (editor) *The Psychotherapy of Perversions*, Citadel, 1964; (editor) *Psychoanalysis and Literature*, Dutton, 1964; (editor) *Varieties of Personality Theory*, Dutton, 1964; (editor) *The Creative Imagination*, Quadrangle, 1965; (editor) *The Literary Imagination*, Quadrangle, 1965; *Freud and America*, Macmillan, 1966; (editor) *Psychoanalysis and Female Sexuality,* College & University Press, 1966; (editor) *Psychoanalysis and Male Sexuality,* College & University Press, 1966; (editor) *Heirs to Freud: Essays in Freudian Psychology,* Grove, 1966, published as *The First Freudians,* Jason Aronson, 1973; (editor) *Death and Mourning: Psychological Interpretations,* Dell, 1967, published as *The Interpretation of Death,* Jason Aronson, 1973; (compiler) *The Psychotherapy of Perversions,* Citadel, 1967; (editor) *Homosexuality and Creative Genius,* Astor-Honor, 1967; *The Male Myth,* Dell, 1967; (editor) *Group Therapy Today: Styles, Methods, and Techniques,* Atherton, 1969.

The New Group Therapies, Discus Books, 1970; (editor) *Sexuality and Identity,* Dell, 1971; (editor) *Going Crazy: The Radical Therapy of R. D. Laing and Others,* Bantam, 1972; (editor) *The Analytic Situation: How Patient and Therapist Communicate,* Aldine, 1973; (editor) *Freud As We Knew Him,* Wayne State University Press, 1973; (editor) *Homosexuality: A Changing Picture,* Souvenir Press, 1973; *The New Sexuality,* New Viewpoints, 1974; *Psychotherapy: What It's All About,* Avon, 1976. Contributor to journals.†

* * *

RUSH, Anne Kent 1945-

PERSONAL: Born July 28, 1945, in Mobile, Ala.; daughter of George Le Grand and Cynthia (Boyd Williams) Rush. *Education:* Wayne State University, B.A., 1967. *Politics:* Feminist. *Address:* 1150 High Ct., Berkeley, Calif. 94708. *Office address:* Moon Books, P.O. Box 9223, Berkeley, Calif. 94709.

CAREER: Little, Brown & Co. (publishers), Boston, Mass., trade copywriter, 1968; Esalen Institute, San Francisco, Calif., staff teacher, 1970-72; Bookworks (publishers), Berkeley, Calif., art editor, 1970-73; Alyssum: Center for Feminist Consciousness, San Francisco, member of organizing collective, 1973-75; Moon Books (publishers), Berkeley, partner, 1974—. Partner in feminist theatre company, Amazon Grace, San Francisco, 1974.

WRITINGS—All self-illustrated: (Editor) George Downing, *The Massage Book,* Bookworks/Random House, 1972; *Getting Clear: Body Work for Women,* Bookworks/n Books/Random House, 1973; (with Anica Vesel Mander) *Feminism as Therapy,* Random House, 1974; *Moon, Moon,* Random House, 1976; *The Basic Back Book,* Summit/Simon & Schuster, 1979. Contributor to *Issues in Radical Therapy.*

WORK IN PROGRESS: Exploration into feminist politics and body therapy.

* * *

RUSSELL, D(iana) E(lizabeth) H(amilton) 1938-

PERSONAL: Born November 6, 1938, in Cape Town, South Africa; naturalized U.S. citizen; daughter of James Hamilton and Kathleen Mary (Gibson) Russell. *Education:* University of Cape Town, B.A., 1958; London School of Economics and Political Science, postgraduate diploma (with distinction), 1961; Harvard University, M.A., 1967, Ph.D., 1970. *Politics:* "Feminist." *Religion:* Agnostic. *Home:* 2432 Grant St., Berkeley, Calif. 94703. *Office:* Division of Social Science, Mills College, Oakland, Calif. 94613.

CAREER: London School of Economics and Political Science, London, England, research assistant in department of social anthropology, 1961-62; University of Cape Town, Cape Town, South Africa, research assistant, 1963; Princeton University, Center of International Studies, Princeton, N.J., research associate, 1967-68; Mills College, Oakland, Calif., assistant professor of sociology, 1975—. Lecturer on feminism, rape, and violence against women in United States, Canada, Belgium, and West Germany. Research associate, Institute for Scientific Analysis, 1974—; principal investigator of research projects, National Center for the Prevention and Control of Rape, 1977-79, Institute for Scientific Analysis, 1977-79, and National Center on Child Abuse and Neglect. Member, coordinating committee, International Tribunal on Crimes against Women, 1974-76. Participant and speaker at international conferences; U.S. delegate, International Women's Year World Congress, 1975; narrator of presentation, "Crimes against Women," at National International Women's Year Conference, 1977. Research consultant to California Commission on Crime Control and Violence Prevention, 1981-82. *Member:* Feminist Writer's Guild, Women against Violence in Pornography and Media (member of board of directors, 1978—), Sociologists for Women in Society, Anti-Slavery Society.

WRITINGS: Rebellion, Revolution, and Armed Force: A Comparative Study of Fifteen Countries with Special Emphasis on Cuba and South Africa, Academic Press, 1974; *The Politics of Rape: The Victim's Perspective,* Stein & Day, 1975; (editor with N. Van de Ven and contributor) *Crimes against Women: The Proceedings of the International Tribunal,* Les Femmes, 1976; (author of introduction) Del Martin, *Battered Wives,* Glide Publications, 1976; (contributor) Lorenne M.G. Clark, editor, *New Theoretical Perspectives on Rape,* University of Toronto Press, 1977; (contributor) Laura Lederer and Lynn Campbell, editors, *First Feminist Papers on Pornography,* Morrow, 1980; (editor with R. Linden, D. Pagano, and L. Star) *Against Sadomasochism: A Radical Feminist Perspective,* Frog in the Well, 1982; *Rape in Marriage,* Macmillan, 1982; *Rape and Other Forms of Sexual Abuse,* California Commission on Crime Control and Violence Prevention, 1982.

Also author and editor of text for dramatic reading, "Crimes against Women," first produced at National International Women's Year Conference, Houston, Tex., November 18, 1977. Contributor to *Arete* encyclopedia, 1980. Also contributor of articles and reviews to journals, including *Signs: Journal of Women in Culture and Society, Contemporary Sociology, Victimology: An International Journal, Sex Roles: A Journal of Research,* and *Ms. Magazine.* Contributing editor of *Chrysalis,* 1977—.

WORK IN PROGRESS: The Sexual Abuse of Female Children.

* * *

RUSSELL, Letty M(andeville) 1929-

PERSONAL: Born September 20, 1929, in Westfield, N.J.; daughter of Ricketson Borden (an engineer) and Miriam (Towl) Russell; married Johannes Christiann Hoekendijk (a professor), January 3, 1970 (died, 1975). *Education:* Wellesley College, B.A., 1951; Harvard University, S.T.B. (cum laude), 1958; Union Theological Seminary, New York, N.Y., S.T.M., 1967, Th.D., 1969. *Politics:* Democrat. *Home:* 116 River St., Guilford, Conn. 06437. *Office:* Divinity School, Yale University, 409 Prospect St., New Haven, Conn. 06510.

CAREER: Ordained minister of United Presbyterian Church, 1958. East Harlem Protestant Parish, New York, N.Y., director of Christian education, 1952-55, pastor, 1958-68; Manhattan College, Bronx, N.Y., assistant professor of religious studies, 1969-74; Yale University, Divinity School, New Haven, Conn., lecturer, 1973-74, assistant professor, 1974-77, associate professor of theology, 1977—. Adjunct professor at New York Theological Seminary, 1969-72; visiting professor at United Theological College, Bangalore, India, 1972. World Council of Churches, member of working committee on studies in evangelism, 1962-73, consultant to U.S. working group on participation of women, 1974-75; member of special committee on membership of United Presbyterian Church, U.S.A., 1971-75. Religious consultant to national board of Young Women's Christian Association, 1970-73.

MEMBER: American Association of University Professors, American Academy of Religion (member of the Women's Caucus, 1973—), Professors of Religious Education, Association for Professional Education for Ministry. *Awards, honors:* S.T.D., Dickinson College, 1982.

WRITINGS: (With Clyde Allison and Daniel C. Little) *The City: God's Gift to the Church*, United Presbyterian Church, 1960; *Christian Education in Mission*, Westminster, 1967.

Women's Liberation in a Biblical Perspective (study guide), National Board of YWCA, 1971; (contributor) John Westerhoff, editor, *Colloquy on Christian Education*, United Church Press, 1972; *Ferment of Freedom*, National Board of YWCA, 1972; *Unfinished Dimensions of the YWCA*, Young Men's Christian Association, 1973; *Human Liberation in a Feminist Perspective: A Theology*, Westminster, 1974; (contributor) Alice Hageman, editor, *Sexist Religion and Women in the Church*, Association Press, 1974; (contributor) Thomas McFadden, editor, *Liberation, Revolution and Freedom: Theological Perspectives*, Seabury, 1975; (editor) *The Liberating Word*, Westminster, 1976; *The Future of Partnership*, Westminster, 1979.

Growth in Partnership, Westminster, 1981; *Becoming Human*, Westminster, 1982. Author of *Bible Study Guide*, 1960-68, and *Christian Education Handbook*, 1966, both for East Harlem Protestant Parish. Contributor to theological and church journals.

WORK IN PROGRESS: Researching the relation of feminist theology and black theology, issues in liberation theology, and theology of vocation.

* * *

RUZIC, Neil P. 1930-

PERSONAL: Surname rhymes with "music"; born May 12, 1930, in Chicago, Ill.; son of Joseph F. (an oral surgeon) and Ida (Pierce) Ruzic; married Carol W. Kalsbeek, April 14, 1950; children: David Neil. *Education:* Attended Loyola University, Chicago, Ill., 1946-47; Northwestern University, B.S., 1950. *Politics:* Independent. *Office address:* P.O. 527, Beverly Shores, Ind. 46301.

CAREER: Former foreign correspondent in Central America, professional photographer, and building contractor; Illinois Institute of Technology Research Institute, Chicago, Ill., director of publications, 1954-58; Industrial Research, Inc. (publishers of *Industrial Research* and other publications), Chicago, founder and president, 1958-72; Neil Ruzic & Co. (consultants to National Aeronautics and Space Administration), Chicago, founder and president, 1972-78; Island for Science, Inc., Beverly Shores, Ind., founder and president, 1978—. Founder and director of National Space Institute. *Military service:* U.S. Army, 1952-54.

MEMBER: Institute of Electrical and Electronics Engineers (senior member), American Vacuum Society, Sigma Delta Chi. *Awards, honors:* Three "best magazine" awards from Industrial Marketing Association, 1958-65.

WRITINGS: *There's Adventure in Civil Engineering*, Popular Mechanics, 1958; *There's Adventure in Meteorology*, Popular Mechanics, 1958; (editor) *Stimulus*, Scientific Research, 1960; *The Case for Going to the Moon*, Putnam, 1965; *Where the Winds Sleep* (Literary Guild selection), Doubleday, 1970; *Spinoff 1976*, National Aeronautics and Space Administration, 1976; *A Blueprint for an Island for Science*, two volumes, privately printed, 1977; *Open-Ocean Polyculture*, privately printed, 1979. Contributor of two hundred or more articles and short stories to technical, business, and science fiction magazines.

SIDELIGHTS: In 1967 Ruzic patented the "Ruzic Shield," the first U.S. patent to be granted for a device to be used exclusively on the moon. He is currently developing Little Stirrup Cay (Bahamas) as a cruise-ship port-of-call and is planning a seaweed-shrimp farm on land in Florida.

* * *

RYERSON, Martin 1907-

PERSONAL: Born January 28, 1907, in New York, N.Y.; son of Frank Stephen (a mortician) and Ethel (Vinicombe) Smith; married Marilyn Reiss (in sales promotion), December 9, 1936; children: Lois Jean. *Education:* Attended schools in New York, N.Y. *Politics:* Republican. *Religion:* Protestant. *Home and office:* 4540 Vandever, Apt. 8, San Diego, Calif. 92120. *Agent:* Jay Garon-Brooke Associates, Inc., 415 Central Park West, 17D., New York, N.Y. 10025.

CAREER: Radio writer and director of several stage shows, New York City, in 1930s; free-lance writer for pulp magazines, 1940-43; associate editor, McCann-Erickson Advertising Agency, New York City, and writer of network radio and television scripts, 1945-53; copy director at KMJ-TV and KFRE-TV, Fresno, Calif., 1953-59; editor of *Fresno Star* (weekly newspaper), Fresno, 1959-64; editor of *Pasadena Courier*, Pasadena, Calif., 1965-70; full-time writer. Actor in television series, "O'Henry from Brooklyn," 1955, in other radio and television programs, and in Fresno Community Theatre productions. *Military service:* U.S. Army, 1943-45; news editor, and broadcaster, American Forces Network, London, 1943-45; became technical sergeant.

WRITINGS—Novels: *Thunder in the Badlands*, Bouregy, 1964; *Sudden Rage at War's Rim*, Sunset Books, 1964; *Showdown at Devil's Fork*, Sunset Books, 1964; *Press Agent for Murder*, Sunset Books, 1964; *Gunfire at Big Needles*, Sunset Books, 1964; *Doctor vs. Murder*, Sunset Books, 1964; *Star-Studded Murder*, Playtime Books, 1965; *No Time for Angels*, Novel Books, 1965; *Border Justice*, Bouregy, 1965; *Golden Venus*, Award Books, 1968.

Gunfighter, Award Books, 1970; *Sex Goddess*, Award Books, 1970; *Gamecock*, Midwood, 1970; *Baseball Playboy*, Midwood, 1971; *Sugar Baby*, Greenleaf Books, 1973; *Mafia Mistress*, Midwood, 1973; *Fantasy Girl*, Liverpool, 1973; *Beauty in Bondage*, Manchester, 1974; *Golden Mermaid*, Midwood, 1974; *Gunfire at Purgatory Gate*, Major Books, 1976; *Bitter Breed*, Major Books, 1977; *Sheriff without a Gun*, Major Books, 1978.

Canyon Fire, Leisure Books, 1980; *Quick Badge*, Leisure Books, 1981; *A Nest of Rattlers*, Leisure Books, 1981. Also author of over 100 other novels under various pseudonyms; author of unpublished manuscript, "Moman—The Monkey Man."

Author of three one-act plays, produced at Attic Theatre, New York, N.Y., two three-act plays, "Old Mother Hubbard's" and "Revenge Without Music," produced in New York and New Jersey, 1936-37, and "First Stop to Nowhere," produced in Fresno, Calif., 1959. Author of one-act play, "Accidentally on Purpose," produced on Sears Radio Theater, 1980. Also author of more than one hundred network radio and television scripts for such programs as "Suspense," "Lights Out," "Gangbusters," "Molle Mystery Theatre," "Grand Central Station," "Stars Over Hollywood," and "Death Valley Days," 1945-53. Author of two weekly dramatic shows for WEVD, New York, N.Y., 1936-39, and of radio scripts for British Broadcasting Corp., 1945; also author of radio play, "The Wolf Ship."

Regular contributor to Standard Magazines, Columbia Publications, and Popular Publications, 1940-43, with stories in *Thrilling Magazine, Exciting Detective, Black Mask, Detective Tales, Thrilling Sports,* and other magazines.

WORK IN PROGRESS: Two novels, *Crack Shot* and *The Scorched Star.*

SIDELIGHTS: Martin Ryerson told *CA:* "Over and over people ask: 'How did you start to write?' The answer: With a beginner's innocence, I believed I could write a better adventure novel than Edgar Rice Burrough's *Tarzan.* So with a ream of lined paper and a few sharp pencils, I sat down and hand-wrote more than one-hundred pages of a novel I called, 'Moman—The Monkey Man.' Unfortunately, 'Moman' never got out of the rejection slip jungle, never even made it to the presses, let alone the book racks.

"For book number two, I decided to try to 'improve' on *Dracula,* which came out in the form of a radio play called 'The Wolf Ship.' This attained slightly better 'success,' running thirteen weeks on a local New York radio station. Then 'The Wolf Ship' sailed into oblivion.

"By then, of course, I had been badly bitten by the 'literary bug' for which there is no antidote—except more writing. Three or four more novels, then some slight encouragement when my three-act play, 'Old Mother Hubbard's' was produced at the Park Palace in New York City, the City Park Theatre in Newark and the Rialto Theatre in Hoboken. 'Old Mother Hubbard's' never reached Broadway.

"Through the thirties, forties and fifties, I wrote for most of the top dramatic radio shows, then spent six years writing television copy. Finally I decided to go back to my first love—novel writing. Since then I've had more than a hundred books published. None ever reached the bestseller list because most of my books have been paperbacks. More recently I've concentrated on westerns.

"What does all this mean to the writer who is just starting out? It means because your first efforts don't jell, don't get discouraged. You might be in the wrong medium. Keep trying until you find one that suits your own particular style of writing. As they say in real estate: There's a buyer for every house, and a house for every prospective buyer. The important thing is—never stop trying!"

While stationed in London, England during World War II, Ryerson "voiced the blow-by-blow" of more than 500 boxing bouts from Rainbow Corner, Picadilly. He also acted in dramatic programs for the British Broadcasting Corp. at that time.

S

SAATY, Thomas L(orie) 1926-

PERSONAL: Born July 18, 1926, in Mosul, Iraq; came to United States in 1946; son of David M. and Dola (Hayali) Saaty; married Rozann Waldron, December 9, 1964; children: Linda, Michael, Emily, John, Daniel. *Education:* Columbia Union College, B.A., 1948; Catholic University of America, M.S., 1949; Sorbonne, University of Paris, graduate study, 1952-53; Yale University, Ph.D., 1953. *Home:* 4922 Ellsworth Ave., Pittsburgh, Pa. 15213. *Office:* Graduate School of Business, University of Pittsburgh, Pittsburgh, Pa. 15260.

CAREER: Melpar, Inc., Alexandria, Va., mathematician, 1953-54; Massachusetts Institute of Technology, Cambridge, scientific analyst with Operations Evaluation Group, 1954-57; U.S. Department of the Navy, Washington, D.C., mathematician in Management Office, 1957-58; Office of Naval Research, London, England, mathematician, 1958-59, director of advanced planning of Naval Analysis Group, 1959-61, head of Mathematics Branch, 1961-63; U.S. Arms Control & Disarmament Agency, Washington, D.C., research scientist, 1963-69; University of Pennsylvania, Warton School of Commerce and Finance, Philadelphia, professor of applied mathematics, 1969-79, chairman of Operations Research, 1969-71; University of Pittsburgh, Pittsburgh, Pa., professor and department chairman, 1979—. Visiting lecturer at a number of colleges and universities, including U.S. Department of Agriculture Graduate School, 1954-69, Catholic University of America, 1960, George Washington University, 1962-65, and University of California, Los Angeles, 1963-69. Executive director, Conference Board of Math Sciences, 1965-67. Consultant to governmental and private agencies.

MEMBER: International Institute for Strategic Studies, American Mathematical Society, Mathematical Association of America, Operations Research Society of America, American Association for the Advancement of Science (fellow), World Future Society, Pi Mu Epsilon. *Awards, honors:* Award from Office of Naval Research, 1959, for contributions to the advancement of international scientific cooperation; Lester R. Ford Award from Mathematical Association of America, 1973; award from Institute of Management Sciences, 1977.

WRITINGS: Mathematical Methods of Operations Research, McGraw, 1959; *Elements of Queueing Theory with Applications,* McGraw, 1961; (with Joseph Bram) *Non-Linear Mathematics,* McGraw, 1964; (editor) *Lectures on Modern Mathematics,* three volumes, Wiley, 1964-65; (with Robert Busacker) *Finite Graphs and Networks,* McGraw, 1965; *Modern Non-Linear Equations,* McGraw, 1967; *Mathematical Models of Arms Control and Disarmament,* Wiley, 1968; (editor with F. J. Weyl) *The Spirit and Use of the Mathematical Sciences,* McGraw, 1969.

Optimization in Integers and Related External Problems, McGraw, 1970; *Topics on Behavioral Mathematics,* Mathematical Association of America, 1973; (with George Dantzig) *Compact City,* W. H. Freeman, 1973; *Mathematical Models in Physical, Biological and Social Sciences,* American Association for the Advancement of Science, 1975; *The Analytic Hierarchy Process,* McGraw, 1980; *Decision Making for Leaders,* Wodsworth, 1981; (with Luis Vargas) *The Logic of Priorities,* Kluwer Nijhoff, 1981.

Contributor to journals in his field. Assistant editor, *Operations Research,* 1958-63, *Naval Research Logistics Quarterly,* 1964—; editor, *Newsletter for the Mathematical Science,* 1965-67.

WORK IN PROGRESS: Research on priorities for energy distribution hierarchies, fuzzy sets, quantitative methods in the social sciences, transport planning for the Sudan, and the construction of a regional energy game.

*　*　*

SABLOFF, Jeremy A(rac) 1944-

PERSONAL: Born April 16, 1944, in New York, N.Y.; son of Louis (a dentist) and Helen (Arac) Sabloff; married Paula Lynne Weinberg, May 26, 1968; children: Joshua Marc. *Education:* University of Pennsylvania, B.A., 1964; Harvard University, M.A., 1969, Ph.D., 1969. *Home:* 1630 Cornell N.E., Albuquerque, N.M. 87106. *Office:* Department of Anthropology, University of New Mexico, Albuquerque, N.M. 87131.

CAREER: Harvard University, Cambridge, Mass., assistant professor, 1969-74, associate professor of anthropology, 1974-76, Peabody Museum, assistant curator, 1970-74, associate curator of Middle American archaeology, 1974-76; University of Utah, Salt Lake City, associate professor of anthropology, 1976-77; University of New Mexico, Albuquerque, professor of anthropology, 1978—, chairperson of department, 1980—. *Member:* American Anthropological Association (fellow), Society for American Archaeology, American Association for the Advancement of Science, Sigma Xi. *Awards, honors:* National Geographical Society grant to Cozumel, Mexico, 1972-74.

WRITINGS: (With G. R. Willey) *A History of American Archaeology*, W. H. Freeman, 1974, 2nd edition, 1980; (editor with C. C. Lamberg-Karlovsky) *The Rise and Fall of Civilizations*, Cummings, 1974; (editor with Lamberg-Karlovsky) *Ancient Civilization and Trade*, University of New Mexico Press, 1975; *Excavations at Seibal: Ceramics*, Peabody Museum, Harvard University, 1975; (editor with W. L. Rathje) *Ancient Maya Commercial Systems*, Peabody Museum, Harvard University, 1975; (with Gair Tourtellot and Robert Sharrick) *A Reconnaissance of Cancuen, Peten, Guatemala*, Peabody Museum, Harvard University, 1977; (with Lamberg-Karlovsky) *Ancient Civilizations: The Near East and Mesoamerica*, Benjamin-Cummings, 1979.

(Editor with Willey) *Readings in Pre-Columbian Archaeology*, W. J. Freeman, 1980; (editor) *Simulations in Archaeology*, University of New Mexico Press, 1981; (editor) *Supplement to the Handbook of Middle American Indians, Volume I: Archaeology*, University of Texas Press, 1981; (editor) *Archaeology: Myth and Reality*, W. H. Freeman, 1982; (editor) *Analyses of Fine Paste Ceramics*, Peabody Museum, Harvard University, 1982.

Contributor: J. Harte and R. Socolow, editors, *The Patient Earth*, Holt, 1971; R. Brill, editor, *Science and Archaeology*, M.I.T. Press, 1971; T. P. Culbert, editor, *The Classic Maya Collapse*, University of New Mexico Press, 1973; N. Hammond, editor, *Mesoamerican Archaeology: New Approaches*, University of Texas Press, 1974; E. Benson, editor, *The Sea in the Pre-Columbian World*, Dumbarton Oaks, 1977; N. Hammond, editor, *Social Process in Maya Prehistory*, Academic Press, 1977; P. H. Oehser, John S. Lea, and N. L. Powers, editors, *National Geographic Society Research Reports, 1971 Projects*, National Geographic Society, 1980; E. A. Hoebel, editor, *Crisis in American Anthropology: A View from Spring Hill*, Garland Publishing, 1982.

Editor of *American Antiquity*, 1977-81.

* * *

SAHAKIAN, William S(ahak) 1921-

PERSONAL: Surname is pronounced Sar-*hark*-ian; born October 7, 1921, in Boston, Mass.; son of Jacob and Anna (Pakchoian) Sahakian; married Mabel Marie Lewis (a professor of philosophy and psychology), 1945; children: James William, Richard Lewis, Barbara Jacquelyn, Paula Leslie. *Education:* Northeastern University, B.S., 1944; Boston University, M.Div., 1947, Ph.D., 1951; additional study of Harvard University, 1948-55. *Politics:* Independent. *Home:* 49 Eisenhower Cir., Wellesley, Mass. 02181. *Office:* Suffolk University, Beacon Hill, Boston, Mass. 02114.

CAREER: Licensed psychologist, Commonwealth of Massachusetts; psychotherapist in private practice; Suffolk University, Boston, Mass., 1946—, professor of psychology and philosophy, 1951—, chairman of department, 1951-73. Lecturer in psychology, Graduate School, Northeastern University, 1951-70, and Harvard University extension courses; lecturer, Curry College, 1955-57, and Lasell College, 1960-61; professorial lecturer in psychology, Massachusetts College of Pharmacy. Assisted in preparation of Graduate Record Examination in psychology; conducted psychological testing of police recruits for Massachusetts Metropolitan District Commission. Critical reviewer of book and journal manuscripts for several publishing companies; consultant to Mendota Research Group, 1960-65, and National Association on Standard Medical Vocabulary; member of advisory board of American Institute of Logotherapy; advisor to president of Curry College.

MEMBER: American Psychological Association (fellow), American Philosophical Association (fellow), American Association for the Advancement of Science, Britannica Society, Human Factors Society, Personalist Group, Association for Realistic Philosophy, New England Philosophy of Education Society, Massachusetts Philosophical Association (fellow), New York Academy of Sciences, Northeastern University Honor Society, Kappa Sigma, Phi Sigma Tau, Kappa Psi. *Awards, honors:* D.Sc., Curry College, 1956; numerous awards for achievements in psychology and philosophy.

WRITINGS: *Systems of Ethics and Value Theory*, Philosophical Library, 1963, revised edition, 1968; *Outline of Philosophers*, privately printed, 1963; (with wife, Mabel Lewis Sahakian) *Realms of Philosophy*, Shenkman, 1965, 3rd edition, 1981; (editor) *Philosophies of Religion*, Shenkman, 1965; (editor) *Psychology of Personality: Readings in Theory*, Rand McNally, 1965, 3rd edition, 1977; (with M. L. Sahakian) *Ideas of the Great Philosophers*, Barnes & Noble, 1966, 2nd edition, Harper, 1974; *Philosophy Simplified: Keynotes*, Barnes & Noble, 1968; *History of Psychology*, F. E. Peacock, 1968, revised edition, 1981; *History of Philosophy*, Harper, 1968; *Philosophy*, Cliffs, 1968; *Psychotherapy and Counseling*, Rand McNally, 1969, revised edition, 1976.

Psychopathology Today: The Current Status of Abnormal Psychology, F. E. Peacock, 1970, revised edition, 1978; *Psychology of Learning*, Rand McNally, 1970, revised edition, 1976; *Social Psychology: Experimentation, Theory, and Research*, Intext Educational, 1972; *Systematic Social Psychology*, Chandler Publishing, 1972, 2nd edition published as *History and Systems of Social Psychology*, Hemisphere, 1980; *Ethics: Theories and Problems*, Harper, 1974; (with M. L. Sahakian) *Rousseau as Educator*, Twayne, 1974; (with M. L. Sahakian) *John Locke*, Twayne, 1975; *History and Systems of Psychology*, Halsted, 1975; (with M. L. Sahakian) *Plato*, Twayne, 1977; (contributor) R. J. Corsini, editor, *Current Personality Theories*, F. E. Peacock, 1977; (editor with J. Fabry and R. Bulka and contributor) *Logotherapy in Action*, Aronson, 1979.

(Contributor) Richie Herink, editor, *Psychotherapy Handbook*, New American Library, 1980. Advisory editor of psychology books for Rand McNally College Publishing Co. Contributor to *Psychology Handbook*, edited by J. Jones, Aronson, and to *Analecta Frankliana*; also contributor to *International Encyclopedia of Neurology, Psychiatry, Psychoanalysis, and Psychology, Encyclopaedia Britannica, Collier's Encyclopedia*, and *Wiley's Encyclopedia of Psychology*. Contributor of book reviews and articles to psychology journals and newspapers, including *Journal of Individual Psychology, Israel Annals of Psychiatry and Related Disciplines, American Psychologist*, and *Boston Globe*. Associate editor, *Wiley Encyclopedia of Psychology;* member of editorial board, *International Forum for Logotherapy*.

SIDELIGHTS: William S. Sahakian told *CA*: "I address my books to students, not professors; to the general reader, not professionals, and curiously they have become accepted by both. My entry into the world of writing began in spending months, and even years, looking for an appropriate text for students in my philosophy of life class, and, finding none, I began writing a text of my own designed specifically for them. I wrote at a leisurely pace, expecting to find a suitable text long before finishing mine. But none appeared, and it came as a surprise to find that a publisher saw fit to accept mine. Oddly, what began as a hobby fructified into a professional career. Book upon book appeared. Even a manuscript that was discarded, one firm rescued from my wastebasket and published. Ironically, it became one of his top sellers for a decade and is currently being readied for its third edition.

"The only secret I know in successfully publishing is the love of research and writing, making a hobby pay, being paid for enjoying oneself. Coupled to that is self-discipline, the budgeting of one's time, and the determination to see the manuscript through to completion, an experience not too different from the marathon runner bent on finishing his grueling race, except that writing need not be exhausting. And yes, rejections and setbacks must be taken in stride, considered and then set aside, for the only element that counts is the successful publication and acceptance by the general public of one's book. It is not the negatives, but the positives that will see you through . . . not only to publication but successfully through life itself."

* * *

St. JOHN, Beth
See JOHN, Elizabeth Beaman

* * *

St. JOHN, Elizabeth
See JOHN, Elizabeth Beaman

* * *

SALISBURY, Frank B(oyer) 1926-

PERSONAL: Born August 3, 1926, in Provo, Utah; son of Frank M. (in insurance) and Catherine (Boyer) Salisbury; married Lois Marilyn Olson, September 1, 1949; children: Frank Clark, Stephen Scott, Michael James, Cynthia Kay, Phillip Boyer (deceased), Rebecca Lynn, Blake Charles. *Education*: University of Utah, B.S., 1951, M.A., 1952; California Institute of Technology, Ph.D., 1955. *Politics*: Republican. *Religion*: Church of Jesus Christ of Latter-day Saints. *Home*: 2020 Country Estates, North Logan, Utah 84321. *Office*: Plant Science Department, UMC 48, Utah State University, Logan, Utah 84322.

CAREER: Missionary for Church of Jesus Christ of Latter-day Saints in Switzerland, 1946-49; photographer, Boyart Studio, 1949-50; Pomona College, Claremont, Calif., assistant professor of botany, 1954-55; Colorado State University, Fort Collins, assistant professor, 1955-61, professor of plant physiology, 1955-61; Utah State University, Logan, professor of plant physiology, 1966—, professor of botany, 1968—, head of department of plant sciences, 1966-70. Speaker at colleges, universities, and at a variety of organizations. Member of board of trustees, Colorado State University Research Foundation, 1959-62; technical representative in plant physiology, U.S. Atomic Energy Commission (now U.S. Department of Energy), 1973-74; National Aeronautics and Space Administration and American Institute of Biological Sciences, member of committee to study biological experiments in an orbiting laboratory and of panel to evaluate research proposals, both 1974-79, and chairman of committee to investigate possible uses of Lunar Receiving Laboratory for research on extreme environments. Part-time commercial portrait photographer, 1950—. Consultant to National Aeronautics and Space Administration; former consultant to Aerial Phenomena Research Organization. *Military service*: U.S. Army Air Forces, 1945.

MEMBER: American Association for the Advancement of Science (fellow), American Institute of Biological Sciences (member-at-large of governing board, 1975-78), American Society of Plant Physiologists, Ecological Society of America, Botanical Society of America, Western Society of Naturalists, Utah Academy of Science, Arts, and Letters, Sigma Xi, Phi Kappa Phi. *Awards, honors*: National Science Foundation senior postdoctoral fellow in Tuebingen and Innsbruck, 1962-63.

WRITINGS: *The Flowering Process*, Pergamon, 1963; (with R. V. Parke) *Vascular Plants: Form and Function*, Wadsworth, 1964, 2nd edition, 1970; *Truth by Reason and by Revelation*, Deseret, 1965; (with Cleon Ross) *Plant Physiology*, Wadsworth, 1969, 2nd edition, 1978; *The Biology of Flowering*, Natural History Press, 1971; (with William Jensen) *Botany: An Ecological Approach*, Wadsworth, 1972; *The Utah UFO Display: A Biologist's Report*, Devin-Adair, 1974; *The Creation*, Deseret, 1976; (with Edward J. Kurmondy, Thomas F. Sherman, Nelson T. Spratt, Jr., and Garvin McCain) *Biology*, Wadsworth, 1977. Contributor of technical and popular articles on plant physiology, physiological ecology and space biology (especially the question of life on Mars), unidentified flying objects, and science and religion to U.S. and German periodicals. Member of editorial board, *Plant Physiology*, 1967—, and *BioScience*, 1972-78.

WORK IN PROGRESS: A second edition of *Botany: An Ecological Approach*, with Jensen; *Decisions, Decisions: The Challenge of Agency*, an examination of some of the problems of free will in the context of the Church of Jesus Christ of Latter-day Saints; research on the physiology of flowering, plant responses to gravity and mechanical stresses, maximum yields of plants in controlled environments, photoperiodism in plants, and growth of plants in extreme environmental conditions.

SIDELIGHTS: Frank B. Salisbury told *CA*: "Although I find little time to pursue the matter (except for publication of *The Creation*), I am increasingly impressed with the idea that the findings of science can not only contribute to one's belief in God but can help one to better understand the nature of the Creator. I am not a creationist in the contemporary sense of the word—I fully accept an ancient age for the earth and demonstrated processes of evolution—but I find many reasons to believe in God, and some of those reasons appear in modern science." *Plant Physiology* has been translated into Chinese, Polish, and Bahasa Malaysis.

AVOCATIONAL INTERESTS: Photography, mountaineering, sculpture, and running.

* * *

SALMON, Margaret Belais 1921-

PERSONAL: Born March 16, 1921, in New York, N.Y.; daughter of Arnold and Hortense Belais; married Douglas A. Salmon (a chemical engineer), October 19, 1945; children: Robert, Betty Lynn, Donald. *Education*: University of California, Berkeley, B.S., 1941, graduate study, 1941-42; Duke University, Certificate of Hospital Dietetics, 1943; Columbia University, M.S., 1964, professional diploma, 1967. *Religion*: Unitarian Universalist. *Office*: Salmon Consultants, 435 Lynn St., Harrington Park, N.J. 07640.

CAREER: Columbia-Presbyterian Medical Center, New York City, therapeutic dietitian, 1943-45, research dietitian, 1957-66; University of California, Berkeley, food technologist, 1945; therapeutic and teaching dietitian at Englewood Hospital, Englewood, N.J., Hackensack Hospital, Hackensack, N.J., and Holy Name Hospital, Teaneck, N.J., 1954-66; St. Luke's Hospital Center, New York City, administrative dietitian and therapeutic dietician, 1966-70; Bronx-Lebanon Hospital Center, Bronx, N.Y., associate director, 1970-71; St. Joseph's Hospital and Medical Center, Paterson, N.J., chief therapeutic dietitian, 1971—. President, Salmon Consultants (nutrition consultants), Harrington Park, N.J., 1957—. Director of school lunch programs at Moriah Academy, Englewood, and Yavneh Academy, Paterson, 1962-66; consulting dietician, prenatal program, American Red Cross; member of nutrition committee, Bergen County Heart Association; lecturer at colleges and universities, including Bergen Community College, Passiac County Community College, Montclair State College and Rutgers University Extension Division; also lecturer for Visiting Homemaker Service and Federal Women, Infants and Children's Program, both for New Jersey State Department of Health, and for various women's clubs, church groups, and schools; keynote speaker, spring conference, Nursing Mothers, Inc., 1981. Has appeared on various television programs and educational videotapes as a nutrition educator. Recipe judge for *Record* newspaper, Hackensack, and for Future Homemakers of America. Science Club advisor, Harrington Park Junior High School; leader and volunteer for Boy Scouts of America and Girl Scouts of U.S.A.; program chairwoman, Parent-Teachers Association.

MEMBER: American Dietetic Association (speaker at Bicentennial Convention, 1976), League of Women Voters (Englewood chapter; treasurer), Northern New Jersey Dietetic Association (president, 1966-68), Kappa Delta Pi, Pi Lambda Theta, Omicron Nu.

WRITINGS: Food Facts for Teenagers, C. C Thomas, 1965; (editor) *Enjoying Your Restricted Diet,* C. C Thomas, 1972; (contributor) *Easy and Delicious Rice Flour Recipes,* C. C Thomas, 1973; (contributor) *Career Guidance for Young Women,* C. C Thomas, 1974; (editor) *Physician's Diet Handbook,* Harrington Press, 1975, revised edition, Techkits, 1978; *Diabetic Diet Exchange Handbook,* Techkits, 1977; (editor) *St. Joseph's Hospital and Medical Center Diet Manual,* St. Joseph's Hospital and Medical Center, 1977, revised edition, 1981; *The Joy of Breastfeeding,* Techkits, 1977, 2nd edition, 1979; *A Professional Dietician's Natural Fiber Diet,* Parker Publishing, 1979, revised edition, 1981; *Diabetic Diet Exchange Handbook for Low Sodium Diets,* Techkits, 1980.

WORK IN PROGRESS: Continuing research on teenage nutrition.

AVOCATIONAL INTERESTS: Swimming, diving, competition dancing, reading.

*   *   *

SALMON, Wesley C(harles) 1925-

PERSONAL: Born August 9, 1925, in Detroit, Mich.; son of Wallis Samuel (an engineer) and Ruth (Springer) Salmon; married Nancy Pilson, November 26, 1949 (divorced, 1970); married Merrilee Hollenkamp Ashby, July 24, 1971; children: (first marriage) Victoria Anne. *Education:* Attended Wayne State University, 1943-44; University of Chicago, M.A., 1947; University of California, Los Angeles, Ph.D., 1950. *Office:* Department of Philosophy, University of Pittsburgh, Pittsburgh, Pa. 15260.

CAREER: University of California, Los Angeles, instructor in philosophy, 1950-51; Washington State University, Pullman, instructor, 1951-53, assistant professor of philosophy, 1953-54; Northwestern University, Evanston, Ill., lecturer, 1954-55; Brown University, Providence, R.I., assistant professor, 1955-59, associate professor of philosophy, 1959-63; Indiana University at Bloomington, professor of the philosophy of science, 1963-67, Norwood Russell Hanson Professor of Philosophy of Science, 1967-73; University of Arizona, Tucson, professor of philosophy, 1973-81; University of Pittsburgh, Pittsburgh, Pa., professor of philosophy, 1981—. Visiting lecturer, University of Bristol, 1959; visiting professor, University of Minnesota Center for Philosophy of Science, 1963, University of Pittsburgh, 1968-69, University of Melbourne, 1978.

MEMBER: International Union for the History and Philosophy of Science (chairman of U.S. national committee, 1967-68; first vice-president of Division of Logic, Methodology, and Philosophy of Science, 1979-83), American Academy of Arts and Sciences (fellow), American Association for the Advancement of Sciences (fellow), American Philosophical Association (member of executive committee of Western Division, 1969-71; Pacific Division, vice-president, 1976-77, president, 1977-78), Philosophy of Science Association (vice-president, 1968-70; president, 1971-72), Sigma Xi. *Awards, honors:* Fund for the Advancement of Science faculty fellow, 1953-54; M.A., Brown University, 1959.

WRITINGS: Logic, Prentice-Hall, 1963, 2nd edition, 1973; *The Foundations of Scientific Inference,* University of Pittsburgh Press, 1967; (editor) *Zeno's Paradoxes,* Bobbs-Merrill, 1970; (with others) *Statistical Explanation and Statistical Relevance,* University of Pittsburgh Press, 1971; *Space, Time, and Motion: A Philosophical Introduction,* Dickenson, 1975, 2nd edition, University of Minnesota Press, 1980; (editor) *Hans Reichenbach: Logical Empiricist,* D. Reidel, 1979.

Contributor: Sidney Hook, editor, *Psychoanalysis, Scientific Method, and Philosophy,* New York University Press, 1959; Herbert Feigl and Grover Maxwell, editors, *Current Issues in the Philosophy of Science,* Holt, 1961; Bernard H. Baumrin, editor, *Philosophy of Science: The Delaware Seminar II,* Wiley, 1963; Henry E. Kyburg, Jr. and Ernest Nagel, editors, *Induction: Some Current Issues,* Wesleyan University Press, 1963; Paul Feyerabend and Maxwell, editors, *Mind, Matter, and Method,* University of Minnesota Press, 1966; Robert G. Colodny, editor, *Mind and Cosmos,* University of Pittsburgh Press, 1966; Imre Lakatos, editor, *The Problem of Inductive Logic,* North-Holland Publishing, 1968; David L. Arm, editor, *Vistas in Science,* University of New Mexico Press, 1968; Nicholas Rescher, *Essays in Honor of Carl G. Hempel,* D. Reidel, 1969.

Colodny, editor, *The Nature and Function of Scientific Theories,* University of Pittsburgh Press, 1970; Roger H. Stuewer, editor, *Historical and Philosophical Perspectives of Science,* University of Minnesota Press, 1970; Joel Feinberg, editor, *Reason and Responsibility,* Dickenson, 2nd edition, 1971, 3rd edition, 1975 (Salmon was not associated with 1st edition); George Nakhnikian, editor, *Bertrand Russell's Philosophy,* Duckworth, 1974; Maxwell and Robert M. Anderson, Jr., editors, *Induction, Probability, and Confirmation,* University of Minnesota Press, 1975; S. Koerner, editor, *Explanation,* Yale University Press, 1975; Peter Machamer and Robert G. Turnbull, editors, *Motion and Time, Space and Matter,* Ohio State University Press, 1976; John S. Earman, Clark N. Glymour, and John Stachel, editors, *Foundations of Space-Time Theories,* University of Minnesota Press, 1977; R. E. Butts and Jaakko Hintikka, editors, *Basic Problems in Methodology and Linguistics,* D. Reidel, 1977.

Hintikka, David Gruender, and Evando Agazzi, editors, *Probabilistic Thinking, Thermodynamics and the Interaction of the History and Philosophy of Science,* D. Reidel, 1981; Robert McLaughlin, editor, *What? Where? When? Why?,* D. Reidel, 1982.

Editor with Joel Feinberg of Prentice-Hall's "Contemporary Prospectives in Philosophy Series." Contributor to *Encyclo-*

pedia Americana. Also contributor to philosophy journals. Member of editorial board, *Journal of Philosophical Logic, Erkenntnis, American Philosophical Quarterly, Synthese, Synthese Library,* and *Pacific Philosophical Quarterly.*

* * *

SALTER, Mary D.
See AINSWORTH, Mary D(insmore) Salter

* * *

SARGENT, Pamela

PERSONAL: Born in Ithaca, N.Y. *Education:* State University of New York at Binghamton, B.A., 1968, M.A., 1970. *Residence:* Johnson City, N.Y.

CAREER: Honigsbaum's, Albany, N.Y., sales clerk and model, 1964-65; Endicott Coil Co., Inc., Binghamton, N.Y., solderer on assembly line, 1965; Towne Distributors, Binghamton, N.Y., sales clerk, 1965; State University of New York at Binghamton, typist in cataloging department of library, 1965-66, teaching assistant in philosophy, 1969-71; Webster Paper Co., Albany, N.Y., office worker, 1969; writer, 1969—. *Member:* Science Fiction Writers of America.

WRITINGS—Science fiction, except as indicated: *Cloned Lives* (novel), Fawcett, 1976; (author of afterword) *The Fifth Head of Cerberus,* Ace Books, 1976; *Starshadows* (short stories), Ace Books, 1977; *The Sudden Star* (novel), Fawcett, 1979; *Watchstar* (novel), Pocket Books, 1980; (author of afterword) Terry Carr, editor, *Fantasy Annual V,* Timescape, 1982; (author of afterword) James Gunn editor, *The Road to Science Fiction: From Here to Forever,* Volume IV, Signet, 1982; *The Golden Space* (novel), Timescape, 1981; *The Alien Upstairs* (novel), Doubleday, 1983; *Earthseed* (novel), Harper, in press.

Editor and contributor; all published by Vintage Books: *Women of Wonder: Science Fiction Stories by Women about Women,* 1975; *Bio-Futures: Science Fiction Stories about Biological Metamorphosis,* 1976; *More Women of Wonder: Science Fiction Novelettes by Women about Women,* 1976; *The New Women of Wonder: Recent Science Fiction Stories by Women about Women,* 1978.

Contributor to anthologies: David Gerrold, editor, *Protostars,* Ballantine, 1971; Michael Moorcock, editor, *New Worlds Quarterly Three,* Berkeley Books, 1972; Carr, editor, *Universe Two,* Ace Books, 1972; Jack Dann, editor, *Wandering Stars* (Science Fiction Book Club selection), Harper, 1972; Roger Elwood, editor, *Ten Tomorrows,* Fawcett, 1973; Elwood, editor, *And Walk Now Gently through the Fire* (Science Fiction Book Club selection), Chilton, 1973; Joseph Elder, editor, *Eros in Orbit,* Trident, 1973; Thomas N. Scortia and Chelsea Quinn Yarbo, editors, *Two Views of Wonder,* Ballantine, 1973; Carr, editor, *Universe Four* (Science Fiction Book Club selection), Random House, 1974; Elwood, editor, *Continuum Three,* Putnam, 1974; Carr, editor, *Fellowship of the Stars* (Science Fiction Book Club selection), Simon & Schuster, 1974; Elwood, editor, *The Missing World and Other Stories* (juvenile), Lerner, 1974; Elwood, editor, *The Killer Plants and Other Stories* (juvenile), Lerner, 1974; Elwood, editor, *Night of the Sphinx and Other Stories* (juvenile), Lerner, 1974.

Elwood, editor, *Dystopian Visions,* Prentice-Hall, 1975; Damon Knight, editor, *Orbit 20,* Harper, 1978; Jack Dann, editor, *Immortal,* Harper, 1978; Patricia Warrick and others, editors, *Contemporary Mythology* (nonfiction), Harper, 1978; C. C. Smith, editor, *Twentieth Century Science Fiction Writers* (nonfiction), in press. Also contributor to science fiction and fantasy magazines.

WORK IN PROGRESS: Two novels, *Venus of Dreams,* for Timescape, and *Migratory Dreams;* short stories.

SIDELIGHTS: "Although I write science fiction, my primary interest is in characters—people," Pamela Sargent writes to *CA.* "Through them I try to explore possible future societies." Joanna Russ, in a *Magazine of Fantasy and Science Fiction* review of *Cloned Lives,* observes that Sargent "reveals a talent for tracing the psychology and human relations of her characters, projecting a kind of ideal decency that is pleasant and refreshing."

Sargent's concern with characterization is evident in her ambition to introduce well-rounded female protagonists into the male-dominated genre of science fiction. Gerald Jonas in a *New York Times Book Review* article comments that "the great mass of [science fiction] has been written by males and for males; and the role of women in most S.F. stories has been limited to decoration, breeding, and a dash of what old-time pulp editors referred to as 'human interest'. . . . One wonders why S.F. writers who can blithely dispatch hyperspace ships to the ends of the universe cannot conceive of putting a few interesting women on board." In an attempt to ameliorate the sexism that she believes is reflected in science fiction, Sargent has edited several volumes of "science fiction stories by women about women." In the introduction to the first of these anthologies, *Women of Wonder,* Sargent states: "If more women begin to take an interest in SF and the scientific and futurological ideas involved, publishers will have an interest in publishing and writers in writing novels exploring such ideas from different perspectives. If, however, publishers and writers can do better with the old stereotypes and have little reason to believe that readers want anything else, women will remain minor characters, and familiar roles and prejudices will be a major part of the literature."

According to a *Washington Post Book World* critic, *Women of Wonder* "shows a broadening perspective" in the field of science fiction. Sargent's introduction, the reviewer notes, is "excellent" and contains "some acute observations about sex roles in traditional science fiction." However, despite Sargent's claim that *Women of Wonder* attempts to introduce a feminist perspective by portraying female characters in dominant and responsible roles, some reviewers feel that she falls short of her goal. Algis Budrys in *Magazine of Fantasy and Science Fiction* says that *Women of Wonder* "contains few clinkers and many stories well worth reading," but also asserts that the volume "is not an excellent anthology. Some of the selections . . . are highly questionable." In a later review, Budrys calls the anthology a "contrafeminist assemblage," noting that *Women of Wonder* ignores numerous well-established female science fiction writers who write stories with strong female protagonists. In the earlier review, Budrys says: "Sargent's editorial motive is to be polemical, rather than entertaining. The stories here [in *Women of Wonder*] are only incidentally to divert, empathize with, or parade before the reader. They are blows against the masculine SF establishment [and Sargent] uses the sledgehammer approach as basic to her method of argument."

Budrys also argues that "Sargent's introduction seems to indicate that she . . . does not distinguish between the quality of being female and that display of culturally defined attributes which comprises 'femininity.'" As a result, claims Budrys, Sargent presents the reader with "a series of inaccuracies, of injustices not only to SF but to several female writers." Jonas also notes weaknesses in the stories included in *Women of*

Wonder: "Sargent's introduction notwithstanding, no more than one or two stories in her collection could be categorized as serious 'Women's lib S.F.'"

However, critics feel that Sargent came closer to the mark in the succeeding "Women of Wonder" volumes. An *English Journal* critic praises the "realistic" characters in *New Women of Wonder*. And *More Women of Wonder,* says Budrys, is "everything [*Women of Wonder*] claimed to be. . . . Its selections, while not always excellent, are exactly representative of what has been available in the field. . . . This is a good book, a valuable book, and in the bargain a very nice collection of reading."

BIOGRAPHICAL/CRITICAL SOURCES: Pamela Sargent, editor, *Women of Wonder: Science Fiction Stories by Women about Women,* Vintage Books, 1975; *Washington Post Book World,* February 16, 1975; *Psychology Today,* April, 1975; *New York Times Book Review,* May 4, 1975, May 11, 1980; *Magazine of Fantasy and Science Fiction,* November, 1975, November, 1976, June, 1977; *English Journal,* May, 1978; *Analog Science Fiction/Science Fact,* October, 1979; *Fantasy Newsletter,* October, 1982.

* * *

SARNOFF, Irving 1922-

PERSONAL: Born May 5, 1922, in Brooklyn, N.Y.; son of Nathan and Rose (Gelfand) Sarnoff; married Suzanne Fischbach (an artist, writer, and teacher), November 28, 1946; children: David, Sara. *Education:* Brooklyn College (now Brooklyn College of the City University of New York), B.A., 1946; University of Michigan, M.A., 1949, Ph.D., 1951. *Home:* 100 Bleecker St., New York, N.Y. 10012. *Office:* Department of Psychology, New York University, 10 Washington Pl., New York, N.Y. 10003.

CAREER: University of Michigan, Ann Arbor, research associate and extension service lecturer, 1951-54; University of London, University College, London, England, Fulbright advanced research scholar, 1954-55; Yale University, New Haven, Conn., assistant professor of psychology, 1955-60; Western Reserve University (now Case Western Reserve University), Cleveland, Ohio, professor of social work and psychology, 1960-62; New York University, New York, N.Y., professor of psychology, 1962—. Senior stipend, National Institute of Mental Health, 1968-69. *Military service:* U.S. Army, Signal Corps, 1943-46. *Member:* American Psychological Association.

WRITINGS: (Contributor) D. Katz and others, editors, *Public Opinion and Propaganda,* Dryden, 1954; *Personality Dynamics and Development,* Wiley, 1962; *Society with Tears,* Citadel, 1966; (contributor) R. Abelson and others, editors, *Theories of Cognitive Consistency: A Sourcebook,* Rand McNally, 1968; I. Katz and H. Silver, editors, *The University and Social Welfare,* Magnes Press, 1969; *Testing Freudian Concepts: An Experimental Social Approach,* Springer Publishing, 1971; (with wife, Suzanne Sarnoff) *Sexual Excitement/Sexual Peace: The Place of Masturbation in Adult Relationships,* M. Evans, 1979. Editorial advisor, *Encyclopaedia Britannica,* 1969—. Contributor of more than thirty articles and reviews to professional journals in America and England.

WORK IN PROGRESS: A book on love in lifelong marriage, with S. Sarnoff.

SIDELIGHTS: "For many years, I wrote about many subjects, expressing the diversification of my interests in the psychology of the individual and in the relationship between individuals and society," Irving Sarnoff told *CA*. "This writing helped me to discover and to clarify my thoughts and feelings about the topics I addressed. Meanwhile, it gave me the utterly playful delight of entering the bubble of my own mind and of remaining there day after day—year after year—without having to feel like an autistic madman for doing so. Indeed, even as a young child, I learned that writing is so revered in our culture that it is entirely possible to immerse oneself in it—that is, to withdraw from the world and into oneself—without running the risk of being considered deranged by other people. On the contrary, whenever people heard that I was writing—or going off to write—a hush of respect crept into their attitude toward me. So, far from being suspected as a rather benign lunatic—which, of course, all writers essentially are—I was regarded as someone who engaged in a supremely valued process: I was a wordgiver—evidently, in the archetypical consciousness of most people, a special person who is carrying out a sacred mission that they knew *somebody* ought to be doing, yet weren't moved to do themselves.

"Of course, I have thoroughly enjoyed the esteem attached to being an author. I probably would stop writing if I were convinced that *nobody* would ever read what I first communicated to myself in the privacy and silence of my scribbled ruminations. In fact, I am always secretly hoping, as I write, that some people—no, ultimately, a *lot* of people—will find that I have helped them to build a bridge between their potentials for awareness and their actual consciousness; that my words help them to cross over an invisible line between what they have already thought about some subject and what lies just below the threshold of their insight into its deeper meanings.

"I do have something to 'push'—something so good and true and right that I have no doubt about my efforts to get its facets and implications across to others. That 'something' is the psychology of love. For love is the one topic—of all I have ever approached—that inspires me to write, even when I feel the gravest lack of faith in myself; even when I feel totally fed up at the prospect of dancing in words for others to tell me that I'm O.K. or have some talent or have opened their eyes to something.

"I didn't 'discover' love as my topic until . . . my career as a psychologist was already long-established. Luckily, I finally realized that love was what I had been living for more than anything else—even more than the prestige I had been driving myself to attain as a writer and professor.

"In fact, it took me almost fifty years to feel, at last, the empty and illusory nature of the egoism I had been pursuing so avidly. It was only then that I could admit how completely my morale, happiness, well-being, and creativity depended not on any individual accomplishment but on the loving relationship my wife and I had developed in the course of our married life. And it was only then that I recognized how much I had taken the gratifications of our relationship for granted as my basic source of sustenance while immersing myself in the various professional and literary trips I had taken—presumably on 'my own.'

"With the dawning of this awareness, I decided to collaborate with my wife, Suzanne, in writing on the psychology of love; and our joint work is, in its very duality of creation, a medium that expresses the message of loving. Indeed, the challenge of submerging our separate egos for the greater good of our collaboration has been one of the most trying proofs of the genuiness of our marital relationship."

* * *

SATZ, Ronald Norman 1944-

PERSONAL: Surname rhymes with "cats"; born February 8,

1944, in Chicago, Ill.; son of David Harold (a master locksmith and salesman) and Gertrude (Smith) Satz; married Christa Grete Ilgaudas, July 4, 1969; children: Ani Berta, Jakob Samuel. *Education:* Illinois Institute of Technology, B.S., 1965; Illinois State University, M.A., 1967; University of Maryland, Ph.D., 1972. *Home address:* Route 6, Box 92, Martin, Tenn. 38237. *Office:* Office of Graduate Studies and Research, University of Tennessee, Martin, Tenn. 38238.

CAREER: University of Tennessee at Martin, assistant professor, 1971-75, associate professor, 1975-80, professor of history, 1980—, dean of graduate studies, 1976—, dean of research, 1977—. Visiting professor at University of Maryland, summer, 1973. Member of board of directors of University of Tennessee Research Corp., 1981. Member of editorial board of University of Tennessee Press, 1975-78; editorial referee and consultant to scholarly presses.

MEMBER: National Council of University Research Administrators, Society for American Indian Studies and Research, Society for Historians of the Early American Republic, Society of Research Administrators, Council of Graduate Schools in the United States, American Historical Association, Organization of American Historians, National Association of Interdisciplinary Ethnic Studies, American Association of University Professors (president of Martin chapter, 1974-76), Western History Association, Southern Historical Association, Conference of Southern Graduate Schools, Midwestern Association of Graduate Schools, Tennessee Historical Association, Tennessee Conference of Graduate Schools (secretary-treasurer, 1977-78; vice-president, 1980-81; president, 1981-82), Northwest Tennessee Humanities Council, Pi Gamma Mu, Delta Tau Kappa, Phi Alpha Theta, Phi Kappa Phi. *Awards, honors:* Ford Foundation fellow in ethnic studies, 1971; The University of Tennessee at Martin research grants, 1973, 1974; National Endowment for the Humanities younger humanist research fellow, 1974.

WRITINGS: American Indian Policy in the Jacksonian Era, University of Nebraska Press, 1975; *Tennessee's Indian Peoples: From White Contact to Removal, 1540 to 1840,* University of Tennessee Press, 1976; (contributor) Leonard Dinnestein and Kenneth T. Jackson, editors, *American Vistas, 1607-1877,* Oxford University Press, 1979; (contributor) Billy M. Jones, editor, *Heroes of Tennessee,* Memphis State University Press, 1979; (contributor) Robert M. Kvasnicka and Herman J. Viola, editors, *The Commissioners of Indian Affairs, 1824-1977,* University of Nebraska Press, 1979; (with Charles Dollar, Joan Gunderson, H. Viscount Nelson, Jr., and Gary Reichard) *America: Changing Times—A Brief History,* Wiley, 1980, 2nd edition, 1982; *Recruitment, Admission and Retention of Black Students in Graduate and Professional Education,* Tennessee Conference of Graduate Schools, 1982; (contributor) Wilcomb Washburn, editor, *Handbook of North American Indians,* Volume IV, Smithsonian Insitution Press, in press.

Contributor of articles and reviews to history journals. Member of editorial board of *Maryland Historian,* 1970-71, and *American Indian Quarterly,* 1977. Editorial referee and consultant to scholarly journals.

WORK IN PROGRESS: The Impact of Protestant Evangelism upon the Traditional Religious Beliefs of the Southern Indians; The Mississippi Choctaws after Removal; research on the Bureau of Indian Affairs, on ethnic minorities in America, and on congressional efforts to thwart native American self-government in the trans-Mississippi West.

SIDELIGHTS: Ronald Norman Satz told *CA:* "Although my primary research, teaching, and writing interests are in nineteenth-century America, I believe that a study of past events can provide helpful insights into some of today's problems. Hopefully, objective studies of the sources and results of ethnic conflicts in our nation's past will provide some clues as to how Americans can deal more effectively with such tensions in contemporary times. In any event, historians have an obligation to be objective reporters of the past, not propagandists. Generally, my research has focused on the wide gap between political rhetoric and reality in the area of government-minority relations in the nineteenth century. The present gap between such rhetoric and American realities is one of my deep and abiding concerns.

"I find that the social sciences and other disciplines offer many important insights and helpful conceptual tools for historians. During the past several years, I have taken a special interest in preparing students to teach about minority groups in American life."

AVOCATIONAL INTERESTS: Jazz (plays tenor saxophone).

BIOGRAPHICAL/CRITICAL SOURCES: American Indian Quarterly, autumn, 1974.

* * *

SAVITZ, Leonard D. 1926-

PERSONAL: Born June 7, 1926, in Philadelphia, Pa.; son of Harry (a clerk) and Minnie (Aaronson) Savitz; married Faye Weiss, June 25, 1961 (died April, 1978); children: Steven M., Jonathan L., Ruth L. *Education:* Temple University, B.S., 1949, M.S., 1950; University of Pennsylvania, Ph.D., 1960. *Politics:* Democrat. *Religion:* Jewish. *Home:* 615 Anthony Rd., Elkins Park, Pa. 19117. *Office:* Department of Sociology, Temple University, Philadelphia, Pa. 19122.

CAREER: Temple University, Philadelphia, Pa., instructor, 1955-60, assistant professor, 1960-68, professor of sociology, 1968—. *Military service:* U.S. Army, 1944-46. *Member:* American Sociological Association, American Society of Criminology, Society for the Study of Social Problems.

WRITINGS: (With N. Johnston and M. Wolfgang) *Sociology of Crime and Delinquency,* Wiley, 1964; (with Johnston and Wolfgang) *Sociology of Punishment and Correction,* Wiley, 1964; *Dilemmas in Criminology,* McGraw, 1967; *Delinquency and Migration,* R & E Research Associates, 1975; (with M. Lalli and L. Rosen) *City Life and Delinquency,* U.S. Government Printing Office, 1977; (with Johnston) *Crime in America,* Wiley, 1978; *Criminology,* Wiley, 1981; (with Johnston) *Legal Processes and Corrections,* Wiley, 1981.

WORK IN PROGRESS: The Fear of Rape; Obscene Phone Calls; The Rules for Enhancing Sexual Attractiveness.

* * *

SCANNELL, Vernon 1922-

PERSONAL: Born January 23, 1922, in Lincolnshire, England; married Josephine Higson, October, 1954; children: John, Tobias, Nancy, Jane. *Education:* Attended University of Leeds, 1946-47. *Politics:* "Romantic Radical." *Home:* Flat 2, 28 Spencer Pl., Leeds LS7 4BR, England.

CAREER: Author. Professional boxer for brief period; teacher of English, Hazelwood School, Limpsfield, Surrey, England, 1955-62. Broadcasts talks and poetry. *Military service:* British Army, 1941-46. *Member:* Royal Society of Literature (fellow). *Awards, honors:* Heinemann Award for Literature from the Royal Society of Literature, 1960, for *The Masks of Love;* Cholmondeley Poetry Prize, 1974.

WRITINGS—Novels: *The Fight,* Nevill, 1953; *The Wound and the Scar,* Nevill, 1954; *The Big Chance,* John Long, 1960; *The Shadowed Place,* John Long, 1961; *The Face of the Enemy,* Putnam, 1961; *The Dividing Night,* Putnam, 1962; *The Big Time,* Longmans, Green, 1965.

Poems: *Graves and Resurrections,* Fortune Press, 1948; *A Mortal Pitch,* Villiers Publications, 1957; *The Masks of Love,* Putnam, 1960; *A Sense of Danger,* Putnam, 1962; *Walking Wounded,* Eyre & Spottiswoode, 1965; *Selected Poems,* Allison, 1971; *The Winter Man,* Allison, 1973; *The Loving Game,* Robson Books, 1975; *Collected Poems,* Robson Books, 1980; *Winterlude,* Robson Books, 1982.

Other: *Edward Thomas* (criticism), Longmans, Green, for the British Council, 1963; *The Tiger and the Rose* (autobiography), Hamish Hamilton, 1971; *A Proper Gentleman* (autobiography), Robson Books, 1977. Editor with Ted Hughes and Patricia Beer, *New Poems 1962: The P.E.N. Anthology.* Also author of radio scripts, "A Man's Game," and "A Door with One Eye," and of radio opera, "The Cancelling Dark," with music by Christopher Whellen, performed December 5, 1965. Contributor to *Listener, Encounter, London Magazine, Spectator,* and *Times Literary Supplement.*

SIDELIGHTS: At one time a professional boxer, Vernon Scannell has been described by a critic for *New Statesman* as "egalitarian, empirical and often funny." It has been suggested that his earlier career may have influenced his writings. The recurring themes in Scannell's work are fear, death, soldiering and what a reviewer for the *Times Literary Supplement* describes as "the vulnerability of seemingly-strong characters."

Although he is more widely known in England for his autobiographies and novels, Scannell is also praised for his ability to write clean, unburdened poetry. For example, Simon Curtis writes in the *Times Literary Supplement* that Scannell's "*Collected Poems* demonstrate much that is right with the plain presentation of mood and reflection, linked to incident and episode; poems that limit themselves to saying something clear. He belongs to a fraternity of poets who have 'soldiered on' independently, without great praise or fuss."

BIOGRAPHICAL/CRITICAL SOURCES: *New Statesman,* October 21, 1977; *Times Literary Supplement,* August 1, 1980.

* * *

SCHAKOVSKOY, Zinaida 1908-
(Jacques Croise)

PERSONAL: Born August 30, 1908, in Moscow, Russia; daughter of Alexis and Ann (von Kninen) Schakovskoy, married Sviatislav de Malewsky-Malevitch (a painter), November 21, 1926. *Education:* Attended American College for Girls, Turkey, 1921-23, Monastere de Berlaymont, Brussels, Belgium, 1923-25, and College de France, Paris, 1925-26. *Politics:* "I do not belong to any party, but I am anti-Marxist." *Religion:* Russian Orthodox. *Home:* 16, rue Faraday, Paris 75017, France.

CAREER: Writer and poet. Contributor to Russian emigre journals, 1932—; special correspondent for Belgian newspapers in Poland, Lithuania, Estonia and Latvia, 1937-38; literary critic for Belgian newspapers and reviews, 1937-40; Agence Francaise d'Information, London, England, editor, 1942-45; correspondent with Allied forces in Italy, Greece, Germany, and at Nuremberg Trials, 1945-47; Radio Television Francaise, Paris, France, head of cultural broadcasts in French and Russian, beginning 1955; *Rousskaya Mysl* (Russian-language newspaper), Paris, editor-in-chief, 1968-78; president, VL. Dahl (literary organization), 1979-81. *Military service:* Army Red Cross, 1940; received Croix des Evades (Belgium) and Chevalier de la Legion d'Honneur (France).

MEMBER: Societaire des Geus de Lettres de France, Syndicate of Literary Critics, P.E.N. (France). *Awards, honors:* Prix de Paris, 1949, for *Europe et Valerius;* Prix Therouanne de l'Academie Francaise, 1964, for *La Vie quotidienne a Moscou au XVII siecle,* and for *La Vie quotidienne a Saint-Petersbourg a l'epoque romantique;* Officier de la legion d'honneur, 1981; Officer des Arts et Lettres.

WRITINGS—In English translation: *Ma Russie habille en U.S.S.R.: Retour au pays natal,* Grasset, 1958, translation by Peter Wiles published as *The Privilege Was Mine: A Russian Princess Returns to the Soviet Union,* Putnam, 1959; *The Fall of Eagles: Precursors of Peter the Great,* translation by J. Maxwell Browjohn, Harcourt, 1964.

In Russian: *Ouhod* (poems), Polyglotte (Brussels), 1934; *Doroga* (poems), Polyglotte, 1935; *Pered Snom* (poems), La Pense Russe, 1970; *Otrajenia I* (memoirs; title means "Reflections"), YMCA-Press, 1975; *Rasskazi, statji, stihi* (short stories, articles, and poetry), Editeurs Reunis, 1978; *V poiskah Nabokova* (memoirs, critical essays, and excerpts from correspondence; title means "In Search of Nabokov"), La Presse Libre, 1979. Editor, with R. Guerra and E. Ternovsky, of *Russki Almanach.*

In French: *Vie d'Alexandre Pouchkine,* Cite Chretienne (Brussels), 1937; *Hommage a Pouchkine* (anthology), Journal des Poetes (Brussels), 1937; *Insomnies* (poems), Journal des Poetes, 1939; *Une Enfance* (autobiography), La Renaissance du Livre, 1939; *La Vie quotidienne a Moscou au XVII siecle,* Hachette, 1963; *Tel est mon siecle* (memoirs), Les Presses de la Cite, Volume I: *Lumieres et Ombres,* 1964, Volume II: *Une Maniere de vivre,* 1965, Volume III: *La Folle Clio,* 1966, Volume IV: *La Drole de paix,* 1967; *La vie quotidienne a Saint-Petersbourg a l'epoque romantique,* Hachette, 1967.

Under pseudonym Jacques Croise; all novels: *Europe et Valerius,* Flammarion et Cie, 1949; *Sortie de secours,* Plon, 1953; *La Dialogue des aveugles,* Amiot-Dumont, 1955; *Jeu de massacres,* Grasset, 1956; (translator from Russian into French) Alexandre Grine, *Celle qui court sur les vagues,* Laffont, 1959.

Contributor of poetry, articles, and criticism to literary journals in England and France.

WORK IN PROGRESS: *Otrajenia II,* recollections of the ten years as editor of *Rousskaya Mysl; Otrajenia III: Ne-Vstrecha* (subtitle means "The Non-encounter"), recollections of meetings with new Russian emigre writers; annotations on personal archive material.

SIDELIGHTS: Born a princess in czarist Russia, Zinaida Schakovskoy fled the country during the Russian Revolution when she was ten years old. Although she did not return to her homeland until she accompanied her husband on a diplomatic assignment forty years later, Schakovskoy's works have focused on the culture, traditions, and history of Russia and on the Russian emigre experience in Western Europe.

It is Schakovskoy's account of her return to Moscow in 1958 that has received the most critical attention in the United States. Published during the post-Stalinist "thaw" in Soviet-American relations, *The Privilege Was Mine: A Russian Princess Returns to the Soviet Union* addressed the growing curiosity Americans had about Soviet citizens. The book, writes Evelyn Eaton in *Chicago Sunday Tribune,* is a "moving, authoritative account of life in Russia [and] does more to make us understand the Russian people and their rulers than a host of recent impressions and travelogs hastily concocted by foreign visitors." *New York Herald Tribune*'s William Attwood comments that "at this moment in history [*The Privilege Was Mine*] is a wonderfully easy yet important book for Americans to read."

Many critics feel that Schakovskoy's background made her particularly sensitive to the Soviet people. Harrison Salisbury states in *New York Times Book Review* that "because Princess Schakovskoy knew the Russian language perfectly, because she had lived with her family in Moscow, St. Petersburg and on the family estate near Tula until she was ten years old and because she was raised in the rich tradition of Russian culture, she brought to the Soviet Union an unusually perceptive eye. . . . At no moment does . . . Schakovskoy permit emotional attachment to the old way of life in Russia to blind her to the realities of present day Soviet society." H. C. Wolfe notes in *Saturday Review* that Schakovskoy, "at home in the language and steeped in the culture and history of Russia, is in a unique position to interpret her homeland."

While E. V. Valkenier in *Library Journal* finds that the best parts of *The Privilege Was Mine* are Schakovskoy's "encounters with ordinary people which show the high degree to which Russians have resisted brainwashing and retained independence of mind," some reviewers feel that Schakovskoy's presentation of Soviet life is too strongly influenced by her anti-communist politics. "One cannot blame Princess Schakovskoy for her strong ties with the past," contends E. S. Pisko in *Christian Science Monitor,* "but one may regret that she failed to write the better balanced comparison between the past and the present for which her upbringing, intelligence, and warm emotions uniquely qualify her." According to a reviewer for *Times Literary Supplement,* "It is unfortunate that a record of this kind should so frequently be spoiled by digressions and occasional inconsistencies. So long as the author deals with her own first-hand impressions, brings ordinary men and women to the foreground, lifts a corner of the drab curtain to reveal the even more shoddy interior, she keeps her readers spellbound. But when she allows her narrative to become impersonal, factual, and even didactic, we get the sense of an old, old story retold in no remarkable manner. Churches turned into anti-religious museums, villages still leading a primitive life, the inadequacy of transport and all the rest of it are familiar enough, and [Schakovskoy] has little to add."

Attwood, however, does not agree with the *Times Literary Supplement* critic's assessment. "This is not the angry, superficial, bitter book that one might expect from a Russian princess," he says. "The indictment of the [Communist] regime comes mostly from the people who are forced to live under it—in their own words. As a Russian . . . Schakovskoy loves and understands her people; as a perceptive writer she also makes them come alive."

AVOCATIONAL INTERESTS: Reading, history, travel (Europe, United States, Canada, Mexico, and Africa), art, people, and animals (especially dogs).

BIOGRAPHICAL/CRITICAL SOURCES: *Kirkus Reviews,* November 15, 1958; *Library Journal,* December 15, 1958; *Booklist,* December 15, 1958, February 1, 1959; *Times Literary Supplement,* January 16, 1959, April 16, 1964; *Spectator,* January 23, 1959; *Chicago Sunday Tribune,* February 1, 1959; *New York Herald Tribune,* February 1, 1959; *Time,* February 9, 1959; *Christian Science Monitor,* February 12, 1959; *Saturday Review,* February 28, 1959; *New York Times,* March 1, 1959; *New Yorker,* November 14, 1964; *Best Sellers,* December 1, 1964.

SCHMIDT, Stanley (Albert) 1944-

PERSONAL: Born March 7, 1944, in Cincinnati, Ohio; son of Otto E. W. (an electrical engineer) and Georgia (Metcalf) Schmidt; married Joyce Tokarz, June 9, 1979. *Education:* University of Cincinnati, B.S. (with high honors), 1966; Case Western Reserve University, M.A., 1968, Ph.D., 1969. *Agent:* Scott Meredith Literary Agency, Inc., 845 Third Ave., New York, N.Y. 10022. *Office:* Analog, 380 Lexington Ave., New York, N.Y. 10017.

CAREER: Heidelberg College, Tiffin, Ohio, assistant professor of physics, 1969-78, also taught courses in astronomy, science fiction, and biology; Davis Publications, Inc., New York, N.Y., editor of *Analog Science Fiction/Science Fact,* 1978—; freelance writer, musician, and photographer. *Member:* American Association of Physics Teachers, Science Fiction Writers of America, Appalachian Trail Conference, Cleveland Philharmonic Orchestra, Phi Beta Kappa, Sigma Xi.

WRITINGS: *Newton and the Quasi-Apple* (science fiction novel), Doubleday, 1975; (contributor) Jack Williamson, editor, *Teaching Science Fiction: Education for Tomorrow,* Mirage Press, 1975; *The Sins of the Fathers* (science fiction novel; first serialized in *Analog,* 1973-74). Berkley Publishing, 1976; (contributor) Thomas D. Clareson, editor, *Many Futures, Many Worlds,* Kent State University Press, 1976; *Lifeboat Earth* (science fiction novel), Berkley Publishing, 1981.

Anthologies: (Contributor) *Anthropology Through Science Fiction,* edited by Martin H. Greenberg and others, St. Martin's, 1974; (contributor) *Sociology Through Science Fiction,* edited by Greenberg and others, St. Martin's, 1974; (contributor) *American Government Through Science Fiction,* edited by Joseph Olander and others, Rand McNally, 1974; (editor and contributor) *Analog's Golden Anniversary Anthology,* Dial, 1980; (editor) *Analog Yearbook II,* Ace Books, 1981; (editor) *Analog: Readers' Choice,* Davis Publications, 1982. Contributor to science fiction, camping, and physics journals.

WORK IN PROGRESS: Two novels; short stories; articles.

SIDELIGHTS: Stanley Schmidt reads Spanish, German, Russian, Portuguese, French, Italian, Dutch, and Swahili. *Avocational interests:* Music (Schmidt plays several instruments and composes music), travel, camping, hiking, backpacking, photography, flying, cooking, and linguistics.

BIOGRAPHICAL/CRITICAL SOURCES: *Toledo Blade,* January 31, 1975; *Analog Science Fiction/Science Fact,* December, 1977.

* * *

SCHRAG, Peter 1931-

PERSONAL: Born July 24, 1931, in Karlsruhe, Germany; son of Otto (a businessman) and Judith (Haas) Schrag; married Jane Mowrer, June 9, 1953 (divorced, 1969); married Diane Divoky (a writer), May 24, 1969; children: (first marriage) Mitzi, Erin Andrew; (second marriage) David, Benaiah. *Education:* Amherst College, B.A., 1953; graduate study at Amherst College and University of Massachusetts, 1957-59. *Home:* 1500 Seventh St., Sacramento, Calif. 95814. *Office: Sacramento Bee,* 21 and Q Sts., Sacramento, Calif. 95813. *Agent:* Curtis Brown, Ltd., 575 Madison Ave., New York, N.Y. 10022.

CAREER: *El Paso Herald Post,* El Paso, Tex., reporter, 1953-55; Amherst College, Amherst, Mass., assistant secretary, 1955-

66, instructor in American studies, 1960-64; *Saturday Review,* New York City, associate education editor, 1966-68, executive editor, 1968-69, contributing editor, 1970-73; *Change Magazine,* New York City, editor, 1969-70; full-time writer, 1970-78; *Sacramento Bee,* Sacramento, Calif., editorial page editor, 1978—. Lecturer at University of Massachusetts, 1970-72, and University of California, Berkeley, 1974-78. Member, Committee on the Study of History. Consultant to Science Research Associates, 1960-61, U.S. Office of Education, and U.S. Information Service.

AWARDS, HONORS: Guggenheim fellow, 1971-72; professional journalism fellow, Stanford University, 1973-74.

WRITINGS: (Editor) *The Ratification of the Constitution and the Bill of Rights,* Heath, 1964; *Voices in the Classroom: Public Schools and Public Attitudes,* Beacon, 1965; (editor) *The European Mind and the Discovery of a New World,* Heath, 1965; *Village School Downtown,* Beacon, 1967; *Out of Place in America,* Random House, 1970; *Decline of the WASP,* Simon & Schuster, 1972; *The End of the American Future,* Simon & Schuster, 1973; *Test of Loyalty,* Simon & Schuster, 1974; (with wife, Diane Divoky) *Myth of the Hyperactive Child,* Pantheon, 1975; *Mind Control,* Pantheon, 1978.

Contributor to periodicals, including *Saturday Review, New Republic, Commonweal, Progressive, College Board Review, Playboy, New West, New York Review, Atlantic, New York Times Education Supplement, Nation,* and *Harper's.*

AVOCATIONAL INTERESTS: Travel and sailing.

*   *   *

SCHUL, Bill D(ean) 1928-

PERSONAL: Born March 16, 1928, in Winfield, Kan.; son of Fred M. (a teacher and farmer) and Mildred (Miles) Schul; married Jeanne Duboise, August 3, 1952; children: Robert Dean, Deva Elizabeth (Mrs. Mark Randel). *Education:* Southwestern College, B.A., 1952; University of Denver, M.A., 1954; Clayton University, Ph.D., 1977. *Politics:* "Republican—but actually bipartisan." *Religion:* "Eclectic." *Address:* R.R. 3, Winfield, Kan. 67156.

CAREER: Augusta Daily Gazette, Augusta, Kan., reporter and editor, 1954-57; *St. Petersburg Independent,* St. Petersburg, Fla., reporter, 1957-58; *Wichita Eagle-Beacon,* Wichita, Kan., reporter and columnist, 1958-61; Attorney General's Office, Topeka, Kan., director of juvenile affairs, 1961-65; Seventh Step Foundation, Topeka, state director, 1965-66; Menninger Foundation, Topeka, editorial consultant, 1966-71; full-time writer, 1971—. President, Kansas Council for Children and Youth, 1965; executive director, Shawnee City Mental Health Corp., Topeka, 1966-67; founder, Kansas Youth Council, 1969; founder and first president, Association for Strengthening the Higher Realities and Aspirations of Man, 1970. Member of board of directors of Olive Garvey Center for the Improvement of Human Functioning, and Monroe Institute of Applied Sciences. *Military service:* U.S. Navy, 1945-46. *Member:* American Academy of Parapsychology and Medicine. *Awards, honors:* Editorial award, Freedoms Foundation, 1966; John H. McGinnis Memorial Award, Southern Methodist University, 1972, for the essay, "Exploration of Inner Space."

WRITINGS—Published by Fawcett, except as indicated: *Community Planning for Youth,* State of Kansas, 1964; *Let Me Do This Thing* (a book-length poem), Rubert, 1969; (with Ed Pettit) *The Secret Powers of Pyramids,* 1975; *How To Be An Effective Group Leader,* Nelson-Hall, 1975; (with Pettit) *The Psychic Power of Pyramids,* 1976; *Psychic Frontiers of Medicine,* 1977; *The Psychic Power of Animals,* 1977; (with Pettit) *Pyramids and the Second Reality,* 1979. Also author of weekly column, "Accent on Youth," published in 116 Kansas newspapers, 1961-65. Contributor of over two hundred articles to periodicals, including *Intellectual Digest, Town and Country, 'Teen, Catholic Digest, Science of Mind, Psychic,* and *Probe the Unknown.*

WORK IN PROGRESS: Research on the effects of sound on brain waves.

SIDELIGHTS: Bill Schul wrote *CA:* "I find myself involved from time to time in organic gardening, sports, and oil painting, but my current priorities have to do with methods or techniques—philosophies, if you will—of expanding human consciousness and the resulting social applications; this I am trying to do through my writing, lecturing, and my teaching of Raja Yoga and meditation, the latter of which I have done for many years. I have been deeply affected by the philosophy and life of Gandhi. Disenchanted by traditional methods of social control, I believe that change must come from the individual understanding of the inner life or inner awareness."

*   *   *

SCHULBERG, Herbert C(harles) 1934-

PERSONAL: Born February 10, 1934, in New York, N.Y.; married Phyllis Gitelman (a teacher), June 23, 1957; children: Mark Ira, Michelle Toby. *Education:* Yeshiva College (now University), B.A., 1955; Columbia University, M.A., 1956, Ph.D., 1960; Harvard University, M.S.Hyg., 1963. *Home:* 144 Oak Park Pl., Pittsburgh, Pa. 15243. *Office:* Western Psychiatric Institute and Clinic, 3811 O'Hara St., Pittsburgh, Pa. 15261.

CAREER: Certified psychologist in Connecticut, 1961, and Massachusetts, 1964, licensed in Massachusetts, 1974. Veterans Administration Hospital, Lyons, N.J., psychology trainee, 1956-57; Veterans Administration Hospital, Brooklyn, N.Y., psychology trainee, 1957-58; Veterans Administration Mental Hygiene Clinic, Brooklyn, psychology trainee, 1958-60; Fairfield State Hospital, Newtown, Conn., clinical psychologist, 1960-62; Massachusetts Mental Health Planning Project, Boston, director of research, 1963-65; South Shore Mental Health Center, Quincy, Mass., clinical psychologist, 1964; Professional Counseling Center, Quincy, clinical psychologist, 1964-66; Attleboro Area Mental Health Center, Attleboro, Mass., clinical psychologist, 1966-67; private practice of clinical psychology in Norwood, Mass., 1967-76; University of Pittsburgh, School of Medicine, Pittsburgh, Pa., professor of psychology, 1976—. Harvard University, research associate, 1964-66, associate, 1966-69, assistant clinical professor, 1969-73, associate clinical professor, 1973-76, head of program research unit at community psychiatry laboratory, 1965-69. Lecturer at University of Bridgeport, 1960-61, Boston University, 1965-66, and University of Massachusetts, 1973-74. Associate executive vice-president of United Community Planning Corp., 1969—.

MEMBER: American Psychological Association (fellow), American College of Mental Health Administration, Eastern Psychological Association, Pennsylvania Mental Health Administration. *Awards, honors:* U.S. Public Health Service grant, 1962-63.

WRITINGS: (With Alexander Tolor) *An Evaluation of the Bender-Gestalt Test,* C. C Thomas, 1963; (with Frank Baker) *The Baker-Schulberg CMHI Scale,* Behavioral Publications, 1967; (editor with Baker and Alan Sheldon) *Program Evaluation in the Health Fields,* Behavioral Publications, 1970; (editor with Baker and Sheldon Roen and contributor) *Developments in Human Services,* Behavioral Publications, Volume I, 1973, Volume II, 1975; (with Baker) *The Mental Hospital and Human Services,* Behavioral Publications, 1975; (editor with Jeanette Jerrell) *The Evaluator and Management,* Sage Publications, 1979; (with Marie Killilea) *Principles and Practices of Community Mental Health,* Jossey-Bass, 1982.

Contributor: Roy Penchansky, editor, *Health Services Administration: Policy Cases and the Case Method,* Harvard University Press, 1968; Henry Grunebaum, editor, *The Practice of Community Mental Health,* Little, Brown, 1970; Sheldon, Baker, and Curtis McLaughlin, editors, *Systems and Medical Care,* M.I.T. Press, 1970; Baker, editor, *Organizational Systems,* Irwin, 1973; Harold Demone and Dwight Harshbarger, editors, *A Handbook of Human Service Organizations,* Behavioral Publications, 1974; Jack Zusman and Elmer Bertsch, editors, *The Future Role of the State Hospital,* Heath, 1975; Clifford Attkisson, William Hargreaves, and Mardi Horowitz, editors, *Evaluation of Human Service Programs,* Academic Press, 1978. Contributor to *Encyclopedia of Social Work.* Also contributor of about sixty articles and reviews to psychology and medical journals.

* * *

SCHULL, (John) Joseph 1916-1980

PERSONAL: Born February 6, 1916, in Watertown, S.D.; died of leukemia, May 19, 1980; son of Charles Henry (a lawyer) and Aveline Alice (Travers) Schull; married Helene Gougeon (a journalist), January 8, 1955; children: Christiane, Joseph, Michael. *Education:* Attended Queen's University and University of Saskatchewan. *Religion:* Roman Catholic. *Home:* 180 Grande Cote Rd., Rosemere, Quebec, Canada.

CAREER: Employed in banking and advertising. *Military service:* Royal Canadian Naval Volunteer Reserve, 1941-45; became lieutenant commander. *Awards, honors:* University of British Columbia Gold Medal, 1966, for *Laurier: The First Canadian;* officer, Order of Canada, 1980.

WRITINGS: The Legend of Ghost Lagoon (narrative poem), Macmillan (Toronto), 1937; *I, Jones, Soldier* (poetry), Macmillan (Toronto), 1944; *The Far Distant Ships,* E. Cloutier, 1952, abridged edition published as *Ships of the Great Days: Canada's Navy in World War II,* St. Martin's, 1962; *The Salt Water Men: Canada's Deep Sea Sailors,* St. Martin's, 1957; *100 Years of Banking in Canada: A History of the Toronto-Dominion Bank,* Copp, 1958.

Battle for the Rock: The Story of Wolfe and Montcalm, St. Martin's, 1960; *Laurier: The First Canadian,* Macmillan (Toronto), 1965, St. Martin's, 1966; *The Nation Makers,* Macmillan (Toronto), 1967; *The Jinker* (novel), Macmillan (Toronto), 1968, Dodd, 1969; *Rebellion: The Rising in French Canada, 1837,* Macmillan (Toronto), 1971; *The Century of the Sun: The First Hundred Years of Sun Life Assurance Company of Canada,* Macmillan (Toronto), 1971; *Veneration for Valour: An Assessment of the Veterans Charter—Its Impact on Canadian Veterans and on Canada as a Whole,* Information Canada, 1973; *The Vice President* (play), Simon & Pierre, 1973; *Edward Blake: The Man of the Other Way,* Macmillan (Toronto), 1975; *Ontario since 1867,* McClelland & Stewart, 1978; *The Great Scot: A Biography of Donald Gordon,* McGill-Queen's University Press, 1979. Also author of over 200 radio plays and 30 television plays.

WORK IN PROGRESS: A history of the Bank of Nova Scotia.†

SCHUSKY, Ernest L(ester) 1931-

PERSONAL: Born October 13, 1931, in Portsmouth, Ohio; son of Ernest L. (an editor) and Leona (a nurse; maiden name, Davis) Schusky; married June, 1953; wife's name, Jane (divorced, 1965); married Mary Sue Dillard (a professor), June 14, 1968; children: Read Eric, Mark Elliott. *Education:* Miami University, Oxford, Ohio, A.B., 1952; University of Chicago, M.A., 1957, Ph.D., 1960; postdoctoral study at London School of Economics and Political Science, 1967-68. *Politics:* Independent. *Religion:* None. *Home:* 412 Willowbrook, Collinsville, Ill. 62234. *Office:* Department of Anthropology, Southern Illinois University, Edwardsville, Ill. 62901.

CAREER: South Dakota State College (now University), Brookings, instructor in sociology, 1958-60; Southern Illinois University at Edwardsville, assistant professor, 1960-64, associate professor, 1964-69, professor of anthropology, 1969—, director of graduate program in behavioral science, 1977. *Military service:* U.S. Army, 1953-54. *Member:* American Anthropological Association (fellow), Society for Applied Anthropology, American Ethnological Society, Royal Anthropological Society (London), Central States Anthropological Society (president, 1974). *Awards, honors:* Fulbright fellowship, 1964, for study in India.

WRITINGS: A Manual for Kinship Analysis, Holt, 1965, 2nd edition, 1972; *The Right to be Indian: Civil Rights Problems of American Indians,* Institute for Indian Studies, 1964, 2nd edition, Indian Historian Press, 1970; (with T. Patrick Culbert) *Introducing Culture,* Prentice-Hall, 1967, 3rd edition, 1978; (contributor) Ethel Nurge, editor, *The Modern Sioux: Social Systems and Reservation Culture,* University of Nebraska Press, 1970; *Variation in Kinship,* Holt, 1974; *Study in Cultural Anthropology,* Holt, 1975; *The Forgotten Sioux: An Ethnohistory of the Lower Brule Sioux Reservation,* Nelson-Hall, 1975; (editor) *Political Organization of Native North Americans,* University Press of America, 1980; *Introduction to Social Science,* Prentice-Hall, 1981.

SIDELIGHTS: Ernest L. Schusky told *CA:* "I have always considered my writing to reflect interest in both the theoretical and applied aspects of social science. My early work concentrated on American Indians and while this interest continues, I have expanded my concern to the Third World." *A Manual for Kinship Analysis* has been translated into Portuguese; *Introducing Culture* has been translated into Korean.

* * *

SCHWARTZ, Arthur Nathaniel 1922-

PERSONAL: Born June 14, 1922, in Chicago, Ill.; son of Isadore (a clergyman) and Faye (Garfinkle) Schwartz; married Cherie Louise Snyder, 1981; children: (prior marriages) Andrew Christopher, Andrea Thompson, David Paul, Brian Jeremy, Cynthia Osborne, Jonathan Matthew. *Education:* Concordia Seminary, St. Louis, Mo., B.A., 1944; graduate study at University of Houston, 1950-51, and Eastern Washington State College (now University), 1957; Washington University, Ph.D., 1962. *Home:* 112 East Alhambra Rd., Alhambra, Calif. 91801. *Office:* California Lutheran Homes, 2312 South Fremont Ave., Alhambra, Calif. 91803.

CAREER: Veterans Administration Hospital, American Lake, Tacoma, Wash., staff clinical psychologist, 1962-65; Veterans Administration Center, Los Angeles, Calif., chief of clinical psychology section, 1965-72, clinical researcher on aging, 1967-

72; University of Southern California, Los Angeles, lecturer on aging, 1970—, adjunct professor of psychology, 1973-79, assistant clinical professor of preventive and family medicine at School of Medicine, 1982—, director of long term care education, 1972—, director of adult counseling training program, 1973-79; California Lutheran Homes, Alhambra, Calif., director of training and research, 1981—. Elementary school teacher in Seymour, Ind., 1942-43. Instructor at University of Puget Sound, 1962-64, Pacific Lutheran University, 1963-65, and University of California, Los Angeles, 1967-70; associate professor at California State University, Los Angeles, 1969-73; member of faculty at California School of Professional Psychology, 1970-72; professor of clinical geropsychology and director of gerontology program, Caribbean Center for Advanced Studies, Puerto Rico, 1979-80. Private practice in clinical psychology in Tacoma, Wash. Therapist and director of gerontological training programs at Peterson-Guedel Family Center, 1969—. Chairman of Los Angeles County Affiliated Committee on Aging, 1969-71; member of board of directors of Los Angeles County Psychology Center, 1971—; member of California State White House Conference on Aging, 1971; member of board of examiners of nursing home administrators of California, 1972-77. Consultant to Ethel Percy Andrus Gerontology Center, University of Southern California, 1968—.

MEMBER: American Psychological Association, Gerontological Society (fellow). *Awards, honors:* National Institute of Mental Health fellowship, 1972—; Outstanding Service Award, Veterans Administration, 1971; Better Life Award for Education, California Association of Mental Health Facilities, 1979; Meritorious Service Award, California Association of Homes for the Aging, 1980; Jessie L. Terry Community Service Award.

WRITINGS: (Editor with I. N. Mensh) *Professional Obligations and Approaches to the Aged*, C. C Thomas, 1964, revised edition, 1973; (contributor) P. Woodruff and J. Birren, editors, *Aging: Scientific Perspectives and Social Issues*, Van Nostrand, 1975; *Survival Handbook for Children with Aging Parents*, Follett, 1977; (with J. Peterson) *Introduction to Gerontology*, Holt, 1979; (contributor) P. Ragan, editor, *Aging Parents*, University of Southern California Press, 1979; (contributor) S. S. Sargent, editor, *Nontraditional Therapy and Counseling with the Aged*, Springer Publishing, 1980.

WORK IN PROGRESS: A second edition of *Introduction to Gerontology*, for Holt.

SIDELIGHTS: Arthur Nathaniel Schwartz told *CA:* "Generally speaking, I write about aging (gerontology) because I am uncomfortable—sometimes incensed—about the appalling attitudes of American society toward the old—negative attitudes that are in many instances subtly reinforced by professional helpers and researchers in the field. Writing about aging is, for me, the kind of arduous exercise, like early morning running or wood-chopping, found to relieve tension. It helps maintain intellectual 'tone' and often makes me sleep better."

* * *

SEGAL, Marilyn 1927-

PERSONAL: Born August 9, 1927, in Utica, N.Y.; daughter of Abraham L. (a financier) and Alice (Lyons) Mailman; children: Betty, Wendy, Richard, Patricia, Debra. *Education:* Wellesley College, B.A., 1948; McGill University, B.S., 1949; Nova University, Ph.D., 1969. *Politics:* Democrat. *Religion:* Jewish. *Home:* 919 S.S. Lake Dr., Hollywood, Fla. 33020. *Office:* Family Center, Nova University, 3301 College Ave., Fort Lauderdale, Fla. 33314.

CAREER: Social worker in Boston, Mass., 1959, 1969; The Pre-School, Hollywood, Fla., administrator, 1965-68; Nova University, Fort Lauderdale, Fla., director of University School, 1970-71, assistant professor of early childhood, 1971-79, professor of developmental psychology, 1979—, director of Institute of Early Childhood and Open Education, 1971-72, chief investigator, School for Parents program, 1971-72, director of Family Center, 1979—. Member of board of trustees, University of Miami, 1969-82; member of board of governors, University School, 1969-82.

WRITINGS: Run Away Little Girl, Random House, 1965; (contributor) *You Are Your Baby's First Teachers*, Nova University Press, 1973; *"Play and Learn" for Parents and Infants*, Nova University Press, 1974; *From Birth to One Year: Play and Learn*, Nova University Press, 1974, published as *From Birth to One Year*, B. L. Winch, 1978; (with Don Adcock) *From One to Two Years: Play and Learn*, Nova University Press, 1976, published as *From One to Two Years*, B. L. Winch, 1978; (with Adcock) *From Two to Three Years: Social Competence* (also see below), B. L. Winch, 1979; (with Adcock) *From Two to Three Years: Play and Learning* (also see below), B. L. Winch, 1979; (with Adcock) *Feelings: Social and Emotional Development in the Preschool Years*, Humanics, 1980; (with Adcock) *Play and Learn Volume I and II and III* (includes revised editions of *From Two to Three Years: Social Competence* and *From Two to Three Years: Play and Learning*), Oak Tree Publications, 1981; (with Adcock) *Just Pretending*, Prentice-Hall, 1981. Author of scripts for "To Reach a Child," television series for the Office of Child Development, 1973. Contributor to *Reader's Digest, Research in Education, Journal of Reading Behavior,* and *Inquiry*.

* * *

SEIDEL, Frederick (Lewis) 1936-

PERSONAL: Born February 19, 1936, in St. Louis, Mo.; son of Jerome Jay (a business executive) and Thelma (Cartun) Seidel; married Phyllis Munro Ferguson, June 7, 1960 (divorced, 1969); children: Felicity, Samuel. *Education:* Harvard University, A.B., 1957. *Home:* 251 West 92nd St., New York, N.Y. 10028.

CAREER: Poet. Occasional lecturer, Rutgers University, 1964—. *Awards, honors:* Lamont Poetry Prize, Academy of American Poets, 1980, for *Sunrise;* book award for poetry, National Book Critics Circle, 1981, for *Sunrise;* poetry prize, *American Poetry Review,* for *Sunrise.*

WRITINGS—Poems: *Final Solutions*, Random House, 1963; *Sunrise*, Viking, 1979. *Paris Review*, Paris editor, 1961, advisory editor, 1962.

SIDELIGHTS: Rarely has a poet's first book created as much controversy as Frederick Seidel's *Final Solutions*. As William Jay Smith notes in *Harper's*, "Mr. Seidel's first collection has already caused quite a stir, largely because it was banned even before publication, a distinction that few poets achieve." The book was awarded a literary prize, but the prize was withdrawn when the poems were judged to be libelous. Seidel, according to Smith, "attempts the grotesque on a grand scale . . . and at times he succeeds. . . . [But] the failure of much of Mr. Seidel's book for me lies . . . in the lack of . . . adequate images, in a too heavy reliance on Robert Lowell's meters, and a theatricality that . . . does not ultimately ring true."

Several reviewers have commented on the similarity of Seidel's poetry to Robert Lowell's, especially in regards to style and meter. "In Frederick Seidel's case," James Dickey writes in the *New York Times Book Review*, "his relationship to the poetry of Robert Lowell amounts not so much to influence as to slavery. The diction is the same as Lowell's, as are the historical references, and the inflated, hortatory style." In a review of *Final Solutions*, Dickey concludes: "Imitation and shock tactics are no substitute for personal creativity. . . . Mr. Seidel's talents are by no means imposing." In a review of the same collection for *Book World*, Charles Berger finds that "Seidel seems to have been testing the premises and the ordinary language of poetry. . . . The result is an extremely savvy book of poems, reminiscent of Lowell as social prophet, but without the latter's deep moral affiliations." And Denis Donoghue, reviewing *Sunrise* for the *New York Review of Books*, believes Seidel is "loyal to his first book, as well he may be. Even then he had a gift of style, though in some poems it seemed mostly a gift of Robert Lowell's style. . . . A remarkably gifted and serious poet, [Seidel] gives me the impression, in some poems, of having lost or given up his confidence in the official forms seriousness has been supposed to take. . . . Despite that, *Sunrise* is an even stronger book than *Final Solutions*. Seidel's voice is now securely his own. . . . 'The Soul Mate' is the most beautiful poem in the book, a love poem as touching as anything I have read in years."

Despite the influence of Lowell, Seidel speaks with a unique voice. His poetry is intense and pessimistic, born of a "sensibility made raw by experience, uneasy by history," William Logan writes in *Library Journal*. Reviewing *Sunrise*, Logan comments, "Beyond the small tragedies of personal life he finds the mocking disasters of the great, from Vietnam to our assassinated presidents, and with an ear for the flux of literature and politics he exploits their varied mythologies." In a review of *Final Solutions* for the *New Yorker*, Louise Bogan states: "Seidel is angry, and his anger, ultimately, is directed less against evils apparent in this or that person or society than against the basic stupidities and depravities of mankind itself. . . . The terrifying aspects of the experiences he describes are outlined with clinical precision. . . . Whether or not Seidel's talent will come into the full power it now suggests it is impossible to predict. But how extraordinary if it should." Stephen Stepanchev, in a *New York Herald Tribune Books* article on *Final Solutions*, believes that in Seidel's poetry "the world seems a place of predicaments of cruelty and madness. . . . But the structure of the poems is relatively weak and tends to disintegrate in the 'meaninglessness' that is at the center of the poet's vision." And Jerome Mazzaro says of Seidel in a review of *Sunrise* for the *Hudson Review:* "Writers know the power of words, and . . . Seidel is not beyond painting a desert to get his effects. Readers have only to turn to '1968,' 'Men and Women,' 'Wanting to Live in Harlem,' and the title poem to recognize the importance of Seidel's concerns and talent and be reassured that, although not now venturous enough, Seidel has the power to be an important visionary."

BIOGRAPHICAL/CRITICAL SOURCES: New York Herald Tribune Books, August 11, 1963; *New York Times Book Review*, September 1, 1963, September 21, 1980; *Harper's*, September, 1963; *New Yorker*, October 12, 1963; *Library Journal*, March 1, 1980; *Book World*, July 6, 1980; *New York Review of Books*, August 14, 1980; *Hudson Review*, autumn, 1980; *Contemporary Literary Criticism*, Volume XVIII, Gale, 1981.

* * *

SENDER, Ramon (Jose) 1902-1982

PERSONAL: Born February 3, 1902, in Alcolea de Cinca, Spain; came to United States in 1942, naturalized in 1946; died of emphysema, January 15, 1982, in San Diego Calif.; son of Jose (a farmer) and Andrea (Garces) Sender; married Amparo Barayon, January 7, 1934 (died October 11, 1936); married Florence Hall, August 12, 1943 (divorced September 3, 1963); children: (first marriage) Ramon, Andrea. *Education:* Instituto de Segunda Ensenanza de Teruel, Bachillerato, 1917; University of Madrid, Licenciado en filosofia y letras, 1924. *Residence:* San Diego, Calif. *Agent:* American Literary Agency, 11 Riverside Dr., New York, N.Y. 10023.

CAREER: El Sol, Madrid, Spain, editor and literary critic, 1924-30; free-lance writer in Madrid, 1930-36, and in Mexico, 1939-41; Amherst College, Amherst, Mass., professor of Spanish literature, 1943; Metro-Goldwyn-Mayer, Inc., New York, N.Y., translator and adapter, 1943-45; University of Denver, Denver, Colo., professor of Spanish literature, 1946; University of New Mexico, Albuquerque, professor of Spanish literature, 1947-63; University of Southern California, Los Angeles, professor of Spanish literature, until 1973. Visiting professor, Ohio State University, 1950, University of California, Los Angeles, 1962, and University of Southern California, 1965. *Military service:* Served as reserve officer on Spanish infantry mission to Morocco, 1923-24; received Medal of Morocco and Military Cross of Merit. Spanish Republican Army, 1936-39; became major on general staff.

MEMBER: Hispanic Society of America, Spanish Confederated Societies (New York; honorary member), Ateneo (Spain; member of governing board and secretary of Ibero-American section), National Council on Culture (Spain), Alliance of Intellectuals for the Defense of Democracy (Spain), Phi Sigma Iota, Alpha Mu Gamma. *Awards, honors:* National Prize for Literature (Spain), 1935, for *Mister Witt en el canton;* Guggenheim fellow, 1942-43; Planeta Prize (Spain), 1969, for *En la vida de Ignacio Morel;* D.Litt., University of New Mexico and University of Southern California; nominated for Nobel Prize for Literature, 1979.

WRITINGS: El Problema religioso en Mejico (nonfiction), preface by Ramon del Valle-Inclan, Imprenta Argis (Madrid), 1928; *Iman* (novel), Editorial Cenit (Madrid), 1930, reprinted, Ediciones Destino (Barcelona), 1976, translation by James Cleugh published as *Earmarked for Hell*, Wishart, 1934, published as *Pro Patria*, Houghton, 1935; *Teresa de Jesus*, Editorial Zeus (Madrid), 1931; *El Verbo se hizo sexo* (nonfiction), Sociedad Anonima Editorial (Madrid), 1931; *Siete domingos rojos* (novel), Coleccion Balague (Barcelona), 1932, revised edition, Editorial Proyeccion (Barcelona), 1973, translation by Sir Peter Chalmers Mitchell published as *Seven Red Sundays*, Liveright, 1936, reprinted, Collier, 1961; *La Noche de las cien cabezas* (novel), Imprenta de J. Pueyo (Madrid), 1934; *Viaje a la aldea del crimen* (nonfiction), Imprenta de J. Pueyo, 1934; *Mister Witt en el canton* (novel), Espasa-Calpe (Madrid), 1936, reprinted, Alianza Editorial (Madrid), 1976, translation by Mitchell published as *Mr. Witt among the Rebels*, Faber, 1937, Houghton, 1938; *Counter-attack in Spain* (nonfiction), translated from the original Spanish manuscript by Mitchell, Houghton, 1937 (published in England as *The War in Spain: A Personal Narrative*, Faber, 1937); *Proverbio de la muerte* (novel), Ediciones Quetzal (Mexico), 1939, published as *La Esfera*, Aguilar (Madrid), 1969, translation by F. Giovanelli published as *The Sphere*, Hellman, Williams (New York), 1949; *El Lugar del hombre* (novel), Ediciones Quetzal, 1939, reprinted, Ediciones Destino, 1960, translation by Oliver La Farge published as *A Man's Place*, Duell, 1940, revised Spanish edition published as *El Lugar de un hombre*, Ediciones CNT (Mexico), 1958, reprinted, Ediciones Destino, 1976.

Hernan Cortes (nonfiction), Ediciones Quetzal, 1940; *Mexicayotl* (nonfiction), Ediciones Quetzal, 1940; *O. P.: Orden publico* (novel), Publicaciones Panamericanas (Mexico), 1941; *Epitalamio del prieto Trinidad* (novel), Ediciones Quetzal, 1942, reprinted, Ediciones Destino, 1973, translation by Eleanor Clark published as *Dark Wedding*, Doubleday, 1943; *Cronica del alba*, Editorial Nuevo Mundo (Mexico), 1942, translation by Willard R. Trask published as *Chronicle of Dawn* (also see below), Doubleday, 1944, annotated Spanish edition, edited and introduced by Florence Hall, Crofts, 1946; *El Rey y la reina* (novel), Editorial Jackson, 1949, reprinted, Ediciones Destino, 1972, translation by Mary Low published as *The King and the Queen*, Vanguard, 1948.

El Verdugo afable (novel), Nascimento (Santiago, Chile), 1952, translation by Hall published as *The Affable Hangman*, J. Cape, 1954, Las Americas Publishing Co., 1963; *Mosen Millan* (novel), [Mexico], 1953, Heath, 1964, published as *Requiem por un campesino espanol/Requiem for a Spanish Peasant* (parallel English and Spanish texts), translated by Elinor Randall, Las Americas Publishing Co., 1960, Spanish text reprinted, Ediciones Destino, 1976; *Hipogrifo violento* (novel), [Mexico], 1954, translation by F. W. Sender published as *Violent Griffin* in *Before Noon: A Novel in Three Parts* (also see below), University of New Mexico Press, 1957; *Ariadna* (novel), [Mexico], 1955, published as *Los Cinco Libros de Ariadna*, Ediciones Iberica (New York), 1957, reprinted, Ediciones Destino, 1977; *Unamuno, Valle-Inclan, Baroja y Santayana* (critical essays), Ediciones de Andrea (Mexico), 1955; *Before Noon: A Novel in Three Parts* (contains *Chronicle of Dawn*, *Violent Griffin*, and *The Villa Julieta* [translation by F. W. Sender from original Spanish manuscript *La Quinta Julieta*]), University of New Mexico Press, 1957; *El Diantre: Tragicomedia para el cine segun un cuento de Andreiev*, Ediciones de Andrea, 1958; *Los Laureles de Anselmo* (novel), Ediciones Atenea (Mexico), 1958; *Emen hetan* (novel), Libro Mex (Mexico), 1958.

El Mancebo y los heroes (novel), Ediciones Atenea, 1960; *Las imagenes migratorias* (poems), Ediciones Atenea, 1960; *La Llave* (novel; also see below), Editorial Alfa (Montevideo, Uruguay), 1960; (with Ramon del Valle-Inclan) *Memorias del marques de Bradomin*, Las Americas Publishing Co., 1961; *Examen de ingenios: Los Noventayochos* (critical essays), Las Americas Publishing Co., 1961; *Novelas ejemplares de Cibola*, Las Americas Publishing Co., 1961, translation by Hall and others published as *Tales of Cibola*, 1964; *La Tesis de Nancy* (novel), Ediciones Atenea, 1962; *La Luna de los perros*, Las Americas Publishing Co., 1962; *Los Tontos de la concepcion* (nonfiction), Editorial Coronado (Sandoval, New Mexico), 1963; *Carolus Rex* (historical novel), Editores Mexicanos Unidos (Mexico), 1963; *Jubileo en el Zocalo: Retablo commemorativo*, edited by Hall, Appleton, 1964, *La Aventura equinoccial de Lope de Aguirre, antiepopeya* (novel), Las Americas Publishing Co., 1964.

Cabrerizas altas, Editores Mexicanos Unidos, 1965; *El Bandido adolescente*, Ediciones Destino (Barcelona), 1965; *Valle-Inclan y la dificultad de la tragedia* (nonfiction), Editorial Gredos (Madrid), 1965; *El Sosia y los delegados* (nonfiction), B. Costa-Amic (Mexico), 1965; *Tres novelas teresianas* (fiction), Ediciones Destino, 1967; *Las Gallinas de Cervantes y otras narraciones parabolicas* (nonfiction), Editores Mexicanos Unidos, 1967; *Ensayos sobre el infringimiento cristiano*, Editores Mexicanos Unidos, 1967; *La Llave y otras narraciones* (fiction), Editorial Magisterio Espanol (Madrid), 1967; *Las Criaturas saturnianas*, Ediciones Destino, 1968; *Don Juan en la mancebia: Drama liturgico en cuatro actos*, Editores Mexicanos Unidos, 1968; *El extrano Senor Photynos y otras novelas* (fiction), Ayma (Barcelona), 1968; *Novelas de otro jueves*, Aguilar, 1969; *Comedia del Diantre y otras dos*, Ediciones Destino, 1969; *En la vida de Ignacio Morel* (novel), Editorial Planeta (Barcelona), 1969; *Nocturno de los 14* (novel), Iberama Publishing Co. (New York), 1969; *Tres ejemplos de amor y una teoria* (nonfiction), Alianza Editorial, 1969.

Ensayos del otro mundo, Ediciones Destino, 1970; *Relatos fronterizos*, Editores Mexicanos Unidos, 1970; *Tanit* (novel), Editorial Planeta, 1970; *Zu, el angel anfibio* (novel), Editorial Planeta, 1970; *La Antesala*, Ediciones Destino, 1971; *El Fugitivo*, Editorial Planeta, 1972; *Paginas escogidas*, edited and introduced by Marcelino C. Penuelas, Editorial Gredos (Madrid), 1972; *Donde crece la marihuana: Drama en cuatro actos*, Escelicer (Madrid), 1973; *Tupac Amaru*, Ediciones Destino, 1973; *Una Virgen llama a tu puerta*, Ediciones Destino, 1973; *Libro armilar de poesia y memorias bisiestas*, Aguilar, 1974; *La Mesa de las tres moiras* (novel), Editorial Planeta, 1974; *Nancy, doctora en gitaneria*, Editorial Magisterio Espanol, 1974; *Nancy y el bato loco*, Editorial Magisterio Espanol, 1974; *Las tres sorores*, Ediciones Destino, 1974; *Cronus y la senora con rabo*, AKAL (Madrid), 1974.

El Futuro comenzo ayer, CVS Ediciones (Madrid), 1975; *La Efermerides* (novel), Sedmay Ediciones (Madrid), 1976; *El pez de oro*, Ediciones Destino, 1976; *Obra completa*, Ediciones Destino, 1976; *El Alarido de Yauri*, Ediciones Destino, 1977; *Gloria y vejamen de Nancy*, Editorial Magisterio Espanol, 1977; *El Mechudo y la llorona*, Ediciones Destino, 1977; *Adela y yo*, Ediciones Destino, 1978; *El Superviviente*, Ediciones Destino, 1978; *Solanar y lucernario aragones*, Heraldo de Aragon (Saragossa, Spain), 1978; *La Mirada inmovil*, Editorial Argos Vergara, 1979.

Also author of novel *La Quinta Julieta*, B. Costa-Amic, and of one-act plays "The House of Lot," "The Secret," and "The Photograph"; author of introduction to *Reflejos de Espana* by A. Monros, Federacion Social de Montreal. Contributor to magazines and literary periodicals.

WORK IN PROGRESS: Poetry; works in philosophy and history.

SIDELIGHTS: Though Ramon Sender was forced to spend more than half his life in countries other than his native Spain, he was nevertheless regarded as one of that nation's most distinguished novelists. Sender's path to exile began during his years at the University of Madrid, where his political activities on behalf of various reformist causes angered school authorities and ultimately led to his expulsion and even to a brief period of imprisonment. Sender did, however, manage to earn a degree, and in 1924 he went to work as an editor and literary critic for the liberal publication *El Sol*. Six years later he severed his official ties with *El Sol* and became a free-lance writer, contributing to many different newspapers and journals and publishing novels, essays, and plays.

When civil war broke out in Spain in the summer of 1936, Sender was among the first to join the army of the Republic in its fight against the forces of Generalissimo Francisco Franco. But the young writer's military career was brief; Sender left Spain in 1937, not long after learning that his wife and brother had been executed by the Fascists for sympathizing with the republican cause. In an attempt to garner support for the beleaguered government, Sender then set out on a speaking tour of Europe and the United States as a representative of the Republic. The victory of Franco's troops in 1939, however, meant that Sender faced the prospect of permanent exile. After traveling and writing in Mexico for several years, he settled in the United States, spending most of the remaining forty years of his life in the Southwest and writing (in Spanish) about the world he had left behind in 1937.

Critics have tended to divide Sender's best-known works of fiction into two categories that correspond to these two major periods in his life. In the first category are novels Sender wrote *before* leaving Spain, such as *Pro Patria* and *Seven Red Sundays;* in the second category are novels he wrote *after* leaving Spain, including *The Sphere* and *Chronicle of Dawn* and its sequels, a series many believe is his greatest achievement. For the most part, noted John Devlin in his book *Spanish Anticlericalism: A Study in Modern Alienation,* "the earlier group evokes the fights, illusions and hardships of [Sender's] fellow Spaniards before and during the Republic. . . . [The] latter works reveal a continual philosophic evolution and search for values in the twentieth century world of turmoil."

Pro Patria, Sender's first novel, is one of those works concerned with the political and social atmosphere of pre-civil war Spain. A fictionalized account of events the author witnessed during the Spanish military's attempt to suppress a revolt among the Moors in Morocco in the early 1920s, *Pro Patria* reflects on the uselessness of the campaign and the brutal sacrifices expected of the lower classes in the name of patriotism and economic gain. Charles L. King, commenting in his critical study of Sender, found this particular novel significant not only because it is Sender's first, "but also because in style and human content it accurately foreshadows [his] prolific . . . novelistic production of the next four decades." Viance, the army private who serves as the principal narrator of the story, is, according to King, "both an individual soldier and a symbol of the Spanish underprivileged masses. . . . There is a parallel between the treatment meted out to Viance by his officers and the treatment of the Spanish lower classes by the upper classes through the centuries. . . . In the end Viance breaks national boundaries, becoming a universal symbol of the common man as victim of injustice and man's inhumanity to man." In addition, wrote the critic, *Pro Patria* resembles subsequent Sender novels in that it displays "a direct, sober, verbal style, an impersonal distancing of the author from the work, the same grim—sometimes gruesome—humor. . . , the same interweaving of objective and subjective realities to create the novel's own private world, the harshest of visual detail alongside lyrical and metaphysical fantasy, the flight into delirium and dreams which sometimes cast a surrealistic spell over the action, and the everpresent probing of ultimate reality, mystery."

In a review written at the time of the book's publication (1935), a *Times Literary Supplement* critic remarked that it is appropriate to regard *Pro Patria* "less as a work of fiction than as an impressive piece of journalism contributing an unpublished page to the detailed history of the present." But as Paul Allen observed in *Books,* Sender was not entirely successful at blending the two genres. Observed the critic: "All this is not for the squeamish certainly. Nor for the strong. For it seems hardly possible that any one can have stomach or nerves strong enough to read it unmoved. Nor can one take refuge in doubt. Senor Sender was on the scene. . . . But so intense was his desire to cram into the book all the searing things he had felt and seen he forgot he was writing a novel."

The *Christian Century*'s Raymond Kresensky also noted that *Pro Patria* lacks many of the qualities of a good novel. "There is no romance, no sentiment, and very little humaneness [in this book]," he began. "Not once is it lightened by even a glimmer of humor. . . . Those with weak stomachs will not be able to read through the three hundred pages of ghastly experiences."

Though Otis Ferguson of the *New Republic* agreed that "as a novel [*Pro Patria*] is confusing and incomplete, half this, half that," he went on to state that it is nevertheless "more valuable, in what it has to tell us of things we could not imagine, than any five-foot shelf of Life and Death in Recent Leading Fiction." V. S. Pritchett expressed a similar view, declaring in the *New Statesman and Nation* that "*Pro Patria* has dignity but no great distinction, and the attempt to create a symbolical Spanish soldier type is not very successful. . . . [Yet] it would be a pity if, after our glut of war books, this intelligent and sensitive Spanish document were put aside."

A few reviewers were somewhat more generous in their praise of Sender's first novel. Commented a *Saturday Review of Literature* critic: "[*Pro Patria*] is as full of humanity as it is of terror. It is like so many current war stories, a narrative of futility. . . . If it makes the reader shudder, [it] also inevitably makes him think." William Plomer of the *Spectator* noted that "only a man of rare imaginative power and literary skill, a man both honest and brilliant, could have produced this record of a prolonged and complicated nightmare. Senor Sender makes it clear that he had no need to invent anything. . . . Private Viance has as great a significance as any character in recent fiction."

Unlike those reviewers who did not like the author's documentary approach, the *Nation*'s Florence Codman was pleased to see that Sender disclaimed all "literary and aesthetic prejudices" before beginning *Pro Patria.* "The agreeable thing about this book," Codman stated, "is its total lack of pretenses—sentimental, egotistic, social, or artistic. In fact, I recall no recent examples of war fiction in which there is so little attitude and so generous a permission to let bare incidents, within their context, speak for themselves. It is Sender's compliment to his subject to have realized that no inflation could make it more ghastly or render his hero more pitiable or more dignified."

Sender's second novel, *Seven Red Sundays,* continued the examination of politics and society in pre-civil war Spain, this time from the point of view of a group of communists, anarchists, and trade unionists who stage an unsuccessful general strike in Madrid. Though this book also struck many critics at the time of its publication as more documentary than literary in style, it nevertheless demonstrated the author's growing preoccupation with experimental philosophies and different ways of perceiving reality. In *The Modern Spanish Novel,* for instance, Sherman H. Eoff suggested that Sender's interest in "the mysterious 'presence' that lurks behind commonplace existence" and in "the notion that the heart of human reality is concealed in a nonrational and phantomlike quality" foreshadowed the French existentialists in some ways. Explained Eoff: "Bolder—and less organized—than the French in his expression of ideas, and less dedicated to novelistic technique as a goal in itself, [Sender] evinces a lusty primitivism whose existentialist affinity is an aspect rather than a systematic trend of thought." King observed that "Sender uses external or ordinary reality in *Seven Red Sundays* as a solid base of operations, as a kind of trampoline from which to launch his leaps to 'higher' realities. The chapter in which the moon becomes a character is an example of unrestrained imagination which clearly violates the usual norms for a 'realistic' work. . . . [Thus,] the 'realism' of *Seven Red Sundays* is a strange fusion of ordinary reality with other 'realities,' imaginative 'realities' that sometimes add an intellectual dimension, at others a lyrical or metaphysical overtone."

Perhaps the most philosophical of Sender's many works is *The Sphere,* the first novel he wrote after leaving Spain. Described by King as "an ambitious attempt to fuse into an artistic unity the realistic, the lyrical-metaphysical, the fantastic, and the symbolic," *The Sphere* follows a Spanish refugee on a transatlantic voyage that is marred by several murders, a mutiny, and a shipwreck. In this complex story, Sender explored a variety of universal opposites—life and death, love and hate—and tried to synthesize them into higher unities or "spheres" that incorporated elements of the purely rational and conventional "everyday" world as well as the chaotic and fragmented world of the subconscious and the unconscious. According to King, "the dramatic tension of *The Sphere,* as it is in all of Sender's fiction, is . . . between [these] two worlds. . . . Sender seeks ever to write in the twilight zone where [they] merge."

One of the more unusual, yet significant, "opposites" the author discussed in *The Sphere* was "man" and "person." As Sender himself explained in a passage from the novel, a man is (in a somewhat mystical sense) "the source of all truth, of each universal and innate truth," and "an integral part of *the infinite intellect of God.*" A "person," on the other hand, is the individualized "mask" that begins to develop soon after birth and continues to grow and change throughout life—in essence, the sum of those qualities that makes one man different from another. In Sender's view, this process of individualization isolates a man from his fellow man and gradually takes him farther and farther away from his instinctive nature.

In his essay on *The Sphere,* King pointed to this man-person antithesis as the source of Sender's major philosophical convictions. It was, for instance, the basis for his belief in the "natural unity of all created objects" and his "deep faith in the value of man *simply because he is man*"; it also led him ultimately to deny the existence of death. (According to Sender, man, the "eternal substance," is immortal; what "dies" is the person, "that growing individualization of the human being.")

Sender demonstrated his preoccupation with these and other thought-provoking concepts in many of his subsequent works of fiction, including *A Man's Place, Dark Wedding, The King and the Queen,* and *The Affable Hangman.* For the most part, critics found these books bewildering yet fascinating in their symbolic complexity and blend of reality and fantasy. One particular group of post-exile novels, however, did not exhibit quite the same abstruseness. Known by the general title of the first work in the series, *Chronicle of Dawn,* these novels depict early twentieth-century Spain in a tenderly nostalgic light, primarily through the eyes of a republican refugee, Pepe Garces, as he lies dying in a French prison camp during the final months of the civil war. Though Sender's series is, as Bertram Wolfe observed in *New York Herald Tribune Books,* first and foremost "a remarkably beautiful tale of romantic and heroic childhood which will take its place alongside the very best in its genre," it is also, declared the *New York Times*'s Marjorie Farber, a war story unlike any other in its portrayal of "what happens to the good men, and to all men, in the course of the fight."

Nearly all the critics who were familiar with the English translations of three novels in the series—*Chronicle of Dawn, Violent Griffin,* and *The Villa Julieta* (published together as the trilogy *Before Noon*)—were charmed as well as saddened by the author's simple narrative of youth. In his *Nation* review, for example, Paul Blackburn called *Before Noon* "one of the sweetest-tempered books I have read in a long time. In fact, I can recall no book of prose at all with which to set it. I thought that only poetry could be this warm. This does not seem to be so much a result of Mr. Sender's style (an enviable clarity in itself), as of his attitude toward his character, Pepe Garces. I don't think Pepe can avoid being mostly Ramon Sender, ages ten to twelve. I do not know what Mr. Sender thinks of himself as man, but he adores that boy! I am grateful; you will be too. . . . The fabric of the book will catch you up, both in its gross take and in its delicacies, so that you will read, impatient for the next development."

Isaac Rosenfeld of the *New Republic* found that the technique of beginning the story in the present and then returning to the past creates "an idyllic effect. . . . But it is the tone in which remembered experience is set down and the purpose these scenes serve which give *Chronicle of Dawn* its quality of delight." The critic was also impressed by "the renewed ease" with which the author handled symbolism in the book. Remarked Rosenfeld: "[In previous novels Sender's] symbolism appeared to be getting out of hand, even at times symbolizing nothing so much as itself in an iconography run riot, religious in its overtones but wary of the reality to which it owed some final commitment. *Chronicle of Dawn* is to my mind a very welcome reconstruction of the symbol."

Farber applauded Sender for at last writing "an astonishingly true and moving" book which examines "the total truth of our tragedy"—in short, "the whole monstrous discrepancy between human potential and the inhuman, mechanized result: the love perverted or corrupted, the courage exploited, the nobility thrown away." She was also pleased to note Sender's "tone of respect" and "unusual honesty and clarity" in recording "the physical details and the passionate emotions of childhood," explaining that "Sender's humor contains none of the underlying contempt of Tarkington's attitude toward Penrod; nor does he ever allow nostalgia to falsify his memories into the pastel prettiness of Saroyan. Pepe may be young, but he is a human being—a young man in the most dignified literal sense."

Unlike Farber, however, *Nation* critic Diana Trilling did not find Sender's portrait of Pepe particularly dignified. "For all Mr. Sender's good prose," she stated, "[*Chronicle of Dawn*] was marred for me by the fatal coyness with which Mr. Sender reproduces the mind of a ten-year-old." Others, too, had some less-than-flattering observations to make about the book. As Edwin Honig commented in the *Saturday Review:* "Despite the delicacy and charm of its details, the novel is somber and bare, and at times appears too far removed from the sources of feeling it exploits. . . . After the first true heat and *vraisemblance* are struck in *Chronicle of Dawn,* the novel seems to jerk along without developing characters or situations beyond the passing events themselves." In his *Commonweal* review, Paule Berault described *Chronicle of Dawn* as a childhood memory "with all the weaknesses and the charm of this form" and expressed his disappointment with Sender's all-too-brief mention of that "drama [the Spanish civil war] which was the forerunner of that which spread all over the world." As far as Berault was concerned, Sender's sober yet powerful explanation of how and why the dying Pepe came to tell his story "far surpasses the rest of the book."

At least two critics believed that Sender did not err in downplaying the political and social realities of the 1930s in his novel. The *Saturday Review*'s Ralph Bates, for example, speculated that the author, "driven out of his own land with memories too horrible for contemplation," probably felt "compelled to reorder his thinking [and thus] deliberately returned to that [time when] the spirit was whole and hard and pure." Continued the critic: "Sender must go back, as [Pepe] must do, not in order to comfort the heart with dreams of a Golden Epoch, but in order to collect and concentrate himself, to pare off the impurities, particularly the uncleanness of the political world of compromise and ungodly tolerance. . . . This return to childhood is a kind of voluntary seclusion, a monasticism of the spirit that is far more rigorous than the imprisonments which have been made to serve the same purpose by other writers. . . . That is the significance of this simple, astonishing book. That is why it is so singularly pure, for against its one banal memory there are set within it scores of startling and altogether beautiful things.''

Rosenfeld agreed that Sender's "reconstruction of [Pepe's] childhood is . . . not an escape from political responsibility, nor even a simple flight from hopelessness. It is, rather, a justification of the hopeless. . . . Only through the reconstruction of the times and experiences in which the ideal had meaning—the childhood of hope—can one examine, with the most unsparing honesty, the significance of the ideal, and know, without delusion, precisely what was lost when 'all was lost.'''

Sender's lifelong desire to determine "precisely what was lost when 'all was lost''' did not, however, leave him bitter or pessimistic. It is true, noted critic John Devlin, that as "a novelist with philosophical inclinations" Sender did continually seek out the "explanations behind reality—not only the reality of Spain of his day, but of human existence, as well." Nevertheless, concluded Devlin, "an examination of [his] first novel reveals, under literary symbols, that he discovered in the worst of situations and people a small light shining in the midst of the surrounding darkness of chaos and cruelty. This note is [Sender's] saving grace; it pervades and becomes the touchstone of all his major works."

BIOGRAPHICAL/CRITICAL SOURCES—Books: Ramon Sender, *Chronicle of Dawn*, annotated Spanish edition, edited and introduced by Florence Hall, Crofts, 1946; Sherman H. Eoff, *The Modern Spanish Novel*, New York University Press, 1961; John Devlin, *Spanish Anticlericalism: A Study in Modern Alienation*, Las Americas Publishing Co., 1966; Charles C. King, *Ramon J. Sender*, Twayne, 1974; *Contemporary Literary Criticism*, Volume VIII, Gale, 1978.

Periodicals: *New Statesman and Nation*, September 8, 1934, January 16, 1937, April 10, 1937; *Times Literary Supplement*, October 25, 1934, May 2, 1936, April 17, 1937; *Spectator*, September 14, 1935, April 16, 1937; *New York Times*, September 22, 1935, October 18, 1936, January 30, 1938, November 3, 1940, March 28, 1943, February 20, 1944, June 27, 1948, May 1, 1949, January 19, 1958; *Nation*, October 2, 1935, October 24, 1936, November 2, 1940, April 24, 1943, March 18, 1944, April 19, 1958; *Books*, October 6, 1935, October 11, 1936; *New Republic*, October 16, 1935, October 14, 1936, February 3, 1941, April 5, 1943, April 24, 1944, May 31, 1948, November 30, 1963; *Saturday Review of Literature*, October 19, 1935, September 26, 1936, January 29, 1938, December 21, 1940, May 15, 1943, April 15, 1944, June 4, 1949, April 12, 1958, September 7, 1963; *Christian Century*, November 6, 1935; *Manchester Guardian*, May 1, 1936, April 23, 1937; *Christian Science Monitor*, May 12, 1937, May 24, 1949; *New York Herald Tribune Weekly Book Review*, March 28, 1943, March 12, 1944, May 16, 1948; *Commonweal*, May 26, 1944; *San Francisco Chronicle*, June 19, 1949, February 16, 1958; *New Yorker*, April 19, 1958; *Book Week*, September 29, 1963.

OBITUARIES: *Chicago Tribune*, January 19, 1982; *London Times*, January 19, 1982; *AB Bookman's Weekly*, February 22, 1982.†

—Sketch by Deborah A. Straub

* * *

SEULING, Barbara 1937-

PERSONAL: Surname pronounced Soo-ling; born July 22, 1937, in Brooklyn, N.Y.; daughter of Kaspar Joseph (a postman) and Helen Veronica (Gadie) Seuling. *Education:* Attended Hunter College (now Hunter College of the City University of New York), 1955-57, Columbia University, 1957-59, New School for Social Research, and School of Visual Arts. *Home and office:* 320 Central Park W., New York, N.Y. 10025. *Agent:* Harriet Wasserman Literary Agency, Inc., 230 East 48th St., New York, N.Y. 10017.

CAREER: Freelance writer and illustrator, 1966—. Has worked for an investment firm, insurance companies, a university, and at the General Electric Co. exhibit at the New York World's Fair; Dell Publishing Co., New York City, children's book editor, 1965-71; J. B. Lippincott Co., New York City, children's book editor, 1971-73. Lecturer on books at local schools. Consultant to New York Foundlings Hospital.

MEMBER: Society of Children's Book Writers (member of board of directors). *Awards, honors:* Award from American Institute of Graphic Arts, 1979, for *The Teeny Tiny Woman*; Christopher Award, The Christophers, 1979, for *The New York Kids' Book;* first place, Harold Marshall Solstad Prize, Cameron University Children's Short Story Competition, 1982.

WRITINGS—All juveniles; all self-illustrated: *Abracadbra!: Creating Your Own Magic Show from Beginning to End*, Messner, 1975; *The Teeny Tiny Woman*, Viking, 1976; *The Great Big Elephant and the Very Small Elephant*, Crown, 1977; *The Triplets*, Clarion, 1980; *Just Me*, Harcourt, 1982.

Published by Doubleday: *The Last Legal Spitball and Other Little Known Facts about Sports*, 1975; *You Can't Eat Peanuts in Church and Other Little Known Laws*, 1975; *The Loudest Screen Kiss and Other Little Known Facts about the Movies*, 1976; *The Last Cow on the White House Lawn and Other Little Known Facts about the Presidency*, 1978; *The New York Kids' Book*, 1979; *You Can't Count a Billion Dollars and Other Little Known Facts about Money*, 1979; *You Can't Show Kids in Underwear and Other Little Known Facts about T.V.*, 1982.

Illustrator: Wilma Thompson, *That Barbara!*, Delacorte, 1969; Nan Hayden Agle, *Tarr of Belway Smith*, Seabury Press, 1969; Stella Pevsner, *Break a Leg!*, Crown, 1969; Antonia Barber, *The Affair of the Rockerbye Baby*, Delacorte, 1970; Pevsner, *Footsteps on the Stairs*, Crown, 1970; Moses Howard, *The Ostrich Chase*, Holt, 1974.

Contributor to books for and about children. Also contributor to journals for and about children, including *Cricket*.

WORK IN PROGRESS: Picture books for children; an adult book on writing for children; a novel.

SIDELIGHTS: "I love both writing and illustrating, but I find that writing takes much more discipline and a different sort of mental energy," Barbara Seuling told CA. "After an hour or two of steady writing, I am truly tired. With drawing, I can go on all day and tune in to my favorite radio station at the same time. Someone can interrupt me, talk to me, and I am still involved in my drawing without losing ground. A distraction when I'm writing, however, is serious, and often I cannot go back to work once this happens. I know a lot of it has to do with concentration, but I also wonder if a large part of it isn't the security I feel with drawing, which came naturally and was recognized early, and writing, which I discovered later, and with which I feel less on solid ground.

"My purpose is different for each book I create. With my novel I mean to share an emotional experience. I like to think of picture books as tools for growing—growing in some way to understand the world better and to find a way to fit into it— and yet all this must be kept carefully hidden so that it doesn't frighten children away. So, on the surface, I want to make children laugh, to entertain them, tell them a good story. My fact books are meant purely as entertainment because I feel there is a real need for fun. That doesn't mean one cannot learn from them, but that is not their purpose.

"This is a very exciting time to be writing for children. Never before have so many areas opened up for exploration through writing. With few exceptions (and they are decreasing), writers are free to write about whatever they choose. Young people want to know more and more about the life around them, about people and relationships and feelings, and, at last, we [writers] can feel a direct line to them, since [young people] are buying their own books.

"My advice to new writers is: be persistent. The saddest part of writing is the defeatism that is felt so early by writers. One's first work rarely gets published, but that is when our hopes and ideals are so high that they are easily dashed by rejection. It is a rough process, and if one can weather the first years, and keep writing in spite of the obstacles, the chances of success keep growing. A writer is a growing thing; we grow with each page we write, and therefore the more we write the more we learn and the better we become."

AVOCATIONAL INTERESTS: Movies (silent to modern).

* * *

SEWARD, Jack
See SEWARD, John Neil

* * *

SEWARD, John Neil 1924-
(Jack Seward)

PERSONAL: Born October 11, 1924, in Houston, Tex.; son of John Neil and LaNelle (Denny) Seward; married Jean Aiko Morimoto, January 14, 1963; children: John Neil III, William Kenneth. Education: Attended University of Oklahoma, 1941-43; University of Michigan, A.B., 1945; graduate study at University of Hawaii, 1950-51. Religion: Protestant. Home: 10507 Brinwood, Houston, Tex. 10507.

CAREER: U.S. Civil Censorship Detachment, Osaka, Japan, censor, 1947-49; Pan-Pacific Trading Co., Tokyo, Japan, branch manager, 1950; affiliated with U.S. Central Intelligence Agency, stationed in Far East, 1951-56; Yashica Camera Co., Tokyo, export sales manager, 1957-60; Sunbeam Corp., Tokyo, Far East representative, 1960-66; full-time writer, 1966-70; Far East representative, Scholastic Magazines, Inc., 1970-72; University of Texas at Dallas, professor of Japanese, 1973-75; director of international operations, Ecology and Environment, Inc., 1975-78; International Consulting Services, Inc., Houston, Tex., president, 1978—. Military service: U.S. Army, 1943-47.

WRITINGS—Under name Jack Seward: *Cave of the Chinese Skeletons,* Tuttle, 1964; *Japan Guide,* American-Oriental Associates (Hong Kong), 1964; *Hara-Kiri: Japanese Ritual Suicide,* Tuttle, 1967; *Japanese in Action,* Weatherhill, 1968; *The Frogman Assassination,* Tower, 1968; *The Eurasian Virgins,* Tower, 1968; *Assignment: Find Cherry,* Tower, 1969; *The Chinese Pleasure Girl,* Tower, 1969.

The Diplomat, Lotus Press, 1971; *The Japanese* (Reader's Digest Condensed Book), Morrow, 1972; *More About the Japanese,* Lotus Press, 1972; *The Darned Nuisances,* Lotus Press, 1972; *Tekisasu no Koinobori* (in Japanese), Shin-Takeuchi Shoten, 1974; *Nihonjin no Bijinesu Kankaku* (in Japanese), Daiyamondo-sha, 1976; *Suwado-san no Nippongo Noto* (in Japanese), Eichosha, 1976; *The Japanese and the Americans,* Eichosha, 1977; *An American's America,* Eichosha, 1978.

Words across the Pacific, Eichosha, 1980; *On Japan Again,* Eichosha, 1981; *Common Sense* (in Japanese), Mikasa Shobo, 1981; *America and Japan: The Twain Meet,* Lotus Press, 1981.

Also author of several other books on the Japanese.

SIDELIGHTS: John Neil Seward told CA: "When I first studied how to write, I was told that to succeed, a writer should write about what he knows best. Having lived half my life in Japan and being (then and now) fascinated by that country, I went on to write twenty-five books about it. The most successful I suppose, was *The Japanese,* . . . the most widely read book about the people of Japan ever written. Even so, I now doubt the validity of this advice, at least as it applies to me. Americans simply are not that interested in Japan or any other foreign country. They'll buy light entertainment like *Shogun.* Serious works, no.

"I have, therefore, changed my objectives. From now on, I will write about Americans for American readers.

"I would like to write humor more than anything else, but since I sometimes find myself laughing alone in a movie theater, while those around me look at me askance, my readers may be limited in number. Besides, ours is not an age that appreciates humor. We strive too hard to become 'involved' in 'relevant issues.'"

* * *

SHAN, Yeh
See WANG, C(hing) H(sien)

* * *

SHANKS, Michael (James) 1927-

PERSONAL: Born April 12, 1927, in London, England; son of Alan James (a businessman) and Margaret (Lee) Shanks; married Elizabeth Juliet Richardson, April 4, 1953 (died, 1972); married Patricia Jaffe, 1973; children: (first marriage) Andrew, Helena, Christopher, Roland; (second marriage) six stepchildren. Education: Balliol College, Oxford, B.A. (with honors), 1950; graduate study, 1951-52. Politics: Labour. Religion: Church of England. Home: Clapton Revel, Wooburn Moor, Buckinghamshire HP10 0NH, England.

CAREER: Williams College, Williamstown, Mass., instructor in economics, 1950-51; *Economist,* Intelligence Unit, London, England, research worker, 1952-53; *Financial Times,* London, leader and feature writer, 1953-54, labor correspondent, 1954-57, industrial editor, 1957-64; *Sunday Times,* London, economic correspondent, 1964-65; Department of Economic Affairs, London, industrial adviser, 1965-66, industrial policy coordinator, 1966-67; British Leyland Motor Corp., London, group economic adviser, 1967-68, director of marketing services and economic planning, 1968-71; British Oxygen Co., chief executive of finance and planning, 1971-72, director of group strategy, 1973; Commission of the European Economic Community, Brussels, Belgium, director general for social affairs, 1973-76; currently chairman or director of National Consumer Council, Datastream PLC, Geo. Bassett Holdings PLC, Barratt & Co. Ltd., Bassett Confectionery Ltd., Bassett Exports Ltd., BOC International PLC, Henley Centre for Forecasting, P-E Consultants Ltd., Environmental Resources Ltd., and Barmel Associates Ltd. Member, Distributive Trades Economic Development Committee, 1965-73, Electrical Engineering Economic Development Committee, 1965-67, and National Economic Development Council, 1977-81; member of executive committee, Warwick University Centre on Industrial and Business Studies, 1968-71; member of advisory council,

Business Graduates Association, 1968-73; Confederation of British Industry, member of grand council and economic committee, 1968-73, member of employment policy committee, 1976-77, member of council, 1976-77, currently member of Europe committee; member of council, Society for Long Range Planning and Society of Business Economists, 1969-73, and Institute of Directors, 1976-77; member of management board, European Foundation for Living and Working Conditions, 1975-76; chairman of management board, European Centre for Vocational Training, 1975-76; director, Royal Ordnance Factories, 1976-80; member of executive board, British Standards Institution, 1977-81; currently member of Academic Council of Wilton Park, Council of the Foundation for Management Education, European advisory council of Tenneco, Inc., and advisory council of Science Policy Foundation; United Kingdom Program director, Jobs in the 80s Programme. Visiting professor, University of Brunel and European Business School; visiting fellow, University of Lancaster; fellow, British Institute of Management. Editorial advisor, Penguin Books, beginning 1963; member of editorial board, Times Management Library, 1968-72. Treasurer, Fabian Society, 1964-65, and Great Britain/East Europe Centre, 1968-70. Governor, Wycombe Abbey Girls School, 1970-73. Founder and member, Campaign for Democratic Socialism. *Military service:* British Army, Royal Artillery, 1945-48; became lieutenant. *Member:* Labour Committee for Europe, Reform Club.

WRITINGS: *Poems,* Fantasy Press, 1953; *The Stagnant Society,* Penguin, 1961, revised edition, 1972; (with John Lambert) *The Common Market Today—and Tomorrow,* Praeger, 1962 (published in England as *Britain and the New Europe: The Future of the Common Market,* Chatto & Windus, 1962); *Incomes Policy and the Professional Employee* (pamphlet), National Union of Teachers, 1962; (contributor) B. C. Roberts, editor, *Industrial Relations: Contemporary Problems and Perspectives,* Methuen, 1962; (editor) *The Lessons of Public Enterprise: A Fabian Society Study,* J. Cape, 1963; (contributor) *Suicide of a Nation?,* Hutchinson, 1963; *ABC of Economics* (pamphlet), BBC Publications, 1965; *The Innovators: The Economics of Technology,* Penguin, 1967; *The Quest for Growth,* Macmillan (London), 1973; *European Social Policy, Today and Tomorrow,* Pergamon, 1977; *Planning and Politics: The British Experience, 1960-1976,* Allen & Unwin, 1977; *What's Wrong with the Modern World?: Agenda for a New Society,* Bodley Head, 1978, Merrimack Book Service, 1979.

Author of additional pamphlets, including *How to Export,* United Kingdom Board of Trade. Commissioning editor of Penguin series on economics. Contributor to *Encounter, Banker, Political Quarterly, Punch, Listener, New Statesman, Time and Tide, Geographical Magazine, Sunday Times,* and other publications.

* * *

SHANNON, Doris 1924-

PERSONAL: Born August 7, 1924, in Elmira, N.Y.; daughter of Edwin (an engineer) and Elizabeth (a telephone operator; maiden name, Graham) Giroux; married Frank Shannon (a customs officer), August 1, 1947; children: Patricia Anne, Deborah Elizabeth. *Education:* Attended Napanee Collegiate Institute, 1939-42. *Home:* 10580 154A St., Surrey, British Columbia, Canada. *Agent:* Kirby McCauley, 425 Park Ave. S., New York, N.Y. 10016.

CAREER: Writer, 1969—. Royal Bank of Canada, teller in Napanee, Ontario, 1942-47, in Vancouver, British Columbia, 1948-49. *Member:* Authors League of America. *Awards, honors: Writer's Digest* creative writing award, 1969, for short story "And Then There Was the Youngest."

WRITINGS—Novels: *The Whispering Runes,* Lenox Hill, 1972; *Twenty-two Hallowfield,* Fawcett, 1974; *The Seekers,* Fawcett, 1975; *Hawthorn Hill,* St. Martin's, 1976; *The Lodestar Legacy,* Popular Library, 1976; *Cain's Daughters,* St. Martin's, 1978; *Beyond the Shining Mountains,* St. Martin's, 1979; *The Punishment,* St. Martin's, 1981.

WORK IN PROGRESS: A historical New York saga, tentatively entitled *Family Money.*

SIDELIGHTS: Doris Shannon writes that at the age of forty, "without quite realizing my own motivation I turned to writing. Much to my surprise . . . editors expressed . . . confidence in a talent I had never realized I possessed. . . . Writing appears to be a profession where gray hair and age are not signals that one's working life is over. I share with many writers the desire to write that special book, the fine one, and also eventually I should like to teach creative writing."

* * *

SHAW, George
See BICKHAM, Jack M(iles)

* * *

SHAYNE, Gordon
See WINTER, Bevis (Peter)

* * *

SHEBL, James M(ichael) 1942-

PERSONAL: Born July 1, 1942, in Tacoma, Wash.; son of Joseph J. (a physician) and Mary Ellen (Hurley) Shebl; married Patricia A. Pedroni, August 22, 1964; children: Bonnie Marie, Catherine Theresa. *Education:* Creighton University, B.A., 1965; University of Nebraska, M.A., 1969; University of the Pacific, Ph.D., 1974. *Politics:* "Left Conservative." *Religion:* Roman Catholic. *Home:* 3517 Stone River Cir., Stockton, Calif. 95209. *Office:* University of the Pacific, Stockton, Calif. 95211.

CAREER: Worked as U.S. Air Force civilian instructor in swimming and diving, 1964-65, and as inspector of agricultural crops in California, 1969-70; University of the Pacific, Stockton, Calif., director of university townhouse, 1970-73, assistant to academic vice-president, 1972-78, assistant professor of humanities, 1975—, associate director of Pacific Center for Western Historical Studies, 1975-80, assistant dean of Raymond-Callison College, 1978-79, director of foundation support, 1980—. Consultant to Knotts Berry Farm and Cahuilla Indian Reservation. *Member:* Modern Language Association of America, American Association of University Professors, Western Literature Association, Westerners, Western History Association, Southwestern American Literature Association, Southwest Mission Research Center, Phi Kappa Psi (past president), Phi Kappa Phi (president). *Awards, honors:* Nominated for gold medallion for western writing by Commonwealth Club of California, 1974, for *King, of the Mountains.*

WRITINGS: (Author of introduction) Clarence King, *Mountaineering in the Sierra Nevada,* University of Nebraska Press, 1969; *King, of the Mountains,* University of the Pacific Press, 1974; (co-editor and contributor) *Daddy Boy: Jack London's Inscriptions to His Wife Bessie,* Pacific Center for Western Studies, University of the Pacific, 1976; (contributor) *Pioneer or Perish: A History of the University of the Pacific, 1947-1972,* University of the Pacific, 1976; *In This Wild Water: The*

Suppressed Poems of Robinson Jeffers, Ritchie, 1976; (editor) *The Tulebreakers: The Story of the California Dredge,* Westerners (Stockton), 1982.

Contributor to *Valley Trails* (Westerners annual), 1980, and to *Arizona and the West, Pacific Historian, California Historian,* and *Far Westerner.* Editor, *Far Westerner.*

WORK IN PROGRESS: *Pike County West; Green Gold,* a historical novel of the Salinas Valley; *Dear Una,* a drama of the early years of Robinson Jeffers.

SIDELIGHTS: James M. Shebl explained to *CA:* "I write to bring to our people a taste of what went before. Hopefully, there is a lesson to be learned, hope to be gained, pride to be restored. This is very important, you know—that we, as a people, have a sense of pride in what we have accomplished. I am convinced that this is prerequisite to our being able to grasp our potential. The beauty of this is that individuals and the society can maintain a personality. Hopefully a contributing one. Perhaps, then, my aesthetic is like that of an impressionistic painter wherein individuals are the subject of pointillism and the fabric of the culture is viewed by stepping back. I suspect literary history and fictionalized history—which is not to say untrue accounts—shall always be my way."

AVOCATIONAL INTERESTS: International travel (Spain, Italy, Mexico), reading, athletics, Spanish California missions, the Sierra Nevada, horse-packing.

* * *

SHEPARD, Leslie (Alan)   1917-

PERSONAL: Born June 21, 1917, in West Ham, London, England; son of Robert William George and Annie Elizabeth (Williams) Shepard; married (wife deceased); children: one son, one daughter. *Education:* Attended elementary school at Harold Road, Upton Park, London, and Day Continuation School for Commercial Subjects, London, 1922-33. *Politics:* "Unpolitical, humanitarian.' *Religion:* "No formal religious grading, but sympathetic to basic truths of many religions; usually class as Vedantist." *Home:* 1 Lakelands Close, Stillorgan, Blackrock, County Dublin, Irish Republic. *Office:* Gale Research Co., Book Tower, Detroit, Mich. 48226.

CAREER: Paul Rotha Productions Ltd., London, England, assistant organizer of bi-monthly newsreel for Ministry of Information and scriptwriter, 1942-44; Data Film Productions Ltd., London, 1945-58, founder-member, assistant director of various industrial and educational films for Central Office of Information and for industry, 1945-48, member of board of management, 1947, joint production manager-organizer of "Mining Review" (monthly news film), 1948-50, associate producer, 1950-57, scriptwriter, editor, director of other productions; Central Office of Information, London, production controlling officer, supervisor of documentary films and Public Service Television items for British Broadcasting Corp. and Independent Television, 1960-62; University Books, New York, N.Y., London editor, 1965-66; Gale Research Co., Detroit, Mich., editor and researcher, 1966—. Presented lecture, "John Jacob Niles, American Folk Singer," on British Broadcasting Corp. Third Programme, 1965. Founding member, Standing Committee of Jews, Christians and Moslems. Active in ecumenical conferences. Script advisor for dance-drama, "Nritya Nahika Ramayana," 1981; senior resource consultant for Center for Scientific Anomalies Research. *Wartime service:* Served with Civil Defense stretcher party during World War II.

MEMBER: International Folk Music Council, Association of Cinematograph, Television and Allied Technicians, English Folk Dance and Song Society, Private Libraries Association, British Society of Dowsers, College of Psychic Science, Fairy Investigation Society, Dracula Society, Printing Historical Society, Ephemera Society, Society for Psychical Research.

WRITINGS: *The Broadside Ballad: A Study in Origins and Meaning,* Folklore Associates, 1962; *John Pitts, Ballad Printer of Seven Dials, London, 1765-1844, with a Short Account of His Predecessors in the Ballad & Chapbook Trade,* Singing Tree Press, 1969; *The History of Street Literature,* Singing Tree Press, 1973; (editor and reviser) H. T. Dave, *The Life and Philosophy of Shree Swaminaravan,* Allen & Unwin, 1974; (editor) *The Dracula Book of Great Vampire Stories* (Book-of-the-Month Club selection), Citadel, 1977; (editor) *Encyclopedia of Occultism and Parapsychology,* Gale, 1978, supplements published as *Occultism Update,* 1978-81; *How to Protect Yourself against Black Magic and Witchcraft,* Citadel, 1978; (editor) *The Dracula Book of Great Horror Stories,* Citadel, 1981.

Author of forewords for more than seventy reprints, including the following; published by University Books, except as indicated: Rupert T. Gould, *Oddities,* 1965; Ralph Shirley, *The Mystery of the Human Double,* 1965; W. J. Kilner, *The Human Aura,* 1965; (postface to Volume II) Godfrey Higgins, *Anacalypsis,* 1965; A. E. (pseudonym of George William Russell), *The Candle of Vision,* 1965; G.R.S. Mead, *Apollonius of Tyana,* 1966; W. Y. Evans-Wentz, *The Fairy-Faith in Celtic Countries,* 1966; Nandor Fodor, *Encyclopedia of Psychic Science,* 1966; H. E. Rollins, *An Analytical Index to the Ballad Entries, 1557-1709, in the Registers of the Company of Stationers of London,* Folklore Associates, 1967; S. Baring-Gould, *Curious Myths of the Middle Ages,* 1967; Charles Hindley, *Curiosities of Street Literature,* John Foreman, 1967; F. E. Willard and M. A. Livermore, *A Woman of the Century,* Gale, 1967; *The Works of William Hone,* Gale, 1967; *English as She Is Spoke,* Gale, 1967. Also author of foreword of other books published by Gale.

Recordings; all released by Folkways Records: (Compiler and author of booklet and notes) "Vox Humana: Experiments of Alfred Wolfsohn in Extension of Human Vocal Range"; (compiler and author of booklet and notes) "Yoga Vedanta: Documentary of Life in an Indian Ashram"; (author of booklet) "John Jacob Niles Sings".

Contributor of articles to *Film and Television Technician, Books* (journal of National Book League), *New Society, Mountain Life and Work,* and to various folk music magazines. Member of editorial board of *Kundalini.*

WORK IN PROGRESS: *Popular Broadside Ballads;* books on yoga and on occultism; editing an English translation of the Hindu scripture *Vachanamrita,* and encyclopedias of allusions.

SIDELIGHTS: In 1958 and 1959, Leslie Shepard studied Yoga and Hindu metaphysics in India, living in an old temple on the banks of the Ganges River in the foothills of the Himalayas. He has worked closely with the Hindu community in Great Britain and is also connected with the work of modern mystic Pandit Gopi Krishna. In 1959 he joined David Regan in his unsuccessful attempt to cross the Atlantic in a 28-foot cutter via the earliest known sea route to America (the Viking route). During the voyage, Shepard acted as cinematographer, cook, and carpenter. Shepard owns a unique collection of broadside ballads "and related ephemera" and was an early populariser of the Kentucky Mountain dulcimer in Britain. In the field of the occult and the paranormal, Shepard believes that there is a proportion of genuine phenomena but is concerned to "strike a fair balance between extreme attitudes of credulous acceptance and over-skeptical rejection."

SHEPPARD, Joseph 1930-

PERSONAL: Born December 20, 1930, in Owings Mills, Md.; son of Joseph E. and Edna (Marquiss) Sheppard; married Nina Akamu; children: (previous marriage) Jonathan, William, Joseph. *Education:* Maryland Institute of Art, fine art certificate, 1952; studied privately with Jacques Maroger. *Home:* Via Terzano 54, San Donato in Collina, Florence, Italy.

CAREER: Artist. Artist-in-residence and instructor in oil painting, Dickinson College, 1955-57; instructor in oil painting, Maryland Institute of Art, 1963-75. One-man shows at Butler Institute of American Art, 1964 and 1972, Westmoreland County Museum, 1966 and 1972, and Davenport Municipal Art Gallery, 1967; work included in many public and private collections including Baltimore Museum of Art, Columbus Museum of Fine Arts, and University of Arizona Museum. *Member:* Allied Artists of America, Artists' Fellowship, National Sculpture Society.

AWARDS, HONORS: Emily Lowe Prize from Allied Artists exhibition, 1956; Guggenheim fellowship, 1957-58; John F. and Anna Lee Stacy Award, 1958; Bronze Medal of Honor, Allied Artists of America Exhibition, 1959; Prize for Figure Painting, Allied Artists of America, 1963; first purchase award, Butler Institute of American Art, 1963; John McDonough Prize, Butler Institute of American Art, 1967; Governor's Prize, Maryland Artists' Exhibition, 1971.

WRITINGS—Published by Watson-Guptill, except as indicated: *Anatomy: A Complete Guide for Artists,* 1975; *Drawing the Female Figure,* 1975; *Illustrations for Socrates,* Stemmer House, 1975; *Drawing the Male Figure,* 1976; *Learning from the Masters,* 1979; *Illustrations for Keeping Christmas,* Stemmer House, 1981; *The Work of Joseph Sheppard,* Georgi & Gambi, 1982.

SIDELIGHTS: Anatomy: A Complete Guide for Artists, Drawing the Female Figure, and *Drawing the Male Figure* have been translated into Japanese.

* * *

SHERMAN, D(enis) R(onald) 1934-

PERSONAL: Born December 20, 1934, in Calcutta, India; son of Denis Basil (a printer) and Marjorie (Clayton) Sherman; married Sylvaine Dingwall, November 6, 1961. *Education:* Received primary education in India and secondary education in England; British School of Wireless Telegraphy, London, P.M.G. Certificate, 1952. *Residence:* Praslin Island, Seychelles. *Agent:* A. M. Heath & Co. Ltd., 40-42 William IV St., London WC2N 4DD, England.

CAREER: Marconi Marine, Chelmsford, Essex, England, radio officer, 1952-54; station foreman in Africa for Rhodesia Railways, beginning 1956. *Military service:* Royal Navy, 1954-56.

WRITINGS: Old Mali and the Boy (novel), Little, Brown, 1964; *Into the Noonday Sun* (novel), Little, Brown, 1966; *Brothers of the Sea,* Little, Brown, 1966; *The Sinners,* Cassel, 1970; *Ryan,* Ace Books, 1973; *The Boat,* Cassel, 1973; *The Lion's Paw,* Doubleday, 1974. Occasional contributor of short stories to magazines.

SIDELIGHTS: D. R. Sherman told *CA:* "[I] hope to be able to write well enough one day to earn my living at it. I really like to write, but most days it's an effort to make the start, and usually after two thousand words or so I get tired and begin to lose interest." Sherman adds that he has not written anything at all since 1978, but "maybe the fire will come back. I don't know, but in any case, I've learned to live without it."

AVOCATIONAL INTERESTS: Horseback riding, hunting, drinking.

* * *

SHOOK, Robert L. 1938-

PERSONAL: Born April 7, 1938, in Pittsburgh, Pa.; son of Herbert M. (an insurance executive) and Belle (Slutsky) Shook; married Roberta Gay Wolk, April 18, 1962; children: Faith Caroline, Robert James, Michael David. *Education:* Ohio State University, B.S., 1959. *Religion:* Jewish. *Home:* 201 South Drexel Ave., Columbus, Ohio 43209. *Office:* Shook Associates Corp., 3140 East Broad St., Columbus, Ohio 43209.

CAREER: Shook Associates Corp., Columbus, Ohio, chairman of board, 1961—, partner in Atlantic Division, 1964-78; American Executive Corp., Columbus, chairman of board, 1973-78; American Executive Life Insurance Co., Phoenix, Ariz., chairman of board, 1973-78; full-time writer, 1978—. Director, J. Ashburn Youth Center, 1974—; member of board, Columbus Film Association, 1980-82. *Military service:* U.S. Army, 1960; U.S. Army Reserves, 1960-61.

WRITINGS—Published by Harper, except as indicated: (With father, Herbert M. Shook) *How to Be the Complete Professional Salesman,* Fell, 1974; (with Ronald L. Bingaman) *Total Commitment,* Fell, 1975; *Winning Images: Nothing Succeeds Like the Appearance of Success,* Macmillan, 1977; *Ten Greatest Salespersons* (Fortune Book-of-the-Month selection), 1978; *The Entrepreneurs,* 1980; *The Real Estate People,* 1980; *The Chief Executive Officers,* 1981; (ghostwriter) *Mary Kay* (autobiography), 1981; (with Martin Shafiroff) *Successful Telephone Selling in the 80's,* 1982; *Why Didn't I Think of That?,* New American Library, 1982; *The Shaklee Story,* 1982.

WORK IN PROGRESS: Women in Non-Traditional Work; The Survivors: A Profile of Long-Term Cancer Patients.

SIDELIGHTS: Robert L. Shook writes: "I have a business background, and have always been sales-oriented. In considering an idea for a book I always address myself to the questions: What is my market? Who will want to buy a book on this subject? After all, like any other businessperson, an author has a product that must be sold. In negotiating with publishers, I always offer to help market the book in many non-traditional ways (outside retail book stores). I believe that an author must make every effort to help sell his book. My motto is, 'Nothing happens until something is sold.'"

BIOGRAPHICAL/CRITICAL SOURCES: New York Times Book Review, April 13, 1980; *Washington Post,* October 23, 1981; *Los Angeles Times Book Review,* July 18, 1982.

* * *

SHORES, Louis 1904-1981

PERSONAL: Born September 14, 1904, in Buffalo, N.Y.; died June 19, 1981; son of Paul (a painter) and Ernestine (Lutenberg) Shores; married Geraldine Urist, November 19, 1931. *Education:* University of Toledo, B.A., 1926; City College (now City College of the City University of New York), M.S., 1927; Columbia University, B.S. in L.S., 1928; attended University of Chicago, 1929-30; George Peabody College for Teachers (now George Peabody College for Teachers of Vanderbilt University), Ph.D., 1934. *Politics:* Democrat. *Religion:* Baptist. *Home:* 2013 W. Randolph Circle, Tallahassee, Fla. 32303.

Office: Room 304, Strozier Library, Florida State University, Tallahassee, Fla.

CAREER: New York Public Library, New York, N.Y., reference assistant, 1926-28; Fisk University, Nashville, Tenn., professor of library science and librarian, 1928-33; George Peabody College for Teachers (now George Peabody College for Teachers of Vanderbilt University), Nashville, Tenn., librarian, 1933-37, director of library school, 1933-46; Florida State University, Tallahassee, professor and dean of library school, 1946-67, professor emeritus and dean emeritus, 1967-81. Special lecturer in library science, McGill University, Montreal, Quebec, Canada, 1930, University of Dayton, Dayton, Ohio, 1931, and Colorado State College of Education (now University of Northern Colorado), Greeley, 1936; visiting professor, Southern Illinois University, University of Colorado, Dalhousie University, University of Georgia, Morehead State University, and Johnson C. Smith University. Director, Tex-Tec, 1967-68. Chairman of Governor's Commission on Works Progress Administration Community Service Projects, 1939-41; member of literary advisory board, Air University, Maxwell Air Force Base, 1952-56. *Military service:* U.S. Army Air Forces, 1942-46; became major. Air Corps Reserve, 1946-53. Awarded Legion of Merit.

MEMBER: Association of College and Reference Librarians (director), American Library Association, American Library History Roundtable (founder), National Education Association, Southeastern Library Association (president, 1950-52), Phi Kappa Phi, Phi Delta Kappa, Kappa Delta Pi, Pi Gamma Mu, President's Club (charter member), Lions Club. *Awards, honors:* Senior Fulbright research fellow, 1951-52; Beta Phi Mu Award in Library Education, 1967; Library-College Associates, Isadore Gilbert Mudge Citation, 1967, and citation for founding library-college movement, 1971; D.H.L., Dallas Baptist College, 1970.

WRITINGS: *How to Use Your Library: A Series of Articles on Libraries for High School and College Students* (pamphlet), Scholastic Publishing Co., 1928; *Origins of the American College Library, 1638-1800,* George Peabody College for Teachers, 1934, reprinted, Gregg, 1972; *The Library Arts College: A Possibility in 1954?* (pamphlet), School and Society, 1935; (with Walter Scott Monroe) *Bibliographies and Summaries in Education to July 1935: A Catalog of More Than 4000 Annotated Bibliographies and Summaries Listed under Author and Subject in One Alphabet,* H. W. Wilson, 1936; *Basic Reference Books: An Introduction to the Evaluation, Study, and Use of Reference Materials with Special Emphasis on Some 200 Titles,* American Library Association, 1937, 2nd edition, 1939; *Know Your Encyclopedia: A Unit of Library Instruction Based on "Compton's Pictured Encyclopedia"* (pamphlet), F. E. Compton, 1937; (with Joseph E. Moore) *Peabody Library Information Test: Elementary Level Form A* (pamphlet), Educational Publishers, 1940; (with Moore) *Peabody Library Information Test: High School Level Form A* (pamphlet), Educational Publishers, 1940; (with Moore) *Peabody Library Information Test: College Level Form A* (pamphlet), Educational Publishers, 1940; *Highways in the Sky: The Story of the AACS,* Barnes & Noble, 1947; *Libraries in Florida: A Survey of Library Opportunities in the State* (pamphlet), Florida Library Association Survey Committee, 1948; *Not for Tourists* (pamphlet), Florida Library Association Library Action Committee, 1948.

(Editor with W. Hugh Strickler and James P. Stoakes) *General Education: A University Program in Action,* W. C. Brown, c. 1950; (editor) *Challenges to Librarianship,* Florida State University, c. 1953; *Basic Reference Sources: An Introduction to Materials and Methods,* American Library Association, 1954, reprinted, Libraries Unlimited, 1973; (editor with John D. Marshall and Wayne Shirley) *Books-Libraries-Librarians,* Shoe String, 1955; *A Profession of Faith* (pamphlet), State University (Geneseo, N.Y.), 1958; (editor) *Basic Materials for Florida Junior College Libraries: Reference Books,* Florida State Department of Education, 1960; *Instructional Materials: An Introduction for Teachers,* Ronald, 1960; *Mark Hopkins' Log, and Other Essays,* selected by John D. Marshall, Shoe String, 1965; (editor with Robert Jordan and John Harvey) *The Library-College: Contributions for American Higher Education at the Jamestown College Workshop, 1965,* Drexel Press, 1966; (with others) *The Tex-Tec Syllabi: Courses of Study for the Texas State Library,* Communication Service Corp., 1968; *Library-College USA: Essays on a Prototype for an American Higher Education,* South Pass Press, 1970; *Library Education,* Libraries Unlimited, 1972; *Looking forward to 1999,* South Pass Press, 1972; *Audiovisual Librarianship: The Crusade for Media Unity (1946-1969),* Libraries Unlimited, 1973; *Quiet World: A Librarian's Crusade for Destiny—The Professional Autobiography of Louis Shores,* Linnet Books, 1975; *Reference as the Promotion of Free Inquiry,* Libraries Unlimited, 1976; *The Generic Book: What It Is and How It Works,* Library-College Associates, 1977.

Contributor: Samuel Smith, *Best Methods of Study,* Barnes & Noble, 1938, 3rd revised edition, 1958; Bernard Berelson, editor, *Education for Librarianship,* American Library Association, 1949; Alfred Stefferud, editor, *The Wonderful Wolrd of Books,* Houghton, c. 1952; (with Mary Alice Hunt) Laurence R. Campbell, editor, *Careers in Journalism,* Quill and Scroll Foundation, 1955; Harry Shaw, editor, *A Collection of Readings for Writers: Book Three of a Complete Course in Freshman English,* 4th edition, Harper, 1955; John D. Marshall, compiler, *Of, by, and for Librarians,* Shoe String, 1960; Marshall, compiler, *An American Library History Reader,* Shoe String, 1961; LaNelle Vandiver, editor, *University of Tennessee Library Lectures,* University of Tennessee, 1961; (with Helen Danford and Lila Eubanks) Marshall, editor, *In Pursuit of Library History,* Library School, Florida State University, 1961; Leslie Whitaker Dunlap, *The Story of Our Libraries,* [New York], 1962; Arthur R. Rowland, compiler, *Reference Services,* Shoe String, 1963. Contributor to *The Library in General Education: National Society for the Study of Education Forty-Second Yearbook, Part II,* Society for the Study of Education, 1943.

Author of introduction: Mabel E. Wiloughby, editor, *SELA Directory of Member Libraries and Librarians in the Southeast,* Southeastern Library Association, 1952; Robert W. Murphey, *How and Where to Look It Up: A Guide to Standard Sources of Information,* McGraw, 1958; (with Loutrell Cavin) *Strategic Air Command Library Workshop,* Library School, Florida State University, 1959; Allen Morris, compiler, *The Florida Handbook,* Peninsula Publishing Co., 1962, new edition, 1963.

Also author of *Speculation: Concerns with Ultimates,* 1977, and *Encyclopedia: A Commonplace Book,* 1977. Editorial advisor and contributor, *Compton's Pictured Encyclopedia,* 1934-41; *Collier's Encyclopedia,* associate editor, 1946-60, editor-in-chief, beginning 1960; editor, *Merit Students Encyclopedia,* beginning 1967. Editor, *Annual Reference Check List of Library Journals,* 1954-58. Editorial director, "Harvard Classics Home Study Program" series, eleven volumes, Crowell-Collier, 1961.

Contributor to professional journals and popular magazines. Editor, *Current Reference Books, Current Reference Aids,* and *Journal of Library History,* 1965-68; contributing editor and advisory editor, *Learning Today.*

WORK IN PROGRESS: The Quiet Force; College Educate Yourself; Of Media and Man, a book on communications.

SIDELIGHTS: Louis Shores once told *CA:* "Steadily, a faith in librarianship as the profession of destiny grew mystically. Perhaps four years of war, especially the first two rough years in the CBI theatre away from library work, strenghthened my belief in what I have titled my next book, *The Quiet Force.* Possibly my growing concern with the meaning of death . . . and a mounting concern that the devotion to research (a la the scientific method) may be a principal obstacle to coming to grips with the ultimate are lashing me to rouse my colleagues against the ancillary 'retriever' outlook that has shaped the librarian image of the past. In short, I long to balance our national passion for 'where the action is' with a bit of meditation and introspection, to rescue a few hours from the discotheque for reading in the bibliotheque.

"The quest continues for an extrasensory solution to the 'Riddle of the Universe.' Library quiet, I am convinced, is a necessary prelude—the climate that will enable us to devote ourselves to some ultimates. *Looking forward to 1999* dissented with the activists of the sixties, the groovies, who despite their hypothetical claims of idealism were engaged in proximates. Their noise and bombast must be replaced with quiet; their corny 'explosions' with implosions."

BIOGRAPHICAL/CRITICAL SOURCES: John D. Marshall, *Louis Shores: A Bibliography,* Beta Phi Mu (Gamma Chapter), Florida State University Library School, 1964; *Quiet World: A Librarian's Crusade for Destiny—The Professional Autobiography of Louis Shores,* Linnet Books, 1975.†

* * *

SHORT, James F(ranklin, Jr.) 1924-

PERSONAL: Born June 22, 1924, in Sangamon County, Ill.; son of James Franklin and Ruth (Walbaum) Short; married Kelma Hegberg, December 27, 1947. *Education:* Attended Shurtleff College, 1942-43; Denison University, B.A., 1947; University of Chicago, M.A., 1949, Ph.D., 1951. *Politics:* Democrat. *Religion:* Unitarian Universalist. *Home:* 425 Dexter St. S.E., Pullman, Wash. 99163. *Office:* Graduate School, Washington State University, Pullman, Wash.

CAREER: Washington State University, Pullman, 1951—, began as instructor, became professor of sociology, dean of Graduate School, 1964-68, director of Social Research Center, 1970—. Visiting associate professor of sociology, University of Chicago, 1959-62; visiting professor at University of Hawaii, 1969, and Stanford University, 1975. Cecil and Ida Green Visiting Professor Chair, Texas Christian University, 1979. Fellow of Institute of Criminology and King's College, University of Cambridge, 1976. Director of research, National Commission on the Cause and Prevention of Violence, 1968-69. Consultant to National Institute of Mental Health, Ford Foundation, National Science Foundation, Behavior Science Section, President's Committee on Juvenile Delinquency and Youth Crime, Chicago Youth Development Program, and many other institutions and organizations. *Military service:* U.S. Marine Corps Reserve, 1943-46, became second lieutenant.

MEMBER: American Sociological Association (fellow; member of council, section on criminology, 1960-63; member of research committee, 1962-64; chairman of research committee, 1963; council member-at-large, 1967-70; secretary-elect, 1977; secretary, 1978-80), Society for the Study of Social Problems (membership chairman, 1957-58; member of executive committee, 1965, 1966), National Council on Crime and Delinquency (member of research council, 1968—), Law and Society Association (trustee, 1981-83), Pacific Sociological Association (Northern vice-president, 1965; president, 1966).

AWARDS, HONORS: Faculty research fellowship from Social Science Research Council, 1953-56; National Institute of Mental Health grant, 1959-65, special fellowship, 1969-70; Ford Foundation grant, 1961-67; Curriculum Development Grant from President's Committee on Juvenile Delinquency and Youth Crime, 1962-65; honorary degree recipient from Denison University, 1975; Guggenheim fellow, 1975-76; Paul W. Tappan Award from Western Society of Criminology, 1977; Edwin H. Sutherland Award from American Society of Criminology, 1979.

WRITINGS: (With Andrew F. Henry) *Suicide and Homicide,* Free Press of Glencoe, 1954, 2nd edition, 1964; (with Fred L. Strodtbeck) *Group Process and Gang Delinquency,* University of Chicago Press, 1965, 2nd edition, 1974; *The State of Sociology: Problems and Prospects,* Sage Publications, 1981.

Editor: *The Gang: A Study of 1,313 Gangs in Chicago,* University of Chicago Press, 1963; *Gang Delinquency and Delinquent Subcultures,* Harper, 1968; *Delinquency and Urban Areas,* revised edition (Short was not associated with earlier edition), University of Chicago Press, 1969; (and contributor) *Modern Criminals,* Aldine, 1970, 2nd edition, Dutton, 1973; *The Social Fabric of the Metropolis,* University of Chicago Press, 1971; (with Marvin E. Wolfgang; and contributor) *Collective Violence,* Aldine-Atherton, 1972; *Crime, Delinquency, and Society,* University of Chicago Press, 1976.

Contributor: E. S. Schneidman and N. S. Farberow, editors, *Clues to Suicide,* McGraw, 1957; Robert A. Nisbet and Robert K. Merton, editors, *Contemporary Social Problems,* 2nd edition, Harcourt, 1961, 5th edition, 1976; Marshal Clinard, editor, *Anomie and Deviant Behavior,* Free Press of Glencoe, 1964, 2nd edition, 1971; Carolyn Sherif and Mazafer Sherif, editors, *Problems of Youth: Transition to Adulthood in a Changing World,* Aldine, 1965; Malcolm W. Klein, editor, *Juvenile Gangs in Context: Theory, Research and Action,* Prentice-Hall, 1967; Irving Louis Horowitz, editor, *Sociological Self-Images: A Collective Portrait,* Sage Publications, 1969; Daniel Glaser, editor, *Handbook of Criminology,* Rand McNally, 1974; N. J. Demerath III, Otto Larsen, and Karl F. Schuessler, editors, *Social Policy,* Academic Press, 1975; Mirra Komarovsky, editor, *Sociology and Social Policy,* Elsevier Press, 1975; Duncan Chappell and John Monahan, editors, *Violence and Criminal Justice,* Heath, 1975; LaMar T. Empey, editor, *The Future of Childhood and Juvenile Justice,* University Press of Virginia, 1979; David Shichor and Delos Kelly, editors, *Critical Issues in Juvenile Delinquency: Facing the Last Quarter of the Twentieth Century,* Heath, 1980; Klein and Katherine S. Teilman, editors, *Handbook of Criminal Justice Evaluation,* Sage Publications, 1980.

Contributor to numerous professional publications and to encyclopedias. Associate editor, *Social Problems,* 1958-61, 1967-69, *American Sociologist,* 1968-69, and *Criminology Review Yearbook,* 1972—. *Journal of Research in Crime and Delinquency,* special issue editor, January, 1967, member of board of editors, 1968—; *American Sociological Review,* associate editor, 1960-63, 1970-71, editor, 1972-74; *Annual Review of Sociology,* member of editorial committee, 1978—, associate editor, 1980—. Advisory editor of *Transaction,* 1963-69, and *American Journal of Sociology,* 1964-72; consulting editor, *Suicide and Life Threatening Behavior,* 1970-75; editorial consultant, *Journal of Criminal Law and Criminology,* 1976—.

WORK IN PROGRESS: "Research on the social impact of crime and natural disasters and on 'acceptable risk.'"

SHRYOCK, (Edwin) Harold 1906-

PERSONAL: Born April 14, 1906, in Seattle, Wash.; son of Alfred Quimby (a physician) and Stella (Tefft) Shryock; married Daisy May Bagwell (a registered nurse), April 30, 1929; children: Patricia Helen (Mrs. G. Carleton Wallace), Edwin F. Education: Pacific Union College, B.S., 1930; Loma Linda University, M.D., 1934; University of Southern California, M.A., 1939. Religion: Seventh-day Adventist. Home: 11593 Acacia St., Box 638, Loma Linda, Calif. 92354.

CAREER: Pacific Union College, Angwin, Calif., instructor in chemistry, 1930-31; Loma Linda University, School of Medicine, Loma Linda, Calif., instructor, 1934-39, assistant professor, 1939-45, associate professor, 1945-57, professor of anatomy and chairman of department, 1957-75, associate dean, 1950-51, dean, 1951-54. Personal counselor. Member: American Association of Anatomists, American Association for the Advancement of Science, Sigma Xi, Alpha Omega Alpha.

WRITINGS: Happiness for Husbands and Wives, Review & Herald, 1949; Happiness and Health, Pacific Press Publishing Association, 1950; On Becoming a Man, Review & Herald, 1951; On Becoming a Woman, Review & Herald, 1951; Highways to Health, Review & Herald, 1953; Living, Pacific Press Publishing Association, 1958; Mind If I Smoke?, Pacific Press Publishing Association, 1959, revised edition, 1965; On Being Sweethearts, Review & Herald, 1966; On Being Married Soon, Review & Herald, 1968; You and Your Health, Pacific Press Publishing Association, 1970, revised edition, 1984; Your Amazing Body, Southern Publishing, 1971; What to Do in an Emergency, Pacific Press Publishing Association, 1978; Modern Medical Guide, Pacific Press Publishing Association, 1979; We've Come a Long Way, Maybe, Pacific Press Publishing Association, 1981. Contributor of about a dozen articles to medical journals.

* * *

SICHEL, Werner 1934-

PERSONAL: Born September 23, 1934, in Munich, Germany; son of Joseph and Lilly (Greenwood) Sichel; married Beatrice Bonne, February 22, 1959; children: Lawrence, Linda. Education: New York University, B.S., 1956; Northwestern University, M.A., 1960, Ph.D., 1964. Home: 5046 Merryview Dr., Kalamazoo, Mich. 49008. Office: Department of Economics, Western Michigan University, Kalamazoo, Mich. 49008.

CAREER: Roosevelt University, Chicago, Ill., assistant professor, 1959-60; Western Michigan University, Kalamazoo, instructor, 1960-64, assistant professor, 1964-66, associate professor, 1966-72, professor of economics, 1972—. Instructor, Lake Forest College, 1959-62; Fulbright senior lecturer, University of Belgrade, 1968-69. Member: American Economic Association.

WRITINGS: (With Peter Eckstein) Basic Economic Concepts: An Aid to the Study of Economic Problems, Rand McNally, 1974, 2nd edition, 1977, Volume I: Microeconomics, Volume II: Macroeconomics.

Editor: Industrial Organization and Public Policy: Selected Readings, Houghton, 1967; Antitrust Policy and Economic Welfare, Bureau of Business Research, University of Michigan, 1970; (with Thomas G. Gies) Public Utility Regulation: Change and Scope, Heath, 1975; The Economic Effects of Multinational Corporations, Bureau of Business Research, University of Michigan, 1975; Salvaging Public Utility Regulation, Lexington Books, 1976; Economic Advice and Executive Policy: Recommendations from Past Members of the Council of Economics Advisers, Praeger, 1978; Public Utility Rate Making in an Energy Conscious Environment, Westview, 1979; (with Gies) Applications of Economic Principles in Public Utility Industries, Division of Research, Graduate School of Business Administration, University of Michigan, 1981; (with Gies) Deregulation: Appraisal before the Fact, Division of Research, Graduate School of Business Administration, University of Michigan, 1982.

Contributor of articles to professional journals, including Journal of Risk and Insurance, St. John's Law Review, Antitrust Bulletin, and Journal of Economic Issues.

* * *

SILLITOE, Alan 1928-

PERSONAL: Born March 4, 1928, in Nottingham, England; son of Christopher Archibald (a tannery laborer) and Sylvina (Burton) Sillitoe; married Ruth Esther Fainlight (a poet, writer, and translator), November 19, 1959; children: David Nimrod, Susan (adopted). Education: Left school at the age of fourteen. Home: 21 The Street, Wittersham, Kent, England. Agent: Tessa Sayle, 11 Jubilee Pl., London SW3 3TE, England.

CAREER: Worked in a bicycle plant, in a plywood mill, and as a capstan-lathe operator; free-lance writer, 1948—. Military service: Royal Air Force, radio operator in Malaya, 1946-49. Member: Society of Authors, Royal Geographical Society (fellow), Writers Action Group, Savage Club. Awards, honors: Author's Club prize, 1958, for Saturday Night and Sunday Morning; Hawthornden Prize for Literature, 1960, for The Loneliness of the Long-Distance Runner; honorary fellow, Manchester Polytechnic, 1977.

WRITINGS—Poems: Without Beer or Bread, Outpost Publications (London), 1957; The Rats, and Other Poems, W. H. Allen, 1960; A Falling out of Love, and Other Poems, W. H. Allen, 1964; Shaman, and Other Poems, Turret Books, 1968; Love in the Environs of Voronezh, and Other Poems, Macmillan (London), 1968, Doubleday, 1969; (contributor) Poems [by] Ruth Fainlight, Ted Hughes, Alan Sillitoe, Rainbow Press, 1971; Storm, and Other Poems, W. H. Allen, 1974; Barbarians, and Other Poems, Turret Books, 1974; Snow on the North Side of Lucifer, W. H. Allen, 1979.

Novels: Saturday Night and Sunday Morning, W. H. Allen, 1958, Knopf, 1959, revised edition, with an introduction by the author and commentary and notes by David Craig, Longmans, Green, 1968; The General, W. H. Allen, 1960, Knopf, 1961; Key to the Door, W. H. Allen, 1961, Knopf, 1962; The Death of William Posters, Knopf, 1965; A Tree on Fire, Macmillan (London), 1967, Doubleday, 1968; A Start in Life, W. H. Allen, 1970, Scribner, 1971; Travel in Nihilon, W. H. Allen, 1971, Scribner, 1972; The Flame of Life, W. H. Allen, 1974; The Widower's Son, W. H. Allen, 1976, Harper, 1977; The Storyteller, W. H. Allen, 1979, Simon & Schuster, 1980; Her Victory, F. Watts, 1982.

Short stories: The Loneliness of the Long-Distance Runner, W. H. Allen, 1959, Knopf, 1960, bound with Sanctuary, by Theodore Dreiser, and related poems, edited by Roy Bentley, Book Society of Canada, 1967; The Ragman's Daughter, W. H. Allen, 1961, Knopf, 1964; Guzman Go Home, and Other Stories, Macmillan (London), 1968, Doubleday, 1969; A Sillitoe Selection, Longmans, Green, 1968; Men, Women and Children, W. H. Allen, 1973, Scribner, 1974; The Second Chance, Simon & Schuster, 1981.

Plays: (Translator and adapter with Ruth Fainlight) Lope de Vega, *All Citizens Are Soldiers* (two-act; first produced in Stratford, England, at Theatre Royal, 1967), Macmillan (London), 1969, Dufour, 1970; "This Foreign Field," first produced in London at Round House, 1970, published in *Three Plays* (also see below) as "The Slot Machine," W. H. Allen, 1978; *Three Plays: The Slot Machine, The Interview, Pit Strike* (*The Interview* was produced at the Almost Free Theatre, 1978), W. H. Allen, 1978.

Other: *Road to Volgograd* (travel), Knopf, 1964; (author of introduction) Arnold Bennett, *Riceyman Steps,* Pan Books, 1964; (author of introduction) Bennett, *The Old Wives' Tale,* Pan Books, 1964; *The City Adventures of Marmalade Jim* (juvenile), Macmillan, 1967; *Raw Material* (memoir), W. H. Allen, 1972, Scribner, 1973; *Mountains and Caverns* (essays), W. H. Allen, 1975; *Big John and the Stars* (juvenile), Robson Books, 1977; *The Incredible Fencing Fleas* (juvenile), Robson Books, 1978; *Marmalade Jim on the Farm* (juvenile), Robson Books, 1979. Also author of film script adaptations of his novel *Saturday Night and Sunday Morning* and of his short stories "The Loneliness of the Long-Distance Runner" and "The Ragman's Daughter"; author of film script "Che Guevara," 1968.

WORK IN PROGRESS: A novel; a new collection of poems.

SIDELIGHTS: "I was twenty years old when I first tried to write, and it took ten years before I learned how to do it." Thus remarked Alan Sillitoe in reference to *Saturday Night and Sunday Morning,* the novel that catapulted the thirty-year-old self-educated Briton into the literary limelight. Described by the *New Yorker*'s Anthony West as a "brilliant first book," *Saturday Night and Sunday Morning* broke new ground with its portrayal of "the true robust and earthy quality characteristic of English working-class life." Only one year later, Sillitoe was again the center of critical attention, this time for "The Loneliness of the Long-Distance Runner," the title novella in a collection of short stories which also contained some frank representations of working-class life in Britain. Although he has since written numerous novels and short stories, as well as several poems and plays, Sillitoe has almost always been evaluated in terms of these first two works. Both, in fact, are the focus of a debate that has yet to be resolved: is Alan Sillitoe a traditionalist, a sentimental throwback to writers of an earlier age, or is he a genuine "revolutionary," an Angry Young Man of the modern age?

On a thematic level, Sillitoe seems to draw inspiration from both the old and the new. As is true of many contemporary writers, he often centers his stories around an individual isolated from society, studying what the *Guardian*'s Roy Perrot calls "the spirit of the outsider, the dissenter, the man apart." But instead of limiting himself strictly to the psychological confines of this one person and allowing the rest of the world to remain somewhat shadowy, Sillitoe places his rebellious outsider in a gritty, distinctive milieu—Nottingham, an English industrial town (and the author's birthplace) where, as Charles Champlin explains in the *Los Angeles Times,* "the lower-middle and working classes rub, where breaking even looks like victory, and London is a long way South." This strong regionalism, reminiscent of the regionalism common in nineteenth-century British fiction, is one of the most striking features of Sillitoe's writing.

Sillitoe populates his rather grim world with factory workers, shop girls, and other types not often depicted from the inside in English literature. Whether they are at home, at work, or relaxing in the pubs, these characters reveal themselves to be "unfamiliar with the great world of London or country houses or what is called high culture," says the *Chicago Tribune Book World*'s Kendall Mitchell. "And they don't care—they have their lives to live, their marriages to make and wreck, their passions to pursue." "The cumulative impression of Sillitoe's people," notes Champlin, "is of their strength and will to survive, however forces beyond their control blunt their prospects."

These "forces beyond their control" play a major role in the author's fiction; Sillitoe's conception of fate, however, differs from the classical one in that economic and social factors, not the whim of the gods, determine one's destiny. As James Gindin writes in *Postwar British Fiction*: "Nothing really changes Sillitoe's jungle world. A man may win or lose, depending on the wheel of chance, but he cannot control the wheel or change his position. Often, too, the wheel is rigged, for the same numbers keep coming up as privilege and power keep reinforcing themselves." In short, comments Saul Maloff in *Contemporary British Novelists*, "for Sillitoe, class is fate."

John W. Aldridge expands on this idea in the book *Time to Murder and Create* but suggests that Sillitoe's belief in the power of fate hinders rather than helps the reader to understand his characters and their motivations. States the critic: "To the extent that his people are the victims of their economic situation, they are people without the power of moral freedom. And to the extent that they are unfree, and lack even the opportunity to be enticed to choose freedom and to be damned by it, they are grossly oversimplified as fictional characters, pawns in a chess game in which every move is necessary and therefore none is possible. . . . Hence, nothing they think is interesting, nothing they do is finally worth doing, and nothing they want will in the end be of any value whatever to them. There can be no doubt that one may be impressed by this and frequently moved to compassion. But one is emphatically not moved to understanding."

Yet as even Aldridge admits, Sillitoe is a master at presenting his material in such a way that compassion, and not disgust, is what most readers feel for his rough-edged characters. Several critics, including the *Washington Post*'s Daniel O'Neill, credit the author with an "ability to blend cold-blooded rendering of the exterior world with insightful and sensitive representation of the inner workings of the characters' minds." According to Max Cosman of *Commonweal,* "such is Mr. Sillitoe's interest in his fellow man and such his skill in compelling attention, that ignoble, or subnormal as his Nottinghamites are, they can [bring] forth compassion even in the midst of disapproval."

Others, however, feel that this emphasis on compassion makes Sillitoe less an Angry Young Man with a special talent for describing the plight of the proletariat than a sentimentalist who idealizes the lives of his working-class heroes. Though the *New Republic*'s Irving Howe is pleased by the lack of romanticization, "moral nagging [and] political exhortation" in *Saturday Night and Sunday Morning,* for instance, he nevertheless concludes that "in its hard-headed and undeluded way it is not quite free from sentimentality." The *New York Review of Books*'s Stanley Kauffmann is especially critical of what he feels is Sillitoe's mishandling of pathos, pointing out that "often he appeals for sympathy with music-hall blatancy." David Boroff of the *Saturday Review* agrees that Sillitoe is "sometimes betrayed by his own sentimentality," as does a *Times Literary Supplement* critic, who suggests that such lapses may stem not from the author's attitude toward his subject but from "the difficulties presented by the use of a fictitious narrator who is not supposed to be as articulate or as sophisticated as the writer himself."

Sillitoe's practice of speaking through a narrator who is less articulate and sophisticated than himself has resulted in a style many critics have trouble classifying. As Champlin notes, "at times the essayist, social historian and social reporter in Sillitoe seems simply to have chosen fiction as the best carrier of impressions he wants to leave and points he wants to make." Consequently, remarks Kauffmann, his writing "fluctuates from straight hard prose to Nottingham slang to the most literary effusions, often all on the same page." In most other respects, comment a number of reviewers, including the *Times Literary Supplement*'s John Lucas, Sillitoe's style is "peculiarly artless" in that "even the best of [the stories] work in a manner that is unusual or unorthodox." There is, for example, no particularly strong emphasis on plot in a Sillitoe story, no "half hidden thread than can be traced," no sudden flash or insight that makes everything clear; as Lucas states, "nothing happens: there is no revelation, the story hardly seems to be a story at all." West also notices that Sillitoe's stories are "so firmly rooted in experience, and so ably handled, that they do not seem to have been written at all; they seem to be occurrences of a most engrossing and absorbing kind." Gene Baro agrees with this assessment of the author, writing in the *New York Herald Tribune Book Review* that "Sillitoe exhibits . . . lucid design, pace, a gift for salty vernacular, an unerring eye for the telling gesture, a robust and yet a restrained sense of the comic. . . . All is achieved simply, matter-of-factly, without apparent striving for effect."

A *Times Literary Supplement* critic is especially impressed by Sillitoe's "integrity of style that never falsifies the writer's role—which is why, for instance, he refuses to go on 'like a penny-a-liner to force an ending' if inspiration stops before he knows what to do with the character he has created. There may not even *be* an ending to a Sillitoe story." John Updike notices this same feature in Sillitoe's writing, pointing out in a *New Republic* article that his stories "have a wonderful way of going on, of not stopping short . . . that lifts us twice, and shows enviable assurance and abundance in the writer."

P. H. Johnson of the *New Statesman* also regards Sillitoe as "highly gifted technically: he is an excellent story-teller, and his style is perfectly adapted to his subject-matter; he has literary tact and a sense of design." The *Saturday Review*'s James Yaffe reports that among Sillitoe's "many wonderful qualities" are "a fluent, often brilliant command of language, an acute ear for dialect, [and] a virtuoso ability to describe the sight, sound, and smell of things."

What reviewers cannot agree upon in their evaluations of Sillitoe's work is whether he writes in the tradition of an earlier age (notably the American proletarian novelists of the 1930s) or in the tradition of certain British authors of the 1950s and 1960s whose bitter attacks on the political and social establishment earned them the name "Angry Young Men." Kauffmann, for one, feels Sillitoe is a victim of the cultural "'time-lag'" that exists between the United States and England and is therefore merely rediscovering the themes that once preoccupied American writers such as John Steinbeck, Erskine Caldwell, Theodore Dreiser, and John Dos Passos. Maloff shares this view, commenting: "Sillitoe is a throwback, an old-fashioned realist—in fact, a regionalist. He has attempted to make viable as art what was called, without embarrassment or sneering, the 'proletarian novel' in the 1930's. His protagonists are profoundly rooted in their class, and draw such strengths as they possess—or come finally to possess—from that identification. . . . In this central respect, Sillitoe is almost a solitary figure among the writers of the post-war generation. . . . [He] is a historical surprise. In the utterly changed circumstances of the fifties and sixties, he has partially validated as art the 'proletarian novel' of the thirties; and standing eccentrically against the current driven by his defter contemporaries, he has made possible a working-class novel."

Aldridge suggests that part of Sillitoe's inspiration may date back even earlier than the 1930s. States the critic: "Sillitoe stands as a comforting reminder to the English that the grand old roistering 'low life' tradition of Fielding and Dickens may have lost its sting, but is not yet dead. . . . Although [the author] does have his grievances, he seems basically content to keep the working man in his place, and as a writer he evidently wants to remain a working man. . . . [But other writers] did all that he has done first and better than he. It might be objected that working-class life is, after all, Sillitoe's material, and that he ought to have a perfect right to use it if he so chooses. But there is little virtue in repeating the discoveries or the mistakes of one's predecessors, or in trying to make literature out of a cultural lag that merely social reform and the payment of some money can rectify."

Allen R. Penner of *Contemporary Literature* also sees traces of an old-fashioned literary tradition in Sillitoe's works—but with a modern twist. Explains Penner: "'The Loneliness of the Long-Distance Runner' . . . is written in a tradition in English fiction which dates at least from Elizabethan times, in . . . the rogue's tale, or thief's autobiography. . . . [But Sillitoe] has reversed the formula of the popular crime tale of fiction, wherein the reader enjoys vicariously witnessing the exploits of the outlaw and then has the morally reassuring pleasure of seeing the doors of the prison close upon him in the conclusion. Sillitoe begins his tale in prison, and he ends it before the doors have opened again, leaving us with the unsettling realization that the doors will indeed open and that the criminal will be released unreformed." This emphasis on unrepentant rebellion, says Penner, proves that "Sillitoe was never, really, simply an 'angry young man.' His hostility was not a transitory emotion of youth, but a permanent rancor well grounded in class hatred. 'The Loneliness of the Long-Distance Runner' contains the seeds of the revolutionary philosophy which would eventually attain full growth in his works."

On the other hand, some critics see nothing but youthful anger in Sillitoe's writings. Commenting in the *New York Times Book Review*, Malcolm Bradbury notes that "if the heroes of some . . . English novels are angry young men, Mr. Sillitoe is raging; and though he doesn't know it, he is raging for much the same reasons." Champlin remarks that Sillitoe's emergence was "a sharp signaling of an end to quiet acceptance of the way things are. It was a protest, fueled by the war, against the stratified status quo. . . . Unlike some of Britain's angry young men who have matured and prospered into more conservative postures, Sillitoe remains the poet of the anonymous millions in the council flats and the cold-water attached houses, noting the ignored, remembering the half-forgotten."

Though John R. Clark of the *Saturday Review* also sees Sillitoe as an Angry Young Man, he feels that "his anger and fictions have altered with time. In [his] early work there was something single-minded and intense in the actions and scenes, particularly in the shorter novels. . . . Later novels reveal a broader social and political horizon. Sillitoe's characters not only privately rebel but become dedicated to larger 'movements.'"

Prairie Schooner's Robert S. Haller rejects the notion that Sillitoe is an Angry Young Man. "If this title is justified for any writers," he begins, "it would be so for [those] men with university training who wanted room at the top but who resented the moral and aesthetic cost of getting there. But it hardly applies to Sillitoe [and others] who are authentically of the working class, self-educated, and uninterested in the matter of rising to the upper classes. . . . Anger is the resentment of frustrated ambition; neither Sillitoe nor his early heroes see in established values and styles anything to aspire to."

Nor is Sillitoe's style based on that of any grand literary tradition, Haller goes on to state. In fact, declares the critic, the author's "commitment to his [Nottinghamite] people has been an expression of a refusal to mimic the educated literary man." Consequently, books like *Saturday Night and Sunday Morning* and *The Loneliness of the Long-Distance Runner* "have been continuous best sellers because they provide a mirror for working-class readers and a window for others into a culture with its own richness of circumstance and its own integrity."

Sillitoe himself sees little merit in arguing about whether he is traditional or modern, sentimental or angry. As he told Igor Hajek in a *Nation* interview: "I cannot understand why people are always looking for trends and movements. Writers work just as all others: miners, engineers, psychologists. From their point [of view] trends do not exist. Why should they exist in writing? Although I admit that looking from a distance some similarities may appear, the writer himself usually does not realize it."

In this same interview, Sillitoe reveals that he is not at all dismayed by the fact that he is best known for his earliest works, especially "The Loneliness of the Long-Distance Runner." "I think those people [who remember me primarily as the author of 'The Loneliness of the Long-Distance Runner'] are absolutely right," he says. "This story of a working-class youth is at the same time the statement of my artistic integrity. I shall never write anything to uphold this Establishment and this society. And I'm ready to stick to my principles even to a self-damaging extent."

Continues the author: "Whatever I have against [English society] I say through my characters: every character in my books has an opinion, and they are all mine. On the other hand, it is very difficult to write about something you hate, you have to try to understand and even show some sympathies. That is why people, who consider writers from a political rather than artistic viewpoint, accuse them of being treacherous: they take this for sympathizing with enemy. . . . If they ask me what I am, a Communist or Socialist, etc., I can only answer that I'm on the Left, beyond that I can't say much. . . . A writer never stands still. When you are young, everything is simple, but I am not young any more, [which] means that I am leaving a lot of simplicities behind. Basic beliefs stay, but things now look more complex."

In short, concludes Sillitoe, "Each individual has to make a choice: either to accept this society or stand up against it. . . . In this country, as in any other, a writer is liked if he is loyal to the system. But it is the writer's duty in a sense to be disloyal. In the modern world, he is one of the few people who are listened to, and his primary loyalty should be to his integrity and to his talent. He can speak up in many ways; the best way is to write a book."

MEDIA ADAPTATIONS: Continental filmed *Saturday Night and Sunday Morning* in 1960 and "The Loneliness of the Long-Distance Runner" in 1961; *The General* was filmed by Universal in 1968 and released under the title "Counterpoint."

BIOGRAPHICAL/CRITICAL SOURCES—Books: James Gindin, *Postwar British Fiction: New Accents and Attitudes,* University of California Press, 1962; Charles Shapiro, editor, *Contemporary British Novelists,* Southern Illinois University Press, 1965; John W. Aldridge, *Time to Murder and Create: The Contemporary Novel in Crisis,* McKay, 1966; *Contemporary Literary Criticism,* Gale, Volume I, 1973, Volume III, 1975, Volume VI, 1976, Volume X, 1979, Volume XIX, 1981; *Authors in the News,* Volume I, Gale, 1976.

Periodicals: *New York Herald Tribune Book Review,* August 16, 1959, May 29, 1960; *New York Times Book Review,* August 16, 1959, April 10, 1960, September 28, 1980, April 19, 1981; *New Republic,* August 24, 1959, May 9, 1960; *Yale Review,* September, 1959; *Commonweal,* September 4, 1959, April 29, 1960, March 27, 1964; *New Yorker,* September 5, 1959, June 11, 1960; *Saturday Review,* September 5, 1959, April 16, 1960, January 25, 1964, October 16, 1971; *Guardian,* September 25, 1959; *Spectator,* September 25, 1959; *Times Literary Supplement,* October 2, 1959, October 19, 1973, January 15, 1981, January 23, 1981; *New Statesman,* October 3, 1959; *San Francisco Chronicle,* November 29, 1959, May 1, 1960; *Time,* April 18, 1960; *New York Review of Books,* March 5, 1964; *Nation,* January 27, 1969; *Contemporary Literature,* Volume X, number 2, 1969; *Milwaukee Journal,* November 10, 1974; *Prairie Schooner,* winter, 1974/75; *Sewanee Review,* summer, 1975; *Los Angeles Times,* October 1, 1980, April 21, 1981; *Chicago Tribune Book World,* October 26, 1980, August 31, 1981; *Washington Post Book World,* October 26, 1980; *Washington Post,* June 2, 1981.

—Sketch by Deborah A. Straub

* * *

SIMINI, Joseph Peter 1921-

PERSONAL: Surname is pronounced See-*mee*-knee; born February 15, 1921, in Buffalo, N.Y.; son of Paul (a bakery owner) and Ida (Moro) Simini; married second wife, Marcelline T. McDermott, 1968; children: (first marriage) Paul. *Education:* St. Bonaventure University, B.S., 1940, B.B.A., 1949; University of California, Berkeley, M.B.A., 1957; Western Colorado University, D.B.A., 1981. *Politics:* Republican. *Religion:* Roman Catholic. *Home:* 2 Mountain Springs Rd., San Francisco, Calif. 94114. *Mailing address:* P.O. Box 31420, San Francisco, Calif. 94131.

CAREER: Inspector in war plants, 1940-41; U.S. Navy Department, Bureau of Ordnance, Buffalo and Rochester, N.Y., senior inspector of optical material, 1942-44; Paul Simini Bakery, Buffalo, manager and partner, 1946-48; St. Bonaventure University, St. Bonaventure, N.Y., part-time instructor in mathematics, 1948-49; auditor and accountant in San Francisco, Calif., with Di Giorgio Corp., 1950-52, Keaton & Miller, 1952-53, Price Waterhouse & Co., 1953-54; R. L. Hanlin (certified public accountants), San Francisco, senior accountant, 1954-55; University of San Francisco, San Francisco, instructor, 1955-57, assistant professor, 1957-62, associate professor, 1962-66, professor of accounting and business systems, 1966-79; writer, consultant, lecturer, and real estate developer, 1979—. Certified public accountant, state of California, 1954. Examiner, California State Board of Accountancy, 1964-69. Holder of patent on Dial-a-Trig, a trigonometric formula-finding device; inventor of Verbum Est, a word-building card game. *Military service:* U.S. Naval Reserve, 1944-46; became ensign.

MEMBER: American Institute of Certified Public Accountants, American Accounting Association, National Association of Accountants (president of San Francisco chapter, 1974-75; member of national education committee, 1975-77), American Management Associations (course developer, 1966—), American Arbitration Association (member of commercial panel), American Association of University Professors (past president of University of San Francisco chapter), California Society of Certified Public Accountants, Beta Alpha Psi, Delta Sigma Pi,

Beta Gamma Sigma, Knights of Columbus, Leonardo da Vinci Society (vice-president, 1981—), Il Cenacolo (president, 1979—), Olympic Club, Serra Club.

AWARDS, HONORS: Scouters' Key, Boy Scouts of America, 1960; Crown Zellerbach Foundation fellowship, 1968; Outstanding Teacher Award, College of Business Administration, University of San Francisco, 1973; Distinguished Teacher Award, University of San Francisco, 1975; Joseph Peter Simini Award created in his honor by University of San Francisco Student Accounting Association.

WRITINGS: (Co-author) *Principles of Accounting*, Pitman, 1959; *Accounting Made Simple*, Doubleday, 1966; (technical consultant) *Accounting Essentials*, Wiley, 1972; *Cost Accounting Concepts for Nonfinancial Executives*, American Management Associations, 1976; *Become Wealthy!*, Bottom Line Press, 1982. Contributor to *Navy Civil Engineer* and to newspapers and accounting journals.

WORK IN PROGRESS: *The Shroud of Christ*, a book about the shroud of Turin; a book on how non-profit organizations can increase their funds using tax rules.

SIDELIGHTS: "After a quarter of a century in the classroom," Joseph Peter Simini told *CA*, "writing is a logical way to extend the expanding of minds. Now the students don't have to be in the same room—they can be anywhere and my words are available day or night."

* * *

SIMON, Rita James 1931-

PERSONAL: Born November 26, 1931, in Brooklyn, N.Y.; daughter of Abraham (a businessman) and Irene (Waldman) Mintz; married Julian L. Simon (a professor), June 25, 1961; children: David, Judith, Daniel. *Education:* University of Wisconsin, B.A., 1952; Cornell University, graduate study, 1952-54; University of Chicago, Ph.D., 1957. *Religion:* Jewish. *Office:* Department of Sociology, University of Illinois, Urbana, Ill. 61822.

CAREER: University of Chicago, Chicago, Ill., research associate in Law School, 1958-61, assistant professor of sociology, 1959-61; Columbia University, School of Social Work, New York, N.Y., research associate, 1961-63; University of Illinois at Urbana-Champaign, associate professor, 1963-68, professor of sociology, 1968—, research professor of communications and professor in College of Law, 1971-74, professor of law and communications research, 1980—, head of department of sociology, 1968-70, director of law and society program, 1975-80. Annie W. Goodrich Visiting Professor, Graduate School of Nursing, Yale University, 1962-63; Hebrew University of Jerusalem, visiting lecturer, 1967-68, visiting professor, 1970-71 and 1974-75. Fellow, Center for Advanced Study, University of Illinois, 1980-81. Member of governor's committee on competency to stand trial, 1967-68; member of president's commission on the causes and prevention of violence, 1968-69; member of National Institute for Mental Health crime and delinquency review council, 1971-74; member of advisory screening committee in sociology for Fulbright-Hays applications, 1972-74. Consulting editor in sociology, JAI Press, Inc., 1976-81; consultant to PRC Public Management Services, Inc., 1977-79, and KOBA Associates, Inc., 1979—. *Member:* American Sociological Association (member of council, 1971-73), Phi Kappa Phi. *Awards, honors:* Guggenheim fellow, 1966; Ford Foundation fellow, 1971.

WRITINGS: *The Jury and the Defense of Insanity*, Little, Brown, 1967; (editor) *As We Saw the Thirties*, University of Illinois Press, 1967; (editor) *Readings in the Sociology of Law*, Chandler Publishing, 1968; (with Jeffrey O'Connell) *Payment for Pain and Suffering*, Insurers Press, 1972; *American Public Opinion, 1937-1970*, Rand McNally, 1974; (editor) *The Jury System*, Sage Publications, 1975; *Women and Crime*, Lexington Books, 1975; (with Howard Altstein) *Transracial Adoption*, Wiley, 1977; *Continuity and Change: A Study in Two Ethnic Communities in Israel*, Cambridge University Press, 1978; (editor) *Research in Law and Sociology*, JAI Press, 1978; (author of foreword) Barbara Heyl, *Madam as Entrepreneur*, Transaction Books, 1978; (editor with Freda Adler) *The Criminology of Deviant Women*, Houghton, 1979; *The American Jury*, Lexington Books, 1980; *Transracial Adoption: A Followup*, Lexington Books, 1981; (editor with Steven Spitzer) *Research in Law, Deviance and Social Control*, JAI Press, 1981.

Contributor: S. M. Miller and A. Gouldner, editors, *Applied Sociology: Opportunities and Problems*, Free Press, 1965; Philip Hauser, editor, *Social Statistics in Use*, Russell Sage, 1975; F. Cooke, editor, *The Role of the Forensic Psychologist*, C. C Thomas, 1980; Malcolm Klein and Kathie Teilman, editors, *Handbook of Criminal Justice Evaluation*, Sage Publications, 1980.

Contributor to newspapers, magazines, and professional journals. Associate editor, *American Journal of Sociology*, 1969-72; editor, *American Sociological Review*, 1978-80; consulting editor, *Journal of Criminal Law and Criminology*, 1982—.

* * *

SIMPER, Robert 1937-

PERSONAL: Born December 12, 1937, in Blaxhall, Suffolk, England; son of Norman Edward (a farmer) and Lillian (Turner) Simper; married Pearl Bater (a potter), July 18, 1959; children: Caroline Sara, Joanna Eleanor, Jonathan Robert. *Education:* Attended Royal Agricultural College, 1957-58. *Politics:* "Middle of the road." *Home:* Sluice Cottage, Ramsholt, Woodbridge, Suffolk 1P12 3AD, England.

CAREER: Worker on family farm, 1953—, partner, 1981—; N. E. Simper & Son (farm management company), Suffolk, England, director, 1962—; sailor and writer on agriculture, sailing, traditional vessels, and travel, 1962—. *Member:* Society for Nautical Research, American National Maritime Historical Society, Old Gaffers Association (vice-president, 1977—).

WRITINGS: *Over Snape Bridge*, East Anglian Magazine, 1967; *Woodbridge and Beyond*, East Anglian Magazine, 1972; *East Coast Sail*, David & Charles, 1972; *Scottish Sail*, David & Charles, 1974; *North East Sail*, David & Charles, 1976; *British Sail*, David & Charles, 1977; (contributor) Spencer Smith, editor, *Yachtsman's Winterbook*, McKay, 1978; *Victorian and Edwardian Yachting from Old Photographs*, Batsford, 1978; *Gaff Sail*, Argus Books, 1979; *Traditions of East Anglia*, Boydell Press, 1980; *Suffolk Show*, East Anglian Daily Times, 1981; *Britain's Maritime Heritage*, David & Charles, 1982; *Sail in the Orwell*, Maritime Ipswich, 1982.

Author of column "Sail Review" in *Sea Breezes*, 1966—. Contributor to agriculture and sailing magazines and newspapers.

WORK IN PROGRESS: *Beach Boats of Britain*.

SIDELIGHTS: Robert Simper told *CA*: "I began writing accidentally because of a prolonged back injury. The result has been that my living has remained in farming, an occupation I get a great deal of pleasure from, but writing satisfies the creative side of my nature. Much of my writing is intended to encourage people to preserve traditional working craft. I have researched, so far, throughout the British Isles, Western Europe, the West Indies, the eastern United States and Canada.

"I am a believer in democracy and working towards some form of stable world peace. Every area should retain its own individual identity and culture, but co-exist with its neighbour. This belief means that Britain should stay firmly united and part of the Western European community."

AVOCATIONAL INTERESTS: Photography (has used several of own photographs to illustrate books), meeting people, travel.

* * *

SIMPSON, Lewis P(earson) 1916-

PERSONAL: Born July 18, 1916, in Jacksboro, Tex.; son of John Pearson (a lawyer) and Grace (Sidebottom) Simpson; married Mary Elizabeth Ellis, July 14, 1941; children: Lewis David. *Education:* Attended North Texas Junior Agricultural, Mechanical, and Industrial College (now University of Texas at Arlington), 1933-35; University of Texas, B.A., 1938, M.A., 1939, Ph.D., 1948. *Religion:* Episcopal. *Home:* 965 Aberdeen Ave., Baton Rouge, La. 70808. *Office:* Department of English, Louisiana State University, Baton Rouge, La. 70803.

CAREER: University of Texas, Main University (now University of Texas at Austin), tutor, 1941-42, instructor in English, 1944-45 and 1946-48; Louisiana State University, Baton Rouge, assistant professor, 1948-53, associate professor, 1953-60, professor of English, 1960-71, William A. Read Professor of English Literature, 1971-80, Boyd Professor of English, 1980—. Lamar Memorial Lecturer, Mercer University, 1973. Consultant, National Endowment for the Humanities, 1970-74.

MEMBER: Thoreau Society, Modern Language Association of America, American Studies Association, Organization of American Historians, American Association of University Professors, Southern Historical Association, South Central Modern Language Association. *Awards, honors:* Guggenheim fellowship, 1954-55; Louisiana State University Foundation faculty fellowship, 1971-72; Distinguished Research Master Award and University Medal, Louisiana State University, 1977; National Endowment for the Humanities fellowship for independent study and research, 1977-78.

WRITINGS: (Editor and author of introduction, notes, and bibliography) *The Federalist Literary Mind,* Louisiana State University Press, 1962; (author of introduction) Murry C. Falkner, *The Faulkners of Mississippi,* Louisiana State University Press, 1967; (editor and author of introduction) *Profile of Robert Frost,* C. E. Merrill, 1971; (editor and author of introduction) *The Poetry of Community: Essays on the Southern Sensibility of History and Literature,* School of Arts and Sciences, Georgia State University, 1972; (author of introduction) Donald Davidson, *Still Rebels, Still Yankees,* Louisiana State University Press, 1972; *The Man of Letters in New England and the South: Essays on the History of the Literary Vocation in America,* Louisiana State University Press, 1973; (author of foreword) John Tyree Fain and Thomas Daniel Young, *The Literary Correspondence of Donald Davidson and Allen Tate,* University of Georgia Press, 1974; *The Dispossessed Garden: Pastoral and History in Southern Literature,* University of Georgia Press, 1975; (editor and author of introduction) *The Possibilities of Order: Cleanth Brooks and His Work,* Louisiana State University Press, 1975; *The Brazen Face of History: Studies in the Literary Consciousness in America,* Louisiana State University Press, 1980.

Contributor: Waldo McNeir and Leo B. Levy, editors, *Studies in American Literature,* Louisiana State University Press, 1960; Donald E. Stanford, editor, *Nine Essays in Modern Literature,* Louisiana State University Press, 1965.

Thomas A. Kirby and W. J. Olive, editors, *Essays in Honor of Esmond Linworth Marilla,* Louisiana State University Press, 1970; Francis Lee Utley, Lynn Z. Bloom, and Arthur F. Kinney, editors, *Bear, Man, and God: Eight Approaches to William Faulkner's "The Bear,"* Random House, 1971; Eric W. Carlson and T. Lasley Dameron, editors, *Emerson's Relevance Today,* Transcendental, 1971; A. Owen Aldridge, *The Ibero-American Enlightenment,* University of Illinois Press, 1971; H. Ernest Lewald, editor, *The Cry of Home: Cultural Nationalism and the Modern Writer,* University of Tennessee Press, 1972; Louis D. Rubin, Jr., editor, *The Comic Imagination in American Literature,* Rutgers University Press, 1973; John Loos, editor, *Great Events in American History,* Salem Press, 1974; Rubin and C. Hugh Holman, editors, *Southern Literary Study: Problems and Possibilities,* University of North Carolina Press, 1975; J. Leo Lemay, editor, *The Oldest Revolutionary: Essays on Benjamin Franklin,* University of Pennsylvania Press, 1976; George H. Wolfe, editor, *Fifty Years after "The Marble Faun,"* University of Alabama Press, 1976; William C. Havard and Joseph L. Bernd, editors, *200 Years of the Republic in Retrospect,* University Press of Virginia, 1976; Evans Harrington and Ann J. Abadie, editors, *The Maker and the Myth: Faulkner and Yoknapatawpha,* University Press of Mississippi, 1978; Donald Pizer, editor, *Essays in American Literature in Memory of Richard P. Adams,* Tulane University, 1978; Eliott Anderson and Mary Kinzie, editors, *The Little Magazine in America,* Pushcart Press, 1978; Daniel Hoffman, editor, *Harvard Guide to Contemporary American Writing,* Harvard University Press, 1979.

Louis J. Budd, Edwin Cady, and Carl L. Anderson, editors, *Toward a New American Literary History: Essays in Honor of Arlin Turner,* Duke University Press, 1980; Rubin, editor, *The American South: Portrait of a Culture,* Louisiana State University Press, 1980; Havard and Walter Sullivan, editors, *A Band of Prophets: The Nashville Agrarians Fifty Years After,* Louisiana State University Press, 1982. Also contributor to *Prospects: An Annual Journal of American Culture,* edited by Jack Salzman, 1982.

General editor, "Library of Southern Civilization" series, 1969—; member of selection board and consultant, "Library of America" series, Viking-Time-Life, 1980-82. Contributor of articles and reviews to literature and history journals. Co-editor, *Southern Review,* 1963—; member of editorial board, *American Literature,* 1969-72; advisory editor, *Southern Studies: An Interdisciplinary Journal of the South,* 1972—.

* * *

SINGER, Peter (Albert David) 1946-

PERSONAL: Born July 6, 1946, in Melbourne, Australia; son of Ernest (a businessman) and Cora (a doctor; maiden name, Oppenheim) Singer; married Renata Diamond (a teacher), December 16, 1969; children: Ruth, Lee, Esther. *Education:* University of Melbourne, B.A. (with honors), 1967, M.A., 1969; University College, Oxford, B.Phil., 1971. *Politics:* Australian Labor Party. *Religion:* None. *Home:* 14 Auburn Grove, East Hawthorn, Victoria, Australia. *Office:* Department of Philosophy, Monash University, Clayton, Victoria, Australia.

CAREER: Oxford University, University College, Oxford, England, lecturer in philosophy, 1971-73; New York University, New York, N.Y., visiting assistant professor of philosophy,

1973-74; La Trobe University, Bundoora, Victoria, Australia, senior lecturer in philosophy, 1974-76; Monash University, Clayton, Victoria, professor of philosophy, 1977—.

WRITINGS: Democracy and Disobedience, Clarendon Press, 1973, Oxford University Press (New York), 1974; (editor with Thomas Regan) *Animal Rights and Human Obligations,* Prentice-Hall, 1975; *Animal Liberation: A New Ethics for Our Treatment of Animals,* Random House, 1975; *Practical Ethics,* Cambridge University Press, 1979; *Marx,* Oxford University Press, 1980; *The Expanding Circle,* Farrar, Straus, 1981; (editor with William Walters) *Test-Tube Babies,* Oxford University Press (Melbourne), 1982. Contributor to *New York Review of Books* and to philosophy journals.

WORK IN PROGRESS: Research in ethics, applied ethics, and bio-ethics.

SIDELIGHTS: While teaching at England's Oxford University in the early 1970s, Peter Singer encountered a group of people who were vegetarians not because of any personal distaste for meat, but because they felt, as Singer later wrote, that "there was no way in which [maltreatment of animals by humans] could be justified ethically." Impressed by their arguments, the young Australian philosopher soon joined their ranks. Out of his growing concern for the rights of animals came the book *Animal Liberation,* a study of the suffering we inflict upon animals in the name of scientific experimentation and food production.

Singer attributes most of this lack of respect for non-human life to "speciesism," a concept he defines as "a prejudice or attitude of bias toward the interests of members of one's own species and against those of members of other species." In *Animal Liberation,* explains the *New York Times Book Review*'s C. G. Luckhardt, Singer attempts to prove that "only in rare cases" is the speciesism mankind displays "either necessary or moral." For example, says the critic, Singer believes that many of the experiments performed on laboratory animals are unnecessary due to the fact that they often "duplicate experiments already performed . . . , tell us what we already know . . . , cause medical problems in animals that could for the most part be avoided by humans . . . , and create data that are useless because inapplicable to humans." It is also unnecessary for humans to eat meat, the author maintains, especially when it means that animals must suffer during nearly every stage of their lives in order to provide us with protein that can be obtained from other sources. And as Luckhardt concludes in his summary of Singer's position, our treatment of animals is ultimately immoral because "there is every reason to believe, and no good reason to deny, that animals feel pain. . . . Whatever reasons we have for not inflicting pain on innocent and helpless humans extend equally well to animals."

Luckhardt praises Singer for writing a work of philosophy that is so "refreshing and well-argued; as a book intended for the mass market it is quite unhysterical yet engagingly written. [His] documentation is unrhetorical and unemotional, his arguments tight and formidable, for he bases his case on neither personal nor religious nor highly abstract philosophical principles, but on moral positions most of us already accept. The strength of this book lies in shifting the burden of argument to those who would maintain that animals ought to be excluded from our sphere of moral concern."

John Naughton of the *Listener* calls *Animal Liberation* "a sombre, challenging and somewhat harrowing book, which deserves to be widely read and 'inwardly digested,' if that is not too gruesome a phrase. . . . [Singer] is supported in [his] claims, not by the gooey affirmations of little old ladies, but by the sober deliberations of some of the most eminent scientists in Britain." Though Naughton finds that Singer "occasionally rides roughshod over his opponents," he declares that *Animal Liberation* "is one of the most thoughtful and persuasive books that I have read in a long time."

Despite assessments of the book which are otherwise quite favorable, both the *Spectator*'s Nick Totton and the *Village Voice*'s Richard Goldstein detect a hint of naivete in Singer's philosophy. As Totton observes: "Mr. Singer's main shortcoming as a propagandist is that he believes in the naked light of human reason. He is a philosopher, and a utilitarian at that; for him, a logical demonstration that meat-eating or vivisection increases the overall quotient of sentient suffering on this planet is conclusive. . . . [His] arguments are lucid, but really quite beside the point: they depend firstly on the axiom that there is a network of ethical values somehow built into the universe, and secondly upon the fond hope that conformity with such values is the primary intention of human beings."

Goldstein also notes a tendency towards what he terms "social obliviousness" in *Animal Liberation.* Comments the critic: "Because [Singer] does not make the necessary connection between intensive farming and the price of food, between the use of leather and the planned obsolescence of synthetics; because he never considers the changes in the way people treat each other which would have to accompany animal liberation, we cannot offer him more than sympathy in return for his obliviousness. . . . Aside from the havoc such reforms as Singer suggests would wreck on crucial institutions such as agribusiness and manufacturing, how can a government which declares itself devoted to free enterprise attempt to regulate so fundamental a pursuit of happiness as the ingestion of protein? Hindus believe certain animals are holy, but it is asking much more of people to give up meat simply because animals are sentient."

Nevertheless, Goldstein concludes, "I am willing to forgive Peter Singer his social obliviousness and more. [*Animal Liberation*] is an important book, first, because it reveals . . . the rough beast of self-interest which motivates all human society. Second, because it offers its solutions . . . in a spirit of mercy so touching and disquieting that one can only marvel at the persistent power of compassion. And third, because it questions, unintentionally perhaps, the sectarian organization of the world's people into competing states, and the brutality we extend to all those (animals, and the people who are denied the protein we feed to animals) beyond the pale."

BIOGRAPHICAL/CRITICAL SOURCES: Peter Singer, *Animal Liberation: A New Ethics for Our Treatment of Animals,* Random House, 1975; *New York Times Book Review,* January 4, 1976, March 1, 1981; *Village Voice,* March 22, 1976; *New Republic,* May 29, 1976, February 7, 1981; *Spectator,* June 5, 1976; *Listener,* June 17, 1976; *New York Review of Books,* May 15, 1980; *Washington Post Book World,* June 7, 1981; *Times Literary Supplement,* January 15, 1982.

—Sketch by Deborah A. Straub

* * *

SINJUN
See JOHN, Elizabeth Beaman

* * *

SKEEL, Dorothy J(une)

PERSONAL: Born in Erie, Pa.; daughter of Kenneth Selby and Cora (Gidner) Skeel. *Education:* Edinboro State College, B.S.; Pennsylvania State University, M.Ed., 1961, D.Ed., 1966;

postdoctoral study at University of Washington, Seattle, 1968-69. *Home:* 981 General George Patton Rd., Nashville, Tenn. 37221. *Office:* Department of Education, Vanderbilt University, Nashville, Tenn. 37203.

CAREER: Elementary and high school teacher at public schools in Pennsylvania; Kutztown State College, Kutztown, Pa., assistant professor of education, 1961-64; Pennsylvania State University, University Park, associate instructor in education, 1964-66; Indiana University at Bloomington, associate professor of education, 1966-76, director of TEAM experimental program, and coordinator for social studies; Vanderbilt University, Nashville, Tenn., professor of education, 1976—, director of Peabody Center for Economic and Social Studies Education. Visiting professor at University of Southern Nevada, summer, 1968, and University of Washington, summer, 1969. Secretary of Indiana Sponsors' Coordinating Council of the State Education Agency, 1969.

MEMBER: National Council for the Social Studies, National Society for the Study of Education, Association for Supervision and Curriculum Development, Indiana Council for the Social Studies (member of board of directors, 1971-73), Pi Lambda Theta, Delta Kappa Gamma (vice-president, 1972-74; president, 1974-76), Beta Beta Beta, Pi Gamma Mu, Kappa Delta Pi (counselor, 1978—).

WRITINGS: (With Oscar A. Rogers) *Objectives and Evaluation* (monograph), Tri-University Project, University of Washington, 1969; (contributor) James L. Olivero and E. G. Buffie, editors, *Educational Manpower: From Aides to Differentiated Staff Patterns,* Indiana University Press, 1970; *The Challenge of Teaching Social Studies in the Elementary School,* Goodyear Publishing, 1970, 3rd edition, 1979; (with Owen A. Hagen) *Process of Curriculum Change,* Goodyear Publishing, 1971; *Children of the Street: Teaching in the Inner-City,* Goodyear Publishing, 1971; (contributor) D. W. Beggs and Buffie, editors, *Non-graded Schools in Action: Bold New Venture,* Indiana University Press, revised edition (Skeel was not associated with earlier edition), 1971; *The Challenge of Teaching Social Studies: A Book of Readings,* Goodyear Publishing, 1972; *The People of United States and Canada* (juvenile), Sadlier, 1972; *The People of Latin America* (juvenile), Sadlier, 1972.

Self (textbook), American Book, 1979, revised edition, 1982; *Others* (textbook), American Book, 1979, revised edition, 1982; (contributor) Jack Allen, editor, *Education in the Eighties,* National Education Association, 1981. Also author of *Behavioral Objectives;* also contributor to Charlotte Anderson, editor, *Daring to Dream: Law-Related Education and the Humanities in the Elementary School,* 1981. Author of two records, "Developing Language Arts Skills" and "Developing Creative Ability," produced by H. W. Wilson. Contributor to education journals, including *NEA Journal* and *Intercom.*

WORK IN PROGRESS: Fourth edition of *The Challenge of Teaching Social Studies in the Elementary School;* research project, "How Do Children in Various Geographic Areas of the United States Rank Values?"

* * *

SKLAR, Robert 1936-

PERSONAL: Born December 3, 1936, in New Brunswick, N.J.; son of Leon (a junior high school principal) and Lilyn (Fuchs) Sklar; married Kathryn Kish, November 27, 1958 (divorced, 1979); married Adrienne Harris, June 11, 1982; children: (first marriage) Leonard, Susan. *Education:* Princeton University, A.B., 1958; University of Bonn, graduate study, 1959-60; Harvard University, Ph.D., 1965. *Office:* Department of Cinema Studies, New York University, New York, N.Y. 10003.

CAREER: Associated Press, Newark, N.J., worked on rewrite desk, 1958-59; *Los Angeles Times,* Los Angeles, Calif., staff writer, 1959; University of Michigan, Ann Arbor, assistant professor, 1965-69, associate professor, 1969-75, professor of history, 1975-76; New York University, New York, N.Y., professor of cinema studies, 1977—, chairman of department, 1977-81. Visiting associate professor, University of Auckland, New Zealand, 1970; Fulbright lecturer, University of Tokyo and Sophia University, Japan, 1971; Distinguished Visiting Professor of American Studies, Bard College, 1975-76. *Awards, honors:* Guggenheim fellow, 1970-71; Theatre Library Association prize, 1975, for *Movie-Made America: A Cultural History of American Movies;* Rockefeller Foundation humanities fellowship, 1976-77.

WRITINGS: F. Scott Fitzgerald: The Last Laocoon, Oxford University Press, 1967; (contributor) Werner M. Mendel, editor, *A Celebration of Laughter,* Mara Books, 1970; (editor) *The Plastic Age: 1917-1930,* Braziller, 1970; *Movie-Made America: A Cultural History of American Movies,* Random House, 1975; (contributor) Richard Glatzer and John Raeburn, editors, *Frank Capra: The Man and His Films,* University of Michigan Press, 1975; *Prime-Time America: Life on and behind the Television Screen,* Oxford University Press, 1980; (contributor) John R. O'Connor and Martin Jackson, editors, *American History/American Film,* Ungar, 1980. Contributor to *Encyclopaedia Britannica,* and *Dictionary of American Biography;* also contributor of articles, essays, and reviews to periodicals.

* * *

SLOSSON, Preston (William) 1892-

PERSONAL: Born September 2, 1892, in Laramie, Wyo.; son of Edwin Emory (a journalist and chemist) and May (Preston) Slosson; married Lucy Denny Wright, June 21, 1927 (died, 1974); children: Flora May (Mrs. Wilhelm Wuellner), Edith Denny (Mrs. Ivan Aron); (stepdaughters) Lucy Chase (Mrs. Jim Bob Stephenson), Mary Elizabeth (Mrs. George Fearnehough). *Education:* Columbia University, B.S., 1912, M.A., 1913, Ph.D., 1916. *Religion:* Congregationalist. *Home address:* R.D. 2, Church Rd., Knox, Pa. 16232.

CAREER: New York Independent, New York City, junior editor, 1917; U.S. Department of State, Washington, D.C., assistant in New York City, 1917-18; American Commission to Negotiate Peace, Paris, France, assistant librarian, 1918-19; *New York Independent,* literary editor, 1920-21; University of Michigan, Ann Arbor, instructor, 1921-23, assistant professor, 1923-27, associate professor, 1927-37, professor of history, 1937-62, professor emeritus, 1962—. Carnegie Foundation visiting professor at Universities of Bristol, Manchester, and Glasgow, 1932-33, and Universities of Bristol, Sheffield, and Aberystwyth, 1938-39; Haynes fellow at Redlands University, 1954-55; distinguished professor at Kansas State University, 1960; also taught at Baldwin-Wallace College, Columbia University, University of Minnesota, University of Wyoming, University of North Carolina at Greensboro, and University of South Carolina. Broadcaster on current events for WWJ-Radio, 1941-45. Democratic candidate for U.S. House of Representatives, 1948; member of Washtenaw County Committee.

MEMBER: American Historical Association, American Association of University Professors, American Civil Liberties

Union, Atlantic Union, United World Federalists, Research Club (University of Michigan), Phi Beta Kappa. *Awards, honors:* LL.D., Hillsdale College, 1944.

WRITINGS: Fated or Free?: A Dialogue on Destiny, Sherman, French, 1914; *Peace with Honor* (pamphlet), New York Independent, 1915; *The Decline of the Chartist Movement,* Columbia University Press, 1916, International Scholastic Book Service, 1967; *Twentieth Century Europe,* edited by J. T. Shotwell, Houghton, 1927; *The Problems of Austro-German Union,* Carnegie Endowment for International Peace, 1929; *America and the Anschluss Question* (pamphlet), Braumiller, 1930; (editor and contributor) Edwin E. Slosson, *A Number of Things,* Harcourt, 1930; *The Great Crusade and After, 1914-1928: A History of American Life,* Macmillan, 1930, F. Watts, 1971; *Europe since 1870,* Houghton, 1935; (with Arthur E. R. Boak and Albert Hyma) *The Growth of European Civilization,* Crofts, 1938.

War Returns to the World, 1938-41, Crofts, 1941; *Why We Are at War,* Houghton, 1942; (with Boak and H. R. Anderson) *World History,* Houghton, 1942, revised edition (with Boak, Anderson, and Bartlett) published as *The History of Our World,* 1959; (with Robert B. Mowat) *History of the English-Speaking Peoples,* Oxford University Press, 1943; *After the War—What?,* Houghton, 1943, revised edition, 1945; *Swords of Peace: Problems of Disarmament,* Foreign Policy Association, 1947; (with wife, Lucy Slosson) *From Washington to Roosevelt,* Ginn, 1949; *Europe since 1815,* Scribner, 1954; *A Teacher's Report Card,* Wahr, 1975; *Pitt and Fox,* Wahr, 1978; *Bright and Cobden,* Sweet Arrow Lake Press, 1980; *A Flight of Fifty* (essays), Sweet Arrow Lake Press, 1981. Contributor of several hundred articles and reviews to history journals and newspapers.

WORK IN PROGRESS: Writing captions for an illustrated history of the United States, for Bison Press.

AVOCATIONAL INTERESTS: International government.

*   *   *

SMALL, Dwight Hervey 1919-

PERSONAL: Born March 1, 1919, in Oakland, Calif.; son of Benjamin (an engineer and salesman) and Ragnhild (Ostrom) Small; married Ruth Ida Elizabeth Stone, June 13, 1942; children: Lynne Tahmisian, Sharon Cudworth. *Education:* University of California, Berkeley, B.A., 1940; San Francisco Theological Seminary, M.Div., 1943. *Home:* 142 La Vista Grande, Santa Barbara, Calif. 93108. *Office:* Department of Sociology, Westmont College, 955 La Paz Rd., Santa Barbara, Calif. 93108.

CAREER: Ordained Presbyterian minister, 1943; pastor of Presbyterian churches in Fresno, Calif., San Jose, Calif., Philadelphia, Pa., and Chicago, Ill., 1943-60; ordained minister of the Evangelical Covenant Church of the United States, 1960; pastor of Evangelical Covenant church in Redwood City, Calif., 1960-70; Westmont College, Santa Barbara, Calif., assistant professor, 1970-75, associate professor of sociology, 1975—.

WRITINGS—Published by Revell, except as indicated: *Design for Christian Marriage,* 1958; *The Biblical Basis for Infant Baptism,* 1959; *The High Cost of Holy Living,* 1964; *After You've Said I Do,* 1968; *Christian, Celebrate Your Sexuality,* 1974; *The Right to Remarry,* 1975; *Marriage As Equal Partnership,* Baker Book, 1978; *Your Marriage Is God's Affair,* 1979; *How Should I Love You?,* Harper, 1979; *No Rival Love,* Christian Literature Crusade, 1982. Contributor to religious periodicals.

SIDELIGHTS: Dwight Hervey Small writes *CA:* "The majority of my writing over [the] years, has to do with the Christian perspective on marriage and sexuality. *Christian, Celebrate Your Sexuality* is recognized as one of the first attempts by an American writer to produce a theology of sexuality from the perspective of conservative Protestantism."

*   *   *

SMART, James D(ick) 1906-1982

PERSONAL: Born March 1, 1906, in Alton, Ontario, Canada; died January 23, 1982, in Rosedale, Ontario, Canada; son of John George (a railway agent) and Janet Elizabeth (Dick) Smart; married Christine McKillop, September 24, 1931; children: Margaret Jean (Mrs. R. J. Watson), Mary Eleanor, Janet Ann (Mrs. Paul Young). *Education:* University of Toronto, B.A., 1926, M.A., 1927, Ph.D., 1931; Knox College, Lic. in Theology, 1929; graduate study at University of Marburg and University of Berlin, 1929-30. *Politics:* Liberal. *Religion:* Presbyterian. *Residence:* Rosedale, Ontario, Canada.

CAREER: Ordained to ministry of the Presbyterian Church in Canada, 1931; pastor of churches in Alisa Craig, Ontario, 1931-34; Knox's Church, Galt, Ontario, pastor, 1934-41; St. Paul's Church, Peterborough, Ontario, pastor, 1941-44; Presbyterian Church in the U.S.A., Board of Christian Education, Philadelphia, Pa., editor-in-chief of curriculum materials, 1944-50; Rosedale Presbyterian Church, Toronto, Ontario, pastor, 1950-57, minister, 1970-74; Union Theological Seminary, New York, N.Y., Jessup Foundation Professor of Biblical Interpretation, 1957-71; lecturer at Toronto School of Theology, 1971-76. Lecturer in homiletics and Christian education, Knox College, 1951-57; Carnahan Lecturer in Buenos Aires, 1963. *Member:* Society of Biblical Literature and Exegesis, American Theological Society. *Awards, honors:* D.D., Knox College, 1956.

WRITINGS—Published by Westminster Press, except as indicated: *What a Man Can Believe,* 1943; (with David Noel Freedman) *God Has Spoken: An Introduction to the Old Testament for Young People,* 1948; *A Promise to Keep,* 1948; *The Recovery of Humanity,* 1953; *The Teaching Ministry of the Church: An Examination of Basic Principles of Christian Education,* 1954.

The Rebirth of Ministry: A Study of the Biblical Character of the Church's Ministry, 1960, reprinted, 1978; *Servants of the Word,* 1960; *The Interpretation of Scripture,* 1961; *The Creed in Christian Teaching,* 1962; *The Old Testament in Dialogue with Modern Man,* 1964; (translator) Karl Barth and Eduard Thurneysen, *Revolutionary Theology in the Making: Correspondence 1914-1925,* Epworth, 1964; *History and Theology in Second Isaiah: A Commentary on Isaiah 35, 40-66,* 1965; *The Divided Mind of Modern Theology: Karl Barth and Rudolph Bultmann, 1908-1933,* 1967; *The ABC's of Christian Faith,* 1968; *The Quiet Revolution: The Radical Impact of Jesus on the Men of His Time,* 1969; (co-editor) *Luther, Erasmus, and the Reformation,* Fordham University Press, 1969; *The Strange Silence of the Bible in the Church: A Study in Hermeneutics,* 1970; *Doorway to a New Age: A Study of Paul's Letter to the Romans,* 1972; *One Israel or Two* (phonotape), Thesis Theological Cassettes, 1972; *The Cultural Subversion of the Biblical Faith: Life in the Twentieth Century under the Sign of the Cross,* 1977; *The Past, Present, and Future of Biblical Theology,* 1979. Contributor of articles to journals. Co-editor, *Westminster Study Bible,* 1949.

WORK IN PROGRESS: Work on the future of Biblical theology.

SIDELIGHTS: Reviewing James D. Smart's *History and Theology in Second Isaiah: A Commentary on Isaiah 35, 40-66,* a *Times Literary Supplement* critic stated, "Professor Smart has produced a brilliant and provocative book." Commenting on the work's "brilliant originality," the reviewer admired Smart's theological premises, which refute many popular interpretations of these verses. The reviewer criticized the lack of indexes, yet concluded: "Professor Smart has written a very striking book, which deserves the most respectful consideration."

BIOGRAPHICAL/CRITICAL SOURCES: *Times Literary Supplement,* August 8, 1967.

OBITUARIES: *New York Times,* January 27, 1982.†

* * *

SMELSER, Neil J(oseph) 1930-

PERSONAL: Born July 22, 1930, in Kahoka, Mo.; son of Joseph Nelson (a teacher) and Susie (Hess) Smelser; married Helen Margolis, July 10, 1954 (divorced, 1965); married Sharin Fately, December 20, 1967; children: (first marriage) Eric Jonathan, Tina Rachel; (second marriage) Joseph Neil, Sarah Joanne. *Education:* Harvard University, B.A. (summa cum laude), 1952, Ph.D., 1958; Oxford University, B.A. (with first class honors), 1954, M.A., 1959; San Francisco Psychoanalytic Institute, graduate, 1971. *Home:* 109 Hillcrest Rd., Berkeley, Calif. 94705. *Office:* Department of Sociology, 410 Barrows Hall, University of California, Berkeley, Calif. 94720.

CAREER: University of California, Berkeley, assistant professor, 1958-60, associate professor, 1960-62, professor, 1962-72, University Professor of Sociology, 1972—. Social Science Research Council, member of committee on economic growth, 1961-65, member of board of directors, 1968-73, chairman of board, 1971-73. Junior fellow, Society of Fellows, Harvard University, 1955-58.

MEMBER: American Sociological Association (member of council, 1968-71 and 1973-75; vice-president, 1971-73), American Philosophical Society, American Association for the Advancement of Science, American Academy of Arts and Sciences (fellow), Pacific Sociological Association, Phi Beta Kappa. *Awards, honors:* Rhodes scholarship, Oxford University, 1952-54; Social Science Research Council, faculty research fellow, 1961-63, auxiliary award of $4,000, 1962; research grants from National Science Foundation, 1965-66, Ford Foundation, 1970-71, Russell Sage Foundation, 1978-80, and National Institute of Education, 1980-82; Guggenheim fellowship, 1973-74.

WRITINGS: (With Talcott Parsons) *Economy and Society,* Free Press of Glencoe, 1956; *Social Change in the Industrial Revolution,* University of Chicago Press, 1959; (editor with Seymour M. Lipset) *Sociology: The Progress of a Decade,* Prentice-Hall, 1961; *Theory of Collective Behavior,* Free Press of Glencoe, 1963; (editor with brother, William T. Smelser, and co-author of introduction) *Personality and Social Systems,* Wiley, 1963, 2nd edition, 1970; *The Sociology of Economic Life* (college textbook), Prentice-Hall, 1963; (editor) *Readings on Economic Sociology,* Prentice-Hall, 1964; (editor with Lipset and co-author of introductory chapter) *Social Structure, Mobility, and Economic Development,* Aldine, 1966; (editor) *Sociology,* Wiley, 1967, 2nd edition, 1973; *Essays in Sociological Explanation,* Prentice-Hall, 1968.

Sociological Theory: A Contemporary View, General Learning Press, 1971; (editor) *Karl Marx on Society and Social Change,* University of Chicago Press, 1973; (editor with Gabriel Almond and contributor) *Public Higher Education in California, 1950-70,* University of California Press, 1974; *Comparative Methods in the Social Sciences,* Prentice-Hall, 1976; (with Robin Content) *The Changing Academic Market,* University of California Press, 1979; (editor with Erik H. Erikson and contributor) *Themes of Love and Work in Adulthood,* Harvard University Press, 1980; *Sociology,* Prentice-Hall, 1981.

Contributor: Wilbert E. Moore and Bert F. Hoselitz, editors, *Industrialization and Society,* Mouton, 1963; Amitai Etzioni and Eve Etzioni, editors, *Social Change: Sources, Patterns, and Consequences,* Basic Books, 1964; Milton L. Barron, *Contemporary Sociology: An Introductory Textbook of Readings,* Dodd, 1964; Alex Inkeles and Bernard Barber, editors, *Stability and Social Change,* Little, Brown, 1971; Ivan Vallier, editor, *Comparative Methods in Sociology,* University of California Press, 1971; Donald P. Warwick and Samuel Osherson, *Comparative Research Methods,* Prentice-Hall, 1973; David Riesman and Verne Stadtman, editors, *Academic Transformation,* McGraw, 1973; Talcott Parsons and Gerald Platt, *The American University,* Harvard University Press, 1973; Carl Kaysen, editor, *Content and Context: Essays on College Education,* 1973. Also contributor to *International Encyclopaedia of the Social Sciences.* Series editor in sociology, Prentice-Hall, 1966—. Advisory editor, *American Journal of Sociology,* 1960-62; editor, *American Sociological Review,* 1962-65.

WORK IN PROGRESS: Research on kinship structure and economic development; research on the methodology of comparative analysis.

* * *

SMITH, Clodus R(ay) 1928-

PERSONAL: Born May 15, 1928, in Blanchard, Okla.; son of William Thomas (a farmer) and Rachel (Hale) Smith; married Pauline Chaat, June 25, 1950; children: Martha Lynn, William Paul, Paula Diane. *Education:* Cameron State Agricultural College, A.A., 1948; Oklahoma Agricultural and Mechanical College (now Oklahoma State University of Agriculture and Applied Sciences), B.S., 1950, M.S., 1955; Cornell University, Ed.D., 1960. *Religion:* Methodist. *Home:* 3174 Onaway Rd., Shaker Heights, Ohio 44120. *Office:* Cleveland State University, Cleveland, Ohio 44115.

CAREER: Teacher of agriculture at high schools in Oklahoma, 1949-52, and in Texas, 1952-57; University of Maryland, College Park, assistant professor, 1959-61, associate professor of agriculture and extension education, 1962-73, director of summer school, 1963-72, administrative dean of summer programs, 1972-73; Cleveland State University, Cleveland, Ohio, special assistant to the president, 1973-74, vice-president for university relations and executive director of university development foundation, 1974—. Member, Danforth Associates, 1962—; member of board, Maryland Chamber of Commerce, 1971-73; director, Prince George's County, Md., human resources and community development program, human relations commission, community action committee, and county demonstration agency, 1972-73; member of steering committee, YWCA career women of achievement program, 1981—; American Cancer Society, Cleveland, member of board, 1981—, member of budget committee and nominating committee, 1982; director of interdisciplinary approach to leadership development, Leadership Development Seminar series, U.S. Office of Education. Consultant to industrial, educational, and government groups.

MEMBER: American Association of Teacher Educators in Agriculture (regional vice-president, 1962-66), National Association of College and University Summer Sessions (founder;

president, 1964-65), American Vocational Association (life member), American Vocational Research Association (charter member), Council for the Advancement and Support of Education, American Association of University Administrators, Association of University Summer Sessions, American Public Health Association, American Association for Higher Education, American Alumni Council/American College Public Relations Association, National Society for the Study of Education, American Association of University Professors, Inter-University Council of Ohio (chairman, 1977-78), Northern Ohio Association of Fund Raisers, Phi Kappa Phi (secretary, 1966-67; president, 1968-69), Phi Delta Kappa, Lions Club, Masons.

AWARDS, HONORS: Honorary Lone Star Farmer degree, 1955; National Project in Agricultural Communications research award, 1959; Danforth faculty fellow, 1962; honorary Maryland State Farmer degree, 1968; Prince George's Chamber of Commerce Education Award, 1971; North American Association of Summer Sessions Recognition Award, 1979.

WRITINGS: (With Lloyd Partain and James Champlin) *Rural Recreation for Profit*, Interstate, 1966, 2nd edition, 1968; *Planning and Paying for College*, Crowell-Collier, 1968; *A Strategy for University Relations*, Division of University Relations, Cleveland State University, 1975, revised edition, 1980; *A Marketing Communication Plan for 1980-1981*, Division of University Relations, Cleveland State University, 1980; *State Relations for the 1980 Decade: The Campus-Capitol Connection*, Division of University Relations, Cleveland State University, 1982. Also contributor to *Theoretical Considerations in Indian Education*, 1974. Contributor to education and agriculture journals. Editor, *Maryland Vocational Agricultural News* and *Collegiate Reporter*, 1960-63.

AVOCATIONAL INTERESTS: Hunting, fishing.

* * *

SMITH, Daniel M(alloy) 1922-1976

PERSONAL: Born July 12, 1922, in Sanford, N.C.; died July 28, 1976; son of D. M. (a salesman) and Alma (Bruton) Smith; married Carolyn Aladeen Brown, January 11, 1946; children: Stephanie Ann, Daniel Bennett, Gregory Malloy. *Education:* University of California, Berkeley, A.B., 1949, M.A., 1950, Ph.D., 1954. *Home:* 315 Hopi Place, Boulder, Colo. *Office:* Department of History, University of Colorado, Boulder, Colo. 80302.

CAREER: Stanford University, Stanford, Calif., instructor in history, 1953-57; University of Colorado, Boulder, assistant professor, 1957-60, associate professor, 1960-64, professor of history, beginning 1964, chairman of history department, beginning 1968. Visiting instructor, University of California, Berkeley, summer, 1954; visiting professor, University of Oregon, summer, 1965. *Military service:* U.S. Navy, 1942-46. *Member:* Organization of American Historians, American Historical Association, Phi Beta Kappa, Phi Alpha Theta.

WRITINGS: Robert Lansing and American Neutrality, 1914-1917, University of California Press, 1958; (editor) *Major Problems in American Diplomatic History: Documents and Readings*, Heath, Volume I, 1964, Volume II, 1965; *The Great Departure: The United States and World War I, 1914-1920*, Wiley, 1965; (editor) *American Intervention, 1917: Sentiment, Self-Interest, or Ideals?*, Houghton, 1966; *Aftermath of War: Bainbridge Colby and Wilsonian Diplomacy*, American Philosophical Society, 1970; *The American Diplomatic Experience*, Houghton, 1972; *War and Depression: America 1914-1939*, Forum Press, 1972; (with Joseph M. Siracusa) *The Testing of America, 1914-1945*, Forum Press, 1978, revised edition, 1979. Contributor of articles on U.S. diplomacy to American history journals.†

* * *

SMITH, Duane A(llan) 1937-

PERSONAL: Born April 20, 1937, in San Diego, Calif.; son of Stanley W. (a dentist) and Ila (Bark) Smith; married Gay Woodruff, August 20, 1960; children: Laralee Ellen. *Education:* University of Colorado, B.A., 1959, M.A., 1961, Ph.D., 1964. *Home:* 2911 Cedar Ave., Durango, Colo. 81301. *Office:* Department of History, Fort Lewis College, Durango, Colo. 81301.

CAREER: Fort Lewis College, Durango, Colo., assistant professor, 1964-67, associate professor, 1967-72, professor of history, 1972—. *Member:* North American Society for Sport History, Organization of American Historians, Western History Association, Colorado Historical Society, Montana Historical Society, Phi Alpha Theta. *Awards, honors:* Huntington Library research grants, 1968, 1973, and 1978; Hafen Award, 1971, for outstanding magazine article; Certificate of Commendation, 1974, for *Horace Tabor*, and Award of Merit, 1981, both from American Association for State and Local History; Westerners' Little Joe Award, 1977, for *Colorado Mining;* Society for Technical Communication Award of Distinction, 1980, for *Secure the Shadow.*

WRITINGS: Rocky Mountain Mining Camps: The Urban Frontier, Indiana University Press, 1967; (with M. Benson and C. Ubbelohde) *A Colorado History*, Pruett, 1972, revised edition, 1982; *Horace Tabor: His Life and the Legend*, Colorado Associated University Press, 1973; *Silver Saga: The Story of Caribou, Colorado*, Pruett, 1974; *Colorado Mining: A Photographic History*, University of New Mexico Press, 1977; (with D. Weber) *Fortunes Are for the Few: Letters of a Forty-Niner*, San Diego Historical Society, 1977; *Rocky Mountain Boom Town: A History of Durango*, University of New Mexico Press, 1980; *Secure the Shadow: Lachlan McLean, Colorado Mining Photographer*, Colorado School of Mines Press, 1980; (with D. Vandenbusche) *A Land Alone: Colorado's Western Slope*, Pruett, 1981; *Song of the Hammer and Drill: The Colorado San Juans, 1860-1914*, Colorado School of Mines Press, 1982.

WORK IN PROGRESS: Research on Colorado during the Civil War years and on the 8th Illinois Cavalry.

SIDELIGHTS: Duane A. Smith told *CA:* "Probably the most important motivation for research on mining camps was the desire to uncover a more realistic and honest history as opposed to much of the literature which passes for the true history of the mining frontier."

AVOCATIONAL INTERESTS: Jogging and other sports, conservation, politics.

* * *

SMITH, M. Estellie 1935-

PERSONAL: Born December 1, 1935, in Buffalo, N.Y.; daughter of O. Roy (a businessman) and Marietta C. Perry (a businesswoman; maiden name, Pereira) Smith; married Charles A. Bishop (an anthropologist), September 16, 1968. *Education:* State University of New York at Buffalo, B.A. (magna cum laude), 1962, M.A. (with honors), 1964, Ph.D. (with highest honors), 1967. *Politics:* Republican. *Religion:* Episcopalian.

Home: 51 East Main St., Ontario, N.Y. 14519. *Office:* Department of Anthropology, State University of New York College, Oswego, N.Y. 13126.

CAREER: Florida State University, Tallahassee, assistant professor of anthropology, 1966-69; Eastern New Mexico University, Portales, assistant professor of anthropology, 1969-70; State University of New York College at Brockport, associate professor of anthropology, 1970-76; State University of New York College at Oswego, professor of anthropology, 1976—. Visiting professor at Southern Methodist University, 1970; adjunct professor at Texas Tech University, 1970; visiting lecturer at Erie Community College, 1973. Permanent research associate at Fort Burgwyn Research Center, 1968—; permanent research professor at Eastern New Mexico University, 1972—.

MEMBER: American Ethnological Society, American Anthropological Association (fellow), Ethnologica European (associate member), Linguistic Society of America, Society for American Archeology, American Association for the Advancement of Science, Royal Anthropological Institute (fellow), Society for Applied Anthropology (fellow), Society for American Ethnohistory, Current Anthropology (associate member), Northeast Anthropological Association (president, 1983-84), Southern Anthropological Society, Phi Beta Kappa, Sigma Xi.

AWARDS, HONORS: American Philosophical Society research grant, 1968; National Foundation in the Humanities and Arts fellow, 1968; Sigma Xi research grant, 1969, and grant-in-aid of research, 1974; National Science Foundation, two research grants, 1970, travel grant to Rome, Italy, 1972.

WRITINGS: Governing at Taos Pueblo (monograph), Eastern New Mexico University Press, 1969; (editor) *Studies in Linguistics: Papers in Honor of George L. Trager,* Mouton, 1972; (contributor) Roger Wescott, editor, *Language Origins,* Linstok, 1974, 2nd edition, Mouton, 1975; *Those Who Live from the Sea,* Westview, 1977; (editor with Irwin Press) *Urb and Urbanism,* Macmillan, 1980.

Monograph series editor, Association for Political and Legal Anthropology, 1982—. Contributor to proceedings; contributor to anthropology journals, including *Current Anthropology. Abstracts in Anthropology,* founder and editor, 1969-72, senior advisory editor, 1969-73; book review editor for *Urban Anthropology,* 1972—, and *Studies in European Society,* 1972-75; associate editor of *Political Anthropology Newsletter,* 1974—, and *Ethnohistory,* 1980-82.

WORK IN PROGRESS: Studies of the theory of the state/city-state and of cultural continuity; maritime studies; Portugese ethnic studies.

* * *

SMITH, Robert Kimmel 1930-
(Peter Marks)

PERSONAL: Born July 31, 1930, in Brooklyn, N.Y.; son of Theodore (in civil service) and Sally (Kimmel) Smith; married Claire Medney (a literary agent), September 4, 1954; children: Heidi, Roger. *Education:* Attended Brooklyn College (now Brooklyn College of the City University of New York), 1947-48. *Residence:* Brooklyn, N.Y. *Agent:* (Literary) Harold Ober Associates, 40 E. 49th St., New York, N.Y. 10017; (television/plays) Lois Berman, WB Agency, 156 E. 52 St., New York, N.Y.

CAREER: Doyle, Dane, Bernbach (advertising agency), New York City, copywriter, 1957-61; Grey Advertising, New York City, copy chief, 1963-65; Smith & Toback (advertising agency), New York City, partner and writer, 1967-70; full-time writer, 1970—. *Military service:* U.S. Army, 1951-53. *Member:* Authors League of America, Writers Guild, Dramatists Guild, Leukemia Society of America, Eugene O'Neill Theatre Center, Eugene O'Neill Playwrights (co-chairman, 1974-75), Kayoodle Club (president, 1969), Knickerbocker Field Club. *Awards, honors:* Named Eugene O'Neill Playwright, 1971, for "A Little Singing, A Little Dancing"; Massachusetts Children's Book Award, 1980, for *Chocolate Fever.*

WRITINGS: Ransom (novel), McKay, 1971; "A Little Singing, A Little Dancing" (play; produced at O'Neill Memorial Theatre, July, 1971), published as "A Little Dancing" in *Best Short Plays of 1975,* edited by Stanley Richards, Chilton, 1975; *Chocolate Fever* (juvenile), Coward, 1972; *Sadie Shapiro's Knitting Book* (novel), Simon & Schuster, 1973; *Sadie Shapiro in Miami,* Simon & Schuster, 1977; *Sadie Shapiro, Matchmaker,* Simon & Schuster, 1979; *Jelly Belly* (juvenile), Delacorte, 1981; *Jane's House* (novel), Morrow, 1982.

Also author of two other plays and several television scripts. Contributor of short fiction to periodicals, writing under pseudonym Peter Marks prior to 1970.

WORK IN PROGRESS: A children's book, for Delacorte; a novel.

SIDELIGHTS: Robert K. Smith told *CA:* "In 1970, at the age of forty, I decided to give full-time writing a shot and haven't looked back since. I published four novels and a juvenile within the next decade, wrote three plays and a number of television scripts. Most of my work turned out to be on the humorous side; some of it may last more than a week and a half. *Sadie Shapiro's Knitting Book* has now been published in ten languages and twenty-seven countries. *Chocolate Fever* is in its thirteenth printing with Dell.

"In 1980 I decided to try something bigger, which turned out to be the novel *Jane's House.* I think this book will mark a turning point for me. I want to write in a more serious way, with humor as a counterpoint instead of being *the* point. Writing juveniles has been very rewarding. Kids are a responsive audience. I'll continue to be funny for them. I have given up on television, however, having found it impossible to do work there which meets my standards.

"After a dozen years I think I'm beginning to know myself. I write about love (the center of my life) and what it means to be human. But also, being human, I realize that all of the above is subject to change without notice."

BIOGRAPHICAL/CRITICAL SOURCES: New York Times Book Review, May 13, 1973; *Times Literary Supplement,* November 16, 1973.

* * *

SMITH, Vivian (Brian) 1933-

PERSONAL: Born June 3, 1933, in Hobart, Tasmania, Australia; son of Vivian and Sibyl (Daniels) Smith; married Sybille Gottwald, February 15, 1960; children: Vanessa, Gabrielle, Nicholas. *Education:* University of Tasmania, M.A., 1956; University of Sydney, Ph.D., 1971. *Home:* 19 McLeod St., Mosman, New South Wales 2088, Australia. *Office:* Department of English, University of Sydney, Sydney, New South Wales 2006, Australia.

CAREER: University of Tasmania, Hobart, lecturer in French, 1955-67; University of Sydney, Sydney, Australia, lecturer, 1967-74, senior lecturer, 1974-82, reader in English, 1982—;

poet. *Member:* Poetry Society of Australia, Australian Society of Authors.

WRITINGS: The Other Meaning (poems), Edwards & Shaw, 1956; *James McAuley,* Lansdowne Press, 1965; *An Island South,* Angus & Robertson, 1967; *Les Vige en Australie* (juvenile; title means "The Vige Family in Australia"), Longmans, Green (Melbourne), 1967; (editor) *Australian Poetry,* Angus & Robertson, 1969; *The Poetry of Robert Lowell,* University of Sydney Press, 1974; *Vance and Nettie Palmer,* Twayne, 1975; *Letters of Vance and Nettie Palmer,* National Library (Canberra), 1977; *Familiar Places* (poems), Angus & Robertson, 1978; *Tide Country* (poems), Angus & Robertson, 1982.

Contributor of poems to anthologies: *Young Commonwealth Poets '65,* edited by Howard Sergeant, Heinemann, 1965; *Modern Australian Writing,* edited by G. P. Dutton, Fontana, 1966; *Commonwealth Poems of Today,* edited by Sergeant, John Murray, 1967; *Modern Australian Poetry,* edited by David Campbell, Sun Books, 1974; *A Map of Australian Verse,* edited by James McAuley, Oxford University Press, 1975; *Modern Australian Poetry,* edited by H. P. Heselline, Penguin, 1980; *Collins Book of Australian Verse,* edited by R. Hall, Collins, 1981; *Oxford History of Australian Literature,* Oxford University Press, 1981.

Contributor to Australian newspapers and literary journals. Literary editor of *Quadrant,* 1975—.

AVOCATIONAL INTERESTS: Translating from French and German.

* * *

SMYTH, Paul 1944-

PERSONAL: Born January 31, 1944, in Boston, Mass.; son of Paul and Nona (Long) Smyth. *Education:* Harvard University, B.A., 1968. *Home address:* P.O. Box 531, Village Station, New York, N.Y. 10014.

CAREER: Poet.

WRITINGS—Poetry: *Native Grass,* Windy Row Press, 1972; *Fifty Sonnets,* Windy Row Press, 1973; *Shadowed Leaves,* Press Porcepic, 1973; *Conversions,* University of Georgia Press, 1974; *Thistles and Thorns,* Abattoir Editions, 1977; *Antibodies,* Cedar Creek Press, 1979; *The Cardinal Sins: A Bestiary,* Pennyroyal Press, 1981.

* * *

SOBEL, Robert 1931-

PERSONAL: Born February 19, 1931, in New York, N.Y.; son of Philip (an artist) and Blanche (Levinson) Sobel; married Carole Ritter (a teacher), June 30, 1958; children: David. *Education:* City College (now City College of the City University of New York), B.S.S., 1951; New York University, M.A., 1952, Ph.D., 1957. *Politics:* Democrat. *Religion:* Jewish. *Home:* 21 Division Ave., Massapequa, N.Y. *Office:* Department of History, New College, Hofstra University, Hempstead, N.Y. 11550.

CAREER: New York University, New York, N.Y., instructor, 1956-57; Hofstra University, Hempstead, N.Y., 1957—, began as assistant professor, professor of history, 1976—. Business history editor, Greenwood Press, 1966—; consulting editor, Year, Inc. *Military service:* U.S. Army, 1953-55. *Member:* American Historical Association, American Economic Association, Business History Association, American Association of University Professors, Phi Alpha Theta. *Awards, honors:* Cordell Mull fellow, 1961-63; Economics-in-Action fellow, 1962; New York State fellow in African history, 1966-67.

WRITINGS: The Origins of Interventionism: The United States and the Russo-Finnish War, Bookman Associates, 1961; *The Collier Quick and Easy Guide to American History,* Collier, 1962; *Basic Facts of U.S. History,* Collier, 1963; *Review Notes and Study Guide to "The Peleponnesian War" by Thucydides,* Monarch, 1964; *The Big Board: A History of the New York Stock Market,* Free Press, 1965; *The Putnam Collegiate Guide to American History,* two volumes, Putnam, 1965, published as *American History: College Level,* American R.D.M. Corp., 1968; *Niccolo Machiavelli's "The Prince"; also "The Discourses," and Other Works,* Monarch, 1965; *Voltaire, including "Candide" and "The Philosophes,"* Monarch, 1965; *The Federalist Papers,* Monarch, 1965; *The Putnam Collegiate Guide to Western Civilization,* Volume II, Putnam, 1966, published as *World History,* Volume II, American R.D.M. Corp., 1968; (editor) D. N. Alloway, *Economic History of the United States,* Monarch, 1966; *The American Revolution: A Concise History and Interpretation,* Ardmore, 1967; *The French Revolution: A Concise History and Interpretation,* Ardmore, 1967; *The Great Bull Market: Wall Street in the 1920s,* Norton, 1968; *Panic on Wall Street: A History of America's Financial Disasters,* Macmillan, 1968; *Study Master Notes in American History,* American R.D.M. Corp., 1968; *Study Master Notes in the History of Western Civilization,* American R.D.M. Corp., 1968; (with Paul Sarnoff) *The Automobile Makers,* Putnam, 1969.

The Curbstone Brokers: The Origins of the American Stock Exchange, Macmillan, 1970; *Conquest and Conscience: The 1840s,* Crowell, 1971; (editor-in-chief) *Biographical Directory of the United States Executive Branch, 1774-1971,* Greenwood Press, 1971, 2nd edition published as *Biographical Directory of the United States Executive Branch, 1774-1977,* 1977; *The Age of Giant Corporations: A Microeconomic History of American Business, 1914-1970,* Greenwood Press, 1972; *Amex: A History of the American Stock Exchange, 1921-1971,* Weybright & Talley, 1972; *For Want of a Nail . . . : If Burgoyne Had Won at Saratoga,* Macmillan, 1973; *Machines and Morality: The 1850s,* Crowell, 1974; *The Money Manias: The Eras of Great Speculation in America, 1770-1970,* Weybright & Talley, 1974; *The Entrepreneurs: Explorations within the American Business Tradition,* Weybright & Talley, 1974; *Herbert Hoover at the Onset of the Great Depression, 1929-1930,* Lippincott, 1975; *N.Y.S.E.: A History of the New York Stock Exchange, 1935-1975,* Weybright & Talley, 1975; *The Manipulators: America in the Media Age,* Doubleday, 1976; *The Fallen Colossus,* Weybright & Talley, 1977; *Inside Wall Street: Continuity and Change in the Financial District,* Norton, 1977; (editor with John Raimo) *Biographical Directory of the Governors of the United States, 1789-1978,* Meckler, 1978; *They Satisfy: The Cigarette in American Life,* Doubleday, 1978.

The Last Bull Market: Wall Street in the 1960s, Norton, 1980; *The Worldly Economists,* Macmillan, 1980; *IBM: Colossus in Transition,* Times Books, 1981; *ITT: The Management of Opportunity,* Times Books, 1982. Contributing editor, *Newsfront.*

SIDELIGHTS: Though Robert Sobel's academic specialty is American financial history, his books on that subject are written with a popular (rather than scholarly) audience in mind. Downplaying the role of complex analysis and detailed statistical evidence, Sobel instead relies on biographical vignettes, anecdotes, and reminiscences to produce studies many find unusually brisk and entertaining. Commenting in the *New York Times Book Review* on *Panic on Wall Street,* for example, Gerald Carson notes "the author's eye for the revealing anecdote and his evident gift for projecting social history," talents that "enliven matters that might otherwise remain somewhat abstract." Fellow *New York Times Book Review* critic Andrew Tobias has similar words of praise for *The Last Bull Market*. "You might not think that a history of the United States whose principal figure is the Dow Jones Industrial Average would hold a reader's interest," he begins. "But [*The Last Bull Market*] does this and more. . . . Mr. Sobel has managed to weave a fine narrative. It is as though you are walking through a historical theme park, with this engaging man at your side pointing out the sights."

BIOGRAPHICAL/CRITICAL SOURCES: *Choice,* February, 1966, January, 1969, December, 1975, March, 1977, June, 1978; *American Historical Review,* July, 1966; *New York Times Book Review,* February 9, 1969, October 27, 1974, September 7, 1975, November 6, 1977, February 19, 1978, June 15, 1980; *Newsday,* November 28, 1970; *Journal of American History,* December, 1973, September, 1977; *Christian Science Monitor,* November 5, 1976; *New Yorker,* February 20, 1978; *Washington Post,* November 24, 1978; *Chicago Tribune,* December 6, 1978.

* * *

SOBLE, Jennie
   See CAVIN, Ruth (Brodie)

* * *

SOBOL, Harriet Langsam 1936-

PERSONAL: Born April 30, 1936, in New York, N.Y.; daughter of Morris (an investments broker) and Rose (a teacher; maiden name, Hirschtritt) Kaye; married Barry Langsam, June 15, 1958 (divorced March, 1973); married Thomas Sobol (a school administrator), June 24, 1973; children: (first marriage) Gregory, Jennifer, Jeffrey. *Education:* Attended Skidmore College, 1953-55; Boston University, B.A., 1957; New York University, M.A., 1958. *Home:* 10 Claremont Rd., Scarsdale, N.Y. 10583.

CAREER: Sixth grade teacher in Cherry Hill, N.J., 1958-61; Scarsdale Alternative High School, Scarsdale, N.Y., substitute and volunteer English teacher, 1972-74; creative writing instructor, White Plains Adult School, White Plains, N.Y., 1976—, Scarsdale Adult School, Scarsdale, and Mamaroneck Adult School, Mamaroneck, N.Y., 1978—, and College of New Resources, College of New Rochelle, 1979-80. Writer. *Member:* League of Women Voters (vice-president of local chapter, 1970-71). *Awards, honors: My Brother Steven Is Retarded* was named one of the best books of 1977 by *School Library Journal.*

WRITINGS: *Jeff's Hospital Book* (nonfiction), Walck, 1975; *My Brother Steven Is Retarded,* Macmillan, 1977; *Pete's House,* Macmillan, 1977; *Cosmo's Restaurant,* Macmillan, 1978; *My Other-Mother, My Other-Father,* Macmillan, 1979; *Grandpa: A Young Man Grown Old,* Coward, 1980; *The Interns,* Coward, 1982; *Clowns,* Coward, 1983.

WORK IN PROGRESS: A book about college.

* * *

SOLOTAROFF, Ted
   See SOLOTAROFF, Theodore

* * *

SOLOTAROFF, Theodore 1928-
   (Ted Solotaroff)

PERSONAL: Born October 9, 1928, in Elizabeth, N.J.; son of Ben (a contractor) and Rose (Weiss) Solotaroff; married Lynn Friedman, 1950 (divorced); married Shirley Fingerhood (a lawyer), 1965 (divorced); married Ghislaine Boulanger, 1972 (divorced, 1980); married Virginia Heiserman, 1981; children: (first marriage) Paul, Ivan; (second marriage) Jason; (third marriage) Isaac. *Education:* University of Michigan, B.A., 1952; University of Chicago, M.A., 1956. *Politics:* Independent. *Religion:* Jewish. *Home:* 54 Morningside Dr., New York, N.Y. 10025.

CAREER: Member of College English teaching staff, University of Chicago, Chicago, Ill.; *Commentary* (magazine), New York City, associate editor, 1960-66; *New York Herald Tribune,* New York City, editor of *Book Week,* 1966; editor, *New American Review,* New American Library, New York City, 1966-70, and Simon & Schuster, Inc., New York City, 1970-72; Bantam Books, Inc., New York City, editor of *American Review,* 1972-77, senior editor, 1977-79; Harper & Row Publishers, Inc., New York City, senior editor, 1979—. Jules and Avery Hopwood Awards Lecturer, University of Michigan, 1971; lecturer and teacher of English and creative writing at colleges and universities, including Yale University, City College of City University of New York, University of California, Berkeley, and Columbia University. *Military service:* U.S. Navy, 1946-48. *Member:* Phi Beta Kappa.

AWARDS, HONORS: Jules and Avery Hopwood Awards in fiction and criticism, University of Michigan; Irita Van Doren Book Award, American Booksellers Association, 1973; Brandeis University Creative Arts Awards citation in literature, 1973; Lucille J. Medwick Memorial Award, P.E.N. American Center, 1979; National Endowment for the Arts fellowship.

WRITINGS: (Editor) Isaac Rosenfeld, *An Age of Enormity,* World Publishing, 1962; (editor and author of introduction) *Writers and Issues,* New American Library, 1969; *The Red Hot Vacuum, and Other Pieces on the Writing of the Sixties,* Atheneum, 1970; (editor, with Shannon Ravenel, and author of introduction) *Best American Short Stories of 1978,* Houghton, 1978; (editor, under name Ted Solotaroff) *Many Windows: Twenty-two Stories from "American Review,"* Harper, 1982. Contributor of reviews to periodicals, including *Esquire, Book Week, Commentary, New Republic,* and *New York Times Book Review.*

WORK IN PROGRESS: An autobiography.

SIDELIGHTS: "There is a great deal of creative expression in America today that does not flow in strictly literary channels," wrote Theodore Solotaroff in the first issue of *New American Review* in 1967. "At the same time, literature at present is so inextricably tied to the fearful, bewildering, and controversial state of our 'post-modern' culture that more and more of its interest lies in its social, political and moral bearings. This should not be construed as another way of saying that literature in general and fiction in particular is declining in its intrinsic vitality and relevance. I think it is a good deal less likely that the novel has gone dead than that our critical apparatus has."

Solotaroff has been instrumental in evaluating and shaping literature in America. Former editor of one of the United States' most prestigious literary quarterlies, *New American Review* (later renamed *American Review*), Solotaroff "displays rare skill in evoking the spirit and elucidating the ideas of a literary work," wrote Henry Halpern in *Library Journal.* John Romano in the *New York Times Book Review* declared, "Ted Solotaroff's taste in fiction has proved to be something of a national resource."

Solotaroff came to the forefront of the American literary scene in 1967 when he began editing *New American Review* for New

American Library. Brom Weber in *Saturday Review* called the publication "one of the most interesting literary magazines of our time." The journal is a work of "overall excellence [and offers a] continuing challenge to thought and feeling," Robert K. Morris said in *Nation*. "It is a paperback of substance, both sensitive and significant, and one that will be read and referred to long after its newness has worn off."

When Solotaroff began editing *New American Review/American Review*, he was following in the path of New American Library's highly regarded paperback literary periodical *New World Writing*, which ended publication in 1959. *New World Writing*, Solotaroff noted in his introduction to *New American Review*, Number 1, "supported no school of fiction, poetry or criticism, had no editorial policies except those of taste, relevance, freshness. It was not a magazine that belonged very much to its editors. From its cover . . . to its closing pages, . . . it was a journal that belonged primarily to the writers." It is that tradition, Solotaroff continued, that *New American Review* "now renews and attempts to extend."

"I want [*New American Review*] to be a vehicle for what *writers* have to say," Solotaroff told *Publishers Weekly* before the first issue of the journal was released. "I'll find the writers, but I'll let them do the talking. I do not want to edit the magazine too heavily, to make it go any one way. I want it to go where the best writing is." In the first issue of *New American Review*, Solotaroff assured his readers that the journal would eschew "the tendencies toward cult and coterie" and make "a virtue of catholicity."

The attempt to make *New American Review/American Review* a "writers' magazine" met with some criticism. Robert Hatch in *Nation* questioned Solotaroff's criteria for selecting material for the magazine. Solotaroff, wrote Hatch, "adopts a generally laissez-faire position in which excellence is the non-constrictive criterion. This permissiveness runs so counter to the magazine editor's typical claim to a directive, persuasive role that one suspects the perplexities of assembling an occasional periodical in book form may have suggested it." Hatch then concluded: "Given a clean slate, but only one, on which to record what exercised writers in 1967, who would not resort to discriminating opportunism? Lacking the haven of a pigeonhole, what will you choose from this bewildering activity [of modern fiction]? In the event, it looks very much as though you choose whatever comes conveniently to hand."

Reed Whittemore in a *New York Times Book Review* article also examined the validity and workability of the selection criteria that Solotaroff set forth: "If I have any bone to pick with Mr. Solotaroff, it is his apparent unawareness of the 'tendencies toward cult and coterie' that his authors do reflect. No author can avoid reflecting them, but an editor needs to see them; he needs to know what is and is not represented by his selections, especially if he aspires to 'catholicity.' Catholicity is almost impossible to achieve anyway, but protestations of catholicity abound, and they muddy the air badly. Our literary culture is much more hemmed in than its inhabitants acknowledge, or even realize. The first issue of *New American Review* is a remarkably fine collection, but it is also, despite its movement away from narrow literary concerns, cultish."

In the introductory notes to the second issue of *New American Review*, Solotaroff stated, "We are more interested in publishing writers who are arriving rather than those who are departing or standing still"; that issue featured Guenter Grass, Robert Coover, John Barth, and Richard Hugo, among others. *New American Review/American Review* published works by both "well-known writers who have made landmark contributions [to the periodical] over the years, and some by those young or otherwise unknown writers who have dropped into its pages from out of the blue to give the magazine its Heraclitean flow," Solotaroff observed in *American Review*'s final issue. Solotaroff is now credited with promoting and encouraging numerous writers, including Philip Roth, E. L. Doctorow, and Donald Barthelme. "As an editor," commented Morris, "Mr. Solotaroff is generally happy and provocative in his choices, adept at sighting the rising stars of young writers, and above all resolute in integrity; he refuses to make his review a forum for literary cults, coteries and cabals. His guiding principle is to keep the journal open to the 'flow of fresh, articulate, good writing and thought'; his credo, that good writing is good writing no matter where it comes from."

In addition to outstanding writing, a major aspect of *New American Review/American Review*'s popularity and impact was its sensitivity to the cultural and societal changes of the 1960s and 1970s. As Solotaroff observed in the foreword to *The Best American Short Stories of 1978*, the literary establishment suddenly found that it could no longer isolate itself from the "here and now, particularly in cultures like ours in which the new, the perplexing, the ominous, the random is our central universal." It was this philosophy that was reflected in *New American Review/American Review*. In the original issue of *New American Review*, Solotaroff indicated that the journal would differ from its predecessor *New World Writing* by "providing somewhat more explicit topical connections between contemporary literature and the culture-at-large." Solotaroff stated in *Publishers Weekly*: "I think a strong literary mind can have very valuable things to say about society. Literature remains fresh by maintaining its contacts with society."

Hence, *New American Review/American Review* included not only short fiction and poetry, but each issue also featured a number of nonfiction pieces. "Obviously Mr. Solotaroff is depressed by the word 'literature' as it is defined or confined these days; so he has balanced the seven stories in his first issue with eight interestingly hybrid essays—mixtures of reminiscences, literary criticism, and social commentary," wrote Whittemore. "[Solotaroff] has commissioned his authors to think big and they have; about Broadway, youth, homosexuality, anti-Johnsonism, the irresponsibility of academies; about Norman Mailer, Karl Marx, and Edmund Burke. The essays are miscellaneous, but of a piece in earnestness, intelligence, and, oddly enough, idealism."

The trends in culture and the trends in literature are interwoven, Solotaroff believes, each one influencing the other. In his *Saturday Review* article on *New American Review*, Number 11, Morris described this interrelationship: "Perhaps the best means of defining the sensibilities and aims shared among [the counter-culture] writers . . . are provided by Michael Rossman's essay, 'The Day We Named Our Child, We Had Fish for Dinner,' which weaves Kent State, the [Vietnam] war, racism, campus revolutions, environmental problems—in short, all the threads of the shroud smothering our dying system—with the day-to-day business of living and the continuing dream of renewal." Morris continued: "Unlike the writers of the forties and fifties, lone voices in the wilderness of isolation and alienation, those [writers] of the sixties and seventies know where there is a community of people who think and feel the same way they do; people whom they can touch, speak with, love, write for."

As an editor, Solotaroff found it necessary to defend *New American Review/American Review*, his views of good writing, and indeed, twentieth-century American literature itself. "I like to think . . . the magazine has made an important historical point," Solotaroff wrote in *American Review*'s final issue. "The conventional wisdom of the literary authorities is that we are passing through a relatively sterile and minor literary era. The main evidence for this view is the absence of the towering figures who bestride the age and take their place in this or that Great Tradition. . . . In short, few if any certifiable geniuses and masterpieces. Instead we are living, as it were, in the aftermath of modernism, acting out T. S. Eliot's prophesy that the second half of the century would be a mopping-up operation following the tremendous advances made in the first half. . . . [However,] I sometimes even find myself with the sacrilegious notion that Joyce would have had his hands full with the Irish history being unleashed in comtemporary Dublin, or Faulkner with the kaelidescopic vistas of the New South, or Kafka with the heavier burdens of alienation in today's Prague, or D. H. Lawrence with a sexual revolution that outflanks even his visions.''

However, Solotaroff's defense of the literature of the 1960s and 1970s did not maintain an ingratiating stance to all that was new and different, nor did it manifest itself in a literarily, politically, or socially radical perspective. The essays in the first issue of *New American Review* contained ''a great deal of low-keyed pleading for such archaisms as responsibility, rationality, historical perspective and truth,'' observed Whittemore. ''I don't know that one could find in print now a better small collection than this of sensible literary minds on the loose, determinedly confronting the sundry wild revolutions around us.''

Although Solotaroff appreciated the innovations in literary form, structure, and style made during the decade of *New American Review/American Review*'s publication, he also rejected experimentation for its own sake. ''Typically an issue [of the magazine] contained an 'experimental' story or two, but rarely was the experiment unfelt, solipsistic,'' Romano wrote in the *New York Times Book Review*. ''One of the mistakes we make is in thinking that new writing has to be *avant garde* in its immediate appearance, with wildly different syntax or a shocking vocabulary,'' Solotaroff told *Publishers Weekly*. ''There is an awful lot of good, new fiction being written today that is relatively nonexperimental, but presents a fresh, original point of view.'' In the introduction to *New American Review*, Number 2, Solotaroff declared: ''We are . . . committed to good writing and do not plan to whore after the young and the wild or to publish material merely because its like has never before been seen on land or sea. We believe the cultural tradition needs to be reinstated, not abandoned.''

Solotaroff's view of literature garnered criticism. A *Choice* critic in a review of *New American Review*, Number 1, hoped later issues of the journal would be ''less 'establishment' oriented.'' *Village Voice* critic Eric Oatman found the pieces in *New American Review/American Review* staid and uninspiring: ''My gut reaction to the first two issues of *New American Review* was tempered rage. . . . In retrospect, I suppose I should have anticipated the lack-luster competence of the first issue, with its fiction seldom rising above the level of 'good writing,' with its intelligently carpentered, spiritless verse, and with its essays, virtuoso performances by Concerned Men, extremely pleasant to read but too gracefully conceived and executed to trigger any permanent alteration of vision. It was a satisfactory arrangement; nothing hallowed got too bruised, and the writers got paid.'' A reader and contributor also found fault with the magazine; Weber recounted the argument in *Saturday Review*: ''Solotaroff made it clear [in *New American Review*, Number 6] that he preferred 'the reasoned social thought of Paul Goodman and Herbert Marcuse' to the ''sluttish antinomianism'' . . . of the Jerry Rubins and the Mark Rudds.' Ironically enough, a contributor who had extolled Rubin in the same issue wrote a scathing letter [in the next issue] derogating the periodical as a 'liberal intellectual journal' and informing Solotaroff that her conception of literary 'responsibility' did not include his 'judiciousness,' 'intellectual respectability or . . . balanced view.' '' Concluded Weber: ''The American scene owes a great deal to Solotaroff for his maintenance of that necessary intellectual stance.''

Solotaroff's ''judiciousness'' and ''intellectual respectability'' are also evident in his critical work. Solotaroff ''is always acutely sensitive to the historical matrix of literature,'' *New York Times'* Christopher Lehmann-Haupt commented in his review of *The Red Hot Vacuum, and Other Pieces on the Writing of the Sixties*. ''At the same time, [Solotaroff] never fails to respect the integrity of the text, presumably the legacy of his years as a graduate student and teaching English literature.'' Leo Braudy in the *New York Times Book Review* believed that *The Red Hot Vacuum* maintained ''a steady level of responsible brilliance.''

A major focus of the essays collected in *The Red Hot Vacuum* was the shifting aesthetic and ethical values in American literature and the concomitant changes in standards for evaluating contemporary writing. In the preface to *The Red Hot Vacuum*, Solotaroff articulated the impact those literary and critical changes have had: ''The market for serious writing cracked open in the Sixties and soon became a kind of howling forum where all manners of ideas, styles and standards contended for attention. As the literary climate altered radically, there was a distinct shift among writers and editors from a preoccupation with values as the ground of experience to a preoccupation with experience as the ground of values—a shift that was, of course, to be felt everywhere in America as the decade of opposition and revision careened along.''

Critics of *The Red Hot Vacuum* observed that Solotaroff, too, was engaged in the preoccupation with ''experience as the ground of values.'' Weber called *The Red Hot Vacuum* ''a probing survey of the American literary imagination in the Sixties, one that grapples with the radical novelty and difficulty of the contemporary writer and attempts to elucidate whatever underlying humanistic value his enterprise contains.'' However, Braudy challenged the assumption that Solotaroff's chief concern was with ''defining a decade [or] recreating the spume and dust of literary-political controversy.'' ''The reader who is looking for a semi-caustic, semi-hip chronicle of the Sixties will be disappointed by *The Red Hot Vacuum*,'' stated Braudy. ''The true energy of *The Red Hot Vacuum* is not in the explication of books. It is in the attempt to define what it means to be a critic.''

Solotaroff's critical perspective as an editor and a writer shifted during the 1960s, as is evident in the essays contained in *The Red Hot Vacuum* and in the introductory notes to *New American Review/American Review*. Weber traced ''the drift in Solotaroff's thought . . . from 'academic liberalism and humanism' through 'radical humanism' to . . . 'libertarianism.' This particular transvaluation of values is not an unfamiliar pattern nowadays.'' According to Weber, the changes in Solotaroff's attitudes are displayed in his critical works: ''Returning literature to its full human context has not been either a quick or easy undertaking for Solotaroff or others. The reticence concerning himself in the 1962 essay on [Issac] Rosenfeld [in *The Red Hot Vacuum*] is only gradually transformed into the unremitting autobiographical involvement that guides his treatment in 1969 of Roth's career and writings.'' *The Red Hot Vacuum*, said a critic for *Antioch Review*, showed Solotaroff to be ''a writer engaged in a semi-private quest for character.''

In the articles published in *The Red Hot Vacuum*, Solotaroff ''seems increasingly . . . to employ the fist person singular pronoun, to introduce his essays with personal anecdotes, and to gauge his judgements by his own experience instead of by a set of theoretical rules," said *New York Times*' Lehmann-Haupt. "It is almost as if he were saying 'I no longer know what rules to go by, but anyway, here is what touches me.'" In the preface to the volume, Solotaroff reflected on the alterations in his critical perspective: "My own literary journalism became a way of responding somewhat more directly and individually to the altered environment of letters, and, inevitably, to the political, social and cultural developments that related to it. [The articles in *The Red Hot Vacuum*] became a way of letting into my work some of the impact of the drastic changes that took place in my private life, some of the truths that have come with the blows. . . . Often I didn't succeed very well, but near the end I began to get a firmer grip on this conflict of approach, and to come a little cleaner, a little clearer, I think, in learning how to use that most difficult word in the writer's vocabulary, according to Gide—the word 'I.'"

CA INTERVIEW

CA interviewed Theodore Solotaroff by phone August 4, 1981, at his office at Harper & Row Publishers, Inc. in New York, N.Y.

CA: You've described your childhood as "mostly one long angry struggle to escape from my parents' designs on it." Is this what led you to an interest in writing and writers?

SOLOTAROFF: That was one view of it. I've since been thinking a lot about it, because I'm working on an essay about my earlier years. Like most poeple, I began writing for my mother, as one does at four or five. I wrote poems and drew pictures and so on. The mother is the first audience. My mother, an artistic woman, was a pianist, and I think she encouraged my aesthetic tendencies. What really led me directly to writing was, when I was a college freshman I submitted a story to the Hopwood Awards at the University of Michigan. It was the first real story I'd ever written, and it won and that made me think, "Gee, if I can win a prize the first time I ever write a story, this is easy." It's like getting a home run the first time you're up at bat. That's how I started. I thought of myself essentially as a fiction writer, as you can tell from my essay "The Practical Critic: A Personal View," in the summer, 1972 *Michigan Quarterly Review*.

CA: In "Silence, Exile and Cunning," an article in New American Review, *Number 8, you wrote about being stuck in your writing and being unable to utilize the real experiences of your own life. Do you think this is a problem for many beginning writers?*

SOLOTAROFF: I think so. I think there's the idea that literary experience is somehow beyond their own experience, that they have to live the kind of life Hemingway or Fitzgerald or Faulkner did. I think that idea was more prevalent in my formative period because those figures were much more dominating than they are now. A lot of writers have since proven that their own experience is quite good enough. You don't tend to mythologize Updike or Roth or Bellow and other writers who obviously write pretty directly from their lives. There's been a whole change about what makes literature, and I think now it's less a matter of great imaginative constructs than of limited reports of one's being in the world.

CA: From your own experiences, what advice would you give aspiring writers?

SOLOTAROFF: I would say don't be faked out by *Literature*—write about what you know or feel strongly about: don't worry about whether it's worthy of *Literature* or not. Let literature judge that for itself. I often tell young writers that I think the best way to prepare themselves to write is to write a journal and develop a style that's very personal, as you can with a journal because no one's looking over your shoulder except yourself. That kind of training—writing without any pressure—is excellent for developing personal style.

CA: You went to Commentary *as an editor in 1960. Was that your first experience with editing?*

SOLOTAROFF: Actually, the only prior experience I had had with manuscripts was as a freshman English teacher, which stood me in good stead.

CA: Did you find Commentary *a good training ground?*

SOLOTAROFF: Excellent. It was very strong on fundamentals.

CA: As editor of New American Review *and* American Review, *you've published some very select writing. Has it been hard to make choices about what to include?*

SOLOTAROFF: Oh yes. There was usually a good deal more to include than I had room for. We received enormous numbers of manuscripts and published very few of them. I figured out we published about four-tenths of one percent of what we received. A lot of what we received, of course, were not really eligible. They were simply not mature enough, not accomplished enough. There were almost always three or four manuscripts that we could well have published for every one that we did publish, if we had had room for them.

CA: Did you just return those or did you direct them somewhere else?

SOLOTAROFF: I would often try to direct them to other places like the *New Yorker, Esquire,* or one of the little magazines.

CA: What have you found to be the greatest difficulties in editing the review?

SOLOTAROFF: I think the main difficulty was keeping it going. It really was meant to have a fairly large readership, so I was very involved in the whole distributing of it, advertising it, developing a subscription program—all those things. It was really sort of a one-man show.

CA: What problems do you find foremost in editing now?

SOLOTAROFF: Some manuscripts are certainly more problematic than others; some require a lot more work. I suppose the main problem now is to know what to publish, know what to acquire. The market is extremely selective. Books that might have succeeded a few years ago are having a hard time now. Just choosing something because it's the work of a very promising writer doesn't necessarily fill the bill. You have to choose a book that has a real chance of catching on, that has some sort of commercial ingredient built into it. Finding those two together can be difficult.

CA: It seems very hard now for new novelists to get published.

SOLOTAROFF: I'm not too sure the new novelist has as much trouble as the novelist who has had a couple of books published that haven't caught on. The really good first novel has much more of a chance simply because there is no track record. If someone has written two very gifted novels that have sold two thousand copies each, it's very hard to find a publisher to do a third one.

CA: In your preface to The Red Hot Vacuum *you said of writing in the 1960s, "As the literary climate altered radically there was a distinct shift among writers and editors from a preoccupation with values as the ground of experience to a preoccupation with experience as the ground for values." As a critic, do you see or foresee a shift back to fiction rooted in the earlier values?*

SOLOTAROFF: I think so, I think that's happening now. I think that's part of the reactionary trend of the age, the return to the basics, the return to history. What I was really referring to was the whole sense of the 1960s that had turned over everyone's expectations and made you try to pay attention to what was happening here and now. The whole question of *relevance* became so prominent, and that's really what I was referring to.

CA: You've commented on the journalistic novel. Do you think this genre will continue to gain in importance?

SOLOTAROFF: I think so. A lot of the bloom is off the rose, of course. I think the age we live in is so confusing and perplexing and repellent that it exerts a continual fascination for the writer, and also the readers are anxious to know just what it is they're living in. There don't seem to be any boundaries or precedents. Each decade seems like a century in a way—how far away the 1960s seem from us now, for example. I think that anyone who can offer some kind of promise of describing or defining the age in a more immediate way has a good leg up, and that's what journalism tends to do.

CA: Do you think the electronic media have much influenced the novelist's outlook and approach to writing?

SOLOTAROFF: In a couple of cases obviously, like Burroughs and Barth, who have been using tapes. I think they much more influence readers. I think McLuhan is right, that for the most part people who grow up with television and the other media lose the habit of reading for imagination, and even for information. I can remember how important *Life* magazine used to be, which was about as close as a magazine could come to a television program. *Life* now is a very minor magazine. My own sons, however, who grew up watching television, are still inveterate readers. But I do find more and more people telling me that they don't read or their friends don't read. This means, of course, that the kind of publishing I do, where serious reading is required to make these books work, becomes that much more precarious.

CA: Are you teaching at all or otherwise in touch with universities or writing workshops?

SOLOTAROFF: Yes, I've been teaching a fiction workshop at Columbia off and on.

CA: Do you have pretty good students?

SOLOTAROFF: They vary. The good ones are very good. It usually works out that way; in any class of sixteen there are four or five good writers. The difference really tends to be in the rest. In a place like Columbia, the next five or six are also very good, and there's maybe only a few who shouldn't be there. I don't know that they have any more outstanding writers than in other places, but they tend to have more competent ones.

CA: How do you feel about academic critical writing?

SOLOTAROFF: I'm not terribly interested in it. It seems to me kind of an enterprise of its own that doesn't have too much to do with the books or the writers it addresses itself to. It keeps a lot of academics working and thinking and so on. It's just not my kind of criticism.

CA: Are there periodicals that you read for good topical writing or fiction?

SOLOTAROFF: I read the *New York Review* fairly steadily; I read the *Nation* and the *New York Review of Books*. As for fiction, I read the *New Yorker* stories, though not every time. I read so much fiction in my work that it's kind of a pleasure not to read it. I do like to read nineteenth-century fiction. And I also write a fair amount about fiction. A first-rate writer is still as thrilling as ever, but I don't really read that much fiction for recreation. I like to read something unlike what I'm publishing.

CA: You said in 1972 that you believed American literature was in one of its more creative periods. What about now?

SOLOTAROFF: I don't know how much of that was due to my own perspective. I saw a lot more writing then, of course, than I do now. My own access has narrowed considerably from editing books instead of magazines. I work with fewer writers on much longer projects. Still, I think there is an awful lot of talent; I see a lot of polished, professional writing, particularly poetry. Poetry is in a boom period, although it doesn't seem to be producing many major figures. Maybe we no longer live in an age when major figures are produced. As I said elsewhere: it's true of history, physics, chemistry, and mathematics. We don't have any giants. We don't have an Einstein today or a Freud or a Toynbee or a Fermi or a Marx. Maybe that's true of literature too.

CA: To this point, what's been most gratifying about your career?

SOLOTAROFF: That's hard to answer because a lot of things have been gratifying. Being an editor in itself was gratifying, for *Commentary* and particularly *Book Week* and *American Review*. The work I do now is gratifying. I suppose on the whole my own writing has been the most gratifying since it's been my own. I still find a lot of satisfaction in writing reviews and essays.

CA: You said some years ago that you were writing an autobiography. Are you still working on that?

SOLOTAROFF: Yes and no. It's hard to sustain a longer work, and some of the material that was going to be in that is now becoming the essay I mentioned earlier. I don't know if I'll get around to doing a full-fledged autobiography until I retire. But much of my writing is autobiographical in one way or another, as everyone's is really.

CA: Do you think you'll ever try fiction again?

SOLOTAROFF: Yes. I'm writing a story now. That's what I do for R & R sometimes. It's fun to write fiction. I did a story in 1979 for *TriQuarterly* called "The Amorist." One of the things that really gave me satisfaction was a story I wrote with my two younger sons that appeared recently in a Rolling Stone Press anthology called *Wonders*. It's a swell story called "Hector Leaves Home" about a mouse that lives at Cathedral School, which is where one of my sons went to school. Working with the kids on writing the story was a terrific kick, not just because of the story itself, but because I managed to be a writer without spooking them away from it. All four of my sons are quite literary; all of them write. That gives me a lot of satisfaction. I guess I must have done something right.

CA: How did you and the boys collaborate on the story?

SOLOTAROFF: We were together on vacation, and I'd been asked to write a story for this anthology, and I said, "Why don't you write it with me?" and they said, "Oh, come on. It's vacation." And I said, "Well, if you do, you'll each get half the advance." It came to a hundred dollars each; that was very big money for an eight-year-old and even a thirteen-year-old. Now they tell me they feel as if they're writers too.

BIOGRAPHICAL/CRITICAL SOURCES: New American Review, Number 1, September, 1967, Number 2, January, 1968, Number 3, April, 1968; *Time*, September 1, 1967; *Saturday Review*, September 9, 1967, October 5, 1968, January 16, 1971; *New York Times Book Review*, September 17, 1967, June 29, 1970, December 4, 1972; *Nation*, October 23, 1967, May 31, 1971, February 9, 1974, June 3, 1978; *New York Review of Books*, October 26, 1967; *Choice*, November, 1967; *Christian Century*, November 29, 1967; *Village Voice*, February 29, 1968; *Washington Post*, January 23, 1969; Theodore Solotaroff, *The Red Hot Vacuum, and Other Pieces on the Writing of the Sixties*, Atheneum, 1970; *Antioch Review*, fall-winter, 1970-71; *Library Journal*, October 1, 1970; *Newsweek*, November 16, 1970, April 17, 1972; *New York Times*, December 4, 1970; *New York*, May 17, 1971; *American Review*, Number 26, November, 1977; Theodore Solotaroff and Shannon Ravenel, editors, *Best American Short Stories of 1978*, Houghton, 1978.

—Sketch by Heidi A. Tietjen

—Interview by Jean W. Ross

*   *   *

SPECHT, Harry 1929-

PERSONAL: Born August 1, 1929, in New York, N.Y.; son of Joseph (a gambler) and Helen (a pianist; maiden name, Frankele) Specht; married Riva Genfan (a social worker), June 5, 1954; children: Daniel Joseph, Eliot David. *Education:* City College (now City College of the City University of New York), B.A., 1951; Western Reserve University (now Case Western Reserve University), M.S.S.W., 1951; Brandeis University, Ph.D., 1962. *Politics:* Socialist. *Religion:* Jewish. *Home:* 807 Oxford, Berkeley, Calif. 94707. *Office:* School of Social Welfare, University of California, Berkeley, Calif. 94720.

CAREER: Mobilization for Youth, New York, N.Y., director of community organization, 1962-64; Contra Costa Council of Community Services, Walnut Creek, Calif., associate director, 1964-66; San Francisco State College (now University), San Francisco, Calif., associate professor, 1966-67; University of California, Berkeley, lecturer, 1967-69, associate professor, 1969-73, professor of social work, 1973—, dean of School of Social Welfare, 1977—. *Awards, honors:* Senior Fulbright scholarship, London, England, 1973-74.

WRITINGS: Young Adults in Groups, National Jewish Welfare Board, 1964; *Urban Community Development: A Social Work Process*, Contra Costa Council of Community Services, 1966; (with Anatole Shaffer) *Training the Poor for New Careers*, Contra Costa Council of Community Services, 1966; (editor with Ralph Kramer) *Readings in Community Organization Practice*, Prentice-Hall, 1969, 2nd edition, 1975; (with George Brager) *Community Organizing*, Columbia University Press, 1973; (with Neil Gilbert) *Dimensions of Social Welfare Policy*, Prentice-Hall, 1974; (with Gilbert) *The Model Cities Program*, U.S. Government Printing Office, 1974; (editor with Gilbert) *Planning for Social Welfare: Issues, Models, and Tasks*, Prentice-Hall, 1977; (with Anne Vickery) *Integrating Social Work Methods*, Allen & Unwin, 1977; (with Gilbert) *Handbook of the Social Services*, Prentice-Hall, 1981; (with Gilbert) *The Emergence of Social Welfare and Social Work*, 2nd edition, F. E. Peacock, 1981.

WORK IN PROGRESS: Practice in Social Planning; Social Welfare Perspectives.

*   *   *

SPENCER, William 1922-

PERSONAL: Born June 1, 1922, in Erie, Pa.; son of Herbert Reynolds (a manufacturer) and Rachel (Davis) Spencer; married Martha Jane Brown, February 6, 1948 (divorced); married Elizabeth Bouvier (an artist and teacher), May 18, 1969; children: (first marriage) Christopher, Meredith, Anne. *Education:* Princeton University, A.B., 1948; Duke University, A.M., 1950; American University, Ph.D., 1965. *Politics:* Democrat. *Religion:* Presbyterian. *Home address:* P.O. Box 25, Micanopy, Fla.

CAREER: Middle East Journal, Washington, D.C., assistant editor, 1956-57; George Washington University, Washington, D.C., associate professor of political science, 1957-60; U.S. Office of Education, Washington, D.C., international programs specialist, 1960-62; UNESCO, Paris, France, chief of publications, 1962-64; American University, Washington, D.C., director of Institute of Non-Western Studies, 1965-68; Florida State University, Tallahassee, professor of Middle East history, 1968-80; writer, 1980—. Member of board of directors, Florida Heritage Foundation, Santa Fe Regional Library Advisory, Alachua County Human Services Advisory Board, and Islam Centennial Fourteen National Committee. Consultant to Historical Evaluation and Research Organization and Special Operations Research Office; adviser to Government of Morocco (for UNESCO). Elder, McIntosh Presbyterian Church. *Military service:* U.S. Army, 1943-46; cryptanalyst in India; received Presidential Citation. *Member:* Middle East Studies Association (fellow), Phi Kappa Phi, Pi Sigma Alpha, Phi Alpha Theta. *Awards, honors:* Distinguished Service Award, U.S. Junior Chamber of Commerce, 1958; Carnegie fellowship; U.S. Office of Education Title V grant; Fulbright-Hays Award; Florida State University research grant.

WRITINGS: The Land and People of Turkey, Lippincott, 1958, revised edition, 1972; *Political Evolution in the Middle East*, Lippincott, 1962; *The Land and People of Morocco*, Lippincott, 1965, revised edition, 1973; *The Land and People of Tunisia*, Lippincott, 1967, revised edition, 1972; *The Land and People of Algeria*, Lippincott, 1969; *The Story of North Africa*, McCormick-Mathers, 1975; *Algiers in the Age of the Corsairs*, University of Oklahoma Press, 1976; *Historical Dictionary of Morocco*, Scarecrow Press, 1980; *Conflict in the Middle East: The Islamic States*, F. Watts, in press. Also author of several government reports.

Author of weekly column, "Micanopy," in *Gainesville Sun*, 1980—. Contributor to *World Book Encyclopedia*, *World Book Year Book*, and *Grolier Encyclopedia Year Book*. Contributor of over 500 articles and book reviews to newspapers, magazines, and journals.

WORK IN PROGRESS: A comic novel, *The CIA and the Twelfth Imam;* a book about ship travel experiences with a Mediterranean setting; a nonfiction book interweaving experiences running a small farm in the middle of the city with those of early retirement, *Our Urban Farm.*

SIDELIGHTS: William Spencer told *CA:* "Since my retirement from university teaching, writing has become a full-time vocation, a craft to be learned, and a challenge as I work with strict discipline toward new goals. My thirty-year professional career now becomes a backdrop for drawing together a variety of experiences and knowledge of a particular area into a 'statement' of my beliefs, what I've learned, what truths are relevant out of my life to the lives of others. I'm excited about these new projects, and excited about *Conflict in the Middle East: The Islamic States.* Although it's written for young people, I think it tells a story for all ages."

* * *

**SPRIGEL, Olivier
See AVICE, Claude**

* * *

SPYERS-DURAN, Peter 1932-

PERSONAL: Born January 26, 1932, in Budapest, Hungary; son of Alfred (a colonel) and Maria Balogh (Almassy) Spyers-Duran; married Jane F. Cumber, March 21, 1964; children: Kimberly, Hilary, Peter II. *Education:* University of Budapest, certificate, 1955; University of Chicago, M.A.L.S., 1960; Nova University, Ed.D., 1975. *Home:* 11221 Weatherby Rd., Los Alamitos, Calif. 90720. *Office:* California State University, Long Beach, Calif. 90840.

CAREER: Chicago Public Library, Chicago, Ill., reference librarian, 1959-60; University of Wichita, Wichita, Kan., head of circulation department, 1960-62; American Library Association, Chicago, Ill., assistant executive secretary, 1962-63; University of Wisconsin—Milwaukee, assistant director of libraries and assistant professor, 1963-67, associate director of libraries and associate professor, 1967; Western Michigan University, Kalamazoo, associate professor, 1967-69, professor, 1969-70, director of libraries, 1967-70; Florida Atlantic University, Boca Raton, professor and director of libraries and chairman of library science program, 1970-76; California State University, Long Beach, executive director of library and learning resources, 1976—. Institutional representative to Center for Research Libraries and International Federation of Library Associations. *Member:* American Library Association, Southeastern Library Association, Florida Library Association, Florida Association of Public Junior Colleges, California Library Association, California Academic and Research Libraries.

WRITINGS: Moving Library Materials, University of Wisconsin—Milwaukee Library Associates, 1964, revised edition, American Library Association, 1965; *A Survey of Fringe Benefits Offered by Public Libraries in the United States,* American Library Association, 1966; *Basic Fringe Benefits for Public Libraries in the United States,* Libraries Unlimited, 1967; (contributor) Theodore Samore, editor, *Problems in Library Classification, Dewey 17 and Conversion,* University of Wisconsin, 1968.

(Editor) *Approval and Gathering Plans in Academic Libraries,* Western Michigan University, 1970; (editor) *Advances in Understanding Approval Plans in Academic Libraries,* Western Michigan University, 1970; *Economics of Approval Plans,* Greenwood Press, 1972; (co-editor) *Management Problems in Serials Work,* Greenwood Press, 1973; *Prediction of Resource Needs: A Model Formula Budgeting System for Upper Division University Libraries,* Nova University Press, 1975; *Issues in Automated Cataloging,* Greenwood Press, 1979; *Shaping Library Collections for the 1980's,* Oryx, 1981; *Austerity Management in Academic Libraries,* Scarecrow, 1983.

Contributor of reviews and articles to professional journals, including *Wilson Library Bulletin, Incipit, Library Quarterly,* and *College Research Libraries.*

AVOCATIONAL INTERESTS: Riding, tennis, swimming, the theater, music, deep-sea fishing, and boating.

* * *

**STACHYS, Dimitris
See CONSTANTELOS, Demetrios J.**

* * *

STALLWORTHY, Jon (Howie) 1935-

PERSONAL: Born January 18, 1935, in London, England; son of John Arthur (a surgeon) and Margaret (Howie) Stallworthy; married Gillian Waldock, June 25, 1960; children: Jonathan Meredith, Philippa Margaret, Nicolas Kyd. *Education:* Magdalen College, Oxford, B.A., 1958, B. Litt., 1961. *Religion:* Church of England. *Home:* 1456 Hanshaw Rd., Ithaca, N.Y. 14850; and Long Farm, Old Marston, Oxford, England (summer). *Office:* Department of English, Cornell University, Ithaca, N.Y. 14853.

CAREER: Oxford University Press, London, England, editor, 1959-77; Cornell University, Ithaca, N.Y., John Wendell Anderson Professor of English Literature, 1977—. *Military service:* British Army, Oxfordshire and Buckinghamshire Light Infantry, 1953-55; became lieutenant. *Awards, honors:* Newdigate Prize, 1958, for English verse; Duff Cooper Memorial Prize, 1974, W.H. Smith & Son Literary Award, 1975, and National Institute and American Academy of Arts and Sciences E.M. Forster Award, 1976, all for *Wilfred Owen.*

WRITINGS: The Earthly Paradise (poem), privately printed, 1958; *The Astronomy of Love* (poems), Oxford University Press, 1961; *Between the Lines: W. B. Yeats's Poetry in the Making,* Clarendon Press, 1963; *Out of Bounds* (poems), Oxford University Press, 1963; *Vision and Revision in Yeats's Last Poems,* Clarendon Press, 1963; *The Almond Tree* (poem), Turret Books, 1967; (editor) *Yeats: Last Poems* (collection of critical essays), Macmillan (London), 1968; *Root and Branch* (poems), Oxford University Press, 1969.

(Translator with Jerzy Peterkiewicz and Burns Singer) Peterkiewicz and Singer, editors, *Five Centuries of Polish Poetry, 1450-1970,* enlarged edition, Oxford University Press, 1970; (translator) Alexander Blok, *The Twelve, and Other Poems,* Oxford University Press, 1970; (editor) Alan Brownjohn, *New Poems, 1970-1971,* Hutchinson, 1971; *Hand in Hand* (poems), Oxford University Press, 1974; *The Apple Barrel: Selected Poems, 1955-1963,* Oxford University Press, 1974; (editor and author of introduction) *The Penguin Book of Love Poetry,* Allen Lane, 1973, published as *A Book of Love Poetry,* Oxford University Press, 1974; *Wilfred Owen* (biography), Oxford University Press, 1974; (translator) Blok, *Selected Poems,* Penguin, 1974; *A Familiar Tree* (poems), Oxford University Press, 1978; (translator) Boris Pasternak, *Selected Poems,* Allen Lane, 1982; (editor and author of introduction) *The Complete Poems and Fragments of Wilfred Owen,* Oxford University Press, 1983.

Contributor of poems and articles to periodicals, including the *New York Times, London Magazine, Critical Quarterly, Review of English Studies, Times Literary Supplement,* and *Review of English Literature.* Editor, *Workshop,* summer, 1968.

WORK IN PROGRESS: Literary criticism; translations; poems; a biography of Louis MacNeice.

SIDELIGHTS: A departure from his previous volumes of poetry and criticism, Jon Stallworthy's biographical study *Wilfred Owen* retraces the brief life of the English poet who was killed in action some seven days before the end of World War I. Now regarded as one of his country's finest war poets, Owen was an "unmistakably adolescent" Romanticist until the last months of his life, maintains the *Listener*'s Denis Thomas; his current reputation is derived from a legacy of thirty or so poems he wrote as he reflected on scenes of death and mutilation he witnessed on the front. In order to discover what pre-war experiences might have influenced Owen's work, Stallworthy sought out the poet's few remaining relatives and friends and analyzed numerous letters, unpublished manuscripts, and even annotations the young soldier had made in his favorite books. The resulting biography, many critics note, provides a welcome and warmly sympathetic synthesis of the numerous portraits of Owen that have appeared in the decades since his death.

Though several reviewers, including one from the *New Yorker,* point out that the three-volume memoir of Owen's brother Harold has "already provided a basis that no formal biographer is likely to surpass," others, like the *Times Literary Supplement*'s John Bayley, note that Stallworthy takes this source and "recreates a rich domestic density of felt and feeling existence. Harold Owen's edition of his brother's letters is made good use of, and so are such pioneer critical studies as that of D.S.R. Welland. Mr. Stallworthy has a gift for biography which evokes the period, the ideology and the background from which Owen came, with something like the fullness and the deliberation with which Lawrence and Joyce wrote up their own early years in *Sons and Lovers* and *Portrait of the Artist*." Kingsley Amis, writing in the *Observer,* also praises Stallworthy's "fully detailed, irreplaceable biography" and its many "additions to our knowledge of the period." The *Sewanee Review* critic is especially pleased to note that the author's "superb and exemplary narrative" is such "a model of intelligent selectivity and balance. . . . Stallworthy gives us all the relevant facts and details of Owen's life without lapsing into the conventional gestures of judgmental intrusion."

Several critics, however, would have preferred to see the author do a bit *more* interpreting. Though the *Encounter*'s Philip Larkin believes Stallworthy does a good job of sorting his material and arranging it in a manner the reviewer describes as "alert, unprejudiced and vivid," Larkin nevertheless goes on to write: "Where [Stallworthy's] book is less satisfactory is in its lack of emphases and its general suspension of judgment on the kind of person we now know Owen to have been, and how this new knowledge relates to his work. The evidence is there, but perhaps through the very scrupulousness that ensures its accurate presentation Stallworthy refrains from interpreting it." In particular, some reviewers point to Stallworthy's discussion of the poet's work as well as his restrained approach to the subject of Owen's "latent homosexuality" as areas that might have been explored in more detail.

Regarding Owen's apparent homosexuality, for example, Thomas remarks that it is a topic Stallworthy "does not shrink from, but on which he does not enlarge." Bernard Jones, commenting in *Books and Bookmen,* speculates that the author felt bound to discuss Owen's extremely close relationship with his mother in terms of homosexuality, since "modern psychological thinking would have it that such relationships drive the young persons into homosexuality. . . . Earlier generations, however, found nothing strange in such relationships nor in homosexuality itself. . . . [Thus, it appears that Stallworthy] is so much of his own time that he fails to bring Owen's values to the reading of Owen's words." Amis, for one, is glad to see that Stallworthy downplays the subject. "No doubt this is the wisest course," he states, "especially since I should guess Mr. Stallworthy shares my own conviction that those feelings never ran as far as being translated into practice. Their presence in Owen, however, deserves recognition, because. . . . they were an essential part of his artistic nature, causing him perhaps to experience a peculiar agony on the battlefield and to convey a peculiar tenderness in his work."

Stallworthy's criticism of the poems, which the *New York Review of Books*'s Karl Miller characterizes as "sensible but rather unforthcoming," strikes a few reviewers as inadequate. Calvin Bedient of the *New York Times Book Review,* for instance, labels it "sparse," and both Jones and Amis wish Stallworthy had devoted more time and effort to discussing the technical aspects of Owen's poetry. Remarks Amis: "Stallworthy's critical comments are both sensitive and sensible, but he has little to say about Owen's major technical innovation, the use of chime or pararhyme or consonantal rhyme or alliterative assonance." Jones, too, believes that "the whole question of Owen's technical virtuosity called for a more sustained examination than it has received. . . . Stallworthy may have been inhibited here by [previous studies], but the subject is not one that is easily exhausted. . . . Likewise there is still much noting to be done of affinities with other poets."

For the most part, though, reviewers feel Stallworthy includes just the right amount of critical interpretation in his biography. *Commonweal*'s Jeffrey Meyers declares that the author, "himself a considerable poet and experienced soldier, provides a sensitive reading of the poems, emphasizes Owen's development and shows how he evolved from the derivative . . . to the confident and characteristic." The *Sewanee Review* critic points out that "the critical materials are not defensive; nor are they advertisements for Owen's work. . . . Stallworthy simply assumes that Owen is a poet of the first rank and devotes his central critical attention to the way in which the poems were composed and the materials out of which they were made." Bayley finds that "one of the many good things about Jon Stallworthy's really admirable and scholarly biography is his unobtrusive slipping in of quick comparison, nuances of critical perception done without much emphasis or weight of commentary."

In short, concludes Jones, *Wilfred Owen* "is a model of self-effacement in the service of a fine poet. Here and there it will probably betray the time and society in which it was composed, . . . but there can be little doubt that the book belongs with the first rank of biographical works and that it can be studied profitably by any one who cares to know Wilfred Owen and his work. . . . Stallworthy's biography is a brilliant attempt to convey a portrait of a shy poet whose private world confronted unafraid the breaking of nations. It is a book of quality that is not equalled once a year, a book that leaves one feeling for the Owens."

BIOGRAPHICAL/CRITICAL SOURCES: Punch, February 26, 1969; *New Statesman,* February 28, 1969, July 5, 1974, November 8, 1974; *Times Literary Supplement,* April 24, 1969, August 9, 1974, November 15, 1974, July 4, 1980; *Books and*

Bookmen, June, 1969, September, 1976, October, 1976; *Virginia Quarterly Review,* autumn, 1969, spring, 1979; *London Magazine,* October, 1969; *Observer,* November 10, 1974; *Spectator,* November 30, 1974; *Listener,* January 9, 1975, March 15, 1979; *Encounter,* March, 1975; *Commonweal,* May 23, 1975; *Saturday Review,* July 26, 1975; *Washington Post Book World,* August 3, 1975; *New York Times Book Review,* September 14, 1975, April 1, 1979; *New York Review of Books,* October 16, 1975; *Poetry,* November, 1975; *New Yorker,* January 26, 1976; *Sewanee Review,* summer, 1976; *Contemporary Literature,* winter, 1980.

—Sketch by Deborah A. Straub

* * *

STANG, Judit 1921-1977
(Judy Stang; Judy Varga, a pseudonym)

PERSONAL: Born August 14, 1921, in Hungary; died August 28, 1977; daughter of Varga and Cecilia (Valdmari) Jeno; married Soren Stang (an executive), June 27, 1947; children: Erik. *Education:* Attended Hungarian Royal School of Commercial Art, 1939, and Alma College, St. Thomas, Ontario, Canada, 1942. *Religion:* High Episcopalian. *Address:* Box 195, Montego Bay, Jamaica, West Indies. *Agent:* Mary Gerard, 8 Jane St., New York, N.Y.

CAREER: National Film Board of Canada, Ottawa, Ontario, artist, 1942-45; free-lance writer and artist, 1945-77.

WRITINGS—Under pseudonym Judy Varga, except as indicated, all self-illustrated; published by Morrow, except as indicated: *Gremlins on the Job,* [Canada], 1942; *The Dragon Who Liked to Spit Fire,* 1961; *Miss Lollipop's Lion,* 1963; *Pig in the Parlor,* 1963; *The Sociable Seal,* 1965; *The Crow Who Came to Stay,* 1967; *The Puppy Who Liked to Chew Things,* 1968; *Janko's Wish,* 1969; *The Magic Wall,* 1970; *The Monster behind the Black Rock,* 1971; *The Mare's Egg,* 1972; *Once-a-Year Witch,* 1973; *The Battle of the Wind Gods,* 1974; *Circus Cannonball,* 1975; (under name Judy Stang) *The Pet in the Jar,* Western Publishing, 1975.

Illustrator: Jane Hart, *Let's Think about Time,* Hart Publishing, 1965; (under name Judy Stang) Dorothea Tostrud, *A Dragon for Danny Dennis,* Dean, 1980. Also illustrator, under name Judy Stang, of *Mother Goose,* Wonder-Treasure Books.

WORK IN PROGRESS: A book, tentatively entitled *Silly Bear: The Dog Who Liked Everybody.*

SIDELIGHTS: Judit Stang lived in France, England, and Norway from 1945 until 1951. An animal lover, she once owned four dogs and several tame rabbits, hens, roosters, and hamsters, all of which had the run of the house. Her books were often written from an animal's point of view.†

* * *

STANG, Judy
See STANG, Judit

* * *

STANLEY, Julian C(ecil), Jr. 1918-

PERSONAL: Born July 9, 1918, in Macon, Ga.; son of Julian C. (a real estate broker) and Ethel (Cheney) Stanley; married Rose Sanders (a part-time child psychologist and textbook author), August 18, 1946 (died November 15, 1978); married Barbara S. Kerr, January 1, 1980; children: (first marriage) Susan R. *Education:* South Georgia Teachers College (now Georgia Southern College), B.S., 1937; Harvard University, Ed.M., 1946, Ed.D., 1950. *Politics:* Democrat. *Office:* Department of Psychology, Johns Hopkins University, Baltimore, Md. 21218.

CAREER: High school teacher of science and mathematics in Atlanta, Ga., 1937-42; Newton Junior College, Newton, Mass., instructor in psychology, 1946-48; Harvard University, Cambridge, Mass., instructor in education, 1948-49; George Peabody College for Teachers (now George Peabody College for Teachers of Vanderbilt University), Nashville, Tenn., associate professor of educational psychology, 1949-53; University of Wisconsin—Madison, associate professor, later professor of education, 1953-62, professor of educational psychology, 1962-67, director of laboratory of experimental design, 1961-67; Johns Hopkins University, Baltimore, Md., professor of education and psychology, 1967-71, professor of psychology, 1971—. Fulbright lecturer in New Zealand and Australia, 1974. Member of advisory council, Cooperative Research Branch, U.S. Office of Education, 1962-64; College Entrance Examination Board, member of committee of examiners for aptitude test, 1961-65, chairman of committee, 1965-68. *Military service:* U.S. Army Air Forces, 1942-45; became staff sergeant.

MEMBER: American Educational Research Association (president, 1966-67), American Psychological Association (fellow; president of division of educational psychology, 1965-66; president of division of evaulation and measurement, 1972-73), National Council on Measurement in Education (president, 1963-64), American Association for the Advancement of Science (fellow), Psychometric Society (director, 1962-65), American Statistical Association (fellow), Institute of Mathematical Statistics, Tennessee Psychological Association (president, 1951) *Awards, honors:* Social Science Research Council fellow, University of Michigan, 1955; Rockefeller Foundation postdoctoral fellow in statistics, University of Chicago, 1955-56; Fulbright research scholar in educational psychology, University of Louvain, 1958-59; National Institute of Mental Health special postdoctoral fellow, 1965-67; Center for Advanced Study in the Behavioral Sciences fellow, 1965-67.

WRITINGS: Measurement in Today's Schools, with workbook, 3rd edition (Stanley was not associated with earlier editions), Prentice-Hall, 1954, 4th edition, 1964; (with Donald T. Campbell) *Experimental and Quasi-Experimental Designs for Research,* Rand McNally, 1966; (editor and contributor) *Improving Experimental Design and Statistical Analysis,* Rand McNally, 1967.

(With Gene V. Glass) *Statistical Methods in Education and Psychology,* Prentice-Hall, 1970; (with Kenneth D. Hopkins) *Measurement and Evaluation in Education and Psychology,* Prentice-Hall, 1972; (editor with Glenn H. Bracht and Kenneth D. Hopkins) *Perspectives in Educational and Psychological Measurement,* Prentice-Hall, 1972; (editor) *Preschool Programs for the Disadvantaged,* Johns Hopkins University Press, 1972; (editor and contributor) *Compensatory Education for Children, Ages 2 to 8,* Johns Hopkins University Press, 1973; (editor and contributor with David P. Keating and Lynn H. Fox) *Mathematical Talent: Discovery, Description, and Development,* Johns Hopkins University Press, 1974.

(Editor and contributor with William C. George and Cecilia H. Solano) *The Gifted and the Creative: A Fifty-Year Perspective,* Johns Hopkins Press, 1977; (editor with George and Solano) *Educational Programs and Intellectual Prodigies,* SMPY, Department of Psychology, John Hopkins University, 1978; (editor and contributor with George and Sanford J. Cohn) *Educating the Gifted: Acceleration and Enrichment,* John Hopkins Press, 1979; (editor and contributor with Camilla P. Benbow) *Academic Precocity: Aspects of Its Development,* Johns Hopkins Press, in press. Also co-author of two project reports for the U.S. Office of Education, 1962, and of two for the National Service Foundation, 1982.

Contributor: Frederick C. Gruber, editor, *Partners in Education,* University of Pennsylvania Press, 1958; Raymond O. Collier, Jr., and Stanley M. Elam, editors, *Research Design and Analysis,* Phi Delta Kappa, 1961; Jerome M. Seidman, editor, *Educating for Mental Health,* Crowell, 1963; N. L. Gage, editor, *Handbook of Research on Teaching,* Rand McNally, 1963; Ellis B. Page, editor, *Readings for Educational Psychology,* Harcourt, 1964; Egon Guba and Elam, editors, *The Training and Nurture of Educational Researchers,* Phi Delta Kappa, 1965; Keating, editor, *Intellectual Talent: Research and Development,* Johns Hopkins University Press, 1976. Contributor to other books and symposia and to the *International Encyclopedia of the Social Sciences.* Contributor of more than 300 articles, abstracts, and reviews to psychology and education journals.

SIDELIGHTS: Julian C. Stanley, Jr., told *CA:* "Since 1971 I have written mainly to help educationally, via my Study of Mathematically Precocious Youth (SMPY), those youths who reason extremely well mathematically."

* * *

STARR, Martin Kenneth 1927-

PERSONAL: Born May 21, 1927, in New York, N.Y.; son of Harry and Melanie (Krauss) Starr; married Polly Exner, April 5, 1955; children: Christopher H., Loren M. *Education:* Massachusetts Institute of Technology, B.S., 1948; Columbia University, M.S., 1951, Ph.D., 1953. *Home:* 512 TT Peconk Cres., Hampton Bays, N.Y. 11946. *Office:* Graduate School of Business, Columbia University, New York, N.Y. 10027.

CAREER: Columbia University, Graduate School of Business, New York, N.Y., associate professor, 1961-65, professor of management science, 1965—, vice-dean, 1974-75. Consultant in production, operations research, management science, and systems analysis, 1961—. *Military service:* U.S. Navy, 1945-47. *Member:* Academy of Management, American Association for the Advancement of Science, Institute of Management Sciences (president, 1974-75), Operations Research Society of America, American Institute of Decision Sciences, Beta Gamma Sigma.

WRITINGS: (With David Miller) *Executive Decisions and Operations Research,* Prentice-Hall, 1960, 2nd edition, 1969; (with Miller) *Inventory Control: Theory and Practice,* Prentice-Hall, 1962; *Product Design and Decision Theory,* Prentice-Hall, 1963; *Production Management: Systems and Synthesis,* Prentice-Hall, 1964, 2nd edition, 1972; (contributor) *Models, Measurement and Marketing,* Prentice-Hall, 1965; (editor) *Executive Readings in Management Science,* Institute of Management Sciences and Macmillan, 1965; (with Miller) *The Structure of Human Decisions,* Prentice-Hall, 1967; (editor) *Management of Production,* Penguin, 1970; *System Management of Operations,* Prentice-Hall, 1971; *Management: A Modern Approach,* Harcourt, 1971; *Operations Management,* Prentice-Hall, 1978; (with David G. Dannenbring) *Management Science: An Introduction,* McGraw, 1981; (with Earl K. Bowen) *Basic Statistics for Business and Economics,* McGraw, 1982.

Member of editorial board, *Journal of Operations Research Society of America,* 1960—, *Columbia Journal of World Business,* 1964-70, *American Production and Inventory Control Society,* 1968-70, *Behavioral Science,* 1970—, and *Operational Research Quarterly,* 1970—; editor-in-chief, *Management Science: Application,* 1967-68 and 1969—, *Management Science: Theory,* 1969—, and combined sections, 1970—; member of editorial advisory board, *Design Methods Group Newsletter,* University of California, Berkeley, 1968-70; member of advisory board, *Marketing Science,* 1981—.

* * *

STATERA, Gianni 1943-

PERSONAL: Born November 27, 1943, in Rome, Italy; son of Vittorio (a journalist) and Vera (Vania) Statera; children: Daniele. *Education:* University of Rome, Laurea in Filosofia, 1966, Libera Docenza in Sociology, 1971. *Home:* Via Bisagno 28, Rome, Italy. *Office:* Instituto Di Sociologia, University of Rome, Via Parigi 11, Rome, Italy.

CAREER: University of Rome, Rome, Italy, assistant professor of sociology, 1966-69; University of Siena, Siena, Italy, associate professor of sociology, 1970-71; University of Rome, professor of sociology and methodology of social research, 1970—, head of department, 1976. Visiting professor at University of Connecticut, 1969-70. Vice-president, E.R.I. Publishing House, 1977. Consultant to Ministry of Labor, 1966. *Member:* International Sociological Association, Italian Association of Social Sciences, Center for Communication Research, Italian Philosophical Society. *Awards, honors:* Premio Della Cultura (Italian Prize for Culture), 1971.

WRITINGS: Logica, Linguaggio e Sociologia: Studio su O. Neurath e il Neopositivismo (title means "Logic, Language and Sociology: A Study on O. Neurath and Logical Positivism"), Taylor, 1967; *La Conoscenza Sociologica: Aspetti e Problemi* (title means "Sociological Knowledge: Dimensions and Problems"), Carucci, 1968, revised edition, 1970; (editor) Otto Neurath, *Sociologia e Neopositivismo* (title means "Sociology and Neopositivism"), Ubaldini, 1968; (editor) Elihu Katz and Paul Lazarsfeld, *L'Influenza Personale nelle Comunicazioni di Massa* (title means "Personal Influence: The Part Played by People"), E.R.I., 1968; (editor) Alfred McClung Lee, *L'Uomo Polivalente* (title means "Multivalent Man"), U.T.E.T., 1969.

Societa' e Comunicazioni di Massa (title means "Society and Mass Communications"), Palumbo, 1972; *Storia di una Utopia: Ascesa e Declino dei Movimenti Studenteschi Europei,* Rizzoli, 1973, translation published as *Death of a Utopia: The Development and Decline of Student Movements in Europe,* Oxford University Press, 1974; *La Conoscenza Sociologica: Problemi e Metodo* (title means "Sociological Knowledge: Problems and Method;;), Liguori, 1974; *Analisi Metodologica e Ricerca Sociale* (title means "Methodological Analysis and Social Research"), Elia, 1974; *Il Destino Sociale dei laureati dell'Universita di massa* (title means "The Destiny of Mass University Graduates"), Liguori, 1977; *Problemi della Sociologia* (title means "Problems of Sociology"), Palumbo, 1978; *Sociologia della Scienza,* Liguori, 1978.

Metodologia e tecnica della Ricerca Sociale, Palumbo, 1982. Contributor to sociology journals. Editor, *Sociologia e ricerca sociale,* 1980.

WORK IN PROGRESS: Research on unemployment of Italian graduates; research projects in the sociology of science.

* * *

STERN, Stuart
See RAE, Hugh C(rauford)

STERNLIEB, George 1928-

PERSONAL: Born August 16, 1928, in New York, N.Y.; son of Bernard J. and Golda (Mayer) Sternlieb; married Phyllis Fox (a mathematician), April 23, 1958; children: David, Benjamin. *Education:* Brooklyn College (now Brooklyn College of the City University of New York), B.A., 1950; Harvard University, M.B.A., 1953, D.B.A., 1962; postdoctoral study at Harvard University and Columbia University. *Home:* 66 Old Short Hills Rd., Short Hills, N.J. *Office:* Center for Urban Policy Research, Rutgers University, New Brunswick, N.J. 08903.

CAREER: Bloomingdale's, New York, N.Y., merchandising executive, 1953-58; Harvard University, Harvard Business School, Boston, Mass., research associate, 1958-59; Adams Associates (business consultants), Bedford, Mass., co-founder and treasurer, 1959-66; Rutgers University, Graduate School of Business Administration, Newark Campus, Newark, N.J., associate professor, 1962-65, professor of marketing, 1965-68, New Brunswick Campus, New Brunswick, N.J., professor of urban and regional planning, 1968—, director of Center for Urban Policy Research, 1969—. Member of federal, state, and local urban development and planning committees. Consultant to Boston Redevelopment Authority and Westinghouse Advance Systems.

WRITINGS: *The Future of the Downtown Department Store*, Harvard University Press, 1962; *Garden Apartment Houses: A Municipal Cost-Revenue Analysis*, Bureau of Economic Research, Rutgers University, 1964; *The Tenement Landlord*, Urban Studies Center, Rutgers University, 1966; (co-author) *Social Needs and Social Resources—Newark: 1967*, Research Center, Rutgers Center, Rutgers University, 1967; *Newark, New Jersey: Population and Labor Force*, Institute of Management Labor Relations, Rutgers University, 1967; (co-author) *Leisure Market Studies*, two volumes, Urban Studies Center, Rutgers University, 1967.

The Urban Housing Dilemma, New York City Housing Development Administration and Rutgers University, 1970; (co-author) *Housing in an Affluent Suburb: Princeton, New Jersey*, Transaction Books, 1971; (with Patrick Beaton) *The Zone of Emergence*, Transaction Books, 1972; (co-author) *New York City: Housing and People*, New York City Housing Development Administration, 1973; (with Bernard P. Indik) *The Ecology of Welfare*, Transaction Books, 1973.

All published by Center for Urban Policy Research, Rutgers University: (Co-author) *Housing Development and Municipal Costs*, 1973; (with Lynne B. Sagalyn) *Zoning and Housing Costs: The Impact of Land Use Controls on Housing Price*, 1973; (with Robert W. Burchell) *Residential Abandonment: The Tenement Landlord Revisited*, 1973; (with James W. Hughes) *Post-Industrial America: Metropolitan Decline and Inter-Regional Job Shifts*, 1975; (with Hughes) *Housing and Economic Reality: New York City*, 1976; (with Hughes and others) *Tax Subsidies and Housing Investment: A Fiscal Cost-Benefit Analysis*, 1976; (with Hughes) *Jobs and People: New York City 1985*, 1978; (with Hughes) *Revitalizing the Northeast*, 1978; (with Hughes) *Current Population Trends*, 1978; (with Burchell) *Planning Theory in the 1980s*, 1979; (with Hughes and others) *America's Housing: Prospects and Problems*, 1980; (with Hughes) *Shopping Centers: USA*, 1981; (with Hughes) *New Tools for Economic Development: The Enterprise Zone, Development Bank, and RFC*, 1981; (with Hughes) *The Future of Rental Housing*, 1981.

Contributor: *The Impact of Sales Taxes as a Function of Family Income*, Graduate School of Business Administration, Rutgers University, 1965; *Some Aspects of the Abandoned House Problem*, Department of Housing and Urban Development, 1970; *Society*, Transaction Books, 1972. Contributor to planning, business, and marketing journals.

* * *

STIGUM, Marcia (Lee) 1934-

PERSONAL: Born August 26, 1934, in Oyster Bay, N.Y.; daughter of Peter N. (an arborist) and Helen (a secretary; maiden name, Hill) Hanson; married Bernt Petter Stigum (a professor), August 4, 1956; children: Tove, Erik. *Education:* Middlebury College, B.A. (cum laude), 1956; Massachusetts Institute of Technology, Ph.D., 1961. *Politics:* Independent. *Home:* 300 Intracostal Pl., Tequesta, Fla. *Office:* Stigum & Associates, Ltd., 360 Coolidge Ave., Fort Lee, N.J. 07024.

CAREER: New England Mutual Life Insurance Co., Boston, Mass., member of economic research staff, 1961; Northeastern University, Boston, instructor in economics, 1961-62; Wellesley College, Wellesley, Mass., instructor in economics, 1961-63; Cornell University, Ithaca, N.Y., assistant professor of economics, 1963-66; Loyola University of Chicago, Chicago, Ill., assistant professor, 1971-74, associate professor of economics, 1974-77; money market specialist at Carroll, McEntee & McGinley, 1978-79; currently president of Stigum & Associates, Ltd. (money market consulting firm). Visiting associate professor of finance at Northwestern University, 1977-78; visiting lecturer at Yale University. Financial consultant to several firms, including Bermuda Monetary Authority, Merrill Lynch, Pearce, Fenner, & Smith, Citicorp, AMR International, Astley & Pearce, and Allen & Overy (London).

WRITINGS—Published by Dow Jones-Irwin, except as indicated: (With husband, Bernt P. Stigum) *Economics* (textbook), Addison-Wesley, 1968, 2nd edition, 1972, study guide, 1969, 2nd edition, 1972; *Problems in Microeconomics*, Irwin, 1975; *How to Turn Your Money into More Money*, 1976; *The Money Market: Myth, Reality and Practice*, 1978; (contributor) Sumner Levine, editor, *Investment Manager's Handbook*, 1980; *Money Market Calculations: Yields, Break-Evens and Arbitrage*, 1981; (contributor) Frank Frabozzi and Frank Zarb, editors, *Handbook of Financial Markets*, 1981; *Managing Bank Assets and Liabilities: For Risk Control and Profit*, 1982; *Bond Market Calculations: Cash and Futures*, 1983. Contributor of articles to finance journals, including *Journal of Finance*, *The Money Manager*, *The Cash Manager*, and *Pensions & Investment Age*. Member of board of advisors and contributing editor of *Financial Services Review*.

SIDELIGHTS: Marcia Stigum speaks fluent French and Norwegian. *Avocational interests:* International travel, skiing, tennis, raquetball.

* * *

STINCHCOMBE, Arthur L. 1933-

PERSONAL: Born May 16, 1933, in Clare County, Mich.; son of Frank Homer (a high school counselor) and Christina (Stratton) Stinchcombe; married Barbara E. Bifoss, July 1, 1953 (divorced); married Carol A. Heimer, December 30, 1980; children: (first marriage) Maxwell Benjamin, Amy Lenore, Adam Michael, Kirk Thomas. *Education:* Central Michigan University, A.B., 1953; University of California, Berkeley, Ph.D., 1960. *Politics:* Socialist. *Office:* Department of Sociology, Social Science Bldg., University of Arizona, Tucson, Ariz. 85721.

CAREER: Johns Hopkins University, Baltimore, Md., assistant professor, 1959-65, associate professor of social relations and chairman of department, 1965-67; University of California, Berkeley, 1967-75, began as associate professor, became professor of sociology, chairman of department, 1971-73; University of Chicago, Chicago, Ill., professor of sociology and senior study director of National Opinion Research Center, 1975-80; University of Arizona, Tucson, professor of sociology, 1980—. Visiting professor, University of Essex, 1968-69, and University of Bergen, 1979-80. Member of staff and researcher in Venezuela and elsewhere, Harvard University-Massachusetts Institute of Technology Joint Center for Urban Studies, 1964-65; fellow, Netherlands Institute for Advanced Study, 1973-74; senior research sociologist, Institute of Industrial Economics, Bergen, 1979-80. *Military service:* U.S. Army, Medical Corps, 1953-55. *Member:* American Sociological Association, American Academy of Arts and Sciences (fellow), American Civil Liberties Union.

WRITINGS: Rebellion in a High School, Quadrangle, 1965; *Constructing Social Theories,* Harcourt, 1968; (with Rene Marder and Zahava Blum) *Creating Efficient Industrial Administration,* Academic Press, 1974; *Theoretical Methods in Social History,* Academic Press, 1978; (with Calvin Jones and Paul Sheatsley) *Dakota Farmers Evaluate Crop and Livestock Surveys,* National Opinion Research Center, 1979; (with others) *Crime and Punishment: Changing Attitudes in America,* Jossey-Bass, 1980.

Contributor: James G. March, editor, *Handbook of Organizations,* Rand McNally, 1965; Neil J. Smelser, editor, *Sociology: An Introduction,* Wiley, 1967, revised edition, 1973; *Instructor's Guide to Sociology Today,* CRM Books, 1971; K. Land and S. Spilerman, editors, *Social Indicator Models,* Russell Sage, 1975; Nelson Polsby and Frederick Greenstein, editors, *Handbook of Political Science,* Volume III, Addison-Wesley, 1975; Louis A. Coser, editor, *The Idea of Social Structure,* Harcourt, 1975; Coser and Otto N. Larsen, editors, *The Uses of Controversy in Sociology,* Free Press, 1976; Dwight Perkins, editor, *Small Scale Industry in China,* University of California Press, 1978; Walter G. Stepahn and Joe R. Feagin, *School Desegregation: Past, Present and Future,* Plenum, 1980; *Social Science Information,* Sage Publications, 1980.

Contributor to *Encyclopedia of the Social Sciences.* Contributor of articles and reviews to professional journals.

* * *

STODDARD, Sandol 1927-
(Sandol Stoddard Warburg)

PERSONAL: Born December 16, 1927, in Birmingham, Ala.; daughter of Carlos French and Caroline (Harris) Stoddard; married Felix M. Warburg, April 2, 1949 (divorced June 14, 1963); married Frank Drew Dollard (a professor of English), June 19, 1966; married William A. Atchley (a physician), June 1, 1974; children: (first marriage) Anthony, Peter, Gerald, Jason; Katherine, Suzanne (stepdaughters). *Education:* Bryn Mawr College, A.B. (magna cum laude), 1959; graduate study at San Francisco State College (now University).

CAREER: Writer. *Awards, honors:* New York Herald Tribune selected *The Thinking Book* as one of the ten best picture-books of 1960; American Library Association named *Saint George and the Dragon* a distinguished book of 1963.

WRITINGS—Juvenile books, except as indicated: *Free,* Houghton, 1976; *The Hospice Movement: A Better Way of Caring for the Dying* (adult), Stein & Day, 1977.

Under name Sandol Stoddard Warburg; published by Houghton, except as indicated: *The Thinking Book,* Atlantic-Little, Brown, 1960; *Keep It Like a Secret,* Atlantic-Little, Brown, 1961; (adaptor) *Saint George and the Dragon: Being the Legend of the Red Cross Knight from "The Faerie Queene,"* by Edmund Spenser, 1963; *My Very Own Special Particular Private and Personal Cat,* 1963; *Curl Up Small!,* 1964; *I Like You,* 1965; *From Ambledee to Zumbledee: An A-B-C of Rather Special Bugs,* 1968; *Growing Time,* 1969; *Hooray for Us,* 1970; *On the Way Home,* 1973.

WORK IN PROGRESS: A filmscript of *I Like You.*

SIDELIGHTS: In *Books Are by People,* Lee Bennett Hopkins records Sandol Stoddard's motivation for writing *Saint George and the Dragon:* "'This one I did because I itch for mid-century America, California particularly, because people go around not having the least idea of their heritage, their identity, or their obligation to the human race. An American can't know who he really is unless he makes some viable connection between himself and the mainstream of America. *Saint George and the Dragon* deals with the basic image of our civilization and what's left of it. So, by putting it into a form comprehensible to the young, I hoped to perform a useful service by helping children, including my own, to know better who they are and where they're at.'"

MEDIA ADAPTATIONS: The Thinking Book was filmed by Bank Street College's Communication Laboratories. *Curl Up Small!* is a John Korty film. *Growing Time* has been translated into Japanese and was made into a Japanese film in 1975.

BIOGRAPHICAL/CRITICAL SOURCES: Lee Bennett Hopkins, *Books Are by People,* Citation Press, 1969.†

* * *

STOKER, H(oward) Stephen 1939-

PERSONAL: Born April 16, 1939, in Salt Lake City, Utah; son of Howard Seymour (an electrician) and Alice Maud (Child) Stoker; married Sharon Rosella Stevenson, June 16, 1964; children: Rebecca Elizabeth, Deborah Rosella, Howard Scott, Henry Stephen, Howard Spencer, Alice Colleen, Hyrum Stevenson. *Education:* University of Utah, B.A., 1963, University of Wisconsin, Ph.D., 1968. *Religion:* Church of Jesus Christ of Latter-day Saints. *Home:* 765 Ben Lomond Dr., Ogden, Utah 84403. *Office:* Department of Chemistry, Weber State College, Ogden, Utah 84408.

CAREER: Weber State College, Ogden, Utah, professor of inorganic chemistry, 1968—. *Member:* American Chemical Society, Sigma Xi.

WRITINGS—Published by Scott, Foresman, except as indicated: (With Spencer L. Seager) *Environmental Chemistry: Air and Water Pollution,* 1972, 2nd edition, 1976; (with Seager) *Chemistry: A Science for Today,* 1973; (with Seager and R. L. Capener) *Energy: From Source to Use,* 1975; (with Joseph C. Muren) *Testimony,* Bookcraft, 1980; (with Michael R. Slabaugh) *General Organic, and Biochemistry: A Brief Introduction,* 1981; *Introduction to Chemical Principles,* Macmillan, 1983.

* * *

STONE, Albert E(dward) 1924-
(Albert E. Stone, Jr.)

PERSONAL: Born January 1, 1924, in New London, Conn.; son of Albert E. (a Navy officer) and Rebecca (Rollins) Stone; married Grace Woodbury, July 5, 1954; children: Albert Edward, Jr., Rebecca Rollins. *Education:* Yale University, B.A., 1949, Ph.D., 1957; Columbia University, M.A., 1955. *Politics:* Democrat. *Religion:* Episcopalian. *Home address:* R.R. 2, Box 171, Oxford, Iowa. *Office:* Department of American Studies, 302 English-Philosophy Bldg., University of Iowa, Iowa City, Iowa 52242.

CAREER: Casady School, Oklahoma City, Okla., instructor in English, 1949-52; Yale University, New Haven, Conn., instructor, 1955-59, assistant professor of English, 1959-62; Emory University, Atlanta, Ga., professor of English and chairman of department, 1962-68, professor of English and American studies, 1968-77; University of Iowa, Iowa City, professor of American studies and chairman of department, 1977—. Fulbright lecturer, Charles University, Prague, Czechoslovakia, 1968-69. Member of advisory council, Danforth Foundation graduate fellowship program, 1965-68. *Military service:* U.S. Army, Military Intelligence, 1943-46; served in Southwest Pacific; became master sergeant; received Purple Heart and Bronze Star.

MEMBER: Modern Language Association of America, American Studies Association, American Civil Liberties Union, Phi Beta Kappa, Elizabethan Club, Elihu Club. *Awards, honors:* Morse fellowship, Yale University, 1960-61; E. Harris Harbison Award for distinguished teaching, 1965-66; National Endowment for the Humanities fellowship, 1976-77.

WRITINGS: (Under name Albert E. Stone, Jr.) *The Innocent Eye: Childhood in Mark Twain's Imagination,* Yale University Press, 1961; (editor and author of introduction under name Albert E. Stone, Jr.) St. John de Crevecoeur, *Letters from an American Farmer,* New American Library, 1963, revised edition (under name Albert E. Stone) published as *Letters from an American Farmer* [and] *Sketches of Eighteenth-Century America,* Penguin, 1981; (editor under name Albert E. Stone, Jr.) *Twentieth-Century Interpretations of "The Ambassadors,"* Prentice-Hall, 1969; (editor) *The American Autobiography: A Collection of Critical Essays,* Prentice-Hall, 1981; *Autobiographical Occasions and Original Acts: Versions of American Identity from Henry Adams to Nate Shaw,* University of Pennsylvania Press, 1982.

Contributor to *Prospects: An Annual of American Cultural Studies* and to *American Heritage, American Literature, American Quarterly, Genre, New England Quarterly, College Language Association Journal,* and other periodicals.

WORK IN PROGRESS: Editions of Mark Twain's *Personal Recollections of Joan of Arc* and *A Tramp Abroad;* a book on history, literature and American culture.

* * *

STONE, Albert E., Jr.
    See STONE, Albert E(dward)

* * *

STONE, Frank A(ndrews) 1929-

PERSONAL: Born January 12, 1929, in Wilmington, Del.; son of Royal Amidon (a mechanical engineer) and Ruth Sherman (Andrews) Stone; married Barbara May Tinkham (an educator), June 14, 1957; children: David, Ruth, Beth, Priscilla. *Education:* Heidelberg College, A.B., 1949; Oberlin College, M.Div., 1952, D.Min., 1953; Western Michigan University, M.A., 1960; University of Ankara, additional study, 1962-63; Boston University, Ed.D., 1968. *Politics:* Democrat. *Religion:* United Church of Christ. *Home:* 3 Westgate Lane, Storrs, Conn. 06268. *Office address:* Box U-32, University of Connecticut, Storrs, Conn. 06268.

CAREER: American School, Tarsus, Turkey, 1953-66, began as teacher, became director; University of Connecticut, Storrs, assistant professor, 1968-69, associate professor, 1970-75, professor of international education, 1975—, director of I.N. Thut World Education Center, 1971—. Visiting professor at Hacettepe University, 1969-70. Member, Turkey Schools Council, 1957-66; member of board of visitors, Near East School of Theology, 1958-70; member of Connecticut/Paraiba Partners of the Americas.

MEMBER: World Education Fellowship (president of Connecticut chapter, 1974-76; president of U.S. section, 1981—), American Educational Studies Association, Comparative and International Education Society, History of Education Society, Middle East Institute (fellow), Middle East Studies Association (fellow), Philosophy of Education Society (fellow), Society for Educational Reconstruction (national chairperson).

WRITINGS: Translate: A Casebook of Texts and Projects for Learning to Translate between Turkish and English, Tarsus College (Tarsus, Turkey), 1965; *Emphases in Modern Turkish Literature,* Redhouse Press (Istanbul), 1969.

The Impact of Culture on Education in Modern Turkey, Redhouse Press, 1970; *Communities of Learning: People and Their Programs,* Redhouse Press, 1970; *Modern Turkish Educational Thought: A Bibliographic Introduction,* Hacettepe University Press (Ankara), 1971; *The Rub of Cultures in Modern Turkey: Literary Views of Education,* Indiana University, 1973; (editor) *The New World of Educational Thought,* Mss Information, 1973; *Armenian Studies for Secondary Students,* World Education Project, University of Connecticut, 1975; *The Irish: In Their Homeland, In America, In Connecticut,* World Education Project, University of Connecticut, 1975; *Scots and Scotch Irish in Connecticut: A History,* World Education Project, University of Connecticut, 1978.

(Editor) *The Peoples of Connecticut: Studies of Cultural Pluralism by Connecticut High School Students,* I.N. Thut World Education Center, 1981. Also author of *Historic Tarsus: A Day and the Centuries,* 1957.

Work represented in numerous anthologies. Contributor of over fourteen reviews and of forty-five articles to journals. Editor, *Current Turkish Thought,* 1968-71, *Cutting Edge* (journal of the Society for Educational Reconstruction), 1974-78.

WORK IN PROGRESS: Academies for Anatolia, a study of the American board schools in Turkey from 1820 to the 1980's; *Methods of Qualitative Educational Research; Approaches to Critical Thinking: Philosophical Tools for Educators; Strategies for International Development Education.*

SIDELIGHTS: Frank A. Stone wrote *CA:* "Cross-cultural communication has been my chief motive for writing since I prepared a little tourist guide *Historic Tarsus: A Day and the Centuries* for the local Turkish tourist bureau in 1957. I have tried to help North Americans understand Armenian and Turkish cultural and educational affairs.

"Writing about ethnic groups in Connecticut has been another long-term interest. More recently I have been engaged in applying methodologies from specialized fields such as ethnography, phenomenology, and international development planning to attempt to resolve some educational problems."

* * *

STOTT, D(enis) H(erbert) 1909-

PERSONAL: Born December 31, 1909, in London, England;

son of Augustus Parker and Margaret (Smith) Stott; married Jane Brook (a teacher), July 30, 1937; children: Marion Davidson, Peter. *Education:* Cambridge University, B.A., 1932, M.A., 1941; University of London, Ph.D., 1950. *Home:* 30 Colborn St., Guelph, Ontario, Canada N1G 2M5.

CAREER: Teacher of modern languages at schools in England, 1932-46; Carnegie United Kingdom Trust, Dumfermline, Scotland, research officer, 1946-51; University of Bristol, Bristol, England, research fellow, 1951-57; University of Glasgow, Glasgow, Scotland, lecturer in psychology, 1957-66; University of Guelph, Guelph, Ontario, professor of psychology and director of Center for Educational Disabilities, 1966-75, professor emeritus, 1975—. Charles Russell Memorial Lecturer, 1957. *Member:* Canadian Psychological Association (honorary life fellow), British Psychological Society (fellow).

WRITINGS: A School German Course Using Inductive and Other Active Methods, Methuen, 1944; *Language Teaching in the New Education,* University of London Press, 1946; *Delinquency and Human Nature,* Carnegie United Kingdom Trust, 1950; *Saving Children from Delinquency,* Philosophical Library, 1952; *Unsettled Children and Their Families,* Philosophical Library, 1956; (with E. G. Sykes) *The Bristol Society Adjustment Guides,* University of London Press, 1956, 4th edition (with N. C. Marston), 1971; *The Social Adjustment of Children* (manual to *The Bristol Society Adjustment Guides*), University of London Press, 1958, 4th edition, 1972; (contributor) Ashley Montagu, editor, *Culture and the Evolution of Man,* Oxford University Press, 1962; *Studies of Troublesome Children,* Humanities, 1966; *The Parent as Teacher,* Fearon, 1974; (contributor) Maurice F. Freehill, editor, *Disturbed and Troubled Children,* Spectrum, 1974; (with N. C. Marston and S. D. Neill) *Taxonomy of Behaviour Disturbance,* University of London Press, 1975; *The Hard-to-Teach Child,* University Park Press, 1978; *Helping the Maladjusted Child,* Prentice-Hall, 1982; *Delinquency: The Problem and Its Prevention,* Spectrum, 1982.

Also author of "Day-of-the-Week Books" series and "Micky Books" series, Holmes McDougall, 1961, and of "Programmed Reading Kit," 1962, "Flying Start: Learn to Learn Kit," 1972, "Flying Start Extension Kit," 1973, "Learning about Number," 1973, and "Math Activity Kits," 1974, all Holmes McDougall. Script writer for film "We Learn to Read." Contributor of more than thirty articles to *British Journal of Delinquency, New Scientist, Lancet,* and other psychology and education journals.

WORK IN PROGRESS: Research in learning disabilities, maladjustment, and the teaching of reading.

AVOCATIONAL INTERESTS: Ceramics, gardening.

* * *

STRELKA, Joseph P(eter) 1927-

PERSONAL: Listed in some sources as Josef Strelka; born May 3, 1927, in Wiener Neustadt, Austria; came to United States, 1964; son of Josef and Maria (Lisetz) Strelka; married Lucy Zambal, 1951 (divorced, 1957); married Brigitte Vollmer, July 13, 1963; children: Alexandra. *Education:* University of Vienna, Ph.D., 1950. *Home:* 1188 Avon Rd., Schenectady, N.Y. 12308. *Office:* Department of German, State University of New York, 1400 Washington Ave., Albany, N.Y. 12222.

CAREER: Municipal Office of Cultural Activities, Wiener Neustadt, Austria, director, 1950-51; free-lance critic in Vienna, Austria, 1951-64; University of Southern California, Los Angeles, visiting associate professor, 1964, assistant director of program at University of Vienna, 1964-65, professor of German literature, 1965-66; Pennsylvania State University, University Park, professor of German, 1966-71; State University of New York, Albany, professor of German and comparative literature, 1971—. Visiting professor at Free University of Berlin, 1980, University of Augsburg, 1981, and University of the Witwatersrand, 1981.

MEMBER: International Robert Musil Society, International Association of Germanic Studies, P.E.N., Modern Language Association of America, American Comparative Literature Association, Vienna Goethe Society. *Awards, honors:* Theodor Koerner Foundation award, 1955-57; City of Vienna award, 1958; Austrian Institute of Cultural Affairs research fellow in Paris, 1958-59; Austrian Cross of Honor for the Arts and Sciences, First Class, 1978.

WRITINGS: Georg Forsters literarhistorische Bedeutung (title means "Georg Forster's Literary-Historical Significance"), F. Berger, 1955; *Der burgundische Renaissancehof Margarethes von Oesterreich und seine literarhistorische Bedeutung* (title means "The Burgundian Renaissance Court of Margaret of Austria and Its Literary-Historical Significance"), A. Sexl, 1957; *Kafka, Musil, Broch und die Entwicklung des modernen Romans* (title means "Kafka, Musil, Broch, and the Development of the Modern Novel"), Forum Verlag, 1959.

Rilke, Benn, Schoenwiese und die Entwicklung der modernen Lyrik (title means "Rilke, Benn, Schoenwiese, and the Development of Modern Poetry"), Forum Verlag, 1960; *Brecht, Horvath, Duerrenmatt: Wege und Abwege des modernen Dramas* (title means "Brecht, Horvarth, Durrenmatt: Paths and Deviations of Modern Drama"), Forum Verlag, 1962; *Bruecke zu vielen Ufern* (title means "Bridges to Many Shores"), Europa Verlag, 1966; (with Harold von Hofe) *Luegendichtung* (title means "Tall Tales"), Scribner, 1966; (with von Hofe) *Vorboten der Gegenwart: Marx, Nietzsche, Freud, Einstein* (title means "Precursors to the Present: Marx, Nietzsche, Freud, Einstein"), Holt, 1967.

Vergleichende Literaturkritik (title means "Comparative Literary Criticism"), Francke, 1970; *Die gelenkten Musen* (title means "The Bound Muses"), Europa Verlag, 1971; *Auf der Suche nach dem verlorenen Selbst,* Francke Verlag, 1977; *Werk, Werkverstaendnis, Wertung,* Francke Verlag, 1978; *Methodologie der Literaturwissenschaft,* Niemayer, 1978; *Esoterik bei Goethe,* Niemayer, 1980; *Stefan Zweig: Freier Geist der Menschlichkeit,* Osterreichischer Bundesverlag, 1981.

Editor or compiler: *Gedichte Margarethe's von Oesterreich* (title means "Poems of Margaret of Austria"), A. Sexl, 1954; (and author of introduction) Alfred Kubin, *Dichtungen* (title means "Collected Works"), Bergland Verlag, 1961; (and author of introduction) *Das zeitlose Wort: Eine Anthologie oesterreichischer Lyrik von Peter Altenberg bis zur Gegenwart* (title means "The Timeless Word: An Anthology of Austrian Verse from Peter Attenberg Up to the Present"), Stiasny Verlag, 1964; (with Robert Stauffer and Paul Wimmer) *Aufruf zur Wende: Eine Anthologie neuer Dichtung, Ernst Schoenwiese zum 60* (title means "A Call to Change: An Anthology of Modern Literature"), Oesterreichische Verlagsanstalt, 1965; (and author of introduction) Gustav Meyrink, *Der Engle vom westlichen Fenster* (title means "Angle of the Western Window"), Stiasny Verlag, 1966; (with Walter Hinderer) *Moderne amerikanische Literaturtheorien* (title means "Modern American Theories of Literature"), S. Fischer Verlag, 1970.

Editor: "Yearbook of Comparative Criticism" series, Pennsylvania State University Press, Volume I: *Perspectives in Literary Symbolism,* 1968, Volume II: *Problems of Literary Eval-*

uation, 1969, Volume III: *Patterns of Literary Style,* 1971, Volume IV: *Anagogic Qualities of Literature,* 1971, Volume V: *Literary Criticism and Sociology,* 1973, Volume VI: *The Personality of the Critic,* 1973, Volume VII: *Literary Criticism and Psychology,* 1976; "Penn State Series in German Literature," Pennsylvania State University Press, Volume I, 1971, Volume II, 1971, Volume III, 1974, Volume IV, 1975; "New Yorker Beitraege zur Vergleichenden Literaturwissenschaft" series, Verlag Peter Lang, 1982—; "New Yorker Studien zur Neueren Deutschen Literaturgeschichte" series, Verlag Peter Lang, 1982—.

Contributor of articles to journals in his field, including *Wort in Zeit* and *German Quarterly.* Co-editor, *Deutsche Exilliteratur,* 1976—; member of editorial board, *Colloquia Germanica,* 1971—, *North Carolina Studies in Comparative Literature,* 1972—, and *Michigan Germanic Studies,* 1975—.

WORK IN PROGRESS: Exilliteratur; Zwischen Traum und Wirklichkeit; Literarische Textanalyse.

* * *

STRODE, Hudson 1892-1976

PERSONAL: Born October 31, 1892, in Cairo, Ill.; died September 22, 1976, in Tuscaloosa, Ala.; son of Thomas Fuller and Hope (Hudson) Strode; married Therese Cory, December 20, 1924. *Education:* University of Alabama, A.B., 1913; Columbia University, M.A., 1914; Harvard University, special study, 1916. *Politics:* Independent. *Religion:* Episcopalian. *Home:* 49 Cherokee Rd., Tuscaloosa, Ala. 35401.

CAREER: Syracuse University, Syracuse, N.Y., instructor in English, 1914-16; University of Alabama, University, associate professor, 1916-24, professor of English, 1924-63, professor emeritus, 1963-76. Writer and lecturer. *Member:* P.E.N., Newcomen Society, Phi Beta Kappa, Delta Kappa Epsilon. *Awards, honors:* First prize, National Little Theater Contest, 1929, for one-act play "The End of the Dance"; D.Litt., University of Alabama, 1952, and University of the South, 1960; named Knight of the Royal Order of the North Star by King Gustaf Adolf of Sweden, 1961.

WRITINGS: The End of the Dance (one-act play), Samuel French, 1929; *The Story of Bermuda,* Smith & Haas, 1932, new and enlarged edition, Harcourt, 1946; *The Pageant of Cuba,* Smith & Haas, 1934; *South by Thunderbird,* Random House, 1937, revised edition, Harcourt, 1945; (editor and author of introduction) *Immortal Lyrics: An Anthology of English Lyric Poetry,* Random House, 1939; *Finland Forever,* Harcourt, 1941; *Timeless Mexico: A History,* Harcourt, 1944, reprinted, 1960; (editor and author of introduction) *Spring Harvest: A Collection of Stories from Alabama,* Knopf, 1944; *Now in Mexico: A Book of Travel,* Harcourt, 1947; *Sweden: Model for a World,* Harcourt, 1949, revised edition, 1965; *Denmark Is a Lovely Land,* Harcourt, 1951; *Jefferson Davis,* Harcourt, Volume I: *American Patriot,* 1955, Volume II: *Confederate President,* 1959, Volume III: *Tragic Hero,* 1964; (editor) *Jefferson Davis: Private Letters, 1823-1889,* Harcourt, 1966; *Ultimates in the Far East: Travels in the Orient and India,* Harcourt, 1970; *The Eleventh House: Memoirs,* Harcourt, 1975.

Contributor of articles, stories, poetry, and reviews to *Forum, New Republic, Harper's Bazaar, Reader's Digest, New York Times Magazine,* and other periodicals in the United States and abroad.

SIDELIGHTS: Though widely known for his interpretive accounts of his travels in such countries as Mexico, Sweden, Finland, and Denmark, Hudson Strode also achieved recognition as the author of what many regard as the definitive biography of Confederate president Jefferson Davis. The three-volume work details major events in Davis's life, paying special attention to his early years and to the Civil War period. Writing from what he himself called "the Southern viewpoint," Strode intended *Jefferson Davis* to counter the effects of more than a century's worth of harsh criticism of the rebel leader.

The first volume of the biography, *American Patriot,* was well-received by the critics, most of whom welcomed its sympathetic approach. Commenting in the *New York Times,* for example, Dumas Malone observed that readers of Strode's "well told" biography "will gain much new information about Jefferson Davis, and most of them probably will like him." A. N. Chamberlain declared in the *San Francisco Chronicle* that "Strode's writing skill, his use of manuscript material and hitherto unpublished letters, and his own obvious feeling for his subject have produced a volume which will make the reader aware of Jefferson Davis as a leading American prior to the Civil War." *American Historical Review* critic Clement Eaton agreed with this assessment, stating that "Strode has made a contribution to our knowledge of Jefferson Davis as a human being.... This fresh and entirely credible portrait marks a turning away from the trend of caustic criticism of Davis that has characterized much of the writing on the Civil War." And as Margaret Coit declared in the *New York Herald Book Review,* "In *Jefferson Davis: American Patriot,* the man and the biographer have met. The book is authoritative and well documented. It is highly readable. And it is temperate in tone. Although sympathetic to Davis, it does not minimize his faults."

Writing in the *Saturday Review,* T. Harry Williams also noted that Strode "views his subject with reverence, sympathy, and condonation," sometimes to the extent that "it is not going too far to say that his point of view is that of an admiring Southerner of Davis's own time who could admit a few mild faults in the object of his adoration." Nevertheless, Williams concluded, this "bias or slant ... is not in itself a serious drawback. There is value in having Davis presented as his own people saw him."

The second volume of the Davis biography, *Confederate President,* elicited similar comments. In an *American Historical Review* article, R. S. Henry praised the "new and more appealing dimension" of Davis that Strode offered readers, while Coit wrote: "Probably no book ... will recount this 'tragic journey into history' more vividly or movingly.... [Strode] deserves much credit for righting these historical misconceptions, and restoring Davis the tragic dignity his character deserves."

Admitting to some Northern partisanship of his own, E. S. Miers stated in the *Saturday Review* that "Strode demonstrates exceptional literary accomplishment, and with the second volume, easily emerges as the commanding general of that militant band of rebel penmen dedicated to winning the war for the South whether it takes one century or two.... Yet some ... years after the stillness fell at Appomattox, who can resist a fascination for the fresh confidence and enthusiasm which Mr. Strode injects into what has long been the official Confederate party line? ... [He] writes [his version of history] with the skill of an old master, achieving in those passages where he deals with Davis as father, husband, and human being a compelling vitality."

Some reviewers were not so sure that Strode's lack of objectivity worked to his advantage in writing about Jefferson Davis. As Avery Craven observed in the *Chicago Sunday Tribune:* "[Strode's] picture of Davis is a fairer one than we have heretofore had. It does not, however, reveal a man with the greater qualities which trial brings out, nor one with the capacity for growth into a folk hero." J. K. Bettersworth speculated in the *New York Times Book Review* that "it could be that Mr. Strode will only add to the legion of mythical Davises. Perhaps in rescuing the bones of the Confederate President from the infidels he may, indeed, be guilty of an indefensible defensiveness.... In Hudson Strode, Davis has a charming and literate advocate on his side, a man who will probably be able to convince the jury."

The third volume of the biography, *Tragic Hero*, recounts the last twenty-five years of Davis's life, including the Southern defeat and the former president's return to private life. In the case of this final volume, however, reviewers were somewhat more critical of Strode's work. Commenting in the *New York Times Book Review*, for example, David Donald called the entire biography "badly proportioned" in that the author paid only brief attention to Davis's pre-Civil War political career but found room for "endless detail on Davis's later years." In addition, wrote Donald, Strode seemed "either unaware of [those historians who have questioned Davis's intelligence and ability] or unable to meet their arguments." Despite these faults, the critic concluded, *Jefferson Davis* "is much superior to all previously published [biographies].... This third volume especially sustains a superb narrative pace."

A *Time* reviewer, observing that Davis "was neither a great chief nor a tragic hero," suggested that "a more measured appraisal would have done him more justice." This view was seconded by William B. Catton, who stated in the *Saturday Review* that Strode's attempts "to prove that Davis belongs high among the ranks of America's greatest men" made for "fascinating biography but inferior history." Explained Catton: "[*Jefferson Davis* is] badly flawed because it ignores all complexity, contradiction, subtlety, inconsistency, ambiguity, or uncertainty in human affairs or historical interpretation where such elements would detract from the heroic human portrait. For all its merit and wealth of detail the result is a two-dimensional study, needlessly partisan and limited in value."

Though *Best Sellers* reviewer Paul Kiniery agreed that Strode's "treatment is admittedly sympathetic," he insisted that this "does not necessarily lessen the value or the reliability of the volume." Concluded the critic: "Here [in *Jefferson Davis*] we have biographical writing at its best.... It is difficult to see how anyone could feel anything save deep respect for Jefferson Davis after reading this continuously interesting account."

BIOGRAPHICAL/CRITICAL SOURCES: *New York Herald Tribune Book Review*, September 11, 1955, October 18, 1959; *New York Times*, September 11, 1955; *New Yorker*, September 24, 1955; *Saturday Review*, September 24, 1955, October 31, 1959, November 28, 1964; *San Francisco Chronicle*, November 27, 1955; *American Historical Review*, January, 1956, July, 1960; *Annals of the American Academy of Political and Social Science*, March, 1956, July, 1960; *Atlantic*, June, 1956; *Political Science Quarterly*, September, 1956; *New York Times Book Review*, October 18, 1959, September 27, 1964; *Chicago Sunday Tribune*, October 25, 1959; *Christian Science Monitor*, December 17, 1959; *Time*, October 16, 1964; *Best Sellers*, November 1, 1964.†

—Sketch by Deborah A. Straub

* * *

STUART, Dabney 1937-

PERSONAL: Born November 4, 1937, in Richmond, Va.; son of Walker Dabney, Jr., and Martha (von Schilling) Stuart; married Martha Varney, August 14, 1965 (divorced, 1977); children: Martha, Nathan von Schilling, Darren Wayne. *Education:* Davidson College, A.B., 1960; Harvard University, A.M., 1962. *Office:* Department of English, Washington and Lee University, Lexington, Va. 24450.

CAREER: College of William and Mary, Williamsburg, Va., instructor in English, 1961-65; Washington and Lee University, Lexington, Va., instructor, 1965-66, assistant professor, 1966-69, associate professor, 1969-74, professor of English, 1974—. Visiting assistant professor of English, Middlebury College, 1968-69; McGuffey Professor of Creative Writing, Ohio University, spring, 1975; lecturer in creative writing, University of Virginia, fall, 1981. Resident poet, Trinity College, Hartford, Conn., spring, 1978. Has given poetry readings at numerous colleges and universities throughout the United States.

MEMBER: Authors League of America, Authors Guild, American Association of University Professors. *Awards, honors:* Dylan Thomas Award, Poetry Society of America, for "The Two Lindens"; Howard Willett Research Prize, for poetry manuscript; Borestone Mountain Poetry Awards, 1969, 1974, and 1977; National Endowment for the Humanities summer stipend, 1969; National Endowment for the Arts fellow, 1974 and 1982; first Governor's Award for the Arts (Virginia), 1979.

WRITINGS—Poems, except as indicated: *The Diving Bell*, Knopf, 1966; *A Particular Place*, Knopf, 1969; *The Other Hand*, Louisiana State University Press, 1974; *Friends of Yours, Friends of Mine* (poems for children), Rainmaker Press, 1974; *Round and Round*, Louisiana State University Press, 1977; *Nabokov: The Dimensions of Parody* (nonfiction), Louisiana State University Press, 1978; *Rockbridge Poems*, Iron Mountain Press, 1981; *Common Ground*, Louisiana State University Press, 1982.

Work is represented in about sixty anthologies. Contributor of essays, reviews, and poetry to journals. Poetry editor, *Shenandoah*, 1966-76; advisory editor, *Poets in the South* and *New Virginia Review*.

WORK IN PROGRESS: A new book of poems, tentatively entitled *Heroes; Selected Poems;* a series of short stories, *Sweet Lucy Wine*.

* * *

SWANBERG, W(illiam) A(ndrew) 1907-

PERSONAL: Born November 23, 1907, in St. Paul, Minn.; son of Charles Henning and Valborg (Larsen) Swanberg; married Dorothy Upham Green, March 21, 1936; children: John William, Sara Valborg. *Education:* University of Minnesota, B.A., 1930, graduate study, 1931; New York University, special study, 1944. *Home and office:* Route 3, Taunton Lane, Newtown, Conn. *Agent:* McIntosh & Otis, 475 Fifth Ave., New York, N.Y. 10017.

CAREER: Worked at diverse jobs in various places, 1931-35; Dell Publishing Co., New York, N.Y., assistant editor, 1935-36, editor, 1936-44; writer in Europe for U.S. Office of War Information, 1944-45; free-lance writer, 1945—. Member, Newtown (Conn.) Library Board. *Member:* International P.E.N., Society of American Historians (fellow), New York Historical Society, Authors League of America. *Awards, honors:* Christopher Award and Minnesota Centennial Award for *First Blood;* Guggenheim fellow, 1960; Frank Luther Mott-Kappa Tau Alpha Award, 1961, for *Citizen Hearst;* Van Wyck Brooks Award for nonfiction, 1967; Pulitzer Prize for biography, 1973, for

Luce and His Empire; National Book Award for biography, 1977, for *Norman Thomas: The Last Idealist.*

WRITINGS—All published by Scribner: *Sickles the Incredible,* 1956; *First Blood: The Story of Ft. Sumter* (Book-of-the-Month Club selection), 1957; *Jim Fisk: The Career of an Improbable Rascal,* 1959; *Citizen Hearst: A Biography of William Randolph Hearst* (Book-of-the-Month Club alternate selection), 1961, reprinted, 1981; *Dreiser,* 1965; *Pulitzer* (Literary Guild selection), 1967; *The Rector and the Rogue,* 1969; *Luce and His Empire,* 1972; *Norman Thomas: The Last Idealist* (Book-of-the-Month Club alternate selection), 1976; *Whitney Father, Whitney Heiress* (Book-of-the-Month Club alternate selection), 1980.

Contributor of narratives to "The Image of War: 1861-1865" series, Doubleday, 1981— . Contributor of articles to *True, Yankee, Redbook, Saga, Woman's Home Companion, This Week, Cavalier, New Yorker, Life,* and *American Heritage.*

SIDELIGHTS: A professional biographer for over twenty-five years, W. A. Swanberg has a well-established reputation for writing scrupulously detailed yet highly entertaining studies of people he terms "controversial"—in short, "people about whose careers there may be considerable disagreement." As Jason Epstein further explains in the *New York Review of Books:* "Swanberg is attracted by American grotesques. . . . [He writes of] men of vast and shallow appetites who rose and fell with their ability to celebrate the tastes and passions of their times; tribunes of the people whose special and largely unselfconscious gift was the power to satisfy in the populace its desire for justification, no matter what its sins, and to provide those images of virtue and success which an energetic and uncertain people require."

Among Swanberg's favorite "grotesques" are those nineteenth- and early twentieth-century American entrepreneurs whose colorful exploits and accomplishments are mentioned only briefly (if at all) in conventional history books. In his biographies of publishing giants William Randolph Hearst, Joseph Pulitzer, and Henry Luce, for example, the author examines in depth how the influence of these men extended far beyond the boundaries of their respective press empires.

Citizen Hearst, the first of Swanberg's studies of American tycoons, analyzes "the Jekyll and Hyde sides of Hearst," according to E. D. Canham of the *Christian Science Monitor.* "[It] is a big step forward from the several biased biographies which have preceded it," Canham adds. *Saturday Review* critic L.L.L. Golden agrees, declaring that "to any student of American politics and press this is a highly informative and even exciting book. It shows not only long and painstaking research but a refusal to take the say-so of those who were so totally blinded by hatred of Hearst that they pictured him as a monster with no human attributes." In a *New York Times Book Review* article on *Citizen Hearst,* E. F. Goldman also observes that Swanberg "seeks not to judge but to understand [his] complex subject and to present Hearst against a fullness of setting that will make him come authentically alive. The book goes a long way toward achieving its objectives. . . . For reading pleasure, no biography has topped *Citizen Hearst* in quite a few seasons." Canham, while pointing out that the Hearst family's refusal to grant the author access to certain material makes it impossible to label the biography "definitive," nevertheless concludes that "it will do for a while. . . . Swanberg has done an absolutely first-rate job."

Though a few reviewers believe Swanberg tends to overestimate the historical importance of his subject in *Pulitzer,* most agree that it is an even better book than *Citizen Hearst.* In the *New York Times Book Review,* Oliver Knight declares *Pulitzer* to be "a splendid biography. With much new information at his command from the Pulitzer papers—which he has combed as no previous writer has done—Mr. Swanberg treats his subject sympathetically and, on the whole, circumspectly. . . . [This is] the first Pulitzer biography of any depth, breadth and judiciousness." Writing in the *Saturday Review,* Stuart W. Little predicts that "*Pulitzer* will be studied almost as a basic text of American newspapering. Few books reveal so much of what makes for success in that uncertain world. . . . *Pulitzer* is a remarkably rich and detailed biography of a remarkable life." The *Nation's* Carl Dreha particularly admires the "ease and clarity" with which Swanberg presents his material, "making the reader quite unconscious of the enormous labor that went into the book." In short, remarks Courtney R. Sheldon in the *Christian Science Monitor,* "it seems doubtful if any biographer will ever do a more definitive and gripping biography of [Pulitzer]."

For the most part, reviewers judge *Luce and His Empire* to be as entertaining and informative as Swanberg's earlier biographies. It strikes a few of them, however, as somewhat less objective than it could have been. Comments Cecil King in *Books and Bookmen:* "[*Luce and His Empire*] is an interesting and important book. . . . The style is clear without being distinguished; it is fully researched and documented but I think it would be fair to say that the general tone of the book is hostile rather than critical of its subject." *Newsweek's* Walter Clemons expresses a similar view, stating: "Both as biography and as corporate history, *Luce and His Empire* is riveting. . . . Swanberg is both amusing and humane about Luce's personality. . . . [But] good as it is, [this biography] is disfigured by polemic. While Swanberg says it would be 'excessive' to say that without Luce there would have been no China Lobby, no Sen. Joseph McCarthy, no national hysteria over Asian Communism, in effect he seems to attribute every national mistake in more than three decades to Luce's unascertainable power over the American mind." Epstein points out in the *New York Review of Books* that Luce's biographer "never considers that *Time* may merely have reflected, occasionally magnified, and generally confirmed [the prejudices of its readers]." The *Saturday Review* critic believes that Swanberg spends so much time and effort fitting in the "amusingly deflating material" he discovered that "the real substance and meaning of the story of Henry Luce and the empire he built and ran are only barely discernible."

On the other hand, R. Daniel Evans reports in *Best Sellers* that the author is "quite fair to his subject." Continues the reviewer: "Swanberg does not hesitate to give his own frank opinions of Luce, and those to the extreme right of the political spectrum will be unhappy with this candid biography. The research for this book is impeccable, and must have been enormous. . . . Sometimes *Luce and His Empire* seems almost too detailed for the casual reader, probably because is is so inclusive. At its best it is a fascinating account not only of Luce, but also of American and world history from 1923 until almost the present. This will remain, no doubt, the definitive biography of Henry R. Luce; it is colorful, frightening in political implications, and at all times eventful."

Despite the emotional responses they provoke among many readers and critics, controversial people will probably always be Swanberg's favorite subjects; as he told *CA,* he finds the disputes they inspire "not only interesting but calculated to clarify the issues involved." And at least in the cases of Hearst and Pulitzer, declares Knight in the *New York Times Book Review,* Swanberg does succeed in demonstrating "what made them tick." "[These men] have met the same perceptive biographer in W. A. Swanberg," the critic concludes. "In each case, a hitherto puzzling man emerges as a much more understandable whole man."

BIOGRAPHICAL/CRITICAL SOURCES: *Saturday Review,* April 28, 1956, February 14, 1959, September 16, 1961, October 14, 1967, October 21, 1972; *New Yorker,* April 28, 1956, September 9, 1961, June 23, 1980; *New York Herald Tribune Book Review,* April 29, 1956; *New York Times,* April 29, 1956, February 22, 1959, July 19, 1980; *San Francisco Chronicle,* April 29, 1956, February 18, 1959; *Atlantic,* May, 1956; *American Historical Review,* October, 1956; *Christian Science Monitor,* February 19, 1959, September 14, 1961, October 12, 1967; *Chicago Sunday Tribune,* March 8, 1959, September 10, 1961; *Spectator,* January 22, 1960; *Times Literary Supplement,* January 29, 1960; *New York Herald Tribune Books,* September 3, 1961; *New York Times Book Review,* September 10, 1961, October 1, 1967, November 10, 1968, October 1, 1972, November 7, 1976, July 27, 1980; *New York Review of Books,* June 3, 1965, November 2, 1972, March 3, 1977; *New Republic,* September 30, 1967, September 30, 1972, January 1, 1977; *Best Sellers,* October 1, 1967, November 1, 1968, October 1, 1972, March, 1977; *Christian Century,* October 4, 1967; *Nation,* November 13, 1967, October 30, 1972, January 22, 1977; *Saturday Night,* January, 1968; *Newsweek,* October 2, 1972, November 8, 1976; *National Review,* October 27, 1972, January 7, 1977; *Books and Bookmen,* February, 1973; *Washington Post Book World,* November 21, 1976, June 15, 1980; *Commentary,* February, 1977; *Chicago Tribune Book World,* May 18, 1980; *Detroit News,* July 20, 1980.

—Sketch by Deborah A. Straub

* * *

SWINGLEHURST, Edmund 1917-

PERSONAL: Born March 14, 1917, in Chile; son of Edward (a banker) and Lydia Jones; married Janice Anderson; children: (previous marriage) Julian, Mark, Elissa. *Education:* Attended school in Devon, England. *Politics:* None. *Religion:* Christian. *Office:* Thomas Cook, 45 Berkeley St., London W1A1, England.

CAREER: Headmaster of school in Chile, 1939-44; Grant Advertising, Buenos Aires, Argentina, account executive, 1944-46; E. R. Squibb, Buenos Aires, publicity manager, 1947-50; artist in Paris, France, 1950-53; Thomas Cook, London, England, member of public relations staff, 1953—. *Member:* Press Club, Overseas Press Club.

WRITINGS: (Self-illustrated) *How! The Whole Truth about the Wild West* (humor), Parrish, 1957; (editor) *French Lovers Are Lovely* (cartoons), Arco, 1957; (self-illustrated) *All Abroad!* (travel humor), Parrish, 1958; (with Willy Trebich) *The Broken Swastika,* Cooper, 1971; *The Romantic Journey: The Story of Thomas Cook and Victorian Travel,* Pica, 1973; *England,* WHS Distributors, 1980; *Scottish Walks and Legends,* Granada, 1981; *Outdoor and Activity Holidays in Britain (Wish You Were Here Guide),* Magnum Books, 1981; *Cook's Tours,* Blandford Press, 1981.

Published by Hamlyn: *The Victorian and Edwardian Seaside,* 1978; *Wonders of the World,* 1978; *French Phrase Book,* 1979; *German Phrase Book,* 1979; *Italian Phrase Book,* 1979; *Spanish Phrase Book,* 1979; *Guide to the Channel Islands,* 1979; *Greek Phrase Book,* 1981; *Portuguese Phrase Book,* 1981. Also author of *Paris, Rome, Florence, Hong Kong, Los Angeles,* and *San Francisco.*

SIDELIGHTS: Some of Edmund Swinglehurst's books have been published in French, German, Italian, Spanish, Greek, and Portuguese. *Avocational interests:* Travel, art.

T

TAETZSCH, Lyn 1941-

PERSONAL: Surname is pronounced "taych"; born September 24, 1941, in East Orange, N.J.; daughter of William Kilpatrick and Ella (Kroupa) Taetzsch; married Adrian Epstein; children: Blixy. *Education:* Attended Cooper Union Art School; Rutgers University, B.A. (with honors), 1971. *Home:* 1165 Long Hill Rd., Stirling, N.J. 07980. *Agent:* Dominick Abel, 498 West End Ave., New York, N.Y. 10024.

CAREER: Blue Cross-Blue Shield, Newark, N.J., manager and trainer, 1968-70; Holy Cow Leather (leather accessories manufacturer), Newfield, N.Y., owner and president, 1971-74; part-time lecturer on small business management, Ithaca College, Ithaca, N.Y., 1974-75, Tompkins-Cortland Community College, Dryden, N.Y., 1975-76, Fairleigh Dickinson University, Madison, N.J., 1976; senior editor and creative director, Economics Press, 1976-81; owner and president, Information Plus (publishing firm), 1979—. Consultant, Automated Instruction, Inc.

WRITINGS: (With Sandra Z. Taetzsch) *Preschool Games and Activities*, Fearon, 1974; (with Herb Genfan) *How to Start Your Own Craft Business*, Watson-Guptill, 1974; (with Genfan) *Leather Decoration*, Watson-Guptill, 1975; (with Genfan) *Latigo Leather*, Watson-Guptill, 1976; *How to Open and Operate a Retail Store*, Regnery, 1976; (with Enid Littman) *Out of Work: The Complete Job Hunter's Guide*, Regnery, 1976; (with Laura Taetzsch) *Practical Accounting for Small Businesses*, Van Nostrand, 1977; *Winning Methods of Betting and Bluffing in Poker*, Drake, 1977; (with Eileen Benson) *Taking Charge on the Job: Techniques for Management Assertiveness*, Executives Enterprises Publications, 1978. Editor of *Better Communication* (newsletter), and *Computer Basics* (study course), both published by Information Plus. Contributor to American Society for Training and Development *Training and Development Journal*.

WORK IN PROGRESS: Revised edition of *Practical Accounting for Small Businesses*.

AVOCATIONAL INTERESTS: Art (had a one-woman show of her paintings in New York, 1965).

* * *

TALBOT, Charlene Joy 1928-
(Lucy Lee)

PERSONAL: Born November 14, 1928, in Frankfort, Kan.; daughter of Charles Henry (a laborer) and Helen (Jillson) Talbot. *Education:* Kansas State College of Agriculture and Applied Science (now Kansas State University), B.S., 1950. *Home:* 568 Van Duzer St., Staten Island, N.Y. 10304.

CAREER: After college wandered to New York, California, Mexico, and Europe, working as typist, secretary, waitress, and classified ad-taker; in 1958 found a cheap apartment in the market district of Manhattan, worked part-time as a secretary, began to write, and finally sold a children's story to a Sunday school paper. *Awards, honors:* Fellowship in juvenile literature to Bread Loaf Writers' Conference, 1966.

WRITINGS—Juveniles: *Tomas Takes Charge*, Lothrop, 1966; *A Home with Aunt Florry*, Atheneum, 1974; *The Great Rat Island Adventure*, Atheneum, 1977; *An Orphan for Nebraska*, Atheneum, 1979; *The Sodbuster Venture*, Atheneum, 1982.

Adult books; under pseudonym Lucy Lee; published by Harlequin: *Heart's Fury*, 1981; *The Rite of Love*, 1982.

WORK IN PROGRESS: *Heart's Paradise*, a contemporary romance set in Hawaii, for Worldwide Books.

SIDELIGHTS: Charlene Joy Talbot told *CA*: "The wonderful thing about writing for children is that they're interested in everything. You can do all the things you wanted to do as a child, and then write about them as though you still were. The wonderful thing about writing romances is researching the fascinating backgrounds."

* * *

TALLON, Robert 1935-

PERSONAL: Born September 21, 1935, in New York, N.Y.; son of Charles A. and Anne E. Tallon. *Education:* Attended art school for two years, college for three years, and studied voice at Metropolitan Opera Studios for two years.

CAREER: Artist in oil, watercolor, and mixed mediums, with four one-man shows in New York, N.Y. *Military service:* U.S. Army.

WRITINGS—Most books self-illustrated: *Conversations: Cries, Croaks, and Calls*, Holt, 1963; (illustrator) Ruth Leslie Smith, *Hurry!*, *Dinner Is at Six*, Bobbs-Merrill, 1969.

A.B.C. . . . in English and Spanish, Lion Press, 1970; *The Thing in Dolores' Piano*, Bobbs-Merrill, 1970; *Zoophabets*, Bobbs-Merrill, 1971; *Handella*, Bobbs-Merrill, 1972; *Rhoda's*

Restaurant, Bobbs-Merrill, 1973; *Rotten Kidphabets,* Holt, 1975; *ZAG: A Search through the Alphabet,* Holt, 1976; *Fish Story,* Holt, 1976; *Flea Story,* Holt, 1977; *Worm Story,* Holt, 1978; *Little Cloud,* Parents Magazine Press, 1979.

The Alligator's Song, Parents Magazine Press, 1981.

WORK IN PROGRESS: A movie script.†

* * *

TARR, Yvonne Young 1929-

PERSONAL: Born December 10, 1929, in Covington, Ky.; daughter of Elwood Stinson (an architect) and Margaret (Linehan) Young; married William Tarr (a sculptor), March 7, 1952; children: Jonathon Young, Nicolas Joseph. *Politics:* None. *Religion:* None. *Residence:* East Hampton, N.Y.

CAREER: Writer. *Awards, honors:* New play of the year award, Southeast Theatre Conference, for "Clap Hands 'Til Daddy Comes Home."

WRITINGS: *The Ten-Minute Gourmet Cookbook,* Lyle Stuart, 1965; *The Ten-Minute Gourmet Diet Cookbook,* Lyle Stuart, 1967; *A Hundred and One Desserts to Make You Famous,* Lyle Stuart, 1971; *The New York Times Bread and Soup Cookbook,* Quadrangle, 1972; *Love Portions,* Citadel, 1972; *The Complete Outdoor Cookbook,* Quadrangle, 1973; *The Farmhouse Cookbook,* Quadrangle, 1973; *The New York Times Natural Foods Dieting Book,* Quadrangle, 1973; *The New Ten-Minute Gourmet Cookbook,* Lyle Stuart, 1975; *The Up with Wholesome, Down with Storebought, Book of Recipes and Household Formulas,* Random House, 1975; *The Great Food Processor Cookbook,* Random House, 1976.

All published by Vintage: *The Supereasy Sausagemaking Book,* 1975; *The Supereasy Winemaking Book,* 1975; *The Supereasy Cheesemaking Book,* 1975; *The Supereasy Book of Special Breads,* 1975; *The Tomato Book,* 1977; *The Squash Cookbook,* 1979; *The Great East Coast Seafood Book,* 1982.

Also author of "Clap Hands 'Til Daddy Comes Home," a play, and "The Decameron," a musical drama. Author of United Features syndicated columns, "The Quick Gourmet" and "The Diet Gourmet." Contributor to magazines.

* * *

TAVES, Isabella 1915-

PERSONAL: Born September 20, 1915, in Lincoln, Neb.; daughter of Cornelius William and Blanche (Roberts) Taves; married Daniel D. Mich, November 4, 1944 (deceased). *Education:* Northwestern University, B.S., 1932. *Home:* 137 East 38th St., New York, N.Y. 11016.

CAREER: Free-lance magazine writer. *Member:* Women in Communications, Phi Beta Kappa, Alpha Phi. *Awards, honors:* Merit Award, Northwestern University; Headliner Award, Women in Communications, 1974.

WRITINGS—Juveniles: *Successful Women,* Dutton, 1943; (with Margaret Hubbard Ayer) *The Three Lives of Harriet Hubbard Ayer,* Lippincott, 1953; *Not Bad for a Girl,* M. Evans, 1972; *True Ghost Stories,* F. Watts, 1978.

Adult: *The Quick Rich Fox,* Random House, 1960; *I Learned about Women from Them,* McKay, 1963; *Women Alone,* Funk, 1968; *Destiny Times Six,* M. Evans, 1970; *Love Must Not Be Wasted,* Crowell, 1974; (with Madame Wellington Koo) *No Feast Lasts Forever,* Quadrangle, 1975; *A Widow's Guide,* Schocken, 1982.

SIDELIGHTS: Isabella Taves says of *Women Alone*: "I started the book as therapy when I was a widow of seven months after twenty-one years of marriage. Later, after gaining perspective, I took a fresh and more detached look at the state of widowhood in *A Widow's Guide*."

BIOGRAPHICAL/CRITICAL SOURCES: *Washington Post,* July 1, 1968.

* * *

TAYLOR, Kenneth N(athaniel) 1917-

PERSONAL: Born May 8, 1917, in Portland, Ore.; son of George N. (a minister) and Charlotte B. (Huff) Taylor; married Margaret Louise West, September 13, 1940; children: Rebecca, John, Martha, Peter, Janet, Cynthia, Mark, Gretchen, Mary Lee, Alison. *Education:* Wheaton College, Wheaton, Ill., B.S., 1938; attended Dallas Theological Seminary, 1940-42; Northern Baptist Theological Seminary, Th.M., 1944. *Office address:* Tyndale House Publishers, 336 Gundersen Dr., Box 80, Wheaton, Ill. 60187.

CAREER: Moody Press, Chicago, Ill., director, 1947-62, director of Moody Literature Mission, 1948-62; Tyndale House Publishers, Wheaton, Ill., founder and president, 1962—; Living Bibles International, president, 1968-77, international president, 1977—. President, Tyndale House Foundation, 1964-80; chairman, Living Bibles Foundation, 1973-79. Member of board of directors, Inter-Varsity Christian Fellowship, 1950-59, and InterSkrift Forlage Aktiebolag, Sweden, 1974-79; chairman of board, Evangelical Literature Overseas, 1951-70, Coverdale House Publishers, London, England, 1969-79, and UNILIT, Inc., 1972-73; director, Short Terms Abroad, 1963-77, and Christian Library Service, 1972-76. Member of advisory board, Campus Crusade for Christ Christian Embassy, 1976—; member of board of reference, Association of Christian Prison Workers, 1978—, and Eurovangelism of Canada, 1978—. Member of board of visitors, Gordon-Conwell Theological Seminary, 1974; trustee, Fuller Theological Seminary, 1974-80. Elder, College Church, Wheaton, 1958-61 and 1964-67. *Member:* Wheaton College Alumni Association (vice-president and chairman of alumni fund, 1944; president, 1945-46).

AWARDS, HONORS: Litt.D., Wheaton College, 1965, and Trinity Evangelical Divinity School, 1972; citation from Layman's National Bible Committee, 1971; special award from Religious Heritage of America, 1972; Distinguished Service Citation, International Society of Christian Endeavor, 1973; Nelson Bible Award, Thomas Nelson, Inc., 1973; Better World Award, National VFW Auxiliary, 1974; Distinguished Public Service Award, Messiah College, 1974; Doctor of Humane Letters, Huntington College, 1974; Recognition Award, Urban Ministries, Inc., 1977; Service Award, Wheaton College Alumni Association, 1977; Christian Service Contribution Award, Crusader Club, Wheaton College, 1980; Achievement Award, Christian Booksellers Association, 1980; Achievement Award, Allied Paper, 1980; Gutenberg Award, 1981.

WRITINGS—Adult; published by Tyndale, except as indicated: *Is Christianity Credible?,* Inter-Varsity, 1948; *Living Letters* (also see below), 1962; *Living Prophecies* (also see below), 1965; *Living Gospels* (also see below), 1966; *The Living New Testament* (also see below; contains *Living Letters, Living Prophecies,* and *Living Gospels*), 1967, illustrated edition published as *The Greatest Is Love: An Illustrated Edition of "The Living New Testament,"* World Home Bible League, 1971, condensed edition, edited by David Wilkerson, published as *David Wilkerson Presents the End Times New Testament,* Chosen Books, 1975; *Living Psalms and Proverbs* (also see below),

1967; *Living Lessons of Life and Love* (also see below), 1968; *Living Books of Moses* (also see below), 1969; *Living History of Israel* (also see below), 1970; *The Living Bible* (also see below; contains *Living Letters, Living Prophecies, Living Gospels, Living Psalms and Proverbs, Living Lessons of Live and Love, Living Books of Moses,* and *Living History of Israel*), 1971, illustrated edition published as *The Way: An Illustrated Edition of "The Living Bible,"* 1972, Catholic edition, 1976, excerpt illustrated with photographs published as *The Life of Christ,* 1974; *Who Is This Man Jesus?: "The Living New Testament,"* 1973; *Soul Food,* 1973; *Responsive Readings from "The Living Bible,"* 1973; *"The Living New Testament" Notebook,* 1977.

Juvenile; published by Moody, except as indicated: *Stories for the Children's Hour,* 1953, revised edition, 1968; *Devotions for the Children's Hour,* 1954; *I See What God Wants Me to Know,* 1955, revised edition, 1958, published as *Living Thoughts for the Children's Hour,* 1972; *Bible in Pictures for Little Eyes,* 1956; *Lost on the Trail,* 1959, reprinted, Tyndale, 1980; *Romans for the Children's Hour,* 1959, published as *Living Letters for the Children's Hour,* 1968; *Almost Twelve,* Tyndale, 1968; *Creation and the High School Student,* Tyndale, 1969; *Evolution and the High School Student,* Tyndale, 1969; *Taylor's Bible Story Book,* Tyndale, 1970, revised edition, 1976; *Reach Out: An Illustrated Edition of "The Living New Testament,"* Tyndale, 1971; *The Children's Living Bible,* Tyndale, 1972; *"The Living Bible" Story Book,* Tyndale, 1979.

Contributor of Bible paraphrases: George M. Wilson, compiler, *Words of Wisdom from "Living Psalms and Proverbs,"* World Wide Publications, 1967; Don W. Hillis, compiler, *Living Words for Today: A Bible Reading for Each Day of the Year,* Tyndale, 1967; Edythe Draper, compiler, *Living Light: Daily Light in Today's Language,* Tyndale, 1972; Perry Tanksley, editor, *Light from "The Living Bible,"* Revell, 1973; Jack Atkeson Speer, *"The Living Bible" Concordance Complete,* Poolesville Presbyterian Church (Poolesville, Md.), 1973; Dave Grant, *Would You Believe: "The Living New Testament,"* Regal Books, 1974; Alice Zillman Chapin, editor, *"Let "The Living Bible" Help You,* Harper, 1975; H. Norman Wright, compiler, *The Living Marriage: Lessons in Love from "The Living Bible,"* Revell, 1975; Don De Welt, *Leviticus,* College Press, 1975; Tanksley, editor, *Love from "The Living Bible,"* Revell, 1978.

SIDELIGHTS: *The Living Bible,* a modern English paraphrase of the entire Bible, took Kenneth N. Taylor fourteen years to complete; more than twenty-five million copies are now in print. Taylor credits his children with providing the inspiration needed to accomplish such a difficult task. As he explained to *CA:* "Our family devotions were tough going because of the difficulty we had understanding the King James Version, which we were then using, or the Revised Standard Version, which we used later. All too often I would ask questions to be sure the children understood, and they would shrug their shoulders—they didn't know what the passage was talking about. So I would explain it. I would paraphrase it for them and give them the thought. It suddenly occurred to me one afternoon that I should write out the reading for that evening thought by thought, rather than doing it on the spot during our devotional time. So I did, and read the chapter to the family that evening with exciting results—they knew the answers to all the questions I asked! So that was the beginning of my work on paraphrasing *The Living Bible.* My greatest prayer is that *The Living Bible* will bring people closer to God and give them more knowledge of the way He works and of the tremendous privilege they have in being children of God through Christ the Savior."

BIOGRAPHICAL/CRITICAL SOURCES: *Authors in the News,* Volume II, Gale, 1976.

* * *

TEGNER, Bruce 1928-

PERSONAL: Born October 28, 1928, in Chicago, Ill. *Education:* LaVerne College, B.A., 1975. *Address:* P.O. Box 1782, Ventura, Calif. 93001.

CAREER: Specialist in self-defense and sport forms of weaponless fighting; has trained actors and devised fight scenes for films and television. Operator of Bruce Tegner School, 1952-67; Moorpark College, Moorpark, Calif., instructor in defense tactics, beginning 1970; currently teacher in Physical Education Division, Ventura College, Ventura, Calif. *Military service:* U.S. Army, 1950-52; trained instructors to teach weaponless fighting, taught military police tactics, and coached sport judo teams.

WRITINGS—Published by Thor Publishing, except as indicated: *Karate,* Volume I: *The Open Hand and Foot Fighting,* 1959, 3rd edition, 1965, Volume II: *Traditional Forms for Sport,* 1959, 3rd edition, 1963.

Bruce Tegner Method of Self-Defense: The Best of Judo, Jiujitsu, Karate, Savate, Yawara, Aikido, Ate-waza, 1960, 3rd edition, 1971; *Savate: French Foot Fighting, Self-Defense, Sport,* 1960, 3rd revised edition, 1982; *Aikido Self-Defense: Holds and Locks for Modern Use,* 1961; *Judo for Fun: Sport Techniques Made Easy,* 1961; *Self-Defense for Women: A Simple Method,* 1961, 2nd edition (with Alice McGrath), 1969; *Stick Fighting for Self-Defense: Yawara, Police Club, Aikido, Cane, Quarter-Staff,* 1961, 3rd edition, 1972; *Teach Your Boy Self-Defense and Self-Confidence,* 1961; *Judo-Karate for Police Officers: Defense and Control, a Simple Method,* 1962; *Bruce Tegner's Complete Book of Self Defense,* Stein & Day, 1963, revised edition, Thor Publishing, 1975; *Judo and Karate Belt Degrees: Requirements, Rules, Regulations,* 1963, revised edition, 1967; *Judo and Karate Exercises: Physical Conditioning for the Un-Armed Fighting Arts,* 1963, revised edition published as *Karate and Judo Exercises,* 1981; *Karate: Self Defense and Sport,* Dell, 1963; *Isometric Power Exercises,* Dell, 1964.

Instant Self-Defense, Grosset, 1965; *Bruce Tegner's Complete Book of Karate,* Bantam, 1966, 3rd edition, Thor Publishing, 1970; *Black Belt Judo, Karate, and Jukado: Advanced Techniques for Experts,* 1967; *Complete Book of Judo,* 1967; *Complete Book of Karate,* 1967, 3rd edition, 1970; (with McGrath) *Self-Defense for Girls: A Secondary School and College Manual,* 1967, revised edition, Grosset, 1969; *Complete Book of Jukado Self-Defense: Judo, Karate, Aikido (Jiu-jitsu Modernized),* 1968; *Kung Fu and Tai Chi: Chinese Karate and Classical Exercises,* 1968, revised edition, 1981; *Self-Defense: Nerve Centers and Pressure Points for Atemiwaza, Jukado, and Karate,* 1968, revised edition, 1978; *Self-Defense for Boys and Men: A Secondary School and College Manual,* 1968, revised edition, 1969; *Aikido and Jiu Jitsu Holds and Locks,* 1969.

Bruce Tegner's Complete Book of Aikido and Holds and Locks, Grosset, 1970; *Judo for Fun: Sport Techniques,* 1970; *Self-Defense You Can Teach Your Boy: A Confidence-Building Course,* 1970; *Defense Tactics for Law Enforcement,* Volume I: *Weaponless Defense and Control,* 1972, revised edition, 1978; *Stick Fighting: Sport Forms,* 1973.

Judo: Sport Techniques for Physical Fitness and Tournament, 1976; (with McGrath) *Self-Defense for Your Child,* 1976; *Bruce Tegner's Complete Book of Jujitsu,* 1977; (with McGrath) *Self-*

Defense and Assault Prevention for Girls and Women, 1977; *Self-Defense: A Basic Course,* 1979.

(With McGrath) *Solo Forms of Karate, Tai Chi, Aikido, and Kung Fu,* 1981; *Judo: Beginner to Black Belt,* 1982; *Karate: Beginner to Black Belt,* 1982; (with McGrath) *The Survival Book,* 1982.

SIDELIGHTS: Bruce Tegner, who holds black belts in judo and karate, was born to the teaching of unarmed fighting skills. Both his parents were professional teachers of judo and jiujutsu and began to train him when he was two years old. After the age of eight, Tegner was instructed by Oriental and European experts, receiving instruction in sword and stick fighting as well as the various forms of weaponless fighting.

Before he gave up competitive judo, Tegner became the California state judo champion. He has taught men, women, and children, exceptionally gifted students, and blind and disabled people.

* * *

TESTER, Sylvia Root 1939-

PERSONAL: Born October 6, 1939; daughter of Ralph Orrin (an editor) and Thelma (Aldridge) Root; married N. Eugene Tester (a teacher), July 18, 1959; children: Rachael Anne, Julia Linette. *Education:* Attended Cincinnati Bible College, 1958-60, and Elgin Community College, 1978-80. *Religion:* Christian. *Home:* 1001 Cedar St., Elgin, Ill. 60120.

CAREER: Standard Publishing Co., Cincinnati, Ohio, assistant editor, 1959-60; David C. Cook Publishing Co., Elgin, Ill., 1963-68, school products editor, 1968-74; free-lance writer, 1974-77; The Child's World, Inc. (publisher), Elgin, editor, 1977-80, 1981-82; free-lance writer, 1982—.

WRITINGS: *The Life of Jesus in Pictures,* Standard Publishing, 1962; *Jesus Is Born,* Standard Publishing, 1963; *Jesus Lives,* Standard Publishing, 1963; *Gifts for Baby Jesus,* David Cook, 1963; *Let Me Help,* David Cook, 1963; *Where Are You Going Today?,* Standard Publishing, 1964; *Baby Jesus,* Standard Publishing, 1964; *Happy Sunday Morning,* Standard Publishing, 1964; *God's Children Help,* David Cook, 1964; (with Betty Freedy Larsen) *The Birth of Jesus,* David Cook, 1964; *But I Can't See Him,* David Cook, 1966; *Teachers' Manual for Health and Cleanliness,* David Cook, 1966; *Plants and Seeds* (teaching pictures), David Cook, 1967; *My Friend, the Doctor,* David Cook, 1967; *My Friend, the Policeman,* David Cook, 1967; *My Friend, the Fireman,* David Cook, 1968; *Teachers' Manual for Moods and Emotions,* David Cook, 1970; *Teachers' Manual for Creative Adventures,* David Cook, 1972.

Published by Childrens Press, except as indicated: *Carla-Too-Little,* 1976; *Billy's Basketball,* 1976; *A World of Color,* 1976; *That Big Bruno,* 1976; *Tell Me a Tale about Trolls,* 1976; *Rover, Jr.'s Baseball Career,* 1976; *The Parade of Shapes,* 1976; *Feeling Angry,* 1976; *Melinda,* 1977; *Mr. and Mrs. Opposite,* 1977; *Never Monkey with a Monkey,* 1977; *What Did You Say: A Book of Homophones,* 1977; *One Unicorn: A Counting Book,* 1977; *Over, Under, and All Around: Relationships in Space,* 1977; *The Loud-Noisy, Dirty-Grimy, Bad and Naughty Twins: A Book of Synonyms,* 1977; *Opposite Odelia: A Book of Antonyms,* 1978; *You Dance Like an Ostrich!: A Book of Similes,* 1978; *A Day of Surprises,* 1979; *The Great Big Boat,* 1979; *Sandy's New Home,* 1979; *Sometimes I'm Afraid,* 1979; *We Laughed a Lot: My First Day of School,* 1979.

Frustrated, 1980; *Traffic Jam!,* 1980; *Chase!,* 1980; *Parade!,* 1980; *Family!,* 1980; *Jealous,* 1980; *Sad,* 1980; *Learning about Ghosts,* Child's World, 1981; *The World into Which Jesus Came,* Child's World, 1982.

"Magic Monsters" series, published by Child's World: *What Is a Monster,* 1979; *Magic Monsters Around the Year,* 1979; *Magic Monsters Learn about Safety,* 1979; *Magic Monsters' Halloween,* 1980; *Magic Monsters Learn about Weather,* 1980.

WORK IN PROGRESS: Articles on suicide and on the Ku Klux Klan.

* * *

THIMM, Alfred L. 1923-

PERSONAL: Born December 10, 1923; married; children: two. *Education:* New York University, B.A. (cum laude), 1948, M.A., 1949, Ph.D., 1959; summer post-doctoral study at University of Wyoming, 1959, and University of Iowa, 1961. *Home:* 7 Chelsea Circle, South Burlington, Vt. 05401. *Office:* School of Business Administration, University of Vermont, Burlington, Vt. 05405.

CAREER: Industrial engineer for American Can Co., 1951-52; St. Lawrence University, Canton, N.Y., assistant professor of economics, 1953-55; New York University, Department of Economics, New York, N.Y., research fellow, 1955-56; Clarkson College, Potsdam, N.Y., associate professor of business administration and mechanical engineering, 1956-59; Union College, Schenectady, N.Y., associate professor, 1960-68, professor of economics and industrial administration, 1968-81, director of graduate program of industrial administration, 1962-68, director of Institute of Administration and Management, 1968-80, director of Ph.D. program in administration and engineering systems, 1980-81; University of Vermont, Burlington, Vt., director of School of Business, 1981—. Visiting professor at University of Munich, 1972, 1974-75, and at Wirtschafts Universitat, 1980. Management consultant to New York State Bureau of the Budget, New York State Department of Transportation, and other public and private agencies; associate with Stochos, Inc. (management consulting firm), 1973-76. *Awards, honors:* National Science Foundation grants, 1959, 1961; Ford Foundation summer research grants, 1960, 1962; Fulbright research scholar at Technische Hochschule, Graz, Austria, 1967-68.

WRITINGS: (Contributor) L. R. Robinson and Adams, editors, *Introduction to Modern Economics,* Dryden, 1959; (contributor) John M. Champion and Francis J. Bridges, editors, *Critical Incidents in Management,* Irwin, 1963; (with J. Finkelstein) *Economists and Society: From Aquinas to Keynes,* Harper, 1973, 2nd revised edition, Union College Press, 1981; *The Dynamics of Project Management,* Administrative and Engineering Systems Monograph, Union College, 1974; *American Business Opinion,* University of Alabama Press, 1975; (with Eberhard Witte) *Neue Richtlinien in der Amerikanischen Managment Theorie,* Westdeutscher Press, 1976; *Business Ideologies in the Reform-Progressive Era, 1880-1914,* University of Alabama Press, 1976; (with Witte) *Entscheidungstheorie: Texte und Analysen,* Th. Gabler, 1977; *The False Promise of Codetermination,* Heath, 1980. Contributor of articles to numerous journals, including *Bell Telephone Magazine, Business and Society Review, Columbia Journal of World Business,* and *Journal of Systems Management.*

WORK IN PROGRESS: With J. Finkelstein, *The Political Economy of Planning and Control; The Foundations of Systems Analysis;* research on the dynamics of economic planning in the Soviet Union and Eastern Europe and the impact of administrative and political behavior on the planning-decision process.

SIDELIGHTS: Alfred L. Thimm is bilingual in English and German and has a working knowledge of Spanish, French, and Italian. *Economists and Society* has been translated into Spanish.

* * *

THOMAS, Bill 1934-

PERSONAL: Born November 11, 1934, in Elizabethtown, Ky.; son of William Roy (a farmer) and Elizabeth (Crabtree) Thomas; married Joan McBroom, February 2, 1954 (divorced, 1965); married Phyllis Newkirk, 1965; children: (first marriage) David, Dianne, Lisa; (second marriage) Alan Lowell. *Education:* Western Kentucky State University (now Western Kentucky University), A.B., 1958. *Politics:* "May the best man win." *Religion:* "Sometimes." *Home and office address:* Route 4, Box 387, Nashville, Ind. 47448.

CAREER: *Park City Daily News,* Bowling Green, Ky., reporter, 1955-58; United Press International, Louisville, Ky., staff writer, 1959-62; *Cincinnati Enquirer,* Cincinnati, Ohio, bureau chief in Lebanon, Ohio, 1962-63, travel editor, 1964-66; free-lance magazine photojournalist, 1966—. *Military service:* U.S. Army, Intelligence, 1958-59; became captain.

MEMBER: Society of American Travel Writers, Outdoor Writers of America, American Society of Magazine Photographers, Hoosier Outdoor Writers. *Awards, honors:* Writer's Digest Award, 1967, for nonfiction magazine article; Ohio Governor's Award, 1972.

WRITINGS: *Tripping in America: Off the Beaten Track,* Chilton, 1974; *Eastern Trips and Trails,* Stackpole, 1975; *Mid-America Trips and Trails,* Stackpole, 1975; *The Swamp,* Norton, 1976; *The Complete World of Kites,* Lippincott, 1977; *Lakeside Recreation Areas,* Stackpole, 1977; *American Rivers: A Natural History,* Norton, 1978; *Natural Washington,* Holt, 1980; *The Island,* Norton, 1980; *The Brown County Book,* Indiana University Press, 1981. Contributor to popular magazines, including *Outdoor Life, Argosy, Field & Stream, Saga, Sports Afield, Popular Science, Good Housekeeping, Parent's* and *Redbook.* Editor of *Travel Writer,* 1964-66.

WORK IN PROGRESS: *Natural New York* and *Natural Chicago,* both for Holt; *Natural Los Angeles,* for Dial.

SIDELIGHTS: Bill Thomas's first book, on outdoor recreation in America, was written in 1972 under contract to the U.S. Information Agency. It was published in color and presented as a gift to the peoples of the Soviet Union as an educational and goodwill gesture. *Avocational interests:* Bicycling, jogging, swimming, mountain climbing, camping, boating, canoeing, fishing, backpacking.

* * *

THORPE, Michael 1932-

PERSONAL: Born September 18, 1932, in Great Yarmouth, Norfolk, England; son of Ernest Gordon (a brewery manager) and Muriel Florence (Bateman) Thorpe; married Pauline Constance Keith, February 11, 1956; married second wife, Elin Elgaard Berg, July, 1971; children: (first marriage) Lucy, Edmund Keith Gordon; (second marriage) Jacob Johan. *Education:* University College (now University of Leicester), B.A. (with honors), 1954; University of Singapore, M.A., 1964. *Politics:* "A personal variety of Socialism." *Address:* P.O. Box 1456, 73 Salem St., Sackville, New Brunswick, Canada. *Office:* Department of English, Mount Allison University, Sackville, New Brunswick, Canada.

CAREER: During his early career taught English at colleges in Turkey and Nigeria; Nayang University, Singapore, lecturer in English, 1962-64; University of Leiden, Leiden, Netherlands, senior lecturer in English, 1965-70; University of Calgary, Calgary, Alberta, 1970-74, began as associate professor, became professor of English; Mount Allison University, Sackville, New Brunswick, professor of English and head of department, 1974—. *Military service:* British Army, 1955-57; became sergeant. *Member:* English Association.

WRITINGS: (Editor) *Modern Poems,* Oxford University Press, 1963; *Siegfried Sassoon: A Critical Study,* University Press (Leiden) and Oxford University Press (London), 1966, Oxford University Press (New York), 1967; (editor) *Modern Prose,* Oxford University Press, 1968; *By the Niger and Other Poems,* Fortune Press, 1969; *A Choice of Clough's Verse,* Faber & Faber, 1969; *Matthew Arnold,* Evans Brothers, 1969, Arco, 1971; *The Poetry of Edmund Blunden,* Bridge Books, 1971; *Clough: The Critical Heritage,* Routledge & Kegan Paul, 1972; *Doris Lessing,* Longman, 1973; (editor) Siegfried Sassoon, *Letters to a Critic,* Bridge Books, 1976; *V. S. Naipaul,* Longman, 1976; *Doris Lessing's Africa,* Evans Brothers, 1978; *John Fowles,* Profile Books, 1982, *V. S. Naipaul: A House for Mr. Biswas,* Nexus Books, 1982. Contributor of poems and reviews to *Times* (London), and other publications.

WORK IN PROGRESS: *19 Dorset Poems,* for Word & Action; *Out of the Storm,* a book of poems.

AVOCATIONAL INTERESTS: Travel, gardening, walking.

* * *

THRASHER, Crystal (Faye) 1921-

PERSONAL: Born December 5, 1921, in Oolitic, Ind.; daughter of Virgil Leroy (a stonecutter) and Rozella (Bennett) Knight; married Joseph Martin Thrasher, April 22, 1939; children: Carol (Mrs. Rex Hatfield), Joseph, Jr., Janis. *Education:* Attended Indiana University, 1972-73. *Politics:* "Mixed emotions." *Religion:* "A little." *Residence:* Roanoke, Ind. 46783.

CAREER: Fort Wayne Country Club, Fort Wayne, Ind., waitress, 1957-75. Writer, 1975—. Part-time office worker and model, Sears, Fort Wayne, 1960-61. *Member:* Greater Fort Wayne Writer's Club. *Awards, honors:* Friends of American Writers award, 1980, for *Between Dark and Daylight.*

WRITINGS—Juveniles; all published by Atheneum: *The Dark Didn't Catch Me,* 1975; *Between Dark and Daylight,* 1979; *Julie's Summer,* 1981; *End of a Dark Road,* 1982.

WORK IN PROGRESS: *Seely,* a young adult novel, for Atheneum.

SIDELIGHTS: Crystal Thrasher told *CA:* "Corny as it may seem, love got me into the habit of writing. Love for my family and friends, my love of life, and the need to put it all into words brought forth my first book. My family, who loves me and understands my need to write, and my good friends, who sometimes think my oars don't quite reach the water but love me anyway, encouraged me to go on with my writing. It was my good fortune that the books appealed to children, to the child in all of us, and the books are being received with love. Just the way I wrote them."

AVOCATIONAL INTERESTS: Walking through the forest, travel, reading.

* * *

TIERNEY, Tom 1928-

PERSONAL: Born October 8, 1928, in Beaumont, Tex.; son

of John Taylor (an accountant) and Mary Lou (Gripon) Tierney. *Education:* University of Texas, B.F.A., 1949; attended Pratt Institute, 1953, Art Students League, 1955, School of Visual Arts (N.Y.), 1955. *Politics:* "Not committed." *Religion:* "Not committed." *Home:* 151 West 74th St., New York, N.Y. 10023. *Office address:* Tom Tierney Studio, Inc., Drawer D, Hopewell Jct., N.Y. 12533.

CAREER: Tom Tierney Studio, Inc., New York, N.Y., freelance illustrator. *Military service:* U.S. Army, 1951-52; became sergeant. *Member:* "None (I am a rabid non-joiner!)"

WRITINGS—Published by Dover, except as indicated: *Thirty from the Thirties,* Prentice-Hall, 1974; *Glamorous Movie Stars of the Thirties Paper Dolls,* 1978; *Attitude: An Adult Paper Doll Book,* St. Martin's, 1979; *Marilyn Monroe Paper Dolls,* 1979; *Rudolph Valentino Paper Dolls,* 1979; *John Wayne Paper Dolls,* 1981; *Pavlova and Nijinsky Papers Dolls in Full Color,* 1981; *Vivien Leigh Paper Dolls in Full Color,* 1981; *Cut and Assemble a Toy Theater/The Nutcracker Ballet: A Complete Production in Full Color,* 1981.

WORK IN PROGRESS—All paper doll books; all for Dover: *Carmen Miranda; Mae West; Glamorous Men of the Thirties; Judy Garland; Famous Modern Dancers; Famous Queens and Empresses; Famous Movie Cowboys; St. Nicholas; A Colonial Family; Betty Grable; Personality Kids; Peter Pan Toy Theater.*

SIDELIGHTS: Tom Tierney told *CA:* "My training has been as a visual artist, painting, sculpture, etc., so most of my interests have been in these areas. I have always been a film enthusiast—this, coupled with my fashion art career, led to *Thirty from the Thirties.* The success of this book led to a series of paper doll books for Dover. These paper doll books are unique in that they are designed for the serious collector or nostalgia buff. They include biographical data and notes while the costumes are researched and rendered for maximum accuracy. The series seems assured of success."

AVOCATIONAL INTERESTS: Ballet, singing.

* * *

TIGER, John
See WAGER, Walter H(erman)

* * *

TIPTON, James 1942-

PERSONAL: Born January 18, 1942, in Ashland, Ohio; son of J. Robert (a businessman) and Ruth (Burcher) Tipton; married Lynn Ellen Johnson (a teacher), September 5, 1965; children: Jennifer Lynn, James Daniel. *Education:* Purdue University, B.A., 1964, M.A., 1968. *Home:* 1007 Falkirk St., Alma, Mich. 48801. *Office:* Department of English, Alma College, Alma, Mich. 48801.

CAREER: Kalamazoo College, Kalamazoo, Mich., writer-in-residence, 1969-70; Alma College, Alma, Mich., assistant professor of English, 1970—. *Awards, honors:* Grant from National Endowment for the Humanities, 1972, to study ritual in contemporary poetry; first prize from Birmingham, Ala., Festival of the Arts, 1973, for story "Baby Jesus."

WRITINGS: *Bittersweet* (poems), Cold Mountain Press, 1975; (editor with Herbert Scott and Conrad Hilberry and contributor) *The Third Coast: Contemporary Michigan Poetry,* Wayne State University Press, 1976; (editor with Robert Wegner) *The Third Coast: Contemporary Michigan Fiction,* Wayne State University Press, 1982.

Work is anthologized in *The Haiku Anthology,* Doubleday, 1974, *Heartland II: Poets of the Midwest,* Northern Illinois University Press, 1975, and *The Other Voice,* W. W. Norton, 1976. Contributor of poems, stories, translations, and reviews to literary journals and magazines, including *Nation, Esquire, South Dakota Review, Carolina Quarterly, Contemporary Poetry,* and *Southern Humanities Review.*

WORK IN PROGRESS: Editing an anthology of contemporary love stories; working on a manuscript about Michigan.

* * *

TOMKINS, Calvin 1925-

PERSONAL: Born December 17, 1925, in Orange, N.J.; son of Frederick (a manufacturer) and Laura (Graves) Tomkins; married Susan Cheever, October 1, 1981; children: (first marriage) Anne, Susan, Spencer; (second marriage) Sarah. *Education:* Princeton University, A.B., 1948. *Home:* 257 Central Park W., New York, N.Y. 10028. *Office:* New Yorker, 25 West 43rd St., New York, N. Y. 10036.

CAREER: Radio Free Europe, New York City, reporter, 1953-57; *Newsweek,* New York City, writer and editor, 1957-61; *New Yorker,* New York City, staff writer, 1961—. *Military service:* U.S. Navy, 1944-46. *Member:* Century Association, Society of American Historians.

WRITINGS: *Intermission* (novel), Viking, 1951; *The Bride and the Bachelors: The Heretical Courtship in Modern Art,* Viking, 1965; *The Lewis and Clark Trail,* Harper, 1965; *The World of Marcel Duchamp,* Time-Life, 1966; *Eric Hoffer: An American Odyssey,* Dutton, 1968; *Merchants and Masterpieces: The Story of the Metropolitan Museum of Art,* Dutton, 1970; *Living Well Is the Best Revenge,* Viking, 1971; (with former wife, Judy Tomkins) *The Other Hampton,* Viking-Grossman, 1974; *The Scene: Reports on Post-Modern Art,* Viking, 1976; (with David Bourdon) *Christo: Running Fence,* Abrams, 1979; *Off the Wall: Robert Rauschenberg and the Art World of Our Time,* Doubleday, 1980.

Also author of television documentary, "The Journals of Lewis and Clark," National Broadcasting Co., 1965. Contributor to *Harper's, Life,* and other publications.

SIDELIGHTS: "As chronicler of the avant-garde for the *New Yorker,* Calvin Tomkins has specialized in rendering the esoteric doings of artists comprehensible to a reader whose initial reaction to the art might be suspicion or hostility," writes Mary Ann Tighe in the *Washington Post Book World.* "His quiet, meticulously detailed prose is the voice of reason calmly explaining the work of madmen."

Tomkins' explorations of the New York avant-garde have been critically well received. A *Book Week* reviewer finds *The Bride and the Bachelors,* for example, "a lively and intelligent book that easily and competently unriddles the avant-garde." Writing in *Best Sellers,* Edward Gueresche judges *The Scene* to be "an engaging source book that categorizes and lucidly explains the puzzling social and aesthetic involvements of modern art." In a review of *The Scene* for *New Republic,* Tighe defines the factors that make Tomkins' writings so effective. "Tomkins," she states, "explains his complex material admirably. He even makes the material enjoyable: the restraint and decorum of his prose style is often a delightful counterpoint to his content. . . .By reporting rather than commenting on post-modern art, Tomkins is free to cover territory that is foreign to criticism. Unencumbered by aspirations to higher significance, he deals with the practical problems of making art today." Speaking of *Merchants and Masterpieces,* Henry Halpern of *Library*

Journal comments: "This is definitely one of the best written and most consistently fascinating books about art that I have read in a decade. . . .This book is indispensable reading for anyone interested in where American culture has been and where it hopes to go."

CA INTERVIEW

CA interviewed Calvin Tomkins by phone October 9, 1981, at his *New Yorker* office in New York City.

CA: Your first published book was a novel, Intermission, *in 1951. Were you writing only fiction then, or had you started to do some reporting as well?*

TOMKINS: I was just writing fiction. Actually, I hadn't written anything else except for some stories in college.

CA: Working for Radio Free Europe from 1953 to 1957, did you do a variety of jobs, or was your work concentrated on a specific kind of reporting?

TOMKINS: I was working in a newsroom there that provided material for use by the various Eastern European language desks as the basis of their programs. It was basically a news operation. We put out a daily bulletin.

CA: Then you did some editing and writing at Newsweek?

TOMKINS: Yes, I began as a writer in the foreign-news department and later moved to the back of the magazine as a writer, and then I spent about a year as an editor of the sections on music, art, and religion, and a section called "Life and Leisure."

CA: So much of your writing, especially your work as a staff writer at the New Yorker, *reflects your interest in art. Was that an early interest for you?*

TOMKINS: It wasn't really. It came about more or less by accident because in that period at *Newsweek* there was no regular art writer; there was an art researcher but no writer. They hardly ever ran any stories on art, but when one came up, they would have to get somebody from another department to write it. I did a number of them, and as a result became increasingly interested in art.

CA: Do you paint or collect art?

TOMKINS: No, I never have done anything of that nature.

CA: When you report on the avant-garde artists and the "happenings" they create, your tone is usually quite objective, nonjudgmental. Doesn't it take a great sense of humor to observe and write about some of these happenings?

TOMKINS: Well, I hope so, yes. I think of my predecessor in the *New Yorker* art column, Harold Rosenberg. I was talking with him a year before he died—I was writing a book about the art world—and he said, "The only way to write about the art world is as a comedy." And I think I do see it in somewhat humorous terms, but that doesn't mean I don't see it seriously too. The mistake of a lot of art writers is that they are a great deal more solemn than the artists they're writing about.

CA: I especially enjoyed the piece you did on John Cage in The Bride and the Bachelors. *Did you talk with Cage a lot when you were writing that?*

TOMKINS: Yes, I did. I spent probably more time with John Cage than I spent with any of the other profile subjects in that book. It was partly because of John himself; I don't think he had ever really looked back over his life in that way before, but when he started doing it, it came out in great detail. Every day for about three or four months I spent several hours with him, and it was as if we were writing a novel—a chapter every day as he would take up a phase of his life; and every day there would be a beginning, a middle, and an end, like a continuing story.

CA: Was he willing to talk about all sorts of things without any special persuading?

TOMKINS: Yes, he was extremely open. He talked about a lot of things that I didn't use. For example, he opened up completely about the homosexual aspects of his life and work; I guess he thought he'd rather do that and trust to my judgment what should be used. His life has been very interesting; but also his thinking—his interpretation of earlier art, particularly Duchamp—has been absolutely crucial to a lot of other artists. Whether they actively realize it or not, they've been influenced enormously by the way the ideas of the surrealists and of Duchamp and people like that have been filtered through his mind.

CA: There are always so many things going on in New York at the same time. Is it hard for you to see everything you want to see?

TOMKINS: Oh, it's impossible, it's out of the question. There are more than three hundred galleries in New York now. And that's one of the big changes. When I began writing in this field it was possible to see everything—every art show or event of any importance—in a couple of days. But now it's impossible for anybody to keep up with all of it.

CA: Is it hard to decide what to write about in your New Yorker *column?*

TOMKINS: Yes, but that's because the column appears infrequently, not more than once a month and sometimes less than that. I don't try so much to cover individual shows; I go around and get a sense of what's going on and then write about something that interests me. It's highly selective and personal in that sense.

CA: Merchants and Masterpieces *provides not only a history of the Metropolitan Museum of Art but a kind of social history as well. Was it an especially tough research job?*

TOMKINS: There was a lot of research, but it was all more or less in the museum. Its library and archives were open to me, and I was given complete freedom to go through correspondence files and previous records. The real problem was I didn't have an awful lot of time. Al Gardner, a curator at the Metropolitan, had planned for years to write the centennial history, but he died before anything was down on paper. By the time I took over the job it was only about eighteen months before the museum's hundredth anniversary, and the book was planned to come out in 1970 to coincide with the anniversary. So in a way it was a rush, and I easily could have spent more time on it.

CA: A conflict-of-interests question was raised at the Greenville, South Carolina, museum recently over commissions received by its director at the time through a patron's acquisition of Andrew Wyeth paintings that were then donated to the museum. What do you think about the ethics of this kind of situation?

TOMKINS: At almost all museums there's a great effort to avoid anything that would smack of conflict of interests. At the Metropolitan, for instance, the curators always have been discouraged from having collections themselves in their own field. If you're a curator of Greek and Roman, it's definitely frowned upon for you to have a collection of Greek and Roman; but if you want to collect Japanese prints or something, it's all right. I don't know of another case where a museum official has been involved with commissions in this way; it certainly is to be avoided.

CA: You noted in a New Yorker *piece this past June that Americans were buying heavily in the May art auctions in New York. A few years back you said German buyers dominated the American art market. Is there any discernible cause for this shift?*

TOMKINS: Yes, I think it's part of the general expansion of the American art market that's been going on for ten years or so and accelerating in recent years. It's become a much more desirable activity for young Americans with money to start collecting—people who, maybe ten years ago, would have bought another automobile or a house or something as soon as they got a little affluent. I think they are much more inclined now to buy works of art, partly because of the enormous amount of publicity that has attached itself to auction sales, but partly also because of a general broadening of the market that all the dealers talk about. For example, Arnold Glimcher at the Pace Gallery, one of the most successful dealers of the moment, told me that five years ago he knew personally three quarters of the people who bought pictures in his gallery, but that now it's completely reversed: three quarters are total strangers to him. And this is indicative: a lot more people have decided that art collecting is something interesting and they want to get involved with it.

CA: How much of this interest is speculation?

TOMKINS: I think a good deal of it is. There has been such enormous publicity about the rise in prices and the fact that they say the art market has outperformed the stock market. I don't know if it's true, but it's often said. I'm sure a lot of people are buying with that at least partially in mind—that, if necessary, they can sell it in ten years for a lot more.

CA: What do you think about the strong interest in photography now? Do you think that will continue to be a major trend?

TOMKINS: That's kind of a tricky market because the high prices being asked for a photograph right now are almost exclusively confined to photographs by the old masters, by people who are dead. It's very, very difficult for a contemporary photographer to support himself by selling prints. Most of the photography shows are of contemporary prints, but they're basically unsuccessful: they don't sell out. So it's been a hard market to pin down. There are a lot more photography galleries all the time, but there's quite a feeling of uncertainty in that market. I think it may not hold up; it might be in for a rather spectacular decline.

CA: Did you meet Gerald Murphy before you decided to write Living Well Is the Best Revenge?

TOMKINS: Yes, I did. I had known him for several years.

CA: Is that how the book evolved?

TOMKINS: Yes. Actually, I was a neighbor of his in the country and became extremely fond of him, and I began trying to persuade him to write a book about his life in the 1920s and his association with the Fitzgeralds and other expatriates. He kept telling me he wouldn't dream of it, and so finally the idea just evolved that I would put down some of these stories without any particular idea of how it would work out. Almost all of the material came from my talking with him.

CA: The section of the book in which you discussed his paintings was interesting. Were you able to see the remaining paintings?

TOMKINS: Yes, I did. I saw some of them at his house, where he kept them rolled up in the attic, and others at the houses of people he had given them to. Later, in 1974, there was a show that collected them all together at the Museum of Modern Art.

CA: In doing "Raggedy Andy," your profile on Andy Warhol that's in the collection The Scene, *did you see him a great deal?*

TOMKINS: Not nearly as much as I saw John Cage for his profile. I guess I spent a week or so talking with him. I did more talking with other people about Andy because Andy's made a point of not really telling you anything about himself. I met people who had known him before he became an artist.

CA: You've recently written Off the Wall, *a book on Robert Rauschenberg, whom you had written about earlier as well. You seem to have had a continuing interest in his work.*

TOMKINS: Yes. I met Rauschenberg pretty early in his career, in 1961. My *New Yorker* profile of him came out in 1964, and a piece on his winning the Venice Biennale appeared in *Harper's* in 1965. And I've written a couple of other little things about him. I had kept up with his career because, of all of the artists I've met, he's the one that I feel personally the closest to, in terms of both his work and his personality. So when I was approached by Doubleday with the idea of doing a book about the art world, it seemed to me that Rauschenberg provided a point of focus for a book of that kind. Using him was a good way to structure the experience of the art world that I had had. He seemed to be the most representative figure in that world.

CA: You've written about other things besides art. You wrote The Lewis and Clark Trail *in 1965, and you did the television documentary on that exploration. Do you plan to take on any new topics?*

TOMKINS: At the moment, in addition to *New Yorker* things, I'm doing research for a major biography on Buckminster Fuller, whom I've already written a profile on for the *New Yorker*. I plan to do other things that are not connected with the art world and that I hope will take me into new areas.

CA: Do you plan ever to do another novel?

TOMKINS: I have it in mind, yes.

BIOGRAPHICAL/CRITICAL SOURCES: *Library Journal,* August, 1951, April 15, 1967, April 15, 1970; *Chicago Tribune,* August 12, 1951; *New York Times,* August 12, 1951, June 25, 1971, May 31, 1980; *New York Times Book Review,* August 26, 1951, July 18, 1971, July 25, 1976, May 25, 1980, June 28, 1981; *Book Week,* May 9, 1965; *New York Review of*

Books, June 17, 1965, May 8, 1969, January 27, 1972; *Nation,* December 20, 1965; *Natural History,* November, 1966; *Choice,* September, 1967.

Best Sellers, April 15, 1970, November, 1976; *New Yorker,* April 18, 1970; *Newsweek,* June 22, 1970, July 19, 1971, December 10, 1979; *Washington Post Book World,* June 27, 1971, August 5, 1979, August 10, 1980; *Christian Science Monitor,* July 15, 1971, September 8, 1976; *Time,* July 19, 1971; *Saturday Review,* July 24, 1971; *Harper's,* September, 1971; *New Republic,* October 23, 1976, June 21, 1980; *Chicago Tribune Book World,* May 15, 1980; *Art in America,* September, 1980; *Virginia Quarterly Review,* autumn, 1980.

—Interview by Jean W. Ross

* * *

TONG, Te-kong 1920-

PERSONAL: Born August 24, 1920, in Hofei, Anhwei, China; became a U.S. citizen; son of Mon-fu and Jo-hsia (Liu) Tong; married Sharon Chao-wen Woo, December 22, 1957; children: Ray Kuang-yi, June Kuang-pei. *Education:* National Central University, Chungking, China, B.A., 1943; Columbia University, M.A., 1952, Ph.D., 1959. *Home:* Apartment 7F, 100 La Salle St., New York, N.Y. 10027. *Office:* Department of Asian Studies, City College of the City University of New York, New York, N.Y. 10033.

CAREER: Staff writer, *Chinese Navy Monthly,* 1941-43; editorial writer, *Anhwei Daily,* 1943-47; National Anhui University, Li-huang and Hofei, China, instructor in history, 1945-47; research assistant on Chinese history project jointly sponsored by Columbia University, New York City, and University of Washington, Seattle, Wash., 1955-57; Columbia University, research associate on Chinese and oral history projects, East Asian Institute, 1958-62, assistant professor of Chinese history, 1963-67, adjunct associate professor, 1968-71, curator, Chinese collection, East Asian Library, 1963-70; State University of New York College at Oneonta, professor, 1971-72, chairman of department of Asian studies, 1972-73; City College of the City University of New York, New York City, professor of Asian studies, 1972—, chairman of department, 1981—. Lecturer in Asian history, Brooklyn College of the City University of New York, 1961-62; honorary distinguished professor of history, Northwest University, Xian, People's Republic of China, honorary university professor of history, Shandong University, Jinan, People's Republic of China, and Hau-Kang Professor of History, Chinese Culture University, Taipei, Taiwan, 1981. Advisor to Ministry of Education, Republic of Singapore, 1982. *Member:* American Historical Association, Association for Asian Studies. *Awards, honors:* Social Science Research Council grant, 1963-65; U.S. Department of Health, Education and Welfare research grants, 1974 and 1975.

WRITINGS: United States Diplomacy in China, 1844-60, University of Washington Press, 1964; (compiler) *Modern China, 1912-1949: A Bibliographical Study,* East Asian Library, Columbia University, 1965; (with Hu Shih) *The Reminiscences of Dr. Hu Shih,* Microfilming Corp., 1975; (editor with Li Tsung-Jen) *The Memoirs of Li Tsung-Jen,* Westview, 1979; (with Robert Wu) *The Third Americans: A Selected Bibliography of Asians in America with Annotations,* Chinese Culture, 1980.

Also author of books in Chinese. Editor, *Bulletin of National Defense,* 1947-48; chief editor, *China Life Semi-Monthly,* 1955-56; editor, *World Forum Monthly,* 1959-62.

WORK IN PROGRESS: A book on modern China.

SIDELIGHTS: Many of Te-kong Tong's books have been published in Chinese. Over one million copies of *The Memoirs of Li Tsung-Jen* have been sold in China and overseas in two editions.

* * *

TOOMBS, Lawrence Edmund 1919-

PERSONAL: Born April 1, 1919, on Prince Edward Island, Canada; son of Edmund and Amelia Elizabeth (Luther) Toombs; married, June 25, 1945; children: Millicent Ann, Edmund Mark. *Education:* Acadia University, B.A., 1941, B.S., 1942; Pine Hill Divinity Hall, B.D., 1948; Drew University, Ph.D., 1952; attended University of London, 1961-62. *Religion:* Methodist. *Office:* Department of Religion, Wilfrid Laurier University, Waterloo, Ontario, Canada N2L 3C5.

CAREER: Meteorologist, Canadian Department of Transport, 1943-45; St. Stephen's College, Edmonton, Alberta, professor of Old Testament, 1951-53; Drew University, Madison, N.J., professor of Old Testament, 1953-68; Wilfrid Laurier University, Waterloo, Ontario, professor of religion and culture, 1969—. Associate director, Drew McCormick Archaeological expedition in Jordan, 1957, 1960, and 1962. *Military service:* Royal Canadian Air Force; served as meteorologist. *Member:* Society of Biblical Literature, Biblical Colloquium. *Awards, honors:* Fellow, American Schools of Oriental Research.

WRITINGS: A Year with the Bible, United Church of Canada, 1952; *The Threshold of Christianity,* Westminster, 1960; *Nation Making,* Lutterworth, 1961; *The Old Testament in Christian Preaching,* Westminster, 1961; *God's People among the Nations,* Association Press, 1963; (contributor) *Archaeological Discoveries in the Holy Land,* Crowell, 1967; (with Norman E. Wagner and Eduard R. Riegart) *The Moyer Site: A Prehistoric Village in Waterloo County,* Wilfrid Laurier University, 1973; (with Jeffrey A. Blakely) *The Tell el-Hesi Field Manual,* American Schools of Oriental Research, 1980. Contributor to professional journals.†

* * *

TOWNS, James Edward 1944-

PERSONAL: Born February 27, 1944, in Clovis, N.M.; son of Verney Edward (a businessman) and Mona (Hancock) Towns. *Education:* Hardin-Simmons University, B.A., 1965; Southern Illinois University, M.A., 1966, Ph.D., 1970. *Politics:* Democrat. *Religion:* Baptist. *Home address:* Box 6174, S.F.A. Station, Nacogdoches, Tex. 75691. *Office:* Department of Communication, Stephen F. Austin State University, Nacogdoches, Tex. 75961.

CAREER: Stephen F. Austin State University, Nacogdoches, Tex., instructor, 1966-68, assistant professor, 1970-77, associate professor of communication, 1977—. Speaker at religious conferences and retreats; conducts workshops for families and single adults. Communication consultant for businesses and local churches. *Member:* Speech Communication Association of America, Southern Speech Communication Association, Texas Speech Communication Association, Phi Kappa Phi.

WRITINGS: Faith Stronger Than Death: How to Communicate with a Person in Sorrow, Warner Press, 1975; *The Social Conscience of W. A. Criswell,* Crescendo, 1976; *One Is Not a Lonely Number,* Crescendo, 1977; *Solo Flight,* Tyndale, 1980; *Life: Joy in Being,* Broadman, 1981.

WORK IN PROGRESS: Research and writing on the subjects of death education, single adult life, and interpersonal communication.

* * *

TRACY, Honor Lilbush Wingfield 1913-

PERSONAL: Born October 19, 1913, in Bury St. Edmunds, East Anglia, England; daughter of Humphrey Wingfield (a surgeon) and Christabel May Clare (Miller) Tracy. *Education:* Educated privately in London, England. *Home:* Four Chimneys, Achill Sound, County Mayo, Ireland.

CAREER: Simpkin Marshall Ltd. (publishers), London, England, general assistant, 1934-37; free-lance writer, 1937-39; Ministry of Information, London, Japanese specialist, 1941-45; *Observer,* London, special correspondent, 1946, 1947-48 (from Japan in 1947); *Sunday Times,* London, Dublin correspondent, 1950; British Broadcasting Corp., Third Programme, contributor of talks and features, 1950-68, roving correspondent, 1951-52; novelist, 1968—. *Military service:* British Women's Auxiliary Air Force, Intelligence, 1939-41; became sergeant. *Member:* Royal Irish Automobile Club. *Awards, honors:* Award from British Writers Guild, 1968, for radio feature script "Sorrows of Ireland."

WRITINGS: (Translator) B. de Ligt, *The Conquest of Violence,* Dutton, 1937; *Kakemono: A Sketch Book of Post-War Japan,* Methuen, 1950; *Mind You, I've Said Nothing!: Forays in the Irish Republic* (essays), Methuen, 1953, British Book Centre, 1958; *Silk Hats and No Breakfast: Notes on a Spanish Journey,* Methuen, 1957, Random House, 1958; *Spanish Leaves,* Random House, 1964; *Winter in Castile,* Random House, 1975.

Fiction; published by Random House, except as indicated: *The Deserters,* Methuen, 1954; *The Straight and Narrow Path,* 1956; *The Prospects Are Pleasing,* 1958; *A Number of Things,* 1960; *A Season of Mists,* 1961; *The First Day of Friday,* 1963; *Men at Work,* Methuen, 1966, Random House, 1967; *The Beauty of the World,* Methuen, 1967, published as *Settled in Chambers,* Random House, 1968; *The Butterflies of the Province,* 1970; *The Quiet End of Evening,* 1972; *In a Year of Grace,* 1974; *The Man from Next Door,* 1977; *The Ballad of Castle Reef,* 1979. Contributor to *Daily Telegraph* (London), 1973—.

SIDELIGHTS: An English woman residing in Ireland, Honor Tracy is well known as both a novelist and a travel writer. She has written extensively about traveling in Spain, much to the delight of critics who praise the wit and charm of these nonfiction accounts. Of her fictive efforts, however, reviewers are more critical. Though she aims at satire, critics maintain that she frequently misses her mark, particularly in her later novels which poke fun at British-Irish antagonisms.

A case in point is Tracy's tenth novel, *The Man from Next Door.* Set in London, the story pits a naive English schoolmistress against an unscrupulous Irishman. "The result," observes *America* reviewer Terrence A. McVeigh, "is a totally uneven contest and a nasty little story of victim and victimizer. So biased is the characterization that it is difficult not to interpret the tale as blatant chauvinism." McVeigh concludes that the stereotyping of the Irish bank clerk as "instinctively hostile to all things British," including his hapless victim, works against the novel's early promise of suspense. Instead of satire, the result is pathos that evokes "pity rather than amusement or scorn."

While agreeing that *The Man from Next Door* misses its mark, the *New York Times Book Review* critic tempers this negative evaluation with praise for Tracy's travel books: "In . . . *Winter in Castile,* she showed an infallible eye for the defining image. Her favorite bootblack parlor in Madrid is now a fancy dog-boutique, after a short career as a milk-bar. There is smog at last over the city, and it is a source of pride to the inhabitants—proof of their modernity. In a restaurant, Miss Tracy eats what she describes as 'a chicken of experience.'" Her vivid depiction of events such as these leads the reviewer to conclude that "Honor Tracy is one of the best travel writers alive today."

AVOCATIONAL INTERESTS: International travel, music, wildlife, gardening.

BIOGRAPHICAL/CRITICAL SOURCES: New York Times Book Review, March 10, 1968, May 8, 1977; *Time,* April 5, 1968; *America,* March 4, 1978, February 2, 1980; *National Observer,* August 12, 1968; *New York Times,* December 26, 1979.

* * *

TREDEZ, Denise 1930-
(Denise Trez)

PERSONAL: Born in 1930, in Marseille, France; married Alain Tredez (an author and illustrator), 1950; children: Isabelle, Corinne, Florence.

CAREER: Author of books for children. Co-editor, *Dominique* (children's magazine), Paris, France, 1952—.

WRITINGS—Under pseudonym Denise Trez; with Alain Trez, pseudonym of husband, Alain Tredez; published by World Publishing, except as indicated: *Circus in the Jungle,* 1958; *Fifi,* 1959; *The Butterfly Chase,* 1960; *Le Petit Chien,* 1961, translation by Douglas McKee and Donine Mouche published as *The Little Dog,* Faber, 1962; *The Magic Paintbox,* 1962; *The Little Knight's Dragon,* 1963; *Sophie,* 1963, published in England as *Sophie Runs Away,* Faber, 1964); *Le Vilain Chat,* 1965, translation by McKee published as *The Mischievous Cat,* Faber, 1966; *The Royal Hiccups,* Viking, 1965; *Rabbit Country,* Viking, 1966; *Good Night, Veronica,* Viking, 1968; *Maila and the Flying Carpet,* Viking, 1969; *The Three Little Mermaids,* 1969; *The Smallest Pirate,* Viking, 1970; *Pourquoi Pas?,* L'Ecole des loisirs, 1971.†

* * *

TREZ, Denise
See TREDEZ, Denise

* * *

TRITON, A. N.
See BARCLAY, Oliver R(ainsford)

* * *

TSOU, Tang 1918-

PERSONAL: Born December 10, 1918, in Canton, China; son of Lu Tsou (an educator) and Chien-yun Hsu; married Yi-chuang Lu (a research sociologist), January 29, 1943. *Education:* National Southwest Associated University, Kunming, China, B.A., 1940; University of Chicago, Ph.D., 1951. *Home:* 5608 Harper Ave., Chicago, Ill. 60637. *Office:* Department of Political Science, University of Chicago, Chicago, Ill. 60637.

CAREER: Illinois Institute of Technology, Chicago, instructor, 1951-52; University of Utah, Salt Lake City, lecturer, 1953-54; University of Chicago, Chicago, research associate, 1955-63, assistant professor, 1959-62, associate professor, 1962-66, professor of political science, 1966—. *Member:* American Political Science Association, Association for Asian Studies. *Awards, honors:* Social Science Research Council grant; Gordon J. Laing prize, 1963, for *America's Failure in China, 1941-1950;* Rockefeller Foundation grant, 1965.

WRITINGS: *The Embroilment Over Quemoy: Mao, Chiang, and Dulles,* University of Utah Press, 1959; *America's Failure in China, 1941-1950,* two volumes, University of Chicago Press, 1963; (contributor) Robert Goldwin, editor, *Beyond the Cold War,* Rand McNally, 1966; *Revolution, Integration, and Crisis in Communist China: A Framework for Analysis,* Center for Policy Study, University of Chicago, 1967; (editor with Ping-ti Ho) *China in Crisis,* University of Chicago Press, Volume I: *China's Heritage and the Communist Political System,* two books, 1968, (sole editor) Volume II: *China's Policies in Asia and America's Alternatives,* 1968. Contributor to journals.

SIDELIGHTS: Jonathan Spence writes in the *New York Times Book Review* that "the value of *China in Crisis,* edited by Ping-ti Ho and Tang Tsou of the University of Chicago, is that it constitutes the most comprehensive and the most intelligent attempt yet made to survey the ramifications of the current Chinese Communist political system."

BIOGRAPHICAL/CRITICAL SOURCES: *Spectator,* January 3, 1968; *New York Times Book Review,* January 12, 1969; *Times Literary Supplement,* July 17, 1969.†

*   *   *

TUDOR, Dean 1943-

PERSONAL: Born May 26, 1943, in Toronto, Ontario, Canada; son of Frederick (a radio engineer) and Jean (Pasquantonio) Tudor; married Nancy Rice (a librarian), June 3, 1967 (divorced May, 1978); married Ann J. Harwell (an editor), June 17, 1978. *Education:* University of Toronto, B.A., 1965; McGill University, M.L.S., 1967. *Politics:* Socialist (New Democratic Party). *Religion:* Humanist. *Home:* 51 Gothic Ave., Toronto, Ontario, Canada M6P 2V8. *Office:* Ryerson Polytechnical Institute, 50 Gould St., Toronto, Ontario, Canada M5B 1E8.

CAREER: York University Libraries, Downsview, Ontario, reference librarian, 1967-68; Ontario Department of Revenue Library (now Ministry of Treasury, Economics and Intergovernmental Affairs Library), Toronto, Ontario, director of library branch, 1968-73; Ryerson Polytechnical Institute, Toronto, chairman of library arts department, 1974-80, professor in department of library arts and in School of Journalism, 1980—. Director, Peter Martin Associates, 1973-82. Consultant to Treasury Board of Survey of Ontario Government Libraries, 1969-72; editorial manuscript consultant to Libraries Unlimited, R. R. Bowker, Special Libraries Association, Canadian Library Association, University of Toronto Press, Oryx Press, Books for Cooks, Ragtime Society of Canada, and International Wine and Food Society.

MEMBER: Canadian Association for Information Sciences, Canadian Library Association, American Library Association, Ragtime Society of Canada, Special Library Association (treasurer of Toronto branch, 1969-71, executive director, 1971-72), Institute of Professional Librarians of Ontario (member of board of directors, 1971-73), Ontario Government Librarians Council (member of board of directors, 1970-72), Ontario Library Association, International Wine and Food Society, Les Compagnons des Vins de France, Les Amis du Tastevin, Amici dell' Enotria. *Awards, honors:* Outstanding Reference Book award, American Library Association, 1976, for *Cooking for Entertainment.*

WRITINGS: *Regional Development and Regional Government in Ontario* (annotated bibliography), Council of Planning Librarians, 1970; *Wine, Beer and Spirits,* Libraries Unlimited, 1975; (editor) *The Compleat Library Guide to Toronto,* Canadian Library Association, 1975; *Cooking for Entertainment,* Bowker, 1976; (with Nancy Tudor) *Black Music,* Libraries Unlimited, 1979; (with N. Tudor) *Contemporary Popular Music,* Libraries Unlimited, 1979; (with N. Tudor) *Grass Roots Music,* Libraries Unlimited, 1979; (with N. Tudor) *Jazz,* Libraries Unlimited, 1979; *Popular Music Recordings for Libraries: A Retrospective Guide,* Libraries Unlimited, 1983.

Also compiler, with others, of *Popular Music Periodicals Index,* Scarecrow, 1973-76, and of *Annual Index to Popular Music Record Review,* Scarecrow, 1973-79; editor, *Canadian Book Review Annual,* Peter Martin Associates, 1975—. Food editor and restaurant reviewer for Toronto *Downtown,* 1979—. Editorial consultant to *Canadian Essay and Literature Index,* University of Toronto Press, 1973-76, *Canadian Serials Directory,* University of Toronto Press, 1974, *Canadian Historical Calendar and Day Book,* Peter Martin Associates, 1974-76. Contributor of articles and reviews to *Ragtimer, Coda,* and library journals. Editor, *OGLE* (Ontario Government Librarians Exchange), 1969-72; *Grapevine* (publication of International Wine and Food Society), 1976—, and *Ragtimer,* 1979-80; contributing editor, *LJ/SLJ Previews,* 1972-73, *Blues Link,* 1973-74, and *Blues Is—,* 1975; music editor, *Ontario Library Review,* 1972—.

WORK IN PROGRESS: *Canadian Record Catalogue; Library Standards* (four volumes); *Subject Information Profiles,* Volume I: *Journalism.*

SIDELIGHTS: Dean Tudor told *CA:* "Most of my work involves either short, crisp descriptions, such as annotated reviews and bibliographies, or the routine world of copy editing, proofreading, indexing, etc. My major loves are music, food, and wines. I view my loves and writing skills as one package, subject to enjoyment as well as something to write about, to index, to proofread, etc. I prefer to work in a complete editorial environment, that is, to have sole responsibility for creating an information package, from conception to research to writing to editing to proofing to indexing. Thus, I am able to spin off my knowledge in so many ways; to produce true information packages. It is the only way to be a one-stop writer, with vast knowledge of a few subject areas, and with vast knowledge of all the communication skills needed to produce access to that information in a readable, indexed form."

*   *   *

TURKEL, Pauline
See K-TURKEL, Judi

U

ULYATT, Kenneth 1920-

PERSONAL: Born March 16, 1920, in London, England; married Patricia Brealey, 1945; children: Susan, Keith. *Education:* Educated in England; attended art school. *Politics:* S.D.P. *Home and office:* 13 Market St., Poole, Dorsetshire, England.

CAREER: Has worked for advertising agencies and for publishers, as designer and writer; currently affiliated with Book Club Associates in England. *Military service:* Royal Air Force, 1940-45; served in North Africa. *Member:* English Westerners, Western History Association of America, Poole Museum Society.

WRITINGS—All juveniles: *North against the Sioux* (first book in Portugee Phillips trilogy), Collins, 1965, Prentice-Hall, 1967; *The Longhorn Trail* (second book in Portugee Phillips trilogy), Collins, 1967, Prentice-Hall, 1968; *Custer's Gold* (third book in Portugee Phillips trilogy), Collins, 1971; *The Day of the Cowboy,* Penguin, 1973; *The Time of the Indian,* Penguin, 1975; *Outlaws,* Penguin, 1976, Lippincott, 1978; *Cowboys of the American West,* Flammarion, 1977; *Hussars of the Napoleonic Wars,* Flammarion, 1981; *King Arthur and His Knights of the Round Table,* Flammarion, 1983. Contributor of articles and stories to magazines.

WORK IN PROGRESS: The Adventures of Robin Hood; Stories of the Old West, with illustrations by Gino d'Achille, for Flammarion

SIDELIGHTS: "I have always been lucky enough to earn my living at the two things I most like doing—writing and drawing," Kenneth Ulyatt told *CA*. "And I have always been interested in the frontier days in America; both as a boy, when I was a keen scout and camper, and later, when I began reading the history of the West rather than its fiction. When TV came along and we watched westerns, my children would ask me: 'Was it really like that?' and as often as not I would have to say 'no.' So I began to write my first western: a story in which the Indians did not bite the dust and the cavalry were defeated. It was a true story.

"And I think that it was because I tried hard to make that past, which I found so exciting, vibrant for young readers that the Portugee Phillips trilogy became so successful. The subject of the West, too, transcends frontiers. Portugee Phillips now rides in nine European countries, from Finland to Italy."

UNKELBACH, Kurt 1913-

PERSONAL: Born November 21, 1913, in New Britain, Conn.; son of Max J. (an architect) and Louise (Gunther) Unkelbach; married Evelyn Haskell; children: Evenlyn P. and L. Cary (daughters). *Education:* Attended Wesleyan University, Middletown, Conn., 1932-34, and studied at Pasadena Playhouse, 1934-36. *Religion:* Protestant. *Home address:* Starks Rd., R.F.D. 3, Winsted, Conn. 06098. *Agent:* Knox Burger, Knox Burger Associates, Ltd., 39½ Washington Square S., New York, N.Y. 10012.

CAREER: Radio writer for various independent stations and networks, 1936-41; account executive with advertising and public relations agencies in New York, N.Y., 1947-64; full-time writer, 1965—. *Military service:* U.S. Army, 1941-46; served in South Pacific; became captain. *Member:* Dramatist Guild of the Authors League of America, Dog Writers' Association of America. *Awards, honors:* Named Dog Writer of the Year, 1975.

WRITINGS: Love on a Leash, Prentice-Hall, 1964; *The Dog in My Life,* Four Winds, 1966; *The Winning of Westminster,* Prentice-Hall, 1966; *Murphy,* Prentice-Hall, 1967; *Ruffian: International Champion,* Prentice-Hall, 1967; *The Dog Who Never Knew,* Four Winds, 1968; *Both Ends of the Leash,* Prentice-Hall, 1968; *A Cat and His Dogs,* Prentice-Hall, 1969; *Catnip: Selecting and Training Your Cat,* Prentice-Hall, 1970; (with wife, Evelyn Unkelbach) *The Pleasures of Dog Ownership,* Prentice-Hall, 1971; *You're a Good Dog, Joe,* Prentice-Hall, 1971; *The Love That Shook the World,* C & B Book House, 1971; *Winning Ways,* F. Watts, 1972; *Albert Payson Terhune: A Centennial Biography,* Charterhouse, 1972; *How to Bring Up Your Pet Dog,* Dodd, 1972; *Those Lovable Retrievers,* McGraw, 1973; *Tiger Up a Tree,* Prentice-Hall, 1973; *How to Make Money in Dogs,* Dodd, 1974; *Uncle Charlie's Poodle,* Dodd, 1975; *The American Dog Book,* Dutton, 1976; *How to Show Your Dog and Win,* F. Watts, 1976; *Best of Breeds Guide for Young Dog Lovers,* Putnam, 1978; *How to Teach an Old Dog New Tricks,* Dodd, 1979. Ghost writer of other books.

Author of "Straw Hat," play produced on Broadway, 1937, and of 150 radio plays, 1936-41; also wrote scripts for twenty commercial films, 1948-56. Columnist and free-lance contributor to dog magazines, including *Dog World, Dogs in Canada,* and *American Kennel Gazette.* Contributing editor, *Dogs,*

1970—; canine editor, *On the Sound,* 1971-74; pet editor, *American Home,* 1974-76.

WORK IN PROGRESS: A novel about dog lovers; two nonfiction children's books on puppies and kittens; one ghosting assignment; a series of magazine articles.

SIDELIGHTS: Kurt Unkelbach told *CA:* "What I write about reflects my lifelong avocations of the dog and cat worlds, animals in general, nature, ornithology, ecology, biology, and fishing. In a sense, these avocations have become vocations, since they provide the fuel for my typewriter." Unkelbach breeds, trains, and exhibits Labrador Retrievers.

Two of Unkelbach's books, *The Dog in My Life* and *A Cat and His Dogs,* have been translated into Swedish.

* * *

UPSON, Norma 1919-
(Nancy Kimball)

PERSONAL: Born December 23, 1919, in New Britain, Conn.; daughter of Orrin E. (a golf course architect) and Letty E. (Lewis) Smith; married Robert A. Upson (a territorial sales manager; deceased); children: William S., Daniel W. *Education:* Graduated from high school in East Northfield, Mass. *Home address:* Route 5, Box 596, Portland, Ore. 97231. *Agent:* Maxwell Aley Associates, 145 East 35th St., New York, N.Y. 10016.

CAREER: Writer and public speaker; has appeared on television programs. Teacher of creative writing in department of continuing education at Portland State University. Established Haystack pilot program in writing, 1969; co-founder, director, and teacher for Braille Teens; director of Sun Country Writer's Roundup. *Member:* Denver Women's Press Club, Williamette Writers.

WRITINGS—Published by Pacific Search Press, except as indicated: *How to Survive as a Corporate Wife,* Doubleday, 1974; *The Crawfish Cookbook,* 1977; *The Eggplant Cookbook,* 1979; *The Bean Cookbook,* 1982. Author, under pseudonym, of "Nancy Kimball's Column," in *American Salesman,* 1964-75. Contributor of articles and juvenile stories to national magazines.

WORK IN PROGRESS: Boat Is a Four-Letter Word.

SIDELIGHTS: Norma Upson lives on a houseboat on the Willamette River. *Avocational interests:* Natural sciences, fishing, boating, collecting and polishing gemstones, early American history, music, biography, crafts, hiking, golf, camping.

V

VAID, Krishna Baldev 1927-

PERSONAL: Born July 27, 1927, in Dinga, India; son of Ishar Dass (a civil servant) and Ramrakhi Vaid; married Champa Bali, December 12, 1952; children: Rachna, Jyotsna, Urvashi (all daughters). *Education:* Panjab University, B.A. (with honors), 1946, M.A., 1949; Harvard University, Ph.D., 1961. *Home:* 3 Pierrepont Ave., Potsdam, N.Y. 13676. *Agent:* Gunther Stuhlmann, Box 276, Becket, Mass. 01223. *Office:* Department of English, State University of New York College, Potsdam, N.Y. 13676.

CAREER: Delhi University, Delhi, India, lecturer in English, 1950-62; Panjab University, Chandigarh, India, reader in English, 1962-66; State University of New York College at Potsdam, professor of English, 1966—, acting chairman of department, 1971-72. Visiting professor at Case Western Reserve University, summer, 1968, and at Brandeis University, 1968-69; has lectured at University of Chicago, Harvard University, University of Iowa, University of Rochester, University of Mysore, Osmania University, and Jadavpur University. Member of Indian delegation, P.E.N. International Conferences, 1966; director of Star Lake Writing Conference, summers, 1967-68. Consultant to (Indian) National Academy of Letters and Indian Institute of American Studies. *Awards, honors:* Smith-Mundt Fulbright fellowship, 1958-61; Rockefeller Foundation fellowship, 1959-61; State University of New York Research Foundation grants, summers, 1970, 1977, 1980.

WRITINGS: Steps in Darkness, Orion Press, 1962; *Technique in the Tales of Henry James,* Harvard University Press, 1964; *Silence and Other Stories,* InterCulture Associates, 1972; *Bimal in Bog,* two volumes, InterCulture Associates, 1972; (translator from Hindi) Nirmal Verma, *Days of Longing,* InterCulture Associates, 1972; (translator from Hindi) Srikant Varma, *Bitter Sweet Desire,* Vikas, 1975.

Books in Hindi: *Us Ka Bachpan* (title means "His Childhood"), Saraswati, 1957, revised edition, Radhakrishna, 1981; *Beech Ka Darvaza* (title means "The Connecting Door"), Neelabh, 1962; *Mera Dushman* (title means "My Enemy"), Rajkamal, 1966; *Doosre Kinare Se* (title means "From the Other Shore"), Radhakrishna, 1970; *Lapata* (title means "Incognito"), Sindhu, 1973; *Bimal,* Kalpana, 1974; *Us Ke Bayan* (title means "His Statements"), Rajpal, 1974; *Nasreen,* Sambhavna, 1975; *Doosra Na Koi* (title means "None Other"), Sambhavna, 1978; *Dard La Dava* (title means "Pain No Panacea"), Sambhavna, 1980; *Voh Aur Mein* (title means "He and I"), Prabhat, 1980; *Guzara Hua Zamana* (title means "Time Past"), Radhakrishna, 1981.

Translator into Hindi: Samuel Beckett, *Waiting for Godot,* Radhakrishna, 1970; Beckett, *Endgame,* Radhakrishna, 1971.

Contributor to anthologies: *Span: An Anthology of Asian and Australian Writing,* Canberra Fellowship of Writers (Canberra, Australia), 1959; *A Death in Delhi,* edited by Gordon Roadermel, University of California Press, 1972. Contributor of stories, articles, and reviews to literary journals in the United States and abroad, including *Books Abroad, Botteghe Oscure, TriQuarterly, Encounter, PRISM International,* and *Western Humanities Review.*

SIDELIGHTS: Krishna Baldev Vaid writes: "I spent the most formative years of my life in India where I was born. Transplantation to the U.S.A. where I now live more or less permanently has had a tremendous influence on my writing. I take it as an intense experience of a self-imposed exile. This experience has given me an insight into alienation, marginal living, transience, void, pain, and one's capacity to transcend all this. I write primarily in Hindi and am my own translator into English. In India I am a controversial figure because of my style." Vaid's work has been translated into Italian, German, Spanish, Polish, Japanese, Gujarati, French, Urdu, Panjabi, Bengali, and Marathi.

BIOGRAPHICAL/CRITICAL SOURCES: Vagartha (New Delhi), October, 1973.

* * *

VALETTE, Rebecca M(arianne Loose) 1938-

PERSONAL: Born December 21, 1938; daughter of Gerhard (a professor) and Ruth A. (Bischoff) Loose; married Jean-Paul Valette (a writer), August 6, 1959; children: Jean-Michel, Nathalie Marie, Pierre Alexis. *Education:* Mount Holyoke College, B.A. (cum laude), 1959; University of Colorado, Ph.D., 1963. *Religion:* Roman Catholic. *Home:* 16 Mt. Alvernia Rd., Chestnut Hill, Mass. 02167. *Office:* Boston College, Chestnut Hill, Mass. 02167.

CAREER: University of South Florida, Tampa, examiner and instructor in French and German, 1961-63; North Atlantic Treaty Organization Defense College, Paris, France, instructor in English, 1963-64; Wellesley College, Wellesley, Mass., instructor in French, 1964-65; Boston College, Chestnut Hill, Mass., assistant professor, 1965-68, associate professor, 1968-73, professor of French and education, 1973—. Fulbright senior lecturer in West Germany, 1974. *Member:* American Council on the Teaching of Foreign Languages, Modern Language Association of America (chairman, Division of the Teaching of Language, 1980-81), American Association of Teachers of French (vice-president, 1980-83), American Association of Teachers of German, American Association of Teachers of Spanish and Portuguese, National Association of Language Laboratory Directors, Teachers of English to Speakers of Other Languages.

WRITINGS: Modern Language Testing, Harcourt, 1967, revised edition, 1977; (with husband, Jean-Paul Valette) *Lisons,* McGraw, 1967; (editor with Robert Morgenroth) *C'est de la Prose,* Harcourt, 1968; (editor) *Lectures libres,* Harcourt, 1969; *Arthur de Gobineau and the Short Story,* University of North Carolina Press, 1969; *Directions in Foreign Language Testing,* Modern Language Association of America, 1969; (with Edward D. Allen) *Modern Language Classroom Techniques,* Harcourt, 1973; (with Renee S. Disnick) *Modern Langauge Performance Objectives and Individualization,* Harcourt, 1973; (with J. Valette) *France: A Cultural Review Grammar,* Harcourt, 1973; (with J. Valette) *French for Mastery 1: Salut, les amis!,* Heath, 1975, 2nd edition, 1981; (with J. Valette) *French for Mastery 2: Tous Ensemble,* Heath, 1975, 2nd edition, 1982.

(With J. Valette) *Contacts: Langue et culture francaises,* Houghton, 1976, 2nd edition, 1981; (with Allen) *Classroom Techniques: Foreign Languages and English Second Language,* Harcourt, 1977; (with J. Valette) *C'est comme ca,* Heath, 1978; (with J. Valette) *Spanish for Mastery 1,* Heath, 1980; (with J. Valette) *Spanish for Mastery 2,* Heath, 1980; (with J. Valette and Gene S. Kupferschmid) *Con Mucho Gusto: Lengua y Cultura del Mundo Hispanico,* Holt, 1980; (with J. Valette) *Spanish for Mastery: Dia a Dia,* Heath, 1981; (with J. Valette) *Spanish for Mastery: Bienvenidos,* Heath, 1981; *Nouvelles Lectures Libres,* Heath, 1982; (with J. Valette) *Panorama 2: Lectures faciles,* Heath, 1982.

WORK IN PROGRESS: Research into second-language acquisition.

SIDELIGHTS: Rebecca M. Valette told *CA:* "The recent President's Commission on Foreign Langauge and International Studies stated that 'Americans' incompetence in foreign languages is nothing short of scandalous and is becoming worse.' My husband and I are striving to reverse that trend through our popular French and Spanish texts which combine a carefully sequenced presentation of new vocabulary and structures with learning activities based on interpersonal communication. Students can only acquire a new language if they have the frequent opportunity to use that language for self-expression."

* * *

VANCIL, Richard F(ranklin) 1931-

PERSONAL: Born September 17, 1931, in St. Louis, Mo.; son of George K. and Pearl (Cochran) Vancil; married Emily C. Robinson, June 17, 1955; children: Richard C., Robinson C., Virginia C. *Education:* Northwestern University, B.S., 1953; Harvard University, M.B.A., 1955, D.B.A., 1960.

CAREER: Harvard University, Harvard Business School, Boston, Mass., instructor in control, 1958-60, assistant professor, 1960-64, associate professor of business administration, beginning 1964. Certified public accountant, Illinois and Massachusetts. Chairman of the board, Management Analysis Center, Inc., Cambridge, Mass.; management consultant to various businesses. *Military service:* U.S. Army, Finance Corps, 1955-58; became first lieutenant. *Member:* American Institute of Certified Public Accountants, American Accounting Association, Financial Executives Institute, Institute of Management Sciences, Beta Gamma Sigma, Beta Alpha Psi.

WRITINGS: (With J. L. Treynor) *Machine Tool Leasing,* Management Analysis Center, 1956; (with Neil E. Harlan) *Cases in Accounting Policy,* Prentice-Hall, 1961; (with Harlan and Charles Christenson) *Managerial Economics: Text and Cases,* Irwin, 1962; (with Robert F. Vandell) *Cases in Capital Budgeting,* Irwin, 1962; *Leasing of Industrial Equipment,* McGraw, 1963; (with Robert D. Buzzell and Walter J. Salmon) *Product Profitability and Merchandising Decisions,* Harvard Business School, 1965; (with Robert N. Anthony and John Dearden) *Management Control Systems: Cases and Readings,* Irwin, 1965, revised edition, 1972; (with John Desmond Glover) *Management of Transformation: A Report to Top Management of the Telephone Industry,* International Business Machines Corp., 1968.

Financial Executive's Handbook, Irwin, 1970; (with Roman L. Weil) *Replacement Cost Accounting: Readings on Concepts, Uses, and Methods,* Thomas Horton, 1976; (with William J. Bruns) *A Primer on Replacement Cost Accounting,* Thomas Horton, 1976; (with Peter Lorange) *What Kind of Strategic Planning System Do You Need?,* Alfred P. Sloan School of Management, Massachusetts Institute of Technology, 1976; (editor with Lorange) *Strategic Planning Systems,* Prentice-Hall, 1977; *Decentralization: Managerial Ambiguity by Design,* Dow Jones-Irwin, 1979. Editor, *Formal Planning Systems.*†

* * *

VANDENBERG, Philipp 1941-
(Klaus Dieter Hartel)

PERSONAL: Original name Klaus Dieter Hartel; name legally changed in 1972; born September 20, 1941, in Breslau, Germany; son of Josef (a gynecologist) and Dorothea Hartel; married Doris Priske, 1964 (divorced, 1976); children: Sascha. *Education:* Attended University of Munich, 1963-64. *Politics:* None. *Religion:* None. *Home:* D 8157 Baiernrain, Villa Vandenberg, Germany.

CAREER: Passauer Neue Presse (newspaper), Passau, Bavaria, local editor, 1964-67; *Abendzeitung,* Munich, Germany, news editor, 1967-69; *Quick* (magazine), Munich, editor and writer, 1969-74; *Playboy*—Germany, Munich, non-fiction editor, 1974-76; full-time writer, 1976—.

WRITINGS—In English translation: *Der Fluch der Pharaonen,* Scherz, 1973, translation by Thomas Weyr published as *The Curse of the Pharaohs,* Lippincott, 1975; *Nofretete: eine archaeologische Biographie,* Scherz, 1975, translation by Ruth Hein published as *Nefertiti: An Archaeological Biography,* Lippincott, 1978; *Der vergessene Pharao: Unternehmen Tut-ench-Amun,* Bertelsmann, 1978, translation published as *The Golden Pharaoh,* Macmillan, 1980.

In German: (Under name Klaus Dieter Hartel) *Martin Luther King: Vorkaempfer fur Frieden und Menschenwuerde,* Brunnen, c. 1968; *Auf den Spuren unserer Vergangenheit,* Goldmann, 1977; *Ramses der Grosse: eine archaeologische Biographie,* Scherz, 1977; *Das Geheimnis Orakel* (title means "The Secret of the Oracles"), Bertelsmann, 1979. Also author of *Nero,* 1981, *Der Gladiator* (fiction), 1982, and *Das Tal,* 1983.

SIDELIGHTS: Philipp Vandenberg's books have been published in twenty-five languages, including Japanese, Turkish,

Spanish, Finnish, Swedish, Polish, Rumanian, Italian, and French.

* * *

Van TASSEL, Dennie L(ee) 1939-

PERSONAL: Born July 8, 1939, in South Dakota; son of Rush and Gladys Van Tassel; married Cynthia L. Sokolowski. *Education:* University of Southern California, B.A., 1965; California State College (now University), Los Angeles, M.A., 1967. *Office:* Computer Center, University of California, Santa Cruz, Calif. 95064.

CAREER: Employed with Statistical Tabulation Corp., 1959-68, and San Jose State College (now University), San Jose, Calif., 1968-70; University of California, Santa Cruz, user liaison in Computer Center, 1970—. *Military service:* U.S. Marines, 1957-59. *Member:* Association of Computing Machinery.

WRITINGS: Computer Security Management, Prentice-Hall, 1972; *Program Style, Design, Efficiency, Debugging, Testing,* Prentice-Hall, 1974; *The Compleat Computer,* Science Research Associates, 1976; *Computer, Computer, Computer: The Computer in Fiction and Verse,* Elsevier-Dutton, 1978; *Introductory COBOL,* Holden-Day, 1980; *BASIC-PACK: Statistics Programs for Small Computers,* Prentice-Hall, 1981.

SIDELIGHTS: Dennie L. Van Tassel told *CA:* "I write computer books for beginners. I enjoy writing at a level that new computer users will find understandable. I try to make the books enjoyable and fun. My other motivation is to write books that will be useful for a long period of time. Finally, I write to learn. If I want to learn all about a subject, I write a book about it."

* * *

VARGA, Judy
See STANG, Judit

* * *

VERHOEVEN, Cornelis 1928-

PERSONAL: Born February 2, 1928, in Udenhout, Netherlands; son of Johannes (a farmer) and Johanna Verhoeven; married Janine Van de Kamp (a teacher), July 10, 1965. *Education:* University Nymegen, Ph.D., 1956. *Home:* Uilenburg 30, 5211 EV 's Hertogenbosch, Netherlands.

CAREER: Jeroen Bosch College, 's Hertogenbosch, Netherlands, teacher of Greek and Latin, 1955-1982; University of Amsterdam, Amsterdam, Netherlands, professor of Greek philosophy, 1982—. *Member:* Maatschappy der Nederlandse Letterkunde. *Awards, honors:* Anne Frank Prize, Dutch Government, 1964; Pieter Cornelisz Hooft Prize, Dutch Government, 1979.

WRITINGS—Published by Ambo, except as indicated: *Symboliek van de Voet* (title means "The Symbolism of the Foot"), Van Gorcum, 1957; *Symboliek van de Sluier* (title means "The Symbolism of the Veil"), Standaard, 1961; *Rondom de Leegte* (title means "Around Emptiness"), 1965; *Het grote gebeuren* (title means "The Great Event"), 1966; *Tegen het geweld* (title means "Against Violence"), 1967; *Inleiding tot de verwondering,* 1967, translation by Mary Foran published as *The Philosophy of Wonder,* Macmillan, 1972; *Omzien naar het heden: De mythe van de vooruitgang* (title means "Look Back at the Present"), 1968; *Afscheid van Brabant?* (title means "A Farewell to Brabant?"), 1968; *Voor eigen gebruik* (title means "For the Use of Myself"), 1969; (with Frederik Jacobus Johannes Buytendijk) *Taal en gezondheid* (title means "Language and Health"), Spectrum, 1969.

Bijna niets (title means "Hardly Anything"), 1970; (with Cas Eijsbouts) *Zakelijkheid en ethiek* (title means "Facts and Ethics"), 1971; *Het Leedwezen: Beschouwingen over troost en verdriet, leven en dood* (title means "Mourning: Essays about Consolation and Sorrow"), 1971; *Het gewicht van de Buitenstaander* (title means "The Importance of the Outsider"), 1972; *Het axioma van Geulincx* (title means "The Axiom of Geulincx"), 1973; *Parafilosofen* (title means "Paraphilosophers"), 1974; *De Resten van het vaderschap* (title means "The Rests of Fatherhood"), 1975; *Een Vogeltje in myn buik* (title means "A Little Bird in My Belly"), 1976; *Een verleden als bezit* (title means "A Past as a Property"), Deventer, 1977; *Folteren om bestwil* (title means "Torture for the Good"), 1977; *Herinneringen aan mijn moedertaal* (title means "Memories of my Vernacular Language"), 1978; *De schaduw van een haar* (title means "The Shadow of One Hair"), 1979.

Tractaat over het spieken (title means "An Essay about Cribbing"), 1980; *Merg en Been* (title means "Marrow and Bone"), 1981; *Weerloos Denken* (title means "Defenseless Thinking").

Weekly columnist, 1966—; editor, *Raam,* 1961-1975.

* * *

VIERECK, Phillip 1925-

PERSONAL: Born June 2, 1925, in New Bedford, Mass.; son of Raymond (a civil engineer) and Marion (Neagus) Viereck; married Ellen Kingsbury (now an illustrator), December 18, 1949; children: four. *Education:* Dartmouth College, B.A., 1948; Plymouth Teachers College, M.Ed., 1957. *Politics:* Independent. *Religion:* Unitarian Universalist.

CAREER: Teacher for Alaska Native Service on King Island, 1949-52, in Cordova, Alaska, 1952-54, and in Bennington, Vt., 1954-66; Molly Stark School, Bennington, Vt., supervising principal, beginning 1966; North Bennington Graded School District, North Bennington, Vt., principal, 1974—. *Military service:* U.S. Naval Air Corps, 1943-45. *Member:* National Education Association, Vermont Education Association (chairman of instructional committee, 1963-65), Green Mountain Club. *Awards, honors:* Dorothy Canfield Fisher Memorial Children's Book Award, 1967, for *The Summer I Was Lost.*

WRITINGS—Published by John Day, except as indicated: *Eskimo Island,* 1962; *Independence Must Be Won,* 1964; *The Summer I Was Lost,* 1965; (editor) *The New Land,* 1967; *Let Me Tell You about My Dad,* 1971; *The Third Planet,* Macmillan, 1971; (with Bertha Davis) *Web of the World,* Macmillan, 1971; *Sue's Secondhand Horse,* 1973. Contributor to journals.

AVOCATIONAL INTERESTS: Hunting, fishing, hiking, gardening. †

* * *

VILAR, Esther 1935-

PERSONAL: Born September 16, 1935, in Buenos Aires, Argentina; daughter of Federico (a farmer) and Anna (Schindler) Vilar; married Klaus Wagn (a philosopher), 1961 (divorced, 1963); children: Martin. *Education:* University of Buenos Aires, M.D., 1958. *Religion:* None.

CAREER: Physician in Munich, West Germany, 1960-61; freelance writer.

WRITINGS—Published by Caann Verlag (Munich), except as indicated: *Der Sommer nach dem Tod von Picasso* (play), 1969; *Man und Puppe*, 1969; *Der Dressierte Mann*, 1971, translation by Eva Borneman published as *The Manipulated Man*, Abelard, 1972, revised edition, Farrar, Straus, 1972; *Die Lust an der Unfreiheit: Erlaeuterungen zur Theorie des Genetivismus*, 1971; *Das polygame Geschlect*, 1974, translation by Sophie Wilkins published as *The Polygamous Sex: A Man's Right to the Other Woman*, W. H. Allen, 1976; *Das Ende der Dresser: Modell fuer eine neue Maennlichkeit*, Druckenmueller, 1977.

SIDELIGHTS: In her controversial book *The Manipulated Man*, Esther Vilar maintains that feminists are completely wrong in their assessment of male-female relationships. "They're getting nowhere because they have the male idea about women," she declares in a *New York Times* article. "They make women the objects of male charity." Instead, Vilar insists, it is men who are slaves to women. "Men have been trained and conditioned by women not unlike the way Pavlov conditioned his dogs," she once told a *Publishers Weekly* interviewer. "A woman will make use of a man whenever there is an opportunity."

Vilar levels her criticism at all types of women—working or non-working, married or single—for she finds their faults to be the same: laziness, selfishness, stupidity, and an inability to feel. As she notes in the *New York Times*: "A married woman always has the choice to work or not. Men never do.... Women always work with a net under them; they can let themselves fall. Women work for luxuries.... Men work because it's their responsibility to support a family. What I want to see is even one woman who is permanently willing to let her husband stay home to look after the children, while she goes out to work." Women who are already working and who view themselves as "liberated" rate little better in Vilar's eyes; the work such a woman usually chooses to do, she feels, "rarely involves effort or responsibility, although she makes herself believe it involves both."

According to the author, women manage to get away with being so manipulative because men allow them to. "What a man fears most is freedom," she asserts. "He needs some kind of system to tell him he is worth something. A woman is a man's scale of values, but if he doesn't have a woman to manipulate him, he will find another system." Vilar explains this concept further in the *Publishers Weekly* interview, in which she contends that there is no such thing as a "male chauvinist." "Men love to be called that by women because it makes them feel big and strong, which women have always told them they must be. Its use by women is just another kind of trick to make men do what they want them to do. Women get so many advantages out of the system as it works for them today that I do not have much hope for many of them wanting to change things and really liberate themselves from the manipulation of men."

Reactions to the theories, Vilar reports, "are either very positive or very negative" among women readers; during a publicity tour in England, for instance, she was confronted by a group of middle-aged women who knocked on her hotel room door and invited her to leave the country because she was "insulting" them. Men, on the other hand, tend to be "more in between in their reactions, more cautious. I do get a certain number of letters from men who say, 'of course, it's all true what you write about men being manipulated by women—but I'm the exception.'"

Vilar does not appear to be at all concerned about the commotion she has caused. Freely admitting that *The Manipulated Man* "is a very rude book," she concludes: "I meant it to be. Otherwise nobody would have listened. I'm not interested in revolution. I don't want to change all the rules; people must find their own solutions. I just wanted to bring it to consciousness that it is men who are enslaved—not women."

The *New Republic*'s Doris Grumbach agrees that "there are grains of partial truth in [Vilar's] thesis." In the end, however, continues the critic, "it fails to persuade when it talks of American male/female relations because it is a from-the-other-side-of-the-ocean view of American life, and upper-class American life at that. So much of it is wrong-headed, short-sighted, and limited to vast, undocumented generalizations." Mary Ellman of the *New York Review of Books* also mentions that Vilar's observations are confined to the middle class, as does Raymond Durgnat of *Books and Bookmen*, who feels that her terms are "especially appropriate to the Latin American bourgeoisie; they don't even seem to apply, in Britain's sexually and socially less segregated society."

Despite these reservations about Vilar's failure to examine a broader sector of world society, few critics dispute the fact that *The Manipulated Man* is a thought-provoking book. Though he declares that it "reads like the work of a long-winded pixie," Durgnat writes that "all the same, there are some neat and pointed passages." Ellman is pleased to see Vilar pursue her idea "by hard work, not by swishy emotionalism.... I didn't like [the] book at first. But as I went on, I reluctantly liked it better. [Vilar] is a legitimate cynic. Her argument is slapdash and unsubstantiated, but pointed. The common defects of women are quite neatly isolated and excised."

The *Washington Post Book World*'s Ann Birstein is less complimentary in her review of *The Manipulated Man*. Dismissing the book as a "piece of tripe," she declares that its "only possible value" is that it "does sell." Continues the critic: "For all of its opinionated opinions, *The Manipulated Man* contains no index, no bibliography, not even a simple 'I believe' as justification for its statements. And last, and saddest of all, a book like this only confirms what too many of us already know, that women are only too ready to be cruel to other women. As men are cruel to men. As all of us often are to each other."

Ingrid Bengis, commenting in the *New York Times Book Review*, is also not very impressed by *The Manipulated Man* but still finds it thought-provoking for a reason she is sure Vilar did not intend. Like her colleagues, Bengis agrees that "the women whom Vilar describes are not unknown to us." But the reviewer goes on to point out that the author, after having portrayed women as "rotten and unbearable" creatures, then "completely avoids the problem of self-hatred, and avoids as well the conflicts of identity she creates for herself by asserting that all women are unalterably 'imbecilic,' etc." In short, concludes Bengis, "instead of being a description of women, [*The Manipulated Man*] thus becomes a bitter, vituperative, yet particularly eloquent testimony to the inner damage that takes place in so many women who split themselves in order to avoid confronting their feelings.... [Yet] never has the hollowness of our old definitions seemed so chilling as Vilar makes them through the distorting lens of her contempt. Having written what is in some way a cruelly inhumane and viciously over-generalized book, she has also, probably without knowing why, written a searing one."

BIOGRAPHICAL/CRITICAL SOURCES: New York Times, June 13, 1972; *Books and Bookmen*, December, 1972; *Publishers Weekly*, January 29, 1973; *New Republic*, February 3, 1973;

Washington Post Book World, February 4, 1973; *New York Review of Books,* November 1, 1973; *New York Times Book Review,* March 24, 1974.†

—Sketch by Deborah A. Straub

* * *

VIOLA, Herman J(oseph) 1938-

PERSONAL: Born February 24, 1938, in Chicago, Ill.; son of Joseph (a carpenter) and Mary (Incollingo) Viola; married Susan Bennett (a librarian), June 13, 1964; children: Joseph, Paul, Peter. *Education:* Marquette University, B.A., 1960, M.A., 1964; Indiana University, Ph.D., 1970. *Office:* National Anthropological Archives, Smithsonian Institution, Washington, D.C. 20560.

CAREER: National Archives, Washington, D.C., archivist, 1966-68; *Prologue: Journal of the National Archives,* Washington, D.C., founding editor, 1968-72; Smithsonian Institution, National Anthropological Archives, Washington, D.C., director, 1972—. *Military service:* U.S. Navy, 1962-64. *Member:* Society of American Archivists, Organization of American Historians, Western History Association.

WRITINGS: Thomas L. McKenney: Architect of America's Early Indian Policy, 1816-1830, Swallow Press, 1974; (editor) Charles Royce, *The Cherokee Nation of Indians,* Beresford Book Service, 1975; *The Indian Legacy of Charles Bird King,* Smithsonian Institution Press, 1976; (editor with Robert Kvasnicka) *The Commissioners of Indian Affairs,* University of Nebraska Press, 1979; *Diplomats in Buckskins: A History of Indian Delegations in Washington City,* Smithsonian Institution Press, 1981.

BIOGRAPHICAL/CRITICAL SOURCES: Washington Post Book World, August 23, 1981.

* * *

von CASTELHUN, Friedl
See MARION, Frieda

W

WAGER, Walter H(erman) 1924-
(Walter Herman, John Tiger)

PERSONAL: Born September 4, 1924, in New York, N.Y.; son of Max Louis (a doctor) and Jessie (Smith) Wager; married Sylvia Leonard (a writer), May 6, 1951 (divorced May, 1975); married Winifred McIvor (a goldsmith and jewelry designer), June 4, 1975; children: (first marriage) Lisa Wendy. *Education:* Columbia College, B.A., 1943; Harvard University, LL.B., 1946; Northwestern University, LL.M., 1949; additional study at Institut des Hautes Etudes Internationales, 1949-50. *Politics:* Democrat. *Religion:* Jewish. *Home:* 200 West 79th St., New York, N.Y. 10024. *Agent:* Curtis Brown Ltd., 575 Madison Ave., New York, N.Y. 10022. *Office:* National Music Publishers' Association, 110 East 59th St., New York, N.Y. 10022.

CAREER: Aeroutes, Inc., New York City, director of editorial research, 1947; *Journal of Air Law and Commerce,* Chicago, Ill., federal department editor, 1948-49; Israeli Department of Civil Aviation, Lydda Airport, Tel Aviv, Israel, international affairs and law advisor, 1951-52; free-lance writer in New York City, 1952-54; United Nations Secretariat, New York City, senior editor, 1954-56; Columbia Broadcasting System, Inc. (CBS), New York City, writer for radio and television, 1956; National Broadcasting Co., Inc. (NBC-TV), New York City, writer and producer, 1957; free-lance writer for magazines, radio, and television, 1958-63; *Playbill,* New York City, editor-in-chief, 1963-66; American Society of Composers, Authors, and Publishers, New York City, public relations consultant and editor of *ASCAP Today,* 1966-72, director of public relations, 1972-78; National Music Publishers' Association, New York City, public relations counselor, 1978—. Lecturer at Northwestern University, 1949, and at Columbia University, 1955-56; special assistant to Attorney General of the State of New York for investigation of hate literature in elections, 1962. *Member:* Writers Guild of America, Authors League of America, National Academy of Popular Music (member of governing board). *Awards, honors:* Fulbright fellow at University of Paris, 1949-50.

WRITINGS—Novels, except as indicated: *Frontier Formalities for International Airlines* (nonfiction), [Chicago], 1949; (editor) *Some Selected Readings on International Air Transportation* (nonfiction), [Chicago], 1949; (under pseudonym Walter Herman) *Operation Intrigue,* Avon, 1956; *Camp Century: City under the Ice* (nonfiction), Chilton, 1962; (editor) *The Playwrights Speak* (interviews), Delacourte, 1967; *The Girl Who Split,* Dell, 1969; *Sledgehammer,* Macmillan, 1970; *Viper Three,* Macmillan, 1971; *Swap,* Macmillan, 1972; *Telefon,* Macmillan, 1975; *My Side, by King Kong* (farce), Macmillan, 1976; *Time of Reckoning,* Playboy Press, 1979; *Blue Leader,* Arbor House, 1979; *Blue Moon,* Arbor House, 1980; *Blue Murder,* Arbor House, 1981.

Under pseudonym John Tiger; published by Popular Library, except as indicated: *Death Hits the Jackpot,* Avon, 1954; *I Spy,* 1965; *Masterstroke,* 1966; *Wipeout,* 1967; *Countertrap,* 1967; *Mission Impossible,* 1967; *Death Twist,* 1968; *Doomdate,* 1968; *Mission Impossible Number Four: Code Name Little Ivan,* 1969.

Also author of screenplay "Swap," based on his novel, 1974; author of documentary films of jazz, spirituals, guerrilla warfare, organzied crime in America, U.S. disarmament policy. Alliance for Progress in Colombia and Venezuela, the U.S. decision to use the atomic bomb against Japan, and the life of a Roman legionary and that of an American soldier. Contributor of articles on theater and music to periodicals. Senior editor, *Show,* 1965.

SIDELIGHTS: Walter Wager told *CA:* "I have written for pleasure since I was ten but never thought that one could make a living at it. I had no idea how to get started in the writing world and really wandered in casually as a source of income while waiting for a security clearance to become a UN editor. I've been very lucky, and I've enjoyed what I do. I'm still surprised by all the people who 1) want to be novelists, 2) consider writing/writers exotic and superior. Fortunately, writers themselves are not as arrogant as lawyers, doctors, or movie producers—but who is? On the other hand, I'm bored with cry-baby novelists who write irate articles about their horrid experiences with 'boorish' movie or television folk. I am also dismayed by certain defensive/hostile types who resent anyone who 1) creates personally, 2) works at home. However, I'm generally in a cheery mood, doing my thing. I don't see writers as competing with each other or with anyone else. None of us writes like any other writer, thank God. The best things for writers to do are 1) write, 2) stay off talk shows unless the hosts are genuinely amusing.

"I try to assist young writers by introducing them to agents and editors, and by encouraging them if/when they are temporarily uncertain. I tell them of the 'luck' factor and how a 'real' writer will go on writing no matter what. I joke about how I literally stumbled into hard cover fiction. In June 1967,

I was in [Washington,] D.C. autographing paperbacks at an American Booksellers Association convention. There were many parties, and I was among those who imbibed conscientiously. Somewhat tipsy, I was struggling through a throng in the crowded Harper & Row suite when I stumbled and bumped into a good-natured chap. We exchanged boozy witticisms, and later my good friend and super editor, James A. Bryans, told me that the stranger was impressed. Bryans urged me to send that man a book. The fellow was Richard Oldenberg, then managing editor at Macmillan and now head of the Museum of Modern Art. I sent him a proposal for an anthology, was directed to another bright Macmillan editor, Bob Markel—now vice-president at Grossett & Dunlap—who urged me to do a novel. I did—quite a few. I never did get to thank Oldenberg, but I certainly will if we ever meet again."

MEDIA ADAPTATIONS: Metro-Goldwyn-Mayer filmed *Telefon* in 1977, and Lorimar's production of *Viper Three* was released in 1977 as "The Twilight's Last Gleaming."

AVOCATIONAL INTERESTS: Travel (has been to twenty-six countries in North, Central, and South America, Asia, Africa, and Europe).

BIOGRAPHICAL/CRITICAL SOURCES: New York Times, January 27, 1977, August 22, 1982.

* * *

WAGNER, Francis S(tephen) 1911-

PERSONAL: Born February 28, 1911, in Krupina, Austria-Hungary (now Czechoslovakia); came to United States, 1949; naturalized, 1956; son of Ferenc (a restauranteur) and Maria (Miko) Wagner; married Irene Trefny, February 2, 1947; children: Christina Maria Teresa. *Education:* University of Szeged, Hungary, high school teacher's diploma (summa cum laude), 1935, college teacher's diploma (summa cum laude), 1937, Ph.D. (summa cum laude), 1940. *Religion:* Roman Catholic. *Home:* 4610 Franklin St., Kensington, Md. 20895.

CAREER: Budapest State College, Budapest, Hungary, professor of history and of Hungarian and Slavic languages, 1938-45; Ministry of Foreign Affairs, Budapest, head of Czechoslovak division, 1945-46; Hungarian Consulate General, Bratislava, Czechoslovakia, consul general, 1946-48; Library of Congress, Washington, D.C., staff member of East European accessions index project, 1953-61, of Cyrillic bibliography project, 1962-65, of subject cataloging division, 1965-81.

MEMBER: International Platform Association, American Historical Association, American Studies Association, Helicon Society (Toronto, Ontario), Philosophy Club (Washington, D.C.), Civil War Round Table of the District of Columbia, Harry S. Truman Library Institute for National and International Affairs (honorary fellow).

WRITINGS: A csehszlovak nacionalizmus tortenetirasa (title means "Historiography of Czechoslovak Nationalism"), Tortenetiras, 1938; *Citanka* (title means "Primer"), Egyetemi Nyomda, 1939; *A szlovak nacionalizmus elso korszaka* (title means "First Period of Slovak Nationalism"), Ferenc Jozsef Tudomanyegyetem, 1940; *Cultural Revolution in East Europe,* Danubian Research Service, 1955; *A magyar tortenetiras uj utjai* (title means "New Ways of Hungarian Historiography"), privately printed, 1956.

Szechenyi and the Nationality Problem in the Hapsburg Empire, privately printed, 1960; (editor and author of introduction) *The Hungarian Revolution in Perspective,* Freedom Fighters Memorial Foundation, 1967; (editor) *Toward a New Central Europe: A Symposium on the Problems of the Danubian Nations,* Danubian Press, 1970; *A magyar kisebbsegek helyzete a szomszed allamokban* (title means "The Situation of Hungarian Minorities in the Neighboring Countries"), privately printed, 1975; *Hungarian Contributions to World Civilization,* Alpha Publications, 1977; *Fifty Years in the Laboratory: Survey of the Research Activities of Physicist Zoltan Bay,* Alpha Publications, 1977; *Eugene P. Wigner: An Architect of the Atomic Age,* Rakoczi Foundation, 1981; *Atomic Physicist Zoltan L. Bay: A Pioneer of Space Research,* Rakoczi Foundation, 1982.

Contributor: *Hungarians in Czechoslovakia,* Research Institute for Minority Studies, 1959; *Guide to Historical Literature,* American Historical Association, 1961; Eric H. Boehm, editor, *Historical Periodicals: An Annotated World List of Historical and Related Serial Publications,* Clio Press, 1961; Boris V. Kit and Frederick I. Ordway, editors, *U.S.S.R. Space Program: Manpower, Training, and Research Developments,* Department of Physics and Astronomy, University of Maryland, 1964; Thomas T. Taylor, editor, *Soviet Foreign Relations and World Communism: A Selected, Annotated Bibliography of 7,000 Books in Thirty Languages,* Princeton University Press, 1965; Joseph Roucek, editor, *Contemporary Sociology,* Philosophical Library, 1968; Eugene P. Wigner, editor, *Survival and the Bomb: Methods of Civil Defense,* Indiana University Press, 1969; Paul L. Horecky, editor, *East Central Europe: A Guide to Basic Publications,* University of California Press, 1969.

Contributor to *Collier's Encyclopedia.* Contributor of over 250 articles in six languages to professional journals and magazines. Consulting editor, *Historical Abstracts,* 1955, and *America: History and Life,* 1965-81; member of editorial board, *Foreign Areas Survey,* 1965-72; member of advisory board, *Historical Abstracts,* 1971-81, editor, *Studies for a New Central Europe,* Volume 3, number 1, 1972.

WORK IN PROGRESS: A world guide to nationality and racial problems; *U.S. Foreign Prestige: 1776 to the Present; Philosophy of History; Nation-Building in the United States: The American Concept of Nationhood in Perspective;* research on historical knowledge and dialectical materialism, the diplomatic history of World War II, and on global analysis of the concept of nationalism.

SIDELIGHTS: Francis S. Wagner, who knows, in order of proficiency, Hungarian, Slovak, Czech, German, Russian, Polish, Serbo-Croatian, Bulgarian, French, Slovenian, and Latin, told *CA* that since his college years he has been interested in the possibility of peaceful coexistence among different ethnic groups. He sincerely believes "that after so many failures, mankind will find the ways and methods to develop relatively well-functioning systems of peaceful coexistence based upon the principle of human dignity stemming from the immortal standard: 'Whatsoever you would that men should do to you, do also to them.'"

AVOCATIONAL INTERESTS: Research, publishing, lecturing, music, sports (chiefly walking and gymnastics).

* * *

WALKER, Dale L(ee) 1935-

PERSONAL: Born August 3, 1935, in Decatur, Ill.; son of Russell Dale (a career soldier) and Eileen M. (Guysinger) Walker; married Alice McCord, September 30, 1960; children: Dianne, Eric, Christopher, Michael, John. *Education:* Texas Western College (now University of Texas at El Paso), B.A., 1962. *Politics:* Democrat. *Religion:* Protestant. *Home:* 800 Green

Cove, El Paso, Tex. 79932. *Office:* News-Information Office, University of Texas, El Paso, Tex. 79968.

CAREER: KTSM-TV, El Paso, Tex., reporter, 1962-66; University of Texas at El Paso, director of News-Information Office, 1966—. *Military service:* U.S. Navy, 1955-59. *Member:* National Historical Society, Society of WWI Aero Historians, Western Writers of America.

WRITINGS: (Author of introductory essay) George Sterling, *Wine of Wizardry,* Pinion Press, 1962; (with Richard O'Connor) *The Lost Revolutionary: A Biography of John Reed,* Harcourt, 1967; *The Fiction of Jack London,* Texas Western Press, 1972; *C. L. Sonnichsen: Grassroots Historian,* Texas Western Press, 1972; *The Alien Worlds of Jack London* (monograph), Wolf House Books, 1973; (editor) Howard A. Craig, *Sunward I've Climbed,* Texas Western Press, 1974; *Jack London, Sherlock Holmes, and Sir Arthur Conan Doyle* (monograph), Alvin S. Fick, 1974; (contributor) W. Burns Taylor and Richard Santelli, editor, *Passing Through,* Santay Publishers, 1974; *Death Was the Black Horse: The Story of Rough Rider, Buckey O'Neill,* Madrona Press, 1975; (editor and author of introduction) *Curious Fragments: Jack London's Tales of Fantasy Fiction,* Kennikat, 1975; (contributor) Howard Lamar, editor, *The Reader's Encyclopedia of the American West,* Crowell, 1977; *No Mentor but Myself: Jack London, the Writer's Writer,* Kennikat, 1979.

Only the Clouds Remain: Ted Parsons of the Lafayette Escadrille, Alandale, 1980; *Jack London and Conan Doyle: A Literary Kinship,* Gaslight, 1981; (author of introductory essay) *An American for Lafayette: The Diaries of E.C.C. Genet,* University of Virginia Press, 1981. Contributor to newspapers and magazines. Books editor, *El Paso Times,* 1979—; editor, *The Roundup,* 1980—.

WORK IN PROGRESS: Disputed Barricades, a work on Americans in the French Foreign Legion, 1914-1918.

SIDELIGHTS: Dale L. Walker writes: "My principal areas of reading and writing interest are: 1) American and British biographical subjects, nineteenth century; 2) Victorian era, 1839-1900, military history; 3) Jack London studies."

* * *

WALLACH, Paul I. 1927-

PERSONAL: Born July 29, 1927, in Los Angeles, Calif.; son of Lewis J. and Ann (Krinitt) Wallach; divorced; children: Bruce John, Bret Richard, Robin Lianne, Adam Joseph. *Education:* University of California, Santa Barbara, B.A., 1951; Los Angeles State College of Applied Arts and Sciences (now California State University, Los Angeles), M.A., 1956. *Politics:* Democrat. *Religion:* Jewish. *Home:* 826 Morningside Dr., Millbrae, Calif. 94030.

CAREER: Teacher of drafting and architecture in Los Angeles, Calif., public schools, 1951-64, Sequoia Union High School District, 1964-80; Canada College, Redwood City, Calif., instructor in architecture, 1969-80; currently part-time instructor in architecture at Fashion Institute of Design and Merchandising, San Francisco, Calif. Teacher at U.S. Air Force dependent schools in Europe, 1958-60. *Military service:* U.S. Navy, 1945-46. *Member:* Epsilon Phi Tau.

WRITINGS: (With Hepler) *Architecture: Drafting and Design,* McGraw, 1965, 4th edition, 1982; (with Hepler) *Housing Today,* McGraw, 1965; (with Hepler) *Home Planning,* McGraw, 1966; *Study Guides for Architectural References,* Pierce Publishing, 1968; *Architectural Drafting Study Guides Workbook,* McGraw, 1972; *Metric Study Guide,* Pierce Publishing, 1975; *The Basic Book of Drafting,* American Technical Publications, 1979; *Metric Drafting,* Glencoe, 1979; *Reading Construction Drawing,* McGraw, 1979; *Meet the Metric System,* Pitman Learning, 1980; *Drafting,* Glencoe, 1981; *Visualized Basic Mechanical Drafting,* Glencoe, 1981; *Basic Architectural Drafting,* Southwestern, 1982; *Interior Design Kit,* Southwestern, 1983; *Fundamentals of Interior Design,* Southwestern, 1983; *Home Planners Design Fundamentals,* McGraw, in press.

WORK IN PROGRESS: Architectural transparencies for the overhead projector.

AVOCATIONAL INTERESTS: Handball, tennis, and cycling.

* * *

WALLIS, Charles L(angworthy)

PERSONAL: Born in Hamilton, N.Y.; son of Robert Scott (a clergyman) and Caroline (Langworthy) Wallis; married Betty Watson (a college English instructor), August 16, 1947. *Education:* University of Redlands, B.A., 1943, M.A., 1945; Colgate Rochester Divinity School, B.D., 1945. *Politics:* Republican. *Home and office:* Keuka College, P.O. Box 1, Keuka Park, N.Y.

CAREER: Ordained Baptist minister, 1944. First Baptist Church, Canandaigua, N.Y., minister, 1943-47; U.S. Veterans' Administration Hospital, Canandaigua, N.Y., chaplain, 1944-46; Keuka College, Keuka Park, N.Y., started as instructor in English, 1945, professor of English and chairman of department, 1959-70, minister of college church, beginning 1947, special lecturer in philosophy, 1954-60, coordinator of publications, beginning 1975. Reader, Harper & Row, Inc. Editorial fellow, Ministers Research Foundation, 1956-59. *Member:* American Baptist Historical Society (member of board of managers, beginning 1961), College English Association, American Folklore Society, Poetry Society of America, American Association of University Professors, New York English Council, New York State Historical Association, New York Folklore Society (vice-president, 1954-55), Rotary Club (Penn Yan, N.Y.; president, 1962-63), Yates County Republican Committee (chairman, beginning 1965), Masons (Penn Yan, N.Y.; master, 1965), Sigma Tau Delta, Pi Delta Epsilon, Delta Alpha. *Awards, honors:* Civil War Centennial Medallion, 1962.

WRITINGS: Stories on Stone: A Book of American Epitaphs, Oxford University Press, 1954, published as *American Epitaphs: Grave and Humorous,* Dover, 1973; (with G. Henton Davies and Alan Richardson) *Twentieth Century Bible Commentary,* Harper, 1955; (with Charles L. Allen) *Christmas in Our Hearts,* Revell, 1957; (with Allen) *Candle, Star, and Christmas Tree,* Revell, 1959; (with Allen) *When Christmas Came to Bethlehem,* Revell, 1963; *365 Table Graces for the Christian Home,* Harper, 1966; (with Allen) *Christmas,* Revell, 1977.

Editor: *Selected Poems of John Oxenham,* Harper, 1948, reprinted, Books for Libraries, 1971; *Poems of Edwin Markham,* Harper, 1950; *A Treasury of Sermon Illustrations,* Abingdon, 1950; *The Funeral Encyclopedia,* Harper, 1953, reprinted, Baker Book, 1973; *Worship Resources for the Christian Year,* Harper, 1954; *Autobiography of Peter Cartwright,* Abingdon, 1956; *Speakers' Illustrations for Special Days,* Abingdon, 1956; *A Treasury of Sermons for Children,* Harper, 1957; Harry Emerson Fosdick, *Riverside Sermons,* Harper, 1958; James Ferguson, *Prayers for Public Worship,* Harper, 1958; *Notable Sermons from Protestant Pulpits,* Abingdon, 1958; *The Table of the Lord,* Harper, 1958, published as *A Complete Source*

Book for the Lord's Prayer, Baker Book, 1978; *The Greatest Sermons of George H. Morrison*, Harper, 1959; *A Treasury of Poems for Worship and Devotion*, Harper, 1959.

Lenten-Easter Sourcebook, Abingdon, 1961, reprinted, Baker Book, 1978; *1010 Sermon Illustrations from the Bible*, Harper, 1963; *Eighty-Eight Evangelistic Sermons*, Harper, 1964; *The Treasure Chest*, Harper, 1965; *Speakers' Resources from Contemporary Literature*, Harper, 1965; *Words of Life*, Harper, 1966; V. C. Hudson, *Flapdoodle, Trust, and Obey*, Harper, 1966; *Holy, Holy Land: A Devotional Anthology*, Harper, 1969; *Our American Heritage*, Harper, 1970.

General editor, "New Anvil" series and "Church Life" series, Harper. Editor, *The Minister's Manual* (annual), Harper, 1968—. Contributor to *World Book Encyclopedia*. Contributor of articles and reviews to *Saturday Evening Post* and other publications. Member of editorial staff, *The Interpreter's Bible*, 1953-57; editor, *Pulpit Preaching*, 1948—, and *New York Folklore Quarterly*, 1955-62.†

*　*　*

WALSER, Martin 1927-

PERSONAL: Born March 24, 1927, in Wasserburg, Germany; son of Martin (an innkeeper) and Augusta (Schmid) Walser; married Jehle Kaethe, October 20, 1950; children: Franziska, Katharina, Alissa, Theresia. *Education:* Attended University of Regensburg; University of Tuebingen, Ph.D., 1951. *Religion:* Catholic. *Home:* Hecht 36, Ueberlingen, Germany 777.

CAREER: Writer, 1951—. *Member:* P.E.N., Deutsche Akademie fuer Sprache und Dichtung, Akademie der Kuenste. *Awards, honors:* Gruppe 47 Prize, 1955; Hermann Hesse Prize, 1957; Gerhart-Hauptmann Prize, 1962; Schiller Foerder Prize, 1965; Bodensee Literature Prize, 1967; Schiller Gedaechtnis Prize, 1980; Buechner Prize, 1981.

WRITINGS—Published by Suhrkamp, except as indicated: *Ein Flugzeug ueber dem Haus and andere Geschichten* (title means "An Airplane over the Roof and Other Stories"), 1955, 2nd edition, 1966; *Ehen in Philippsburg* (novel), 1957, reprinted, 1977, translation by Eva Figes published as *The Gadarene Clubs*, Longmans, Green, 1960, adaptation of Figes' translation by J. Laughlin published as *Marriage in Philippsburg*, New Directions, 1961.

Halbzeit (novel; title means "Half-Time"), 1960, reprinted, 1973; *Hoelderlin auf dem Dachboden* (title means "Hoelderlin in the Attic"), 1960; (editor) *Die alternative; oder, Brauchen wir eine neue regierung?* (title means "The Alternative: or, Do We Need a New Government?"), Rowohlt (Hamburg), 1961; *Beschreibung einer Form: Kafka* (title means "Description of a Form: Kafka"), C. Hanser (Munich), 1961, 3rd edition, 1968; (editor and author of introduction) *Vorzeichen II: Neun neue deutsche Autoren* (title means "Omens: Nine New German Authors"), 1963; (editor) Franz Kafka, *Er: Prosa*, 1963.

Luegengeschichten (title means "Lying Stories"), 1965; (author of essay) Jonathan Swift, *Satiren*, Insel-Verlag (Frankfurt), 1965; *Erfahrungen und Leseerfahrungen* (essays; title means "Experiences and Reading Experiences"), 1965, 3rd edition, 1969; *Das Einhorn* (novel), 1966, translation by Barrie Ellis-Jones published as *The Unicorn*, Calder & Boyars, 1971; (with Karl Chargesheimer) *Theater, Theater*, Friedrich (Hanover, Germany), 1967; *Heimatkunde* (essays and addresses; title means "Topography"), 1968; (author of foreword) Ursula Trauberg, *Vorleben*, 1968; (with others) *Ueber Ernst Bloch*, 1968.

Hoelderlin zu entsprechen (address; title means "To Meet Hoelderlin"), K. Thomae (Biberach an der Riss, Germany), 1970; *Fiction* (stories), 1970; *Die Gallistl'sche Krankheit* (novel; title means "Gallistl's disease"), 1972; *Der Sturz* (novel; title means "The Fall"), 1973; *Wie und wovon handelt Literatur* (essays and addresses; title means "How and On What Does Literature Act"), 1973.

Das Sauspiel: Szenen aus dem 16. Jahrhundert, 1975; *Jenseits der Liebe: Roman*, 1976; *Was zu bezweifeln war: Aufsaetze und Reden 1958-1975*, Aufbau-Verlag, 1976; *Ein fliehendes Pferd*, 1978, translation by Leila Vennewitz published as *Runaway Horse*, Holt, 1980; *Der Grund zur Freude: 99 Sprueche zur Erbauung d. Bewusstseins*, Verlag Eremiten-Presse, 1978; *Heimatlob: Ein Bodenseebuch mit Bildern von Andre Ficus*, Gessler, 1978; *Wer ist ein Schriftsteller?: Aufsaetze und Reden Seelenarbeit*, 1979; *Das Schwanenhaus*, 1980; *Selbstbewusstein und Ironie*, Vorlesungen, 1981.

Plays: *Der Abstecher* (also see below), 1961, translation by R. Grunberger published as *The Detour* in *The Rabbit* [and] *The Detour*, J. Calder, 1963; *Eiche und Angora: Eine Deutsche Chronik*, 1962, 3rd edition, 1966, reprinted with English introduction and notes by A. E. Stubbs, Harrap, 1973, adaptation by R. Ducan published as *The Rabbit* in *The Rabbit* [and] *The Detour*, J. Calder, 1963; *Ueberlebensgross Herr Knott: Requiem fuer einen Unsterblichen* (title means "More Than Life Size, Mr. Knott"), 1964, 2nd edition, 1969; *Der Schwarze Schwan* (title means "The Black Swan"), 1964; *Der Abstecher* [and] *Die Zimmerschlacht* (latter title means "Homefront"), 1967; *Ein Kinderspiel* (title means "A Children's Play"), 1970; *Aus dem Wortschatz unserer Kaempfe* (title means "From the Vocabulary of Our Fights"), Verlag Eremiten-Presse (Stierstadt, Germany), 1971; *Gesammelte Stuecke* (collected plays), 1971.

BIOGRAPHICAL/CRITICAL SOURCES: Anthony Edward Waine, *Martin Walser: The Development as Dramatist, 1950-1970*, Bouvier Verlag, 1978; *Times Literary Supplement*, July 25, 1980, October 3, 1980.

*　*　*

WALTHER, Regis (Hills) 1917-

PERSONAL: Born November 24, 1917, in Chicago, Ill.; son of George Jacob (a nurseryman) and Margaret (Durmody) Walther; married Ferne Essene, August 14, 1939; children: Frances, Margaret, Linda; Richard (stepson). *Education:* University of California, Los Angeles, B.A., 1941; George Washington University, Ph.D., 1963. *Politics:* Democrat. *Home:* 1808 Collingwood Rd., Alexandria, Va. 22308. *Office:* Department of Management Sciences, George Washington University, Washington, D.C.

CAREER: U.S. Office of Price Administration, Washington, D.C., personnel officer, 1942-47; U.S. Department of State, Washington, D.C., medical administrator, 1948-56, personnel research officer, 1956-64; George Washington University, Washington, D.C., professorial lecturer in psychology research methods, 1960—, director of Center for Behavioral Sciences and Manpower Research Projects, 1964—, research professor of management science, 1971—. *Member:* American Psychological Association, American Association for the Advancement of Science, Society for the Psychological Study of Social Issues, Sigma Xi.

WRITINGS: Psychological Dimension of Work, George Washington University Center for Behavioral Sciences, 1964; *Orientations and Behavioral Styles of Foreign Service Officers*,

Carnegie Endowment for International Peace, 1965; *Socialization Principles and Work Styles of the Juvenile Court*, George Washington University Center for Behavioral Sciences, 1965; *Human Factors Related to Quality and Reliability of Unmanned Spacecraft Components*, George Washington University Center for Behavioral Sciences, 1965; (with Margaret L. Magnusson) *A Retrospective Study of the Effectiveness of Out-of-School Neighborhood Youth Corps Programs in Four Urban Sites*, George Washington University Social Research Group, 1967; *Job Adjustment and Health*, George Washington University Manpower Research Projects, 1968; *The Accelerated Learning Experiment: An Approach to the Remedial Education of Out-of-School Youth*, George Washington University Social Research Group, 1969.

The Measurement of Work Relevant Attitudes: A Report on the Development of a Measuring Instrument, George Washington University Manpower Research Projects, 1970; *A Study of Negro Male High School Dropouts Who Are Not Reached by Federal Work-Training Programs*, George Washington University Social Research Group, 1970; *A Study of the Effectiveness of Selected Out-of-School Neighborhood Youth Corps Programs*, George Washington University Social Research Group, 1971; *An Educational Model for Manpower Programs: A Manual of Recommended Practices*, George Washington University Manpower Research Projects, 1975; *A Longitudinal Study of Selected Out-of-School Neighborhood Youth Corps Programs: Two Programs in Four Cities*, George Washington University Manpower Research Projects, 1975; *The Measurement of Work Relevant Attitudes: Final Report*, George Washington University Manpower Research Projects, 1975; *Analysis and Synthesis of Department of Labor Experience in Youth Transition to Work Programs*, Manpower Research Projects, Inc., 1977; *The Manual for the Job Analysis and Interest Measurement*, JAIM Research, 1977.

WORK IN PROGRESS: *Federal Employment and Training Programs for Youth: A Critique*, for U.S. Department of Labor; *Psychological Factors in Occupations and Work*.

* * *

WANG, C(hing) H(sien) 1940-
(Yang Mu, Yeh Shan)

PERSONAL: Born September 6, 1940, in Taiwan, China (now seat of Nationalist Chinese Government); son of Shui-sheng Yang (a printer) and Pao-hsiu Wang; married Nora Chen (an instructor), September 3, 1966 (divorced, 1977); married Ying-ying Hsia, January 2, 1979; children: (second marriage) Bruce. *Education:* Tunghai University, Taiwan, B.A., 1963; University of Iowa, M.F.A., 1966; University of California, Berkeley, Ph.D., 1971. *Home:* 10400 32nd Ave., Seattle, Wash. 98125. *Office:* Department of Asian Languages and Literature, University of Washington, Seattle, Wash. 98195.

CAREER: University of Massachusetts—Amherst, instructor, 1970-71, assistant professor of Chinese and comparative literature, 1971; University of Washington, Seattle, assistant professor, 1971-74, associate professor, 1974-81, professor of Chinese and comparative literature, 1981—. *Military service:* Army of the Republic of China, 1963-64. *Member:* American Oriental Society, Association for Asian Studies.

AWARDS, HONORS: Time-Life Award for poetry translation, 1965; first prize for lyrical essay from Republic of China, 1966; Mainstream Prize for poetry, 1971; Asia Society award for Chinese epic project, 1971; University of Washington research grants, summers, 1972-75; American Council of Learned Societies-Social Science Research Council grant, 1975-76; Sun Yat-sen Prize for poetry, 1980; China Times Literary Prize for Narrative Poetry, 1980.

WRITINGS: *The Bell and the Drum: Shih Ching as Formulaic Poetry in an Oral Tradition*, University of California Press, 1974.

Under pseudonym Yeh Shan: *Shui chih mei* (poems; title means "On the Water Margin"), Lan-hsing Poetry Association (Taipei), 1960; *Hua chi* (poems; title means "Flower Season"), Lan-hsing Poetry Association, 1963; *Yeh Shan san-wen chi* (title means "First Essays"), Wen-hsing Bookstore (Taipei), 1966; *Teng ch'uan* (poems; title means "Lantern Boat"), Wen-hsing Bookstore, 1966; (translator) Federico Garcia Lorca, *Hsi-pan-ya lang-jen yin* (translation of *Romancero gitano*), Hsien-tai Wen-hsueh (Taipei), 1966; (translator with others) *Mei-kuo hsien-tai ch'i ta hsio-shuo-chia* (translation of *Seven Modern American Novelists*, edited by William Van O'Connor), Chin-jih Shih-chieh Press (Hong Kong), 1969; *Fei tu chi* (title means "Selected Poems, 1956-1960"), Hsien-jen-chang Press (Taipei), 1969; *Ch'uan shuo* (poems; title means "Legends"), Chih-wen Press (Taipei), 1971.

Under pseudonym Yang Mu; published by Hung-fan Press (Taipei), except as indicated: *Ch'uan-t'ung-ti yu hsien-taiti* (essays; title means "Traditional and Modern"), Chih-wen Press, 1974; *Yang Mu tsu-hsuan chi* (title means "Selected Essays, 1960-1975"), Li-ming Enterprise (Taipei), 1975; *P'ing Chung Kao* (poems; title means "Manuscripts Sealed in a Bottle"), Chin-wen Press, 1975; *Nien-lun* (poems; title means "Rings of the Tree"), Four Seasons Press (Taipei), 1976; *Po-k'e-lai Ching-shen* (essays; title means "The Spirit of Berkeley"), 1977; *Pei-tou hsing* (poems; title means "Song of the Dipper"), 1978; *Wen-hsueh chih-shih* (essays; title means "Literary Knowledge"), 1979; *Wu feng* (play), 1979; *Chin-chi ti yu-hsi* (poems; title means "Games of Taboo"), 1980; *Hai-an ch'i-tieh* (poems; title means "The Seven Turns of the Screw"), 1980; *Sou-shuo che* (essays; title means "The Searcher"), 1982.

Contributor to anthologies: *New Chinese Poetry*, edited and translated by Yu Kwang-chung, Heritage Press (Hong Kong), 1960; *New Voices 1961*, edited and translated by Nancy Chang, Heritage Press, 1961; *Modern Chinese Poetry: Twenty Poets from the Republic of China*, edited and translated by Wai-lim Yip, University of Iowa Press, 1970; *Modern Verse from Taiwan*, edited and translated by Angela Jung Palandri, University of California Press, 1972; *Anthology of Chinese Literature, Volume II: From the 14th Century to the Present Day*, edited by Cyril Birch, Grove Press, 1972; *An Anthology of Contemporary Chinese Literature*, Volume I (also includes essays and translations by Wang), edited by Ch'i Pang-yuan and others, National Office of Compilation and Translation (Taipei), 1975.

Editor of "Hung-fan Wen-hsueh ts'ung-shu" (title means "Hung-fan Literature" series), 1975—. Contributor of articles, reviews, and poems to *The Chinese Pen, China Times Literary Supplement, Journal of the Oriental Society, Tri-Quarterly, Tamkang Review, Literature East and West, Metaphrasis, Tsing Hua Journal of Chinese Studies, Journal of Asian Studies*, and numerous other Chinese and American publications. Co-editor, *Hai-ou* (title means "Sea Gull Poetry Weekly"), 1957-59; contributing editor, *Ts'uang-shih-chi* (title means "Epoch Poetry Quarterly"), 1962-68, *Hsien-tai wen-hsueh* (title means "Modern Literature"), 1965-72, *Chung-wai wen-hsueh* (title means "Chung-wai Literary Monthly"), 1973—; editor, *Tung-feng* (title means "East Wind"), 1961-62, *Hsin-ch'ao ts'ung-shu* (title means "New Currents Series"), 1969—.

WORK IN PROGRESS: A sequel to *The Bell and the Drum,* on ancient Chinese verse as epic; a book in Chinese about American experience.

SIDELIGHTS: Although he is a permanent resident in the United States, C. H. Wang retains his Chinese citizenship and does his writing in both English and Chinese. He finds his bilingual writing in both scholarly and creative areas "a challenge, sometimes exciting and sometimes frustrating." Some of Wang's poems have been translated into Korean, French, and Japanese.

* * *

WARBURG, Sandol Stoddard
See STODDARD, Sandol

* * *

WARK, Robert R(odger) 1924-

PERSONAL: Born October 7, 1924, in Edmonton, Alberta, Canada; came to United States, 1948; naturalized, 1970; son of Joseph Henry (a grain inspector) and Louise (Rodger) Wark. *Education:* University of Alberta, B.A., 1944, M.A., 1946; Harvard University, A.M., 1949, Ph.D., 1952. *Religion:* Episcopalian. *Home:* 1330 Lombardy Rd., Pasadena, Calif. 91106. *Office:* Henry E. Huntington Library and Art Gallery, San Marino, Calif. 91108.

CAREER: Harvard University, Cambridge, Mass., instructor, 1952-54; Yale University, New Haven, Conn., instructor, 1954-56; Henry E. Huntington Library and Art Gallery, San Marino, Calif., curator of art, 1956—. Lecturer in art at California Institute of Technology, 1960—, and at University of California, Los Angeles, 1966—. *Military service:* Royal Canadian Air Force, 1944-45; Royal Canadian Naval Volunteer Reserve, 1945. *Member:* College Art Association, Association of Art Museum Directors, American Museum Association, American Society for Eighteenth-Century Studies, Twilight Club.

WRITINGS—All published by Henry E. Huntington Library and Art Gallery, except as indicated: (Editor) C. Collins Baker, *Catalogue of William Blake's Drawings and Paintings in the Huntington Library,* 2nd edition (Wark was not associated with earlier edition), 1957; (editor) Joshua Reynolds, *Discourses on Art,* 1959, reprinted, Yale University Press, 1975; *Sculpture in the Huntington Collection,* 1959; *French Decorative Art in the Huntington Collection,* 1961, 2nd edition, 1968; (author of introduction and notes) Thomas Rowlandson, *Drawings for a Tour in a Post Chaise,* 1963; (author of introduction and notes) Rowlandson, *Drawings for the English Dance of Death,* 1966; (author of introduction and notes) Isaac Cruikshank, *Drawings for Drolls,* 1968; *Early British Drawings in the Huntington Collection, 1600-1750,* 1969.

Drawings by John Flaxman in the Huntington Collection, 1970; *The Huntington Art Collection* (handbook), 1970; *Ten British Pictures, 1740-1840,* 1971; *Meet the Ladies: Personalities in Huntington Portraits,* 1972; *Drawings from the Turner Shakespeare,* 1973; *Drawings by Thomas Rowlandson in the Huntington Collection,* 1975; *British Silver in the Huntington Collection,* 1978; *Charles Doyle's Fairyland,* 1980; *British Landscape Drawings and Watercolors, 1750-1850,* 1981. Also author of art history papers on English painting and catalogs of art exhibitions.

WORK IN PROGRESS: British Drawings of the Late Eighteenth Century.

* * *

WARNOCK, Mary (Wilson) 1924-

PERSONAL: Born April 14, 1924, in Winchester, England; daughter of Archibald Edward (a teacher) and Ethel (Schuster) Wilson; married Geoffrey James Warnock (a fellow of Magdalen College, Oxford University), July 2, 1949; children: Kitty, Felix Geoffrey, James Marcus Alexander, Stephana, Grizel Maria. *Education:* Lady Margaret Hall, Oxford, B.A., 1948, B.Phil., 1949. *Politics:* Conservative Party. *Office:* St. Hugh's College, Oxford University, Oxford, England.

CAREER: Oxford University, St. Hugh's College, Oxford, England, fellow and tutor, 1949-66; Oxford High School for Girls, Oxford, headmistress, 1966-72; Oxford University, St. Hugh's College, senior research fellow, 1972—. *Awards, honors:* Greene Moral Philosophy Prize, 1956, for unpublished work.

WRITINGS: Ethics since 1900, Oxford University Press, 1960; (editor) John Stuart Mill, *Utilitarianism,* Meridian, 1962; *The Philosophy of Jean Paul Sartre,* Hutchinson, 1965; *Existentialist Ethics,* St. Martin's, 1967; *Imagination,* Faber, 1974; *Schools of Thought,* Faber, 1976; *Education,* Basil Blackwell, 1979. Editor, *Oxford Magazine,* 1959-61.

* * *

WARREN, Betsy
See WARREN, Elizabeth Avery

* * *

WARREN, Elizabeth Avery 1916-
(Betsy Warren)

PERSONAL: Born January 27, 1916, in St. Louis, Mo.; daughter of Albert James (a coal merchant) and Ethel (Mitchell) Avery; married William Warren (news editor of *American Statesman*), March 18, 1942; children: William, Stephen, Mark, Melissa. *Education:* Miami University, Oxford, Ohio, B.S. in Art Education, 1937. *Politics:* Republican. *Religion:* Presbyterian. *Home:* 2409 Dormarion St., Austin, Tex. 78703.

CAREER: Teacher of organ and piano and free-lance artist, mainly as illustrator for children's books. Westminster Presbyterian Church, Austin, Tex., organist, 1951—. *Awards, honors:* Texas Institute of Letters award, 1971, for *Indians Who Lived in Texas.*

WRITINGS: I Can Read about Baby Animals, Troll, 1975; *I Can Read about Bats,* Troll, 1975; *I Can Read about Indians,* Troll, 1975; *I Can Read about Trees and Plants,* Troll, 1975.

Under name Betsy Warren; published by Steck, except as indicated: *The Donkey Sat Down,* 1955; *Make a Joyful Noise,* Augsburg, 1963; (illustrator) Dorothy E. Prince, *Speedy Gets Around,* 1965; (illustrator) Joan Potter Elwart, *Daisy Tells,* 1966; (illustrator) Doris J. Chaconas, *A Hat for Lilly,* 1967; (illustrator) David P. Butts, *Watermelon,* 1968; (illustrator) Elwart, *Right Foot, Wrong Foot,* 1968; *Papacito and His Family,* 1969; *Indians Who Lived in Texas,* 1970; *The Queen Cat,* 1972; (illustrator) Eleanor Eisenberg, *The Pretty House That Found Happiness,* revised edition, 1974; *Let's Remember When Texas Belonged to Spain,* Hendrick-Long, 1982.†

* * *

WARRICK, Patricia Scott 1925-

PERSONAL: Born February 6, 1925, in La Grange, Ind.; daughter of Ross B. (a beekeeper) and DeEtte (Ulman) Scott; children: Scott McArt, David McArt, Kristin McArt. *Education:* Indiana University, B.S., 1946; Goshen College, B.A., 1964; Purdue University, M.A., 1965; University of Wisconsin—Milwaukee, Ph.D., 1977. *Home:* 3308 Scarlet Oak Lane, Appleton, Wis. 59411. *Office:* Department of English, University of Wisconsin—Fox Valley, Menasha, Wis. 54952.

CAREER: Long Island University, Brooklyn, N.Y., employed in Office of Development, 1946-48; St. Elizabeth's Hospital, Indianapolis, Ind., director of technicians-medical laboratory, 1948-52; Lawrence University, Appleton, Wis., instructor in English, 1965-66; University of Wisconsin—Fox Valley, Menasha, instructor, 1966-71, assistant professor, 1971-74, associate professor, 1974-77, professor of English, 1977—, director of technology and culture program, 1975-80. *Member:* Modern Language Association of America, National Council of Teachers of English, World Future Society, Science Fiction Research Association.

WRITINGS: (Editor with Carol Mason and Martin Greenberg) *Anthropology through Science Fiction,* St. Martin's, 1974; (editor with Greenberg and Joseph Olander) *American Government through Science Fiction,* Rand McNally, 1974; (editor with Greenberg and Harvey Katz) *Introductory Psychology through Science Fiction,* Rand McNally, 1974; (editor with Greenberg) *Political Science Fiction,* Prentice-Hall, 1974; (editor with Greenberg, Olander, and John Milstead) *Sociology through Science Fiction,* St. Martin's, 1974; (editor with Greenberg and Milstead) *Social Problems through Science Fiction,* St. Martin's, 1974; (editor with Greenberg and Olander) *School and Society through Science Fiction,* Rand McNally, 1974; (editor with Greenberg) *The New Awareness,* Dell, 1975; (contributor) Thomas Clareson, editor, *Many Futures, Many Worlds: Theme and Form in Science Fiction,* Kent State University Press, 1977; *Science Fiction: Contemporary Mythology,* Harper, 1978; *The Cybernetic Imagination in Science Fiction,* MIT Press, 1980; (editor with Issac Asimov) *Machines That Think: Robots and Computers in Science Fiction,* Holt, 1983. Also contributor to *Teaching the Future,* edited by Jack Williamson. Contributor to periodicals, including *Science Fiction Studies, Extrapolation,* and *Critique.*

WORK IN PROGRESS: A critical study of the fiction of Philip K. Dick; a novel about contemporary women.

SIDELIGHTS: Patricia Scott Warrick writes: "We literary scholars are a strange breed with eyes in the back of our heads. We are always peering with fascination into the past. No century intrigues us as much as the sixteenth century, when our English ancestors began a tempestuous crossing from the medieval into the modern world. Running a close second is the seventeenth century, when Newton created the mechanistic paradigm of classical physics that would replace medieval cosmology, although Milton chose to ignore Newton's model when he wrote *Paradise Lost.*

"Then along came the eighteenth century, the age that gave us the steam engine and the industrial world. Change. Change. Change. The patterns all seem so clear to us when we look back.

"But another tempestuous crossing is under way right now, moving us into a world so new we critics have not even named it yet—except to occasionally call it postmodern. Mostly we ignore it. Science calls it the Information Age. The paradigm of classical physics is being replaced by the model of quantum mechanics and relativity physics. Physicists now understand that when we move to the macro world of galaxies or the micro world of particles, cause/effect logic is meaningless. It just doesn't apply. Those worlds turn out to be very, very strange. The logic of our middle realm, where our senses perceive the material world, provides no useful explanations in the universe described by quantum physics.

"Neither is mainstream realistic fiction very useful in comprehending the universe according to the model of twentieth-century physics. The literature born of these new world views is contemporary science fiction. As Doris Lessing noted several years ago when she stopped writing mainstream novels and turned to science fiction, it is the only significant literary form today.

"I read science fiction and I write criticism about it because I think it is important. Science fiction breaks down the fossilized structures in our minds and asks us to look afresh at our mysterious universe which is eternally and restlessly transforming itself. Science fiction creates the ship of the imagination that carries us as we cross over into a new cultural paradigm. Our journey is quite as dramatic as that of the Renaissance, and far more significant to us because it is happening right now. Undoubtedly if Shakespeare were alive today, he would be writing science fiction. That's where the action is.

"Science fiction points the way into the future and I find it more interesting to look ahead than to look back. The road into the future is less crowded and the horizons are more tempting. Traveling this new road, I can always count on running into something I didn't know before. That keeps life interesting."

AVOCATIONAL INTERESTS: "Prowling through the Wisconsin woods on horseback."

BIOGRAPHICAL/CRITICAL SOURCES: Times Literary Supplement, November 7, 1980.

* * *

WASSER, Henry H. 1919-

PERSONAL: Born April 13, 1919, in Pittsburgh, Pa.; son of Nathan (a merchant) and Mollie (Mendelson) Wasser; married Solidelle Fortier, August 20, 1942; children: Frederick Anthony, Felicity Louise. *Education:* Ohio State University, B.A. (cum laude) and M.A., 1940; Columbia University, Ph.D., 1951. *Home:* 5517 Fieldston Rd., New York, N.Y. 10471. *Office:* Department of English, College of Staten Island of the City University of New York, 130 Stuyvesant Pl., Staten Island, N.Y. 10301.

CAREER: Instructor at University of Akron, Akron, Ohio, 1943-44, and New York University, New York City, 1945-46; City College of the City University of New York, New York City, instructor, 1946-53, assistant professor, 1953-61, associate professor of English, 1961-66; Richmond College (now College of Staten Island) of the City University of New York, Staten Island, N.Y., professor of English and dean of faculty, 1966-73; California State University, Sacramento, professor of English and vice-president for academic affairs, 1973-74; City University of New York, professor of English at College of Staten Island, 1974—, director of Center for European Studies at Graduate School and University Center, New York City, 1979—. Fulbright professor of American literature, University of Salonika, 1955-56; lecturer at universities in England, Germany, Norway, Poland, Sweden, Yugoslavia, and Italy, 1961-64, Norway, 1972, Sweden, 1979, and Germany, 1980; University of Oslo, Fulbright professor of American literature, 1962-64, and director of American Institute, 1963-64; visiting professor at University of Sussex, 1972. Columbia University, seminar associate in American civilization, 1961—, seminar associate in higher education, 1969—; conductor of seminars on American literature at University of Urbino, University of Ljubljana, and University of Warsaw, 1964, and for teachers in Sweden and Norway. Member of advisory board,

General Electric "College Bowl" (television quiz show), 1960-61; City University of New York, secretary and member of board of directors of Scandinavian Seminar, 1979—, chairman of faculty senate and member of board of trustees, 1981—.

MEMBER: International Association of University Professors of English, Modern Language Association of America, American Studies Association (member of executive council, 1968-74), Melville Society of America (historian, 1969-74), Association of Upper Level Colleges and Universities (second vice-president, 1971-72), English Graduate Union (Columbia University), English Round Table (New York University), Phi Beta Kappa. *Awards, honors:* American Scandinavian Foundation award, 1969 and 1971; German Academy Exchange Service award, 1973 and 1980; Swedish Information Service award, 1979.

WRITINGS: *The Scientific Thought of Henry Adams* [Salonika, Greece], 1956; (contributor) *American Studies in Transition,* University of Pennsylvania Press, 1964; (editor with Sigmund Skard and contributor) *Americana Norvegica: Norwegian Contributions to American Studies,* University of Pennsylvania Press, 1966; (contributor) *U.S.A. in Focus,* Scandinavian University Press (Oslo), 1966; (editor with J. Fomerand and others) *Higher Education in Western Europe and North America,* Council for European Studies, Columbia University, 1979; (editor) *Economics of Higher Education: A Comparative Perspective,* Council for European Studies, Columbia University, 1980; (editor) *American Literature and Language: An Annotated Bibliography,* Council for European Studies, Columbia University, 1981. Columnist, *Times Higher Education Supplement* (London), 1973—. Contributor to *Encyclopedia Americana* and *Encyclopedia Americana Annual,* and to professional journals.

* * *

WATERMAN, John Thomas 1918-

PERSONAL: Born August 1, 1918, in Council Bluffs, Iowa; son of Charles Murray and Edith Stowe (Clark) Waterman; married Mary Catherine Adams, October 10, 1942; children: John Robert, Teresa Kathleen. *Education:* Concordia Theological Seminary, St. Louis, Mo., B.A., 1940; Washington University, St. Louis, Mo., M.A., 1945; graduate study at Yale University, 1947-48; University of California, Ph.D., 1949. *Home:* 1830 Eucalyptus Hill Rd., Santa Barbara, Calif. 93108. *Office:* Department of Germanic and Slavic Languages, University of California, Santa Barbara, Calif. 93106.

CAREER: University of Southern California, Los Angeles, 1948-68, became professor of linguistics and German, chairman of department of German, 1955-68, chairman of department of linguistics, 1960; University of California, Santa Barbara, professor of German and chairman of department of Germanic and Slavic Languages, 1968—. Visiting professor of linguistics, University of British Columbia, 1967. Prepared and conducted sixteen-week television program, "Language and You," for Columbia Broadcasting System (CBS-TV), 1961. Language consultant to Los Angeles City School System, 1955—, and Ventura County School System, 1958—; linguistics consultant to Columbia Broadcasting System, 1963—. *Military service:* U.S. Army Air Forces, 1940-43. *Member:* Linguistic Society of America, Modern Language Association of America, Philological Association of the Pacific Coast, Linguistic Circle of New York, Order of St. Lazarus of Jerusalem, Delta Phi Alpha. *Awards, honors:* American Council of Learned Societies fellow, 1947-48; Ford Foundation fellow, 1954-55; University of Southern California award for research and scholarship, 1967.

WRITINGS: *Perspectives in Linguistics,* University of Chicago Press, 1963, 2nd edition, 1970; *A History of the German Language, with Special Reference to the Cultural and Social Forces That Shaped the Standard Literary Language,* University of Washington Press, 1966, revised edition, 1976; *Leibniz and Ludolf on Things Linguistic: Excerpts from Their Correspondence, 1688-1703,* University of California Press, 1978.†

* * *

WATSON, Jane Werner 1915-
(Elsa Jane Werner, Jane Werner; pseudonyms: A. N. Bedford, Annie North Bedford, Monica Hill, W. K. Jasner, Elsa Ruth Nast)

PERSONAL: Born July 11, 1915, in Fond du Lac, Wis.; daughter of Henry Charles (a physician) and Elsa (Nast) Werner; married Ernest Charles Watson (a professor), October 6, 1954 (died December 5, 1970). *Education:* University of Wisconsin, B.A., 1936. *Home:* 166 Eucalyptus Hill Circle, Santa Barbara, Calif. 93108.

CAREER: Whitman Publishing Co., Racine, Wis., editorial assistant, 1938-42; Artists and Writers Guild, New York, N.Y., editor and staff writer, 1942-54; part-time instructor in creative writing and cultural geography, Continuing Education Division, Santa Barbara Community College, 1966—. Trustee, Santa Barbara Museum of Art; member of board of directors, Santa Barbara Friends of the Library. *Member:* Authors Guild, Authors League of America. *Awards, honors:* Junior book award, Boys' Clubs of America, 1954, for *The Golden Geography: A Child's Introduction to the World;* named Woman of the Year in Literature by *Los Angeles Times,* 1958; Best Book for Neo-Literates in Hindi Award, Government of India, 1964, for *Aab Hom Azad Hung;* L.H.D., University of Wisconsin, 1975; Outstanding Science Books for Children award, National Science Teachers Association and Children's Book Council, 1975, for *Whales,* and 1981, for *Deserts of the World.*

WRITINGS: *The Tall Book of Make-believe,* Harper, 1950, reprinted, 1980; (under name Elsa Jane Werner) *The Golden Geography: A Child's Introduction to the World,* Simon & Schuster, 1952, revised edition, Golden Press, 1964; (under name Elsa Jane Werner, with Charles Hartman) *A Catholic Child's Bible,* Volume I: *Stories from the Old Testament,* Volume II: *The New Testament,* Simon & Schuster, 1958, published in a single volume as *The Holy Bible,* Guild Press, 1960; *The Everyday Atom,* Peterson, 1959; *Man in Flight,* L. W. Singer, 1959; *The Seaver Story,* Pomona College, 1960; *Aab Hom Azad Hung* (title means "Now We Are Free"), [India], 1964; *Words to Know and Learn: My First Dictionary in Colour,* Hamlyn, 1969.

Living Together in Tomorrow's World: A Challenging Preview of Future Developments in Community Living, Transportation, and Communication, Abelard, 1976; *Conservation of Energy,* F. Watts, 1978; *Alternate Energy Sources,* F. Watts, 1979; *The Case of the Semi-Human Beans,* Coward, 1979; *The First Americans: Tribes of North America,* Pantheon, 1980; *Deserts of the World: Future Threat or Promise?,* Philomel, 1981; *The Case of the Vanishing Space Ship,* Coward, 1982. Also author of ten beginning readers on Indian subjects, Rajkamal Prakashan (Delhi).

Published by Simon & Schuster: (Editor) *The Golden Book of Poetry,* 1947; *Good Morning and Good Night,* 1948; *Mr. Noah and His Family,* 1948; *Christopher Bunny, and Other Animal Stories,* 1949; *The Fuzzy Duckling,* 1949; *The Golden Book of Words: How They Look and What They Tell,* 1949, published as *The Golden Picture Book of Words: How They Look and What They Tell*, 1954.

Chatterly Squirrel, and Other Animal Stories, 1950; *The Marvelous Merry-go-round*, 1950; *Pets for Peter*, 1950; *Albert's Zoo*, 1951; *The Golden Book of Trains*, 1953; *The Little Golden Christmas Manger*, 1953; *The Golden History of the World*, 1955; *Heroes of the Bible*, 1955; *Houses*, 1955; *Our World: A Beginner's Introduction to Geography*, 1955; *Smokey, the Bear*, 1955; *The True Story of Smokey the Bear*, 1955; (adaptor) *The Iliad and the Odyssey: The Heroic Story of the Trojan War and the Fabulous Adventures of Odysseus*, 1956; *My Little Golden Book about God*, 1956; *How to Tell Time*, 1957; *My First Book about God*, 1957; *Walt Disney's Sleeping Beauty* (based on the film "Sleeping Beauty"), 1957; *Wonders of Nature*, 1957, published as *Wonders of Nature: A Child's First Book about Our Wonderful World*, 1958; *A Catholic Child's Book about God*, 1958; *A Giant Little Golden Book about Plants and Animals*, 1958; *A Giant Little Golden Book of Birds*, 1958; *Plants and Animals*, 1958; *The World of Science: Scientists at Work Today in Many Challenging Fields*, 1958.

Published by Golden Press: (Adaptor) Lincoln Barnett, *The World We Live In*, 1956; *Birds*, 1958; *This World of Ours*, 1959; *Walt Disney's People and Places*, 1959; (adaptor) *Walt Disney's True-Life Adventures: Nature's Half-acre, Bear Country, Seal Island*, 1959.

The Giant Golden Book of Dinosaurs and Other Prehistoric Reptiles, 1960; *The Lion's Paw: A Tale of African Animals*, 1960; *The Sciences of Mankind: Social Scientists at Work Today in Many Challenging Fields*, 1960; (with Kenneth Stafford Norris) *The Whale Hunt*, 1960; *Animal Dictionary*, 1960; (editor) Dorothy Agnes Bennett, *The New Golden Encyclopedia*, revised edition, 1963; *Walt Disney's Mary Poppins*, 1964; *My First Golden Learning Library*, 1965; (with Norris) *The Happy Little Whale*, 1968; *My First Golden Encyclopedia*, 1969.

(With Robert E. Switzer and J. Cotter Hirschberg) *Sometimes I'm Afraid*, 1971; (with Switzer and Hirschberg) *Sometimes I Get Angry*, 1971; (with Switzer and Hirschberg) *My Friend the Babysitter*, 1971; (with Switzer and Hirschberg) *Look at Me Now!*, 1971; (with Switzer and Hirschberg) *My Body: How It Works*, 1972; (with Switzer and Hirschberg) *My Friend the Dentist*, 1972; (with Switzer and Hirschberg) *My Friend the Doctor*, 1972; (with Switzer and Hirschberg) *Sometimes I'm Jealous*, 1972; *Our World Tomorrow*, 1973; *Toward a Better Environment for Our World Tomorrow*, 1973; *Whales: Friendly Dolphins and Mighty Giants of the Sea*, 1975; *The Golden Book of the Mysterious*, 1976; *Disney's Numbers Are Fun*, 1977.

Published by Garrard: *India: Old Land, New Nation*, 1966; *Iran: Crossroads of Caravans*, 1966; *Ethiopia: Mountain Kingdom*, 1966; *Thailand: Rice Bowl of Asia*, 1966; *Nigeria: Republic of a Hundred Kings*, 1967; *Peru: Land Astride the Andes*, 1967; *Egypt: Child of the Nile*, 1967; *Greece: Land of Golden Light*, 1967; (with C. L. Grant) *Mexico: Land of the Plumed Serpent*, 1968; *Canada: Giant Nation of the North*, 1968; *Japan: Islands of the Rising Sun*, 1968; (with L. C. Paloheimo) *Finland: Champion of Independence*, 1969.

The Indus: South Asia's Highway of History, 1970; *Rama of the Golden Age: An Epic of India*, 1971; *The Niger: Africa's River of Mystery*, 1971; (editor) *Castles in Spain*, 1971; *The Volga: Russia's River of Five Seas*, 1972; *The Mysterious Gold and Purple Box*, 1972; *Dance to a Happy Song*, 1973; *The Soviet Union: Land of Many Peoples*, 1973; *India Celebrates!*, 1974; *A Parade of Soviet Holidays*, 1974; *Tanya and the Geese*, 1974; *The People's Republic of China: Red Star of the East*, 1976, revised edition, in press.

Under name Jane Werner; published by Simon & Schuster, except as indicated: *Noah's Ark*, Grosset, 1943; *A Child's Book of Bible Stories: From the Garden of Eden to the Promised Land*, Random House, 1944; (editor) *Wings of the Morning: A Child's Own Treasury of Bible Sayings*, Grosset, 1946; *The Golden Bible: From the King James Version of the Old Testament*, 1947; *The Golden Book of Poetry*, 1947, reprinted, Golden Press, 1964; *Joseph and His Brethren*, 1947; *The Little Golden Book of Hymns*, 1947; *The Golden Book of Nursery Tales*, 1948, published as *Nursery Tales*, Golden Press, 1963; *The Golden Mother Goose*, 1948, published as *The Giant Golden Mother Goose*, Golden Press, 1963.

Mickey Mouse's Picnic, 1950; (adaptor) *Walt Disney's Cinderella*, 1950; *Walt Disney's Cinderella's Friends*, 1950; *Walt Disney's Donald Duck's Toy Train*, 1950; *Animal Friends*, 1951; *The Giant Golden Book of Elves and Fairies with Assorted Pixies, Mermaids, Brownies, Witches, and Leprechauns*, 1951; *Mad Hatter's Tea Party*, 1951; *Walt Disney's Alice in Wonderland Finds the Garden of Live Flowers*, 1951; *Walt Disney's Alice in Wonderland Meets the White Rabbit*, 1951; *Walt Disney's Grandpa Bunny*, 1951; *The Christmas Story*, 1952; (adaptor) *Walt Disney's Snow White and the Seven Dwarfs*, 1952; *Bible Stories of Boys and Girls*, 1953; (editor) *The Golden Bible for Children: The New Testament*, 1953; *Uncle Mistletoe*, 1953; *Walt Disney's Living Desert*, 1954; *Walt Disney's Vanishing Prairie*, 1955.

Under pseudonym A. N. Bedford: *Roy Rogers and the New Cowboy*, Simon & Schuster, 1953.

Under pseudonym Annie North Bedford; published by Simon & Schuster, except as indicated: *The Jolly Barnyard*, 1950, reprinted, Golden Press, 1974; *Susie's New Stove*, 1950; *Walt Disney's Donald Duck's Adventure*, 1950; *Bugs Bunny and the Indians*, 1951; *Bugs Bunny's Book*, 1951; (adaptor) *Frosty the Snow Man*, 1951; *Bugs Bunny Gets a Job*, 1952; *Walt Disney's Noah's Ark*, 1952; *Walt Disney's Peter Pan and the Indians*, 1952; *Walt Disney's Peter Pan and Wendy*, 1952; *Walt Disney's Pluto Pup Goes to Sea*, 1952; *Walt Disney's Seven Dwarfs Find a House*, 1952; *Walt Disney's "The Ugly Duckling,"* 1952; *Donald Duck and the Witch*, 1953; *Walt Disney's Mickey Mouse Birthday Book*, 1953; *Walt Disney's Mickey Mouse Goes Christmas Shopping*, 1953; (adaptor) *Walt Disney's Story Book of Peter Pan*, 1953; *Walt Disney's Chip 'n' Dale at the Zoo*, 1954.

Walt Disney's Disneyland on the Air, 1955; *Walt Disney's Dumbo*, 1955; *Walt Disney's Little Man of Disneyland*, 1955; *Walt Disney's Robin Hood*, 1955; *Walt Disney's Donald Duck and the Mouseketeers*, 1956; *Walt Disney's Donald Duck: Prize Driver*, 1956; *Walt Disney's Goofy: Movie Star*, 1956; *Walt Disney's Jiminy Cricket: Fire Fighter*, 1956; *Walt Disney's Mickey Mouse and the Missing Mouseketeers*, 1956, reprinted, Golden Press, 1978; *Walt Disney's Mickey Mouse Flies the Christmas Mail*, 1956; (adaptor) *Walt Disney's Perri and Her Friends* (based on *Perri*, by Felix Salten), 1956.

Walt Disney's Donald Duck Treasury, Golden Press, 1960; *Walt Disney Presents "The Jungle Book"* (based on the Mowgli stories by Rudyard Kipling), Golden Press, 1967; *Walt Disney Presents Legends of America*, Golden Press, 1969.

Under pseudonym Monica Hill; published by Simon & Schuster: *Dale Evans and the Lost Gold Mine*, 1954; *Rin Tin Tin and Rusty*, 1955; *Gene Autry and Champion*, 1956; *Lassie Shows the Way*, 1956; *Rin Tin Tin and the Lost Indian*, 1956; *The Life and Legend of Wyatt Earp*, 1958.

Under pseudonym W. K. Jasner: *Which Is the Witch?*, Pantheon, 1979; *Witch's Shop*, Xerox Education Publications, 1979.

Under pseudonym Elsa Ruth Nast: *A Woods Story*, Harper, 1945; *A Farm Story*, Harper, 1946; (compiler) *Little Steps: Children's Poems of Thanks*, Grosset, 1947; *Our Puppy*, Simon & Schuster, 1948; *The Magic Wish, and Other Johnny and Jane Stories*, Simon & Schuster, 1949; *How to Have a Happy Birthday: A Party Cut-out Book*, Simon & Schuster, 1952; *Tex and His Toys*, Simon & Schuster, 1952; *Fun with Decals*, Simon & Schuster, 1953.

SIDELIGHTS: Jane Werner Watson lived in India for several years and has traveled extensively in the Middle East, Africa, Asia, South America, and Europe. *Avocational interests:* Archaeology, ancient history, collecting Indian miniature paintings, photography.

* * *

WATSON, Lyall 1939-

PERSONAL: Born April 12, 1939, in Johannesburg, South Africa; son of Douglas (an architect) and Mary (Morkel) Watson. *Education:* University of Witwatersrand, B.S., 1958; University of Natal, M.S., 1959; University of London, Ph.D., 1963. *Politics:* "Absolutely none." *Religion:* "Animist." *Agent:* Murray Pollinger, 4 Garrick St., London WC2 9BH, England. *Office:* BCM-Biologic of London, London WC1, England.

CAREER: Zoological Garden of Johannesburg, Johannesburg, South Africa, director, 1964-65; British Broadcasting Corp., London, England, producer of documentary films, 1966-67; expedition leader and researcher in Antarctica, in Amazon River area, in Seychelles, and in Indonesia, 1968-72; BCM-Biologic of London (consultants), London, founder and director, 1967—.

WRITINGS: *The Omnivorous Ape*, Coward, 1971; *Supernature*, Doubleday, 1973; *The Romeo Error*, Doubleday, 1974; *Gifts of Unknown Things*, Simon & Schuster, 1977; *Lifetide: The Biology of the Unconscious*, Simon & Schuster, 1978; *Whales of the World*, Dutton, 1981; *Lightning Bird: The Story of One Man's Journey into Africa* (biography), Dutton, 1982. Contributor to Reader's Digest Services' "Living World of Animals" series, 1970. Contributor to professional journals.

WORK IN PROGRESS: Research on the building of a bridge between scientific investigation and mystic revelation; a novel; a screenplay.

SIDELIGHTS: "Since 1967 I have travelled constantly," writes biologist Lyall Watson, "looking and listening, collecting bits and pieces of apparently useless and unconnected information, stopping every two years to put the fragments together into some sort of meaningful pattern. [I] never plan ahead [but] simply follow whichever strange god calls the loudest. Now [I am] totally unemployable but very happy."

Gifts of Unknown Things is an account of Watson's brief visit to Nus Tarian, a small Indonesian island, and the seemingly supernatural occurrences he witnessed there. Many of the paranormal phenomena in the book center on a young girl called Tia, and several of the book's reviewers find the events incredible. John Naughton, for example, writes in the *New Statesman* that Watson's "chronicle of [Tia's] more spectacular exploits stretches the reader's credulity to breaking point and beyond." Christopher Lehmann-Haupt of the *New York Times* elaborates: "I don't believe that Tia, the young orphan girl of the island, learned to heal burns by touching them with her hand, to cure schizophrenia by drawing out bad chemicals, to raise a man from the dead, and, finally, when the Muslim natives begin to find Tia's powers too disturbing to their orthodoxy, to transform herself into a porpoise. . . . Now it may well be, as Mr. Watson argues, that my Western rationalism is woefully limited—that it fails to perceive what children and poets and Eastern mystics and with-it physicists see with the greatest of ease, which is that 'There are levels of reality far too mysterious for totally objective common sense. There are things that cannot be known by exercise only of the scientific method.' Fair enough. But just because Newton has turned out to be wrong doesn't make *all* things possible. . . . Yet this is how Mr. Watson reasons."

In *Lifetide: The Biology of the Unconscious*, Watson attempts to construct a unified model of life and the universe that accounts for phenomena currently unexplained by modern science. Using a plethora of examples from biology—his own area of expertise—as well as such disciplines as physics, anthropology, medicine, psychology, and paleontology, Watson argues that evolution and everything else in the cosmos is deliberately directed by a kind of collective unconscious of all living things (including biological components). He calls this "contingent system" the Lifetide and describes it as "the whole panoply of hidden forces that shape life in all its miraculous guises, . . . the eddies and vortices of nature that flow together to form the living stream." Reviewing the book in the *Washington Post Book World*, Dan Sperling declares: "Watson builds an admirable case in favor of the existence of such a contingent system, and believes that the eventual discovery of its parameters and properties will reveal it to be the source of much that we now call the paranormal, . . . [though] even this, he feels, will not solve the underlying mysteries of the Lifetide." Sperling also points out that Watson's description of this system contains "language so rich and lively that at times the book seems as though it were written by a poet rather than a scientist."

BIOGRAPHICAL/CRITICAL SOURCES: *New Statesman*, July 2, 1976; *New York Times*, April 13, 1977; Lyall Watson, *Lifetide: The Biology of the Unconscious*, Simon & Schuster, 1978; *New York Times Book Review*, June 3, 1979; *Washington Post Book World*, July 15, 1979, May 23, 1982; *Times Literary Supplement*, August 20, 1982.

* * *

WATTERS, (Walter) Pat(terson) 1927-

PERSONAL: Born February 28, 1927, in Spartanburg, S.C.; son of Walter Patterson (an army officer) and Mary (Bookout) Watters; married Cecile Rhinehart, June 6, 1952 (divorced, 1969); married Glenda Herbert Bartley, March 10, 1971; children: (first marriage) Patrick John, Ellen Leslie. *Education:* Emory University, B.A., 1951; University of Iowa, M.A., 1953. *Home:* 532 St. Charles Ave. N.E., Atlanta, Ga. 30308.

CAREER: *Atlanta Journal*, Atlanta, Ga., reporter, 1952-59, city editor, 1959-61, columnist, 1961-63; Southern Regional Council (human relations organization), Atlanta, director of information, 1963-75; free-lance writer, 1975—.

WRITINGS: (With Reese Cleghorn) *Climbing Jacob's Ladder: The Arrival of Negroes in Southern Politics*, Harcourt, 1967; (contributor) Theodore Solotaroff, editor, *New American Review #5*, New American Library, 1969; *The South and the Nation*, Pantheon, 1970; *Down to Now: Reflections on the Southern Civil Rights Movement*, Pantheon, 1971; (editor with Stephen Gillers) *Investigating the FBI*, Doubleday, 1973; *The Angry Middle-Aged Man*, Grossman, 1976; *Coca-Cola: An Illustrated History*, Doubleday, 1978; *Fifty Years of Pleasure: The Illustrated History of Publix Super Markets, Inc.*, Publix, 1980. Contributor to *New South, New York Times Magazine, Atlanta, Reporter, Dissent, New Republic,* and *Nation*.

SIDELIGHTS: Pat Watters told *CA* that he is "rather deeply committed to writing about the South, its people and problems, out of various motivations, including the belief that most of the crucial concerns of the world today are in sharp psychological focus here."

* * *

WEATHERS, Winston 1926-
(Tobias Palmer)

PERSONAL: Born December 25, 1926, in Pawhuska, Okla.; son of Russell O. (a building contractor) and Edith (Casey) Weathers. *Education:* University of Oklahoma, B.A., 1950, M.A., 1951, Ph.D., 1964; Middlebury College, Bread Load School of English, graduate study, summer, 1952. *Home:* 100 Center Plaza, Tulsa, Okla. 74119. *Office:* Department of English, University of Tulsa, Tulsa, Okla. 74104.

CAREER: University of Tulsa, Tulsa, Okla., lecturer, 1957-59, instructor, 1959-62, assistant professor, 1962-66, associate professor, 1966-69, professor of English, 1969—. *Member:* Phi Beta Kappa.

WRITINGS: *On the Air,* Northwestern Press, 1945; *Mysteries for Radio,* Eldridge Entertainment House, 1946; *Adventures in Radio,* Northwestern Press, 1947; *The Big Broadcast,* Northwestern Press, 1948; (with Otis Winchester) *The Strategy of Style,* McGraw, 1967, 2nd edition published as *The New Strategy of Style,* 1978; (with Winchester) *The Prevalent Forms of Prose,* Houghton, 1968; *The Archetype and the Psyche: Essays in World Literature,* University of Tulsa Press, 1968; *Par Lagerkvist,* Eerdmans, 1968; (with Winchester) *Copy and Compose,* Prentice-Hall, 1969; *William Blake's "The Tyger": A Casebook,* C. E. Merrill, 1969.

(With Winchester) *The Attitudes of Rhetoric,* Prentice-Hall, 1970; *Indian and White: Sixteen Eclogues,* University of Nebraska Press, 1970; *The Lonesome Game,* David Lewis, 1970; (under pseudonym Tobias Palmer) *An Angel in My House,* Ave Maria Press, 1975; *An Alternative Style: Options in Composition,* Hayden, 1980; *The Broken Word: Communication Pathos in Modern Literature,* Gordon, 1981.

Published by Joseph Nichols: *Messages from the Asylum,* 1970; *The Island,* 1974; *The Creative Spirit,* 1975; *The Gifts That We Bear,* 1976; *The Chevrolet Garden,* 1978; *The Dancing Goat,* 1979; *Monday Nights at Mrs. Gasperi's,* 1979; *Persimmon Wine,* 1979; *Mezzo Cammin: Poems from the Middle of My Life,* 1981.

* * *

WEAVER, Ward
See MASON, F(rancis) van Wyck

* * *

WEBB, Pauline M(ary) 1927-

PERSONAL: Born June 28, 1927, in London, England; daughter of Leonard F. (a Methodist minister) and Daisy (Barnes) Webb. *Education:* King's College, London, B.A. (with honors), 1948; London Institute of Education, teaching diploma, 1949; Union Theological Seminary, New York, N.Y., S.T.M., 1965. *Office address:* British Broadcasting Corp. World Service, P.O. Box 76, London WC2B 4PH, England.

CAREER: Teacher and assistant mistress of grammar school in Twickenham, England, 1949-52; Methodist Missionary Society, London, England, youth officer, 1952-54, editor, 1954-64, director of lay training, 1967-73, executive secretary, 1973-79; British Broadcasting Corp. World Service, London, organizer of religious broadcasting, 1979—. Became accredited local preacher of Methodist Church, 1953. Vice-president of Methodist Conference, 1965-66; member of World Methodist Executive Committee, 1966-74. Teacher at Adult Evening Institute of Westminster College of Commerce, 1952-54; member of Anglican-Methodist Negotiating Commission, 1965-68; World Council of Churches, vice-chairman of central committee, 1968-75, moderator of Assembly Preparation committee, 1981-83.

WRITINGS: *Women of Our Company,* Cargate, 1958; *Women of Our Time,* Cargate, 1960; *Operation Healing: Stories of the Work of Medical Missions throughout the World, with Bible Links and Things to Do,* Edinburgh House Press, 1964; *All God's Children,* Oliphants, 1965; *Are We Yet Alive?: Addresses on the Mission of the Church in the Modern World,* Epworth, 1966; *Agenda for the Churches,* S.C.M. Press, 1968; (contributor) Rupert E. Davies, editor, *We Believe in God,* Allen & Unwin, 1968; *Salvation Today,* S.C.M. Press, 1974; (contributor) David Hasborn, editor, *Agenda for Prophets,* Bowerham Press, 1980; *Where Are the Women,* Epworth, 1980.

Also author of pageants "Kingdoms Ablaze," 1958, "Set My People Free," 1960, and "Bring Them to Me," 1964, film scripts "Bright Diadem" (on southern India), "The Road to Dabou," "New Life in Nigeria," and "Beauty for Ashes," and television scripts "Man on Fire," "Let Loose in the World," "A Women's Place?," and "A Death Reported."

SIDELIGHTS: Pauline Webb told *CA* her primary concerns are "the mission and unity of the Church, the ministry of the laity, race relations, world poverty, and the contribution of women in Church and community." She has traveled in Sri Lanka, India, Burma, Nigeria, Kenya, Zambia, the United States, the Caribbean, and most of western Europe.

* * *

WECHSLER, Judith Glatzer 1940-

PERSONAL: Born December 28, 1940, in Chicago, Ill.; daughter of Nahum Norbert (a historian, writer, and professor) and Anne (a teacher; maiden name, Stiebel) Glatzer; married Benson R. Snyder, 1976; children: (previous marriage) Johanna. *Education:* Brandeis University, B.A., 1962; Columbia University, M.A., 1967; University of California, Los Angeles, Ph.D., 1972. *Religion:* Jewish. *Home:* 68 Fuller St., Brookline, Mass. 02146. *Office:* Department of Liberal Arts, Rhode Island School of Design, Providence, R.I. 02903.

CAREER: Member of Alwin Nikolais Dance Co., 1957; Schocken Books, New York, N.Y., assistant editor, 1963-65; Massachusetts Institute of Technology, Cambridge, assistant professor, 1970-74, associate professor of art, 1974-77, fellow, Center for Advanced Visual Studies, 1977-79; Tufts University, Medford, Mass., associate professor of art, 1979-81; Rhode Island School of Design, Providence, associate professor of art, 1981—. Lecturer at Brown University, 1970, and Harvard University, 1981-82. *Member:* College Art Association.

WRITINGS: (Editor and author of introduction) *Cezanne in Perspective,* Prentice-Hall, 1975; (editor and author of introduction) *On Aesthetics in Science,* M.I.T. Press, 1978; *The Interpretation of Cezanne,* UMI Research Press, 1981; *A Human Comedy: Physiognomy and Caricature in Nineteenth Century Paris,* Thames & Hudson, 1982.

Author, producer, and director of film, "Pissarro: At the Heart of Impressionism," 1981. Contributor of articles to journals, including *Artforum, Art News, Aperture, Gazette des Beaux*

Arts, Studies in Visual Communication, and *Technology Review.*

WORK IN PROGRESS: A film series, "The Changing Constants of Art."

SIDELIGHTS: Judith Wechsler has directed two other films, both with Charles Eames, "Daumier, Paris, and the Spectator," 1977, and "Cezanne: The Late Work," 1978.

* * *

WEHMEYER, Lillian (Mabel) Biermann 1933-(Lillian Biermann)

PERSONAL: Born October 29, 1933, in Milwaukee, Wis.; daughter of William Alfred (an electrical engineer) and Mabel (Knippel) Biermann; married Gerald C. Edson, August 29, 1953 (divorced, 1957); married Werner F. Wehmeyer (a real estate broker), August 28, 1962; children: (first marriage) Paula Nancy. *Education:* Wisconsin Conservatory of Music, piano teacher's diploma, 1951; additional study at Alverno College, 1956-62; University of California, Berkeley, B.A. (with great distinction), 1965, M.L.S., 1969, Ph.D., 1978. *Religion:* Lutheran. *Home:* 1333 37th Ave., San Francisco, Calif. 94122. *Office address:* San Mateo City School District, P.O. Box K, San Mateo, Calif. 94402.

CAREER: Comptometer operator in Milwaukee, Wis., 1950-51; library aide at Milwaukee Public Library, 1951-54; Industrial Writers and Illustrators, Wauwatosa, Wis., typist, 1957-58; instrumental music teacher in Milwaukee public schools, 1958-59; junior high school librarian in Elm Grove, Wis., 1959-62; Lafayette School District, Lafayette, Calif., junior high school librarian, 1965-69, district librarian, 1969-73, administrative assistant for curriculum and library services, 1973-75, curriculum director, 1975-77, assistant superintendent for instruction, 1977-79; San Mateo City School District, San Mateo, Calif., assistant superintendent for instruction, 1979—. Private music teacher, 1955-59, 1963-68; church choir director, 1957-60, 1963-64; piano accompanist for Damenchor Liederkranz Women's Chorus; vocal soloist.

MEMBER: World Future Society, American Library Association, National Council of Teachers of English, Association for Supervision and Curriculum Development, California Library and Media Educators Association, California Network for Educational Futures, Association of California School Administrators, Phi Beta Kappa, Beta Phi Mu, Pi Lambda Theta, Phi Delta Kappa.

WRITINGS: (Under name Lillian Biermann) *Your Library: How to Use It,* Harper, 1962; *The School Library Volunteer,* Libraries Unlimited, 1975; *The School Librarian as Educator,* Libraries Unlimited, 1976; *Images in a Crystal Ball: World Futures in Novels for Young People,* Libraries Unlimited, 1981. Contributor to juvenile, education, and library journals.

WORK IN PROGRESS: Revising *The School Librarian as Educator;* a book for young people, *Futuristics.*

* * *

WELLEK, Rene 1903-

PERSONAL: Born August 22, 1903, in Vienna, Austria; naturalized American citizen, 1946; son of Bronislav (a lawyer) and Gabriele (von Zelewsky) Wellek; married Olga Brodska, December 22, 1932 (died September 11, 1967); married Nonna Dolodarenko, May 21, 1968; children: Alexander Ivan. *Education:* Charles University, Prague, Czechoslovakia, Ph.D., 1926; Princeton University, graduate study, 1927-28. *Religion:* Protestant. *Home:* 45 Fairgrounds Rd., Woodbridge, Conn. 06525. *Office:* Department of Comparative Literature, Yale University, New Haven, Conn. 06520.

CAREER: Smith College, Northampton, Mass., instructor, 1928-29; Princeton University, Princeton, N.J., instructor, 1929-30; Charles University, Prague, Czechoslovakia, privatdocent in English literature, 1930-35; University of London, London, England, lecturer in Czech language and literature, 1935-39; University of Iowa, Iowa City, associate professor, 1939-44, professor of English, 1944-46; Yale University, New Haven, Conn., professor of Slavic and comparative literature, 1946-52, Sterling Professor of Comparative Literature, 1952-72, professor emeritus, 1972—, chairman of Slavic Department, 1948-59, chairman of Department of Comparative Literature, 1960-72. Visiting professor at Harvard University, 1950, 1953-54, Indiana University, 1976, Princeton University, 1977, University of California, San Diego, 1979, University of Washington, 1979, State University of New York at Albany, 1980, and University of California, Riverside, 1982. Visiting summer professor at University of Minnesota, 1947, Columbia University, 1948, University of Hawaii, 1961, and University of California, Berkeley, 1963. Fellow, Huntington Library, San Marino, Calif., 1942, Kenyon School of English, 1949, and Indiana School of Letters, 1950-80; senior fellow, National Endowment for the Humanities, 1972-73.

MEMBER: International and American Comparative Literature Association (president, 1961-64), Czechoslovak Society of Arts and Sciences in America (president, 1962-66), Modern Language Association of America (former member of editorial board; former member of executive council; vice-president, 1964), Linguistic Society of America, Modern Humanities Research Association (president, 1974), American Academy of Arts and Sciences, Royal Netherlands Academy, Italian National Academy, Bavarian Academy, Connecticut Academy, P.E.N.

AWARDS, HONORS: M.A., Yale University, 1946; Guggenheim fellow, 1951-52, 1957, 1966-67; L.H.D., Lawrence College, 1958; American Council of Learned Societies award for distinguished service to humanities, 1959; Fulbright research scholar, Italy, 1959-60; D.Litt. from Harvard University, 1960, Oxford University, 1960, University of Rome, 1961, University of Maryland, 1964, Boston College, 1965, Columbia University, 1968, University of Montreal, 1970, University of Louvain, 1970, University of Munich, 1972, University of Michigan, 1972, and University of East Anglia.

WRITINGS: Immanuel Kant in England, 1793-1838, Princeton University Press, 1931, University Microfilms, 1975; (with Norman Foerster and others) *Literary Scholarship,* University of North Carolina Press, 1941; *The Rise of English Literary History,* University of North Carolina Press, 1941; (with Austin Warren) *Theory of Literature,* Harcourt, 1949, 3rd edition, Penguin, 1974; (translator with Lowry Nelson) Pavel Eisner, *Franz Kafka and Prague,* Golden Griffen Books, 1950; *A History of Modern Criticism,* Yale University Press, Volume I: *The Late Eighteenth Century,* 1955, Volume II: *The Romantic Age,* 1955, Volume III: *The Age of Transition,* 1965, Volume IV: *The Later Nineteenth Century,* 1965.

The Concept of Realism in Literary Scholarship, J. B. Wolters, 1961; *Essays on Czech Literature,* Mouton, 1963; *Concepts of Criticism,* edited by Stephen G. Nichols, Jr., Yale University Press, 1963; *Czech Literature at the Crossroads of Europe* (booklet), Toronto Chapter of the Czechoslovak Society of Arts and Sciences, 1963; *Confrontations: Studies in the Intellectual and Literary Relations between Germany, England, and the United States during the Nineteenth Century,* Princeton University Press, 1965; *The Literary Theory and Aesthetics of the Prague School,* Department of Slavic Languages and Literatures, University of Michigan, 1969; *Discriminations: Further Concepts of Criticism,* Yale University Press, 1970; *Four Critics: Croce, Valery, Lukacs, Ingarden,* Washington University Press, 1981; *The Attack on Literature, and Other Essays,* University of North Carolina Press, 1982.

Editor: (With Thomas M. Raysor and others) *The English Romantic Poets,* Modern Language Association of America, 1950; *Dostoyevsky: A Collection of Critical Essays,* Prentice-Hall, 1962; Tomas G. Masaryk, *The Meaning of Czech History,* University of North Carolina Press, 1974; (with Alvaro Ribeiro) *Evidence in Literary Scholarship: Essays in Memory of James Marshall Osborn,* Oxford University Press, 1979.

Contributor: *The Importance of Scrutiny,* Stewart, 1948; Frank Brady, John Palmer, and Martin Price, editors, *Literary Theory and Structure: Essays in Honor of William K. Wimsatt,* Yale University Press, 1973. Also contributor to *World Masterpieces,* Norton.

General editor, "English Literary Criticism of the Eighteenth Century" series, 208 volumes, and "British Philosophers and Theologians of the Seventeenth and Eighteenth Centuries" series, 38 volumes, all published by Garland Publishing. Member of editorial board, *Comparative Literature, Slavic Review,* and *Studies in English Literature.* Contributor to *Sewanee Review, Southern Review, Denver Quarterly, Yale Quarterly Review,* and other journals.

WORK IN PROGRESS: Fifth volume of *A History of Modern Criticism,* which will concentrate on English and American criticism in the early twentieth century.

SIDELIGHTS: Rene Wellek is a scholar whose theories of literary criticism have been immensely influential. Wellek, according to Christopher Ricks in the *New Statesman,* sees "'the central task of criticism [as] the definition and description of the nature of poetry and literature.'" Perhaps his most famous works are *Theory of Literature,* which A. Walton Litz describes in *The Harvard Guide to Contemporary American Writing* as a "learned and highly influential survey of the various methodologies of literary study," and *A History of Modern Criticism.*

In *Theory of Literature,* Wellek distinguishes extrinsic from intrinsic approaches to a literary work in an effort to develop a proper critical method. Extrinsic approaches, according to Wellek, are those employed by literary biographers, psychologists, sociologists, and philosophers who concern themselves primarily with the personal lives and psychological dispositions of authors, with the political, social, and intellectual influences on literary creation, or with the work's psychological effects on the reader. Wellek argues that these approaches are limited and reductive, for by inappropriately focusing on the work's causes and effects, extrinsic approaches foster a sense of determinism in literary creation and encourage relativity in interpretation. Intrinsic approaches, on the other hand, deal with the work itself as a system of meaningful signs and are therefore, Wellek says, better suited to the study of literature. He sees the proper critical method as one of describing, analyzing, and evaluating a work solely in terms of the problems it poses for itself and how well the writer solves them; biographical, historical, and psychological information is incidental. Thus, while Wellek and co-author Austin Warren acknowledge "the relative or partial quality of any one critical reading," summarizes Litz, "[they] insist that there is a substantial element common to all readings, and claim that our best access to this common center is through close study of the work's formal structure."

When *Theory of Literature* appeared in 1949, according to Litz, it helped institutionalize the developing New Criticism of such analytical critics as William K. Wimsatt, Jr. and Monroe C. Beardsley, who called for the recognition of the literary work of art as an autonomous object, one completely independent of its maker. But Wellek, himself, was not a member of the school. Though sharing the New Critics' belief that the study of literature should focus on the work itself, Wellek rejected their more formalistic tendencies and pointed out that literary study cannot be reduced to stylistics; it must go beyond language to the world of the poet.

Theory of Literature has, at times, drawn criticism from psychoanalytic and other subjectivist critics who maintain that the reader "creates" to some degree the meaning of a literary work, but for the most part, Litz states, the book has had "a profound impact on a whole generation of teachers and students." Praising the book, Harriet Zinnes writes in *Poetry* that "*Theory of Literature* is a brilliant *Poetics* of the twentieth century. It details the peculiar 'mode of existence' of a work of art as it has been understood by working critics." She concludes that, through the text, "there emerge new answers to age-old critical questions." G. F. Whicher of the *New York Herald Tribune Book Review* sees the book's value in how "it puts in order the often confused elements of literary study. Here in one system are combined literary theory . . . , evaluations of literature . . . , techniques of research . . . , and the dynamics of literature." In similar terms, D. A. Stauffer states in the *New York Times* that *Theory of Literature* is "the most ordered, ranging, and purposeful attempt that has been made in some time toward keeping the study of literature at once intelligent and liberal." *Theory of Literature* has been translated into 22 languages.

Similar praise has greeted the publication of each new volume of Wellek's *A History of Modern Criticism,* a wide-ranging work covering literary criticism since 1750. Several critics voice the opinion that Wellek is uniquely qualified to write such a history. "Wellek," writes L. T. Lemon in the *Journal of Aesthetics,* "is quite probably the only scholar on either side of the Atlantic with a sufficiently detailed knowledge of modern European and American criticism to write an adequate history of the subject." David Daiches in *Saturday Review* agrees, "I can think of no one better qualified than Mr. Wellek for the task of writing the history of modern European criticism."

Critics find *A History of Modern Criticism* an essential work. R. J. Willingham of *Library Journal,* for example, calls it a work of "unquestioned value for any serious student of literature." "One may make minor reservations," Daiches states, "but there can be no doubt of the importance of this work. The combination of scholarly and critical apparatus is formidable. There is no other history of criticism like it, none which combines its scope with its sense of contemporary relevance." "Wellek's history," writes a reviewer for the *Times Literary Supplement,* "is a distinguished work of scholarship, which will become an indispensable work of reference."

Wellek, a critic for the *Virginia Quarterly Review* maintains, "is rightly considered one of the leading authorities in matters of literary theory." W. B. Fleischmann of *Modern Language Journal* simply calls Wellek "a very great scholar."

CA INTERVIEW

CA interviewed Rene Wellek by phone at his home in Woodbridge, Conn. on June 29, 1981.

CA: Did you first come to this country as a student?

WELLEK: Originally I came to Princeton University in 1927 on a fellowship, and I remained in the United States until 1930, when I returned to Czechoslovakia. In 1939 I came back to this country for good after accepting a teaching position at the University of Iowa.

CA: Was the intellectual atmosphere at Princeton at all stimulating?

WELLEK: At Princeton I had little contact with criticism because all instruction was purely in literary history. The only professor who had any aesthetic interest was Morris W. Croll. I remember reading at that time the *American Mercury* and the American New Humanists, who were very popular in the late 1920s. I called on Paul Elmer More, who lived in Princeton, and he loaned me copies of the Cambridge Platonists.

CA: What was literary criticism like when you got to the University of Iowa in 1939?

WELLEK: There was a conflict between literary history and criticism. It was quite an issue on the campus. I was surprised and somewhat shocked by the lack of theoretical awareness in this country. I had myself reacted long ago in Europe to the historical scholarship which was dominant at that time. Norman Foerster, who was director of the School of Letters at Iowa, appointed me partly because I was on the critical side. I'll never forget the time when Austin Warren and I met one of the literary historians on the campus. Mr. Warren pointed out to him that in his study of *Paradise Lost*—I think it was the last cantos—he had made some sound criticism. All of a sudden the professor get red in the face and said: "The worst insult that anybody could give me is that I am a critic. I am a historian." And that is a true story.

CA: Didn't you begin work on your famous Theory of Literature *while you were at Iowa?*

WELLEK: Yes. Mr. Warren and I agreed to write *Theory of Literature* which, in many ways, I conceived of as an attempt to bring knowledge of continental critical developments to the United States. Mr. Warren brought his interest in the New Criticism to our book. The book was delayed because of the war—I was involved in a Language and Area program in Czech for the army—and also because Warren's wife became ill and died. The book came out at the beginning of 1949, but actually it was written in the years 1945 to 1947. It has made a great impact. There exist translations in twenty-two languages. In this country it has become a basic textbook, although it wasn't designed as a textbook at all.

CA: Were you instrumental in starting the first comparative literature department at Yale?

WELLEK: Yes. When I came to Yale in 1946, I was asked to establish a department of comparative literature. Originally it was only a program, but then it developed into a department. Yale did not have the first department in that field. There existed a department at Columbia University as far back as 1903. It was abolished in 1910 and merged with the English Department where it is since only a marginal activity.

CA: In your essay on Leo Spitzer you write about his feeling of isolation, his few friends, and how he felt uprooted when he first came to the United States. Did you feel the same way when you first came here?

WELLEK: No, I think I got very quickly acclimatized when I arrived. Many of the emigres, you know, were living in a kind of enclave because they couldn't write in English, but I wrote in English from the very beginning. Of course, I had been a docent—which is something like an assistant professor—in English literature at the University of Prague, and that had been my professional interest.

CA: Do you think that the place of your birth, at the crossroads of Europe, has provided you with a detachment in studying and writing about literature?

WELLEK: I do, but I also think that America does the same because it makes you look at Europe as a totality. I feel rather strongly that one should take one's uprootedness not only as something negative but also as something positive. It allows you to look at Europe in perspective.

CA: Many people, rightly or wrongly, consider you a member of the school of New Criticism. Do you look upon yourself as a New Critic?

WELLEK: No, I think this is a misunderstanding, and I've tried to explain it when I was called a New Critic by Wayne Booth in the *Critical Inquiry*. I came to this country in 1939 with a fully formulated view about literature and a doctrine largely shaped by the Prague Linguistic Circle, of which I was a junior member. I was also very impressed by the phenomenology of Roman Ingarden. I do not think of myself as a New Critic, though I do have great sympathy with much of the New Criticism.

CA: In what ways do you differ from the New Critics?

WELLEK: I think I have a different conception of the nature of the literary work. I disapprove of their psychologism. I hold a phenomenological point of view, and I have no use at all for I. A. Richards, whose ideas clash with my own. I also don't share T. S. Eliot's view of the history of English poetry.

CA: In your 1969 article "A Map of Contemporary Criticism in Europe," you said that after traveling in Europe and talking with authorities, you came away with one overriding impression—namely, that there was an almost unbridgeable chasm dividing schools, ideologies, and individuals. Do you anticipate there will ever be a change in these divisions?

WELLEK: There are still great differences, but there are international movements which are changing this. For example, much of the psychoanalytical criticism, Marxist inquiry, and now also the whole semiotic movement and what is called French structuralism are in part international movements. These movements have broken down the differences between the Anglo-American and the continental, particularly French, tradition. Still, the differences are very marked. Probably internationalism cannot overcome linguistic and geographical barriers and the barriers of different academic organizations.

CA: Do you think our technological age is producing a less literate people than was true a generation or two ago?

WELLEK: That seems to be true in many ways. Certainly in the United States, I think television has had a bad influence on the younger generation, but I don't think it can really affect the status of criticism. I'm sure that technology has brought about less understanding of traditional knowledge than was true earlier. In Germany after the 1970 revolt there has been a repudiation of the classics. Students are no longer required to read Goethe and Schiller and many other standard writers. But of course it is not all that bad. There are academics and other critical establishments which are still in contact with the past. So it is not as dangerous as it may seem.

CA: Do you think the permissive attitude of the late 1960s and early 1970s exercised a pernicious effect on education?

WELLEK: Oh, I'm sure. Even a place like Yale, which, of course, is able to maintain some standards and be more selective in its students, gave in to certain pressures. For instance, this was especially true in foreign languages and the lack of emphasis on traditional subjects. But it was much worse in other places. Friends tell me if you teach at the City University of New York, you are no longer a teacher, you are simply a social worker.

CA: When you came to this country in the late 1930s, you must have been appalled that so few Americans knew foreign languages.

WELLEK: I think that is a real catastrophe. It is a superstition that Americans can't learn foreign languages. They can learn them just like everyone else. Not having a knowledge of foreign languages is a real handicap in international business and foreign relations.

CA: Do you keep up with the writings of the leading novelists and poets of the last twenty years?

WELLEK: Only in a haphazard fashion. I do read some of them. I have read some of the writings of my friend Robert Penn Warren; I have read Saul Bellow and some of the other current novelists. On the whole, I have little time for reading current fiction.

CA: You have devoted most of your life to the study and interpretation of literature. Have you ever seriously thought of writing fiction yourself?

WELLEK: Only in my youth. It is sometimes said that I am a "critic of critics," that I write only criticism of criticism. Actually I did write a good deal of criticism about particular works of fiction. In the Norton Anthology, *World Masterpieces,* a number of interpretations, mainly works of nineteenth-century writers, were written by me. The works reprinted and commented on vary from edition to edition: if the little essays were collected, they would make up a good number. When I was young, in Czechoslovakia, I wrote a great many reviews of English books as they came out and, off and on, I've written straightforward criticism of texts. The new book by Martin Bucco in the Twayne series about me gives a full account.

CA: Can a person learn literary criticism in the same way he might learn how to write?

WELLEK: To a certain extent. I think practice in writing book reviews could help. I suppose one can be trained in the same way as one can be trained in creative writing. It's not a substitute, of course, for talent. There must be some native ability.

CA: You have now written four volumes of your history of modern literary criticism. You have two volumes to go?

WELLEK: Yes. The fifth volume is almost ready now. It's all about English and American criticism in the first part of the twentieth century. It is still unfinished partly because I discovered that there are some gaps in the book. It will be published in the next year or so. The sixth volume, on criticism on the continent of Europe, is still far from complete.

CA: Any other books coming along?

WELLEK: I have two books forthcoming, a collection of eleven essays called *The Attack on Literature, and Other Essays.* The manuscript has been accepted by the University of North Carolina Press. And then a little volume called *Four Critics,* which comprises Croce, Valery, Ingarden, and Lukacs. This book comes from a series of lectures that I gave at the University of Washington in Seattle.

BIOGRAPHICAL/CRITICAL SOURCES—Books: F. R. Leavis, *Common Pursuit,* Chatto & Windus, 1952; Lowry Nelson, *Yearbook of Comparative and General Literature,* Volume VI, University of North Carolina Press, 1957; Peter Demetz, *Essays on Czech Literature,* Mouton, 1963; B. R. Tilghman, editor, *Language and Aesthetics,* University Press of Kansas, 1973; Louise M. Rosenblatt, *The Reader, the Text, the Poem: The Transactional Theory of the Literary Work,* Southern Illinois University Press, 1978; Daniel Hoffman, editor, *Harvard Guide to Contemporary American Writing,* Belknap Press, 1979; Martin Bucco, *Rene Wellek,* Twayne, 1981.

Periodicals: *Modern Philosophy,* August, 1932; *Journal of Philosophy,* November 10, 1932; *New York Times,* January 30, 1949, July 10, 1955; *New York Herald Tribune Book Review,* March 27, 1949; *Poetry,* February, 1950; *Saturday Review,* July 16, 1955; *Times Literary Supplement,* July 26, 1963, August 31, 1967, December 21, 1979; *Virginia Quarterly Review,* autumn, 1963; *Comparative Literature,* spring, 1965; *Modern Language Journal,* October, 1965; *Library Journal,* November 1, 1965; *Journal of Aesthetics,* winter, 1966; *New Statesman,* January 6, 1967; *Criticism,* spring, 1967; *Washington Post Book World,* August 2, 1970; *Books Abroad,* spring, 1971; *Spectator,* July 28, 1973; *Modern Language Review,* January, 1982.

—*Interview by Walter W. Ross*

*   *   *

WELS, Byron G(erald) 1924-

PERSONAL: Born April 20, 1924, in New York, N.Y.; son of Joseph and Henrietta (Schreiber) Wels; divorced; children: Joshua, Deborah, Heather. *Education:* Attended Brooklyn College of the City University of New York; also attended Cleveland Institute of Electronics and various military radio and radar schools. *Home:* 32-L Riverview Gardens, North Arlington, N.J. 07032. *Office:* Gar Schmitt & Associates, 388 Pompton Ave., Cedar Grove, N.J. 07009.

CAREER: Prior to 1963 worked as advanced research and developmental electronics technician for such firms as Potter Instruments, Amperex, and Fairchild Engine Division, and in publications departments of other firms, including Radio Engineering Laboratories, Westbury Electronics, and Eldico Electronics; *Popular Mechanics,* electronics editor based in New York City, and Chicago, Ill., 1963-66; Davis Publications, Inc., New York City, editor-in-chief of *Radio-TV Experimenter* and *Elementary Electronics* and electronics editor of sister magazine, *Science and Mechanics,* 1964-66; *Popular Electronics,* New York City, feature editor, 1966-67; Conover-Mast, Inc., New York City, began as engineering editor for *Mill & Factory,* managing editor of *Construction Equipment* 1967-69; *Data Products News,* New York City, editor-in-chief, 1969-70; writer or executive for public relations firms in New York

City, and Princeton, N.J., 1970-72; Singer Communcations Corp., Little Falls, N.J., public relations and advertising and writer of correspondence courses, 1972-75; former editor-in-chief of *Magic* magazine; currently vice-president of Gar Schmitt & Associates, Cedar Grove, N.J. Holds Federal Communications Commission second class radiotelephone license, amateur radio operator's license, and pilot certificate. *Military service:* U.S. Army Air Forces; received Air Medal. *Member:* Flying Engineers, New York Advertising Sportsmen's Club, Masons.

WRITINGS: Layman's Guide to Hi-Fi, American Electronics Co., 1959; *Getting the Most from Your Hi-Fi and Stereo System,* Editors and Engineers, 1966; *Here Is Your Hobby: Magic* (juvenile), Putnam, 1967; *Here Is Your Hobby: Amateur Radio* (juvenile), Putnam, 1968; *Transistor Circuit Guidebook,* TAB Books, 1968; *Electronics in Photography,* Sams, 1968; *Fell's Guide to Guns and How to Use Them Safely—Legally—Responsibly,* Fell, 1969.

Computer Circuits and How They Work, TAB Books, 1970; *Fire and Theft Security Systems,* TAB Books, 1971, 2nd edition, 1976; *Magic Made Easy,* Wilshire, 1971; *How to Build Clocks and Watches,* Auerbach, 1971; *Science Fair Experiments* (juvenile), Auerbach, 1971; *Simple Wall Paneling,* Doubleday, 1971; *How to Repair Musical Instrument Amplifiers,* TAB Books, 1973; *The Medicine Cabinet,* Hammond, 1978; *Personal Computers: What They Are and How to Use Them,* Prentice-Hall, 1978; *Animal Heroes: Stories of Courageous Family Pets and Animals in the Wild,* Macmillan, 1979. Also author of *The Great Illusions of Magic,* Tannens, and *The Big Book of Magic,* Waldman.

Contributor to about eighty popular, technical, and trade magazines, including *Argosy, Popular Photography, Reader's Digest, National Wildlife, American Sportsman,* and *Civil Engineering.*

WORK IN PROGRESS: A book on how to upholster furniture, for TAB Books; a book on candle making, for Putnam; a book on hot air balloons, for Drake.

SIDELIGHTS: Byron G. Wels told *CA:* "Mort Persky, of *Family Weekly,* calls me his 'man of perilous adventure,' and continually gives me assignments that his staffers won't touch. It was Mort that got me to solo in a ballon for the first time, and has had me in race cars at Daytona, and Lord knows what he'll have for me in the future. I'm a licensed pilot, and love to use my writing skills to explore new and different areas that I might never have been able to expose myself to had I to depend on my own finances.

"Writing is not a suitable career for anybody, as there are so few who are howlingly successful. I've received royalty checks for as little as 68¢, and would actively discourage any who would pursue this as a full-time career. Once, I tried freelancing on a full-time basis, was writing a book, and my daughter was approached by a nosy neighbor who asked, 'Honey, what does your daddy do?' Debbie knew I was writing a book, so she said, 'He's a book-maker!' Try to live THAT down!

"But the *cacothes scrivendi* is a strong urge, and once you start, you can't stop. I simply stumble along, doing my best, and wishing I could do better."

* * *

WERNER, Elsa Jane
See WATSON, Jane Werner

WERNER, Jane
See WATSON, Jane Werner

* * *

WERTSMAN, Vladimir 1929-

PERSONAL: Born April 6, 1929, in Secureni, Romania; came to the United States, 1967; naturalized U.S. citizen, 1972; son of Filip and Anna Wertsman. *Education:* University A.I. Cuza, diploma in legal sciences (LL.M.; summa cum laude), 1953; Columbia University, M.S.L.S., 1969. *Home:* 330 West 55th St., Apt. 3G, New York, N.Y. 10019. *Office:* New York Public Library, Donnell Library Center, Foreign Langauge Library, 20 West 53rd St., New York, N.Y. 10019.

CAREER: Lawyer with practice in criminal and civil law in Romania, 1953-67; First National City Bank, New York City, stock certificates examiner, 1967-68; Brooklyn Public Library, Brooklyn, N.Y., reference librarian in Science and Industry Division, 1969-74, assistant branch librarian at Canarsie Branch, 1974-77, assistant branch librarian at Greenpoint Branch, 1977-80, branch librarian at Leonard Branch, 1980-82; New York Public Library, Donnell Library Center, New York City, head librarian and foreign language specialist, 1982—.

MEMBER: American Library Association, National Writers Club, American Society of Writers, American Lodge of Research, Independent Press Association, Ethnic Materials Information Exchange Task Force (director of public relations), Slavic American Cultural Association (member of board of directors), Delta Tau Kappa.

WRITINGS: The Romanians in America, 1748-1974, Oceana, 1975; *The Ukrainians in America, 1608-1975,* Oceana, 1976; *The Russians in America, 1727-1970,* Oceana, 1977; *The Armenians in America,* 1618-1976, Oceana, 1978; *The Romanians in America and Canada,* Gale, 1980; (co-author) *The Ukrainians in Canada and the United States,* Gale, 1981. Contributor of more than forty articles and papers to law, library, and philately journals.

SIDELIGHTS: "American history is in essence ethnic history," Vladimir Wertsman told *CA.* "I view ethnicity as the spice of America." Wertsman is fluent in Romanian, Russian, and Ukrainian, and has working knowledge of German, French, and Spanish. *Avocational interests:* Chess, stamp-collecting, music, travel (including visits to Europe, Asia, South America, and Central America).

BIOGRAPHICAL/CRITICAL SOURCES: Ethnic American News, October, 1975; *Who's Who in Romanian America,* 1976; *American Romanian Review,* May, 1980; *Solia,* May, 1980; *Unirea,* May, 1980; *National Genealogical Inquirer,* summer, 1980; *National Genealogical Society Quarterly,* June, 1981; *Ethnic Forum,* spring, 1982.

* * *

WHEELER, Richard 1922-

PERSONAL: Born January 8, 1922, in Reading, Pa.; son of Clarence E. and Margaret (Wenrich) Wheeler. *Education:* Attended public school in Laureldale, Pa. *Politics:* Nonpartisan. *Home:* Route 1, Pine Grove, Pa. 17963 (summer); and 328 Pilgrim Rd., West Palm Beach, Fla. 33405 (winter). *Agent:* McIntosh & Otis, Inc., 475 Fifth Ave., New York, N.Y. 10017.

CAREER: Worked on a small weekly newspaper, now defunct, for several years after World War II; full-time writer, 1949—, doing light verse for magazines for about fifteen years before switching to prose. *Military service:* U.S. Marines, 1942-45; received Purple Heart for wounds received on Iwo Jima. *Awards, honors:* Christopher Award, 1973, for *Voices of 1776;* Fletcher Pratt Award, 1977, for *Voices of the Civil War.*

WRITINGS—Published by Crowell: *The Bloody Battle for Suribachi,* 1965; *In Pirate Waters,* 1969; *Voices of 1776,* 1972; *Voices of the Civil War* (Book-of-the-Month alternate selection), 1976; *We Knew Stonewall Jackson,* 1977; *We Knew William Tecumseh Sherman,* 1977; *The Siege of Vicksburg,* 1978; *Sherman's March,* 1978; *Iwo* (Military Book Club main selection), 1980. Contributor to thirty magazines of about eight hundred pieces of verse, including one hundred twenty-five in *Saturday Evening Post.*

WORK IN PROGRESS: A history of U.S. Marine Corps operations in World War II, for Harper.

SIDELIGHTS: "I began writing at age five in 1927," writes Richard Wheeler, "and still have my very first manuscript, a little tale with a sylvan setting entitled, 'A Day in the Woos (sic).' All I ever wanted to do was write, and, except for time out during the war years, I have done little else. Handicapped by a lack of brilliance, I had to tackle the job wholly as a craft. It has been extremely hard work, and I am still a plodder. My best efforts net me only a page or two a day. But I have persisted and am now working on my tenth book. All have been concerned with presenting the human side of American military history. My rewards? The convenience of working at home; the privilege of living North in summer and South in winter; a great many letters from readers who seem to have understood what I've been trying to do; and generally happy reviews, including two cherished ones in the *New Yorker.* Money? Well, it's been a living—which, considering the odds against me, I suppose is saying pretty much."

During the battle for Mount Suribachi, Wheeler's platoon lost forty-two of its original forty-six men. While recuperating in the hospital from his injuries, he wrote a long account of what actually had happened and used it for his first magazine article, "The First Flag Raising on Iwo Jima," which appeared in *American Heritage,* June, 1964, as well as for his book, *The Bloody Battle for Suribachi.* He says of his part in the battle, "I was a very scared marine surrounded by heroes."

BIOGRAPHICAL/CRITICAL SOURCES: *Saturday Review,* November 6, 1965; *New Yorker,* July 26, 1976, May 12, 1980; *Time,* August 30, 1976.

*   *   *

WHELAN, Elizabeth M(urphy) 1943-

PERSONAL: Born December 4, 1943, in New York, N.Y.; daughter of Joseph F. (an attorney) and Marion (Barrett) Murphy; married Stephen Thomas Whelan (an attorney), April 3, 1971. *Education:* Connecticut College, B.A., 1965; Yale University, M.P.H., 1967; Harvard University, M.S., 1968, Sc.D., 1971. *Home:* 165 West End Ave., 11R, New York, N.Y. 10023. *Agent:* Rhoda Weyr, William Morris Agency, 1350 Avenue of the Americas, New York, N.Y. 10019. *Office:* American Council on Science and Health, 1995 Broadway, New York, N.Y. 10023.

CAREER: New Haven Health Department, New Haven, Conn., member of staff, 1966-67; Massachusetts Department of Public Health, Boston, epidemiologist/vital statistician, 1968-71; Planned Parenthood-World Population, New York City, county study coordinator, 1971-72; American Council on Science and Health, New York City, executive director, 1975—. Moderator of nationally syndicated radio program "Healthline." Consultant to Cable News Network (CNN-TV), Child Welfare League of America, Population Council, and other organizations. *Member:* American Public Health Association, American Medical Writers Association, Population Association of America.

WRITINGS: *Sex and Sensibility: A New Look at Being a Woman,* McGraw, 1974; *A Baby?—Maybe: A Guide to Making the Most Fateful Decision of Your Life,* Bobbs-Merrill, 1975, revised edition, 1980; (with father-in-law, Stephen T. Whelan) *Making Sense out of Sex: A New Look at Being a Man,* McGraw, 1975; (with Frederick J. Stare) *Panic in the Pantry: Food Facts and Fallacies,* Atheneum, 1975; *Boy or Girl?: The Sex Selection Technique That Makes All Others Obsolete,* Bobbs-Merrill, 1977; *The Pregnancy Experience: The Psychology of Expectant Parenthood,* Norton, 1978; *Preventing Cancer,* Norton, 1978; (with Stare) *Eat OK Feel OK!: Food Facts and Your Health,* Christopher, 1978.

Contributor to periodicals, including *Social Biology, Studies in Family Planning, Journal of Marriage and the Family, Demography, Glamour, Cosmopolitan, Bride, National Review, Weight Watchers, American Baby, Reader's Digest, Reason, Vogue,* and *Harper's.* Member of editorial board, *Connecticut College Alumni News,* 1972—.

WORK IN PROGRESS: A book on nutritional needs during pregnancy; *The Nutrition Hoax,* with F. J. Stare.

*   *   *

WHITCOMB, Ian 1941-
(Mel Bubb, Buck Murphy, Stu Newton, Arthur Nouveau)

PERSONAL: Born July 10, 1941, in Woking, Surrey, England; son of Patrick (a builder's merchant) and Eileen (Burningham) Whitcomb. *Education:* Trinity College, Dublin, honors degree in modern history and political science, 1965. *Politics:* Apolitical. *Residence:* London, England; and Hollywood, Calif. *Office address:* P.O. Box 451, Altadena, Calif. 91001.

CAREER: Writer on music; singer, composer, lyricist, and producer of recordings. Producer of albums "Mae West—'Great Balls of Fire,'" Metro-Goldwyn-Mayer (MGM), 1972; "Red Hot Blue Heaven," Warner Bros., 1977; "Crooner Tunes," First American, 1977; "Treasures of Tin Pan Alley," Audiophile, 1977; "Pianomelt," Sierra Briar, 1980; "Don't Say Goodbye, Miss Ragtime," Stomp Off, 1981; and "In Hollywood," First American, 1981. Consultant to British Broadcasting Corp. television arts features.

WRITINGS: *After the Ball,* Allen Lane, 1972, Simon & Schuster, 1974; *Tin Pan Alley* (also see below), Two Continents, 1975; "Tin Pan Alley" (television script based on book of same title), produced by KCET Public Television, 1975; "Chasing Rainbows" (television script), produced by EMI Theater Projects Television, 1975; *Lotusland,* Wildwood House, 1979; *Whole Lotta Shakin' Going On,* Arrow, 1981; *The Rock Chronicles,* Doubleday-Anchor, 1981.

Singer, composer, lyricist, and producer of L.P. albums: "You Turn Me On," Tower, 1965; "Ian Whitcomb's Mod, Mod, Music Hall," Tower, 1966; "Yellow Underground," Tower, 1967; "Sock Me Some Rock," Tower, 1968; "On the Pier," EMI, 1970; "Under the Ragtime Moon," United Artists, 1972; "Hip Horray Neville Chamberlain," Argo, 1974.

Also author of script "L.A.—My Home Town," for British Broadcasting Corp. Television; composer of score for "Doo Dah Gang" show, produced in Las Vegas, 1975. Contributor to periodicals, including *Listener, Los Angeles Times, Let It Rock,* and *Radio Times.*

* * *

WHITE, Irvin L(inwood) 1932-

PERSONAL: Born March 15, 1932, in Hertford, N.C.; son of Irvin Linwood and Katherine (Winslow) White; married second wife, Mary Ruth Hamilton, May 6, 1978; children: (first marriage) two sons. *Education:* Pennsylvania State University, B.A., 1954; University of Arizona, Ph.D., 1967. *Home:* 4458 Elan Ct., Annandale, Va. 22003. *Office:* U.S. Bureau of Land Management, Washington, D.C. 20240.

CAREER: University of Arizona, Tucson, visiting assistant professor of political science, 1967-68; Purdue University, Lafayette, Ind., assistant professor of political science, 1968-70; University of Oklahoma, Norman, associate professor, 1970-74, professor of political science, 1974-80, assistant director of Science and Public Policy Program, 1970-80; U.S. Bureau of Land Management, Washington, D.C., assistant director of Energy and Mineral Resources Program, 1980—. Acting director, Office of Strategic Assessment, U.S. Environmental Protection Agency, 1978-80. *Military service:* U.S. Navy, 1954-62; became lieutenant.

MEMBER: International Technology Assessment Association, International Studies Association, American Political Science Association, American Association for the Advancement of Science, American Association of University Professors, Policies Studies Organization, Southwestern Social Sciences Association. *Awards, honors:* Research grants from National Science Foundation, 1971, 1972, from Council on Environmental Quality, 1973, and from U.S. Environmental Protection Agency, 1975.

WRITINGS: Decision-Making for Space: Law and Politics in Air, Sea, and Outer Space, Purdue University Studies, 1970; *Planning and Organizing for Research: A Guide for Beginners,* Institute of Government Research, University of Arizona, 1970; (compiler with Clifton E. Wilson and John A. Vosburgh, and contributor) *Law and Politics in Outer Space: A Bibliography,* University of Arizona Press, 1972; (contributor) Richard S. Lewis and Bernard I. Spinrod, editors, *The Energy Crisis,* Educational Foundation for Nuclear Science, 1972; (contributor) Michael Haas, editor, *International Systems: A Behavioral Approach,* Intext, 1973; (with others) *Energy under the Oceans: A Technology Assessment of Outer Continental Shelf Oil and Gas Operations,* University of Oklahoma Press, 1973; (with others) *North Sea Oil and Gas: Implications for Future U.S. Development,* University of Oklahoma Press, 1973; (contributor) Walter F. Scheffer, editor, *Energy Impacts on Public Policy and Administration,* University of Oklahoma Press, 1974.

(With others) *Energy Alternatives: A Comparative Analysis,* U.S. Government Printing Office, 1975; (contributor) Sherry Arnstein and Alexander Christakis, *Perspectives on Technology Assessment,* Science and Technology Press, 1975; (contributor) Alfred J. Van Tassel, editor, *The Environmental Price of Energy,* Heath, 1975; (with others) *Energy Policy-Making: A Selected Bibliography,* University of Oklahoma Press, 1977; (with others) *Energy from the West: Energy Resource Development Systems,* U.S. Environmental Protection Agency, 1978; (with others) *Energy from the West: Policy Analysis Report,* U.S. Environmental Protection Agency, 1978; (with others) *Energy from the West: Impact Analysis Report,* U.S. Environmental Protection Agency, 1978.

(With others) *Environmental Outlook 1980,* U.S. Environmental Protection Agency, 1980; (with others) *Energy from the West: Technology Assessment of Western Energy Resource Development,* University of Oklahoma Press, in press. Contributor to proceedings and to professional journals, including *Science, Chemical and Engineering News, Western Political Quarterly, International Studies Quarterly, Energy Policy, American Behavioral Scientist, Policy Studies Journal,* and *Environmental Professional.*

* * *

WHITEHEAD, G(eorge) Kenneth 1913-

PERSONAL: Born May 16, 1913, in Bury, Lancashire, England; son of Percy Kay (a dyer) and Dorothy Myrtle (Wike) Whitehead; married Nancy Bagot, 1965 (divorced, 1972). *Education:* Attended Uppingham School, 1927-31. *Religion:* Church of England. *Home:* Old House, Withnell Fold, Chorley, Lancashire PR6 8A2, England.

CAREER: Withnell Fold Paper Mill, Chorley, Lancashire, England, manager, 1947-68, raw material buyer, 1968-80. Former director of Liverpool Storage Co. Ltd. *Military service:* British Army, Royal Artillery, 1940-45; became major. *Member:* Conseil International de la Chasse, Fauna Preservation Society, British Deer Society, Zoological Society of London (fellow). *Awards, honors:* Prix Litteraire, Conseil International de la Chasse, 1975, for *Deer of the World.*

WRITINGS: Deer and Their Management, Country Life, 1950; *The Ancient White Cattle of Great Britain,* Faber, 1953; *The Deer-Stalking Grounds of Great Britain and Ireland,* Hollis & Carter, 1960; *Deerstalking in Scotland,* Percival Marshall & Co., 1964; *The Deer of Great Britain and Ireland,* Routledge & Kegan Paul, 1964; *Wild Goats of Great Britain and Ireland,* David & Charles, 1972; *Deer of the World,* Viking, 1972; *Hunting and Stalking Deer in Britain through the Ages,* Batsford, 1980; (editor with others) *The Game-Trophies of the World,* Paul Parey, 1981; *Hunting and Stalking Deer throughout the World,* Batsford, 1982. Contributor to *Country Life, Field, Shooting Times,* and other outdoor magazines.

SIDELIGHTS: G. Kenneth Whitehead has studied ruminants and collected specimens in most European countries, Australasia, the United States, Canada, Morocco, and West Africa for a private museum. As an amateur, he played in all of England's Association Football (soccer) team matches, 1938-39, and he formerly played tennis for the Lancashire county team.

AVOCATIONAL INTERESTS: Nature filmmaking.

* * *

WIEDER, Laurance 1946-

PERSONAL: Born June 28, 1946, in New York, N.Y.; son of Herbert Wieder (a physician) and Gloria (an office manager; maiden name, Cohen) Wieder Sinclair; married Christine Brueckner, November 1, 1969 (divorced February, 1973); married Martha Yates, 1976 (divorced, 1978); married Andrea Korotky, 1982. *Education:* Columbia University, B.A., 1968; Cornell University, M.A., 1970. *Residence:* New York, N.Y. *Office address: Camera Arts* Magazine, Number One Park Ave., New York, N.Y. 10016.

CAREER: Cornell University, Ithaca, N.Y., instructor in English, 1970; University of Colorado, Boulder, associate in English department, 1970-71; Cornell University, lecturer in English, 1971-73; free-lance writer and editor, 1973-74; Harcourt, Brace, Jovanovich, New York City, assistant to co-publisher, 1974; Winchester Press, New York City, editor, 1974-76; Lincoln Center Institute, New York City, staff artist, 1976-77; Yale University, New Haven, Conn., Sanford Professor of Poetics and Music, 1977-78; Princeton University, Princeton, N.J., Faber Lecturer in Poetics and Music, 1978; *American Craft* Magazine, New York City, associate editor, 1978-80; *Camera Arts* Magazine, New York City, associate editor, 1980—. Has given poetry readings on radio and at colleges and universities; part-time ski instructor and professional horse trainer and rider. *Awards, honors:* Ingram Merrill Foundation grant in poetry, 1974-75.

WRITINGS: The Coronet of Tours, Ithaca House, 1972; *No Harm Done,* Ardis, 1975; *Garden Intelligence,* Nobodaddy Press, 1976; (with William Wegman) *Man's Best Friend,* Abrams, 1982. Contributor to *Paris Review, Poetry, Epoch, New Yorker,* and other periodicals.

WORK IN PROGRESS: Blind Astronomy, a book of poems.

* * *

WIESEL, Elie(zer) 1928-

PERSONAL: Born September 30, 1928, in Sighet, Romania; came to United States in 1956, naturalized in 1963; son of Shlomo (a grocer) and Sarah (Feig) Wiesel; married Marion Erster Rose, 1969; children: Shlomo Elisha. *Education:* Attended Sorbonne, University of Paris, 1948-51. *Religion:* Jewish. *Address:* University Professors, Boston University, 745 Commonwealth Ave., Boston, Mass. 02215. *Agent:* Georges Borchardt, 136 East 57th St., New York, N.Y. 10022.

CAREER: Foreign correspondent at various times for *Yedioth Ahronoth,* Tel Aviv, Israel, *L'Arche,* Paris, France, and *Jewish Daily Forward,* New York City, 1949—; City College of the City University of New York, New York City, Distinguished Professor, beginning 1972; Boston University, Boston, Mass., Andrew Mellon Professor in the Humanities, 1976—. Chairman, U.S. Holocaust Memorial Council. *Member:* Authors League, Foreign Correspondents Association, U.N. Correspondents Association.

AWARDS, HONORS: Prix Rivarol, 1963; Remembrance Award, 1965, for *The Town beyond the Wall* and all other writings; William and Janice Epstein Fiction Award, Jewish Book Council, 1965, for *The Town beyond the Wall;* Jewish Heritage Award, 1966, for excellence in literature; Litt.D., Jewish Theological Seminary, 1967, Marquette University, 1975, Simmons College, 1976, St. Scholastica College, 1978, Yale University, 1981, and Hobart and William Smith Colleges, 1982; D.H.L., Hebrew Union College, 1968, Manhattanville College, 1972, Yeshiva University, 1973, Boston University, 1974, Wesleyan University, 1979, Notre Dame University, 1980, Anna Maria College, 1980, Brandeis University, 1980, and Kenyon College, 1982; Prix Medicis, 1969, for *Le Mendiant de Jerusalem;* Prix Bordin, French Academy, 1972; Eleanor Roosevelt Memorial Award, 1972; American Liberties Medallion, American Jewish Committee, 1972; Doctor of Hebrew Letters, Spertus College of Judaica, 1973; Frank and Ethel S. Cohen Award, Jewish Book Council, 1973, for *Souls on Fire;* Martin Luther King, Jr., Award, City College of the City University of New York, 1973; Doctor of Philosophy, Bar-Ilan University, 1973; Faculty Distinguished Scholar Award, 1973-74, and LL.D., 1975, both from Hofstra University; LL.D., Talmudic University, 1979; Prix Livre-International, 1980, and Prix des Bibliothecaires, 1981, both for *Le Testament d'un poete juif assassine;* Joseph Prize for Human Rights, Anti-Defamation League of B'nai B'rith; S. Y. Agnon Gold Medal; Jabotinsky Award; Shazar Award.

WRITINGS—French editions published by Editions du Seuil, except as indicated: *Un Di Velt Hot Geshvign* (in Yiddish; title means "And the World Has Remained Silent"), [Buenos Aires], 1956, abridged French translation published as *La Nuit* (also see below), foreword by Francois Mauriac, Editions de Minuit, 1958, translation by Stella Rodway published as *Night* (also see below), Hill & Wang, 1960; *L'Aube* (also see below), 1961, translation by Frances Frenaye published as *Dawn* (also see below), Hill & Wang, 1961; *Le Jour* (also see below), 1961, translation by Anne Borchardt published as *The Accident* (also see below), Hill & Wang, 1962; *La Ville de la chance,* 1962, translation by Stephen Becker published as *The Town beyond the Wall,* Atheneum, 1964, new edition, Holt, 1967; *Les Portes de la foret,* 1964, translation by Frenaye published as *The Gates of the Forest,* Holt, 1966; *Le Chant des morts,* 1966, translation published as *Legends of Our Time,* Holt, 1968; *The Jews of Silence: A Personal Report on Soviet Jewry* (originally published in Hebrew as a series of articles for newspaper *Yedioth Ahronoth*), translated and with an afterword by Neal Kozodoy, Holt, 1966, 2nd edition, Vallentine, Mitchell, 1973; *Zalmen; ou, La Folie de Dieu* (play), 1966, translation by Lily Edelman and Nathan Edelman published as *Zalmen; or, The Madness of God,* Holt, 1968; *Le Mendiant de Jerusalem,* 1968, translation by the author and L. Edelman published as *A Beggar in Jerusalem,* Random House, 1970; *La Nuit, L'Aube,* [and] *Le Jour,* 1969.

Entre Deux Soleils, 1970, translation by the author and L. Edelman published as *One Generation After,* Random House, 1970; *Celebration hassidique: Portraits et legendes,* 1972, translation by wife, Marion Wiesel, published as *Souls on Fire: Portraits and Legends of Hasidic Masters,* Random House, 1972; *Night, Dawn,* [and] *The Accident: Three Tales,* Hill & Wang, 1972; *Le Serment de Kolvillag,* 1973, translation by M. Wiesel published as *The Oath,* Random House, 1973; *Ani maamin: A Song Lost and Found Again* (cantata), music composed by Darius Milhaud, Random House, 1974; *Celebration biblique: Portraits et legendes,* 1975, translation by M. Wiesel published as *Messengers of God: Biblical Portraits and Legends,* Random House, 1976; *Un Juif aujourd'hui: Recits, essais, dialogues,* 1977, translation by M. Wiesel published as *A Jew Today,* Random House, 1978; *Four Hasidic Masters and Their Struggle against Melancholy,* University of Notre Dame Press, 1978; (with others) *Dimensions of the Holocaust,* Indiana University Press, 1978; *Le Proces de Shamgorod tel qu'il se deroula le 25 fevrier 1649: Piece en trois actes,* 1979, translation by M. Wiesel published as *The Trial of God (as It Was Held on February 25, 1649, in Shamgorod): A Play in Three Acts,* Random House, 1979; *Images from the Bible,* illustrated with paintings by Shalom of Safed, Overlook Press, 1980; *Le Testament d'un poete juif assassine,* 1980, translation by M. Wiesel published as *The Testament,* Simon & Schuster, 1981; *Five Biblical Portraits,* University of Notre Dame Press, 1981; *Somewhere a Master,* Simon & Schuster, 1982; *Paroles d'etranger,* 1982. Contributor to numerous periodicals.

SIDELIGHTS: In the spring of 1944, the Nazis entered the Transylvanian village of Sighet, Romania, until then a relatively safe and peaceful enclave in the middle of a war-torn continent. Arriving with orders to exterminate an estimated 600,000 Jews in six weeks or less, Adolf Eichmann, chief of the Gestapo's Jewish section, began making arrangements for a mass deportation program. Among those forced to leave their homes was fifteen-year-old Elie Wiesel, the only son of a grocer and his wife. A serious and devoted student of the Talmud and the mystical teachings of Hasidism and the Cabala, the young man had always assumed he would spend his entire life in Sighet, quietly contemplating the religious texts and helping out in the family's store from time to time. Instead, along with his father, mother, and three sisters, Wiesel was herded onto a train bound for Birkenau, the reception center for the infamous death camp, Auschwitz.

For reasons he still finds impossible to comprehend, Wiesel survived Birkenau and later Auschwitz and Buna and Buchenwald; his father, mother, and youngest sister did not. (He did not learn until after the war that his older sisters also survived.) With nothing and no one in Sighet for him to go back to, Wiesel boarded a train for Belgium with four hundred other orphans who, like him, had no reason or desire to return to their former homes. On orders of General Charles de Gaulle, the train was diverted to France, where border officials asked the children to raise their hands if they wanted to become French citizens. As Wiesel (who at that time neither spoke nor understood French) recalls in the *Washington Post*, "A lot of them did. They thought they were going to get bread or something; they would reach out for anything. I didn't, so I remained stateless."

Wiesel chose to stay in France for a while, settling first in Normandy and later in Paris, doing whatever he could to earn a living: tutoring, directing a choir, translating. Eventually he began working as a reporter for various French and Jewish publications. But he could not quite bring himself to write about what he had seen and felt at Auschwitz and Buchenwald. Doubtful of his—or of anyone's—ability to convey the horrible truth without diminishing it, Wiesel vowed never to make the attempt.

The young journalist's self-imposed silence came to an end in the mid-1950s, however, after he met and interviewed the Nobel Prize-winning novelist Francois Mauriac. Deeply moved upon learning of Wiesel's tragic youth, Mauriac urged him to speak out and tell the world of his experiences, to "bear witness" for the millions of men, women, and children whom death, and not despair, had silenced. The result was *Night*, the story of a teen-age boy plagued with guilt for having survived the camps and devastated by the realization that the God he had once worshipped so devoutly allowed his people to be destroyed. For the most part autobiographical, it was, says Richard M. Elman in the *New Republic*, "a document as well as a work of literature—journalism which emerged, coincidentally, as a work of art."

Described by the *Nation*'s Daniel Stern as "undoubtably the single most powerful literary relic of the holocaust," *Night* is the first in a series of nonfiction books and autobiographical novels this "lyricist of lamentation" has written that deal, either directly or indirectly, with the Holocaust. "He sees the present always refracted through the prism of these earlier days," comments James Finn in the *New Republic*. The *New York Times*'s Thomas Lask agrees, stating: "For [more than] twenty-five years, Elie Wiesel has been in one form or another a witness—a witness to the range, bestiality and completeness of the destruction of European Jewry by the Germans. . . . Auschwitz informs everything he writes—novels, legends, dialogues. He is not belligerent about it, only unyielding. Nothing he can say measures up to the enormity of what he saw, what others endured. The implications these experiences have for mankind terrify him. . . . He is part conscience, part quivering needle of response and part warning signal. His writing is singular in the disparate elements it has unified, in the peculiar effect of remoteness and immediacy it conveys. He is his own mold."

The elements that have shaped that mold are by no means unique to Wiesel; the Holocaust and the Jewish religious and philosophical tradition involve experiences and beliefs shared by a great many people, including other writers. But as Kenneth Turan declares in the *Washington Post Book World*, Elie Wiesel has become "much more than just a writer. He is a symbol, a banner, and a beacon, perhaps *the* survivor of the Holocaust. . . . He seems to own the horror of the death camps, or, rather, the horror owns him." But it is a moral and spiritual, not a physical, horror that obsesses Wiesel and obliges him to compose what Dan Isaac of the *Nation* calls "an angry message to God, filled with both insane rage and stoical acceptance; calculated to stir God's wrath, but careful not to trigger an apocalypse." Explains Isaac's *Nation* colleague Laurence Goldstein: "For Elie Wiesel memory is an instrument of revelation. Each word he uses to document the past transforms both the work and the memory into an act of faith. The writings of Elie Wiesel are a journey into the past blackened by the Nazi death camps where the charred souls of its victims possess the sum of guilt and endurance that mark the progress of man. It is a compulsive, fevered, single-minded search among the ashes for a spark that can be thrust before the silent eyes of God himself."

Unlike those who dwell primarily on the physical horror, then, Wiesel writes from the perspective of a passionately religious man whose faith has been profoundly shaken by what he has witnessed. As Goldstein remarks, "He must rediscover himself. . . . Although he has not lost God, he must create out of the pain and numbness a new experience that will keep his God from vanishing among the unforgettable faces of the thousands whose bodies he saw." According to Maurice Friedman of *Commonweal*, Wiesel is, in fact, "the most moving embodiment of the Modern Job": a man who questions—in books that "form one unified outcry, one sustained protest, one sobbing and singing prayer"—why the just must suffer while the wicked flourish. This debate with God is one of the central themes of what a *Newsweek* critic refers to as Wiesel's "God-tormented, God-intoxicated" fiction.

In addition to his intense preoccupation with ancient Jewish philosophy, mythology, and history, Wiesel displays a certain affinity with modern French existentialists, an affinity Josephine Knopp believes is a direct consequence of the Holocaust. Writes Knopp in *Contemporary Literature:* "To the young Wiesel the notion of an 'absurd' universe would have been a completely alien one. . . . The traditional Jewish view holds that life's structure and meaning are fully explained and indeed derive from the divinely granted Torah. . . . Against this background the reality of Auschwitz confronts the Jew with a dilemma, an 'absurdity' which cannot be dismissed easily and which stubbornly refuses to dissipate of its own accord. . . . The only possible response that remains within the framework of Judaism is denunciation of God and a demand that He fulfill His contractual obligation [to protect those who worship Him]. This is the religious and moral context within which Wiesel attempts to apprehend and assimilate the events of the Holocaust. [He seeks] to reconcile Auschwitz with Judaism, to confront and perhaps wring meaning from the absurd."

The strong emphasis on *Jewish* tradition and *Jewish* suffering in Wiesel's works does not mean, however, that he speaks only to and for Jews. In fact, maintains Robert McAfee Brown in *Christian Century*, "writing out of the particularity of his own Jewishness . . . is how [Wiesel] touches universal chords. He does not write about 'the human condition,' but about 'the Jewish condition.' Correction: in writing about the Jewish condition, he thereby writes about the human condition. For the human condition is not generalized existence; it is a huge, crazy-quilt sum of particularized existences all woven together."

To Stern, this time commenting in the *Washington Post Book World,* it seems that "Wiesel has taken the Jew as his metaphor—and his reality—in order to unite a moral and aesthetic vision in terms of all men." Manes Sperber of the *New York Times Book Review* expresses a similar view, stating that "Wiesel is one of the few writers who, without any plaintiveness, has succeeded in revealing in the Jewish tragedy those features by which it has become again and again a paradigm of the human condition."

According to Michael J. Bandler in the *Christian Science Monitor,* Wiesel conveys his angry message to God "with a force and stylistic drive that leaves the reader stunned." Concise and uncluttered, yet infused with a highly emotional biblical mysticism, the author's prose "gleams again and again with the metaphor of the poet," writes Clifford A. Ridley in the *National Observer.* Though it "never abandons its tender intimacy," reports Sperber, "[Wiesel's] voice comes from far away in space and time. It is the voice of the Talmudic teachers of Jerusalem and Babylon; of medieval mystics; of Rabbi Nachman of Bratzlav whose tales have inspired generations of Hasidim and so many writers." As Lask observes, "[Wiesel] has made the form of the telling his own. The surreal and the supernatural combine abrasively with the harsh fact; the parable, the rabbinic tale support and sometimes substitute for narrative. The written law and oral tradition support, explain and expand the twentieth-century event." Goldstein, noting the author's "remarkably compassionate tone," declares that "he writes with that possessive reverence for language that celebrates, as much as describes, experience. The written word becomes a powerful assertion, the triumph of life over death and indifference. . . . Words carved on gravestones, legend torn from the pit where millions of broken bodies lie. This is the inheritance which Elie Wiesel brings to us. His voice claims us with its urgency. His vision lights the mystery of human endurance."

Several critics, however, feel Wiesel's prose does not quite live up to the demands of his subject. Commenting in the *New York Times Book Review,* for example, Jeffrey Burke states that the author occasionally "slips into triteness or purple prose or redundancy," and a reviewer for the *New Yorker* finds that Wiesel becomes "nearly delirious" in his intensity. *Newsweek's* Geoffrey Wolff believes that Wiesel's work at times "suffers from unnecessary confusions, linguistic cliches, dense and purple thickets, and false mystifications. Ideas tend to hobble about . . . on stilts. . . . The language, seeking to transport us to another world, collapses beneath the weight of its burden much too often." Concludes Burke: "No one can or would deny the seriousness and necessity of Elie Wiesel's role as witness. . . . It is natural that such a mission would remain uppermost in the writer's mind, but that the requirements of art should proportionately diminish in significance is not an acceptable corollary. [Wiesel tends] to sacrifice the demands of craft to those of conscience."

In defense of Wiesel, Turan states that "his is a deliberate, elegant style, consciously elevated and poetic, and if he occasionally tries to pack too much into a sentence, to jam it too full of significance and meaning, it is an error easy to forgive." Elman, this time writing in the *New York Times Book Review,* also finds that "some of Wiesel's existentialist parables are deeply flawed by an opacity of language and construction, which may confirm that 'the event was so heavy with horror . . . that words could not really contain it.' But Wiesel's work is not diminished by his failure to make his shattering theme— God's betrayal of man—consistently explicit." Thus, according to Jonathan Brent in the *Chicago Tribune Book World,* Wiesel is "the type of writer distinguished by his subject rather than his handling of it. . . . Such writers must be read not for themselves but for the knowledge they transmit of events, personalities, and social conditions outside their fiction itself. They do not master their material esthetically, but remain faithful to it; and this constitutes the principle value of their work."

Few would agree with these assessments of Wiesel's stylistic abilities, but many would support Brent's conclusion that the author is almost compulsively faithful to his subject. As Lawrence L. Langer observes in the *Washington Post Book World:* "Although Elie Wiesel has announced many times in recent years that he is finished with the Holocaust as a subject for public discourse, it is clear . . . that the Holocaust has not yet finished with him. Almost from his first volume to his last, his writing has been an act of homage, a ritual of remembrance in response to a dreadful challenge 'to unite the language of man with the silence of the dead.' . . . If Elie Wiesel returns compulsively to the ruins of the Holocaust world, it is not because he has nothing new to say. . . . [It is simply that] the man he did not become beseiges his imagination and compels him to confirm his appointments with the past that holds him prisoner."

Wiesel expresses what *Commonweal's* Irving Halpern calls "the anguish of a survivor who is unable to exorcise the past or to live with lucidity and grace in the present" in the book *Night,* his first attempt to bear witness for the dead. Wiesel writes: "Never shall I forget that night, the first night in camp, which has turned my life into one long night, seven times cursed and seven times sealed. Never shall I forget that smoke. Never shall I forget the little faces of the children, whose bodies I saw turned into wreaths of smoke beneath a silent blue sky. Never shall I forget those flames which consumed my Faith forever. Never shall I forget that nocturnal silence which deprived me, for all eternity, of the desire to live. Never shall I forget those moments which murdered my God and my soul and turned my dreams to dust. Never shall I forget these things, even if I am condemned to live as long as God Himself. Never."

Many years after this painful passage was first written, Wiesel is still torn between words and silence. "You must speak," he told a *People* magazine interviewer, "but how can you, when the full story is beyond language?" Furthermore, he once remarked in the *Washington Post,* "there is the fear of not being believed, . . . the fear that the experience will be reduced, made into something acceptable, perhaps forgotten." But as he went on to explain in *People:* "We [survivors] believe that if we survived, we must do something with our lives. The first task is to tell the tale." In short, concluded Wiesel, "The only way to stop the next holocaust—the nuclear holocaust— is to remember the last one. If the Jews were singled out then, in the next one we are all victims."

CA INTERVIEW

CA interviewed Elie Wiesel by phone April 13, 1981, at his office at Boston University.

CA: In One Generation After *(1970), you wrote of the new, post-Holocaust generation, "The past interests them only to the extent that they can reject it." Do you find that still as true now, even though much attention has been focused on the Holocaust in the decade since that book was published?*

WIESEL: No, I think today the Holocaust has become a household word. Whether it's good or bad I don't know. People hear the word, speak the word, reflect on its meaning, meditate on its implications. So on the surface I think things have changed. But whether we are ready to delve into ourselves or into the subject and see really what it means, what it was, I don't know. My feeling is that the word has been commercialized, cheapened, and trivialized, unfortunately, in so many quarters that people don't know much more now than they did then. The only difference is that now they think they know.

CA: Are there exceptions, writings or productions that haven't betrayed and distorted the message?

WIESEL: My first, foremost conviction is that the survivors are important, *their* documents are important, their testimony is essential. The other books—some are good, some are not, but the survivors' books must be read, their voice must be heard.

CA: When did you first begin to think of being a writer?

WIESEL: I knew I would write when I was a child, but I didn't imagine I would write this kind of books. I grew up in a religious family and I wrote commentary on the Bible at a young age. What I wrote wasn't good, but I wrote.

CA: Why do you prefer to write in French?

WIESEL: It's my language. Once you acquire a language at a certain age, then it becomes your vehicle, it becomes your shelter, it turns into a home.

CA: Your wife does the translations of some of your books into English. Do you work closely with her on the translations?

WIESEL: No, she does them all by herself. Occasionally, we discuss a specific term.

CA: You've written about the plight of the Jews in Russia. What can be done to help them?

WIESEL: What can we do? Alert public opinion, educate the people that there is a problem, that somewhere minorities are oppressed and need help, that's all we can do. That's all we must do. For when we do apply pressure, usually it helps. We must not wait. Because of the pressure, because of public opinion, because of the protest, many Jews and non-Jews have already been saved.

CA: Do you have much personal contact with other Holocaust survivors?

WIESEL: Yes, I do. I meet them in New York or Boston. Their children often come to be my students. We share a code. A secret. We are members of a vanishing species: nobody will ever totally understand us. We do not belong here. We belong to another universe.

CA: Do you still have close contact with the Hasidic community in New York?

WIESEL: Of course. I study and occasionally teach Hasidic texts and stories. I like to spend time with Hasidim. I like to hear them sing. I like to sing with them—and remember. . . .

CA: Are you teaching Jewish studies now?

WIESEL: I teach humanities now; I have been given a chair in the humanities. I taught Jewish studies when I was at the City College of New York for a long time. Even now, I bring back Jewish themes into general studies. How could I speak of Kafka and not mention Rabbi Nachman of Bratzlav?

CA: When you were teaching Jewish studies, did you have many non-Jewish students in your classes?

WIESEL: I always had many non-Jewish students. They come either for literary or for personal reasons. In most cases, they come from Christian theological schools.

CA: Where does the legend of the Just Men come from?

WIESEL: From the Talmud. The Talmud tells the legend of thirty-six Just Men thanks to whom the world can exist. According to Hasidic legend, they are unknown, forever disguised as wanderers, beggars, peasants, or madmen.

CA: Yale University is conducting a campaign to expand its Jewish studies program. Last fall you spoke there at a ceremony initiating the Judaic studies major. How is that project coming along?

WIESEL: I think it's going well. President Bart Giamatti is committed to it. Professor Geoffrey Hartmann is working hard on putting it together.

CA: How did you decide to live primarily in New York City?

WIESEL: I came to New York first as a journalist. Then I had an accident and spent a whole year in the hospital in a wheelchair and I couldn't go back to Paris; so I stayed.

CA: Do you spend much time abroad now?

WIESEL: No, I am committed to teaching; I can't go away often. But I go to Israel once a year.

CA: Are you able to spend much time there when you go?

WIESEL: No, unfortunately not. A week or two. Mainly in Jerusalem.

CA: Are you optimistic about the future of Israel?

WIESEL: Yes, in the long run. I am worried about the present, but not about the future.

CA: What do you think the main problems are?

WIESEL: The hostility of surrounding countries. Egypt is the only one that accepts Israel. The others should too.

CA: But there's a good spirit within?

WIESEL: Yes. Israel generates hope and lives with faith.

CA: You were chairman of the Presidential Commission on the Holocaust during President Carter's term in office. Is that still active?

WIESEL: Naturally. Now it's a permanent agency, and it's called the United States Holocaust Memorial Council. I serve as its chairman.

CA: How are the plans progressing for a national museum to stand as a monument to the Holocaust?

WIESEL: Working well. Numerous committees devote countless days and weeks exploring various projects. The difficulties seem insurmountable: how can we *show* what must be remembered as an ontological event? How can we speak of the unspeakable? There *are* problems—there must be.

CA: Do you have a lot of support for the project?

WIESEL: We hope. At this stage we don't know yet, but we hope we'll get support. In Congress, especially. The funds must be raised from private sources. We shall begin soon.

CA: You wrote a second play, The Trial of God, *in 1979. I've read that you intended* The Madness of God *(1974) to be your only play. Why did you change your mind?*

WIESEL: Some themes can be explored only as novels; others only as plays.

CA: Are there present or future plans you'd like to talk about?

WIESEL: I am concerned with the nuclear threat. It has grown into an obsession. Unless we wake up, mankind may vanish simply because, somewhere, one ruler may press the button. Our writings must be warnings.

BIOGRAPHICAL/CRITICAL SOURCES: Elie Wiesel, *Night*, translated by Stella Rodway, Hill & Wang, 1960; *Times Literary Supplement*, August 19, 1960, November 20, 1981; *Commonweal*, December 9, 1960, January 6, 1961, March 13, 1964, October 14, 1966; *Saturday Review*, December 17, 1960, July 8, 1961, July 25, 1964, May 28, 1966, October 19, 1968, January 31, 1970, November 21, 1970; *New York Herald Tribune Lively Arts*, January 1, 1961, April 30, 1961; *Christian Century*, January 18, 1961, June 17, 1970, June 3, 1981; *New Yorker*, March 18, 1961, January 9, 1965, August 20, 1966, July 6, 1970, July 12, 1976; *New York Times Book Review*, July 16, 1961, April 15, 1962, July 5, 1964, June 12, 1966, January 12, 1969, January 25, 1970, January 20, 1976, January 21, 1979, April 12, 1981, August 15, 1982; *Newsweek*, May 25, 1964, February 9, 1970; *New Republic*, July 5, 1964, December 14, 1968.

Book Week, May 29, 1966; *New York Review of Books*, July 28, 1966, January 2, 1969, May 7, 1970; *Nation*, October 17, 1966, February 24, 1969, March 16, 1970, January 5, 1974; *Washington Post Book World*, October 20, 1968, January 18, 1970, August 8, 1976, October 29, 1978, April 12, 1981; *Washington Post*, October 26, 1968, February 6, 1970; *Atlantic*, November, 1968; *Christian Science Monitor*, November 21, 1968, February 19, 1970, November 22, 1978; *New Leader*, December 30, 1968, June 15, 1981; *TV Guide*, February 15, 1969.

National Observer, February 2, 1970; *Best Sellers*, March 15, 1970, May, 1981; *Time*, March 16, 1970, May 8, 1972, July 12, 1976, December 25, 1978, April 20, 1981; *New York Times*, December 15, 1970, March 10, 1972, April 3, 1981; *Contemporary Literature*, spring, 1974; *Contemporary Literary Criticism*, Gale, Volume III, 1975, Volume V, 1976, Volume XI, 1979; *Authors in the News*, Volume I, Gale, 1976; Alvin Rosenfeld, *Confronting the Holocaust*, Indiana University Press, 1978; *Chicago Tribune Book World*, October 29, 1978, March 29, 1981; *People*, October 22, 1979; *National Review*, June 12, 1981; *London Times*, September 3, 1981; *Contemporary Issues Criticism*, Volume I, Gale, 1982.

—Sketch by Deborah A. Straub

—Interview by Jean W. Ross

* * *

WIESENFARTH, Joseph (John) 1933-

PERSONAL: Born August 20, 1933, in Brooklyn, N.Y.; son of Charles Adam (a bank official) and Elizabeth (Koechler) Wiesenfarth. *Education:* Catholic University of America, B.A. (magna cum laude), 1956, Ph.D., 1962; University of Detroit, M.A., 1959. *Office:* Department of English, 600 North Park St., University of Wisconsin—Madison, Madison, Wis. 53706.

CAREER: St. Joseph's High School, Detroit, Mich., teacher, 1956-58; De La Salle College, Washington, D.C., lecturer in English, 1958-62; La Salle College, Philadelphia, Pa., assistant professor of English, 1962-64; Manhattan College, Bronx, N.Y., assistant professor, 1964-67, associate professor of English, 1967-70; University of Wisconsin—Madison, associate professor, 1970-76, professor of English, 1976—. *Member:* American Association of University Professors, Modern Language Association of America, English Institute, Phi Beta Kappa.

WRITINGS: *Henry James and the Dramatic Analogy: A Study of the Major Novels of the Middle Period*, Fordham University Press, 1963; *The Errand of Form: An Assay of Jane Austen's Art*, Fordham University Press, 1967; (adaptor) *The Meanest Animal in the Whole Wide World*, [Madison], 1972; *Plane Words: Three Poems Written in the Jet Stream*, Halfpenny Press, 1975; *George Eliot's Mythmaking*, Carl Winter, 1977; *George Eliot: A Writer's Notebook, 1854-1879, Collected Writings*, University Press of Virginia, 1981. Contributor of articles on Nathaniel Hawthorne, Graham Greene, Katherine Anne Porter, Ford Madox Ford, and Henry James to professional journals.

* * *

WILEY, Jack 1936-

PERSONAL: Born December 4, 1936, in Fresno, Calif. *Education:* University of Illinois, Ph.D., 1968. *Residence:* Stockton, Calif.

CAREER: Writer. University of South Alabama, Mobile, assistant professor and director of Human Performance Laboratory, 1968-70; University of Illinois at Urbana-Champaign, assistant professor, 1970-71; University of California, Santa Barbara, assistant research physiologist at Institute of Environmental Research, 1971-72.

WRITINGS: *The Unicycle Book*, Stackpole, 1973; *Fiberglass Kit Boats*, International Marine Publishing Co., 1973; *Basic Circus Skills*, Stackpole, 1974; *Modifying Fiberglass Boats*, International Marine Publishing Co., 1975; *Boat Living*, International Marine Publishing Co., 1976; *The Tumbling Book*, McKay, 1978; *Acrobatics Book*, Anderson World, 1978; *Men's Gymnastics*, Anderson World, 1980; *Women's Gymnastics*, Anderson World, 1980.

All published by TAB Books: *The Bicycle Builder's Bible*, 1980; *How to Fix Up an Old Boat on a Small Budget*, 1981; *The Fiberglass Repair and Construction Handbook*, 1982; *Boat and Recreational Vehicle Canvas and Upholstery Work*, in press; *The Fiberglass Boat Handbook*, in press; *Collecting and Restoring Antique Typewriters*, in press; *The How-To Book of Collecting of Collectibles*, in press; *Whittling and Wood Carving*, in press; *The Kite Building and Kite Flying Handbook*, in press.

Contributor to magazines, including *Mechanix Illustrated*, *Popular Mechanics*, and *Popular Science*.

SIDELIGHTS: Jack Wiley competed in gymnastics during high school and college and placed second in tumbling at the 1959 NCAA National Gymnastics Championships. He presently lives and writes aboard his sailboat, *Go for It*, in Stockton, California. *Avocational interests:* Travel (has been to Buenos Aires).

BIOGRAPHICAL/CRITICAL SOURCES: *Newsletter of Unicycling Society of America*, July, 1975.

WILLIAMS, Jonathan (Chamberlain) 1929-

PERSONAL: Born March 8, 1929, in Asheville, N.C.; son of Thomas Benjamin and Georgette (Chamberlain) Williams. *Education:* Attended St. Albans School, Washington, D.C., 1941-47; studied art history at Princeton University, 1947-49, painting with Karl Knaths at Phillips Memorial Gallery, 1949, and etching and engraving with Stanley William Hayter at Atelier 17, 1949-50; attended Chicago Institute of Design, 1950-51, and Black Mountain College, intermittently, 1951-56. *Residence:* Highlands, N.C. 28741; and Corn Close, Dentdale, Sedbergh, Cumbria, England.

CAREER: The Jargon Society, Inc. ("a poet's press"), Highlands, N.C., founder, executive director, editor, publisher, and designer, 1951—; The Nantahala Foundation, Highlands, president, 1960—. Poet-in-residence at Aspen Institute for Humanistic Studies, summer, 1962, Maryland Institute College of Art, 1968-69, University of Kansas, 1971, and University of Delaware, 1977; scholar-in-residence, Aspen Institute for Humanistic Studies, 1967-68; visiting poet at Wake Forest University, North Carolina School of the Arts, Salem Academy, and Winston-Salem State University, all 1973. Has given over 950 readings, lectures, seminars, and slide shows at universities and organizations throughout the world, 1954-80. *Military service:* U.S. Army Medical Corps, 1952-54; conscientious objector. *Member:* P.E.N., Bruckner Society of America, Congress of Racial Equality, Appalachian Trail Conference, Sierra Club, Youth Hostel Association, Society for Individual Rights, Campaign for Homosexual Equality, National Trust of Great Britain, Elgar Society, Delius Society.

AWARDS, HONORS: Guggenheim fellowship for poetry, 1957-58; Longview Foundation grant, 1960, for editing of Jargon Society books; National Endowment for the Arts grants, 1968-70, 1972, 1974-76, 1978, and 1979; D.H.L., Maryland Institute College of Art, 1969; named member of Order of Kentucky Colonels, 1974, for "services to the arts of Kentucky"; Coordinating Council of Literary Magazines award, 1974, for essay writing; *Publishers Weekly* Carey-Thomas Citation, 1977, for creative small press publishing; North Carolina Award in Fine Arts Gold Medal, 1977, for "services to the arts of North Carolina and the United States."

WRITINGS—Poetry, except as indicated: *In England's Green & (A Garland & Clyster)*, drawings by Philip Van Aver, Auerhahn, 1962; *LTDG (Lullabies Twisters Gibbers Drags)*, covers by R. B. Kitaj, Jargon Society, 1963, reprinted with new introduction, Design Department, Indiana University, 1967; *Lines about Hills above Lakes* (prose), foreword by John Wain, drawings by Barry Hall, Roman Books, 1964.

Petite Country Concrete Suite, Fenian Head Centre Press, 1965; *Twelve Jargonelles from the Herbalist's Notebook*, graphic design by Ann Wilkinson, Design Department, Indiana University, 1965; *Ten Jargonelles from the Herbalist's Notebook*, graphic design by Arthur Korant, Graduate Graphic Design Program, University of Illinois, 1966; *Four Jargonelles from the Herbalist's Notebook*, Lowell House Printers, Harvard University, 1966; *Paean to Dvorak, Deemer & McClure*, Dave Haselwood, 1966; *Eight Jargonelles from the Herbalist's Notebook*, graphic design by Dave Ahlsted, Design Department, Indiana University, 1967; *Affilati attrezzi per i giardini di Catullo* (selected poems in English and Italian), translations by Leda Sartini Mussio, drawings by James McGarrell, Roberto Lerici Editori (Milan), 1967, published as *Sharp Tools for Catullan Gardens*, introductory note by Guy Davenport, Fine Arts Department, Indiana University, 1968; *Mahler Becomes Politics . . . Beisbol*, silk-screen prints by Kitaj, Marlborough Fine Arts (London), 1967, revised and enlarged edition published as *Mahler*, Grossman, 1969; *50! EPIphytes, -taphs, -tomes, -grams, -thets! 50!*, Poet & Printer (London), 1967; *Les Six Pak* ("disposable six-pak xerox edition"), Aspen Institute, 1967; *A French 75! (Salut Milhaudious)*, Dave Haselwood, 1967; *Futura 15: Polycotyledonous Poems*, Edition Hansjoerg Mayer (Stuttgart), 1967; *The Luciditties: Sixteen in Visionary Company*, drawings by John Furnival, Turret Books, 1968; *Ripostes*, silk-screen print and design by William Katz, Edition Domberger (Stuttgart), 1969; *An Ear in Bartram's Tree: Selected Poems, 1957-1967*, introduction by Davenport, University of North Carolina Press, 1969; *Six Rusticated, Wall-Eyed Poems*, graphic realizations by Dana Atchley, Press of the Maryland Institute of Art, 1969.

The New Architectural Monuments of Baltimore City, lithographs by John Sparks, typography by Robert Gotsch, Press of the Maryland Institute of Art, 1970; *The Apocryphal, Oracular Yeah-Sayings of the Ersatz Mae West*, lithographs by Raoul Middleman, Press of the Maryland Institute of Art, 1970 (not released); (editor) *Edward Dahlberg: A Tribute* (prose and poetry collection; festschrift for Dahlberg's seventieth birthday), David Lewis, 1970; *Blues & Roots/Rue & Bluets: A Garland for the Appalachians*, photographs by Nicholas Dean, graphic realizations by Atchley, Grossman, 1971; *The Loco-Logodaedalist in Situ: Selected Poems, 1968-1970*, embellishments by Joe Tilson, Grossman, 1972; *Pairidaeza* ("a celebration for the garden at Levens Hall"), lithographs by Ian Gardner, typography by Ronald Pearson, Blue Funnel Press, 1973; *Imaginary Postcards (Clints Grikes Gripes Glints)*, drawings by Tom Phillips, typography by Asa Benvensite, Trigram Press, 1973; *Much Further Out Than You Thought* ("Stevie Smith in conversation and celebration"), drawings by Furnival, Turret Books, 1973; (with Thomas Meyer) *Gone into When* (seven epitaphs), William Katz, 1973; *Selected Essays (Poeticules Criticasters Kitschdiggers & Just-folks)*, edited by Herbert Leibowitz, [New York], 1973; *Hasidic Exclamation upon Stevie Smith's Poem "Not Waving but Drowning,"* University of Connecticut Library, 1974; *My Quaker-Atheist Friend*, drawings by Gardner, privately printed, 1974; (author of introduction) John Clarence Laughlin, *The Personal Eye*, Aperture, 1974.

(Contributor) *The Land: Twentieth-Century Landscape Photographs*, Fraser, 1975; *Hot What?* (prose), Mole Press, 1975; *A Wee Tot for Catullus*, Moschatel Press, 1975; *A Celestial Centennial Reverie for Charles E. Ives*, Donald B. Anderson, 1975; *Untinears & Antennae for Maurice Ravel*, Truck Press, 1977; *An Omen for Stevie Smith*, Sterling Memorial Library, Yale University, 1977; *Super-Duper Zuppa Inglese (and Other Trifles from the Land of Stodge)*, drawings by Barbara Jones, Aggie Weston's Editions, 1977; *A Hairy Coat Near Yanworth Yat*, North Carolina Wesleyan College Press, 1978; *Shankum Naggum*, Friends of the Library, North Carolina Wesleyan College, 1979; *The Delian Seasons*, Topia Press, 1979; *St. Swithin's Swivet*, Circle Press, 1979; *Glees, Swarthy Monotonies, Rince Cochon, and Chozzerai for Simon*, drawings by Furnival, DBA Editions, 1979; *Homage Umbrage Quibble and Chicane*, drawings by Furnival, DBA Editions, 1980.

Published by Jargon Society: *Garbage Litters the Iron Face of the Sun's Child*, engraving by David Ruff, 1951; *Red/Gray*, drawings by Paul Ellsworth, 1951; *Four Stoppages: A Configuration*, drawings by Charles Oscar, 1953; *The Empire Finals at Verona*, collages and drawings by Fielding Dawson, 1959; *Lord! Lord! Lord!*, 1959; *Amen/Huzza/Selah*, preface by Louis Zukofsky, photographs by Williams, 1960; *Elegies and Cel-*

ebrations, preface by Robert Duncan, photographs by Aaron Siskind and Williams, 1962; *Emblems for the Little Dells, & Nooks & Corners of Paradise* (includes a reproduction of a page of Samuel Palmer's sketchbook of 1824), 1962; (author of preface) *The Appalachian Photographs of Doris Ulmann,* 1971; (with Meyer) *EPitaph,* typography by Benvensite, 1972; (with Meyer) *Fruits Confits,* decorations by Gardner, 1972; (editor and contributor) *Epitaphs for Lorine,* 1973; *Who Is Little Enis?,* 1974; (contributor) Ralph Eugene Meatyard, *The Family Album of Lucybelle Crater,* 1974; (editor and author of preface) Lyle Bonge, *The Sleep of Reason,* 1974; *Gists from a Presidential Report on Hardcornponeography,* 1975; (editor with Allen Ginsberg and contributor) *Madeira and Toasts for Basil Bunting's Seventy-fifth Birthday,* 1977; *Elite/Elate Poems: Selected Poems, 1971-1975,* photographs by Guy Mendes, 1979.

Published by Gnomon Press: *Descant on Rawthey's Madrigal: Conversations with Basil Bunting,* 1968; *A Blue Ridge Weather Prophet Makes Twelve Stitches in Time on the Twelfth Day of Christmas,* illustrations by Carolyn Whitesel, 1977; (editor and author of introduction) *"I Shall Save One Land Unvisited": Eleven Southern Photographers,* 1978; *Portrait Photographs* (photographs and prose commentary), 1979.

Published by Finial Press: *On Arriving at the Same Age as Jack Benny,* 1969; *Strung out with Elgar on a Hill,* plates by Peter Bodner, 1971; *Adventures with a Twelve-Inch Pianist beyond the Blue Horizon,* photographs by David Colley, 1973; *Five from up T'Dale,* 1974; *gAy BCs,* 1976; *In the Field at the Solstice,* 1976.

Also author of *Jammin' the Greek Scene.* Work represented in many anthologies, including *New Directions in Prose and Poetry,* New Directions, Volume XVI, 1957, Volume XVII, edited by James Laughlin, 1961; *The Beat Scene,* edited by Elias Wilentz, Corinth Books, 1960; *The New American Poetry, 1945-1960,* edited by Donald Allen, Grove, 1960; *Beat Poets,* Vista Books, 1963; *Erotic Poetry,* edited by William Cole, Random House, 1963; *A Controversy of Poets,* edited by Paris Leary and Robert Kelly, Doubleday-Anchor, 1965; *Poets of North Carolina,* edited by Richard Gaither Walser, University of North Carolina Press, 1965; *The Voice That Is Great within Us,* edited by Hayden Carruth, Bantam, 1970; and anthologies of concrete poetry edited by Mary Ellen Solt, Stephen Bann, Emmett Williams, Jerry G. Bowles, and Milton Klonsky. Author of recording "Blues & Roots/Rue & Bluets," Folkways Records, 1964.

Contributor to *Evergreen Review, Contact, Vogue, Nation, Aperture, Black Mountain Review, Monk's Pond, Kulchur, Origin, Jazz Monthly* (St. Ives), *Poor. Old. Tired. Horse.* (Dunsyre, Lanarkshire), *Vou* (Tokyo), *I Quattro Soli* (Turin), *Cimaise* (Paris), *Art International* (Zurich), *Cultural Affairs, Art in Society, Craft Horizons, Poetry Review* (London), *Parnassus: Poetry in Review, Prose,* and other periodicals. Contributing editor, *Aperture;* member of advisory board, *Foxfire.*

WORK IN PROGRESS: *Corbel & Misericord,* with drawings by John Furnival; *I (Also) Remember,* a homage to Joe Brainard; *Letters to the Great Dead,* with details by R. B. Kitaj; *A Man Standing by His Word,* a year of letters.

SIDELIGHTS: Often associated with the Black Mountain School and the beat poets, Jonathan Williams is a self-proclaimed ecologist of the word, "an imagistic mystic, a disciple of W[illiam] C[arlos] Williams ('my spiritual grandfather'), and a hip Pound who stayed home," according to Alan Helms in the *Partisan Review.* A versatile stylistic experimenter, he often mingles elements of word play with "found" poems—bits of overheard conversations, slogans from billboards, and graffiti scrawled on buildings—and his work frequently blends the rhythms of music and everyday speech. "He takes the language eroding right now in our mouths," writes Robert Morgan in *Nation,* "and cultivates it, shapes it, and speaks it to life. For Williams more than anyone I know, poetry is an active art, the language being spoken." William's poetic attention, however, is not completely focused on the sense of sound, for as the founder, editor, and publisher of the Jargon Society ("a poet's press"), he has helped design books that are as aesthetically pleasing to the eye as to the ear. "More than any other poet," says Morgan, "Williams has used the Objectivist principle, the idea that a poem is first of all a linguistic, phonetic, graphic object."

"Like John Clare, I tend to find poems in fields," Williams told *CA.* "To recover from confinement in the little world of poetry," Williams has hiked 1,408 miles of the Appalachian Trail, and over 5,000 miles in England and America, including routes along Hadrian's Wall, the Pennine Way, the Lake District, North York Moors, the Wye River, Offla's Dyke, and the North Cornish and Devon coasts. Edward Grier says in *Vort* that Williams "knows his home terrain, the Appalachians, intimately, its contours, its flora and fauna, and its people," and that this knowledge is apparent in his poetry. Ralph J. Mills, writing in *Poetry,* assents: "Perhaps the most obviously striking quality in Williams' work, aside from the erudition and bookishness (which are of the delightful, never the pedantic variety), is the extraordinary acuteness of his ear. As a perpetual traveler, . . . he has attuned his sensitive powers of listening to every nuance of speech and sound, and given them back to his readers beautifully articulated."

Williams gives poetry readings and lectures to support himself and the Jargon Society, a non-profit corporation devoted to charitable, educational, and literary purposes. He told *CA:* "I am in the position of having no income except what I snare by these readings and the few book sales. This isn't very much, it could not be, but it allows other money to go into book production. It is a consistent juggling act, and, like they say, how is it really possible? Since my image seems often that of 'southern gentlemen and deepcountry publisher,' counting endless amounts of lucre from the slave market, I would like the picture to be apparent. The *modus operandi* is thus more than a private matter: I am able to use the family place, which sits on a mountain in western North Carolina. It is the requisite, occasional sanctuary. Without it, no such hopeless vocational mission as Jargon could persist. I prefer it to institutional sanctuaries; i.e., I don't need a job in teaching or in commercial bookmaking. . . . The poems are constructed with vocal intentions; the books are made to be looked at, etc., and I must act as my own agent. It is simple enough, if not simple at all.

"There are certain kindred spirits at work in the country," Williams explains, "and it is to make coherence of these that Jargon exists. It does not represent an armed camp. The *avant-garde* is never anything but a community of particular sympathy. I have attempted to know it in a number of areas because it is the total locale of America that produces the culture. [Poet Edward] Dahlberg asks whether a civilization can be produced on a landscape vaster than the body of a Titan. It is our business to try."

Concerning his lectures, Williams says: "It is very rarely that an English Department will sponsor me. This may be because: (1) I do not wear a Confederate uniform; (2) I do not play the Beat/Square Game, or other forms of the old American Pushme/Pullyou, like Brainwashed/Great Unwashed, In/Out, SF/NYC, Queer/Straight—these are peculiar ways to con people and sell them things; (3) I am involved in an area which is, has been, always will be 'outside the Academy.' It is where all them idiosyncratic, autochthonous injuns live in the thickets of disinterest, etc. And so, Jargon and its poet get confused with some kind of Chaos by some sitting there by the campfires, martinis loaded in readiness. However, there are many ways to get on a campus, and I shall not forget an inventive friend who got me to Earlham College on a Tuesday afternoon, under the auspices of the Friday Tea Committee of the Humanities & Social Sciences Division. . . . I would prefer, frankly, to be sponsored by the Ecology Department, since poetry is a matter of making the viable connections between written things. . . . I dress and behave *only* as one who almost entered the Anglican ministry; viz., let us keep our attention on the poetry and one or two of the major tendencies for writing it, as I see it now in America.

"About my poems—my business is to make them, not to obfuscate or clarify them. A few people have said a few very decent things. James Laughlin writes me that 'nobody who is writing today has a more individual style, or more vitality, or a more salty wit.' I hope, but, like they say, I don't know. Also Hugh Kenner has written well of the poems in (hang on) *The National Review*. Otherwise, it has been 'just friends': Zukofsky, WCW [William Carlos Williams], Creeley, Layton, Levertov, Turnbull, Metcalf, Edelstein, Niedecker. So be it. I am not running in a competition for public office. The poems and the books . . . are made for one person at a time. I hope to keep finding him and her.''

BIOGRAPHICAL/CRITICAL SOURCES: Jonathan Williams, *Amen/Huzza/Selah*, preface by Louis Zukofsky, Jargon Society, 1960; Kenneth Rexroth, *Assays*, New Directions, 1962; *Books at Brown*, Volume XIX, John Hay Library of Brown University, 1963; Williams, *An Ear in Bartram's Tree: Selected Poems, 1957-1967*, introduction by Guy Davenport, University of North Carolina Press, 1969; *Library Journal*, June 1, 1969, May 1, 1970; *Saturday Review*, September 6, 1969; *New Statesman*, September 12, 1969; *Virginia Quarterly Review*, autumn, 1969; *Poetry*, February, 1971; *Nation*, August 16, 1971; *New York Times Book Review*, November 21, 1971; *Manchester Guardian*, July 3, 1972; *Studio International*, September, 1972; *Parnassus*, fall/winter, 1972; *Vort*, fall, 1973; *Partisan Review*, Volume VI, number 1, 1974; *Contemporary Literary Criticism*, Volume XIII, Gale, 1980; *Dictionary of Literary Biography*, Volume V: *American Poets since World War II, Part 2*, Gale, 1980.

* * *

WILLIAMS, Pete
See FAULKNOR, Cliff(ord Vernon)

* * *

WINDSOR, Philip 1935-

PERSONAL: Born September 14, 1935, in New Delhi, India. *Education:* Merton College, Oxford, B.A., 1957; St. Antony's College, Oxford, B.Phil., 1959. *Office:* International Institute for Strategic Studies, 23 Tavistock St., London WC2E 7NQ, England.

CAREER: International Institute for Strategic Studies, London, England, research associate, 1961—. Occasional commentator on current affairs for British Broadcasting Corp. *Awards, honors:* Ford Foundation fellow at Free University of Berlin, 1959-60.

WRITINGS: City on Leave: A History of Berlin, 1945-1962, Praeger, 1963; (with Alistair Buchan) *Arms and Stability in Europe*, Praeger, 1963 (published in England as *Arms and Stability in Europe: A British-French-German Enquiry*, Chatto & Windus, 1963); (with Adam Roberts) *Czechoslovakia, 1968: Reform, Repression, and Resistance*, Columbia University Press, 1969; *German Reunification*, Beekman, 1969; *Germany and the Management of Detente*, Praeger, 1971; *Oil: A Plain Man's Guide to the World's Energy Crisis*, Temple Smith, 1975; *Change in Eastern Europe*, Royal Institute of International Affairs, 1980. Co-author with Peter Calvocoressi of recording ''The New Alignments,'' BFA Educational Media, 1972. Contributor to *Encyclopaedia Britannica Yearbook*. Assistant editor and reviewer, *Survival;* occasional correspondent for *Het Parool* (Amsterdam) and *Le Monde Diplomatique* (Paris); contributor to *History Today*.

WORK IN PROGRESS: A study of current Soviet strategy; studies of France, DeGaulle, and Europe.

BIOGRAPHICAL/CRITICAL SOURCES: New York Times, April 28, 1969.†

* * *

WINN, Alison (Osborn) [a pseudonym]

PERSONAL: Born in England; married; children: David, Martin, Alison, Philip. *Home:* Cherry Burton, 3 Powys Ave., Leicester, England.

WRITINGS—All juveniles; published by Hodder & Stoughton, except as indicated: *Roundabout*, 1961; *Swings and Things*, illustrations by Jennie Corbett and Peggy Fortnum, 1963, Rand McNally, 1965; *Helter Skelter*, illustrations by Janina Ede, 1966; *A First Cinderella*, 1966; *Aunt Isabella's Umbrella*, illustrations by Glenys Ambrus, 1976, Children's Press, 1977; *Charley's Iron Horse*, 1979.

Translator from the Swedish; all juveniles; all published by Hodder & Stoughton: Gunilla Wolde, ''The Thomas Books'' series, ten volumes, 1971-75; Ulf Loefgren, *Who Holds Up the Traffic?*, 1973; Loefgren, *One, Two, Three, Four*, 1973; Loefgren, *The Flying Orchestra*, 1973; Loefgren, *The Magic Kite*, 1973; Loefgren, *The Color Trumpet*, 1973; Wolde, ''The Emma Books'' series, ten volumes, 1975-77; Loefgren, *Harlequin*, 1978; Babro Lindgren, *The Wild Baby*, 1981.

* * *

WINTER, Bevis (Peter) 1918-
(Al Bocca, Peter Cagney, Gordon Shayne)

PERSONAL: Born August 27, 1918, in Birmingham, Warwickshire, England; son of Jack and Freda (Abramson) Winter; married Deirdre Clifton, September 8, 1949; children: Pennie Sharmon, Stephen Clifton, Alayne Kathryn. *Education:* Educated in England at King Edward's School. *Politics:* Liberal. *Home:* 23 Second Ave., Hove, Sussex BN3 2LL, England. *Agent:* Howard Moorepark, 444 East 82nd St., New York, N.Y. 10028. *Office:* Peter Cagney Associates, 17 Second Ave., Hove, Sussex BN3 2LL, England.

CAREER: National School of Authorship, London, England, literary consultant, 1947-49; W.B. Press Ltd., Birmingham, England, editor, 1947-50; Peter Cagney Script Service (scripts for radio, television, stage, cabaret) and subsidiary, Cagney Publications, Hove, Sussex, England, director, 1949—; formed Peter Cagney Entertainments Agency Ltd. (managing and booking), a subsidiary of Peter Cagney Script Service, 1965. Director of Peter Cagney Associates and of variety programs. *Wartime service:* Aircraft testing. *Member:* International Radio-TV Scripts Association (chairman).

WRITINGS—Published by Jenkins, except as indicated: *Sad Laughter*, Mortimer, 1946; *The Truth about Writing*, Stagbooks, 1947; *Redheads Cool Fast*, 1952; (with Eric Maschwitz) *Little Red Monkey*, 1953; *The Dead Sleep for Keeps*, 1953; *Darker Grows the Street*, 1955; *Next Stop—The Morgue*, 1955; *A Noose of Emeralds*, Mystery House, 1956; *Let the Lady Die*, 1957; *The Night Was Made for Murder*, 1958; *Sleep Long My Lovely*, 1958; *Blondes End Up Dead*, 1959; *The Dark and the Deadly*, 1961.

Under pseudonym Al Bocca: *Dressed To Kill*, Milestone, 1952; *Ticket to San Diego*, Scion, 1952; *No Room at the Morgue*, Milestone, 1952; *Trouble Calling*, Milestone, 1953; *All or Nothing*, Milestone, 1953; *A Corner in Corpses*, Milestone, 1953.

Under pseudonym Peter Cagney: *No Diamonds for a Doll*, 1960; *Hear the Stripper Scream*, 1960; *A Grave for Madam*, 1961; (editor) *Treasury of Wit and Humour*, A. Thomas, 1966; *Comedy Scripts for Tape Recording*, Queen Anne Press, 1967; *Peter Cagney's Second Treasury of Wit and Humour*, A. Thomas, 1967; *The Big Book of Wit and Laughter*, Wolfe, 1972; *Five Hundred Quickfire Gags*, Wolfe, 1974; *One Thousand Jokes for Holidays*, Wolfe, 1975; *The Book of Wit and Humour: A Public Speaker's Treasury*, A. Thomas, 1976; (editor) *Official Irish Joke Book Number Four*, Futura Publications, 1979; (editor) *Positively the Last Irish Joke Book*, Futura Publications, 1979; (editor) *Official Aussie Joke Book*, Futura Publications, 1979; (editor) *Official Graffiti Joke Book*, Futura Publications, 1980; (editor) *Official Salesman's Joke Book*, Futura Publications, 1980.

Under pseudonym Gordon Shayne: *Ticket to Eternity*, Jasmit, 1952.

Also author of radio and television plays and comedy shows for British Broadcasting Corp., Associated-Rediffusion, and Granada Television; writer of other scripts, mainly comedy shows, for radio and television, revues, cabaret, and other entertainment media in a dozen countries, including Australia, Sweden, and the United States. Contributor of over five hundred short stories and articles to periodicals, including *Sketch*, *Spotlight* (South Africa), *Courier*, *Coronet*, *Weekly Pocket Book* (Australia), *Aftonbladet* (Sweden), and *Mike Shayne Detective Magazine*.

WORK IN PROGRESS: Research into psychiatric and hypnotic methods of treating stress conditions and advanced neuroses; shooting-script for a comedy-thriller motion picture.

SIDELIGHTS: Bevis Winter says his outlook is mainly liberal and that he abhors intolerance in social, religious, and political life. He studies human nature clinically, for serious research, and objectively, for writing comedy. He has a working knowledge of languages—primarily French, German, and Swedish—necessary to prepare scripts for overseas.

AVOCATIONAL INTERESTS: Psychology, ju-jitsu, and hi-fi (makes his own equipment).

BIOGRAPHICAL/CRITICAL SOURCES: *Writer*, June-July, 1949; *Men Only*, October, 1961.†

* * *

WISEMAN, B(ernard) 1922-

PERSONAL: Born August 26, 1922, in Brooklyn, N.Y.; son of Abraham Z. and Yetta (Goldstein) Wiseman; married second wife, Susan Nadine Levin Cranis, May 9, 1970; children: Michael Avram, Andrew Lee; Peter Franklin Cranis (stepson). *Education:* Attended Art Students League. 1946. *Politics:* "Independent with conservative bias." *Religion:* Hebrew. *Home:* 2640 Lake Hill Rd., West Eau Gallie, Melbourne, Fla. 32935.

CAREER: Cartoonist, writer, and illustrator of books for children and adults, 1948—. Contract cartoonist for *New Yorker* (magazine), New York City, and *Punch* (magazine), London, England, 1948-59; cartoonist for Spadea Syndicate, 1965-66, and for McNaught Syndicate, 1967-69; became partner and art director of Crown Syndicate. Creator of cartoons and comic illustrations for *Saturday Evening Post*, *True*, *Look*, *This Week*, *Playboy*, *Rogue*, *Cosmopolitan*, and other periodicals; creator of advertising illustrations for American Airlines, New York Transport Authority, Woolite, and other companies and organizations. *Military service:* U.S. Coast Guard, 1941-46. *Member:* Young Men's Hebrew Association, New York Dojo Club, Mas Oyama's Karate Dojo.

WRITINGS—All self-illustrated: *Cartoon Countdown*, Ballantine, 1959; *Morris the Moose*, Harper, 1959, reprinted, Scholastic Book Services, 1973; *Morris Is a Cowboy, a Policeman, and a Baby Sitter*, Harper, 1960; *The Log and Admiral Frog*. Harper, 1961; *Irwin the Intern*, Dell, 1962; *Boatniks*, Dell, 1962; (with Sandy Brier) *Sadness Is a Back View*, Citadel, 1964; (with Brier) *Since I Quit Smoking I Don't Know What to Do with My Hands*, Citadel, 1964; *The Hat That Grew*, E. M. Hale, 1965.

Morris Goes to School, Harper, 1970, published as *Morris the Moose Goes to School*, Scholastic Book Services, 1972; *Ninety-Six Cats*, E. M. Hale, 1970; *Detective Dog*, Platt, 1971; *Hats and Coats, Cows and Goats*, Platt, 1971; *Nutty Nature Book*, Platt, 1971; *Silly Science Book*, Platt, 1971; *Sex-Ed*, Dell, 1971; *Little New Kangaroo*, Macmillan, 1973; *Morris and Boris: Three Stories*, Dodd, 1974, published as *Three Stories about Morris and Boris*, Scholastic Book Services, 1976; *Halloween with Morris and Boris*, Dodd, 1975; *Billy Learns Karate*, Holt, 1976; *Iglook's Seal*, Dodd, 1977; *Bobby and Boo, the Little Spaceman*, Holt, 1978; *Morris Has a Cold*, Dodd, 1978; *The Lucky Runner*, Garrard. 1979; *Morris Tells Boris Mother Moose Stories and Rhymes*, Dodd, 1979; *My Googoo*, Holt, 1979; *Quick Quackers*, Garrard, 1979.

Hooray for Patsy's Oink!, Garrard, 1980; *Oscar Is a Mama!*, Garrard, 1980; *Penny's Poodle Puppy, Pickle*, Garrard, 1980; *Tails Are Not for Painting*, Garrard, 1980; *Don't Make Fun!*, Houghton, 1982; *Very Bumpy Bus Ride*, Parents Magazine Press, 1982.

Illustrator of stories, including "The Boy Who Found Xmas," 1966, by James A. Michener. Contributor of "Sir Nervous Norman" stories to *Boys' Life*, 1968—; contributor of numerous cartoons to periodicals in the United States and England.

SIDELIGHTS: Booklets that Bernard Wiseman illustrated for Radio Free Europe were dropped by balloons in Communist satellite countries.

* * *

WITTKOWSKI, Wolfgang 1925-

PERSONAL: Born August 15, 1925, in Halle, Germany; came to United States in 1963; son of Gerhard (an economist) and Margarete (Linckelmann) Wittkowski; married Maria Jokiel (divorced, 1972); married Charlotte Korner, 1977; children: (first marriage) Mechtild, Ute, Isa, Albrecht, *Education:* Attended University of Goettingen, 1944-50; University of Frankfurt, staatsexamen, 1953, Ph.D., 1964. *Office:* Department of German, State University of New York, Albany, N.Y. 12222.

CAREER: Assistant master of secondary school in Bad Nauheim, Germany, 1956-63; Ohio State University, Columbus, associate professor, 1963-66, professor of German, 1966-77; State University of New York at Albany, professor of German, 1977—. Currently preparing an International Goethe Symposium. *Military service:* German Army, 1943-45. *Member:* Modern Language Association of America, American Association of Teachers of German, Hebbel und Lessing Gesellschaft.

WRITINGS: (Contributor) H. Kreuzer, editor, *Hebbel in neuer Sicht,* Kohlhammer (Stuttgart), 1963; *Der Junge Hebbel,* De Gruyter (Berlin), 1969; (with Claude David and Lawrence Ryan) *Kleist und Frankreich,* E. Schmidt (Berlin), 1969; (contributor) Klaus Berghahn, editor, *Friedrich Schiller: Theorie und Praxis der Dramen,* Wege der Forschung (Darmstadt), 1972; *Das Drama in der Weimarer Klassik,* scriptor, 1977; *Heinrich von Kleist's "Amphitryon"* De Gruyter, 1978; *Georg Buchner: Personlichkeit, Weltbild, Werk,* Winter (Heidelberg), 1978; (editor) *Friedrich Schiller: Kunst, Humanitoet und Politik in der Spaeten Aufklaerung—Ein Symposium,* Niemeyer (Tubingen), 1982. Contributor of articles on Hoffmann, Grillparzer, Stifter, Raabe, Fontane, S. Kirsch, and Hemingway to German literature journals.

WORK IN PROGRESS: Research on Goethe's and Schiller's dramas, and on tragedy and poetry.

* * *

WOLFE, Peter 1933-

PERSONAL: Born August 25, 1933, in New York, N.Y.; son of Milton B. (an optician) and Mae (Salius) Wolfe; married Marie Paley, December 22, 1962 (divorced, 1969); children: Philip Graham, John Bennett. *Education:* City College (now City College of the City University of New York), B.A., 1955; Leigh University, M.A., 1957; University of Wisconsin, Ph.D., 1965. *Politics:* Democrat. *Home:* 4466 West Pine, Apt. 18B, St. Louis, Mo. 63108. *Office:* Department of English, University of Missouri, St. Louis, Mo. 63121.

CAREER: University of Nebraska, Lincoln, assistant professor of English, 1964-67; University of Missouri, St. Louis, assistant professor, 1967-68, associate professor, 1968-76, professor of English, 1976—. Visiting professor, University of Windsor, 1971, University of California, Los Angeles, 1975, University of Waikato, New Zealand, and University of Queensland, Australia, 1980, and National Taiwan Normal University, 1982. *Military service:* U.S. Army, Ordnance Corps, 1957-59. *Member:* Modern Language Association of America (president, Modern Literature Section, 1972, 1976), American Association of University Professors, Kipling Society, James Joyce Society, Arnold Bennett Society. *Awards, honors:* National Endowment for the Humanities summer fellow, 1974.

WRITINGS: *The Disciplined Heart: Iris Murdoch and Her Novels,* University of Missouri Press, 1966; *Mary Renault,* Twayne, 1969; *Rebecca West: Artist and Thinker,* Southern Illinois University Press, 1971; *Graham Greene: The Entertainer,* Southern Illinois University Press, 1972; *John Fowles: Magus and Moralist,* Bucknell University Press, 1976; *Dreamers Who Live Their Dreams: The World of Ross Macdonald's Novels,* Bowling Green University Press, 1977; *Jean Rhys,* Twayne, 1980; *Beams Falling: The Art of Dashiell Hammett,* Bowling Green University Press, 1980; *Laden Choirs: The Novels of Patrick White,* University Press of Kentucky, 1983. Editor of *Graham Greene Annual* and *Virginia Woolf Quarterly.*

WORK IN PROGRESS: Books on Raymond Chandler and John le Carre, both for Bowling Green University Press.

AVOCATIONAL INTERESTS: Music (particularly modern jazz), sports (especially hockey, basketball, and racquetball).

* * *

WOOD, James L(eslie) 1941-

PERSONAL: Born August 30, 1941, in Oakland, Calif.; son of James L. (a physician) and Maxine E. Wood; married Patricia A. Taylor (a health information director), June 13, 1964; children: Ann M., Jeffrey J. *Education:* University of California, Beeley, B.A., 1963, M.A., 1966, Ph.D., 1973; attended Hastings College of Law, 1963-64. *Home:* 5021 Tierra Baja Way, San Diego, Calif. 92115. *Office:* Department of Sociology, San Diego State University, San Diego, Calif. 92182.

CAREER: Holy Names College, Oakland, Calif., instructor in sociology, 1971-73; University of California, Riverside, lecturer in sociology, 1973-75; San Diego State University, San Diego, Calif., lecturer, 1975-76, assistant professor, 1976-78, associate professor, 1978-81, professor of sociology, 1981—. Assistant professor of sociology, California State University, San Francisco, summer, 1972; lecturer and consultant. *Member:* American Sociological Association (member of Collective Behavior/Social Movements Section), Pacific Sociological Association. *Awards, honors:* Grants from University of California, 1975, 1976, 1979, and 1981.

WRITINGS: (With Willie Thompson) *A Handbook for Block Clubs,* Bay Area Urban Extension, University of California, 1967; *The Sources of American Student Activism,* Lexington Books, 1974; (with Wing-Cheung Ng and wife, Patricia A. Wood) *Urban Sociology Bibliography,* Council of Planning Librarians, 1977; (with Wing-Cheung Ng and P. A. Wood) *Political Sociology Bibliography,* Vance Bibliographies, 1979; (author of foreword) Richard G. Braungart, *Family Status, Socialization and Student Politics,* University Microfilms, 1979; (with Howard J. Sherman) *Sociology: Traditional and Radical Perspectives,* Harper, 1980; (with Maurice Jackson) *Social Movements: Development, Participation, and Dynamics,* Wadsworth, 1982.

Monographs: *Political Consciousness and Student Activism,* Sage Publications, 1974; *New Left Ideology: Its Dimensions and Development,* Sage Publications, 1975; (with Jackson) *Aging in America: Implications for the Black Aged,* National Council on the Aging, 1976; (with Phillip T. Gay) *Empirical Tests of Paradigms and Theories for Module in Social Movements,* American Political Science Association, 1978; (with Gay) *Modules in Social Movements,* American Political Science Association, 1978.

Contributor: (With Gary T. Marx) *Annual Review of Sociology,* Annual Reviews, Inc., 1975; David W. Swift, editor, *American Education: A Sociological View,* Houghton, 1976; (with Bohdan Kolody and Jackson) Ron C. Manuel, editor, *Minority Aging,* Greenwood Press, in press.

Author of papers presented at meetings of professional organizations, including American Sociological Association and American Political Science Association; contributor to *Footnotes* of American Sociological Association, 1980. Contributor of articles and reviews to professional journals, including *Human Organization, Sociological Focus, American Journal of Sociology,* and *Contemporary Sociology.* Co-editor, *Berkeley Journal of Sociology,* 1969.

WORK IN PROGRESS: Editing *The Politics of the Working Class;* papers; statistical analysis, with Jackson and Kolody, of black aging in America.

BIOGRAPHICAL/CRITICAL SOURCES: Kenneth Keniston, *Radicals and Militants: An Annotated Bibliography of Empirical Research on Campus Unrest,* Lexington Books, 1973.

* * *

WOODMAN, Anthony John 1945-

PERSONAL: Born April 11, 1945, in Newcastle upon Tyne, England. *Education:* University of Newcastle upon Tyne, B.A., 1965; King's College, Cambridge, Ph.D., 1970. *Office:* School of Classics, University of Leeds, Leeds LS2 9JT, England.

CAREER: University of Newcastle upon Tyne, Newcastle upon Tyne, England, lecturer in classics, 1968-79, reader in Latin literature, 1979-80; University of Leeds, Leeds, England, professor of Latin, 1980—. *Member:* Classical Association of England and Wales, Society for the Promotion of Roman Studies, Cambridge Philological Society.

WRITINGS: (Contributor) Jacqueline Bibauw, editor, *Hommages a Marcel Renard* (title means "Studies in Honor of Marcel Renard"), Latomus (Brussels), 1968; (editor with David West and contributor) *Quality and Pleasure in Latin Poetry,* Cambridge University Press, 1975; (contributor) T. A. Dorey, editor, *Empire and Aftermath: Silver Latin II,* Routledge & Kegan Paul, 1975; *Velleius Paterculus,* Cambridge University Press, Volume I: *The Tiberian Narrative,* 1977, Volume II: *The Caesarian and Augustan Narrative,* 1983; (editor with West and contributor) *Creative Imitation and Latin Literature,* Cambridge University Press, 1979; (editor with West and contributor) *Poetry and Politics in the Augustan Age,* Cambridge University Press, 1983. Contributor to classical journals.

WORK IN PROGRESS: A book on Roman historiography.

AVOCATIONAL INTERESTS: Football, mountains, poetry, table tennis, and "the Great War, World War II."

* * *

WRAGG, E(dward) C(onrad) 1938-

PERSONAL: Born June 26, 1938, in Sheffield, England; son of George William (a florist) and Maria (Brandstetter) Wragg; married Judith King, December 29, 1960; children: Josephine, Caroline, Christopher. *Education:* University of Durham, B.A. (first class honors), 1959, diploma in education, 1960; University of Leicester, M.Ed., 1967; University of Exeter, Ph.D., 1972. *Office:* School of Education, University of Exeter, Exeter EX1 2LU, England.

CAREER: Teacher in grammar school in Wakefield, England, 1960-63; teacher of German and head of department in boys' school in Leicester, England, 1964-66; University of Exeter, Exeter, England, lecturer in education, 1966-73; University of Nottingham, Nottingham, England, professor of education, 1973-78; University of Exeter, professor of education, 1978—, director of School of Education, 1978—. Chairman, BBC School Broadcasting Council; specialist adviser, Parliamentary Select Committee on Education; director, Teacher Education Project, Department of Education and Science, 1976-81; member, Council for National Academic Awards. *Member:* British Educational Research Association (president), Universities Council for the Education of Teachers.

WRITINGS: (Author of adaptation) Wolfgang Ecke, *Krimis,* Longmans, Green, 1967; *Life in Germany,* Longmans, Green, 1968; *Teaching Teaching,* David & Charles, 1974; *Classroom Interaction,* Open University, 1976; *Teaching Mixed Ability Groups,* David & Charles, 1976; *A Handbook for School Governors,* Methuen, 1980; *Class Management and Control,* Macmillan, 1981; *A Review of Research in Teacher Education,* National Foundation for Educational Research, 1982; *Inside Education,* Trentham, 1982. Editor of teaching series for David & Charles. Regular Columnist for *Times Educational Supplement.* Contributor to language and education journals.

WORK IN PROGRESS: Research on teacher education, classroom interaction, and curriculum development.

SIDELIGHTS: E. C. Wragg told *CA:* "Writing a regular column for a national newspaper in which I try to bring out the humorous side of education has made me realise how hilarious human behavior is. I think of all those wasted years I took it seriously." *Avocational interests:* Sport, reading, travel, media.

* * *

WRIGHT, Barton A(llen) 1920-

PERSONAL: Born December 21, 1920, in Bisbee Ariz.; son of Roy Joline and Anna Harris Wright; married Margaret Anna Nickelson, April 16, 1949; children: Frances Elena, Matthew Allen. *Education:* University of Arizona, B.A., 1952, M.A., 1954. *Home:* 6254 Rose Lake Ave., San Diego, Calif. 92119. *Office:* Museum of Man, 1350 El Prado, San Diego, Calif. 92101.

CAREER: Town Creek Indian Mound State Park, Mt. Gilead, N.C., state archaeological assistant, 1949-51; Arizona State Museum, Tucson, museum assistant, 1951-52; Amerind Foundation, Dragoon, Ariz., archaeologist, 1952-55; Museum of Northern Arizona, Flagstaff, curator of arts and exhibits, 1955-58, museum curator, 1958-77; Museum of Man, San Diego, Calif., scientific director, 1977—. Artist and illustrator; commissioned for display at Wupatki National Monument, 1962; work exhibited throughout southwestern United States, 1967—. *Military service:* U.S. Army, 1943-45. *Member:* American Archaeological Society, American Association of Museums, Western Museum League, Southwestern Museums Association, Arizona Academy of Science.

WRITINGS—All published by Northland Press: *Kachinas: A Hopi Artist's Documentary,* 1973; *The Unchanging Hopi,* 1975; *Pueblo Shields,* 1976; *Hopi Kachinas: The Complete Guide to Collecting Kachina Dolls,* 1977; *Hopi Material Culture,* 1979. Also author of *Shalakos,* and of pamphlets, *This Is a Hopi Kachina,* with Evelyn Roat, and *Age of Dinosaurs in Northern Arizona,* with William Breed. Contributor of articles to southwestern periodicals and to *American Indian.*

WORK IN PROGRESS: Pueblo Religion.

* * *

WRIGHT, H(arry) Norman 1937-

PERSONAL: Born July 25, 1937, in Hollywood, Calif.; son of Harry N. (a salesman) and Amelia (Cornelius) Wright; married Joycelin Archinal, August 22, 1959; children: Sheryl, Matthew. *Education:* Westmont College, B.A., 1959; Fuller Seminary, M.R.E., 1961; Pepperdine University, M.A., 1965. *Religion:* Christian. *Residence:* Long Beach, Calif. *Office:* Biola College, 13800 Biola Ave., La Mirada, Calif. 90639.

CAREER: Licensed marriage and family counselor; Biola College, La Mirada, Calif., professor of marriage and family counseling, 1965—. Founder and director, Christian Marriage Enrichment, Family Counseling and Enrichment. Christian education consultant, Gospel Light Publications, 1963—. *Member:* American Association for Marriage and Family Therapy, California Association of Marriage counselors.

WRITINGS: *Help! I'm a Camp Counselor,* Regal Books, 1967; *Ways to Help Them Learn: Adults,* Regal Books, 1972; *Christian Marriage and Family Relationships,* Christian Marriage Enrichment, 1972; *The Christian Use of Emotional Power,* Revell, 1974; *Communication: Key to Your Marriage,* Regal Books, 1974; *The Living Marriage,* Revell, 1975; *Pre-Marital Counseling,* Moody, 1977, revised edition, 1981; *The Family that Listens,* Victor Books, 1978; (with Rex Johnson) *Characteristics of a Caring Home,* Vision House, 1979; *Into the High Country,* Multnomah, 1979; *Pillars of Marriage,* Regal Books, 1979; *Preparing for Parenthood,* Regal Books, 1980; *Marital Counseling: A Biblically Based Behavioral Cognitive Approach,* Christian Marriage Enrichment, 1981; *How to Be a Better than Average In-Law,* Victor Books, 1981; *Seasons of a Marriage,* Regal Books, 1982.

"Answer" series, published by Harvest House: *An Answer to Worry and Anxiety,* 1976; *. . . the Fulfilled Marriage,* 1976; *. . . Frustration and Anger,* 1977; *. . . Divorce,* 1977; *. . . In-Laws,* 1977; *. . . Building Your Self Image,* 1977; *. . . Parent-Teen Relationships,* 1977. Also author of *An Answer to Depression, . . . Discipline, . . . Loneliness, . . . Family Communication, . . . Submission and Decision Making.*

Author of *The Christian Faces Emotions, Marriage and Family Relationships, Marriage and Family Enrichment Resource Manual,* and *Training Christians to Counsel,* all published by Christian Marriage Enrichment, and of *Communication and Conflict Resolution,* David Cook; also author of *Communication: Key to Your Teens, Building Positive Parent-Teen Relationships, A Guidebook for Dating, Waiting and Choosing a Mate, Preparing Youth for Dating, Courtship and Marriage, Living beyond Worry and Anger, Living with Your Emotions, Self Image and Depression, Before You Say "I Do",* and *After You Say "I Do",* all published by Harvest House.

Contributor to religious publications and journals in his field.

* * *

WROBLEWSKI, Sergius C(harles) 1918-

PERSONAL: Born March 8, 1918, in Chicago, Ill.; son of Francis (a janitor) and Angela (Faikiel) Wroblewski. *Education:* St. Francis College, Burlington, Wis., A.B., 1943; Catholic University of America, S.T.L., 1952. *Office:* Department of Religion, St. Bonaventure University, St. Bonaventure, N.Y. 14778.

CAREER: Ordained Roman Catholic priest, member of Franciscan Order; Christ the King Seminary, West Chicago, Ill., professor for eighteen years, became director; currently member of religion department, St. Bonaventure University, St. Bonaventure, N.Y. Former director of the Third Order of St. Francis Secular, and instructor in theology at Franciscan Institute for Sisters, St. Francis College, Joliet, Ill., and Immaculata College, Bartlett, Ill.

WRITINGS: Following Francis: Commentary on the Third Order General Constitutions, Franciscan Herald, 1961; *Christian Perfection for the Layman,* Franciscan Herald, 1963; (contributor) James Michael Lee and Louis J. Putz, editors, *Seminary Education in a Time of Change,* Fides, 1965; *Updating Franciscan Communities,* Franciscan Publishers, 1966; *Christ-Centered Spirituality,* Alba, 1967; *Bonaventurian Theology of Prayer,* Franciscan Publishers, 1967; *The Real Francis,* Franciscan Publishers, 1967; *A Prophetic History of the West,* Alba, 1968; *Growth in Christ,* Franciscan Publishers, 1969; *St. Francis: Yesterday and Today,* Franciscan Publishers, 1974. Contributor to religious journals.†

* * *

WUCHERER, Ruth Marie 1948-

PERSONAL: Born June 17, 1948, in Milwaukee, Wis.; daughter of Frank Edward (a machinist) and Helen Antoinette (Wieczorek) Wucherer. *Education:* University of Wisconsin—Milwaukee, B.A., 1970. *Home:* 3045 South Ninth Pl., Milwaukee, Wis. 53215. *Office:* School of Education, Enderis Hall 555, University of Wisconsin, Milwaukee, Wis. 53201.

CAREER: Gimbel's Department Store, Milwaukee, Wis., advertising copywriter, 1971-78; University of Wisconsin—Milwaukee, program assistant in School of Education, 1979—. *Member:* Associated Business Writers of America, American Medical Writers Association, Women in Communications (publicity chairman of Southeastern chapter, 1975-76), Wisconsin Regional Writers Association, Council for Wisconsin Writers.

WRITINGS: How to Sell Your Crafts, Drake, 1976; *What You Should Know about Credit,* Pamphlet Publications, 1977; *Make Money Selling Your Crafts,* Pamphlet Publications, 1977; *The Fascinating World of Advertising,* Pamphlet Publications, 1979. Contributor of travel, business, and feature articles to magazines and newspapers.

WORK IN PROGRESS: A book on travel writing.

AVOCATIONAL INTERESTS: Travel, bicycling, bowling, reading, attending the theater and concerts.

Y

YANNELLA, Donald 1934-

PERSONAL: Born May 12, 1934, in New York, N.Y.; son of Donald J. (a senior executive) and Johanna (Meehan) Yannella; married Kathleen Malone, May 23, 1959; children: Susan, Katherine, Donald, Christopher, Clare. *Education:* Fordham University, B.S., 1956, M.A., 1963, Ph.D., 1971. *Home:* 66 Sharmont Dr., Hattiesburg, Miss. 39401. *Office:* Department of English, University of Southern Mississippi, Hattiesburg, Miss. 39406-5037.

CAREER: Auburn University, Auburn, Ala., teaching fellow, 1956-57; Westchester Community College, Valhalla, N.Y., assistant professor of English, 1964; Glassboro State College, Glassboro, N.H., assistant professor, 1964-68, associate professor, 1968-71, professor of English, 1971-81; University of Southern Mississippi, Hattiesburg, professor of English and chairman of department, 1981—. Member of National Project on Film and the Humanities Advisory Committee, 1974—. *Military service:* U.S. Army, 1957-58. *Member:* Melville Society (secretary-treasurer, 1975—), Modern Language Association of America (secretary-treasurer, American Literature Section, 1982—).

WRITINGS: (Editor of reprint) Cornelius Mathews, *Behemoth* (novel), Garrett Press, 1970; (editor of reprint) Matthews, *The Career of Puffer Hopkins and Big Abel and the Little Manhattan* (novel), Garrett Press, 1970; (editor) *Romanticism in American Literature: 1820-1960*, Transcendental, 1973; (with John H. Roch) *American Prose to 1820*, Gale, 1979; *Ralph Waldo Emerson*, Twayne, 1982. Contributor of reviews to journals in his field. Editor of *Melville Society Extracts*, 1973-74, 1976—.

WORK IN PROGRESS: The Diary and Letters of E. A. Duyckinck.

YOHN, Rick 1937-

PERSONAL: Born April 16, 1937, in Fresno, Calif.; son of Henry M. (an engineer) and Ada A. Yohn; married Linda H. Anderson (a high school teacher), June 18, 1960; children: Ricky, Steven. *Education:* Attended Franklin & Marshall College, 1955-56; Philadelphia College of Bible, B.S., 1960; Dallas Theological Seminary, Th.M., 1964. *Office:* Fresno Evangelical Free Church, 3438 East Ashlan Ave., Fresno, Calif. 93726.

CAREER: Christian education director of Presbyterian church in Minneapolis, Minn., 1964-67; pastor of Evangelical Free Church in Winnipeg, Manitoba, 1967-71; Fresno Evangelical Free Church, Fresno, Calif., pastor, 1971—. President of Twin Cities Directors of Christian Education, 1969; soccer coach for young boys in Fresno, Calif., 1973, 1974. *Awards, honors:* Award of Excellence, *Campus Life* magazine, 1975, for *Discover Your Spiritual Gift and Use It*.

WRITINGS—Published by Harvest House, except as indicated: *Discover Your Spiritual Gift and Use It*, Tyndale, 1974; *What Every Christian Should Know about God*, 1976; *God's Answers to Life's Problems*, 1976; *Now That I'm a Disciple*, 1976; *What Every Christian Should Know about Bible Prophecy*, 1976; *God's Holy Spirit for Christian Living*, 1977; *Character Growth: Priority for Christian Living*, Tyndale, 1977; *God's Answers to Financial Problems*, 1978; *How to Overcome Temptation*, Thomas Nelson, 1978.

* * *

YORK, Jeremy
See CREASEY, John

Z

ZALD, Mayer N(athan) 1931-

PERSONAL: Born June 17, 1931, in Detroit, Mich.; son of Harold and Ann (Levitt) Zald; married Joan Kadri (a social worker), June 15, 1958; children: Ann, David, Harold. *Education:* Attended Wayne State University, 1949-51; University of Michigan, B.A., 1953, Ph.D., 1960; University of Hawaii, M.A., 1955. *Home:* 2110 Vinewood, Ann Arbor, Mich. 48104. *Office:* Department of Sociology, University of Michigan, Ann Arbor, Mich. 48104.

CAREER: University of Chicago, Chicago, Ill., instructor, 1960-61, assistant professor of sociology and psychology, 1961-64; Vanderbilt University, Nashville, Tenn., associate professor, 1964-68, professor of sociology, 1968-77, chairman of department, 1971-75; University of Michigan, Ann Arbor, professor of sociology and social work, 1977—, chairman of department, 1981-83. Member of committee of examiners in sociology for Graduate Record Examination, 1972-74. *Military service:* U.S. Army, 1955-56. *Member:* American Sociological Association, Society for the Scientific Study of Social Problems, American Association of University Professors, American Civil Liberties Union, Southern Sociological Society (chairman, 1968-69; member of executive committee, 1973-76). *Awards, honors:* Career Development Award grants, National Institute of Mental Health, 1967-72.

WRITINGS: (Editor) *Social Welfare Institutions: A Sociological Reader*, Wiley, 1965; (editor) *Organizing for Community Welfare*, Quadrangle, 1967; *Organizational Change: The Political Economy of the YMCA*, University of Chicago Press, 1970; (editor) *Power in Organizations*, Vanderbilt University Press, 1970; *Occupations and Organizations in American Life: The Organization-Dominated Man?*, Markham, 1971; (author of foreword) Robert Mayer, *Social Planning and Social Change*, Prentice-Hall, 1972; (with John Ehnes) *Handbook of Organizational Statistics*, Department of Sociology, Vanderbilt University, 1975; (with Gary L. Wamsley) *The Political Economy of Public Organizations*, Heath, 1976; (editor with William Rushing) *Organizations and Beyond: Selected Essays of James D. Thompson*, Heath, 1976; (editor) *Dynamics of Social Movements*, Winthrop, 1979.

Contributor: Morris Janowitz, editor, *The New Military: Changing Patterns of Organization*, Russell Sage, 1964; E. Sampson, editor, *Approaches, Problems, and Context of Social Psychology*, Prentice-Hall, 1964; Robert T. Golembiewski and others, editors, *Public Administration: Readings in Institutions, Processes, and Behavior*, Rand McNally, 1966; Rose Giallombardo, editor, *Juvenile Delinquency Reader*, Wiley, 1966; W. Coplin, editor, *Simulation in Political Science*, Markham, 1968; L. Hazelrigg, editor, *Prison and Society*, Doubleday, 1968; A. Etzioni, editor, *Readings on Modern Organizations*, Prentice-Hall, 1969; Fremont Lyden, G. Shipman, and M. Kroll, editors, *Policies, Decisions and Organizations*, Appleton-Century-Crofts, 1969; R. Kramer and H. Specht, editors, *Community Organization Reader*, Prentice-Hall, 1969; J. Gusfield, editor, *Protest, Reform and Revolt: A Reader in Social Movements and Collective Action*, Wiley, 1969.

Michael Aiken and Paul E. Mott, editors, *The Structure of Community Power: Readings*, Random House, 1970; Carl Bersani, editor, *Crime and Delinquency: Selected Readings*, Macmillan, 1970; L. Ruchelman, editor, *Big City Mayors: Readings on the Crisis of Urban Politics*, Indiana University Press, 1970; F. Cox, John Erlich, Jack Rothman, and J. Tropman, editors, *Strategies of Community Organization*, Peacock, 1970; Alan Booth and John N. Edwards, editors, *Social Participation in Urban Areas*, Schenkman, 1970; Polsky, Claster, and Goldberg, editors, *Social System Perspectives in Residential Institutions*, Michigan State University Press, 1970; Charles Bonjean and Louis Zurcher, editors, *Planned Social Intervention: An Inter-Disciplinary Anthology*, Chandler, 1970; Sandor Halebsky, editor, *The Sociology of the City*, Scribner, 1972; Boge and Coleman, editors, *Readings in Business Policy*, Macmillan, 1972; (with Feather Davis Hair) Basil Georgopoulos, editor, *Organization Research on Health Institutions*, Institute on Social Research, University of Michigan, 1972; Robert Evans, editor, *Social Movements*, Rand McNally, 1974; Richard English and Yehenskel Hasenfeld, editors, *Human Services Organizations*, University of Michigan Press, 1974; Candice Piaget, editor, *Criminal Justice and the Democratic State*, W. H. Anderson, 1976; R. A. Rossum, editor, *Urban Administration: Management, Politics, and Change*, Dunellen, 1976; Alberto Melucci, editor, *Movimenti Sociali E Azione Colle Hiva*, Societa per Azioni (Milan, Italy), 1977.

Contributor of articles and reviews to periodicals, including *American Journal of Sociology*, *American Sociological Review*, *Social Forces*, *Human Relations*, *Contemporary Sociology*, *Sociological Quarterly*, *Social Work*, *Crime and Delinquency*, *Urban Affairs Quarterly*, and *Sociology of Education*. *American Journal of Sociology*, member of editorial board, 1960-74, associate editor, 1962-63; member of editorial board,

Social Problems, 1965-68, *Journal of Health and Human Behavior,* 1967-70, and *Journal of Voluntary Action Research,* 1972—; advisory editor, *Social Forces,* 1974—, and *Administration and Society,* 1976—.

WORK IN PROGRESS: Research on social control of institutions.

* * *

ZEMACH, Kaethe 1958-

PERSONAL: Born March 18, 1958, in Boston, Mass.; daughter of Harvey Fischtrom (a writer of children's books) and Margot (an illustrator of children's books) Zemach; married Ray Bird (a musician). *Education:* Attended schools in England, Denmark, and the United States. *Home:* 2423 Oregon St., Berkeley, Calif. 94705.

CAREER: Artist; writer.

WRITINGS: (With Harve Zemach, pseudonym of father, Harvey Fischstrom) *The Princess and Froggie* (juvenile; short stories), Farrar, Straus, 1975; (illustrator) Norman Rosten, *The Wineglass,* Walker & Co., 1978; (adapter and illustrator) *The Beautiful Rat* (Japanese folk tale), Four Winds Press, 1979; (illustrator) Yuri Suhl, *The Purim Goat,* Four Winds Press, 1980.

SIDELIGHTS: Kaethe Zemach told *CA:* "I feel that my work with children's books is still in an experimental stage, and I hope that in the future it will blossom into the stories and illustrations which will stand strong and be entertaining for children and adults alike."